THE
OXFORD COMPANION TO
POLITICS OF THE WORLD

THE OXFORD
COMPANION TO
POLITICS OF THE WORLD

Editor in Chief

Joel Krieger

Editors

William A. Joseph   Miles Kahler

Georges Nzongola-Ntalaja

Barbara B. Stallings   Margaret Weir

Consulting Editor

James A. Paul

New York Oxford
OXFORD UNIVERSITY PRESS
1993

OXFORD UNIVERSITY PRESS

Oxford   New York   Toronto
Delhi   Bombay   Calcutta   Madras   Karachi
Kuala Lumpur   Singapore   Hong Kong   Tokyo
Nairobi   Dar es Salaam   Cape Town
Melbourne   Auckland   Madrid

and associated companies in
Berlin   Ibadan

Library of Congress Cataloging-in-Publication Data
The Oxford companion to politics of the world / Joel Krieger,
editor in chief ; William Joseph . . . [et al.], editors ;
James A. Paul, consulting editor.
p.   cm.   Includes bibliographical references and index.
ISBN 0-19-505934-4
1. Political science—Encyclopedias.   2. World politics—
Encyclopedias.   I. Krieger, Joel, 1951–
JA61.095   1993
320'.03—dc20   92-25043   CIP

Printing (last digit): 9 8 7 6 5 4 3 2 1

Printed in the United States of America
on acid-free paper

EDITORS AND ADVISERS

CONTENTS

PREFACE

We are living through extraordinary times in which the world of politics has been buffeted by unlikely events and transformed in remarkable ways. East-West political rivalries have faded and military alliances have receded in significance. Within a broader pattern of global interdependence, Japan and the new East Asian economic powers compete with a resurgent (if troubled) European Community and with the emerging United States–led North American free trade zone. The sovereignty of the nation-state is eroded simultaneously from above and below, by regional and global forces outside, and by ethnic-nationalist, separatist, and religious forces within. For the time, at least, the democratic ideal has swept away authoritarian regimes throughout much of the world. The very language of politics and the sources of collective identity—how individuals and groups understand their condition and come together to advance political aims—have been recast. Solidarities based on gender, race, ethnicity, religion, and sexual identity, and animated by concerns like immigration and the environment, challenge an understanding of politics defined by economic interest and traditional Left/Right political oppositions.

Much has changed since we began this project. *The Oxford Companion to Politics of the World* was conceived while Nelson Mandela languished in prison in South Africa, international politics was dominated by United States–Soviet superpower rivalry, the Iran-Iraq War lingered in the Middle East, and Europe remained divided into Eastern and Western blocs. The *Companion* took shape as 1989 ushered in democratic transitions throughout Eastern and Central Europe, the hopes of perestroika faded, Iraq's invasion of Kuwait led to the Gulf War, and the African National Congress and the de Klerk government began often interrupted power-sharing talks to dismantle apartheid.

By the time the project came to fruition, the Soviet Union had dissolved. The euphoria that greeted German reunification had faded, and the fragments of Yugoslavia were rocked by a terrifying war. Russia and the other post-Soviet successor states struggled desperately to stabilize their economies and unify peoples torn by ethnic and nationalist strife. No one knew how long Saddam Hussein would hold power, or the shape of South Africa's future.

APPROACH

Such upheavals make it tempting to view world politics as a rapidly moving target. But the changes, however dramatic, come into focus with a full appreciation of more enduring themes and issues: the social bases of politics; the organizations and institutions of politics at the international and national levels; law, foreign policy, and economic and social policy; the linkage between international and domestic developments; and the recurring patterns of change in diverse societies (political development, modernization, revolution, reform, and racial, class, and ethnic conflict). Designed to explain political developments through article-by-article discussion of themes such as these, the *Companion* gives perspective and depth to the contemporary political moment.

In a single volume, *The Oxford Companion to Politics of the World* provides a comprehensive guide to international relations and national domestic politics throughout the world. It does so through the alphabetical arrangement of 650 articles that represent the contributions of nearly 500 scholars from more than 40 countries, thereby offering the reader a diverse sampling of critical insights about contemporary world politics.

Today, world affairs encompasses an exceptionally rich and varied tableau of powerful social forces outside government that give rise to rapidly proliferating and often colliding political identities and social movements. Politics has blurred the boundaries; it has absorbed economics and cultural studies, commingled the public and the private. Writing about politics cannot be separated from interpreting politics. We intend in the *Companion* to recognize—and communicate—the range of significant interpretations, Western and non-Western, national and international in scope, European and Third World, Left and Right, green and feminist.

In keeping with this vision of the terrain of politics and these ambitious goals, the contributors to the work have been drawn from a host of disciplines in the social sciences and humanities, including political science, economics, women's studies, sociology, anthropology, philosophy, law, history, international studies, and business. All are specialists chosen for the originality and importance of their contributions to the study of world politics. The contributors, a distinguished group of scholars from across the globe, ensure the vital interaction of diverse national and international perspectives.

The selection of authors and the mix of articles represent an attempt to strike a balance among regions of the world, varieties of subject matter, and schools of interpretation. They also reflect a concerted effort to transcend the formal binary divisions (First World/Third World, North/South, domestic politics/world politics) that sometimes constrain innovative scholarship by narrowing the field of vision. Reference books are expected to provide accurate, definitive treatments of important subjects consistent with the highest standards of scholarship, and we trust that *The Oxford Companion to Politics of the World* will satisfy this expectation. But we hope to go further, to convey something of the vitality and excitement of world politics, to contribute to understandings that challenge parochialism and transcend narrow disciplinary divisions, and to offer the reader many and varied examples of vibrant, cutting-edge interpretation and analysis.

ORGANIZATION AND USE

Guided by an international advisory board of preeminent scholars, the editors devised a conceptual scheme for the book that would allow an enormous amount of information about politics throughout the world to be conveyed in a single volume. All told, the 650 articles are distributed among ten substantive categories, and vary in length from short factual pieces of several hundred words to major essays of 4,000 words or more. Written with a diverse array of readers in mind, the articles should appeal to general readers fascinated by politics, students from high school through graduate study, and scholars throughout the social science disciplines, philosophy, religion, women's studies, law, and business. In addition, the *Companion* is intended to meet the professional needs of journalists, diplomats, people working in foundations, government offices, and international organizations, and those engaged in international business or law.

Inevitably, in a project of this scope, principles of selectivity are crucial. Rather than dispersing information through a multitude of short, dry articles on narrowly defined topics, the editors devised a system of coverage in which recurring patterns of information are uniformly located within particular types of articles. For example, the *Companion* contains articles on virtually every country in the world. These articles convey extensive information about national institutions and organizations, political leaders, parties, political economy, the social bases of politics and political divisions (class, race, ethnicity, iedology, religion, gender, traditional forces), patterns of internal conflict and prospects for change, and foreign affairs.

Also included in the *Companion* are biographies of leaders and intellectual figures who have shaped the political world as we know it. These articles include biographical information and assessments of the national and international significance of figures as diverse as Mohandas Gandhi, Eva Perón, Mao Zedong, David Ben-Gurion, Margaret Thatcher, Aleksandr Solzhenitsyn, Charles de Gaulle, Hannah Arendt, Michel Foucault, Martin Luther King, Jr., Boris Yeltsin, and some seventy-five other persons who have played exceptionally significant roles in contemporary political life.

In addition, the *Companion* features twenty-one interpretive essays. These are major analytic treatments of particularly significant and far-reaching themes written by eminent scholars. Addressing such topics as ethnicity, nationalism, gender and politics, development and underdevelopment, war, democracy, class and politics, political parties and party competition, race and racism, and environmentalism, the interpretive essays provide a thematic scaffold for the work as a whole. We also include three interpretive essays that identify debates, analyze directions, and assess the contributions of the academic fields that frame the *Companion*: comparative politics, international relations, and international law.

Along with the country articles, biographies, and interpretive essays, the *Companion* includes seven other categories for communicating critical information about world affairs and conveying the range and depth of contemporary interpretation:

- concepts (e.g., sovereignty, political violence, citizenship, postindustrial society)
- conventions, treaties, and developments in international law (e.g., Balfour Declaration, law of the sea, Treaty of Rome, Lomé Convention)
- forms of government and institutions (e.g., apartheid, military rule, U.S. Congress, totalitarianism)
- historical events (e.g., World War II, Chernobyl nuclear accident, Cuban missile crisis, Holocaust)
- international issues (e.g., AIDS, antisemitism, liberation theology, security)
- international organizations (e.g., Roman Catholic church, European Community, Amnesty International, Organization of Petroleum Exporting Countries, Organization of African Unity)
- domestic political, economic, and social issues (e.g., elections and voting behavior, reproductive rights, psychology and politics, literacy, green parties, taxes and taxation)

The *Companion* relies on several cross-referencing schemes to guide readers from their initial point of entry to related articles throughout the volume. At the highest level of organization are blind entries. Blind entries appear within the alphabetical range of entry terms and, for synonyms, related subjects, and inverted terms, refer the reader to the actual entry under which the topic is discussed. For example, the blind entry "Guest Workers" refers the reader to the entry "Foreign Workers." In some cases, a blind entry will send the user to another entry that discusses the topic within a larger context. For example, "Botswana" appears as a blind entry that directs the reader to the entry "BLS States."

Within the body of an article, cross-references may also be indicated by insertion of an asterisk. Topics marked in this way will be found elsewhere in the volume as separate entries. For example, in the entry "Elections and Voting Behavior," the terms *class, state,* and *proportional representation* are preceded by asterisks, meaning that the reader may wish to refer to the entries "Class and Politics," "State," and "Proportional Representation." Finally, when the use of an asterisk would be misleading or unclear, or when the entry term of a related article does not appear within the body of text, cross-references are listed within parentheses at the end of the article.

More generally, the cross-referencing scheme will help users gain an in-depth understanding of comprehensive themes. For example, cross-references will direct readers interested in women's studies to an ensemble of articles on topics including feminism, feminist theory, gender and politics, partriarchy, women and development, the Equal Rights Amendment, and reproductive rights. They will be led from any one of these articles to the others, and in turn to articles on topics such as gay and lesbian politics, gender gap, and *Roe* v. *Wade,* which in turn draw the reader's attention to articles treating new social movements, elections and voting behavior, and the New Right. Similarly, readers interested in business and economics will be led from articles on international finance, political economy, and international debt to related articles discussing balance of payments, the International Monetary Fund, and protection, and in turn to articles on North-South relations, newly industrializing economies, and many others.

In addition, the index will help readers pursuing a line of reasoning, looking to locate particular information, or seeking references to political figures not covered by independent articles. The bibliographies at the end of articles suggest sources that may prove helpful for those wanting to pursue more intensive research into an area of interest or professional concern. The Directory of Contributors (pages xiii–xxxi) identifies all the articles by a particular author. Finally, despite the boundary disputes that beset contemporary world politics and the uncertain future of quite a few countries, six regional maps are included in the *Companion*. The maps reflect the balance of international consensus and common usage in the fall of 1992, and are presented with the knowledge that country names and borders are subject to change.

With considerations of space and focus in mind, coverage has been limited, with a few significant exceptions, to the issues and personalities of the twentieth century; a vast majority of the articles treat the period since World War II.

The *Companion* is the work of many people. With the assistance of an international advisory board, the project was conceived and directed by an editorial board consisting of William A. Joseph, Miles Kahler, Georges Nzongola-Ntalaja, James A. Paul, Barbara B. Stallings, and Margaret Weir. They worked tirelessly through every phase of the project with enormous intelligence and skill, for which I am immensely grateful. Of course, the ultimate value of the *Companion* depends on the commitment and talent of the contributors, some of whom worked on their articles under extraordinarily difficult conditions, and all of whom graciously invested their wisdom and scholarship in the project. I am very grateful for all their efforts and the interest which sustained the project. Several friends and colleagues were unstinting in the advice and encouragement they provided: Martin Brody, Richard Gordon, David Held, Martín Sánchez Jankowski, Mark Kesselman, Joanne Landy, Lars Lih, Craig Murphy, George Ross, Lois Wasserspring. The idea for the *Companion* emerged spontaneously in conversations with Linda Halvorson Morse at Oxford University Press. From the beginning, she has provided tremendous encouragement and inspiration. Her faith in the project and the direction she has provided the editors proved invaluable throughout.

Many others at Oxford University Press have helped in various phases of the project, including Mark Cummings, Nancy Davis, Liza Ewell, and Karen Hirning. Thanks are due to David Gombac, who copyedited the manuscript with exceptional skill and sensitivity. I also thank Claude Conyers, who shared his experience and enthusiasm with me throughout.

I wish especially to thank Stephen Chasteen, who has had day-to-day responsibility for shepherding the *Companion* to publication. His combination of perseverance, intelligence, diplomatic skills, and good humor have been without peer. I will miss our almost daily contact. Finally, I thank Kris Glen, who threw herself into the *Companion* with her characteristic passion and commitment. She not only sustained my efforts, but tapped her endless networks to unearth some of the finest contributors to the *Companion*.

Sadly, I must also note that the *Companion* was touched by tragedy when David Trimmer-Smith, who was to take responsibility for the international marketing of the book, perished over Lockerbie, Scotland. His infectious enthusiasm for the project and intellectual vitality were very much missed.

History provided an extraordinary backdrop to our work on the *Companion,* and a challenge to editors and authors alike, as each set of breathtaking changes in the world prompted another cycle of reflection and revision. The contemporary moment of politics gives unusual significance to the project; it offers a unique opportunity to present a timely and much-needed resource for in-depth understanding of the complex and ever-shifting terrain of world affairs. I hope the reader will share our sense of excitement and join us in this challenging effort to grasp the world of politics.

Joel Krieger
New York
October 1992

DIRECTORY OF CONTRIBUTORS

Philip Abbott, *Professor of Political Science, Wayne State University*
  Roosevelt, Franklin Delano

Olayiwola Abegunrin, *Associate Professor of International Relations, Howard University*
  African Regional Organizations

Lévon Abrahamian, *Visiting Professor of Cultural Anthropology, Institute of Archaeology and Ethnography, Academy of Sciences of Armenia, Yerevan*
  Armenia

Joan R. Acker, *Professor of Sociology, University of Oregon*
  Comparable Worth

John A. Agnew, *Professor of Geography, Maxwell School, Syracuse University*
  Geopolitics

Feroz Ahmad, *Professor of History and University Research Professor, University of Massachusetts at Boston*
  Atatürk, Kemal; Kemalism; Turkey

Claude Ake, *Director, Centre for Advanced Social Science, Port Harcourt, Nigeria*
  Development and Underdevelopment; Nigeria

Mateo Alaluf, *Professor of Labor and Social Thought, Université Libre de Bruxelles*
  Belgium; Luxembourg

Syed Hussein Alatas, *Formerly Vice-Chancellor, Universiti Malaya*
  Corruption

Glenn H. Alcalay, *Ph.D. Candidate, Department of Anthropology, Graduate Faculty, New School for Social Research*
  Pacific Islands

Herbert E. Alexander, *Professor of Political Science, University of Southern California*
  Political Action Committees

Hayward R. Alker, Jr., *Professor of Political Science, Massachusetts Institute of Technology*
  International Systems; Thucydides

Erik Allardt, *Professor of Sociology and University Chancellor, Åbo Akademi*
  Finland

Christopher S. Allen, *Associate Professor of Political Science, University of Georgia*
  Codetermination; Kohl, Helmut; Proportional Representation; Social Market Economy

Stephen E. Ambrose, *Thomas Boyd Professor of History and Director, The Eisenhower Center, University of New Orleans*
  Eisenhower, Dwight D.

Benedict R. O'Gorman Anderson, *Aaron L. Binenkorb Professor of International Studies and Director, Cornell Modern Indonesia Project, Cornell University*
  Nationalism

Lamis Andoni, *Journalist, Amman*
  Jordan

Peggy Antrobus, *Tutor/Co-ordinator, Women and Development Unit, University of the West Indies*
  Women and Development

Peter Anyang'-Nyong'o, *Associate Professor of Political Science and Secretary General, African Association of Political Science, Nairobi*
  Mau Mau Anticolonial Struggle

Cynthia J. Arnson, *Associate Director, Americas Watch, Washington, D.C.*
  Contras

Robert J. Art, *Christian A. Herter Professor of International Relations, Brandeis University*
  Bureaucratic Politics; Security

G. Pope Atkins, *Professor of Political Science, United States Naval Academy*
  Inter-American Development Bank; Latin American Regional Organizations; Monroe Doctrine; Organization of American States; Rio Treaty

Don Babai, *Associate, Center for International Affairs, Harvard University*
General Agreement on Tariffs and Trade; International Monetary Fund; World Bank

Les Back, *Birkbeck College, University of London*
Race and Racism

John H. Badgley, *Curator, John M. Echols Southeast Asia Collection, Cornell University*
Burma

Bruce M. Bagley, *Associate Dean, Graduate School of International Studies; Director, Interamerican Studies Program, Graduate School of International Studies; and Director, Drug Trafficking Task Force, North-South Center, University of Miami*
Drugs

Raymond William Baker, *Fred Greene Third Century Professor of International Relations and Director, Africa and Middle East Studies Program, Williams College; and Adjunct Professor of Political Science, American University in Cairo*
Sadat, Anwar

Sudeshna Baksi-Lahiri, *Ph.D. Candidate in Anthropology, Cornell University*
Maldives; South Asian Association for Regional Cooperation

Ivo Banac, *Professor of History, Yale University*
Tito; Yugoslavia

Lok Raj Baral, *Professor of Political Science, Tribhuvan University*
Nepal

Zoltan D. Barany, *Assistant Professor of Government, University of Texas at Austin*
Soviet–East European Relations

William J. Barber, *Andrews Professor of Economics, Wesleyan University*
Keynesianism

Zygmunt Bauman, *Professor of Sociology, Emeritus, University of Leeds*
Holocaust; Modernity

Edna G. Bay, *Associate Professor, Institute of Liberal Arts, and Executive Director, African Studies Association, Emory University*
Benin

Kenneth Baynes, *Assistant Professor of Philosophy, State University of New York at Stony Brook*
Legitimacy

David Beetham, *Professor of Politics, University of Leeds*
Weber, Max

Joel Beinin, *Associate Professor of History, Stanford University*
Nasser, Gamal Abdel; Nasserism

Mark R. Beissinger, *Associate Professor of Political Science, University of Wisconsin–Madison*
Baltic Republics; Commonwealth of Independent States; Russia

Getinet Belay, *Assistant Professor of Communication Studies, Rutgers University*
Information Society

Thomas J. Bellows, *Professor of Political Science, University of Texas at San Antonio*
Singapore

Shlomo Ben-Ami, *Ambassador of Israel to Spain*
Franco, Francisco; Spanish Civil War

Larry Berman, *Professor of Political Science, University of California, Davis*
Reagan, Ronald Wilson

Marshall Berman, *Professor of Political Science, City College, City University of New York*
Postmodernism

Serge Berstein, *University Professor and Director, Cycle Supérieur d'Histoire du XXᵉ Siècle, Institut d'Etudes Politiques de Paris*
Gaullism

M. R. Bhagavan, *Swedish Agency for Research Cooperation with Developing Countries, Stockholm*
Angola

Ashok Bhargava, *Professor of Economics and Coordinator of Research, College of Business and Economics, University of Wisconsin–Whitewater*
Bhopal Disaster

Lucien Bianco, *Director of Studies, Centre de Recherches et de Documentation sur la Chine Contemporaine, Ecole des Hautes Etudes en Sciences Sociales, Paris*
Chinese Revolution

Henry S. Bienen, *Dean, Woodrow Wilson School of Public and International Affairs, Princeton University*
Military Rule

Laura Bigman, *Director, Africans in Washington Project, Washington, D.C.*
    Cape Verde; Guinea-Bissau; São Tomé and Príncipe

Harry W. Blair, *Professor of Political Science, Bucknell University*
    Bangladesh

Heraclio Bonilla, *Coordinator, History Section, Facultad Latinoamericana de Ciencias Sociales, Quito*
    Bolívar, Simón; Haya de la Torre, Víctor Raúl; Mariátegui, José Carlos; Martí, José

John A. Booth, *Regents Professor of Political Science, University of North Texas*
    Nicaragua; Nicaraguan Revolution

Sylvia Borren, *Amsterdam*
    Gay and Lesbian Politics

Juan Botella Corral, *Professor of Political Science and Dean, Faculty of Political and Social Sciences, Universitat Autónoma de Barcelona*
    Andorra

Kenneth E. Boulding, *Distinguished Professor of Economics, Emeritus, Institute of Behavioral Science, University of Colorado at Boulder*
    Power

Steven J. Brams, *Professor of Politics, New York University*
    Game Theory

Jacqueline Anne Braveboy-Wagner, *Associate Professor of Political Science, Graduate School and University Center, City University of New York*
    English-Speaking Caribbean; Grenada; Trinidad and Tobago

George W. Breslauer, *Professor of Political Science, University of California, Berkeley*
    Khrushchev, Nikita

Judith Brett, *Lecturer, Politics, La Trobe University*
    Australia

Alan Brinkley, *Professor of History, Columbia University*
    New Deal

Festus Brotherson, Jr., *Assistant Professor of Political Science, Baldwin-Wallace College*
    Guyana

Archie Brown, *Professor of Politics, University of Oxford, and Director, Russian and East European Centre, St. Antony's College, University of Oxford*
    Gorbachev, Mikhail

Martin van Bruinessen, *Senior Lecturer, Social Science, Rijksuniversiteit Leiden and State Institute of Islamic Studies, Yogyakarta, Indonesia*
    Kurdistan

Robert Buijtenhuijs, *Director of Research, Department of Political and Historical Studies, Afrika-Studiecentrum, Leiden*
    Chad

Valerie Bunce, *Professor of Government and Director, Slavic and Eastern European Studies, Cornell University*
    Council for Mutual Economic Assistance

Charlotte Bunch, *Professor, School of Planning, and Director, Center for Women's Global Leadership, Rutgers University*
    Feminism

Stephen G. Bunker, *Professor of Sociology, University of Wisconsin–Madison*
    Amazon Development

David P. Calleo, *Dean Acheson Professor and Director, European Studies, Paul H. Nitze School of Advanced International Studies, Johns Hopkins University*
    German Reunification

Horace Campbell, *Professor of African Politics, Syracuse University*
    Cabral, Amílcar; Nyerere, Julius; Pan-Africanism; Soweto Rebellion

George W. Carey, *Professor of Government, Georgetown University*
    Separation of Powers

Clayborne Carson, *Professor of History and Editor, The Papers of Martin Luther King, Jr., Stanford University*
    African Americans

Antonio Cassese, *Professor of International Law, European University Institute, Florence*
    International Law; Self-Determination

David Chalmers, *Distinguished Service Professor of History, University of Florida*
    Ku Klux Klan

Parris H. Chang, *Professor of Political Science and Director, Center for East Asian Studies, Pennsylvania State University*
    Zhou Enlai

Margaret Chatterjee, *Professor of Philosophy, University of Delhi*
  Gandhi, Mohandas

Fantu Cheru, *Associate Professor of African and Development Studies, American University*
  Kenya

Daniel Chirot, *Professor of International Studies, Henry M. Jackson School of International Studies, University of Washington*
  Romania

Nazli Choucri, *Professor of Political Science, Massachusetts Institute of Technology*
  Environmentalism

Christopher Clapham, *Professor and Chair, Department of Politics and International Relations, University of Lancaster*
  One-Party System; Patron-Client Politics

James W. Clarke, *Professor of Political Science, University of Arizona*
  Assassination

Gregory Cleva, *Arlington, Va.*
  Kissinger, Henry

Helena Cobban, *Director of Research and Staff Coordinator, Initiative for Peace and Cooperation in the Middle East, Search for Common Ground, Washington, D.C.*
  Arafat, Yasir

David Collier, *Professor of Political Science and Chair, Department of Political Science, University of California, Berkeley*
  Bureaucratic Authoritarianism

Michael L. Conniff, *Professor of History, Auburn University*
  Vargas, Getúlio

Allan D. Cooper, *Associate Professor of Political Science, St. Augustine's College*
  Namibia

Michael Coppedge, *Assistant Professor, Latin American Studies Program, Paul H. Nitze School of Advanced International Studies, Johns Hopkins University*
  Venezuela

Stephen Cornell, *Associate Professor of Sociology, University of California, San Diego*
  Native Americans

Margaret E. Crahan, *Henry R. Luce Professor of Religion, Power and Political Process, Occidental College*
  Arias, Oscar

Barbara B. Crane, *International Population Fellow, University of Michigan*
  Population Policy

Robert Cribb, *Lecturer, Modern Southeast Asian History, University of Queensland*
  Timor

Donald K. Crone, *Dean of Faculty and Professor of International Relations, Scripps College*
  Association of Southeast Asian Nations; Southeast Asia Treaty Organization

Selwyn R. Cudjoe, *Professor of Africana Studies, Wellesley College*
  James, C. L. R.

Bruce Cumings, *Harris Professor of International Studies, Northwestern University*
  Korea, Democratic People's Republic of; Korean War

Michael Curtis, *Professor of Political Science, Rutgers University*
  Antisemitism

Robert A. Dahl, *Sterling Professor of Political Science, Emeritus, Yale University*
  Pluralism

Richard Dale, *Associate Professor of Political Science, Southern Illinois University at Carbondale*
  BLS States

Dana G. Dalrymple, *Research Adviser, International Agricultural Research Center Staff, Office of Agriculture, Bureau for Research and Development, Agency for International Development, Washington, D.C.*
  Green Revolution

Russell J. Dalton, *Professor of Political Science, University of California, Irvine*
  New Social Movements

Robert V. Daniels, *Professor of History, Emeritus, University of Vermont*
  Stalin, Joseph

Roger H. Davidson, *Professor of Government and Politics, University of Maryland at College Park*
  Congress, U.S.

Thomas M. Davies, Jr., *Professor of History and Director, Center for Latin American Studies, San Diego State University*
  Guevara, Ernesto

Richard B. Day, *Professor of Political Science, University of Toronto*
  Trotsky, Lev

Samuel Decalo, *Professor of African Politics, University of Natal*
Central African Republic; Togo

Mark W. DeLancey, *Professor of Political Science, University of South Carolina*
Cameroon

Lual Acuek Deng, *The World Bank, Washington, D.C.*
African Development Bank

Jacques Depelchin, *Associate Professor of African Studies, Universidade Eduardo Mondlane, and Visiting Associate Professor, University of California, Berkeley*
Mozambique

James Der Derian, *Associate Professor of Political Science, University of Massachusetts at Amherst*
Diplomacy

Meghnad Desai, *Professor of Economics, London School of Economics and Political Science*
Capitalism

Edward M. Dew, *Professor of Politics and Director, International Relations Program, Fairfield University*
Suriname

Yoram Dinstein, *Yanowicz Professor of Human Rights and President, Tel Aviv University; Member, Institute of International Law, Geneva*
Nuremberg Trials; War Crimes; War, Rules of

Lowell Dittmer, *Professor of Political Science, University of California, Berkeley*
Deng Xiaoping

George W. Downs, *Class of 1942 Professor of Peace and War, Department of Politics, and Woodrow Wilson School of Public and International Affairs, Princeton University*
Arms Race

Margaret P. Doxey, *Professor of Political Studies, Trent University*
Commonwealth; Treaty

Paul W. Drake, *Institute of the Americas Professor of Inter-American Affairs, University of California, San Diego*
Allende, Salvador; Chile; Pinochet, Augusto

Alasdair Drysdale, *Associate Professor of Geography, University of New Hampshire*
Syria

Peter D. Drysdale, *Professor of Economics, Research School of Pacific Studies, and Executive Director, Australia-Japan Research Centre, Australian National University*
Pacific Region

William J. Duiker, *Professor of East Asian History, Pennsylvania State University*
Ho Chi Minh

Alex Dupuy, *Professor of Sociology, Wesleyan University*
Haiti

Ronald S. Edari, *Associate Professor of Sociology, University of Wisconsin–Milwaukee*
Urbanization

S. N. Eisenstadt, *Rose Isaacs Professor of Sociology, Hebrew University of Jerusalem*
Modernization

Zillah Eisenstein, *Professor of Politics, Ithaca College*
Feminist Theory

Samuel J. Eldersveld, *Professor of Political Science, Emeritus, University of Michigan*
Elites

Charlotte Elton, *Research Coordinator, Centro de Estudios y Acción Social Panameño, Panama*
Panama

Donald K. Emmerson, *Professor of Political Science, University of Wisconsin–Madison*
Indonesia

Cynthia H. Enloe, *Professor of Government, Clark University*
Gender and Politics

Steven P. Erie, *Associate Professor of Political Science, University of California, San Diego*
Political Machine

Peter B. Evans, *Professor of Sociology, University of California, Berkeley*
Dependency

Richard R. Fagen, *Professor of Political Science, Stanford University*
Cuban Revolution

Richard Falk, *Albert G. Milbank Professor of International Law and Practice, Princeton University*
Hiroshima; International Court of Justice; Rights; Sovereignty

Richard E. Feinberg, *President, Inter-American Dialogue, Washington, D.C.*
Foreign Aid

M. Patricia Fernández Kelly, *Research Scientist and Associate Professor of Sociology, Institute for Policy Studies, Johns Hopkins University*
Maquiladoras

Kenneth Finegold, *Assistant Professor of Political Science, Rutgers University*
New Deal Coalition; Progressive Movement, U.S.

E. V. K. FitzGerald, *Director of Financial Studies, International Development Centre, University of Oxford*
Economic Commission for Latin America and the Caribbean

Michael Fleet, *Associate Professor of Political Science, Marquette University*
Christian Democracy

David P. Forsythe, *Professor of Political Science, University of Nebraska–Lincoln*
Conference on Security and Cooperation in Europe; Helsinki Accords

Jeffry A. Frieden, *Professor of Political Science, University of California, Los Angeles*
International Debt

Jonathan Friedland, *Finance Correspondent, Far Eastern Economic Review, Hong Kong*
Asian Development Bank; Economic and Social Commission for Asia and the Pacific

Haruhiro Fukui, *Professor of Political Science, University of California, Santa Barbara*
Hirohito; Japan

Johan Galtung, *Professor of Peace Studies, University of Hawaii*
Peace

Eduardo A. Gamarra, *Associate Professor of Political Science, Florida International University*
Bolivia

F. Chris Garcia, *Professor of Political Science, University of New Mexico*
Hispanic Americans

David E. Gardinier, *Professor of History, Marquette University*
Gabon

Raymond L. Garthoff, *Senior Fellow, Foreign Policy Studies, Brookings Institution, Washington, D.C.*
Warsaw Treaty Organization

Joyce Gelb, *Professor of Political Science and Director, Rosenberg/Humphrey Program in Public Policy, City College of New York and Graduate School and University Center, City University of New York*
Gender Gap

Stephen George, *Reader, Politics, University of Sheffield*
European Community; European Free Trade Association; European Parliament; Rome, Treaty of

Ashraf Ghani, *Adjunct Associate Professor of Anthropology, Johns Hopkins University*
Soviet-Afghanistan War

David N. Gibbs, *Assistant Professor of Political Science, University of Arizona*
Mauritania

Hashim T. Gibrill, *Associate Professor of Political Science, Clark Atlanta University*
Economic Commission for Africa; South-South Cooperation

Dennis Gilbert, *Professor of Sociology, Hamilton College*
Sandinistas

Martin Gilbert, *London*
Churchill, Winston

Stephen Gill, *Associate Professor of Political Science, York University*
Group of 7; Hegemony; Trilateral Commission

Charles Guy Gillespie, *Assistant Professor of Political Science, University of Wisconsin–Madison (deceased)*
Paraguay; Uruguay

Michael Gilsenan, *Khalid bin Abdullah al Saud Professor for the Study of the Contemporary Arab World, Magdalen College, University of Oxford*
Islam; Jihad

Benjamin Ginsberg, *David Bernstein Professor of Political Science and Director, Center for Governmental Studies, Johns Hopkins University*
Elections and Voting Behavior

Todd Gitlin, *Professor of Sociology, University of California, Berkeley*
New Left

Betty Glad, *Professor, Department of Government and International Studies, University of South Carolina*
Carter, Jimmy

Kristin Booth Glen, *Justice, New York State Supreme Court*
  Roe v. Wade

Michael J. Glennon, *Professor of Law, School of Law, University of California, Davis*
  War Powers Resolution

Helmut Goerlich, *Professor of Public Law, Bergische Universität–Gesamthochschule Wuppertal*
  European Court of Justice

Thomas B. Gold, *Associate Professor of Sociology and Chair, Center for Chinese Studies, University of California, Berkeley*
  Taiwan

Jack A. Goldstone, *Professor of Sociology, University of California, Davis*
  Revolution

Pablo Gonzáles Casanova, *Director, Center for Interdisciplinary Research in the Humanities, Universidad Nacional Autónoma de México*
  Imperialism

Richard Gordon, *Associate Professor of Politics, University of California, Santa Cruz*
  Fordism; Postindustrial Society

Lewis L. Gould, *Eugene C. Barker Centennial Professor in American History, University of Texas at Austin*
  Johnson, Lyndon Baines

Peter A. Gourevitch, *Dean, Graduate School of International Relations and Pacific Studies, University of California, San Diego*
  Political Economy

Doris A. Graber, *Professor of Political Science, University of Illinois at Chicago*
  Psychology and Politics

Norman A. Graebner, *Randolph P. Compton Professor of History and Public Affairs, Emeritus, University of Virginia*
  Isolationism

Sarah Graham-Brown, *Co-ordinator, Gulf Information Project, British Refugee Council, London*
  Palestine

Deborah A. Green, *Political Director, Rainbow Lobby, Inc., Washington, D.C.*
  Zaire

Beverly Grier, *Assistant Professor of Government and International Relations, Clark University*
  Niger

Merilee S. Grindle, *Research Associate, Harvard Institute for International Development, Harvard University*
  Rural Development

Bertram Gross, *Distinguished Professor Emeritus, City University of New York, and Visiting Professor of World Classics, Saint Mary's College of California*
  Planning

Jan T. Gross, *Professor of Politics, New York University*
  Central Europe

Isebill V. Gruhn, *Professor of Politics, University of California, Santa Cruz*
  Technology Transfer

A. Tom Grunfeld, *Associate Professor of History, Empire State College, State University of New York*
  Tibet

Richard Gunther, *Professor of Political Science, Ohio State University*
  Spain

Ted Robert Gurr, *Professor of Government and Politics and Distinguished Scholar, Center for International Development and Conflict Management, University of Maryland at College Park*
  Political Violence

Stephan Haggard, *Professor, Graduate School of International Relations and Pacific Studies, University of California, San Diego*
  Export-Led Growth; Import-Substitution Industrialization; Newly Industrializing Economies

John A. Hall, *Professor of Sociology, McGill University*
  Liberalism; State

Kermit L. Hall, *Dean, Henry Kendall College of Arts and Sciences, and Professor of History and Law, University of Tulsa*
  Supreme Court of the United States

Peter A. Hall, *Professor of Government, Harvard University*
  Monetarism

Fred Halliday, *Professor of International Relations, London School of Economics and Political Science*
  Cold War; Iranian Revolution; Terrorism; Yemen

Nora Hamilton, *Associate Professor of Political Science, University of Southern California*
  Cárdenas, Lázaro

Phillip Hansen, *Associate Professor of Political Science, University of Regina*
Arendt, Hannah

B. E. Harrell-Bond, *Director, Refugee Studies Programme, University of Oxford*
Refugees

Jonathan Hartlyn, *Associate Professor of Political Science, University of North Carolina at Chapel Hill*
Colombia; Dominican Republic

Fareed Mohamed Ahmed Hassan, *Assistant Professor of Econometrics, University of Khartoum, and Sabbatical Faculty Scholar, Department of Economics, University of Connecticut*
Sudan

Fred M. Hayward, *Consultant, International Initiatives, American Council on Education, Washington, D.C.*
Sierra Leone

Michael Hechter, *Professor of Sociology, University of Arizona*
Internal Colonialism; Peripheral Nationalism

J. Bryan Hehir, *Research Professor of Ethics and International Politics, Edmund A. Walsh School of Foreign Service, Georgetown University*
Roman Catholic Church

David Held, *Professor of Politics and Sociology, The Open University*
Democracy

Suzette Hemberger, *Assistant Professor of Political Science, Johns Hopkins University*
Constitution

Phillip G. Henderson, *Associate Professor of Political Science, Catholic University of America*
Bush, George Herbert Walker

Charles F. Hermann, *Director, Mershon Center, and Professor of Political Science, Ohio State University*
Crisis

Carolina G. Hernandez, *Center for Integrative and Development Studies, University of the Philippines*
Aquino, Corazon; Marcos, Ferdinand; Philippines

Danièle Hervieu-Léger, *Director of Research, Groupe de Sociologie des Religions, Centre National de la Recherche Scientifique, Paris*
John Paul II; Vatican II

Christopher Hill, *Montague Burton Professor of International Relations, London School of Economics and Political Science*
Foreign Policy

Enid Hill, *Professor of Political Science, American University in Cairo*
Ibn-Khaldūn

Ronald J. Hill, *Professor of Soviet Government, University of Dublin Trinity College*
Soviet Union

Scott Hill, *Ph.D. Candidate, Political Science, University of California, Davis*
Reagan, Ronald Wilson

Stanley Hoffmann, *Chair, Center for European Studies, and Douglas Dillon Professor of the Civilization of France, Harvard University*
Gaulle, Charles de

Kalevi J. Holsti, *Professor of Political Science, University of British Columbia*
League of Nations

Eric Hooglund, *Editor, Middle East Journal, Washington, D.C.*
Iran; Khomeini, Ruhollah

Michael Hout, *Professor of Sociology and Director, Survey Research Center, University of California, Berkeley*
Social Mobility

Evelyne Huber, *Morehead Alumni Distinguished Professor in Latin American Politics, University of North Carolina at Chapel Hill*
Jamaica

Shirley Hune, *Associate Dean, Graduate Programs, University of California, Los Angeles*
Nonaligned Movement

Richard M. Hunt, *Senior Lecturer, Social Studies, and University Marshal, Harvard University*
Hitler, Adolf

Ronald Inglehart, *Professor of Political Science and Program Director, Center for Political Studies, Institute for Social Research, University of Michigan*
Postmaterialism

Anita Isaacs, *Assistant Professor of Political Science, Haverford College*
Ecuador

Keith Jackson, *Professor of Political Science, University of Canterbury*
ANZUS Treaty; New Zealand

Ayesha Jalal, *Associate Professor of History, Columbia University*
Pakistan

Martín Sánchez Jankowski, *Associate Professor of Sociology, University of California, Berkeley*
Gangs

Barbara Jenkins, *Assistant Professor of Political Science, Carleton University*
Multinational Corporations

Jane Jenson, *Professor of Political Science, Carleton University*
Canada; Trudeau, Pierre

Bruce W. Jentleson, *Director, UC Davis Washington Center, and Associate Professor of Political Science, University of California, Davis*
Domino Theory

Dong Youl Jeong, *Assistant Professor of Library and Information Science, Ewha Woman's University*
Information Society

Bob Jessop, *Professor of Sociology and Head, Department of Sociology, University of Lancaster*
Thatcherism

George Joffé, *Vice-Director, Geo-Politics and International Boundaries Centre, School of Oriental and African Studies, University of London*
Libya; Monarchy; Qaddafi, Muammar

Susanne Jonas, *Lecturer, Latin American Studies, University of California, Santa Cruz*
Guatemala

William A. Joseph, *Associate Professor of Political Science, Wellesley College*
China; Cultural Revolution

Samba Ka, *Assistant Professor of History, Université Cheikh Anta Diop de Dakar, and Ph.D. Candidate, Paul H. Nitze School of Advanced International Studies, Johns Hopkins University*
Senegal

Stephen Kalberg, *Assistant Professor of Sociology, Boston University*
Convergence Thesis

Donna Rich Kaplowitz, *Ph.D. Candidate, Paul H. Nitze School of Advanced International Studies, Johns Hopkins University*
Cuba

Robert Kaufman, *Professor of Political Science, Rutgers University*
Mexico

Dennis Kavanagh, *Professor of Politics, University of Nottingham*
Thatcher, Margaret

John T. S. Keeler, *Associate Professor of Political Science, University of Washington*
Reform

Edmond J. Keller, *Professor of Political Science and Director, Center for African Studies, University of California, Los Angeles*
Afro-Marxism

Robert O. Keohane, *Stanfield Professor of International Peace, Harvard University*
Reciprocity; Regime

Mark Kesselman, *Professor of Political Science, Columbia University*
Mitterrand, François

Moncef M. Khaddar, *Associate Professor of Political Science, Faculté de Droit et des Sciences Politiques de Tunis*
Tunisia

Rashid I. Khalidi, *Associate Professor of Modern Middle Eastern History and Director, Center for Middle Eastern Studies, University of Chicago*
Intifada; Resolution 242

Baruch Kimmerling, *Professor of Sociology of Politics, Hebrew University of Jerusalem*
Israel

Desmond King, *Official Fellow in Politics, St. John's College, University of Oxford*
New Right; Right

Richard S. Kirkendall, *The Scott and Dorothy Bullitt Professor of American History, University of Washington*
Truman, Harry S.

Michael T. Klare, *Five College Associate Professor of Peace and World Security Studies, Hampshire College*
Militarism

Amy Knight, *Senior Research Specialist, Federal Research Division, Library of Congress, Washington, D.C.*
KGB

Jack Knight, *Assistant Professor of Political Science, Washington University*
Public Good

Atul Kohli, *Professor of Politics and International Affairs, Woodrow Wilson School of Public and International Affairs, Princeton University*
Gandhi, Indira; India; Nehru, Jawaharlal

Walter S. G. Kohn, *Professor of Political Science, Emeritus, Illinois State University*
Liechtenstein; Switzerland

George Kolankiewicz, *Co-ordinator, Economic and Social Research Council, East-West Research Programme, University of Essex*
Poland; Wałęsa, Lech

E. W. Kolinsky, *Professor of Modern German Studies, University of Keele*
Green Parties

Bennett Kovrig, *Professor of Political Science, Trinity College, University of Toronto*
Hungary

Stephen D. Krasner, *Graham H. Stuart Professor of International Relations, Stanford University*
International Political Economy

Joel Krieger, *Professor of Political Science and Chair, Department of Political Science, Wellesley College*
Britain

Jacek Kugler, *Elizabeth Rosencranz Professor of International Relations, Center for Politics and Policy, Claremont Graduate School*
War

Charles Kupchan, *Assistant Professor of Politics, Princeton University*
Strategy; Superpower

James Kurth, *Professor of Political Science, Swarthmore College*
Military-Industrial Complex

Walter LaFeber, *Noll Professor of American History, Cornell University*
Truman Doctrine

Anthony Lake, *Five College Professor in International Relations, Mount Holyoke College*
Vietnam War

David A. Lake, *Professor of Political Science and Research Director, Institute on Global Conflict and Cooperation, University of California, San Diego*
Balance of Power; Realism

Carol Lancaster, *African Studies, Edmund A. Walsh School of Foreign Service, Georgetown University*
Paris Club

Joanne Landy, *Executive Director, Campaign for Peace and Democracy, New York*
Nineteen Eighty-Nine

Emily Lau, *Hong Kong*
Hong Kong; Macao

Fred H. Lawson, *Associate Professor of Government, Mills College*
Arab League; Gulf States; Kuwait

Kay Lawson, *Professor of Political Science and International Relations, San Francisco State University*
Political Parties and Party Competition

Margaret C. Lee, *Associate Professor of Political Science, Tennessee Technological University*
Southern African Development Co-ordination Conference

Christiane Lemke, *Lecturer, Political Science, Freie Universität Berlin*
German Democratic Republic

Ann M. Lesch, *Professor of Political Science and Associate Director, Center for Arab and Islamic Studies, Villanova University*
Palestine Liberation Organization

Steven I. Levine, *Senior Research Associate, Boulder Run Research, Hillsborough, N.C.*
Sino-American Relations

David Levering Lewis, *Martin Luther King, Jr., Professor of History, Rutgers University*
Du Bois, W. E. B.

Margot Light, *Senior Lecturer, Department of International Relations, London School of Economics and Political Science*
Soviet Foreign Policy

Lars T. Lih, *Assistant Professor of Political Science, Wellesley College*
Bukharin, Nikolai; New Economic Policy, U.S.S.R.; Stalinism; Yeltsin, Boris

Arend Lijphart, *Professor of Political Science, University of California, San Diego*
Consociational Democracy

Juan J. Linz, *Sterling Professor of Political and Social Science, Yale University*
Authoritarianism

Seymour Martin Lipset, *Virginia E. Hazel and John T. Hazel, Jr., Professor of Public Policy, George Mason University, and Senior Fellow, Hoover Institution on War, Revolution and Peace, Stanford University*
United States

Charles Lipson, *Associate Professor of Political Science; Chair, Committee on International Relations; and Director, Program on International Politics, Economics, and Security, University of Chicago*
Finance, International; Nationalization

Robert S. Litwak, *Director of International Studies, Woodrow Wilson International Center for Scholars, Washington, D.C.*
Containment; Détente

Zachary Lockman, *Associate Professor of History, Harvard University*
Balfour Declaration; Ben-Gurion, David; Zionism

Tom Lodge, *Associate Professor of Political Studies, University of the Witwatersrand, Johannesburg*
Mandela, Nelson; Sharpeville Massacre

John M. Logsdon, *Director, Space Policy Institute, George Washington University*
Space

John Logue, *Professor of Political Science, Kent State University*
Denmark

Joseph L. Love, *Professor of History, University of Illinois at Urbana-Champaign*
Prebisch, Raúl

Brian Loveman, *Professor of Political Science, San Diego State University*
Guerrilla Warfare; Guevara, Ernesto

S. Neil MacFarlane, *Associate Professor and Director, Center for Russian and East European Studies, University of Virginia*
National Liberation Movements

Henri Madelin, *Associate Professor of Political Science, Institut d'Etudes Politiques de Paris*
Vatican City State

A. B. M. Mafeje, *Department of Sociology, American University in Cairo*
Tribalism

Victor V. Magagna, *Associate Professor of Political Science, University of California, San Diego*
Peasants

Bernard Magubane, *Professor of Anthropology, University of Connecticut*
African National Congress; Apartheid; South Africa

John Maher, *Lecturer, Spanish Studies, University of Salford*
González, Felipe

Ku-Ntima Makidi, *Director of Political Science and History Degree Programs and Associate Professor of Political Science and International Affairs, Morris Brown College*
Congo

Chibli Mallat, *Lecturer, Islamic Law, School of Oriental and African Studies, University of Longon*
Sharīʿa

Patrick Manning, *Professor of History and African-American Studies, Northeastern University*
Francophone Africa

Jane J. Mansbridge, *Jane W. Long Professor of the Arts and Sciences, Northwestern University*
Equal Rights Amendment

Otwin Marenin, *Associate Professor of Criminal Justice, Washington State University*
Biafra

John Markakis, *Professor of African Studies, University of Crete*
Ethiopia

Andrei S. Markovits, *Professor of Political Science and Chair, Board of Studies in Politics, University of California, Santa Cruz*
Austria; Germany, Federal Republic of; Ostpolitik; Socialist International

Guy Martin, *Associate Professor of International Service, School of International Service, American University*
Burkina Faso; Lomé Convention; Mali

J. Paul Martin, *Executive Director, Center for the Study of Human Rights, Columbia University*
Amnesty International

Lisa L. Martin, *Associate Professor of Government, Harvard University*
International Cooperation; Sanctions

Michael Mastanduno, *Associate Professor of Political Science, Dartmouth College*
Coordinating Committee

James Mayall, *Professor of International Relations and Chair, Centre for International Studies, London School of Economics and Political Science*
Mercantilism

David Mayers, *Associate Professor of History and Political Science, Boston University*
Kennan, George

Robert J. McIntyre, *Associate Professor of Economics, Smith College*
Bulgaria

Timothy J. McKeown, *Associate Professor of Political Science, University of North Carolina at Chapel Hill*
Protection

David McLellan, *Professor of Political Theory, University of Kent at Canterbury*
Acheson, Dean; Communism; Marx, Karl

Kenneth McRoberts, *Professor of Political Science and Director, Robarts Centre for Canadian Studies, York University*
Quebec

Zhores A. Medvedev, *National Institute for Medical Research, Medical Research Council, London*
Chernobyl Nuclear Accident

Pratap Mehta, *Assistant Professor of Government, Harvard University*
Gandhi, Indira; India; Nehru, Jawaharlal

Maurice Meisner, *Harvey Goldberg Professor of History, University of Wisconsin–Madison*
Mao Zedong

Berhanu Mengistu, *Associate Professor and Chair, Department of Urban Studies and Public Administration, Old Dominion University*
Parastatals

Anthony M. Messina, *Associate Professor of Political Science, Tufts University*
Foreign Workers

Alfred G. Meyer, *Professor of Political Science, Emeritus, University of Michigan*
Leninism; Totalitarianism

Michael L. Mezey, *Professor of Political Science and Associate Dean, College of Liberal Arts and Sciences, DePaul University*
Legislature

William Minter, *Scholar-in-Residence, Comparative and Regional Studies, School of International Service, American University*
Angolan Conflict

Bruce Miroff, *Associate Professor of Political Science, State University of New York at Albany*
Kennedy, John Fitzgerald

Timothy Mitchell, *Associate Professor of Politics, New York University*
Egypt

William C. Mitchell, *Professor of Political Science, University of Oregon*
Public Choice Theory

James H. Mittelman, *Professor of International Relations and Chair, Department of Comparative and Regional Studies, School of International Service, American University*
Third World

Lars Mjøset, *Research Director, Comparative Studies, Institute for Samfunns Forskning, Oslo*
Iceland; Norway; Scandinavia

Tommie Sue Montgomery, *Formerly Associate Professor of Latin American Studies, Agnes Scott College*
El Salvador

Patrick M. Morgan, *Tierney Professor of Peace Research, University of California, Irvine*
Arms Control; Disarmament

Aldon Morris, *Professor of Sociology; Chair, Department of Sociology; and Professor, Center for Urban Affairs and Policy Research, Northwestern University*
Civil Rights Movement

Robert A. Mortimer, *Professor of Political Science, Haverford College*
Algeria; Algerian War of Independence

Chantal Mouffe, *Director, Citizenship and Modern Democracy Program, Collège International de Philosophie*
Citizenship

Gary Mucciaroni, *Assistant Professor of Government, College of William and Mary in Virginia*
Political Business Cycle; Watergate

Craig N. Murphy, *Associate Professor of Political Science, Wellesley College*
Council of Europe; Gramsci, Antonio; International Labor Organization; Organization for Economic Co-operation and Development; San Marino

Walusako A. Mwalilino, *Freelance Journalist and former Associate Officer, Department of Political and General Assembly Affairs, United Nations*
Malawi

Musifiky Mwanasali, *Lecturer, African Politics, Lake Forest College*
Burundi; Congo Crisis; Lumumba, Patrice

Richard P. Nathan, *Distinguished Professor and Provost, Nelson A. Rockefeller College of Public Affairs and Policy, State University of New York at Albany*
Federalism

Marysa Navarro-Aranguren, *Professor of History, Dartmouth College*
  Perón, María Eva Duarte de

Clark D. Neher, *Professor of Political Science, Northern Illinois University*
  Thailand

Aryeh Neier, *Executive Director, Human Rights Watch, New York*
  Human Rights

Joan M. Nelson, *Senior Associate, Overseas Development Council, Washington, D.C.*
  Political Participation

Michael Nelson, *Professor of Political Science, Rhodes College*
  Presidency, U.S.

Catharine Newbury, *Associate Professor of Political Science and African Studies, University of North Carolina at Chapel Hill*
  Rwanda

August H. Nimtz, Jr., *Associate Professor of Political Science, University of Minnesota*
  Marxism

Okwudiba Nnoli, *Professor of Political Science and Co-ordinator General, Pan-African Centre for Research on Peace, Development and Human Rights, University of Nigeria*
  Ethnicity

Emile Noël, *President, European University Institute, Florence*
  Monnet, Jean

Philip Norton, *Professor of Government, University of Hull*
  Cabinet Government; Constitutional Monarchy; Parliamentary Democracy; Parliamentary Sovereignty

Sulayman S. Nyang, *Professor and Chair, African Studies and Research Program, Howard University*
  Gambia

Georges Nzongola-Ntalaja, *Professor of African Studies, Howard University*
  Zaire

Rowena Olegario, *Ph.D. Candidate, Department of History, Harvard University*
  Malcolm X

Amii Omara-Otunnu, *Associate Professor of History and Director, Center for Contemporary African Studies, University of Connecticut*
  Uganda

Akwasi P. Osei, *Assistant Professor of Black Studies and Political Science, The College of Wooster*
  Ghana; Nkrumah, Kwame

David Ost, *Assistant Professor of Political Science, Hobart and William Smith Colleges*
  Solidarity

René Otayek, *Chargé de Recherche au Centre National de la Recherche Scientifique, Centre d'Etude d'Afriqué Noire, Institut d'Etudes Politiques de Bordeaux*
  Djibouti

Roger Owen, *Lecturer, Recent Economic History of the Middle East, and Director, Middle East Center, St. Antony's College, University of Oxford*
  Suez Crisis

Robert Paarlberg, *Professor of Political Science, Wellesley College*
  Food Politics

David Scott Palmer, *Professor of International Relations and Political Science and Director, Latin American Studies Program, Boston University*
  Peru

Nicholas C. Pano, *Professor of History and Associate Dean, College of Arts and Sciences, Western Illinois University*
  Albania; Balkanization; Balkans

Peter Paret, *Andrew W. Mellon Professor in the Humanities, School of Historical Studies, Institute for Advanced Study, Princeton*
  Clausewitz, Carl von

Jane L. Parpart, *Professor of History, Women's Studies, and International Development Studies, Dalhousie University*
  Zambia

Gianfranco Pasquino, *Professor of Political Science, Università degli Studi, Bologna*
  Historic Compromise; Italy; Secularization

Robert A. Pastor, *Director, Latin American and Caribbean Program, Carter Center, and Professor of Political Science, Emory University*
  Panama Canal Treaty

James A. Paul, *Independent Scholar and Consultant, Middle East and International Affairs, New York*
  Gulf War; Lebanon; Middle East; Morocco; Tunisia

J. Roland Pennock, *Richter Professor of Political Science, Emeritus, Swarthmore College*
  Equality and Inequality

Don Peretz, *Professor of Political Science, State University of New York at Binghamton*
  Arab-Israeli Conflict

B. Marie Perinbam, *Associate Professor of History, University of Maryland at College Park*
  Fanon, Frantz

Rosalind Pollack Petchesky, *Professor of Political Science, Hunter College, City University of New York*
  Reproductive Politics

M. J. Peterson, *Associate Professor of Political Science, University of Massachusetts at Amherst*
  Antarctica; Law of the Sea

Karen Pfeifer, *Associate Professor of Economics, Smith College*
  Infitah

Gail Pheterson, *Independent Scholar, Paris*
  Prostitution

Stuart D. B. Picken, *Professor, Division of Humanities, International Christian University*
  Shinto

Adamantia Pollis, *Professor of Political Science, Graduate Faculty, New School for Social Research*
  Cyprus; Greece

Jonas Pontusson, *Associate Professor of Government, Cornell University*
  Sweden

Mark Poster, *Professor of History, University of California, Irvine*
  Foucault, Michel

Alex Pravda, *St. Antony's College, University of Oxford*
  Prague Spring

Victor Prescott, *Professor of Geography, University of Melbourne*
  Boundary Disputes

Roy L. Prosterman, *John and Marguerite Walker Corbally Professor in Public Service and Professor of Law, University of Washington*
  Land Reform

Adam Przeworski, *Martin A. Ryerson Distinguished Service Professor, University of Chicago*
  Socialism and Social Democracy

Louis Putterman, *Professor of Economics, Brown University*
  Collectivization

Lucian W. Pye, *Ford Professor of Political Science, Massachusetts Institute of Technology*
  Political Culture

George H. Quester, *Professor of Government and Politics, University of Maryland at College Park*
  American Foreign Policy

Paul J. Quirk, *Associate Professor, Department of Political Science and Institute of Government and Public Affairs, University of Illinois at Urbana-Champaign*
  Deregulation

Jeremy A. Rabkin, *Associate Professor of Government, Cornell University*
  Conservatism

John Ranelagh, *Cambridge*
  Central Intelligence Agency

Arati Rao, *Assistant Professor of Political Science, Wellesley College*
  Patriarchy

Thomas C. Reeves, *Professor of History, University of Wisconsin–Parkside*
  McCarthyism

Robert B. Reich, *U.S. Secretary of Labor*
  Deindustrialization

Mitchell Reiss, *Guest Scholar, Woodrow Wilson International Center for Scholars, Washington, D.C.*
  Nonproliferation, Nuclear

Robert B. Marks Ridinger, *Associate Professor, University Libraries, Northern Illinois University*
  Peace Corps

T. H. Rigby, *Professor of Political Science, Emeritus, and University Fellow, Australian National University*
  Communist Party of the Soviet Union

Mitchell S. Ritchie, *College of Law, University of Florida*
  Supreme Court of the United States

Adam Roberts, *Montague Burton Professor of International Relations, University of Oxford; Fellow, Balliol College, University of Oxford; Fellow, British Academy*
  Grotius, Hugo; United Nations

Richard A. H. Robinson, *Reader, Iberian History, University of Birmingham*
  Portugal

Thomas R. Rochon, *Associate Professor of Politics, Center for Politics and Policy, Claremont Graduate School*
  Peace Movement

Luis G. Rodríguez, *Professor of Political and Social Sciences, Cayey University College, University of Puerto Rico*
  Puerto Rico

Riordan Roett, *Sarita and Don Johnston Professor and Director, Latin American Studies Program, Paul H. Nitze School of Advanced International Studies, Johns Hopkins University*
  Brazil

John D. Rogers, *Visiting Research Fellow, Center of South Asian and Indian Ocean Studies, Tufts University*
  Sri Lanka

Leo E. Rose, *Professor of Political Science, University of California, Berkeley, retired, and Editor, Asian Survey*
  Bhutan

Richard Rosecrance, *Professor of Political Science and Director, Center for International Relations, University of California, Los Angeles*
  Interdependence

James N. Rosenau, *University Professor of International Affairs, George Washington University*
  International Relations

Mark B. Rosenberg, *Professor of Political Science and Director, Latin American and Caribbean Center, Florida International University*
  Honduras

George Ross, *Morris Hillquit Professor in Labor and Social Thought, Brandeis University, and Senior Associate, Center for European Studies, Harvard University*
  Eurocommunism; France; Labor Movement; May 1968; Monaco

Donald Rothchild, *Professor of Political Science, University of California, Davis*
  Secessionist Movements

Robert L. Rothstein, *Harvey Picker Distinguished Professor of International Relations, Colgate University*
  Group of 77; New International Economic Order; North-South Relations; United Nations Conference on Trade and Development

Joshua Rubenstein, *Northeast Regional Director, Amnesty International USA, Cambridge, Mass.*
  Solzhenitsyn, Aleksandr; Soviet Dissent

Barnett R. Rubin, *Associate Professor of Political Science and Director, Center for the Study of Central Asia, Columbia University*
  Afghanistan

Bruce Russett, *Dean Acheson Professor of International Relations and Political Science, Yale University*
  Deterrence; Security Dilemma

Peter Rutland, *Professor of Political Science, Wesleyan University*
  Command Economy

Tony Saich, *Professor of the Politics and Administration of Contemporary China, Sinologisch Instituut, Rijksuniversiteit te Leiden*
  Chinese Communist Party; Tiananmen Square

Ghassan Salame, *Director of Studies, Centre National de la Recherche Scientifique, Université de Paris I (Panthéon-Sorbonne)*
  Arab Nationalism; Saudi Arabia

Ahmed I. Samatar, *Associate Professor of Government, St. Lawrence University*
  Somalia

Joel Samoff, *Visiting Scholar, Center for African Studies, Stanford University*
  Tanzania

Alan J. K. Sanders, *Lecturer, Mongolian Studies, School of Oriental and African Studies, University of London*
  Mongolia

Deborah A. Sanders, *Associate Professor of African/Afro-American Studies and Director, African/Afro-American Studies Program, Jersey City State College*
  Southern Africa; Zimbabwe

Ellis Sandoz, *Professor of Political Science and Director, Eric Voegelin Institute, Louisiana State University*
  Bill of Rights

S. N. Sangmpam, *Assistant Professor of Political Science and African American Studies, Syracuse University*
  Shaba Wars

John S. Saul, *Professor of Social Science, Atkinson College, York University, and Professor of Political Science, Graduate Faculty, York University*
  African Socialism

Martin A. Schain, *Professor of Politics and Associate Director, Center for European Studies, New York University*
  Poujadism

Jorge Reina Schement, *Associate Professor of Communication, Information, and Hispanic Studies, Rutgers University*
Information Society

Thomas Schierholz, *Paul H. Nitze School of Advanced International Studies, Johns Hopkins University*
Brazil

Jennifer Schirmer, *Assistant Professor of Women's Studies, Wellesley College*
Torture

Kay Lehman Schlozman, *Professor of Political Science, Boston College*
Interest Groups; Public Interest Movement

Elizabeth S. Schmidt, *Assistant Professor of History, Loyola College*
Disinvestment; Guinea

Philippe C. Schmitter, *Professor of Political Science, Stanford University*
Comparative Politics; Corporatism

Brooke Grundfest Schoepf, *Director, Project CONNISSIDA, Woods Hole, Mass.*
AIDS

Lars Schoultz, *William Rand Kenan, Jr., Professor of Political Science, University of North Carolina at Chapel Hill*
U.S.–Latin American Relations

Joseph M. Schwartz, *Assistant Professor of Political Science, Temple University*
Left

Thomas Alan Schwartz, *Associate Professor of History, Vanderbilt University*
Marshall Plan; Potsdam Conference; Yalta Conference

Katherine O'Sullivan See, *Professor of Sociology, James Madison College, Michigan State University*
Northern Ireland

Gerald Segal, *Senior Fellow, International Institute for Strategic Studies, and Editor, The Pacific Review, London*
Sino-Soviet Relations

Claudio G. Segrè, *Professor of History, University of Texas at Austin*
Fascism; Mussolini, Benito

Bereket Habte Selassie, *Professor of African Studies and Law, Howard University, and Distinguished Fellow, United States Institute of Peace*
Eritrean War of Independence; Haile Selassie I; Horn of Africa; Organization of African Unity

Mitchell A. Seligson, *Professor of Political Science, University of Pittsburgh*
Costa Rica

Andrew Shacknove, *Joyce Pearce Fellow, Refugee Studies Programme, University of Oxford*
Refugees

D. Michael Shafer, *Associate Professor of Political Science, Rutgers University*
Counterinsurgency

Robert Y. Shapiro, *Associate Professor of Political Science, Columbia University*
Public Opinion

Gene Sharp, *Senior Scholar-in-Residence, The Albert Einstein Institution, Cambridge, Mass.*
Civil Disobedience; Nonviolent Action

Jeremy Shearmur, *Research Associate Professor, Institute for Humane Studies, George Mason University*
Libertarianism

Andrew Shennan, *Assistant Professor of History, Wellesley College*
World War II

Paul E. Sigmund, *Professor of Politics and Director, Program in Latin American Studies, Princeton University*
Liberation Theology

Joel H. Silbey, *President White Professor of History, Cornell University*
Political Realignment

Jon Simons, *Ph.D. Candidate in Political Science, Hebrew University of Jerusalem, and Visiting Scholar, Department of Government, Harvard University*
Israel

D. S. Ranjit Singh, *Universiti Malaya*
Brunei

A. W. Singham, *Professor of Political Science, Brooklyn College, City University of New York (deceased)*
Nonaligned Movement

Richard Sinnott, *Director, Centre for European Economic and Public Affairs, University College, Dublin*
Ireland

Carmen Sirianni, *Associate Professor of Sociology, Brandeis University*
Industrial Democracy; Workers' Control

Ian Skeet, *Consultant, Oxford Institute for Energy Studies*
  Organization of Petroleum Exporting Countries

Marion Sluglett, *Lecturer, Politics, University College of Swansea*
  Hussein, Saddam; Iraq

Peter Sluglett, *Lecturer, Modern Middle Eastern History, Centre for Middle Eastern and Islamic Studies, University of Durham*
  Hussein, Saddam; Iraq

Ninian Smart, *J. F. Rowny Professor of Comparative Religions and Chair, Religious Studies Department, University of California, Santa Barbara*
  Religion and Politics

Dan Smith, *Director, Transnational Institute, Amsterdam*
  Foreign Military Bases

Michael Joseph Smith, *Associate Professor of Government and Foreign Affairs, University of Virginia*
  Anarchy; Idealism

Tony Smith, *Cornelia Jackson Professor of Political Science, Tufts University*
  Decolonization; Political Development

Wayne S. Smith, *Director, Cuban Studies, Paul H. Nitze School of Advanced International Studies, Johns Hopkins University*
  Cuba

William C. Smith, *Associate Professor of Political Science, University of Miami*
  Argentina

Richard Smoke, *Professor of Political Science and Research Director, Center for Foreign Policy Development, Watson Institute, Brown University*
  Nuclear Weapons; Strategic Arms Limitation Treaties

Pamela A. Solo, *Executive Director, Cultural Survival, Inc., Cambridge, Mass.*
  Nuclear Freeze

John Solomos, *Reader, Public Policy, Birkbeck College, University of London*
  Race and Racism

Carolyn M. Somerville, *Associate Professor of Political Science, Hunter College, City University of New York*
  Sahel

James M. SoRelle, *Associate Professor of History, Baylor University*
  King, Martin Luther, Jr.

Donald L. Sparks, *Associate Professor of International Economics, The Citadel, Charleston, S.C.*
  Indian Ocean Region; Madagascar

Barbara B. Stallings, *Professor of Political Science and Director, Global Studies Research Program, University of Wisconsin–Madison*
  Balance of Payments

Sven Steinmo, *Assistant Professor of Political Science, University of Colorado at Boulder*
  Taxes and Taxation

John D. Stephens, *Professor of Political Science and Sociology, University of North Carolina at Chapel Hill*
  Jamaica

Joe Stork, *Editor, Middle East Report, Middle East Research & Information Project, Washington, D.C.*
  Eisenhower Doctrine; Iran-Iraq War

Susan Strange, *Professor of International Relations and Director, European Policy Unit, European University Institute, Florence*
  Gold Standard

Paul Streeten, *Spencertown, N.Y.*
  Basic Needs; Brain Drain

Martin Stuart-Fox, *Reader, History, University of Queensland*
  Laos

Jomo Kwame Sundaram, *Professor, Faculty of Economics and Administration, Universiti Malaya*
  Malaysia

Ibrahim K. Sundiata, *Professor and Chair, Department of African and Afro-American Studies, Brandeis University*
  Equatorial Guinea

Ronald Grigor Suny, *Alex Manoogian Professor of Modern Armenian History, University of Michigan*
  Russian Revolution

Abram De Swaan, *Dean, Amsterdam School for Social Research*
  Welfare State

Donald K. Swearer, *Professor of Asian Religions, Swarthmore College*
  Buddhism

Hung-chao Tai, *Professor of Political Science, University of Detroit*
  Confucianism

John Richard Thackrah, *History Master, British Army Sixth Form College, Worksop, U.K.*
  Malta

Carlyle A. Thayer, *Associate Professor of Politics, Australian Defence Force Academy, Canberra*
  Vietnam

Carol B. Thompson, *Senior Research Associate, Political Studies, University of Zimbabwe*
  Destabilization

John B. Thompson, *Lecturer, Sociology, and Fellow, Jesus College, University of Cambridge*
  Ideology

Hugh Tinker, *Department of Politics, University of Lancaster*
  Colonial Empires

Jeanne Maddox Toungara, *Assistant Professor of History, University of Virginia*
  Côte d'Ivoire

Gregory F. Treverton, *Senior Fellow, Council on Foreign Relations, Inc., New York*
  Intelligence

Yoshi Tsurumi, *Professor of International Business, Baruch College, The City University of New York*
  Japan-U.S. Relations

Danilo Türk, *Professor of International Law, Univerza v Ljubljani, and Permanent Representative of Slovenia to the United Nations*
  Genocide

Blair P. Turner, *Professor of History and Political Science, Virginia Military Institute*
  Malvinas/Falklands War

Frederick C. Turner, *Professor of Political Science, University of Connecticut*
  Perón, Juan Domingo

Thomas Turner, *Professor of Political Science, Wheeling Jesuit College*
  Mercenaries

Meredeth Turshen, *Associate Professor of Urban Studies and Community Health, Rutgers University*
  World Health Organization

Brian Urquhart, *Scholar-in-Residence, International Affairs Program, Ford Foundation, New York*
  Hammarskjöld, Dag

Aldo C. Vacs, *Associate Professor of Government, Skidmore College*
  Argentina

Nelson P. Valdés, *Director, Latin America Data Base, University of New Mexico*
  Castro, Fidel

Peter van der Veer, *Professor of Comparative Religion, Centre for Asian Studies, Universiteit van Amsterdam*
  Hinduism

Michael Vickery, *Associate Professor of History, Universiti Sains Malaysia*
  Cambodia

John R. Vile, *Professor and Chair, Department of Political Science, Middle Tennessee State University*
  Judicial Review

R. John Vincent, *Montague Burton Professor of International Relations, London School of Economics and Political Science (deceased)*
  Intervention

Paul R. Viotti, *Professor of Political Science, University of Denver*
  Force, Use of; North Atlantic Treaty Organization

Stephen M. Walt, *Associate Professor of Political Science, University of Chicago*
  Alliance

Ronald Walters, *Professor and Chair, Political Science Department, Howard University*
  U.S.-Africa Relations

M. Stephen Weatherford, *Professor of Political Science, University of California, Santa Barbara*
  Policy Coordination, Economic

Brian Weinstein, *Professor of Political Science, Howard University*
  Literacy

Margaret Weir, *Senior Fellow, Brookings Institution, Washington, D.C.*
  Community Control; Entitlements; Great Society; Underclass

Claude E. Welch, Jr., *SUNY Distinguished Service Professor, Department of Political Science, State University of New York at Buffalo*
  Coup d'État

David A. Welch, *Assistant Professor of Political Science, University of Toronto*
  Bay of Pigs Invasion; Cuban Missile Crisis

Stephen White, *Professor of Politics, University of Glasgow*
  Communist Party States; Perestroika

Laurence Whitehead, *Official Fellow, Nuffield College, University of Oxford*
  Democratic Transitions

Robert C. Williams, *Dean of Faculty, Vice-President for Academic Affairs, and Professor of History, Davidson College*
  Lenin, Vladimir Ilich

Ife Williams-Andoh, *Postdoctoral Fellow in Political Science/Afro-American Studies, University of Illinois at Urbana-Champaign*
  Liberia

Samuel R. Williamson, Jr., *Vice-Chancellor and President, The University of the South*
  World War I

Garry Wills, *Adjunct Professor of History, Northwestern University*
  Nixon, Richard Milhous

Ernest J. Wilson III, *Associate Professor of Government and Politics, University of Maryland at College Park*
  Privatization

Graham K. Wilson, *Professor of Political Science, University of Wisconsin–Madison*
  American Federation of Labor and Congress of Industrial Organizations

Gilbert R. Winham, *Eric Dennis Memorial Professor of Government and Political Science, Dalhousie University*
  U.S.-Canada Free Trade Agreement

Ann Withorn, *Professor of Social Policy, College of Public and Community Service, University of Massachusetts at Boston*
  Feminization of Poverty

Sharon L. Wolchik, *Professor of Political Science and Director, Russian and East European Studies Program, George Washington University*
  Charter 77; Czechoslovakia; Havel, Václav

Robert Paul Wolff, *Professor of Philosophy and of Afro-American Studies, University of Massachusetts at Amherst*
  Anarchism

Steven B. Wolinetz, *Professor of Political Science, Memorial University of Newfoundland*
  Netherlands

Meredith Woo-Cumings, *Associate Professor of Political Science, Northwestern University*
  Korea, Republic of

Peter Worsley, *Professor Emeritus, Victoria University of Manchester*
  Populism

Erik Olin Wright, *C. Wright Mills Professor of Sociology and Director, Havens Center for the Study of Social Structure and Social Change, University of Wisconsin–Madison*
  Class and Politics

Mark W. Zacher, *Professor of Political Science, University of British Columbia*
  International Organizations

Aristide R. Zolberg, *University-in-Exile Professor, Graduate Faculty, New School for Social Research*
  International Migration

Yahia H. Zoubir, *Associate Professor of Political Science and International Relations, American Graduate School of Business, Montreux*
  Western Sahara

A

ABDEL NASSER, Gamal. See NASSER, GAMAL ABDEL.

ABORTION. See REPRODUCTIVE POLITICS.

ACHESON, Dean. Born in 1893 in Middletown, Connecticut, Dean Acheson trained as a lawyer and developed formidable administrative talents. He first entered the State Department in the mid-1930s, as a protégé of Felix Frankfurter, and became under secretary of state in Franklin D. *Roosevelt's last administration. But it was while occupying the same position under Harry S. *Truman, with whom he enjoyed a close affinity, and later, as secretary of state in Truman's second administration, that Acheson reached the height of his influence.

As under secretary he represented the United States in establishing a number of international economic organizations immediately after World War II. With the Secretaries of State James F. Byrnes and his successor George C. Marshall abroad much of the time, Acheson was probably the main influence on the conduct of U.S. foreign policy in the crucial years of 1946 and 1947. During that period, and as secretary of state during Truman's second administration (1949–1953), Acheson probably exercised more influence on U.S. foreign policy than any of his predecessors at that office. In addition to the formulation of the *Truman Doctrine, he was particularly closely connected with U.S. proposals in March 1946 for international control of trade in fusionable materials, with the policy of the *containment of the Soviet Union through the *North Atlantic Treaty Organization (NATO), and with the apparent exclusion of Korea from the list of countries on the Asian periphery that the United States was prepared to defend. He was convinced that the active wielding of American political, economic, and military power was necessary for the preservation of world peace and that the United States should assume the duties of empire that had previously devolved upon Britain. In such areas as Greece, Indochina, and the Middle East, Acheson was prominent in advising Truman to assert boldly the newfound power and influence of the United States in the postwar world. Indeed, he was one of the main architects of the Truman Doctrine, which, in its more radical formulations, committed the United States to supporting anticommunist regimes everywhere in the world in a dangerously open-ended manner.

With the landslide victory of Eisenhower in 1953, Acheson returned to his law practice but continued to frame the foreign policy plank of the Democratic platform until the Kennedy era. He published his political memoirs, entitled *Present at the Creation*, in 1969, and died in 1971.

(See also AMERICAN FOREIGN POLICY; COLD WAR.)

Dean Acheson, *Present at the Creation: My Years in the State Department* (New York, 1969). Gaddis Smith, *Dean Acheson* (New York, 1972).

DAVID MCLELLAN

AFGHANISTAN. A mountainous, sparsely populated, landlocked country of about 15.5 million people, Afghanistan entered the modern international system through a treaty signed with Britain in 1879. Britain and Russia subsequently agreed to make the country a buffer state between their empires. Afghanistan lost this status with the intervention of Soviet troops on 24–27 December 1979. After nine years of devastating but inconclusive war, the approximately 100,000 troops completed their withdrawal on 15 February 1989. The government they continued to support collapsed in April 1992, barely one hundred days after the dissolution of the Soviet Union. A shaky coalition of Islamic insurgents (*mujahidin*) took power.

The dynasties that ruled Afghanistan until 1973 originated in an empire founded by Ahmad Shah Durrani in 1747. This ruler united the Pashtun ("Afghan") tribes, but after his death the state lost its imperial territories.

In the nineteenth century the Eurocentric *international system entered the region. British concerns over Russian advances in Central Asia led to two Anglo-Afghan Wars (1839–1842 and 1878–1880). The first ended in a defeat for the British, but the second allowed them to obtain control of Afghanistan's foreign affairs and deprive it of important territories. These lands, between the Indus River and the "Durand Line" (which today divides Pakistan from Afghanistan), included about half of the Pashtuns.

Strengthened by British subsidies, Emir Abdul

Rahman Khan, who reigned from 1880 to 1901, began the construction of an absolutist state. His grandson, King Amanullah Khan, tried to modernize Afghanistan during his reign from 1919 to 1929. He won independence in the Third Anglo-Afghan War (1919) but consequently lost the British subsidy and failed to establish a reliable resource base or an effective army. Peasant rebels supported by fundamentalist clergy seized the capital, Kabul, in January 1929. After nine months of rule by a rebel leader from the Tajik ethnic minority, Kabul fell again in October 1929 to Pashtun tribes led by Nadir Khan, a senior member of the royal clan. His family ruled Afghanistan until April 1978.

Nadir was assassinated in 1933. The throne passed to his son, Zahir Shah. In 1953 Daud Khan, Zahir's cousin, launched a *modernization program as prime minister. He resigned in 1963, and Zahir Shah promulgated a constitution that provided for an elected consultative parliament and freer public expression. In July 1973, Daud staged a *coup, abolished the monarchy, and proclaimed himself president of the Republic of Afghanistan. On 27 April 1978, he was overthrown and killed by the same officers who had helped him to power in 1973, but this time they turned over power to the Marxist-Leninist People's Democratic Party of Afghanistan (PDPA).

The roots of the turmoil lay in Daud's reforms. Using foreign aid from both superpowers as a substitute for domestic resources he could not extract, Daud built an army, paved roads, invested in economic projects, and expanded education. The elite was trained in the West, military officers studied in the Soviet Union, and Islamic legal officials were trained at Egypt's al-Azhar University.

Soviet aid to the military developed from Afghanistan's situation in the *Cold War system. The United States had refused military assistance in 1954 out of deference to Pakistan, which had joined two of the anti-Soviet pacts the United States was sponsoring. Pakistan opposed aid to Afghanistan because the latter demanded self-determination for "Pashtunistan," the Pashtun lands across the Durand Line. Daud then accepted a Soviet offer to build his armed forces.

The newly educated groups transformed politics in Afghanistan. Previously the main struggles were for the autonomy of the state from the Pashtun tribes. There were also challenges from Persian-speaking (Tajik, Hazara) and Turki-speaking (Uzbek, Turkoman) minorities. These conflicts could become sectarian, as when the Sunni government (representing eighty-five percent of the over ninety-nine percent Muslim population) fought the Shi'i Hazaras. Only the tribal elite, however, sought state power.

The intellectuals also identified with the state but were excluded from power. Frustrated intellectuals joined radical groups, both Marxist and Islamic. The PDPA was founded in 1965 and split into two factions in 1967. Khalq ("Masses"), led by Nur Muhammad Taraki and Hafizullah Amin, appealed to the newly educated from rural, mainly Pashtun backgrounds. Parcham ("Banner"), led by Babrak Karmal, drew from the lower ranks of the Persian-speaking Kabuli elite.

Led by teachers from the Islamic Law (Shar'iyyat) faculty of Kabul University, who were influenced by the Egyptian Muslim Brotherhood, the Islamists organized the Jam'iyyat-i Islami-yi Afghanistan (Islamic Society of Afghanistan). In Pakistani exile during the late 1970s, this group split, largely on ethnic lines, into Jam'iyyat, led by Burhanuddin Rabbani, a Tajik lecturer from the Shar'iyyat faculty, and the Hizb-i Islami (Islamic Party), led by Gulbuddin Hikmatyar, a Pashtun former engineering student.

These groups began to contend for state power in the 1970s. The 1973 coup was carried out by army officers belonging to Parcham, whose members also served in Daud's initial cabinet. The Islamists fled to Pakistan, where the government gave them refuge and training to counter Daud's militancy on Pashtunistan. In 1975, with Pakistani support, the Islamists tried to stage a rural uprising, but they received no support and were suppressed easily.

Analysts disagree about covert Soviet involvement in the 1978 coup. Daud had begun to distance himself from the Soviet Union and move closer to the oil-rich states of the Persian Gulf. He removed Parchamis from his cabinet, and the Soviet Union did press the PDPA factions to reunite in 1977. It appears, however, that the coup was carried out by Afghan military units.

Once in power, the Khalqis soon expelled the Parchamis and embarked on a revolution by decree and mass terror. Lacking experienced cadres, mass organizations, or popular support, the Khalqis succeeded in driving the countryside into revolt rather than in implementing their program. Resistance fighters (mujahidin) and refugees began to flee to Pakistan, where the Islamists, now joined by traditional religious and other leaders, competed for leadership.

The Soviets viewed the growing revolt against a "progressive" regime on their border with increasing alarm and finally sent troops to control the situation. In a botched operation, they killed Amin, who had become president after killing his rival, Taraki, in September 1979, and installed a Parchami-dominated PDPA leadership in power.

The result was a generalized uprising throughout the country and worldwide condemnation of the Soviet actions. The United States, Saudi Arabia, Pakistan, and China expanded material support to the resistance; the support increased greatly after 1985, reaching $600 million a year from the United States. The Soviet Union tried various strategies to defeat the resistance and stabilize the government, including building up a KGB-style secret police headed by Najibullah, who became the PDPA leader in 1986, and massive bombing of rural areas, which drove over 5 million refugees into Pakistan and Iran. One survey concluded that by 1987 1.24 million people, mostly civilians, had been killed.

The collapse of both government administration and traditional institutions provided an opportunity for the Islamists, aided by strong support from the Pakistani military, to build the support they had previously lacked. Pakistan hoped for a pan-Islamic government in Afghanistan that would abandon the nationalist Pashtunistan demand. The traditionalist forces remained strong, however, especially in Pashtun tribal areas, and the Islamists also had to use traditional tribal and ethnic loyalties to gain rural followings. The Soviet presence enabled the government to hold the cities and border.

In 1986 Mikhail *Gorbachev decided to seek an exit from Afghanistan. On 14 April 1988, the Soviet Union, the United States, Pakistan, and Afghanistan signed four agreements in Geneva providing for the withdrawal of Soviet troops. No agreement was reached, however, on the composition of a future government. As Soviet troops withdrew, the government lost control of several provincial capitals and much of the border, but the resistance was unable to capture the center. The United States and the Soviet Union continued to aid their clients, the Pakistani military continued to support the Islamists, especially Hikmatyar, and Saudi Arabia and Iran continued their proxy battle for leadership of the Islamic world in Afghanistan. Factional, tribal, and ethnic conflicts reemerged within both the resistance and the government. Najibullah defeated a coup led by the Khalqi defense minister in March 1990. In June of that year, the PDPA followed the example of other Communist parties in the age of *perestroika: it renamed itself the Hizb-i Watan (Homeland Party); renounced Marxism-Leninism, the monopoly of power, and socialism; and embraced *Islam, political pluralism, and the market economy. A few individuals from the old elite joined the government, and some resistance leaders tentatively opened secret talks with Najibullah. The major forces of the resistance, however, continued to oppose both the government in Kabul and Pakistan's plans to replace it with one to Islamabad's liking. After the failed Moscow coup of August 1991, the United States and Soviet Union agreed to end aid to all parties and to support a UN plan for an interim government. The end of Soviet aid and of the Soviet Union itself, however, deprived Najibullah of his major prop. Uzbek and Tajik militias and Homeland Party leaders revolted against him and his Pushtan allies. In the resulting turmoil, the UN plan was bypassed, and a shaky coalition of *mujahidin* leaders proclaimed the establishment of the Islamic State of Afghanistan as of 6 May 1992.

(See also SOVIET-AFGHANISTAN WAR; SOVIET FOREIGN POLICY.)

Louis Dupree, *Afghanistan*, 2d ed. (Princeton, N.J., 1980). Henry S. Bradsher, *Afghanistan and the Soviet Union* (Durham, N.C., 1983). Olivier Roy, *Islam and Resistance in Afghanistan* (Cambridge, U.K., 1986).

BARNETT R. RUBIN

AFL-CIO. See AMERICAN FEDERATION OF LABOR AND CONGRESS OF INDUSTRIAL ORGANIZATIONS.

AFRICAN AMERICANS. More than 10 million people brought as slaves to the Americas during the period from the sixteenth to the nineteenth centuries confronted a situation that was historically unprecedented. Never before had such a large group of people been driven from their homelands and forced to labor for the remainder of their lives in distant societies dominated by culturally and racially different people. Deprived of their freedom and torn from their cultural roots, slaves and their descendants responded to their enslavement in varied ways.

Slaves born in African societies initially relied upon their cultural traditions as they struggled against chattel slavery, but life in Africa had not prepared them to challenge European technological superiority. Some slaves saw their situation as hopeless and committed suicide rather than endure the passage to the Americas or the harsh process of slave breaking once they arrived. Others fought their enslavers, rebelling aboard slave ships or in the Americas. Few rebellions succeeded, however, because slaves were closely supervised, unfamiliar with their new surroundings, often divided by linguistic and religious differences, and subjected to brutal punishments when disobedient. In addition, disease and malnutrition killed many slaves and weakened the ability of others to rebel. Most Africans who came to the Americas, particularly those brought to the sugar plantations of Brazil or the Caribbean islands, died before they could bear children.

Those who survived found it necessary to undergo a cultural transformation. Africans from diverse cultural backgrounds became African Americans, a group defined by the color of their skin and bound together by the common experience of being dominated by Europeans. The most basic aspect of this cultural transformation was the adoption of European languages, which not only enabled slaves to communicate with their masters but also, in some cases, with each other. The transformation also involved the adoption of other European cultural, social, and political practices, but this did not constitute a complete abandonment of African cultural values, some of which persisted in the Americas. Nor did African slaves simply become Europeanized, because they simultaneously transformed European culture as they infused it with their own insights. African Americans not only endured under oppression; over time they also established families, churches, schools, self-help groups, fraternal orders, and other institutions as they sought to improve their lives collectively and individually. These institutions conformed somewhat to European-American models, but they also reflected the distinctive common experiences and aspirations of slaves and their descendants.

The tendency of African Americans to utilize European cultural forms increased during the eighteenth and nineteenth centuries as a result of the religious "awakenings" and democratic revolutions that occurred in many European-dominated societies. Emerging forms of African-American Christianity combined residual elements of African religions and those aspects of Christianity that appealed to slaves and freed blacks. From the beginning of the slave era, conversion to Christianity sometimes offered a means for slaves to improve their lives or simply to find a degree of psychological solace, but conversion rarely led directly to emancipation for slaves. Instead, most slave masters saw slavery as compatible with or even justified by Christianity. In the British colonies of North America, however, the spread of evangelical Christianity during the eighteenth and nineteenth centuries fostered democratic ideals. Methodist and Baptist religious practices were especially appealing to African Americans, because they encouraged individuals to assert control over their spiritual lives as well as over congregational decision making.

The formation in 1793 of Philadelphia's Bethel African Methodist Episcopal (AME) church was an important step in the institutionalization of African-American culture and society. Bethel's minister, Richard Allen (1760–1831), initially remained within the Episcopal church hierarchy, but in 1816, when the AME church became fully autonomous, he became the denomination's first bishop. Other blacks would join the AME Zion denomination or one of hundreds of Baptist and Methodist churches that gained members as a result of the religious revivals of the decades before the Civil War. Such religious institutions provided training grounds for the development of black leadership. Moreover, Christianity became a source of insights for African Americans seeking understanding of their history and plight. They could identify their enslavement with that of the Jews and see the Ethiopians mentioned in the Bible as their ancient ancestors. Prayer and prophecy became means for expressing African-American aspirations. As transformed by blacks struggling to free themselves, Christianity became a theology of liberation at least partially outside the control of whites.

While African Americans adapted Christianity to serve new purposes, they also transformed modern concepts of *nationalism into a set of political ideas that gave them a collective identity and informed their movements for freedom and justice. Both the American and the French revolutions of the late eighteenth century encouraged African Americans to hope that they might enjoy the *rights that were being obtained by white people. The gradual movement in Europe and the Americas toward the ideal of universal rights influenced and was influenced by African-American struggles for advancement. After the British colonies of North America gained their independence, blacks in the *United States petitioned white leaders to end slavery and racial discrimination by pointing to the egalitarian sentiments expressed in revolutionary documents such as the Declaration of Independence. The U.S. Constitution reflected the postrevolutionary decline of democratic idealism, however, reinforcing the legal rights of slaveholders and providing few mechanisms for effective political action against the proslavery state governments. The French Revolution of 1789 strengthened antislavery sentiment in the Americas and prompted a successful slave rebellion, led by Toussaint L'Ouverture (1743–1803), in the colony that became *Haiti. Taken together, the American and the French revolutions provided democratic ideals for many subsequent African-American political movements.

Whether slaves could free themselves and then gain full *citizenship rights in white-dominated societies became central questions for nineteenth- and twentieth-century African-American political movements. In the United States, the strengthening of the slave economy after the invention of the cotton gin in 1793 lessened the possibility that slavery would be abolished peacefully. Although some emancipated blacks became politically active during the early nineteenth century, most states imposed special restrictions on their political freedom. After the exposure of major slave conspiracies in Virginia in 1800 and South Carolina in 1822, and the crushing of the Nat Turner (1800–1831) slave rebellion in Virginia in 1831, southern whites severely restricted the ability of southern slaves and free blacks to assemble. In addition, the desire of African Americans to emigrate back to Africa or at least out of the United States gathered strength during the antebellum years. In 1815 Paul Cuffe (1759–1817), a wealthy African-American merchant mariner, brought a small group of settlers to Sierra Leone on the west coast of Africa. Most emancipated blacks found emigration to Africa impractical and undesirable, however, for they had been born in America and had little knowledge of life elsewhere. In 1817 a national meeting of black leaders rejected the efforts of white leaders of the American Colonization Society to encourage freed blacks to go to Africa.

The formation of the American Anti-Slavery Society in 1833 further encouraged African-American antislavery agitation. Although the society's leader, William Lloyd Garrison, was a white abolitionist who believed in "moral suasion" as the best means of ending slavery, by the 1840s many black abolitionists had begun to attack slavery politically by supporting antislavery parties and candidates for political office. The most well-known black abolitionist, Frederick Douglass (1817–1895), initially allied himself with Garrison, but by the end of the 1840s had become a proponent of political strategies. Other black leaders such as Henry Highland Garnet and Martin Delany urged not only political action but also slave rebellions as the best means of abolishing slavery. Garnet and Delany became advocates of black nationalism, believing that there was little hope for black advancement in the United States. Delany's *Condition, Elevation, Emigration and Destiny of the Colored People of the United States, Politically Considered* (1852) argued that African Americans were "a nation within a nation" and recommended emigration to Central America or Africa. Pessimism increased among African Americans about their prospects in the United States after the Supreme Court's Dred Scott decision of 1857, which concluded that blacks were not citizens but were "a subordinate and inferior class of beings."

The Civil War marked a major turning point in African-American politics. Although President Abraham Lincoln initially did not see the war as a struggle against slavery, the increasing reliance of the Union army on black soldiers altered war objectives. In 1863, Lincoln's Emancipation Proclamation promised freedom to slaves in areas still held by the Confederacy. After the defeat of the Confederacy, Republican leaders recognized that citizenship rights for freed slaves were necessary for the party's success in the South during the Reconstruction period. They drafted and obtained ratification by the states of three constitutional amendments designed to free all slaves (Thirteenth Amendment) and to eliminate racial discrimination in the administration of laws (Fourteenth) and voting (Fifteenth). During the Reconstruction period, African Americans participated in the southern political system, but black-supported Republican state governments in the region faced strong opposition from recalcitrant white segregationists, and none survived after the last federal troops were removed in 1877.

The end of Reconstruction led to a rapid decline in black political activity, and by the early twentieth century most southern states had enacted racially discriminatory laws that segregated blacks and prevented them from voting. Black political leaders responded to the imposition of this "Jim Crow" system in a variety of ways. Some leaders, including AME bishop Henry McNeal Turner (1834–1915), advocated black separatism and even emigration to Africa. Others, notably Booker T. Washington (1856–1915), head of Tuskegee Institute in Alabama, urged blacks to forgo agitation for civil rights and instead develop skills that would be useful for white employers. Washington garnered the financial backing of white philanthropists, particularly after his conciliatory address at the Atlanta Exposition of 1895, and he dominated African-American politics at the national level at the beginning of the twentieth century.

The most innovative political thinker of the period was W. E. B. *Du Bois (1868–1963), who combined elements of earlier nationalist thought, particularly an appreciation of the African roots of African-American culture, with a strong commitment to ending racial discrimination. In 1900, Du Bois, influenced by the earlier efforts of Alexander Crummell (1819–1898) and Edward Wilmot Blyden (1832–1912), participated in the first Pan-African Conference in London, which advocated unity among all people of African ancestry. In 1905, Du Bois became a founding member of the Niagara movement, formed to promote protest activity on behalf of black civil rights, and four years later he joined with white reformers to establish the National Association for the Advancement of Colored People (NAACP).

Twentieth-century African-American politics were greatly affected by the migration of millions of blacks from the rural South to urban areas. A massive influx of blacks to northern cities during World War I strengthened existing African American urban religious and fraternal institutions, and led to increasing political militancy in the growing black communities. Marcus Garvey (1887–1940) organized the most substantial manifestation of the new militancy, the Universal Negro Improvement Association, which, according to some estimates, attracted several million followers. Garvey's ultimate goal was to create a strong, independent African nation that would advance the interests of black people throughout the world. Garvey's caustic criticisms of civil rights leaders such as Du Bois made him a controversial figure among blacks and a target of government persecution. He was convicted of mail fraud in connection with his fund-raising for the Black Star steamship line, and his movement declined rapidly after his deportation in 1927 to Jamaica.

Despite the imprisonment of Garvey, African-American cultural distinctiveness continued to flourish through the movement known as the Harlem Renaissance. Poets, essayists, dramatists, novelists, and artists of the 1920s became increasingly concerned with depicting the lives of African Americans. Langston Hughes (1902–1967), the most popular and prolific of the poets of the period, summarized the sentiments of other writers when he announced in a 1926 article: "We younger Negro artists who create now intend to express our individual dark-skinned selves without fear or shame." Other major intellectual figures of the movement included Alain Locke (1886–1954), Claude McKay (1890–1948), and Zora Neale Hurston (1901–1960). Innovative forms of African-American music also appeared during the 1920s as blues and jazz became increasingly popular in urban centers.

The worldwide economic depression of the 1930s strengthened the tendency of African Americans to seek advancement through interracial political movements and civil rights reform. A small minority of blacks, including a number of prominent artists and intellectuals, was drawn to the Communist Party, which identified itself with the ideal of universal rights and which fostered the notion that blacks could play a major role in radically transforming American society. Du Bois and Paul Robeson (1898–1976), a famed singer and actor, were prominent among blacks who remained close to the Communist Party during the 1940s and 1950s, even as other blacks, such as Hughes and novelist Richard Wright (1908–1960), became disillusioned with the party. The dominant direction of African-American political activity outside the South involved electoral participation and efforts to combat racial discrimination through litigation, lobbying efforts, and, to an increasing extent, protest activity. After 1932, black voters generally supported the Democratic Party in national elections, and most black leaders at the national level participated in interracial coalitions favoring civil rights reforms. The 1941 March on Washington movement under the leadership of A. Philip Randolph demonstrated the potential for mass protest activity as a means of bringing about civil rights reform, but the strategy of nonviolent direct action had few practitioners outside of the Congress of Racial Equality (CORE), an interracial group without much support among blacks.

During the two decades following World War II, the generalized political and cultural conformity that characterized Cold War America also affected African-American life. Both socialist and black nationalist radicalism had little impact on black politics, particularly at the national level. Instead, encouraged by the Supreme Court's *Brown v. Board of Education* (1954) decision, civil rights organizations and their leaders sought to strengthen federal and state antidiscrimination policies. The NAACP largely shaped the national civil rights agenda, but, after the Montgomery bus boycott movement of 1955–56, this organization faced competition from more militant local groups inspired by African independence movements, linked to black colleges and churches, as well as skilled in the use of nonviolent protest tactics. The Southern Christian Leadership Conference (SCLC), formed in 1957 and led by Montgomery protest leader Martin Luther *King, Jr. (1929–1968), was particularly effective in organizing massive protest campaigns in southern communities such as Birmingham in 1963 and Selma in 1965. CORE initiated a Freedom Ride campaign in 1961, pressuring the federal government to act against racial discrimination in interstate travel. The Student Nonviolent Coordinating Committee (SNCC), formed by student leaders of the sit-in movement of 1960, spearheaded the effort to achieve voting rights for blacks in Mississippi, Alabama, and southwest Georgia. The southern protest movement prodded the federal government to enact the Civil Rights Act of 1964, which outlawed segregation in most public facilities, and the Voting Rights Act of 1965.

Even as the southern protest movement achieved its civil rights goals, it also fostered revived feelings of racial consciousness among African Americans. Black nationalist sentiments were evident among urban blacks during the early 1960s, but the most effective proponent of these ideas, *Malcolm X (1925–1965), had little impact on national African-American politics until 1964 when he broke with the religious separatist group the Nation of Islam. In the months before his assassination in 1965, Malcolm began to establish ties with militants who had been active in the *civil rights movement. By 1966, both SNCC, under the leadership of Stokely Carmichael (b. 1944), and CORE became identified with the "Black Power" slogan, which symbolized the increasingly militant racial consciousness of African Americans. During the decade from 1965 to 1975, many new black-controlled cultural, social, political, educational, and economic institutions came into existence. The Black Panther Party, based in Oakland, California, reflected the widespread discontent of young northern blacks through the brash willingness of armed Panthers to confront police. For the most part, however, the majority of African-American institutions did not pose direct political challenges to the state but instead emphasized African-American cultural distinctiveness. During the late 1960s and early 1970s internal ideological conflicts and external repression led to the decline of militant political groups. The National Black Political Assembly, founded at a 1972 convention in Gary, Indiana, could not reverse the disintegration of black nationalist political activity. Instead, black political activity increasingly focused on efforts to elect black politicians in predominantly black areas. The most enduring outgrowths of the militancy of the 1960s were the black studies academic programs, businesses selling products designed for blacks, and associations formed to protect the interests of black professionals.

The overall dominance of conservative, Republican political leaders during the 1970s and 1980s discouraged African-American political militancy. Nevertheless, many of the insights and institutional outgrowths of earlier mass struggles endured, and African-American racial consciousness continued to be affected by the widespread availability of publications on African-American life and history. National black leaders largely focused their efforts on the consolidation of the civil rights gains of the 1960s, but many incorporated aspects of black nationalism and Pan-Africanism into their political perspectives. Jesse Jackson's (b. 1941) campaigns for the presidency in 1984 and 1988 demonstrated the potential strength of the black electorate. Jackson and other African-American leaders were unable, however, to implement successful strategies to deal with the serious economic problems of blacks who did not receive material benefits as a result of civil rights legislation and affirmative action programs. The persistence of poverty, the increasing deterioration of black families, and the reluctance of white Americans to support major new governmental social programs to deal with these problems led to a revival of strategies for African-American institutional and cultural uplift. Advocates of such strategies included not only community leaders but also black neoconservative intellectuals tied to conservative institutions. In addition, during the period after 1970, black women have increasingly won election to public office and assumed leadership roles in racial policy discussions. After centuries of institutional development and movements for collective advancement, African Americans continue to be concerned with unresolved questions of group identity and destiny.

(See also NONVIOLENT ACTION; RACE AND RACISM; RELIGION AND POLITICS.)

W. E. B. Du Bois, *The Souls of Black Folk* (New York, 1903). Herbert Aptheker, ed., *A Documentary History of the Negro People in the United States* (New York, 1974). Vincent Harding, *There Is a River* (Orlando, Fla., 1981). Jacqueline Jones, *Labor of Love, Labor of Sorrow: Black Women, Work, and the Family from Slavery to the Present* (New York 1985). Eric Foner, *Reconstruction: America's Unfinished Revolution, 1863–1877* (New York, 1988). John Hope Franklin, *From Slavery to Freedom: A History of Negro Americans*, 6th ed., with Alfred A. Moss, Jr. (New York, 1988).

CLAYBORNE CARSON

AFRICAN DEVELOPMENT BANK. The African Development Bank (ADB) was established in 1964 by thirty-two independent African states. Article 1 of the agreement establishing it states that "the purpose of the Bank shall be to contribute to the economic development and social progress of its regional members—individually and jointly." Ten years later, its membership was extended to twenty-six non-African states through the creation of the African Development Fund (ADF). Resources of ADF are lent to poorer African countries at zero interest rates, with principal repayments spread over fifty years including a ten-year grace period. Moreover, a Nigerian Trust Fund (NTF) was established in 1976 to assist African states severely hit by the first oil shock.

The Bank Group—ADB, ADF, and NTF—currently has seventy-seven member states, of which fifty-one are African. This expansion in membership has led to a substantial increase in the authorized capital of the bank from US$1.6 billion in 1979 to US$21.8 billion in 1988. It has also led to a significant increase in the volume of concessional lending, with two-thirds of the total number of loans now being funded through ADF.

Bank resources are managed by an executive president, assisted by five vice-presidents and 500 professional staff. Moreover, there is an eighteen-person Board of Executive Directors representing its shareholders. Since 1986 the bank has enjoyed a triple-A rating in the international capital markets, which is a significant recognition.

The founders of the bank envisaged it as having a dual role of financing "investment projects and programmes relating to the economic and social development of its regional members" and of providing technical know-how in their design, implementation, and management. In this regard, the Bank Group has collaborated with a majority of multilateral and bilateral donors in cofinancing projects and programs in Africa.

The bank financed only investment projects during the first nineteen years (1967–1985) of its operations. With the African economic crisis at its peak in the mid-1980s, the Bank Group has added a new and quick disbursing instrument to the investment project financing device. Hence, as of 1986 it has allocated twenty-five percent of its annual lending to finance, with the *World Bank, policy-based operations in the framework of structural adjustment programs. This has resulted in a significant increase in the annual volume of loans as well as disbursements. For instance, loans worth about US$6.0 billion were approved during the period 1986–1988, compared to approximately US$7.0 billion during 1967–1985. By sectoral allocation, agriculture is the leading sector with about thirty-one percent of cumulative lending, followed by public utilities, transport, and industry with twenty-three percent, nineteen percent, and fourteen percent respectively. The share of education and health is only 8.2 percent.

In recognition of the challenges facing African economies, the bank is currently reorganizing its internal organizational structures to better serve Africa. In this regard, it is reorienting its lending operations in support of strategies that focus on economic growth and poverty reduction.

(See also AFRICAN REGIONAL ORGANIZATIONS; ASIAN DEVELOPMENT BANK; INTER-AMERICAN DEVELOPMENT BANK.)

African Development Bank, *Agreement Establishing The African Development Bank*, 2d ed. (Abidjan, Ivory Coast, 1988).

LUAL ACUEK DENG

AFRICAN NATIONAL CONGRESS. In 1652 Jan Van Riebeeck, a representative of the Dutch East India Company, established a refreshment station at what the Europeans called the Cape of Good Hope. From then on, the indigenous peoples and their descendants became the victims of colonial conquest, exploitation, and racial domination. The San and Khoikhoi, the Nguni, and the Sotho chiefdoms and kingdoms fought heroically to defend their sovereignty. The arrival of the British with their superior military technology finally broke African resistance. Following the Anglo-Boer War of 1900–1902, the Union of *South Africa was constituted as a white dominion within the British Empire.

With the passage in the British Parliament of the South African Act—which would be ratified by the white South African Parliament on 31 May 1910, or exactly eight years after the signing of the treaty that ended the Anglo-Boer War—it became obvious that Britain meant to betray African interests in its pursuit of Anglo-Boer reconciliation and that Africans must unite in the face of a common enemy. On 8 January 1912, at a unity conference at Bloemfontein attended by chiefs and kings, professionals and intellectuals, workers and peasants from all parts of the country, including the British protectorates, the African Native Congress—later the African National Congress, or ANC—was founded. The emergent ANC was to represent African aspirations for independence and equality, and to transcend ethnic, linguistic, religious, and class barriers in the fight for freedom. African *nationalism, as represented by the ANC, was inclusive rather than narrow and exclusive. From the 1920s, it began to work with the Communist Party of South Africa (later, the South African Communist Party), the Coloured People's Organisation, and the South African Indian Congress.

For the first fifty years, the ANC waged peaceful campaigns against segregation. Mass meetings, demonstrations, deputations, protest, passive resistance, and strikes were the hallmarks of its struggle. Because of its commitment to nonviolence, in 1960 President General Chief Albert Luthuli was awarded the Nobel Peace Prize.

In 1953, to underline its commitment to a nonracist South Africa, the ANC convened a Congress of the People. In 1955, 3,000 delegates gathered in Kliptown and adopted the Freedom Charter, which declared, "South Africa belongs to all who live in it, black and white," and affirmed that "no government can justly claim authority unless it is based on the will of all the people." In 1956, 156 leaders of the Congress movement were arrested and charged with high treason. After four years the case was finally dismissed.

In March 1960, the police killed 69 protesters and wounded 157 people at *Sharpeville. The ANC and the Pan-African Congress were banned and a state of emergency was declared. In 1961 the ANC formed Umkhonto Wesizwe (Spear of the Nation). From then on political and armed resistance combined to undermine *apartheid.

Nelson *Mandela, leader of the underground struggle, was captured in 1963 by the South African police. At the Rivonia Trial, Mandela and several others were sentenced to life imprisonment. In 1967, ANC guerrillas, traveling with guerrillas of the Zimbabwe African People's Union (ZAPU), were intercepted in the Wankie Game Reserve in Rhodesia (now Zimbabwe). The clashes alarmed the South African government but encouraged the black African communities. The 1972–1973 strikes in Natal were followed in 1976 by student revolts against Bantu education in *Soweto. In the upheaval, many were killed and many crossed into Mozambique, where they joined the ANC. At each decisive juncture the regime failed to return the country to a state of normalcy.

In 1978 then-president P. W. Botha said that the nation faced "a total onslaught" and "must develop a total strategy." To meet the threat, he initiated "reforms," tightened the legal infrastructure of oppression, and devoted a larger budget to armed forces and police—all of which failed to subdue the rising tide of resistance. In 1983, the United Democratic Front was formed to oppose the new constitutional dispensation for Coloureds and Indians, and in 1985 the South African Congress of Trade Unions was formed, linking factory issues with community struggle. The 1984–1986 countrywide rebellion made South Africa ungovernable as strikes, school boycotts, acts of sabotage, and countless demonstrations and rallies were organized. A state of emergency was imposed in 1985 and has since been renewed four times. The release of Walter Sisulu and his compatriots in September 1989 and of Nelson Mandela on 11 February 1990, along with the unbanning of the ANC and other organizations, demonstrated the power of united mass action inside South Africa, complemented by the struggle of Umkhonto Wesizwe. When the South African government sat across the table from an ANC delegation in May 1990 to discuss negotiations toward a new constitution, it acknowledged not only the premier role of the ANC but also the changed political climate. The symbolism of the talks was as important as their substance.

(See also SOUTHERN AFRICA; ASIAN DEVELOPMENT BANK; INTER-AMERICAN DEVELOPMENT BANK.)

Bernard Magubane, *The Ties That Bind: African American Consciousness of Africa* (Trenton, N.J., 1987). Bernard Magubane, *The Political Economy of Race and Class in South Africa* (New York, 1989).

BERNARD MAGUBANE

AFRICAN REGIONAL ORGANIZATIONS. Many regional organizations have developed in Africa since the independence movements of the 1950s and 1960s. Of these, only the major past and present organizations will be discussed.

The *Organization of African Unity (OAU) is the leading African regional organization, and the largest in membership. The OAU emerged in 1963 as an amalgamation of several former subregional groupings of states in Africa. From its inception in 1963 with an original membership of thirty, it has grown to include fifty-one states. Only independent and sovereign nations are eligible, and admission is by simple majority of the members after notice is given by the applicant country of its intention to accede to the charter.

The objectives of the OAU are: 1) to promote the unity and solidarity of the African countries; 2) to cooperate and coordinate efforts to achieve a better life for the peoples of Africa; 3) to defend their sovereignty, territorial integrity, and independence; 4) to eradicate all forms of colonialism in Africa; and 5) to promote international cooperation with due regard to the UN Charter and the Universal Declaration of Human Rights. In addition to those implicit in its objectives, the basic principles of the organization include: 1) peaceful settlement of disputes by negotiation, mediation, conciliation, or arbitration; 2) the sovereign equality of all member states; 3) unreserved condemnation of political assassination and subversive activities; and 4) affirmation of a policy of nonalignment with respect to all blocs.

At the inception of the OAU in 1963, Ghana led an effort to establish a central political organization with power to formulate a common *foreign policy, common planning for economic *development, a common currency, and a common defense system. These suggestions for the surrender of national sovereignty were unacceptable to most of the heads of states and governments that approved the charter. The Ghanaian proposal for organic political union was rejected in favor of a loose organization with a limited functional approach to unity.

The OAU's quest to consolidate Africa's political independence and to assure Africa's economic future found support and encouragement in an organization with similar objectives—the UN *Economic Commission for Africa (ECA). The ECA, created by the UN General Assembly Resolution 1155(xii) of 26 November 1957 and the UN Economic and Social Council's Resolution 671A(xxv) of 29 April 1958, provided the first opportunity for the articulation of African social-economic aspiration on a continental scale. The ECA in its multifaceted operations in Africa has served as an African think tank.

Besides the OAU and ECA, the other major African regional organizations are the West African Economic Community (CEAO), 1973; the Economic Community of West African States (ECOWAS), 1975; the *Southern African Development Co-ordination Conference (SADCC), 1980; and the Preferential Trade Area for East and Southern African States (PTA), 1981.

One of the earliest regional organizations for economic cooperation in Africa was the East African Community, established by the Treaty for East African Cooperation between Kenya, Tanzania, and Uganda. The community, which formally came into existence on 1 December 1967, disbanded early in 1977, soon after an outside authority completed a review of the treaty, upon which Kenya set up its own airline and Tanzania closed its border with Kenya. The disruptive effects of diverging ideologies in the East African Community (with Tanzania committed to *African Socialism or Ujamaa and Kenya to a capitalist economy), combined with Uganda's

political instability, led to the failure of the organization. However, the existence of different economic systems probably caused fewer problems than the growing tendency of states to give priority to local interests rather than to the common East African cause. Dissatisfaction over the distribution issue, coupled with the difficulties resulting from disastrous mismanagement of some of the common services, clearly played a significant role.

With a total population of 150 million and a GNP of US$85 billion, and representing sixteen West African countries, ECOWAS was formally established in 1975 on the initiative of Nigeria and Togo. It aims at a common market with free movement of goods, capital, and labor.

The CEAO, which comprises only Francophone West African countries, was established in 1973, reportedly upon a French initiative designed purposely to kill the West African Community founded in 1968. Like ECOWAS, CEAO seeks a fundamental restructuring of the economies of its member states. It aimed to institute a common external tariff by 1985. All its members also belong to ECOWAS, and it remains to be seen whether the two economic communities will ultimately merge.

The establishment of SADCC, and to a lesser extent the initiation of the 1981 Preferential Trade Area for East and Southern African States, were ostensibly encouraged by the prospect of an independent Zimbabwe which the 1970s war of national liberation in Southern Africa engendered. On 1 April 1980 the five Frontline states (Angola, Botswana, Mozambique, Zambia, and Tanzania), joined by Lesotho, Malawi, and Swaziland as well as the newly independent Zimbabwe, signed the Lusaka Declaration on Economic Liberation, which formally brought SADCC into existence. The main objectives of SADCC as a regional organization are to integrate economic development in the areas of agriculture, industry, energy conservation, security, transport and communication, and human resource development. The SADCC states' strategies of integration are based on the need to devise a collective strategy to lessen their economic dependence on South Africa. The Lusaka Declaration noted that "future development must aim at the reduction of economic dependence not only on the Republic of South Africa, but also on any single external state or group of states."

Given the necessary political will and sacrifices on the part of Africa's leaders, the continent's future is promising. Therefore, regional organizations in Africa have an important future.

(See also AFRICAN DEVELOPMENT BANK; EUROPEAN COMMUNITY; LATIN AMERICAN REGIONAL ORGANIZATIONS.)

R. I. Onwuka and A. Sesay, eds., *The Future of Regionalism in Africa* (New York, 1985). Leroy A. Bennett, *International Organizations: Principles and Issues* (Englewood Cliffs, N.J., 1988). Olayiwola Abegunrin, *Economic Dependence* and Regional Cooperation in Southern Africa: SADCC and South Africa in Confrontation (Lewiston, N.Y., 1990).

OLAYIWOLA ABEGUNRIN

AFRICAN SOCIALISM. The term *African Socialism* has come to connote something very different, in continental parlance, from a mere shorthand for "*socialism in Africa." Instead it has been used to summarize a claim—heard more in the 1960s and 1970s than in recent years when the formulation has become much discredited—that there is a "socialism" distinctive to Africa, a socialism surfacing, quite spontaneously, from egalitarian cultural predispositions and communal social practices which antedate the European penetration of Africa. These predispositions and practices, it has been argued by the protagonists of the *ideology of African Socialism, were not effaced by colonialism and are said to reemerge, more or less unproblematically, in the independence period to give a promisingly collectivist tilt to the policies of postcolonial governments.

Sometimes these notions reflected the cultural-nationalist preoccupations of certain of the first generation of successful African nationalists, less eager to advance a deeply critical analysis of their own societies than to develop an indigenous alternative to left-wing discourses they considered too Eurocentric. Léopold Senghor of Senegal is an example, although it should also be noted that this perspective was already, from the very earliest days of African independence, viewed with suspicion by other, putatively socialist, leaders like Kwame *Nkrumah of Ghana and Sékou Touré of Guinea. Such leaders employed a rather more universalistic, if still hazily defined, "progressive" discourse in outlining their own (ultimately unrealized) left-populist goals for their societies.

More often, the project of African Socialism was put forward quite cynically by opportunistic elites, on the rise everywhere in Africa, to give a veneer of progressiveness and apparent concern for popular aspirations to their otherwise self-interested and increasingly capitalist policies. By means of this ideological rationale, these elites sought to mask the workings of new *class structures and continuing imperial linkages that a more "scientific" socialist discourse could more readily have revealed to popular scrutiny. A particularly notorious example of this manipulative use of the concept was the Kenya government's "Sessional Paper #10" on "African Socialism and its Application to Planning in Kenya" (1965) which, substantively, had almost nothing to do with any recognizably socialist intent. It was not long before the Kenyan leadership itself had begun to rationalize its policies in much more straightforwardly capitalist terms. Yet certain other much-touted variants on African Socialist themes—the "humanism" of Zambia's Kenneth Kaunda, for example—proved to have little more genuine socialist content.

Probably the least cynical and most developed of all variants of African Socialism was the philosophy and practice of *Ujamaa* ("familyhood") generated by Julius *Nyerere in Tanzania. Suspicious, in part on religious grounds, of *Marxism and of notions of "class struggle," Nyerere evinced a high moral tone and a genuine concern for the fate of the mass of the population in his impoverished country. Nyerere first exemplified his position in a seminal 1962 essay, "Ujamaa: The Basis of African Socialism": "Socialism . . . is an attitude of mind. . . . We in Africa have no more need of being 'converted' to socialism than we have of being 'taught' democracy. Both are rooted in our own past—in the traditional society which produced us." As Nyerere sought to balance this (rather romantic) perspective against his own deepening awareness of the profound contradictions inherent in modern African society, he produced a series of widely quoted analyses of rural questions *(Ujamaa Vijijini/Socialism and Rural Development)*, education *(Education for Self-Reliance)*, and leadership and *democracy. Unfortunately, his overall project did not prove to be notably successful in practice. Soon, too, it was found wanting analytically by a subsequent generation of socialists in Africa, many of them linked to the liberation movements and post-liberation governments of Southern Africa such as that of Mozambique's President Samora Machel.

When the latter have, in turn, rejected *capitalism's claim to developmental promise, they have tended to seek more systematic premises than any of their predecessors in some variant of Marxism. There was an awareness (on the part of Machel, for example) that this must be a Marxism effectively rooted in the concrete realities of Africa, and, indeed, some advance beyond the nostrums of African Socialism did prove possible via this route. But Marxism in Africa (especially in the inflexible and stereotyped form of Eastern European–style Marxism-*Leninism) too often has itself become a legitimating ideology for those in power rather than a tool for effective socialist practice. Moreover, the external *destabilization of radical regimes (e.g., Mozambique) and the ongoing process of Western economic recolonization of the African continent as a whole have meant that the scope for socialist achievement of any sort has proven to be exceptionally narrow.

It remains to be seen whether "socialism in Africa" in any form can revive itself in the near future. The scant success and high social costs of alternative capitalist *development strategies and the deepening impoverishment of most of Africa do suggest that aspirations grounded in the socialist tradition will eventually reassert themselves. For the moment, a post-apartheid South Africa may provide the best promise of clearer theory and more effective practice in this respect. In South Africa communalist themes that parallel the thrust of African Socialism have indeed surfaced from time to time, notably in some of the initial (late 1960s, early 1970s) formulations of the Black Consciousness movement. More recently, however, the key protagonists for socialism have sprung from South Africa's vibrant trade union movement and, albeit unevenly, from within the resurgent "Congress Alliance" (an alliance centered on the *African National Congress and including, prominently, the South African Communist Party). Such actors have ensured that class analysis and various Marxist emphases are now the more prominent features of left-wing thinking about that country's socioeconomic future.

(See also AFRO-MARXISM; PAN-AFRICANISM.)

William H. Friedland and Carl G. Rosberg, Jr., eds., *African Socialism* (Stanford, Calif., 1964). Julius K. Nyerere, *Freedom and Socialism/Uhuru na Ujamaa* (Dar es Salaam and London, 1968). John S. Saul, *Socialist Ideology and the Struggle for Southern Africa* (Trenton, N.J., 1990).

JOHN S. SAUL

AFRO-MARXISM. The term *Afro-Marxism* was coined by B. D. G. Folson in his article "Afro-Marxism: A Preliminary View" (*African Review,* 1976). Folson identified two types of Marxists in Africa: 1) African Marxists and 2) Afro-Marxists. African Marxists were described as individuals (i.e., African intellectuals and political leaders) who rigorously applied the principles of scientific socialism to Africa. (In 1976, when he wrote his article, Folson could find not even one African Marxist regime.) Afro-Marxists were described as those leaders who attempted to adapt the principles of scientific *socialism to African conditions. The first explicitly Afro-Marxist regime appeared in 1969 in Congo-Brazzaville. By 1987, six African regimes could be classified as Afro-Marxist (*Angola, *Mozambique, *Ethiopia, *Congo, *Benin, *Madagascar); by 1990 Afro-Marxism was in retreat throughout the continent.

Afro-Marxist regimes tended to be hybrids with both Leninist and populist traits. The most well-articulated among them grew out of *national liberation movements in the name of the "African people" of their respective countries (Angola, Mozambique) or from a social *revolution in the name of the "toiling masses" who were liberated from their "feudal chains" (Ethiopia). These regimes were attracted to the Soviet-style Leninist model because of the organizational power it seemed to promise more than because of the dogma which undergirded the model. This model justified a top-down *development strategy led by a small oligarchy that also defined the moral or normative principles of the order.

Some features of the Soviet model were wholeheartedly endorsed (e.g., central *planning, the vanguard party, state control of the economy), whereas other features were ignored or rejected outright (e.g., *class struggle). The tenets of Afro-Marxist doctrine were fleshed out according to local conditions. However, the most well-articulated Afro-Marxist regimes attempted to follow Marxist-Leninist doctrine more closely than did those self-proclaimed but more politically and economically heterodox Afro-Marxist regimes like those in Benin, Congo, and Madagascar.

By the end of the 1980s it was clear that the various attempts to establish Afro-Marxist regimes had failed. *Ideology and central control were not enough to allow the governments that engaged in such experiments to overcome the deeply rooted problems of poverty, underdevelopment, and *dependency. Afro-Marxist regimes, like other African regimes, continued to lack the economic, technological, and skilled workforce necessary to lead self-sustained development. Desperate for foreign economic and technical assistance, one after the other, leaders of Afro-Marxist regimes decided to admit failure and to do what was necessary to attract the foreign capital needed for reconstruction and development. By the early 1990s, either prodded by "civil society" or independently choosing reform, all previously Afro-Marxist regimes were forced to be responsive to yearnings for democracy in their respective countries. To the extent that Afro-Marxism as a concept continues to exist it can mostly be found in the ideas and political writings of African intellectuals.

(See also AFRICAN SOCIALISM; LENINISM; MARXISM.)

Crawford Young, *Ideology and Development in Africa* (New Haven, Conn., 1982). Edmond J. Keller and Donald Rothchild, eds., *Afro-Marxist Regimes: Ideology and Public Policy* (Boulder, Colo., 1987).

EDMOND J. KELLER

AGGRESSION. See FORCE, USE OF.

AGRARIAN REFORM. See LAND REFORM.

AIDS. Acquired immunodeficiency syndrome (AIDS) is a new fatal disease syndrome which poses a significant threat to the health and survival of millions in developed and less-developed countries. The human immunodeficiency virus (HIV) which causes immune system damage leading to AIDS is transmitted through sexual intercourse, blood, and from mother to infant during pregnancy and birth. The impact of AIDS is increasing in less-developed countries where health and social infrastructures, already inadequate and further weakened by economic crisis, are unable to cope with severe new burdens of disease. These burdens are being shifted to the shoulders of women caretakers.

HIV infection spread widely in the late 1970s, before the first cases were identified in the United States in 1981. By now, the slow-acting virus has become pandemic, with AIDS cases reported from 162 countries. Some areas of the world are more affected than others, and in some the epidemic is just beginning. However, no area will be spared; most of those now infected, and ninety percent of the 15 to 30 million new infections expected to occur during the 1990s, will be in less-developed countries.

Spread of HIV in less-developed countries is propelled by socioeconomic factors which disrupt families, increase disparities in wealth and power, and alter behavioral norms. These set the stage for sex with multiple partners, and make it difficult for youth and women to reduce their HIV risk. The survival strategies of many families depend on labor migration, long-distance trade, smuggling, and exchange of sex for the means of subsistence. Deepening economic crisis, wars, and military occupation lead to violence against civilian populations and population displacement. Many are deprived of hope for the future.

In many countries, powerful interest groups have treated AIDS (and classic sexually transmitted diseases before them) as a moral and political, rather than a health issue. This makes it difficult for some governments to conduct rational prevention campaigns. When national, community, and nongovernmental organization leaders share these perspectives, the moralist stance may inhibit the activities of other groups to act in a more effective manner.

Nearly 447,000 cumulative cases of AIDS had been reported to the *World Health Organization (WHO) by the end of 1991. One-third of these were newly reported during 1991. However, the true figure is likely to be much higher. About 2 million cases of AIDS are believed to have occurred, the majority in the United States and in ten countries in Africa, with nearly one-third among children. About 10 million people are estimated to have been infected worldwide, about half in the last three years. By the year 2000 some 30 to 40 million people will have been infected, including 12 to 18 million children. Another 10 to 15 million children under 15 years of age will have been orphaned by the death of one or both parents.

AIDS is not just another disease; the HIV virus is not just one among many new microorganisms affecting humans. While AIDS currently causes fewer deaths than malaria and diarrheal or infectious diseases, its impact upon families and societies in less-developed countries will be far greater. The biological processes involved are complex and difficult for lay people to understand. The virus uses the body's own immune system to reproduce itself, and damages its defenses against other diseases. These include virulent forms of tuberculosis, pneumonia, wasting diarrheas, and various neurological disorders. Major diseases of the AIDS syndrome may be culturally stigmatized; because it is incurable, AIDS may be attributed to supernatural causes.

The virus is slow-acting, one of a growing family of "lentiviruses." In the United States about half of those found to be infected have developed disease symptoms within ten years; reasons for the variable rates of progression are not now known. Some strains of the virus appear to be more virulent than others; reinfection with different strains may be involved in some cases. To date, no HIV-infected person has yet recovered a healthy immune system. Most are expected to progress to AIDS eventually, but only time will tell if this is actually the case. The prolonged disease process is extremely painful in its later stages, and most of the sick require extensive care. Death generally occurs within two years following the onset of AIDS; the time depends upon availability of expensive drugs and skilled biomedical treatment. At present there is no cure for AIDS and no vaccine to prevent HIV infection. These are not likely to be discovered in the near future, and when they do become available, access will be limited by inability to pay, especially in the Third World.

Different transmission patterns predominate in different parts of the world and in different population subgroups within countries. These patterns are changing over time. Currently, about seventy percent of infections are believed to have been acquired during sexual intercourse with an infected partner. Although AIDS was first detected in Western gay men, globally, one-third or more of the infected are women. Some are women forced by poverty to exchange sex for the means of subsistence. Most are women who were infected by men who had sex with multiple partners. This proportion is rising rapidly; young adolescent women are especially vulnerable to infection by older men. AIDS underscores the powerlessness of many women to refuse risky sexual relations.

The virus continues to spread, not only in cities where the epidemic has become established, but to rural areas and to countries where infection was absent in the 1980s. Between 6 and 8 million Africans (as many as thirty percent of youths and young adults in some cities) are believed to be infected. WHO forecasters believe that by mid-decade this number may be exceeded in Asia. Some countries in Latin America and the Caribbean also will be heavily affected.

AIDS is invariably fatal. In high-prevalence areas of Central Africa and the poverty-stricken ghettos of U.S. cities, AIDS is the leading cause of death in people aged 20 to 44. With the majority of infected women in their childbearing years, AIDS is "an impending catastrophe" for children. One in ten children in U.S. ghettos is infected. In the Third World the gains made by child survival programs have been overtaken in high prevalence areas where AIDS has increased infant mortality by fifteen to twenty percent. By mid-decade, more African children will die from AIDS than from either malaria or measles, with deaths of those under age five expected to rise by twenty to forty-three percent. Deaths of productive adults will leave orphaned many children and elders who depended upon them for survival.

AIDS often provokes fear and hostility toward the afflicted. Families unable to dissemble the nature of the illness may find themselves isolated; AIDS orphans may be shunned and left to roam the streets, where they are particularly vulnerable to HIV infection. With numerous people falling sick and others demoralized by seeing so much death around them, the impact on all economic activities—particularly on season-sensitive, labor-intensive agriculture and food-processing—and on all social groups in the affected areas is likely to be severe.

Blaming others leads to denial of risk and failure to take realistic steps to protect oneself and others. Where AIDS is attributed to the behavior of women, or to supernatural agency, scapegoating and social unrest are likely to compound socioeconomic disruption and to undermine both the capacity to govern and the capacity to build more democratic societies.

An epidemic is essentially a social process, shaped by political economy and culture. Globally, AIDS is best regarded as a disease of *development and underdevelopment. It has struck with particular severity in communities struggling under the burdens of economic crisis, the roots of which lie deep in a combination of internal and external processes. These include stagnation in the global economy, distorted internal production structures inherited from colonialism, unfavorable terms of trade, rapid class formation, and widening disparities in wealth fueled by channeling public funds into private pockets. Africa is the first, but not the only, continent to experience the effects of prolonged, multiplex crisis. However, it is the most vulnerable region, heavily indebted and dependent upon exports of a limited number of tropical products.

The only immediate hope of limiting sexual transmission is to empower substantial numbers of people to alter behavior which is highly valued and considered normal and natural by many. There are numerous cultural constraints to AIDS prevention. However, many of these can be overcome by posing the problems with people at risk.

Social empowerment strategies which incorporate deep understanding of local cultures and small group dynamics have the potential to bring about changes in sexual behavior and the social relations in which they are embedded. Problem-posing methods can be used by community groups to address broader issues of gender relations and to model more egalitarian behaviors, placing these within the context of social action in support of development and social change.

This account has relied chiefly upon data from Africa. However, rapidly rising seroprevalence in South and Southeast Asia spotlights distorted development, poverty, and landlessness along with the subordination of women. The understandings on which the gender relations and development perspective is based, and the conclusions with respect to the need for global redistribution of power and wealth which follow, have not been readily accepted by policymakers. Instead, there is a tendency to seek panaceas in the form of limited interventions which appear to offer hope of interrupting the epidemic without threatening vested interests. However, unless the underlying struggles of millions to survive in the midst of poverty, powerlessness, and hopelessness are addressed, HIV infection will continue to spread. Because social structures circumscribe the choices people make, stopping AIDS requires eliminating the barriers that deny women control over sexual decisions.

(See also GAY AND LESBIAN POLITICS; GENDER AND POLITICS; REPRODUCTIVE POLITICS.)

African Urban Quarterly 5, no. 1-2, 1991. Special issue on AIDS, sexually transmitted diseases, and urbanization in Africa. *Journal of Sex Research* 28, no. 2 (1991). Special issue on anthropology and sexuality and AIDS. B. G. Schoepf, "Ethical, Methodological and Political Issues of AIDS Research in Central Africa," *Social Science and Medicine* 33, no. 7 (1991): 749–763. B. G. Schoepf, "Women and AIDS: A Gender Relations and Development Approach," in *Women and International Development Annual, Volume 3,* edited by Rita Gallin and Ann Ferguson (Boulder, Colo., 1992). B. G. Schoepf with E. Walu, N. Rukarangira, N. Payanzo, and C. Schoepf, "Action-Research on AIDS with Women in Kinshasa: Community-Based Risk Reduction Support," *Social Science and Medicine* forthcoming (1992).

BROOKE GRUNDFEST SCHOEPF

ALBANIA. The Republic of Albania is located in the southwestern quadrant of the Balkan Peninsula. With an area of 28,750 square kilometers (11,000 sq. mi.) and a population in 1991 of approximately 3.3 million, Albania is the smallest of the Balkan states in size and population. Albania is one of the most ethnically homogeneous countries in Europe with Albanians in 1989 comprising ninety-eight percent of the population. Prior to World War II, about seventy percent of Albanians were Muslims, twenty percent Eastern Orthodox, and ten percent Roman Catholic. Albania is thus the only predominantly Muslim country in Europe. With an estimated per capita GNP US$930 in 1986, Albania is Europe's least developed nation.

Albania was part of the Ottoman Empire for nearly 450 years prior to winning its independence in November 1912. After a period of political instability between 1912 and 1924, Ahmet Zogu (1895–1961) became president in 1925. In 1928, he transformed Albania into a monarchy and ruled as King Zog until 1939, when he fled the country following its invasion and occupation by Italy. After a power struggle between communist and noncommunist resistance groups during *World War II, the Albanian Communist Party under the leadership of Enver Hoxha (1908–1985) emerged victorious in 1945.

Hoxha ruled Albania from 1945 until his death in April 1985. He was a staunch disciple of the

Soviet dictator Joseph *Stalin and continued to pursue hard-line Stalinist policies even after they had been repudiated by the Soviet Union and its Eastern European allies. Within Albania, Hoxha owed his success in charting his own course to the ironclad control he exercised over the army, secret police, and Communist Party—the mainstays of his regime. Externally, he was able to exploit divisions in the world communist movement at critical points in Albania's history. The 1948 Soviet-Yugoslav dispute, for example, saved Albania from incorporation into Yugoslavia, and the Sino-Soviet rift of the early 1960s enabled Hoxha to resist Soviet pressures for de-Stalinization as a consequence of the political and economic support received from China.

Following the collapse of the Sino-Albanian alliance in 1978 and the loss of Chinese economic aid, the Albanian economic situation began to deteriorate and its diplomatic isolation became apparent. Hoxha nevertheless refused to alter his policies and continued to purge associates whose loyalty he questioned.

Ramiz Alia (b. 1925), Hoxha's successor as party leader, recognized the need for change, but hesitated to advocate more than modest reform of the economic *planning and management systems and an expansion of Albania's international contacts. After the overthrow of the Eastern and Central European communist regimes in late 1989, Alia was compelled by growing popular pressure to enact a broad program of political, economic, legal, and social reforms. These culminated in December 1990 in the legalization of opposition political parties. In March 1991, Albania held the first genuinely contested election in its history. The following month a temporary "Constitutional Ordinance" was adopted and the name of the country changed to the Republic of Albania. Since that time, the country has experienced political instability, social unrest, and economic decline as its new leaders strive to establish a market economy within the frame work of a democratic multiparty system.

(See also COMMUNIST PARTY STATES; NINETEEN EIGHTY-NINE; SOVIET–EAST EUROPEAN RELATIONS.)

Elez Biberaj, *Albania: A Socialist Maverick* (Boulder, Colo., 1990). Nicholas C. Pano, "Albania," in *The Columbia History of Eastern Europe*, edited by Joseph Held (New York, 1992): 16–64.

NICHOLAS C. PANO

ALGERIA. For a quarter-century after independence in 1962, Algeria's political system was strongly marked by the ideological and institutional heritage of the *Algerian War of Independence (1954–1962). The wartime conception of a "party-nation" was transformed into a hegemonic party-state in an effort to overcome the heterogeneity of Algerian society. The postwar elite, especially as led by Colonel Houari Boumédienne, who held power from 1965

to 1978, erected an authoritarian state on the dual foundation of army and single party, the Front de Libération Nationale (FLN), purveyor of a militantly socialist and anti-imperialist ideology. As that elite faltered in the face of burgeoning social problems and sinking oil revenues, a populist Islamic movement emerged in the 1980s to challenge the power holders.

The army was the first arbiter in postwar Algerian politics, installing Ahmed Ben Bella, one of the nine founders of the FLN, as head of government in a power struggle among wartime leaders during the summer of 1962. A charismatic politician, Ben Bella gained the support of the general staff of the Armée de Libération Nationale led by Boumédienne. The army itself was divided between a centralized external command under Boumédienne and a decentralized internal guerrilla force. The early alliance of party leader and military officer laid the foundation for the postcolonial state, codified as a *one-party system with a strong head of state in the 1963 constitution. The principle of a single party guiding the action of the state remained in force until the 1989 constitutional revision.

Boumédienne suspended the 1963 constitution when he seized power in 1965, but governed through the same tripartite structure of army, state, and party that Ben Bella had utilized. In theory the party through its congress, central committee, and political bureau guided national decision making; in practice the bureaucracy of the state governed, led by a handful of powerful ministers commanding the levers of the economy (finance, energy, heavy industry, *planning) and society (information, justice, culture, youth, religious affairs).

The legislature, suspended in 1965 and reinstituted in 1977, has played a secondary role to the state and party. The political preeminence of the party was reaffirmed in the 1976 constitution, promulgated by the state only after a national charter had first been approved. The charter represented the official ideological orientation of the state, committing Algeria to a socialist model of development. Although the charter called for active citizen participation at the grass-roots level of the party, in reality a strong executive at the pinnacle of the state controlled appointments in both the government and the party (as well as the army). Likewise, interests such as labor, farmers, women, and students were largely controlled by the party apparatus. Elections to local and national assemblies were conducted under a system of multiple candidacies within the single party.

Although Chadli Benjedid, another military officer elected to the presidency in 1979 as the sole candidate named by the FLN, continued to operate within the same institutional environment, he incrementally chipped away at the ideological foundations of Algerian *socialism. He broke up many of the state firms into smaller enterprises and encouraged a gradual shift toward private-sector initiatives. As Benjedid diluted the ideological militance of the regime without narrowing the FLN's prerogatives, disadvantaged social groups turned increasingly toward Islamist ideas for an alternative regime model. Accumulated disaffections forced the rulers to revise the constitution in 1989, terminating the FLN's monopoly status. In Algeria's first multiparty elections in June 1990, the Front Islamique du Salut (FIS) ran well ahead of the FLN and captured control of numerous cities, towns, and regional assemblies. A sharp cleavage between secular and religious models of society emerged. Sharp tensions between the rising Islamist movement and entrenched secular elite plagued the emergent multiparty system throughout 1991. With the FIS on the verge of gaining control of the National Assembly in December 1991 elections, the army reasserted its power in January 1992 by canceling the election results, obliging Benjedid to resign, instituting a new five-member High State Committee, and subsequently banning the FIS.

Algeria's development strategy has emphasized national self-sufficiency and state ownership of the principal means of production. During the war for independence, Algerian intellectuals formulated a critique of the colonialist/capitalist economic structures erected during 130 years of French rule and settlement. Ben Bella's government undertook the recovery of national resources by nationalizing abandoned French properties and some large colonial estates. It created the first state company, SONATRACH (Société Nationale de Transport et Commercialisation des Hydrocarbures), in 1963 to build a pipeline; over two decades, SONATRACH grew into a huge enterprise managing Algeria's substantial oil and natural gas resources. By 1971, the state nationalized all foreign energy holdings and embarked on massive investments in this and other industrial sectors. Eighteen large national firms (sociétés nationales) in such domains as iron and steel, mechanical engineering, industrial vehicles, mining and metallurgy, and construction materials were established. A succession of three-year, four-year, and five-year plans directed state investment policy in both heavy and light industries. Until the late 1970s, the state shunned foreign private investment in its pursuit of national autonomy, but it went heavily into debt as oil prices, and hence state revenues, declined.

While industrializing the country and providing free health care and education, the state-managed economy failed to keep pace with the consumption and employment needs of a rapidly growing population (which increased from 10 to 23 million between 1962 and 1987). Despite some land redistribution and agricultural development initiatives, the rural sector received inadequate public investment; food imports rose accordingly. During the 1980s, Benjedid began to shift toward free-market policies in an attempt to stimulate production, but shortages and social inequalities sparked massive riots in October 1988 that led to the constitutional reforms of 1989 and the electoral repudiation of the FLN in 1990-1991.

Algeria's model of self-reliant national development was grounded in a strategy of collective Third World action. From 1962 through 1983, Algeria played an unusually active role in efforts to organize African states, oil-producing states, raw materials producers, and the *Third World as a whole. The country organized a series of major conferences of developing countries including the first conference of the *Group of 77 in 1967, the fourth summit meeting of nonaligned states in 1973, and the first Organization of Petroleum Exporting Countries (OPEC) summit in 1975, all convened in Algiers. It also played a major role in such major North-South negotiations as the Conference on International Economic Cooperation and the Sixth and Eleventh Special Sessions of the UN. This pronounced engagement in the international debate on global economic structures was one of the distinguishing characteristics of Algerian diplomacy.

In the years following its own independence, Algeria trained Africans from countries such as Angola, Mozambique, and South Africa in techniques of *guerrilla warfare. It established particularly cordial relations with other Third World states—Cuba, Vietnam, and Nicaragua, for example—that were perceived as allies in a common struggle against external hegemony. Closer to home, it supported the right of self-determination in *Western Sahara, producing strained relations with Morocco. However ambitious its goal of organizing a large Third World coalition, Algeria's power was objectively limited. As oil prices fell and material constraints grew, the voluntarism of the first two decades of Algerian foreign policy gave way to a narrower conception of national interest, namely regional stability and economic integration in the Maghreb.

For more than two decades after independence, power holders drew their political legitimacy from their service in the revolution against *France or from their role as managers of Algeria's development model. As a leading Algerian political scientist, Abdelkader Djeghloul, pointed out in the mid-1980s (Annuaire de l'Afrique du Nord, 1985, Paris, 1987), these two modes of legitimization gradually lost their force as a consequence of the passage of time, the rise of a postwar generation, and economic setbacks. The attempt to refashion legitimacy through competitive electoral politics broke down under the Islamist challenge, leaving Algeria's military/secular regime in search of a new formula to restore political stability.

(See also DECOLONIZATION; ISLAM; NATIONALIZATION; NATIONAL LIBERATION MOVEMENTS; NONALIGNED MOVEMENT; RELIGION AND POLITICS.)

David and Marina Ottaway, *Algeria: The Politics of a Socialist Revolution* (Berkeley, Calif., 1970). Jean Leca and Jean-Claude Vatin, *L'Algérie politique: Institutions et régime* (Paris, 1975). John Entelis, *Algeria: The Revolution Institutionalized* (Boulder, Colo., 1986). Jean Leca, "Etat et société en Algérie," in Bassma Kodmani-Darwish and May Chartouni-Dubarry, eds., *Maghreb: Les Années de transition* (Paris, 1990).

ROBERT A. MORTIMER

ALGERIAN WAR OF INDEPENDENCE. The Algerian war (November 1954–March 1962) was a major event in the history of *decolonization in Africa. The war mobilized the Algerian nation and deeply divided the French people. It impelled *France's president, Charles de *Gaulle, himself carried to power by a revolt of the European population of *Algeria in May 1958, to grant independence to the colonies of black Africa. Unable to stem the tide of indigenous Algerian support for the nationalist movement, de Gaulle eventually negotiated the terms of Algerian independence, bringing to power in July 1962 a militant anti-imperialist government that became a major actor in Arab, African, and *Nonaligned Movement affairs.

Nine "historic chiefs," young men who had been active in legal and clandestine political activity and who in several cases had served in the French army during World War II, formed the Comité Revolutionnaire de l'Unité et de l'Action (CRUA) early in 1954. This committee organized a network of resistants into the Front de Libération Nationale (FLN) and Armée de Libération Nationale, which launched the insurrection with some seventy attacks across the country on 1 November 1954. France progressively committed hundreds of thousands of troops to the "pacification" of Algeria, a colony that some 1 million European settlers considered their home. The FLN recruited a corps of rural and urban guerrilla fighters who tied down this large French military contingent. Terrible instances of *torture and *terrorism marked the conduct of the war. Although France largely succeeded in containing the insurgency on a strictly military plane, it could not extinguish the political force of the *revolution. The FLN moreover capitalized upon the accession of Morocco and Tunisia to independence in 1956 (itself attributable in part to the insecurity in Algeria) to assemble a sizable military force on Algeria's borders. The two countries provided bases of operations and gave ample logistic and diplomatic support to the FLN.

The institutions of the Algerian revolution evolved steadily as the rebellion gained force. In August 1956, the top internal guerrilla leadership met in the Soummam Valley. This congress constituted the first meeting of the Conseil National de la Révolution Algérienne (CNRA), an organ that met periodically to fix broad policy; after the cease-fire in 1962, the CNRA adopted the Tripoli Program, the first comprehensive statement of the FLN's intention to carry out a "democratic popular revolution" after independence. The CNRA created an executive committee, transformed in September 1958 into the Gouvernement Provisoire de la République Algérienne (GPRA), which henceforth assumed the functions of a government in exile, representing the nationalist movement in its relations with France and other governments. Meanwhile, as he explored avenues of a negotiated settlement, de Gaulle had to contend with an army-settler rebellion in January 1960 and an attempted military coup in April 1961.

Ferhat Abbas and Ben Youssef Ben Khedda served successively as prime ministers of the GPRA while the future leader of independent Algeria, Ahmed Ben Bella—a founder of the CRUA captured by France along with several other leaders in 1956— was an honorary minister of state in the GPRA. The provisional government was recognized by many Arab and other *Third World governments, and it maintained an effective lobbying presence at the UN, where French policy was strongly criticized. Ultimately the war was won not so much on the battlefield as in the arena of politics and *diplomacy where the FLN/GPRA captured the support of the great majority of Algerians and of international opinion. During the final phase of the war, as negotiations took place in Europe, the Organisation de l'Armée Secrète, created by extremist proponents of French Algeria, conducted a savage rearguard scorched earth campaign.

As the first sustained armed uprising against colonial rule in Africa, the Algerian war had a major effect on movements of national liberation throughout the continent and beyond. The Algerian struggle prompted assertions of the right of independence elsewhere in Africa, and the cost of the war discouraged France and other colonial powers from seriously resisting the anti-imperialist tide. Algeria gave military training to the fledgling *national liberation movements of Angola, Mozambique, and South Africa, and Algiers became a haven for political exiles. Even before acquiring national sovereignty, the GPRA participated in numerous anticolonial conferences including the founding meeting of the Nonaligned Movement in which independent Algeria became a driving force. The militant ideology of national self-sustaining development forged by the Algerian intelligentsia during the war made Algiers a notable pole of attraction in Third World politics through the 1960s and 1970s. The war stirred deep passions on both shores of the Mediterranean and shaped the new era of post-colonial politics.

(See also GUERRILLA WARFARE; POLITICAL VIOLENCE.)

Alistair Horne, *A Savage War of Peace: Algeria, 1954–1962* (Harmondsworth, U.K., 1977). Slimane Chikh, *L'Algérie en armes ou le temps des certitudes* (Paris, 1981).

ROBERT A. MORTIMER

ALLENDE, Salvador. Salvador Allende Gossens became an international symbol of the attempt to create *socialism through nonviolent, democratic means. As a politician, Allende always exhibited a Marxist orientation, but he excelled as a practitioner rather than an ideologist or intellectual. He achieved fame in 1970 as the first Marxist ever freely elected president. Then a violent military *coup d'état on 11 September 1973 cut short his six-year term. The resultant death of Allende and *Chile's socialist experiment have stirred controversy ever since.

Born 26 July 1908 in the port city of Valparaíso, Allende entered medical studies in 1926. He became a student leader against a military dictatorship, and then received his medical degree in 1932. The following year he helped found the Partido Socialista of Chile. After working for the public health service, Allende won election to the national Chamber of Deputies in 1937. His career prospered in 1939 when he became minister of health in the Frente Popular government (1938–1942), based on a coalition among the Partido Socialista, the Partido Comunista, and the Partido Radical.

After serving as secretary general of the Socialist Party in 1943, Allende devoted his energies to the national Senate. He won election to that body in 1945, 1953, 1961, 1965, and 1969. A consummate congressional politician, he also served as the Senate's vice president in the 1940s and president in the 1960s.

In those same decades, Allende ran for president of Chile four times as the candidate of an alliance of the Socialist and Communist parties, usually known as the Frente de Acción Popular (FRAP). Those campaigns, mainly backed by organized labor, featured increasingly bold programs against the local upper class and the United States. Allende captured six percent of the total national votes in 1952, twenty-nine percent in 1958, thirty-nine percent in 1964, and thirty-six percent in 1970. Elected a minority president in a multiparty contest, Allende nonetheless tried to carry out his long-standing commitment to a democratic transition toward socialism. He headed a coalition government known as the Unidad Popular (UP), which encompassed Radicals, social democrats, and defectors from the left wing of the Christian Democrats, along with the dominant Socialists and Communists.

As president, Allende socialized the major means of production. Although the opposition complained about illegal measures, he enacted most of his reforms within the constitutional framework. The main targets for expropriation and redistribution were U.S. copper mines and other foreign-owned industries, banks, large corporations, and great estates. The government also recognized extensive private and mixed public-private sectors of the economy but failed to clearly demarcate those domains.

State intervention mainly benefited workers and peasants, whose share of national income rose. After Allende's first year in office, however, investment and production fell while inflation soared, exacer-

bated by cutoffs of U.S. aid and credits. Amid economic shortages, *class conflict escalated. The middle class increasingly reacted against the degree to which Allende's project favored the proletariat at their expense.

Politics polarized between Allende's leftist coalition and his centrist and rightist opponents, backed by the United States. The president was unable to discipline his own supporters, who quarreled over offices, ideologies, and strategies. Some demanded and initiated on their own more rapid changes than Allende desired, especially in property transfers. Allende vacillated between compromise and confrontation with the increasingly disloyal opposition. His adversaries mobilized strikes and lockouts, mainly by truckers, shopkeepers, and professionals. They also launched media campaigns accusing the government of illegitimacy and totalitarian intentions.

Allende tried to restore order by appointing military commanders to top cabinet posts, but they did not want to take responsibility for his besieged government. In the showdown midterm congressional elections of March 1973, the opposition unified nearly all the centrist and rightist parties. They hoped that deteriorating economic conditions would allow them to win two-thirds of the congressional seats and thus impeach Allende. However, the UP increased its electoral share to forty-four percent.

Although civil liberties were still intact, representative *democracy was strained by the deadlock between the executive and legislature. Allende's decisions to resolve that stalemate through a plebiscite in September 1973 was blocked by the takeover by a junta led by Army General Augusto *Pinochet Ugarte. According to most accounts, Allende committed suicide during the attack on the presidential palace, but others maintain he was murdered. In any case, the military interred Allende's remains in an unmarked grave. The security forces also imprisoned, tortured, and assassinated or exiled thousands of Allende sympathizers. The subsequent dictatorship of the armed forces pledged to extirpate democracy as well as *Marxism.

Controversy has continued to swirl around the Allende government as to why it failed to construct socialism and why it failed to preserve democracy. On the first question of socialism, most analysts agree that the goal was too ambitious for the means. Whether Allende should have moderated his objectives or radicalized his methods remains in dispute. Equally debatable is the issue of whether the Chilean tragedy proved that there cannot be a peaceful path to socialism or merely showed that it was impossible under a minority government in the specific conditions in Chile in the early 1970s.

On the second question of democracy, scholars still argue as to whether the right, center, or left were primarily to blame for the inability to negotiate differences and avoid a breakdown. At the same time, most experts continue to criticize the United

States for destabilizing the UP government through economic pressures and support for the subversive opposition. Virtually no one, however, assigns primary responsibility to the United States for the overthrow of Allende. Some early analysts contended that the clash within Chile of irreconcilable social and ideological forces made Allende's downfall inevitable. By contrast, subsequent research has suggested that greater political skill and flexibility on the part of the UP and its opponents might have averted Armageddon.

After harsh rule by the armed forces finally ended in a restoration of electoral democracy in 1990, most Chileans hoped to avoid any repetition of the conflicts of the Allende years. Polls showed that a majority looked back on his presidency as a disastrous period of economic crisis, social strife, and political extremism. A minority, however, still viewed Allende as a noble figure; they honored him as a leader who never forsook his dedication to both socialism and representative democracy—however incompatible—and who gave his life fighting for the working class.

(See also U.S.–Latin American Relations.)

Paul W. Drake, *Socialism and Populism in Chile, 1932–52* (Urbana, Ill., 1978). Edy Kaufman, *Crisis in Allende's Chile* (New York, 1988).

Paul W. Drake

ALLIANCE. An alliance is a cooperative *security relationship between two or more states, usually taking the form of a written military commitment. In practice, however, the presence of a formal treaty says relatively little about the level of commitment or the extent of cooperation. Less formal arrangements—variously known as alignments, ententes, or coalitions—perform similar functions and can exert equally significant effects.

Efforts to explain why alliances form fall into two basic families. Within the realist tradition, alliances are seen as a way for states to increase their security in response to an external threat. The greater the threat—a function of relative power, geographic proximity, and aggressive intentions—the greater the tendency for states to ally against it.

The strong tendency for states to balance threats is the main barrier to *hegemony in the *international system. As Louis XIV, Napoleon Bonaparte, and Adolf Hitler discovered, states that seek to dominate the system eventually provoke a powerful countervailing alliance. Similarly, the creation of the *North Atlantic Treaty Organization (NATO) in 1949 was a response to the military power of the Soviet Union, its geographic proximity to Western Europe, and Western concerns about Soviet intentions.

Liberal or idealist approaches argue that alliances result from the natural affinity of states with similar domestic characteristics. From this perspective, NATO's durability reflects its members' commitment to democracy and market economies. Although alliance members often emphasize common values in their public rhetoric, ideological affinities are less important than security concerns in most alliances. States facing a common enemy usually overlook ideological differences (as the United States and Soviet Union did during World War II), while states proclaiming similar ideologies may be bitter rivals (as in the Sino-Soviet conflict or the various quarrels within the pan-Arab movement).

Alliances are often seen as a cause of *war, but repeated efforts to verify this hypothesis have been unsuccessful. If anything, war is more likely when alliance formation does not proceed efficiently. If balancing coalitions form slowly or if alliance members try to exploit their partners by excessive "free-riding," aggressors are more likely to underestimate the opposition they will face and thus may be more inclined to use force.

Ending the *Cold War will alter existing alliances dramatically. Within Europe, the disintegration of the Soviet Union and the *Warsaw Treaty Organization has removed NATO's principal *raison d'être*. Proposals to transform NATO into a collective security arrangement should be viewed with skepticism, however, given the dismal record of previous attempts (such as the *League of Nations) and the likelihood of increased tensions within Europe as the *superpowers gradually withdraw. The demise of the Soviet Union will bring superpower competition in the developing world to an end as well, and lesser powers will be forced to rely more on their own resources or on regional security arrangements such as the Gulf Cooperation Council. These developments may also tempt some states to acquire their own *nuclear weapons. Such a step would simultaneously reduce their need for allied support and make potential partners more fearful of being drawn into a nuclear confrontation. For all of these reasons, alliance commitments are likely to become more flexible, short-lived, and limited as the Cold War recedes.

(See also Balance of Power; Idealism; Ideology; Liberalism; Realism.)

Glenn Snyder, "The Security Dilemma in Alliance Politics" *World Politics* 36, no. 4 (1984): 461–495. Stephen M. Walt, *The Origins of Alliances* (Ithaca, N.Y., 1987).

Stephen M. Walt

ALLIANCE FOR PROGRESS. See U.S.–Latin American Relations.

AMAZON DEVELOPMENT. Natural resource extraction has dominated regional economies of the Brazilian Amazon. During the rubber boom and other, briefer episodes of prosperity, regional business elites and politicians proposed diversification as a shelter against the violent market fluctuations, high infrastructural costs of expansion, and heavy debt load occasioned by their dependence on natural resource exports. Sporadic attempts to promote manufacturing and agriculture in the region have succumbed to scanty budgets, topographic and climatological obstacles, and the allure of new extractive export booms.

A new effort began in the 1960s, with the Superintendência do Desenvolvimento da Amazônia (SUDAM) and the Banco da Amazônia (BASA) administering a program of fiscal incentives based on tax exemptions and tax holidays for investments in the region. Originally designed to promote industry, the fiscal incentives were soon expanded to include cattle ranching, an activity that dominated the agencies' agendas and budgets, vastly accelerated deforestation, speculation, and land conflicts, but engendered little permanent economic growth or employment. Only in the controversial free trade zone in Manaus did manufacturing dominate development budgets.

In 1970, agricultural development returned briefly to the fore. The Programa de Integração Nacional (PIN) stressed road building and colonization, with a strong emphasis on small farms, agricultural extension, and integrated rural development. By 1973 business criticisms of PIN's social welfare provisions and of the agencies assigned to implement them, a growing government deficit combined with expanding foreign debt, and the administrative difficulties of the colonization programs led to substantial reductions in PIN budgets.

POLAMAZONIA, a plan established the following year, was committed to large-scale extraction around sites chosen as "growth poles." POLAMAZONIA aimed to promote specific developmental projects, in priority order: 1) mining, 2) lumbering, 3) ranching, 4) fishing, 5) agriculture, and 6) hydroelectric energy. Whereas PIN had professed to develop by distributing access to resources and infrastructure around domestic markets, POLAMAZONIA aimed to concentrate capital investments and resources in order to accelerate Amazonian exports, both to the rest of *Brazil and to external markets.

The greatest numbers of subsidies were applied around three large mineral deposits, the pole around the huge Carajas iron ore deposits receiving by far the greatest share. The Tocantins River, which flowed nearby, was dammed at Tucurui to provide electricity to a joint venture in aluminum smelting between a Japanese consortium and the state firm that was developing the Carajas mine and the railroad that would take the ore to the coast. Local business interests, politicians, and intellectuals protested against the environmental, demographic, and political consequences of granting huge tracts of land and extensive rights-of-way to mining companies and of damming a river whose navigability had been crucial to older local economies. These critical voices had little impact on the central state, however, whose centralizing policies since 1968 had been particularly debilitating for the poor, sparsely populated local states in the Amazon. In 1980, it mounted a massive

new fiscal incentives project, the Projeto Grande Carajas (PGC), to attract investment in the 900,000-square-kilometer (350,000 sq. mi.) area around the mine, the dam, and the railroad. PGC granted corporate tax exemptions on profits earned within its jurisdiction, so its main beneficiaries were the mining companies and the large construction companies that were engaged in infrastructural development.

Meanwhile, migrants had been flowing into the area around Carajas, encouraged by the prospects of jobs in the area and by the certainty that the necessary roads and railroads would open up new lands for settlement. This migration intensified land conflicts. Indigenous groups in the area were also clearly at risk of invasion owing to the minerals projects. The impoverished local state could not deal with the increased demands on its social welfare and order budgets, especially in an area so far from its own administrative center. Its failure was used to justify further usurpations by the federal state and by the mining company, even though the mining project itself had not yet achieved the international financing it had been seeking since 1977.

By 1982, some national intellectuals and politicians mounted opposition to the huge investment required for the mine and in the PGC, as well as to their environmental impact. By this time it was clear that the Brazilian government had succumbed to a highly unfavorable deal when it assumed the entire cost of building the Tucurui dam and other infrastructure with no firm commitment by the Japanese on the scale of the aluminum smelter. There was also nationalist protest against the direct involvement of the Japanese International Cooperation Agency in planning the PGC. Environmentalists in the European Parliament threatened to oppose European Community (EC) credits to the Carajas project. When the *World Bank coordinated the eventual Carajas loan agreement, it incorporated protections for both environment and indigenous groups into the agreement, but as the loan was made to the mining company rather than to the state, these did not extend to the entire PGC region.

In Brazil, environmental and political debate about the PGC has been intense. International concern has focused more on another World Bank–supported project, POLONOROESTE, in the south central Amazon, and on the plight of the indigenous groups in the northern Amazon whose lands are being invaded by gold miners. In negotiating the POLONOROESTE loan to asphalt a highway into Rondonia and to support small-scale colonization there, the World Bank was far more timid in demanding environmental and indigenous rights guarantees than it was in Carajas. It conceded to the protests by Brazilian officials that making international groups beholden to the bank rather than to the nation would violate national sovereignty.

The deforestation, the massive social upheavals, and the violence that attended the building and asphalting of the road BR-364 from Cuiaba to Porto Velho and the flood of migrants and lumber mills along it, together with the clear failure of the Brazilian government to implement any of the controls the World Bank had demanded, greatly strengthened the hand of the international critics of the large, highly capitalized projects in the Amazon. Though continuing to protest that international criticism challenges its sovereignty, the central state has begun to respond to pressure from environmentalists and advocates of indigenous rights. The fiscal crisis Brazil confronts, however, and its continued susceptibility to intromission by business and political groups have limited the governmental response to highly publicized proclamations and occasional dramatic sanctions. A new constitution returns some powers over resource extraction and the environment to the local states, but they have neither the organization nor the revenues at this time to exercise their new powers. Individual firms are doing well with the minerals boom and with the incentives that accompany it, but the local political systems have received little additional revenue to offset the social and ecological problems that mineral wealth under external control has brought them.

(See also ENVIRONMENTALISM.)

Stephen G. Bunker, *Underdeveloping the Amazon: Extraction, Unequal Exchange, and the Failure of the Modern State* (Urbana, Ill., 1985). Susanna B. Hecht, "Environment, Development, and Politics: Capital Accumulation and the Livestock Sector in Eastern Amazonia" *World Development* 13 (June 1985). Dennis Mahar, *Government Policies and Deforestation in Brazil's Amazon Region* (Washington, D.C., 1989).

STEPHEN G. BUNKER

AMERICAN FEDERATION OF LABOR AND CONGRESS OF INDUSTRIAL ORGANIZATIONS. The American Federation of Labor and Congress of Industrial Organizations (AFL-CIO) is the umbrella organization to which most unions in the United States belong. Its membership consists of unions, not individual workers. Not all unions belong to the AFL-CIO, however. Unions as diverse and important as the United Auto Workers, the Teamsters, and the Steelworkers have spent long periods outside the organization for different reasons. The National Education Association, which has functioned in part as a union and which can claim to be one of the nation's largest unions, has never belonged.

The organization has the power to expel individual unions for breaches of its policies or constitution, a power exercised in the late 1950s when the Teamsters were expelled for failure to cooperate with inquiries into corruption in the union. As the unwieldy title of the organization itself suggests, the AFL-CIO is not a strongly centralized organization. Important conflicts about the nature and role of unions take place within it. The AFL part of the title refers to the craft unions that after many false starts established a permanent organization in the United States in the late nineteenth century. The AFL unions emphasized "unionism pure and simple," a strategy that stressed the pursuit of the immediate material benefits of union members primarily through collective bargaining. Political involvement was limited, and was geared by and large to the protection of unions and furtherance of their industrial relations objectives. Little effort was made to expand union membership beyond the labor aristocracy of craft workers. The CIO unions emerged in the 1930s, with some protection and encouragement from the federal government. CIO unions represented workers of different types in single industries such as steel and automobiles. CIO unions tended to give politics greater importance, perhaps reflecting the importance of government cooperation in their creation, and to pursue a much broader range of policies politically than the AFL unions. The tensions between the AFL and CIO traditions have continued since the merger of the two organizations in 1955. The craft unions have tended to be more bipartisan in their approach, showing a willingness to support administrations that appeal to them, whether Republican or Democratic; the old CIO unions, joined by the growing public sector unions, have been committed to more liberal causes and greater identification with the Democratic Party.

The AFL-CIO as an organization has almost no role in labor negotiations. It is probably not surprising, therefore, that its leaders—even those from an AFL background—have attached much importance to politics. Contrary to the belief that U.S. unions are less political than European counterparts, the AFL-CIO long has been recognized in Washington as a major political force. Its Committee on Political Education (COPE), which was founded in the 1950s, can be regarded as the oldest major *political action committee. COPE has been a major source of support for Democratic candidates, especially liberal Democrats in Congress. Very little money is given to Republicans. The AFL-CIO has also been known in Washington for the quality of the lobbyists it employs.

The AFL-CIO has a poor reputation with some liberals because of its "hawkish" *foreign policies. The AFL-CIO backed U.S. involvement in the *Vietnam War, for example, almost to the end. Somewhat less well known is the important support that the AFL-CIO has given liberal domestic policies. AFL-CIO support was important in securing the adoption of the 1964 Civil Rights Act, the 1965 Voting Rights Act, the creation of Medicare, and much consumer legislation.

Ironically, the AFL-CIO has not been able to secure many of the changes in *labor* legislation that it has seen as essential for ending the dramatic decline in union membership in the United States, which was down to sixteen percent of the work force by 1990. The AFL-CIO's last chance to secure legislation to make it easier to recruit union members came in the 1970s, when Democrats controlled both Congress and the White House; Republicans have a clear tendency to side with management in union/management disputes. Yet the AFL-CIO was unable to push labor law reform through a supposedly sympathetic Congress.

The AFL-CIO's political position has declined in the Democratic Party in part because the proportion of workers who belong to unions grows ever smaller and in part because the modern Democratic Party is uncongenial to AFL-CIO leaders. Prior to reforms of the early 1970s, AFL-CIO leaders had considerable behind-the-scenes influence over the selection of the Democratic Party's presidential nominee, a choice made by political professionals who ran the party. Since the early 1970s, the Democratic Party nominee is in effect chosen in primaries. The AFL-CIO leaders, who resisted this change bitterly, have failed to find an effective method for exerting influence in the primaries. In consequence, the impact of the organization on presidential selection has diminished.

Unions are still regarded with hostility by most Republicans, but have in addition lost their natural support from liberal Democrats. The failure of unions in the United States to maintain their membership has also made them less politically important to liberal Democrats, who instead seek the support of women's organizations, environmentalists, and other groups composed mostly of middle-class professionals. In consequence, the AFL-CIO is less important in American politics today than at any time since its creation.

(See also LABOR MOVEMENT.)

J. David Greenstone, *Labor in American Politics* (Chicago, 1977). Graham K. Wilson, *Unions in American National Politics* (London, 1979). Michael J. Goldfield, *The Decline of Organized Labor in the United States* (Chicago, 1989).
GRAHAM K. WILSON

AMERICAN FOREIGN POLICY. Because the *United States is one of the most powerful nations in the world, analyses of its *foreign policy have tended to be wrapped in controversy. Thus Americans may see their foreign policy very differently from the foreigners affected by such policy, and academic analysts may see it differently from ordinary voters. At the risk of oversimplification and missing some of the more complicated disputes, I will outline three major contending interpretations of U.S. foreign policy.

Most Americans consciously (or more subliminally) endorse a *liberal* or "bourgeois-liberal" view of their own foreign policy; in such a view, the institutions of political *democracy in domestic affairs lead to peaceful *international relations, and

the United States is thus seen as an unusually moral actor in world affairs, fighting only when it is first attacked by someone else (as at Pearl Harbor in 1941), offering economic and political assistance to others (as in the *Marshall Plan after *World War II), a nation generally motivated by altruistic and generous motives, a "model for the world." The *Monroe Doctrine, enunciated in 1823, and U.S. participation in two world wars and in the *Cold War, are thus seen as the United States protecting the freedom and self-determination of other nations, simply because Americans identify with the well-being and happiness of human beings in general.

In opposition to this view, some American critics of U.S. foreign policy are joined by many others around the world in adopting a Marxist or *radical* view. In this view, the economic structures of *capitalism are interpreted as causing the United States (as the preeminent capitalist country in the world) to be an unusually expansionist country, a nation launching more than its share of gunboat diplomacy and armed invasions, provoking international tensions and arms races. This view has captured a wide audience among the academics of Western Europe and of the *Third World, and it is intuitively endorsed by many of the poor throughout the world. It has also, of course, been the official interpretation of U.S. foreign policy taught in *communist party states. The phrase *dollar diplomacy* thus has unpleasant connotations for many Latin Americans, for it is retrospectively seen as having brought the U.S. Marines into Nicaragua or Haiti in the 1920s to protect American investments, and as producing many other forms of intervention.

A third view holds that the United States is neither an unusually moral country nor an unusually avaricious country, but simply an ordinary country, pursuing self-interest and *power as every other major power has done. This is a power-politics or *realist* interpretation that would attach relatively little importance to either political democracy or capitalist economics as explanations for the conduct of foreign policy, but would rather see the anarchic character of world politics as dictating the basic behavior of *any* international actor: all such actors are driven to behave in the same fashion. Such an interpretation became fashionable after World War II among those U.S. academics analyzing international relations. The writings of Hans Morgenthau played a major role in introducing students in the United States to the realist school of analysis. This is also more or less the interpretation of American foreign policy that would have been found persuasive by European diplomats and political *elites through much of the nineteenth century, as they regarded the American declarations of a "different" approach to the world as largely hypocritical and saw the Monroe Doctrine as nothing more than the assertion of a sphere of influence. Most European political elites (perhaps rationalizing their own positions) thus sympathized with Spain in the 1898 Spanish-American War, for they saw the United States as embarking on an *imperialism no different from European imperialisms.

It is significant to note that these interpretations emphasize very different factors in the prediction or explanation of American foreign policy behavior. The realist focus will emphasize military power and will often broaden this (sometimes at the risk of tautology) to include all components of national power, especially international economic power. Whatever a nation seeks, it will have to have power to obtain it, so the analysis goes; and the primary object of choice and analysis will thus be whether a nation can maintain its power and influence. In the increasingly interdependent world emerging since the 1960s, economic leverage may count for more, and military capacity for less, but the significance of coercive military power will never disappear. The 1947 Marshall Plan, and the delivery of *foreign aid in general, are interpreted as tools of power, rather than as generous and humane gestures in their own right.

The history of U.S. isolation and nonentaglement in the years before the Spanish-American War and the American entry in 1917 into *World War I are thus seen, in this realist power-politics interpretation, as simply an application of the rules of *balance of power. As long as Europe was divided against itself, and as long as the Atlantic Ocean offered the United States the protection of a very wide moat (much more secure than the moat offered Britain by the English Channel), it made sense for the United States to forgo heavy investments in armies and fleets. Any other country blessed with the same natural reassurance against invasion would have done the same. But the United States' "Manifest Destiny" conquest of Mexican territory in 1845 and general expansion to the Pacific is similarly seen as what any other state would do, exploiting the central position on a continent to expand to its edges, just as tsarist Russia expanded across Siberia.

Such Morgenthau-type realists see the United States as no different from Britain or other countries, but have lamented the self-assessments by which Americans, Woodrow Wilson being a most important example, have foolishly and idealistically convinced themselves that they were somehow above power politics, i.e., that American foreign policy was in some way more high-minded and generous and unselfish than the foreign policy of the more traditional powers. At times, the realists almost seem to be insisting that it is impossible for any country to have a different foreign policy, and to be angry with anyone for trying to do so, as if it were somehow unnatural for a country to be interested in goals other than power. For the realists, *idealism is seen as a dangerous self-delusion, causing interventions for noble causes where the beneficiary allies (as in

Vietnam or El Salvador) are actually not so noble, causing the United States to be naive sometimes about "open covenants, openly arrived at," and then to be cruelly disappointed when the results, as in the Treaty of Versailles, do not match such high standards. The American attempt to return self-consciously to isolation between 1919 and 1939 is interpreted by such realists as a misguided reaction to the discovery that Britain and France had imperialistically negotiated secret treaties during World War I, i.e., that the Allies were not much more moral than imperial Germany had been in its conduct of foreign policy.

The power-politics believer in the significance of international *anarchy thus sees all nations trapped in a "prisoner's dilemma," in which none can trust the other states to be restrained, and in which each thus has to reach for power for itself, as a reassurance against what other states would do with untrammeled power. As noted, the most modern of such realist analysts recognize that power can have many dimensions beyond the military, but they still would interpret economic factors mostly in terms of the influence it gives state A over state B, or vice versa.

A quite different emphasis on economic considerations emerges in the radical or Marxist interpretation. This view rejects the centrality of state-centered power rivalries and instead sees the economic workings of capitalism as the root cause, rather than a secondary dimension of international competition. Capitalist states are burdened by great inequalities of wealth, by periods of dangerously high unemployment and by endemic crises of profitability caused by overproduction of commodities relative to their marketability (or underconsumption). Political elites are concerned that economic crises will spill over into the political realm. By this interpretation, countries like the United States therefore become desperate to find markets abroad. Navies are built that would otherwise never be needed, in part to put the unemployed to work as sailors, marines, and shipbuilders, but in larger part to force the underdeveloped countries of the world to open themselves up to U.S. investment and to the importation of surplus manufactures. Thus, expansionist foreign policy flows from underlying economic causes.

This view considers it "no accident" that the United States began a more active foreign policy, for the first time building a large navy, after 1890, because until then the open frontier and an expanding economy had amounted to a "safety valve" for any periodic cycles of unemployment or underconsumption. The further capitalist industrialization proceeded in the United States, by this interpretation, the more the United States felt driven to expand out into the world, doing a great deal of harm by this expansion.

This radical-Marxist interpretation thus attaches great significance to the domestic political-economic structures of the United States, but at the same time often neglects the empirical details of political behavior. It is enough to know that U.S. policy is determined by the linkages between state and class interests. Little attention therefore is assigned to elections and political or cultural trends. The triumph of "internationalist" Republicans like Vandenberg and *Eisenhower over the "isolationists" like Taft at the end of the 1940s is regarded as almost foreordained by economic drives, and explanations for interventionist policy from the *Vietnam War to the *Gulf War are sought in economic motivations.

Finally, the interpretation the majority of Americans would find the most plausible views foreign policy as a projection basically of the advantages of their domestic regime. The details of whether democratic processes have been properly executed, and how they have functioned, thus become central in the liberal view, and the *process* of foreign policy making has to be analyzed alongside the *substance* of that policy.

A typical attitude of U.S. policy makers has been that the citizens of other countries would be happier if they were free to adopt the same system of self-government and political democracy that applies in the United States, and that such democratic countries would then have no real difficulty in getting along internationally. The Monroe Doctrine illustrates this faith, and so do Woodrow Wilson's proposals for Europe in 1918 and Franklin ' Roosevelt's vision of the world to follow World War II. And it is indeed difficult to find an example of any *war between two countries as democratically governed as the United States.

This model of free compact and self-government has not just seemed appropriate for other nations in their domestic affairs but has also been applied as a model for relations among all nations. It is not surprising that the *League of Nations was the brainchild of U.S. President Woodrow Wilson. Just as Americans have confidence in the voluntary contracts of domestic law, as long as this is part of government by the consent of the governed, so they long had great confidence in *international law, and in international organizations such as the League of Nations and the UN.

If American foreign policy is criticized abroad as being driven by capitalism, most adherents of the liberal view would respond that U.S. policy is not intended to advance any particular economic system but rather to advance free elections, free press, and free speech, the crucial ingredients for political democracy. If democratic voters then have voted for a form of socialism, as in Sweden for much of the past half-century, this creates no tension with the United States. Capitalism, in this view, is the product of a free political system, and not the other way around.

The crucial variables for the liberal interpretation (as for the realist power-politics interpretation) are thus *political* and not economic. Although still the dominant view of American foreign policy within the United States, the tenets of American *liberalism have been strained in recent decades. One of the shocks of the Vietnam War (which all around the globe worked to increase the appeal of the Marxist interpretation, and very much shook American liberal self-confidence) was that many analysts began in the 1960s to question whether democracy could so easily be exported to the poorer countries of the Third World.

Perhaps one had to be economically rich to benefit from freedom of the press. Or perhaps one had to be conditioned by specific cultural traditions to make free elections work well. Perhaps the dominant American self-analysis of U.S. foreign policy simply reflected a peculiar cultural tradition dating back to New England town meetings, and to the free-and-equal style of the American frontier.

Thus, Americans have entered the world arena with a profound trust in the processes by which they have participated in and checked their own governments. They have a Lockean confidence in the power of voluntary organizations and in the mechanisms of self-government, and they have a great faith in the workings of *federalism. Rather than opposing the unification of Europe (out of a fear of losing power or losing markets), Americans have tended to support European integration since 1945, on the premise that the model of the union of the American states ought to be adopted elsewhere to help prevent dangerous traditional rivalries and arms races (and wars) among the European powers.

Professional political scientists sometimes scoff at the idealism and optimism of this liberal interpretation of American foreign policy. In fact, the most realist of analysts may share with typical citizens a great awareness of power. Americans have spent two centuries distrusting and checking the uses of political power in domestic life, worrying that governments might shoot, imprison, and coerce individuals. The power-politics outlook merely shifts the concern about the abuse of power to foreign governments, and to what they might do if their armies were more powerful than ours. Whereas the Marxist would regard issues of economic interrelationship as much more significant than these arrangements of political and military power, the average liberal American thus shares with the power-oriented political scientist a fascination with the political arrangements by which citizens are governed and coerced. More than any other, a perspective that emphasizes issues of power in their institutional contexts pulls the fields of American government, *comparative politics, and international relations (and, for that matter, even political philosophy) closer together, a perspective that treats foreign policy making as a more complicated variant of the policy process.

(See also GAME THEORY; ISOLATIONISM; JAPAN-

U.S. Relations; Realism; Soviet Foreign Policy; United Nations; U.S.-Africa Relations; U.S.-Latin American Relations.)

Frank Klingberg, "The Historical Alternation of Moods in American Foreign Policy" *World Politics* 4, no. 2 (January, 1952): 239–273. Louis Hartz, *The Liberal Tradition in America* (New York, 1955). Hans Morgenthau, *Politics Among Nations* (New York, 1967). Gabriel Kolko, *The Roots of American Foreign Policy* (Boston, 1969). Philip Quigg, *America, the Dutiful* (New York, 1971). Richard Rosecrance, ed., *America as an Ordinary Country* (Ithaca, N.Y., 1976).

George H. Quester

AMERICAN INDIANS. See Native Americans.

AMNESTY INTERNATIONAL. Founded in 1961 in London by the British lawyer Peter Benenson, Amnesty International is a nongovernmental *human rights organization which works for the release of prisoners of conscience, fair and prompt trials for political prisoners (defined as persons in prison for their beliefs who have not practiced or preached violence), and the abolition of the death penalty, extrajudicial killings, and all forms of *torture. The organization took root quickly in Europe and the United States, but it was not until the mid-1970s that its numerical and geographical growth became remarkable.

Compared with other human rights nongovernmental organizations (NGOs), Amnesty International has set the standards for research and organizational expertise. It is also by far the largest. In 1990 it claimed 700,000 active or dues-paying members in more than 150 countries, as well as a headquarters staff of more than 250.

Amnesty International seeks to remain independent of external influences, particularly of governments and ideologies. Collaboration with other NGOs is governed by strict guidelines. Seeking to avoid charges of bias, Amnesty covers human rights violations throughout the world. It has also adopted fund-raising guidelines designed to avoid compromising its independence. Amnesty International maintains an active and successful lobbying presence on issues within its mandate at the UN, the United Nations Educational, Scientific and Cultural Organization, and the *Council of Europe, as well as with the Inter-American Commission on Human Rights and the *Organization of African Unity.

Amnesty's advocacy methods have evolved from Benenson's original idea, namely that exposure to public view, especially through the media, can persuade nation-states to improve their human rights practices. The organization sends missions to investigate violations in individual countries, and it issues carefully documented reports and other publications as well as an annual nation-by-nation survey of human rights violations. It conducts public campaigns on such themes as the death penalty, the abolition of torture, and human rights abuses in specific countries. It has also organized an urgent action network to mobilize worldwide appeals for specific prisoners. Local groups of Amnesty members participate in the campaigns, but devote special attention to work for the release of two or three individual political prisoners whom they have "adopted."

Amnesty is governed by an International Council. An International Secretariat in London, under a secretary general, runs the day-to-day affairs of the organization and operates an extensive research unit. The administrative and policy-making structures of national sections vary in form from country to country.

The significance of Amnesty International has been less in its individual initiatives than in its success in mobilizing popular support for human rights, even, to some degree, in Third World countries. Its work has contributed significantly to the current world human rights climate. Three hundred million men, women, and children from over 130 countries, for example, signed one Amnesty International petition to the UN. Amnesty also broke new ground in establishing the credibility of human rights reporting, thus assuring that national governments take such reports seriously.

(See also United Nations.)

J. Paul Martin

ANARCHISM. Anarchism is the political philosophy which holds that the putative authority of the *state is illegitimate, and therefore either *may* be, or *ought* to be, ignored, resisted, or undermined. The doctrine has antecedents in the teachings of the Skeptic philosophers of the classical period but finds its modern origins in the reaction to the modern theory of state authority advanced by sixteenth-, seventeenth-, and eighteenth-century social contract theorists and theorists of the absolute state.

There are two traditions of anarchist thought—libertarian, or extreme individualist, and communitarian—and each appears in three distinctively different variations, which may be labeled philosophical anarchism, ideal anarchism, and revolutionary anarchism. Philosophical anarchism is the thesis that there is not, and cannot be, a legitimate state—a state that has the moral right to demand the obedience of its subjects or citizens—because that demand by the state violates the moral autonomy of the individual. Ideal anarchism holds that, in addition to being illegitimate, the state is suboptimal—it performs less well the tasks of maintaining social order and providing essential services than would an association of free men and women without coercive state *power to compel their behavior. Revolutionary anarchism goes a step further and argues that the state is so immediately destructive of human well-being that it must be destroyed by force, so that a more humane and constructive social order can take its place. It is revolutionary anarchism that is associated in the popular mind with the term *anarchism*. In the United States, anarchists are popularly imagined to speak with Eastern European accents, to wear beards, and to favor the use of bombs.

Libertarian, or individualistic, anarchism is grounded in the laissez-faire theory of the capitalist economy. It holds that states are illegitimate interferences with the individual's *rights of contract; that the police power of the state is a violation of natural rights; and that all of the functions now performed by states, such as maintenance of public order, provision of public services, even defense against foreign invasion, can be performed more efficiently and more legitimately by voluntary associations of free individuals. This line of attack on the *legitimacy of state authority can be found in such popular authors as the nineteenth-century U.S. lawyer Lysander Spooner and the twentieth-century Hungarian-American novelist Ayn Rand, as well as in the philosophical writings of the nineteenth-century German Max Stirner and the twentieth-century U.S. philosopher Robert Nozick and others.

Communitarian anarchism holds that in the absence of a coercive state, social life is most efficiently and humanely organized by means of cooperative communities in which the collective good, rather than one's own individual interest, is the primary motivating concern. (See Jean-Jacques Rousseau for a classic development of the distinction between the General, or Common, Good and Individual Interest.) Communitarian anarchists reject the libertarian anarchists' emphasis on mutually self-interested contractual agreements, and emphasize instead discussion, collective deliberation, and mutual understanding as a basis for social order. In the writings of some communitarian anarchists, such as the nineteenth-century Englishman William Godwin, the great Russian novelist Leo Tolstoy, and the Indian pacifist leader Mohandas *Gandhi, this doctrine is combined with the teaching of the natural goodness and sympathy of human beings. According to Godwin and other communitarians, it is modern civilization, *capitalism, and the state that corrupt human beings and turn them against one another.

The nineteenth and twentieth centuries have seen a number of important communitarian anarchist experimental communities in which a substantial effort was made to live out the ideals of the doctrine. These include New Lanark in England and New Harmony in Indiana, both organized by nineteenth-century Welsh industrialist Robert Owen; Brook Farm, a communitarian anarchist experimental community started by George Ripley outside Boston and inhabited, at one time or another, by such nineteenth-century literary figures as Ralph Waldo Emerson and Henry David Thoreau; and the kibbutzim, or collective agricultural experimental communities, started in Israel by early twentieth-century European émigrés.

The central theme of all strains of anarchist doctrine is the illegitimacy of the state. The central theme of all nonanarchist political philosophy is the legitimacy of the state—the right of the state to rule. Anarchism thus stands as the permanent Other in the discourse of political philosophy. As such, it is reviled, condemned, ignored, but always present as a challenge to established political authority.

(See also CITIZENSHIP.)

ROBERT PAUL WOLFF

ANARCHY. As applied to *international relations, anarchy refers to the absence of authoritative institutions or norms above independent sovereign *states. Both the empirical and normative consequences of this international anarchy are subjects of debate. To adherents of *realism, anarchy is the defining feature of relations among states. Following *Thucydides and Hobbes, authors like Hans Morgenthau and Kenneth Waltz emphasize the permanent insecurity that follows from the absence of any institution to protect states from one another. No state can be secure in its borders from the ambitions of other states; trust among states is impossible because promises can be enforced only by self-help. The result is a permanent "*security-*power dilemma." Each state seeks greater security by adding to its military power; but in so doing it creates fear among other states that this power will be used against them, so they too seek to add to their power. A vicious circle of power and insecurity is thus established because there exists no authority above states to enforce order. Every state must permanently prepare for *war—or face extinction.

According to this view of international anarchy, states can mitigate, but never escape, the effects of their permanent rivalry. They may enter into *alliances with other states to prevent any one actor from becoming dominant; they may seek the protection of a single, powerful state at some cost to their external autonomy; they may seek to avoid permanent alliances altogether so as to maintain some degree of flexibility. All these strategies may help a state to survive, but they cannot negate the permanent structural feature of the *international system, i.e., anarchy. Depending on the skill, prudence, and ambitions of states making up the international system at a given historical moment, the competition among states may or may not result in general war; but general war is a permanent possibility. "Structural realists" therefore emphasize continuity in international relations and regard most schemes for institutionalized *international cooperation to be futile and utopian. States guard their independence; they will not willingly cede their sovereign authority to some higher institution, however "rational" such a scheme may be.

A consequence of this view of international anarchy is a tendency to treat individual states as unitary, rational actors competing in a fixed universe of power. Domestic determinants of *foreign policy are deprecated or largely ignored; the theoretical demands of the international structure are regarded in themselves as providing a parsimonious explanation of a given state's foreign policy. Anarchy in this sense becomes more than a description of the international milieu; it is a fundamental reality upon which to base a theory of international relations. Perhaps the best-known recent theory taking this approach is that of Kenneth Waltz in *Theory of International Politics*.

Other authors treat international anarchy less literally and as less important. In *The Anarchical Society* Hedley Bull argues that international relations resembles a society at least as much as it resembles Hobbesian anarchy—hence his oxymoronic title. Bull points out that international anarchy has not prevented the growth of trade and industry, and that it has not made life for individuals "solitary, poor, nasty, brutish, and short." Hobbes himself did not apply his description of the state of nature to the international milieu; he thought individual sovereign states would learn to control their disposition to go to war with one another. For thinkers like Bull, the absence of authoritative supranational organization or law does not necessarily rule out all forms of international society. International anarchy, in short, not only can be distinguished from domestic anarchy, but its consequences are not as deleterious.

On the normative level, thinkers who regard international anarchy as a primary and determining feature of international political life are usually pessimistic about the possibilities of taming the competition among states by means other than deterrent strategies based on military power. (Authors who share this diagnosis but are more sanguine about the possibilities of creating viable international organizations are normally classed as "idealists.") The best hope for moderation in the international system is a prudent calculation of the power interests of the state; theorists disagree about whether a bipolar or a multipolar system is more conducive to stability. Those who regard anarchy as less all-encompassing point to the increased possibilities of existing international institutions and believe that states can learn to guarantee their security by means other than war and the preparation for war. They are also more likely to regard differences in domestic regime to be key for an understanding of policy.

(See also DETERRENCE; IDEALISM; SECURITY DILEMMA; SOVEREIGNTY.)

Hedley Bull, *The Anarchical Society* (New York, 1977). Kenneth W. Waltz, *Theory of International Politics* (Reading, Mass., 1979). Stanley Hoffman, *Janus and Minerva* (Boulder, Colo., 1987).

MICHAEL JOSEPH SMITH

ANDORRA. The Principality of Andorra is located in the Pyrenees, bordering both Spain and France.

Catalan is the official language. Owing to a feudal agreement (called the *Pareatges*) entered into in 1278 by the Spanish bishop of Seu d'Urgell and the count of Foix, Andorra today is in the peculiar position of being governed not by a head of state but by two co-princes *(coprinceps)* with equal rights and powers—the bishop of Seu and the president of the French Republic (successor to the French monarchs, themselves successors to the count of Foix). This situation is more complex than that of the other European microstates, given the duality of co-princes, each directing his own administration (including, essentially, the *veguers,* who carry out police and executive functions, and the *batlles,* who are responsible for judicial functions), directed by the respective "permanent delegates." The only independent Andorran institution has traditionally been the *Consell General* (General Council), formed by representatives of the Andorran local councils, or *parròquies* (parishes), on an equalitarian basis (four delegates for each of the seven *parròquies,* irrespective of population).

This anachronistic structure might have been feasible in a predominantly rural society, but social and economic *modernization necessitated changes in the way in which Andorra is governed. In the 1950s, the Andorran economy began to develop thanks to winter sports tourism and the arrival of French and Spanish consumers who, given the principality's low levels of taxation, could purchase imported goods at comparatively low prices. This development attracted a large number of Spanish (and, to a lesser extent, French) immigrants who, because of the restrictive Andorran nationality code, are excluded from civil rights; in 1991, only 8,000 of the approximately 50,000 inhabitants of the principality had the right to vote. More recently, the development of the *European Community and, specifically, the entry of Spain into the community implied the suppression of tariff frontiers between Spain and France; Andorra thus lost its attractiveness as a fiscal paradise for citizens of those two countries.

Calls for popular participation and the need to establish relations with the European Community (which outstripped the traditional French claim to exercise a protectorate on Andorran international relations) led to the realization that institutional reforms were necessary. They are intended, in the long run, to turn Andorra into a modern, democratic, and independent state. In 1981, the co-princes agreed to a program of reforms, which has included the creation of an Andorran government (Consell *Executiu*), the transformation of the *Consell General* into a Parliament, and other minor reforms. In 1989, the co-princes and the government agreed to start the process of drafting a constitution as well. The pace of reforms, however, has been very slow: as of 1991, political parties and trade unions had not yet been legalized. Traditional sectors (supported by the bishop co-prince) oppose the more ambitious proposals forwarded by the government and the French president. With the creation of a tax system and the enlargement of *citizenship (still restricted to twenty percent of the population) as other major issues, Andorra faces a difficult process in becoming a full state before the end of the century.

B. Berlinguier, *La condition juridique des vallées d'Andorre* (Paris, 1970). Universitat Catalana d'Estiu, *Andorra: estat, institucions, societat* (Andorra, 1990).

Juan Botella Corral

ANGOLA. Although the Portuguese arrived in Angola by the late fifteenth century, it was not until the middle of the twentieth century that they seriously turned their attention to making Angola into a "settler colony." By the mid-1970s, the number of Portuguese settlers had climbed to nearly 350,000, constituting roughly six percent of the population.

Peaceful and nonviolent attempts by Angolans at acquiring political independence were put down ruthlessly by the colonial authorities. The armed struggle that ensued in the early 1960s soon split into three main movements: The Movimento Popular de Libertação de Angola (MPLA), the Frente Nacional para a Libertação de Angola (FNLA), and the União Nacional para a Independência Total de Angola (UNITA). Although ideological and ethnic differences were responsible for this division, the conflicting personal ambitions of the leaderships played an equally important role. FNLA was based among the Bakongo people in the north and UNITA among the Ovimbundu in the central and southern regions, both being extremely hostile to the involvement of white and *mestiço* (mixed-race) Angolans in the independence movement. While FNLA was antisocialist from the very beginning, UNITA became so after a confused and confusing interlude with Maoist rhetoric. With some exceptions, MPLA's leadership has, by and large, advocated and practiced a nonracial, nonethnic, and socialist approach to Angolan independence and development.

In 1974, the Portuguese Armed Forces Movement, which overthrew the fascist regime in Lisbon, committed itself to rapid *decolonization. As the end of Portuguese rule drew near in 1975, the simmering armed conflict between the three movements intensified rapidly. With *South Africa, *Zaire, France, and the United States backing FNLA and UNITA with substantial military, logistical, and financial support, MPLA turned to the Soviet Union and *Cuba for help. The deployment of Cuban soldiers was decisive in stopping the advance of the South African, Zairian, FNLA, and UNITA troops and forcing them into deep retreat. Seizing the initiative that this provided, MPLA proclaimed its one-party state, the People's Republic of Angola (PRA), in November 1975. Two years later, it adopted *Marxism-*Leninism as its official creed and imposed Leninist "democratic centralist" structures. The PRA soon won diplomatic recognition by a large number of governments, including the West, the singular exception to date being the United States.

Angola is a member of the *Organization of African Unity (OAU), the *Southern African Development Coordination Conference (SADCC), and the Preferential Trade Area for East and Southern Africa (PTA). It joined the *Lomé Convention in 1985. In 1989, despite U.S. opposition, it gained entry into the World Bank and the *International Monetary Fund (IMF).

Ending the War and Ensuring the Peace. Following its setbacks in 1976, the FNLA declined rapidly and ceased to exist as a viable force by the late 1970s. But UNITA recouped its strength under the protective umbrella of South Africa and the United States to carry on its attacks against the Angolan army, the noncombatant civilian population, and the infrastructure.

The war between South Africa and Angola, which had gone on intermittently since 1975, came to an end in September 1988, with the total withdrawal of South African troops from Angola. The United States and the Soviet Union actively promoted the negotiations that led to this accord. In a linked agreement, Cuba began a phased withdrawal of its troops in January 1989. By the end of May 1991, all Cuban troops had left Angola.

After a series of talks held in 1990 and 1991 under the aegis of *Portugal, with the very active involvement again of the United States and the Soviet Union, a peace agreement between the Angolan government and UNITA was signed and ratified in May 1991. The cease-fire that came into effect at the same time has held thus far.

Under the terms of the May 1991 agreement, all foreign military support to both sides is to cease, the greater part of the troops on both sides are to be disarmed and demobilized and a national army is to be formed with the remainder, and multiparty elections are to be held between September and November 1992. A Joint Political-Military Commission (CCPM) and its sub-bodies have been charged with the responsibility of ensuring that the cease-fire holds and that all the other components of the peace agreement are implemented. The CCPM comprises equal numbers of Angolan government and UNITA officials, as well as observers from the United States, the Soviet Union, and Portugal. A UN team of 600 will monitor the whole peace process.

Meanwhile, U.S. assistance to UNITA continues, with the House of Representatives approving a $30 million covert aid program in June 1991. The UNITA chief of staff has spoken openly of requesting funds from the U.S. government to contest the 1992 elections. The parallel with *Nicaragua is obvious.

Changes in the Constitution and Moves toward a Multiparty Democracy. In October 1990, the Central Committee of the MPLA discarded the party's

Marxist-Leninist *ideology, replacing it with a vague "democratic *socialism." In March 1991, the national legislature (which was elected in 1986 under the then-existing *one-party system) passed a number of laws amending the constitution in consonance with the move toward a pluralist democratic society. The amended Constitution enshrines the principles of multiparty politics, universal suffrage, and the secret ballot. It incorporates civil liberties and fundamental rights, including the freedoms of assembly, expression, the press, and the trade unions. It grants the right to strike. It omits all references to socialism, committing itself to a mixed economy, with the right to private property.

In parallel with these changes, nearly twenty-five new political parties have sprung up. Most of them, however, are minuscule in size. The real electoral contest will be between MPLA and UNITA. The former has some strength in the urban areas, which hold one-third of the population. The leader of UNITA, Dr. Jonas Savimbi, is expecting massive electoral support from his ethnic group, the Ovimbundu—the country's largest. And both MPLA and UNITA are courting the support of a resurrected FNLA, with its base among the Bakongo, the third-largest ethnic group, after the Mbundu. Meanwhile, pending the outcome of the general elections in the latter half of 1992, the MPLA government continues to operate with near-total concentration of powers in the hands of the president, the highly educated, urbane, and soft-spoken José Eduardo dos Santos.

Promises of Radical Changes in the Economy. Angola is a vast country with a very small population, estimated at 10 million in 1991. It is extremely well endowed with all sorts of natural resources, including important minerals. Despite the country's immense potential wealth, the economy is in ruins because of the voluntary mass exodus of Portuguese skills and assets after independence in 1975 and the ravages of fifteen years of postcolonial war.

Under these formidably difficult conditions, it is not surprising that the Angolan government's attempts at reviving the ruined economy through state ownership and control should have proved so futile. Among other things, the lack of skills, the general incompetence, and the *corruption of the state bureaucracy condemned the efforts to failure.

The one bright spot in this otherwise dismal picture is the petroleum sector, run by foreign firms. It is doing very well. Petroleum exports generate over ninety percent of the hard currency income, which pays for the indispensable imports of essential food and consumer goods, machines and intermediate goods, vehicles and spare parts, and defense requirements.

Notwithstanding its substantial income from petroleum and diamond exports (estimated at US$3.85 billion in 1990), Angola has borrowed heavily from abroad, its total external debt estimated at US$7 billion in 1990. Like most other countries in Africa, it too is firmly caught in the debt trap and has appealed for the rescheduling of its debt repayments.

Since 1987 the Angolan government has issued statements and announced plans (and passed some laws) whose intentions are to liberalize the economy in the free market direction. In principle, the government has pledged to devalue the currency massively; reduce government wages; fight the astronomical inflation; privatize parts of the public sector; cut its subsidies to urban consumers, the defense forces, and public sector enterprises; create favorable conditions for domestic private enterprise; and provide strong inducements to foreign investors. In practice, however, the one significant measure taken so far was to introduce a new national currency, the New Kwanza, in September 1990, and to devalue it by a factor of two against the U.S. dollar in March 1991. Most of the other measures remain declarations on paper.

The Structural Adjustment Programme (SAP) demanded by the IMF and the *World Bank has been deferred several times. It is highly unlikely that MPLA and its government will risk imposing further hardships through the SAP on an already exhausted population until the elections are over late in 1992.

(See also ETHNICITY; INTERNATIONAL DEBT; SOUTHERN AFRICA.)

B. Davidson, *In the Eye of the Storm: Angola's People* (London, 1972). G. J. Bender, *Angola Under the Portuguese: the Myth and the Reality* (London, 1978). F. W. Heimer, *The Decolonization Conflict in Angola, 1974–76* (Geneva, 1979). M. Wolfers and J. Bergerol, *Angola in the Front Line* (London, 1983). M. R. Bhagavan, *Angola's Political Economy, 1975–1985* (Uppsala, 1986). G. Walker, *Angola: The Promise of Riches* (London, 1990).

M. R. BHAGAVAN

ANGOLAN CONFLICT. Contention over *Angola since Portuguese control began to crumble in April 1974 has reflected an intricate interaction of international, regional, and domestic components. In the first phase, until March 1976, three Angolan parties vied for power. The Frente Nacional para a Libertação de Angola (FNLA), headed by Holden Roberto, was based among Kikongo-speaking people in the north, and backed by Mobuto Sese Seko of *Zaire and the U.S. *Central Intelligence Agency (CIA). Jonas Savimbi's União Nacional para a Independência Total de Angola (UNITA), which had collaborated with the Portuguese army during the last years of the anticolonial war, claimed leadership of Umbundu-speaking Angolans and others of the south and east. During 1975 it was assisted both by the CIA and by the presence of troops from *South Africa. The Movimento Popular de Libertação de Angola (MPLA), which proclaimed the People's Republic of Angola under President Agostinho Neto in November 1975, based its political appeals on national rather than ethnic grounds and gained support particularly among urban Angolans around the country. Its strongest base, however, was among

Kimbundu-speaking people and *mestiços* in and around the capital, Luanda; its closest international ally was *Cuba.

There is still dispute over responsibility for the armed conflict that erupted in early 1975, only months after an agreement on elections and a peaceful transition to independence. The process of mistrust and escalation was clearly reciprocal. But most analysts agree that one decisive factor was the U.S. policy of eliminating the MPLA, which was considered unacceptably radical. U.S., Zairian, and South African intervention was matched step-by-step by Cuban advisers and troops, with the aid of the Soviet Union, until the U.S. Congress barred further U.S. involvement and African opinion coalesced against South African intervention. By April 1976 both Zairian and South African troops had withdrawn, the FNLA was a spent force, and UNITA was dispersed in the bush.

In the second phase, since March 1976, the MPLA-led People's Republic of Angola was the target both of *guerrilla warfare and of direct South African attacks. In the north a détente with Zaire was reached in 1978, and significant numbers of FNLA members were reconciled with the Angolan government. From 1979 through 1985, when the U.S. Congress lifted restrictions on U.S. military involvement in Angola, Zaire's hostility to Angola was muted. Thereafter CIA aid to UNITA was resumed through Zaire. To the south, however, Angola provided support for guerrillas seeking the independence of South African–occupied *Namibia, and South Africa backed UNITA on a massive scale until the independence of Namibia in 1990.

After an initial period of limited guerrilla actions, from 1979 UNITA occupied part of southeastern Angola with the aid of South African troops, using this sparsely populated zone as a base for attacks on more densely populated central areas. Conflict over the supply routes in the southeast led to several large-scale battles involving South African and Cuban troops as well as Angolan government and UNITA forces, culminating in a setback for South Africa in the 1987–1988 period.

The December 1988 agreements on Namibian independence and withdrawal of Cuban troops from Angola resulted in cessation of large-scale South African military involvement with UNITA. The United States, however, had never recognized the Angolan government and had encouraged South African and other support for UNITA even while U.S. involvement was prohibited by Congress. It escalated direct military aid to UNITA in 1989, and a military stalemate ensued.

Peace negotiations to reconcile UNITA and the Angolan government began in 1989 and continued into 1990. Prospects were enhanced by war-weariness on both sides in Angola, by improved U.S-Soviet relations, and by the absence of South African motives for intervention. After extended

negotiations in Portugal, mediated by the Portuguese government with the assistance of the United States and the Soviet Union, the two sides reached agreement on a cease-fire in May 1991. The peace plan called for merger of the two armies into a nonpartisan national army, and for multiparty elections to be held by November 1992.

Hostility between Savimbi and the MPLA leadership probably would have prolonged conflict after independence in any case. But the scale and longevity of the UNITA insurgency were largely due to South Africa's aggressive efforts to maintain its position in Namibia and the region, and to the ideologically inspired U.S. campaign to punish the MPLA and Cuba by promoting a model Reagan-doctrine anticommunist insurgency.

John A. Marcum, *The Angolan Revolution* (Boston, 1969, 1978). John Stockwell, *In Search of Enemies: A CIA Story* (New York, 1978). F. W. Heimer, *The Decolonization Conflict in Angola, 1974–76* (Geneva, 1979).

WILLIAM MINTER

ANTARCTICA. The international *regime covering activity in Antarctica and the Southern Ocean is defined by the 1959 Antarctic Treaty, as supplemented by the 1972 Convention on the Conservation of Antarctic Seals, the 1980 Convention on the Conservation of Antarctic Marine Living Resources, the 1991 Protocol on Environmental Protection plus Annexes, and a large set of consultative parties' recommendations. The 1988 Convention on the Regulation of Antarctic Mineral Resource Activities has been set aside in favor of a fifty-year moratorium on mineral and hydrocarbon exploitation.

The Antarctic Treaty was negotiated among the twelve states—seven territorial claimants (Argentina, Australia, Chile, France, New Zealand, Norway, and the United Kingdom), two superpowers, and three others (Belgium, Japan, and South Africa)—operating Antarctic research stations during the International Geophysical Year (IGY) in 1957–1958. It created a regime based on four shared principles and one compromise. The shared principles are 1) existence of an "Antarctic community" using and managing the area jointly, 2) scientific cooperation, 3) nonmilitarization, and 4) environmental protection. The compromise allows parties to avoid disputes about territorial *sovereignty by putting claims into abeyance for the treaty's duration.

The Antarctic regime is unusual in many respects. Though "regional" in its focus on a particular geographical area, participating states are self-selected from around the world on the functional criterion of supporting scientific research. Like regional regimes, but unlike global functional ones, it was created and still operates outside the UN. It is also unusual in having two distinct classes of members. The twelve original members plus any other state sponsoring "substantial scientific research" on the continent hold voting rights as "consultative parties." Twenty-six states now hold such status. The other fourteen participating states, the "nonconsultative parties," have sent observers to meetings since 1983 but have no vote. Increasing the number of consultative parties, particularly by including major Third World states like Brazil, China, and India, buttresses the regime's political strength vis-à-vis outsiders, but also increases the probability of intragroup stalemate because most decisions must be made unanimously.

The low intensity and almost exclusively scientific focus of Antarctic activity in the 1960s and 1970s allowed participating states to manage Antarctic affairs through biennial consultative meetings. The Scientific Committee on Antarctic Research (SCAR)—a transnational committee of scientists initially created by the International Congress of Scientific Unions to coordinate IGY programs—provided expert advice as needed. Increased activity has led to the creation of three standing bodies—the Commission on Antarctic Marine Living Resources in 1980, the Council of Managers of National Antarctic Programs within SCAR in 1988, and the Committee on Environmental Protection in 1991—and to proposals for creating a small secretariat for the consultative parties.

In recent years the Antarctic regime has been questioned by two sets of external challengers. The first, a coalition of nonmember states led by Malaysia, has sought to replace the Antarctic Treaty system by a regime based on the "common heritage of mankind" principle. Both the initial idea of vesting management in a UN body operating under one state—one vote and majority rules, and the fallback proposals for some form of global participation in management of resource activity within the Antarctic Treaty framework quickly stalled because of united consultative party opposition and lack of consensus among the Malaysia group. The second set of challengers, a coalition of private environmentalist organizations, has sought to prevent resource activity by having the Antarctic declared a "world park" or "wilderness preserve."

Maintaining the Antarctic regime required settling the disagreements on resource and environmental questions that divided participating states. These differences became public in early 1989 when the Australian and French governments announced support for banning mineral and hydrocarbon exploitation. Both were among the nine states (the seven claimants plus the United States and the Soviet Union) able unilaterally to keep the 1988 minerals convention from entering into force. Other consultative parties, particularly the U.S. and British governments, felt that the minerals agreement should be retained but supplemented by agreements on environmental issues. Lengthy discussions at several meetings in 1989, 1990, and 1991 yielded the protocol on environmental protection. It requires parties to give priority to science over other activities, meet certain environmental standards in all activities, assess environmental impact before commencing activities, participate in environmental monitoring, and respect the fifty-year moratorium.

(See also ENVIRONMENTALISM.)

Peter J. Beck, *The International Politics of Antarctica* (New York, 1986). Arnfinn Jorgensen-Dahl and Willy Ostreng, eds., *The Antarctic Treaty System in World Politics* (London, 1991).

M. J. PETERSON

ANTIGUA AND BARBUDA. See ENGLISH-SPEAKING CARIBBEAN.

ANTISEMITISM. Discrimination, prejudice, bigotry, racism, and xenophobia have existed in all historical eras and in all countries, yet there is something distinctive in the extraordinary persistence of antisemitism, or hatred of Jews, historically and spatially. A wholly disproportionate amount of the attention given to the existence of Jews has been critical in character, irrespective of any specific behavior. Or it has focused for varied and often contradictory reasons on the alleged negative qualities of Jews. No other group of people has suffered from a regime like that of Nazi Germany, whose leaders had the total extermination of a whole people as a defining ideological motivation. Throughout history Jews have suffered from massacres, burning, expropriation of property, expulsions, wearing of special badges, imposition of quotas, legal and social discrimination, and denial of and limits on freedom.

Antisemitism has emanated from all political persuasions, from holders of all religious beliefs, from those critical of Christianity or Judaism, and from all social groups. Hatred of Jews has been manifested when they lived in segregated ghettoes and when they shared emancipated environments with non-Jews. It has persisted in an age of universal suffrage and change in the nature of economic systems.

What distinguishes antisemitism from the ever-present prejudice or hostility directed against other (non-Jewish) people and groups is not so much the strength and passion of this hatred and its many-faceted character and the range of arguments and doctrines that see Jews at best as peripheral in society and at worst as destructive monsters and forces of evil. Some arguments—whether of a political, economic, social, religious, or psychological nature—make a claim to rationality. The claim is that the Jews, because of their religious customs, insistence on monotheism, dietary habits, or tribal exclusiveness, are alien to the traditions and ways of life of the societies in which they live, try to subvert those societies, or are able to control both these societies and other diabolical forces in the world.

The uniqueness of antisemitism is that no other

group of people in the world has been charged simultaneously with alienation from society and with cosmopolitanism; with being capitalist exploiters and agents of international finance and also revolutionary agitators; with having a materialist mentality and with being people of the Book; with acting as militant aggressors and with being cowardly; with adherence to a superstitious religion and with being agents of modernism; with upholding a rigid law and also being morally decadent; with being a chosen people and also having an inferior human nature; with both arrogance and timidity; with both individualism and communal adherence; with being guilty of the crucifixion of Christ and at the same time held to account for the invention of Christianity. Even in ancient Greece and Rome, the refusal of Jews to recognize pagan gods and their different rituals, their practice of circumcision, their observance of the Sabbath, their dietary laws, and intermarriage among Jews set them apart. Christian hostility was based on the responsibility of Jews, who rejected Christianity and the Messiah, for the crucifixion of Jesus, which justified their "perpetual servitude." From early modern European history on, Jews were castigated for their ethnic separation, culture, and autonomous community.

Logically, it might have been expected that the criticism of Jewish particularity would cease in the era of European emancipation and the gradual removal of many traditional restrictions and forms of discrimination. Emancipation would, it was believed, bring with it assimilation, if not religious conversion, and the elimination of supposedly Jewish behavioral characteristics.

The religious element of antisemitism, resting on Jewish rejection of the true faith, may indeed have been reduced, if not eliminated. But in its place greater prominence was given to Jewish characteristics, which were partly genetic in nature and partly the result of alien cultural and ethnic traditions. Purported characteristics such as moral insensitivity, superstitious habits, lack of social graces, and cultural inferiority now rendered Jews incapable of true citizenship.

Unexpectedly, the Enlightenment helped produce a new rationale for antisemitism. Some of its major figures, especially Voltaire, were instrumental in providing a secular anti-Jewish rhetoric in the name of European culture rather than religion.

Not surprisingly, the visibility of the Jewish community, especially in central Europe, buttressed the argument that Jews were cultural aliens who were disproportionately prominent in elite positions. Envy of economic success by Jews, resentment of their position in certain businesses and professions, criticism of their central role in the sphere of distribution and of their crucial situation as intermediaries, and jealousy of their conspicuous role in cultural and intellectual life led to the charge that Jews were subverting the economic basis of society and were responsible for its problems, economic crises, dislocation of individuals, and any reduction in the standard of living.

Reinforcing this charge of the alien nature of Jews has been a second, more recent one of racial inferiority. The very coining of the term *antisemitism* by Wilhelm Marr in 1879 suggested that opposition was being registered to racial characteristics rather than religious beliefs. Secular racial antisemitism has never really been anything other than antagonism to Jews. The myth of Jewish biological inferiority justified the continuing attacks in a more secular age because evils in society supposedly were traceable to the presence of the Jewish race. The argument of biological differences marks the emergence of the genocidal strain in modern antisemitism. The world, it was concluded, must be saved from Judaization.

In other words, Jews were considered a threat to culture itself, as the materialist spirit of their race presumably eroded true values. Much of the original support for Nazism rested on its claim that it was defending the true European values against the threat to Aryan virility—a claim that stemmed from the inculcation of the nineteenth-century and twentieth-century German ideology of the *Volk* in both racial and nonracial forms. The *Volk* must overcome and reject the materialism and capitalism symbolized by the urban and rationalistic Jew.

Paradoxically, the charge that Jews were a separate ethnic group, thus justifying denial of their individual rights, did not lead to a recognition that they were also members of a collective entity with its own self-consciousness and interest in collective self-determination as a nation-state. The price of civil and political equality in this view was renunciation of any collective identification by Jews. For two centuries this argument has been made, but in the present it has another dimension. The question of Jewish nationhood or collective identity is now linked with the state of Israel.

In world politics, the principle of Jewish self-determination as people with the right to form its own state has often been regarded less sympathetically than in the case of other peoples. Not only has the creation of *Israel been opposed by Arab and Muslim countries, but its claim to legitimacy as a sovereign state also troubles left-wing Western intellectuals who have no similar difficulty with the claims of other groups.

The establishment of the state led in part to the transformation of the traditionally perceived image of Jews. That image—of the sinister economic force, usurer, moneylender, landlord, parasite—still survives, if in much-reduced fashion, but it has now been superseded by that of the Israelis, or Zionists, who are criticized as arrogant, colonialist, imperialist, and racist. Political anti-Zionism is not synonymous with traditional antisemitism. Nevertheless, many current examples show that one belief is not readily distinguishable from the other.

In addition to the criticism of Jewish particularity, a historical source of antagonism has proceeded from the concept of Jews as the "chosen people." The concept was meaningful for the early leaders of the Church and of Islam. For antisemites the chosen people embody fanaticism, evil, or an attitude of superiority to other peoples. They perceive the Old Testament as the source of Jewish fanaticism, tribal nationalism, and communal exclusivism, and now as the basis for the aggressive attitude of the state of Israel.

To explain the pathological obsession with Jews some have resorted to psychological factors, as did Jean-Paul Sartre in his famous definition of the antisemite as a person who is afraid. Troubled people project their own anxieties, drives, impulses of which they are ashamed, and negative self-images onto Jews, who are then seen as aggressive, competitive, and secretive; are resented as a "chosen people"; and are made a scapegoat for the failures of society and themselves.

Fear of a worldwide Jewish plot or conspiracy has been manifested in a variety of ways, whether Christian, Enlightenment, socialist, Marxist, Third World, or Nazi in form. The Nazi version was that Jews were destroyers of culture and constituted the basis of a worldwide conspiracy. The conclusion was that the Jewish race was a microbe or bacillus that had to be eliminated so that purification could be obtained. Thus the Nazis justified the policy of total extermination or *Holocaust of an entire people.

Today, the virus of antisemitism continues to infect the rhetoric and actions of heterogeneous groups: religious fundamentalists, elements of the Right, blacks, Arab and Islamic countries, the Third World, the Soviet Union, the political Left, and those who are critical of liberal democratic systems. Christian hostility toward Jews has declined considerably. But the 2,000-year-old Christian prejudice, with its negative moral and spiritual conception of Jews, has still not ended. In Western societies, now that Jews, the former pariahs, have moved into the center of society and compete on equal terms for its key positions, prejudice has become alloyed with resentment.

Yet hostility toward Jews has also come from the political Left. With the Socialist movement in the nineteenth century came sharp criticism of the role of Jews in capitalist systems. In this criticism Karl Marx (among others) was an influential figure in arguing that Judaism constituted the essence of capitalism. The contemporary hostility to Israel of the Left, which has associated it with imperialism, pronounced it a racist state, and regarded *Zionism as the only national liberation movement that is "reactionary" rather than progressive, suggests deeper emotions.

Antisemitic attitudes in the United States are higher in the African-American community than among whites. Contrary to the situation with American whites, black antisemitism is inversely related both to age (the strongest antisemitism is expressed by young blacks) and to educational level, as better-educated blacks are more negative than the less educated. Typically, black leaders (other than members of Congress) and the more politically conscious African-Americans are more frequently negative than the majority of blacks. Although analytically quite distinct, this more negative attitude toward Jews overlaps in general with a less sympathetic attitude to Israel than that held by whites.

To the Islamic world, Jews no longer conform to the stereotype of a tolerated but subordinated minority. Muslim treatment of Jews has historically been less harsh than that in Western countries or that accorded Christians in Muslim countries, partly because Jews did not challenge the political supremacy of Muslims. But now Jews rule over Muslims. To this has been added the growing antisemitism first introduced by diplomatic and Christian missions to Arab countries and by antisemitic European works such as the *Protocols of the Elders of Zion*. Antisemitism in the Islamic world has dramatically increased since the formation of the state of Israel in 1948.

In the Soviet Union antisemitism flourished for a variety of reasons: resentment of Jewish overrepresentation in certain occupations, annoyance at Jews who were critical of the system or who struggled for human rights, inherited prejudice from tsarist times, rancor at the desire of Jews to emigrate, and the use of antisemitism as an instrument for the regime to gain popularity among the population and to deflect attention from the country's pressing problems. Soviet antisemitism directly infected current thought in the rest of the world through its criticism of Jewish traits and behavior; moreover, until they abated during the Gorbachev era, Soviet attacks on the actions of Israel affected the international community, especially the UN, which reached its lowest point with the 1975 "Zionism is racism" resolution.

In the postwar period there has been a significant decline in democratic countries in discriminatory attitudes and in the numbers of those who are strongly prejudiced against Jews. Antisemitism is now not politically or intellectually respectable. No important political organization in the United States or in other democratic countries openly advocates antisemitic views, nor are Jews denied civil or political rights in those countries. But the phenomenon of antisemitism has still not disappeared either in attitudes and beliefs or in patterns of behavior.

(See also RACE AND RACISM; ZIONISM.)

Jacob Katz, *From Prejudice to Destruction* (Cambridge, Mass., 1980). Norman Cohn, *Warrant for Genocide* (Decatur, Ga., 1981). Michael Curtis, ed., *Antisemitism in the Contemporary World* (Boulder, Colo., 1985). Bernard Lewis, *Semites and Anti-Semites* (New York, 1987). Leon Poliakov, *The History of Antisemitism* (New York, 1987).
MICHAEL CURTIS

ANZUS TREATY. The ANZUS Treaty between *Australia, *New Zealand, and the United States was signed in San Francisco in September 1951. Although designed originally to afford United States *security backing for Australia and New Zealand against any future threat posed by a resurgent Japan, it is a very generalized document containing loose guarantees of support with no specific threat enumerated. The key article, Article IV, stipulates that "each Party recognises that an armed attack in the Pacific area on any of the Parties would be dangerous to its own peace and safety and declares that it would act to meet the common danger in accordance with its constitutional processes." The treaty was designed to remain in force indefinitely although any party could "cease to be a member of the Council" following one year's notice (Art. X). There is no provision for expulsion.

For more than a decade after it was signed ANZUS did not provide the primary basis for Australian and New Zealand defense. It was only with the advent of the *Vietnam War and the British policy of withdrawal east of Suez that ANZUS came to the forefront. Technically, Vietnam fell more under the *Southeast Asia Treaty Organization (SEATO) arrangements than under ANZUS, but the ANZUS link was used to bring influence to bear upon New Zealand in particular.

In practice, the United States tended to regard Australia and New Zealand as one, and any important differences in approach between the two needed to be settled in advance in Canberra, or they tended to be ignored. Yet in reality Australia and New Zealand had divergent regional interests. The Australian focus was on neighboring *Indonesia, on its security concerns in the divided island of New Guinea, and on the potentially troubled area of the Indian Ocean. New Zealand meanwhile tended to concentrate on the world of micro- or ministates in the Southwest Pacific. Also, New Zealand was not keyed into the U.S. global deterrence network through such facilities as the important communications and relay facilities at North West Cape, Pine Gap, or Nurrungar in Australia.

Strains in the alliance emerged in the late 1960s and early 1970s. Opposition to nuclear power in New Zealand came into conflict with a resumption of visits by nuclear-powered U.S. warships, which had been suspended pending acceptance of insurance liability for nuclear accident. By 1984, three of the four leading New Zealand political parties contesting the general election of that year advocated a ban on nuclear-ship visits. The ban covered both ships carrying—or likely to be carrying—*nuclear weapons and those that were nuclear-propelled. The remaining party, the National Party, adopted a similar policy before being returned to power in 1990, by which time the ban had been enshrined in legislation.

Subsequently, with the U.S. decision to remove nuclear weapons from its warships, a major obstacle was removed, but, despite a softening of the attitude on the part of the national government, the legislation ensured that problems continued to exist over the prohibition of nuclear propulsion. The ban was not intended as a rejection of ANZUS for, in effect, New Zealanders wanted both the ban and retention of the alliance. The United States claimed that the ban amounted to a nonfulfillment of New Zealand's obligations under the treaty and declared its security guarantee for New Zealand nonoperative.

In formal terms, the ANZUS Treaty continues, with one partner nonoperative. In practice, Australia and the United States have always been the dominant partners. New Zealand's relations with the United States have been downgraded from ally to friendly country while Australia continues to maintain close defense cooperation with both countries, only separately rather than as part of a tripartite *alliance.

(See also INDIAN OCEAN REGION.)

Jacob Bercovitch, ed., *ANZUS in Crisis: Alliance Management in International Affairs* (London, 1988).
                                                    KEITH JACKSON

APARTHEID. In 1948 the Nationalist Party (NP) was swept into power by the crisis of "segregation" policies that had guided "native policy" in *South Africa since the formation of the Union in 1910. The NP program was summed up in the concept of "apartheid," or "apartness." The policy of segregation which excluded all people who were not white from the organs of power, except for a handful of Coloureds, and especially after the elimination of the Cape Africans' qualified franchise in 1936, had become, by 1948, nothing more than a pragmatic plugging of the leaks in the structures of segregation as they occurred and were judged to undermine white domination.

The policy of apartheid represented a qualitatively new stage to entrench and guarantee white minority rule, exploitation, and oppression. It was racism unbridled and unrestrained; it was blatant at home and it was terroristic at home and abroad. It made racism and anticommunism the main principles of state policy.

The milestones on the political road to an apartheid state had been laid down systematically beginning with the Act of Union in 1909 which, by excluding the black majority from participation in politics, guaranteed them powerlessness. The Land Act of 1913 ensured that mine owners would have a regular supply of cheap black labor. The overrepresentation of rural white voters who were mostly Afrikaner farmers in the whites-only Parliament ensured that the farming interest would be guaranteed their labor needs. The "civilized" labor policies made certain that white workers kept all skilled and semiskilled jobs. In other words, the NP did not invent the policy of white supremacy and black political powerlessness. What they did was to give the policy of white domination and African exploitation a sense of finality. Indeed, its assumptions were simple: white power and disciplined, cheap black labor.

On this premise the NP, which claimed to represent Afrikanerdom, built the edifice of apartheid. The essential difference between the policy of apartheid and that of segregation is that, for the advocates of apartheid, white domination and African subservience were not a matter for discussion or negotiation. Africans had to accept ultimate submission or prepare for revolution. In 1960, rather than negotiate African grievances, the regime banned the *African National Congress (ANC), which had been formed in 1912, and the Pan-African Congress, which had split from the ANC in 1958.

The years 1948 to 1988 were characterized by the NP's attempt to forcibly subjugate all independent political expression by the African people, Indians, Coloureds, and progressive whites. The first political organization to be proscribed was the South African Communist Party in 1950. Later, especially in the 1970s and 1980s, the Black Consciousness movement and the United Democratic Front fell victims to the ban. By the 1960s a battery of laws decided who belonged to what "racial" group, who could live in a particular area, who could attend what university, who could have sex with whom, and so on. And, to prevent a breach in these statutes and regulations, a fearsome police and informer system was put in place to control every aspect of life of the people of South Africa. There were laws that reminded whites that their privileges depended on their observance of the etiquette of white supremacy.

The whites-only franchise made it possible from 1910 to the 1970s for whites of different classes to unite and to maintain black subservience by keeping the latter divided along ethnic, linguistic, and other lines. From 1948, through the policy of apartheid, the regime reinforced the political and social divisions among Africans by further restricting their rights to urban residence and by developing the reserves into independent "homelands" where Africans could enjoy their "freedom" and exercise their "democratic rights." The reserves, always reservoirs of cheap labor, by the 1970s began to be granted independence. But the very success of building the white economy on cheap, black labor had undermined the very basis of apartheid. The influx control laws could not stem the tide of African *urbanization. Today across the urban landscape are huge concentrations of African townships and slums whose residents have united across ethnic lines, the very development that apartheid was supposed to stop.

In 1961, Hendrik Verwoerd, the architect of apartheid's native policy who had become prime minister in 1958, withdrew South Africa from the *Commonwealth and declared a republic. This was a crowning moment; the Afrikaner struggle for absolute control of South Africa had been achieved. It

remained for the English-speaking section of the white population to reconcile itself to this political fact.

The fifth anniversary of the declaration of South Africa as a white republic was celebrated at the Voortrekker Monument in Pretoria with all its attendant pomp and circumstance. Verwoerd, who made the main speech, with great sentiment recapitulated the steps the Afrikaner had taken to achieve the republic. He paid tribute to previous Afrikaner leaders who had helped achieve this. Turning to the English speakers, he reminded them (in English) of the economic prosperity they had enjoyed under apartheid rule. In September 1966, Verwoerd was assassinated in the House of Parliament.

The *assassination was the turning point; Afrikaner self-confidence was replaced by doubt. In the final analysis, South Africa's racial policy was based on the determination of the white minority to retain all political power and economic and social privilege in white hands. These goals, whites believed, necessitated that they have exclusive control of the state. The brutality with which apartheid was maintained had led the UN in the early 1960s to declare it a crime against humanity. In 1961 the *Organization of African Unity had been formed, and one of its goals was to fight against white colonial enclaves in Africa and especially against apartheid. In the 1970s and 1980s South Africa's international position had so deteriorated that the Western powers were forced by world public opinion to introduce various sanctions against their once-favored offspring. In 1976 the Soweto uprising underlined the fact that the methods of apartheid rule had lost their potency, and the collapse of Portuguese colonial rule in 1975 and the independence of *Zimbabwe in 1980 left the apartheid regime without an overall strategy to control the political agenda. The theological foundations of apartheid also collapsed in the 1980s.

Recognizing that political arrangements that were considered natural in 1910 were now, in the second half of the twentieth century, considered offensive abroad and an insult at home, the NP began to take steps to reform apartheid. The debate about the future of apartheid pitted the *Verkampte* camp (the "narrow ones") against the *Verligtes* (the "enlightened ones"). By the 1980s the debate was no longer an idle intellectual exercise about this or that aspect of apartheid but about the best way to share political power between blacks and whites. The tumultuous events unleashed by the constitutional dispensation to the Coloureds and Indians saw the NP split into various factions ranging from the extreme right to those on the left. The release of Nelson *Mandela from prison in February 1990 and the unbanning of the ANC and other organizations meant that the political circle had turned one hundred and eighty degrees. President de Klerk has now accepted that South Africa is a unitary state and the majority will rule. The issue in the negotiations between the ANC and the NP involves the modalities of how majority rule should guarantee political *pluralism in the future.

(See also Race and Racism; Sharpeville Massacre; Soweto Rebellion.)

A. Hepple, *Verwoerd* (London,1967). Bernard Magubane, *The Political Economy of Race and Class in South Africa* (New York, 1969, 1989). Dunbar Moodie, *The Rise of Afrikanerdom, Power, Apartheid, and the Afrikaner Civil Religion* (Berkeley, Calif., 1975). Dan O'Meara, *Volkskapitalisme, Class, Capital and Ideology in the Development of Afrikaner Nationalism, 1934–1948* (Johannesburg, 1983).

                                    Bernard Magubane

AQUINO, Corazon. On 25 February 1986 Corazon ("Cory") Cojuangco Aquino became the first woman president of the Philippines through a popular revolt following a failed coup attempt against Ferdinand *Marcos, her predecessor in office. Widow of former Senator Benigno ("Ninoy") Aquino, Marcos's principal political rival, she participated in the snap elections in February 1986 after more than one million Filipinos signed their names endorsing her candidacy.

She was born on 25 January 1933 of wealthy and politically prominent families in Luzon. Her father was a Filipino Chinese businessman and politician from Tarlac, her mother a member of a political clan in Rizal. Cory was educated in Catholic schools in Manila and the United States, receiving a bachelor's degree from the College of Mount St. Vincent in New York City.

Her marriage to Ninoy Aquino in 1954 brought two politically prominent Tarlac families together. He was an impressive journalist-politician—young, articulate, witty, dynamic—who went on to become his town's youngest mayor, his province's youngest vice-governor and governor, and, by 1967, the youngest Philippine senator.

When martial law was declared on 21 September 1972, Marcos ordered the arrest and prolonged imprisonment of his opponents, led by Ninoy Aquino. Aquino's seven-year detention was followed by exile in the United States on humanitarian grounds. His *assassination on his return to Manila on 21 August 1983 triggered middle-class protest against Marcos, culminating in the "People Power Revolt" that led to Marcos's fall and Cory Aquino's rise to power.

Her presidency began with overwhelming popularity. It was marked, however, by constant threat from military factions loyal to Marcos and closely identified with his former defense minister, Juan Ponce Enrile. Enrile, General Fidel V. Ramos, the vice chief of staff, and an organization called the Reform the Armed Forces of the Philippines Movement (RAM) had led a mutiny amid mass protest against the fraudulent February 1986 elections. Enlisting popular support, they claimed electoral victory for Cory Aquino. Since 1986, however, Enrile and RAM have continued plotting against the government.

Cory Aquino saw her role simply as a transition president whose tasks were to restore democracy and to revive the country's devastated economy. She was constrained, however, by the tenacity of inherited socioeconomic and politico-military problems. Her abhorrence of patronage and party politics caused her shaky coalition to fragment, thereby costing her a vehicle for effective governance. Reluctant to wield power, she sacrificed the opportunity to institute socioeconomic measures as lasting foundations for meaningful economic progress and political stability.

Aware of her country's vulnerabilities and cognizant of the imperative of national independence, she sought in 1990 to restructure her country's relations with the United States by serving notice of termination of the agreement on military basing rights. In mid-1992 she was succeeded as president of the Philippines by former defense secretary Fidel Ramos, whom Aquino had endorsed in a hotly contested multiparty election. Her legacy of uniting Filipinos against authoritarian rule and defending the transition to democracy against its enemies became an inspiration for subsequent prodemocracy movements elsewhere in the world. She will be remembered as the frail, bespectacled widow in yellow courageously leading her people in nonviolent resistance against dictatorship.

(See also Democratic Transitions.)

Claude A. Buss, *Cory Aquino and the People of the Philippines* (Stanford, Calif., 1987).

                                    Carolina G. Hernandez

ARAB-ISRAELI CONFLICT. Since 1948, when Jewish inhabitants of the former colonial mandate of *Palestine established the state of *Israel, the Arab-Israeli conflict has appeared on the agenda of every session of the UN General Assembly and was discussed at nearly every summit conference between leaders of the United States and the Soviet Union.

The conflict has roots which go back to the 1890s when numerous Jewish settlers first came from Europe into Palestine and the Zionist movement began to lay the foundations for a future Jewish homeland in a territory with an overwhelmingly Arab population. The clash of this Jewish state-building project with the emerging nationalist sentiment of the indigenous Palestinian Arabs gave rise to bitter intercommunal struggles during the mandate period and led to the deep conflict that lay ahead. Though only a small territory was at stake—with few natural resources—the conflict was eventually magnified in international significance by the fact that the territory is sacred to three of the world's great religions, by the intersection of the conflict with politics in the world's most important oil-producing region, and by the connection of the conflict to the emerging *Cold War between the Soviet Union and the United States.

In November 1947, to the shock and dismay of the Arabs, the UN partitioned Palestine into two states (as well as an international enclave for Jerusalem), giving fifty-five percent of the territory to the Jewish state. As British forces withdrew, a civil war broke out between Jews and Arabs. When Israel declared its independence in May of 1948, several *Arab League members sent units of their regular armies to join Arab guerrilla forces fighting in Palestine. Israel eventually won this *war, aided by weapons it received from the Soviet bloc. The poorly armed Arab armies and Palestinian irregulars, badly led and unable to coordinate their operations, were no match for the Jewish forces.

After the fighting stopped in 1949, Israel gained about 5,200 square kilometers (2,000 sq. mi.) beyond the area allocated in the UN partition plan, and it now occupied over seventy-five percent of Palestine. The UN-sponsored armistice agreements, signed between Israel and the Arab belligerents (*Egypt, *Jordan, *Lebanon, and *Syria), gave Egypt control of the Gaza Strip and gave Jordan control over some 5,200 square kilometers (2,000 sq. mi.) of eastern Palestine on the west bank of the Jordan River, including the Old City of Jerusalem. In spite of efforts by the UN Conciliation Commission for Palestine (CCP), which met separately with Arab and Israeli delegations in Lausanne, the parties made no lasting *peace agreement.

Over 700,000 Palestinian Arabs had fled or were driven from their homes to surrounding Arab countries, mostly to Jordan, the Gaza Strip, Lebanon, and Syria. Both the host countries and the *refugees themselves insisted that those who left Palestine be permitted to return to their homes before direct negotiations with Israel. In its Resolution 194(III) of 11 December 1948 establishing the CCP, the UN General Assembly resolved "that the refugees wishing to return to their homes and live at peace with their neighbors should be permitted to do so at the earliest practicable date, and that compensation should be paid for the property of those choosing not to return. . . ." During the interim period the refugees were to be assisted by the UN Relief and Works Agency for Palestine Refugees in the Near East (UNRWA).

International efforts to resolve the conflict attempted to find a compromise between the position of Israel, which insisted on the status quo, and Arab demands for refugee repatriation and/or compensation and Israeli withdrawal from land beyond the partition borders. Absent a settlement, the Arab states refused to recognize Israel or to have any diplomatic relations with it.

The United States offered several proposals, including plans for regional economic development that would have integrated refugees into the countries to which they had fled. All such proposals failed, however, because of political obstacles.

Political change in the Arab world sharpened the conflict between Israel and its neighbors during the 1950s. New military regimes came to power—in Syria in 1949 and in Egypt in 1952. Both sought to throw off Western tutelage and to affirm Arab national identity. Gamal Abdel *Nasser of Egypt in particular symbolized the new radical nationalist leadership and the growing military, economic, and political strength of the Arab world.

Israeli leaders saw Nasser as a threat. In 1954, in an effort to undermine relations between Egypt and the West, Israeli agents set off a series of bombs at U.S. and Egyptian properties in Cairo and Alexandria. Israel also encroached on the demilitarized zone with Syria and carried out many punitive raids against villages in Jordan. In February 1955, Israel carried out a large-scale attack on Gaza, in retaliation for infiltrators and guerrillas coming across the border.

For its part, Egypt contributed to heightened tensions by continuing to refuse passage through the Suez Canal to Israeli shipping. Nasser was also inclined to use a bellicose public rhetoric that sharpened Israeli insecurity.

In 1954, Israel began to purchase advanced aircraft from France, and it shortly made deals with Paris for other major arms as well. Nasser tried unsuccessfully to obtain arms from Western sources and finally made a deal in 1955 to buy arms from the Soviet bloc. Soviet support had shifted away from Israel and began to favor Syria as well as Egypt.

In July of 1956, Nasser nationalized the Suez Canal, after the United States and the West rejected his requests for assistance in constructing the Aswan High Dam. Both Britain and France saw the Egyptian move as an unsupportable blow to their international interests. Soon after, at secret meetings in Europe, Israeli, French, and British leaders agreed to launch a joint military action against Egypt to regain control of the canal and overthrow the Egyptian leader. Israel began the attack in October. After its forces seized the Gaza Strip and the Sinai Peninsula, and reached the Suez Canal, British and French forces occupied the northern Canal Zone.

With uncharacteristic unity, both the United States and the Soviet Union denounced the tripartite attack and joined in a call through the UN for immediate withdrawal of the invading forces. The Soviets threatened military action against Britain and France and the United States withheld vital oil supplies from both countries. Such moves soon forced the invaders to withdraw.

In November the General Assembly established the UN Emergency Force (UNEF) to supervise the withdrawal and to patrol the frontiers between Egypt and Israel. Israel left Gaza in March 1957 after receiving assurances that UNEF would remain in the Strip and in southern Sinai to guarantee free passage from the Gulf of Akaba through the Straits of Tiran to the Red Sea.

Following the Suez War, UNEF assured relatively stable conditions on the frontier between Egypt and

Israel, although the two countries remained officially at war. More serious were Israeli border clashes with Syria and Jordan, some over the Jordan River and its sources. The Arab states opposed Israeli plans to divert Jordan waters to the arid Negev in southern Israel, plans that would diminish the scarce water supplies at their disposal. In 1960 the Arab League charged that Israel's water scheme was "an act of aggression," and in 1963 the League adopted its own diversion blueprint. Israel nevertheless went ahead with its plan.

Israel's strategic doctrine required that it develop and maintain overwhelming military superiority over all its potential Arab enemies. Close relations with France enabled the Israeli military to purchase very advanced weapons; French experts helped Israel set up a nuclear reactor and what is widely believed to be a *nuclear weapons program. During this time, Israel also developed a sophisticated weapons manufacturing capability of its own.

By 1967 tensions caused by the water dispute and by border incidents led to a number of military clashes. During May the situation reached crisis dimensions. Syria protested that Israel was massing troops on its border. Nasser threatened to prevent Israel's passage through the Straits of Tiran, demanded that all UNEF forces leave Egyptian territory, and moved troops towards the Sinai border with Israel. Bellicose statements were made on all sides.

In early June the situation led to a political crisis in Israel where the first national unity government was formed. On 5 June, Israeli leaders decided to make a "preemptive" strike against Egypt, Syria, and Iraq. After firing on Israeli-controlled Jerusalem, Jordanian forces were involved in the fighting as well. The fate of the Arab armies was determined in the first few hours of war when Israeli planes destroyed most of the opposing air fleets while they were still on the ground. The war lasted just six days. Israel conquered the Sinai Peninsula from Egypt, the West Bank and East Jerusalem from Jordan, and the Golan Heights from Syria.

As a result of the war, Israel emerged as the dominant regional power, the Arab states were thrown into disarray, and tensions deepened between the United States and the Soviet Union in the region. After the war, the Soviet Union greatly increased support for Egypt, Syria, and Iraq, while the United States began for the first time to provide Israel with major arms and large aid packages. A regional arms race began in earnest. With Israeli forces on the east bank of the Suez Canal, Egypt shut the waterway, badly damaging its own economy. Some 300,000 more Palestinians had been driven into exile as refugees as well as nearly 100,000 Syrians who had lost their homes in the Golan Heights.

Differences between the Soviet Union and the United States blocked efforts to end the twenty years of conflict through the UN. Moscow supported UN resolutions condemning Israel and calling on it to return territory gained in the war, while Washington supported Israel's insistence that territory could be returned only through direct negotiations and a final peace settlement guaranteeing Israel's security.

The diplomatic stalemate was broken in November 1967 when both the United States and the Soviet Union agreed to a British-sponsored compromise, Security Council *Resolution 242. Its principal components included "the inadmissability of the acquisition of territory by war and the need to work for a just and lasting peace. . . . Withdrawal of Israeli armed forces from territories of recent conflict; Termination of all claims or states of belligerency and respect for and acknowledgement of the sovereignty, territorial integrity and political independence of every State in the area . . . [and] a just settlement of the refugee problem. . . ."

Parts of the resolution were ambiguous, but it remained the basis of future proposals and negotiations. Although the United States, the Soviet Union, Israel, and most Arab states accepted the resolution, they disagreed over the phrase, "withdrawal of Israeli armed forces from territories" occupied during the war. The Arab states, supported by the Soviet Union and many other UN members, insisted that withdrawal had to be complete, whereas Israel and the United States argued that partial withdrawal could satisfy the resolution.

The war led to major changes in the conflict: most Arab states scaled down their terms for a peace settlement. Few demanded that Israel retreat to the 1947 partition borders or repatriate all the refugees. They now based their demands on Resolution 242: withdrawal to the 1949 armistice frontiers and a solution of the refugee problem that could include alternatives to repatriation.

An important consequence of the 1967 war was revival of Palestinian *Arab nationalism. Palestinians now became disenchanted with leaders of the defeated Arab states and gave their support to Palestinian groups, recently founded, that proposed to liberate the country by means of *guerrilla warfare. The largest such organization was Fatah; one of its leaders, Yasir *Arafat, soon became leader of the new umbrella group representing Palestinian nationalism—the *Palestine Liberation Organization (PLO).

The focus now shifted from conflict between Israel and Arab governments to conflict between Israel and Palestinian nationalists. The diverse Palestinian factions devised their own strategies for defeating Israel and establishing an independent state. Until the 1970s, most Palestinian groups sought total victory over Israel, though they insisted that Jews resident in Palestine before Israel was established would be welcome in the "secular, democratic state" they sought to found. Palestinian groups tried to infiltrate guerrillas into Israel for raids against military and civilian targets, they sometimes struck at Israeli targets outside of Israel, and some even hijacked civilian aircraft in an effort to advance their cause. Palestinian groups and Israeli security services also waged a long underground war in Europe.

The Palestinian movement won formal support and even financial backing from most Arab states, but many Arab leaders also viewed the Palestinians as dangerous antagonists. By striking militarily at states that harbored Palestinian guerrillas, Israel sought to sharpen this conflict. In 1970, Jordan was the principal Palestinian base and their armed groups had become a state within a state, threatening the royal government. In September, Jordan's King Hussein attacked the Palestinians with his army, reimposing control over the border zones. Because neither Syria nor Egypt had permitted autonomous Palestinian presence and guerrilla bases, most Palestinian organizations withdrew to Lebanon, and all but Israel's northern border was now relatively secure from guerrilla raids.

When years passed and Israel continued to occupy the territories it had conquered in 1967, Egyptian and Syrian leaders concluded they could not regain their territory through *diplomacy alone. In 1972, Egyptian President Anwar *Sadat sent away his Soviet military advisers in hopes that closer ties with the West would lead to an agreement for Israeli withdrawal. But he was disappointed. Finally he decided to force the issue by war. In secret negotiations, Egypt and Syria decided to open a two-front surprise attack in October 1973. Initially, Egyptian and Syrian forces drove back the Israelis, recapturing large sectors of Sinai and the Golan. Eventually, the tide of battle turned and Israel regained most of the territories it had occupied before.

The war, known as the October, Yom Kippur, or Ramadan War, shattered the myth of the invincible Israeli army. It nearly became a confrontation between the United States and the Soviet Union when the Soviets threatened to send troops to assist Egypt; the United States then declared a high-level military alert. Both *superpowers sent airborne resupplies of arms to their allies during the heat of battle. But as the fighting ended, tensions were diffused and the two countries agreed on another Security Council Resolution—338, reaffirming Resolution 242.

An international peace conference convened in Geneva under UN auspices during December of 1973, but it broke up after two days. The United States then began a "step-by-step" approach mediated by Secretary of State Henry *Kissinger, who arranged a series of disengagement agreements, two with Egypt and one with Syria, providing for gradual Israeli withdrawal from parts of Sinai and the Golan.

President Sadat of Egypt turned again to diplomacy with a surprise announcement on 9 November 1977 declaring his desire to visit Jerusalem for peace talks with Israel. The Jerusalem visit opened a new phase in Arab-Israeli relations: it was the first time an Arab head of state traveled to Israel and entered into direct negotiations with the Israelis. The subsequent talks faltered, but U.S. President Jimmy *Carter convened the Israeli and Egyptian leaders at Camp David in September 1978. After thirteen days of often acrimonious debate, Carter convinced Sadat and Israeli Prime Minister Menachem Begin to sign accords on a framework for peace.

Following further difficult negotiations, Israel and Egypt signed a peace treaty in Washington, D.C., on 26 March 1979 providing for phased withdrawal of Israeli forces from Sinai and establishing normal diplomatic and economic ties between the two countries. Because Syrian and Palestinian territories remained occupied, Arab opinion was incensed at the Egyptian step and the country stood isolated in the region for many years.

Relations between Egypt and Israel remained strained, worsened by disputes over interpretation and implementation of the Camp David Accords and by Israel's hostile relations with other Arab states, especially its attack on Lebanon in 1982. Egypt interpreted the pact to mean full rights of self-government for the Palestinians; the Israeli government insisted that it was responsible only to offer them "autonomy."

Between 1967 and 1987, Palestinians increasingly resisted Israeli rule in the occupied territories. Israel's leaders believed that Palestinian acts of rebellion were instigated by the PLO and struck at the organization's base in Lebanon. Israel supported anti-Palestinian Maronite forces in the Lebanese civil war which began in 1975. It also mounted air attacks against southern Lebanese towns and villages, culminating in an invasion in 1978 that took Israeli forces up to the Litani River. When its forces later withdrew, Israel maintained control over a ten-mile-deep territory north of its border by means of Lebanese Christian surrogate militias and continued its air raids against Palestinian bases in Lebanon.

In June 1982, Israel struck at Lebanon with a full-scale invasion by 40,000 Israeli troops, supported by massive armor, paratroop drops, and heavy air raids. Neither the small Lebanese army, nor the Syrians (who occupied part of Lebanon), nor the Palestinian fighters were any match for this force. Israel soon laid siege to Beirut, a phase of the fighting that caused worldwide condemnation. Eventually, the United States persuaded Israel to withdraw from the city, provided Palestinian and Syrian troops also left. The evacuation culminated in the Sabra and Chatilla incident in which right-wing Lebanese Christian militia forces allied with Israel slaughtered hundreds of Palestinian civilians in the two refugee camps.

The Sabra and Chatilla incident sharpened opposition in Israel to the invasion of Lebanon, and it became a major issue in the 1982 election. After the election, Israeli forces began a phased withdrawal, but they left a fifteen-mile-wide strip in south Lebanon under their control and continued to carry out occasional air strikes against Lebanese and Palestinian targets.

Unrest in the West Bank and Gaza erupted again in December 1987 with widespread strikes and demonstrations aimed at Israeli occupation forces. Unlike previous occasions, the disturbances did not end in a few days, but escalated into a unified uprising called the *intifada. The uprising refocused Israeli, Arab, and international attention on the Palestine question. The central issue was the Palestinian demand for an independent state in the West Bank and Gaza alongside Israel. More and more, international opinion favored this outcome, which was supported by members of the European Community and Japan.

As a result of the intifada and the confidence it inspired, the PLO recognized UN Resolutions 242 and 338 as the basis for peace discussions. It also renounced the use of *terrorism and agreed to mutual recognition between Palestine and Israel. This led to a public dialogue between the United States and the PLO which soon broke down. By the end of the decade, attempts to reach a compromise remained stymied. The Arabs continued to call for a return of all territories occupied in 1967, including East Jerusalem and the Golan Heights. They also insisted on direct talks between Israel and the PLO and on the creation of an independent Palestinian state. Israel refused to talk to the PLO and insisted that it would not give up any occupied territories—building Jewish settlements in the territories instead. Migrations of hundreds of thousands of Soviet Jews to Israel, beginning in 1989, further sharpened controversy over the land.

After the *Gulf War of 1990–1991, the United States undertook yet another major effort to broker a peace agreement. A conference convened in Madrid during October 1991 to initiate bilateral negotiations between Israel and Syria, Lebanon, and Jordan. Israel agreed to Palestinian participation in the conference as part of the Jordanian delegation, provided no members or individuals affiliated with the PLO were represented. After a two-day formal opening session, the conference was to reconvene into three bilateral series of meetings which were to deal with issues in dispute between Israel and its neighbors. A third phase of the conference brought together parties concerned and others interested in regional issues including water, environment, development, refugees, and disarmament and regional security. The Israeli election for the thirteenth Knesset in June 1992 led to replacement of the hard-line Likud bloc by a new government headed by Labor Party leader Yitzhak Rabin, raising hopes that further settlement in the West Bank and Gaza would be suspended, thus removing a major obstacle to future progress in peace negotiations.

(See also NATIONALISM; NATIONALIZATION; RE-

LIGION AND POLITICS; SUEZ CRISIS; UNITED NATIONS; ZIONISM.)

Martin Gilbert, *The Arab-Israeli Conflict, Its History in Maps,* 2d ed. (London, 1976). Walter Laqueur and Barry Rubin, eds., *The Israel-Arab Reader: A Documentary History* (New York, 1984). Fred J. Khouri, *The Arab-Israeli Dilemma,* 3d ed. (Syracuse, N.Y., 1985). Don Peretz, *The Middle East Today,* 5th ed. (New York, London, 1988). Don Peretz, *Intifada: The Palestinian Uprising* (Boulder, Colo., London, 1990).

DON PERETZ

ARAB LEAGUE. On 25 September 1944, representatives from Egypt, Iraq, Syria, Lebanon, and Transjordan met in Alexandria to draw up plans to enhance the level of cooperation among Arab states through the creation of a General Arab Congress. The Alexandria Protocol, issued on 7 October, proposed the formation of a League of Arab States whose primary institutions would be a council, in which all Arab states would participate on an equal basis, and a number of specialized subcommittees charged with facilitating joint policies on such issues as economic *development, nationality and immigration, and Palestinian rights. The treaty formally establishing the League was signed on 22 March 1945 by the governments of Egypt, Iraq, Syria, Lebanon, Transjordan, Saudi Arabia, and (North) Yemen. It provided for a council in which each member-state would have a single vote; special standing committees to promote cooperation in economic and financial affairs, communications, cultural affairs, legal matters, social affairs, and public health; and a secretariat, consisting of a secretary general appointed by the council and confirmed by a two-thirds majority of the member-states along with supporting staff. Palestine was granted representation on the council, while Cairo was designated "the permanent seat of the League of Arab States." Membership in the organization was open to "any independent Arab State" upon application to the secretariat. Algeria, Bahrain, Kuwait, Libya, Morocco, Oman, Qatar, Tunisia, the United Arab Emirates, and the People's Democratic Republic of Yemen joined the League immediately after becoming independent; Djibouti, Mauritania, Somalia, and the Sudan made up the remainder of the League's twenty-two members.

League efforts to settle disputes among member-states have for the most part proven unsuccessful. Conflict between Egypt and Iraq over the latter's participation in the Baghdad Pact paralyzed the organization throughout the 1950s; attempts to mediate the fighting between Egypt and Saudi Arabia that attended the Yemeni civil war of 1962 foundered; calls for arbitration between the Jordanian government and the Palestinian national movement in the months leading up to the civil war of September 1970 went unheeded; successive plans to end the fighting in Lebanon after 1975 could not be

implemented. In March 1979, following Cairo's signing a peace treaty with Israel, the council suspended Egypt's membership in the League and moved the secretariat to Tunis. Egypt was readmitted to full membership ten years later, but joined Saudi Arabia in sponsoring a resolution that condemned the Iraqi occupation of Kuwait in August 1990 and authorized Arab League forces to collaborate with U.S. and British troops in the Gulf. Tensions resulting from this decision led to the resignations of Secretary General Chadhli Klibi and the League's long-standing ambassador to the United Nations, Clovis Maksoud; ten member-states, led by Iraq, then boycotted an extraordinary council meeting in September 1990 that approved the transfer of the secretariat back to Cairo. By early 1991, Iraq, Jordan, Yemen, Tunisia, Algeria, and the Palestine Liberation Organization had joined in accusing Egypt of abandoning the principles and procedures of the League. The overall inactivity of the new Egyptian secretary general, Esmat ʿAbd al-Majid, underlined the organization's postwar dormancy.

(See also ARAB NATIONALISM.)

Ahmad M. Gomaa, *The Foundation of the League of Arab States* (London, 1977).

FRED H. LAWSON

ARAB NATIONALISM. The concept of *Arab nationalism* has been invoked by Arab monarchs as well as revolutionists; pro-Westerners and anti-Westerners; advocates of secularism and exponents of religion; capitalists and socialists; democrats and dictators. In fact, it has been put to so many contradictory uses that its meaning is far from clear. One thing is clear, however: *nationalism is a potent factor in Arab *political culture. *Public opinion surveys show that most Arabs feel an "Arab identity," though the meaning of such identity can range from a diffuse feeling of cultural belonging to a commitment to creating a unified Arab state.

Like other kinds of nationalism throughout the globe, Arab nationalism is quite recent, going back only to the late nineteenth century. Its earliest advocates worked to create a new "national" language by modernizing and purifying literary Arabic. That language is now standard throughout the Arab world in the mass media and most literature. But separate and quite distinct dialects are still used for ordinary discourse in the various Arab countries—a reminder that a unified Arab state was never created.

Early nationalists also created the myth of "Arabism," an ethnic and cultural unity that supposedly binds all people in the Arabic-speaking world. Arabism plays down the differences (and conflicts) between various Arab communities: Shiʿi and Sunni, Copt and Muslim, for example. And it does not adequately account for the place of many non-Arabs like Kurds, Berbers, and Armenians who live in various Arab states.

Arab nationalism created myths about its ancient roots and past glories. Just as the French believe that modern France is the lineal descendant of Charlemagne's empire (a dubious proposition), so Arabs came to believe that the Arab Nation is the inheritor of the great Islamic empires of the past. The important role of Islam in this construct has created difficulty for secular Arab nationalists, including Christian Arabs who have often been active in the secular nationalist movements.

Arab nationalism was the invention of schoolteachers, journalists, and other intellectuals of the late Ottoman Empire. To this project they eventually won over the wealthy classes of merchants and landowners as well as large sections of the urban populace and even many rural dwellers. Socialist and religious movements also bid for mass support during this very turbulent time, but nationalism won out over its rivals.

Arab nationalism never successfully solved the problem as to what territory would constitute the Arab state. Early nationalists had only local ambitions, but there soon emerged pan-Arabists who called for unity of all the Arabic-speaking peoples—"from Baghdad to Tetouan," as a famous song went. A popular early poem by the Lebanese-born Ibrahim al-Yazigi caught the yearning of these early nationalist intellectuals and their sense that national identity was the safest psychic harbor in a stormy world: "Awaken, O Arabs and leave slumber aside/As danger's flood washes your knees in its tide!"

In the late nineteenth century, most Arabic-speaking lands were ruled by the Ottoman Empire, whose sultans and central bureaucracy were Turkish. Emerging Arab nationalism called for new relations of equality within the empire. Nationalists founded societies for literary revival and administrative autonomy and some younger radicals set up clandestine groups that began to work for independence. In 1908, reforms of the Young Turks in Istanbul further Turkified the empire (nationalism was emerging in Turkey, too). Arab nationalists responded with sharpened demands and they convened their first general congress in Paris in June 1913.

The British enlisted the aid of Arab nationalism during World War I. In return for Arab military aid against the Ottomans, they promised to support Arab independence after victory in the war. Simultaneously, however, the British gave assurances for a "Jewish National Home" in *Palestine, and they secretly planned to divide most of the area into British and French colonies. After the war, Arab nationalists tried to create a unified Arab Kingdom based in Damascus. It effectively governed only a small area, and after less than two years was snuffed out by the French military.

Arab nationalism then encountered a new and more powerful antagonist: European colonialism. The Arab world had been divided up, rather arbitrarily, into a number of colonial states. Nationalist anticolonial movements sprang up in nearly every one. Alongside pan-Arab national identity was born an identity based on the colonial units: Syrian, Lebanese, Iraqi, and Palestinian nationalism.

Throughout the colonial period, the nationalist movements grew in strength, though sometimes they faced cruel repression. European rulers made every effort to split up and isolate the nationalists, appealing especially to minority groups like Kurds, Berbers, Armenians, Jews, Druze, ʿAlawis, and the like. These efforts at divide and rule, though ultimately unsuccessful, created animosities between communities that left a legacy of mutual suspicion and intolerance for the independence period.

After World War II, most Arab countries successfully gained their independence and assumed their separate places in the UN and the international state system. Though nationalism had won, many Arab nationalists were discontent. They were unhappy that the Arab world remained divided into some twenty states, that the new state of Israel had taken Arab land in 1948, and that most of the independent states were still dominated economically and politically by the former colonial powers. A new brand of postcolonial nationalism sought to battle against all three of these problems, while within each country, governments promoted a new nationalist identity—*citizenship in the new states.

In the 1950s and 1960s, a number of movements came into being to promote Arab nationalism throughout the region. The best-known and perhaps the most influential was *Nasserism, inspired by the Egyptian leader Gamal Abdel *Nasser. The Movement of Arab Nationalists was especially influential in Lebanon and among the Palestinians, while the Baʿth Party came to play an important role in Syria and Iraq. In the early 1960s, all of these groups gave greater emphasis to secularism and especially to socialism.

As the individual Arab states built up their structures of power and *ideology, reinforced in many cases by oil wealth, the potential and support for larger Arab unity began to fade. Egypt and Syria merged but then split again (1958–1961), creating further skepticism about the project of unity. Other abortive unity efforts, especially those proclaimed by Libyan leader Muammar *Qaddafi in the 1970s and 1980s, began to seem almost comical.

But the earlier spirit of militant nationalism remained alive, kindled most often by the *Arab-Israeli conflict and the wars which it regularly produced. Some regimes, like those in Syria, Iraq, and Libya, used pan-Arabism in their official ideology. More common symbols, like a map of a pan-Arab state, appeared regularly throughout the region, even in such moderate venues as Egypt's semiofficial newspaper, *al-Ahram*. But for all the symbolic and rhetorical flourish, Arab nationalism failed to prevail over its Israeli antagonist, and no amount of talk about national unity could obscure the record of *authoritarianism and economic difficulties of the

nationalist regimes. Feuds between Arab governments further weakened the pan-Arabist impulse, and even the *Arab League, the strongest inter-Arab organization, nearly disintegrated in 1990 under the pressure of the Iraqi invasion of Kuwait.

A different view of Arab nationalism gained ground in the 1980s, one based on regional economic integration and the free movement of people and capital. Local groupings of states took shape in this period, notably the Gulf Cooperation Council (1981) and the Arab Maghreb Union (1988). Such projects had none of the ideological fire of the earlier movements, but their gradualism appealed to many Arab intellectuals, business executives, and politicians, especially in light of the successes of European integration. This trend was slow to bear fruit, however, and by the end of the decade, inter-Arab trade, investment, and cooperation remained quite limited.

The most formidable challenge to Arab nationalism in the late 1970s and 1980s came from Islamic revivalism. Islamic groups bitterly opposed Arab nationalism because of its secularist approach to politics. During this period, secular governments cracked down harshly on their Islamic rivals in a number of countries, most notably in Syria during the Hama uprising of 1982. By 1990, however, as limited democratic openings led to elections in Jordan, Tunisia, and Algeria, the challenge of the Islamists reemerged in electoral successes. The ballot box seemed to show that sentiments of religious solidarity had at least partly replaced sentiments of nationalist identity.

As Arab nationalism reconstructs once again, a synthesis with Islamic revivalism seems likely, at least in the short run and among the opposition movements. The regional integrationist project is an appealing alternative, a path which would permit greater autonomy and self-expression for important minorities like the Kurds. As long as deep social crises afflict the region, however, dogmatic ideologies like authoritarian nationalism and Islamic fundamentalism will remain strong contenders for power.

(See also COLONIAL EMPIRES; DECOLONIZATION; GULF WAR; ISLAM; RELIGION AND POLITICS; SECULARIZATION.)

Albert Hourani, *Arabic Thought in the Liberal Age, 1798–1939* (Cambridge, U.K., 1983). Giacomo Lucian and Ghassan Salame, eds., *The Politics of Arab Integration* (London, 1988).

GHASSAN SALAME

ARAFAT, Yasir. Born in Cairo in August 1929, Yasir Arafat was the sixth child of a Palestinian wholesale merchant. His mother died when he was 4 years old, and he was sent to Jerusalem to live with an uncle. As a 7-year-old, he observed at close hand the Arab Revolt of 1936. Returning to Cairo in 1937, he pursued his education and became involved in the Palestinian national movement at an early age.

Like other members of his generation, Arafat was deeply influenced by events of 1948, when 700,000 Palestinians lost their homes and Israel was created. While studying in Cairo, he became increasingly involved in the politics of the Egyptian capital, forming close ties to the Muslim Brotherhood and coming under the influence of radical *Arab nationalism. He soon joined with Salah Khalaf and others to form the Palestinian Student Union and was elected its first president.

After receiving his engineering degree from Cairo University in 1956, Arafat and some friends found work in the booming oil city of Kuwait. There, he took a post with the Kuwaiti Public Works Department, but politics continued to be his real vocation. During meetings held in Kuwait in 1958 and 1959, he joined with Salah Khalaf, Khalil al-Wazir, and others to found the Palestinian Liberation Movement—known as Fatah. For the next five years he devoted himself increasingly to organizing this movement, traveling throughout the *Middle East to contact potential supporters and adherents.

In December 1964, Arafat persuaded his comrades that the time had come to launch an armed struggle against Israel, as Algerians had done against French colonial power ten years before. He quit his job to work full-time for Fatah, and in January 1965, with scant resources, he organized the first guerrilla attacks on Israel from across the Jordanian border.

During this time, he lived on the move between Beirut, Damascus, and Palestinian camps in Jordan, traveling incognito, wearing disguises, and narrowly escaping danger. The guerrilla raids he organized did not affect Israel much—many were intercepted by Israeli security forces—but they won great approval and support among Palestinians and throughout the Arab world. Some Arab governments offered financial aid, although they were very wary of the new movement. In 1966, Arafat was arrested twice in Damascus on orders of Syrian Defense Minister Hafiz al-Asad.

After the Arab-Israeli war of 1967, in which the remainder of Palestine fell under Israeli rule, Arafat infiltrated across the border into the occupied West Bank and tried to build networks and train cadres to foment an uprising. But the population did not respond, and soon Arafat escaped back to Jordan.

In March 1968, hearing of an impending Israeli army attack on a Palestinian camp at Karameh in Jordan, Arafat and some of his Fatah comrades decided to disregard classic guerrilla strategy and engage the Israeli forces. With help from units of the Jordanian army, the Palestinian fighters inflicted heavy casualties on the Israelis. This broadly advertised victory brought Fatah a flood of support; thousands joined the guerrillas, and contributions of money and arms flowed in. Arafat then emerged from the anonymity of Fatah's collective leadership

and soon was named the movement's "official spokesman."

On 3 February 1969, the Palestine National Council elected Arafat chairman of the Executive Committee of the newly reorganized *Palestine Liberation Organization (PLO). Arafat then presided over the rapid development of the PLO, including the buildup of several thousand armed guerrillas in camps in Jordan. In 1970, Arafat was pushed by the most radical factions into an ill-judged confrontation with the monarchy there; the PLO armed presence in the country was then destroyed by King Hussein's army.

The PLO regrouped in Lebanon, and Arafat sought to build his forces anew. He presided over the organization as it created a state within a state, with military forces as well as many economic and social service organizations. He also gave some support to international terror operations designed to bring pressure on Israel and call attention to the Palestinian cause.

After Israel's victory in the October War of 1973, Arafat won unanimous support for the PLO from Arab heads of state, and in November 1974 he addressed the UN General Assembly. That same year, the PLO took steps toward accepting the existence of Israel and shifted its goals toward creating an independent Palestinian state in the territories occupied by Israel since 1967.

As civil war engulfed Lebanon in 1975, Arafat built the PLO fighters into a standing army outfitted with heavy weapons and even a few old tanks. When the Israeli army moved massively into Lebanon in 1982, PLO military installations in the south were quickly defeated, but Arafat nonetheless led his forces in an epic defense of Beirut. Eventually, he agreed to lead an evacuation of PLO forces from the city.

Shifting headquarters to Tunis, far from Israel's borders, Arafat led the PLO in an increasingly diplomatic strategy for Palestinian *rights, first seeking a joint strategy with his old enemy King Hussein. For several years he faced fierce opposition to his leadership from a Syrian-sponsored breakaway group led by Abu Musa, but continuing efforts to evict him from the PLO leadership proved unavailing.

In 1983 he repaired relations with Cairo and began to develop more ties to European governments and improved relations with the United States. The *intifadah, or Palestinian uprising in the Occupied Territories, gave new force to the Palestinian cause beginning in late 1987, but it also created an alternative potential center of leadership and power based within the territories.

In November 1988, Arafat led the Palestine National Congress to support more conciliatory policies, and in December he announced recognition of Israel after addressing the UN General Assembly in Geneva. He was not able to establish a lasting dialogue with the United States, however, and was personally excluded from the Palestinian-Israeli *peace talks that began in Madrid in November 1991 because the Israelis refused to negotiate with the PLO.

Over the years, Arafat has constantly worked to forge consensus among widely divergent PLO factions and also between the PLO and various Arab states. Under these constraints, he has frequently been criticized for lacking a clear personal political position. Some critics have accused him of being too autocratic and too personalistic. Others have faulted him for being too influenced by Saudi Arabia (the largest financial supporter of the PLO), and they have pointed out his tendency to tolerate corruption among his lieutenants. However, Arafat has faced almost insuperable odds, and he has overcome setbacks with shrewd political tactics and a tough survivor instinct. He has held together his movement during many difficult times and always attracted far broader support among Palestinians than any other leader.

After nearly a half-century of effort, Arafat's hopes for Palestinian self-determination remained far from being realized. Though widely excoriated in the West as a terrorist and man of violence, Arafat has been more a diplomat than a warrior, especially in his later years. He has left a lasting mark with his role in affirming Palestinian identity and in mobilizing the world community in support of Palestinian rights.

(See also ARAB-ISRAELI CONFLICT; PALESTINE.)

Helena Cobban, *The Palestinian Liberation Movement* (New York, 1984). John Wallach and Janet Wallach, *Arafat: In the Eyes of the Beholder* (New York, 1990). Andrew Gowers and Tony Walker, *Yasser Arafat and the Palestinian Revolution* (London, 1991).

HELENA COBBAN

ARENDT, Hannah. Born in Hanover, Germany, in 1906, Hannah Arendt was educated at the universities of Marburg and Heidelberg. At Marburg she studied with Martin Heidegger and Edmund Husserl. At Heidelberg she worked with Karl Jaspers, completing a doctorate on the concept of love in the work of Saint Augustine in 1929. Following Hitler's rise to power in Germany in 1933, she moved to Paris, where she was active in Jewish refugee organizations. In 1941, she escaped Nazi-occupied France and emigrated to the United States, eventually becoming a U.S. citizen. In the United States she taught and lectured at a number of institutions, notably the University of Chicago and the New School for Social Research in New York City, and produced her best-known work in political thought. She died in New York in 1975.

Arendt was influenced by her teachers as well as by the central figures in German philosophy and culture, notably Immanuel Kant. However, she was no disciple of any of them, instead using their ideas to develop her own distinctive political and philosophical analysis. This has made it difficult to slot her in the ranks of political theorists and has contributed to widely divergent interpretations of her work.

The most powerful image raised by Arendt's work is her own: thinking without a banister. The banister is the Western tradition of political thought as it shaped Western experience from Greek antiquity until the late nineteenth century. Thinking without a banister means starting with the traditional framework and thinking through its limits. That is, one deals with radically new phenomena, especially *totalitarianism and *revolution, in new ways, while respecting the humanist concerns of traditional thought. This involves recovering the original meaning and significance of concepts and issues that the tradition itself has covered up.

Arendt's approach is evident in her account in *The Human Condition* (Chicago, 1950) of "public" and "private" realms. She provocatively argues that what we call "public" and "private" are in reality neither, but that there has emerged in the modern era a new sphere, the "social." In this realm, private economic matters have become public political ones, to the detriment of both. People are reduced to the status of means to the satisfaction of material ends. Fueled by the requirements of labor, once the most despised but now the most honored of human activities, individuals increasingly relate to each other as interchangeable and dispensable parts of a complex division of labor rather than as citizens consciously sharing a common situation. Both totalitarianism and revolution express these developments (*On Revolution*, New York, 1965; *The Origins of Totalitarianism*, 3d ed., New York, 1973).

Arendt finds widespread in the twentieth century a "normal" kind of thoughtlessness that could lead to political evil. The relation between thoughtlessness and the politically unconscionable is given its sharpest statement in Arendt's most controversial work, *Eichmann in Jerusalem* (New York, 1965). In it, she makes a distinctive contribution to political thought by confronting the question of what it means to think politically and the consequences of our failure to do so.

Thinking politically requires above all a strong sense of personal responsibility. *Citizenship involves a concern for a world that was here before we were born and will remain after we have died, a network of common involvements that do not simply serve the reproduction of life. Judging, for Arendt the most political of our mental faculties, allows us to rule on those things that should or should not inhabit this world. The capacity to judge has been seriously eroded in modern society and with it the ability to make distinctions important for both political theory and political practice.

Because she wrote with a broad sweep about large-scale historical and philosophical developments, and because she criticized an obsessive focus on the self in modern life, Arendt's concern for the personal in a plural world of many persons can easily be missed. Arendt's "person" is no mere isolated individual. A person exists necessarily in, through, and for others, and they for him or her. Thus to assess or judge a person is to assess or judge the polity of which this person is a member—and vice versa. The speculative treatment of Adolf Eichmann's motivations or the essays on specific individuals that are collected in *Men in Dark Times* (New York, 1968) are not simply biographical fragments but concrete political analyses whose very specificity brings the larger picture into a new, clearer light.

Hannah Arendt's political thought asks us to think about fundamental political distinctions without the assurance of a generally accepted tradition of cultural norms. It asks us to exercise our reason without assuming the possibility of transparent truths about social and political life. In defending a critical reason and personal responsibility, while at the same time stressing the limits of this reason, Arendt speaks powerfully to an age in which many of the utopian hopes of *modernity and the Enlightenment have been called into question, but which remains inescapably modern.

George Kateb, *Hannah Arendt: Politics, Conscience, Evil* (Totowa, N.J., 1983). Leah Bradshaw, *Acting and Thinking: The Political Thought of Hannah Arendt* (Toronto, 1989). Phillip Hansen, *Hannah Arendt: History, Politics and Citizenship* (Cambridge, U.K., 1991).

PHILLIP HANSEN

ARGENTINA. At the beginning of the twentieth century, Argentina ranked among the privileged nations of the world. Its population enjoyed European levels of per capita income, *urbanization, and literacy. Its sophisticated entrepreneurial class, large and prosperous middle class, relatively well-paid urban working class, and the absence of an oppressed peasantry differentiated Argentina's semiperipheral political economy from most other Latin American societies. The rich endowment of agricultural resources, the absence of ethnic, racial, and religious cleavages, and the nation's early prosperity pointed toward a promising future—a promise that has not been fulfilled. It is the puzzling contrast between Argentina's impressive socioeconomic potential and its contemporary political instability and economic stagnation that has led to the frequent characterization of Argentina as a "riddle" or "paradox."

Historical Background. For the Spanish Crown, the territory currently occupied by the Argentine Republic had negligible economic importance. There were no precious metals or other valuable raw materials and few sedentary Indians to provide labor for agriculture. As a defensive outpost against Portuguese expansionism, however, the strategic and commercial importance of the Río de la Plata region was considerable. In 1776 the viceroyalty of the Río de la Plata was created with the port city of Buenos Aires as the seat of government. Meanwhile, taking advantage of the multiplication of wild cattle in the pampas, the production and exports of hides and salted meat expanded rapidly. This commercial expansion further enhanced the coastal region's significance and sharpened conflicts between the elites of the interior and the dominant groups in Buenos Aires.

Independence from Spain in 1816 led to a succession of civil wars. On one side were the Buenos Aires–based "Unitarians" who controlled the vast fertile pampa grasslands and the main port, favoring free trade with Europe and a powerful centralized national state. Against them were the regional elites, known as the "Federalists," who steadfastly defended regional autonomy and economic protectionism as the foundations of their patrimonial influence. This violent stalemate was temporarily broken after 1829 by the populist and authoritarian brand of *federalism imposed by Juan Manuel de Rosas.

Following the overthrow of Rosas in 1852, the adroit use of military force, electoral fraud, political concessions, and economic might established the hegemony of the agro-export elite and allied commercial interests of Buenos Aires. These groups created conditions that favored Argentina's rapid economic *modernization and insertion in the world economy as a major producer of beef and grains between 1862 and 1916. By the end of this period, Argentina had consolidated its status as prosperous semiperipheral society and had become a major exporter of temperate agricultural goods to the advanced core nations of the world economy. The population had increased five-fold thanks to massive immigration from Europe. Per capita income and levels of conspicuous consumption by the upper classes surpassed those of several European countries.

This economic boom, however, contained the seeds of the destruction of the oligarchical order. The growth of the urban middle class and the resentment of those regional elites excluded from the economic bonanza led in 1891 to the creation of the Unión Cívica Radical (UCR), Argentina's first mass political party. At the same time, the extraordinary growth in the number of immigrants and urban workers spurred the emergence of an anarchist movement and the creation in 1894 of the Partido Socialista. The rise of militant labor and political organizations, the growing pressure from the moderate opposition, and the realization by the ruling conservative elites that the largely middle-class UCR had no revolutionary intentions facilitated liberalization of the oligarchical system and paved the way for the Radical caudillo Hipólito Yrigoyen to win the presidency in 1916.

During the period of democratic political stability from 1916 to 1930, the conservative groups were partially displaced from political power but only minor changes were introduced in the socioeconomic domain. Key to political liberalization was the fact that agrarian elites could not control a pliable peasantry, a class that was practically nonexistent in modern Argentina. The moderate redistribution of income and wealth carried out under the Radicals was tolerated by the agro-export bourgeoisie as long as the economy continued to prosper. The crash of 1929 and the ensuing disruption of international trade ended this tolerance, however, and the struggle for economic shares among rival classes and socioeconomic sectors became acute. The *coup d'état of September 1930 orchestrated by the landed and commercial elites, implemented by the army, and supported by middle-class groups marked a watershed in the country's modern history, inaugurating six decades of political upheaval.

Rise and Decline of Populist Political Economy. The use of coercion and fraud following the coup of 1930 ushered in the long "infamous decade" (1930–1943) of conservative rule. The attempt to re-create the traditional export economy and the oligarchic republic was a chimera in the changed domestic and international circumstances engendered by the Great Depression.

The emergence of an entrepreneurial class based on *import-substitution industrialization, combined with the stagnation of the export-oriented rural economy and the ensuing massive rural-urban migration, sparked fundamental transformations of Argentina's class structure and hastened a rapid expansion of state intervention in the economy. The onset of World War II accelerated these structural trends and also gave rise to a virulent antinationalism that propelled the armed forces toward a coup against the conservative administration in 1943. Colonel Juan Domingo *Perón emerged as the most skillful of the new generation of politically inclined military officers. Taking full advantage of his ascendance within the military and using state patronage, Perón moved rapidly to consolidate his popular support and to defeat his conservative and leftist opponents. He won the presidency in the 1946 elections with fifty-four percent of the popular vote, while his supporters carried most provinces and obtained majorities in both legislative houses.

The triumph of Perón and his Justicialista movement signaled the end of the UCR's electoral dominance. More broadly, the support Perón received from the new urban working class, the rural population, inhabitants of poorer provinces, and substantial sectors of the lower middle class foreshadowed a remarkable transformation of the Argentine political arena. Perón successfully organized a state-controlled corporatist alliance whose fundamental pillars were organized labor, industrialists producing for the domestic market, and nationalistic military officers in favor of industrialization. Peronist economic policy consisted of strong state intervention to promote light industrialization; income distribu-

tion (in favor of workers, middle classes, and civilian and military bureaucracies); and the *nationalization of public utilities, railroads, and foreign trade. While the Peronist regime maintained democratic forms, it did not hesitate to utilize a broad array of authoritarian practices, including the manipulation of the mass media and the educational system and the imposition of political constraints on public employees and union members, to harass its political adversaries and restrict opposition parties' chances to compete successfully for power.

The combination of populist economic policies and authoritarian political practices was relatively successful in the early postwar years. In the early 1950s, however, the regime began to crumble in the face of economic stagnation engendered by severe balance-of-payments problems, a swollen public sector deficit, and mounting inflationary pressures. Renewed struggles over income shares among members of the Peronist coalition, plus growing resistance by the military, rural producers and urban entrepreneurial interests, and the Catholic church to Perón's increasingly authoritarian and repressive policies, led to a military coup in September 1955 that toppled the regime and sent its leader into exile.

Stalemate, Cyclical Crises, and Modern Authoritarianism. During the decade following Perón's overthrow, unable to cope with renewed international competition and rapid technological change, successive semidemocratic and dictatorial governments found it virtually impossible to implement the coherent macroeconomic policies necessary to modernize Argentina's semiclosed economy. Cyclical economic crises and electoral stalemates weakened civilian governments and deepened public cynicism regarding the efficacy of democracy. Many politicians and powerful local and transnational industrial and financial interests, as well as Peronist union leaders and politicians, began to yearn for top-down authoritarian solutions to deepening social conflicts.

In June 1966 a military coup overthrew the elected Radical government of Arturo Illia and imposed an authoritarian regime presided over by General Juan Carlos Onganía. The self-proclaimed "Argentine revolution" sought to implement a new strategy of state-led development designed to "deepen" import-substitution industrialization by promoting domestic production of intermediate and capital goods and providing incentives for the export of nontraditional manufactured goods. Following the 1969 Cordobazo, an unprecedented mass uprising, a confluence of factors, including military factionalism, the evaporation of entrepreneurial support, mounting mass mobilization, and increasingly radical opposition from revolutionary guerrilla groups, led to Onganía's ouster in 1970.

A looming spiral of *political violence and popular protests and the rebirth of the civilian opposition spearheaded by Peronists and Radicals led General Alejandro Lanusse to extricate the military from the direct exercise of state power. The armed forces' reluctant acceptance of the transition to civilian rule facilitated Juan Perón's return to Argentina in 1972 and paved the way for Peronism's sweeping electoral victory in 1973.

Hopes for a return to *democracy and economic growth were dashed by Perón's death in 1974, the escalation of revolutionary and counterrevolutionary violence, and the vacillating performance of the government headed by his widow, María Estela Martínez de Perón. The discredited Peronist government was overthrown in March 1976, and a new cycle of *militarism and dictatorship was launched.

The military conducted a "dirty war" of state *terrorism against a wide array of regime opponents. The official number of reported deaths was nearly 10,000, while the unofficial tally of killed and "disappeared" was estimated at 25,000–30,000. Headed by General Jorge Rafael Videla, the military and their business and technocratic allies attempted to restructure the state, society, and economy in a veritable "capitalist revolution" following the tenets of "free-market" *monetarism. The economic policies enacted under the aegis of the military provoked rampant financial speculation and triple-digit inflation, while much of the country's industrial base was dismantled and tens of thousands of blue- and white-collar jobs were eliminated in the manufacturing sector. This economic disaster was fueled by a massive foreign debt, which soared from US$7 billion to over US$43 billion under the dictatorship.

General Videla left power in 1981 as the enormity of the debacle was becoming evident, but the subsequent collapse of the military dictatorship was less the result of the economic crisis than the consequence of the disastrous April 1982 decision to invade the Malvinas/Falkland Islands. The ensuing humiliating defeat at the hands of *Britain left the military regime with a bankrupt economy perched on the precipice of international financial insolvency. Deep divisions within the armed forces themselves, coupled with the resurgence of civilian opposition, forced the military to accede to elections.

Travails of Democratic Consolidation. Raúl Alfonsín and his Radical Party came to power in late 1983 following Peronism's surprising electoral defeat. Under Alfonsín's leadership, Argentines demonstrated a new appreciation of democratic values and representative government. The difficulties of reconciling growth, monetary stability, and service on the huge external debt of more than US$60 billion with popular expectations for income redistribution and social justice proved impossible for the Alfonsín administration. The failure of the Radical "heterodox shock" economic policies led to catastrophic hyperinflation and secured the victory of the Peronist Carlos Saúl Menem in the May 1989 presidential election.

Menem's government embarked on an ambitious project of neoliberal free-market restructuring (*privatization of state enterprises, liberalization of international trade, and promotion of foreign investment) that explicitly repudiated the populist and statist economic policies defended by Peronism since the 1940s. The immediate consequences of Menem's allegiance to marketplace logic included a costly recession and the exacerbation of tendencies toward deepening inequality and growing concentration of income and wealth. Consequently, a nation that had long prided itself on its relative affluence entered the 1990s with approximately one-third of the population of 32 million living below the poverty line.

The specter of authoritarianism receded considerably with the return to civilian rule in 1983 and the peaceful transfer of power in 1989 between the two majoritarian parties, the Radicals and the Peronists. Nevertheless, the legacy of decades of unabated economic decline, combined with sharpening distributional conflicts, still make Argentina's prospects for long-term democratic consolidation problematic.

(See also AUTHORITARIANISM; BALANCE OF PAYMENTS; CORPORATISM; DEMOCRATIC TRANSITIONS; EQUALITY AND INEQUALITY; MALVINAS/FALKLANDS WAR; MILITARY RULE; PERÓN, MARÍA EVA DUARTE DE; POPULISM.)

Carlos F. Díaz Alejandro, *Essays on the Economic History of the Argentine Republic* (New Haven, Conn., 1970). James R. Scobie, *Argentina: A City and a Nation,* 2d ed. (New York, 1971). David Rock, *Argentina 1516–1987: From Spanish Colonization to Alfonsín,* 2d ed. (Berkeley, Calif., 1987). Carlos H. Waisman, *Reversal of Development in Argentina: Postwar Counterrevolutionary Policies and Their Structural Consequences* (Princeton, N.J., 1987). Guillermo O'Donnell, *Bureaucratic Authoritarianism: Argentina, 1966–1973, in Comparative Perspective* (Berkeley, Calif., 1988). William C. Smith, *Authoritarianism and the Crisis of the Argentine Political Economy* (Stanford, Calif., 1989).

WILLIAM C. SMITH
ALDO C. VACS

ARIAS, Oscar. President of *Costa Rica from 1986 to 1990, Oscar Arias Sánchez received the Nobel Peace Prize in 1987 for his efforts to develop a *peace plan to end the warfare that plagued Nicaragua, El Salvador, and Guatemala in the 1980s. His proposal, commonly known as Esquipulas II, was originally sketched out on a napkin in the cafeteria of Washington's Mayflower Hotel in September 1985, eight months prior to Arias's election as president. Aimed at building on the efforts of the Contadora countries (Colombia, Mexico, Panama, and Venezuela), who had initiated a peace process in 1984, it called for internal dialogue within each country between the government and the opposition, a cease-fire and amnesty for guerrillas and political prisoners, freedom of speech, and free elections. It also called on foreign governments to stop aiding the guerrillas.

As president of the most democratic country in

the region, which had eliminated its army in 1948, Arias used his moral authority, bolstered by the Nobel Peace Prize, to pressure the Central American presidents to abide by the plan. Ultimately it contributed to the end of warfare in Nicaragua in 1989 and in El Salvador in 1992. The plan also emphasized greater regional political and economic cooperation and was regarded as a Central American declaration of independence from the superpowers.

Born into a wealthy coffee-growing family that had a long history of public service, Arias received degrees in law and economics from the University of Costa Rica in 1967 and a doctorate in political science from the University of Essex in England in 1974. Arias entered government service in 1970 as a member of the economic council of President José Figueres (1970–1974) and as vice president of the Board of Directors of the Central Bank. From 1972 to 1975 he served as minister of national *planning and economic policy. In this post he followed a pragmatic course admitting the limits of state planning, particularly in small open economies such as Costa Rica's.

In February 1978 Arias was elected to the National Assembly where he promoted constitutional and electoral reform. In July 1979 he was chosen general secretary of the Partido de Liberación Nacional and was reelected in 1983. That post provided a base for his eventual campaign for his party's nomination for the presidency. During the campaign Arias portrayed himself as the candidate who was most likely to promote peace in the region.

As president Arias renegotiated Costa Rica's foreign debt—which in 1986 was estimated to be the highest per capita debt in the world (US$1,800)—providing some short-term relief. Efforts to deemphasize Costa Rica's dependence on coffee for export earnings by encouraging an expansion of nontraditional exports such as flowers and textiles had limited success. The government also encouraged a substantial expansion of tourist facilities to generate foreign exchange. Attempts to deal with deficit spending via cutbacks in government social welfare programs and reduction of consumer price subsidies brought dissension within Arias's cabinet as well as public opposition. Arias's administration was, however, successful in implementing a program to finance low- and middle-income housing and spent more than twenty times as much on education and health care as on security.

Arias nevertheless continues to be best known for his assiduousness in convincing the Central American presidents to sign the Esquipulas II agreement on 7 August 1987 and then pressuring them, as well as the United States, Cuba, and the Soviet Union, to support the peace process. While President *Reagan initially categorized the agreement as fatally flawed, it garnered considerable support in the U.S. Congress and ultimately undercut funding for the counterrevolutionary forces (*contras) attempting to overthrow the *Sandinista government in Nicaragua. The State Department and some members of *Congress attempted to pressure Arias by intimating that U.S. economic aid might be cut. Once Arias received the Nobel Peace Prize, however, such pressures diminished.

Arias used the money from the Peace Prize to establish the Arias Foundation for Peace and Human Progress, which focuses on promoting nonviolent conflict resolution, demilitarization, ecological preservation, and the reduction of socioeconomic injustice. Arias himself was involved in promoting a 1992 plebiscite in Panama to determine whether to abolish the armed forces in that country as Costa Rica did in 1948. To those who have accused Arias of rampant idealism, he has replied: "Politicians have an obligation to be dreamers, to be idealists, to be Quixotes. It is our obligation to want to change things. Nobody in Central America can be satisfied with the status quo. There is too much poverty, violence, hunger, and misery."

(See also U.S.–LATIN AMERICAN RELATIONS.)

Oscar Arias Sánchez, *Nuevos rumbos para el desarrollo costarricense,* 2d ed. (San José, Costa Rica, 1984). Oscar Arias Sánchez, *¿Quién gobierna en Costa Rica?* (San José, Costa Rica, 1984). Guido Fernández, *El primer domingo de febrero: crónica interior de la elección de Oscar Arias* (San José, Costa Rica, 1986). Lowell Gudmundson, "Costa Rica's Arias at Mid-term" *Current History* (December 1987): 417, 420, 431–432. Edward J. Heubal, "Costa Rican Interpretations of Costa Rican Politics" *Latin American Research Review,* 25, no. 2 (1990): 217–225.

MARGARET E. CRAHAN

ARMENIA. Premodern Armenian society existed on the Anatolian plateau in the region of Lake Van as early as 2000 B.C.E. It gave rise to several important kingdoms and eventually produced a distinct language and alphabet and a distinct religious institution, the Armenian Orthodox church. Armenian territory passed under the rule of a number of foreign conquerors and was fought over between rival empires: Arabs and Byzantines, Ottomans and Persians. Thanks to their geographic position, Armenians played an important role in trade between Europe and Asia.

Modern Armenian *nationalism arose in the late nineteenth century, when the territory was under Ottoman and Russian rule. Armenian nationalists formed parties and secret societies to press for Ottoman reforms and for concessions from the Russians. Two major parties were formed during this period, the socialist Hunchak and the nationalist Dashnak.

All such reform efforts were forcibly repressed, with large-scale massacres of Armenians taking place in Ottoman Armenia in 1895 and in Istanbul in 1896. Armed groups then sprang up to defend Armenian communities. Also, between 1897 and 1903, the Russian tsar closed many Armenian schools and cultural institutions and confiscated the property of the Armenian church.

During World War I, the Istanbul government regarded its Armenian population as unreliable and potentially subversive, despite Armenian declarations of loyalty. Consequently, in 1915 the government decided to deport the entire Armenian population—nearly 2 million people—to Syria and Mesopotamia. Deportations continued until 1918; it has been estimated that as many as 1.5 million Armenians died or were killed en route, in what is often referred to as the Armenian genocide. A final wave of massacres occurred in the Russian Transcaucusus, notably in Baku (1918) and Shushi (1920). As a result of continuing persecution, Armenians emigrated throughout the world, and today form significant communities in the United States (more than 800,000), Syria, Lebanon, and Israel (600,000), France (300,000), and Latin America (100,000).

In May 1918, in the final phase of World War I, Armenians established an independent republic, with the capital at Yerevan, in lands of the former Russian Empire. In late 1920 the Armenian government surrendered authority to the Communists as Turkey pressed Armenia at its western border. By 1990 the population of Soviet Armenia had grown to about 3 million, and the republic had become relatively prosperous, with an industrialized economy and many cultural institutions. In the diaspora Armenians also donated funds for research centers and university chairs to develop the field of Armenian studies.

During the 1970s and 1980s, an international Armenian movement sought to gain worldwide recognition of the Armenian genocide, an effort which was vigorously opposed by the Turkish government. In addition, a terrorist organization—the Armenian Secret Army for the Liberation of Armenia—became active.

The tumultuous changes occurring throughout the Soviet Union beginning in the 1980s inevitably had repercussions in Armenia. A movement to unite the republic with the Armenian enclave in the Nagorno-Karabakh autonomous region inside neighboring Soviet Azerbaijan resulted in outbreaks of interethnic violence that drove some 300,000 Armenians from Azerbaijan between 1988 and 1990. There was widespread political ferment: the Hunchak and the Dashnak, which had been kept alive thanks to the Armenian diaspora, resumed their activities inside Armenia in 1990; so did the liberal Ramgavar Party, which had been formed in 1921. In 1990, in the first democratic election held in Armenia during the Soviet era, non-Communist parties, notably the Armenian Pan-National Movement, won a majority of seats in the legislature and formed a government with its leader, Levon Ter-Petrossian, as president. In March 1991 the government announced Armenia's intention to withdraw from the Soviet Union, a process which was accomplished after the collapse of Soviet authority in August 1991. On 16 October

1991, after constitutional changes mandated the direct election of the president, Ter-Petrossian retained his office with a decisive electoral victory.

(See also COMMONWEALTH OF INDEPENDENT STATES; TURKEY.)

Richard G. Hovannisian, *Armenia on the Road to Independence* (Berkeley, Calif., 1967).

LEVON ABRAHAMIAN

ARMS CONTROL. The precise origin of the term *arms control* is unclear, although what would now be termed arms control endeavors can be found throughout recorded history. The term came into wide use in the 1950s and early 1960s as a way to distinguish efforts toward various types of limitations on arms and military forces from the search for *disarmament. The most influential definition, very widely used and cited, is the functional one offered by Thomas Schelling and Morton Halperin in *Strategy and Arms Control:* "all the forms of military cooperation between potential enemies in the interest of reducing the likelihood of war, its scope and violence if it occurs, and the political and economic costs of being prepared for it." This falls short of encompassing all of the activities now involved because some are not cooperative in nature and one or two are not military related (such as the Hot Line). It is also worth emphasizing that arms control is intended to enhance *security, and it is not uncommon to find assertions that it can fulfill other functions as well, such as strengthening political relationships among states or helping governments to better manage or control the domestic influence of their military establishments.

Although arms control can include selective reductions in, or the outright elimination of, some weapons and forces, it differs from disarmament. Arms control activities derive from the assumption that states will continue to see military forces as useful, or vital, in international politics and that therefore they will continue to exist and be used. Disarmament is pursued in the belief that military forces are pernicious and should be eliminated so that they cannot be used. Thus the two overlap in terms of some actions but not in conception or objective. From an arms control perspective certain conditions may make it wise to increase military forces or weapons and, by the same token, cutting forces can sometimes be deemed undesirable. Arms control advocates are partial to the view that disarmament is an unrealistic quest whereas arms control is an eminently realistic and attainable route to greater security.

In the history of warfare, the urge to get *war and the burdens of preparing for it under a degree of control can be traced to two broad impulses. One is a military distaste for weapons that discount martial values such as the courage and honor displayed in personal combat. For instance, some in the military opposed the crossbow, the use of gunpowder, and the submarine, and modern soldiers have been known to condemn *nuclear weapons at least partly because they cancel the meaning and presence of traditional values in armed combat and call into question the use of military forces as instruments of *foreign policy. The other impulse is civilian repugnance for the emergence and elaboration of steadily more destructive weapons and wars. In this century, and particularly with regard to contemporary arms control in theory and practice, the latter has been predominant—the theory was largely developed by civilian analysts, and arms control proposals have generally received less support in military circles than in civilian ones.

Each impulse competes with offsetting ones. Military distaste and civilian repugnance clash with the compelling desire to survive and be victorious should war occur—restraint risks defeat and death—and arms limitations are particularly difficult to sustain in time of war. Arms limitations are further compromised by suspicion about other governments' intentions, including the fear that these governments will either evade or cheat on any cooperative arrangements. Arms control thus becomes, for the most part, a variant of the problem of cooperation under anarchy—a dilemma in which potentially quite beneficial cooperative limitations leave open the possibility of gaining advantage by evading the limitations; suspicion that this is what others will do and temptations to do the same oneself lead to difficulty both in reaching acceptable arrangements and then sustaining them.

Modern arms control theory was primarily developed in a brief period (roughly 1958–1962) in conjunction with *deterrence theory. It suggested that overcoming the cooperation-under-anarchy dilemma was both necessary and feasible in the context of nuclear deterrence. States had an immense and mutual interest in limiting the arms race, preventing nuclear deterrence from breaking down (in keeping it "stable"), and limiting any war that occurred. Thus even quite hostile states could and should cooperate in pursuit of this interest at the same time that a stable nuclear deterrence would curb the incentive to defect from cooperation and ease suspicion about this as a possibility. Although the cooperation envisioned was to pertain to nuclear forces in particular, it was but a short step to suggest cooperation below the nuclear level as well, because it was plausible that conventional arms buildups and force deployments, also costly, could readily lead to instability, confrontations, and fighting that might escalate to the nuclear level. The point of the theory was to assist governments in seeing the virtue and necessity of arms control and to help identify what steps should (and should not) be taken. Given the overwhelming concern with the threat of nuclear weapons, the theory did not rest on a thorough analysis of parallel ideas and previous experience with arms control activities in the prenuclear era,

and to this day no comprehensive history of arms control has been written.

Arms control measures can be unilateral (such as taking steps to prevent accidental or unauthorized firing of one's own nuclear weapons), bilateral, or multilateral. Those involving more than one government can derive from informal agreement or the creation of and adherence to a negotiated treaty or convention. The measures can be designed to take effect at any stage in the life cycle of weapons and forces: development, deployment, decision to use, and use. Quite common is categorization by the nature of the weapons and forces involved or the functional purpose of the measures, as in the following typology and accompanying descriptions and examples:

- Control of strategic nuclear weapons: The SALT I ABM treaty (1972) banned Soviet and American development and deployment of dense, nationwide antiballistic missile defenses, with the intent of stabilizing deterrence so as to reduce the chances of war. The Interim Offensive Arms Agreement (1972) limited the number of Soviet and U.S. intercontinental ballistic missiles and submarine-based ballistic missiles. The SALT II agreement (1979), which was never ratified but was generally observed, set limits on the numbers of each type of existing Soviet and American strategic bombers and missiles and on the number of nuclear weapons each delivery vehicle could carry.
- Control of intermediate-range or tactical nuclear weapons: The Intermediate Nuclear Forces (INF) Treaty (1987) banned the future development and deployment of ballistic and cruise (land-based) missiles with a range of 300 to 3,400 miles and ordered the destruction of all existing ones in the Soviet, U.S., and West German arsenals.
- Control of nuclear proliferation: The Nuclear Nonproliferation Treaty (1968) sought to prevent the development and deployment of nuclear weapons by states that do not already possess them.
- Control of nuclear testing: Proposals to ban nuclear testing sought to prevent any further development of nuclear weapons; the Limited Test Ban Treaty (1963) sought to prevent testing that would adversely affect people's health through radioactive fallout.
- Establishment of nuclear-free zones: The Antarctic Treaty (1959), the Treaty for the Prohibition of Nuclear Weapons in Latin America (1967), the Outer Space Treaty (1967), and the Seabed Treaty (1971) barred nuclear weapons from their respective areas.
- Control of conventional forces: The Paris Treaty on Conventional Armed Forces in Europe (1990) limited deployments of forces in Europe so as to enhance deterrence stability by curbing the capability to launch swift and decisive military attacks.

- Control of chemical weapons: The Geneva Protocol (1925) banned the use of chemical weapons in war; a proposed treaty would ban development and deployment, and order destruction of existing weapons.
- Control of biological weapons: The Biological Weapons Convention (1972) banned deployment and use of the weapons and ordered the destruction of existing weapons.
- Preventing accidental or unauthorized use: "Permissive Action Links" on nuclear weapons make them inoperable when tampered with and unusable without inserting a code sent from the national command center.
- Avoidance or management of tense or dangerous situations: The U.S.-Soviet Agreement on Measures to Reduce the Risk of Outbreak of Nuclear War (1971) called for immediate notification by one party of the other in the event of an accidental or unauthorized incident of a serious nature involving nuclear weapons. Hot Line agreements created continuous communication channels among major states for use in emergencies or crises.
- Limiting wars: Refusal to resort to the most destructive weapons available is one way states keep within the bounds of limited war. The Geneva Convention (latest version 1949) on the treatment of prisoners of war mandated that they be treated humanely.

Numerous other actual or proposed arms control measures could be listed, but it is worth noting that four concerns have been preeminent in shaping arms control endeavors since World War II. One has been a desire to limit or outlaw weapons considered particularly horrendous—nuclear, chemical, and biological. A second has been to stabilize deterrence by restricting the development and deployment of "provocative" weapons and forces, ones which could readily increase the incentives to initiate a war, particularly in a crisis. This includes nuclear weapons ideal for a war-winning initial attack, defensive systems that could undermine a nation's deterrence threats, highly offense-oriented conventional forces, weapons and forces unusually vulnerable to attack, and, recently, command and control systems very vulnerable to attack. A third has been to prevent accidental or unauthorized use of weapons by terrorists and unbalanced individuals or due to mechanical malfunctions. The final one has been to limit nuclear proliferation, with concern about both the weapons and suitable delivery systems.

The fact that arms control is an issue between states involved in a competitive, sometimes severely hostile relationship, making national security a major concern in foreign policy and domestic politics, has meant that in the practice of arms control certain features have been consistently prominent. To begin with, the pursuit of arms control is normally affected by the tenor of the political relationships among the states involved, and its status is often taken as a barometer of those relationships. There has been a debate about the necessity and wisdom of this linkage. One view holds that the mutual interests that are the basis of arms control should and can override a bad, even deteriorating, adversarial relationship—especially with respect to nuclear weapons. The opposite view, now fairly widely accepted, is that when political relations are poor (and especially if they are getting worse) it is unrealistic to expect any serious cooperation to limit arms. If the political relationship is an important factor, then a case can be made that arms control is really possible mainly when it is unnecessary.

Next, arms control is normally pursued in keeping with a strong concern for verification, and agreement often is confined to what states believe they can verify and what they will permit others to verify. This adds greatly to the contention and complexities involved in negotiations, ratification, and implementation. Another limiting factor is that arms control has rarely restricted weapons and forces to which the parties attached great importance and which they strongly wished to refine or expand. Along these lines, states have commonly taken steps to design around agreements they have signed, thereby circumventing them. This incites complaints that arms control is a peripheral matter, used only at the margins, and too often pursued to create an illusion of restraint that is politically useful at home and abroad.

Finally, arms control is politically popular in principle but often controversial when it comes to actual agreements and practices. This makes it difficult for one or more states to arrive at and sustain a sufficient domestic consensus, especially within the same time frame. It is often said that the negotiations at home to develop bargaining positions or secure ratification of agreements can be at least as difficult as the ones with other states.

With these features in mind, the crafting of acceptable agreements has often been exceedingly complex and time consuming, with a good probability of failure or of the results being outmoded by political developments or technological change. Some analysts believe that, under suitable conditions, it is better to go for the speed and flexibility of informal unilateral (but parallel) steps to limit arms to avoid these problems.

The contemporary significance of arms control for international politics is a matter of continuing debate. Clearly international politics is now conducted within an elaborate web of arms control practices and agreements, and in tandem with nuclear deterrence arms control has been the foremost route to security adopted by major states during the past half century. The 1990 Paris Agreement, signed by virtually all national governments in Europe and North America, involves the most significant conventional forces limitations ever undertaken, including prospective destruction of over 100,000 pieces of equipment and elaborate restraints on deployments. The proposed chemical weapons treaty would eliminate these items, with plans having been announced by the United States and the Soviet Union to destroy most of them in advance of its signing and ratification. The INF Treaty has led to the elimination of 2,767 missiles. The Strategic Arms Reduction Agreement (July 1991), as revised by subsequent pacts, will slash U.S. and post-Soviet strategic nuclear weapons to 3,500 and 3,000, respectively (from roughly 10,000 to 12,000 each). The United States and Russia have also announced the unilateral elimination or storage of most of their many thousands of short-range nuclear weapons. All this has come after a period, from 1975 to 1985, when optimism about and support for arms control had been greatly reduced, and suggests that it is a durable and significant phenomenon.

However, its significance is limited by the fact that the arms control web is fragile, incomplete, and not of fine mesh. Ballistic missiles and other potential nuclear delivery systems have widely proliferated, and the resumption of outright nuclear proliferation is anticipated by many analysts in the near future. Conventional arms continue to spread, as does the ability to produce them, with almost no restraints in place. Technological change has produced numerous new weapons systems which could be destabilizing to deterrence and which make verification more complicated. Chemical weapons have recently been used on a scale not seen for many years and may have spread too widely to be controlled. Modern wars have amply displayed the enormous pressures to override restraints on weapons and targets.

The theory of arms control is well developed for explaining what it is, why and how it can be useful, and why it is possible. The theory is much weaker concerning when and why it is actually attained or fails, with continuing disagreement about what important factors are involved (international system structure, technological change, bureaucratic interests, domestic politics, etc.) and their relative impact. There is also more interest among governments, for the first time in years, in steps more like disarmament than arms control. Thus consensus is missing about whether arms control is of independent significance in international politics or derivative in impact, having its effects only because key prerequisites are present.

(See also ARMS RACE; STRATEGIC ARMS LIMITATION TREATIES; STRATEGY.)

Hedley Bull, *The Control of the Arms Race: Disarmament and Arms Control in the Missile Age* (New York, 1961). U.S. Arms Control and Disarmament Agency, *Arms Control and Disarmament Agreements: Texts and History of Negotiations* (Washington, D.C., 1982). Bernard F. Halloran, *Essays on Arms Control and National Security* (Washington, D.C., 1984). Thomas C. Schelling and Morton Halperin, *Strategy and Arms Control*, 2d ed. (Washington, D.C., 1985). Albert Carnesdale and Richard N. Haass, *Superpower Arms Control: Setting the Record Straight* (Cambridge, Mass., 1987). Patrick M. Morgan, "On Strategic Arms Control and International Security," in Edward A. Kolodziej and Patrick M. Morgan, eds., *Security and Arms Control: A Guide to International Policymaking, Volume Two* (New York, 1989): 299–318. William C. Potter, "On Nuclear Proliferation," in Edward A. Kolodziej and Patrick M. Morgan, eds., *Security and Arms Control: A Guide to International Policymaking, Volume Two* (New York, 1989): 319–355.

PATRICK M. MORGAN

ARMS RACE. The precise origin of the term *arms race* is obscure, but it seems to have first appeared in England during the late 1850s when journalists and politicians began to use it to describe the competitive, interstate accumulation of naval combat vessels by Britain and France. The timing of the term's appearance can probably be explained by the fact that it was around this time that technologically advanced and expensive weapons began to assume greater importance. A large number of infantry could be mobilized and sent into the field in a matter of months. The same thing could not be said about ironclad frigates. This meant that the nation with the largest number of such vessels at the outset of a *war possessed an important and potentially critical advantage. Not surprisingly, nations soon found themselves in a race to have the most modern as well as the largest navies. No less predictably, they turned to the technologies created by the emerging industrial revolution to help them accomplish their ends.

Both the scholarly and popular literatures have continued the tradition of applying the term *arms race* to describe a competition involving major weapons systems and technological innovations. A simpler troop buildup has rarely been viewed as an arms race. The Anglo-French arms race of 1859–1860 was precipitated by the French construction of the ironclad *La Gloire* and its plan to build sixteen others. The arms race between the United States and the Soviet Union focused on the development of *nuclear weapons and missile systems. The close historical relationship between arms races and technology explains why the arms race literature has had what might appear to be a myopic and discriminatory preoccupation with the arms races between European nations and those involving major world powers such as Japan and the United States. This situation has been changed somewhat in recent years with the growing technological character of the arms buildups in the Middle East and South Asia.

What Is an Arms Race? The 1850s common language definition of an arms race as an "intense competition over the rapid accumulation of weaponry that requires a significant amount of time and/or money to produce" is as relevant today as it was a century and a half ago, but scholars have disagreed about the degree of competition that must be present to justify the use of the term *arms race*. For example, the United States and Iran both initiated major new arms programs in the 1980s. However, no one would argue that they were in an arms race because it is obvious that neither program was inspired by the other. The buildups were not competitive. The same thing can be said of parts of the apparent arms race between the United States and the Soviet Union during a substantial portion of the *Cold War. For example, a close examination of the historical record during the years of the Reagan administration reveals that much of the increase in the defense budget of United States was inspired more by the domestic imperatives of the campaign strategy that Ronald *Reagan used against Jimmy *Carter than by the rate of Soviet arms procurement or the desire to establish strategic superiority. One important implication of the multitude of rationales that underlie arms races is that the dream of game theorists to characterize all arms races by reference to a single game such as the Prisoner's Dilemma will probably not be realized.

The pattern of arms growth that must be present is also problematic. Lewis Richardson, the best-known arms race theorist, argued that the rate of arms accumulation in an arms race either converges to a stable growth rate or continues to accelerate. This model provides an adequate description of the arms race preceding *World War I, the inspiration for much of Richardson's work, but it is now clear that most arms races do not fit this neat pattern. The arms race between the United States and Soviet Union provides one of the clearest exceptions. Over its forty-year history there were periods when both nations were accelerating their rates of arms acquisitions, periods when they both were reducing the rate of acquisition, and periods when the growth in arms stocks of one nation was accelerating while that of the other was declining. This complexity characterizes any group of arms races as well. If one examines ten different arms races, it becomes clear that the pattern of growth rate varies across the races. While the arms race that culminated in World War I was characterized both by large increases in the number of weapons (an absolute measure of arms race intensity) and a proportionate increase in the number of weapons available in each nation's stockpile (a relative measure), this is not always the case. Many naval arms races of the nineteenth century involved only modest increases in absolute number of weapons, and some of those in the late twentieth century involve only modest relative increases in available forces.

Do Arms Races Cause Wars? After decades of systematic study, the relationship between arms races and wars remains a contentious issue. There is a general recognition that many wars have not been preceded by arms races (e.g., Boer War, *Vietnam War) and many arms races have not led to war (e.g., Anglo-French naval race of 1859, postwar arms race between the United States and Soviet Union). However, there is little agreement on whether the existence of an arms race increases or decreases the chances that an antagonism between two states will erupt into war. One tradition of scholarship believes that arms races increase the probability of war by mutually exacerbating the perception of hostility. This occurs because each nation sees the other as more aggressive because of its arms policy. Another tradition believes that arms races often reduce the probability by mutually increasing the cost of aggression.

Since 1970, a growing number of social scientists have begun to believe that there is no simple answer to the question of whether or not arms races cause wars. They argue that the empirical record reveals that there are times when arms races have increased the likelihood of conflict and other times when they have reduced it. Whether or not a particular arms race will increase the risk of war depends on a host of factors. These include national goals, strategic choices, the current technology of war, and the level of misperception and uncertainty that exist. Because these factors vary from case to case, the likelihood that an arms race will lead to war varies as well. If correct, this helps to account for why previous scholars from each competing tradition have been able to find evidence in support of their positions. To complicate matters still further, this third school believes that any estimate of the "average" likelihood that an arms race will lead to war can be expected to vary from decade to decade as technologies and the distribution of other key factors such as goals and resources change.

Despite the evolution of this more contingent vision of the relationship between arms races and war, policymakers faced with the choice of whether or not to develop a new weapons system can still find themselves in a quandary. The question is not whether the development of the system will increase the price that a rival perceives that it must pay for initiating conflict or whether it will increase the rival's perception of the offensive threat that can be mounted against it—except in rare cases it will do both. What matters is the precise tradeoff between the *security induced by increasing the cost of aggression and the insecurity induced by increasing the perception of hostile intent. In some contexts this trade-off is fairly obvious. A nation in a situation of highly redundant mutually assured destruction (MAD) is unlikely to have its security threatened by a modest increase in the capabilities of its rival. On the other hand, a non-nuclear power with a significant arms advantage might be tempted to initiate a preventive war in order to stave off the impact of an arms race that it feels it will lose. Unfortunately, most intent/cost trade-offs are not so clear.

For now, two prescriptions are believed to hold across the widest variety of contexts. Decision makers should: 1) respond to an arms increase on the part of an adversary with a slightly smaller increase; and 2) concentrate on defense. It is recognized that few weapons will be viewed as being entirely defensive, but it is also true that some weapons will be viewed by a rival as much more defensive than others. These two prescriptions both possess the twin virtues of minimizing the chances that the action will be interpreted as indicating aggressive intent without signaling weakness or the willingness to be exploited.

(See also ARMS CONTROL; GAME THEORY; STRATEGIC ARMS LIMITATION TREATIES.)

Lewis F. Richardson, *Arms and Insecurity* (Pittsburgh, Pa., 1960). Matthew Evangelista, *Innovation and the Arms Race* (Ithaca, N.Y., 1988). George W. Downs and David M. Rocke, *Tacit Bargaining, Arms Races, and Arms Control* (Ann Arbor, Mich., 1990).

GEORGE W. DOWNS

ASIAN DEVELOPMENT BANK. Established in December 1966 and headquartered in Manila, the Asian Development Bank (ADB) seeks to contribute to the economic development and social progress of its regional members. As of April 1991, the ADB had fifty member nations, including thirty-five from the Asia-Pacific region and fifteen countries from Europe and North America. The bank is run by 606 professional staff members reporting to a twelve-member board of directors headed by the ADB's president. To date, all ADB presidents have been Japanese nationals.

The bank's principal functions are to make loans and equity investments to developing countries in the Asia-Pacific region. In addition to its ordinary capital resources, which account for sixty-six percent of its cumulative lending, the ADB administers the Asian Development Fund (ADF), which makes zero-interest-rate, fifty-year loans to the poorest Asian countries. The ADB also provides substantial technical assistance to its member countries. According to the ADB's last annual report, the bank had committed a total of US$32.7 billion in loans and investments for 1,020 projects between 1966–1990.

The ADB raises money on international capital markets to supplement contributions provided by its developed member countries. As of 31 December 1991, the ADB had authorized capital of US$23.9 billion. A total of US$10 billion had been borrowed from international capital markets for lending from ordinary capital resources. About US$13.4 billion had been made available for concessional loans from the ADF between 1966 and 1990.

Among the bank's biggest borrowers are China, India, Indonesia, and Pakistan. Several *newly industrializing economies, including the Republic of Korea and Singapore, have been elevated from the ranks of borrowers to become net lenders to the institution.

In line with other regional development banks, the ADB has moved in recent years to reorient its lending operations in support of country strategies that focus on economic growth and poverty alleviation. It has also provided more direct support to the private sector at the insistence of the United States and other donors. Since 1983, private sector lending has accounted for US$440 million committed to sixty-four projects. A thirty-percent-owned subsidiary, the Asian Finance and Investment Corporation, was established in August 1989 by the ADB in conjunction with commercial banks to provide direct private sector finance.

(See also AFRICAN DEVELOPMENT BANK; INTER-AMERICAN DEVELOPMENT BANK; PACIFIC REGION.)

Asian Development Bank, *Annual Report 1990* (Manila, 1990). Jonathan Friedland, "Enter Mr. Nice Guy" and "Private Solutions," *The Far Eastern Economic Review* 29 (March 1990), pp. 57–58.

JONATHAN FRIEDLAND

ASSASSINATION. The premeditated murder of a political figure for reasons associated with the victim's prominence, political perspective, or some combination of both is known as assassination. As a formal means of political action, assassination is usually traced historically to a secret Islamic order known as Nizaris that emerged (ca. 1090) in the region south of the Caspian Sea that is now encompassed by Syria and Iran. The members of this radical sect were distinguished by a fanatical devotion to their cause and a willingness to kill selectively on command to eliminate political opposition. The term *assassin* is derived from an Arabic word meaning "user of hashish," the substance members of the sect used to prepare themselves psychologically for a politically inspired murder. In modern times, assassination occurs throughout the world and is not restricted to any particular religious sect, ethnic group, nationality, or culture. The distinction between assassination and lethal acts of *terrorism is based on the political prominence of the actual, or intended, victim(s). For example, the Irish Republican Army's (IRA) clandestine killings of British troops and Protestant civilians are often described as acts of terrorism, whereas the death of Lord Louis Mountbatten, killed by an IRA bomb in 1979, is considered an assassination.

Transnational research suggests that social and economic factors are not associated with assassinations in any interpretable way. Contrary to popular belief, assassination is *less* likely to occur in non-Western developing nations than it is in Western developed nations. Assassination is a much more frequent event in Italy, France, and the United States, for example, than it is in any African nation. Several other tentative conclusions are possible. Assassinations are more likely during times of political instability and domestic strife. Such acts are less frequent in the most permissive, democratic societies (e.g., the Scandinavian nations) as well as the most restrictive, authoritarian societies (e.g., China and the pre-perestroika East European bloc). Heads of state and high government officials remain the most frequent targets, but in recent years the attention of political extremist groups has shifted sharply to multinational business executives and members of the diplomatic corps (who are also more likely than heads of state to be killed when an attempt is made). Heads of state remain the preferred targets of lone assassins. Before 1970, most assassination attempts were carried out by lone assassins. The pattern has changed since then with political extremist groups accounting for the majority of assassination attempts, except in the United States where the earlier lone assassin pattern continues.

When a political figure does fall victim to a single assassin, attention necessarily shifts to the assailant's mental state. A psychological study of assassins and would-be assassins (James W. Clarke, *American Assassins: The Darker Side of Politics,* rev. ed., Princeton, N.J., 1990) identifies certain themes that define the motives of lone assassins in the United States that may have more universal applicability. Most assassins in the United States acted alone and were motivated primarily by personal problems (e.g., failed relationships and careers, or completely delusionary grievances) having little to do with political ideology or, for that matter, the public figures they attacked. This persistent, and possibly peculiar, American motivational strain, combined with the dramatic increase in successful and attempted assassinations from 1963 to 1990 (eight, which was one more than the number of presidential elections during the same period), the world prominence of the victims, and the corresponding sharp increase in the normally high levels of ordinary homicide, set the United States apart from other nations.

(See also POLITICAL VIOLENCE.)

Thomas H. Snitch, "Terrorism and Political Assassinations: A Transnational Assessment, 1968–80" *Annals of the American Academy of Political and Social Sciences* 463 (September 1982): 54–66. Franklin L. Ford, *Political Murder: From Tyrannicide to Terrorism* (Cambridge, Mass., 1985).

JAMES W. CLARKE

ASSOCIATION OF SOUTHEAST ASIAN NATIONS. A change of government in Indonesia in 1965 that ended hostilities with Malaysia and a sense of external security threats to the region from China and the *Vietnam War combined to allow the creation of the Association of Southeast Asian Nations (ASEAN) in August 1967 through the Bangkok Declaration. The original members, *Indonesia, *Malaysia, the *Philippines, *Singapore, and *Thailand, were joined by *Brunei on its independence in January 1984; several other states may join in the future. ASEAN replaced the Association of Southeast Asia, founded in 1961 by Thailand, Malaysia, and the Philippines. Its work is conducted through intergovernmental committees, assisted since 1976

by a small secretariat established in Jakarta (Indonesia). All decisions must be approved by the foreign ministers, representing national governments.

Formally a mechanism for regional coordination, ASEAN serves as one channel among its members and between them and a wide range of other international organizations, without replacing the members' own representations in those organizations. The range of issues considered by ASEAN has slowly grown to encompass almost all areas of policy, from international *refugees and the drug trade to trade liberalization and transportation. Summit meetings at Bali (Indonesia) and Kuala Lumpur (Malaysia) in 1976 and 1977 emphasized economic cooperation, especially in reducing trade barriers and increasing industry, but with small effect. A third summit, in Manila (Philippines) in 1987, reemphasized these issues, improving chances for modest growth of ASEAN influence in regional economic affairs. A wide network of nongovernmental organizations among business, government, and professional groups provides another level of regional cooperation that leads some to speak of an ASEAN Community. Official and unofficial exchange of information about economic policies and problems has become extensive and is of great value to states primarily concerned with accelerating their economic development. But Southeast Asian nations' economic ties are so much more extensive outside the region than within that integration like that advanced in Europe by the *European Community is unlikely. This is considered by some to be ASEAN's signal failure.

The Treaty of Amity and Co-operation in Southeast Asia and the Declaration of ASEAN Concord, both signed in 1976, effectively established peaceful relations among the members. These treaties allow other states to extend a successful peace zone further in Southeast Asia and the South Pacific. A concern to prevent intervention by outside powers resulted in the Declaration of a Zone of Peace, Freedom and Neutrality in Southeast Asia in 1971, and a nuclear-free zone has been proposed to buttress this effort. Although ASEAN formally avoids the image of a security alliance, bilateral military exercises and exchanges of intelligence are commonplace among the members, providing the ability to coordinate defense, if needed.

ASEAN is probably best known globally for its leading role, both within and outside the UN, in efforts to end the Vietnamese occupation of *Cambodia, which lasted from 1979 until 1989. But the aspect most valued by the members is coordination of economic diplomacy with Japan, the United States, Europe, and other partners. ASEAN's annual meetings have become a central focus of Pacific economic discussions. As the only intergovernmental economic organization in the Pacific Basin until the formation of Asia-Pacific Economic Cooperation in late 1989, ASEAN played a critical role in the evolution of Pacific economic cooperation. ASEAN is considered the most successful regional organization among Third World states.

Linda Martin, ed., *The ASEAN Success Story* (Honolulu, 1987).

DONALD K. CRONE

ATATÜRK, Kemal. Turkish nationalist leader and founder of modern *Turkey, Kemal Atatürk (originally Mustafa Kemal) was born in 1881 in what is now the Greek city of Salonika. He went to military school, one of the few options open to a lower-middle-class Muslim youth seeking a modern education and a career. Graduating as staff captain in 1905, he joined the Young Turk movement whose goal was to reform the Ottoman Empire. When the Young Turk revolution took place in July 1908, he pursued a military rather than a political career, serving in Albania (1910), Libya (1911–1912), and in the Balkans (1912–1913). He was military attaché to Sofia in October 1913 but returned to active command at Gallipoli where he made his reputation. Promoted to the rank of pasha (general) in April 1916, he was virtually exiled by his Young Turk rivals to the eastern front. Subsequently he recaptured the towns of Bitlis and Muş from the Russians and fought a defensive campaign in Palestine and Syria.

In October 1918 the Turks were forced to sign an armistice and await their fate. In May 1919 the sultan sent Kemal to disband Ottoman armies in Anatolia; instead Kemal decided to unify a fragmented resistance movement and reorganize the army. The Greek landing at Izmir on 15 May aroused passions throughout Anatolia and facilitated Kemal's task. He summoned nationalist congresses in Erzurum (July 1919) and Sivas (September 1919) where he was elected the chair. The sultan (and the Allies occupying Istanbul) responded with massive repression, and a court-martial in Istanbul sentenced Kemal to death in absentia. But the sultan's acceptance of the Treaty of Sèvres (August 1920) left the nationalists as sole guardians of national rights. After signing agreements with the Soviets and thus ending his isolation, Kemal concentrated on defeating the Greek invasion, finally succeeding in September 1922. The discredited sultan's attempt to participate in peace negotiations enabled Kemal to abolish the sultanate in November, and the Treaty of Lausanne (July 1923) gave European recognition of an independent sovereign Turkey.

Kemal now dealt with conservatives in his own ranks, most of whom were generals popular with the army. Because of their higher social status, they preferred an Islamist regime under the caliph. Kemal outflanked them by having the Assembly declare a republic on 29 October with himself as president. The caliphate was abolished in 1924 and the Kurdish rebellion of 1925 provided Kemal with the opportunity to crush all opposition. He then carried out a program of radical reform which transformed the entire institutional structure of the new state. Kemal had become the unrivaled master of the new state, ruling through the Republican People's Party and mediating between various factions. He strove to create a Turkey with a modern social structure and economy. He experimented briefly with an opposition in 1930 but abandoned the project when he found that conservative forces were aroused. That made him even more radical, for he assumed that the people needed to be educated in the values of the new Turkey. His radical ideas were formulated in an ideology known as *Kemalism. He was reelected president in 1927, 1931, and 1935, and the Assembly bestowed upon him the name *Atatürk* ("Father Turk") in 1934; soon after his death on 10 November 1938 he was proclaimed "eternal leader."

Lord Kinross, *Ataturk: The Rebirth of a Nation* (London, 1964). Bernard Lewis, *The Emergence of Modern Turkey*, 2d ed. (London, 1968). Turkish National Commission for UNESCO, *Atatürk* (Ankara, 1981). Vamik Volkan and Norman Itzkowitz, *The Immortal Atatürk: A Psychobiography* (Chicago, 1984).

FEROZ AHMAD

ATOMIC BOMB. See NUCLEAR WEAPONS.

AUSTRALIA. With its legal, cultural, and political institutions modeled on those of the mother country, Australia developed as a British outpost in the South Pacific, with an economy based on the export of primary commodities, primarily wool and gold. A British penal colony was established at Sydney Cove in 1788, followed by the establishment of five more colonies during the first half of the nineteenth century, peopled predominantly with settlers from the British Isles. From the middle of the nineteenth century immigration restrictions were imposed, particularly with respect to Asians, to maintain a white Australia.

The effect of British settlement on the Australian Aborigines was devastating. The land was annexed under the doctrine of *terra nullius*—that Australia was an empty land belonging to no one. European infectious diseases, destruction of food sources, and armed conflict decimated the population, and those who survived were subject to restrictive and discriminatory legislation until the middle of this century. Since the early 1970s many Australians of aboriginal descent have been agitating both for land rights and for some form of retrospective recognition of their prior occupancy, as well as for improved living conditions.

In 1901 the six colonies federated to form the Commonwealth of Australia. The resulting political institutions combined the conventions of the Westminster system of responsible cabinet government with a federal system in which the colonies became states, retaining their own parliaments and bureaucracies and a considerable degree of *sovereignty.

The federal Parliament is a two-chamber legislature, elected on a universal franchise. The lower house (House of Representatives) employs a preferential voting system, the upper house (the Senate) a proportional system. Although designed as a state's house, with equal representation from each state, the Senate's operations have followed party lines for most of its history. Voting in elections at both federal and state level is compulsory.

The constitution formally divided powers between the two levels of government and established the High Court of Australia to adjudicate disputes. The initial powers given to the new federal government seemed limited—mainly to do with external affairs such as defense and immigration and with matters such as currency and marriage laws on which uniformity seemed desirable. During the twentieth century, however, the scope of the federal government's powers has increased enormously, both because of judicial interpretation and because of the financial dominance held by the federal government since World War II. Friction between the two levels of government is a continuing feature of Australian political life, and the division of power has proved frustrating to reforming governments. Although the Australian federal system is unsupported by marked regional or ethnic differences, it is deeply embedded in the organizational life of Australian society and is unlikely to be seriously challenged in the foreseeable future.

The Commonwealth of Australia also includes the Northern Territory, which now has limited self-government, and the Australian Capital Territory, which is the location of Canberra, the federal capital. Apart from some islands in the Indian and Pacific oceans and the Australian Antarctic Territory, Australia has no external territories. Papua New Guinea, which had been administered by Australia since World War II as a United Nations Trust Territory, became an independent nation in 1975.

Since 1910 the Australian party system has been dominated by three parties: the Australian Labor Party, formed in the 1890s as the political wing of the trade union movement; a non-Labor party committed to private enterprise and liberalism which has undergone several changes of identity and which was re-formed by Robert Menzies (1894–1978) in 1944 as the Liberal Party of Australia; and a rural-based party (originally the Country Party, now the National Party) which has regularly participated in coalition governments with the major non-Labor party. Until the early 1970s Australian patterns of party identification were relatively stable, but since then the electorate has become more volatile. The rural-based National Party has continued to exert considerable influence, despite a decline in the farm-based population. A new center-left party with a strong environmental policy, the Australia Democrats, has achieved some success in Senate elections, and it is now unlikely that the governing party will also control the Senate.

Historically the two major parties have differed most markedly in the class orientation of their social outlook and in their attitude to government intervention in the economy, although both supported the postwar expansion of the government's role in the regulation of the economy and provision of social welfare, and both have retreated from this since the mid-1970s out of a concern to reduce the size and scope of government. Skills at economic management rather than sharp differences in political values are now the main ground of party competition.

Australia only slowly sought legal independence from Britain. Authority was increasingly delegated to governors and parliaments in Australia throughout the nineteenth century, although the British monarch and parliament possessed the theoretical legal power to rule Australia until 1986 when the U.K. Australia Act was proclaimed. Australia did not begin to assume independence in foreign affairs until 1917 and did not adopt the 1931 U.K. Statute of Westminster until 1942. Elizabeth II, the queen of England, is also queen of Australia, and is represented in Australia by six state governors and by the governor general of the Commonwealth.

Although on paper these governors have enormous power, they have rarely exercised it. An exception to this occurred in 1975 when the incumbent governor general, Sir John Kerr, dismissed the Labor government led by Gough Whitlam in order to resolve a deadlock between the two houses of parliament caused by the Senate's refusal to pass appropriation bills. This remains a controversial incident in recent Australian politics, with continuing disagreement over the propriety of both Kerr's actions and of the behavior of the Liberal and National parties in the Senate.

Until World War II, Australia looked to Britain for defense, for markets for its primary produce, for capital, for immigrants, and for its cultural standards. While Australia has remained a member of the *Commonwealth, the wartime alliance with the United States in the Pacific war, together with the latter's dominance of the postwar Western world, drew Australia closer to the United States, as a source of capital and cultural standards and as a major ally. In 1951 the *ANZUS Treaty was signed by Australia, New Zealand, and the United States. Australia fought with the United States in the *Vietnam War and has allowed it to establish military bases on its soil. Some controversy surrounds the U.S. bases, as well as the degree of dependence manifested in Australia's continuing, if somewhat less insistent, reliance on powerful allies for its defense.

After World War II Australia embarked on a massive immigration program that has radically altered its demographic composition. More than half of the population increase since the war, from 7.5 million in 1947 to 17 million in 1990, has been due to immigration and to children born to immigrant parents. While migrants continued to come from Britain and Ireland, they were also drawn from most parts of Europe, particularly Greece and Italy, and from the Middle East. Since the end of the 1960s with the dismantling of the white Australia policy there has been increasing immigration from Asia; this has met with some opposition, as have previous waves of immigration. The Australian population has moved in less than fifty years from being one of the most homogeneous to one of the most diverse in the world, and an official policy of assimilation has been replaced, with some tension, by one of multiculturalism, which recognizes people's rights to maintain their separate cultural identities within a shared political and legal framework.

Australia has a mixed economy in which the government historically has played a large role in the development of infrastructure. Encouraged by the strength of the labor movement, Australia, like New Zealand, developed a system of industrial tribunals to settle disputes between employers and unions and to fix conditions of labor. Australia continues to have a highly unionized workforce by Western standards. Throughout the twentieth century the Australian economy has relied heavily on the export of primary commodities, particularly wool and minerals. The manufacturing sector has been weak, developed for the domestic market rather than for export. It has been highly protected, dependent on imported technology, and has high levels of foreign ownership. In the 1980s problems of the economy came to dominate political debate, in particular the need to develop competitive and more export-oriented industries to improve Australia's rapidly deteriorating terms of trade and escalating *international debt. One response has been to intensify the argument that Australia needs to develop closer economic and cultural links with Asia. Japan is now the third-largest source of foreign investment.

The economic pressures on Australia have been increasing since the 1970s, and Australia has responded by attempting to develop defense, foreign, immigration, trade, and investment policies appropriate to its position in the region of Asia and the Pacific.

(See also FEDERALISM; INTERNATIONAL MIGRATION; PACIFIC REGION.)

Geoffrey Sawer, *Australian Government Today*, 13th ed., (Melbourne, 1987). Bruce Grant, *What Kind of Country? Australia and the Twenty-First Century* (Melbourne, 1988). Geoffrey Bolton, *The Oxford History of Australia*, vol. 5, (Melbourne, 1990).

JUDITH BRETT

AUSTRIA. With an area of 84,372 square kilometers (32,576 sq. mi.) and a population of about 7.5 million, the Second Austrian Republic must be judged one of contemporary Europe's success stories. Compared to its ill-fated predecessor of the interwar years (the First Republic, 1918–1934) and other European countries, both East and West, Austria's postwar existence has been characterized by political stability buttressed by economic prosperity and a careful management of formerly divisive social cleavages. This domestic equilibrium found helpful international support thanks to Austria's postwar neutrality, which gave the country—together with Switzerland, Sweden, and Finland—a distinct status in Europe's political order.

In the case of Austria, informal understandings among the major political players, an altered international context, and societal *secularization—instead of formal institutional and legal arrangements—account for the virtually opposite political outcomes in the two republics. Both republics had a bicameral legislature. Both used proportional representation to elect their representatives. Both were dominated by distinct blocs representing deep-seated cleavages. Yet in the First Republic this scenario led to civil war and the destruction of the republic in 1934, followed by the disappearance of Austria as a sovereign country in 1938 via the *Anschluß* to Nazi Germany. In contrast, virtually the same constellation led to moderation, prosperity, and stability after 1945.

In both republics, Austria's party system revolved around the cleavages of "*class," nation," and "*religion," perhaps the most ubiquitous dividing lines informing all modern politics. Until its destruction at the hands of Austrian Fascists—thus ending the First Republic—the Sozialistische Partei Österreichs (SPÖ) embodied the prototypical European class-based party. Controlling Vienna and other industrial centers, the SPÖ provided its extensive membership and loyal supporters with a cradle-to-grave society featuring its own housing, educational institutions, welfare agencies, recreational facilities, and paramilitary guard. Opposing social democracy on issues of class were two bourgeois "camps" *(Lager)* representing opposite sides of the national and religious cleavages. The Christian Social Party, rechristened the Österreichische Volkspartei (ÖVP) in the Second Republic, was roughly equal in size to the SPÖ (approximately forty percent of the population). It was the home of political Catholicism and Austrians who identified their national allegiance predominantly with a sovereign Austria as opposed to a merger with Germany. As the third, and somewhat smaller, force, the Landbund and the Pan-German People's Party (First-Republic predecessors to the contemporary Freiheitliche Partei Österreichs [FPÖ]) represented that segment of the Austrian middle class that was at best indifferent, and usually actively hostile, to Catholicism, and whose affinity with things German extended to wanting to see Austria forgo its national sovereignty and become part of a Greater Germany.

Following the destructive contests among these three camps during the 1930s and the ensuing war experience, the leaders of the two dominant blocs—Social and Christian Democracy—emerged after World War II with the fundamental commitment never to destroy each other. Thus was born a paragon of *consociational democracy in which the two parties jointly governed Austria in a grand coalition during the all-important formative years between 1945 and 1966. During these two decades the formal institutions of consociationalism as well as the informal channels of social partnership were put in place. As a consequence, the single most prominent feature of the Second Austrian Republic is its finely tuned and extensive web of conflict management in which the guiding principle for all players is compromise.

In contemporary Austria, the political parties and their ancillary interest organizations—the trade union federation and the chamber of labor on the "red" side, and the industrialists' association and the chamber of commerce as their "black" counterparts—have continued to permeate all aspects of Austrian public life, as they did during the interwar period. However, postwar economic prosperity and the overall *modernization of Austrian society encouraged a secularization process that brought the parties into a cooperative public space. The two camps became increasingly blurred and thus less exclusive and hostile to each other. Socialist voters did not necessarily come from the industrial working class anymore. Nor did they live ghetto-style in particular working-class districts or belong to party-sponsored sports clubs. Conversely, ÖVP voters developed considerable autonomy in relation to a weakened Catholic church and the less strident business associations. The cleavages of class and religion have lost their previously hostile edges.

The class-religion cleavage become even more muted over time. With *Germany divided and politically emasculated, joining Germany in any kind of political union was neither attractive nor possible for Austrians in a postwar Europe controlled by the Soviet Union and the Western powers. Indeed, with the Allies' declaration of Austria as Nazi Germany's first victim, the foundation for Austria's separate identity was laid in 1943. However, it was mainly Austria's neutrality—reaffirmed in the state treaty of 1955—that severed all realistic possibilities of any Anschluß-type arrangement between the two countries. The respect accorded neutrality by the global community and a general perception of its benefits gave Austria a political identity that made its citizens feel increasingly "Austrian" instead of "German." The "German question"—so much in the forefront of the First Republic—receded to relative harmlessness in the Second.

In distinguishing Austria from Germany, neutrality also helped foster Austria's amnesia vis-à-vis its role in the Third Reich. Accepting history's verdict as Nazi Germany's first victim, Austrians could blame the Holocaust's horrors on the "evil" Germans and avoid the painful process of coming to terms with their own complicitous past. Paradoxically, it was the international controversy surrounding the election of Kurt Waldheim to the Austrian presidency in 1986 that for the first time led to broad-based debates in Austria about the country's role under National Socialism.

The secularization and Europeanization process continues to diminish the parties' dominance in Austrian life. By the mid-1980s Austria, too, had its citizens' movements and "nontraditional" protest politics that found uneasy parliamentary expression in vocal and active green and other "alternative" parties. With the opening of Europe's hitherto sequestered eastern half, Austria's importance as a bridge between East and West will most certainly be enhanced. Indeed, Austria is well placed to become the geographic center of a renewed *Mitteleuropa* that, in contrast to its pre-1945 situation, will be run neither by feudal aristocrats nor by a fascist middle class but by secularized capitalists and pragmatic labor leaders always on the lookout for deals.

(See also CENTRAL EUROPE.)

Kurt Steiner, *Politics in Austria* (Boston, 1972). WIlliam T. Bluhm, *Building an Austrian Nation: The Political Integration of a Western State* (New Haven, Conn., 1973). Peter J. Katzenstein, *Corporatism and Change: Austria, Switzerland and the Politics of Industry* (Ithaca, N.Y., 1984). Anton Pelinka and Fritz Plasser, eds., *The Austrian Party System* (Boulder, Colo., 1989).

ANDREI S. MARKOVITS

AUTHORITARIANISM. While authority refers to legitimate power, authoritarianism is associated with "arbitrary," illegitimate authority, at least according to liberal and democratic values. Nondemocratic regimes share the following characteristics: those governing are self-appointed and, even if elected, cannot be displaced by citizens' free choice among competitors; and there is no freedom to create a broad range of groups, organizations, and political parties to compete for power or question the decisions of the rulers.

This essay deals with authoritarian regimes, which may be contrasted with competitive *democracies (which enjoy almost *unlimited* rather than very confined *pluralism) and with totalitarian systems (where pluralism is entirely absent and mobilizational *ideologies, rather than the more fluid and formless mentalities, sustain the regime). We have previously defined authoritarian regimes as "political systems with limited, not responsible, political pluralism, without elaborate and guiding ideology, but with distinctive mentalities, without extensive nor intensive political mobilization, except at some points in their development, and in which a leader or occasionally a small group exercises power within formally ill-defined limits but actually quite predictable ones."

Operating with neither the resources of *legitimacy associated with competitive democracies nor the mobilizational capacities of totalitarian systems, the authoritarian regimes on the periphery of ideological centers feel the pressure to imitate, incorporate, and manipulate dominant ideological styles. Generic values like patriotism, *nationalism, economic development, social justice, and order and the pragmatic incorporation of ideological elements derived from the dominant political centers allow rulers without mobilized mass support to neutralize opponents, co-opt a variety of supporters, and decide policies pragmatically.

The lack of ideology limits the capacity to mobilize people, to create the psychological and emotional identification of the masses. Indeed, limited political mobilization is a characteristic of authoritarian regimes. In some, the depoliticization of the masses corresponds to the intent of the rulers; in others, the rulers initially intended to mobilize their supporters and the population. The struggle for national independence from a colonial power, the desire to incorporate into the political process sectors of the society untapped by any previous political leadership, or the defeat of a highly mobilized opponent in societies in which democracy had allowed and encouraged such a mobilization lead to the emergence of mobilizational authoritarian regimes of a nationalist, populist, or fascist variety. The maintenance of equilibrium between limited pluralisms limits the effectiveness of the mobilization and leads to apathy.

If our definition is useful, it should allow us to develop subtypes. Authoritarian regimes include 1) bureaucratic-military regimes; 2) organic statist regimes; 3) mobilizational regimes, including postdemocratic and postcolonial; 4) personal rulership; and 5) post-totalitarian regimes.

Bureaucratic-Military Regimes. The most frequent subtype are regimes in which a coalition predominantly but not exclusively controlled by army officers, bureaucrats, and technocrats establishes control of government and excludes or includes other groups without commitment to a specific ideology, acts pragmatically within the limits of their bureaucratic mentality, and neither creates nor allows a mass single party to play a dominant role. They may operate without parties, but frequently they have created an official government-sponsored single party. In a few cases they allow a multiparty system but make sure that the elections do not offer an opportunity for a free competition for popular support.

Organic Statism. Quite different in form from bureaucratic-military-technocratic authoritarian regimes, organic statism presupposes a corporatist mode of interest representation and participation or mobilization. Theorists of the organic statist authoritarian model contrast the natural (or organic) development of business and professional organizations, trade unions, universities, churches, workplace associations, neighborhood groups, etc., to the artificial formation of political parties and other institutions for interest representation and the organization of political life in competitive democracies.

A set of false assumptions pervades the model, beginning from the expectation that natural primary associations will not be troubled by internal conflicts of ideology or interest. Moreover, in historical terms, no political system has employed an exclusively organic or corporatist institutional format. Nevertheless, ideologies derived from organic statism and *corporatism have significantly influenced twentieth-century authoritarian regimes.

*Mussolini, linked originally with the syndicalist tradition, reinforced by the intellectual heritage of rightist nationalists, and searching for the approval of Catholics, built a corporatist superstructure that served conservative interests by disenfranchising a highly mobilized working *class and providing a channel for the complex interest structure of a relatively developed society. The strong totalitarian tendencies of many fascist leaders and the conception of an "ethical *state" above interests derived from an idealistic tradition, however, created an uneasy balance between the corporatist and the single-party mobilizational components of the regime. The military in Peru attempted a similar experiment by the creation of the Sistema Nacional de Apoyo a la Movilización Social (Sinamos).

Mobilizational Regimes: Postdemocratic and Postcolonial Societies. It is well known that in the crises in Europe following the end of World War I, *Leninism and *fascism emerged as antidemocratic and illiberal mobilizational regimes, both based on elite representation of the majority and driven by overarching historical goals, whether to liberate the proletariat or affirm a vision of national grandeur. Mobilizational authoritarian states emerged also with considerable frequency among postcolonial states where the struggle for independence would often become associated with an individual leader. In a context of arbitrary and often externally imposed national boundaries, fierce ethnic rivalries, religious and linguistic diversity, and the weak institutionalization of political representation and administration, the dilemmas of underdevelopment and state-building were met with authoritarian responses. *One-party systems and personalized charismatic leadership emerged as alternative authoritarian systems characterized by mass mobilization.

Personal Rulership. Independently of the Euromorphic disguises (constitutional forms, single party, bureaucratic organization) and the symbolic attempts to link with tradition, many postcolonial African states can best be characterized as regimes of personal rulership. Personal rule is a system of relations linking rulers not with the "public" or even the ruled (at least not directly), but with patrons, associates, clients, supporters, and rivals, who constitute the "system." The system is structured not by institutions but by the politicians themselves, and this dependence on persons accounts for its essential vulnerability. It is severely restrictive with regard to political liberties while being generally tolerant of nonpolitical * rights (except in the tyrannical regimes). Rulers exercise nearly unlimited legal competence. They use: 1) co-optation and consultation, 2) patronage, 3) agreement and accord, and 4) intimidation and coercion in different mixes. The fate of the ruler affects that of the political class that supports him and often the welfare of the political order. If we add the restraints and uncertainties posed by foreign political and economic factors, poor countries dependent on a few primary exports, with crop fluctuations due to the weather, we can understand the instability of personal rule. Foreign economic and military assistance, including that given by neighboring countries to the ruler or to the exiles and rebels, is another factor. Personal rule therefore presents the paradox of relatively autonomous, even arbitrary power, but one marked by coercion and the inability to implement policies owing to the lack of resources and trained officials.

Jackson and Rosberg distinguish four ideal types of personal rulership: princely, autocratic, prophetic, and tyrannical (the last we discuss as sultanism). The prophetic was more characteristic of some of the founding leaders like *Nkrumah and *Nyerere and comes closer to the ideals if not the realities of the single-party mobilization type of regimes. The distinction between princes and autocrats provides insight into this type of authoritarian regime. The prince is an astute observer and manipulator of lieutenants and clients; he tends to rule jointly with other oligarchs and to cultivate their loyalty presiding over the struggle for preferment without allowing it to get out of hand. Some of them were founders like Kenyatta or Kaunda; the most distinguished representative was Léopold Senghor. The autocrat is distinguished by the greater freedom to act as he sees fit and an antagonism to "politicians' politics" and the autonomous power and authority of others, forcing those who refuse to become his dependents to become conspirators or exiles. The autocrat's power is based on his own abilities and experience, specifically personal and unlikely to be transferred to another leader. This and the lesser likelihood that capable and experienced politicians will be available to insure a peaceful succession will lead to instability until someone consolidates himself in power and learns the skills of personal rulership. Personal rulership is more unpredictable, more paternalistic or arbitrary (even potentially oppressive), tyrannical, and corrupting, but ultimately weaker and more unstable than more "formed" authoritarian regimes.

A number of highly arbitrary, personalistic, and nondemocratic but nontotalitarian regimes have been labeled authoritarian regimes. One of their most distinctive forms may be termed *sultanistic* (borrowed from Max *Weber's description of extreme forms of patrimonialism).

A rule not based on tradition, nor on ideology or sense of mission, nor on charismatic appeal, nor on the purpose of defending a particular social order (class structure, conception of the nation, religious traditions), sultanistic rule benefits the ruler and his family, friends, cronies, and praetorian guards. It blurs the boundaries between the public treasury and the ruler's wealth, establishing profit-oriented monopolies, demanding gifts and payoffs in exchange for opportunities to contract with the state or even to engage in business activities. The power is based on the loyalty of henchmen, a praetorian guard, and clients, handsomely rewarded and licensed to use arbitrary power, but also at his mercy, one day in his grace, another persecuted, and sometimes rehabilitated.

Officers and bureaucrats have no regular careers, no distinctive training, and no status honor; business elites cannot base their decisions on the market or the formal legal system, but only on the good will of the ruler, although his self-interest might lead him to respect foreign companies. Power is neither institutionalized nor oriented toward the achievement of collective goals of a society or even a class. Class position is derived from the relation to the ruler, and the wealthy may be the object of extortion and arbitrary actions, as may anyone. This does not mean that the ruler may not show his generosity to his subjects and engage in public enterprises contributing to his glory. All kinds of institutional and ideological facades, from elections (sometimes, as in the case of Trujillo, of a stand-in) to a single party (like Mobutu), from modern ideological language to pseudo-traditionalism, serve the ruler. We speak of rule rather than regime on account of the lack of institutionalization, and of sultanism rather than patrimonialism, because office holders do not have rights to their office, there is no secure appropriation, and rulers are not bound by traditional norms or custom.

Post-Totalitarian Regimes. Few problems lead to more discussion than how to conceptualize the changes in the Soviet Union and some East European communist countries (with the exception of Poland) after de-Stalinization. After some theoretical efforts in the early post-Stalin period, some of the contemporary works were largely descriptive, avoiding the debates on *totalitarianism although explicitly or implicitly rejecting the applicability of the ideal type.

Those systems approached the authoritarian model, but with some significant differences we indicate by the term post-totalitarian. The fact that those regimes came after the transformation of society by totalitarianism, that the institutions and organization that sustained it—particularly the single party—had not been dismantled (except the extensive terror machine and the gulags), the use of the wooden language of "frozen ideology," and the memory of the recent past made them different from authoritarian systems. Totalitarianism can be said to have failed in its most positive ambitions to change people, to provide a sense of purpose and meaning. But it succeeded in changing societies and largely destroying the bases of the social-cultural pluralism of civil society, the autonomy and self-assertiveness of churches, the distinctive ethos of professions and their corporate groups, and (in socialist societies) the independence of economic actors.

The result was that the social pluralism that could give rise to a latent and perhaps politically relevant pluralism did not exist. In addition, the relative closure of those societies and the control of the mass media made it impossible for the broader population to think about alternative political models (as in most authoritarian regimes). There was room for *privatization and dissidence on a scale intolerable under totalitarianism, but not for the wide range of nonlegal and illegal oppositions as under most authoritarian regimes, partly because the civil society that might protect or encourage them did not exist. An exception is Poland. Even before the rise of * Solidarity as a nonlegal but powerful political actor, Poland was an authoritarian regime, owing to the special position retained by the Catholic church.

The following changes favored a move toward post-totalitarianism: the ossification of an ideology mechanically repeated, the growing acceptance of programmatic or rational criteria in policy-making not derived from or even compatible with the ideological tenets, the ritualization of indoctrination, the growing lack of support by intellectuals, and the tolerance for esthetic expressions not subject to ideological dictates. Only the articulation and diffusion of dangerous ideas was still limited. Ideology, accepted in a diffuse and inarticulated way, could serve as a "mentality" to the apparatchiks but did not occupy the central place it once did. The single party and its top leadership continued to be the central decision-making structure, but changes in the activities of the party organizations, in recruitment and promotion through nomenclature, and the composition of the top leadership could not be ignored. Bureaucratization and gerontocratic tendencies characterized the party. These changes resulted from the reconsideration by the elite of the cost, including to themselves, of the totalitarian model, particularly the insecurity (such as purges and the * Cultural Revolution) and considerations of efficacy in the competitive world system of economies, technology, and military capability. Without question, de-Stalinization, the liquidation of massive and indiscrimate terror, and the introduction of socialist legality (even when, for dissidents, a repressive legality) have contributed to the transformation of totalitarian systems.

Crises, Breakdown of Authoritarian Regimes, and Transition to Democracy. Since the 1970s a "third wave" of democratization has led to transitions to democracy in many authoritarian regimes, first in Southern Europe, then in Latin America and the Republic of Korea (South Korea), and most recently in the post-totalitarian communist countries of Eastern Europe and parts of the former Soviet Union. These developments have led to a growing literature that analyzes the crisis or breakdown of authoritarian regimes and the different paths to democratization. Those changes range from negotiated transitions imposed from above, *reforma pactada–ruptura pactada,* to overthrow by coup, abdication, or disintegration of the regime.

Although each transition has its own distinctive characteristics, the type of nondemocratic rule can make a difference in the path followed in the transition and the legacy to the new * democracy. In a number of authoritarian military regimes, the military decided to end authoritarian rule, allowing free elections that transferred power to democratic presidents, but sometimes retaining certain privileges and the implicit threat to contest decisions affecting the armed forces. The limited changes in the society often led to the restoration of the old constitution and reemergence of the old party system and patterns of politics. More institutionalized authoritarian regimes did not lead to the restoration of the predictatorship democratic regimes but to a new democratic regime owing to the social change that had taken place. In the case of civilian or civilianized regimes, the transition often was negotiated between reformist incumbents and the opposition.

The regimes we have characterized as sultanistic have not led to such peaceful, orderly, and negotiated transitions, but to a broad and heterogenous coalition that gains power violently and establishes a provisional government. Such a government in a number of cases has led to the establishment of a new authoritarian (sometimes revolutionary rule) rather than democracy, or to continued instability.

Despite the wave of democratization, totalitarian, or at least post-totalitarian and authoritarian, regimes still exist. But the crisis of the ideologies that have supported these regimes (*Marxism-Leninism, communism, fascism, authoritarian corporatism and derivatives like "*African socialism" or the "national security state"), the recognition by intellectuals of the value of liberal democracy as something more than "formal" or "bourgeois" democracy, and the failure in performance of centrally planned socialist economies make the establishment of nondemocratic regimes less attractive. Nonetheless, the failure of new democracies to satisfy popular expectations, social and economic conflict, ethnic violence, and aggressive nationalism may well lead to authoritarian rule.

(See also COMMAND ECONOMY; COMMUNIST PARTY STATES; DECOLONIZATION; DEMOCRATIC

Transitions; Military Rule; Nineteen Eighty-Nine; Patron-Client Politics; Populism; Roman Catholic Church.)

Samuel P. Huntington, and Clement H. Moore, eds., *Authoritarian Politics in Modern Society* (New York, 1970). Guillermo O'Donnell, *Modernization and Bureaucratic Authoritarianism* (Berkeley, Calif., 1973). Philippe Schmitter, "Still the Century of Corporatism?" *Review of Politics* 36 (1974): 85–131. Juan Linz, "Totalitarian and Authoritarian Regimes," in Fred Greenstein and Nelson Polsby, eds., *Handbook of Political Science,* vol. 3 (Reading, Mass., 1975), pp. 175–411. Juan Linz and Alfred Stepan, eds., *The Breakdown of Democratic Regimes* (Baltimore, 1978). Alfred Stepan, *The State and Society* (Princeton, N.J., 1978). David Collier, ed., *The New Authoritarianism in Latin America* (Princeton, N.J., 1979). Robert H. Jackson, and Carl G. Rosberg, *Personal Rule in Black Africa* (Berkeley, 1982).

Juan J. Linz

AUTHORITY. See Legitimacy; Sovereignty.

AZERBAIJAN. See Commonwealth of Independent States.

B

BAHAMAS. See English-Speaking Caribbean.

BAHRAIN. See Gulf States.

BALANCE OF PAYMENTS. The balance of payments is an accounting device for recording a country's economic transactions over a given period with the rest of the world. Although there are no universally accepted categories for constructing the balance of payments, the International Monetary Fund (IMF) has tried to establish a uniform set of criteria. In addition, the IMF's annual publication, *Balance of Payments Statistics,* is the main international source of data on the balance of payments.

The balance of payments is usually divided into three sets of categories. The first is the "current account": exports and imports of goods (the "trade balance"), exports and imports of services, investment income, and unrequited transfers. The current account mirrors a country's domestic accounts, i.e., a current account deficit reflects more domestic spending than saving and vice versa. The second set of categories is the "capital account": inward and outward flows of direct investment, portfolio investment, long-term loans, and short-term capital. The third set involves the items constituting a country's reserves: monetary gold, special drawing rights (SDRs), IMF credit, and foreign exchange assets. In principle, changes in a country's reserves must offset any difference between the current and capital account balances. In practice, since not all transactions are recorded, there is a residual item called "net errors and omissions."

Far from being only an accounting device, the balance of payments has crucial economic and even political consequences. Since the difference between the current and capital accounts must be offset by a country's reserves, the balance of payments represents a limit on a country's ability to obtain resources from the rest of the world. When that limit is reached, domestic economic policy must be changed in order to adjust. For example, a devaluation could be decreed in order to increase exports and lower imports, or domestic spending could be cut in order to achieve the same goals. A country could also try to increase capital inflows through higher interest rates or more favorable treatment of foreign capital. (While the need for adjustment theoretically applies to both surplus and deficit countries, there is no economic mechanism to force the former to change policy.)

The political consequences of the balance of payments arise in part because there are always winners and losers from the economic policy changes to deal with a balance-of-payments deficit. For example, a devaluation will favor exporters, while increasing costs for consumers and for producers who use imported inputs. Likewise, a rise in interests rates to attract foreign capital will mean that domestic savers will also increase their return while borrowers will have to pay more. The IMF itself frequently becomes involved in political conflicts over the balance of payments, since it has strong views on appropriate types of adjustment and considerable influence over lenders.

An overall pattern is supposed to characterize the balance of payments. A "mature economy" is expected to have a current account surplus offset by capital exports, meaning that it produces more than it uses domestically. A "developing economy" is supposed to have the opposite: it consumes more than it can produce, thus running a current account deficit financed through capital imports. This pattern has frequently been violated in recent years as the United States has run the world's largest current account deficit and absorbed a substantial share of the world's capital. The trade and investment dynamics underlying this situation have been another source of political friction, in this case among industrial countries, especially the United States and Japan.

International Monetary Fund, *Balance of Payments Statistics* (Washington, D.C., various years). Rudiger Dornbusch, *Open Economy Macroeconomics* (New York, 1980).

BARBARA B. STALLINGS

BALANCE OF POWER. The balance of power is one of the oldest concepts in *international relations. Apparently practiced since organized human societies first began to interact, and with certainty since the time of ancient Greece, it is said by some to be a universal law of history. Yet the term is used in a variety of different and occasionally incompatible ways—often by the same author. Descriptively, it can refer to any distribution of *power, an equality of power, a preponderance of power, a policy of equilibrium, or a policy of preponderance. Analytically, it can denote either a specific theory of *state behavior or *realism and other general theories that utilize power as a central organizing concept. Prescriptively, it is usually—but not always—invoked in support of national goals or policies associated with expanded military capabilities.

Although considerable ambiguity remains, the balance of power has come to mean, at least among scholars of international relations, an international process that, when operative, tends to create roughly equal distributions of power between opposing states or coalitions of states or a situation characterized by such a distribution. Balance of power theory is a set of logical statements specifying when and how this process or situation is likely to arise. Preponderances of power, once confusingly referred to as "balances," are now commonly, but not universally, referred to as situations or structures of *hegemony.

By checking power with power—often through the formation of flexible, temporary *alliances—the balance of power purportedly works to limit expansionism, preserve the independence of states, and maintain the status quo. If scholars now generally agree on this more delimited conception of the balance of power process, they disagree over whether it works automatically, as an inherent feature of *international systems, or only through conscious efforts to manage international politics. In other words, while they share a general consensus on the nature of the process, they subscribe to different theories of the balance of power.

In *System and Process in International Politics* (New York, 1957), Morton A. Kaplan develops a theory of conscious state action and balancing behavior. Assuming that actors have limited aims and seek to maintain the system itself, he identifies six "essential rules" that, when followed by at least five "essential actors" (or states), characterize a balance of power system:

1. Act to increase capabilities but negotiate rather than fight.
2. Fight rather than pass up an opportunity to increase capabilities.
3. Stop fighting rather than eliminate an essential national actor.
4. Act to oppose any coalition or single actor which tends to assume a position of predominance with respect to the rest of the system.
5. Act to constrain actors who subscribe to supranational organizing principles.
6. Permit defeated or constrained essential national actors to re-enter the system as acceptable role partners or act to bring some previously inessential actor within the essential actor classification. Treat all essential actors as acceptable role partners.

By following these rules, Kaplan argues, states guard against the ambitions of others. By rehabilitating the losers as potential allies, states also preserve the necessary conditions for the balance of power system to operate. Any failure by an essential national actor to follow one or more of these rules, for whatever reason, may destabilize the system and transform it into one of five other possible systems. It is this ability of states to choose whether to follow these rules, and especially the implied self-restraint required in rules three and six, that necessitates conscious management and creates a need for states to be socialized into the system. A balance of power system as described by these rules, Kaplan argues, existed in Europe during the eighteenth, nineteenth, and early twentieth centuries.

Other scholars see the balance of power as driven by the unconscious motivations and interests of states—with the exception of a "balancer" that throws its weight into one scale, and then the other, opposing whichever side appears to possess the greatest ambitions. This semiautomatic theory assumes that whereas every other state strives to enhance its power and resources, the balancer is curiously immune from this otherwise universal law. Motivated not by national egoism but by international altruism, the balancer forgoes potential national gains to preserve the stability of the system. Built largely on the experience of Britain in the eighteenth and nineteenth centuries, this theory also draws some support from the balancing behavior of the United States in the first and second world *wars. By attributing a special position to the pivotal power, however, the semiautomatic balance of power theory blurs the distinction between balance and hegemony—for if its weight is enough to tip the scales against the expansionist power, the result may be not a balance but a preponderance of power under the leadership of the pivot.

In terms reminiscent of the operation and description of physical laws and purely competitive economic markets, the balance of power is understood by still other scholars as an automatic process. That is, it tends to produce roughly equal distributions of power without any state deliberately willing this result. In this view, all states strive for predominance and, by doing so, naturally tend to check the aspirations and counter the successes of others. If one state threatens to rise above the rest, its competitors will redouble their own efforts, form countervailing alliances, or initiate preemptive *war. Although this equilibrating mechanism may be thwarted by the fortunes of economic growth or ineptitude of political leaders, the competition between states nonetheless tends to prevent any single state or coalition of states from dominating others.

Although most scholars are aware that states can augment their power through a variety of means, such as increasing their independent military capabilities or raising their levels of economic growth, they have treated the balance of power, *in practice,* as essentially a study in alliance formation. States balance power, according to this view, by forming countervailing coalitions. As a result, many scholars assert—as does Kaplan above—that the balance of power requires at least three, and preferably five, states to function effectively.

This tendency to restrict the balance of power to questions of alliance formation unduly restricts the scope of the theory. Distinguishing between internal balancing strategies, such as increasing one's economic or military capability, and external strategies, defined in more traditional terms as expanding one's own alliance or weakening an opponent's, Kenneth Waltz (*Theory of International Politics,* Reading, Mass., 1979) suggests that relatively equal distributions of power, properly conceived, will tend to arise in all international systems irrespective of the number of essential actors. His subsequent hypothesis that internal strategies will predominate in bipolar international systems is empirically dubious—given the importance of the *North Atlantic Treaty Organization and the *Warsaw Treaty Organization (Warsaw Pact) in American and Soviet foreign policy, respectively, after 1949. Nonetheless, constructing a more complete theory of the balance of power that incorporates the full range of instruments available to states promises to significantly enhance the explanatory power of the theory.

While balance of power theory is often accepted as true, both because of its logical consistency and wide acceptance among policymakers, there is some debate as to whether roughly equal distributions of power do in fact tend to form within the international system—whether automatically or as the result of conscious efforts. In part, this debate is rooted in the different theories discussed above: proponents of theories based on conscious state action who assume that the balance of power requires at least three actors to function would exclude the period since 1945 as a potential case, but it is central, say, to Waltz's modified version of the automatic balance of power theory. It also stems from inadequate definitions and measures of power; nineteenth-century Britain, for instance, is classified by some as a balancer and others as a hegemon.

Although exceptions do not disprove the rule, important empirical anomalies do exist. During the first and second world wars, for instance, the Allies possessed overwhelming power—whether measured by GNP, industrial production, or military expenditures, all standard indicators. "Bandwagoning" rather than balancing appears to have characterized the foreign policies of European states at these times. Working within the context of the theory but seeking to address such anomalies, Stephen M. Walt (*The Origins of Alliances,* Ithaca, N.Y., 1987) has hypothesized that states balance threats, not power—but this merely substitutes one ambiguous term for another without increasing our ability to test or falsify the theory.

While the balance of power if widely seen as a process that regulates international conflict and thereby preserves national independence and the status quo, analysts disagree over whether the balance of power promotes *peace or war. For some, war is often necessary to counter drives for hegemony, and power—in the end—is measured only on the battlefield; war, in this view, is an inherent part of the balancing process. For others, balances of power deter war, as risk-adverse states are normally reluctant to initiate hostilities in situations of approximate equality.

The gap between these positions is not as large as it seems. Both hold that the balance of power creates and preserves relatively equal distributions of power within the international system. For the former group, war is, on occasion, a necessary means toward this end. For the latter, balances typically inhibit aggressive action. It is not inconsistent to suggest that war may be required to establish a balance of power that subsequently will prevent war. This offers relatively little hope, however, for controlling or reducing the frequency of war; given the dynamic nature of the international system, propelled forward by varying rates of economic growth and military expenditures, states may be constantly moving toward but only occasionally reaching balances of power.

(See also FORCE, USE OF; FOREIGN POLICY; SECURITY.)

Ernst B. Haas, "The Balance of Power: Prescription, Concept, or Propaganda?" *World Politics* 5, no. 4 (July 1953): 442–477. Edward Vose Gulik, *Europe's Classical Balance of Power* (Ithaca, N.Y., 1955). Emerson M. S. Niou, Peter C. Ordeshook, and Gregory F. Rose, *The Balance of Power* (New York, 1989).

DAVID A. LAKE

BALFOUR DECLARATION. On 2 November 1917, Arthur Balfour, the British secretary of state for foreign affairs, announced that "His Majesty's Government view with favour the establishment in Palestine of a national home for the Jewish people, and will use their best endeavours to facilitate the achievement of this object." This declaration, which came as British forces were conquering *Palestine, hitherto part of the Ottoman Empire, marked the first time that a major European power had extended official support to the Zionist movement's goal of making Palestine (ninety percent of whose population was at that time Arab) into a Jewish homeland.

In later years there would be considerable dispute about the extent of the commitment to *Zionism which the Balfour Declaration entailed, and about how to reconcile its promise to foster the development of the Jewish "national home" with its promise that "nothing shall be done which may prejudice the civil and religious rights of the existing non-Jewish communities in Palestine." Nonetheless, for two decades the Balfour Declaration stood as official policy, underlying British support for Jewish immigration, settlement, and state-building in Palestine. It was thus a tremendous achievement for Zionism, giving it the powerful patron without whose protection and support it could not have overcome the opposition of the indigenous Arab majority and laid the demographic, economic, political, and military foundations of the future State of *Israel.

Several considerations contributed to the British decision to endorse Zionism in 1917. Many imperial policymakers believed that a Jewish Palestine under British tutelage would strengthen British power in the postwar Middle East, protect the Suez Canal, and help secure control of the eastern Mediterranean. Foreign Office officials were convinced that the declaration would induce Jews in the United States and in Russia to support the Allied cause in World War I. Zionist leaders in Britain tirelessly and effectively lobbied the British government to adopt this new policy, with the support of a number of prominent Christian Zionists, including Prime Minister Lloyd George.

The Balfour Declaration was one of several mutually irreconcilable commitments which Britain made regarding the postwar disposition of the Arab provinces of the Ottoman Empire. In 1915–1916 Britain negotiated an agreement with Hussein, the sharif of Mecca, who with his Hashemite family wanted to break free of Ottoman rule (the so-called Hussein-McMahon Correspondence). Assured of British arms and money, and what they took to be a British commitment to support the postwar establishment of an independent Arab state in virtually all the former Ottoman Arab provinces, Hussein and his Arab nationalist allies launched a revolt against Ottoman rule. At the same time, however, Britain was secretly negotiating a treaty with France (the Sykes-Picot Agreement of May 1916) which divided the region between them.

After the war the British reneged on their promise to the Arabs: although two of Hussein's sons were ultimately installed on the thrones of the newly created British client-states of Iraq and Transjordan, France assumed control of Syria and Lebanon while Palestine came under British rule. Despite strong Palestinian Arab nationalist opposition, the Balfour Declaration's commitment to Zionism was incorporated into the mandate which Britain received from the *League of Nations. In 1939, however, anxious to win Arab support as war approached, Britain declared that it had fulfilled its commitments under the Balfour Declaration and imposed restrictions on Jewish immigration and land purchases. The resulting rupture of the British-Zionist alliance turned into open conflict after the war, leading ultimately to British withdrawal from Palestine and the establishment of the State of Israel in 1948.

(See also ARAB NATIONALISM; COLONIAL EMPIRES.)

Leonard Stein, *The Balfour Declaration* (New York, 1961). Christopher Sykes, *Crossroads to Israel, 1917–1948* (Bloomington, Ind., 1965).

ZACHARY LOCKMAN

BALKANIZATION. Balkanization refers to the process by which the territory of a political or geographic unit is divided into smaller units. In its most common usage the term has a negative connotation. It implies that political fragmentation results from mutually antagonistic relationships between or among groups or political units, that it is an undesirable political outcome, and that relations of the newly created political unit(s) with other states will be hostile.

The term was coined during the second decade of the twentieth century to describe the breakup of the Ottoman Empire during the nineteenth and early twentieth centuries and the resulting quarrels among the successor states to the empire. It was subsequently employed to characterize such developments as the division of Africa into independent states following the breakup of the European colonial empires during the 1950s and 1960s. By the early 1990s, the process of Balkanization was most apparent in the former *Soviet Union, where the fifteen constituent union republics of the USSR declared their independence and began to function as sovereign states. The prevalence of separatist political tendencies among national groups in the successor states to the former Soviet Union and in the multiethnic states of Eastern Europe and Asia suggests that Balkanization will continue to be a factor in world politics for the foreseeable future.

It is uncertain whether the most recent manifestations of Balkanization will be accompanied by the international tensions and hostilities that have characterized this process in the past or whether it will serve as a constructive force for dissolving nonvoluntary political unions and federations, and establishing a more cooperative international environment.

(See also COMMONWEALTH OF INDEPENDENT STATES; DECOLONIZATION.)

NICHOLAS C. PANO

BALKANS. The Balkans refers to both the Balkan Peninsula located in southeastern Europe and the five countries of *Albania, *Bulgaria, *Greece, *Romania, and *Yugoslavia (and its successor states) situated in this region. The term *Balkan* is derived from the Turkish word for "forested mountain." Beginning in the nineteenth century, the expression *Balkans* was used to describe the area in Europe dominated by the Ottoman Empire, and since the end of World War I, it has applied to the five states of the region.

The Balkan states have a combined area of 765,000 square kilometers (295,350 sq. mi.), slightly larger than the state of Texas. In 1991, the population of the region was approximately 70 million. There are three major religions practiced in the area: Eastern Orthodoxy, Roman Catholicism, and Islam, with the Eastern Orthodox divided into self-governing national churches. Reflecting the ethnic diversity of the Balkans, eight major languages (Albanian, Bulgarian, Croatian, Greek, Macedonian, Romanian, Serbian, and Slovene) are used by the peoples of the region. Until the 1960s, when they began to develop and diversify, the economies of the Balkan states were predominantly based on agriculture.

The strategic location of the Balkan Peninsula at the juncture of Europe and Asia has made it a "cockpit" for competing empires, peoples, and cultures. During the fourteenth and fifteenth centuries, most of the Balkans fell under the control of the Ottoman Empire.

With the decline of the Ottoman Empire and the growth of national consciousness on the part of the Balkan peoples during the nineteenth century, the region became a major focal point in European international relations between 1815 and 1914. During this period, the Eastern Question, the problem of determining the disposition of the European territories of the empire, occupied much of the attention of the major European powers of the era. The conflicting interests of the European powers in the Balkans coupled with the territorial disputes among the emerging Balkan states combined to transform the region into the so-called "powder keg" of Europe, and they were contributing factors to the outbreak of *World War I in 1914.

Prior to World War I, Serbia, Greece, Romania, Bulgaria, and Albania had in turn succeeded in winning their independence from the Ottoman Empire. Following the war, a Yugoslav state was created through the union of Serbia, Montenegro, Croatia, and Slovenia.

During World War II, Romania and Bulgaria were allied with the Axis powers while Albania, Greece, and Yugoslavia resisted Axis occupation. After the war communist regimes were established in all the countries but Greece. Yugoslavia was expelled from the Soviet bloc in 1948 following a dispute with the Soviet Union. Similarly, the Soviet Union served diplomatic and party ties with Albania in 1961. Romania began to pursue an independent *foreign policy in the mid-1960s, leaving Bulgaria as Moscow's most faithful Balkan ally.

In 1989 Bulgaria and Romania repudiated *communism, as did Albania in 1991. The unity of Yugoslavia was destroyed when the Republics of Croatia and Slovenia declared their independence in 1991 following a civil war. Given the subsequent recognition of the Republic of Bosnia and Herzegovina and the expressed desire for independence of Macedonia as well as of the Albanians of Kosovo, the end of the fragmentation of the former Yugoslavia is not yet in sight. The political instability of the new Balkan regimes and the revival of ethnic conflicts in the region suggest that the Balkans may again become the "powder keg" of Europe.

Barbara Jelavich, *History of the Balkans,* 2 vols. (Cambridge, U.K., 1983).

NICHOLAS C. PANO

BALTIC REPUBLICS. The central fact of modern Baltic history has been prolonged occupation. Even before the tsarist empire extended its control over the region in the eighteenth century, the Baltic littoral had experienced Prussian, Swedish, and Polish rule. The Balts have often been cited as examples of what John Armstrong (in Erich Goldhagen, ed., *Ethnic Minorities in the Soviet Union,* New York, 1968) called "state-nations"—i.e., peoples with a long history of independent statehood. This is certainly true of Lithuanians, whose kings successfully defended their independence from the thirteenth to the sixteenth centuries, when Lithuania formed a dynastic union with Poland that roughly lasted until the advent of Russian rule. It is less true of Estonians and Latvians, who lacked a history of independent statehood until the twentieth century and were traditionally ruled by a German landowning nobility. As in the rest of Europe, nationalist movements arose in the Baltic in the latter half of the nineteenth century. The collapse of the Russian Empire in 1917 gave rise to a twenty-two-year interlude of independence in the Baltic. Originally established as parliamentary democracies, all three interwar Baltic governments fell prey to fascist dictatorships by the 1930s.

The fates of the interwar Baltic states were sealed by the secret protocols of the Molotov-Ribbentrop Pact in August 1939, which were followed by invasion by the Red Army in 1940. *Hitler's attack on the *Soviet Union in 1941 cut short Sovietization of the region and led to a three-year German occupation. The consolidation of Soviet rule after *World War II brought the imposition of totalitarian controls, violent agricultural *collectivization, mass deportations, and a huge influx of outsiders. But throughout Soviet rule, national resistance was highly visible. Guerrilla movements continued to operate into the 1950s, and acts of mass protest (at times involving as many as 100,000 people) occurred periodically even before glasnost arrived on the scene. It was therefore little surprise that secessionist *nationalism quickly emerged in the Baltic as Soviet politics liberalized in the late 1980s. By fall 1988 popular fronts had been formed in all three republics, organizing huge protest demonstrations in favor of sovereignty and overturning entrenched communist leaders.

Noncommunist governments emerged in the three Baltic republics as a result of elections for republican legislatures in late 1989 and early 1990. In spite of the exceptional importance of the elections, voter participation was moderate: eighty percent in Latvia, seventy-eight percent in Estonia, and seventy percent in Lithuania. In Lithuania Sajudis-backed candidates won eighty-nine of 141 seats, while Latvian Popular Front candidates won 121 of 201 seats. The Estonian Popular Front won only forty-three of 105 seats, but more radical nationalist parties won an additional thirty seats, providing proponents of independence with a majority. In 1990 these newly formed governments openly proclaimed their intentions to secede from the Soviet Union. Lithuania declared its independence in March 1990, suspending it temporarily after Moscow imposed an economic blockade. Only with the collapse of Soviet central institutions after the aborted *coup d'état of August 1991 did the Soviet Union officially recognize Baltic independence.

All three Baltic governments are *parliamentary democracies, with lawmaking authority vested in their legislatures, the Supreme Councils. As such, the legislatures select their presidents and approve the presidents' choices for prime minister and cabinet posts. A curious aspect of Estonian government has been the existence of a shadow legislature, the Congress of Estonia, formed in March 1990 by 499 delegates elected by 600,000 descendants of the citizens of interwar Estonia. Tensions between the more radical Congress and the Supreme Council over how restrictive *citizenship policy should be have plagued Estonian politics.

The popular fronts that played so prominent a role in the independence politics of the Baltic were originally organized as umbrella social movements in which various groups supporting independence could participate. The Estonian Popular Front and Sajudis did not have formal membership, while the Latvian Popular Front counted 180,000 members in 1991. The Latvian Popular Front, though represented by the majority faction within the Supreme Council, has most strongly resisted the temptation to constitute itself as a political party, but is widely expected to split into parties. The Estonian Popular Front, similarly composed of a coalition of parties, disintegrated into its constituent groups in January 1992, when it lost control of the government in the wake of Prime Minister Edgar Savisaar's divisive attempts to obtain emergency powers. Since December 1990, when Prime Minister Kazimiera Prunskiene was forced to resign and the faction of President Vytautas Landsbergis gained full control over the government, Sajudis has functioned largely as a Lithuanian governmental party.

The main cleavages in Baltic politics revolve around *ethnicity. In 1989 eighty percent of the 3.7 million inhabitants of Lithuania were Lithuanian; fifty-two percent of the 2.7 million inhabitants of Latvia were Latvian; and sixty-two percent of the 1.6 million inhabitants of Estonia were Estonian. Particularly in Latvia and Estonia, large Russian-speaking communities were created as a result of massive inmigration during the Soviet period. Indeed, in 1989 only forty-seven percent of the population of Tallinn was Estonian, thirty-six percent of the population of Riga was Latvian, and fifty-one percent of the population of Vilnius was Lithuanian. Mass movements defending the Russian-speaking community's language rights and opposing independence and restrictive citizenship policies emerged in each of the Baltic republics. Such movements have been strongest in Latvia, where the Russian-speaking population is the largest and the regional headquarters of the former Soviet military are located. Even after independence the former Soviet military maintained a substantial presence in the Baltic and acted outside of local government control. At the same time, the high rate of ethnic intermarriage in Latvia (approximately a quarter of all marriages) has worked to mitigate conflict. In Estonia, mobilization of the Russian-speaking community has occurred in northern Estonia around the area of Narva, where Russians were in the majority in some areas. There, a movement developed to detach the region from Estonia and incorporate it into *Russia. In Lithuania, where the Russian-speaking community is smaller, a Polish minority of 260,000 is concentrated in the east around the Vilnius region, which belonged jto interwar Poland. Their attempts to gain self-government have brought them into conflict with Lithuanian authorities and fostered tensions between Lithuania and neighboring Poland.

Ethnic and class politics are intertwined in the Baltic, where a large portion of the working class consists of Russian-speaking immigrants. Indeed, one means by which the Russian-speaking community supported its demands was through strike activity. Baltic governments are attempting to traverse the divide between state socialism and a market economy with substantial private ownership. As elsewhere in the former Soviet bloc, these policies have been accompanied by massive inflation and sharp conflicts over economic strategies. Large-scale unemployment is expected in the future as well. These factors, along with the pervasive shortages and disruptions in energy supply that resulted from severed economic ties after independence, caused the region to slip into deep economic crisis.

The Baltic states are generally considered to have a better chance at establishing stable *democracy than other former republics of the Soviet Union, in part because of the educated character of their populations, their higher standards of living, and their prior traditions of democratic government. Yet, interwar Baltic democracy ultimately gave way to dictatorship. Ethnic conflict was as salient in interwar Baltic politics as it is in post-Soviet Baltic politics, and the stresses that will be generated by the transition from state socialism are expected to be at least as severe as those unleashed by the Great Depression. Should post-Soviet Baltic democracy survive these pressures when interwar Baltic democracy could not, it could tell us much about the factors that sustain and undermine democratic government.

(See also COMMONWEALTH OF INDEPENDENT STATES; SECESSIONIST MOVEMENTS.)

Romuald J. Misiunas and Rein Taagepera, *The Baltic States: Years of Dependence, 1940–1980* (Berkeley, Calif., 1983). Alfred Erich Senn, *Lithuania Awakening* (Berkeley, Calif.,

1990). John Hiden and Patrick Salmon, *The Baltic Nations and Europe* (New York, 1991). Toivo Raun, *The Estonians*, 2d ed. (Bloomington, Ind., 1991).

MARK R. BEISSINGER

BANGLADESH. One of the world's poorest nations, Bangladesh is also among the most populous and most densely populated. At the beginning of the 1990s, its per capita income placed it among the bottom ten nations ranked by the World Bank, while its more than 110 million people occupied an area only ten percent larger than Czechoslovakia's. In addition, Bangladesh has a larger portion of its population at risk of flood and famine under normal conditions than virtually any other country.

Although it is rapidly urbanizing, at about eight percent per year over the 1965–1985 period, the country is still overwhelmingly rural, with roughly fifteen percent of its population in urban areas in the late 1980s. Correspondingly, perhaps seventy percent of the labor force is in agriculture, producing about forty-five percent of GDP.

Ethnically, Bangladesh is remarkably homogeneous, with more than ninety-seven percent Bengalis (defined essentially as those who speak the Bengali language) and a scattering of tribal groups mostly in the mountainous southeast. The country is also predominantly of one religion, being some eighty-five to ninety percent Muslim, with Hindus making up most of the remainder.

Bangladesh has in a sense achieved independence twice, first in 1947 when it emerged from British rule as the "eastern wing" of *Pakistan, separated from its western counterpart by 1,500 kilometers (930 miles) of *India, and then again in 1971 when, with Indian help, it broke away from Pakistan to become a separate country in its own right after a bloody civil war.

Its politics have been primarily authoritarian since 1971, with the Parliament serving largely as a creature of the executive. Changes of regime have come through assassination and military coup. Major leaders include the country's founding father, Sheikh Muijibur Rahman, usually referred to as "Mujib" (1972–1975), Ziaur Rahman or "Zia" (1976–1981), and Hussein Muhammad Ershad (1982–1990).

Although the pattern of government has been a single-party system with political support based largely on patronage from the regime, three major political parties exist, each the creation of one of the country's major rulers. Ideologically there is some differentiation, with Mujib's party, the Awami League, professing a moderately socialist, secular, pro-India stance. Zia's legacy, the Bangladesh National Party (BNP), is more capitalist and less secular in its orientation, but it differs from the Awami League mainly in its anti-India position. The Jatiya Party, Ershad's organization and the newest of the three, has sought to establish its identity through a mildly pro-Islamic posture. In addition there are scores of smaller parties, several of which have grouped themselves together as an Islamic alliance, which acts as a fourth element in the party spectrum, distinctly weaker than the first three.

Since 1972, elections at the national level for president and Parliament, as well as occasional forays into a plebiscitary model, have been subject to varying degrees of fraud and manipulation, while those at the local level have been considerably more open, although marred by considerable violence. Freedom of speech has for the most part been respected, but freedom of assembly has been restricted in various ways, including frequent martial law.

In late 1990 a tide of unrest began in an oft-repeated pattern of opposition demonstration and harsh regime reaction, but to the surprise of almost everyone this time the political dynamic emulated the overthrow of Ferdinand *Marcos in the Philippines in 1986 rather than the customary course of military repression. The army, called upon to impose martial law, instead instructed President Ershad to resign immediately, which he then did. An acting president was installed and elections, widely regarded as honest, were held in February 1991, returning the BNP to power with a hairline majority and leaving the Awami League in a very distant second place, with about one-third of the seats, and the other parties even further behind. The new Parliament quickly scrapped the presidential system for a Westminster-style parliamentary model, and Prime Minister Khaleda Zia embarked on an uncertain and probably unsteady path of leading an economy that was, in the end, the same low performer that Ershad had guided.

Stemming from its experience as the central actor during the coups and countercoups of the 1970s and 1980s and the overthrow of 1990, the military remains the major locus of power in the political system. Well-treated by the Ershad regime, it received some ten to eleven percent of total central government expenditures and numbered about 100,000 members. This largesse can be expected to continue.

The political economy at all levels has centered around a patron-client system in which the beneficiaries of government spending provide the regime with their support. In the urban areas contracting, trading, and licensing are major sources of income for the regime's supporters, while in the countryside development project monies form the basis of linkage. The patron-client process is funded in large part by a national development budget that receives more than eighty-five percent of its revenues from external donors. Such large quantities of external aid (e.g., US$1.5 billion net flow in 1989) have greatly facilitated corruption, which has become increasingly institutionalized since independence, especially since 1982.

*Development strategy has focused mainly on infrastructure, with emphasis on power, water control, and industries. In the 1980s the government launched a major rural development initiative, decentralizing funding and discretionary power to elected bodies at the *upazila* level (about 200,000 population). The net effect thus far, however, has been to reinforce the patron-client structure linking the central government with the rural areas.

Despite its authoritarian past, Bangladesh has been relatively open to experiments in *rural development, and although the majority of projects have done no better than those elsewhere, several nongovernmental organizations, such as the Grameen Bank and the Bangladesh Rural Advancement Committee (BRAC), have gained world-class reputations for their innovative strategies. The Grameen Bank, specializing in small loans to landless people without collateral, had by the end of the 1980s expanded to about 600,000 members (of whom more than eighty-five percent were women, a significant achievement in a Muslim country) and had a default rate of less than two percent, a unique record for a rural credit institution so large. BRAC has evolved a "conscientization" approach to rural development in which village-level groups are encouraged to construct their own strategies for promoting increased income and control over their own lives.

Foreign relations for Bangladesh focus primarily in three directions. India, with roughly eight times its population and more than twelve times its GDP, is inevitably the major concern. Disputes over sharing water from the Ganges River have persistently been the main conflict with India, followed by long-festering insurrectionary movements among tribal groups on both sides of Bangladesh's southeastern border, in which the two countries have continually accused each other of complicity. The Bangladesh government hopes that the *South Asian Association for Regional Cooperation (SAARC), formed in 1983, will serve to alleviate some of its problems with India.

A second foreign policy concern has been dealing with international aid donors, led by the *World Bank and the United States, which have pressed for such policies as *privatization, reducing subsidies, encouraging export industries, and the like. The third major focus in foreign policy has been the Middle Eastern countries, chiefly Saudi Arabia, which has given significant aid in recent years while also encouraging Islamic fundamentalism in Bangladesh.

(See also HINDUISM; ISLAM; MILITARY RULE; PATRON-CLIENT POLITICS.)

James Heitzman and Robert L. Worden, eds., *Bangladesh: A Country Study* (Washington, D.C., 1989). *Asian Survey*, political assessment of Bangladesh appearing each year in February, e.g., Craig Baxter, "Bangladesh in 1991: A Parliamentary System," 32, no. 2 (February 1992): 162–167.

HARRY W. BLAIR

BARBADOS. See ENGLISH-SPEAKING CARIBBEAN.

BASIC NEEDS. The basic needs approach grew out of disappointment with policies for economic growth in the *Third World, which had left poverty and unemployment largely untouched. Basic needs emphasizes the need for concern for the poor by defining development as "*of* the people, *for* the people, and *by* the people." The simplest definition of the basic needs approach is "incomes plus social services plus participation." *Incomes* covers the creation of productive and remunerative jobs. *Social services* covers the provision of public goods such as health and education, as well as food subsidies. These raise the earning power of the poor. Transfer payments out of public revenue, charitable donations or gifts by the family, and payments in kind to temporarily or chronically unemployed (the latter include the handicapped, disabled, infirm, old, and chronically sick) are necessary to meet the needs of the unemployable.

Participation in its widest sense covers the non-material aspects of basic needs: self-reliance, freedom, recognition of one's work, cultural identity, participation in the life of the community. Although this component is much more difficult to include in an economic analysis, it is nonetheless important—material basic needs may well be provided for in, for example, a well-run prison, yet we would not say that basic human needs are met there. Participation is both an end in itself and a means for the delivery of basic needs in an affordable way.

The basic needs sectors are normally regarded to be food and nutrition, education, health, water and sanitation, and shelter. To these one may wish to add, in some circumstances, fuel and transport. There is controversy over who should determine what are basic needs: experts or the consumers themselves. When is there a case for intervening with free consumers' choices? What is the correct policy if people prefer circuses to bread?

An important lesson of work on the subject has been to show the absence of a rigid link between income per head and basic needs fulfillment. Countries such as Sri Lanka, Cuba, Chile, China, Costa Rica, and the state of Kerala in India have registered basic needs indicators, such as life expectancy, infant mortality, and literacy rates, that are similar to those of much more economically advanced countries, whereas countries such as South Africa, Saudi Arabia, and Brazil show poor basic needs performance despite much higher average incomes. This is, of course, partly a function of unequal income distribution, but other factors are also important. Among these are political organization (although many types of political regimes have shown good basic needs performance), whether the poor participate in the process of decision making, proportion of government budget spent on health and education, and whether this expenditure is directed to the poor.

Although there are technical and economic problems to be faced in the basic needs approach, the principal obstacles are administrative and political. The international community can help by supporting regimes that are intent on giving high priority to basic needs. The governments of some low-income countries are not always willing to devote resources to this purpose and have therefore objected to basic needs being introduced into the international development dialogue. They have charged donors with being intrusive and diversionary. On the other hand, donor countries have occasionally used basic needs as a way of reducing commitments by claiming that the ability to meet basic needs is largely a matter of local resources and action.

(See also DEVELOPMENT AND UNDERDEVELOPMENT; EQUALITY AND INEQUALITY; FOOD POLITICS.)

Paul Streeten et al., *First Things First: Meeting Basic Human Needs in Developing Countries* (New York, 1981).

PAUL STREETEN

BAY OF PIGS INVASION. The Bay of Pigs Invasion, launched on 17–19 April 1961, was the most serious attempt by the U.S. *Central Intelligence Agency to overthrow Fidel *Castro. Castro's rise to power in *Cuba upset a long-standing hemispheric status quo built upon a U.S. claim to an exclusive sphere of influence in Latin America and a prohibition against the spread of *communism into the region. U.S. opinion, both in the government and in the country at large, gradually turned to the conclusion that Castro had to be removed.

The scheme was hatched during the *Eisenhower administration, and called for training and equipping a force of Cuban exiles in Guatemala that would land, with U.S. air support, on the southern coast of the island near the Escambray mountains, move into the hills, and rally the Cuban people against the new dictator. The essence of the plan was to repeat the success of a similar operation against Guatemalan President Jacobo Arbenz Guzmán in July 1954. But the CIA grossly underestimated Castro's popularity, and the size, equipment, and training of the invasion force proved wholly inadequate to the task at hand. Moreover, the plan underwent a series of changes, right up until the day of the invasion itself, virtually guaranteeing its failure. The landing site was moved westward from Trinidad to Playa Girón, a flat, swampy area far away from the Escambray, affording no cover and no escape; the number of bombing runs on Cuban airfields authorized for the small exile air force was scaled back to the point where it failed to knock out Castro's air power; and at the last minute, President John F. *Kennedy decided to withhold the American air support needed to cover the landing. The invasion was quickly defeated by superior Cuban forces.

Kennedy had, in fact, inherited an almost impossible predicament from Eisenhower. Kennedy was reluctant to use U.S. military might directly against Castro because of the ill will it would generate in Latin America. He had high hopes that the Alliance for Progress would lead to an improvement in U.S. relations with its Latin American neighbors, and overt intervention against Cuba would frustrate that aim. At the same time, as CIA director Allen Dulles vehemently argued, once preparations for an exile invasion were under way in Guatemala, it would be difficult to turn back. If the invaders were brought back to the United States or dispersed, they would blow the cover on the operation and alienate the Right (who would conclude that the president lacked nerve), the Left (who would object to the very idea of intervention), and the Latin Americans (who would question the president's commitment to nonintervention). Perhaps most importantly, the Soviet Union would conclude that Kennedy was soft on communism, and Dulles worried that canceling the operation might trigger Communist takeovers throughout the hemisphere. It was also possible, Dulles noted, that the exile force would resist being disarmed.

Kennedy was well aware of the faults of the plan, and it met strong and vocal opposition from many of the administration's Latin American specialists and top military advisers. But Kennedy allowed himself to be persuaded that the landing should go ahead, with the United States distancing itself from it as far as possible. He would later take full public responsibility for the disaster.

The invasion generated considerable ill will in Latin America and exposed President Kennedy to severe criticism from both Right and Left. But the most important short-run effect of the invasion was to convince Castro of the United States' unrelenting hostility and drive Cuba further into the Soviet camp. It was partly to forestall a more decisive military assault that the Soviet Union attempted to deploy nuclear missiles to Cuba in 1962, although, ironically, the experience convinced Kennedy that a military solution to the Cuban problem was imprudent.

(See also COLD WAR; CUBAN MISSILE CRISIS; U.S.–LATIN AMERICAN RELATIONS.)

Peter Wyden, *Bay of Pigs: The Untold Story* (New York, 1979). Trumbull Higgins, *The Perfect Failure: Kennedy, Eisenhower, and the CIA at the Bay of Pigs* (New York, 1987).

DAVID A. WELCH

BELARUS. See COMMONWEALTH OF INDEPENDENT STATES.

BELGIUM. From the time of its independence in 1830 until 1970, the Belgian state was a centralized parliamentary monarchy; then, its history rife with tension, Belgium was transformed from a unitary into a federal state. Belgium presently has around 10 million inhabitants, forty percent of whom are French-speaking and sixty percent Dutch-speaking. There is also a small German-speaking community.

The tensions running through Belgian society arise from what V. R. Lorwin termed "segmented *pluralism"—in other words, the gradual institutionalization of philosophical (Christian versus secular), socioeconomic (social classes), and linguistic (French-speaking versus Dutch-speaking) divisions within a pillar-like system that splits society into Christian, socialist, and liberal "worlds."

The type of compromise that enabled the gradual separation of church and state set the pattern for the institutionalization of conflicts. Since the end of the nineteenth century, each of the different "worlds" that make up Belgian society has established its own network of institutions: political parties, trade unions, health insurance funds, cooperatives, schools, hospitals, day care center, and so on. Each of these worlds, through these organizations, controls a part of society and keeps under control, through a range of compromises, the conflicts running through it.

Universal suffrage was introduced in 1919 for men and 1948 for women. Usually, no party has an absolute majority. Since 1945, governments have nearly always been coalitions. The Parti Social Chrétien (PSC) and Christelijke Volkspartij (CVP) have been present in all the governments (except 1954–1958), in coalition with the liberals or, more frequently, with the socialists, and occasionally with certain regionalist parties.

The economic crisis in the middle of the 1970s called into question the entire framework of the dialogue between labor representatives, employers' organizations, and the state. This dialogue extended from the company (Works Councils, health and safety committees, trade union delegations) to the economic sector (joint commissions), to the economy as whole (Central Council on the Economy, National Labor Council). The clout of all these bodies was considerably reduced as a consequence of the crisis.

The integration of the highly representative trade unions (which enjoy membership of seventy-five percent of the work force) in the different worlds or pillars of Belgian society includes association with the political parties: trade unions thus have a voice in the political decision-making system. But the capacity of labor organizations to influence decisions has been severely restricted by the government's austerity policies.

Even before the aging of the industrial structures, Belgian society and each of its pillars was infused by language-based tension. Since the creation of the Belgian state, the "collective conscience" has been linguistically and culturally divided. As long as the state was controlled by a French-speaking ruling class, it embodied for the French-speaking population the expression of a national community, with Flemish appearing simply as a local dialect. But the birth and growth of the Flemish movement signaled the failure of this type of integration. Within the Flemish movement, language acted as a cultural catalyst, defining and strengthening Flemish tradition and specificity. Initially, the movement saw the Belgian state as imposed from outside. In a second phase, once it had established itself in the various spheres of society and had won the adoption of language laws defining the Flemish region as Dutch-speaking and giving Brussels bilingual status, it used the instruments placed at its disposal by the state to assume a role appropriate to its force within it.

A sense of identity developed in the French-speaking region of Wallonia as crisis gripped Walloon industry and industrial development moved to the port regions in the north of the country. The distinction between the two communities goes much deeper than just language; it is also socioeconomic, political, and ideological. In the north, Catholic influence is much stronger. The Dutch-speaking CVP is the dominant party in Flanders, and the Confédération des Syndicats Chrétiens (CSC) is the majority union. In the south, on the other hand, the socialists and secular union traditions are much stronger.

The nature of these two nationalist movements is specific to Belgium. They are not minority nationalities seeking greater autonomy or independence, but social movements struggling for control of the state itself. The Flemish claim is first and foremost cultural, the Walloon claim socioeconomic. Brussels, in the Flemish part of the country but with a majority French-speaking population, is a permanent source of conflict despite its bilingual status.

The constitutional changes implemented since 1970 are therefore the combined result of 1) an economic crisis that has hit the south of the country harder and 2) the sustained Flemish and Walloon movements, each with its own aims. The outcome has been an asymmetrical institutional reform process. On the one hand, a Flemish nation has emerged around the Flemish movement, inspired by linguistic and cultural demands. On the other hand, the people of Wallonia and Brussels have mobilized primarily against economic decline, and only secondarily as defenders of the French-speaking majority in Brussels.

The constitutional revisions of 1970 and 1980 were a compromise: they established three communities—two large Flemish and French-speaking communities and a German-speaking community, with special status for its 65,000 members—and three regions (Wallonia, Flanders, and Brussels). Flanders, Wallonia, and the French-speaking community have their own institutions, executive bodies, and councils. The Brussels region also has its own specific institutions. The regions and the communities now have decision-making powers on such vital matters as education, the economy, regional development, and health, and manage around forty percent of public expenditure. A new phase of state evolution, with the reform of the two-chamber system, is under way in the framework of the 1987 government program.

Considerable progress has been made along the road to federalism. However, there are a number of outstanding problems. State reform would appear to have fallen short of creating a stable situation, as demonstrated by the conflict over the Fourons area: villages situated on the linguistic boundary, in the Flemish province of Limburg, but with a majority of French-speaking inhabitants who are calling for attachment to the Walloon province of Liège. The Fourons is currently an emotionally charged symbol for the two communities.

On the international front, external factors have continually influenced Belgium's foreign policy. After separation from Holland in 1830, the new Belgian state was granted the status of permanent neutrality and was intended to be a buffer state that would keep the balance within Europe. This status did not survive the two world wars, for on each occasion Germany violated Belgian neutrality and invaded the country. Occupied Belgium took up the cause of the Allied camp in both instances.

World War II had important consequences. After capitulation on 28 May 1940, King Léopold III decided in his capacity as commander-in-chief of the army to stay in occupied Belgium and refused to follow his ministers to France or Britain to carry on the struggle. This refusal was the origin of the "royal question," which divided the country just after the war. After a period of regency from 1944 to 1950, Léopold III abdicated in favor of his son, Baudouin.

In 1944, Belgium joined with the Netherlands and Luxembourg to found an economic union, the Benelux. During the Cold War, volunteers were sent to Korea, and Belgium was hurriedly integrated into a Western economic, political, and military union considerably different from the "free hand" policy advocated in the interwar period. Belgium became a member of the North Atlantic Treaty Organization (NATO) and participated in the institutional founding of the *European Community (EC). Belgium plays an active role in the EC, and Brussels is vying with Strasbourg to become its "capital."

*Zaire has also played a central role in Belgian foreign policy. From being under the personal rule of King Léopold II from 1885 onwards, it became a Belgian colony, the Belgian Congo, in 1908 and finally won independence on 30 June 1960. However, Belgium remained involved in the country both in the form of military intervention (in the province of Katanga, now Shaba, which seceded immediately after independence and during the 1965 rebellion) and through civil and military assistance agreements and considerable trade flows. Crisis and conflict have, however, upset Belgian relations with Zaire, notably in 1988 and then again in 1990, following Belgium's call, after the Lubumbashi events, for an international inquiry into the human rights situation in Zaire, which is one of the conditions of the cooperation agreement between the two countries. Zaire then broke off these agreements, accusing Belgium of interference in its domestic affairs.

Each of the questions that have united or divided Belgian society must be understood through the prism of its underlying structural divisions, which are socioeconomic, philosophic, and community related. However, these are not the only issues dividing the Belgian people. As elsewhere in Europe, ecological concern among the population is considerable, seen in the existence of two green parties: the French-speaking Ecolo and the Dutch-speaking Agalev, both represented in Parliament. In addition, the process of secularization has generated significant tensions. For example, following the 1991 elections, a resurgence of the far-right parties occurred in the northern part of the country.

The complex interplay of these sources of division, simultaneously engendered by the conflicts, the causes of them, and the objects of compromise, has given rise to a form of consensus unique to Belgium. In socioeconomic terms, the "social solidarity pact" concluded by representatives of employers and trade unions just after World War II would appear to lay firm foundations for lasting peaceful labor relations. However, the tradition of general strikes (for universal suffrage, over the royal question in 1950, against a government bill in 1960–1961) and the effects of the economic crisis have demonstrated the precariousness of these foundations.

The state-church division focuses mainly on the question of school provision. It was also fueled for many years by the abortion debate. The adoption in 1990 of a law partially legalizing abortion led to a constitutional crisis, although this was rapidly resolved.

The division between the two language communities has given rise to the emergence of community parties: the Volksunie, represented in several governments; the Vlaams Blok, a small extreme right-wing party in Flanders; and the French-speaking Front Démocratique des Francophones (FDF) in Brussels. In Wallonia, the Rassemblement Wallon proved to be short-lived, with French-speaking socialists taking on the Walloon call for radical federalism. But the main effect of the division has been to cut in two the traditional parties. The Christian Socialists, socialists, and liberals are now organized into totally separate French-speaking and Dutch-speaking parties.

The divisions and compromises arising from the existence of distinct communities have consistently taken the form of institutional pluralism, with the coexistence at the national level of compartmentalized educational, health care, social, and cultural networks, rather than ideological pluralism. This has made possible their coexistence within the same structures. The new institutions resulting from the constitutional revisions of 1970 and 1980 provide decision-making autonomy for the communities and regions, which should reduce the potential for community conflict. The question remains, however, as to what will become of the old compromises within the new federal structures.

(See also CONGO CRISIS; FEDERALISM; INTERNAL COLONIALISM; PERIPHERAL NATIONALISM.)

Val R. Lorwin, 'Segmented Pluralism: Ideological Cleavages and Cohesion in the Smaller European Democracies," in K. McRae, ed., *Consociational Democracy: Political Accommodation in Segmented Societies* (Toronto, 1974), pp. 33–69. Xavier Mabille, *Histoire politique de la Belgique* (Brussels, 1986). Els Witte and Jan Craeybeckx, *La Belgique politique de 1830 à nos jours* (Brussels, 1987). Hervé Hasquin, ed., *Dictionnaire d'histoire de Belgique* (Brussels, 1988).

MATEO ALALUF

BELIZE. See ENGLISH-SPEAKING CARIBBEAN.

BEN-GURION, David. For more than four decades David Ben-Gurion was one of the preeminent leaders of the Zionist labor movement in *Palestine, of that country's Jewish community (the *Yishuv*), of the international Zionist movement, and then of *Israel, whose political life he dominated for a decade and a half. He can safely be ranked foremost among the founders of the State of Israel.

David Ben-Gurion was born David Gruen in 1886 in the small town of Plonsk in Russian Poland. His father, an uncertified lawyer, was a secular Jew and fervent adherent of the proto-Zionist "Love of Zion" movement. While still an adolescent, young Gruen became an activist of the socialist-Zionist "Workers of Zion" party. Emigrating to Palestine in 1906, he adopted the Hebrew name Ben-Gurion and for a brief period worked in agriculture, after which he devoted himself to party work and several years of legal studies.

Deported by the Ottoman authorities when World War I broke out, Ben-Gurion spent most of the war years in the United States, where he married. In 1918 he made his way back to Palestine as a volunteer with the Jewish Legion, a unit of the British army created after the *Balfour Declaration of November 1917. Although away on a mission for his party when the *Histadrut* ("General Organization of Jewish Workers in the Land of Israel") was established in 1920, he became its secretary and leading figure soon after his return at the end of 1921.

The *Histadrut* was the vehicle through which Ben-Gurion built up not only his own personal power but also the power of the labor-Zionist movement (dominated by his party) within the broader *Yishuv* and the Zionist Organization. Ben-Gurion and his party struggled to have the Jewish working class in Palestine, organized in the highly centralized *Histadrut*, assume the role of state-building vanguard in the Zionist project by taking charge of immigration and settlement and creating its own network of economic enterprises in agriculture, industry, construction, and distribution, and its own social, educational, and cultural institutions. As part of the same strategy, Ben-Gurion and the *Histadrut* fought to compel Jewish employers to hire only Jewish workers, to the exclusion of cheaper Arab labor. In the 1920s, while advocating cooperation between Arab and Jewish workers, Ben-Gurion strongly rejected the authenticity of Palestinian *Arab nationalism and insisted on the Jews' superior claim to Palestine.

By the early 1930s Ben-Gurion's party, by then known as MAPAI (Workers' Party of the Land of Israel), had become the leading force within the *Yishuv* and the Zionist movement, a development signaled by Ben-Gurion's elevation in 1935 from the leadership of the *Histadrut* to the positions of chair of the Zionist Executive and of the Jewish Agency, the de facto political leadership of the *Yishuv*. From then until 1948 Ben-Gurion would be at the center of Zionist politics and diplomacy. While publicly calling for peace and reconciliation with Palestine's Arab majority, and favoring acceptance of a 1937 British proposal to establish a Jewish state in only a small part of Palestine, he insisted in private that ultimately all of Palestine must be Jewish, a position whose formal endorsement by the Zionist movement he secured in 1942. After World War II Ben-Gurion directed the Zionist political and military struggle, first to compel the British to open Palestine to Jewish immigration and then to secure the establishment of a Jewish state.

Ben-Gurion presided over the establishment of the State of Israel in May 1948 and became its first prime minister and defense minister, suppressing challenges to the authority of the new government and supervising military operations during the war that ensued. A skillful politician, Ben-Gurion held together fractious coalition governments severely tested by the new state's economic difficulties, the massive influx of Jewish immigrants, conflicts between secular and religious Jews, and the acceptance of reparations payments from the Federal Republic of Germany (FRG).

As the *Cold War got under way, Ben-Gurion aligned Israel with the Western camp. In the 1950s, with the United States declining to assume the role of Israel's big-power patron, he established close ties with France, based on a common interest in suppressing Arab nationalism. Convinced that Arabs understood only the language of power, Ben-Gurion opposed Israeli concessions and advocated an "activist" policy of large-scale military retaliation in response to border incidents.

In December 1953 Ben-Gurion abruptly resigned and, proposing to set an example to Israeli youth, "retired" to a desert kibbutz. Rising border tensions aggravated by Israeli raids paved the way for his return to power in 1955, whereupon he began (in collusion with Britain and France) to plan an attack on Egypt aimed at bringing down the nationalist regime of President *Nasser. A military success for Israel, the Suez War of October–November 1956 brought few lasting gains: under U.S. pressure Israel was soon forced to withdraw from the territories it had conquered.

Ben-Gurion remained prime minister until 1963 when, exhausted by party infighting, he again abruptly "retired" to his kibbutz. He soon returned to political life, however, and when his old party MAPAI refused to accommodate his demands, he and his younger protégés broke away to form a new party, RAFI (Israel Workers' List). Ben-Gurion now advocated "statism," which rejected MAPAI's social democratic ethos in favor of a nonclass ideology, proposed that the state assume many *Histadrut* functions, and demanded electoral reform. RAFI did poorly in the 1965 elections, however, and a few years later it merged with MAPAI into the new Israeli Labor Party. Old, in declining health, and no longer a serious candidate for national leadership, Ben-Gurion finally left political life for good in 1970. He died in December 1973 at the age of 87.

Ben-Gurion combined an unquestioning devotion to the achievement of his ultimate goal, the establishment and strengthening of the Jewish state, with considerable tactical flexibility. He possessed tremendous willpower, first-rate organizational ability, and a talent for political maneuvering. Ben-Gurion's critics on both left and right not inaccurately saw him as overbearing, self-righteous, and stubborn, while his supporters insisted that he was precisely the kind of tough and realistic leader *Zionism and later Israel needed. Certainly Ben-Gurion left a deep and enduring imprint on Israeli politics and policy.

(See also ARAB-ISRAELI CONFLICT; INTERNATIONAL MIGRATION; SUEZ CRISIS.)

Shabtai Teveth, *Ben-Gurion and the Palestinian Arabs* (Oxford, 1985). Shabtai Teveth, *Ben-Gurion: The Burning Ground, 1886–1948* (Boston, 1987).

ZACHARY LOCKMAN

BENIN. The Republic of Benin (Dahomey until 1975) has an outward-looking character shaped by its well-educated elite and by geographical factors promoting contacts with neighboring states.

The elite originated with Africans returned from Brazil to the West African "Slave Coast." These literate "Brazilians" and others in southern Dahomey were drawn into the colonial civil service, and the country became known for intellectuals who worked throughout French Africa. The intelligentsia was active in opposing colonialism, building nationalism, and, thirty years after independence, forcing national leadership toward democratization.

Long, narrow Benin lies between Nigeria and Togo. The French promoted cross-border commerce by building a coastal road across its 125-kilometer (74-mile) width and a railroad and road along its 675-kilometer (420-mile) length. Independent Benin enlarged the port of Cotonou and created small industries for Nigerian markets. Smuggling became commonplace, with luxury imports and food moving east in exchange for cocoa and oil.

Colonial boundaries incorporated dozens of ethnicities, though culturally and geographically the greatest contrast was between north and south. In the south, several culturally related groups were dominated by the Fon kingdom of Dahomey. The north contained three-fourths of the land, far fewer people, and far more ethnic diversity. People remained faithful to African religions with only small numbers adopting Christianity (fifteen percent) and Islam (thirteen percent).

Independence in 1960 left the nation with an area of 112,622 square kilometers (43,484 sq. mi.), few natural resources, and a population that would grow to 4.2 million by 1990. Industry remained small-scale, employing seven percent of the population by 1985. Palm products, cotton, and peanuts were exports, though food crops kept the country self-sufficient.

Three regional parties competed in a system of clientelist politics to control state resources. During the country's first twelve years Dahomey became infamous for instability (five coups d'état, six presidents, and government by nearly a dozen combinations of civilian and military leaders).

A sixth coup in 1972 brought Mathieu Kerekou to power. Strongly anti-French, the new government in 1974–1975 adopted *Marxism-*Leninism as state *ideology and changed the country's name to the People's Republic of Benin.

Benin's revolution tended less to pure Marxism-Leninism and more to pragmatic socialism. Dramatic reforms in the late 1970s attempted to increase mass access to education, health, and local government. Businesses were nationalized into state companies, while one-party government lodged control in a handful of leaders. Numbers of intellectuals fled. By 1980 failures of poorly conceived projects led Benin to seek private investments.

Economic decline, corruption, and mismanagement left the country bankrupt by the end of the 1980s. Crippled by strikes and unable to pay the bloated civil service (up from 9,236 in 1972 to 47,163 in 1989), the government slowed to a halt. Under pressure from international financial institutions and France, Benin adopted a program of structural adjustment. In 1989 unrest forced Kerekou to amnesty exiled opponents and political prisoners, renounce Marxism-Leninism, and call a national assembly to discuss the nation's future. Over fifty parties appeared as open political activity resumed. The national assembly convened in 1990, established a one-year transition government, but allowed Kerekou to remain nominally in power. A new constitution provided for the democratic election of a unicameral assembly and a president limited to two five-year terms. Nicephore Soglo, the transition prime minister, was elected president and took office in 1991.

(See also FRANCOPHONE AFRICA.)

Chris Allen, "Benin," in Bogdan Szajkowski, ed., *Benin, The Congo, Burkina Faso: Economics, Politics and Society* (London and New York, 1989), pp. 1–144.

EDNA G. BAY

BHOPAL DISASTER. On the night of 2–3 December 1984 highly toxic gas leaked from a contaminated methylisocyanate storage tank at the Union Carbide Corporation (UCC) plant at Bhopal, India, leading to the worst industrial disaster in history. Methylisocyanate is a highly reactive, flammable chemical that generates several toxic products when released. Safety systems did not work, and no alarm was sounded for the general public. The accident caused colossal human suffering, ecological damage, and financial loss to the citizens of Bhopal. The death toll was at least 3,500, another 60,000 had serious health problems, and the total population affected was between 150,000 and 250,000. Many victims were permanently disabled, while others still suffer from physical and psychological problems. Deaths attributable to the accident continue.

The disaster highlights the dilemmas that developing countries face in their drive for rapid change and their dealings with *multinational corporations (MNCs). The Indian government of Prime Minister Rajiv Gandhi wanted to appear to be a champion of the victims without giving the appearance of being hostile to MNCs. It refused UCC's initial offer for a settlement, passed a law to make itself the sole representative of the victims, and sued in U.S. courts, which sent the case back to India. The government suspended its effort to establish a new law on multinational enterprise liability when it backed down and settled out of court in 1989. Gandhi's successors have attempted to overturn the settlement, which they consider inadequate and a sellout to UCC. Despite the litigation with UCC, the Gandhi government continued its policy of investment liberalization and reduction of controls on MNCs in order to promote *modernization. The Bhopal plant was closed after the disaster, but there were no reprisals against UCC's subsidiary, Union Carbide India, Ltd., or any other MNC. Bhopal did not lead to any direct political changes at the state or federal level. The disaster did not significantly affect organizations, institutions, law, or politics.

Bhopal highlighted the dangers worldwide of chemicals and the chemical industry despite efforts to blame the disaster on restrictive Indian laws relating to MNCs. The immediate reaction to Bhopal was to raise safety issues in chemical plants all over the world, with the chemical industry spending large amounts of resources to upgrade safety measures. In some developing countries governments passed more comprehensive legislation to ensure the safe operation of hazardous industries. However, new laws did not solve the underlying problem of limited financial and human resources to police chemical industries nor address the dependence of developing countries on MNCs.

Ward Morehouse and M. Arun Subramaniam, *The Bhopal Tragedy: What Really Happened and What It Means for American Workers and Communities at Risk. A Preliminary Report for the Citizens' Commission on Bhopal* (New York, 1986).

ASHOK BHARGAVA

BHUTAN. The Kingdom of Bhutan is located on the southeast slope of the Himalayas. It is bordered on the north and east by Tibet and on the south and west by India. The population as of mid-1990 was about 700,000. Historically, Bhutan had a theocratic system of government similar to that in Tibet, dominated by the Druk ("dragon") Buddhist sect of Mahayana Buddhism. The Druk leaders assiduously followed an isolationist policy toward all their neighbors, including Tibet. By the late nineteenth century the system had fallen apart, and it was replaced by a hereditary monarchy in 1907. The first two rulers of the Wangchuk dynasty gradually extended their control over the disparate collection of monastic and local landed elites. On this foundation, Jigme Dorji Wangchuk (1952–1972) introduced basic political and economic reforms: a *Tshogdu* (elected national assembly); a *Lhengyel Tsok* (council of ministers), but with the king serving as prime minister; land reforms; and the opening of Bhutan to the outside world.

The present ruler, Jigme Singye Wangchuk, came to the throne in 1972 and continued his father's *modernization programs. The central administrative system was greatly expanded and given a broad range of powers and responsibilities. An autonomous judiciary was established, with a high court in the capital, Thimphu, and courts in each district. A new legal code, based upon both modern principles of jurisprudence and Bhutan's customary Buddhist laws, was introduced.

By the mid-1980s, King Jigme Singye was concerned with the excessive concentration of power in the center and sought to introduce an ambitious decentralization program. But this was superseded in the late 1980s by a broad range of new policies— termed the *Drigham Namza,* or national culture principle, program—that had as its objective the preservation of Bhutan's national identity and traditional Buddhist culture. All Bhutanese, whatever their ethnic and religious background, were ordered to wear only "Bhutanese dress" in public—defined to mean the *glos* and *kiras* worn by officials in office but not, normally, by large segments of the public outside Thimphu. Dzongka, the official language, became the national language by decree, replacing the various Tibetan dialects in eastern Bhutan and the Nepali spoken in southern Bhutan. These programs elicited a negative response from the large Hindu Nepali minority in the south and the various other ethnic and linguistic minorities in the middle hills.

Some changes were also evident in Bhutan's external relations by 1990. The friendly, close relationship with India has been maintained in form, but measures have been introduced to lessen economic dependence on India. About half of the foreign (mainly Indian) labor force has been expelled; new trade permits have not been issued to Indian businesses; and Thimphu announced that its budget would be funded from internal revenues by 1991, thus ending the heavy reliance on Indian aid. This has not yet constituted a reintroduction of the old isolationist policy, as extensive contacts with the outside world have been maintained and even expanded—e.g., new Bhutanese (Druk Airlines) flights to New Delhi, Kathmandu, and Bangkok. But it is indicative of a new attitude toward foreign powers and alien cultures, and this is bound to have a major impact on Bhutan internally as well as internationally over the next decade.

(See also SOUTH ASIAN ASSOCIATION FOR REGIONAL COOPERATION.)

P. P. Karan, *Bhutan: Environment, Culture and Development Strategy* (New Delhi, 1990).

LEO E. ROSE

BIAFRA. The eastern region of *Nigeria, renamed the Republic of Biafra, declared its independence on 30 May 1967, with Lieutenant Colonel Chukwuemeka Odumegwu Ojukwu as head of state. Secession followed prolonged political instability, two coups, changes in the federal structure of the country, and the massacre of Igbo people living in northern Nigeria. (About 1.5 million Igbos fled back to their homeland.) Diplomatic attempts to bring Biafra back into the fold failed, and fighting broke out in July 1967. By May 1968, after early successes, Biafra was encircled and cut off from the sea and lost control over oil production. Two years of fighting threw a slowly tightening blockade around Biafran territory. The war ended on 12 January 1970 when a plane carrying General Ojukwu lifted into the night sky from Uli airport, the last enclave left the Igbos, on its way to the general's new home in Côte d'Ivoire. A formal surrender was signed the next day in Lagos. An estimated 600,000 to 1.5 million people had lost their lives. The economy of the eastern region lay in shambles. Fears of an impending genocide lay like smoke on the landscape.

The federal government was supported by arms and diplomacy from the Soviet Union and its clients, the Organization of African Unity, and Arab countries. The United States and Britain, although on the side of the central government, also urged an end to the war and supported humanitarian relief efforts. Biafra received international recognition and support from France, four African states (Gabon, Côte d'Ivoire, Tanzania, and Zambia), China, Israel, and the white-controlled Southern African states. Mercenaries were drawn to the war on both sides. Private relief organizations flew medical supplies and food into Biafra and maintained personnel on the ground to the very end. Superpower considerations, ideological rivalries, the degrading image of an African state in the throes of self-destruction, and the humanitarian urge to alleviate civilian suffering led to these decisions.

The origins of secession arose from three factors: a political structure that fragmented power among regions each dominated by a major ethnic group; traditional subnational fears and rivalries; and an increasing differentiation of political and economic power among groups, regions, and classes. The question whether Biafra was essentially a "tribal" or a class and *elite conflict has no clear answer. Elements of *ethnicity and *class reinforced each other. Views of "the other" reflected both cultural stereotypes and economic fears, and economic and elite competition fueled ethnic recriminations.

The eastern region was reintegrated politically and economically into Nigeria, in a remarkable example of compassion and political wisdom, without major persecutions. The war caused a profound change in nationalist thinking. Nigerians had been forced to confront their country's arbitrary origins, imposed political structures, and the divisive nature of their political conflicts. The massive economic, social, and human costs of the war were sacrifices to the idea of One Nigeria that, once made, could not be cast aside. To prevent another Biafra has been a leitmotif of succeeding governments and political and military elites.

(See also SECESSIONIST MOVEMENTS; TRIBALISM.)

John de St. Jorre, *The Brothers' War: Biafra and Nigeria* (Boston, 1972). John J. Stremlau, *The International Politics of the Nigerian Civil War, 1967–1970* (Princeton, N.J., 1977).

OTWIN MARENIN

BILL OF RIGHTS. The Bill of Rights of the U.S. *Constitution consists of the first ten amendments taken together, especially the first eight of these which identify specific individual *rights. These were proposed in 1789 by Representative James Madison, who was solidly backed by President George Washington during the First Congress. Ten of the twelve congressionally approved amendments were ratified by ten states so as to take effect on 15 December 1791. Their general tenor is to protect individual personal, political, and religious liberties against infringement by government, principally by the national government in the original conception and down to 1925, when a process of "nationalization" gradually began that has brought protection against invasion by the states of most of the rights listed and of a number only implied by (or "penumbral" to) the rights specified. The philosophical foundation of the Bill of Rights is set forth in the Declaration of Independence's first sentences, especially the announcement of "certain unalienable rights" grounded in the "laws of nature and of nature's God." The effectiveness of the provisions of the Bill of Rights in protecting fundamental personal liberties through American law is uniquely dependent upon the power of *judicial review as exercised by the federal judiciary, with a last resort in the *Supreme Court of the United States. The judiciary determines with finality, on a case-by-case adversary basis, the meaning and force of laws under the Constitution considered as the "supreme Law of the Land" (Art. VI).

The origins of the liberties protected and general theory of rights undergirding that protection are of great antiquity and grounded in immemorial usage (or *prescription*) and natural right, although their meaning and importance were sharpened by the debate leading to American independence and Revolution and gained impetus from the eighteenth-century Enlightenment with its emphasis upon reason and the individual. It remains generally true, however, that the rights protected substantively were part and parcel of an inherited tradition of common law liberty and rule of law that emerged in medieval England from the time of King Edward the Confessor (d. 1066), last of the Saxon kings, to Magna Carta (1215) as developed in the jurisprudence of Henry de Bracton (d. 1268), refined in the Lancastrian constitutional jurisprudence of Sir John Fortescue (lord chief justice and lord chancellor under Henry VI, d. 1479?). This tradition was recovered, vivified, and perfected in seventeenth-century England especially by Sir Edward Coke (1584–1634) in the House of Commons during the long contest between Parliament and the Stuart kings memorialized in the Petition of Right (1628), the beheading of Charles I (1649), and eventuating in the Glorious Revolution of 1688, the Settlement of 1689, and parliamentary enactment of the Declaration of Rights as the English Bill of Rights of the same year, thus giving its name to the genre. The constitutional form authoritative at the time of the American founding (1760–1790) was powerfully shaped by Coke, former attorney general and lord chief justice of England, who led a successful resistance against extension of the royal prerogative and the attendant establishment of absolutism and rule by divine right that saved rule of law and constitutionalism for England and the modern world, as Sir William Holdsworth observed (*Some Makers of English Law: Tagore Lectures of 1937–38*, Cambridge, U.K., 1938). Decisive for the continuity of this vision of liberty through law and limited government was the education of subsequent generations of lawyers, including the American revolutionary generation and

beyond, by Coke's *Institutes* and *Reports*. Thus, although the bill of rights concept may primarily be American, the liberties protected, and institutional modes devised for their protection, are deeply moored in Anglo-American political and constitutional history, especially in those passages in which the absolutism was narrowly averted that swept over almost all of Western civilization in the seventeenth century with consequences into the present. Indeed, the securing of personal liberty and free government through rule of law is a legacy quite self-consciously reaching back to distant antiquity, to Cicero in Rome and Aristotle in Hellas.

Well before 1789 when, under heavy political pressure from the Anti-Federalists and public sentiment fearful that personal liberties might be imperiled by the new Constitution, Madison proposed his amendments, virtually *all* of the rights to be included in the federal Bill of Rights already had been set out in bills of rights ratified by eleven of the original thirteen states plus Vermont. The inventory of such rights already adopted by one or another of the new American states thus included the following: no establishment of religion, free exercise of religion, free speech, free press, assembly, petition, bearing of arms, no quartering of soldiers, searches and seizures protection, requirement of grand jury indictment, protection against double jeopardy and self-incrimination, guarantee of due process of law, just compensation, public trial, jury trial, accusation and confrontation, witnesses, guarantee of counsel, and protection against excessive bail, fines, and punishment. The only major provision not found in the earlier state documents is the retained rights provision of the Ninth Amendment. The Massachusetts Declaration of Rights (1780), drafted by John Adams, even included a reserved powers clause (Art. IV) analogous to the Tenth Amendment's provision. The Massachusetts document also had the merit of partly replacing the admonitory language of *ought* used by George Mason in drafting the 1776 Virginia Declaration of Rights (the model for eight other states' bills of rights) with the imperative *shall* of legal command found (along with *shall not*) in Madison's Bill of Rights.

There was virtually no judicial construction of the meaning of the various provisions of the Bill of Rights until well after adoption of the Civil War amendments, the Thirteenth, Fourteenth, and Fifteenth. A voluminous litigatory process of "absorption," "selective incorporation," and identification of liberties occupying a "preferred position" (First Amendment rights) or as being "fundamental rights" has accelerated, however, since the ruling in the 1947 *Adamson* case which resulted in the Bill of Rights being applied to state governments, and even to private actions, no less than to actions of the federal government. Today the *liberty* protected (against invasion by the states) under the Due Process Clause of the Fourteenth Amendment embraces all provisions of the First Amendment and nearly all provisions of the Fourth, Fifth, Sixth, Seventh, and Eighth Amendments. The principal exceptions are the Fifth Amendment right to a grand jury indictment in criminal cases and the Seventh Amendment guarantee of a jury trial in civil cases. In addition, there is a substantial expanse of additional personal liberty, especially race-related civil rights, protected by the Equal Protection Clause, and as strictly extraconstitutional rights (such as privacy and the right to travel) that an activist judiciary has discovered in "penumbras" of the express rights, or has construed as being included in the Retained Rights Clause of the Ninth Amendment and even, perhaps, as being among the "Blessings of Liberty" mentioned in the Preamble to the Constitution.

Bernard Schwartz, *The Great Rights of Mankind: A History of the American Bill of Rights* (New York, 1977). Ellis Sandoz, *A Government of Laws: Political Theory, Religion and the American Founding* (Baton Rouge, La., 1990).

ELLIS SANDOZ

BLS STATES. Botswana, Lesotho, and Swaziland, referred to jointly as the BLS states, are three landlocked Southern African states that border on the Republic of *South Africa. They would have become part of South Africa and none would have had a separate existence had it not been for the British government, which administered them from the late nineteenth or early twentieth century until their independence in 1966 (Botswana and Lesotho) and 1968 (Swaziland). The constitution of the Union of South Africa, drawn up less than a decade after Britain defeated the two Boer republics in the 1899–1902 war, anticipated that the three British protectorates would be incorporated into the Union, provided the inhabitants of the three territories were consulted. African opinion, when sought, tended to oppose the incorporation, and the incorporation issue served to fuel the feelings of nationalism.

Two of the BLS states have monarchical forms of government; the third (Botswana) is a republic not so much because the people of Botswana are not royalists but because the nation never had an all-inclusive monarchy aggregating its eight tribal units. The first prime minister (and subsequent president) of Botswana, Sir Seretse Khama, was heir to the Ngwato throne, but the British colonial authorities made him renounce his claim after he had married Ruth Williams, a white Briton. Interracial marriage at that time (1948) in *Southern Africa ran counter to the mores of the white residents of Southern Rhodesia and South Africa. President Khama died in office in 1980 and was succeeded by Quett Masire, then vice-president. Sir Seretse was the most able of the political leaders of the BLS states and made full use of his traditional (Ngwato) *legitimacy to solidify the modern political system of Botswana, which was never seriously challenged by the chiefs of the seven other tribes who have suffered a loss of some functions and prestige.

In the other two states, the monarchy has been a relatively effective symbol of unity and a vibrant political force. Swaziland not only enjoyed the world's longest-reigning monarch, King Sobhuza II (monarch from 1921 until his death in 1982), but also experienced the growth of a royally inspired political movement (known as the Imbokodvo National Movement) that outmaneuvered more overtly modern political parties in the immediate pre-independence and post-independence periods. Five years after independence, the king suspended the democratic constitution, and the system reverted to a more autocratic style, although there was no loss of legitimacy. Following the death of King Sobhuza II, a period of severe political turbulence followed in which royal factions intrigued for control in the palace. The Swazi monarchical system did not provide for an equivalent to the heir apparent who could be groomed while the monarch was still alive. In 1986, the second-youngest son of King Sobhuza II, an eighteen-year-old away at boarding school in England, became the new sovereign as King Mswati III. Although he has authorized parliamentary elections and has expressed his distaste for the corruption that marred the interregnum period, observers sense that he will not act very forcefully to restore modern democratic practice to Swaziland. Although he does not lack legitimacy, he seems to be one of the weaker leaders in the BLS states.

Lesotho has probably suffered the greatest legitimacy deflation of all the three BLS states because it has been under military rule since early 1986, when Prime Minister Leabua Jonathan's government was ousted by the security forces. The new rulers, headed by Lieutenant General Justin Lekhanya of the Royal Lesotho Defense Force, revamped the political system by establishing a ruling Military Council that made sure that the reigning monarch, King Moshoeshoe II, was the final executive and legislative authority in the realm. Ever since colonial Basutoland became the Kingdom of Lesotho in 1966, the king has been tethered and forced to accept a very secondary political role. Recently he clashed with the Military Council and, for the second time, went into exile. In 1970 he went to the Netherlands, and in 1990 he went to Britain. Late in 1990, the king was removed from his throne and replaced by his eldest son, David Bereng Seeiso Mohato, who took the title of Letsie III. In April 1991, Major General Lekhanya, in turn, was replaced by Colonel Elias Ramaema as head of the governing Military Council. As in Swaziland, there was a royalist political movement, the Marema Tlou Freedom Party, but it was never an exceptionally effective force in Lesotho. The monarchy has been visibly weakened, and the political dissensus within the system has not been satisfactorily addressed since the late Prime Minister Jonathan, fearing that the opposition Basutoland Congress Party would defeat his own Basutoland National Party, canceled the 1970 general election as it was in progress. The minister of constitutional affairs expects that a new constitution will be ready shortly, and in May 1991 Colonel Ramaema ended the ban on political party activity in anticipation of a June 1992 general election.

Of the three BLS states, Botswana has been the least encumbered by South African hegemonic policy, in large measure because of the international stature of President Khama whose moderate, nonracial policies earned him international respect and access to Western power and resources. He was able to exert moral leadership and to avoid the debilitating costs of a sanctions war against neighboring white-ruled Rhodesia. Along with the other two states, Botswana was able to secure a beneficial restructuring of the Southern Africa Customs Union (embracing South Africa, Namibia, and the BLS states) in 1969, and thereafter Botswana left the Rand Monetary Area to develop its own currency and national bank. Its economic position improved enormously once diamonds were discovered and effectively mined by De Beers, the South African multinational mining house. This has enabled it to withstand years of drought and to build up its foreign exchange reserves. The currencies of the other two states are linked to the South African rand through the Tripartite Monetary Area, which was initiated in 1986. All three send migrant workers to South Africa, with Lesotho being the most dependent upon the monies sent home by migrant laborers, and all three offer asylum to South African refugees, which invites South African retaliation from time to time. Only Swaziland has signed a non-aggression treaty with South Africa and only Swaziland permits a South African trade mission on its territory. None exchanges ambassadors with Pretoria, and all three belong to the *Commonwealth, the *Organization of African Unity, and the *Southern African Development Co-ordination Conference. All, in varying degrees, have been subject to South African destabilization pressure, and Swaziland has sometimes been thought to engage in sanctions-busting commercial operations.

Richard P. Stevens, *Lesotho, Botswana, and Swaziland: The Former High Commission Territories in Southern Africa* (London, 1967). Alan Booth, *Swaziland: Tradition and Change in a Southern African Kingdom* (Boulder, Colo., 1984). John E. Bardill and James H. Cobbe, *Lesotho: Dilemmas of Dependence in Southern Africa* (Boulder, Colo., 1985). Jack D. Parson, ed., *Succession to High Office in Botswana,* Monographs in International Studies, Africa Series No. 54 (Athens, Ohio, 1990).

RICHARD DALE

BOLÍVAR, Simón. Best known of the heroes of the Latin American independence movement, Simón Bolívar was a brilliant military strategist and was responsible for the liberation of the five Andean countries from Spanish control. Equally important, Bolívar is remembered for his prophetic views about Latin American political problems and his aborted attempts to form a continent-wide federation rather than a proliferation of small nations.

Born in Caracas, *Venezuela, on 24 July 1783, Bolívar's wealthy background enabled him to combine military expertise with a broad general culture, frequently expressed through bitter statements regarding the present and future of Latin America. At a young age, he went to Spain and elsewhere in Europe. Back in Caracas in 1807, he began to militate for the independence of Latin America. He first participated in agitation and propaganda organizations such as the Sociedad Patriótica. Later he organized a liberation army that won the decisive battles leading to the independence of Venezuela, Colombia, Ecuador, Peru, and Bolivia.

After the military period was over, Bolívar became active as a political leader in several of the countries he had liberated. Unlike José de San Martín, leader of the independence movement in the southern part of the continent, Bolívar was a staunch republican. From the beginning, however, he argued that only a strong and centralized government could control the factional forces in the new republics and prevent national disintegration. For example, he was one of the first to suggest that the failure of the first republic in Venezuela did not result from the superiority of the monarchic forces but the establishment of a weak government in 1811. In his famous speech at the Congress of Angostura in February 1819, Bolívar voiced his preference for a central and unitary government as well as a hereditary senate; this anticipated his idea of a life-term president, which he elaborated for Bolivia's constitution. Latin America was not yet ready, he thought, for representative government.

In international terms, Bolívar also supported centralism. He tried to persuade his contemporaries to form a large, unified nation rather than many small ones. This would provide a defensive mechanism against external aggression, he argued. Although his vision was adopted at the Congress of Panama in 1826, it was never implemented. Latin America fragmented, while its neighbor to the north followed the Bolivarian prescription. Partly as a consequence, the United States came to dominate Latin America, just as Bolívar had feared.

After twenty years of involvement in political and military struggles, and of controlling the public affairs of several countries, Bolívar admitted that "America is ungovernable for us." These words, written a month before his death in December 1830, summarized his profound pessimism. The next 150 years of history can be seen as confirmation of Bolívar's prophecies about domestic and international problems in the Western Hemisphere.

Simón Bolívar, *Cartas de Bolívar, 1799–1822* (Paris, 1912). Gerhard Masur, *Simón Bolívar* (Albuquerque, N.Mex., 1948).

HERACLIO BONILLA

BOLIVIA. Bolivia's turbulent political history is rooted in its racial, geographic, and ethnic diversity. Approximately sixty percent of the country's 6.5 million inhabitants are Indians; another thirty percent are racially mixed. Bolivia's political life, however, has always been dominated by whites, who constitute less than ten percent of the population. Moreover, Bolivia's geographic diversity has contributed to a profound sense of regional rivalry. Political conflict in Bolivia has been characterized by regional disputes, pitting the residents of the eastern lowlands against those of the Andean highlands. This pattern of regional and racial conflict has been largely responsible for undermining the effectiveness of national governments.

Owing largely to these factors, for the first fifty years after Bolivian independence in 1825, the country plunged into a period of strongman (*caudillo*) rule. The War of the Pacific in 1879 ended the *caudillo* period as the combined forces of Peru and Bolivia were defeated by Chile; as a result, Bolivia became a landlocked nation. The end of the war also coincided with Bolivia's integration into the world economy through the export of tin. For most of the next fifty years, Bolivia was ruled by a formally democratic system controlled by the country's powerful tin barons. The Chaco War (1932–1935) pitted Bolivia against Paraguay in a bloody struggle that ended the prolonged period of civilian rule. The war unleashed a number of social forces and generated a period of intense questioning that culminated in revolutionary upheaval in 1952.

Led by the Movimiento Nacionalista Revolucionario (MNR), Bolivian workers, middle sectors, and peasants overthrew the old order on 9 April 1952. For the next twelve years, the MNR carried out one of the most far-reaching social revolutions of the twentieth century. The MNR nationalized the nation's tin industry, introduced a broad agrarian reform, and declared universal suffrage. In the process, thirty years of state-led economic development began.

In November 1964, the Bolivian military overthrew the MNR and governed for nearly two decades. The military period consisted of several different military governments, ranging from the populist experiments of General Juan José Torres (1970) to the repressive right-wing government of General Hugo Banzer Suárez (1971–1978) and the corrupt government of "Narco General" Luis García Meza (1980–1981). Following a dramatic institutional breakdown, the military transferred power to the civilians in October 1982.

Since the transition from military-authoritarian rule, Bolivia has held two national elections. The results, however, have been determined by the Congress, which serves as an electoral college when the winning candidate fails to obtain a majority of the vote. Coalitions between governing and opposition parties have become the basic form of contemporary Bolivian politics. To govern, especially to implement their economic programs, recent democratic governments have entered into pacts with the principal opposition parties. In 1985, President Víctor Paz Estenssoro's MNR joined forces with General Hugo Banzer's right-wing party; the current Paz Zamora government has also entered into a ruling pact with Banzer.

The main political actors in recent Bolivian history have been the political parties, labor, and the military. The largest party is the MNR, founded by Paz Estenssoro in 1941. Responsible for carrying out the 1952 revolution, the party switched positions when it returned to power in 1985. It imposed an economic program that ended hyperinflation and stabilized Bolivia's economy. It also ended state capitalism by decentralizing and privatizing state firms and opening up the economy through a neoliberal economic program known as the "new economic policy."

General Hugo Banzer's Acción Democrática y Nacionalista (ADN) was founded after Banzer was overthrown in 1978. In 1985, the ADN won the presidential election but failed to reach the required fifty percent and was outmaneuvered in the Congress by Paz Estenssoro and the MNR. The third party is the Movimiento de Izquierda Revolucionaria (MIR), founded in 1971 to combat the Banzer dictatorship. In August 1989, the MIR's leader Jaime Paz Zamora was elected president by the Congress. In one of the most ironic twists in Bolivian politics Paz Zamora was elected through a pact with Banzer's ADN. The MIR-ADN pact is likely to remain operative into the 1990s and may support General Banzer in the 1993 presidential election.

Historically, labor has been among Bolivia's most powerful institutions. Under the direction of the Central Obrera Boliviana (COB), labor was able to challenge the imposition of austerity measures while simultaneously obtaining concessions for the working classes. But years of struggle culminated pitifully in 1985 with the decimation of the COB when the government launched its new economic policy. Mass firings of mine workers, who constituted the backbone of organized labor in Bolivia, proved to be the COB's downfall. After five years of rebuilding, however, the COB appears to be making a slow comeback.

Finally, the military have been powerful both in government and behind the scenes. At the time of the transition to civilian government in 1982, the Bolivian armed forces were discredited by their institution's corruption, factionalism, and widespread *human rights abuses committed in the nearly twenty years of controlling state power. Democratic governments refused to investigate atrocities committed by the military; instead, they attempted to rebuild the institution without challenging the workings of the military. With U.S. military aid, Bolivian governments have satisfied demands from officers for better equipment and training. Moreover, the armed forces have taken on an active role in combating the drug trade in the Bolivian lowlands and coca leaf–producing valleys. Concern has been raised that this may serve to catapult the military back into politics in the near future. For the moment, however, the armed forces have sworn to uphold civilian rule and the constitution.

(See also DEMOCRATIC TRANSITIONS; LAND REFORM; MILITARY RULE; NATIONALIZATION; PRIVATIZATION.)

James Dunkerley, *Rebellion in the Veins: Political Struggle in Bolivia, 1952–1982* (London, 1984). James M. Malloy and Eduardo Gamarra, *Revolution and Reaction: Bolivia, 1964–1985* (New Brunswick, N.J., 1988).

EDUARDO A. GAMARRA

BOLSHEVIK REVOLUTION. See RUSSIAN REVOLUTION.

BOSNIA AND HERZEGOVINA. See YUGOSLAVIA.

BOTSWANA. See BLS STATES.

BOUNDARY DISPUTES. Except in the eastern half of the Arabian Peninsula, where the territory of Saudi Arabia joins the lands of Yemen, Oman, the United Arab Emirates, and Qatar, the nineteenth and early twentieth centuries witnessed the replacement of frontiers by boundaries. Everywhere else frontiers, which are zones of varying widths, were replaced by boundaries, which are lines. Unfortunately this improvement in the precise definition of national territory has not ended disputes associated with international boundaries, as the war following the Iraqi invasion of Kuwait in August 1990 readily attests. They exist in every continent except Australia, where there are instead boundary disputes between some of the states making up the federation.

The study of international boundary disputes provides an interdisciplinary focus for geographers, lawyers, and political scientists. Although there will be different approaches within and between disciplines, there is general agreement that there are four types of boundary disputes. Territorial disputes arise when one country claims adjoining land across the boundary because of some special quality that that area possesses. The qualities might relate, for example, to the history of the region, the population that occupies it, or its strategic character. The persistent dispute between Chile and Bolivia stems from the desire of the latter, landlocked country to regain access to the Pacific Ocean that was lost in 1879.

Positional disputes relate to some defect in the definition of the boundary. The Sino-Russian dispute over the island at the confluence of the Amur and Ussuri rivers in eastern Asia is based in the ambiguous description of their common boundary in the treaty of 1860. Other positional disputes occur when a river in which the international boundary is located changes its course suddenly, perhaps by cutting through the neck of a meander in its course. Such events bedeviled U.S.-Mexican relations along the Rio Grande until 1964, when a comprehensive treaty ended the uncertainty about the proper location of the boundary. In both territorial and positional disputes at least one side is arguing that the boundary should be moved either so that it can acquire territory to which it has a solid claim or so that the boundary will occupy the correct position fixed by an earlier treaty.

The other two kinds of boundary disputes can be solved without moving the line. Resource disputes occur when the boundary intersects some unitary resource, such as a lake or oil field, and the two neighbors disagree on how the resource should be exploited. In 1975 Bangladesh and India were involved in a resource development dispute when India built a barrage across the Ganges River, which reaches the sea on the coast of Bangladesh, in order to divert waters into the Hooghly River so that sediments silting the port of Calcutta could be flushed into the Bay of Bengal. Bangladesh was convinced that the scale of diversion proposed would adversely affect its coastal environments and its agricultural and fishing industries. The issue was resolved when India agreed to let a larger proportion of the Ganges' flow continue unimpeded to Bangladesh.

Functional boundary disputes occur when one country perceives that it is being adversely affected by rules and regulations being applied by its neighbor along the boundary and especially at crossing points. The detriment might be suffered by the people who live in the borderland or by the country's import and export industries. In the period between 1964 and 1977 there were twenty-four occasions when one African country closed its boundary, prompting strenuous objections, especially when the country affected was landlocked. Functional disputes can be solved by the designation of new regulations or the provision of exemptions from their operation in critical cases.

When scholars working on boundary disputes have decided into which category a particular dispute falls, the comprehensive analysis of the topic involves the following elements. First, it is necessary to identify the trigger action that persuaded the claimant country to initiate the dispute at that particular time. Some disputes, especially territorial disputes, last for long periods and pass through periods of intense activity and quiescence. The Iranian claim to three islands in the Persian Gulf was executed, at the expense of Sharjah, when British forces were withdrawn from the Gulf in November 1971.

Second, it is important to establish the aims of the government initiating the dispute. In most cases the desire will be for additional territory or relief from some administrative irritation connected with the boundary. However, apparently hopeless claims have been launched, to generate national cohesion when governments are facing serious domestic problems, for example, or for other reasons, as in the case of the Philippines' claim to North Sabah in 1960 to delay the inclusion of Sabah and Sarawak into Malaysia.

Third, the arguments deployed to justify the dispute and the policies designed to secure success must be identified and assessed. Finally the results of the dispute need to be cataloged. Do they relate directly to some aspect of the boundary or to some facet of bilateral relations or domestic politics?

Although it is rarely possible to predict when any particular boundary dispute will develop, there have been historical periods during the last two centuries when boundary disputes were more common than at other times. The acquisition of colonies by European powers in North America, Africa, and Asia prompted a rash of disputes as efforts were made to secure the best possible areas, sometimes with only imperfect knowledge of the human and physical geography of the regions involved. These unknown areas were often divided by straight lines or the course of a river or a watershed. The rectification of these lines once the area had been thoroughly explored created serious friction in the bilateral relations of Britain, France, and Germany. At the end of colonial periods boundary disputes will often erupt. In the 1820s, as Spanish rule was replaced by independent states in South America, disputes arose over the correct location of Spanish administrative boundaries, which were the lines of cleavage along which independence movements separated. In Africa in the 1960s, several African states found that colonial administrators had failed to correct evident positional problems on their boundaries.

In Europe the conclusions of wars have been marked by outbreaks of territorial claims by the victorious states against those defeated. The Congress of Vienna in 1815, the Congress of Berlin in 1878, the London Conference in 1913, and the Paris peace conferences in 1919 and 1945 were the events when territorial disputes were tackled and solved in large numbers.

Since 1945, when the United States laid claim to its continental margin, coastal states have made claims to a suite of maritime zones in addition to the long-standing territorial waters. The new areas consist of the continental margin and an exclusive economic zone. Because the latter zone is 200 nautical miles wide, adjacent coastal states and states separated by less than 400 nautical miles of sea have been faced with the need to fix common maritime limits. Whereas boundary disputes on land involve a boundary that already exists, maritime boundary disputes arise through overlapping claims to areas of the sea and seabed. Once the boundary is drawn, the dispute is settled; to date, the resulting boundary

has never been challenged by either party. There seem to be three main reasons for this. First, both states ensure that they have complete and detailed knowledge about the physical, resource, and strategic qualities of the seas and seabed to be divided. Second, the selected line is often a compromise between the two extreme claims. Third, provisions in the boundary treaty deal with questions of developing resources intersected by the line and settling any future disagreements that might arise over interpretation.

(See also DECOLONIZATION; GULF WAR; LAW OF THE SEA)

A. J. Day, ed., *Borders and Territorial Disputes* (Detroit, 1982). J. R. V. Prescott, *The Maritime Political Boundaries of the World* (New York, 1986). J. R. V. Prescott, *Political Frontiers and Boundaries* (London, 1987).

VICTOR PRESCOTT

BRAIN DRAIN. The debate about the benefits and damage of the brain drain, or the outflow of professional people trained in low-income countries to higher-income countries, has distinguished among three groups: the migrants, those they join, and those they leave behind. It is usually agreed that the first two groups gain, but controversy arises over the third.

On one side are those who point to benefits of the free movement of human beings. Above all, the migrating individuals and their families gain. In addition, migrants' contribution to knowledge is often greater abroad, where better facilities for work are available. This greater contribution to knowledge is often available to the whole world.

Occasionally migrant professionals return, after a period of self-improvement, to their own country; while away, they may send remittances to their family at home. And although they deprive their country of taxable capacity, the migrants relieve it of burdens such as educating their children. The home country may enjoy political benefits from having ex-nationals (if they have not been driven out), in positions of power and influence abroad. Worldwide living standards are improved by permitting talent to go to its highest-yielding activity, and equality is promoted by the weakening of monopoly positions.

Although this cosmopolitan line of reasoning has appeal, some qualifications are necessary. First, the home country has borne (some of) the costs of educating the migrants but loses the tax revenue from their incomes.

Second, there are intellectual as well as technical economies of scale, external economies, and complementarities. The emigration of leading professionals (e.g., teachers) can deprive those left behind of guidance and stimulus. There is also the loss of employment opportunities for less highly trained people, such as assistants.

Third, the problem is aggravated by the fact that

the mobility is partial. Trained and skilled people move, while the unskilled and semiskilled, on the whole, do not. Although it may be best to permit both skilled and unskilled people to move freely, it does not follow that any step toward greater freedom of movement is good. If the skilled can move and the unskilled cannot, it may be better also to restrict the movement of the skilled.

Fourth, possibly the most important impact of the brain drain, or rather of attempts to plug it, is the impact on internal income distribution. In order to prevent skilled people from leaving, salary differentials have to be raised, reinforcing an initial inegalitarian income distribution. This adds obstacles to national integration, and retarded development adds to the temptations of the brain drain. This creates additional incentives to perpetuate inequalities, and so on in a vicious circle.

Fifth, the external brain drain is matched by an internal drain: the reference group for the professionals who remain is the group of their peers in the rich countries. For example, doctors go to the cities to practice expensive, private, curative medicine instead of to rural areas to provide preventive health services.

(See also DEVELOPMENT AND UNDERDEVELOPMENT; INTERNATIONAL MIGRATION.)

Walter Adams, ed., *The Brain Drain* (New York, 1968).
PAUL STREETEN

BRAZIL. The largest and most populous country in South America, with 150 million inhabitants and enormous natural resources, by the early 1990s Brazil had become the world's tenth biggest economy. Its automobile, computer, and other manufacturing industries, although uncompetitive by international standards, are among the most developed in the *Third World. This impressive industrialization, though, masks a very uneven distribution of wealth and income that contributes to political divisiveness.

Brazil's political system, rooted in a strong and sometimes paternalistic state structure, has acted both as a creative force in the country's *development as a nation and as an obstacle to change. In various incarnations from colonial administration to monarchy, from early presidentialism to military authoritarianism, the aggregate values of the state apparatus have guided political decision making as much or more than any individual political actor or group of actors. Indeed, the state has rarely, if ever, ceded power to the majority.

Historical Background. Unlike any other Latin American country, Brazil was colonized by Portugal. In 1530, the Portuguese crown sent an expedition to establish fifteen captaincies to be administered by hereditary rulers. These local landowners enjoyed considerable autonomy from the Portuguese government in Lisbon until King João VI and his court were forced to flee to Brazil in 1808, fugitives from Napoleon's armies. Consolidation and centraliza-

tion of economic life in the colony resulted. In 1821, the king returned to Portugal, and the following year his son Pedro, the regent whom he had left behind, declared himself emperor of an independent Brazil.

Confrontations between Emperor Pedro I and the local Brazilian aristocracy over the degree of centralization became common occurrences. Indeed, it was one such clash—over the issue of slavery—which catalyzed Pedro's eventual downfall. The slave trade, which had begun in the mid-sixteenth century, was outlawed in 1850 and legal ownership of slaves was abolished in 1888. Growing discontent among the landed elites over this issue, as well as the emperor's administrative abilities and the prospect of his daughter Isabel taking the throne, provoked the creation of a political alternative: military leaders ousted the emperor in a bloodless coup in 1889 and ushered in Brazil's first attempt at republican government.

The political era that emerged after the monarchy, known as the "Old Republic," was characterized by a federalism in which two states, Minas Gerais and São Paulo, were first among equals. The elites of those areas—by custom, economic prowess, and geography—had grown close to the power center in the national capital at Rio de Janeiro. With the end of the monarchy and the beginning of the *política dos governadores* (polity of the governors), they were allowed to assume preeminent responsibility in fashioning the economic policies of the nation. In exchange, the leaders of the two dominant states agreed not to interfere in the internal politics of the other states. Political participation in the Old Republic remained in the hands of regional oligarchies. Although the immigration of non-Portuguese Europeans to Brazil had quickened following the abolition of slavery—with colonies of Swiss, Germans, and Italians settling principally in the country's south—the new peoples enjoyed few civil rights or privileges. Expanded participation in politics was only given force when an iconoclast from the country's deep south emerged to challenge the rules of the game.

When political bosses in Minas Gerais and São Paulo failed to agree on the presidential succession in 1930, the time was right for a renegade candidate to seize power amid the confusion. With the tacit support of the armed forces and the church, the Old Republic was dissolved and Getúlio *Vargas became provisional president.

A political populist as well as opportunist, Vargas succeeded in perpetuating his rule by skillfully using political institutions so long as they contributed to his designs and abandoning them when they did not. In 1934, delegates approved a new constitution and elected Vargas their first president. Three years later, Vargas ignored the constitution's one-term limit on the presidency, canceled the 1938 elections, and declared the *Estado Novo* (New State).

During the *Estado Novo,* Vargas concluded a consolidation of the patrimonial state. Labor, which had been occasionally organized since colonial times but never united in anything resembling a class consciousness, was successfully drawn under direct control. Political parties—few of which had survived by 1937—were not allowed to operate. Whatever remnant of the *política dos governadores* that might have existed was swallowed up in the central powers accorded to the presidency.

Although Vargas was able to rule the country as a virtual dictator for another six years, by 1943 there was considerable pressure among social elites and the military for a return to democratic government. Vargas acceded to the pressure and called elections for 1945, but when it looked like he would again subvert the electoral process, the military removed him from office.

Vargas would eventually return to the presidency for a final five-year term, although his legacy in political terms was largely concluded by the end of the *Estado Novo.* The central powers of the presidency, the weak and constantly shifting landscape of political parties, the co-optation and suppression of labor and other class-based movements, the consolidation of the patrimonial state in a national corporatist bureaucracy: these phenomena continue to channel, if not dictate, the progress of the Brazilian state today.

Postwar Politics. The end of the *Estado Novo* ushered in an era of ever-increasing military participation in national politics. Military candidates ran in every presidential election between 1945 and 1960, although only the first contender, Eurico Gaspar Dutra, ever won. The losers in the subsequent contests remained nominally on sidelines, but a military coup in 1954 and attempted coups in 1955 and 1961 presaged the eventual 1964 coup that installed a military regime for more than two decades.

In the years before that takeover, however, the country experienced a series of populist presidents: Vargas won election in 1950, followed by Juscelino Kubitschek in 1955 and Jahio Quadros in 1960. With no strong ideological movements and a weak party tradition, the presidents of the 1946 Republic tended to be little more than clientelist leaders, using the presidency to dole out favors to political supporters. Although social mobilization increased as the country's urban centers grew during this period, political participation remained firmly in the hands of elites, which used the state apparatus to their own political and economic advantage.

It was a challenge to the perquisites of those political and economic elites that spurred the military to break decisively with constitutional democratic rule in 1964. João Goulart, who had assumed the presidency following the untimely resignation of Quadros, was perceived by the traditional power centers as a reformer with a leftist bent. Before any major reform project even got under way, the military toppled his civilian regime. Commanders installed General Humberto Castello Branco as the first of five military presidents.

Although the ideological predilections of the armed forces were hardly homogenous throughout the military corps, the administrations between 1964 and 1985 were united in their determination to advance Brazilian economic development and to reorder (and at times brutally suppress) civil society to the extent necessary to sustain the economic project. Military leaders ruled by decree law, the so-called Institutional Acts.

Following an era of increasing repression under Castello Branco's two immediate successors, when the national Congress ceased to exist even as a rubber stamp for military directives, the armed forces began a program of *abertura* or political opening. The government reestablished habeas corpus protections, initiated a political amnesty, granted increased press freedoms, and laid the groundwork for popular elections of regional and local officials as well as a civilian president.

An important part of the *abertura* process was the contest between two political parties: the pro-military Partido Democrático Social (PDS) and the catch-all opposition Partido Movimento Democrático Brasileiro (PMDB). When the first direct elections were held in 1982, the PMBD won resounding victories in the important southern states. Encouraged by these results, the party united around the popular governor of Minas Gerais, Tancredo Neves, as its candidate for the presidency in 1985. It was aided by factional fighting within PDS, which culminated in the formation of a splinter party, Partido da Frente Liberal (PFL); this group threw its support to Neves, thus enabling him to win an electoral-college victory.

Neves, however, never took office. He died within weeks of his scheduled inauguration, leaving the vice president, José Sarney from the PFL, to become president. Since Sarney had been a military supporter until shortly before the election, he was unable to gain the full backing of the antimilitary forces. He also proved to be an inept leader and spent a good deal of his political capital fighting for a five-year term as opposed to the originally prescribed four years. The Sarney period saw public support for the traditional parties and politicians erode substantially. Thus, in the November 1989 presidential election, the two run-off candidates were political newcomers. Fernando Collor de Mello, wealthy former governor of a small northeastern state, advocated the neoliberal policies that were becoming increasingly popular in Latin America. Luis Ignacio ("Lula") da Silva, a well-known labor leader and candidate of the Partido dos Trabalhadores (PT), ran on a populist platform reminiscent of Brazil's past. In a highly polarized situation, Collor won a narrow victory, but governing proved difficult because he had no party to back him in Congress and had to improvise coalitions for each issue.

Political Economy. With its vast size, wealth of natural resources, and combination of tropical and temperate climates, during its entire history as an independent nation Brazil has had pretensions of being a world economic power.

From colonial times well into the twentieth century, the country's economy was driven by a steady flow of exports: sugar production, concentrated in the humid northeast, began as early as 1520 and thrived well into the seventeenth century; gold production took off with the discovery of major deposits in 1695 and, with diamond finds, dominated the export sector until the end of the eighteenth century; coffee production in the country's center-south emerged in the early nineteenth century. Although coffee fortunes were increasingly invested in industrial ventures, as late as the 1920s coffee still constituted seventy-five percent of Brazil's exports.

With the Great Depression of the 1930s, Brazil experienced difficulty in purchasing manufactured goods abroad and so began its first experiment with *import-substitution industrialization. The program was expanded after World War II as a new generation of economic planners sought to overcome the lagging expansion of primary product export markets with a major state-sponsored industrialization push. President Juscelino Kubitschek (1956–1961) captured the ethos of Brazilian economic pretensions in his promise to complete "Fifty Years of Progress in Five."

Between 1945 and 1962, Brazilian industrial production grew an average of eight percent per annum—although not without economic dislocations and major social costs. The economic incentives awarded to industrial producers effectively penalized the primary product sector, leaving agricultural producers and workers demoralized and vulnerable in the face of a soft world market. The attempts of the Quadros and Goulart regimes to reconcile these competing economic interests were further complicated by the frustration of a growing urban working class at the continuing social and political inequities in Brazilian life, and the determination of landowners to forestall any major income redistribution. The resulting fissures in political society led to the military takeover.

Fiscal and monetary discipline imposed during the military years, together with high rates of investment, paid off with impressive rates of economic growth. GDP rose at an annual average of 10.9 percent from 1968 through 1974, the industrial sector flourished (but at the expense of agriculture), and the country's foreign exchange reserves expanded from US$656 million in 1969 to US$6.417 billion in 1973. Despite inflation averaging seventeen percent during the same period, observers nonetheless refer to those years as the "economic miracle."

In the latter half of the 1970s, however, growth began to wane and inflation surged higher. Negative real interest rates and an overvalued currency put extreme pressure on the nation's *balance of payments. Rather than curtail imports and possibly undercut growth, economic planners decided to borrow abroad to finance the current account deficit.

When it came time to repay, Brazil was ill equipped to do so. The oil shocks of 1973 and 1979 had led to a worldwide economic slump, and demand for Brazilian exports had fallen. In addition, international banks had become extremely reticent about making new loans to Third World countries following Mexico's announcement in August 1982 that it could no longer service its foreign debt. The better part of the 1980s was spent seeking new ways out of the debt crisis in which Brazil found itself.

The external debt problems were combined with internal mismanagement as the Sarney government proposed various economic "packages" to deal with runaway inflation. Some innovative "heterodox" policies were put forward, but they all failed, helping to pave the way for the Collor victory in 1989. Collor's own policies were an odd mix of traditional statist-nationalist policies with attempts to reduce the role of the state and open the Brazilian economy to international forces. His lack of support in Congress further reduced his chances to return the country to the dynamic growth seen in the 1960s and 1970s.

Social Bases of Politics and Catalysts for Change. Amid the economic turmoil, political relations among various sectors found new dynamics during the 1980s. While the state retained preeminence as the broker of civil discourse, the reshaping, if not remaking, of major civil institutions outside the patrimonial state—organized labor, the church, and the military, in particular—is worth noting. Although none of these extrastate actors has sufficient autonomous power to reshape the civil society of modern Brazil on its own, each contends for public attention and national power, and each, working alongside the patrimonial state, stands to influence the shape of contemporary Brazil.

Beginning in 1979, with major strikes in the industrial heartland of São Paulo state, Brazilian labor came to win an increasing level of autonomy. Hamstrung since the Vargas years by labor laws that made the government the final arbiter of labor relations, by the early 1980s *independent* union leaders—especially Lula da Silva—were increasingly able to bargain directly with employers. Initially imprisoned for his activism, as generations of aspiring nonstate labor and political organizers had been, Lula came to symbolize a "New Unionism," in which independent labor syndicates could hold legitimacy and contend vociferously for economic power. Furthermore, the political gains in the quest for such power were subsequently consolidated into the Partido dos Trabalhadores, or Workers' Party, an organization remarkable for its relative cohesion amid a weak political party tradition.

The *Roman Catholic church, traditionally a social activist in Brazil, has faced challenges to its vitality from both within and without. Although historically it has been one of the most liberal churches in Latin America, the conservatization of the world church in the time of *John Paul II brought the installation in Brazil of clerical leaders more ideologically aligned with the papacy. The doctrine of *liberation theology, which found some of its most ardent proponents in Brazil, has been the object of broad censure. Leading Brazilian theologians have been silenced and church leaders stripped of their responsibilities. In addition, the church faces the ongoing doctrinal challenge of Afro-Brazilian sects, which mingle pagan religious rites with Catholic dogma, as well as the more recent, vigorous, and largely successful push of evangelical movements to win converts away from Rome.

While military officers maintain a low public profile with respect to the day-to-day operation of the Brazilian bureaucracy, considerable evidence can be adduced to show that the armed forces maintain as their prerogative a substantial influence over contemporary policy making. Military ministers from the army, navy, and air force continue to hold cabinet rank, and there is no civilian chief of the armed forces below the president. During the effort to draft a new constitution in 1987, military leaders made clear their desire that the new document retain provisions designating the armed forces as responsible for guaranteeing the normal operation of the executive, legislative, and judicial branches of the government.

Moving into the 1990s, Brazil seems caught between its powerful state, which has traditionally dominated both economic and political life, and a set of new international trends toward more emphasis on private business and autonomous political groups. Those opposing tendencies must be resolved in some way if the country is to move toward the world power status that its people have always sought.

(See also BUREAUCRATIC AUTHORITARIANISM; DEMOCRATIC TRANSITIONS; INTERNATIONAL DEBT; MILITARY RULE; U.S.–LATIN AMERICAN RELATIONS.)

Thomas E. Skidmore, *Politics in Brazil, 1930–1964* (New York, 1967). Thomas E. Skidmore, *The Politics of Military Rule in Brazil, 1964–1985* (New York, 1988). Werner Baer, *The Brazilian Economy: Growth and Development* (New York, 1989). Alfred Stepan, ed., *Democratizing Brazil: Problems of Transition and Consolidation* (New York, 1989). Riordan Roett, *Brazil: Politics in a Patrimonial Society* (New York, 1992).

RIORDAN ROETT
THOMAS SCHIERHOLZ

BRETTON WOODS SYSTEM. See FINANCE, INTERNATIONAL; INTERNATIONAL MONETARY FUND.

BRITAIN. By contrast to Germany, the states of Eastern and Central Europe, or the post-Soviet republics, Britain in the 1990s continues to enjoy a reputation for stability and continuity. Nevertheless, British politics and society have experienced some unsettling developments in the postwar period, and in both domestic and international terms difficult adjustments lie ahead.

In domestic terms, the premiership of Margaret *Thatcher from 1979 to 1990 marked a dramatic departure in the consensus politics that Britain's two leading parties (Labour and Conservative) had shared throughout the postwar period. Until she was abruptly replaced by John Major as Conservative Party leader and prime minister in November 1990, Thatcher challenged fundamental principles of British politics including the egalitarian ethos of the *welfare state, commitment to a full employment economy, an accepted role for trade unions in the formation of economic and social policy, a significant public sector economy based in nationalized industries, and state economic management to secure growth, stable prices, and desirable exchange rates and balance of payments through Keynesian demand management. *Thatcherism challenged both the policy agenda and the broader political ethos in Britain, advancing a neoliberalism and an "enterprise culture" that challenged the principles (but continued most of the policies) of the welfare state, preferred *monetarism to *Keynesianism, shifted the balance of resources from the public sector to the private sector through *privatization and the contracting out of municipal services, and, in addition, helped forge a *political culture that exalts individualism, selectivity, and competition.

In international terms, Britain has experienced far greater changes and a longer-term and perhaps more enduring transition. From hegemonic power in the nineteenth century, Britain has dropped toward the bottom of the second-level powers. Moreover, Britain's continuing reluctance to participate fully in the *European Community's agenda of economic and political integration heightens perceptions that there is more than geography to the United Kingdom's position as a European outsider. Many wonder what role Britain will enjoy in an increasingly powerful regional bloc dominated by Germany.

Thatcher set out to redraw the domestic political map as the geopolitical map of Europe was transformed. Occurring in tandem, these developments have contributed to increased tensions between social groups and vastly complicated party competition and electoral behavior. They have also raised fundamental questions about where Britain is (or should be) headed, and contributed an unexpected air of volatility to Britain, a nation-state held up traditionally as a model of a stable polity.

The Dilemmas of State Formation. As a shorthand, *Britain* refers to the United Kingdom of Great Britain and Northern Ireland, or UK, a territory of some 244,000 square kilometers (94,000 sq. mi.), comparable in size to Uganda or the Federal Republic of Germany (FRG) before unification. The equally common name, *Great Britain,* in law excludes *Northern Ireland. Although outsiders sometimes use *England* interchangeably with *Britain* or *UK,* as a state or nation-state the UK in fact comprises several culturally and historically separate countries or nations. Of the approximately 57 million persons residing in the UK in 1990, just over 47.5 million were English, slightly under 3 million were Welsh, just over 5 million were Scottish, and some 1.6 million lived in Northern Ireland.

Despite the longevity of Britain's constitutional order, dating from the Constitutional Settlement of 1688, complications remain with the identity of the nation-state. Although formal political divisions among England, Scotland, and Wales were resolved centuries ago, tensions flared far more recently, in the 1970s. Declining economic fortunes deepened the pattern of uneven development in regional and national terms within Britain, in which England prospered in relative terms, when compared with Scotland and Wales. The discovery of oil reserves off Scotland's northern coast increased Scottish demands for greater autonomy, and at the same time culturally based nationalism flared in Wales. Movements for devolution, the transferral of specified powers from the UK Parliament in Westminster to national bodies, gained considerable momentum, and the growth of national parties in Scotland (the Scottish National Party) and Wales (the Plaid Cymru) contributed to the realignment of the British party system and the weakening of the two-class, two-party (Labour and Conservative) model of British party competition.

The relationship between Northern Ireland and Britain remains far more complicated. Soon after the failed Easter Rebellion in 1916, Britain partitioned Ireland (in 1920): the six northern counties which make up Northern Ireland today were split from the remaining twenty-six counties which became the Irish Free State and later the Republic of *Ireland. The majority Protestant population of Northern Ireland is descended from English and Scottish settlers, dominates political and economic affairs, and endorses continued union with Britain (hence they are called *unionists*). The minority population of Northern Ireland are Catholic descendants from the original Irish inhabitants (like the vast majority in the Irish Republic), many of whom are nationalists who, in one form or another, want to sever or reduce ties with Britain and increase ties or unify with the Republic of Ireland (hence they are called *republicans*). The British government rushed troops to Northern Ireland in 1969, after Catholic demands for economic and political equality pro-

voked Protestant riots. Despite a series of efforts at negotiated agreements between the Northern Irish communities, the UK, and Ireland—including a series of much-anticipated, on-again, off-again talks beginning in the spring of 1991—the political deadlock endures and troops remain in Northern Ireland.

Thus, contemporary Britain has yet to resolve some fundamental problems linked to its formation as a nation-state. In addition to the complex of nationalist and religious pressures within the UK, Britain's imperial legacy and the historic role of the City of London (the financial district) in international finance continue to shape contemporary affairs. One legacy of empire, *decolonization, has contributed to a multiracial society in Britain, but black Britons whose roots go back to Britain's colonies face continued discrimination, violent attacks, and cultural isolation. A series of nationality and immigration acts have reduced the rights of former colonial subjects or current *Commonwealth citizens to residency in the UK, and Britain has witnessed the politicization of race, notably in the 1979 general election, in which Margaret Thatcher first became prime minister.

Another imperial legacy, governmental obsession through the 1960s with preserving the role of British sterling as a reserve and transaction currency in international exchange, led to a series of economic maneuvers that weakened the British economy. More generally, comparatively high rates of overseas investment and low rates of domestic investment, and the strength of finance as compared with domestic industry (notably regarding the ability of interests and institutions to influence governmental policy), have contributed to Britain's comparatively weak performance in the postwar period.

Finally, in geopolitical terms, Britain is still adjusting with some difficulty to its declining fortunes as a global power ever since World War I shattered its century-long dominance dating from the end of the Napoleonic Wars (the period called Pax Britannica). Declining influence has created *foreign policy dilemmas. How will Britain reconcile its European identity with its historic commitment as former colonial power within the Commonwealth and continued special relationship with the United States? Even what many would consider successes—an aggressive defeat of Argentina in the *Malvinas/Falklands War in 1982 and its determined stance as U.S. partner in the *Gulf War—suggest to others the relative futility of its foreign policy. The processes of adjustment are unfinished, with significant institutional and broader political ramifications.

Institutions and Political Behavior. Owing to its exceptional regime continuity, Britain must apply constitutional traditions and institutional arrangements that were developed in a very different age. In addition, the British Constitution remains a patchwork of common law, convention, statutory law, and works of authority rather than a single document of preeminent authority. Fundamental constitutional principles are few, and even they are subject to change induced both by historical processes of *modernization and by the strategic interpretations of governments.

First, by contrast to the United States or the FRG, which have federal systems of government, all powers are reserved for central government, and none for other tiers of government whether at the national level (e.g., Scotland, England, Wales) or at the level of municipalities (there are no states). The preeminent authority of central government was illustrated by the perfectly lawful, if surprising, abolition of the Greater London Council, or GLC (London's city government), and a set of six metropolitan county councils in 1986.

Second, in a system based on parliamentary supremacy (often called parliamentary sovereignty), no act of Parliament can be lawfully countermanded by any executive or judicial action. Because Britain is a constitutional monarchy, sovereignty rests with the Queen-in-Parliament (the formal term for Parliament), but the House of Commons, the lower, elected chamber of Parliament (whose members are referred to as members of Parliament, or MPs) is controlling. Bills not concerning taxation or budgetary matters may be amended by the unelected House of Lords (which can delay but not defeat legislation). Nevertheless, the preeminence of prime minister and cabinet in promulgating policy and presenting legislation, the process of forming a government (administration) after a general election which requires that the governing party possess a working majority in the Commons, and the power of party loyalty result in a very limited legislative function for the Commons.

In practice, Parliament no longer enjoys the power it wielded in the mid-nineteenth century (and still retains in principle) to withdraw confidence in governments by the defeat of critical legislation, leading to cabinet resignation or triggering immediate general elections. Despite recent structural changes, notably the revitalization of select (watchdog) committees since 1979, the balance of power remains with the executive. Paradoxically, despite its very circumscribed powers and the long period of Conservative governments beginning in 1979, the Lords has become more significant and querulous in recent years, serving as a lightning rod for anti-Thatcher rebellion, but ministers retain inordinate power.

Third, Britain operates under a system of fusion of powers: Parliament is the supreme legislative, executive, and judicial authority. The fusion is expressed most palpably in the cabinet, some twenty ministers selected by the leader of the victorious party in a general election. Normally, ministers are drawn from the ranks of MPs of the prime minister's party, although lords may be included. The pivot of the system, the cabinet bridges the legislative and executive functions of the state, is empowered with collective responsibility for government policy and may therefore act as a check on the "presidential" power of the prime minister, and retains legal responsibility for the conduct of state administrative agencies (although in practice responsibilities devolve increasingly on civil servants).

Thus, British politics operates by a fusion of legislature and executive expressed in the cabinet, with the prime minister much more than the first among cabinet equals but less autonomously powerful than the chief executive in a presidential system. The British chief executive is the head of government and leader of the party with a working majority in the Commons. Programmatically oriented and powerful (if perhaps not inspiring) parties still dominate the landscape of British politics, play a critical constitutional role in the formation of governments, and determine parliamentary behavior of MPs to a degree unimaginable in the United States.

Just as the term *parliamentary sovereignty* obscures the practical limits of its influence, the term *two-party system* which is commonly applied to British politics is somewhat misleading. It is true that two parties have competed for governance for a century and a half (although not the same two parties), and that since 1945 Conservative and Labour have monopolized the office of prime minister. With the Conservative Party's victory at the polls in April 1992, the Conservatives had won eight general elections and Labour six during the postwar period, and routinely divided ninety percent or more of the seats in the House of Commons.

Nevertheless, divisions within the two major parties and a changing roster of other parties—center, nationalist, environmental, and even neofascist—complicate the contemporary picture of party competition. For example, several ideological orientations have developed within the Conservative Party, and, not surprisingly, quite different interpretations of these divisions have also emerged. Some scholars stress the distinction between traditional paternalistic and hierarchical values and a modernizing current that emphasizes individualism and entrepreneurship. Others suggest that the party represents the interests of a class (the bourgeoisie) rather than the nation, and identify ideological currents with factions of capital (for example, financial versus manufacturing interests or domestic versus international business). Still other interpretations stress the distinction between "one-nation Tories" (consensus-oriented Conservatives committed to political regulation of the market, the principles of the welfare state, full employment, and the political integration of diverse class and social groups) and "two-nation Tories" (ideologically driven Conservatives who advance laissez-faire, reject the principles of comprehensive welfare provision and governmental responsibility for employment levels, assault trade union rights, and advance controversial and divisive policies on race and nationality).

For its part, throughout the 1970s, the Labour Party was increasingly torn by disputes over the relative independence of MPs from trade unionists, how candidates should be selected, and who should draft and approve the party programs and electoral manifestoes. These organizational disputes reflected powerful ideological differences about Britain's relationship to the European Community, the meaning of *socialism and social democracy in Britain, and whether the party should serve as a vehicle to represent the interests of the working *class (which in practice meant orienting policy toward white male laborers employed in manufacturing) or distance itself from the trade unions and move to the electoral center. By the early 1980s, the internal organizational and programmatic issues were for the most part resolved in favor of a centrist strategy, and under Neil Kinnock's leadership (1983–1992) Labour moved in a decidedly pragmatic direction.

Nevertheless, Labour's relative calm occurred only after the disputes resulted in a breakaway centrist party, the Social Democratic Party (SDP), which was launched in 1981. Through the 1987 general election, the SDP was electorally significant: it helped press Labour toward the center; it formed an alliance with Britain's long-standing center party, the Liberals, which reinvigorated debate and challenged the two-party system; and the SDP/Liberal alliance enjoyed considerable electoral success, gaining 25.4 percent of the popular vote in 1983 and 22.6 percent in 1987. Early in 1988, most of the SDP merged with the Liberal Party to form the Social and Liberal Democratic Party (now called the Liberal Democrats, or LD), and the remaining portion of the SPD which refused merger dissolved in June 1990.

Britain's political center also includes a environmental party formed in 1973, the Green Party, which after a long period of political invisibility burst on the scene with a quite unexpected showing of fifteen percent in the 1989 elections to the European Parliament. Party competition in Britain also includes a neofascist and xenophobic party (the National Front) which peaked in the late 1970s in electoral terms but remains a cultural force, and a host of nationalist parties: the Scottish National Party (SNP), founded in 1934; the Plaid Cymru, which dates from 1925; and a set of parties in Northern Ireland with denominational and either Irish nationalist or pro-English (unionist) appeal (except for the Alliance, which includes Catholics and Protestants).

In the end, Britain is far from a two-party system. Parties other than Conservative and Labour have played an increasingly important role in setting political agendas, and only once (1979) in the six general elections between 1974 and 1992 did a combination of center and nationalist parties fail to take a fifth of the vote. Moreover, as many have suggested, different regions in the UK involve different two-party competitions: Conservative-Labour competition in English urban and northern seats; Conservative–center party competition in England's rural and southern seats; and Labour-nationalist competition in Welsh and Scottish seats.

Britain in the 1990s. With Thatcher gone, in the early 1990s Britain is in the midst of a more modest transition. Eager to change the ethos of government and party and to jettison or soften unpopular and divisive policies—the anti-EC stance, the much-reviled community charge (or "poll tax"), market-based reforms in the National Health Service—Major's premiership nonetheless continues critical elements of Thatcher's project (privatization, welfare retrenchment, and the enterprise culture). Meanwhile, the modernized and pragmatic Labour Party, which eagerly awaited the election it lost in April 1992, must once again face difficult choices under the new leadership of John Smith. Whatever its decisions and the moderating influence of John Major, the policy agenda and the deeper political-cultural legacy of Thatcherism will continue to shape British politics throughout the 1990s.

(See also CONSERVATISM; GREEN PARTIES; IMPERIALISM; INTERNATIONAL POLITICAL ECONOMY; LIBERALISM; NATIONALISM; RELIGION AND POLITICS.)

Keith Middlemas, *Politics in Industrial Society: The Experience of the British System since 1911* (London, 1979). Samuel H. Beer, *Britain against Itself: The Political Contradictions of Collectivism* (New York, 1982). Peter A. Hall, *Governing the Economy: The Politics of State Intervention in Britain and France* (New York, 1986). Joel Krieger, *Reagan, Thatcher and the Politics of Decline* (New York, 1986). Bob Jessop et al., eds., *Thatcherism* (Cambridge, U.K., 1988). Peter Riddell, *The Thatcher Decade* (Oxford, 1989). Stuart Hall and Martin Jacques, eds., *New Times: The Changing Face of Politics in the 1990s* (London, 1990).
JOEL KRIEGER

BRUNEI. Brunei, or Brunei Darussalam (Abode of Peace), became an independent nation on 1 January 1984. Once a sprawling empire, but threatened with extinction in the nineteenth century, this tiny state of 5,788 square kilometers (2,226 sq. mi.) on the northwestern portion of the island of Borneo has survived under British protection since 1888. After World War II, the rapid increase in wealth from the petroleum industry, the British desire to withdraw, and unpleasant experiences with mass political parties—notably an abortive revolt in 1962—led to the entrenchment of royal absolutism during the reign (1950–1967) of Sultan Omar Ali Saifuddin III.

In 1967, Omar abdicated in favor of his son, Hassanal Bolkiah. On independence day in 1984, Brunei emerged as an absolute monarchy with a ministerial form of government in which members of the royal family and the Malay nobility *(pengiran)* were given key portfolios. Very little has changed since then. (The Brunei National Democratic Party, permitted since 1985, was dissolved in 1988 when it became too vocal in demanding reforms.) The sultan maintains his power through an alliance with the nobility by appeasing economically the Malays, who form sixty percent of a population of 230,000, and by invoking the precepts of the Malay monarchy and *Islam, both of which call for unquestioned loyalty to the ruler.

The government has benefited by having been able to install a *welfare state as a result of the rapid development of the petroleum industry. Brunei today has accumulated over US$25 billion in reserves, and although petroleum reserves may last only another thirty years, income from foreign investment is sufficient to maintain the welfare state for a long time beyond that. The benefits, however, accrue mainly to the Malays rather than to the Chinese, who make up twenty percent of the population but are considered noncitizens.

Given past trends, the policy of keeping the Malays economically happy but politically starved may not last forever. The monarchy is apprehensive about a recurrence of political unrest. An additional stimulus to discontent is the extravagance of the royal family and the fact that there is no distinction between the private purse of the sultan and state revenues. The sultan has surrounded himself with extensive security forces including the Royal Brunei Armed Forces (about 3,500 strong), the Royal Brunei Police, the Gurkha Reserve Unit (900), and the British Army Gurkha Battalion (1,000). Evolutionary change might be encouraged by the educated elite and the technocrats who are becoming increasingly powerful in the civil service.

Brunei's main fear externally is encroachment by its larger neighbors, especially Malaysia and Indonesia. To some extent it has immunized itself against external threat by becoming a member in 1984 of the *Association of Southeast Asian Nations (ASEAN), the Organization of the Islamic Conference (OIC), and the UN. More important, since 1987 it has sought to play a more dynamic role in ASEAN economies. Its interest-free loan of US$100 million to Indonesia in 1987 gave Brunei the greatest unwritten guarantee of all for its security.

D. S. Ranjit Singh, *Brunei 1839–1983: The Problems of Political Survival* (Singapore, 1984). David Leake, Jr., *Brunei: The Modern Southeast-Asian Islamic Sultanate* (Kuala Lumpur, 1990).

D. S. Ranjit Singh

BUDDHISM. The term *Buddhism* is derived from the title of the founder of the tradition, the Buddha, meaning "the Enlightened One." From its beginnings in north India in the fifth century B.C.E. as a mendicant/monastic-based religion Buddhism spread throughout the rest of Asia during the early centuries of the present era, becoming a major cultural, social, economic, and political force. In many cases Buddhism broadened local, animistically defined conceptions of political leadership. In particular, it formulated classical conceptions of kingship in the Indianized states of *Sri Lanka, Myanmar (*Burma),

*Thailand, *Laos, and *Cambodia. The Buddhist worldview legitimated the king as maintainer of the political, economic, social, and moral orders. The historical model for the mythic Buddhist world ruler was the great Indian monarch Asoka (third century B.C.E.), who established hegemony over virtually the entire Indian subcontinent. The quality of later Buddhist rulers—Sinhalese, Burmese, Thai, Lao—was measured by the idealized rule of this strong, righteous, benevolent monarch who, according to the Buddhist chronicles, created a welfare state dedicated to the pursuit of religious and humanitarian goals. This ideal has also been operative in the development of the modern nation-state, and still functions as a moral norm for political leadership.

In *China, Korea, and *Japan Buddhism competed with *Confucianism for influence in defining policy as well as influencing court politics. By the end of the ninth century in China the political and economic power of Buddhist monasteries led to an attempt to disestablish the tradition; in eighth-century Japan the disruptive political and military power of the Buddhist monasteries in the hills surrounding the ancient city of Nara prompted the emperor to move the capital to Kyoto; and by the thirteenth century *Tibet had become a Buddhist theocratic state. In short, Buddhism was a major factor in the historical development of the classical states in virtually all mainland South, Southeast, Central, and East Asian countries. Its worldview and its institutions have both legitimated and challenged traditional political structures and statuses. While various Buddhist religious ideals, e.g., nirvana, do not fit comfortably with power politics, throughout the centuries Buddhism has generally supported the state and been supported by it. In the twentieth century this traditional symbiotic relationship has been evolving and, in some cases, undergoing dramatic changes.

The fortunes of Buddhism in various Asian countries have been determined by three major factors: the policies of political regimes, economic and social change, and educational and cultural transformation. Buddhism played a major role in the nationalist resistance to Western colonialism in Sri Lanka and Burma in the late nineteenth and early twentieth centuries. In both cases Buddhism fueled pride in national identity. In Sri Lanka, S. W. R. D. Bandaranaike won election as prime minister in 1957 on a Buddhist ticket. His victory was arguably a key factor in the development of the chauvinistic Buddhist fundamentalism which has been such a potent political force in Sri Lanka's racial strife since the mid-1980s. In Burma, U Nu's attempt to create a Buddhist state in the decade after the end of World War II led to his ouster in 1962 by his colleague, General Ne Win. Ne Win's road to Burmese socialism has been an economic disaster. The government's recent attempts to bolster Buddhism seem to be a ploy to win support for an unpopular regime.

In *Vietnam Buddhist protest against the Diem regime as a "Catholic police state" contributed to Diem's downfall in 1963. The creation of a Unified Buddhist church in 1964 and the Buddhist effort to forge a middle path between policies of China, the Soviet Union, and the United States proved to be politically naive and ineffective. In Thailand support of Buddhism has been a major element in the Thai government's efforts to fashion various nation-building programs ranging from hill tribe resettlement to rural development. A counterpoint to Japan's secular political and economic climate is the Kometo Party's affiliation with the Nichiren Shoshu sect of Japanese Buddhism.

Politically repressive states have undermined Buddhist institutions as in the case of *Mao's China and Pol Pot's Cambodia, although they have also supported them as in the case of Ne Win's Myanmar. Mao and Pol Pot saw Buddhism in traditional Marxist terms as a justification of class exploitation and, therefore, as something to be attacked or, in the extreme case of Cambodia, to be destroyed. Buddhist leaders in Tibet have been in exile in India since the Chinese occupation of that country in 1959. The Dalai Lama has appealed to Western democracies to exert pressure on China to stop what he considers to be the cultural genocide of his country. In 1980 Ne Win created a national organizational structure for Burmese Buddhism which provided more state support for Buddhism. At the same time, the government has exercised greater control over Buddhist institutions. Recalcitrant Buddhist monks, especially in the Mandalay area, resisted the Burmese military regime in 1989 and 1990. They were arrested and imprisoned.

Classical Asian Buddhism defined itself institutionally in relationship to the monarchical state, on the one hand, and a village, agricultural economy on the other. Buddhism has had some difficulty in redefining itself in a modern nation-state, urban, increasingly industrialized, world-market economic environment. Buddhist leaders have sought to create a viable social ethic which speaks to such a modern environment. Western-educated laypersons have played an important role in redefining Buddhist thought for the modern world. As a consequence, in the monastic-oriented Buddhist countries of Southeast Asia, the central place of the monk is being challenged. Furthermore, as increasing attention is being devoted to such issues as Buddhism and race relations, Buddhism and peace, Buddhism and nuclear development, Buddhism and the destruction of the environment and so on, critics argue that the specifically religious orientation of Buddhism is at risk. Yet a new international Buddhist leadership is emerging—both lay and monastic—which is fashioning a relevant Buddhist spirituality rooted in personal disciplines like meditation coupled with a Buddhist social ethic focused on particular economic, social, and political issues. Generally speaking, this international "engaged Buddhism" has been critical of the exploitation of the *Third World by Western nations. Its proponents have argued for balanced, humane, and less exploitative forms of development which are more respectful of the cultural, religious, and natural environments of Asian countries. Currently, this critical role appears to be Buddhism's most important contribution to the political and economic climates not only of Asia but also of the West.

(See also RELIGION AND POLITICS; SECULARIZATION.)

Heinz Bechert and Richard Gombrich, eds., *The World of Buddhism* (New York, 1984). Joseph H. Kitagawa and Mark D. Cummings, eds., *Buddhism and Asian History* (New York, 1989).

DONALD K. SWEARER

BUKHARIN, Nikolai Ivanovich. Born in Moscow, Nikolai Ivanovich Bukharin (1888–1938) joined the Bolshevik Party in 1906 after participating in the revolutionary events of the year before. In 1917 he was one of the leaders of the Bolshevik party organization in Moscow. Shortly after the Bolshevik takeover in October 1917, Bukharin became one of the leaders of the "Left Communists," who opposed *Lenin over industrial policy and especially over the failure to continue the war with Germany. Bukharin soon returned to the fold and took over the editorship of the party newspaper, *Pravda*, a post he retained throughout the 1920s.

During this period, Bukharin became the chief theorist of the *New Economic Policy (NEP) introduced in 1921. Bukharin saw NEP as a strategy for managing the transition to socialism in a peasant country. NEP was based on the realization that the market was the only available mechanism for managing economic relations with millions of scattered single-owner peasant farms. Relying on Lenin's 1923 article "On Cooperation," Bukharin argued that the cooperatives could be used to transform peasant agriculture gradually by appealing to the peasant's direct material interest. In this way the market would prepare the ground for its self-negation. In 1925, he wrote: "How will we be able to draw [the peasant] into our socialist organization? . . . We will provide him with material incentives as a small property-owner. . . . On the basis of this very same economic growth, the peasant will be moved along the path of a transformation of both himself and his enterprise into a particle of our general state socialist system."

During the NEP period, Bukharin was a political ally of *Stalin and served as the polemical heavy artillery against the leaders of the opposition within the Bolshevik Party, especially *Trotsky, Evgenii Preobrazhenskii, Grigorii Zinoviev, and Lev Kamenev. In the late twenties, however, when Stalin broke with NEP and moved toward collectivization and breakneck industrialization, Bukharin continued to defend the policy. Stalin quickly branded him a "right deviationist." Because of his concern for party unity, Bukharin never took his case beyond the confines of high party institutions such as the Central Committee. The ensuing struggle was sharp but short and ended in Bukharin's complete political defeat.

Bukharin later admitted his errors, and in 1934 he was allowed to become editor of the government newspaper, *Izvestia*. Soon thereafter, however, he fell victim to Stalin's murderous assault on the Bolshevik elite, and in March 1938 he confessed his guilt in one of the last great public trials of the Stalin era. (Some analysts have argued that Bukharin managed to use his confession to deliver a veiled indictment of Stalin.) The court found Bukharin guilty of high treason, and he was immediately executed.

In the early years of the *Gorbachev era, when the reforms were still portrayed as a return to *Leninism, Bukharin was regarded by many reform-minded intellectuals almost as the patron saint of *perestroika. In 1988, Bukharin was officially cleared of all charges and posthumously readmitted into the party. He operated as a powerful symbol not only because of his reputation as a defender of NEP but also because he was widely viewed as a representative of the best aspects of the Bolshevik tradition, and his execution by Stalin gave him an aura of martyrdom. Efforts by reformers to portray Bukharin as a prophet of market socialism were less successful, for Bukharin clearly meant what he said about the market negating itself.

Bukharin's large literary output includes popularizations of Marxist and Bolshevik theory, analyses of developments in the capitalist world, discussions of literary figures, theses on science and technology, and many other topics. In the final analysis, however, his primary importance rests on his role as a spokesman for the Soviet NEP period, with all its hopes and contradictions.

(See also COMMUNIST PARTY OF THE SOVIET UNION; RUSSIAN REVOLUTION; SOVIET UNION; STALINISM.)

Nikolai Bukharin, *Selected Writings on the State and the Transition to Socialism*, ed. Richard B. Day (New York, 1982). Nikolai Bukharin, *Put' k sotsializmu* (Novosibirsk, 1990).

LARS T. LIH

BULGARIA. The liberation of Bulgaria from Turkish control by the Russian Army in 1878 and the arrival of the Red Army in August 1944 set the parameters for a relatively favorable post–World War II experience with the *Soviet Union. Popular russophile attitudes and the autonomous development of an extraordinarily radical Agrarian government under Alexander Stamboliski, which ruled from 1919 until it was overthrown by an explicitly fascist coup in 1923, explain broad popular support for a Soviet model. The Bulgarian Communist Party (BCP)

in alliance with the surviving radical splinter of the Agrarian Party set about establishing a comprehensive set of Soviet-type political, economic, and social institutions.

Starting from a particularly low material and cultural level as well as unfavorable resource and energy endowments, Bulgaria achieved relatively dynamic and successful growth within Soviet forms. Comprehensive state ownership and physical central planning characterized the rapidly expanding urban, industrial core. The rural economy was collectivized in a manner that led to rapid mechanization, high rural incomes, and generally good results, aided by effective integration of the family garden plots with the collective sector.

Fast structural transformation, rapid growth in incomes, and improvement in quality and quantity of consumer goods availability during the 1945–1975 period produced a widespread view that the country was well governed and little pressure for economic or political reform. Less satisfactory economic results in the following decade and severe problems from 1983 to 1985 were accompanied by rising political discontent. Bulgaria was deeply committed to the *Council for Mutual Economic Assistance (CMEA) bilateral trade patterns, especially the Soviet Union as its major market for manufactured and agricultural output and principal source of raw materials. The decay of trade relationships beginning in the Andropov period sharply depressed Bulgarian economic performance. Soviet trade retrenchment after 1986 compounded the Bulgarian problem and it began to borrow heavily abroad. A crisis atmosphere developed in which mass expulsion of the Turkish minority took place.

The political effects of *perestroika and glasnost were late in arriving in Bulgaria, but struck with particular force since the collapse of the coordinating function of the BCP parallel hierarchy occurred in the context of already-existing economic difficulties. The absence of historical anti-Soviet feeling and the successful creation of a political order following after that of the *Communist Party of the Soviet Union (CPSU) contributed to the lack of an experienced and coherent opposition. The political crisis in the fall of 1989 produced the abrupt resignation of Todor Zhivkov after thirty-five years in power but left Bulgaria with a leadership vacuum when no alternative structures of coordination and control emerged. From a position of relative prosperity and seemingly successful development, Bulgarians suddenly faced the possibility of real deprivation at the same time that the creation of entirely new forms of economic organization was required.

The strong showing of the renamed Bulgarian Socialist Party (BSP) in the June 1990 parliamentary elections and the lack of a coherent program by the sixteen-party United Democratic Front (UDF) suggest little support for a complete recasting of the system regardless of what happens elsewhere in

Eastern Europe. After a six-month political impasse, a coalition government dominated by the BSP and the Agrarians (eight and four ministers, respectively) was formed in December 1990 with an unaffiliated prime minister, Dimitar Popov, joined by three UDF and four independent members. New elections in November 1991 saw the BSP share of the vote fall to thirty-four percent, slightly less than the coalition total for the UDF. UDF Prime Minister Filip Dimitrov governs in tenuous coalition with the Turkish minority party, which drew barely seven percent of the vote but is the only other participant in Parliament. The narrow 54–46 margin for the UDF candidate Zhelyu Zhelev over the BSP candidate in the January 1992 presidential election showed that the socialist party has long-term strength. Although pressures for smaller-scale production, decentralization, and marketization are strong, they are not necessarily consistent with Western understandings of *privatization, and the contours of postcommunist political and economic development in Bulgaria remain uncertain.

(See also COLLECTIVIZATION; COMMUNIST PARTY STATES; NINETEEN EIGHTY-NINE; SOVIET–EAST EUROPEAN RELATIONS.)

R. J. McIntyre, *Bulgaria: Politics, Economics and Society* (London, 1988). R. J. Crampton, *A Short History of Modern Bulgaria* (Cambridge, U.K., 1989).

ROBERT J. MCINTYRE

BUREAUCRATIC AUTHORITARIANISM. The concept of bureaucratic authoritarianism arose from the study of major episodes of authoritarian rule in South America between the 1960s and the 1980s: Brazil from 1964 to 1985, Argentina from 1966 to 1973 and later from 1976 to 1983, Chile from 1973 to 1990, and Uruguay from 1973 to 1985. This body of analysis is closely identified with the writings of Guillermo O'Donnell.

Bureaucratic *authoritarianism is a type of *military rule often interpreted as novel in relation to the earlier history of Latin America. It was generally led by the military as an institution, in contrast to the personalistic rule of individual officers. Rotation in the presidency among military leaders was a common, though not universal, trait. This form of rule has been interpreted as distinctively bureaucratic because national leadership was dominated by individuals who had risen to prominence not through political careers but through bureaucratic careers in large public and private organizations, including international agencies and transnational corporations. Decision-making styles among these leaders were commonly technocratic.

This bureaucratic, technocratic orientation was generally accompanied by intense repression, which in most of the cases reached levels unprecedented in the region. Repression was unleashed against the *labor movement, political parties associated with labor, and other social sectors whose prior mobilization had seemed to threaten the existing political and economic system.

The phenomenon of bureaucratic authoritarianism commanded wide analytic interest, in part because its emergence seemed to contradict the hypothesis that socioeconomic *modernization might be supportive of *democracy. In terms of per capita indicators, Argentina, Chile, and Uruguay were among the most modernized countries in Latin America. Brazil was less modernized on a per capita basis, yet in absolute terms it had a large modern sector and its economic difficulties prior to the 1964 coup were in important respects those of an industrial economy. The appearance in these countries of an authoritarianism of unprecedented harshness thus challenged this earlier hypothesis.

Analysts explained this outcome by suggesting that the process of modernization had two consequences which collided: it intensified certain types of economic problems, and it augmented the capacity of the popular classes to resist an important spectrum of proposed solutions to these problems. It was argued that this collision increased pressures to inaugurate bureaucratic authoritarianism, both as a means of pursuing these proposed solutions and of controlling resistance to them.

The rise of authoritarianism must be seen against the backdrop of abiding dilemmas in Latin American development: serious inequalities, which governments periodically sought to remedy through redistributive policies; inefficient industrial structures, sheltered from international competition by a high level of state protection which was strongly supported by a larger framework of economic nationalism; and the contradictory role of labor movements that favored redistribution and protection, were able to confront governments when they abandoned such policies, and yet were often unable to enter coalitions that provided a stable basis for pursuing these policies.

The cases of bureaucratic authoritarianism shared a common approach to addressing these dilemmas. This approach included: 1) postponing redistribution, or even reversing it, in order to foster economic growth; 2) seeking to create a more efficient, internationally competitive economy and cultivating international economic actors as partners in the development model; and 3) attempting to control or destroy the labor movement, which in the past had often undermined these other policies. This policy mix had long been an option on the Latin American development agenda, and the initial success experienced by some of these new governments in implementing these policies commanded great attention, evoking both condemnation and praise.

The Concept. Bureaucratic authoritarianism has thus been understood as a form of bureaucratic and technocratic military rule that seeks to curtail popular mobilization and is built on a political coalition and a policy orientation that entails strong ties to international economic actors. It contrasts with *fascism, which is mobilizational and nationalistic. It lacks the comprehensive domination of *totalitarianism, notwithstanding the scope of repression in Chile and Uruguay, as well as Argentina in the 1970s. As a subtype of authoritarian rule, it may be distinguished from other subtypes: populist authoritarianism, which promotes popular mobilization rather than demobilization; and traditional authoritarianism, which is found prior to any extensive popular mobilization.

As occurs with many concepts, scholars debated both the fit with the initial cases and the extension to other cases. In response to the evolving interpretations of the original four countries, analysts refined their definitions, and the question arose whether the concept really corresponded to these cases. A useful way to view this debate is to understand bureaucratic authoritarianism as an analytic construct referring to a syndrome of attributes, all of which may not be present in every case.

In the debate over extension to other cases, one candidate was Peru, which experienced institutional military rule around the same time—between 1968 and 1980. Yet many analysts interpret Peru, especially up to 1975, as a case of populist authoritarianism, owing to the scope of popular mobilization. The inclusion of Mexico was suggested in light of its conjunction of authoritarianism and technocratic policy-making. However, it is misleading to add Mexico because organized labor was not excluded from the country's governing coalition and because the Mexican system during this period was not the outgrowth of an immediate prior polarization and was not a military regime.

With reference to non–Latin American cases, the concept has been applied to authoritarian Spain; to Poland, Hungary, and Austria during the interwar period; to Greece in the late 1960s and early 1970s; and to authoritarian experiences in East and Southeast Asia and in the Middle East. In these cases, many traits that Latin American specialists associate with the original four countries may not be present, and hence the concept has served more generically to refer to modern (rather than traditional) authoritarianism that has a major bureaucratic dimension.

Explaining the Rise of Bureaucratic Authoritarianism. Economic issues were a contributing condition in the original four cases, though not a sufficient explanation. An initial hypothesis suggested that military and economic elites established bureaucratic authoritarianism with the specific goal of promoting long-term economic and political stability, which in turn would promote the vertical integration ("deepening") of the economy, i.e., increase the domestic production of industrial inputs. Although this specific hypothesis was not well supported, the broader set of economic priorities discussed above—within which vertical integration was sometimes an element—did represent both a source of pressure, and

(for some actors) a political opportunity, for inaugurating bureaucratic authoritarianism. A global process of economic internationalization reinforced these economic priorities, and hence also the incentives for this new form of rule.

Three other contributing conditions merit note. One is the demonstration effect of the opposition movements, social protests, and new alternatives on the left that arose in Western Europe, the Communist world, and the Americas in the 1960s and early 1970s. In Latin America, this demonstration effect was intensified by the emergence of socialist Cuba. The survival of a socialist state in the region dramatically extended the political horizon of the Latin American Left, and combined with the larger international context of political ferment, it played a role in escalating opposition and protest in the original four countries. This escalation also fueled conservative suspicions of popular mobilization, thereby intensifying polarization and subsequent repression.

Second, the structure of domestic politics had an impact. Its role can be seen in the contrast between the four cases discussed above and the experience of Venezuela and Mexico. Venezuela had a high level of modernization in per capita terms, and Mexico had one of the largest modern sectors in Latin America. In light of the modernization arguments noted above, these two countries might have experienced bureaucratic authoritarianism yet they did not. This occurred partly because during an earlier period in Mexico and Venezuela, a cohesive political center had been constituted that commanded an electoral majority and incorporated organized labor. In the subsequent period of crisis and polarization, this broad center provided a basis for stable rule and mitigated some of the difficulties experienced in Argentina, Brazil, Chile, and Uruguay—none of which had formed an equivalent centrist bloc.

Third, in Venezuela, and in Mexico late in the period under discussion, this political resource was supplemented by an important economic resource: massive oil revenues, which gave the state greater capacity to address distributional issues and hence may have reduced pressure for the measures entailed in bureaucratic authoritarianism.

Demise and Impact. As of the early 1990s, bureaucratic authoritarianism had disappeared in South America. Various factors contributed to this outcome. First, many Latin American countries have had difficulty establishing stable, legitimate political rule and have experienced long-term cycles of alternation between competitive and authoritarian regimes. Hence, this disappearance is part of a recurring pattern, the causes of which remain a matter of scholarly debate. Second, damaging tensions emerged within bureaucratic-authoritarian rule, for instance, between the internationalization promoted by the economic model and the *nationalism of the military and of other sectors capable of mounting serious opposition. Third, severe economic problems, experienced throughout the region as part of the *international debt crisis, helped discredit authoritarianism. Finally, domestic and international protest against *human rights abuses, and somewhat later, the demonstration effect of a worldwide process of democratization, further debilitated authoritarian rule.

What was the impact of this authoritarian experience? The economic record is diverse. Notwithstanding ongoing economic difficulties, Brazil unquestionably saw a dramatic advance toward a modern industrial economy. In Chile a far more open economy was created, a transformation which a subsequent democratically elected government sought to build upon, not reverse. Argentina, by contrast, produced dramatic failures. The post-1966 government achieved initial economic success and then collapsed in an explosion of social protest. The post-1976 government imposed far more draconian economic measures and repression, yet it was unable to overcome a myriad of economic difficulties and left a deeply troubled economy. Uruguay experienced a revival of economic growth in the 1970s, reversing two decades of stagnation. These gains eroded in the early 1980s, however, owing to the combined effects of internal policy failure and the larger debt crisis.

Although the political record is likewise diverse, in two important respects the political legacies are convergent. Among substantial sectors of the population, the experience of preauthoritarian polarization and crisis, followed by the trauma of authoritarian rule, led to a greater appreciation of electoral democracy. In addition, the experience of this cycle of authoritarianism—along with the debt crisis, other economic difficulties, and later the collapse of socialism in Eastern Europe and the Soviet Union— lowered developmental expectations and eroded the credibility of socialist and progressive political alternatives in these four countries. Consequently, in the aftermath of bureaucratic authoritarianism, there was evidence of greater support for democracy and a reduced likelihood of any immediate renewal of polarization.

(See also DEVELOPMENT AND UNDERDEVELOPMENT.)

Guillermo O'Donnell, *Modernization and Bureaucratic-Authoritarianism: Studies in South American Politics*, Politics of Modernization Series No. 9, Institute of International Studies, University of California, Berkeley (Berkeley, Calif., 1973). David Collier, ed., *The New Authoritarianism in Latin America* (Princeton, N.J., 1979). Karen L. Remmer and Gilbert W. Merkx, "Bureaucratic-Authoritarianism Revisited," with a reply by O'Donnell, *Latin American Research Review* 17, no. 2 (1982): 3–50. Guillermo O'Donnell, *Bureaucratic Authoritarianism: Argentina, 1966–1973, in Comparative Perspective* (Berkeley, Calif., and Los Angeles, 1988). Ruth Berins Collier and David Collier, *Shaping the Political Arena: Critical Junctures, the Labor Movement, and Regime Dynamics in Latin America* (Princeton, N.J., 1991).

DAVID COLLIER

BUREAUCRATIC POLITICS. A term that came into vogue in the late 1960s in American political science, *bureaucratic politics* has become an accepted concept for the analysis of *foreign policy decision-making. The "bureaucratic politics model" purports to explain how bureaucracies affect both the formulation and implementation of a state's foreign policy. Proponents of the model claim that bargaining among foreign policy bureaucracies is the key to understanding a state's foreign policy output. Critics of the model claim that a focus solely on bureaucratic conflict is insufficient to explain a state's foreign policy, although such behavior must be taken into account.

At the outset, it would be absurd to deny either that bureaucracies exist or that they have influence. The modern *state is, above all else, the bureaucratic state. That is, bureaucracies are essential to both domestic and foreign policies. The earliest student of bureaucratic behavior, Max *Weber, applauded the bureaucratic mode of political organization as the most advanced and the form best suited to the administration of complex societies. Selection for a position within a bureaucracy would come through testing and merit, not favoritism or connections. Decisions would be made on the basis of expertise, not personal whim. Behavior would be predictable and regularized and occur within well-proscribed channels and procedures. In short, for Weber the bureaucratic mode was a clear advance on its predecessors.

What Weber saw as virtues, however, became vices in the eyes of later observers. What Weber found predictable and regularized others found deadening and stifling. Rules to provide regularized channels had become ends in themselves, not means to other goals. Advancement on the basics of merit had too easily become a lifelong sinecure for unimaginative bureaucrats. Injecting fresh approaches became difficult because elected leaders could not break the stranglehold that bureaucrats had on policy. The marshaling of expertise to solve difficult problems became a cover for bureaucrats to serve the interests of their own organizations at the expense of the public interest and other bureaucracies with which they competed for resources and influence. What for Weber had been the pinnacle of modern political organization had become the logjam in the machinery of government to successor observers.

In the late 1960s, students of foreign policy analysis in the United States built upon the basic insight these earliest critics had advanced about the pernicious effects of the bureaucratic mode and developed three propositions about how bureaucracies affected foreign policy. Their first proposition held that organizational position determined policy stance, that "where you stand (your policy stance on a given issue) depends on where you sit (your institutional position and responsibilities)." The best predictor of what position a bureaucrat would take on an issue was the interests of the organization that he or she represented. Their second proposition was that the foreign policy decisions and actions of a government do not represent the intent of any one figure, but rather are the unintended result of bargaining, pulling, hauling, and tugging by bureaucratic competitors in their ceaseless quest for more funds, resources, and influence. The policy a government might adopt is unpredictable because it is the result of a fierce bureaucratic struggle for power. The third proposition of the bureaucratic politics model asserted that there was a difference between formulating and implementing a policy. Even if top political decision makers prevailed over the bureaucrats in the formulation stage, they would lose out to them in the implementation stage because the bureaucrats implement the policy. There would be considerable slippage between governmental intent (the policy as formulated) and governmental action (what actually was done). Bureaucrats, in short, appeared to be both powerful and pernicious.

Accepted uncritically, the bureaucratic paradigm would lead one to look at bureaucrats, not elected political leaders, for the major initiatives in foreign policy; to focus on the internecine struggles among bureaucrats, not on the views and images that are held in common by them; and to look within a government to predict its actions, rather than observing the policies of other governments and how those actions affect the balance of competition among competing bureaucracies.

Critics of the bureaucratic politics model reacted to its exclusive focus on bureaucratic politics and its neglect of both domestic and international politics. Their criticisms did not imply that bureaucracies were irrelevant in explaining foreign policy outcomes, only that their role was circumscribed. The critics held that heads of government and top political leaders set the terms within which bureaucrats work, and that it was important to look at how top political decision makers constrained the bureaucrats below them, not simply at how the bureaucrats fought with one another. In this view bureaucrats derived their power, not from their bureaucratic position per se, but from the larger interests within society that they represented and especially from their close alliances with members of Congress. Shared images often characterized the top-level decision makers; where differences of opinion occurred, they were as often as not due to differences in intellectual outlook and past experiences rather than to bureaucratic position. Events in the international realm also constrained bureaucratic behavior by altering the balance of political power among the bureaucracies. In sum, critics of the bureaucratic politics school argued that more often than not bureaucratic factors took second place to both domestic and international politics as determinants of foreign policy. Bureaucratic politics was a necessary supplement to those two, but could never make much sense without them.

Ironically, the bureaucratic politics approach experienced its greatest popularity in the United States, a country where executive branch bureaucrats are subject to powerful presidential and congressional pressures. In a presidential system such as that of the United States, where power is shared between the executive and the Congress, bureaucratic power is severely constrained. In parliamentary systems, where parliaments are weak in relation to executives, bureaucrats have considerable power vis-à-vis the legislature; but even in these cases they are subject to prime ministers and cabinets whom they must serve, whatever the party or policy. Bureaucrats may thus retain more power in parliamentary than in presidential systems, but in both they are subject to popularly elected executives. Bureaucratic politics is important in modern government, but only within the parameters set by both domestic and international politics.

Graham T. Allison, *Essence of Decision* (Boston, 1971). I. M. Destler, *President, Bureaucrats, and Foreign Policy* (Princeton, N.J., 1972). Morton H. Halperin, *Bureaucracy and Foreign Policy* (Washington, D.C., 1974). Robert J. Art, "Bureaucratic Politics and American Foreign Policy—A Critique," reprinted in G. John Ikenberry, ed., *American Foreign Policy—Theoretical Essays* (New York, 1989): 433–457. Stephen C. Krasner, "Are Bureaucracies Important? (or Allison Wonderland)," reprinted in G. John Ikenberry, ed., *American Foreign Policy—Theoretical Essays* (New York, 1989): 419–433.

ROBERT J. ART

BURKINA FASO. A Sahelian, land-locked former French colony in West Africa, Burkina Faso (formerly Upper Volta) has a land area of 274,200 square kilometres (105,870 sq. mi.) and a population estimated at 8.7 million in 1990. During that year the GDP stood at US$3.2 billion, while GNP per capita was $326. The capital city is Ouagadougou (population 450,000), and traditional African religion is dominant.

In March 1959, the Upper Volta section of the interterritorial West African nationalist party, the Rassemblement Démocratique Africain (RDA), won an overwhelming victory in the legislative elections and brought Maurice Yaméogo, a moderate, pro-French leader, to power as prime minister (and later president) of the country. After independence from France was formally proclaimed on 5 August 1960, politics took the form of power struggles among contending factions and personalities within the RDA, with the trade unions playing a mediating role. Indeed, labor strikes contributed to the downfall of the corrupt Yaméogo regime, which was toppled on 3 January 1966 by a military *coup d'état led by General Sangoulé Lamizana. The RDA continued to dominate the country's political life under the military regime and was back in power by 1971. However, in February 1974, Lamizana and the military suspended the Constitution and resumed power. The constitutional referendum of November 1977 and the legislative and presidential elections of April–May 1978 marked a return to traditional party politics characterized by increased factionalism and personal rivalries within the RDA.

The military coup of 25 November 1980 which overthrew Lamizana and brought Colonel Sayé Zerbo to power marked the end of the dominance of the RDA in Upper Volta's political life. The loose coalition of nationalist and reformist-minded army officers led by Sayé Zerbo ruled through the Comité Militaire de Redressement pour le Progrès National (CMRPN). The CMRPN immediately embarked on a program of economic and financial austerity, coupled with restrictions on civil liberties, which put it on a collision course with the trade unions. This conflict resulted in yet another military coup on 7 November 1982, led by a group of younger, more radical junior army officers. The new governing body, the 120-member Conseil de Salut du Peuple (CSP), headed by Major Jean-Baptiste Ouédraogo, clearly indicated its intention to reinstate political freedom and to initiate a policy of social justice. Very soon a major politico-ideological cleavage developed within the CSP and culminated in a third coup which, on 4 August 1983, brought to power the left-wing faction, led by a popular and charismatic young captain, Thomas Sankara. Designed to empower the disenfranchised people to the detriment of the urban national bourgeoisie, the Burkinabè revolution institutionalized new instruments of popular power (the Conseil National de la Révolution, or CNR, and the Comités de Défense de la Révolution, or CDRs). A *basic needs–oriented economic and social development strategy was initiated, and a genuinely nonaligned foreign policy was launched. The various Marxist-Leninist political parties which had contributed to the seizure of power by the Sankara faction of the army were absorbed into the new revolutionary politico-bureaucratic structure. Intraleftist factional struggles soon developed between the Marxist Ligue Patriotique pour le Développement (LIPAD), the pro-Chinese Union de Lutte Communiste (ULC), the Parti Communiste Révolutionnaire Voltaïque (PCRV), and the country's most powerful leftist trade union, the Confédération Syndicale Voltaïque (CSV). This led Sankara to initiate a progressive unification process of all the extreme-leftist political factions under the banner of a new party, the Union of Burkinabè Communists (UCB), which was to constitute the nucleus of the future single party. As the CNR progressively deprived itself of the traditional social basis of previous regimes (the urban petite bourgeoisie) without gaining the total support of the peasantry, it became increasingly isolated, and the Sankara faction itself became marginalized within both the CNR and the army. Growing disagreement on *ideology, strategy, tactics, and security issues culminated in a bloody

coup on 15 October 1987 engineered by Blaise Compaoré, leading to the violent death of Sankara, thirteen of his associates, and up to 100 other persons, and to the subsequent seizure of power by Compaoré and his faction.

Soon after coming to power, the Compaoré regime embarked on a rectification process designed to redress the perceived excesses of the previous government. The Front Populaire (FP)—the organ which now replaced the CNR as the regime's main ruling body—embarked on a witch hunt designed to neutralize the extreme-leftist factions. In March 1988, the Comités Révolutionnaires (CRs) replaced the CDRs, with a somewhat reduced political role. On 19 September 1989 former Sankara associates Jean-Baptiste Lingani and Henri Zongo were arrested and executed on account of their "antirevolutionary" activities. On 2 June 1991 a new Constitution was adopted by referendum.

Meanwhile, growing opposition to Compaoré and his party, the Organisation pour la Démocratie Populaire/Mouvement du Travail (ODP/MT) led to the creation in September 1991 of a loose coalition of democratic forces, the Coordination des Forces Démocratiques (CFD). On behalf of some twenty political parties, the CFD called for a popular and sovereign national conference to be convened at the earliest opportunity. In October 1991 Compaoré responded by creating yet another support group, the Alliance pour le Respect et la Défense de la Constitution (ARDC). Presidential elections were held on 1 December 1991. The four opposition candidates (Pierre-Claver Damiba, Ram Ouédraogo, Herman Yaméogo, and Gérard Kango Ouédraogo) pointedly refused to take part in what they perceived to be a predetermined electoral process. Thus Compaoré was voted back in office with 84.4 percent of the vote (but with only twenty-five percent of the electorate voting). In spite of its new-found (but limited) legitimacy, the Compaoré regime is now confronted with a vibrant and dynamic Burkinabè democratic opposition which constitutes a constant challenge and permanent threat to its quasimonopoly on Burkinabè politics and institutions.

(See also FRANCOPHONE AFRICA; SAHEL.)

Claudette Savonnet-Guyot, *Etat et Sociétés au Burkina* (Paris, 1986). Pierre Englebert, *La Revolution Burkinabè* (Paris, 1987). Ludo Martens, *Sankara, Campaoré et la Révolution Burkinabè* (Antwerp, 1989). Guy Martin, "Revolutionary Democracy, Socio-political Conflict and Militarization in Burkina Faso, 1983–1988," in Peter Meyns and Dan W. Nabudere, eds., *Democracy and the One-Party State in Africa* (Hamburg, 1989).

GUY MARTIN

BURMA. A military junta, the State Law and Order Restoration Council (SLORC), seized power on 18 September 1988 in Burma (Myanmar). The junta consists of senior military officers chaired by the commanding general of the army and includes commanders of the navy, air force, and the chief of intelligence, who functions as secretary of the SLORC. The People's Assembly was disbanded at the time of the coup d'état, and the SLORC governs under martial law based on the 1974 constitution. An election for representatives to design a new constitution was held on 27 May 1990, and an opposition party, the National League for Democracy (NLD), won eighty percent of the seats; however, the SLORC refused to accept the election as legitimate and has not allowed the representatives to meet.

The judiciary, police, and civil service are under martial law, and no independent branch of government remains. Likewise, all private organizations and institutions, including nearly one hundred political parties registered for the elections, are subject to review and investigation by the SLORC. Buddhist religious bodies, known as the Sangha, are also subject to the same control, as are other religious organizations in this largely Theravada Buddhist land

Burma is in Southeast Asia and is located west of China, Laos, and Thailand and east of Bangladesh and India. Its 40 million people (1990) are known as Burmese, two-thirds of whom are Burmans—the remainder consist of Shan, Karen, Arakanese, Kachins, Chin, Mon, Palaung, Wa, Lisu, Lahu, Akha, and numerous smaller language groups of fewer than 100,000 people. These many languages fall into two families, Tibeto-Burman and Mon-Khmer. Minorities inhabit the hills surrounding the central plain and delta of the Irrawaddy River, although many Karens also live in the delta region. Cities and larger towns also have Chinese and Indian communities, consisting of Muslim, Hindu, and Mahayana Buddhist faiths. Over four-fifths of the Burmese live in villages, and their per capita income ranks among those of the least developed countries. The annual population growth has hovered at two percent for the past three decades.

Socialism was the prevailing *ideology among intellectuals and political activists following independence on 4 January 1948 until the collapse of the Burma Socialist Program Party (BSPP) in 1988. At that time, U Ne Win, Burma's leader since he seized power in 1962, declared socialism to be a bankrupt ideology. He resigned from the BSPP, which had been his political base for a quarter-century, and recommended reestablishment of a multiparty system. Parliamentary democracy was developed during the British colonial period, with elections held in the 1920s and home rule introduced in the 1930s.

The electorate in 1990 who voted for candidates opposed to the military regime were supporting a coalition of parties headed by Aung San Suu Kyi, daughter of General Aung San. He had negotiated independence from Britain within three years of Japan's surrender, then was himself assassinated six months before independence. Before his death Aung San had also negotiated agreements with the minorities who had been administered separately under the British since 1886.

Aung San's agreement was ignored by his successors, U Nu and U Ne Win, and insurgent warfare has been integral to Burmese politics since. The civil war has had a racial cast, as the Burmese army is constituted mostly of Burmans who fight armed factions of Karens, Kachins, Mon, Arakanese, Shans, and Wa. However, for the first four decades the Burma Communist Party (BCP) led a separate insurgency that waxed and waned as a threat, in part because it successfully recruited Burmans. In 1968 and again in 1989 the BCP turned on its leadership and self-destructed. In the complicated ethnic politics of Burma, the more recent episode involved a battalion of Wa tribesmen, supplied with Chinese arms, who turned against their Burmese leadership—a spasm of involuted warfare having little to do with Lenin, Mao, or the class struggle but much to do with control of profits from the opium trade.

Until the 1988 coup, economic development was staged in four-year plans formulated by government economists. As in all socialist countries, Burmese leaders assumed the state should play the leading role in *planning and implementing change. Political development was measured by membership in parties—the Anti-Fascist People's Freedom League (AFPFL) during the first fourteen years, the BSPP in the subsequent quarter century. A million and a half members and candidates were in the BSPP when it collapsed; overnight it became a liability to be affiliated with the BSPP, despite its substantial assets. Likewise, membership in the NLD, reportedly in excess of a half-million within eight months of its formation, became dangerous after the 1990 election as its leaders and organizers were detained by the SLORC on suspicion of crimes against the state.

The rhetoric of free enterprise replaced socialism as the SLORC leaders joined with foreign investors in joint ventures designed to exploit Burma's abundant natural resources. Large license and lease fees from investors permitted the government to rebuild depleted foreign exchange reserves, acquire new military and medical supplies, and stabilize their position; however, caution in the face of continuing political unrest keeps investors from helping Burma move toward sustained economic growth.

The SLORC has fractured Burma's classic nonaligned, neutralist foreign policy and opened the country to substantial influence from old adversaries. Thai and Chinese are particularly evident among the joint ventures, and a US$1 billion arms agreement with China confirms a commonality of purpose between leaders in both nations. Such a relationship was unthinkable in the past, as the cornerstone of Burmese foreign policy has been nonalignment since U Nu, Nehru, Tito, Sukarno, and Zhou Enlai founded the movement in 1954. From the outset, Burmese leaders were advocates of the UN and supporters of its charter. Indeed, U Thant, the third secretary-general of the UN, was U Nu's protégé. But in recent years Ne Win and his protégés have resisted the liberal reforms stemming from the 1975 Helsinki Accords and share with the leaderships in China, Pakistan, and Vietnam an antipathy toward pluralistic trends.

Burma has joined no regional political bodies, such as the Association of Southeast Asian Nations (ASEAN) or the Southeast Asia Treaty Organization (SEATO), but has received substantial *foreign aid. Japan has contributed as much as all other sources combined, both bilaterally and through the *Asian Development Bank, the *World Bank, the Colombo Plan, and key UN technical assistance agencies. While Ne Win's and the SLORC's policies have been insular, recent economic openings are changing the nature of Burma's relations with the rest of the world. Korean investors have joined Chinese, Japanese, and Thai entrepreneurs, hoping to benefit from the turnabout, and although these linkages are not yet secure, they suggest a pattern akin to that of neighboring Southeast Asian countries. The SLORC junta seems to draw its model from the South Korean experience, where military leaders worked closely with select family corporations to introduce modern manufacturing techniques and competitive productivity. However, because Burma has such a diverse population and has suffered such disruption from insurgency since independence, it seems likely that the country will continue to experience considerable hardship until greater domestic tranquillity is established.

(See also BUDDHISM; MILITARY RULE.)

Victor Lieberman, *Burmese Administrative Cycles* (Princeton, N.J., 1984). Michael Aung Thwin, *Pagan: The Origins of Modern Burma* (Honolulu, 1985). Robert Taylor, *The State in Burma* (Honolulu, 1987). Mya Than and J. L. H. Tan, eds., *Myanmar Dilemmas and Options* (Singapore, 1990). David Steinberg, *The Future of Burma* (New York, 1990).

JOHN H. BADGLEY

BURUNDI. The Republic of Burundi is a small, landlocked country located in the Great Lakes region in Africa. It is surrounded by Zaire to the west, *Rwanda to the north, and Tanzania to the south and the east. Once nicknamed the "Hilly Country" because of the prominence of hills and luxuriant landscape, Burundi covers 27,834 square kilometers (10,747 sq. mi.) on which live approximately 5 million people. With 170 persons per square kilometer, Burundi is ranked among the most densely populated areas in the world. Almost half the population is aged 18 or less. Bujumbura is the political and economic center.

Most Burundians are agriculturalists and pastoralists. Coffee is the major cash crop, whereas cattle serve as symbol of both material wealth and social status. With the exception of tin and some gold, Burundi imports all necessary industrial goods, including oil.

Burundi is an old sixteenth-century monarchy. Mwami (King) Ntare I is credited as the founder of this polity whose history was to be marked by many vicissitudes. In the early nineteenth century, his successors further unified and expanded it roughly to its present borders. By 1850, Uburundi, as the country was then called, was a very powerful nation in East and Central Africa, with a homogeneous, though socially variegated, population speaking one language (Kirundi) and bound by the same culture. Ethnic conflicts, which became the staple of its politics in the postcolonial era, were almost nonexistent then, since both Hutu and Tutsi, the two major contemporary ethnic groups, held various titles at different levels in the monarchy. Ethnic *nationalism in contemporary Burundi is actually the result not of long-standing ethnic hatred, as is usually presented, but of favoritism and new ethnic identities brought about by European occupation.

German officers were the first Europeans to control Burundi, imposing a treaty in 1903 that made Burundi part of German East Africa. After World War I, Belgium took over and, in 1924, began a series of changes that still affect Burundi. The most important was the dismantlement of precolonial ethnic arrangements and the replacement of the old power structure with colonially appointed chiefs.

At independence on 1 July 1962, Mwami Mwambutsa IV briefly returned to power. Soon, however, a period of social turmoil ensued that ultimately led Colonel Micombero to stage a coup and establish the first republic in November 1968. Micombero was overthrown a few years later by an officer who, in turn, was toppled in 1989.

Three main issues seem to haunt Burundians and their leaders. One is political openness and the participation of all citizens in the governing process. Another is the pressure of a rapidly increasing population on a small country with very limited resources. A third is an enclaved economy which depends on the goodwill of less developed neighbors and the fluctuations of the world market for its survival. Ultimately, the future directions of Burundi are still in the making.

(See also ETHNICITY; FRANCOPHONE AFRICA.)

René Lemarchand, *Rwanda and Burundi:* (New York, 1970). E. Mworoha, *Histoire du Burundi: Des Origines à la fin du XIXe siècle* (Paris, 1987).

MUSIFIKY MWANASALI

BUSH, George Herbert Walker. Forty-first president of the *United States, George Herbert Walker Bush was born on 12 June 1924 into a prosperous and politically active family. (His father, a partner in a Wall Street investment firm, served as a U.S. senator from Connecticut from 1952 until 1963.) Upon graduation from Phillips Academy, Andover, Bush entered the U.S. Navy, where he won the Distinguished Flying Cross and three air medals during World War II. At the end of the war, Bush attended Yale University, graduating Phi Beta Kappa in 1948.

In 1963, having made his own fortune in the Texas oil industry, Bush entered Texas politics by winning election as a moderate candidate running against a conservative faction for the Republican Party chair of Harris County, Texas. In 1966, he was elected to represent the Seventh District of Houston, Texas, in the U.S. *Congress. In Congress, Bush was a moderate Republican, supporting such measures as a 1968 national open housing bill despite the strong opposition of his constituents.

Bush made unsuccessful bids for a U.S. Senate seat in Texas in 1964 and in 1970. In 1971, President Richard *Nixon appointed Bush the U.S. ambassador to the UN. In 1974 he was appointed chief of the U.S. Liaison Office in China. Upon returning to the United States, Bush became chair of the Republican National Committee, a position which he held at the peak of the Watergate crisis. With the unpleasant task of presiding over Nixon's resignation behind him, Bush was asked by President Gerald Ford to assume the director's post at the *Central Intelligence Agency in 1976.

In 1980, with James Baker as his manager, Bush campaigned against Ronald *Reagan for the Republican presidential nomination. Bush positioned himself as the moderate challenger to Reagan but withdrew from the race late in the primaries after Reagan appeared to have the nomination locked up. Bush accepted Reagan's invitation to become the vice-presidential running mate on the 1980 ticket. As vice president, Bush chaired several task forces, including those on *drugs and *terrorism, traveled to seventy-four nations as the representative of the United States, and was designated by the president to chair the crisis management team in the White House.

After defeating Senator Robert Dole of Kansas in early contests for the Republican presidential nomination in 1988, Bush began to put some distance between himself and the Reagan administration with regard to his policy views on the environment, civil rights, and ethics in government. Bush, however, reiterated the Reagan philosophy of maintaining a strong national defense and pledged "no new taxes" during the 1988 election campaign on his way to defeating Democratic nominee Michael Dukakis by a margin of forty states to ten in the electoral college.

Bush's early reputation as a moderate, pragmatic politician resurfaced in 1990 when he broke his tax pledge and supported non–income tax increases in order to curb the growing deficit. Bush's sponsorship of a comprehensive clean air program enacted by Congress also served to indicate a different policy perspective from that of his predecessor.

On the whole, however, foreign affairs dominated Bush's policy interests during the first two years of his presidency. He met with Soviet leader Mikhail *Gorbachev three times to discuss a wide array of issues including potential agreements on the reduction of strategic and chemical weapons and the issuance of a joint communiqué condemning *Iraq for the invasion of neighboring *Kuwait on 2 August 1990.

The joint communiqué on Iraq reinforced earlier U.S.-Soviet cooperation in forging a UN Security Council resolution authorizing the use of military force by U.S.-led coalition powers if economic sanctions and diplomacy failed to bring about a withdrawal of Iraqi forces from Kuwait by 15 January 1991. President Bush ordered a U.S.-led attack on military targets in Iraq and Kuwait when the government of Saddam Hussein showed no intention of abiding by the UN decree, and on 17 January a forty-three-day war erupted.

The war with Iraq marked the second occasion in which the Bush administration had resorted to the use of military force after diplomacy had failed to bring about a successful resolution to an international problem. On 20 December 1989, Bush ordered 10,000 American troops into *Panama to restore order after General Manuel Noriega annulled the May 1989 elections, which had been won by U.S.-backed opposition candidate Guillermo Endara.

Bush's leadership was characterized by most observers as collegial, broadly consultative, and flexible. Friendship and loyalty were hallmarks of Bush's personal style and were central to his conduct of *foreign policy, upon which his success as president will likely be judged to a considerable degree.

(See also GULF WAR; PRESIDENCY, U.S.)

Fitzhugh Green, *George Bush: An Intimate Portrait* (New York, 1989).

PHILLIP G. HENDERSON

C

CABINET GOVERNMENT. In its origins, cabinet government is an English concept, denoting government by a small collective decision-making body, answerable for its actions to—and, often, formally removable from office by—the legislature. The term *cabinet* derives from English practice in the seventeenth century, when the king found his principal body of advisers, the privy council, to be too large to assist effectively in the governing of the country and turned instead to a small group of council members. This group became known by different names, including the cabinet council, and in the following century the king's principal body of ministers became recognized as "the cabinet."

The nineteenth century witnessed the emergence of mass franchise and the recognition of the need for the cabinet to maintain the support of the elected chamber. The century saw the confirmation of the concept of collective responsibility as a convention of the constitution, ministers remaining legally answerable to the monarch but politically answerable to Parliament. The convention entailed 1) that decisions must be collectively arrived at, with ministers then accepting decisions once made (or else resigning their seals of office) and 2) that the government must resign or request a dissolution of Parliament if defeated on a vote of confidence in the House of Commons. The body for collective decision-making was the cabinet, though all ministers (those outside as well as within the cabinet) were—and remain—bound by the convention of collective responsibility.

The functions of the British cabinet were delineated by the Machinery of Government Committee in 1918 as: 1) the final determination of the policy to be submitted to Parliament; 2) the supreme control of the national executive in accordance with the policy prescribed by Parliament; and 3) the continuous coordination and delimitation of the activities of the several departments of state. Although the growth of political parties largely ensured parliamentary approval for measures presented by cabinet, the nexus between cabinet and the legislature is central to the concept of cabinet government. A political system may have a cabinet, but there is no cabinet government if the cabinet itself is not the decision-making body and is not collectively answerable to the legislature for its measures and conduct of government.

Cabinet government is common in *Commonwealth and West European countries. Many of the Commonwealth countries replicate British experience with two-party systems and strong cabinets (the Westminster model), whereas many West European countries have multiparty and weak cabinet systems (Continental model). *France has a hybrid system in which executive power is shared by an elected president and a cabinet drawn from a separately elected national assembly.

The extent to which cabinets remain able to govern is a subject of contemporary debate. The demands made of government make it increasingly difficult for a cabinet collectively, and with dispatch, to reach decisions, decision-making competence flowing instead upward to the head of government ("prime ministerial government") or downward to cabinet committees, individual ministers, and civil servants. (See also BRITAIN.)

John P. Mackintosh, *The British Cabinet*, 3d ed. (London, 1977).

PHILIP NORTON

CABRAL, Amílcar. The preeminent theorist and guerrilla fighter in the period of the *decolonization of Africa, Amílcar Cabral was born on 12 September 1924 at Bafata in *Guinea-Bissau. Brought up in the period of the Second World War, he saw firsthand the impact of colonialism, especially at the hands of the poorest country in Europe. Amílcar Cabral went to Portugal to be educated in 1944 and later graduated as an agricultural engineer. In 1952 he returned to Guinea-Bissau to work as a colonial agronomy engineer. Having been trained at the agronomy center in *Portugal, Cabral was instructed to plan and execute the agricultural census of Guinea-Bissau in 1953. This study gave Cabral insight into the conditions of the majority of the population in Guinea-Bissau. This provided the raw material which was to be the basis of the theoretical, contributions of Cabral on the social structure of Guinea-Bissau. This study also gave him the opportunity to travel throughout the rural areas and gave him historical, racial, and cultural data on the ethnic makeup of Guinea-Bissau.

A job transfer to *Angola in 1955 brought him into direct contact with those elements in that society who were in the embryonic stages of forming the Movimento Popular de Libertação de Angola (MPLA). It was this sojourn in Angola along with his experience in Guinea-Bissau and São Tomé which made Cabral a pivotal person in drawing up a plan for a coordinated struggle against Portuguese colonialism in Angola, Guinea-Bissau, *Mozambique, and *São Tomé.

Cabral was one of the founding members of the Partido Áfricano da Indêpendencia da Guiné-Bissau e Cabo Verde (PAIGC). As the secretary-general of the organization, he molded a small guerrilla army into a fighting force that tied down the Portuguese army in Guinea-Bissau.

As a theoretician, diplomat, writer, and spokesperson for the forces of liberation, Amílcar Cabral distinguished himself inside and outside Africa. At the Tri-Continental Conference in Havana in 1966 Cabral delivered a major statement on the peculiarities of the historical process in Africa and made a unique contribution to the understanding of historical materialism in Africa. Cabral's position as a theorist of the African condition was reinforced by his analysis of the role of cultural resistance in the struggle for African liberation. His affirmation of African culture's important place in the universal culture of humanity was based in a conception of liberation not only for political sovereignty but also as true cultural liberation. In this context, he affirmed that national liberation was an act of culture.

Amílcar Cabral was assassinated in Conakry, *Guinea, on the night of 20 January 1973. Prior to his assassination, he had proclaimed that Guinea-Bissau would declare its independence from Portugal in that year. It was the protracted struggles of the Africans in Guinea-Bissau, Angola, and Mozambique which precipitated the coup in Portugal in April 1974. This change sped the process of decolonization in Africa in a very fundamental way. Cabral's writings and speeches have provided the basis for a new direction in the study of Africa.

(See also CAPE VERDE; GUERRILLA WARFARE; NATIONAL LIBERATION MOVEMENTS.)

Amílcar Cabral, *Unity and Struggle: Speeches and Writings* (New York, 1979).

HORACE CAMPBELL

CAMBODIA. The transformation of the ancient Southeast Asian Kingdom of Cambodia into a modern nation-state began in 1863, when its king signed the first protectorate treaty with France. It had in theory been an absolute Buddhist monarchy, based on peasant agriculture and ownership of land in principle by the king. Commerce was undeveloped and in the hands of foreign Asians. Over eighty percent of the population was ethnic Khmer.

The French protectorate preserved the Cambodian state structure, including royalty and the traditional bureaucracy, but privatized land ownership, tightened the tax system, and encouraged commerce, still largely controlled by French and Chinese. The few

modern schools that were established served the local elites, and because they were assured places in the bureaucracy they had little incentive to revolt. Nationalist movements were notably lacking until after World War II.

By agreement with Japan the French administration survived World War II until March 1945, when the Japanese interned the French and offered formal independence. King Sihanouk abrogated the treaties that had been signed with France, but no resistance was offered when the French returned to reestablish their protectorate in October 1945.

France then instituted a constitutional regime with elections, political parties, and a strong national assembly. The first three elections, in 1946, 1947, and 1951, were won by a party whose goal was independence and some degree of social change, and which opposed Sihanouk and sympathized with the anti-French struggle in *Vietnam. At the same time, that struggle attracted grass-roots Cambodian support and in 1951 the first Cambodian communist organization was formed, consisting mostly of peasants with a small core of leaders from the petty bourgeoisie.

The combined pressure of anticolonialist sentiment in parliament and the rapidly developing rural insurgency forced King Sihanouk to campaign for independence in order not to lose credibility. The French, who were by then near defeat in Vietnam, granted independence to Sihanouk's government in November 1953.

The Geneva Accords of 1954 required that elections be held in Cambodia in 1955 according to the existing constitution. Sihanouk, who abdicated in favor of his father in order to play a more active political role, would again be in danger of defeat at the hands of enemies who had won all previous elections, strengthened by former guerrillas who, according to the terms of Geneva, were to have full political rights.

Unexpectedly, and probably unfairly, a newly organized Sihanoukist party won all assembly seats in the 1955 election, and from then until 1970, through single-party elections in 1958, 1962, and 1966, Sihanouk ruled as a dictatorial chief of state, with his policies legalized by a rubber-stamp national assembly.

During this period, there was an explosive expansion of schooling, not an unmixed blessing, for it encouraged rural children in unrealistic dreams of bureaucratic careers and wealth. Commerce developed rapidly, along with some industry, and was increasingly controlled by Cambodians, either as capitalists or as bureaucrats in state agencies. Agriculture at first prospered but declined after 1964 as the state pumped more out of the countryside to finance budgets that favored the urban elite who dominated the bureaucracy and national assembly.

Three significant factions coexisted within the national assembly. The Left supported the communist struggle in Vietnam, wanted changes in domestic society, and a neutralist foreign policy, a matter on which they were formally in agreement with Sihanouk. The other two factions were both politically conservative, but one was modernizing capitalist while the other was made up of courtier-bureaucrats who favored Prince Sihanouk's "Royal Buddhist Socialism" and who sought control of the economy through appointment of themselves and their allies as heads of economic agencies and state enterprises.

By 1967 most of the Left had gone underground, emerging after 1970 as leaders of the revolution; and by 1970 rivalry between the other two factions led to the deposition of Sihanouk, seemingly in favor of the capitalists, but ultimately in favor of the old-style bureaucrats led by General Lon Nol, who assumed the presidency of the new Khmer Republic in 1972.

The Khmer Republic had almost no support in the countryside, and it was weakened by involvement in the *Vietnam War. In April 1975 communist insurgents (the Khmer Rouge) led by Pol Pot gained power and established the government of Democratic Kampuchea. The Khmer Rouge made little attempt to establish formal political institutions. Economic policy involved a return to poor peasant agricultural life, organized in large collective units, for the entire country. Town populations were evacuated to rural areas, with a minimum of essential manufacturing maintained. The result was great loss of life and alienation of the population; but what was fatal to the regime was its anti-Vietnamese policy and attacks on Vietnam, resulting in a Vietnamese invasion and change of regime in January 1979.

The government of the new People's Republic of Kampuchea (renamed State of Cambodia in May 1989), was formed at first from former Democratic Kampuchean personnel who had broken with that regime before 1978 and from older communists who had lived in Vietnam since 1954. But soon the administration was fleshed out, particularly at sub-ministerial and provincial levels, with people who had not been part of any previous communist faction. Many of them had already served the kingdom and the Khmer Republic. The State of Cambodia, in the socioeconomic background of its political elite, differs little from pre-1975 regimes, although few of the highest strata of the old ruling groups have survived.

A constitution was promulgated and a single-party election held in 1981, and since that year there has been a national assembly, with an executive state council and president chosen from it, and a ministerial government responsible to it. A monopoly of political power rests with the People's Revolutionary Party, renamed People's Party in October 1991, which traces its history from the first communist organization of 1951.

Normal urban life was restored, and the population has recovered to a total of 8–8.5 million, more than in 1975. Until 1989 there was orthodox socialist emphasis on industry, although private commerce developed rapidly at all levels, and by 1991 it was decided to privatize nearly all state enterprises and convert to a free-market economy. Agriculture too, after a period during which *collectivization was encouraged (although not enforced), has been almost completely decentralized to private family farming, and by late 1991 land was being transferred to cultivators as private property.

Major problems have been security and foreign affairs. Cambodia has been threatened by attacks from survivors of the Khmer Rouge, the Khmer Republic of Lon Nol, and Sihanouk's kingdom, based on the Thai border. In 1982 these groups formed the Coalition Government of Democratic Kampuchea, which has been supported militarily, financially, and diplomatically by China, the United States, and the *Association of Southeast Asian Nations (ASEAN). Soviet and Vietnamese aid enabled Cambodia to build up an army of over 100,000 regular troops plus local militia. Until September 1990 Cambodia's UN seat was occupied by Democratic Kampuchea, and no capitalist state except India recognized the Phnom Penh government. Normal international trade and financing were blocked, forcing the country to exist at an abnormally low economic level.

A peace agreement signed in October 1991 provides for demobilization, political party pluralism, and a UN-supervised election in 1993. The UN exercises its supervisory role through a Supreme National Council with six representatives from Phnom Penh and two each from the other three factions. This council also occupies Cambodia's UN seat and accepts accreditation from foreign diplomats; but internal administration is still carried out by the Phnom Penh government, which has proclaimed Prince Sihanouk as chief of state.

Liberalization of the economy has resulted in rapid inflation since 1989 after a previously rather stable currency. This has alienated administrative cadres who exist on exiguous salaries, urban workers, students, and peasants. They might again, as in the 1970s, find sympathy for the radical policies of the Khmer Rouge, giving them an unexpected advantage in the election scheduled for April 1993.

(See also BUDDHISM; COMMUNISM; DECOLONIZATION.)

David P. Chandler, *A History of Cambodia* (Boulder, Colo., 1983). Ben Kiernan, *How Pol Pot Came to Power* (London, 1985). Michael Vickery, *Cambodia 1975–1982* (Boston, 1984). Michael Vickery, *Kampuchea, Politics, Economics and Society* (London, 1986).

MICHAEL VICKERY

CAMEROON. A highly centralized state, Cameroon is located in west-central Africa. Once a German colony (1884–1916), then French (in the east) and British (in the west) mandate and trust territories, the majority of the state gained independence on 1 January 1960. On 1 October 1961 the southern portion of the British trust joined to form the Federal Republic of Cameroon. The name was changed to the United Republic of Cameroon in 1972 and to the Republic of Cameroon in 1984.

The first president, Ahmadou Ahidjo (1924–1989), accepted a constitution similar to that of de *Gaulle's France but quickly modified it, creating an authoritarian state where the president was the center of power and where arbitrary force exercised through the police and the secret police (or Service de Documentation and the Brigades Mixtes Mobiles) was the ultimate arbiter of conflict. Ahidjo was replaced by Paul Biya in a constitutional transfer of power in 1982.

The executive is the dominant political institution. Elected for a five-year term, the president is reelectable without limit. As head of state and government, with vast powers of appointment and dismissal combined with the presidency of the dominant party, the president is a superpatron with the resources of the government to maintain a clientele linking leaders from ethnic, regional, religious, and other groups directly to the president. The judiciary, the legislature, and the dominant party (the Cameroon People's Democratic Party [CPDM]) are subservient. Only the bureaucracy and—after a violent coup attempt on 6 April 1984—the military have been capable of exerting pressure on or deflecting the impact of the president's policies.

The CPDM operates by a cell structure. These are organized into branches, subsections, and sections. The latter coincide with *départements,* the basic administrative structure of the government. The Party Congress, Central Committee, and Political Bureau top the structure. The Congress meets every five years in a gala celebration, but the Political Bureau is the most significant body. Allied to the CPDM are the Women's Organization (WCPDM), the Youth (YCPDM) and the National Union of Cameroon Workers. Although other parties have formed, party competition has proved exceedingly difficult owing to government's patronage resources and use of the security forces. Perhaps over time, one of these parties may gain sufficient strength to challenge the CPDM.

The most obvious source of cleavage is the more than 200 ethnic groups, but these are not the most significant divisions. The dual colonial inheritance is the base of the most powerful cleavage: between Anglophones, about twenty percent of the population, and Francophones, eighty percent. This split was manipulated by Ahidjo to prevent the emergence of the potentially more dangerous north-south conflict, a mixture of religious (*Islam in the north, Christianity in the south), cultural (pastoral versus agricultural), and historical divisions. But the Anglophone-Francophone issue subdivides the south, allowing a skillful politician to downplay the potentially greater regional division. The second president, Paul Biya, continued this tactic, but with less success than Ahidjo. Almost all those implicated in the 1984 coup attempt against Biya, who had come to power as constitutional successor in 1982, were northerners. Ahidjo was from the north, Biya the south.

Class conflict is successfully smothered by the other cleavages. Although a substantial gap in income and life-style exists between the majority and a tiny elite of high-level bureaucrats, politicians, military officers, businesspeople, and a few traditional rulers, this gap has found little political meaning.

Organizations representing these differences in society came into existence only in the early 1990s. The Cameroon Action Movement focused on Anglophone sentiment and called for a confederation. A coalition of Anglophone, northern, and commercial leaders formed the Social Democratic Front. The most long-lasting opposition movement has been the Union des Populations du Cameroun (UPC), led by Woungly Massaga. Founded in the 1950s, the UPC fought the French and the Ahidjo government in a violent struggle in the late 1950s and early 1960s. When Biya became president there were expectations that the UPC, a radical nationalist movement espousing socialism and nonalignment, would be allowed to return from exile, but several years passed before this took place. Numerous other small parties have come into existence.

Ahidjo and Biya followed similar policies. At independence the French suppressed the UPC, the true nationalist party, and gave power to Ahidjo, a moderately conservative northerner. Both by his predilection and because of a series of secret treaties, independence came with close ties to France. Since then, foreign policy, officially nonaligned, has been based on a pro-France, pro-West, procapitalist orientation. Trade diversification, mostly involving other Western nations, has reduced the significance of France, which nevertheless remains the predominant trade partner.

The major regional *foreign policy issue is the relationship with *Nigeria, seen as a giant imperial power to the west. Trade issues and smuggling, border demarcation, and the treatment of foreign nationals are key sources of conflict. Major attention is paid to regional affairs in the Union Douanière et Economique de l'Afrique Centrale (UDEAC). Of the six members, Cameroon has the most to gain from an enlarged market and as the hub of transportation and administration.

*Development policy, or "Planned Liberalism," is based on a free-market orientation and a centrally planned economy. Foreign investment has been welcomed, but under the concept of "Self-reliance" there has also been emphasis on domestic capital and personnel. "Balanced Development" emphasized the even distribution of economic improvement to all regions and classes, although the results have not fulfilled the concept. Development policy, enunciated in five-year plans, now focuses on agriculture and small industry. In general, Cameroon has gained a reputation as a fiscally conservative government.

Agricultural expansion has shown some success as export crops have generally increased, and the country remains largely food self-sufficient. Food is also exported to neighboring countries. However, *import-substitution industrialization and large-scale industrial development have generally not succeeded. The limits were made clear in the 1980s, when a drop in commodity prices for key exports—petroleum, cocoa, coffee, and others—led to an economic crisis, followed by increasing political discontent.

(See also ETHNICITY; FRANCOPHONE AFRICA.)

Jean-François Bayart, *L'Etat au Cameroun* (Paris, 1979). Michael G. Schatzberg and I. William Zartman, eds., *The Political Economy of Cameroon* (New York, 1986). Mark W. DeLancey, *Cameroon: Dependence and Independence.* Profiles/Nations of Contemporary Africa Series (Boulder, Colo., 1989).

                                        MARK W. DeLANCEY

CANADA. Its immense landmass makes Canada the second-largest country in the world, but its population of 26 million as of 1990 leaves it only sparsely populated. Moreover, ninety percent of that population lives in a narrow 320-kilometer (200-mile) band along the border with the *United States, with sixty-two percent concentrated in the two central provinces of Ontario and *Quebec. Such proximity to its southern neighbor and close cultural ties have made the Canada-U.S. relationship one of the most important factors in post-1945 economics and politics. Of equal importance, however, are the legacies of its colonial ties to France and Britain.

Much of the area that now is Canada was first explored and settled by the French in the sixteenth century. France controlled most of that territory until 1759 when British forces attacked Quebec City. Although the elite and colonial administrators returned to France after the conquest, the ordinary population of farmers and traders remained in place. Canada's first steps toward nationhood in the nineteenth century followed more than 100 years of political conflict between French and English colonists.

Canada's existence as an independent nation-state began with the British North America (BNA) Act, passed by the Parliament of the United Kingdom in 1867. That act set out the terms of unification of four British colonies in North America—Nova Scotia, New Brunswick, Lower Canada (Quebec), and Upper Canada (Ontario). Subsequent acts expanded the national territory by incorporating western lands belonging to the Hudson's Bay Company (much of Saskatchewan and Alberta), the Red River Colony (Manitoba), and the colony of British Columbia on the Pacific coast. A federal system of government with nine provinces was in place by 1905. The tenth province, Newfoundland and Labrador, joined the confederation in 1949.

Political institutions were modeled on those of the United Kingdom, albeit within a federal system. The central government (termed the federal government in Canadian political discourse) and all provinces have popularly elected assemblies whose business is organized by a system of competitive parties. The Parliament of Canada consists of the House of Commons and an appointed upper chamber, the Senate. The executive, comprising the prime minister and cabinet, is responsible to the House in accordance with the procedures of a responsible party system. The Senate was designed to provide provincial representation at the federal level. Its seats are apportioned unequally among the provinces, and it is appointed by the governor-general, on the recommendation of the prime minister. This procedure, as well as the unequal distribution of seats, has been a matter of great controversy for several decades. The head of state remains the British monarch, represented in Canada by a governor-general and ten lieutenant-governors.

Full independence from the British Parliament was achieved slowly and in recent years only with a great deal of domestic controversy. Created as a dominion in 1867, autonomy in international affairs came with Canada's participation in World War I and its separate signature of the Treaty of Versailles. The Statute of Westminster of 1931 confirmed this independence. The fundamental constitutional document—the BNA Act—set out, *inter alia,* the division of powers between the federal government and the provinces. The final court of appeal for disputes over this division of powers remained the Judicial Committee of the Privy Council of the British Parliament until 1949. That body quite systematically favored the powers of the provinces over those of the central government. Since 1949 the Supreme Court has been the final court of appeal. The final act severing the vestiges of colonial ties came only in 1982, with the patriation of the constitution. The British Parliament, at the request of Canadian government, passed the Constitution Act, which established new constitutional arrangements, including a Charter of Rights and Freedoms and a procedure for amending Canadian constitutional documents domestically.

Dispute over constitutional arrangements has been deeply divisive since the 1960s, and the 1982 arrangements did not settle the matter. Indeed they exacerbated the issue, because the new arrangements were put into place over the objections of the province of Quebec. That province was not willing to accept the constitutional compromise worked out in the negotiations leading to the Constitution Act, but the prime minister and nine provincial premiers made the request to the British Parliament nonetheless.

Two fundamental social cleavages of Canadian society are language and culture. These issues have had profound effects on political conflict and the evolution of the federal institutions. The place in the Canadian community of the one-third of the citizens whose language is French has dominated political debate since the nineteenth century. At the heart of the dispute are differing visions or models of Canadian society. For many Francophones the model is that of two founding peoples—French and English—whose status is one of equality. Moreover, they consider the province of Quebec to be their homeland where they have constituted a distinct society and whose protection depends upon a powerful provincial government. Beginning in the 1960s a Québécois nationalist movement pressed for the recognition of this vision of society. An important test of the model occurred in a 1980 referendum organized by the nationalist government of the province of Quebec on the issue of changing Quebec's status within Canada to one of sovereignty-association. This referendum was defeated, but in subsequent years popular support within the province for such a change grew.

An alternative model of society, actively promoted from the late 1960s under the leadership of Prime Minister Pierre *Trudeau (1968–1979; 1980–1982), describes Canada as a bilingual and bicultural society, organized as ten equal provinces. Language rights are to be protected by the constitution and through the political process. By implication, the federal government has responsibility for guaranteeing that all Canadians, whether Francophone or Anglophone, may live and receive services anywhere in the country.

A third and competing alternative emerged out of the politics of the 1960s, in part as a result of the high rates of postwar immigration from Europe and the Third World and official encouragement to ethnic groups to retain their cultural distinctiveness. In this view Canada is a multicultural society in which no group merits being singled out for distinction. Canada is one of the three main immigrant-receiving countries of the world and has a continually high ratio of immigrants to population (sixteen percent in 1981). A new immigration policy instituted in the 1970s dropped a long-standing concern with whether newcomers could be "assimilated" to Canadian society and instituted an official policy of nondiscrimination, favoring entrepreneurs and family members, and recognizing the special needs of refugees. Sources of immigration have changed as a result. In the 1980s, the proportion of Europeans dropped below thirty percent, with more than two-fifths of immigrants coming from Asia and another fifth from the

Americas, including the Caribbean. These patterns have strengthened the multicultural policy thrust and have led to new demands for state responses to discrimination and disadvantages suffered by "visible minorities."

The first two models of society had clear implications for constitutional politics and the division of powers in *federalism. Quebec, after 1960, demanded greater control over spending and policy-making in jurisdictions shared with the federal government. The response of the federal government was a compromise, which throughout the 1970s and 1980s gave greater powers to all provinces. These actions involved the federal government divesting itself of the ability to control the major levers of social and economic policy, devolving them to the provinces or to intergovernmental institutions.

Conflict between models came to a head in the constitutional negotiations of 1981. The federal government's document constitutionally entrenched the Trudeauian model by establishing language rights of French and English throughout the country and by establishing for the first time a Charter of Rights in fundamental law. There was no recognition of a distinct status for Quebec.

Premier René Lévesque of Quebec refused to approve the document and after 1982 that province rejected Canada's constitutional arrangements. New negotiations completed in 1987 produced a constitutional amendment—the Meech Lake Accord—which would have set out a definition of Quebec as a "distinct society" in the preamble to the 1982 document. Two provincial legislatures refused to ratify this accord, however, by the 1990 deadline, because of opposition to the notion of special status for Quebec. The leaders of all parties in the province of Quebec then began to prepare the way for a unilateral restructuring of the constitutional arrangements, in the direction of greater autonomy.

The long conflict over constitutional forms and institutional relations, reflecting the historic conflict over Canadian identity in a linguistically divided society moving from colony to nationhood, has provided a constant source of political division. The other constant pole, also derivative of a powerful external force, is the relationship with the United States. With World War II and postwar reconstruction, the Canadian economy moved increasingly into the orbit of the U.S. economy. The development strategy of the federal government, supported by both the Liberals and Progressive Conservatives—the two major political parties—was moderately Keynesian in fiscal policy, modestly committed to social spending, and centered around the encouragement of both primary and secondary production via investment by foreign as well as Canadian firms. The economy grew, albeit unevenly, in the first postwar decades. One central aspect of the unevenness reflected profound regional differences in the distribution of resources and population. The province of Ontario was the only one that consistently benefited from the modern economy, while all others suffered from the lack of modern manufacturing or natural resources or both. Programs for regional development and redistribution of income from the richer provinces to the poorer began in the late 1950s. In the 1960s, in addition, new social programs (universal health care, state-funded old-age pensions, workforce training programs, etc.) were instituted jointly by the federal and provincial governments. Nevertheless, state spending for social programs still ranks behind levels observed in many European countries with a comparable political history.

Throughout the postwar decades the Canadian and U.S. economies integrated. Trade patterns intensified so that by 1987 seventy-five percent of Canadian exports went to the United States. Only forty-four percent of Canadian exports were fully manufactured goods (the bulk of these were products which fell under an agreement made in the 1960s for free trade in automobiles and parts); the rest were unprocessed or semiprocessed primary goods. Fully two-thirds of imports were manufactured goods, sixty-eight percent of which came from the United States.

Opposition to North American economic integration because of its political consequences, described as a threat to Canadian political and cultural sovereignty, and its economic consequences, described as job loss, weakening of research and development, and *deindustrialization, provided a major focus for political conflict from the late 1960s. A nationalist movement in English Canada played a role in organizing such politics as well as helping to foster the institutional supports in communication and other arenas to sustain a distinct Canadian identity. Social democrats from the New Democratic Party consistently opposed the state's development strategy, as did a wing of the Liberal Party. Opposition also grew among intellectuals and trade unionists.

Nevertheless, despite widespread opposition in Anglophone Canada, in 1987–1988 the Canadian government, led by the Progressive Conservatives, negotiated the *U.S.-Canada Free Trade Agreement. All tariffs fell and there was a substantial weakening of nontariff barriers. The establishment of free trade in the service sector was of particular importance both for economic restructuring in North America and as a model for international economic negotiations.

With this important step toward the constitution of a regional bloc, Canada clearly dedicated its economic future to North America. It remains, however, involved in the international economic and political community through its membership in *North Atlantic Treaty Organization (NATO), the *Commonwealth, la Francophonie, the UN, and the *Group of 7. The country came out of World War II with a clear and active commitment to multilateral

economic and political institutions. It played an important role in the founding of the UN and the *General Agreement on Tariffs and Trade (GATT) and in the institutionalization of the Commonwealth and la Francophonie for a postcolonial world. Being a rich middle power with long-standing ties to the United States, two different European nations, and the Third World, Canada has preferred multilateral negotiations and peacekeeping activities. Recent political changes have brought a substantial reduction in Canada's role in providing development aid to the Third World. Military expenditures in recent decades have been restrained, concentrating on forces for peacekeeping and for defense of the sovereignty of the Canadian Arctic, including against incursions by the United States.

(See also INTERNAL COLONIALISM; INTERNATIONAL MIGRATION; NATIONALISM.)

Michael S. Cross and Gregory S. Kealey, eds., *Modern Canada: 1930–1980's,* Readings in Canadian Social History, vol. 5 (Toronto, 1984). Robert Bothwell, Ian Drummond, and John English, *Canada: 1900–1945* (Toronto, 1987). Janine Brodie and Jane Jenson, *Crisis, Challenge and Change: Party and Class in Canada Revisited* (Ottawa, 1988). Wallace Clement and Glen Williams, eds., *The New Canadian Political Economy* (Montreal, 1989). Michael Whittington and Glen Williams, eds., *Canadian Politics in the 1990s* (Toronto, 1990).

JANE JENSON

CAPE VERDE. Located off the coast of Senegal in the Atlantic Ocean, the Cape Verde Islands achieved political independence from Portugal in 1975. The archipelago was uninhabited prior to the 1460s. There is now a single ethnolinguistic group descended from both Africans and Europeans; ninety percent of the islanders consider themselves Catholic. In addition to its history as a slaving entrepôt and Portuguese colony, Cape Verdian reality has been shaped by periodic drought, horrific famine, and massive emigration. The resident population is estimated at 400,000, with 600,000 emigrants, 300,000 in the United States alone.

Between 1975 and 1990, the Republic of Cape Verde was a one-party state. In the republic's first multiparty elections in 1991, the Movimento para a Democracia (MpD), a social-democratic party led by Carlos Viega and supported by the Catholic church, ousted the Partido Africano da Independência de Cabo Verde (PAICV). The União Caboverdiana Independente e Democrática (UCID), a Christian social-democratic group founded by emigrants in the Netherlands in 1977, also has legal party standing.

Traditionally, Cape Verdians have made a living by growing rain-fed crops or raising animals, but both the climate and sharecropping relations have hindered the economy. Confronting the consequences of years of drought, the country has relied for food and income on foreign aid, fees generated by its international airport on Sal Island, and emigrant remittances. Food donations have been used to employ farmers in public works projects such as building dams and planting trees.

During the 1980s, imports were valued at twenty times exports, and studies predicted that Cape Verde could never be self-sufficient in staple grains. Owing partly to high rates of emigration, eighty percent of the islands' children are born to single mothers, many of whom have no means of support.

Under the 1985 constitution, the public sector dominated the economy, but by 1989, constitutional reform had been undertaken to encourage private investment by both domestic and foreign capital. Debate accompanied plans to promote tourism, offshore financial institutions, and export of seafood, fruit, and vegetables.

The exceptionally stable government of Aristedes Pereira (1975–1991) was led by PAICV militants active since the 1960s, when there was a single movement, the Partido Áfricano da Independência da Guiné-Bissau e Cabo Verde (PAIGC), representing both colonies. In the 1950s, national hero Amílcar *Cabral, a Cape Verdian born in *Guinea-Bissau, founded the PAIGC, which assumed power in both countries after an armed struggle in Guinea-Bissau. In 1981, the Cape Verdian wing of the PAIGC reestablished itself as the PAICV, following an anti–Cape Verdian coup on the mainland.

In its international relations, Cape Verde maintains strong ties with former Portuguese colonies in Africa. Under the PAICV, the government gained a reputation for its skilled *diplomacy, especially regarding problems in *Southern Africa. Cape Verde is active in regional organizations such as the *Economic Community of West African States (ECOWAS) and the Permanent Inter-State Committee on Drought Control in the Sahel (CILSS).

(See also SAHEL.)

Basil Davidson, *The Fortunate Isles: A Study in African Transformation* (Trenton, 1989).

LAURA BIGMAN

CAPITALISM. Despite the suffix -*ism,* capitalism refers neither to an *ideology nor a movement. It refers, if anything, to a set of economic and legal institutions which together make the production of things for private profit the normal course of economic organization. In short, it is a mode of production, a way of organizing economic activity.

The word itself is of recent vintage, having been coined by William Makepeace Thackeray in the mid-nineteenth century. Capitalism may be said to have originated in Western Europe sometime in the 200 years or so following the Black Death of 1349. Like much else about the subject, this is a controversial assertion, for exactly what constitutes capitalism—certain features of which existed in earlier periods of history and on other continents—is open to debate. Capitalism as we now know it, however, arose

in Western Europe between four and six centuries ago.

Capitalism is a system marked by 1) private property in the means of production, whether land, tools, machines, or ideas; 2) a legal framework entitling the owner of those means to the profits they generate subject only to nonarbitrary taxation; 3) a framework of contracts within which sales and purchases relevant to the production activity can be carried out, especially the right to hire and fire workers; and 4) the legal right of the owner to dispose of the profits as well as the property generating those profits in any way he or she chooses, subject to well-specified and justiciable limits.

The use of money and the existence of markets becomes ubiquitous as capitalism spreads, limited only by what individuals may hold property rights in. For its sustained growth capitalism requires investment on a continuing basis, either out of profits previously earned or from credit provided by financial intermediaries. But money, markets, and investment are necessary only inasmuch as they are instrumental to generating profits. The necessary conditions are profits in a system of private property with contractual rights.

Although money and markets have existed at least since the early Phoenicians and sophisticated credit markets have existed in India and China for centuries, the identification of the rise of modern capitalism with Western Europe is beyond dispute. Why capitalism should have originated there rather than in the more prosperous and economically sophisticated (as of 1350) regions of Arabia or Asia, on the other hand, is a much-debated topic. The debate has been particularly strong among Marxists given that the transition from feudalism to capitalism forms a major part of *Marx's theory of history as well as a rehearsal for the presumed future transition from capitalism to *socialism.

The lines of debate are drawn according to whether forces internal to Western European societies or those external are said to form the crucial element. Thus advocates of the internal explanation stress the loosening of feudal bonds on serfs via the spread of monetization and the rise of absolutist monarchies dominating the feudal baronage, along with the development of urban settlements peopled by traders and artisans. The external explanation emphasizes the shock of the encounter with Islamic civilizations during the Crusades, the search for alternate trade routes in response to the capture of overland routes by the Arabs, and the innovation of the maneuverable cannon which fitted on to sailing ships and extended the capacity of European navies to sail farther away from their home base.

Each of these explanations is conditional upon the other, and a synthesis is needed. Any explanation must place Western Europe in a global context and must account for the force of ideas (especially religious) and technological innovations (especially in the military sphere). As yet, no theory has satisfactorily explained not only why the advent of capitalism was in Western Europe but also why other regions which may have stood a better chance in terms of prior conditions failed to develop anything similar. Explanations of the origins of capitalism have thus far taken its advent in Western Europe as a given rather than a contingent fact to be explained.

Until the eighteenth century capitalism existed side by side with feudal structures. Especially in the realm of the technology of production, changes, if any, had been gradual over the centuries, and in some areas even ancient Roman standards had not been reattained. Money, markets, contracts, and property rights were all more or less in place by the beginning of the eighteenth century, although much more development was yet to come here as well. It was the development of the steam engine during the eighteenth century that irreversibly set capitalism on its path of growth. Industrialism came to be synonymous with capitalism. The first Industrial Revolution of the 1770s in England was followed by several others over the next 200 years, each setting off a half-century wave of expansion and contraction only to be renewed by the next revolution. The key to capitalism seemed to lie in its releasing the potential of labor for infinite rises in productivity.

Population growth expanded in parallel with the Industrial Revolution and has been a major complementary feature wherever capitalism has developed. Factory production with large concentrations of workers in one place, the growth of rapid transport and of communications on a global scale, the growth of cities and the desertion of villages, and the breakdown of the household as a major center of production of consumables all gave capitalism a dynamism and a facility for "creative destruction" of all that was old or merely recent. Complaints of attendant social breakdown, of anomie and alienation, of the dissolution of marriage and households, of the decline of religion, were commonly—and perhaps too glibly—voiced.

It was in this combination of alienation from the rural, precontractual life and the concentration of large numbers in factories and towns that the first articulate opposition to capitalism arose in the form of socialism. Different schools of socialism combined the nostalgic and the futuristic elements in various ways, but as an ideology and as a movement socialism became a powerful force of resistance and reform in capitalism. Alongside these developments arose trade unions, a form of association hitherto unknown. While trade unions were not always socialist, their interest was in regulating the growth of capitalism in ways that would enhance the workers' share in the total surplus. The collectivism of trade unions was eminently adaptable to mass politics, which increasingly became the norm in advanced capitalist countries, and these led to major qualifications to laissez-faire in capitalist countries—pensions, social security, and other social provisions associated with the *welfare state. It was from these roots that in the course of the first half of the twentieth century the *state came to play a major role in the spheres of the economy involved with the welfare of the labor force.

In the period between World War I and World War II, capitalism faced its most severe challenge. Hyperinflation following upon war, the triumph of Bolshevism in Russia, the long depression of the 1930s, and the rise of *fascism in Germany and Italy were seen as demonstrating the weakness of individualist capitalism and the success of collectivist alternatives. The rise of welfare capitalism in the United States during the *New Deal and in Britain during World War II was a successful social innovation that revived the prospects of capitalism in the postwar period. The rise of mass consumerism with full employment was seen as a permanent solution to the problems of capitalism.

As full employment became the norm, however, the strength of the trade unions as well as the permanence of the welfare state threatened the sustainability of profits. By the 1970s everywhere in advanced capitalism the crisis of profitability led to stagflation. Reacting to these pressures, capitalism emerged in the late twentieth century renewed by new innovations in electronics and telecommunications and with a reduced commitment to the collectivist institutions of previous years. *Multinational corporations which had arisen in the early twentieth century became the major shaping force of the newly emerging global capitalism. Capitalism seems to proceed through alternating cycles of inward-looking and outward-looking developments, and the 1980s and 1990s suggest a return to the nineteenth century when an earlier phase of capitalism became entwined with *imperialism.

In its preindustrial phase Western European capitalism had already spread its trade network to all parts of the globe, and *colonial empires had been established in America, Africa, and Asia. At the outset these empires were sources for plunder of gold and silver and slaves. The influx of gold from South America into the Iberian empires may even have been the cause of the first century of sustained inflation in Western Europe. But after the Industrial Revolution the network of formal and informal empires established through trade and credit offered ready markets for the industrial products of Western European capitalism. In return these peripheral regions became suppliers of (nonslave but still relatively unfree) labor and raw materials.

As informal trade links gave way to territorial conquest across Africa and Southeast and South Asia during the late nineteenth century, capitalism began to be widely identified with imperialism. Especially in South America, informal networks were just as influential as were formal networks. As growth spread, many former peripheral regions—North America, southern Europe, and finally during the late twentieth century East Asia—became fully capitalist and part of the advanced core.

Throughout its 200-year history industrial capitalism has continued to be productive at ever-increasing levels, despite prolonged periods of depression. The capacity of the system for sustained growth is often underestimated and does not seem to have diminished. What is more difficult is to establish the reasons for this sustained growth. Some attribute it to the innovating entrepreneur, ever seeking fabulous profits and willing to take enormous risks. Others attribute it to the combination of competition in the private sphere and the self-denying practice of laissez-faire on the part of the state. Others assign the state a more prominent role, especially in the earlier phases of industrial growth. Military expansionism, the Protestant ethic, gold discoveries, universalization of education and training, discoveries of science and technology—all these have been given their due prominence. The possibility of achieving large and sustained profits and the guarantee that these profits can be kept, augmented, and/or enjoyed would seem to be the one constant characteristic of capitalism. A variety of institutional arrangements have existed at different times within capitalism—competition and monopoly, inflation and stable prices, laissez-faire and interventionism, *authoritarianism and *democracy. In the end, as long as profits can be made and spent as the profit maker wishes within a nonarbitrary legal framework, capitalism—no matter how unclear its workings—will flourish.

(See also DEVELOPMENT AND UNDERDEVELOPMENT; LABOR MOVEMENT; MARXISM.)

MEGHNAD DESAI

CÁRDENAS, Lázaro. President of *Mexico between 1934 and 1940, Lázaro Cárdenas is widely recognized as the most progressive president of Mexico's postrevolutionary period. Born in 1895, of Damaso Cárdenas and Felicitas del Río, in Jiquilpán, Michoacán, Cárdenas joined the Constitutionalist army at age 18, during the Mexican Revolution, and eventually rose to the rank of division general. In 1928 he was elected governor of Michoacán, where he promoted the organization of workers and peasants and carried out an extensive agrarian reform. In 1930 he became president of the executive committee of the governing Partido Nacional Revolucionario, and in 1931, secretary of government in the Ortiz Rubio administration.

The election of Cárdenas as president of Mexico in 1934 led to a decisive shift in government policy in the areas of labor relations, agrarian reform, and national control over natural resources. Throughout his campaign, Cárdenas had urged workers to organize and unite, and while he was president he supported workers in their strikes and other conflicts with both foreign and national capital. He also

encouraged the formation of the Mexican Labor Confederation, which continued to be the major labor federation in Mexico for several decades.

Under Cárdenas, an extensive agrarian reform was implemented that distributed 18 million hectares (44.5 million acres), twice as much as all previous governments combined, to 810,000 peasants, generally in the form of ejidos—community-owned plots that could be farmed individually or collectively. The agrarian reform was innovative in that it was applied not only to traditional and often inefficient holdings but also to highly productive commercial estates, and collective ejidos were established as a means to maintain high levels of productivity (by maintaining economies of scale) while achieving the social goals of giving land to *peasants and rural workers.

In 1938, following a lengthy dispute between the newly organized confederation of petroleum workers and the U.S.- and British-owned petroleum companies, Cárdenas expropriated the companies, turning their administration over to a state-owned company, Petroleos Mexicanos (PEMEX), which became the largest company in Mexico's extensive *parastatal sector. The expropriation and *nationalization of the oil industry marked a significant step in eliminating foreign control of the export sector, affirmed the right of the Mexican *state to exercise control over critical resources, and positioned the state for more effective intervention in the economy.

Although the Cárdenas administration was a period of intense confrontation between the state and the private sector over such issues as agrarian reform and the rights of labor, groups within the private sector also benefited from government efforts to promote manufacturing and from loans by state development banks, as well as the expansion of the market resulting from wage increases and reforms in the rural areas. Nevertheless, polarization grew between an increasingly militant and organized urban and rural labor force, on the one hand, and business groups and landowners, often supported by state governors, military officers, and party officials, on the other. The growing polarization and fear of a split within the government were factors in what many have seen as a shift in the last years of the Cárdenas administration toward a moderation of reform efforts and attempts to control the militancy of labor and peasant groups.

In 1938 the government restructured the governing party on a corporate basis, changing its name to the Partido de la Revolución Mexicana. The party was composed of four sectors: labor, peasants, the military (later dropped), and the "popular sector" (consisting of organizations of state workers, teachers, small landowners, students, professionals, and women's groups). Ostensibly organized to institutionalize the influence of these sectors on the party and government, the party structure in fact reinforced hierarchical structures within the constituent organizations and eventually became a mechanism for the co-option and control of these sectors.

The election of General Manuel Avila Camacho as president in 1940 brought a formal end to the most progressive phase of Mexico's postrevolutionary history, and several of the reforms of the Cárdenas administration were subsequently reversed. Nevertheless, the Cárdenas government had an enduring effect on Mexican social, economic, and political life. The agrarian reform effectively eliminated traditional forms of labor exploitation in the countryside, curtailed the political power of the landowning class, and provided land to a significant sector of the peasantry. The nationalization of the petroleum industry eliminated foreign control and confirmed that of the Mexican state over a critical resource, setting the stage for the growth of Mexico's public sector. The new corporate party structure institutionalized the relationship between the state and popular sector. At the same time, the reforms of the Cárdenas government reinforced the legitimacy of the state as heir of the Mexican Revolution, an important factor in Mexico's political stability over the next several decades.

Cárdenas continued to have a role in Mexican politics, holding several positions in government, including that of minister of defense in the Avila Camacho administration, and informally representing the left wing within the government party until his death in 1970. Recognition of his record in government and his continued support for reform, especially in issues affecting the peasantry, is evident in the general use of the term *cardenismo* to refer to progressive currents within the Mexican political system.

(See also LAND REFORM.)

Arnaldo Córdova, *La política de masas del cardenismo* (Mexico City, 1974). Fernando Benítez, *Lázaro Cárdenas y la Revolución Mexicana* (Mexico City, 1977). Nora Hamilton, *The Limits of State Autonomy: Post-Revolutionary Mexico* (Princeton, N.J., 1982).

NORA HAMILTON

CARIBBEAN REGION. See ENGLISH-SPEAKING CARIBBEAN.

CARTER, Jimmy. Thirty-ninth president of the *United States, Jimmy Carter was born in the small town of Plains, Georgia, on 21 October 1924. He was the eldest of four children born to James Earl Carter, Sr., and Lillian Gordy Carter. After graduating from Plains High School (1941), he attended Georgia Southwestern College (1941–1942), the Georgia Institute of Technology (1942–1943), and the U.S. Naval Academy at Annapolis (1943–1946). In 1946 he married Rosalynn Smith and graduated from the Naval Academy. Between 1946 and 1953, he served primarily in the submarine service of the U.S. Navy and obtained the rank of lieutenant, senior grade.

Upon the death of his father in 1953, Jimmy Carter returned to Plains to manage the family farm and peanut processing business. His political career began in 1962, when he won a seat in the Georgia legislature. In 1966 he undertook an unsuccessful gubernatorial campaign. Four years later he defeated the popular and moderate former governor Carl Sanders in the Democratic primaries and won the governorship. Despite a stylistically "populist" campaign that contained some covert appeals to white racist sentiment, Carter proved to be a racial moderate and progressive in office. He reorganized the Georgia state government, reformed the state's mental health and environmental programs, hung Martin Luther King's portrait in the state capitol, and increased the number of black state employees.

A short-lived attempt to secure the Democratic vice-presidential nomination in 1972 was followed by a four-year campaign for the Democratic presidential nomination. Not only did Carter outflank and outmaneuver his more prominent opponents, he used symbols to great advantage. His emphasis on his religious commitments (Baptist), regional base (southern, small-town), and good relations with Georgia blacks appealed to voters wearied of *Watergate, big government, and racial divisions. His appeals, however, were sufficiently broad that his Republican opponent in the general election, incumbent President Gerald Ford, was able to cut into his strength with claims that he waffled on the issues. Despite polls in the late summer of 1976 showing him winning approximately seventy percent of the vote, Carter was elected by only a two-percent margin.

As president, Carter showed energy and intelligence in tackling several problems of his day. In his *foreign policy he went beyond a mere concern with U.S.-Soviet relations to attempts to deal with new world order problems. Thus he secured Senate approval of the treaty returning the Panama Canal to Panama, played a key role in securing the Camp David Accords between *Egypt and *Israel, and curbed the export of *nuclear weapons technology to countries that did not possess them. He also put *human rights near the top of his foreign policy agenda and tried to adapt to revolutionary movements in the *Third World (e.g., to the *Sandinistas in *Nicaragua).

Domestically, his presidency marked the turn of the Democratic Party away from the *New Deal to a neoliberal program emphasizing *deregulation and the conservation of energy and the environment. His successes included the deregulation of the airline industry and interstate trucking, the creation of the Departments of Energy and Education, and the passage of several conservation measures, including the Strip Mining Control and Reclamation Act of 1977 and the Alaska Land Act of 1980. After a long struggle, he also secured portions of his energy program, including measures providing for the decontrol of natural gas and crude oil prices, tax credits for the installation of fuel conservation measures, and provisions for a synthetic fuels program. In a more conservative direction, he resisted calls by the *American Federation of Labor and Congress of Industrial Organizations (AFL-CIO) to raise the minimum wage to $3.00 per hour and deferred action for several months on the full employment provisions of the proposed Humphrey-Hawkins bill.

Several of his major policy goals, however, never were accomplished. His *Strategic Arms Limitation Treaty (SALT) agreement was not concluded until June 1979, and whatever chances it had for passage in the U.S. Senate were ended when the Soviets invaded *Afghanistan in December 1979. He also failed in his attempts at welfare reform, as well as in his endeavors to create a national no-fault insurance program and to establish a federal consumer protection agency.

Despite Carter's intelligence and energy and his skills at running certain kinds of campaigns, his popular support as president was shallow, and other Democratic politicians had ambivalent feelings toward him. A precipitous decline in his popularity toward the end of 1979 led Senator Edward Kennedy of the Democratic Party's liberal wing to compete with him for the party's nomination in 1980. Having fended off that challenge, Carter lost the general election of 1980 to the Republican candidate, Ronald *Reagan, by a vote of fifty-one to forty-one percent. Independent candidate John B. Anderson carried seven percent of the popular vote. It was the first time since Herbert Hoover that an elected president had run for and failed to win a second term.

The reasons for Carter's shallow support in the country and in the Democratic Party have been widely debated. Some scholars argue that his problems were due to one or more of the following forces: the growing factionalism in the U.S. *Congress, the lack of programmatic cohesion in the Democratic Party, the difficulties traditional Democrats had in adapting to a more conservative political climate, and the intractable nature of the problems facing the country. Other scholars see Carter as bearing more responsibility for his political problems. They note that he lacked the kinds of political skills requisite to successful governance. He had difficulties in determining his programmatic priorities and dealing with political tradeoffs, his congressional liaison operation was amateurish at the beginning, and he often failed to consult influential people in the relevant policy networks as a part of the coalition-building process.

Certainly factors over which Carter had no clear control contributed to his failure to win reelection. The administration's inability to secure the release of the U.S. hostages held in Iran caused some voters to shift toward Reagan. But most important was the double-digit inflation of the economy. Voters, as most exit polls showed, had not turned to the polit-

ical right. But many of them saw Carter as an ineffective president, and public opinion polls showed that a plurality of the voters, for the first time since the New Deal, saw the Republican Party as the more likely to manage the economy in constructive ways.

(See also AMERICAN FOREIGN POLICY; NEW DEAL COALITION; PANAMA CANAL TREATY; PRESIDENCY, U.S.; SOVIET-AFGHANISTAN WAR.)

Betty Glad, *Jimmy Carter: In Search of the Great White House* (New York, 1980). Gaddis Smith, *Morality, Reason and Power: American Diplomacy in the Carter Years* (New York, 1986). Erwin C. Hargrove, *Jimmy Carter as President: Leadership and the Practice of the Public Good* (Baton Rouge, La., 1988).

BETTY GLAD

CASTRO, Fidel. Because of his role in *Cuba, Latin America, and the *Third World, Fidel Castro occupies a special place in twentieth-century history. He represented a wave of revolutionary experiments and tried to integrate Cuban historical tradition with European revolutionay theory. He made important contributions to revolutionary strategy and tactics, while elucidating a Third World perspective on world affairs.

Born 13 August 1926 into a prosperous landowning family, Castro was educated in private Catholic schools, where he was greatly influenced by Spanish priests who instilled in him a sense of discipline, dedication, and assertiveness. He arrived at the University of Havana in 1945. Although he studied little, he excelled thanks to a remarkable memory. His major academic interests were politics, sociology, history, and agriculture, but he received a law degree, which would later aid his political career. He also was active in student politics. Immersed in the polemical climate of Cuban politics, *nationalism, anti-imperialism, and *socialism became his standard themes.

By 1951, Castro was a leader of the populist-oriented Partido del Pueblo Cubano (the Ortodoxos), an anticommunist nationalist group that promised major social, economic, and political reforms and expected to gain the presidency through electoral politics. Castro planned to run for Congress, but on 10 March 1952, Fulgencio Batista overthrew the constitutional government. Together with other Ortodoxos, Castro began to organize an insurrection. He led a civilian armed attack against the Moncada military barracks on 26 July 1953. The attack failed and Castro landed in prison.

Granted political amnesty in May 1955, he went into exile in Mexico and began to train an expeditionary force. In late 1956, he landed in eastern Cuba with a force of eighty-two to initiate a guerrilla war. The movement grew, and from the Sierra Maestra mountains Fidel organized a parallel government, carried out a small-scale agrarian reform, established controlled territories with agricultural and manufacturing production, set up a radio station, and even created a small air force. He proved to be a skillful political and military strategist, and his guerrilla movement was the first in Latin America to defeat the military. On 1 January 1959, as Batista fled, Castro marched into Havana with the largest popular support of any political movement in Cuban history.

Once in power, Castro proved to be a persuasive and moving speaker, and a leader who had the affection and support of the population. He was the critical factor in defining the future direction of the *revolution. Scholars, analysts, supporters, and enemies agree on at least one feature of the *Cuban Revolution: Fidel Castro has been the unquestioned political and ideological leader. He holds a number of formal titles: Maximum Leader of the Revolution, commander-in-chief of the Cuban Armed Forces, president of the Republic, chairman of the Council of State, chairman of the Council of Ministers, first secretary of the Communist Party, and member of the National Assembly.

Fidel Castro is action oriented, even if the action is dangerous. This characteristic is closely tied to a strong character, determination, and persistence. He has an iron discipline accompanied by an inordinate self-assurance. He tends to consider alternative views erroneous and wrongheaded. Self-assurance and strong will are accompanied by keen intelligence. Even opponents concede that Castro is bright, insightful, and well read. Like any good strategist or actor, he has an uncanny sense of timing. His public speaking is the work of a craftsperson who understands and uses well the psychology of Cubans. One author has called his ability a "rare oratorical virtuosity." Castro educates, instructs, explains, criticizes, persuades, attacks. His oratory attempts to inspire confidence, to stir to action, to move. A dedicated student of Cuban history, he uses history as a weapon and guide.

Certain core values and ideas characterize his speeches and the policies he sponsors. He is certainly a nationalist. Fidel's unique contribution linked the defense of national independence with the necessity of socialism. This integration has meant that the revolution and the nation have become inseparable in his view. Thus, revolutionary survival requires revolutionary unity, which may be translated into national unity. If persuasion does not work, the law and the mass mobilization of intolerance assures unity through imposed public uniformity. In such a milieu, to question, dissent, or oppose revolutionary policies inexorably leads to the charge of treason.

Castro's revolutionary philosophy can be summed up as a set of simple axioms: collective needs rank higher than individual rights; revolutionary consciousness rather than money should motivate; selflessness is a positive value while greed is not; the state can make rational choices while the market is irrational; an underdeveloped country should be more concerned with production than consumption;

political needs precede economic rationality; mass political participation is more important than political choice; unity is necessary and superior to a plurality of views; central control is preferable to administrative autonomy; mass mobilization is more important than administrative methods; direct contact with the population by the political leadership is a true measure of democracy; *equality and justice take precedence over individual civil and political rights. It is on the basis of such ranking that decisions have been made, and a new society created.

The Cuban political system set up by Castro is an uneasy balance of formal institutions and charismatic authority. His leadership is based not on constitutional rule but on the permanent reaffirmation of authority that he receives from the mobilization of the population. His contact with the population is his very claim to power. Castro earned popular esteem in this fashion in 1959, and has continued that mode since. From the mid-1970s to 1986, he allowed a process of institutionalization to gain ground, while his own personal touch diminished. But as problems mounted, he went back to the charismatic approach. Just as the charismatic leader goes directly to the people, the people reciprocate by calling on him. Letters are received, in the thousands, from all over the island. Each and every letter is answered, by a special team that answers to Fidel. When everything else fails, there is Fidel. Charismatic authority is a demanding task.

Yet, a charismatic leader does not make decisions entirely on his own. He has an inner circle made up of specialists who are there mainly because Fidel trusts them, secondly because of their special knowledge. They are charged, among other things, with keeping him well informed. They are expected to be hard working and versatile. Over the years, the support group has changed. The older guerrillas have been supplanted by the university educated.

Castro's greatest accomplishment is to have remained in power longer than any other Cuban ruler, despite the opposition of the United States. In the domestic arena he led the radical transformation of Cuban politics, economy, and society, including the introduction of a socialist system. His *legitimacy cannot be separated from the benefits that the population received through the distributionist policies of the regime. He led the process of establishing new institutions. He introduced the method of mass mobilization, whatever the task may be. He also defined the pattern of concentrating resources away from the urban areas, and instilled in the population the belief that they have an inherent right to a job, health care, and education. Under his direction the revolution dared to nationalize foreign property and then challenged the Soviet Union on the proper way to build socialism.

In *foreign policy, from the very outset, Castro's relations with the United States were strained. In 1961, a U.S.-organized force of exiles was defeated by Cuba in the *Bay of Pigs invasion, which Fidel Castro proclaimed the "first defeat of American imperialism" in the Western Hemisphere. The United States retaliated by imposing an economic embargo on Cuba. The conflict escalated into the 1962 missile crisis, bringing the world to the brink of war. Castro defined the need for a global foreign policy in order to escape the U.S.-imposed isolation in the Western Hemisphere. Cuba established ties with Africa and Asia, while Castro began to play a major role in representing the Third World in international fora and Cuban personnel went to a number of countries.

From 1961 Cuba developed a special relationship with the Soviet Union. Castro played a critical role in linking the two countries and in obtaining unusually beneficial terms of trade from the Soviets. With the accession to power of *Gorbachev and the new policy directions in the Soviet Union, Cuba's special relation with the Soviets ended. The subsequent breakup of the Soviet Union and efforts by the members of the Commonwealth of Independent States, led by *Yeltsin's Russia, to distance themselves from the special relationship has placed Cuba at its most difficult juncture since Fidel Castro seized power. In the early 1990s, the prospects for the survival of the Cuban Revolution seem dim. With a shortage of oil, spare parts, raw materials, and consumer goods, the population confronts ever more drastic austerity measures. And this is happening precisely as the demands for political liberalization gain force.

Unquestionably, the greatest challenge that ever confronted Fidel Castro lies just ahead. Like his guerrilla fighters, Castro has aged. The élan and magic of earlier heroism does not touch the young as it did their parents. It is doubtful that Fidel Castro will relinquish power. If he does not, it remains an open question whether he will have created the means by which the nation and the revolution will survive his death.

(See also CUBAN MISSILE CRISIS; GUERRILLA WARFARE; LAND REFORM; U.S.–LATIN AMERICAN RELATIONS.)

NELSON P. VALDÉS

CENTRAL AFRICAN REPUBLIC. The Central African Republic (CAR) is one of Africa's less-developed and least-known countries. A 600- to 900-meter-high (2,000 to 3,000 ft.) landlocked plateau, the CAR is ecologically a transitional zone, its 625,000 square kilometers (240,000 sq. mi.) stretching from savannah lands in the north to dense rain forests in the extreme south. The country possesses rich timber (hardwoods) and mineral resources (including diamonds, uranium, iron, and copper) and grows cash crops (cotton, coffee); however, poor roads and distance to the coast (all goods must travel via the shallow Oubangui River to Brazzaville) keep the economy depressed, resources underexploited, and imports costly.

The country's estimated population of 2 million is a complex mosaic of some eighty ethnic groups, the largest being the Gbaya, Banda, Zande, and Sara. Few are indigenous to the CAR, most arriving during the last 200 years. The northeast is depopulated, a heritage of brutal sweeps by the great slave-raider, Rabah, and sultanates in Chad and Sudan. As a consequence only a few small precolonial kingdoms developed in the region. Interethnic relations are poor, and resentments exist against the power monopoly of the "Riverines"—a collective name for small groups residing along the Oubangui River—who advanced rapidly owing to their earlier contact with the French colonial administration.

Prior to independence known as Oubangui-Chari (after two of its rivers) and part of French Equatorial Africa, at the outset the colony was carved into concessions and harshly exploited by private companies. Outcries in Paris (spearheaded by author André Gide) in due course alleviated some of the worst abuses. Still, to pay for its upkeep a poll tax forced farmers to grow cash crops, especially cotton, resulting in new abuses and unrest. Stagnating during the colonial era, the CAR emerged independent on 13 August 1960 under David Dacko, its charismatic founding father, Barthélemy Boganda, having just died in an air crash. Social and budgetary stresses, Dacko's weak leadership, and interelite frictions set the stage for the coup of 31 December 1965, led by Chief of Staff Colonel Jean-Bedel Bokassa, a relative of both Boganda and Dacko—all three Riverines.

Bokassa's bizarre fourteen-year rule was a vain tyranny with all domestic and foreign policy dictated by whim, culminating in his grandiose Napoleon-style coronation as emperor. National resources were looted; the CAR's minimal infrastructure fell into disrepair; the economy ground to a halt. Having directly sustained the regime owing to the CAR's mineral wealth and strategic location, France finally flew in troops to the capital, Bangui, to oust Bokassa on 20 September 1979 after he crushed student riots with great bloodshed and (personal) cruelty. (In 1986 Bokassa stunningly returned from exile to stand trial.) Dacko, reelevated to power by France, and "confirmed" in office in rigged presidential elections, again proved inept in governing the by-now-seething country. On 1 September 1981 he was himself ousted by General André Kolingba in a coup countenanced by France.

Though Kolingba civilianized and constitutionalized his regime, set up a (single) political party and National Assembly, and held elections, stability and legitimacy elude him. He is viewed as yet another Riverine under the overlordship of France. Ethnicity continues to polarize an increasingly urban and radical populace with pressing societal needs in an economy in shambles, rampant with corruption, and providing few employment prospects. The changed global context of the 1990s saw a dramatic shift in France's African policy and a decline in the commitment to sustain Kolingba. Civilianization, multiparty elections, and democratization are in the process of being implemented.

(See also FRANCOPHONE AFRICA.)

Yarisse Zactizoum, *Histoire de la Centrafrique*, 2 vols. (Paris, 1983). Thomas O'Toole, *The Central African Republic* (Boulder, Colo., 1986). Samuel Decalo, "Jean-Bedel Bokassa," in *Psychoses of Power: African Personal Dictatorships* (Boulder, Colo., 1989).

SAMUEL DECALO

CENTRAL EUROPE. Central Europe cannot be sharply delimited on a map. Although it is situated on the east-west axis of the continent—the adjective *central* here signifies an in-between (as in Central America) rather than a being at the hub (as in the center-periphery distinction)—Central Europe is less a geographical entity than an intellectual construct. Occasionally an alternative name—East-Central Europe—has been applied to it. And indeed, while the countries comprising it—with *Poland, *Hungary, and *Czechoslovakia at the core—were part of the Soviet bloc, it used to be called Eastern Europe. Thus the term itself, its meaning, as well as the territory to which it corresponds, are all somewhat amorphous.

In its original, German form, the term first gained wide currency beginning in 1915 with the publication of Friedrich Naumann's book *Mitteleuropa*. In *Mitteleuropa*—100,000 copies of which were sold within six months—Naumann evoked the idea of the common destiny of smaller European nations whose variety and distinct identities could be preserved in a supranational, federative organism with Germany and Austria at the core. Thus, although it was robbed of its immediate political relevance by the defeat of the Central Powers in *World War I, the idea of Central Europe (a literal translation of the German original) has always carried with it the notion of organized variety. It points toward a search for arrangements tolerant of local diversity, yet strong enough to deny powerful neighbors the ability to impose their will unilaterally. The Austro-Hungarian monarchy might have played this role if it had not disintegrated. A body of writings refers to the Danube as a geographical linchpin and cultural metaphor of identity *cum* variety embedded in the idea of Central Europe.

After World War I the map of Central Europe was redrawn to include a number of new or restored state entities: the so-called successor states. Following the lofty principles introduced at the Versailles peace conference (1919) by the U.S. President Woodrow Wilson, the inhabitants of reconstructed Europe were to live under self-government in their own nation-states. Accordingly, the new states were to have ethnically-derived boundaries and republican, democratic institutions. Neither ideal could be successfully implemented, however, because of the patchwork of ethnic settlements throughout Central Europe.

With the advent of *fascism in Italy and in Germany, aggressive *nationalism and authoritarian rule came to dominate politics in Central Europe. This brought the gradual erosion of democratic institutions in all countries of the region with the exception of Czechoslovakia. In the words of a contemporary historian, it was an epoch characterized by the rule of "little dictators." Appeasement of *Hitler's territorial claims against Czechoslovakia by the Western powers at the Munich Conference (1938) revealed how defenseless small European countries were against more powerful and aggressive neighbors. After the conclusion of the Nazi-Soviet pact in August 1939 and the outbreak of *World War II in September, some were directly occupied, some joined the Axis, and some were created anew (notably Slovakia and Croatia) under Nazi sponsorship eager to exploit ethnic resentments.

Central Europe suffered staggering material and human losses during World War II, the most devastating being the *Holocaust of European Jewry. But other national groups—notably Poles, Serbs, and Croats—lost several million people as well. Moreover, the war brought population transfers and boundary shifts to the region. Thus the Central Europe that emerged from the conflict was virtually uninhabited by Jews or Germans, two groups which until then had been a ubiquitous and essential component of its urban landscape. At the conference tables of Tehran (1943) and Yalta (1945), arrangements for the postwar world order made by Winston *Churchill, Franklin D. *Roosevelt, and Joseph *Stalin recognized Central Europe as the *Soviet Union's buffer zone. In the political vocabulary the term *Yalta* soon replaced *Munich* as a symbol of unprincipled and shortsighted Western realpolitik.

By 1948 in all countries of the region political *pluralism was eradicated, Socialist parties were absorbed by local Communist parties, and an effective *one-party system was installed under the close supervision of networks of Soviet advisers and a ubiquitous security police. The Iron Curtain fell over what was now known as Eastern Europe while local regimes proceeded to emulate the Soviet model. The state took ownership of material resources and control over production. Economic *planning and *collectivization of agriculture were implemented. *Secularization and indoctrination in Marxist ideology proceeded apace. The legal and constitutional order was amended to institutionalize the regime of "people's democracy." In slavish replication of the Soviet paradigm, indigenous Communist Party leaders were idolized as "little Stalins," while many eminent Communists were purged in a series of show trials.

Thus, the European satellites of the Soviet Union—with the exception of Yugoslavia, whose Communist leader, Josip Broz *Tito, was branded a renegade by Stalin—became a part of "the Soviet bloc." Their economic integration was safeguarded through the *Council for Mutual Economic Assistance (1949–1991), and military integration through membership in the *Warsaw Treaty Organization, or Warsaw Pact (1955–1991). In all international fora they always followed guidelines dictated by the Soviet leadership. Their sovereignty was in effect very limited.

The mid-1950s, the years following Stalin's death, brought significant political change to Central Europe. Austrian sovereignty was restored in 1955 and Allied forces, including the Red Army contingent, withdrew from the country. Stalin's "personality cult" was denounced in the Soviet Union and a "thaw," a liberalization, followed in the Soviet bloc. In Hungary this led to the proclamation of neutrality by Imre Nagy, a Communist leader turned patriot, and a bloody military intervention by the Red Army to suppress the national uprising. In Poland a similar tragedy was narrowly avoided as a new team of reform-minded Communists led by Władysław Gomulka ascended to power. In Czechoslovakia the process of de-Stalinization lasted longer and culminated only in 1968, when Alexander Dubček committed the Communist Party to a reform policy dubbed "Socialism with a Human Face." Yet another military intervention by the Soviet Union (this time assisted by the other Warsaw Pact armies) cut the process short in August 1968.

In the 1970s there was *détente with the West and mounting social tensions in the Soviet-bloc countries. In accordance with the "third basket" provisions of the *Helsinki Accords (1976) *human rights began to be invoked in political discourse. Human rights activists in Central Europe openly challenged the ruling Communist regimes. Opposition milieus evolved a new strategy of social action practicing freedom of speech, openly addressing their fellow citizens, and promoting civil society. In the summer of 1980 *Solidarity was born in the Gdansk shipyards under the charismatic leadership of Lech *Wałesa.

Even though suffering organizational setbacks and imprisonment of their leaders in the 1980s, Solidarity in Poland and *Charter 77 in Czechoslovakia eventually prevailed and transformed East European politics. Ideas of empowered *citizenship, emancipated society, political and cultural pluralism, elaborated in the writings of numerous talented writers and essayists (Václav *Havel among them), brought forth the strength of spiritual links with European politics and tradition. The concept of Central Europe made its comeback.

In the climate induced by pursuit of glasnost and *perestroika in the Soviet Union the 1989 "refolution" (akin simultaneously to reform and revolution) took place in Central Europe. With the exception of Romania, and until civil war broke out in Yugoslavia in 1991, it was a nonviolent, negotiated process of regime change. Popular protests led to roundtable negotiations and then to free elections, and instead of "people's democracies" there were by the end of 1990 multiparty parliamentary republics in Central Europe. To be sure, institutionalization of political democracy was only slowly taking root there, but, surprisingly, it proved easier to accomplish than transformation of the economic system. In another development, dormant ethnic antagonisms came to the surface with surprising strength.

At the time of the 1989 revolution, the economies of all the countries in the region were in deep crisis. And to the extent that they had been interconnected, heavily dependent on each other and on the economy of the Soviet Union, their individual economic failures reinforced one another, compounding difficulties on the road to recovery.

There was broad agreement that market institutions and private property ought to replace central planning and state ownership in economy. But the sheer scale of changes required to implement this transition was unprecedented. Poland and Hungary were crippled by an enormous foreign debt accumulated in the 1970s and 1980s. All of the Soviet-bloc countries suffered widespread environmental devastation. The industrial base of local economies was obsolete, and technologies backward. Banking systems, financial markets, unemployment services—infrastructure that was indispensable to the transition—were nonexistent. Resources necessary to sustain a capitalist economy—institutions, procedures, managerial skills, adequately trained work force, capital—were sorely lacking.

Despite ethnic antagonisms, a sense of common destiny and common purpose pervades Central Europe. All countries of the region desire rapid integration with institutions of the *European Community. But they also share a sense of unexpectedly steep challenges lying ahead on the road to sovereignty, freedom, and prosperity which will have to be carved out between a unified Germany and a disintegrating Soviet Union.

(See also NINETEEN EIGHTY-NINE; PRAGUE SPRING; SOVIET–EAST EUROPEAN RELATIONS.)

Anthony Polonsky, *The Little Dictators: The History of Eastern Europe Since 1918* (London, 1975). Jacques Rupnik, *The Other Europe* (London, 1988). Timothy Garton-Ash, *The Uses of Adversity: Essays on the Fate of Central Europe* (New York, 1989). Joseph Rothschild, *Return to Diversity: A Political History of East Central Europe Since World War II* (New York, 1989).

JAN T. GROSS

CENTRAL INTELLIGENCE AGENCY. The shock of Pearl Harbor and the realization of the *Cold War prompted the 1947 National Security Act, which created the Central Intelligence Agency (CIA) as the United States' first peacetime foreign *intelligence organization, covering espionage, counterespionage, and intelligence analysis. The agency was prohibited from operating inside the United States and was placed under the direction of the president through the National Security Council (NSC). It coordinates intelligence from all sources and from all departments of U.S. government. The 1949 Central Intelligence Agency Act empowered the director of central intelligence (DCI) to spend agency money "without regard to the provisions of law and regulation": this provides the legal authority for covert actions (e.g., support for foreign political parties and trade unions) and operations (e.g., organizing the overthrow of a foreign government). In 1976 President Gerald Ford issued an executive order prohibiting the agency from conducting assassinations. In 1981 President Ronald *Reagan authorized the agency to operate within the United States to collect "significant" foreign intelligence as long as spying on the domestic operations of U.S. citizens and corporations is not involved. In 1982 the Boland amendment forbade the CIA to engage in or fund activities aimed at the overthrow of the Sandinista government in Nicaragua. In 1990 a congressional inspector general was appointed.

Extraordinary technical achievements characterized the CIA's first decades. Richard Bissell (deputy director responsible for operations, 1958–1962), a genius at intelligence management, developed the U-2 and SR-71 spy planes and the first spy satellites. The U-2 moved from the drawing board in 1954 to first flight in less than a year. It was at the experimental edge of aviation technology, flying higher and longer than any other airplane. U-2 photographs caused the U.S. Air Force to retarget and remap the USSR before Francis Gary Powers was shot down in a U-2 over the Soviet Union on 1 May 1960. The SR-71, operational from 1965, officially broke the world's speed and altitude records in 1990. Spy satellites became the principal means of intelligence collection from the early 1960s and remain so in the present day.

Until the mid-1970s, individual congressional leaders, rather than committees, exercised oversight of the CIA. With the *Vietnam War and *Watergate, attitudes changed, and the place—if any—for secrecy in the democracy became a political issue. President Ford's Rockefeller Commission (1975) and the Pike and Church congressional committees (1975–1976) revealed assassination plots against foreign leaders, notably Patrice *Lumumba in the Congo (1960) and Fidel *Castro (1961–1964); domestic surveillance of a number of U.S. citizens and journalists; mail opening; and possession of lethal toxins and devices. The investigations found that the agency had not been a "rogue elephant," but concluded that stricter authority and control were required. A new understanding developed between Congress, the presidency and the agency, and a place for secrets was acknowledged by implication. The CIA began to report not only to the president and the NSC but also to many congressional committees, in particular the Intelligence Oversight and the Appropriations committees, which in turn raised questions about

CIA secrecy and security. A consequence of this, and of the Boland amendment, was that support for anti-Sandinista forces was organized by the NSC staff, resulting in the Iran-Contra scandal, which marred the end of Ronald Reagan's presidency.

The CIA organization consists of four directorates—operations (DDO), science and technology (DDS&T), intelligence (DDI), and administration (DDA)—reporting through an executive director and deputy director of central intelligence to the DCI. A public affairs office and a comptroller report similarly. A general counsel, CIA inspector general, legislative liaison and director of intelligence community staff, as well as national intelligence officers, report directly to the DCI. The DCI, while being head of the agency, is also nominally the head of all U.S. intelligence and the president's chief intelligence officer.

The relationship between the DCI and the president has been the key element in the influence of the agency. Allen Dulles (DCI 1953–1961) was close to Dwight *Eisenhower, and oversaw many of the agency's most famous exploits, including the overthrow of Jacobo Arbenz in *Guatemala (1954), the Berlin Tunnel tapping into Soviet land lines (1955), and the public failure to overthrow Castro via the *Bay of Pigs Invasion (1961). Richard Helms (DCI 1966–1973) used his influence with Lyndon *Johnson to warn about the growing dangers of U.S. involvement in Vietnam, and despite pressure from Richard Nixon, kept the agency out of the *Watergate scandal. William Colby (DCI 1973–1976) consciously created the modern agency by revealing controversial secrets, forcing Congress, the presidency, and the population at large to accept the reality of an intelligence agency. William Casey (DCI 1981–1987) was the only DCI to achieve cabinet rank.

(See also CONGRESS, U.S.; KGB; PRESIDENCY, U.S.; SECURITY.)

John Ranelagh, *The Agency* (New York, 1987). Rhodri Jeffreys-Jones, *The CIA and American Democracy* (New Haven, Conn., 1989).

JOHN RANELAGH

CENTRALLY PLANNED ECONOMY. See COMMAND ECONOMY.

CHAD. The recent history of Chad has been quite exceptional compared with that of other African polities south of the Sahara. When the country became independent in August 1960, after slightly more than half a century of French colonization, internal tensions were already building. Chad's first president, François (later N'Garta) Tombalbaye, came to power in the late 1950s as head of the then-dominant Parti Progressiste Tchadien, a party whose membership was drawn chiefly from the more developed south (about one-quarter of the national territory, comprising slightly less than fifty percent of the population, estimated in 1990 at 5.6 million). The inhabitants of the north, almost entirely Muslim, were politically divided among themselves, but soon became antagonized by the increasingly authoritarian rule of President Tombalbaye. The antagonism was deepened by the presence in the northern provinces of a large number of civil servants from the south. Some of this stratum of officials were corrupt, and many, being Christians or believers in traditional African religions, did not understand local cultures and customs.

This uneasy situation led, in 1965–1968, to a series of grass-roots peasant revolts in several of the northern provinces and to the creation of a nominally radical and anti-imperialist exile political movement, the Front de Libération Nationale du Tchad (FROLINAT), that endeavored to unite the various local peasant movements. At first the FROLINAT rebellion did not constitute a real menace to the Chadian state, although the Tombalbaye regime lost control over part of the north and had to turn to France for military assistance during 1969–1972. In 1977, however, branches of FROLINAT began to receive extensive support from *Libya, which claimed Chad's northern Aozou Strip as Libyan territory and, more generally, wanted to exercise greater influence over the Saharan and Sahelian regions of Chad. FROLINAT now represented a truly formidable rebel force. In the meantime, the Chadian army, headed by General Félix Malloum, had taken power in April 1975; Tombalbaye was killed in the coup.

A series of bloody battles and several rounds of diplomatic negotiations led to the formation in late 1979 of a national coalition government headed by Goukouni Weddeye, a FROLINAT leader. Soon afterward, in April 1980, new tensions developed when FROLINAT leaders quarreled among themselves about the proper extent of Libyan aid and influence in Chadian affairs. Hissein Habré, then minister of defense and a staunch anti-Qaddafi politician, left the government; another civil war erupted, ending in victory for Habré and his Forces Armées du Nord in June 1982 (marking, incidentally, the first time a guerrilla movement had ever come to power in independent Africa). The Libyan-backed forces of Weddeye managed to retain control over the Saharan provinces.

The protracted civil war had several important consequences. First, with the Libyan intervention, the conflict became fully internationalized. Habré received support from the Sudan, Egypt, Saudi Arabia, and the United States in his anti-Qaddafi crusade, while France came to his rescue in 1983 by sending troops in response to a thinly disguised Libyan invasion (a contingent of French troops remained into the 1990s). Chad's strategic position in the heart of Africa, bordering important and mutually hostile countries such as Libya and the Sudan, explains the intervention of non-African powers.

Second, during the turmoils of the civil war, Chad nearly ceased to exist as a political entity. From February 1979 until the summer of 1982, Chad's southern provinces functioned as an independent state in all but name, while various FROLINAT "warlords" exercised autonomous control over northern provinces. Only with Habré's military victory was central authority reestablished. Habré first reconquered the southern provinces; then, with the support of several former opponents of the regime, he managed to drive the Libyan army out of all but the Aozou Strip.

Third, the civil war virtually destroyed the economy of a country that, already at independence, had been counted among the poorest in the world, with virtually no resources except agriculture and animal husbandry. (Cotton is the main export crop; oil has been discovered in the south, but as of June 1990 exploitation had not yet begun.) The stabilization of Habré's regime led to lavish economic aid, principally from France and the United States, but Chad nevertheless remains a poor and undeveloped country.

At the end of 1989, Habré's regime seemed rather stable: in December, a new Constitution was overwhelmingly adopted by referendum, the same referendum confirming Habré as Chad's president. However, a split within the regime brought renewed warfare. In April 1989, several military commanders, led by Colonel Idriss Déby, had fled to the Sudan denouncing Habré's dictatorial rule. They represented two ethnic groups from the center-east, the Zaghawa and the Hadjeraï, that had backed Habré when he came to power in 1982 but that now withdrew their allegiance.

In exile, Déby founded a new political movement, the Mouvement Patriotique du Salut (MPS), and started to build up his armed forces with limited help from Libya and the Sudan. Although he seemed at first no real menace to Habré (several attacks by MPS forces failed over 1989 and 1990), a surprise offensive in late 1990 led to the unexpected breakdown of the incumbent regime. On 1 December 1990 Habré went into exile in Senegal and Idriss Déby became Chad's new ruler.

The new regime's political record is rather contradictory. A provisional constitution, the Charte Nationale, adopted in February 1991, is strongly presidential in nature and does not allow for popular participation in politics: President Déby was nominated by the Conseil National du Salut, the leading body of the MPS, and is responsible only to this council. At the same time, Déby promised that the Charte Nationale would be valid only for a thirty-month period during which democracy would gradually be introduced in Chad. Since the end of 1991 political parties have been officially allowed to function and a National Conference is scheduled for May 1992. This conference will draft a new constitution, after which presidential and parliamentary elections will be held. Because the regime does not really control its own armed forces—which has led to acute security problems all over the country—the outcome of this democratization process remains uncertain.

(See also CORRUPTION; FRANCOPHONE AFRICA.)

Virginia Thompson and Richard Adlof, *Conflict in Chad* (Berkeley, Calif., 1981). Michael P. Kelley, *A State in Disarray: Conditions of Chad's Survival* (Boulder, Colo., 1986). Robert Buijtenhuijs, *Le Frolinat et les guerres civiles du Tchad (1977–1984)* (Paris, 1987).

ROBERT BUIJTENHUIJS

CHARTER 77. The most important dissident organization in *Czechoslovakia, Charter 77 was founded in January 1977. It was established by dissident writers, philosophers, and other professionals, including Václav *Havel, currently president of Czechoslovakia, to protest against the systematic violation of *human rights in Czechoslovakia. Originally a small group of some 200 intellectuals, the charter came to have over 1,300 signatories. The influence of the charter proved to be far greater than the number of those who formally adhered to its principles. Charter activities helped to keep alive a spirit of free thought during the communist period, when the charter also served as a moral referent for many people. Charter activists were also instrumental in founding the Civic Forum, the umbrella group that emerged in November 1989 to lead the Velvet Revolution that ousted the communist system.

Outraged by the harsh sentences meted out to a group of Czech rock musicians, the Plastic People of the Universe, and inspired by the *Helsinki Accords, the charter originally functioned as a human rights group. Its spokespersons called on Czech and Slovak leaders to observe the international agreements they had signed, as well as Czech and Slovak law, and brought violations of human rights to the attention of world opinion. Despite frequent harassment by the authorities, who interrogated all of the original signatories and deprived many of them of the right to work in their professions, the charter continued its activities throughout the rest of the communist period in Czechoslovakia.

Beginning in the early 1980s, the emphasis of the charter's activities shifted. Charter spokespersons continued to defend human rights, but they also began issuing a series of position papers that provided alternative perspectives on pressing economic, political, and social problems. They also discussed issues that the communist authorities wished to ignore, such as problems with nuclear reactors and environmental problems. The charter thus came to serve as a focus of a second, independent intellectual community. Charter activists inspired and encouraged independent activities on the part of young people, artists, and others. Charter documents also came to be known to large circles of people who were still part of the official world.

The charter's immediate impact on policy-making was extremely limited during the communist period, owing in part to the small number of activists and the social composition of charter supporters. Although the signatories of the charter included people from all walks of life, most were well-educated professionals or former professionals. Similarly, although there were Slovaks and members of other national groups among the signatories of the charter, most were Czechs. The impact of the charter was further inhibited by the harsh response of the regime to its activities.

At the same time, the continued existence of the charter was important not only to later developments in Czechoslovakia but throughout Central and Eastern Europe. Dissidents in *Poland, *Hungary, and elsewhere drew inspiration from the charter. As the Communist Party leadership hesitatingly implemented certain aspects of *Gorbachev's policies in Czechoslovakia, the ground that the charter's activities had helped to prepare bore fruit in the increased willingness of the population, including young people, to challenge the regime by engaging in open protests and founding illegal groups. In the early days after the brutal police attack on peaceful student demonstrators in November 1989, charter activists took the lead in organizing Civic Forum and in the negotiations that led to the renunciation of the leading role of the Communist Party and the eventual restoration of a multiparty, democratic political system in Czechoslovakia.

The charter continues to exist in postcommunist Czechoslovakia. Many charter activists hold crucial positions in the new government and in other areas of public life. At a summer 1990 conference, charter activists decided to continue to serve as a watchdog to see that the new, democratic regime in Czechoslovakia respects human rights.

(See also CENTRAL EUROPE; COMMUNIST PARTY STATES; NINETEEN EIGHTY-NINE; PRAGUE SPRING.)

SHARON L. WOLCHIK

CHERNOBYL NUCLEAR ACCIDENT. The nuclear accident that occurred on 26 April 1986 at Chernobyl, a town in Ukraine situated approximately 100 kilometers (60 mi.) north of Kiev, is an event that seems to become increasingly important with time. The reason is that its impact on human health and on agriculture, the environment, the economy, and future energy strategies continues to mount each year. Moreover, its effects have extended beyond the former *Soviet Union to all states that use nuclear energy. For this reason, and because of public sensitivity about nuclear issues, neither the Soviet government nor other governments were eager to publish information about the accident and its consequences. As a result, new facts are still emerging, and assessments of the accident keep changing.

Most of the studies that have been made of the

medical and environmental impact of the accident remain classified. The continued lack of openness about Chernobyl reflects the fact that the Soviet authorities did not have a consistent, rational policy and were unable to respond to the challenges that the accident produced. On the positive side, however, after Chernobyl there was more frankness about other accidents, both before and after, and the disaster can be seen as one of the triggers that stimulated *glasnost in the USSR.

There is no doubt that the Chernobyl accident dealt a crushing blow to the prestige of Soviet science and technology. It also ruined the nuclear energy program in the Soviet Union and Eastern and Central Europe. It turned the embryonic Soviet environmental movement into a strong political force that formed links with local nationalist movements in key Soviet republics. Internationally it served as a stark warning that pollution cannot be contained within one country and that greater international cooperation is required to deal with it and other global problems. Furthermore, it demonstrated the need for stricter international supervision of nuclear facilities. As a result, the International Atomic Energy Agency (IAEA) gained prominence and became more effective.

Economic Cost and Impact on World Nuclear Industry. In purely financial terms the cost of the accident, initially estimated in July 1986 at 2 billion rubles (US$3 billion), increased to 8 billion rubles in 1987. By 1990, when the Soviet government allocated special funds to the most affected regions, the cost had escalated to 50 billion rubles. If one adds the costs of the tasks that remain to be done, together with those of canceled or frozen nuclear energy projects, the cost will rise to nearly 200 billion rubles by the year 2000, and it will continue to rise well into the next century.

The world nuclear energy industry was severely affected by the accident. Before 1986 it was assumed that in the unlikely event that a maximum nuclear reactor accident occurred, it would involve the meltdown of the reactor core owing to the accumulation of fission radionuclides. If this occurred at the end of the reactor cycle, the fission radionuclides would generate about four percent of the total thermal power of a working reactor. Most safety devices, therefore, were designed to protect the environment from such an accident.

What happened at Chernobyl was far worse. The total power of the reactor surged to about 100 and then to 440 times its normal full power within four seconds, provoking a "prompt criticality" explosion. The fuel channels ruptured, the reactor core was destroyed, and the 2,000-ton, three-meter-thick upper plate was displaced, shearing off more than 1,000 steel pipes attached to the primary circuit. The bottom 1,000-ton concrete plate was pressed down, smashing the metal structures beneath it. The local release of thermal energy in the reactor core was about 10,000 times higher than in the Three Mile Island nuclear accident in Pennsylvania in March 1979. Neither the safety regulations nor risk factor calculations had envisaged the possibility of this type of accident.

Although Western authorities insisted that the design flaws that made the accident possible were unique to that type of graphite-moderated, high-power, boiling channel type and were not to be found in Western or Japanese reactors, nuclear power everywhere was affected. The new safety regulations recommended by the IAEA made nuclear energy far more expensive. In 1986, 430 reactors in twenty-six countries generated nearly sixteen percent of the world's electricity. A further 149 reactors were planned or under construction. Within two years this number had fallen to ninety-six. The Soviet energy program suffered most, but many projects in Eastern and Western Europe and in the developing countries were also canceled. All older Magnox-type, graphite-moderated reactors in Britain were shut down.

Impact on Soviet and East European Energy Programs. Because Soviet oil production had declined, nuclear power was given priority in the economic development plan proposed by Mikhail *Gorbachev for the period 1985–2000. Nuclear-generated electricity was expected to reach forty percent of the total energy requirement toward the end of the century. Nearly half of the new capacity was planned to come from graphite-moderated, high-power, boiling channel reactors of the Chernobyl type. Studies of the causes of the accident, however, identified several fundamental design flaws in the reactor model. As a result, it was eliminated from the nuclear energy program and extensive modifications had to be made to the thirteen existing reactors of this type.

Several pressurized water reactors and five military plutonium-producing reactors were shut down for good. Others already under construction were canceled or temporarily halted for safety reasons. Levels of production of nuclear-generated electricity remained stagnant, causing an acute energy crisis that set back Soviet industrial development in 1986–1990. Energy shortages, compounded by a shortage of investment capital (owing both to the cost of Chernobyl and to reduced oil revenues) gradually caused the total failure of the "administrative-command" economy, contributing significantly to the decision to adopt market-oriented economic principles as part of a new *perestroika package.

The use of crude oil and oil fuel to generate electricity and for heating increased. Soviet per capita oil consumption, already high (twelve barrels a year), rose even further. The result was a reduction in the amount of oil available for export. Eastern and Central European countries, heavily dependent on Soviet oil, were severely affected (they were further hit by the decision to charge them world prices in hard currency from the beginning of 1991) both by oil shortages and by the problems in the Soviet nuclear energy program: forty-nine percent of Hungarian, thirty-six percent of Bulgarian, twenty-six percent of Czechoslovakian, and thirty-seven percent of Finnish electricity was produced by nuclear power stations built by the Soviet Union, as of 1989. Furthermore, in the future they will have to dispose of their own spent nuclear fuel and nuclear waste.

In the German Democratic Republic (GDR) there were four Soviet pressurized water reactors of the old type in 1990, producing ten percent of the country's electricity. Five new units were under construction at the time of reunification. None of them met the safety standards of the Federal Republic of Germany (FRG). Because no alternative energy sources exist (except highly polluting lignite coal), it has been decided to close down the old reactors and to put the new models into operation after reequipping them.

Health Impact. After the accident 116,000 people were evacuated from the so-called exclusion zone, i.e., areas lying within a radius of 30 kilometers (18.6 mi.) of the power station. Later, new areas of radioactive contamination were discovered to the west, north, and south of the exclusion zone, some with levels of radioactive cesium 137 well above 40 curies per square kilometer (above 1,500,000 Bq/m^2). These were designated "special areas of strict radiological control," and about 600,000 inhabitants were registered to undergo periodic medical examinations for the rest of their lives. Their offspring would also be subject to lifelong medical checkups.

The permissible whole-life radiation exposure for these people was raised to 35 rem, higher than the permissible whole-life exposure for those working in the nuclear industry. But by 1990 some groups were already approaching the maximum level, and nearly 100,000 people from Byelorussia, the Ukraine, and the Bryansk region of the Russian Republic had to be resettled.

Nearly 500,000 people who had taken part in the initial stages of cleaning up, decontaminating the accident site and villages in the area, conducting dosimetry for radiation maps, patrolling the area, constructing protective dams and the cover for the damaged reactor, and so forth, had been exposed to high levels of radiation. They have established the Chernobyl Society to lobby for better medical care and financial compensation for health damage.

According to unofficial reports, radiation-linked health problems are affecting three groups in particular: evacuees from the exclusion zone, inhabitants of the special areas of strict radiological control, and people who were involved in dealing with the consequences of the accident. They are said to suffer both from specific conditions (increased incidence of thyroid deficiency and leukemia) and from nonspecific problems (especially nervous and respiratory disorders). However, there have been no official scientific or statistical reports of these problems.

The main delayed effect of radiation exposure—the increased incidence of cancer—will emerge twenty to forty years after the accident and will carry the problems of Chernobyl victims well into the next century. No information has been released about the incidence of genetic defects among newborn children or about the genetic effects on plants and animals in the exclusion zone and on farm animals near it.

Environmental and Antinuclear Movements. Before the Chernobyl disaster the Soviet environmental movement was weak and divided and there was no independent Soviet antinuclear movement. Officially sponsored groups campaigned against *nuclear weapons and nuclear war, not against nuclear power. After the accident antinuclear environmental groups began to emerge, and in some republics they combined nationalist grievances with their environmental concerns. The strongest opposition to nuclear power developed in the Ukraine and Byelorussia, the two republics that had suffered most from the accident.

There were more working and planned nuclear power stations in the Ukraine than in any other republic. The plan of the central government was to use nuclear-generated heat directly in some metallurgical technologies and to sell electricity from these power stations to Bulgaria, Hungary, and Romania. The planning, design, and implementation of all nuclear projects was done in Moscow, and there was little consultation with local communities about their need for power or the location of stations. When freely contested elections were held in 1989 and 1990, environmental movements used the opportunity to organize political campaigns and to elect representatives to the central and republican parliaments. In 1990 the Ukrainian Supreme Soviet declared the republic an "ecological disaster area" and demanded that the three remaining working reactors at Chernobyl be closed. The first *green party was officially registered in the Ukraine in 1990. In Lithuania antinuclear groups campaigned successfully against the construction of the third and fourth units at the Ignalina plant.

In 1988 the antinuclear movement also began to campaign against underground nuclear tests in the Semipalatinsk region of Kazakhstan, the main nuclear test site since the first Soviet atomic bomb was exploded in 1949. Despite strong resistance from the ministry of defense, the Semipalatinsk test site was closed in 1990.

Future Tasks. Recent calculations show that nearly 70 million curies of radioactivity were released by the Chernobyl accident. Half of them were deposited within the then Soviet Union. By 1990 only the long-lived radionuclides (cesium 137, strontium 90, and plutonium) were creating problems. The first maps published in 1990 showed the uneven, almost random distribution of these radionuclides. About half of the cesium and strontium and most of the plutonium remain inside the exclusion zone, which has now been converted into an ecological study area for research into plants and animals. A significant proportion (probably about 1 million curies) is located in hundreds of temporary waste disposal facilities where the topsoil that was scraped from a million hectares (2.5 million acres) of land in and around the Chernobyl station, asphalt and concrete from the roads, vehicles, and trees that were killed by the initial fallout have been stored.

There are about 700 kilograms (1,540 lbs.) of plutonium, 43 kilograms (95 lbs.) of strontium 90, 81 kilograms (179 lbs.) of cesium 137, and nearly 170 metric tons (187 tons) of uranium, totaling about 7 million curies of radioactivity, in the hastily constructed sarcophagus that covers the damaged reactor. But the metal structures inside the cover are rusting and becoming brittle, and volatile dust composed of "hot particles" from the melted fuel materials is building up. There is therefore a danger that some structures within the sarcophagus will collapse, allowing radioactivity to be released through holes in the cement. The present plan is to build a huge, solid cover that will seal the existing sarcophagus hermetically and serve as a safe tomb for at least 300 years.

Because of the very slow natural process of decontamination of soil tainted by strontium 90, cesium 137, and plutonium, the agricultural consequences will persist for forty to fifty years. About 1 million hectares (2.5 million acres) have been taken out of agricultural use and will be reforested. Field, meat, and dairy products from a further 2 million hectares (5 million acres) must checked for contamination and subjected to special processing methods to reduce radioactivity before consumption.

The Chernobyl accident was a turning point in Soviet history and in public perceptions of nuclear power. It reversed the trend toward wider reliance on nuclear power and discredited the belief that this was the ultimate answer to the world's energy needs.

(See also ENVIRONMENTALISM; NUCLEAR FREEZE.)

Report of the U.S. Department of Energy's Team Analyses of the Chernobyl-4 Atomic Energy Station Accident Sequence, U.S. Department of Energy (Washington, D.C., 1986). *Summary Report on the Post-Accident Review Meeting on the Chernobyl Accident,* INSAG-I Report, International Atomic Energy Agency, Safety Series (Vienna, 1986). Viktor Haynes and Marko Bojcun, *The Chernobyl Disaster* (London, 1988). Zhores A. Medvedev, *The Legacy of Chernobyl* (New York, 1990).

ZHORES A. MEDVEDEV

CHILE. Chile is a long, thin country on the west coast of South America, stretching 4,150 kilometers (2,600 mi.) from Peru to the Antarctic. Numbering approximately 13 million, its Spanish-speaking population is almost ninety percent *Roman Catholic.

Chile has been distinctive in Latin America because it boasted one of the most stable, progressive constitutional democracies prior to 1973 and experienced one of the most durable, conservative military dictatorships from 1973 until the return of *democracy in 1990. In the closing years of the twentieth century, its ability to consolidate civilian rule was a litmus test of the democratic trend that had engulfed Latin America.

After independence from Spain in 1818, Chile suffered the civil strife typical of the liberated colonies. Unlike its neighbors, however, it quickly established a stable republic under the constitution of 1833, which lasted until 1925. That oligarchic system concentrated power in the hands of the president, the landowning families, the merchants, and the Roman Catholic church. It nevertheless sustained civilian rule and gradually incorporated new social groups and parties through peaceful elections. The only disruption of regular presidential turnover occurred during the brief civil war of 1891. That conflict between the legislative and executive branches resulted in a semiparliamentary republic in which congressional authority outweighed that of the presidency.

The constitution of 1925, which lasted until 1973, restored a strong presidential system, separated church and state, and codified rights for labor. After its enactment, a military dictatorship ruled from 1927 to 1931, toppled by the Great Depression of the 1930s. From 1932 until 1973, Chile maintained an unusually open, sturdy representative democracy. It was noteworthy for its multiparty system reminiscent of West European polities. That spectrum included three poles clearly defined by *ideology and *class: a conservative Right based among the economic elites, a reformist center rooted in the middle strata, and a Marxist left anchored in the proletariat. From the 1930s through the 1960s, centrist coalition governments dedicated to *import-substitution industrialization and to welfare for the urban middle and working classes prevailed. In Chilean politics, this system was referred to as the "compromise state," because it incorporated newly mobilized social sectors and reformist parties without damaging traditional political and economic elites.

An erratic but persistent leftward trend in voting and policies culminated in the first free election anywhere of a Marxist president, Salvador *Allende Gossens in 1970. Mainly backed by the Socialist and Communist parties, he won with thirty-six percent of the popular vote in a three-way race. He greatly accelerated the reforms—especially *nationalization of U.S. copper mines and redistribution of agricultural lands—begun under his Christian Democrat predecessor, Eduardo Frei Montalva. In order to move the country from state capitalism toward state socialism, Allende expropriated the major means of production and promoted massive redistribution to urban and rural workers.

Backed by the United States, centrist forces (the Partido Demócrata Cristiano) joined rightists (the Partido Nacional) in an alliance against Allende's socialist project. Class conflict and political polarization escalated. In the showdown midterm congressional elections of March 1973, the electorate divided between forty-four percent for the government and fifty-four percent for the opposition. Thereafter, on 11 September 1973, President Allende died defending his government—democracy and socialism—against a coup d'état led by Army General Augusto *Pinochet Ugarte.

For nearly a decade, Pinochet reigned without significant challenge. After exterminating, exiling, or imprisoning thousands of leaders of the left and labor, Pinochet relied on a coalition of military officers, technocrats, and capitalists. He constructed an extremely repressive system of one-man rule, giving the president iron control over both the government and the armed forces. While he governed as chief executive, the junta representing the four branches of the armed forces (army, navy, air force, and national police) performed legislative functions.

Pinochet ended not only democratic politics but also statist economic policies designed to subsidize manufacturing and social welfare. The Pinochet government brought inflation under control from the triple-digit levels it had reached under Allende. Guided by economists enamored of the neoliberal model associated with the University of Chicago, the government shrank the role of the state in favor of the market. It liberalized trade, promoted nontraditional exports, slashed fiscal outlays, privatized public enterprises, pruned social services, and crippled labor unions. An economic boom from 1977 to 1981 was called the Chilean "miracle," purchased at the cost of regressive income distribution and high unemployment.

At the pinnacle of success of his authoritarian politics and free-market economics, Pinochet convoked a noncompetitive plebiscite in 1980. It was designed to approve a constitution to continue him in office through 1988, when a subsequent plebiscite would be held to ratify his mandate for another eight years. That 1980 charter was intended to create a "protected democracy," monitored by the armed forces and excluding Marxist groups. At the start of the 1980s, Pinochet looked invincible against his divided and demoralized opponents.

In the decade of the 1980s, however, Chile evolved from *authoritarianism to democracy through five profound transformations. First, the international recession and debt crisis of 1981–1982 provoked modifications in the neoliberal economic model. After recovery began in 1985, the essential elements of the free enterprise approach were retained. Second, although most military and business leaders remained loyal to Pinochet, dissent broke out in the previously solid ranks of regime supporters. Third, economic dislocations sparked massive social pro-

tests from 1983 to 1986. That mobilization of civil society spread from organized labor through the middle classes to end up concentrated in the urban shantytowns. Fourth, the previously shackled and dormant political parties recaptured center stage and took charge of the campaign to defeat Pinochet in the 1988 plebiscite. Those parties began to absorb or displace the *new social movements—such as *human rights organizations and women's groups—that had arisen to resist Pinochet in their absence. And fifth, the democratization contagion that swept the Western Hemisphere left the Pinochet regime isolated and defensive, particularly vis-à-vis pressures for liberalization from the United States.

Despite government control of the media and other resources, an uneasy coalition of centrist and leftist parties defeated Pinochet in the 1988 plebiscite, fifty-five percent to forty-three percent. As a result, the government convened competitive presidential and congressional contests in 1989, won by the opposition by an identical margin. The opposition standard-bearer, Christian Democrat Patricio Aylwin, took office in March 1990. Thus ended seventeen years of harsh military rule peacefully and within the legal framework erected by the dictatorship.

The Aylwin administration was an unusual post-authoritarian government, representing desires for social reform as well as determination to reconstruct democratic procedures. The new civilian administration faced four daunting tasks. First, it wanted to deliver truth and justice to the victims of human rights abuses under Pinochet without enraging the armed forces. Second, it sought to reform the constitution and key political institutions to eradicate vestiges of authoritarianism without arousing the wrath of the military and its right-wing sympathizers. Third, it needed to reestablish civilian control over the armed forces with Pinochet retaining his post as commander of the army. Fourth, it had to address the pent-up demands for social justice of a majority of poorer Chileans without upsetting the macroeconomic stability and growth bequeathed by Pinochet. Chile also remained vulnerable to shocks from the world economy, such as a drop in the price of its copper exports, contamination of its fruit shipments overseas, or a jump in the cost of its imported oil.

In contrast with 1973, one legacy of the authoritarian period was a stronger right, an enduring center, and a smaller, more moderate left. The Christian Democrats and the Socialists, bitter enemies under Allende who coalesced against Pinochet, dominated the governing coalition. Outside official circles, the government also received support from the shrunken Communist Party, disoriented and divided by years of vain struggle against the dictatorship. Particularly supportive of the administration were labor unions, students, and intellectuals. Torn between more democratic and more authoritarian elements, the rightist opposition was captained by two offshoots of the old National Party and the Pinochet camp: the Renovación Nacional and the Union Democrática Independiente. The most ardent backers of the opposition were the business magnates.

At the start of the 1990s, Chile possessed a constitutional democracy dominated by a president elected directly by popular vote. To avoid a repetition of a minority chief executive like Allende, candidates had to win by a majority or face a runoff. The House of Deputies was controlled by the Aylwin coalition, but the Senate was held by rightists because the 1980 constitution gave nine senatorial seats to conservatives without being elected. Having lost its autonomy under Pinochet, the judiciary was slated for reform. Applauded by the international community, the Aylwin government also took steps to end the diplomatic isolation suffered by Chile under Pinochet because of human rights violations.

Despite obstacles, conditions seemed optimistic for the reinvigoration of Chilean democracy. In contrast with most Latin American cases, Chile's transition took place under favorable economic circumstances: inflation was down, employment and export sales were up, growth was high, and painful structural adjustments to reduce the role of the state, expand the purview of the market, and honor the foreign debt had already been carried out, with all the incumbent social costs. Equally important, Chile's democratization entailed a return to deeply rooted values and institutions.

(See also DEMOCRATIC TRANSITIONS; MILITARY RULE; SOCIALISM AND SOCIAL DEMOCRACY; U.S.– LATIN AMERICAN RELATIONS.)

J. Samuel Valenzuela and Arturo Valenzuela, eds., *Military Rule in Chile: Dictatorship and Oppositions* (Baltimore, 1986). Brian Loveman, *Chile: The Legacy of Hispanic Capitalism* (New York, 1988). Manuel Antonio Garretón, *The Chilean Political Process* (Boston, 1989). Paul W. Drake and Iván Jaksic, eds., *The Struggle for Democracy in Chile, 1982–1990* (Lincoln, Neb., 1991).

PAUL W. DRAKE

CHINA. China approaches the twenty-first century in much the same way it entered the twentieth: on the precipice of a political crisis that portends epochal change for the Chinese state and the Chinese people. Many of the dilemmas that fueled China's crisis at the end of the last century also shape its contemporary predicament: a frustrated quest for national wealth and power; an uneasy relationship with the West and a deep ambivalence about China's role in the *international system; the crumbling *legitimacy of the country's rulers; the pressure to incorporate new social forces into the nation's political life; an alienated intelligentsia who question the validity of Chinese cultural norms in a rapidly changing world. In many ways, these issues are as relevant to understanding China in the 1990s as they were in the 1890s.

Yet to see China as unchanged would be a woeful misperception. The country has been through a century not only of terrible trauma but also of profound transformation. It is a far more modern, unified, and sovereign nation than it was a hundred years ago. China's tragedy is that its leaders have largely squandered the promise of these achievements amid internecine power struggles that have—once again—brought China to the brink of crisis.

Geography, Demography, and Administration. In terms of area, the People's Republic of China (PRC) is slightly bigger than the United States, making it the world's third largest nation, after the Soviet Union and Canada. It is the most populous country, with more than 1.1 billion people as of mid-1991. Owing to an aggressive—and sometimes coercive— family planning program, the population growth rate has been brought down to around 1.4 percent per year; nevertheless, China's population is expected to reach 1.3 billion by the year 2000. China still faces its age-old quandary of the race between the number of people and the availability of food: the country currently has about twenty percent of the world's population and only seven percent of its arable land.

Despite enormous economic progress since 1980, China remains one of the poorest nations in the world. The GNP per capita, according to World Bank calculations, was US$350 as of 1989. Other indicators, however, suggest that the physical quality of life in China may be better than in many countries at a comparable level of economic *development; for example, life expectancy in China is 70 years (compared with 58 in India). Such figures reflect the relative priority that the Chinese government has given to basic health care and other welfare measures over the last several decades.

The PRC is made up of twenty-two provinces, five autonomous regions, and three centrally administered municipalities (including Beijing, the capital of the country). The autonomous regions are areas of the country with high concentrations of non-Chinese ethnic minorities (they constitute approximately six percent of the total population). These regions (for example, *Tibet) are, according to the constitution, entitled to some measure of self-government in order to meet their special needs and to preserve their cultural identities; in reality, such autonomy is extremely superficial.

The PRC is a *unitary* state in which the subnational levels are subordinate in all important matters to the center. Growing regional economic differentiation, ethnic assertiveness, and the complexity of modern administration in a continental-sized nation may increase centrifugal pressures on the PRC in the years ahead; movement toward a federal system with more power sharing between the center and its constituent units might ease some of these tensions, but such a trend would run against the grain of age-old patterns formed when China was a highly centralized empire.

From Empire to People's Republic. Any analysis of China's contemporary political system must begin with an understanding of the major events that have shaped Chinese history in the twentieth century. Ideological conflicts, power struggles, and individual leaders have been far more important than institutional evolution or constitutional processes in defining the basic character of government and politics in China. China has had five fundamentally different constitutions in the last forty years, reflecting the fact that the most persistent crisis of the Chinese state in this century has been the failure to replace autocracy with the rule of law.

China's birth as a modern nation-state was a painful one. The 2,000-year-old imperial system was destroyed by a combination of internal decline and external pressures that culminated in the 1911 *revolution and the establishment of the Republic of China, whose first president was Sun Yat-sen. But, in some ways, the collapse of the empire was only the beginning of the *Chinese Revolution. Though the republic survived in name, the country disintegrated into regional warlordism and ultimately civil war between two major claimants to national power, the Kuomintang (or Nationalist) Party and the *Chinese Communist Party (CCP). The CCP, under the leadership of *Mao Zedong, prevailed in this struggle, and, in October 1949, proclaimed the establishment of the People's Republic of China.

The first years of communist rule in China were dominated by the tasks of political consolidation, economic reconstruction, and social transformation. The early 1950s was a period of significant achievement for the new regime: a strong, effective central government was in place for the first time in nearly a century; industrial and agricultural production quickly reached and then surpassed prewar levels; and popular support was secured via successful campaigns to redistribute land to poor *peasants and eradicate long-standing social ills such as *prostitution and opium addiction. Internationally, China asserted its reclaimed sovereignty by fighting the United States and its allies to a stalemate in the *Korean War; although this engagement was costly in economic and military terms, it bolstered the nation's pride and international prestige.

At the same time, there were signs that political repression and ideological dogmatism would be hallmarks of communist power. The party quickly backtracked from its initial pledges to go slow in the transition to socialism and to preside over a mixed economy and an inclusive polity. The socialization of the means of production in both industry and agriculture was set in motion and essentially completed by the mid-1950s, while substantial violence was unleashed against those judged to be enemies or doubters of the new order. The new state—with Mao Zedong in firm control of the party and *Zhou Enlai overseeing the government bureaucracy as premier—was structured in such a way as to ensure communist domination of the economy, politics, and cultural life.

In 1953, the PRC adopted its First Five-Year Plan. Based largely on the Soviet model, this plan put the greatest emphasis on the rapid expansion of heavy industry and the *collectivization of agriculture. The results of the plan in the industrial sector were quite impressive with overall output exceeding the target and rising more than 130 percent by 1957, the last year of the plan. In agriculture, the figures were less striking, although production did achieve a critical measure of success in outstripping population growth. However, the Chinese countryside was transformed during this period by the coercive establishment of large-scale cooperative farms (averaging 250 families) that expanded the scope of collective agriculture far beyond the more modest efforts that had been carried out in the wake of the earlier *land reform.

The central political event of this period—and one of the major turning points in the history of the PRC—was the "Hundred Flowers" movement of 1956, an ill-fated attempt by Mao Zedong to liberalize China's political life and shake up the bureaucracy. Responding to what he perceived as the first manifestations of ideological retrogression in the Soviet Union and a flagging of revolutionary élan within the CCP, Mao let it be known that he welcomed public criticism of his regime's shortcomings ("Let a hundred flowers bloom"); but when the criticism became more intense than he expected and challenged the very nature of communist authority, he joined with the bureaucracy in sanctioning a vicious crackdown on all dissent. The subsequent "Anti-Rightist Campaign" of 1957 had the immediate result that hundreds of thousands of intellectuals were labeled as traitors; many of these were dismissed from their jobs or demoted, sent to jail, or banished to remote labor reform camps. More broadly, the campaign had the effect of casting a pall over China's intellectual life that would not be lifted until after the death of Mao Zedong two decades later.

Radicalism Ascendent. The Hundred Flowers movement had occurred in the context of a debate within the CCP about China's future economic development. More conservative party leaders held to the view that the pattern established by the First Five-Year Plan was essentially correct and that, with moderate modifications stressing greater material incentives and technical assistance for the peasantry, agricultural production could be effectively stimulated to reach satisfactory levels. However, in the highly charged ideological milieu that followed the Anti-Rightist Campaign, Mao was able to prevail upon his colleagues to endorse his more radical vision for a thorough break with the Soviet model of cautious planning and technocratic management. The result was the "Great Leap Forward" of 1958–1960.

This utopian campaign, with its stress on mass

mobilization and moral incentives, was intended to be a great leap into both prosperity and *communism; in just a few years, it was hoped, China would jump into the forefront of industrial nations while at the same time completing the building of socialism to enter the more egalitarian communist stage of social development. The countryside was once more subjected to a precipitous reorganization when the agricultural cooperatives were merged into gigantic and unmanageable communes that encompassed between 5,000 and 20,000 families each. Fantastically high production targets were set for all sectors of the economy. More than a million backyard steel furnaces sprang up across the land in the effort to meet the goal of quickly overtaking Britain in steel production; steel output did surge, but most of what was produced in these small-scale enterprises was useless. As the Leap unfolded, critics were silenced, either afraid to speak out or censured when they did, as happened to Peng Dehuai, the defense minister, who dared to call some of the movement's basic premises into question.

The Great Leap turned into a great disaster. Agricultural production plummeted as resources were wasted, the land was exhausted, and the labor force pushed beyond endurance. One result was the largest famine in human history, which directly or indirectly claimed between 20 and 30 million Chinese lives. Industrial production also collapsed, plunging the country into a deep depression. Poor weather and the withdrawal of Soviet advisers and technical assistance (a result of increasing tensions in *Sino-Soviet relations) played a role in exacerbating China's economic misfortunes during this time, but the major blame for the catastrophe must lie with the flawed vision and the political intolerance of China's leaders—principally Mao Zedong.

The early 1960s was a time of recovery for the PRC. The Leap was abandoned and replaced by a more incremental development strategy that partook of elements of the First Five-Year Plan but allowed more leeway for market forces that had been squelched by both the Soviet model and the Maoist alternative. The communes were sharply reduced in size and function; bureaucratization supplanted mobilization; and meritocracy rather than equality was promoted as the guiding principle of China's *modernization. Although Mao retained significant power as chairman of the party during this period, his prestige was considerably diminished and day-to-day administration rested with other leaders, including Liu Shaoqi (president of the PRC), Zhou Enlai (premier of the PRC), and *Deng Xiaoping (secretary-general of the CCP).

By 1965, Chairman Mao had concluded that both he and China had been betrayed by some of the highest-ranking members of the CCP (especially Liu and Deng), and, indeed, that the whole party and country were in need of a reinfusion of revolutionary spirit. His solution was the "Great Proletarian Cultural Revolution," an engineered mass movement to isolate and remove those leaders who were seen to be leading China down the same "capitalist road" that the Soviet Union had already traversed. At the outset of the *Cultural Revolution, Mao forged an alliance of radical party ideologues, loyal military commanders, and tens of millions of student Red Guards to carry out his crusade against revisionism. From 1966 to 1969 (when the army stepped in to restore order), China was plunged into near anarchy: the economy was disrupted, the polity paralyzed, and society torn by a violent and vindictive witch-hunt for *class enemies. Many of China's leaders were toppled from power and, along with numerous intellectuals, were publicly humiliated, physically abused, and imprisoned or sent into internal exile, where some (including President Liu Shaoqi) died of maltreatment.

During the next few years, the People's Liberation Army, under the command of a sycophantic Maoist, Lin Biao, dominated the Chinese political scene. A new wave of extreme leftist policies were implemented across a wide range of areas of life, including education, the arts, factory management, income distribution, and health care. Radicalism appeared triumphant.

But the 1970s turned out to be another decade of intense political and ideological struggle within China's elite. In 1971, Lin Biao—Mao's closest ally during the Cultural Revolution and his chosen heir—allegedly attempted to have the chairman assassinated after the two parted ways on a number of issues including the new trend toward *détente in *Sino-American relations and the political role of the military. The mid-1970s witnessed a cataclysmic confrontation between defenders of the legacies of the Cultural Revolution and more conservative leaders (including Zhou Enlai and the rehabilitated Deng Xiaoping) who urged that the nation's priorities be shifted from class struggle politics to economic modernization.

Reform and Repression in Post-Mao China. The death of Mao Zedong in September 1976 set the stage for the denouement of radical power in the PRC. In October, Hua Guofeng, who had risen from relative obscurity as a compromise candidate to become premier following Zhou's death in January 1976, ordered the arrest of his radical rivals in the top leadership (the so-called Gang of Four, which included Mao's widow, Jiang Qing). Shortly thereafter, Hua was named to succeed Mao as chairman of the CCP.

But Hua himself was pushed aside in a few years. He was outmaneuvered by Deng Xiaoping after Deng had come back to the center of power from a second spell in political purgatory that had begun in mid-1976 after he had again incurred Mao's wrath. By the late 1970s, Deng Xiaoping was firmly installed as China's paramount leader, though he never took any of the highest positions in either the party or state hierarchy.

Under the rubric of building "*socialism with Chinese characteristics," Deng used his position to launch China on an ambitious effort to modernize the nation. Eschewing many of the radical policies of the Maoist era, Deng oversaw the introduction of far-reaching reforms in the 1980s that touched nearly every aspect of life in the PRC. Agriculture was decollectivized and authority for managing farm work devolved to the individual peasant household. Market mechanisms were allowed to supplement a greatly relaxed central *planning system. Enterprise management was decentralized and workers were induced to increase productivity by a host of material incentive schemes. Science, education, and cultural life in general were depoliticized in order to encourage China's intellectuals to devote their energies and talents to the country's modernization. A policy of "opening to the outside world" was introduced to encourage expanded trade, foreign investment, and cultural exchange. The overall effect of these reforms on the economy was tremendous, with GNP growth rates averaging ten percent per year for most of the 1980s.

Political *reform was also on Deng's agenda. Curbs were placed on the arbitrary exercise of power and steps were taken to give some measure of regularity to the legal system. But change in the political realm never proceeded as far as it did in the economy. Deng made it clear from the start of his reform effort that the supremacy of the Communist Party and its "cardinal principles" were to remain sacrosanct. He proved his inflexibility on this point by the ruthless suppression of a series of popular movements for greater democracy in 1979, 1986, and, most dramatically, in the crisis of June 1989, when hundreds of demonstrators were killed by army troops in the area around Beijing's *Tiananmen Square.

The 1989 Beijing protests reflected the accumulation of a number of pressures that had been building in China during the late 1980s. Serious problems had emerged in the Chinese economy, including high rates of inflation, that led to a paralyzing split in the party leadership over the speed and direction of further reform. Mounting public anger at official corruption and deteriorating livelihoods created a restive situation among the urban populace. These tensions, when joined with frustrations of many of China's university students and other intellectuals over the slow pace of meaningful political change, created a volatile mix that exploded in the spring of 1989.

The brutal crushing of the Tiananmen protests ushered in a period of uneasy quiet in Chinese politics. Leaders considered too soft on the question of political reform (including party chief, Zhao Zi-yang) were removed or demoted. Power was held by a coalition of octogenarians, many of whom had made a pretense of retiring from active involvement in politics, and their underlings who held the more formal positions of state and party authority. Political repression and economic retrenchment characterized government policy in the early 1990s, while anger, cynicism, and apathy best described the public mood.

China's Political System in the 1990s. The PRC is one of the few remaining *Communist party states. Its political system in many ways can be described as classically Leninist. The Communist Party asserts the right to exercise the "leading role" in China, which is defined in the PRC constitution as "a socialist state under the people's democratic dictatorship led by the working class and based on an alliance of workers and peasants." This formula effectively gives the CCP a monopoly on formal power and ostensibly legitimizes the proscription of meaningful opposition. Other political parties do exist (for example, the China Democratic League), but they are politically impotent and are allowed to function only so long as they abide by strict guidelines set down by the CCP. Although there is somewhat more latitude for the pursuit of independent nonpolitical interests than there was during the Maoist era, most social organizations and professional or occupational associations serve as transmission belts for party policy; indeed, one of the leadership's greatest fears during the Tiananmen crisis of 1989 was the possibility of the emergence of a Solidarity-like movement among China's workers.

The constitutional structure of the PRC vests formal state authority in a hierarchically arranged system of people's congresses; these begin at the local level of the urban district and the rural township and culminate in the "highest organ of state power," the National People's Congress (NPC), which meets once a year for about two weeks. The NPC chooses the highest officials of the state, the premier, who presides over the government's functional ministries and commissions, and the president, a largely ceremonial position that has always been held and used as a base of personal power by an influential individual.

Elections to the people's congresses at the grassroots level have become more democratic in recent years, and the constitutionally specified powers of the congresses at all levels are impressive. However, the scope of these powers is in practice greatly circumscribed by the reality of Communist Party oversight of elections to ensure the ideological acceptability of all candidates and the fact that most high-ranking state officials are also party members.

Although CCP membership comprises less than five percent of the total population, the party is organized so that it penetrates society at every level, including places of work and residence through its weblike network of branches, committees, and congresses. There have been efforts to reduce the amount of political interference in economic, academic, and administrative matters, but little of importance is decided by factory managers, mayors, university presidents, or other responsible authorities without the concurrence of the ubiquitous party secretary. But the image of the omnipresent party is belied by the CCP's low public legitimacy in the aftermath of Tiananmen. The capacity of the regime to influence the lives of its citizens has diminished considerably, reflecting the fact that China's political system is no longer as totalitarian as it was during the Maoist period and has evolved toward a less intrusive, though still repressive, *bureaucratic authoritarianism under Deng.

According to the CCP constitution, the National Party Congress and the Central Committee are the party's "highest leading bodies"; but because of their large size and infrequent meetings, these organizations are relatively insignificant in terms of important decision-making. Much greater power resides in the relatively small Politburo and its even more exclusive Standing Committee. The position of "chairman" as head of the party, which was held by Mao Zedong for more than three decades, was replaced by a "general secretary," in 1982 as part of a broader effort to routinize party leadership following the extreme personalism of Mao's rule.

China's state and party constitutions depict a complex arrangement for the institutions and processes of government. But the realities of power in the PRC are more accurately, if less precisely, described by the workings of informal patterns of influence and decision-making. *Guanxi* (or "connections") are more important for getting things done than is reliance on specified bureaucratic procedure; *patron-client relations and nepotism still dominate both elite and local politics, as does factionalism based as much on personal links as on ideological affinities. This situation reflects the profound lack of institutionalization that continues to plague the Chinese political system. The dominance of individuals over institutions in Chinese politics was tragically illustrated by the fact that the CCP's leading bodies did not convene during the height of the 1989 Tiananmen crisis and that the critical decisions about how to respond to the protests were made by Deng Xiaoping and his cronies who had ostensibly retired. In this regard, Deng has made little progress in overcoming one of the most destructive legacies of the Maoist era.

Toward the Twenty-First Century. The PRC's political system in the early 1990s could be called a "gerontocracy" since the handful of men who hold ultimate power are all in their seventies and eighties. Any significant change in China is unlikely before the deaths of Deng Xiaoping and the other party elders. The PRC seems poised for yet another in a series of debilitating succession struggles, again reminiscent of one of the major failings of the politics of the Maoist era. Deng, like Mao, has shown no propensity to prepare an orderly, institutionalized succession process, preferring instead to groom heirs apparent based on personal loyalty; also like Mao, Deng has discarded such heirs when they have lost his favor for political or ideological reasons. Thus, as China nears the twenty-first century, much depends on who prevails in the succession sweepstakes to come.

The passing of the "gerontocrats" may bring about a revival of the trend toward a more open economy and free polity—perhaps in the direction of democratic socialism—if leaders committed to bold reform succeed to positions of power. On the other hand, power may fall to those whose preference is for bureaucratic caution—although in the long run technocratic tinkering is not likely to provide a remedy for the pathologies that plague what appears to be a mortally ill system. Protracted chaos cannot be ruled out of any scenario about what may happen next in China. Economic distress could bring social tensions beyond the boiling point, while leadership splits could spill over into a civil war or military coup.

There may also be a resurgence of antiregime protests in post-Deng China. But many factors would make it difficult for a popular movement to bring about the collapse of the regime as in Eastern Europe. China simply has no equivalent to the church, semiautonomous trade unions, or organized dissident movements to provide focal points for effective opposition; furthermore, the coercive power of the CCP remains formidable and is not dependent on outside support as were the military and security forces of the East European communist regimes. However, given the scale of the Tiananmen demonstrations, the level of pent-up anger and frustration in Chinese society, and the tarnished legitimacy of the ruling party and the official *ideology, it would be imprudent to dismiss entirely the possibility that "people power" will prevail in China.

The economic reforms of the last decade have also brought the seeds of potential political change to China. New groups, including entrepreneurs, technocrats, and a more informed and consumer-oriented general public, may well become more politically demanding. Similarly, Deng's policy of opening China to the outside world may prove to be a double-edged sword from the viewpoint of Beijing's rulers. On the one hand, it has profitably integrated the PRC more fully into the global economic system; on the other hand, the opening policy makes Chinese politics increasingly susceptible to external influences (such as international human rights standards) and the experiences of the tens of thousands of Chinese students, scholars, and officials who have traveled or studied abroad.

China will both be influenced by and be an influence on the international system in the last years of the twentieth century. The PRC occupies a rather anomalous position internationally. By many measures (e.g., GNP per capita, level of technological development), it is still very much a Third World nation. In fact, the government in Beijing often proclaims itself to be the champion of Third World causes in international organizations. By other measures (e.g., natural resources, military might), China can be considered a *superpower or at least a potential superpower. In any case, the PRC is a very significant player in East Asian and global affairs and will undoubtedly play a major role in shaping the post–Cold War world order.

China's vast peasantry, which still makes up a large majority of the population, will also have decisive influence in shaping the country's destiny. In some ways, economic reform has made them into a force for conservatism; the desire to protect and expand their share of China's new prosperity gives peasants a material reason to respond favorably to the regime's argument that, above all else, China needs stability and order. But change has come to much of the Chinese countryside, too. A sharply declining percentage of the rural labor force earns its income directly from agriculture owing to the expansion of rural industry and other means of nonfarm employment. China's new "open door" has also reached the countryside as an increasing number of rural enterprises are linked to the export economy. The relaxation of restraints on internal migration has created a "floating population" of some 60–80 million former rural dwellers who seek better economic opportunities in the cities. These migrants could bring an element of instability to urban politics; they might also forge a link between city and countryside that, along with the expansion of telecommunications into the rural areas, may have the effect of broadening the political horizons of China's peasantry.

The irony of politics in China in the post-Tiananmen period is that although the CCP still rules, communism seems dead. The party maintains it grip on power through a combination of inertia and coercion, but its claim to govern as the guardian of an ideology that represents the interests of the Chinese people has been shattered by, to use Barbara Tuchman's phrase, "the march of folly" that has marked the CCP's stewardship of the Chinese state. The PRC's next generation of leaders will confront an enormous challenge both in repairing the damage of the past and in preparing their nation for the coming century.

(See also COMMAND ECONOMY; CONFUCIANISM; DEVELOPMENT AND UNDERDEVELOPMENT; HONG KONG; LENINISM; MACAO; MODERNIZATION; TAIWAN.)

Roderick MacFarquhar and John K. Fairbank, eds., *The Cambridge History of China, Volume 14: The People's Republic of China, Part I: The Emergence of Revolutionary China, 1949–1965* (Cambridge, U.K., 1987). Carl Riskin, *China's Political Economy: The Quest for Development Since 1949* (Oxford, 1987). John Gittings, *China Changes Face: The Road from Revolution, 1949–1989* (Oxford, 1990). Jonathan D. Spence, *The Search for Modern China* (New York, 1990). Joint Economic Committee, Congress of the United States, *China's Economic Dilemmas in the 1990s: The Problems of Reform, Modernization, and Interdependence* (Washington, D.C., 1991). Roderick MacFarquhar and John K. Fairbank, eds., *The Cambridge History of China, Volume 15: The People's Republic of China, Part II: Revolutions within the Chinese Revolution, 1966–1982,* (Cambridge, U.K., 1991). James C. F. Wang, *Contemporary Chinese Politics: An Introduction,* 4th ed. (Englewood Cliffs, N.J., 1991).

WILLIAM A. JOSEPH

CHINESE COMMUNIST PARTY. The Chinese Communist Party (CCP) is one of the last ruling communist parties in the world. Founded in 1921, the CCP gained power in 1949 and has ruled the People's Republic of *China ever since.

Before seizing national power, the CCP had fought an extensive guerrilla war against the Japanese (1937–1945) and later a civil war with the Kuomintang, or Nationalist Party (1945–1949). During this period, the CCP ruled a number of base areas with a total population of some 80 to 100 million people. This experience had a number of important consequences for post-1949 CCP rule. First, the CCP was able to form an alternative state structure in the base areas and use them as laboratories for policies for social and economic change. This is quite distinct from the Soviet experience and that of Eastern and Central Europe where most parties were imported from the Soviet Union after World War II. Second, the nature of the struggle and the fact that all senior party leaders were also military leaders has meant that the military has always been held in high esteem and has played an important part in the political process. The words of *war and struggle dominate the vocabulary of the CCP. Further, when *Mao Zedong felt that the party had become corrupt in the early 1960s, he turned to the military as the repository of the virtues of plain living and struggle inherited from the revolutionary period. Third, to survive the Japanese invasion, the CCP had to use the tactic of a united front to appeal to a broad section of the population for support. This policy of class collaboration guided the initial years after 1949 and has formed the basis of policy since economic modernization became the key focus of party work from 1978 onward. Fourth, the CCP-led revolution was an indigenous one. Mao Zedong made it quite clear that the CCP was not fighting a war of liberation in order to become the "slaves of Moscow." The CCP was willing to ignore Soviet advice when it ran counter to national interests and to abandon the Soviet approach to development once its inadequacies and inapplicability to the Chinese situation became apparent.

In 1989, party membership numbered some 49

million, making it the largest, but still most exclusive, ruling communist party in the world. The actual criteria for membership have changed over the years, reflecting shifts in *ideology and recruitment policies. Currently, the stress is on recruiting better-educated members to help oversee the policies of economic modernization. Previous recruitment policies that stressed workers, peasants, and soldiers now hinder the party's self-ascribed role as an agent of modernization. In the mid-1980s only four percent of party members had received higher education and over fifty percent were illiterate or had only been to primary school. Whereas it is probably true to say that, in the past, young people were attracted to join the party because of its prestige, now they join because it is indispensable for a good career. The party is still the locus of political power, and few can achieve real political influence without membership and a record of political activism.

In theory, the party is organized in accordance with the principles of democratic centralism that subordinate the lower to the higher levels. The result is a hierarchical pattern of organization with 3 million party organizations at the bottom based on work units or neighborhoods and the national bodies in Beijing at the top. Nominally, the supreme decision-making body is the National Party Congress, which meets once every five years. However, real power lines cannot be divined from official party documents.

The formal power structure competes with individual patron-client relationships where real power often lies. Individual prestige based on relationships built up over decades can be more important than any official position held. Although *Deng Xiaoping has retired from all formal positions, he remains the most important decision maker in China. The inability to institutionalize leadership and leadership change suggests another round of debilitating struggle in the near future. No one in the present leadership has either the stature or the power base to play Deng's part. Yet the system desperately needs a Deng-like figure, one who can arbitrate policy disputes in the manner of Mao Zedong. (There are many examples of Mao Zedong circumventing formal party organs to implement his own policy preferences, most dramatically when he turned against the party apparatus in launching the *Cultural Revolution in 1966.)

Overreliance on the individual and the cavalier way in which formal structures are treated have hindered the process of institutionalization. Thus the party, dependent on purge as its only mechanism for dealing with succession and policy change, is extremely unstable.

Finally, the party has ascribed to itself a position of almost complete domination of state and society. This domination has been threatened by the program of economic modernization launched by the party itself in 1978. At the same time, the party has been unwilling to come to terms with the social and political consequences of this program. The party has tried to shift the legitimacy for its continued rule from one based on the correct interpretation of ideology to one that is based more on economic competence. However, its economic failings have served to undermine further its *legitimacy to rule in the eyes of many.

Certain powerful elderly leaders have insisted that the party continue to dominate state and society as before, refusing to come to terms with the increasing diversity of the society over which they rule. With the party thus unable to redefine its relationship to other organizations in society and to institutionalize the political process, much political activity now takes place outside formal structures—and this activity has become increasingly anti-systemic. Unless the party can devise a political system that is not only an efficient managerial machine but also one that can accommodate the demands of an increasingly complex society, it will have to resort continually to the use of force to maintain its "leading role."

(See also COMMUNIST PARTY STATES; PATRON-CLIENT POLITICS; GUERRILLA WARFARE; ZHOU ENLAI.)

Frederick C. Teiwes, *Leadership, Legitimacy, and Conflict in China: From a Charismatic Mao to the Politics of Succession* (Armonk, N.Y., 1984). Tony Saich, "Much Ado About Nothing: Party Reform in the Eighties," in Gordon White, ed., *From Crisis to Crisis: The Chinese State in the Era of Economic Reform* (Armonk, N.Y., 1991).

TONY SAICH

CHINESE REVOLUTION. At first glance, the Chinese Revolution looks like a younger sibling of the *Russian Revolution. It is true that the latter provided a revolutionary model to be followed, and that the nascent Chinese Communist movement was aided by its Russian counterpart. The ultimate victory of the Communists over their competitors within China does not imply, however, that the Chinese Revolution was merely a manifestation of an international movement inspired by Marxist *ideology. In a more fundamental sense, it was an indigenous *revolution with roots far back in the Chinese past.

External forces undoubtedly played a part in *China's century of turmoil and revolutionary change. Beginning with the Opium War (1839–1842), Western powers compelled a secluded Chinese Empire to open several ports to foreign merchants and missionaries. As suggested by *Japan's quick and successful response to the same challenge from the West, however, dramatic intrusion from abroad need not invariably lead to the kind of convulsive, painful, and protracted revolutionary process undergone by China between the mid-nineteenth and mid-twentieth centuries. Even before the West became a factor, the Chinese Empire was beset by internal troubles that by themselves might have brought about a traditional revolution in the form of a change of dynasty. When the last imperial dynasty was eventually overthrown in 1911, its fall resulted from the conjunction of growing external pressure and a host of long-unsolved and steadily accumulating domestic problems ranging from demographic imbalance and economic stagnation to administrative breakdown and growing assertiveness by autonomous social forces.

The 1911 revolution accomplished little beyond changing the form of the political system from an imperial to a republican one. The most obvious result was an accentuation of China's internal divisions and a further weakening of its ability to resist imperialist encroachments. For more than a decade, the country was so torn apart by the struggles of competing warlords that frustrated radical intellectuals deemed a political revolution like the one that had just overthrown the empire insufficient to solve China's ills. In their eyes, nothing less than a cultural revolution was needed to purge the Chinese people of some of their most ingrained habits and cherished values. In order to ensure the survival of the Chinese nation in a world dominated by an apparently more advanced civilization, they did not hesitate to repudiate Chinese cultural identity, and they relentlessly attacked *Confucianism as its symbol. Radical ideas found an outlet in the May Fourth Movement, named after an anti-imperialist student demonstration staged in Beijing on 4 May 1919. The choice of that date as a name underlines the nationalist devotion that impelled Chinese patriots to imitate the West in order to overcome its hegemony.

The *Chinese Communist Party (CCP) was founded in 1921 in the wake of the May Fourth Movement. Following the orders of the Soviet-centered Comintern, the CCP merged with the main Chinese revolutionary party, the Kuomintang (KMT), led by the veteran revolutionary Sun Yat-sen (1866–1925); this alliance helped to promote the CCP from a tiny group of radical intellectuals into a mass movement able to foment labor strikes and urban insurrections in just a few years. Success came mostly in the wake of a new wave of anti-imperialist demonstrations. However, when the KMT-CCP United Revolutionary Front launched a military campaign in 1926 against old-style warlords and reunified the country in 1927–1928, the decisive victory belonged not to the CCP but to the KMT, the senior partner of the coalition. Chiang Kai-shek (1887–1975), the overall commander of the revolutionary armies, destroyed his Communist one-time allies before establishing his own personal rule over the country.

The Chinese Revolution thus was ushered into a new phase, one of protracted struggle between former revolutionary partners, between those who held that the revolution had been betrayed and those who claimed it had been won. Defeated and slaughtered in the cities, the Communists took refuge in the countryside. There they could agitate the poorer and much more numerous rural masses instead of the tiny urban proletariat who had been the main target of their mobilization efforts until 1927. Despite early success in establishing rural bases—by *Mao Zedong (1893–1976) in the southeast and by others elsewhere—the Communists proved no match for the armies of the KMT. The famous Long March (1934–1935) was at best a victorious retreat: victorious only in that the defeated Communist armies escaped annihilation and found a haven in the distant northwest. They might very well have been destroyed there if Japanese expansionism had not provided them with an opportunity to regroup and expand.

The Sino-Japanese War (1937–1945) was the single most decisive period in the building of the Communist victory. Playing the card of patriotic resistance against foreign invaders, the Communists established so-called "liberated areas," mostly in northern China. Within these areas they won over a peasant constituency, partly by shielding villagers from Japanese troops, party by undermining the influence of the traditional rural elite and distributing some of its possessions and revenues to the rural poor. By 1944–45, solidly entrenched Communist areas threatened a much-weakened central government. This government's military strength, support, and overall legitimacy had declined dramatically during the course of the war, as the KMT proved no more able to stand the test of war than had the tsarist government of Russia between 1914 and 1917.

Both the Russian and the Chinese communist revolutions therefore sprang from a world war. During the last phase of the Chinese civil war (1946–1949), the CCP was able to parlay the advances it had already won thanks to World War II into further gains. In Manchuria, where most of the civil war was fought, the CCP implemented the same kind of rural mobilization policies that had succeeded elsewhere between 1937 and 1945. At first outnumbered by better-equipped armies, the CCP aptly exploited the poor command and steadily deteriorating morale of KMT forces. Hyperinflation accelerated the KMT's inability to cope with a protracted state of war. The Communist victory and the subsequent founding of the People's Republic of China on 1 October 1949 were a result of both the CCP's sweeping military successes and the internal crumbling of the KMT regime.

The timing and impact of the Japanese invasion of China and internal failings help explain the KMT's defeat. Efficient mass mobilization policies and clever military strategies and tactics enabled the Communist challengers to exploit opportunities created by foreign aggression and indigenous weakness. The weakness of the KMT regime resulted largely from inherited problems. In fact, China's long-standing weakness may very well have been the fundamental cause of the Chinese Revolution.

In a sense, the revolution of 1949 grew out of the failure of the revolution of 1911. Latter-day Chinese revolutionaries—the Communists—contributed much of substance to the mostly nationalist, anti-imperialist program of their forerunners; they addressed social problems and eventually directed their attention to the plight of the rural as opposed to urban masses. Yet the often-heard characterization of the Chinese Revolution as a *peasant revolution requires at least two qualifications.

First, although northern Chinese peasants played a more decisive role in the 1940s than that played by Petrograd's proletariat in Russia in 1917, in both cases Lenin's "professional revolutionaries" were firmly in charge. Agrarian reform was a means to an end, its goal to attract and organize enough peasants to win power. Whenever the imperatives of social revolution contradicted the requirements of military victory, the revolutionary elite regularly sacrificed the former to the latter. As for the rank and file, the peasant masses, only those villagers who happened to live in Communist-held areas, or more precisely some of those villagers (and not all of them willingly), rallied to the Communist side. Elsewhere peasants did not care or simply did not know about the revolution going on in their country. What limits the significance of the above qualification is that most revolutions are, after all, the work of a minority, and very few of them are accomplished for the sake of the poor majority—a fact illustrated in the Chinese case by the post-1949 gap between rural and urban incomes.

Second, although Communist leaders assigned special importance to both imperialism and the peasant condition as targets of their revolution, their discovery of the second was far from spontaneous. Only a tiny minority of those radical intellectuals who embraced *communism in the early 1920s did so because they were moved by the sorry plight of the rural (or urban) masses. The social concerns and devotion to class struggle of most others, the huge majority of whom were essentially nationalist revolutionaries, were acquired—or, more exactly, provided as an afterthought. These concerns were basic ingredients in the Leninist recipe for the conquest of power in a "backward" country, which led to the CCP's initial, more orthodox emphasis on the urban worker rather than the peasant movement.

While Lenin never hesitated to speak of "backward Russia," his Chinese disciples proved more reluctant to apply the epithet to their own country. They were certainly not unaware of China's backwardness; they had suffered from it and were anxious to overcome the basic conditions that prevented their country from succeeding in the international system. Even when publicly indicting imperialist *oppression,* many of them remained painfully conscious of the imperialist *challenge* as a model to imitate or emulate. Beyond the openly acknowledged goal of anti-imperialism, the revolutionary

crusaders barely dissimulated their undeclared but more basic goal, namely the modernization of a society lagging behind in a world that was rapidly moving ahead.

(See also IMPERIALISM; LENINISM; MARXISM; NATIONALISM; TAIWAN.)

Lucien Bianco, *Origins of the Chinese Revolution, 1915–1949* (Stanford, Calif., 1971). John K. Fairbank, ed., *The Cambridge History of China,* Vol. 10: *Late Ch'ing, 1800–1911,* Part 1 (Cambridge, U.K., 1978). John K. Fairbank and Kwang-ching Liu, eds., *The Cambridge History of China,* Vol. 11: *Late Ch'ing, 1800–1911,* Part 2 (Cambridge, U.K. 1980). John K. Fairbank, ed., *The Cambridge History of China,* Vol. 12: *Republican China, 1912–1949,* Part 1 (Cambridge, U.K., 1983). John K. Fairbank and Albert Feuerwerker, eds., *The Cambridge History of China,* Vol. 13: *Republican China, 1912–1949,* Part 2 (Cambridge, U.K., 1986).

LUCIEN BIANCO

CHRISTIAN DEMOCRACY. A contemporary political movement with a substantial following in Europe and Latin America, Christian Democracy arose in the early twentieth century as a progressive alternative to the socioeconomic and political conservatism with which Roman Catholicism had been associated from the sixteenth through the nineteenth centuries. Most Christian Democratic parties were initially concerned with religious values and issues, but came to stress them less as time and *secularization proceeded apace. Today all parties embrace liberal democracy, and virtually all advocate a reform or welfare version of capitalism that provides for basic needs and for some worker participation in decision making. The German (Christlich-Demokratische Union/Christlich-Soziale Union) and Italian (Democrazia Cristiana) are among the most successful of the European parties, while the Chilean, Venezuelan, and Salvadoran parties have been leading political forces in Latin America.

Most Christian Democratic parties set out to capture the middle or moderate conservative ground between ideologically defined parties of the Right and socialist Left. They hoped to supersede both by appealing to consciously Christian (Catholic and Protestant) constituents across a sociological spectrum. Their success in attracting business interests, middle-class elements, and non-Communist workers soon made them an "enlightened" alternative to the socialist left. Where they have come to power, whether alone or in coalition with others, it has generally been as a right-of-center force. This has been difficult for some party intellectuals and trade unionists to accept. In Germany and Italy, these groups have constituted a permanent, minority left wing within the party. Elsewhere, they have formed rival Catholic left parties (as in Chile) or joined forces with erstwhile leftist adversaries (as in France, El Salvador, and Venezuela).

Division and dissension among Christian Democrats during the 1960s, 1970s, and early 1980s were a consequence of their socially diverse followings, their lack of common sociological reading of historical experience, and the ease with which their social Christian principles could therefore be variously interpreted and applied. In countries (the Federal Republic of Germany and Italy) where sustained economic growth and prosperity provided them with an additional margin for error, such divisions caused little or no political damage. In other instances, however, economic decline fueled social and political polarization, forced parties to choose between right and left, and led to the alienation of important constituencies.

During the late 1980s, Christian Democratic movements and parties were political and electoral beneficiaries of the breakdown of the economies and political systems in Eastern and Central Europe. In Latin America, Christian Democracy's "third way" has also enjoyed a renaissance of sorts, thanks to a new willingness on the part of Marxists and other leftists to form alliances with "democratic" centrists and rightists as an alternative to continued *military rule, and to the imposition of neoliberal economic criteria by national governments and international financial institutions.

Christian Democratic parties coordinate with one another through loosely structured supranational mechanisms such as the International Union of Christian Democratic Parties, the (Latin) American Christian Democratic Organization, and a Christian Democratic caucus within the *European Parliament.

(See also RELIGION AND POLITICS; SOCIALISM AND SOCIAL DEMOCRACY.)

R. E. M. Irving, *The Christian Democratic Parties of Western Europe* (London, 1979). Michael Fleet, *The Rise and Fall of Chilean Christian Democracy* (Princeton, N.J., 1985). Gregory Baum and John Coleman, eds., *The Church and Christian Democracy* (Edinburgh, 1987).

MICHAEL FLEET

CHURCHILL, Winston. Winston Churchill was born in 1874 and died in 1965. After five years as a soldier and war correspondent, he entered the British Parliament in 1900 as a Conservative. Four years later he joined the Liberal Party, returning to the Conservatives twenty years later, and becoming Conservative Party leader in 1940, five months after he had been appointed prime minister of a national coalition government. This all-party administration, which he headed for five years, had been formed on the day of the German invasion of France, Belgium, and the Netherlands on 10 May 1940. He served a second time as prime minister, in peacetime, from 1951 to 1955.

Churchill's long career was often marked by controversy and dogged by political antagonism, for he was always outspoken and independent, expressing his views without prevarication; and his criticisms of others acquired all the more force thanks to his breadth of knowledge and his vivid, adept, and penetrating language. The controversies were understandably many in a public life that spanned more than fifty years and saw him hold eight cabinet posts even before he became prime minister.

The range of Churchill's activities and experiences was extraordinary. He received his Army commission during the reign of Queen Victoria, fought in the Northwest Frontier province of India in 1897, took part in the cavalry charge at Omdurman in the Sudan in 1898, and was taken prisoner of war during the Boer War in South Africa in 1899. Strategy and tactics fascinated him and engaged his attention from his earliest days; he was also closely involved in the early development of aviation—learning to fly before World War I—and established the Royal Naval Air Service. He was an active participant in the inception of the tank. He was a pioneer in the advocacy and preparation of anti-aircraft defense and in the evolution of aerial warfare. In the 1920s he foresaw the building of weapons of mass destruction, and in his last speech to Parliament, in 1955, he proposed using the existence of the hydrogen bomb and its deterrent power as the basis for world disarmament.

From his early years, Churchill had an uncanny understanding and vision of the future unfolding of events. His early military training and his natural inventiveness gave him great insight into the nature of *war and society. He was also someone whose personal courage, whether on the battlefields of empire at the turn of the century, during his mission to Antwerp to try to stiffen the resolve of its defenders in 1914, during his command of a battalion in the trenches on the western front in 1916, or during his dash to an Athens beset by civil war in 1944, was matched by a deep understanding of the horrors of war and the devastation of battle. "Much as war attracts my mind with its tremendous situations," he wrote to his wife Clementine from German army maneuvers in 1909, "I feel more deeply every year, and can measure the feeling here in the midst of arms, what vile and utter folly and barbarism it all is."

Both in his Liberal and Conservative years Churchill was a radical, a believer in the need for the state to take an active part, both by legislation and finance, in ensuring minimum standards of life, labor, and social well-being for all citizens. Among the areas of social reform in which he took a leading part both before and after World War I, including the drafting of substantial legislation, were prison reform, unemployment insurance, state-aided pensions for widows and orphans, a permanent arbitration mechanism for labor disputes, state assistance for those in search of employment, shorter hours of work, and improved conditions on the shop and factory floor. He was also an advocate of a national health service, of wider access to education, of the taxation of excess profits, and of profit sharing by employees. In his first public speech, in 1897, three years before he entered Parliament, he looked forward to the day when the laborer would become "a shareholder in the business in which he worked."

At times of national stress, Churchill was a persistent advocate of conciliation, even of coalition; he shunned the paths of division and unnecessary confrontation. In international affairs he consistently sought the settlement of the grievances of those who had been defeated and the building up of meaningful associations for the reconciliation of former enemies. After two world wars he argued in favor of maintaining the strength of the victors in order to redress the grievances of the vanquished and to preserve peace. In the 1920s and 1930s he was one of the leading advocates of collective security to deter war. In 1950 it was he who first used the word *summit* to refer to a meeting of the leaders of the Western and communist worlds, and subsequently he did his utmost to set up such meetings to end the dangerous confrontations of the *Cold War. Among the agreements that he negotiated with patience and understanding were the constitutional settlements in South Africa and Ireland and the war debt repayment schemes after World War I.

A perceptive, shrewd commentator on the events taking place around him, Churchill was always an advocate of bold, farsighted courses of action. The genesis of the British naval attack on the Dardanelles in 1915 was Churchill's determination to find a way to end the stalemate and bloodshed of the war of trenches and attrition in France; throughout the following years he begged the government not to embark on futile frontal assaults against the heavily fortified German trench line without first securing superiority, including air superiority. Between the wars, confronted by German rearmament, he insisted that only a well-armed Britain with superior air power to Germany's could deter Hitler from aggression; his warnings were mocked as alarmist and went largely unheeded.

Churchill had a complete and extraordinary faith in his own abilities and in his destiny. When he went to the western front in December 1915, with every possibility of being killed, he wrote to Clementine, "My conviction that the greatest of my work is still to be done is strong within me, and I ride reposefully along the gale." After nearly being killed by a German shell in March 1916 he wrote to his wife that, had he been killed, it would have been "a loss to the war-making power of Britain that no one will ever know or measure or mourn."

One of Churchill's greatest gifts, evident in several thousand public speeches as well as in his many broadcasts, was his ability to use his exceptional mastery of words and love of language to convey detailed arguments and essential truths; to inform, to convince, and to inspire. He was a person of great humor and warmth, of magnanimity; a consistent and lifelong liberal in outlook; someone often turned to by successive prime ministers between 1905 and 1929 for his skill as a conciliator. His dislike of unfairness, of victimization, and of bullying—whether at home or abroad—was the foundation stone of much of his thinking. His finest hour was the leadership of Britain when it was most isolated, most threatened, and most weak; when his own courage, determination, and belief in democracy became one with that of a beleaguered nation.

(See also POTSDAM CONFERENCE; WORLD WAR II.)

Randolph S. Churchill, *Winston S. Churchill*, vols. 1–2 (Boston, 1967–8). Martin Gilbert, *Winston S. Churchill*, vols. 3–8 (Boston, 1971–88). Martin Gilbert, *Churchill: A Life* (New York, 1991).

MARTIN GILBERT

CIA. See CENTRAL INTELLIGENCE AGENCY.

CITIZENSHIP. The term *citizenship,* meaning membership in a political community, comes to us from the classical Greek and Roman conception of man as a political being. Ancient citizenship was understood as the capacity to govern and to be governed. It implied the idea of equality before the law and active political participation, and its emergence is concomitant with the birth of *democracy. However, citizenship in the Greek democratic city-states was restricted to free and native-born men, and citizens only represented a minority of the population, even in Athens. Their participation in public life was only possible because of the existence of slaves, who were responsible for performing the main economic functions.

In Rome we can witness the beginning of a new dynamic. Although citizenship was still defined in terms of office holding, its extension during the empire, first to plebeians and then to conquered peoples, produced a much more heterogeneous body of citizens, and the term began to refer more to protection under the law than to active participation in its execution. From being the assertion of a political identity indicating allegiance and active participation in a political community, citizenship became a legal and juridical status. By edict of the emperor Caracalla in 212 C.E., citizenship was granted to the great majority of imperial subjects; only the very lowest classes and women were excluded.

After a long eclipse during the Middle Ages, the tradition of Greek and Roman republicanism was revived in the Italian republics of the Renaissance, finding its champion in Niccolò Machiavelli. It was also reformulated in England by James Harrington, John Milton, and other republicans in the course of the constitutional revolution of the seventeenth century. Later it traveled to the New World through the work of the neo-Harringtonians and was influential during the American Revolution.

The universalistic ideal of citizenship culminated in the French Revolution and the Declaration of the

Rights of Man and Citizen. The main theoretical referent in this case is Jean-Jacques Rousseau, who in *The Social Contract* (1762) established the modern figure of the citizen by connecting it to the theory of consent. The citizen for Rousseau is a free and autonomous individual who is entitled to take part in making decisions that all are required to obey. Rousseau's conception of citizenship, which draws on both the classical republican tradition and on modern contractualism, attempts to link the republican conception of political community with the premises of individualism. Writing in the context of an emerging commercial society, Rousseau was aware of the tension between the common good and private interests, and saw in the dominance of organized group interests the main threat to the well-being of the body politic.

With the development of market relations and the growing hegemony of *liberalism during the nineteenth century, the republican conception of the active citizen was displaced by a view of citizenship expressed in the language of natural *rights. The ideas of civic activity, public spiritedness, and political participation in a community of equals appeared as nostalgic relics to be discarded by most liberal writers who, following Benjamin Constant, declared that in order to preserve the "liberties of the moderns," it was necessary to renounce the "liberties of the ancients." Citizenship was reduced to a mere legal status, indicating the possession of rights that the individual holds against the *state. Defined in terms of rights, citizenship nevertheless played a very important and progressive role in shaping liberal democratic societies. As T. H. Marshall has shown in the case of Britain in his *Citizenship and Social Class* (Cambridge, U.K., 1950), one can delineate a progression from civil to political and finally to social rights. Obviously the situation is not the same in all countries. In the United States, for instance, citizenship is mainly identified with civil rights. But there is no doubt that there is a strong connection between the institutions and practices of pluralistic liberal democracies and the liberal language of the citizen as a bearer of rights. Slowly, and through bitter struggles, it made possible the inclusion of women and later blacks into citizenship.

Today the liberal model of citizenship has gained a new momentum in countries where the main task is to establish the basic conditions for civil society and pluralistic democracy. However, it has increasingly been criticized in Western democracies for its individualistic bias, which is deemed responsible for the lack of cohesion and the destruction of common purpose and community values endemic in those societies. A school of so-called communitarians has emerged who argue for the revival of the civic republican conception of citizenship with its strong emphasis on the notion of a public good, prior to and independent of individual desires and interests. Authors like Michael Sandel and Alasdair MacIntyre

have taken issue with the work of John Rawls in order to criticize the liberal conception of the citizen and its view of the individual as someone who can have rights independently of the community to which she or he belongs. What is at stake in this debate is the possibility and desirability of a return to a tradition that many liberals see as premodern and incompatible with the *pluralism that is constitutive of modern democracy. According to Isaiah Berlin, ideas about the "common good" today can only have totalitarian implications and are incompatible with the modern idea of liberty. Is it possible to combine democratic institutions with the sense of common purpose that premodern societies enjoyed? If politics in a modern democracy must accept division and conflict as unavoidable, what can be the status of a notion like the "common good"?

At the moment, one of the most discussed questions in many countries is how to establish a notion of citizenship that makes room for the increasingly multiethnic and multicultural character of the population. Such a problem has long existed in North America, but satisfactory solutions have yet to be found there as well. The difficulty seems to lie in the need to create unity without denying multiplicity. How might one combine an effective pluralism as far as cultural, linguistic, ethnic, religious, and other identities are concerned while constructing a common political identity around an allegiance to shared political principles? This is the contemporary challenge associated with citizenship for both communitarians and liberals.

(See also POLITICAL PARTICIPATION.)

Moses I. Finley, *Democracy Ancient and Modern* (New Brunswick, N.J., and London, 1973). Michael Sandel, ed., *Liberalism and Its Critics* (New York, 1984). Bryan S. Turner, *Citizenship and Capitalism* (London, 1986). Ralf Dahrendorf, *The Modern Social Conflict* (London, 1988).
                                              CHANTAL MOUFFE

CIVIL DISOBEDIENCE. The open, deliberate, nonviolent breaking of a law, regulation, or order, including those of governments, courts, police, and military officials, is known as civil disobedience. Usually, the disobeyed command is seen to be illegitimate because of its content or origin. The command may also be believed to contradict a "higher" moral or religious principle. Disobedience of "illegitimate" laws may be practiced by individuals, small groups, or masses of people.

Civil disobedience may be practiced solely with the intent of refusing to participate in activities believed to be evil, without wider objectives. Or, it may be practiced as part of an organized campaign planned to achieve a specific objective, such as the repeal of racial segregation laws. Organized civil disobedience may have reformatory, revolutionary, or defensive objectives.

While the names of Socrates, Henry David Thoreau, Mohandas K. *Gandhi, and Martin Luther

*King, Jr., are often best known in relation to civil disobedience, this method of nonviolent action has been widely practiced. These cases include American colonial resisters in 1766, London newspapers in 1768–1771 publishing prohibited reports of parliamentary debates, the breaking of the British Salt Laws in the 1930–1931 Indian independence satyagraha campaign, and the 1951 defiance campaign in South Africa in which *apartheid laws were deliberately broken to achieve their repeal.

Sometimes, however, certain commands of a strictly regulatory nature, seen to be morally neutral, may be disobeyed. This may occur when the disobedient group wishes strongly to protest a government policy against which it is difficult to find a clear point of resistance. Civil disobedience of morally neutral laws and regulations can also be practiced in an advanced stage of a strong nonviolent movement with revolutionary objectives. The aim is then to weaken further the government's control in order to hasten its full collapse. This stage was partially reached at certain points in the 1930–1931 Indian independence campaign. Gandhi regarded this action as at times morally justified but also as "a most dangerous weapon."

These types of civil disobedience are among nearly forty methods of political noncooperation. Some related but different methods of disobedience are withholding or withdrawal of allegiance, reluctant and slow compliance, nonobedience in absence of direct supervision, popular nonobedience, disguised disobedience, refusal of an assemblage or meeting to disperse, and noncooperation with conscription and deportation.

Issues prominent in the discussion of civil disobedience include: How does one determine when a law, order, etc., should be civilly disobeyed? Is civil disobedience justifiable within a liberal *democracy which provides opportunities to repeal morally offensive laws or policies? What are the distinctions between civil disobedience by individuals acting out of a personal moral decision and organized civil disobedience conducted by groups? Should established laws receive an assumption of obligation to obey them regardless of their content or purpose? Considerations include comparison of the consequences of civil disobedience with the consequences of passive obedience, and with the results of violence in the expression of strong dissent. In addition, discussions consider the issue of whether the willful breaking of law, albeit selectively and nonviolently, contributes to the indiscriminate breaking of laws, perpetration of violence, and social chaos. Finally, those concerned with the issues of civil disobedience consider how civil disobedience within a state relates to *international law.

(See also CIVIL RIGHTS MOVEMENT; NONVIOLENT ACTION; POLITICAL VIOLENCE; REVOLUTION.)

Henry David Thoreau, "On the Duty of Civil Disobedience," in *Walden and Other Writings of Henry David* *Thoreau* (New York, 1937), pp. 635–663. Paul Harris, ed., *Civil Disobedience* (Lanham, Md., 1989).

GENE SHARP

CIVIL RIGHTS MOVEMENT. The modern U.S. Civil Rights Movement was one of the most important freedom struggles of the twentieth century. As late as the 1950s, millions of U.S. citizens were oppressed and disenfranchised on the basis of skin color. This reality was especially shocking because it endured in a nation believed by many throughout the world to be the leading *democracy and promoted by white leaders as the shining model for other countries wishing to break free from their past histories of human oppression.

The historic treatment of black people in the United States stood in sharp contrast to the American image of democracy. From the very beginning U.S. democracy was not extended to people of African descent. In fact, *African Americans were forcibly transported to America as slaves, and the institution of black slavery lasted well over two centuries, during which time slave labor helped fuel the United States' enormous economic growth. Throughout this period, the democratic *rights heralded by the Declaration of Independence and guaranteed by the U.S. Constitution did not apply to black people, since the framers of those documents, as well as their white contemporaries, defined African Americans as chattel, not human beings.

In both moral and economic terms, the U.S. Civil War (1861–1865) was fought over the issue of slavery. With the triumph of Union forces in 1865, the formal institution of slavery was defeated. At this juncture, the United States had the chance to extend full democratic rights to black people. For approximately a decade following the Civil War—the Reconstruction period—it appeared that black people might be allowed to exercise much-expanded *citizenship rights, such as freedom of movement in public facilities and equal access to employment. Such an outcome would have erased a system of privilege based on skin color and created a society on principles of racial *equality.

By the turn of the twentieth century, however, it had become clear that the system of privilege based on skin color was to remain triumphant. By the early 1900s, a formal system of racial segregation known as Jim Crow was hammered into place. The Jim Crow system required that black and white people be segregated on the basis of race. The two races were not allowed to attend the same schools; eat in the same restaurants; attend the same movie theaters; sit on the same side of a courtroom or be sworn in using the same Bible; occupy the same place on a public bus or train; or participate equally in the political process. Although the Jim Crow system was especially entrenched in the South, it was not limited to any region, and in many respects racial segregation was national in scope. Thus an

1896 *Supreme Court ruling, *Plessy* v. *Ferguson,* declared that the system of racial segregation was constitutional, enshrining the blatantly discriminatory doctrine of separate-but-equal facilities. The national scope of Jim Crow was also evident in the U.S. military, where black soldiers served in racially segregated combat units until the post–World War II era.

Throughout U.S. history, the system of racial segregation allowed the concept of white superiority to triumph over the democratic rights of African Americans. By the 1950s, the overwhelming majority of blacks throughout the South were disenfranchised; as a result, no blacks held any significant political offices there. Terror and violence, including lynchings, were routinely used by whites to keep blacks subjugated. In the labor market only low-paying, undesirable jobs were usually available to African Americans. Under this arrangement white economic exploitation of blacks continued unabated. In less material but equally pervasive ways, African Americans also experienced personal humiliation on a daily basis. Indeed, racial segregation was an arrangement whereby black people were set off from the rest of humanity and labeled as an inferior race. Human dignity was stripped from African Americans: simple titles of respect such as "Mr." or "Mrs." were withheld, and even white youngsters held authority over all blacks, however elderly or eminent.

African Americans, like human beings throughout history, have rebelled and protested against their oppressors. These protests began during slavery and have endured over the succeeding generations. At times, resistance has been collective and quite public, while at other times it has remained less visible and more limited in scope. Therefore, by the 1950s African Americans had a long, rich history of social protest to draw upon in confronting the oppression they faced. In short, the modern Civil Rights Movement was part of the ongoing historic struggle for black liberation. As scholars are increasingly coming to realize, great social movements do not have clear-cut beginnings, middles and ends. On the contrary, they are more like an uneven terrain with both peaks and valleys, and the Civil Rights Movement is no exception.

The modern Civil Rights Movement, which took root in the mid-1950s, was clearly one of the peaks of the historic black freedom struggle. This movement emerged in the Deep South, where black oppression was most intense and where the system of racial segregation was firmly entrenched. With oppression dating to the era of slavery and the pattern of subjugation ingrained in U.S. democracy, why did such a powerful and galvanizing Civil Rights Movement erupt when it did?

The movement was able to take off during this period for several reasons. First, by the 1950s large numbers of African Americans had migrated to southern cities. This *urbanization of the black masses provided them with new strength derived from tightly knit urban communities and dense, effective communication networks. Second, by the 1950s major black institutions—especially black churches and colleges—had become powerful, indigenous institutions capable of sustaining large volumes of black protest. Third, by the 1950s the National Association for the Advancement of Colored People (NAACP) had won successful legal battles against the Jim Crow system, especially in the 1954 Supreme Court decision *Brown* v. *Board of Education,* which overturned *Plessy* v. *Ferguson* and determined that separate schooling based on race was unconstitutional. This ruling, along with others, served to delegitimize the entire system of racial segregation in the eyes of African Americans, encouraging struggles for implementation of court orders and for wider legislative reform and catalyzing massive campaigns of resistance.

Finally, the international picture was changing in the late 1950s as African nations were gaining their independence through anticolonial struggles. African Americans identified with those freedom struggles, which intensified their own thirst for freedom. Moreover, the context of *decolonization and *Cold War rivalry made the federal government more susceptible to pressure from the Civil Rights Movement because the United States was determined to persuade these new African nations to model themselves after U.S. democracy, not the Soviet alternative. Segregation and racial oppression were obstacles standing in the path of harmonious relations between the United States and the newly independent African nations. Thus, the federal government came under increased international pressure to support visible efforts to overthrow institutionalized racial segregation at home, and it was unusually vulnerable to such pressure.

The convergence of these factors created the fertile soil in which the modern Civil Rights Movement took root. Applying the strategy of mass, nonviolent, direct action, the movement galvanized widespread social protest in the streets and within oppressive institutions. For such a strategy to succeed, white communities, businesses, and institutions would have to be disrupted. To do so, the leaders and organizers of the movement had to persuade tens of thousands of African Americans to bear witness to their oppression and to become directly involved in dangerous social protest. Strategies had to be devised to execute widespread social disruption, all the while maintaining morale in the black community despite setbacks, hardship, and recriminations.

The Civil Rights Movement succeeded in mobilizing massive nonviolent direct action. Innovative tactics included economic boycotts (beginning with the year-long boycott of a bus company in Montgomery, Alabama, begun in December 1955 and led by Martin Luther *King, Jr.); sit-in demonstrations (started in February 1960 by black college students at a lunch counter in Greensboro, North Carolina); and mass marches (including a massive mobilization of whites and blacks in the August 1963 March on Washington, which culminated in King's "I have a dream" speech, and protest marches led by King that met with police violence in Selma, Alabama, in January 1965).

The goal of this massive protest activity was to overthrow the entire system of legalized racial segregation and to empower African Americans in the South by seizing the franchise. Of course, southern elected officials utilized their governmental power and the resistance by the larger white community in a spirited (and often brutal) effort to defeat the Civil Rights Movement and to maintain legally enforced racial segregation. Participants of the Civil Rights Movement—many of them children and college students—were often beaten and brutalized by southern law officials, and thousands were arrested and jailed for their protest activities. Some leaders and participants—such as Medgar Evers, chair of the Mississippi state chapter of the NAACP in 1963, and three civil rights workers in Mississippi in 1964—were killed.

Nevertheless, an endless stream of highly visible confrontations in the streets, which contrasted the brutality and the inhumanity of the white segregationists with the dignity and resolve of black protesters, made the cause of black civil rights the major issue in the United States for over a decade during the 1950s and 1960s. The nation and its leaders were forced to decide publicly whether to grant African Americans their citizenship rights or to side with white segregationists who advocated racial superiority and the undemocratic subjugation of black people.

The movement could not be ignored. Eloquent leaders sustained the pressure on local elites and the federal government, and countless heroic figures inspired a massive following, among them: Rosa Parks, a dignified older woman and secretary for the local NAACP, who sparked the Montgomery bus boycott when she defied an order to move to the back; Martin Luther King, Jr., who emerged from the Montgomery bus boycott and the Southern Christian Leadership Conference (SCLC) to assume a position of preeminent moral leadership and national influence; James Forman, executive secretary of the more militant Student Nonviolent Coordinating Committee (SNCC), who was to raise questions about SCLC's and King's strategy; SNCC's leader, Stokely Carmichael (now Kwame Toure), who introduced the slogan "black power"; and Fannie Lou Hamer, daughter of a sharecropper who lived on a plantation, who went to a voter registration meeting run by Forman and other SNCC members, was arrested at the courthouse in Indianola, Mississippi, when she tried to register to vote, and then was beaten with a blackjack in prison.

These leading figures and countless other participants in the Civil Rights Movement articulated the oppression and democratic aspirations of African Americans of every generation and circumstance. In addition, thousands of whites (students, lawyers, and other civil rights workers from all walks of life) were inspired to join the Civil Rights Movement. They participated in lunch-counter sit-ins, mass demonstrations, and campaigns such as the 1964 Mississippi Freedom Summer Project, a campaign that involved hundreds of volunteers in voter registration drives and the creation of "freedom schools." Some, like Andrew Goodman and Michael Schwerner, who were involved in the Freedom Summer campaign, and Viola Liuzzo, a Michigan homemaker shot by Klansmen after a rally in support of the march from Selma to Montgomery, lost their lives in the Civil Rights Movement and, in turn, helped inspire others.

Inevitable differences of *ideology, leadership style, and approach emerged within the movement as the SCLC, SNCC, the Congress of Racial Equality (CORE), and other organizations reached different judgments about the value of *nonviolent action, the role of whites in the movement, and the influence of *Malcolm X. Whatever these controversies, the moral challenge and the widespread social disruption caused by the economic boycotts, the marches, the sit-ins, and other forms of nonviolent direct action, coupled with international pressure, created an impasse in the nation that had to be resolved in order for the country to return to business as usual.

As a result, the Civil Rights Movement achieved several important legislative victories in Congress. The landmark Civil Rights Act of 1964 outlawed discrimination in public accommodations on the basis of race, color, religion, or national origin; it granted authority to the attorney general to force the integration of schools through litigation; and it barred discrimination in employment practices on grounds of race, color, religion, national origin, or sex. The 1965 Voting Rights Act suspended the use of literacy tests, authorized the attorney general to challenge the constitutionality of poll taxes, and introduced procedures and provided for the appointment of examiners to ensure that all restrictions on black voter registration be ended. In short, it enfranchised the southern black population.

Beyond specific legislative relief, the Civil Rights Movements has affected U.S. politics in fundamental ways. The movement taught those Americans who were oppressed and excluded from the political process how to pursue empowerment effectively. The Civil Rights Movement demonstrated to the oppressed black community how such protest could be successful, and it made social protest more respectable. The Civil Rights Movement also proved that at times significant *reform can occur through nonviolent action.

Yet it is often overlooked that the significance of the Civil Rights Movement extends beyond the rights and freedoms of blacks. The movement also broadened the scope of politics and inspired diverse movements for citizenship rights and social justice in the United States and throughout the world. Before the Civil Rights Movement, many groups in U.S. society—women, *Hispanics, *Native Americans, the physically disabled, *gays and lesbians, etc.—were oppressed but unaware of how to resist or galvanize support. The Civil Rights Movement provided an example of successful social protest and a host of new tactics. Moreover, the Civil Rights Movement had an influence on freedom struggles around the world. Participants in movements in Africa, Eastern Europe, the Middle East, Latin America, and China have made it very clear that they were inspired by and learned important lessons from the U.S. Civil Rights Movement.

For all its success and influences, however, the Civil Rights Movement did not solve the problem of racism in the United States. In the closing decade of the twentieth century African Americans and many other nonwhite groups are at the bottom of the social and economic order, where they continue to experience excruciating suffering. These conditions are exacerbated by a mean political climate in which the poor and oppressed are blamed for their own suffering and oppression. It may be that protest remains the only viable means to achieve greater empowerment. If this is the case, the Civil Rights Movement has left a rich legacy to inspire and inform future struggles.

(See also CIVIL DISOBEDIENCE; DU BOIS, W. E. B.; RACE AND RACISM.)

Clayborne Carson, *In Struggle: SNCC and the Black Awakening of the 1960s* (Cambridge, Mass., 1981). Aldon Morris, *Origins of the Civil Rights Movement* (New York, 1984). David Garrow, *Bearing the Cross* (New York, 1986). Taylor Branch, *Parting The Waters* (New York, 1988). Doug McAdam, *Freedom Summer* (New York, 1988). Clayborne Carson, David J. Garrow, Gerald Gill, Vincent Harding, and Darlene Clark Hine, eds., *The Eyes on the Prize Civil Rights Reader* (New York, 1991).

ALDON MORRIS

CLASS AND POLITICS

The concept of class has had an erratic career in the contemporary analysis of politics. There was a time, not so long ago, when class played at best a marginal role in explanations of political phenomena. In the 1950s and early 1960s the dominant approach to politics was *pluralism. Political outcomes in democratic societies were viewed as resulting from the interplay of many crosscutting forces interacting in an environment of bargaining, voting, coalition building, and consensus formation. While some of the organized *interest groups on this playing field may have been based in constituencies with a particular class character—most notably unions and business associations—nevertheless, such organizations were given no special analytical status by virtue of this.

From the late 1960s through the early 1980s, with the renaissance of the Marxist tradition in the social sciences, class suddenly moved to the core of many analyses of the *state and politics. Much discussion occurred over such things as the "class character" of state apparatuses and the importance of instrumental manipulation of state institutions by powerful class-based actors. Even among scholars whose theoretical perspective was not built around class, class was taken seriously and accorded an importance in the analysis of politics rarely found in the previous period.

While class analysis never became the dominant paradigm for the analysis of politics, it was a theoretical force to be reckoned with in the 1970s. Ironically, perhaps, in the course of the 1980s, as U.S. national politics took on a particularly blatant class character, the academic popularity of class analysis as a framework for understanding politics steadily declined. The center of gravity of critical work on the state shifted toward a variety of theoretical perspectives which explicitly distanced themselves from a preoccupation with class, in particular "state-centered" approaches to politics which emphasize the causal importance of the institutional properties of the state and the interests of state managers and cultural theories which place discourses and symbolic systems at the center of political analysis. While the class analysis of politics has by no means retreated to the marginal status it was accorded in the 1950s, it is no longer the center of debate the way it was a decade ago.

This is, therefore, a good time to take stock of the theoretical accomplishments and unresolved issues of the class analysis of politics. As a prologue to the discussion, in the next section we will briefly look at the concept of class itself. This will be followed in section 2 by an examination of three different kinds of mechanisms through which class has an impact on politics. Using terminology adapted from the work of Robert Alford and Roger Friedland, I will refer to these as the *situational, institutional,* and *systemic* political effects of class. Section 3 will then briefly examine the problem of variability in the patterns of class effects on politics. The essay will then conclude in section 4 with a discussion of the problem of explanatory primacy of class relative to other causal processes.

The Concept of Class. The word *class* has been used to designate a variety of quite distinct theoretical concepts. In particular, it is important to distinguish between what are sometimes called *gradational* and *relational* class concepts. As has often been noted, for many sociologists as well as media commentators, "class" is simply a way of talking about strata within the income distribution. The frequent references in contemporary U.S. politics to "middle-class taxpayers" is equivalent to "middle-income taxpayers." Classes are simply rungs on a ladder of inequalities. For others, particularly analysts working in the Marxian and Weberian theoretical traditions, the concept of class is not meant to designate a distributional *outcome* as such, but rather the nature of the underlying social relations which generate such outcomes. To speak of a person's class position is thus to identify that person's relationship to specific kinds of mechanisms which generate inequalities of income and power. In a relational class concept, capitalists and workers do not simply differ in the amount of income they acquire, but in the mechanism through which they acquire that income.

It is possible to deploy both gradational and relational concepts of class in the analysis of politics. Many people, for example, use a basically gradational concept of class to examine the different political attitudes and voting behaviors of the poor, the middle class, the rich. However, most of the systematic work on class and politics has revolved around relational class concepts. There are two basic reasons for this: First, relational concepts are generally seen as designating more fundamental aspects of social structure than gradational concepts, since the relational concepts are anchored in the causal mechanisms which generate the gradational inequalities. To analyze the determinants of political phenomena in terms of relational class concepts is therefore to dig deeper into the causal process than to simply link politics to distributionally defined class categories. Second, relational class categories have the analytical advantage of generating categories of actors who live in real interactive social relations to each other. The "rich," "middle," and "poor" are arbitrary divisions on a continuum; the individuals defined by these categories may not systematically interact with each other in any particular way. Capitalists and workers, on the other hand, are inherently mutually interdependent. They are real categories whose respective interests are defined, at least in part, by the nature of the relations which bind them together. Building the concept of class around these relations, then, greatly facilitates the analysis of the formation of organized collectivities engaged in political conflict over material interests.

Adopting a relational perspective on class, of course, is only a point of departure. There are many ways of elaborating such a concept. In particular, much has been made of the distinction between the Marxian and Weberian traditions of class analysis. Weberians, as has often been noted, define classes primarily in terms of *market* relations, whereas Marxists define classes by the social relations of *production*. Why is this contrast of theoretical importance? After all, both Marxists and Weberians recognize capitalists and workers as the two fundamental classes of capitalist societies, and both define these classes in essentially the same way—capitalists are owners of the means of production who employ wage earners; workers are nonowners of the means of production who sell their labor power to capitalists. What difference does it make that Weberians define these classes by the exchange relation into which they enter, whereas Marxists emphasize the social relations of production?

First, the restriction of classes to market relations means, for Weberians, that classes only really exist in capitalist societies. The relationship between lords and serfs might be oppressive and the source of considerable conflict, but Weberians would not treat this as a class relation since it is structured around relations of personal dependence and domination, not market relations. Marxists, in contrast, see conflicts over the control of productive resources in both feudalism and *capitalism as instances of class struggle. This is not simply a nominal shift in labels, for it is part of the effort within *Marxism to construct a general theory of historical change built around class analysis. Aphorisms such as "class struggle is the motor of history" only make sense if the concept of "class" is built around the social relations of production rather than restricted to market relations.

Second, the elaboration of the concept of class in terms of production relations underwrites the linkage between class and exploitation that is central to Marxist theory. In the traditional Marxist account, exploitation occurs primarily within production itself, for it is in production that labor is actually performed and embodied in the social product. Exploitation, roughly, consists in the appropriation by one class of the "surplus labor" performed by another. While the exchange relation between workers and capitalists may create the *opportunity* for capitalists to exploit workers, it is only when the labor of workers is actually deployed in the labor process and the resulting products appropriated by capitalists that exploitation actually occurs. The characteristic lack of discussion of exploitation by Weberian class analysts thus, at least in part, reflects their restriction of the concept of class to the exchange relation.

While these differences between the Marxian and Weberian concept of class are important for the broader theory of society within which these class concepts are used, in practical terms for the analysis of capitalist society the actual descriptive class maps generated by scholars in the two traditions may not be so divergent. As already noted, both traditions see the capital-labor relation as defining the principal axis of class relations in capitalism. Furthermore, scholars in both traditions acknowledge the importance of a variety of social categories, loosely labeled the "new middle class(es)"—professionals, managers and executives, bureaucratic officials and perhaps highly educated white-collar employees—who do not fit neatly into the polarized class relation between capitalists and workers. There is little consensus either among Weberian or among Marxist scholars on precisely how these new middle classes should be conceptualized. As a result, particularly as Marxist accounts of these "middle class" categories has become more sophisticated, the line of demarcation between these two traditions has become somewhat less sharply drawn.

While Marxist and Weberian pictures of the class structure of capitalist society may not differ dramatically, their use of the concept of class in the analysis of political phenomena is generally sharply different. Weberians typically regard class as one among a variety of salient determinants of politics. In specific problems this means that class might assume considerable importance, but there is no general presumption that class is a more pervasive or powerful determinant of political phenomena than other causal processes. Marxists, in contrast, characteristically give class a privileged status in the analysis. In the most orthodox treatments, class (and closely related concepts like "capitalism" or "mode of production") may become virtually the exclusive systematic explanatory principles, but in all Marxist accounts of politics class plays a central, if not necessarily all-encompassing, explanatory role. In the final section of this paper we will examine the problem of explanatory primacy for class. Before we engage that issue, however, we will examine the various ways in which Marxist class analysts see class shaping politics.

How Class Shapes Politics. Robert Alford and Roger Friedland, building on the analysis of Steven Lukes and others, have elaborated a tripartite typology of "levels of *power" that will be useful in examining the causal role of class on politics: 1) *Situational* power refers to power relations of direct command and obedience between actors, as in Weber's celebrated definition of power as the ability of one actor to get another to do something even in the face of resistance. This is the characteristic form of power analyzed in various behavioral studies of power. 2) *Institutional* power refers to the characteristics of different institutional settings which shape the decision-making agenda in ways which serve the interests of particular groups. This is also referred to as "negative power" or the "second face of power" (see Bachrach and Baratz)—power which excludes certain alternatives from a decision-making agenda without, as in situational power, actually commanding a specific behavior. 3) *Systemic* power is perhaps the most difficult (and contentious) conceptually. It refers to the power to realize one's interests by virtue of the overall structure of a social system rather than by virtue of commanding the behavior of others or of controlling the agendas of specific organizations. This corresponds to what Lukes calls the "third face of power."

Alford and Friedland discuss this typology of power in an interesting way using a loose game theory metaphor: Systemic power is power embedded in the fundamental nature of the game itself; institu-

tional power is power embodied in the specific rules of the game; and situational power is power deployed in specific moves within a given set of rules. When actors use specific resources strategically to accomplish their goals, they are exercising situational power. The procedural rules which govern how they use those resources reflect institutional power. And the nature of the social system which determines the range of possible rules and achievable goals reflects systemic power. There is thus a kind of cybernetic relationship among these levels of power: the system level imposes limits on the institutional level which imposes limits on actors' strategies at the situational level. Conflicts at the situational level, in turn, can modify the rules at the institutional level, which cumulatively can lead to the transformation of the system itself.

The class analysis of politics is implicated in each of these domains of power and politics. Although class theorists of politics do not explicitly frame their analyses in terms of these three levels of power, nevertheless the distinctions are implicit in many discussions.

Class and Situational Power. Much of the theoretical debate over the relative explanatory importance of class has occurred at the situational level of political analysis. Marxists (and non-Marxists heavily influenced by the Marxian tradition) typically argue that actors whose interests and resources are derived from their link to the class structure generally play the decisive role in actively shaping political conflicts and state policies. Sometimes the emphasis is on the strategic action of the dominant class, on the ability of capitalists to manipulate the state in their interests. Other times the emphasis is on the political effects of class struggle as such, in which case popular action as well as ruling class machinations are seen as shaping state policies. In either case, class is seen as shaping politics through its effects on the behavioral interactions among political actors.

The theoretical reasoning behind such treatments of the class basis of situational power is fairly straightforward. Class structures, among other things, distribute resources which are useful in political struggles. In particular, in capitalist societies capitalists have two crucial resources available to them to be deployed politically: enormous financial resources and personal connections to people in positions of governmental authority. Through a wide variety of concrete mechanisms—financing politicians, political parties, and policy think tanks; financially controlling the main organs of the mass media; offering lucrative jobs to high-level political officials after they leave state employment; extensive lobbying—capitalists are in a position to use their wealth to directly shape the direction of state policies. When combined with the dense pattern of personal networks which give capitalists easy access to the sites of immediate political power, such use of financial resources gives the bourgeoisie vastly disproportionate direct leverage over politics.

Few theorists deny the empirical facts of the use of politically important resources in this way by members of the capitalist class in pursuit of their interests. What is often questioned is the general efficacy and coherence of such actions in sustaining the class interests of the bourgeoisie. Because individual capitalists are frequently preoccupied by their immediate, particularistic interests (e.g., in specific markets, technologies, or regulations), when they deploy their class-derived resources politically some scholars argue that they are unlikely to do so in ways which place the class interests of the bourgeoisie as a whole above their own particularistic interests. As Fred Block among others has noted, the capitalist class is often very divided politically, lacking a coherent vision and sense of priorities. Thus, even if capitalists try to manipulate politics in various ways, such manipulations often work against each other and do not generate a consistent set of policy outcomes.

The fact that capitalists have considerable power resources by virtue of their control over capital thus does not ensure a capacity to translate those resources into a coherent class direction of politics. What is more, in terms of situational power, capitalists are not the only actors with effective political resources. In particular, as Theda Skocpol, Anthony Giddens, and others have stressed, state managers—the top-level politicians and officials within state apparatuses—have direct control of considerable resources to pursue political objectives. Although in many instances the interests and objectives of state managers may be congruent with the interests of the capitalist class, this is not universally the case, and when overt conflicts between state managers and the bourgeoisie occur there is no inherent reason why capitalists will always prevail. Even more to the point, in many situations, because of the disorganization, myopia, and apathy of the capitalist class, state managers will have considerable room to initiate state policies independently of pressures from the capitalist class.

These kinds of arguments do not discredit the claim that class structures do shape both the interests of actors and the political resources they can deploy in struggles over situational power. However, the blanket claim that class-derived interests and power resources are always the most salient is called into question.

Class and Institutional Power. It was at least in part because of a recognition that at the level of situational power capitalists are not always present as the predominant active political actors that much class analysis of politics has centered around the problem of the institutional dimensions of power. The argument is basically this: the state should be viewed not simply as a state *in* capitalist society, but rather as a *capitalist* state. This implies that there are certain institutional properties of the very form of the state that can be treated as having a specific class character to them. The idea here is not simply that there are certain policies of the state which embody the interests of a specific class, but rather that the very structure of the apparatuses through which those policies are made embodies those class interests.

Claims about the class character of the institutional level of power involve what is sometimes called non-decision-making power or negative power. The basic argument was crisply laid out in an early essay by Claus Offe. Offe argued that the class character of the state was inscribed in a series of negative filter mechanisms which imparted a systematic class bias to state actions. "Class bias," in this context, means that the property in question tends to filter out state actions which would be inimical to the interests of the dominant class. The form of the state, in effect, systematically determines what does not happen rather than simply what does.

An example, emphasized by Claus Offe and Volker Ronge as well as by Goran Therborn, would be the institutional rules by which the capitalist state acquires financial resources—through taxation and borrowing from the privately produced surplus rather than through the state's direct appropriation of the surplus generated by its own productive activity. By restricting the state's access to funds in this way the state is rendered dependent upon capitalist production, and this in turn acts as a mechanism which filters out state policies which would seriously undermine the profitability of private accumulation. Or, to take another example, given considerable emphasis by Nicos Poulantzas (1973), the electoral rules of capitalist representative democracies (in which people cast votes as individual citizens within territorial units of representation rather than as members of functioning groups) have the effect of transforming people from members of a class into atomized individuals (the "juridical citizen"). This atomization, in turn, serves to filter out state policies that would only be viable if people were systematically organized into durable collectivities or associations. To the extent that this filter can be viewed as stabilizing capitalism and thus serving the basic interests of the capitalist class, then exclusive reliance on purely territorial, individualized voting can be viewed as having a class character.

This way of understanding the class character of an apparatus suggests a certain functionalist logic to the thesis that the state is a capitalist state: its form is capitalist insofar as these institutional features contribute to the reproduction of the interests of the capitalist class. This functional logic has been most systematically elaborated in Goran Therborn's *What Does the Ruling Class Do When It Rules?* Therborn stresses that the real analytical bite of the thesis that the state has a distinctive class character occurs when the state is analyzed comparatively, particularly across historical epochs. The class character of the state apparatus is a variable; state apparatuses corresponding to different class structures will have distinctively different properties which impart different class biases on state actions. If this "correspondence principle" is correct, then it should be possible to define the specific class properties of the feudal state, the capitalist state, and—perhaps—the socialist state. Take the example already cited of the mechanism through which the state acquires resources. In the capitalist state this occurs primarily through taxation, thus insuring the fiscal subordination of the state to private capital accumulation. In the feudal state revenues are acquired through the direct appropriation of surplus from the personal vassals of the king. And in the socialist state, state revenues are acquired through the appropriation of the surplus product of state enterprises. In each case, the argument goes, these class forms of revenue acquisition selectively filter out political practices which might threaten the existing class structure.

Many critics of the thesis that the state has a distinctive class character have argued that this claim implies a functionalist theory of the state. This accusation is certainly appropriate in some cases. In the early work on the state by Nicos Poulantzas (1973), for example, and even more in the work of Louis Althusser, there was very little room for genuinely contradictory elements in the state. The class properties of the capitalist state were explained by the functions they served for reproducing capitalism. The functional correspondence principle for identifying the class character of aspects of the state slid into a principle for explaining the properties of the state. This kind of functionalism, however, is not an inherent feature of the class analysis of the institutional level of political power. While the thesis that state apparatuses have a class character does follow a functional logic (i.e., what makes a given property have a given "class character" is its functional relation to the class structure), this does not necessarily imply a full-fledged functionalist theory of the state.

Class and Systemic Power. To say that capitalists have *situational* power is to say that they command a range of resources which they can deploy to get their way. To say that they have *institutional* power is to argue that various institutions are designed in such a way as to selectively exclude alternatives which are antithetical to their interests from the political agenda. To say that they have *systemic* power is to say that the logic of the social system itself affirms their interests quite apart from their conscious strategies and the internal organization of political apparatuses.

The idea that capitalists have such systemic power has been forcefully argued by Adam Przeworski, building on the work of Antonio *Gramsci. Przeworski argues that so long as capitalism is intact as a social order, all actors in the system have an interest in capitalists making a profit. What this means is that unless a group has the capacity to overthrow the system completely, then at least in terms of material interests even groups opposed to capitalism have an interest in sustaining capitalist accumulation and profitability.

This kind of system-level power has been recognized by many scholars, not just those working firmly within the Marxist tradition. Charles Lindblom's well-known study *Politics and Markets,* for example, is built around the problem of how the interests of capitalists are imposed on political institutions by the operation of markets even without any direct, instrumental manipulation of those institutions by individual capitalists. Indeed, this essential point, wrapped in quite different rhetoric, is also at the core of neoconservative supply-side economics arguments about the need to reduce government spending in order to spur economic growth.

There are two critical differences between Marxist treatments of this systemic level of analysis and most mainstream treatments. First, Marxists characterize these system-level constraints on politics as having a distinctive *class* character. Neoconservatives do not regard the private investment constraint on the state as an instance of "class power," because they regard markets as the "natural" form of economic interaction. The constraint comes from the universal laws of economics rooted in human nature. In contrast, the Marxist characterization of these constraints in class terms rests on the general claim that capitalism is a historically distinct form of economy.

The second important difference between Marxist and mainstream perspectives on the constraints capitalism imposes on the state is that most liberal and neoconservative analysts see this system-level logic as much less closely tied to the institutional and situational levels of analysis than do Marxists. Neoconservatives in particular grant the state considerably more autonomy to muck up the functioning of the capitalist economy than do Marxists. For neoconservatives, even though the political system is clearly dependent on the private economy for resources and growth, nevertheless politically motivated actors are quite capable of persisting in high levels of excessive state spending in spite of the economic constraints. The state, being pushed by ideological agendas of actors wielding situational power, can, through myopia, "kill the goose that lays the golden egg." Marxists tend to see state spending and state policies as less likely to deviate persistently from the functional requirements of capitalism because they see the levels of situational and institutional power as generally congruent with the level of systemic power. The structure of state apparatuses and the strategies of capitalists, therefore, generally prevent too much deviation from occurring. Neoconservatives, on the other hand, see the three levels of politics as having much greater potential for divergence. They believe that the democratic form of institutions and the excessive mobilization of popular forces systematically generates dysfunctional levels of state spending which are not necessarily corrected by the exercise of capitalist situational power or the negative feedback.

Variability in the Effects of Class on Politics. We have reviewed three clusters of mechanisms through which class shapes politics: the class-based access to resources which can be strategically deployed for political purposes; the institutionalization of certain class biases into the design of state apparatuses; and the way in which the operation of the system as a whole universalizes certain class interests. Frequently, in the more theoretical discussions of these mechanisms, the class character of these mechanisms is treated as largely invariant within a given kind of class society. Abstract discussions of "the capitalist state," for example, emphasize what all capitalist states have in common by virtue of being capitalist states. Relatively less attention has been given to the problem of variability. In many empirical contexts, however, the central issue is precisely the ways in which class effects concretely vary across cases. Let us look briefly at such variability in class effects at the situational, institutional, and systemic levels of political analysis.

One of the central themes of much Marxist historical research is the shifting "balance of class forces" between workers and capitalists (and sometimes other classes) in various kinds of social and political conflicts. Generally, expressions like "balance of forces" refer to the relative situational power of the contending organized collectivities—i.e., their relative capacity to actively pursue their interests in various political arenas. The task of an analysis of variability in the class character of situational power is thus to explain the social determinants of these varying capacities. Generally this involves invoking mechanisms at the institutional and systemic levels of analysis. Thus, for example, the enduring weakness of the U.S. working class within electoral politics has been explained by such institutional factors as the existence of a winner-take-all electoral system which undermines the viability of small parties, the lack of public financing of elections which enhances the political influence of financial contributors, and voter registration laws which make voter mobilization difficult, as well as such systemic factors as the location of U.S. capitalism in the world capitalist system. Each of these factors undermines the potential situational power of the working class within electoral politics. This enduring situational weakness, in turn, blocks the capacity of the popular forces to alter the institutional properties of the state in ways which would enhance their power. While in all capitalist societies it may be the case that capitalists have disproportionate situational power, capitalist societies can vary considerably in power of different subordinate groups relative to the bourgeoisie.

The same kind of variation is possible in terms of power embodied in the institutional properties of the state. In various ways, noncapitalist elements can be embodied in the institutional structure of capitalist states. Consider the example of workplace safety regulations. A variety of institutional forms can be established for implementing safety regulations. The conventional device in most capitalist states is to have a hierarchical bureaucratic agency responsible for such regulations with actual enforcement organized through official inspections, licensing requirements, and various other aspects of bureaucratic due process. An alternative structure would be to establish workplace occupational safety committees within factories controlled by employees with powers to monitor compliance and enforce regulations. Such administration procedures built around principles of what Joshua Cohen and Joel Rogers call "associational democracy" violate the class logic of the capitalist state by encouraging the collective organization rather than atomization of the affected people. To the extent that such noncapitalist elements can be incorporated into the institutional structure of the capitalist state, then the class character of those apparatuses can vary *even within capitalism.*

Finally, some theoretical work entertains the possibilities of variation in the class character of systemic power within capitalist societies. The essential issue here is whether the overall relationship between state and economy within capitalism can significantly modify the dynamics of the system itself. Do all instances of capitalism have fundamentally the same system logic simply by virtue of the private ownership of the means of production, or can this logic be significantly modified in various ways? Most Marxists have insisted that there is relatively little variation in such system logic across capitalisms, at least as it relates to the basic class character of system-level power. The transition from competitive to "monopoly" capitalism, for example, may greatly affect the *situational* power of different classes and fractions of classes, and it might even be reflected in changes in the class character of the institutional form of the state (for example, petit bourgeois elements in state apparatuses might disappear as capitalism advances). But the basic system-level class logic, Marxists have traditionally argued, remains organized around the interests of capital in both cases.

There has been some challenge to this view by scholars generally sympathetic to Marxian perspectives. Gosta Esping-Andersen, for example, argues that differences in the forms of the *welfare state (which he refers to as conservative, liberal, and socialist welfare state regimes) can have a basic effect on the system logic of capitalism, creating different developmental tendencies and different matrices of interests for various classes.

Joel Rogers has forcefully argued a similar view with respect to the specific issue of industrial relations. He argues that there is an "inverse-J" relationship between the interests of capital and the degree of unionization of the working class. Increasing unionization hurts the interests of capitalists up to a certain point. Beyond that point, however, further increases in unionization are beneficial to capitalists, because they make possible higher levels of coordination and cooperation between labor and capital. This means that if, for example, the legal regime of industrial relations prevents unionization from passing the trough threshold in the curve (as, he argues, is the case in the United States), then unions will be constantly on the defensive as they confront the interests of capital, whereas if the legal order facilitates unionization moving beyond the trough (as in Sweden), then the system logic will sustain unionization. High unionization and low unionization capitalisms, therefore, embody qualitatively different system patterns of class power within what remains an overall capitalist framework.

Conclusion. Few scholars today would argue that class is irrelevant to the analysis of political phenomena, but there is much contention over how important class might be. The characteristic form of this debate is for the critic of class analysis to attack class reductionism, i.e., the thesis that political phenomena (state policies, institutional properties, political behavior, party strategies, etc.) can be fully explained by class-based causal processes. Defenders of class analysis, on the other hand, attack their critics for claiming that political phenomena are completely autonomous from class determinants. Both of these positions, when stated in this form, have no real defenders. Even relatively orthodox Marxists introduce many nonclass factors in their explanations of any given example of state policy and thus are not guilty of class reductionism; and even the most state-centered critic of class analysis admits that class relations play some role in shaping political outcomes.

The issue, then, is not really explanatory reductionism vs. absolute political autonomy, but rather the relative salience of different causal factors and how they fit together. A good example is the recent discussions of the development of the welfare state sparked by the work of Theda Skocpol and others advocating a "state-centered" approach to the study of politics. In an influential paper published in the mid-1980s Ann Orloff and Skocpol argue that the specific temporal sequence of the introduction of social security laws in Britain, Canada, and the United States cannot be explained by economic or class factors. Rather, they argue, this sequence is primarily the result of causal processes located within the political realm itself, specifically the bureaucratic capacities of the state and the legacies of prior state policies.

The empirical arguments of Orloff and Skocpol are quite convincing given the specific way they have

defined their object of explanation. But suppose there was a slight shift in the question. Instead of asking, "why was social security introduced in Britain before World War I, in Canada in the 1920s, and the United States in the 1930s?" suppose the question were, "why did no industrialized capitalist society have social security in the 1850s while all industrialized capitalist societies had such programs by the 1950s?" The nature of class relations and class conflicts in capitalism and the transformations of the capitalist economy would surely figure more prominently in the answer to this reformulated explanatory problem.

In general, then, the issue of causal primacy is sensitive to the precise formulation of what is to be explained *(explanandum)*. It is certainly implausible that class (or anything else) could be "the most important" cause of all political phenomena. For claims of causal primacy to have any force, therefore, it is essential that the domain of the explanations over which the claims are being made be well defined. Can we, then, specify the domain of *explananda* for which class is likely to be the most important causal factor? Implicit in most class analyses of politics are two very general hypotheses about the range of explanatory problems for which class analysis is likely to provide the most powerful explanations:

Hypothesis 1. The more coarse-grained and abstract the *explanandum,* the more likely it is that general systemic factors, such as class structure or the dynamics of capitalism, will play an important explanatory role. The more fine-grained and concrete the object of explanation, on the other hand, the more likely it is that relatively contingent causal processes—such as the specific legislative histories of different states or the detailed rules of electoral competition—will loom large in the explanation. All things being equal, therefore, the decision to examine relatively nuanced concrete variations in political outcomes across cases with broadly similar class structures is likely to reduce the salience of class relative to other causal processes.

Hypothesis 2. The more the reproduction of the class structure and the interests of dominant classes are directly implicated in the *explanandum,* the more likely it is that class factors—at the situational, institutional, and systemic levels—will constitute important causes in the explanation. This is not a tautology, for there is no logical reason why class mechanisms must be causally important for explaining class-relevant outcomes. Such a hypothesis also does not reject the possibility that causal processes unconnected to class might play a decisive role in specific instances. But it does argue that one should be surprised if class-based causal processes do not play a significant role in explaining political phenomena closely connected to the reproduction of class structures and the interests of dominant classes.

Taken together, these two hypotheses help specify the applicability of class to the analysis of politics.

(See also MARX, KARL; SOCIALISM AND SOCIAL DEMOCRACY; WEBER, MAX.)

Ralf Dahrendorf, *Class and Class Conflict in Industrial Societies* (Stanford, Calif., 1959). Ralph Miliband, *The State in Capitalist Society* (New York, 1969). Peter Bachrach and Morton S. Baratz, *Power and Poverty* (New York, 1970). Louis Althusser, "Ideology and Ideological State Apparatuses," in Louis Althusser, *Lenin and Philosophy* (New York, 1971). Nicos Poulantzas, *Political Power and Social Classes* (London, 1973). Steven Lukes, *Power: A Radical View* (London, 1974). Claus Offe, "Structural Problems of the Capitalist State: Class Rule and the Political System. On the Selectiveness of Political Institutions," in Klaus Von Beyme, ed., *German Political Studies,* vol. 1 (London, 1974). Claus Offe and Volker Ronge, "Theses on the Theory of the State" *New German Critique* 6 (Fall 1975): 139–147. Nicos Poulantzas, *Classes in Contemporary Capitalism* (London, 1975). Charles Lindblom, *Politics and Markets* (New York, 1977). Goran Therborn, *What Does the Ruling Class Do When It Rules?* (London, 1978). Frank Parkin, *Marxist Class Theory: A Bourgeois Critique* (New York, 1979). Anthony Giddens, *A Contemporary Critique of Historical Materialism* (Berkeley, Calif., 1981). John Roemer, *A General Theory of Exploitation and Class* (Cambridge, Mass., 1982). Ann Orloff and Theda Skocpol, "Why Not Equal Equal Protection? Explaining the Politics of Public Social Spending in Britain, 1900–1911, and the United States, 1880s–1920" *American Sociological Review* 49, no. 6 (1984): 726–750. Robert Alford and Roger Friedland, *The Powers of Theory* (Cambridge, U.K., 1985). Adam Przeworski, *Capitalism and Social Democracy* (Cambridge, U.K., 1985). Theda Skocpol, "Bringing the State Back In: False Leads and Promising Starts in Current Theories and Research," in Peter Evans, Theda Skocpol, and Dieter Reuschmeyer, eds., *Bringing the State Back In* (Cambridge, U.K., 1985), pp. 3–37. Erik Olin Wright, *Classes* (London, 1985). Fred Block, *Revising State Theory: Essays in Politics and Postindustrialism* (Philadelphia, 1987). Gosta Esping-Andersen, *The Three Worlds of Welfare Capitalism* (Princeton, N.J., 1990). Erik Olin Wright, *The Debate on Classes* (London, 1990). Joel Rogers, *Silenced Majority* (New York, forthcoming).

ERIK OLIN WRIGHT

CLAUSEWITZ, Carl von. The first modern writer to develop a nondidactic theory of *war, the primary intention of Carl von Clausewitz (1780–1831) was not to teach soldiers how to wage war effectively, but to analyze war as a permanent phenomenon of the human condition with its own elements and dynamic. He entered the Prussian army at the age of 12, and served both as an infantry officer and in staff positions in the Revolutionary and Napoleonic wars. Between 1818 and 1830 he was director of the War Academy in Berlin, an undemanding administrative post that enabled him to devote much of his time to scholarship. His major theoretical work, *On War,* was written during these years; he died before completing the extensive revisions he had planned.

Clausewitz believed that although war, like art, was not a science, it could be studied scientifically. His approach combined intensive historical research with the experience of contemporary wars into a broad evidentiary base, to which he applied the analytic methods of German idealist philosophy. He developed his arguments dialectically and by means of comparisons between present and past, which alone, he thought, made possible the discovery of universal elements and processes. The theoretical results were then tested against actual events, which called for further historical study. Not coincidentally, history rather than theory makes up the largest share of his writings.

According to Clausewitz, theory should identify the military and nonmilitary elements of war, explain how they function and interact, and place war in its political context. The hypotheses and explanations must be intellectually valid, logical, and consistent; they must also reflect as closely as possible the reality they seek to explain. Reality will always differ from its theoretical reflection, if only because reality contains imponderables. Theory must build chance and accident into its structure, but will never be truly comprehensive. Theory, in Clausewitz's view, cannot provide laws for action, but by helping people think logically and realistically about war it might indirectly improve performance.

War is distinguished from other social activities by its element of large-scale, organized violence. Because violence is its only essential property, the ideal conflict contains the highest degree of violence—absolute war. Not only are extremes of violence a logical necessity, but war in the real world tends to approach the absolute as the result of technological development and of the dynamic process Clausewitz termed "escalation," in which the two antagonists will try to outdo each other.

The concept of absolute war is logically valid, supported by some historical evidence, and helps us analyze all wars. But real wars have usually fallen short of the highest level of violence. This contradiction between theory and reality is partly explained by the concept of "friction," which Clausewitz developed as a means of analyzing chance and the accidents that occur in war. Its basic explanation, however, is discovered when an antithesis is joined to the thesis of absolute war. War is always influenced by forces external to it: by its political goals and by the characteristics of the societies and governments in conflict. War is a continuation of policy by other means. If a particular war does not seek the opponent's annihilation but a lesser goal—defense of a border area, for instance—then even theory does not demand the extreme. The concept of absolute war and the concept of war limited by friction, policy, and other factors, jointly form the dual nature of war.

It is a consequence of war's dual nature that a purely military evaluation of a strategic decision or operational act is inappropriate. In a rational context the use of violence should always agree with the political motive and take account of the likely political result.

These central tenets of Clausewitz's theory are supported by concepts such as friction, escalation, and "moral elements"—psychological qualities in society, the armed forces, and the military leadership, which are particularly difficult to analyze and quantify, but are of supreme significance. Lesser propositions address specifics of actual warfare, an example being the assertion that a demonstration is a weaker use of force than a real attack, and must therefore be justified by particularly compelling motives.

Clausewitz wrote with great precision, but readers have often found it difficult to follow the dialectical line of his arguments or have misinterpreted his use of operational and even tactical examples as advocacy. Despite numerous attempts, it has never been possible to show that his writings have affected the strategic planning and operations of modern war. His true influence is intellectual. His work holds out a model—so far unequaled—of systematic, realistic thinking about war as a timeless agent of ideologies and of state policy.

(See also FORCE, USE OF; STRATEGY.)

Carl von Clausewitz, *On War,* trans. and ed. Michael Howard and Peter Paret, rev. ed. (Princeton, N.J., 1984). Peter Paret, *Clausewitz and the State,* rev. ed. (Princeton, N.J., 1985). Carl von Clausewitz, *Historical and Political Writings,* trans. and ed. Peter Paret and Daniel Moran (Princeton, N.J., 1991).

PETER PARET

CLIENTALISM. See PATRON-CLIENT POLITICS.

CODETERMINATION. As an institutional relationship between organized labor and business, codetermination gives labor movements the opportunity and right to participate with their employers in major decisions that jointly affect their firm and/or industry. Common throughout northern Europe— including the Netherlands, Scandinavia, and particularly the Federal Republic of *Germany (FRG)— codetermination (*Mitbestimmung* in German) allows representatives of workers and trade unions to obtain voting seats on the supervisory board of directors *(Aufsichtsrat)* of large firms.

The roots of codetermination lie in the guild structures of feudal Europe where handicraft traditions encouraged the transmission of worker skills in a master-journeyman-apprentice system that deeply embedded participatory traditions among skilled workers. More modern roots of codetermination include a resurgence of worker participation during the period of the Weimar Republic in Germany (1918–1933) when workers demanded increased rights in a newly democratic society. Partially eroded by increasingly conservative governments in the 1920s, and cut short by the Nazis' suppression of independent worker representation, codetermination in its present form did not reappear until the formation of the FRG in 1949.

German codetermination has two official forms, one for the coal and steel industries and one for all other industries. The former provides full parity for worker representatives in all decisions of the supervisory board, while the latter provides nearly full parity between worker and employer representatives, as a representative of management always has the tie-breaking vote. The push for codetermination in the postwar years was attributable to the anger of German workers toward the complicity of German industrialists with the Nazi war machine. This was especially true of the coal and steel barons, hence the full parity in those industries. Thus, after World War II, the idea of placing workers and union representatives on the boards of directors of these firms was seen by many as an opportunity to provide increased accountability to German capitalism.

The laws governing codetermination were first passed in the early 1950s and expanded in the 1970s and thus represent the powerful role of the trade unions in the politics of the postwar FRG. They give the workers—and indirectly their unions, in the case of those firms so organized—a form of institutionalized participation via membership on the supervisory board of German firms. This participation, rather than making German firms uncompetitive, actually has had the opposite effect. Workers—and unions—can comprehend if not unilaterally determine corporate decisions regarding investment and the introduction of new technologies. Codetermination has allowed German workers a broader and deeper knowledge of the goals and strategies of the firms for which they work.

Codetermination has not been free of conflict in the FRG. In 1976, at the time of the broadening of some of the unions' powers, the Constitutional Court ruled that worker representatives could never attain majority representation on supervisory boards. The court argued that such a provision could compromise private property rights. This ruling caused the unions to break away from a more structured process of consultation on macroeconomic policy— called "concerted action"—with the government and organized business. Despite this residual tension, however, codetermination has provided substantial benefits to German business, workers, and to the entire society.

(See also LABOR MOVEMENT; SOCIAL MARKET ECONOMY.)

Andrei S. Markovits, *The Politics of the West German Trade Unions: Strategies of Class and Interest Representation in Growth and Crisis* (New York, 1986).

CHRISTOPHER S. ALLEN

COLD WAR. The term *Cold War* is used to describe the protracted conflict between the Soviet and Western worlds that, while falling short of "hot" *war, nonetheless involved a comprehensive military, political, and ideological rivalry. Originally used in the fourteenth century to denote the long-running conflict between Muslims and Christians in Spain, it entered modern political vocabulary after *World War II, as a description, popularized by the columnist Walter Lippmann, of the conflict between the Soviet and Western blocs. It was initially used to describe a historical period—the Cold War—that began with the breakdown of the wartime alliance in 1946–1947. Some writers saw an end to the Cold War in the 1950s, after the death of *Stalin; others saw its demise in the 1970s with *détente. The term *Second Cold War* was widely used to refer to the period after the collapse of détente in the late 1970s.

Cold War was, however, also used in a more analytic sense, not to denote a particular phase of East-West rivalry but rather to denote the very fact of the rivalry between the communist and capitalist systems itself, one that involved competition and confrontation but not all-out, "hot" war. In this sense, the Cold War began not in 1945 but in 1917, with the accession of the Bolsheviks to power, and their proclamation of a worldwide challenge to capitalism, and continued until the late 1980s. The communist revolutionary challenge, and the Western response to it, were checked by a variety of factors— the fragmentation of the world into separate societies and states, the power of *nationalism, the fear of *nuclear weapons, the limits on the power of each side—but it nevertheless endured for more than seven decades. Whatever the periodicity or meaning adopted, most writers agreed that the Cold War, in the sense of a global rivalry between two competing and roughly equal blocs, ended, after *Gorbachev's accession to power in 1985, with the collapse of Soviet power and the end of the Soviet ideological challenge to the West.

The development of East-West rivalry was marked by a set of crises, in both Europe and the *Third World, and by an enduring competition in arms, especially nuclear weapons. Central as the *arms race was to Cold War, however, the latter comprised a broader strategic and political contest. After the end of World War II, Europe was soon divided by the "Iron Curtain" of communist border controls into the Soviet and Western blocs, which led to the Berlin blockade of 1948–1949 and to the formation, in 1949 and 1955, respectively, of the *North Atlantic Treaty Organization and the *Warsaw Treaty Organization. Further crises over Berlin followed in 1959 and 1961, and attempts by states under Soviet control to assert their independence were crushed by force—the German Democratic Republic (East Germany) in 1953, Hungary in 1956, Czechoslovakia in 1968, Poland in 1981. Yugoslavia, Albania, and Romania were able to evade Soviet domination but remained ruled by Communist parties until they, like the Soviet allies, were overwhelmed by the democratic revolutions of the late 1980s.

The rivalry of East and West was also fought out in the Third World. After the Azerbaidzhan crisis of March 1946, a dispute over Soviet reluctance to pull forces out of Iran that marked the first major dispute of the Cold War, there followed the *Chinese Revolution of 1949, the *Korean War of 1950–1953, the *Suez crisis of 1956, the *Cuban Revolution of 1959 and, in its aftermath, the missile crisis of 1962, and the U.S. involvement in Vietnam of 1965–1973. In the latter part of the 1970s the collapse of détente and onset of the so-called Second Cold War was in part the result of U.S. concern at the advent to power of pro-Soviet revolutionary regimes in a dozen Third World states, notably South Vietnam, Afghanistan, Ethiopia, Mozambique, Angola, and Nicaragua.

The Second Cold War came after the lessening of tensions that was evident in the 1970s with the Strategic Arms Limitation Talks of 1972 and the Helsinki Accords of thirty-three European nations, the United States, and Canada on European security in 1975. This amelioration had ended by the late 1970s and appeared dead when Soviet forces occupied Afghanistan in December 1979. The period after 1980 initially saw an intensification of East-West confrontation: an increased emphasis in the West on the arms race, with the deployment of intermediate-range cruise missiles in Europe and the Strategic Defense Initiative, and an encouragement by the United States of anticommunist guerrillas in Cambodia, Afghanistan, Angola, and Nicaragua.

In the Second Cold War the Soviet leadership appeared to have retreated behind the defensive positions of the earlier cold war: but from 1985 onwards, under Gorbachev's leadership, the Soviet Union made wide-ranging concessions that brought the earlier confrontation and the Cold War as a whole to an end. The Soviet Union withdrew support for most Third World revolutionary regimes and for the Eastern European Communist parties it had kept in power for forty years, signed wide-ranging agreements on arms control and reduction with the United States, and abandoned its global ideological rivalry with the capitalist West. Frictions between the Soviet Union and the West certainly continued, but the Cold War, in both its historical and analytic senses, was to all intents and purposes over.

Writing on the Cold War has revolved around two broad questions. The first has been that of historical responsibility, of which side caused the cold wars of the late 1940s and late 1970s. Whereas earlier writings tended to polarize around a Western view that the Soviet Union was responsible and a Soviet view that the "imperialist" countries were to blame, a later school of "revisionist" Western writing stressed forms of U.S. responsibility. In the 1980s a "postrevisionist" school emerged, locating responsibility in both the Soviet and U.S. blocs, while, with the advent of glasnost in the Soviet Union after

1988, Soviet writers began for the first time to concede that the policies of Stalin and Brezhnev had contributed to exacerbating East-West tensions.

The second broad set of questions concern what the Cold War was and what the sources of the conflict were. Here four broad schools of explanation have emerged. The first, a traditional application of power politics, sees it as a continuation under new ideological guises of the kind of great power rivalry for empire, influence, and domination seen in earlier epochs. A second school stresses the cognitive and subjective factors, the degree of misperception involved in the failure of the two sides to maintain their wartime alliance and resolve subsequent disputes, and to extricate themselves from the reinforcing anxieties of the arms race. A third school views the Cold War as only apparently a rivalry between two blocs, and more as a means by which the dominant states within each bloc controlled and disciplined their own populations and clients, and by which those who stood to benefit from increased arms production and political anxiety promoted a mythical rivalry. Fourth, there are those who see the Cold War not primarily as a conflict between states or as a merely military rivalry but more as a conflict between two distinct, competing social and political systems, each committed to prevailing over the other at the global level.

(See also ARMS CONTROL; CONTAINMENT; MARSHALL PLAN; PERESTROIKA; POTSDAM CONFERENCE; SOVIET-AFGHANISTAN WAR; STRATEGIC ARMS LIMITATION TREATIES; SUPERPOWER; YALTA CONFERENCE.)

Walter LaFeber, *America, Russia and the Cold War, 1945–1980* (New York, 1980). Raymond Garthoff, *Detente and Confrontation* (Washington, D.C., 1985). Fred Halliday, *The Making of the Second Cold War*, 2d ed. (London and New York, 1986).

FRED HALLIDAY

COLLECTIVIZATION. In the *Soviet Union and other countries under Marxist-Leninist rule, collectivization was a response to problems posed by agriculture for economic and social transformation. The ruling parties in these countries adopted rapid industrialization and transition to a socialist institutional order as their primary goals. After substantial debate in the 1920s, the question of the role of agriculture in the industrialization process was resolved in the Soviet Union in favor of an extractive approach. Under it, agriculture was to be a source of new recruits to the industrial labor force, of inexpensive food for the nonfarm population, and of raw materials for industry, while consuming as little as possible of the investment resources made available by this unequal transfer. However, further issues were raised by the question of the appropriate *institutional* model for agriculture under *socialism as understood by the Soviets.

*Marx had viewed *peasants as a declining *class

and had focused most of his analysis of *capitalism and of its eventual demise on the conflict between the owners of industry and the industrial working class. Whereas the transformation of the latter actors into participants in a planned industrial economy under state ownership seemed a logical consequence of Marx's historical scheme, the prospects for any remaining tillers were unclear.

The fraction of the population still engaged in agriculture at the time of the *Russian Revolution in 1917, and in some countries coming under similar regimes in the years after World War II, was much larger than that in the northern European industrial societies that were Marx's primary referents. Cultivation in these countries was mainly on a small scale and by owner-operators or tenant farmers, not large-scale labor-hiring farms. Rather than attempt to transform these farms into state enterprises, the Communist leaders of the Soviet Union favored the establishment of "semisocialist" institutions called collective farms, in which output would be produced under joint management, with distribution of the net proceeds among participants in proportion to their labor contributions. A few such institutions were established on a voluntary basis following the Russian Revolution, and Soviet leader V. I. *Lenin advocated their gradual popularization through provision of state assistance and preference in commercial dealings. However, Joseph *Stalin opted for compulsory collectivization, a process that began in 1928 and was completed by 1937 despite resistance resulting in the slaughter of about half the country's livestock and an unknown number of deaths by starvation. The institutions thus formed, called *kolkhozy* (singular *kolkhoz*), were subject to tight state controls in the forms of output targets, compulsory sales quotas, regulations on internal institutional structure, and intervention in the choice of officials.

The main economic difference between a collective farm and a state enterprise lay not in the degree of autonomy of the farm workers but rather in the fact that, unlike state employees, workers were not paid guaranteed wages but had to survive on the net income produced by their unit. (A minimum wage for collective farmers was introduced in the Soviet Union in the 1960s.) Although destructive of lives and productive potential, the system allowed the state to eliminate open opposition in the countryside, to meet its targets for extracting output from agriculture, to induce a large labor transfer to the cities, and to avoid directly bearing agricultural risk by forcing the farmers to be residual income claimants.

In comparison with private farms, collective farms held income differentiation in check and allowed the nonfarm sector to obtain farm products without relying on the existence of a stratum of more successful commercial farmers and without having to offer the farmers economically attractive prices for their products. Turning the terms of trade against farmers required replacing market exchange by mandatory state procurement, the implementation of which was facilitated by the grouping of farmers into larger entities (the *kolkhozy*) over which officials could maintain effective control. The relatively large scale of the *kolkhozy* was also consistent with Marxist beliefs in the existence of economies of scale in agriculture and in the desirability of mechanization—beliefs that were disputed by later Western students of agricultural development. However, partly to pacify farmer resistance and partly to rid the collective farms of the burden of producing labor-intensive products for which scale was clearly unimportant, collective farmers were permitted to maintain small private plots and to raise animals for meat, dairy products, and eggs.

The Soviet pattern was copied by other *Communist Party states, with the exception of *Poland and *Yugoslavia, the governments of which permitted perpetuation of private farms in the face of strong farmer resistance. Most of these countries also established a certain number of state farms, organized along the lines of state factories. *China attempted to amalgamate its collective farms into still larger communes in 1958, but the move resulted in massive famine, and the system was reorganized in 1962 with small production teams as basic farm units. Between 1979 and 1983, China decollectivized in the sense of restoring individual households to the status of production units, although considerable intervention by local government and the state continued in such areas as pricing and obligatory sales. Farm liberalization movements also occurred in other countries, including *Hungary and *Vietnam; the Soviet Union was preparing for related reforms in the late 1980s. Collective farms were widely viewed as having depressed agricultural performance by reducing production incentives. Chief culprits appear to have been internal egalitarianism, problems of supervision, and the role of the collectives as enforcers of the extractive policies of the state.

(See also COMMAND ECONOMY; COMMUNISM; RURAL DEVELOPMENT.)

Alec Nove, *An Economic History of the U.S.S.R.* (Harmondsworth, U.K., 1969). Peter Nolan, *The Political Economy of Collective Farms: An Analysis of China's Post-Mao Rural Reforms* (Boulder, Colo., 1988). Louis Putterman, "Agricultural Producers' Cooperatives," in Pranab Bardhan, ed., *The Economic Theory of Agrarian Institutions* (Oxford, 1989), pp. 319–339.

LOUIS PUTTERMAN

COLOMBIA. Located in the northwestern corner of South America, Colombia is the third most populous country in Latin America (approximately 33 million people) and has the fifth largest economy. The country has a rugged topography, with three Andean mountain ranges traversing the western half, although the country's highest peaks are located off the Caribbean coast in the Sierra Nevada. South and east from the eastern plains are the scarcely populated Amazon territories. These geographical features had important political consequences through fostering decentralization and regionalism.

In 1830, some ten years after Gran Colombia gained its independence from Spain, Venezuela and Ecuador broke away. (Panama gained independence in 1903.) By the 1850s, the country's two political parties, dominant to this day, the Partido Liberal and the Partido Conservador, were established. Their history includes periods of hegemonic one-party rule, civil wars, and coalition government. The parties often mobilized armed bands larger than the national army, indicating the weakness of the state and the military.

Numerous civil confrontations from 1851 to 1903 generated sectarian identification with the two parties. Liberals dominated national politics from 1863 to 1885, enacting antichurch reforms and federalist, secularist, and politically liberal constitutions. A centralizing reaction ultimately controlled by the Conservatives led to the 1886 Constitution, the basic text in effect until 1991, and to an 1887 concordat with the Vatican reestablishing church centrality. Conservatives controlled national politics until 1930, when the Great Depression and party divisions facilitated a Liberal victory.

In his first term in office, Liberal President Alfonso López Pumarejo (1934–1938) enacted constitutional, administrative, electoral, fiscal, and agrarian reforms known as the "Revolution on the March." They helped the Liberals become the country's majority party by limiting church influence, expanding the urban electorate where the party was stronger, and increasing the party's support base within labor. However, intraparty divisions permitted a narrow Conservative victory in the 1946 presidential elections even as the Liberals retained congressional control. Local violence exploded into a national conflagration following the assassination of the populist Liberal leader Jorge Eliécer Gaitán in 1948. The country's oligarchic democracy ended as an undeclared civil war, *la violencia,* between adherents of the two parties took the lives of some 200,000 people, ushering in the military government of General Gustavo Rojas Pinilla (1953–1957).

In 1957–1958, to facilitate a return to civilian rule and end partisan violence, leaders of the two parties agreed to join together in a Frente Nacional. Under the Frente Nacional agreement, the two parties shared equally in executive, legislative, and judicial posts; they also agreed that from 1958 to 1974 the presidency would alternate between the two parties.

The Frente Nacional coalition governments contributed to the country's transformation. Colombia became more urbanized and educated as the population doubled, and the sectarian party identities that had justified coalition rule disappeared. However, regional political leaders and economic elites urged retention of coalition rule, and efforts to open up the political system failed. During the 1970s, nonelectoral opposition in the form of labor protest, civic strikes, and guerrilla violence grew. Conservative President Belisario Betancur (1982–1986) sought peace agreements with the country's various guerrilla groups and enacted limited political reforms. Violence began to grow as state authority was also challenged by *drug trafficking groups. This violence accelerated under Liberal President Virgilio Barco (1986–1990), who confronted "narco-terrorism" while reaching accommodation with some of the guerrilla groups. Under Liberal President César Gaviria (1990–), reincorporated guerrilla groups remained politically active, several major drug traffickers surrendered to authorities under a plea-bargaining agreement, and a democratizing constitution was enacted in July 1991.

With a long history of liberal constitutional government, Colombia today is a political *democracy. The nature of Colombian democracy, however, has been qualified by the exclusionary restrictions of coalition rule, only fully dismantled in 1991; by state of siege restrictions; and currently by extensive violence. Colombia has a unitary form of government. Until 1991, the president was elected in a single round for a four-year term, with no immediate reelection. Under the new Constitution, there will be a second round if no candidate receives an absolute majority, and reelection is prohibited. The 1991 Constitution places new limits on the president's formerly expansive formal powers. Departmental governors, previously appointed, are now elected popularly, as mayors have been since 1988.

Congress consists of a Senate and a Chamber of Deputies, with four-year terms. Elections are based on proportional representation by departments, parties are allowed to present multiple lists, and abstention rates have been high; this has encouraged factionalization and reinforced the role of the two traditional parties. Party discipline has been low, forcing the presidents to continually renegotiate governing legislative majorities. The judiciary is weak, owing to budgetary neglect and, currently, intimidation and violence associated with drug trafficking.

Since competitive presidential elections began anew in 1974, the Partido Liberal has always obtained a congressional majority and won the presidency, except in 1982. Both the Partido Liberal and Partido Social Conservador are mainstream, "catchall" parties. Weak electorally, the Partido Comunista de Colombia has close ties with the country's largest guerrilla organization, the Fuerzas Armadas Revolucionarias de Colombia (FARC), created in 1964. After a truce was signed between the FARC and the Betancur administration in 1984, the FARC created a political party, Unión Patriótica (UP), which had increasingly overshadowed the Communist Party. It has competed in elections since 1986, but many of its activists, including two presidential candidates, have been assassinated. The strongest third party in 1990 emerged from the Movimiento del 19 de Abril (M-19), which has had considerable electoral success since agreeing to lay down its arms.

Colombia is a highly stratified society, and many, especially in rural areas, live in absolute poverty. Business organizations seek regional balance and are well represented in both traditional parties. Organized labor is a declining percentage of the economically active population (around nine percent in 1990) and is divided into competing confederations. Public-sector unions are among the most organized and radical. As the links of the traditional parties to societal groups have declined, independent neighborhood associations and civic movements have increased. Historically strong, the influence of the *Roman Catholic church—one of the most conservative on the continent—has been declining.

Colombia's economic record has been steady but not spectacular. The country's per capita GDP growth rate between 1961 and 1980 was 2.8 percent (the continent's average was 3.1 percent), and in the 1980s Colombia retained 1.5 percent average growth (while the rest of Latin America suffered declines). The country's inflation rates of between twenty percent and thirty percent over the past two decades have been lower than those of most of its neighbors. Populist policies have been attenuated, and initial *import-substitution industrialization, which began in the 1930s, was not as protectionist as it had been among the early Latin American industrializers. During the Frente Nacional period, coalition rule by two multiclass elitist parties inhibited radical policy shifts, reassuring investors and international financial institutions. In the 1970s, experiencing a strong coffee boom and an influx of foreign exchange owing to marijuana and then cocaine exports, the country borrowed little from private commercial banks. Thus, the negative consequences of the *debt crisis of the 1980s were felt less than in other Latin American countries. Recent discoveries of coal and oil have permitted the country to reduce further its dependence on coffee, historically its major export crop. Responding to the globalization of the world economy and seeking increasing flows of foreign investment, recent governments have implemented market-oriented reforms and sought to revive free trade and integration schemes with several of the country's neighbors.

Colombia's central challenge in the 1990s is the rebuilding of state institutions, threatened by growing violence linked to drug trafficking groups—occasionally in collaboration with regional landowners and elements of the armed forces—and to guerrilla forces. Over the last half of the 1980s, 15,000 to 20,000 people suffered violent deaths each year, of which ten to fifteen percent were associated with guerrilla activity, drug trafficking, or political conflict. Although the Colombian state may be able to reduce narco-terrorism in the short term, drug trafficking is a long-term problem that will only be resolved, if at all, with substantial international collaboration.

Under President Gaviria, efforts to reincorporate remaining guerrilla groups into peaceful political competition have continued, even as the 1991 Constitution has opened up the political process. By banning extradition, the new Constitution has also facilitated a decline in terrorism by drug traffickers, although their illegal business activities largely continue. Major challenges remain in these areas and in rebuilding the country's judicial apparatus. In addition, civilian leadership—which largely abdicated responsibility over the insurgency struggle to the armed forces—must seek to assert greater democratic control over the military, which has become a more corporate and professionalized entity over the past three decades. In 1991, a civilian minister of defense was named for the first time in nearly four decades, and civil-military relations are likely to remain a delicate issue throughout the 1990s.

(See also GUERRILLA WARFARE; U.S.–LATIN AMERICAN RELATIONS.)

Francisco Leal Buitrago, *Estado y política en Colombia* (Bogotá, 1984). Daniel Pécaut, *Crónica de dos décadas de política colombiana, 1968–1988* (Bogotá, 1987). Jonathan Hartlyn, *The Politics of Coalition Rule in Colombia* (Cambridge, U.K., 1988).

JONATHAN HARTLYN

COLONIAL EMPIRES. This form of political organization, bringing a number of different cultures or tribes or nationalities under a superior central authority, has a history infinitely older than that of the nation-state. In modern times most empires were under European control, apart from the Chinese Empire (with origins in antiquity) and the ephemeral Japanese Empire. Modern empires have taken two main forms: the acquisition of territories overseas and their acquisition by landward expansion—although only the Russian Empire was in this latter category. The Portuguese and Spanish regarded their acquisitions as contributing to the greater glory of God. In more secular terms France invoked the *mission civilisatrice;* the United States appealed to Manifest Destiny; the pragmatic British spoke of the White Man's Burden. Each power insisted that empire building was, in part, unselfish, even noble. However, there was a tacit acceptance that empires contributed material benefits and also national prestige. This was the main reason why, after their defeat by Prussia in 1870, the French plunged into colonial adventures in Africa and Southeast Asia. For these conquests no solid economic motive could be adduced, but French esteem was enhanced: in the words of Léon Gambetta, France had become a great power again.

How did the Europeans come to dominate Asia and Africa? They had acquired technology more advanced than those they came to conquer. Their ships were more maneuverable, they deployed greater firepower. Their military forces operated under stricter discipline: and this was the crucial factor—discipline, or systematic control—that enabled them to take on much greater numbers of opponents. They came to trade: first in luxury goods (spices, ivory, silks) previously monopolized by Arab and other commercial intermediaries, then in looking for markets for their own industrial products, and to exploit natural resources and cheap labor. There remained the intangible factor of national prestige, which led to the "scramble" for Africa and the "forward movement" in Southeast Asia.

This expansion was justified by pseudoscientific argument, grounded in a vulgarized version of Darwin, the "survival of the fittest." The principal authority on French colonial expansion, Paul Leroy-Beaulieu, noted in *De la colonisation chez les peuples modernes* that the world could be divided between the Western civilizations, others moving toward the same destination (principally Japan), a third category groping forward but unable to attain stability, hence (like India) necessitating a Western takeover—and then the major part of the world, containing "tribes barbarous and savage, addicted to conflict without end, knowing little of culture or technology." The West possessed the "right of intervention" in both of these latter cases.

Rivalry between Western colonial powers threatened, between 1890 and 1914, to develop into war on several occasions. However, the only open conflict was between Spain in its colonial twilight and the United States. This led to the cession of the Philippines and Puerto Rico from Spain to America. After World War I the German colonies were distributed among the victorious Allies as "mandates" (as were the Arab regions of the Ottoman empire). World War II saw the former Italian colonies in Africa placed under the British as "trust territories" before attaining independence. Similarly, the Pacific islands held by Japan were annexed by the United States: the Marianas were given self-government in 1986. Only Namibia remained under white rule until 1989 as a colonial fossil. Whereas colonies had previously been a symbol of world-class status, by the 1960s they symbolized backwardness. Portugal, the first European state to enter the colonial race, was nearly the last to leave, relinquishing its colonies only under pressure from the superpowers.

As an issue in the rivalries of the Great Powers, the colonies featured mainly in the period 1880–1914 when the Afro-Asian world was almost wholly under Western dominance. Between 1918 and 1939 two cases of expansion became international issues: the Italian takeover of Ethiopia and Japanese intervention in China. Both were raised in the League of Nations, which proved unable to influence the course of events. The UN was originally mainly a Western body, like the League of Nations, but from about 1960 it became a forum for the newly independent states protesting the remnants of colonialism, as in Dutch New Guinea and most persistently in Namibia, which South Africa continued to refuse to relinquish.

The heyday of the colonial empires was very brief, from about 1890 to 1950. Nevertheless, the legacy of Western colonialism (which some termed neocolonialism) could not be shaken off as rapidly as the formal colonial structure.

(See also Decolonization; Imperialism.)

J. S. Furnivall, *Colonial Policy and Practice* (Cambridge, U.K., 1948). Rupert Emerson, *From Empire to Nation* (Cambridge, Mass., 1960). D. K. Fieldhouse, *The Colonial Empires: A Comparative Survey* (London, 1966). Hugh Tinker, *Men Who Overturned Empires* (Madison, Wis., 1987).

Hugh Tinker

COMMAND ECONOMY. At least until the transformations in the Soviet Union and Central and Eastern Europe that began in the late 1980s, students of comparative economics were traditionally presented with two alternative systems for organizing economic activity: the market economy and the command economy. Unfortunately, this crude dichotomy draws attention away from hybrid forms of economic organization, such as the regulated economies of France and Japan, where *state management was crucial to economic development. Their reliance on indicative planning of mostly privately-owned corporations means that their economies fit neither the market nor command economy models, yet they lack a clear "ideal type" of their own.

The command economy is nevertheless a form of economic and political organization that can be conceptually distinguished from a market or regulated economy. In a command economy the state tries to attain as high a degree of control over economic activity as is practically feasible. This involves taking the major factors of production (land, natural resources, and capital) into state ownership and trying to enforce strict controls over all economic activity.

The command economy cannot be understood in purely economic terms, because only regimes of a certain type—typically, *Communist Party states—seek that particular type of maximal economic control. First, there are no cases of a Communist Party staying in power in the absence of a command economy. Second, there are no clear cases of a non–Communist Party regime maintaining a command economy outside of wartime.

Even in authoritarian and social democratic regimes with a large public sector, such as Argentina or Sweden, state employment is usually only around twenty-five percent of the labor force outside agriculture. Moreover, in these hybrid systems, state intervention takes place against a background of capitalist market forces, domestic and international. In contrast, in command economies state employment typically embraces ninety percent or more of the nonagricultural labor force.

States with command economies differ in the degree of effective control over the economy that they are able to establish. One can distinguish three broad categories: 1) the Stalinist command economy (*Soviet Union 1929–1953, Albania 1945–1990, Eastern Europe 1948–1953, *Cuba and North Korea); 2) the "normal" command economy (Soviet Union 1953–1988, Eastern Europe 1953–1989); 3) the fragmented command economy (*China since 1957, *Yugoslavia between 1964 and its collapse into civil war in 1991). Almost all the command economies have gone through a Stalinist phase where the state tried to squeeze independent economic activity to a minimum and then retreated when such policies proved increasingly counterproductive. This Stalinist phase even included efforts to establish tight state control over the supply of labor. In the Soviet Union, for example, after 1932 police permission was required to change one's residence, and between 1940 and 1956 workers could only quit their jobs with management approval. Food and consumer goods were distributed by rationing between 1928 and 1956 (and again, progressively, since 1978).

Perhaps the most sustained example of a Stalinist command economy is provided by Ceauşescu's *Romania, where domestic consumption was bled white to pay for a thirty year industrialization drive. In Romania state control even extended to the reproduction of labor, through the infamous four-child-per-family policy. As of the early 1990s, Cuba and North Korea had also failed to progress beyond this Stalinist phase.

Most command economies (*Poland and Yugoslavia being exceptions) introduced new forms of collective ownership in agriculture during their Stalinist phase, although some such as China and *Tanzania eventually broke up their collective farms and reverted to household agriculture. Similarly, some command economies tried to ban all forms of private entrepreneurial activity in the services sector, whereas others (e.g., Poland, *Hungary, and the *German Democratic Republic [East Germany]) tolerated a small private service sector, typically amounting to roughly five percent of the total national work force. From 1986 until its demise, relaxations in Soviet regulations allowed the private and cooperative sector in the Soviet Union to spread to about five percent of the labor force. Even where private activity was allowed, however, strict limits were imposed on labor hiring, price setting, the purchase of land and equipment, and the range of activities permitted, in order to prevent the private sector from spreading through the whole economy. These restrictions were partially relaxed after 1988.

The command economies developed a distinctive set of institutions and practices for managing the industrial sector, designed to achieve the maximum feasible centralization of strategic decision making.

These planning institutions were established during the Stalinist phase, but lived on through the "normal" phase, and have proved remarkably resistant to reform.

In the classic model of the command economy, the central planning board (Gosplan, in the USSR) draws up a plan of output targets for the forthcoming year, measured in physical terms. These output targets are then allocated to industrial enterprises through the hierarchy of industrial ministries, along with instructions detailing to whom the output is to be delivered.

The main advantage of this system is that it enables the state to mobilize resources from the rural sector, to hold down the wages of urban workers, and to concentrate the nation's efforts on the development of a few key strategic sectors for its industrialization drive. This advantage usually proves short-lived, however, as within five, ten, or twenty years the state sector sucks in the underutilized labor resources; it then faces the task of shifting from an extensive growth path based on mobilizing additional factors of production to an intensive growth path based on improved efficiency.

The disadvantages stem from the fact that the command economy relies on a vast and cumbersome bureaucratic system in which there are few incentives for efficiency and innovation. Labor and capital productivity is low, as is product quality and responsiveness to consumer demand. Firms face what the Hungarian economist János Kornai termed a "soft budget constraint," meaning that managers pay scant regard to costs and revenues and instead devote their energies to getting hold of scarce supplies and producing their planned output. This dependence on physical targets, and the weak role played by money and prices, has persisted despite efforts to strengthen the role of profits.

A further drawback of the command economies is their inability to take advantage of the international division of labor. Exports and imports as a proportion of GNP are about one-third the level they would be in a comparable market economy (looking at Czechoslovakia and Austria, for example). Two-thirds of their trade takes place with other command economies, and because of low product quality they are generally only able to export raw materials and semifinished products to market economies. Countries like Poland and Hungary that tried to expand their trade with the West in the 1970s ended up with huge hard currency debts.

The rigidities of the command economy are such that in several cases the national planning system collapsed, to be replaced by a network of regional command economies. This has happened in China since the mid-1950s, and began in Yugoslavia in 1964. It began in the Soviet Union in 1988, a process that contributed to the subsequent dissolution of the USSR. In a fragmented command economy regional political elites continue to enforce state control of economic activity, although some regions will be more willing to experiment with market forces than will others (e.g., Slovenia, or the Chinese coastal zones). The national political elite no longer has the unchallenged authority to run the economy from the center. (That is why it is more accurate to describe these as "command" and not "centrally planned" economies.) Instead it has to rely on political bargaining with the regional elites—backed up, on occasion, by threats of military force. Problems of macroeconomic stabilization such as inflation and unemployment, which are not particularly prominent in a "normal" command economy, come to the fore in a fragmented command economy.

(See also COLLECTIVIZATION; COMMUNISM; MARXISM; NATIONALIZATION; NINETEEN EIGHTY-NINE; STALINISM.)

Jan S. Prybyla, *Market and Plan Under Socialism: The Bird in the Cage* (Stanford, Calif., 1987). Anders Åslund, *Gorbachev's Struggle for Economic Reform* (Ithaca, N.Y., 1989).

PETER RUTLAND

COMMON AGRICULTURAL POLICY. See EUROPEAN COMMUNITY.

COMMON MARKET. See EUROPEAN COMMUNITY.

COMMONWEALTH. The modern Commonwealth, which evolved from the British Empire, has fifty members, forty-six located in the developing world. Most British colonies opted to remain within the Commonwealth on attaining independence, and its survival reflects remarkable adaptability to changing circumstances in the twentieth century. Landmarks were the Statute of Westminster (1931), which confirmed the sovereignty of the "white" dominions; the formula, agreed in 1949, that allowed India—and thus other members—to be a republic within the Commonwealth while acknowledging the British monarch as its symbolic head; the forced withdrawal of *South Africa in 1961; and the establishment of the Commonwealth Secretariat in 1965. The Secretariat, which replaced the British Commonwealth Relations Office as the center for coordination of the association's activities, is headed by a secretary-general who has considerable scope for personal diplomacy through access to all heads of government and can also act as Commonwealth spokesperson. There have been three incumbents: Arnold Smith (Canada), 1965–1975; Shridath Ramphal (Guyana), 1975–1990; Emeka Anyaoku (Nigeria), 1990–.

The Commonwealth is primarily an intergovernmental organization offering forum and service facilities to its members. It has no formal charter or governing structure, but heads of government meet biennially and there are regular meetings of ministers of education, finance, health, labor, law, and women's affairs. A Declaration of Principles adopted in

1971 was updated in 1991, and a number of functional agencies linked to the Secretariat are responsible for technical cooperation, scientific cooperation, youth affairs, and distance education. The Commonwealth also has an unofficial dimension, encompassing numerous nongovernmental bodies.

Major concerns for the majority of members have been *decolonization, economic *development, and the end of white minority rule in *Southern Africa. The latter issue proved politically divisive, bringing intense pressure on Britain from other members, led by the African group. Consensus was maintained with difficulty in the period following Rhodesia's illegal declaration of independence in 1965 until its emergence as *Zimbabwe in 1980, but British opposition to sanctions against South Africa brought heated debates and, in 1986, a clear policy split between *Britain and the rest. Reforms in South Africa have eased strains on this issue.

Less controversially, the Commonwealth contributed to the North-South dialogue, mainly through expert studies, and in a reversal of its former imperial ethos now offers a useful range of services to developing members, particularly small states. Twenty-seven Commonwealth countries have populations of less than one million.

In 1989 Commonwealth heads of government initiated a high-level appraisal of directions and structure which was reviewed at their meeting in 1991. The agenda for the future includes the reinforcement of *democracy and *human rights—which may challenge the convention that internal affairs of members are not matters for discussion. Other issues are the environment, drug trafficking, the *security needs of small states, and a continuing concern for political and economic development in Southern Africa.

Membership in 1990 included Antigua and Barbuda, Australia, Bahamas, Bangladesh, Barbados, Belize, Botswana, Britain, Brunei, Canada, Cyprus, Dominica, The Gambia, Ghana, Grenada, Guyana, India, Jamaica, Kenya, Kiribati, Lesotho, Malawi, Malaysia, Maldives, Malta, Mauritius, Namibia, Nauru, New Zealand, Nigeria, Pakistan, Papua New Guinea, St. Kitts, St. Lucia, St. Vincent, Seychelles, Sierra Leone, Singapore, Solomon Islands, Sri Lanka, Swaziland, Tanzania, Tonga, Trinidad and Tobago, Tuvalu, Uganda, Vanuatu, Western Samoa, Zambia, Zimbabwe.

(See also ENVIRONMENTALISM; NORTH-SOUTH RELATIONS.)

Arnold Smith, *Stitches in Time: The Commonwealth in World Politics* (Don Mills, Ont., 1981). Margaret P. Doxey, *The Commonwealth Secretariat and the Contemporary Commonwealth* (London and New York, 1989).
MARGARET P. DOXEY

COMMONWEALTH OF INDEPENDENT STATES. The Commonwealth of Independent States was established in December 1991 as an international organization of sovereign states after negotiations to preserve the *Soviet Union as a federal or confederal entity failed. Founded by the presidents of the three Slavic republics of the Russian Federation (or *Russia), Ukraine, and Belarus, it was later joined by the former Soviet republics of *Armenia, Azerbaijan, Kazakhstan, Kyrgyzstan, Moldova, Tajikistan, Turkmenistan, and Uzbekistan. Georgia originally did not join, but sent observer delegations to some commonwealth meetings.

The commonwealth agreement provided for a unified command over the strategic forces of the former Soviet military and committed its members to cooperate in the development of a common Eurasian market, recognize existing borders, and guarantee political and cultural rights for all citizens, regardless of nationality. A Council of Heads of State, meeting at least twice a year with decisions to be reached through consensus, was established as the supreme body of the organization. In addition, a Council of Heads of Governments was set up for coordinating policies. Headquarters of the commonwealth are in Minsk, the capital of Belarus.

Shortly after its establishment the commonwealth was entangled in a web of conflicts that raised doubts about its ability to survive. These revolved around the division of the former Soviet military among member states, rival territorial claims, control over former Soviet property, responsibility for paying Soviet debt obligations, and the impact of economic policies of member states on other member states. Two member states, Armenia and Azerbaijan, remained at *war over control of the disputed territory of Nagorno-Karabakh. In addition, Russia's claim to Crimea and Ukraine's claims to the Black Sea Fleet brought these two key members of the commonwealth into conflict.

In spite of their shared Soviet experience, the commonwealth states differ enormously in their histories, cultures, ideological orientations, and internal politics. What follows is a brief survey of the governments of member states, with the exception of the Russian Federation.

Armenia. In modern Armenia (population 3.3 million), politics have been shaped by two demographic and historical facts: the Armenian diaspora (in the former Soviet Union, for instance, a third of Armenians lived outside the republic) and the 1915 genocide against Armenians in Turkey, in which up to a million Armenians are said to have died. As the first nation to adopt Christianity as its official religion, the Armenians have long struggled to preserve their ancient culture.

By the early nineteenth century Armenia was under joint Russian and Ottoman control. The rise of an Armenian independence movement ultimately led to an armed uprising against the Ottoman Empire and to violent Turkish retaliations against the Armenian community. An independent Armenian state briefly existed from 1918 to 1920 under the guidance of the Dashnak party, but was conquered by the Red Army and eventually incorporated into the Soviet Union.

As Soviet politics liberalized under *Gorbachev, the fate of the predominantly Armenian population of Nagorno-Karabakh (a mountainous enclave ceded to Azerbaijan in the 1920 Treaty of Kars between Soviet Russia and Turkey) dominated Armenian politics. After more than a year of massive protests in favor of incorporating the territory into Armenia and sporadic pogroms against minorities in both Azerbaijan and Armenia, the conflict erupted into a protracted war between Armenian partisans operating inside Azerbaijan and Azerbaijani militia troops. Large numbers of *refugees flowed between the two republics.

Voter turnout was low (less than fifty percent) in the May 1990 elections to the 259-seat Armenian Supreme Soviet. After several rounds of voting, a majority developed for a coalition led by the moderate Armenian Pan-National Movement, which itself controlled only sixty-two seats. Its leader, Levon Ter-Petrossian, was selected by the legislature as president. After constitutional changes introducing an elected presidency, Ter-Petrossian ran in a contested election for the office in October 1991, defeating his rivals with over eighty percent of the vote (with a sixty-nine percent turnout). In March 1991 the Armenian government indicated its desire to secede from the Soviet Union. With the collapse of the Soviet Union in August 1991, Armenia issued a declaration of independence and nationalized the property of the Armenian Communist Party. The major opposition party in Armenia is the radically nationalist Union for National Self-Determination.

Azerbaijan. Azerbaijan (population 7 million)—formerly the Azerbaidzhan Soviet Socialist Republic (SSR)—was incorporated into the tsarist empire from Persia in the nineteenth century. While most Muslims of the former USSR belong to the Sunni branch of *Islam, the Azerbaijanis are primarily Shi'i and enjoy close cultural and historical ties with both Turkey and Iran. The Azeri language is a dialect of Turkish, and 9 million Azerbaijanis live across the border in Iran. Under the leadership of the Musavat Party, Azerbaijan experienced a brief period of independence from 1918 to 1920, but was occupied by the Red Army and eventually incorporated into the USSR.

Nationalist ferment engulfed Azerbaijan in response to efforts by the Armenian population of Nagorno-Karabakh to secede and join Armenia. The failure of the Soviet government to establish order in the territory became a focal point for protest by the Azerbaijani Popular Front in the fall of 1989. In December 1989 the Popular Front led an uprising against Soviet power that was brutally crushed, with hundreds killed and martial law imposed. Under these conditions, the Azerbaijani Communist Party dominated elections in September 1990 to the 350-seat Azerbaidzhani Supreme Soviet, the Popular Front winning only forty seats. Accusations of electoral fraud were rampant. President Ayaz Mutalibov, who was simultaneously first secretary of the Azerbaidzhani Communist Party, pursued a conservative national-communist line, defending the sovereignty of the republic while suppressing opposition. He supported the *coup d'état against Soviet President Mikhail Gorbachev in August 1991; once the coup failed, Mutalibov declared his republic independent and transformed the Communist Party into the Democratic Party of Azerbaijan. In September 1991 he ran in an uncontested election for president in which he received ninety-nine percent of the vote (with an eighty-four percent electoral turnout). Once again, there were widespread accusations of electoral fraud. However, in March 1992 Mutalibov was forced to resign as a result of Azerbaijani military setbacks in Nagorno-Karabakh.

Belarus. Belorussian politics have always been characterized by a low level of national consciousness. Until 1991, Belorussians had never experienced any significant period of independent statehood, having instead come under the sustained influence of Polish, Lithuanian, and Russian rule. In 1989 Belorussians constituted seventy-eight percent of the 10.2 million population. But owing to the educational and language policies of the Soviet regime, urban Belorussians were subjected to considerable linguistic Russification. Perhaps for these reasons, while much of the rest of the Soviet Union was racked by nationalist turmoil, Belarus (formerly the Belorussian SSR) earned a reputation as a stronghold of communist conservatism in the Gorbachev era.

In elections to the republican Supreme Soviet in 1990, candidates backed by the nationalist-minded Belarusian Popular Front captured only 30 seats of 340 seats. Candidates of the Belorussian Communist Party won the remainder. When a mass awakening did come to Belarusian politics, it came primarily in the form of class action over economic issues. The general strike of April 1991, which protested Soviet government price rises and called for the resignation of republican leaders, paralyzed the republic for almost a month. The chair of the Belorussian Supreme Soviet, Mikalai Dzemyantsei, closely connected with the local Communist Party apparatus, supported the overthrow of Gorbachev in August 1991 and was removed from power after the collapse of the coup. At that time, the legislature declared the republic's independence from the Soviet Union, temporarily suspended the activities of the Belorussian Communist Party, and elected Stanislau Shushkevich, a reformist communist, as its chair. Belarus is the only commonwealth state with a parliamentary rather than a presidential system of government.

Kazakhstan. The Kazakhs are the descendants of Muslim Turkic nomads who came under Russian domination in the eighteenth and nineteenth centuries as Russian settlers moved into the vast Kazakh steppes in search of land. The Kazakhs revolted against Russian colonization on a number of occasions, the most serious occurring in 1916. The region was incorporated into the Russian republic after the revolution, but was made a separate union republic in 1936. Soviet rule brought an end to Kazakh nomad culture. *Collectivization was carried out with particular brutality, resulting in the deaths of up to a third of all Kazakhs in a four-year period. By the end of the 1930s, more Russians lived in Kazakhstan than Kazakhs. By 1989, however, owing to a high Kazakh birthrate, the Kazkhs constituted forty percent of the total population of 16.5 million, while Russians had dropped to thirty-eight percent.

In December 1986 the removal of longtime Kazakh Communist Party chief Dinmukhamed Kunaev and his replacement by the Russian Gennady Kolbin sparked student demonstrations that were violently suppressed. Kolbin himself was replaced in June 1989 by Nursultan Nazarbaev, who initiated policies of liberalization and economic reform. Semicompetitive elections to the 360-seat Supreme Soviet were held in March 1990. Kazakhstan was the only former Soviet republic which reserved a portion (ninety) of seats in its legislature for so-called "public organizations," a form of corporate representation that favored communist-dominated organizations. The result was a communist-dominated legislature which overrepresented Kazakhs relative to their population size. After the collapse of the August 1991 coup in Moscow, the Communist Party of Kazakhstan broke from the *Communist Party of the Soviet Union and renamed itself the Socialist Party of Kazakhstan. Kazakhstan was the last Soviet republic to declare its independence, waiting until after the creation of the Commonwealth of Independent States in December 1991 to do so. Nazarbaev has championed market reforms and foreign investment in the mineral-rich republic. He ran in an uncontested presidential election in December 1991 in which he received ninety-nine percent of the vote, with eighty-eight percent of eligible voters participating.

While opposition parties in Kazakhstan have been weak, Kazakh politics is rich in social movements. The largest has been the antinuclear movement Nevada-Semipalatinsk, created in February 1989; it has mobilized up to 100,000 citizens in protests against nuclear testing in the region. The popular front Azat, composed primarily of Kazakh intellectuals, received support from the moderate wing of the Communist Party; the group has favored interethnic harmony in addition to Kazakh independence. Northern Kazakhstan has been the site of massive miner strikes, as well as of vigilante Cossack movements among the Russian population.

Kyrgyzstan. The Kirgiz are closely related culturally, linguistically, and historically to the Kazakhs, traditionally having been seasonal instead of steppe nomads. That small detail, however, meant that the Kirgiz would suffer fewer losses during the collectivization drives of the 1930s. Like Kazakhstan, Kirgizia was originally incorporated into the Russian republic after the revolution and was later established as the Kirgiz SSR in 1936. Large-scale Russian migration to Kirgizia was confined to urban areas, where Russians comprised half of the population. In 1989 Kirgiz made up only fifty-two percent of a total population of 4.3 million, Russians twenty-two percent, and Uzbeks thirteen percent.

The first semicompetitive elections to the 350-seat legislature in February 1990 were firmly under the control of the local Communist Party apparatus. But the Kirgiz political landscape was transformed in the summer of 1990 by the outbreak of violence in the Osh valley between Kirgiz and Uzbeks over access to land and housing, leaving 230 dead. The violence led to a split within the Supreme Soviet between conservative communists and an emerging Group for Democratic Renewal, consisting of over 120 deputies. Dissatisfaction with the conservative rule of Kirgiz Communist Party leader Absamat Masaliev led in October 1990 to the election of Askar Akaev, a liberal scientist, to the office of president after Masaliev fell four votes short of a majority in the legislature.

Akaev turned Kirgizia into the main outpost of liberalism in Central Asia, championing ideas of political pluralism and market-oriented reforms and asserting his republic's sovereignty vis-à-vis Moscow. In December 1990 the name of the republic was changed to Kyrgyzstan. Following the failure of the August 1991 coup, Akaev declared Kyrgyzstan independent, banned the Kirgiz Communist Party, and nationalized its property. After an elected presidency was introduced, Akaev ran in an uncontested presidential election in October 1991, in which he received ninety-five percent of the vote, with eighty-nine percent of eligible voters participating. Shortly afterwards, Akaev supporters split into two groups: the Democratic Kyrgyzstan movement, which criticized Akaev for manipulating the electoral process and whose following was chiefly among the Kirgiz population; and the National Unity movement, a multinational organization supported by Akaev.

Moldova. The Moldavians are Romanians whose ancestors inhabited Bessarabia, which was conquered by the Russian Empire in 1812 from the Ottoman Empire. In 1918 most of the territory reverted back to Romania, only to be annexed by the Soviet Union in 1940. Soviet authorities sought to create a separate Moldavian identity distinct from Romanian, even though the other half of Moldavia lay across the border in Romania and within Romania Moldavian was a regional designation rather than an *ethnicity. An agricultural region, the Moldavian SSR remained one of the most backward parts of the Soviet Union. Only sixty-four percent of the total population of 4.3 million is Moldavian, the rest consisting primarily of Ukrainians (fourteen percent), Russians (thirteen percent), and Gagauzy (four percent).

Nationalist ferment over language issues engulfed the republic at the end of 1988. As a result, in September 1989 the identity of the Romanian and Moldavian languages was recognized, and the Latin alphabet was adopted. The Moldavian Popular Front emerged as the main vehicle for the nationalist movement. In competitive elections to the Moldavian Parliament in March 1990, with eighty-four percent of eligible voters participating, the Popular Front won thirty-seven percent of the 380 seats, while associated groups won another thirty percent. The Parliament elected Mircea Snegur, a Communist Party official with nationalist sympathies, as president. After the demise of the August 1991 coup, Snegur proclaimed the republic's independence and banned the Moldavian Communist Party. In December 1991, following the introduction of an elected presidency, Snegur received ninety-eight percent of the vote in an uncontested election for president, with an eighty-two percent electoral turnout.

In addition to the severe economic problems connected with the transition from state socialism, the main battles of Moldovan politics revolve around the issues of reunification with Romania and relations with Moldova's minorities. The Moldavian Popular Front's insistence on a quick reunification caused it to break with Snegur in the fall of 1991, though Snegur's position was highly popular. As a result, the Popular Front's parliamentary faction largely disintegrated. Fearful of their minority status in the new Moldova, the Russian-speaking population of the Dnestr region and the Gagauz have at various times declared independence, leading to significant interethnic bloodshed.

Tajikistan. The Tajiks are the descendants of the ancient Iranian population of Central Asia. The region they inhabit came under Russian control in the mid-nineteenth century, when the emirates of Bukhara and Khiva became protectorates of the tsar. After the dissolution of the tsarist empire, the territory was conquered by the Red Army and incorporated into the Russian republic, eventually becoming a separate union republic, the Tadzhik SSR, in 1929. Only sixty-two percent of the 5.1 million inhabitants of Tajikistan are Tajik. Uzbeks make up a quarter of the population. Moreover, close to a million Tajiks live in Uzbekistan. The lack of fit between ethnicities and borders is one of the chief characteristics of Central Asian politics and a cause of considerable interethnic friction; it is largely the result of Bolshevik policies in the 1920s aimed at creating national states in a region where none had existed before. The Tajik economy, like those of other Central Asian republics, is based primarily on cotton growing, creating a dependence that began

under tsarist rule and was reinforced during the Soviet period.

Violence erupted in the capital city of Dushanbe in February 1990 in response to rumors that Armenians fleeing Azerbaijan would be resettled in the republic. Twenty-two people died, and the republic was placed under martial law. Two weeks later, elections were held to the 230-seat Tadzhik Supreme Soviet, allowing the conservative Communist Party apparatus to establish its firm control over the legislature. This sequence of events later played a determining role in the politics surrounding Tajik independence. After the failure of the August 1991 coup, the Tajik Parliament declared independence and forced the resignation of President Kakhar Makhamov for his support of emergency committee rule. But within several weeks the predominantly conservative Parliament had removed Makhamov's successor for attempting to ban the Tajik Communist Party and nationalize its property, electing in his place the old Tajik Communist Party boss Rakhman Nabiev, who had been removed in 1985. This in turn unleashed a massive campaign of *civil disobedience in the republic, led by the main opposition movement, Rastokhez. Amid widespread charges of electoral fraud, in November 1991 Nabiev ran in a contested election for president, winning with fifty-eight percent of the vote.

Turkmenistan. The Turkmen are the descendants of Turkic tribes who migrated to Central Asia from the eighth to tenth centuries. The area they inhabit became part of the Russian Empire in the mid-nineteenth century, when the emirates of Bukhara and Khiva were made protectorates of the tsar. In 1924 the territory of these emirates was distributed to create the union republics of Turkmenia and Uzbekistan. Turkmen constitute seventy-two percent of the total population of 3.5 million; ten percent are Russians, and nine percent are Uzbeks. Clan loyalties continue to play a key role in Turkmen politics, penetrating deeply into governmental structures.

No major opposition movements have been able to emerge on Turkmen soil, in part owing to the repressive policies of the authorities. Indeed, of all the Central Asian republics, Turkmenistan remains the most firmly under communist control. The only significant unrest to occur in Turkmenistan since the initiation of glasnost was a series of anti-Armenian riots that took place in May 1989. Elections to the 175-seat Turkmen Supreme Soviet in January 1990 were entirely controlled by the Communist Party apparatus, and the legislature elected Communist Party chief Saparmurad Niyazov as president. Unlike what occurred in most republics, Niyazov did not declare his republic independent after the failure of the August 1991 coup, but rather waited until October 1991. In December 1991, the ruling Turkmen Communist Party changed its name to the Democratic Party of Turkmenistan. Turkmenistan's economy is dominated by cotton and natural gas production.

Ukraine. Kievan Rus, located in present-day Ukraine, was the center of East Slavic civilization from the ninth through the twelfth centuries. The Kievan state collapsed into a series of smaller principalities on the eve of the Mongol invasions in the thirteenth century, and out of the East Slavic tribes a slow differentiation gave rise to three separate identities: Russians, Ukrainians, and Belorussians. From the fourteenth to the eighteenth centuries, the Ukrainians and Belorussians came under the influence of the Polish-Lithuanian Commonwealth. In the seventeenth century, Ukrainian Cossacks revolted, their leaders swearing allegiance to the Muscovite tsar in exchange for autonomy and protection. That autonomy was subsequently eliminated, and most of Ukraine fell to Russian control. Western Ukraine, however, remained outside the Russian Empire under Austro-Hungarian rule. Not until 1940, when *Stalin incorporated western Ukraine into the Soviet Union from Poland, were Ukrainians united within a single political entity.

With the collapse of the tsarist regime in 1917, Ukraine became a major battleground of the civil war. Nine successive governments attempted to rule Ukraine, none capable of establishing itself until the Red Army consolidated its control over the territory in 1919. Ukraine suffered tremendous losses during collectivization; it is estimated that up to 5 million inhabitants starved to death in the famine that engulfed the region in 1932 and 1933. Both under the tsars and under the Soviet government, Ukrainians were subjected to policies of cultural and linguistic Russification; indeed, a significant number of Ukrainians today do not know their native language. John Armstrong (in Erich Goldhagen, ed., *Ethnic Minorities in the Soviet Union,* New York, 1968) referred to the Ukrainians under Soviet rule as "younger brothers," largely because of Soviet attempts to recruit Russified Ukrainians into elite positions as mediators of imperial control.

Glasnost came late to Ukraine, where tight control over expressions of nationalist dissent was maintained until the retirement of Ukrainian Communist Party leader Volodymyr Shcherbitsky in September 1988. In competitive elections held in March 1990, the Ukrainian popular front Rukh, which counted over 630,000 members, captured local governments in western Ukraine, but was able to win only 125 out of 450 seats in the republican Supreme Soviet, where the Ukrainian Communist Party commanded a majority (239 seats). But over the course of 1990 and 1991 Ukrainian politics radicalized, as strong anti-Moscow sentiments spread throughout the republic. In July 1990 the Supreme Soviet, following the lead of other republics, voted sovereignty for Ukraine. Gradually, attitudes within the Ukrainian

Parliament shifted toward support for full Ukrainian independence. On the eve of the August 1991 coup, the Ukrainian Parliament voted to postpone participation in a new union treaty and to print its own currency. After the collapse of the coup, the Ukrainian government declared independence. A referendum held in December 1991 in which eighty-four percent of eligible voters participated resulted in a ninety percent vote in favor of independence. Competitive presidential elections were held at the same time; Leonid Kravchuk, chair of the Supreme Soviet, won with sixty-two percent of the vote.

Ukrainian politics are characterized by sharp divisions along regional, religious, ethnic, and class lines. Western Ukraine, where support for Rukh has been strong, is the traditional center of Ukrainian *nationalism. It is also predominately Uniate Catholic, as opposed to Orthodox eastern and southern Ukraine. The Uniate church was officially abolished by Stalin in 1946 and forced to operate underground until 1989. Relations between Uniates and Orthodox have been marked by conflict (and occasional violence) over ownership of church property. Russians constitute a significant proportion (twenty-two percent) of the total population of 51.5 million; they are concentrated in the south and east, constituting a majority of the population in Crimea, which was ceded to Ukraine by Russia in 1954. Some Russians have agitated for return of the territory, although the area historically was neither Russian nor Ukrainian, but Crimean Tatar—a group exiled by Stalin to Central Asia in 1944, and which has been allowed to return to its homeland since 1989. The Donbass area of Ukraine has also been the scene of major labor unrest, the region having been gripped by massive coal miner strikes on several occasions since 1989.

Uzbekistan. For centuries the area of modern Uzbekistan constituted a major center for trade along the land routes to China, its inhabitants being a sedentary population, unlike the nomads to the north and east. In the fourteenth century, Samarkand became the hub of Tamerlane's world empire, a temporary military conquest that stretched across most of Asia and Russia. In the sixteenth century the Uzbeks invaded, conquered most of the area, and established a series of khanates and emirates. The Central Asian region came under Russian control in the 1860s, as the emirates of Bukhara and Khiva became protectorates of the tsar; the region was then known as the province of Turkestan.

After a series of revolts, Turkestan was conquered by the Red Army in 1920 and incorporated into the Russian republic. In 1924 Moscow divided part of the region into the republics of Turkmenia and Uzbekistan. Soviet policy in Central Asia aimed at strengthening local ethnic identities in order to prevent the emergence of Pan-Turkic movements that might threaten Soviet rule. This policy largely proved effective, but Soviet institutions never succeeded in fully penetrating Uzbek society. Local patronage networks pervaded Central Asian politics and, to a large extent, remained intact through the glasnost period. Semicompetitive elections for the 500 seats of the Supreme Soviet, held in February 1990, were tightly controlled from above, producing a legislature dominated by the local Communist Party apparatus. In September 1991, after the failure of the August coup, the Uzbek government declared independence, largely in fear that the liberalism emanating from the Yeltsin government might undermine local control. Shortly afterwards, the Uzbek Communist Party renamed itself the Popular Democratic Party of Uzbekistan. The main opposition movement, Birlik, has been subjected to government harassment and has not been allowed to register as a legal political party.

Cotton production, first introduced by the tsarist government in the nineteenth century, dominates the Uzbek economy, soaking up much of the limited water resources of the region. Underdevelopment, a single-crop agriculture, an elevated population growth, significant rural unemployment, a growing water shortage, and a major ecological crisis in the Aral Sea basin have combined to produce high rates of poverty and disease. Uzbeks make up seventy-one percent of the total population of 19.8 million, while Russians, confined largely to urban areas, constitute eight percent. But the most violent interethnic conflicts have revolved around competition over jobs, land, water, and markets between the Uzbeks and other Muslim groups: the Tajiks (five percent of the population), and the approximately 100,000 Meskhetian Turks exiled by Stalin from the Caucasus to Central Asia.

Georgia. While Georgia did not sign the commonwealth agreement, some discussion of its tumultuous politics is appropriate. This ancient mountain kingdom maintained its independence through the end of the eighteenth century, when, in order to avoid capture by Persian and Turkish forces, it accepted Russian rule. With the disintegration of the Russian Empire, the Georgians set up a republic in 1918 under a Menshevik government. However, in 1921 Soviet forces invaded; Georgia was incorporated into the Transcaucasian Federation (a constituent republic of the Soviet Union), but was later made into a union republic in 1936. Throughout Soviet rule, Georgia was the scene of periodic mass unrest: in the mid-1920s over forced entrance into the Transcaucasian Federation; in the mid-1950s over de-Stalinization and the denigration of Georgia's most famous son, Joseph Stalin; and in the mid-1970s over language policy and the treatment of minorities. In April 1989 twenty people were killed and more than 4,000 injured when Soviet troops went on a rampage against Georgian protestors advocating independence. The event radicalized Georgian politics, giving rise to strong seces-

sionist sentiments throughout the republic. The Georgian government officially declared its independence in April 1991, after a referendum demonstrated overwhelming support for the idea.

In October 1990 the first multiparty elections were held. They brought Zviad Gamsakhurdia (a nationalist dissident and a leader of the Georgian *human rights movement) and his Round Table/Free Georgia coalition to power with a majority of 155 of 250 seats. Gamsakhurdia ran in a contested presidential election in May 1991, receiving eighty-seven percent of the vote. But his coalition soon began to crumble owing to his erratic and authoritarian policies. In the months following his election, he arrested opposition leaders, shut down opposition parties, imposed martial law, waged a bloody war against Georgia's Ossetian minority after abolishing its autonomy, and accused all opponents of being traitors to the Georgian cause. In December 1991 he was overthrown in an armed uprising led by the paramilitary Georgian National Guard, which set up a state council to run the country until competitive elections could be held. In March 1992 Eduard Shevardnadze, former Soviet foreign minister under Gorbachev, returned to his native Georgia and was made head of the state council. In addition to clashes between Gamsakhurdia supporters and opponents, Georgia has been the site of considerable interethnic violence between Georgians (who constitute seventy percent of the total population of 5.4 million) and the republic's minorities (in particular, the Abkhaz and the Ossetians), who claim to have been victims of policies of Georgianization.

Prospects. By most accounts, the collapse of the Commonwealth of Independent States is imminent. There are, of course, strong reasons why the post-Soviet states need a transnational community to deal with the common interdependencies among them. But the major preoccupation of all commonwealth states since gaining independence has been the consolidation of the trappings of statehood. It was perhaps inevitable that this overriding concern would bring them into serious conflict, crippling the capacity of the commonwealth to act as an effective link among them. Moreover, having declared itself the legal successor to the Soviet state, Russia is widely viewed by non-Russians as the successor to the Soviet empire as well. Until the post-Soviet states feel secure in their *sovereignty, it is doubtful that any post-Soviet transnational community can function successfully.

(See also INTERNATIONAL MIGRATION; NATIONALIZATION; PERESTROIKA; SECESSIONIST MOVEMENTS.)

Richard Pipes, *The Formation of the Soviet Union* (Cambridge, Mass., 1964). Edward Allworth, ed., *Soviet Nationality Problems* (New York, 1971). Hélène Carrère d'Encausse, *Decline of an Empire* (New York, 1979). Robert Conquest, ed., *The Last Empire: Nationality and the Soviet Future* (Stanford, Calif., 1986). Lubomyr Hajda and Mark Beissinger, eds., *The Nationalities Factor in Soviet Politics and Society* (Boulder, Colo., 1990). Bohdan Nahaylo and Victor Swoboda, *Soviet Disunion: A History of the Nationalities Problem in the USSR* (New York, 1990). Michael Mandelbaum, ed., *The Rise of Nations in the Soviet Union* (New York, 1991).

MARK R. BEISSINGER

COMMUNICATIONS. See INFORMATION SOCIETY.

COMMUNISM. The term *communism* originated among revolutionary societies in the Paris of the 1830s, where it combined two meanings. The first designated a political movement, of or on behalf of the working *class, that was dedicated to the overthrow of emerging capitalist society. The second sense referred to the kind of society that such a movement wished to inaugurate. In the first sense communism was seen as an extreme and violent form of socialism, more fundamental in its approach to the abolition of private property than that advocated by socialists, who favored a relatively peaceful political stance and gradual social reform. This contrast finds its classic expression in the 1848 *Communist Manifesto* of *Marx and Engels.

In the latter half of the nineteenth century, however, the terms *socialism* and *communism* tended to be used virtually synonymously to designate the working-class movement as a whole: most Marxist parties, including the two largest (in Germany and Austria), used the title "Social Democratic." The *Russian Revolution of 1917, the adoption by the Bolsheviks of the term *Communist* to describe their party, and, above all, the creation of the Third (Communist) International in 1921 gave the term a much more specific meaning. The aftermath of the Bolshevik revolution and the founding of the Third International involved the emergence of separate Communist parties sharply opposed to socialist or social democratic parties and advocating policies reminiscent of early European communists. These new Communist parties were organized, along Leninist "democratic centralist" lines, where power resided, formally as well as in practice, in the hands of a small Politburo. It was *Lenin, too, in his *State and Revolution,* who formalized the difference between communism and socialism as a project of social reorganization. Marx had already drawn a distinction between an immediately postrevolutionary society, in which reward would be according to merit, and a "higher stage of communist society" that would put into practice the famous slogan "from each according to his abilities, to each according to his needs." Lenin called the first of these societies "socialist" and the second "communist." Thus the parties of the Third International, although Communist, were running societies which were, as yet, only socialist.

With the consolidation of *Stalinism in the *Soviet Union, a third sense of *communism* emerged: a worldwide network of doctrinaire parties organized along authoritarian lines, propagating a worldview known as dialectical materialism and more or less completely subordinate to the political line laid down by the *Communist Party of the Soviet Union (CPSU) through the operations of the Communist International. After the death of Stalin, this Communist movement entered a historical decline, the first serious symptom of which was the split between the Soviet and Chinese Communist parties in 1960, accompanied by the increasing unpopularity and difficulties of the Communist regimes in Eastern and Central Europe. In Western Europe, the long postwar boom and the lack of progress made by the Communist parties there led in the 1970s to the emergence of a trend known as *Eurocommunism. The Eurocommunists, led by the Italian Communist Party, adopted a much more conciliatory attitude to parliamentary institutions and advocated what seemed to be *reforms rather than *revolution—to such an extent that the post-1917 distinction between socialism and communism as opposed political tendencies seemed to be disappearing.

The 1989 revolutions in Eastern and Central Europe and the reforms in the Soviet Union inaugurated by Mikhail *Gorbachev marked the end of this decline of European communism and its reassimilation into the general socialist movement. The anti-Stalinist communist movement represented by Trotsky and his followers continues to exist but is numerically small and politically insignificant. The vanguard parties constructed along the Leninist model still operate in such places as China, Cuba, and South Africa, but their future seems far from assured. The two central ideas of Stalinist communism—the Leninist vanguard party and an economy planned by a centralized bureaucracy—have gone into terminal decline. However, communism in the very different sense of a more principled version of socialism, an aspiration to a society in which resources are divided primarily according to human need, is likely to have a future every bit as long as its past.

(See also CAPITALISM; CHINESE COMMUNIST PARTY; COMMAND ECONOMY; COMMUNIST PARTY STATES; LENINISM; MARXISM; NINETEEN EIGHTY-NINE; SINO-SOVIET RELATIONS; TROTSKYISM.)

Fernando Claudin, *The Communist Movement: From Comintern to Cominform* (New York, 1975). Leslie Holmes, *Politics in the Communist World* (New York, 1986).

DAVID MCLELLAN

COMMUNIST PARTY OF THE SOVIET UNION. The Communist Party of the Soviet Union (CPSU) grew out of the Bolshevik ("Majority") wing of the (Marxist) Russian Social-Democratic Labor Party (founded in 1898). The Bolsheviks were followers of Vladimir Ilich *Lenin, who sought to weld them into a centralized, disciplined, conspiratorial organization of professional revolutionaries. From small beginnings, the Bolsheviks won a mass following in the chaos following the February 1917 *revolution, and on 7 November overthrew the provisional government and established a "worker-peasant government" in the name of the Second Congress of Soviets ("Councils"). After a brief partnership with the Left Socialist-Revolutionaries, the Bolsheviks ruled the Soviet Union from March 1918 as a single-party dictatorship. In 1918 they changed their name from the "Russian Social-Democratic Labor Party (of Bolsheviks)" to the "All-Russia Communist Party (of Bolsheviks)"—"All-Union" from 1922—and the name "Communist Party of the Soviet Union" was adopted in 1952.

Goals and Sociopolitical Role. As Marxists, the Bolsheviks believed the basic source of all social evils was private ownership of the means of production and that its abolition would pave the way to *communism, a society of truly free individuals without exploitation, oppression, or alienation. As Leninists, they believed this could be achieved only by a "dictatorship of the proletariat"—which, Lenin acknowledged, meant in practice a dictatorship of the Communist Party, whose leaders were theoretically equipped to guide the revolutionary process and who must be unhampered by either legal or moral scruples. To this end they nationalized the factories and land and subjected all other institutions to party direction. Every sphere of life became the monopoly of a designated organization run by a command hierarchy of party members, and these were all integrated into a single organizational whole by the command-hierarchy of the Communist Party, which assigned their tasks, appointed their key staff, and monitored their performance. This "mono-organizational" system began to take shape under Lenin, but by 1921 he started to doubt its effectiveness, and his resulting *New Economic Policy could have led Soviet society in a radically different direction. With his death and the subsequent consolidation of *Stalin's power, however, the transition to the "mono-organizational system," officially described as socialism, the "lower stage of communism," was completed during the 1930s, and its essentials persisted through the 1980s.

The Bolsheviks took seriously the Marxist view that *class loyalties should prevail over national loyalties and saw their revolution as the first victory in the world transition from *capitalism to *socialism, a transition they should do all they could to foster. To this end they founded in 1919 a Communist International (Comintern) of affiliated communist parties around the world, which were committed to implementing the policies of the Comintern, determined in practice by the CPSU. Under Stalin, with his policy of "socialism in one country" and increasing reliance on Russian nationalism, the Comintern served largely as an instrument of *Soviet foreign policy. It was abolished in 1943, and although between 1947 and 1956 some of its functions were entrusted to a new Communist Information Bureau (Cominform), Soviet efforts to control and direct foreign communist parties were henceforth pursued mainly through the International Department of the CPSU Central Committee (CC). From the 1960s, however, these efforts were increasingly impeded by the split with Maoist China, *Eurocommunism, and other fissiparous developments.

Structures, Leadership, and Membership. The CPSU's basic organizational principle has always been "democratic centralism," but the democratic element, a partial reality at first, was progressively ritualized. From Stalin's time the party was totally dominated by its *apparat* ("machine") of full-time officials, who stage-managed party congresses, local conferences, and committee meetings and reduced elections to the unanimous endorsement of "candidates" bureaucratically selected under the *nomenklatura* ("job-schedule") system. At each level the party machine was run by a small bureau of key officials, who exercised authority over all governmental and nongovernmental bodies in their area, and the key figure in the bureau was the first secretary. At the top was the Political Bureau (Politburo) of the CC, whose roughly fifteen to twenty full and "candidate" (nonvoting) members included not only the chief figures in the CC Secretariat, directing the party machine, but also key state officials responsible for the economy, armed forces, political police (*KGB), etc. The Politburo, rather than the constitutionally designated Council of Ministers, was the true government of the Soviet Union, and the hierarchy of district, city, regional, and republic first secretaries, culminating in the general secretary of the CPSU, constituted the political and administrative backbone of the country.

The supreme leadership usually operated as an oligarchy, and Stalin alone succeeded in converting the general secretaryship into a personal dictatorship. Lenin was never general secretary, and his primacy rested on his personal authority and role as founding head of the Soviet government. Stalin (general secretary 1922–1953) and Nikita S. *Khrushchev (general secretary 1953–1964) both also assumed the top government post of chairman of the Council of Ministers, while Leonid I. Brezhnev (1906–1982; general secretary 1964–1982) became instead head of state (chairman of the Presidium of the Supreme Soviet), as did his successors Yury V. Andropov (1914–1984; general secretary 1982–1984), Konstantin U. Chernenko (1911–1985; general secretary 1984–1985), and Mikhail S. *Gorbachev (general secretary 1985–1991).

In March 1990 the CPSU's salaried officialdom numbered 213,000. At each echelon they worked in departments and sectors responsible for different branches of the economy, ideology (including the media, science, arts), the soviets, trade unions and other mass organizations, and subordinate levels of the CPSU itself. Their task was to provide "guiding directions" to sectors throughout society, to monitor and correct their activities, and to choose their key officials, operating both through these officials and the secretaries of the primary organizations of party members formed in every workplace. In the army and police the CPSU maintained a hierarchy of political officers.

The CPSU was always viewed as a vanguard rather than a mass party, and membership was not just a formality or a privilege but entailed sometimes onerous demands on one's time, energies, and conscience. Nevertheless, CPSU membership grew from 24,000 in March 1917 to perhaps a quarter million in November 1917, rose to 730,000 in 1921, 3 million in 1932, nearly 6 million in 1945, 11 million in 1964, 16 million in 1977, and 19 million in 1990. Although these figures conceal massive losses due to purges and war and indicate a tapering off since the 1970s, they graphically reflect the CPSU's concern to penetrate all levels and sectors of society. Throughout its history the CPSU endeavored to place members in all posts of authority or influence and to attain a dominant presence in the burgeoning administrative, managerial, intellectual, and other elites as well as in the soviets, trade unions, and other mass organizations. Men always predominated in the CPSU and virtually monopolized its upper levels, although women gradually rose to over a quarter of the rank-and-file members. All Soviet nationalities came to be represented in the CPSU, but in sharply differing proportions, owing to socioeconomic, cultural, and historical factors, and Russians dominated the central apparatus.

Impact of Gorbachev's Reforms. *Perestroika, fueled by the disastrously flagging performance of the Soviet economy and the fading legitimating force of communism and aiming at a pluralistic, democratized society with a market economy, undermined the rationale for the CPSU's historical role and functions. It lost its politico-administrative control first over ideology and then over the economy, and in March 1990 lost its constitutional monopoly of power when supreme authority passed from the Politburo to the state presidency. President Gorbachev remained general secretary until 1991, but the Politburo and Secretariat were reconstituted to focus on internal party matters and party policy development. Factional splits appeared, there were numerous resignations (including the heralded departure of Boris *Yeltsin, chairman of the Russian Republic's Supreme Soviet), and rival political parties mushroomed. The defeat of the conservative coup of August 1991 doomed any chance of reversing these changes and led the governments of Russia and the other former Soviet republics to ban the CPSU and confiscate its property.

(See also CHINESE COMMUNIST PARTY; COMMUNIST PARTY STATES; LENINISM; MARXISM; RUSSIAN REVOLUTION; SINO-SOVIET RELATIONS.)

Leonard Schapiro, *The Communist Party of the Soviet Union*, 2d (rev.) ed. (London, 1975). Jerry F. Hough and Merle Fainsod, *How the Soviet Union Is Governed* (Cambridge, Mass., and London, 1979). Ronald J. Hill and Peter Frank, *The Soviet Communist Party*, 3d ed. (Boston and London, 1986).

T. H. RIGBY

COMMUNIST PARTY STATES. When World War I broke out in 1914 there were no communist party states. For many years after the *Russian Revolution of 1917 there were only three, the *Soviet Union itself and two Asian outposts, Mongolia and Tuva; and as late as the end of World War II there were only five such states, located for the most part in Eastern Europe (Albania and Yugoslavia as well as the Soviet Union). Since then communist party states have come into existence elsewhere in Eastern and Central Europe (Bulgaria, Romania, Poland, Czechoslovakia, Hungary, and the German Democratic Republic, or GDR), in Latin America (Cuba), and also in Asia (China, Vietnam, the Democratic People's Republic of Korea [North Korea], Laos, and Cambodia). By the late 1980s there were at least sixteen states that claimed allegiance to *Marxism-*Leninism and were ruled by communist parties, and these were known, in Soviet terminology, as the "world socialist system." A wider group of states, ruled by "vanguard" or "revolutionary-democratic" parties or movements, included Afghanistan, Angola, Congo (Brazzaville), Mozambique, Ethiopia, Madagascar, and Yemen. More broadly, a network of about 100 ruling or nonruling parties constituted what was known as the world communist movement.

Communist party states, however broadly defined, are accordingly a small minority of the 150 or so states that are members of the UN. Their importance, however, is much greater than these limited numbers might suggest. Communist-ruled states, in the 1980s, accounted for about a third of the world's population and for more than forty percent of the world's industrial production. The world's largest state, the Soviet Union, was (until 1991) under communist rule, and so too is its most populous state, the People's Republic of *China. Communist party states have been included in one of the world's main trading blocs, the *Council for Mutual Economic Assistance or COMECON (established in 1949), and one of the world's two major military alliances, the *Warsaw Treaty Organization (or Warsaw Pact), established for a period of thirty years in 1955 and extended for a further twenty in 1985. (Both of these organizations were dissolved in 1991 following the political changes in Eastern Europe.) Above all, for the student of politics, communist party states represent one of the most important types of political system in the modern world, one that is different from and opposed to liberal *democracy and one that has been of considerable influence on developing and other nations whether or not they have adopted any of its characteristic forms.

At least until the late 1980s, when a far-reaching process of systemic change began to affect them, communist party states could be defined in terms of four related characteristics. In the first place, all of the communist-ruled states based themselves on an official ideology, Marxism-Leninism, which was derived from the theories of Marx, Engels, Lenin, and (in China) *Mao Zedong, and which provided the vocabulary of politics in these states as well as the basis on which their rulers claimed to exercise authority. Second, the economy was largely or entirely in public ownership, in line with the Marxist doctrine that private ownership of productive resources involved the exploitation of workers by those who employed them. There were some exceptions, even before the changes of the 1980s and 1990s: in Poland, for instance, agriculture remained in private hands, and in the GDR and China there was a tiny group of "people's capitalists" for some years after communist rule had been established. In all these countries, however, the dominant sectors of the economy—industry, finance, and transport—were in public ownership, and production was typically organized by means of national economic plans.

The third distinguishing feature of communist party states, at least until the late 1980s, is that they were ruled, in all but exceptional circumstances, by a single or at least dominant communist party, within which power was highly centralized. This was ensured by the application of the principle of "democratic centralism," by which each level in the hierarchy had to accept the decisions of the level immediately above it, and by the "ban on factions," which forbade any attempt to organize an opposition within these parties. (This did not, of course, mean that there were no differences of opinion or even informal groupings within them.) And finally, the range of institutions which in Western democracies are more or less independent of the political authorities, such as the press, the trade unions, and the courts, came and often still come under the direct control of the party leadership at all levels. This wide-ranging control over virtually all areas of society, from economic management and government to sports and stamp collecting, was known as the party's "leading role," and for the communist authorities themselves it was of particular importance (it was, for instance, to recover this "leading role" for the communist party that the Warsaw Pact powers justified their intervention in Czechoslovakia in 1968).

The states that were organized on these principles shared a number of characteristic political forms, some of which survived the transition to noncommunist rule in Eastern and Central Europe at the end of the 1980s. In all of these states political power, under their constitutions, was formally vested in "the people," and that power was nominally exercised through elected councils, or Soviets, at all levels of government. In fact the representative character of communist party states was—and is—more illusory than real. The electoral system, in the first place, was largely or entirely controlled by the party authorities. Although a movement toward partly competitive polls began in Eastern Europe in the 1950s, at least until the late 1980s there was no opportunity to reject the regime itself at the ballot box. Candidates typically were nominated by public organizations, including the communist party, rather than by individual citizens, and a negative vote was strongly discouraged in various ways. In Poland, for instance, officially favored candidates were placed at the top of the ballot paper, and in the Soviet Union voters had to make use of a screened-off booth in the polling station if they wished to exercise their nominal right to reject the single candidate. For many critics, within as well as outside the countries concerned, exercises of this kind were a form of mobilization rather than elections in the ordinary meaning of the word.

The legislatures to which deputies were elected, in any case, met very infrequently, their votes were normally unanimous, and there was no direct criticism of party policy as distinct from the performance of individual members of the government. The USSR Supreme Soviet, which was reasonably representative, met just three or four days a year from the 1950s to the 1980s. From its establishment in 1937 up to 1988, when it was comprehensively remodeled, there was no vote against government proposals and only a single recorded abstention, in 1955 when an elderly woman deputy was overcome by shock when Georgy Malenkov's resignation as prime minister was announced without prior warning. The spring or summer session reviewed a variety of policy areas, while the winter session normally considered the annual plan and budget. At best, however, only thirty or forty of the 1,500 deputies could take the floor during these sessions. Deputies enjoyed rather better opportunities to hold government to account through an elaborate network of committees, which scrutinized legislation while still in draft and also monitored the performance of ministers. The Soviet legislature, despite these opportunities, was nonetheless regarded as a rubber stamp both in the Soviet Union and elsewhere. The Polish and Yugoslav assemblies enjoyed a considerably greater degree of influence; but at the other extreme, there were no meetings of the legislature in China and Cuba for at least ten years during the 1960s and 1970s.

The key feature of communist systems, however, was and (in the 1990s) still is the presence of a Marxist-Leninist party at the center of public life, directing all aspects of the life of the society on the basis of a supposedly superior knowledge of the nature of social development conferred on it by the ideology. The notion of the "leading role" of the communist party derives most obviously from Lenin, particularly from his doctrine of the "vanguard party" set out in works such as *What Is to Be Done?* (1902). In this and other writings Lenin argued that *socialism would not come about through the automatic extension of trade union and other forms of working-class activism. What was necessary, for Lenin, was a theoretical understanding of the nature of such activity; and such an understanding would have to be brought to the workers "from the outside," by the educated intelligentsia—a notion that had obvious elitist potential. Lenin's views on party organization and structure were no less influential. For Lenin, as for the other Bolsheviks, the revolutionary party must be centralized and secretive; equally important, it should consist of "professional revolutionaries" whose occupation consisted largely or entirely of political activity.

These principles, intended originally to apply to tsarist conditions, have since served as the organizational basis of ruling communist parties throughout the world. Membership is typically selective— in the Soviet party (until its suspension in 1991) for instance, a new member was recommended by three existing members and would be expected if necessary to serve a year-long probationary or candidate period before full membership was conferred. Members were attached to branches or (in the Soviet Union) "primary party organizations" throughout the country, and these in turn were elected to district, regional, republican, and national party institutions.

At the national level a congress was convened every five years to lay down the broad outlines of party and state policy for the following period. It elected a Central Committee, a smaller group of (in the Soviet Union) 400-odd senior officials who served as a sounding board for policy initiatives. They in turn elected the leadership institutions, the Politburo, Secretariat, and first or general secretary. The leadership operated through a full-time bureaucracy or *apparat,* with counterparts at the local level. At least until the party's suspension in 1991 this full-time apparatus, and the party bodies that supervised it, was the central institution in the political system, directing the party itself and (through a variety of mechanisms) the wider life of the society. The party, in particular, directed the councils or Soviets through a caucus of activists within them, and it regulated appointments to leading positions at all levels through the *nomenklatura* (a list of positions the filling of which required party approval).

Communist party states have periodically been affected by patterns of reform or even radical change—in the Soviet Union under Khrushchev, for instance, or in China during the Cultural Revolution, when Mao Zedong with the support of the army led a movement against "capitalist roaders" in the party itself. The processes of change that took place in the late 1980s and early 1990s were nonetheless unprecedented. In Poland, Hungary, Romania, the GDR, and Czechoslovakia, most dramatically, a series of demonstrations led to the collapse of communist authority and the formation of non-communist administrations. In Bulgaria and Yugoslavia the ruling party abandoned its constitutionally guaranteed leading role. Mongolia, and even Albania, began to move toward limited forms of political *pluralism. In the former Soviet Union, Mikhail *Gorbachev's program of *perestroika (restructuring) both inspired and made possible this wider process of change. Cuba (where Fidel *Castro insisted on communist orthodoxy), China (where a student-led movement was brutally crushed at *Tiananmen Square in 1989), and North Korea (where Kim Il Sung has remained entrenched in power for more than forty years)—and to a somewhat lesser degree Vietnam, Laos, and Cambodia— held out against the trend. Entering the 1990s, it was clear that all communist party states would eventually have to reform their inefficient economies and accommodate at least a limited degree of political pluralism. What was less clear was whether these changes would represent the reform of communist rule or its replacement by capitalist democracy—ironically, the very system that communism had been originally designed to supersede.

(See also CHINESE COMMUNIST PARTY; COLLECTIVIZATION; COMMAND ECONOMY; COMMUNISM; COMMUNIST PARTY OF THE SOVIET UNION; STALINISM.)

Leslie Holmes, *Politics in the Communist World* (Oxford, 1986). Ronald J. Hill, *Communist Politics under the Knife: Surgery or Autopsy?* (London, 1990). Stephen White et al., *Communist and Postcommunist Political Systems: An Introduction,* 3d ed. (London, 1990). J. F. Brown, *Surge to Freedom: The End of Communist Rule in Eastern Europe* (Durham, N.C., 1991).

STEPHEN WHITE

COMMUNITY CONTROL. An outgrowth of the *civil rights movement and the War on Poverty in the United States during the 1960s, proponents of community control urged that city services be decentralized and that local residents be given greater influence over services. Community control reflected black dissatisfaction with white-run social institutions and it expressed the desire for black control of such institutions. Community control had its greatest impact in the administration of urban education, police, and social services.

Although it appeared as a new demand in the late 1960s, community control reflected a deeply rooted American preference for local control. The War on Poverty extended this principle to urban black ghettos with the community action program and its call for "maximum feasible participation" of the poor in administering the social programs initiated during the 1960s. Community participation subsequently became a requirement of many other federal programs.

The desire for local control was also fueled by black discontent with city services. This dissatisfaction stemmed in part from conflicts with the police, which often led to the urban riots of the 1960s. But concern about the quality of services and the accountability of service workers extended to many areas including education and social services. Growing nationalism, expressed in the black power movement, distilled these discontents into a critique called *internal colonialism. Black ghettos were likened to colonies governed by white rulers who ran institutions for their own benefit.

Several experiments in community control were launched in the late 1960s. One of the most visible and contentious occurred in the Ocean Hill–Brownsville section of New York City, where a community board was granted limited control over education. The board's attempts to remove some teachers and administrators led to a bitter strike by the teachers' union and aroused deep racial and ethnic antagonisms.

Despite the militant rhetoric attached to community control and the controversy that accompanied the Ocean Hill–Brownsville experiment, many mayors saw local control as a way of defusing and channeling the urban tensions of the 1960s. Moreover, these mayors saw decentralization as a way of establishing institutionalized links with black and Hispanic residents, who had not been incorporated into local party politics as white ethnics had. Thus, in many large cities, the demand for community control combined with mayors' objectives to create an array of decentralized institutions and new forums for participation. Among the most important were decentralized school systems; "little city halls," where neighborhood grievances could be voiced; and civilian review boards, charged with considering complaints against police activity.

Although the demand for community control was particularly American, it had counterparts in European movements to decentralize the large bureaucracies of the *welfare state. Efforts to make bureaucrats more accountable and to increase local participation in administering social services are an enduring feature of welfare state politics in Europe.

The movement for community control created new institutions and forms of participation, but it was not able to address the substantive problems of ghetto neighborhoods. In many cases, local institutions simply provided a means of funneling limited patronage into poor minority neighborhoods; at worst these institutions became sources of corruption and mismanagement of public funds. Despite the ambiguous legacy of community control, decentralization and local control remain potent issues in U.S. politics.

(See also GREAT SOCIETY; POLITICAL PARTICIPATION.)

Alan A. Altshuler, *Community Control* (New York, 1970).
MARGARET WEIR

COMOROS. See INDIAN OCEAN REGION.

COMPARABLE WORTH. Pay equity, or comparable worth, is a reform strategy to reduce gender- and race-based wage discrimination, advocated since the mid-1970s, first in the United States, and then Canada, Britain, and other countries. Proponents argue that the wage gap between jobs held primarily by women and those held primarily by men (or by members of minority and majority groups) is caused by the undervaluation of women's jobs, which results from a long history of employers' and male workers' actions or beliefs that devalue women's skills. Comparable worth projects employ a technical strategy to eliminate this wage gap. Job evaluation, an established management tool, identifies the undervaluation and measures the amount of wage inequality by assessing levels of skill, complexity, responsibility, and adverse working conditions in various job classifications. Jobs with varying content, such as nursing and engineering, are evaluated according to these factors and given numerical scores, the wages of jobs with similar evaluation scores are compared, and inequity is identified when comparably scored jobs have different levels of pay. Implementation allocates wage increases to undervalued jobs.

Comparable worth is also a social movement that works for pay equity policies through legislation, collective bargaining, and litigation. In the United States, efforts have been made primarily in the public sector, including, by 1990, forty-four state governments and 1,739 local jurisdictions. First used in the state of Washington in the early 1970s, the strategy spread rapidly thanks to the activities of women's organizations, labor unions, and feminist state legislators. The movement was assisted by a feasibility study published by the National Research Council in 1981 (Donald J. Treiman and Heidi I. Hartmann, *Women, Work, and Wages: Equal Pay for Jobs of Equal Value*, Committee on Occupational Classification and Analysis, Washington, D.C.). The most comprehensive effort has been in Ontario, Canada, where Parliament passed a Pay Equity Act in 1987 covering employers in both private and public sectors. The Ontario Pay Equity Commission provides information, education, and dispute resolution. By 1990, public organizations had started implementation, with private organizations scheduled to begin adjustments in 1991.

The cost of equity adjustments, the effectiveness of comparable worth in eliminating the wage gap, and the persistence of gender bias in job evaluation are current issues. In spite of predictions of great cost, pay equity adjustments have been inexpensive. In Minnesota, for example, adjustments from 1983 to 1986 cost four percent of the state's payroll. Women's pay increased 10.7 percent, but women still earned only eighty-one cents to every dollar earned by men ("Pay Equity in Minnesota: Women's Wages Increased, State Economy Remained Sound" *Newsnotes,* National Committee on Pay Equity, vol.

11, no. 1, October, 1990). The wage gap continues because it is not caused solely by undervaluation. Job evaluation systems often incorporate the negative beliefs about women's skills that pay equity intends to erase. Efforts to develop gender-neutral job evaluation are ongoing in many projects, raising fundamental questions about the nature of skill and work values.

(See also EQUALITY AND INEQUALITY; FEMINIZATION OF POVERTY; GENDER AND POLITICS; RACE AND RACISM.)

Joan Acker, *Doing Comparable Worth: Gender, Class, and Pay Equity* (Philadelphia, 1989).

JOAN R. ACKER

COMPARATIVE POLITICS

The term *comparative politics* refers to both a subject matter and a method of analysis. In principle, the two should complement each other; in practice, they frequently do not.

As a subject, comparative politics is the special field of teaching and research within the discipline of political science that is customarily devoted to "the politics of other countries or peoples." At least in the United States, its academic position has usually been somewhat marginal, flanked on the one side by U.S. politics (which are implicitly treated as incomparable) and, on the other, by *international relations (which are explicitly regarded as more consequential). Despite the number and variety of "other countries and peoples," vastly more political scientists are employed in studying the domestic politics and foreign relations of the United States.

The situation elsewhere used not to be very different. However, in recent years, teaching and research involving comparisons among European countries have increased significantly, and there are encouraging signs that a similar trend is emerging within Latin America and parts of Asia. For example, it has become almost inconceivable that a German, Italian, Dutch, or Spaniard would seriously attempt to understand his or her politics without at least some reference to the politics of neighboring states—if only because of the high levels of interdependence and joint policy-making embedded in the *European Community. Scholars from France and Britain may still be convinced, along with the Americans, of the uniqueness of their brand of politics, but that too may be waning. Only in these countries could one imagine that an introductory course in politics would refer just to the country in which it was being given.

As a method, comparative politics involves an analytical effort to exploit the similarities and differences between political units as a basis for developing "grounded theory," testing hypotheses, inferring causality, and producing reliable generalizations. As John Stuart Mill observed some 150 years ago, the practical difficulty of applying experimental

techniques to political matters makes comparison of observed variance across "natural" units the most feasible—if still the second-best—technique for developing scientific knowledge in this field. Recourse to it is as old as political inquiry itself. Plato and, especially, Aristotle not only made systematic use of it but developed core concepts, typologies, and hypotheses that are still of great utility. As we shall see, the "fashion for comparison" has waxed and waned over the subsequent centuries, but the "urge to compare" has never completely disappeared.

If and when the subject and the method are successfully blended to produce reliable and cumulative generalizations across a wide range of settings, then comparative politics would cease being an exotic subfield and become virtually synonymous with the scientific study of politics. American politics would provide material for just another case; international relations would enrich our understanding of the broader contexts in which the cases are located. All systematic political inquiry—except for those few areas appropriate for controlled experimentation—would be explicitly or implicitly comparative.

Despite considerable effort by a distinguished group of scholars over the past four decades, such a synthesis is still on the distant horizon. As we shall see, there are some formidable obstacles to be overcome.

The Dependence on Theory and Concepts. "Comparativists" bear a double burden. Their topic demands that they produce useful information about foreign polities, but their method requires that they develop and apply analytical categories that are equivalent across the units they are examining. "Theory" is indispensable for establishing this comparability, but its tendency to rely on general and abstract concepts interferes with easy comprehension by nonspecialists and often generates understandings that are far removed from the explanations actors themselves use to describe and justify what they are doing.

Some original practitioners of the subdiscipline could afford to ignore this difficult issue. By confining their attention to those Euro-American polities with a common politico-cultural heritage and similar range of socioeconomic development, they could unself-consciously rely on everyday labels and assumptions. James Bryce, A. Lawrence Lowell, and Woodrow Wilson are examples of learned scholars around the turn of the century who felt no need for elaborate and explicit conceptualization in going about their task of describing the institutions and norms of political life in Britain, the United States, and "the Continental Powers." To the extent that they had a theory, it was rooted in the comfortable assumption that eventually all countries would evolve toward a similar set of liberal democratic practices.

The Impact of Events. World War I, the Russian Revolution, and the rise of Fascist and National Socialist regimes during the 1920s and 1930s radically shattered this assumption of benevolent convergence. The range of variation within Europe in institutions, behaviors, and justifications increased with dramatic and tragic consequences. After World War II, when the Western European polities seemed to be returning to a common evolutionary path, the worldwide process of *decolonization and attendant struggles for national independence introduced new sources of diversity into the field. Indeed, the excitement that accompanied these changes—plus the policy needs for information coming from the U.S. government and the financial incentives for research coming from major foundations—produced a significant shift in the attention of comparativists away from the First World of Europe toward the "communizing nations" of the Second World and, especially, the "developing nations" of the *Third World. Coping with this extraordinary increase in the number of units and the diversity of their situations demanded a major effort in explicit and elaborate theory-building. Much of this focused on the concept of "*political development" and the search for "functional equivalences" beneath the bewildering variety of new institutions, practices, norms, and beliefs.

The "Golden Age." During the 1960s and 1970s, comparative politics became *the* major locus of theory-building within the discipline as a whole, and its innovations subsequently affected the more established fields of U.S. politics and international relations. Faced with explaining the "*constitution" of the Soviet Union, "elections" in Albania, "parliaments" in Ghana, "professional associations" in Libya, "ministerial selection" in Sri Lanka, "*federalism" in Argentina—not to mention "civil-military relations" in Ecuador or "budgeting" in Zaire—one could not simply apply the usual labels without serious risk of distortion. The similarity in rhetoric hid an obvious absence of analogous behavior, intent, or consequence. But what could replace the old, comfortable rubrics? What makes a concept "transcultural" and "transportable"—hence, utilizable across polities of otherwise great diversity?

The answer to these questions led postwar comparativists to rely increasingly on general theory. Their first reaction was to postulate a universalistic characteristic of all polities, namely, their tendency to form systems whose components were interdependent and homeostatic. Then they defined the system components not as institutions but as functions, i.e., generic tasks that must be performed if the postulated equilibrium were to be reached and sustained. As these initially diverse systems were affected by a generic similar process: *modernization (i.e., economic development, urbanization, *secularization, literacy, industrialization, rationalization, bureaucratization, and so forth), the result would be *political development.

With these fundamental notions at hand (taken largely from social anthropology and biology, often via the sociology of Talcott Parsons), they courageously sallied forth not just to explain what was going on in an extraordinary diversity of settings, but also to create a new "universalistic" understanding of what politics was all about and why political development was bound to occur.

The results of this ambitious venture were mixed. Quantities of new, and often very useful, data were gathered about "exotic" places. Novel (or long-forgotten) aspects of *state-society relations such as clientelism and patrimonialism were opened up to inquiry. Sensitivity certainly grew with regard to the variety of ways in which political business could be conducted and institutions could be exploited. The exclusive emphasis on comparisons between "advanced polities" was irrevocably altered. Nevertheless, already by the early 1970s serious doubts about the paradigm had begun to arise, and by the 1980s the field had lost its unity of purpose. Complaints accumulated that the systemic functionalism was excessively abstract, weak in providing specific and researchable hypotheses, and incapable of orienting the collection of empirical data. Moreover, its Americocentric aspects became increasingly apparent. Equilibrium did not always set in. Functional tasks were not so nicely differentiated or performed so complementarily. Political systems on the "periphery" proved to be less autonomous and more subject to dependency and domination effects. Assumptions about the coherence and identity of "national" societies and their corresponding polities turned out to be overoptimistic. Traditional cultures were more varied and resilient than anticipated. They did not give way so easily to the "imperatives" of modernization. Autocracy rather than *democracy became the more probable outcome. Instead of the expected political development, something much more akin to political decay emerged in much of the Third World—and in the Second World of communism a very different pattern of domination installed and consolidated itself.

The Reaction of Area Specialists. Meanwhile, the "American" promotion of comparative politics had spread to Europe. Practitioners there also tended to chafe at the limitations and assumptions of systemic functionalism, but for different reasons. European polities may have been manifestly more self-equilibrating than those of the Third World (after an initial decade of postwar uncertainty in some countries); however, the interdependence of components and, hence, the configuration of institutions often differed markedly from the paradigm case of the United States. Contrary to the prevalent view from America, it was not specialized performance of functions, overlapping cleavage patterns, broadly aggregative parties, and limited state interventions that could account for the relatively high degree of order that emerged. Also for Europeans, the flagrantly "ahistorical" nature of the general paradigm contradicted the abundant evidence for the persistent role of different historical residues, sequences, and trajectories in the region.

During the 1960s individual European scholars began to elaborate alternative models of political order and political change. Basically, they took the case they knew best (usually the one in which they lived and taught), summarized it, and generalized its characteristics to other settings. Stein Rokkan used his native Norway to produce an elaborate theory of historical cleavages and center-periphery relations; Giovanni Sartori analyzed the party system of Italy to challenge the American assumption of centrist-centripetal tendencies by showing how polarized-centrifugal patterns of competition could emerge; Gerhard Lehmbruch and Leonard Neidhart came up with models of *Proporz-* or *Pluralitäre-demokratie* to explain the special features of Swiss and Austrian politics; Arend Lijphart, Hans Daalder, and Val Lorwin exploited the cases of the Netherlands and Belgium to show how "segmented" rather than "overlapping *pluralism*" could produce stability through a consociational form of democracy. While all the above were (at least initially) intended only to make sense out of the peculiar characteristics of continental European polities, Juan Linz abstracted the characteristics of what was a markedly deviant case in this context, Spain, and came up with the definition of a distinctive type, the authoritarian regime, that very quickly was picked up by scholars working on other parts of the world. Joseph Lapalombara's appropriation of *parentela* and *clientela* from the Italian political jargon to explain certain peculiarities of that country's interest politics enjoyed a similar, if less successful, fate.

For Europeanists were not the only ones who resisted the universalistic appeal of systemic functionalism. From the start, specialists on such foreign areas as Latin America, Africa, Asia, and the Middle East regarded the pretensions of comparative politics with considerable skepticism. Their domain of expertise was being invaded by outsiders (some of whom, it must be admitted, did possess detailed knowledge of specific cultures, languages, and histories). The concepts being thrown at "their" societies seemed excessively abstract, insufficiently informative, and hardly value-neutral. Not only were the concepts biased toward the rational utilitarianism of Western societies, but they also seemed to justify various forms of policy intervention—not to say imperialist manipulation—by the already-developed powers that were sponsoring and consuming comparative research.

In addition to the general, culturally and historically based objections mentioned above, scholars working on and/or coming from these Third World countries began to develop alternative concepts and theories. The most significant of these focused on the international context within which politics was being conducted—particularly the unequal exchange between central and peripheral economies, owing to the differential historical development of a single world capitalist system. In a broader sense, it was argued that the conditions of late development and dependency upon external sources of demand, investment capital, ownership of enterprises, *elite values, and models of mass consumption altered the basic parameters of policy choice and led to different political outcomes. Guillermo O'Donnell drew the conclusion that under these conditions of delayed, dependent development through import substitution the most likely result would not be democracy but protracted bureaucratic authoritarian rule. This thesis produced a great deal of critical discussion and had an impact far beyond the South American context from which it originated. A related conceptual innovation was the notion that *corporatism, not pluralism, was the most probable response in the realm of interest associations to such differences in patterns of development. This idea was very quickly diffused across national, regional, and cultural boundaries and, suitably reformulated, led to a major revision in the way that Europeans conceptualized their interest politics.

One group of area specialists paid little or no attention to all this ferment and controversy: those who worked on the Soviet Union, Eastern Europe, and China. With very few exceptions, they easily agreed that what was going on in their bailiwicks was incomparable and required a different approach. *Totalitarianism both provided an overarching concept and served to justify a unique set of methods of observation and inference that could cope with its secretive and sinister nature. The static and isolated character of this subfield left its practitioners quite unprepared for explaining the remarkable (and unanticipated) changes that emerged during the late 1980s, and they have since been busy trying to join their long-lost comparativist colleagues.

The Proliferation of Methods, Levels, and Designs. If this dispersion of critiques and innovations were not enough, the subdiscipline of comparative politics has also been buffeted in recent decades by a proliferation of methods, levels, and designs. The original comparativists were scholars (all DWEMs: Dead, White, European Men—but not Boring) who worked alone, mainly used publicly available information about the public leaders and institutions of sovereign states in multiple settings (often mixed with a good deal of "itinerant wandering" and "participant observation"), and drew their conclusions based on prevailing standards of logic and inference (even if, occasionally, reaching unusual and counterintuitive conclusions). They made extensive use of typologies as simplifying devices to establish equivalences and differences. For example, Aristotle first separated Greek city-states into three descriptive categories: rule by one person, rule by a few persons, and rule by all citizens, and then further divided them normatively into good and corrupt versions of each. Machiavelli relied heavily on the dichotomy between republican and princely government, Montesquieu on a trichotomy of republics, monarchies, and despotisms. Tocqueville broadened the focus to include private as well as public institutions, masterfully exploited the contrast between aristocratic and democratic societies, and offered the field a new *telos,* the ineluctable drive toward equality. Since these promising beginnings, the classification systems have multiplied and the thematic foci have shifted from one putative goal or end state to another—without producing much in the way of accumulated wisdom or conceptual convergence.

As mentioned above, comparativists have always supplemented "official" sources of information with a good deal of data gathering on their own. Through travel, personal experience in politics, and access to primary sources, as well as the reading of history, they have attempted to get beyond constitutional forms and legal categories to get at what "really" determines similarities and differences. Field research abroad for an extended period is still an obligatory *rite de passage* for all its practitioners.

The Behavioral Revolution. What is distinctive about recent practice is the reliance on new forms of data, new means of compilation, and new techniques of analysis. *Public opinion polling developed in the study of American politics and soon spread to comparative politics. The first efforts were relatively crude attempts to find out "if foreigners think like us," but with the spread of survey research facilities across the world and increasing sophistication in the conceptualization and translation of items, it became possible to design and execute multinational projects based on the attitudes of individuals. Gabriel Almond and Sidney Verba's *The Civic Culture* was a particularly ambitious, "landmark" study that analyzed the opinions of mass publics in Britain, Italy, the Federal Republic of Germany (FRG), and Mexico. Since then, the volume of research on "comparative political behavior" has grown almost exponentially. Research is now conducted routinely on such items as voting preference, electoral turnout, citizen tolerance and subjective competence, confidence in institutions, modes of participation, salience of class and other bases of cleavage, party identification, difference in elite-mass values, etc., in a wide range of polities. It has even proved possible to study comparatively the emergence of new, allegedly postmaterialist, values and citizens' dispositions for engaging in "unconventional" political actions. Within the European Community, mass surveys covering all twelve member states are routinely conducted and reported in its *Eurobarometre* publications. Sizable collections of these attitudinal data have been assembled, such as the one at the Inter-University Consortium for Political and Social Research at the University of Michigan, or registered, for example, through the Data Information Service of the European Consortium

for Political Research in Bergen, Norway, which allow researchers easy and inexpensive access for the purpose of secondary analysis.

The Appearance of Aggregate Data. But the explosion of sources and archives was not confined to surveys. With the independent development of national accounting systems and statistical services—and the growing availability of computers—scholars began to collect and manipulate large quantities of aggregate data. International organizations contributed to the standardization of many of these measures of national performance, and comparativists were soon adding indicators of their own. The publication of this information in "handbooks" that covered virtually the entire universe of national states added a further stimulus. By now, machine-readable data sets on a wide range of subjects are available from commercial sources, and more will be available on CD-ROM disks.

The impact of this explosion of aggregate data has been at least as profound as that of survey data. It has permitted researchers for the first time to examine the full range of variance, "the universe," on a given subject. Previously, time, expense, and human limitations restricted the number of cases that a comparativist could deal with. These compilations have allowed analysts to bring the powerful tools of statistical estimation to bear and to incorporate many variables simultaneously in their analyses. The first efforts focused on relatively simple correlations such as that between "social mobilization and political *development*" and "economic development and democracy." Subsequently, the scope of inquiry widened and the complexity of the models increased to tackle issues such as the political determinants of mass violence, industrial conflict, welfare policy, growth of state expenditures, social equality, "regime governability," and rebellion. The burgeoning field of comparative public policy owes a great deal to the stimulus of these new data sets and statistical techniques.

But these "gifts" have not been unmitigated blessings for comparativists. Much of the work ignored elementary problems of conceptual equivalence across units (not to mention empirical validity in the data); depended on crude inductive methods and *ex post facto* theorizing; neglected to measure concepts with adequate indicators; relied on static cross-sections and ignored time-dependent, dynamic relations; used statistical tools that were inappropriate for testing the postulated relationships; and failed to distinguish between correlation and causality. Nevertheless, the quality of both data and inference has improved consistently over time, and new techniques of statistical estimation are being introduced which should correct many of the analytical errors.

The Problem with Units. Both survey and aggregate data initially reinforced the already firmly entrenched tendency to use the nation-state as the exclusive unit of analysis for most comparative purposes. This was unfortunate for three reasons. 1) Most newly independent states had much less coherence and autonomy than did the established states of Europe, North America, and the "White *Commonwealth." This violated a basic assumption of the comparative method that the units should be equivalent in their capacity to act with regard to the properties being examined. 2) All comparisons are jeopardized by Galton's problem, namely the possibility that the observations of a given variable are not "really" independent, but caused by an underlying process of diffusion. With the "trade, investment, and communications revolution" that emerged during the postwar period, especially within certain, highly interdependent, regional contexts such as Western Europe, national states effectively lost their sovereign control over many policy processes. 3) The figures generated as national frequencies or averages often masked very substantial differences between unevenly developed regions and sectors within these countries. At times, this internal variation could be greater than that between the polities being compared. The national datum became an artifact of a nonexistent unit.

Growing sensitivity to these issues has resulted in several modifications of the method. Universal "samples" have been abandoned in favor of smaller and more homogeneous subsets of units. Some of these are geocultural areas, but many are based on new analytical categories that cut across these regions: "advanced industrial countries," "newly industrialized countries," and, perhaps, if the proper euphemism can be found, "really backward countries." Another trend is to exploit the infranational variation by comparing systematically the conditions and performances of *municipios, départements, provincias, regioni, Länder, estados autonómicos,* Soviet republics, etc. This approach began with U.S. states and cities, but now covers a wide range of polities where subunits have some significant degree of autonomy. Another strategy has been to focus on the meso-level of economic sectors. There is even an embryonic literature dealing comparatively with the emergent properties of supranational authorities and international organizations.

The Choice of Design. The classic format was for a scholar to study two or more units explicitly selected for their mix of common and contrasting features. Much of the production of comparativists, however, consists of "single country monographs" in which only one unit is ostensibly analyzed. The most famous and enduring of these is Tocqueville's *Democracy in America.* What accounts for its comparative status is both the way in which it is conceptualized, i.e., as a contrast between two types of societies, the democratic and the aristocratic, and the consistent, if often implicit, contrast which is made with an "absent" case, i.e., France. This casestudy method has been used extensively in the postwar period, especially for dissertation research given the limited means at the disposal of young scholars. Not only have these monographs contributed heuristically to the eventual development of "grounded theory," examined critically "deviant cases," and served as "proving grounds" for new techniques, but they have also been replicated in other settings. It is important to remember that comparison is not just an event, but a process. As such, it can involve the same scholar subsequently extending his or her coverage to other cases or other scholars picking up the original conceptualization and operationalization and applying them again.

The advent of aggregate data and, to a lesser extent, survey data encouraged a shift from "small N" strategies of single or paired cases to "large N" strategies which might even include the total relevant universe. Comparativists found themselves analyzing units whose language, culture, and history—even whose location—they did not know, simply because they were available in some data series of the United Nations Educational, Scientific and Cultural Organization or of the International Labor Organization. When the issues of incommensurability and unintelligibility became more salient, the enthusiasm for this design declined rapidly and researchers reverted to working on selected subsets of units where they were more familiar with the quality of the data and where they could bring more variables into the analysis—especially the effects of historical time, sequence, and memory.

Much intelligent discussion has focused on whether it is preferable, when comparing a small number of cases, to use a "most similar systems" design in which as many variables as possible can (putatively) be held constant, allowing only those under surveillance to vary—say, to study the impact of revenue windfalls on the party system by comparing Norway and Sweden—or a "most different system" design in which the effect of the same variable is traced by comparing two systems which otherwise have as little in common as possible—say, the impact of petroleum booms on Norway and Nigeria. Both have their generic advantages and disadvantages, and the choice hinges largely on whether one is seeking to maximize the specificity or the generalizability of one's findings.

One major limitation on the design of comparative research in the past has been definitively broken. Most studies were carried out by a single scholar, almost invariably an American or a European, working in relative isolation. With the increase in resources and the diffusion of competence in the social and political sciences around the globe, it has become possible to put together teams of scholars working on different countries from different disciplines. Originally, these were staffed, funded, conceptualized, and carried out almost exclusively by American academics—the Committee on Comparative Politics of the Social Science Research Council was the prototype—but this is now less likely to be

the case. Most of the recently edited and multiau-
thored volumes cited in the bibliography of this
essay were produced by collaborative efforts which
were international in every aspect. Moreover, around
the European Consortium for Political Research
(ECPR) in Europe and the Consejo Latinoamericano
de Ciencias Sociales (CLASCO) in Latin America,
important new concentrations have formed to promote comparative research.

The State of the Art. It has been alleged that the
personality of scholars tends to resemble the characteristics of the unit or units they study. If this
were the case, most comparativists would risk
schizophrenia as they are caught between the conflicting demands for providing specific and accurate
information and searching for reliable and verifiable
generalizations. Instead, they seem to have avoided
such a collective pathology by vacillating over time
between the two objectives—although individual
practitioners have occasionally proved that it is possible to satisfy both simultaneously.

Their response to the postwar demand for a universalistic and relevant "science of politics" was
initially enthusiastic and then increasingly skeptical.
To the excesses of systemic functionalism, they reacted by stressing the specificities of culture, geographic location, economic exploitation, and social
structure, while seeking to avoid excessive reliance
on the idiosyncrasies of each case. The need for
"history," "thick description," and "bringing the
state back in" were among the slogans bandied
about. Of course, some eminent students of comparative politics had long been speaking this sort of
prose without knowing or proclaiming it. Even the
more "mainstream" practitioners associated with
development theory responded to the critiques. Samuel P. Huntington consistently stressed the longer-
term cultural and institutional aspects of political
change and arrived at much less sanguine conclusions about the likely outcome. The Social Science
Research Council (SSRC) Committee on Comparative Politics in its later years turned its attention
back toward Europe and recuperated a more historical perspective.

But comparative politics has not merely returned
to its point of departure. Along the tortuous route,
it picked up new concerns, new concepts, and a lot
of new converts. It may have momentarily lost a
clear sense of direction, but there are definite signs
of movement, even of enthusiasm, among its contemporary practitioners. Few would question, however, that the subdiscipline is at an important crossroads.

Three challenges are looming on the horizon for
comparativists: one to their theoretical foundations;
one to their basic units of analysis; one to their
subject matter. 1) The current fashion for rational
choice and game-theoretic explanations raises the
specter of a possible return to universalistic premises—based this time not on unconscious adjustment

and functional equilibration at the macro level, but
on stable solutions worked out through repeated
exchanges between individual actors at the micro
level. If completely successful, this approach would
not only convert entire departments of political science into dependencies of neoclassical economics,
but it would also wipe out the accumulated stock
of comparativists' assumptions about the significance of cultural, institutional, and obligational factors. History would be reduced to the passage of
time and the iteration of exchanges; institutions
would be contingent on continuous calculation;
preferences would be given rather than socially constructed; maximizing self-interest would be the only
admissible norm. 2) Unprecedented increases in interdependence—through trade, investment, production, diffusion of images and tastes, spread of international regimes and obligations, etc.—have greatly
eroded the autonomy (not to mention the sovereignty) of the national states that have so far provided the subdiscipline with its principal units of
observation and analysis. Galton's dilemma has run
wild. In such a globalized context, no polity can
choose and act independently. Will comparativists
be able to shift their bases of inference, as well as
their units of inquiry? Or will they be confined in
the future to analyzing intertemporal and regional
variations of a single "world system"? 3) The wave
of democratization that has swept across the world
since 1974 offers to comparativists the attractive
prospect of once again being able to focus on a
common topic. They looked on with dismay at the
"praetorian politics" and "breakdown of democracy" in the 1960s and early 1970s; now they are
turning their attention to the more heartening processes of "transition from authoritarian rule" and
"consolidation of democracy." Whether this will
trigger a resurgence in theoretical speculation about
evolutionary convergence, or a greater conceptual
sophistication about differences in the types of democracy that are emerging, remains to be seen. If
the past is any guide, two things are certain: comparativists will divide into "generalizers" and "spe-
cifiers" in response to these issues, and the debate
between them will contribute to keeping their subdiscipline lively, controversial, and consequential.

(See also AUTHORITARIANISM; BUREAUCRATIC
AUTHORITARIANISM; COMMUNIST PARTY STATES;
CONSOCIATIONAL DEMOCRACY; DEMOCRATIC TRAN-
SITIONS; GAME THEORY; IMPORT-SUBSTITUTION IN-
DUSTRIALIZATION; POLITICAL CULTURE; POLITICAL
ECONOMY; POLITICAL PARTICIPATION; PUBLIC
CHOICE THEORY.)

Carl Friedrich and Zbigniew Brzezinski, *Totalitarian Dictatorship and Autocracy* (New York, 1956). Gabriel Almond and James Coleman, eds., *The Politics of Developing
Areas* (Princeton, N.J., 1960). Alexander Gerschenkron,
Economic Backwardness in Historical Perspective (Cambridge, Mass., 1962). Gabriel Almond and Sidney Verba,
The Civic Culture (Boston, 1963). Arthur Banks and Robert

Textor, *A Cross-Polity Survey* (Ann Arbor, Mich., 1963). Bruce Russett et al., *World Handbook of Political and Social Indicators* (New Haven, Conn., 1964). Samuel Huntington, *Political Order in Changing Societies* (New Haven, Conn., 1968). Adam Przeworski and Henry Teune, *The Logic of Comparative Social Inquiry* (New York, 1970). Leonard Binder, ed., *Crises and Sequences in Political Development* (Princeton, N.J., 1971). Philippe C. Schmitter, "Still the Century of Corporatism?" in F. B. Pike and T. Stitch, eds., *The New Corporatism: Social-Political Structures in the Iberian World* (London, 1974). Charles Tilly, ed., *The Formation of National States in Western Europe* (Princeton, N.J., 1975). Juan Linz and Alfred Stepan, eds., *The Breakdown of Democratic Regimes*, 4 vols. (Baltimore, 1978). Fernando Henrique Cardoso and Enzo Falletto, *Dependency and Development in Latin America* (Berkeley and Los Angeles, 1979). Guillermo O'Donnell, Philippe C. Schmitter, and Laurence Whitehead, eds., *Transitions from Authoritarian Rule*, 4 vols. (Baltimore, 1986). Charles Ragin, *The Comparative Method* (Berkeley, Calif., 1987).

PHILIPPE C. SCHMITTER

CONFERENCE ON SECURITY AND COOPERATION IN EUROPE. A grouping of European and North American states, the Conference on Security and Cooperation in Europe (CSCE) has an uncertain future about which one can only speculate. Created out of the waning *Cold War in the mid-1970s, the CSCE has outlasted that bipolar structure of power. A product both of Soviet desires to reinforce the geostrategic status quo and of Western desires to engage the countries of the *Warsaw Treaty Organization (Warsaw Pact) in a reform process, the conference has witnessed a redrawing of the political map of Europe and an expansion of the principles of democratic capitalism. The conference continues although the status quo has been swept away and the European communist world has collapsed. These changes happened more rapidly than anyone could have imagined at the time of the 1975 *Helsinki Accord—the basic framework statement about European cooperation emanating from the conference. Given the rapidity and breadth of changes in all of Europe since 1985 when Mikhail *Gorbachev became first secretary of the Communist Party of the Soviet Union, and especially since 1989 when a series of mostly peaceful revolutions swept Eastern and *Central Europe, it is no wonder that disparate views have arisen concerning the future of the CSCE. It is not clear what the role of the CSCE should be economically, socially, or strategically.

One view holds that the CSCE will be marginal to the future of Europe. In this view the conference, with its unwieldy membership of more than fifty states, will take a backseat to strictly European organizations. Advocates of this view insist that the *European Community (EC) will gradually absorb most of the Eastern and Central states economically, that the *Council of Europe will absorb them socially, especially concerning human rights standards and procedures, and that the *North Atlantic Treaty Organization (NATO) will remain as an important security guarantee. It is said NATO will survive

primarily in order to ensure German restraint and as a safeguard against any renewed Russian machinations.

This school of thought emphasizes the reemergence of Europe as an independent power center, with reduced influence for both the United States and Russia. This change is symbolized by the tendency toward growing regional integration associated with the EC's plan for a single European market after 1992. This view emphasizes the reduced role in Europe already accepted by the United States in deferring to Western European states in the new international bank for European reconstruction and in other financial assistance to the East. Thus it is said the United States will increasingly limit itself to a role in NATO while European states work out their destiny through existing organizations. This first view of the CSCE amounts to a forecast of the conference as a periodic consulting framework—a pale image of the 1815 Concert of Europe which faded after seven years.

A second view, which assumes NATO's demise, sees an enhanced role for the CSCE operating out of its new headquarters in Prague, Czechoslovakia. Given the obvious decline of any Russian threat of territorial expansion westward and the collapse of the Warsaw Pact, the basic rationale for the alliance has disappeared. Supporters of this view believe the CSCE will have an important security role to play in a post-NATO, post–Warsaw Pact world. They look to the confidence-building measures such as quite intrusive inspection of security agreements, which came out of the 1985 Stockholm meeting, as a model for the future. They also see the CSCE as a source of peacekeeping in the troubled *Balkans and perhaps in the states of the former Soviet Union. The CSCE Conflict-Prevention Center has already been established in Vienna.

This second school of thought also sees the CSCE playing a large role in the international protection of minorities in Eastern and Central Europe, the Balkans, and the former Soviet Union. These advocates note that the European Convention on Human Rights is silent on minority protection and that in any event many former communist states cannot meet the rigorous standards of human rights necessary for membership in the Council of Europe. Hence this second school of thought sees a continuing human rights role for the CSCE and notes that the CSCE Office of Free Elections has already been set up in Warsaw, Poland.

Finally, those who see an enhanced role for the CSCE argue that even with a dynamic EC, there will be broader economic forces at work in Europe. The economic influence of the United States and Russia will, in different ways, continue to be felt in Europe, it is said, making necessary some larger system of cooperation. Moreover, some believe that an EC dominated by a unified Germany will create considerable interest in a larger framework that sets the rules of economic cooperation and economic justice. Given that there is no prospect of either the United States or Russia joining the EC, some believe a broader framework of economic cooperation will be required.

This second view of the CSCE amounts to a forecast of a new and important regional organization. There is already agreement on a Council of Ministers and on a second-tier meeting of important state officials, and there are plans for further specialized organs plus some type of elected assembly, or perhaps a linkage to the existing *European Parliament.

At present there are too many variables in flux for confident prediction. One set of factors involves the former Soviet Union. There must be stable states emerging from the former Soviet Union, interested in moderate policies toward the West, for Europe as a whole to be secure and for any type of CSCE to generate influence. A large area in more or less constant upheaval over nationalities, minorities, and federal schemes will not be a reliable partner for the rest of Europe or a reliable building block for any type of useful CSCE.

Germany, too, is a question mark. The Federal Republic has been preoccupied with a surprisingly rapid but difficult and expensive unification. How it will utilize its new power within and without the EC remains to be seen. Whether the French will feel secure in the face of anticipated German hegemony by relying on the economic web of the EC, whether the Germans will seek to break out of NATO sooner rather than later, whether they will show sensitivity about their anticipated economic expansion into Eastern and Central Europe, as the Japanese have shown about Asia, remain to be seen.

Still another set of uncertain factors pertains to the United States. Will it gracefully agree to abandon NATO, one of the most successful military alliances in history, at the same time as its partners? Will it abandon or at least reduce the special relationship with a United Kingdom more drawn to the continent by economic ties? Will it—after the preoccupation with the Persian Gulf—find the burdens of policing the world too onerous and retire more into itself, or focus more on the Pacific rim? Or, conversely, will it unilaterally project itself into the myriad ethnic and other disputes emerging in the new Europe, as it did with disastrous results in Lebanon in the 1980s?

Some actors can be expected to push for an active CSCE. Particularly the neutral and nonaligned states found that the framework of the CSCE allowed them to play an enlarged mediating role between East and West during the decade from 1975 to 1985. Neutrals like Austria, Finland, Sweden, and Switzerland and some of the nonaligned like Yugoslavia helped produce the international agreements emanating from the CSCE. But East and West are no longer so sharply delineated, and the former greater Yugosla-via needs more CSCE help than it can provide to the conference.

In the very short term, the CSCE is likely to coexist with other regional bodies in an untidy mix. NATO, the EC, the Council of Europe, and the CSCE are all likely to operate without clear relationships in the near future. In the longer term, the CSCE will be shaped by uncertain political forces. The ending of the Cold War in Europe removed much stability and predictability, however dangerous it may have seemed. The aftermath, while bringing welcomed change, also brought with it unanswered questions about the "New Europe," "Europe as a Common Home," or "Europe from the Atlantic to the Urals." All we know for sure is that the CSCE continues as an institutional process rather than as a well-developed formal organization with precise tasks.

(See also COMMUNISM; GERMAN REUNIFICATION; HUMAN RIGHTS; INTERNATIONAL COOPERATION; NINETEEN EIGHTY-NINE; SECURITY.)

James E. Goodby, "A New European Concert: Settling Disputes in CSCE" *Arms Control Today* 21, no. 1 (January–February 1991): 3. Niles H. Wessell, ed., *The New Europe: Revolution in East–West Relations* (Montpelier, Vt., 1991).

DAVID P. FORSYTHE

CONFUCIANISM. A system of ethics applicable to Chinese society, state, and culture, Confucianism was formulated by Confucius and his disciples and appeared primarily in *The Analects, The Great Learning, The Doctrine of the Mean,* and *The Book of Mencius* (known collectively as *The Four Books*). In some of these works, Confucius identified "five sets of relationships: [those] between the sovereign and ministers, father and son, husband and wife, elder and younger brothers, and between friends." He specified the ethical properties of some of these relationships as follows: "Father, kindness; son, filial piety; elder brother, goodness; younger brother, respect; husband, righteousness; wife, compliance; the sovereign, benevolence; ministers, loyalty." For more than 2,000 years, this system of ethics has been continuously and universally followed by the Chinese.

Confucian thought is characterized by a spirit of humanism, rationalism, and moralism. It is concerned with human relations, upholding *ren* (humanity or love) as its highest value; it relies on human experience—rather than any religious doctrine—to justify its beliefs; it emphasizes the regulation of all human conduct through ethical precepts. This spirit remained unchanged throughout Chinese history despite its frequent interactions with many other systems of thought, notably Legalism, *Buddhism, and Taoism.

In traditional *China, Confucianism exerted its influence primarily through two means. First, from 136 B.C.E. during the Western Han dynasty to the end of the Qing dynasty in 1911, Confucianism was accepted as the state orthodoxy by which the political conduct of all individuals, from the sovereign to the commoners, was regulated. Moreover, from 606 to 1905 C.E., most Chinese political and bureaucratic leaders were recruited through an examination system based in Confucianism.

Second, the Chinese have firmly accepted the Confucian belief in the perfectibility and educability of the common person. An ideal society could be realized, Confucius emphasized, because every individual was capable of acquiring virtues through self-cultivation, and the society should help individuals with this task by providing education to all. Confucian classics and their interpretations constituted the exclusive curricula in all Chinese private and state schools.

In contemporary times, Confucianism has been subject both to challenge and affirmation. In the early twentieth century, the Chinese New Culture movement argued that Confucian ethics were feudalistic in content and served the interests of monarchical absolutism; Confucianism was seen as responsible for the social and cultural stagnation of the nation. The *Chinese Communist Party, following this line of thought, has generally rejected Confucianism as being inimical to *Marxism-*Leninism, yet on occasion it has acknowledged, for reasons of expediency, certain progressive features of Confucianism, such as the emphasis on popular education and the application of a common set of ethics to all individuals.

Many scholars, both in China and overseas, have come to the defense of Confucianism. Liang Souming, Hsiung Shih-li, and Hsu Fu-kuan, for example, saw Confucianism as possessing certain transcendental qualities that characterized Chinese civilization, differentiating it from the world's other great civilizations. In the last three decades, a school of New Confucianism has emerged, with Mou Tsung-san, T'ang Chun-i, Tu Wei-ming, Thomas A. Metzger, and Yu Ying-shih as its leading advocates. They believe that the Confucian emphasis on *junzi* (the virtuous person) gives followers of Confucianism a common mission: to seek virtuous individuals, harmonious families, an orderly state, and a peaceful world. Some of these scholars have suggested that this mission has endowed modern Confucianism with a "transformative force" for social and economic changes—an idea opposite to Max *Weber's argument that Confucianism lacked an innate driving force for the betterment of life.

More recently, other scholars have suggested that Confucianism has contributed to the spectacular economic performance of the East Asian countries. In Japan, Taiwan, the Republic of Korea, Hong Kong, and Singapore, these scholars believe, the economic impact of Confucianism is manifested in the organizational characteristics of businesses, management-labor relations, the saving rate, and the strong emphasis on education. These conditions are linked to expanded foreign trade and investment opportunities as an explanation for why the Pacific Basin region has been the fastest-growing area of the world in economic terms over the last three decades.

In the 1980s Singapore proposed to incorporate Confucianism into school curricula and initiated Confucian-based social policies. Only a concern to maintain interethnic harmony among the Chinese, the Malays, and the Indians of the country persuaded the government to discontinue these efforts. (See also NEWLY INDUSTRIALIZING ECONOMIES.)

H. G. Creel, *Confucius: The Man and the Myth* (New York, 1949). Hung-chao Tai, ed., *Confucianism and Economic Development: An Oriental Alternative?* (Washington, D.C., 1989).

HUNG-CHAO TAI

CONGO. Once known as the Middle Congo (under French rule), the Republic of the Congo is a 349,000-square-kilometer (134,750-sq.-mi.) territory on the equatorial line, located northwest of Zaire. The total population is estimated at 2.1 million. Although French is the official language, many other languages are spoken. Chief among them are Kikongo, Lari, Mboshi, and Lingala. Brazzaville (the capital), Pointe-Noire, Loubomo, Nkayi, Madingou, Sibiti, Djambala, Owando, Ouesso, and Impfondo are the major urban centers.

Since the advent of independence on 15 August 1960, the Congo has undergone serious political mood swings—from l'Abbé Fulbert Youlou's conservative and neocolonial regime to the current (1992) transitional government of Andre Milongo, via Denis Sassou-Nguesso's fuzzy socialism and Marien Ngouabi's scientific socialism. Under both Ngouabi and Sassou-Nguesso, the Constitution defined the Congo as a united people's republic whose supreme organ was the Parti Congolais du Travail (PCT), the only party in the country up until 1991, the year of the National Conference. In theory the PCT was a proletarian party guided by the dictates of *Marxism-*Leninism and committed to the principles of proletarian internationalism. According to its declared goals, "on the social level, the Party's mission is to solve the contradictions which underlie and divide the Congolese societal fabric." The party went on to identify those key contradictions. Accordingly, the party viewed the principal contradiction as that opposing the Congolese people to international *imperialism—in Congolese experience, principally French. In decreasing order of importance, secondary contradictions were identified: 1) the contradiction opposing the most exploited classes to the national bourgeoisie; 2) the contradiction between intellectuals and laborers; and 3) the contradiction between national unity and *tribalism qua regionalism. In the final analysis, the party's aim was to dismantle the colonial state and build a revolutionary people's democracy. This, in part, may help explain the Congo's embrace of left-wing or left-leaning regimes in the world as well as its support of *national liberation movements. All this altered with the National Conference, which changed the official name of the country from People's Republic of the Congo to the original, pre-1969 name of Republic of the Congo.

On the economic front, it is safe to characterize the pre–National Conference Congo as a mixed economy dominated by a colonial capitalist mode of production. Indeed, a quick glance at the country's economic structure reveals the following salient features: 1) the rural sector, in which the vast majority of the population (eighty percent) operates, is still by and large a subsistence economy; 2) the modern agricultural sector, introduced by foreign capitalists under colonial rule, is still dominated by them—particularly the lumber industry—despite a serious increase of the state's participation and control; 3) the industrial sector, which is very limited, is spearheaded by the extractive industries, particularly petroleum—although here, too, the state's share of ownership is considerable and increasing; and 4) the banking and insurance sectors are also controlled by foreign capitalist interests. Since 1986, thanks to an *International Monetary Fund-*World Bank–inspired structural adjustment program, the political discourse has acquired a new vocabulary as well as new slogans for the 1990s, such as "Back to the land," "We must encourage the private national initiative," etc. Concretely, this rhetoric has translated into a series of reforms, particularly in agriculture, whose share in the investment budget has increased considerably. The same applies to agricultural commodities prices. The government's ultimate goal is food self-sufficiency by the turn of the century.

Overall, the double objective of economic independence and political national integration is still a dream. Indeed, the contradictions that separate the intellectuals from the common masses and laborers and the regions from one another, the fall of the once-mighty PTC, the struggle for control between the prime minister and the president since the National Conference, and the emergence of a multiparty system combine to produce an image of the Congo as a sleeping volcano, ready to erupt at any moment. Economically, the Congo seems to be committed irreversibly to *privatization and *capitalism. Ironically, however, most of the once state-owned and state-controlled business ventures that have been privatized are now in foreign hands. Whether privatization is the way to development remains to be seen. In the meantime, the rapidly deteriorating living conditions of the average wage earner, the increasing number of unemployed college graduates, the alarming increase in crime, etc., seem to suggest that neither privatization nor the structural adjust-

ment program can provide the necessary remedies for the Congo's ills.

(See also FRANCOPHONE AFRICA.)

S. Amin and C. Coquery-Vidrovitch, *Histoire Economique du Congo, 1880–1968,* (Dakar, 1969). René Gauze, *The Politics of Congo-Brazzaville,* trans. Virginia Thompson and Richard Adloff (Stanford, Calif., 1973).

KU-NTIMA MAKIDI

CONGO CRISIS. The term *Congo Crisis* is used to describe the political turmoil which erupted in *Zaire (then the Republic of the Congo) in the wake of its independence on 30 June 1960. Though domestic, the conflict was heightened by the *Cold War and by the continuous interference of foreign interests with a stake in the newly independent country. The Congo Crisis emerged from three sets of factors: the historical conditions surrounding *Belgium's colonial policy, the rivalries among various foreign powers which had always coveted this rich and massive land, and the internal manipulation of its numerous ethnic divisions.

With an area of nearly 2.35 million square kilometers (900,000 sq. mi.), Zaire is roughly equal to the size of Western Europe. Strategically located, it is the third-largest country on the continent and one of the richest in mineral resources and farming land. Its population of nearly 40 million is divided into over 200 major ethnic groups. Kinshasa is the capital city. The main economic centers are the mineral-rich Shaba (former Katanga) and Kasai, the Kivu, and the Upper Zaire provinces.

Zaire has a long history. In 1482, the Portuguese Diego Cao was the first to explore the Kingdom of Kongo, one of the famous precolonial states. Explorations were further intensified by people like the Scottish missionary David Livingstone and the Welsh-born Henry Morton Stanley, a reporter for the *New York Herald.*

Through the latter's travel accounts, King Leopold II of Belgium became interested in this land. He convened a conference of European geographers in Brussels, created the International Congo Association to further the exploration of Central Africa, and was finally granted by the Berlin Conference of 1884–1885 the right to establish the Congo Free State as a personal estate. Later, faced with an international outcry against his ruthless colonization, Leopold II reluctantly turned his asset over to Belgium in 1908. Thus was born the Belgian Congo.

Belgian colonialism was utterly paternalistic and geared primarily toward the extraction of natural resources. Influenced by a triumvirate of large corporations, Catholic missions, and the colonial apparatus, Belgium exerted tight control over a colony that, until 1955, was seen as an "empire of silence" and a model of prosperity. It was relatively calm politically and, because of the comprehensive welfare program in public health and primary education, the native population was seen as well-off economically.

Yet, Belgium prohibited *political participation by the native population and denied them equal rights. For example, secondary and postsecondary education was discouraged on the grounds that training an indigenous elite would create political troubles for the colonizer. Instead of higher education, the colonial regime created a "middle class" of *évolués,* natives who, through some Western education, Christianity, and clerical jobs in the colonial apparatus, were regarded as the new urbanized and detribalized elite.

The *évolués* founded various cultural associations concerned with issues regarding their status. However, the publication of a thirty-year *decolonization plan by a Belgian academic in 1956 stirred controversy among them and marked the political awakening of the colony. With the rise of popular resentment against its rule, Belgium was forced to consider political emancipation.

The rise, particularly since 1959, of indigenous political activism was the utmost catalyst for radical change in the colony. It forced Belgium to recognize the first political parties which recruited mainly among ethnic members. The only exception was Patrice *Lumumba's Mouvement National Congolais (MNC), which combined a nationalist ideology with a broad interethnic base. A year later, Belgium drafted the constitution of the future sovereign country and, five months before independence, oversaw the first national elections. These were won by the MNC, whose leader became the head of the first and only democratic government in the entire history of Zaire.

A few weeks after independence, troubles erupted all over the country and threatened its unity. The national army mutinied against its Belgian officers, which prompted the Belgian armed forces to intervene. In the mineral-rich Katanga province, Moise Tshombe, with the support of major Belgian interests and mercenary troops, declared independence while the Kasai and the four remaining provinces slowly broke into smaller pieces. Interethnic conflicts were exacerbated and the former colonial expatriates publicly humiliated.

The deteriorating situation forced the new government to request UN intervention. It also led to a face-off between the prime minister, Lumumba, and the head of state, Joseph Kasavubu. Lumumba eventually lost, was arrested, and was murdered in 1961.

When the UN intervened in 1960, it faced ambiguous and contradictory goals. For the host government, its purpose was to help restore law and order, end Belgium's ongoing military presence, and preserve national unity. Within the Security Council, however, East-West ideological alignments, the United States' aversion for and UN Secretary-General Dag *Hammarskjöld's dislike of Lumumba, and continuous external interference in Zaire's affairs greatly affected the UN decision-making process. Moreover, the lack of a legal framework to justify its action and the parallel goals pursued by individual countries contributing to the UN force further complicated its task and undermined its credibility. For example, its neutralist position toward internal rivalries, such as its refusal to press for the release of Lumumba and its pre-1963 decision not to quell the Katanga secession, was seen as support for the anti-Lumumba forces and for the Katanga secessionists.

The Congo Crisis left a mark on the UN and all the parties involved. It is uncertain whether the UN was successful in ending the crisis or in preventing further foreign interference in Zaire's affairs. When it withdrew in 1964, a rebellious "movement for the second independence" was already in progress, whereas external intrusions never stopped. Besides, political developments since 1964 suggest that, though not unique in this respect, Zaire's long-term stability has been an elusive goal.

(See also COLONIAL EMPIRES; ETHNICITY; UNITED NATIONS.)

Ernest Lefever, *Crisis in the Congo: A United Nations Force in Action* (Washington, D.C., 1965). Thomas Kanza, *The Rise and Fall of Patrice Lumumba: Conflict in the Congo* (London, 1978).

MUSIFIKY MWANASALI

CONGRESS, U.S. The U.S. Congress remains as distinctive a legislative body as when it first convened in the spring of 1789. Almost alone among the world's legislatures, it writes its own legislation and monitors the vast governmental apparatus. Its powers, enumerated in the 1787 Constitution, are quite expansive. It has protected these powers largely by resorting to division of labor (creating standing committees and subcommittees) and by adding to its staff resources.

In reality there are two Congresses, not just one. By design and by historical experience, Congress is not only a lawmaking body; it is also an assembly of disparate representatives who owe primary allegiance to voters who are hundreds or even thousands of miles away from the nation's capital. These lawmaking and representative duties clash uneasily within the same institution.

Congress as a Representative Assembly. "All politics are local," remarked former House Speaker Thomas P. ("Tip") O'Neill. Although national tides influence elections, congressional candidates, their voters, and often their issues and styles, are deeply rooted in local states and districts. States are represented equally in the Senate (two for each state). The 435 members of the House of Representatives represent separate districts based on population (the decennial census is held to apportion seats among states); the House also has four delegates and one resident commissioner from the District of Columbia and U.S. territories.

Formal constitutional requirements for office are few and simple: age (25 years of age for the House, 30 for the Senate); citizenship (7 years for the House, 9 for the Senate); and residency in the state from which the person is elected. But de facto rules favor candidates with long-standing, intimate ties to the state or district. Once elected, senators and representatives tend to be judged by voters according to their stewardship regarding local issues. Members are vulnerable to the charge of ignoring "home folks" or becoming overly fond of Washington life.

In most congressional elections, incumbents run for reelection, and they usually prevail. Since World War II, an average of ninety-two percent of all incumbent representatives and seventy-five percent of incumbent senators running for reelection have been returned to office. Short of a major scandal or misstep, it is nearly impossible to topple a House incumbent—and nearly as difficult to dislodge a senator.

Incumbents have resources that ensure visibility and promote support: through speeches, statements, press releases, press coverage, newsletters and mailings, staff assistance, and constituency services. The average House member enjoys perquisites valued at well over $1 million over a two-year term: senators' resources are valued at between $4 million and $7 million. And although incumbents need less money than do challengers, they receive more from outside sources that rightly view them as better investments than their opponents. Incumbents capture nine out of every ten dollars given by political action committees (PACs) to congressional candidates. Most incumbents, in fact, finish their campaign with a surplus.

Incumbent legislators fashion effective "home styles"—ways of projecting themselves and their records to constituents. Ingredients of their home styles include: a cultivated image of trust; plausible explanations of behavior in office; and shrewd use of the perquisites of office. Legislators' messages are conveyed through personal appearances, radio or television spots, press releases, and responses to constituents' requests for help ("casework").

Staff aides extend senators' and representatives' constituent outreach. About 12,000 people work in members' offices. Senators' staffs range in size from thirteen to seventy-one, depending on the state's population; the average is about thirty-six. Representatives' staffs average about seventeen. Constituent relations are their most time-consuming job. Members of Congress have from one to six local offices in key home-state locations; increasingly, casework and voter contacts are handled there.

Congress as Policymaker: Committees and Parties. Congress has retained an active legislative role by delegating its workload to committees (and subcommittees) which write, revise, and oversee laws, programs, and agencies. Most bills and resolutions are referred to the relevant committee(s) of jurisdiction. It is very difficult, especially in the House, to bypass a committee that refuses to act upon a measure. "Congressional government is committee government," wrote Woodrow Wilson (*Congressional Government,* 1885). "Congress in session is Congress on display, but Congress in committee is Congress at work."

House and Senate committee structures are complicated: the Senate has twenty committees, and these have eighty-seven subcommittees; the House has twenty-seven committees with 152 subcommittees. There also four joint committees (with eight subcommittees), not to mention temporary panels, boards, and commissions.

Most standing committees are authorizing committees: they draft the substance of policies and oversee executive agencies' implementation of laws. There are also appropriations committees that draft bills empowering agencies to spend money for programs; revenue committees draft revenue bills to pay for the programs. In 1974 Congress created an elaborate internal budget process for setting guidelines (proposed by House and Senate budget committees) and regulating revenues and expenditures that are supposed to be followed by all committees: income and spending levels are brought into balance by reconciliation bills.

Committees usually exert decisive control over legislative proposals: nine out of every ten measures referred to committee go no farther in the legislative process. Promising bills may be accorded staff research and public nearings—giving executive officials, lobbyists, and citizens a chance to speak publicly on the issue. If the bill has enough support, the committee will hold meetings to revise the text ("markups") and may eventually report the measure to the full chamber.

Each committee is a unique mixture of members, viewpoints, and decision-making styles. They differ in levels of conflict, partisanship, or public visibility. Many committees or subcommittees form ongoing alliances with executive agencies and relevant pressure groups, forming the so-called "iron triangles," or subgovernments, that dominate much routine domestic policy making.

Whereas committees provide expertise for legislating, the political parties manage the legislative process. The parties organize the two chambers, supply their leaders, shape the legislative agenda, and superintend the scheduling of business. Partisan control hinges on the size of the parties' ranks in the two bodies. The majority party (at least fifty-one senators or 218 representatives) organizes the respective houses; the party's size and unity determine how effective its control will be.

The House has a tradition of vigorous leadership. The Speaker combines the duties of presiding officer with those of party leader; historically, Speakers like Henry Clay (1811–1814, 1815–1820, 1823–1825), Thomas B. ("Czar") Reed (1889–1890, 1895–1899),

Joseph G. ("Uncle Joe") Cannon (1903–1911), and Sam Rayburn (1940–1947, 1949–1953, 1955–1961) bent the unruly chamber to their will through procedural skills and the force of their personalities.

In the Senate, strong leadership is the exception rather than the rule. Not until the twentieth century did visible party leaders emerge; even then they were no match for powerful House Speakers. The conspicuous exception was Lyndon B. *Johnson, who as majority leader (1955–1961) worked with the Senate's conservative clique to dominate the chamber as no leader has done before or since. Recent leaders have acted more as facilitators for individual senators' legislative goals and schedules.

Parties are the most stable and significant coalitions on Capitol Hill. Although party discipline is lax, party loyalty runs deep and is the leading determinant of voting in the two chambers. Indeed, party-line voting has been higher in recent years than at any time since the 1930s. Elected lawmakers are, in fact, more partisan than their constituents, whose declining party loyalties constitute a leading trend in contemporary U.S. politics.

At least three distinct periods, or eras, define the recent history of Congress. The first (roughly 1937–1964) was dominated by the conservative coalition of southern Democrats and conservative Republicans; the second was an era of liberal activism (1965–1978), marked by heavy Democratic majorities; the third is an era of fiscal restraint (1979–), characterized by a lagging economy and divided government.

The results of this modern era of "cutback politics" define the characteristics of today's postreform Congress. 1) Fewer measures are sponsored by individual senators and representatives. 2) Key policy decisions are packaged into huge "megabills," permitting lawmakers to combine their initiatives and escape adverse reactions to individual provisions. 3) Techniques of blame avoidance are employed to protect lawmakers from adverse effects of cutback policies. 4) Noncontroversial commemorative resolutions are passed into law—nearly half of all laws produced by recent Congresses. 5) Driven by budgetary concerns, party-line voting is at or nearly at modern-day highs on Capitol Hill. 6) Senate and (especially) House leadership is markedly stronger now than at any time since the 1910 revolt against Speaker Cannon. Today's leaders benefit not only from powers conferred by reform-era innovations of the 1960s and 1970s—for example, controls over legislative scheduling and, in the House, domination of the Rules Committee. They also respond to widespread expectations that they are the only people who can manage the legislative schedule.

"Americans are especially fond of running down their congressmen," observed Lord Bryce (*The American Commonwealth*, New York, 1888). Political pundits and humorists find in Congress's foibles ample material for ridicule. Serious scholarly and journalistic critics fault Congress for its disorder, inertia, and corruption. Congress gets only mediocre marks from the public at large. Public approval of the institution rises or falls with economic conditions, wars and crises, scandals, and waves of satisfaction or cynicism. Congressional approval also follows public approval of presidents. Although extensively reported by the media, Congress remains poorly understood and underappreciated by the average citizen.

In contrast, most individual senators and representatives are given high marks by their constituents. If voters think that elected officials as a class are rascals, they do not feel that way about their own elected officials. Nor do they show sustained eagerness to "throw the rascals out." Modern-day legislators tend to be handsomely rewarded at the polls, and to enjoy extended careers on Capitol Hill. This dichotomy is one more reminder of the "two Congresses" phenomenon: the dual character of the U.S. Congress as a collective maker of public policy and a collection of locally oriented politicians.

(See also LEGISLATURE; POLITICAL ACTION COMMITTEE; POLITICAL PARTIES AND PARTY COMPETITION; PRESIDENCY, U.S.; UNITED STATES.)

Richard F. Fenno, Jr., *Home Style: House Members in Their Districts* (Boston, 1978). Gary C. Jacobson, *The Politics of Congressional Elections*, 2d ed. (Boston, 1987). David W. Brady, *Critical Elections and Congressional Policy Making* (Stanford, Calif., 1988). Roger H. Davidson and Walter J. Oleszek, *Congress and Its Members*, 3d ed. (Washington, D.C., 1990). Steven S. Smith and Christopher J. Deering, *Committees in Congress*, 2d ed. (Washington, D.C., 1990). Roger H. Davidson, *The Postreform Congress* (New York, 1992).

ROGER H. DAVIDSON

CONSERVATISM. Like *liberalism* or *socialism* or *democracy, conservatism* is one of those blanket terms that has been stretched to cover very diverse political terrain over the past 150 years. Even in comparison with other broad labels of this sort, conservatism may seem a particularly elastic or evasive creed. In seeking to conserve existing traditions, after all, conservatism seems to commit itself to all the variety of traditions that have existed in different nations in successive eras.

In fact, the vagueness or ambiguity of conservatism as a political label seems, from the outset, to have been a large part of its appeal. Although the term was apparently coined by Chateaubriand in the 1820s (to describe the more moderate supporters of the restorationist monarchy in France), "conservative" only came into general use a few years later, when it was taken up by the leaders of the Tory Party in Britain. The Tories officially renamed themselves the Conservative Party following the enactment of the parliamentary Reform Act of 1832—toward which, for all its liberalizing implications, newly named Conservatives were anxious to appear accommodating. Thus one of the earliest English literary references to conservatism is the disparaging remark of the young Disraeli that a "conservative government" is an "organized hypocrisy," supporting Whig measures under the cover of traditional rhetoric.

Definitional Quandaries. Something that might be described as conservatism is surely as old as change. In the third century B.C.E. the Roman consul Cato the Elder—popularly known as Cato the Censor and from whom we derive the term *censorious*—was continually berating Romans for betraying their venerable ancestors. Aristotle had already derided this sort of ancestral piety in the previous century, remarking that "the primeval inhabitants" of the ancient city-states "may be supposed to have been no better than ordinary or even foolish people among ourselves." Yet on prudential grounds even Aristotle cautioned against the "evil" of "lightly changing the laws," because "the law has no power to command obedience except that of habit which can only be given by time. . . ."

But conservatism as an independent doctrine is generally regarded as a reaction to the French Revolution and to that atmosphere of rationalist and "enlightened" thought which gave the French Revolution its peculiar force and resonance. Some interpretations, notably that of Karl Mannheim in his pioneering work on the sociology of modern *ideologies, insist on the immediate connection between conservatism and the defense of aristocracy and the "precapitalist social attitudes" of the ancien régime. This interpretation certainly captures a central aspect of nineteenth-century politics in many European countries, whereby defenders of "tradition" (associated with aristocracy, monarchy, and an established church) denounced "liberal" ideals as subversive of honor, patriotism, and piety.

The problem with confining conservatism to the early opponents of the French Revolution is that it leaves the term with little relevance to the twentieth century—and little relevance to the United States in any period—when conservatives have made their peace with *capitalism and liberal *democracy. Critics of modern conservatives are often drawn to this localized, historical definition precisely as a way of questioning the relevance or integrity of conservatism in the late twentieth century. But the fact is that major parties and millions of voters around the world continue to embrace this term without imagining that it commits them to the politics of Metternich.

Nevertheless, periodic efforts to link modern conservative beliefs to a philosophic tradition beginning with Plato and Aristotle have not been very persuasive or influential. In fact, the most learned and penetrating "conservative" reflections on the history of political thought in the West, most notably *Natural Right and History* (Chicago, 1953) by Leo Strauss, have been at pains to emphasize the essential difference between all modern thought, even that conventionally labeled conservative, and the premises of medieval and classical thought.

A third interpretation of conservatism has tried to make a virtue of this confusion by insisting that conservatism is not really a substantive social or political outlook at all, but simply a posture of resistance to change. Samuel Huntington offered a classic expression of this interpretation ("Conservatism as an Ideology" *American Political Science Review* 51, no. 2, June 1957, p. 45), when he described "conservatism as essentially a situational ideology." In this view, conservatism is a response to fundamental challenges which seeks to defend existing institutions "qua institutions"; thus it necessarily refuses to defend any broader, substantive theory on which the institutions were founded, lest the existing institutions be judged deficient by these very theories.

The appeal of this interpretation is that it allows the same label to be fastened on the champions of extraordinarily diverse doctrines and causes. And some notion of this sort seems to account for the current convention of describing Communist apparatchiks, resisting the dismantling of totalitarian controls, as conservative. Yet a definition that links conservatism to the defense of existing institutions per se must exclude energetic *state builders like Bismarck and Cavour or such figures among the American founders as John Adams and Alexander Hamilton, all of whom plainly acted to forestall what they regarded as unacceptable democratic or populist alternatives. Similarly, a definition that restricts conservatism to the defense of the existing order must exclude such contemporary figures as Ronald *Reagan and Margaret *Thatcher, who conceived themselves to be reversing institutional trends and patterns of at least the previous two generations. Though opponents of such ambitious conservative programs have indeed tried to stigmatize them as radical or reactionary rather than properly conservative, this sort of name calling smacks more of partisan polemics than of serious analysis.

Perhaps the most useful approach is to acknowledge that conservatism has indeed been a situational or reactive ideology, aroused and defined by differing challenges in varying contexts. Conservatism has not simply reacted against violent or convulsive change, however, but against the general momentum of modern thought, which continually inspires ambitions to reconstruct social life, as science and technology expand the range of human powers. At bottom, conservatism has expressed a distrust of human willfulness and insisted that enlightenment and technology can never altogether transform the human condition or supersede the wisdom of the past. In this sense, conservatism has sought to conserve not so much particular institutions but the human virtues or the social benefits of older institutions and older patterns of social life. The jibe that conservatives are always defending the achievements of past generations of reformers is as old as the term *conservative* itself; the characteristic conservative aversion to systematic doctrines or causes (at least in non-Catholic countries) has indeed facilitated the conservative embrace of previously resisted doctrines or causes. But it is equally true that egalitarian or liberationist doctrines have continually outrun the expectations of their initial adherents. Disdaining eighteenth-century doctrines of constitutional liberty and equality, much opinion in the modern West now seriously looks to liberate human beings from the links between achievement and reward or from the differences between manliness and femininity. In broader terms, then, one can say that conservatism has as much continuity as the doctrines of liberalism or socialism or progress against which conservatives have contended in particular disputes over the past 150 years.

Three themes of conservative thought continue to have relevance in modern political disputes. First and perhaps most important is a resistance to utopian thinking. This stand is fortified by conservative insistence on the complexity of human nature and the concomitant fear that radically new political projects will unloose savage impulses or smother spiritual strivings. A second theme, which follows in a way from the first, is a respect for tradition and continuity as embodying more "latent wisdom" than any embracing rational plan of a single mind or a single generation; conservatives have also praised lived traditions for securing a fuller adherence among their followers than mere abstract or rational argument. Finally, conservatives have sought to defend particular institutions—a traditional conception of the family, a traditional sense of patriotic obligation, religious and moral traditions—which are difficult to defend in a liberal framework that reduces all obligations to choice. Conservatism has stood, most fundamentally, for the notion that the most valuable elements of life lose most of their force and significance when regarded merely as private or personal choices. Given that much in modern life runs contrary to this attitude, conservatives seem to have been losing big battles since the term came into vogue. But the perpetuation of the term—and the wreckage of many social reform schemes along the way—suggests that conservatism responds to enduring human concerns.

Conservatism in Party Politics. Contemporary accounts of conservative party politics often seek to distinguish economic conservatism from social conservatism as appealing to different constituencies and often implying different policies. Thus in the late 1960s the American sociologist Seymour Martin Lipset ("Class, Politics and Religion in Modern Society: The Dilemma of the Conservatives," in *Revolution and Counter-Revolution: Change and Persistence in Social Structure*, New Brunswick, N.J., 1988), stressing the persistence of voting by (economic) *class in almost all Western democracies,

concluded that "conservative parties must seek to reduce the saliency of class voting by appealing to lower classes on non-economic issues."

The British Conservative Party was indeed able to survive extensions of the franchise in the nineteenth century and appeal to a significant fraction of non-affluent voters as the defender of the established church, of traditional institutions like the monarchy, and of national and imperial prestige. But in historical terms, as Lipset and others have emphasized, the British experience is more the exception than the rule. In most Western countries, more traumatic political evolution in the nineteenth century generated sharp cleavages in the potential constituencies of social conservatism. In much of Catholic Europe, bitter divisions between clerical and anticlerical opinion left conservative religious voters hostile to existing regimes, most notably in France and Italy after 1870, yet their anticlerical opponents were often quite preoccupied with maintaining "bourgeois respectability" and in many ways quite socially conservative.

Elsewhere, regional or ethnic divisions divided the potential constituencies of social conservative appeals in the nineteenth century. The empires of central and eastern Europe were wracked by ethnic tensions, which often carried national minorities to the left. At the same time, the Irish in Britain, the French in Canada, and white southerners in the United States all gravitated toward the more liberal parties, in spite of being more socially conservative in their own regions than the dominant conservative parties at the national level.

In the twentieth century, however, general liberalizing trends—and the impact of horrors in Europe beyond anything experienced in the French Revolution—have worked to soften many old divisions. In France, de *Gaulle's Fifth Republic finally rallied clerical and republican conservatives under common conservative banners; in Italy, a revived, somewhat less clerically dominated and much more nationally minded Christian Democratic Party emerged as the dominant party in postwar politics; the Christian Democratic Party in the Federal Republic of Germany, or FRG (attracting a broad Protestant constituency), has done still better in bridging old social divisions. In the United States, southern whites began voting in large numbers for Republicans in the 1960s, as the Democratic Party embraced a more systematically liberal program and as the suppression of racial segregation by the national government eliminated one of the central aspects of southern regional exceptionalism. Similarly, whereas the Republican Party had been closely identified with "heartland" Yankee Protestantism in the past, it was increasingly successful, from the 1960s onward, in attracting the assimilated descendants of Catholic immigrants in the eastern cities. Paradoxically, such broader liberalizing trends in social life, by weakening old particularist commitments, have made it easier in most countries for social conservatives to come together in party politics.

Economic conservatism, on the other hand, even if frequently seen as a major force in conservative coalitions, is not a concept of any clear meaning in historical terms, unless it is simply identified with resistance to forcible redistribution of property. Otherwise, a remarkable variety of economic policies have historically been associated with conservative governments. Even in the nineteenth century, conservative governments frequently favored protective tariffs and state subsidies to promote the growth of strategic industries. Conservative governments could also favor paternalist schemes of protection for workers in order to promote social harmony and national unity. Bismarck pioneered both sorts of measures in imperial Germany in the 1880s. Parties more suspicious of state intervention in the economy thus continued to call themselves liberal in many countries—though self-described liberals also came to endorse many schemes of state intervention in the twentieth century.

In the first three decades after World War II, socially conservative parties in most European countries, as well as in North America, embraced a large degree of governmental involvement in stimulating production and ensuring social welfare—in what has been called a "social democratic consensus." Since the mid-1970s, however, there has been a general shift among conservative parties toward favoring a retrenchment of governmental involvement in the economy. The shift was stimulated by the persistence of inflation amid slow growth in the 1970s; conservatives decried inflation as the product of excessive demands on government and slow growth as stemming from the diversion of private capital into unproductive government expenditures. What seems most salient in the conservative revolt against the social democratic consensus is the greater concern with growth than with equality—both because growth appealed to national pride and to hopes of dissipating class conflict in the long run.

The swing of conservative opinion away from government involvement in the economy seems to have been strongest—and most contentious—in Britain and the United States. But the trend toward renewed respect for the market has been evident in many countries. In the FRG, for example, the Christian Democrats, who in the immediate postwar decades had stressed their own commitment to a *social market economy, became much more openly identified with protecting the scope of maneuver for business. In the 1976 federal elections, the Christian Social Union of Bavaria, the most socially conservative segment of *Christian Democracy in the FRG, successfully persuaded its coalition partners to adopt the campaign slogan *Freedom or Socialism?*, a slogan endorsed by most other conservative parties in Western Europe at an international conference that year.

It is certainly possible to favor a severely limited state in economic matters and an equally limited role for the state in all other matters as well. The most extreme libertarians—who proudly style themselves "anarcho-capitalists"—flaunt their consistent individualism by opposing state power even to defend the nation against military aggression from abroad and championing individual freedom even when it abuses the most helpless members of society. Murray Rothbard, a leading libertarian theoretician, thus has argued that the libertarian ideal is not only unrestricted access to abortion but also the right to sell children to the highest bidder. But in fact this outlook is rare outside the United States and not of much importance even in the United States.

Strong currents of opinion in many Western countries have been hostile to military preparedness and to traditional moral norms. Ronald Inglehart popularized the notion that these currents, which gathered considerable momentum in the 1970s and 1980s, were defined by a "postbourgeois" ethos emphasizing personal "self-actualization" rather than material improvement. But as Inglehart's own studies suggest, adherents of the postbourgeois ethos almost always gravitate to the left in economic policy as well—as the evolution of the *Green Party in the FRG illustrates.

Social Conservatism and Economic Liberalism. For all its evident tensions, the marriage of classical liberal economics with social conservatism is far from recent. The conservative English political philosopher Edmund Burke was filled with praise for Adam Smith's *Wealth of Nations*, and Smith declared that Burke was the one person in England who thought as he did on economic questions. In the mid-nineteenth century, not only were British Conservatives won over to free trade, but many other conservative parties sought alliances with economic liberals (in the classical sense). In some countries, parties previously calling themselves liberal and conservative were merged as "national" parties, and in some cases even gave themselves new names retaining both terms (as did the Liberal-Conservative Party in the German state of Hesse in the 1860s and the Liberal-Conservative Party of Canada in the same period, which campaigned in the early twentieth century as the National Liberal and Conservative Party). By the late nineteenth century, many would-be conservatives were drawn to liberal doctrines concerning limitations on state power as the best means of forestalling radical or socialist attacks on churches, schools, and private wealth.

The renewal of this convergence in the past twenty years owes much to the pressures of recent history, however. In the first place, much conservative opinion has been drawn to market economics as a means of enforcing an ethos of personal responsibility and promoting other "Victorian" virtues. Protests against "welfare cheats" and "social permissiveness" were a major theme of Reaganite rhetoric, and similar denunciations of "permissiveness" and "self-indulgence" figured centrally in that of Margaret Thatcher. The 1970s witnessed dramatic increases in drug addiction and births out of wedlock, along with increases in crime and vandalism in many Western countries. Conservatives often blamed these trends on a decline in the ethic of responsibility, which they traced in turn to the ethos—and in some cases to the immediate perverse incentives—of social welfare policies that treated poverty and failure as a social responsibility rather than a challenge to individual effort. At the same time, conservatives came to admire the initiative and energy of entrepreneurs in a world that seemed increasingly bland and petty. Few went so far as George Gilder, whose 1980 best-seller *Wealth and Poverty* (New York, 1981) argued that the entrepreneurial spirit rested on "faith" and the spirit of giving. But even the austere British conservative Roger Scruton decried the "feeling that would people the world with invalids, in order to lavish upon it the luxury of 'social justice' " (*The Meaning of Conservatism,* London, 1981).

A second point of convergence derived from the traditional conservative disdain for the politics of mass mobilization. This attitude goes deeper than the fear of demagoguery—though that has certainly been a continuing strain in conservative thought. Beyond that, conservative thought has always tended to celebrate private life. Lord Hailsham insisted in his 1947 manifesto *The Case for Conservatism* (London, 1947) that "[t]he man who puts politics first is not fit to be called a civilized human being, let alone a Christian." Michael Oakeshott argued a few years later that a "disposition to be conservative would seem to be preeminently appropriate to men who have something to do and something to think about on their own account . . . to people whose passions do not need to be inflamed, whose desires do not need to be provoked and whose dreams of a better world need no prompting" ("On Being Conservative," in *Rationalism in Politics and Other Essays,* London, 1962).

Something of this disdain for politics is reflected in the characteristic organizational patterns of conservative parties. Whereas parties of the *Left in Europe have almost always sought to organize a mass base, conservative parties have generally had a much smaller membership and much less intraparty democracy. They have presented themselves as potential instruments of government, rather than ongoing movements. At the same time, conservatives have worried about the excesses of interest group politics and longed for a state somewhat removed from the clamor of factions. This outlook has a long tradition in the more statist countries of Western Europe, well illustrated by de Gaulle's disdain for parliamentary wrangling. Since the 1970s, however, this outlook has increasingly been linked to a perception that a state committed to so many areas of

economic subsidy or protection could not possibly maintain sufficient distance from organized interests to uphold its own separate authority. Thus Thatcher's program of denationalization and retrenchment appealed to many Tories as a way of strengthening the authority of the state in other areas. In a somewhat similar vein, Reagan Republicans continually urged constitutional amendments to limit spending or deficit financing—while continually complaining about congressional "micromanagement" of government programs through restrictions or directives in appropriations bills.

In more theoretical terms, there is also an evident affinity between liberal respect for market processes, responding to the diverse insights, circumstances, and concerns of vast numbers of individuals, and the conservative regard for traditions that embody the accumulated insights of generations. Both appeal to the wisdom of unplanned outcomes, both respect the discipline of constraints that are not dependent on any single directing will. Michael Oakeshott's celebrated conservative attack on "rationalism in politics" thus shares much common ground with F. A. Hayek's praise of unplanned, market "evolution"—even though Oakeshott, characteristically, questioned Hayek's reduction of his argument to a "doctrine" ("a plan to resist all planning") while Hayek subsequently complained that conservatives were too readily carried along by prevailing trends and insufficiently committed to the principles of liberal order.

Even in practical politics, evident differences remain between market enthusiasts and social conservatives. In Europe, perhaps particularly in Britain, conservatives have worried about the threat to national sovereignty and national traditions from European integration. Other conservatives broke with market enthusiasts in protesting the threat to national character posed by open labor markets and extensive immigration. Still others have worried about threats to family life from commercial pandering to lust and from the difficulties of accommodating women in the work force—where conservatives have been much less inclined to trust to the beneficent workings of the free market.

Special Cases and General Conclusions. The United States presents a special case with regard to conservatism. In many ways an extremely individualist country, it has a highly fragmented political system, aggravated in some areas by racial conflicts. Liberal policies—the suppression of religious symbols in public schools, the legalization of abortion, the imposition of racial integration, reform of the criminal justice system—were consequently pursued to a large extent through the courts, which often imposed more extreme policies than political bargaining would ever have settled upon. A revitalized movement of social conservatism in the 1970s was—in a way characteristic of the United States, but uncharacteristic of conservative politics generally—spurred by grass-roots organizations rather than political parties. Thus a proposed Equal Rights Amendment to the Constitution, supposed to guarantee equal treatment for women, was launched with very broad bipartisan support in the mid-1970s and fought to a standstill by an opposition group organized by Phyllis Schlafly, until then a little-known conservative activist based in Alton, Illinois. In more conservative Canada, a similar provision was included in the new Constitution in 1982, with almost no organized opposition.

Similarly, the movement toward tax cutting, which came to be identified with the Reagan administration in the 1980s, actually began with state-level referenda which were organized at the grass roots in the late 1970s. Protests against abortion had continued to draw larger crowds in the past decade than any other cause. The "right-to-life" movement, which established important new links between Catholic and Protestant strands of social conservatism, seems to have had a significant influence on appointments to the U.S. *Supreme Court, through which it is likely to have a considerable impact on constitutional law in the 1990s. This sort of populist conservatism has not always been admired by European conservatives nor indeed by an older generation of conservatives in the United States. But it may be the natural counterpart to a liberal-individualist current in American social policy that is more ideological in some ways than in any European country.

One might place Japan at the other extreme. Its Liberal-Democratic Party (formed in 1954 by the merger of the two older parties) has stressed business growth and the preservation of national traditions, and on both counts is widely regarded as a very conservative party. For most of the postwar period, this party (or its predecessors in coalition) has retained such broad electoral hegemony that it has not had to engage in significant political mobilization. Japan's economic performance has been widely admired in the West—and, characteristically, has often been attributed by left-liberals to governmental programs to promote or coordinate business and attributed by social conservatives to social discipline and cohesion. But a noticeable reluctance to tout Japan as any sort of conservative model suggests that conservatives in most Western countries have valued a degree of spiritual energy and diversity which they regard as lacking in Japan.

In Latin America there have been parties calling themselves conservative since the early nineteenth century. As in Catholic Europe, however, these parties were so strongly identified with traditional landed elites and with the immediate, proprietary concerns of the *Roman Catholic church that they were ill equipped to cope with liberalizing trends, even in the nineteenth century. In recent decades, several Latin countries have seen the growth of Christian Democratic parties, which have generally been far more committed than their European counterparts to activist programs of state intervention in economic development. Still more recently, however, there has been a trend toward withdrawal of state subsidies and protectionist schemes, and parties urging this path, while styling themselves "liberal" or "national" rather than "conservative," have often been at pains to establish their respectability with Catholic leaders.

Western conservatives have generally seen little to admire in the politics of new nations in the Third World, dominated by modern utopian rhetoric and modern instruments of tyranny. The success of market-oriented authoritarian regimes in several Asian countries, however, is often taken as a sign of hope that economic growth can eventually foster a degree of stability that will allow for a more democratic future. In the meantime, Western conservatives have tended to be a good deal more patient with the undemocratic character of such regimes than have their opponents on the left. At the same time, threats to conservative modernizing regimes from Islamic fundamentalism may be a reminder of how much the success of conservatism in the West has depended on establishing a certain distance between politics (even conservative politics) and premodern orthodoxies.

It has often been argued that in modern Western countries, the continuing strength of conservative parties or political tendencies reflects the success of liberal or social-welfare measures in securing broad popular acceptance of the existing order. But the converse may be equally true and equally important—that a broader framework of conservative constraints has helped to make liberalizing measures socially tolerable. Wealth and freedom, if they often induce broad contentedness, can as well include hubristic political ambition and furious impatience with remaining inequalities and constraints. So long as this is so, some form of conservative politics is likely to remain of considerable importance in the modern world.

(See also LIBERTARIANISM; MODERNITY; NEW RIGHT; POLITICAL ECONOMY; POLITICAL PARTIES AND PARTY COMPETITION; POPULISM; RELIGION AND POLITICS; REPRODUCTIVE RIGHTS; RIGHT; WELFARE STATES.)

JEREMY A. RABKIN

CONSOCIATIONAL DEMOCRACY. Found in several countries that are deeply divided into distinct religious, ethnic, racial, or regional segments, the two principal and complementary characteristics of consociational *democracy are grand coalition and segmental autonomy: shared decision making by representatives of all significant segments with regard to matters of common concern and autonomous decision making by and for each separate segment on all other issues. Two additional characteristics are proportionality in political representation, civil service appointments, and the allocation of public funds, and the minority veto for the protection of vital minority interests. A possible variant of strict proportionality is deliberate minority over-representation. In all four respects, consociational democracy contrasts sharply with majority-rule democracy.

The first political theorist to use the term *consociation* was the early federalist thinker Johannes Althusius in his *Politica Methodice Digesta* (1603). It was revived by David E. Apter (*The Political Kingdom in Uganda*, Princeton, N.J., 1961) who, like Althusius, used it mainly to refer to a territorial-federal form of decentralized decision making. The first modern scholar to use the concept in the more specific sense given above—although he did not use the actual term—was the economist Sir Arthur Lewis (*Politics in West Africa*, London, 1965). Lewis also presented the first explicit argument that for deeply divided societies the consociational form of democracy is both more democratic and likely to be more effective than majority rule. From the late 1960s on, consociational theory has been developed and applied further by political scientists, sociologists, and historians like Hans Daalder, Edward Dew, Robert H. Dix, Theodor Hanf, Luc Huyse, Gerhard Lehmbruch, Arend Lijphart, Val R. Lorwin, Kenneth D. McRae, Eric A. Nordlinger, G. Bingham Powell, Jr., F. van Zyl Slabbert, Jürg Steiner, and David Welsh.

Examples of consociational democracy can be found all over the world. In Europe, it has established a very successful record: in Switzerland since 1943; in Belgium after World War I and, with even better results, from 1970 on; in Austria from 1945 to 1966; in the Netherlands from 1917 to about 1967; and in Luxembourg during the same period of about half a century. Where, as in the last three cases, consociational democracy has declined or ended, the reason has not been that it failed but that it worked so well that it was no longer needed. On the other hand, the British government's attempts to introduce consociational democracy in Northern Ireland since 1972 have been unsuccessful.

In Africa, Asia, and Latin America, the record is mixed. Only Colombia (1958–1974) and Malaysia (from 1955 on) can be counted as largely successful examples. In Cyprus, the consociational experiment adopted upon independence in 1960 ended in civil war in 1963. The other cases are more ambiguous. Lebanon's consociational democracy collapsed in brutal civil strife in 1975, but it had worked remarkably well for almost a third of a century (1943–1975); moreover, the civil war was caused more by external forces than by weaknesses in the internal consociational system. Nigeria's democracy degenerated into *military rule in 1966, but its government was only partly consociational. Aruba's secession marked the end of consociationalism in the Netherlands Antilles (1950–1985), but secession was achieved by an entirely peaceful, negotiated process.

Military rule came to Uruguay in 1973 and to Suriname in 1980, but by then the system of each—semi-consociational in Uruguay (1952–1967) and consociational in Suriname (1958–1973)—had already shifted to largely majoritarian patterns; hence in each case the failure was one of majority rule rather than consociationalism.

Pure consociationalism and pure majoritarianism are ideal types; actual political systems can be located along a range between the pure forms. Examples of countries in approximately the middle of the range, in addition to the Nigerian and Uruguayan cases mentioned above, are Canada and Israel. Consociational practices can also be found in nondemocratic and predemocratic regimes, such as the United Province of Canada from 1840 to 1867 and Belgium after independence in 1830.

The comparative analysis of these cases has led to the formulation of several factors that are conducive to the establishment and maintenance of consociational democracy. The two most important of these are the absence of a majority segment and the absence of large socioeconomic inequalities. Others are segments of approximately equal size, a small population, foreign threats, countrywide loyalties that counteract segmental loyalties, and preexisting traditions of consensus.

Consociational democracy has made two important contributions to democratic theory. First, it challenges the traditional narrow equation of democracy with majority rule. Second, it extends the applicability of democracy to societies that were traditionally regarded as ill suited for democratic government.

Gerhard Lehmbruch, *Proporzdemokratie: Politisches System and Politische Kultur in der Schweiz und in Österreich* (Tübingen, 1986). Arend Lijphart, *Democracy in Plural Societies: A Comparative Exploration* (New Haven, Conn., 1977).

AREND LIJPHART

CONSTITUTION. The term *constitution* refers both to the institutions, practices, and principles that define and structure a system of government and to the written document that establishes or articulates such a system. Every *state has a constitution in the first sense and, since World War II, virtually every state—Britain, New Zealand, and Israel are among the exceptions—has a written constitution as well.

Constitutionalism denotes not merely the existence of either a written or an unwritten constitution, but a commitment to limited government. Some scholars argue that constitutions inherently limit government—either by regularizing the governmental process and thus prohibiting capricious action or by establishing policies or procedures that cannot be modified by ordinary legislative action. Others see limitation as the result of specific constitutional provisions, such as a bill of rights or the *separation of powers.

Both the ambiguity in the term *constitution* and the fact that not every nation with a constitution is committed to constitutionalism have fostered an academic discourse in which some constitutional documents are labeled nominal, sham, fictive, or facade constitutions. Within this rhetoric, a constitution is called nominal when its text accurately describes, but does not limit, governmental behavior. In other words, a nominal constitution is a written constitution that faithfully articulates the nation's unwritten constitution but does not subscribe to the principles of constitutionalism. A sham, fictive, or facade constitution, on the other hand, is a text whose provisions do not correspond to actual governmental practice. Such labeling assumes that a government publicly professes its commitment to constitutionalism in a written constitution in order to deflect attention from the arbitrary exercises of power that characterize the nation's unwritten constitution.

The exclusive focus on constitutions as a means of limiting governmental power is somewhat deceptive. Historically, constitutions have been made to empower states rather than to limit them. The first written constitutions were made during the American and French *revolutions. These constitutions restructured governmental institutions, articulated political principles, and, in the case of the United States, proclaimed independence from colonial rule. In both France and the United States, written constitutions attempted to establish governments based on popular consent and respect for individual *rights.

These eighteenth-century French and American constitutions came to define the genre as a whole. Constitution making was a recurrent feature of both nationalist and bourgeois revolutions in the nineteenth century. Coercion, as well as intellectual influence, spread the practice of writing constitutions. After World War II, colonial and occupying powers sometimes refused to relinquish sovereignty to indigenous peoples until "acceptable" constitutions were adopted. Now, a written constitution has become almost a prerequisite to international recognition for new nations.

A constitution constitutes a polity in a variety of ways. First, a constitution marks the existence of a polity that claims its own sphere of authority. This authority may be defined in terms of a particular region, particular people, and/or particular issues. Such authority need not be national. In federal systems, for example, each subnational government may have its own constitution.

Secondly, a constitution not only asserts that there *is* a polity, it also describes how that polity will be governed. Constitutions typically enumerate the institutions that comprise the state. Because institutional design affects both the distribution of political power and the making of governmental policy, the structure of the state is often hotly contested in debates over making or amending a constitution.

Finally, a constitution provides a vocabulary for politics. Both the identities one can claim and the claims one can make in the political sphere are, at least in part, constitutionally constructed. By privileging one set of identities over another, a constitution shapes political discourse. For example, the U.S. Constitution encourages poor people of color to frame their grievances in terms of race rather than class because it restricts governmental discrimination based on race while allowing discrimination based on wealth. Similarly, even revolutionary politics may be articulated in terms of constitutional categories. Czechoslovakia's *Charter 77 movement chose to fight political repression by publicizing the state's violation of constitutional provisions. Members of the movement did not believe that the best form of government for Czechoslovakia would be one that implemented the guarantees of the existing constitution. But they knew that couching their criticisms in constitutional terms would give the movement the *legitimacy (both at home and abroad) that it would have lacked if it had attempted to challenge the constitutive principles of the regime more directly.

Constitutions are attempts to construct politics, both institutionally and rhetorically. To understand the significance of constitutions in *comparative politics, then, we have to look beyond the question of whether constitutions limit governmental power and investigate the variety of ways in which constitutions shape both the state and *political culture.

(See also Decolonization; Federalism.)

Giovanni Sartori, "Constitutionalism: A Preliminary Discussion" *American Political Science Review* 56 (1962): 853–864. Carl J. Friedrich, "Constitutions and Constitutionalism" *International Encyclopedia of the Social Sciences* (New York, 1968). J. Roland Pennock and John W. Chapman, *Constitutionalism, Nomos XX* (New York, 1979). Vernon Bogdanor, *Constitutions in Democratic Politics* (Aldershot, U.K., 1988). Jon Elster and Rune Slagstad, *Constitutionalism and Democracy* (Cambridge, U.K., 1988).

Suzette Hemberger

CONSTITUTIONAL MONARCHY. *Monarchy —literally "rule by one"—denotes a system of government in which the head of state ascends to his or her position by hereditary succession. (Examples have been recorded of elective monarchies, but no such arrangement has survived.) On accession the monarch may take any of a number of titles— usually that of king or queen, but in some cases emperor, prince, emir, or sultan. The distinction is often made between absolute and constitutional monarchies. Absolute monarchy is one in which the head of state is not constrained by provisions of the *constitution; constitutional monarchy is one in which the head of state is so constrained.

The basis of authority of absolute monarchies was essentially religious, and the nineteenth and early twentieth centuries witnessed the disappearance of most such monarchies as their claims to rule were variously contested. They were replaced by republican forms of government or, less commonly, by constitutional monarchies. In 1987, just under fifty countries were ruled by monarchs, and of these all but seven were constitutional monarchies. Seventeen actually shared the same head of state—Queen Elizabeth II, head of state of the United Kingdom and of sixteen Commonwealth countries and British colonies. The largest single concentration of constitutional monarchies (ten) was in Western Europe. The characteristic feature of such monarchies is that policy-making resides with the elected government, the monarch fulfilling largely ceremonial and symbolic duties. Occasionally, though, the role of the monarch may be pivotal—for example, in breaking a constitutional deadlock or in attempting—either successfully, as in the case of King Juan Carlos I of Spain in 1981, or unsuccessfully, as in that of King Constantine II of Greece in 1967—to prevent a military *coup.

Frank Hardie, *The Political Influence of the British Monarchy* (London, 1970).

PHILIP NORTON

CONTAINMENT. U.S. diplomat George F. *Kennan coined the term *containment* to describe the appropriate American strategy to counter the threat of Soviet expansionism in the aftermath of *World War II and the advent of the *Cold War. In February 1946, Kennan, then the relatively obscure chargé d'affaires in the Moscow embassy, was asked by the State Department for an "interpretive analysis" of Soviet intentions. His "long telegram" in response was the first comprehensive American report on the evolving state of postwar relations between the *United States and the *Soviet Union. Kennan's assessment of Soviet intentions arrived in Washington at a moment when Soviet pressures on Iran and Turkey were being viewed as an immediate threat to the global *balance of power. In recognition of his incisive cables from Moscow, Kennan was brought to Washington and asked to assume the directorship of the State Department's newly founded Policy Planning Staff. Kennan's writings provided an important part of the intellectual context within which the March 1947 *Truman Doctrine (authorizing emergency military and economic assistance to Greece and Turkey) was formulated.

The initial public expression of Kennan's containment doctrine came in the July 1947 issue of *Foreign Affairs* in an article, published anonymously, on "The Sources of Soviet Conduct." In the "X" article, Kennan observed that "the political personality" of Soviet power under *Stalin was "the product of ideology and circumstances." Whereas Marxist *ideology postulated continuous struggle with the capitalist world, Soviet history provided a backdrop of civil war, foreign intervention, and internal dictatorship. Kennan advocated the adoption of a "long-term, patient but firm and vigilant" policy of "containment" to thwart Soviet expansionist tendencies. This would entail "the adroit and vigilant application of counter-force at a series of constantly shifting geographical and political points corresponding to the shifts and maneuvers of Soviet policy. . . ." Kennan believed that the implementation of a containment policy would remain necessary until such time that the inherent contradictions of the Soviet Union's totalitarian system led to significant, if not profound, internal changes and a consequent moderation in Soviet external behavior.

Domestic critics of Kennan's relatively ambiguous counterforce strategy spanned the U.S. political spectrum. The most detailed and sustained critique of the "X" article came from the journalist Walter Lippmann, who argued that containment was a "strategic monstrosity" because its essentially reactive nature would leave the United States responding indefinitely to probes whose timing and location would be determined by the Kremlin. In the public mind, there was a clear link between the "X" article and the Truman Doctrine. Hailed as a grand new formula for *American foreign policy, it was perceived as the intellectual justification for the Truman Doctrine. This was denied by Kennan, who rejected the undifferentiated globalism suggested by the rhetoric of the Truman Doctrine. In his *Memoirs*, Kennan wrote that what he meant by "the containment of Soviet power was not the containment by military means of a military threat, but the political containment of a political threat."

The Berlin blockade, the Soviet Union's detonation of an atomic bomb and the Chinese Communists' seizure of power in 1948–1949 reinforced the image of global confrontation and provided added impetus to the militarization of containment. A high-level policy review commissioned by the Truman administration in response to these events recommended the modernization and expansion of U.S. military capabilities. Following the outbreak of the *Korean War in June 1950, this document—NSC-68—provided a blueprint for the buildup of U.S. forces. The Korean conflict, which confirmed Kennan's prediction that the Soviet Union might use proxy forces for probes on the Eurasian periphery, marked the geographical extension of containment from Europe to Asia and beyond. This process received further impetus during the *Eisenhower administration with the creation of a global *alliance system to complement the *North Atlantic Treaty Organization (NATO), the first peacetime alliance entered into by the United States.

The Eisenhower administration's desire to conduct a global containment strategy at lower economic cost led to a renewed emphasis on the U.S. nuclear deterrent and increased reliance on allies to provide conventional forces for local defense. In a January 1954 speech, Secretary of State John Foster Dulles advocated the threatened use of the United States' "massive retaliatory power" to deter Soviet expansionism. The press immediately seized upon the slogan of "massive retaliation" and portrayed it as a formula for turning every border skirmish into a nuclear showdown. Prominent academic specialists, noting that this asymmetrical response to Soviet-backed aggression lacked credibility, argued for the continuing need for limited war capabilities. The Eisenhower administration maintained that its "New Look" strategy was a comprehensive approach in which *nuclear weapons, both strategic and tactical, were a complement to other policy instruments (such as alliances, covert operations, and negotiation).

President John *Kennedy, who assumed office in 1961 at a time when the *Third World was rapidly becoming the principal arena of *superpower competition, favored decreased reliance on nuclear weapons for local defense. The expansion of conventional forces was a central component of his administration's move to a strategy of "flexible response" under which the United States sought to meet the Soviet challenge across the entire spectrum of threat from guerrilla insurgency to thermonuclear war. The Kennedy administration placed greater emphasis on nonmilitary dimensions of containment (e.g., the use of economic assistance to win "hearts and minds" in the developing world), but did little, contrary to Kennan's long-standing recommendation, to exploit fissures within the Communist bloc (e.g., the Sino-Soviet rift).

The globalization of U.S. containment policy reached its zenith with the large-scale deployment of U.S. ground forces to Vietnam following the 1965 Gulf of Tonkin incident. This move derived from a worldview that drew no distinction between vital and peripheral interests. The *Johnson administration steadfastly contended that Vietnam was a symbol of U.S. resolve and that the failure to meet the Communist challenge there would undermine the credibility of American commitments elsewhere. Vietnam became a key test case of "flexible response." This strategy, which emphasized gradual escalation and the calibrated application of U.S. military power, was intended to demonstrate to the North Vietnamese that there was no alternative to a negotiated settlement. U.S. policymakers, however, underestimated the determination of an adversary who saw itself engaged not in limited, but total *war.

The *Nixon administration came to power in 1969 amid widespread public calls for a major retrenchment of U.S. overseas commitments as a consequence of the Vietnam debacle. Operating within this domestic context, President Richard Nixon and National Security Adviser Henry *Kissinger developed an approach to containment whose main element was a policy of *détente toward the Soviet Union. At the heart of this *strategy was the concept of "linkage" under which the United States sought to create a system of incentives and penalties to foster more cooperative Soviet behavior (e.g., assistance in the resolution of the *Vietnam War). The Soviets rejected the U.S. preference for linkage in favor of a compartmentalized approach in which *arms control, regional conflicts, and economic relations were considered as discrete issues. During the late 1970s, Soviet interventionist policies in the Third World, culminating in the 1979 invasion of Afghanistan, undermined U.S. public support for détente and led to the *Reagan administration's return to a more militarized version of containment following the 1980 presidential election. The Reagan strategy featured a major rearmament program (including the Strategic Defense Initiative, or SDI) and support for anti-Communist insurgents in the Third World (e.g., the Afghan mujahidin).

In the mid-1980s, Soviet President Mikhail *Gorbachev, faced with intractable economic and social problems at home and a hostile external environment, initiated a sweeping internal reform program (i.e, *perestroika). These profound domestic changes were accompanied by correspondingly dramatic changes in Soviet external behavior (e.g., the 1988 decision to withdraw from Afghanistan and acquiescence to the collapse of Communist regimes in Eastern and Central Europe in 1989). In April 1989 testimony before the Senate Foreign Relations Committee, George Kennan, who had argued in his "X" article that profound Soviet domestic change (specifically the demise of a world-revolutionary ideology) would obviate the need for containment, stated that the Soviet Union "should now be regarded essentially as another great power, like other great powers. . . ."

(See also DETERRENCE; SOVIET FOREIGN POLICY.)

"X" [George F. Kennan], "The Sources of Soviet Conduct" *Foreign Affairs* 25 (July 1947): 566–582. Adam B. Ulam, *The Rivals: America and Russia since World War II* (London, 1973). John Lewis Gaddis, *Strategies of Containment: A Critical Appraisal of Postwar American National Security Policy* (New York, 1982).

ROBERT S. LITWAK

CONTRAS. From 1980 until their disbanding in early 1990, Nicaraguan counterrevolutionaries, or contras, waged a military and, to a lesser extent, political struggle against the *Sandinista government that had taken power in *Nicaragua in July 1979. Drawn from remnants of the defeated Nicaraguan National Guard of President Anastasio Somoza, the contras grew from a handful of exiles operating out of Honduras and Miami in 1980 to a force of approximately 15,000 combatants by the end of the decade. The contras, by then operating under the name of the Resistencia Nicaragüense, were disbanded in the context of a 1987 Central American peace plan and 1990 presidential elections in Nicaragua.

U.S. support for the contras began in mid-1981, when the *Central Intelligence Agency (CIA) enlisted Argentine intelligence officers to begin training ex-National Guardsmen based largely in Honduras. CIA involvement expanded in late 1981, following presidential authorization of covert operations against the Sandinista government. Such operations were described as necessary to halt Sandinista support for leftist rebels in neighboring El Salvador, but the rebels themselves spoke of their desire to overthrow the Sandinista government, an objective apparently shared by some U.S. officials. Dubious of the goals of the contra program, the U.S. *Congress provided on-again, off-again funding for the rebels, cutting off aid in late 1984 and renewing full military support in 1986. Congress restricted aid once again when a 1987 Central American peace plan called for an end to external support for regional insurgencies and when it was revealed in late 1986 that funds from the U.S. sale of arms to Iran had been illegally diverted to the contras.

The contras were divided into several groups with diverse political orientations. The most important of the groups were the Fuerza Democrática Nicaragüense (FDN), founded in mid-1981; the Alianza Revolucionaria Democrática (ARDE), founded in late 1982 by a Sandinista guerrilla hero; and MIS-URA (an acronym formed from the names of three indigenous tribes: Miskito, Sumo, Rama), one of two factions of Miskito Indian rebels residing on Nicaragua's Atlantic coast. The FDN was the largest and most militarily significant of the groups, and the one most associated with former National Guardsmen, who constituted the FDN's high command. Enrique Bermúdez, the top FDN military commander, was a senior National Guard officer under Somoza.

In the early years of the war, the contras staged brutal attacks against civilians inside Nicaragua, executing, torturing, and kidnapping suspected Sandinista sympathizers. Reforming and democratizing the contra movement and purging ex-National Guardsmen from its military leadership were major goals of civilian members of a rebel political umbrella organization known as Unidad Nicaragüense Opositora (UNO), formed in 1985. By then, the contra army consisted largely of peasants disaffected with Sandinista rule. Midlevel field commanders and contra rank and file also waged internal struggles to purge the movement of corrupt and brutal leaders. The contras underwent four major reorganizations between 1982 and 1987 before younger officers succeeded in pushing Bermúdez aside in late 1988.

Following presidential elections in February 1990 in which the Sandinistas were defeated, the contras demobilized under the auspices of the UN. They were promised land and other forms of economic assistance, and several prominent field commanders accepted posts in the new government. Bermúdez

was assassinated in Managua in early 1991. Later in the year, groups of rearmed rebels, or recontras, took to the hills, primarily demanding an end to Sandinista dominance of the military and police.

(See also GUERRILLA WARFARE; NICARAGUAN REVOLUTION; U.S.–LATIN AMERICAN RELATIONS.)

Sam Dillon, *Commandos: The CIA and Nicaragua's Contra Rebels* (New York, 1991).

CYNTHIA J. ARNSON

CONVERGENCE THESIS. The notion of a convergence across societies stems originally from Karl *Marx. Marx contended that, driven by underlying economic forces, capitalist societies follow a single path of *development that culminates in *communism. In the late 1950s and 1960s an intense debate arose regarding the long-term convergence, on the one hand, of U.S. *capitalism and Soviet communism and, on the other hand, of all industrializing societies. Whereas economists dominated the former debate, the voices of sociologists held sway in the latter discussion. Some participants predicted a new, hybrid society and an "end of *ideology."

Economic historians such as W. W. Rostow (*The Stages of Economic Growth,* Cambridge, Mass., 1960) and John Kenneth Galbraith (*The New Industrial State,* New York, 1964) and economists such as Simon Kuznets (*Economic Growth and Structure,* New York, 1965) and Jan Tinbergen ("Do Communist and Free Economies Show a Converging Pattern?" *Soviet Studies,* vol. 12, April 1961, pp. 333–341) argued that, irrespective of political ideologies, economic growth constitutes a uniform process and that industrial economies evolve through several common stages. Moreover, a number of common features characterize these economies: the demand to utilize technology efficiently; the increasing specialization of tasks; the necessity for a highly skilled and educated labor force; an increasing percentage of the labor force in nonagricultural occupations; a growing significance of material incentives; an expansion of ever more complex organizations; and similar planning procedures, problems of economic management, and policy aims. In essence, the social organization of industrialism was viewed as unvarying and sufficiently powerful to impose its "logic" upon all societies undergoing industrialization. Convergence theorists predicted that as prosperity increased and a still greater emphasis was placed on technological innovation and economic productivity, ideological differences would decline in significance and a gradual convergence of Soviet communism toward the political *pluralism of the United States would take place.

Critics argued that the entire debate remained at a far too global level. They also pointed to an inadequate acknowledgment of culturally distinct values. Empirical studies have led to the conclusion, for example, that factory organization varies across cultures (Ronald Dore, *British Factory—Japanese Factory,* London, 1973) and that a distinction must be made between formal structures and the values and social relationships that infuse organizations.

A sociological version of the convergence thesis centered around the concept of *modernization. Sociologists such as Marion J. Levy, Jr. (*Modernization and the Structure of Society,* Princeton, N.J., 1966) and Talcott Parsons (*The System of Modern Societies,* Englewood Cliffs, N.J., 1971) asserted that universal structural constraints indigenous to industrialism *level* differences and impose a commonality upon heretofore very different societies. Common indicators of social and economic modernization—*urbanization, expanding education systems, increasingly similar occupational prestige and mobility patterns, falling birth and death rates, widespread electronic communication networks—reduce crosssocietal differences. "Functional prerequisites" of the advanced industrial society are often identified; e.g., a dominance of scientific rationalism over superstition, universalism over particularism, individualism over collectivism, decision-making in reference to standards of achievement rather than ascriptive, or kinship, criteria, and the dominance of a state that defines rights and obligations. As countries rise on the social modernization scales, they converge: differentiated forms of social organization appear and impose a structural uniformity upon diversity; even values become more homogeneous. This version of the convergence thesis also assumes that the extension of *citizenship, increased *political participation, and the expansion of individual liberties will follow universally upon industrialization.

Critics particularly focused their attacks on this latter tenet. Pointing to the Soviet Union or Eastern and Central Europe, nearly all found little evidence of a universal increase in political freedoms or equality with modernization. Others contended that the rise of "experts" and "technocrats" typical in modern societies in many ways tends to restrict political pluralism. Still others take a "corporatist" position: interest groups become highly organized and visible in modern societies and strongly capable of influencing the state, thus bypassing parliamentary processes.

Other features of the "convergence with modernization" thesis have also been questioned. Many have been very specific; John Goldthorpe, for example ("Social Stratification in Industrial Society," in R. Bendix and S. M. Lipset, eds., *Class, Status and Power,* New York, 1966, pp. 648–649), found little convergence of social stratification between the United States and the Soviet Union. Critics also deplored the downplaying of cultural differences. By the early 1970s, it became widely accepted that "becoming modern" involved processes far more complex and obstacle-ridden than those anticipated by the convergence theorists.

The fading of the convergence thesis can be in part attributed to the acknowledgment of complexity and particularity and to a subsequent emphasis on sharply delineated comparative studies. In addition, a new perspective—the "world systems theory," most forcefully articulated by Immanuel Wallerstein (*The Modern World-System,* New York, 1974)—called into question the assumption of an independent evolution of societies. In this perspective, an advanced world market is viewed as pivotal. In part, by subjugating all countries to similar economic pressures, this market produces convergence; however, by coercing societies to take a specific position within a "world stratification system" and an "international division of labor," it also calls forth divergence. In very recent years, the appearance in diverse regions of religious fundamentalism, anti-Westernism, and overt ethnic rivalries has called into question all theories that postulate a smooth and uniform pathway toward industrial and modern societies, as has the fall of Eastern and Central European and Soviet communism as well as the general contraction of the world economy.

(See also CORPORATISM; INTERNATIONAL SYSTEMS.)

Clark Kerr, John T. Dunlop, Frederick H. Harbison, and Charles A. Myers, *Industrialism and Industrial Man* (Cambridge, Mass., 1960). Arnold S. Feldman and Wilbert E. Moore, "Industrialization and Industrialism: Convergence and Differentiation," in William A. Faunce, ed., *Comparative Perspectives on Industrial Society* (Boston, 1969): 244–279.

STEPHEN KALBERG

COOPERATION, INTERNATIONAL. See INTERNATIONAL COOPERATION.

COORDINATING COMMITTEE. The Coordinating Committee on Multilateral Export Controls (CoCom) was created in 1949 and has been functioning since January 1950. Its members include the countries of the *North Atlantic Treaty Organization (NATO), minus Iceland, plus Japan and Australia. Its purpose has been to regulate the flow of equipment and technologies with potential military significance to the former Soviet Union, other members of the former *Warsaw Treaty Organization (Warsaw Pact), China, Albania, Mongolia, Vietnam, and the Democratic People's Republic of Korea (North Korea).

CoCom has neither treaty status nor a charter. It has functioned as an informal "gentlemen's agreement" among the participating governments, with a tradition of confidentiality regarding its deliberations and decisions. CoCom has no formal relationship to NATO, the *Organization for Economic Cooperation and Development (OECD), or any other postwar *international organization.

Member governments draw up and administer three embargo lists, covering munitions, atomic energy items, and industrial or "dual-use" items. Private firms in participating countries must obtain permission from their government and in some cases from CoCom prior to exporting controlled items to proscribed destinations. While CoCom members construct the control lists by multilateral consensus, the administration and enforcement of controls, including the sanctioning of violators, have been left to the national discretion of member governments.

Much of CoCom's history has involved a conflict between the U.S. government, which has favored more extensive controls, and those of Western Europe and Japan, which have sought to minimize the extent to which controls interfere with the pursuit of economic interests in East-West trade. During the *Korean War, the CoCom control lists were expanded to cover items of general economic as well as specific military significance to the Soviet Union and its allies. The lists were reduced significantly after major negotiations in 1954 and 1958. In 1957, CoCom abandoned its policy of requiring stricter controls on trade with China than on that with the Soviet Union and Eastern Europe.

As East-West *détente took hold during the 1970s, CoCom controls were relaxed. Following the Soviet invasion of Afghanistan, the United States made the revitalization of CoCom a national *security priority. It adopted a policy of not granting exceptions for the export of controlled items to the Soviet Union. A high-level meeting was held in January 1982 to consider U.S. initiatives to expand the control list, improve enforcement, and bring "third-country" suppliers such as Sweden, Austria, and the Republic of Korea (South Korea) into greater conformity with CoCom controls. U.S. efforts bore fruit, yet also created considerable diplomatic friction. Some governments were reluctant to extend controls or improve enforcement to the extent desired by the United States, and the U.S. government responded by restricting U.S. exports to those countries. A compromise was reached at a high-level CoCom meeting in January 1988. The United States agreed to relax export controls, and other members pledged to improve the enforcement of remaining controls.

Since 1989, CoCom has sought to adjust to the end of the *Cold War and the dramatic transformations of the Soviet Union and Eastern and Central Europe. Members agreed at a historic meeting in June 1990 to restructure the control system. They decided to create a highly selective "core list" of controlled items, and to allow former target states—initially, Poland, Czechoslovakia, and Hungary—to be removed from the list of proscribed destinations in exchange for observing CoCom controls. CoCom members introduced the core list in September 1991.

The precise impact of CoCom controls on the military capabilities of its targets is difficult to determine. Although CoCom could not prevent the Soviet Union from becoming a formidable military power, many analysts believe that the controls contributed to the ability of the United States and NATO to maintain a lead over the former Soviet Union and Warsaw Pact countries in the application of advanced technologies to military purposes. That the Soviet Union deemed it necessary, beginning in the 1960s, to organize and fund a systematic campaign to acquire CoCom-controlled items illegally testifies to the significance of the multilateral export control regime.

The future of CoCom is uncertain. The end of the Cold War and the diminution of East-West military competition have led some governments and private firms to question the need to maintain CoCom. As of 1991, member governments felt it was still necessary to maintain controls, in particular on trade with the former Soviet Union in advanced telecommunications and computers. How long CoCom will continue, and whether it will be restructured to meet emerging security threats, such as the proliferation of weapons of mass destruction to developing countries, remains to be seen.

(See also ARMS CONTROL; INTERNATIONAL COOPERATION; SANCTIONS; TECHNOLOGY TRANSFER.)

Gunnar Adler-Karlson, *Western Economic Warfare, 1947–1967* (Stockholm, 1968). Michael Mastanduno, *Economic Containment: CoCom and the Politics of East-West Trade* (Ithaca, N.Y., 1992).

MICHAEL MASTANDUNO

CORPORATISM. Corporatism, or corporativism—the spelling varies by author, country, and period—is a distinctive way of organizing interests and influencing public policy. It has had an erratic history. As a practice, it is ancient. The Roman Republic had professional *collegia* with a distinctive public role; medieval city-states had elaborate systems of representation and self-government through monopolistic guilds. As a concept in the active vocabulary of political life or scholarly debate, however, it is of relatively recent origin. The first explicit references emerged in Europe during the latter third of the nineteenth century.

By some, corporatism was hailed as a novel and promising way for ensuring social harmony, even as a "third way" between *capitalism and *communism; by others, it has been roundly condemned as an illusory and reactionary effort to suppress political demands and impose authoritarian rule. It reached its greatest visibility under the *Estado Corporativo* of *Mussolini's Italy after 1928 and was much imitated by other autocratic regimes of the interwar period. With the defeat of *Fascism and *Nazism, the concept more or less disappeared from polite political discourse—except in Antonio Salazar's Portugal and Franco's Spain, where it remained on public display until their transitions to *democracy in the mid-1970s. Some of these "anachronistic" practices still characterize the interest politics of such countries as Argentina, Brazil, Greece, Indonesia, and Turkey.

In the mid-1970s, a group of scholars revived the concept to describe and explain certain puzzling features of advanced industrial democracies that could not be understood by the heretofore dominant paradigm, *pluralism. To differentiate the new variety from discredited previous experiences, these scholars usually added a prefix such as "liberal," "societal," or "neo-" to the corporatist root. Empirically, they drew special attention to developments during the late 1930s and the postwar period in a number of small European democracies and to emerging properties in some of the larger ones, such as the Federal Republic of Germany (FRG) and Britain, that indicated a very different structure of organized *class, sectoral, and professional interests and a very different pattern of interaction with state agencies. From their diverse perspectives, these U.S., British, and German scholars began to identify an alternative model of state-society relations that was, nonetheless, compatible with democracy. The "corporatism debate" became the "growth industry" of the subsequent decade, especially in Western Europe.

Confusing Variety of Definitions. Given this checkered history, the concept of corporatism has been defined in many different ways. In the minds of some, it never managed to divest itself completely of its prior association with Fascism and authoritarian rule. Its practice has almost always been controversial. In contemporary politics, the term remains largely polemical—a label to be avoided even if one is practicing it, or something to accuse one's opponent of doing—despite the effort of many scholars to give it a more objective or, at least, less pejorative connotation.

Corporatism can be, and has been, defined as referring to a distinctive *ideology, variety of political culture, type of *state, form of economy, or, even, kind of society. The most productive usage has been to consider it as one of several possible arrangements through which interest associations can intermediate between their members (individuals, families, firms, groups of all kinds) and their interlocutors (especially agencies of the state with authority and other resources to satisfy their demands). When these associations are configured in a certain way or when they participate in decision making in a certain way, then it is appropriate to use the label *corporatist* to indicate their nature. It should be stressed that corporatism is not the only way to institutionalize such exchanges of influence. Except for the long-extinct practices of medieval cities and, more recently, those of the interwar autocracies, it has been relatively rare. Pluralism is a much more widespread "solution" to this problem among advanced industrial polities. Indeed, given its greater frequency and its allegedly strong link to

forms of modern democracy, pluralism has enjoyed a virtual hegemony within the social sciences. Open advocates of corporatism in recent years have been few. Those who found some merit in its practices have often been compelled to disguise their advocacy behind other labels, such as "social partnership," "concertation," "coordinated market economy," or "societal bargaining." Even those who have merely studied it have labored under the accusation that they were promoting something intrinsically undemocratic.

Both pluralism and corporatism must involve themselves in two contrasting aspects of the political process: 1) they must communicate and transform member preferences into claims on others, especially public authorities; and 2) they must monitor and influence the subsequent behavior of their members with regard to realizing these claims. In the language of systems theory, intermediary associations have both input and output functions. In the language of political theory, they are simultaneously engaged in representation and control. An association that represents its members but cannot influence their subsequent behavior will be unlikely to command the attention of its interlocutors; conversely, one that only seeks to control behavior without reflecting member opinion risks being treated as a state agency and being rejected as illegitimate by those it claims to represent.

Behind the rival labels of pluralism and corporatism lie very different assumptions about how representation and control are mixed and embodied in associations. Figure 1 specifies the elements of the "pure" corporatist and the "pure" pluralist models. No existing polity exactly replicates the arrangement summarized in either column, although Austria comes closest to the former and the United States to the latter. Moreover, a good deal of research has demonstrated that within a given polity the configuration of organized interests may vary considerably across policy arenas and sectors. The same association may operate sequentially or simultaneously in a more pluralist or a more corporatist fashion as it interacts with different agencies or levels of government.

The right-hand column in Figure 1 summarizes the characteristics of a pure corporatist system with regard to both members and interlocutors. It begins with the input side of politics. Interests are organized into monopolistic units with nonoverlapping domains of representation, coordinated hierarchically by more encompassing, "peak associations" and supported by involuntary contributions. In exchange for this, the state grants explicit recognition to one association per category, incorporates that organization directly and reliably within the decision-making process, and negotiates its agreement with relevant measures. These usually involve comprehensive package deals across several issues. Seen from the output perspective, corporatist associations

Figure 1. Properties Distinguishing Pure Pluralist and Pure Corporatist Modes of Intermediation

I. REPRESENTATION (INPUT)

	PLURALIST	CORPORATIST
I. In relation to members	Multiple units	Monopolistic units
	Overlapping claims	Differentiated domains
	Autonomous interaction	Hierarchical coordination
	Voluntary adherence	Involuntary contribution
II. In relation to interlocutors	Mutual tolerance	Explicit recognition
	Opportunistic access	Structured incorporation
	Consultative role	Negotiative role
	Shifting alliances (log-rolling)	Stable compromises (package dealing)

II. CONTROL (OUTPUT)

I. In relation to members	Persuasive conviction	Interest indoctrination
	Leader prestige	Organizational authority
	Discriminate treatment	Coercive sanctions
	Selective goods	Monopolistic goods
II. In relation to interlocutors	Provision of information	Organization of compliance
	Irresponsibility for decisions	Co-responsibility for decisions
	Autonomous monitoring	Devolved implementation
	Mobilization of pressure	Withdrawal from concentration

are actively engaged in defining and indoctrinating the interests of members and in exercising authority over the behavior of members, if necessary through the application of coercive sanctions and the withdrawal of services that members cannot do without, such as licenses, certifications, trademarks, etc. In return, the state receives the assured compliance of the entire category and devolves part of the responsibility for policy implementation upon the association.

Uneven Distribution of Cases. Much effort has been expended in labeling countries as more or less "corporatist." Less attention has been paid to specific sectors. The usual ordering places Austria, Sweden, Norway, Finland, and the Netherlands at the top; Denmark, Ireland, Switzerland, Belgium, and the FRG somewhere in the middle; Britain, France, and Italy further down in the category of "weak and unsuccessful" corporatisms; and the United States and Canada at the "pluralist" bottom of the list. Australia is an interesting case of a non-European country where "social contracting" between the state and peak associations has become a regular (if controversial) feature of its politics. Spain offers a fascinating example of how voluntary corporatist arrangements can be used to stabilize the transition from authoritarian rule to democracy. Japan has proven a very difficult country to classify along this continuum.

Ambiguity about Consequences. But what difference does it make if a country or sector is corporatist or pluralist? The relative "social peace" of Scandinavia, Switzerland, and Austria in the postwar era is one obvious consequence, but it takes considerable

econometric work to tease out other probable socio-economic effects. For example, analyses of data on Organization for Economic Co-operation and Development (OECD) member-states show significantly lower rates of inflation and unemployment in the more corporatist countries but not much difference in economic growth. For the 1960s and 1970s, comprehensive agreements between organized social classes and the state seemed to resolve a central dilemma of welfare capitalism: how to prevent full employment from generating inflation via union militancy. In such negotiations, workers could exchange short-term power advantage for long-term concessions in welfare and other policies. Macrocorporatism also offered a solution to growth-inhibiting "distributive coalitions." It shifted the calculus of interest to more encompassing organizations, thereby diminishing the likelihood of passing on the costs to others.

The consequences for politics have been more controversial. Although the finding that corporatist arrangements contribute to "governability" through greater citizen compliance and fiscal effectiveness seems widely accepted, the suspicion persists that they surreptitiously undermine democracy. Organizations replace persons as the principal participants; specialized professionals gain at the expense of citizen amateurs; direct functional channels of representation to state agencies displace territorially based legislative decision-making; monopolies and privileged access are recognized at the expense of overlapping and competing associations; comprehensive national hierarchies diminish the autonomy of local and specialized organizations.

Nevertheless, one cannot deny that the most corporatist countries have also been stable democracies. Some of them, e.g. the Scandinavian polities, have even been in the forefront of experimentation with such measures as worker participation in management, open disclosure, ombudsman arrangements, public financing of parties, and so on. The spontaneous, voluntaristic, and autonomous features of pluralism may seem freer in principle, but in practice they reproduce greater inequality of access to power, especially across social classes. Corporatism evens out the distribution of resources across interest categories and guarantees formal parity in the decision-making process. The incorporation of associations in policy implementation seems to ensure greater responsiveness to group needs than the "arm's-length" relation separating the public and the private under pluralism. One may conclude that democracy is being transformed by modern corporatism (see P. C. Schmitter, "Democratic Theory and Neo-Corporatist Practice" *Social Research* 50, no. 4 (Winter 1983): 885–928). Organizations are becoming citizens alongside individuals. Accountability and responsiveness are increasing, but at the expense of citizen participation and access for all groups. Competition is less interorganizational and more intraorganizational. Across advanced industrial societies, the pace of these changes is uneven; their acceptance is uncertain; their outcome by no means unequivocal—but all modern democracies are becoming more "interested," organized, and vicarious.

(See also AUTHORITARIANISM; CONSOCIATIONAL DEMOCRACY; INTEREST GROUPS; POLITICAL ECONOMY; POLITICAL PARTICIPATION.)

P. C. Schmitter, "Still the Century of Corporatism?" *Review of Politics* 36, no. 1 (1974): 85–131. P. C. Schmitter and G. Lehmbruch, eds., *Trends toward Corporatist Intermediation* (Beverly Hills, Calif., and London, 1979). S. D. Berger, ed., *Organizing Interests in Western Europe: Pluralism, Corporatism, and the Transformation of Politics* (Cambridge, U.K., 1981). G. Lehmbruch and P. C. Schmitter, eds., *Patterns of Corporatist Policy-Making* (Beverly Hills, Calif., and London, 1982). J. H. Goldthorpe, ed., *Order and Conflict in Contemporary Capitalism: Studies in the Political Economy of Western European Nations* (Oxford, 1984).

PHILIPPE C. SCHMITTER

CORRUPTION. Throughout history, corruption has appeared in societies displaying a relatively developed social and economic organization. The greater the complexity and development of society, the more striking is the corruption. Thus it is already observable in ancient times in, for example, China, Greece, and Rome.

Corruption is distinct from crime or certain customary cultural practices. Essentially it is the abuse of public trust for private gain. The characteristics of corruption are as follows: 1) Deliberate subordination of public or common interests to personal ones; 2) secrecy of execution except in situations that allow powerful individuals or those under their protection to be open about it; 3) the presence of mutual obligations and benefits, in pecuniary or other forms; 4) the interaction of those who want certain decisions and those who can influence them in a mutually reciprocating framework; 5) the attempt to camouflage the corrupt act by some forms of lawful justification; and 6) involvement in contradictory dual functions by those committing the act.

The last characteristic is significant to distinguish corruption from other types of criminal behavior. When a bribed official issues a business license according to established rules and procedures, the act of issuing is a function of his or her position. The self-interest, the bribe, is obtained through the fulfillment of an official function. He or she acts in a dual and contradictory manner, both official and corrupt, which sets corruption apart from theft, burglary, or embezzlement.

Early records of political corruption refer to the bribery of judges and actions of public officials. In ancient Egypt, Babylon, India, China, Greece, and Rome, corruption often surfaced as a problem. It was clearly condemned both in the Old Testament Book of Exodus and in India since at least 1000 B.C.E. The Laws of Manu contained severe punishment for corrupt officials. Corruption was an important issue in the conflict between factions in ancient Greece.

In extent and variety, however, corruption probably was greater still in imperial Rome, given its vastness; and the Roman administrative system partly contributed to the abuse of office by provincial governors whose authority was exercised with little or no control from the capital. As the empire grew, so did corruption, and it figured no less prominently in the decline and fall of the empire.

From these ancient roots, the problem of corruption remains an important political issue today. It appears in both developed and developing countries and distorts the political process both in democratic and dictatorial systems. Although the pattern of distortion differs, its consequences are essentially the same: 1) Increased economic burden for the public because the cost of corruption is transferred to the consumer; 2) negligence in all aspects of administration, particularly that affecting public welfare; 3) a tendency toward subordination of efficiency norms to the norms of the graft transaction; and 4) general loss of respect for the constituted authority with regard to observance of rules and regulations.

Corruption can be classified into at least two broad categories. One is the secret, isolated corruption that happens everywhere without infecting the entire body politic. The other is what can be called tidal corruption. It floods the entire state apparatus, including those at the center of power. It immerses everything in its path. It distorts and debilitates administrative efforts and dampens the enthusiasm of genuine and capable public officials.

Corruption distorts the political system in the sense that it deflects it from its avowed objectives. It negates general objectives such as social welfare and justice as well as the particular objectives of the various institutions and organizations of the state. A corruption-ridden democracy might practice bribery on a colossal scale during elections. In a system where there are no periodic general elections corruption follows other channels of distortion. For example, in the Soviet Union, corruption centered around black market activity, the allocation of rations and privileges, and the buying of party positions. Those who amassed millions remained underground, as there was no legitimate means of becoming a millionaire. In the United States, on the other hand, the combination of politics and business is the wellspring of corruption. Whatever is the avowed objective of the system, it is distorted by corruption, the pattern of which is determined by the particular configurations of the system.

Corruption may be divided into three types: extortive, manipulative, and nepotistic. The first refers to a situation where one is forced to bribe in order to gain or protect one's rights or needs. The second refers to the attempt to influence decisions in one's favor in any area of life. The third refers to preferential treatment of relatives and friends in appointments to positions, which can also include organizational nepotism, that is, special favors given to political parties or social organizations.

The functional theory of corruption suggests that there may be some positive contributions of corruption to social development. It is said that corruption helps to redistribute wealth, develop the middle class, and cut through bureaucratic red tape. This theory misses the focus of concern in that it does not differentiate between corruption as voluntary interaction and corruption as extortion.

Extortive corruption is desired by only one party, the taker; the giver is the victim. For the victim certain acts of corruption can have a beneficial effect, however. A case in point was the philosopher Wittgenstein. When Germany annexed Austria in March 1938, he was in England; his two sisters were in Vienna. To avoid having the Nazi laws on race applied to them, Wittgenstein went to Germany, negotiated with the authorities, and put at the disposal of the German state bank a certain sum of money from his family fortune in Switzerland; in turn, his sisters escaped persecution. Wittgenstein bribed the Germans to protect his sisters against oppressive and inhumane laws. Certainly Wittgenstein's bribery had a positive function in saving his sisters. However, the other side of the transaction, the Nazi side, was extortive and definitely not positively functional in the morally approved sense.

In societies where corruption is rampant, the over-all effect is always negative. Important decisions are determined by ulterior motives regardless of their effect on the community at large. The administrative machine does not respond to direction, making it impossible for honest leaders to achieve results, and thus parasitism, negligence, and inefficiency become yet more solidly entrenched. In developing societies it contributes greatly to *brain drain. It increases the psychological stress of life in big cities and in business circles owing to the tension a corrupt environment generates. It demoralizes people in situations where norms and standards are subverted, as for example when an examination result is affected by bribery. It fosters criminal activity and undermines the judiciary. Perhaps most invidious, however, is the manipulation of elections by parties in power. Once this takes root in a political order, force comes to be seen as the only possible engine of change. Thus, by corroding respect for authority, corruption eventually endangers political stability.

Arnold J. Heidenheimer, ed., *Political Corruption* (New York, 1976). Syed Hussein Alatas, *The Problem of Corruption* (Singapore, 1986).

SYED HUSSEIN ALATAS

COSTA RICA. Many Costa Ricans believe that they are victims of a geographical error. Costa Rica, according to this view, is a European nation that by mistake found itself located in Central America. There is a grain of truth to this joke because Costa Rica is so different from its neighbors. Central America chronically suffers from brutal military rule, political instability, economic underdevelopment, and extremes in the distribution of income, wealth, and land. Costa Rica, while having experienced all of these symptoms of political and economic underdevelopment, has done so to a far more limited extent than other countries in the region and has made considerable progress in overcoming all of them.

No single feature of Costa Rica sets it apart from the rest of Central America more than its system of political *democracy. Like its neighbors, Costa Rica was a colony of Spain until it was granted independence in 1821. Of all of the Spanish colonies in Central America, Costa Rica was probably the poorest and certainly the most isolated. This geographic isolation, however, may have proved to be an advantage because it seems to have helped to insulate the country from the politics of violence and military rule that came to dominate the rest of the region. Throughout the nineteenth century there is evidence of domination by military strongmen, but at the same time, there were also signs of the growth of responsible, representative government.

It was not until the twentieth century, however, that the last vestiges of instability and authoritarian rule were fully overcome. With one brief exception, the first half of the century was characterized by elected, civilian governments dedicated to social and economic development. While the right to vote remained restricted to property-owning males, in 1925 the secret ballot was institutionalized, and in the years that followed an increasingly sophisticated voter-registration system was developed that has become the envy of even highly advanced industrialized nations. Perhaps the major turning point occurred in 1940 with the election to the presidency of Rafael Angel Calderón Guardia. Despite having been selected by the coffee-growing economic elite, once in office Calderón instituted a series of reforms that granted rights to workers (e.g., social security protection, minimum wages, eight-hour day). He proved to be a very popular president, but began to run into serious opposition from both the economic elite as well as sectors of the middle class when he formed an electoral alliance with the Costa Rican Community Party in 1943. The alliance helped elect Calderón's handpicked candidate in the 1944 elections, but in the 1948 election, when Calderón ran again, he was defeated. The pro-Calderón legislature reacted by annulling the election, an act that enraged the populace and was the catalyst that set off a popular uprising led by José (Pepe) Figueres Ferrer. A brief but violent civil war erupted, thereby marring the tradition of domestic peace that had been developing. The rebels were victorious and under Figueres' guidance rewrote the constitution, which granted universal suffrage and other key rights and, perhaps most importantly, abolished the army. Unlike other victors in Latin American uprisings, Figueres voluntarily relinquished rule after holding dictatorial power for eighteen months. He successfully ran for election in 1953 under the banner of his newly established Partido de Liberación Nacional (PLN). In time, the PLN became institutionalized as the nation's best-organized, most electorally successful political party.

Since the 1948 Civil War, political stability and democracy have not been seriously threatened in Costa Rica. Every four years the PLN has competed against a coalition of opposition forces and has won more often than it has lost. It appears that the losses are more a function of the electorate's demand for "a new broom" to sweep out politicians who seem to have become corrupt than they are of any deep discontent about the way the system of government is run. There has emerged a broad consensus that democratic politics is desirable and that human and civil rights must be respected by those in power.

Political democracy has not protected Costa Rica from economic hardships, however. Although economic development was impressive throughout the 1950s, 1960s, and 1970s, with the emergence of modern infrastructure in the form of roads, a nationwide telephone system, and the widespread availability of health and education facilities, by the late 1970s the economic model of state-promoted development seemed to run out of steam. Beginning in the early 1980s a severe economic crisis developed: high inflation, unemployment, economic contraction, and the explosive growth of foreign debt. Costa Rica seemed to be slipping into the pattern experienced so often by its neighbors in the region. To some extent the economic crisis can be attributed to external factors, especially the destabilization of Central America resulting from the *Nicaraguan Revolution, the outbreak of protracted civil war in El Salvador, and the breakdown of the Central American Common Market. But a large factor in the equation was that Costa Rica, with its total population of less than 3 million inhabitants, was not economically capable of financing the state-supported social service net that had been woven since the 1940s.

The collapse of the economy was prevented by a large dose of foreign aid, most of it coming from the United States. This assistance enabled Costa Rica to begin a process of structural adjustment. The democratic nature of the system initially limited the capacity of the government to impose adjustment measures, such as the reform of the banking system, but as Costa Rica moved into the 1990s many of the reforms had been put in place. Economic growth was restored as government spending was limited and the production of nontraditional exports was stimulated.

Costa Rica's traditional aloofness from events in Central America was affected as a result of the regional political and military crisis of the 1980s. President Oscar *Arias (1986–1990) played a major role in the efforts to negotiate a peace settlement in the region, for which he won the Nobel Prize. Once the peace process was well along, Central American leaders turned to the issue of restructuring the moribund Central American Common Market and creating durable regional institutions that would both help avoid international conflicts and stimulate regional economic growth. Many Costa Ricans, however, were reluctant to join this process for fear of being drawn into regional conflicts. Symptomatic of that fear was the reluctance of the Costa Rican legislative assembly to ratify the agreement to establish a Central American Parliament even after all of the other nations of the region had done so. The challenge for Costa Rica is to maintain its democratic system while joining its neighbors in the search for sustained economic growth.

(See also U.S.–LATIN AMERICAN RELATIONS.)

Mitchell A. Seligson, *Peasants of Costa Rica and the Development of Agrarian Capitalism* (Madison, Wis., 1980). Lowell Gudmundson, *Costa Rica Before Coffee: Society and Economy on the Eve of the Export Boom* (Baton Rouge, La., 1986). Marc Edelman and Joanne Kenan, eds., *The Costa Rica Reader* (New York, 1989).
                                    MITCHELL A. SELIGSON

CÔTE D'IVOIRE. With an area of 322,460 square kilometers (124,500 sq. mi.), Côte d'Ivoire is bordered by Liberia, Guinea, Mali, Burkina Faso, and

Ghana. There are over sixty ethnic groups, classified into four main linguistic divisions: Akan, forty-three percent (Baulé, Agni), in the southeast; Kru, seventeen percent (Bété, Guéré), in the southwest; Mandé, twenty-seven percent (Malinké, Dan, Gouro), in the northwest; Voltaic, thirteen percent (Senufo), in the northeast and central savannas. About twenty-five percent of the estimated 12.5 million inhabitants are foreigners, predominately Mossi peoples from Burkina Faso (who work as domestics and field laborers), followed by Africans from nearby coastal states, French, and Lebanese. There are three main religious branches: Christianity, thirty-two percent; Islam, twenty-four percent; African religions, forty-four percent. The president declared his commitment to Catholicism by constructing the Basilica of Our Lady of Peace in 1989.

Under the leadership of Félix Houphouët-Boigny (b. 1905), the Parti Démocratique de la Côte d'Ivoire (PDCI) was imposed as the nation's sole political party until 1990. The one-party state reflected Houphouët's notion of unity within diversity. In 1944, Houphouët successfully organized a group of bourgeois African planters, which included several administrative elites, to form the Syndicat Agricole Africain (SAA). Its primary goal was to acquire laborers, which French administrators supplied to colonial planters but denied to Africans. The SAA was quickly transformed into a political party, the PDCI, in order to present candidates in local elections. The Bloc Africain, an all-African slate headed by the PDCI candidate, Houphouët, won all seats on the municipal council in the 1945 elections. Houphouët represented Côte d'Ivoire in the First Constituent Assembly of France, where he initiated the Houphouët-Boigny Law abolishing forced labor throughout the French territories. In 1946, he extended PDCI influence by founding the Rassemblement Démocratique Africain (RDA), an umbrella organization for political parties throughout Francophone Africa.

In the 1950s, French repression of the Communist Party and its affiliates caused Houphouët to renounce *communism and declare his loyalty to France. This act, called a "tactical retreat," compromised the anticolonial struggle and prepared the way for nonviolent collaboration with the French. (Houphouët was rewarded and served as French minister of health in 1956.) By referendum, in 1958, Côte d'Ivoire declined independence, in favor of semiautonomy within the French Union. Full independence was granted anyway, on 7 August 1960, after the reorganization of France by de Gaulle.

Through patron-client relations Houphouët garnered support from the next generation of technocrats whose loyalty he secured in return for jobs, higher salaries, and opportunities to invest in the private sector. Student groups, trade unionists, women activists, and politicians were alienated, suppressed, or co-opted under the banner of the PDCI. A con-spiracy to overthrow the government was fabricated in 1963 as an excuse to imprison and torture dissidents. Further, in October 1970, repression of Bété in Gagnoa, after Houphouët refused to recognize the Parti Nationaliste (PANA), is said to have resulted in 3,000–4,000 deaths.

In 1989, while the country was suffering a severe economic recession, the patron-client system broke down, and political processes underwent a dramatic transformation. Massive street demonstrations marked widespread dissatisfaction with the one-party state. Teachers, students, doctors, and workers in crucial sectors of energy and communications organized strikes. Cleavages were exacerbated by competition for scarce resources. To preserve the system, Houphouët accepted a complete renovation of the PDCI and named Alassane Ouattara as interministerial coordinator to reorganize the government. But pressure from opposition groups and the international financial community, in addition to worldwide trends toward democratization, forced Houphouët to announce a return to the multiparty system (30 April 1990). The most important parties to challenge the PDCI in the 1990 elections were the Front Populaire Ivoirien (FPI), the Union des Sociaux-Démocrates (USD), the Parti Ivoirien des Travailleurs (PIT), and the Parti Socialiste Ivoirien (PSI). Laurent Gbagbo (FPI), the only candidate to oppose Houphouët, won eighteen percent of the vote. In the contest for 175 seats in the legislature, the results were: PDCI 163, opposition parties 10, and independents 2. In municipal elections, opposition candidates won 6 out of 135 cities. Some forty opposition parties have been officially recognized.

The constitution established the republic, recognized equal rights for all, and allowed citizens to form political parties. But, because loyalty to Houphouët and PDCI activism had become the bases for gaining political offices and administrative posts, democratic elections were repressed. Every five years Ivoirians simply confirmed a single list of PDCI candidates for the National Assembly. Houphouët ran uncontested. After the Seventh Party Congress in 1980, PDCI candidates competed against one another and were elected by direct suffrage. Article 11 of the constitution, which pertains to succession, has been amended several times. In 1990, it was amended again to permit the head of the National Assembly to assume leadership until the end of the presidential mandate. Two new Articles, 12 and 24, allow the president to nominate and delegate powers to a prime minister. The number of ministerial portfolios changes according to need. (They reached a record high of thirty-nine under Houphouët.) Ouattara, the first prime minister, appointed twenty ministers.

The PDCI was restructured in 1990. Houphouët is president of the PDCI. A general secretary, who is nominated by Houphouët and approved by the Political Bureau, manages the party. Membership in the party hierarchy is determined by loyalty, age, ethnicity, regional origin, and national affiliations, e.g., trade unions and professional associations. The Comité Central (eighty members) serves as an advisory body and steering committee for the national leadership. The Bureau Politique (400 members), largely composed of a younger generation of cadres and administrative elites, deliberates issues of national interest. The secrétaires généraux (235) implement PDCI directives and mobilize the membership. The comités de base, organized in neighborhoods and villages, have about 100 members each. Opposition parties are also creating comités de base.

Côte d'Ivoire's liberal economy is fueled by cash crop–growing *peasants. They were guaranteed a minimum price of 400 CFA (Communauté Financière Africaine) francs per kilogram for cocoa and 200 CFA francs for coffee regardless of market fluctuations. In thirty years, annual production of cocoa increased ten times to 800,000 tons, coffee production doubled to reach 300,000 tons, and cotton production quadrupled to 300,000 tons. Côte d'Ivoire was among the world's top three producers of each commodity until 1989, when its inability to continue to pay peasants at rates higher than the market forced the Caisse de Stabilisation (Stabilization Fund) to reduce payments. Other export crops are pineapples, oil palm, coconuts, timber, latex, and sugar. Petroleum production from two offshore wells reached nearly 1.5 million metric tons in the mid-1980s, but was insufficient to alleviate strains on the budget or prevent the rescheduling of international debts.

High revenues from export production and political stability facilitated access to loans which financed infrastructure, such as roads, ports, housing, schools, and office buildings in Abidjan and Yamoussoukro. About one-third of the national budget goes toward public education. The "miracle" of economic *development, for which Côte d'Ivoire was known, disguised a weak industrial sector. Ivoirian bureaucrats and French investors have profited most from marketing and transporting export products, banking, and private investments.

The armed forces have been kept to a minimum with an estimated 6,000 infantry (approximately sixty percent are young conscripts), 450 air force, and 500 navy personnel. About 3,600 persons make up the Gendarmerie Nationale. Incidents in 1973 and 1980 were interpreted as attempted coups, but, in each case, the charges were reversed and no one was executed. Since 1961, a detachment of about 600 French marines have been stationed at Port-Bouët, near the main airport.

Côte d'Ivoire emerged as one of the most developed, stable, and influential of the former French colonies in West Africa. Houphouët, called the "wise man of Africa," is a leader in interregional organizations, such as the Conseil de l' Entente, the Communauté Economique de l'Afrique de l'Ouest (CEAO),

and the Economic Community of West African States (ECOWAS).

(See also AFRICAN REGIONAL ORGANIZATIONS; FRANCOPHONE AFRICA.)

Aristide R. Zolberg, One-Party Government in the Ivory Coast, rev. ed. (Princeton, N.J., 1969). I. William Zartman and Christopher L. Delgado, eds., The Political Economy of Ivory Coast (New York, 1984). Robert E. Handloff, ed., Côte d'Ivoire: a country study, 3d ed. (Washington, D.C., 1991).

JEANNE MADDOX TOUNGARA

COUNCIL FOR MUTUAL ECONOMIC ASSISTANCE. The Council for Mutual Economic Assistance (CMEA or COMECON) was the regional organization that structured economic relations between the Soviet Union and its socialist allies in the postwar period. CMEA was founded in 1949 at the initiative of the Soviet Union. Its purpose was both economic and political. On the economic side, CMEA was to serve two functions. First, CMEA was to integrate the centrally planned economies of the Soviet bloc; that is, the Soviet Union, the socialist states in Eastern and *Central Europe (excepting Albania and Yugoslavia—the latter having "special," but nonmember, status), and, finally, Mongolia, Cuba, and Vietnam. In practice, this did not mean that CMEA had the capacity to dictate domestic production and international trade. Rather, the process of coordination was more informal—for example, regular meetings among national representatives to CMEA were held in order to draft various bilateral agreements and to coordinate and plan production, trade, and (by the 1970s) research and development in the bloc. The second economic function of CMEA was to create a socialist regional economy that was to be self-sufficient and therefore separate from, if not in opposition to, the global capitalist economy. As a result, trade outside of CMEA was discouraged. For instance, the currencies of the CMEA countries were nonconvertible, and members of CMEA were not members of the *General Agreement on Tariffs and Trade (GATT).

The major political function of CMEA was to provide the Soviet Union with more control over its allies. With more control, the Soviets could convert their regional base of power into stronger claims for international power. What CMEA did, in particular, was to give the Soviets a regional economic monopoly. This occurred both because of the structure of CMEA—that is, its isolation from the global economy, its capacity to link domestic economies with the regional economy, and its emphasis on bilateral trade—and because of the regional dominance of the Soviet economy—for instance, the much larger size of the Soviet economy and the dependence of the smaller economies of the bloc on the Soviet Union as a consequence of their derivative structures and their primary product dependence.

CMEA added economic control to the already

considerable political and military control the Soviet Union exercised over its allies. Just as the *Warsaw Treaty Organization (Warsaw Pact) created a military monopoly and the dependence of these Communist parties on the Soviet Union for political authority created a political monopoly, so the structure of CMEA created for the Soviet Union a regional economic monopoly. As a result, the Soviet bloc became a hierarchical regional system; that is, a genuine economic, political, and military bloc with the Soviet Union serving as the regional hegemon.

By 1990, however, it was clear that CMEA was in the process of disintegration. It was not just that the revolutions in Eastern Europe in 1989 created systems that, because of economic and political liberalization, were no longer able to fit into the structure of CMEA. The Soviets also had decided to dismantle CMEA, primarily because it was no longer in Soviet interests to hold onto a bloc which interfered with their desires to ally with the West and to make the Soviet economy more productive. Although this became a formal decision in the spring of 1990 when the Soviet prime minister announced that starting in 1991 Soviet–East European trade would be hard currency trade only, there were a number of prior decisions from 1986 onward that suggested that the Soviets were no longer interested in continuing CMEA. For example, during this period the Soviets applied for membership in GATT, they began the process of creating a convertible ruble, and they went about systematically deregulating politics and economics—at home and in the bloc. As a result, CMEA, like so much that defined the postwar order, has withered.

(See also NINETEEN EIGHTY-NINE; SOVIET–EAST EUROPEAN RELATIONS.)

VALERIE BUNCE

COUNCIL OF EUROPE. An intergovernmental organization created by Western European democracies at the beginning of the *Cold War, the Council of Europe had grown by 1990 to include twenty-three states. Most members remain parliamentary democracies within Western Europe. The council includes all the members of the *European Community (EC) and the *European Free Trade Agreement (EFTA) as well as Turkey, most of Western Europe's microstates, and the Mediterranean island nations of Cyprus and Malta.

The organization focuses on issues of European civil society, although not issues of economic cooperation, which are dealt with in the EC, EFTA, and other forums. The council is principally concerned with issues of *human rights, social welfare, environmental protection, and relations between Europe and the less industrialized world. Although the council is governed, as almost all intergovernmental organizations are, by a periodic diplomatic conference of member governments, the council's meetings and working groups, often at its headquarters in Strasbourg, serve as a means for parliamentarians throughout Europe to meet. Whereas key meetings of the EC bring together the most important ministers of the various member governments, the council in some respects can be characterized as a European organization of backbenchers.

The council established a European human rights regime, the European Convention on Human Rights (ECHR) and the European Court of Justice on Human Rights (ECJHR), which administers it, in 1950. The regime has played a significant role in standardizing civil rights across Europe, especially the rights of women. The court's decisions generally are respected. In 1965 the council extended human rights work with the European Social Charter and Convention on Social Security, which establishes a regionwide labor regime and the means to enforce it as well as a regime of reciprocity in social services. The convention also establishes a regionwide system of economic rights for citizens of member states. In a 1983 convention the European human rights regime was extended to migrant workers and *refugees. The rights of noncitizens are made explicit and consistent across signatory states, although noncitizens are not granted the same rights as citizens.

The council has also commissioned working groups and studies of other social issues—health, education, sports, the concerns of youth, crime, and the preservation of cultural heritage. In each case the aim has been to establish regionwide norms reflecting the common expectations developed in prosperous, democratic societies whose economic futures increasingly are linked through other organizations.

Throughout the 1980s a major focus of council meetings and studies was on environmental conservation and protection. Its broad membership makes the council a better place to address these transborder issues than the EC or the EFTA. Some commentators believe that the environment will be the major emphasis of the council's work in the 1990s, providing a strong reason for the new multiparty democracies of Eastern Europe to seek membership.

(See also ENVIRONMENTALISM; FOREIGN WORKERS.)

Council of Europe, *Third Medium Term Plan, 1987–1991: Democratic Europe, Humanism, Diversity, Universality* (Strasbourg, 1986).

CRAIG N. MURPHY

COUNTERINSURGENCY. A government's combined politico-military program to defeat an organized, revolutionary movement dedicated to its overthrow and to eliminate the conditions that gave rise to that movement is known as counterinsurgency. Given its political dimension, counterinsurgency is broader than anti-guerrilla warfare; at the same time, it is narrower than low-intensity conflict, which is a category including everything from counterterror operations to small conventional wars as well.

During the *Cold War counterinsurgency assistance to weak *Third World allies became an essential element in *containment as the Western powers confronted a bipolar world in an era marked by a stable nuclear balance between the *superpowers that shifted competition to the periphery, by a normative attachment to self-determination that constrained traditional imperial forms of that competition, and by tumultuous change in the Third World that made it a tempting target for superpower meddling. In particular, Western powers feared Soviet-backed wars of national liberation, which, they believed, exploited the trauma of modernization to subvert newly independent governments. Thus, "as a strategy," the United States Department of State declared in terms French and British practitioners would also accept, outside counterinsurgency assistance offered "a technique for tiding weak and unstable governments over periods of internal upheaval until the constructive forces of political and economic development are strong enough to control the situation without external assistance." (See "Our Internal Defense Policy—A Reappraisal," *Foreign Policy Journal,* January 1969, by Charles Maechling, Jr., the State Department coordinator for "internal defense," or counterinsurgency, for much of the 1960s.)

Insurgents threaten governments only when they draw on widespread and popular discontent, confront weak political institutions, and can challenge government military forces. Counterinsurgency programs therefore seek to help governments 1) secure the population from insurgent attack, 2) provide competent, legal, responsive administration that is free from abuses and broad in domain, scope, and vigor, and 3) ameliorate popular discontent by raising living standards. In each case, programs aim both to build institutions and improve their output so as to provide more and better government. *Security assistance programs aim to improve the state's capacity to identify, target, and defeat insurgents and to reduce attacks on citizens by renegade security forces. Political development programs attack the two basic political problems behind insurgency —bad administration and underadministration—by reducing *corruption; addressing distributional, racial, and communal problems; and penetrating national authority into the hinterland. Economic development programs seek to eliminate the discontent underlying insurgency by bringing the material benefits of modernity to all citizens.

Counterinsurgency programs may help a friendly government defeat an illegitimate challenge by improving its institutional capabilities and winning the hearts and minds of the population. Conversely, they may simply strengthen the hand of an oppressive government and so block needed reforms.

Before World War II counterinsurgency seldom attracted public attention; since 1945, however, the suppression of insurgent challenges to Third World allies has received recurring high-level attention by Western governments. Such efforts, both successful and unsuccessful, have been among the most important and controversial foreign policy undertakings of the Cold War. France developed a formal counterinsurgency doctrine and fought two painful, losing counterinsurgency campaigns in Indochina and Algeria that deeply divided France and were widely condemned internationally. Britain defeated Malaysian Chinese insurgents and Kenyan insurgents in the *Mau Mau Anticolonial Struggle, two model counterinsurgency campaigns that culminated in peaceful transitions to independence for both colonies. American counterinsurgency assistance helped allies such as Greece, the Philippines, Bolivia, Peru, and Thailand crush insurgent threats, but failed disastrously in the Republic of South Vietnam in what became the worst defeat in American history.

(See also ALGERIAN WAR OF INDEPENDENCE; GUERRILLA WARFARE; NATIONAL LIBERATION MOVEMENTS; REVOLUTION; VIETNAM WAR.)

Sir Robert Thompson, *Defeating Communist Insurgency: Experiences from Malaya and Vietnam* (London, 1966). Douglas Blaufarb, *The Counterinsurgency Era: U. S. Doctrine and Performance* (New York, 1977). D. Michael Shafer, *Deadly Paradigms: The Failure of U.S. Counterinsurgency Policy* (Princeton, N.J., 1988).

D. MICHAEL SHAFER

COUP D'ÉTAT. A nonconstitutional change of governmental leadership carried out with the use or threatened use of violence is known as a coup d'état. It has served historically in many African, Asian, and Latin American states as the major form of regime change. A coup d'état results in the formation of a governmental junta either dominated directly by the members of the armed services who seized political control or controlled indirectly by them through closely aligned civilians.

Explanations for coups d'état fall into three broad schools: factors internal to armed forces (corporate and personal grievances); factors marking the environment of the political system as a whole; and international or extra-systemic factors. Corporate grievances include budget, policy autonomy, and potential threats to military identity resulting from creation or expansion of paramilitary units. Personal grievances refer to concerns of individual officers who, for various reasons, are disaffected from the current national political and/or military leaders and who seek rectification by seizure of power and ouster of those in control. Environmental factors refer to domestic economic, political, and social settings. In general, certain levels of ethnic fragmentation, political mobilization, and domestic violence have been correlated with coups. International factors include changes outside the domestic political and economic arena such as trends in world prices, direct or indirect encouragement of military intervention by outside groups, and financial and technical assistance that enhances the political and coercive strength of armed forces.

The success of a coup d'état depends largely on surprise and total commitment of resources by the insurgents. In broad terms, planners of coups rely on a total commitment of resources to achieve speedy success. Their desire is to displace the existing government as rapidly as possible. Planning of a coup d'état is confined to a small number of military officers. The risks of discovery and punishment preclude involvement of more than a handful of officers, themselves generally linked by ethnicity, rank, age, or other ties, until a few hours prior to execution. The new junta must seek some degree of popular legitimation. As the overall levels of *modernization rise within societies, the obstacles to gaining such legitimation seem to have increased, with consequent shifts in the major types of coups d'état.

Coups d'état can be classified into four groups: oligarchic, modernizing, radical, and guardian. Oligarchic coups are largely of historic interest. Characteristic particularly of nineteenth-century Latin America, they took place within pre-industrial settings in which the officer corps showed little professionalization and levels of popular political awareness were minimal. Modernizing coups reflect increased professionalization of the officer corps and greater modernization of society. Such seizures of power are customarily led by military officers aware of the gap separating their societies from more developed ones, and ease the transition from traditional or oligarchic rule to rule by the urban middle classes and their allies. Radical coups introduce potentially revolutionary changes into society and place members of the armed forces into positions of unquestioned control. This intense politicization of the military, and the sweeping alterations undertaken in the distribution of power and resources, create widespread social tensions. The usual consequences have been either control falling into the hands of the military head of state and a reduction in the armed forces' direct political roles, or some form of military guardianship. Guardian coups occur in societies in which lower-class politicization has been encouraged and in which the armed forces have heritages of direct political involvement. Weaknesses of civilian governments, often manifested in uncontrolled domestic violence or runaway inflation, encourage such military takeovers; on the other hand, traditions of professionalism within the officer corps and a distaste for politics among officers inhibit long-term exercise of power. The juntas develop close ties with middle-class and technocratic groups, occasionally leading to the emergence of *bureaucratic authoritarianism.

Disengagement of armed forces from direct political roles poses many problems. The usual impetus comes from divisions within the governing junta between hard-liners and soft-liners, the latter preferring to return to the barracks to reduce intramilitary tensions, the former pressing for intensification of the military's role. Such tensions also often lead to further coups d'état, thus continuing a cycle of "praetorian" politics. The rapid pace of liberalization and democratization in Latin America during the 1980s, and pressures against several African and Asian military juntas, suggest the importance of emerging norms of governmental control over the armed forces.

(See also AUTHORITARIANISM; DEMOCRATIC TRANSITIONS; MILITARISM; MILITARY RULE; POLITICAL VIOLENCE; REVOLUTION.)

Edward Luttwak, *Coup d'Etat: A Practical Handbook* (Cambridge, Mass., 1979). Claude E. Welch, Jr., *No Farewell to Arms? Military Disengagement from Politics in Africa and Latin America* (Boulder, Colo., 1987). S. E. Finer, *The Man on Horseback: The Role of the Military in Politics*, 2d ed. (Boulder, Colo., 1988).

CLAUDE E. WELCH, JR.

CRISIS. The term *crisis* comes from the Greek *krinein*, meaning to separate. A medical crisis is a turning point in a serious illness toward either recovery or death. In international politics, the turning point may be between *war and *peace.

Scholarship and analysis in world politics has stipulated more specific meanings for crisis. At least three alternative definitions deserve attention. They represent not only definitional distinctions but also different levels of analysis and alternative theoretical and practical concerns. Thus it is possible to distinguish between systemic crises, international confrontation crises, and governmental decision-making crises.

*International systems consist of a set of actors regularly interacting according to some structure that is maintained by norms, laws, or the distribution of capabilities. From a systemic perspective, a crisis is a strong shock to the structure that holds the system together. Thus a systemic crisis threatens the stability of the international system and creates the possibility of a system transformation. For example, the bipolar international system led by the opposing *superpowers that prevailed after *World War II has experienced a crisis with the collapse of the Soviet Union and the *Warsaw Treaty Organization.

A core question to those, such as Kenneth Waltz (*Theory of International Politics*, New York, 1979), concerned with systemic crises is: When does a crisis lead to the *destabilization of the international system? Some scholarship has inquired whether one kind of international system (e.g., mulipolar vs. bipolar) is more susceptible to crises and the conditions under which they destabilize the system. Descriptive studies have sought to determine the conditions that trigger systemic crises. Typically these have been envisioned as wars or *revolutions that dramatically alter the power distribution among actors in international politics. In the increasingly economically interdependent international system that prevails today, other types of events (e.g., national currency collapse, depression) may be future crisis triggers.

Not all systemic crises need be dysfunctional for a system, particularly if it has leaders with a capacity to adapt and learn from the shocks. Leaders in systems or subsystems may actually use crises as a means of forcing member governments to take initiatives they otherwise might not take. The leadership of the *European Community has repeatedly used deadline crises as a means of forcing member governments to take further integrative steps or risk collapse of that subsystem, which produces beneficial results no party wishes to forgo.

A second type of crisis is an international confrontational crisis that typically, but not always, is bilateral. Whereas systemic crises concern the fate of the system as whole, crises between actors focus only on the consequences for nations confronting one another. These crises are defined as a major challenge by one actor to the status quo position of another. After an initial escalatory challenge that triggers the situation, the fundamental dynamic involves bargaining—either directly or by means of some form of tacit signaling.

Analysts using the actor confrontation perspective on crisis frequently rely on one of two methods of inquiry—comparative case studies or the theory of games. Researchers applying *game theory generally address the conditions under which a stable solution to the crisis can be found. Analysts using case studies have focused on such issues as types of *strategy, third-party intervention, and the conditions governing escalation. Glenn Snyder and Paul Diesing (Conflict Among Nations, Princeton, N.J., 1977) have effectively illustrated both approaches. Like other students of international confrontation crises, they pose the basic question: What bargaining strategies produce a successful outcome without escalation to greater violence or war?

In the third orientation to crisis, the focus is on a single country. Governmental or decision-making crises involve an event or other stimulus that poses a severe problem for the policymakers and possibly their constituents. Definitions of crisis emphasize properties of the situation facing the policymakers, usually as they are perceived by the decision makers. My own definition (Charles F. Hermann, "International Crisis as a Situational Variable," in James N. Rosenau, ed., International Politics and Foreign Policy, New York, 1969) involved three properties: high threat, short time, and surprise. More specifically a crisis involves the combination of high threat to basic goals of the policymakers, short time before the situation evolves in a manner undesired by them,

and appearance as a surprise (i.e., a lack of expectation that the situation would occur).

From a decision-making perspective a basic question is: What effects do crises have on the quality of decisions? A decision-making crisis need not involve an international problem. Unless one of the defining characteristics is the probability of war, a crisis may include domestic events that threaten the government as well as those emerging in world affairs. Thus in *comparative politics a governmental crisis refers to a pending vote of no confidence in a parliamentary regime that challenges the continuation of the government.

Prescriptive studies seek to advance means to avoid crises or to manage them without severe consequences. Such studies can be undertaken at any of the three levels of crisis, but they tend to be concentrated at that of governmental decision making. Crisis management research establishes a standard for the quality of decisions (e.g., rationality, adaptation, avoidance of war) and then identifies circumstances in policy-making that tend to produce a deviation from that standard. Proposals for avoiding these crisis-induced difficulties are then recommended. For example, Irving Janis (Victims of Groupthink, Boston, 1972) contends that decision groups in crisis tend to engage in excessive concurrence seeking that erodes the quality of decisions. He proposes steps to reduce this concurrence-seeking behavior.

Each of the three levels (and definitions) of crisis concerns different questions. In systemic crises, when do such events lead to destabilization? In international confrontation crises, when do bargaining strategies produce successful outcomes without war? In governmental crises, what effects do such events have on the quality of decisions? Thus, the definition of crisis and the level of analysis used depend upon the problems to be addressed. At all levels, the overriding question is how the affected actor(s) deals with an acutely threatening situation.

(See also COLD WAR; DETERRENCE; DIPLOMACY; INTERDEPENDENCE.)

Richard N. Lebow, Nuclear Crisis Management (Ithaca, N.Y., 1987). Michael Brecher, Jonathan Wilkenfeld, and Sheila Moser, Crises in the Twentieth Century, 2 vols. (New York, 1988).

CHARLES F. HERMANN

CROATIA. See YUGOSLAVIA.

CUBA. Lying 145 kilometers (90 mi.) off the U.S. coast, Cuba is situated at the entrance to the Gulf of Mexico. Consequently, despite its small size (about 11 million people in 1992), it has always been of strategic interest to the United States, which has tried many ways to acquire control over Cuba or to assure its allegiance. The Cubans, however, have had other ideas.

Historical Background. Cuba gained its independence from Spain in 1898, as a consequence of the so-called Spanish-American War. As Spain was about to lose the struggle, the United States intervened under the guise of helping Cuba and quickly defeated Spain. Although Cuba was theoretically granted full sovereignty after the war, in fact the United States imposed protectorate status and ruled through proxy between 1901 and 1933. Legal justification derived from the Platt Amendment, which authorized the United States to intervene to protect life and property and to "assure Cuban independence." Over the years, U.S. marines did intervene frequently to restore order and protect growing American economic interests on the island.

In 1933, Gerardo Machado, the corrupt president since 1925, was forced to resign by a surge of student-led opposition. He was replaced by liberal reformer Dr. Ramón Grau San Martín. The newly elected Roosevelt administration charged that Grau's government had "communistic tendencies," and backed a coup by Colonel Fulgencio Batista (1934–1944). A mulatto of humble origins, Batista gained a reputation as a populist by enacting liberal social and labor legislation, but he also relied heavily on force to pursue his goals.

The years 1944–1952, Cuba's only experience with liberal democracy, were a period of disillusion. The country was governed by the Partido Auténtico, first under Grau San Martín and later Carlos Prío Socarrás. Although the period began with a spirit of optimism inspired by the reform platform of the party, the two leaders abused their positions and ushered in an avalanche of corruption and graft. Hungry to return to power, and citing fraudulent elections, Batista's men in the army staged a coup and the colonel returned to power. This time he was more unscrupulous and more closely aligned with the United States.

Led by a young university student named Fidel *Castro, a handful of Cubans refused to acquiesce to Batista's seizure of power. They began their struggle for power with the assault on the Moncada garrison in 1953, a military failure but a political success. Taken prisoner, Fidel culminated his defense with the provocative speech, "History Will Absolve Me," a rallying cry for the revolution. Castro and his men were amnestied and they fled to Mexico where they plotted their return. In November 1956, they set sail for Cuba aboard the *Granma*. During the next two years, the Batista army fought the revolutionaries in the countryside and the cities, and on 1 January 1959, with the army in shambles, Batista fled Cuba. Fidel Castro marched into Havana, cheered as a national hero.

The *Cuban Revolution of 1959 did not begin as a socialist revolution. First and foremost a nationalist, Castro's reform program provoked U.S. opposition. Fearing *nationalization, U.S. companies pulled out, and the government imposed a partial trade embargo against Cuba. Within a year, Washington broke diplomatic relations with Havana, and on the eve of the U.S.-sponsored *Bay of Pigs invasion of Cuba in April 1961, Castro declared the Cuban Revolution to be socialist. Recognizing that a split with the United States was inevitable and invasion probably imminent, Castro turned to the Soviet Union, the only source that could guarantee his survival. Over the next three decades, Castro instituted a socialist government with Soviet assistance.

Political Institutions. The Partido Comunista de Cuba (PCC) was formed in 1965, by merging the early revolutionary parties. The only legal party in Cuba, the PCC was patterned on the *Communist Party of the Soviet Union, with a Central Committee and Politburo. PCC membership is highly selective: members constitute about five percent of the population. Castro also reorganized the Cuban state along Soviet lines, with a Council of Ministers and a system of popular assemblies roughly equivalent to the soviets in the USSR. Cuba's assemblies begin at the municipal level and culminate in the National Assembly of People's Power. The first nationwide, secret-ballot, direct elections for the municipal assemblies were held in 1976. Direct elections for the National Assembly took place in 1992. The National Assembly has little real power; its principal function has been to rubber-stamp decisions taken by the Politburo of the PCC. In spite of this bureaucracy, true power in Cuba remains almost exclusively in the hands of Fidel Castro, who is the first secretary of the Politburo, president of the Council of State of the National Assembly, and president of the Council of Ministers.

The Cuban armed forces (Fuerzas Armadas Revolucionarias; FAR) are also a crucial component of the governing structure. Led by Fidel Castro's brother, Raúl, the FAR is the most powerful military force in the hemisphere after the United States and Brazil. Cuba spends more money per capita on its armed forces than any other Latin American nation; much of its equipment, as well as its professional training, has come from the Soviet Union. With the changes in the former Soviet states, however, Soviet military aid is being steadily reduced, and the Russian leadership is planning a full troop withdrawal as soon as an agreement is reached with Cuba. The FAR not only serves to protect Cuba from external enemies and maintain order domestically, it has also come to the aid of fellow socialist regimes all over the Third World. Over 300,000 Cubans have served in military and civilian assistance programs in *Angola, where Cuba had its largest military mission. Tens of thousands of Cubans have also served in over a dozen African and Latin American countries.

Cuban citizens participate in politics through mass organizations. The Comités de Defensa de la Revolución, the Confederación de Trabajores de Cuba, the Federación de Mujeres Cubanas, and the Asociación Nacional de Agricultores Pequeños constitute the four most important mass organizations. The Cuban government does not recognize independent public organizations. In recent years, a number of *human rights monitoring groups have sprung up in Cuba and operate illegally.

Economic and Social Goals. The main goals of the revolution were social and economic: increased housing, improved health care, universal education and literacy, land reform, and an end to malnutrition and unemployment. The revolutionary leaders believed that after sixty years of a semicolonial relationship with the United States, their commitment to meeting *basic needs could be accomplished only though a radical transformation of the island's economy. As they began dismantling the foreign monopoly in Cuba, the United States responded by imposing an economic embargo against Cuba that continues today. Revolutionary goals and U.S. opposition worked in tandem to push the Cubans closer to the Soviet orbit, and by the mid-1960s, the Soviet Union had become Cuba's primary aid and trade partner.

The Cuban economy has performed respectably, if unevenly, over the years. Cuba's annual growth rate over the last thirty years averaged around five percent, considerably above that of most other Latin American nations. A major economic problem is the continued dependence on sugar, which represents about seventy-five percent of Cuban exports. Nevertheless, some success has been achieved in the areas of import substitution and export diversification. By the early 1980s, Cuban nontraditional exports (citrus products, shellfish, medicines, nickel, and cement) outstripped those of other Caribbean Basin countries. Tourism has also expanded significantly.

Most impressively, the Cuban revolution ended illiteracy, eradicated unemployment, and made education universal. Medical care is free for all, and it is so advanced that Cuba is recognized as a "medical power" by the World Health Organization. Cuba exports medicines, medical equipment, doctors, and treats foreigners under its medical tourism program. In 1991, Cuba's infant mortality rate stood at 11 per 1,000, lower than any other *Third World country and, indeed, lower than in many parts of the United States.

There is no doubt that Cuba was able to accomplish these achievements because of Soviet aid. In the first decades of the revolution, cut off from traditional trading partners, Soviet project aid, military assistance, and trade were crucial to the very survival of the Cuban economy. In the 1980s, however, project aid nearly ended, and the balance of trade swung in favor of the Soviets. Economic and political change in the former Soviet Union altered the relationship substantially. Trade is taking place in hard currency rather than the former barter basis, and deliveries of goods have been sporadic at best.

The changes in the former Soviet Union are causing enormous problems for the Castro government, which has responded with a severe austerity program.

Foreign Policy. It is said that Cuba is a little country with a big foreign policy. The *ideology of proletarian internationalism—assisting socialist regimes to attain and maintain power—has guided Cuban foreign policy since the revolution. Cuba has had economic and military aid programs in seventeen African countries, the largest in Angola and Ethiopia. In the 1960s, Cuba also provided support for revolutionaries in many Latin American countries. The best-known was Bolivia, where Ernesto ("Che") *Guevara died leading a guerrilla movement.

The effect of Cuban assistance to antigovernment movements in Latin America was to isolate Cuba from the rest of the hemisphere. The United States played a major role in this isolation, leading the move to have Cuba thrown out of regional organizations and encouraging governments to break diplomatic ties with the island. At the same time, the U.S. government itself has maintained a policy of almost constant economic and political hostility to Cuba. The only exception was a brief warming of relations during the *Carter years, when the two countries opened "interest sections" in each other's capitals.

Despite the hostility of its giant neighbor, the revolutionary government has managed to survive for three decades, with Castro now one of the longest-sitting leaders in the world. Moreover, its Latin American neighbors have gradually begun to normalize relations with Cuba. Ironically, then, in the 1990s, Cuba's biggest problems come from its former Soviet patron: both ideological attacks and a substantial cut in economic assistance. Castro has responded defiantly, insisting the Cuba will never abandon *socialism as he sees his former allies doing. The outcome remains uncertain, but the island nation seems destined to continue in the international spotlight for some time to come.

(See also AMERICAN FOREIGN POLICY; ANGOLAN CONFLICT; COMMUNIST PARTY STATES; CUBAN MISSILE CRISIS; GUERRILLA WARFARE; U.S.–LATIN AMERICAN RELATIONS.)

Wayne Smith, *The Closest of Enemies* (New York, 1987). Philip Brenner, William M. Leogrande, Donna Rich, and Daniel Siegel, eds., *The Cuba Reader: The Making of a Revolutionary Society* (New York, 1989). Jorge Dominguez, *To Make a World Safe for Revolution: Cuba's Foreign Policy* (Cambridge, Mass., 1989).

WAYNE S. SMITH
DONNA RICH KAPLOWITZ

CUBAN MISSILE CRISIS. On 15 October 1962, American *intelligence discovered the first of six Soviet nuclear missile bases under construction in *Cuba. After a week of deliberation with a group of close advisers that would later become known as the Executive Committee of the National Security Council, or "ExComm," President John F. *Kennedy announced the discovery to the world in a televised address at 7:00 P.M. on 22 October. Stressing that the deployment had been undertaken secretly and in flagrant violation of his own warnings against such a move, Kennedy demanded that the missiles be withdrawn, and announced his intention to impose a naval "quarantine" on shipments of "offensive" weapons to Cuba. He warned Soviet Chairman Nikita *Khrushchev that any missile launched from Cuban territory against any nation of the Western Hemisphere would be considered an attack by the Soviet Union on the United States, requiring a full retaliatory response upon the Soviet Union. To back up his threat, Kennedy ordered a massive redeployment of forces to the Caribbean and placed the Strategic Air Command on heightened alert. Thus began the Cuban missile *crisis, widely regarded as the closest the world has yet come to nuclear war between the *superpowers.

Furious, Khrushchev immediately ordered construction at the missile sites accelerated, and denounced the quarantine as piracy—a flagrant interference with Soviet freedom of navigation and a gross violation of the Soviet Union's right to enter into military arrangements with friendly sovereign states. But by the time the quarantine took effect on the morning of Wednesday, 24 October—after a unanimous vote of support from the *Organization of American States—Khrushchev had ordered Soviet ships carrying suspect cargo not to challenge the U.S. blockade. An immediate confrontation on the high seas was thereby avoided. Still, for several days a settlement of the dispute eluded U.S. and Soviet diplomats. As the crisis dragged on, pressure began to build on both sides for more decisive action.

Neither Kennedy nor Khrushchev was prepared to risk nuclear war over the issue, and both became increasingly preoccupied with the danger that an accident or inadvertent military action might push them over the brink. An apparent break came on Friday, 26 October, when, in a long and emotional letter, Khrushchev vaguely offered to withdraw the missiles in return for a U.S. pledge not to invade Cuba. But in a letter received the following morning, Khrushchev seemed to back away from this position, offering instead to remove the missiles in return for the withdrawal of the fifteen U.S. Jupiter missiles from Turkey—obsolete medium-range nuclear missiles deployed under the aegis of the *North Atlantic Treaty Organization (NATO). The ExComm as a whole argued strongly against such a deal on the grounds that it was politically unacceptable: it would be interpreted by the Soviets as evidence of U.S. weakness; it would be regarded as a betrayal of Turkey, a NATO ally, for whose benefit the Jupiters had been deployed; and it would be extremely unpopular domestically. The president decided to ig-

nore Khrushchev's latest demand and "accept" his "offer" of 26 October.

As the ExComm deliberated on Saturday, 27 October, word reached the White House that an American U-2 reconnaissance plane had been shot down over Cuba, and that another had inadvertently strayed over Siberian airspace, narrowly avoiding a similar fate. At this point, Kennedy evidently resolved to bring the crisis to an end. Ignoring the ExComm's advice, he secretly instructed Secretary of State Dean Rusk to lay the groundwork for a contingency by which the secretary general of the UN would propose the Cuba-Turkey missile swap. Knowing this to be acceptable to Khrushchev, Kennedy therefore knew that it would provide a quick resolution to the crisis should events get out of hand. But Kennedy was saved from having to decide whether or not to execute his demarche by Khrushchev's sudden agreement on 28 October to withdraw the missiles from Cuba in return for a noninvasion pledge.

While Khrushchev's agreement proved to be the decisive break in the crisis, it did not immediately resolve the confrontation. Khrushchev had failed to consult Fidel *Castro on the matter, and Castro understandably felt betrayed by his Soviet patron. He therefore refused to allow UN inspectors to examine the missile sites to verify the withdrawal, forcing the U.S. Navy to make do by inspecting outbound Soviet ships from the air. Kennedy also insisted that the Soviets withdraw a handful of Il-28 light bombers, because these were believed to have a nuclear capability. But the Il-28s had been supplied to Cuba for coastal defense purposes wholly independently of the missile deployment, and it would take Khrushchev's special envoy, Anastas Mikoyan, a full three weeks to persuade Castro to comply. On 19 November, Castro finally relented, and on 21 November, Kennedy issued a proclamation terminating the quarantine.

Causes. The causes of the Cuban missile crisis continue to spark controversy. Evidence and testimony currently available indicate that Khrushchev decided on the deployment in the late spring of 1962, after a hasty and uncritical decision-making process involving only a small group of advisers. One of his main motivations seems to have been to deter a U.S. invasion of Cuba, which seemed inevitable to the Soviets and Cubans given the U.S. role in the *Bay of Pigs invasion the previous year, and in light of Operation Mongoose, the *Central Intelligence Agency's energetic covert campaign to topple the Castro regime. Another important goal was to counterbalance the United States' massive superiority in strategic *nuclear weapons, publicly revealed to the world by Deputy Secretary of Defense Roswell Gilpatric in an October 1961 speech exploding the myth of a "missile gap" favoring the Soviet Union. It is impossible to know which of these (if either) was the more important motivation—they were mutually reinforcing, and there is no evidence to suggest that Khrushchev asked the question of himself. A third and evidently subsidiary consideration was the desire to counterbalance the U.S. deployment of Jupiter missiles on the Soviet periphery, for reasons of prestige.

Conduct. The Cuban missile crisis is considered by many a classic case of prudent crisis management. Kennedy and Khrushchev managed to prevent the conflict from escalating while they sought and eventually found a solution satisfactory to both. They did so by avoiding irreversible steps, curtailing unwarranted bluster, and refraining from ultimatums. But others have criticized their handling of the crisis for being too timid or too bold. Kennedy's critics on the Right lament his unwillingness to seize the opportunity provided by the pretext of the Soviet deployment to deal decisively with Castro once and for all, while the United States enjoyed a massive advantage in strategic nuclear weapons and unquestioned local conventional superiority. His critics on the Left condemn his willingness to risk nuclear war merely to delay the inevitable—the vulnerability of the United States to Soviet nuclear weapons. Khrushchev's handling of the crisis has been largely criticized by hard-liners who condemn his willingness to yield to U.S. pressure. Others in the Soviet Union applaud his cautious handling of the situation and his willingness to compromise while condemning him for recklessly provoking the crisis in the first place.

Consequences. Almost paradoxically, the Cuban missile crisis was the immediate cause of a considerable improvement in U.S.-Soviet relations. A series of agreements intended to restrain the *arms race and improve crisis stability followed closely on its heels, of which perhaps the most important were the 1963 Limited Test Ban Treaty and Hot-Line Agreement. The crisis severely strained, but did not disrupt, Soviet-Cuban relations. Sources close to Kennedy insist that if he had won a second term as president, as seems likely given his popularity after the crisis itself, he would have ventured a reconciliation with Cuba. Kennedy's *assassination in November 1963 and his succession by Lyndon *Johnson, and Khrushchev's ouster in 1964 by Leonid Brezhnev, marked the end of their two countries' brief *détente, and forestalled any improvement in U.S.-Cuban relations.

In a technical sense, the Cuban missile crisis was never fully resolved. No treaty was ever concluded governing the settlement, and the exchange of letters between Kennedy and Khrushchev formalizing the terms of their agreement has not been made public. It is questionable whether they contain the firm guarantees against an invasion of Cuba that the Soviet Union trumpeted publicly as Kennedy's major concession. Indeed, while in office, one U.S. president—Ronald *Reagan—publicly denied being bound by any such obligation. Nevertheless, the United

States and the Soviet Union crafted and scrupulously followed a modus vivendi in which the purported terms on which the crisis was resolved played a pivotal role. The Soviet Union refrained from deploying military equipment with offensive capabilities to Cuba, and the United States acquiesced in a Communist-controlled Cuba with close ties to the Soviet Union. But even more importantly, the United States and the Soviet Union worked out rules of the road limiting provocative initiatives in areas each regarded as being within its sphere of vital interest. Thus the Cuban missile crisis performed the valuable service of helping to immunize against a similar event.

(See also LATIN AMERICAN REGIONAL ORGANIZATIONS; U.S.–LATIN AMERICAN RELATIONS.)

David L. Larson, ed., *The "Cuban Crisis" of 1962: Selected Documents, Chronology and Bibliography,* 2d ed. (Lanham, Md., 1986). Raymond L. Garthoff, *Reflections on the Cuban Missile Crisis,* rev. ed. (Washington, D.C., 1989). James G. Blight and David A. Welch, *On the Brink: Americans and Soviets Reexamine the Cuban Missile Crisis,* 2d ed. (New York, 1990).

DAVID A. WELCH

CUBAN REVOLUTION. The roots of the Cuban Revolution lie in the early twentieth century, when the island was occupied by the United States at the end of the Spanish-American War. Fierce *nationalism coupled with a determination to rid *Cuba of President Fulgencio Batista's corruption and brutality led Fidel *Castro to attack the Moncada Army Barracks on 26 July 1953. Captured, imprisoned, and then exiled to Mexico, Castro and his followers subsequently landed on Cuba's eastern shore in November 1956, fought a twenty-five-month guerrilla war, and forced Batista to flee on New Year's Eve 1958.

The first three years of the Cuban Revolution defined its main characteristics to date: the preeminent place of Fidel Castro (first as leader of the 26th of July Movement, and later as Cuban president, prime minister, and first secretary of the Communist Party), the Leninist political system, the highly socialized economy, the deep antagonism from and toward the United States, and the special—although not always easy—relationship with the Soviet Union. From the radical nationalization and reform measures of the first years to the U.S. economic embargo, the *Bay of Pigs invasion in April 1961, and the missile crisis of October 1962, the Cuban Revolution established itself as the most dramatic and conflictual (and some would say most dangerous) example of revolutionary nationalism in the history of modern Latin America.

Cuban revolutionary support for Latin American guerrilla movements in the 1960s—always a source of friction with the Soviet Union—was much reduced after the death of Ernesto ("Che") *Guevara in Bolivia in October 1967. Subsequently, in the 1970s the *revolution overcame some of its most serious economic problems owing in large measure to very significant material and technical aid from the Soviet Union. The seventies also saw profound Cuban involvement with liberation movements in Africa, culminating in the armed defense of Angolan independence in 1975. Increasingly in the 1980s, however, despite continued Soviet aid and some experimentation with free markets, the Cuban economy performed poorly. The country is still dependent largely on agricultural and mineral exports, and ambitious plans to develop tourism and high technology industries have met with only modest success. In the 1990s, faced with declining support from the former Soviet Union and Eastern Europe, Cuba faces its most acute economic crisis in over two decades.

Despite its multiple economic difficulties, the Cuban Revolution has nevertheless managed to secure impressive social gains for its citizens, particularly in the areas of health and education. Even more dramatically, this small island and its revolution—made in the shadow of the United States—have left a mark on the history of the Americas far beyond what would have been predicted when Fidel Castro and his followers came to power in 1959. Castro himself was, at the outset of 1992, the longest-sitting head of state in the world. And the Cuban regime, seemingly firm in its commitment to socialism—while the former Soviet Union, Eastern Europe, and many of Africa's revolutionary states are divesting themselves of both the economic and political trappings of Marxism—remains, as many have called it, "the last revolution."

(See also GUERRILLA WARFARE; LENINISM; U.S.–LATIN AMERICAN RELATIONS.)

Sandor Halebsky and John M. Kirk, eds., *Cuba: Twenty-Five Years of Revolution, 1959–1984* (New York, 1985). Philip Brenner et al., eds., *The Cuba Reader: The Making of a Revolutionary Society* (New York, 1989).

RICHARD R. FAGEN

CULTURAL REVOLUTION. *China's Cultural Revolution (1966–1976), or "Great Proletarian Cultural Revolution" as it was formally called, was a movement launched by *Chinese Communist Party (CCP) chairman *Mao Zedong to stem what he perceived as the country's drift away from *socialism and toward the "restoration of *capitalism." The campaign, which was euphorically described at its inception by its progenitors as "a great *revolution that touches people to their very souls" and which inspired radical students from Paris to Berkeley, is now regarded as having been a terrible catastrophe for the Chinese nation.

The origins of the Cultural Revolution can be traced to the mid-1950s when Mao first became seriously concerned about the path that China's socialist transition had taken in the years since the CCP had come to power in 1949. His anxieties about the bureaucratization of the party, ideological

degeneration in society as a whole, and the glaring socioeconomic inequalities that had emerged as China modernized escalated through the early 1960s and propelled him to embark on a crusade to expunge the "revisionism" that he believed was contaminating the party and the nation.

Mao concluded that the source of China's retrogression lay in the false and self-serving view of many of his party colleagues that class struggle ceased under socialism. On the contrary, the chairman concluded, the struggle between proletarian and bourgeois ideologies took on new, insidious forms even after the landlord and capitalist classes had been eliminated. The principal targets of Mao's ire were party and government officials who he felt had become a "new class" divorced from the masses and intellectuals who, in his view, were the repository of bourgeois and even feudal values.

Mao's decision to undertake the Cultural Revolution was strongly influenced by his analysis that the Soviet Union had already abandoned socialism for capitalism. The Cultural Revolution may also have been a power struggle in which Mao fought to recapture from his political rivals some of the authority and prestige that he had lost as a result of earlier policy failures. Futhermore, Mao saw the Cultural Revolution as an opportunity to forge a "generation of revolutionary successors" by preparing China's youth to inherit the mantle of those who had originally brought the CCP to power.

There was also a policy dimension to the Cultural Revolution: once the "capitalist roaders" had been dislodged from power at all levels of society, a wide range of truly socialist institutions and processes were to be put in place to give life to the vision of the Cultural Revolution. For example, elitism in education was to be replaced by schools with revamped, politicized curricula, mass-based administration, and advancement criteria that stressed good class background and ideological correctness.

The complex and convoluted history of the Cultural Revolution can be roughly divided into three major phases. The mass phase (1966–1969) was dominated by the Red Guards, the more than 20 million high-school and college students who responded to Mao's call to "make revolution," and their often-vicious efforts to ferret out "class enemies" wherever they were suspected to lurk; during this stage, most of Mao's rivals in the top leadership were deposed. The military phase (1969–1971) began after the People's Liberation Army had gained ascendancy in Chinese politics by suppressing the anarchy of the Red Guards; it ended with the alleged coup attempt in September 1971 by Mao's disgruntled heir, Defense Minister Lin Biao, who had also been one of Mao's main allies in launching the Cultural Revolution. The succession phase (1972–1976) was an intense political and ideological tug-of-war between radical ideologues and veteran cadres over whether to continue or curtail the policies of the Cultural Revolution. Underlying this conflict was a bitter struggle over which group would control the succession to the two paramount leaders of the CCP, Chairman Mao and Premier *Zhou Enlai, both of whom were in deteriorating health by the early 1970s. The decisive lot in this struggle was cast when the most prominent radicals (the "Gang of Four," which included Mao's widow, Jiang Qing) were preemptively arrested in October 1976, a month after the chairman's death, by a coalition of more moderate leaders. The arrest of the Gang of Four is said to mark the official end of China's Cultural Revolution.

The Cultural Revolution is now referred to in China as the "decade of chaos" and is generally regarded as one of the bleakest periods in the country's modern history. The movement's noble ideals were betrayed at every turn by its destructive impulses. Hundreds of thousands, if not millions, of officials and intellectuals were physically and mentally persecuted. The much-vaunted initiatives that were to transform the nation often had disastrous consequences for China's education and cultural life. Economic development was disrupted by factional strife and misguided "ultraleftist" policies.

The policies that have been followed in China since the late 1970s represent a thorough repudiation of everything the Cultural Revolution stood for. Nevertheless the memory of the movement still casts an ominous shadow over Chinese politics. *Deng Xiaoping and the other elderly leaders who made the decision to crush the *Tiananmen protests in June 1989 feared that, left unchecked, the demonstrations would snowball into Cultural Revolution–like disorder. For Deng, who was one of the Cultural Revolution's foremost victims and whose son was permanently paralyzed after being thrown off a roof by Red Guards, the Cultural Revolution is very much a living and a painful memory—as it is for the Chinese people as a whole.

(See also IDEOLOGY.)

Roderick MacFarquhar, *The Origins of the Cultural Revolution, Volume 1: Contradictions Among the People, 1956–1957* (New York, 1974). Roderick MacFarquhar, *The Origins of the Cultural Revolution, Volume 2: The Great Leap Forward, 1958–1960* (New York, 1983). William A. Joseph, Christine P. W. Wong, and David Zweig, *New Perspectives on the Cultural Revolution* (Cambridge, Mass., 1991).

WILLIAM A. JOSEPH

CYPRUS. The modern state of Cyprus became independent in 1960 after eighty years of British colonial rule (1879–1959). Earlier it had been part of the Ottoman Empire, ruled by the *millet* system in which religious leaders, under the broad authority of the Ottoman administrators, exercised considerable autonomy in governing their coreligionists. The population was predominantly Eastern Orthodox Christian with a sizable Muslim minority, largely a result of migration during the centuries of Ottoman rule.

The imposition by the British of separate political and educational institutions for Greeks and Turks began the process of a shift in identity from religion to *ethnicity. Moreover the rise of nationalist movements and their respective terrorist bands—the National Organization of Cypriot Fighters (EOKA) for the Greeks and the Turkish Resistance Organization (TMT) for the Turks—reinforced segregation and enmity. During the 1950s the Greek Cypriot anticolonial movement for *enosis* (union) with Greece, spearheaded by the charismatic leader Archbishop Makarios, led to protracted negotiations among Britain, *Greece, and *Turkey, with the Cypriots in a subordinate role. The compromise was independence, but the terms of the new constitution structurally segregated the two communities while the treaty signed by the interested parties limited Cyprus's sovereignty. Greece and Turkey were authorized to station a limited number of their troops on the island ostensibly to protect their respective communities.

Although a multiparty democracy, the state of Cyprus has fragmented, leaving the constitutional order inoperative. In 1960 two communal chambers, one Greek and one Turkish, were created and given broad policy-making powers, while the small minorities had to opt for membership in one of the two communities. The authority of the national government was limited, governmental positions were divided between Greeks and Turks with a Greek president and a Turkish vice president, each with the power of veto, and a separate majority vote of Greek and Turkish representatives in the national legislature was required for the passage of bills on crucial issues such as taxation and defense. As a consequence the government was stalemated, and President Makarios proposed majoritarian constitutional revisions, which led to ethnic violence.

The sequence of events that followed resulted in the de facto division of the island in 1974: the Turkish Cypriots rule the northern thirty percent of the island and the Greek Cypriot government controls the remainder. In the north, Turkish troops from the mainland remain, having first invaded in response to the overthrow of President Makarios by Greek Cypriot elements seeking union with Greece. Greek Cypriots fled south and Turkish Cypriots north, a "green line" was established demarking the two sectors, population movement between the sectors was prohibited, and a UN peacekeeping force was sent to maintain peace. Interminable, inconclusive talks have taken place between the leaders of the two communities under the aegis of the UN secretary-general. In the intervening years the Greek Cypriot sector has prospered through commerce, shipping, and finance; the north remains largely agricultural as the Turkish Cypriot leadership settles the area with rural Turks from Turkey. Thanks to the emigration of Turkish Cypriots, the estimated 80,000 settlers from Turkey now nearly balance the estimated 105,000 indigenous Turkish Cypriots who remain. The number of Greek Cypriots is estimated to be 600,000.

For Greece and Turkey, Cyprus is one of the conflicting issue areas between them, while U.S. policy is set by its overall strategic interests in the region. Greece and Turkey claim to speak for the welfare of their conationals in Cyprus, and the Greek and Turkish Cypriot political leaderships in turn expect support from Greece and Turkey. Turkish Cypriots have declared themselves an independent state, the "Turkish Republic of Northern Cyprus," and have adopted several measures integrating themselves with Turkey (the only nation that has recognized their claim to sovereignty). U.S. policy, driven by its interests in the Middle East and the Mediterranean, in the past favored partition of the island. After the Turkish invasion of the island in 1974, in light of Turkey's greater strategic and political importance, it has tilted toward Turkey. UN efforts to resolve the issue of Cyprus's future have reached a stalemate.

(See also NATIONALISM; RELIGION AND POLITICS.)

Kyriacos C. Markides, *The Rise and Fall of the Cypriot Republic* (New Haven, Conn., 1977). Christopher Hitchens, *Cyprus* (London, 1984).

ADAMANTIA POLLIS

CZECHOSLOVAKIA. Created as an independent state in the aftermath of *World War I, the history of Czechoslovakia reflects its position at the heart of Europe as well as its ethnic composition. Thus, this state of approximately 17 million inhabitants has experienced several major changes in political structure and values in the twentieth century. The result of efforts by Czech and Slovak leaders as well as Allied desires to fill the vacuum created in the region by the demise of the Austro-Hungarian Empire, the new state brought together groups that differed from each other in many respects. In contrast to the other states in the region, in Czechoslovakia democratic government survived until it was ended by outside forces. The persistence of *democracy resulted in part from the fact that Czechoslovakia, and in particular the Czech lands, were more developed economically than many of the country's neighbors, had a stable and sizable middle class, and had an educated population. Many of the country's political leaders, including Tomas Masaryk, the first president, were deeply committed to democratic ideals. The ability of the leaders of the country's major political parties to form coalitions and the impact of progressive social and economic policies also contributed to political stability.

The country's leaders were less successful in dealing with ethnic issues. The dissatisfaction of the Sudeten Germans provided the pretext for *Hitler's occupation of Czechoslovakia after the Munich agreement of 1938. The creation of the Slovak state under Hitler's tutelage in March 1939 and the *Soviet Union's annexation of the Subcarpathian Ruthene completed the dismemberment of the interwar Czechoslovak state.

Most political forces recognized the need to have a special relationship with the Soviet Union in the aftermath of *World War II. However, Edvard Beneš returned from exile to serve as president. Although the Communist Party had certain advantages, several other political parties also were active.

This period of modified *pluralism ended in February 1948, when the Communist Party provoked a political crisis that led to the resignation of the democratic ministers and the formation of a government clearly dominated by the Communist Party. The country's communist leaders took steps to reshape values and institutions to conform to those in place in the Soviet Union at the time. All political forces not under the control of the Communist Party were banned, and a system of unified mass organizations was established to mobilize the population to support elite objectives. Private ownership of industry and agricultural land was virtually eliminated, and central economic *planning was instituted. The country's new leaders established a system of censorship; as the Stalinist system was consolidated, they came to rely increasingly on coercion.

Little changed in Czechoslovakia after *Stalin's death. The authorities quickly put down protests in Plzeň in 1953. Although the leadership paid lip service to the need to de-Stalinize, particularly after the Twentieth Party Congress of the *Communist Party of the Soviet Union in 1956, little changed until the 1960s, when declining economic performance and a new wave of reform in the Soviet Union after the Twenty-second Party Congress led to economic and, later, political reform.

The effort to create "Socialism with a Human Face," or the *Prague Spring, that came into the open after January 1968 had its roots in the process of theoretical renewal that took place at the elite level from the early 1960s. Growing Slovak dissatisfaction with what many Slovaks perceived to be continued inequalities in their position in the common state also fueled desires for change. After Alexander Dubček's selection to replace Antonín Novotný as head of the Communist Party in January 1968 and the effective end of censorship in March 1968, ordinary citizens began to press for more dramatic changes. As the Action Program of the Communist Party adopted in April 1968 makes clear, the reformers whose views came to be symbolized by Dubček clearly intended to keep the process under the control of the Communist Party. But, although the leading role of the party was not to be abandoned, they did envision a larger role for noncommunist groups and ordinary citizens.

The Dubček leadership's inability to reassure the conservative leaders of the Soviet Union and several of its European socialist allies led to the *Warsaw Treaty Organization (Warsaw Pact) invasion of Czechoslovakia on 21 August 1968. This step ended what had been the most ambitious program of *reform to date and ushered in a period of political orthodoxy that persisted until the late 1980s. Led by Gustáv Husák, the Communist Party restored censorship and tight political control. Its leaders also instituted a massive personnel purge and renounced the effort made in 1968 to gain popular support. Instead, they relied on a mixture of material benefits and coercion to keep the population in line. As developments in the next twenty years illustrated, this strategy succeeded in maintaining political stability. Writers and other intellectuals occasionally opposed the policies of the post-1968 leadership and, in 1977, *Charter 77 was formed. One of the most important dissident groupings in Central and Eastern Europe, the Charter served as a focus for independent activity and helped to keep independent thought and activity alive.

*Gorbachev's rise to power in the Soviet Union initially had little impact in Czechoslovakia. Afraid that *perestroika and glasnost would re-create a movement for change similar to that of 1968, the Czechoslovak leadership, which had been among the Soviet Union's most loyal allies in the region, did little to implement Gorbachev's policies in Czechoslovakia.

However, despite the surface stability, Czechoslovakia's leaders faced many of the same political and economic problems as other communist leaders. Although the standard of living remained among the highest in the region, economic performance declined. In the last two years of communist rule, there was a marked increase in the willingness of the population to openly challenge the regime. There were also important changes in the leadership of the Communist Party after Miloš Jakeš replaced Gustáv Husák in December 1987.

The fall of the communist system in Czechoslovakia was precipitated by external factors, including the ouster of the hard-line Honecker regime in the German Democratic Republic (GDR), and the move to a negotiated end of communist rule in Hungary and Poland. But, while developments in the Soviet Union under Gorbachev and changes in Soviet policies toward Central and Eastern Europe provided the catalyst, internal factors set the stage and influenced the way in which the communist government was ousted.

When hundreds of thousands of Czech and Slovak citizens took to the streets after the brutal beating of peaceful student demonstrators by police on 17 November 1989, the old regime was swept away very quickly. The resignation of the Communist Party leadership and the renunciation of the party's leading role were followed in early December by the creation of Czechoslovakia's first noncommunist government in forty-one years. The selection of the dissident playwright Václav *Havel, who quickly emerged as the moral leader of what came to be termed the "Velvet Revolution," as president of the country in late December sealed the victory of the opposition.

The new government took immediate steps to re-create democracy. Drawing on the dominant democratic tradition of the country during the interwar period, its new leaders began the arduous process of returning to the rule of law, revising the Constitution, preparing for free elections, and dealing with the legacy of communist rule in areas as diverse as culture and the environment. There has been a re-pluralization of political, associational, and cultural life and a proliferation of independent sources of information.

The free parliamentary and local elections of June and November 1990 legitimated the new government and led to substantial change in political leaders. After initial hesitation owing to divisions among top economic officials, the country's new leaders began economic reforms designed to re-create a market economy and reorient the country's trade. They also reasserted Czechoslovakia's independence in foreign policy. As in other postcommunist societies, Czech and Slovak leaders were soon forced to deal with external disruptions, including the collapse of the *Council for Mutual Economic Assistance trading system, persistent turmoil in the Soviet Union, and, in 1990 and early 1991, the situation in the Persian Gulf.

As in other postcommunist states in the region, the transition to postcommunist rule has led to the reemergence of old problems and the emergence of new public issues. In Czechoslovakia, the most important of these are ethnic issues. In the period after November 1989, ethnic issues complicated steps toward economic reform and constitutional revision. The leaders of the major political parties in both the Czech Republic and Slovakia supported the continuation of some form of common state. However, support for greater autonomy for Slovakia or a separate Slovak state increased after the end of communist rule, and conflict over ethnic issues led to several political crises. Other groups, such as the Moravians, gypsies, Hungarians, and Ukrainians, also began to assert their rights as ethnic groups more forcefully.

The country's leaders were able to contain conflict over ethnic issues within the framework of the existing political system until the June 1992 parliamentary elections. The victory of Vladimir Meciar's Movement for a Democratic Slovakia and the subsequent inability of Czech and Slovak leaders to agree on the proper role of the federal and republic level governments led to a downgrading of the role of the federal government and an agreement to take steps to realize a break-up of the common state by

September 1992. In protest of this plan, Václav Havel resigned his post as president in July 1992. There is little likelihood that the end of the common state will result in violence. However, both parts of the country will be affected by the economic dislocations that will follow, at least in the short run. The break-up of the groups that led the revolution in 1989, Civic Forum and Public Against Violence, into several organizations, and the continued support for the successors to the Communist Party in certain quarters, also complicate the political situation at present.

(See also CENTRAL EUROPE; ETHNICITY; NINE-TEEN EIGHTY-NINE; SOVIET–EAST EUROPEAN RELATIONS; STALINISM.)

Timothy G. Ash, *The Magic Lantern: The Revolution of '89 Witnessed in Warsaw, Budapest, Berlin & Prague* (New York, 1990). Sharon L. Wolchik, *Czechoslovakia in Transition: Politics, Society, and Economics* (London, 1991).

SHARON L. WOLCHIK

D

DEBT CRISIS. See International Debt.

DECOLONIZATION. The term *decolonization* is commonly defined as a change in *sovereignty, in which a *state recognizes the independence of a segment of the people formerly under its rule and their right to a government formed according to procedures determined by them. A new state acting under its own volition, free from the direct control of foreign actors, comes into existence as a part of the international community. In this sense, the separation of India and Ireland from Britain; of Zaire from Belgium; of Indonesia from the Netherlands; of Bangladesh from Pakistan are clear-cut examples of decolonization.

The difficulty with such a definition comes from the ambiguity inherent in the concept of sovereignty. Simply because a country is nominally independent does not mean that it is immune to foreign influence—at times to such an extent that it is part of an informal empire. Thus, until recently the countries of Eastern and *Central Europe were treated as sovereign by the international community while in fact the policies of the governments there were determined in most important respects by Moscow. In this sense, the events of 1989–1990 constituted the "decolonization" of this region every bit as much as, say, the independence of Algeria from France in 1962 can be covered by the term. Similarly, the United States has long enjoyed enormous influence in Central America. Yet if El Salvador may today be treated as a sovereign state, in all probability its government could not last a month without the backing of Washington. In a world of states with grossly unequal amounts of power, what constitutes sovereignty? In the 1960s, an African leader such as Kwame *Nkrumah of Ghana talked of "neocolonialism" as if decolonization were a flag-and-anthem ceremony signifying nothing more than the replacement of white bourgeois rule by a black bourgeoisie dedicated to the continued exploitation of the people allegedly given their independence.

If we agree that the concept of sovereignty is inherently ambiguous, we may more easily see decolonization in a broader, if less precise, light and use the term to refer not only to the independence of peoples once under formal imperial control but also to the increased independence of peoples never subjected directly to such rule. We may then see decolonization as related to such significant developments as the Young Turk movement in the Ottoman Empire at the turn of this century, to the Mexican Revolution of 1910, and to the rise of *nationalism and *communism in China. From this perspective, decolonization refers to the general process of nationalist uprising against European (including Soviet), U.S., and Japanese imperialism since about 1880, of which the story of the formal decolonization of European empires in Africa and Asia after 1945 is but one chapter (although often the only history included under the term).

If the definition of decolonization is no easy task, the elucidation of the forces that have created this process is an even more daunting challenge. On the one hand, each case is individual with its own specific character; on the other hand, decolonization is just as clearly a global phenomenon, linked historically to the character of the international political and economic system since about 1880, when a new round of European *imperialism began. To see developments during this period as a series of discrete case studies, each isolated by its own individual characteristics, would be to ignore the powerful worldwide trends that have molded local forces in terms that have a general identity.

The juxtaposition of specific cases of decolonization with the general process bearing this name can perhaps best be made by seeing the global process largely in terms of the dynamics of imperialism while analyzing decolonization in more local terms. In this sense, the history of modern decolonization is inextricably linked to that of modern imperialism.

Decolonization obviously refers to the inability or unwillingness of the previously powerful to continue to exercise their imperial rule. On the one hand, the imperialists could weaken themselves as occurred in the two world wars, which weakened Britain, France, Belgium, and the Netherlands. The rise of the United States and the Soviet Union as two self-proclaimed anti-imperialist superpowers after 1945 noticeably accelerated the process of European decolonization. On the other, the subject or weaker peoples were not assimilated or destroyed, and over time they developed a political capacity to ward off the imperialists. In countries as diverse as India and Vietnam the decisive development was the organization of powerful nationalist political movements whose first aim was to secure the independence of their countries and their effective sovereignty in world affairs. In the case of the end of the Soviet empire, similar distinctions between internal and international developments must be appreciated.

The character of these nationalist movements varied widely in terms of local conditions. In India, a national bourgeoisie dominated the Congress Party, headed by *Gandhi and *Nehru. In Vietnam, *Ho Chi Minh's Communist Party led the nationalist struggle. In Algeria, dispossessed Muslim peasants organized the Front de Libération Nationale and attacked French rule. In *Poland, workers and intellectuals joined *Solidarity and pledged to remove the Soviet-controlled Polish Communist Party from rule in Warsaw. In much of sub-Saharan Africa, by contrast, the Europeans prepared to leave power before it was actually demanded by well-organized nationalist groups. It is thus not surprising that the character of the particular local groups that took power during the decolonization process explains a good measure of the different experiences previously colonized peoples have had since independence. Just as very distinct interests, *ideologies, and organizations constituted the various nationalist movements, so the new governments have quite unique identities. Nevertheless, decolonization remains a general historical process, in good measure because the fortunes of imperialism are the stuff of which global history is made.

Given the variety of forces contributing to decolonization it is evident why no single theory can hope to explain more than a part of what occurred. Thus, the particular character of British, and later U.S., *hegemony over the *international system since about 1815 was of great significance. Both countries based their influence on an opposition to formal imperialism (even if they both engaged in it extensively) and the doctrine of free trade. By the twentieth century, the Anglo-Americans had decided that democratic government was the only legitimate form of state and that the claim of nationalist movements for independence was morally irrefutable. In sum, the international system dominated by London or Washington was relatively favorable to the growth of local nationalisms. An order primarily controlled by Germany, Japan, or the Soviet Union would presumably have made for a very different set of forces acting on the weaker peoples of the globe.

The structure of international politics played its role as well. A multipolar world promoted a scramble for colonies in the late nineteenth century, much as the rise of a bipolar world after 1945 brought powerful influences to favor the decolonization of the West European empires thereafter.

Yet another force influencing the character of decolonization was socioeconomic change among the previously colonized peoples. Technological development in the economically weaker regions tended to create urban cultures, new bureaucracies, and higher levels of education in a way that stimulated the rise of new political demands on the parts of colonial subjects. New forms of political organization there created a heightened sense of place and person—so giving rise not only to nationalism but to a tangible ability to engage in political expression. Just as political, military, economic, and cultural factors gave rise to imperialism, so too did changes in these various dimensions of social life lead eventually to decolonization.

The paradox of decolonization is that it has occurred in a century marked by a growing interdependence of nations. The resolution of the paradox of simultaneously increasing interdependence and independence among peoples at the end of the twentieth century may perhaps be found in concepts of *political development. As specific local functions increase in activity—as economic productivity increases, or as previously separated class or ethnic groups are brought into closer political contact—so too does the need arise for governing mechanisms designed to promote coherence and alleviate conflict. In this sense the increasing self-consciousness of distinct peoples can be understood as part of the very process of their growing interdependence. A heightened localism and a greater feeling of internationalism are therefore not necessarily contradictory developments but aspects of economic, cultural, and political life that are the result of more than two hundred years of development, beginning in the latter half of the eighteenth century, with the Industrial Revolution in Britain and the rise of nationalism concurrent with the French Revolution. Thus the study of decolonization obliges us at one and the same time to respect the vigor of local political forces, yet not to lose sight of the global changes of which they are a part.

(See also COLONIAL EMPIRES; NINETEEN EIGHTY-NINE.)

Tony Smith, ed., *The End of European Empire: Decolonization after World War II* (Lexington, Mass., 1975). Tony Smith, *The Pattern of Imperialism: The United States, Great Britain and the Late-Industrializing World since 1815* (Cambridge, 1981). Rudolf von Albertini, *Decolonization: The Administration and Future of the Colonies, 1919–1960*, 2d ed. (New York, 1982). Miles Kahler, *Decolonization in Britain and France: The Domestic Consequences of International Relations* (Princeton, N.J., 1984). Brian Lapping, *End of Empire* (New York, 1985). Stephen D. Krasner, "Sovereignty: An Institutional Perspective" *Comparative Political Studies* 21, no. 1 (April 1988).

TONY SMITH

DEFENSE. See SECURITY.

DE GAULLE, Charles. See GAULLE, CHARLES DE.

DEINDUSTRIALIZATION. The term *deindustrialization* came into vogue in the 1980s, to describe the loss of relatively high-paying factory jobs in advanced industrial nations. From the onset, there was confusion abut what was being claimed, and about the appropriate government policies for remedying the presumed problem. While the "deindustrializers" fretted over the loss of these jobs, their critics argued that advanced nations were not really "deindustrializing" at all, since manufacturing output in the 1980s was not substantially lower, as a percentage of GNP, than it had been in previous decades. The reason for the decline in manufacturing employment, they said, was that manufacturers had become so productive that they now needed fewer workers. The shift from manufacturing to services within all advanced economies was an inevitable stage of development, much like the shift in the previous century from agriculture to manufacturing. The "deindustrializers" responded that, such explanations notwithstanding, well-paying manufacturing jobs were being replaced by low-paying service jobs, with the result that the United States was losing its middle class.

Most researchers have come to agree that the middle class is shrinking in the United States, although there is no consensus that "deindustrialization" is the culprit. Controlling for family size, geography, and other changes, the average income of the poorest fifth in the United States declined between 1977 and 1990 by about nine percent, while the richest fifth became about nineteen percent wealthier. That left the poorest fifth with 3.7 percent of the nation's total income in 1990, down from 5.5 percent twenty years before—the lowest portion they had received since 1954; and it left the richest fifth with a bit over half the nation's income—the highest portion ever recorded by the top twenty percent. The top five percent commanded twenty-six percent of the nation's income, another record. Some researchers, selecting different years and using different measurements, have found the divergence to be somewhat less pronounced than this, but they note the same trend.

Proposals for what to do about this widening gap are related to its presumed cause. The "deindustrializers" seek measures to preserve, protect, subsidize, or otherwise encourage the creation of well-paying manufacturing jobs that would supposedly restore middle-class incomes. Their critics—who attribute the divergence in incomes to factors such as the growth in single-parent, lower-income families, or the influx of young, unskilled, and inexperienced baby boomers and women into the work force—argue that such measures would be pointless. To the extent that the "deindustrializers" want to protect U.S. manufacturing jobs against foreign competition, moreover, critics contend that others would bear the burden of paying substantially higher prices for the goods they purchased, and that such policies also would invite foreign nations to bar American-made goods, resulting in losses for everyone.

The argument will continue to rage, but there is mounting evidence that the widening income gap is more related to changes in the global demand for labor than to changes in U.S. labor supply. Increases in the number of single-parent families, and in the number of baby-boomer and women job entrants, actually slowed after the late 1970s, just as the income gap in the United States began to widen precipitously. Moreover, other nations have experienced similarly diverging incomes, even without these demographic changes. This is not to suggest that the "deindustrializers" are entirely correct in attributing the widening gap to the loss of good manufacturing jobs, however. Other, broader trends are at work, involving services as well as manufacturing.

What has happened, it seems, is that national economies have become so integrated into a single global economy that labor supply and demand now operate worldwide. Highly skilled and talented workers in economically advanced nations confront an ever-larger world market for their services; thus the earnings of software engineers, lawyers, investment bankers, architects, management consultants, movie producers, and other professionals are on the rise. At the other extreme, unskilled workers—whether in traditional manufacturing industries or in services that are traded internationally, such as data processing—find themselves competing with a growing number of unskilled workers around the world, many of whom are eager to work for a fraction of the wages of unskilled workers in advanced nations. Thus are relatively unskilled workers in advanced industrial countries pushed into local service occupations where they must compete with labor-saving machinery, immigrants, and all the other unskilled workers who can no longer compete internationally. Their earnings are thus stagnating or declining.

The consequences for public policy are profound. The United States and other nations face three policy choices. They can attempt to preserve or protect older manufacturing jobs, or, alternatively, they can abdicate all responsibility to the magic of the global marketplace. Finally, industrialized nations may seek to enhance the capacities of their citizens to add value to the global economy, and thus command a higher standard of living from the world. Toward this end, they would increase expenditures on education, training, and infrastructure (roads, bridges, airports, and other forms of public capital), and on subsidies to global corporations that provide on-the-job training in advanced technologies.

(See also DEVELOPMENT AND UNDERDEVELOPMENT; FOREIGN WORKERS; FORDISM; POLITICAL ECONOMY; POSTINDUSTRIAL SOCIETY.)

Barry Bluestone and Bennett Harrison, *The Deindustrialization of America* (New York, 1982). Robert Z. Lawrence, *Can America Compete?* (Washington, D.C., 1984). Robert B. Reich, *The Work of Nations* (New York, 1991).
ROBERT B. REICH

DEMOCRACY

Recently, democracy seems to have scored a historic victory over alternative forms of governance. Nearly everyone today, whether of the *Left, Center, or *Right, claims adherence to democratic principles. Political regimes of all kinds throughout the world style themselves democracies—albeit that there may be vast differences between statement and execution. Democracy seems to bestow an aura of *legitimacy on modern political life: rules, laws, policies, and decisions appear justified when they are "democratic." This was not always so. The great majority of political thinkers from ancient Greece to the present day have been highly critical of the theory and practice of democracy. A uniform commitment to democracy is a very recent phenomenon.

The record contains little about democracy from ancient Greece to eighteenth-century Europe and North America. The widespread turn to democracy as a suitable form for organizing political life is less than a hundred years old. In addition, while many states today may be democratic, the history of their political institutions reveals the fragility and vulnerability of democratic arrangements. The remarkable difficulty of creating and sustaining democratic forms is borne out by the flowering of *Fascism and Nazism in twentieth-century Western Europe. Democracy has evolved in intensive social struggles and is frequently sacrificed in such struggles. This brief essay is about the idea of democracy, but in exploring the idea one cannot escape aspects of its history in theory and in practice. It will be evident that the concept of democracy and the nature of democratic arrangements are a fundamentally contested terrain.

The word *democracy* entered English in the sixteenth century from the French *démocratie;* the word is Greek in origin, having been derived from *dēmokratia,* the root meanings of which are *dēmos* (people) and *kratos* (rule). Democracy refers to a form of government in which, in contradistinction to monarchies and aristocracies, the people rule. It entails a state in which there is some form of political equality among the people. But to recognize this is not yet to say very much. For not only is the history of the idea of democracy marked by conflicting interpretations, but Greek, Roman, medieval, and Renaissance notions intermingle to produce ambiguous and inconsistent accounts of the key terms of democracy today: the nature of "rule," the connotation of "rule by," and the meaning of "the people."

Among the questions that require examination are: Who are "the people"? What constitutes a "people" entitled to rule themselves? What kind of participation is envisaged for them? How broadly or narrowly is the scope of rule to be construed? Is democracy a set of political institutions or a process? How does the size of a political community affect the nature and dynamics of democracy? Must the

rules of "the people" be obeyed? What is the place of obligation and dissent? Under what circumstances, if any, are democracies entitled to resort to coercion of an element of "the people" or of those outside the sphere of legitimate rule?

Within the history of the clash of interpretations about these and related questions lies a deeply rooted struggle to determine whether democracy will mean some kind of popular *power (a form of life in which citizens are engaged in self-government and self-regulation) or an aid to decision making (a means to legitimate decisions of those voted into power—representatives—from time to time). This basic struggle has given rise to three basic variants or models of democracy. First, there is direct or participatory democracy, a system of decision making about public affairs in which citizens are directly involved. This was the original type of democracy found in ancient Athens, among other places. Second, there is liberal or representative democracy, a system of rule embracing elected officers who undertake to represent the interests or views of citizens within the framework of the rule of law. Representative democracy means that decisions affecting a community are not taken by its members as a whole but by a group of people whom "the people" have elected for this purpose. In the arena of national politics, representative democracy takes the form of elections to congresses, parliaments, or similar national bodies, and is associated with the system of government in countries as far afield as the United States, Britain, Germany, Japan, Australia, New Zealand, Costa Rica, Senegal, and elsewhere. Third, there is a variant of democracy based on a one-party model (although some may doubt whether this is a form of democracy at all). Until recently, the Soviet Union, many East European societies, and some *Third World countries have been dominated by this conception. The principle underlying one-party democracy is that a single party can be the legitimate expression of the overall will of the community. Voters choose among different candidates, putatively proposing divergent policies within an overall framework, not among different parties. The following expands on each of these models in turn.

In the fifth century B.C.E., Athens emerged as the preeminent city-state, or *polis,* among many rival Greek powers; the development of democracy in Athens has been taken as a fundamental source of inspiration for modern Western political thought. The political ideals of Athens—equality among citizens, liberty, respect for the law, and justice—have shaped political thinking through the ages, although there are some central ideas (for instance, the modern liberal notion that human beings are individuals with rights) that notably cannot be traced directly to ancient thought.

The Athenian city-state did not differentiate between state and society, ruled as it was by citizen-governors. In ancient Athens citizens were at one and the same time subjects of state authority and the creators of public rules and regulations. The people *(dēmos)* engaged in legislative and judicial functions, for the Athenian concept of *citizenship entailed sharing in these functions, participating directly in the affairs of the state. Athenian democracy required a general commitment to the principle of civic virtue: dedication to the republican city-state and the subordination of private life to public affairs and the common good. The public and the private were intertwined. Citizens could only properly fulfill themselves and live honorably in and through the *polis.* Of course, who was to count as a citizen was a tightly restricted matter. Those who were excluded included women and a substantial slave population.

The Athenian city-state—eclipsed ultimately by the rise of empires, stronger states, and military regimes—shared features with republican Rome. Both were predominantly face-to-face societies, oral cultures, and both had elements of popular participation in governmental affairs and little, if any, centralized bureaucratic control. Both sought to foster a deep sense of public duty, a tradition of civic virtue or responsibility to the republic—to the distinctive matters of the public realm. In both polities, the claims of the state were given a unique priority over those of the individual citizen. However, if Athens was a democratic republic, contemporary scholarship generally affirms that Rome was by comparison an essentially oligarchic system. Accordingly, from antiquity, the heritage of the classical Greek tradition, and of the model of Athenian democracy in particular, is especially important in the history of democratic thought and practice. Although the heritage of Athens received its clearest and most robust defense in the early Renaissance period, especially in the city-states of Italy, it retained a force throughout the early modern period.

In ancient Greece a citizen was someone who participated in "giving judgment and holding office." Citizenship meant participation in public affairs. This classical definition is noteworthy in two respects. First, it suggests that the ancient Greeks would have found it hard to locate citizens in modern democracies, except perhaps as representatives and officeholders. The limited scope in contemporary politics for active involvement would have been regarded as most undemocratic. Second, the classical Greek idea of citizenship would have found resonance in few communities before, during, or after its initial elaboration. The ancient democracies are quite atypical regimes in recorded political history. The idea that human beings could be active citizens of a political order, something more than mere dutiful subjects, has had few advocates from the earliest human associations to the early Renaissance and the demise of absolutism.

The eclipse in the West of the idea of the active citizen, one whose very being is affirmed in and through political action, is hard to explain fully. But it is clear enough that the antithesis of *Homo politicus* is the *Homo credens* of the Christian faith: the citizen who exercised active judgment was displaced by the true believer. Although it would be quite misleading to suggest that the rise of Christianity effectively banished secular considerations from the lives of rulers and ruled, it unquestionably shifted the source of authority and wisdom from this-worldly to otherworldly representatives. The Christian worldview transformed the rationale of political action from that of the *polis* or empire to a theological framework. The Hellenic view of humanity was replaced by a preoccupation with how humans could live in communion with God. The Christian worldview insisted that the good lay in submission to God's will.

The integration of Christian Europe came to depend on two theocratic authorities above all: the Roman Catholic church and the Holy Roman Empire. During the Middle Ages there was no theoretical alternative. The entire fabric of medieval thought had to be torn asunder before the idea of democracy could reemerge. Not until the end of the sixteenth century did the nature and limits of political authority, law, rights, and obedience once again become objects of European political thought. The Protestant Reformation, the most significant of all the developments that triggered new ways of thinking about political authority, did more than just challenge papal jurisdiction and authority across Europe; it raised the starkest questions about political obligation and obedience. Whether allegiance was owed to the Catholic church, a Protestant ruler, or particular religious sects was not an issue easily resolved. The bitter struggles that spread across Europe during the last half of the sixteenth century, culminating in the Thirty Years' War in Germany, testified to the increasing divisiveness of religious belief. Competing religions, all seeking to secure for themselves the kinds of privileges claimed by the medieval church, had engendered a political crisis whose only solution would be to disconnect the powers of the state from the duty of rulers to uphold a particular faith.

The impetus to reexamine the nature of the relationship between society and state was given added force by a growing awareness in Europe of the variety of possible social and political arrangements that followed in the wake of the discovery of the non-European world. The relationship between Europe and the "New World" and the nature of the rights (if any) of non-Europeans became a major focus of discussion. It sharpened the sense of a plurality of possible interpretations of political life. The direction these interpretations took was, of course, directly related to the context and traditions of particular countries: the changing nature of politics was experienced differently throughout the early modern period. But it is hard to overestimate the significance of the events and processes that ushered in a new era of political reflection, marked as it was by such dramatic occurrences as the English Revolution (1640–1688), the American Declaration of Independence (1776), and the French Revolution (1789).

Modern liberal and liberal democratic theory has constantly sought to justify the sovereign power of the state while at the same time justifying limits on that power. The history of this attempt since Niccolò Machiavelli (1469–1527) and Thomas Hobbes (1588–1679) is the history of arguments to balance might and right, *power and law, duties and *rights. On the one hand, *states must have a monopoly of coercive power in order to provide a secure basis on which trade, commerce, and family life can prosper. On the other hand, by granting the state a regulatory and coercive capability, political theorists were aware that they had accepted a force that could, and frequently did, deprive citizens of political and social freedoms.

Liberal democrats provided the key institutional innovation to try to overcome this dilemma—representative democracy. The liberal concern with reason, law, and freedom of choice could only be upheld properly by recognizing the political equality of all mature individuals. Such equality would ensure not only a secure social environment in which people would be free to pursue their private activities and interests, but also that the state would do what was best in the general and public interest—for example, pursue the greatest satisfaction of the greatest number. Thus, liberal democrats argued that the democratic constitutional state, linked to other key institutional mechanisms, above all the free market, resolved the problems of ensuring both authority and liberty.

Two classical statements of the new position can be found in the philosophy of James Madison (1751–1836) and in the works of two of the key figures of nineteenth-century English *liberalism: Jeremy Bentham (1748–1832) and James Mill (1773–1836). In their hands the theory of liberal democracy received a most important elaboration: the governors must be held accountable to the governed through political mechanisms (the secret ballot, regular voting, competition between potential representatives, the struggle among factions) that alone can give citizens satisfactory means to choose, authorize, and control political decisions. And by these means, it was further contended, a balance could finally be obtained between might and right, authority and liberty. But who exactly was to count as a "citizen" or an "individual," and what his or her exact role was to be, remained either unclear or unsettled. Even in the work of James Mill's radical son, John Stuart Mill (1806–1873), ambiguities remained: the idea that all citizens should have equal weight in the political system remained outside his actual doctrine.

It was left by and large to the extensive and often violently repressed struggles of working-class and feminist activists in the nineteenth and twentieth centuries to achieve in some countries a genuinely universal suffrage. This achievement was to remain fragile in countries such as Germany, Italy, and Spain, and was in practice denied to some groups—for instance, many *African Americans in the United States before the civil rights movement in the 1950s and 1960s. Through these struggles the idea that citizenship rights should apply to all adults became slowly established; many of the arguments of the liberal democrats could be turned against existing institutions to reveal the extent to which the principle and aspirations of equal *political participation and equal human development remained unfulfilled. It was only with the actual achievement of citizenship for all adult men and women that liberal democracy took on its distinctively contemporary form: a cluster of rules permitting the broadest participation of the majority of citizens in the selection of representatives who alone can make political decisions (i.e., decisions affecting the whole of society).

The idea of democracy remains complex and contested. The liberal democratic tradition itself comprises a heterogeneous body of thought. However, the entire liberal democratic tradition stands apart from an alternative perspective—the theory of single-party democracy. It is worth saying something more about this, because it is associated with one of the key counterpoints to liberal democracy—the Marxist tradition.

The struggle of liberalism against tyranny and the struggle by liberal democrats for political equality represented, according to Karl *Marx (1818–1883) and Friedrich Engels (1820–1895), a major step forward in the history of human emancipation. But for them, and for the Marxist tradition more broadly, the great universal ideals of "liberty, equality and justice" could not be realized simply by the "free" struggle for votes in the political system and by the "free" struggle for profit in the marketplace. Advocates of the democratic state and the market economy present them as the only institutions under which liberty can be sustained and inequalities minimized. However, the Marxist critique suggests that, by virtue of its internal dynamics, the capitalist economy inevitably produces systematic inequality and massive restrictions on real freedom. Although each step toward formal political equality is an advance, its liberating potential is severely curtailed by inequalities of *class.

In class societies the state cannot become the vehicle for the pursuit of the common good or public interest. Far from playing the role of emancipator, protective knight, umpire, or judge in the face of disorder, the agencies of the liberal representative state are meshed in the struggles of civil society. Marxists conceive of the state as an extension of civil society, reinforcing the social order for the enhancement of particular interests—in capitalist society, the long-run interests of the capitalist class. Marx and Engels argue that political emancipation is only a step toward human emancipation, that is, the complete democratization of society as well as the state. In their view, liberal democratic society fails when judged by its own principles—and to take these principles seriously is to become a communist.

Marx himself envisaged the replacement of the "machinery" of the liberal democratic state by a "commune structure": the smallest communities, which were to administer their own affairs, would elect delegates to larger administrative units (districts, towns); these in turn would elect candidates to still-larger areas of administration (the national delegation). This arrangement is known as the "pyramid" structure of direct democracy: all delegates are revocable, bound by the instructions of their constituency, and organized into a pyramid of directly elected committees. In the Marxist-Leninist model, this system of delegation is, in principle, complemented by a separate, but somewhat similar, system at the levels of the Communist Party. In practice, however, complementarity has meant party domination. It was only during the *Gorbachev era that a pyramid of councils, or soviets, from the central authority to those at local village and neighborhood level, were given anything more than a symbolic or ritualistic role.

What should be made of these various models of democracy today? The classical Athenian model, which developed in a tightly knit community, cannot be adapted to stretch across space and time. Its emergence in the context of city-states and under conditions of social exclusivity (no female participation, a slave economy, many other marginalized groups) was integral to its successful development. In contemporary circumstances, marked by a high degree of social, economic, and political differentiation, it is very hard to envisage how a democracy of this kind could succeed. The significance of these reflections is reinforced by examining the fate of the model of democracy advocated by Marx, Engels, and their followers. The suitability of their model as an institutional arrangement that allows for mediation, negotiation, and compromise among struggling factions, groups, or movements, does not stand up well under scrutiny, especially in its Marxist-Leninist variant. A system of institutions to promote discussion, debate, and competition among divergent views—a system encompassing the formation of movements, pressure groups, and/or political parties with leaderships to help press their cases— appears both necessary and desirable. Further, the events in Central and Eastern Europe beginning in 1989 seem to provide remarkable confirmatory evidence of this.

Inevitably, then, one must recognize the importance of a number of fundamental liberal tenets

concerning the centrality, in principle, of an impersonal structure of public power; of a constitution to help guarantee and protect rights; of a diversity of power centers within and outside the state; and of mechanisms to promote competition and debate among alternative political platforms. What this amounts to, among other things, is confirmation of the fundamental liberal notion that the separation of state from civil society must be an essential feature of any democratic political order. Conceptions of democracy that depend on the assumption that the state could ever replace civil society, or vice versa, must be treated with the utmost caution.

However, to make these points is not to affirm any one liberal democratic model as it stands. It is one thing to accept the arguments concerning the necessary protective, conflict-mediating, and redistributive functions of the democratic state; quite another to accept these as prescribed in the model of liberal democracy from Madison or Bentham onward. Advocates of liberal democracy have tended to be concerned, above all else, with the proper principles and procedures of democratic government. By focusing on government, they have diverted attention from a thorough examination of such issues as: formal rights vs. actual rights; commitments to treat citizens as free and equal vs. disparities of treatment in practice; concepts of the state as, in principle, an independent authority vs. involvements of the state in the reproduction of the inequalities of everyday life; notions of political parties as appropriate structures for bridging the gap between state and society vs. the array of power centers that are beyond reach of parties.

The implications of these points are profound. For democracy to flourish today it has to be reconceived as a double-sided phenomenon concerned, on the one hand, with the *reform of state power and, on the other hand, with the restructuring of civil society. This entails recognizing the indispensability of a process of "double democratization": the interdependent transformation of both state and civil society. Such a process must be premised on the acceptance of the principle that the division between state and civil society must be a central feature of democratic life, and on the notion that the power to make decisions must be free of the inequalities and constraints that can be imposed by an unregulated system of private capital, as Marx foresaw. But, of course, to recognize the importance of both these points is to recognize the necessity of recasting substantially their traditional connotation.

If this leaves many questions open, it should not come as a surprise. The history of democratic theory and practice is coterminous with conflicts of interpretation and struggles for position—and this state of affairs is inevitable when politics is free of the constraints of authoritarianism in all its forms. Democratic politics is bound to the terrain of dispute and contestation. Democracy is an ingenious political arrangement for the articulation, expression, and mediation of difference. It is a testimony to the idea of democracy itself that the battle over its constitutive elements will, in all likelihood, continue.

One area where the battle will continue connects the idea of democracy to the larger framework of *international relations. The modern theory of the democratic state presupposes the idea of a "national community of fate"—a community that rightly governs itself and determines its own future. But national communities by no means exclusively program the actions, decisions, and policies of their governments, and governments by no means determine what is right or appropriate for their own citizens. For example, a decision to build a nuclear plant near the borders of a neighboring country is likely to be a decision taken without consulting those in the nearby country (or countries). Or the decision to permit the building of a chemical factory making toxic or other noxious substances may contribute to ecological damage which does not acknowledge national boundaries or frontiers. In a world of global interconnectedness—mediated by modern communication systems and information technology—there are pressing questions about the very future and viability of national democracies. Regional and global interconnectedness contests the traditional national resolutions of the key questions of democratic theory and practice.

Therefore, one ought not to be perplexed to hear more insistent demands that the international form and structure of politics and civil society be built into the foundations of democracy. At issue is the problem of specifying how democracy can be secured within a series of interconnected power and authority centers. Also at issue is rethinking the territorial boundaries of systems of accountability and how the pressing problems that escape the control of a nation-state—aspects of monetary management, environmental questions, elements of health, new forms of communications—can be brought under better control.

If the history and practice of democracy has focused up until now on the idea of locality (the city-state, the community, the nation), it is likely that in the future it will be centered on the international or global domain. There are no immediate solutions to the problems posed by global interconnectedness and its complex and often profoundly uneven effects—yet an important series of questions inescapably must be addressed. Certainly, one can find many good reasons for being optimistic about finding a path forward, and many good reasons for thinking that at this juncture democracy will face a critical test.

(See also CONSOCIATIONAL DEMOCRACY; EQUALITY AND INEQUALITY; INDUSTRIAL DEMOCRACY; INFORMATION SOCIETY; MARXISM; NINETEEN EIGHTY-NINE; PLURALISM; POLITICAL PARTIES AND PARTY COMPETITION.)

John Stuart Mill, *Considerations on Representative Government* (London, 1951). Karl Marx, *The Civil War in France* (Peking, 1970). John Pocock, *The Machiavellian Moment* (Princeton, N.J., 1975). Joseph A. Schumpeter, *Capitalism, Socialism and Democracy* (London, 1976). Aristotle, *The Politics* (Harmondsworth, U.K., 1981). Moses I. Finley, *Politics in the Ancient World* (Cambridge, U.K., 1983). David Held, *Models of Democracy* (Cambridge, U.K., 1987). John Keane, *Democracy and Civil Society* (London, 1988). Robert A. Dahl, *Democracy and its Critics* (New Haven, Conn., 1989). David Held, "Democracy, the Nation-State and the Global System," in David Held, ed., *Political Theory Today* (Cambridge, U.K., 1991). Patricia Springborg, *Western Republicanism and the Oriental Prince* (Cambridge, U.K., 1991).

DAVID HELD

DEMOCRATIC TRANSITIONS. The democratic transitions of the 1980s replicated processes that had occurred in more isolated fashion in earlier decades. Indeed, Dankwart Rustow's seminal 1970 article "Transitions to Democracy: Towards a Dynamic Model" was published at a time when the predominant trend in the Third World was toward apparently entrenched forms of authoritarian rule: conservative military dictatorships in Latin America; one-party states often clothed with vaguely socialist rhetoric in most of Africa and parts of the *Middle East; and *national liberation movements of communist inspiration in Southeast Asia. Rustow had worked on Turkey and Japan, and also drew on European experiences, and he broke with an earlier tradition that had explained the rise of democracy largely as a function of certain "social correlates" of *modernization—*urbanization, the spread of literacy, etc. Instead he directed attention toward the political conflicts and dynamic interactions through which a democratic compromise (or "pact") might emerge, and he suggested that democracies not forged in conflict might prove ephemeral. This perspective proved fruitful when interpreting the subsequent emergence and consolidation of democratic regimes in southern Europe—in Greece and Portugal in 1974, and in Spain two years later. All these three authoritarian regimes were the product of intense social and ideological conflict, and seemed set in a rigid mold of anticommunism, antiliberalism, and police repression that appeared impervious to the supposedly liberalizing effects of modernization. In all three cases bitter memories of earlier conflicts were invoked by the incumbents to justify repression, on the argument that any concessions would be seized on by a vengeful opposition seeking to reverse the verdict of history.

The southern European transitions of the 1970s, however, revealed the extensive scope for compromise and democratic institution-building once artificial restraints on political expression and negotiation were lifted. The trigger for democratic transition differed from country to country—in Greece the discredit arising from a military defeat by Turkey; in Portugal the demoralization and radicalization arising from a protracted stalemate in a colonial war; in Spain the death of *Franco. In all cases the fading of the *Cold War, the need to participate in a process of European integration premised on liberal capitalism, and the emergence of a new generation of politicians wishing to distance themselves from an archaic past, all contributed to subsequent processes of democratic consolidation.

These southern European precedents exerted a powerful influence over the transitions of the 1980s. Just as the *Spanish Civil War had contributed to ideological polarization in Latin America (with *Marxism and militant Catholicism as the two competing poles), the disappearance of the Salazar and Franco regimes and their replacement by modern and consensually-based political systems rather than by new upheavals, caused intransigents in Latin America to reconsider the scope for accommodation with their rivals. Other international factors also reinforced this tendency. Thus the romance of the *Cuban Revolution had faded (except perhaps in parts of Central America) and the "national security" reflex inspired by the threat of more Cubas had also run its course. Following *Watergate and the *Vietnam War the *Carter administration took up the cause of *human rights, distancing itself from some of its most unsavory allies notably in Argentina, Chile, Guatemala, and Uruguay. The evident failures of authoritarian politics—in Velasco's Peru, in Somoza's Nicaragua, and in Argentina after the *Malvinas/Falklands War—reinforced the demonstration effect coming from southern Europe.

Nevertheless, more than an inchoate sympathy would be required to turn tentative, and often quite opportunistic, flirtations with *democracy into a continent-wide commitment to abide by the constraining rules of constitutional government. The democratic transitions of the 1980s took multiple routes and passed through a series of stages. In the beginning, the initiative was generally taken by liberalizing elements within the authoritarian ruling group. Perhaps influenced by external models, or perhaps simply seeking to buttress their own bargaining power within a regime conscious both of its strength and its social isolation, they advocated measures of *abertura,* or controlled liberalization, at least partly with the aim of dividing the opposition. But liberalizing measures tended to gather their own momentum as increased freedom of expression and organization led to the emergence of newly permitted organizations and demands. In due course, part of the political initiative would pass to these interests, which generally lacked the strength to bring down the existing order, but which could continually press for further extensions of the political realm. The "transition" process consisted of a series

of improvisations under pressure, through which the composition and objectives of the authoritarian coalition were shifted toward cooperation and convergence with the more temperate elements of the opposition. "Liberalization" passed into "democratization" where this interaction resulted in an agreement (a "pact") to allow open contestation for public office, without a preordained victor. If the voters, rather than the incumbents, controlled the final outcome of this contestation, then the transition could be called democratic. Not all transitions took this form, however. In Mexico, for example, the incumbent president remains the "great elector" despite extensive liberalization of the media and the party system. In Brazil the transition was dragged out for so long, and the moment of uncontrolled choice was so delayed and manipulated, that popular enthusiasm for a regime change became dissipated. In Argentina and Bolivia there was no solid "pact," but rather a collapse of the military regime, which paved the way for an uncontrolled transition.

Despite all these complications, the outcome of the 1980s is remarkably clear. Almost all countries in Latin America have witnessed some form of transition to a broadly democratic (civilian constitutional) political regime. These regimes may not be fully consolidated (they often remain institutionally fragile and politically ineffective), but their medium-term prospects of survival are surprisingly good.

On the whole the evidence from election turnout survey research and some data on social movements suggests that support for transitional democracies in southern Europe and Latin America is surprisingly wide. It is not so clear whether it is correspondingly deep. This may seem surprising, given that most Latin American democracies (in contrast to those of southern Europe) have undergone a "lost decade" of economic decline and demoralization. The fiscal crisis of the state, and the related burden of external indebtedness, has obstructed the provision of material benefits to the mass of the newly enfranchised electorate, and indeed in many cases previously existing social programs have been eroded or dismantled. But in Argentina, Bolivia, and Mexico, to cite only the most vivid examples, voters appear willing to reward the authors of austerity plans with renewals of their mandates, and previously militant and aggressive "antisystem" forces appear to have been tamed. Social support for such regimes may be more volatile than in the cases of the rather successful and consolidated democracies of southern Europe, but so far explicit sources of opposition are remarkably muted. Tentatively, two lines of interpretation suggest themselves. On the one hand, the organized minorities that formerly articulated coherent antidemocratic projects capable of destabilizing fragile democracies no longer possess the self-confidence and unity to act in this way. The collapse of the Soviet bloc has destroyed one image of an alternative society, and the lingering failures of *military rule still discredit the other. A new generation of military officers, business leaders, and popular activists has discovered that constitutionalism offers an alternative within which some modest gain may eventually be secured. On the other hand, the debt crisis, the experience of hyperinflation, and the discredit of the old economic model of inward-looking development have affected popular attitudes, drastically lowering the electorate's expectations of what can be achieved through political action. If the capture of state power no longer offers a realistic hope of providing lasting solutions to the problems of daily life, then a much more "disenchanted" attitude toward politics may come to prevail. This could allow fragile and unsatisfactory democratic regimes to remain in place, and even to reproduce themselves within a climate of fairly generalized indifference. "Democracy by default" could be the outcome of such transitions.

A few fully consolidated, reasonably autonomous, and conventionally "liberal" democracies may well emerge in Latin America over the next few years. But at least for the near future the normal result of democratic transition will be a more provisional and unsatisfactory form of constitutional rule. The limitations on these democracies will vary from country to country: restrictions on national sovereignty; curtailment of political choice by market mechanisms; "facade" arrangements intended to project an external image of *pluralism without disturbing traditional power relations; the persistence of undemocratic structures in rural areas; policy paralysis derived from fiscal crisis; misguided design of institutional arrangements; a fragmented civil society incapable of generating legitimacy or social consensus. In Eastern and *Central Europe, there will also be limitations arising from insecurity over national boundaries, and from the difficulty of converting centrally planned into market economies. Thus most transitional democracies are likely to remain provisional, incomplete, and unconsolidated, at least for the next few years. This should not be considered particularly surprising or shocking. The consolidation of democracy is a process that must take at least a generation or longer. So long as the framework of representative institutions is kept intact the prospect remains open that a future government, under pressure from the citizenry, will rectify the omission, correct the errors, or enlarge the rights as required to complete and entrench the democratization process.

Of course, at the end of the 1980s, many countries of Eastern and Central Europe and sub-Saharan Africa have inaugurated their own processes of democratic transition. The Eastern and Central European "transitions" of 1989–1990 bear some intriguing resemblances to earlier southern European and Latin American processes, but the contrasts are sharp enough to raise the doubt that the use of prepackaged terminology could conflate the two distinct

logics. The parallels work best for Poland and Hungary, where internally generated processes of liberalization and reform created some space for negotiation between weakening governments and resurgent oppositions. Poland's "roundtable" negotiations of spring 1989 fit surprisingly well within the framework of preexisting transition literature, and quite a few of the constitution-writing and election-inaugurating events of 1990 were entirely familiar in form. For example, Latin American debates over the relative merits of presidentialism and parliamentarism were taken up with a keen interest in various parts of Eastern and Central Europe. A striking similarity with southern Europe concerns the way in which prospective (or at least hoped-for) membership in the *European Community may have stimulated a consensus favoring liberal forms of political organization linked with market-based economic reforms.

Taking the ex-Soviet bloc as a whole and adopting a rather longer time horizon, however, these could prove relatively superficial resemblances that are overshadowed by more striking contrasts. The Eastern and Central European transformations all occurred very rapidly and were bunched together within a few months. The "contagion" effect was much more powerful and direct than elsewhere. Moreover, it can reasonably be argued that the dominant force at work was a Moscow-centered initiative (whether by decision or miscalculation) to dismantle the Soviet empire. The term "peaceful anticommunist revolutions" suggests itself as an alternative to the language of "democratic transitions." Such a shift in focus would have major implications for the subsequent outcomes. All other democratic transitions were directed against authoritarian regimes which fostered or sheltered certain minority capitalist interests, and the democratic opposition nominally embraced a range of anticapitalist or broadly "left-wing" orientations. For most East and Central Europeans, by contrast, capitalism was equated with liberty and anticapitalism with state monopolization of political and economic power. Both in ideological and in material terms the task of forging a "pluralist" political system was therefore quite different from elsewhere, especially in those parts of Eastern and Central Europe where the collapse of Soviet control also put national boundaries in question.

In Africa the collapse of the Soviet bloc and the consequent cessation of Cold War rivalries coincided with the decision of the South African regime to dismantle the formal structures of *apartheid and to seek a constitutional settlement to enfranchise the African majority. As externally promoted civil wars were steered toward more or less negotiated settlements, international pressure was brought to bear on sub-Saharan Africa's large array of one-party states. Put more cynically, Western donors no longer had much interest in providing further aid to client regimes whose corruption and mismanagement seemed inexpungeable. The resulting Western demand for "democracy" could prove, in various cases, just an excuse for budget cutting. However that may be, nearly a score of African states have responded by lifting restraints on political opposition and convoking competitive elections. On the face of it, "transitions to democracy" have swept through Africa almost as abruptly as through Eastern and Central Europe.

Transitions there have certainly been, in the sense that thirty-year-old structures of political administration have been shaken and reformed. In a *few* cases, the eventual outcome could prove to be relatively durable multiparty democracies. Botswana shows that this is at least *possible* in an African setting; for some time Sierra Leone gave the same impression; and Senegal also offers some encouragement. The former white minority regimes of Southern Africa also possess various advantages that *could* assist democratization—diversified economies, relatively better educational endowments (though provision is extremely unequal), some elements of efficient and impartial administration under some kind of rule of law. It is difficult to believe, however, that viable democracies will prove to be the norm in Africa as a whole, since for the most part national political communities are extremely fragile; patrimonial forms of administration dominate economic and political life; and the socioeconomic bases for civilized coexistence have all too often been blocked or destroyed by those accustomed to wield absolute power.

(See also AUTHORITARIANISM; INTERNATIONAL DEBT; NINETEEN EIGHTY-NINE; ONE-PARTY SYSTEM.)

Guillermo O'Donnell, Philippe Schmitter, and Laurence Whitehead, eds., *Transitions from Authoritarian Rule* (Baltimore, Md., 1986). Larry Diamond, Juan Linz, and Seymour Martin Lipset, eds., *Democracy in Developing Countries* (Boulder, Colo., 1988). Adam Przeworski, *Democracy and the Market: Political and Economic Reforms in Eastern Europe and Latin America* (Cambridge, U.K., 1991). David Held, ed., *Prospects for Democracy: North, South, East, West* (Cambridge, U.K., 1992). John Higley and Richard Gunther, eds., *Elites and Democratic Consolidation in Latin America and Southern Europe* (Cambridge, U.K., 1992).

LAURENCE WHITEHEAD

DENG Xiaoping. As the leader of one of the largest and potentially most powerful countries in the world during a period of major reorientation and accelerated economic growth, *China's Deng Xiaoping ranks among the most noteworthy political figures of the second half of the twentieth century. Apparently bluff, candid, and straightforward, the man actually abounds in hidden contradictions that complicate any attempt at summation. After spending much of his life in the shrewd and aggressive pursuit of personal power, he steadfastly refused the highest offices of the party and government when they were easily within his grasp, preferring to pull strings from behind the scenes. Although never a Marxist theorist, his pragmatic admixture of Marxist and market principles seemed to many to bespeak a tacit repudiation of Maoist dogmatism—yet he reacted ruthlessly to any attempt to expand the reforms beyond certain vaguely defined ideological limits, ultimately reaffirming official adherence to "*Marxism–*Leninism–*Mao Zedong Thought." An ardent advocate of institutionalization, Deng was not above distorting China's embryonic legal system in political show trials or upsetting routinized succession arrangements because he had changed his mind about his successor. Yet despite these inconsistencies his place in history seems reasonably firm.

Deng was born 22 August 1904 in a village in Sichuan province, the eldest son of a wealthy landowner. His relationship to his father was (in contrast to Mao Zedong's early rebelliousness) correct and respectful. The roots of his turn to radicalism may thus be more plausibly sought in his youthful coming of age than in his childhood.

After middle school, Deng took a preparatory course for candidates to be selected for studies in France as worker-students and embarked in the fall of 1920 to study at the University of Lyon. Thus he entered an elite fraternity of young people who saw themselves as future leaders and whose experiences in the outside world had a broadening, politicizing effect. Although he remained in France for five years Deng led a highly peripatetic life, living on the margin and seldom staying anywhere for more than a few months. He later commented that he had not studied in France at all but worked as a laborer, but even this seems generous; despite stints at several jobs, most of his time and attention were dedicated to revolutionary activities. In 1922 he joined the Chinese Socialist Youth League branch in France, and the French branch of the *Chinese Communist Party (CCP) upon its founding in 1924.

Deng's energy, intelligence, and ambition quickly propelled him to positions near, but not at the pinnacle of, both the Youth League and the CCP—a political vantage point he was to prefer for the remainder of his career. His positions in these organizations brought him into his first contact with *Zhou Enlai, secretary of the Youth League and then the CCP. Deng built a reputation on his willingness to make himself indispensable in whatever capacity he was needed.

Thereafter, Deng studied at the Sun Yatsen University in Moscow from January to August 1926. When he returned to China Deng's first post was as an instructor in the political department of the communist-oriented Sun Yatsen Military Academy in Xian. Following a rightward shift in the *Chinese Revolution, Deng was thrown out of his positions in Xian.

On 1 August 1927, Deng helped launch the abortive Nanchang uprising, which officially marked the birth of the Red Army. Subsequently Deng worked in the CCP Central Organization in Shanghai and then was sent to Guangxi province to mobilize the peasantry, an effort that turned out disastrously in the face of extreme pressure by Chiang Kai-shek's Nationalist forces. Deng abandoned his troops and made his way to Shanghai to report to the Central Committee.

This was perhaps the nadir of Deng's personal career, as well as that of the CCP. In early 1933 Deng was criticized and blamed for CCP setbacks. This criticism notwithstanding, Deng was given a lectureship on the history of the Communist Party at the Red Army Academy in one of the communist base areas only a few months later.

Deng participated in the Long March in 1934–1935 that followed CCP defeat by the Nationalists. During the march Deng threw his lot in with Mao, and his political career began to ascend with that of his new patron. He held a number of important posts in the CCP, but his most historically redeeming assignment was that of political commissar with the Second Field Army under Liu Bocheng, which inflicted a costly loss on Japanese troops in August–October 1940, and waged the decisive Huaihai battle against the Nationalist forces in January 1949.

Deng came into his own after the CCP victory. He was appointed a member of key provisional central organs and also assumed effective control of the southwest region of China. He seems to have been a competent, even zealous regional implementer of central policies including *land reform. Beginning in 1952 he also became vice-premier, and in 1953 minister of finance and chair of the Central Economic Affairs Committee under Zhou Enlai. By the mid-1950s he had shifted his base of operations almost entirely to the central level. In May 1954 he was first identified as secretary-general of the CCP Central Committee; in April 1955, he was elected to the Politburo, and in 1956 was elected junior member of the newly established elite Standing Committee of the Politburo.

Upon his arrival in the highest leadership circles, Deng soon gravitated into a coalition with veteran party leader Liu Shaoqi, whose views and general approach he shared, an alliance that would lead him into a series of conflicts with Mao. Deng joined with Liu Shaoqi in a repudiation of Mao's "cult of personality" in September 1956 by endorsing the deletion of pledges of allegiance to "Mao Zedong's Thought" in the CCP constitution. Deng erected bureaucratic hurdles to Mao's bold experiment with liberalism, the "Hundred Flowers" movement of 1956–1957, and led the subsequent highly repressive "antirightist movement" against dissidents. In the early 1960s, Liu and Deng again cooperated in rescinding various components of Mao's "Great Leap Forward" in the wake of the devastating economic depression caused by the Leap. Deng's Secretariat advocated such un-Maoist policies as the allocation of agricultural production quotas to individual *peasant households rather than to the collectives and the implementation of piecework wages for factory workers, the "chopping down" of unproductive industries, and a shift of investment priorities to light industry.

This "Liu-Deng" alignment soon evolved into a self-sufficient alternative policy-making center within the CCP. Mao seemed at first to accede to this arrangement. But beginning in the summer of 1962 he reversed course, calling for a revival of radicalism and class struggle. Mao complained of a rift, noting Deng's failure to brief him often and his tendency to distance himself physically at meetings. Policy-making became more complicated as politics became more factionalized and as each side sought to thwart or modify the other's initiatives while guarding its own. Finally, with the help of his wife, Jiang Qing, and the "Kitchen Cabinet" of radical intellectuals she had assembled, Mao launched the "Great Proletarian *Cultural Revolution," building momentum at the mass level to "topple" the party-state apparatus controlled by Liu and Deng. After more than two years of chaotic factionalism and mass criticism, Liu and Deng (and most of their known disciples) were purged from all leadership positions and "sent down" to do manual work in penance for their errors.

Unlike Liu, Deng was never evicted from the party or criticized by name in the official press, perhaps because he was not perceived to pose a threat to Mao's leadership position. Liu died in captivity in 1969, while Deng survived his banishment to rise again. In 1972 Mao accepted Deng's self-criticism, and Deng first reappeared publicly in April 1973. He quickly made himself invaluable to Mao and the ailing Zhou Enlai. By January 1975 he had become acting premier as well as first vice-chairman of the CCP. He used the power he had recovered to launch an ambitious *modernization program that flew directly in the face of the radical party leaders known as the "Gang of Four." When Zhou Enlai died in January 1975 the Gang lost no time launching a vigorous counterattack, and with Mao's backing engineered Deng's second purge from all leadership positions (although he again was not expelled from the party).

Deng spent the next six months under ostensible house arrest in south China, reportedly involving himself in the scheming that eventually resulted in the Gang of Four's arrest in October 1976 following Mao's death a month earlier. By July 1977 Deng had been restored to his previous positions. The reform program he launched upon his rehabilitation was double-edged, aimed both at enhancing the efficiency of the economy and at undermining his more radical political adversaries. Deng achieved his objectives over the next several years through a medley of clever tactics, including the wholesale rehabilitation of veteran cadres, an uncharacteristic liberalism toward prodemocracy demonstrators, continuing criticism of Mao Zedong, and a public trial of the Gang of Four.

After he consolidated his hold on power in the late 1970s and early 1980s, Deng's reform program surged ahead. Communes were dissolved and replaced by a "household responsibility system," markets proliferated in both rural and urban venues, and central financial controls devolved to local or factory levels. Essentially reversing Mao's emphasis on "self-reliance" for China, Deng launched a policy of "opening to the outside world" by inviting extensive foreign investment; Chinese students were also allowed to study abroad, resulting in a mounting exodus of the brightest young people. Repression of intellectuals was greatly eased. Ideology gave way to productivity. Under Deng's tutelage, the nation experienced a vigorous economic revival, as GDP growth averaged about ten percent per annum in the 1978–1988 period.

In the late 1980s, Deng's reform coalition began to fall apart. Deng began to turn against the veteran cadres who had helped him to reconsolidate power in the wake of the Cultural Revolution but now showed increasing misgivings about pushing liberal reforms through to the end. In dealing with these opponents Deng used an elaborately phased scheme in which veterans would become "advisers" before retiring with relatively generous benefits. He curtailed the political role of the military top commanders by steadily trimming the army budget and manpower allotment.

However, he had not reckoned with the consequences of the reforms he had unleashed. The attempt to introduce price reform and other urban reforms in 1986 caused inflation to spiral, generating discontent in the cities; the attempt to cap the prices of farm products allowed grain harvests to stagnate after the record 1984 crop. Discontent manifested itself among young people in demands for political reform, which Deng saw as an unacceptable challenge to the authority of the CCP. These demands first surfaced in a spontaneous student movement in the fall of 1986, and then in a far more extensive mass movement in favor of democracy in April 1989, which culminated in the June 4 *Tiananmen massacre. The subsequent purge depleted the reform forces and left Deng's legacy hanging uneasily in the balance.

(See also SINO-AMERICAN RELATIONS.)

Deng Xiaoping, *Built Socialism with Chinese Characteristics* (Beijing, 1985). Uli Franz, *Deng Xiaoping* (Boston, 1988).

LOWELL DITTMER

DENMARK. Danish *democracy dates to the beginning of this century. The country's sudden leap from royal absolutism to a liberal *constitutional monarchy in 1849 was partly reversed when the loss of the war with Prussia led, in 1866, to a retreat from the relatively democratic provisions of the 1849 constitution. Subsequent royal cabinets based on the privileged upper house of Parliament governed against growing opposition in the popularly elected lower chamber, the *Folketing*. The supremacy of the lower house and the right of its majority to form a government were established in 1901, and constitutional reform in 1915 completed the transition by universalizing suffrage and democratizing the upper house. The 1953 Constitution abolished the upper chamber entirely.

Danish political institutions today fit the model of parliamentary government. There are a few peculiarities, however. Although there is no tradition of *judicial review, officials' arbitrary acts are restrained by the ombudsman system established in the 1953 Constitution and Parliament itself is checked by regular resort to referenda. Policy-making powers are centralized in the unitary national government, but implementation of many policies has been decentralized to municipal and county governments since consolidation of local governments in 1970 increased their capacity. Moreover, the Faeroe Islands and Greenland—"North Atlantic Denmark"—have enjoyed far-reaching autonomy since, respectively, 1948 and 1979.

The Party System. Danish politics are characterized by a multiparty system with strong and disciplined parties, frequent elections (on the average every two and a half years in the postwar period), an absence of single-party majorities (the last was before World War I), high voter participation (turnout has averaged over eighty percent since 1960), and stable coalition governments.

In the formative stage of the Danish party system, two groups developed in Parliament after 1866: the agrarian Liberals *(Venstre),* supported by farmers and the urban middle class, rolled up increasing majorities in the lower house, and the Conservatives *(Højre,* renamed *Det konservative Folkeparti* in 1915), supported by the well-to-do and the old aristocracy, controlled the upper house. The former were the proponents of expansion of the suffrage and of the *Folketing's* supremacy; the latter opposed both. The organization of the Social Democratic Party in 1871 added a new type of mass-membership party outside Parliament; the party organized the growing urban working class, and elected its first member of Parliament in 1884.

Both agrarian Liberals and Social Democrats conceived of themselves as the political wing of broader popular movements of farmers and workers respectively, and each developed an elaborate organizational infrastructure that included economic groups (agricultural cooperatives and trade unions), newspapers, youth groups, and educational societies. Centrifugal forces ultimately divided both. The left wing of the Liberal Party organized the Radical Liberals (Det radikale Venstre) in 1905 and the left wing of the Social Democratic youth organization established a small Communist Party (CP) after the Bolshevik Revolution.

From the 1920s until the 1970s, this five-party system with its clear class division characterized Danish political competition. The Social Democrats predominated with an average vote of over forty percent between 1929 and 1971; since 1932, the party has typically polled as many votes as the next two parties combined. Together the agrarian Liberals, Radical Liberals, and Conservatives averaged about forty-five percent of the vote in this period; a secular decline in the farming population strengthened the Conservatives at the expense of the other two. Although the Communists emerged from the Resistance with considerable working-class support, the party declined in the 1950s and, after expelling long-time party leader Aksel Larsen (1897–1972), was replaced in Parliament by Larsen's new Socialist People's Party (SPP) in 1960; the CP or SPP polled five percent to ten percent between 1945 and 1971. The two-percent threshold for *proportional representation permitted other groups to win seats, but, for half a century, the lines of partisan cleavage established by 1920 dominated the parliamentary landscape. Despite the multiparty system, Denmark enjoyed stable *cabinet government because of the stability in party coalition patterns. The long-lived Social Democratic–Radical Liberal alliance formed the foundation of Social Democratic dominance in government (thirty-three of forty years between 1929 and 1968) during this period.

The 1973 "earthquake election" ended that era. The number of parties in Parliament doubled from five to ten as every third Danish voter cast a ballot for a party not represented in the previous Parliament. While additional parties won seats on the left and in the center, the bulk of the protest vote went to two anti-tax parties, most notably Mogens Glistrup's Progress Party which ran second to the Social Democrats and outpolled the established nonsocialist parties. Though the Progress Party's support eventually ebbed, fragmentation persisted as eight to eleven parties won seats in each subsequent election of the 1970s and 1980s, reflecting mobility among the growing white-collar strata and a general partisan dealignment in voting patterns that affected working-class and old middle-class voters alike. Although party fragmentation after 1973 complicated cabinet formation, minority Social Democratic governments between 1975 and 1982 and minority Conservative-led governments since 1982 have governed effectively. Both have maintained the characteristic Danish *welfare state policies developed under Social Democratic auspices.

The Welfare State. Since the establishment of political democracy and recovery of Danish Schleswig after World War I, Danish politics have revolved primarily around economic issues. The degree of national ethnic and religious homogeneity (Denmark is more than ninety-five-percent ethnically Danish and religiously Lutheran) restricted other lines of cleavage, and the structure of the party system offered easy articulation of economic demands.

The foundation for the modern Danish welfare state was laid in the "red-green" agreement of 30 January 1933 between the Social Democratic–Radical Liberal cabinet of Social Democratic Prime Minister Thorvald Stauning (1873–1942) and the agrarian Liberal opposition. The "Kanslergade compromise" provided emergency employment for the unemployed, price supports for farmers, extension of existing labor agreements without wage reductions, and the overhaul of the patchwork of welfare measures and the poor law. It set a pattern for active state intervention in the economy and for a consensus commitment to redistribution through the public sector. For the Social Democrats, the welfare state became a surrogate for socialism; for the bourgeois parties, a means to stabilize capitalism. Successive Danish governments developed a complex system of transfer payments and social services to raise the level of those worst off and to maintain economic security for all. Universalistic criteria for access helped eliminate the stigma previously attached to welfare measures. Most recently, in the 1970s and 1980s, measures providing home assistance for the elderly and high-quality public day care for children eased women's entry into the labor market; women's labor force participation rates increased steadily from forty-four percent in 1960 to seventy-five percent in 1985.

In the postwar period, policy making has increasingly become corporatist. Major interest organizations—labor, employers, and farmers—participate in policy deliberation and implementation. Indeed, these organizations have become so universal in membership and their policy involvement so significant that they constitute new channels of functional representation and democracy.

Despite the success of welfare measures in providing shared affluence (Danes have the highest living standard in the *European Community), the period since the 1973–1974 oil price shock has been one of challenges: unemployment has remained stubbornly high; high tax rates have distorted economic behavior and undermined support for welfare policies; welfare spending has risen, partly because of rising take-up rates for some benefits, without improving actual welfare; and immigration has diminished the sense of social solidarity.

Denmark in the International Arena. The German invasion of 9 April 1940 ended faith in neutrality which had served Denmark well during World War I. After World War II, Denmark participated in negotiations to form a Scandinavian defense pact and, after these efforts failed, joined the *North Atlantic Treaty Organization. As a founding member of the Nordic Council (1952), Denmark has combined its Atlantic and Nordic orientations with a European orientation (Danes voted to join the European Community in 1972), and a global perspective through active membership in the UN. International economic integration has impinged on growing areas of domestic policy to the discomfit of many, yet despite nostalgia for the days when national policies were hammered out in Copenhagen, most Danes recognize that Denmark, with little more than 5 million inhabitants, is simply too small to go it alone. Nevertheless, Denmark sent shock waves throughout the European Community in June 1992 by voting "no" in a referendum on the Maastricht Treaty designed to advance economic and monetary union and set the foundations for a common *security policy. Issues of international economic and security policy have regularly been bones of political contention, yet, apart from the unexpected treaty defeat, Denmark has served successfully as a political—as well as geographical—bridge between *Scandinavia and the rest of Europe.

(See also CORPORATISM.)

Gwyn Jones, *Denmark: A Modern History* (London, 1986). Mogens N. Pedersen, "The Danish 'Working Multiparty System': Breakdown or Adaptation?" in Hans Daalder, ed., *Party Systems in Denmark, Austria, Switzerland, the Netherlands and Belgium* (New York, 1987), pp. 1–60. Eric S. Einhorn and John Logue, *Modern Welfare States: Politics and Policies in Social Democratic Scandinavia* (New York, 1989).

JOHN LOGUE

DEPENDENCY. In the 1960s and 1970s, the originators of the dependency approach insisted that *Third World *development should be treated as a historically distinctive problem. They argued that diffusion of culture, technology, and resources from advanced industrial countries would not cause poor industrializing countries to replicate the developmental trajectories of Western Europe or the United States. In their view, industrializing in a global political economy already populated with industrial powers is a new kind of challenge, one that could not be analyzed in purely domestic terms or reduced to a reflection of structural change at the international level. Instead, the projects and struggles of local groups and classes interacted with constraints and opportunities generated by the global political economy to produce historically distinctive patterns of social, political, and economic change.

These assertions set practitioners of the dependency approach apart from earlier development theorists. *Modernization theorists saw the future of the Third World as shaped primarily by the global diffusion of the complex of "modern" values, attitudes, and social structures that prevailed in northwestern Europe and the United States. In this view the persistence of traditional local cultures was the principal obstacle to development. Neoclassical economists had a similar vision, except that they focused on entrepreneurship as the key value and the free market as the master institution. Marxists denied that the free market was the endpoint of the development, but still argued that the essence of change in the Third World lay in the diffusion of *capitalism. As long as the diffusion of global patterns was seen as the driving force of change, analysis naturally began with the dynamics of the metropole or "core" (the advanced industrial countries of Western Europe and the United States). Predictions regarding the future of the "periphery" (the poor nations of Asia, Africa, and Latin America) were essentially extrapolations from the experience of the core.

The idea of dependency emerged out of an intellectual tradition whose primary concern was to provide a convincing analysis of what was going on in the developing countries themselves. The cornerstone of the dependency literature was an essay produced by Fernando Henrique Cardoso, a Brazilian sociologist, and Enzo Faletto, a Chilean historian, in Santiago in the mid-1960s. Their essay had its roots in a long series of scholarly efforts by Latin Americans trying to understand why, after 200 years of pervasive political, economic, and cultural interchange with Europe and the United States, the degree of Latin America's "underdevelopment" vis-à-vis the advanced industrial countries had changed so little. Raúl *Prebisch and his colleagues working in Santiago for the UN *Economic Commission for Latin America and the Caribbean (ECLAC) had questioned the long-term benefits of pursuing comparative advantage by concentrating on the export of agricultural products and minerals. Celso Furtado, Caio Prado, Sergio Bagu, and others had dissected the historical connections between class structure and developmental trajectories. Florestan Fernandes, Pablo González Casanova, and Osvaldo Sunkel had examined the social and political implications of the local social structures that emerged from the long history of Latin America's interaction with the metropole. Cardoso and Faletto used the concept of dependency to recast and focus the debate. They offered a historical analysis of the transformations that had occurred in Latin America over the 150 years since the end of colonial rule and proposed that further efforts to analyze these transformations should use what they later came to call a "historical-structural" approach.

The historical-structural approach began the comprehensive analysis of economic and political actors reminiscent of classical political economy and set it in the context of a global system in which the fortunes of nations at different levels of development were bound together. It combined an analysis of the way in which relatively stable global structures conditioned the developmental possibilities of the various countries of Latin America with an appreciation of the way in which these structures had been transformed by historically specific conflicts and movements. Viewed through the lens of the historical-structural approach, the interweaving of interests across the divide that separates rich and poor countries cannot be reduced to a foreordained structural logic. The politics of development are full of contradictory combinations and unexpected twists and turns. Structures of domination meet with resistance from below. Those trying to maintain themselves in a position of dominance adopt new strategies that in turn yield unexpected opportunities for transformation. Social movements devise new definitions of what is politically possible and new organizational forms at the local level, while improvements in technology and communication make transnational mechanisms of control more effective. These contradictory trends do not just cancel each other out, they result in directions of change that could not have been spelled out in advance. Because they see development as historically open-ended, those who use the idea of dependency have, on the whole, preferred to think of it as a "methodology for the analysis of concrete situations of underdevelopment" rather than as a formal theory.

The dependency approach rejected the idea that the dynamics of diffusion drove the process of social change in Latin America, but it did not deny that the influence of the core was a critical force in shaping developments on the periphery of the world economy. The very term *dependency* highlights the extent to which the movement of economics and politics in poor countries is conditioned by a global economy dominated by others. Dependency flows from asymmetrical ties between nations, but it is not simply a relationship between countries. It involves an ensemble of ties among groups and classes both between and within nations. Groups and classes in the core have interests with respect to the course of development in the periphery. These resonate with the interests of some local groups and classes and conflict with those of others in ways that are contingent on historical circumstance.

Even during the period of "outward-oriented growth" in the late nineteenth century when all Latin American countries were relying on the export of primary products, there was variation. In countries where exports consisted primarily of minerals under the control of foreign capital, strategies of capital accumulation, political alliances, and possibilities for the emergence of local industry were different from those in countries where the production of agrarian exports was undertaken on locally-owned haciendas or latifundia. Such variation affected domestic responses to changes in the global economy. All the countries of Latin America were affected by the traumatic economic consequences of the Great Depression, but the growth of the nascent manufacturing sector was stimulated only in some of them. Once local manufacturing began to emerge, the situation became even more complicated. Landowners producing export crops in the periphery (Argentine cattle ranchers, for example) shared an interest in liberal trade agreements with exporters of industrial goods based in the core (Manchester textile merchants, for example). Local manufacturers whose interests were threatened by this local-foreign alliance sometimes turned to workers and middle-class groups in their search for political allies. The state apparatus became an arena of contestation. Later, when transnational corporations had been drawn into the process of local industrialization, local entrepreneurs suffered from their competition within the domestic market but were at the same time beneficiaries of the industrial societies that the transnationals were helping to create.

Although there is general agreement within the dependency tradition that prospects for development must be analyzed by looking at the interweaving of local interests and political strategies with those of groups and classes in the advanced industrial countries, there is a range of opinion with regard to developmental consequences. Early arguments seemed to imply that local agrarian and commercial interests allied with metropolitan manufacturers and foreign investors in extractive industries would be able to block industrialization in peripheral countries indefinitely. Even after it was clear that substantial industrialization was occurring in the countries of the periphery, some argued that powerful metropolitan interests would block the transfer to the periphery of full capacity to produce technologically innovative products and processes and that this would in turn force local industrialists to rely on wage-repressive strategies, undercutting the growth of domestic markets and the possibility for self-sustained growth. Others have focused on the possibility of an alliance of transnational and local capital constructed around a project of local industrialization. The "dependent development" that results from this sort of alliance may not carry with it the political and social consequences associated with industrialization in the core but, as cases like Brazil illustrate, it has produced substantial economic growth.

During the 1970s, the dependency approach gained adherents not just in Latin America but in North America and Europe as well. It provided the impetus for a rich outpouring of research, ranging from quantitative cross-national analyses of direct foreign investment (for example in the work of Volker Bornschier, Christopher Chase-Dunn, and Richard Rubinson) to detailed studies of the interplay of foreign and local actors in particular countries and sectors (as, for example, David Becker's work on copper mining in Peru or Gary Gereffi's study of the pharmaceutical industry). At the same time, the dependency approach was subject to a barrage of criticism. It was accused of focusing too much attention on the role of external ties and distracting attention from the dynamics of internal conflict and of not providing an adequate account of the dynamics of interaction between local and international groups and classes in other regions of the world, such as the newly industrializing countries of East Asia.

Nonetheless, the dependency approach remained an important point of departure for cross-regional analyses, and Cardoso and Faletto's historical-structural methodology continued to serve as a guide for those working on the comparative study of development. As the century draws to a close, the issues raised by the dependency approach remain as relevant as ever. International debt and its local consequences, the opening of domestic markets to new competition from imports, the return to an emphasis on outward-oriented growth all offer opportunities for the sort of analysis that Cardoso and Faletto proposed. Looking back over the decades since it emerged, dependency continues to stand out as one of the rare cases in which an approach generated primarily by scholars in the Third World subsequently came to have a pervasive influence on the perspectives of scholars working the core.

(See also CLASS AND POLITICS; IMPERIALISM; INTERNATIONAL POLITICAL ECONOMY; INTERNATIONAL SYSTEMS; MULTINATIONAL CORPORATIONS; NEWLY INDUSTRIALIZING ECONOMIES; POLITICAL DEVELOPMENT; TECHNOLOGY TRANSFER.)

Fernando Henrique Cardoso and Enzo Faletto, *Dependencia y Desarollo en América Latina* (Santiago, 1967); published in English as *Dependency and Development in Latin America* (Berkeley, Calif., 1979). Gabriel Palma, "Dependency: A Formal Theory of Development or a Methodology for the Analysis of Concrete Situations of Underdevelopment" *World Development* (1978): 881–894.

PETER B. EVANS

DEREGULATION. A wide-ranging deregulation of economic activity in the Western democracies has been one of the notable developments of contemporary *political economy. With the exception of the dismantling of wartime controls, the essentially uniform trend throughout the twentieth century had been toward more detailed and extensive regulation of business. Since the mid-1970s, however, most of the democracies have scaled down or abolished important regulatory programs. Along with the *privatization of municipal services and state enterprises in the democracies and the liberalization of planned economies in Eastern and *Central Europe, deregulation represents a sharp rise in the worldwide prominence of free-market economic policies in the last quarter of the century.

Some commentators have traced deregulation to economic and technological changes that caused strains under existing regulations and led regulated industries or other powerful groups to demand reform. Such changes did account for certain cases of deregulation. In the United States, for example, the introduction of new savings instruments in the 1970s caused severe competitive pressures in the banking industry and led to the deregulation of deposit interest.

Nevertheless, the rise of a broad deregulation movement, affecting a wide range of programs in several countries, mainly reflected intellectual and political developments. Academic economists had concluded by the 1960s that much regulation was unnecessary or ill conceived and, in particular, that public utility–type regulation of pricing and entry in multifirm industries was almost always unwarranted. By the mid-1970s, prominent attitudes and concerns of mass publics were adding political weight to the economists' critique; these included anxiety about inflation, an increasing skepticism about the efficacy of government programs, and (especially in the United States) a moralistic consumerism that often focused on allegations of improper collusion between government and business.

These forces converged and promoted deregulation primarily in one class of regulatory programs—those that controlled entry into markets or set minimum prices in potentially competitive industries. Such regulation has been widespread in the developed democracies in transportation (including railroads, trucking, airlines, intercity buses); financial services (banking, securities brokerage); communications (telephone equipment, long-distance service, broadcasting, cable television); agriculture (price supports, marketing orders); and many other industries and occupations. These programs restrain competition, usually with the rationale of protecting consumers from instability. Instead of benefiting consumers, however, they almost inevitably raise prices and reduce service. Although there were also efforts to reduce the cost or increase the efficiency of other regulatory programs (environmental protection, equal opportunity requirements, public utility regulation, and so on), these programs generally did not come under severe attack. Among the principal exceptions, the United States and Canada phased out maximum price controls on natural gas and petroleum products, and the *Reagan administration launched a general effort to trim federal regulation, mostly without long-term success.

Support for deregulation cut across political lines. In the United States, early sponsorship was provided by a liberal Democratic senator, Edward M. Kennedy, and a conservative Republican president, Gerald R. Ford. In Britain, deregulation was a central commitment of the conservative *Thatcher government. In France, broadcast deregulation was implemented by the socialist *Mitterrand government. The principal opposition generally came from regulated industries and their labor unions, which sought to preserve protection from competition; additional opposition sometimes came from narrow groups of consumers or business customers, often in rural areas, who believed they received subsidized service under regulation. The ability to adopt deregulatory policy changes, therefore, typically depended on government's capacity to resist pressure from narrow groups and vindicate widely shared interests—for example, the interest in economic efficiency. Despite the ideological breadth of the reform movement, the scope and intensity of deregulation also reflected national dispositions toward market-oriented economic policies. The most wide-ranging deregulation occurred in the United States, Britain, and Australia; Canada, Italy, France, and the Federal Republic of Germany took more moderate steps toward deregulation; Japan, Denmark, and Austria adopted very limited measures.

For the most part, deregulation has delivered on its promise of economic benefits: lower rates and more flexible service in freight transportation, accelerated technological progress in communications, expanded entertainment and information services, lower average airfares, smaller commissions for the execution of stock transactions, and higher interest rates on savings deposits, among others. In a few cases, however, there have also been adverse consequences. These have included, in the United States, fare instability in the airline industry and, most important, the collapse of the savings and loan industry in the late 1980s. But these difficulties have been largely the result of incompatible collateral policies (such as inadequate investment in airport facilities and overly liberal deposit insurance), and there is little evidence that they will lead to widespread reregulation of pricing or entry in deregulated industries.

(See also PLANNING; THATCHERISM.)

Martha Derthick and Paul J. Quirk, *The Politics of Deregulation* (Washington, D.C., 1985). Kenneth Button and Dennis Swann, eds., *The Age of Regulatory Reform* (Oxford, 1989).

PAUL J. QUIRK

DESTABILIZATION. The use of ideological, economic, and military sabotage to prevent a target state from providing basic security or necessities to its population is known as destabilization. The goal is not always to take control of the country but to destroy or cripple its economy, its infrastructure, and thereby undermine popular support for the government. Destabilization seeks to render the country ungovernable, engendering a collapse of the state from within, a form of political-economic implosion. The objective is to change the behavior of a weaker state without incurring the high cost that a direct invasion might entail.

Behavior unacceptable to the destabilizer might be actions to assert national authority or interests (against an ex-colonial regime or a regional power), developing a military capacity independent of a dominant power, or exercising political power outside the control of economic elites supported by the destabilizer. Success may be attained when the target state accepts specified political (e.g., alignment or alliance) or economic (e.g., dependence) conditions.

Destabilization has been chosen as a strategy when a government judges it cannot coexist with another, but also cannot invade, because the costs might be too high. To appear legitimate and to reduce cost, sabotage is often carried out by disaffected nationals

of the target country or by mercenaries, not by the army of the destabilizer. It differs from other forms of intervention, therefore, in avoiding a direct confrontation of regular armies; rather, guerrilla tactics prevail, with the destabilizing forces often operating against civilians and avoiding confrontation with other military forces.

The "low-cost" component of destabilization also distinguishes this strategy from other forms of intervention. Because it does not engage very many regular troops (mainly trainers), the destabilizer's expenditures can be small enough to be hidden in diverse budget categories, not requiring direct new taxes to fund a foreign war. Politically costly conscription may be avoided, and fewer young men return home as casualties. The operations appear not to be a burden, and therefore, popular domestic opposition may be confined and minimized.

Destabilization is often conducted in the context of a regional strategy in that the surrogate forces need a secure base, most likely in a neighboring state, and it is important that the neighbors of the target state agree that its political economy is unacceptable. This strategy can, therefore, escalate regional tensions and hostilities.

Destabilization, a contemporary term for a familiar strategy known previously in this century as "small wars" (U.S. Marine Corps, "Small Wars Manual," 1940) or "roll-back," today comprises one aspect of "low-intensity conflict" (others include *counterinsurgency and antidrug operations, according to the U.S. Department of Defense, "Proceedings of the Low-Intensity Warfare Conference," Washington, D.C., 14–15 January 1986). Distinct from counterinsurgency, destabilization is an assault against an established state, while counterinsurgency tries to impede an incipient revolt.

Although the United States engaged in 215 conflicts below the level of war from 1946 to 1975, destabilization really became a preferred strategy of the United States for more than a decade after its defeat in Vietnam (Jochen Hippler, "Low-Intensity Warfare: Key Strategy for the Third World Theater" *Middle East Reports* [Jan.–Feb. 1987]: 32–38). In 1984, the Heritage Foundation encouraged President Ronald Reagan to "employ paramilitary assets to weaken those communist and noncommunist regimes that may already be facing the early stages of insurgency within their borders and which threaten US interests." The United States employed destabilization most in Central America (especially against *Nicaragua, 1981–1989) and in the Caribbean. However, the strategy has also been used by Israel in the Middle East (especially against Lebanon, 1981–1989) and by South Africa against its neighbors (especially Angola, 1975–1988, and Mozambique, 1981–present). In Asia, the United States tried to destabilize the Afghanistan regime supported by the Soviet Union (1979–1989) and harassed the Corazon *Aquino government in the

Philippines (late 1980s). Both the People's Republic of China and the United States supported forces to destabilize the Vietnamese-backed Cambodian government during the 1980–1990s.

Because destabilization in often protracted, the essential first condition for success in the effort to reverse policies is to gain ideological hegemony by stigmatizing the target government with such labels as "terrorist" or "totalitarian." Every effort is made to tarnish the international reputation by exaggerating mistakes of the target state, in agriculture, industry, or in whatever sector it is vulnerable to accusations of ineptitude. The government loses moral authority. It then becomes "acceptable" to the citizens of the destabilizing state and the international community to escalate to the second stage, which is economic delinking, to change behavior. Both overt and covert propaganda are, therefore, equally important within the destabilizing country, to make the tactics acceptable, and within the target country to make the state unacceptable.

Economic delinking, purposefully disrupting long-term relations, ranges from threats which are not carried out (delaying shipments of food instead of cutting them off), to disruption of crucial economic links, to sanctions, to total embargo. The destabilizer may also demand that other states also delink, enforcing international isolation.

Economic delinking escalates to economic sabotage, attacking infrastructure to disrupt the economy, such as telecommunications, transport links, and ports. Factories and warehouses may be bombed at night as a warning, destroying the productive and income-earning capacity not only of the state, but of the population.

The final escalation involves attacking the producers directly. The first targeted are those relatively skilled: union leaders, health workers, teachers, agricultural extension workers. Not only is this to disrupt production, but to attack morale, as it becomes clear that the first killed are those who have benefited by the status quo through education and leadership. In Mozambique in the 1980s, for example, the forces of destabilization cut off the ears of village leaders to demonstrate that one "should not listen to Frelimo [the government]." Finally, any civilian becomes a target: peasants are killed in the fields and their crops are burned, forcing massive displacement.

The major tactic is *terrorism as people are kidnapped and brutalized into acquiescence; by this stage, there are no rules, no restrictions and no restraints at all, for it becomes total war at the grassroots level (Central Intelligence Agency, Nicaragua Manual, *Psychological Operations in Guerrilla Warfare*, New York, 1985). Most people break down under *torture, and this stage involves torture of a whole nation through managed terror. The 1987 report of the human rights organization Americas Watch described the Nicaraguan *contra violations of the laws of war as "so prevalent that these may be said to be their principal means of waging war." South Africa's surrogates in Mozambique have brutalized (mutilation and rape) young children (U.S. Department of State, Gersony Report, 1988). Therefore, destabilization is not "low-intensity" at all for the victims, simply for the perpetrator because it does not engage its regular forces.

Demobilizing the population, and virtually halting production, destabilization cripples the government so it cannot serve the people. It disrupts and destroys any efforts at development. Eventually, people turn away from a government which cannot provide basic protection, let alone basic necessities. The destabilizer can then move in with donor food, with efficient deliveries, and with equipment for water supplies and tools for production in refugee areas; development aid rewards those who support the destabilizing state's goals. The message is clear: the target government failed to provide the most fundamental needs, and the destabilizer can "remedy" the problems.

(See also GUERRILLA WARFARE; SOUTHERN AFRICA; VIETNAM WAR.)

Secretary of Defense, *Proceedings of the Low-Intensity Warfare Conference, January 1986* (Washington, D.C., 1986). Michael T. Clare and Peter Kornbluh, eds., *Low-Intensity Warfare: Counter-insurgency, Proinsurgency, and Antiterrorism in the Eighties* (New York, 1988). United States Department of State Bureau for Refugee Programs, *Summary of Mozambican Accounts of Principally Conflict-Related Experience in Mozambique* (Washington, D.C., 1988). Elling Njal Tjonneland, *Pax Pretoriana: The Fall of Apartheid and the Politics of Destabilization* (Uppsala, 1989). Lawrence A. Yates, "From Small Wars to Counterinsurgency: US Military Interventions in Latin America since 1898" *Military Review* (February 1989): 74–86.

CAROL B. THOMPSON

DÉTENTE. Derived from the French verb "to slacken," détente denotes an easing of strained relations between states. In medieval French, a *destente* was the mechanism that tightened or loosened the tension of a crossbow string. Although the term has a long tradition in diplomatic parlance, its contemporary usage is identified primarily with the brief period of improved U.S.-Soviet relations during the 1970s. The chief architects of the *superpower détente were President Richard *Nixon and National Security Adviser Henry *Kissinger.

In his 1969 inaugural address, Nixon proclaimed an end to the "era of confrontation" with the *Soviet Union and the advent of an "era of negotiation." This move toward a less confrontational approach to relations with the Soviet Union came at a time of widespread public calls for a radical scaling down in U.S. overseas commitments following the Vietnam War. Operating within the constraints of this domestic political context, Nixon and Kissinger developed their détente policy as a realistic variation of George *Kennan's *containment doctrine. At the heart of this strategy was the concept of "linkage" under which the *United States sought to create a system of incentives and penalties to moderate Soviet behavior. Tangible economic benefits, such as *technology transfers or financial credits, were to be granted to promote more cooperative Soviet policies—for example, Moscow's assistance in resolving regional conflicts in Southeast Asia and the Middle East. The obverse, of course, was that such positive inducements would be withheld if the Soviet Union continued to pursue *Cold War policies. U.S. officials hoped that an expanding web of economic, political, and cultural relations between East and West would not only moderate Soviet external behavior but might also help foster a process of political liberalization within the Soviet Union itself. While acknowledging that the superpower relationship remained essentially competitive, Kissinger believed the long-term success of détente could lead to the creation of a new "structure of peace" and the end of the Cold War.

Détente diplomacy produced a range of bilateral accords, most notably on *arms control. The May 1972 summit meeting in Moscow between Nixon and Soviet leader Leonid Brezhnev yielded agreements on the limitation of strategic nuclear weapons (SALT I) and antiballistic missiles (ABM). In addition, a statement of "Basic Principles" was concluded that committed both sides to "exercise restraint" and eschew "efforts to obtain unilateral advantage at the expense of the other." These principles, likened by Nixon to a "road map," were to be a code of conduct regulating superpower behavior.

In practice, the implementation of the 1972 "Basic Principles" agreement was hindered by competing Soviet and U.S. conceptions of détente. If Nixon and Kissinger saw détente as a variation of containment, the Soviet leadership viewed it as an updated version of Nikita *Khrushchev's "peaceful coexistence" doctrine. Brezhnev asserted that while there was no alternative to détente in the nuclear age, it did not negate the Marxist tenets of international *class struggle. From Moscow's perspective, détente diplomacy offered mechanisms for keeping East-West competition within acceptable bounds to avert *war. The Soviets rejected the U.S. preference for linkage in favor of a compartmentalized approach in which arms control, regional conflicts, and economic relations were considered as discrete issues. In its efforts to impose its conception of détente on the Soviet Union, the U.S. administration found linkage difficult to achieve on issues where there existed a strong mutuality of superpower interest. During the *Angolan conflict of 1975–1976, for example, the Ford administration, despite Kissinger's warning that Soviet military assistance to one of the warring factions was incompatible with détente, did not suspend the SALT II negotiations given the powerful

U.S. interest in completing a strategic arms limitation agreement.

An important milestone in détente diplomacy was the signing of the 1975 *Helsinki Accords by the thirty-five member states of the *Conference on Security and Cooperation in Europe (CSCE). Among its provisions, this agreement declared the inviolability of Europe's postwar borders and committed the signatories to the maintenance of fundamental *human rights. The Kremlin's failure to comply fully with the Helsinki Accords—notably, the continued suppression of political dissidents and Jewish activists—intensified public criticism of the U.S. administration's détente policy. This sentiment had been fueled in April 1975 by the humiliating defeat of the U.S.-backed regime in South Vietnam at the hands of Communist guerrilla forces supported by the Soviet Union. Conservative critics charged that détente had become a "one-way street" of U.S. economic and political concessions to the Moscow regime without any corresponding change in Soviet behavior. Under this domestic pressure, President Gerald Ford, who had succeeded Nixon in August 1974, was prompted to drop détente from his political lexicon in favor of the phrase "peace through strength" during the 1976 election campaign.

President Jimmy *Carter came to office in January 1977 with the avowed intention to continue his Republican predecessors' policy of détente toward the Soviet Union, albeit with greater assertiveness on the issue of Soviet human rights abuses. During the late 1970s, increased Soviet activism in the Third World (e.g., Angola, Ethiopia) was a major factor undermining superpower détente. This pattern of behavior culminated in the Soviet invasion of Afghanistan in December 1979—an act prompting Carter to withdraw the unratified SALT II treaty from Senate consideration. The Afghan invasion marked the end of the détente era and ushered in the return to a more militarized approach to containment under President Ronald *Reagan following the 1980 presidential election.

The Soviet-U.S. experience of the 1970s demonstrated that détente is a condition, not structure, of *international relations. While the superpowers acknowledged a common interest in the prevention of nuclear war, both remained committed to the pursuit of unilateral advantage. The Nixon administration's hyperbolic rhetoric about a "structure of peace" created public expectations that détente marked the end of Cold War competition. The 1970s détente ultimately unraveled because the reality of political linkage made it impossible to isolate continued competition in the *Third World from other aspects of the superpower relationship, such as arms control.

The late 1980s did not witness the revival of the term *détente* during the improvement of Soviet-U.S. relations under Reagan and Soviet President Mikhail *Gorbachev. This stemmed not only from the desire to avoid unfavorable political connotations from the past; it also reflected the belief that profound Soviet societal changes—Kennan's key precondition for the end of the Cold War—might lead not to renewed détente but to a fundamental transformation in the structure of international relations.

(See also AMERICAN FOREIGN POLICY; INTERNATIONAL COOPERATION; SOVIET-AFGHANISTAN WAR; SOVIET FOREIGN POLICY; STRATEGIC ARMS LIMITATION TREATIES.)

Henry A. Kissinger, *White House Years* (Boston, 1979). Robert S. Litwak, *Détente and the Nixon Doctrine: American Foreign Policy and the Pursuit of Stability, 1969–1976* (Cambridge, U.K., 1984).

ROBERT S. LITWAK

DETERRENCE. Most simply, deterrence is dissuasion by means of threat. Individuals and states have practiced policies of deterrence for millennia. The term, with French roots, means "to frighten from." States try to deter one another from attacking, police try to deter criminals, and parents try to deter children from undertaking acts that may harm themselves or others. As an explicit policy, justified and guided by theory, the most developed form of deterrence originates in the special case of the *international relations of the nuclear era.

Elements of deterrence theory can be found in early writings on aerial warfare. For example, the mathematician F. W. Lanchester (*Aircraft in Warfare,* London, 1916) wrote: "The power of reprisal and the knowledge that the means of reprisal exists will ever be a far greater deterrent than any pseudo-legal contract." Its prominence, however, dates from the nuclear era, and especially U.S. efforts to deter perceived threats to itself and its allies by the Soviet Union and its allies. In 1946 Bernard Brodie published in *The Absolute Weapon* (New York) his famous statement which, without using the term deterrence, expressed the essence of subsequent policy: "Thus far the chief purpose of our military establishment has been to win wars. From now on its chief purpose must be to avert them."

U.S. Secretary of State John Foster Dulles articulated the policy as nuclear deterrence by threat of "massive" retaliation in 1954, when he declared an intent "to depend primarily upon a great capacity to retaliate instantly by means and at places of our own choosing." This threat was issued in response to the perceived continuing danger of Soviet aggression and, to Americans, the unacceptable costs of meeting that "aggression" with large-scale conventional forces as had been done in the *Korean War. It represents an example of "extended" deterrence, wherein the deterrer wishes to prevent not a direct attack on itself but an attack on some third party (ally or neutral). Whereas the ability of a nuclear-armed superpower to deter a direct attack on itself was deemed to be high, extended deterrence—although practiced widely—has been thought to be more problematic, as the stakes to the deterrer were less and its willingness to use force therefore more in doubt.

In the emphasis on threat, deterrence is often distinguished from more general forms of persuasion, including those based principally on the offer of rewards. A more general theory of influence includes rewards, as do some deterrence theorists; nevertheless rewards are often neglected by such theorists. Moreover, as an exercise of dissuasion deterrence aims to prevent another party (typically an adversary) from taking certain actions, rather than to induce the adversary to undertake a particular action or to cease an action already underway. In strategic parlance the latter is often called compellence. Policies of deterrence and compellence both utilize coercion, but compellence typically is the more difficult as it demands an actual change in policy.

Deterrence is often conceptualized as a function of capability and will. That is, it is posited to succeed to the degree that the adversary perceives the deterrer as both able to inflict severe punishment and willing to do so—even perhaps at substantial cost to the deterrer. A deterrer may undertake various military or diplomatic actions to try to enhance an adversary's assessment of its capability and/or will. Deterrent threats may be expressed as a readiness to deny the adversary the ability to carry out or benefit from its action, as well as to punish the adversary (without necessarily denying it immediate benefits of the action). U.S. strategic nuclear deterrence policy typically has taken the latter form; Soviet policy somewhat more often the former.

A formulation emphasizing capability and will is embedded in rational deterrence theory, which assumes that the adversary will be able to make a well-informed means-end calculation of the damage which the deterrer can inflict and of the likelihood that the deterrer will actually carry out its threat. It thus forms part of a more general model of rational choice based on expected utilities. A more general model, however, also includes terms for those incentives of the adversary that are beyond ready manipulation by the deterrer; that is, it includes the adversary's subjective calculation of the likely costs and benefits not only of disregarding the deterrer's threat but also of those it may incur or forgo if it does allow itself to be deterred. These costs, in terms of missed opportunities or subsequent vulnerabilities, may be severe. The limited formulation of rational deterrence theory, by ignoring them, may give an erroneous prediction of behavior. For example, a leader faced with an internal political threat to power may be motivated to take risks internationally that would otherwise be deemed unacceptable.

Another limitation is simply that the adversary may not behave "rationally" even in the limited sense of rationality used here. Cognitive and social psychologists often challenge deterrence theory on its adequacy as an empirical predictor and therefore on its adequacy as a guide to policy formulation. Especially under conditions of severe crisis—surprise, finite decision time, and threat to major values perhaps magnified by deterrent threats—decisionmakers may make a very inadequate search for information and alternatives, may make very inaccurate estimates of the intentions or capabilities of the deterrer, and may even be unable to make ordered means-ends calculations of their own desired outcomes. Decision-makers may be led, by their biases or "motivated misperceptions," to exaggerate their chances of success, especially if they are simultaneously faced with other threats to vital interests (e.g., such as internal political threats to power). Decisions taken by complex organizations lacking a strong leader may further deviate from the basic model of rationality as applied to the decisions of a single individual.

Academic scholarship has reached little consensus on the conditions and degree to which a theory of rational deterrence provides a reasonable explanation or prediction of behavior. Systematic empirical study of cases of extended deterrence indicates that it is more likely to succeed when the local balance of forces and the active and readily mobilizable balances of military force favor the deterrer (capability). Deterrence is also more likely to succeed when the deterrer's *crisis bargaining behavior is firm but flexible, and it has neither bullied nor appeased in a previous crisis (will, tempered by elements of reassurance as discussed below). These findings suggest that rational deterrence theory offers a useful guide to the interpretation of many cases; nevertheless there are many circumstances it does not adequately explain, and it is difficult to know in advance when its predictions will prove satisfactory.

Evaluation of the success of a deterrent threat is often difficult, as it requires an assessment of the adversary's prior intentions, and hence of the role of the threat in changing those intentions. It demands a counterfactual assessment of how an adversary would have acted in the absence of the deterrent threat. Decision-makers' intentions are rarely known with certainty, either at the time of the threat or in their subsequent statements. Political decision-makers often have incentives to disguise the degree to which they may have allowed themselves to be dissuaded, or to expose their readiness to run great risks. Moreover, the manipulation of uncertainty, and thus of deception, is inherent in a deterrent situation. Both the deterrer and the adversary have incentives to appear more determined to fight than they really may be, and their intentions may change as they seem to gather more complete information on each other's incentives. Thus an observer may erroneously say deterrence has succeeded under conditions in which the adversary in fact had little intention to attack (deterrence was really irrelevant) or may erroneously treat a retreat as evidence of an initial lack of resolve when in fact the adversary did probe the deterrer's apparent resolve and then changed its intentions (deterrence really did succeed). These difficulties both hinder academic assessment and contribute to disagreements over desirable policy.

The analytical and empirical problems may be most severe in situations of "general" rather than "immediate" deterrence, i.e., in which there is no crisis of explicit threat and counterthreat, but merely a long-term deterrent threat not matched with any overt military or political action by the adversary. Thus many Western observers often claimed that U.S. nuclear deterrence of Soviet attack on Western Europe succeeded, while Eastern or neutral observers questioned whether the Soviet Union ever had an intention to attack Europe that needed to be deterred by military threat.

Such considerations make it difficult to evaluate the success of U.S. massive retaliation policy in the 1950s, or to determine whether it was more successful than merely the threat of taking non-nuclear action might have been. Whereas the United States manifestly had the capability to inflict severe damage on the Soviet Union with *nuclear weapons, its willingness to do so remained in doubt, given the Soviet Union's emerging ability, in return, to inflict damage on the United States and/or its allies. The United States might have been perceived as more willing to take non-nuclear military actions that, although less punishing to the Soviet Union, also carried less danger of severe Soviet retaliation.

Doubts over the credibility of U.S. threats were inherent in the earliest policy formulations, and grew in subsequent years as Soviet capabilities grew. In the application to modern nuclear deterrence they came to illustrate a fundamental paradox of deterrence theory; the deterrer often is making a threat that would not be in its own interest actually to carry out. Policy attempts to grapple with this problem involved various statements about "graduated" or "flexible" response, leaving the adversary uncertain about what specific responses might be forthcoming to particular actions. As major powers have come to achieve relatively secure, invulnerable nuclear deterrent forces, the ability of other nuclear powers to make credible threats to use nuclear weapons against them has become more constrained, especially in situations of extended deterrence. Under these circumstances, however, mutual direct nuclear deterrence (sometimes called mutual assured destruction) is often regarded as relatively stable, except perhaps under conditions of crisis. Policies that attempt to deter by threatening to strike the adversary's "values" (loosely, its population centers) are often thought to be more stable than those directed toward the adversary's forces (specifically, its retaliatory capabilities), but in operational details the strategies and their likely consequences become highly complex.

Uncertainty about intentions has been magnified by uncertainty about the deterring state's ability to completely control the use of force by its own military units; that is, by the possibility of unauthorized action by military commanders that would not necessarily be desired by the high-level leaders. Thus evolved some application of a strategy of the "threat that leaves something to chance."

Uncertainty may serve to undermine deterrence as well as to enhance it. Successful deterrence policies must combine threats with some measure of reassurance that dire consequences will not follow if the adversary does in fact abstain from an undesired action. A threat that leaves something to chance may help to deter the emergence of a political-military crisis, but should the crisis occur anyway, an adversary may feel compelled to make a "preemptive" strike if it fears that for one reason or another the deterrer may use force in any case. This, as well as the social-psychological conditions of crisis that may distort decision-making, is why a policy of deterrence may become especially problematic in crises.

Policies of deterrence always entail some risk of failure—a potentially catastrophic failure when weapons of mass destruction are employed. In the recent era of markedly improved East-West relations military deterrence has come to be regarded as less necessary: the incentives of both sides to encroach on each other's territory or vital interests seem reduced by the diminished ideological hostility and the mutual rewards of cooperative relations under peacetime conditions. The dangers of crisis instability are further reduced by various measures of arms reduction, information gathering, and communication. Nevertheless large numbers of nuclear weapons remain and policies of military deterrence are not entirely superseded.

(See also AMERICAN FOREIGN POLICY; FORCE, USE OF; SOVIET FOREIGN POLICY; STRATEGY; SUPERPOWER.)

Glenn H. Snyder, *Deterrence and Defense: Toward a Theory of National Security* (Princeton, N.J., 1961). Patrick M. Morgan, *Deterrence: A Conceptual Analysis*, 2d ed. (Beverly Hills, Calif., 1983). Barry Buzan, ed., *The International Politics of Deterrence* (London, 1987). Paul K. Huth, *Extended Deterrence and the Prevention of War* (New Haven, Conn., 1988). Robert Jervis, *The Meaning of the Nuclear Revolution: Statecraft and the Prospect of Armageddon* (Ithaca, N.Y., 1988).

BRUCE RUSSETT

DEVELOPMENT AND UNDERDEVELOPMENT

From its very beginning the science of economics has been preoccupied with economic development. But the theory of development as distinct from economic development came into vogue in the wake of World War II at the height of the nationalist movement in the *Third World. Third World countries embraced development in order to secure their independence from colonialism, to meet rising expectations of material betterment, and to become a going concern in the *international system. The West supported Third World aspirations to development in what was called "partnership in development." This support was apparently motivated by the need to maintain a presence in the Third World and to facilitate the fight against the spread of communism, which the West feared might get new impetus from the rapid industrialization of the Soviet Union. The earlier Western writings on development issues were interested in the problems of industrialization in Eastern and Southeastern Europe.

Development theory emerged as a variant of a notable Western model of social transformation, *modernization theory. Modernization theory takes its point of departure from the evolutionary paradigm which dominated classical sociology. This paradigm extracted ideal characteristics of forms of society and posited a movement from lower ones to higher ones. The paradigms were also a theory of progress, which invariably represented the Western societies as the apex of historical evolution. For instance, Ferdinand Toennies thought in terms of a movement from *gemeinschaft* to *gesellschaft*, Henry Maine from status to contract, Max *Weber from traditional forms of authority to the rational bureaucratic, and Emile Durkheim from mechanical to organic solidarity.

As Westerners looked around for a way of making sense of the evolution of the Third World countries and relating them to their own experience and vision of the world, they fell back on the evolutionary theories of the past, using the terms of modernization to describe the movement of societies. They took for granted a theory of progress by which all societies are on a continuum moving from a state of backwardness to one of *modernity.

In its most characteristic form, modernization theory posits an original state of underdevelopment characterized by, among other things, a low rate of economic growth which is amenable at least potentially to a change for the better, that is, development. This original state of backwardness is initially universal, but some countries in the West have managed to overcome it. Others would overcome it too. The spatial distribution of progress, however polarized it may appear to be at any point, is never static, but dynamic. By proximity and interaction, progress is diffused. Uneven development is essentially a transitional phenomenon which can be removed by creating certain favorable conditions within the underdeveloped regions and by ensuring the appropriate interactions between the underdeveloped regions and the developed ones. The evolutionary schema which modernization theory used to hang these ideas invariably made the desired end of societal evolution (modernity) the ideal characteristics of the West, so modernization could easily be construed as Westernization. The other side of this was the representation of premodern society as "backward," in an undesirable state of being or a "problem."

There were specific disciplinary versions of modernization theory, and it was these disciplinary versions which were developed in the wake of the World War II for the comparison of the Third World societies that form the corpus of development theory. In economics one of the notable works of development theory was Rostow's *Stages of Economic Growth*. Rostow held that all societies evolve through five stages to self-sustaining economic growth: traditional society with a characteristically low level of technology and productivity; a transitional stage for satisfying the "preconditions" for change; the "takeoff" stage when structural constraints to industrialization have been removed and an entrepreneurial class has emerged; the drive to maturity when industrialization is well under way and the levels of technological development and productivity are high; and the society of high mass consumption when there is general abundance and society has moved beyond basic needs to the consumption of durable goods. A rather more sophisticated if less well known theory of economic growth is Alexander Gerschenkron's *Economic Backwardness in Historical Perspective*. Gerschenkron regards his stages of economic growth not so much as universal but as historical; he allows for the possibility of skipping stages and for multilinearity.

The sociological development theories mainly restated the dichotomous evolutionary schema of classical sociology, such as Durkheim's mechanical and organic solidarity in *The Division of Labor in Society* and Weber's traditional and rational-bureaucratic authority in *Economy and Society*. One of the most influential classical sources of sociological theories of development was Talcott Parsons's *Social System* which was famous for his pattern variables, a more complex version of the dichotomous schemes found in Durkheim and Toennies: particularism-universalism, ascription-achievement, diffuseness-specificity. This was widely applied to societal development by theorists such as Edward Shils in *Political Development in New States* and Bert Hoselitz in *Theories of Economic Growth*.

In political science the pioneering work of political development theory was *The Politics of Developing Areas*, edited by Gabriel Almond and James S. Coleman (1960). This study in comparative politics was highly suggestive of what became known as the developmental approach. Perhaps the best known work in the theory of *political development was Almond and Powell's *Comparative Politics: A De-

velopmental Approach*. The work theorized that political systems are developed to the extent that they are characterized by structural differentiation, subsystem autonomy, and cultural *secularization. A more conventional stages approach was Organski's *Stages of Political Development*, which was much like a political science version of Rostow's *Stages of Economic Growth*. The theory of political development was treated in depth in the multivolume Princeton Series in Political Development, which was sponsored by the Committee on Comparative Politics of the Social Science Research Council of the United States.

Limitations. The development theories were at best heuristic devices. With minor exceptions they were too general and too vague to be taken seriously as scientific theories and paradigms even by the standards of the social sciences. Their major concepts could not be operationalized and their empirical referents were unclear; they could not be refuted or corroborated. They tended to be ahistorical because they assumed that the state of underdevelopment was initially universal; their teleologism distracted them from paying close attention to the realities on the ground in the developing societies. Finally they were too ethnocentric. They used evolutionary schema that made the desired end of social evolution the ideal characteristics of the West, which meant that in the final analysis development was confused with Westernization.

Marxism and Development. It is interesting to note that for all its concern with the emancipation of the oppressed and apparent appeal in the Third World, *Marxism does not have a theory of development. *Marx was not interested in the study of *capitalism in the less developed countries. He focused on the genesis of capitalism in Western Europe. To be sure, Marx understood capitalism to be a global phenomenon and treated it as such. Here and there, there are indications of the impact of the development of capitalism in less developed or preindustrial societies, notably in the *Communist Manifesto, Das Kapital,* and in the letters and articles for the *New York Herald Tribune* from 1853 to 1859. But these are passing references and not a treatment of the topic.

This was by no means a matter of chance. There is a legacy of hostility and contempt for peasant societies in Marxism dating back to Marx himself. He considered peasants a reactionary force and peasant societies a drag on historical progress. The attitude to peasants in the *Communist Manifesto*, where peasants are referred to as barbarians, is typical. *Peasants and peasant societies were consigned to the role of objects of history whose fate was to be determined by what happened in the industrialized West. Peasant societies lacked internally generated dynamism, and there were no dialectics of development specific to them.

This attitude did not encourage any serious study

of the so-called backward societies or their development. It was assumed that while the impact of the globalization of capitalism was devastating for these societies, it was essentially progressive, the engine of their incorporation and development.

Underdevelopment. While development theory took underdevelopment for granted as an initially universal state and focused on explaining how development occurs, underdevelopment theory problematized underdevelopment as a historically constituted reality and concerned itself with theorizing its persistence.

Underdevelopment theory arose from two sources: theoretical debates within Marxism and the concrete development experience of Latin America. As we have seen, Marx had assumed the desirability and feasibility of capitalist development in the non-European countries and insisted that their development as part of the process of the globalization of capitalism would be no different from capitalist development in the West. But these assumptions had become a matter of dispute within the Russian *Left. In particular the Narodniks disputed the view that capitalism was a desirable, feasible, or even a necessary option for preindustrial societies. The Narodniks saw in the Russian commune the possibility of a direct transition from a precapitalist mode of production to socialism. It was this debate that inspired *Lenin's great study *The Development of Capitalism in Russia,* which came down on the side of orthodoxy.

But that was not the end of the matter. The classic Marxist studies of *imperialism were to raise the questions of the progressive role of capitalism again and again. Unfortunately the questions were often obscured or deflated by more pressing issues which Marxist theorists had to deal with, namely the revolution of 1905, the war, the collapse of international socialist solidarity, and the surprising ability of capitalism to increase real wages.

But from the end of the 1950s the classical Marxist view was effectively challenged by a series of influential writings which argued that capitalist development in underdeveloped countries was neither feasible nor progressive. The first major work to break ground in this direction was Paul Baran's *Political Economy of Growth.* Baran argued that far from being an asset to progress, capitalism was, in prevailing conditions, inimical to it. The reactionary character of capitalism worldwide was particularly so in the underdeveloped countries, where it was incapable of developing the productive forces because of the opposition of the interests of capital in the developed countries:

. . . economic development in underdeveloped countries is profoundly inimical to the dominant interests in the advanced capitalist countries. Supplying many important raw materials to the industrialized countries, providing their corporations with vast profits and investment outlets, the backward world has always represented the indispensable hinterland of the highly developed capitalist West. Thus the ruling class in the United States (and elsewhere) is bitterly opposed to the industrialization of the so-called "source countries" and to the emergence of integrated processing economies in the colonial and semi-colonial world. (Baran, pp. 11–12)

Latin American social scientists, notably *Prebisch, Cardoso, Sunkel, and Dos Santos, challenged the thesis that capitalism fosters development (the progressive thesis) and enunciated an alternative theory of underdevelopment; their particular version came to be known as *dependency theory because of its emphasis on the dominance of Western economies and the satellite status of Latin American economies. Initially the focal interest of the work done by the UN Economic Commission for Latin America (ECLA) under Prebisch was on international trade, particularly terms of trade. It opposed the classical standard theory of international trade developed from Smith and Ricardo through Heckshen, Ohlin, and Samuelson.

ECLA argued that the world economy had been polarized into a center and a periphery. The former is characterized by a production structure which is homogeneous and diversified and the latter by a structure which is heterogeneous and specialized. The periphery is specialized in the sense that production is confined to a few primary commodities and to enclaves which have little or no linkages to the rest of the economy. It is heterogeneous on account of its dualism. Because of these features, the economies of the periphery cannot benefit much from the international division of labor and international trade. Low levels of productivity and unfavorable terms of trade add up to sustained unequal development.

Building on the work of Baran and ECLA, André Gunder Frank came to represent the full development of dependency theory and to epitomize the left-wing challenge to the progressive thesis of classical Marxism. In his main work, *Capitalism and Underdevelopment in Latin America,* and through several writings, Frank developed his thesis that "underdevelopment as we know it today, and economic development as well, are the simultaneous and related products of the development on a world-scale and over a history of more than four centuries, at least, of a single integrated economic system: capitalism." He maintained that capitalisms at the center and the periphery are dynamically related and the dynamics produce development at both ends; the problem is that at the end of the periphery, what occurs is the development of underdevelopment. The underdevelopment of the periphery is a condition of the development of the center. Thus there is no way of eliminating underdevelopment at the periphery apart from delinking from capitalism.

Another major contribution to underdevelopment theory, this time from Africa, came from Samir Amin. In numerous writings, particularly *Accumu-*

lation on a World Scale, Samir Amin argued that the industrialized countries and the less developed countries are integrated in a manner which inhibits capitalism from performing its historical role of developing the productive forces in the underdeveloped countries. He asserted that from the beginning of the imperialistic period, the less developed countries were no longer capable of attaining autonomous self-sustaining growth, whatever their level of per capita output might be. One aspect of this state of affairs is that the periphery seeks development in competition with the center, which dominates it and distorts its structures, rendering them unsuitable for self-sustaining development. This competition leads to a distortion toward export activities, the choice of light industries and low technology, and toward tertiary activities, all of which transfer multiplier effects from the periphery to the center and block economic growth.

Immanuel Wallerstein, whose monumental studies of the history of capitalism epitomize the world system perspective, contributed another very significant version of underdevelopment theory. In *The Capitalist World System* Wallerstein traced the major institutions of the modern world—classes, ethnic and national groups, households, and states—as effects of the development of the capitalist world system. He argued that the world system is unequal and that this is related to its capitalist character. The inequality resolves into a hierarchy of three kinds of *states or regions—the periphery, the semi-periphery, and the core—and the dynamics of economic forces, reinforced by the disparities of state power, ensures a steady flow of resources from the periphery to the core. Where a state or region is located in this hierarchic system is, for Wallerstein, essentially conjunctural, related to a number of contingent forces coming together in time and place. But once located it tends to become fixed thanks to the operation of world market forces which not only accentuate the differences but also institutionalize them.

The Spread of Dependency Theory. Dependency theory was particularly influential in Latin America, whose historical experience played a major part in the invention of the theory. The empirical studies of international trade and the terms of trade in ECLA under the leadership of Prebisch led to doubts about the beneficial assumptions of the classical theory of international trade and later to suggestions about the differential effects of exchange in center and periphery. Through Prebisch, Furtado, Sunkel, Paz, Cardoso, Faletto, Dos Santos, and Marini, Latin America contributed more than any other region to the development of underdevelopment theory, in this case the dependency version. Through the ECLA and the radical movements the theory exerted considerable influence on government policies in the region. No wonder underdevelopment theory is largely associated with Latin America and regarded as Latin America's major contribution to the social sciences.

Owing perhaps to geographical proximity, the rising radicalism in the Caribbean in the 1960s quickly adopted dependency theory. Some of the young scholars at the University of the West Indies were opposed to the ideas of the distinguished West Indian economist Arthur Lewis and were frustrated by his international and local influence. Lewis was not only a strong advocate of the crucial role of foreign capital, but his ideas ran in the direction of the neoclassical orthodoxies of the *International Monetary Fund (IMF)–type policy reform, such as devaluation, export promotion, and keeping wages low. Younger scholars, especially Owen Jefferson, Rex Nettleford, and Norman Girvan, used dependency theory to challenge him and to orient their own political practice. Academic radicalism in the Caribbean met and fused with the political and cultural radicalism of, for instance, the Rastafarian movement, the New World Group formed in Georgetown, Guyana, in 1962, the Black Power movement, and Michael Manley's Peoples National Party (PNP) of Jamaica. Thus Walter Rodney, a celebrated young historian from Guyana and a black nationalist, wrote one of the most famous treatises of underdevelopment theory, *How Europe Underdeveloped Africa;* Michael Manley, the leader of the PNP, was a scholar of some repute, and his book *The Politics of Change: A Jamaican Testament* took a dependency perspective. When Manley's PNP came to power, he took some of the dependency theorists into government with him. Owen Jefferson joined the Central Bank, Norman Girvan went into Planning, and Rex Nettleford became a special adviser to the prime minister. Manley himself quickly became a Third World leader and helped to spread underdevelopment theory in the Third World.

In Asia, underdevelopment theory in general, and the dependency approach in particular, was not so influential, but it has enjoyed a visible presence. It owed its development in India initially to the Indian Marxist intellectuals Dadobhai Naoroji and M. N. Roy. The development continued through the writings of a group of able theoreticians, especially Alavi and Banaji. Although it has a considerable presence in India, underdevelopment theory does not appear to have had the broad appeal and influence which it had in Latin America and the Caribbean.

In Africa underdevelopment theory grew in three centers: the Institute for Economic Development and Planning (IDEP), which assumed a dependency orientation in the 1970s when it was headed by Samir Amin; the Council for the Development of Economic and Social Research (CODESRIA), the umbrella social science organization of Africa which, like IDEP, is based in Dakar, Senegal; and the University of Dar es Salaam's Faculty of Arts and Social Sciences, especially between 1966 to 1978. As in India, underdevelopment theory in Africa developed independently of Latin America. The social sciences were established very late in Africa, long after the nationalist movement was in full swing. So from the beginning the social sciences were impregnated with the values of the nationalist struggle against colonialism and imperialism. In these circumstances the dialectics of domination and satellization did not have to be invented; they were, so to speak, a matter of course. It is not surprising that one of the first major works by an African scholar on underdevelopment theory, *Social Science as Imperialism: The Theory of Political Development* (Ake), was a discourse on how Western social science constitutes the satellization and underdevelopment of Africa. Apart from Samir Amin, African scholars were self-absorbed; they did not take much interest in the Latin American debates or the debates on the Left in the West. They simply continued to develop the nationalist social science with its fixity on domination, satellization, and exploitation and evolved, in a natural progression, a corpus of underdevelopment theories which were more sensitive to issues of methodology and epistemology than the dependency literature of Latin America, but sharing rather similar political and policy commitments: Dan Nabudere, *The Political Economy of Imperialism;* I. Shivji, *The Silent Class Struggle in Tanzania;* Claude Ake, *Revolutionary Pressures in Africa* (1969); and others.

Underdevelopment theory was very influential in policy circles in Africa—probably more so than in Latin America. This was due partly to the influence of CODESRIA on African social science and the African intelligentsia. Just as important was the influence of Dar es Salaam as a revolutionary capital of Africa from the mid-sixties. As the base of the Liberation Committee of the *Organization of African Unity (OAU), it was a gathering center for the leaders of the more radical nationalist and liberation movements from Angola, Mozambique, South Africa, Zimbabwe, Namibia—all of whom had their own home-grown theories of underdevelopment which emerged from their fixation on exploitative imperialism. At the same time all the leading theorists of underdevelopment theory in Africa except Amin were teaching at the University of Dar es Salaam. It was this group which founded the influential African Association for Political Science and the *African Journal of Political Economy*. Finally, underdevelopment theory was popularized by Julius *Nyerere, the president of Tanzania, and became part of the official *ideology in independent Mozambique and Angola. Not surprisingly the development strategy which the OAU adopted in 1980—the Lagos Plan of Action—is heavily infused with the values and concepts of underdevelopment theory.

Criticisms of Underdevelopment Theory. It has been all but impossible to produce a scientific evaluation of underdevelopment theory. Its assumptions were so different from and so diametrically opposed

to those of classical economics and modernization theory that it was not so much criticized as caricatured and dismissed. Much the same thing happened on the Left, where underdevelopment theories were also a frontal attack on the Marxist dogma of the desirability and feasibility of capitalism in the Third World. Also, both Western mainstream and left-wing social science appear to have rejected, on political grounds, the tendency of underdevelopment theory to hold the West responsible for the underdevelopment of the Third World. It is now common to proclaim that underdevelopment theory has been decisively refuted although just how this has been done is unclear, though not entirely implausible, given the performance of the Republic of Korea (South Korea), Thailand, Singapore, Taiwan, and the other *newly industrializing economies. What is clear is that underdevelopment theory is less influential today. It has been largely defeated—politically, not scientifically—by the collapse of the Soviet bloc, the Westernization of the former Soviet empire, and the renewed hegemonization of the market. More importantly, it has been largely defeated by the economic crisis of the Third World, which has forced many Third World countries to accept more dependence and adopt neoclassical solutions, notably the IMF-type structural adjustment programs, especially in Latin America and Africa. The paradox is that in its demise, underdevelopment theory is getting its most significant corroboration.

(See also COLONIAL EMPIRES; DECOLONIZATION; ECONOMIC COMMISSION FOR LATIN AMERICA AND THE CARIBBEAN; EQUALITY AND INEQUALITY; EXPORT-LED GROWTH; IMPORT-SUBSTITUTION INDUSTRIALIZATION; INTERNATIONAL DEBT; INTERNATIONAL SYSTEMS; NATIONALISM; NORTH-SOUTH RELATIONS; POLITICAL ECONOMY.)

Paul Baran, *The Political Economy of Growth* (New York, 1957). Bert Hoselitz et al., *Theories of Economics* (New York, 1960). Alexander Gerschenkron, *Economic Backwardness in Historical Perspective* (Cambridge, Mass., 1962). Edward Shils, *Political Development in the New States* (The Hague, 1962). Gabriel Almond and G. Bingham Powell, Jr., *Comparative Politics: A Developmental Approach* (Boston, 1966). André Gunder Frank, *Capitalism and Underdevelopment in Latin America* (New York, 1967). A. F. Organski, *The Stages of Political Development* (New York, 1967). Samir Amin, *Accumulation on a World Scale: A Critique of the Theory of Underdevelopment*, 2 vol. (New York, 1974). Issa G. Shivji, *Class Struggles in Tanzania* (London, 1976). Claude Ake, *Social Science as Imperialism: The Theory of Political Development* (Ibadan, 1979). Immanuel Wallerstein, *The Capitalist World Economy* (Cambridge, U.K., 1979). Dan Nabudere, *The Political Economy of Imperialism*, 2d ed. (London, 1980). Walter Rodney, *How Europe Underdeveloped Africa*, rev. ed. (Washington, D.C., 1982). Michael Manley, *The Politics of Change: A Jamaican Testament*, rev. ed. (Washington, D.C., 1990). W. W. Rostow, *The Stages of Economic Growth*, 3d ed. (New York, 1991).

CLAUDE AKE

DICTATORSHIP. See AUTHORITARIANISM.

DIPLOMACY. Above and before all else, diplomacy is a system of communication between strangers. It is the formal means by which the self-identity of the sovereign *state is constituted and articulated through external relations with other states. Like the dialogue from which it is constructed, diplomacy requires and seeks to mediate otherness through the use of persuasion and *force, promises and threats, codes and symbols. It is also, according to the American humorist Will Rogers, "the art of saying 'Nice doggie' until you can find a rock."

The linguistic origins of diplomacy are fairly easy to ascertain, its historical beginnings less so. The word itself comes from the Greek verb *diploun,* referring to a folded document such as a tax receipt or passport. When these "diploma" began to accumulate in state archives, specialists were needed to organize and conduct *res diplomatica,* or diplomatic affairs. Indeed, the "paper" origins of Western diplomacy coincide with the development of centralized empires requiring reliable communication with the periphery. From the early days of imperial Rome and the Holy See to the last days of the Holy Roman Empire, the figure who kept the keys to the diplomatic archives, that is, the *chancellor,* occupied a position of power comparable to the figureheads of empire.

It was not until late into the eighteenth century that the meaning of diplomacy was extended from the management of archives to the management of *international relations in general. The *Oxford English Dictionary* gives credit to Edmund Burke for first using the term in this modern sense in 1796. It could well be the case, however, that Burke cribbed this usage from his revolutionary rival Thomas Paine, who referred four years earlier in *The Rights of Man* (1792) to Benjamin Franklin as "not the diplomat of a Court, but of MAN." Obviously diplomacy, defined by the *OED* as "the management of international relations by negotiation," did not *begin* in 1792—unless, of course, one takes the pedantic view that it could *only* begin in 1792, the year in which the first nation-state emerged (France) and the word *international* itself was coined (by Jeremy Bentham).

Long before ambassadors were cloaked with the robes of *sovereignty (of king and queen, then nation-state), the earliest diplomats were thought to be the winged (of foot, then shoulder) representatives of the gods. The heralds of the Greek city-states operated under the protection of Hermes, the messenger of Zeus as well as patron of travelers (and thieves). The *missi* ("messengers"), the proto-diplomats of the Carolingian Empire in the early Middle Ages, carried a caduceus as did Hermes, relying on the Holy and Roman aspect of the Empire for personal protection as they transmitted oaths of fealty, settled terms of disputes, and acted as the eyes and ears of Charlemagne and his successors. Well into the sixteenth century the mythological origins of diplomacy were cited for good effect. For instance, in *De Legationibus* (1584) the Italian jurist Alberico Gentili establishes the inviolability of envoys by tracing the origins of diplomacy back to God and His legates, the angels.

One should not, however, paint too hallowed a portrait of the first diplomats. The British ambassador Sir Henry Wotton failed to amuse King James when he remarked that "an ambassador is an honest man who is sent to lie abroad for the good of his country"; but he did provide an apt aphorism for the often conflicting duties of the diplomats of the period. Abraham de Wicquefort, who wrote one of the first manuals on diplomacy, *The Ambassador and His Functions* (1682), earned his diplomatic credentials in the service of Richelieu, Mazarin, and de Witt. He expressed the prevailing sentiments of the time when he defined the diplomat as "an honorable spy." Indeed, the rash of new treatises on diplomacy in the sixteenth and seventeenth century seemed intent on rescuing diplomacy from its Byzantine and Italianate origins—and less than pristine reputation. In these works (with over fifty written between 1430 and 1630) diplomacy is presented as a culture, in terms of a body of thought of how civilized behavior was to be propagated among "ideal ambassadors," and in terms of a body of individuals through which civilized behavior was to be reproduced in the fledgling institutions of a states-system.

The culmination of this textual civilizing process is François de Callières's *On the Manner of Negotiation with Princes* (1716). Drawing on his experience as an able negotiator for France, he acknowledges the rather low esteem in which diplomacy was held at the time, and proceeds to provide sound advice on how to redeem the profession. First and foremost of the diplomatic virtues should be honesty: although momentary advantage may be gained by deceit, "honest is the best policy . . . a lie always leaves in its wake a drop of poison." Second is civility, the art of dignified court behavior which was to be cultivated for the creation of a cosmopolitan diplomatic corps. And third is prudence, the necessary mix of intelligence, foresight, and flexibility in action that would allow the diplomat to best represent the interests of his prince.

The effort to capture the essence of diplomacy reaches its zenith in the classic text *Diplomacy* (1939) by the British diplomat and historian Sir Harold Nicolson. He modernizes de Callières by taking into account (and mildly regretting) the popularizing and often propagandizing effects of democracy and revolution on traditional diplomacy, while maintaining the classical belief that the "essence" of diplomacy is "common sense and charity applied to international relations." What Nicolson has in common with de Callières (as well as de Wicquefort and many other ex-diplomats who took up the pen) is that they were both serving governments at the apogee of imperial power, and understandably not too interested in looking too critically or deeply into alternative beginnings and future possibilities of diplomacy. The question must be asked, then, whether the dominant view of diplomacy as practical wisdom, working in combination with the expectation of reciprocal actions, was a moral prejudice of the European great powers.

There have been, after all, other diplomacies. In his book *The Beginnings of Diplomacy* (1950), Ragnar Numelin takes the reader on an ethnological voyage from Stone-Age Australia to pre-Columbian America to demonstrate that many of the fundamental practices of diplomacy predated modern Europe. Adam Watson, in *Diplomacy: The Dialogue Between States* (1982), is even more adept at identifying early diplomatic conventions of immunity, negotiation, and communication that were developed by Egyptians and Hittites, Greeks city-states and Hellenistic kingdoms, ancient China and India.

Yet the historical fact remains that the European model of diplomacy emerged triumphant. In *System of States* (1977) Martin Wight provides in erudite detail the history of how estrangement between Western Christendom and the Turks promoted the conferences and intercourse among the European powers which prefigured the establishment of a diplomatic system. In *Renaissance Diplomacy* (1955) Garrett Mattingly traces the development of the residential form of diplomacy among the five Italian city-states that eventually made its way into transalpine Europe. With the end of the Thirty Years' War (1618–1648)—and with it the threat of a universal monarchy under the Hapsburgs—the exchange of officially accredited agents, the establishment of permanent embassies, and the codification of a secular system of immunities became the standard form of diplomacy throughout Europe.

The golden age of diplomacy followed. From the eighteenth to the twentieth century a homogeneous yet cosmopolitan elite made up the diplomatic corps of Europe. They shared a common culture (aristocratic), a common language (French), and a common vision of order (*balance of power). World War I, however, brought revolutions, national democratic movements, and the first wave of anti-imperialism: the aristocratic veneer of the diplomatic corps began to wear thin. The "new diplomacy" of open negotiation and popular accountability, advocated if rarely practiced by Woodrow Wilson, Lenin, and Trotsky, left its mark on the consanguinity and conservatism of the *ancien régime*. The diplomatic corps, long an elite enclave, increasingly gave way to a meritocracy—taking into account, of course, the right schools, gender, and political affiliations. "Tact and intelligence," rather than the civil behavior of the court, is offered by Sir Ernest Satow in his *Guide to Diplomatic Practice* (London, 1922) as the proper qualification of the diplomat.

Not to be ignored, *imperialism played an important role in the spread and transformation of the diplomatic system. As great power politics expanded in an orderly if sometimes genocidal fashion into the Americas, Africa, and Asia, diplomacy went with it. Perhaps the most important artifact of the age of imperialism is the formation of a diplomatic culture, in the sense of a system of symbolic power and social codes that brings cohesiveness to the international society. Born of the European experience, the diplomatic culture found in the colonial encounter a new self-consciousness. Diplomacy was once again invoked as a civilizing process, but this time on a global scale in which a very large gap in development encouraged a unilateral form of diplomacy that to this day favors the West.

Diplomacy is now considered to be an essential international institution which provides the norms, protocols, and practices for the reconciliation of differences between sovereign states. The international relations scholar Hedley Bull believes that "the diplomatic profession itself is a custodian of the idea of international society," and he marvels at the integrating power of the diplomatic culture at a time when its elitist European underpinnings were coming under intense attack: "The remarkable willingness of states of all regions, cultures, persuasions and states of development to embrace often strange and archaic diplomatic procedures that arose in Europe in another age is today one of the few visible indications of universal acceptance of the idea of international society" (*Anarchical Society,* 1977).

Diplomacy remains, however, the institution by which states pursue their own particular interests. At the systemic level diplomacy might well seek to maintain an international order and general *peace. Yet that very order is often seen by individual states to be an obstacle to justice, or to the equitable distribution of wealth, or to the dissemination of a preferred ideology. Diplomacy's most difficult task continues to be the management of changes in relative power and ideological beliefs in the international system. One need not subscribe to a Machiavellian view of the world to find some truth in Frederick the Great's statement that diplomacy without power is like an orchestra without a score. When power and diplomacy fall out of kilter, diplomacy tends toward coercion, propaganda, and intervention. The dialogue of diplomacy then carries the threat of *war rather than the promise of peace.

In a time of rapid change in the states-system, what lies ahead for diplomacy? Many of the conditions which made diplomacy necessary and possible in the classical age of Europe still obtain. Strangers persist in the *international system. The bipolar estrangement of the *Cold War may have ended, and with it some of the worst excesses of "megaphone diplomacy," but disturbingly familiar sources of conflict have arisen in what once was the Soviet Union, the Balkans, Africa, and many other places where ethnic, religious, economic, and nationalist hostilities continue to surface. Indeed, as the number of powers increases, as power itself disperses and diffuses in the contemporary states-system, and as diplomatic utterances multiply and speed up in the international communication web, one must ask whether the dialogue of diplomacy has become a cacophony. Global developments—from multilateral summitry to a transnational CNN—have diminished the independence and significance of the individual diplomat whose home now more than ever is everywhere and nowhere.

Diplomacy as an institution endures, nevertheless. States continue to construct, confront, and sometimes cooperate with their alien others. As long as there is a need to communicate with strangers and to manage the movement of ideas, goods, people, and even armies across boundaries, there will be a need for diplomacy.

(See also FOREIGN POLICY; INFORMATION SOCIETY; INTERNATIONAL COOPERATION.)

Sir Ernest Satow, *Guide to Diplomatic Practice* (London, 1922). Sir Harold Nicolson, *Diplomacy* (Oxford, 1939). Hedley Bull, *The Anarchical Society: A Study of Order in World Politics* (London, 1977). Adam Watson, *Diplomacy: The Dialogue Between States* (London, 1982). François de Callières, *The Art of Diplomacy*, M. A. Keens-Soper and Karl Schweizer, eds. (Leicester, 1983). James Der Derian, *On Diplomacy: A Genealogy of Western Estrangement* (Oxford, 1987).

JAMES DER DERIAN

DISARMAMENT. An ancient ideal, disarmament, properly understood, is the near elimination of arms and military forces by one or more states, as opposed to *arms control in which weapons and forces continue to exist but are subjected to restraints on their number, nature, or use. What is referred to as partial or selective disarmament is really arms control, but the terms are often used interchangeably. Thus elimination of offensively oriented forces—an arms control measure—was the focus of the *League of Nations disarmament conference in 1932–1933, and the UN Special Session on Disarmament (1978) was devoted to arms control proposals.

Although disarmament can be imposed on the losing state after a *war (Japan in 1945) or adopted by a single state voluntarily (Costa Rica some years ago), it is mainly envisioned as a bilateral or multilateral endeavor. States could make parallel cuts on their own, and significant reductions sometimes occur this way—usually after a major war—but effective disarmament is normally felt to require formal treaties and elaborate inspection provisions.

Disarmament is expected to contribute greatly to *peace by erasing the tools of war, easing interstate conflicts, and curbing the willingness or ability of governments to treat the threat or use of *force as legitimate. An additional objective is diversion of resources from military preparations and war to other purposes.

One source of support for disarmament is pacifism; renunciation of the use of force, even in self-defense, makes possession of arms pointless. Another is the view, reinforced by *nuclear weapons, that the potential destructiveness of modern war exceeds tolerable limits in terms of sanity, morality, or any reasonable political objective.

Do arms cause wars? Disarmament supporters often assert that military capabilities encourage war by making it a constantly available option—otherwise using force would require rearming, a substantial undertaking. In an intense political conflict disarmament would provide time for emotions to subside and for attention to other options. Supporters also contend that the presence of military capabilities means participation in decision making by officials responsible for those capabilities, who are likely to urge or endorse the use of force and regard it as a proper and feasible step. The most influential view is that even forces intended solely for defense incite reciprocal fears of attack. The result is a *security dilemma—each state's individual pursuit of *security by arming adds to everyone's insecurity, inciting spirals of mistrust and arms racing that can culminate in war. Finally, supporters suggest that military capabilities provoke phenomena that promote the legitimacy of war, such as holding military forces and leaders in high esteem, celebration of past military achievements, dehumanizing enemies, and inciting intense feelings of *nationalism.

Opponents of disarmament begin by contending that states have consistently been willing to carry political conflicts to lethal levels and to resort to force—their arming is the result, not the cause, of this. Hence even if disarmament were achieved, ubiquitous conflicts among states would eventually provoke rearming. Many opponents further assert that, in the nuclear age, the only reliable way to prevent war is *deterrence, i.e., disarmament would be disastrous. Usually added is the argument that in the anarchical *international system nothing prevents states from resorting to force and that states must therefore arm to protect themselves. Disarmament is thus impossible without transforming international politics (many supporters of disarmament readily agree) through new institutions and processes for managing change, settling disputes, and policing agreements. This means either a supranational authority or concerted efforts of national governments motivated by a well-developed sense of global community and interdependent security. Either would entail prior political adjustments and agreements that are quite improbable in view of the entire history of international politics.

Governments ultimately side with the opponents, and disarmament has been of little significance. The League conference was soon followed by the military buildups leading to World War II. In 1961, under the rubric of "General and Complete Disarmament," the United States and the Soviet Union reached agreement on broad principles, and there was a flurry of popular and academic interest in disarmament. This had no discernible impact as each *superpower initiated a large military buildup in the 1960s. The UN "disarmament decade" (the 1970s) coincided with unprecedented conventional arms transfers and the burgeoning of nuclear arsenals, followed by President *Reagan's huge military buildup. Despite recent revival of the goal of eliminating nuclear weapons and the serious attention that proposals to demilitarize Europe now receive, alongside continued interests in civilian-based defense (via complete noncooperation and civil disobedience) as a substitute for arming, the outlook for anything like general disarmament remains bleak.

(See also STRATEGIC ARMS LIMITATION TREATIES; UNITED NATIONS.)

Richard J. Barnet and Richard A. Falk, eds., *Security in Disarmament* (Princeton, N.J., 1965). James E. Dougherty, *How to Think About Arms Control and Disarmament* (New York, 1973). Trevor N. Dupuy and Guy Hammerman, eds., *A Documentary History of Arms Control and Disarmament* (New York, 1973).

PATRICK M. MORGAN

DISINVESTMENT. In U.S. political parlance, disinvestment refers to the severance of all economic ties to *South Africa by foreign banks and corporations. Complete disinvestment includes the termination of all licensing and franchise agreements as well as the withdrawal of all direct investments (i.e., corporate subsidiaries). Disinvestment is a tactic that constitutes part of a larger strategy of economically isolating the *apartheid regime. In order to fully comprehend the significance of disinvestment, the objectives of the broader strategy must first be addressed.

Since the end of World War II, U.S. and Western European corporations have dominated the most strategic sectors of the South African economy. Investments and taxes paid by these companies, together with the transfer of their technology and expertise, have helped to strengthen the economy and contributed to Pretoria's program of strategic self-sufficiency. Because South Africa is the only country in the world where racism is not only institutionalized but constitutionally entrenched, it has been singled out by the international community.

Since the early 1960s, domestic and international opponents of apartheid, including the *African National Congress, the Pan-Africanist Congress, the UN General Assembly, and the *Organization of African Unity, have called for the complete economic isolation of South Africa through the imposition of comprehensive economic sanctions. Proponents of such measures argue that the constraints imposed by sanctions, compounded by internal political mobilization, will force the white minority regime to dismantle apartheid and negotiate a transition to majority rule.

Likewise, anti-apartheid activists inside South Africa have insisted that the economic isolation of South Africa is the last hope for achieving funda-

mental change, short of an all-out military conflict. Advocates of this view include South Africa's largest labor federation, the Congress of South African Trade Unions, the 13-million-member South African Council of Churches, the Azanian People's Organization, and one of South Africa's largest grass-roots organizations, the 3-million-strong United Democratic Front.

The strategy of economically isolating South Africa has itself been composed of a series of tactical actions. Since the late 1960s, divestment—the sale of stocks, bonds, or other financial interests in banks and corporations doing business in or with South Africa—has been a major tactic of the U.S. anti-apartheid movement. The immediate goal of divestment has been to pressure U.S. businesses and financial institutions to disinvest, or withdraw, from South Africa. By 1989, divestment actions taken by state and local governments, educational institutions, religious bodies, foundations, trade unions, and community organizations had resulted in the sale of billions of dollars' worth of investments in South Africa-linked firms. These grass-roots actions, together with mounting pressure inside South Africa, precipitated the sale of scores of U.S. subsidiaries in South Africa, including 179 (of a total of some 350) between January 1984 and January 1989. More than half of these have maintained nonequity links to South Africa through contracts of licensing, distribution, franchise, trademark, or technological agreements with their former affiliates.

Although partial, disinvestment, along with other forms of economic sanctions, has had a devastating impact on the South African economy. These actions have in large measure been responsible for recent reforms in South Africa, including the release of Nelson *Mandela and other political prisoners, the unbanning of several important political organizations, and discussions between high-level delegations of African National Congress and South African government officials.

Janice Love, *The U.S. Anti-Apartheid Movement. Local Activism in Global Politics* (New York, 1985).

ELIZABETH S. SCHMIDT

DISSENT, SOVIET. See SOVIET DISSENT.

DJIBOUTI. Formerly a French colony known as the Territory of the Afars and Issas, Djibouti achieved its independence on 27 June 1977. Since that time, this state of 23,200 square kilometers (9,000 sq. mi.) and, as of 1991, some 394,000 people, has been led by President Hassan Gouled Aptidon. The head of state is also the head of the sole party, the Rassemblement Populaire pour le Progrès (RPP), and the regime may be characterized as presidential and authoritarian. Both the president of the Republic and the National Assembly are elected by direct and universal suffrage.

The stability of Djibouti is largely a consequence

of the ethnic equilibrium between the Issas and the Afars, who make up most of the population. (These groups may be found on either side of Djibouti's borders as well, the Afars in *Ethiopia and the Issas in *Somalia.) Officially, Gouled affirms his desire to "detribalize" political life by involving all ethnic groups in the conduct of public affairs. The reality is otherwise. Although Afars do hold high positions within the government, there is nonetheless a genuine feeling of frustration at the heart of this community, certain important members of which are in opposition to the regime. The fragility of the Gouled regime is heightened by the inability of the RPP to mobilize the population in any meaningful way.

The political uncertainty facing Djibouti is in direct proportion to its economic weakness. In the absence of significant natural resources, the country lives essentially off the activity of its port. At one time one of the most active on the Red Sea, it is showing signs of decline. Another important source of revenue is from the spending of the French military contingent of about 3,500 stationed in Djibouti.

Situated in an extremely sensitive area, Djibouti is dependent on its external environment. Ethiopia on one side and Somalia on the other pay close attention to the political evolution of this microstate. For its part, Djibouti pays constant attention to the maintenance of good relations with these two powerful neighbors: for example, Gouled abstained from taking sides during the Ogaden war, instead playing the role of mediator between the two warring factions. In spite of this prudence, the Djiboutian government faced *destabilization maneuvers by Somalia, always haunted by the pan-Somalian dream. In this context, cooperation with France appeared to be the surest guarantee. At the same time, Djibouti plays the card of moderate *Islam and develops its rapport with the Arab world, notably the conservative states, carefully preserving an equilibrium between Arabness and Frenchness. Finally, the Djiboutian state attempts to be the agency of increased multilateral cooperation in the *Horn of Africa.

(See also ETHNICITY; FRANCOPHONE AFRICA; ONE-PARTY SYSTEM.)

Brigitte Nouaille-Degorce, "Djibouti: l'accession à l'indépendance," in *Année africaine 1977* (Paris, 1977), pp. 267–331.

RENÉ OTAYEK

DOMINICA. See ENGLISH-SPEAKING CARIBBEAN.

DOMINICAN REPUBLIC. The Dominican Republic occupies the eastern two-thirds of the island of Hispaniola, which it shares with *Haiti. With approximately 7 million people, it has the second-largest population in the Caribbean.

Initial independence from Spain in 1821 lasted only a few months owing to an invasion from Haiti, which occupied the country until 1844. Fear of renewed invasion led Dominicans to seek protection, chiefly from France, Spain, and the United States. Historically, the government revolved largely around *caudillo* strongmen and their intrigues involving foreign powers; Spain reannexed the country from 1861 to 1865. External debt, political instability, and U.S. involvement in Dominican affairs expanded in the last half of the nineteenth century. Upheaval followed the assassination of Ulíses Heureaux in 1899, ending a seventeen-year reign. By 1907, the United States controlled Dominican customs and became the country's sole foreign creditor. The country fell under direct U.S. military occupation from 1916 to 1924. Improvements in transportation and communications and particularly the formation of a constabulary force under the occupation facilitated the rise to power six years later of Rafael Leónidas Trujillo Molina (1930–1961).

Trujillo's regime involved personal rule, large-scale corruption, arbitrary decisions combined with attention to legal forms, and ruthless violence (including a 1937 massacre of some 18,000 Haitians in the border area). These were juxtaposed with the forging of national integration, the establishment of state institutions, reduction in the extent of direct control by foreigners (e.g., the U.S. administration of Dominican customs finally ended in 1940), and the beginnings of industrialization, however distorted. In the wake of the 1959 *Cuban Revolution, intervention by the United States and sanctions by the Organization of American States preceded and followed Trujillo's assassination on 30 May 1961. These actions helped prevent family members from continuing in power and paved the way for democratic elections in 1962, which were won by Juan Bosch and his Partido Revolucionario Dominicano (PRD).

*Democracy, however, was not to come easily. Bosch was overthrown by conservative forces only seven months after assuming office. The discovery of a civil-military conspiracy to try to bring him back to power led in April 1965 to a U.S. intervention out of an exaggerated fear of a "second Cuba." Elections in 1966 pitted the former Trujillo puppet president, Joaquín Balaguer, against Bosch, who only left his house twice for campaign appearances. Disillusioned with liberal democracy, Bosch left the PRD in 1973 to found a more radical, disciplined, cadre-style Partido de la Liberación Dominicana (PLD). Balaguer gained reelection with overt military pressure against his opposition in 1970 and 1974. In a democratic transition, however, Balaguer lost in open elections to a more moderate PRD in 1978, although domestic and international pressure was important in blocking a coup in the making. Following the inauguration of the PRD government, a purge of top military officers occurred; with forced retirements in the subsequent administration, the fear of military coups in the country has diminished significantly from the 1960s. The PRD won again in 1982, but economic crisis, charges of corruption, and increased strength by Bosch and his PLD facilitated a victory by Balaguer and his Partido Reformista Social Cristiano (PRSC) in 1986. In 1990, the two octogenarians, Balaguer and Bosch, were the primary contenders; with Bosch claiming fraud, Balaguer won by a narrow plurality.

The country's current constitution dates from November 1966. The constitution grants extensive powers to the president, who is elected for a four-year term and can stand for reelection indefinitely. Senators, deputies, mayors, and members of municipal councils are also elected for four-year terms at the same time as the president. The Chamber of Deputies has 120 members elected by *proportional representation; the senate has thirty members, one from each province. It names all judges as well as members of the Central Electoral Board, which is responsible for overseeing elections. As the judges' terms are coterminous with those of the president and Senate, and judges depend on the executive for disbursement of funds, both the judiciary and the election board are perceived as politicized. This has helped fuel widespread allegations of irregularities and fraud in each election since 1966. The country has no civil service legislation, and government patronage and jobs play major roles in the elections.

Balaguer's PRSC is affiliated with the international Christian Democratic Union, but the party is largely his personalist vehicle. It has been strongest in rural areas, although it has gained strength in Santo Domingo. The PRD is affiliated with the Socialist International. Bosch's PLD has made an effort to educate its party cadres with quasi-Marxist, nationalist, and populist material, but the party has moderated considerably since 1973. The PLD has had its greatest electoral successes in previous PRD strongholds in urban and eastern sugar-growing areas of the country. Many other parties are largely personalist vehicles, although there are several small parties of the left, including a Dominican Communist Party currently in ideological disarray owing to the collapse of the Soviet bloc.

The Dominican Republic is a highly stratified society, with extensive poverty. Over the past decade, economic crisis, public sector deficits, and government policy decisions have led to further declines in the provision of health, education, and utility services. Extensive migration, both to Dominican cities and abroad, has resulted; urbanization has increased from thirty-five percent of the population in 1960 to sixty-two percent in 1989, while approximately ten percent of Dominicans live overseas, particularly in the United States. At the same time, Haitian migration into the country is extensive, and Haitian labor is exploited in the sugar fields and other agricultural areas.

The strongest interest groups reflect business interests, as organized labor is weak, bitterly divided, and restrained by Trujillo-era legislation. In recent years neighborhood associations have played prominent roles in civic strikes. The Catholic church has sought to play a mediating role in political and economic crises and faces a stiff challenge from the growing strength of Protestant and evangelical churches, which now represent some ten to twenty-five percent of the country's population.

Historically, the economy has revolved around sugar. In the late 1960s and early 1970s, the country experienced high levels of growth stimulated by extensive economic aid, public sector construction, and *import-substitution industrialization. During the 1970s and 1980s, oil price increases and the sharp decline in world sugar markets caused problems, which were exacerbated by the debt build-up of the late 1970s. Poor implementation of an overdue but painful stabilization plan in 1984 led to "IMF riots"; subsequent governments have therefore postponed adjustments as much as possible. At the same time, the country has begun to diversify economically, into tourism, light assembly manufacturing free trade zones, and export of fruits and vegetables. It also depends heavily on the remittances of overseas Dominicans.

The major political challenge of the 1990s will be to reaccommodate the party system once Balaguer and Bosch pass from the scene. Neither will leave an obvious heir, and their parties may well divide and could join with parts of other parties. At the same time, the country continues to face a difficult economic transition away from sugar as well as the need to strengthen and trim its state sector and improve basic services for its population.

(See also DEMOCRATIC TRANSITIONS; INTERNATIONAL DEBT; INTERNATIONAL MIGRATION; INTERNATIONAL MONETARY FUND; U.S.–LATIN AMERICAN RELATIONS.)

Howard Wiarda, *Dictatorship, Development and Disintegration: Politics and Social Change in the Dominican Republic,* 3 vols. (Ann Arbor, Mich., 1975). Frank Moya Pons, "The Politics of Import-Substituting Industrialization in the Dominican Republic, 1925–1982" (Ph.D. diss., Columbia University, 1987). Jonathan Hartlyn, "The Dominican Republic: The Legacy of Intervention," in Abraham F. Lowenthal, ed., *Exporting Democracy: The United States and Latin America* (Baltimore, 1991).

JONATHAN HARTLYN

DOMINO THEORY. The domino theory is most familiar as one of the principal justifications for the *Vietnam War. The term itself traces to a 1954 press conference in which President Dwight D. *Eisenhower explained the strategic importance of Vietnam to the United States in terms of "a row of dominoes set up; you knock over the first one and what will happen to the last one is the certainty that it will go over very quickly . . . the loss of Indochina, of Burma, of Thailand, of the Peninsula [Malaysia] and Indonesia following . . . Japan, Formosa, the Philippines and to the southward; it moves in to threaten Australia and New Zealand. . . . So the possible consequences of the loss are just incalculable to the free world."

Every president from Eisenhower to Gerald Ford based his commitment to Vietnam in large part on the domino theory. The same was true for U.S. commitments in many other parts of the *Third World, in particular in Central America in the 1980s. Unless the Nicaraguan *Sandinistas were removed, the *Reagan administration warned, all the nations of Central America would tumble, U.S. credibility around the world would be weakened, and even "the last domino"—the United States itself—would be threatened by Soviet and Cuban bases as well as by masses of refugees fleeing across U.S. borders.

Critics of such commitments, however, rejected the foreboding chain of events forecast by the falling dominoes metaphor, and thus questioned whether the interests at stake justified both the scope and types of commitments that were made. In Southeast Asia, for example, they argued that the eventual fall of both South Vietnam and Cambodia was less a substantiation of the domino theory than a highly destructive self-fulfilling prophecy.

With the waning of the *Cold War, the domino theory has lost its traditional centrality to debates over U.S. foreign policy. Somewhat ironically, though, the revolutions that swept Eastern and *Central Europe in 1989 might be seen as the domino theory in reverse: the rebellion against *communism in one country did help foment rebellion against communism in other countries, and the old communist regimes fell one on top of the other.

(See also AMERICAN FOREIGN POLICY; DETERRENCE; NINETEEN EIGHTY-NINE.)

John Lewis Gaddis, *Strategies of Containment* (New York, 1982). Bruce W. Jentleson, "American Commitments in the Third World: Theory vs. Practice" *International Organization* 41 (Autumn 1987): 667–704.

BRUCE W. JENTLESON

DRUGS. The political, social, and economic problems surrounding drug production and use date back centuries and have a worldwide scope. Beginning in the 1980s, however, these problems became especially severe with respect to production in Latin America and use in the United States. Indeed, in both areas, drugs have become a major force of concern at the governmental as well as the private level. And, as a consequence, they have come to have a heavy weight in *U.S.–Latin American relations.

Perceptions of the causes, costs, and consequences of the "drug problem," both in the United States and in Latin America, changed during the 1980s. At the outset of the decade, U.S. policymakers typically viewed drug trafficking and consumption primarily as criminal and public health issues whose solutions lay in the reduction or cutoff of "supply" at the source in Latin American producing and refining countries. Latin American and Caribbean officials,

in contrast, either ignored drug issues altogether or saw them as basically U.S. problems that had to be resolved in the United States by U.S. authorities. As of 1990, however, there was widespread consensus in the Americas that drug production, smuggling, and consumption constituted significant threats to national *security and societal well-being throughout the hemisphere.

Despite the emergence of this new consensus, U.S. efforts to impose an "antidrug" national security regime and to curtail cultivation, processing, and trafficking of illicit drugs (principally marijuana, cocaine, and heroin) in the region were unsuccessful, in large part because Washington's U.S.-centric supply-side strategy and tactics during the *Reagan administration did not offer a legitimate, credible, and symmetrical approach to the multiple problems stemming from the region's burgeoning drug trade.

Despite some hopeful signs in the *Bush administration's initial emphasis on reduction of U.S. demand, in practice U.S. policy priorities and actions during the Bush presidency added up to little more than a reaffirmation of the widely discredited longstanding U.S. emphasis on supply-side control, interdiction, and enhanced law enforcement in Latin American source countries without any counterpart intensification of U.S. efforts to reduce demand. Indeed, the Bush White House accelerated the trend toward increased militarization of U.S. antinarcotics policies abroad begun during the Reagan years, despite regionwide civilian fears that increased military participation in hemispheric drug control programs could increase *political violence and narco-terrorism, decrease civilian control over the armed forces, and foment military intervention and usurpation of democratic power and authority. The Bush administration's linkage of increased U.S. drug assistance to broader military involvement, especially in the Andean countries, provoked intense resentments and frictions. In light of its continuing supply-side bias, U.S. attempts to escalate the ineffective strategies and tactics of the Reagan administration were clearly predestined to fail. To enlist sustained and effective cooperation from Latin American and Caribbean governments, modification of strategies (from supply-side to demand-side approaches) and tactics (from unilateral pressures and sanctions to multilateral cooperation) will be necessary to make real progress in the fight against drug trafficking and abuse in the hemisphere.

In essence, the U.S.–Latin American drug trade epitomizes the type of issue (environmental problems are another) that cannot be resolved through unilateral or bilateral approaches alone. Indeed, rather than curtailing the hemispheric drug trade in the 1980s and early 1990s, supply-side policies systematically exacerbated drug-related violence and instability in the region and undermined possibilities for greater multilateral cooperation against the expanding flow of illicit drugs into the United States and the attendant economic, social, and political consequences throughout the hemisphere.

There are, of course, inherent limits to effective national and regional action in this issue area, whether such actions are undertaken unilaterally or collectively. It is unrealistic to expect, for example, that the hemispheric drug trade could be effectively curbed in the short or even medium term no matter what approach is adopted to reduce either supply or demand. Reducing U.S. demand will unquestionably be a difficult, expensive, and time-consuming process under even the most optimistic assumptions. Moreover, in view of the fact that governments of advanced capitalist countries, such as the United States or Italy, have proved unable to eliminate organized crime in their societies despite repeated attempts to do so throughout the twentieth century, the less developed and institutionalized nation-states of Latin America and the Caribbean cannot be expected to do much better, especially against the immensely wealthy and well-armed international drug trafficking rings they presently face.

Progress in the drug-trafficking realm does not require the total fulfillment of utopian goals such as a "drug-free" society. Measurable movement toward the more modest and feasible objectives of effective containment and gradual reversal of the negative economic, social, and political ramifications of drug trafficking and consumption would certainly constitute real gains. From this perspective, rather than evaluating the effectiveness of the Bush administration or other governments of Latin America and the Caribbean in terms of their ability to "win" the "war on drugs" or to "end" the region's drug scourge once and for all, the standards for judging state performance in this issue area should be more pragmatic and realistic. Incremental progress is a more realistic scale against which to measure the general effectiveness of drug control efforts in the Western Hemisphere.

Five questions can be used to measure progress. First, in the 1990s will the political leaders of the hemisphere manage to move away from the counterproductive cycles of rhetorical denunciations and periodic tensions that characterized U.S.-Latin American narco-diplomacy during the 1980s? Second, will these leaders be able to develop and sustain the policy coordination required to address the hemisphere's multifaceted drug problems seriously? Third, will the U.S. government—still the regional hegemon—prove willing and able to mobilize the leadership and resources required to reduce U.S. drug consumption and attendant violence or to reduce U.S.-based money laundering, chemical exports, and arms trafficking? Fourth, will the Latin American and Caribbean governments in source or transit countries prove willing and able to commit the resources necessary to strengthen their legal systems and law enforcement agencies, reduce their endemic institutional corruption, and lower economic dependence on drug exports? Fifth, will the international community provide the levels of economic and technical assistance that the nation-states of Latin America and the Caribbean require to institute and sustain economic and institutional reforms needed to combat the powerful and corrosive effects of the region's illicit drug trade on their social and governmental structures?

If U.S. administrations and their counterparts in Latin America and the Caribbean make even modest progress in these five areas during the 1990s, they will justifiably be able to claim that they have achieved progress in the hemisphere's war on drugs; for they will have at least laid the foundation of a more functional and effective regional antidrug regime. Conversely, retrogression in these very areas will signal failure in the hemisphere's war on drugs.

(See also TERRORISM.)

Bruce M. Bagley, guest ed., "Assessing the Americas' War on Drugs," *Journal of Interamerican Studies and World Affairs* 30, nos. 2 and 3 (Special Issue, Summer/Fall 1988). Bruce M. Bagley, *Myths of Militarization: The Role of the Military in the War on Drugs in the Americas,* Drug Trafficking in the Americas Series (Coral Gables, Fla., 1991). Christina Jacqueline Johns, *Power, Ideology, and the War on Drugs: Nothing Succeeds like Failure* (New York, 1992). William O. Walker III, *Drug Control in the Americas,* 2nd ed. (Albuquerque, N.M., 1992).

BRUCE M. BAGLEY

DU BOIS, W. E. B. Born in Great Barrington, Massachusetts on 23 February 1868, William Edward Burghardt Du Bois died in Accra, Ghana, on 27 August 1963, on the eve of the March on Washington. His mother, Mary Silvina Burghardt, was a domestic whose family had lived in the Berkshire Hills since the early eighteenth century. Alfred Du Bois, the father he never knew, was an itinerant mulatto barber of French-Haitian extraction. Du Bois attended Fisk University in Nashville, Tennessee, from which he graduated in 1888, after three years. Further scholarship assistance permitted him to attend Harvard College, where he earned a second bachelor of arts degree in philosophy in 1890. In 1895, Du Bois was awarded a doctorate of philosophy in history, the first African American to achieve this distinction at Harvard. His dissertation, *The Suppression of the African Slave Trade to the United States of America,* was selected as the first monograph of the influential Harvard Historical Series (1896). After completing course work for the doctorate, Du Bois pursued two years of graduate work in economics at the University of Berlin (1892–1894).

Unable to secure a position at a major American research university in the United States, Du Bois taught assorted subjects at Wilberforce University (Ohio). There were several tentative offers from Booker T. Washington of a professorship at Tuskegee Institute (Alabama) during the period when Du Bois held positions at the University of Pennsylvania (1896–1897) and Atlanta University (from 1898). Although he had applauded Washington's famous 1895 racial compromise address at the Atlanta and Cotton States Exposition, Du Bois rapidly evolved into an opponent of what he eventually termed the "Tuskegee Machine." The years 1900 to 1910 saw Du Bois achieve worldwide recognition for his scholarship (*The Philadelphia Negro*, 1899; the eighteen Atlanta University Studies publications) while simultaneously assuming the role of civil rights militant and propagandist. Publication of his most famous work, *The Souls of Black Folk* (1903), in which Du Bois repeated remarks first made in London in 1900—that the "problem of the 20th century is the problem of the color line"—decisively established his leadership role.

In 1905, he was a principal organizer of the Niagara Movement (comprising African Americans Du Bois memorably dubbed the "Talented Tenth"). In 1910, with a group of white progressives outraged by increasing antiblack violence in the urban North Du Bois became cofounder of the National Association for the Advancement of Colored People (NAACP). His fiery, opinionated editorship of *The Crisis* (1910–1934) propelled the monthly NAACP magazine to a circulation of 100,000 by 1919. Scholarship was not neglected, however: his publications included the biography *John Brown* (1909) and the interpretive histories *The Negro* (1915), *The Gift of Black Folk* (1924), and *Africa* (1930). Two novels, *The Quest of the Silver Fleece* (1911) and *Dark Princess* (1928), and a collection of essays, *Darkwater* (1920), significantly influenced the arts and letters movement of the 1920s (the Harlem Renaissance and its analogues) as well as the Black Aesthetic of the 1960s.

Du Bois's espousal of a socialist scheme for separate racial development led to his resignation from the NAACP in 1934 and return to Atlanta University. *Black Reconstruction* (1936), his most important monograph, and the founding of the scholarly journal, *Phylon*, as well as the abortive attempt to obtain foundation financing for *The Encyclopedia of the Negro*, were the main undertakings of that period. Du Bois returned to the NAACP after his enforced retirement from Atlanta University at age 75 and promptly embroiled himself in the Progressive Party controversy, supporting Henry Wallace in defiance of NAACP policy. Invited to depart again, Du Bois joined Paul Robeson's Council on African Affairs, participated in the 1949 Cultural and Scientific Conference for World Peace at the Waldorf-Astoria Hotel, became an officer of the Justice Department–disapproved Peace Information Center in 1950, and ran a vigorous campaign for the U.S. Senate from New York on the American Labor Party ticket. At age 83, he was indicted and unsuccessfully tried by the Justice Department under the Foreign Agents Registration Act. Du Bois's interesting account of the "Second Red Scare" appeared in the 1952 book, *In Battle for Peace*.

In 1958, Du Bois's passport was restored. Accompanied by his second wife, the novelist and musicologist Shirley Graham, he traveled widely in the Soviet Union and China. His recommendation to Premier Nikita *Khrushchev to create the Institute of African Studies in the Academy of Sciences was quickly implemented. The Lenin Prize was awarded in 1959. On 1 October 1961 (in honor of the Russian Revolution), Du Bois joined the American Communist Party, stating that "capitalism cannot reform itself." The Du Boises departed for Ghana immediately, where he spent his remaining years at work on the *Encyclopaedia Africana*, a project supported by the *Nkrumah government. He was given a state funeral, and is buried in Accra.

(See also AFRICAN AMERICANS; CIVIL RIGHTS MOVEMENT; RACE AND RACISM; SOCIALISM AND SOCIAL DEMOCRACY.)

Julius Lester, ed., *The Seventh Son: The Thought and Writings of W. E. B. Du Bois*, 2 vols. (New York, 1971). Arnold Rampersad, *The Art and Imagination of W. E. B. Du Bois* (Cambridge, Mass., 1976). Joseph P. DeMarco, *The Social Thought of W. E. B. Du Bois* (Lanham, Md., 1983). Manning Marable, *W. E. B. Du Bois: Black Radical Democrat* (Boston, 1986).

DAVID LEVERING LEWIS

E

EAST GERMANY. See German Democratic Republic.

EASTERN EUROPE. See Central Europe.

ECOLOGY. See Environmentalism; Green Parties.

ECONOMIC AND SOCIAL COMMISSION FOR ASIA AND THE PACIFIC. The UN Economic and Social Commission for Asia and the Pacific (ESCAP) was established in 1947 under a slightly different name to stimulate development in the Asia-Pacific region. Headquartered in Bangkok, ESCAP now has thirty-eight nations as full members and ten associate members, including Hong Kong and some of the smaller Pacific island nations. ESCAP is the largest of the five UN regional commissions in terms of both land area and people served.

For the 1990–91 fiscal year, ESCAP had a regular budget of US$39.4 million, a permanent professional staff of 182 and a support staff of 315. It also was set to disburse an additional US$50.7 million for the fiscal year in project financing provided by the UN Development Program and by individual countries.

ESCAP serves as an advisory body to its members, organizes meetings on themes ranging from family planning to remote sensing, provides seed money for some projects, and publishes books and periodicals on issues it believes need to be addressed, including an annual economic and social survey of the Asia-Pacific region. ESCAP also hosts an annual conference and has seven committees that concentrate on specific issue areas: rural development and the environment; development planning; industry and technology, natural resources, and energy; population; trade; and transport.

Among ESCAP's most successful regional initiatives have been the founding of the * Asian Development Bank in 1966 and the establishment of a committee to oversee the development of the Mekong River in 1957. Less successful has been its plan for a trans-Asian highway running from Singapore to Iran. Burma has failed to build the link to complete the highway and other nations do not have the money to improve the sections of the road that exist.

Like other UN agencies, ESCAP has been criticized by some of its members for inefficiency. Australia has been among the most vocal critics. Japan, which is ESCAP's largest donor, and the Republic of Korea, its largest donor among developing nations, have been reticent on this issue.

(See also Development and Underdevelopment; Economic Commission for Africa; Economic Commission for Latin America and the Caribbean; Southern African Development Coordination Conference; United Nations.)

N. Balakrishnan, "ESCAP, Very Pacific" *The Far Eastern Economic Review* 12 (July 1990), pp. 72–73.

Jonathan Friedland

ECONOMIC COMMISSION FOR AFRICA. The Economic Commission for Africa (ECA) was established in April 1958 as a regional commission of the UN. It has become a leading participant in the effort to devise effective * development strategies for the African continent, and provides an array of technical assistance, socioeconomic information, and applied research. The commission has also emerged as a sharp critic of the "structural adjustment" programs adopted by a majority of African states during the 1980s at the insistence of the International Monetary Fund (IMF), the World Bank, and other multilateral development finance institutions and donor countries.

The ECA's broad mandate is to facilitate concerted action for the economic and social development of Africa. In carrying out this mandate the ECA cooperates closely with the * Organization of African Unity (OAU), the Food and Agricultural Organization of the UN, and the UN Industrial Development Organization. And under the commission's auspices over thirty African interstate finance, management, trade, transportation, environmental, and social and economic *planning organizations have been founded. These organizations are providing economic analyses, international negotiating positions and strategies, country and regional development plans, technical and management training, cartographic and remote-sensing data, and demographic data and population policies. The ECA has also spurred the development of regional economic integration groupings such as the Economic Community of West African States, the *Southern African Development Co-ordination Conference, and the Preferential Trade Area for East and Southern African States.

In collaboration with the OAU, the ECA has produced comprehensive development blueprints and position papers seeking to bring about fundamental economic restructuring in Africa. These include the Lagos Plan of Action (1980), Africa's Priority Program for Economic Recovery 1986–1990 (1985), and the Khartoum Declaration: Towards a Human Focused Approach to Socio-Economic Recovery and Development in Africa (1988). And in 1989, in a direct challenge to economic adjustment policies designed by the IMF, the ECA presented its African Alternative Framework to Structural Adjustment Programs for Socio-Economic Recovery and Transformation (AAF-SAP). The underlying philosophy of development of this alternative strategy and the earlier plans and declarations is regional self-reliance through regional economic cooperation and eventual integration, with more equitable distribution of scarce resources between the rural and urban and agricultural and industrial sectors and among socioeconomic groups, within a mixed economy. The ECA envisions economic development as being driven increasingly by private capital, yet it retains a clear role for government ownership and overall direction of the economy. Specifically AAF-SAP calls for increased investment in agriculture and rural infrastructure; increased rural credit facilities; more efficient, equitable, and ethical taxation systems; the redirection of government expenditure from defense and nonessential parastatals to education, health, and the integration of women in development; financial encouragement for the production of essential commodities and the consumption of domestic goods; the strengthening of intra-African financial and trade cooperation; and greater mass participation in decision making and program implementation.

Increasingly the ECA has become the articulator of Africa's concerns about the inequities of the international economic order, a critic of the internal constraints to economic growth with equity and respect for human dignity, and the proponent of new development initiatives. As Africa searches for appropriate strategies to overcome its entrenched underdevelopment, the ECA will continue its role as a font of ideas, facilitator of continental cooperation, and challenger of development strategies that ignore the plight of Africa's poor masses.

(See also AFRICAN REGIONAL ORGANIZATIONS; ECONOMIC AND SOCIAL COMMISSION FOR ASIA AND THE PACIFIC; ECONOMIC COMMISSION FOR LATIN AMERICA AND THE CARIBBEAN; UNITED NATIONS.)

"30 Years of the ECA" *West Africa* 3690 (May 2, 1988): 789–796.

HASHIM T. GIBRILL

ECONOMIC COMMISSION FOR LATIN AMERICA AND THE CARIBBEAN. The Economic Commission for Latin America and the Caribbean (ECLAC), often known by its Spanish acronym, CEPAL, was founded by the UN in 1948 to coordinate policies for the promotion of economic *development in the Latin American region; the Caribbean was added in 1984. The thirty-three countries of the region are full members, as are the United States, Canada, France, Netherlands, Portugal, Spain, and Britain. The function of ECLAC is to research regional and national economic problems and provide expert advice on the formulation of development plans. The Latin American Institute for Economic and Social Planning (ILPES) was founded by ECLAC in 1962 in order to provide training and advisory services for the development planning bodies in the region. Both ECLAC and ILPES are located in Santiago, Chile.

The considerable influence of the ECLAC on public policy–making in Latin America is mainly exercised through its central contribution to regional discourse on industrialization and trade issues, in the form of an economic doctrine known as "structuralism." This doctrine holds that markets are embedded in historically specific institutional structures which lead to supply rigidities, response lags, and demand disequilibria (at both national and international levels), and in turn determine the form of economic adjustment and the appropriate choice of development policy (Chenery, 1973). The ECLAC *Economic Survey,* published annually since 1948, is the authoritative source on the region, combining rigorous statistical analysis with independent policy evaluation. The commission also publishes major studies on topics such as regional trade integration, industrial development, external debt, poverty, and social problems. The ECLAC staff and associated experts present their more polemical research results under their own names in the semiannual journal *Cepal Review.*

Since its foundation, ECLAC has led a more active and independent life than its counterparts in other regions, such as the *Economic Commission for Africa or the *Economic and Social Commission for Asia and the Pacific. This appears to reflect both a strong regional tradition of independent thought on industrialization and trade and the nationalist sentiments of Latin American states, which have led in turn to a tradition of confrontation with Washington which is unusual for UN institutions. Unfortunately, no direct link seems to have been established with the other regional commissions. Internationally, ECLAC has more affinity with the *United Nations Conference on Trade and Development (UNCTAD) and the International Labor Organization (ILO), whose Latin American program has made major contributions to the structuralist approach in the fields of employment and technology. Within

Latin America, and arising from its emphasis on domestic markets as the basis for scale economies and subsequent industrial exports, ECLAC significantly influenced several regional organizations: the Andean Pact, the Central American Common Market, and the Sistema Económico Latinoamericano (SELA). In consequence, it is hardly surprising that ECLAC has entered into implicit (and at times explicit) conflict with the *World Bank and the *International Monetary Fund (and to a lesser extent the *Inter-American Development Bank) over issues of macroeconomic management and trade liberalization.

The considerable political influence of ECLAC in the region was originally derived from its articulation of a critical approach to the problems of late industrialization and disadvantageous trade relations worked out by its first executive secretary, Raúl *Prebisch (Prebisch, 1984). This doctrine was subsequently extended to encompass problems of *technology transfer, agrarian reform, inflation, and employment, and involved the leading Latin American economists of the postwar decades. Structuralist theory undoubtedly had a major influence on the widespread policies of import substitution and public investment applied throughout the region during the 1950s and 1960s. This influence was not just confined to state bureaucracies (where it was mainly adopted by ministries of industry and *planning, and often opposed by ministries of finance and central banks) but became standard teaching material in Latin American social science faculties and spread further into civil society to enter the agendas of industrial associations, trade unions, and even church activists. ECLAC doctrine also became a major component of the international debate on underdevelopment in the *Third World as a whole—although its misuse in dependency and world-systems theories did little to further the commission's reputation. During the early 1970s, more radical experiments such as that of Chile under Allende, Peru under Velasco, and Mexico under Echeverría also applied ECLAC propositions on national autonomy and social expenditure—with unfortunate consequences that were due more to incompetent economic management and U.S. disapproval than to inadequacies of the doctrine itself.

The 1980s were a difficult time for ECLAC, as *monetarism and liberalization became the dominant economic doctrines in the region due to both domestic and international political changes as well as the economic evidence of the limits of state intervention. This loss of authority was exacerbated by the widespread collapse of Latin American universities and increased influence of neoclassical economics. Nonetheless, ECLAC continued to produce important work on the debt crisis (particularly its fiscal and social consequences), technology transfer, and regional integration. Structuralist doctrine was

also central to two major political experiments of the 1980s: the attempt by the Sandinistas in Nicaragua to integrate *basic needs provision with mixed-economy planning in Nicaragua, and the implementation by various Brazilian administrations of heterodox stabilization policies as a socially acceptable alternative to monetarism.

The future role of ECLAC—beyond its continuing institutional functions within the UN system—depends to a great extent on the way in which economic management itself develops in the region. To the extent that the United States is successful in extending the North American Free Trade Area southward from Mexico and the leading Latin American governments maintain a liberal stance on economic and social policy, the role for interventionist strategy of the kind identified with ECLAC will clearly be limited. But if the current trends toward political cooperation between regional states lead to a greater capacity for financial negotiation with Washington and growing concern about poverty and social collapse lead to a return to economic management and longer-term planning, the space for a neostructuralist doctrine could open up again. The autonomy of economic discourse in a region where civil society is not only historically weak but in profound *crisis presents an opportunity to ECLAC not dissimilar to that of the postwar circumstances of its birth.

(See also IMPORT-SUBSTITUTION INDUSTRIALIZATION; LAND REFORM; LATIN AMERICAN REGIONAL ORGANIZATIONS; SOUTHERN AFRICAN DEVELOPMENT CO-ORDINATION CONFERENCE.)

H. B. Chenery, "The Structural Approach to Development Policy" *American Economic Review* 65, no. 2 (1975): 310–322. David H. Pollock, "Some Changes in US Attitudes towards CEPAL over the Past Thirty Years" *Cepal Review* no. 6 (second half of 1978): 57–80. Octavio Rodríguez, *La teoría del subdesarrollo de la Cepal* (Mexico City, 1980). Raul Prebisch, "Five Stages in My Thinking on Development," in G. Meier and D. Seers, eds., *Pioneers in Development* (New York, 1984). Hans W. Arndt, "The Origins of Structuralism" *World Development* 13, no. 2 (1985): 151–159. Cristóbal Kay, *Latin American Theories of Development and Underdevelopment* (London, 1989). José A. Ocampo, "New Economic Thinking in Latin America" *Journal of Latin American Studies* 22, no. 1 (1990): 169–181.

E. V. K. FITZGERALD

ECONOMIC COMMUNITY OF CENTRAL AFRICAN STATES. See AFRICAN REGIONAL ORGANIZATIONS.

ECONOMIC COMMUNITY OF WEST AFRICAN STATES. See AFRICAN REGIONAL ORGANIZATIONS.

ECONOMIC PLANNING. See PLANNING.

ECONOMIC POLICY COORDINATION. See POLICY COORDINATION, ECONOMIC.

ECONOMICS. See POLITICAL ECONOMY.

ECUADOR. Located at the equator, from which it derives its name, Ecuador gained its freedom from Spain in 1822, initially joining with Colombia and Venezuela to form the federation of Gran Colombia. With the dissolution of that union in 1830, Ecuador became an independent republic.

The history of Ecuador has been marked by an absence of national integration, as barriers imposed by geography have served to perpetuate regional differences. The traditionally conservative Andean region, home to the country's forty percent Indian population and the nation's capital, Quito, remained, until the 1970s, largely rural and maintained only weak links to the international or even coastal economies. By contrast, the fertile coastal plain, where the bustling port city of Guayaquil is located, is the commercial center of the country and the region where a majority of the country's primary exports are produced, including bananas, cacao, coffee, and fish products.

Regional fragmentation, a historic dependence on primary agricultural exports at the expense of industrial development, and the economic dominance of a coastal export elite have had implications for Ecuadorian *political development. The economy has been highly vulnerable to shifts in international prices, the state has remained weak by comparison with other countries in the region, and the absence of a numerically significant middle or working class has militated against the emergence of mass-based political institutions. As a result, politics in Ecuador have been highly unstable, with coastal and sierra elites competing for power without strong political institutions to mediate their conflicts, and with boom-bust cycles in export agriculture punctuated by military intervention.

The advent of a reformist military regime (1972–1979) on the eve of an anticipated petroleum boom triggered widespread economic, social, and political changes. With the gradual assumption of state control over the oil industry, the power of the coastal agricultural elite was undermined as the locus of economic power shifted to the sierra-based capital. Relying on petroleum wealth to finance a development effort, the military leadership promoted agrarian reform and state-sponsored industrial development. Their accomplishments were particularly noteworthy in the manufacturing sector, which expanded rapidly (roughly ten percent per annum) during the decade. Those changes were responsible in turn for the emergence of a new entrepreneurial elite and for the growth of the middle and working classes. As a further by-product, the 1970s also witnessed the development of middle-class reformist parties, with a strong grass-roots base among the newly emergent sierra social groups. In the years that followed, those parties have posed an increasingly effective challenge to coastal-based parties and more populistic movements.

The changes introduced during the military regime notwithstanding, the recent democratically elected civilian regimes have had to confront a number of challenges. Heavy dependence on petroleum revenue has perpetuated Ecuador's vulnerability to shifts in the international economy, as the drops in the price of oil in the 1980s have plunged the economy into recession and forced renegotiation of the country's large foreign debt. Politics continues to be plagued by conflicts, owing as much to personality as policy clashes; on more than one occasion, these have paralyzed the policy-making process. The military continues to monitor politics from the sidelines, a reluctant player in the context of economic austerity, but one that retains significant legitimacy because of its credible performance in office during the 1970s.

(See also DEMOCRATIC TRANSITIONS; INTERNATIONAL DEBT; MILITARY RULE.)

David Schodt, *Ecuador: An Andean Enigma* (Boulder, Colo., 1987).

ANITA ISAACS

EDUCATION. See LITERACY; WELFARE STATE.

EGYPT. In the early nineteenth century, Egypt was formed as a centralized state out of a province of the Ottoman Empire. Muhammad Ali, an Ottoman commander sent to Egypt to help end the French occupation of 1798–1801, built a modern mass army to establish control of the Nile valley. The new state promoted the development of agriculture and modern industry, and expanded its empire abroad from the Sudan to Syria. In 1839, however, European states intervened to reestablish the nominal power of the Ottoman Empire, forcing Egypt to disarm itself and remove restrictions on the penetration of European commerce and capital.

The building of the Suez Canal and a modern transport and irrigation network during the 1850s and 1860s accelerated Egypt's incorporation into the European world economy, principally as a producer of raw cotton. Export agriculture concentrated landownership in the hands of a Turkish-speaking elite and produced a new stratum of European and Levantine financiers and merchants tied to powerful European banks and enterprises. In 1881 a reformist movement of landowners, intellectuals, and army officers attempted to replace absolutist rule subservient to European creditors with parliamentary government, but within a year British troops invaded Egypt, overthrew the reformers, and reestablished a client regime.

Britain's colonial rule lasted until Egyptian independence in 1922, which followed a second nationalist revolt in 1919. Egypt became a *constitutional monarchy, although the British retained their military presence, control of Egyptian foreign policy, and considerable influence over domestic affairs. In

1936 Britain withdrew its troops to the Suez Canal zone, but the economic hardships of World War II and Egypt's defeat in the Palestine war of 1948–1949 led to violent popular protest against the British presence and the corruption and incompetence of the monarchy. In 1952, junior nationalist army officers led by Gamal Abdel *Nasser seized power, abolished the *monarchy, and negotiated Britain's final withdrawal from Suez.

Today, Egypt is a constitutional republic, ruled by a president who is nominated to a six-year, renewable term of office by the People's Assembly and approved by the electorate. The president appoints the prime minister and other members of the government, lays down the general policies of the state, issues decrees with the force of law, declares states of emergency and *war, and is the supreme head of the armed forces and the police. The judiciary is protected by the constitution from political interference and in practice has maintained significant independence, to the extent that the regime has been forced to evade its powers by the use of martial law and military courts.

Following the 1952 coup Egypt became a *one-party system. The new regime suppressed existing parties and replaced them with the Liberation Rally, which was renamed the Arab Socialist Union (ASU) in 1962 and organized in communities and workplaces as an agency of popular political mobilization. The ASU leadership weakened after the death of President Nasser in 1970 and after landowners and other conservative forces reasserted themselves under his successor, President Anwar *Sadat. In 1976 Sadat permitted rival political organizations to form, first as platforms within the ASU and from 1978 as separate parties.

The ASU itself became the National Democratic Party, remaining the ruling political party. Closely linked to the government and the state-controlled media and security forces, it has been assured of large electoral majorities. *Left-leaning intellectuals and Nasserists organized the National Progressive Unionist Party, whose support was strong among industrial workers and whose criticisms prompted the regime to establish the religious-nationalist Socialist Labor Party as a more loyal opposition. The center-right New Wafd, successor to the popular pre-1952 nationalist party, emerged as the most influential opposition party.

Communist, Nasserist, and Islamic political parties continued to be banned. However, the Muslim Brotherhood, a mass political movement formed in 1929 and suppressed after 1954, was allowed to renew its activities in the 1970s as an alternative to the Left. After the assassination of President Sadat in 1981 by members of a militant Islamic cell, the Brotherhood was also seen as a conservative alternative to religious extremism. Forbidden to function as a party, the Brotherhood forms alliances with nonreligious parties and fields election candidates

under their name. Islamic candidates also dominate elections to many professional syndicates, which, along with business associations, operate as pressure groups articulating the interests of their members. Under Sadat's successor, Husni Mubarak, opposition newspapers were allowed more freedom. Given the restrictions on the holding of public meetings, the press provides a major forum for criticism of government policy. Labor unions, an important political force before 1952, remain under close government control.

Support for the regime lies among medium and large landowners, an urban capitalist class, and the upper ranks of the bureaucracy, state-run economic enterprises, and the armed forces. These groups and classes benefited from the regime's policies of *land reform, industrialization, and military growth and remain dependent on the state for price controls, protected markets, contracts, and commissions.

Almost half the country's population is now urban, concentrated in the two major cities of Cairo and Alexandria. Although the efforts at industrialization produced an industrial work force more than a million strong, most of the urban population is employed in the service sector, including the overstaffed state bureaucracy. The rural population remains predominantly agricultural, but despite reform measures land is still concentrated in few hands. In 1982, forty-three percent of farmland was held in farms of more than five acres, the maximum size of a family farm, by the top ten percent of landholders. This stratum holds social and political power in the countryside. The rest of the land is shared in small plots by the remaining ninety percent of landholders, while a significant proportion of the rural population remains landless.

Egypt's population is largely Muslim, with Christians a minority estimated at ten percent. During the colonial period parts of the Christian community prospered as intermediaries for European capital and political power, but since the 1950s their position of relative privilege has declined. This has contributed to Christian-Muslim animosity and sometimes violence, especially in areas where the Islamic movement is strong.

Women in Egypt benefited from the emergence of a feminist movement early in the twentieth century, in the context of the nationalist struggle. After 1952 they gained the right to vote and to stand for election as well as wider access to education and employment. As education moved them into the workplace, many women adopted a modern form of veiling, with motives ranging from piety and political activism to dealing with the discomforts of a male-dominated public space. At the same time, the wider growth of the Islamic movement carried with it a reassertion of the male prerogatives weakened by these economic and social changes.

The Nasser regime undertook a program of state-controlled capitalist development labeled "Arab

*Socialism." The 1952 agrarian reforms dispossessed the small landed aristocracy and guaranteed the security of tenant farmers but otherwise left capitalist agriculture intact. The regime initially sought international investment to finance agricultural and industrial development, but when the United States refused to finance the keystone of this program, the Aswan High Dam, the state was forced into a more active economic role. The Suez Canal was nationalized, and, after the abortive Suez invasion by Britain, France, and Israel in 1956, the regime Egyptianized European banks and enterprises. Egyptian financiers, industrialists, business elites, and landowners prospered, in alliance with the new military elite. Yet they were unwilling to invest in rapid industrialization to promote wider prosperity and reduce pressure from the left, which was subject to growing political repression.

In the 1960s the military regime moved against the power of private Egyptian capital, nationalizing banks, major companies, and industries, and passed laws giving workers shares of profits, a minimum wage, and free health care and education. Five-year *planning focused on a program of *import-substitution industrialization in iron and steel, aluminum, chemicals, and other heavy industry, and efforts were made to extend the land reform. Egypt's defeat in the June 1967 Arab-Israeli war weakened the regime, however, and enabled the emergent bureaucratic and military elite, together with large landowners and surviving elements of the urban bourgeoisie, to resist further reform.

The Sadat regime reflected these interests, and reoriented Egypt into alliance with the United States. The 1974 economic "opening" (*infitah) encouraged foreign investment in collaboration with local capital, but the boom occurred in construction, property speculation, consumer imports, tourism, and other services, rather than renewed industrial growth. By the end of the 1980s services accounted for more than fifty percent of the country's GDP, while industry contributed only thirty percent and agriculture less than twenty percent.

Unable to promote self-sustaining growth or further redistribution, the regime preserved social order with a program of price subsidies for food, fuel, and other necessities. This was financed with the income from Suez Canal tolls and oil exports, together with subsidized U.S. loans and grain sales on a scale that exceeded U.S. aid to all the rest of Africa combined. Combined with extensive purchases of U.S. arms, these loans drew the government heavily into debt and diverted further resources abroad for interest payments. Although part of the debt was later forgiven, Egypt had to seek international aid to refinance its obligations. In exchange, the government gradually accepted a program of financial restructuring, aimed at encouraging exports and reducing the system of subsidies. It remained unclear, however, whether export markets could be developed or

capital found to invest in productive assets, and unlikely that the Egyptian bourgeoisie would allow a significant redistribution of those assets to alleviate poverty and inequality. Millions of Egyptian workers sought employment abroad, especially in Iraq and the Gulf, and their remittances temporarily kept up living standards, until the oil price collapse of the mid-1980s.

Egyptians live with poverty, inflation, rising unemployment, and declining access to adequate housing, nutrition, health care, and education. Poverty in turn sustains high birth rates, as poor families seek to increase the number of potential breadwinners. Egypt's total population grew from 40 million in 1980 to 55 million in 1990, and continues to increase at a rate of more than 2.5 percent a year. Efforts to extend political freedoms and electoral competition may shore up the regime's *legitimacy, which it can no longer afford to purchase through populist programs of social welfare or food subsidies, but such efforts aim to forestall rather than facilitate a more far-reaching social and economic transformation. Persistent, occasionally violent challenges come from lower-middle-class youth, industrial workers, conscript soldiers, and others. Martial law and the repression of leftist and militant Islamic organizations continue.

Egypt's economic and military dependence on the United States since the mid-1970s has reduced its international role. Until oil wealth financed the growth of Saudi Arabia and Iraq, Egypt was the predominant Arab power and a leader in wider anti-imperialist coalitions such as the *Nonaligned Movement and the *Organization of African Unity. Israel's unsuccessful 1956 Suez invasion affirmed Nasser's leadership of a populist *Arab nationalism, and was followed in 1958 by political union with Syria to form the short-lived United Arab Republic. The United States opposed Arab nationalism, which threatened its more oligarchic Arab allies, forcing Egypt and other populist states to depend increasingly on the Soviet Union. In 1967 Israel again invaded Egypt, this time with U.S. support, after Israeli-Syrian clashes had led Egypt to reimpose its pre-1956 blockade of Israeli shipping in the Gulf of Aqaba. In response to a humiliating defeat, Egypt began realigning itself to gain U.S. support. The October 1973 war forced Israel into military disengagement talks. Sadat's November 1977 trip to Jerusalem led to the 1979 Camp David peace accords by which Israel withdrew in stages from Egyptian territory and promised some form of autonomy to the Palestinians in the West Bank and Gaza Strip.

The other Arab states opposed a peace treaty that left Israel holding the West Bank and Gaza under military occupation, and broke diplomatic relations with Cairo. Egypt's formal isolation lasted a decade, interrupting aid from the Gulf states and increasing Cairo's dependence on Washington. The *Iran-Iraq War (1980–1988), however, drew Egypt closer to

Saudi Arabia and Jordan in joint support of Iraq, and after the war ties with Syria and Libya were remade. The *Gulf War (1991), following Iraq's invasion of Kuwait, divided the Arab world again. Egypt confirmed its post-1967 alliance with the oil oligarchies of the Gulf and their collective dependence on the United States, while the exodus of more than a million Egyptian migrant workers from Iraq placed new strains on the domestic economy.

(See also ARAB-ISRAELI CONFLICT; COLONIAL EMPIRES; DECOLONIZATION; FOREIGN WORKERS; INTERNATIONAL MIGRATION; ISLAM; NASSERISM; NATIONALIZATION; SUEZ CRISIS.)

Anouar Abdel Malek, *Egypt: Military Society* (New York, 1968). Derek Hopwood, *Egypt: Politics and Society, 1945–1984* (New York, 1985). Afaf Marsot, *A Short History of Modern Egypt* (Cambridge, U.K., 1985). Robert Springborg, *Mubarak's Egypt* (Boulder, Colo., 1989). Arlene MacLeod, *Accommodating Protest: Working Women, the New Veiling, and Change in Cairo* (New Haven, Conn., 1991).

TIMOTHY MITCHELL

EISENHOWER, Dwight D. Born in Denison, Texas, on 14 October 1890, Dwight D. Eisenhower was the son of a section hand on the railroad. The family moved to Abilene, Kansas, in 1891; there he grew up and graduated from high school in 1911. He won an appointment to the U.S. Military Academy at West Point, where he graduated and received a commission as a second lieutenant in the U.S. Army. His army career was marked by slow promotion and high praise from his superiors, one of whom was General Douglas MacArthur.

In December 1941, Chief of Staff George C. Marshall brought Lieutenant Colonel Eisenhower to Washington, gave him a temporary promotion to major general, and put him in charge of the Operations Division of the War Department. In June 1942, Marshall sent Eisenhower to England to take command of the European Anglo-American invasion of North Africa; in May 1943, he forced the surrender of the German-Italian military units in Africa; in July, he commanded the Anglo-American invasion of Sicily; in September, forces under his command invaded Italy at Salerno. In December 1943, President Franklin *Roosevelt selected him to command Operation Overlord, the invasion of France in Normandy.

In June 1944, Eisenhower launched the assault. By late August, his troops liberated France from the Germans. In December, his forces met and hurled back the last great German offensive of the war, in Belgium, known as the Battle of the Bulge. In March 1945, British, U.S., and Canadian troops crossed the Rhine River and overran Germany. On 7 May 1945, at his headquarters in Reims, France, Eisenhower presided over the unconditional surrender of Germany.

Eisenhower emerged from *World War II as the most successful and famous general in the world.

He was also immensely popular personally. A political career seemed natural and inevitable. In 1948, Democrats and Republicans alike wanted to nominate him for the *presidency, but he declared that a professional soldier ought not get involved in partisan politics. He retired as chief of staff and took the position of president of Columbia University.

In 1951, at President Harry *Truman's request, he left Columbia to become the first Supreme Allied Commander, Europe, head of the military arm of the *North Atlantic Treaty Organization (NATO). The Republicans, desperate after losing five presidential elections in a row, were eager to nominate him in 1952. Party leaders convinced him that if he did not run, Senator Robert Taft would be the Republican nominee; Taft was an isolationist who had voted against NATO, and would pull the United States out of NATO if he became president. If the Democrats won, the leaders predicted it would be the end of the two-party system and the beginning of *socialism in the United States. To avert such calamities, Eisenhower reluctantly agreed to accept the nomination.

He won a landslide victory over Democratic nominee Adlai Stevenson in 1952, and again for reelection in 1956. As president, he was extremely popular. Partly this was a result of his sunny disposition, his big grin, his "there's nothing to worry about" manner, his ability to project himself as "just plain folks." Mainly, however, his popularity was a product of his policies.

He was a political conservative who always sought the middle of the road. His philosophy was that the extremes on any political debate were always wrong. He wanted a balanced budget, but not at the expense of the social programs created by the *New Deal Democrats in the 1930s. He was a moderate on civil rights, willing to enforce the law as laid down by the Supreme Court in *Brown v. Topeka* (1954) but unwilling to move aggressively to integrate the schools. He wanted to eliminate communist influence in the schools and in government, but was opposed to the methods used by Senator Joseph *McCarthy.

Eisenhower was a great builder. More schools were built during his administration than any other (they were, admittedly, necessary because of the baby boom). The St. Lawrence Seaway was one of his achievements. His proudest boast was that he initiated and carried through the Interstate Highway System, the greatest public works project in history.

He was a general who hated war. He ended the *Korean War with an armistice six months after taking office, and entered no others, in a decade in which the *Cold War was at its most dangerous. Nearly all his advisors wanted him to save the French position in *Vietnam in 1954, but he refused to commit U.S. troops. War with China seemed all but certain on three occasions during his presidency, but he always managed to find a peaceful solution.

In 1955, he went to Geneva for a summit with Nikita *Khrushchev, the first time a U.S. president met with a Soviet leader since the end of World War II, to establish a system of peaceful coexistence.

Eisenhower held down the costs and dangers of the *arms race through the 1950s in a way that no one else could have done. Both political parties demanded more defense spending, especially after the Soviets launched the first satellite, Sputnik, in 1957, but Eisenhower consistently held that building more weapons would not create more security, and that a balanced budget was more important than defense spending.

Eisenhower was no reformer. Except for his appointment of Earl Warren as chief justice, black Americans had little to thank him for; neither did women, or the poor, or other minorities. He opposed McCarthy's witch-hunting methods, but did almost nothing personally to stop the senator. Nor was he a risk-taker. The counterpoint to his success in achieving and maintaining peace was his failure to "roll back" *communism in Central and Eastern Europe (as he had promised to do in the 1952 campaign), or to stop the spread of communism to Vietnam and Cuba. To his critics, he appeared to be a do-nothing president, content to "stand pat" and preside over a rich, happy, self-satisfied nation. He left his party vulnerable to Senator John F. *Kennedy's 1960 presidential campaign charges that he had allowed the nation to "fall behind" the Soviets.

Eisenhower gave the nation eight years of peace and prosperity, a claim no other president in the twentieth century could make. In 1961, he retired to his farm in Gettysburg, Pennsylvania. He died on 28 March 1969. He was survived by his wife Mamie and his son John.

(See also AMERICAN FOREIGN POLICY; CIVIL RIGHTS MOVEMENT; EISENHOWER DOCTRINE.)

Dwight D. Eisenhower, *Crusade in Europe* (New York, 1948). Dwight D. Eisenhower, *The White House Years*, 2 vols. (Garden City, N.Y. 1962–3). Stephen E. Ambrose, *Eisenhower: Soldier and President* (New York, 1990).

STEPHEN E. AMBROSE

EISENHOWER DOCTRINE. On 5 January 1957, U.S. President Dwight D. *Eisenhower delivered a major *foreign policy address in which he asked Congress to authorize the use of armed *force to aid any country requesting help "against overt armed aggression from any nation controlled by international communism." On 9 March, the lawmakers ratified what is known as the Eisenhower Doctrine, a rationale for U.S. intervention directed primarily at the *Middle East, where radical nationalist opposition to the West had sharpened in the aftermath of the *Suez Crisis.

The Eisenhower Doctrine affirmed U.S. determination to become the leading power in the region. Eisenhower had just blocked a military campaign by Britain and France, the former colonial powers, who, along with Israel, hoped to recapture the nationalized Suez Canal and overthrow Egypt's president *Nasser. The U.S. president now made it clear that the *United States itself reserved the right to intervene in this oil-rich zone if it perceived its vital interests threatened.

The Eisenhower Doctrine was in some sense a continuation of the *Truman Doctrine of ten years earlier (March 1947), which had provided U.S. military aid to Turkey and Greece to block any extension of Soviet influence into the Mediterranean and the Middle East. The Eisenhower Doctrine reflected the same *Cold War imperatives, but it was broader, aimed in large measure at containing radical *nationalism.

Washington identified radical nationalism with the Soviet Union for three main reasons. First, it considered nationalist demands for control over resources like oil to be the practical equivalent of *communism in terms of interfering with corporate control and access. U.S. oil companies were consolidating their interests in the region at the time, and Washington wanted to make it clear that it would combat nationalizations or other interference in these highly profitable enterprises.

Second, radical nationalists had rejected a proposed anti-Soviet military alliance, known as the Baghdad Pact, and they had taken a leading role in the emerging movement of "nonalignment." Secretary of State John Foster Dulles believed that countries who refused to be allies were virtual enemies, and he viewed nonalignment as thinly disguised support for communism.

Third, radical nationalist regimes in Egypt and Syria had recently established direct military and economic relations with Moscow. In fact, such steps had been less ideological than pragmatic, and the regimes domestically were anticommunist. But Washington was inclined to see these governments as extremely vulnerable to Soviet "penetration" and subversion, if not as functional Soviet allies. The Eisenhower Doctrine, then, was a means to hold these governments in check, to pressure them toward accommodation, and to sanction direct military *intervention if absolutely necessary.

Eisenhower's proclamation coincided with a visit to Washington by King Saud of Saudi Arabia, whom the United States wanted to build up as a conservative regional ally and counterweight to Egypt's Nasser. In fact, the U.S. government invoked the Eisenhower Doctrine only twice, and never in circumstances of external aggression. In April 1957, Washington sent emergency aid to Jordan and moved the Sixth Fleet to the eastern Mediterranean to support King Hussein, whose throne had been threatened by an abortive military coup. And in July 1958, U.S. marines landed in Lebanon to defend the Lebanese government of Camille Chamoun in the midst of a civil war and in the wake of a nationalist military coup in Iraq. Soviet involvement was absent in both cases, as U.S. policymakers were well aware.

After the Eisenhower administration left office in January 1961, the U.S. government no longer invoked the doctrine. The new Kennedy administration sought greater accommodation with nationalists in the Middle East. Later in the decade, the Nixon Doctrine expressed a policy of relying on regional surrogates (like Iran and Israel in the Middle East) to protect and advance U.S. interests. But in 1980, the *Carter Doctrine returned to the idea of direct U.S. military intervention—now focused on the oil-rich Persian Gulf and Arabian Peninsula area. That doctrine, and the military preparations it called into being, laid the groundwork for the massive intervention of U.S. forces in the *Gulf War of 1991.

(See also ARAB NATIONALISM; CONTAINMENT; NASSERISM; NONALIGNED MOVEMENT.)

Alan Dowty, *Middle East Crisis: US Decision-Making in 1958, 1970, and 1973*, Part I (Berkeley, Calif., 1984). Douglas Little, "Cold War and Covert Action: The United States and Syria, 1945–1958," *The Middle East Journal* 44, no. 1 (Winter 1990).

JOE STORK

ELECTIONS AND VOTING BEHAVIOR. Over the past two centuries, electoral institutions have come to play a role in the governmental structures and political processes of most nations. The forms that these institutions take, and the precise role that they play, however, vary enormously from place to place and over time. The most fundamental dimension on which national electoral systems vary is the opportunity for opposition within the formal electoral framework. Democratic electoral processes permit opposing forces to depose and replace current officeholders. What could be called authoritarian electoral systems, by contrast, do not permit the electoral defeat of those in power and serve primarily as instruments of mass mobilization and legitimation for the regime.

The Emergence of Democratic Elections. In general, democratic electoral systems are most likely to evolve and persist in societies where politically relevant resources, including the capacity to employ armed force or violence, are distributed relatively widely outside the control of the central government. Generally, electoral processes are introduced when governments face economic difficulties, military demands, or internal political challenges that require them to seek popular support and to create formal channels of participation and opposition. Few ruling groups, however, are anxious to see these channels effectively used by their political foes. At some point in every nation's electoral history, incumbent *elites have sought to use military force to suppress their electoral opponents.

But military force is by no means the only important factor. Where other politically relevant resources and skills, such as wealth, education, com-

munications, and organization, are relatively widely diffused and outside the state's control, the likelihood that incumbent elites can successfully eliminate their opponents is lessened. It is for this very reason that economic development, as Seymour Martin Lipset and others have shown (*Political Man,* New York, 1963), was historically conducive to the evolution of democratic electoral institutions. Industrialization and urbanization, especially under capitalist auspices, entailed the creation and dissemination of private wealth, organizational expertise, communications, literacy, and a host of other resources that facilitated political action and increased citizens' capacities for sustained political opposition. The relative absence of these resources helps to explain why democratic electoral institutions have not usually persisted in the nations of the *Third World and raises questions about the prospects for their persistence in some of the nations of Eastern and *Central Europe that have recently sought to introduce democratic reforms.

Where democratic electoral processes become entrenched, contending political forces typically build party organizations and seek to develop appeals that will help them to mobilize popular followings. In general, political forces that attempt to win elections on the basis of working-class support find it necessary to build coherent and disciplined party organizations in order to make the most effective use of their adherents' numerical strength and to compensate for their supporters' lack of economic, institutional, and social resources. By contrast, political forces that have access to the social and economic resources controlled by the middle and upper classes— the Republican Party in the United States and the Conservative Party in Britain, for example—typically rely less on mass organization and more on media campaigns that employ expensive political technologies such as polling, television advertising, computerized phone bank and direct mail operations. These campaigns are "capital-intensive," as contrasted with the more "labor-intensive" organizational efforts upon which their opponents more often depend.

Voter Mobilization. In most nations, contending forces have sought to make use of a variety of different appeals to link themselves to popular followings. The most effective and durable appeals are those based on voters' *class, religious, or ethnic identifications and regional attachments. Whether and how any particular social group or stratum will participate in electoral politics, however, cannot be directly inferred from some characteristic of the group itself. The relative political significance of race, class, religion, and so forth depends in large measure on when, how, on what basis, and by whom a group is electorally mobilized.

For example, in the United States in the early twentieth century the Republicans mobilized northeastern workers partly on the basis of their religious and ethnic affiliations. In the 1930s, however, by sponsoring welfare, economic, and labor programs, Franklin D. *Roosevelt was able to bring most of these same voters into the Democratic Party on the basis of their class identification. Thus, it is not surprising that in a variety of national and historical settings, individuals with very similar social origins and life conditions have been mobilized by political forces that differed substantially from one another in aims and methods. For example, as Martin Shefter observes ("Party and Patronage: Germany, England and Italy" *Politics and Society* 7, no. 4 [1977]: 403–451), southern Italian peasants who migrated to northern Italian cities were recruited by Socialist and, later, Communist parties while their cousins who migrated to American cities became the mainstays of conservative patronage machines. Conversely, individuals with very different social characteristics have been mobilized by the same or similar parties. For example, conservative parties in all the Western democracies have been able to use patriotic and ethnic appeals to recruit large numbers of working-class voters to stand alongside their middle-class compatriots.

Elections and Popular Influence. The evolution and persistence of democratic electoral institutions can substantially alter the relationship between citizens and the *state. In particular, democratic electoral processes can transform the relationship between popular influence and state power. Even in the absence of elections or formal mechanisms for their expression, citizens' wishes almost always have some impact upon governments' conduct. Even the most autocratic regime must, at the very least, concern itself with popular disorder.

In the absence, however, of formal mechanisms for its expression, popular influence tends to be inversely related to governmental power. So long as they command military forces and an administrative apparatus sufficiently powerful to compel popular obedience and deal with threats to their rule, governments can afford a measure of indifference to popular pressure. If, on the other hand, the state's military and administrative institutions are too weak, then those in power are likely to become more concerned with citizens' needs and preferences. The advent of the democratic election, however, meant that even when governments possessed the military and administrative capacity to compel obedience, popular influence was no longer necessarily reduced. Popular influence and state power could coexist.

At the same time that they potentially strengthen popular influence over governments' conduct, elections also serve as important institutions of governance. Elections are among the principal mechanisms through which contemporary states regulate mass political action and strengthen their own power and authority. First, elections socialize political activity. Elections make how, when, where, and which citizens take part in political life a matter of public policy rather than simply a matter of individual choice, transforming what might otherwise consist of sporadic, citizen-initiated acts into a routine public function. This helps to preserve governments' stability by containing and channeling away potentially more dangerous or disruptive forms of political activity. Second, elections can bolster governments' power and authority. The opportunity to participate in elections can help to persuade citizens that the government is responsive to their needs and wishes and can help to persuade citizens to obey, to pay taxes, to accept military service, and so on.

Finally, to the extent that elections take the place of other, more spontaneous forms of popular *political participation, they allow incumbent elites an opportunity to regulate popular intervention into policy-making processes. Thus, those in power often seek, through election laws, to regulate the composition of the electorate in order to diminish the weight of groups they deem to be undesirable. Historically, nearly everywhere electoral laws denied participation on the basis of gender and frequently on racial or ethnic-nationalist grounds. During the nineteenth century, property requirements and weighted voting schemes were employed throughout Europe. In the United States, today, unusually cumbersome registration requirements help to inhibit voting by the poor and uneducated.

Similarly, regimes may undertake to manipulate the translation of voters' choices into electoral outcomes through regulation of the criteria for victory (i.e., the selection of majority, plurality, or proportional voting systems) and through the organization of electoral districts (gerrymandering). In general, majority and plurality voting systems create higher thresholds for legislative representation than do proportional systems; as a result, they are generally preferred by more established forces. In nineteenth century Europe, entrenched conservative parties usually preferred majority and plurality voting systems to reduce the representation of emerging working-class groups. However, as working-class parties gained in strength and threatened to win electoral majorities, conservative groups came to see *proportional representation as a barrier against *socialism. By the same token, many ruling groups have attempted to insulate some institutions and policy-making processes from electoral control by limiting the impact of elections on the composition of the government and administration. The most obvious forms of insulation are the confinement of popular election to only some governmental agencies, various modes of indirect election, and lengthy tenure in office for elected officials.

Democratic elections are a regulated and constrained form of popular intervention into governmental processes. Indeed, often elections are introduced or the suffrage expanded because spontaneous forms of mass political action threaten to have too great an impact on governments' actions. Walter

Lippmann once observed that "new numbers were enfranchised because they had power, and giving them the vote was the least disturbing way of letting them exercise their power" (Clinton Rossiter and James Lare, eds., *The Essential Lippmann,* New York, 1965). Over time, the vote can provide the "least disturbing way" of allowing ordinary people to exercise power because elections can formally delimit mass influence that rulers are unable forcibly to contain.

(See also CITIZENSHIP; DEMOCRACY; ETHNICITY; POLITICAL BUSINESS CYCLE; POLITICAL PARTIES AND PARTY COMPETITION; POLITICAL REALIGNMENT; RELIGION AND POLITICS.)

Angus Campbell, Philip E. Converse, Warren E. Miller, and Donald E. Stokes, *The American Voter* (New York, 1960). Robert A. Dahl, ed., *Political Oppositions in Western Democracies* (New Haven, Conn., 1966). Seymour Martin Lipset and Stein Rokkan, eds., *Party Systems and Voter Alignments: Cross-National Perspectives* (New York, 1967). Benjamin Ginsberg, *The Consequences of Consent* (New York, 1982). Bernard Grofman and Arend Lijphart, eds., *Electoral Laws and Their Political Consequences* (New York, 1986). A. James Reichley, ed., *Elections American Style* (Washington, D.C., 1987).

BENJAMIN GINSBERG

ELITES. The term *political elites* has different uses. Elites are leaders who perform important roles in the governance of society; they make the important decisions or have influence in decisions at the national and local levels of government. There are many types of elites—presidents or prime ministers, parliamentary deputies, judges, administrators, political activists. There are elites who hold no formal position at all: policy specialists, campaign consultants, and political financiers, for example. Elites have been the subject of much writing, from Plato to the present. Many controversies have developed about their characteristics and their functions. Two conflicting positions have been argued: 1) elites do play, and should play, a dominant role in operating political systems, with the public having only a minimal or subordinate role, perhaps only in the periodic election of leaders; 2) elites do share, and should share, power with their publics if they are to survive, be effective and responsive, and if we are to realize the goal of a democratically based political order. Which of these two positions is valid?

In terms of social and economic background, political elites are unrepresentative of the public. For example, over eighty percent of the national elites of the United States and Western *democracies have a university education, compared with twenty percent or less of the adult populations (although higher in the United States). Elites are much more likely to have learned about politics in their families than is true of the public. Because of social class status and family exposure, they have much better chances to enter political careers. Hence there is a social bias in elite selection. However, considerable opportunity exists for those with lesser education and those from working-class families to become active in politics at the local level and to take positions in local government. From forty percent to sixty percent of city elites in Western democracies do not have a university education, and forty percent come from working-class families.

Many paths to political elite status exist. Political parties are important recruiters, as are civic groups, labor unions, and business associations. Such groups are often the channels to political careers. In them elites develop an interest in politics, as well as experience, and undergo a process of screening and grooming for political positions. Each community and each country constitutes a special context, or elite culture, within which this grooming takes place.

Political elites vary greatly in their beliefs. In one study of the national elites of six countries, it was found that twenty-three percent favored extensive governmental control over the economy, nineteen percent favored very minimal control, and the remainder took differing intermediate positions. The values of elites also differ. When these same elites were asked what their value priorities were for the future, thirty-five percent mentioned social justice and equality, thirty percent mentioned economic security or economic welfare, and the remainder had a mixture of responses. Elites are not homogeneous. Indeed, research demonstrates the pluralism of elites and their heterogeneity in social backgrounds, interests, attitudes, and values. There is no unified power elite or ruling class that runs cities or nations in democratic societies.

The study of elites deals with their performance, that is, their impact on policy, on voters, and on change or stability in the system. The new leadership that emerges after elections can, and often will, change the direction of public policy. Thus, elections can have consequences. Similarly, parties, through their activists, can affect election outcomes if they mobilize their vote. New elites can change, even revolutionize, societies in liberal or reactionary directions, as the sweeping changes in Eastern and Central Europe attest.

A major question is, under what conditions can elites be made more responsive to the public? We know that political activism through community groups results in closer linkage of elites' views to public views. We know that the defeat of elites at the polls can produce policy change. We also know, however, that voter turnout is often low (particularly in the United States) and that citizen apathy is high. We also know elites are very entrenched—for example, over ninety percent of incumbent U.S. congressional representatives are regularly victorious in elections. But research has also shown that the possibility of defeat can make leaders more responsive and that electoral competition therefore is crucial. Thus neither the model of elite dominance nor the model of citizen control over elites represents complete reality. Both models are useful. Elites exercise *power, but they are also constrained by the potential, and actual, power of political organizations, public opinion, and mass protests.

(See also POLITICAL PARTICIPATION; POLITICAL PARTIES AND PARTY COMPETITION.)

Joel D. Aberbach, Robert D. Putnam, and Bert A. Rockman, *Bureaucrats and Politicians in Western Democracies* (Cambridge, Mass., 1981). Samuel J. Eldersveld, *Political Elites in Modern Societies: Empirical Research and Democratic Theory* (Ann Arbor, Mich., 1989).

SAMUEL J. ELDERSVELD

EL SALVADOR. With a population approaching 5 million, El Salvador, physically the smallest mainland country in the Western Hemisphere, has the highest population density. Unlike most of Central America it has no African-American population; the few thousand slaves who arrived during the colonial period and the indigenous and European populations intermingled to produce an overwhelmingly mestizo people. This homogeneity, however, has not prevented extreme violence over the course of Salvadorean history.

Socioeconomic-political conditions are rooted in the colonial and early national periods. Lacking natural resources, El Salvador's wealth lay in the rich volcanic soil that supported a monocrop export economy after the conquest. Cacao, which was being cultivated by the Indians when the Spanish arrived in 1524, was followed by indigo and then, in the nineteenth century, coffee. Only after World War II was there some effort to diversify export crops and to industrialize. Still, coffee continued to dominate, accounting for sixty-one percent of exports in the 1980s even as the civil war reduced production eighteen percent between 1980 and 1987. Meanwhile, the value of exports declined twenty-three percent during the decade and the overall standard of living regressed a quarter-century.

The agro-economic pattern led to a growing concentration of land and wealth, a decreasing number of landowners (the "oligarchy"), and the extreme deprivation and political repression of the peasant majority. The oligarchy adopted a laissez-faire economic philosophy and a classical liberal belief in the sanctity of private property and the purpose of government—to maintain order. it created an army, National Guard, and its own private forces to keep a periodically rebellious peasantry in line.

El Salvador became a part of the Central American Federation following independence from Spain in 1821, then an independent republic when the federation collapsed in 1839. All the country's presidents came from the oligarchy until a *coup d'état in December 1931 created a division of labor: the army took control of the state while the oligarchy continued to run the economy. The arrangement, which was punctuated by occasional coups d'état and periodic elections, lasted until October 1979,

when a coup led by young, progressive officers ended this symbiotic relationship.

The military-oligarchic control of the country was increasingly challenged in the 1970s by the Catholic church and five revolutionary organizations. The church, heeding the call of the 1968 Latin American bishops' conference, aggressively began pastoral work among the peasantry and urban poor. The result was a new consciousness among thousands of poor Salvadoreans. The army and death squads responded by torturing, murdering, or "disappearing" hundreds of religious leaders, including Archbishop Oscar Romero. This, in turn, produced growing political radicalization among the affected groups.

The revolutionary organizations, with roots in nineteenth-century peasant uprisings, 1920s labor organizing, and the Salvadorean Community Party, began working among peasants and urban laborers in 1970. Divided over *ideology and strategy for a decade, the five began moving toward unity in 1980 and created the Frente Farabundo Martí para la Liberación Nacional (FMLN) in October. Three months later the FMLN began military operations that, until 1984, threatened to defeat the army. Thereafter, the armed forces' increased air power halted the guerrillas' advances and forced them to alter their strategy. Still, the FMLN expanded their operations from five provinces to all fourteen by 1988.

The October 1979 coup was an effort to derail the revolutionary movement and institute long-overdue socioeconomic reforms. The United States, fearing a second leftist revolution on the heels of *Nicaragua, increased its involvement through a Janus-headed policy: politically, reforms and elections were emphasized; militarily, the Salvadorean armed forces were trained in *counterinsurgency.

In March 1980 an agrarian reform was promulgated, the banks were nationalized, and export sales of coffee, cotton, and sugar were placed under state control. The Reagan administration considered these reforms socialist, but while congressional pressure prevented their rollback, the pace of implementation slowed markedly. The political emphasis shifted to sponsoring elections, which would ostensibly put El Salvador on the road to *democracy and rob the revolutionary movement of any remaining raison d'être.

These elections gave El Salvador a "democratic government" that rarely exhibited the conditions of a functioning democracy: freedom of speech, the media, and party organization; freedom for interest groups; the absence of state-sponsored terror; and the absence of fear and coercion among the population.

Nor was the military subordinated to civilian rule. The most powerful institution in Salvadorean society since 1931, the armed forces was enlarged, enriched, and reinforced by over $2 billion in U.S. military assistance. Indeed, increasing the military and training it to fight guerrillas became the primary focus of U.S. policy.

While the war continued, other developments changed the internal dynamics of El Salvador. One was the emergence of an extreme right-wing political party, the Alianza Republicana Nacionalista (ARENA), in 1981, whose shadowy origins and direct ties to death squads are well documented. Another was unanticipated: the electoral process opened political space that repression had closed in the early 1980s. New grass-roots organizations and existing labor unions began organizing and demanding better wages and working conditions, economic reforms, and peace. Leaders of center-left political parties allied with the FMLN, who had been forced into exile by the repression in 1980, quietly began returning in 1985 and increased their activities in subsequent years. Third, after 1983 the church played a growing role as messenger, mediator, and then leader in the search for peace.

El Salvador's first civilian president in fifty-three years, Christian Democrat José Napoleón Duarte, was elected in 1984 on a platform promising economic reforms and peace negotiations with the FMLN. In 1989, having delivered on neither while presiding over one of the most corrupt governments in Salvadorean history, his party lost to ARENA. The new president, Alfredo Cristiani, promised to seek peace and responded positively to an FMLN initiative to begin peace talks.

After Cristiani's inauguration, however, repression against the unions and other mass organizations escalated. The bombing of the headquarters of El Salvador's largest union federation convinced the FMLN that the government was not serious about negotiations. Two weeks later the FMLN opened a countrywide offensive and brought the war to the capital.

In 1990 government and guerrillas returned to the negotiating table under the aegis of the UN. The main stumbling block was the future of the armed forces, which, the FMLN insisted, had to be significantly reduced and purged of officers implicated in human rights abuses. By late 1991, under extraordinary international pressure, including, finally, the United States, agreements were reached on all issues. The signing of the peace accords in Mexico City on 16 January 1992 and a ceasefire on 1 February ended eleven years of civil war and paved the way for the FMLN to emerge as a legal political party and prepare to compete in the 1994 elections.

(See also GUERRILLA WARFARE; LAND REFORM; RELIGION AND POLITICS; ROMAN CATHOLIC CHURCH; TERRORISM; TORTURE; U.S.–LATIN AMERICAN RELATIONS.)

Tommie Sue Montgomery, *Revolution in El Salvador: Origins and Evolution* (Boulder, Colo., 1982, 1992). Raymond Bonner, *Weakness and Deceit: U.S. Policy and El Salvador* (New York, 1984).

TOMMIE SUE MONTGOMERY

EMPIRE. See IMPERIALISM.

EMPIRES, COLONIAL. See COLONIAL EMPIRES.

ENGLAND. See BRITAIN.

ENGLISH-SPEAKING CARIBBEAN. The English-speaking Caribbean, or the *Commonwealth Caribbean, includes twelve independent countries and six dependent territories. The former are Belize (on the Central American mainland), Antigua and Barbuda, Bahamas, Barbados, Dominica, *Grenada, *Guyana (on the South American mainland), *Jamaica, St. Christopher and Nevis (St. Kitts/Nevis), St. Lucia, St. Vincent and the Grenadines, and *Trinidad and Tobago. The latter are Bermuda, British Virgin Islands, Cayman Islands, Anguilla, Turks and Caicos Islands, and Montserrat. All are past or current British colonies.

Together the English-speaking territories (including the dependent states) have a population of about 5.6 million people. The overall figure, however, covers great variety. Population size ranges from St. Kitts with 43,000 people to Trinidad and Tobago (1.2 million) and Jamaica (2.4 million). All the others have populations below 1 million.

After a period of representative rule based on a limited franchise, these territories became Crown Colonies with nominated or mixed nominated-elected legislatures. Minor reforms were instituted over time, but it was not until social disturbances swept the region in the late 1930s that political parties were allowed and universal suffrage was introduced. The growth of *nationalism and the effects of World War II led to increasing pressures on the British, who proposed a West Indies federation as a prelude to independence. A federation was instituted in 1958, comprising all the countries except Bahamas, Belize, and Guyana, but federal negotiations were bogged down. In particular, major disagreements occurred between Jamaica (the largest country) and Trinidad and Tobago (the wealthiest). In 1962, the two countries pulled out of the federation and became independent.

Barbados sought and gained its independence in 1966. Since the seven smaller islands of the eastern Caribbean were considered too small to go it alone, Britain devised a new constitutional status for them. "Associated statehood" allowed them to be self-governing in all but their external affairs and defense. Eventually, world acceptance of the imperative of *decolonization, even for very small states, facilitated the emergence of the eastern Caribbean states to independence: Grenada in 1974; Dominica in 1978; St. Lucia and St. Vincent in 1979; Antigua and Barbuda in 1981; and St. Kitts/Nevis in 1983. Of the other English-speaking countries, Guyana gained its independence in 1966, and the Bahamas in 1974. Belize's independence was delayed by Guatemala's claim to its territory, but was achieved in 1981 with British *security guarantees.

The English-speaking Caribbean states inherited certain political institutions and norms from *Britain that have given them their reputation for democracy and stability: a two-party system, *parliamentary democracy, *cabinet government, bicameral legislatures, *constitutional monarchy (with the monarchy represented by a governor-general), and general elections every five years. Over time, most of these institutional and constitutional norms have been modified either by design or by chance. Democracy in the region has been highly personalistic: strong leaders have dominated their countries, and most have remained in power for several terms of office. Related to this has been the tendency toward one-party legislative dominance: in almost all these countries (Barbados and Jamaica are notable exceptions), one party has consistently won elections, usually on the strength of the leadership and the capacity of the party to organize and reward the masses.

Despite the English-speaking Caribbean's reputation for stability, various sources of societal and political tensions can be identified. Ethnic tensions exist in Guyana and Trinidad and Tobago between Africans and East Indians. A mix of racial and ideological politics has been even more destabilizing. The rise of a postcolonial generation concerned about neocolonialism and social and economic inequalities was largely responsible for widespread "Black Power" antigovernment disturbances in Trinidad and Tobago in 1970. They established left-wing parties throughout the Caribbean, and effected the rise of Michael Manley's *socialism in Jamaica in the 1970s and the New Jewel movement in Grenada.

The region's record of stability was marred by violence in Jamaica in the 1970s, in Grenada in 1983, and in Trinidad and Tobago in 1990 when a group of Islamic militants, concerned about declining socioeconomic conditions and perceived government insensitivities, attempted to overthrow the government. The governments of Dominica and Barbados were also the objects of aborted mercenary coup attempts in the 1970s. Other sources of regional instability have included: threats of secession from smaller island-partners such as Anguilla (successful), Nevis, Barbuda, Union Island in the Grenadines, and Tobago; and more recent social pressures (including *drug trafficking, smuggling, illegal migration, and *refugee problems).

The countries of the English-speaking Caribbean, with the exception of Guyana, are classified by the *World Bank as middle income (GNP per capita above US$545 in 1988) and high income (US$6,000 and above) countries. They are mainly primary producers: of minerals and fuels (oil in the case of Trinidad and Tobago, bauxite in Jamaica and Guyana); sugar (especially Jamaica, Barbados, Trinidad

and Tobago, Guyana, and St. Kitts); bananas (Dominica, St. Lucia, St. Vincent); cocoa and spices (Grenada); and citrus products (Belize). They are also in varying degrees dependent on tourism. Industry is generally light industry and assembly operations (particularly important in Barbados). Trinidad and Tobago is the only country with major heavy industries (steel, natural gas, ammonia and urea plants, petrochemicals).

Like all primary-product producers, the countries of the English-speaking Caribbean are highly vulnerable to fluctuations in world market prices. This problem is compounded by the small size of their markets. One of the ways that they have tried to overcome the limitations of small market size has been through regional integration. The Caribbean Free Trade Act (Carifta) was initiated in 1968; in 1973 it became the Caribbean Community (Caricom), combining a common market with a level of foreign policy coordination. Regional integration scored initial gains as intraregional trade expanded sharply, but in the 1970s Caricom almost collapsed as a result of quarrels over the unequal distribution of benefits, balance-of-payment problems caused by the increase in oil prices, and ideological polarization between the socialist Caribbean (Jamaica, Guyana, and Grenada) and the more conservative states of the eastern Caribbean. After the U.S. intervention in Grenada, Caricom leaders moved to heal rifts and worked toward deeper integration. With an eye to European integration efforts, Caricom hopes to eliminate all barriers to trade in the early 1990s. Meanwhile, the Organization of Eastern Caribbean States (OECS) has initiated plans for political union.

Because of their geographical proximity to the United States, the Caribbean countries have established close political, economic, and security links with this superpower. The United States is the major trading partner for these nations, although there are strong links to the *European Community through preferential arrangements negotiated by the African-Caribbean-Pacific (ACP) group.

The end of the *Cold War presents these countries with difficulties as their leverage as friends of the United States has been removed. Like other small states, the focus of their global activity remains the UN and (except for St. Vincent and St. Kitts) the *nonaligned movement. They have also recognized the geopolitical ramifications of their proximity to Latin America, and all are members of the hemispheric organization, the *Organization of American States (OAS).

(See also ECONOMIC COMMISSION FOR LATIN AMERICA AND THE CARIBBEAN; LATIN AMERICAN REGIONAL ORGANIZATIONS.)

Commonwealth Secretariat, *Vulnerability: Small States in the Global Society,* Report of a Commonwealth Consultative Group (London, 1985). Jacqueline Braveboy-Wagner,

The Caribbean in World Affairs: The Foreign Policies of the English-Speaking States (Boulder, Colo., 1989).

JACQUELINE ANNE BRAVEBOY-WAGNER

ENTITLEMENTS. Social protections and benefits that a *state owes to is citizens are known as entitlements. In the most general sense, entitlements are akin to social *rights, in which a government promises to ensure its citizens access to various goods and services, such as minimum income, housing, health care, or employment. The notion of entitlements became particularly important in advanced industrial societies, which created *welfare states of varying kinds after World War II.

The use of the term *entitlement* varies across nations. In most Western European nations, entitlement expresses a general political commitment by the state to provide social benefits. In the United States, entitlement has taken on a more specific meaning. Reflecting the importance of legal mechanisms in U.S. policy-making and the absence of a tradition of social rights, entitlements have been enumerated in detail and defined as legal claims in the United States. This way of defining entitlements grew out of the legal movements of the 1960s that sought to define social policy benefits as a form of property. Although the Supreme Court has declined to endorse formally this view of policy, in practice courts have struck down numerous administrative barriers that reduced access to social benefits and have guaranteed clients the right to appeal decisions altering the benefits.

This legal defense of access to social policy benefits has been accompanied by an increasingly detailed description of the components of an entitlement in the United States. The value of itemizing entitlements in this way is debated among theorists of the welfare state. American liberals, who tend to favor this approach, argue that it ensures access to social benefits. Critics, such as the British social theorist Richard Titmuss, charge that the "fragmentation of entitlement" removes needed discretion and deprives beneficiaries of choice (Brian Abel-Smith and Kay Titmuss, eds., *Selected Writings of Richard Titmuss: The Philosophy of Welfare,* London, 1987). At the same time, critics fear that itemizing entitlements creates a ceiling defining the maximum level of benefits.

Entitlements became the subject of considerable contention in U.S. budgetary politics during the 1970s. Because the benefits of entitlement programs must be made available to all who are eligible for them, the costs of these policies are difficult to control. As administrative barriers fell and new programs were established, expenditures for entitlement programs expanded rapidly from 1965 to 1974. When the American economy stagnated in the 1970s, government officials expressed strong concern about the uncontrollable nature of spending for entitlement programs, which comprised nearly half the national budget. In subsequent years, the costs of entitlement programs leveled off as new procedures made it more difficult to enact entitlements and marginal cutbacks reduced existing programs. Nonetheless, entitlement programs remain the central components of American social provision.

During the 1980s, conservatives questioned the very notion of entitlements, arguing that the concept stresses the responsibility of the government but ignores the obligations of citizens. Although such criticisms have not prompted the elimination of entitlements in Western societies, they have in many cases justified the imposition of conditions and reciprocal obligations on the part of beneficiaries.

(See also CITIZENSHIP; CONSERVATISM.)

R. Kent Weaver, "Controlling Entitlements," in John E. Chubb and Paul E. Peterson, eds., *The New Direction in American Politics* (Washington, D.C., 1985), pp. 307–341.

MARGARET WEIR

ENVIRONMENTALISM

As an emerging political platform or *ideology and as the basis for social and political movements, environmentalism is based on a view of humanity as integral to nature, of nature as empowering humans, and of the relationship between both as uneasy at best, and perhaps even threatening to the integrity and viability of nature and hence of humans. In this view, a symbiotic relationship between human beings and nature must be restored, and any such restoration will entail fundamental alterations in human behavior and in the characteristics of social institutions.

The concept of environmentalism has important analytical implications: it calls for an integrated conception of life on earth that addresses the coherence of environmental and social processes. It seeks an explanation of the *interdependence among all elements necessary for life. It addresses the vulnerabilities and susceptibilities of life-sustaining properties as humans press their claims on nature.

At both the conceptual and the programmatic levels, environmentalism affirms the connectedness between the smallest and largest social units. The environmental cliché of the 1990s—"think local, act global"—reflects the unique, integrated domain of environmentalism in its vision of scale and scope.

Among the properties of the "smallest" unit—the individual in a household—environmentalism suggests that human beings are trapped in a fundamental paradox: 1) every implementation of knowledge and skills results in a degradation of resources from a "more usable" to a "less usable" form with consequent production of "wastes"; 2) technology itself requires resources—energy and other materials; the more advanced the knowledge and skills, moreover, the greater the amount and range of energy and other resources required; and 3) the more advanced the technology, the greater the amount and range of resources that people have believed are necessary. Thus, individual patterns of innovation and consumption have profound global consequences.

At the planetary level, environmentalism highlights the following: 1) While the basic biogeochemical characteristics are generally understood, there are major uncertainties about the *feedback effects* on both physical and social processes. 2) Environmental as well as social processes operate along multiple, unequal, and sometimes overlapping *time horizons*. Variability in time increments complicates assessments of the underlying processes, and often blunts policy responses. Fundamentally the long lead times in both social and environmental processes—and the separation of cause and consequences—become major sources of uncertainty. 3) There are crucial *intergenerational* impacts of environmental change whereby future generations incur the environmental costs of the actions of past and present generations. 4) It may well be that some patterns of environmental alterations are *irreversible* and that the underlying causes of these patterns cannot be eliminated—at least not within the frame of historical (as opposed to geological) time. 5) Unevenness in both the sources of environmental disturbances and in the consequences raise critical questions of *equity*. Countries do not contribute equally to the global imbalances, nor are they affected uniformly. Some regions may even benefit from climate alteration. (For example, global warming could alter the Siberian climate, enhancing agricultural prospects.) This unevenness may be a significant constraint in the development of international responses.

These features characterize some crucial uncertainties associated with environmental change, from the individual to the global dimension. Because human activities are incremental in historical time and therefore minuscule in geological time, they confound assessments of complex feedback, time horizon, and differentials in sources and in consequences. Together these factors influence the political issues and the policy responses of the international community, as they serve also to frame conceptions of the complex and shifting terrain of environmentalism.

Environmentalism involves ideas of nature, ecological balances, and ecological growth as central to the survival of the human species. It also stresses how humans influence and alter nature and, in the domain of economics and politics, how this influences social relations, both national and international. Environmentalism is also a political program, an ideology, and a plan of action.

Environmentalism in all senses recognizes that the global climate may well be inexorably altered by human action, and this provides the basis for the emergence of environmentalism as a public policy and a political issue. This approach to environmentalism involves an action-oriented view of humanity-nature interactions intended to improve the relationship or, at a minimum, to limit the damage inflicted on nature by humanity.

A large number of *states have gradually become aware of the environmental consequences of growth and *development. It is fair to say that there has been concurrently both an expansion of awareness and coordination of response as well as a remarkable insensitivity to the full implications of anthropogenic sources of global change. At all levels of development the states of the contemporary *international system also vary extensively regarding perception and policies toward the environment. If there is one trend that can be identified clearly, it is the expansion of environmental concerns and a sharper delineation of the trade-offs between environmental protection, on the one hand, and growth and development, on the other. This trade-off is intimately tied to a new recognition of the tension between the concerted pursuit of national objectives and national *security and the resulting threats to the global environment, thereby generating global insecurities.

Coordinated response among states has evolved through three phases during the postwar period, reflecting different degrees of awareness and different levels of institutionalization of policy response. The first phase began with the establishment of functional international agencies in the postwar period and culminated in the World Environment Conference held in Stockholm in 1972. The second spanned the period from 1972 to the organization of the World Economic Commission (the Brundtland Commission) of 1983. The third phase, beginning with the Brundtland Report to the UN General Assembly that introduced and focused on the concept (and objective) of sustainable development, continued through the 1992 UN Conference on Environment and Development in Rio de Janeiro, the overall results of which proved a disappointment to environmental activists.

In retrospect, the 1972 Stockholm conference was a landmark in the formulation of an international consensus recognizing the protection of the environment as an important objective. Prior to that time international institutions were developed explicitly for the pursuit of political, economic, strategic, and developmental purposes, abstracted from, or exclusive of, the context of the natural environment. The environment-development connection had been made as early as 1971 in the preparatory meetings held at Fournex, Switzerland. Consensus on the interconnection facilitated the eventual formation of the UN Environment Program (UNEP), the major institutional outcome of the Stockholm conference.

At Stockholm the international community set in place the "Institutional and Financial Arrangements for International Environmental Cooperation" to facilitate implementation of the Action Plan on the environment, which led to the creation of UNEP. In the course of this process the UN General Assembly identified four institutional mechanisms for the protection of the environment: a governing council composed of fifty-eight states elected by the General Assembly; a secretariat; an environment fund; and an environment coordination board. By this concerted action, the General Assembly established precedents for the management of the natural environment, legitimizing the principle and providing the attendant institutional requirements.

The Action Plan from the Stockholm conference focused on functions, the specific activities deemed necessary for interventions in environmental assessment, management, and supporting measures. The management function—treaties, norm formulation, policies, guidelines, recommended practices, etc.—addressed changes in state behavior directly. Non-binding in character, nonetheless these management functions were considered at the time as being instrumental in the articulation of new norms. In this process nongovernmental organizations (NGOs) played an increasingly important role. The NGOs, as later became apparent, assumed a stronger, even determinative, role in subsequent decades. The Protocol for the Protection of the Ozone Layer, concluded fifteen years later, owed much of its existence to the persistence and pressures of the NGOs—research institutions, scientific organizations, public policy groups, etc.

The first effective result of the Stockholm conference was the establishment of the Mediterranean Action Plan (1975) through the aegis of UNEP, signed by all countries bordering on the Mediterranean. The Med Plan, as it became known, is significant for the following reasons: it was the first instance in which collaboration on environmental factors transcended conflicts on political objectives. Despite the fact that several of the Mediterranean countries were (and continue to be) in conflict with each other, engaged in overt hostilities, or otherwise involved in diplomatic disputes, consensus was reached on management of the Mediterranean.

Enhanced awareness of the global nature of human impacts on the environment is due largely to the accumulation of scientific evidence. Despite acknowledged uncertainty, disagreements in the scientific community, and conflicts among scientific disciplines in interpretation and assessment of evidence, the fact remains that the international community has become more sensitive, more aware, and more concerned. None of this, however, translates yet into international and effective policies for environmental protection. Scientific evidence regarding risk to the stratospheric ozone due to human action (initially thought to be as a result of supersonic transport; more recently recognized as the outcome of manufactured chemicals, the chlorofluorocarbons) and assessments of potential consequences of doubling atmospheric carbon dioxide were crucial factors shaping the evolution of a global consensus.

The notion of development itself has undergone considerable change—from an earlier definition centering on growth, to a greater emphasis on welfare and distribution, to a concern for the empowerment of developing countries as agents of their own development. The World Economic Commission, established in 1983 and designed to explore the environment-development linkages, resulted in the Brundtland Report of 1987. By introducing and identifying the concept of "sustainable development," the report placed human activities in the context of the natural and social environment. It conceived of sustainable development as the management of necessary change while preventing excessive erosion of the environment and of its life-sustaining properties for future generations. In this conception the interdependence of humans and nature was formally acknowledged by the international community.

Despite the principles established and legitimized internationally by the UN General Assembly, two new obstacles to a full international consensus developed: difficulty in reaching agreement on the operational *definition* of sustainable development; and difficulty in agreement among nations, at various levels of development, regarding the national *priority* to be accorded to sustainable development. Both obstacles reflected the increasing salience of environmental issues and the extent that they are becoming perceived as *political*—affecting who *gets* what, when, how, and who *does* what, when, how.

The evolution of environmental problem-solving may be construed as a process of learning. International decision-makers have gradually come to accept a broader, interdependent, symbiotic, and holistic conception of the environmental system for their pollution control efforts and have adapted their policies accordingly. Still, most arrangements remained remedial rather than preventive, e.g., coordinating policies to regulate emissions rather than addressing the underlying conditions which give rise to emissions.

The full implications of these broad developments can best be seen in the changing characteristics of international agreement over the past decades. Over 140 multilateral environmental treaties have been concluded on environmental matters. In this process precedents were being set in place to shape a new treaty-making process. The establishment of framework agreements has provided the basis for consensus on more specific and more binding efforts. Binding agreements are now in place with respect to marine pollution, acid rain, the UNEP regional seas program, and, of course, on the ozone layer. This type of treaty making is quite different from formal agreements in other areas salient to the international community, such as *arms control, where great attention to detail defines the general approach from the outset. This mode of treaty making also creates political constituency. It is more flexible and allows for convergence on more effective results. Equally important is the fact that it enables accomplishment of two contradictory goals: reaffirmation of sovereign rights and reaffirmation of international constraints on national activities.

The entire UN system has begun to accommodate the new demands of environmental politics. Most organizations have developed new programs to cope with the organizational needs of most of these issues. Many of the interlinking elements of these issues have been partially met by UNEP, which was created with a "catalytic" mission to spur and coordinate action on specific issues elsewhere in the UN system. Since its inception in 1973, UNEP has expanded its focus to incorporate the activities of NGOs as well.

There is evidence that the conventional international institutions are beginning to develop more specific policy responses. For example, a growing appreciation of the interlinks between the environmental domain and the domain of economic development has emerged in the World Bank. Published in September 1989, "World Bank Support for the Environment: A Progress Report" outlined a broadened environmental strategy intended to "blur the lines between environmental activities and the rest of the Bank's work—to make them one." In 1989, thirty-eight percent of World Bank loans included an "environmental element." Whether this directive in fact has a significant impact remains to be seen. It is noteworthy that the 1992 issue of *World Development Report* focused on environment and development.

The importance of science to policy responses in the area of global warming is compelling. The political and economic costs of international responses are much greater than for other issues, and there is little technical consensus—but the stakes are much higher. The issue is already politicized—news of climate change appears in the press nearly every day—and it is nearly impossible to separate scientific from political discussions. International negotiation toward accord on the global environment is a complex and ongoing process; however, the international community has made considerable progress in framing a set of accords for managing the global environment. At the UN Conference on Environment and Development in Rio de Janeiro in June 1992, the international community reached a set of agreements on principles as well as practices designed to shape future modes of global environmental management: the Rio Declaration on Environment and Development; Agenda 21; the UN Framework Convention on Climate Change; the Convention on Biological Biodiversity; and a Statement of Principles on the Management, Conservation and Sustainable Development of All Types of Forests. These accords are likely to affect global policy and international institutions as well as both national and regional policy. In addition, corporate strategy and policy worldwide are expected to be affected as global accords evolve.

Just as the UN Charter of 1945 put in place the basic principles governing international relations following a cataclysmic war, so, too, the events of 1992 have begun to set in place new principles for environmental management. Implicit in the 1992 accords are new premises and procedures for a global order based on enhanced environmental responsibility at all levels. The fiftieth anniversary of the UN Charter in 1995 may emerge as the occasion for additions and expansions of the charter to take account of new principles for management of the global environment.

As the twenty-first century approaches, there is evidence of diffusion of power concerning environmental policy away from the state. Although the state remains the legitimate source of authority, its behavior is increasingly influenced and constrained by cross-boundary, transnational forces. There is also a substantive change toward more comprehensive efforts at regulating and managing the environment, possibly reflecting a deeper recognition of environmental interdependence and a nascent willingness to subordinate *sovereignty, to some extent, and other autonomous national concerns to such ends. Finally, at both the national and the global levels there is an emergent awareness of the dilemma that actions considered normal and legitimate, in both ends and means, could be detrimental to the environment or have environmentally threatening consequences. Action, to some extent, is increasingly being scrutinized for the implicit environmental costs.

There is an emerging constituency for global environmental protection at the international level. Some elements are located in the state; others transcend territorial boundaries; still others have supranational status. With respect to legal responses, increasingly it appears that new techniques of *international law are being codified. Foremost among these developments is the fact that broad conventions appear to be giving rise to more precise protocols. And future generations are recognized as bearing legitimate interests as issues of intergenerational equity begin to assume formal legal significance.

Despite these positive signs of institutionalized commitments and responses to environmental issues, these developments also spawn new complications. There are major differences in the imperatives or priorities of environmental decision-making and governance at the national, international, and global levels. At the national level two procedural considerations regarding policy making must be set in place to begin responding to the challenges posed by environmental changes. First, domestic ecological conditions must be explicitly incorporated in the decision-making process. In other words, economic, strategic, and other policies may no longer be pursued without taking into account cross-border and global environmental ramifications. Second, external environmental impacts of national actions must be introduced as a constraint on national decision-making. In other words, states must alter their priorities, ceasing to behave as if they were truly sovereign, rather than highly interdependent, both ecologically and organizationally.

From the perspective of *international relations, the problem is that management of national environmental adjustments may entail generating dislocating effects or creating costs that must be borne by others. When states are confronted with resource scarcity and pressure for making resource allocation decisions, sometimes the use of *force is resorted to in order to constrain domestic demand and limit political dissent. In cases where resource bases and environmental conditions are allowed to deteriorate further, countries may respond in ways that could adversely affect not only the internal population/resource balances but also relations with neighbors and with the international community. Furthermore the action of *international organizations often influences the range of acceptable policies domestically. For example, involvement with the International Monetary Fund on the debt issue generally entails explicit demands for state policy changes.

On the global level there is a need for an identification of underlying principles for guiding the international community's strategies for the management of environmental issues. These principles are: 1) *legitimacy*—intervention strategies must be viewed as legitimate by all actors; 2) *equity*—interventions must be fair, appropriate, and equitable; 3) *volition*—policy must be adopted through noncoercive procedures predicated on voluntary measures, not coercive ones; 4) *universality*—coverage must be global in scope, encompassing all sovereign states; and 5) *efficacy*—implementation must be effective (bearing results) and not necessarily efficient (in economic terms). Significant violations of any one or more of these will undoubtedly undermine the effectiveness of evolving global environmental management strategies. In the last analysis, it will be politics rather than principles alone that will shape effective action. However, to the extent that the above shared principles prevail, the evolution of effective political interactions, bargaining, and negotiations will be facilitated.

(See also GREEN PARTIES; TREATY; UNITED NATIONS.)

Kenneth J. Arrow and A. C. Fisher, "Environmental Preservation, Uncertainty, and Irreversibility" *Quarterly Journal of Economics* 88 (1974): 312–19. World Commission on Environment and Development, *Our Common Future* (Oxford, 1987). Norman L. Rosenburg et al., eds., *Greenhouse Warming: Abatement and Adaptation* (Washington, D.C., 1989). Jeremy Warford and Zeinab Partow, "Evolution of the World Bank's Environmental Policy" *Finance and Development* 26, no. 4 (December 1989): 6. Edith Brown Weiss, *In Fairness to Future Generations* (New York, 1990). Nazli Choucri, "Population and the Global Environment," in Jefferson W. Tester, David O. Wood, and Nancy A. Ferrari, eds., *Energy and the Environment in the 21st Century* (Cambridge, Mass., 1991). Peter Haas with Jan Sundgren, "Evolving International Environmental Law," in Nazli Choucri, ed., *Global Accord: Environmental Challenges and International Responses* (Cambridge, Mass., 1993). Nazli Choucri, ed., *Global Accord: Environmental Challenges and International Responses* (Cambridge, Mass., 1993).

NAZLI CHOUCRI

EQUALITY AND INEQUALITY

The politics of the world today are beset by tensions arising from inequality. Whether it be within a country or between countries or both, the privileges and valuables enjoyed by some have provoked conflicts, violent or nonviolent, with those who are, or who feel themselves to be, less favored. These privileges and valuables—which may relate to prestige, respect, power, or wealth and income—are often distributed according to race, gender, religion, or culture. In 1990, inequality was cited as a basis for conflicts in nations as diverse as South Africa, the Soviet Union, the United States, and India. Unequal women's rights were of particular political concern in Africa and the Muslim world. Unequal income among countries is a major source of global tensions. Inequality is especially important for understanding the ferment in the Middle East where the oil wealth of some, coupled with state-sanctioned racial and religious privileges, saturate the popular outlook, providing the ever-present foundation for political and violent struggle.

Indeed, inequality, actual or perceived, is, throughout the world, the greatest motivating force in politics. The emphasis here is on *inequality* rather than *equality* simply because equality, literally, is not to be found outside of the world of mathematics. It means identity. When people cry out for equality, they are actually demanding equality with respect to some particular thing or things. They may not express their demands in terms of "equality." They merely demand *more,* or they may seek legislative or administrative action that they believe will give them more, of something they desire, whether it be an economic or a psychic good. But most of the time they have their eyes on how others in their reference group, or in other categories not far removed in status or monetary income, are faring. It is relative rather than absolute equality that they are seeking.

No doubt this proposition about inequality could be contested. It might be claimed that persons, above all, seek power, whether it be the *power accruing to a ruler or "power to the people." But they generally desire power either to gain more than they have (perhaps material things, perhaps recognition) or to preserve what they already possess. It is some perceived equality or inequality that they wish to maintain or obtain.

True, this is not always the case. People may seek "more" of something not to attain equality, either generally or with regard to those who have more of that commodity than they do, but because they enjoy excelling, being, if possible, "number one." In short, it is superiority (a special kind of inequality), rather than equality, that they are striving for.

Another possible claimant for priority as a political motivating force is liberty. After all, it was the modern demand for liberty (the overthrow of existing authorities) that, in succeeding, led to relatively greater equality, especially of political power—and this process is ongoing. Those who demand more money claim that without it they are deprived of effective liberty (to supply their needs and satisfy their desires). But in every society some have more effective liberty than others, and this inequality is a major source of discontent that finds expression in politics.

None of this constitutes proof of the proposition that either resentment of inequality or the desire to attain it is the primary motivating force in the world of politics. That statement is not capable of proof or disproof. But it seems beyond rational doubt that it is one of the small number of candidates to be the mainspring of politics. Whether it be the world of *states, a state of tribes, racial or ethnic groups, or indeed any group, even the family, questions of sharing (whether of power, rank, prestige, income, wealth, welfare, well-being, or whatever) are bound to arise—sharing in what proportions and in proportion to what? The examination of the agenda of almost any legislative body will give abundant support to this proposition.

It is not that all of us are out to maximize only our own personal goods. Many seek and pursue a common good and the good of others; probably most of us do so much of the time, especially when our own good is not too much endangered; but, in a world of scarcity, even a society of altruists would be divided over the relative priority to be given to various goods and over who were the most deserving. In any case, that is a problem more remote than need be considered here.

The demand to minimize inequality seems to have been on the rise for a long while. Alexis de Tocqueville, over a century and a half ago (in his monumental *Democracy in America* [New York, 1945], vol. 1, p. 6), declared that "the gradual development of the principle of equality is a providential fact. It has all the chief characteristics of such a fact. It is universal, it is lasting, it constantly eludes all human interference, and all events as well as all men contribute to its progress." As monarchies, dictatorships, even oligarchies gradually are replaced by some form of government that is at least struggling to become democratic, we have all become aware of Tocqueville's prescience. The movement toward democracy and the advance of the principle of equality in other aspects of social life have not been without setbacks, nor will they be in the future. These may be severe and far from brief, but the overall direction of change seems undeniable. Even dictatorial regimes claim to be essentially democratic, and they do indeed partake of some of the characteristics of *democracy. In general, the responsiveness of government to the views of citizens increases unabated. Slavery has been virtually abolished. *Apartheid is slowly dying. Greater equality in political rights and economic conditions flow from these developments.

This trend toward greater equality is by no means confined to the spread of political democracy; it appears to characterize all hierarchical structures, public or private—even the military, although probably least evident there. The flattening of social pyramids is observable in all walks of life. What has become of the family patriarch? Committee chairpersons no longer enjoy the predominant position once occupied by chairmen. The same tendency, in varying degrees and by no means universally, is observable in business organizations. Where the spread of equality began, whether in the social or the political realm, is of no consequence, for, in the United States especially, it has become so ingrained in society generally that it is bound to be reflected in politics more narrowly defined. In some parts of the world it may take centuries for this episodic movement, enduring many reversals, to reach a stage comparable to that of the industrial democracies.

As "natural law" tended to be superseded by "natural rights," and the latter in turn by "*human rights" (rights that are the same and equal for all persons), the individual gained in stature and in dignity. "Subjects" became "citizens," and citizens had rights that must be respected. The crumbling of dictatorial power in the Soviet Union and other communist regimes owes much to their adherence to the *Helsinki Accords. This clarion call for human rights and, even more importantly, this authorization to monitor nations with respect to their observance of these rights provided *legitimacy for demands that could previously be ignored.

The concept of *rights, although unknown to the ancient world, is far from new. What is at least modern is the contention that, with respect to many of the most critical rights, all persons are equal. This proposition is enunciated in the Universal Declaration of Human Rights, and the implementation of these rights is reduced to *treaty form in a series of covenants of various rights subscribed to by most of the nations of the world. Equality of the races and of the sexes have become continuing battlegrounds. "Equality" is today a "virtue word." Like "justice" or "love," no one is against it; but people may mean different things by it.

It is not only individuals who assert equal rights, a fact that leads to problems. From the early days of *international law, at least from the time of *Grotius, sovereign states have been held to possess equal rights, a claim that leads to difficulties. The *League of Nations foundered on the obvious issue:

should the tiniest legally independent principality, such as Monaco, have a vote of equal weight to those of states hundreds of times larger, more populous, more powerful, and wealthier than it? The unsupportable nature of this claim was recognized, in a rough sort of way, when the UN was brought into being. The Security Council of the UN, its only organ that can make legally binding decisions, is composed of but a handful of its total membership. This might not be incompatible with the equality principle if all members of the council were elected in a way that provided equal power to each of the member states; but this is not the case. A small number (five) of the council members are "permanent." They cannot be replaced, nor is provision made for adding to their number. Moreover, the permanent and nonpermanent members are not created equal: each of the permanent members has an absolute veto over all substantive actions of the council.

In yet another way the UN charter runs into difficulties with the equality principle. How does it accord with the rights of individuals? If the vote of a state of 10 million is to count the same as that of a country with a population of 200 million, what becomes of the equal rights of citizens? Here it would appear that the ideas of the equality of humankind and that of states are in head-on conflict. The U.S. Constitution, in the case of the Senate, provides an example of the same problem, rendered less serious in a unit as politically homogeneous as is the United States as compared with the UN.

The case of *international organizations only casts in larger form a more fundamental problem that theories of human equality have always encountered. It is simply this: given that human beings cannot be identical, in what respects can they be equal? Even when it is a single element, such as income or wealth, serious difficulties arise, as has been noted above. When it comes to the ethical validity of competing claims, the problem becomes much more difficult. Aristotle cast it in terms of "numerical" versus "proportionate" equality. If, for instance, it is income that is in question, numerical equality would be achieved if every person or household received exactly the same amount. Proportionate equality would mean that income would be distributed in proportion to merit. But what is merit? Need, capability, work, production, ability to do what the public is willing to pay for (as in the cases of football players and film stars)? The list is long and the problem of selection is daunting. The difficulty is further complicated if we ask the question, What should count as income? Money only, or psychic income, or all that contributes to happiness? Further, should the comparison be made at a given point in time, or longitudinally, looking at the experience of a person through his or her lifetime? And what about generational equity? How much should youth be taxed for the benefit of the elderly?

It is easy to see why Aristotle concluded that the "passion for equality" is "at the root of sedition"; and why we are considering the proposition originally enunciated.

It is also apparent that the quarrels over absolute equality and relative equality challenge Tocqueville's thesis regarding the onward march of equality, as though it were a simple, unambiguous goal. No society is truly egalitarian. *Elites are omnipresent; but in many countries elites have changed in three important respects: degree of power, privilege, or status; unity; and continuity. For instance, the British elite today (whether measured in terms of political power, economic domination, or social *class) by no means has influence comparable to its eighteenth-century counterpart. This, in no small measure, reflects the decline of deference, itself the effect of numerous factors, such as the growth of the bourgeoisie at the expense of the landed aristocracy, the development of the professional and skilled classes, and the enlarged electorate following electoral reforms. Japan stands out as a country in which an elite has maintained a dominant position for a long time, in spite of striking technological development; but even there signs of its declining power are evident. The significance of elites also depends greatly upon their unity. The power of an elite united by common interests and life-style is likely to be much greater than that of one that is highly dispersed among such elements as big business, scientists, the military, union leaders, and so on. Finally, what about continuity? To what extent are elites able to pass along their privileges to their descendants? It is notable that in highly industrialized countries mobility is much greater than in societies where agriculture predominates: a fact that interferes with the continuity of elites.

Another pertinent aspect of inequality is its distribution. The importance of a large middle class as a protection against *revolution has long been recognized. In a healthy society the inequalities, whether of political or of economic power, pose much less of a threat to stability if they are virtually continuous from the lowest to the highest category and if the gap between rich and poor, between powerful and powerless, is mediated by a large and easily permeable middle class. The very fact that "middle class" is today so much more difficult to define and identify than was the "bourgeoisie" even in Marx's day, is testimony to its diversity, its lack of homogeneity. While this feature makes for difficulty in obtaining consensus, by the same token it blurs the distinction between elites and masses, with its threat of either exploitation or revolution. Those at the bottom can see the possibility of step-by-step improvement, especially for their children.

If to economic differences one adds ethnic, linguistic, racial, or gender inequalities, the case obviously becomes much more complicated. Just how complicated and resistant to broad generalization the matter can be is illustrated by the Canadian case. In Quebec, the French-speaking population a decade or so ago was economically less well-off than the English-speaking minority and, rightly or wrongly, perceived themselves to be discriminated against. A strong separatist movement developed, although it did not succeed and the threat of secession subsided. Today, however, in spite of the fact that many of the more well-to-do English-speaking people have left the province and many of the French-speaking ones enjoy an improved position both economically and socially, the move for separation has once more become a federation-threatening force. In this case, at least, it appears that economic differentials, while not insignificant, are not necessarily determinant. Matters of culture, including a common language, and of race (especially exemplified in the United States) may be even more important than economic inequalities. And, even without regard to their relative importance, inequalities are cumulative in their effect. One person's grievance about unequal treatment arising out of cultural differences may combine with another person's grievance attributable to economic inequality, contributing cumulatively to discontent.

We have spoken of a trend toward equality, then shown how that leads to a discussion of kinds of equality, especially numerical and proportionate, which, as some would see it, is really a matter of equality versus inequality, and thence have been led to consideration of related political issues. Now let us turn to another aspect of the problem, one that is introduced by the concept of equality of opportunity. It will become apparent that it, too, leads directly to many of the central issues of politics and of public policy.

"Equality of opportunity" is easily seized upon as a phrase well designed to capture at once the virtues of equality and of liberty. Liberty without opportunity would come close to being a contradiction in terms, and equality without opportunity sounds like the equality of slaves or prisoners. It might be said that the phrase marries equality and liberty; but divorce, as will appear, is by no means impossible. The importance of this concept and its value are great, but so are its pitfalls. How to provide all with equal opportunities? If it is taken to mean only that no laws shall bar anyone from pursuing legitimate goals to the best of her or his abilities, few would disagree. But also few would find it sufficient. What about bars imposed by lack of education, prejudice, inadequate home background? What, indeed, about differences in income as effective limits to the exercise of liberty? Some would go further and say, What about genetic handicaps, mental or physical? Many steps have already been taken in the United States and elsewhere along the lines that these remarks suggest. For instance, in the United States conditions largely associated with race are addressed by such programs as Head Start, Upward Bound,

and affirmative action. The latter in particular, especially when it leads to the requirement of racial quotas, has led to serious political dispute.

Pushed to its logical conclusion, the concept of equality of opportunity would seem to demand the prohibition of all bars to the freedom of migration from country to country, the abolition of inheritance and, indeed, of the family itself. Probably few would wish to go that far even if (improbably) all this could be done without drastically reducing the standard of living. An even greater problem: at what point must opportunities be equal? Throughout life? Even these few lines are probably enough to demonstrate that the ideal of equality of opportunity, splendid starting point for discussion as it may be, is no more than a beginning. Even the brief analysis above shows how it leads, step by step, to virtual equality of condition, something that could not be attained or maintained without great intrusions on liberty. Hence the "divorce" referred to above of liberty from equality. Indeed, this tension between equality and liberty largely accounts for the fact that quarrels over the ideal of equality comprise the mainspring of politics and the source of the major dilemmas of public policy, as neoconservatives insist on the priority of individual liberty and U.S. liberals and European social democrats press for greater equality.

The subject of equality of opportunity does, however, invite consideration of another topic that is both virtually endless and yet too relevant to our topic to be avoided: the market. Communist societies worldwide, which sought to minimize unjust inequalities by instituting state control of both production and distribution, were driven to attempt to move to a market system. They discovered that in practice state control did not eliminate great economic inequalities, did produce great political inequality (at the expense of liberty), and vastly decreased total production; but the postcommunist societies that have emerged are finding the transition extremely difficult.

Use of a market system, giving individual liberty priority over equality in the distribution of both capital goods and consumer goods, both in theory and practice, has a strong claim to being more efficient than central *planning and control. It increases the size of the pie that is to be distributed, so that it is possible for the economically worst off to be better off than they would be under a more egalitarian system that suffers from greater scarcity. This advantage may be more assured if appropriate steps are taken to place a floor under impoverishment. Without the latter, the market system leads to gross economic inequalities, which in turn may translate into political inequalities. Both of these are widely seen as unjust; when they become intolerably so, they are answered by governmental regulations of the market or by systems that are mixtures of private and public enterprise, "mixed economies."

Moreover, relying as it must upon competition, upon individual self-interest, the market tends to encourage greed and exploitation, and to discourage the social aspect of human nature, altruism, and fellow-feeling, which it is the aim of *socialism and *communism to encourage, and on which to an important degree the political stability of all modern states depends. Here again regulatory measures are called for.

Can the market system be so modified and regulated as to escape the worst of its bad tendencies? Most of the nations of the world, especially those that are substantially industrialized, are constantly wrestling with this problem. It is not one to which a single solution is likely to be found.

The second, related question has to do with human nature. Is it fixed or can it be altered? If the latter, how and how much? Can human self-interest be so qualified as to make human sympathy, altruism, fellow-feeling, or commitment to certain ideas of justice prevail to the extent that what might be a golden mean, an optimum mixture of free markets and political controls (the latter including redistributive taxation), would cease to be so, even though other relevant conditions remained the same? The record of past and present strongly suggests that human nature is ambivalent between self-seeking and benevolence, and, within certain limits, is likely to remain so for the foreseeable future, even despite heroic attempts to produce radical change.

By no means are all of the inequalities that prevail under a market system attributable to the market, however. The evidence seems conclusive that the largest part of inequalities arises out of family background; whether by nature, nurture, genes, training, or example, personal success is largely determined during the first five years of life. By this time one's mental and physical abilities, energy level, propensity to save, and other important factors have already been firmly implanted, subject in most cases to only relatively minor modification, as has been well documented by Sir Henry Phelps Brown in *The Inequality of Pay* (London, 1977).

Are we then condemned to remain in a vicious circle, with underclass breeding underclass? Such a grim outlook is not justified, for two reasons. First, even minor modifications in distribution through regulation and public policy initiatives can be pyramided in succeeding generations and, in time, result in not insignificant improvements in equality of opportunity. Second, the evidence refutes the notion that the underclass syndrome is ironclad. If it were, we would have a caste system, whereas in reality we have quite considerable class mobility, a fact that we owe in important degree to the phenomenon of genetic combinations and permutations, as well as to pure luck after birth. These factors can and should be supplemented by improved schooling, especially in the early years, directed precisely toward overcoming the handicaps produced by an inferior home

environment. This would be costly, involving a large amount of one-on-one instruction, and progress would be painfully slow, but it would eventuate in a more productive society, even paying for itself financially in the long run.

As for the international scene, I must venture into a more speculative realm. By now we are all familiar with the term *multinational*. IBM is a prime example; it operates worldwide, but it is a U.S. firm. What, though, of Visa International, which, Alvin Toffler tells us (*PowerShift*, New York, 1990), "is owned by 21,000 financial institutions in 187 countries and territories," while "its governing board and regional boards are set up to prevent any one nation having 51 percent of the votes" (p. 460). The significance of this development for present purposes is that the nation-state is thereby weakened as an independent entity. Power is dispersed. *Imperialism and neocolonialism are upstaged. If guerrillas or even hostile nations threaten such entities, to whom will they turn for help? Possibly to an enlarged and renamed UN, where it is no longer one-nation, one-vote, but where such entities as a truly *World Bank unite with other global entities to share power on an equal footing.

The world of two great superpowers may never be repeated. Change, perhaps ever more rapid, will certainly continue. It will be accompanied by turmoil and probably by violence. One can envisage a world in which Europe, America (the Western Hemisphere?), and Asia (Africa?), along with such transnational entities as those suggested above, are the players: even one in which the players operate on less unequal terms than they do today and whose constituents likewise share power more equally than is now the case. But by this point we surely have moved at least into the twenty-second century, and must recognize that a starkly different scenario might be quite possible—equally possible?

(See also CITIZENSHIP; CONSERVATISM; ETHNICITY; GENDER AND POLITICS; LIBERALISM; MODERNITY; RACE AND RACISM; SOCIAL MOBILITY; UNITED NATIONS; WELFARE STATE.)

R. H. Tawney, *Equality* (New York, 1931). J. Roland Pennock and John W. Chapman, eds., NOMOS IX, *Equality* (New York, 1967). J. Roland Pennock, *Democratic Political Theory*, chap. 1 (Princeton, N.J., 1979). Amy Gutmann, *Liberal Democracy* (Cambridge, U.K., 1980). Douglas Rae et al., *Equalities* (Cambridge, Mass., 1981). Giovanni Sartori, *The Theory of Democracy Revisited*, chap. 12 (Chatham, N.J., 1987). Lloyd L. Weinreb, *National Law and Justice* (Cambridge, Mass., 1987). Ian Shapiro and Grant Reeher, eds., *Power, Inequality, and Democratic Politics* (Boulder, Colo., and London, 1988). J. Roland Pennock, "Normative Political Theory," in *Annual Review of Political Science*, vol. 3, ed. Samuel Long (Norwood, N.J., 1990). Peter Weston, *Speaking of Equality* (Princeton, N.J., 1990).

J. ROLAND PENNOCK

EQUAL RIGHTS AMENDMENT. In 1923, three years after women won the suffrage in the United

States, the first Equal Rights Amendment (ERA) to the Constitution of the United States was introduced in the U.S. *Congress. Its primary proponents were the professional and upper-middle-class suffragist militants of the National Women's Party. The amendment was opposed by "social feminists," Progressives, and union leaders, who, in the absence of a strong labor movement in the United States, were trying to institute protections for at least women workers—special protections that would have had to be dropped or extended to men by an ERA's requirement of formal equality.

By the 1960s, a number of professional associations and both political parties supported the ERA; however, Democratic President John *Kennedy's Commission on the Status of Women concluded that such a "constitutional amendment need not now be sought." One year later, opponents of the Civil Rights Act added "sex" as a protected category to the proposed act, hoping to induce some representatives to vote against it. But the act passed as amended. By 1970, the federal Equal Employment Opportunity Commission had interpreted the 1964 act to forbid precisely the special protections for women (in most cases extending the protections to men) that had made the unions oppose the ERA.

In 1970, therefore, the Pittsburgh chapter of the newly formed National Organization for Women (NOW) took direct action to promote the ERA, which NOW had given first place on its Bill of Rights for Women. After two years of controversy, the ERA passed the House of Representatives with a vote of 354 to 23, and the Senate with a vote of 84 to 8. The amendment's substantive clause read: "Equality of rights under the law shall not be denied or abridged by the United States or by any State on account of sex."

The ERA then went immediately to the states, Hawaii ratifying on 22 March 1972, the day the Senate passed the amendment. Twenty-nine more states ratified in 1972 and early 1973, the earliest with unanimous or nearly unanimous votes. By 1973, however, the opposition had begun to organize, led by Phyllis Schlafly, a maverick from the right wing of the Republican Party. A skilled political entrepreneur, Schlafly tied the ERA to homemakers' fears of the changes entailed by the growing number of women in the paid labor force, the increasing number of divorces, and other larger social changes that had emerged along with the growing women's liberation movement in the United States. She tied the ERA as well to conservative and mainstream legislators' anger at the *Supreme Court's liberal decisions, and to state legislators' fears of losing control over most issues regarding women, which the U.S. federal system allocates primarily to the states. Five more states ratified in 1974, 1975, and 1977. None ratified after 1977 despite the triumph of ERA proponents in 1978 in getting Congress to extend the original 1979 deadline to 1982. On 30 June, the final deadline for ratifying the ERA passed, with only thirty-five of the required thirty-eight states having ratified.

In *public opinion polls, a majority of the U.S. public (fifty-seven percent in the "average" survey) always supported the ERA. Men were as likely to support it as women, the working class as likely as the middle class, blacks somewhat more than whites, and Catholics somewhat more than Protestants. Fundamentalists, frequent churchgoers, parents with large families, older people, and rural residents tended to oppose the amendment. The amendment lost because it came to be linked with abortion (the Supreme Court decision of *Roe v. Wade had legalized abortion in 1973), could be portrayed as dividing women (homemakers versus women in the paid labor force), its proponents failed to meet objections that the amendment would force changes that most Americans disapproved (e.g., drafting women for combat in the armed forces), it stopped being a nonpartisan issue (the right wing having come to power in the Republican Party with the candidacy of Ronald Reagan, and withdrawn the ERA from its platform), and it had to be ratified by states with fewer than fifteen percent women legislators (in the unratified states seventy-nine percent of the women legislators but only thirty-nine percent of the men favored the amendment).

Although feminists criticized it for detracting from other causes, in the long run the struggle for the ERA helped build the prestige and budget of NOW (the budget rose from $700,000 in 1977 to $8.5 million in 1982), making the organization the strongest independent feminist organization in the world and putting it in a position to demand successfully that the Democratic Party run a woman for vice president of the United States in the 1986 election. The ERA struggle also helped build the feminist movement in the United States to the point at which by 1989 one out of three women in the United States was reporting to poll takers that she considered herself a "feminist"—about the same percentage as considered themselves Democrats or Republicans.

Argentina (1853) and Iran (1907) were the first countries to guarantee in their constitutions equality for "all inhabitants," including women. After 1945, when the UN Charter affirmed the "equal rights of men and women," many of the world's nations adopted similar clauses in their constitutions. In 1982, the Charter of Rights in Canada's new constitution guaranteed "the right to the equal protection and equal benefit of the law without discrimination and, in particular, without discrimination based on . . . sex," generating litigation under that clause that has greatly extended women's rights. The impact of each of these constitutional clauses, including the "equal protection" clause of the U.S.

constitution, which now governs legislation affecting women in the absence of an ERA, must be judged by the policy decisions reached under it.

(See also FEDERALISM; FEMINISM; FEMINIZATION OF POVERTY; GENDER AND POLITICS; GENDER GAP.)

Janet K. Boles, *The Politics of the Equal Rights Amendment: Conflict and the Decision Process* (New York, 1979). Mary Frances Berry, *Why ERA Failed* (Bloomington, Ind., 1986). Jane Mansbridge, *Why We Lost the ERA* (Chicago, 1986).

JANE J. MANSBRIDGE

EQUATORIAL GUINEA. The Republic of Equatorial Guinea, formerly Spanish Guinea, has as its major components the mainland province of Río Muni (approx. 26,000 sq. km.; 10,000 sq. mi.) and the island of Bioko (approx. 2,100 sq. km.; 800 sq. mi.).

The population is approximately 390,000. Río Muni, with its capital in Bata, is inhabited by a number of ethnic groups, including the Ndowe of the coast. The Fang are the largest group and spill over into neighboring Gabon. They make up approximately eighty percent of the republic's population. Spain claimed Río Muni definitively in 1900; the Fang resisted into the 1920s. Even afterwards, most Fang remained outside the colonial economy.

Malabo, the national capital, is on the island of Bioko, formerly called Fernando Po. Spain claimed the island in 1778, but it was not until 1910 that its Bubi inhabitants recognized Spanish suzerainty. For most of the twentieth century the island has been dominated by a thriving cocoa monoculture.

The regime of the first president of independent Equatorial Guinea, Francisco Macias Nguema (1968–1979), went a long way toward destroying the colonial economy. During his tenure at least a third of the population was killed or went into exile.

Macias Nguema was executed after a coup. Under his successor and nephew, Teodoro Obiang Nguema, a new constitution was drafted in 1982. By its terms, the president has a seven-year term. In 1987 Obiang Nguema formed the Partido Democrático de Guinea Ecuatorial. In 1989 he was elected to a second term in a one-party race.

The president can make laws by decree, dissolve the legislature, negotiate and ratify treaties, and fire cabinet members. There is also a prime minister and a state council. The Chamber of the People's Representatives is made up of fifteen members appointed by the president and forty-five chosen indirectly by the citizenry. Traditional laws are honored within the national court system provided that they do not conflict with state statutes.

Fang from the Esangui subgroup at Mongomo have provided the core of state leadership. The "Mongomo clique" is in practice far more important than the institutions established in the written constitution. Tensions within the regime persist; the Mongomo group at some points has acted as a check on the presidency and has been suspected of plotting coups.

A look at the present state of the economy reveals halting development despite high inputs of foreign aid. Major products are cocoa, coffee, and lumber (okume wood). France and Spain have taken the lead in petroleum exploration. The country has granted exploration rights to Spanish, French, Gabonese, and U.S. companies. Río Muni has other subsoil wealth as well: copper, uranium, iron ore, rutile, tantalum, and manganese.

Labor shortage is a major problem. In the 1960s the majority of the population on Bioko consisted of migrant workers. In 1975 most of the Nigerian migrant workers were repatriated. They have not returned in great numbers.

The country's closest relationships are with Spain and France. Entrance into the Communauté Financière Africaine (CFA) zone increased links with *Francophone Africa, especially Cameroon. Trouble with Nigeria erupted in 1985 over a South African presence on Bioko. It is not certain that, even with massive amounts of assistance, the country can overcome the handicaps imposed by underpopulation, small size, and a heritage of authoritarian rule.

I. K. Sundiata, *Equatorial Guinea, Colonialism, State Terror and the Search for Stability* (Boulder, Colo., 1990).

IBRAHIM K. SUNDIATA

ERITREAN WAR OF INDEPENDENCE. Fought since 1961, the war in Eritrea would have earned the dubious distinction of beating Vietnam's record as the longest *war in the modern world, had it not ended in May 1991. Why this war, and how have the Eritreans managed to wage it for so long?

*Clausewitz's dictum that war is the continuation of politics by other means applies in the Eritrean case with tragic poignancy. The politics of Eritrean self-determination from British occupation (1941–1952), following Italian colonial rule (1889–1941), and subsequently from Ethiopian encroachment came to a head in 1961–1962.

With its defeat in World War II, Italy relinquished its legal right to its colonies in a treaty signed in 1947, under which the Four Powers (France, the United Kingdom, the United States, and the Soviet Union) would dispose of the former Italian colonies by agreement, failing which they would submit the matter to the UN General Assembly. Libya's and Somalia's cases were determined without much ado at the UN; Eritrea proved to be difficult, principally because of Emperor *Haile Selassie's interest in acquiring it and U.S. strategic and geopolitical interest in the Red Sea region. The convergence of these two interests and the dominant U.S. position sealed the fate of Eritrean self-determination.

Instead of gaining independence, as demanded by the majority of its inhabitants, Eritrea was joined with *Ethiopia in a lopsided federation under "the Sovereignty of the Ethiopian Crown." It was lopsided because a basic principle of *federalism was absent: a neutral arbiter between the Eritrean entity and Ethiopia. It was also imposed by a U.S.-engineered resolution instead of by a freely expressed referendum as practiced in other cases of self-determination of colonized peoples. Moreover, the emperor's government began encroaching on Eritrean autonomy soon after the federation came into force in 1952. Eritrean protests were ignored by the UN, which bore responsibility for the integrity of the federation. Finally, emboldened by the impunity with which he had violated the UN arrangement, Emperor Haile Selassie abolished the federation in 1962.

A year earlier, in September 1961, the Eritrean Liberation Front (ELF) declared armed struggle, galvanizing a disappointed nation. By 1970, when the Eritrean People's Liberation Front (EPLF) was established, the Eritrean War had become Haile Selassie's principal preoccupation. Indeed, it was a major cause for his demise four years later. His successors adopted his policy of a military solution to the "Eritrean problem," vowing to "liquidate the secessionist rebels." Sixteen years later, Haile Selassie's successors, who had increased their armed forces by eightfold to 250,000, not only failed in their objective, but also lost ground. The EPLF (now the sole front) controls all Eritrea, having defeated the Ethiopian army on 26 May 1991.

The essence of the Eritrean case is that it represents denied *decolonization, not a secession. It is analogous to those of *Namibia and *Western Sahara. Ethiopian diplomacy, first backed by the United States (1953–1976), then by the Soviet Union, miscast it as a secession, thus turning African opinion against Eritrean independence. Military victories by the EPLF and a reappraisal of the basis of Eritrean claims have begun to sway international opinion in favor of Eritrean independence.

Despite the incalculable cost, the Eritreans have proved that a nation determined to win its rightful place in the family of nations is capable of surviving overwhelming odds. The Eritreans, led by the EPLF, have triumphed against a much bigger Ethiopian army that is backed by external powers. The primary source of this triumph is the support of the population which has sacrificed life and property for its cause. The second is the nature of the guerrilla army, its experience, its resilience and tenacity, its adeptness at the use of weapons, and its knowledge and mastery of the terrain. Its creation of a disciplined organization and impressive social infrastructure, notably in education and health, help secure and maintain very wide popular support.

The end of the war in Eritrea was followed by an agreement reached between the EPLF (now a provisional government) and the transitional government of Ethiopia to a peaceful settlement of the "Eritrean question" through an internationally supervised referendum.

(See also DECOLONIZATION; GUERRILLA WARFARE; SECESSIONIST MOVEMENTS.)

Bereket Habte Selassie, *Eritrea and the United Nations and Other Essays* (Trenton, 1989). Georges Nzongola-Ntalaja, ed., *Conflict in the Horn of Africa* (Atlanta, 1991).

BEREKET HABTE SELASSIE

ESTONIA. See BALTIC REPUBLICS.

ETHIOPIA. The historical antecedents of Ethiopia are found in the Christian kingdom of Abyssinia, whose own history links it to the Axumite empire that flourished in the northern part of the Ethiopian plateau in ancient times. The emergence of the modern state begins in the reign of Menelik II, the Abyssinian ruler who not only repelled an Italian invasion in 1896 and spared his country the experience of colonialism, but also expanded his domain prodigiously through conquest and gave the state, henceforth called Ethiopia, its present borders. Unlike Abyssinia, Ethiopia was a heterogeneous empire impossible to rule through the feudal Abyssinian political system. Consequently, a process of modernization was launched by *Haile Selassie, who became regent in 1917, king in 1928, emperor in 1930, and ruled Ethiopia until he was overthrown in 1974. Under him, the power of the Abyssinian aristocracy was broken, the governmental process was centralized, the state was reinforced with bureaucratic, military, and security apparatuses, and Haile Selassie ruled as an absolute monarch in a state where conventional political life had not yet appeared.

Nevertheless, powerful forces opposed to the regime emerged among dissident ethnic groups and social classes. Dissidence grew among groups that had been forcibly incorporated into the state by Menelik's expansion. Opposition also mounted among the Eritreans in the former Italian colony, who had been deprived of self-government by Haile Selassie when he dismantled a federal scheme that had linked Eritrea with Ethiopia during 1952–1962. Generally such groups inhabited the arid lowland periphery of Ethiopia where no sign of development had appeared, and many were Muslim pastoralists, ignored and alienated by a state dependent on cultivation and ruled by Christians. Denied normal political outlets, some of these groups were driven to armed rebellion beginning in the early 1960s.

Dissidence bred also among the new social groups spawned by the system of modern education installed in the 1940s and by the process of economic change that began the following decade. The intelligentsia was alienated by its exclusion from power and the domination of the economy by foreign capital, which limited the scope for native enterprise. Ethiopia's nascent working class was alienated by the regime's collusion with foreign employers to reduce labor costs, which resulted in harsh exploitation. Dissidence also affected the junior army officer corps whose members shared the outlook of the intelligentsia, and the soldiers who bore the burden of fighting against oppositional *guerrilla movements in various parts of the country. The regime's most militant opponents were the students from the university and secondary schools. Having espoused *Marxism as their ideological guide, they succeeded in making it the only credible political alternative to the *ancien régime*.

A devastating famine in 1972–1974 that was largely ignored by the government galvanized the dissident social groups into simultaneous, albeit uncoordinated, action that caused the collapse of the imperial regime in 1974. A group of 112 junior and noncomissioned officers and plain soldiers representing units of the military establishment seized power. Influenced by the radicalism of the intelligentsia and wishing to secure its support, this group, known as the Dergue (Committee), itself espoused Marxism, and decreed a series of basic socioeconomic reforms that revolutionized Ethiopian society. Among these were the nationalization of rural land and its distribution equally among working peasants, the nationalization of industry, finance, large-scale trade, and other sectors of the economy, and the nationalization of urban land and extra housing. The reforms effectively wiped out the economic base of the old ruling class.

The Dergue's espousal of Marxism did not appease the radicals who demanded civilian rule and attacked the regime, provoking a violent reaction that claimed many victims and effectively silenced all opposition to military rule from that quarter. However, armed opposition from dissident ethnic and regional groups proliferated and became a serious threat both to the regime and the state. The Eritrean rebels nearly overran their province in 1977, and Somali irredentism (a policy aimed at recovering land from foreign control) provoked an invasion from neighboring *Somalia the same year. A new movement sprang up in the northern Abyssinian province of Tigzay, an impoverished, desiccated land, tormented by drought and famine. Yet another movement claimed to represent the Oromo, Ethiopia's most populous group. The goals of these movements ranged from secession and independence in the case of Eritrea, to secession and union with Somalia in the case of the Somali living in Ethiopia, to regional self-rule for Tigzay.

The Dergue's response to this challenge was devoid of political substance. Its choice was suppression, and for that purpose it increased the size of the military establishment tenfold and fought civil wars on several fronts. The regime's *ideology and reforms alienated the United States, heretofore Ethiopia's chief patron and provider of military aid. Its place was eagerly taken by the Soviet Union,

which provided the weaponry needed to expel the Somali invaders and to regain control of Eritrea. The revolution in that province was contained but not extinguished, and it flared up again spectacularly in the 1980s when, in concert with the Tigzayan rebels, the Eritreans routed the Ethiopian army from the northern part of the country and brought the regime to the brink of collapse.

While *war raged, Ethiopia's economy stagnated, but its population grew at the rate of 2.9 percent per year and reached 42 million in 1984, when the first census was taken. Food production hardly kept up, and the country faced a serious problem of food insufficiency. The marketing process was dislocated by the imposition of compulsory purchasing at low prices by the state. The establishment of state farms to boost food production proved a failure, even though they absorbed the bulk of the state's investment in agriculture. When drought revisited northern and eastern Ethiopia in the early 1980s, a biblical famine ensued, claiming lives by the hundreds of thousands and making the country a ward of international charity. In the midst of the disaster, the regime launched a massive resettlement program to move the stricken peasantry from the drought-affected region and a villagization campaign to move peasants from their isolated homesteads into villages.

While battling on several fronts, the regime also sought to institutionlize itself by creating political structures based superficially on the Soviet model. Ten years after it came to power, the Dergue set up the Workers' Party of Ethiopia to be the political vanguard in the People's Democratic Republic of Ethiopia, as the state was called in the constitution adopted in 1987. The constitution sought to address the problem of ethnic and regional dissidence by offering self-government to various ethnic and regional units, although it defined Ethiopia as a unitary state. It also provided for an elected legislative assembly and a president elected by it. The president in turn appointed a ministerial council and a prime minister. The presidency was designed for and promptly occupied by Colonel Mengistu Haile Mariam who, after a series of bloody purges, had emerged as the undisputed leader of a much-depleted Dergue. Although elections for the assembly were held in 1987 and many civilians held high office in the party and the government, Colonel Mengistu's military faction was the dominant force in both. In essence, the regime remained a rigid military dictatorship.

(See also AFRO-MARXISM; ERITREAN WAR OF INDEPENDENCE; FOOD POLITICS; HORN OF AFRICA; SECESSIONIST MOVEMENTS.)

Christopher Clapham, *Haile Selassie's Government* (London, 1968). John Markakis, *Ethiopia: Anatomy of a Traditional Polity* (Oxford, 1974). John Markakis and Nega Ayele, *Class and Revolution in Ethiopia* (Nottingham, 1978). John Markakis, *National and Class Conflict in the Horn of Africa* (Cambridge, U.K., 1987). Christopher Clapham,

Transformation and Continuity in Revolutionary Ethiopia (Cambridge, U.K., 1988). Edmond J. Keller, *Revolutionary Ethiopia* (Bloomington, Ind., 1988). John Harbeson, *The Ethiopian Transformation: The Quest for the Post-Imperial State* (Boulder, Colo., 1989).

JOHN MARKAKIS

ETHNICITY

A phenomenon associated with contact between cultural-linguistic communal groups within societies, ethnicity is characterized by cultural prejudice and social discrimination. Underlying these characteristics are the feelings of pride in the in-group, common consciousness and identity of the group, and the exclusiveness of its members. It is a phenomenon linked directly or indirectly to forms of affiliation and identification built around ties of real or punitive kinship.

In reality ethnicity is a very complex phenomenon and, like other social phenomena, it is subject to change. Its form, place, and role in society may alter. Its links with other social phenomena such as politics, *religion, and *class relations may change, posing new questions. In fact, ethnicity hardly exists in a pure form. It is always closely associated with political, juridical, religious, and other social views and forms of interaction which constitute important ingredients of the ethnic phenomenon. Hence ethnicity sometimes finds expression in political domination, economic exploitation, and psychological oppression.

The nature, intensity, and forms of expression of ethnicity are determined by various factors. These include the size and location of the various linguistic-cultural groups in the society; the strength and cohesion of their leaderships; the courage, determination, and nature of the leadership of the underprivileged classes; the degree of foreign influence in the society; the nature, pervasiveness, and power of the dominant ideology; the prevailing social custom, tradition, and culture of the various linguistic groups; and the form of government of the society. Other factors include historical patterns of relations between different cultural groups, the level of development of the groups, the socioeconomic context in which the groups make contact, and the pattern of group migration to the place of contact. Thus ethnicity must vary from place to place depending on the existence and significance of these factors and combinations of them. It is found in both developed and underdeveloped countries, in societies with differing ideologies, and in societies with different historical-cultural backgrounds.

Potentially, ethnicity embodies both positive and negative elements. On the positive side it involves an appreciation of one's own social roots in a community and cultural group without necessarily disparaging other groups. As a reference phenomenon it provides a material as well as an emotional support network for individuals in society. This func-tion is particularly important as the society becomes more complex, massified, bureaucratized, impersonal, and alienating. It fosters a sense of belonging as part of an intermediate level of social relations between the individual and society. Thus ethnicity may serve as an adaptive mechanism which enables the individual to adjust successfully to the increasing alienation of mass societies. It enables the individual to overcome the socioeconomic insecurity consequent on divisive competition in market-oriented societies. In this regard, ethnicity binds individuals together, gives them internal cohesion, encourages them to provide for each other's security, promotes their sense of identity and therefore their sense of direction. Ethnicity offers a personal solution to the generic problems of exploitation and oppression.

On the other hand, the negative aspects of ethnicity make it problematic for social harmony in multicultural societies. Under conditions of intense socioeconomic competition in the society ethnicity is associated with conflict and violence. It embodies passionate, symbolic, and apprehensive aspects which promote not only direct and potentially violent conflict but also intense conflict in the competition of members of ethnic groups for socioeconomic advantages. By investing group entitlement with comparative worth and legitimacy it encourages the ethnic in-group to be willing to incur costs to maximize beneficial intergroup differentials in resource competition.

This situation of group interests and pride in interethnic competition is illustrated by tension between "middlemen minorities" and their host societies, as in the case of the Asian community in Uganda. The "middlemen minorities" concentrate in trade and commerce, and often act as intermediaries between producer and consumer, employer and employee, owner and renter. Conflict occurs not merely because of ordinary business rivalries but also because these minorities often undercut their rivals by the use of their own credit institutions, their guildlike technique of restraining competition among themselves, and their use of cheap, usually family, labor. At the same time they have contradictory interests with those with whom they transact business such as consumers, tenants, and clients. Economically and organizationally powerful, the "middlemen" ethnic groups are extremely hard to dislodge competitively. Ethnic sentiments can be easily mobilized against them or even hysterically whipped up in response to imaginary threats from them. Conversely, they have little else than nepotism on which they can rely for self-protection in a hostile social environment. Politically powerless and culturally marginalized, they are quite vulnerable to attack. Similarly, if employers use the labor of one ethnic group to undercut the price of labor of another group, intra-working-class competition ensues along ethnic lines because higher-paid laborers are threatened by the introduction of cheaper labor into the market. If the labor market is thus split ethnically, the resultant class antagonism takes the form of ethnic antagonism. Then ethnicity is not an artificial diversion from economic interests but a faithful reflection of those interests.

In another respect ethnicity promotes hostility and violence. Within the in-group, and especially during competition with out-groups, hostility among individuals is usually met with a united hostile front by all the other members through the process of socialization. If necessary, it is forcibly suppressed. But the internal restraints against hostility are relaxed at times of interethnic rivalry which stresses economic competition. Such a relaxation permits hostility toward the out-group. Such hostility is again socially legitimate against the out-group where there is an actual threat to the dominance of the in-group. The in-group accepts rivalry manifestations as legitimate modes of keeping the outsiders in their place.

Two types of hostility are fomented by ethnicity—direct aggression and indirect aggression. In the former case, intense competition and the resultant deprivation and frustration lead to pervasive insecurity. This condition produces hostility and aggression which are designed to restore a balanced situation. The individual or group imposing the frustration and inciting the hostility is identified and made the object of the aggressive response. In indirect aggression, however, the real target of the aggressive response is not the victim of hostility. The aggression cannot be directed at the individual or group that caused it because of its remoteness or the danger involved. The aggrieved party finds a substitute. Hostility to an out-group is more fully actualized for direct than indirect aggression because of the lack of inhibitions and tender ties toward it. Therefore, ethnic hostility would tend to be quite vehement even without the admixture of displaced aggression. Often, however, direct and indirect victimization coincide, further exacerbating interethnic hostility. Difficulties within the in-group caused by one of its members tend to be displaced onto the traditional rival or rivals. Thus, during periods of stress, ethnic hostility and aggression are the result of the rational motive of competition.

Irrationality in interethnic antagonism is sometimes related to the emergence and escalation of an interethnic conflict spiral. This arises when an ethnic group correctly or incorrectly perceives itself threatened by another group. The former responds with a threat or hostile action which elicits a hostile and "defensive" reaction from the latter. Thus the former's original perception of threat and danger is confirmed, and it increases its own "defensive" hostile activity. Soon the exchanges between the two groups are caught in an increasingly intense spiral of self-confirming hostile suspicions, actions, counteractions, and expectations which are virtually unrelated to the initial cause of the antagonism, and which open the possibility for interethnic violence.

It is no longer a question of excluding out-group members from jobs and the enjoyment of various social services but of ruthlessly eliminating them in violent preemptive actions. The history of interethnic tension in Nigeria between 1964 and 1967 illustrates the nature and consequences of this process of escalation.

Thus ethnicity produces adverse effects on the peace, harmony, and integration of national societies. This explains why a great deal of effort is put into combating ethnicity in spite of its positive aspects. These negative aspects are more dramatic both in their dynamics and effects than the positive ones. These negative aspects are reflected in the political instability which has plagued a number of multiethnic societies around the world and which contributed, with dramatic effect, to the breakup of the Soviet Union and Yugoslavia and to endemic political tensions in countries such as Britain, Spain, Sri Lanka, Czechoslovakia, Canada, and Belgium, to name a few. The negative effects of ethnicity overshadow the positive ones because they are usually more dramatic and have grave consequences for the survival of the nation-state concerned.

The Emergence of Ethnicity. The worldwide existence of ethnicity suggests that it is not the result of some barbarous heritage peculiar to any group of people, or the consequence of the precolonial pattern of conflict between members of different ethnic groups within the same political society or state. It is a social phenomenon involving relations among individuals and is influenced by several factors.

Among these factors are the memories of similar interactions which individuals learn from the history of their respective groups and then bring to the contact situation. The consequent ethnicity is often referred to as primordial ethnicity. It is unalloyed by occupational, political, and other identities and is focused essentially on blood ties, the accompanying emotional bonds, and the consciousness of the historical pattern of association with other groups. In Kenya, for example, the traditional enemies of the Kikuyu during precolonial times were the Masai. Therefore, ethnicity arising from relations between members of the two groups that is traceable to this precolonial enmity would be classified as primordial ethnicity. The same holds true for Hausa-Fulani relations in northern Nigeria.

On the other hand, there is ample evidence to show that patterns of ethnicity have changed over time, that boundaries of ethnic groups tend to change, and that some groups may wish to mask their ethnic identity or submerge it under other ethnic identities. For example, in precolonial Kenya there was no enmity between the Luo and Kikuyu groups. But by 1960 a strong ethnicity had developed in their relations. In Nigeria immediately after the civil war members of the Igbo ethnic group in riverine southern Nigeria, fearing reprisals at the hands of a state machinery that was rife with anti-Igbo sentiment, denied their Igbo ethnic identity and assumed an Ikwere identity as manifested by the addition of the prefix *ru-* to all the names in their communities.

Thus contact alone is not sufficient for ethnicity to emerge. In fact, not every case of interethnic contact has produced ethnicity. It all depends on the context of the contact. In the case of the Reindeer Tungus and the Cossacks of Manchuria, contact did not produce ethnicity; nor did relations between the Yoruba and the migrant laborers in the cocoa belt of Nigeria. The critical factor in the contact situation is the degree of socioeconomic competition that is involved. Both the Reindeer Tungus and the Cossacks remained racially and culturally dissimilar and characterized by a general ethnocentric preference for the in-group. However, their two economies were complementary, and therefore there was no socioeconomic competition among them. In the case of the Puyallup Indians of North America, the complementarity of interests between them and the early white migrants to their territory led to a quick and peaceful social interaction and economic transaction. But when other whites came and acquired Indian land and exploited Indian timber they entered into destructive competition with the Puyallup for these scarce resources. Relations between the two groups became strained and ethnicity emerged. More convincing still is the effect of socioeconomic competition within the same ethnic group. Ethnicity also emerges. This has been observed in a study of Japanese-Americans as reported in Carey McWilliams, *Prejudice: Japanese-Americans* (Boston, 1943). It is also observable in subethnic hostility and antagonism among the Yoruba and Igbo of Nigeria.

The net effect of intense socioeconomic competition in the interethnic contact situation is the insecurity of the individual regarding its outcome. Ethnicity acts as an instrument to ameliorate the adverse effects of this competition, and to enable the individual to compete better. For example, once the members of a particular group gain access to the best jobs and other resources they use their positions to find jobs for others or at least to pass on the news of job opportunities to them. The unsuccessful competitors find it easy and convenient to blame their plight on advantages possessed by members of other groups. The repercussions are felt in unequal levels of unemployment and income, as well as in different degrees of social status among ethnic groups. Attempts by each to escape the negative consequences of this competition lead to the further strengthening of ethnicity. In the face of such competitions one ethnic group may submerge its identity under another that is more efficient in the competition or it may change its identity in order to gain advantage.

This factor of socioeconomic competition is reinforced by the degree of social distance among groups, especially the social distance arising from differences in language. Since language is the major means of communication among human beings, it is the essential precursor of social interaction and behavior. It is also a symbolic medium. When it is not shared by individuals, frustration, stress, anxiety, lack of trust, and insecurity tend to characterize social relations. In a society where different and mutually unintelligible languages are spoken there is a tendency for individuals to confine their initial pattern of communication and, therefore, their social relations to members of the same language group, at least until they are able to learn the other languages. The situation is worsened if such lack of communication occurs in an atmosphere of intense socioeconomic competition. It is for this reason that the adoption of a lingua franca is often suggested as a solution for the problem of ethnicity in multiethnic states. However, the impact of such a lingua franca is bound to be limited in view of the emergence of ethnicity within the same language group, as in the case of the Hutu and Tutsi in Rwanda and Burundi. And there is the problem of which language to choose.

Other forms of social distance that are relevant for ethnicity include the difference in the level of socioeconomic development of the various ethnic groups. Antipathy often exists between groups at different levels of development which coexist in the same society. The one may look down on the other, thereby increasing the latter's hostility; or the latter may be jealous of the former, thereby generating the same hostility. For example, ethnic consciousness among the Kikuyu developed during the colonial period not, as is popularly believed, primarily as a result of their loss of land to the white settlers, because the Masai and the Giriama lost equal or more land, but essentially because forced Kikuyu participation in colonial activities led to the early growth of socioeconomic fortune among them. Entering the colonial economy earlier than the other ethnic groups, they took advantage of opportunities in the emergent economy out of proportion to their share of the total population. Other groups in competition for these opportunities began to resent this Kikuyu advantage. Hence in Kenya ethnicity has been characterized by the hostility of all the other groups to the Kikuyu.

Another factor which is significant for the emergence and persistence of ethnicity is the manipulation of ethnic sentiments by the leaders of ethnic groups and the state for ethnic, class, economic, or political reasons. Colonial rulers manipulated ethnic sentiments in order to secure their rule over the various colonies of Africa and elsewhere. They encouraged ethnic sentiments among the Africans by spreading the myth and propaganda that Africans were separated from one another by great social distance, by differences of history and traditions, and by ethnological, political, and socio-religious barriers. Therefore the colonialists sought to secure for each African group the right to maintain its identity, its individuality, its chosen form of government, and the peculiar political and social institutions which it had evolved over the years. This objective was made concrete in the administrative system of indirect rule. Even the French, although they ostensibly applied direct rule, used it. By expanding and strengthening the precolonial traditional authorities this system ensured that a linguistic-cultural focus existed for ethnic identification.

The colonialists' emphasis on differences among the ethnic groups to the utter neglect of similarities among them, and the pervasive colonial bureaucratic requirement that official forms should contain information about the ethnic origin of the African population, also helped to general and keep alive ethnic identity and consciousness. In addition, fearing the revolutionary potential of the African working class, the colonial rulers used ethnicity as a weapon to destroy effective working-class collective action. Finally, they employed ethnicity in order to curb African *nationalism by sponsoring ethnic political parties and manipulating elections along ethnic lines.

Many African leaders have followed in the footsteps of the colonialists in manipulating ethnicity for their own selfish ends. They convince the people that the backwardness of communities arises from mystical, inherent differences among them or, worse still, from the machinations of other groups in the use of the society's resources. Deceived in this way, various communities are set against one another. They are told that to perform their communal duty and defend their community rights they should be mindless of the needs of the other people and seize whatever privileges they can, and hold smaller communities under subjugation. In their struggle for wealth and power these leaders build a system of preferences based on ethnic groups. In-group–out-group boundaries are created around these parochial communities which serve to exclude others from enjoying the privileges of the society. Thus members of an ethnic group believe that members of other groups would discriminate against them in the competition for resources, that they can expect preferences only from members of their own group in a position to help them, that it is in their interest to promote the activities of their own group in competition with others, and that no one of the other groups would give them preference over their own people. As a result anyone who finds himself or herself outside the system of ethnic preference is lost.

As this happens, members of an ethnic group tend to look more and more toward their group for support. The consequent intragroup cohesion acts to further separate it from the other ethnic groups. Its members begin to develop common experiences in relation to others and, therefore, a common history, tradition, and set of interests. Under the circumstance, further conflicts of interest increase their social distance in economic and security considerations as well as in *ideology. If ethnic group lines coincide with regional geographical boundaries, the resultant territorial cohesion acts to convert ethnic group boundaries into cultural, economic, and, as a prelude to secession, military barriers.

This dynamic is reinforced by competition for political power. Within the same ruling class it is often difficult for an opposition political party to justify its separate existence from the ruling party on the basis of appeals to socioeconomic programs. Nevertheless, it must justify its separate existence on the basis of some important and viable indicator. Ethnicity provides one of the most convenient and appealing of such criteria. Political constituencies are often geographical in nature and quite often ethnically homogeneous, and therefore to win the support of an ethnic group is to win a political constituency. Such parliamentary candidates tend to become entrenched because of the political gains likely to accrue to them from appeals to ethnic sentiments, and their presence acts to perpetuate ethnicity because they continually fan the embers of ethnic identification.

As ethnic consciousness thus increases in scope and intensity, the socioeconomic and political atmosphere becomes charged with tension. Ethnic hostility, loyalty, and identification are passed on to successive generations through the family, press, and public and private conversations. Therefore, even when the original bases of ethnicity, such as socioeconomic competition, social distance, and manipulation, have been eliminated, the problems posed by the internationalized dimension remain. Under such conditions the persistence—and sometimes growth—of ethnicity is assured. An adequate solution to the ethnic problem must therefore come to grips with individual insecurity and the internalized dimension of ethnic sentiments.

Resolving the Ethnic Problem. Often associated with ethnicity and underlying it are fears concerning injustice, oppression, and inequality in relations among ethnic groups. Such fears include those regarding injustice in the maintenance of law and order, nepotistic distribution of jobs, social services, contracts, the siting of public industries and other projects, and the possible imposition of the culture of one ethnic group on the other. Therefore, there is a democratic side to ethnicity. It concerns the right of the members of each ethnic group to be secure in their lives and property, as well as secure from arbitrary arrest and punishment, and for them to enjoy equal opportunity in real terms in trade, business, employment, schooling, and the enjoyment of social amenities. It encourages the recognition of the equal rights of all ethnic groups, and is a tool in the fight against privilege and nepotism. Ethnicity can only be attenuated by the consistent application of democratic principles, norms, values, and procedures in socioeconomic and political life.

Therefore, only a policy that is based on clear, consistent, and democratic principles is realistic in the search for solutions to the ethnic problem. Such a policy must appraise each concrete ethnic demand from the perspective of removing all inequality, all privileges, and all exclusiveness. In concrete terms, for example, such a policy means that the socioeconomic imbalance between ethnic groups should be corrected by extending employment facilities, educational institutions, and other welfare services on a disproportionate basis to the areas occupied by the disadvantaged ethnic groups. Nevertheless, all citizens of the country residing in the areas, and not just the indigenes of these areas, must be equally eligible to benefit from these activities. Furthermore, such programs must include a built-in mechanism for phasing themselves out as soon as their mission is fulfilled—otherwise the benefiting ethnic groups may become the privileged communities of the future. *Democracy is vital for interethnic harmony.

(See also COLONIAL EMPIRES; EQUALITY AND IN-EQUALITY; FOREIGN WORKERS; INTERNAL COLONIALISM; INTERNATIONAL MIGRATION; PERIPHERAL NATIONALISM; SECESSIONIST MOVEMENTS.)

Nathan Glazer and Daniel P. Moynihan, eds., *Ethnicity: Theory and Experience* (Cambridge, Mass., 1975). Archie Mafeje, "The Ideology of Tribalism" *Journal of Modern Africa Studies* 9, no. 2 (1977): 253–262. Regina E. Holloman and S. A. Arutinov, *Perspectives on Ethnicity* (The Hague, 1978). P. Brass, ed., *Ethnic Groups and the State* (London, 1985). Donald Horowitz, *Ethnic Groups in Conflict* (Berkeley, Calif., 1985). D. L. Thompson and D. R. Roneou, eds., *Ethnicity, Politics and Development* (Boulder, Colo., 1986). Frederick Barth, *Ethnic Groups and Boundaries* (London, 1989). Okwudiba Nnoli, *Ethnic Politics in Africa* (Ibadan, 1989).

OKWUDIBA NNOLI

ETHNIC NATIONALISM. See INTERNAL COLONIALISM; PERIPHERAL NATIONALISM.

EUROCOMMUNISM. The term applied to the liberalizing movements which developed in many Communist parties (CPs) in capitalist democracies in the 1970s was Eurocommunism. At that moment the Italian, French, Spanish, and many smaller CPs confronted changed political settings following the events of 1956 in the Communist world—the Twentieth, "de-Stalinizing" Party Congress of the *Communist Party of the Soviet Union and revolts in East Europe, *détente in East-West relations, and social changes in capitalist societies themselves following from postwar economic successes. The rising political importance of the new middle classes which accompanied the occupational postindustrialization of social structures called in particular for a revision of communist doctrine about sociopolitical alliances with non-working-class groups.

Taking new distance from the organizational and

political roots of the Third (Communist) International was the core of Eurocommunist change. The Eurocommunist "road to *socialism" was to be national, not international. Socialism itself was to be democratic. Soviet institutional patterns were rejected—one-party dictatorships of the proletariat in particular—and the Soviet model was no longer considered to be a guide. To varying degrees "de-Stalinization" and limited democratization of party internal life were advocated. Finally, attenuating or renouncing Soviet international leadership was high on the Eurocommunist agenda.

The specific contents of national Eurocommunism were a function of the domestic situations of the different parties. The Italian CP, the Eurocommunist pioneer, elaborated its perspective in the context of its "*historic compromise" strategy for coming to power in alliance with the ruling Christian Democrats. The leader of the Spanish CP in the 1970s, Santiago Carrillo, formulated his particular vision in anticipation of the tasks of Spanish democratization after Franco. The French Communists, whose Eurocommunism was of very brief duration, needed new ways of maneuvering politically inside their perilous programmatic and electoral alliance with the renascent French Socialists.

Commonality of approach among different Eurocommunist parties never emerged. Under the pressures of the renewed *Cold War, some parties, the French in particular, rallied to the Brezhnevite Soviet cause and downplayed their revisionism. Others, like the Italians, completely rejected Soviet approaches and actions in Afghanistan and Poland in the first instance. Domestic trajectories also pushed the parties in varied directions. "Historic compromise" failed in Italy and this had the effect of pushing Italian *communism ever more toward self-conscious reconfiguration as a social democratic movement. The process was crowned by the party's rechristening in 1990 as the "Democratic Party of the Left." The Spanish party had a more complex history, largely owing to its inability to discard authoritarian leadership patterns, and suffered a cascade of internal splits in consequence. By the 1990s it, too, was engaged in a quasi–social democratic quest to create a "united Left" in which the persistence of the CP as an autonomous organization was in question. The French CP, faced with coalitional hard times beginning in the later 1970s, beat a hasty retreat from Eurocommunist innovation toward more traditional "workerist" and pro-Soviet postures.

All of the large ex-Eurocommunist parties lost a great deal of their strength in the 1980s. The Italians, most consistent in their liberalization, fared best and maintained the support of more than one-fifth of the electorate (compared to approximately one-third in the 1970s). The Spanish party never made a post-Franco electoral breakthrough and now hover around ten percent. The French party had lost two-thirds of its voting strength—from twenty-one percent to seven percent—and most of its plausibility by 1990. In smaller parties like the British, conflict between "Euros" and pro-Soviets divided party members to such a degree that the very existence of the parties was threatened. Thus Eurocommunism was already history well before *perestroika in the Soviet Union, the collapse of "existing socialism" throughout Central and Eastern Europe, and the end of the Cold War.

(See also STALINISM.)

Nicos Poulantzas, *State, Power, Socialism* (London, 1978). Peter Lange and Maurizio Vannicelli, *Eurocommunism: A Casebook* (London, 1981).

GEORGE ROSS

EUROPEAN COMMUNITY. In 1952 the European Coal and Steel Community (ECSC) came into existence, aiming to create a common market in coal, iron, and steel products between Belgium, the Federal Republic of Germany (FRG), France, Italy, Luxembourg, and the Netherlands. So successful was this first experiment in European economic integration that in 1957 two more communities began operation, the European Atomic Energy Community (Euratom) and the European Economic Community (EEC), with the same six states participating.

The EEC soon emerged as the most important of these three communities. It made rapid advances in eliminating tariffs on industrial goods between the members and in creating a Common Agricultural Policy (CAP). All of this was completed by the late 1960s, by which time agreement had also been reached on fusing the institutions of the three communities, so that they are now known collectively as the European Community (EC). The main common institutions are the supranational European Commission, which proposes community legislation, and the Council of Ministers, which consists of the representatives of national governments and accepts or rejects the commission's proposals. There is also a *European Parliament, which since 1979 has been directly elected but has limited legislative powers.

Impressed by the record of the EC in expanding trade between the members and raising their rates of economic growth, other European states soon applied for membership, notably Britain. However, French President Charles de *Gaulle twice vetoed British membership, in 1963 and 1966, on the grounds that Britain was not ready to assume a European vocation and was too strongly oriented towards the Atlantic alliance and its special relationship with the United States.

This French attitude caused some strain within the EC, the smaller states in particular favoring British entry to provide a counterweight to French dominance. Further problems were caused by de Gaulle in 1965 when he withdrew France from participation in the work of the EC for six months in protest at attempts to increase the powers of the European Parliament. As well as wanting an EC that was independent of the United States, de Gaulle also wanted to avoid surrendering national *sovereignty to the community's central institutions. Eventually a settlement of the dispute was reached in January 1966 in Luxembourg, but only at the price of abandoning the scheduled movement to majority voting in the Council of Ministers. According to this "Luxembourg compromise," any state that considered its vital national interest to be threatened by proposed community legislation could exercise a veto, which made it very difficult to get agreement on any new measures.

Further progress had to await the resignation of de Gaulle in 1969. His successor, Georges Pompidou, called for an EC summit, which met in The Hague in December 1969. In what was described as the "relaunching of Europe," the summit agreed to complete the budgetary arrangements that had been blocked by de Gaulle in 1965, to reopen negotiations with the applicant states, and to proceed rapidly to economic and monetary union. Eventually Britain was admitted to the EC from the start of 1973, along with Ireland and Denmark. (Norway negotiated terms for membership at the same time, but the Norwegian people rejected entry in a referendum.)

Shortly after this first enlargement of the EC the world was plunged into recession by the December 1973 oil price rises, and hopes of following enlargement with economic and monetary union were dashed by major divergences in rates of growth and rates of inflation between the member states. It also proved impossible to arrive at other significant common policies to complement the CAP. Although the European Regional Development Fund was set up in December 1974, it was small in comparison with the amounts spent on agricultural support. In addition to these disappointments, the recession produced a proliferation of nontariff barriers to trade between the member states. Restrictions such as health and safety standards were manipulated by governments in an attempt to reserve domestic markets for domestic producers, and public subsidies to national manufacturers increased.

Despite these internal difficulties, the EC was already a major international actor by the 1980s. It was the world's largest importer and exporter (even when trade between the member states themselves is excluded); it had concluded preferential trading agreements with a number of other European and Middle Eastern states; and it had a special economic relationship with forty-six African, Caribbean, and Pacific states through the 1975 *Lomé Convention.

Both the preferential trading agreements and, especially, the Lomé Convention were regarded with some suspicion by the United States as departures from the principle of multilateral world free trade. Nevertheless, the United States was prepared to tolerate these agreements because it saw the EC as potentially an important partner in ensuring stability.

Yet the United States and the EC remained economic rivals, and increasingly as time went by the EC came to have interests that differed from those of the United States in various parts of the world. In the Middle East the dependence of the EC on the Arab oil producers for energy encouraged a more balanced perspective on the Arab-Israeli disputes than the strongly pro-Israeli line often adopted by the United States. In relations with the Soviet Union and Eastern Europe, the natural tendency of the West Europeans to favor peaceful coexistence was reinforced by trade and investment links that grew during the period of *détente, benefiting West European industry more than that of the United States. This divergence of views gave impetus to the process known as European Political Cooperation (EPC), whereby the EC members coordinated their foreign policies. EPC was seen as one of the major success stories for the EC in the 1970s.

The other success was the setting up of the European Monetary System (EMS) in 1978. This system was essentially a relaunching of the experiment in economic and monetary union that had foundered in the early 1970s. An initiative of Chancellor Helmut Schmidt of the FRG, it was taken up and supported by the French President Valéry Giscard d'Estaing. It involved the creation of a European currency unit (Ecu) and an exchange rate mechanism that fixed the values of the participating national currencies against each other, allowing for a limited percentage fluctuation either side of parity.

The EMS was designed to create, according to Schmidt, "a zone of monetary stability in Europe." This idea has two aspects: on the one hand it could be seen as a contribution to the building of a new world monetary order; on the other it could be seen as an attempt to insulate internal EC trade from the disruptions caused by frequent fluctuations in the value of the dollar in the 1970s.

Against expectations, the EMS held together. In its early years this was largely because the 1979 oil crisis weakened the deutsche mark and made it easier for the currencies of the other members to hold their parity against it. Subsequently it worked because of the recognition by all the participating states that the control of inflation had to be their highest priority in economic policy, and so the spread in rates of inflation gradually narrowed. However, there were two factors that weakened the claims of the EMS to be an unqualified success. First, until 1990 Britain declined to take sterling into the exchange rate mechanism. Secondly, unemployment remained too high for comfort in the EC as a whole.

Concern about unemployment was heightened when the economy of the EC proved slow to recover from the post-1979 recession. The success of the United States and Japan in riding out this recession and returning to high rates of investment in the early 1980s caused a serious reassessment of the condition of the EC. Net investment flows had become negative; in addition, the recovery in the United States and Japan was based on the development and exploitation of innovations in the areas of computers, robotics, aerospace, laser technology, and biotechnology. The EC faced the prospect of technological obsolescence.

It was in these circumstances that in 1985 the European Commission proposed a project to free the internal market of the EC by the end of 1992. Freeing the market meant getting rid of the nontariff barriers to trade in industrial goods that had proliferated in the recession years, extending free trade to the services sector, removing the remaining barriers to the free movement of labor, and abolishing controls on the free movement of capital. This ambitious program to create a single European market was accepted by the member states. Project 1992, as it was called, captured worldwide attention and imbued the EC with a new spirit of confidence. To facilitate progress the voting rules of the Council of Ministers were changed by the 1987 Single European Act to allow the acceptance of measures related to this 1992 project by a qualified majority instead of by unanimity. Majority voting was made more necessary because by this time there were twelve members, Greece having acceded in 1982 and Spain and Portugal in 1986.

Although there was agreement on the vital necessity of freeing the market, there was dissension on the other related programs that were brought forward by the commission, with Britain being the most awkward partner, especially under Prime Minister Margaret *Thatcher, who took over de Gaulle's role as the leading opponent of supranationalism, although she did not share his anti-Americanism.

First, the commission proposed a number of framework programs in technological research and development. Britain accepted that some such programs should exist but was reluctant to commit large amounts of public funding to them. This was in line with the neoliberal economic philosophy of the Conservative government under Thatcher. The consequence was that the programs were underfunded in the view of the commission and those member states, particularly France, that were most anxious to close the technological gap that had opened between the EC on the one hand and the United States and Japan on the other. However, the British government became an enthusiastic supporter of French President François *Mitterrand's initiative regarding a research program, to be called EUREKA, that would encourage collaboration in technological research between private corporations and institutions of higher education in all West European states. This appealed to Britain because it was not limited to the EC, would not increase the sphere of competence of the commission, and would involve relatively little public as opposed to private money.

Second, the commission argued, with the support of most of the member states, that the internal market program needed a social dimension if it were to be acceptable to all the citizens of the EC, especially workers. In 1988 the commission produced a social charter that laid down nonobligatory guidelines on issues such as health and safety at work, hours of work, social security benefits, training, and the rights of workers to be consulted on management decisions. The commission also made clear its intention to propose legislative measures on some, although not all, of these issues. With regard to all but health and safety measures, the British government objected. This again reflected its contention that the commission was encroaching on areas that were properly the preserve of the member states; it also reflected the very market-oriented philosophy of the British government, which saw most of these measures as an unjustified interference with the proper functioning of the labor market.

Third, the commission proposed rapid movement toward a monetary union. Again, most member states supported the creation of a single currency as an important corollary of the creation of the internal market. But Thatcher took particularly strong exception to this step as an intolerable interference with national sovereignty. Not all of her government agreed with her, however, particularly because the determination of the other member states to proceed threatened to leave Britain isolated as a second-class member of the post-1992 EC, with damaging consequences for industrial investment and for the position of the City of London as Europe's leading financial center. Eventually Thatcher was pushed into resigning in part over this issue and was replaced by the more pragmatic John Major, a development which encouraged prospects that British policy might be less at odds with EC developments.

However, partnership had its limits. The United States and the EC remained commercial rivals, as was demonstrated in 1990 in the *General Agreement on Tariffs and Trade (GATT) negotiations on a package of measures to extend world free trade in a number of sectors, including agriculture. The political strength of farmers in the EC, particularly in France, Germany, and Ireland, prevented agreement on the reduction of agricultural subsidies. This had been a central demand of the United States, and it became an major obstacle to an overall agreement.

At the beginning of the 1990s the EC faced tremendous challenges to its position as a central actor in world economic and political systems; however, tremendous opportunities were available to consolidate that position as well. The movement toward further integration on both the economic and political planes was accelerating in response. This inevitably meant the continued erosion of the sovereignty of the member states, something that Britain in

particular regretted and tried to minimize. But increasingly the process seemed inexorable. The December 1991 Treaty on European Union (often called the Maastricht Treaty) reflected an EC determination to expand the scope of economic and monetary union and set the framework for a common *security policy. Although a "no" vote in a June 1992 Danish referendum placed the treaty's future in doubt, increased integration (and expanded membership to include applicants from the *European Free Trade Association and, perhaps, from *Central Europe and the Mediterranean) remained high on the agenda of the EC.

What the consequences of these developments would mean for the internal political and economic systems of member states remained a matter for speculation at the start of the 1990s. Success in creating the single market would clearly lead to further economic restructuring within the EC, with member states having to cope with the political consequences of the decline of some economic sectors and, it was hoped, the growth of new ones. Such changes would inevitably affect the social cleavages that form the basis of political behavior, including electoral behavior. More significantly, perhaps, the single market seemed to imply that a great many more decisions of political significance would be taken at the EC level. In July 1988 Jacques Delors, president of the European Commission, predicted that in ten years' time eighty percent of economic legislation, and perhaps tax and social legislation, would be directed from the community. The prospect of a new political system forming at community level, added to the predicted economic strength of the post-1992 EC, led some people to see a new superpower emerging in Europe.

(See also EUROPEAN COURT OF JUSTICE; ROME, TREATY OF.)

Stephen George, *Politics and Policy in the European Community* (Oxford, 1991). Jacques Pelkmans and Alan Winters, *Europe's Domestic Market* (London, 1988). Juliet Lodge, ed., *The European Community and the Challenge of the Future* (London, 1989). Stephen George, *An Awkward Partner: Britain in the European Community* (Oxford, 1990).

STEPHEN GEORGE

EUROPEAN COURT OF JUSTICE. The European Court of Justice (ECJ), located in Luxembourg, is a body of the *European Community (EC). It is not to be confused with the European Court of Justice on Human Rights (ECJHR) at Strasbourg; the ECJHR is the judicial branch of the *Council of Europe (not to be confused with the European Community); the ECJHR resolves conflicts arising under the European Convention on Human Rights of 1950 (ECHR), which is a separate regional instrument of *international law, even though basic principles of the ECHR are at the same time an intrinsic part of the background of the Treaty of Rome of 1957. The

ECJ of the EC was established under the Treaty of Rome. It is composed of thirteen judges appointed by the member states; the appointments are for a term of six years and are renewable. A judge may be removed from office if in the unanimous opinion of the other judges and the advocates-general attached to the court he or she no longer fulfills the requisite conditions or meets the obligations arising from judicial office. From among themselves the judges appoint a president of the ECJ. Usually the ECJ sits in plenary sessions, but for certain purposes it may sit in separate chambers of three or five judges.

The ECJ is assisted by six advocates-general whose principal function is to consider the issues of each case independently of the judges and to make a reasoned submission in open court after the parties have done so. They do not participate in the formation of the judgment and their submissions are not binding to the court. Until 1989 the ECJ was the sole judicial organ of the EC. In 1989 an additional court called the European Court of First Instance was established for the purpose of adjudicating certain enumerated matters. In such cases the ECJ acts as a court of appeal.

Proceedings in the ECJ may be initiated either by individuals or by juridical persons such as corporations. The proceedings are of several kinds. Basically, the ECJ may declare an act or behavior of any member state illegal if it violates the EC treaties or subsequent European law. Proceedings may also be brought to establish liability. In addition, the ECJ adjudicates institutional conflicts arising from allegations that a body of the EC has violated the EC law. Also, any court from a member state may request that the ECJ render a preliminary ruling.

In the exercise of its multiple powers and functions the ECJ applies and develops law as an independent institution of the EC on the basis of written law and the general common principles of law emanating from the EC and its member states. For example, it has adopted the European Convention on Human Rights as an expression of these general principles of law. Through its interpretation of the basic liberties under the Treaty of Rome, the ECJ has widened its jurisdiction with respect to issues of freedom, equality, nondiscrimination, trade, capital, the work force, and services. Moreover, the Single European Act, which took force in 1987, gave the ECJ jurisdiction over various mental, cultural, social, and scientific matters, thus vastly expanding its scope.

The effectiveness and success of the ECJ depends upon the acceptance of the democratic base of law within the EC. So far this has been the case, even though the lawgiving bodies of the EC are still dominated by the national executives of the member states, by the European Commission (the EC's executive), and by the Council of Ministers (representing national governments).

(See also HUMAN RIGHTS; INTERNATIONAL COURT OF JUSTICE.)

Office for Official Publications of the European Community, *The Court of Justice of the European Community,* 4th ed. and later eds. (Luxembourg, 1986 et seq.).

HELMUT GOERLICH

EUROPEAN FREE TRADE ASSOCIATION. When the European Economic Community (EEC) was set up in the mid-1950s, Britain tried to persuade the six states that became members to adopt instead a less ambitious project for a European free trade area. When negotiations on this idea broke down in 1960, a number of West European states that had not joined the EEC formed the European Free Trade Association (EFTA). The original members were Britain, Austria, Denmark, Norway, Portugal, Sweden, and Switzerland. Finland became an associate member in 1961, and subsequently a full member, and Iceland joined in 1970.

The future of EFTA was put in some doubt when Britain and Denmark left in 1972 to join the *European Community (EC). (Portugal also left to join the EC in 1985). However, EFTA remained viable by negotiating a special trading relationship with the EC.

Following the decision of the EC in 1985 to create a single internal market by the end of 1992, the EFTA states opened negotiations to ensure that their economies did not suffer as a result. However, the negotiations made slow progress, because the EC was not prepared to offer EFTA any voice in the drafting of EC legislation that EFTA members would have to adopt domestically, as participants in the internal market.

One result of these difficulties was that although investment boomed in the member states of the EC as firms geared up for the post-1992 single market, investment stagnated in the EFTA states. Even their own companies preferred to invest in the member states of the EC. This prompted Austria to file an application for membership in the EC in 1989; it was followed by Sweden in 1991 and Finland in 1992.

Neutrality had been a barrier to membership for these states in the past. It was felt that the EC was too closely aligned with the *North Atlantic Treaty Organization (NATO) and that membership would therefore compromise their neutrality. However, the end of the *Cold War made it easier for that aspect of membership to be glossed over.

Although an agreement was signed with the EC in October 1991, the prospects for EFTA at the beginning of the 1990s were poor. However, a possible future role had emerged at the same time. Some of the states of Eastern and *Central Europe (particularly Czechoslovakia, Hungary, and Poland) indicated that they hoped for membership in the EC in the future. It was clear that this future was some distance away, and the idea gained currency that membership in EFTA might serve as a halfway stage that would demonstrate tangible progress. For other East European states EC membership might prove an impossible dream, but some link to the Single Market would be necessary. It seemed possible, therefore, that EFTA would continue to have a role in the architecture of the new Europe.

J. Jamar and H. Wallace, eds., *EEC–EFTA: More Than Just Good Friends?* (Bruges, 1988).

STEPHEN GEORGE

EUROPEAN MONETARY UNION. See EURO-PEAN COMMUNITY.

EUROPEAN PARLIAMENT. In 1962 the Assembly of the *European Community (EC) unilaterally adopted the name European Parliament (EP), though some questioned its appropriateness. The Assembly was not at that time directly elected, consisting of national parliamentarians holding a dual mandate. Further, the budgetary and legislative powers of the Assembly were extremely limited.

In 1987 the Single European Act (SEA) made the new name of the Assembly official. By that time the EP had been directly elected since 1979 (with elections every five years), and its budgetary and legislative powers had been increased: but it still fell far short of being the democratic legislature that it aspired to be.

Since the enlargement of the EC to twelve states, there have been 518 Members of the European Parliament (MEPs). The number allocated to each member state corresponds approximately to its population. France, Germany, Italy, and the United Kingdom each have 81; Spain, 60; the Netherlands, 25; Belgium, Greece, and Portugal, 24 each; Denmark, 16; Ireland, 15; and Luxembourg, 6. However, MEPs sit in party groups, not by nationality. The largest groups are the Socialists and the European People's Party; there were nine other groups in the EP that was elected in 1989.

The EP has the right to reject the budget of the EC as a whole, and it has the last word on amendments, subject to a maximum rate of increase, over what are described as "noncompulsory" items of expenditure. However, two-thirds of the budget consists of "compulsory" expenditure, including money spent on the common agricultural policy, and here the EP can only propose amendments; the Council of Ministers, which represents the member states, has the last word.

The council also has the last word on most EC legislation. It must receive a formal opinion from the EP before it can act on a legislative proposal from the European Commission (the executive body), but it can ignore that opinion. However, the SEA introduced weighted majority voting into the council for items connected with the freeing of the internal market of the EC (on other items voting is by unanimity), and on these items the EP was given a right of second reading, after which, if its proposed amendments are adopted by the commission, the council can reject them only if it acts unanimously.

The EP has a watchdog role over the workings of the *Lomé Convention, which links the EC with sixty-nine developing countries. According to the SEA, moreover, international agreements arrived at by the EC must be approved by the EP. It is to be expected, then, that in time the EP will acquire greater influence.

In 1991 a further small increase in the powers of the EP was agreed to in the Maastricht Treaty. For some national parliaments this was seen as a threat to their own position; others took the view that national parliaments were unable effectively to control EC decisions, especially with majority voting in the council, and that the only solution to the EC's "democratic deficit" was to increase the powers of the EP.

(See also EUROPEAN COURT OF JUSTICE; ROME, TREATY OF.)

Neill Nugent, *The Government and Politics of the European Community* (London, 1989).

STEPHEN GEORGE

EXPORT-LED GROWTH. Classical and neoclassical economists have consistently emphasized the gains from international trade. Adam Smith argued that trade provided a "vent" for surplus productive capacity, and David Ricardo's model of comparative advantage showed the advantages of economic specialization. Trade was also held to have a number of dynamic effects, contributing to growth in the long run. Export industries could be the leading sector in the economy, growing more rapidly than other sectors and thereby serving as an "engine" of growth.

The first theory of export-led growth emerged from studies of the economic history of the land-abundant "countries of recent settlement," particularly Canada, Australia, and Argentina. This "staple" theory held that the discovery of a primary product in which a country has comparative advantage would have a number of positive effects on the exporting country: attracting capital inflows and labor; establishing linkages with other sectors; inducing innovation, increases in productivity, and infrastructural development; opening the economy to the transfer of technology and skills; and contributing to higher levels of capital accumulation.

Critics argued that these beneficial mechanisms had not operated for a majority of developing countries. Export-led growth did not create dynamic linkages within the economy, in part because foreign ownership of export activities, such as mining or plantation agriculture, resulted in a transfer of profits out of the exporting country. The expected dynamic effects of trade also depended on the product being exported. Learning, technological innovation, and linkages were considered more likely in manufacturing than in agriculture or mining.

Second, an export orientation exposed developing countries to adverse international shocks and increased their dependence on the international system. Declining terms of trade for tropical products were held to perpetuate or even increase international economic inequality. In the short run, dependence on exports exposed countries to price volatility, which was particularly damaging in countries specialized in one or a narrow range of export products. Finally, dependence on exports created possible political vulnerabilities because more powerful developed-country importers could manipulate trade relations as a means of exercising political influence.

These arguments were not without merit, and helped explain why some countries had not benefited from trade to the expected extent. Moreover, they had a profound political and ideological influence in the *Third World, providing the justification for the pursuit of *import-substitution industrialization through protectionist trade policies. These arguments also provided the rationale for political efforts in the 1970s to institutionalize a *New International Economic Order (NIEO) that would offset the disadvantages of export dependence through trade preferences and international commodity agreements.

Yet as general propositions, the critical arguments did not hold up well. The applicability of the staple theory was admittedly limited, but it did demonstrate that agricultural exports contributed to growth in some circumstances. The commodity boom and oil price increases of the early 1970s showed that international price trends could favor producers of primary products as well as disfavor them. As developing countries learned to exploit their bargaining power, they were often able to rewrite contracts to their advantage. The establishment of linkages through the processing of tropical products was also not ruled out. Nor were countries as vulnerable to short-run price fluctuations as had been thought; the critical issue was how to design international and national mechanisms, such as compensatory schemes or domestic savings programs, for smoothing the financial impact of price fluctuations.

Through the 1960s, the debate about export-led growth centered almost exclusively on the advantages and disadvantages of trade in traditional tropical products: foodstuffs, agricultural raw materials, and ores, minerals, and metals. Yet by the mid-1960s, a number of developing countries began to expand their exports of manufactured products, setting in motion a new round of debate about trade policy.

These countries fell into two groups. In the first were large Latin American countries that had industrialized through import-substituting policies, including Argentina, Brazil, and Mexico. In response to *balance-of-payments problems, these countries sought at different times to expand their exports of manufactured goods. The policies used to accomplish this objective varied from country to country, but included exchange rate devaluation, selective import liberalization for exporters, subsidies and tax rebates, and incentives for foreign firms to expand their exports. Some countries, such as Brazil, were successful in diversifying their export structures, not only in light, labor-intensive manufactures but in intermediate and processed raw materials.

In general, however, these policy reforms did not result in a shift toward an export-led growth model. Incentives remained biased toward import-substituting activities, and export-promotion policies were applied inconsistently. Although there was some increase in trade, these economies remained relatively closed and did not generate adequate foreign exchange through exports to service their mounting external debt.

The second group of countries were the East Asian newly industrializing countries (NICs): the Republic of Korea (South Korea), Taiwan, Hong Kong, and Singapore. These countries developed dynamic export sectors beginning in the 1960s, and fit much more closely the export-led growth model. The transition to an export orientation varied somewhat from country to country. Hong Kong and Singapore were historically entrepôt economies, dominated by commerce and service industries. When export growth began in the 1950s in Hong Kong, it came mainly from textile and apparel firms that had fled the Communist revolution in China. In Singapore, by contrast, the export takeoff did not begin until the late 1960s and was almost completely dependent on export-oriented foreign firms.

Korea and Taiwan both had developed fledgling manufacturing sectors during the period of Japanese occupation and through import-substituting policies in the 1950s. Both countries undertook important policy reforms in the early 1960s that marked a change of strategy, including exchange rate devaluations, selective import liberalization, efforts to attract foreign direct investment, as well as other government supports to exporters.

Despite their differences, these four countries shared a number of common features. All were resource-poor countries with relatively abundant supplies of well-educated labor. All exploited their comparative advantage in light, labor-intensive manufactures, but over time gradually diversified into technology-, skill-, and even capital-intensive goods in response to rising labor costs, international competitive pressures, and growing protection in their advanced country markets. All depended heavily on the U.S. market. Most significantly, all grew extremely rapidly and managed to do so while maintaining relatively egalitarian distributions of income.

The success of East Asian newly industrializing countries has generated a number of important controversies. The most central one concerns the role of policy in their rapid economic growth. Two basic positions can be identified. On the one hand, neoclassical economists have stressed the pursuit of market-oriented policy reforms and a stable macroeconomic environment as the most important sources of growth. The export takeoff followed changes of trade policy in South Korea and Taiwan, generating a virtuous cycle from higher exports to higher savings and investment, technological innovation and learning, and higher growth.

The critique of the neoclassical position has come from a diverse group of political scientists, economists, and sociologists who place greater emphasis on the institutional setting. They have underlined that export-led growth was not a function of the market alone but was accompanied in Korea, Taiwan, and Singapore by a variety of state interventions, including continuing state ownership of industry, trade protection in a number of sectors, subsidies and special incentives to exporters, and the development of substantial trade bureaucracies to monitor performance and provide information to exporters. Second, it has been noted that all shared a number of particular political features that may have facilitated the transition to export-oriented policies, including weak or repressed labor movements, weak leftist parties, strong "developmentalist" bureaucracies, and authoritarian political leaderships.

A second controversy surrounds the role of foreign direct investment in NIC growth and exports. Critics have contended that the new export-led growth models based on manufactures resulted in dual economies just as the old export-led growth had, with export enclaves dominated by foreign firms. Lowered transport costs allowed mutinational corporations to transfer the labor-intensive portion of the production chain "offshore" to low-wage countries. This "new international division of labor" had minimal effects in terms of technology transfer or linkages with the domestic economy. This observation has some merit for the export-processing zones of East Asia, for the Border Industrialization Program in Mexico, and perhaps for Singapore. Generally, however, export-led growth in East Asia has not been the result of foreign investment but of domestic firms, and the share of foreign firms in total exports has fallen.

A third controversy concerns the revival of export pessimism. Skeptics have argued that the East Asian NICs grew rapidly because of buoyant international conditions. With slowed world trade growth and the effort by more and more developing countries to expand their exports, export-led growth may be less viable or profitable than it was in the past. A particular concern is the growth of protectionist barriers. The term *new protectionism* is often used loosely to encompass legitimate retaliation against unfair trade practices such as dumping, but there has been a trend toward the imposition of barriers that violate the spirit, if not the letter, of international commercial law. The export-oriented NICs have been the major targets of this new protectionism.

Critics of the new export pessimism have responded by noting that the NICs have generally been able to circumvent protectionist restrictions through industrial upgrading, and that exports from the NICs have continued to exhibit dynamism even in the face of external adversity. This is taken as proof that an outward-oriented economic strategy is superior regardless of external conditions.

By the end of the 1980s, there were substantial pressures on most developing countries to expand their exports, including large debt burdens, the unavailability of commercial lending, and the inefficiencies associated with previous import-substituting patterns of industrialization. A second tier of export-oriented countries has emerged, such as Thailand and Turkey, and a number of Latin American countries, including Mexico and Chile, have undertaken dramatic reforms of their trade policy systems. The unique conditions operating in the East Asian NICs make it unlikely that many countries will be able to fully replicate their success with export-led growth, but the gains from exporting will continue to pull countries toward export-led growth strategies.

(See also DEVELOPMENT AND UNDERDEVELOPMENT; NEWLY INDUSTRIALIZING ECONOMIES; PROTECTION.)

Bela Balassa, *The Newly Industrializing Countries in the World Economy* (New York, 1981). David Yoffie, *Power and Protectionism: Strategies of the Newly Industrializing Countries* (New York, 1983). Stephan Haggard, *Pathways from the Periphery: The Politics of Growth in the Newly Industrializing Countries* (Ithaca, N.Y., 1990).

STEPHAN HAGGARD

F

FALKLANDS WAR. See MALVINAS/FALKLANDS WAR.

FANON, Frantz. Medical doctor and psychiatrist, Frantz Fanon (1925–1961) was born in Fort-de-France, Martinique, one of France's "old colonies." Educated there and in the metropole, he served with the Ninth French Division in France (1944–1946), receiving the Croix de Guerre for bravery. Graduating as a psychiatrist (1952) from the Faculty of Medicine and Pharmacy at Lyon, Fanon later accepted an appointment at the Saint-Alban-de-Lozère hospital near Mende in central France (1952–1953). In the early 1950s, he married Marie-Josephe Dublé from Lyon, who bore him a son.

Subsequently becoming a divisional director at the psychiatric hospital in Blida-Joinville in *Algeria (1953–1957), Fanon was eventually expelled by Algeria's French authorities for his work with the Front de Libération Nationale (FLN)—the principal nationalist organization formed by Algerians in their anticolonial or liberation war against France (1954–1962). Based in Tunis (1957–1960), he carried his revolutionary mission to Europe and to West Africa, while as part of his local war effort he placed his skills and scientific findings at the disposal of the sick and war-weary *mujahidin* or freedom fighters of the FLN, and the Armée de Libération Nationale (ALN).

In the course of his relatively short lifetime, and in conjunction with medical and psychiatric colleagues, Fanon published no less than sixteen scientific articles, in addition to numerous political communications, letters, and articles, appearing in journals such as *Esprit,* a liberal French journal published in Paris, and newspapers such as *El Moudjahid,* the official mouthpiece of the FLN. He likewise published *Black Skin, White Masks* (New York, 1967); *A Dying Colonialism* (New York, 1968), his last book, owing much to his field work in Algeria; *The Wretched of the Earth* (New York, 1965); and the posthumous volume *For the African Revolution* (New York, 1967).

Fanon's contributions to an understanding of the psychology of colonialism are considerable. To date few have gone beyond his findings or insights. First, as a politicized psychiatrist, he was among the early pioneers to recognize that individual and collective emotional disorders were associated on a large scale with the social pathology of colonialism, which, by its very nature, denied validity to indigenous peoples and their cultures. More specifically, the syndrome fostered widespread social diseases such as feelings of rage, alienation, inferiority, self-hatred, and withdrawal—all products, he believed, of a conflict-ridden colonial pathology. Second, as a revolutionary theorist and participant in the *Algerian War of Independence, Fanon was also among the first to identify the revolutionary potential of the peasantry. In conflict with Marxist revolutionary theories which denigrated *peasants, equating them with "rural idiocy," Fanon's theory of the revolutionary peasantry met with considerable criticism. However, far from attributing a leadership role to peasants during the Algerian War of Independence (which critics frequently charged), Fanon recognized instead their limited ability to initiate, manage, and sustain a revolutionary endeavor, thereby advising nationalist leaders that peasant historical propensities for violence and opposition to outsiders, in this case the French, should not be ignored; and that through appropriate revolutionary indoctrination and leadership from nationalist cadres, amorphous peasant violence could be channeled into nationalist and revolutionary aims. This is exactly what happened. On the morning of 1 November 1954, sounding the first tocsins, it was the peasants of the Aurès Mountains under the direction of nationalist cadres who were the first to rise against the French settlers and army in Algeria.

Finally, as a revolutionary propagandist with a profound understanding of changes likely to occur in human behavior under certain types of wartime stresses, Fanon was among the first to identify and explain that phenomenon in the developing world. Fanon argued that involvement in an anticolonial struggle, reinforced by supportive networks composed of groups sharing the same revolutionary ideals, could enable the alienated and emotionally fraught individual to recover from destructive colonial disorders. On becoming a new person (if only temporarily) in the heat of struggle, the depressed, cowardly, and inferior feelings, together with the alienation, frustration, and rage, could give way to courage, self-renewal, and an enhanced self-appraisal. The "cure" was not always permanent, and not all colonized Algerians were "restored" to emotional health as a consequence of their revolutionary endeavors; yet some oral and written accounts testify to some of these effects.

Fanon died in residence at the National Institutes of Health in Bethesda, Maryland, a suburb of Washington, D.C., while being treated for leukemia. His remains lie buried in Tunisia, near the Algerian frontier.

(See also COLONIAL EMPIRES; DECOLONIZATION; POLITICAL VIOLENCE; PSYCHOLOGY AND POLITICS; REVOLUTION.)

B. Marie Perinbam, *Holy Violence: The Revolutionary Thought of Frantz Fanon* (Washington, D.C., 1982).
B. MARIE PERINBAM

FASCISM. The term *fascism* was first used to identify the political system by which Italy was ruled from 1922 to 1945. It now also refers to a prototype of *totalitarianism and is applied to variations of political systems thought to parallel the Italian model.

The term derives from the Italian *fascio,* a perfectly ordinary word with no more sinister meaning than "bundle," "weight," "group," or "grouping." When used in a political context, the English equivalent would be *league, alliance,* or *union;* the German might be *Bund.*

Contemporaries found fascism difficult to define. Scholars have not fared better: too often they have agreed to use the term without agreeing on what it means. Depending on their viewpoint, scholars have traced fascism's origins to such varied sources as Plato's *Republic,* to Romantic radicals like Rousseau, to conservative philosophers who idealized a strong *state like Fichte and Carlyle, Hegel and Nietzsche. Other scholars have identified protofascist regimes ranging from the French Revolutionary Terror to Napoléon III's Second Empire.

These precedents are useful to indicate that fascism was a unique blend of earlier *ideologies and institutions. Nevertheless, fascism was essentially a creature of *World War I, a response to the revolutionary changes which that conflict brought to European politics, culture, and society. The term came into use at that time, and the two decades between World War I and *World War II have often been described as the "Era of Fascism." With the defeat of the fascist regimes in World War II, fascism has apparently disappeared as a major political phenomenon, a threat to the international order. Yet, given the right crisis, fascism, or at least fascist-style regimes, could once again emerge.

Fascism has been difficult to define in part because its ideology varied so widely. It was often easier to understand what fascism was against than what it stood for. Fatherland, flag and country, old-fashioned patriotism against the threats of internationalism and the Bolshevik menace constituted the core of fascism's appeal. This fanatic "blood-and-soil" *nationalism was often transmuted into racism, ranging from a generic ethnic pride to a violent, biological racism and *antisemitism, as in the case of Nazi Germany. Fascist ideology also included a romantic, antirational allure, an appeal to the emotions, to a quasi-religious longing for a mystic union of peoples and their prophetic leader. In reaction to the utilitarian liberal state, fascism revived aspirations toward the normative or "ethical state." According to this view, the community existed not simply as a practical convenience but in order to fulfill the individual's ethical and moral potential.

How people perceived these themes depended on the eye of the beholder. Conservatives viewed fascism as a bulwark against Bolshevism or as a middle way between a worn-out liberal capitalism and the communist horror. Radicals viewed fascism as a genuinely revolutionary ideology that would sweep away discredited ideals and institutions and replace them with a new, disciplined, cohesive society.

If fascism is difficult to define as an ideal, it is no easier to delimit in practice. In defining fascism, it is useful to recall the movement's genesis. Fascism originated in Italy after the end of World War I and scored its first big success with *Mussolini's "March on Rome" in 1922. In Italy, fascism was primarily a response to the crisis of the liberal state's political institutions. The Italian prototype spawned wide variations. Every major European country developed at least a fascist party or movement. José Antonio Primo de Rivera's Falangists in Spain, Corneliu Codreanu's Legion of the Archangel Michael in Romania, Action Française and the Croix de Feu in France, Léon Degrelle's Rexists in Belgium, Oswald Mosley's British Union of Fascists in England, Ferencz Szalasi's Arrow Cross movement in Hungary, all claimed to find inspiration in fascism. They drew on the Italian model, or, as often in Eastern Europe, on the Nazis, or a combination of both. Movements or parties, however, did not always blossom into full-blown regimes. In some cases, as in Romania and Hungary, fascism came to power only under the aegis of the World War II Nazi occupation.

Looming as the dominant model after 1933 was the example of Nazi Germany. But the extreme violence, brutality, and racism of the Nazi regime set it apart, and scholars today are still uncertain whether to include the Nazi example under the general rubric of fascism. How little the fascist regimes had in common became evident when Italy and Germany attempted to create a bloc of fascist powers with the Axis (1936) and then contracted a formal *alliance with the Pact of Steel (1939). The union proved to be notoriously awkward and quickly foundered during World War II. Thus, rather than a generic "fascism," it would be more accurate to speak of "fascist-style regimes."

Nevertheless, within wide national variations, fascist states had certain characteristics and aspirations in common. In their political systems, they created police states, *one-party systems led by a charismatic dictator. Their economic systems aimed to develop some form of national *socialism. The government was to play an active role in controlling the economy, but unlike Marxian socialism, the state was not to take over the means of production. Fascist socialism was directed at the interests of the nation, not a particular *class. Fascism also aspired to some form of the corporativist (or corporatist) state. The antagonism between labor and capital, fostered under the liberal state, was to be bridged in the form of corporations. Through these guildlike structures, labor and capital were to find common ground in developing their particular economic sector. Economic interest would submerge or supersede class interest. In *foreign policy, fascist regimes were unabashedly expansionist and imperialist. Mussolini revived Italy's vision of African colonial empire. *Hitler's Third Reich aspired to a great *Volkisch* empire in Poland, Russia, and the Ukraine. Hungarian fascists dreamed of dominating the Danube basin; Spanish Falangists coveted African possessions and perhaps even hoped to reannex Portugal.

Given its many forms in ideology and practice, interpretations of fascism have also varied widely. Historically, four major interpretations can be distinguished: fascism as the crisis of the liberal state, as *totalitarianism, as the radical right, as a revolt against *modernity.

In the 1920s and 1930s, many contemporaries quite naturally viewed fascism as a crisis of the old liberal system. Liberal political values and institutions had failed. In their place, fascism surfaced: a series of brutal, barbaric, violent dictatorships, led by charismatic tyrants, bereft of ideas or plans for the future. Communists, in particular, viewed fascism as a last, desperate authoritarian phase of capitalism. But such interpretations ignored the genuine mass appeal of fascism and minimized the fascist vision, no matter how confused, of a disciplined, cohesive society.

A second major interpretation, popular during the Cold War, saw fascism as totalitarianism. Proponents of this view were deeply influenced by the apparent identity of fascism, in its last stages, with communism. The Nazi-Soviet Pact of 1939, combined with the disclosures of *Stalin's purges and mass murders and postwar revelations of the *Holocaust, suggested that fascists and communists were cut from the same cloth.

A cornerstone of this interpretation is the importance of terror and the repressive apparatus of the modern state. Certainly fascism was a prototype of the modern totalitarian state—in the words of Mussolini, "Everything within the state, nothing outside the state, nothing against the state." Fascism aspired to total control over its citizens, leaving them with no island of privacy. With the aid of twentieth-century mass media, fascist states could reach and control their citizenry in a way that earlier regimes could not. Yet there were wide variations in the repressive powers and the totalitarian reach of fascist or fascist-style regimes. The control of a Mussolini or a *Franco was never comparable to that of Hitler or Stalin.

The equation of fascism and *communism also minimizes the ideological differences and the social and institutional bases of fascist and communist regimes. In its crudeness and violence, fascist ideology cannot be easily compared to the sophistication of *Marxism. Nor were the social and institutional bases of fascist and communist societies comparable. Fascist regimes protected middle class interests and preserved and compromised with traditional institutions like the church and the military far more than the communists did. Mussolini signed the Lateran Pacts and protected Italian big business. Stalin repressed the church and murdered kulaks.

In the 1960s, a third major interpretation of fascism as "a radicalism of the right," as traditional conservative ideas pushed to an extreme, emerged. Fascism as totalitarianism emphasized the novelty of fascism; fascism as a "radicalism of the right" emphasized its continuities with the past. Such an interpretation, however, lays too much stress on political ideology. Moreover, such a view, with its accent on the "conservative" or "reactionary" aspects of fascism, ignores the genuinely revolutionary and innovative goals to which fascists often aspired.

With a lessening of the *Cold War and increasing stability in international relations, fascism has been viewed as "a revolt against modernity," a protest against the pace of social and cultural change wrought by rapid industrialization. Such an interpretation focuses less on political systems than on paths to social development. In this view, fascism appears as one of several possible routes, together with liberal *capitalism and socialism, to modern society. Fascist regimes mobilized and disciplined societies to transform themselves far more rapidly than would have been the case under a laissez-faire system. Under fascism, however, direction came "from above" in such a way as to avoid upsetting the social structure.

In perspective, however, the transformation under fascist regimes appears to have been ambivalent and often superficial. Fascist regimes froze or retarded development more than they sped it up. Italy's transformation into the West's fourth major industrial power occurred during the postwar decades after the fall of fascism. Germany was already a modern, industrialized society when the Nazis came to power, and some scholars have argued that Nazism was in fact a reaction to *modernization, a desire to return to a simpler preindustrial past.

World War II totally discredited fascism as an ideology with mass appeal. These days the term applies to anything from right-wing terrorist groups in Italy to *Third World military dictatorships, from ordinary police to motorcycle gangs. Most commonly, the term is used as a label for Third World military dictatorships ranging from the latest juntas in Africa or Latin America to Saddam *Hussein's Iraq. Following the events of 1989 and the end of Soviet influence in Eastern Europe and the Balkans, fascist-style movements and popular outbursts have surfaced in these regions. Observers have commented that if democratic regimes do not develop there, fascist-style regimes might arise. They would feed on the conflicting nationalisms in the area, and they might be spearheaded by the military. Even if such regimes were to emerge, however, it appears unlikely that they would pose a threat to the international order in the way that the fascism of the interwar period, led by Nazi Germany, precipitated the crisis of World War II.

Thus fascism is probably more dormant than dead. Old-style fascism of the interwar period is unlikely to reemerge. Nevertheless, the fascist ideology appeals to our deepest longings for community, for solidarity, for safety in the face of a seething world. Scenarios that might bring forth fascist-style regimes in Europe or the United States are not difficult to imagine. What if the tide of immigrant workers and refugees from the Third World appeared to overwhelm Europe or the United States? What if the *AIDS epidemic continues to spread uncontrollably? What if a stock market crash set off a worldwide economic panic? Any such prolonged *crisis might condition people to respond to fascist-style appeals: ultranationalism, revolutionary fever, antirationalism, a mystic faith in a strong leader. Future fascisms, like the earlier ones, would vary with local political traditions and circumstances. With the development of mass media and computers such future fascist regimes would have new totalitarian capacities.

(See also AUTHORITARIANISM; CORPORATISM; IMPERIALISM; MILITARY RULE; POLITICAL VIOLENCE; RACE AND RACISM; TERRORISM.)

Eugen Weber, *Varieties of Fascism* (New York, 1964). Ernst Nolte, *Three Faces of Fascism* (New York, 1966). S. J. Woolf, ed., *European Fascism* (New York, 1969). Walter Laqueur, ed., *Fascism: A Reader's Guide, Analyses, Interpretations, Bibliography* (Berkeley, Calif., 1976). Stanley G. Payne, *Fascism: Comparison and Definition* (Madison, Wis., 1980).

CLAUDIO G. SEGRÈ

FEDERALISM. Modern federalism, according to British political scientist K. C. Wheare (*Federal Government*, 4th ed., New York, 1964), was invented in Philadelphia, Pennsylvania, 200 years ago by the authors of the U.S. Constitution. Until then, a federal country had been seen as a league or club of member states. Under the U.S. Constitution, each citizen is a citizen of two governments, national and state.

There is general agreement among experts that a functioning federal system, composed of a number of regional governments, must have a democratic and pluralist political system that provides opportunities for access and participation by citizens at both the national and state levels. Otherwise, the idea of self-expression by the states would not be meaningful. Most experts also agree that an effective federal form needs to operate under a written *constitution that stipulates the responsibilities of the central and state governments, the role of the states in the amendatory process, and the rights of *citizenship.

Advocates of federalism see it as a way to protect against central tyranny, increase citizen participation, encourage innovation (the states as "laboratories"), and strengthen community identity and values. Opponents of the federal form criticize its slowness to respond to new challenges, its perceived inability to take advantage of technological advances, and the allegedly cumbersome nature of its governmental decision-making and implementation processes.

The basic objective of federalism is to reconcile unity and diversity. In particular, federalism has been adopted in various forms by many nations as a way to balance the interests of different ethnic and language groups, although this was not the purpose of the founders of U.S. federalism, where former British colonies covering a large territory with a vast unsettled frontier were joined together. The Swiss federation, founded in 1848, has twenty-three cantons (the equivalent of states in the United States). For over 100 years, it has balanced the interests of three major ethnic and language groups (German, French, and Italian). Federalism in India and Canada likewise seeks to reconcile the interests of different ethnic and language groups, although the tensions in these countries have at various times caused serious problems for the federalism bargain.

Among political scientists, there are debates about the nature of federalism. One school stresses the amorphous nature of federalism and its operational complexity. U.S. political scientist Morton Grodzins, a leading exponent of this position, likened modern federalism to a marble cake (rather than a layer cake) characterized by constantly shifting, swirling patterns of functions, finances, and administrative arrangements. Some members of the Grodzins school describe federalism as inevitably progressing toward a centralized governmental system. According to this view, federalism is, in effect, a way station to unitary government.

A second school highlights the distinctive role of regional governments in federal systems, however designated—states, provinces, republics, cantons, *Länder*. (The term *state* is used for all of these regional entities in this essay.) Some members of this second school view federalism as cyclical in nature, noting that the role of states tends to increase in some periods and contract in others. According to this model, the role of the central government tends to expand in liberal periods (that is, periods in which progovernmental views are strong) and to contract in conservative periods (in which, in turn, the role of the states expands).

Many nations have attempted to institute a federal form, sometimes copying the actual wording of the U.S. Constitution. Often, however, they either have not carried out the intent or have tried to do so but were unable to establish or maintain a federal form. The Caribbean Federation and the East African Federation are recent examples of failed federations. The Soviet Union, which was federal in its formal constitution but not in actual behavior, has now been replaced by a far looser federal association, the Commonwealth of Independent States. The emergence of a unified market among the member nations of the *European Community (EC) raises the interesting prospect of a movement toward a federal system in Europe.

A useful way to view the federal bargain is to focus on major aspects of the role of state governments including, for example: 1) the political and constitutional aspect of the federal relationship, referring to the powers of the states to determine, organize, and control their own legal and electoral systems; 2) their fiscal role, referring to the way in which, and the degree to which, the states can set and levy their own taxes; 3) the programmatic dimension of federalism, referring to the functional areas of governmental activity over which the states have sole or predominant responsibility; 4) the role of state governments in the policy-setting process of the central government (for example, in the upper house of the legislature); and 5) the role of the states in determining the form, functions, and finances of local units of government.

Countries currently and frequently classified as federal are: Australia, Canada, Brazil, the Federal Republic of Germany, India, Malaysia, Nigeria, Switzerland, and the United States.

(See also PLURALISM; POLITICAL PARTICIPATION.)

Thomas J. Anton, *American Federalism and Public Policy* (Philadelphia, 1989). Richard P. Nathan and Margaret M. Balmaceda, "Comparing Federal Systems of Government," in Robert J. Bennett, ed., *Decentralization, Local Governments and Markets: Towards a Post-Welfare Agenda* (Oxford, 1990).

RICHARD P. NATHAN

FEDERATED STATES OF MICRONESIA. See PACIFIC ISLANDS.

FEMINISM. The term *feminism* refers to diverse theories and movements that critique male bias and female subordination and are committed to eliminating gender inequity. Feminism is not simply a list of women's issues or synonymous with the constituency of women. Rather feminism is a transformative perspective on any question that women and men can take by looking specifically at how something affects women and challenging how gender is socially constructed. The activity this constitutes varies by context, time, and place; as the leading *Third World women's organization, Development Alternatives with Women for a New Era (DAWN) states: "There is and must be a diversity of feminisms, responsive to the different needs and concerns of different women, and defined by them for themselves. This diversity builds on a common opposition to gender oppression and hierarchy which, however, is only the first step in articulating and acting upon a political agenda" (Gita Sen and Caren Grown, *Development, Crisis, and Alternative Visions: Third World Women's Perspectives,* Stavanger, Norway, p. 13).

Over the past two decades, a vast number of projects and treatises have developed globally that address how gender constructs and constricts our lives daily, reflecting the vitality of current exploration of the implications of feminism for our world. Gender is increasingly recognized as a central category for understanding politics that has policy implications in most areas and affects men as well as women. As feminism is examined in relation to various fields, it transforms the way knowledge is constructed and how we conceive of society and politics.

Development of Feminism. Individuals and groups in different eras have opposed female subordination and sought to fashion a better life for women. But the concept of a modern women's movement took shape in the nineteenth century, and use of the term *feminism* to describe such activity began in Europe at the end of that century. Late-nineteenth-century and early-twentieth-century women's movements focused primarily on education, individual political and legal *rights (including voting and property rights in the West and participation in independence struggles in the East), or on women's special needs as mothers and keepers of society's virtue.

Contemporary Western feminism began its theoretical revival with the 1949 publication of *The Second Sex* by Simone de Beauvoir. She challenged the secondary "other" status of women in a society that assumed men as the subject and maleness as the norm. De Beauvoir asserted that women are made subordinate by *patriarchy, not born that way naturally. The activist resurgence of feminism in the West came with the 1960s black rights, national liberation, antiwar, and student movements.

This resurgence had two major strands: women's rights and women's liberation. Women's rights (also called liberal feminism) emphasizes the demand for equality of women with men in the mainstream of society. Based on the tradition of liberal *democracy, it seeks equal opportunity for women as individuals with rights to be obtained through legislation, rational enlightenment, and reform.

Women's liberation arose primarily among young

women in *New Left movements who fought for equality in "the revolution" and sought women's freedom from mainstream patriarchal structures. This strand spawned various feminisms offering radical interpretations of women's oppression and what was necessary for liberation: socialist, radical, lesbian, and cultural feminism were the most visible.

Socialist feminism, stronger in Europe than the United States, has many variations depending on which Left traditions it draws on. It fuses these theories by bringing gender perspectives to Marxist analysis, asking new questions that alter, not abandon, that framework's emphasis on *class. Radical feminism, asserting the primacy of sex/gender as categories of analysis, views relations between the sexes as political—a concept pioneered by Kate Millett's *Sexual Politics* in 1969. Recognizing sexuality as central to women's oppression, it concentrates on issues involving the control of women's bodies such as reproduction, heterosexuality, and sexual violence. Lesbian feminism is both a movement for lesbian rights and a theory analyzing heterosexism (the domination of and compulsory demand for heterosexuality) and how that maintains sex roles and adds to the oppression of all women. Cultural feminism posits the importance (and some claim superiority) of women's different nature and values, but is primarily expressed through women's art, music, spirituality, and other cultural forms.

These broad categories describe the evolution of contemporary Western feminism in relation to the century's dominant political theories, but feminist developments often move beyond such boundaries. Feminism today has many specialized fields that draw on all of these theories, and discussion often focuses on identity politics and the question of differences between women as well as between women and men. In the 1980s, movements and writing from the Third World and women of color in the West provided the most significant influences on feminist development.

Global Feminism. Feminists have been active in Asia, Africa, Latin America, and the Middle East at different points in the nineteenth and twentieth centuries prior to today's movements. According to Kumari Jayawardena's study of twelve Eastern countries (*Feminism and Nationalism in the Third World,* New Delhi, 1986), movements for women's emancipation and *political participation took place within a context of nationalist struggles "aimed at achieving political independence, asserting a national identity, and modernizing society." In Latin America, early-twentieth-century feminists focused primarily on gaining the vote and women's education.

Contemporary feminism in the Third World got a boost from the UN International Women's Year in 1975 and the Decade for Women from 1976–1985. The UN decade's theme, "Equality, Development, and Peace," reflected Western emphasis on equality, Third World preoccupation with development, and the Eastern bloc's focus on peace. Most women's advocates in Africa and Asia linked improvement in women's status to bringing them into the economic development process. Latin American and Caribbean feminists sought to enhance women's participation in movements for change and viewed imperialism and class as causing female poverty.

The UN decade created a global dialogue that gave space and legitimacy to exploring women's lives and provided context and funding for women's projects in developing countries. As those working for women in the Third World encountered multiple obstacles, many turned to feminism to interpret the web of gender, race, class, and cultural biases women faced.

The UN held three world conferences on women (Mexico City, 1975; Copenhagen, 1980; Nairobi, 1985)—all accompanied by nongovernmental forums, which enabled women to make global connections, as did the nongovernmental Tribunal on Crimes Against Women in Brussels 1977. The Mexico City and Copenhagen conferences saw conflict between Western and Third World women, especially over what were "women's issues," but they still provided common ground for learning from each other.

By 1985, many were moving beyond old divisions and making connections between demands for equality, development, and peace. More Third World women had become feminist, finding a need to act autonomously from other political groups and seeing the key role of gender discrimination in issues killing women, like poverty, sexual violence, and lack of reproductive health care. Western feminists understood better the importance of race, class, and economic development in shaping women's oppression. This was a result of both decade activities and women of color calling for more attention to such questions in the West. Feminists who had struggled to establish "women's issues" such as equal pay and reproductive rights as serious public and political matters had begun to understand the need also to broaden feminism and assert that all issues concern women. Thus the Nairobi conferences, attended by over 15,000 (at least half from the Third World), were characterized by constructive debate demonstrating that out of the ferment of the decade, global feminism was emerging.

There are many differences among women, and priorities vary, but commonality exists in broad feminist goals, such as those articulated by the International Workshop on Feminist Ideology and Structures sponsored by the Asian and Pacific Centre for Women and Development, Bangkok, 1979: "1.) Freedom from oppression for women involves not only equity, but also the right of women to freedom of choice, and the power to control their own lives within and outside of the home. Having control over our lives and our bodies is essential to ensure a sense of dignity and autonomy for every woman. . . . 2.) The second goal of feminism is the removal of all forms of inequity and oppression through the creation of a more just social and economic order, nationally and internationally," a process that involves women in national liberation struggles and as active participants in national development plans.

Global feminism means not only that activity is occurring around the world but also that women in each setting are part of an interconnected picture affected by global forces. Further it calls for a holistic approach which understands that domination by sex is linked to domination over people based on other differences and that sociopolitical and economic issues such as poverty, militarism, and sexism are interrelated.

Global feminism has not produced large international organizations but is characterized by networks and clearinghouses for information sharing and coordinating strategies. Key multipurpose groups that conduct training, serve as resource centers, and publish internationally are the International Women's Tribune Centre (IWTC) in New York, ISIS International in Santiago and Manila, and ISIS:WICCE in Geneva. Many global networks and events focus on topics like health, women's studies, reproductive rights, and development; others are area-specific, like the Network for Solidarity with Women Living Under Muslim Laws or the Latin American Lesbian Feminist Network. Solidarity and strategies for feminist action globally are built around concrete issues. This work is based on respecting diversity of needs and approaches in each locale while recognizing common concerns, like violence, which take different cultural forms but disrupt women's lives everywhere.

Feminism often emerges out of national independence or social change movements, but usually becomes autonomous in order to develop theory and action that is not submerged by other interests and can articulate women's perspectives forcefully. Currently, feminists in many places are addressing the need to transform basic social concepts such as development and democracy from feminist perspectives and are interacting with other movements in so doing. For example, Latin American feminists call for extending democracy to the private sphere, rallying around a Chilean slogan coined in the struggle against dictatorship: "Democracia en el país y en la casa" (Democracy in the country and in the home.) Ecofeminists analyze connections between treatment of the earth and of women and contribute such insights to ecological movements that question society's attitudes toward industry, science, and nature. Other feminists revise traditional approaches to human rights, development, and peace, trying to incorporate women's realities into these concepts and utilizing women's perspectives as a basis for generating new approaches to change. Feminism's promise then is both to improve women's lives and

to seek a better future for the human race and for the planet.

(See also DEVELOPMENT AND UNDERDEVELOPMENT; EQUALITY AND INEQUALITY; FEMINIST THEORY; GAY AND LESBIAN POLITICS; GENDER AND POLITICS; IDEOLOGY; IMPERIALISM; MARXISM; NEW SOCIAL MOVEMENTS; REPRODUCTIVE POLITICS; SOCIALISM AND SOCIAL DEMOCRACY; WOMEN AND DEVELOPMENT.)

Miranda Davies, ed., *Third World, Second Sex*, vols. 1 and 2, (London, 1981 and 1987). Bell Hooks, *Feminist Theory: From Margin to Center* (Boston, 1984). Robin Morgan, ed., *Sisterhood Is Global: International Women's Movement Anthology* (New York, 1984). Kamla Bhasin and Nighat Said Khan, *Some Questions on Feminism and Its Relevance in South Asia* (New Delhi, 1986). Joni Seager and Ann Olson, *Women in the World: An International Atlas* (London, 1986). Sonia Kruks, Rayna Rapp, and Marilyn B. Young, eds., *Promissory Notes: Women in the Transition to Socialism* (New York, 1989).

CHARLOTTE BUNCH

FEMINIST THEORY. Western feminist theory locates and names power as it defines the lives of women in the home and in the market (as mothers, daughters, sisters, wives, and lovers) and the ways they bring their gender along with them from the home to the market and back again. At its best feminist theory reinvents the way we think about * power itself because it directs us to the politics of sex. It requires that we reimagine the relationship between the personal and political realms of life; the public and the private; the family and the economy; the domestic and the waged spheres of work. In its more limited scope it is a corrective to a "generalized" viewing of political theory that presumes the male standard as the referent.

Feminist theory examines and critiques the relations of power that are defined in and through the sex/gender system that "unnaturally" differentiates women from men. The feminist viewing of this problematic system of power, which privileges men while denying women legal and political equality and sexual freedom, has shifted over time. Different theorists of feminism reflect the changing times, histories, and varied conceptions of women's power and oppression.

Western feminist theory first developed in eighteenth-century England both as a critique and extension of bourgeois democratic rights. Mary Wollstonecraft argued in *A Vindication of the Rights of Woman* (1792) that women had the same capacity for rationality as men and therefore should be included in ongoing societal changes. She very specifically argued for women's right to an education. There were many variations of this liberal equal rights theme that called for women's *rights to be similar to men's in terms of property, contracts, etc. The articulation of liberal *feminism—which both endorsed the discourse of *liberalism and indicted it for its exclusion of women—was the center of

Western feminist theory through the early twentieth century.

Modern Western feminist theory emerged in 1970 via its roots in this earlier liberal feminism, its roots in the *civil rights movement of the 1960s, and its embrace and critique of *New Left politics. Feminist theory, through the 1970s, was articulated by a series of critical dialogues between feminism, liberalism, and radically leftist and Marxist theory. As such, the naming of feminist theory is done through "other" political identities: socialist feminists define the problem for women as the system of capitalism and its intersections with *patriarchy and/or male privilege; radical feminists theorize the system of patriarchy as the central problem of women's domination; radical lesbian feminists focus on the problem of heterosexuality as the pivotal core of women's oppression; anarcha-feminists highlight the problem of structure within the systems of capitalism and patriarchy. By the late 1970s black and *Third World feminism emerged as a critique of the white privilege inherent in feminist theory itself.

Contemporary Western feminist theory in the 1980s moved beyond the dialogues that sought to differentiate feminisms from each other and instead began to articulate a more pluralized notion of feminism at its core. Feminist theory emerged with an understanding of gender and its sexual *class structure that cuts through the differences of *race and economic class while recognizing its semi-autonomous political status. There is no uncontested agreement about how the various systems of oppression intersect with the gender system. But feminist theory has mapped and charted patriarchal privilege as a key political/power relation to be threaded through these other systems of power.

Theory always develops in dialogue with other theory and with the particular historical and political contexts of the moment. Whereas feminist theory in the 1970s established its epistemological identity through multiple construction of patriarchal privilege, the contemporary period is one of cross-dialogue and critique of the various feminisms themselves. The focus of the 1970s was on Western society and its structural barriers toward women. The focus of the 1980s for feminist theory was a critique of feminism itself and the ways it reproduces aspects of a racist and patriarchal society. In the 1990s this dialogue continues with a specific focus on the concept of difference. This is in large part due to the influence of women of color within feminist theory, in part due to a dialogue with postmodernist and French feminist theory, and in part a reaction to the neoconservative antifeminist discourse that dominates the U.S. state and policy arenas.

Feminist theory has always had to contend with the "problem" or difference, particularly women's supposed difference from men. This notion of difference focuses on women as homogeneous; as though they all are alike, and different from men in the same way. In reaction, liberal feminism takes the stance that women are not different from men, that they are the same, or more similar than different. Cultural feminism, often also termed "essentialism," argues that women are different and the difference is positive, i.e., women are more caring, less competitive, more likely to be peaceful. Women of color take the concern with difference in other directions and demand a recognition of racial and economic class diversity as a starting point for any discussion about similarities and variations among "women" considered both as a group by itself *and* as distinct from men. These developments continue to keep feminist theory open to new invention and theorization.

There is no one feminist theory, but this is different from saying that feminism has a problematic theoretical status. Rather it means that there are a variety of ways to theorize the key institutions and relations of patriarchy. There are various interpretations of the institution of motherhood (the conflation of bearing and rearing children and domestic labor) as distinguished from biological motherhood; the dichotomization of public and private life and the personal from the political; and the intersections of patriarchy, economic class, racism, and heterosexism. As a result feminist theory theorizes women's lives in the ways they interact with the relations of power. Because systems of power are always shifting and being reconstituted, feminist theory must continually redefine itself from the multiple sites of women's oppression. Hopefully this creates the possibility of using feminist theory to change and reconstruct systems of power.

(See also GAY AND LESBIAN POLITICS; GENDER AND POLITICS; MARXISM; POSTMODERNISM; REPRODUCTIVE POLITICS; WOMEN AND DEVELOPMENT.)

Shulamith Firestone, *The Dialectic of Sex* (New York, 1970). Kate Millett, *Sexual Politics* (Garden City, N.Y., 1970). Juliet Mitchell, *Woman's Estate* (New York, 1971). Ti-Grace Atkinson, *Amazon Odyssey* (New York, 1974). Adrienne Rich, *Of Woman Born* (New York, 1976). Zillah Eisenstein, *The Radical Future of Liberal Feminism* (New York, 1981). Gloria T. Hull, Patricia Bell Scott, and Barbara Smith, eds., *All the Women Are White, All the Blacks Are Men, But Some of Us Are Brave* (New York, 1982). Catharine A. MacKinnon, *Feminism Unmodified* (Cambridge, Mass., 1987). Hazel Carby, *Reconstructing Womanhood: The Emergence of the Afro-American Woman Novelist* (New York, 1987). Linda Nicholson, *Feminism/Postmodernism* (New York, 1990).

ZILLAH EISENSTEIN

FEMINIZATION OF POVERTY. The term *feminization of poverty* came into use in the late 1970s as an expression encapsulating the phenomenon of women's increasing presence among the ranks of the poor. U.S. sociologist Diana Pearce coined the phrase in 1978 and the popular media began to mention it by the early 1980s. In 1981, the President's National Advisory Council on Economic Opportunity made the prediction that, "All other things being equal, if the proportion of the poor in female headed families were to continue to increase at the same rate as it did from 1967 to 1978, the poverty population would be composed solely of women and their children by the year 2000." This prognosis was widely mentioned in discussions of domestic policy during the 1984 presidential election. By 1990, the feminization of poverty was commonly cited whenever poverty and gender were discussed together.

Although there are analytic problems with the term, its popularity served the important purpose of bringing the particularities of women's poverty to political attention. There are two major reasons why women in most societies have been historically and are currently vulnerable to poverty. First, women's access to breadwinner's wages, and the social benefits accruing to them, have been limited by cultural expectations, discrimination, and employment and educational segregation. Second, most cultures have assigned women the bulk of society's unpaid caregiving work: childcare, care for elderly and infirm family members, and general family maintenance duties. Such nurturing obligations compete for women's time and attention when they enter the waged labor market, and yield the label "dependence" when they are supported economically by the paid employment of husbands, by government transfer payments, or by private charity.

Several social changes of the late twentieth century have caused women's long-standing poverty to represent an increasing proportion of the entire poverty population, increasing from fifty percent of all poor adults in the United States in 1960 to sixty-four percent by 1987. Most important has been that the growing acceptability of women's participation in the labor market has contributed to a dramatic rise in the numbers of two-parent families with both adults employed outside the home. Consequently, more two-parent families have been able to escape poverty status—even as the related overall lessening of the "family wage" has left families or households with only one wage earner more vulnerable to poverty. At the same time, a complex set of social forces, including the increased cultural tolerance of divorce and the expansion of social welfare benefits, has led to a dramatic increase in the number of divorced and never-married mothers: in the United States families headed by women have doubled in proportion to all families over the past thirty years. In addition, gender differences in longevity within the expanding elderly segment of the population mean that more older women live longer as singles and are therefore in greater jeopardy of poverty.

Taken together, these trends yield a poverty population in most Western industrial nations that is increasingly composed of single women and their children. Policy advocates, politicians, and feminists have viewed this situation with alarm and have called for a wide array of responses aimed at both changing the nature of the problem and responding directly to the needs of poor women and their families. The most widespread political response has been to call for more assistance to preserve two-parent families, so that women and their children will not face the "inevitable" problems associated with single parenthood. Many mainstream politicians and policy advocates have begun to propose a series of specific "family policies" at both the state and federal levels (e.g., child care subsidies, employment supports, health insurance supplements, parental leave guarantees, and mandated child support). Other policy responses have been aimed at those single women already poor and receiving public assistance, i.e., mandated work programs, job training programs, pursuit of noncustodial parents, and child care and health care guarantees while a woman is "in transition" from welfare to employment.

Sharp ideological debate, across party lines, has characterized the discussions of the feminization of poverty and proposed measures to affect it. Many commentators, especially those representing *African-American interests or influenced by Marxist analysis, have stressed the concern that race and class dynamics are neglected in the discussions. Women from poor communities are most likely to be poor or near poor regardless of their marital status, such critics argue, so the focus on women's poverty underestimates the role that racial discrimination and class boundaries play in producing poverty, and disregards the needs of poor men. Such critics call for more universal employment policies as well as for certain programs targeted at poor communities, viewing the combination as a better way to address the needs of the poorest women—both directly and by providing an economic base for the men they may marry.

Some feminist critics have worried that initiatives to support the family neglect poor single women, whose need to receive adequate income and other social programs is no less immediate. They have called for increased and less punitive income supports, for nonmandatory employment programs, and for more child and health care benefits regardless of employment or marital status.

Conservatives, in Congress and in research centers such as the Heritage Foundation, have feared that social expenditures to help families would create more "dependence" on government and thereby ultimately weaken family independence, and even foster increases in welfare rolls. In general, they have favored programs aimed at forcing women off welfare into low-paying jobs and at developing disincentives for single parenthood.

But most critics would agree that, thus far, significant policy solutions to women's poverty remain to be found. In 1988, the Family Support (Welfare Reform) Act was passed amid much argument about which policy plans would actually help poor families. It expanded the more politically popular employment mandates as a way to remove women from welfare rolls but offered no new program initiatives to lessen single mothers' vulnerability to poverty within the low-waged job sector. Since President *Bush's election, domestic policy controversies have occurred in regard to child care, health care, and parental leave legislation. Such debates indicate the continuing U.S. concern for addressing issues flagged by recognition of the "feminization of poverty." In Europe, as the *European Community begins to consider the prospect of common social policies, a series of similar discussions are occurring, albeit building upon a more long-standing set of social policy commitments, because women and children also remain disproportionately present among the European poor.

(See also CLASS AND POLITICS; FEMINISM; GENDER AND POLITICS; RACE AND RACISM; WELFARE STATE.)

Hilda Scott, *Working Your Way to the Bottom: The Feminization of Poverty* (London, 1984). Rochelle Lefkowitz and Ann Withorn, eds., *For Crying Out Loud: Women and Poverty in the United States* (New York, 1986).
ANN WITHORN

FIJI. See PACIFIC ISLANDS.

FINANCE, INTERNATIONAL. Monetary transactions across political borders, usually involving the exchange of currencies, is known as international finance. Because different economies use different currencies, basic transactions such as trade, loans, and asset sales are all more complicated when conducted internationally.

Arrangements for setting exchange rates are the core of the international monetary system. The rates themselves and their volatility are crucial to traders, investors, and policymakers. At one extreme, nations can fix the price of their money. They choose to make it convertible, on demand, into a recognized standard (gold, for example, in the nineteenth century). That creates a more predictable environment for transactions (and may curb inflation in some states), but at the cost of national monetary autonomy. At the other extreme, currency rates are simply determined in the marketplace. They fluctuate (or "float") as supply and demand changes. Monetary authorities may still intervene, either to dampen short-term volatility or to influence the long-term direction of rates (so-called managed floating), but they are not committed either to fixed rates or to specific target zones.

These varied monetary arrangements have all been tried since World War II. As the war drew to a close, the United States and Britain organized a multilateral conference to reconstruct the world financial system. Meeting at Bretton Woods, New Hampshire, they devised a new system of pegged exchange rates based in practice on the dollar. Once established, exchange rates were to be changed only rarely to cope with fundamental balance-of-payments problems. The conference established the *International Monetary Fund (IMF) to monitor the system and to oversee the return to currency convertibility. The *World Bank was also established to finance postwar reconstruction in Europe, although it was never given adequate resources. The key to Bretton Woods was an informal U.S. pledge to redeem dollars for gold at $35 per ounce. Foreign central banks could then hold dollars as well as gold to settle their balance-of-payments shortfalls. World trade could grow on a base of expanding dollar reserves. That, at least, was the plan.

It actually took Western Europe fifteen years to return to full currency convertibility. One overriding worry was how to earn enough hard currency to overcome the "dollar shortage" of the 1940s and 1950s. Economist Robert Triffin looked further ahead and saw that the real crisis would not be too few dollars, but too many (Triffin, *Gold and the Dollar Crisis,* New Haven, Conn., 1960). As dollars slowly accumulated in foreign central banks, they would eventually exceed U.S. gold holdings. The U.S. pledge to redeem them would become untenable and the system itself unstable. Triffin's point and its implications were soon acknowledged by experts, but the structural problems were never solved.

The Bretton Woods arrangements suffered another fundamental problem that emerged in the 1960s: its uneven impact on *balance-of-payment adjustment. While deficit countries faced clear pressures to deflate in order to maintain exchange rates, surplus countries such as the Federal Republic of Germany (FRG) did not face similar constraints and were not forced to revalue. The dollar, linchpin of the system, also faced mounting difficulties. Although the United States had unique advantages as the creator of dollar reserves, it had no effective way to depreciate a currency that was becoming increasingly overvalued.

The strong dollar profoundly affected the U.S. role in the world economy. It stimulated vast increases in U.S. foreign investment, which became a contentious issue in Western Europe, especially in France. At home, it damaged exports and encouraged imports, hurting all traded-good industries. U.S. international deficits were growing, and the Bretton Woods system offered no clear avenue to limit them. Unlike other deficit countries, the United States could simply fund its shortfall by printing the world's reserve currency, and it did so. Private speculators added to the pressures to realign exchange rates. With capital markets now closely linked, they could move large sums into stronger currencies, such as the deutsche mark, instantly and at low risk.

The Bretton Woods system finally collapsed in August 1971 when the U.S. abandoned its convertibility pledge. Efforts to restore a fixed-rate system using new parities (the 1971 Smithsonian Agreement) ultimately failed. By default, the world's major currencies began floating. (Most less developed economies continued to peg their exchange rates to one or two large trading partners).

This unplanned system has persisted for nearly two decades, combining floating rates and ad hoc intervention by monetary authorities. The major economic powers have sometimes intervened jointly as they did after the 1985 Plaza Agreement and the 1987 Louvre Accord. The aim of this informal (and often short-lived) cooperation is to manage the crucial nexus of the dollar, yen, and deutsche mark.

Since the breakdown of Bretton Woods, the only sustained institutional effort to fix exchange rates has been a regional one: the European Monetary System (EMS). Beginning in 1972, the *European Community (EC), led by France and the FRG, sought to facilitate trade and investment by narrowing their regional currency movements. Their cooperation was formalized in 1979 against the backdrop of continued dollar instability. The stated goal was to create "a zone of monetary stability in Europe." Not only has the EMS succeeded, in December 1991 a treaty was negotiated in Maastricht, Netherlands, that stipulated much closer coordination, including economic and monetary union, a common currency, and a central bank, all complementing the larger process of European integration. (A rejection of the treaty in a June 1992 referendum in Denmark raised grave questions about the future course of economic cooperation within the EC.)

Outside Western Europe, monetary authorities have found it extremely difficult to manage exchange rates. Private financial markets now determine currency rates on a day-to-day basis. To affect these rates directly, central banks buy and sell foreign exchange in the markets. They hope to shift private agents' expectations and thus the composition of their currency portfolios. It is a difficult task and often an unsuccessful one. The markets dwarf the scale of intervention by monetary authorities, even joint intervention. Ironically, the markets are so large partly because floating rates are so volatile. To control their exposure to currency movements, multinational corporations hedge with foreign-exchange contracts and use international capital markets to match longer-term assets and liabilities in multiple currencies.

The growth of these interdependent markets for capital and foreign exchange represents an important shift in international financial structure. The world's largest capital market, the London-based Euromarket, is now an essentially unregulated one. Along with other "offshore" banking centers, it eliminates many of the costs and constraints of domestic banking.

The offshore markets began in the early 1960s, fostered by U.S. restrictions on interest rates and a tax on foreign borrowing. Major U.S. banks responded by allowing their London subsidiaries to accept deposits and grant loans denominated in dollars. The Euromarkets grew rapidly because of their cost advantages for large-scale depositors and borrowers. They benefited from low regulatory overhead and intense competition among international banks. These offshore markets, from London to Hong Kong, became centers of global finance, increasing the pressures to deregulate national financial markets in Western Europe, Japan, and North America.

The Euromarket's largest participants are multinational corporations, but the most controversial have been *Third World states. Their borrowing started in the early 1970s, aimed at sustaining rapid growth without dependence on direct foreign investment. Debts grew dramatically after the oil shock of 1973–1974, funded, ironically, by bank deposits from oil-producing states ("petrodollar recycling"). Lending standards seemed relaxed, at least in retrospect, but commercial credits were still limited to larger economies in Latin America and Asia, plus a few states with rich natural resources. Weaker economies, such as most sub-Saharan African states, relied on aid donors.

Banking syndicates lent on standard commercial terms, usually for five to ten years, with principal due at the conclusion. Interest rates were recalculated periodically to reflect the banks' cost of funds. Profits came from initial fees and negotiated "spreads" above interest costs.

These arrangements marked a substantial change from foreign lending practices over the past 150 years. In earlier periods, loans took the form of bonds, sold by banking houses to individual investors. Defaults were not uncommon, but they generally harmed bondholders and not the banking system. The quality of Euromarket loans, on the other hand, directly affects the solvency of large banks. National monetary authorities are thus drawn into foreign loan problems and their renegotiation.

After a second oil shock in the early 1980s, these loan problems proliferated. The world economy contracted and commodity prices fell sharply. Real interest rates soared and remained high. As a result, debt burdens rose while debt-servicing capacity plummeted. In August 1982, Mexico announced its inability to meet current debts. It was soon followed by most other major developing country debtors, including Brazil, Argentina, and Venezuela.

The debt crisis was initially understood as a short-term emergency, requiring an infusion of liquidity and a sharp contraction of imports. The banks moved to reschedule immediate obligations but offered no debt forgiveness. Before any rescheduling, they insisted that debtors agree to austerity programs supervised by the IMF.

Perceptions of the debt crisis gradually changed as it persisted through the 1980s and early 1990s. Debtors paid a high price in political instability, foregone income, and lower future productivity, but seldom returned to creditworthiness. Commercial banks, export-credit agencies, and aid donors finally began to set aside major loan-loss reserves and to write down their impaired credits. Official U.S. policies also changed. The banking system's stability remains important, but by 1985, the United States also began to promote structural adjustment and economic growth as longer-term solutions. The Baker Plan, developed under U.S. Treasury Secretary James Baker, was underfunded and unsuccessful, but it did signal a policy shift. The 1989 Brady Plan goes further and encourages debt reduction. Although several new debt packages have been negotiated to lower debt service significantly, the largest debtors continue to face heavy payments and cannot attract voluntary lending. With credit markets effectively closed, a number of developing countries have changed their approach to international finance. They have reversed their long-standing opposition to multinational firms and invited new equity investments.

(See also DEVELOPMENT AND UNDERDEVELOPMENT; INTERDEPENDENCE; INTERNATIONAL DEBT; INTERNATIONAL POLITICAL ECONOMY; MULTINATIONAL CORPORATIONS.)

Charles Lipson, *Standing Guard: Protecting Foreign Capital in the Nineteenth and Twentieth Centuries* (Berkeley, Calif., 1985). Miles Kahler, ed., *The Politics of International Debt* (Ithaca, N.Y., 1986). Robert Z. Aliber, ed., *The Reconstruction of International Monetary Arrangements* (Houndmills, U.K., 1987). Jeffrey D. Sachs, *Developing Country Debt and Economic Performance* (Chicago, 1989).

CHARLES LIPSON

FINLAND. Located on the Baltic Sea between Sweden and Russia, Finland has seen its historical development being profoundly affected, both internally and internationally, by each neighbor in turn. In size, political system, institutions, and social structure, however, Finland is a Scandinavian country. Although geographically the country straddles the border between East and West, Finland, with its *parliamentary democracy, unicameral parliament, and multiparty system, clearly is a Western society.

From the Middle Ages until 1809 Finland formed part of the Swedish kingdom. Absorbed by the Russian Empire as a result of the war of 1808–1809, the country became an autonomous grand duchy with the Russian tsar as grand duke, operating under the Swedish legal system. This arrangement lasted until 6 December 1917, when Finland was able to gain its independence from a Russia weakened by revolution and civil war.

Another prerequisite for the gaining of independence, however, was that economic conditions had developed rapidly during the closing years of the nineteenth century. Owing to extensive forests and the greatly increased demand worldwide for paper products, toward the end of the nineteenth century Finland was quickly drawn into the world economy. (The paper and pulp industries are still dominant in the Finnish economy and provide the backbone of Finnish foreign export.)

The rapid integration of Finnish farmers into the capitalist economy also explains why land owning peasants came to represent a crucial nation-building force in Finnish society. Peasants and their political organizations were decisive at all turning points and great domestic crises during the hundred years between 1880 and 1980. Independent *peasants made up the core of the victorious White army during the Finnish civil war of 1918, defeating the Reds at the same time that the Reds were defeating the Whites in Russia. Later, in the aftermath of World War II (in which Finland had participated from 1941 to 1944, fighting on the side of Germany and against the Soviet Union), the peasant-dominated Agrarian Party—later renamed the Center Party—was instrumental in adjusting Finnish *foreign policy to new postwar conditions.

Political antagonisms in Finnish society traditionally have had their origin in 1) class conflicts, 2) ideological struggles within the working class between Social Democrats and Communists, 3) tensions between town and countryside, and 4) tensions between the Finnish-speaking majority and the Swedish-speaking minority. During the first decades after World War II Finland had a strong Communist Party, which in the 1950s and 1960s was supported by almost a quarter of the total electorate. Communist support was partly located in the countryside. An "industrial *communism" and a "backwoods communism" were identifiable as distinct types. Since the middle of the 1970s Communist support has dwindled. The Communist decline has been due to improved social conditions and to structural changes as a result of which the poor rural, Communist voting blocs have ceased to exist. In the 1980s all the major historical divisions lost their former strength and appeal. In 1987–1990 the Conservatives and the Social Democrats formed the two dominant parties in a coalition government undoubtedly reflecting an increasing dominance of the middle class. The Social Democrats represent the middle class of the public sector, whereas the Conservatives are supported mainly by the middle class or the private sector.

During World War II Finland fought two wars against the Soviet Union, was for a time a cobelligerent with Germany, and made a separate truce with the Soviet Union in September 1944. It was condemned to pay heavy war reparations to the Soviet Union, but Finland was never occupied by foreign forces, and it maintained its system of market economy and parliamentary democracy throughout. After the war Finland readjusted its foreign policy and aimed at building peaceful relations with the Soviet Union. Neutrality and integration into *Scandinavia were emphasized as well. Because of Finland's particular brand of neutrality, the foreign press coined the term *Finlandization* to allude to submissiveness to Soviet demands, but the Soviet impact on Finnish everyday life and culture was very small. In March 1992, with the strictures of neutrality in the post–Cold War, post-Soviet era somewhat relaxed and the pressures for regional economic integration growing, Finland applied for membership in the *European Community.

Erik Allardt, *Finnish Society: Relationship between Geopolitical Situation and the Development of Society* (Helsinki, 1985). Risto Alapuro, *State and Revolution in Finland* (Berkeley, Calif., 1988). Max Engman and David Kirby, eds., *Finland: People, Nation, State* (London, 1989).

ERIK ALLARDT

FOOD POLITICS. The politics of food and agriculture can vary dramatically from country to country, depending most of all on the level of industrial development. Governments in nonindustrial developing countries (and also in *command economies) have tended to tax rural agricultural producers and to subsidize urban consumers. By contrast, governments in industrial countries tend to subsidize rural producers and tax urban food consumers. When nations undergo rapid industrial development, they tend to switch the bias in their food and agricultural policies accordingly. In this century, Japan, Taiwan, and the Republic of Korea (South Korea) have all switched from taxing farmers and subsidizing consumers to taxing consumers and subsidizing farmers.

Why these contradictory policy patterns? The tendency of nonindustrial countries to subsidize food consumers is a part of what Michael Lipton has called "urban bias" (*Why Poor People Stay Poor*, Cambridge, Mass., 1977). The political sources of urban bias have included 1) a pro-industry, anti-agriculture bias among elites in postcolonial developing countries (likewise among Marxist-Leninist *elites in centrally planned societies); 2) the political disorganization and low social status of remote rural villagers in most developing countries; and 3) the political threat to regime survival that can be presented by urban food consumers, rich and poor alike. These consumers in developing countries are especially sensitive to food prices because a relatively larger share of their total income tends to be spent on food purchases (often more than fifty percent).

The policies of taxing farmers and subsidizing consumers has frequently gone wrong in the developing world (and also in the command economies). Where implicit taxes on farmers have been steepest—for example, in much of sub-Saharan Africa, and also historically in the Soviet Union—food production has failed to keep pace with either population growth or demands for dietary enrichment. In most African countries, food crop production has declined on a per capita basis since independence. It is popular to blame this adverse trend on cash cropping, but in most of Africa nonfood cash crop production has actually declined more rapidly than food crop production.

In order to keep food consumption increasing in these circumstances, the supply gap must be made up through expensive imports. To ensure low food prices in urban areas, developing country governments have also been obliged to spend beyond their means on direct consumer food subsidies. When these governments subsequently try to cut back on these food subsidies (often a condition for obtaining new lending from the *International Monetary Fund), they have found themselves politically challenged in the streets by rioting mobs.

The contrasting tendency of governments in wealthy industrial countries to provide generous subsidies to rural food producers (rather than to urban food consumers) is attributable to 1) the price support demands that farmers in rich countries make when personal income growth in the agricultural sector begins to lag behind rapidly growing income in the industrial sector, and 2) the willingness of urban consumers to accept these price support demands, both because their share of personal income spent on food shrinks with affluence and because productivity growth in the farming sector (owing to the mechanization of production, increased chemical fertilizer use, and the adoption of high-yield *green revolution seed varieties) results in lower real commodity prices for consumers even when price supports are factored in. It also becomes more affordable for rich industrialized countries to subsidize farmers because the total number of farmers in such countries will be shrinking. Over the last thirty years, the number of full-time farmers in Japan, for example, has declined by seventy percent. As this process continues in the most advanced industrial countries, political disputes over farm subsidies may eventually become less divisive than new issues such as consumer food safety, biotechnology, and farm chemical use.

Still, if commodity prices in rich countries are set too high above market-clearing levels (as in the *European Community, under the Common Agricultural Policy), the result can be a burdensome surplus of high-priced farm products that are hard to dispose of except through wasteful and costly export subsidies. The use of such export subsidies (recently by the United States as well as in the European Community) can bring industrial country governments into direct trade conflicts with each other. Past efforts in the *General Agreement on Tariffs and Trade (GATT) to negotiate away these rich country export subsidies have been unavailing, in large part because food trade measures are impossible to disentangle from domestic price supports, which farm lobbies often consider nonnegotiable.

One of the most controversial aspects of the international politics of food has been the question of "food power"—the hypothetical international power advantage enjoyed by food-exporting nations over food-importing nations. Political leaders in some food-importing countries have at times argued for the importance of "food self-sufficiency" so as to reduce the vulnerability associated with import dependence.

This hypothetical vulnerability to food power has seldom been tested, mostly because food-exporting nations are constrained by domestic producers from ever withholding exported supplies. Moreover, on those occasions when "food power" has been attempted, the exporter's advantage has not been confirmed. In 1980–1981, when the United States imposed a partial grain embargo on the Soviet Union following the Soviet invasion of Afghanistan, the Soviet Union had little trouble finding alternative grain suppliers in Argentina, Australia, Canada, and the European Community. Total Soviet grain imports actually increased during the period that the U.S. embargo was in place. In 1990, following the Iraqi invasion of Kuwait, a food embargo was imposed by the UN Security Council, but a full-scale war against Iraq soon overtook this more comprehensive food exercise. So long as rich countries continue to subsidize food production, international markets are likely to remain—in most years—a setting in which buyers rather than sellers enjoy a political and commercial advantage.

(See also LAND REFORM; RURAL DEVELOPMENT; SANCTIONS; TAXES AND TAXATION.)

Amartya Sen, *Poverty and Famines: An Essay on Entitlement and Deprivation* (Oxford, 1981). Robert Paarlberg, *Food Trade and Foreign Policy* (Ithaca, N.Y., 1985).
ROBERT PAARLBERG

FORCE, USE OF. *International relations are often described as being *anarchic*—that is, there is no central authority in world politics, much less one with the power necessary to assure order and prevent the use of force among *states. Unlike activities *within* a state's borders that normally are subject to the authority of the state enforced by its government agencies, the relations *among* states are not subject to any external governance or enforcing authority. There is no authority in international relations superior to that claimed by any single sovereign state. Indeed, states claim by virtue of their *sovereignty, which is recognized formally by other sovereign states, not only the right to exercise complete authority over matters on territory within their jurisdiction, but also the *right* to be independent or autonomous in relation to other states in the formulation and execution of *foreign policy.

Although there is no enforcing authority in international relations, there are internationally recognized rules and norms for state behavior, some of which have acquired the force of law. The 1928 Pact of Paris or "Kellogg-Briand" Treaty outlawed *war "as an instrument of policy" and called exclusively for "pacific means" for dealing with "all disputes or conflicts" among states. Nevertheless, states continued to use force in their relations with other states during the 1930s even if only in self-defense. The UN Charter (1945) asserts that states "shall settle their disputes by peaceful means" (Article 3) and that they "shall refrain in their international relations from the threat or use of force against the territorial integrity or political independence of any state" (Article 4). At the same time, however, Article 51 describes self-defense against an attack for states acting individually or collectively as an "inherent right." Moreover, it provided for a collective security machinery under the UN Security Council (UNSC) with authority to impose *sanctions and take other measures including the use of force. (By contrast, the earlier *League of Nations, which was established after World War I, had authority to impose economic sanctions against an aggressor but lacked authority to use force.)

In practice, exercise of this authority by the UNSC has proven difficult in the absence of consensus among the great powers or permanent members of the Security Council, any one of which can exercise a veto and thus block collective UN action. The Soviet Union did not vote (and thus did not exercise its veto) in the UNSC's authorization in 1950 for a collective response to the invasion of the Republic of Korea (South Korea); however, the UN was blocked from taking so central a role in many subsequent situations when some members sought a similar response. For a time, the UN General Assembly tried to assume this role under "Uniting for Peace" resolutions. Even this rather weak mechanism fell into disuse in the 1960s when an expanded UN membership was less prone to support such action. Although peacekeeping eventually became a significant UN contribution to conflict management in the Middle East, Africa, Cyprus, Korea, and elsewhere, the absence of consensus among the permanent UNSC members precluded the UN from using its collective security machinery as originally intended. By contrast, UN actions in 1990 and 1991 to redress Iraq's aggression against Kuwait were a demonstration of how a consensus among the great powers and other states can make collective and effective UN action possible.

One approach to maintaining order in an anarchic international system of states is agreed rules or norms that are followed by states typically because it is in their enlightened self-interest to do so. Rules or norms concerning the use of force that may have the binding or obligatory character of *international law are those that have become established by formal agreement (treaties or covenants), have come into being through customary practice, conform to generally accepted principles, or have been established through the interpretations or writings of jurists such as those on the *International Court of Justice (ICJ). Beyond resort to the ICJ, imposition of sanctions, or other nonlethal methods, when states choose to use force aggressively, thus violating international law, there frequently is no remedy for the victimized state or states except the use of force in self-defense or collective self-defense. In this sense, then, the world remains a self-help system of relations among states.

International law concerning war draws heavily from the just war doctrine in Western political thought. One finds this concern about justice and war in Cicero, but developed further over the centuries by Augustine, Aquinas, Gentilis, Vitoria, Suarez, and others. The writings of *Grotius on war and those who would follow him gave legal character to what previously had been moral doctrine concerning right conduct in war *(jus in bello)* and the right to use force or go to war in the first place *(jus ad bellum)*.

As they have evolved over the centuries, the principles of "just war" may be summarized today as including the following: 1) there must be a *just cause* (such as self-defense against an aggressor); 2) decisions to go to war and conduct the war are to be made by *legitimate authority;* 3) *proportionality* must be observed between means and ends in going to war and in conducting the war; 4) there must be some chance of success in attaining legitimate objectives through resort to use of force; 5) the use of force should be a last resort after efforts to use peaceful means have been exhausted; 6) weapons immoral in themselves (indiscriminate weapons or those causing needless suffering) must not be used; and 7) decisions on going to war and how the war is to be conducted should be taken with the right intention—an important provision because any abstract set of principles can be misused by the unprincipled to "justify" actions taken for illegal or immoral purposes.

In contrast to a purely pacifistic position, whether on religious or secular grounds, that would renounce any use of force, the just war doctrine attempts to set limits on resort to (and actual use of) force in international relations. There has been considerable debate on the present-day applicability of just war principles, given the presence of nuclear and other weapons of mass destruction. The morality of threats to use mass-destructive force, even if the intent is to deter or effectively preclude such wars, has been hotly disputed. Most concede, however, that just war principles remain relevant at least in relation to smaller-scale wars. Indeed, the overall intent in just war thinking about conduct in war is to moderate or limit the death (particularly of noncombatants) and destruction that would occur in the absence of such rules.

Short of hostilities, the threat of force—"saber rattling" or what has been referred to more formally as "coercive *diplomacy" or "compellence"—may be employed to influence the behavior or compel actions by other states. Alert and readiness levels may be increased, reserves mobilized, standing forces redeployed to new locations, or other actions may be taken to signal to an adversary both the capability and the resolve to use force. Even though no forces or weapons may engage in actual hostile fire, the threat to do so may be understood nevertheless as equivalent to a use of force. In coercive diplomacy the attempt is to induce actions or changes in the actual behavior of other states. *Deterrence policies, by contrast, are somewhat more passive; the effort is to deliver a credible threat that there will be a response to include the use of force if certain actions are taken by another state or group of states. Threats to use force can thus be considered a use of force even if no hostilities actually take place. However passive, the mere presence of military forces postured to defend a country and thus dissuade a would-be aggressor is a use of force.

Efforts have been undertaken in recent years to inhibit the use of force through arms reductions (of "conventional" or non-nuclear forces and nuclear, chemical, biological, and any other mass-destructive categories of weaponry) and through establishing various confidence- and security-building measures. Thus, notifications in advance of military exercises and provision for observers from other countries attempt to reduce the likelihood that these events will be misperceived as having hostile intent. In an effort to reduce the threat or risk of war or lesser uses of force considerable attention also has been paid to the numbers, types, and peacetime stationing and readiness of forces.

Notwithstanding all of these efforts, resort to the use of force by states remains part of international relations. Some have sought to delegitimize war as an instrument of state policy by changing over time the attitude toward war by leadership elites or masses of peoples. Nevertheless, the use of force persists. Indeed, in an anarchic world that lacks central authority with the power to enforce international law and global norms, there are few obstacles to a state's use of force other than the threat or actual use of countervailing force by other states.

(See also ANARCHY; ARMS CONTROL; GULF WAR; NUCLEAR WEAPONS; UNITED NATIONS.)

Kenneth N. Waltz, *Man, the State and War* (New York, 1959). Robert J. Art and Kenneth N. Waltz, eds., *The Use of Force: Military Power and International Politics,* 3d ed. (New York, 1971, 1988). Michael Walzer, *Just and Unjust Wars* (New York, 1977).

PAUL R. VIOTTI

FORDISM. A remarkable fusion of incremental technological change and radical social innovation, a synthesis first achieved in the Ford Company's Highland Park plant immediately prior to World War I, established Fordism as a world-historical force with the stunning immediacy of a natural upheaval. The chasm that separated traditional craft methods of automobile manufacture from the new Fordist mass production system appeared almost without warning, although the fault lines which coalesced to produce it often traced their origins a considerable distance into the past. Evolutionary improvements to established practice in component manufacturability, product design, equipment specialization, materials flow, work coordination, and business organization had already expanded annual output of Ford's Model T automobile more than thirtyfold in the five years before the moving assembly line was introduced in 1912–1913. With even more fundamental changes in the social organization of production accompanying the imposition of line-paced continuous manufacture, labor time for constructing each automobile was further reduced from 12.5 hours only a few months earlier to just ninety minutes.

Ford's system not only revolutionized automobile production (within a few years, Ford had captured fifty-five percent of the U.S. auto market) but, in successfully applying mass production methods to so complex an object, it established a universal logic of industrial production, portending fundamental transformation in many areas of manufacturing and the potential historical regression of societies unable to deploy the new techniques effectively. Its economic and cultural implications were so vast that, even at its inception, contemporaries recognized that Fordism laid claim to defining the epoch.

Thus freighted with historical significance, it is inevitable that Fordism should become interpretively overburdened. In stark contrast with its most famous product, a single model appealing to a range of desires ("available in any color a customer wants so long as it is black"), Fordism is in fact a broad term masquerading as a singular concept. Some equate it with the scientific fragmentation of tasks and specialized division of labor characteristic of Taylorism. For others, Fordism is synonymous with the assembly line. Somewhat more inclusively, Fordism is identified with mass production, the use of specialized machinery and semiskilled labor to manufacture standardized products in large volumes. Fordism has also been conceptualized as an "accumulation regime," a growth path governed by positive feedback loops connecting mass production and mass consumption. At the other end of the spectrum, Fordism achieves a meaning as nebulous as it is all-encompassing when it is understood as definitive of American culture or, still more broadly, as the essence of a particular stage in the development of industrial civilization. The contemporary catchphrase intended to suggest its eclipse—post-Fordism—suffers from a similar problem of diverse and often noncommunicating applications.

Fordism proper involved a refinement and synthesis of disparate, if intersecting, trends within the realm of production method and industrial organization, that is, something rather more than a single element of the production process and rather less than a totalistic cultural form.

The essential precondition for the possibility of Fordist mass production was the practical manufacture of precisely interchangeable parts first accomplished in small arms production under the auspices of the U.S. Ordnance Department and diffusing to the fabrication of sewing machines, agricultural equipment, bicycles, and, eventually, automobiles. The very idea of exactly duplicated components eliminated the craft worker's raison d'être, the ability to create a wide variety of different products or models and to provide experience-based solutions to fabrication problems. Ford pushed this idea to its limit: "There cannot be much hand work or fitting if you are going to accomplish great things."

With parts interchangeability, tasks and processes can be disconnected from each other (and from the same worker) and, thus decomposed, they can be reordered in new configurations. As a consequence, substantial experimentation in task rationalization had already occurred in Ford's plants independently of F. W. Taylor's application of the "armory system"'s norms of precise measurement and exact replication to the practice of human labor itself. The central tenets of Taylorism—the analytical decomposition, separation, and standardization of movements and tasks to their smallest efficient scope; functional specialization or the assignment of discrete tasks to distinct workers; scientific selection of the work force; a clear division of labor between the tasks of conception and execution—were all manifest in Fordist production. Yet Fordism and Taylorism were quite divergent in that Taylor's system focused on individual conformity to objective task requirements whereas Ford was far more concerned with the coordination of tasks or posts and the flow of work between them.

The constant refinement of parts interchangeability, machine specialization, and work standardization compelled engineering concern for the systemic integration of machine operations, materials circulation, the distribution of labor, and work organization. Constant, if pragmatic, exploration of integrative techniques and practices culminated in the moving assembly line and the concomitant organization of large-scale manufacture as an integrated, continuous flow, a genuine social innovation.

This same preoccupation led Ford also to build on tendencies toward vertical integration already advanced in other industrial sectors. The "visible hand" of industrial organization was pushed to its logical conclusion at Ford's gigantic River Rouge complex which constituted a virtually self-contained manufacturing system, from the production of raw materials to shipping of the finished product, at a single location. The final step in this extensive nesting process—the integration of discrete work stages into a coherent manufacturing process and of the manufacturing process into a sequentially coordinated production system—was to link the production system directly with the economy as a whole. This connection was established through Ford's distinctive concern to cheapen final product price as opposed to sustaining high-price monopolistic market control, a strategy that presupposed a combination of mass production and mass consumption.

Despite its extraordinary achievements, the inherent rigidity of the supply-driven Fordist system rendered it rapidly obsolete: in less than two decades, Ford's market share declined from three-fifths to less than one-fifth as the company was bested by more flexible rivals. Ford's commitment to specialization was so rigorous and its production system so tightly interdependent that significant engineering improvements (battery-powered ignition, electric starters, shock absorbers) could not be accommodated. Model redesigns were resisted as long as possible and the coordination of sales levels and output became increasingly difficult. When substantive model overhauls occurred, as with the replacement of the fifteen-year-old Model T with the Model A, they required long-term plant closures and equipment scrapping and retooling on a massive scale. High levels of vertical integration proved counterproductive when declines in demand increased unit costs more rapidly for Ford than for its competitors. Henry Ford's propensity for maintaining personal leadership of the firm further reduced organizational responsiveness and innovative capabilities. The impact of employment security and high wages on workers was undermined by the constant acceleration of the assembly line, the only possible Fordist response to deteriorating competitiveness.

Far from monolithically defining industrial society in general or even particular national economies, Fordism remained one logic of production among others: indeed, imperial conceptualizations of Fordism have left largely unexplored its relationship to, and integral dependence on, non-Fordist sectors of the economy. Insofar as Fordism diffused beyond the United States, it was modified substantially by existing institutional structures and industrial cultures. It is not clear that skill-based manufacturing in Germany or Japanese forms of collaborative manufacturing owe much to Fordism at all. The growth of mass consumption certainly preceded the advent of Fordism, and rapid advances in national income levels, such as those occurring in postwar Europe, owe as much to factors like urbanization and the conversion of traditional sectors to capitalist techniques as to national adaptations of Fordist practice.

In this context, the question of "post-Fordism" also seems quite misplaced. To the extent that mass production was not defined by Fordism alone, the reality of post-Fordism long preceded its conceptual formulation. On the other hand, to the degree that post-Fordism denotes the end of of mass production, it neglects the continuing salience of Fordist principles in the movement toward more flexible forms of manufacturing. These include large-scale organization and economies of scale, the capital cost constraints inherent in flexible automation, and the ability of mass production firms to achieve greater flexibility, as in contemporary forms of modular production (the achievement of high levels of product customization on the basis of extensive component and subassembly standardization), through simultaneous refinement and transcendence of Fordist techniques.

(See also DEINDUSTRIALIZATION; POLITICAL ECONOMY.)

H. Arnold and F. Faurote, Ford Methods and Ford Shops (New York, 1915). D. Hounshell, From the American System to Mass Production, 1800–1932 (Baltimore, 1984). C. Maier, In Search of Stability: Explorations in Historical Political Economy (Cambridge, U.K., 1987). Bob Jessop, "Fordism and Post-Fordism: A Critical Reformulation," in A. J. Scott and M. Storper, eds., Pathways to Industrialization and Regional Development in the 1990s (Boston and London, 1992).

RICHARD GORDON

FOREIGN AID. Initially created to assist in the recovery of the war-torn economies of Western Europe following World War II, during the 1960s foreign aid became an integral component of *North-South relations. Designed to promote economic *development through a transfer of resources and knowledge from industrialized to developing countries, foreign assistance has traditionally been promoted as a tool to bridge the economic gap between rich and poor nations. Many argue, however, that political, structural, and institutional obstacles on both sides have hampered aid effectiveness. Although such barriers are likely to persist, deepening global economic *interdependence suggests a future of enhanced multilateral action and donor coordination to improve foreign assistance efforts.

The strictest definition of foreign aid, "official development assistance" (ODA) (as provided by the Development Assistance Committee [DAC] of the *Organization for Economic Co-operation and Development [OECD]), is based on three criteria: administration by official agencies, promotion of economic development as its main objective, and a subsidy or "grant element" of twenty-five percent or more. Such a definition encompasses food aid and technical cooperation for training and education but excludes other types of assistance such as military aid and "other official flows" of little or no concessionality (i.e, export credits, equity, and portfolio investment).

While other private and official capital flows faltered during the 1980s, DAC ODA has expanded in line with aggregate DAC GNP to reach approximately US$46 billion in 1989. Japan led aid donors in absolute terms, contributing $8.9 billion. The United States, the traditional leader, trailed closely behind with $7.6 billion in DAC net aid outlays. On a relative scale, however, European countries have been larger donors, allocating an average of 0.57 percent of their GNP to foreign assistance in 1989, versus 0.32 percent for Japan and 0.15 percent for the United States. The regional distribution of aid in 1948 was as follows: Africa received $17.5 billion net ODA, Asia $15 billion, and Latin America $5.1 billion. Eastern Europe has also recently qualified as a recipient.

Foreign aid has undergone significant changes in both format and purpose during the postwar period. Throughout the 1950s and 1960s, donors focused on the financing of investment projects suitable to promote long-term growth in developing countries. In the 1970s, the growing human costs of development prompted lending aimed at poverty alleviation, although foreign exchange was still perceived as the primary restriction on development. The onslaught of the debt crisis in the early 1980s precipitated yet another type of foreign assistance. Designed specifically to satisfy immediate balance-of-payment requirements, these quick-disbursement credits also promote more prudent macroeconomic policies and more efficient, market-oriented policies at the sectoral level.

Clearly one vital determinant of aid effectiveness is the ability and willingness of the recipient governments to adopt sound policy aimed at promoting growth with equity. However, such initiatives may be hampered by shortages of professional expertise, fragmentation of policy planning, or inadequate accountability of government to the people. Effectiveness may also be inhibited by structural weaknesses within the local economy itself, such as a limited domestic market, technological backwardness, inadequate infrastructure, and rapid population growth. To redress these institutional and structural impediments, donor countries frequently tied lending in the 1980s to the adoption of market-oriented development strategies, such as deregulation of capital and labor markets, trade liberalization, and privatization of production. By the close of the decade, willingness to engage in these reforms became the new litmus test of eligibility for this "policy-based" lending.

The success of development assistance programs is not uniquely dependent on host country conditions. Donor countries may distort aid allocations in antidevelopment directions through trade protectionism, tied aid (i.e., required import purchases), and overriding security and commercial objectives. Likewise, donor agency weaknesses such as inadequate staffing, insufficient knowledge of host country conditions, and biases toward large capital-intensive projects can impinge upon aid's effectiveness. Finally, a proliferation of donors, projects, and policy restrictions without sufficient coordination can also impede smooth, efficient implementation.

The future shape of foreign assistance promises to be no less complex nor controversial than in the past. Throughout the 1980s, the pace of global change molded a political and commercial landscape marked by declining global tensions, greater global interdependence, and increasing diversity among developing nations.

The impact of the debt crisis on developing economies was far from uniform. The low-income nations of sub-Saharan Africa experienced stagnant or even negative growth as the supply of commercial credit dried up and demand for primary commodities stagnated. Many middle-income countries, primarily in Latin America, rectified their trade imbalances but suffered severe internal dislocations as domestic demand was choked off in order to meet debt-servicing obligations. In contrast, the rapid growth in exports of the newly industrializing countries (NICs) of Asia allowed for measured improvements in living standards.

Seen in this light, it is probable that future foreign assistance programs will tailor the mix of aid instruments to match the recipient's level of development. The poorest nations, lacking the fundamental institutions and infrastructure for development, will undoubtedly require ODA for some time. However, export revenues, foreign investment, and debt reduction figure more prominently with "graduates" or near graduates of concessional assistance programs. As such, potential forms of "aid" for middle-income and upper-income developing countries could involve such varied measures as encouragement of a strong system of open multilateral trade or improvements in access to capital and technology.

Firmer support for these types of policy measures on the part of industrialized nations appears more likely in the wake of the recent decline in global tensions. The easing of East-West hostilities has both facilitated and complicated the North-South aid process. On the one hand, movements toward reduction in arms and military personnel have opened the door to increases in economic and humanitarian assistance. On the other, domestic issues have assumed rising prominence within donor nations just as new aid requests have skyrocketed in conjunction with the global upsurge in democratic and economic reforms. Consequently, difficult choices have sprung up regarding who "merits" aid and to what degree external needs should supersede pressing internal concerns.

Nevertheless, the distinction between internal and external needs is often amorphous. Linkages between developed and developing countries have become increasingly pronounced in recent years. Industrial nations are clearly not immune to the repercussions of *Third World dilemmas such as environmental deterioration, narcotics trafficking, and unsustainable debt burdens that shake global financial markets and choke off export opportunities.

In view of the cross-border nature of these problems, donor nations have indicated growing interest in strengthening multilateral aid institutions and stepping up bilateral aid coordination. Multilateral agencies such as the *World Bank and the regional development banks, although not completely apolitical in nature, can boast greater impartiality in the execution of their assistance programs than individual donor states whose policies are intrinsically colored by foreign policy and commercial objectives. Moreover, the international character of these institutions as well as their access to substantial resources permit them to exert considerable pressure on recipient nations to undertake recommended policy reforms. Despite strong donor support for multilateral agencies, about seventy-five percent of total ODA is still channeled through bilateral programs. Given the variance between aid policies and procedures of individual states, enhanced coordination among national agencies is also likely to become a more salient feature of the foreign aid process.

(See also International Debt; Newly Industrializing Economies; Technology Transfer.)

John Eatwell et al., eds., *The New Polgrave: Economic Development* (New York, 1989). Organization for Economic Co-operation and Development, *Development Co-operation in the 1990s* (Paris, 1989). U.S. House of Representatives, *Report of the Task Force on Foreign Assistance to the Committee on Foreign Affairs* (Washington, D.C., 1989). Richard E. Feinberg and Rachik M. Avakov, eds., *From Confrontation to Cooperation? U.S. and Soviet Aid to Developing Countries* (Washington, D.C., 1990).

RICHARD E. FEINBERG

FOREIGN INVESTMENT. See Finance, International; Multinational Corporations.

FOREIGN MILITARY BASES. The term *foreign military base* signifies many things, ranging from *alliance to conquest. It can imply partnership or domination, sometimes both simultaneously. Foreign military bases are a source of influence, yet also of political and financial burdens.

In the past, great empires were commonly built around systems of military control, with bases or garrisons to maintain authority over far-flung lands. Rome, the Ottoman Empire, and the British Empire all depended on such arrangements, as well as on related systems of communication and control over seaborne routes.

In the second half of the twentieth century, in spite of the decline of the old territorial empires, foreign military bases remained a common way for powerful states to project their power on a regional or global basis. The United States and the Soviet Union deployed many troops overseas and established large networks of bases in their forty-five years of global competition. In 1989, as the *Cold War between these *superpowers ended, the Soviet Union had over 600,000 military personnel based in eleven foreign countries, while the United States—counting all military installations including communications and electronic intelligence stations—had about half a million personnel in thirty-seven foreign countries. The superpowers were far ahead of the field: twenty-six other states deployed about

400,000 military personnel abroad, but only Britain and France had anything like a global system of overseas bases. In all, there were over 3,000 foreign bases in eighty-five foreign states and territories.

At the beginning of the 1990s, the end of the Cold War added to already-growing economic and political pressures to prompt the Soviet Union and the United States to reduce their foreign forces and bases. About the same time, a number of long-standing conflicts were resolved or diminished in intensity as some states withdrew their forces from foreign combat: the Soviet Union from Afghanistan, South Africa from Namibia, Cuba from Angola, Vietnam from Cambodia, and India from Sri Lanka. Despite this trend, the United States and several of its allies deployed large forces in the Persian Gulf in the fall of 1990 and, following the short but devastating war against Iraq in January and February 1991, the United States contemplated permanently locating forces and bases in that region.

The United States first set up overseas military bases in the late nineteenth century—in Puerto Rico, Hawaii, Panama, the Philippines, and China, among other places. But the United States gained most of its overseas bases during or soon after *World War II, when it became the dominant world power. In addition to its military occupation of Germany and Japan, the United States deployed major forces to Korea during the *Korean War and after (1950–), to Vietnam during the final phase of the *Vietnam War (1963–1973), and to the Persian Gulf during the war against Iraq (1990–1991). Though some major bases have been closed over the years, others have been opened. With the exception of war-related changes, the system of U.S. overseas bases has remained fairly stable over time.

Soviet foreign military deployment was largely concentrated in Eastern Europe—the states of the *Warsaw Treaty Organization (Warsaw Pact). Soviet forces there confronted the forces of the *North Atlantic Treaty Organization and kept unpopular East European rulers in power. From the early 1960s, the Soviets also acquired bases in the *Third World. Eventually, the most important of these bases were in Cuba, South Yemen, and Cambodia. But Soviet forces in the Third World were always less numerous and less widespread than those of the United States. In 1990, as the Warsaw Pact disintegrated, the Soviets announced that all their forces would be withdrawn from the German Democratic Republic, Czechoslovakia, and Hungary.

In 1991 Soviet military forces also withdrew from a number of territories formerly under Soviet *sovereignty—territories that declared their independence such as the Baltic states. By the end of 1991, the disintegration of the Soviet Union placed a query against the status and future location of all formerly Soviet bases. This development highlights the fact that even within a national territory, troops and bases under the authority of a central government may be considered "foreign" by local nationalists (Spanish army bases in Basque country would be another case in point).

Britain and France maintained substantial overseas bases and forces in the period immediately following World War II, including large occupation forces in Germany and forces stationed in their colonial empires. As the colonies fought for their independence, the number of occupying forces temporarily increased, most notably during the *Algerian War of Independence (1954–1962). Eventually, however, most of the colonial forces withdrew or were disbanded. By 1990, British forces in the former empire numbered just 30,000, their French counterparts just 37,000.

Most other states which based forces abroad in the late twentieth century did so in nearby and often contiguous countries; this was often done as straightforward military occupation: South Africa in Namibia; Israel in the Golan Heights, southern Lebanon, the West Bank, and Gaza; Syria in Lebanon; Turkey in northern Cyprus; Morocco in Western Sahara; Vietnam in Cambodia. One major exception was Cuba, which deployed troops at considerable distance, in Angola and Ethiopia.

Among the most curious types of overseas bases are those associated with extraterritorial enclaves—small pockets of foreign control, typically a colonial vestige—usually on the shore of another country or an offshore island. Ceuta and Melilla are Spanish enclaves in northern Morocco protected by garrisons. The British enclave and base at Gibraltar in southern Spain is similar. Yet another case is the large U.S. naval base at Guantánamo on the east coast of Cuba.

Foreign bases are invariably controversial. Even when they do not represent a clear-cut case of military occupation, those in the "host" country who oppose their presence invariably do so in the discourse of resistance to occupation. This has sometimes led to major political controversies in host states, such as the controversy in the Philippines in 1991 over whether the government should renew the leases for two large U.S. bases.

Foreign forces cannot be wholly subject to the control of the host state. Their presence invariably constrains and limits the host state's sovereignty. Sometimes base agreements go quite far in this direction—for example, limiting the jurisdiction of local courts over foreign military personnel. The exemption of U.S. military personnel from the jurisdiction of courts in Iran under the Shah was a major source of popular discontent, not only directed at the United States but also at the Shah, who was considered responsible for the agreement. U.S. forces in Britain are also largely exempt from British legal jurisdiction.

Opposition to foreign bases is strengthened by a variety of issues—by the noise of aircraft, by the threat of accidents with nuclear or chemical weapons, and by the damage done to farmland by armies on maneuver. Financial compensation, even when added to the contribution some bases make to the local economy, does not balance the cost of the bases, especially if the value of the real estate set aside for military use is taken into account.

There are other, more visceral issues. Not far from many bases are clusters of nightclubs and brothels; the local area is often dominated by this kind of low-life service economy. In Cómiso, Sicily, where a U.S. missile base was constructed in the early 1980s, the Mafia bought up land in the vicinity so it could control such enterprises. In the Philippines, the huge Clark Field and former Subic Bay bases have been accused of attracting thousands of young women to prostitution and of spreading HIV infection and *AIDS.

While political and military leaders view bases in relatively abstract strategic terms, the responses of those directly affected by them are more often moral and personal. Foreign bases are not simply strategic assets; they are also foreign intrusions into local culture and society. In a world of sovereign states, such bases may seem like anachronisms. But judging from recent history, the phenomenon does not seem likely to disappear soon.

(See also AMERICAN FOREIGN POLICY; COLONIAL EMPIRES; DECOLONIZATION; FOREIGN POLICY; GULF WAR; MILITARISM; SOVIET FOREIGN POLICY.)

Robert E. Harkavy, *Bases Abroad: The Global Foreign Military Presence* (Oxford, 1989). Michael Kidron and Dan Smith, *The New State of War and Peace: An International Atlas* (London, 1991). The International Institute for Strategic Studies, *The Military Balance* (London, annual).

DAN SMITH

FOREIGN POLICY. The term *foreign policy* is a nineteenth-century expansion of the idea of *policy*, which had been in use since Chaucer to denote a government's conduct of affairs. The phrase *foreign affairs* was increasingly common from the seventeenth century, as the growing volume of *state business began to compel a clearer organizational distinction between home and abroad in the secretariats of royal households. But the idea of a coherent set of positions toward the outside world, or a foreign policy, seems to have been a product of the bureaucracy and systematization of the industrial age.

For modern observers, foreign policy is at once a phenomenon, a concept, and a major area of study. No definition can do full justice to all three of these aspects of the term, but it is still possible to establish a starting point from which the arguments about interpretation can develop. For there are almost as many views of foreign policy as there are different schools of thought on *international relations, or types of political *ideology in the world.

Foreign policy, then, can be said to be the sum of official external relations conducted by an independent actor (usually a state) in international relations.

Such a definition is short enough to be of practical use, while retaining sufficient flexibility to incorporate the changes which have occurred and continue to occur in the nature of modern international politics. To take the components of the definition: *international relations* refers to the web of transactions across state boundaries by all kinds of groups and individuals, and *external relations* to the same activities from the point of view of these actors as they move outside their own society into dealings with others. Neither is restricted to politics in the narrow sense, as almost any act can be political if it relates to fundamental issues like the distribution of *power or the setting of social values and priorities. On the other hand relations must be *official* to qualify as foreign policy because otherwise all transactions could be included and there would be no inherent sense of agency or purposive action, which is what the term *policy* always implies. In this sense all external relations conducted by the legitimate officeholders of the entity express and contribute to foreign policy: defense ministers, foreign trade ministers, and environment ministers may be almost as involved as their colleagues in charge of the diplomatic service. To the extent that senior bureaucrats also take part directly in high-level international transactions, they too will be conducting foreign policy, although their margin of maneuver will vary enormously from state to state and issue to issue.

The *sum* of external relations is important because although we talk properly about a country's specific foreign policy toward this state or that, the use of the term *tout court* must always be holistic—it represents the entire package of actions and attitudes toward the outside world. Lastly, it is important to define foreign policy as issuing from *independent actors* rather than the more conventional restrictive definition, so as to avoid chaining ourselves to the state in an era when it is evident both that foreign and domestic policy often blur into each other, and that nonstate actors are major participants in international relations. So although it has to be admitted that the great majority of foreign policies belong to states, which still monopolize the business of global politics, there is no intrinsic reason why other actors, such as churches or political groups, which transcend on a transnational basis much of the control theoretically exercised by states, should not be deemed to have foreign policies. For they, like nation-states, naturally distinguish between their internal character and the external world. We may need to qualify their actions as *private* foreign policies, but they remain foreign policies nonetheless.

Independence is the crucial quality to possess, however, as most nonstate actors have neither the reach nor the motivation to go beyond mere external relations into foreign policy proper. The average sporting federation or municipality can rarely defy government-to-government structures, let alone transcend them. But some can, at the level of oil companies, regions, and political groupings, and if they choose to assert themselves in the realm of international politics, they may qualify as independent actors with the potential for foreign policy behavior. Judgments about claims to such a status will therefore be largely empirical, on a case-by-case basis, according to the criteria set out above. Claims on behalf of a given class of actor (other than states) whether churches or governments-in-exile, cannot be admitted as such. But particular entities like the *African National Congress or the Anglican church may reasonably be described as having foreign policies.

A comparatively wide definition, such as that used here, has its own problems. Diplomatic practitioners, for example, are unlikely to accept a view of foreign policy which goes beyond state-to-state relations, and the gap between academic concepts and practical usage should not be allowed to grow too large. For foreign policy, like many others in political science, is at once a term of both action and analysis. Yet scholarship is often able to pinpoint trends before they have become institutionalized, and the literature which has burgeoned on foreign policy since 1960 provides us with the means to understand both the underlying forces which shape a country's foreign policy and the evolution of the phenomenon itself.

This literature has produced a major subarea of international relations, known variously as foreign policy analysis (FPA) or comparative foreign policy (CFP). This takes the micro, or actor, perspective on international relations, as opposed to the macro, or system, perspective in which patterns are identified without going into the motivations of the actors who produce them. Views differ on what can be achieved at the micro level of analysis. The CFP school, which became well established in the United States, has preferred a behavioral methodology, and has operated on the assumption that it should be possible to generalize about the behavior of states and foreign policies, as classes of phenomena, once sufficient data have been generated by rigorously scientific methods. This positivist approach did not catch on in most European or Commonwealth universities, or in the more traditionalist U.S. faculties. There are also now signs that after the expenditure of considerable effort, money, and ingenuity, some of the main proponents of the school have come to realize its limitations. Quite apart from the general debate about positivism, foreign policy is an insufficiently discrete phenomenon to be able to bear the weight of extensive cross-cultural comparisons and generalizations.

This is to say that because foreign policy as an activity is not sharply different from other kinds of public policy, it cannot generate an exclusive theory of behavior to fit it; also, that the variations over countries and time periods are large enough to enforce damaging qualifications on attempts to derive general laws. More than a wholly distinctive universe of human behavior, foreign policy represents an arena in which various forms of explanation may be brought together, enabling us to say a great deal about the nature of foreign policy, its making, its interaction with domestic politics, and its place in our understanding of international politics as a whole.

This more eclectic approach, which has established itself as the most fruitful in the study of foreign policy, employs the dialectical approach of critically testing generalizations and case studies against each other. It uses theory without being enslaved to it, in the sense of concentrating on what are known as middle-range theories. At one end of the spectrum this means rigorously constructed hypotheses about closely defined particular aspects of foreign policy (or "structured empiricism" in Michael Brecher's words), of which the best example is Brecher's own work on decisions under conditions of crisis. At the other end of the same scale of middle-range theories are sets of insights, more loosely organized but not less valuable for that, on such matters as the tendency of decision makers to lean on historical analogies, or the impact of geopolitical and other environmental constraints on choice. In the middle is a good deal of impressive work on the domestic sources of foreign policy, perception and misperception, *bureaucratic politics, and the problems attending on the notion of rational conduct in the context of foreign policy.

The comparative spirit informs most of this writing, even if a tendency toward the case study method sometimes obscures the fact. Indeed, the foreign policy characteristics of certain types and groups of states have attracted a good deal of attention from those wishing to link the study of foreign policy-making to the broader patterns of international relations. Small states, middle-range powers, developing countries, Islamic states, and West European states all come into this category. In this sense comparative foreign policy is often conducted on traditionalist lines and is not to be associated exclusively with the behavioral school referred to above.

Thus the study of foreign policy as it has evolved over more than thirty years, despite continuing differences over methodology and scope, deals in essence with the content of policy on the one hand and the process of foreign policy-making on the other. Most often, however, it focuses on the interactions between the two, starting from the premise that *what* is done will be partially determined by *how* it is done, and allowing for the possibility of human beings asserting their existential rights to choice, even in the most constricted circumstances. Moreover the environments in which action takes place are to be regarded as crucial but not given; the interplay of domestic and international factors is an endlessly varied and elastic process.

For the most part the contemporary analysis of foreign policy has been driven by a dispassionate desire to open up previously neglected questions. But the spirit of scientific enquiry should not be allowed to obscure the points of connection between the concerns of policy analysis with rationality and perception, and that long-standing normative approach which dwells on such subjects as the extent to which law or morality should affect *diplomacy, and the tension between short-term and long-term considerations in foreign policy. *Realism, with its black boxing of the state and its reductionist emphasis on interests as the basis of foreign policy, cannot match foreign policy analysis in this respect as a meeting place for the empirical and philosophical aspects of states' activities toward each other.

Yet the study of foreign policy, for all its now-extensive literature and the transparency of its basic concepts for nonspecialists, is facing an important challenge for the future. For the very need to define foreign policy broadly enough so as to cater to a wider range of actions than those encompassed by traditional diplomacy, shows how it is becoming difficult to distinguish the aspects of public policy which are directed toward foreigners from those which are primarily in the domestic domain. To the extent that such a distinction will become increasingly unsustainable, the study of foreign policy will merge with that of *comparative politics to form a new, broader focus on the politics and policies of states (or whatever systems for mobilizing decisions may replace states) within the complex web of global *interdependence. The disappearance of foreign policy that this would represent, however, is still many decades into the future, and even then the concept would probably need reinventing under another name. Whenever foreign policy seems on the point of losing its contemporary relevance, it has the habit of bouncing back to the center of our concerns, whoever and wherever we are.

(See also AMERICAN FOREIGN POLICY; IDEALISM; SOVIET FOREIGN POLICY.)

Arnold Wolfers, *Discord and Collaboration: Essays in International Politics* (Baltimore, 1962). Harold Sprout and Margaret Sprout, *The Ecological Perspective in Human Affairs* (Princeton, N.J., 1965). Michael Brecher, ed., *Studies in Crisis Behavior* (New Brunswick, N.J., 1979). James N. Rosenau, *The Scientific Study of Foreign Policy*, 2d ed. (London, 1980). Michael Clarke and Brian White, eds., *Understanding Foreign Policy: The Foreign Policy Systems Approach* (Aldershot, U.K., 1989).

CHRISTOPHER HILL

FOREIGN WORKERS. The mass migration of foreign workers since 1945 and the evolution of a global labor market inevitably result from the modernization of both the advanced industrial and developing countries and their increasing *interdependence within the international economy. Although virtually every region has been affected—in 1980, for instance, three-quarters of workers in Kuwait were aliens—the advanced industrial countries have especially benefited from and borne the unique costs of postwar labor migration. Of the approximately 30 million foreign workers and illegal aliens in the world, more than half reside in the industrial countries. These predominantly nonwhite populations comprise up to four percent of the total population of the United Kingdom, six percent of Germany, seven percent of the United States, eight percent of France, and thirteen percent of Switzerland. In Australia, the most ethnically diverse industrial society, twenty percent of the population are immigrants.

The primary catalyst of this mass migration from the economically developing to the industrial countries is quite evident. The economic boom generated within the industrial countries between 1945 and 1969, the greatest production boom in history, created acute labor shortages and rigidities in domestic labor markets. To remedy these problems and to sustain economic growth, private employers and governments recruited foreign workers from the *Third World and Eastern Europe. These efforts were unambiguously successful. During the period of the boom, economic growth, an abundant supply of labor, and productivity gains were strongly correlated in the advanced industrial countries.

While the economic benefits of postwar labor migration were always apparent, its political and social implications were not. Policymakers in the industrial countries did not anticipate three eventual outcomes: the postwar boom would end during the early 1970s and precipitate mass unemployment; many foreign workers would settle permanently in their host country; and the settlement of these workers would stimulate a secondary migration of family members. It is primarily this latter migration wave that has altered the content of political discourse and public policy in the industrial countries.

These changes are evident on several levels. First, the settlement of the new ethnic and racial minorities has reinforced the salience of *ethnicity as a major cleavage within the industrial countries. All the industrial countries have been plagued historically by ethnic conflict. The interests of majority populations and traditional ethnoregional and ethnonational groups, like the Basque minority in Spain, have inevitably collided. However, the influx of new minority groups has seriously shaken the monocultural foundations of the nation-state. As a result, ethnic-related issues are now more important in influencing individual political behavior and deciding electoral outcomes than during any period since World War II.

Second, the presence of the new minorities has altered the character of many political institutions in the industrial countries. The established political parties in particular have been affected. The influx of new minorities has stimulated a nativist backlash that has fed the growth of numerous xenophobic groups. Groups like the Front National in France are pressuring the established parties to curtail all new immigration and to adopt anti-assimilation policies toward settled immigrants. Their modest popularity has spurred the established right and center-right parties to become more ideological and nationalistic. Meanwhile, problems of integrating the new minorities into the political and social mainstream have divided the leaderships and core political constituencies of the social democratic Left. These difficulties have undermined the ability of the Left to maintain the political support of blue-collar voters who hold xenophobic views.

Third, the presence of the new minorities has eroded the political foundations of the welfare state in the industrial countries by sowing dissension among the social forces that historically have benefited most from welfare spending. Organized labor especially has been divided on the question of foreign workers and their access to both the labor market and to welfare services. These conflicts have permitted right and center-right governments since the mid-1970s to reduce the growth of welfare expenditures with electoral impunity. Under current conditions of fiscal stress in the industrial countries, reductions in government welfare spending will be difficult to restore.

Finally, the presence of foreign workers and illegal aliens imperils the *European Community's long-standing commitment to the unrestricted movement of labor across national boundaries. Most Community governments want to ensure that the elimination of internal borders associated with Project 1992 does not give foreign workers legally resident in one country unrestricted access to labor markets in others. Unless and until this issue is resolved, the creation of a true European common market will be indefinitely delayed.

(See also INTERNATIONAL MIGRATION; INTERNATIONAL POLITICAL ECONOMY; LABOR MOVEMENT; RACE AND RACISM.)

Stephen Castles, *Here for Good: Western Europe's New Ethnic Minorities* (London, 1984). Rosemarie Rogers, ed., *Guests Come to Stay: The Effects of European Labor Migration on Sending and Receiving Countries* (Boulder, Colo., 1985).

ANTHONY M. MESSINA

FOUCAULT, Michel. Having taken his degrees in philosophy and psychology and taught in Sweden, Poland, the Federal Republic of Germany, and Tunisia, Michel Foucault (1926–1984) finally, in 1970, occupied a chair in the History of Systems of Thought in France's most prestigious institution of higher learning, the Collège de France. During the 1960s, Foucault's work was associated with structuralism and antipsychiatry, but he denied kinship with either group. In the 1970s and 1980s he was known in the United States as a poststructuralist, and again he was unhappy with the designation. He acknowledged an affinity with the work of Gilles Deleuze for both political and philosophical similarities. Politically he participated in the Groupe Information Prisons (GIP) and was active in various causes, such as gay rights, *feminism, and anticolonialism, that emerged in the wake of *May 1968 and the *New Left. As an intellectual with a concern for the victims of domination he may be compared to Voltaire and Jean-Paul Sartre. But he strove to redefine the stance of the intellectual in important ways.

Foucault's writings may be characterized as "post-Marxist" in the sense that he attempted to develop strategies of interpretation that define mechanisms of domination outside the workplace, or, better, outside the category of the mode of production. Each of his books addresses a historical topic or field, discovering how that realm of experience was colonized or controlled by hierarchical apparatuses. These domains are madness in *Madness and Civilization* (1961), medicine in *The Birth of the Clinic* (1963), the human sciences in *The Order of Things* (1966), punishment in *Discipline and Punish* (1975), and sexuality in *The History of Sexuality* (1976–1984). He also wrote a treatise on his methodology, *The Archaeology of Knowledge* (1969). In addition Foucault wrote important books on art, especially on René Magritte (*This Is Not a Pipe* [1973]) and on Raymond Roussel (*Death and the Labyrinth* [1963]). Finally, important articles and interviews have been collected in Donald Bouchard, ed., *Language and Counter-Memory, Practice* (1977); Colin Gordon, *Power/Knowledge* (1980); and Lawrence Kritzman, *Foucault: Politics, Philosophy, Culture* (1988).

Much of this work betrays the influence of Friedrich Nietzsche: Foucault follows a genealogical paradigm, one that searches backward in history for a point of difference and, once locating that, deploys that difference as a critical lever for the analytical critique of the phenomenon in the modern period. This principle is opposed to all forms of evolutionism that trace the rise and development of a phenomenon that culminates in the present. Foucault also looks for the interplay of discourse and practice in the topic, rather than assuming a split between opinion and action. The specific combination of discourse and practice that he identifies he calls a "technology of *power" or "microphysics of power." He treats these configurations as mechanisms of power that have positive effects of constituting subjects or individuals rather than negative effects of restricting or constraining their action. Taken together, these innovations construct a model for a new kind of cultural history, a history that is neither intellectual nor social but a startling combination of them. Foucault's historical paradigm, which connects very well with certain new directions in the history of women and minority groups and in *feminist theory and anticolonialism, offers a new departure for critical studies in the social sciences.

The salient theme of Foucault's work is the critique of the Cartesian subject, the autonomous, rational individual. He attempts to show how the Cartesian individual is a faulty starting point for theory and politics, how it is a historical phenomenon that requires investigation, not affirmation. He has been most concerned to examine the forms of rationality generated in a culture characterized by this sort of subject-position. In this sense his work intersects that of Teresa de Lauretis in *Technologies of Gender* (Bloomington, Ind., 1987). In this sense also it bears a resemblance to the sociology of Max *Weber and to those such as Georg Lukács and the Frankfurt School whose work elaborates his study of instrumental rationality and bureaucracy. But Foucault's position deviates from theirs in the degree that it reflects upon the configuration of the author in scientific studies and refuses to allow the author a privileged stance of objectivity or authority. Thus Foucault rejects what he calls "the universal intellectual," someone whose scientific work affords a position of authority either as objectivity or within a movement of emancipation. Instead he proposes a category of "the specific intellectual," one whose discourse may be taken up by those seeking to protest domination but which derives its power only from within defined institutional and historical contexts.

(See also MARXISM; MODERNITY; POSTMODERNISM.)

Mark Poster, *Foucault, Marxism and History* (New York, 1974). Hubert Dreyfus and Paul Rabinow, *Michel Foucault: Beyond Structuralism and Hermeneutics* (Chicago, 1982).

MARK POSTER

FRANCE. Modern France is a product of centuries of historical sedimentation. French, theretofore regarded as a debased form of Latin, became the official language in 1539, under François I. Under the seventeenth-century royal absolutism of Louis XIV, *Colbertiste* (after Jean-Baptiste Colbert, Louis's chief minister) state-led patterns of economic development were firmly set out, Catholicism universalized at the expense of France's Protestants, and France's ambitious international role defined. The revolution of 1789 added new layers, vividly prefiguring subsequent debates over the *monarchy, desirable forms of political representation, and more radical proposals for a centralized Jacobin *democracy. Moreover, the image of revolutionary upheaval was deeply imprinted on France's collective memory in ways which fed later revolutionary socialist traditions. Finally, in the revolution and its Napoleonic aftermath, France—then Europe's largest nation with a population of 28 million—reconfigured its imperialist international vocation.

Nineteenth-century France had extraordinary difficulty in making basic constitutional choices. There were thus episodic alternations of monarchy and revolutionary crisis (1830, 1848, 1871) until the foundation of the Third Republic, modern France's hardiest constitutional arrangement, which lasted from 1871 to World War II. Dramatic political cleavages nonetheless persisted. Republican central

France struggled against Catholic and rural France through centralizing programs of public education to endow every young Frenchperson with uniform tools for republican *citizenship. Monarchists and the antirepublican nationalists who slowly replaced them struck back with agitation of which the Dreyfus affair of the 1890s was but one important episode. (Dreyfus, a Jewish officer unjustly accused of treason, became the center of an intense struggle between reactionaries and republicans.) When the *labor movement emerged from France's comparatively slow capitalist expansion, it, too, was ideologically riven between moderate tendencies and strong revolutionary urges, whether Marxist or syndicalist. The early Third Republic also reformulated French imperialism into a system in which high protectionist walls protected the economy while connecting it in privileged ways to French colonies all over the globe.

Modernization: 1918–1958. World War I began another half-century of political turbulence in which disagreements about constitutional forms overlapped, and were slowly changed by, the social changes of modernization. As a result of the Great War the nation had lost a substantial minority of its male population and gained a new set of divisive ideological themes. The *Left, growing in importance as industrialization progressed, split between Socialists and pro-Soviet Communists. France's twentieth-century labor movement would thus be marked by factional infighting which both weakened it and strongly politicized French industrial relations.

Institutional, ideological, and social blockages made the process of French *modernization slow and turbulent in the interwar period. Third Republic institutions, built on social "stalemate" between the rural, provincial, and protected world of the nineteenth century and more dynamic urban capitalism, made important choices extremely difficult to make. In addition, politically conservative and socially paternalistic capitalists would not seek common ground with radicalized labor interests. The result, fed by the Great Depression and a newly ominous international context, was growing delegitimation of the republic itself. Reformist Popular Front governments after 1936, supported by Socialists, Radicals, and Communists, were unable to survive long enough to institute needed reforms. Divided, France was quite unable to confront the rise of *fascism elsewhere in Europe. Moreover, the shock of the first modern experience of Left government precipitated much of the *Right toward antirepublicanism.

France's wartime disgrace ironically prodded modernization forward. Defeat by the Germans in June 1940 led to political capitulation and the authoritarian, backward-looking Vichy regime of Marshal Pétain, supported by much of the traditional French Right. The resistance movement which emerged contained, in very uneasy coexistence, most of France's modernizing elements. Given the discredit of the Right and the commitment of the Resistance to significant change, the two-year life of the post-Liberation coalition after November 1944 allowed a wide range of reforms. Extensive *nationalizations endowed the state with new power over the direction of France's economy. France's *welfare state was greatly expanded. A caste of modernizing technocrats, symbolized by Jean *Monnet and his *planning commission, were eager to use these new state levers for a rejuvenated *Colbertisme* which would distinguish France's postwar development trajectory from those of other European societies.

Post-Liberation governments did less well at building new political institutions. Disputes between General Charles de *Gaulle, Resistance leader and first postwar prime minister, and the Left over the place of the executive led to de Gaulle's angry resignation and denunciation of the emerging "regime of the parties." In the new Fourth Republic Constitution—barely approved by the electorate—the National Assembly became the seat of all power. Its majority coalitions, made volatile given a new system of *proportional representation, became even more changeable after the *Cold War came in 1947. France's strong alignment on the side of the United States forced the Communists, who represented twenty-five percent of the electorate, into quasi-permanent sectarian isolation. Governments had thenceforth to be constructed from among Center-Left and Center-Right groups who rarely agreed on anything important. The Fourth Republic thus drifted rightward and progressively was taken hostage by forces determined to preserve colonialism at all cost. Thus from 1946 until 1958 there was costly and divisive warfare first in Indochina and then in Algeria.

Despite political confusion socioeconomic modernization continued. Modernizing elites continued to encourage change from behind the scenes and were clearly visible in the founding of the European Coal and Steel Community in 1951 and subsequent steps toward the 1957 Treaty of Rome which founded the European Economic Community (EEC). The EEC, so central to later European and French economic growth, was constructed around common Franco-German interests. On quite another plane, the same elites also quietly laid the foundations of France's nuclear weapons programs in this period.

Modernity: 1958–1981. The Fourth Republic did not survive to reap the fruits of modernization. Instead, a quasi-coup in May 1958 based in extremist procolonial groups and the military brought Charles de Gaulle to power, first as legal prime minister and then, later in 1958, as president of a new Fifth Republic. The new Constitution adopted by popular referendum in September 1958 announced a very great increase in the power of the executive. The president, who was independently elected (indirectly, to begin with, and then by universal suffrage after a 1962 amendment), could appoint and dismiss the prime minister and his or her government, preside over the government, dissolve the National Assembly, call referenda under certain circumstances, and speak for the country in international affairs (beginning with de Gaulle, the president acquired a "reserved domain" in foreign and military affairs). The government appointed by the president, in turn, was strengthened over parliament by provisions which allowed it to control the National Assembly's agenda, making it difficult for governmental legislation to be defeated. The determination of the Constitution's framers to grant the president extensive new powers initiated the process of presidentializing French politics which has been the most important dynamic in recent French institutional history. A long, slow decline in the importance of parliament thus began. Finally, on certain matters a Constitutional Council could review governmental actions.

The Constitution was nonetheless an ambiguous document. The directly elected presidency, with a seven-year renewable term (which may soon be shortened to five years), and the National Assembly emanate from two separate electoral consultations. For much of the Fifth Republic there was an unspoken assumption that the political influence of the presidency would elicit a parliamentary majority in support of presidential policies. Indeed, the parliamentary electoral law chosen by de Gaulle after 1958—single-member constituencies with a runoff in the event no majority emerges at the first round—was designed to promote this. Yet the Constitution also held out the theoretical possibility of a president from one side of the political spectrum and a parliamentary majority from the opposition. In these circumstances, which had begun to seem increasingly plausible by the later 1970s, the president would be obliged to seek a modus vivendi with his opposition in ways which could severely limit the enhanced executive power which de Gaulle had meant to build into the new order.

President de Gaulle himself had a reliable parliamentary majority for nearly eleven years after 1958, as various factions of the French Center and Right massed behind his charisma. Thus he was able to accomplish his first major task, ending the *Algerian War, by June 1962 when the Evian Accords made Algeria an independent nation and ended France's colonial era. In the peacetime years which ensued, de Gaulle, fortified by the autonomy granted by France's new nuclear *force de dissuasion*, took his distance from the United States in Europe and the *North Atlantic Treaty Organization, in relations with the Soviet Union and the *Third World, and in financial policy. In Europe he promoted the implementation of a customs-free Common Market, while insisting that the European Economic Community (EEC) take on an essentially intergovernmental cast—a *Europe des patries*—and vetoing

Britain's membership on the grounds that the British were not sufficiently European.

Domestically, the Gaullist 1960s were the culminating point of what the French came to call the "thirty glorious years" of economic growth. In this period, which also coincided with a massive demographic boom in which the French population expanded from 40 million to well over 50 million in slightly more than two decades, France urbanized. It was transformed from being the most rural of all advanced societies after 1945, reconstructed its cities, purchased vast numbers of new consumer durable goods, learned to watch television and buy new cars, and began to send its youth to universities in unprecedented numbers. Such processes had been under way before 1958, but energetic Gaullist efforts helped them along, in particular through the state-*dirigiste* programs contained in France's periodic "indicative" economic plans. Quite as important, the 1960s saw the end of an earlier highly protected and empire-oriented economic outlook. France turned instead to the new EEC, while the growth-producing effects of increased intra-European trade helped France prosper.

The social complications of this economic success ended de Gaulle's brilliant career, however. De Gaulle was a genuinely charismatic leader, confident in his ability to speak directly to "France." Thus the general's regime came to be characterized by a certain disdain for the desires of intermediary social groupings like unions and for the social protest which rapid modernization incited. It was the general's inept handling of massive protests by students and workers in May–June 1968 which led to his resignation in April 1969.

De Gaulle's presidential successors until 1981, Georges Pompidou (elected in 1969, died in office in 1974) and Valéry Giscard d'Estaing (from 1974 to 1981), were obliged to temper their conservative proclivities with new concern for social policy. Initially this was due to aftereffects of the "May events." It became even more urgent, however, when in the early 1970s the previously divided Left—Communists and resurgent Socialists around François *Mitterrand—signed a programmatic pact which quickly brought them close to an electoral majority. Giscard d'Estaing was elected president over Mitterrand by a bare one percent of the vote, and subsequent elections in the 1970s remained that close. The dramatic change in economic circumstances after the first oil shock in the mid-1970s further complicated this precarious political situation. The end of the "thirty glorious years" in stagflation made economic policy making a treacherous affair. Right-of-center governments knew that the policies needed to restore profitability and investment would cost them their electoral majority. In the policy stalemate which followed, growth declined, inflation rose rapidly, and unemployment, which had been very low in the boom years, shot up.

The political and economic tensions of post-Gaullism took a lasting toll on the French Right. The 1974 presidential election first announced the disaggregation of the Gaullist coalition. Giscard, the first non-Gaullist president of the Fifth Republic, introduced new policy packages which antagonized his Gaullist coalition partners, tried to move the Gaullists out of entrenched positions in the state, and founded his own presidential vehicle, the Union Pour la Démocratie Française (UDF). Open conflict on the right developed when, in summer 1976, Gaullist leader Jacques Chirac dramatically resigned as prime minister to reconstitute the Gaullists in a Rassemblement Pour la République (RPR), a barely hidden declaration of war on Giscard. New rivalries on the right were as much about economics as politics. The relative shift in loci of economic regulation from national to international levels made 1960s-style Gaullist *dirigisme* less and less appropriate. Unable to agree upon a new program, the Right lost its socioeconomic compass and began to degenerate into warring clans.

The End of French Exceptionalism. The Left finally came to power when Socialist leader François Mitterrand defeated Giscard in the 1981 presidential elections. The Socialists won an absolute majority of seats in parliament shortly thereafter and formed a coalition government with the Communists. For the first two years of Left power after 1981, the Mitterrand presidency attempted to implement a project derived from the Communist-Socialist "Common Program" of 1972. At its heart was a reassertion of nationalist and reformist *Colbertisme* involving massive nationalizations, the strategic use of public funds for investment, state economic planning, and *dirigiste* industrial policy. There were also important reforms to give workers and unions more power in the workplace and to establish a degree of governmental decentralization. In the harsh economic circumstances of the early 1980s, the project led straight to impasse. Inflation rose, imports flooded the domestic market, and the franc weakened.

By 1983 Mitterrand and the Socialists, henceforth the dominant force on the left, had begun a cultural revolution. By mid-1984 the Communist junior partners in the coalition, unhappy with the Socialists' new directions, had left the government. The Socialists' agenda subsequently has been redefining the French Left's traditional outlooks to position themselves as promoters of a new project of national economic restructuring, or "modernization," as Mitterrand called it. In this project a mixed economy, coordinated by Socialist leaders, would rebuild France's competitiveness in the international economy. Henceforth the state would be an important facilitator for private-sector profitability and innovation while destatizing and deregulating an economic environment in which the firm would be the locus of social creativity. In concrete terms deflation and the maintenance of a strong franc—*monetar-ism, in fact—drove policy. Unemployment rose in consequence, even if the Socialists maintained a strong commitment to the existing French welfare state. As the Socialists changed, the Communists declined. By the end of the decade the once-powerful Parti Communiste Français—which had attracted twenty-six percent of the vote in 1946—had become a sect receiving between seven and eight percent.

The Right initially took the Left's 1981 success badly, but events were soon kinder. By the municipal elections of 1983 the Right had largely recovered, but by this point it was no longer quite the same Right. The Front National (FN), led by Jean-Marie Le Pen, a skillful demagogue focusing on racist anti-immigrant discontents, had appeared and won nearly eleven percent of the vote in the 1984 Europarliamentary elections. Its presence placed the moderate Right, which had already lost its sense of political project in the 1970s, in a situation where it could not win without dealing with the FN yet was unlikely to win if it did.

In 1985, faced with a virtually certain Left defeat in upcoming legislative elections, François Mitterrand changed the electoral law to proportional representation to cut down the size of any Right majority and magnify the strength of the FN. Mitterrand's ploy worked remarkably well. The FN won thirty-five deputies in the 1986 legislative elections while the moderate Right could only come up with a bare parliamentary majority. For the first time in the Fifth Republic, *cohabitation* between a president and government on opposite sides of the Left-Right divide occurred. Jacques Chirac, the Gaullist leader who became the first prime minister of *cohabitation*, was poorly armed to deal with it. *Cohabitation* thus ultimately favored Mitterrand. The Right's *privatization and deregulation were anticlimactic after the Left's earlier about-face. Moreover, the Right's neoliberal rhetoric barely concealed simple *conservatism and a transparent effort to reinforce privileged groups. A massive 1986 student movement against a timid university reform and the 1987 stock market crash ended the Right's policy pretensions. Mitterrand thus won reelection in the May 1988 presidential election by a margin of nearly ten percent, the first president of the Fifth Republic ever to do so. After new legislative elections, the Socialists, although a minority in Parliament, formed a new government around Prime Minister Michel Rocard.

By the early 1990s France had entered an unprecedented situation. The Socialists' new identity, constructed around an austere quest for international competitiveness "with a human face" to preserve the welfare state, allowed the Left to stay in power. Persistent austerity did not stir French souls, however. At the same time the Right was sinking further into a maelstrom. The Right's elders—Chirac, Raymond Barre, and Giscard—spend the bulk of their time engaged in trying to diminish their rivals' prospects rather than devising new ideas. In the meantime the FN continued to grow, winning 14.4 percent in the first round of the 1988 presidential elections and settling thereafter at around fifteen percent in the polls.

The economic changes of the 1980s, despite enhanced market internationalization and the restructuring of production, did not lead to a strengthened Right or to neoliberal triumph in France. They nonetheless did promote certain basic changes in French approaches—the end of nationalist *Colbertisme,* increased attention to the market, and, as discussions around the 1989 bicentenary of the French Revolution showed, the end of mythologies about the possibilities of dramatic social and political change. In these new circumstances France became less "exceptional" and more an ordinary middle-sized nation-state. Still, neither Left nor Right seemed able to resolve the policy dilemmas which France faced. Instead, political elites resorted to complex infighting covered over transparently by public relations exercises. The resulting disenchantment of the electorate was manifested not only in rising levels of political indifference and abstentionism but also in successes by new political groups like the Verts (Greens) and the racist FN.

The wrenching period after 1981 saw an important, and perhaps more promising, adjustment in France's international positions. After the Left's change in focus in 1983–1984 President Mitterrand took the lead in relaunching European integration. The *European Community's program to complete the Single Market by demolishing all remaining internal barriers to the free movement of goods, services, capital, and people by 1 January 1993 was then energetically promoted by Jacques Delors, president of the European Commission after 1985 (and former Socialist minister of finance). To the degree to which the Single Market and subsequent European "state-building" efforts like Economic and Monetary Union, Social Europe, and the construction of a Common European Foreign and Defense Policy (following a Franco-German initiative prompted by the end of the Cold War in Europe) succeeded, France's destiny would henceforth be tied to those of a larger Europe. France had come full circle. In the sixteenth and seventeenth centuries it had been a founding, and quite imperious, member of the quarrelsome universe of European nation-states. By the end of the twentieth century, France's future greatness seemed bound tightly to that of a united Europe.

(See also COLONIAL EMPIRES; DECOLONIZATION; EUROCOMMUNISM; GAULLISM; MAY 1968; RACE AND RACISM; REFORM; SOCIALISM AND SOCIAL DEMOCRACY.)

Stanley Hoffmann et al., *In Search of France* (Cambridge, Mass., 1963). Theodore Zeldin, *France 1848–1945,* 2 vols. (New York, 1979). George Ross, *Workers and Communists in France: From Popular Front to Eurocommunism* (Berkeley, Calif., 1982). Peter A. Hall, *Governing the Economy: The Politics of State Intervention in Britain and France* (New York, 1986). George Ross, Stanley Hoffmann, and Sylvia Malzacher, *The Mitterrand Experiment* (New York, 1987). François Borella, *Les Partis politiques dans la France d'aujourd'hui* (Paris, 1990). Pierre Favier and Michel Martin-Roland, *La Décennie Mitterrand,* 2 vols. (Paris, 1990, 1991). James Hollifield and George Ross, eds., *Searching for the New France* (New York, 1991).

GEORGE ROSS

FRANCO, Francisco. Born in El Ferrol, a port town in the province of La Coruña, on 4 December 1892, Francisco Franco Bahamonde was the son of a lower-middle-class family. He was the youngest of three brothers, short in stature, with delicate features and a soft, somewhat shrill, voice. At the age of 15 he enlisted in the Toledo Military Academy, where the decisive features of his character took shape. There, he identified with the frustrations of the Spanish army, which was torn between a mystic belief in its destiny—to save *Spain from the inefficiency of its politicians—and the humiliation suffered during the war against the United States in 1898. At the age of 17 Franco was made an officer and volunteered to serve in Morocco; this was the best means toward quick promotion.

Franco joined the Spanish Foreign Legion in 1920. In 1923 he married Carmen Polo, the daughter of a wealthy businessman. She instilled in his life bourgeois order and Catholic piety. At the age of 33 he was promoted to colonel, and it was then (February 1925) that he took command of the Foreign Legion. One year later he became the youngest general in Europe, and in 1928 he was appointed head of the Zaragoza Military Academy.

The coming of the Second Republic, following the April 1931 elections, curbed Franco's military career. But in 1933, when the conservative Right took over the government of the republic, Franco returned to active service and within a year was promoted to major general. His staunch loyalty to the conservative forces of the republic was revealed when he was called to quell the Asturian miners' rebellion in October 1934. His services were rewarded in May 1935 when he was appointed Army Head of Staff.

Thanks to his military prestige and notable political skill, which enabled him to obtain military aid from both *Hitler and *Mussolini, Franco became head of the conservative forces, rebelling against the Republic on 18 July 1936. On 1 November of that same year he was elected head of state of Nationalist Spain and generalissimo of its armies, but General Franco's rebel regime needed three long years of civil war to gain control of the whole nation. During *World War II the new nationalist regime was saved thanks to Franco's astute *diplomacy; he knew how to support the cause of the Axis powers without taking on irreversible military or diplomatic commitments.

Franco's regime started as a military dictatorship but later adopted a civil structure, reflecting its middle-class social base. On 19 April 1937 the Falange (the Spanish fascist party) merged with other right-wing political forces and became the regime's official political party, known as the Movimiento. Unlike Nazism and *fascism, "Francoism" was not based on a revolutionary party of the masses nor on a patriotic youth movement, but on conservative forces such as the army, the church, and the *caudillo* (leader). In other words, before the regime began to rely on economic prosperity and the seductions of a consumer society—a policy that, from the 1960s onward, would create a gradually unsustainable tension between *development and *modernization on the one hand and political *authoritarianism on the other—it rested on the traditional forces of Spanish society. Until the late 1950s, the social foundations of Francoism were the large landowners of the south, the Castilian middle-class peasantry, the new bourgeoisie that had sprung up in the shadow of the black market, and the bureaucracy of a country of "red tape" and hierarchies.

Ideology and the party never played a central role in Francoism; the party was an instrument of the government, not the other way round. The structure of Franco's governments was always flexible owing both to his practice of adapting his policies to changing conditions—provided that such "adaptation" would not undermine political authority—and his insistence on constantly restructuring the balance of forces within his conservative coalition. The army and the church—the latter providing the main ideological cement of Franco's regime—were the pillars that sustained the unity of the new Spain. Although a negative facet of the regime was that it excluded those who did not share the ideals of Franco's crusade against *parliamentary democracy and *liberalism, a positive facet of the regime was that it channeled conservative interests into evolutionary forms.

Francoism was more than just the personal rule of a dictator, although it was not a completely totalitarian regime, either. Juan Linz defined Franco's government as an institutionalized authoritarian system, that is, a political system with limited political *pluralism, devoid of a coherent or clearly defined ideology.

Franco's regime received very little international backing until 1953, when it managed to break its diplomatic isolation thanks to the concordat with the Holy See and a cooperation treaty with the United States. Until then, the regime was able to ignore any reactions that its domestic policy might provoke in Europe; it even managed to profit politically from international hostility. Franco reacted to this hostility toward his regime by presenting it to the Spanish people, who closed ranks around him, as a manifestation of the supposed international conspiracy against Spain.

Franco was head of state and prime minister until 1973, and carried out official duties such as presiding over important cabinet meetings and receiving ambassadors. He was head of the Movimiento—Spain's only political organization—and generalissimo, supreme commander of all the armed forces.

Franco died on 20 November 1975, connected to an array of sophisticated medical devices, and with Saint Teresa's arm at his side and the cloak of the Virgin on his bed. His death was symbolic of the Spain he had ruled: a modern, industrial nation and consumer society obsessed by the relics of a traditional Catholic state.

(See also ROMAN CATHOLIC CHURCH; SPANISH CIVIL WAR.)

Stanley Payne, *Franco's Spain* (London, 1968). Edouard de Blaye, *Franco and the Politics of Spain* (Harmondsworth, U.K., 1976). Paul Preston, ed., *Spain in Crisis: The Evolution and Decline of the Franco Regime* (Hassocks, U.K., 1976). José Amodia, *Franco's Political Legacy: From Fascism to Facade Democracy* (London, 1977). Raymond Carr and Juan Pablo Fusi, *España, de la dictadura a la democracia* (Barcelona, 1979).

SHLOMO BEN-AMI

FRANCOPHONE AFRICA. Comprising the sub-Saharan nations for which French is the language of government all of which were colonies of France or Belgium, Francophone Africa consists of seventeen countries that form a contiguous bloc in West and Central Africa; to them may be added Madagascar and the Comoros of the Indian Ocean and Djibouti on the Horn of Africa.

Francophone Africa includes nearly half the area of sub-Saharan Africa, and its population of more than 100 million is one-third of the sub-Saharan African total. Zaire, with 30 million inhabitants, is the largest and most populous country of the group; Cameroon, Madagascar, and Côte d'Ivoire follow with just over 10 million each. In West Africa, Islam is the dominant religion, although Christianity and local religions are important in Côte d'Ivoire, Togo, and Benin. In Central Africa and Madagascar, Christianity is dominant, with Catholics outnumbering Protestants.

These political units were formed through European conquest in the period 1880–1920. France organized most of its conquests into two large federations: French West Africa was formed in 1905 with its capital in Dakar; French Equatorial Africa was formed in 1910 with its capital in Brazzaville. French Madagascar had a separate government-general. Zaire has its origin in the Congo Independent State, founded by King Leopold II of Belgium in 1885; it became the Belgian Congo in 1908. The conquest of German colonies during World War I led to the creation of additional Francophone territories, French Togo and Cameroon, and Belgian Ruanda-Urundi, under mandate from the League of Nations and then the UN. Independence came to almost all of Francophone Africa in 1960: Guinea gained independence in 1958; Rwanda, Burundi, the Comoros, and Djibouti later.

The term *Francophone Africa* came into usage in the years after independence, when it was no longer appropriate to refer to *French Africa*. Thereafter, the tenuous unity of the Francophone countries was reinforced by political and cultural developments. Most obvious among these was the emergent role of France as neocolonial power, providing economic, military, and technical aid, and linking the Francophone nations in a series of international groupings, beginning with the Organisation Commune Africaine et Malgache, founded in 1960.

In addition to the French presence, some African factors serve to sustain the identity of Francophone Africa. Use of the French language in Africa expanded greatly with the growth of public education after independence. The elites of the Francophone countries are united by a common cosmopolitan culture, based on the French system of higher education, and reaffirmed by such institutions as the newsmagazine *Jeune Afrique* and the Libreville-based radio station Africa No. 1. Further, the commonality of the Francophone states serves them, in continental politics, as a counterweight to the relative power and wealth of such English-speaking states as Nigeria, Kenya, Zimbabwe, and, ultimately, South Africa. The Francophone countries participate actively in the *Organization of African Unity: recent presidents have included Abdou Diouf of Senegal, Moussa Traoré of Mali, and Denis Sassou-Nguesso of Congo; Idé Oumarou of Niger has served as secretary-general.

Most Francophone African nations are governed as republics with single-party regimes; exceptions include the military regimes of Burundi, Guinea, Mauritania, and Niger. Several are or have been Marxist-Leninist people's republics: Madagascar, Mali, Guinea, Benin, and Congo. Senegal has been most consistent in sustaining the forms of multiparty, *parliamentary democracy. In most cases, however, the practical form of government has been relatively standard: a strong presidency, a ministerial system of government, a strong party structure, and a relatively powerless national legislature. In a number of countries—Zaire, Chad, and Niger, for instance—the balance of regional and ethnic interests has been an important element in national politics. Local elections have been a significant arena of political struggle.

Armed forces range from a low of 4,000 for Togo to over 50,000 for Zaire. They average two persons in the armed forces for every 1,000 in population throughout the region. Civil war dominated Zaire in the 1960s; in Chad two decades of civil war led to several years of war with Libya over the Aozou Strip.

The former French colonies of West and Central Africa are almost all members of the franc zone, with the Communauté Financière Africaine (CFA) franc pegged at 0.02 French franc. Zaire, Rwanda, Burundi, Mauritania, and Madagascar have autonomous currencies, as did Mali and Guinea before they rejoined the franc zone. The domestic economies of the desert-edge countries and of Madagascar have been hard hit by drought. The leading agricultural exports of Francophone Africa have been cocoa, coffee, peanuts, and cotton. Prices for all these exports fell during the 1980s. Gabon, Congo, and Cameroon benefited from an oil boom during the early 1980s, then suffered from the decline in oil prices thereafter. Zaire is rich in agricultural and mineral resources, but is compromised by heavy debt. Two major regional economic unions involve Francophone states. The Union Douanière et Economique de l'Afrique Centrale (UDEAC)—linking Chad, the Central African Republic, Cameroon, Gabon, Congo, and Equatorial Guinea—functions successfully despite ideological differences among national governments. The Economic Community of Central African States, founded in 1985, is dominantly Francophone. The Economic Community of West African States (ECOWAS) includes all West African states, and has been somewhat less successful.

Structural adjustment programs of the *International Monetary Fund have influenced virtually every Francophone African country, but particularly Zaire and Côte d'Ivoire, which have the largest debts. These programs caused the launching of *privatization campaigns by most governments, most notably by those that had followed socialist policies. For Francophone Africa—more so than Anglophone Africa—expansion of the state sector of the economy was an inheritance from the colonial era.

Soviet influence in Francophone Africa rose with the emergence of radical regimes—first in Guinea and Mali in the 1960s, and during the 1970s in Madagascar, Benin, and Congo. More significantly, the United States developed very close relations with President Mobutu Sese Seko of Zaire and with Félix Houphouët-Boigny of Côte d'Ivoire, and exercised influence over African international relations through those ties.

French influence in Africa was limited for a time by the rise of radical regimes, but in the 1980s France regained influence in all its ex-colonies, and grew to influence the ex-Belgian colonies; Soviet influence with the socialist regimes declined accordingly. The French president meets annually with African heads of state. In 1986 France acted on the proposal of Léopold Sédar Senghor of Senegal regarding creation of an organization of Francophone states.

France is also deeply involved in military supply and assistance in Africa and has intervened militarily in Chad, Zaire, Gabon, the Central African Republic, Rwanda, and the Comoros. French interests in Europe, however, have progressively limited the depth of military commitment to Africa.

Two presidents, Senghor of Senegal and Ahidjo of Cameroon, stepped down voluntarily during the 1980s. Since then there have been some moves toward institutionalization of party politics and regular succession and limits on presidential power in Francophone African states. Francophone Africa participated fully in the wave of democratization movements of 1989–1990.

(See also AFRICAN REGIONAL ORGANIZATIONS; COLONIAL EMPIRES.)

Colin Legum, ed., *Africa Contemporary Record* (New York, annual). Patrick Manning, *Francophone Sub-Saharan Africa, 1880–1985* (Cambridge, U.K., 1988).

PATRICK MANNING

FUNDAMENTALISM. See SECULARIZATION.

G

GABON. A heavily forested country created by France in western equatorial Africa between the 1840s and 1880s, Gabon achieved national independence on 13 August 1960. Its constitution of 21 February 1961 established a presidential form of government within a democratic republic. The attempts of the first president, Léon Mba (1902–1967), to gain control of the National Assembly through the establishment of a single political party provoked the coup of 17–20 February 1964 by young military officers.

French military intervention restored Mba to power and eliminated his opponents from public life. Intervention allowed Mba to install a dictatorship which he transferred to his chosen successor, Omar Bongo (b. 1935). Bongo, supported by the French government and French interests doing business in Gabon, was able to establish a single party, the Parti Démocratique Gabonais (PDG), on 12 March 1968. The National Assembly no longer initiated legislation; instead it merely discussed the implementation of measures already decided by the party executive directed by Bongo. By this time Bongo headed not only the state and the government but also several key ministries, including defense. Bongo practiced a clientism or patrimonialism that offered members of the French-educated elite (numbering about 2,000) well-paying positions in government and administration. Those who refused his terms for incorporation into the ruling class became exiles; internal critics met death. The unprecedented expansion of petroleum revenues from the early 1970s gave Bongo and the ruling class unexpected opportunities for increased power and personal enrichment.

The petroleum-based economy transformed Gabon in other ways. It led to the neglect of food crops and to the emptying of the countryside where the bulk of the 800,000 Gabonese had previously lived. Given the low rate of population growth, 30,000 Europeans provided most of the technical and managerial skills for the economy while 100,000 Africans from other countries predominated as petty retailers, local transporters, and unskilled laborers. But the oil boom and related activities gave rise to a larger wage-earning class, thereby increasing the influence of socioeconomic factors in a society hitherto shaped more by ethnic, regional, and religious factors.

The Bongo regime built the Transgabonese Railway from Owendo on the Gabon Estuary to Franceville in the Upper Ogooué River Valley in order further to develop manganese, uranium, timber, and other resources of the interior. It improved health and education for the ordinary citizen. But its extravagance, wastefulness, and corruption contributed to a severe financial crisis in the late 1980s when world demand for petroleum declined. The austerity measures taken to deal with this crisis contributed to the upheaval that Gabon has been experiencing since January 1990. Opposition groups that had emerged in the 1980s to demand the end of corruption, respect for civil liberties, and restoration of democracy, gained legal recognition in May 1990.

In the Assembly elections of September–October 1990, which were marred by irregularities, the PDG won 62 of the 120 seats. But the emergence of both a leftist party based at Port-Gentil, the Parti Gabonais du Progrès (PGP), and a heavily Fang party, the Rassemblement des Bûcherons, in the Estuary, gave Gabon's politics new and unpredictable dimensions.

(See also Francophone Africa.)

David E. Gardinier, *Historical Dictionary of Gabon* (Metuchen, N.J., 1992).

DAVID E. GARDINIER

GAMBIA. The Republic of the Gambia is approximately 10,500 square kilometers (4,000 sq. mi.) in area and has a population of about 800,000. It became an independent country on 18 February 1965. The first Europeans to visit the area were Portuguese who arrived in the mid-fifteenth century. They were later replaced by the French and British. In 1900 the British brought the whole country under one imperial roof. For the next sixty-five years the Gambia witnessed constitutional changes which gradually gave the franchise to the peoples of the former colony and the former protectorate. Political parties emerged in the early 1950s. Between 1951 and 1962 the arena was dominated by the People's Progressive Party (PPP) of Dr. D. K. Jawara and the United Party (UP) of the Gambian lawyer Pierre Sarr Njie. Because of the polarization between the urban politicians of the capital city of Banjul and their rural counterparts, "a green revolution took place," according to Gambia scholar Arnold Hughes ("From Green Uprising to National Reconciliation: The People's Progressive Party in the Gambia" *Canadian Journal of African Studies* 9, no. 1, 1975). The capturing of political power by the PPP changed the political landscape of the country.

When the Gambia became independent, it inherited a Westminster model of government from the British. There was a Parliament with thirty-two representatives drawn from single district contituencies and four chiefs elected by their peers. A judiciary patterned after that of Britain facilitated the administration of justice, while a bureaucracy built during colonial rule became the instrument of administration for the political class that captured power at the time of *decolonization. The Gambia underwent a constitutional change in 1970, after a referendum approved the adoption of a republican constitution that replaced the office of prime minister with that of the presidency.

Between 1970 and 1990 the Republic of the Gambia witnessed three major events. The first was the abortive coup d'état of July 1981; the second was the 1982 decision of the Gambia and *Senegal to form the confederation of Senegambia; the third was the breakup of the confederacy in 1989, following a row between the two countries over the question of rotational leadership of the confederation. The 1981 coup d'état was significant because it disrupted the democratic process in the Gambia and brought in Senegalese troops to maintain law and order.

The postcolonial political life of the country has been largely peaceful except for the 1981 coup attempt. From 1965 to 1975 the PPP and the UP dominated the political landscape. By 1972, however, the UP was virtually a spent force, and it performed badly in that year's general elections. This pattern of decline among opposition forces was repeated in 1987 when the Gambia went to the polls. The ruling PPP has continued to gain strength.

Since independence, the Gambia has developed a number of diplomatic relations with other states in the African and international arenas. Being a small country with limited resources, the Gambia has a small diplomatic service with embassies in London, Brussels, Paris, Washington, Freetown, Riyadh, and Lagos. The country is a member of the *Organization of African Unity (OAU), the *Commonwealth, the Organization of Islamic Conference (OIC), the UN, and the Economic Community of West African States (ECOWAS).

Sulayman S. Nyang, "The Gambia: Between Internal and External Foes" *African Concord* (25 February 1985). John A. Wiseman, *Democracy in Black Africa* (New York, 1990).
SULAYMAN S. NYANG

GAME THEORY. A branch of mathematics, game theory is used to analyze competitive situations whose outcomes depend not only on one's own choices, and perhaps chance, but also on the choices made by other parties, or "players." Because the outcome of a game is dependent on what *all* players do, each player tries to anticipate the choices of other players in order to determine its own best choice. How these interdependent strategic calculations are made is the subject of the theory.

Game theory was created in practically one stroke with the publication of *Theory of Games and Economic Behavior* (Princeton, N.J., 1944; 3d ed., 1953) by the mathematician John von Neumann and the economist Oskar Morgenstern. This was a monumental intellectual achievement and has given rise to scores of books and thousands of articles in a variety of fields.

The theory has several major divisions, the following being the most important:

- 2-person versus *n*-person: the 2-person theory deals with the optimal strategic choices of two players, whereas the *n*-person theory ($n > 2$) mostly concerns what coalitions, or subsets of players, will form and be stable, and what constitute reasonable payments to their members.

- zero-sum versus nonzero-sum: the payoffs to all players sum to zero (or some other constant) at each outcome in zero-sum (or constant-sum) games but not in nonzero-sum games, wherein the sums are variable; zero-sum games are games of total conflict, in which what one player gains the others lose, whereas nonzero-sum games permit the players to gain or lose simultaneously.

- cooperative versus noncooperative: cooperative games are those in which players can make binding and enforceable agreements, whereas noncooperative games may or may not allow for communication among the players but always assume that any agreement reached is in equilibrium—that is, it is rational for a player not to violate it if other players do not, because it would be worse off, or at least not better off, if it did.

Games can be described by several different forms, the three most common being: 1) *extensive (game tree)*—indicates sequences of choices that players (and possibly chance, according to nature or some random device) can make, with payoffs defined at the end of each sequence of choices; 2) *normal/ strategic (payoff matrix)*—indicates strategies, or complete plans contingent on other players' choices, for each player, with payoffs defined at the intersection of each set of strategies in a matrix; 3) *characteristic function*—indicates values that all possible coalitions (subsets) of players can ensure for their members, whatever the other players do. These different game forms, or representations, give less and less detailed information about a game—with the sequences in form 1 dropped from form 2, and the strategies to implement particular outcomes in form 2 dropped from form 3—to highlight different aspects of a strategic situation.

Common to all areas of game theory is the assumption that players are rational: they have goals, can rank outcomes (or, more stringently, attach utilities, or values, to them), and choose better over worse outcomes. Complications arise from the fact that there is generally no straightforwardly best strategy for a player because of the interdependency of player choices. (Games in which there is only one player are sometimes called "games against nature" and are the subject of decision theory.)

A game is sometimes defined as the sum total of its rules. Common parlor games, like chess or poker, have well-specified rules and are generally zero-sum games, making cooperation with the other player(s) unproductive. Poker differs from chess in being not only an *n*-person game (although only two players can play it) but also a game of incomplete information, because the players do not have full knowledge of each other's hands, which depend in part on chance.

The rules of most real-life games are equivocal; indeed, the "game" may be about the rules to be used (or abrogated). Thus, international politics is considered to be quite anarchistic, though there is certainly some constancy in the way conflicts develop and may, or may not, be resolved. *Arms races, for instance, are almost always nonzero-sum games in which two competitors can benefit if they reach some agreement on limiting weapons, but such agreements are often hard to verify or enforce and, consequently, may be unstable.

With the diminution of *superpower conflict, interest has focused on whether a new "*balance of power"—reminiscent of the political juggling acts of European countries in the nineteenth and early twentieth century—may emerge in different regions or even worldwide. Game theory offers tools for studying the stability of new alignments, including those that might develop on issues of *political economy.

Consider, for example, the *General Agreement on Tariffs and Trade (GATT), whose durability is now being tested by regional trading agreements that have sprung up among countries in the Americas, Europe, and Asia. The rationality of supporting GATT or joining a regional trading bloc is very much a strategic question that can be illuminated by game theory. Game theory also provides insight into how the domestic politics of a country impinges on its foreign policy, and vice versa, which has led to a renewed interest in the interconnections between these two levels of politics.

Other applications of game theory have been made to strategic voting in committees and elections, the formation and disintegration of parliamentary coalitions, and the distribution of power in weighted voting bodies. On the normative side, electoral reforms have been proposed to lessen the power of certain parties (e.g., the religious parties in Israel), based on game-theoretic analysis. Similarly, the voting weights of members of the *European Com-

munity Council of Ministers, and its decision rule for taking action (e.g., simple majority or qualified majority), have been studied with an eye to making the body both representative of individual members' interests and capable of taking collective action. In sum, game theory can be used both to analyze existing strategic situations and to shed light on new situations that might arise were there a change in the rules, the preferences of the players, or the information available to them.

(See also INTERDEPENDENCE; PUBLIC CHOICE THEORY; STRATEGY.)

Steven J. Brams and D. Marc Kilgour, *Game Theory and National Security* (New York, 1988). Emerson M. S. Niou, Peter C. Ordeshook, and Gregory F. Rose, *The Balance of Power: Stability in International Systems* (Cambridge, U.K., 1989). George Tsebelis, *Nested Games: Rational Choice in Comparative Politics* (Berkeley, Calif., 1990).

STEVEN J. BRAMS

GANDHI, Indira. One of modern *India's important political leaders, Indira Gandhi was born in 1917. She was the daughter of Jawaharlal *Nehru. Born to politics, she took an intermittent part in the nationalist movement, headed by Mohandas *Gandhi and her father. After India gained independence, she became president of the Congress Party during 1959–1960. She subsequently served as a cabinet minister from 1964 to 1966 and eventually became prime minister of India in 1966. She remained India's prime minister until 1977, when her Congress Party suffered defeat at the elections. She regained the office of prime minister in the 1980 parliamentary elections and retained that office until her *assassination in 1984.

Indira Gandhi's political legacy is ambiguous. The proximity of her reign, moreover, makes an overall assessment difficult. On the economic front, she continued the policies of previous Congress governments, emphasizing self-reliance, capital-intensive industrialization, an inward-looking trade policy, and a large role for the public sector. India's industrial performance during these years was, at best, sluggish. Where she did make changes, they tended to be ideologically disparate. On the one hand, she nationalized the banking industry. Conversely, she pushed the *green revolution and a turn to commercial agriculture, leading India toward self-sufficiency in food. After regaining power in 1980, she also attempted to liberalize India's economy and to relax state controls.

Where Indira Gandhi left an indelible mark was in the field of politics. She introduced a genuinely populist style to Indian politics and sought to address the issue of poverty through public sector programs. Her slogan *Garibi Hatao* (Out with Poverty) set a viable strategy for electoral mobilization. The populist tone also helped lay out a political agenda to which all her opponents had to respond.

Indira Gandhi had little success in actually alleviating poverty. Her efforts were constrained by a lack of resources on the one hand and a reluctance and inability to engage in such structural reforms as land redistribution on the other. Nevertheless, her style of leadership deeply affected the nature of India's political system. She centralized decision making and created a personalized regime that bypassed the institutions of both party and state. This weakened India's political institutions—such as the Parliament, *federalism, and the Congress Party—and diminished the country's capacity to resolve political conflicts without violence.

Indira Gandhi was both a cause and a consequence of India's growing political problems. By the late 1960s, social and economic changes had considerably weakened the regional elites on which Congress under Nehru had relied. Indira Gandhi sought to salvage Congress's political position by creating a personalistic and populist rule. Her style, however, also weakened the principal political institutions of India. Pressed by growing political opposition, she declared a state of emergency in 1975, which led to a two-year period of authoritarian rule. She did, however, call—and ultimately lost—a general election in 1977.

During the 1980s, she increasingly turned to religious and ethnic issues to mobilize the electorate. An important consequence of this approach was the exacerbation of a religious-based secessionist movement in India's northwestern state of Punjab. Growing turmoil in that state led her to order a major army operation in 1984 against the Sikhs (a religious minority) and eventually resulted in her assassination.

In foreign relations, Indira Gandhi kept India on the path of nonalignment, and she became chairperson of that movement in 1982. She was, on balance, more sympathetic to the Soviet Union, and Indo-U.S. relations during her reign remained strained. Indira Gandhi also played a decisive role in the 1971 war with *Pakistan that led to the creation of *Bangladesh.

(See also NONALIGNED MOVEMENT; RELIGION AND POLITICS.)

Inder Malhotra, *Indira Gandhi: A Personal and Political Biography* (London, 1989).

PRATAP MEHTA
ATUL KOHLI

GANDHI, Mohandas. On 2 October 1869 at Porbandar, a small town in what was then one of the princely states in Kathiawar in Gujarat, *India, Mohandas Karamchand Gandhi was born to a family that belonged to the Vaishya (trading) community and were Vaishnavas of the Vallabhacharya Hindu tradition. Jainism was strong in Gujarat, and Gandhi was accustomed to an atmosphere that combined both the devotional and the ascetic tempers. Thanks to his father, who was a high government official first in Porbandar and then in Rajkot, he was no

less used to regarding moral and political questions as interrelated. He was married to Easturba Makanji in 1882 when both were thirteen years old. From 1889 to 1891 he studied law in London. During that period he became friendly with vegetarians and theosophists and familiarized himself with the *Bhagavadgita,* Edwin Arnold's *The Light of Asia,* and the New Testament. Unable to establish himself as a lawyer on his return to India, in 1893 he accepted an assignment as legal adviser to Dada Abdullah & Company in Durban, South Africa, remaining in that country until 1914.

During those twenty-one years his interests extended from those of his mainly Muslim merchant clientele to the general cause of the Indian immigrants in South Africa, more particularly the cause of the indentured laborers. In the course of his work at this stage he used the following techniques: the amicable settlement of disputes whenever possible, various means of rousing *public opinion (constitutional agitation in law courts, petitions, journalistic campaigns, deputations to Parliament), and the new strategy of nonviolent resistance known as *satyagraha* (literally "grasp of truth"). In South Africa Gandhi was not a full-time politician, as he continued to earn his living as a lawyer and, moreover, organized two model communities, called Tolstoy Farm and Phoenix Settlement. It was during his South Africa days that he developed his belief in an across-the-board approach, combining socioeconomic, ethico-religious, and political concerns. He suspended his nonviolent campaign for Indian civil rights during the Boer War of 1899–1902 and the Zulu rebellion of 1906–1907, organizing an ambulance corps for noncombatant duties. This signified two new steps in his political thinking, namely, that resisters should not take advantage of an enemy's predicament and that those who claim rights should be prepared to undertake duties. By 1914 his efforts in South Africa were largely successful, and his attention shifted to India, with which he had been in touch over the years through periodic visits and contacts.

From 1915 on he gradually acquired the status of a national leader in India's struggle against British rule. Politically he was different both from the moderates, who believed in constitutional methods, and from extremists or terrorists, who were willing to resort to violence. Gandhi's role as a political figure includes his building up of the Indian National Congress (which was already in existence at the time) as the main vehicle of the independence movement, the organizing of a mass movement beyond the control of the party, and the nurturing of a network of voluntary institutions that would serve both as a training ground for volunteers and as a nucleus of the new society that he believed would come into existence when independence came.

His own life history—which ended with his assassination by a Hindu fanatic on 30 January 1948—

is scarcely distinguishable from his involvement in the political and other events that took place in his country at the same time. A series of *satyagraha* campaigns of varying scales showed that nonviolent resistance could be effective against injustice and in resolving conflicts and could be used as a tool in the fight for national liberation. The first campaign on Indian soil was in Champaran in Bihar in 1917. It was carried out by Indian cultivators against the British indigo factory owners. The campaign was notable for the fact-finding engaged in by Gandhi and his associates, the bringing in of volunteers from other parts of India, and the beginning of "constructive work" in the village, the last of these being regarded by him as an indispensable part of any *satyagraha* campaign. In Ahmedabad in 1918 Gandhi entered into a labor dispute in which textile workers confronted an enlightened family of mill owners, the Sarabhais. It was Gandhi's first experience with India's industrial proletariat. The conflict in the Kheda district in the Bombay Presidency the same year was yet again of a different kind: between the peasants and the local administration. The method resorted to was a no-tax campaign.

The next stage of Gandhi's political career had as its target the repeal of the Rowlett Act, which continued wartime measures to put down political violence. Such measures were indubitably repressive in peacetime. The campaign took the form of a strike; but sporadic violence broke out, and crowds were fired on in Jallianwala Bagh in April 1919.The combined effect of the killing of innocent people on Baisakhi festival day and Gandhi's sympathy with Indian Muslim support for pan-Islamic efforts were major factors leading to the noncooperation movement against the British, proposed by Gandhi and adopted by the Indian National Congress in a special session in September 1920. The movement involved the boycott of educational institutions and the founding of parallel ones, the adoption of *swadeshi* (homemade goods, including *khadi* or homespun cloth), and the boycott of legislative councils and courts. The moral component of this political attempt to paralyze the administration was the shedding of fear of the rulers and a self-purification that aimed at the promotion of Hindu-Muslim unity, the removal of untouchability, abstention from alcohol, and the purging from Indian society of forced labor and other evils. However, the involvement of congress workers in a violent incident at Chauri Chaura in 1922 led Gandhi to suspend the plan to embark on massive civil disobedience. Gandhi believed that all political activity must be peaceful and that the outbreak of violence was a sign that the people were not yet ready for mass action.

As a political educator Gandhi sought to channel the energies of ordinary people in constructive ways so that neither anger aroused by local grievances nor the innate explosive force of *nationalism would lead to violence. He continued to negotiate with the British government and to lead the nationalist movement even when he was in jail. He resigned from the Congress Party in 1934 but remained the chief figure on the Indian political scene. The civil disobedience movement he launched in 1930 to protest the Salt Laws showed once again his flair for symbolic acts. Gandhi's combination of negotiation, courting arrest, direct action, and constructive work provided a new form of political activity at a time when constitutionalists, socialists, and extremists were each advocating different lines of action. His tutelage of Congress Party workers was always fraught with difficulty because those who believed that politics could be moralized were in a minority. India attained freedom at the end of World War II, and the partition of the country went through despite Gandhi's own wishes. Having encouraged the Congress Working Committee to come to its own decisions, he felt unable to use his personal influence to achieve a different end. Instead, in an attempt to bring about peace, he visited parts of the country where sectarian violence had broken out. The goal of *swaraj* (self-rule) would not be attained as long as conflict remained.

Gandhi's key concepts of *satyagraha* (nonviolent resistance), *swadeshi* (homemade goods), and *swaraj* (self-rule) have become part of the political vocabulary of the twentieth century. Of these it was the first that captured the imaginations of leaders such as Martin Luther *King, Jr., and Nelson *Mandela. His "oceanic circle" metaphor for the relationship between the individual and collectivities, with the individual firmly at the center, provided a nonhierarchical model for a changed society. If there was a touch of propheticism in his political style, this was balanced by his practical sense in giving importance to the restructuring of socioeconomic affairs. Some of Gandhi's ideas became incorporated into Indian state policy, including constitutional safeguards for the scheduled castes (formerly known as "untouchables") and the promotion of cottage industries.

(See also DECOLONIZATION; HINDUISM; ISLAM; NEHRU, JAWAHARLAL; NONVIOLENT ACTION.)

MARGARET CHATTERJEE

GANGS. The term *gang* has generally been used to identify a grouping of individuals involved in some type of antisocial behavior. To use the term so loosely, however, presents an inaccurate picture of gangs and their actual relationship with other people or institutions in society. Sociologically, gangs have been and continue to be collectives of individuals who are associated with each other through some formal organizational structure, and who are involved in both legal and illegal activities. It is precisely because of their organizational dimension (leadership structure and codes regulating behavior) and illegal activities that historically the term became synonymous with "Mob," "Syndicate," and Mafia. While the term *gang* has been used interchangeably with each of these terms, since the 1950s it has been used to identify groups whose membership are composed primarily of adolescents or young adults.

In regard to their social basis, gangs display two general characteristics. First, they are composed of individuals from low-income families. In essence, gangs represent an organizational response by those from low-income backgrounds to secure the material possessions that they lack. Second, gangs are generally, although not exclusively, composed of adolescents or young adults. One significant demographic development since the 1970s has been that the age level of gangs has steadily risen, with increasing numbers of individuals 30 years of age or older participating in them.

Politically, gangs have been used throughout the world by a wide variety of political actors as resources to achieve their goals. The political use of gangs has assumed a number of forms. First, in many countries, and especially in the United States, gangs have been used by politicians (or political parties) to assist in the mobilization of voters. To this end gangs help to disseminate information, transport individuals to the polls for election, and pressure individuals to support the political position they have been solicited to proselytize—assuming some of the duties, in other words, once handled by urban political machines. In effect, the gang is simply an independent organization for hire on an ad hoc basis. However, elsewhere, particularly in the *Third World, gangs have been directly integrated into the various *political machine organizations. Because political machines are more salient in many of these countries, the gang becomes an enduring element within that organizational form.

Second, in countries like El Salvador, Mexico, and Argentina, gangs have been used by individual politicians and governments alike to help enforce desired policies and/or suppress opposition. While the use of gangs to eliminate political opponents by intimidation or murder is mostly a Third World phenomenon, it has also occurred in the United States (the El Rukns gang in Chicago, for example) and South Africa.

Third, gangs may act as an unofficial arm of the state or, conversely, a countervailing force against a particular form of state action. At times gangs serve as a local police force, at others as a guardian against police harassment. In low-income communities throughout the world, and among middle-income communities primarily in the Third World, gangs provide protection that the police either cannot (for lack of efficiency or power) or will not (for personal or class interests) provide. Cases in which gangs deter police abuse have occurred to a limited degree in the United States but are more widespread in low-income communities of the Third World. However, such gangs are also able to, and often do, impose an alternative form of tyranny on the individuals within their control.

Fourth, politicians and government officials have used gangs symbolically as part of a strategy to achieve a particular political objective. In this regard, gangs are depicted as an impending physical, social, or economic threat to the larger community and must, it is argued, be effectively deterred. Such appeals have been used throughout the United States and have been generally successful in winning support for a particular candidate, policy, or program.

Finally, various political insurgency groups—for example, in Nicaragua, El Salvador, Vietnam, South Africa, and the United States—have actively recruited gangs for their military operations. In such cases, gangs are seen as having both the skills to perform violent acts and the advantage of being familiar with the social and physical geography that is being contested. However, while they may be active in insurgency groups, gangs lack the organizational capacity and the ideological will to become central actors in the establishment of a social movement. They are essentially organizations whose goals are limited to maintaining the organization and maximizing the benefits of its members, rather than organizations possessing a broad social vision.

In conclusion, then, gangs arise in response to a particular economic situation and as such are primarily economic, not political, organizations. Nonetheless, despite the fact that gangs are rarely pivotal actors in the political arena, they can and do influence the political dynamics within the local communities where they are active.

(See also POLITICAL VIOLENCE.)

C. Ronald Huff, ed., *Gangs in America* (Newbury Park, Calif., 1990). Martín Sánchez Jankowski, *Islands in the Street: Gangs and American Urban Society* (Berkeley, Calif., 1991).

MARTÍN SÁNCHEZ JANKOWSKI

GATT. See GENERAL AGREEMENT ON TARIFFS AND TRADE.

GAULLE, Charles de. The French military and political leader Charles de Gaulle was born in Lille on 22 November 1890 and educated in Paris. His father came from an old family of soldiers, lawyers, and writers belonging to the small nobility, his mother from a bourgeois small business family; both were ardent Catholics and monarchists. The third of five children, Charles decided early to become a soldier, and at 15 wrote an essay in which he saw himself saving France from defeat as military commander against Germany. After graduating from the military school of Saint-Cyr, he served in the regiment of Colonel Philippe Pétain. Wounded in *World War I, he spent almost two-and-a-half years in captivity in Germany. After taking part in the defense of Warsaw against the Russians in 1920, he returned to France, married Yvonne Vendroux, lectured at the Ecole de Guerre, served on Marshal Pétain's staff, and wrote several books, including a study of the causes of Germany's defeat (among which the abdication of civilian control over the military was crucial) and the *Edge of the Sword,* an essay on leadership that was also a self-portrait. In the 1930s, he became the champion of the idea of a motorized, professional army capable of offensive action. Despite his efforts, and those of his political mentor Paul Reynaud, the cult of the defensive prevailed in a tired nation, and his warnings were disregarded even after *World War II began.

After fighting with some success as the commander of an armored division, he served briefly in Reynaud's last cabinet of the Third Republic in June 1940, and decided not to accept defeat. When Marshal Pétain replaced Reynaud and called for an armistice, de Gaulle flew to London and, on 18 June 1940, at the BBC, called on the French to continue to fight and to join him. Few did, but he obtained Winston *Churchill's help, and despite many setbacks, difficult relations with the British, and Franklin D. *Roosevelt's hostility, he set up what was in effect a French government in exile and succeeded in obtaining the support of the parties and movements of the Resistance in occupied France. He organized, from London and Algiers, the restoration of the republican state in France, and was greeted with enthusiasm as liberator by the French in the summer of 1944.

As head of the provisional government of the republic, he soon ran into conflicts with the old and new political parties over a variety of issues, and particularly over their preference for a parliamentary system they would dominate. He resigned in January 1946, hoping to be called back soon. He had to wait for twelve-and-a-half years, during which the Fourth Republic staggered from crisis to crisis. He set up the Rassemblement du Peuple Français (RPF) against it in 1947. Its program was intensely anticommunist, nationalist in foreign and colonial affairs, and sought "association" as a third way between *capitalism and *socialism in social affairs. The RPF had a very successful start but soon got bogged down and divided, and de Gaulle retired to his country home at Colombey-les-deux-Eglises, where he wrote his *War Memoirs.* The settlers' revolt in Algiers in May 1958, however, provided him with the opportunity to return to active politics; receiving a legally valid delegation of power from the dying Fourth Republic, he was able to create the constitutional system, centered on a strong presidency, he had advocated openly since 1946.

As president of the Fifth Republic from January 1959 on, he undertook the painful liquidation of the *Algerian War of Independence, leading to Algerian independence in 1962. He had to overcome two military rebellions in Algiers, and to proceed in stages, leaning on French support through referendums. After a failed *assassination attempt, he called again for a referendum on a constitutional amendment in October 1962 so as to ensure the popular election of the president, and won. He embarked on a domestic policy of economic *modernization and on a grandiose *foreign policy aimed at providing French military autonomy through the development of a nuclear strike force, at turning the European Economic Community into a "Europe of states," and at reducing the influence of the superpowers in the world. This led him to challenge the United States repeatedly (he converted French dollar reserves into gold and took France out of the military-political structure of the *North Atlantic Treaty Organization) and to initiate a policy of *détente toward the Soviet Union. His authority was seriously weakened by the students' revolt and workers' strike in *May 1968, but he prevailed at the end of the month, after having "disappeared" for a day. However, when he staked his power once more on the success of a referendum (on regional decentralization and a reform of the Senate), he lost and resigned on 27 April 1969. He again retired to Colombey and worked on his new memoirs; these were left unfinished when he died of a stroke on 9 November 1970.

De Gaulle was the most important French political leader since Napoleon. To many of his compatriots, this intransigent defender of French grandeur saved the honor of the nation during World War II and restored its institutions and status. Although his role as founder and leader of the Fifth Republic was more controversial, his ambitious if often unsuccessful diplomatic activism, his extraordinary dramatic sense—demonstrated in his press conferences, TV speeches, journeys at home and abroad, and many public ceremonies—his mastery of the French language, and his success in establishing a regime that was strong without being dictatorial—a novelty in French history—earned him the admiration even of many of his opponents. His vision of a Europe "from the Atlantic to the Urals," with a reunited Germany, seemed utopian in the 1960s but turned out to have been prophetic in 1989. His main legacy is a constitutional system that has proved to be far more flexible than many observers had believed and that has erased the image of a weak executive, parliamentary division, and party impotence which the two previous republics had created.

De Gaulle disdained dogmas and believed in the exploitation of circumstances. He knew how to adapt: his colonial policies were prudent during World War II, far more rigid in 1945, and reactionary in the days of the RPF, but he became a worldwide champion of national self-determination in the Fifth Republic, just as he became the champion of reconciliation with the Federal Republic of Germany even though he had tried to impose a repressive policy after the defeat of *Hitler in 1945. He knew the necessity and merits of *international cooperation, but the two fixed stars in his constellation were his will to preserve French independence and grandeur (thus excluding any possibility of a supranational Europe) and his insistence on strong executive leadership appealing to national unity and the common good above factions and interests. In this respect, he appears to have (finally) synthesized the different and conflicting traditions of the Old Regime, plebiscitarian leadership, Jacobin republicanism, and *parliamentary democracy. He reminded the French of the greatness of their past, appealed both to the classical and to the romantic "families of thought," and owed much of his prestige to his literary gifts and intellectual incisiveness—another traditional source of political authority in France. But in his policies he also prepared the French for the future, and while realizing that France was no longer a superpower, refused to accept mediocrity and passivity. Twenty years after his death, his greatness is recognized by almost all the French, even if it is perhaps more a source of nostalgia and less an inspiration than he had hoped.

(See also EUROPEAN COMMUNITY; GAULLISM; GERMAN REUNIFICATION.)

Stanley Hoffmann and Inge Hoffmann, de Gaulle artiste de la politique (Paris, 1973); English version in Stanley Hoffmann, Decline or Renewal? France since the 30s, New York, 1974). De Gaulle et le service de l'Etat (Paris, 1977). Bernard Ledwidge, de Gaulle (London, 1982). Jean Lacouture, de Gaulle, 3 vols. (Paris, 1984–1986; English abridged version of vol. 1, London, 1990). Pierre-Louis Blanc, de Gaulle au soir de sa vie (Paris, 1990).

STANLEY HOFFMANN

GAULLISM. In contemporary French history, the term Gaullism has had three distinct meanings. From 1940 to 1945, during *World War II, the term designated the attitude of those who, rejecting the armistice signed with Germany by Marshal Pétain in June 1940, rejoined General Charles de *Gaulle in order to put *France back in the war on the side of the Allies. Between 1946 and 1958, Gaullism was a form of opposition to the Fourth Republic, whose unstable parliamentary regime was challenged in favor of institutions whose keystone would be a president of the republic with preeminent constitutional powers. Finally, in the third period, Gaullism was nothing other than the support given to the general's own politics after he returned to power in 1958 and served as president of the newly formed Fifth Republic from 1959 until his resignation in 1969. Since then the term has been used in reference to those who declared themselves his heirs. By reference to these three periods, one may attempt to define Gaullism.

In examining the evidence, one must conclude that Gaullism is neither a doctrine nor a political *ideology. No text defines its content; it tends neither to the *Left nor *Right. Considering its historical progression, it is a pragmatic exercise of power that is neither free from contradictions nor of concessions to momentary necessity, even if the imperious word of the general gives to the practice of Gaullism the allure of a program that seems profound and fully realized.

A Strong State. Flexibility aside, Gaullism relies on a fundamental principle on which everything else follows: the "certain idea of France," which opens de Gaulle's War Memoirs. France appeared to him to be an indomitable entity, a "person" with whom a mystical dialogue was maintained throughout history. The goal of Gaullism, therefore, is to give precedence to its interests, to ensure that the voice is heard, to make it respected, and to assure its survival.

To achieve this aim, according to de Gaulle, it is first necessary that France become strong from within; parties are attacked as representing divisive interests and the French people are urged to regroup, to overcome their partisan quarrels within a larger unity. The historical heritage of the country is accepted in its entirety, the monarchy of the Old Regime that built France no less than the revolution that led it to dominate Europe. To remain worthy of its past, the nation must endow itself with a powerful *state. By affirming in 1946 the necessity of resting the institutions of the state on a strong executive, de Gaulle flew in the face of the "republican tradition," according to which power must reside chiefly in the elected assembly made up of representatives of the sovereign nation. In addition, his desires to establish authority by direct universal vote; to speak to the country over the heads of the parliamentarians via radio broadcasts, press conferences, and trips to the provinces; and to elicit direct voter input via referendums were perceived by republicans as proof of a tendency toward dictatorial power. It took his resignation following the negative referendum of April 1969 to show that his lofty respect for *democracy was more than a mere rhetorical ploy.

Gaullists assume that a strong France must be based on a strong economy and a stable society; they believe that France can play a role in the world only if it possesses economic and financial means. From the Gaullists perspective, it is the imperative of the state, as guardian of the national interest, to give impetus to economic growth and to guide it. Liberal opinion is accepted if it promises more efficiency than planning. As for social justice, so long as its natural distrust of big business can be allayed, it is less a matter of doctrine than a means of upholding stability. To put an end to *class struggle, Gaullists hope to make use of participation, a nineteenth-century concept of which the general spoke frequently, but which he allowed his associates to ignore.

Vision of the World. If the aim of Gaullism is a strong France, this is above all in order to give it the power to strongly influence the world's future. According to de Gaulle, history consists of the rivalry between nations struggling to realize their own ambitions. To enable France to fulfill its international role, the first imperative was to overcome the factors that restrict its latitude internationally—for example, by freeing it, through *decolonization, "of constraints, henceforth without counterpart, imposed on it by the empire." It was no less important that it assure itself of ways to guarantee its national independence without resorting to allies whose interests might not coincide with those of France. This imperative required an independent nuclear capability whose realization was relentlessly pursued despite obstacles and criticism.

In short, from a Gaullist perspective, France could not hope to play a world role if it remained a slave of its U.S. ally. Refusing a bipolar world bequeathed, in their view, by the *Yalta Conference, Gaullists sought *alliances founded on partnership and equality, refusing to acknowledge any system of protection by the *superpowers. For France, placed in the U.S. orbit, this conception would lead to its distancing itself from the military policies of the *North Atlantic Treaty Organization and to its rejection of the technical and economic domination of overseas interests exemplified by the control exerted by U.S. investors and the controversial role of the U.S. dollar in the international monetary system. Nevertheless, regaining national independence did not enable France, a middle-ranked power, to determine the destiny of the planet. To counterbalance the two superpowers, Gaullism counted on Europe, conceived not as a supranational entity but rather as a confederation of sovereign states whose members engage in common policy, autonomous from the superpowers, and significantly politically influenced by France. But all attempts to create such confederation failed in the face of the desire of the other European powers to remain closely allied to the United States.

Heritage. Gaullism has had a profound influence on the history of the Fifth Republic after de Gaulle. President Georges Pompidou, from 1969 to 1974, referred explicitly to "continuity" with regard to the Gaullist way of doing things. Thereafter, those political parties that are heirs to Gaullism—the Union des Démocrates Pour la République (UDR) until 1976, and later the Rassemblement Pour la République (RPR)—wished to remain faithful to the inspiration of the general. Above all, throughout the 1980s, Gaullism became an integral part of the national heritage. Thus Gaullism has contributed to a consensus that, since 1984, has been establishing itself in a country whose *political culture was, until then, made up of divisions and relentless antagonisms.

The institutions founded by de Gaulle and consolidated by Pompidou are no longer the focus of political controversy. Presidential domination, so decried at the time of its inception, has been reinforced by all of the general's successors, including the socialist François *Mitterrand. The policy of national independence founded on an independent nuclear military capability has achieved consensus. As for Gaullist *foreign policy, since 1969 it has become the guiding force of French *international relations, even if presidents since de Gaulle have expressed it in more flexible terms.

It is no exaggeration to say that Gaullism has molded postwar France. At the same time, considering that the essence of Gaullist ideas are now accepted by everyone, those who wish to be the legitimate heirs of de Gaulle (e.g., Jacques Chirac of the RPR) now have an identity crisis. It is difficult for them to distinguish themselves from other political perspectives.

Gaullism for Export? Does Gaullism, a tempered *nationalism adapted to the late twentieth century, have any significance beyond the borders of France? It has often been poorly understood and pejoratively judged, as foreign observers and French adversaries of Gaullism have emphasized the appearances (monarchical attitudes, abrupt words, harsh statements) over the realities. It is undeniable, however, that Gaullism has identified a number of real problems that have aggravated international affairs for many years and that continue to do so: the dysfunction of the international monetary system, the problems of the *Third World, the dominance of the superpowers, the dangers of hegemonic powers, and the continuing strength of national sentiment. All in all, it appears unfair to liken Gaullists to national leaders such as Amintore Fanfani in Italy who are determined to advance the parochial interests of their countries in the international community, for none has exceeded de Gaulle himself in promoting the conditions designed to accomplish his objectives or in understanding the consequences of those objectives. Gaullism appears to be a peculiarly French phenomenon, without doubt the quintessential French political phenomenon of the twentieth century.

(See also EUROPEAN COMMUNITY.)

Jean Charlot, *Le gaullisme* (Paris, 1970). Jean Touchard, *Le gaullisme 1940–1969* (Paris, 1978). Jean Charlot, *Le gaullisme d'opposition 1946–1958* (Paris, 1983). Serge Berstein, *La France de l'expansion I: La République gaullienne 1958–1969,* Nouvelle histoire de la France contemporaine, No. 17 (Paris, 1989).

SERGE BERSTEIN

GAY AND LESBIAN POLITICS. Within every age, culture, nation, and people in the world, women have loved women and men have loved men. Social contexts and constructs may differ, as have interpretations and assumptions. Lifestyles have differed, and the question of identity has had varied responses. But (some) women emotionally and physically love women and (some) men emotionally and physically love men. They always have and they always will.

Gay and Lesbian History. Lesbian and gay politics are in an early stage of development. Much "her-" and "history" still needs to be uncovered. Experiences from Greek and Roman times, accounts in Buddhist writings, the antilesbian elements of witch hunting in Europe, the same-sex lifestyles in some Indian and African tribes—all await historical recovery. Organized efforts to understand homosexuality and encourage tolerance started around the turn of the century. The Wissenschaftlich Humanitäre Komitee was founded in 1897 in Germany, and a Dutch branch began its work in 1911. The committee was founded to prove scientifically that homosexuality is a biological phenomenon. Members argued that homosexuals are born as they are—and therefore love between people of the same sex (then called uranism or homosexuality) should be seen as one of the God-given variations of nature. C. H. Ulrichs and M. Hirschfeld of Germany and J. A. Schorer of the Netherlands were among the scientific leaders. They organized support among liberal thinkers, artists, and industrialists, and fought against laws criminalizing homosexual behavior (successfully in Norway). An active and fairly open European lesbian and gay subculture thrived at the time, especially in Paris and Berlin. Discussions about decriminalizing homosexual relations were held in many European countries—and Poland, for example, passed a new penal code in 1932 which fixed the age of consent at 15 years for both heterosexual and homosexual acts.

With the advance of *fascism in Europe, the situation for lesbians and gays was transformed dramatically. In the 1930s the Nazis in Germany closed lesbian and gay bars and sent up to 7,000 gays a year to jails and later to camps. During World War II many lesbians and gays died in concentration camps: estimates vary from 20,000 to 80,000. Gay men, mainly, were forced to wear a pink triangle, and lesbians may well have been categorized with prostitutes and forced to wear a black triangle. In the 1980s Dutch lesbians and gays collected funds and political support for the Pink Triangle Monument in Amsterdam in order to draw attention to this forgotten group of Nazi victims.

The postwar period brought the return of some progressive initiatives. In 1946 the COC (its name stands for Cultural Relaxation Center) was founded in the Netherlands. It is now the oldest lesbian and gay organization in the world. From 1951 to 1959 the International Committee for Sexual Equality (ISCE), a continuation of prewar initiatives, worked to encourage advances with respect to legal protections.

The more recent history of the movement is framed by the famous Stonewall riots, which took place in New York City on 28 June 1968. In a legal context where anal and oral sex between persons of the same sex was considered a crime in all U.S. states until 1961 (and still in nearly thirty states in the 1990s), the thriving gay subculture was an easy target for police forces out to enjoy some action. During the Stonewall riots gay men fought back against physical assaults. This became the start and symbol of a wave of political activities among lesbians and gays. Every year in many countries all over the world international Gay Pride demonstrations celebrate the Stonewall riots and the subsequent growth in political stature of lesbian and gay organizations.

Gay and Lesbian Political Ideology. The political *ideology of the many lesbian and gay groups that began to emerge in the West in the 1970s was relatively straightforward. Lesbians and gay should be able to live openly and freely and should not be discriminated against—in law, at their jobs, or in any social context. Homosexual women and men should be proud of their sexuality, and should not try to hide it or change it. The concept of Gay Pride was popularized. Discussions about the origins of homosexual orientation (whether there is a biological or a social basis) were considered irrelevant. Modern (Western) homosexuals should be proud of their sexuality and lifestyle, demand equal *rights, and show the world who and what they are. The process of informing others and achieving a positive self-image was advanced by public affirmation of sexual and affectional preferences and identity (a process called "coming out").

It was lesbian *feminism that took the political ideology beyond the equal rights issue. Lesbians not only want to claim their own rights and political space—they challenge the basic assumptions, the social construct, of male and female gender roles. They understand that lesbianism is threatening because it challenges male domination, the traditional division of labor between the sexes. Lesbian separatists choose to spend their energy within a women's context only, and have created a wide range of choices for women who want to develop privately or professionally through interaction with other women.

By the 1980s, earlier utopian thinking about a lesbian world with its own universal culture had made room for a more realistic view of the diversity of social and cultural backgrounds, of the range of lesbian political opinions, and of the variety of personal choices and lifestyles. By the start of the 1990s, finding ways to recognize and come to terms with such differences and to communicate across the barriers of class, race, culture, age, and physical, mental, and economic conditions has become a major challenge for the lesbian community. In addition, political activities against discrimination (such as sexual violence against lesbians and gays) and for equal rights (for example, to have and keep children) continue.

International Lesbian and Gay Politics. The International Lesbian and Gay Association (ILGA, or IGA as it was called in its first years) was founded in 1978. It aims to exchange information and to coordinate political action. At approximately thirty international and regional conferences the ILGA has inaugurated more than 100 political actions/projects and has helped to produce many reforms:

- The *World Health Organization deleted homosexuality from the tenth edition of its *International Classification of Diseases.*
- The *Council of Europe passed a fourteen-point proposal to combat discrimination against homosexuality.
- New Zealand reformed its laws (1986) so that homosexuality is no longer a criminal offense.
- *Amnesty International decided in 1990, after a decade of discussions and much lobbying by ILGA members, to include in their target groups men and women who are imprisoned because of their sexual preferences.

In addition, the ILGA aided in the publication of two international *Pink Books,* which provide an inventory of the legal and social position of lesbians and gays throughout the world. The work of the ILGA has been recognized by the UN, which is expected to grant the ILGA observer status. This will permit the organization to participate in the ongoing debate about *human rights.

Lesbians have organized internationally within the ILGA, as well as in the ILIS (International Lesbian Information Service). A basic ideology is that enforced heterosexuality is a problem for every woman who has not had the opportunity to choose how she wants to live. Thus the ILIS demands that girls and women have the right to control their own bodies, to receive information/education about lesbian lifestyles, and to organize and be protected from criminalization and discrimination. The increased information about violence (mental, physical, and sexual) and the oppression of women helps dramatize the struggle lesbians face when they try to live autonomously or to organize. In addition to its European-based conferences, ILIS (and thus lesbian) visibility was increased during the UN Women's Conference and the NGO forum in Nairobi (1985). The ILIS made contact with a number of Latin American lesbian groups (Brazil, Chile, Peru) who supported the first lesbian conference in Mexico (1987). Since then lesbian organizing in the region has increased considerably.

A more recent development was the first Asian lesbian conference in Bangkok (1990). Lesbian visibility within the Asian context has proved to be difficult and dangerous, but networking has begun. In Africa, where in some cultures marriages between women are recognized and where emotional and physical contact between girls is fairly common without its being defined as homosexuality, the first lesbian groups also are emerging, although they usually operate underground.

Recent Developments. The *AIDS crisis has had a profound effect on the gay community. The gay community, especially in the United States, has lost many of its leaders, but it has rallied. Organized support, such as buddy systems, has been impressive and is having a more general effect on health services. In countries where (homo)sexuality was a taboo topic (such as Peru), AIDS prevention projects are having a much wider social effect. Sexual choice has become part of the public and political debate and, for instance, the Peruvian organization Movimiento Homosexual de Lima enjoys an unusual popularity at all levels of society.

As more information about violence against women is collected, the right of women to self-determination is becoming a recognized human rights issue. In this area, and in efforts to increase awareness of the need for international cooperation to understand cultural difference as a positive force, individual lesbians and the lesbian movement are strongly and visibly represented. The enormous changes in Eastern and *Central Europe and the unification of much of Western Europe in the *European Community provide important opportunities for the strengthening of the lesbian/gay movement.

The movement can grow—but only if its political clout increases. In order to increase political recognition of the rights of lesbian women and gay men and bring their ideas to the forefront of public awareness, the lesbian and gay political movement is slowly professionalizing. In the last few decades most of the organizational work was voluntary—and in many lesbian and gay organizations this is still the case. But as the lesbian and gay agenda receives more recognition as an important *civil rights movement, funding is also being made available, and the political impact of the lesbian and gay lobby should become even more noticeable.

(See also GENDER AND POLITICS; NEW SOCIAL MOVEMENTS.)

SYLVIA BORREN

GENDER AND POLITICS

During the 1990–1991 Persian Gulf crisis many people learned for the first time that Kuwaiti women had organized a suffrage movement. This news joggled conventional minds. For Muslim women, especially those in the conservative states surrounding the oil-rich gulf, typically were imagined to be secluded, banned from the public arena. Yet here were Kuwaiti women calling their own rallies, building alliances with men in the prodemocracy movement, organizing resistance against the Iraqi invaders, and holding exile strategy sessions in London. This new information about Kuwaiti women's suffrage campaign forced many outside observers not only to reimagine Muslim women but to rethink Kuwaiti politics and perhaps the entire political landscape of the Persian Gulf crisis.

Movements to demand the vote have been the most visible site of women in politics. For many, it is the only time they take women's impact on politics seriously. It is also one of the few moments when men's presumptions about their own place in politics—as men—are thrown into sharp relief. The spotlight, however, usually is turned on women suffragists only in the final phase of their campaign, when the men in power are being forced to revise their ideas about *political participation, when glasses are raised (by some) upon women's victory. Then the stage of gendered political drama goes dark, to be lit up again only briefly when the "first woman" is elected to parliament or chosen to head a national party or is tapped for prime minister. This sort of superficial coverage ignores the ripple effects that women's struggle to vote sends through the whole political system. It also overlooks the ways that women's suffrage campaigning challenges men's lives, in the *state and in the home. Kuwaiti women, like their suffragist predecessors in Finland, the Philippines, the United States, and Mexico, know that one of the reasons so many men—and not a few women—object to women being allowed to vote is that granting such a right will alter ideas not only about what it means to be "womanly" in Kuwaiti society but what it means to be "manly" as well. More is, and always has been, at stake than merely the ballot box.

For "gender and politics" is never just about women; it is about the ways in which relations between women and men shape public *power. Maybe it is more useful to think of the topic as "the gendering of politics," that is, the processes by which public life is infused with presumptions about what it means to be a woman and what it means to be a man. Every time the definition of "femininity" is changed—for instance, by women insisting that "woman voter" is not an oxymoron—the meaning of "masculinity" must be reconsidered as well. Once women can vote on the same terms as men, to be manly no longer can be deemed coterminous with exercising public responsibility. Individual men indeed may still be considered responsible public actors, but that mantle of political seriousness will have to be earned; it no longer simply comes with the hormonal territory. Therefore, when women win the vote, powerful character attributes such as "mature," "adult," "rational," and "serious" will lose at least some of their masculinized undertones. Not all, however: if women are allowed into the voting booth but are kept out of the legislature, cabinet, treasury, and the war room, masculinity's special relationship to those valued human qualities may survive. And, as a consequence, the *state itself will continue to be intimately related to masculinity, giving men a privileged relationship to any government that they will be reluctant to surrender.

One has only to look at the collective portrait of the thirty-four heads of government gathered in Paris in November 1990 to sign the historic Charter of Paris for the New Europe. The gathering marked the end of the *Cold War. Newspaper headlines heralded the meeting as the "end of an era." But a reader with any gender consciousness could not help but be struck by not what was new but what was persistent. The ceremonial photograph was full of men in dark suits. One had to squint to find the two women among the thirty-four heads of government: Gro Brundtland, prime minister of Norway, and Margaret *Thatcher, prime minister of Britain. If the historic photograph had been taken just two days later, Gro Brundtland would have been the lone woman head of government; Margaret Thatcher had by then resigned, and all three contestants for her job were men. Decades after most of these societies had accorded women full *citizenship, the most serious and powerful posts in public life remained masculinized, that is, defined in such a way that women were not considered fit to hold them. The post–Cold War era might be dawning, but it was with an old gender formula still in place.

Gender refers to the meanings we assign to being a woman or being a man. This act of assigning politicizes gender. Since the eighteenth century feminists, scholars, and activists together have taken up the task of revealing just how much of political life has been built on presumptions about the meanings of femininity and masculinity. While often resistant, many people have found it easier to acknowledge that political institutions and ideas have been constructed out of ideas about race and about social class than to admit that ideas about gender have been just as crucial. One reason for this analytical stubbornness may be that ideas about what it means to be manly or feminine strike very close to individuals' own sense of identity, and few people want to admit that their personal identities might rest on manipulations of political power. Furthermore, to accept this *feminist theory about how political life works would mean acknowledging that seemingly personal relations between women and men—including the most intimate emotional and sexual relations—do not occur in a protected private sphere; rather, according to feminist analysis, these relationships among friends, lovers, and relatives are seen to be building blocks of the wider public sphere and thus fraught with power and *ideology. If one accepts this premise, then one's political consciousness remains active when figuring out which parent should take time off work to care for a sick child or whose sense of pleasure should structure heterosexual lovemaking. Given the cost of this intellectual leap, perhaps it is not surprising that most political commentators prefer to talk of *class and *race while ignoring gender.

Feminists are not advocating the linkage between public power and private relationships. They simply are pulling back the curtain on a reality they believe has been denied because such a denial serves to privilege masculinity in political affairs. In doing so, in showing how politics has been gendered, they are revealing two realities of political life: first, anyone or any group seeking to control public affairs will try to control private spheres of human activity as well; second, consequently, most conventional explanations of how governments work have grossly understated the amount of power operating in politics. These two assertions are the radical elaborations of the now-familiar feminist analytical assertion, "The personal is political," a concept whose meaning has changed with the changing dynamics of *patriarchy.

The term *patriarchy* harks back to relationships controlled by a certain kind of fatherhood, a male parenting whose authority over children and adult women in the household derives from presumptions that adult men are more rational, more capable of looking after the well-being of the other members, and thus better suited to speak on their behalf to the outside world. In eighteenth-century France and nineteenth-century China, this model of fathering was considered a microcosm of the entire political system: as the patriarchal father's authority was over his wife and children, so the monarch's authority was over his subjects. Thus these monarchies have a vital stake in preserving patriarchal family relations; they were thought to be essential to the maintenance of the larger political order. Although today that analogy has been subverted in most countries by the spread of republican notions of popular sovereignty, patriarchal principles nonetheless have proved adaptable and persistent.

Any country's political system is patriarchal insofar as it depends on the existence of three conditions. First, a patriarchy is a social or political order in which people who are feminine—women—are thought to be naturally, automatically, inevitably best suited to certain tasks (listening, caring, weeding, taking shorthand, hauling water, assembling microchips), while people who are masculine—men— are thought naturally inclined to perform other tasks (talking, exploring, planning, plowing, welding, fighting). In other words, a patriarchal society rests on a sexual division of labor. In their *Divided Britain* (London, 1989), for example, Ray Hudson and Allan Williams provide evidence to support their assertion that Britain remains patriarchal. They note that in 1984, within British Rail, one of the largest government-owned enterprises, men constituted 589 of the 591 senior managers and 20,201 of the 20,201 track repair workers. The British civil service's reliance on the sexual division of labor was no less remarkable: in 1987, women made up seventy-six percent of the low-level administrative assistants but a mere four percent of the personnel in the elite grades that included the influential permanent secretaries and directors.

Second, a patriarchy is a social or political order in which the things that masculine people do are deemed of greater social value—more "productive," more "serious," more "skilled"—than the things

that feminine people do. Thus the woman who weeds is less likely to be talked to by the UN agricultural development officer than the man who plows; the woman who cares for children is less likely to be called as a witness before a legislative committee than the man who does child care planning. Third, and this makes clear the centrality of power to patriarchy, in a society that has remained patriarchal the people who perform the allegedly more valued, masculine tasks are deemed to have the responsibility of looking after, protecting, and controlling the people who perform the less valued, feminine tasks.

That is, a patriarchy is more than a sexual division of labor arranged hierarchically. A patriarchy is a system of control of one sector of society over another. As fraught with questions about the relationships between gender, race, and class and about the character of the state as any women's campaign may be, women's demand for the right to participate in the political arena in a meaningful fashion chips away at all three legs of the patriarchal structure: the sexual division of labor; the accompanying political and social hierarchy; and the system of control patriarchy fosters.

In doing so, women's campaigns—campaigns for the vote, education, and equal pay, against dowry burnings, for land titles, for divorce and abortion rights, against domestic violence, for criminalization of marital rape—reveal how and why so many political regimes and the state structures supporting them have become so invested in patriarchy. To make sense of the often entrenched, even violent resistance to women's rights, one has to understand that patriarchy has its benefits not only for individual men, but for entire governmental systems. Many commentators have been slow to admit this—that the state has a profound stake in women weeding and men plowing, that the state is invested in men's pleasure being able to define heterosexual sex, that the state benefits from the feminization of the home and the masculinization of reason. It has been easier for these conventional commentators to think of political systems resting solely on skewed—ungendered—distributions of capital and weaponry.

But there is abundant evidence now that regimes and the states beneath them in fact have taken deliberate steps to sustain a sort of sexual division of labor that provides them with cheap, often completely unpaid, women's productive labor. This is most blatantly visible in the *Third World export processing zones (EPZs) established with international agency assistance and local government public services and tax breaks. On average these light industry factory zones depend on a labor force that is seventy percent female precisely because both the factory owners and the government believe that women will accept lower wages, thus allowing products from the EPZs to compete more effectively on the international market. If ideas about femininity were turned upside down, if women's work were considered as important to those women as men's work were to men, both the local regimes and their international agency backers would have to surrender one of their chief means of sustaining domestic political stability and international economic order.

Likewise, there is convincing documentation revealing that governments make policy choices with an eye to sustaining men's control of women's reproductive capacities, insofar as this ensures that women will produce the numbers of children governments need to generate tax revenue, perform productive work, and serve in its militaries. Finally, researchers are providing impressive proof that governments deploy gendered resources in order to cultivate and then maintain the very concept of the "nation" on which modern states depend for their *legitimacy. That is, in most countries, industrialized and industrializing, national identity has been built out of notions of women's subordination to men: women's "traditional" seclusion in the home or "traditional" identities as self-sacrificing mothers have been turned by governmental officials and their nationalist supporters into essential elements that glue the "nation" together. If women rejected these roles and values, nationalists in countries as otherwise dissimilar as Iraq, Poland, Israel, and Singapore appear to believe, this fragile creature, the nation, would fall apart and the state in turn quickly would lose its foundation of legitimation: without "motherhood," the nation-state would deteriorate into a mere state.

The sites to watch in order to determine whether any particular regime in the world is taking active steps to sustain its patriarchal foundations are not always the most visible or newsworthy. In fact, if a country's president, its cabinet, or even its national legislature has to take decisive action to shore up the three legs of patriarchy, it is probably a signal that patriarchal relationships between women and men are in jeopardy. Given the unnaturalness of so many aspects of a patriarchal order, it is indeed unstable and filled with daily struggle, though that struggle—of women in abusive marriages, of women workers coping with the double burden of job and home responsibilities, of women politicians trying to overcome sexism in party nomination processes— is often imagined as outside the arena of "real politics" and thus not taken into account by those assessing the dynamics of power in any political system. But the final stages of any women's campaign, while dramatic and thus impossible for even the most gender-unconscious commentator to overlook, are not necessarily the most representative of patriarchy at work. Rather, the sites to monitor are more mundane: lower courts, housing authorities, race relations boards, public hospitals, tourism and immigration offices, secondary schools, land reform tribunals, police and welfare departments, military field commands.

In the late twentieth century, one must add to this list of sites those institutions that operate outside state boundaries: the *World Bank, the Commission of the *European Community, the *International Monetary Fund, the UN Development Program, the UN High Commission for Refugees, the *North Atlantic Treaty Organization, the *Organization of African States, the South Pacific Forum, and the *Conference on Security and Cooperation in Europe. In their everyday operations these supranational authorities also are making decisions which either weaken or prop up patriarchal pillars of gendered politics. Their decisions are nearly always gendered—sometimes in their motivations, sometimes in their consequences, sometimes in both.

For example, the UN High Commission for Refugees (UNHCR) must constantly decide in the administration of any of its camps—in Afghanistan, Thailand, Somalia, or Turkey—whether to allow people within the camp to administer their own social relations or to interfere directly in ordering those relations. Although women and their dependent children constitute at least seventy percent of all refugees, it is usually male refugees within the camps who presume to have authority, often using it to prevent women from gaining access to UN literacy classes or other resources that would enhance women's economic and political status. How the UNHCR decides on this seemingly "administrative" question will have serious and long-range implications for women displaced by war or famine.

On the other hand, patriarchal relationships between men and women do benefit specific men, not simply governments. It is for this reason that many political institutions and movements claiming to be in opposition to the current regime may in practice support that regime's efforts to sustain sexual divisions of labor and gendered inequalities. Business associations harshly critical of a socialist regime's policies on investment or welfare may nonetheless share with that regime the assumption that men, not women, are the natural participants in business-government bargaining sessions. Leftist parties may seize every chance to point out the failings of the current conservative government and yet be no less defensive in the face of women's charges that all the country's political parties, left, center, and right, operate as if they were men's clubs. Thus it is because patriarchal beliefs about masculinity and femininity benefit both individual men and a masculinized state that the specifically patriarchal character of any given government is so hard to discern— or transform.

Thus when women in any country do manage to gain some genuine influence in any sector of the opposition, it becomes significant: it serves to highlight the specifically patriarchal foundations of the government in power and perhaps even the state as a whole. In the Federal Republic of Germany in the 1980s, for example, the success of women in constructing a green party that not only adopted an internal leadership process that reduced the privileging of masculinity but also accorded women's issues and feminist analysis at least more seriousness than any other German political party had the effect of making clear just how masculinist both the process and the platform of the ruling Christian Democratic Party and the opposition Social Democrats are. Similarly, the ascendance to party leadership of Takako Doi in the principal Japanese opposition party, the Japanese Socialist Party, in the late 1980s, along with her deliberate appeal to women voters in the 1990 elections, awarded press significance for the first time to the long-entrenched Liberal Democratic Party's all-male senior leadership's belief that it could continue to rule without nominating a single woman candidate for a seat that year in the lower house of the Diet.

In the 1980s, observers in a number of countries began to note an occasional patterned difference between women's voting and men's voting; they called it the "*gender gap." The belief that men and women are always likely to cast their ballots differently, regardless of their variations in regional interests, their generational experiences, or their economic circumstance, in fact is not all that new. Mexican and French male political leaders who claimed to espouse revolutionary republican principles nonetheless blocked female suffrage for decades because they were convinced that women in these two Catholic countries would be more prone than men to vote for conservative candidates backed by their local priests. Still, the gender gap is different. It is not presumed to dictate differences between men and women political participants on all issues as a result of biologically ingrained feminine conservatism. Rather, where it has appeared in recent years, this electoral gender gap has been less tied to specific candidates than to their parties' platforms and to the particular issues that have gained saliency in the electoral campaign.

Thus, for example, in the United States during the 1980s the national Republican Party began to rely on its popularity among white men. Men of color and women of all racial groups became less inclined than white men to vote for Republican presidential candidates. This gendered—and racial—voting pattern in turn began to shape partisan policy decisions. In 1990, two years into his administration, President George *Bush vetoed a congressionally passed civil rights bill that would have strengthened minority and women's rights in employment. The National Public Radio correspondent Nina Totenberg reported ("All Things Considered," 25 October 1990) that the president made this decision at least in part because his White House advisers, with one eye on the voting booth, sought to solidify President Bush's support among his most solid constituency, white male voters.

The emergence of *public opinion polling has meant that voting preferences are being constantly monitored, even when an election is several years in the future. Polling is fueling interest in possible "gender gaps." But it is because women now have the vote in all but a handful of countries that political polling data on their policy opinions carry such weight among the still largely male officialdom. In those countries where popular elections carry the most influence in distributing public power, polling has been most institutionalized as an instrument for decision-making, and in those same countries the gender gap has become most discussed: e.g., the United States, Canada, Britain, Japan, Australia. As polling companies such as Gallup, MORI, and Lou Harris are hired more widely by politicians in the Third World and in the newly democratized countries of Eastern and *Central Europe, there too the gender gap, where it appears, is likely to be assigned more political saliency.

The concept of the gender gap, however, is not just a tool used by policymakers to determine the costs and rewards of one policy option over another. Polls that show a marked difference between women's and men's voting or policy preferences, if widely publicized, can strengthen or weaken the women's movement in that country. If women can see that, despite their racial and class differences, as women, they collectively hold views on taxes, abortion, child care, or war that are quite distinct from those held by most men in their society, there is a greater likelihood that they can imagine organizing politically as women. Thus Molly Yard, head of the largest U.S. feminist organization, the National Organization for Women, was heartened when polls were published in November 1990 showing that women's attitudes toward military operations in the Persian Gulf were strikingly different from those of men. This had not always been true. During the *Vietnam War, when the women's movement was still in its infancy, polls showed almost no difference in U.S. women's and men's attitudes toward the war. But twenty years later one of the reasons that George Bush's presidential advisors were so eager to bolster his support among white males in October of 1990 was that the polls showed his popularity slipping because of the drawn-out nature of the Persian Gulf crisis. It was especially women voters who were telling pollsters that they disapproved of the president's policies toward Iraq. In one poll, when men and women were asked whether they would support a U.S. invasion of Iraq, the gap yawned to twenty-five percent: seventy-three percent of women were opposed, compared with just forty-eight percent of men.

Women's differences with men over questions of military policy have provoked analytical and strategic discussion in countries as socially and politically dissimilar as Papua New Guinea and Sri Lanka, where women have organized to press their governments' male officials to take more energetic steps to end civil wars and their accompanying military violence, and Chile and Britain, where women developed feminist strategies to confront what they believed were patriarchal causes of *militarism. Are women by nature less violent than men? Is this international prominence of women in *peace movements to be explained hormonally? Women themselves disagree. However, as the understanding of the subtle processes of constructing masculinity and femininity becomes more sophisticated there is waning confidence in essentialist explanations. Scholars instead are pointing to childhood socialization differences in many cultures that encourage little girls to resort to talking, listening, and compromise as ways to resolve conflict while those same cultures encourage little boys to see outcomes in terms of clear-cut victories and losses. Other scholars have investigated gendered socialization differences among adults. For instance, male national *security intellectuals have been shown to have adopted forms of language that allow them to distance their feelings from the destructive formulas they are designing; similarly, military officials have not presumed that 20-year-old men are natural soldiers and thus deliberately have employed rewards and punishments to instill those attitudes in new recruits. At the same time, investigations into the militaristic attitudes of some women, including prominent political figures such as Margaret Thatcher and Indira *Gandhi, make it clear that antiwar attitudes are the product of socialization and experience, not genetic makeup. That is, they are gendered. If women do express notably less enthusiasm for their government's military solutions to conflicts, the reasons lie in the ways they have been taught to be feminine in their cultures.

This of course makes it difficult to critique societies' patriarchal *ideologies: should the antimilitaristic attitudes be thrown out with the patriarchy that fosters such gendered differences in attitude and perspective? Many have rejected this as a false choice. It is necessary instead to deconstruct ideas that have been packaged monolithically as "femininity." Those ideas that are socially valuable, feminist antimilitarists argue, should be perpetuated; they should be taught to men as well as to women; no woman who espouses such an attitude should be marginalized in public affairs for being "naive"; no man who promotes such an idea should have his manliness questioned; no man who rejects such antimilitaristic ideas should be considered the model of masculinity and thus treated as if he were the standard-bearer of public responsibility.

Demilitarization and democratization have provided settings in Eastern and Central Europe, Latin America, Africa, and Asia for monitoring the gendered implications of political change. If militarization does privilege not just men but conventional masculine values in many cultures, then steps taken toward demilitarization should provide a more se-

rious hearing to people, usually women, espousing nonmasculinist ideas. If patriarchy thrives on hierarchical pyramids of authority, then democratization should open doors to women's wider political participation. The limited evidence suggests that the relationships may be more complicated.

In Chile, the overthrow of the military junta led by General Augusto *Pinochet was in no small measure due to women's organizing all-women's campaigns during the 1980s. As Chilean anthropologist Ximena Bunster has described in her articles on women and torture and the politics of Chilean military wives (in June Nash and Helen Safa, eds., *Women and Change in Latin America*, Hadley, Mass., 1986; in Eva Isaksson, ed., *Women and the Military*, New York, 1988), the Pinochet regime's hold over public life was profoundly gendered, and thus the loosening of that grip would have to be gendered. However, despite women's self-conscious reconstructing of femininity as part of their antijunta and *human rights campaigns, it proved difficult to turn the eventual demilitarization movement into a genuinely antipatriarchal movement, for the civilian men leading the prodemocracy political parties, while opposing the military, still had a stake in defining electoral politics in masculinist terms. As a result, although women gained new bureaucratic footholds in the new government and became more mobilized within both the leading center and left parties, the post-Pinochet government produced by the popular elections in 1989 remains overwhelmingly male: President Patricio Aylwin appointed an all-male cabinet; only three of the newly elected senators and six of the lower house representatives were women.

Likewise the historic democratization of Eastern and Central Europe in the early 1990s, which brought with it the end of the Cold War militarization of Europe, had very mixed results for women's relationships both to men and to the state. Communist regimes in Eastern and Central Europe, like their Soviet model, had made the emancipation of women a pillar of their political legitimation. In practice, although women did gain social security and reproductive rights, this emancipation did not mean the demasculinization of Soviet or Eastern and Central European politics. Rather, it meant that women gained access to the waged labor force while still being treated as the primary caretakers of men and children in the home. The "double burden" was as crucial as state ownership of industry to the post-1945 political systems of Czechoslovakia, Poland, the German Democratic Republic, and Hungary. Yet the collapse of these Communist systems in the face of popular pressure during 1989 did not translate into the demasculinization of politics. If Eastern and Central Europe's newly elected officials encourage women to see in the market economies a chance to lighten their double burdens without confronting men by exchanging full-time jobs for part-time jobs, then the transition to a free market form of democratic polity may encourage women's further withdrawal from the political arena. If, in addition, as is especially evident in Poland, the rejection of Soviet-backed Communist regimes is fueled by a *nationalism rooted in presumptions about women's patriotic motherhood, then democratization is likely to be accompanied by state policies aimed at reducing women's reproductive rights.

Drusilla Menaker reported (*Boston Globe*, 2 December 1990) that a survey by the Inter-Parliamentary Council in Geneva showed that in every one of the legislatures in the former Soviet bloc women lost seats in the first post-Communist open elections. Women comprised twelve percent of the Polish parliament after the popular elections, compared with twenty percent when the Communist Party chose all the candidates; in Hungary women's representation dropped from twenty-one percent to seven percent; Bulgaria's postdemocratization parliament was only 3.5 percent women, a fall from the earlier twenty-one percent; Czechoslovakia's was down to six percent from 29.5 percent. The newly unified German parliament replicated the same masculinist pattern, celebrating its debut with less than ten percent women representatives. In the Soviet Union the more openly elected Congress of People's Deputies, the flagship of glasnost politics, in 1990 included just fifteen percent women. It is not that the legislatures under the formerly Communist systems had political power; they did not. But it appears that once the legislative arms of these now-democratized states have gained meaningful influence, women are marginalized by men.

These developments in Latin America and Eastern and Central Europe reflect broader patterns in gendered politics on the eve of the twenty-first century. First, states may undergo seemingly radical changes in their left-right associations and yet remain dependent on patriarchal concepts of masculine and feminine roles in those states. Second, genuine alterations in gendered political systems will not come until men's relationships to women in the allegedly "private" spheres of domestic life are deemed serious political objectives. Those movements that have the greatest chance of demasculinizing political life, consequently, are those in which women's diverse experiences of power are taken seriously as the basis of both political theorizing and strategizing; they are those in which at the same time all men's stake in maintaining the three legs of patriarchal society is openly acknowledged.

(See also FEMINISM; FEMINIZATION OF POVERTY; GAY AND LESBIAN POLITICS; NEW SOCIAL MOVEMENTS; REPRODUCTIVE POLITICS; WOMEN AND DEVELOPMENT.)

Kumari Jayawardena, *Feminism and Nationalism in the Third World* (London, 1986). Joni Seager and Ann Olson, *Women in the World: An International Atlas* (London and New York, 1986). R. W. Connell, *Gender and Power* (Stanford, Calif., 1987). Cynthia Enloe, *Bananas, Beaches and Bases: Making Feminist Sense of International Politics* (London, 1989, and Berkeley, Calif., 1990). Nira Yuval-Davis and Floya Anthias, eds., *Woman—Nation—State* (London and New York, 1989). Bell Hooks, *Yearning: Race, Gender and Cultural Politics* (Boston, 1990). The JUNIC/NGO Programme Group on Women and Development, *Women and the World Economic Crisis*, United Nations Non-Governmental Liaison Service (Geneva, 1990). Christine Sylvester, *Feminist Theory and International Relations in a Postmodern Era* (Cambridge, U.K., 1992).

CYNTHIA H. ENLOE

GENDER GAP. The gender gap refers to a growing divergence in attitudes and behavior between men and women, primarily related to candidate selection and approval and partisan preference. This process has been reinforced by the creation of new political resources deriving from women's increased *political participation, the differentiation of women's electoral priorities from those of men, and efforts by organized feminists to influence the allocation of resources in order to achieve particular political outcomes. In the United States, gender differences in political evaluations first appeared in the 1980 presidential election campaign, and have persisted ever since. In that year, it first became evident that while men supported Ronald *Reagan by a large majority, women split their vote more evenly between the Democratic and Republican candidates. Other gender-based differences, including voter turnout, partisan identification, and assessment of presidential effectiveness, have also been observed. With regard to partisan identification, the Democrats have a higher level of support among women. This preference has manifested itself in congressional and statewide elections, as well as the presidential contests. Another dimension of the gap involves support by women for female candidates if their nomination is accompanied by policy commitments that incorporate or emphasize women's concerns.

Perhaps even more important than the gender gap has been the so-called "marital gap." This phenomenon reflects distinctive voting patterns among married and single political participants. The marital gap is greatest between married men and single women. Another dimension of the gap that has been identified is that dividing working or "independent" women from housewives; differences among them on some issues are as great as differences between men and women.

Origins of the gender gap are to be found in greater liberalism among women. Differences between men and women are found on issues related to foreign policy (opposition to war and defense spending), specifically feminist concerns such as *Equal Rights Amendment, abortion rights, and *comparable worth, support for public spending for the poor and the environment, and also equitable allocation of social welfare programs. However, there is no consensus regarding the sources of gender-based political behavior. Some argue for a female perspective based on economic self-interest, contending that women's increased dependence on the state for welfare and employment accounts for gender-based political differences between men and women. Others support the view that women's roles as wives and mothers have given them a more humanitarian political perspective. For other analysts, the women's movement helped to reinforce and articulate the notion that women's interests are fundamentally different from those of men. This trend accelerated as more women identified with their gender and came to appreciate its political significance. Growing awareness of politics as important and the linkages created by group membership and identification brought about by the expansion of *feminism and the women's movement thus helped to create the gender gap. However, issues related to women's equality seem to be less salient than others in explaining the gender gap.

Outside of the United States, a cross-national perspective reveals some similar trends with regard to the gender gap and women's political behavior. Evidence from Canada, Sweden, Norway, France, and Britain shows a modest, if less marked and documented, trend related to gender-based attitudes and voting. Similarities have been documented in the voting patterns of European men and women, although gender-based policy differences provide evidence of a potential gap concerning such issues as nuclear energy, unemployment, and defense, as well as issues related to women's concerns. The extent to which a more left-wing or liberal women's vote becomes operational may depend on the interest of parties in stressing relevant issues related to gender gap concerns and the capacity of gender-based movements to mobilize women for electoral purposes.

(See also ELECTIONS AND VOTING BEHAVIOR; FEMINIZATION OF POVERTY; GENDER AND POLITICS; NEW SOCIAL MOVEMENTS; REPRODUCTIVE POLITICS.)

Carol Mueller, ed. *The Politics of the Gender Gap: The Social Construction of Political Influence* (Berkeley, Calif., 1988).

JOYCE GELB

GENERAL AGREEMENT ON TARIFFS AND TRADE.

The General Agreement on Tariffs and Trade (GATT) is the institutional focus of the closest thing the world has to a global *regime for trade. As purists are wont to note, it is not an *international organization in the strict sense of the term. Rather, it is a *treaty that binds its members to a body of rules in certain facets of commercial exchange. It also provides those members a forum for striking deals and settling disputes on trade. Its overall purpose has remained constant: to boost the growth in world trade by reducing commercial barriers in a nondiscriminatory fashion. Momentous as this task might be, it is not one that has sufficed to

endow GATT with universal endearment. Indeed, the authority and even the legitimacy of GATT have been subject to frequent questioning. Much of GATT's agenda is arcane and soporific; its procedures are at best cumbersome and often ineffectual; its pace is glacial. To many seasoned diplomats who have been subjected to the rituals of GATT, its acronym stands for the General Agreement to Talk and Talk. Nevertheless, it is in those talks that GATT has been particularly instrumental. GATT has facilitated the construction of package agreements involving complex trade-offs on matters that impinge on some of the most vital economic concerns of states, rich and poor alike. It also has insinuated a measure of international accountability into areas once confined to sovereign prerogatives.

As was the case with the other institutions that underpinned the postwar international economic order, GATT reflected the preponderance and preferences of the United States. It also embodied a conviction of avoiding a relapse into the beggar-thy-neighbor policies that led to the disintegration of the world economy in the 1930s. Yet the agreement, originally envisaged as an interim treaty and signed by twenty-odd countries in 1947, was not intended to stand alone. Rather, it was designed to be part of a comprehensive International Trade Organization (ITO) which, in turn, would have formed the third leg of the Bretton Woods tripod—along with the *International Monetary Fund (IMF) and the International Bank for Reconstruction and Development (IBRD). The ITO would have had a broad mandate covering not only trade barriers but also economic development, commodity agreements, employment policy, foreign investment, and restrictive business practices. It also would have had strong enforcement powers to ensure compliance with its rules. The charter of the ITO drew the ire of the U.S. Congress and was not even submitted to it for ratification. The ITO, therefore, never came into existence. GATT emerged by default as the overseer of the rules for world trade. But it was given no teeth to perform such a role. Its scope, moreover, was limited largely to one among the multiplicity of trade-related issues: commercial barriers on industrial products.

Freer and Fairer Trade. At the heart of GATT is a code of prescriptions and proscriptions for the behavior of states in trade. The dominant thrust of the code is liberal, albeit not of the classical nineteenth-century version of *liberalism. Hence, measures to liberalize and increase the flow of goods were not tethered entirely to ideals of aggregate growth and aggregate efficiency. There was a common recognition that those measures also would have to respect goals of domestic employment and price stability and, more generally, the greater responsibilities assumed by governments in protecting their economies against external disturbances. The occasional recitations of the idiom of laissez-faire orthodoxy notwithstanding, GATT was to dedicate itself not so much to free trade as to freer and fairer trade.

The cornerstone of GATT is the principle of non-discrimination, embodied in the rule of unconditional "most-favored-nation" (MFN) treatment for all its signatories. Accordingly, any concession granted by one member to another member has to be extended automatically to all others, the so-called "contracting parties" of GATT. The rule, in effect, is intended to ensure that a country's products can enter foreign markets according to terms no less favorable than those enjoyed by any other country. Hence, any reduction or increase in trading barriers would have to be generalized to all members of the regime. At the same time, according to the principles of GATT, liberalization of trade would have to be based on *reciprocity: market-opening measures negotiated between any two parties would have to involve concessions by both sides. In the jargon of GATT, liberalization would have to be mutually advantageous and substantially equivalent. While the economic justification behind reciprocity is dubious, the norm has an eminently political calculus: to deflect the domestic opposition that inevitably would crystallize against unilateral and unrequited reductions in trade barriers. The agreement also urged its members to make the instrument of *protection transparent. In general, nontariff barriers (NTBs), such as quantitative restrictions, were to be prohibited. Hence, states were to confine themselves to tariffs, which operate by price rather than by volume, and are more predictable, less arbitrary, and easier to negotiate downward.

From the outset, GATT was strewn with escape clauses. The MFN rule can be suspended for customs unions and free trade areas. Thus the European Common Market, the forerunner to the *European Community (EC), was free to engage in reductions in trade barriers among its members that would not have to be multilateralized across GATT. Exemptions from MFN were also tolerated for preferential arrangements existing before the formation of GATT, e.g., British and French imperial relations. Quantitative restrictions could be used to cope with *balance of payments difficulties. They also could be invoked for reasons of national *security. Subject to certain strictures, temporary safeguards in the form of higher tariffs or import quotas could be imposed in order to protect domestic industries threatened with a surge of imports attributable to previous concessions. Also codified in the rules, at the insistence of the United States, were allowances for a panoply of illiberal practices in agriculture, including export subsidies and import controls. These loopholes and exceptions grew over the years. Some of them were expected to provide an incentive to move toward greater openness; many were intended to temper the costs of international adjustments on national economies and societies; all bore the imprint of politically influential domestic interests pushing for protection.

Nominally in charge of this code was an entity with marginal powers. In fact, GATT was run as a club by and for the world's largest trading nations: the United States, the EC, and Japan. To this day, they have ceded no autonomy to GATT. As a global agency, GATT has a small secretariat and a minuscule budget. Some of its directors-general have been influential in brokering agreements among states, but ultimately states have been the source of all major initiatives in GATT. GATT does not have an arm to police the rules that are decided under its aegis. Therefore, it can neither offer the material inducements nor impose the punitive sanctions that are at the command of the IMF and the *World Bank. GATT's principal function has been to provide a setting for two activities.

The first is dispute settlement. The mechanisms GATT provides for this purpose are weak; the processes are slow, sometimes dragging on for years; and rarely have the outcomes enhanced the credibility of the institution. In the main, GATT has relied on expert panels to handle complaints about violations of its trade rules that cannot be resolved through more routine consultation procedures. The consensual decision-making requirement that has prevailed across GATT allows disputants to block panel findings. In any event, the rulings, which may authorize retaliation by the injured party, are not binding, while the means of securing compliance are effectively nonexistent.

The second activity is one in which GATT has had a greater measure of success: conference *diplomacy. The highlight of this diplomacy has been successive rounds of multilateral trade negotiations (MTNs). The six rounds of MTNs held between the late 1940s and the 1960s, culminating in the Kennedy Round of 1962–1967, paved the way for a remarkable decline in tariff barriers and an equally remarkable increase in world trade and prosperity. Like the institution as a whole, the bargains struck through GATT in these years rested on the ability and willingness of the United States to underwrite the costs of creating a more open trade order. GATT was of limited utility in addressing the concerns of the *Third World: for most developing countries, the norms and rules of GATT, and the preoccupation of MTNs with tariff barriers on industrial products, were hardly relevant to their immediate concerns. Once the charter for the ITO was shelved, many of them chose to stay clear of GATT, while even those that did join for the most part remained outside the MFN process. On the other hand, GATT was instrumental in absorbing the Europeans and the Japanese into the emerging economic order. U.S. toleration of asymmetric benefits—specifically, its willingness to forgo an insistence on reciprocal concessions by Western Europe and Japan and, more generally, to accommodate a measure of cheating by its trading partners—helped to lower the resistance to liberalization under GATT. At the same time, despite resistance from a variety of economic and political constituencies, there was little in the GATT process that posed a serious threat to material interests at home. The United States was the driving force behind all the multilateral negotiations. It remains so today. But for the United States and the rest of the world—and for GATT itself—the issues at stake in the enterprise of liberalization, and more generally in the international management of trade, have become markedly different.

The Erosion of GATT Rules. In the 1970s and 1980s, the GATT-based regime was shaken at its foundations by protectionism. Protectionism did not emerge full blown in these decades. Even in prior years, the industrial countries shielded a variety of domestic producers from the pressures of foreign competition. Moreover, there has not been a wholesale and inexorable retreat from liberalization. By and large, protectionism has remained a selective affair and has not precluded further measures toward openness. Nevertheless, there is no mistaking the overall trend of the 1970s and 1980s: mercantilist practices proliferated, reaching levels that dwarfed those in preceding decades, with the consequence that an increasing proportion of world trade has fallen outside the rules of GATT. "Voluntary export restraints" (VERs) and "orderly marketing arrangements" (OMAs)—market-restricting agreements that are often quotas in all but name and that are outright evasions of the MFN requirement—have become pervasive in numerous industries, including steel, automobiles, textiles, footwear, semiconductors, electronic products, and machine tools. By some counts, as much as one-half of world trade consists of such forms of "managed trade." Most of them have been imposed by the United States and the EC and have been directed against Japan and the developing countries, especially the newly industrializing countries (NICs) of East Asia. A variety of other NTBs—ranging from government procurement practices and customs procedures to health standards and environmental protection requirements—have been added to the arsenal of trade policy. Often such NTBs have been deployed for few purposes other than shutting out or slowing down foreign competition. However, despite their trade-distorting effects, many NTBs are part of the economic and social fabric of industrial countries; consequently, the obstacles they have posed for GATT negotiators have been far more intractable than those associated with tariffs. A variety of other practices have eroded the principle of nondiscrimination in GATT. Antidumping actions and countervailing duty measures have become favorite weapons against individual suppliers. The EC has even pressed for institutionalizing the principle of "selectivity" in the application of industrial safeguards, which would give a legal imprimatur to the practice of penalizing particular competitors and thereby further chip away at the MFN rule.

In short, the behavior of many states in world trade in recent decades has violated both the letter and the spirit of GATT. At the same time, GATT was helpless and virtually irrelevant in defusing conflicts that erupted among its leading members. Some of these conflicts were especially pronounced in areas that had not been brought under the scope of GATT. At one end of the spectrum is a set of policies that are not even readily subsumable under the issue of trade: industrial policies aimed at developing and maintaining a comparative advantage in high technology. The amalgam of government interventions orchestrated to enhance international competitiveness are embedded in a welter of macroeconomic and microeconomic policies that surface in the form of trade disputes yet cannot be designated by the labels of tariff or nontariff barriers that are the stock-in-trade of GATT. At the other end of the spectrum is an area that was deliberately left out of the pale of GATT: agriculture. Both the economic and the political toll exacted by agricultural protection has been heavy. Production support to farmers in the industrial countries, as measured by producer subsidy equivalents, reached US$180 billion in 1990. The total cost to taxpayers and consumers in that same year was even higher—around US$300 billion (Organization for Economic Cooperation and Development, *Agricultural Policies, Markets and Trade: Monitoring and Outlook, 1991*, Paris, 1991). The supreme practitioner of agricultural protection has been the EC, whose Common Agricultural Policy, through a combination of internal supports and import levies, has reduced foreign competition and generated large surpluses that are dumped on world markets through export subsidies. Although more egregiously mercantilist than its trading rivals, the EC has been far from alone in agricultural protectionism. The United States, too, has maintained high levels of support for its farming sector and in the 1980s countered the EC by sharply boosting its own export subsidies, helping to pave the way for a full-scale trade war.

The causes behind the new protectionism and the attendant erosion of GATT rules are both numerous and complex. They include the harsh economic environment of the 1970s and 1980s, particularly the dislocations brought about by the oil price shocks, by bouts of recession and inflation, by unemployment in beleaguered industries, and by massive trade and payments imbalances. They also include the rapid changes in international competitiveness manifested in the rise of Japan and the NICs and the loss of a good part of the traditional manufacturing base of Western countries to these newcomers. The relative decline of the United States in the world economy has played its part, too: the erosion of U.S. dominance in world trade at the hands of rising powers across both the Atlantic and the Pacific has led not only to a more aggressive trade policy, as suggested by the strenuous demands for creating "level playing fields" and for wresting unilateral concessions from others in the name of reciprocity, but also to a questioning of the costs and benefits of GATT itself. GATT has come close to being abandoned by its founder and patron. Even the consensus about the cause of free trade has become frayed. Instead, the case for government intervention has received a new intellectual respectability from such quarters as the advocates of "strategic trade" theory, who give pride of place to activist policies geared toward tilting the terms of competition in favor of domestic producers. (See, e.g., Paul Krugman, *Rethinking International Trade,* Cambridge, Mass., 1990.)

To all these factors must be added one that lies at the doorstep of GATT itself. Unwittingly, GATT became the victim of its own success. Its one indisputable achievement has been to negotiate tariffs virtually out of existence: the average tariff in industrial countries was brought down from a level of more than forty percent in 1947 to less than five percent by 1990. But once tariffs were no longer a usable instrument of trade policy, governments came under intense pressure to deploy other means—particularly "gray-area" measures such as VERs and OMAs—in order to circumvent GATT rules. Unsurprisingly, nearly all such market-restricting agreements have been negotiated outside the framework of GATT. In a more general sense, the rise in protectionism has been an antidote to the realization of one of GATT's hallowed objectives: the rapid growth in world trade. This growth has meant a sharp increase in *interdependence, which has increased sensitivity to external disturbances, accentuated the pressures on domestic industries, and complicated the management of the trade regime.

The Tokyo and Uruguay Rounds. The seventh and eighth sets of MTNs under GATT, respectively the Tokyo and Uruguay rounds, have been the most concerted attempts to restore a measure of coherence and stability to the trade regime. The Tokyo Round (1973–1979) was the first systematic effort to tackle the proliferation of NTBs. The negotiations produced codes of conduct on NTBs in a variety of areas, including export subsidies, countervailing duties, government procurement, customs valuation, product standards, and import licensing. In each case, the objective was to increase the degree of transparency and to limit the element of arbitrariness in government interventions. The extension of the scope of GATT to include the management of NTBs represented an important advance. However, the effort to devise a code that would limit the widespread evasions of GATT's safeguard provisions, and thereby bring under multilateral surveillance the rash of VERs and OMAs, foundered over the issue of selectivity. This failure to agree on rules that would reaffirm the principle of nondiscrimination underscored a further weakening of the regime. Moreover, even the status of the codes that were agreed upon signified a retreat from the multilateralism originally programmed in GATT: the codes apply only to countries that ratify them, and as most developing countries have chosen not to ratify them, they are not legally entitled to the benefits. A less than universal application of the rules of GATT may contribute to institutional flexibility and also check the tendency to free ride, but it also points to the fractured nature of the regime. On the whole, the Tokyo Round was an exercise in damage limitation. The negotiations brought about further reductions in tariffs on manufactures. However, the primary object of the Tokyo Round was less one of continuing liberalization than containing the drift toward protectionism. The attempt to nail down more liberal rules for trade in agricultural products made little headway.

The Uruguay Round opened in Punta del Este in 1986 with an agenda that, in its complexity and ambitiousness, rivaled that of the Bretton Woods Conference of 1944. The negotiations were divided into fifteen negotiating committees; the number of participating countries was 108. The task was nothing less than to tackle anew the unfinished business of the Tokyo Round and, simultaneously, to bring under GATT's wing a new set of trade issues. Besides tariffs, the older issues on the agenda included the uses and abuses of safeguards, subsidies, and antidumping. Each of the latter issues became increasingly contentious over the course of the 1980s. Developing countries succeeded in inserting onto the agenda the restrictions on their exports of clothing and textiles to the industrial countries. For three decades, these exports have been governed by a regime—in its latest incarnation, the Multifiber Arrangement (MFA)—that, under the guise of a voluntary export restraint, imposes a series of bilaterally negotiated quotas which are a breach of the MFN rule and widely regarded as the epitome of managed trade. The most important new issue to be included in the Uruguay Round is services, a vast sector that embraces banking, insurance, telecommunications, construction, aviation, shipping, tourism, advertising, consultancy, and broadcasting. Services represent the fastest-growing area of world trade. Writing joint rules for them is an activity that is likely to take decades. Two other new areas in the Uruguay Round are trade-related intellectual property rights (TRIPs) and trade-related investment measures (TRIMs). The former involves an effort by the industrial countries to tighten the rules that protect patents, licenses, trademarks, and copyrights against piracy. The focus of the latter is guidelines on trade-restricting investment restrictions such as rules about local content, export performance, foreign exchange, and domestic sales. In addition to these old and new areas is one that straddles the two and that proved to be most troublesome: agriculture. And added to this bundle of issues was the question of the future of GATT itself—its role in dispute settlement and its status as an international institution.

The tortuous progress made at the Uruguay Round by the end of 1990, the original deadline imposed on the negotiators, underscored the increasing difficulties in dealing with trade issues. If the experience of similar encounters in conference diplomacy, such as the Third United Nations Conference on the *Law of the Sea, is a guide, the prospects of a sustainable breakthrough on a package as enormous and disparate as that before the Uruguay Round are not favorable. Nevertheless, after four years of negotiations, several important elements of an agreement were in place. These included 1) the creation of a General Agreement on Trade in Services (GATS) based on norms of nondiscrimination, reciprocity, and equality of treatment for domestic and foreign suppliers; 2) the gradual phaseout of the MFA and the integration of textiles and clothing into GATT; 3) the harmonization of rules on property rights in ways that would balance the demands of developed countries for protection against counterfeiting with those of developing countries for avoidance of monopoly charges on patent rights; and 4) the enhancement of GATT's capacity in the resolution of disputes through such steps as giving more force to panels by making the adoption of their findings automatic. All the bargains that were reached in each of these and other areas were qualified and tentative. Nevertheless, the outlines of a package agreement were in place when the negotiations broke down in December 1990 over a dispute about agricultural protection between the United States and the EC. The United States, backed by a fourteen-member "Cairns Group" of agricultural exporters, pressed for cutbacks in export subsidies and internal supports so drastic that they would have meant the dismantlement of the EC's Common Agricultural Policy. Although the United States later scaled down its maximalist demands and although the EC did offer significant concessions, the gap in the negotiating positions was too large to prevent the Uruguay Round from collapsing in 1990 or from remaining deadlocked into 1992.

The tribulations of the Uruguay Round will not be fatal for world trade and, regardless of the final script, they are not likely to be fatal for GATT, either. Nevertheless, the experience of the latest round does not augur well for the collective management of trade issues. It also signals a hardening of postures on the part of the powers with the greatest capacity to either destroy or rescue the regime. The United States was the main force behind the Uruguay Round: the Reagan administration, confronted with a soaring trade deficit, sought the

talks in an effort to deflect protectionist pressures at home and to pry open markets abroad. The construction of the agenda also was the work of the United States, which had taken the lead in putting such items as services and agriculture on the table. But the United States also was a prime mover in the breakdown of 1990, having played a game of double-or-nothing against the EC even though the talks had succeeded in crafting a package deal that, even on the issue of farm trade, surpassed all its original objectives. The United States insisted on the linkage of all the issues in the package that it considered to be critical, with the consequence that a partial agreement was precluded and failure to agree on one item meant derailment of the entire package. GATT may well turn out to be a beneficiary of these stratagems—if the United States succeeds in simultaneously furthering the goals of liberalization and multilateralism. However, since this task has long ceased to be a consuming concern for the United States and others in world trade, the outcomes for GATT could be altogether different.

The attractiveness of bilateral and regional trade agreements has grown in recent years and could grow even more in coming years, especially if there is continued stalemate in GATT. Many already foresee the emergence of three giant trade blocs: the EC single market, eventually swollen well beyond its borders of 1992; an Asian group with Japan at its center; and a North American free trade zone among the United States, Canada, and Mexico. For GATT, the worry is that such blocs, by leading to a *balkanization of the world trading system, will render it obsolete. The years of the Uruguay Round also saw a growing tendency to resort to aggressive unilateralism in coping with trade problems. For example, the Omnibus Trade and Competitiveness Act of 1988 strengthened legislation that already gives the United States potent weapons to employ in retaliation against countries it judges to be unfair traders. Reliance on such devices poses extensive dangers for the trade regime.

The defection by the leading powers from the multilateral regime embodied in GATT, although far from total, represents one of the profound ironies in the history of the institution. Over the course of the Uruguay Round, a long queue of countries sought entry into GATT: initially, holdouts among developing countries, and subsequently more than a score of socialist and ex-socialist countries. Aside from the fact that they once regarded GATT with suspicion, if not outright hostility, most of these countries had one thing in common: a strong interest in acquiring or maintaining access to the markets of the advanced industrial countries. This interest, reinforced by an acute sense that they had the most to lose from closure of the trade system, helped to trigger a major shift in attitudes toward GATT. Many of these countries instituted sweeping market-oriented reforms, shedding decades of statist policies that had isolated them from the trading system. These reforms owed much to revisions in economic convictions and to the exhaustion of economic alternatives, but they also were part of the price of entry into GATT.

Developing countries, which had been marginal in previous MTNs, emerged as full participants in the Uruguay Round. And their stances went beyond the dogmatic insistence on "special and differential" treatment. The latter principle, enshrined in GATT in 1965 as part of a concession to its poorer members, exempted them from obligations such as reciprocity but also diminished their bargaining power by reducing their role to that of supplicants. While there were profound differences between the developed and developing countries on numerous issues, both old and new, the Uruguay Round did not fragment along *North-South lines. Instead, both interests and coalitions cut across the traditional divisions. For example, on the liberalization of services, there were striking divergences between the export-oriented NICs and the more autarkic countries such as India and Brazil. The Cairns Group, which pressed for freer farm trade, comprised not only affluent exporters such as Australia and Canada but also ten developing countries—including Argentina, Brazil, Malaysia, and Thailand—along with Hungary.

The Prospects for GATT. In the lore of GATT, there is a metaphor that is invoked by officials in the agency's headquarters in Geneva whenever the enterprise of multilateral liberalization appears to be faltering: the bicycle must keep moving; otherwise, it will tip over. To many who surveyed the world trade system at the beginning of the 1990s, the bicycle may have toppled already. Indeed, pronouncements of the death of GATT became commonplace. The proliferation of trade restrictions, the subversion of the norms and rules that are the bedrock of an open order, the eruption of trade wars among the leading economies and their growing penchant for settling squabbles bilaterally—these developments, at the very least, point to a regime that is more wobbly than at any other period since its creation.

In several important respects, however, the bicycle metaphor may be misleading, for it rests on two unwarranted assumptions: first, that liberalization and protectionism are mutually exclusive; and, second, that it is the momentum of trade talks that checks the slide toward protectionism. The experience of the years since World War II in fact suggests that protectionism in some areas has proceeded in tandem with liberalization in other areas. And the bulwarks against protectionism are not confined to MTNs, which remain an affair among bureaucrats. The internationalization of production—spurred by corporate strategies that are spinning a complex web of transnational alliances, mergers, and cooperative agreements—is in part a response to protectionist pressures and also a brake on the acceleration of such pressures. Protectionism no doubt has reduced the volume of world trade, but world trade has continued to grow at robust levels, typically twice as high as those of output.

But if the bicycle has not fallen, for GATT two nagging questions remain: Who is the rider? And is there a destination? That neither question can be answered with certainty is testimony to the travails of GATT in recent years. The identity of the rider is unclear because the principal players in the world economy are disengaging from many aspects of the multilateral regime represented by GATT. It may not be easy for them to continue both to maintain a leadership stronghold in GATT and develop institutional alternatives to GATT. The destination is unclear because liberalization, the objective presumed in the bicycle metaphor—and by GATT since its inception—itself entails different projects. GATT's image of world trade tends to assume a realm of buyers and sellers interacting at arm's length across national borders on the basis of comparative advantage and disadvantage. In this image trade policy consists of formal barriers imposed by the importing country at the border, and the task of trade negotiations and trade agreements is to reduce those barriers. In fact, an increasing proportion of world trade now takes the form of intrafirm trade in components and services produced in many different countries, often importing and exporting the same product; and the essence of trade policy is not import restrictions but a variety of policies and structures that affect the capacity to acquire strategic advantage in advanced technology or to secure access to foreign markets for specific sectors or firms. Devising rules to govern interactions in this area is increasingly recognized by GATT to be an essential task, albeit one that does not easily fall under the label of liberalization, as it is less than clear what ought to be the target of liberalization. It is also a task that may be elusive for GATT; for, unlike the case with the liberalization of tariffs, it implies a substantial intrusion into the workings of domestic policies and institutions.

Most of the world's trading nations are likely to continue to maintain a major stake in GATT if only because GATT remains the only rules-based regime for trade with universal applicability. There is strong support for measures to increase GATT's role in such areas as dispute settlement and policy surveillance. It is even possible that GATT will be transformed into a World Trade Organization with a role in trade comparable to that of the IMF in money and that of the World Bank in development. An organization of this kind, discussed in passing at the Uruguay Round, would bring all the multilateral trade treaties under one roof. However, the prospect that such an organization would provide the exclusive moorings of a regime for world trade are not bright. The more likely outcome is a multilayered regime with multilateral rules coexisting and even contending with regional and bilateral rules.

(See also DEVELOPMENT AND UNDERDEVELOPMENT; INTERNATIONAL POLITICAL ECONOMY; MERCANTILISM; MULTINATIONAL CORPORATIONS; NEWLY INDUSTRIALIZING ECONOMIES.)

Clair Wilcox, *A Charter for World Trade* (New York, 1949). Robert E. Hudec, *The GATT Legal System and World Trade Diplomacy* (New York, 1975). William R. Cline, ed., *Trade Policy in the 1980s* (Washington, D.C., 1983). Gilbert R. Winham, *International Trade and the Tokyo Round* (Princeton, N.J., 1986). John H. Jackson, *Restructuring the GATT System* (New York, 1990). Jagdish Bhagwati, *The World Trading System at Risk* (Princeton, N.J., 1991).

DON BABAI

GENOCIDE. Despite the fact that genocide, i.e., the use of deliberate measures taken with the intent to physically destroy a racial, ethnic, religious, or other similar group, has taken place throughout human history, it was only recently that such atrocious practices became a matter of specific and explicit prohibition by *international law. Today, however, it is universally recognized that genocide is the gravest international crime and the most dangerous violation of *human rights and that the international community is morally and politically responsible to take steps to prevent its occurrence and to punish persons responsible for crimes amounting to genocide.

Such recognition arose in response to a number of episodes of genocide during the first half of this century, in particular the Nazi *Holocaust during *World War II. The genocidal policies of *Hitler's Germany stand above all comparisons because they were a part of a carefully calculated plan to systematically annihilate particular nations, races, religions, and political groups.

The tragedy of the Nazi holocaust led a Polish jurist, Raphael Lemkin, to coin the word *genocide* from the Greek word *genos* (race, people) and the Latin *caedere* (to kill) and to begin action aimed at the international prohibition of genocide, which would in turn provide the necessary international legal basis for action against this crime. One result of this initiative was the Convention on the Prevention and Punishment of the Crime of Genocide, which was adopted unanimously by the UN General Assembly on 9 December 1949 (UN Treaty Series, vol. 78, p. 278) and which entered into force on 12 January 1951. The convention was subsequently ratified or acceded to by more than 100 states, and it is now universally accepted that prohibition of the crime of genocide as defined in that convention belongs to peremptory norms (*ius cogens*) of international law.

In the terms of the convention "genocide means any of the following acts committed with the intent to destroy, in whole or in part, a national, ethnical, racial or religious group, such as (a) Killing members of the group; (b) Causing serious bodily or mental harm to members of the group; (c) Deliberately inflicting on the group conditions of life calculated to bring about its physical destruction in whole or in part; (d) Imposing measures intended to prevent births within the group; (e) Forcibly transferring children of the group to another group." Punishment for acts of genocide and associated acts such as complicity in genocide, whether committed in time of peace or in time of war, applies to "constitutionally responsible rulers, public officials or private individuals." The contracting parties to the convention are obliged to enact legislation that makes genocide a crime within their territories and to provide effective penalties for persons guilty of genocide or of associated acts. Persons charged with any of these acts shall be tried "by a competent tribunal of the State in the territory of which the act was committed, or by such international tribunal as may have jurisdiction. . . ."

The provisions relating to the question of jurisdiction reflect the major deficiency of the convention and, indeed, of the entire international legal system in regard to prosecution of international crimes: the absence of compulsory international criminal jurisdiction. In the case of genocide this problem poses particular difficulties. The crime of genocide can hardly be committed without at least indirect involvement of a government, and it is unlikely that such a government would bring before the court individuals directly responsible for such crimes. The only real solution to this problem would be the establishment of an international tribunal with an appropriate jurisdiction in criminal matters relating to international crimes such as genocide. An additional problem of the convention is that it does not specifically provide for protection of political and cultural groups that are in reality often exposed to the same danger of physical destruction as groups named in the convention.

Notwithstanding such problems of interpretation and application, the convention and, more generally, the acceptance of express prohibition of genocide in international law represent a fundamental contribution to the international protection of human rights. Acts of commission or omission with respect to genocide can no longer be considered as a matter exclusively within the domestic jurisdiction of the states concerned. In all situations involving genocide the UN has the moral and legal right to intervene. Moreover, the compulsory international jurisdiction and prosecution of persons responsible for acts of genocide may become possible in the future.

(See also WAR CRIMES.)

Raphael Lemkin, *Axis Rule in Occupied Europe* (Washington, D.C., 1944). Leo Kuper, *The Prevention of Genocide* (New Haven, Conn., 1985).

DANILO TÜRK

GEOPOLITICS. Originally coined by the Swede Rudolf Kjellen in 1899, geopolitics was popularized in the early twentieth century by the British geographer Halford Mackinder as part of his effort to promote the field of geography as an aid to British statecraft. It was intended to signify the impact of geographical factors such as the spatial disposition of the continents and oceans and the distribution of natural and human resources upon international politics at a time when the whole world was finally available for state territorial and economic expansion.

During the 1920s and 1930s Mackinder's formal model of a Eurasian "heartland" rising to global dominance if not checked by cohesive reaction from the encircling "outer or insular crescent" was adopted by certain Nazi apologists to justify Germany expansionism. In German *Geopolitik* the heartland model was added to concepts of movable frontiers, autarky, *Lebensraum* (living space or room to expand), and *Panideen* (panideas such as Pan-Americanism, as expressed in the *Monroe Doctrine in the United States). Some of these ideas were directly inspired by the writing of the German geographer Friedrich Ratzel on the "laws of the spatial growth of states." There is still controversy over whether German *Geopolitik* directly influenced Nazi policies.

In the aftermath of *World War II the term fell into disuse, especially among professional geographers, because of its association with Nazi policies and ideas of environmental determinism from which geographers were in retreat. Formal geopolitical models, especially Mackinder's heartland model, continued to appear in geography textbooks, and some academics made "adjustments" by allowing for changes in military technology (airpower, nuclear weapons, etc.) and changes in regional "ecology" resulting from the disintegration of the European colonial empires. However, in the absence of much explicit continuity with the prewar period geopolitics acquired two new meanings: 1) as a synonym for geostrategy in the pursuit of particular diplomatic and military goals and 2) as the equivalent of political geography, in the sense of areal variation in political phenomena at all scales, including the global.

The more classical usage returned to prominence in U.S. debates over international politics in the late 1970s and early 1980s. Interest groups such as the Committee on the Present Danger and ideological elements strong in the first *Reagan administration argued that the United States must redouble its efforts at "containing" the Soviet Union after the détente and "idealism" of the United States following the *Vietnam War. They used explicit geopolitical language about the "domino effect" of revolutions in Central America, Soviet desire for warm-water ports and oil deposits in the Middle East, and the key role of the U.S. Navy in denying the world's sea-lanes to the Soviet Union. From this perspective the United States and the Soviet Union were seen as successor states to, respectively, Britain's nineteenth-century maritime empire and French and German attempts to assemble an overwhelming "continental bloc."

In this context some geographers began to question whether geopolitics, in the sense of the geographical ordering of the world into a hierarchy of "strategic regions," "spheres of influence," "buffer zones," and "strategic locations," existed in *foreign policy only when the term was used in reference to formal geopolitical models (such as Mackinder's). Rather, geopolitics could be viewed as any discourse about geographically defined interests including particular models privileging fixed geographical "facts" about the world. From this point of view geopolitics did not disappear after World War II or when moral rhetoric replaced *Realpolitik* in the pronouncements of politicians. It is implicit in the practice of foreign policy.

In line with this dynamic conception of geopolitics, as the world political economy changes the criteria used for ordering the world geographically change. Currently, economic rather than military-territorial considerations are becoming more central to discussions about geopolitics in the United States and the Pacific Basin is challenging Europe as the highest-priority region for U.S. policymakers. But older themes from the height of U.S.-Soviet competition in the 1950s persist even as their real-world basis is undermined. Geopolitical discourse can lag behind the world it purports to explain.

Since the nineteenth century the geopolitics of, first, Britain, and, second, the United States, have been hegemonic at the global scale because of the dominant position of these states. Other states could either consent or pose a challenge. In this century a succession of challenges, both global (for example, Nazi Germany and Japan in the 1930s and 1940s; the Soviet Union during the *Cold War) and regional (for example, Gaullist France in Europe; India in South Asia; Iran and Iraq in the Middle East), have been made to the global status quo but as yet without international success.

(See also DOMINO THEORY.)

John Agnew and Stuart Corbridge, "The New Geopolitics: The Dynamics of Geopolitical Disorder," in Ronald J. Johnston and Peter J. Taylor, eds., *A World in Crisis? Geographical Perspectives*, 2d ed. (Oxford, 1989), pp. 266–288. Simon Dalby, "American Security Discourse: The Persistence of Geopolitics" *Political Geography Quarterly* 9 (April 1990): 171–188.

JOHN A. AGNEW

GEORGIA. See COMMONWEALTH OF INDEPENDENT STATES.

GERMAN DEMOCRATIC REPUBLIC. The German Democratic Republic (GDR)—also known as East Germany—was created in the Soviet-occupied zone after *World War II as a separate German state next to the Federal Republic of *Germany (FRG). Founded on 7 October 1949, the GDR (population 16 million) ceased to exist on 3 October 1990, upon its unification with the FRG (which until then had also been known as West Germany) following the peaceful revolution of fall 1989. Thus the political history of the GDR can be divided into three periods: the formative stage in the postwar years, the four decades of communist rule, and the transition period beginning with the peaceful *revolution.

After the defeat of Nazism the wartime Allies determined the political restructuring of Germany in accordance with the *Potsdam Agreement of 1945 in their respective zones. The Soviet military administration allowed the rebuilding of political parties and unions, favoring, however, the Kommunistische Partei Deutschlands (KPD). In April 1946, the larger party on the Left, the Sozialdemokratische Partei Deuschlands (SPD), was pressed into merging with the KPD to form the Sozialistische Einheitspartei Deutschlands (SED). The new party became a mechanism for the communists to control the political process. The distance between the occupation zones widened during the *Cold War and the division of Germany led to the formation of the GDR as a *communist party state with a centrally planned economy.

Even though four other political parties existed—the Christlich-Demokratische Union (CDU), the Demokratische Bauernpartei Deutschlands (DBD), the Liberal-Demokratische Partei Deutschlands (LDPD), and the National-Demokratische Partei Deutschlands (NDPD)—the SED kept tight control of all other so-called bloc parties that were part of the Nationale Front. Elections to the parliament were held every four years, allowing only one unified list. A fixed distribution of seats among the political parties and other organizations, such as the Freier Deutscher Gewerkschaftsbund (FDGB), the Youth Organization, and the Women's Federation, was prearranged before the elections.

Political decision making was highly concentrated and centralized. In 1952, the *Länder,* or states, were abolished, allowing the central government in the capital, East Berlin, to control and administer policies uniformly in the entire country. The most important body politically was the Communist Party, with power concentrated in the politburo of the SED (first secretary, 1951–1971: Walter Ulbricht; 1971–1989: Erich Honecker). The SED became one of the most tightly controlled and organized Communist parties in the Soviet bloc. In 1988 it had 2.1 million members. Based on a *nomenklatura* system, all key positions in the state administration, the economy, education, the media, and the military were controlled by the party. Even the judiciary was dependent on SED directives and policies, neglecting opportunities to claim individual rights while favoring state power and control. The powerful secret police, the Stasi (Staatssicherheit) or state security, monitored and controlled the population, keeping files on over 6 million people. Before the collapse of communist rule it had some 106,000 employees; additionally, between 1.6 and 2 million citizens were unpaid "informers" for the regime.

Economic policies in the GDR were molded largely upon those of the *Soviet Union. Production targets were set by five-year plans and economic *planning was directed by the politburo. More than eighty-five percent of the GDR's economy was run by nationalized enterprises, agriculture was collectivized, and even small-scale industries, crafts, and services were almost entirely socialized. Unlike the Soviet Union, however, the GDR could draw upon its fairly advanced industrial as well as human resources. Under the Honecker regime, the development of microelectronics and other new technologies was aggressively promoted, but results were modest. To enhance political *legitimacy the SED also introduced social policies in the 1970s, including a housing program and benefits for mothers.

The SED firmly rejected the reform ideas proposed by the Soviet Communist Party leader Mikhail *Gorbachev in 1985–1986. As conditions in the *international political economy became increasingly unfavorable for the *command economies in Eastern and *Central Europe and the Soviet Union—leading to declining growth rates, deterioration of the standard of living, increasing pollution, and foreign debts—the GDR withstood the squeeze longer than other countries in the region, largely owing to favorable trade conditions and economic relations with the Federal Republic.

Mass migration of East Germans to the West through the open border between *Hungary and *Austria in the fall of 1989 led to mounting popular pressure and increased oppositional activity including the forming of the Neues Forum in September 1989, the refounding of the SPD, and actions by small civil rights, women's, and environmentalist groups, some of which had existed for some years, mostly under the shelter of the Protestant church. Almost two percent of the population emigrated to the Federal Republic in the second half of 1989. Mass demonstrations in Leipzig, Berlin, Dresden, and other cities under the slogan "We are the people" led to hectic leadership change in the SED. The dramatic and unexpected opening of the Berlin Wall on 9 November 1989 accelerated the collapse of the communist regime. Only a few weeks later, the party was forced to give up its "leading role," agree to roundtable negotiations with oppositional groups, and schedule free elections. But insufficient attempts were made to abolish the power of the secret police and to reform the economy.

The first and last free elections to the GDR parliament, the *Volkskammer,* which took place on 18 March 1990, were a mandate for quick unification with the Federal Republic. Supported by West German Chancellor *Kohl, the CDU-led Alliance for Germany, which had called for quick unification, won forty-eight percent of the vote; the SPD, which had favored a slower, more cautious approach to unification, received twenty-one percent; the Partei des Demokratischen Sozialismus (PDS), successor to the SED, received sixteen percent; while the civil groups that had helped carry out the peaceful revolution were clearly marginalized. The GDR government moved to accomplish unification as quickly as possible. After the currency union that introduced the West German deutsche mark into the GDR on 1 July 1990, the GDR parliament decided to join the Federal Republic by accession under Article 23 of the West German Basic Law, and reunification occurred on 3 October 1990.

Given the lack of reliable empirical data, it is difficult to assess to what extent citizens in the GDR had developed identification with and support for their state. Orientation toward the Federal Republic had always been a powerful underlying pattern of popular attitudes, and the attempt of the SED regime to foster identification with a "socialist nation" has clearly failed. However, for years to come significant political cultural differences between citizens in the west and the east of Germany will prevail.

(See also COLLECTIVIZATION; COMMUNISM; ENVIRONMENTALISM; GERMAN REUNIFICATION; NINETEEN EIGHTY-NINE; POTSDAM CONFERENCE; POLITICAL CULTURE; SOVIET–EAST EUROPEAN RELATIONS.)

James McAdams, *East Germany and the West: Surviving Détente* (New York, 1985). Marilyn Rueschemeyer and Christiane Lemke, eds., *The Quality of Life in the German Democratic Republic: Changes and Developments in a State Socialist Society* (New York, 1989). Elizabeth Pond, *After the Wall: American Policy Toward Germany* (New York, 1990.)

CHRISTIANE LEMKE

GERMAN REUNIFICATION. German reunification came as a surprise. Thanks to broadly shared views of recent European history, feelings were mixed about achieving it, even among Germans themselves. Bismarck's Germany seemed to have been too big for the European state system and unstable internally. The Nazi regime was often seen as only a monstrous caricature of the repression at home and adventurism abroad feared to be inherent in any unified German state. By contrast, the western Federal Republic of *Germany, or FRG (West Germany), was a manageable partner for France in a European confederation and a particularly faithful ally for the United States in the *North Atlantic Treaty Organization (NATO). Without the eastern regions, the Federal Republic achieved an internal political and cultural balance that made it a model of democratic civility. Meanwhile, the *German Democratic Republic, or GDR (East Germany), appeared to encapsulate the more repugnant traits of both *communism and the old imperial *authoritarianism.

These sentiments were difficult to express openly. Officially, the Federal Republic awaited the inclusion of the east and welcomed refugees as citizens. But other policies suggested a different view. In the early *Cold War, the Federal Republic chose a posture of unremitting hostility toward the East German state. *Democracy, *capitalism, and a Western orientation generally had clear priority over reunification. As wary coexistence stabilized, the Federal Republic began to imagine more intimate relations—perhaps leading to some confederal structure. But a single centralized state was thought unlikely in the foreseeable future, both because the Soviet Union would never permit it and because the GDR would be strong enough to reject it. Reunification could only be achieved as "two states in one nation," the formula popularized by Willy Brandt in the 1970s. Meanwhile, the Federal Republic would continue as the principal U.S. ally in NATO and France's principal partner in the *European Community (EC).

It was changing Soviet policy that permitted Germany's sudden reunification. With the Soviet leader Mikhail *Gorbachev dedicating himself to reform and a "common European home," Soviet force was no longer ready to buttress the communist regime in East Germany. Reunification grew imminently possible. The United States blessed it and no other Western power felt able to oppose it.

In October 1989, huge demonstrations forced the communist leader Erich Honecker to resign. East Germans had begun streaming to the West over the summer. To restore confidence, and unable to prevent the exodus anyway, the communist government itself began dismantling the Berlin Wall on 9 November 1989. As the flow continued, the GDR began to break down. The Federal Republic, welcoming refugees with automatic *citizenship and economic aid, faced enormous disruption. Nothing would resolve the situation, it was widely argued, short of complete reunification. Chancellor Helmut *Kohl's coalition of his own party, the Christlich-Demokratische Union (CDU), the Bavarian Christlich-Soziale Union (CSU), and Foreign Minister Genscher's Freie Demokratische Partei (FDP) gradually came to favor rapid absorption of the GDR. The Sozialdemokratische Partei Deutschlands (SPD) opposition inclined toward delay and confederation. By February 1990, it was agreed that negotiations for the new Germany would take place in a "two-plus-four" format, which meant bilateral German talks in parallel with collective talks adding Britain, France, the Soviet Union, and the United States.

Hopes for avoiding a reborn single Germany lay with the GDR. If it could reform rapidly enough to gain *legitimacy from its own population, reunification could be confederal. The GDR scheduled elections for 18 March. The principal contenders proved to be the well-financed affiliates of the West German parties rather than either the indigenous reformist coalition or the reconstituted communist party, transformed into the Partei des Demokratische Sozialismus (PDS). The East German CDU won a near majority (48.1 percent) and headed a coalition pledged to entering the Federal Republic. By early May, the two German states reached final arrangements for a currency union—on terms generous to holders of eastern marks. Economic union took place on 1 July. A formal treaty, signed on 31 August, set the terms for reunification. The GDR would be dismantled into five *Länder* (states), which would accede to the Federal Republic under Article 23 of its Basic Law. Both parliaments ratified the treaty on 20 September, and reunification occurred on 3 October.

The two-plus-four talks resolved Germany's international status. The new Federal Republic was to continue the formal relationships of the old. Gorbachev and Kohl met in the Soviet Union and confirmed that the Federal Republic would remain in NATO, and that Soviet troops would leave Germany by 1994. The Federal Republic would permit no foreign troops in the old East German territory, continue to renounce biological, chemical, and nuclear weapons, and cut its army to 370,000. On 12 September in Moscow, a final settlement ended the special rights and responsibilities of the Four Powers and guaranteed the Oder-Neisse border between Poland and Germany.

The new Germany also reaffirmed its links to the EC. German reunification was not to deflect plans for European integration. Successive summit meetings gave priority to "deepening" the EC's institutions over widening its membership. Formal negotiations opened to strengthen the EC in general and, among other things, to give it a common currency and a greater capacity for coordinated foreign and security policies. Pan-European institutions also progressed. At a *Conference for Security and Cooperation in Europe (CSCE) summit in Paris opening on 19 November, member states signed a treaty limiting conventional forces in Europe, formally proclaimed the end of Europe's military and economic division, and affirmed Europe's adherence to democratic freedoms and *human rights.

In December, the first all–German Federal elections gave Chancellor Kohl's CDU/CSU forty-four percent of the vote. Foreign Minister Genscher's FDP was also a big winner—with eleven percent. The SPD, whose leader, Oskar Lafontaine, had campaigned for a confederal structure, took only 33.5 percent. The Kohl coalition had triumphed on all sides. The Federal Republic had swallowed the GDR. Germany was once more a single state, despite all the misgivings. This new Germany was mostly free from the trammels of the postwar system, and the Federal Republic seemed, more than ever, Europe's leading power.

Celebration was brief. Rapid economic union collapsed much of East Germany's uncompetitive economy. While long-term economic prospects may have been highly promising, the Kohl government had seriously understated the immediate costs of absorbing the GDR. Unemployment in the five new *Länder* quickly reached frightening levels. Private business was diffident about providing the huge capital needed to modernize the east, let alone clean up its acute environmental mess. Heavy new welfare and pension costs helped push the federal budget into deep deficit, projected unofficially at 100 billion deutsche marks for 1991—up a third from earlier official estimates. The Bundesbank resisted monetizing the deficit and interest rates jumped to record levels. By February 1991, the chancellor, despite election promises, asked for a large tax increase. By March, the chairman of the Bundesbank, Karl-Otto Pöhl, having opposed monetary union in the first place, declared it an ongoing disaster.

Kohl's momentary popularity had only briefly obscured Germany's new volatility. West Germany's political stability and economic strength had been outstanding, and its political, social, and economic structures exceptionally robust. Reunification would create a new social and economic profile and different cultural balances. No one could say how the changing situation would translate into party politics, particularly in the east with its unpromising heritage. A strong majority coalition might grow more difficult to sustain.

Germany's internal challenges would probably absorb its energies for several years. Worries declined about any outsized external influence. Germany's domestic difficulties meant new problems and opportunities for the EC, long accustomed to relying heavily on German monetary stability, budgetary contributions, and private capital flows. A more troubled and weaker Germany, feeling vulnerable to eastern turmoil, could grow more solicitous of its EC ties. Germany's internal struggles might be transposed into European struggles—with German elements looking for allies within the EC. The Bundesbank, for example, might come to see European monetary union, once a way for Germany to reinforce monetary discipline on the rest of Europe, as a way to reinforce monetary stability in a suddenly much less disciplined Germany. Or, a federal government mired in debt might use European monetary union to liberate itself from the Bundesbank. Whether the new German politics would strengthen or weaken the EC remained to be seen.

Neither Germany nor the EC was likely to settle its problems undisturbed. By early 1991, increasingly troubled Balkan, Central European, and Soviet politics plus the *Gulf War indicated that Europe would not long enjoy a vacation from security problems. France and others were pressing to give European political cooperation a military dimension through the West European Union. The United States, victorious in the Gulf but beset by economic problems and concerned about its future role in Europe, seemed wary and ambivalent, even about a more

Europeanized NATO. Germany, meanwhile, was severely criticized in the United States and Britain for not sending troops to the Gulf.

Unified Germany would have to rethink its security policy. A more European NATO might raise old problems about nuclear *deterrence. The Soviet withdrawal, and the Gulf experience, pointed toward a smaller and perhaps more professional military force. The chancellor was pressing for constitutional changes to permit forces to be sent outside the country. The SPD was resisting, and the public showed little enthusiasm for military obligations— old or new. A new consensus would not be easy to obtain. Postwar Germans, loaded with guilt and restrictions, had developed an aversion to military interventions and power politics generally. The new Germany might not be allowed the same luxury. But a German *political culture more favorable to exerting military power would make some people wonder if history were not repeating itself.

In short, unity had brought new and old problems, as well as great new resources to Germany and to Europe. Germany and Europe as a whole were on their way to release from the confines of the postwar order. Pessimists, predicting the future, could draw on the experiences of Germany and Europe before World War II. Optimists could note the remarkable accomplishments of the Federal Republic and the EC thereafter.

(See also NINETEEN EIGHTY-NINE.)

David P. Calleo, *The German Problem Reconsidered* (Cambridge, U.K., 1978). David P. Calleo, "Deutschland und Amerika: Eine amerikanische Sicht," in *Geteiltes Land— halbes Land?* (Frankfurt am Main and Berlin, 1986). Wolfram F. Hanrieder, *Germany, America, Europe* (New Haven, Conn., 1989).

DAVID P. CALLEO

GERMANY, FEDERAL REPUBLIC OF. One of the hallmarks of German politics has been a peculiar mixture of social stability and political instability. The latter manifested itself in Germany's inability to establish a coherent center, a solid nation-state until 1870. Even then, one can argue, the newly forged political unity was far from stable. Social *authoritarianism and conservative domination of domestic politics were merely the mirror images of a highly restless polity that felt insecure and unaccomplished as a nation-state. Never was this more obvious than with Germany's leading role in initiating *World War I, and, subsequently, in the tragic failure of the Weimar Republic. The total destruction of the Third Reich ended this brief eighty-year episode of German political unity. Once again, Germany would revert to political fragmentation. Put differently, in notable contrast to its West European neighbors, what exactly embodied and constituted "Germany" still remained unclear. Thus, one of the most contentious and unresolved questions since the European Middle Ages—what is Germany?— continued to dominate European politics after 1945.

With *Austria finally going its own way, thus leaving the contentious realm of the "German question," and the westward relocation of many of Eastern Europe's German speakers, the unresolved German problem was narrowed to the rivalry and hostile relations between the Federal Republic of Germany, or FRG (West Germany), a creation of the Western Allies, and the *German Democratic Republic, or GDR (East Germany), its Soviet bloc counterpart. From the very beginning, it was clear that the former enjoyed something that eluded the latter until its demise: the political system's *legitimacy in the eyes of the governed. This, more than its economic prowess, rendered the Federal Republic immeasurably superior to and more powerful than the GDR, whose entire existence was ultimately predicated on the readiness of the Soviet army to use force. Once this readiness was denied by Mikhail *Gorbachev in the early fall of 1989, it was only a matter of weeks until the GDR was relegated to the dustbin of history. Underlining the Federal Republic's economic strength and political legitimacy vis-à-vis all Germans—east and west—as well as vis-à-vis the international community has been the fact that the unification of the two Germanys has *de facto* and *de jure* amounted to an extension of the Federal Republic eastward. Tellingly, the new entity continues to bear the name *the Federal Republic of Germany,* thus denoting a political and structural continuity that has been very rare in German history. Rarer still has been the fact that this "takeover"—some have called it an *Anschluß*—has occurred via entirely peaceful means.

To be sure, major difficulties plague the transition process. Largely because of the immense uncertainties accompanying this process and the daily changes besetting it, much of the ensuing analysis will focus on the FRG during its forty-year history as West Germany. But there can be no doubt that the new Federal Republic, though surely changed from the old, will represent an extension of the country as it existed between May 1949 and October 1990. Institutionally, culturally, politically, and economically, the former West Germany will remain hegemonic in the new united Germany.

Covering 153,498 square kilometers (95,936 sq. mi.), the FRG, with its 61 million people, represented one of the world's most densely populated areas. As decreed by its constitution (the Basic Law), the Federal Republic consisted of ten rather autonomous states *(Länder)* and West Berlin. The Basic Law created a *parliamentary democracy for the Federal Republic. The central institution of the federal government has been a bicameral parliament consisting of a lower house, the Bundestag, and an upper house, the Bundesrat. This parliament passes legislation, elects the federal chancellor and president, debates government policies, and oversees the activities of the federal ministries. To avoid the problems of the past, however, the Federal Republic's parliamentary system has an extensive set of checks and balances both to strengthen and control government action. As with much else in the Federal Republic, its political system was clearly designed with Germany's recent past in mind.

Given the vicissitudes and violence of modern German history, and measured by a direct comparison with other European countries, the FRG has to be classified by virtually all criteria as a highly successful liberal *democracy. Three interrelated developments form the basis of this success.

First, the Federal Republic has been thoroughly bourgeoisified and completely incorporated into Western Europe by virtue of its institutional attachments and memberships in *international organizations such as the *North Atlantic Treaty Organization (NATO) and the *European Community (EC). More prominently still, this Westernization is the result of major changes in values and attitudes on the part of a solid majority of West German citizens who came to cherish Western-style constitutionalism and parliamentary democracy. Jürgen Habermas's well-known concept of "constitutional patriotism" *(Verfassungspatriotismus)* aptly characterizes this accepted set of values on the part of a substantial majority of the FRG's population. Beginning with decisive efforts by Konrad Adenauer (the FRG's first chancellor, 1949–1963) to anchor the fate of this new German republic irrevocably in the West, West Germany's consistent Atlanticism and active pro-Europeanism exorcised from the body politic once and for all any remnants of Germany's previously pernicious "special development" *(Sonderweg)*.

Second, as part of this embourgeoisement and Westernization, the Federal Republic's success rests on an economic prosperity that has made it one of the richest countries in the world. With the exception of the rather high level of unemployment throughout the 1980s (hovering consistently around 8.5 percent of the work force), virtually every economic indicator conveys the formidable prowess of the FRG economy. Be it the FRG's per capita income, which has steadily ranked alongside that of the United States and the Scandinavian countries—and well ahead of its French and British counterparts—as one of the world's highest, or its status as the "export world champion" (i.e., the largest exporter in absolute numbers) by 1987, one would be hard pressed to find a blemish in the Federal Republic's overall economic performance.

Lastly, the third development ensuring the FRG's success consists in the inordinate stability and predictability of the country's political arrangements. The FRG has been governed by a three-party system that is basically devoid of political extremes either of the right or the left and whose main protagonists are unmitigated centrists in virtual agreement concerning all matters of fundamental political significance. Thus, all three democratic parties—the Christlich-Demokratische Union (CDU), the Sozial-demokratische Partei Deutschlands (SPD), and the much smaller Freie Demokratische Partei (FDP)—uphold parliamentarism, the Federal Republic's integration into the West, and the tenets of a managed (i.e., socially mitigated) capitalism. The Federal Republic's political stability has been such that no government had ever been voted out of office by the electorate. Differently put, elections never displaced rulers in the country's forty-one-year history. The three governmental changes that occurred in 1966, 1969, and 1982 each resulted from interparty coalition shifts yielding new parliamentary majorities rather than electoral verdicts by the public.

In notable contrast to the Weimar Republic (1919–1933) when it was the *Right's and *Left's respective extremes that defined their relationship, moderation has been the main characteristic in organizing the political competition between Right and Left in the Federal Republic. The Right, very much influenced by Konrad Adenauer's Western orientation and Ludwig Erhard's success in building a modern capitalist economy, shed its racist, antidemocratic, and authoritarian past in favor of an inclusive capitalism that cushioned the demise of its losers with the help of an extensive *welfare state. The Left, in turn, having relegated its communist wing to the former East Germany, accepted this managed capitalism provided it was to have a "human face" through constant progressive reforms initiated, if not necessarily implemented, by the Left's main political representatives, the SPD. This broadly accepted arrangement came to be known as the "social market economy." Both the CDU and the SPD developed into centrist "catch all" parties that encompassed virtually all social strata of the Federal Republic. Acerbic class conflict, the Weimar Republic's death knell, metamorphosed into an inclusive system of "democratic *corporatism" in West Germany where moderation, gradualism, and an atmosphere of mutual acceptance have defined Right-Left relations.

Nowhere has this system of inclusion been more successfully practiced than in the country's industrial relations. Whereas labor's internal cleavages along occupational, ideological, and religious lines contributed to the Left's demise in the Weimar Republic, West Germany's trade unions vigorously practiced a politics of comprehensive universalism. To avoid interunion rivalries, in principle each plant had one union represent all its workers, regardless of rank, skill, occupation, or political conviction. Furthermore, workers in each industrial sector were represented by one union, thereby yielding a centralized, bureaucratic, but all-inclusive system of sixteen large unions for the West German economy as a whole. With capital organized along similar institutional lines, labor and capital developed a highly elaborate system of checks and balances, aspects of which attained world fame under the rubric *codetermination (Mitbestimmung)*. The Federal Republic's political economy employed a conflict-regulating mechanism that defused arguments and fostered cooperation.

This is not to say that West Germany remained immune to serious political disagreements and discord. Perhaps in no other advanced capitalist country did the forces advocating industrial accommodation, parliamentary politics, and economic growth clash as severely and as consistently with the proponents of "postmaterial" politics as in the Federal Republic. Nowhere has the political legacy and intellectual relevance of the student rebellion of the late 1960s remained as vibrant as in the FRG, where it spawned the most successful institutionalization of "new" politics in the form of the Green Party and movement.

In contrast to most other industrial societies where in retrospect the ferment of 1968 produced little more than transitory fads, the date represents the most conspicuous political turning point in the Federal Republic's existence. Following the FRG's first two decades in which the mechanisms of political accommodation were successfully institutionalized, a new generation of baby boomers, taking the material abundance of their environment as a given rather than as a virtue, initiated a fundamental challenge to *"Modell Deutschland."* Criticizing the silence of their parents concerning their involvement in Germany's national socialist past, the students and their allies dismissed the Federal Republic's manifest achievements as window dressing in a morally bankrupt society. For the "sixty-eighters," material comfort meant little without moral self-evaluation, economic growth seemed downright dangerous because it inevitably entailed the destruction of the environment, and parliamentarism was nothing but a veneer devoid of real (i.e., participatory) *democracy because it meant rule by *elites, committees, and—worst of all—bureaucracies.

Although the sixty-eighters were obviously no match for the large consensual base of the West German establishment, they became ensconced in an "alternative milieu" that changed the dominant *political culture in the Federal Republic throughout the 1970s and 1980s. Issues related to peace, disarmament, the environment, nuclear energy, women's rights, North-South relations, human empowerment, and the homeless entered the discourse of West German politics. Indeed, their acceptance is best characterized by their being co-opted by the established parties.

Ultimately, 1968 and its legacy rendered the Federal Republic a more democratic country. Formerly accepted authoritarian structures became a bit less authoritarian, opposition was not immediately associated with irreverence, and the citizen and civil society, *not* the state, assumed, perhaps for the first time in German history, definite pride of place. Never was this democratizing influence more obvious than through a direct comparison between West and East Germany, made possible by the fall of the Berlin Wall in November 1989. If there was one thing that the GDR clearly lacked vis-à-vis the Federal Republic, it was a democratic culture that, through a healthy synthesis of the founding generation's affirmative posture and its subsequent critique on the part of the sixty-eighters, had developed into a commonplace in West Germany.

The *annus mirabilis* of 1989 was miraculous not least because it witnessed Germany's political unification "from below." For the first time in German history, the German people took matters into their own hands and completed a successful revolution against illegitimate and despised authority. Adding to their accomplishment is the fact that they performed this revolution without any serious violence. This successful revolution from below could never have happened had liberal democracy as a governing system not become completely entrenched and accepted in the Federal Republic. There can be no doubt that liberal democracy will be put to severe tests in the new Germany's political future. Yet, precisely because the new Germany is merely an extension of the old Federal Republic, there also can be little doubt that liberal democracy will prove successful as a legitimate and effective political arrangement in unified Germany.

(See also GERMAN REUNIFICATION; GREEN PARTIES; MAY 1968; NINETEEN EIGHTY-NINE; SOCIAL MARKET ECONOMY.)

Andrei S. Markovits, *The Politics of the West German Trade Unions: Strategies of Class and Interest Representation in Growth and Crisis* (Cambridge, U.K., 1986). Peter J. Katzenstein, *Policy and Politics in West Germany: The Growth of a Semisovereign State* (Philadelphia, 1987). Russell J. Dalton, *Politics in West Germany* (Glenview, Ill., 1989). M. Donald Hancock, *West Germany: The Politics of Democratic Corporatism* (Chatham, N.J., 1989).

ANDREI S. MARKOVITS

GHANA. Although its relatively small size (238,536 sq. km., or 92,099 sq. mi.) has belied its role in African political development over the last ninety years, Ghana was in the forefront of the anticolonial struggle. In the postcolonial era, Ghana has gone from being a bastion against neocolonialism to becoming a showpiece for international finance.

The First Republic (1957–1966) was notable for two reasons. First, it had a decidedly Pan-Africanist and anticolonial posture. Ghana under Kwame *Nkrumah was placed at the service of nationalists and liberation movements, and it became the refuge for people of African descent.

Second, it made attempts at economic *development financed by local reserves, building a credible social and economic infrastructural base. Unfortunately, the regime was limited in its ability to sustain genuine development, becoming heavily dependent on external sources. Even as it proclaimed a socialist state in 1960, it was relying on these sources for half of its development funds. *Socialism implied a determining role for the state: ninety percent of total public revenues was invested in newly created state enterprises whose direct beneficiaries were an alliance of party activists, businesspeople, and bureaucrats. Investment in the public good resulted in a culture in which public service became an opportunity for wealth accumulation.

No other regime, with the possible exception of the present one, has come close to matching the potential and promise of the Nkrumah era. In 1966, the National Liberation Council (NLC), an army-police alliance, overthrew Nkrumah. It opened up the economy to vigorous external influence. The predominant role of the state was curtailed through the sale of public enterprises to foreign and local private concerns.

The NLC installed a new civilian government in 1969 after organizing an election significant for its prohibition of ideas and people associated with Nkrumah and his party, the Convention People's Party (CPP). This government, headed by Prime Minister Kofi Busia, followed the policies of the NLC, especially in its efforts to stop a mounting external debt. To do this, the regime found itself implementing policies largely dictated from external sources. In its *foreign policy, it adopted a policy of dialogue with *apartheid South Africa that alienated supporters at home and abroad. Unable to deal with balance of payment problems, high unemployment, labor disputes, high prices of goods, and low export prices, the regime succumbed to the armed forces in 1972.

Since its foray into active politics, the Ghanaian military has become highly politicized and protective of its corporate interests. Indeed, since 1972, it has remained the prime mover behind state power. Its 10,600 members (9,000 army, 800 navy, and 800 air force) enjoy generous government expenditure, ranked fifth behind education, public services, economic services, and health.

During its rule between 1972 and 1979, under General I. K. Acheampong (1931–1979), the military reached its nadir, mismanaging the economy and alienating almost all segments of the society. In this sense it had performed much like its predecessors. Not by accident, the lower ranks and junior officers took steps to "discipline" their superior officers, assuming state power in 1979 and again in 1981. In the interim, a civilian government headed by Dr. H. Limann (b. 1934) also succeeded in incurring the wrath of Ghanaians with its inability to govern.

Perhaps the most significant point regarding the military was its ability to spawn a quasi-revolution, both within its ranks and among Ghanaians—a populist uprising that has had revolutionary tendencies. The Provisional National Defense Council (PNDC) assumed power in December 1981 under Flight Lieutenant Jerry John Rawlings (b. 1947). For most of the 1980s, the government attempted to create conditions for necessary changes in the economy. Initially, the Rawlings government was populist, open, and determined to demystify government and politics—indeed, it had as members two military men (a junior officer and a noncommissioned officer), a priest, a factory worker, and a university student. It encouraged people and workers to organize themselves and held the view that achieving economic progress entailed a policy of self-reliance and national control of resources.

Initiating change while seeking a semblance of socioeconomic sanity has proved to be a daunting task. First, the PNDC has had to face the real problem of managing a neocolonial, dependent economy. Second, it has had to face divisions within its ranks and serious opposition from entrenched local and external interests. Third, between 1982 and 1984 Ghana experienced a prolonged, severe drought and extensive bush fires that at times wiped out large quantities of food and export produce.

In 1983, the PNDC reached an agreement with the international financial community on an Economic Recovery Program (ERP). Since then there have been some upward signs of improvement: positive growth rates and a decent effort at reducing a burdensome external debt. By far the severest impact of the ERP has been on the majority of Ghanaians: declining wages, less food, deteriorating health care, fewer jobs, more expensive goods, and increasing privatization of the economy. Aware of the need to cushion the impact, the PNDC has pressed its financiers to provide funds to alleviate the social and political costs of the ERP.

As the longest-serving regime since Nkrumah's, the PNDC clearly intends to tough it out. Against the odds (no ERP-type strategy has been known to succeed anywhere), it is rallying Ghanaians around new efforts toward a politically open and participatory society and effective management: better tax collection, improved fiscal management, lower deficits, and low inflation.

K. B. Dickson, *A Historical Geography of Ghana* (Cambridge, U.K., 1969). Geoffrey Kay, ed., *The Political Economy of Colonialism in Ghana: A Collection of Documents and Statistics, 1900–1960* (Cambridge, U.K., 1972). Adu Boahen, *Ghana: Evolution and Change in the Nineteenth and Twentieth Centuries* (London, 1975). Rhoda Howard, *Colonialism and Underdevelopment in Ghana* (New York, 1978). M. M. Hug, *The Economy of Ghana: The First 25 Years Since Independence* (London, 1988).

AKWASI P. OSEI

GLASNOST. See GORBACHEV, MIKHAIL; PERESTROIKA; SOVIET UNION.

GOLD STANDARD. More a myth than a working monetary system for the international economy, the gold standard has to be understood as a declaration of faith in an ideal world rather than an accurate description of monetary relations between states before World War I. For two centuries, most liberal economists have advocated the adoption of some system that would provide stable money for the world market economy. Most of them have extolled the virtues of the gold standard as the theoretical model for such a system. Its supposed automaticity, divorcing monetary management from political interference by governments, and thus depoliticizing economic policy-making, was what has always particularly recommended it to them.

The key features of a gold standard system were, first, that the central banks of countries considered to be party to the system were pledged freely to buy and sell gold (and only gold) at a fixed price in terms of the home currency; and second, that private residents in such countries were legally entitled to possess gold and to export and import it freely. Fixed exchange rates resulted from the use of gold as the common *numéraire* of international transactions, in which the prices of different national currencies were expressed. Differences that might develop from time to time in the market values of these currencies, reflecting for example unequal rates of inflation, would result in—and be automatically corrected by—either inflows or outflows of gold. Adjustment was supposed to work by the impact of such gold flows on the monetary base of the country, either expanding or contracting the money supply and thus influencing the general price level. It was a system, in short, that (if theory were applied in practice) would allow the general preference for national political autonomy for the *state to be reconciled with the preference of ruling classes of the industrial countries for an open, efficient market economy aided by a minimum degree of monetary stability.

In practice, an approximation to such a system only prevailed from the 1870s to the outbreak of war in 1914. (Some would argue for an even shorter heyday, of two decades from the early 1890s—only slightly longer than the duration of the working Bretton Woods system, from 1958 to 1971.) Even then, for good political reasons and to preserve the coherence of civil society and the stability of the state, governments resisted the deflationary imperatives of adjustment under the gold standard. Especially in later years, they used their reserves of foreign exchange to finance deficits, prudently conserving gold as the ultimate war chest for national security in an increasingly unstable political system.

Moreover, the vaunted stability of this golden age of international monetary relations rested on, first, the relatively immobile real value of gold as compared with silver; and second, on the stability of the value of the British pound sterling in terms of gold from 1817 to 1914. This stability, in turn, was maintained thanks to a British statute—the Bank Charter Act of 1844—that limited severely the power of government to expand the money supply and thus to finance deficit spending. The system also may be said to have rested on a third factor, the

involuntary compliance of peripheral developing countries, who needed the capital provided by the core, with its uneven availability and price—a kind of dependence also experienced by indebted developing countries in the 1980s.

(See also FINANCE, INTERNATIONAL; INTERDEPENDENCE; INTERNATIONAL POLITICAL ECONOMY.)

R. Triffin, *The Evolution of the International Monetary System* (Princeton, N.J., 1964). B. J. Cohen, *Organizing the World's Money: The Political Economy and International Monetary Relations* (London, 1978). M. De Cecco, *Money and Empire* (Oxford, 1982; reprint London, 1987).

SUSAN STRANGE

GONZÁLEZ, Felipe. Born in Seville in 1942, Felipe González was a little-known provincial labor lawyer when elected in 1974, at the age of thirty-two, to the leadership of the Partido Socialista Obrero Español (PSOE). He headed a new executive, replacing an old guard that had left the exiled party in a critical state: internally divided and overshadowed in the clandestine opposition to the *Franco dictatorship by the more dynamic and better-organized Partido Comunista de España. Fifteen years later, González led his party to a third consecutive general election victory. He has been prime minister of *Spain since 1982.

His achievement can be divided into two phases. The first entailed the molding of the PSOE into a modern mass-based party. The party's radicalism was diluted, culminating in the jettisoning of its formal adherence to *Marxism in a tense 1979 battle. This consolidated the dominance of González and his team within the party, now projected in his image as youthful, open, and forward-looking rather than rooted in Spain's divisive recent history.

The second phase covers the period in office. The successful overhaul of the PSOE was confirmed by a landslide victory in the 1982 election, when the new government was confronted with a critical political situation—there had been an attempted military coup in 1981—and with sharply rising inflation and unemployment. Once in power, González remained pragmatic. Social *reform was subordinated to a policy of economic austerity and industrial renewal. *Democracy was to be confirmed by Spain's integration into Western Europe. In 1986 Spain joined the *European Community, and continued membership in NATO was confirmed by referendum. This fulfilled a promise made during the PSOE's strong criticism of Spain's entry in 1981. Now the PSOE government placed its resources and status behind a vote in favor of Spain's continued presence, which was narrowly achieved in defiance of poll predictions.

This enhanced González's prestige with other European leaders and his domestic status, contributing to a convincing second election victory in the same year. The second administration pursued a similar economic policy to the first, but against a background of an increasingly discontented work force, which bore the brunt of its cost. Criticism emerged from within the party, and especially from the traditionally loyal socialist trade union, culminating in massive support for a twenty-four-hour general strike in December 1988. Since then, González and his government have been criticized for being isolated in government, detached from the grass roots of the PSOE and the mass of the population. Nevertheless, in 1989 a third, though less convincing, election victory was obtained.

González's significance should be judged in its Spanish context. The consolidation of democracy and the renewal of the economy were responses to problems inherited from and exaggerated by the Franco dictatorship. Equally, González's transformation of the PSOE consisted in aligning the party with contemporary European *socialism and social democracy rather than in any original ideological contribution.

By combining a charismatic personality with the construction of a powerful political machine, González has gained the most incontrovertible political reward bestowed by a democracy—longevity. For Spain this has represented stability, *modernization, and an enhanced role in a changing Europe.

John Hooper, *The Spaniards: A Portrait of the New Spain* (London, 1986). Paul Preston, *The Triumph of Democracy in Spain* (London, 1986).

JOHN MAHER

GORBACHEV, Mikhail. The leader of the Soviet Union from 11 March 1985 until 25 December 1991 and the initiator of the most far-reaching *reforms in Soviet history, Mikhail Sergeevich Gorbachev was born into a peasant family in the village of Privolnoe in the Stavropol region of southern Russia on 2 March 1931. He had to combine work in the fields with study at school during and after World War II; it was the award of the Order of Red Banner of Labor for his achievements as an agricultural worker in 1949, together with scholastic success, that made possible his admission to the Law Faculty of Moscow University in 1950.

Gorbachev made the most of this unusual opportunity for a boy from a peasant family. He was active in the Law Faculty Komsomol organization and he graduated with distinction in 1955. It was at the university in 1951 that he met his wife, Raisa Maksimovna Titorenko, a student in the Philosophical Faculty; they were married in 1953.

Having obtained a law degree, Gorbachev returned to his native Stavropol region and embarked on a political career, first in the Komsomol apparatus and later as a Communist Party official. (He had joined the party in 1952, the year before *Stalin's death.) By 1966—just four years after moving from the Komsomol apparatus to the party organization—Gorbachev was party first secretary in the city of Stavropol, and by 1970 he had become the first secretary of the regional party committee *(kraikom)*, a post which led to entry to the Central Committee of the *Communist Party of the Soviet Union (CPSU) in 1971.

Gorbachev, who had added a degree in agriculture from the Stavropol Agricultural Institute in 1967 to his 1955 Moscow law degree, was in charge of one of Russia's most important grain-growing areas and, as such, maintained his links with a former first secretary of that region, Fedor Kulakov, who had helped to advance Gorbachev's early career, and who was the secretary responsible for agriculture within the party leadership in Moscow. It was, however, Kulakov's sudden death in 1978 that led to Gorbachev's being brought to Moscow to join the Soviet leadership and to take over agricultural administration. By 1980 Gorbachev was a full member of the Politburo as well as a secretary of the Central Committee, a combination of posts which made him a potentially powerful figure, although as long as Leonid Brezhnev was alive and his conservative Communist entourage remained in control, Gorbachev's opportunities were limited.

Gorbachev supported Yury Andropov as successor to Brezhnev in 1982, and during Andropov's leadership Gorbachev's responsibilities were widened. However, the backlash against Andropov's disciplinarian and anticorruption crackdown and tentative placing of economic reform on the political agenda led the Politburo selectorate on Andropov's death to opt for a return to a safer and more predictable leadership style, choosing Brezhnev's ally of long standing, Konstantin Chernenko, in preference to his younger and much better qualified rival, Mikhail Gorbachev.

Chernenko's death in March 1985, only thirteen months after he succeeded Andropov, meant that Gorbachev's wait was over, and just a week after his fifty-fourth birthday he became general secretary of the Central Committee of the Soviet Communist Party and leader of his country. Although the choice of Gorbachev was anathema to some of the old guard, thanks partly to the support of Andrei Gromyko his nomination got through the Politburo and was endorsed by the Central Committee within twenty-four hours of Chernenko's death.

What followed was one of the most dramatic periods of change in Russian as well as Soviet history, culminating in the demise of the Communist system and the disintegration of the Soviet state. There is still debate on how far Gorbachev wished to go in changing the Soviet Union and the character of its relations with other countries, but there can be no doubt that it was he, above all, who put radical political and economic reform on the Soviet agenda. His intentions were signaled by his political appointments. By promoting Eduard Shevardnadze to full membership of the Politburo and appointing him foreign minister in succession to Gromyko in the summer of 1985 and by bringing Aleksandr

Yakovlev into the Secretariat of the Central Committee and the Politburo, Gorbachev demonstrated his own readiness to embrace what became known as *novoe politicheskoe myshlenie* ("new political thinking") on both foreign and domestic policy. It was, accordingly, worrying for radical reformers when Yakovlev lost his positions of power in 1990 and when in December of that year Shevardnadze resigned his post as foreign minister.

In the meantime Gorbachev's international diplomacy had earned him the Nobel Peace Prize in 1990 after relations with the United States and Western Europe had been put on a new, cooperative footing, and the Soviet Union had accepted the political autonomy of the countries of Eastern and Central Europe (most of which ceased to be Communist states during 1989 and 1990) and had agreed to the unification of Germany within the North Atlantic Treaty Organization (NATO) and the European Community (EC). Whereas Gorbachev had hoped initially to see reformed Communist regimes in East Europe, he made the crucial decision to abandon the "Brezhnev doctrine" and accept free elections, which, in turn, meant accepting noncommunist systems in what had formerly been called "the Soviet bloc."

Domestically, there was also a contrast between Gorbachev's reform initiatives—which were remarkably bold in the Soviet context—and some of their unintended consequences. The latter included interethnic violence, large-scale independence movements in almost half of the Soviet Union's fifteen republics, and the threat of the breakup of the multinational Soviet state (which became a reality in the aftermath of the failed coup of August 1991).

Soon after he became general secretary, Gorbachev began the process of replacing conservative Communists in the leadership and of promoting both political and economic reform. His personal telephone call in December 1986 to Andrei Sakharov, who had been exiled to the provincial city of Gorky (now restored to its old name of Nizhny Novgorod) by the Brezhnev leadership in 1980, symbolized a new willingness to tolerate the expression of dissident opinions and was doubtless intended to make a positive impact both on the Soviet intelligentsia and the West. Gorbachev's policy of glasnost led to the gradual publication of numerous books previously taboo, including some—such as Solzhenitsyn's *Gulag Archipelago* and Orwell's *Nineteen Eighty-Four* and *Animal Farm*—which called into question the foundations of the Soviet system.

The term *perestroika,* which Gorbachev had introduced at the outset of his general secretaryship, came to signify the comprehensive reform of the Soviet political and economic system. Radical reform was placed on the political agenda by Gorbachev at important Central Committee meetings in January and June 1987 and at the Nineteenth Conference of the Communist Party in 1988. In 1989 competitive elections for a new Soviet legislature—the Congress of People's Deputies of the USSR (which elected an inner body, the Supreme Soviet)—took place, and this representative assembly became one in which criticism could be voiced and the executive could no longer rely on getting its every proposal accepted.

Gorbachev was a proponent of competitive elections, but initially he aimed at a one-party *pluralism in which electoral choice would be linked to democratization of the Communist Party and the legitimation of different opinion groupings and regional interests within it. It was only in early 1990 that he publicly accepted the need to legalize the creation of other political parties and to take the reference to the "leading role" of the Communist Party out of Article 6 of the Soviet Constitution. When elections took place in the various Soviet republics in 1990, several of them produced non-Communist majorities. Most embarrassing initially for Gorbachev was the choice of Boris *Yeltsin in May 1990 as chairman of the Supreme Soviet of the Russian Republic. Yeltsin, who left the Communist Party in July of the same year, had become a more popular politician within *Russia than Gorbachev himself, whose domestic prestige was by this time significantly lower than his international standing.

Faced by mounting problems, Gorbachev attempted in 1990 to increase his personal power not within the Communist Party, whose institutions (including that of the Politburo) he downgraded, but in a new state presidency. In March 1990 he became the Soviet Union's first *president* and later in the year acquired the power to rule by decree. Those reformers who supported these moves hoped that Gorbachev would now be able to take more resolute steps toward the introduction of a market economy, which he had embraced in principle but which was extraordinarily difficult to introduce in practice in a society lacking experience of markets and the most basic market institutions. Gorbachev was criticized, however, both by those who feared a return to capitalism and by those who felt that he was moving too slowly with economic reform. He was caught similarly in cross fire between those who complained about growing disorder and anarchy within Soviet society and others who argued that he was leading their country back to dictatorship.

After a period of half a year during the winter of 1990–1991 in which he made significant concessions to those who were pressing for a more conservative approach to the Soviet Union's economic and interethnic problems, Gorbachev established a new modus vivendi with the more radical proponents of change, including those from a majority of the Soviet republics, when he initiated a series of "nine-plus-one" meetings in April 1991. This involved an effort to agree on a new union treaty with the nine republics willing to remain in a renewed and decentralized Soviet federation. Over the next few months he took steps also to mend fences with Yeltsin, who had acquired substantially increased power and authority through his election as president of the Russian Republic in June 1991. By this time Gorbachev could speak for the Soviet Union only after a prior process of negotiation and accommodation with the leaders of the major Soviet republics.

The draft Union Treaty which emerged from the protracted negotiations between Gorbachev and a majority of republican leaders, including Yeltsin, not only devolved a great deal of federal power to the republics (renamed "states" in what was intended to become a Union of Sovereign States) but came close to creating a confederation. It was, above all, to pre-empt this further diminution of central power that the leaders of the Soviet army, government, KGB, Ministry of Interior, and military industry joined forces in an attempted coup which began on 18 August 1991 when Gorbachev was put under house arrest in his holiday home on the Crimean coast. The coup was over by the evening of 21 August. Widespread resistance in Moscow, led by Boris Yeltsin in the Russian White House, played a crucial part in the defeat of the putschists, but every bit as important was the refusal of Gorbachev to have any truck with the coup leaders. Deprived of a constitutional fig-leaf to cover their seizure of power, the putschists were soon to learn that the years of perestroika and glasnost had made Russia a different country from what it had been before, one in which a sufficient number of people were prepared to come on to the streets to defend their recently won liberties.

For Gorbachev the coup was the beginning of the end of the main part of his political career. Insofar as it accelerated the break-up of the Soviet Union (for, in their ineptitude, the plotters had promoted that which they had aimed to prevent), it called into question the office of President of the Soviet Union. Gorbachev, weakened by the fact that he had himself appointed the senior politicians and officials who in August 1991 betrayed him, strove to preserve a renewed union and warned of the dangers ahead if the Soviet Union split into fifteen separate states (with the prospect of further interethnic conflict and fissiparous movements to follow). Nevertheless, a Ukrainian referendum vote for independence on 1 December 1991 was followed by a meeting on 8 December of the presidents of Russia, Ukraine, and Belarus at which they declared that the Soviet Union was "ceasing its existence" and at which they announced they would be establishing a *Commonwealth of Independent States. On 25 December 1991 Gorbachev made a televised speech, announcing his resignation as President of the Soviet Union, and on the same day he handed over his functions as commander-in-chief of the armed forces (and control over the use of nuclear weapons) to Boris Yeltsin.

By the end of the month, the Soviet Union had formally ceased to exist.

In the perspective of Russian and Soviet history, Gorbachev must be counted a great reformer. The system he inherited, however, required comprehensive transformation rather than mere reform. Gorbachev increasingly recognized this, but he had to take account of powerful conservative interests as well as of radical centrifugal tendencies. Moreover, the dual challenge of democratization and marketization in the face of growing and competing nationalisms and of "left"–"right" ideological polarization made the task of a transition leader in the Soviet Union far more daunting than in any other European country. Given the national tensions that had been suppressed for so long within the Soviet state, it is far from clear that any other leader could have accomplished the enormously difficult task of making liberalization of the system compatible with preservation of the union. Domestically, for better or worse (and mostly for better), Gorbachev's impact on Russian history has been immense. Internationally, he did more than anyone else to end the Cold War by allowing the East European states to regain their national independence and by breaking with much of Soviet traditional foreign policy. In retirement Gorbachev has continued to make pronouncements on policy issues, and, although the odds must be against his holding high office again in Russia, he himself has not ruled out all possibility of a political comeback.

(See also COMMUNIST PARTY STATES; SOVIET–EAST EUROPEAN RELATIONS; SOVIET FOREIGN POLICY.)

Dusko Doder and Louise Branson, *Gorbachev: Heretic in the Kremlin* (New York, 1990). Stephen White, *Gorbachev and After* (Cambridge, UK, 1991). Archie Brown, *The Gorbachev Factor in Soviet Politics* (Oxford, 1993).

ARCHIE BROWN

GRAMSCI, Antonio. Although born in 1891 into the family of a seamstress and a minor Sardinian civil servant on the periphery of Italian society, by 1924 Antonio Gramsci had moved to the center of Italian political life as a leader of the Communist Party and of the democratic opposition to *fascism. Jailed in 1926 by *Mussolini's government, Gramsci spent ten years in prison and died in 1937, soon after his release; but his writings throughout that decade, collected as the *Prison Notebooks,* assured that his influence on Italian, European, and world politics would continue to grow. In them Gramsci developed an original and nuanced Marxist theory of society and political change that has had significant impact on political practice and on both Marxist and non-Marxist scholarship.

Gramsci's turn toward an intellectual life was influenced by a crippling accident he suffered as boy. Scholarly accomplishments allowed him to escape a backward rural society that persecuted him as a hunchback. Yet, Gramsci always defended the interests of the rural masses along with those of industrial workers. He became a socialist journalist soon after entering the university in Turin in 1911. Turin was then the Italian hub of the second industrial revolution, a center of assembly line, mass production industries. Throughout the period of Italian labor militancy that lasted through World War I, Gramsci championed the spontaneous factory council movement, fearing however that the councils' insufficient political realism and their disunity would make them ultimately ineffectual.

Gramsci was impressed by the success of the *Communist Party of the Soviet Union and, in 1921, helped found its Italian counterpart. He worked for the Comintern in Moscow for two years, until May of 1924, when he returned to Italy as a leader of the parliamentary opposition to the Fascist government. Mussolini signaled the end of his toleration of that opposition two years later when, ignoring parliamentary immunity, he had Gramsci and other Communist leaders arrested.

Despite the privations of prison, Gramsci was able to keep his mind active. He received books from the Cambridge economist Piero Sraffa, and the two corresponded—albeit obliquely and somewhat haphazardly—through Gramsci's sister-in-law. Gramsci, like Sraffa (who worked with the Cambridge Keynesians and who never treated *Marx's economics as dogma), was an open-minded and creative thinker. Gramsci's prison writings reevaluated the social "superstructure"—politics, law, culture, religion, art, and science—that had been given little systematic attention in contemporary Marxist theorizing owing to its focus on the determining role of the "economic base." Using a similar architectural metaphor, Gramsci emphasized the importance of the superstructures. He suggested that they were like a building's walls, windows, doors, and staircases, built upon the economic base and forming with it a "historical bloc," which had to be understood in its entirety.

Gramsci saw the political activity of different social classes as directed toward establishing, maintaining, or undermining particular historical blocs. The establishment and maintenance of a historical bloc represents the "supremacy" of a *class, which involves both force and consent. Opposing social forces must be dominated, but supremacy cannot be achieved without "*hegemony," noncoercive leadership over a coalition of allied social forces. To establish hegemony a class must sacrifice some of its narrow, often purely material goods in order to serve some of its allies' interests.

Gramsci understood hegemony as being established within "civil society," by which he meant the realm of voluntary social action, the realm in which collective identities are formed. In societies with effective parliamentary systems, where the realm of civil society is extensive, Gramsci saw the role of

the socialist movement as waging a "war of position," unifying social forces that could oppose *capitalism (thus forestalling the divide-and-conquer tactics of the capitalists) and disputing mystifications offered to suggest a unity of interests between capitalists and the masses. Gramsci saw communist parties in advanced capitalist societies as contributing to the general political role played by progressive "intellectuals" at any time of social change. Intellectuals help form collective identities; they help overcome the limits of our "common sense," our everyday beliefs. Gramsci argued that the usual problem with the common sense of the masses is not a "false consciousness," or a deep belief in the mystifications that promote an exploitative society, but a "contradictory consciousness," an incoherent mix of beliefs, that contains the germ of the coherent, self-reflective "good sense" that should guide a socialist and democratic society.

Gramsci's ideas influenced the Eurocommunist movement in Western Europe after World War II. They also have had an impact on activists in the *Third World, especially when they have tried to define the proper role for progressive, often Westernized intellectuals in the movements against colonialism and neocolonialism.

Gramsci's work has also had an impact on more academic studies of society. In sociology, in some parts of the world, he has joined the canon of masters that includes Marx and *Weber. His theories have guided studies of the historical sociology of individual *states, the role of culture in social change, and the role of the peasantry in industrial societies, among other topics. Recently Gramsci's political theory has had a significant impact on the study of *international relations, primarily because his central concepts focus on a process of statecraft and do not require scholars to treat all juridical nation-states as fundamentally similar. For example, Gramsci's theory allows us to consider *decolonization and the extension of legal sovereignty as a control structure, a means of maintaining the hegemony of the ruling classes in the advanced industrialized states.

(See also EUROCOMMUNISM; MARXISM; PEASANTS; SOCIALISM AND SOCIAL DEMOCRACY.)

Anne Showstack Sassoon, ed., *Approaches to Gramsci* (London, 1982). David Forgacs, ed., *An Antonio Gramsci Reader: Selected Writings, 1916–1935* (London, 1988).
CRAIG N. MURPHY

GREAT BRITAIN. See BRITAIN.

GREAT SOCIETY. The Great Society is the name that President Lyndon Baines *Johnson gave to the outpouring of social and economic policies enacted in the United States during the 1960s. New initiatives increased the federal government's role in the domains of health care for the poor and elderly, education, and low-income housing. These policies were complemented by Keynesian macroeconomic management to promote full employment; civil rights measures to ensure equal opportunity for *African Americans; and a highly visible "War on Poverty," which sought to end poverty in the United States.

The Great Society represented a completion of many initiatives first contemplated in the 1930s during the *New Deal. With it, the U.S. federal government took a role in promoting the social welfare of its citizens akin to that assumed by many European nations immediately after World War II. However, the Great Society featured distinctly American approaches to social policy and remained less far-reaching than most European *welfare states. The programs inaugurated during the Great Society sought to promote equal opportunity rather than to redistribute income or to guarantee social rights.

A variety of economic, political, and social factors created a favorable environment for social *reform in the 1960s. Postwar growth had boosted the U.S. economy, but "pockets of poverty" continued to exist in areas left behind by industrial transformation. Some groups were more economically vulnerable than others: the elderly and African Americans had particularly high rates of poverty as the United States entered the 1960s. Although the decade began with a sluggish economy, by the mid-1960s, unprecedented prosperity allowed the federal government to increase spending on social programs without raising taxes. As James T. Patterson (*America's Struggle Against Poverty, 1900–1980,* Cambridge, Mass., 1981) has noted, this secure economic climate took the sting out of increased public spending; social reform could be accomplished without redistributing wealth.

Politics, too, moved in directions favorable to social reform in the 1960s. Since the 1950s, congressional Democrats had been pressing for action on a range of social policy issues including education, health care, and unemployment. And, after a decade of struggle, the southern *civil rights movement succeeded in drawing national attention to the exclusion of African Americans from the economic prosperity and political rights enjoyed by the majority of whites.

The shock of President John F. *Kennedy's *assassination in 1963 finally jolted Congress into action. The unfulfilled promise of the Kennedy administration, which had vowed to get the country "moving again," provided renewed impetus for reformers. When combined with President Johnson's considerable legislative skill, these circumstances made Congress more amenable to social legislation than it had been in several decades. This predilection to increase the federal role in ensuring social welfare was strongly reinforced in 1964, when Americans elected the most liberal Congress since 1936.

Many of the Great Society programs had been on the nation's agenda for decades. The Medicaid and Medicare programs, which established health insurance for the poor and the elderly respectively, represented a compromise that established a federal role in ensuring the nation's health but fell short of the national health insurance proposed since the 1930s. The panoply of low-income housing programs enacted in the late 1960s and the establishment of a Department of Housing and Urban Development in 1965 extended federal activity in the field of housing beyond the small public housing programs authorized in the 1930s. The Keynesian tax cut enacted in 1964, which aimed to stimulate the economy and reduce unemployment, represented the triumph of an economic strategy first tried in 1938.

Other initiatives reflected concerns that had grown during the 1950s. Support for federal aid to education, traditionally the province of states and localities, mounted as localities struggled to accommodate the explosive demands on public education created by the postwar baby boom and as concern about the different capacities of local governments grew. Although federal aid to education actually increased by very little during the 1960s, the acknowledgment of a federal role in funding public education represented a new departure. A second new area of federal activism was civil rights. In 1964, the Civil Rights Act outlawed discrimination in public facilities, ending over a half century of legally sanctioned racial segregation in the South. The Voting Rights Act passed a year later sought to ensure black political rights and laid the foundation for the conquest of political power by a generation of black politicians in the following decade.

The newest and most visible element of the Great Society was the War on Poverty. Although many of the components of the attack on poverty were not new, the effort to package them into a concerted effort to end poverty was novel. The charter legislation for the War on Poverty, the Economic Opportunity Act of 1964, created programs for youth job training, public service employment for youth, a volunteer national services corps, and a new Office of Equal Opportunity, operating out of the Executive Office of the President. The most innovative aspect of the War on Poverty were community action agencies, which were established in localities across the country to administer the new programs with the "maximum feasible participation" of the poor. In creating these agencies, the federal government bypassed state and city government to establish the first direct relationship between community groups and the federal government.

Despite its flamboyant rhetoric, the War on Poverty did not commit the federal government to major spending to reduce poverty; its greatest gains were in promoting black political empowerment. Although the War on Poverty was officially race-neutral, in practice it focused on urban minorities. Local black communities seized on community action programs to challenge the exclusionary practices of local governments and service bureaucracies. As black riots spread across urban America in the 1960s, the federal government used community action agencies to funnel resources into these troubled communities.

The social reform launched by the Great Society lost its momentum in the late 1960s as spending on the *Vietnam War limited funds for domestic social purposes. Equally important was dwindling support for the War on Poverty in the wake of urban rioting. Although federal social spending would rise under the Nixon administration, the emphasis on federal activity and the focus on the poor that characterized the War on Poverty diminished in the 1970s. And, as inflation and unemployment grew in the 1970s, confidence that government could solve economic and social problems declined.

The Great Society left an uneven institutional legacy. Some of the policy innovations of the 1960s have survived over a decade of conservative administrations: the federal government continues to help finance health care for the poor and elderly and provides modest aid to education. Many of the neighborhood community organizations created by the community action programs still deliver social services to poor neighborhoods. Some of the programs pioneered in the War on Poverty, including early childhood education provided by Head Start, have survived attempts to eliminate them. But the programs that have survived, particularly those aimed at the poor, are poorly funded and struggle for resources. Other policy innovations, including most of the job training and employment efforts of the Great Society, have been abandoned altogether.

The intellectual and policy legacy of the Great Society remains hotly contested. Liberal supporters point to successes in reducing poverty levels and call for extensions of many programs including health care, job training, and education. Critics from the Left blame the limited focus of the Great Society for its failure to sustain political support and call for broader policies that can appeal to both the middle class and the poor. Conservatives, by contrast, argue that the social policies of the 1960s distorted the work incentives of the poor and are consequently responsible for the growth of an urban *underclass dependent on government subsidies.

The central vision of the Great Society, that federal government should provide equal opportunity for all citizens, unraveled as funds grew tight and new policies proved unable to sustain public support. But, because of its bold ambitions, the Great Society will continue to provide the touchstone for future debates about social policy in the United States.

(See also KEYNESIANISM; POLITICAL PARTICIPATION.)

Henry J. Aaron, *Politics and the Professors: The Great Society in Perspective* (Washington, D.C., 1978). James T. Patterson, *America's Struggle Against Poverty, 1900–1980* (Cambridge, Mass., 1981). Allen J. Matusow, *The Unraveling of America: A History of Liberalism in the 1960s* (New York, 1984).

MARGARET WEIR

GREECE. In 1829 Greece became an independent, sovereign state after a seven-year nationalist war to gain independence from Ottoman rule. But is sovereignty was limited. Three "protecting powers"—Britain, France, and Russia—imposed a foreign absolute monarchy and restricted Greece's autonomy. Furthermore, the boundaries of the new state excluded areas populated by "Greeks," such as Thessaly, northern Greece, and most Ionian and Aegean islands. Consequently, for nearly a century Greece pursued an irredentist *foreign policy—the Megali Idea—only renouncing it in 1923, when Greek troops suffered defeat in Asia Minor at the hands of Kemal *Atatürk's forces. The current boundaries of Greece—from Crete to the southern tip of the Balkan peninsula to Macedonia, along with the majority of the Aegean, Dodecanese, and Ionian islands—were finalized at the end of World War II with the addition of the island of Rhodes. Its population has increased from approximately 750,000 in 1830 to 10 million at present, largely owing to territorial expansion and partly to the refugee influx from Asia Minor after the 1920s population exchange with *Turkey.

Although ancient Greece was seen by the West as the cradle of *democracy, its subsequent historical experience was the spiritual religiosity of Byzantium followed by incorporation into the Ottoman Empire. Greek society was not influenced by the Enlightenment and the socioeconomic transformations in the West during the seventeenth and eighteenth centuries, except for a few intellectuals and a merchant class living outside the new Greek state. As a consequence of its historical legacy, its traditional culture, and the imposition of a foreign authoritarian regime at the time of independence, the foundations of liberalism and democracy in modern Greece have been shaky. Military intervention and military coups, *authoritarianism, and dependence on a foreign patron have punctuated its history. The underlying principles of a liberal democratic polity, individual *rights and liberties, have not been integral to its *political culture. The state has been perceived as the communal, organic embodiment of the Greek nation. Even in periods of democratic regimes, severe restrictions have existed on the exercise of rights. In fact, rights are not seen as inherent or inalienable but as grants given by the state.

Prior to World War II Greece was ruled by the dictator Ioannis Metaxas (1936–1940) who modeled his reign on European *fascism. Italian and German occupation during the war was succeeded by a devastating civil war (1945–1950), prompting the *Truman Doctrine for the defense of Greece and Turkey against communism and the Soviet Union. After the defeat of the guerrilla forces, an authoritarian, repressive regime, albeit within a parliamentary framework, was established in 1950. Power was lodged in the military, the monarchy, and the United States, the latter being instrumental, if not decisive, in the selection of Greece's political leadership. By the early 1960s social discontent was widespread, demands for democratization were mounting, and the ruling oligarchy felt threatened, while Greece's policy on *Cyprus antagonized the United States. In response a military coup was executed in 1967 by colonels active in a paramilitary organization dedicated to protecting Greece from communism, a coup supported by Greece's patron, the United States. Seven years of repressive military rule under the slogan "Greece for Christian Greeks" collapsed in 1974 as a result of the fiasco of an attempted coup against President Makarios of Cyprus.

The transition to democracy in Greece, as in *Portugal (1975), was precipitated by a specific military event, whereas in *Spain (1974) the process was gradual. Within a few years all three had consolidated democratic regimes. In 1975 a new Greek constitution reestablished a parliamentary system, a far more democratic one than in the past, modeled initially on the French Fifth Republic. The powers of the president (elected by the legislature) were diminished and transferred to the prime minister by a 1983 constitutional amendment. In this modified parliamentary system, independent executive power is vested in the prime minister. A perennially contentious issue is the independence of the judiciary. Although constitutionally independent, Greece's two highest courts, the Council of State (administrative) and the Supreme Court (civil and criminal), tend to be politicized.

Politics in Greece are clientelist, lacking until recently significant *class, ideological, or programmatic conflict. The current multiparty system which took form after 1975 was a continuation of precoup political alignments, with the exception of the newly organized Panhellenic Socialist Movement (PASOK) led by Andreas Papandreou. Campaigning on anti-Americanism, his anti-junta credentials, *populism, and democratic *socialism (more participatory and less corporatist than social democracy), Papandreou and PASOK won a resounding electoral victory in 1981. The political landscape changed—PASOK replaced the traditional center; the electoral support of the traditional *Left declined; smaller Marxist parties, appealing primarily to intellectuals, were formed; and the traditional *Right, renamed New Democracy, espoused neoliberalism. Simultaneously, both an environmental and a women's movement appeared, challenging the traditional parameters of Greek politics. A neofascist party has little support. Once in power, while maintaining populism, Papandreou modified or reversed his stance on numerous issues, and clientelist politics became his hallmark. Opposition to Greece's membership

in the *European Community (EC) dissolved, anti-Americanism remained a rhetorical devise, U.S. base agreements were renegotiated, and domestic reforms were minimal. Legislation on women's rights was the most significant reform. In 1989, under a cloud of major financial scandals implicating Papandreou and several advisors and ministers in his government, PASOK lost the elections. For the first time in its modern history Greece experienced coalition government, initially of the Right and Left, followed by an electoral victory for New Democracy and its leader, Constantine Mitsotakis, in 1990.

Throughout its modern history Greece has been a peripheral or semiperipheral state. On the one hand it has been a political client of one or another great power, on the other an economic dependency of the more advanced economies of the West. Dependent on foreign loans, most recently from various international financial and regional institutions, for financing its external debt, for meeting budget deficits, and for aid in industrialization, it has failed to industrialize. Unemployment and underemployment have been perennial problems that have been alleviated only by emigration from Greece, the latest large exodus being the "guest workers" in Western Europe during the 1960s and early 1970s. Agricultural products and low-technology manufactured goods are Greece's principal exports; it imports industrial and consumer goods, including foodstuff. Despite an ideological commitment to *capitalism, the small industrial and manufacturing sector is heavily government-controlled or state-owned. Recent efforts to privatize have met with little success.

Historically prominent for their merchant and shipping activities, Greek shipowners remain a dominant, internationally oriented class, although many keep their main offices overseas and their ships and tankers often fly foreign flags. The highly bureaucratized Greek state has created a middle class largely composed of public sector employees who in turn are members of powerful trade unions. The industrial labor force in the private sector is small by comparison to the petty bourgeoisie, which is composed of small-scale traders and shopkeepers. The ruling class in Greece is largely a social and political *elite characterized by intra-elite conflict for political power. Hereditary political families have dominated Greek politics. The numerically small economic oligarchy exercises little direct political power, but its alliance with the political elites enables it to further its interests.

The Greek Orthodox church and the military have been powerful political institutions in Greece. The latter has had a history of intervention, at times in alliance with a political faction, at times, as in 1967, on its own. In the aftermath of the military junta's brutal rule, its ignominious action against the president of Cyprus, and its subsequent disintegration, there appears to have been a "return to the barracks" and a restoration of civilian control. By contrast, the church, financed largely by the state, remains powerful, partly because legally Eastern Orthodoxy is the established religion in Greece, partly because it is a critical component of Greek nationality.

Membership in the EC (1981) has not modernized the Greek economy; in fact, membership was sought primarily for political reasons, as a protection against the resurgence of *military rule. With the accession of Portugal and Spain (1986), whose motivations were similar, the three constitute the southern European periphery. Membership is considered economically beneficial to Greece, which obtains loans for economic development projects and whose farmers benefit from the community's Common Agricultural Policy. Greece has had little foreign investment, but moves toward greater economic integration have resulted in significant European buyouts of the few successful Greek enterprises. Despite economic benefits, Greek policy is ambivalent with regard to moves for greater integration. Intensely nationalistic, it is reluctant to lose sovereignty or delegate authority to community organs, particularly as the EC moves toward greater political integration.

While the Greek political leadership struggles domestically with recurrent pressures for modernization and development of its society and economy, foreign policy remains a major concern. Greece has been a member of the *North Atlantic Treaty Organization (NATO) since 1952 and is an ally of the United States. Its principal foreign policy issue has been relations with Turkey. Conflict over the continental shelf, over territorial waters, over the Turkish minority in Greece and the Greek minority in Turkey, and over Cyprus (populated by Greeks and Turks) has been ongoing, and the issues remain unresolved. With the collapse of communism in Eastern Europe and particularly the breakup of Yugoslavia, new foreign policy issues have come to the fore: Macedonia (formerly part of Yugoslavia) and southern Albania inflame Greek *nationalism.

(See also DEMOCRATIC TRANSITIONS; FOREIGN WORKERS; PATRON-CLIENT POLITICS.)

Nicos P. Mouzelis, *Modern Greece: Facets of Underdevelopment* (London, 1978). Martin Blinkhorn and Thanos Veremis, *Modern Greece: Nationalism and Nationality* (Athens, 1990; first published as a special issue of *European History Quarterly* 19, London, 1989.)

ADAMANTIA POLLIS

GREEN PARTIES. In contemporary politics, *green* refers to political parties whose programs emphasize environmental protection and ecological concerns to curtail what they regard as the self-destruction of the earth and human life through the detrimental effects of technology, *modernization, and unlimited economic growth. Most green parties started as electoral lists in the 1970s or 1980s, often at the local or regional level and in close association with citizens' initiatives and *new social movements; in some countries (Italy, Sweden) existing small parties adopted green programs. Green parties can be conservative or left-wing in their interpretation of environmentalism and their party organization. Conservative greens are single-issue parties. They warn of an imminent ecological crisis and advocate a way of life and use of technology that would restore a balance between people, economic activity, and nature. Conservative greens have adopted conventional hierarchical structures in their party organizations, and recasting *political participation or the internal structure of democratic institutions does not interest them. The second type of green party is characterized by a left-wing orientation that links ecology with demands for fundamental changes of policy and procedure. For left-wing green parties, politics based on ecological principles would mean redefining the relationship between people and their living environment: in society, ecological principles imply equal opportunities for men and women, foreigners, and the socially disadvantaged; in the economy, ecological socialism aims at small firms, safe technologies, and state-enforced bans of pollution; in politics, green parties of the *Left advocate grassroots democracy with various patterns of direct involvement in decision making of party members and citizens in general. A core aim of left-wing green parties is recasting hierarchical practices in *parliamentary democracies.

The majority of green parties are on the left of the political spectrum. They perceive themselves and have been regarded as parties of the New Politics. New Politics refers to the changes in the value orientations in advanced industrial societies since the 1960s: as material needs declined as the dominant force in people's lives, nonmaterial issues assumed more importance. This process has been called *postmaterialism. Issues such as environmental protection, concern about nuclear power or nuclear weapons, but also self-realization and equality emerged as priority issues among the young, well-educated generations. It has been suggested that a new protest milieu has developed in Western democracies which constitutes the social basis of the green vote. This milieu consists of middle-class city dwellers, relatively well educated and often trained or employed in teaching or health care, whose pressing concerns—about, for example, the environment and *peace—differ from those of the average citizen. Green parties have seen themselves as correctives to mainstream parties and their neglect of environmental and related issues. In the 1980s, however, green issues have shaped the programs of most political parties and governments; environmental concerns are no longer the sole domain of green parties. The general relevance of green issues reduced the electoral chances of most conservative green parties while New Politics green parties defined themselves more clearly as left-wing in order to remain distinctive. These green parties could draw on the critical views in the New Politics milieu of the political agendas and institutions of the "old politics." This social basis of green party support has been particularly evident in the Federal Republic of *Germany (FRG), where those voting for Die Grünen tend to be academics, critical of the democratic system, of economic competition and success, often unemployed and not seeking conventional employment, and strongly concentrated in university towns and middle-class areas of large cities. Prior to unification, over seventy percent of the electorate of Die Grünen belonged to the 25–45 age cohort; among older voters, support has been weak, and among the youngest it has been declining since the mid-1980s. Unification added a more conservative grouping, the Bündnis 90/Grüne, but did not extend the social basis of green parties in Germany.

Green parties have successfully competed in elections at the local, district, regional, national, and European level. With the exception of local government elections where voters' preferences are often tied to specific local concerns, green parties have suffered the fate of small parties in general and won parliamentary representation only in political systems with *proportional representation. Green parties have held seats in the national parliaments of Austria, Belgium, Finland, Italy, Luxembourg, Sweden, Switzerland, and the FRG. In Germany, Die Grünen have been members of coalition governments with the Sozialdemokratische Partei Deutschlands (SPD) in the regions of Hesse (1985–1987), Berlin (1989–1990), Lower Saxony (1990 to date), and of many local and district coalitions, also usually with the SPD. In the *European Parliament, elected members for green (and some left-wing) parties from Belgium, Denmark, Italy, the Netherlands, Spain (since 1987), the FRG, and France (since 1989) have formed the Rainbow Faction. In the 1989 European elections, the British greens polled the highest percentage (fifteen percent) but failed to win a seat owing to the winner-take-all electoral system. In the election in March 1990 in the German Democratic Republic, a newly founded green party won less than two percent of the vote but eight seats in the national parliament. Electoral successes of green parties depend on proportional representation. Moreover, Die Grünen in the FRG benefited from state funding for all parties that poll at least 0.5 percent of the popular vote.

In contemporary societies, environmental protection is gaining ground as a priority issue among electorates and as a core policy area for all political parties. The left-wing orientation of most successful green parties (Switzerland and Sweden are exceptions) have inspired policy debates on the future of the Western alliance and the *North Atlantic Treaty Organization, on the stationing of nuclear missiles and armament policies, on the need for more equal treatment of women in politics and employment, and on the participation of citizens in public life and party organizations. In party systems where electoral support for a green party may threaten the overall majority of an established party, green parties have been catalysts of policy change. Despite electoral support of less than ten percent on average, weak party organizations, and relatively low membership numbers (no more than 30,000 in the whole of Germany) green parties have emerged as effective oppositions at the parliamentary and extraparliamentary levels in several European countries and in the European Parliament. They have also begun to contribute to government. Green parties have revitalized the role of small parties as policy innovators and brought environmental concerns to the top of contemporary policy agendas.

(See also ENVIRONMENTALISM; GERMAN REUNIFICATION.)

Eva Kolinsky, ed., *The Greens in West Germany* (Oxford, 1989). Ferdinand Müller-Rommel, ed., *New Politics in Western Europe: The Rise and Success of Green Parties and Alternative Lists* (Boulder, Colo., 1989).

E. W. KOLINSKY

GREEN REVOLUTION. The green revolution, strictly defined, refers to the introduction and adoption of high-yielding varieties of wheat and rice, along with improved production practices, in the less developed nations in Asia and to a lesser extent in Latin America and Africa, beginning in the mid-1960s. These varieties were generally developed by international agricultural research centers in cooperation with national agricultural research programs. They were usually short or semidwarf in growth habit and responded to fertilization without lodging or falling over. They also usually were not sensitive to day length and consequently had shorter growing seasons.

High-yielding varieties were originally introduced in South and Southeast Asia and have found their greatest use there, particularly in irrigated or well-watered regions. By the 1982–83 crop year in the noncommunist developing nations, about sixty-one percent of the wheat area and nearly forty-two percent of the rice area were planted with these varieties. Additional areas were also planted in the communist nations of Asia, especially the People's Republic of China (which largely developed its own high-yielding varieties of rice). All told, the high-yielding varieties have spread more widely and more quickly than any other technological innovation in the history of agriculture in the developing nations.

This green revolution has brought about significant changes—generally quite positive—in the countries and regions where the new varieties have been adopted. The economic and social changes have been relatively well monitored. Political effects have not been so closely studied and remain somewhat more speculative. The economic and social impacts have undoubtedly influenced political issues and will be considered first.

The principal immediate effect of the high-yielding varieties is to increase grain production. Their shorter growing season also facilitates more intensive multiple cropping systems, some of which involve non-grain crops. The result is that more food is produced at lower cost per unit than would otherwise be the case. This means that farmers, especially early adopters, receive higher incomes. Consumers—rural and urban—are able to buy more food at lower cost; low-income consumers, who spend a large percentage of their income on food, are particularly benefited. Employment of farm workers is often expanded, and their wages are usually increased. The direct and indirect increases in incomes in turn have multiplier effects among merchants and others in the local community and in the region.

The benefits are, however, not always shared equally among producers. And some groups—especially farmers and regions that are late to adopt the technology or unable to do so—may actually be disadvantaged as expanded production elsewhere brings prices down. But the extent of this disadvantage in some areas is, it is becoming evident, being moderated by shifts in the labor force and by changes in production patterns.

Views of the economic and social effects of the green revolution have shifted over time. At first there was concern that the new technology would largely be adopted by larger and wealthier farmers and that this would widen class differences in the countryside. But the reality has been rather different: the highly divisible biological technology embodied in the high-yielding varieties—in contrast to large-scale mechanical technology—has proved to be quite accessible to smaller farmers and has been widely adopted by them, although sometimes at a slower pace. Government policies, social structure, and the degree of development of infrastructure also influence the rate of adoption and the distribution of benefits.

The generally widespread and equitable adoption of the high-yielding varieties has also changed perceptions of their political effects. In the early years of the green revolution, especially in the early 1970s, there was substantial concern about political destabilization—that the green revolution would turn red. This has not turned out to be the case. If anything, the effect has been just the opposite. The green revolution may well have lessened the potential for revolutionary change and thus somewhat strengthened the political position of those in power. This outcome may not please everyone, especially radicals who want political change. The biggest political problems may come in areas that have not experienced a green revolution.

As for the future, the big challenges are to broaden the spread of the improved technologies into commodities and areas where they have not already been adopted (which may not be easy, feasible, or possible in some cases), to sustain and/or further increase yields in areas where the green revolution has occurred, and to give more attention to ecological interactions and sustainability of improved technologies. All will provide a substantial challenge for research.

(See also DEVELOPMENT AND UNDERDEVELOPMENT; FOOD POLITICS; LAND REFORM; RURAL DEVELOPMENT; TECHNOLOGY TRANSFER.)

Dana G. Dalrymple, "The Adoption of High-Yielding Grain Varieties in Developing Nations" *Agricultural History* 53, no. 4 (October 1979): 704–726. Dana G. Dalrymple, "The Development and Adoption of High-Yielding Varieties of Wheat and Rice in Developing Countries" *American Journal of Agricultural Economics* 67, no. 5 (December 1985): 1067–1073. Jock R. Anderson, Robert W. Herdt, and Grant M. Scobie, *Science and Food: the CGIAR and Its Partners* (Washington, D.C., 1988): 74–87. Michael Lipton with Richard Longhurst, *New Seeds and Poor People* (Baltimore, 1989).

DANA G. DALRYMPLE

GRENADA. The most southerly of the Windward Island chain of West Indian Islands, Grenada is part of the *English-speaking Caribbean. Its population of 100,000 is relatively homogeneous: ninety percent of African origin, with a white or mixed minority and a small number of Portuguese and East Indian descendants. Despite its small size, Grenada became known internationally in the early 1980s as the result of a *Cold War skirmish leading to a U.S. invasion.

The island was the scene of colonial rivalry between France and Britain until it was ceded to Britain in 1763. It became a British Crown Colony in 1877, with a limited representative system that was slowly liberalized as the Crown came under pressure from local and regional labor activists. After World War II, universal adult suffrage was introduced and a party system was developed.

In 1950, Eric Gairy, a populist leader who had been a labor organizer among West Indian oil workers in Aruba, formed the Grenada United Labor Party (GULP) and quickly gained a strong following among the rural proletariat. The Grenada National Party, formed in 1953, attracted support from the middle and upper classes. Except for a few brief intervals, the GULP dominated Grenada's politics from the first general elections in 1951 through independence in 1974, until it was dislodged by a coup in 1979. Although Gairy initially championed the cause of the masses, his extended tenure was marked by the growth of strong personalist government, widespread patronage, and corruption.

In 1973 a new political movement, the New Jewel movement (NJM), was formed. NJM tapped the discontent of the young and unemployed and the energies of some elements of the middle class. After independence, NJM became part of the parliamentary opposition. In 1979 NJM leaders staged the English-speaking Caribbean's first successful coup.

The People's Revolutionary Government that came to power, led by Maurice Bishop, implemented a socialist popular *democracy combined with a mixed economy.

Its links with Cuba and the Eastern bloc, its high level of militarization, *human rights violations, and the regime's refusal to schedule elections alarmed the United States and Grenada's eastern Caribbean neighbors. In 1983, a dispute between governmental factions resulted in the execution of the prime minister and members of his cabinet and the death of many civilians. The eastern Caribbean countries formally requested U.S. intervention in Grenada, and, with Barbados and Jamaica, lent military support. The invasion restored order, but at the cost of many Grenadian lives and a few deaths among Cuban and U.S. military personnel.

Since 1984 Grenadian politics has been marked by elite instability. Political unrest and uncertainty have had an adverse effect on the economy, but relatively strong growth has occurred in recent years. With a per capita income of US$1720, Grenada's main exports are cocoa, nutmeg, and spices. Small-scale agriculture has been the backbone of the economy, and industry is mainly handicraft and light garment production. Various governments have sought to improve agro-industry with limited success. Tourism has also been an important source of revenue for Grenada.

Since 1984 the economy has been heavily dependent on U.S. aid, but U.S. investment has been courted with little success. Small size has limited the opportunities for investors. The country has expanded its market somewhat through membership in the Eastern Caribbean Common Market within the Organization of Eastern Caribbean States (OECS), and in the wider Caribbean Community (Caricom).

(See also SOCIALISM AND SOCIAL DEMOCRACY; U.S.–LATIN AMERICAN RELATIONS.)

Anthony Payne, Paul Sutton, and Tony Thorndike, *Grenada: Revolution and Invasion* (New York, 1984). Jorge Heine, ed., *A Revolution Aborted: The Lessons of Grenada* (Pittsburgh, 1990).

JACQUELINE ANNE BRAVEBOY-WAGNER

GROTIUS, Hugo. Huig de Groot (Hugo Grotius is the Latinized version of his name, used in his major works) is most widely remembered as a leading intellectual figure of the seventeenth century and an important writer on *international law and *international relations. Grotius was born in 1583 at Delft in the United Provinces of the Netherlands or Dutch Republic. His early career was marked by an astonishing range of achievement. A child prodigy, he entered the University of Leiden at age 11. When he visited Paris at the age of 15 he was acclaimed by King Henri IV as "the miracle of Holland." In 1599 he was admitted to the bar of The Hague, and in 1607 he was appointed to the high legal office of advocate-fiscal of Holland.

Already the author of several volumes on the history of the Dutch Republic, which was a new and in many ways insecure state, in 1609 he published his first legal work, *Mare Liberum*. This classic exposition of the freedom of the seas defended the activities of the Dutch East India Company when threatened by the Spanish and Portuguese empires.

In 1613 Grotius was appointed pensionary of Rotterdam—a more important post than its name might suggest. However, within five years his political career in Holland came to an end. Like many in Holland, he had coupled his Protestantism with support for toleration both at home and abroad. In 1618 Prince Maurice, the commander of the Dutch Republic's armies, imposed a more militant and less tolerant regime on Holland. Grotius's patron, Johan van Oldenbarnevelt, was arrested and executed, while Grotius himself was sentenced to life imprisonment. In 1621 he made a celebrated escape from the castle of Loevestein in a chest of books.

He was in exile for almost all the rest of his life—mainly in Paris, where he spent two ten-year periods. In the first, sustained by a small pension from the king and by literary earnings, he wrote and published (in 1625) *De Jure Belli ac Pacis* (On the Law of War and Peace)—his major, and last, work in the field of international law. He also dreamed of a triumphant return to Holland, but when he did go back, in 1631–1632, he could not resume his previous career in Dutch politics. He had once more to flee abroad, and from 1634 to 1644 was again in Paris, this time in the important post of Swedish ambassador at the French court. He had been appointed by the Swedish chancellor, Axel Oxenstierna, and when in 1644 Oxenstierna's influence temporarily declined, Grotius was recalled to Sweden and relieved of his post. The following year, on his way back to Paris, Grotius was shipwrecked in the Baltic, and died two days later at Rostock.

Grotius wrote many books, including poetry, translations, and studies on theological and historical topics. He is most remembered today for *De Jure Belli ac Pacis,* which addresses perennial problems of international relations: justifications for *war and military intervention; restraints in war; the *legitimacy or otherwise of rebellion; the treatment of the vanquished after a war.

Grotius has often been seen as the "father of international law." This description points to his achievement as a systematic writer who drew together strands from an eclectic variety of sources of law. His work had a special significance because, in his day, the society of independent sovereign states was beginning to emerge in its modern form—a development symbolized three years after his death by the 1648 Peace of Westphalia. Grotius provided a guide to the operations of this new system of sovereign states. However, he cannot properly be seen as the begetter of international law. Not only did his writing draw heavily on classical writers, and on recent predecessors such as Alberico Gentili (1552–1608), but also the very idea that international law—deriving as it does from long tradition, and from the interests and practices of states—can have a single "father" is doubtful.

Grotius is associated with a "Grotian" tradition of thought about international relations—one that accepts the *sovereignty of *states, and even their right in certain circumstances to wage war, but at the same time stresses the existence of shared values and the necessity of international rules. A lawyer who took fully into account the practice of states, his thinking had considerable influence in many countries long after his death and provided the basis for a flexible tradition of thought about international law and relations, capable of being adapted to a variety of conditions and causes.

Hugo Grotius, *De Jure Belli ac Pacis Libri Tres* (1625), translated by Francis W. Kelsey (Oxford, 1925). Hedley Bull, Benedict Kingsbury, and Adam Roberts, eds., *Hugo Grotius and International Relations* (Oxford, 1990).

ADAM ROBERTS

GROUP OF 7. The term *Group of 7* (G7) refers to two different, but closely related processes of high-level economic *diplomacy among the most powerful capitalist nations (the United States, Japan, the Federal Republic of Germany (FRG), Britain, France, Italy, Canada), and between them and the rest of the world. The first involves heads of state, their staffs, and key ministers (the annual seven-power "economic summits," which include the president of the European Commission). The second, which is the major focus of this essay, is a more specific process of meetings and communication among the finance ministers and central bankers of the summit nations, as well as the managing director of the *International Monetary Fund (IMF). This "G7" forum was formalized at the Tokyo Economic Summit of 1986.

Since the first summit in 1975, agendas have become less and less economic and increasingly political in nature, including, for example, East-West *security, energy and the Middle East, responses to the invasion of Afghanistan, and changes in China, Central and Eastern Europe, and the Soviet Union. For example, the Houston summit in June 1990 involved proposals for a collective G7 strategy for the economic (and social) reconstruction of the former communist states and the Soviet Union, as well as debate on the global environment challenge.

The more narrowly economic G7 process involves formal and informal meetings of finance ministers and central bankers. These meetings have been shrouded in secrecy and possess the peculiar mystique associated with the world of high finance and monetary policy. Similar meetings have sometimes involved only Japan and the United States (G2); these two and the FRG (G3 meetings have all been informal and unreported); these three and Britain and France (G5); these five plus Canada (G6) and Italy (G7). The formal meetings of the G7 are often for public (market) consumption and only reflect a small part of the continual communication and, occasionally, coordination and synchronization of intervention in the markets. One recent G7 meeting discussed the global financial implications of the Gulf War and the organization of international transfers to pay for U.S. and British expenditures in the Gulf War, and another, held in 1991, discussed G7 strategy toward Soviet debt and economic and political restructuring.

The wider setting of the G7 process includes international economic organizations such as the *Organization for Economic Co-operation and Development (G24), the *World Bank, the IMF, and the Bank for International Settlements. Think tanks and research institutes (and informal organizations which combine perspectives from the private sector [especially financial] and the academy with those of officials, politicians, and regulators, such as the Group of 30) also contribute. Taken together, these processes are designed to steer financial markets and underpin the stability of the system, for example, through developing common standards of capital adequacy and prudential practice for banks and other firms providing financial services and products. The summits and the G7 are indicative of "the internationalization of the *state": a still-embryonic process of the internationalization of economic policy-making, and the changing relations within and between state structures that are bound up with this.

The G7 process of policy coordination has proved to be controversial. Its main limitations appear to relate to the incomplete internationalization of political authority in a world of massive, almost instantaneous flows of mobile capital in globally integrated, round-the-clock financial markets.

For example, smooth international coordination of macroeconomic policies presupposes the relinquishing of economic sovereignty, whereas G7 governments are most concerned with domestic economic activity, for which they require policy autonomy. Few are willing to yield their prerogatives to any international process, especially (and most crucially) the United States. Although the Louvre Agreement of February 1987 announced a commitment to sustain (publicly unspecified) exchange rate target zones and the coordination of domestic monetary and fiscal policies to ensure this, only Japan of the major parties kept its pledge, expanding domestic demand by fiscal stimulus. The FRG refused to stimulate, for fear of inflation, and attempts to reduce the U.S. budget deficit were blocked in Congress. Cooperation disintegrated, and private investors, anticipating a depreciation of the dollar, reduced the supply of finance to the United States. Fearing a free-fall in the dollar, central banks bought dollars to sustain its parity. The bond market began to decline rapidly, followed by a collapse in values on the international equity markets in October 1987. The authorities them pumped liquidity into the system to prevent the collapse from triggering a worldwide economic depression as occurred following the Wall Street crash of 1929.

Since 1987, G7 cooperation has appeared to lose momentum, leading some to suggest that domestic obstacles can only be overcome in times of severe crisis or systemic threat. Critics argue that the Louvre/crash period showed the dangers of G7 coordination; advocates argue that it reflected a new collective capacity to sustain the system under new global conditions, in a new policy process. As the case of the 1987 crash illustrates, however, the knowledge level and resources needed to steer the brave new world of global capitalism are still far from sufficient.

(See also FINANCE, INTERNATIONAL; GROUP OF 77; INTERNATIONAL COOPERATION; INTERNATIONAL POLITICAL ECONOMY; NORTH-SOUTH RELATIONS; POLICY COORDINATION, ECONOMIC; TRILATERAL COMMISSION.)

Robert Putnam and Nicholas Bayne, *Hanging Together: the Seven-power Summits* (London, 1987). Yoichi Funabashi, *Managing the Dollar: From Plaza to the Louvre* (Washington, D.C., 1988).

STEPHEN GILL

GROUP OF 77. Emerging during the first meeting of the UN Conference on Trade and Development (UNCTAD) in 1964, the Group of 77 became the main caucusing organization of the countries of the *Third World in the UN system. The group, which retained its name despite the addition of many more members, came to operate in a number of other multilateral settings of the North-South dialogue, but the group's efforts within UNCTAD—the Third World's "own" institution—have always been primary. This is largely because UNCTAD's broad mandate and its identification with the struggle to establish the *New International Economic Order in the 1970s gave the group unusual prominence and the power (limited but not irrelevant) to discuss and take positions on a wide array of issues.

The Group of 77 was also the strongest manifestation of the Third World's belief that, if it were to be successful in creating international economic *regimes biased in its favor, unity was its strongest weapon. Unity meant that agendas could be set, that common positions could be enunciated, and that sustained pressures against the developed countries could be maintained. Given the fact that the developing countries, while sharing common grievances and perspectives and some shared interests, were also deeply divided, the question was raised as to how unity was to be achieved and maintained. The answer was the institutionalization of the group system.

The group system was defended as the only means to avoid chaos, to permit many developing countries to negotiate with many developed countries. For the Group of 77, regional caucusing was followed by the establishment of a common position at a leadership caucus. The professional staff at UNCTAD was usually instrumental in ensuring that the position made some technical sense; nonetheless, when presented to the developed countries, the proposals were usually rejected or left unresolved.

Failure to reach compromise agreements was due, in part, to characteristics of the proposals developed by the group. The proposals were very complex because they had to satisfy many interests; they were too ambitious in promising too much to too many; and they were frequently badly designed as they sought primarily a single goal (restructuring in favor of developing countries). In addition, compromise was difficult because compromises could unravel unity. Staff members were influential in framing proposals but powerless to affect crucial political decisions by the developed countries. The proposals produced were also usually incompatible ideologically with Western market values as they tended to seek large increases in central guidance of international economic activity: nothing else would guarantee sufficient benefits to enough developing countries to maintain unity.

The group was not as politicized as the *nonaligned movement, but it still did not achieve any of its restructuring goals. It insisted for too long that agreement on new principles must precede more pragmatic bargaining on specifics. Stalemate resulted in the 1970s. Subsequently, as economic conditions worsened, the group's influence declined, despite moderation in demands and ideology, as attention shifted to domestic reform and bilateral or regional negotiations.

(See also DEVELOPMENT AND UNDERDEVELOPMENT; GROUP OF 7; NORTH-SOUTH RELATIONS.)

Robert L. Rothstein, *Global Bargaining* (Princeton, N.J., 1979).

ROBERT L. ROTHSTEIN

GUATEMALA. The most populous Central American country, with a population of over 9 million, Guatemala has had a particularly turbulent history. The extreme polarization of Guatemala's social structure stems largely from the compounding of *class with ethnic divisions: even today, over fifty percent of the population is Indian.

The Spanish Conquest, a violent clash of two socioeconomic systems and two cultures, forcibly "integrated" Guatemala's Indians into "Western civilization": several million were killed immediately, and by 1650, two-thirds to six-sevenths of the Indian population in Central America and Mexico had died (largely through disease epidemics). The conquest also integrated Guatemala into an expanding capitalist world market that determined the colony's production priorities and systematically channeled its surplus to foreign economic *elites. This dependent relationship left internal legacies that have endured far longer than colonial status itself: agricultural mono-export (at the expense of food production), concentration of landholding in the hands of a small minority, and forced Indian labor as the underpinning of the entire socioeconomic structure.

Independence in 1821 brought little change in the internal structures, although it began a diversification of Guatemala's external contacts, replacing the Spanish monopoly with Britain, and later Germany and the United States. Within Guatemala, power alternated between Liberals and Conservatives until the Liberal "Revolution" of 1871. The triumph of the Liberals, who ruled with an iron hand until 1944, coincided with the rise of coffee as the dominant export: at the same time, three U.S. corporations (most notably the United Fruit Company) began monopolistic operations there. These developments greatly intensified the concentration of land as well as the levels of coercion applied to the subjugated Indian labor force, with the army becoming the principal labor mobilizer and enforcer. This period also saw the rise of the United States as a world power and a great expansion of U.S. influence over internal Guatemalan affairs, in alliance with the local landed oligarchy.

Under the weight of the crises caused by the world depression of the 1930s, the old neocolonial order finally cracked in 1944, when a broad-based coalition of middle- and working-class groups overthrew Liberal dictator Jorge Ubico. Thus began the Revolution of 1944–1954, the only genuinely democratic experience in Guatemala's entire history. The *revolution—under the governments of Juan José Arévalo (1945–1950) and Jacobo Arbenz (1951–1954)—guaranteed basic democratic liberties (including free elections), abolished forced labor, granted minimum wages and basic rights for workers and *peasants, and increased social welfare and equality. In addition, the revolution modernized Guatemalan capitalism and increased agricultural diversification and industrialization programs; the new regimes also encouraged the growth of national enterprises and regulated foreign investment to serve Guatemalan priorities. Most significant was Arbenz's far-reaching—but capitalist—agrarian reform, which distributed land to over 100,000 peasant families.

Coming on top of other nationalistic moves by Arbenz, the expropriation of some United Fruit land prompted an angry response from the U.S. government. Unwilling to countenance an independent-minded nationalistic government, the United States charged Guatemala with serving as a "beachhead for Soviet expansion" in the Western Hemisphere, despite the adherence of the Arbenz government to the principles of capitalist economic development and *democracy. The *Central Intelligence Agency organized the overthrow of the Arbenz government in June 1954 and installed in its place a pro-U.S. counterrevolutionary regime. This regime immediately reversed the democratic and progressive legislation of the revolution and unleashed wide-scale repression.

The legacy of the revolution and its violent end was to compound the social polarization already characteristic of Guatemala and abruptly ended the country's only democratic regime. Nevertheless, the counterrevolution was unable to literally "reverse history" because the same underlying structural dynamics and contradictions continued to develop. The Guatemalan economy, like that of all Central America, enjoyed a thirty-year period (1950–1980) of growth based on the expansion of agricultural exports. But even *export-led growth generated turmoil because of extreme inequities in resource distribution. For example, in the 1970s, the diversification of exports brought significant new land expropriations (from peasants) and concentrations (largely in the hands of army generals using their control over the state to accumulate wealth): thus, impoverishment stemming from land concentration intensified geometrically.

The land crisis in Guatemala—ironically, a crisis of growth—was compounded in the 1980s when pressures emanating from the world economy hit Central America as severely as the depression of the 1930s. As a consequence of this combination of domestic and international factors, the Guatemalan economy contracted during the 1980s; inflation and unemployment reached unprecedented proportions; and purchasing power plummeted. As of the late 1980s, over eighty-seven percent of the population lived below the poverty line, over two-thirds in "absolute poverty" (unable to afford a basic minimum diet). On numerous welfare indicators, Guatemala's record was the worst in the hemisphere, particularly for Indians and women.

Politically, post-1954 Guatemala has been ruled primarily by military regimes: even during the two periods of civilian government (1966–1970 and since 1985), the army has dominated politics from behind the scenes. But these hard-line regimes have faced constant challenges: indeed, Guatemala since the 1960s has undergone a thirty-year-long civil war, the longest and bloodiest in the hemisphere. The first wave of guerrilla insurgency, during the 1960s, was centered in the eastern region. Although small and without support from the indigenous communities, it was contained only after a major *counterinsurgency effort, organized, financed, and run directly by the United States. This first "dirty war" cost the lives of over 8,000 civilians. Government *counterinsurgency also introduced to Latin America the phenomena of semiofficial death squads (spawned by security forces) and the "disappearance" of civilian opposition figures.

Defeated temporarily in 1968, the insurgents reorganized and reinitiated their struggle in the 1970s in the western Indian highlands. The active involvement of up to half a million Indians in the uprising of the late 1970s and early 1980s was without precedent. Coming in the wake of the victory of the *Sandinistas in *Nicaragua and the outbreak of civil war in *El Salvador, this remarkable awakening in the Indian highlands threatened the army's century-old domination over rural Guatemala. The army's "scorched earth" methods in smashing the insurgency left over 440 villages totally destroyed, 100,000–150,000 civilians dead, and over a million uprooted and displaced. Having "won" the war, the army then militarized the entire Guatemalan countryside in an effort to prevent any future uprising. Despite these very harsh means of controlling the population, by the late 1980s, Guatemala's rulers faced a third challenge from the insurgents, now united in the Unidad Revolucionaria Nacional Guatemalteca (URNG).

Even as the war continued, all major players in Guatemala and the United States came to understand the necessity for a return to formal civilian rule. The 1985 election brought to power the first civilian president in twenty years, but that government did very little to control the army or address the country's underlying problems. There was another election in 1990, but abstention was extremely high, and no real opposition parties were permitted. By 1991, negotiations between the government and the insurgents had begun, reflecting a national consensus (articulated by top church officials, among others) that Guatemala could not be truly democratized until the civil war was ended through political negotiations (rather than a military victory by either side), until the country was demilitarized, and until the underlying problems of structural inequality and ethnic oppression were addressed.

(See also ETHNICITY; GUERRILLA WARFARE; LAND REFORM; MILITARY RULE; MULTINATIONAL CORPORATIONS; U.S.–LATIN AMERICAN RELATIONS.)

Richard Adams, *Crucifixion by Power* (Austin, Tex., 1970). Susanne Jonas, *The Battle for Guatemala: Rebels, Death Squads and U.S. Power* (Boulder, Colo., 1991).

SUSANNE JONAS

GUERRILLA WARFARE. A method utilized by small, mobile units to harass, weaken, demoralize, and combat larger conventional forces, guerrilla warfare antedates modern history. References to irregular forces appear in the Hittite *Anastas Papyrus* of the fifteenth century B.C.E.; in ancient Chinese military writings; in biblical stories depicting Jewish resistance to Syrian forces; in Roman military history against North Africans, Iberians, Germans, and Gauls; and in medieval accounts of ethnic, religious, and dynastic *wars. There is no major part of the world in which some sort of guerrilla warfare has not been utilized by the weak against the strong, by resistance forces against foreign invaders, by technically or numerically inferior armies against better-equipped, larger, or more powerful forces.

No single theater of operations or mode of combat

defines guerrilla warfare. Historically, guerrilla fighters operated in rural areas, forests, mountains, and deserts. As the world's population concentrated more in cities in the nineteenth and twentieth centuries, urban guerrilla warfare became more common. Indicative of this was the publication in 1966 of the Uruguayan Abraham Guillen's *Strategy of the Urban Guerrilla*. Guillen's work synthesized the consensus of revolutionary writers on guerrilla warfare by the 1960s: "In a war of liberation, final victory is not military but political; the victorious side will destroy the enemy's morale and outlast the enemy in a war of attrition. . . ."

At times guerrilla warfare varies little in appearance from banditry; at other times it involves a relatively large number of light infantry units operating independently but in communication with one another or even with conventional forces. Typical operations involve surprise attacks and ambush; destruction of enemy supplies; cutting of transportation and communication links; attacks on advance units or stragglers; assassinations of political leaders, military officers, and police; and hostage taking. Guerrilla units often live off the land, attempt to make allies and intelligence assets of local populations, or may even be local residents who carry out guerrilla raids and then return to their lives as peasants or workers. Sanctuary in neighboring countries sometimes makes guerrillas even more effective. Examples include Greek guerrilla bases in Albania, Yugoslavia, and Bulgaria (1946–1949); Vietnamese sanctuaries in Cambodia and Laos (1950–1970); Nicaraguan *contra camps in Honduras and Costa Rica (1980s); and Afghan rebel retreats in Pakistan (1980s).

Civil wars, insurgencies, and independence movements often include elements of guerrilla warfare; American independence struggles against the British in the late eighteenth century, Haitian liberation from France (1804), and the independence movements in Spanish America (1810–1825) all found irregular forces combating regular armies. Guerrilla forces often obtain support from conventional forces, whether domestic or foreign, engaged in combat against common enemies. Thus insurgencies, independence movements, and revolutionary struggles utilizing guerrilla techniques have found support from "enemies of enemies." This occurred throughout European history; in anticolonial struggles in the nineteenth century in Asia, Africa, and the Americas; and it continues in the twentieth century.

While irregular warfare has a history practically as old as human conflict, the term *guerrilla* warfare was popularized in modern military history by the actions of Spanish irregulars resisting Napoleon's invasion of the Iberian peninsula in 1807. Hit-and-run attacks by small Spanish units supported with matériel and advisers by British and Portuguese conventional forces introduced the *guerrilla,* or "little war," into the military lexicon. (The word was formed by adding the diminutive suffix to the Spanish word for war, *guerra*.)

In the nineteenth century, guerrilla warfare played a role in a number of European conflicts, including the Greek War of Independence (1821–1827) and the Italian *Risorgimento* (1848–1871). European colonialism in Asia and Africa induced guerrilla resistance from Burma to New Zealand and South Africa. British, French, Italian, and Portuguese armies faced periodic guerrilla struggles throughout their imperial domains.

Twentieth-century writing on guerrilla warfare has paid increasing attention to its political significance. T. E. Lawrence (*The Seven Pillars of Wisdom*, 1935) is often credited with the first theoretical contribution to understanding guerrilla warfare not as a military tactic supporting conventional military operations but as a *political* movement utilizing irregular warfare as a tactic. After World War I and the success of the Russian revolutionaries (1917), Marxist-Leninist theorists also incorporated doctrine concerning guerrilla warfare into their writings. *Lenin introduced the concept of "protracted revolutionary war"; Trotsky and *Stalin also accepted partisan warfare as an instrument of revolutionary struggle, providing a doctrinal foundation for Soviet assistance to *national liberation movements later in the century.

In China (1930s and 1940s) *Mao Zedong systematized and attempted to universalize the method of rural guerrilla warfare, blending classical Chinese military writings, Marxist-Leninist doctrine, and the experiences of Chinese resistance and civil war. Relying heavily on Mao and the experience of Vietnamese resistance against the Japanese and French, the great Vietnamese General Vo Nguyen Giap sought to extend the international revolutionary appeal of guerrilla warfare as "people's war" in *People's War, People's Army* (1962): "Guerrillas rely upon heroic spirit to triumph over modern weapons, avoiding the enemy when he is stronger, and attacking him when he is the weaker."

Guerrilla warfare as a technique, however, is as useful to counterrevolutionary forces, ethnic and religious minorities, nationalists, or brigands as it is to revolutionaries. Likewise it may be used as an instrument of foreign policy by nations supporting irregular forces for their own policy objectives. Examples include Cuban support for guerrillas throughout Latin America in the 1960s and early 1970s; U.S. support for Afghan Muslim irregulars and Nicaraguan contras (1980s); East German support for Chilean resistance fighters (1970s, 1980s); and South African support for Angolan guerrilla forces (1970s–1990s).

Guerrilla warfare frustrates conventional armies by making "victory" impossible in the traditional sense. Because guerrillas attack in small numbers, by surprise or ambush, and disappear into the surrounding countryside or towns, it is extremely difficult to achieve military success, that is, destruction of enemy forces. Inability to distinguish between guerrilla fighters and local populations generates tension between military personnel and civilians. The desire for intelligence concerning guerrilla organization, operations, and location frequently leads conventional forces to adopt repressive measures that alienate noncombatants. Historically these measures have included interrogation by *torture, collective punishment of populations where guerrilla activity or presence is suspected, concentration of populations into "protected zones" in the hope of denying resources to guerrillas, forcing local populations to join in combat against guerrillas, and requisitioning supplies or animals from peasant populations.

Twentieth-century *counterinsurgency techniques became somewhat more sophisticated as a result of the lessons learned from a number of guerrilla wars, for example, the British experience in the South African campaigns against the Boers (1899–1902), in Ireland against the Irish Republican Army (IRA) (1919–1921), against African insurgents such as the Mau Mau in Kenya (1952), and in Malaya and Cyprus (1950s). French conflicts in Algeria and Indochina (1952–1954) as well as the U.S. experience in Vietnam (1960s and 1970s) and widespread guerrilla wars in Latin America (1960s–1970s, some ongoing) also contributed to modern counterinsurgency methods. These experiences have led to a growing awareness of the political as well as military dimension of guerrilla warfare. Nevertheless, nationalists, revolutionary movements, and opponents of incumbent regimes around the globe continued to utilize guerrilla warfare effectively into the 1990s. Sendero Luminoso (Shining Path) in Peru, the New People's Army in the Philippines, the *Palestine Liberation Organization in the Mideast, and the ongoing war waged by the IRA in Northern Ireland exemplify the pervasive influence and challenge of guerrilla movements in the early 1990s.

(See also ALGERIAN WAR OF INDEPENDENCE; CHINESE REVOLUTION; DECOLONIZATION; GUEVARA, ERNESTO; MAU MAU ANTICOLONIAL STRUGGLE; REVOLUTION; SOVIET-AFGHANISTAN WAR; VIETNAM WAR.)

Gerard Chaliand, ed., *Guerrilla Strategies, An Historical Anthology from the Long March to Afghanistan* (Berkeley, Calif., 1982). Brian Loveman and Thomas M. Davies, Jr., *Che Guevara on Guerrilla Warfare* (Lincoln, Nebr., 1985).
BRIAN LOVEMAN

GUEST WORKERS. See FOREIGN WORKERS.

GUEVARA, Ernesto. With the victory over Cuban dictator Fulgencio Batista in 1959, Ernesto ("Che") Guevara became the symbol of revolutionary *guerrilla warfare against the old order in Latin America. An advocate of armed struggle to overturn capitalism and create *socialism in the *Third World,

Guevara's portrait on millions of posters and banners served notice of the revolutionary challenge represented by the *Cuban Revolution to Latin American regimes and to the foreign policy of the United States.

Ernesto Guevara was born 14 June 1928 in Rosario, Argentina, the descendant of two old and respected Argentine families. His parents early rejected the conventions of Argentine society and adopted a near bohemian lifestyle, thereby providing Ernesto with a liberal political ambience enjoyed by few youth of his social class. That advantage was offset, however, by the fact that Guevara was stricken early with the asthma that was to debilitate him throughout his life and severely affect his activities as adventurer and guerrilla warrior, particularly in 1967 in Bolivia.

While still in medical school, Guevara traveled widely in South America, and, when he finished, he embarked on the odyssey that was to shape his life and that of the world around him. He was in Guatemala in 1954 when the U.S.-orchestrated coup ousted the government of Jacobo Arbenz Guzmán. After the victory of the Central Intelligence Agency—trained forces in Guatemala, he went to Mexico where he joined a band of young, revolutionary exiles from Peru and *Cuba.

Led by Fidel *Castro, the rebels sailed to Cuba on the ship *Granma* in December 1956. The Cuban Revolution had begun. During the struggle against Batista, Guevara served both as a military commander and as doctor, but it was as the former that he became renowned in the early 1960s. Guevara served in a series of posts, including a disastrous tenure as minister of industry (1961–1965). In 1965, he dropped from public view, and was widely reported to be leading guerrilla movements all over the Third World (Africa, Southeast Asia, etc.). In his famous treatise *Guerrilla Warfare* (1960), Guevara had argued forcefully that revolutionary guerrilla warfare would be successful only in those countries where a "Caribbean-type dictatorship" was present. Later he modified that thesis several times until, in 1966, in a speech to the Tricontinental Congress in Havana, he called for the creation of "many Vietnams" to confront the United States and the rest of the imperialist West. That his initial thesis was the most correct was proved tragically in the Bolivian fiasco of 1966–1967 where he and his followers were captured or killed. Guevara was taken alive, but killed by his captors.

Guevara's political career after Batista's defeat might lead one to conclude that he had failed miserably. But to dismiss Guevara in that way is to miss the true significance of his life and work. His was a call to action, a call to the youth of Latin America to rise up and throw off the shackles of the ages. Even more important, however, was his promise of ultimate victory to those who kept the faith and persevered in their revolutionary tasks and fervor.

His life and his message served as the inspiration and motivating force behind the guerrilla movements that sprang up all over Latin America in the 1960s and 1970s. That inspiration and example also served to galvanize the United States into altering seriously its military posture in the hemisphere, and it pushed the Soviet Union into military, political, and economic positions in Latin America that it would have preferred greatly to avoid.

(See also REVOLUTION.)

John Gerassi, ed., *Venceremos: The Speeches and Writings of Ernesto Che Guevara* (London, 1968). Rolando E. Bonachea and Nelson P. Valdés, *Che: Selected Works of Ernesto Guevara* (Cambridge, Mass., 1969). Donald C. Hodges, *The Legacy of Che Guevara* (London, 1977).

THOMAS M. DAVIES, JR.
BRIAN LOVEMAN

GUINEA. When the army seized power in Guinea in April 1984, the Comité Militaire de Redressement National (CMRN) took control of the government. The CMRN abolished the constitution and banned the Parti Démocratique de Guinée (PDG), the ruling party since independence in 1958 and the only party since 1964. The new president, a general, headed both the government and the state. Advised by a predominantly military council of ministers, the president appointed all government officials, served as commander in chief of the armed forces, and ruled by executive decrees that had the force of law. Through 1990, Guinea had no *constitution, legislature, or political parties, and there had been no elections since the military came to power. Military officers governed the capital city and each of Guinea's four provinces and thirty-five prefectures, while local affairs were directed by a network of prominent families, a system that had been suppressed by the previous government.

Although a new constitution was adopted by referendum in December 1990, the government is not obliged to put it into effect for five years. In the aftermath of the vote, the CMRN was replaced by the Conseil Transitoire de Redressement National (CTRN), a quasi-legislative body appointed by the head of state, who was also president of the CTRN. One-third of the CTRN's members were military officers, as were one-third of the government ministers. Although the formation of political parties has been authorized, national elections have not yet been held.

Prior to the military coup, Guinea was a one-party state headed by Ahmed Sékou Touré, president from independence in 1958 until his death in March 1984. The PDG, also led by Sékou Touré, was the most active nationalist party in the 1950s. Composed of trade unionists, *peasants, market women, and youths, the PDG spearheaded the movement that resulted in independence from France. Choosing autonomy from France rather than membership in the Communauté Française, Guinea was ostracized by France and its Western allies. *Foreign aid was cut and development projects abandoned. Guinea then turned to the East, further antagonizing the Western powers.

Sékou Touré's policies of *nationalization, emphasis on rural versus urban development, abolition of colonial chieftaincies, and emancipation of women antagonized many Guinean elites. Male elders, particularly among the Muslim eighty-five percent of the population, were incensed by the outlawing of polygamy. The government's efforts to promote national unity and equitable development, at the expense of ethnic and regional favoritism, angered groups that had once been privileged. Numerous coup attempts were suppressed, including an invasion by Portuguese troops in collaboration with Guinean exiles. By the late 1970s and early 1980s, however, allegations of plotting against the government had become a means by which Sékou Touré eliminated political opponents.

Since the military coup of 1984, numerous high-level officials from the previous government have disappeared. The nationalist period and first fifteen years of Sékou Touré's rule have been erased from Guinean history books, while the authoritarian practices of the last decade have been highlighted. Most of Sékou Touré's economic and social programs have been reversed. Industry has been reprivatized. Once again in the good graces of the West, Guinea has implemented a drastic program of structural readjustment under the auspices of the *World Bank and the *International Monetary Fund (IMF).

Dependent on the export of a few primary commodities, notably bauxite, Guinea's per capita income is among the lowest in the world. The currency devaluation and massive layoff of government workers, stipulated by the World Bank and the IMF, have resulted in severe economic hardships and growing discontent. The PDG's emancipatory laws and programs promoting women have been either abrogated or ignored. Family name, ethnic and regional affiliation, and the ability to pay have become the key to economic and social advancement.

(See also FRANCOPHONE AFRICA; MILITARY RULE; ONE-PARTY SYSTEM.)

Thomas E. O'Toole, *Historical Dictionary of Guinea (Republic of Guinea/Conakry)*. 2d ed., African Historical Dictionaries, No. 16 (Metuchen, N.J., 1987).

ELIZABETH S. SCHMIDT

GUINEA-BISSAU. Located on the coast of West Africa, Guinea-Bissau declared its independence from Portugal in 1973 following a twelve-year armed struggle led by the Partido Áfricano da Independência da Guiné e Cabo Verde (PAIGC). The first constitution (1980) established the republic as a one-party state with public ownership of natural resources and control of finance, commerce, and communications.

At the national level, veterans of the anticolonial war dominated the party-state into the early 1990s. During the transition period preceding multiparty elections scheduled for 1993, the PAIGC was challenged by the Lisbon-based Movimento Bafatá (MB), the Frente Democrática e Social (FDS), associated with long-time dissident Rafael Barbosa, and the Frente Democrática (FD), as well as grouplets identified with factions or personalities of the PAIGC.

Guinea-Bissau's 900,000 inhabitants include over thirty ethnic groups, the most numerous of which include the Balanta, backbone of the guerrilla army in the anticolonial war; the Islamicized Mandinga and Fulbe, whose leadership collaborated with the colonial regime; and the coastal Manjaco and Papel. During the colonial period, the civil service in Guinea-Bissau was staffed by Cape Verdians; the founders of the PAIGC came from this group—including the national hero, Amílcar *Cabral, who was assassinated in 1973, and his half-brother, Luís Cabral, the republic's first president.

With the end of the armed struggle, party leaders became involved in affairs of state and grass-roots organization suffered. Farmers were dissatisfied with heavy taxes, low prices for their produce, and the lack of food and consumer goods. They responded by emigrating or smuggling their grains and nuts into Senegal, contributing to domestic food deficits and depriving the state of revenue from export crops. Acute commodity shortages along with resentment toward the Cape Verdian role in Guinea-Bissau led to a military coup in 1989 headed by party veteran General João Bernardo Vieira (Nino). Continued political repression and economic regression sparked a coup attempt leading to government execution of six in 1986.

In 1984, Vieira began a radical restructuring of the economy in compliance with conditions imposed by the *International Monetary Fund. Civil servants, many of whom were fired or had their workdays and pay scaled back, began setting up small plantations and going into trade. Economic reforms opened new possibilities for the political consolidation of the urbanized Creole population as well as for strata of the Islamicized groups with experience in long-distance trade.

In the international arena, Guinea-Bissau has been an active member of the group of five former Portuguese African colonies who shared a foreign policy during the 1970s and 1980s. Within the region, the republic has participated in organizations such as the Economic Community of West African States (ECOWAS) and the Permanent Inter-State Committee on Drought Control in the Sahel. Since discovery of offshore oil, there have been disputes with Senegal and Guinea over maritime borders. Early ties with the former socialist bloc have yielded somewhat to broader relations with Portugal and the West.

(See also AFRICAN REGIONAL ORGANIZATIONS; CAPE VERDE; DECOLONIZATION.)

Rosemary E. Galli and Jocelyn Jones, *Guinea-Bissau: Politics, Economics and Society* (Boulder, Colo., 1987).

LAURA BIGMAN

GULF STATES. Before 1971, Bahrain, Qatar, and the seven smaller Arab Gulf emirates—Abu Dhabi, Dubai, Sharjah, Ras al-Khaimah, Fujairah, Umm al-Qaiwain, and Ajman—were all protectorates of Britain, which provided political advisers to each ruling family and overall supervision by a Resident based in the Gulf. Oman enjoyed nominal independence, although British advisers continually intervened in the country's internal affairs to prop up the ruler of the port of Muscat in his struggles with tribal confederations of the interior.

Bahrain and Dubai remained important commercial centers into the 1920s and 1930s, while Sharjah served as headquarters for British military forces in the area during the 1940s and 1950s. Internal politics in each emirate consisted largely of jockeying between the ruling family and prominent merchants for control over the local economy, centered around the harvesting and distribution of pearls. In Dubai, wealthy merchants forced the ruler to recognize a consultative council in 1938, although he disbanded it after only five months. In Bahrain, the beginnings of oil production in the 1930s and the construction of a large-scale oil refinery on the islands created a relatively large and vocal working class, whose leaders joined with discontented tradespeople to form a series of nationalist movements in the 1950s. Omani politics remained insulated from the effects of popular mobilization in neighboring principalities during the 1930s and 1940s.

Throughout the region, the coming of oil reinforced the position of the ruling families and their British-run administrations, providing them with resources to use in suppressing or co-opting their domestic opponents. Abu Dhabi's vast oil revenues and its ruler's willingness to spend them on economic and social projects in the six smaller emirates to the north provided the basis for the formation of the United Arab Emirates at the start of 1972, following Britain's withdrawal from the Gulf. Beginning in the 1960s, oil monies provided the ruler of Oman with the means to achieve both the unification of the coastal enclaves of Muscat and Salalah with the country's tribal hinterland and the suppression of the rebellion in the southern province of Dhofar, bringing a virtually unprecedented degree of stability to Omani politics.

Bahrain, refused a preeminent role in a larger federation of Arab Gulf states, elected to stand alone, becoming independent in August 1971. The ruler, Shaikh Isa bin Sulman Al Khalifah, became head of state, while the heir apparent, his son Shaikh Hamad, became minister of defense and Shaikh Isa's brother, Shaikh Khalifah bin Sulman, took the office of prime minister. Close relatives of the ruler have continued to occupy the most important posts in the cabinet, joined by a limited number of Western-educated notables drawn from the established rich merchant community. The size and scope of the central administration grew throughout the 1970s, as the state initiated industrial projects, promulgated labor laws, and expanded health and other social welfare services. The 1980s saw a burgeoning of the country's armed forces, with major air and naval bases constructed on the islands according to plans drawn up by the U.S. Army Corps of Engineers and sizable weapons purchases from U.S. arms manufacturers.

Trade unionists orchestrated a wave of strikes in Bahrain's larger industrial enterprises in early 1974, prompting severe repression on the part of state security forces. In the wake of these strikes, hardliners within the ruling family pushed through a new security law that authorized the ministry of the interior to arrest and imprison anyone suspected of "endangering or . . . planning to endanger the security of the state or disturb public order."

With the suppression of the trade union movement, the most serious challenges to the regime have come from Bahrain's heterogeneous Islamist movement. The more moderate or reformist wing of this movement, consisting of such organizations as the Sunni Society for Social Reform and the Shiʻi Party of the Call to Islam, advocates limits on state intervention in social and religious affairs; the more radical or militant wing, including the Islamic Action Organization and the Iranian-sponsored Islamic Front for the Liberation of Bahrain, calls for the overthrow of the existing political and social order, by violence if necessary. Mass demonstrations organized by Shiʻi militants broke out repeatedly during 1979–1980. In December 1981, the authorities announced that they had broken up a plot by a group of militants having ties to the Islamic Front to assassinate the ruler and take over key government buildings. Those arrested were handed stiff prison sentences but were not executed, a move that largely defused Islamist activism on the islands.

Qatar also remained outside the Arab Gulf federation and became independent in September 1971. Five months later, the prime minister and de facto ruler, Shaikh Khalifah bin Hamad Al Thani, deposed his cousin and took the title of emir with the overt support of neighboring Saudi Arabia. The new ruler's sons were appointed minister of oil and finance and commander in chief of the armed forces, while his brother became minister of the interior. Factional skirmishing between relatives of the deposed ruler and the new emir continues to shape the country's internal politics, and has led to a proliferation of high government posts as a way of mollifying discontented senior shaikhs. The nationalized oil company makes up the bulk of the public sector, although expanding social welfare agencies have produced a large and costly state apparatus. Declining oil revenues after 1986 generated disaffection both within the ruling family and among the general population, but no organized opposition to the regime.

Abu Dhabi, Dubai, Sharjah, Fujairah, Umm al-Qaiwain, and Ajman merged to form the United Arab Emirates in July 1971. The ruler of Abu Dhabi, Shaikh Zayyid bin Sultan Al Nuhayyan, became president of the federation, while the ruler of Dubai, Shaikh Rashid bin Maktum, became vice president. When Ras al-Khaimah finally joined the union in February 1972, a Supreme Federal Council consisting of the seven rulers was established with authority to elect the president and vice president, ratify federal legislation, and draw up the federal budget. The Supreme Federal Council also approves the appointment of a federal prime minister nominated by the president; the president and prime minister then select the members of a Council of Ministers charged with formulating and implementing laws for the federation as a whole. A Federal National Council meets to debate issues confronting the union, but this body has no power to initiate legislation. The federal bureaucracy is funded primarily by Abu Dhabi and is staffed largely by nationals from Dubai and Sharjah, along with considerable numbers of Arab expatriates. The line demarcating federal administration from individual emirate administrations remains fuzzy despite the dissolution of most emirate cabinets soon after independence.

Each emirate has a history of factionalism among prominent shaikhs within its respective ruling family. Shaikh Zayyid of Abu Dhabi deposed his brother Shaikh Shakhbut to become ruler in 1966, naming a close relative of Shaikh Shakhbut federal minister of the interior as a way of keeping accounts balanced. The ruler of Sharjah was assassinated in 1972 by one of his cousins, who had previously been ousted by the British; the Supreme Federal Council stepped in to appoint the ruler's son, Shaikh Sultan bin Muhammad, to succeed his father. In June 1987, Shaikh Sultan's brother attempted to seize control of the emirate. This putsch was defeated only when the Supreme Federal Council nominated Shaikh Sultan's rival as Sharjah's heir apparent. Dubai, on the other hand, carried out a more peaceful transition in leadership following the death of Shaikh Rashid in September 1990, partly owing to the integration of the ruling family into the local commercial elite.

What little opposition there has been to the regimes that constitute the United Arab Emirates has come from groups impatient with the pace of change in the federation. State employees in the poorer northern emirates struck in May 1981 over the government's failure to peg salaries to the cost of living; students at the federal university in al-Ain have periodically demonstrated and boycotted classes to protest the prohibition against forming a student union and to demand that greater control over university administration be given to federation nationals. A series of isolated bombings in Dubai and Abu Dhabi during the early 1980s prompted local security services to tighten restrictions on and surveillance of foreign nationals, particularly Palestinians, residing in the country.

In Oman, eighty-five years of continual conflict between tribal forces loyal to the Ibadi imamate centered in the valleys and plains of the interior and townspeople subject to the sultan in the port city of Muscat came to an end with Sultan Said bin Taimur's reconquest of the hinterlands around the capital and the resignation of the imam in December 1955. The former imam almost immediately joined his brother in soliciting support from Omani laborers working in Saudi Arabia for an antisultanate organization, the Oman Revolutionary Movement. Armed members of this organization landed along the northern coast in June 1957 and, after pushing the sultan's armed forces out of the area, were in turn defeated by British troops and aircraft seconded to the ruler.

Five years later, discontented inhabitants of the southern province of Dhofar began raiding oil company and military installations around the town of Salalah. These guerrillas held a congress in June 1965 and issued a platform calling for the province's independence from the central government in Muscat. More radical activists took control of a second congress in September 1968, renamed the movement the Popular Front for the Liberation of the Occupied Arab Gulf, and adopted an explicitly anti-imperialist platform. This new organization initiated a campaign of armed struggle against government officials and troops throughout Dhofar, with the assistance of the People's Republic of China, the Soviet Union, and Iraq. Early victories sparked the formation of a companion movement in the north, which carried out unsuccessful attacks on two garrisons in the summer of 1970. The formation of this second organization prompted critics of the sultan within the regime to encourage his son, Qabus, to seize control of the country.

Immediately after taking power, Sultan Qabus adopted a dual policy of granting amnesty to any dissidents who would surrender to the central government and complementing military moves against the Popular Front with development projects in the districts from which it drew its support. This combination put Popular Front activists on the defensive, and a series of government victories on the battlefield during 1972–1973 forced the guerrillas to retreat to the most desolate areas of the south. State forces overran the Front's remaining strongholds during the summer and fall of 1974, and by the end of 1976 the sultan was able to claim that order had been fully restored in Dhofar.

In November 1980, Sultan Qabus ordered a ministerial committee to consider ways of broadening the process of formal consultation within policymaking circles. The deliberations of this committee resulted in a set of decrees creating an appointed

State Consultative Council the following October; the sultan presided over the first session of the new council in early November. This body was given no legislative powers; its mandate was limited to advising the ruler on proposed laws; and its meetings were to be held in secret. At the height of the Gulf crisis of 1990–1991, Omani officials intimated that seats on the council might be put up for popular election, but a year later no steps had been taken to implement this proposal and no formal constitution had been promulgated for the sultanate.

(See also DECOLONIZATION; ISLAM; MIDDLE EAST; RELIGION AND POLITICS.)

John Duke Anthony, *Arab States of the Lower Gulf: People, Politics, Petroleum* (Washington, D.C., 1975). Calvin H. Allen, *Oman: The Modernization of the Sultanate* (Boulder, Colo., 1987). Fred H. Lawson, *Bahrain: The Modernization of Autocracy* (Boulder, Colo., 1989). Jill Crystal, *Oil and Politics in the Gulf: Rulers and Merchants in Kuwait and Qatar* (Cambridge, U.K., 1990).
                                                    FRED H. LAWSON

GULF WAR. The Gulf War, fought between *Iraq and a military coalition led by the United States, lasted just forty-three days—from 17 January through 27 February 1991. Coalition forces launched the war in response to Iraqi leader Saddam *Hussein's invasion and annexation of the small, oil-rich state of *Kuwait on 2 August 1991; the Iraqis claimed historic rights over Kuwait, although such claims had scant historical or legal basis.

The United States and Britain demanded Iraq's withdrawal, and they obtained a strong international consensus, reflected in a series of UN Security Council resolutions. Resolution 660, adopted unanimously within twenty-four hours of the invasion, called for the immediate and unconditional withdrawal of Iraqi forces. Resolution 661 of 6 August imposed severe economic *sanctions against Iraq. And eventually, Resolution 678 of 29 November authorized the use of *force against Iraq.

Although the United States obtained UN backing, it chose to act militarily and diplomatically with considerable autonomy from the world body. Claiming an imminent threat to the *security of *Saudi Arabia and the Persian Gulf oil-producing region, the U.S. administration of President George *Bush rushed U.S. naval and ground units to the Gulf on 7 August, bypassing possible formation of a UN multinational force and preempting the results of *Arab League deliberations. Britain (and later, France) contributed contingents, as did Egypt, Syria, Saudi Arabia, and a number of other Gulf states; several other states in Europe and Asia contributed naval, medical, or other ancillary units; by the time hostilities were engaged, however, U.S. forces accounted for about three-quarters of the combat personnel and an even higher proportion of heavy weapons, aircraft, and naval ships.

In the months leading up to the military conflict, intense diplomatic activity—by UN Secretary-General Pérez de Cuéllar, French President Mitterrand, Soviet President Gorbachev, and others—sought to obtain Iraq's withdrawal from Kuwait before a 15 January deadline specified in UN Resolution 678. At the same time, Iraqi leader Saddam Hussein moved to consolidate his position by taking hostage Western civilians in Iraq and mobilizing Islamic sentiment against the West. He also proposed to link his settlement of the crisis to the withdrawal of Israel from the territories it occupied. Amid mixed signals from Baghdad, efforts to find a diplomatic formula for Iraqi withdrawal were rejected by the United States and its allies, who affirmed that Iraqi withdrawal was not negotiable.

As time went by, the Iraqi leader appeared to soften his position, and some think that the tight economic blockade might sooner or later have forced him to withdraw. However, the United States at an early stage moved toward military resolution of the conflict. On 8 November, President Bush deployed 200,000 additional troops, moving the coalition forces from a defensive to an offensive posture. And on 18 November, U.S. officials stated that "neutralization" of Iraq's military and nuclear capacity had become objectives as well as Iraqi withdrawal from Kuwait. Purely diplomatic means could not achieve these additional goals.

By the time hostilities broke out, the United States and its coalition partners had assembled more than 750,000 military personnel, 1,200 high-performance aircraft, 300 naval vessels including 8 aircraft carriers, and 1,800 tanks. Many of these forces and weapons, drawn from Western Europe, would not have been available had not the *Cold War ended and the Soviet Union given its high-profile accord to the *war plans of its former enemies.

In the combat theater, coalition forces faced approximately 400,000 Iraqi troops, armed with relatively advanced Western and Soviet arms acquired during the long and bloody *Iran-Iraq War (1980–1988). The Iraqi army was not considered to be a particularly high-quality fighting force, however, and its strategic reserves in economic and population terms were extremely small compared to those of the United States and its coalition partners.

The coalition campaign began with a forty-day air war during which aircraft subjected Iraqi targets to intense, round-the-clock bombing, destroying not only military targets but also much of Iraq's civilian infrastructure, including power plants and factories. Iraq responded with Scud missiles aimed at Saudi Arabia and also at Israel, although these attacks caused relatively light damage. The war ended with a brief and devastating four-day ground campaign. Iraqi forces retreated and only occasionally engaged coalition units; exposed to lethal air attacks as they withdrew, they were dealt a crushing defeat by coalition forces under the command of U.S. General Norman Schwarzkopf.

To obtain a cease-fire and armistice, Iraq was

forced to agree to all relevant Security Council resolutions, including renunciation of all claims to Kuwait and agreement to pay heavy reparations for the damage done in Kuwait. Soon thereafter, the Bush administration announced that it was seeking to oust Saddam Hussein. The UN imposed stringent conditions on the lifting of sanctions, and Iraq refused to comply. There followed much additional suffering in Iraq because of abortive antigovernment uprisings and health deprivation suffered by ordinary Iraqis during many months of prolonged sanctions.

The war was very costly. In addition to the great physical destruction suffered by Iraq and Kuwait, coalition direct expenses (including social aid packages) have been estimated at well over US$150 billion. The United States was unable and unwilling to bear more than a small share of these costs, so it obtained financing from various partners. Kuwait and Saudi Arabia made the largest financial contributions. The Saudis have estimated their total war-related expenses as US$54 billion; Kuwait spent at least US$25 billion (and probably far more); Japan and Germany contributed about US$10–20 billion each; and Britain, France, the United States, and some small Gulf states accounted for most of the remainder of the outlays.

Though the war resulted in fewer than 500 casualties among coalition forces, Iraqi military casualties have been estimated at 50,000–100,000, while civilian casualties are thought to have reached at least 10,000, mostly due to the air war. In addition, casualties due to the civil war within Iraq are believed to have reached 50,000.

The crisis also led to massive displacement of people. At least half a million fled from Kuwait, including many *foreign workers who lost homes, savings, and livelihood. Iraq also expelled 1–2 million Egyptians and other foreign workers; Saudi Arabia expelled as many as a million Yemeni workers because Yemen refused to support the coalition. And after the postwar Iraqi uprisings, approximately 2 million people were displaced: Kurds in the north who tried to escape toward Turkey or Iran; Shi'is in the south who fled toward Iran and Saudi Arabia. Altogether, 4–5 million people migrated within an eight-month period, one of the largest population movements in recent history.

The war had a very serious environmental impact as well. The Iraqis released large quantities of crude oil into the Persian Gulf, destroying fish and wildlife on a vast scale. They also set fire to most of the Kuwaiti oil wells before withdrawing from the emirate, leaving plumes of oil smoke from hundreds of fires rising into the upper atmosphere and causing "black rain" over a large area. Coalition bombing, which struck nuclear and chemical weapons installations, also caused serious environmental damage; coalition bombing may also have contributed to the release of oil into the Persian Gulf.

The coalition move toward war was opposed by a substantial segment of *public opinion in most of the involved countries. In the United States, Congress was narrowly divided on the issue and antiwar demonstrations took place in many cities. In France, Defense Minister Jean-Pierre Chevènement resigned. And in many countries throughout the world there were large and sometimes violent public protests. Once the war was under way, however, the U.S. government and most of its Western partners were able to rally overwhelming public support, thanks in part to careful management of mass media coverage. But debate continues as to whether the war was necessary to accomplish Iraqi withdrawal from Kuwait, why the United States went to war with a regime it had armed and supported until just before the crisis, and why the U.S. ambassador to Baghdad implied U.S. disinterest in the mounting crisis in an interview with the Iraqi leader only days before the invasion.

The war was the first major military conflict in the post–Cold War period. As such, the Soviet Union played only a secondary role in the crisis and in general tended to support the United States. The U.S. government succeeded in partially overcoming the "Vietnam syndrome" during the conflict—that is, weakening a section of U.S. public opinion that was opposed to military interventions in the *Third World. The United States emerged from the war as the undisputed leader of the global political and military system.

(See also DIPLOMACY; INTERNATIONAL MIGRATION; REFUGEES; UNITED NATIONS.)

Phyllis Bennis and Michel Moushabeck, *Beyond the Storm: A Gulf Crisis Reader* (New York, 1991). John Bulloch and Harvey Morris, *Saddam's War: The Origins of the Kuwait Conflict and the International Response* (London, 1991). Norman Friedman, *Desert Victory* (Annapolis, Md., 1991). Pierre Salinger, *Secret Dossier* (New York, 1991). Theodore Draper, "The Gulf War Reconsidered" *New York Review of Books* (16 January 1992): 46–53. Theodore Draper, "The True History of the Gulf War" *New York Review of Books* (30 January 1992): 38–45.

JAMES A. PAUL

GUYANA. Part of the * English-speaking Caribbean and a former British colony that gained independence in 1966, Guyana has a population of nearly 1 million people. Constitutionally, Guyana is a *parliamentary democracy, but in reality it is a one-dominant-party authoritarian regime. Since 1964, only the People's National Congress (PNC) has won office. The PNC has maintained power by electoral fraud and tight control over institutional life.

Guyana's evolution as a nation-state has been marked by significant instability rooted in socialist policies and the politics of *race. The two leading figures in the country's history have been Cheddi Jagan and Forbes Burnham, who began as socialist allies in the governing People's Progressive Party (PPP). In the early 1950s, they parted company,

Burnham founded the PNC, and violent racial politics engulfed the colony from 1961 to 1964 as the two men struggled for power on grounds of ethnic support. Burnham was black and Jagan was East Indian. East Indians comprised forty-eight percent of the population, blacks thirty-six percent; Portuguese, native Amerindians, and others made up the remainder. Charges were repeatedly made that the PNC promoted racial policies during the administrations of Jagan (1957–1964), Burnham (1964–1985), and Desmond Hoyte, who assumed office in 1985. Cheddi Jagan's PPP government (1957–1964) was also accused of racial politics.

The dominant political institution remains the PNC because of its authoritarian control. The Parliament is a pliable agency that facilitates the PNC's passage of legislation by a two-thirds majority and allows the three opposition parties with seats some minor debate on major issues. In recent years, the ruling party has lost effective control of the highly politicized trade union movement, and other agencies have become emboldened to pursue fundamental democratic change, e.g., the churches, the independent media, lawyers, consumers, and business interests. The military has played a central role in maintaining the PNC in office.

Socialist political and economic policies were introduced by the PNC in the early 1970s. President Hoyte abandoned these policies in favor of a capitalist development strategy whose mainspring involves divestment and reprivatization, a private enterprise approach, and attracting heavy foreign private capital under a comprehensive Economic Recovery Programme (ERP) bankrolled by the *International Monetary Fund (IMF). However, because most people blame the PNC for the country's woes and see the regime as illegitimate, the government has failed to inspire confidence either in its new ideological image or economic program.

Production is down abysmally in all key sectors, including bauxite, sugar, and rice. Diversification and divestment programs are stalled, and foreign investment has occurred at a pedestrian pace. Basic institutional and physical infrastructure have deteriorated, and the agreement with the IMF is often in jeopardy for unmet requirements. This is unlikely to change under a PNC government. Indeed, the ruling party is expected to lose the 1992 general elections. Guyana used to be a major Caribbean Community (Caricom) player, but this role has greatly diminished owing to the country's domestic problems.

(See also AUTHORITARIANISM; ONE-PARTY SYSTEM; SOCIALISM AND SOCIAL DEMOCRACY.)

Colin Baber and Henry Jeffrey, *Guyana: Politics, Economics and Society* (Boulder, Colo., 1986). Percy C. Hintzen, *The Costs of Regime Survival: Racial Mobilization, Elite Domination and Control of the State in Guyana and Trinidad* (New York, 1989).

FESTUS BROTHERSON, JR.

H

HAILE SELASSIE. Emperor Haile Selassie liked to compare himself to the Roman Emperor Justinian. He considered his revised constitution of 1955 and the European-inspired codes of law that he promulgated in *Ethiopia in the late 1950s and early 1960s as prime achievements. He did not take kindly to criticism of these laws and the *constitution.

The 1955 constitution promised cabinet and parliamentary government with an independent judiciary as guardian of a Bill of Rights. At the same time it proclaimed the sanctity of the emperor's person and the paramountcy of his power. In short, the emperor was a traditional ruler with modern pretensions. The tension between his modernizing agenda, with its wrenching demands, and the resistance of traditional concepts and vested interests marked his fifty-eight-year rule, first as regent (1916–1930), then as emperor until his fall in 1974.

Schooled at a French Catholic mission, Haile Selassie began his career as a young governor of his father's province of Harar, where he had been born in 1892. Harar was a prized governorate among Emperor Menelik's newly conquered territories, and was thus entrusted to Ras Mekonnen, Haile Selassie's father and Menelik's trusted cousin. From his youth in Harar, Haile Selassie (then called Tafari) acquired the empire mentality together with an appetite for business, the result of his European contacts. These contacts also eventually helped him to garner support in his bid for the imperial throne. In 1916 he overthrew Lij Yasu, Emperor Menelik's chosen successor, installed Menelik's daughter, Zewditu, as figurehead queen, and began his long rule at the age of 26.

Upon Zewditu's death in 1930, he ascended the throne under the name Haile Selassie. A year later he promulgated a "modern" constitution to undergird the reforms which he had initiated, undermining the power of the regional potentates. The main reforms concerned the introduction of a national army, taxation, and a paid central bureaucracy.

Haile Selassie attained world renown by events beyond his control. In 1936 *Mussolini's Fascist forces invaded Ethiopia, sending the emperor into exile. His memorable appeal for help at the *League of Nations fell on deaf ears, but received wide coverage, thus starting his career as a world figure of great fascination. Four years later Mussolini's alliance with Hitler came as a boon, enabling the emperor to return home with British and Allied assistance.

Five years of Italian rule left him with an impressive infrastructure and fledgling industrial and commercial enterprises. The emperor lost no time in exploiting these legacies to his benefit and to those of his loyal followers. Meanwhile he also acquired Eritrea with the help of U.S. *diplomacy. His imperial appetite overreached itself, however, when in 1962 he unilaterally abolished the UN-arranged federation of Eritrea with Ethiopia. There is a historical irony: in annexing Eritrea, the emperor flouted the very international law to which he appealed when his own country was invaded. The *Eritrean War of Independence began then and would haunt him to his last days, as it has haunted his successors.

His *modernization programs had also spawned new social forces with the attendant tensions and demands. An abortive coup in 1960 led by the head of his bodyguards broke the ice, ushering in an era of protests and clandestine movements. The emperor ignored these developments, finding refuge in international affairs. In 1963 he hosted the founding meeting of the *Organization of African Unity (OAU), becoming its first chairman. It was to be a short-lived glory.

In 1974 he was overthrown by the armed forces which his modernization created. He died in 1975 under mysterious circumstances. His epitaph might read: "Despite his stature and achievements, few mourned him."

Margery F. Perham, *The Government of Ethiopia,* 2d ed. (London, 1969). Christopher Clapham, *Haile Selassie's Government* (London, 1969).

BEREKET HABTE SELASSIE

HAITI. The poorest country in the Western Hemisphere, Haiti has also been burdened with a political history of oppressive dictatorships and instability. Sharing the Caribbean island of Hispaniola with the Dominican Republic, the country has slightly over 6 million people, three-fourths of whom live in rural areas. Per capita income is less than US$300 per year, and the literacy rate is only thirty-six percent.

Formerly a colony of France, Haiti achieved independence in 1804 after the only successful slave *revolution in modern history. Between independence and the U.S. occupation in 1915, Haiti was ruled by an alliance of merchants and the military. The occupation, partly to counter rising German influence in the country, lasted until 1934. While it increased political stability, it also exacerbated many of Haiti's structural problems such as economic and administrative centralization, monocrop exports, fiscal weakness, and poverty.

Haiti's modern political history can be said to date from 1957, when François ("Papa Doc") Duvalier was elected president. Duvalier quickly began to centralize power through the use of violence against his opponents. The main instrument was his infamous group of armed thugs, the *tontons macoutes*. In 1964, when other institutions had been made subservient to the executive, Duvalier declared himself "President for Life." On his death in 1971, his son, Jean-Claude ("Baby Doc"), inherited his father's position. A less skilled politician living in more difficult economic times, Jean-Claude Duvalier could not maintain control as his father had. Alienated supporters eventually joined the oppressed in popular demonstrations against Duvalier. When the United States withdrew support in 1986, Jean-Claude fled to France.

The provisional governments between 1986 and 1990 were unstable and violent, unable or unwilling to make significant changes in society. This situation led to the election in December 1990 of a liberation theologian, Father Jean-Bertrand Aristide, as president. Representing the desperately poor majority of Haiti's population, Aristide received over sixty-seven percent of the vote. Nonetheless, his presidency lasted less than seven months; he fled to Venezuela on 1 October 1991 following a military *coup d'état. Those seven months caused enormous polarization in Haiti, as Aristide tried to implement reforms to benefit the majority of the population. Although he had substantially moderated his radical views, he nonetheless tried to reform the military and proposed social welfare and agrarian reform policies that conflicted with the interests of the landowners and privileged urban elites. These policies, plus others that were perceived as threatening by the military, led to the coup.

In previous years, Aristide's overthrow would either have been applauded in Washington and many Latin American capitals or at least ignored. In the post–Cold War era and the era of new democracies, however, Aristide's counterparts saw his ouster as potentially undermining their own positions. Thus, the *Organization of American States, backed by the U.S. and European governments, took the lead in attempting to negotiate Aristide's return—although with fewer powers. Aristide's return to power seems increasingly unlikely, and a succession of compromise or interim arrangements may result.

Regardless of the government in power, the social and economic problems facing Haiti are overwhelming. A key fissure is the majority black population versus the small mulatto group, which has existed since before independence. This division overlaps substantially but not completely with the economic gap between a small group of very rich and the overwhelming majority of the poor. These schisms, plus the lack of a viable productive economy, the dependency on imports and foreign aid for basic necessities, and the enormous expectations aroused by Aristide's election, will pose a perhaps insurmountable challenge to him or any successor government.

(See also U.S.–LATIN AMERICAN RELATIONS.)

Alex Dupuy, *Haiti in the World Economy: Class, Race, and Underdevelopment since 1700* (Boulder, Colo., 1989).
ALEX DUPUY

HAMMARSKJÖLD, Dag. Best-known for his achievements as UN secretary-general, Dag Hammarskjöld was born in Jönköping, Sweden, on 29 July 1905 and died at Ndola, Northern Rhodesia, on 18 September 1961. Son of a former prime minister of Sweden and educated at Uppsala and Stockholm universities, he entered public service, becoming under-secretary of the Swedish Ministry of Finance and chair of the governors of the Bank of Sweden in 1935 and secretary-general of the Swedish Foreign Office in 1949. From 1953 until his death in 1961 he served as UN secretary-general.

Hammarskjöld was an intellectual of wide-ranging interest. He was a distinguished economist, diplomat, lawyer, and administrator, and was also passionately interested in art and literature. He chaired the Nobel Literature Prize Committee of the Swedish Academy and translated a number of difficult literary works—*Anabase* by Saint-John Perse and *Antiphon* by Djuna Barnes, for example—into Swedish.

Taking over a UN debilitated by the *Cold War, the *Korean War, and the Joseph McCarthy era in the United States, Hammarskjöld rapidly gained the confidence of governments and restored the morale of the international civil service, and his use of the secretary-generalship to engage in active but quiet personal diplomacy transformed the position from a predominantly administrative one into an important political and diplomatic resource. Among his many achievements were the release of the U.S. prisoners in China in 1955; his work in defusing the *Suez Crisis of 1956 and in setting up the first UN peacekeeping force; his successful management of the 1958 Lebanese crisis; and the UN's activities in the Congo, in the course of which he met his death in a plane crash.

Hammarskjöld developed the secretary-general's diplomatic and mediating role, the doctrines of UN "presences" and "good offices" in conflict areas, and the now well-recognized technique of peacekeeping. He was indefatigable in defending the independence and integrity of the secretary-generalship and of the UN Secretariat. He was extraordinarily courageous in standing up for the principles of the UN Charter with powers both great and small. This approach did not endear him to some powerful leaders, and he ended his life disowned and vilified both by Nikita *Khrushchev and Charles de *Gaulle. By others, however, he was greatly respected and admired.

Hammarskjöld was a highly articulate and imaginative man who wrote most of his own statements and speeches. These have stood the test of time remarkably well and are increasingly referred to as classic expressions of international principle and practice. He believed that, through a process of creating precedents and case law, the UN would be gradually transformed from an *institutional* mechanism into a *constitutional* instrument recognized and respected by all nations. He worked tirelessly to give practical shape to this vision.

Hammarskjöld is perhaps best remembered as a courageous and visionary international leader and a master of multilateral *diplomacy. His posthumously published notebook, *Markings,* is a unique record of the inner life of a public figure.

(See also Congo Crisis; United Nations.)

BRIAN URQUHART

HAVEL, Václav. Czech playwright, longtime champion of human rights, and former president of the Czech and Slovak Federative Republic, Václav Havel was born on 5 October 1936 in Prague of well-to-do parents, Václav M. Havel and Božena Vavrečková Havlová. As the result of communist educational policies that discriminated against children of the former bourgeoisie, he was forced to finish high school through night courses while working as a laboratory assistant. Denied admission to university study, Havel studied briefly at a technological university and eventually completed his studies as an external student at the theater department of the Academy of Arts. After completing his military service, he worked as a stagehand at the ABC theater. He soon moved to the Theater on the Balustrade, and there he played an important role in the innovative developments that took place in the small theaters of Prague in the 1960s. Havel's early plays, *The Garden Party* (1963), *The Memorandum* (1967), and *The Increased Difficulty of Concentration* (1968), established his reputation as the leading exponent of the theater of the absurd in *Czechoslovakia. Active in the circle of young writers involved in the journal *Tvář* in the mid-1960s, Havel also worked for change in the official Writers' Union in 1968, during the *Prague Spring.

Forbidden to take any part in public life after the end of the reform period, Havel nonetheless continued to write. Although the authorities did not allow his work to be published or performed in Czechoslovakia during the period of political orthodoxy that followed the Soviet invasion of Czechoslovakia in August 1968, his plays, including *the Conspirators* (1971), *The Beggar's Opera* (1972), *The Moun-*

tain Hotel (1974), *Audience and Private View* (1975), *Protest* (1978), *Largo Desolato* (1984), *Temptation* (1985), and *Slum Clearance* (1988), and books, including *Living in Truth* (1987) and *Letters to Olga* (1988), received widespread acclaim abroad. In 1969, he was awarded the Austrian State Prize for European Literature. His activities in defense of *human rights led to further honors, including the Jan Palach Prize, the Erasmus Prize, the Olof Palme Prize, and the Frankfurt Book Fair Peace Prize.

Havel was one of the founders of the *Charter 77 movement and the Committee for the Defense of the Unjustly Persecuted (VONS). Arrested numerous times for his independent activities, he was placed under house arrest from 1977 to 1979. In 1979, he was sentenced to four-and-a-half years in prison for alleged antistate activities. Released in March 1983, Havel continued to be a tireless champion of human rights and an advocate of "living in truth," regardless of the personal cost. This commitment was put to the test again in early 1989 when, as the result of his participation in the commemoration of the 1969 suicide of Czech student Jan Palach, Havel was once again imprisoned for several months.

The leading force behind the creation of Civic Forum, the organization that arose to lead the mass protests that overthrew the communist regime in November 1989, Havel quickly emerged as the leader of the revolution and the symbol of his country's hopes for democracy and the future. His selection as president of Czechoslovakia by a Parliament still dominated by communist deputies in December 1989 capped the victory of the "Velvet Revolution" that ousted the communist system. Havel was reelected as president by a wide margin by the Federal Assembly after the June 1990 elections.

As the result of his steadfast refusal to compromise with the communist regime, Havel exercised an authority that went far beyond the powers of his office. Clearly the dominant political figure in Czechoslovakia in the early postcommunist period, Havel's presidency was characterized by an attempt to infuse morality into day-to-day politics. Together with Jiří Dienstbier, the dissident colleague who became his foreign minister, Havel pursued a high-profile strategy designed to reassert Czechoslovakia's independence in *foreign policy and reclaim its place among European nations. In addition to negotiating the withdrawal of Soviet troops from Czechoslovakia, he reestablished Czechoslovakia's traditionally warm relations with the United States and took important steps to rejoin Europe. Czechoslovakia's acceptance as a member of the *Council of Europe, the new association agreement with the *European Community, and the interest and aid offered Czechoslovakia by other democratic states all attest to the success of these efforts. The cornerstone of Czechoslovakia's foreign policy under Havel has been a vision of Europe without blocs, whose security would be guaranteed within the framework of the *Conference on Security and Cooperation in Europe (CSCE) process.

Havel's presidency was less successful in dealing with domestic issues, particularly ethnic tensions between Czechs and Slovaks. Although Havel continues to be revered by most citizens of the Czech and Slovak Federative Republic, he is less popular in Slovakia than in the Czech lands. As a result of the victory of forces supporting Slovak independence in the June 1992 elections, Havel was not reelected by the Federal Assembly to a second term as president. His continued popularity in the Czech lands makes it likely that he will be chosen as Czech president after the impending break-up of the Czech and Slovak federation.

(See also NINETEEN EIGHTY-NINE.)

Jan Vladislav, ed., *Vaclav Havel or Living in Truth* (London, 1986). Vaclav Havel, *Disturbing the Peace* (New York, 1990).

SHARON L. WOLCHIK

HAYA DE LA TORRE, Víctor Raúl. One of a handful of twentieth-century Latin American politicians whose careers were significant beyond the boundaries of their own countries, Víctor Raúl Haya de la Torre was the founder of the American Popular Revolutionary Alliance (APRA). Haya spoke to and for a public beyond his native *Peru when he warned of the dangers of *imperialism and the need for social reform. Indeed, a number of so-called national revolutionary parties in Latin America—such as Democratic Action (AD) in Venezuela, the National Revolutionary Movement (MNR) in Bolivia, and the National Liberation Party (PLN) in Costa Rica—were based on Aprista principles.

Haya de la Torre was born in Trujillo in 1895 into a prominent northern family on his mother's side. He attended the National University of Trujillo and San Marcos University in Lima. At San Marcos, he became active in student politics, being elected president of the Peruvian Student Federation in 1920. Using this position, he worked to build a student-worker coalition to launch his political career. As a result of opposing Peru's dictator, Augusto Leguía, he was deported in 1923 and spent the next eight years in exile, mainly in Mexico and Europe.

The period was devoted to advancing the APRA, which Haya founded in 1924. Although considering himself a Marxist, Haya believed the Latin American path to *socialism would be different from that of Europe. For example, Haya declared that change would only come with the alliance of three sectors: *peasants, the proletariat, and the middle class, this last group being the leading actor. This alliance would control, through the APRA, the harmful effects of foreign investment, a necessary evil, which unlike in Europe was the first not the last stage of capitalism. These views brought him into growing conflict with the Communist Party. At the interna-

tional level, this manifested itself in Haya's refusal to affiliate the APRA with the Third International. Back in Peru in the 1930s, it was seen in Haya's rivalry with Peru's other well-known Marxist, José Carlos *Mariátegui. Nonetheless, the Peruvian establishment—and especially the military—resolutely opposed Haya and the APRA.

In the postwar period, following deportations, persecution, and self-isolation, Haya decided that the U.S. threat to the hemisphere had decreased with Roosevelt's Good Neighbor Policy. This, and a desire to adapt to the changing nature of Peruvian politics, led Haya and the APRA to abandon their radical politics and adopt an approach of compromise, even with those who had persecuted him. *Treinta Años de Aprismo,* the ideological justification for such changes, was acclaimed by some and attacked by others.

These internal transformations allowed the return of the APRA to public life and a small share of power during the 1950s and 1960s, but they never allowed Haya to become president despite his status as Peru's premier politician. The military remained adamantly opposed to the party until too late for Haya's own career. In his eighties, Haya presided over the Constituent Assembly in 1979, which drafted Peru's current *constitution and sent the military back to the barracks. He died on 15 August 1979, six years before the APRA would finally win the presidency under Haya's favorite disciple, Alan García.

(See also MARXISM.)

Harry Cantor, *The Ideology and Program of the Peruvian Aprista Movement* (Washington, D.C., 1966). Robert J. Alexander, ed., *Aprismo: The Ideas and Doctrines of Víctor Raúl Haya de la Torre* (Kent, Ohio, 1973).

HERACLIO BONILLA

HEALTH CARE. See WELFARE STATE.

HEGEMONY. The term *hegemony* is found in *Thucydides' classical Realist *History of the Peloponnesian Wars* (fifth century B.C.E.). The major reconceptualization is attributed to Antonio *Gramsci (1891–1937) in his *Prison Notebooks* (New York, 1971). The concept helps to explain the relationships between *power, stability, and order in *international relations (IR), such as in debates on the question of U.S. hegemonic decline. Other historical instances of hegemony include Britain in the nineteenth century and the Soviet Union in the communist world between 1945 and 1989.

The contested concept of hegemony may be usefully explicated with regard to Robert Cox's (in Robert O. Keohane, *Neo-Realism and Its Critics,* New York, 1986) distinction between "critical" and "problem-solving" theories: the former seek to reveal the social basis of power and potential for transformation of world orders; the latter accept the order largely as it is, developing formulas to manage it.

Critical Theories. Classical Realists (e.g., Machiavelli, E. H. Carr) and Historical Materialists (e.g., Fernand Braudel, Robert W. Cox) identify hegemony as a balance of forces under specific historical conditions. Thus each has a historicist epistemology, but with different ontologies of IR, with Classical Realism's based upon regional or global orders (e.g., the relations between ancient Greek city-states and others in the Levant and North Africa). Marxist ontology is a social totality, its major elements being social forces and social structures (frequently categorized into modes of production, such as feudalism and capitalism). Both approaches stress the dynamics of power, production, and the *state in given orders.

Nonetheless, each perspective defines hegemony with regard to different conceptions of agency. For classical Realism this is a dominant state (e.g., Athens; Rome; Britain; the United States) exerting hegemony over others (respectively: other Greek city-states in the fifth century B.C.E.; the Roman Empire, at least in its Byzantine form, up to its collapse in 1453; the British Empire and Continental Europe in the nineteenth century; the "free world" after 1945). The counterparts in *Marxism are social classes or historical blocs, drawn from one or a combination of states. In both approaches, the ruling classes or *elites exercise hegemony and leadership by articulating and synthesizing conceptions of general interests, so that their material power is embedded in, and strengthened by, political consent.

Gramscian approaches stress the crucial role of ideas in the achievement of hegemony, which occurs when the worldview, social principles and practices, and the intellectual and moral leadership of the ruling group are so internalized by subordinates that the order in which hegemony is exercised appears natural and/or inevitable. Hegemony thus configures the "limits of the possible" as they are conceived by different groups and classes in a civilization or political order. Hegemony can be said to be achieved in a negative sense when no credible alternative has emerged to challenge the prevailing order, that is, when no strong counterhegemonic tendencies or movements have begun to materialize. A hegemonic international order would be achieved when the major institutions and forms of organization—economic, social, and political—as well as the key values of the leading elements in the dominant state(s) become models for emulation in subordinate states (Cox, 1987). In the case of post-1945 capitalism, the patterns of emulation are stronger in the developed states than in the less developed. In the former, liberal *democracy and rule by consent generally characterize political life, with economic policy subordinated to the needs of capital. Hegemony is thus embedded in the ideas, institutions, and practices of a system which formally separates politics and economics, and state from civil society. Nevertheless, the quality and intensity of hegemony changes over time, within and across states and world orders.

Problem-Solving Theory. Neorealism (see Keohane, 1986) has emerged recently as a problem-solving theory to establish a conceptualization of system dynamics and the techniques for the reproduction of the existing order. Using a positivist epistemology, and incorporating aspects of Liberal Institutionalism, it develops a utilitarian calculus of states' costs and benefits as an apparatus to help manage IR. The ontology is an *international system, constituted mainly by interactions of states (or governments) and markets (individuals, firms).

More specifically, the conceptualization of interstate relations is based upon Hobbes's reading of Thucydides' *History* (which he translated). States are assumed to behave like Hobbesian egoistic individualists, as if in a state of nature (or international *anarchy) in a struggle of all against all for survival. Rational constraints are placed on this struggle through the *balance of power or hegemonic domination. However, if hegemony declines and/or the balance of power changes, international conflict may rise, after a period of relative equilibrium.

By contrast with Marxism, Neorealists assume a basic structural continuity in IR, despite cycles of changing power balances, or rise and decline of empires or hegemonies. The best-selling book by Paul Kennedy, *The Rise and Fall of the Great Powers* (New York, 1987), symbolized the widespread recognition of U.S. decline, and of the idea of cycles of rising and declining hegemony, and a transition to a posthegemonic era. Moreover, U.S. writers have frequently associated hegemony with international economic order, openness, and postwar prosperity.

American concerns come together in the hybrid liberal/Neorealist theory of hegemonic stability (THS), which states that hegemony is a necessary, but not a sufficient condition for the creation of an open economic order. However, in the absence of hegemony, international *public goods (e.g., international *security, global macroeconomic stability) and international *regimes (e.g., in trade, money) may be undersupplied. Thus in the 1930s the world economy had no hegemon both willing and able to act as lender of last resort, provide a market for distress goods, and steer the global macroeconomy. Also the United States was the biggest economic power, but a second-rank military power (Kindleberger, 1973). Given that most applications of THS in the post-1945 era assume U.S. decline, they conclude that "after hegemony" (Keohane, 1984) there may be tendencies toward economic closure, disorder and conflict, unless states cooperate rationally. Other powerful nations should be willing to share burdens of collective management and leadership, in their "enlightened self-interest."

Comparison of Perspectives and Conclusion. Various conceptualizations of hegemony and world order can be identified. Each sees the question of hegemony differently.

Since for classical Realists morality is subordinate to power, hegemony is simply the acceptable face of dominance, and it declines when other states have sufficient power to challenge it. Repercussions of hegemonic decline depend upon the specific historical conditions which surround it, which today involve the break-up of the Soviet Union and the collapse of the ability of Russia or other Soviet successor states to act as a global counterweight to U.S. power. This implies not a decline but an increase in U.S. dominance in the security structure.

For Gramscians, the issue is not U.S. power as such, more the balance of social forces which constitute a given world order, its dynamics and propensity to change. Nevertheless, U.S. behavior appears less and less based on the articulation of universal interests and consent, more on unilateral applications of U.S. economic and military force: this change is bound up with the decline in the hegemonic appeal of postwar international arrangements. This approach suggests that cumulative and conjunctural changes have served to transform the conditions of existence of the post-1945 world order. Thus the hegemonic structures associated with the Pax Americana may be eroding, at both domestic and international "levels," creating a "crisis of hegemony" (Gill, 1990). New world order possibilities can be hegemonic or nonhegemonic, progressive (emancipatory, peaceful, democratic, and based upon recognition and acceptance of civilizational differences) or regressive (based on dominance, force, violence).

By contrast, Neorealism's concept of international structure is individualistic and akin to the liberal economic concept of market structure. The practical problem is analogous to managing a shift from stable, monopolistic power relations (duopolistic in the security regime) to the more unstable relations of oligopolistic competition (among the leading states). Liberal, "regime" variants of the THS suggest that improvements in interstate cooperation and collective management can offset the effects of declining hegemony by reducing transaction costs and uncertainties, and by increasing information flows, predictability, and flexibility. *International cooperation is thus a second-best solution to the problem of international order in a system which might otherwise tend toward damaging competition and rivalry.

The THS is thus a "problem-solving" theory. It combines with rational choice analysis, *game theory, and liberal functionalism to clarify the conditions under which public goods and political order are created and maintained under conditions of (ascending or declining) hegemony. Both classical Realism and Historical Materialism develop "critical" theories in that as they identify the nature of and conditions for hegemony, they highlight the inequalities and subordinations of a given order, and indicate counterhegemonic forces perhaps latent in the historical situation.

(See also CLASS AND POLITICS; FORCE, USE OF; INTERNATIONAL POLITICAL ECONOMY; LIBERALISM; PUBLIC CHOICE THEORY.)

Charles P. Kindleberger, *The World in Depression, 1929–39* (Berkeley, Calif., 1973). Robert O. Keohane, *After Hegemony: Co-operation and Discord in the World Political Economy* (Princeton, N.J., 1984). Robert W. Cox, *Production, Power and World Order: Social Forces in the Making of History* (New York, 1987). Stephen Gill, *American Hegemony and the Trilateral Commission* (Cambridge, U.K., 1990).

STEPHEN GILL

HELSINKI ACCORDS. The Helsinki Accords of 1975 are a diplomatic agreement among thirty-five states that exerted significant influence on its communist signatories in the field of *human rights. The Accords are an example of a continuing political process that generated important results despite different initial expectations. They also exemplify the internationalization of human rights issues.

In the 1950s and 1960s the Soviet Union, seeking to legitimate its geopolitical position in Europe, repeatedly called for a European security conference. Broadened, according to conditions set by the Western European states, to include discussions on human rights and economic issues and to include the United States and Canada as participants, such a conference was first held in 1972. The resulting Helsinki Accord (officially the Final Act of the Helsinki Meeting of the *Conference on Security and Cooperation in Europe), which was signed by all European and North American states except Albania, pledged the signatories to certain security, economic, and human rights principles.

The Soviet Union and its allies published the text in full, as called for by the agreement itself, and accepted a series of review or follow-up conferences. Publication combined with review had the effect of spotlighting Soviet and East European human rights practices, which the parties had agreed were proper subjects for international scrutiny. In response to publication and dissemination of the Accord, especially in the Soviet Union and Czechoslovakia, Helsinki monitoring groups sprang up, demanding that their governments implement the principles—which included "the right of the individual to know and act upon" human rights—contained in the Accord. Monitoring groups were ruthlessly crushed in these two states in particular. This accelerated attention to Eastern violations of rights.

Initial Western emphasis on human rights and humanitarian principles, which made up Basket Three (Basket One comprised *security issues, Basket Two economic ones), was the product of West European rather than U.S. *diplomacy. In the mid-1970s U.S.

foreign policy, as greatly influenced by Henry *Kissinger, regarded human rights as basically an internal matter of states and a sentimental impediment to "realistic" geostrategy. Kissinger and others were skeptical about what came to be called the Helsinki process, fearing that the Soviet Union would achieve the legitimization of its control over Eastern Europe without having to give anything significant in return. Hence the United States, like the Soviet Union, only reluctantly agreed to the terms of Basket Three.

By 1977, at the first review conference in Belgrade, the United States assumed the leadership of the Western states in focusing on human rights. The Soviet Union, while reacting strongly to the U.S.-led criticisms, did not abandon the Helsinki process, since the 1975 agreement had been proclaimed by Moscow as one of the great achievements of the Brezhnev era. Moreover, the Soviets were reluctant to abandon Basket One's security principles, even as they came under attack for their violations of human rights in Basket Three. In subsequent review conferences and more specialized follow-up meetings, the West—with increasing unity—continued to devote attention to Eastern violations of Basket Three principles. In return, Eastern states reversed their argument that specific criticisms were an interference in domestic affairs, and began to criticize Western violations of social and economic rights.

The West directed their comments to two audiences: the governments of the Eastern states and those individuals dissenting from prevailing practices in Soviet-bloc states. Both audiences were affected by the Helsinki process. Interviews with released dissidents made clear that they were morally sustained by developments in the Helsinki process, as reported by the Western media and other channels of communication. And although some governmental changes could be traced to Helsinki pressures prior to 1985, after that date and the rise of Mikhail *Gorbachev in the Soviet Union, it was clear that Moscow increasingly accepted the human rights and humanitarian principles of Basket Three. After the Eastern and Central European political revolutions of 1989, Basket Three principles helped to provide standards of behavior for the reform regimes. In 1990 a Helsinki follow-up meeting in Copenhagen unanimously endorsed the ideas of political pluralism, multiparty *democracy, an independent judiciary, separation of the state from political parties, and special protection for minorities.

The Helsinki Accords led to an institutionalized process of diplomacy without a formal organization. The Helsinki process had no charter, no budget, no secretariat. Despite the lack of clear law and organization, the Accords as diplomatic instrument played a major role in East-West relations by helping to transform Stalinist states into states that respected internationally recognized human rights.

(See also AMERICAN FOREIGN POLICY; SOVIET–EAST EUROPEAN RELATIONS; SOVIET FOREIGN POLICY.)

A. Bloed and P. Van Dijk, eds., *Essays on Human Rights in the Helsinki Process* (Dordrecht, 1985). Jonathan Luxmoore, *The Helsinki Agreement: Dialogue or Delusion,* Institute for European Defence and Strategic Studies, Occasional Paper No. 20 (London, 1986).Vojtech Mastny, ed., *Helsinki, Human Rights, and European Security* (Durham, N.C., 1986).

DAVID P. FORSYTHE

HINDUISM. The word *hindu* derives from *sindhu* (*Indus* in the Greek transliteration), the name of the great river of the northwest of the South Asian subcontinent, a region still known as Sindh. It is found in ancient Greek writings and refers to the natives of northern India. The terms *India* and its Persian counterpart *Hindustan* designate the territory around the Indus. In the usage of Muslims who settled in the region, "Hindu" came to refer to the non-Muslim population. (The official Indian term for *India today—Bharat—does not bear reference to this history.)

Hinduism, the modern Western term for the majority religion of India, is not a religion in the Semitic sense, that is, based on prophetic revelation, sacred scripture, monotheism, and ecclesiastic organization. The Indian term that comes closest to "religion" is *dharma,* which might be glossed as "socioreligious order." "Hinduism" can best be defined as a set of ideas and practices of the upper, so-called twice-born castes that are based on the interpretation of the ancient Vedas and auxiliary textual traditions by Brahman priests. In addition, a multiplicity of religious movements and centers have arisen over time that are only partly integrated with Brahmanical discourse and practice.

Since the eighteenth century a number of movements have tried to reformulate the disparate religious traditions of India in terms of a unified Hinduism. They have propagated a mixture of religious and social reforms to revitalize an Indian civilization that is considered to be in disarray. This enterprise has depended heavily on orientalist understandings of Indian traditions that share features with Western development rhetoric concerning "Hinduism as a hindrance to *modernization."

A useful way of understanding the significance of these movements to contemporary Indian politics is to relate them to *nationalism. The notion of "Hindu nation" must be regarded in terms of the comparable notion of "Muslim nation" that led to the founding of *Pakistan, or to that of "Sikh nation," currently one of the major threats to the unity of the Indian state. Nationalists on the Indian subcontinent tend to construe shared religion as the basis of the nation-state, and powerful political movements have endeavored to find common ground for the establishment of a Hinduism that will serve as national religion. These commonalities can be found in a limited set of issues, such as conversion, protection of the sacred cow, or the rebuilding of sacred sites destroyed in periods of Muslim conquest. Such issues create a fragile unity among the majority that depends on strong antagonism toward minorities such as Christians and Muslims. Christian missionaries are portrayed as the "dark forces" behind separatist movements in tribal areas. Muslims are portrayed as "secret agents" for Pakistan. The influence of Hindu nationalism on Hindu-Muslim relations has important implications for the development of international relations between India and Pakistan.

(See also RELIGION AND POLITICS.)

Robert Eric Frykenberg, "The Emergence of Modern 'Hinduism' as a Concept and as an Institution: A Reappraisal with Special Reference to South India," in Gunther D. Sontheimer and Hermann Kulke, eds., *Hinduism Reconsidered* (New Delhi, 1989), pp. 29–49.

PETER VAN DER VEER

HIROHITO. Showa Emperor Hirohito, the 124th in the world's oldest surviving *monarchy, according to legend, was born Taisho Emperor Yoshihito's and Empress Kujo Setsuko's eldest son on 29 April 1901. Known as Prince Michi in his childhood, he was brought up from infancy as *Japan's future sovereign ruler and commander in chief of its armed forces. At the age of 10, he was appointed an officer of the Imperial Army and Navy, as provided in the Imperial Family Members Status Ordinance. He became crown prince in 1916, and Japan's first crown prince ever to go abroad in 1921 when he visited Europe. In that same year, he was named prince regent to assist his ailing father. In 1924, he married Princess Kuni, or Nagako, and succeeded Taisho Emperor upon the latter's death. He formally ascended the Chrysanthemum Throne in November 1928.

Under modern Japan's first *constitution promulgated in 1889, Hirohito was, like his grandfather Meiji and his father, not only Japan's sovereign ruler but also a god in human guise, as most Japanese either believed or pretended to believe. Hirohito himself probably did not believe himself to be divine, but he probably did believe that he descended from gods. In the wake of Japan's defeat in *World War II, he publicly renounced his divinity in January 1946. Under Japan's new constitution drafted by U.S. lawyers and promulgated in November 1946, Hirohito lost his status as Japan's sovereign and became merely its "symbol." He escaped trial by the Tokyo International War Crimes Tribunal, thanks to General Douglas MacArthur's goodwill and favorable testimony by wartime leaders, especially General Tojo Hideki, absolving the emperor of any personal responsibility for the *war and wartime atrocities. In his later life, Hirohito made history by visiting Europe in 1972 and the United States in 1975.

Hirohito's role in Japanese politics before and during World War II, especially his involvement in preparations for and conduct of the war itself, remains controversial. All agree that his personal intervention was a critical factor in the Japanese government's decision to surrender to the Allies in August 1945. Opinion is divided, however, on Hirohito's responsibility for the initiation of the war in 1941 and wartime Japanese conduct. Most Japanese and many non-Japanese authors believe that he was a gentle-mannered, peace-loving, and liberal person who was manipulated by his war-mongering civilian and, especially, military advisers and was kept in the dark on details of the war preparation and execution. A few authors hold him responsible for the beginning and execution, as well as the ending, of the war.

Historical records made public in recent years, especially Hirohito's own testimony heard and recorded by a group of his closest confidants on the eve of the *war crimes trial in 1946 and published in late 1990 and early 1991, tend to support the minority view. These records reveal that the emperor was fully informed of and consulted about every important detail concerning the preparation for and execution of World War II, as well as the war against China that preceded it. Moreover, they indicate that he routinely and authoritatively intervened in decisions not only on broad policy issues but also on specific and detailed operational and personnel problems. The records also show that Hirohito supported the continuation of the war until about June 1945 and that his subsequent decision to support Japan's unconditional surrender was based almost exclusively on his concern to save Japan's throne, rather than its people or territory, from certain and total destruction.

Hirohito survived the war by more than four decades before he died in January 1989. An emotional national wake and mourning followed. His role in World War II notwithstanding, he retained the loyalty and devotion of his erstwhile subjects until the very end.

Edward Behr, *Hirohito: Behind the Myth* (London and New York, 1990). Akira Yamada, *Shōwa tennō no sensō shidō* [The Showa emperor's wartime leadership] (Tokyo, 1990). Hidenari Terasaki and Mariko Terasaki Miller, *Showa tenno dokuhakuroku, Terasaki Hidenari goyogakari nikki* [The Showa emperor's monologue and the diary of the emperor's aide Terasaki Hidenari] (Tokyo, 1991).

HARUHIRO FUKUI

HIROSHIMA. The Japanese city of Hiroshima is known throughout the world as the site of the first atomic attack. On the morning of 6 August 1945 a U.S. B-29 bomber, *Enola Gay,* dropped an atomic bomb on Hiroshima from a height of about 580 meters (1,900 feet). The most authoritative Japanese study concludes that the bomb killed 118,661 persons, left another 30,524 severely injured, with a further 48,606 slightly injured. Of the inhabitants of Hiroshima at the time, 118,613 were reported to have avoided injury. The city was devastated by the attack but was completely rebuilt in the years following *World War II.

A second atomic bomb was dropped on the city of Nagasaki late in the morning of 9 August 1945, causing heavy damage and casualties. The most careful estimates conclude that 73,884 were killed and more than 75,000 injured in the attack on Nagasaki.

Japan had been making peace overtures in various foreign capitals prior to the atomic attacks, but it began to offer formal surrender immediately after the second attack, as early as 10 August. By 15 August, Japan's offer to surrender was accepted by the Allies. Japanese authorities had been promised that the emperor would not be charged with any responsibility for the *war and that the emperor system could continue to operate even during the period of U.S. military occupation.

Mention of Hiroshima represents for people everywhere the dawn of the nuclear age. It is associated in the political imagination with the use of a weapon of mass destruction as a tactic in warfare, and it is understood to signify massive human suffering.

At the time of the attacks, few in the United States or elsewhere raised questions about the propriety of *nuclear weapons. The atomic bombs were perceived as weapons of unsurpassed potency. President Harry *Truman and his close advisers justified the use of atomic bombs at the time by arguing that the alternative would have been an invasion of the main Japanese islands, costing upwards of 1 million American lives. Disclosures over the years, including intelligence estimates in 1945, suggest a far smaller number, and generally anticipated Japanese surrender before the invasion was scheduled to have taken place. Moreover, it is clear that wartime leaders such as Truman and Winston *Churchill, both of whom defended the use of the bomb against Japan, were aware of the apocalyptic implications of atomic weaponry.

After more than four decades the Hiroshima decision remains controversial and hotly debated. Some scholars have argued that the overriding reason for the use of the atomic bomb against Japan was to exert diplomatic leverage on the Soviet Union in the postwar world, or to end the war quickly before Soviet military involvement would give Moscow a greater voice in postwar Pacific peace arrangements.

In subsequent decades Hiroshima has served as a central symbol for *peace movements around the world. More conservative political elements, those committed to strategic roles for nuclear weapons, tend not to look back closely at Hiroshima, except possibly to reanalyze the bureaucratic milieu of the decision. In contrast, those who have objected to the reliance on nuclear weapons in the post-1945 world seek to consider the effects on Hiroshima in the most concrete possible manner, by listening to the voices of the survivors, by detailing the forms of physical and psychological damage, and by invoking images of mass death and suffering.

In 1963, a Japanese court, assisted by three *international law experts, decided the *Shimoda* case involving several survivors. The Tokyo District Court decided that the atomic attacks violated international law, judging the bombs to be indiscriminate weapons used against civilians.

The decision to attack Hiroshima with an atomic bomb has become, if anything, more controversial with the passage of time. Nothing conclusive has yet been established. Recent academic writing has tended to favor the view that the official claim of saving lives was, at best, an exaggeration, while the revisionist claim of seeking diplomatic leverage over the Soviet Union was at least partially correct.

Hiroshima remains a powerful symbol of the catastrophic implications of the nuclear age. The Japanese experience of atomic war, despite greater casualties taken during the fire bomb attacks on Tokyo and the much greater destructiveness of subsequent hydrogen bomb technology, has been responsible for what is sometimes called "a nuclear allergy." Japan has legislated against any use, development, or possession of nuclear weapons. Some critics of Japanese *security policy suggest that such a posture is hypocritical, as Japan has welcomed "the nuclear umbrella" provided by the United States throughout the *Cold War period.

As long as there will be students of international politics, debates about Hiroshima will persist: Was it necessary? Did it really shorten the war? Did it make political leaders and the public aware of the great menace of war in the nuclear age? Should we morally condemn Hiroshima? Should we regard the use of atomic bombs against Hiroshima as a crime of state?

Social science cannot hope to answer these questions definitively, and yet the study of the decision and its effects remains valuable. It brings us closer to the realities of the nuclear age than any other single event, and enables us to clarify for the future our moral and legal attitudes toward relying upon weapons of mass destruction for purposes of either *deterrence or combat.

Gregg Herken, *The Winning Weapon: The Atomic Bomb in the Cold War, 1945–1950* (New York, 1980). *Hiroshima and Nagasaki: The Physical, Medical, and Social Effects of the Atomic Bombings,* Report of the Committee for the Compilation of Materials on Damage Caused by the Atomic Bombs in Hiroshima and Nagasaki (New York, 1981).
RICHARD FALK

HISPANIC AMERICANS. Latinos, or Hispanic Americans, constitute the second-largest and most rapidly growing distinctive ethnic group in the *United States. The impact that this group has had on domestic and international affairs in the United States is substantial and promises to be even more significant in the future. While sharing close ties based on the Spanish heritage and language, Hispanic Americans are of diverse national backgrounds, originating not only from the Iberian Peninsula but from most of the nations of the Western Hemisphere, including the Caribbean and Central and South America. The umbrella terms *Hispanics* or *Latinos* are used to designate this extremely heterogenous group of more than twenty national origin groupings in the United States, which in 1988 included about 12.6 million Mexican Americans, 2.3 million Puerto Ricans, 1.1 million Cuban Americans, 2.5 million from other nations in Central and South America, and 1.6 million "others."

History. Hispanics, particularly Mexican/Spanish Americans, have been one of the longest-established ethnic groups in the United States. Explorers representing Spain made several contacts with the New World in the late fifteenth and early sixteenth centuries, and a number of colonial settlements were established in what would later become the United States, primarily in Florida (St. Augustine), New Mexico (Santa Fe), California, and Texas.

Through its war with Mexico, the United States gained vast new territories in the mid-nineteenth century, including much of what is now Texas, New Mexico, Arizona, Nevada, California, Colorado, and Utah. *International migration from Mexico to the United States, more accurately described as a continuous ebb and flow across a 2,000-mile border, has persisted to the present day. One major wave of migration occurred in the early 1900s when largely unskilled, *peasant immigrants entered the United States from Mexico. Immigration to the United States has continued as economically depressed Mexicans seek to improve their economic condition. The official policy of the United States has at times encouraged this source of labor and at other times, primarily during economic difficulty, has discouraged it, even "repatriating" Mexicans. Major deportations occurred during the depression of the 1920s and the recessions of the 1950s.

Puerto Ricans have been citizens of the United States since the Jones Act of 1917. The island of Puerto Rico has been a U.S. commonwealth since 1952, and Puerto Ricans possess almost all legal privileges of U.S. *citizenship. Puerto Ricans continue to make frequent trips between the island and the major cities of the northeastern United States, especially New York, particularly since the advent of regular air travel between the island and the Eastern Seaboard in the 1950s.

Relatively few Cubans lived in the United States until the *Cuban Revolution and the coming to power of Fidel *Castro in 1959. At that point a large number of Cuban refugees, mostly middle- and upper-class professionals, entered the United States, settling mainly in south Florida. Subsequent waves of immigration occurred in 1965 and again in 1980 when Castro expelled the Marielitos, a group that was of substantially lower economic and social status compared with those that had preceded it.

The other 4 million or so Hispanic Americans have various histories. Migrations to and from the United States from other countries of Central and South America have varied depending on the political and economic situation in their home countries and the fluctuating policies of the United States. In the late 1970s and 1980s there was a tremendous increase in the number of political refugees fleeing the turmoil in the countries of El Salvador, the Dominican Republic, Guatemala, and Panama.

Demographics. The social and economic characteristics of Hispanic Americans are difficult to describe because of the great diversity that is often concealed by summary statistics. The Hispanic population represents about eight percent of total U.S. population and is growing rapidly. In fact, one of the most significant demographic characteristics of Latinos is that their numbers are growing five times as fast as the rest of the nation. The Hispanic population has grown thirty-nine percent since 1980, compared with nine percent for the non-Hispanic population. About half the growth was due to immigration. Hispanics are concentrated in certain regions of the country, with Mexican Americans primarily in the Southwest, Puerto Ricans in the urban centers of the northeast, and Cubans concentrated mostly in Florida.

Latinos are significantly younger than the general population of the United States, averaging 23 years of age as against 31 for the population in general. Socioeconomically, Hispanics are among the most depressed of all U.S. ethnic groups. In 1988, about one-quarter of Hispanic families fell below the poverty line; the figure was less than ten percent among non-Hispanics.

The level of educational attainment among Hispanics improved slightly during the 1970s and 1980s but remains below the level of non-Hispanics. The proportion of non-Hispanics who have completed four years or more of college was twenty-one percent in 1988—twice as high as that of Hispanics. At the precollegiate level, the situation is worse: only fifty-one percent of Hispanics 25 years or older have completed four years of high school.

Political Situation. In addition to being socioeconomically disadvantaged, Latinos as a group are underrepresented in U.S. politics. For example, in 1990, there were no Hispanic senators and only ten Hispanic members of the House of Representatives. In general, Latinos are registered to vote in lower percentages, participate in the electoral process less frequently, attend fewer political rallies, and make fewer campaign contributions than other Americans. One reason for this comparative lack of participation in the electoral process is the youthfulness of the population. Young people generally are less political. Another is that about one-third of the Hispanic population are noncitizens who are not eligible for formal participation. Hispanics have relatively weak organizational bases, both locally and, more importantly, at the national level. One reason for the problem in developing a national base has been the difficulty of reconciling differences among various national origin groups. No national leadership of recognizable stature has emerged.

Because of their concentration and diversity, it is most likely that Hispanics will be most successful in politics at the grass-roots level. Latinos have made some impressive strides on the local and regional levels, particularly since the beginning of the 1960s. Mexican Americans, in particular, have won elections in many predominantly Spanish-speaking areas. Hispanics have been crucial to the victories of African-American mayors in Chicago and New York and are being elected in significantly growing numbers to city councils and school boards. Effective local organizing, including get-out-the-vote campaigns and challenges to discriminatory at-large electoral systems, have produced significant gains. The courts have ordered redistricting and also have mandated more equitable distributions of school funding. Efforts to increase Latino voter registration are being made by such organizations as the National Association of Latino Elected Officials (NALEO) and Southwest Voter Registration and Education Project. Voter registration among Latinos climbed twenty-one percent from 1984 to 1988. However, at the same time voter turnout has dropped slightly.

Numbers are important in politics, and in the coming decade, some 5 million additional Hispanics will become eligible for citizenship, in part owing to an amnesty program that grants legal residency to undocumented immigrants who have lived in the United States for five years. This, along with the maturing of the young population, offers at least the possibility for much greater electoral influence.

Much of the future success of Hispanics gaining proportionate political influence will be the result of the politics of coalition. The coalitions may form among the various Latino groupings as well as with non-Latino groups which share at least a part of a common political agenda. It is most probable that such coalitions will be issue-based. In addition to issues involving economic improvements, two others seem to be of particular importance to Latinos. The first is immigration. Migration back and forth between most Hispanic countries and the United States has been fairly continuous throughout U.S. history. It has provided both a blessing and a curse to Latino citizens, some of whom have been deprived of citizenship rights in the United States because they are perceived as foreigners. Yet cultural ties with native countries by and large are a source of continuing revitalization and strength. Another domestic issue which seems to unite Latino groups is bilingualism. Although this takes many forms and means different things to different people, it generally focuses on the preservation of the Spanish language, which in turn is tied to the preservation of at least some elements of Hispanic culture. Most certainly, the preservation of the Spanish language in some form is of paramount symbolic importance to the vast majority of Hispanics in the United States. Movements to install English as the official language in various jurisdictions have provided one focus for Latino consolidation.

Perhaps the most salient issue around which Latinos unite is their treatment by members of the core American culture. Throughout history, Hispanics have been discriminated against simply on account of their distinctive *ethnicity. For many years there existed laws mandating separation of Hispanics from non-Hispanics in schools and overt discrimination in employment and politics. Although eliminated in many of its legislative forms, discrimination persists and in fact seems to be on the upswing. After the gains of the *civil rights movement and some corresponding improvement in the well-being of many Hispanics, some forms of benign neglect and even attempts to undo developments of the 1960s and 1970s have resulted in partial regression in the areas of affirmative action and equity. The redress of continuing grievances and awareness of new slippage may be very important rallying points for Hispanics in the 1990s.

International Politics. Hispanic Americans are particularly well situated to play an important role in world politics, particularly in the Western Hemisphere. Most of the people of the Western Hemisphere are Spanish-speaking, and Hispanic Americans who share the cultural characteristics of both their mother countries and the United States can play a singularly significant role in bridging the gap between the United States and the countries of Latin America.

As the United States' foreign relations based on the *Cold War diminish, its attention may well be redirected toward the *Third World, including Asia, Africa, and Latin America. As countries in Latin America develop into more industrialized and modern democracies, they can benefit greatly from cooperation with the United States. Reciprocally, the United States needs to be an integral partner in the Pan-American community, treating its neighbors with respect and concern.

Likewise, Latinos in the United States, if brought into the political system, can not only be valuable intermediaries in this nation's dealings with the countries of the Western Hemisphere but also can bring an ever-growing pool of yet untapped talent and human resources to American society itself.

(See also POLITICAL PARTICIPATION; U.S.–LATIN AMERICAN RELATIONS.)

F. Chris Garcia and Rudolph O. de la Garza, *The Chicano Political Experience* (North Scituate, Mass., 1976). Matt S. Meier and Feliciano Rivera, *Dictionary of Mexican Amer-*

ican History (Westport, Conn., 1981). Joan Moore and Harry Pachon, *Hispanics in the United States* (Englewood Cliffs, N.J., 1985). L. H. Gann and Peter J. Duigan, *The Hispanics in the United States,* (Boulder, Colo., 1986). Frank Bean and Marta Tienda, *The Hispanic Population of the United States* (New York, 1987). Maurilio E. Vigil, *Hispanics in American Politics* (Lanham, Md., 1987). F. Chris Garcia, ed., *Latinos and the Political System* (Notre Dame, Ind., 1988). U.S. Department of Commerce, Bureau of the Census, *The Hispanic Population in the United States: March 1989,* Current Population Reports, Series P-20, No. 44 (Washington, D.C., 1989).

F. CHRIS GARCIA

HISTORIC COMPROMISE. Following the dramatic overthrow of Salvador *Allende's Unidad Popular government in Chile and recognizing some similarities between Chilean and Italian politics, Enrico Berlinguer launched the idea of historic compromise. In three articles published in the Communist weekly *Rinascita* in September 1973, the secretary-general of the Partito Comunista Italiano (PCI) elaborated the reasons he considered such a compromise necessary. The transformation of the Italian political system required that a long-term agreement be reached among the three major political cultures that had written the constitution and provided the foundations of Italian *democracy. The Democrazia Cristiana (DC), the Partito Socialista Italiano (PSI), and the PCI had to renew their collaboration in order to reform and strengthen the democratic system. Otherwise, as in Chile, the national and international forces of the Right would destroy the democratic framework.

Significant electoral gains for the PCI seemed to indicate popular support for the strategy. Indeed, in the wake of the 1976 elections, only the benevolent communist parliamentary abstention made it possible to create an all-DC government. Then, on 16 March 1978, immediately after the kidnapping of the DC's Aldo Moro by the Brigate Rosse, the PCI supported the vote of confidence in the government led by the DC leader Giulio Andreotti, thus for the first time since May 1947 joining the parliamentary majority. This parliamentary-governmental translation of the historic compromise was called national solidarity. Both the historic compromise and the period of national solidarity are reminiscent of those grand coalitions that occur in *consociational democracy, which in *Italy are created in order to face major threats. In the Italian case, by 1976, the two major threats were terrorism from the Left and Right and double-digit inflation.

The idea of historic compromise was never accepted by the PSI, which looked for the establishment of a democratic regime based on alternation of government. Moreover, it felt squeezed by an alliance between the DC and the PCI. In theory, the DC also rejected the historic compromise. In practice, however, the party shrewdly exploited all the advantages of the support of a strong and disciplined party such as the PCI. It is a matter of some contro-

versy whether Moro intended eventually to include the PCI in the government or only to stabilize DC rule and erode support for the PCI, which was caught in transition from an antisystem opposition to a credible party of government. Not even all the communists were united in support of the historic compromise. Some thought it a good tactic to displace the DC. Others opposed it in the name of the purity and peculiarity of the PCI tradition not to be implicated in DC patronage practices. Moreover, many observers believed that Italian politics had reached the stage at which alternation among competing coalitions was possible and fruitful. Enacted for a short period of time (1976–1979) in its mild version for the purpose of promoting national solidarity, deprived by the kidnapping and murder of Moro, its potential DC supporter, the historic compromise was abandoned even by Berlinguer in 1980 and replaced by the strategy of the democratic alternative. In the final analysis, the compromise contributed to the stemming of terrorism and the containment of inflation. Probably it has delayed the creation of an alternative to DC power as well.

(See also CHRISTIAN DEMOCRACY; EUROCOMMUNISM; RELIGION AND POLITICS.)

Stephen Hellman, *Italian Communism in Transition: The Rise and Fall of the Historic Compromise in Turin, 1975–1980* (New York and Oxford, 1988).

GIANFRANCO PASQUINO

HITLER, Adolf. Probably no leader in world history has been so despised, adulated, and feared as Adolf Hitler. His responsibility for endless human suffering and vast numbers of deaths is rivaled only by *Stalin. During the twelve years of the Third Reich his charismatic sway enthralled millions of Germans who listened raptly to his words and followed his leadership to the very end. At the height of his power in 1942 he dominated almost all of Europe and western Russia while his armies and Schutzstaffel (SS) units moved from conquest to conquest. To the present time he is virtually the only historical figure whose malignant notoriety has not been subject to significant revisionist interpretations.

The meteoric rise of Adolf Hitler presents an exception to Newton's principle that no effect can be greater than its cause. He was a man who came from out of nowhere. Until the age of 30 he showed no evidence of superior talents, no disciplined work habits, and no capacity for stable relationships. He had little education and few coherent ideas. Before he came to power in 1933, most dismissed him as an eccentric nonentity or an unreliable extremist. Finally, he was not even a German.

Hitler was born in 1889 at Braunau am Inn in Austria. The son of an Austrian customs official, Alois Schickelgruber Hitler, and his third wife, Klara, who came from a peasant background, Hitler was a sullen, rebellious child. The early conflicts with his authoritarian father were soothed by his indulgent mother. When she died of cancer in 1908 he lost an anchor in the stormy seas of his adolescence. By that time he had already abandoned the Catholic church and any pretensions to middle-class respectability.

From 1907 to 1913 he lived a vagrant life in Vienna. Rejected twice by the Academy of Fine Arts, he drifted aimlessly, taking odd jobs and hawking his own sketches on streets and in taverns. Although he claimed impoverishment, it was really self-imposed; he received orphan's benefits from the state and could have lived comfortably if he had wished.

During this period Hitler picked up his basic political ideas, most of them from the seamy netherworld of lower-class Vienna. They included crackpot Aryan racism with a fanatic preoccupation with "purity of blood," a stereotypical *antisemitism set forth in violent sexual imagery, and a polyglot list of enemies: *Marxism, *capitalism, *democracy, pacifism, the stock exchange, and the press. Suffusing all of these ideas was the dream of a Greater *Germany.

After moving to Munich in 1913, he found himself surprised and elated by the outbreak of World War I in 1914. Without delay he joined a Bavarian infantry regiment and served at the front as a message runner. He demonstrated personal courage in battle and was awarded the Iron Cross-First Class, relatively rare for a lance corporal. Twice wounded, the last time temporarily blinded in a mustard gas attack, he was evacuated to a military hospital near Berlin. There he learned the terrible news of Germany's defeat and of revolutions breaking out everywhere. He vowed vengeance and claimed voices called him to rescue Germany from the treasonous grasp of Jews and Bolsheviks. In what he called "the most momentous decision of my life," he resolved "to become a politician."

In the summer of 1919, while still in the army, Hitler was assigned to report on some smaller political groups in Munich. One of these, soon to be renamed the Nationalsozialistische Deutsche Arbeiterpartei (NSDAP), he joined, and soon became its chairman. By November 1921 he led a movement of 3,000 members and began to exhibit remarkable political gifts, especially in the arts of party organization, the selection of political lieutenants, propaganda symbol manipulation, and public speech making.

From the very beginning, Hitler sensed the need to form organizational structures to help the movement expand. Quickly he established units of the brown-shirted Sturmabteilung (SA) and a black-shirted bodyguard battalion, the SS. He also set up many other entities—district offices, newspapers, publishing houses, speakers' schools—all to promote the Nazi message. To lead these units he found the "right people": the war veteran Hermann Göring; a disgruntled intellectual, Joseph Goebbels; and the fanatic Heinrich Himmler. All had in common a personal devotion to Hitler and a lust for power.

Also at an early date Hitler recognized the power of symbols, myths, and rituals to reinforce belief in Nazism and to forge bonds of affiliation to the party. For example, the swastika, the "Heil Hitler" greeting, SS uniform regalia, and party rallies were deliberately introduced by Hitler to stimulate the convictions of true believers. Finally, Hitler's impassioned oratory was crucial to his propaganda triumphs. Hitler often extolled the superiority of the spoken over the written word. His carefully rehearsed speeches, sometimes lasting two hours, were masterful dramatizations of Nazi myths. Amplified by recently invented electrical loudspeaker systems and further extended by radio broadcasts, Hitler's voice began to be heard throughout the country.

In November 1923, at the high point of a disastrous inflation, Hitler attempted the overthrow of the Bavarian government in Munich, but it was poorly planned and was a complete failure. Police bullets stopped his marching columns, sixteen party members were killed, and Hitler was arrested. At his trial for high treason he, typically, denounced the judges and said "the eternal court of history" would set him free.

Convicted by the court, he served only nine months of his five-year sentence. In prison he turned adversity into advantage by writing his first and only major book, *Mein Kampf (My Struggle)*. This sprawling work—two volumes of turgid prose called by critics of his party "Mein Krampf" ("My Cramp")—was a mishmash of convoluted ideas. One chapter gave away his secrets for effective propaganda: "Keep the message simple"; "Repeat it and repeat it again"; "Don't admit doubts or qualifications"; "Always attack"; "Know that the biggest untruths will be believed."

The years 1925 to 1929 were lean ones for Hitler and the Nazi Party. With the introduction of a new currency after the 1923 inflation, the economy recovered and advanced rapidly. Political democracy at home seemed assured. Abroad, Germany was welcomed into the *League of Nations as a good neighbor. Hitler was left with few "fighting issues."

Nevertheless, he and his political lieutenants acted "as if" Germany still had enemies and the Nazis would soon come to power. Abandoning the illegal *putsch,* he decreed street violence, vicious propaganda, and tireless electioneering to subvert the Weimar democracy. Some radical followers demanded more socialism in the party platform. Other Nazis, looking for the financial support of industrialists, were more conservative. As always Hitler was a master of such contradictions. He claimed Nazism rose above the *Left and *Right. "We are for Germany," he cried.

By 1928 the Nazis had won only twelve seats out of 491 in the Reichstag. But their fortunes changed dramatically in the 1930 election. After the worldwide economic depression had hit Germany with particular severity—ultimately unemployment reached thirty-two percent—the Nazis attained 107 seats in the Reichstag. Money now streamed into the party treasury from big business seeking insurance from the Nazis and from the middle classes hoping for the defeat of *socialism and *communism.

In 1932 Hitler officially acquired German citizenship and ran for president. Although he lost to Field Marshal von Hindenburg, he was now a national figure. In the next-to-last free election in Weimar Germany, the Nazi Party gained 37.4 percent of the vote, becoming by far the largest party in the Reichstag. A confident Hitler began a series of "power plays" with nationalists, conservative industrialists, and the military. After months of intrigues, a reluctant von Hindenburg finally appointed "the Bohemian corporal" chancellor of Germany on 30 January 1933. It was a triumphant moment for Hitler; the man from nowhere had at last become someone.

With astonishing energy Hitler moved to consolidate and expand his power. He used the Reichstag fire of 27 February 1933 as an excuse to intimidate his political opponents and suspend civil liberties. The Nazis gained in the quasi-free 5 March 1933 elections, but their 44.5 percent plurality still fell short of the hoped-for majority. So Hitler engineered an "enabling act" to give him dictatorial powers for the next four years. He used this authority immediately to "coordinate" many German institutions; this meant the elimination of unreliable opponents and Jews and the conversion of institutions into Nazi organs. One by one, venerable, proudly independent German institutions succumbed. In 1934, Hitler carried out a "blood purge" against unruly SA leaders who had pressed for a "second, more radical, revolution." After the murder of top SA leaders, the regular army and SS acquired new influence and Hitler created a new post for himself, Führer (Leader). Only the churches remained relatively independent of Nazi control.

The next years of the Third Reich at peace witnessed an extensive transformation of German society. Unemployment disappeared. The economy expanded. Wages increased, and cheap consumer goods filled stores. Part of the reason for the boom was Hitler's rearmament of Germany; war contracts brought jobs and artificial prosperity.

Most Germans felt pride in their country and its leader. Hitler ordered the construction of new public buildings, workers' housing developments, and Autobahnen (highways)—actually planned before 1933. He orchestrated the Berlin Olympics of 1936 into a great propaganda triumph. And the trains were running on time—of course they always had in Germany, but Hitler took credit for everything.

But black clouds also darkened these "achievements." With Hitler's approval, Jewish shops were boycotted, books by Jewish authors were burned, and political opponents and Jews were sent off to concentration camps such as Dachau. The Nürnberg Laws of 1935 defined what constituted Jewishness and denied Jews citizenship. In the 1938 Kristallnacht (Night of Broken Glass), Nazi gangs smashed synagogues and Jewish stores. Most Jews, of course, were loyal, productive citizens of Germany; they posed no conceivable threat. In fact Jews in Germany in 1933 comprised less than one percent of the population.

Germany's *foreign policy preoccupied Hitler more and more in the 1930s. It was as if, having subdued Germany's domestic institutions, Hitler now searched for new worlds beyond Germany's borders to conquer. He found them in Germany's neighbors, and one by one they too fell before his *diplomacy by intimidation. Later on he used his armies.

As early as 1933 it was clear that Hitler would refuse to allow Germany to become a normal European power. In that year he withdrew Germany from the League of Nations. He reintroduced military conscription in 1934 and reoccupied the Rhineland in 1936. The next year, in a secret meeting with his general, Hitler outlined a vast plan for the subjugation of Europe and the Soviet Union. Having annexed Austria and Czechoslovakia, he began *World War II by an unprovoked attack against Poland in 1939.

Thereafter, German armies trampled through Denmark, Norway, the Low Countries, France, the Balkans, and finally the Soviet Union. Only Britain held out as a belligerent. The turn of the tide took place in two decisive battles: the defeat of Germany at El Alamein in North Africa in 1942, and the surrender of the German Sixth Army at Stalingrad two months later. The fiction of German invincibility had been dissolved. Hitler now called for the total mobilization of the German people to win the war, but it was too late. Hitler's promised "secret weapons" never materialized. Soviet armies entered Germany from the east and the remaining Allied armies invaded from the west.

Deep in his Berlin bunker, Hitler directed his war, sometimes deploying nonexistent armies. He cursed his fate, Germany's enemies, especially Jews, and the German people, who had proved unworthy. After marrying, Hitler and Eva Braun committed suicide together on 30 April 1945.

After the war the full extent of Hitler's depravity became known. More than 100 Nazi concentration camps dotted the map of Europe. Even more horrifying were the mass extermination camps in Poland, where countless millions of Jews, Slavs, prisoners of war, Gypsies, and homosexuals were gassed. The names of these "death factories" have become emblems of Nazi barbarism: Auschwitz, Belzec, Chelmno, Majdanek, Sobibor, and Treblinka.

Why does Hitler continue to fascinate the contemporary mind? Perhaps his monomaniacal charismatic leadership presents challenges to conventional categories of rational political analysis. Other controversies swirl around Hitler's career. Did Hitler believe in his ideas or was he a cynical opportunist?

(It would be a dangerous mistake to deny that he was a fanatic, true believer.) Were there limits to Hitler's power in Nazi Germany? (Without doubt there were many limits, often not recognized.) Was Hitler a great military leader? (He had an exceptional memory for tactical detail, and he had great gifts in planning strategic attacks. He was less strong in retreats.) Why did he commit so many mistakes in World War II, such as the needless declaration of war against the United States in 1941? (More often than not his *ideology and *psychology blinded him to reality.) Was the Final Solution intended by Hitler from the early days or did it grow out of functional decisions made during the war? (Most Hitler biographers take the intentionalist side over the functionalist in the debate.) Was Hitler insane? (No, but psychiatrists have diagnosed Hitler after his death as a "borderline personality" with strong paranoid tendencies intensified by monorchidism.)

It is well to admit that interpretations of Hitler's career necessarily serve diverse political ends and constituencies. Some Marxist historians have downplayed Hitler's importance and ascribed to him the role of puppet in the hands of monopoly capitalists. Other historians have seen him as the direct descendant of Martin Luther and Otto von Bismarck, or as "the gutter come to power." Today it is difficult to conceive the historical fact of Nazism without the leadership of Adolf Hitler or the enthrallment of millions of Germans without his spellbinding presence.

(See also FASCISM; GERMAN DEMOCRATIC REPUBLIC; GERMANY, FEDERAL REPUBLIC OF; HOLOCAUST; WAR CRIMES.)

Adolf Hitler, *Mein Kampf,* trans. Ralph Manheim (Cambridge, Mass., 1943). Alan Bullock, *Hitler: A Study in Tyranny,* rev. ed. (New York, 1964). J. P. Stern, *Hitler: The Fuehrer and the People* (Berkeley, Calif., 1975). Robert Waite, *The Psychopathic God: Adolf Hitler* (New York, 1977). Eberhard Jaeckel, *Hitler's World View: A Blueprint for Power* (Cambridge, Mass., 1981). Ian Kershaw, *Hitler* (New York, 1991).

RICHARD M. HUNT

HO Chi Minh. The Vietnamese revolutionary Ho Chi Minh (1890–1969) is one of the most controversial figures of the twentieth century. To some he was a patriotic figure who led his people to victory over the combined forces of French colonialism and U.S. *imperialism. To others he was a hard-bitten agent of international *communism who betrayed the cause of Vietnamese *nationalism in the interests of Moscow.

Ho Chi Minh (whose real name was Nguyen Tat Thanh) was born the son of a minor imperial official in central *Vietnam in 1890. From his father he learned to resent French colonial rule over his country, and in 1911 he accepted employment with a French steamship line in order to learn the secret of Western success at its source.

In 1917 Ho Chi Minh arrived in Paris. Taking the name Nguyen Ai Quoc (Nguyen the Patriot), he became involved in nationalist activities and addressed a petition to the victorious Allied powers, meeting at Versailles to frame the post–World War I order, demanding independence for his country. In 1920 he became a founding member of the French Communist Party and three years later was called to Moscow, where he was trained as an agent by the Communist International and sent to south China with instructions to form the first Marxist revolutionary organization in French Indochina.

In 1930, under Ho's direction, a formal Indochinese Communist Party (ICP) was created. One year later he was arrested in Hong Kong on suspicion of revolutionary activities, and after a short stay in prison returned to Moscow, where he remained for five years, reportedly recovering from illness. In 1938 he returned to south China. After serving two years with Chinese Communist military units, he established contact with leading elements of the party inside Vietnam just as his country was coming under Japanese military occupation.

In May 1941 the party, now again under his leadership, formed a broad national front called the League for the Independence of Vietnam, or Vietminh, to struggle for national independence at the end of the Pacific war. In the so-called August Revolution, launched at the moment of Japanese surrender to the Allies in the summer of 1945, the Vietminh seized power in North Vietnam and declared the formation of an independent Democratic Republic of Vietnam (DRV). Nguyen Ai Quoc, now taking the name Ho Chi Minh, was named president. But the French reoccupied the south, and when efforts to reach a compromise settlement failed, the Franco-Vietminh conflict broke out in December 1946.

In 1954, the French government agreed to a negotiated settlement, the Geneva Accords. The agreement divided Vietnam into two temporary administrative zones, with the DRV in the north and anticommunist forces in the south. Ho had played an active role in persuading his colleagues to accept a compromise.

Ho Chi Minh remained president of the DRV until his death in 1969. In the north, he promoted efforts to create a fully socialist society along Marxist-Leninist lines. Land was collectivized and the urban sector was placed under state ownership. At first, he hoped to complete reunification with the south by peaceful means, but national elections called for by the Geneva Accords did not take place, and in 1959 the DRV decided to resume a strategy of revolutionary war. Ho sought to mobilize international support for the Vietnamese cause by attempting to mediate the Sino-Soviet dispute, but had little success. Six years after his death, however, all of Vietnam was under communist rule.

In his long career as a revolutionary and as president of his country, Ho Chi Minh was both an active leader of his party and a symbol of the Vietnamese struggle for independence and national unity. His genial temperament, simple habits, and collegial style earned him the respect of his adversaries as well as the devotion of many of his compatriots. Although his writings do not display the intellectual grasp of a *Lenin or a *Mao Zedong, his sense of timing was superb and in his actions he displayed a profound sense of history and strategy.

Was he primarily a nationalist or a communist? That may remain forever a matter of speculation. It is clear that he was motivated from childhood by a desire to create a free and prosperous Vietnam. On the other hand, he had a lifelong hatred for colonial oppression and there is no reason to doubt his deep commitment to the Marxist vision of a future communist utopia. Undoubtedly, in his own mind he was both revolutionary and patriot, as communist doctrine and practice, suitably revised to meet local conditions, provided him with a framework to realize his goal of a peaceful, independent, and democratic Vietnam.

(See also DECOLONIZATION; REVOLUTION; VIETNAM WAR.)

Jean Lacouture, *Ho Chi Minh: A Political Biography,* trans. by Peter Wiles (New York, 1968). Ho Chi Minh, *Selected Writings* (Hanoi, 1977).

WILLIAM J. DUIKER

HOLLAND. See NETHERLANDS.

HOLOCAUST. The term *Holocaust* is widely used when referring to the project of physical annihilation of the "Jewish race," conceived and administered by Nazi Germany in the course of *World War II. A special name was felt necessary for the atrocity perpetrated against the Jews (the only other ethnic group which was to share their fate under Nazi rule were Gypsies), for it differed from the much more common cases of *genocide in that it was not aimed at the incapacitation and enslavement of a conquered population nor was it an outburst of communal hostility exacerbated by *war conditions. Rather, the Nazi campaign to exterminate the Jews was the product of a planned, designed, and monitored long-term operation calculated to destroy the marked category to the last man, woman, and child. Thanks to the military defeat of Germany, the project of the Holocaust was not implemented in full; by common estimates, however, up to 6 million European Jews perished during its operation.

The chronicle of the Holocaust was subjected after the war to meticulous historical research and has now been documented in great detail. Even so, efforts to explain the event continue unabated. Scholars agree that, both in its conception and its implementation, the Holocaust escapes understanding; its occurrence in the very center of the civilized world, and in the middle of a century that believed itself to exemplify the ultimate triumph of modern rationalism over cruelty and savage passions, seems to contradict the logic of the civilizing process assumed to guide the development of recent centuries.

As to the course the Holocaust actually took, historians are divided into the intentionalist and functionalist schools. Intentionalists believe that total destruction of the "Jewish race" was envisaged by *Hitler and his immediate entourage from the first moment of their struggle for power and certainly from the very beginning of Nazi rule. Steps leading logically to the "final solution" were taken systematically well before the outbreak of war, yet the last act had to wait until the war provided the necessary cover for deeds that otherwise would have aroused moral outcry and active resistance. Functionalists, on the other hand, maintain (without denying the crucial role played by Hitler's anti-Jewish obsession) that Hitler entertained but a very general idea of "getting rid of the Jews" and making Germany *Judenrein* ("Jew-clean")—the rest being an outcome of the unplanned and unanticipated twists of political/military conditions and of the inner operational logic of the state, party, and martial bureaucracies that undertook the implementation of Hitler's will. According to this view, the practice of the "final solution"—the organized murder of the entire Jewish population with the help of specially formed *Einsatzgruppen* ("Task Units"), gas chambers, and crematoria—arose gradually, as German military victories stretched far and wide the boundaries of the "Thousand-Year Reich," thus rendering increasingly impractical the initially planned forced expulsion of Jews from German territory.

However important—and however unlikely—is the resolution of this hotly debated issue, the task of explaining the Holocaust splits into two partly separate questions. First, why was the destruction of the Jews willed in the first place—or, to put it another way, why were the Jews selected as the targets for destruction? Second, how could the mass murder, once conceived, be perpetrated, given that its implementation needed the cooperation of hundreds of thousands of experts and functionaries (regardless of their personal feelings toward the Jews), and at least the passive consent and nonresistance of the millions of witnesses and bystanders?

As to the first question, long-established Judeophobia, inherited by modern Europe from the millennium of Christendom, is the most common answer. It had its roots in the charge of betrayal and murder of Christ; it was institutionalized in premodern, Christian Europe through the practice of exclusion and repetitive assaults against Jewish populations. It was given new content and promoted through new arguments in the context of a rapidly modernizing Europe, when multifarious yet widespread anxieties born of uncertainty brought about by social change were targeted at the purported morbid influence of Jews recently let out of the ghettos, or explained away with the help of theories of Jewish conspiracy. In a Europe struggling to impose new reassuring certainties Jews were cast as the epitome of chaos and ambiguity and the ultimate source of the most painfully felt afflictions of the modern condition. In accordance with the new, scientific stance, the anti-Jewish charge was shifted from Judaism to Jewishness, from the wrong and dangerous faith the Jews preached to the biologically determined hereditary traits of the race that could not be rectified by reeducation or religious conversion. The old Judeophobia took the form of modern *antisemitism. It was not difficult, therefore, to seek in the baneful traits and sinister deeds of the Jews an explanation for the agonies that befell most of the German nation once the challenges of *modernization were topped by the misery of the loss of World War I. It was not difficult, either, to decide that only a physical estrangement, not another missionary, assimilative effort, would put an end to the corrosive impact of the Jews.

In the memorable phrase of Hannah *Arendt, "antisemitism explains perhaps the choice of the victims, but not the nature of the crime" called the Holocaust. The second question, therefore, confronts the interpreter with greater difficulty than the first. The mass murder of the Jews was not an outcome of a momentary outburst of crowd passion but of a long-term, systematic activity that involved meticulous planning, careful division of labor, and the cooperation of "ordinary" institutions and businesses normally engaged in such neutral operations as running the railway network, designing trucks, developing new chemicals, or building houses. As in all complex operations in which partial tasks must be closely correlated so that they combine in the fulfillment of the overall purpose, the Holocaust required neutralization of all personal motives that could interfere with the master plan: Its success could not be made dependent on such imponderable and unmanageable factors as the emotions and personal beliefs of the actors—for instance, the intensity of Jew-hatred in each of the hundreds of thousands of participants. Its undisturbed performance also had to be made secure from all "outside" interference—for instance, opinions of the laity who might be critical of the plan and the methods used to fulfill it.

Unlike traditional pogroms, the Holocaust was therefore a thoroughly modern operation that availed itself lavishly of the advantages offered not only by the technological equipment that modern industry alone is capable of delivering, but also by the impersonal, efficient logic of modern bureaucracy. The Holocaust was a form of genocide conceivable solely under the conditions of *modernity; by the same token, it revealed the awesome murderous potential created with the advent of modern civilization with its advanced technology and methodology of scientific management. The unholy alliance between the Holocaust and modernity expressed itself also in the unprecedentedly grandiose scale of the enterprise, and above all in its functionality. The Holocaust was conceived and executed as part of a total project toward the construction of a "new order." Jews had to be destroyed because they did not fit into the vision of an artificially designed "better society" (envisaged in the *ideology of National Socialism as a racially clean society, catering to the superior values and historical destiny of the German race). This ambition was itself thoroughly modern and would be unthinkable if not for the modern concern to "remake the world," to bring it into "harmony" with whatever has been defined as the needs of the people for whom the new order is to be built. In this respect, the Holocaust must be classified among other attempts to annihilate whole categories of population in the name of constructing a pure and harmonious society—for instance, the mass murder of "hostile classes" on the territory of the Soviet state in the course of constructing the "classless" communist society.

The availability of technical and managerial resources developed in the advanced stage of modern civilization to societies still struggling with modernizing problems and the attendant psychic anxieties and social tensions made the Holocaust and similar mass crimes possible. This condition is propitious to the spread of chiliastic totalitarian ideologies and totalitarian rule, tantamount to a unique condensation of power by the state and a unique freedom of action for the rulers of the state. The former condition places in the hands of state rulers means of destruction of unprecedented magnitude, allowing them to exploit the condensation of power and freedom from constraint for the pursuit of grandiose social engineering schemes which more often than not involve the thorough "remaking" of the population insofar as it is deemed unsuitable for the perfect society about to be constructed.

The conditions that made the Holocaust possible in Germany half a century ago—the coincidence of modern technology and vision on the one hand and the tensions characteristic of the process of modernization on the other—persist today in many parts of the globe. Therefore, it cannot be assumed that the Holocaust has been in contemporary history a unique event never to be repeated. The exploration of the roots of Holocaust-type phenomena and the conditions under which their recurrence may be prevented therefore figures prominently among current social-scientific and political concerns.

(See also NUREMBERG TRIALS; TOTALITARIANISM.)

George A. Kren and Leon Rappoport, *The Holocaust and the Crisis of Human Behavior* (New York, 1980). Leo Kuper, *Genocide: Its Political Use in the Twentieth Century* (New Haven, Conn., 1981). Raoul Hilberg, *The Destruction of European Jews*, 3 vols. (New York, 1983). Michael R. Marrus, *The Holocaust in History* (London, 1987). Richard L. Rubenstein and John Roth, *Approaches to*

Auschwitz (San Francisco, 1987). Zygmunt Bauman, *Modernity and the Holocaust* (Cambridge, 1989).

ZYGMUNT BAUMAN

HONDURAS. The population of Honduras is about 4.5 million and is largely mestizo; there are small concentrations of African Americans in the North Coast areas as well as in the Bay Islands. Although Roman Catholicism is the dominant religion, Protestantism has made important inroads in the population in recent years. The country's capital is Tegucigalpa, which has a population of about 600,000. San Pedro Sula, located in the steamy North Coast area, has a population that has ballooned to about 300,000 in recent years. It is the economic heart of the country, producing almost forty percent of its national product.

The Honduran economy is heavily dependent on the production of agricultural exports. Bananas and coffee account for about one-half of export income. Industrial production lags far behind other Central American countries. The national currency has been under severe stress because of massive capital flight, government deficit financing, and a high value relative to the U.S. dollar. Just under fifty percent of the population still lives in the countryside, where there is serious pressure for *land reform. Migrants from conflicts in Nicaragua, El Salvador, and Guatemala have taken temporary refuge in the country, placing greater strain on its limited resource base.

The formal organization of Honduras's *labor movement dates from 1954 and the successful strike of workers on the country's foreign owned North Coast banana plantations. The Honduran Workers' Confederation (CTH) is the country's most important and powerful labor organization. Bringing together workers from banana, public-sector, and peasant unions, the CTH has periodically taken a major leadership role in the promotion of political change in Honduras. A Christian-based General Confederation of Workers (CGT) emerged during the early 1960s during a period of intense rural mobilization. A Marxist-oriented Federation of Honduran Workers (FUTH) represents public utility and beverage workers' unions.

Despite the quite significant role of labor confederations, political life in Honduras has been dominated by civilian caudillos and military strongmen. Following nearly twenty years of military rule between 1960 and 1980, a civilian government was elected in 1980. Since then, there have been two other democratically elected presidents. In practice, the executive branch has primacy in the country's decision making. A unicameral legislature has gradually expanded its role but still is subordinate to the president and the military. The country's system of justice is controlled by its Supreme Court, whose nine justices are appointed for four years coinciding with the presidential term. A National Electoral Council administers the country's elections and vot-ing census. However, the politicized nature of the organization has traditionally made it the focal point for intense partisan activity during each electoral campaign.

Honduras has one of the oldest party systems in Latin America. Both the National and Liberal parties trace their antecedents to the late 1800s. The former tended to be a conservative, promilitary party during much of the post–World War II period. The Liberal Party was more oriented toward lower classes and given to social reform efforts. By the mid-1980s, however, the platforms of the two parties were similar in orientation. Personalistic conflict within both parties is heavy and usually divisive; their constituencies are cross-class in nature, although the National Party tends to draw more heavily on rural voters. Two other parties have regularly contested power during the last two decades, but neither the Christian Democratic nor the Innovation and Unity parties have commanded more than ten percent of the votes.

Honduras's key location in the middle of Central America gives it a strategic importance in diplomatic and economic matters. In recent years, the country has been a key ally of the United States in its foreign policy efforts in the region. With the decline of attention to the area, however, Honduras may face hard times.

(See also U.S.–LATIN AMERICAN RELATIONS.)

Mark B. Rosenberg and Philip L. Shepherd, eds., *Honduras Confronts Its Future* (Boulder, Colo., 1986).

MARK B. ROSENBERG

HONG KONG. Hong Kong was acquired by *Britain from *China in the nineteenth century in three stages under what China regarded as "unequal treaties." Hong Kong island was ceded to Britain in perpetuity in 1842, Kowloon peninsula was ceded in 1860, and the New Territories—consisting of ninety-two percent of the area of Hong Kong, including 235 adjacent islands—was given to Britain under a ninety-nine-year lease in 1898.

Hong Kong is situated at the mouth of the Pearl River, 1,000 square kilometers (386 sq. mi.) of land sometimes described as a pimple on the southern tip of China. Ninety-eight percent of its 5.8 million people are Chinese; about half of the population are refugees or recent immigrants from the mainland, and the other half are descendants of refugees and immigrants.

From the 1840s to the 1950s, apart from the Japanese occupation between 1942 and 1945, Hong Kong served as a staging post and transshipment center for trade between China and the Western world. With the *Korean War and a UN embargo on the export of strategic goods to China, most of this trade was cut off, and Hong Kong turned to manufacturing; later it became a financial center.

Beginning in the late 1970s and coinciding with China's economic liberalization, Hong Kong's role as an entrepôt for China trade resumed. Many *multinational corporations operate in Hong Kong; some even use the colony as their regional headquarters because they regard it as a gateway to China. Between 1986 and 1989, the economy grew at an average annual rate of nine percent in real terms. Hong Kong's per capita GDP in 1989 was US$11,000.

Under the British administration's archaic colonial system and laissez-faire policy, Hong Kong flourished. Apart from being denied the right to self-determination and the right to elect political representatives, Hong Kong people enjoy many of the freedoms that Britons enjoy.

Despite the antiquated political system under which universal suffrage is denied and the British government appoints top civil servants, the Hong Kong people have never vigorously demanded *democracy, let alone independence. This is partly because of the refugee mentality—many Hong Kong people do not regard the colony as their home. They look upon it as a refuge from *communism, a place to get rich and then move on.

Between 1982 and 1984 Britain and China held secret talks on the future of the colony. On 19 December 1984 the Sino-British Joint Declaration was signed, under which Britain agreed to hand over Hong Kong to China in 1997. No referendum was held, and the Hong Kong people were told by the British government that if they did not accept the Joint Declaration, they would simply be handed over to China without British assistance in the transition. In the Joint Declaration, the Chinese government promised to give post-1997 Hong Kong "a high degree of autonomy" and agreed that the Hong Kong special administrative region would be "run by local inhabitants." It also promised that Hong Kong's capitalist system and lifestyle would be maintained for fifty years after 1997.

In mid-1984, the British promised to democratize Hong Kong's political system. But the Joint Declaration began to unravel in late 1985 when the Chinese government objected to London's plans to introduce universal suffrage in the colony in 1988. London responded by agreeing with Beijing that all developments during the transition period must "converge" with the Basic Law, a "mini-constitution" for post-1997 Hong Kong. Since then, Britain's policy on Hong Kong has been widely described as appeasement to China for the sake of preserving Sino-British relations and winning commercial contracts.

The Basic Law drafted by Beijing and promulgated by China's National People's Congress (NPC) in April 1990 virtually enshrined a colonial system for post-1997 Hong Kong. Under this law the executive, legislature, and judiciary would be subject to the control of the Chinese central government and the ultimate power to interpret the Basic Law would lie with the standing committee of the NPC. The British have also refused to give Hong Kong residents full British nationality, thus denying them the right to emigrate to Britain prior to the onset of Chinese rule.

The 4 June 1989 *Tiananmen Square massacre in Beijing shattered any lingering hope about the future of Hong Kong, and the exodus of middle-class professionals began in earnest. Although the brutality in China triggered a massive political awakening in the colony, the people quickly reached the conclusion that there was little they could do except look after themselves by planning to emigrate. The general fear was that the people of Hong Kong would lose the freedoms that they enjoy under British rule as soon as the British pull out. It is estimated that about 60,000 people emigrated in 1990 and that between 1984 and 1997, 500,000–700,000 people will have left Hong Kong.

In September 1991, for the first time in the colony's history, a direct election by universal suffrage was held to select eighteen out of sixty-one members of the lawmaking Legislative Council. That represented a small, faltering step toward democracy.

(See also INTERNATIONAL MIGRATION; NEWLY INDUSTRIALIZING ECONOMIES; MACAO.)

G. B. Endacott, *A History of Hong Kong* (Oxford, 1982). Norman J. Miners, *The Government and Politics of Hong Kong* (New York, 1987).

EMILY LAU

HORN OF AFRICA. Associated with *war and famine in recent years, the Horn of Africa is a potentially rich and strategically located region. Lying astride the northwest Indian Ocean and the Red Sea, across the oil-rich Arabian peninsula and the Gulf region, it has been a crossroads of history between Africa and Asia.

The combined effect of history and geography is reflected in the region's demographic makeup, culture, national identities, and religion. Its close proximity to the cradles of Christianity and *Islam facilitated the early spread of these two religions which acted as centralizing and harmonizing factors, and at times as causes of conflict. They have both left an indelible mark on the life and peoples of the region.

More recently, European colonial rule left its mark on the region, notably in the realm of governance, the capitalist market economy, and in the colonially fixed boundaries which cross-cut ethnic/linguistic lines and define the national/state identity of the five countries of the region—*Sudan, Eritrea, *Ethiopia, *Djibouti, and *Somalia.

The postcolonial political economy of the region, as of much of Africa, is a study in squandered resources and missed opportunities caused by disastrous policies and politics. Failed *development models, which were externally oriented and urban-biased, mostly inspired by external sources of finance, have left the populations burdened with huge debts. That in turn has conditioned the policies and behaviors of the governments, leaving the people worse off. The region's economic potential—both human and material—thus remains virtually unrealized.

Sudan and Ethiopia were once considered the breadbaskets for the region and beyond, but have become basket cases. Somalia and Eritrea have marine and other resources that have been barely touched. And Djibouti's deep-sea, natural harbor could make it the "Hong Kong" of the region. The region as a whole can be not only self-sufficient but can produce surplus for export in livestock, dairy products, fruits and vegetables, oil seeds, gum arabic, cotton, coffee, oil, copper, and other resources. This potential can be realized only if present policies are changed in favor of self-sustainable development strategies which can engage the optimal participation of the populations and which benefit the majority, not just narrowly-based urban elites. Moreover, changes in policies will require drastic changes in politics.

As things stand, faulty development policies have been exacerbated by disastrous politics. The latter may be summed up as the politics of domination and exclusion which have engendered conflicts drawing foreign intervention and a massive flow of costly arms into the region. The militarization of the region, and its consequent brutalization of society, have had a destabilizing effect.

Political instability has characterized the region against a grim background of economic stagnation, social unrest, and ethnic cleavage. Until recently, only Djibouti has been relatively stable. Its relative stability can be attributed largely to the wisdom of its leadership, which has maintained a fair balance in governance between its two ethnic groups—the Issa Somalis and the Afars—and which has stayed neutral in the Ethio-Somali conflict over the Ogaden. Recent events are raising questions about Djibouti's stability, as some Afars have revolted on the grounds of what they claim to be an Issa domination of the state. Djibouti adopted a French-style presidential system upon gaining independence in 1977, after over a century of French rule.

In contrast, Somalia began with a Westminster-type parliamentary government in 1960. However, Somali politics proved to be clannish and fractious, precipitating a military coup in 1969. The military regime established one-party rule with "scientific socialism" as its guiding ideology. The promised healing and unifying quality of this ideology was short-lived, overwhelmed as it was by clan politics.

In Ethiopia, Emperor *Haile Selassie's "modernizing" monarchy was overthrown by a radical military group which imposed a Soviet-style one-party rule on the country. *Marxism-*Leninism was written into the 1984 constitution as guide and arbiter of politics and society, with suffocating effect. The overthrow of both the Siad and Mengistu regimes in 1991 raised hopes of *democracy, equal rights, and self-determination. The struggle for these ends continues.

In Sudan, a civilian parliamentary government, to which the departing British transferred power in 1956, was overthrown two years later by a military takeover. Since then civilian and military governments have exchanged power four times. The civilian side of the equation has been dominated by the Umma, a sectarian party, continually challenged by another sectarian party, which facilitated military intervention. The current military regime is backed by a new religious party, the National Islamic Front, which insists on the application of *Shari𝑐a (Islamic law) in all Sudan. Hence the continued rebellion in the south.

The politics of exclusion plays out in the region with variations on a theme, i.e., domination by one group, whether on an ethnic, sectarian, factional, or regional basis. Thus in Sudan, the south (mostly Christian) is excluded from power. In Ethiopia the central Amhara group has dominated the country to the exclusion of the Oromo and others. Rebellions by the southern Sudanese and the Oromo can be explained in terms of this politics of exclusion. In Somalia also, the current rebellion of the northern Somalis was caused by their exclusion from power and allegations of economic discrimination of their region in favor of the south.

Eritrea's case is unique: it is a case of denied *decolonization. The limited autonomy that was imposed on the Eritreans under a UN-arranged federation with Ethiopia was abolished by Emperor Haile Selassie in 1962, provoking the armed struggle which ended in Eritrean victory in May 1991. Following a referendum to be held in April 1993 under international observation, the Eritreans will seek to establish an independent, democratic nation-state. The end of the war in Eritrea and the overthrow of the Mengistu regime in Ethiopia were followed by a conference held in Addis Ababa on 1–5 July 1991 which issued a charter with a framework for the principles of self-determination, democracy, and mutual accommodation.

The above-listed conflicts, in addition to the strategic location of the region, have drawn foreign interventions, from the two superpowers which changed clients as it suited them, to the Israelis, the Cubans, and other surrogates of the superpowers. The changed international climate seems to augur well for a peaceful resolution of the costly wars in the Horn of Africa.

(See also COLONIAL EMPIRES; ERITREAN WAR OF INDEPENDENCE; ETHNICITY; FOOD POLITICS; INTERNATIONAL DEBT; MILITARISM; MODERNIZATION; ONE-PARTY SYSTEM; RELIGION AND POLITICS.)

Bereket Habte Selassie, *Conflict and Intervention in the Horn of Africa* (New York, 1980). Georges Nzongola-Ntalaja, ed., *Conflict in the Horn of Africa* (Atlanta, Ga., 1991).

BEREKET HABTE SELASSIE

HOUSING. See WELFARE STATE.

HUMAN RIGHTS. The human rights practices of governments—that is, their respect for freedom of expression and association, for due process of law, for equality before the law, and for the *rights of their citizens not to be subjected to cruel and degrading punishment—have become a factor in the relations between nations alongside such traditional concerns as *security arrangements and trading practices. The growth in international concern for rights was especially dramatic during the 1980s; indeed, the contrast with just the previous decade was striking.

From the time that they began to be defined systematically in the seventeenth century, rights were thought to relate to *citizenship in a particular *state and that it was the state that owed citizens a duty to respect rights. The English Bill of Rights of 1688 began with a complaint against King James II for attempting to subvert those rights and concluded with a demand that henceforth they should be respected by the Prince of Orange. The American Declaration of Independence of 1776 complained about violations by King George III and asserted independence for a new government to be formed by the united colonies on the grounds that such a "tyrant is unfit to be the ruler of a free people." The French Declaration of Rights of 1789 asserted the inalienability of rights but rested the duty to respect rights in the nation, which it proclaimed to be "the source of all sovereignty." It would not have occurred to the authors of these crucial texts in the history of liberty that the world community could be regarded as the guarantor of rights.

The idea that governments' practices and treatment of their own citizens should matter to the rest of the world gained acceptance in the period following World War II, as the world became conscious of the barbarities that had been practiced by the Nazis. The UN Charter, adopted in 1945, provided in Article 55 that the world body "shall promote universal respect for, and observance of human rights and fundamental freedoms for all," and in Article 56 that member nations "pledge themselves to take joint and separate action in cooperation with the Organization for the achievement of the purposes set forth in Article 55." In 1948, the UN spelled out what was meant by "human rights" in the Universal Declaration of Human Rights, which was adopted without dissent, but with abstentions by the Soviet bloc nations, South Africa, and Saudi Arabia. In subsequent years, the nations of the world further committed themselves to respect human rights through a number of international agreements, among them the European Convention on Human Rights (1950); the International Covenant on Civil and Political Rights (1966); the American Convention on Human Rights (1969); the *Helsinki Accords (1975); and the African Charter on Peoples' and Human Rights

(1981). Citizens in many countries established nongovernmental organizations to seek compliance with the provisions of these agreements, and those organizations became a force in shaping international *public opinion to condemn nations that flagrantly violated human rights. Even so, prior to the 1980s, abuses by governments against their own citizens only infrequently became important factors in the way other governments shaped their international policies.

During the 1970s, for example, a period of relative tolerance for dissent came to an end in the Soviet Union without interfering with East-West détente; the United States established relations with China while *Mao was alive and the extreme repression of the *Cultural Revolution was in progress; military coups, accompanied by severe persecution, took place in the first half of the 1970s in Chile and Uruguay, and military repression intensified in Brazil, yet support for these governments by the international lending agencies and by the United States increased dramatically; similarly, the reformist government of Ferdinand *Marcos in the Philippines became highly repressive during the 1970s but enjoyed substantial international support. The first signs of change in the formulation of *foreign policy appeared later in the decade and were particularly associated with the advent in 1977 of the presidency of Jimmy *Carter in the United States.

The Carter administration was vigorous in its efforts to make human rights a factor in its relations with Latin American nations, including Argentina, where a most brutal military regime had taken power in 1976, and Guatemala, where repression escalated in the late 1970s in response to an insurgency; and in relations with South Africa, whose *apartheid policies it condemned. On the other hand, the Carter administration pursued détente with the Soviet Union, despite a deteriorating human rights situation, until the December 1979 invasion of Afghanistan; did not respond discernibly to the crushing of the "democracy wall" movement in China in 1979; and did not make human rights practices a major concern in its relations with most of the repressive governments in Asia, Africa, or the Middle East.

Despite the Carter administration's failure to implement worldwide its proclaimed commitment to human rights, it had a major impact in legitimizing concern for rights as an important factor in international affairs. At the outset, it appeared that the successor *Reagan administration would repudiate that concern; instead, after a shaky start, the Reagan administration proclaimed its own commitment to the human rights cause, though it redefined it by shifting the emphasis away from a focus on such physical abuses as killings and *torture. In a June 1982 address to the British Parliament, President Reagan committed the United States to the promotion of *democracy worldwide, equating democratic government with human rights.

The Reagan approach reflected an awareness that many governments aligned with the United States that were targets of denunciations for abusing human rights nevertheless could be said to be democratic if the meaning of democracy embraced only their conduct of more or less free and fair elections. In contrast, many governments aligned with the Soviet Union did not permit such elections but nevertheless evaded international criticism for human rights abuses because their means of maintaining control did not require them to resort to such practices as death squads, disappearances, and extreme forms of physical torture. At the time, Central America was considered by the Reagan administration to be a leading *Cold War battleground. Accordingly, in his London speech, the president particularly focused on the distinction between El Salvador, where a widely praised election had been held three months earlier, and Nicaragua, where the Sandinistas were proclaiming that they did not intend to hold elections for another three years—six years after they seized power—and in general were expressing disdain for elections. Up to the time of the elections in El Salvador, the Reagan administration had been on the defensive when comparisons were drawn between the two countries because the level of violent abuses of human rights was so much greater in El Salvador, aligned with the United States, than in Nicaragua, aligned with the Soviet Union.

Although this espousal of elections was largely an opportunistic response to a particular Cold War problem, it came to dominate U.S. policy on human rights worldwide for the rest of the decade. At times, it led the United States to help oust military dictators to whom the Reagan administration had initially displayed great friendship. The United States' role in President Ferdinand Marcos's departure from the Philippines in 1986 and in the termination of the *Pinochet dictatorship in Chile at the end of the decade were in large measure attributable to its embrace of democracy and elections as the essence of human rights.

During the 1980s, a number of other governments joined in embracing human rights as a goal of their foreign policies. The Scandinavian governments and the Netherlands began issuing reports on the human rights practices of governments to which they were donating development assistance. Canada and Australia made promoting human rights an important part of their role in international affairs. The *Council of Europe made Turkey's qualification for membership conditional on an improvement in its human rights practices. The *European Community made human rights practices—such as the crackdown on dissent and the imposition of martial law in Poland at the beginning of the decade (December 1981) and in China at the end (June 1989)—an element in its economic relations with various countries.

The growing significance of human rights in international affairs during the 1980s became a factor in transformations of government that took place in a number of countries during the decade. Fearing worldwide condemnation and economic reprisals, it became more difficult for many governments to respond ruthlessly to domestic dissent, especially to dissent that focused on human rights violations and the denial of democratic opportunities. Though by no means the sole cause, domestic and international pressure concerned with human rights played a part in the installation of democratic governments in a number of countries, such as in Argentina in 1983 to replace a thoroughly discredited military regime; in the similar transition in Uruguay in 1985; in the popular revolts that ousted dictators in Haiti and the Philippines in 1986; in the military accession to democratic elections in the Republic of Korea (South Korea) in 1987; and in the process whereby the Pinochet regime in Chile yielded office peacefully to a democratic government in 1990, seventeen years after it came to power.

The most stunning consequences of international concern for human rights were the revolutions that swept Central and Eastern Europe in 1989. The process of change had begun with the emergence of *Solidarity in Poland at the beginning of the decade. To many observers, the imposition of martial law in December 1981 had an air of finality about it. Yet pressure concerned with human rights—such as economic sanctions by the United States until every last one of the Solidarity prisoners was released—helped to transform that episode into a temporary setback. By 1989, the repressive regime in Poland had been effectively dismantled in stages. Revolutions elsewhere in the region took place at great speed: over a two-week period in Czechoslovakia; over a five-day period in Romania. Of the various causes, domestic demands to respect human rights, reinforced by international pressure on the same behalf, had played a large part.

The revolutionary developments in Central and Eastern Europe stirred demands for change elsewhere. Though the Chinese students who assembled in *Tiananmen Square in the spring of 1989 possessed little information about Eastern Europe, they talked a lot about Poland, Solidarity, and Lech *Wałęsa. Their uprising was put down violently on the night of 3–4 June, but this time the rest of the world did not react with the same lack of concern that had characterized previous periods of repression in China. The student demonstrations had drawn the attention of the world's news media and, as a consequence, the crackdown was watched on television by hundreds of millions around the world. It elicited international outrage, but not a sense of hopelessness. Instead, observers widely predicted that in a few years China would again confront a significant movement for democracy and human rights. The fact that China had for the first time become a focus of international concern for human rights has probably increased the likelihood that these predictions will come true. Moreover, the setback in China did not prevent dramatic changes from taking place during 1989 and 1990 in such neighboring countries as Mongolia, where a *communist party state underwent a peaceful transition to multiparty democracy, and Nepal, where a monarchy in which all political parties had been forbidden was forced to undergo a political opening by huge demonstrations that the government could not suppress even by killing scores of demonstrators.

The revolutions in Central and Eastern Europe also sparked demands for human rights and democracy in other parts of the world, including in such Middle Eastern countries as Algeria and Kuwait, and in such sub-Saharan nations as Kenya, Cameroon, Benin, Togo, and Zambia. It remained to be seen, however, whether the same international pressure to respect human rights would be generated in the West towards single-party African states as had been manifest over the course of the previous decade toward various repressive countries in Europe, Latin America, and Asia. The claims by the leaders of several African nations that *one-party systems served the needs of the countries by suppressing corrosive ethnic divisions, like the claims by the leaders of some Middle Eastern nations that limits on democratic rights in their countries were required to suppress Islamic fundamentalism, struck responsive chords in Western public opinion.

To some extent, the rise of concern with human rights practices as a factor in international affairs had been a concomitant of the Cold War. That is, many in the West had criticized repression by the Soviet Union and Soviet bloc nations as a way of delegitimizing *communism. In turn, others in the West had demanded that the Third World clients of the West should adhere to the standards of respect for human rights that were being demanded in communist nations. Though there seemed little question in the 1990s that concern for human rights as a factor in international affairs would remain a powerful force for a period, the longer-term future was cloudier.

While the Cold War was under way, the Soviet bloc nations had frequently rebutted Western criticism of their human rights practices by claiming that their respect for economic and social rights, such as the right to employment, health care, and housing, contrasted favorably with the refusal of the West to acknowledge that these are rights of citizens. In international gatherings, it was customary for Soviet bloc representatives to respond to Western complaints about such abuses as political imprisonment both by asserting that these were internal affairs and by denouncing such matters as homelessness in the United States.

The view that economic and social questions should also be thought of in terms of rights was not solely confined to the Soviet bloc. It is reflected in several provisions of the Universal Declaration of Human Rights and in an International Covenant on Social, Economic and Cultural Rights that was promulgated by the UN at the same time as the Covenant on Civil and Political Rights. Moreover, human rights activists in a number of Third World countries, especially in Asia, have long held the view that both kinds of concerns are rights. Their argument has not proved persuasive in the West, however, and none of the leading international nongovernmental groups concerned with human rights has become an advocate of economic and social rights.

It seemed possible in the post–Cold War era that strife over ethnic and economic factors within some of the nations affected by the rights revolution of the previous decade would dampen enthusiasm internationally for efforts to condition foreign policy decisions on human rights. Yet the heightened public consciousness of human rights will not dissipate quickly. That, combined with the emergence in many countries of an increasingly well-organized movement of nongovernmental groups concerned with human rights, will undoubtedly continue to generate pressure on governments to make human rights a central factor in international policy.

(See also DEMOCRATIC TRANSITIONS; MILITARY RULE; NINETEEN EIGHTY-NINE; SOVIET DISSENT; UNITED NATIONS.)

Lars Schoultz, *Human Rights and U.S. Policy Toward Latin America* (Princeton, N.J., 1981). Theodor Meron, ed., *Human Rights in International Law* (Oxford, 1984). Ludmilla Alexeyeva, *Soviet Dissent: Contemporary Movements for National, Religious and Human Rights* (Middletown, Conn., 1985). Richard P. Claude and Burns H. Weston, eds., *Human Rights in the World Community* (Philadelphia, 1989). Middle East Watch, *Human Rights in Iraq* (New Haven, Conn., 1990). Americas Watch, *El Salvador's Decade of Terror* (New Haven, Conn., 1991). Middle East Watch, *Syria Unmasked: The Suppression of Human Rights by the Asad Regime* (New Haven, Conn., 1991). Americas Watch, *Peru Under Fire* (New Haven, Conn., 1992).
ARYEH NEIER

HUNGARY. After emerging in the late Middle Ages as a major European power, Hungary came under the domination of the Ottoman and Habsburg empires. The roots of the modern state lie in the national revival movement of the early nineteenth century. The *revolution of 1848 secured autonomy in a new, liberal constitution, only to be crushed by Austrian and Russian arms. The Austro-Hungarian Compromise of 1867 granted Hungary self-government, albeit with joint administration of foreign affairs, defense, and finance. The bicameral legislature consisted of an upper house of civil and religious notables and a lower house elected on the basis of a limited, property-linked suffrage. In a predominantly agrarian society, the peasantry enjoyed no direct political representation. The conservative ruling elite divided mainly over the merits of qualified autonomy and warded off the challenges of democratic *socialism and bourgeois liberalism with measured reforms and industrial development.

The defeat of Austria-Hungary in *World War I unleashed disintegrative ethnonational pressures. Barely half of Hungary's population was ethnically Magyar, and initially liberal nationalities laws had given way to more assimilative policies that fed separatist tendencies. Faced with Allied demands for territorial concessions, an embryonic liberal regime headed by Count Mihaly Karolyi surrendered power to a Communist–Social Democrat directorate that styled Hungary a republic of councils. This "dictatorship of the proletariat," led by the Communist Béla Kun, attempted for four months in 1919 to impose Leninist revolution, then collapsed.

With the restoration of the old constitution in 1920, Hungary became a fully independent kingdom, the actual head of state being Admiral Miklós Horthy. The impartial rule of law generally prevailed, and the franchise was initially extended to two-thirds of the adult population, then trimmed again; only the Communist Party was proscribed. Until 1944 a variable coalition known as the governing party ruled Hungary. The dominant political values were irredentist *nationalism, inspired by the Treaty of Trianon, which reduced the country's territory and population by two-thirds, and a conservatism hostile not only to left and right radicalism but to bourgeois liberalism as well. The political opposition encompassed the Social Democrats, who however had agreed to limit their activity; a populist movement that focused on the needs of the peasantry; and, in the late 1930s, right-wing radicals, including the fascist Arrow Cross party. The government enacted a limited *land reform and social welfare measures and labored to surmount the economic consequences of territorial truncation and the depression; industrialization received a boost from the expansion of German economic influence.

Hungary adhered to the Axis to win the return of some territory at the expense of Czechoslovakia in 1938 and of Romania in 1940. Its participation in the war against the Soviet Union was so grudging that in 1944 Germany occupied the country and imposed an Arrow Cross dictatorship. At year's end, a provisional government of former opposition parties and Communists was created under Soviet auspices.

The political climate in economically devastated Hungary favored moderate change, and a thorough land reform was effected. The Communists nevertheless won barely seventeen percent of the vote in the relatively free elections of November 1945. The center-right Smallholder Party emerged as the principal non-Communist force, winning a clear majority, but at Soviet insistence a coalition government was formed. A democratic constitution adopted in 1946 styled Hungary a republic with a sovereign unicameral parliament; the Paris Peace Treaty restored the prewar borders. Communist subversion and agitation gradually incapacitated the democratic majority. On *Stalin's instructions, the Communists in 1948 forcibly absorbed the Social Democrats into the Hungarian Workers' Party and set course for revolutionary change.

The party, dominated by Mátyás Rákosi and a few other former émigrés, imposed *Stalinism on Hungary. The goal of building socialism was enshrined in a new Soviet-type constitution, and all state institutions and mass organizations were subordinated to the party. Initially, the party won some support from the poorer social strata and some intellectuals with its promise of equality, social justice, and *modernization. All political opposition was suppressed, and the party itself underwent massive purges. To the extent that the new system had enjoyed some popular *legitimacy, this was soon dissipated by the brutality of the dictatorship, a decline in the standard of living, and suppression of nationalism in favor of Sovietization.

After Stalin's death, Rákosi was compelled to share power with a reformer, Imre Nagy, who pursued a more balanced economic strategy while alleviating rule by terror. This "New Course" was soon halted by Rákosi, but "revisionism" gained ground among party intellectuals. *Khrushchev's de-Stalinization and the revolution in Poland galvanized Hungarians to challenge their ruler in October 1956. Over a period of two weeks, a multiparty government formed under Nagy's premiership promised to restore *democracy and a mixed economy and, apprehending Soviet military intervention, renounced the *Warsaw Treaty Organization (Warsaw Pact) and proclaimed Hungary's neutrality.

The revolution was crushed by armed force, and Communist dictatorship reimposed, under the renamed Hungarian Socialist Workers' Party headed by János Kádár. Kádár's immediate task was to rebuild the party and complete the *collectivization of agriculture. This accomplished, in the 1960s he adopted a conciliatory "alliance policy" that relaxed political and social discrimination in access to higher education and official posts and led in 1968 to the adoption of a "New Economic Mechanism." The latter aimed to revive Hungary's faltering economy by introducing some elements of the market. The greatest progress was made in agriculture, where investment and self-management greatly improved productivity. A more tolerant cultural policy and the introduction of multiple candidacies in parliamentary elections (still controlled by the Patriotic People's Front, a party appendage) were other concessions by a regime in quest of legitimacy.

The reform was halted in the mid-1970s as a consequence of Soviet and domestic conservative pressures, then was relaunched with new decentralizing measures and concessions to small-scale private enterprise. Despite partial reforms and Western loans, a declining growth rate and mounting foreign debt precipitated an economic crisis in the mid-1980s. Political dissent, meanwhile, spread among intellectuals and within the party itself.

*Gorbachev's willingness to loosen Soviet *hegemony unleashed a quiet revolution in Hungary. In May 1988 a reformist party leadership dumped Kádár and set course for controlled democratization and a marketized economy. Opposition groups pressed for more radical change, and the demoralized party rapidly lost its grip. In October 1989 party reformers created the avowedly social democratic Hungarian Socialist Party, and the constitution was amended to style Hungary a simple republic (rather than "people's republic"), guarantee full political and civil rights, and allow for free elections.

All the new parties advocated liberal democracy, a market economy with social justice, and full independence. The populist-nationalist Democratic Forum was the decisive winner in the elections of March/April 1990 with forty-two percent of the vote and formed a coalition government under Prime Minister József Antall. The Socialist Party won 8.5 percent. The new assembly's first act was to commemorate the 1956 revolution; it later elected a president.

The withdrawal of Soviet forces had been negotiated before the election, and the new government gave notice of its intention to leave the Warsaw Pact (in which Hungary had the smallest army) and to join the *Council of Europe and seek association with the *European Community. It also voiced concern for the cultural rights of Hungarians in neighboring countries, notably the 2-million-strong minority in Romania. But economic and social issues, such as *privatization, foreign investment, and redistribution remain the bread and butter of politics in democratic Hungary.

(See also COMMUNIST PARTY STATES; NINETEEN EIGHTY-NINE; PERESTROIKA; SOVIET–EAST EUROPEAN RELATIONS.)

Bennett Kovrig, *Communism in Hungary from Kun to Kadar* (Stanford, Calif., 1979). Andrew C. Janos, *The Politics of Backwardness in Hungary, 1825–1945* (Princeton, N.J., 1982). Ivan Volgyes, *Hungary: A Nation of Contradictions* (Boulder, Colo., 1982).

BENNETT KOVRIG

HUSSEIN, Saddam. In 1937, a few weeks after his father's death, Saddam Hussein was born to a peasant family near Takrit, a small country town on the Tigris River about a hundred miles from Baghdad. His stepfather seems to have treated him brutally, and the boy found more affection in the house of his uncle, Khairullah Tulfa, whose daughter Sajida he was to marry.

After his primary schooling, he was sent to Baghdad in the early 1950s to continue his education. In those years, although *Iraq was nominally independent of Britain, it was ruled by a small pro-Western oligarchy; all opposition parties had been proscribed, and political life, dominated by the Communists, was effectively driven underground. In 1955,

Hussein joined the Ba'th, a pan-Arab party which then had only 300 members.

In the aftermath of the revolution that swept away the ancien régime in 1958, the Communists enjoyed a brief period of ascendancy, but they were bitterly opposed by the pan-Arabists (Nasserists and Ba'thists), who, in company with conservative and religious forces, felt threatened by the Communists' potential radicalism. In the struggles of the late 1950s and early 1960s, the Ba'th made their presence felt by means of gangs who roamed the streets of Baghdad, attacking suspected Communists and Communist sympathizers.

On 7 October 1959, Hussein and a group of Ba'thist conspirators tried to assassinate the Iraqi president, 'Abd al-Karim Qasim. The assassins managed to escape and Hussein, just 23 years old, fled to Egypt. He stayed there until a Ba'thist-Nasserist coup overthrew Qasim in February 1963. Back in Baghdad, Hussein attracted the attention of the Ba'th Party's Syrian founder, Michel 'Aflaq, who put him in charge of organizing the civilian wing of the party in 1964. He was also linked, by family connections, to army officers in the party's military wing, most notably General Ahmad Hasan al-Bakr, who had served briefly as vice-president of the republic in 1963.

In 1968, a military coup brought the Ba'th back to power and al-Bakr into the presidency. Hussein worked to consolidate the party's grip on the state machinery and the armed forces. He appointed men whom he trusted to top posts in the army and put himself in charge of the country's internal security services. By 1969, a year after the *coup d'état at the age of 32, he had risen to the post of assistant secretary-general of the Ba'th Party and vice-president of Iraq.

During the 1970s, he won increasing power by forging a close alliance with al-Bakr and by tightening his control over the vast security apparatus and the praetorian Republic Guard. He trusted few beyond his inner circle, which increasingly consisted of relatives and friends from his hometown of Takrit. Among the public, he never achieved a charismatic following, but he did become known for his eloquent, if bombastic and self-adulatory, speeches.

Iraq's apparently progressive orientation convinced a willing Soviet Union to conclude a twenty-year treaty of friendship and to encourage the Iraqi Communist Party to join with the Ba'th in a National Patriotic Front. Soviet oil expertise enabled Iraq to develop its unexploited southern oil fields, and the Iraq Petroleum Company was nationalized, a step which gave the government—now increasingly "Saddam Hussein and his entourage"—full control over the country's substantial oil revenues. The alliance with the Communists gave him vital breathing space in his attempt to muzzle his most persistent opponents, the Kurds; the Kurdish movement was defeated as a result of an agreement negotiated between Saddam Hussein and the shah of Iran at Algiers in March 1975, under which the shah undertook to close Iranian borders to the Kurdish guerrillas. By this time the alliance with the Communists had outlived its purpose, and Saddam Hussein began to inaugurate a merciless campaign against them.

In July 1979, Hussein took over the presidency from al-Bakr. He demonstrated his power a few days later by turning against some of his closest former allies within the Baʿth party; a "plot" was discovered in which a number of members of the ruling Revolutionary Command Council (RCC) were implicated. Those found guilty were executed, with great publicity, by Saddam Hussein and the surviving members of the RCC in person, thus forging a gruesome blood brotherhood between them.

Barely a year after consolidating his power, Saddam Hussein bid for primacy in the region when he launched an invasion of *Iran in September 1980. After initial successes, Iraqi forces were driven back by the Iranians, but the *war continued for nearly eight years, with high casualties and destruction on both sides. In the course of the war, Hussein received considerable assistance in arms, *intelligence, and military training from the United States and other Western countries as well as the Soviet Union. He used chemical weapons against the Iranians—as he was to do against the Kurds in March 1988—and ordered several hundred thousand Iraqi Shiʿis deported to Iran on grounds that they were "really" Iranians and thus enemies of the Iraqi state.

In the 1980s, Hussein's cult of personality reached new heights. Pictures of the "Great Leader" were visible everywhere, and buildings, monuments, and suburbs were renamed after him. Although it was difficult to represent the stalemate at the end of the war with Iran as a victory, Saddam Hussein managed to do so. He commissioned many enormous commemorative monuments, the most well-known being a metal sculpture forming an arch out of swords held in two hands, the latter cast from molds taken from the president's own wrists.

During the middle and late 1980s, the Kurdish population took advantage of the regime's other preoccupations to create virtually independent enclaves in northern Iraq. After the end of the war, Hussein undertook a vast pacification operation against them. During this campaign, government forces murdered some 100,000 Kurdish Iraqis and buried them in mass graves near the Iraqi-Saudi border. Although the regime's major *human rights violations occasioned verbal condemnations from the West from time to time, few more positive actions were taken; many Western countries had advanced huge sums to Iraq during the war and were hoping for rich pickings from postwar reconstruction.

In August 1990 Hussein invaded the small, oil-rich state of *Kuwait in yet another bid for regional supremacy. His attempt to annex Kuwait and appropriate its oil resources met strong international opposition, expressed through the UN. The United States organized a military coalition to oppose the invasion and demanded that Hussein withdraw his forces unconditionally, but he refused. In January and February of 1991, coalition forces dealt a crushing military defeat to the Iraqis, while coalition bombing destroyed much of Iraq's modern infrastructure.

Uprisings within Iraq followed the war, but Hussein put them down with much bloodshed, giving rise to over 2 million refugees, many of them Kurds. In spite of these events and clandestine efforts to oust him, Hussein clung tenaciously to power.

In the 1980s, when Iraq's relations with the West were extremely cordial, it was fashionable to assert that Saddam Hussein's programs of modernization and development were creating a new kind of national consensus in Iraq. The regime might be repressive, but things worked and the population was becoming more literate, more educated, and more united. It is now difficult to characterize Saddam Hussein's "achievement" in anything but negative terms.

(See also ARAB NATIONALISM; GULF WAR; IRAN-IRAQ WAR; KURDISTAN; NASSERISM.)

Samir al-Khalil, *Republic of Fear* (London, 1989). Marion Farouk-Sluglett and Peter Sluglett, *Iraq Since 1958: From Revolution to Dictatorship* (London, 1990). Efraim Karsh and Inar Rautsi, *Saddam Hussein: A Political Biography* (London, 1991). Middle East Watch, *Human Rights in Iraq* (New Haven, Conn., 1991).

PETER SLUGLETT
MARION SLUGLETT

I

IBN-KHALDŪN. Born in Tunis in times of great political turmoil, Ibn-Khaldūn (1332–1406) served variously as political adviser, prime minister, and judge in several North African states and Muslim Spain. In later life he settled in Cairo, where he taught at al-Azhar and was appointed Grand Malaki Judge. The great passion of his later years was writing a "universal history" whereby he sought to explain the chaotic politics of his day by discovering general causes for the rise and decline of *states. His introduction, in English translation *The Mugaddima,* sets forth a theory of history and society together with a method, his "science of culture."

Best known is his notion of the dynamic of new states and political movements, which he calls *asabiyya* or (social) solidarity. It arises in simple societies where economies of necessity produce an ethos of community. Political institutions are rudimentary: the leadership of the most able and respected. As the society grows, subgroups appear, loyalties become divided, and the subgroup with the strongest solidarity becomes dominant. Chieftainship turns into kingship. The king consolidates his power through force. Natural solidarity disappears and decline begins.

Decline leads ultimately to the distintegration of state and civilization if not checked by the appearance of a new group with solidarity. Such a new group is unlikely to rise within the state, however. Rather, a less advanced people with rising solidarity typically takes over the state and changes its manner of life—albeit temporarily. Eventually they also will generate the same processes which led to the decline of the state they conquered.

Although the notion of *asabiyya* is a prominent part of Ibn-Khaldūn's explanation of social and political change, it does not begin to indicate the extraordinary character of his writings, which Toynbee described as "undoubtedly the greatest work of its kind that has ever yet been created by any mind in any time or place."

Ibn-Khaldūn anticipated critical themes in modern political thought. He turned from considering how things ought to be to studying states and societies as they "really are" a full century and a half before Machiavelli. He located the vital force of human behavior and thus society in passions, not reason, two centuries before Hobbes. Only after four cen-

turies did another philosophy of history appear, with Hegel, and even then not based on material-empirical reality. Although Ibn-Khaldūn's theory of history was grounded in material reality, he did not find it necessary to disavow either political philosophy or religion. His thought thus represents a unique instance in the transition from classical to modern theory, and it continues to influence contemporary political and social theory in the Middle East.

Mugaddimat Ibn Khaldūn (Prolégomènes d'Ebn Khaldoun), 3 vols. (Paris, 1858). Ibn Khaldūn, *The Mugaddimah: An Introduction to History,* trans. Franz Rosenthal, Bollingen Series XLIII, 3 vols. (Princeton, N.J., 1958; edited and abridged by N. J. Dawood, 1969). Muhsin Mahdi, *Ibn Khaldūn's Philosophy of History: A Study in the Philosophic Foundations of the Science of Culture* (Chicago, 1964).

ENID HILL

ICELAND. An island in the North Atlantic between Norway and Greenland, Iceland has an ethnically homogeneous population of 250,000. It is a member of the UN, the *North Atlantic Treaty Organization, the Organization for Economic Cooperation and Development, the *European Free Trade Association (EFTA), and a range of Nordic institutions, and has a free trade agreement with the *European Community (EC). It is a *parliamentary democracy and has a constitutional president and a Lutheran Protestant state church. Iceland was under the control of Norway from 1262 to 1523, and then under that of Denmark. In 1845, its Parliament was reestablished as an advisory council to the Danish king. Limited home rule was granted in 1874, limited parliamentarism in 1904, and full *sovereignty (except in foreign policy matters) in 1918. In the nineteenth century, the Icelandic elite emulated Danish politics and culture. But the old language was not displaced, and as part of the independence struggle language was purified and Icelandic culture and institutions revived. Iceland declared neutrality in World War II, but was occupied by British troops in 1940, replaced by U.S. troops in 1941. In the postwar security structure, the Keflavik airport, near Reykjavik, the capital, was a point of strategic importance. U.S. use of the base was granted in a bilateral agreement (1951). The U.S. presence gave rise to protests from the left.

The most important party in the postwar period

has been the Independence Party, which has received on average forty percent of the vote. It is a right-wing party, with support from most employers, but also from all other classes. The Progressive Party has its main base in provincial regions, i.e., agricultural and fishing villages. On the left is the Social Democratic Party (founded in 1946, along with the Federation of Labor). A split in the 1930s produced a Communist Party which in 1958 asserted its independence from Moscow, being absorbed into the socialist People's Alliance, which was established as a party in 1968. A Women's List has held parliamentary seats since 1983.

Iceland is entirely dependent on exports of fish, especially cod. Still, its per capita income is as high as that of the other Nordic countries. Most industries are linked to the fisheries (processing, shipyards), but Iceland also exports aluminum. The state and the cooperative movement have been heavily involved in the fisheries sector. Most savings were allocated through state banks, and there was no stock exchange. However, during the 1980s, *privatization and liberalization changed this.

Economic policies created a devaluation–high inflation cycle, with double-digit inflation since 1972 (reaching a peak of eighty-three percent in 1983). The labor market is very tight, with a high employment rate and long working hours. Unemployment was never above one percent in the 1970s. Union membership is a condition for employment. Indexation has been a main focus in the negotiation of collective agreements. In hard times (low fish prices, lack of foreign currencies), indexation is modified. As conditions improve, large-scale strike activity has restored full indexation. In the late 1980s, Icelandic policy makers have tried to turn to a low inflation, hard currency approach.

A *law of the sea *regime is crucial for Iceland. In 1950–1952, Iceland unilaterally extended its national fishing zone to four nautical miles, escaping European embargoes by exporting processed fish to the United States and the Soviet Union. Iceland has always supported UN efforts to secure an international law of the seas. UN conferences in 1958, 1960, and 1974–1975 produced majorities, but no resolutions on extended national controls over fish resources. Iceland made extensions anyway, to twelve nautical miles in 1958–1960, fifty nautical miles in 1972 (declared unilaterally, with reference to resource depletion), and 200 nautical miles in 1974–1975. On each occasion Britain sent warships. The 1958 dispute was settled in the International Court of Justice. But the 1970s saw two "cod wars": small coast guard vessels would cut the trawls of British trawlers, narrowly escaping larger British navy vessels. No lives were lost. A settlement was reached in 1976. Continued control over fish resources is the main condition for Icelandic participation in the EC-EFTA negotiations of the early 1990s.

(See also SCANDINAVIA.)

Stefán Ólafsson, *Modernization and Social Stratification in Iceland* (Reykjavik, 1991).

LARS MJØSET

IDEALISM. In the context of *international relations, idealism refers to the body of thought that regards fundamental reform of the system of international relations to be both essential and possible. Idealists treat the sovereign independence of *states as a basic cause of *war and its attendant misery. Over centuries they have proposed plans for *international law and organization that would, as Immanuel Kant put it in 1784, cause states to "abandon" their "lawless state of savagery and enter a federation of peoples in which every state could expect to derive its security and rights . . . from a united power and the law-governed decisions of a united will" (*Idea for a Universal History with a Cosmopolitan Purpose,* in Hans Reiss, ed., *Kant's Political Writings,* Cambridge, U.K., 1970).

In Kant's version, idealism expressed a kind of tragic optimism about international relations. After centuries of ever-more-destructive wars, people would finally come to realize "what reason could have suggested to them even without so many sad experiences": that the independence of states must give way to an effective *international organization capable of enforcing genuine *peace. Liberals of the nineteenth century like Jeremy Bentham or John Stuart Mill had a more sanguine view of international reform. As international trade spread, so too would *international law and functional international organization; nationalistic sovereign states would come to be seen as irrelevant and atavistic.

*World War I shattered this painless view of international progress but also created the *League of Nations. Supporters of Woodrow Wilson's vision for the League sought to rally *public opinion around the cause of international organization because they believed it to be the only way to prevent another war. Idealism as term of description came into wide use in the 1920s, as scholars and publicists like G. Lowes Dickinson, Alfred Zimmern, and James T. Shotwell indefatigably urged nations to forsake "their illusions, their cupidity and their pride" in order to build the League of Nations into "a working machine for peace" (Dickinson, *The International Anarchy, 1904–1914,* London, 1925, p. 37). These thinkers shared a belief in the essential goodness of human nature, the primacy of ideas and education, and in the ultimate *power of an aroused world public opinion. The Kellogg-Briand Pact of 1928 outlawing war "as an instrument of national policy" began as an idealist initiative (from James T. Shotwell in New York) and was emblematic of idealist hopes for international reform.

The events of the 1930s were widely interpreted as discrediting the approach of idealism, though, perhaps ironically, idealists like Zimmern or Arnold Toynbee implacably opposed the British policy of appeasement, whereas the "realist" E. H. Carr provided arguments in support of Chamberlain's policy at Munich. After *World War II, idealism did not so much die as migrate to U.S. liberal supporters of the UN. In the early postwar period, a debate between "realists" and "idealists" occurred among intellectuals as the United States settled into the *Cold War with the Soviet Union. Idealists tended to argue for more negotiations and wished to base *American foreign policy on the moral ground of international law and the UN; realists denounced idealism's naïveté and urged a policy based on the national interest defined in terms of power. Echoes of this debate can be heard in disagreements about nuclear *deterrence and intervention in external conflicts. Idealism has always claimed to speak for higher human aspiration and the possibility of peace; more recently it has also embraced the cause of global *environmentalism.

(See also INTERNATIONAL COOPERATION; REALISM; RIGHTS; SECURITY; UNITED NATIONS.)

Sissela Bok, *A Strategy for Peace: Human Values and the Threat of War* (New York, 1990). Terry Nardin and David Mapel, eds., *Traditions of International Ethics* (Cambridge, U.K., 1992).

MICHAEL JOSEPH SMITH

IDEOLOGY. The term *ideology* was coined in the late eighteenth century by the French philosopher Destutt de Tracy (1754–1836). A wealthy and educated nobleman who was strongly influenced by the European Enlightenment, de Tracy sought to develop a new discipline that would be concerned with the systematic analysis of ideas and sensations. It was this discipline that he described as *ideology*—literally, the science of ideas. He believed that this discipline would enable human nature to be understood and hence would enable the social and political order to be rearranged in accordance with the needs and aspirations of human beings. The early project of ideology was thus a natural development of certain themes characteristic of the Enlightenment, such as the capacity of human beings to understand and control the world through systematic, scientific analysis.

In the early nineteenth century, the meaning of the term *ideology* was transformed in complicated ways. This transformation began when the French emperor, Napoleon Bonaparte, turned against Destutt de Tracy and his associates, whom he described as *idéologues*. Napoleon condemned ideology as a vague and abstract doctrine that would confuse people and undermine the rule of law. As his military campaigns ran into difficulties and his position weakened both at home and abroad, Napoleon's attacks on ideology became more sweeping and vehement. Many kinds of religious and philosophical thought were condemned as ideology. Thus the meaning of the term began to change: *ideology* ceased to refer only to the science of ideas and began

to refer also to the ideas themselves, that is, to a body of ideas that were alleged to be erroneous and divorced from the practical realities of political life.

The term was further transformed by *Marx and Engels. In their writings the term acquired a new status as a critical tool and as an integral component of a new theoretical system. But Marx and Engels did not use the term in a clear and consistent way. In *The German Ideology,* written in 1845–1846 but left unpublished, Marx and Engels criticized the views of the so-called "Young Hegelians" such as Ludwig Feuerbach, Bruno Bauer, and Max Stirner. In characterizing the views of these thinkers as "the German ideology," Marx and Engels were following, very broadly, Napoleon's use of the term: the work of the Young Hegelians was the equivalent, in the relatively backward social and political conditions of early nineteenth-century Germany, of the doctrines of de Tracy and his associates. The views of the Young Hegelians were ideological in the sense that they were entirely abstract and unconnected with the material conditions of social and political life.

In other writings Marx laid the foundations for a somewhat different and more innovative notion of ideology. He suggested that, in societies divided into classes, ideas may play an important role in articulating the conflicting aims and interests of different social classes. Ideas may also shape the ways in which individuals perceive the social world and their positions within it, thereby affecting the course of social and political change. In the works where Marx analyzed these phenomena in some detail—such as *The Eighteenth Brumaire of Louis Bonaparte* (1852)—he rarely used the term *ideology,* speaking instead of *ruling ideas, fixed ideas,* etc. But this aspect of Marx's work served as an inspiration for subsequent authors and helped to redefine the nature and scope of ideology.

In the course of the twentieth century there has been a proliferation of writings on ideology, and the term has been used in many different ways. One can draw a broad distinction between two different conceptions of ideology that are prevalent in the literature today. In the first place, some social and political analysts use the term *ideology* to refer to any system of thought or belief that animates social or political action: this is what may be described as the neutral conception of ideology. According to this conception, ideologies are discrete and relatively coherent systems of thought or belief, and the task confronting the analyst is to delineate these systems and describe their main features. (See, for example, Martin Seliger, *Ideology and Politics.*) This line of inquiry is exemplified by the tendency to think of ideologies in terms of "isms"—*conservatism, *liberalism, *socialism, *communism, *fascism, Nazism, etc. Most modern political regimes and parties, as well as social and political movements (e.g., the women's movement, the green movement), are characterized by ideologies in this sense. The capacity of such organizations or movements to mobilize support and secure some form of *legitimacy depends on a continuous process of producing and renewing their respective systems of thought or belief.

This use of the term can be distinguished from a second usage, which may be described as the critical conception of ideology. Unlike the neutral conception, the critical conception implies that the phenomena characterized as ideology are misleading, illusory, or one-sided; the very characterization of something as ideology carries with it an implicit criticism or condemnation. Hence the analysis of ideology is, on this account, inseparable from the critique of ideology. There is considerable disagreement within the literature about exactly how the critical conception of ideology should be understood. Some theorists regard ideologies as sets of ideas about the social world that are in some sense "false" or illusory, whereas other theorists prefer to think in terms of the interrelations between symbolism and *power. An example of the latter approach is the proposal to conceptualize ideology as the ways in which symbolic forms serve, in particular circumstances, to establish and sustain relations of domination. (See John B. Thompson, *Ideology and Modern Culture.*)

One advantage of the critical conception of ideology is that it enables the analyst to broaden the domain of analysis. Although the institutions of organized political power are an important site of ideology, it is also appropriate to consider the ways in which meaning is mobilized by other institutions and in other spheres of social life. The mass media are particularly important in this regard. Among the first authors to study the mass media as a source of ideology in modern societies were the early "critical theorists" linked to the Frankfurt Institute for Social Research. These theorists, including Max Horkheimer (1895–1971) and Theodor Adorno (1903–1969), were interested in the development of the entertainment industry—or "culture industry," as they called it—in the late nineteenth and early twentieth centuries. Writing in the 1930s and 1940s, they argued that this industry has given rise to a new form of ideology in modern societies. By producing large quantities of standardized and stereotyped cultural goods (popular films, magazines, books, etc.), the culture industry was providing individuals with imaginary avenues of escape from the harsh realities of social life and was weakening their capacity to think in a critical and autonomous way. Horkheimer and Adorno suggested that these developments, among others, had rendered individuals more vulnerable to the rhetoric of Nazism and fascism. (See Max Horkheimer and Theodor W. Adorno, "The Culture Industry.")

Other authors have also been concerned with emphasizing the importance of ideology in shaping or forming the individual or subject. Ideology is viewed by some social thinkers as a principal mechanism of socialization: through the diffusion of ideology, individuals acquire a sense of themselves as subjects and acquire the skills and attitudes necessary for the reproduction of the social order. An example of this approach is the work of the French Marxist Louis Althusser. Although Althusser's work has been influential, it has also been sharply criticized for failing to provide, among other things, a satisfactory conception of the human subject.

The concept of ideology is a highly contested notion, and there is no general consensus today concerning the most appropriate way to define the term. Nevertheless, many commentators would agree that the study of ideology is an indispensable part of social and political analysis. Political systems, social and political movements, and relations of power and domination are always interwoven in complex ways with ideas, beliefs, and symbolic forms of various kinds. Power is rarely exercised without some kind of symbolic attribute or support. It is this aspect of power, and of social and political life more generally, that has come to define the distinctive province of the study of ideology.

(See also CLASS AND POLITICS; INFORMATION SOCIETY; PSYCHOLOGY AND POLITICS; PUBLIC OPINION.)

Louis Althusser, "Ideology and Ideological State Apparatuses," in *Lenin and Philosophy and Other Essays*, trans. B. Brewster (London, 1971), pp. 121–173. Max Horkheimer and Theodor W. Adorno, "The Culture Industry," in *Dialectic of Enlightenment*, trans. J. Cumming (New York, 1972), pp. 120–167. Martin Seliger, *Ideology and Politics* (London, 1976). Jorge Larrain, *The Concept of Ideology* (London, 1979). John B. Thompson, *Ideology and Modern Culture* (Cambridge, U.K., 1990).

JOHN B. THOMPSON

IMF. See INTERNATIONAL MONETARY FUND.

IMMIGRATION. See INTERNATIONAL MIGRATION.

IMPERIALISM. The term *imperialism* was originally used as an invective against the expansionist policy of Napoleon I, and a little later against the expansionist policy of Britain. The rhetorical use of this term continues today, appearing frequently in the discourse of *Third World nationalist and Marxist-Leninist leaders. But, like many other political terms, it is a scientifically valid concept, useful in explaining various phenomena in contemporary society.

The pioneer in formulating the scientific concept of imperialism was an English economist, J. A. Hobson (1858–1940), who published *Imperialism: A Study* in 1902, a seminal work for future research on this phenomenon. Hobson's study focused on late-nineteenth-century imperialism, which could be distinguished from previous forms of imperialism in two ways: the existence of several empires in competition with one another, and the predominance of finance capital over mercantile capital.

In his examination of imperialist expansion, Hobson attached particular significance to the competition between empires. He also tried to show that imperialist policies favored financial speculation over production and market expansion. On these and other points, Hobson opposed the followers of Joseph Chamberlain (1830–1886), a famous entrepreneur from Birmingham, who advanced the doctrine of "commercial imperialism," and the supposed advantages it would bring about for English workers. Hobson rejected the notion that imperialism could bring advantages to either workers or capitalists in metropolitan countries. Marxist authors, however, reject Hobson's "reformist" proposal that imperialist expansion be replaced by internal market expansion, through an increase in workers' wages and services that would increase effective demand.

The impossibility of resolving, through *reform, the contradictions created by imperialist expansion, lies at the base of the theories of imperialism elaborated by Rudolf Hilferding (1877–1941), Rosa Luxemburg (1871–1919), and V. I. *Lenin (1870–1924). In 1910 Hilferding published *Finance Capital: A Study of the Latest Phase in Capitalist Development,* in which he agreed with Hobson that imperialist competition led inevitably to violence. Hilferding highlighted the use of violence in the creation of a wage labor force in the colonies. At the same time, he rejected as impossible the reformist proposal to expand internal markets through wage increases, pointing out that such an alternative would necessarily reduce profits. Noting the dominant role of finance capital and the concentration of capital under monopoly ownership of an oligarchy, Hilferding concluded that this extreme polarization of wealth under imperialism presaged the "last stage" of the fight between the bourgeoisie and the proletariat. Once most of the means of production were concentrated in a few hands, the expropriation of the "capitalist oligarchy" would give rise to *socialism—without the need to expropriate the minor and middling entrepreneurs. Hilferding thus linked the fight against imperialism to the fight for socialism, and the fight for political power to the fight for economic power. The relationship between imperialism and national oppression was acknowledged, but subordinated to a *class analysis and the class struggle.

Rosa Luxemburg also viewed imperialism as "the last stage in the historical race of *capitalism." Proceeding from a Marxist class analysis, she described the crucial role played by the unequal exchange between imperialist (capitalist) and colonized (precapitalist) countries in the accumulation of capital. In *The Accumulation of Capital,* she also emphasized the historical role played by *militarism in capital accumulation, and pioneered the study of the relationship among political domination, military occupation, and external debt. Moreover, in addition to describing how militarism is used to ensure the conditions of accumulation (through the subjection of colonies, as a weapon in the competitive struggle between capitalist countries, etc.), Luxemburg argued that militarism "is a pre-eminent means for the realisation of surplus value; it is in itself a province of accumulation," which would later form the basis of the "*military-industrial complex" of the great empires.

In *Imperialism, the Highest Stage of Capitalism,* Lenin began his discussion of imperialism by asking what he called "the main question": "whether it is possible to reform the basis of imperialism, whether to go forward to the accentuation and deepening of the antagonisms which it engenders, or backwards towards allaying these antagonisms." He rejected the possibility of reforming capitalism of its imperialist tendencies, insisting that imperialism was the inevitable "highest stage" of capitalism, which could only be defeated by *revolution. "Imperialism," wrote Lenin, "is capitalism in that stage of development in which the dominance of monopolies and finance capital has established itself; in which the export of capital has acquired pronounced importance; in which the division of all territories of the globe has been completed."

Lenin criticized Kautsky for his theory of "ultra-imperialism," pointing out that it was merely a restatement of Hobson's theory of "inter-imperialism." He accused Kautsky of obscuring the true nature of imperialism by implying that "a union of world imperialism, and not struggle amongst imperialisms," was possible, and that "a phase when war shall cease under capitalism" would come. Lenin also took Kautsky to task for his belief that "the rule of finance capital lessens the unevenness and contradictions in world economy," insisting that, "in reality, it *increases* them" (italics in original). Further on he added: "Monopolies, oligarchy, the striving for domination instead of the striving for liberty, the exploitation of an increasing number of small or weak nations by an extremely small group of the richest or most powerful nations—all these have given birth to those distinctive characteristics of imperialism which compel us to define it as a parasitic or decaying capitalism."

This last statement turned out to be historically incorrect; as for the others, they were not particularly original. According to Georg Lukács, "Lenin's contribution to the understanding of imperialism was more tactical than theoretical: in other words, Lenin connected the struggle against capitalism to the struggle against imperialism, the struggle for national self-determination to the struggle of the proletariat for state power. His theory of anti-capitalist politics and anti-imperialist politics left a mark on a whole epoch" (*Lenin: A Study on the Unity of His Thought,* Boston, 1971). Lenin influenced the strategy of Marxist-Leninist states, which declared themselves anti-imperialist from a class standpoint. He also had a direct or indirect influence on those nationalists who lacked a class analysis. He proposed joining revolutionary civil war to anticolonial war, and the war of the proletariat (constituted as a hegemonic class) to war for national liberation. Fighting against imperialism was equivalent to fighting against monopoly capital, even to fighting for socialism. This was the legacy passed on from *Stalin to Palmiro Togliatti, from *Mao Zedong to *Ho Chi Minh to Fidel *Castro.

The crisis of a whole epoch, and of *Marxism-*Leninism as a theory and practice useful for understanding imperialism and waging the struggle against it, became evident from 1985 onward in Lenin's own country, where it began to be supplanted by *perestroika. In his speech of 2 November 1987, Mikhail *Gorbachev raised what he called "some tough questions." "Given the current stage of world development," Gorbachev asked, "is it possible to influence the nature of imperialism and block its most dangerous manifestations? . . . Can capitalism get rid of militarism and function and develop in the economic sphere without it? . . . Can the capitalist system do without neo-colonialism, which is currently one of the essential factors to its survival?" (*October and Perestroika: The Revolution Continues*, Moscow, 1987, p. 62). Gorbachev's questions would have been inconceivable in the era of Marxist-Leninist orthodoxy, when everybody relied on the answer Lenin himself had given to what he called "the main question." Most damaging of all to the Leninist legacy, the official revelation of contradictions encountered by the Soviet Union included a profound self-criticism concerning the policy of enforcing the hegemony of "state socialism" over neighboring countries as well as within its own borders. Those policies had been labeled as imperialist by Western ideologues. The *Truman administration used these policies to justify the so-called *containment of Soviet "expansionism" or "imperialism," but in Marxist-Leninist circles, the labeling of the Soviet Union as "imperialist" was officially understood as a "class response" of the bourgeoisie bent on spreading lies in order to fan the flames of the *Cold War.

However, the leadership of the People's Republic of *China waged a campaign against the Soviet Union, accusing it of being "social-imperialist." This term had been used by Lenin to attack the leaders of the German Social Democratic Party, "justly called," according to Lenin, "social-imperialist, that is, socialist in words and imperialists in deeds" (Lenin, *Imperialism*, ch. 9). Chinese propagandists defined the characteristics of Soviet "social imperialism" based on the presumed policy of the Soviet Union to compete with the United States for world *hegemony. They also pointed to the Soviet domination and exploitation of Eastern and *Central Europe and *Third World countries, as well as to

their behavior toward the nationalities and ethnic groups of Central Asia within the borders of the Soviet Union. Chinese criticism denounced a series of Soviet policies as presumably identical to those of any modern imperialist state, particularly those of the United States. Chinese rhetoric, loaded with metaphors, examples, and distinctive epithets (such as "revisionist renegade coterie," used to designate the Soviet leadership) obscured what was objectively true about this denunciation.

The resemblance between imperialist and "social-imperialist" policies was remarkable. The insulting character of the criticism, however, prevented some from delving more deeply into the controversy. Nevertheless, the Chinese theory of social imperialism and the struggle against it was limited by its lack of a class analysis, although it claimed to be Marxist-Leninist. Failing to take into account the fundamental class differences between the Soviet Union and the United States, the Chinese equated the "imperialism" of the Soviet Union with the imperialism of the United States. The Chinese analysis thus broke the "Leninist" link between imperialist exploitation and capitalist exploitation. "Imperialism" thus became a class-neutral term and lost explanatory precision.

The denunciation of the main policies of "social imperialism" amounted to a sort of enumerative definition. Among the characteristics were the following: "socialist economic integration," used by the Soviet Union as an instrument of "social imperialism"; an "international division of labor" that furthered "social-imperialist" domination; "economic organizations" or *multinational corporations that dominated by virtue of their control over finance, services, products, and cheap manual labor; irrational exploitation of the natural resources of the dominated countries; "uneven trade" with them; military agreements such as the *Warsaw Treaty Organization (Warsaw Pact) with Soviet lines of command; military integration depending on other armies; control of weapons production by the hegemonic country; enforcement of extraterritorial rights by the Soviet Union; hiring advisers and experts to handle arms and logistics; use of military maneuvers to apply pressure (for instance, in the Balkan countries); punishment of unsubmissive governments by deferral of payments and other aid and through actions to destabilize them; surprise invasions such as that of Czechoslovakia in 1968; long-standing governments of occupation; the ability to launch not only defensive but offensive strikes around the world, but particularly in Central Europe. The Chinese, in their denunciations, adopted the classic language of imperialism, speaking of Soviet "neocolonialist policy" and of the Eastern European countries' "dependency"; of "exploitation" and domination as part of a plot to replace a "defeated imperialism" with a rising one.

The link between imperialism and monopoly capitalism was no longer the essence of the problem for those calling themselves Marxist-Leninists. The "crisis" in the theory of imperialism mirrored the defeat of the Leninist project in general, mired as it was in the bureaucratization of "state socialism."

The end of the Western *colonial empires gave rise to ideological interpretations of the "end of imperialism" similar to those written recently about the "end of history." Bill Warren's *Imperialism: Pioneer of Capitalism* (London, 1980) stands out in this regard. His lack of rigor in the use of statistics and Marxist texts does not deprive Warren's work of a certain importance: he sets up a dialectic by which the defeat of Marxist-Leninist and nationalist struggles supposedly corresponds to that stage in the development of capitalism where, as a result of imperialism, it has become a "supranational" system, thus rendering national working-class struggles unnecessary. Warren contends that global capitalism would not have existed without imperialism, and that socialism is impossible without the previous, global extension of capitalism. But he also insists that the historical phenomenon of imperialism ended once the underdeveloped countries were incorporated into the capitalist system. This notion of a return to classic, premonopoly capitalism, however, is as inaccurate as his central thesis that dependent nation-states have ceased being a necessary feature of the capitalist system. Warren's theses tend to deny the importance of the problem of imperialism. In that sense they correspond to a relatively older tradition which admitted the existence of imperialism or discussed its demise, without acknowledging the importance to capitalism of specifically imperialist exploitation.

Authors such as John Strachey (*The End of Empire,* 1959) advanced the opinion that following World War II imperialism was no longer necessary, given the increase in the standard of living in the metropole. Others such as Michael Barratt Brown (*After Imperialism,* 1963) have contended that the prosperity of countries like Britain no longer depended on colonial ventures, which ceased to have macroeconomic significance. For these authors, such historical and social demarcation of imperialism is important in defining the phenomenon. For instance, according to Brown, the "colonial tribute to the great powers" corresponds to an extremely low percentage, which he calculates as 3.3 percent of the GNP of Britain. His calculation, however, does not take into account the fact that imperialism or "colonial tribute" is a *social relation,* which retains enormous significance for both the monopoly enterprises and "tributary nations." Authors such as Hamza Alavi have even gone so far as to say that, beginning in the 1960s, the "new" imperialism no longer used the exportation of capital as a means for "exploiting cheap labour overseas," but confined itself to the expansion of production in metropolitan markets and to the control of world markets ("Im-

perialism Old and New," *Socialist Register,* 1964). On the contrary, as Paul Sweezy has demonstrated, beginning in the 1960s, the "multinational corporations moved their manufacturing facilities to lower-wage countries" ("Imperialism in the 1990s," *Monthly Review,* October 1989).

The fact that Lenin's prediction that imperialism would be "the eve of socialist revolution" has not been proved correct does not imply that the phenomenon of imperialism—the hegemony of monopoly capital and capitalist nation-states—has ended. Nor has the struggle of workers and peoples in the dominated countries against domination and exploitation ended. On the contrary, there is every indication that the phenomenon of imperialism not only persists in the midst of recent, world-historic changes, but has intensified the control that the great powers exercise over the so-called Third World and the so-called socialist countries.

Among the recent changes in imperialist exploitation, Harry Magdoff has emphasized 1) "The integration of military production with the dominant industrial sectors"; 2) "the rising importance of the multi-national corporations which drive towards worldwide control of the most profitable and newest industries in both the periphery and advanced countries"; and 3) "the priority of the interests of military-multinational industry in the affairs of the State" ("Imperialism: A Historical Survey," *Monthly Review,* May 1972). In other words, the structures and subsystems of exploitation are changing, but the phenomenon has not abated.

In the article quoted above, Paul Sweezy raised the possibility that some "additional empires," such as the Soviet Union and/or China, would share domination of the world market with the United States–Canada, Western European, and Japanese blocs. He went so far as to say that this new collegiate imperialism or imperialist club does not seem to contain "the seed of a violent confrontation." His theses are similar to those of superimperialism, but they may have a greater validity today, as the focus of antagonism shifts from East-West to North-South. The policies of the economic superpowers may result in a more or less lasting distribution of the world's markets and resources among them. This distribution arrangement might be founded on 1) a relative disarmament; 2) financial, monetary, and commercial agreements on a world scale; and 3) measures leading to a more or less unequal redistribution of GNP in the world, and between the North and the South. But this resolution of imperialism's contradictions may be circumvented by other features of late-twentieth-century imperialism which are not easily overcome.

The transfer of "surplus" from the "periphery" to the "center" increased considerably during the 1970s and 1980s, even as neoliberal policies have stressed the effects of disaccumulation and underconsumption of the dependent world as a result of unequal terms of trade, expansion of transnational corporations, and external debt. The apparent victory of capitalism over the Eastern bloc and over the nationalist governments of the South has taken place at the same time as the exploitation of the periphery by world capitalism has intensified. Many studies carried out by international organizations (especially the UN, Food and Agricultural Organization, *International Labor Organization, *World Health Organization, *World Bank, and *International Monetary Fund) present data on capital transfers and declines in standards of living in the countries of the periphery which indicate that the imperialist exploitation and domination of these countries is more thorough than ever.

Many researchers have studied this worldwide phenomenon, focusing on the economic, social, political, and cultural relations of the "center" to the "periphery," of the "metropole" to the "dependent" countries, considering the world as a "system." Among these researchers—of differing ideological and intellectual tendencies, Marxist and structuralist—some stand out for their theoretical and analytical contributions: Paul Baran, Fernando Henrique Cardoso, André Gunder-Frank, Samir Amin, Arrighi Emmanuel, and Immanuel Wallerstein. In their analyses, the imperialist countries appear as a subset, closely articulated to the periphery through transnational corporations and associated dependent bourgeoisies. The *development problems of the periphery assume more importance in their definition of imperialism. Some of the authors, such as Anouar Abdel Malek, approach the phenomenon of imperialism as a dialectic between domination and liberation, as a struggle between dominant states and national movements, where politics, technology, and war occupy the foreground.

(See also NORTH-SOUTH RELATIONS; SOVIET–EAST EUROPEAN RELATIONS.)

PABLO GONZÁLES CASANOVA

IMPORT-SUBSTITUTION INDUSTRIALIZATION.
The term *import substitution* (IS) has two related, yet distinct, meanings. First, it refers to the economic process through which local production displaces, or substitutes for, previously imported goods. This process may be triggered by changes in domestic demand or transport costs that make local production profitable or by the interruption of imports as a result of war, embargo, or depression.

The term *import substitution* is also used to refer to policy interventions, particularly trade restrictions, that have the effect of stimulating local industrialization at the expense of imports. These policies may also arise initially as a result of external economic shocks. For example, governments often respond to *balance-of-payments crises by restricting trade to conserve foreign exchange. Although these restrictions may not have the intention of

increasing the profitability of domestic manufactures, they can have that effect.

IS has also been a more self-conscious component of nationalist economic thinking. IS policies have been adopted by developing countries throughout modern history. To develop an indigenous industrial base required protection against the superior competitive position of more advanced countries. Protection of local manufacturing activities was central to British mercantilism in the seventeenth and eighteenth centuries and was advocated by Alexander Hamilton in the United States in his famous *Report on Manufactures*. Soviet economic thinking consistently championed autarky and self-reliance in international economic relations. This idea exerted a powerful influence in other socialist countries, for example in Eastern Europe, which quickly sought to replicate the entire range of basic industries. Soviet thinking had influence in interwar Turkey and postindependence India as well.

In the postwar period, the justification for import substitution was most highly developed in Latin America, where the Great Depression of the 1930s and two world wars stimulated industrial development in the larger countries, especially Argentina, Brazil, and Mexico. Later, the smaller countries of South and Central America and those of Africa also pursued IS policies as the process of development became inextricably associated with industrialization.

Political leaders and local entrepreneurs feared that local industries would be undermined or impeded by foreign competition. This fear was coupled with substantial pessimism about export prospects. It was believed that a secular decline in the terms of trade would result in "immiserizing growth" for the developing world if it continued to specialize in traditional raw material exports. These ideas were most forcefully argued by Raúl *Prebisch and the UN *Economic Commission for Latin America.

The pursuit of IS usually progressed through several phases, although they necessarily overlapped to some extent. In the first phase, protection was extended to producers of light manufactures, such as textiles, apparel, and food processing. These ventures could be carried out by local entrepreneurs because they involved relatively standardized technologies, were not particularly capital-intensive, and could draw on pools of relatively unskilled labor.

At some point, however, the domestic market for these goods became saturated. At this juncture, policymakers faced difficult choices about which new sectors should be emphasized. Consumer durables and intermediate and capital goods production were typically more demanding of capital, technology, and skilled labor, factors in which most developing countries were deficient.

The decision to pursue "secondary" IS in these sectors had important implications for the ownership patterns of IS industries. In the first phase of

IS, domestic entrepreneurs gained and thus were likely to support IS policies. In the secondary phase of IS, however, state-owned and foreign firms usually played a larger role. Intermediate goods production, particularly in steel and oil refining, was typically carried out by state-owned enterprises. A number of larger Latin American countries became important sources for IS foreign investment in sectors such as chemicals, automobiles, and linked industries such as glass and rubber that were beyond the technological reach of local firms.

As early as the mid-1960s, criticisms of IS industrialization began to appear, particularly among neoclassical economists. First, the protection of domestic industry increased the profitability of the manufacturing sector at the expense of agriculture. This had a number of undesirable implications, favoring the city over the countryside, accelerating rural-to-urban migration, and contributing to an unequal distribution of income. By distorting the allocation of resources, IS introduced tremendous inefficiencies, favoring high-cost sectors in which the country had no comparative advantage.

A second line of criticism concerned the penetration of foreign firms and the role of foreign capital more generally. Although IS was designed to increase self-reliance, in many cases it resulted in greater dependence on foreign firms. These firms occupied powerful positions in highly oligopolistic industries and engaged in a number of practices that were seen as detrimental, including the introduction of inappropriate technologies, production processes, and products. In the 1970s, the forward momentum of industrial deepening was sustained in many countries through extensive foreign borrowing. In the 1980s, governments found themselves saddled with the external debt not only of state-owned enterprises but of inefficient private firms in IS sectors.

A third line of criticism concerned export performance. High levels of protection and overvalued exchange rates designed to reduce the costs of importing capital goods and machinery had the effect of discouraging exports. Countries pursuing IS faced recurrent balance-of-payments problems, often solved in the short run by reliance on more protection.

Finally, there were a number of political criticisms of IS. From the *Left, it was argued that the pattern of secondary IS tended to support an elite consumption profile, particularly by emphasizing the production of costly consumer durables such as automobiles. Instead of emphasizing the deepening of the industrial base through secondary IS, according to this view, it would be preferable to widen the domestic market by improving the distribution of income and focusing production on widely consumed basic goods. From the *Right, it was argued that the institution of protection and various subsidies to industry resulted not only in inefficiencies but in a corruption of political life: entrepreneurs concentrated on securing privileges, or "rent-seeking," rather than on productive activities, and the initiation of trade restrictions necessarily gave rise to black markets in goods and foreign exchange.

These criticisms were often indiscriminate, attributing all problems of development to misguided industrial policies. Some IS industries were relatively efficient or had the potential to become so. This was evident in the fact that many, if not most, industries in the advanced industrial states began initially as IS industries, with trade liberalization and the development of exports coming later. This was even true of the export-oriented East Asian economies: Japan, the Republic of Korea, and Taiwan. All three developed their manufacturing base through a subtle combination of protectionist policies, subsidies, and aggressive promotion of exports. Although they managed to avoid the excesses of IS in other developing countries, they were by no means wholly liberal in their trade policies.

Nonetheless, IS as a general strategy came under increasing pressure in the 1980s. Many countries came to recognize the cumulative inefficiencies and costs associated with IS. The withdrawal of international lending associated with the *debt crisis made capital-intensive investments less viable and increased the importance of developing export industries in order to earn foreign exchange. The rapidity of technological change in major industries such as electronics made "self-reliance" a more costly and complicated goal and made it imperative that developing countries maintain close links with world markets.

The pressures to abandon IS were also political. The international financial institutions, including the *World Bank and the *International Monetary Fund, pressed vigorously for trade liberalization. The United States also launched a more aggressive policy in the mid-1980s by placing greater emphasis on opening markets abroad through the threat of retaliation. Major targets of this campaign were the relatively developed newly industrializing countries that had maintained high levels of protection, including Brazil, India, and even export-oriented Korea.

This combination of domestic and international factors has led to several sharp reversals of import-substituting policies. Mexico, Chile, and Turkey provide three important examples, as do the countries of Eastern and Central Europe. Yet it is unlikely that IS will be abandoned altogether. The adjustment costs of moving toward a new strategy are potentially high for both workers and capitalists and thus are likely to meet domestic political resistance. A more likely outcome is the evolution of more mixed industrial strategies that combine elements of protection and support for domestic industry with greater emphasis on exports and the development of international competitiveness.

(See also DEVELOPMENT AND UNDERDEVELOPMENT; EXPORT-LED GROWTH; NEWLY INDUSTRIALIZING ECONOMIES.)

Raúl Prebisch, *The Economic Development of Latin America and its Principal Problems* (New York, 1950). Raymond Vernon, "International Investment and International Trade in the Product Cycle" *Quarterly Journal of Economics* 80 (May 1966): 190–207. Albert Hirschman, "The Political Economy of Import-Substituting Industrialization in Latin America," in Albert Hirschman, *A Bias for Hope* (New Haven, Conn., 1971), pp. 85–123. Gerald Meier and Dudley Seers, eds., *Pioneers in Development* (New York, 1984).
                                          STEPHAN HAGGARD

INDIA. The Republic of India, the world's largest *democracy, emerged from under British colonial rule as a sovereign nation-state in 1947. Its present Constitution, adopted on 26 January 1950, provides for a Westminster-style parliamentary form of government in a federal union that currently consists of twenty-five states and seven centrally administered union territories. The Constitution was a culmination of a process of evolution toward representative government that began under the British and that successively broadened the participation of Indians in elected legislatures.

The Constitution formally vests almost all executive powers of the government in the president, who is the head of state. The president, however, exercises power, with only rare exceptions, upon the advice of the prime minister and the Council of Ministers. Real power thus rests in the prime minister.

The president is elected for a five-year term by an electoral college consisting of elected members of both the bicameral Parliament and the state legislatures. The upper house of Parliament, the Rajya Sabha (House of the State), consists of members who are elected for six-year terms by an electoral college made up of members of the state legislative assemblies. The lower house, the Lok Sabha (House of the People), is the supreme legislative body in India and consists of 542 members who are directly elected for a five-year term according to a single-member-district system, in which the individual with the highest tally of votes wins the seat. The prime minister is elected by the parliamentary members of the majority party in the Lok Sabha. The conventions of cabinet government are used, and the prime minister and cabinet are collectively responsible to Parliament and must retain the confidence of the majority of the members of the Lok Sabha.

An analogous structure of government exists in each of the states. Each state has a governor, who is appointed by the president for a five-year term, and a popularly elected legislature, which may be bicameral or unicameral and is elected for five years. The leader of the majority party in the legislature is elected chief minister, who, with his or her cabinet colleagues, is responsible to the legislature and must command the confidence of a majority of members. Although the Constitution is federal, it provides for strong unitary features, including the ultimate power of the center to control and take over direct administration of the states under those conditions that it deems fit.

The Constitution also provides for an independent judiciary. The powers of the Indian Supreme Court are comparable to those of the *Supreme Court of the United States and include broad original and appellate jurisdiction and the right to judge the constitutional validity of the laws passed by Parliament. The courts have been important institutions in the political system. The relative balance of *parliamentary sovereignty and *judicial review is imprecisely defined and is constantly being negotiated and contested. The overall balance currently rests in favor of parliamentary sovereignty.

The Indian armed forces, numbering some 4 million, remain largely apolitical, professional, and firmly under civilian control. A disquieting trend, however, is the increased deployment of the army to deal with internal law and order problems and the increasing reliance on it as an instrument of governance in more and more parts of India.

Economy. India's economic record has been mixed. Since independence, it has pursued a *development strategy aimed at self-reliance through *import substitution and capital-intensive industrialization. India has a mixed economy with the state sector dominating the industrial sector, both by direct ownership and by a system of controls regulating private enterprise. The national economy grew between 1950 and 1980 at a modest rate of three to four percent a year. During the 1980s, the growth rate of the economy improved and was approximately five percent. India's manufacturing sector, now the tenth-largest in the world, enables the country to be mostly self-sufficient in the production of many consumer and capital goods; the quality of these domestic products, however, is often low.

Although India's development strategy has been mostly consistent, some attempts were made to liberalize the economy in the 1980s. These were aimed at relaxing some domestic political controls on private activities and trade liberalization but have yet to involve large-scale privatization or openness to foreign investment. In June 1990, as liberalization gathered momentum, a vast array of investment licensing and trade controls were abolished, and even partial privatization is being discussed.

In the agricultural sector, the *green revolution of the late 1960s ushered in some gains in productivity and made the country self-sufficient in food grains. Poverty, however, remains a chronic problem for approximately forty percent of the nation's 800 million people. Life expectancy is 54 years and the annual per capita income is approximately US$300, ranking India among the very poor countries of the world. The paradox of India, however, is that it at the same time possesses a sophisticated scientific, technical, and financial infrastructure.

The most serious problem facing the economy at the beginning of the 1990s is the external debt, which as of 1990 amounted to some US$70 billion. Negotiations with international organizations are underway, and a structural adjustment program is already underway.

Politics and Society. India's political institutions have ensured an open and free democratic process seldom seen in developing countries. There have been ten general elections so far, with India's premier political party, the Congress, retaining power in all but the 1977 and 1989 elections. There was a brief suspension of the democratic process between 1975 and 1977 when Indira *Gandhi declared a state of emergency. The democratic process was resumed in 1977 and, for the most part, has operated relatively smoothly ever since, despite the *assassinations of Indira Gandhi (1984) and her son, Rajiv Gandhi, who also served as prime minister from 1984 to 1989.

The institutions that have sustained political freedoms have been coming under increasing strain. These developments may best be understood in the context of the changes that have taken place in both the party system and in the level of politicalization of the diverse social groups that constitute Indian society.

The Indian National Congress, or now just the Congress, was created in 1885 as an organization of anglicized, Western-educated Indian *elites. During the 1920s, under the leadership of Mohandas *Gandhi, it was transformed from an elite political organization into a mass nationalist movement that deepened its social base by incorporating the peasantry, labor, and other urban groups. This forced upon the Congress the delicate tasks of balancing and reconciling contradictory interests. The Congress in the process developed an accommodating ideology and a diffuse organization that, unlike communist movements, deliberately eschewed *class conflict and emphasized class conciliation.

As the Congress transformed itself from a nationalist, anticolonial movement into a ruling party, it continued to work through, rather than against, powerful social interests. The Congress thus mobilized new political support largely by adapting itself to local *power structures. Below the national level, the Congress came to be run by members of the dominant landowning classes and castes, who in turn mobilized their caste peers and economic dependents. The wider organization of the party was a complex pyramid of such vertical multiclass and caste alliances, knit together by promises of governmental patronage. While the middle-class leadership was in control at the national level, the authority of these local leaders and groups was also considerable. The Congress consequently had a large number of operatives who could arrange compromises between competing groups.

From 1967 onward, when Indira Gandhi took power, Congress's capacity to negotiate social conflict has systematically eroded. This reflects two underlying changes. First, many new groups have been mobilized politically. The capacities of those intermediaries and local notables upon whom the Congress had relied to negotiate conflict have thus eroded. And second, the creation of a personalized and centralized *regime by Indira Gandhi systematically weakened the institutions of both the state and the Congress Party, and rendered them less capable of coping with the tensions and cleavages of a heterogeneous society.

As far as social power is concerned, no single class or classes are collectively in a position to set or control India's political agenda. Many of them, however, are in a position to thwart government policy or twist the system to their own needs. Private capital, for example, has flourished against the backdrop of a large public sector but has never been able to set the public agenda. Middle-class urban professionals, intellectuals, and a sprawling bureaucracy rely heavily on public resources for their sustenance and have grown steadily in size. Richer segments of the self-sufficient peasantry have also placed great demands on the state's budget and are an important factor in political mobilization.

Since independence, both central and state governments have pursued policies of protective discrimination for India's lowest strata, namely, the scheduled castes and tribes. The adoption of preferential treatment in the form of affirmative action was sanctioned specifically by India's constitution. Initially, these policies did not apply to the middle castes. However, the state's recognition of caste as a legitimate basis for bestowing political benefits has provided opportunity for other "backward" (or middle) castes to organize and demand protective treatment. A decision in 1990 by India's national government to expand preferential treatment to include other backward castes became a volatile issue in Indian politics. The resulting conflict between forward (or upper) and backward castes is, in turn, likely to strain further the durability of India's institutions.

India's linguistic, regional, ethnic, and religious diversities are prodigious and have generated important obstacles to nation building. India has some forty-six officially listed mother tongues, seventeen of which have achieved the status of recognized languages. Of these, Hindi is spoken by the largest number of people, though they fail to add up to a majority. Over time, the political system has evolved complex compromises in the face of such diversity and related intermittent protest over language issues, most notably in the states of Tamil Nadu in 1963 and Punjab in the late 1960s. The compromises now provide for the joint use of Hindi and English in parliamentary proceedings, the use of Hindi as a language of communication between the center and the Hindi-speaking states, and the use of English between the center and the non-Hindi-speaking states. Adequate provisions also exist for the teaching of mother tongues in various states. The States Reorganization Act of 1956, and subsequent amendments in 1960 and 1966, also brought the boundaries of the southern states into conformity with traditional linguistic regions. The principal political grievances that arise out of the use of language thus seem to have been resolved.

By contrast, the reorganization of states in 1956 failed to accommodate other regional aspirations, the principal ones being movements for greater self-determination in such states as the Punjab, Kashmir, and Assam. These movements, in addition to being attempts at preserving subnational identities, also represent responses to a growing tendency toward centralization in India. Over the years, the central government has made frequent use of its powers to dismiss state governments and to impose direct rule from the center. Moreover, in order to maintain power at the center, political parties have felt obliged to nationalize issues, and to interfere directly in the selection of chief ministers and other political officers at the state level. Consequently, along with increasing centralization of power have come an increase in regional grievances, *secessionist movements, and the emergence of new regional parties.

Also of contemporary political significance are the demands of tribal groups, concentrated especially in India's northeast, whose grievances result from diminishing traditional rights to land and competition from migrants. Many of these movements in the northeast have been resolved through a mixture of coercion and economic aid, and through the political reorganization of what was formerly the North Eastern Frontier Agency into tribal states. A major exception here, however, is Assam, where a three-cornered rivalry between migrant Muslims from *Bangladesh, Assamese, and local tribal groups has resulted in periodic violent conflict.

The most persistent cleavage in India remains the Hindu-Muslim religious divide. Whereas nearly eighty percent of Indians are Hindu, Muslims constitute 11.4 percent of the country's population. Numerous issues divide the two communities. Periodically, some of these take on political significance. During the 1980s, for example, one issue that attracted considerable attention was that of the future status of Muslim personal law (*sharī'a), which, under a postindependence compromise, Muslims were allowed to retain. Another politically potent and violent dispute was over demands by some Hindus to restore a mosque as a site for Hindu worship. This issue, in turn, became a factor in the mobilizing success of militant Hindu groups, such as the Bharatiya Janata Party, the Rashtriya Swayam Sewak Sangh, and the Vishwa Hindu Parishad. The first of these, though not merely a religious-based party, has also managed to carve out a strong right-wing presence in Indian politics.

The prospects for Indian politics thus seem to point toward the growing politicalization of numerous social cleavages. As group demands grow and such institutions as political parties remain weak, it is likely that the body politic will be characterized by political violence and governmental instability. This is not to suggest that India's democracy is about to crumble. India has a number of political strengths: nearly four decades of experience with democracy, a fairly healthy economy, and a sophisticated civil service. Nevertheless, weak institutions and growing demands spell trouble for most polities; India is not likely to be an exception.

Foreign Policy. India's foreign policy has been governed by a persistent belief in nonalignment with the two blocs, although it has always been somewhat closer to the Soviet Union; with the collapse of superpower rivalry, its foreign policy is in increasing disarray. Relations with the United States have varied from strained to warm but have never been overly warm. Since partition, relations between India and *Pakistan have been especially strained and embittered, principally over the long-standing territorial dispute over Jammu and Kashmir. Armed conflict over that region in 1947–1948 resulted in the division of Kashmir into Pakistani-held and Indian-held sectors. There was renewed armed conflict in 1965 and again in 1971 when, following a political crisis in East Pakistan, Indian intervention led to the creation of Bangladesh. Despite periodic efforts to improve relations, tensions persist. India also has an outstanding territorial dispute with China involving 37,500 square kilometers (14,500 sq. mi.) of territory in the Aksai Chin area of Kashmir and 93,250 square kilometers (36,000 sq. mi.) of territory in Arunachal Pradesh. The dispute escalated into a military conflict in 1962, and relations have been strained ever since. During the 1980s, India emerged as a major actor in South Asia. It intervened in the ethnic conflict in *Sri Lanka and is trying to bring about multilateral cooperation in South Asia under the auspices of the *South Asian Association for Regional Cooperation.

(See also HINDUISM; ISLAM; NEHRU, JAWAHARLAL; NONALIGNED MOVEMENT.)

Pranab Bardhan, *The Political Economy of Development in India* (Oxford, 1984). L. Rudolph and S. Rudolph, *In Pursuit of Lakshmi: The Political Economy of the Indian State* (Chicago, 1987). Francine Frankel and M. S. A. Rao, eds., *Dominance and State Power in Modern India: Decline of a Social Order,* 2 vols. (Delhi, 1989, 1990). Paul R. Brass, *The Politics of India Since Independence,* The New Cambridge History of India, IV.1 (Cambridge, 1990). Atul Kohli, *India's Democracy: An Analysis of Changing State-Society Relations* (Princeton, N.J., 1990). Atul Kohli, *Democracy and Discontent: India's Growing Crisis of Governability* (New York, 1991).

PRATAP MEHTA
ATUL KOHLI

INDIAN OCEAN REGION. The islands of the western Indian Ocean—Comoros, Maldives, Mauritius, Réunion, and Seychelles—have much in common, yet each is different in many ways. They share many economic, social, historical, political, geographical, and geophysical characteristics. Until quite recently they were all isolated, in the backwater of the international political arena, and were colonies or dependencies of either France or Britain. They showed little desire for economic or political independence, and showed little promise as viable nation-states. Except for Réunion, which is an Overseas Department of France, they achieved their independence in the 1960s and 1970s: Comoros in 1975, Maldives in 1965, Mauritius in 1968, and Seychelles in 1976.

The histories of the islands vary. For example, Maldives had great social and economic influences from South Asia. The other islands were uninhabited until the colonization by Western powers during the eighteenth and nineteenth centuries. With British and French rule came indentured workers from India and Africa to supply labor for the plantation-agricultural systems which were established to serve the growing markets of industrializing Europe. The main emphasis was placed on cash crop production of sugarcane, coconuts, palm oil, and tea. These colonial ties—linguistic, religious (Catholicism having taken hold in French areas), and especially economic—formed the cultural and social heritage for these islands at independence. Ethnic cleavages and resulting frictions from ruled-ruler relationships (of imported African and Indian labor and imported European supervisors) have left their mark on many of the states. Cash crops have resulted in each state's being an "international price taker" with very little control over its economic destiny. Instead of building mechanisms and infrastructure for self-sufficiency, these islands were forced to continue to rely on food imports as well as high levels of other imported consumer goods.

Each of the island states is small by international comparisons, and none is larger than 2,500 square kilometers (965 sq. mi.). For example, the Maldives group is less than 300 square kilometers (115 sq. mi.) in total area. Agriculture has little room for expansion and development, and in some islands lack of fresh water is an economic as well as a social problem. Their natural resource bases are very small. There are some mineral resources (including offshore oil), but thus far no state in the region has benefited significantly from fuel or nonfuel minerals.

In terms of population these states are also quite small. Seychelles, with a population of only 65,000, is one of the world's smallest ministates. Maldives has a population of nearly 200,000, Comoros has nearly 400,000, Réunion has over half a million, and Mauritius, the largest, has about 1 million. Populations are rising rapidly, and unemployment is a problem in all the states. Nevertheless, the average population growth rate (1973–1982) is only 2.1 percent, below the less developed country average. Population pressures (i.e., land densities) have increased for virtually every state during the past generation. The states with the highest population densities are Maldives and Mauritius. Mauritius, fortunately, has a more diverse economic base to support increasing and more densely populated areas, while Maldives' resource base is low. For Maldives, population density has been and will remain a serious development problem. The other states, particularly Comoros and Seychelles, have found their density problems worsening, especially since the amount of good land in these two states is quite small, both in relative and absolute terms. Comoros and Maldives are very poor by international standards, and are classified as less developed countries (LDCs) by the UN. Réunion, Seychelles, and Mauritius are moving into "middle-income" status.

Organizations and Political Change. The political structures of these island states vary considerably. At one end of the political spectrum is Mauritius, a multiparty *democracy, a member of the *Commonwealth with the British monarch as head of state. The government is headed by a prime minister. The Legislative Assembly is composed of sixty-two elected members and eight members appointed by the governor-general, the queen's representative in Mauritius. Politics in Mauritius has generally been open. Unlike most of sub-Saharan Africa, the government of Mauritius changes hands via fair and free elections.

Comoros, Maldives, and Seychelles have somewhat less democratic forms of government, certainly relative to Mauritius. Seychelles, also a member of the Commonwealth, is a one-party state, headed by a president who is head of state, government, and commander of the armed forces. The National Assembly, all of whose members must be of the ruling party, is composed of twenty-three elected members and two presidential appointments. After a *coup in 1977 the president was empowered to rule by decree. During the 1970s and 1980s there were several coup attempts, and that explains—at least in part—why there is little political openness in Seychelles.

Comoros is also a one-party state. The president is both head of state and head of government, and is directly elected for six-year terms. The country's recent political history has been turbulent, with several coups and coup attempts. Rule in Comoros has been relatively authoritarian. The island's political structure is complicated by Mayotte (physically a part of the Comoran archipelago), which decided to remain a part of France when the rest of the islands declared independence in 1975. Mayotte is administered by France as an Overseas Collective Territory.

Maldives, a member of the Commonwealth, has no political parties, and the government is led by a president who is head of state and commander of the armed forces. The president is elected by popular vote, and appoints eight of the forty-eight-member elected cabinet. There are elections every five years, but there have been few changes in the government leadership since the mid-1970s.

Réunion is an Overseas Department of France, and as such is administered as an integral part of the Republic. Five representatives are sent to the National Assembly and three to the Senate, both in Paris. The island is run by a general council, composed of forty-four elected members. While there is some movement favoring independence from France, the vast majority of people want to retain the status quo. Elections have been contested by about a dozen political parties.

Output and the Economy. All of the islands share most of the economic problems associated with small island states in general. These problems include relatively and absolutely small populations, absence of economies of scale, limited opportunities for employment or *development, and isolation from world markets. With open economies dependent on the world economic system, they suffer from primary production of one or two agricultural products which are subject to severe price fluctuations, and over which they have little if any control. There is little industrial activity or development. Subsistence activities, either farming or fishing, are widespread in most of the states. Of these states, only Réunion and Mauritius have economies where less than ninety percent of the population is engaged in those subsistence activities.

The islands have retained strong economic linkages with the West, primarily in the trade and aid areas. France, the United Kingdom, and the United States are by far the largest bilateral donors, although multilateral development agencies have increased their levels of disbursements in recent years. In absolute terms, Réunion generally receives the largest amount of Official Development Assistance (ODA), in some years amounting to the fourth largest ODA recipient in all of Africa.

Trade has continued to be geared principally with the industrialized countries, and with Britain and France in particular. Generally, the former British colony of Seychelles has tended to maintain stronger trade ties with Britain, while Comoros and Réunion have retained stronger links with France. Maldives never had particularly strong ties with Britain, and Mauritius (originally ruled by France) has had more of a balance in its trade partner mix.

With the opening of over 2 million square nautical miles of Exclusive Economic Zones (EEZs), these island states will have a number of ocean-related economic development options for the long term, including energy production from waves, ocean thermal energy conversion (OTEC) and oil exploration, deep sea nodules, and other deep sea and offshore minerals. All of these marine-related activities are expensive and would probably require a degree of regional cooperation.

Because of their relatively diversified natural resource bases, diversified economic sectors, and well-developed human and physical infrastructures, Mauritius and Réunion have good long-term economic prospects. For the short and medium term, however, both will have problems. Mauritius will have to maintain its competitiveness with South Asia in cheap manufactured textile exports, keep its import levels down, and diversify further from agricultural production. Mauritius could benefit from increased tourism in the region. Réunion continues to hide its severe structural economic problems by its reliance on French budgetary assistance. Its industries are inefficient and will have to modernize. Because of its relatively high education levels and large amounts of foreign (i.e., French) investment, however, the economic prospects for Réunion are bright. For the short term, however, France will have to deal with some unemployment and rising consumer expectations in Réunion.

Neither Maldives nor Seychelles has many natural resources; nevertheless, if they can maintain economic and political stability they should have fair to good long-term economic prospects owing in large part to their tourism sectors. For Maldives, the short and medium terms appear about the same as the long term. It must continue to receive ODA to keep its economy viable, yet the country will gain increasing foreign exchange from increased tourism. The government's planning and economic policies should allow for greater growth in the long term. For Seychelles, however, the prospects are not as clear. Its government has announced plans to take more control over its economy, against a trend which is now occurring in most of sub-Saharan Africa. Such involvement will probably have significant long-term costs in terms of efficiency and equity. Should the government alter its desire to become more involved in the economy, Seychelles could expect good economic progress, given its large levels of tourism and advanced level of economic and human infrastructure.

Comoros has the lowest level of natural resources in the region. Its prospects for both the medium and long term are not bright. Most of its economy is geared toward the subsistence sector, and what little modern sector activities exist are export-oriented with little local value added. There appears little likelihood of increased tourism in the islands. Until it settles its territorial dispute with France, it cannot be assured of continued and sizeable French economic assistance.

International and Regional Political Affairs. Britain had a strategic monopoly over the area from the end of the nineteenth century until World War II. However, Japan's defeat of the British fleet in the Pacific in 1942 essentially ended that hegemony. After the war Britain did not have the desire or the ability to reassert its dominance. Rather, it was engaged in withdrawing its military forces worldwide. Following World War II France continued its modest-sized military presence, and in 1947 the

United States set up a tiny task force based in Bahrain. The Soviet Union did not yet have a fleet capable of operating so far from its home bases.

During the 1960s interest in the region gradually began to increase as Britain began preparations for granting independence to its remaining colonies or possessions in the area. The United States and Britain made several agreements for the use of former British colonial possessions, including Diégo Garcia. In 1965 Britain formed the British Indian Ocean Territory (BIOT) from several small islands in the Chagos archipelago. These possessions had previously been administered by the Crown Colonies of Mauritius and Seychelles. Resettlement of the native populations to Mauritius has been a sore point between the regional "progressive" states and Britain ever since. These states claim that Britain did not adequately compensate the people it removed. By the mid-1970s the United States had begun to establish a naval communications and an air base on Diégo Garcia, and its Seventh Fleet was authorized to extend well into the western Indian Ocean. A landmark was reached in 1967 when Britain announced its strategy of force withdrawal "east of Suez" by 1971. It was then that the United States and the Soviet Union began to jockey for position in the region. The Soviets began to regularly deploy a small but growing military fleet, and also began to engage in more economic activities, principally fishing. During the 1971 Indo-Pakistan War the Soviets and the United States both sent naval warships into the region, and during the 1970s the two powers remained at about equal strength.

During this period the French maintained and even increased their presence in the region, becoming stronger militarily than either the United States, the Soviet Union, or Britain. France operated from bases in Réunion and Comoros. France has remained committed to maintaining a strong presence, and wants to protect its economic and political interests especially in Mayotte and Réunion.

As the oil crisis of the 1970s intensified, many planners in the West began to reassess the area's strategic value because of the large amount of oil which passes through the region. More than ninety percent of Japan's oil, for example, passes through (or near) Maldives. When the Suez Canal was closed during the 1967 Middle East War, the shipping lanes around South Africa's Cape of Good Hope became more important as the major alternative route. About fifty percent of Western Europe's oil passes around the Cape. Comoros, Mauritius, and Seychelles lie directly within those sea lanes; that route retained its importance even after the reopening of the canal because increased ship sizes (particularly oil tankers known as very large cargo carriers, or VLCCs, and ultralarge cargo carriers, or ULCCs) made passage through the Suez Canal impossible.

Tensions have remained high in the Middle East during the past two decades: armed conflict occurred between a number of nearby states including Somalia-Ethiopia, Iran-Iraq, and Iraq-Kuwait. Tensions have remained high in Southern Africa as well. The United States and the Soviet Union have seen potential advantages of having access to bases in the Middle East's southern flank, i.e., the western Indian Ocean. The Soviets tried to lease a former British base on Gan in Maldives, but Maldives rejected the offer because of its desire to remain neutral in the East-West competition. During the early 1980s the United States established its Rapid Deployment Joint Task Force and signed access agreements with a number of nearby African littoral states. While each superpower maintained an almost permanent naval presence on the high seas, neither had a permanent military presence in the independent island states of the region. There have been repeated calls for an Indian Ocean Zone of Peace made by a number of regional states. In 1971 the UN's General Assembly passed a resolution declaring the Indian Ocean a "zone of peace," with a vote of 61 to 0 (with 55 abstentions—from all permanent members of the Security Council except China).

Although clearly they all are located in a strategic location, none of the island states in the western Indian Ocean are—by themselves—vital to Western economic or geopolitical interests. Even for Seychelles, where the United States maintains a large satellite tracking installation, there are satisfactory substitutes. No one island state supplies the West with an inordinate amount of a valuable commodity (indeed, France and the other European Community countries subsidize much of the sugar they buy from the region). Strategic or critical minerals have yet to be exploited in the area. Individually these island states are not important politically. The states in the region have preferred to maintain their economic ties with the United States and Western Europe, and will most likely continue to do so for the long term.

(See also DECOLONIZATION; ETHNICITY; FOREIGN MILITARY BASES; FRANCOPHONE AFRICA; MADAGASCAR.)

André Scherer, *La Réunion* (Paris, 1980). Alex Kerr, *The Indian Ocean Region: Resources and Development* (Boulder, Colo., 1981). Marion Benedict and Burton Benedict, *Men, Women and Money in the Seychelles* (Berkeley, Calif., 1982). Ashok Kapur, *The Indian Ocean: Regional and International Power Politics* (New York, 1983). World Bank, *The Comoros: Current Economic Situation and Prospects* (Washington, D.C., 1983). International Monetary Fund, *Maldives: Recent Economic Developments* (Washington, D.C., 1985). Larry W. Bowman, *Mauritius: Diversity and Democracy in the Indian Ocean* (Boulder, Colo., 1991).

DONALD L. SPARKS

INDONESIA. The southernmost country in Southeast Asia, Indonesia extends 5,100 kilometers (3,200 miles) west to east, equal to the distance from Seattle to Washington, D.C., or Ireland to Azerbaijan. In 1990 an estimated 182 million people lived on some

6,000 of the more than 16,500 Indonesian islands, making this the fifth most populous country.

In Asia only India is culturally more diverse. Upwards of 250 distinct indigenous languages are spoken in the archipelago. Indonesians consider themselves Muslims, Buddhists, Hindus, Catholics, or Protestants, and these labels conceal degrees of syncretism and *secularization. The fact that Indonesia has remained one unitary state since becoming independent in 1945 is a major political achievement.

One island, Java, is the homeland of the largest ethnic group, the Javanese, who form perhaps half the country's population. The other half spans a congeries of smaller groups, the largest of which—the Sundanese—also calls Java home. Java is the demographic, socioeconomic, and political heartland, its infrastructure and opportunities having made it a magnet for members of the ethnic minorities on the "outer islands." On Java stand Indonesia's three most populous cities, including the capital, Jakarta, with its government departments, corporate headquarters, and prestigious university.

The outer islands are rich in natural resources—oil, gas, timber, minerals—much of whose value in revenues from exports is transferred to Java. Food grains aside, the outer islands tend to produce the raw materials that Java consumes. In the 1950s rebels on Sumatra and other islands took up arms against the central government over this, among other issues. But Jakarta prevailed and has managed since to co-opt or contain regional discontent.

In maintaining national unity, the government has been aided by the tendency for cleavages in Indonesia to cut across one another. Heartland and periphery alike are multiethnic and multireligious. The Javanese are mainly Muslim—in no country do more people identify with Islam—but few are strict about their religion, and Java has long accommodated other faiths, notably the *Buddhism, *Hinduism, and animism already in the archipelago in the eleventh century when *Islam arrived. Christianity further differentiated the Javanese and encompassed parts of other groups, in contrast to neighboring Malaysia where Islam, the religion of almost all Malays and almost no Chinese, reinforced the divisiveness of race.

Further restraining instability is the tendency in Indonesia for *class to cut across culture. Wealthy and poor can be found in roughly similar proportions in most religious and ethnic communities. The chief exception are the Chinese, who constitute two percent of the population, are disproportionately in trade and finance, and whose relative wealth breeds resentment among other Indonesians, especially those committed to Islam. In moments of crisis, the trashing of Chinese properties in major cities, as happened in Bandung in 1963, Jakarta in 1974, and Semarang in 1980, remains a danger.

Also conducive to national unity is the neutrality of the national language, Indonesian. Unlike the official indigenous language of India—Hindi—Indonesian was not the mother tongue of a major ethnic group, but spread as a lingua franca convenient for interethnic commerce, journalism, and politics. The 1945–1949 revolution against Dutch efforts to recolonize the islands after World War II endowed the "1945 generation" of Indonesian leaders with the experience of struggling for the "one country, one people, one language" to which Indonesian patriots had sworn fealty in 1928.

In 1990 the leading exponent of the outlook of the 1945 generation was still Soeharto, the Javanese Muslim army general who replaced the revolutionary hero Sukarno as president of Indonesia in 1968 in the aftermath of the 1965 *assassination of six top army commanders by junior officers with links to the Indonesian Communist Party. Blamed on the party, the killings were used by Soeharto, the officers who sided with him, and militant Muslims, among other anticommunists, as a virtual license to ban *communism and arrest or slaughter its adherents. Perhaps hundreds of thousands died in the pogrom. Reversing the leftist policies of Sukarno's regime, General Soeharto established a "New Order" that underwrote with military force and foreign loans and investments a series of initiatives in political engineering and physical *development that resulted in unprecedented political stability and economic growth.

The revolving-door cabinets of 1950–1959, when Indonesia tried *parliamentary democracy, and the unstable "guided democracy" of 1959–1965, which Sukarno imposed and orchestrated, had given way to the longest-lasting regime of all, called by its architects—Soeharto, the armed forces, and their civilian allies—"Pancasila democracy." The name appropriated the five principles (panca sila) of Indonesian identity enunciated by Sukarno on the eve of the revolution of 1945: monotheism, humanitarianism, unity, democracy, and justice. In 1985 all social or political organizations in the country were required to subscribe to Pancasila.

The army was the backbone of the regime. Active or retired military officers occupied key executive, legislative, and judicial positions at national and provincial levels to secure the leadership against communism and two other perceived enemies: fanatic Muslims on the Right, accused of wanting to replace the explicitly religious but nonsectarian New Order with an intolerantly Islamic state; and Westernized liberals on the Left, charged with wanting to trade "Pancasila democracy" for a naively procedural democracy of the sort that could reopen the cultural and ideological wounds of the 1950s and 1960s. In this setting the New Order could be termed a regime of the "extreme center."

Around its military pillar, constitutionally mandated institutions served to support the New Order while making it seem more democratic. Quinquennially since the 1970s a People's Representative

Council (DPR) and a larger People's Consultative Assembly (MPR), respectively, approved the government's development plans and reacclaimed Soeharto president. Elections to these bodies were held in 1971, 1977, 1982, and 1987. Competing in the last three of these contests were the regime's own Functional Group (Golkar), based in the bureaucracy but extending into industry, agriculture, and services; the Development Unity Party, an attempt to fuse and domesticate Islamic political parties; and the Indonesian Democracy Party, an umbrella for nationalist and Christian parties. Golkar won all four polls with majorities between sixty-two and seventy-three percent, achieving the latter peak in 1987 despite an earlier downturn in economic growth and a lessening of military pressure to vote for the government. Nevertheless, of the 500 seats in the DPR in 1987, only 400 were filled by election, the remainder being reserved for military appointments. Because a majority of the 1,000 seats in the MPR were not competitively elected, even had Golkar been defeated at the polls the government technically could still have controlled the MPR and kept Soeharto in office.

The ability of Soeharto and his technocrats to foster development has bolstered the *legitimacy of the New Order among Golkar's constituencies, including the civil service and a burgeoning middle class. With an average annual 4.3 percent rate of growth in per capita GNP in 1965–1988, Indonesia tied Japan for eighth place in the *World Bank's ranking of 100 countries along this measure. In cross-country comparison the distribution of income also has not seemed particularly unequal. Arguably, since the near bankruptcy of the national oil company in the mid-1970s no other large, poor, and populous exporter of oil and gas has used revenues from these commodities more wisely than Indonesia has. In part by reinvesting receipts from oil and gas in agriculture and manufacturing, Indonesia moved away from dependency on hydrocarbon exports and toward self-sufficiency in food.

The about-face of 1965–1966 resulted in a corresponding reversal of Sukarno's leftist *foreign policies. Soeharto's Indonesia cooperated with its anticommunist neighbors Brunei, Malaysia, Philippines, Singapore, and Thailand in the *Association of Southeast Asian Nations (ASEAN), formed in 1967, and with Japan and Western countries, which have continued to supply aid, loans, and investment. At the same time Soeharto kept an independent stance, for example, by conceding to Vietnam a legitimate security interest in Indochina, notwithstanding the U.S.-Chinese-ASEAN campaign in 1978–1989 to remove Vietnamese troops from Cambodia. In 1986–1987 the value of U.S. direct private investment in Indonesia (mainly in oil and gas) exceeded that of any other ASEAN member, yet no ASEAN member voted less often with the United States in the UN. In 1990 Indonesia further balanced its international position by resuming diplomatic relations with China, having suspended them in 1967 over accusations that Beijing had abetted the conspiracy of 1965.

Indonesia in the early 1990s still faced severe problems: it remained the least developed country in ASEAN. Its debt service ratio, down from a record forty percent in 1988, was still a serious burden. Its armed forces still had to contend with regional, ethnic, and religious unrest on the outer islands, notably in East *Timor, Irian Jaya, and Aceh. Meanwhile the prospect of general and presidential elections in 1992 and 1993, respectively, and Soeharto's advancing age—he was born in 1921—raised the question: Would the New Order outlast its founder?

Observers who predicted the collapse of the regime pointed to corruption, the unpopular wealth of Soeharto's adult children, restrictions on civil liberties, and signs of disaffection among Muslims, students, and retired officers. Others were impressed by the New Order's strengths: Soeharto's success in unifying the armed forces, the economy's performance as supported by Japan and the West, the polity's institutions as enhanced by limited toleration of dissent, and the lack of a realistic or attractive alternative to the regime on the Islamic Right or the liberal, let alone Marxist, Left.

If Soeharto's remarkable experiment did survive without him, that would not preclude its evolution toward something less—or more—authoritarian. Nor, if the New Order were revamped or replaced, would that necessarily prevent Indonesia from fulfilling someday the promise it had already shown to become the leading regional power in Southeast Asia.

Harold Crouch, *The Army and Politics in Indonesia,* rev. ed. (Ithaca, N.Y., 1988). R. William Liddle, *Politics and Culture in Indonesia* (Ann Arbor, Mich., 1988). Benedict R. O'G. Anderson, *Language and Power: Exploring Political Cultures in Indonesia* (Ithaca, N.Y., 1990).

DONALD K. EMMERSON

INDUSTRIAL DEMOCRACY. The meanings of the term *industrial democracy* have varied in complex ways over the course of more than a century since the term began to be used widely, and this has reflected the capacities of different industrial actors to appropriate democratic discourses to their own interests. In the United States of the late nineteenth and early twentieth centuries, for instance, industrial democracy was propagated by employers as a way of introducing worker voice (and sometimes a share in profits), but on terms controlled by the employers themselves. This version stressed trust and cooperation rather than conflict, and was often explicitly directed at keeping unions out. In the 1920s, employers referred to works councils and employee representation plans as industrial democracy, while unions saw them as little more than company unions. During World War I some union leaders saw joint (or tripartite) management of certain firms and industries as a form of industrial democracy, and

Sidney Hillman of the Amalgamated Clothing Workers even managed to articulate a blend of this with the more informal traditions of workers' control from below. The success of the Congress of Industrial Organizations (CIO) in the 1930s decisively shifted the favored uses of the term within the *labor movement to the unions' bargained share of participation in determining job classifications and their distribution within an accepted framework of scientific management. Only with the crisis of mass production in more recent years have some union leaders begun to link industrial democracy to direct participation in the work process and joint union-management projects to reorganize it, but even here the terms used by unions and managers alike— *involvement* and *participation*—have carried a much weaker connotation of citizen *rights than does *democracy*.

In Europe there have been similar variations in the meanings of industrial democracy, although the much more militant and often revolutionary movements on the shop floor in the early part of the century produced decidedly more syndicalist conceptions. The British industrial relations theorist Hugh Clegg argued in an influential work (*A New Approach to Industrial Democracy,* Oxford, 1960) against joint consultation schemes and held that only collective bargaining by unions independent of management and the state could produce genuine industrial democracy. Direct participation in management could even jeopardize the union's capacity to represent worker interests. The Industrial Democracy in Europe Research Group's cross-national study (*Industrial Democracy in Europe,* Oxford, 1981), while also highlighting the importance of formalized bargaining and union mobilization, is much more positive about the outcomes of joint consultation and codetermination, and finds legislation to have been one of the most important factors in expanding worker influence and involvement over the preceding decades.

Labor movements in Sweden and Norway have been most successful in appropriating a rights discourse of industrial democracy both to counter managerial attempts to dominate work reform and to enrich the meaning of the concept itself. The pathbreaking sociotechnical systems theory of work redesign of Fred Emery and Eric Trist of the Tavistock Institute in London introduced an analysis of the labor process itself into the vocabulary of industrial democracy via the Norwegian Industrial Democracy Project of the 1960s. The unions in both countries developed ambitious legislative programs for industrial democracy that were realized under Social Democratic governments in the 1970s. New laws mandated greater representation of unions on boards of directors and greater powers of shop stewards on the shop floor. An innovative approach to health and safety regulation was incorporated into work environment laws that mandated union

participation and local initiative rather than expert-dominated and rule-based strategies. Worker participation in the design of new technologies has been facilitated by laws mandating that employers share information and bargain over design and implementation, and unions have begun to develop their own perspectives and collective resources (data stewards, technology consultants, study circles) to democratize this process. Unions in service sectors have developed innovative ways of incorporating consumer and client voice into the technology and work design process, thus enriching meanings even further in the direction of postindustrial democracy. And the participation of women workers in some of these projects has begun to transform what was previously an almost exclusively male discourse. The self-management of time, fostered by rights to flexible working time options and publicly financed leave policies (e.g., job sharing, parental and educational leaves), further enriches the discourse of industrial democracy with feminist and postindustrial themes.

(See also FEMINISM; POSTINDUSTRIAL SOCIETY; SOCIALISM AND SOCIAL DEMOCRACY; WORKERS' CONTROL.)

Carmen Sirianni, ed., *Worker Participation and the Politics of Reform* (Philadelphia, 1987).

CARMEN SIRIANNI

INDUSTRIALIZATION. See MODERNIZATION; URBANIZATION.

INEQUALITY. See EQUALITY AND INEQUALITY.

INFITAH. The concept of *infitah,* or "opening," blossomed in *Egypt in the early 1970s. It meant a shift toward a more market-based economic system, with fewer planning constraints than had been imposed on the economy under the administration of Gamal Abdel *Nasser from 1954 to 1970. It meant an opening to the West, via Egypt's peace agreement with Israel, brokered by the United States and facilitated by a U.S. commitment to massive amounts of economic and military aid to Egypt. It also meant at least token commitment by the regimes of Anwar *Sadat and his successor, Hosni Mubarak, to multiparty *democracy.

In the 1980s, the concept of *infitah* became generalized throughout the Arab world as other countries adopted policies of economic liberalization and political democratization. The economic transformation was spurred by the shortages of foreign exchange, balance of payments deficits, and mounting debt-service problems of many Arab countries, including Morocco, Tunisia, Algeria, Egypt, the Sudan, Jordan, Syria, the Yemens, and Iraq. Expanded export-promotion and enhanced opportunities for foreign capital have taken priority over production for the domestic markets in these countries. Emphasis has shifted from public to private production and the state's commitment to social welfare programs has contracted. The political transformation has been spurred by the angry response of the populace in many countries to the imposition of crisis-bred economic austerity plans and by the failure of the government-run investment and welfare programs to fulfill their original promise.

John Waterbury, "The Soft State and the Open Door: Egypt's Experience with Economic Liberalization, 1974–1984" *Comparative Politics* 18, no. 1 (October 1985): 65–83.

KAREN PFEIFER

INFORMATION SOCIETY. Throughout the twentieth century, the economic system of the United States has evolved toward the production and distribution of information and away from the production and distribution of material goods. In fact, the United States is now recognized, and has been since the 1970s, as an information society—that is, the U.S. economy now primarily produces and distributes information, and the bulk of its labor force works in information-oriented occupations. Within the frameworks of *capitalism and industrialism, the information society brings changes in all areas of social life, from private to public, from personal to political.

In the first decades of the twentieth century, organizational experts mastered the secrets of running large corporations and governments. They did so by inventing a system dependent on communications technologies and bureaucratic techniques, in order to ensure the smooth and timely flow of information among staffs, departments, and decision makers. When successfully implemented, these advances allowed institutions to grow to unprecedented sizes. The rise of big government, with its threat to the privacy of citizens and potential for controlling their lives, represents the best-known political consequence of this wave of the information revolution. As Winston Smith discovered in George Orwell's classic *1984*, government's capacity for domination depends on sophisticated communications systems. But in comparison with Orwell's Oceania, government today appears less monolithic and omnipotent. Moreover, journalists have actively documented government abuses of communications technology, so that Orwell's warning appears less shocking to contemporary citizens who are naturally skeptical of government's intentions.

The evolution of the information society has consequences both for democratic institutions and for private citizens. Because the socioeconomic patterns associated with these tendencies have been identified most clearly in the United States, much of the data on the subject refer to the American experience. However, because the rise of an information society in the United States catalyzed the growth of global communications networks and information markets, developments in an international context must not be ignored.

Integration and Fragmentation. Increasing recognition, in the years following World War II, of the commercial value of information intensified a transformation of the U.S. economy that had been under way throughout most of the twentieth century. In the early 1960s, the economic exchange of information probably accounted for thirty percent of the GNP, and by 1990 approached fifty percent. In a significant way, the modern U.S. economy spends its resources producing and distributing information. Where early-twentieth-century workers sold the labor of their hands in fields and in factories, late-twentieth-century workers mostly sell the labor of their brains. Approximately half of all workers in the United States hold occupations in the information sector, and similar tendencies can be observed for countries such as Britain, the Federal Republic of Germany, Japan, and Singapore.

Early studies of the information society emphasized new developments apparently leading to a *postindustrial society. However, many scholars now see the information society as deeply rooted in the historic growth of *capitalism and in the expansion of industrialization. According to this interpretation, the information society is seen as a continuation of the social forces that forged industrial capitalism in the United States. The shift from agriculture, to industrial, to information work took place well before World War II. In other words, changes in the economy and in the labor force that led to the information society were well under way before the computer revolution.

The steady evolution of an information environment revolves around the mass media, information technologies, and information work. In the United States, capitalism allowed for an unplanned proliferation of commercial communication channels. These many channels structure private life and become major sources of personal participation in the political process. Certainly, in the United States, people's view of national politics and issues is almost totally constrained by the commercial media. Moreover, in those countries where a significant portion of adults labor as information workers, they may develop a heightened sensitivity to information, and to the value of information, leading to a perception of the democratic process as an information process. Thus, the products of capitalism and the realities of information work may converge in powerful ways to create new attitudes toward political life.

Because the television networks are profit-making organizations, they must adhere to the calculus of commercial news production. The networks minimize costs by maintaining news crews in the largest U.S. cities where, they reason, news stories are most likely to occur. In addition, they seek out scheduled events that can be planned into the day's production decisions. For its part, government speaks the language of big media by crafting messages to conform to the constraints of televised news production. By relying on pseudoevents, big media and big government have turned news conferences and presidents into the premier news stories of the public agenda. Indeed, the commercial and competitive nature of the mass media encourages reliance on politically managed news events and focusing on political personalities. Like entertainment programming, the news is made attractive to the largest number of viewers. Furthermore, national networks typically focus on news stories at the national level, while local stations concentrate attention on the largest city in the media market. Consequently, members of the audience, already receiving little information about complex national issues, receive even less about local issues. Residents of the New York metropolitan area, for example, express greater familiarity with the mayor of New York City than with the mayors of their own home towns. The result is low levels of political knowledge.

However, one countercurrent is visible. The mass communication of political news seems to be changing in response to the proliferation of cable systems throughout the United States, resulting in departures from network news practice. Cable News Network (CNN), for example, offers foreign news organizations the opportunity to present news stories directly to U.S. audiences The availability of political news produced according to different cultural assumptions challenges some of the journalistic conventions created by the networks. Moreover, because of its reciprocation policy, CNN has reached viewers in numerous countries including the former Soviet Union. If CNN is successful, it will surely integrate the world news market into an information system dominated by a few giant suppliers, CNN among them. At the same time, CNN may also lead the way to a television marketplace of diversity closer to that enjoyed by magazine readers.

Because marketing strategy dictates that successful vendors identify discrete market segments and package their product to appeal to the characteristics of one or more segments, the media environment is characterized by a host of programmers, advertisers, publishers, editors, announcers—and a few politicians—competing for the attention of the targeted segments. Contrary to the nation-as-community image depicted during election years, the audience presents a highly fragmented appearance to the message producer. From the point of view of the individual, these integrated markets appear as a blizzard of commercial messages with a few political communications nearly lost in the storm. Moreover, commercial messages dominate the media environment, in quantity and quality. They contribute to the formation of a consumer culture of great power, precisely because individuals derive from it their knowledge of the world beyond their own personal experience. Indeed, most adults in the United States spend as many hours with the mass media as they do at work, while their children spend more hours

watching television than attending school. These patterns appear to extend to other industrial countries as well. For the individual in the information society, information overload generated by consumer culture requires coping skills of a considerably high order.

Consumer culture encourages individuals to meet their needs by purchasing products. It does not advocate community values nor cultivate public discourse with other members of the community. It promotes individualistic purchasing of products and further consumption of commercial media. Consumer culture also influences the form, rhetoric, assumptions, and taboos of all public political discussion, so that political communications have gradually taken on the forms of commercial media, looking and feeling more like commercial ads. The tendency of political candidates in a consumer culture is to adapt the patterns of consumer culture to their political ends. Thus politicians tend to be marketed like commercial products. So powerful is consumer culture that political candidates either conform or lose contact with voters.

When individuals substitute consumer behavior for public political behavior, they bring the identity of the fragmented audience to the political arena. Fragmentation leads to a narrow conceptualization of the political agenda, encouraging single-issue interest and voting. The pervasiveness of messages delivered by big media establishes a daily environment of information overload. Not only must citizens be alert to the occasional political message, but they also contend with the obstacle of sheer volume when they choose to speak out. With a few exceptions, political discourse never takes center stage. The forms of commercial media define the audience's expectations and have come to dominate political communication. Neither commercial nor political messages stress the interrelationship between issues that underlies the political agenda. From the perception of the audience, the media environment appears as a rush of discrete products. In other words, the media encourage individuals to approach the political agenda as a lineup of unconnected issues. Not surprisingly, candidates face a multitude of single-issue voters.

Furthermore, fragmentation leads to withdrawal from political parties and from the political agenda of one's group. As consumerism and fragmentation replace participation in political life, political and consumer choices seem of equal importance. By choosing politicians and groceries according to the same consumer paradigm, individuals force political candidates to take a marketing approach, further trivializing political values. Given the struggle of political communicators to be heard from within the blizzard of commercial messages, it is easy to imagine a fragmented electorate leading to a fragmented democracy. Erosion at the base leaves the democratic process vulnerable.

Political Activism and the New Technologies. To be sure, low rates of voting indicate a level of disinterest in the electoral process, while high involvement with media demonstrates acceptance of the behavior patterns that go with consumer culture. However, fragmentation does not deny the desire for community nor the desire for dialogue. As social, family, and political attachments weaken, individuals achieve interconnectedness through the use of communications technologies. Increasingly, Americans live in communities structured by communications networks. These communities exist as connections without the geographic structures of village or town life. Indeed, in a highly mobile population, the nuclear family stays "together" through frequent telephone calls, shared audiocassettes and videocassettes, and letters, even though actual physical contact seldom occurs. Studies of technology and society have drawn attention to network communities among computer programmers and specialists, emphasizing the special attachments formed by individuals who are not in physical contact. That they potentially challenge centralized elites—both governmental and corporate—leads to a proliferation of networks (not all electronic) that generate communities whose cohesiveness lies in identification with the values shared by other members of the network. With their latent political muscle, it may even be that network communities constitute the basis for new political agendas. Possibly they are the source of a new political force within the information society. As such, network communities constitute both a response to fragmentation and a reification of fragmentation. They are communities of communication.

Observations of these communities provide evidence of continued political involvement at the local level. Although national politics in the United States seems to elicit a limited response among eligible voters, local issues (rather than candidates) occasionally draw intense responses. To an extent, mobilization around a local issue forms a community of communication. Landlords in Santa Monica, California, circulated videotapes showing pro–rent control members of the city council in an unfavorable light and won the next election. Computer bulletin boards urge members to take positions on political issues and offer information on how to make oneself heard. In New Jersey, opponents of a tax hike used a local call-in radio station to air grievances and attract attention to a growing tax revolt. In Eastern Europe, individuals defied governments' control over television by using homemade satellite dishes to receive foreign programming, *Solidarity kept its movement alive in Poland by producing video documentaries with its message distributed for viewing on videocassette recorders.

Nor is politically motivated interconnectedness limited to the industrialized countries. Followers of the Ayatollah *Khomeini delivered his message by distributing hundreds of thousands of audiocassettes and created a movement against the Shah of Iran. During the *democracy movement in spring 1989, dissenting Chinese students maintained contact with the outside world by communicating on many of the 30,000 fax machines available through private businesses. In Latin America, localized media have played critical roles in establishing the legitimacy of every group seeking to control government. For example, during the *Cuban Revolution, *Radio Rebelde,* a portable radio station hidden in the mountains of Oriente Province, kept the voice of *Castro alive, demonstrating the seriousness of his claim to the leadership of the country. Similar low-power stations in Guatemala, El Salvador, and Nicaragua have supported rebel groups' efforts to win the support of the people. Politically motivated people will utilize whatever information technologies they can access, no matter how complex the technology, no matter how underdeveloped the country.

Politics and Information. The tendency toward big news organizations and integrated information markets dominated by a few corporations continues to emerge along with fragmented media environments and communities of communication exploiting small media for political purposes. Integration and fragmentation represent two sides of the same need—to communicate in order to exercise power. However, although the tendency is easily documented, the consequences are not. Concern for the consequences of integration prompted a coalition of developing nations to challenge U.S. dominance of world media markets as constituting cultural domination and a threat to the national sovereignty of those nations where U.S. firms controlled large shares of media markets. From the mid-1970s, UN agencies became arenas for opposing U.S. policies. The *Mass Media Draft Declaration* (UNESCO, 1976), the *Interim Report of the Commission on Communication Problems* (UNESCO, 1978), and the *MacBride Commission Report* (Paris, 1980) argued that the hegemonic nature of U.S. capitalism threatened small nations. The United States, with occasional European support, countered that the dominant role played by the United States in the integration of world media markets resulted from the natural workings of the international marketplace for information. Increased polarization and conflict in the 1980s led to U.S. withdrawal from UNESCO. Neither side disputed the facts with respect to integration. They quarreled over differing interpretations of the consequences. No similar debate concerning the consequences of fragmentation has yet taken place. Only recently have social observers like Montague Kern in *30-Second Politics* (New York, 1989) begun to analyze the repercussions of fragmentation.

At least in the United States, micro participation coexists with macro disengagement. The wealth of interactive information technologies becoming available is certain to strengthen the hands of those few citizens working for political change at the local level. Yet the bulk of the potential electorate drifts beyond the reach of frustrated national candidates. The more American voters remain disengaged, the more political strategists will employ the techniques of commercial advertising. The more commercial the style of national campaigns, the more fragmented will they appear to the individual in the audience. The potential for a negative spiral lies close to the surface. At this point, no resolution— whether leading to reemergence of a common public agenda, balkanized localities, or a nation of television couch potatoes—appears visible. The tension between integration and fragmentation appears endemic to the information society. Moreover, as long as the information society evolves globally, variations of the tension will surface in world political arenas. Coming to grips with the prospect for democracy in an information society depends on our grasp of the many tensions fostered by the contemporary pattern of the production and distribution of information.

(See also ELECTIONS AND VOTING BEHAVIOR; PSYCHOLOGY AND POLITICS; PUBLIC OPINION; TIANANMEN SQUARE.)

Eileen R. Meehan, "Towards a Third Vision of an Information Society" Media, Culture and Society 6 (July 1984): 257–271. Neil Postman, Amusing Ourselves to Death: Public Discourse in the Age of Show Business (New York, 1985). Jorge R. Schement and Leah A. Lievrouw, "A Third Vision: Capitalism and the Industrial Origins of the Information Society," in Jorge R. Schement and Leah Lievrouw, eds., Competing Visions, Complex Realities: Social Aspects of the Information Society (Norwood, N.J., 1988), pp. 33–45. Robert M. Entman, Democracy Without Citizens: Media and the Decay of American Politics (New York, 1989). Terry Curtis, "The Information Society: A Computer-Generated Caste System?" in Vincent Mosco, ed., The Political Economy of Information (Madison, Wis., 1990), pp. 95–107.

JORGE REINA SCHEMENT
GETINET BELAY
DONG YOUL JEONG

INTELLIGENCE. Although spying is as old as humankind—by the seventeenth century in England, "King Charles's cavalry" was a euphemism for money, distributed secretly to purchase influence—peacetime national intelligence services developed out of military staff functions only in the twentieth century. The classic task of foreign intelligence comprises two parts: collecting information and putting it together to see what it means, usually referred to, respectively, as "collection" and "analysis." Raw information comes from a variety of sources. Foreigners provide it, knowingly (and openly, to diplomats or secretly, to intelligence officers abroad) or unwittingly, when communications are intercepted or when assets report on the doings of their contacts. Information also comes from satellite pictures and from foreign media broadcasts monitored openly.

Collection, especially by satellites and other so-called "national technical means," consumes the bulk of the $30 billion annual budget of the U.S. intelligence agencies—together referred to, by custom, as the "intelligence community." Compared to technical collection, analysis and espionage are cheap. The collecting is done by a variety of institutions of the U.S. government; the State Department, the *Central Intelligence Agency (CIA), military attachés, the National Reconnaissance Office, the National Security Agency, and the Foreign Broadcast Information Service are the most significant.

The task of analysis are largely the domain of one half of the CIA—the Directorate of Intelligence—though the Defense Intelligence Agency (DIA) provides analysis of military issues, the State Department has its own small Bureau of Intelligence and Research (INR), and there are still smaller groups of more specialized analysts scattered throughout the government. These analysts work in Washington, D.C., not abroad. Their job is to sift through the piles of information from all sources, secret and not, available to them. These analysts are hardly James Bonds. They tell their friends and neighbors openly that they work for the CIA; by temperament they are more professorial than conspiratorial.

Centralizing intelligence functions, especially analysis, in the CIA was the legacy of Pearl Harbor—the perception that the Army, Navy, and State Department operating separately were unable to sort out warning signals of the impending Japanese attack from surrounding "noise" and unwilling, sometimes for parochial institutional reasons, to press that warning on senior officials of government. Intelligence is more centralized in the U.S. government than in almost any other, although Britain, for example, has a cabinet office assessments staff.

The CIA's "other half"—the Directorate of Operations (which used to be called, in bureaucratic euphemism, the Directorate of Plans)—is the United States' secret intelligence service, usually called the Clandestine Service, the cousin of Israel's Mossad, Britain's MI6, or the foreign operations of the *KGB during the Soviet era. When abroad, the service's officers work under "cover," usually the "light" cover of a U.S. embassy. They are ostensibly diplomats, and thus enjoy diplomatic immunity from prosecution in the countries to which they are accredited, but they are CIA operatives in fact.

Few CIA officers are "spies" in the sense of popular novels. (Indeed, most of those novels are not about spying—that is, espionage—but rather about counterespionage.) The "spying" typically is done by foreigners employed or managed by CIA officers—in the jargon of the trade, foreign "assets" "run" by their CIA "case officers." Those assets are lured to betray their countries for varying combinations of belief and greed. The most famous American spy in the Soviet Union, Oleg Penkovskiy, was a "walk-in" who simply asked to work for the CIA. Besides conducting espionage, CIA officers abroad seek to protect American institutions from penetration by foreign intelligence services, "counterintelligence" in the language of the trade. The task, no mean feat in a world of double and triple agents, was once described by James Angleton, long-time head of counterintelligence for the CIA, as a "wilderness of mirrors." In one well-known case of the 1960s a Soviet defector was kept under virtual house arrest for three years while the intelligence agencies argued about whether he was real or a Soviet "plant."

At home, the Federal Bureau of Investigation (FBI) is charged with both counterintelligence and managing foreign "spies," diplomats on assignment in the United States, for instance. In its domestic intelligence—as distinguished from its law enforcement—the FBI is thus the counterpart of Britain's MI5 or the Russian Ministry of Security (as the reformed domestic security apparatus that replaced the domestic operations of the KGB is called). This division of responsibility between the CIA and the FBI—the CIA is barred from domestic spying—has made for ragged relations between the two from time to time.

During the congressional investigations of intelligence in the 1970s, the FBI was found to have corrupted its authority in spying on U.S. citizens, for instance those engaged in anti–Vietnam War or civil rights protests. One program, called by the FBI "Cointelpro," extended to the secret harassment of civil rights leader Martin Luther *King. Judge William Webster, later the CIA director, was brought in to clean house at the FBI.

The third, and most controversial, CIA function abroad is covert action, or actively trying to influence, in secret, the politics of a foreign nation. The 1947 National Security Act authorized the CIA to "perform such other functions and duties related to intelligence affecting the national security as the National Security Council may from time to time direct"—vague language but the formal authorization for covert action.

The history of covert action might be loosely grouped into three categories. *Propaganda* can be no more than a little money distributed secretly to a few journalists in a foreign country to get them to write articles favorable to the United States. At the other extreme are covert *paramilitary operations,* secret military aid and training, most of them large and hardly secret. Aid to the resistance forces in Afghanistan during the 1980s, like the "secret" war in Laos in the 1960s, was not so much secret as unacknowledged, consuming several million dollars a day.

In between, *political actions* attempt to change the balance of political forces in a particular country, most often by secretly providing money to political parties, trade union or media organizations—to influence elections, or to build political forces or sustain them under pressure from existing governments. Covert CIA support for the Italian Christian Democrats in that country's 1948 elections is regarded in the lore of intelligence as having defeated the Communists—and so became the pattern for later CIA efforts.

At the peak of the *Vietnam War covert action claimed more than half the total budget for the CIA. The agency came to own, in secret and not-so-secret, a string of bases and airlines from Arizona to Thailand. As the war wound down, so did covert action, a trend abetted by *Watergate, the investigations of intelligence and the surrounding climate of the mid-1970s. The change was pronounced during the *Carter administration, but it began with President Ford.

With the Soviet invasion of Afghanistan in 1979, the Carter administration got back in the business of covert action. When Ronald *Reagan acceded to the presidency, the upward move became a rush; covert actions perhaps tripled in number to forty-plus. The increase in money spent was even steeper, largely because of Afghanistan, more than a half billion dollars at its peak in the mid-1980s.

When the government was discovered to have been secretly selling arms to revolutionary Iran during 1985–1986 in return for hostages, the result was public scandal. The ensuing congressional investigations unravelled a complicated, and questionable, skein of Reagan administration efforts to help the Nicaraguan *contras. Support for covert action collapsed again, still more so with the toppling of the Berlin Wall and the demise of the Soviet Union.

(See also DIPLOMACY; SECURITY; SOVIET-AFGHANISTAN WAR.)

Sherman Kent, *Strategic Intelligence for American World Policy* (Princeton, N.J., 1949, 1965). Allen Dulles, *The Craft of Intelligence* (Westport, Conn., 1977). John Ranelagh, *The Agency: The Rise and Decline of the CIA* (New York, 1986).

GREGORY F. TREVERTON

INTER-AMERICAN DEVELOPMENT BANK. The 1959 Charter of the Inter-American Development Bank (IDB) created the world's first regional multilateral lending institution. The IDB is an inter-American financial institution designed to promote the economic and social *development of its Latin American constituents. It has forty-six members; they included twenty-five of the thirty-three sovereign states in Latin America and the Caribbean, the United States, Canada, and nineteen nonregional members. Unlike the *World Bank and the *International Monetary Fund, the borrowing nations have a majority of the votes in the IDB (53.9 percent); the United States, with 34.5 percent, is the biggest shareholder.

The IDB has played key roles in economic and social development programs sponsored by the *Organization of American States (OAS), beginning with a plan adopted in 1960 and subsequently articulated as the Alliance for Progress. The bank has traditionally provided two types of loans: loans from the "ordinary capital account" for productive and infrastructural projects (with near-commercial interest rates and fifteen- to twenty-five-year maturities) and loans from the Fund for Special Operations (FSO) to finance social development projects (with one- to four-percent interest rates and maturities of thirty to forty years). During its first thirty years of operation, from 1961 through 1990, the IDB approved US$47 billion of loans to Latin American and Caribbean nations. About three-quarters were from the ordinary capital account and one-quarter from the FSO.

The issue of U.S. predominance in IDB lending decisions has been constantly debated. The IDB Board of Directors approves loans from the ordinary capital account by simple majority. FSO loans, however, require a two-thirds majority, with voting power weighted according to the relative size of a member's contribution. While U.S. voting power in the FSO declined with the introduction of new member capital contributions, especially after 1976, many Latin Americans continued to complain that the system allowed the United States to impose its preferred development models on the region, which, they said, did not necessarily apply to their needs.

This conflict reached crisis proportions in the 1980s during the negotiations over the seventh replenishment of the IDB's capital. The *Reagan administration insisted that Latin American members give up their right to approve loans with their simple majority of votes. The basic issue was the U.S. contention that the borrower-controlled IDB had failed to attach sufficiently tough conditionality on its loans. After a three-year dispute, an agreement was reached in 1988 to allow nonborrowing members to delay loans for up to a year. Other changes will reduce the IDB bureaucracy and extend its activities to policy-based lending, similar to the World Bank's sectoral loans. In return, the United States agreed to the replenishment, which will almost double the bank's lending capacity to US$22.5 billion between 1990 and 1993.

(See also AFRICAN DEVELOPMENT BANK; ASIAN DEVELOPMENT BANK; U.S.–LATIN AMERICAN RELATIONS.)

Sidney Dell, The Inter-American Development Bank (New York, 1972). Samantha Sparks, "The IDB Prepares for the 1990s" Overseas Development Council Policy Focus, No. 1 (1989).

G. POPE ATKINS

INTERDEPENDENCE. The term interdependence refers to the mutual dependency of *state interests. Isolated, independent states are not affected by what other states do or by what happens to the *international system as a whole. In contrast, interdependent states are affected directly (either positively or negatively) by the national policy of one or more of their number. Thus opponents in *war are highly negatively interdependent (if one wins, the other loses) whereas essential trading partners are positively interdependent (they both gain from trade).

Interdependence can vary in symmetry, degree, and type. Some interdependent relationships are likely to produce cooperation, others conflict.

1. *Symmetry*—Symmetric interdependence means mutual dependence and equality in the relationship. Asymmetric interdependence suggests that one is more dependent on the other than the other is on the one. The second party, then, is in a position to manipulate the dependence of the first. Kenneth Waltz contends that great (or super) powers benefit from the dependence of others on themselves, but are not themselves similarly constrained. Waltz believes that high interdependence is a force for conflict because nations wish to resume full independence and untrammeled sovereignty free from foreign control. Most other analysts argue that high interdependence (of positive, trading ties, for instance) is a potential force for cooperation, as nations come to accept and benefit from that relationship. In Latin America and the *Third World generally, many have come to believe that asymmetric interdependence or dependence on First World capital and markets is a factor causing conflict between the North and the South. Some go so far as to label it "structural imperialism." From this standpoint, a more positive linkage between North and South awaits greater symmetry in the relationship.

2. *Degree*—Interdependence can refer to linkages that are important or only peripheral. It is sometimes said that "vulnerability" interdependence represents a "tie that is costly to break," while "sensitivity" interdependence denotes a tie which either party can easily cast aside. This is because the service or good which a lesser interdependence provides can be obtained elsewhere. These terms, however, are influenced by trends in the international political-economic system. A country with abundant oil reserves (like the United States in the 1950s) may have only a "sensitivity" interdependence with Middle Eastern oil producers. As those reserves are depleted, however, sensitivity yields to "vulnerability" interdependence with foreign suppliers of oil. A country with a small percentage of foreign trade relative to its GNP may have only a modest need for the imports of others and place little emphasis upon its own exports. As its imports increase, however, and trade rises as a fraction of GNP, export markets overseas may become a matter of vulnerability interdependence: they are essential to maintain a strong balance of payments.

3. *Type*—Interdependence will vary with the nature of the international "game" that is being played, as illustrated below.

In Figure 1 (Prisoners' Dilemma game) the pattern of interdependence (suggested by payoffs in the game) is conflictual. Although both parties would be better off if each played "cooperate," each thinks: "If the other plays 'cooperate' and I 'defect,' I do better still." Thus, each "defects" and cooperation is lost. In Figure 1 each player has a dominant strategy of playing "defect" because it gains (4 or 2) if it defects as opposed to (3 or 1) if it cooperates.

Figure 1. Prisoners' Dilemma

	Cooperate	Defect
Cooperate	3, 3	1, 4
Defect	4, 1	2, 2

In Figure 2 (Chicken), there is no dominant strategy given that the outcomes of "cooperate" (3 or 2) are of the same value as the outcomes of "defect" (4 or 1). Everything in this game is contingent: it depends on what the other player does. If one is sure the other will play defect, it is in one's interest to co-operate (yielding 2, 4). If on the other hand, one thinks the other will cooperate, then one's interest is to defect (and derive the 4, 2 payoff). In this case, cooperation is contingent; it may or may not emerge.

Figure 2. Chicken

	Cooperate	Defect
Cooperate	3, 3	2, 4
Defect	4, 2	1, 1

In Figure 3 (Assurance II), however, the interdependent relation is much more benign. In this game the incentive to cooperate is overwhelming and the (4, 4) outcome is achieved. (Each party derives [4 or 3] from a strategy of cooperation and only [2 or 1] from a choice of defection).

Figure 3. Assurance II

	Cooperate	Defect
Cooperate	4, 4	2, 3
Defect	3, 2	1, 1

These three games are characteristic of different aspects of international politics. The second game, Chicken, is frequently claimed to apply to *superpower crisis relations. In the 1962 *Cuban missile crisis, for instance, Secretary of State Dean Rusk was reported to have asserted: "We were eyeball to eyeball and the other guy just blinked." Fearing that the United States might resort to force, the Soviets backed down. More recent information suggests that President John F. Kennedy was equally aware of the dangers of a clash (the 1, 1) payoff and was also ready to make significant concessions to avoid that outcome. In superpower relations mutual defection is likely to be very unfavorable, and, indeed, catastrophic to both sides.

In trade negotiations or *arms control talks, the prisoners' dilemma frequently applies. Under conditions of pure rationality, this condition should always lead to disagreement. In fact, it has not always done so. Studies show that people playing Prisoners' Dilemma against one another eventually work out an agreement on the (3, 3) (cooperative) payoff. Tit-for-tat strategies can contribute to this outcome. Among allies, the Assurance II game typically holds: that is, each side considers its own best payoff to lie where the other partner also benefits. To conclude from these three illustrations: in the most general sense interdependence is neutral; whether it is cooperative or conflictual depends upon the nature of the situation and of the particular game that is being played.

In recent years Harold Kelley and John Thibaut have tried to decompose interdependent game matrices into different components. Without trying to illustrate this complex process here, one should observe that Kelley and Thibaut find three different dimensions in such games: reflexive control, fate control, and behavior control. Reflexive control refers to that amount of the payoff that A can guarantee, no matter what B does. Fate control refers to A's ability to control the payoffs that B gets. Behavior control refers to the amount of the payoff that is dependent upon joint action by A and B. One may hypothesize that in a nuclear deterrent relationship, countries can guarantee an unfavorable outcome for the other state, but they cannot guarantee a favorable outcome for themselves: that is, fate control is very high and reflexive control very low. In trading relationships among countries (usually typified by a Prisoners' Dilemma game), fate control also dominates all other dimensions of the matrix. It is only as one proceeds to coordination games that behavior control becomes dominant, as illustrated by Figure 4 (the Coordination game). Fate control and reflexive control are both zero. The achievement of favorable payoffs for both sides depends entirely on coordinating their responses. Such games are involved in driving on the right-hand side of the street and not, for instance, on the sidewalk. Membership in institutions may also facilitate the development of coordination games. Institutional members are more likely to coordinate on certain courses of action because of procedural regularities, precedent, and the frequency of interaction in an institutional setting.

Figure 4. The Coordination Game

	Strategy 1	Strategy 2
Strategy 1	4, 4	0, 0
Strategy 2	0, 0	4, 4

Since 1945 the international system has become more "interdependent" in the sense of there being a greater "connectedness" among nations. What one nation does now, for good or ill, directly impinges on another. This does not mean, however, that positive interdependence or *international cooperation has grown in equal proportion. Any such development depends in turn on the type, degree, and symmetry of interdependence. It appears that symmetry may be increasing as the result of the transformation of a previously bipolar system into one more multipolar in character. The processes of economic development have enabled a number of less developed states to become new industrial countries. At the same time, the relative economic lead of the United States, Europe, and even Japan is declining, while the growth rates of China (at least until recently) and a number of Pacific Rim countries has been increasing. Under these circumstances, the amount of symmetry in international economic relations will also increase. The acceptance of interdependence has also risen in that military alternatives to enmeshment in an interdependent economic system are progressively less attractive. Because of institutional development and greater interaction, Prisoners' Dilemma games have to some degree been transformed into cooperative ones. At the same time the world is far from achieving the status of an Assurance game or a game of Pure Coordination. Conflictual interdependence, as evidenced in the Persian Gulf, is still quite high.

(See also DEPENDENCY; DETERRENCE; GAME THEORY; INTERNATIONAL POLITICAL ECONOMY; NORTH-SOUTH RELATIONS.)

Johan Galtung, "A Structural Theory of Imperialism" *Journal of Peace Research* (1970). Kenneth Waltz, "The Myth of Interdependence," in C. P. Kindleberger, ed., *The International Corporation* (Cambridge, Mass., 1970). Richard Rosecrance and Arthur Stein, "Interdependence: Myth or Reality" *World Politics* (1973). Robert Keohane and Joseph S. Nye, *Power and Interdependence* (Boston, 1977). Harold Kelley and John W. Thibaut, *Interpersonal Relations: A Theory of Interdependence* (New York, 1978). Herman Schwartz, *Dominions and Dependency* (Ithaca, N.Y., 1990). Arthur Stein, *Why Nations Cooperate* (Ithaca, N.Y., 1991)
RICHARD ROSECRANCE

INTEREST GROUPS. Once the political community grows beyond the manageable dimensions of the town meeting, some kind of representative mechanisms become essential to *democracy. Among the various kinds of social aggregates that serve as political intermediaries between the individual and political institutions are interest groups. This category includes organizations of a variety of kinds—among them unions, trade and other business associations, professional associations, consumer and environmental groups, and groups concerned about political issues ranging from abortion to speed limits to public funding of religious schools. Interest groups are fundamental to the politics of every functioning contemporary democracy; indeed, it is difficult to imagine democracy on a national scale without them.

The boundaries between interest groups and other politically relevant social collectivities are not completely distinct. Interest groups resemble political parties in many of their activities—for example, campaigning for candidates, making campaign contributions, screening appointments for public office, and formulating policy alternatives. Unlike political parties, however, they do not nominate candidates to campaign under their name for the purpose of running the government. Interest groups can be differentiated from social movements by their greater degree of formal organization. However, many social movements—for example, the women's movement in the United States—encompass not only informal groups and individual sympathizers but formal associations as well. Because many of the private organizations that get involved in politics—most notably, corporations—do not have members in the ordinary sense, many students of politics substitute the term *organized interests* for *interest groups*.

Almost inevitably, all interest groups perform certain functions: they provide information to public officials to assist in designing sound policy; they seek to persuade policymakers to pursue courses of action that are congenial to what they construe to be the best interests of the organization and its members, an activity that may be difficult to distinguish in practice from the attempt to inform; they communicate with members—keeping them apprised as to what the government is doing, educating them about the political process, and cultivating support.

In spite of the similarities in their role as intermediaries in a two-way process of communication, there are substantial differences among interest groups within any particular democracy as well as enormous diversity across democracies with respect to the nature of organized interest politics. The groups in any single democratic polity vary considerably in terms of their size, their level of resources, the number and kinds of issues they embrace, and the proportion of the potential constituency they can claim to represent as members or sympathizers. Furthermore, they differ in the extent to which they concentrate solely upon the political or combine political and nonpolitical means of promoting the interests of the organization and its members. In addition, they differ in the extent to which they function as insiders or outsiders—utilizing traditional, low-profile means of achieving political influence or adopting more public tactics of mobilization and protest—and are accepted as legitimate by public officials.

There are substantial differences across democracies in the nature of interest group politics. There is wide variation simply in the number of groups, which is, in turn, related to difference in the proportion of citizens who are members of any group at all; in the Scandinavian countries, where most employees belong to some kind of union or professional association, it is much higher than in, for example, Italy. There are also differences in the relative difficulty faced by emergent interests in getting organized and entering the political fray; the nature and number of the axes of political cleavage encompassed in organized interest politics; the degree to which interest representation is highly aggregated or fragmented in either functional or geographical terms, and the extent to which interest groups have a monopoly on the organization of a particular constituency. In addition, there are marked differences in terms of the relative strength of organizations representing different kinds of interests—in particular, in the vigor of the opposition provided by organized labor or citizens' groups concerned about consumer and environmental issues to business organizations, which always carry weight in interest group politics.

It is not simply that the configurations of groups differ from one democracy to another. There is also substantial variation across democratic polities in the ways in which interest groups get involved in politics. Democracies differ in the extent to which interest groups cooperate as well as compete and in the strength of their links to like-minded political parties; for example, British trade unions have a much closer relationship to the Labour Party than their U.S. counterparts do to the Democrats. In addition, there is substantial diversity with respect to both the overall strength of interest groups and the relationships between interest groups and government. In particular, there is variation in the extent to which interest groups are relatively autonomous actors or are, in contrast, more or less creatures of the state: whether, as in Germany, they are formally recognized by the government; have institutionalized links with the state or relate to parts of the government in a way that is more ad hoc and issue-specific; benefit from government assistance;

and are expected to speak for and deliver support from a particular constituency. Furthermore, democracies differ in terms of the mix of techniques ordinarily employed by interest groups.

Variations along all these dimensions reflect differences among democracies in the nature of formal political institutions, political parties (their number, ideological distinctiveness, and competitiveness), and political traditions and *political culture. While understanding the diversity among nations with respect to organized interest politics, some political scientists have suggested that there are two ideal typical patterns of organized interest interaction with the state, neocorporatist and pluralist. According to the neocorporatist model, mechanisms providing for equal representation of individuals on a geographical basis are supplemented by mechanisms providing for functional representation of organized interests—ordinarily by a relatively limited number of peak associations. Such organizations are recognized and licensed by the state and attain a regularized role in policy-making through delegations of administrative power or participation on public councils or committees. Important government decisions are made only after consultation with major economic interests, most notably workers, employers, and farmers. The organizations involved in such deliberations must be able to guarantee membership compliance with the results.

According to the pluralist model, in contrast, interest groups are much more numerous—less highly aggregated and organized around multiple bases of political conflict—and much more autonomous. Pluralist interest group politics is relatively permeable to the entry of new groups, and groups arise and get involved in politics at their own initiative rather than at the behest of the state. In a politics of *pluralism, interest groups have greater freedom in choosing which political battles to fight in which political arenas. Typically, those battles involve shifting, issue-specific coalitions taking sides on issues of narrower, more limited import.

These alternative models have generated considerable scholarly discussion and some controversy. Most fundamentally, there is consensus that these are ideal types and that no polity actually conforms to either model. There is also considerable agreement that Austria and Sweden most closely approximate neocorporatism and that the United States most closely approximates pluralism—although the characterization of other democracies with respect to this distinction results in much less unanimity. Some scholars argue, however, that the issue is not where to place particular polities on the continuum, but is instead whether pluralism and neocorporatism are indeed the poles of a continuum at all. Certain democracies—France, for example, where a strong, centralized state has meant comparative weakness for interest groups, or Japan, where consultation between business and government in a seemingly neocorporatist mold more or less excludes labor—evidence a pattern that is neither pluralist nor corporatist nor anything in between.

Scholars have also pointed out that many democracies display mixed patterns, with some issue areas relatively neocorporatist and others more pluralistic. In most countries no single pattern obtains for the making of policy in all issue areas: the formulation of *foreign policy, for example, is less likely to entail regularized bargaining with interest groups than is the making of agricultural policy. Hence, there may be pockets of pluralism or *corporatism within a country that cannot be placed easily into either category. Whatever the variations within and across democracies, however, it is clear that no contemporary democracy functions without some form of private associational life.

(See also LABOR MOVEMENT; NEW SOCIAL MOVEMENTS; POLITICAL PARTIES AND PARTY COMPETITION; PUBLIC INTEREST MOVEMENT.)

Philippe C. Schmitter and Gerhard Lehmbruch, eds., *Trends toward Corporatist Intermediation* (Beverly Hills, Calif., 1979). Kay Lehman Schlozman and John T. Tierney, *Organized Interests and American Democracy* (New York, 1986). Frank L. Wilson, *Interest-Group Politics in France* (Cambridge, U.K., 1987).

KAY LEHMAN SCHLOZMAN

INTERNAL COLONIALISM. The term *internal colonialism* has had two somewhat different connotations in the literature. It was initially employed in the late nineteenth century by Russian populists to describe the exploitation of peasants by urban classes. Later, Antonio *Gramsci, V. I. *Lenin, Evgeny Preobrazhensky, and Nikolai *Bukharin used it to characterize the persisting economic underdevelopment of certain Russian and Italian regions. In this connotation, internal colonialism is a process of unequal exchange between the territories of a given state that occurs either as a result of the free play of market forces or of economic policies of the central state that have (intended or unintended) distributional consequences for regions. This conception of internal colonialism is primarily found among economists of *development; the first quantitative model of it was Mihail Maniolescu's, which was inspired by the marked contrast between urban wealth and rural poverty in Depression-era Romania. A second model was developed by Hans Singer and Celso Furtado, after a study of the extensive regional disparities in post–World War II *Brazil (Love, 1989).

Since the 1960s, however, the term has tended to be reserved for regions that are simultaneously economically disadvantaged *and* culturally distinct. The impetus for the new emphasis on culture came from the Mexican sociologists Pablo Gonzáles Casanova and Rodolf Stavenhagen, who observed that the poorest territories in Latin America tended to be those largely inhabited by people adhering to cultural practices that were granted low status by the rulers of the central state.

Even so, this concept was more useful for descriptive than explanatory purposes until it was applied explicitly to the relationship between England and the Celtic and/or nonconformist territories of Wales, Scotland, and Ireland from the sixteenth through the twentieth centuries. This was the first demonstration that internal colonialism (of any variety) could be found in the industrialized heartland—indeed in a state which spawned both the industrial revolution and the doctrine of free trade. Instead of coming to resemble the English core economically in the wake of market diffusion and industrialization, Wales, Scotland, and Ireland tended to develop specialized export economies; instead of assimilating to the core culturally and politically, the inhabitants of these peripheral regions maintained separate cultural and political traditions and often supported nationalist political movements.

Internal colonialism is considered responsible for the establishment of a cultural division of labor, which is a principal determinant of *peripheral nationalism. The cultural division of labor is a social structure that reserves high-status jobs for members of the core culture, or those capable of assimilating to it, relegating all others to lower rungs in the occupational hierarchy. This theory has been applied to historical and contemporary cases of peripheral nationalism in *Canada, *Finland, *France, Alaska, *New Zealand, and other societies, although no systematic empirical review of these studies has yet appeared. The best comparative assessment of the internal colonial theory of peripheral nationalism is Charles C. Ragin's study of ethnic political mobilization in thirteen Western European societies, which concludes that it is applicable to a large number of cases of peripheral nationalism in these societies, but not to all of them.

(See also BRITAIN; NATIONALISM; SECESSIONIST MOVEMENTS.)

Michael Hechter, *Internal Colonialism: The Celtic Fringe in British National Development, 1536–1966* (Berkeley, Calif., and London, 1975). Charles C. Ragin, *The Comparative Method: Moving Beyond Qualitative and Quantitative Strategies* (Berkeley, Calif., 1987). Joseph L. Love, "Modeling Internal Colonialism: History and Prospect" *World Development* 17, no. 6 (June 1989): 905–922.

MICHAEL HECHTER

INTERNATIONAL BANK FOR RECONSTRUCTION AND DEVELOPMENT. See WORLD BANK.

INTERNATIONAL COOPERATION. The issue of international cooperation provides a unifying theme in the study of national *security and *international political economy. International cooperation refers to the mutual adjustment of government policies through a process of policy coordination. Cooperation must be distinguished from harmony, a situation in which unilateral pursuit of self-interest automatically facilitates the ability of others to achieve their goals (Robert O. Keohane, *After Hegemony,* Princeton, N.J., 1984). Thus, cooperation does not require that states confront no conflicts of interest, but addresses how they might be able to overcome these conflicts to their mutual benefit.

This understanding of international cooperation reflects the predominance of the "realist" paradigm in the study of *international relations. Realists, focusing on the anarchic nature of the *international system and the intensity of insecurity fostered by anarchy, argued that these factors presented formidable obstacles to cooperation among states. Labeling authors who focused on the international pursuit of common goals and the role of *international law in constraining conflict "idealists," the realists made a coherent case for the persistence of discord among states.

In recent years, a response to these realist arguments has been mounted by a group of theorists known as neoliberals. Accepting core realist assumptions such as the central role of self-interested, rational states and the condition of anarchy in the *international system, neoliberals argue that, under certain conditions, international cooperation may nevertheless occur. Their analysis begins by addressing collective action problems, i.e., situations in which unilateral, self-interested state action leads to outcomes that leave all actors dissatisfied. These outcomes are suboptimal in the sense that alternatives exist that would benefit all actors, hurting none. National trade policies are commonly used as an example: while all states would prefer a system of free trade to one with high levels of *protection, each has an individual incentive to impose restrictions on trade. Myopic pursuit of self-interest thus leaves all states dissatisfied.

Neoliberals argue that far-sighted governments will search for mechanisms that allow them to cooperate to overcome dilemmas of collective action. Thus, they describe a path to international cooperation that does not require assumptions of altruism or self-abnegation on the part of individual states. Instead, cooperation allows egoistic, rational states to better achieve their policy objectives. In this world, cooperation is unstable because each government faces temptations and domestic pressures to "cheat" or unilaterally change its policies to the detriment of others and its own temporary advantage. For neoliberals, cooperation needs to be explained rather than assumed.

Following this reasoning, and drawing on the insights of economists and others studying problems of strategic interaction, theorists have identified a series of factors that will facilitate international cooperation. Although idiosyncratic factors may weigh heavily in some historical cases, three factors should encourage cooperation in general: the existence of common interests, the participation of a small number of actors, and a long shadow of the future.

Cooperation will not occur unless states perceive some common interest in cooperation. Common and conflicting interests often exist side by side in international politics, so that governments see benefits from cooperation but find it difficult to take the risk of pursuing these mutual benefits. Both the constraints of state survival in a self-help system and the pressures of domestic politics may push governments away from risky cooperative endeavors even if the potential advantages of such endeavors are large. However, the larger the degree of common interest, and the smaller the degree of conflicting interest, the more likely it becomes that governments will find a way to overcome these difficulties.

A second factor conducive to international cooperation is the involvement of a small number of actors. When the number of states involved in an issue area is large, negotiating mutually acceptable agreements and monitoring compliance with such agreements become more difficult. Thus, cooperation is often easier when only a few states need to coordinate their policies to achieve superior outcomes. Small numbers make negotiations less cumbersome, increase the ability of actors to recognize and understand one another's preferences, and make identification and punishment of those breaking cooperative arrangements less problematic.

Thirdly, neoliberals argue that a long "shadow of the future" encourages international cooperation. The more states value future benefits relative to immediate gains, the more willing they will be to take the chance of cooperating today. A state with a short-run perspective will behave myopically, only considering the immediate costs and benefits of its actions, and thus will be tempted to cheat on cooperative agreements. However, such behavior can become costly in the long run, as a myopic state will develop a reputation for unreliability. Thus, a state that cares about the future will be more willing to forgo immediate gains in order to gain future benefits from cooperation.

In what kinds of situations are these three factors—common interests, small numbers, and a long shadow of the future—increased? Theorists have focused on two elements that facilitate cooperation. First, a common explanation of cooperation is "hegemonic stability theory." This theory posits that cooperation requires one dominant state to provide the necessary conditions. Thus, the international system is stabilized during periods when one state, such as Britain or the United States, plays a leadership role. Eras without a hegemon, such as the 1930s or, some suggest, the 1980s, see an upswing in the level of uncooperative state behavior.

A second explanation of cooperation relies on the

impact that international institutions can have on state behavior. Because institutions increase the level of information available to states, create dense patterns of issue linkages, and encourage their members to think about the future, they tend to create the conditions necessary for the emergence of cooperation. Such institutions often include formal organizations, such as the *European Community, but can also take the form of less formal arrangements, such as the *General Agreement on Tariffs and Trade.

(See also HEGEMONY; LIBERALISM; REALISM; REGIME.)

Robert Axelrod, *The Evolution of Cooperation* (New York, 1984). Kenneth A. Oye, ed., *Cooperation Under Anarchy* (Princeton, N.J., 1986).

LISA L. MARTIN

INTERNATIONAL COURT OF JUSTICE. The possibility of substituting law for *force in *international relations is not new, and rests heavily on the reality of reliable mechanisms for resolving international disputes peacefully. The main obstacle to such an approach has been the attachment of governments to a military option and to the modern idea that a *state should never abridge its *sovereignty in relation to conflict resolution. In face of this tension, the idea of adjudication at the international level has advanced haltingly, but advanced it has.

A realistic compromise between these opposing tendencies emerged late in the nineteenth century in the form of mediation and arbitration. Mediation provides states in dispute with auspices for peaceful settlement, but there is no binding decision at the end. Arbitration takes further steps in the direction of a law-oriented solution but generally allows the opposed governments to choose the "judges," to shape the rules of procedure, and to impose limits on what can be appropriately decided. The parties do agree in advance to respect the outcome as binding.

World War I pushed forward the process of committing states to third-party adjudication. Several influential U.S. lawyers ardently believed that establishing courts was virtually equivalent to creating a world peace system. A world court was a minor part of the vision of a reformed international order as championed by Woodrow Wilson. In 1921 the Permanent Court of International Justice was established as an independent international body, with some connections to the *League of Nations. This court decided thirty-two cases (as well as delivered twenty-seven advisory opinions) during its eighteen years of existence, but none touched the major war-threatening issues of the era between the two great wars of the century.

Ironically, the United States never became a party to this first institutional embodiment of a world court. Participation was successfully resisted by the same political forces that opposed U.S. membership

in the League of Nations. At the same time, support for the world court project continued to grow, particularly in the United States. The experience of World War II strengthened these internationalist forces sufficiently so that in the subsequent *peace process the United States became a leading member of the UN and an active participant in the revised version of the World Court, now formally named the International Court of Justice (ICJ).

Despite these steps forward, the reality of an adjudicative alternative to *war remains rudimentary and contested. The U.S. attitude toward adjudication at the global level remains ambivalent, suggesting the persistence of opposing ideas about the place of judicial settlement and law in international relations. In a central respect, the attempt to displace power by law went against the whole realist mindset that became so predominant in the decades after 1945, and nowhere more so than in the United States. The idea of entrusting important disputes, especially in the area of peace and *security, to the ICJ came increasingly to be regarded as "legalistic" and naive, being incompatible with the actualities of international politics.

The ICJ is the main judicial arm of the UN, its role being set forth in Articles 92–96 of the UN Charter. It is located in The Hague, and is available to states seeking a judicial resolution of disputes in accordance with *international law. Members of the UN are automatically parties to the Statute to the ICJ, and nonmember states can arrange adherence by agreement. The ICJ can also be used by the organs of the UN to render "advisory opinions," clarifying points of international law that arise during their operations. Unlike judgments in disputes between states, advisory opinions are truly advisory, although their findings can be adopted as binding by the UN organ in question, but even then only for the occasion. Through 1990 the ICJ had issued fifty-one judgments and twenty-one advisory opinions.

Although all UN members can use the court, none can be required to do so without an additional expression of consent. The issue of consent is closely related to the question of sovereignty. Governments generally affirm that entering agreements with other states is an exercise of sovereignty, but they remain reluctant to entrust the outcome of a dispute with another state, especially on important matters, to the application of international law by the World Court. This is mainly a matter of not losing control over options and is partly an atavistic sense that it is a denial of sovereignty to accept the authority of an international institution on matters of vital state interests.

An exception exists if the moving government is convinced that it is likely to win. The U.S. government went with enthusiasm to the World Court in 1980 during the hostage crisis to bolster its claims that Iran was in violation of international law by its role in occupying the U.S. embassy in Tehran and by seizing diplomatic personnel. The court found unanimously in favor of the United States, a conclusion reinforced by the UN Security Council, yet defiantly repudiated by Iran, whose officials attacked the decision and the institution as corrupt expressions of Western modernism. A quite different result occurred a few years later when the Sandinista government in Nicaragua took advantage of its own acceptance of compulsory jurisdiction to initiate an action in the World Court against the United States, alleging that U.S. military actions by way of mining its harbors and lending assistance to the contra insurgents was in violation of international law. Once again the court sided with the aggrieved state by a large majority vote, but this time the U.S. government denounced the institution as biased in favor of the Third World and Marxist perspectives. The United States expressed its displeasure by refusing to comply with the decision, by withdrawing from its acceptance of compulsory jurisdiction, and by limiting its future participation to disputes and circumstances of its choosing.

These two prominent occasions illustrate several aspects of international adjudication and its limitation. States will make use of the World Court even in big cases if the likelihood is one of success. In addition, states committed to a course of policy are unlikely to give it up in the face of an adverse judicial decision. Moreover, the UN is not in a position to enforce such a decision in the face of defiance, especially if the loser is a major state. At the same time, even a nonimplemented decision can often be valuable in the struggle for *public opinion and in strengthening the legitimacy of claims on the part of the winning side.

There are two possible directions of further development for the idea of an effective World Court that follow from this recent experience. The first is to restrict the activity of the court to technical areas such as clarifying minor *boundary disputes or allocating shares of the continental shelf. In these settings the court has demonstrated its competence and states seem willing to respect the outcome even if it goes against their claims. There is less emphasis on winning and more on stabilizing a relationship. The second direction would be to encourage more states to agree to resolve their disputes before the court by agreeing in advance to accept compulsory jurisdiction, and then to increase pressure for compliance. The United States and Britain seem to prefer, at this point, the first direction, whereas the countries of the South seem more inclined to move in the second direction.

It is possible that the ending of the *Cold War will diminish the tendency to regard disputes as matters of *ideology and will foster a renewed effort to build up the role of the court as part of a larger embrace of *international cooperation as essential in relation to the challenge of an intensifying global complexity. Also the growing importance of functional issues, and the decline of ideological controversy regarding the content of international law, may support an expanding role for the World Court in the years ahead.

(See also EUROPEAN COURT OF JUSTICE; UNITED NATIONS.)

Hersch Lauterpacht, *The Development of International Law by the International Court* (London, 1958). R. P. Anand, *Studies in International Adjudication* (Delhi, 1969). Shabtai Rosenne, *The Law and Practice of the International Court*, 2d ed., 2 vols. (Leyden, Netherlands, 1985). Richard Falk, *Reviving the World Court* (Charlottesville, Va., 1986).

RICHARD FALK

INTERNATIONAL DEBT. International lending is a subset of international investment, and has long been a prominent feature of world economic and political affairs. Cross-border debts have been important to economic activity in many nations and have frequently given rise to domestic and international political conflict.

The economic principles of international lending are relatively straightforward. Loans across national borders normally respond to differences in rates of return: capital flows from where it is plentiful (and interest rates low) to where it is scarce (and interest rates high). From the standpoint of the investor, this difference in rates of return makes foreign lending attractive. However, these higher rates also reflect the generally greater risk of foreign as compared to domestic borrowers. If the foreign debtor refuses to service its debt, the creditor has fewer ways of collecting than domestically—especially if the foreign debtor is a national government, for creditors cannot foreclose on a sovereign state. In return for accepting a higher degree of risk, foreign lenders demand a higher interest rate (risk premium).

From the standpoint of borrowing nations, such as the United States in the nineteenth century or most developing countries in the twentieth century, foreign loans have several interrelated effects. First, they increase the local supply of capital, allowing national investment to exceed savings. Second, they increase the supply of foreign currency, allowing national imports to exceed exports. Third, inasmuch as they are extended to governments, they increase the financial resources of the public sector, allowing the government to spend more than it takes in.

Foreign loans generally make economic sense to the borrower if they serve directly or indirectly to increase national output and ability to export (or to produce previously imported goods). To eventually repay foreign lenders, the country must use loans to contribute to economic growth and the country's earnings of foreign currencies. This process can be indirect, but sooner or later loans must increase growth if they are to justify themselves. For example, borrowing might allow the government to increase spending on transportation infrastructure that is not directly productive, and does not directly increase exports, but that allows private economic agents to increase output and exports (perhaps by opening new agricultural or mining regions).

In addition to the underlying economic relationship, international debt has important institutional features. Typically, a large proportion of international loans is made to governments: from the standpoint of a foreign lender, national governments are generally better credit risks than are national firms, which are themselves in any event subordinate to government control. Before 1965, most long-term loans were made in the form of bond flotations; since then, bank lending has also been important. In either instance the number of creditor financial institutions (investment or commercial banks) is generally small. International loan markets are often characterized by credit rationing, in which some countries are unable to borrow at any interest rate. This is due, among other things, to the fact that the ability of creditors to enforce contractual compliance on foreign governments is very limited in the absence of a binding judicial system such as undergirds domestic financial relations. And, for reasons that are controversial, international lending tends to go in waves or cycles of boom and bust: a ten- or twenty-year period of easy money is followed by an equivalent period of little lending.

The political implications of international debt are generally clearest when debt must be serviced (i.e., interest payments made and principal repaid). At this point the favorable economic effects of capital inflow are reversed. The country must save more than it invests in order to send capital abroad; it must export more than it imports in order to send foreign currencies abroad; and its government must bring in more than it spends. These three adjustments can be painful, especially if they have to be undertaken rapidly.

The two most prominent modern experiences with international lending were in the interwar period and the 1970s and 1980s. In the 1920s, U.S. and British capital markets lent heavily to semi-industrial countries in Central, Eastern, and Southern Europe and in Latin America. When the Great Depression of the1930s hit and prices of these countries' exports plunged, most of them defaulted on their debts amid great domestic and international political turmoil. In the 1970s, international banks lent hundreds of billions of dollars to developing (and some socialist) countries. Such countries as Brazil and Mexico grew very rapidly at least in part because of the availability of ample foreign finance. When interest rates rose dramatically after 1980 amid a generalized recession, many debtors did not make payments, once more amid domestic and international political turmoil. Most of Latin America, indeed, spent the 1980s mired in recession, inflation, and political conflict as the debt burden exacted an enormous socioeconomic and political toll.

The international politics of international debt are dominated by the complexity of enforcing property rights, such as the creditor's contractual right to debt service payments, across national borders and against sovereign governments. Creditors have tried many ways to induce compliance by debtors. One is military force: in the pre–World War II era military intervention by home governments of creditors, up to and including direct colonialism, sometimes served to enforce contracts (although whether debt problems were important causes of such intervention is controversial). China, Egypt, and the Caribbean are among the regions in which foreign military interference was associated with foreign lending. Another is the formation of clubs or committees of a country's creditors, which can collaborate to use such economic threats as a cutoff of future loans or trade credits to bring pressure to bear. A third way, common over the past twenty-five years, is to rely on an international organization such as the *International Monetary Fund to monitor and attempt to enforce loan contracts.

In the final analysis, however, the absence of an international bankruptcy court means that resolution of debt problems depends on the interaction of the two sides. When debt comes due, debtors wish to pay as little as possible, while creditors want as much as possible. Debtors threaten to reduce or halt debt service payments. Creditors threaten to seize assets the debtor may have overseas (the national airline's airplanes, bank deposits), or to exclude the debtor from future borrowing, or to retaliate by other means; sometimes they offer new loans or other side payments as an incentive for the debtor to honor past obligations. Typically, lengthy negotiations ensue as the two sides threaten their way to the best outcome they can secure.

Careful studies have found that over the very long run (decades or more) and on average, debt problems are bargained out to where the final rate of return on the loan, taking into account unpaid interest and principal, ends up being roughly equivalent to the return on domestic financial assets. This is evidence that in the final analysis international loan markets are relatively efficient, in that risk premia charged to borrowers that may default tend to reflect the actual probability of default.

Efficient as international lending markets may be, there is plenty of room for drawn-out hostilities between debtors and creditors. These hostilities can affect broader political relations among nations, and are sometimes blamed for wars both small and global. In the 1930s, the heavy economic burden of foreign debts contributed to the rise of highly nationalistic, often fascistic, movements in Central, Eastern, and Southern Europe, and to the resentment of these countries and their populations toward the creditor nations of Western Europe and North America. The debt crisis of the 1980s was less dramatic, but it did exacerbate North-South political tensions, as many in the developing world felt that they were suffering solely to line the coffers of international banks.

In addition to international conflict over the distribution of costs and benefits involved in international lending, there are many analogous domestic disputes. There is no guarantee that those within a borrowing nation who benefit from foreign loans are the ones who will be asked to sacrifice to repay them. Foreign finance can go to reduce borrowing costs to industry, for example, while the resources to service this debt can be extracted from agriculture. Such domestic distributional patterns are sure to give rise to political struggles.

Just as foreign borrowing tends to increase the domestic supply of capital and foreign exchange, making loans and imports cheaper, the need to service debt reduces this supply, making loans and imports more expensive. By the same token, inasmuch as foreign borrowing by the government allowed it to provide more services with lower taxes, servicing debt requires a curtailment of public services and increased taxes. Those who had, during borrowing, come to rely on inexpensive loans and imports, and on government services, can be expected to protest the reversal, as can those required to pay higher taxes.

The requirements of foreign debt service can impose severe burdens on debtor societies. The need to raise funds for service of the foreign debt is often associated with domestic depressions, severe unemployment, and spiraling inflation. The debt crisis was a major factor in Latin America's dismal economic performance in the 1980s, and issues related to the foreign debt were central to the political turmoil that affected the region in the midst of the collapse of a series of authoritarian regimes.

The domestic and international politics of foreign debt interact. In a country burdened with costly debt service payments, those economic *interest groups hardest hit by the impact of these payments clamor for the government to take a tougher stance against its creditors—to shift some of the burden onto foreigners. Such demands are countered by other domestic economic interest groups who may rely on their ties with overseas markets or who are concerned about the precedent set by government disregard for private property rights. At the same time, creditors press the debtor government for prompt and full debt service payments with whatever means they have at their disposal.

In the midst of a full-fledged debt crisis, such as those involving many semi-industrial countries in the 1930s and the 1980s, a swirling spiral of domestic and international political conflict can cause great political and economic instability. International debt issues exacerbated domestic and international conflict during the Great Depression, while the debt crisis of the 1980s also saw major changes

in domestic politics and foreign policies throughout the developing world.

Foreign loans can be important contributors to economic development. However, international debt is inherently political, and frequently conflictual. Economic and political factors interact to determine whether foreign debt will be an unproblematic contribution to national development or the cause of major domestic and international political strife.

(See also FINANCE, INTERNATIONAL; INTERNATIONAL POLITICAL ECONOMY; NEWLY INDUSTRIALIZING ECONOMIES; NORTH-SOUTH RELATIONS.)

Barry Eichengreen and Peter Lindert, eds., *The International Debt Crisis in Historical Perspective* (Cambridge, Mass., 1989). Jeffrey Sachs, ed., *Developing Country Debt and Economic Performance* (Chicago, 1989). Barbara Stallings and Robert Kaufman, eds., *Debt and Democracy in Latin America* (Boulder, Colo., 1989).

JEFFRY A. FRIEDEN

INTERNATIONAL FINANCE. See FINANCE, INTERNATIONAL.

INTERNATIONAL LABOR ORGANIZATION. The International Labor Organization (ILO) has been a specialized agency of the UN system since 1946. It was founded at the end of the World War I as an independent adjunct to the *League of Nations, both with headquarters in Geneva. The ILO subsumed the International Labor Office, established at the turn of the century to promote what was called then "international labor legislation," and intergovernmental agreements on welfare standards for industrial labor, such as the eight-hour day and restrictions on child labor.

In late-nineteenth-century Europe the movement for international labor legislation argued that governments enforcing benign working conditions would be at a competitive disadvantage vis-à-vis those more willing to exploit laborers. However, if global agreement on improving working conditions could be achieved, any economic disadvantage to more progressive nations would vanish.

The ILO's organization recognizes that the initial impetus for improving labor standards will come first from labor groups and then from industries and states where high standards already have been won. Delegations to the ILO, unlike those to any other major intergovernmental organization, include representatives of national associations of labor unions and of employers. The employers' associations often overrepresent advanced industries in which labor conditions tend to be better. Member governments do not have to adhere to ILO standards, but international benchmarks help domestic interest groups and states with more advanced labor standards to make demands upon laggards.

ILO standard setting was important in the interwar years but become less central during the *Cold War. The tripartite system of representation broke down: Communist bloc states sent seemingly unitary delegations, and noncommunist labor representatives united with their governments to isolate the Soviet Union and its allies. Under the leadership of United States, the ILO advocated the American system of collective bargaining. However, promotion of the U.S. model of resolving disputes between workers and employers was not the same as upgrading of labor standards to the highest followed anywhere in the world, the original ILO goal.

As the importance of the ILO's original activities diminished, its secretariat took on new functions. It expanded activities in the *Third World, providing technical assistance on employment promotion and human resources to African, Asian, and Latin American governments. Since the 1970s, the ILO has become a leader in debates about *development strategy by funding and promoting much of the original research that supported strategies aimed at fulfilling basic human needs.

(See also LABOR MOVEMENT; UNITED NATIONS.)

Carol R. Lubin and Anne Winslow, *Social Justice for Women: The International Labor Organization* (Durham, N.C., 1990).
CRAIG N. MURPHY

INTERNATIONAL LAW

The body of legal standards, procedures, and institutions governing the social intercourse of sovereign *states is known as international law. Its main purpose is to orient and channel the *foreign policy of states so as to further relationships of coexistence and cooperation. To this end it: a) delimits the sphere of authority of every member of the community (each state holds exclusive jurisdiction within the bounds of its territory); b) organizes forms of cooperation (mainly through intergovernmental organizations such as the UN, military pacts, economic institutions, etc.); and c) sets the main goals to be pursued by states (*peace, respect for *human rights, *self-determination of peoples) and accordingly prohibits what is contrary to those goals (aggression, gross breaches of human rights, forcible denial of the right of peoples to self-determination).

Principles of International Law. International law regulates the behavior of states, not that of individuals. States are the principal actors on the international scene. They are aggregates of individuals dominated by an apparatus which exercises authority over them. Their general goals are quite distinct from the goals of each individual or group. Each state controls a separate territory, and each is bound together by particular political, economic, ethnic, cultural, and religious links.

Whereas in states individuals are the principal legal subjects, and legal entities (corporations, associations, etc.) are merely secondary objects whose possible suppression would not result in the demise of the whole legal system, in the international community the reverse holds true: states are the primary subjects, and individuals play a very limited role.

Second, as in all primitive legal systems where groups play a much greater role than individuals, responsibility for violations of the rules governing the behavior of states does not fall upon the transgressing official but on the group to which he or she belongs (the state community). Here again we are confronted with a striking deviation from domestic legal systems. In domestic systems we are accustomed to the notion of individual responsibility: the individual who commits a tort or any other breach of law shall suffer in consequence; the transgressor must either make good the damage or—in the case of crime—is liable to a criminal penalty. There are, however, exceptions, one of which is "vicarious responsibility," when the law provides that someone bear responsibility for actions performed by another person with whom the former has special ties (for example, a parent is legally responsible for damage caused by his or her children); sometimes a whole group is held responsible for the acts performed by one of its representatives on behalf of the group (as in the civil liability of corporations for torts).

In the international legal system the exception (collective responsibility) becomes the rule. If a state official breaks international law (as when a military commander orders his or her pilots to intrude upon the airspace of a neighboring state, or a court disregards an international treaty granting certain rights to foreigners, or a police officer infringes upon diplomatic immunity by arresting or maltreating a diplomat), the wronged state is allowed to take action against the whole community to which the state representative belongs, even though the community has neither carried out nor ordered the infraction. For instance, the state which has become the victim of the international transgression can claim the payment of a sum of money (to be drawn from the state's treasury) or will resort to reprisals damaging individuals other than the actual authors of the offense (for example, the expulsion of foreigners, the suspension of a commercial treaty or of diplomatic immunity, and so on).

Third, while in domestic legal orders the three main functions typical of any legal system (lawmaking, adjudication, and law enforcement) are entrusted to central organs acting on behalf of the whole community (parliaments, courts, and law enforcement officers), in the international community such authority is fragmented and diffuse. Although political and military *alliances have occasionally been set up or a strong convergence of interests between two or more members of the community has evolved, this state of affairs has not been consolidated into a permanent power structure. As a consequence, organizational rules are at an embryonic stage. There is no special machinery for discharging the three functions, nor are they entrusted to any particular body or member of the international community. All three functions are decentralized—it is for each individual state, acting together with other states if need be, to create and change law, to settle disputes, and to impel compliance with the law. Of particular significance is the fact that each state has the "right" to pursue remedies, which necessarily follows from the absence of courts endowed with general and compulsory jurisdiction.

Historical Evolution of International Law. The origin of the international community in its present structure and configuration is usually traced back to the Peace of Westphalia (1648) which concluded the Thirty Years' War. Indeed, it is about this time that the decline of two preexisting structures of power (the Catholic church and the Holy Roman Empire) became final, and the international community took the form of a set of independent entities (sovereign states), each equal to the others and no longer subjected to any superior authority. The subsequent evolution of the international legal community can be divided into two basic periods: from 1648 to World War I, and from World War I to the present day.

In the first period, the community consisted of a relatively small number of subjects, all "Western" and relatively homogeneous. Until the end of the nineteenth century, the dominant members of the international community had a common ideological and religious background and, what is even more important, shared a common socioeconomic outlook: they espoused a market economy and capitalist competition. Second, there were no international political organizations designed to harmonize the actions of the states and establish permanent links of cooperation among them. Third, no legal restrictions were imposed on the use of *force, with the consequence that the bulk of legal rules (for example, those protecting territorial *sovereignty, political independence, the right to protect one's own nationals) were respected only by powerful states and only when this did not run counter to their own interests. It follows that international legal standards afforded a protection which was provisional and precarious, which is why lesser states so often resorted to treaties of alliance and promoted a *balance of power between stronger states. Fourth, responsibility for internationally wrongful acts was a "private affair" involving the offending state and the victim only. To the remainder of international subjects, breaches of international standards of behavior were something extraneous, in which they were not authorized to meddle. Clearly, no joint interest in compliance with law existed. Only those directly and immediately injured by a wrong were entitled to take the remedial steps provided by law.

After 1917, the world community began to lose its homogeneity as a result of the founding of the Soviet Union, and later the emergence of numerous new African and Asian states. Since then the international community has been split into three main segments (Western, socialist, and the developing countries), each with a distinct socioeconomic philosophy, a fairly clear *ideology, and different political motivations.

Another characteristic of the present international community is the mushrooming of *international organizations which, without dethroning sovereign states, have come to play a significant role not only as meeting points for international subjects but also as mechanisms for exercising leverage on individual states. Among these organizations are those with a political mandate: the UN at the world level, several Latin American regional organizations, the *Council of Europe, the *Arab League, and the *Organization of African Unity at the regional level. An important role is also played by specialized bodies working in the fields of labor relations (the *International Labor Organization), economic relations (the *World Bank and the *International Monetary Fund), health (the World Health Organization), culture (the United Nations Educational, Scientific and Cultural Organization), and the peaceful use of atomic energy (the International Atomic Energy Agency), among others.

Other salient traits of the present community are the imposition of sweeping restrictions on the resort to military and even economic force by states and the gradual emergence of values designed to limit at least the broad use of force as the exclusive legitimizing criterion in *international relations. A further distinguishing trait of the present pattern is that certain values have emerged that states have decided to invest with particular legal force: peace, self-determination of peoples, and the protection of human dignity from outrageous manifestations of cruelty such as *genocide, racial discrimination (in particular *apartheid), slavery, *torture, and other large-scale and glaring violations of human rights. One of the consequences of this set of values is that their violation is no longer the private business of the offending state and the victim, but amounts to a "public affair" involving the whole international community; any member state can step in and claim respect for law, even though it has not suffered direct injury from the wrongful act. Furthermore, at least with respect to certain of those values (peace, the prohibition of genocide), international rules now provide for the personal responsibility of the state officials who engage in such prohibited acts, in addition, of course, to the traditional responsibility of the state to which those individuals belong and on whose behalf they act.

All these new developments in the world community have not, however, been so radical as to obliterate the previously described model of the international community. As a result, two different patterns in law, one traditional, the other modern, currently live side by side. The new legal institutions that have developed since World War I (and with greater intensity since 1945) have not uprooted or supplanted the old framework; rather, they appear to have been superimposed on it, even though their main purpose is to attenuate the most conspicuous deficiencies of the old one.

In *The Anarchical Society: A Study of Order in World Politics* (New York, 1977), Hedley Bull draws the distinction between what he considers the three competing traditions of thought put forward throughout the history of modern states: the Hobbesian, or realist, tradition, "which views international politics as a state of war"; the Grotian, or internationalist, conception, which emphasizes the element of cooperation and regulated intercourse among sovereign states; and the Kantian, or universalist, outlook, "which sees at work in international politics a potential community of mankind," and lays stress on the element of "transnational solidarity." Applying Bull's framework, it is difficult to avoid the conclusion that in its first stage of development the international community was shaped according to the pattern of Hobbesian and Grotian traditions. The "new" international legal institutions, however, appear to be largely patterned on the "Kantian" model of thought, trying to mitigate the most striking defects of the old system by introducing certain improvements such as the creation of international organizations and the placing of sweeping restraints on the use of force. In particular, the new "setting" has endeavored to attenuate the shortcomings of the decentralization of the three legal functions (lawmaking, adjudication, and law enforcement) referred to above.

The Effectiveness of International Law. International legal standards play a significant role in the world community. Since every sovereign state needs to communicate day to day with other states, even the most powerful states, such as the United States, cannot estrange themselves from international interaction but need to maintain a certain degree of association. They require such association to protect their nationals living abroad, sell their goods to other states, buy the commodities they need, enter into agreements providing for the stationing of troops in foreign countries, and to attempt to influence the policies of other nations in international institutions. Even more compelling are the reasons for middle-sized and smaller states to engage in international relations and to deal with other countries: more pressing economic and commercial needs and the necessity to combine to create agencies that can provide defensive "umbrellas" in the case of aggression by other states, for example. All of these multiple relations need a medium through which they can be effected. International law plays precisely this role. In spite of its weaknesses and inadequacies, this body of law discharges the important task of providing a channel through which international relations are effected with relative smoothness. In turn, this body of law contributes to making states "system-conscious," in Stanley Hoffmann's terminology (*The State of War: Essays in the Theory and Practice of International Politics* [New York, 1965], p. 91), that is, "aware of the existence and structure of the whole" and by and large cooperative within the framework of preestablished patterns of behavior.

Admittedly, many commentators draw attention to the scant importance of the few international courts that exist and emphasize that unlawful behavior often goes unpunished because "private" self-interest still overrides "public" concern for compliance with the law. Nevertheless, the enormous number of treaties that all states enter into and the number of *international organizations through which they cooperate should constitute sufficient evidence that sovereign states take daily account of legal standards in their daily action, especially in areas where *reciprocity prevails: diplomatic and consular relations, commercial and economic dealings, protection of nationals abroad, safeguarding of investment in other countries, and others. On careful analysis, it often becomes clear that enforcement procedures turn out to be less defective than is normally claimed. On the whole, it can be said that even in those areas where it is more difficult to induce states to abide by law (military and strategic relations, particularly when states' vital interests are at stake), many states proceed with great caution for a number of reasons: the pressure that can be exercised on the delinquent party within the UN; the weight of world public opinion; the need not to damage good relations in the economic, commercial, and political fields; and the necessity not to alienate the sympathy of countries with which the wrongdoer may have political and ideological affiliations.

Nevertheless, it cannot be denied that the present body of international rules suffers from three major flaws. First, it is unable to impose sweeping and effective restraints on military violence: whenever a state feels that its interests are better safeguarded by resort to force, international legal standards (and the international institution which should, in principle, safeguard international peace and collective security, the UN) play a minor role in preventing that state from taking such a step. Second, there is no permanent institution for *disarmament: only those states that freely subject themselves to armament limitations restrain themselves in this area; other states retain almost unqualified freedom. Third, the UN primarily pursues the goal of what Johan Galtung ("Peace," in David L. Sills, ed., *International Encyclopedia of the Social Sciences*, vol. 2 [New York, 1968], p. 487) calls "negative peace," i.e., the absence of armed conflict, while attaching lesser importance to "positive peace," i.e., the introduction of international social justice. (And, in addition, even in the field of "negative peace," it has turned out to be defective.)

Of course, these three flaws should not be attributed to international law as such, but to the majority of states making up the international community. Had they the political will to do away with those weaknesses, it would not be difficult to change the present state of legal affairs.

International Law as the Vanishing Point of Law. In 1952 Sir Hersch Lauterpacht wrote that "international law is the vanishing point of law" ("The Problem of the Revision of the Law of War," in 29 *British Yearbook of International Law* [London, 1952], p. 382). There is much truth in this proposition. Because international legal rules have no solid structural underpinnings (i.e., no centralized bodies producing law, settling legal disputes, and enforcing law), they are bound to prove weak standards of behavior whenever they are not coincident with or supported by converging state interests.

It is precisely this feature of international rules which makes enquiry into this body of law particularly enlightening for any student of law. International legal rules reflect the constellation of state interests very closely. They are not accompanied by those technicalities that one so often finds in municipal law. This latter body of law, being highly sophisticated—as a result of the existence of central bodies of the type mentioned above—often conceals the real relationship between the sociopolitical constellation and the legal framework—the metalegal context and its legal reflection. Too many mediations, subtleties, and legal mechanisms tend to obscure the fact that legal rules and procedures are in the final analysis designed to safeguard certain interests, to promote the specific goals of social groups, or to strike a balance among the competing or conflicting interests of those groups. International law, by contrast, being rudimentary and unsophisticated, makes the relationship between socioeconomic or political interests and legal standards of behavior singularly transparent. This is one of the principal reasons why this branch of law has been a popular subject of investigation by scholars interested in jurisprudence, legal theory, and the sociology of law.

Future Prospects. Three factors are likely to heighten the role of international legal institutions in the world community. First, the tremendous tensions created by the existence of weaponry capable of destroying the earth several times over increase the value of existing international legal machinery for facilitating negotiation and agreement. Permanent international forums of a political nature (particularly those specializing in matters of disarmament such as the Geneva Conference on Disarmament) become crucial council chambers where the fate of the species is determined.

A second trend is the development of powerful centrifugal forces within nation-states. Minorities are becoming more and more vocal; ethnic groups throughout the world vociferously claim respect for their identity as well as for a measure of autonomy, and even international status; groups representing widely divergent causes tend to branch out into the international community and set up their own international networks. These and other collectivities tend to disrupt the fabric of nation-states. For better or worse, they tend to introduce into the world community a new sort of anarchy which in the long run may jeopardize the present framework of international relations. Existing international institutions can serve a very important purpose by channeling and directing all these centrifugal forces; they can make room for peaceful integration by accommodating competing demands within an orderly framework—without, however, doing away completely with the interstate structure of the world community.

A third phenomenon should be emphasized: the increasing resort to *terrorism—whether against state officials or common citizens—by political and even religious groups, intent on asserting "ideals" such as the right of peoples to self-determination or freedom for certain ethnic, political, or religious groups. The causes of terrorism are of course multifarious and often difficult to grasp. One contributing factor is certainly the existence of authoritarian structures within many states, not to mention profound social and economic inequalities among states. Yet another factor is the progressive fragmentation of the various centers of power in the international community and the corresponding proliferation of poles of interest. The international community is no longer crystallized into a few great blocs, each dominated by one Great Power, well able to control any centrifugal tendency. Because the Great Powers, which together could have dominated the world, have for many years found it difficult to reach agreement, the international community has now split into many centers of power of varying size, each with a modicum of authority; these centers tend to protect and aid private groups in other state communities, because they share common ideological, political, and religious roots. Another important factor is the inability of the international community in its organized forms (especially the UN) to offer an adequate response to requests for greater international justice, and to the need for preventive mechanisms to defuse economic and social conflicts both at the national and transnational levels. Yet another factor is the spread of utopian ideologies. These give rise to or strengthen groups that feel—to a greater or lesser degree—oppressed, and encourage them to consider legitimate the resort to violence. As such groups almost invariably lack the means to fight in a "conventional" way, they begin to conduct their battle by way of terrorism. Clearly, individuals and groups who wish to play a part on the international scene must choose another route than terrorism. This can be achieved only by a progressive transfer of power, prerogatives, and opportunities for action to individuals and groups working in harmony with the establishment, and not seeking to bring it down by violence. This is the only way to imbue the international community with nongovernmental, and therefore more "humane," values and exigencies, without undermining the current system of sovereign states and thereby risking the loss of all the current guarantees for restraining centrifugal forces. Obviously, this will be a long and arduous task, but it is equally evident that terrorism, far from disrupting the legal and organizational structures of the world community, has prompted states to step up their cooperation and devise mechanisms based on mutual interest, designed both to prevent terrorist groups from attacking innocent civilians or state officials, and, in case such attacks are carried out, to arrest the culprits and bring them to justice.

In contrast to the three aforementioned trends, a tendency exists in the international community which might, in the very long run, erode the role of international institutions and law: regionalization. It is common knowledge that regional (economic or political) institutions have been created in various areas of the world (e.g., the European Community, the Council of Europe, the Organization of American States, the Organization of African States). The reasons behind the drive toward setting up these institutions are obvious: within areas where states tend to share common political values, economic outlooks, and cultural backgrounds, it is much easier to achieve integration (at the political, economic, and normative and institutional levels) than in the world community at large. Arguably, regional integration might gradually make intergovernmental institutions superfluous. However, it seems more likely that regional bodies will not supplant world organizations but rather will constitute the building blocks for the progressive, if slow, construction of more adequate world institutions and legal rules than the present ones.

(See also DIPLOMACY; GROTIUS, HUGO; INTERNATIONAL COOPERATION; REALISM; TREATY; UNITED NATIONS.)

Wolfgang Friedman, *The Changing Structures of International Law* (London, 1964). Richard A. Falk, *The Status of Law in International Society* (Princeton, N.J., 1970). Eduardo Jiménez de Aréchaga, "International Law in the Last Third of a Century," *Hague Recueil* 159, no. 1 (1978). Antonio Cassese, *International Law in a Divided World* (Oxford, 1986). Richard A. Falk, *Revitalizing International Law* (Ames, Iowa, 1989). Thomas M. Franck, *The Power of Legitimacy among Nations* (New York, 1990). Antonio Cassese, "Violence, War and the Rule of Law in the International Community," in D. Held, ed., *Political Theory Today* (Cambridge, U.K., 1991), p. 255.

ANTONIO CASSESE

INTERNATIONAL MIGRATION. Given a world organized into mutually exclusive national communities that view themselves as family-like bodies with a common ancestry and a common destiny, international migration constitutes a deviation from the normal order of things. It entails not merely physical relocation, but a change of jurisdiction, from one sovereign state to another; and should the move be permanent, also a change in membership, from one political community to another. Both aspects of the process, emigration and immigration, therefore elicit considerable public concern and provoke political contention within and between countries. Yet transnational human flows have received much less attention from analysts of international affairs than have trade or strategic interactions.

Traditionally, social scientists conceptualized migrations as aggregates of individual movements, patterned by choices based on available information regarding economic and social conditions in the places of origin and of putative destination, usually termed "push" and "pull." In the 1970s this was modified by more structural approaches, which reconceptualized the "pull" in terms of the initiatives of capitalists in developed countries, motivated by the singular profitability of foreign labor, and the "push" in terms of displacement effects occasioned by dependent *development.

As this literature suggests, the most basic determinant of contemporary international migrations is the dramatic inequality of social and economic conditions in a world that is more integrated than ever before. No corner of the globe is now left that has not been restructured by market forces, uprooting the last remnants of subsistence economies, and propelling ever-growing numbers to move about in search of work. Information about conditions abroad is universally available, and the secular decline in the cost of long-distance transportation affords mobility to many of the inhabitants of even the poorest countries. Demographic projections suggest a continued expansion of the pool of potential migrants from the developing world. Although some less developed countries are experiencing economic growth, most will remain unable to provide jobs for their large and growing generations. Hence many people will attempt to relocate, whether or not their services are needed in the developed countries.

However, economic dynamics account for only part of international population movements. Approximately half of today's migrants are *refugees, driven out of their country by outright persecution at the hand of the government, or by life-threatening violence. The bulk of them also originate in the developing world, mostly as a by-product of the two major processes that generated waves of refugees in Europe in earlier times: attempts to create unified new states in culturally diverse regions, and confrontations between dominant and subordinate classes in societies marked by extreme inequality, maintained by authoritarian regimes. In the post–World War II era such conflicts have tended to evoke intervention by outside powers, often resulting in an expansion in their scope and duration. Internal wars are more destructive today because governments and their opponents have access to firepower in all its forms; furthermore, the impact of violence on poor and densely populated countries is particularly catastrophic, as it often reduces agricultural production below the subsistence level.

Yet, taken together, these economic and political conditions determine only potential movements. States exercise considerable control over actual movements across their borders. If most countries adopted extremely restrictive policies, such as an emigration policy akin to that of the German Democratic Republic (GDR) between 1961 and 1989, and an immigration policy patterned after that of Japan, there would be hardly any international migration to speak of.

What would occur if borders suddenly ceased to exist? Given the prevailing inequality, there would be a massive movement of people from the worse-off to the better-off countries, lasting until worldwide conditions were largely evened out. Hence it is evident that a primary function of immigration control is to preserve the advantageous conditions of better-off countries. But the impact of unfettered movement would go well beyond economics alone. Control over the inward movement of foreigners was deemed by the founders of *international law to constitute a fundamental attribute of *sovereignty on grounds of *security, because in its absence invaders might merely walk in. Beyond this, as Michael Walzer has emphasized ("The Distribution of Membership," in Peter G. Brown and Henry Shue, eds., *Boundaries: National Autonomy and Its Limits*, Totowa, N.J., 1981), no political community can function without a limit on membership, which today is denoted by *citizenship. From this perspective, immigration control constitutes but the first of a broad array of mechanisms for enforcing political boundaries, encompassing the whole of nationality law.

For these reasons, states normally maintain severely restrictive immigration policies, with little variation between regimes. The major exceptions were the United States and other overseas republics or dominions in the nineteenth century; but even then the United States qualified its laissez-faire by means of regulations designed to keep out those deemed unproductive, particularly "paupers," or considered unsuited for membership in the body politic, notoriously nonwhites and felons.

Today, the most fundamental feature of immigration policy worldwide is a general prohibition of entry for purposes of permanent settlement; it is in relation to this tacit baseline that specific exceptions are made. These commonly include the selective recruitment of foreign labor, often for a limited period; the possibility for members of the community to bring in close relatives; and the granting of asylum to people who qualify as refugees, and have no other place to go.

Within these limits there is some variation. The overseas democracies (United States, Canada, Australia, New Zealand) maintain a somewhat more open door than other industrialized states, especially with regard to family reunion, mostly as a consequence of the weight of earlier waves of immigrants in their political process. A few states have adopted "laws of return" providing for the admission of people who qualify as nationals on the basis of ancestry (Israel, Germany, the United Kingdom, Spain, and Italy). Within each type, countries tend to modify their stance in response to changing times. In the past century, the immigration policies of Western states have displayed a cyclical pattern of relative openness and restriction, shaped by fluctuating labor demand, itself a function of broad movements at the level of the *international political economy. These policies are interactive, in that the actions of any one receiver alter the situation faced by all the others.

The onset of economic expansion generates initiatives by some sectors of business to encourage immigration, and fosters more permissive attitudes toward immigrants and refugees more generally. As the flows increase, more is heard from the groups sensitive to the negative side: cultural conservatives who feel threatened by the arrival of heterogeneous groups, workers suffering from displacement effects, welfare officials faced with an overload. However, little is done until the onset of an economic downturn, when business itself adopts a negative stance. But once flows have begun, they tend to be self-sustaining, and liberal democracies are constrained from resorting to the draconian measures necessary to effectively close borders. Hence illegal immigration tends to rise, precisely at a moment when its impact is deemed most negative. This tends to move immigration to the fore of the political agenda.

The most recent cycle was triggered by the boom of the 1950s; by the early 1970s, the foreign-born constituted about seven percent of the population of the industrialized world as a whole, with the singular exception of Japan, and a much larger proportion of its labor force. The oil shock of 1973 and the ensuing recession prompted attempts to stem the ongoing flows. In the United States the focus was on illegal immigration, resulting in the belated enactment of the Immigration Reform and Control Act of 1986. Most European countries promulgated an immediate freeze on further recruitment and sought to return temporary workers to their countries of origin; but many of them were intent on staying, and massive deportation proved politically unfeasible. While insisting they were not "countries of immigration," the receivers provided for family reunion, which produced over the next two decades a large pool of "immigrants of the second generation," who by and large remain excluded from political participation. These ambiguities have fostered the formation of anti-immigration movements and political parties, among which the National Front in France is currently the most prominent, with a special insistence on the alleged unassimilability of Muslims. Concurrently, in the United States anti-immigration sentiment has focused on the formation of a Hispanic subculture.

Emigration policy ranges more widely. Under conditions of population scarcity and of international strategic and economic competition a generalized prohibition against departure accompanied European state formation. In the seventeenth century illegal emigration was a capital crime, tantamount to treason or desertion, legitimized on the grounds that subjects belonged substantially to their sovereign. But the same states did not hesitate to brutally rid themselves of unwanted populations or individuals such as religious or political dissenters and, later, ethnic minorities. Hence restrictive exit policies are associated with a high incidence of forced emigration, expulsion, and exile. Attempts to enforce cultural or political conformity often also prompted the target minorities to flee abroad.

These policies were incompatible with the emerging doctrines of political *liberalism, in which membership rests on consent. In the early decades of the nineteenth century recognition of the right of individuals to leave their country (and to return freely) became the hallmark of liberal regimes, with few qualifications (for example, the obligation for males to complete their military service). Adoption of a permissive stance was facilitated by soaring population growth, which occasioned what came to be viewed as a burdensome surplus of uprooted poor. Under the new conditions, emigration turned from a problem into a solution.

Twentieth-century authoritarian states adopted the stance of their absolutist predecessors; but thanks to their greater police capacity, they were able to close their borders even more tightly. The classic case was the Soviet Union, whose restrictive emigration policy arose in response to economic and political imperatives: to prevent a dwindling of the labor supply, especially of those with valuable skills, at a time when severe sacrifices were imposed in the name of socialist construction, as well as to prevent citizens from "voting with their feet" and thereby demonstrating lack of support for the regime. In an ideologically divided world, emigration was hailed by the other side as "defection," and thereby became even more problematic. The effectiveness of emigration as a weapon of political protest was well demonstrated by the exodus from the GDR in the 1950s, which prompted the erection of the Berlin Wall, and by the new wave of departures in the fall of 1989, which ultimately brought down the Wall, and with it the East German regime itself.

One of the most immediately perceptible by-products of the political liberalization of the *Warsaw Treaty Organization countries in the late 1980s was the opening of their borders. The international migration regime thus incorporates a fundamental asymmetry between the right to leave one's country,

which has come to be recognized as a fundamental human right, and the absence of an equivalent right to enter. With only a handful of states still preventing their citizens from leaving, movements are being regulated mainly by the states to which people seek admission. But immigration policy worldwide is in the restrictive phase of the cycle; hence the gap between potential and actual migration has grown to huge proportions, resulting in acute immigration pressure, and severe dilemmas at the gate. The one exception to the general trend is the gradual elimination of borders within the *European Community, which if and when completed would be tantamount to the creation of rudimentary European citizenship.

In the 1970s, the developing world was engulfed in an unprecedented refugee crisis; although most of the refugees remained in their region of origin, some (mostly Indochinese) were invited to resettle in Western countries, while others entered into the worldwide migratory stream and came seeking asylum at a time of generalized restriction and growing xenophobia. Concurrently, the proliferation of barriers against ordinary immigration prompted some migrants to try their luck by filing an asylum claim. Existing mechanisms for processing applications were rapidly overwhelmed, and the appearance of large numbers of questionable refugees further fueled xenophobic fires. This led to a tightening of procedures, with deleterious consequences for some genuine refugees. The prevailing restrictionist trend also largely counterbalances the newly gained freedom of citizens of the socialist world to leave their countries.

(See also AUTHORITARIANISM; EQUALITY AND INEQUALITY; FOREIGN WORKERS.)

Aristide R. Zolberg, "Contemporary Transnational Migrations in Historical Perspective: Patterns and Dilemmas," in Mary M. Kritz, ed., *U.S. Immigration and Refugee Policy: Global and Domestic Issues* (Lexington, Mass., 1983). Thomas Hammar, *European Immigration Policy: A Comparative Study* (London, 1985). Robin Cohen, *The New Helots: Migrants in the International Division of Labour* (Aldershot, U.K., 1987). Alan Dowty, *Closed Borders: The Contemporary Assault on Freedom of Movement* (New Haven, Conn., 1987). Aristide R. Zolberg, Astri Suhrke, and Sergio Aguayo, *Escape from Violence: Conflict and the Refugee Crisis in the Developing World* (New York, 1989).

ARISTIDE R. ZOLBERG

INTERNATIONAL MONETARY FUND. A central pillar of the postwar economic order established at the Bretton Woods Conference of 1944, the International Monetary Fund (IMF) was designed to oversee the global rules governing money in general and adherence to orderly currency relations among the industrial countries in particular. It also was intended to be a lender of last resort for rich and poor countries alike. But the world for which the IMF was created has long ceased to exist, and the IMF has found itself thrust into roles that were neither planned nor expected. Its primary mission has become to minister prescriptions to financially beleaguered economies in the *Third World. In the process, it has acquired immense influence over the economic destinies of many countries. It also has acquired a reputation as an unrelenting disciplinarian whose programs and policies produce economic austerity, social unrest, and political instability. In its proclivity for becoming enmeshed in controversy, the IMF is without peer among *international organizations. According to one claim, the IMF has overthrown more governments than *Marx and *Lenin combined.

The creation of the IMF reflected a reaction against the beggar-thy-neighbor practices such as currency restrictions and competitive devaluations that hobbled the world economy in the interwar period. It also represented the triumph of Keynesian ideas, which called for greater activism by the state to maintain growth and employment and to cushion the domestic economy against external dislocations. The IMF's articles of agreement call on it to provide its members "the opportunity to correct maladjustments in their balance of payments without resorting to measures destructive of national or international prosperity." It was enjoined, therefore, to dedicate itself to reducing the duration and intensity of upsets in international payments. Toward these ends, Britain, represented at Bretton Woods by none other than John Maynard Keynes, pushed for rules that would place the burden of adjustment to payments imbalances on surplus as well as deficit countries. Britain also argued for relatively automatic and generous access to a sizable volume of liquidity. These demands, which would be voiced repeatedly by developing countries in subsequent decades, were resisted by the United States, then the largest creditor state and the one with decisive influence over the essential elements of the monetary *regime. Although it became the first global agency to perform such a role, the IMF was endowed with only a modest amount of resources for short-term lending to countries running temporary payments problems. Access to the fund by any member was to be limited by a quota and, beyond a minimal threshold, governed by policy conditions, a principle referred to as "conditionality."

To avert both the rigidities of the gold standard and the turbulence of the experiments with floating rates in the 1920s and 1930s, the architects of the monetary regime decided on relative exchange stability. Each member of the IMF was required to establish a par value for its currency defined in terms of gold. These fixed exchange rates could be altered to correct a "fundamental disequilibrium" (a term never precisely defined), but only upon consultation with and approval of the IMF. The fund, in effect, was made the locus of the collective management of exchange rates. The code of behavior it was assigned to uphold also required liberal rules for international payments: members were to dismantle multiple exchange rates and discriminatory currency arrangements and, after a transitional period, to adopt convertibility for current account transactions.

Evolving Roles in the World Economy. The early years of the IMF are forgettable. As the enormity of the task of postwar recovery became apparent, the IMF was relegated to the sidelines. The United States, rather than the IMF, emerged as the primary source of financing for Western Europe. Moreover, the IMF could do little to induce countries to eliminate currency restrictions—the transition to covertibility was not completed by the major European countries until 1958, and by Japan not until 1964. However, by the end of the 1950s the IMF had become a focal point of international monetary collaboration. It came to occupy a central position in *balance of payments financing and began to exercise, in a more credible fashion, its authority to supervise the exchange practices of its members.

In the 1960s worries about a future liquidity shortage led to efforts to provide an alternative to what had become the number one form of global money, the U.S. dollar. These efforts led to the creation in 1969 by the IMF of the world's first artificial reserve asset, Special Drawing Rights (SDRs), to be allocated to members in proportion to their quotas in the fund. By then, however, the world faced a problem of excessive liquidity, thanks to the outflow of dollars brought about by the large external deficits of the United States. The regime of pegged exchange rates the IMF had been charged with overseeing came under considerable strain and finally collapsed on 15 August 1971 when the United States suspended convertibility of the dollar into gold. The IMF was eclipsed in both the initial but abortive attempts to reform the old regime and in the ensuing struggle to build a successor regime that would give the United States greater freedom of maneuver. That successor, formally sanctioned in the 1978 second amendment of the IMF articles of agreement, legalized what had evolved since 1973: floating exchange rates. The choice of exchange systems was left up to the discretion of each member. The IMF was asked to exercise "firm surveillance" over exchange rate policies but was given few binding rules to enforce this function, let alone any means of shaping the policies of the dominant economies.

In the 1970s, the IMF's role in balance of payments financing was undermined as well. The international capital markets assumed the task of recycling the massive surpluses of the *Organization of Petroleum Exporting Countries (OPEC), thereby becoming for the first time in the postwar years the principal instrument of lending for sovereign borrowers. Developed and developing countries alike, seeking to escape the strictures associated with conditional financing from the IMF, turned to private banks with alacrity. The industrial countries, which traditionally accounted for the bulk of IMF lending, ceased to be borrowers altogether before the end of the decade. On the other hand, most of the developing countries that turned to the fund for conditional lending were not sufficiently creditworthy to qualify for commercial finance. For an organization that already had been stripped of many of its functions in the monetary regime, the prospect of marginalization was very real. The IMF responded by expanding access to its resources, granting multiyear loans to allow longer periods for adjustment, and also by relaxing its conditionality provisions. However, the venture in liberalized lending was short-lived as the IMF, bowing to pressures from the *Reagan administration, reverted to its standard posture.

The predicament of the IMF at the beginning of the 1980s was captured by the title of a survey in *The Economist* of 26 September 1981: "Ministry without Portfolio." From an institutional standpoint, the declaration by Mexico in August 1982 that it was unable to service its external debt was a windfall. The IMF was called upon to assist in mounting a rescue operation that would be repeated as many other developing countries, beset by a convergence of external economic shocks and prolonged fiscal mismanagement, followed Mexico into bankruptcy. The IMF became the pivot in the strategy for managing the debt crisis. The rescheduling of not only official but also private debt was made contingent on the negotiation of an adjustment program with the IMF. For a while, the agency even was able to use its muscle to press commercial banks to extend new financing to debtor states. At the same time, however, it emphasized the sanctity of existing obligations and insisted that the debtors maintain full and timely servicing of their bank debts. Otherwise, recalcitrants were to be denied their own credits. The fund tipped the balance of bargaining power away from the debtors, so much so that it incurred the charge that it was serving as a collection agency for the banks.

The IMF was instrumental in defusing one of the most severe threats to the stability of the international financial system. Its intervention helped to avert a rash of defaults and moratoria, a rupture in relations between creditor and debtor states, and a collapse by any of the major banks. However, the debt crisis also revealed the limits of the influence of the IMF. Its presence was not enough to induce the banks to continue with "concerted"—i.e., involuntary—lending. Instead, the banks gradually reduced their exposure in developing countries and soon went into wholesale retreat. Nor did the tactics orchestrated thorough the IMF enhance the debtors' capabilities for resuming growth or returning to creditworthiness. On the contrary, to service their debts most debtors had to undergo a wrenching adjustment, strangling imports and slashing investment and consumption, thereby shrinking their economies. While the IMF was critical in containing the debt crisis, it did not succeed in resolving it. Unwittingly, by providing the organizational infrastructure for policies of muddling through, it even may have prolonged it. Only toward the end of the decade, as the strategy of debt restructuring began to unravel, was the IMF enlisted to offer financial support for debt reduction. However, the IMF ventured into financing debt reduction schemes with caution, given fears of the transfer of risk from the private creditors. The travails of debtor states left the fund with a worry of a yet more immediate and personal nature: as it began the 1990s, arrears to the IMF reached a record of US$4.5 billion (International Monetary Fund, *Annual Report, 1991*, p. 68).

All in all, therefore, the task of managing the debt crisis posed a mixed blessing for the IMF. On the one hand, it checked the institution's slide toward obsolescence. On the other hand, it dragged it into a quagmire from which it, like the debtors, could not readily disengage. The entanglement of the fund in sub-Saharan Africa, in particular, is conceded by many senior officials in the organization to have been a mistake, albeit not one of their choosing. And by accelerating the transformation of the IMF from a temporary to a permanent source of financing for many countries, the debt crisis took it even further from its original mandate in the world economy.

Organizational and Financial Structure. The IMF has been aptly compared to a credit union: every member makes a contribution to the union's pool of funds and can then draw on them when the need arises (Peter B. Kenen, *Financing, Adjustment, and the International Monetary Fund,* Washington, D.C., 1986, pp. 2–6). Central to its operation is the quota assigned to each member country. Quotas determine the size of a member's financial contribution, known as a subscription; its voting power in the IMF's decision-making bodies; the "access limits," or amounts it is entitled to borrow from the organization's lending facilities; and its share of SDR allocations. The size of individual quotas, in turn, is determined by a complex formula that measures each country's relative weight in the world economy—and by political bargaining. Quotas are adjusted periodically, typically as part of agreements on boosting the IMF's capital base. These have been increasingly protracted and contentious exercises as they entail both fresh outlays of funds and changes in the pecking order.

The stratification of power among states has been a constant, although rankings of power have changed: the IMF remains the preserve of the powerful and the affluent. The most notable changes have consisted of reshuffles within an existing hierarchy—specifically the Group of 5 (the United States, Germany, Japan, France, and Britain)—rather than the installation of a new hierarchy. Even in the formal attributes of power, the United States continues to command a preponderance. Thus, while its voting share has declined from one-third to one-fifth, the United States still has more than enough votes to prevent a change in the structure of the organization or in the distribution of quotas, two decisions that require a majority of eighty-five percent. While voting shares are fought over zealously, the prevailing practice has been not to resort to voting. Decisions typically are adopted by consensus. Moreover, on numerous policy issues, including the design of lending programs, the staff of the agency enjoys substantial autonomy. The staff is headed by the managing director who, as part of a convention that balances the consignment of the presidency of the *World Bank as an American fiefdom, is a European national. There has been one exception to the exclusivity of the North in the inner circle: Saudi Arabia. It has been co-opted by virtue of becoming the IMF's foremost supplier of borrowed resources, which, after paid-in subscriptions, are the primary source of the institution's liquid assets. Along with each of the Group of 5 countries, Saudi Arabia has its own seat on the twenty-two-member board of executive directors, who are responsible for conducting the day-to-day business of the organization. The other eighteen directors are not appointed but elected as representatives of country groupings. The majority of countries, therefore, have no direct representation. The executive directors formally derive their authority from the board of governors, the supreme policy-making organ, composed of the minister of finance or central bank head of each member, which meets annually.

The IMF has crafted a complex amalgam of procedures and mechanisms to govern access to its balance of payments assistance. This access is expressed in terms of tranches, each equivalent to twenty-five percent of a country's quota. The first of these, the so-called "reserve tranche," can be withdrawn automatically, much like a demand deposit. The next, the first of four "credit tranches," also is available with minimal conditions. Access to the next three, referred to as the "higher credit" tranches, is more demanding, as it is conditional on the conclusion of an adjustment program with the IMF. Early in its history, the IMF developed the standby arrangement as its main vehicle of conditional financing. The arrangement authorizes a country to draw, in installments, a line of credit, subject to adherence to measures stipulated in the adjustment program. The loans have a short-term focus, typically of one year, and are repayable within three to five years.

Over the years, the IMF has adapted its financing modalities in an effort to cope with altered circumstances. In 1963, it set up the Compensatory Financing Facility (CFF) to help countries, especially primary producers, experiencing shortfalls in export earnings for reasons beyond their control. In 1969,

it created a Buffer Stock Financing Facility to allow members to contribute to approved agreements designed to stabilize prices of individual commodities. These two facilities established the precedent for increasing access to financing beyond the limits set by credit tranches. In 1981, the CFF was expanded to assist countries facing payments difficulties brought about by higher cereal import costs. The scope of the CFF was broadened yet again in 1988, when it was replaced by the Compensatory and Contingency Financing Facility (CCFF), a mechanism intended to cover additional external shocks, such as higher world interest rates.

The Extended Fund Facility (EFF) was introduced in 1974 to provide balance of payments support for longer periods than those under traditional forms of assistance. EFF loans are intended to support medium-term programs, generally running for over three years, and are repayable over a maximum of ten years. In establishing the EFF, the IMF explicitly acknowledged the principle that the payments problems of many developing countries are "structural" in nature and, hence, that they require longer periods of adjustment. That same principle is embodied in the Structural Adjustment Facility (SAF) and the Enhanced Structural Adjustment Facility (ESAF). Both are geared toward adjustment programs with longer horizons. The programs are drawn up in negotiations with both the IMF and the World Bank. Compared to most IMF loans, which are at market terms, SAF and ESAF credits are extraordinarily concessional, carrying annual interest charges of only one-half percent. The borrowers, therefore, are without exception the poorest countries.

Its frequent disclaimers notwithstanding, over the course of the 1970s and 1980s the IMF evolved into a development institution. Nearly all the adaptations in its financing facilities were oriented toward developing countries. Over these same decades, it selectively loosened the links between quota size and borrowing ceilings to allow countries expanded access to its resources. And it recast its conditionality in significant directions: in the 1970s, loosening it; in the 1980s, tightening it to the point where low-conditionality lending all but vanished. By the end of the 1980s, if not much earlier, one of Keynes's gravest fears had been realized: the IMF had become a "grandmotherly" organization through and through (Sidney Dell, *On Being Grandmotherly: The Evolution of IMF Conditionality*, Essays in International Finance No. 144, Princeton, N.J., 1981).

Conditionality, Adjustment, and Development. Conditionality remains the core of the controversies that have embroiled the IMF. In many ways, it is at the heart of current conflicts between North and South about their respective positions in the world economy. The adjustment program a borrower is expected to undertake in return for a loan is formalized in a letter of intent to the IMF and codified in a set of "performance criteria" expressed in quantitative ceilings and targets. Compliance with these conditions is the test for continued access to the loan; a breach, on the other hand, normally triggers its suspension, an eventuality that often leads to a new round of negotiations over a new adjustment program. While there are variations from case to case, there is remarkable continuity in the contents of the programs. The standard measures—branded by critics as the "bitter medicine"—consist of limitations on credit expansion, reductions in government spending, restrictions on public sector wages and employment, increases in taxes or user fees, and devaluation of the national currency. Overwhelmingly, the focus is on demand restraint. The IMF's foray into structural adjustment has entailed a preoccupation with objectives that go beyond stabilizing balance of payments. Hence, its programs increasingly incorporate supply-side measures such as trade liberalization and financial reform. But such measures, intended to improve the economy's efficiency and expand productive capacity, are a complement to, not a substitute for, macroeconomic stabilization. As such, they do not usually constitute the core of conditionality.

At least five major lines of criticism have been leveled against IMF conditionality. In combination, they constitute a sweeping indictment of the role of the institution in developing countries. First, critics accuse the IMF of applying simplistic, largely monetarist, diagnoses of and prescriptions for the problems facing developing countries. Its policies, they hold, tend to assume that the causes of balance of payments problems are government mismanagement and profligacy; consequently, the IMF downplays both the external origins of payments disturbances and the structural rigidities of developing economies. Second, and relatedly, they charge it with making a fetish of instruments that often are misguided or perverse. For example, it has been shown that, in settings where exports cannot be increased quickly, devaluation can produce recessionary and inflationary outcomes with no benefits to the balance of payments. Third, the fund is castigated for insisting on large and swift changes in policy tools. Instead of more gradual and flexible adjustments, it has shown a strong penchant for shock treatments that, to many, amount to overkill, destabilizing countries both economically and politically. Fourth, the IMF is criticized for resorting to a spurious precision in devising performance criteria. Targets and ceilings tend to be set rigidly, and in pinpoint fashion, even though the analytical foundations may be wobbly. Yet a fifth contention is that the IMF has neglected the distributional implications of its lending policies. In particular, it is taken to task for doing little to cushion the impact on the poorer segments of populations, who are most likely to be hurt by higher prices for staples, cutbacks in health spending, and other hardships that commonly accompany adjustment programs.

In reality, the IMF is less doctrinaire in the application of conditionality than most of its critics would acknowledge. Its thinking about development is more eclectic than the presumed fixation with *monetarism would suggest. It has become more mindful of questions of political sustainability and distributive consequences. Its conditionality has evolved in directions that concede some of the arguments of its critics. However, two additional factors need to be weighed in any consideration of the issue of conditionality. First, the track record of IMF adjustment programs is anything but stellar. A wealth of studies, including some done by the agency itself, have arrived at similar findings: the record of compliance in IMF programs is weak and has grown weaker over time. In the majority of developing countries, failure of implementation has been the norm. Moreover, the economic performance of countries that do adhere to the performance criteria has not been dramatically different from that of countries that do not. The second factor is one that, even more than the first, lies beyond the control of the IMF: the balance between adjustment and conditionality has tilted away from adjustment to conditionality. Ironically, as claims on its loans fell due, during most of the 1980s the IMF took more resources out of the Third World than it put in, thereby itself becoming a net drain for debtor states. It had evolved into the executor of a bargain that struck many of these states as improbable: policy reforms with conditions that were stiffening in return for external support that was dwindling.

Life after Debt. As the IMF approached its fiftieth anniversary, it was a markedly different institution from the one founded at Bretton Woods. In its relations with the developed countries, it was only a shadow of its past self. It was all but reduced to a helpless bystander in the process of macroeconomic coordination among the leading industrial powers, the *Group of 7. These countries showed little enthusiasm about allowing the IMF to insinuate itself into the deals they struck with each other on monetary and fiscal policies. Over these countries, the fund's surveillance function is dead and is destined to remain so as long as they do not need to turn to it as supplicants. For the foreseeable future, the prospect of the IMF's becoming a global central bank—once the hope of some, the fear of others—also is remote at best.

In the developing countries, the IMF continues to act as the guardian of economic orthodoxy, even though it often finds itself preempted in that role by its twin across the street, the World Bank. Even beyond the debt crisis, the IMF is likely to remain the certifier of economic rectitude, providing the seal of approval that other actors have come to demand before lending to most developing countries. However, the agency is painfully aware that the debt crisis has left it a weaker institution in many ways. The inability to pursue a countercyclical lending policy during the worst economic crisis faced by the Third World since the Great Depression ranks among the most notable failures of the IMF, even though this was a failure ultimately decided by the fund's paymasters rather than by its managers. And its vaunted power notwithstanding, the IMF's ability to influence the implementation of adjustment programs has been marginal, despite the fact that developing countries have faced a dearth of alternatives. Even the utility of the IMF as a scapegoat for unpopular decisions has diminished. As one critic, who has sat opposite IMF officials at the negotiating table on numerous occasions, observes, "The epithet that a program is *fondo monetarista* is about as damning as possible in the Latin American political lexicon" (Jeffrey D. Sachs, "Conditionality, Debt Relief, and the Developing Country Debt Crisis," in Jeffrey D. Sachs, ed., *Developing Country Debt and Economic Performance*, vol. 1, Chicago, 1989, p. 267).

In 1990, the IMF had under its tutelage reform programs in more than fifty countries. For many of those countries, the decision to turn to the IMF was an act of desperation and negotiations with it an exercise in brinkmanship. The fund had become a lender of last resort in an unwittingly literal and ironic sense. In both developing and developed countries, there were widespread expressions of dissatisfaction with the IMF. Yet within two years the IMF was confronted with a task whose complexity rivaled anything it had attempted in the past, as *Russia and the other republics of the former Soviet Union were admitted to the institution. The Soviets had signed the Bretton Woods Agreement in 1944 but stayed clear of the fund and the World Bank as the *Cold War erupted. Having already taken the lead in the economic liberalization of the ex-socialist countries of Central and Eastern Europe, the IMF was designated the instrument for "the rescue of the century" (*New York Times*, 4 April 1992): guiding the transition of Russia from communist central *planning to market-based *capitalism. True to form, the IMF quickly became caught in a dispute with Russia as the *Yeltsin government balked at pressures to speed up the decontrol of energy prices and to cut back on subsidies to state enterrises.

(See also DEVELOPMENT AND UNDERDEVELOPMENT; FINANCE, INTERNATIONAL; INTERNATIONAL DEBT; INTERNATIONAL POLITICAL ECONOMY; KEYNESIANISM; NORTH-SOUTH RELATIONS.)

Richard N. Gardner, *Sterling-Dollar Diplomacy in Current Perspective* (New York; 1980). John Williamson, ed., *IMF Conditionality* (Washington, D.C., 1983). Tony Killick, ed., *The Quest for Economic Stabilization: The IMF and the Third World* (New York, 1984). Robert J. Myers, *The Political Morality of the International Monetary Fund* (New York, 1987). Catherine Gwin et. al., *The International Monetary Fund in a Multipolar World: Pulling Together* (Washington, D.C., 1990).

DON BABAI

INTERNATIONAL ORGANIZATIONS. One marked change in *international relations over the past century has been the dramatic increase in the number of international organizations. The advent of intergovernmental organizations (IGOs) is often traced to the founding of the International Telegraph Union in 1865 although there was a small number of limited membership bodies before that date. In 1909 there were only thirty-seven IGOs and 176 international nongovernmental organizations (NGOs); the respective figures today are around 400 and 5,000. There has also been a tremendous increase in the number of congresses and conferences that IGOs sponsor. In the middle of the nineteenth century there were about two to three such meetings a year; today there are close to 4,000 annually.

International organizations are particularly important in international relations because they generally constitute the central decision-making components of international *regimes and influence the development of these regimes. International regimes are systems of norms and rules in particular issue areas that regulate state behavior and decision making. Without the permanent decision-making institutions of international organizations the growth of *international cooperation to manage international *interdependence would be greatly curtailed.

There are four main types of voting arrangements (or requirements for the approval of decisions) in international organizations: unanimity, majority rule, selective majorities, and weighted voting. Throughout most of the nineteenth century IGOs had a voting rule of unanimity, that is, the support of all member states was required for the passage of resolutions. In the latter part of the nineteenth century some organizations began to pass recommendations by qualified majorities (usually two-thirds of the membership). In the twentieth century more organizations have been allowed to pass recommendations by majority votes, but states also have accepted selective-majority or weighted-voting formulas for legally binding resolutions. These formulas have specified that certain powerful states must give their consent to organizational decisions and/or that states' votes in the organizations should be weighted according to their importance in the issue area. For example, the UN Security Council requires that the five permanent members support or do not vote against a resolution, and the *International Monetary Fund (IMF) and *World Bank distribute votes largely according to states' financial contributions and require different majorities depending on the importance of the issues. In other words, power realities are integrated into the decision-making formulas of IGOs when their decisions are binding on member states.

There are four key functions or roles of IGOs in the development of international regimes: the facilitation of agreements, the altering of states' and nongovernmental actors' influence in the formation and implementation of regimes, the promotion of compliance with regime rules, and the legitimation of particular ideologies or international practices.

A central function of international organizations is that they facilitate the development of regimes and particular cooperative activities. Without permanent headquarters and secretariats and regularly scheduled meetings it would be very difficult for states to collaborate to the extent that they do. States could, of course, organize ad hoc meetings to deal with particular problems, but there certainly would not be the volume of meetings and accords that there are as a result of the presence of permanent organizations.

A second function of international organizations is that they alter the distribution of influence in international decision making and hence the nature of acceptable regimes. IGOs provide the large number of small and weak states with the opportunity to use their voting power to secure accords they could not ordinarily achieve. Since the 1960s most of these states have been developing or *Third World countries, and they have used their ability to pass and/or block resolutions to extract concessions from the developed world. Overall the process of coalition building to secure adequate backing for regimes or specific resolutions is now an integral part of international politics. Another notable feature of the decision-making process in many international organizations is the prominence of secretariat personnel. They are often the source of technical information, and they sometimes act in a mediatory capacity.

A third role concerns international organizations' promotion of compliance with accords, and these activities can be divided into explicit and implicit roles. The explicit roles concern the gathering of information on the compliance of states and nongovernmental actors with agreements and the settlement of disputes over the terms of the accords. In some organizations there are permanent dispute settlement institutions and/or procedures for the creation of dispute settlement bodies. International organizations sometimes apply *sanctions against states that do not comply with regime rules or organizational decisions (an example being the UN Security Council), but on the whole the application of sanctions and enforcement activities are left to the informal coordination of policies among member states.

International organizations sometimes perform an implicit role in the promotion of compliance—largely through the regulation of problems that must be managed for a particular regime to be politically acceptable. That is to say, states will be predisposed to violate regimes governing certain aspects of an issue area if other regimes are not created to manage other aspects. An example is what a number of international organizations have done to support the existence of free-access jurisdictional regimes for the oceans, airspace, and outer *space. They have established regulatory systems to prevent damages to the parties involved and to third parties while operating in the three nonterrestrial areas. Without such regulatory arrangements states would extend their jurisdictions into these regions in order to control damages to themselves and others.

International organizations also legitimate particular international practices and ideologies. This particular function is one that has been highlighted by neo-Marxist writers concerned with relations between developed and developing countries, but it is not confined to them. A frequently heard argument is that international organizations under the sway of the developed capitalist powers utilize their control of financial resources and information flows to legitimate particular domestic and international economic practices. In the words of Antonio *Gramsci, they promote "ideological *hegemony."

Proponents of the three major theoretical traditions in international relations (*realism, *liberalism, and neo-Marxism) have different perspectives on these four roles and on the significance of international organizations in global politics. Realists are rather pessimistic about prospects for significant international collaboration and do not attribute to international organizations any significant influence on international regimes. At most they might see such organizations as rather weak facilitators of agreements on regimes and of the most powerful states' hegemony in international relations.

Neo-Marxists for the most part share this perspective on the lack of importance of international organizations in global politics in that they see the hegemony of the most powerful capitalist powers as the central feature of global politics. However, some neo-Marxists are more likely than realists to stress the role of international organizations in facilitating (or legitimating) the hegemony of the most powerful countries—in their case, the dominance of the capitalist powers (the core) over the weaker developing states (the periphery). After the states in the periphery overthrow the hegemony of the core states, some neo-Marxists would probably project an expanded role for international organizations built on common interests among most peoples, but they do not predict such a development in the short run.

Those scholars who are most receptive to attributing important roles to international organizations are liberals. While liberals as a group differ in some important ways, they see international organizations as important in leading states to understand mutualities of interest, to acquire new values, and to learn the benefits of cooperation. Liberals also regard international organizations as important facilitators of the predominance of certain *ideologies—particularly economic liberalism and internationalism. In their view many international organizations that have been created in the post-1945 era (for example, the IMF and World Bank) have had significant impacts on the institutionalization of liberal economic and political values in international regimes.

(See also INTERNATIONAL POLITICAL ECONOMY; LAW OF THE SEA; NORTH-SOUTH RELATIONS; UNITED NATIONS.)

Inis L. Claude, Jr., *Swords into Plowshares: The Problems and Progress of International Organization*, 4th ed. (New York, 1970). Stephen D. Krasner, *International Regimes* (Ithaca, N.Y., 1983). Harold K. Jacobson, *Networks of Interdependence: International Organizations and the Global Political System*, 2d ed. (New York, 1984). Ernst B. Haas, *When Knowledge Is Power: Three Models of Change in International Organizations* (Berkeley, Calif., 1990).
MARK W. ZACHER

INTERNATIONAL POLITICAL ECONOMY.

Concerned with the political determinants of international economic relations, international political economy tries to answer such questions as: How have changes in the international distribution of power among *states affected the degree of openness in the international trading system? Do the domestic political economies of some states allow them to compete more effectively in international markets? Is the relative poverty of the *Third World better explained by indigenous conditions in individual countries or by some attribute of the international economic system? When can international economic ties among states be used for political leverage?

Some History. During the 1950s and 1960s *international relations as a field of study and a matter of public policy was concerned primarily with *security. The *Cold War dominated the interest of scholars and the attention of policymakers. International economic issues were a secondary concern. Between East and West economic transactions were highly politicized and tightly controlled. Among the countries of the West economic disputes were muted. The rules of the game and the patterns of international economic transactions were taken as given. There were only a few isolated scholars working on questions related to the political determinants of international economic relations.

Attention devoted to international political economy increased dramatically after 1970 for several reasons, some intellectual and academic, others related to political events. For the United States, things began to go awry. The U.S. balance of payments deficit increased in the late 1960s under the burden of the *Great Society and the *Vietnam War. The deficit prompted the *Nixon administration to initiate a chain of events that destroyed the postwar international monetary system based on the 1944 Bretton Woods Agreements. The U.S. decision first to suspend gold payments in August 1971, and ultimately to accept a system of flexible exchange rates, made it evident that international economic relations involved political choices and not just technical calculations. The quadrupling of oil prices in 1973–1974 drove home the fact that the United States was inextricably involved in a world economy which it could neither isolate itself from nor unilaterally control.

Attention to international political economy was further reinforced by academic developments. The old agenda of international politics had become exhausted. The study of international organization had not moved beyond an arid formality practiced by specialists in *international law. Economics as an academic discipline increasingly came to emphasize mathematical modeling as opposed to the study of specific empirical developments.

Hence, many developments—the *Organization of Petroleum Exporting Countries (OPEC) and the rise of oil prices, the collapse of the Bretton Woods monetary system, the demands of the Third World for a *New International Economic Order—were not being investigated by either political scientists or economists. This academic gap was a major incentive for the development of international political economy as a distinct field of study.

There is no consensus about how developments in international political economy should be explained. Analysts have pointed to the international distribution of power, the importance of mutual self-interest, class interests, and domestic political structures as explanations for outcomes in the world economy. The four major theoretical approaches to the field have been *realism, *liberalism, *Marxism, and domestic politics.

Realism. Realism makes the following basic assumptions: 1) The constituting actors in the *international system are sovereign states. 2) The international system is in a state of anarchy: there is no accepted political authority; states engage in self-help. 3) States must be primarily concerned with their own security and therefore with relative rather than absolute standing. A state must have the power to, at a minimum, protect its territorial and political integrity. 4) States are rational unified actors. Domestic politics, individual irrationality, or organizational failures have only a marginal impact on policies and outcomes.

The explanatory variable for realism is the distribution of power among states; for instance, *hegemony in which there is one dominant state, bipolarity in which there are two dominant states, or multipolarity in which there are several states of about equal power.

The evidence that realists utilize requires operationalizing the power of states by, for instance, looking at the size of armies, aggregate economic output, or the ability to make credible threats and offer rewards to other states.

The basic claim of realism is that given a particular distribution of power among states it is possible to explain both the characteristics of the system and the behavior of individual states. Realism makes no effort to probe the domestic determinants of foreign policy; what counts is state power and external constraints.

The most prominent argument derived from a realist perspective is the theory of hegemonic stability. Hegemonic stability asserts that a stable open international economic system is most likely when there is a hegemonic distribution of power; that is, when there is one state that is much more influential than any of the others. With regard to trade a hegemon is likely to favor openness because such a trading *regime would increase its economic well-being and economic growth, and provide it with more political leverage. A hegemonic power would also have the resources to entice or coerce other states into participating in an open regime, and to provide the system with collective goods such as financial resources to prevent a collapse of the banking system. International openness has been associated with two periods when there was an economic hegemon—Britain during the last part of the nineteenth century and the United States during the last half of the twentieth century.

Liberalism. The basic assumptions of liberalism are the following: 1) There are a multiplicity of actors in the international system. These include multinational corporations, international organizations, foundations, and terrorists as well as states. 2) These actors are rational and calculating but they pursue a multiplicity of different objectives. Different actors have different power capabilities in different areas. 3) *International relations and especially international political economy both offer opportunities for everyone to gain at the same time. Actors are more concerned with their absolute well-being than with their relative position vis-à-vis others.

The explanatory variable for liberalism is the configuration of interests and capabilities associated with a given issue area.

The evidence that is needed for a liberal perspective involves specifying the relevant actors (states, multinationals, etc.), assessing their resources, and stipulating their objectives.

Liberalism is the international analogue to pluralist analyses of the domestic polity. There are many different actors with different interests. There are opportunities for cross-cutting cleavages. A liberal analysis suggests more of a tendency to system stability than is the case for realism because there are more opportunities to cut deals. Actors are not simply involved in a zero-sum game to maximize their own relative power.

The most important development for a liberal perspective is the growth of *interdependence. As transportation and communications costs have declined, international economic transactions—trade, finance, *technology transfer—have increased dramatically. The benefits of an open world economy have increased. More and more actors have a stake in a stable international economic order.

The most important recent development in the area of international political economy, cooperation theory, is a hybrid between realist and liberal approaches. It is realist in its assumption of unified rational actors but liberal in its assumption of a non-zero-sum world in which absolute gains are more important than relative position. For cooperation theory the basic problem is to resolve collective action problems in which individual choice leads to suboptimal outcomes; for instance, no one state wants to act as a lender of last resort in a financial crisis, but the absence of a lender of last resort could leave every state worse off.

The most important statement of the theory of cooperation in the literature that is explicitly directed to the study of international political economy is Robert Keohane's *After Hegemony* (1984), which argues that cooperation is possible even without a hegemonic state if institutions can overcome problems of market failure. By providing more information, establishing mechanisms for monitoring, and generating shared expectations institutions can create an environment in which interstate cooperation is possible even without a single dominant leader.

Marxism. Marxism makes the following basic assumptions: 1) The basic actors in the social system are classes defined by their relationship to the means of production. 2) In international relations the interests of classes are manifest in the policies of states and other actors.

The explanatory argument for Marxism delineates the way in which capitalism generates inherent contradictions—a declining rate of profit, underconsumption, and a growing tension between the socialization of labor and the continued private concentration of ownership and political power—and the efforts of capitalist states to overcome these contradictions. For *foreign policy this implies that capitalist states must be imperialistic because they need to maximize the opportunities for foreign investment, access to new sources of raw materials, and the use of cheap foreign labor. *Capitalism is inherently a system of exploitation and, in the international system, this implies that the wealthy capitalist core will exploit the Third World periphery.

The evidence utilized by Marxist perspectives involves the concentration of economic power and the sociopolitical characteristics of economic systems.

Marxist analysis of the international political economy has concentrated on the relations between the rich and the poor areas of the world. The most prominent exemplar of this approach has been *dependency theory, which maintained that both the wealth of the capitalist core countries and the poverty of the Third World periphery was a function of the exploitative mechanisms of the world capitalist system. Capitalist states used foreign aid and military assistance to keep conservative regimes in power.

Multinational corporations used their privileged access to external markets to prevent the development of technologically advanced production in the periphery. Raw materials companies despoiled the natural resources of less developed countries.

Developments in the 1980s, not only the collapse of the communist system in Eastern Europe but, more important, the economic success of some Third World countries, raised very serious questions about the empirical validity of dependency theory. If Taiwan and the Republic of Korea (South Korea), which were economically backward areas in the 1950s, could develop so spectacularly in the 1970s and 1980s, could capitalism be seen as an inherently exploitative system? As variation in the performance of Third World states increased over time, dependency theory, with its focus on the world capitalist system as opposed to the indigenous characteristics of individual states, became more problematic.

Domestic Politics. The final theoretical focus of international political economy has been the relationship between domestic political structures and the international system. One of the striking successes of international political economy as a field of study is that it has integrated international relations and *comparative politics, fields that were much more distinct before 1970. There are two important lines of inquiry. The first examines the impact of the international system on domestic political structures. The second investigates how variations in domestic political structures affect foreign economic policies and outcomes.

There is no dominant argument about the impact of the international system on domestic political structures. The works of Peter Katzenstein and Ronald Rogowski are illustrative. In *Small States in the World Economy* (1985), Katzenstein argues that the development of what he calls democratic corporatism in the small European countries (Austria, Sweden, Switzerland, Denmark, the Netherlands, Norway, and Belgium) reflects their heavy involvement in the international economy. In democratic corporatist polities distinctions between state and society are blurred and all important groups are incorporated into political decision making. Such inclusive political institutions are needed to lessen the risk of internecine quarrels that would be economically disastrous because they would preclude swift adjustment to rapidly changing external conditions.

Ronald Rogowski in *Commerce and Coalitions* (1989) shows how changes in the international opportunity for trade can have a dramatic impact on the power of domestic groups within a given political system. More trade strengthens the position of abundant factors of production and weakens that of scarce factors. For instance, in a country with an abundance of labor but a scarcity of capital and land, new trading opportunities would be beneficial

for workers but harmful to the interests of the holders of capital and land because production would shift toward labor-intensive activities and away from capital-intensive and land-intensive activities.

The second line of inquiry relating domestic political structures and the international economic system examines the ways in which different domestic structures affect foreign economic policies. One prominent example of this kind of approach distinguishes between weak and strong states. In weak states political power is fragmented among many institutions—the legislature, public bureaucracies, private pressure groups. It is difficult to formulate a coherent foreign economic policy. The United States is the most obvious example. In polities with strong states power is concentrated in the hands of a small number of actors in the executive branch who can set policy and secure, through coercion or incentives, the support of major groups in civil society. Japan is the illustrative case.

In sum, international political economy has been concerned with developments in the world system that are only likely to become more important in the years to come. International trade and financial flows, which have always been important, are becoming even more salient for the well-being of individual states and their citizens. Because of their saliency, decisions about international economic policy will not be left to the private sector or to faceless technocrats; they will be a matter of concern for political leaders and their constituencies. The challenge of international political economy is how best to understand these concerns and the behaviors and outcomes that they generate.

(See also CLASS; FINANCE, INTERNATIONAL; INTERNATIONAL COOPERATION; INTERNATIONAL ORGANIZATIONS; PLURALISM.)

Charles P. Kindleberger, *The World in Depression* (Berkeley, Calif., 1973). Immanuel Wallerstein, *The Modern World System* (New York, 1974). Peter A. Gourevitch, "Second Image Reversed: The International Sources of Domestic Politics" *International Organization* 32 (Autumn 1978): 881–912. Stephen D. Krasner, ed., *International Regimes* (Ithaca, N.Y., 1983). Richard Rosecrance, *The Rise of the Trading State* (New York, 1985). Robert Gilpin, *The Political Economy of International Relations* (Princeton, N.J., 1988).

STEPHEN D. KRASNER

INTERNATIONAL RELATIONS

A generic concept for a vast array of activities, ideas, and goods that do or can cross national boundaries, international relations (IR) embraces social, cultural, economic, and political exchanges that occur in ad hoc as well as institutionalized contexts. Because communication and transportation technologies continue, relentlessly, to lower the barriers and shrink the distances that separate cultures, societies, economies, and *states, fewer and fewer realms of experience remain outside the domain of IR.

For some researchers the broad array of IR phenomena is viewed as the basis of a "field." A few even see it as the paramount discipline because its scope extends across the globe and because its concerns embrace every dimension of human experience. For a preponderance of those who probe IR, however, its vast empirical domain is regarded as too broad for any one discipline, let alone any one investigator, to probe in its entirety. The facets of individual and collective behavior relevant to any IR problem, it is argued, are too numerous and too diverse for the development of coherent theories and methodologies necessary to the disciplined procedures that comprise a recognizable and viable field.

Whether or not one considers IR a separate field, inquiries into its dynamics might be expected to be profoundly interdisciplinary, with scholars joined in collaborative efforts to unravel the complexities of particular problems, countries, regions, institutions, or processes. Such synthesizing of expertise, however, is more the exception than the rule. Most inquiries into IR tend to be narrowly confined to work in a single discipline. Rarely do these separate endeavors converge. Rather, the practitioners in each discipline tend to hold constant the variables that tap the skills of their disciplines.

This account of a fragmented "nonfield" describes only part of the intellectual framework that has evolved in international studies. A more salient characteristic is that most students of the subject are political scientists and most inquiries focus on one or another political aspect of IR. The number of sociologists, anthropologists, psychologists, economists, and historians who specialize in international exchanges is small, both within each of their disciplines and within international studies itself. Professional societies such as the International Studies Association have long sought to develop a multidisciplinary membership, but their efforts have largely been in vain. Their governing councils and annual meetings continue to be dominated, reluctantly, by political scientists, many of whom frequently voice the hope that colleagues from the other social sciences will join their ranks, or at least focus their analytic skills on international problems.

So predominant are political scientists, in fact, that the domain of IR is often referred to as "international politics." For all practical purposes, this term and IR have become virtually synonymous. Indeed, this terminological ambiguity also extends to labels such as "world politics," "international studies," and "foreign affairs."

Fragmentation and Dominance. However regrettable the fragmentation of IR and its dominance by political scientists, this skewed state of affairs can be readily explained. One reason for it is that the most developed of the social sciences, especially economics and psychology, are so preoccupied with

and confident of their paradigms that their practitioners are disinclined to look for collaborative work with colleagues in the less developed social sciences. Such an attitude is further reinforced by a reward structure wherein advancement tends to go to those who make a mark through disciplinary research rather than to those who engage in interdisciplinary or multidisciplinary inquiry.

Another source of the fragmented state of IR studies is a continuing tendency toward specialization in the various disciplines, a narrowing of foci such that investigators become expert at probing deeply but not broadly into their subject matter. The result is that they are unlikely to encounter interdisciplinary problems.

But perhaps the prime reason for the skewed state of the nonfield is to be found not in the structure of disciplines but in the structures of IR itself and, especially, in the long-standing tendencies of these structures to collapse into destructive *wars. Historically the activities of international actors have neither been subject to a central authority nor governed by widely shared norms. Thus IR does not offer the underlying substantive coherence on which most of the social sciences are founded. Sociology has long derived minimal coherence from the presence of all-encompassing entities called societies, which tend to be national in scope and which, as such, serve to coordinate the hierarchies, value consensuses, habitual practices, policy goals, and institutional arrangements that evolve under their auspices. Likewise, leaving aside for the moment the subfield of international economics, the discipline of economics has maintained coherence by focusing predominantly on economies that are national in scale and that, as such, have managed the practices and institutions whereby markets are created, investments generated, trade flows sustained, and the labor force trained and employed. Much of political science, too, has been organized around a national entity, the polity or the state, which has the sovereign authority to maintain order, provide justice, protect territory, conduct *foreign policy, and otherwise enhance the general welfare.

IR does not fit these disciplinary boundaries. No international or world society subsumes national societies and infuses coherence into the subject. No international or world government exercises authority over national states. No world economy (again ignoring for the moment recent globalizing dynamics) controls national markets and the flow of foreign trade, investments, currencies, and labor. Quite to the contrary, if there is any aspect of IR about which the diverse approaches to the subject fully agree, it is that the systemic properties of IR are best characterized as anarchical—that is, there are no centralized institutions capable of prevailing over any or all international actors. The *anarchy of IR does not amount to sheer disarray because the cooperative and patterned interactions of the actors that do possess authority have resulted in the evolution of international structures. Nevertheless, it is an anarchical system in the sense that an overarching global authority has yet to evolve which coherently links its components into a common system of rule.

It is hardly surprising, therefore, that the analysts who gravitate toward the study of IR have been primarily those relatively few political scientists inclined to gear their disciplinary skills toward the phenomena in which bargaining, coercion, and other techniques of statecraft are used either to maintain cooperation and balance or to sustain conflict and wage war in the absence of an overall authority. Both through default and intellectual concern, in other words, IR has been skewed by the predominance of political scientists who are either not put off by the anarchical nature of IR or who are drawn to the subject by predispositions to explain and avert the devastating effects of war.

The Impact of Change. These characteristics of international studies are now showing signs of transformation because the patterns of boundary-crossing activities that comprise IR have in themselves begun to change profoundly in recent years. Not only have the arrangements for managing international affairs that emerged after World War II—the *Cold War era—come to an end, but the dynamics that underlie the prevailing arrangements appear to be undergoing significant alterations.

In the first place, because of the ways in which diverse technologies have rendered social life ever more complex and interdependent, the repercussions of the boundary-crossing activities that comprise IR are no longer confined to contiguous relationships or even regional affairs. Rather, their reach has become global: intended or not, virtually any interaction that transgresses national boundaries can today precipitate ripple effects everywhere in the world. Second, and no less important, these activities are no longer restricted to nation-states. A wide range of "nonstate" actors—some transnational, others subnational—now engage in these activities in such a way as to have significant consequences for the course of events and the structures of world affairs. Third, the greater density of actors and the greater complexity of their interactions has resulted in a declining utility of military force and an increased preoccupation with the economic dimensions of global life. War is by no means an obsolete instrument of policy, but the ability to achieve goals through threatening or resorting to coercive means has lessened and, accordingly, so has the attractiveness of military action. Fourth, the globalization of IR, the proliferation of its actors, the delegitimation of war, and a host of other dynamics have weakened the competence of national governments, heightened the coherence of subnational governments, expanded the readiness of citizens to join in collective action, and thus brought about authority crises in many parts of the world, sometimes relocating authority either "upwards" in the direction of transnational entities or "downwards" toward subnational collectivities.

All these changes have had the cumulative effect of eroding and obscuring the boundaries that separate countries, that differentiate domestic from foreign affairs, and that distinguish economics from politics. Strictly speaking, in other words, IR as "inter-nation" relations has increasingly become a misnomer. It may not be long, in fact, before the aforementioned terminological ambiguity yields to a new, more accurate set of overall labels such as "transnational relations" or "global affairs."

Among the more obvious indicators of the transformations at work in IR is the emergence of *international political economy (IPE) as a specialized field of inquiry and the advent of international regimes as a concept employed by many investigators. Although still very much the focus of political scientists rather than of collaborative work between them and economists, IPE has mushroomed since the 1970s as the prime subfield of international studies. In addition to a vast outpouring of journal articles and research monographs devoted to one or another aspect of IPE, courses and textbooks on the subject have proliferated, and so have IPE subfields for graduate and undergraduate degrees.

The substantive foci, concepts, and problems of IPE are too diverse, however, to constitute a separate discipline. Like IR, IPE consists of congeries of research interests and theoretical foci that do not derive from a common framework and, indeed, are often contradictory. They share only a concern for the overlap of economic and political dynamics in one or another situation.

Similarly, the turn away from military affairs and toward *political economy has heightened an awareness that international actors can be as cooperative in their relationships as they are potentially conflictful. Given the absence of an overarching global authority structure, this awareness has led to the question of how and why sovereign states and autonomous nonstate actors manage to cooperate sufficiently to move toward their goals and avoid breakdowns in their relationships. In response to this question, the concept of international *regime has emerged to fill the conceptual gap. Most fully set forth in *International Regimes,* edited by Stephen D. Krasner (Ithaca, N.Y., 1983), an international regime is conceived to consist of shared norms, rules, principles, and procedures to which all the actors in a particular issue area subscribe, either tacitly or explicitly, sufficiently to maximize cooperation and minimize conflict in that issue area. Hence, for example, the IR literature is filled with research on the "oil regime," the "monetary regime," the "whaling regime," and so on through all the issues that crowd the global agenda.

Diverse Approaches and Theories. It must quickly be noted that some, perhaps many, IR analysts do not agree with the foregoing discussion of the impact of change. Yes, they concur, the Cold War has ended and the present is in many ways considerably different from the past in IR. But, asserts this line of reasoning, the changes involve shifts within the interstate system that has prevailed for four centuries, not transformations of that system. States may be somewhat weaker and other types of actors may have expanded their capacities, but states still retain their sovereign rights and can still resort to coercive techniques to enforce their will. Consequently, all the changes of recent decades, although not trivial, are occurring in a constant context. The state-centric, anarchical system, this argument concludes, is still functioning as it always has.

Those who stress continuity over change in world politics tend to share a realist or neorealist approach to the subject. Realists and neorealists view history as demonstrating the appropriateness of states as the most encompassing entity capable of maintaining the coherence of societies, protecting the borders of countries, and advancing the collective interests of its citizens. This perspective thus regards states as durable, as capable of resisting any changes that might undermine their core interests. Unlike neorealists, realists presume that the core interests of different states are antithetical to one another and that, accordingly, states endlessly seek to enhance their power in order to serve their national interests. Despite the absence of an overarching global authority, the pursuit of conflictful interests by states is not seen by realists to result necessarily in a war of all against all. War does sometimes occur, but realism posits the conflicts among states as tending toward equilibrium as states shift their *alliance relationships to maintain the balance of power whenever its coherence is threatened.

Although the neorealist perspective also emphasizes the durability of states and their reliance on power to serve their national interests, it differs from realism by virtue of a lesser concern with the diplomatic, military, and strategic sources that sustain or alter the *balance of power and a greater preoccupation with the socioeconomic and political dynamics that enable states to overcome their differences and accommodate to each other. Most neorealists therefore tend to be students of IPE and to see utility in the regime concept as a means for explaining the adaptability of states and the interstate system. Indeed, it is probably the case that neorealism is presently the most widely shared perspective in international studies.

More accurately, neorealism appeals widely to IR analysts in the United States and Europe. Students of the subject in the *Third World are much less concerned with identifying and specifying the overall perspective or paradigm within which they conduct their inquiries. Preoccupied with the dire plight of their country and region, Third World investigators tend to eschew theory, to be highly pragmatic, and

to focus on policy problems. To the extent that some Third World students of IR do turn their attention to tracing and explaining overall patterns, they tend to be attracted to *dependency theory, a perspective that posits the Third World as historically exploited by the rich industrial nations of the Northern Hemisphere. Put differently, realism and neorealism are the most widely held IR perspectives because the study of IR is undertaken mostly in the West and, especially, in the United States.

But a quick review of the history and present status of IR studies in the West clearly reveals that *realism and neorealism are not the only perspectives that organize and sustain teaching and research. Realism was not the first broad approach to IR studies that enjoyed wide acceptance. Previously, during the period between the first and second world wars, *idealism was the dominant perspective. Stimulated by Woodrow Wilson's call for effective international institutions and "open covenants openly arrived at," IR specialists devoted the interwar decades mostly to probing issues of *international law and morality, an effort which was idealist in the sense that questions of power and its utilization tended to be ignored, as if the ascendancy of international organizations and law would be sufficient to prevent war and inappropriate, amoral exercises of power. When *Hitler exercised German power, ignored the constraints of international law and morality, and overran Europe, the ground was laid for the realist perspective to replace idealism as a basis for grasping and researching world politics. Munich—where Britain and France acceded to German demands in 1938, hoping to achieve "peace in our time"—became a symbol of the failure of idealism and a spur to framing a "realistic" approach to the challenges of world politics. World War II could have been averted, the realists claimed, if France and Britain had not let their ideals distort their calculations of national interest and had told Hitler they would contest Germany on the battlefield rather than yield to his demands.

Anticipated by E. H. Carr in The 20 Years' Crisis: 1919–1939 (London, 1939) and subsequently elaborated compellingly by Hans J. Morgenthau in successive editions of his postwar text Politics Among Nations (New York, 1972), realism became the dominant approach to IR in the late 1940s and 1950s. It also served as the prime intellectual foundation for the perceptions of the threats and the framing of the policies that came to be called the Cold War. Indeed, echoes of Hitler and Munich reverberated powerfully through the first post–Cold War crisis as much of the world engaged in collective action to contest Iraq's conquest of Kuwait in 1990.

With the introduction of scientific methods into the social sciences late in the 1950s, some IR analysts were emboldened to question the adequacy of realism and its core assumption that all states conduct themselves similarly in the international arena. The state is not an abstraction, they argued, but rather consists of identifiable decision makers who respond to a variety of internal as well as external stimuli when they define their interests and exercise their power. And because states are dissimilar in their structures, histories, and capabilities, this reasoning emphasized, their officials are bound to vary in their conduct of foreign relations. These reactions to realism thus gave rise to the behavioralist approach to IR, which predominated throughout the 1960s and into the 1970s. To grasp world politics, the behavioralists contended, it is necessary to uncover the patterns whereby the duly constituted decision makers of states perceive the world, respond to challenges, frame problems, and ultimately make the choices embodied in their foreign policies. But the recognition of these patterns involved more than reflection and judicious historical inquiry for the behavioralists. They asserted that better methodologies, those used by scientists, were available to differentiate between recurring patterns and deviant cases in world politics, that through systematic quantification of the relevant variables it was possible to probe beneath the abstractions around which the realist perspective was organized.

For a variety of reasons, the promises of behavioralism were not fulfilled before doubts about its utility set in. Like realism, it too yielded its predominant position. By the 1980s, with the ever-greater *interdependence of world affairs and the continuing shift toward a global economy, the neorealist perspective took hold, as did pluralist and transnational approaches that stressed the importance of nonstate actors and the diversity of the processes through which international affairs unfold. In addition, Marxist and neo-Marxist formulations which emphasized the centrality of the capitalist world economy as a determinant of global life emerged as alternative perspectives that organized the work of numerous IR investigators in Europe and elsewhere. Although distinctly a minority group, some analysts were also attracted to postmodernist philosophy as a means of understanding the "subtexts" of IR.

Still another recent perspective, developed by the present author in Turbulence in World Politics (Princeton, N.J., 1990), posits world politics as bifurcated into two prime structures. According to this view, states in the interstate system are active primarily in the diplomatic-political-military arena; diverse nonstate actors, meanwhile, are seen as forming a "multicentric" system that processes mainly socioeconomic issues. These two broad systems of world politics are conceived to be essentially independent of each other even as they are also competitive and interactive. More importantly, the bifurcated structure of IR is viewed as especially conducive to the management of the tensions between change and continuity that are so acute in the present era: whereas the state-centric system is seen as well suited to coping with the persistent and pervasive pressures

for conducting world politics along long-established lines, the multicentric system is regarded as capable of absorbing the dynamics whereby authority is undergoing relocation in both upward and downward directions. Put differently, this perspective synthesizes the neorealist and transnational approaches in such a way as to infuse coherence into a multiplicity of diverse global processes that otherwise seem discrepant and contradictory.

This account of the recent history of IR studies may leave the impression that the several shifts to new perspectives occurred easily. Such was not the case, however. As documented by K. J. Holsti in The Dividing Discipline: Hegemony and Diversity in International Theory (Boston, 1985), the shifts were the focus of intense debates and an escalated rhetoric about the proper paths to international "truth." This was especially the case when the behavioralists began to challenge the realists: as can be seen in the compendium of essays edited by Klaus Knorr and James N. Rosenau (Contending Approaches to International Politics, Princeton, N.J., 1969), each side was capable of viewing the other as misguided regarding the philosophical premises and research methodologists most suited to discerning, measuring, and assessing the underlying dynamics of world politics. A symposium edited by Robert O. Keohane (Neorealism and Its Critics, New York, 1986) reveals that the neorealist perspective also evoked considerable controversy over its premises and potential as an overall guide to inquiry.

On the other hand, it is perhaps a measure of maturation in the study of IR that more recently both the foci and intensity of such debates have undergone change. Where the controversies once raged around methodological and epistemological issues, today analysts argue mostly about substance—about whether international regimes are in fact operative, about whether the hegemonic leadership of the United States has undergone decline, about whether another country is likely to surface as the hegemon of the twenty-first century, about the extent to which states and the interstate system are undergoing transformation—almost as if a live-and-let-live attitude has set in with respect to methodological questions. Even the substantive debates appear to be conducted within the context of a shared tolerance, a readiness to acknowledge that there are no simple answers, that IR has become extraordinarily complex, and that therefore understanding is best advanced through a variety of approaches.

Notwithstanding the climate of tolerance that presently marks inquiry into IR, as of the 1990s, with competing perspectives continuing to anchor the work of analysts in different parts of the world, the study of the subject is as fragmented as world politics itself. Whether the end of the Cold War, the decline of *superpowers, the upward and downward relocation of authority, the weakening and yet continued viability of states, and the unrelenting pace of change will lead to a convergence around fewer approaches remains to be seen. The history and complexity of IR, however, make it seem very doubtful that any single conception of the dynamics of global politics will come to unify the study and teaching of global affairs.

(See also INTERNATIONAL SYSTEMS; LIBERALISM; MARXISM; MULTINATIONAL CORPORATIONS; PLURALISM; POSTMODERNISM.)

Richard C. Snyder, H. W. Bruck, and Burton Sapin, eds., Foreign Policy Decision-Making: An Approach to the Study of International Politics (New York, 1962). Hedley Bull, The Anarchical Society: A Study of Order in World Politics (New York, 1977). Kenneth N. Waltz, Theory of International Politics (Reading, Mass., 1979). Robert O. Keohane, After Hegemony: Cooperation and Discord in the World Political Economy (Princeton, N.J., 1984). Immanuel Wallerstein, The Politics of the World-Economy: The States, the Movements, and the Civilizations (Cambridge, U.K., 1984). Robert Gilpin, The Political Economy of International Relations (Princeton, N.J., 1987). Ernst-Otto Czempiel and James N. Rosenau, eds., Global Changes and Theoretical Challenges: Approaches to World Politics for the 1990s (Lexington, Mass., 1989). James Der Derian and Michael J. Shapiro, eds., International/Intertextual Relations: Postmodern Readings of World Politics (Lexington, Mass., 1989). James N. Rosenau and Ernst-Otto Czempiel, eds., Governance without Government: Order and Change in World Politics (Cambridge, U.K., 1992).

JAMES N. ROSENAU

INTERNATIONAL SYSTEMS. In a 1947 Princeton speech General George C. Marshall doubted "whether a man can think with full wisdom and with deep convictions regarding certain of the basic issues of today who has not at least reviewed in his mind the period of the Peloponnesian War and the fall of Athens"; he probably had in mind *Thucydides' time-defying claim to have written his history not for momentary popularity, but "for all time." Indeed, Thucydides wished to discover an exact knowledge of the past "which (human nature being what it is) will, at some time or other and in much the same ways, be repeated in the future."

Definitions and Cautions. Although Thucydides would not have used the term, contemporary scholars would attribute the regularities that made such fruitful comparisons possible to the systematicity of *international relations, meaning, in Thucydides' case, the regularized connections between the component units of the Greek-cum-Persian international system, and vis-à-vis its external environment. In the contemporary sense, real international systems consist of the major units of international life, their regularized relationships with each other, and vis-à-vis their internal and external environments.

In the case when the component units are sovereign *states, Martin Wight (Systems of States, Leicester, 1977) characterizes these defining relationships as of four sorts: messengers, including heralds, ambassadors, resident agents, spies, and hostages; conferences and international institutions; a common language (presumably including the cultural and diplomatic meanings that make linguistic communication possible); and trade and commerce, which he argues have been of special importance in the development of state systems. To this may be added the regularities of human-environmental interchanges, among which can be distinguished technological/resource, biochemical/ecological, and cosmological aspects.

Some of the most interesting international systems have not been state systems. Asian and African civilizations and the pre-Columbian Americas have produced a number of hierarchically structured suzerain systems of considerable longevity. Medieval Europe witnessed a complex of interpenetrating transnational political and religious hierarchies within which a variety of local nonsovereign political entities found their place.

As even this brief listing of variant international systems suggests, several cautions are in order with respect to Thucydides' oft-cited search for timeless (and universally valid) truths. Perhaps the better analogical ideal for students of international systems is neither Ptolemy's nor Kepler's nor Newton's nor Einstein's laws of planetary motion, but the kinds of developmental historical processes that have led to the supersession of one of these theoretical accounts by another in human scientific understanding. Then again, such cumulative, developmental thinking may be too modernistic or optimistic. More realistic alternative historical accounts of international systems might look like histories of dynasties or families, living in different contexts. Think of the rise and disintegration of empires or civilizations, or the transition from limited *balance of power equilibria to global hegemonic systems, themselves subject to ecological overextension and exhaustion.

Second, any feminist might legitimately raise the question whether the abstractly inclined men that George Marshall had in mind, and the extremely masculine political world of the Greeks and Persians that Thucydides studied, exhausted the possibilities of human nature. Even Giambattista Vico, a politically conservative Catholic writer of the eighteenth century, doubted that human nature was constant. Like Aristotle, he thought of human institutions as humanly, and thus variably, constructed; and he included the culturally, socially, and historically shaped features of human personalities and institutions within this realm of the variably constructed and changeable.

Third, Martin Wight has cautioned against using supposedly "timeless" (and universally valid) systematicity assumptions as a way of equating historically distinct international systems. Contrasting the modern European balance of power system with Thucydides' era, he argues: "If Thucydides does not provide [a theory of the balance of power], it is because the Greeks did not possess one. Just as they had no diplomatic system and no public international law, so they had no sense of an equilibrium of power being the foundation and as it were the constitution of international society" (Wight, 1977, p. 66).

So modern men and women can be said to be socialized into possibly different internationalized relevant roles, political identifications, beliefs, and feelings than medieval ones; and "postmodern" media/terrorist world politics can be described as made by actors, many of which eighteenth-century European diplomats would have difficulty recognizing. Whether the new players are more civilized and knowledgeable is debatable. At least the historicity of international relationships—the fact that their past is embedded in current, internationally shared memories, definitions, and practices—suggests that both continuity and innovation are informed possibilities in the international arena.

Because systematicity may involve historicity—as in the way states learned, evolved, or developed commonly recognized ways of balancing the power of a state threatening to become hegemonic—it is necessary to add to our conception of international systems a discussion of their historical constitution, reformation, and dissolution processes. International systems may be said to be constituted by the norms, the principles, or the practices engendering and/or embodying these norms or principles. Just as Thucydides saw human nature as constitutive of the distinctive member units and their interrelationships with each other and their environments, so John Ruggie has characterized the early modern state system in terms of an emergent, postmedieval clustering of quasi-mechanical time-space descriptions, territoriality, private property, and sovereignty relationships.

Ruggie, Richard Ashley, Robert Cox, and others have recently joined a debate with Kenneth Waltz, Robert Gilpin, and other "neorealists" about how naturalistically or historically to approach the constitutive processes of international political systems. Thus scholarly discussions of contemporary international relations have joined worldwide discussions of the nature of, and prospects for, modern and postmodern forms of international life.

Alternative Perspectives on the Contemporary International System. With these conceptual distinctions and cautions in mind, one can still make some useful claims about contemporary, past, or future international systems. We shall contrast political-military, economic, and ecological systemic conceptions.

Together, the actions of the European powers, their subjects, and their "significant others" have created, sustained, and modified the institutions of the Westphalia state system. These have included: a) the balance of power (a practice of flexible state realignments against a potentially preeminent power, first formally recognized in the Treaty of Utrecht of 1713); b) a hierarchy of power relations and realms

(the Peace of Cateau-Cambrésis, 1559, treated violent conflicts over resources and territories in the peripheral West Indies as separable from wars in a more central European zone, which suggests redescribing such power hierarchies as *imperialism, when seen from peripheral perspectives; and c) the collective security practices of Great Power conflict management, particularly the regularization of postwar outcomes through diplomatic conference (such as the 1518 Treaty of London between the pope, the Holy Roman Emperor, and the kings of France, Spain, and England). Such conferences were often identified with the Concert of Europe in the nineteenth century, and the *League of Nations and the UN in the twentieth century.

Although subjects were normally treated as obligated to follow the laws of their sovereign, a pattern of diplomatic immunity and extraterritoriality for embassies has evolved in the European state system; this was the historical basis for official Western revulsion at the holding of embassy personnel by revolutionary Iranian students in 1979–1981.

Issues of environmental degradation were generally not recognized as worthy of international action before the twentieth century, but scientific and technical knowledge facilitating the "conquest of nature" was avidly pursued and fairly widely shared by the scientific establishment of those times.

A number of transformations in the modern, European state system have been associated with the contemporary era, usually seen as starting somewhere in the twentieth century. Thus it has been argued that the contemporary world has entered an era of world politics, globalizing the balance of power and transcending the European origins of the interstate system. In that process, the traditional concept of a "Great Power" has continued to have meaning when defined in terms of significant *nuclear weapons delivery capabilities, but newer, sometimes conflicting notions of economic "powers" or "*superpowers" also exist.

Others have argued that the Westphalian system of territorially sovereign nation-states is being even more radically transcended. Somehow, the equal and absolute juridical and territorial sovereignty of each nation-state seems a unit-constituting principle out of phase with a world of "superpowers" and "satellites," *multinational corporations with budgets greater than many states' GNPs, UN peacekeeping forces, *International Monetary Fund loan conditions, and UN development programs. And there is the quite remarkable contemporary growth of supranational institutions in, and associated with, the *European Community. Moreover, many postcolonial states, whose state governments' territorial and juridical sovereignty has been buttressed politically and legally by UN membership, have failed to supersede the transnational or subnational political importance of ethnic groupings whose origins preceded the colonial period.

In the post-1945 period, ideological "East vs. West" politics became highly visible, where both a "capitalist vs. communist" ideological reading and a "United States plus allies vs. the Soviet Union plus allies" geopolitical meaning were intended. East vs. West *Cold War geopolitics forcefully divided Germany, Europe, and Korea in the late 1940s. Similar arrangements later, and temporarily, were imposed by the Great Powers on Vietnam in the 1968 Geneva Conference. But with the end of the Cold War and the breakup of the Soviet Union, "North vs. South" politics became more prominent.

"North-South" or "core-periphery" geopolitical language can also be associated either with the original European Great Power system or with the globalized East-West system of the Cold War era, or the emerging post–Cold War, multipolar arrangement—in which Japan, the United States, and an increasingly united Western Europe are playing important leadership roles.

The exclusion of the People's Republic of China from representation in the UN Security Council for nearly twenty-five years after it consolidated power over mainland China, as well as its identification with other less developed *Third World states, called into question its early acceptance as a Great Power in the "core" of the world's political system. But the ambiguous status of the People's Republic of China for much of the Cold War period supports the more general claim that the less developed and often newly independent states of the global South have been precariously autonomous, with their juridical sovereignty not being matched by a unified, widely accepted, integrated and self-steering polity. With postrevolutionary China and perhaps postindependence India as important, partial exceptions, most "Southern" or Third World states have experienced considerable economic penetration. *Dependency and asymmetric interdependence have been a reality among many pro-Western export-oriented states in regions of the world identified as economic "peripheries" or "semiperipheries."

Quite a number of related arguments have concerned the contest for political and economic *hegemony within the increasingly globalized balance of power system. Hegemonic competition may produce temporary periods of bipolar or multipolar stability, but both historical and simulational studies have suggested a cyclical (but irregular) movement toward long, bloody, hegemonic wars. Holland in the seventeenth century, Britain in the nineteenth, and the United States in the twentieth century have emerged as world hegemons consequent upon victory in such wars. This interpretation had been considerably strengthened—and given a challenging economic interpretation as endemic to the growth and decay dynamics of the capitalist world economy—by the early Kondratiev-inspired literature on long waves of economic growth and (war-

exacerbated) inflation, followed by periods of relative stagnation.

Just as total *war involving total weapons, worldwide conflicts, and totalitarian states have created the most important challenge to the international state system in the twentieth century, so it might be hypothesized that the next century will face its greatest challenges from the worldwide drive to achieve living standards comparable to those of contemporary industrial and postindustrial societies, and the enormous cultural and environmental stresses associated with such modernistic striving. Not only will North-South politics become more important, the ecological consequences of energy and resource intensive forms of industrial development will be felt around the globe.

Perhaps the most startling confirmation of the existence of hard-to-transcend limits to growth of worldwide industrial society has been the discovery of polar ozone holes and the apparent reality of global warming. World system dynamics not completely unlike those surmised by *Ibn-Khaldūn, Jay Forrester, and Fernand Braudel are increasingly recognized as real. The international system is being transformed into an environmentally reactive world system which must be lived with, rather than simply dominated.

(See also DIPLOMACY; INTERNATIONAL LAW; INTERNATIONAL POLITICAL ECONOMY; MODERNITY; NORTH-SOUTH RELATIONS; POSTMODERNISM; REALISM; UNITED NATIONS.)

Morton Kaplan, *System and Process in International Politics* (New York, 1957). Ibn Khaldun, *The Muqaddimah: An Introduction to History* (Princeton, N.J., 1969). Hedley Bull, *The Anarchical Society* (New York, 1977). Sam Cole, *Global Models and the International Economic Order* (New York, 1977). Martin Wight, *Systems of States* (Leicester, U.K., 1977). James Der Derian, *On Diplomacy: A Genealogy of Western Estrangement* (Oxford, 1982). Fernand Braudel, *Civilization and Capitalism, 15th–18th Century* 3 vols. (New York, 1981–1984). Thucydides, *The Peloponnesian War* (Harmondsworth, U.K., 1983). Robert Keohane, ed., *Neorealism and its Critics* (New York, 1986). Joshua Goldstein, *Long Cycles: Prosperity and War in the Modern Age* (New Haven, Conn., 1988). Thomas Cusack and Michael Stoll, *Exploring Realpolitik: Probing International Relations Theory with Computer Simulation* (Boulder, Colo., 1990).

HAYWARD R. ALKER, JR.

INTERVENTION. Defined classically as coercive interference by a state or a group of *states into the domestic jurisdiction of another state (thus applying both to internal and to external affairs), the activity of intervention is controversial because it involves outside meddling together with coercion or dictation. The very idea of "outside meddling" producing coercion smacks of illegality. This derives from the emergence of the modern state system in which the corollary of state *sovereignty was taken to be the principle of nonintervention (see R. J. Vincent,

Nonintervention and International Order, Princeton, N.J., 1974).

The principle of nonintervention received its first clear statement in the work of Christian Wolff, an eighteenth-century German authority on *international law, and that of his Swiss follower Emmerich de Vattel. Since that time it has been taken as a fundamental principle of international law. But legitimate exceptions to the general principle have consistently been argued, such as intervention for self-defense, counterintervention, intervention to facilitate *self-determination, and humanitarian intervention.

In contemporary international law, the principle of nonintervention is underlined in the UN charter (which in Article 2(4) prohibits the threat or use of force between states) and buttressed by several subsequent instruments, for example the Declaration on Principles of International Law Concerning Friendly Relations and Cooperation Among States (1970) and the Final Act of the Helsinki *Conference on Security and Cooperation in Europe (1975). It is also endorsed by state practice, not in the sense that states do not intervene, but in the sense that no alternative principle in regard to intervention has either been agreed or consented to by inference from state practice.

The modern law of intervention is now more likely to be found in the sections of international law dealing with the use of *force by states than as a subject in itself. Intervention as dictatorial interference, however, includes more than the use of force, and one of the difficulties with the *international law of intervention from a political point of view is the decision, in a world of unequal powers and complex *interdependence, about when an intervention can be said precisely to have taken place. Some argue that a great power intervenes in the affairs of its neighbors by its very existence, and that a strong economic power intervenes structurally in the countries dependent on it. But the idea of resident intervention loses the sense of intervention as something that has broken a convention, and might be better dealt with in the language of *imperialism.

In the same world of unequal powers we might expect intervention to be more an option for the great powers than the small. And in contemporary international politics this expectation has been met by the interventionary practice since 1945 of both superpowers in relation to their spheres of influence (e.g., the United States in Guatemala [1954] and the Dominican Republic [1965], and the Soviet Union in Hungary [1959] and Czechoslovakia [1968]). But other powers intervene too (e.g., the Cubans over several years in sub-Saharan Africa, Tanzania in Uganda in 1979, India in East Pakistan in 1971). Thus intervention continues to be part of the general pattern of international politics. In this regard tension is likely to continue between a principle of nonintervention widely acknowledged as legitimate in international society and a principle of self-help widely acknowledged as necessary in self-defense.

(See also HELSINKI ACCORDS.)

Hedley Bull, ed., *Intervention in World Politics* (Oxford, U.K., 1984).

R. JOHN VINCENT

INTIFADA. Twenty years after the West Bank, Gaza Strip, and East Jerusalem were occupied in the June War of 1967, they were shaken by a spontaneous popular upheaval which surprised the Israeli authorities, the *Palestine Liberation Organization (PLO), and most other parties to the conflict. The intifada (the Arabic word means uprising) of the 1.8 million Palestinians of these areas, which began on 9 December 1987, significantly changed the scope and dimensions of the *Arab-Israeli conflict. It restored the primacy of the conflict's Palestinian-Israeli aspect, which was for many years eclipsed by that involving *Israel and neighboring Arab states. The intifada has been notable for its effective use of nonviolent forms of civil resistance to an occupying power and for the extent to which it mobilized the population despite heavy pressure from the occupation forces. As a result, it gained international attention and the term *intifada* has taken its place in the international political lexicon.

During the first four years of the intifada, more than 1,000 Palestinians, over 250 of them children 16 years of age and younger, were killed by the Israeli occupation authorities, and approximately 120,000 wounded. In that same period, 16,000 were administratively detained (i.e., imprisoned without trial) for periods of six months or more, and tens of thousands of others jailed after trial by military courts. In consequence of this dramatic upsurge in the conflict, which was the subject of intense international media attention, the intifada imposed itself, and the conflict between Palestinians and Israelis, on the consciousness of the United States and Europe, Israel, and the Arab world. This was all the more significant in that in the years preceding the uprising, the Palestinian aspect of the conflict had faded from public awareness in all these arenas.

Following the outbreak of the intifada and in large measure because of it, important changes took place in the policies of many of the actors involved in the Arab-Israeli conflict. One of the first and most striking changes was Jordan's abdication of its responsibility for the West Bank in July 1988. In November 1988, at the Nineteenth Palestinian National Council held in Algiers, the PLO launched a peace initiative based on an explicit acceptance of the legitimacy of the 1947 partition of Palestine which had created the state of Israel, and called for a peaceful settlement between a Palestinian state in the West Bank and Gaza Strip and Israel to be based on UN Security

Council *Resolution 242. Soon afterwards, PLO leader Yasser *Arafat explicitly accepted the existence of the state of Israel, renounced *terrorism, and accepted Resolution 242, thereby meeting American conditions for a dialogue with the United States, which began in December of the same year.

In the United States, *public opinion and media coverage for the first time became sympathetic to the Palestinians and critical of Israeli practices in a sustained fashion. This was instrumental in bringing the *Reagan administration into a dialogue with the PLO (it was broken off eighteen months later), and in provoking the first muted criticisms in Congress and elsewhere of the level of U.S. aid to Israel. These shifts in public opinion contributed to the *Bush administration's acceptance of the centrality of the Palestinian-Israeli conflict, which was reflected in its making negotiations between the Palestinians and Israel the centerpiece of its policy for its first two years in office.

In Israel, the impact of the intifada was felt economically, and in a variety of other ways, but was still ignored by many citizens. Nevertheless, thinking in Israeli strategic and policy-making circles was deeply influenced by the intifada. This was evidenced by the Jaffee Center report *The West Bank and Gaza: Israel's Options for Peace* (Tel Aviv, 1989), which was the first authoritative statement by a respected body of Israeli academics and former military and intelligence officials to accept the possibility of creation of a Palestinian state in the occupied territories.

In spite of these and other important effects of the intifada, as time wore on, many Palestinians felt that they had little to show for their efforts against Israeli occupation. A new grass-roots leadership drawn from a younger generation emerged in the occupied territories, linked to the PLO, with deep indigenous roots and apparently with strong popular support. This leadership succeeded for a time in defining the Palestinian agenda, and in giving Palestinians a sense of purpose and pride, as local committees established themselves as the leading force in communities throughout the West Bank and Gaza Strip.

One of the consequences of the intense frustration among Palestinians caused by the failure of the intifada and of the PLO's *peace initiative to generate movement toward a peaceful settlement was an increase in random violence against Israelis involving arms and explosives, which had decreased markedly during the first thirty months of the intifada. Another such consequence was the widespread killing of fellow Palestinians marked as Israeli collaborators. Yet another consequence was an apparent growth in the influence in the occupied territories, especially in the Gaza Strip, of Islamic factions such as Hamas, which did not accept the idea of a negotiated settlement advocated by the PLO, and characterized the conflict in absolute, uncompromising religious terms.

The intifada succeeded in changing, perhaps irrevocably, the outlines of the conflict between Palestinians and Israelis, and had a significant impact on world public opinion. However, the Palestinians still seem far from achieving an Israeli withdrawal from the Palestinian territories occupied in 1967, and the creation there of a Palestinian state, goals for which the intifada was originally launched.

Zachary Lockman and Joel Beinin, eds., *Intifada: The Palestinian Uprising against Israeli Occupation* (Boston, 1989). Ze'ev Schiff and Ehud Ya'ari, *Intifada: The Palestinian Uprising—Israel's Third Front* (New York, 1989). Roger Heacock and Jamal Nassar, eds., *Intifada: Palestine at a Crossroads* (New York, 1990). Don Peretz, *Intifada: The Palestinian Uprising* (New York, 1990).

RASHID I. KHALIDI

INVESTMENT, FOREIGN. See FINANCE, INTERNATIONAL; MULTINATIONAL CORPORATIONS.

IRAN. A relatively large country (1,648,000 sq. km.; 636,000 sq. mi.) in Southwest Asia, Iran's twentieth century political history has been strongly affected by international rivalry for influence over its resources. Prior to World War I, the principal foreign threat came from neighboring Tsarist Russia and the British Empire, each interfering in Iran's domestic politics to promote governments that were sensitive to its respective interests. As early as 1907, Britain and Russia had agreed to divide Iran into spheres of influence, and thenceforth each power dispatched troops into its zone whenever it perceived Iranian governments as failing to protect its interests. Foreign *intervention dramatically declined between 1921 and 1939 when Moscow was preoccupied with creating the Soviet Union and London perceived few threats to its expanding oil interests in southwestern Iran. Although Iran acted more independently in this period, its economy became more integrated into the international market system. The outbreak of World War II thus inevitably revived foreign interest in the country's policies and resources, culminating in a joint Anglo-Soviet invasion in August 1941; British and Soviet troops, joined by American forces in 1942, continued to occupy Iran until 1946.

These persistent foreign interventions prompted intense debates within Iran over the most effective means of securing the country's independence and led to the emergence of two major political currents: secular and religious *nationalism. Secular nationalists, mostly political activists educated in Europe, North America, or, after 1930, Iran's secularized public education system, generally believed their country could successfully confront Europeans by adopting Western political institutions, economic programs, and social policies. In contrast, the religious nationalists believed imitation of the West reinforced the country's dependence and so they advocated a return to traditional cultural values, especially those of Shi'i *Islam, the religion of ninety percent of the population. Despite their different perspectives, both secular and religious nationalists viewed the country's shahs (kings) as compromising with foreign powers in order to maintain royal autocracy. Consequently, secular and religious groups sometimes cooperated to restrict the shah's powers, most notably in the 1905–1907 Constitutional Revolution. More typically, shahs exploited conflicts among secular and religious nationalists to enhance royal prerogatives.

The Pahlavi dynasty (ruled 1926–1979) generally tried to co-opt the secular nationalists by promoting many economic and social *reform policies they advocated. These programs initiated the industrialization and urbanization processes that significantly transformed Iranian society, especially after rising oil prices dramatically increased state revenues. The government's diverse development projects supported a large bureaucracy, national army, and internal security forces—institutions that greatly strengthened the central government. The secular nationalists favorably referred to all reforms as *modernization. Nevertheless, because the first Pahlavi shah (ruled 1926–1941) used his power to rule as a dictator, he failed to develop a political support base among secular nationalists. His social policies, such as secularizing the educational and legal systems, generally antagonized the religious nationalists and cost him support among the clergy as well.

Following World War II, Iran became one of the earliest scenes of the emerging *Cold War struggle between the West and the Soviet bloc, as each sought to incorporate the country within its *alliance system. Iran's efforts to pursue a neutral *foreign policy ended in August 1953 when an American-and British-supported military *coup d'état restored power to a shah committed to a strong relationship with the West. The shah cultivated close ties to the United States and consolidated a royal dictatorship, alienating both secular and religious nationalists, who began gradually to cooperate in opposing his rule. In 1978, several groups formed a broad-based religious-secular coalition under the charismatic leadership of the exiled clergyman Ayatollah Ruhollah *Khomeini. This coalition mobilized Iranians in cities and towns throughout the country to participate in mass anti-shah demonstrations. A popular revolutionary movement grew rapidly, demoralizing the extensive security forces; by February 1979, the movement overthrew the monarchy and established a republic. The new government terminated Iran's long-standing alliance with the United States and began to chart a neutral course vis-à-vis the superpowers.

The secular-religious coalition began to dissolve soon after the initial success of the *revolution. The various secular parties faced a serious disadvantage in the postrevolutionary political contest because they appealed primarily to college students and professionals, a small, urban elite in a society where eighty percent of adults had not completed high school. The religious parties appealed more broadly to shopkeepers and artisans in the urban bazaars, lower-ranking civil servants, industrial workers, and peasants. In general, the religious nationalists successfully portrayed the secularists as Westernized "liberals" who had lost touch with their Islamic cultural roots and wished to create a "democratic" republic that would be un-Islamic and ultimately as dependent upon the West as had been the shah's regime. Through their control of revolutionary organizations that assumed judicial and security functions, the religious nationalists effectively intimidated their secular rivals. Significantly, those religious groups affiliated with Khomeini capitalized on his nationwide popularity to help consolidate a theocracy. They drafted a constitution, approved in a December 1979 referendum, that vests ultimate political authority in a senior Shi'i theologian, or *faqih,* who has broad powers to appoint the chief military and judicial authorities and to approve the qualifications of candidates for elective offices. The constitution designated Khomeini the first *faqih* and provides that his successors be chosen by a special assembly of high-ranking clergy.

The constitution also stipulates that the head of government is an elected president who serves a four-year term and may be reelected once. The president appoints the cabinet, but each minister must be approved by the legislature. The president also selects several vice-presidents, one of whom serves as the de facto prime minister. The constitution preserves the national assembly, or Majlis, that was first created in 1906. In its "Islamicised" version, the Majlis is a single-chamber body of 270 members who are elected every four years. The Majlis is independent of the executive, which has no power to dissolve it. A unique institution, known as the Council of Guardians, reviews all Majlis legislation to ensure that laws conform to Shi'i Islamic principles; it has authority to veto any laws that are deemed to be in conflict. The judiciary is independent of both the executive and the Majlis. The chief judicial authorities must be clergy with advanced training in the codices of Shi'i Islamic law.

Despite the personal popularity of Khomeini, there was significant opposition to the establishment of a theocracy. Those opposed to the clergy's rule included both secular and religious groups, as well as the Kurdish ethnic minority (about eight percent of the total population) living primarily in the western mountains along the borders with Turkey and Iraq. The most serious challenge was posed by religious parties that contested the notion of the Shi'i clergy having any special authority to rule in an Islamic government. The Mojahedin-e Khalq, a prerevolutionary clandestine organization that developed into a mass political movement after 1979, actually launched a major nationwide uprising in June 1981.

The regime crushed the rebellion with a reign of terror that lasted for eighteen months; at least 13,000 Iranians, ninety percent of whom were political dissidents, were killed in this conflict. Since 1981 the leadership of the Mojahedin, as well as that of the various secular opposition parties, has been based outside of the country.

The Islamic republic inherited an economically and socially diverse society. Although the government did not alter the primarily capitalist nature of the economic system, one of its aims has been to distribute wealth from oil revenues more equitably. The country's 70,000 villages, where almost half of the total 60 million population resides, have been the beneficiaries of major development programs that have provided them with roads, electricity, piped water, primary schools, and health clinics. Price support policies for agricultural commodities and interest-free credit to finance crop production has helped transfer more money to rural areas. The regime's policies have been less successful in ameliorating living conditions for the urban poor. City population has increased an average of four percent annually since the revolution because of high migration from the villages. Tehran, the capital and one of Asia's largest and most congested cities, has failed to resolve problems associated with its pollution, inadequate water and sewerage systems, inefficient and poorly maintained public transportation services, and extensive slum neighborhoods. Four other cities with populations over one million, Mashhad in the northeast, Isfahan on the central plateau, Tabriz in the northwest, and Shiraz in the south, face similar problems, albeit on a smaller scale.

Low government revenues have handicapped the regime's efforts to deal with urban problems. Initially, the eight-year (1980–1988) *war with Iraq diverted resources to military expenditures and to reconstruction projects for war-damaged oil production facilities and other industrial property. After hostilities ceased, depressed prices for international oil ensured a continuing budget crunch since oil revenues account for ninety percent of the government's budget. The budget problem has been compounded by a prolonged recession that has plagued the domestic economy since the revolution but has deepened since the 1986 collapse of oil prices, leading to price inflation, wage and salary deflation, inadequate private investment, and high urban unemployment rates.

The question of how to resolve the economic problems opened ideological rifts among Iran's ruling elite. During the first decade of the Islamic Republic, the clergy's preoccupation with foreign policy goals not only deflected its attention from issues pertaining to the domestic economy but also helped to maintain its political unity. Initially, consensus focused on the twin objectives of ending the deposed monarchy's de facto alliance with the United States and presenting Iran as a model of *Third World independence from Western political, economic, and cultural domination. Iraq's September 1980 invasion of Iran enabled the clergy to mobilize popular support around the national cause of defending the country against foreign aggression. After nearly eight years of fighting, however, politicians concluded that the war with Iraq had become stalemated and agreed to a cease-fire. The end of hostilities in August 1988 paved the way for refocusing policy concerns onto long-neglected economic matters. Political leaders who described themselves as pragmatists argued that the government's failure to promote economic growth posed a serious threat to the revolution's future. They used both the Majlis and the press as forums to present their perspective: past policies stressing economic self-sufficiency had contributed to the economic depression in the country; Iran must abandon its isolationist course and cooperate with Western nations in order to obtain resources for creating a just, Islamic society at home. They even advocated the use of foreign loans and investments to stimulate the economy. Their views alarmed those politicians who considered themselves revolutionary purists. The purists argued that extensive diplomatic ties and commercial relations, especially foreign loans and investments, would make Iran dependent upon Western countries, compromise the aims of the revolution, and ultimately undermine the very legitimacy of the Islamic Republic.

The pragmatists' emphasis on programs designed to alleviate immediate economic difficulties had broader appeal than the rhetoric of the purists, even though the latter group included several influential politicians. Thus, following the death of Khomeini in June 1989, the pragmatists consolidated their control over the executive branch of government. During the early 1990s, they increased their support among the political elite by adopting policies that kept Iran out of the *Gulf War, a conflict that pitted the country's enemy, Iraq, against virtually the entire international community. Despite the contentious nature of the debate among the pragmatists and purists, each faction demonstrated tolerance for the other's views. Such tolerance did not extend, however, beyond the political elite of clergy and their lay allies. Iranians whose loyalty to the concept of clerical rule was suspect continued to be excluded from participation in the political process.

(See also IRAN-IRAQ WAR; IRANIAN REVOLUTION; RELIGION AND POLITICS; SECULARIZATION.)

Ervand Abrahamian, *Iran Between Two Revolutions* (Princeton, N.J., 1982). Shaul Bakhash, *The Reign of the Ayatollahs: Iran and the Islamic Revolution* (New York, 1984). Nikki Keddie and Eric Hooglund, eds., *The Iranian Revolution and the Islamic Republic* (Syracuse, N.Y., 1986). Nikki Keddie and Mark Gasiorowski, eds., *Neither East Nor West: Iran, the Soviet Union and the United States* (New Haven, Conn., 1990).

ERIC HOOGLUND

IRANIAN REVOLUTION. The Iranian Revolution of 1978–1979 was one of the most momentous and unique events of the postwar epoch: it challenged the established distribution of power in much of the *Middle East and the Islamic world and provided major international conflicts with the United States and *Iran's neighbor, *Iraq. The *revolution itself began in 1978, at a time when the shah, or Persian king, had been in apparent control for twenty-five years and had used the substantial oil revenues that Iran had been earning in the 1970s to build up his country's economy and international importance. By September 1978 the shah's government was confronted with widespread protests, involving millions of people, in the major cities of Iran. Although the first protests had been led by secular opponents of the regime, leadership had quickly passed to the Islamic clergy under the leadership of Ayatollah *Khomeini, in exile since 1964.

By January 1979 the shah was forced to flee. After Khomeini returned to Iran on 1 February and after a brief armed uprising against the remnants of the shah's army on 11–12 February, he took power. Within weeks he had proclaimed the establishment of the Islamic Republic of Iran, and proceeded to transform the political, social, educational, and cultural life of the country to meet what he regarded as Islamic principles.

Power lay in the hands of the leading clergy and the networks of Islamic committees set up throughout the country. The ministries of state and the armed forces were subjected to clerical control. Opposition to Khomeini's regime continued for several years and led to armed clashes with opponents of the clergy, both left-wing guerrillas in the cities and Kurdish insurgents in the western mountains.

Khomeini proclaimed a policy of militant neutrality, under the slogan "Neither East nor West," and appealed to the Islamic and other oppressed peoples of the world to rise up against their rulers. In many parts of the Islamic world, in particular, underground and opposition groups looked to Iran for support and example against governments seen as secular or tied to the West. Iranian influence was especially strong amongst Shi'a in Lebanon.

Two conflicts in particular came to dominate Iranian foreign policy. The first was with the United States and began on 5 November 1979 when a group of Islamic militants, proclaiming themselves to be students following the Imam's line, seized the staff and buildings of the U.S. embassy in Tehran. The Iranian government swung behind these militants and made a series of demands, including the handing over of the shah, then in the United States, and the return of his wealth. The United States froze all Iranian assets and, unsuccessfully, attempted military action to free the hostages. In January 1981, the hostages were released in return for a financial settlement of U.S.-Iranian claims and counterclaims.

The second major conflict came in September 1980 when Iraq, angered by Iranian calls for the overthrow of the Ba'thist regime in Baghdad, invaded Iran in the hope of toppling the Khomeini government. In the ensuing war, in which over a million people are said to have died, neither side was able to prevail over the other or to overthrow the other's government. In 1987 U.S. and other Western navies, anxious about Iranian influence, entered the war on Iraq's side, and in August 1988 Iran finally accepted a UN Security Council resolution on a cease-fire.

The Iranian Revolution was the first successful upheaval of modern times to justify itself in religious terms and to be led by the clergy. More than any other revolution, it rejected modern ideas of progress, democracy, and material well-being. At the same time it was distinct from most *Third World revolutions in taking place in cities and in involving relatively little armed conflict. Some analyses stress the particular power of radical Islamic *ideology, others the appeals of ideological returns to the past, and others the particular conflict between the shah's state, sustained by oil-based modernization, and society.

(See also IRAN-IRAQ WAR; ISLAM; RELIGION AND POLITICS.)

Nikki Keddie, *Roots of Revolution: An Interpretive History of Modern Iran* (New Haven, Conn., and London, 1981). Ervand Abrahamian, *Iran Between Two Revolutions* (Princeton, N.J., 1982). Shaul Bakhash, *The Reign of the Ayatollahs* (London and New York, 1985). Gary Sick, *All Fall Down* (New Haven, Conn., and London, 1985).
                                                    FRED HALLIDAY

IRAN-IRAQ WAR. In September 1980, *Iraq launched full scale air and ground attacks across the 1,170-kilometer (730-mi.) border it shares with *Iran, initiating a *war that raged intermittently until a cease-fire was declared in August 1988. This protracted contest—the longest conventional interstate war of the twentieth century—recalled the infantry trench warfare of World War I, while its later phases incorporated modern ballistic missile technology to attack cities and economic targets. Some 367,000 Iraqis and Iranians were killed and more than 700,000 wounded, by conservative Western estimates, and the war devastated both economies.

The ostensible causes of the Iran-Iraq War (sometimes referred to as the Gulf War of 1980–1988) included disputed borders and rights to a vital waterway, the Shatt al-Arab. Fundamentally at issue was the question of regional *hegemony. On one level this was the latest episode in a history of contention for regional power between Iran and Iraq. At another level, it pitted the revolutionary Islamism of the new regime in Tehran against the Arab nationalist dictatorship in Baghdad, now backed by most of the major powers.

The outbreak of full-scale armed conflict between the two states was preceded by a series of border clashes, and by Tehran's appeals to Iraq's Shiʿi Muslims (about fifty-five percent of the population) to follow Iran's revolutionary example and overthrow the secular tyranny of President Saddam *Hussein. This campaign included sabotage bombings in Baghdad and at least one attempt to assassinate a major Iraqi government official. Baghdad, for its part, escalated hostilities in order to take advantage of the postrevolutionary disarray in Iranian society, especially in the armed forces, and Iran's international isolation, particularly its estrangement from the United States. Its immediate pretext and goal was to overturn the 1975 Algiers agreement, signed by Saddam Hussein and the shah of Iran, which ratified Iranian demands for sharing sovereignty over the Shatt al-Arab in return for ending Iranian support of Kurdish insurgents in northern Iraq.

Iraq's initial incursion captured some 15,000–21,000 square kilometers (6,000–8,000 sq. mi.) of Iran's oil-rich and Arab-populated Khuzestan province, destroying several cities and numerous towns, but failed to inflict any decisive defeat on Iran's forces. The contest was mainly waged by ground forces, though the opening weeks of the war saw both countries' air forces engaged as well.

After the first six months, by March 1981, Iranian forces had rallied to prevent further Iraqi advances. A second phase of the war began in mid-1982, when Iran took the offensive to push Iraq out of most of the Iranian territory it had occupied and, a year later, carried the ground war into Iraqi territory. The war settled into a pattern of stalemate, as year after year Iran launched seasonal "final offensives" which never successfully broke through Iraqi defenses. This second phase coincided with the emergence of a new regional dimension, as the Iran-Iraq war became an Iranian-Arab war. Iraq secured the financial and political support of Saudi Arabia, Kuwait, and other oil-rich Arab states of the gulf, as well as political and limited military support from Jordan and Egypt. The goal of preventing an Iraqi defeat was also shared by the major powers. The Soviet Union, which had cut off arms shipments to Iraq at the beginning of the war, resumed its role as Iraq's major military supplier; France supplied sophisticated warplanes and missile systems; the United States provided important agricultural shipments and credits.

From the outset, both combatants targeted one another's oil export facilities. Iraqi facilities were closer to the war zone, and thus effectively closed early in the conflict. Iraq's vulnerability was compounded when Syria, in 1982, supported Iran by closing off Iraq's pipeline outlet across Syria to the Mediterranean. This left a pipeline through Turkey as Iraq's only oil export outlet until late in the war, when new pipelines through Saudi Arabia were opened. A third phase, the "tanker war," began in early 1984, when Iraq used French-supplied jets and missiles to interdict Iranian oil exports. Baghdad's

aim was to employ technological superiority to break the Iranian siege on the ground. Because Iraqi oil exports by tanker were already closed down, Iran could retaliate only by attacking the shipping of Iraq's allies, Kuwait and Saudi Arabia, risking Western intervention to impose a cease-fire that would appear to favor Iraq.

Something like this scenario finally occurred by early 1987, when the United States responded to Kuwaiti requests for protection of its tankers by dispatching a naval force that grew to some fifty warships. This corresponded with the fourth and final phase of the war. Iran's last, unsuccessful "final offensive" of January–February 1987 was followed by a series of successful Iraqi campaigns to recover lost territory. The combination of Iraqi ground victories and a series of naval clashes with U.S. forces in the gulf, culminating in the destruction of an Iranian airliner that killed 291 civilians, persuaded Iran to accept UN Security Council Resolution 598 which established a cease-fire more or less on Iraqi terms. Negotiations toward a final settlement proceeded in a desultory fashion until the fall of 1990. Then Iraq, in the context of confrontation with the United States following Baghdad's invasion of Kuwait, accepted Iran's terms for settlement based on the status quo ante—namely, the 1975 Algiers accord.

Several dimensions to this conflict deserve mention. The first is the extent to which this was an "oil war." Without access to oil revenues—their own and in the case of Iraq those of its Arab allies—neither country could have sustained a war of this scope, intensity, and duration. The conflict, moreover, grew out of the *Iranian Revolution, itself profoundly shaped by Iran's oil-based political economy, and both countries had experienced oil-motivated overt and covert interventions by the United States and other powers, interventions that also directly influenced the outcome of this conflict.

A second notable aspect is the durability of the postcolonial nation-state. Iranian appeals to Shiʿi coreligionists had no more impact on Iraqi morale or loyalty than did Iraq's efforts to enlist the ethnically Arab population of southern Iran. National rather than sectarian or ethnic solidarities prevailed.

Finally, in many ways the Iran-Iraq War linked the Iranian Revolution of 1978–1979 to the 1991 *Gulf War, the regional confrontation that followed Iraq's invasion of Kuwait in August 1990. Iraq emerged with its economy exhausted and its political ambitions frustrated, but its military much stronger and more cohesive. Kuwait provided both the provocations and the pretexts for Baghdad to make a new bid for regional hegemony. The war had also facilitated the extension of U.S. military forces in the region, both the important naval combat experience of 1987–1988 and, more significantly, the construction of sophisticated bases and ports in Saudi Arabia, without which the deployment of half of U.S. combat forces worldwide to the gulf in the fall of 1990 would have been impossible.

(See also ISLAM; KHOMEINI, RUHOLLAH; KURDISTAN.)

"The Strange War in the Gulf" *MERIP Reports* 125/126 (July–September 1984). Dilip Hiro, *The Longest War: The Iran-Iraq Military Conflict* (New York, 1991).

JOE STORK

IRAQ. The modern state of Iraq was created in 1920, as part of the peace settlement following World War I. The victorious Allies divided the Arab provinces of the former Ottoman Empire between them, and Britain, which had been in occupation of the provinces of Basra and Baghdad for most of the war, and Mosul by the end of the war, was appointed mandatory power under the new system of international trusteeship established by the *League of Nations.

Although parts of the country had been united under a single government at various times in the past, the entity which emerged in 1920 had had no previous independent existence as a nation-state. Britain imported a king, Faisal, son of Sharif Hussein of Mecca, and endowed Iraq with a constitution and a bicameral legislature. The mandate, a form of indirect rule where Arab ministers and officials were closely supervised by British advisers whose advice had to be taken, came to an end in 1932, when Iraq was admitted to the League of Nations as an independent state. By this time Britain had secured Iraq's present northern boundary, had made sure that the concession for oil exploration and exploitation was given to the Iraq Petroleum Company, a conglomerate of British, Dutch, French, and U.S. oil interests, and had generally tried to create a social base for the monarchy by confirming "suitable" tribal leaders in full possession of what had previously been the customary holdings of "their" tribes. In addition, Britain retained military bases in Iraq and generally continued to exercise strong political and economic influence.

For much of the twenty-six years between the end of the mandate in 1932 and the *revolution of 1958, the country was torn by profound political and socioeconomic tensions, many of which long remained unresolved. In the first place, oil revenues began to rise significantly in the 1940s and 1950s. The concentration of wealth and power in a few hands, and the concentration of economic activity in the cities, caused a flood of rural-to-urban migration, mostly by sharecroppers escaping lives of extreme deprivation on the large estates of the rural south. Their presence in the cities, usually in poor squatter settlements on the outskirts, served to inflame the economic and social tensions already present.

Second, the profoundly unrepresentative nature of the government, and the close association of many of its leading figures with Britain, meant that its

policies were out of step with the aspirations of most of the rest of the population. The opposition included liberal democrats, Arab nationalists, Kurdish nationalists, and communists, the latter having emerged after World War II as the largest and most influential political force in the country. Given that the political system was parliamentary in form only and ensured the dominance of parties acceptable to Britain and the monarchy, the opposition lost all confidence in it and looked for alternative routes to power.

The revolution of July 1958, although widely supported, took the form of a military coup, led by a group of disaffected military officers who had no ties to any particular political party but were committed to national independence, nonalignment in the *Cold War, and a gamut of social, economic, and political reforms. However, within weeks of the revolution, political differences began to surface. The three main groupings, which continued to play a significant role in Iraqi politics over the next three decades, were the communists, the Kurds, and the pan-Arab nationalists, both Nasserist and Ba'thist.

With their roots in the shantytowns, the emerging labor movement, and the new professional middle classes, the communists continued to be the principal political force in the country in the years immediately after the revolution, but their position was ambivalent. They supported the president, the military officer 'Abd al-Karim Qasim, partly because of his progressive social and economic policies—in addition to his housing and welfare programs. Law 80, formulated in 1961, was the first legislation enacted to restrict the activities of foreign oil companies in any Arab country. They also did not believe that external and internal forces would permit them to remain in power even if they were to succeed in seizing it.

In addition, like Qasim, the communists were opposed to the Arab nationalists' demand that Iraq should join the United Arab Republic of Egypt and Syria. Given Egyptian President Abdel *Nasser's known antipathy to political parties, they considered a union as tantamount to a ban, or at least tight restrictions, on their activities. As a result, union became the main rallying point, both for and against, in the struggle between right-wing and left-wing forces which only ended with Qasim's overthrow in 1963. It is worth noting that although some nationalists certainly supported unity from conviction, and not merely as an anticommunist slogan, the depth of nationalist attachment to Arab unity may be gauged by the halfheartedness with which they pursued this goal when they were in power and thus in a position to put it into practice.

The second political force, the Kurdish national movement, was divided into a number of factions, but these were dominated by the *Kurdistan Democratic Party and its leader Mulla Mustafa Barzani, who died in exile in 1979. The Kurds are an ethnic minority within the Iraqi state; although many have migrated to the cities, they originate in the mountainous north and northeast of Iraq, and form some twenty percent of the total population of some 17 million (1990). Most Iraqi Kurdish politicians and parties have sought some form of regional or local autonomy within the Iraqi state, but armed Kurdish organizations and political groupings have been in conflict with the authorities in Baghdad since the inauguration of the state in 1920, largely because of the authorities' refusal to countenance such aspirations.

The party with the greatest long-term success in postrevolutionary Iraq has been the Ba'th. Although the Ba'thists never attracted the level of mass support the communists commanded, they eventually succeeded in taking power and keeping it in their hands by a combination of skillful organization and an alliance with key military officers. Together with the Nasserists they organized a military coup against Qasim and the Left in February 1963, but were edged out of government by their partners after eight months. These months saw some of the most terrible violence hitherto experienced in the postwar *Middle East, directed against the communists and the Left. After five years in the wilderness the Ba'th engineered another coup in July 1968.

Ba'thism is a variety of pan-Arab nationalism, based on the general premise that there is a single Arab nation which has been divided artificially, first by the Ottomans, and subsequently by European and American *imperialism and *Zionism. Once the Arabs are liberated and united, it is believed, social conflicts within particular states (or "regions of the Arab nation") will subside. Ba'thism has three central aspirations: unity, freedom, and *socialism. Unity refers to the unity of the Arab nation, freedom to freedom from imperialism and Zionism, and socialism to a general aspiration toward state-directed economic development supported by a mixed economy.

Since its rise to power the Iraqi Ba'th leadership has attempted to legitimate its rule in these very general terms, and the party has been expanded into an organization with several million members. The Ba'th had less than 1,000 members at the peak of its influence in 1960–1963; hence, in an important sense the party in the form it assumed in the early 1970s was created *after* its advent to power. In July 1968, a small but effective and determined Ba'thist group seized power with support from the military; the Ba'th Party only gained mass membership after the leadership had taken over the state apparatus.

According to the constitution, opposition parties are permitted to operate. A National Patriotic Front—an alliance which the Ba'th concluded with the communists a year after the oil *nationalization in 1972—continued to exist on paper long after it had become completely redundant. In practice the Ba'th did not tolerate any political opposition after 1976.

The leadership developed several well-equipped security services to repress real and potential opposition: from the Kurds, from the Left, or, increasingly after the mid-1970s, from Shi'i political groups and parties, membership in which became a capital offense.

Although there is a National Assembly, real power rests with the president and the Ba'th Party leadership, the Revolutionary Command Council. In the course of the 1970s and 1980s Saddam *Hussein, who became president in 1979, concentrated power more and more in his own hands, and developed—along with his immediate family and a few close associates—an elaborate personality cult. After he launched the war against *Iran in 1980, political power gradually moved away from the Revolutionary Command Council and into the presidential office.

A number of factors contributed to bring about this state of affairs. In the first place, the huge increase in oil revenues since 1973, shortly after the nationalization of oil, went straight into the hands of the state, which, by that time, had become equivalent to Saddam Hussein and his circle. Second, these same revenues made Iraq, with its relatively large population, a major market for Western and Japanese products, including consumer goods, industrial and infrastructural projects, and military hardware; the buildup of the latter in the 1970s and 1980s was instrumental in the decision to attack Iran and later to annex *Kuwait.

In addition, the great apprehension aroused in the West, the Soviet Union, and much of the Arab world by the overthrow of the shah and the establishment of the Islamic Republic of Iran meant that Saddam Hussein was able to attract virtually unchallenged support from most of the rest of the world for more than a decade. In the end, he lost this support by an act which in essence marked a continuation of the attempt to gain regional supremacy which he had initiated with the invasion of Iran in 1980—the attack on Kuwait in August 1990.

Reaction to the invasion was swift. It was condemned by all the principal regional actors, and almost unanimously by the UN. In the five months between the invasion itself and the beginning of the *Gulf War in January 1991, an impressive array of forces from Saudi Arabia, Egypt, Syria, Morocco, Britain, France, Pakistan, and Bangladesh, spearheaded by some 500,000 troops from the United States, mustered in Saudi Arabia, backed by the moral support of the European Community, Japan, and all the states of the *Warsaw Treaty Organization (Warsaw Pact).

At the end of November 1990, the UN, under great pressure from the United States, issued Resolution 678, which authorized member states to use all means necessary to force Iraq to withdraw from Kuwait if it had not done so by 15 January 1991. On 17 January 1991, the United States and its allies began to bomb what were claimed to be strategic targets, causing countless civilian deaths and considerable damage to the country's infrastructure. Iraq retaliated by launching Scud missiles at targets in Israel and Saudi Arabia; Israel did not retaliate. After some five weeks of bombing, a ground offensive was launched on 23 February, which ended with the rout and destruction of much of the regular Iraqi army by 27 February, when a cease-fire was declared.

A few days after the war ended, popular insurrections against the Iraqi government broke out in southern Iraq and in Kurdistan. Although the rebels gained control of large areas between the end of February and the beginning of March, units of the Republican Guard responded with exceptional brutality, and were able to gain the upper hand fairly quickly in Basra, Najaf, and Karbala and in the Kurdish cities, causing widespread loss of life and devastation in the process. A mass exodus of Kurds to the Iraqi-Turkish and Iraqi-Iranian borders began; by the end of April there were some 2.5 million refugees, both Kurds and southerners.

In April and May 1991 U.S. and British troops were briefly dispatched to northern Iraq to encourage the Kurds to return and to protect them when they did so; these had left by the end of the summer. The Kurdish leadership spent several months in Baghdad apparently negotiating Kurdish autonomy with Saddam Hussein, but with no definite result by the end of the year. With all civilian resistance inside the country crushed, it seemed unlikely that the regime could be removed other than by a military coup; defense analysts in the United States were debating if, and how best, the United States might assist in such a process.

(See also ARAB NATIONALISM; IRAN-IRAQ WAR; NASSERISM.)

Hanna Batutu, *The Old Social Classes and the Revolutionary Movements of Iraq: A Study of Iraq's Old Landed and Commercial Classes and of Its Communists, Ba'thists and Free Officers*, Princeton Studies on the Near East (Princeton, N.J., 1978). Marion Farouk-Sluglett and Peter Sluglett, *Iraq Since 1958: From Revolution to Dictatorship* (London, 1987). Samir al-Khalil, *The Republic of Fear: The Politics of Modern Iraq* (London, 1989).

MARION SLUGLETT
PETER SLUGLETT

IRELAND. As a small state on the edge of Western Europe, Ireland (population 3.5 million) has been particularly preoccupied with its relationship to its external environment. Before World War II the dominant feature in that external environment was *Britain and the dominant issue was political, i.e., the assertion of independence. From the late 1950s on, the emphasis switched from politics to economics and from the assertion of *sovereignty to the beginning of a strategy designed to make the most of *interdependence within the wider international environment.

Political History and Institutions. Secession from the United Kingdom was achieved in the Anglo-Irish Treaty of 1921. This was the outcome of a prolonged and mainly constitutional agitation for greater autonomy (ca. 1870–1914), followed by a short, sharp guerrilla struggle aimed at outright secession (a struggle kindled by the 1916 Easter Rising but waged in earnest from 1919 to 1921). From the point of view of the secessionists, the achievement was partial, as it was limited by symbolic ties with the British monarchy, by concessions in regard to the use of naval facilities, and by the fact that the six northeastern counties remained in the United Kingdom as *Northern Ireland. All of this ensured that the issue of relations with the former imperial power continued to dominate the politics of the new state. The division over the treaty caused a brief but bloody civil war (1922–1923) and became the basis of the cleavage between the main political parties (Fianna Fáil and Fine Gael). In fact, there was little potential for any other cleavage. Secession had produced a remarkably homogeneous society—ninety-five percent Catholic, predominantly agrarian with a significant *land reform program already completed, and with a tiny industrial proletariat. The limited scope for the emergence of a capital-labor conflict was symbolized and reinforced by the Labour Party's decision not to contest the 1918 election and has been reflected in Labour's persistent minority status (since 1948 its support has ranged from nine to seventeen percent). The declining salience of the protreaty-versus-antitreaty cleavage in later years did not lead to the emergence of any coherent alternative cleavage system but to two competing catchall parties with residual differences on the nationalist issue. Though both aspire to be catchall parties, they are unevenly matched—Fianna Fáil's average vote over the last forty years has been forty-six percent while that of Fine Gael has been thirty-one percent. Minor parties have appeared from time to time, the current ones including the Democratic Left, the center-right Progressive Democrats, and the Green Party.

That *democracy was successfully established after an armed struggle for independence and a civil war was due in part to the British legacy—a democratic political culture and a set of state institutions (bureaucratic, judicial, and parliamentary) that were either taken over directly or copied from the former colonial power. There were, however, some institutional innovations, including judicial review, *proportional representation, and provision for referendums. A new constitution was enacted under Fianna Fáil in 1937 but the changes were mainly ideological rather than institutional. Nationalist *ideology is forcibly expressed in Articles 2 and 3, which claim jurisdiction over the territory of Northern Ireland. The new constitution also contained a symbolic affirmation of the special position of the *Roman Catholic church (the clause was removed in 1972). In a clause that was far from merely symbolic, divorce was banned. Change to the constitution requires a referendum. The electorate showed itself quite conservative twice in the 1980s by inserting a ban on abortion and by upholding the existing ban on divorce. However, in 1990, the same electorate elected a woman with strong liberal credentials to the symbolically important but largely ceremonial role of president. Moreover, the absoluteness of the 1983 ban on abortion was circumscribed by a Supreme Court judgment in early 1992, and the issue was thrown back into the legislature. Assessment of the likelihood of change in the area of public morality must take into account the possibility of an accelerated rate of intergenerational change due to disproportionate numbers in the younger age cohorts.

The Economy. That same demographic profile has a direct impact on the fate of the economy. The unemployment rate is almost one-fifth of the labor force despite a resumption of emigration in the 1980s. In the prewar period, industrialization strategy had been outrightly protectionist. The failure of the policy as manifested in severe economic crisis and mass emigration led to a dramatic U-turn in 1958 and the adoption of a policy of *export-led growth, free trade, and the encouragement of foreign investment. The strategy to encourage foreign industry has been a considerable success, achieving and maintaining high levels of exports. However, such industry has tended to be in a narrow range of sectors and to be capital- rather than labor-intensive. It is argued that some means must be found to develop indigenous industry.

*European Community (EC) membership was both a corollary of the new strategy and an absolute imperative for the Irish agricultural sector. It was approved by an overwhelming majority in a referendum in 1972. Though the farming sector in particular benefited from EC transfer payments, the high hopes of an era of economic progress resulting from EC membership ran afoul of the oil crises of the seventies. Governments attempted to shore up living standards by increasing public spending. Lacking clear ideological anchorage on such issues, the political parties competed at the spending rather than at opposite ends of the spend-save spectrum. This strategy was particularly evident in the Fianna Fáil election manifesto of 1977. The result was that the national debt/GNP ratio rose by nearly ninety percentage points between 1973 and 1986. Stringent corrective measures were finally undertaken by Fianna Fáil in 1987. The government's recovery strategy was aided by support from among the opposition parties and was buttressed by corporatist-style arrangements which were renewed in 1990. Despite a severe buffeting in the recession of 1991, fiscal control (at least in terms of containing the exchequer borrowing requirement) and positive growth rates have been maintained. Anticipation of the severe fiscal and economic criteria set for participation in European Monetary Union in the late 1990s means that budgetary discipline will remain tight. At the same time, unemployment and the emigration of considerable numbers of generally highly educated young people continue to be daunting challenges.

Foreign Policy. Like the economy, *foreign policy could be seen to be traversing a path from isolation to involvement. Neutrality in *World War II was part and parcel of the preoccupation with the relationship with Britain and with the issue of sovereignty. A policy of neutrality, defined in terms of noninvolvement in military *alliances and an independent foreign policy, was pursued in the postwar period, influencing Ireland's activist UN posture in the 1950s and 1960s. However, Ireland never became involved with the *Nonaligned Movement or cultivated particularly close relations with the other European neutrals. With EC accession it was explicitly recognized that neutrality was conditional, the condition that would trigger change being the achievement of a full European political union with its own defense competence. In the early 1980s, however, neutrality received a boost by being linked in popular attitudes with a rejection of the new *Cold War. In turn, at the end of the 1980s, the basic concept of neutrality was put in question by the collapse of communism and the end of the Cold War. Ireland's emphasis on neutrality had retarded the development of European political cooperation in the 1980s by keeping military aspects out of discussions of *security cooperation. The 1991 Treaty of Maastricht has signalled an end to the exclusion of the defense dimension, though special allowance for Ireland's position is made in the treaty reference to not prejudicing "the specific character of the security and defence policy of certain member states." How this works out in practice will depend on the extent of the development of a defense competence within the new European Union, on the shape of a possible revision of the treaty envisaged for 1996, and on the terms under which other European neutrals may join the union. Within Ireland the neutrality issue was assiduously avoided by the pro-Maastricht side in the 1992 referendum. The European significance of the substantial "yes" vote in that referendum was amplified by the fact that it was the first test for the treaty after the Danish "no" vote, and the Irish decision was widely regarded as having put Maastricht back on the rails.

Northern Ireland and Anglo-Irish Relations. By the mid-1960s, the shift away from narrow nationalist preoccupations was evident in a new flexibility in relations with Northern Ireland. This nascent revisionism was severely tested by the recrudescence of violence within Northern Ireland in 1969. Policy did not revert to irredentism, though there were some pressures in that direction. Rather it became, with the exception of the short-lived Sunningdale Agreement, a matter of crisis management. A longer-term strategic joint approach by the Irish and British governments was mooted in 1980 and, after prolonged and difficult negotiations, was institutionalized in the Anglo-Irish Agreement of 1985. This has not by any means solved the problem but has started a process designed to lead to agreement within Northern Ireland on the government of the area and to structures that take account of the all-Ireland dimension of the problem. The process remains vulnerable to possible veto from several quarters, a point that was never far from the surface in the historic talks between both governments and all constitutional parties in Northern Ireland that took place in the summer of 1992. Furthermore, any settlement could be undermined by the spoiling strategy and tit-for-tat tactics of the terrorists, in particular of the Provisional Irish Republican Army (IRA). However, there is little doubt but that the larger threat to regime stability implied by the latter can almost certainly be contained by the high level of security cooperation between the Irish and British governments.

Ireland has for long wrestled with the imperatives of independence in a world where boundaries are highly permeable in economic, political, and cultural terms. Cultural identity, which in the past was highly salient, inward-looking, and a source of gnawing self-doubt, is probably now more taken for granted, more open, and more secure. Considerable domestic problems exist, and tackling them requires an adequate strategy for dealing with the outside world. Both politically and economically, this strategy is now geared toward making the best of limited sovereignty by positively cultivating interdependence.

(See also CORPORATISM; DECOLONIZATION; NATIONALISM; RELIGION AND POLITICS.)

Patrick Keatinge, *A Place among the Nations: Issues of Irish Foreign Policy* (Dublin, 1978). Kieran A. Kennedy, Thomas Giblin, and Deirdre McHugh, *The Economic Development of Ireland* (London, 1988). J. J. Lee, *Ireland 1912–1985: Politics and Society* (Cambridge, U.K., 1989). John Coakley and Michael Gallagher, eds., *Politics in the Republic of Ireland* (Galway, 1992).

RICHARD SINNOTT

ISLAM. Western views of Islam are structured predominantly by political and cultural antagonisms. Rivalry between Islamic and Christian powers in Europe and the Mediterranean in the medieval period; later political and economic competition with the Ottoman Empire; anticolonial nationalist movements in Muslim countries; and the contemporary emergence of oil-rich sheikhs and the radicals of Khomeinist Iran have contributed in the West to a powerful sense of "Islam" as a unitary and usually corrupt and malignant force. Together with racist stereotypes of "the Turk" and "the Arab," and more recently "the Shi'i fanatic-terrorist," such notions lead to a view of Islam as a politically unified, all-encompassing motive and framework for action.

These images and assumptions impede understanding.

The Prophet Muhammad (d. 632 C.E.) believed that in the Quran he was delivering a direct message from God in the Arabic language but addressed to pagans, Jews, and Christians alike. Membership in the community of Muslims, the *umma*, is in principle open to whoever submits to God, the meaning of *Islam*.

The language of prayer and scripture is Arabic, but the larger proportion of Muslims today is in fact non-Arab. In Asia there are majority or significant communities in Afghanistan, Pakistan, India, Bangladesh, Malaysia, and Indonesia, with minorities in the southern Philippines, the successor states of Soviet Central Asia, and western China; in Africa, major populations are found in the West and Saharan zones from Senegal through northern Nigeria to the Sudan, with an important presence in Tanzania and down the East African coast. The principal modern imperial Muslim power was the Turkish Ottoman Empire, which ended with its defeat in World War I. And one of the most important revolutions of the second half of the twentieth century has been in Iran, where Muslim clerics and Ayatollah Ruhollah *Khomeini's interpretation of Islamic power emerged as dominant.

"Islam" should therefore be thought of in terms of historical, political, and social diversity. It is certainly neither an exclusively Arab phenomenon nor a monolithic unity. Religious forces interact with other factors, whether social, cultural, or economic, in varied ways and by no means always in a major role. There is no centralized religious hierarchy to assert worldwide spiritual or political leadership.

All Muslims are required to perform the five pillars of Islam: a) the profession of faith, the *shehadah*, that "there is no God but Allah and Muhammad is his Prophet"; b) the five daily prayers which may be made in any place but at particular set times (Friday is the day of the communal prayer when sermons are delivered at the major mosques, frequently with a state-backed message; as centers for social gatherings, mosques also act as local political, propaganda, and information points, especially if the government obstructs other public gatherings); c) payment of the *zakat*, or alms tax; d) fasting from dawn to dusk during the holy month of Ramadan (President Bourguiba of Tunisia in the 1960s attempted to abolish this duty as an impediment to modernization); and e) making the *hajj*, the pilgrimage to Mecca, at least once in a lifetime if circumstances permit. Observance varies widely between and within social groups. So does the role of the state. Some, such as Saudi Arabia since its inception, Nimeiri's regime in the Sudan (particularly from 1983 until his fall in 1985), Zia al Haqq's dictatorship in Pakistan (1977–1989), and the Islamic Republic of Iran, seek to identify the state with religious controls, especially on women's dress and social roles, as the most public symbol of collective purity. Libya follows Colonel Muammar *Qaddafi's much-disputed interpretations. Other governments try to appropriate religious observance as national projects, as with Malaysian state supervision of the pilgrimage. Attempts to produce an Islamic banking system (without taking interest, which is forbidden) have so far been unsuccessful in the context of a capitalist world economy.

The nature of authority over the *umma* has been an issue since the Prophet's death. Though ideally community and the Islamic order are one, in practice divisions between state and religious considerations have always occurred. Rulers made competing claims to leadership. Jurists differed over legal interpretations in the *shari'a, the Islamic law. The Quran can be cited to support disparate policies.

Disputes arose over who should become the *khalifa*, or deputy ruling the community. Those who became known as Sunnis, the vast majority of the world Muslim population, accept the right to rule of the first four "rightly guided" caliphs and the Ummayad and Abbasid dynasties after them (661–1258). Caliphs were to be accepted as protectors and agents of the shari'a. Rulers, however unjust, tend to be acknowledged by Sunni jurists as having temporal power over the *umma,* although other elements of a society may rise against oppression.

Shi'i Muslims, on the other hand, believe that the Prophet's son-in-law Ali, fourth of the rightly guided caliphs, was chosen by Muhammad as his successor as Imam, or leader, of the community and that Ali's descendants should rightfully have been at the head of the *umma.* The majority Shi'i view is that the twelfth imam in line from Ali became "hidden" (he vanished in 873 C.E.) and that he will finally return to establish justice on earth. They particularly venerate Ali and one of his sons, the Imam Hussein, who in 681 was killed at the battle of Kerbela in Iraq. His martyrdom is ritually remembered every year and may become a powerful political symbol of the unjustly persecuted Shi'a in times of crisis. At other times a more quietist practice accommodating to worldly powers may prevail.

By far the majority in Iran, Shi'a also constitute just over half of the Iraqi population, where a specifically Shi'i politics has not emerged. It has in the Lebanese "confessional" system where Shi'a are the largest such category. But they divided in the Lebanese wars (which began in 1976) into rival Amal and more radical Iranian-backed Hizbollah groupings. The dynasty ruling the Yemen under an imam until its overthrow in 1962 represented a different branch of Shi'a, the Qaydi. There are other relatively small groups in eastern Saudi Arabia, India, and East Africa.

Forms of authority and their relations to politics are various under Islam. Families known as the *ashraf* or *sadat* claiming descent from the Prophet

and therefore a particular holiness and legitimacy frequently have local political relevance. In Morocco such descent is important in the position of the monarch. In the Kuwaiti crisis of 1990, King Hussein of Jordan referred to his family's sherifian status and President Saddam *Hussein produced a holy genealogy for himself and a call for *jihad. Responses to such claims vary from acceptance to derision.

Sufi orders, or mystical brotherhoods, include members from many strata in society owing loyalty to sheikhs who might have politically important roles. In Algeria such groups often led resistance to the French in rural areas in the nineteenth century. The Sanusi order of Libya gave a focus to the struggle against Italian colonialism, forming the state of modern Libya and becoming an independent monarchy under British tutelage in 1951, before being displaced by Colonel Qaddafi's idiosyncratic blend of "Islamic socialism" in 1969. The Muridiya of Senegal still have an important national and economic position. But Sufi groups were often too divided for political action and were attacked by nationalists, modernists, and radicals of all hues as doctrinally suspect, un-Islamic, and backward. More recently, some conservative regimes have encouraged them, as President Anwar *Sadat did in Egypt in the 1970s, to support a more quietist and apolitical Islam against Islamic and secular radicalism.

The learned men and jurists, the *ulema,* have reproduced the Islamic traditions in educational and legal fields, though they have lost their monopoly to modern state apparatuses. Reformists among them stressing a return to a pure Islam and the role of individual legal interpretation played an important role from the late eighteenth century on. They formulated Islamic responses to the challenge of Western power and claims to scientific truth and superiority, but sought "progress" and the modernizing of religious institutions.

In the Arab world, Africa, India, and Indonesia this trend had a great influence on nationalist ideology and politics. The idea of an Algerian nation owed much to the teaching of the Association of Reformist Ulema led by Ben Badis and founded in 1931 under the inspiration of Egyptian reformism. Modern Nigerian Islam and politics were profoundly influenced by the Usman dan Fodio movement of the early nineteenth century. The creation of Pakistan in 1947 under the leadership of Jinnah and the Muslim League is a major example of political significance, and the continuing importance of the Muhammidiyah Association (founded in 1912) in Indonesia shows the social and welfare significance of such reformist movements.

Reformist *ulema* tended to become subordinated to more secular, liberal, and urban-based nationalist movements in the nationalist struggles of the twentieth century and to be politically sidelined by the newly independent states, as happened in Algeria, Egypt, and most radically of all in Turkey under Kemal *Atatürk.

Traditionalist 'ulema opposed them, distrusting their support of individual interpretation in the shari'a, their alleged openness to the West and concern for change. In Saudi Arabia, with dynastic rule and a strict interpretation of Islamic law, the 'ulema play a larger role than in any other Sunni state. The revival of the Ulema movement in Indonesia (founded in 1926) grew into an important opposition to the Masyumi modernists.

In general, the Sunni traditionalist 'ulema too have been forced into subservience to the state. Iranian Shi'i mullahs, on the other hand, had a historically stronger position and preserved greater social and economic autonomy through their schools, universities, religious endowments, and links with the bazaar. This played a key part in their emergence under the Ayatollah Khomeini as the dominant force in the revolution, together with their capacity to carry the street and urban masses with them in a populist call for social justice. The foundation of an Islamic republic under the "Guardianship of the Jurist" represents a novel attempt to provide a model of what an Islamic state should be.

Modern radical Islamic movements have often attacked popular Sufism, the 'ulema, and regimes alike as corrupt, calling for resistance to "non-Islamic" practices and the influence of foreign powers. They seek to make society an Islamic order based on the Quran and the law on the model of the Prophet's first community of believers in Medina. The Muslim Brothers of Egypt, founded in 1928 among new urban classes, are the leading Sunni example. They were brutally suppressed under Nasser in 1954 and 1965 but occupy a leading oppositional role in the Egyptian National Assembly under Mubarak. This trend became politically important in the late 1980s in Algeria, Tunisia, Jordan, and wings of the Palestinian movement, often in the cities and among students and young people. The Muslim Brotherhood has been suppressed in Syria (particularly in Hama in 1982). All groups operate in a framework of the nation-state and modern party organization.

More extreme and sectarian groups now declare that Muslim society must be entirely re-created from the beginning by jihad as there is no true Islam save that of the group members, everyone else being in a "state of ignorance" (jahiliya). Such a group assassinated President Sadat of Egypt in 1981.

Hostility to "capitalism" and "socialism," the call for a return to communal existence, "authenticity," and the pursuit of social justice and welfare are powerful utopian appeals precisely because they are shorn of political and practical details. In a context of severe economic problems, the disappointments of independence, the growth of bureaucracies, party,

military, and security apparatuses with their surveillance and patronage networks, and the attempt to close off any space for opposition, the language of divine truth can become the only publicly available powerful weapon against the corruption of princes. Disparate oil wealth, massive economic problems, Palestinian-Israeli conflict, and the lack of power in the world system as the "South" seems yet more subjugated to the "North" have created fertile ground for such movements since the 1960s, and their attraction is likely to remain strong.

(See also RELIGION AND POLITICS.)

Hamid Enayat, *Modern Islamic Political Thought* (London, 1982). Edward Mortimer, *Faith and Power: The Politics of Islam* (New York, 1982). Michael Gilsenan, *Recognizing Islam* (London, 1982 and 1990; New York, 1983). James P. Piscatori, ed., *Islam in the Political Process* (Cambridge, U.K., 1983). Edmund Burke, III and Ira M. Lapidus, eds., *Islam, Politics, and Social Movements* (Berkeley, Los Angeles, and London, 1988). John L. Esposito, ed., *Islam in Asia: Religion, Politics and Society* (Oxford, 1988). Sami Zubeida, *Islam, the People and the State* (London and New York, 1988).

MICHAEL GILSENAN

ISOLATIONISM. The term *isolationism* denotes a country's determination to avoid unwanted foreign involvements and the power to compel others to respect that intention. In practice the internal and external *foreign policy environment of the United States permitted an isolationist policy only under uniquely favorable circumstances. U.S. isolationism was never a mere response to geographic factors or a thoughtless preoccupation with internal concerns or self-sufficient pursuits. The United States was never a hermit nation; its isolationism was always military and political, never commercial or intellectual. From its beginning the United States faced the recurrent demands for protection of its commercial and trading interests, the pressures of democratic ideologues to involve the country wherever freedom and self-determination seemed to be at stake, and the necessity to curtail or eliminate competing centers of power in the Western Hemisphere or threats to the *balance of power in Europe. The Founders demanded the freedom of action that would enable the nation, in George Washington's words, to choose "peace or war, as our interests, guided by justice, shall counsel." Together these external pressures permitted little isolation, whether in mind or action, from the major trends and events in world politics. From its founding the United States became involved in every European war that ventured onto the Atlantic.

Behind the isolationism of the Founders was the conviction that the United States would render itself more harm than good by meddling in external affairs that were not its direct concern. Policy, so defined, governed the conduct of nations generally. U.S. non-involvement in the political and military affairs of

Europe in the nineteenth century resulted from the continent's fundamental stability. The perennial *security of the United States from European encroachment in the absence of costly defense measures created the illusion that such security flowed, not from the European equilibrium or British naval dominance of the Atlantic, but from the great ocean itself. For many in the United States, security became synonymous with separation from the politics of Europe under the assumption that no European development could endanger the United States. What began to change after 1900 was the increasing frequency of trends and events that seemed to challenge the country's ever-expanding interests. Interwar isolationists still presumed that German power and expansionism could not endanger the security of a United States properly defended with air and naval power. By the late 1930s U.S. isolationism assumed an Asia-first cast; leading isolationists who opposed any involvement in European affairs from 1939 to 1941 revealed no restraint in their demands for an uncompromising posture toward Japanese expansion in the Far East.

After Pearl Harbor some historians accused the isolationists of poor judgment, sympathy for *fascism, even denying the United States the policies required to prevent war. A determined, if ineffectual, isolationism reappeared in opposition to the *Cold War involvements in Europe from the *Truman Doctrine to the *North Atlantic Treaty Organization (NATO), as well as in the determination of some Republicans, in their response to the China, Indochina, and Korea issues, to return U.S. foreign policy to an Asia-first orientation. Only later amid the globalist policies of the Cold War did many historians and analysts begin to judge that the isolationists of the 1930s were not totally wrong in their efforts to constrain the country's burgeoning commitments that led eventually to a two-front U.S. war during World War II. But isolationism cannot describe the preferences of those in the United States who, since midcentury, have favored a more limited definition of national interests and thus a more restricted use of force than that demanded by concepts of global danger and responsibility.

(See also AMERICAN FOREIGN POLICY.)

Selig Adler, *The Isolationist Impulse: Its Twentieth-Century Reaction* (New York, 1957). Manfred Jonas, *Isolationism in America, 1935–1941* (Ithaca, N.Y., 1966).

NORMAN A. GRAEBNER

ISRAEL. On 14 May 1948, Israel declared its independence, following a UN resolution dividing the former British colonial mandate of *Palestine into a Jewish and an Arab state. Israeli leaders affirmed that the new state belonged to all the Jewish people and invited immigration from Jews worldwide.

Israel's founders began to settle in Palestine in the 1880s, joining a small Jewish population already resident in the biblical lands. Jewish immigrants, inspired by *Zionism and escaping from *anti-semitism, came in increasing numbers, mainly from Eastern Europe. They built a polity, called the yishuv, creating many social and political institutions and developing a new national language: modern Hebrew. However, their goals clashed with those of the indigenous Arab population, causing an intercommunal conflict throughout the British mandate period.

The *Holocaust in Europe greatly increased Jewish migration and strengthened support for the state-building project among the Western Jewish diaspora and among Western opinion generally. The new state, led by the dynamic David *Ben-Gurion, won rapid diplomatic recognition from both the United States and the Soviet Union. But Arab residents of Palestine and many governments of surrounding Arab states remained opposed. The day after Israel's declaration of independence, units of Arab armies entered Palestine and joined Arab irregular forces in an effort to prevent the birth of the new state. Israel soon prevailed and armistices signed with neighboring states in 1949 established its new boundaries. During hostilities, some 700,000 Arabs became *refugees.

The social, political, and economic institutions of the yishuv proved resilient and enduring after 1948, but the Jewish homeland nevertheless changed profoundly. Ben-Gurion and his colleagues set up a strong state, and the population grew rapidly with the influx of new immigrants—Holocaust survivors from Europe and Jews from Muslim countries in Asia and North Africa. Immigrants doubled the population from 650,000 to 1.4 million between 1948 and 1951. By 1990, Israel's population had reached nearly 4.6 million. Immigration of Jews from the Soviet Union, especially strong after 1989, could substantially increase Israel's population in the 1990s.

Israel is a *parliamentary democracy with a *cabinet government accountable to a single-chamber legislature elected by *proportional representation. This system encourages a multiparty system and promotes many different opinions in Israel's legislature, known as the Knesset. Israel's print media express diverse and outspoken opinions and Israelis participate actively in politics and electoral campaigns, enlivening Israeli *democracy.

From the foundation of the state until 1977, the Labor Party and its direct predecessors dominated political life. The party's power rested on its control of key institutions of the yishuv, especially the Histadrut, the central trade union, with its large network of social services, health care facilities, and agricultural and industrial enterprises. Under Labor's influence, Israel's economy and social policy came to be heavily dominated by government institutions, on a social-democratic model.

During the 1970s, however, Labor lost its political preeminence. Some attribute this change to disillusionment among the country's elite with Labor's performance, especially in national defense. The 1977 general election for the first time failed to provide Labor with a governing coalition; in that election, the right-wing Likud bloc surpassed Labor. For the next fifteen years, Likud governed at the head of its own coalition, or in a "national unity" coalition with Labor. Likud's first prime minister, Menachem Begin, won the Nobel Peace Prize jointly with Egypt's President Anwar *Sadat in recognition of the peace agreement of 1979 between the two countries. Likud was not inclined, however, to make further "land for peace" accords. Elections in June 1992 dealt a sharp defeat to Likud and enabled Labor to form a new government, opening the way for new policies, especially toward Middle East peace.

Israeli society has been deeply affected by the *Arab-Israeli conflict and especially by the series of wars that Israel has fought with various Arab countries—in 1948, 1956, 1967, 1973, and 1982. Israel won these conflicts with its powerful military and security system, but the Israeli public has nonetheless felt embattled in a hostile region, a feeling that was accentuated in 1991 when Israel was exposed to Iraqi missile attacks during the *Gulf War.

In the 1980s, Israel's conventional military strength was among the world's most powerful—a standing army of 100,000, backed by an elaborate reserve system of 500,000, and armed with very sophisticated weaponry. Though effective, Israel's defense system has been a burden on the economy. Defense expenditures—about thirty percent of GNP on average—are very high and the compulsory draft and annual reserve duty impose other substantial costs.

Israel has built an advanced industrial economy, which is strong in a number of high-technology fields, especially military equipment. Rapid development of the economy was spurred by the high level of education and technical competence of Israel's immigrants as well as by heavy state spending and large amounts of external capital. Major sources of external capital include reparations from the Federal Republic of Germany, contributions from Jews in the diaspora, funds brought in by immigrants, and—especially since the early 1970s—aid from the United States.

The government not only plays a leading role in the Israeli economy, it is also the country's largest civilian employer. The *security services and armed forces, and the firms that they directly or indirectly control, are also very large employers. So is the Histadrut and its firms and institutions; Koor Industries, a Histadrut company, is Israel's largest corporate employer, with interests ranging from steel and cement to salad oil. These three networks are the core of the Israeli economy, and Likud did not seek to dismantle them. During the 1980s, however, there were growing doubts in Israel about the effectiveness of these institutions and their future economic viability. A banking crisis in 1983 underscored the economic problems. Voices in favor of *privatization or economic restructuring emerged in both Likud and the Labor Party in the 1980s, though such voices remained in the minority. A few important changes have taken place, however. For example, government subsidies to Koor have been cut, Koor has reduced its payroll by a third, and control of the firm has passed out of the hands of the Histadrut.

One of Israel's most difficult economic and development issues is its shortage of water. With a high population density and relatively low rainfall, it has pioneered in water conservation methods, including systems of drip irrigation for agriculture. With a growing population and increasing industrial and agricultural water needs, Israel faces a major challenge to ensure its future water supplies.

Within Israel, political conflicts reflect a number of important social cleavages. The deepest cleavage is between Israel's Jewish and Arab citizens. The latter, numbering 830,000 in 1990 or eighteen percent of the population, are not allowed to serve in the country's armed forces and they face a variety of barriers to their economic and professional advancement. Most Arabs affirm their identity as Israelis, but they tend to feel that their future is uncertain and their rights unprotected in a state which defines itself as Jewish.

Another important cleavage is between Israel's Ashkenazim, or European Jews, and the equal number of "Oriental" Jews who have come from countries in the Middle East and North Africa. The former hold most of the top posts in business, politics, the military, and the professions, while the latter are heavily represented among occupations with lower pay and prestige. Many Oriental Jews feel that they face prejudice and discrimination and that their culture and heritage are not sufficiently respected. Their resentment has been effectively mobilized by the Likud and other right-wing forces.

Israel also faces conflict over the role of Jewish religion in the life of Israel society. Though its active adherents number less than a fifth of the Jewish population, Orthodox Judaism has considerably influenced public policy. Orthodox religious courts govern all Jewish marriage and divorce, for example, and the state subsidizes Orthodox religious schools. Beginning in the 1970s, religious parties held the balance in the Knesset, so their influence grew further, much to the dismay of many secular Jews.

In the West Bank and Gaza, occupied by Israel since the June War of 1967, the 1.7 million Palestinian inhabitants have had practically no civil or political *rights. The Israeli government appropriated much of their land and built many Jewish settlements there. After twenty years of Israeli rule, the Palestinians rose in a popular revolt known as the *intifada, demanding national independence.

The issue of the territories has been a key political division in Israel since 1967. The debate over territories also involves questions about the boundaries and nature of Israel. Hard-liners or "hawks" lay claim to the whole "Land of Israel," referring to biblical, historical rights as well as security concerns. Some hawks even talk of "transfer"—a policy to remove Palestinians from the land, to make it exclusively Jewish. The "doves" place more emphasis on compromise over territory and promotion of a secular, civil state and society, in which all citizens are equal. Territorial issues are also the focus of much extraparliamentary politics; Gush Emunim, a religious millenarian movement, leads the drive to settle the territories, while its secular opponents like Peace Now agitate for withdrawal and territorial compromise.

The Arab-Israeli conflict has dominated Israeli foreign relations. After 1967, Israel developed a particularly close alliance with the United States. Israel has also had close relations with important states in Western Europe, including Britain, France, and Germany. These ties enabled Israel to maintain its economic and military strength, and they paved the way for privileged trade relations in the 1980s: a free-trade link to the United States and status as a special trading partner with the European Community.

After the June War of 1967, Israel faced diplomatic isolation from the Soviet bloc and many countries in the *Third World and it encountered hostility at the UN and in many world gatherings. That isolation began to ease in the late 1980s, particularly as the *Cold War ended; in 1991 the Soviet Union restored diplomatic relations and the Soviet successor states followed suit. In the Middle East, however, to date Israel has gained diplomatic relations with only one Arab country—Egypt.

Peace talks began in the fall of 1991 between Israel and its Arab neighbors, opening up a possibility of regional peace, including possible accords on disarmament, water, environmental protection, and joint efforts of trade and development. Such agreements required lengthy talks and extensive concessions on the part of both Israel and its negotiating partners. In spite of the high cost of continuing hostilities, it remains to be seen whether the parties will be able to summon the political will to reach such historic agreements. The outcome will immeasurably effect Israel in the years ahead.

(See also INTERNATIONAL MIGRATION; RELIGION AND POLITICS.)

Dan Horowitz and Moshe Lissak, *Origins of the Israeli Polity* (Chicago, 1978). Ian Lustick, *Arabs in a Jewish State* (Austin, Tex., 1980). Shmuel N. Eisenstadt, *The Transformation of Israeli Society* (London, 1985). Asher Arian, *Politics in Israel: The Second Generation*, rev. ed. (Chatham, N.J., 1989). Baruch Kimmerling, *Israeli State and Society: Boundaries and Frontiers* (Albany, N.Y., 1989).

BARUCH KIMMERLING
JON SIMONS

ITALY. A nation-state since 1861, Italy has so far experienced three different regimes. It was a constitutional monarchy with limited, but increasing, political participation until 1922, when it fell under Fascist rule. Then, in 1946, three years after the collapse of the Fascist government, it became—as it remains today—a republic with a parliamentary form of government. (It had required prolonged internal opposition, war, and the Resistance struggle against occupying Nazi forces and the remnants of *Fascism to create a new, democratic regime.) Once Italy abolished the *monarchy through a referendum, a constituent assembly drafted a constitution that was very progressive with respect to civil, political, and social rights but rather traditional with respect to the structures of the state. For fear of the reemergence of authoritarian rulers, a weak executive was shaped, a parliament composed of two houses with the same functions and the same powers was created, and *proportional representation was introduced. All this puts Italy in the category of consensual democracies with consociational opportunities and propensities. Since then, all governments have been multiparty coalitions. Until 1981, all prime ministers had been members of the Democrazia Cristiana (DC). Indeed, only three prime ministers (the Republican Giovanni Spadolini and the Socialists Bettino Craxi and Giuliano Amato) have not belonged to the DC. (Craxi holds the record for the longest lasting cabinet: 1,060 days [August 1983–June 1986]).

Backed by the *Roman Catholic church and the business community and enjoying the support of U.S. administrations, the DC has provided both Italy's underlying political stability and the tensions leading to short-term instabilities. Among the democracies, only the DC and the Liberal Democratic Party in Japan have remained in power without interruption since the end of World War II—and in fact the DC has held power for a longer period of time. Without doubt, the DC occupies the center of the Italian political alignment and has consistently been capable of creating coalitions around itself: from 1948 to 1962 with the Partito Liberale Italiano (PLI), the Partito Repubblicano Italiano (PRI), and the Partito Socialista Democratico Italiano (PSDI); from 1962 to 1976, dropping the Liberals and including the Partito Socialista Italiano (PSI); from 1976 to 1979, leading all-DC governments with the favorable abstentions of almost all the other parties including Partito Comunista Italiano (PCI); from 1980 on, with the PLI, the PRI, the PSDI, and the PSI.

With stability of political coalitions since the birth of the Italian Republic in 1946, stability of governmental personnel (fifty-one governments but only thirteen prime ministers, among them the most important DC leaders: Alcide De Gasperi, Amintore Fanfani, Aldo Moro, and Giulio Andreotti, in addition to long tenures by the same ministers in key posts), and even stability of policies, governmental instability represents a sort of safety valve for a political system without alternation. Changes in the relative strength of DC factions are largely responsible for governmental instability, allowing some turnover in governmental personnel and, correspondingly, in the many patronage positions dispensed by the government.

Economic reconstruction and the subsequent economic miracle of the late 1950s and 1960s were achieved thanks to a shrewd, though probably unplanned, combination of two elements: unregulated social change and a mixed economy. The sociopolitical climate created by the DC produced an individualistic mobilization of the Italian population, accompanied by mass migrations from the south to the north, from the agricultural sector to the industrial and the tertiary sectors, and from rural areas to large towns. Moreover, for patronage purposes the DC both inflated the public administration and expanded the public sector of the economy, notably through the Istituto per la Ricostruzione Industriale (IRI), which helped it keep tight control over the banking system. Until recently, the radio and television system was also state controlled.

So long as resources kept growing, this strategy allowed the DC to enlarge and consolidate its power base. Because of its real or perceived subordination to the Soviet Union, the PCI was not considered a legitimate or credible claimant for governmental power. However, the PCI did play the role of a legitimate opposition, gathering votes of protest and for change. At the beginning of the 1970s a series of political, cultural, and socioeconomic changes threatened the continuation of DC rule. The process of disengagement of the PCI from the Soviet Union was finalized by its criticism of the Soviet intervention in Czechoslovakia and acceptance of the *North Atlantic Treaty Organization. At the same time, the Socialists were no longer willing to accept a subordinate role in DC-led coalitions and openly advocated a leftist alliance. The student movement and renewed militancy of industrial workers indicated the need for profound changes in the nature of the social relations and the distribution of social power. In a national referendum on the divorce law, a sizable majority voted against making divorce illegal again. Catholic cultural dominance was defeated for the first time, even though the Church remains an influential actor on the sociopolitical scene. Finally, a long period of economic difficulties began, largely attributed to DC mismanagement of the economy, excessive party patronage in the public sector, a hypertrophied and inefficient public administration, and a crisis over the form of government as shaped by the DC (the so-called "material" constitution).

By no means deprived of its electoral support (oscillating between thirty-three and thirty-nine percent), never abandoned by the Church, the Italian business community or the United States, the DC withstood the crisis of the 1970s thanks also to divisions among the *Left. The controversial PCI

strategy of *historic compromise was never shared by the PSI, which disoriented leftist groups. In the meantime, the shrinking, the diversification, and the fragmentation of the working class seemed to go hand in hand with the fragmentation of the political spectrum. Always divided into three competing factions—the largest, the Confederazione Generale Italiana dei Lavoratori (CGIL), dominated by the PCI but also including the PSI; the second largest, the Confederazione Italiana Sindicati Lavoratori (CISL), fundamentally a voice of the DC; the third, the Unione Italiana del Lavoro (UIL), led by the PSI but also including the PSDI and the PRI—Italian unions pursued a strategy of centralization and wage flattening. Two types of reactions followed: industrial cadres and foremen challenged union policies and created their own unofficial organizations; and workers' groups in specific sectors (for instance, the railway system and state schools) gave birth to special bodies for representation and bargaining called Cobas (grassroots committees). All this severely hampered the official union movement and the Left while making it more difficult to produce coherent governmental policies. Divisions within the union movement also allowed the curtailment of the indexation system (which linked wages to inflation) by decree of Prime Minister Craxi in 1984. In addition, the improvement of economic conditions, almost a new boom toward the end of the 1980s, further reduced the power of the unions. Unemployment, especially among young southerners, was mitigated by various welfare measures. Increasingly the developed regions of the north are coming into conflict with the central government over issues of distribution and power.

Still revolving around the DC, Italian governing coalitions appear incapable of managing the necessary processes of adjustment. Italian institutions have increasingly come under attack. At best they serve as intermediaries among competing interests, an art in which the DC has excelled. The coalitions do not allow for a swift and incisive process of decision making; not even the directives of the *European Community are rapidly transformed into Italian legislation. Although faithful and convinced Europeans, Italian decision makers continue to play a passive role on the European as well as the global scene. Once totally subservient to U.S. policies, now Italian governments remain unable to exploit their newly acquired *foreign policy discretion except, to some extent, on the Mediterranean scene and in commercial dealings with Eastern European countries. A united Europe remains both a goal and a framework in which to play a role and its existence has brought the Italian economy and polity stability, resilience, and positive stimuli. Domestic obstacles to further change continue nevertheless.

Politically, the problem of alternation of government persists. The DC has been in power since 1946, and the alternation of different governing coalitions is deemed desirable and useful in order to produce a circulation of the political class, to break the rigidity of interests, and to curtail the powers of the parties—the *partitocrazia,* or pervasive, exaggerated, and oppressive role of the parties in politics. Institutionally, the goal is to shape a more modern, flexible, dynamic form of government. The solution to the political problem is made both easier and more complicated by the crisis and transformation of the PCI, which changed its name to the Partito Democratico della Sinistra (PDS) in February 1991. What used to be a powerful and threatening alternative is no longer threatening, but is also less powerful than might be necessary to provide for a real alternative (either by leading a non-DC government or throwing its weight behind it).

Somewhat disenchanted and less participatory than in the past, Italian voters are looking for a restructuring of Italian institutions. Two solutions have been suggested. The majority of politicians and commentators advocate a strengthening of the parliamentary form of government through electoral reform to give more power and a more visible democratic mandate to the prime minister. This might streamline relationships between the government and a reformed parliament and redefine and circumscribe the role and power of political parties. The Socialist recipe, a minority solution, favors a change in the form of government: from a parliamentary to a presidential republic, according to either the U.S. or the French model. Advocates of a presidential system emphasize the greater decisional efficacy purportedly associated with this form of government. The advocates of a strengthened parliamentary form of government, on the contrary, underscore the need to allow for a continued representation of diversified interests while giving voters the power to elect their governments. Moreover, a lingering fear from the Fascist period of too much power residing in the hands of one person serves as a barrier against the establishment of a presidential republic.

The erosion of traditional sociopolitical cleavages, especially those based on conflicts between state and Church and between entrepreneurs and industrial workers, has made for a more complex society. As with other European societies but perhaps slightly more so, Italians want to distinguish themselves according to specific styles of life. Always a status-conscious society, Italy is now enjoying both the pleasures and the troubles of differentiation. A mass society needs more and better governance. This is, at least, what Italian citizens believe. Italian institutions, Italian governing coalitions, and Italian political parties no longer seem capable of satisfactorily providing that governance. Forty-five years after its return to the democratic fold, having enjoyed the fruits of pluralism, political competition, freedom, and economic growth, Italy is on the verge of important political and institutional changes. What is at stake is not the existence and persistence of the democratic regime—it is the quality and the performance of Italian democracy, the functioning, the improvement, the dynamism, and the transformation of its political and institutional mechanisms and structures that hang in the balance.

(See also CHRISTIAN DEMOCRACY; EUROCOMMUNISM; LABOR MOVEMENT; RELIGION AND POLITICS.)

Norman Kogan, *A Political History of Postwar Italy* (New York, 1981). Donald Sassoon, *Contemporary Italy: Politics, Economy and Society since 1945* (London and New York, 1986). Peter Lange and Marino Regini, eds., *State, Market, and Social Regulation: New Perspectives on Italy* (New York, 1989). Paul Ginsborg, *A History of Contemporary Italy: Society and Politics, 1943–1988* (Harmondsworth, U.K., 1991).

GIANFRANCO PASQUINO

IVORY COAST. See CÔTE D'IVOIRE.

J

JAMAICA. An island nation in the western Caribbean, Jamaica, with 2.3 million inhabitants, is the most populous of the former British West Indian colonies. The economy is very trade dependent: the country imports over sixty percent of what it consumes. The principal economic activities and primary sources of foreign exchange are bauxite mining and alumina production, tourism, and sugar and banana exports. The value of earnings of the illegal marijuana crop, although disputed, is also undoubtedly significant. In the late 1980s, per capita GDP was somewhat over US$800. Over ninety percent of the population is of African or mixed African and European descent. Color is closely related to *class, the lower classes being black, the upper classes largely white, and the middle classes black or brown. Jamaicans are predominantly Christians with the Anglican, Roman Catholic, and Presbyterian churches being the principal denominations. The indigenous Rastafari religion also has a large following especially in the urban lower classes. Independent since 1962, Jamaica is a *parliamentary democracy fashioned after the British Westminster-Whitehall model. The security forces are comparatively small and have complied with the doctrine of civilian supremacy. The two major parties, the People's National Party (PNP) and the Jamaica Labour Party (JLP), have alternated in government since 1944, with each party serving two consecutive terms and then losing at the polls in bids for a third term.

The nationalist movement emerged out of the West Indies–wide labor unrest of the 1930s. The labor rebellion did much to convince the British to initiate the process of *decolonization, which began with the first election with universal suffrage in 1944 and continued with the gradual introduction of self-government in the 1940s and 1950s. The break between the PNP, led by Norman Manley, and the major trade union, whose leader, Alexander Bustamante, formed his own party, the JLP, in 1943, set the pattern of modern politics. It is a highly competitive two-party system, each party having a union base and cross-class electoral support. Initially the parties differed; the PNP had a Fabian socialist position and the JLP a populist one. The PNP had a strong base in the middle classes, and the JLP in the lower classes. These differences gave way to both ideological and sociological convergence of the parties in the 1950s. Both parties pursued a strategy of industrialization based on foreign investment, primarily in bauxite and alumina. Tourism was another significant growth sector, also heavily based on foreign investment. This strategy resulted in significant economic growth in the 1950s and 1960s, but also a large trade deficit, a highly import-dependent manufacturing sector, growing unemployment, and great income inequality.

After coming to power in 1972 the PNP revived its commitment to democratic *socialism and embarked on a reform process that included expansion of state control over crucial sectors of the economy, improvement of health and educational services, increases in income levels of the lower classes, political mobilization, and a turn in *foreign policy toward nonalignment. This led to a class realignment in the 1976 elections, won by the PNP, with the upper and middle classes moving toward the JLP and the lower classes toward the PNP.

In the 1970s Jamaica's Prime Minister Michael Manley took a leadership role in Third World politics. Jamaica was prominent in the promotion of the *Law of the Sea Conference and the International Bauxite Association. The PNP's nonaligned policy, particularly its close relations with Cuba, resulted in sharply deteriorating relations with the United States. Domestically, the relationship to the transnational bauxite/aluminum companies underwent a significant change; the Jamaican state acquired a stake in the local operations of these companies and strengthened its own capacity for research and management in the industry. A *balance-of-payments crisis forced the government to accept *International Monetary Fund (IMF) agreements in 1977 and 1978, and the ensuing deterioration of popular living standards led to the defeat of the PNP in the 1980 elections. The election campaign was characterized by unprecedented levels of violence, with over 500 people losing their lives in political warfare.

At the outset, the JLP government under the leadership of Edward Seaga quickly established warm relations with the United States and committed itself to a free-market, export-oriented path of development, signing on to a *World Bank structural adjustment loan. Other than deregulating imports, cutting public spending, particularly on social services, and privatizing a small number of public enterprises, however, the government did not greatly reduce the state's role in the economy. For instance, in the important bauxite-alumina sector, the government increased its role in ownership and marketed a growing share of alumina and bauxite to parties other than the four North American multinationals, which had accounted for all of Jamaica's bauxite-alumina exports prior to the PNP government's 1974 initiative. The JLP government's political posture and the good relations with the United States did result in significant amounts of official development loans. By the mid-1980s Jamaica had one of the highest per capita debt burdens in the world, with debt service consuming half of export earnings. Tourism made a spectacular recovery in the 1980s, and production in export platforms made possible by the Caribbean Basin Initiative and other concessionary U.S. legislation increased significantly in the latter half of the decade. But the bauxite industry experienced a decline in the first half of the decade and growth in other sectors remained sluggish.

These problems stimulated several rounds of devaluations, which drastically cut living standards and undermined the government's support, leading to a victory of the PNP in the 1989 elections. Owing in part to the PNP's shift to the center and in part to the constraints of IMF agreements, the new PNP government's policies differed little from those of its predecessor. In fact, the PNP government accelerated the divestment of state enterprises and deregulation of the economy.

(See also ENGLISH-SPEAKING CARIBBEAN; NONALIGNED MOVEMENT; POLITICAL VIOLENCE.)

Owen Jefferson, *The Post-War Economic Development of Jamaica* (Mona, Jamaica, 1972). Trevor Munroe, *The Politics of Constitutional Decolonization: Jamaica 1944–1962* (Mona, Jamaica, 1972). Evelyne Huber Stephens and John D. Stephens, *Democratic Socialism in Jamaica: The Political Movement and Social Transformation in Dependent Capitalism* (Princeton, N.J., 1986).

JOHN D. STEPHENS
EVELYNE HUBER

JAMES, C. L. R. Born in *Trinidad, West Indies, Cyril Lionel Robert James (1901–1989) attended Queen's Royal College (QRC), a local high school, where he taught for a few years after he graduated. He also wrote for *Trinidad* and *The Beacon*, two Trinidadian magazines, before he migrated to England in 1932. Later that year, James published *The Life of Captain Cipriani*, and began to write on cricket for the *Manchester Guardian*. In England James became involved in the Independent Labour Party and later joined the Trotskyist movement, out of which came *World Revolution, 1917–1936* (1937). In 1936 James published *Minty Alley*, his only novel, which he had brought with him from Trinidad. Before leaving London to do political work in the United States in 1938, James published *Black Jacobins*, a major analysis of the Haitian Revolution and

one of the works by which he is best remembered. In England, James also completed two other major intellectual feats: he translated Boris Souvarine's *Stalin* (1939) from French to English and, with the assistance of Ria Stone, translated Karl *Marx's *Economic and Philosophical Manuscripts of 1844*, the first time that this work was translated into English.

In the United States, James continued his work in the socialist movement. In 1939, he met with Leon *Trotsky in Mexico to discuss "the Negro Question," as the political problems of African Americans were labeled at that time. Until 1953 when he was deported to the United Kingdom during the McCarthy trials, James worked to organize the sharecroppers in the South. Together with Raya Dunayevskaya, James formed the Johnson-Forest Tendency (pseudonyms for James and Dunayevskaya, respectively) after breaking with Trotsky's interpretation of *Marxism in 1940. In the United States James authored a number of works. Among them were *The Invading Socialist Society* (1947), an analysis of the mass movement toward new forms of social organization; *Notes on the Dialectics* (1948), an examination of Hegelian dialectics and its application to the proletarian struggle; *State Capitalism and World Revolution* (1950), "the theoretical summation of the work of the Johnson-Forest Tendency"; and *Mariners, Renegades and Castaways* (1953), an examination of Herman Melville's fiction, which he wrote while he was incarcerated on Ellis Island. In this, his American period, James also began a potentially important work, *Notes on American Civilization*, which Anna Grimshaw published in summary form as *The Struggle for Happiness*. His abrupt departure from the United States prevented him from completing this work.

Returning to England, James picked up where he had left off. In the wake of the Hungarian Revolution, together with Grace Lee and Pierre Chaulieu, he wrote *Facing Reality* (1958). In 1958, James returned to Trinidad where he worked with Eric Williams, his former student at QRC and colleague in London in the 1930s, to develop the People's National Movement (PNM), the nationalist party of the country. In Trinidad, James edited *The Nation*, the weekly organ of the PNM, which carried forward the struggle for national independence. After spending two years in Trinidad, James ended his association with the PNM, later formed the Workers and Farmers Party, contested the 1965 general elections, and lost. In that Trinidad period James published the very important *Modern Politics* (1960), a brief discussion of the development of *democracy, and *Beyond a Boundary* (1963), a seminal work that documents the manner in which the dominant culture disseminates its values through sports.

After leaving Trinidad, James kept on writing and working. In 1977, he completed *Nkrumah and the Ghana Revolution* and returned to the United States in the 1970s where he taught at Federal City College, in Washington, D.C., for a number of years. After his teaching stint in Washington, James returned to London where he died in 1989. James was buried in Tunapuna, Trinidad, his birthplace. In the latter period of his life, James returned to Trinidad occasionally, lectured, and wrote a number of pamphlets, among the more important of which was *Walter Rodney and the Question of Power* (1983). In many ways, James remained a Renaissance person. In his long life, he wrote about history, politics, culture, music, philosophy, and sports. To the end of his days, he was a supreme lover of cricket; a compilation of his many articles on the game is contained in *Cricket* (1986).

James's importance lay in his creative application of Marxist principles to the struggle for liberty that took place in the world in which he lived, particularly in the *Third World. He proudly proclaimed himself a Marxist and believed that eventually socialism would triumph. He did not believe in what he called the "state socialism" of the Soviet Union nor in the bureaucracy of Eastern Europe as they existed until recently. As he noted in *Facing Reality:*

The whole world today lives in the shadow of the state power. This state power is an ever-present self-perpetuating body over and above society. It transforms the human personality into a mass of economic needs to be satisfied by decimal points of economic progress. It robs everyone of initiative and clogs the free development of society. This state power, by whatever name it is called, One-Party or Welfare State, destroys all pretense of government *by* the people, *of* the people. All that remains is government *for* the people.

James always believed in the power of the working people and their capacity to organize themselves for their own liberation. To him, the alternative was clear: *socialism or barbarism. He remained optimistic about the eventual triumph of socialism and welcomed the emergence of *Solidarity in Poland. He also believed in the creativity of the masses. "Any cook can govern," he argued, and he saw in the everyday activities of ordinary people the seeds of a new socialist society. This is one reason why he was interested in all new forms of social organization and popular cultural forms such as the U.S. cinema industry of the 1950s or the calypso movement in Trinidad and Tobago. James's legacy remains his belief in the working people and their capacity eventually to triumph.

(See also ENGLISH-SPEAKING CARIBBEAN.)

C. L. R. James, *Black Jacobins* (New York, 1963). C. L. R. James, *Notes on Dialectics* (Westport, Conn., 1980). Paul Buhle, *The Artist as Revolutionary* (London, 1988).

SELWYN R. CUDJOE

JAPAN. Modern Japan was born in the midnineteenth century, like virtually all other contemporary nation-states in Asia, Africa, and Latin America, out of unexpected, unsought, and unwelcome contact with Western powers. But unlike most others, the Japanese escaped direct physical conquest and colonial rule. Nonetheless, Japan's encounter with the West had far-reaching and devastating effects on a nation that had lived in deliberate isolation from the world for nearly two and a half centuries. It triggered an immediate and bloody revolution, known as the Meiji Restoration, and led to a radical transformation of the nation's entire political order and social system. The leaders of the new government were all as fervently nationalist as royalist and saw their primary mission as the preservation and consolidation of Japan's political independence and territorial integrity in a world dominated by predatory Western imperialist powers. That mission called for the creation of modern armed forces equal to the Western powers', and that, in turn, called for the development of a modern industrial economy.

This mission was partially accomplished by the turn of the century when the Japanese economy, while still predominantly agricultural, had a thriving light-industrial sector. By the first decade of the new century, a world-class shipbuilding industry had emerged and railroads crisscrossed the island empire. By the second decade of the century, Japan was building not only all its locomotives but all its naval cruisers as well. By then, its military force had fought and won wars against China and Russia, and attained international status as the third-largest naval power, surpassed only by the United States and Britain.

Democracy and Authoritarian Reaction in Prewar Japan. Prewar Japan, however, experienced much more than just the rapid industrialization of its economy and the rise of its military power. The direct contact with the Western powers led to exposure to a broad range of Western ideas and *ideologies as well as to Western weapons, industrial machinery, and consumer products. As a result, the cultural preferences and ideological beliefs of the Japanese people became considerably more diverse and complex than previously. Moreover, as part of its frantic drive to modernize Japan and catch up with the Western powers, the Meiji government established a national system of compulsory elementary and voluntary middle-school education only a few years after the new government itself was established. Universities and colleges, both public and private and many with American and European professors on their faculty, soon followed.

The imported Western ideologies gave rise to political movements and parties. By the mid-1870s, groups, collectively known as freedom and people's rights movements, had been formed in various parts of the country and had begun to press for the establishment of a Western-style parliament. By the early 1880s, Japan's first political parties were founded and the ruling oligarchs themselves had begun to prepare for the introduction of an at least nominally constitutional and parliamentary form of government. In 1889, a constitution, based on the Prussian model, was promulgated, and the next year the first session of the bicameral parliament—known as the Imperial Diet and composed of a House of Representatives of elected members and a House of Peers of hereditary and appointed members—was convened. Two decades later, in the wake of World War I, the parliamentary system appeared successfully established; during the decade, known as Taisho Democracy, not only did a succession of party-based governments rule the country but also democratic theory prevailed in academia, the popular press espoused liberal ideas, and a variety of interest groups and social movements thrived, from Marxist-inspired labor and *peasant unions to Japan's first feminist organization.

The rise of political parties and the antigovernment mass movement, however, provoked the ruling oligarchy to tighten its control of public opinion through the propagation of Confucian and *Shinto dogmas, especially absolute deference and loyalty to the emperor. The government also used thought police, known as the special higher police, to suppress antigovernment and antimilitary movements. The work by the thought police was complemented by a number of laws setting limits to the freedoms of association and assembly, culminating in the 1925 Peace Preservation Law that banned all organizations opposed to Japan's "polity" or its private-property system and made members of such organizations liable to prosecution and punishment, including the death penalty.

Assisted by these authoritarian measures implemented by the civilian government, the military expanded its power and influence at home as rapidly and effectively as abroad. From the beginning, it enjoyed a privileged political position as an institution directly responsible only to the throne and beyond the effective control of the civilian government, a position formalized under imperial Japan's 1889 constitution. In the early 1930s, as the Japanese economy was mired in a prolonged recession and public disaffection with the civilian government's apparent inability to cope with the situation mounted, the military embarked on a series of plans to take over the government by force and in the name of the throne. Within a decade, the military had achieved virtually all of its main objectives: the military-dominated government had signed a military alliance treaty with Nazi Germany and Fascist Italy, vastly expanded the unprovoked *war against China, enacted a total national mobilization law, published a plan to establish a Greater East Asia Co-Prosperity Sphere, a euphemism for an expanded Japanese *colonial empire, and, finally, led Japan into a suicidal war with the United States.

Within half a year of its highly successful surprise attack on Pearl Harbor in December 1941, Japan began to lose one major naval and air battle after another on and around key Pacific islands. None-theless, the military government managed to keep the nation fighting the destructive and tragic war until August 1945 by feeding it outright lies that consistently exaggerated Japanese gains and enemy losses and promised a victory just around the corner. After mid-1944, however, the centrally orchestrated propaganda campaign lost credibility in the face of increasingly frequent and destructive air raids by Allied bombers against Tokyo and other major Japanese cities, the successful landing in and occupation of Okinawa by Allied troops, and, above all, the instant and nearly total destruction of *Hiroshima and Nagasaki by atomic bombs. Combined with the news of Soviet participation in the war against Japan, the reports of the atomic bombing from Hiroshima and Nagasaki shattered the military-controlled propaganda machine and forced the Japanese government, faced with the specter of either total chaos or revolution at home as well as at battle fronts, to seek immediate peace. Japan unconditionally surrendered to the Allied powers on 15 August 1945, and came under their occupation for nearly seven years.

Japan Demilitarized and Democratized. For all intents and purposes, the postwar occupation of Japan was an American enterprise under the direction of the Supreme Commander for the Allied Powers (SCAP), General Douglas MacArthur, rather than an Allied powers' collective effort. According to an elaborate plan prepared long before the Japanese surrender, SCAP arrived in Japan in the fall of 1945 determined to achieve two basic goals, the demilitarization and democratization of Japan, and a sweeping *reform of the country's political, economic, and social institutions in order to accomplish those goals. The ambitious reform program implemented in the first year and a half of the occupation in fact transformed Japan into a fully demilitarized and democratized nation, at least institutionally. By the end of 1945, the Japanese government had taken steps under SCAP's direction to release all political prisoners, repeal the Peace Preservation Law, abolish the special higher police and all other oppressive institutions, emancipate women, recognize and assist labor unions, liberalize education, and democratize the economy. The last involved a halfhearted and only partially successful attempt to eliminate monopolistic *zaibatsu* power over Japan's urban economy and a far more serious and successful attempt to end landlords' dominance of the nation's rural economy and society. More reforms followed in the next two years in such areas as education, labor, antitrust, local government, the civil service, civil and criminal law, and, above all, the constitution itself.

As a result of these occupation-sponsored reforms, especially the enactment of a new, radically democratic, and uniquely pacifist constitution drafted by U.S. lawyers, Japan was reborn into a virtually new nation. Its sovereign was no longer the emperor but the Japanese people; the people's fundamental human rights were unconditionally and permanently guaranteed, rather than guaranteed "subject to law" as under the old constitution; and, above all, Japan as a nation renounced, in Article Nine of its new constitution, its own right either to maintain any form of military power or to engage in acts of war to settle international disputes. In the meantime, Japan's top wartime leaders, with the conspicuous exception of the emperor, were arrested, twenty-five of them were tried by an international military tribunal established in 1946, and seven of them were subsequently sentenced to death and sixteen to imprisonment for life for their "crimes against humanity." Some 200,000 others were removed from public office on the grounds of their wartime collaboration with the military and its policy. The punitive purge, however, virtually bypassed the central government bureaucracy and, in fact, helped it emerge as the de facto policymaker, as well as policy implementer, in postwar Japan.

In the long run, the postwar reforms also helped, directly or indirectly, the rise in political power and influence of the reformed Diet, political parties, and a variety of special interest groups. By the end of 1945, all the four major national parties—i.e., the Liberals, Democrats, Socialists, and Communists— that would continue to dominate electoral and parliamentary politics in the next forty-five years and beyond had been established. Employer associations, farm organizations, and labor unions soon followed. The last became the main source of electoral and financial support for the Socialists, while the organized employers and farmers constituted two of the most important pillars of support for the Liberals and Democrats.

The occupation-sponsored demilitarization of Japan was not as thorough and successful as it might have been but for a dramatic change in U.S. policy within a few years of its initiation in response to the looming *Cold War. By mid-1947, the priority of the occupation policy shifted to the economic rehabilitation and political stabilization, rather than complete demilitarization and democratization, of Japan. By early 1948, U.S. leaders had begun to call for Japan's new role as an important ally in the struggle against international *communism. Following the outbreak of the *Korean War, a 75,000-strong Police Reserve Force was created at SCAP's order. By 1954 this force had evolved into a full-fledged military force of three services, known euphemistically as the Self-Defense Forces (SDF). As the Cold War unfolded, the de facto rearmament of Japan proceeded at a slow but steady pace until, by the end of the 1980s, the SDF became one of the best-equipped and potentially most capable armed forces in the world.

The democratization program also suffered some setbacks as a result of both the change in U.S. policy and independent Japanese initiatives. The substantial decentralization of political power and control accomplished under the initial occupation policy was reversed to some extent after the end of the occupation, especially in the areas of police and educational administration. The municipal police units created during the occupation to counterbalance the centralized power of the national police were absorbed by the latter in 1954, in the name of efficiency and economy. For similar reasons, the popular election of local education board members instituted in 1948 was abolished in 1956 and replaced by appointment by heads of local governments. More importantly, the central government regained effective control of school education through a system of textbook certification by the Ministry of Education under a 1949 law.

*Democracy in postwar Japan may also be said to suffer from the virtual monopoly of government power by the conservatives and, after 1955, by a single conservative party, the Liberal Democrats. Except briefly during the occupation period, the conservatives have dominated the Diet at the expense of the splintered opposition. This perennial monopoly of power sets Japan apart from other industrial democracies and gives rise to charges of the revival of undemocratic and authoritarian government. Moreover, politics in postwar Japan in general and elections in particular have been as often and as seriously tainted by *corruption as politics and elections in prewar Japan.

Under Japan's 1947 constitution, the party that controls the nation's legislative branch also controls both its executive branch and, less directly, its judiciary. This is so because the prime minister must be a member of and elected by the Diet, and he or she in turn appoints all other members of the cabinet. Moreover, a majority of those cabinet members also must be current Diet members. In practice, nearly all cabinet members appointed since 1947 have been incumbent Diet members. The judiciary enjoys, in principle, complete decision-making autonomy and freedom. In practice, however, it has been susceptible to executive and, indirectly, legislative influence because all judges, except the chief judge, of the Supreme Court are appointed by the cabinet, the chief judge is designated by the cabinet for nominal appointment by the emperor, and judges of all other courts—i.e., higher, district, family, and summary courts—are designated by the Supreme Court but appointed by the cabinet.

Like its prewar antecedent, Japan's postwar Diet is bicameral and consists of a House of Representatives and a House of Councillors. Whereas, however, members of the prewar House of Peers were either hereditary or appointed by the emperor, all members of the postwar House of Councillors are, like those of the House of Representatives, popularly elected. Between the two houses, the House of Representatives is the larger (currently 512 seats) and more powerful than the House of Councillors (252 seats). If the two houses fail to agree on a budget bill or the ratification of an international treaty, the decision of the House of Representatives prevails; any other type of bill that has been passed by the House of Representatives but defeated in the House of Councillors becomes law if passed again by the House of Representatives with the concurrence of two-thirds or more of its members.

All but one of the members of the House of Representatives and a majority (152) of the members of the House of Councillors are currently elected from multimember districts. As a result, two or more candidates from the ruling Liberal Democratic Party (LDP) and, less frequently, those from the Social Democratic Party of Japan (SDPJ) routinely run against each other, as well as against candidates from rival parties. Indistinguishable by ideology or policy, these candidates are often forced to compete on the basis of highly personal service to their constituents. Such service usually calls for expenditure of considerable amounts of money not only at election time but even between elections. In the case of LDP candidates, a substantial portion of this money is provided by intraparty factions rather than by the party treasury. The multimember district system thus encourages factionalism in the LDP and, to a lesser extent, in the SDPJ.

As of the early 1990s, there are five factions in the LDP. While not directly concerned with or involved in intraparty debates and decision making on policy issues, these groups are deeply interested and involved in the distribution not only of political money but also of all important party posts and, by virtue of the LDP's control of both the legislative and the executive branches of government, Diet committee chairmanships, cabinet portfolios, and several scores of subcabinet administrative posts. At every Diet election, they engage in fierce fights among themselves for retention of their incumbents and recruitment of new members. They compete with even greater ferocity over the selection of the LDP president who is, thanks to the party's control of the Diet, virtually guaranteed election to the position of Japan's prime minister. In both instances, huge amounts of money are used to buy votes, whether directly or indirectly.

Over the years, the regime of de facto one-party rule has also given rise to a number of competing coalitions of LDP Diet members, senior civil servants, and leaders of special interest groups, each formed with a particular policy area such as agriculture, construction, telecommunications, defense, and so on. In many cases these coalitions have become so entrenched and influential that they are subgovernments for all practical intents and purposes. The perpetual and often intense competition among these subgovernments is another important factor contributing to the rampant "money politics" and all-too-frequent scandals that mar Japan's image and reputation as a mature democracy.

Japan's Emergence as an Economic Superpower. Postwar Japan achieved a far more unambiguous success in the area of economic growth and development. In the fall of 1945, as the occupation forces landed in Japan, the nation was on the verge of total collapse both morally and economically. Well over 10 million people were jobless in the face of a savage inflation. In the next few years, while SCAP was busy trying to reform the nation from top to bottom, a succession of Japanese governments tried hard, but in vain, to overcome the economic crisis. The devastating inflation finally began to be brought under control by a set of draconian belt-tightening measures taken upon the advice of a Detroit banker and special adviser to SCAP, Joseph M. Dodge. These measures helped kill the inflation, but only at the price of a large number of business failures and increased unemployment. It was, ironically, the Korean War and the unexpected boom brought by it that solved Japan's unemployment problem and thus put an end to its protracted postwar economic woes.

Combined with the delayed effects of the fixed dollar-yen exchange rate set in 1949 as part of the deflationary program devised by Dodge, the special procurement boom of the Korean War period paved the way for a series of long peacetime booms beginning in the mid-1950s. Driven by the still-fresh memory of poverty and hunger and led by thriving export trade, the Japanese economy grew thereafter at a rapid and consistent pace unparalleled among advanced industrial nations, until it became the second-largest market economy in the world by the end of the 1960s. In the next two decades, Japan became the world's leading producer and exporter of increasingly sophisticated industrial goods, from textiles, steel, and ships, to televisions, machine tools, automobiles, and semiconductors. By the early 1990s, it was also the world's largest creditor nation and donor of economic aid.

The Japanese "miracle" owed a great deal to the undervalued yen under the fixed-exchange-rate regime and to the availability of cheap oil from the Middle East which replaced domestic coal as the primary energy for Japan's industry in the mid-1960s. As a result, the Japanese economy experienced a severe shock in the early 1970s when U.S. President Richard *Nixon announced in August 1971 a New Economic Policy, including the suspension of the dollar's convertibility and de facto abandonment of the fixed-exchange-rate regime. This put an end to the 360-yen-per-dollar exchange rate that had significantly helped Japanese exporters rapidly expand market share abroad, especially in the United States. The yen's value relative to the dollar's rose rapidly thereafter; between 1971 and 1991, the yen gained by more than sixty percent against the dollar. This change caused considerable hardships among export-dependent Japanese businesses, driving a large number of small businesses to bankruptcy. The 1973 oil crisis compounded the problem and caused Japan's annual economic growth rate to dip below zero for the first time since the early postwar years.

The exchange rate realignment and the oil crisis of the early 1970s led the Japanese economy out of the period of extraordinarily high growth rates into one of more modest and normal rates. Its average annual growth rate fell by more than fifty percent, from well over ten percent in the decade and a half before the 1973 oil crisis to less than five percent after the crisis. Moreover, Japanese exports met increasing protectionist resistance around the world, especially in the United States, in the 1970s and 1980s. The Japanese economy nonetheless survived these adversities by shifting emphasis away from energy-dependent and pollution-generating heavy and chemical industries toward information-dependent and pollution-free high-technology, high-value-added industries and services. Despite the significant deceleration of its growth rate, the Japanese economy continued to outperform all other advanced industrial economies even after the crisis. By the last decade of the twentieth century, Japan had thus emerged as an economic *superpower.

By then, Japan had also become a significant potential military power. The SDF had grown into one of the best-equipped armed forces in the world, and by the late 1980s its defense budget in dollar terms was exceeded, among market-economy nations, only by that of the United States. Japan, however, had become neither a military superpower nor a militarist power. Its defense budget, very large as it was in absolute dollar terms, amounted to only about one percent of Japan's immense GNP, by far the lowest ratio not only among the advanced industrial nations but even in comparison to most developing *Third World nations. The SDF was equipped with some of the most advanced conventional weapons available, but it had no nuclear arsenal at its disposal, nor did it plan to have one in the foreseeable future.

The state of the SDF and the Japanese government policy behind it accurately reflected the prevailing pacifist mood of a Japanese public still haunted by the memories of the wartime and early postwar hardships and deprivations. While the Japanese government launched a rearmament program in compliance with the new U.S. policy following the outbreak of the Korean War, Japanese public opinion never fully accepted the SDF, and the succession of conservative governments by and large stayed within the bounds of the antimilitary public opinion. As a result, the SDF's mission was officially explained as strictly defensive, as complementary to the role of the U.S. forces, as barring any operations abroad, whether independent or as part of an international effort, and, above all, as requiring no offensive, especially nuclear, weapons.

Following the 1979 Soviet invasion of Afghanistan, the restrictions on the SDF's mission and operational scope were slightly relaxed in the name of more equitable burden-sharing with the United States. The Japanese government thus undertook to defend the sea-lanes vital to its self-defense within 1,000 nautical miles of its territory, permitted SDF units to participate in multinational joint military exercises, and committed slightly more than one percent of GNP to defense. The change was, however, more apparent than real, and postwar Japan's fundamental commitment to a nonmilitary path to prosperity and glory remained intact. Moreover, as the Cold War began to wind down and the Soviet threat began to recede rapidly in the latter half of the 1980s, the justification for Japan's expanded defense capability also began to evaporate. As it entered the last decade of the twentieth century, Japan thus remained an economic superpower with respectable but not commanding military power.

Postwar Japan and the World. Much as before *World War II, Japan developed the closest, though often contentious, economic and political relationships with the United States and nations in East Asia. Its relations with nations in other regions of the world, especially Western Europe, the Middle East, and, more recently, Latin America, gradually expanded, but remained far less important, whether materially or psychologically. Its relationships with the Soviet Union and its Cold War allies in Eastern and Central Europe were particularly remote, until the dramatic changes in these nations in the late 1980s and 1990s gave rise to mutual hopes for significant improvement in economic, if not political, relationships.

After the Allied occupation of Japan ended in 1952, U.S. military bases and troops remained in Japan under the terms of the United States–Japan Mutual Security Treaty that was signed in 1951, simultaneously with the Japanese Peace Treaty. Like the first treaty signed between the two nations in the mid-nineteenth century, this original bilateral treaty was "unequal" in the sense that the United States was granted the right to maintain its armed forces in Japan without accepting an explicit obligation to defend Japan. In order to make it more equal, the treaty was revised in 1960 in the face of intense and widespread opposition by millions of Japanese concerned that the military alliance might lead to Japan's involvement in another, and potentially nuclear, war. As it turned out, the alliance, either under the original or under the revised treaty, did not lead to Japan's direct involvement in another war, but it led to perpetuation of Japan's dependence upon U.S. military power, or the "nuclear umbrella," for its own defense and protection. The revised United States–Japan Mutual Security Treaty, which was "automatically" renewed annually after 1970 by mutual consent, thus also perpetuated the "unequal" relationship between the two nations.

Apart from the mutual security treaty, the U.S. occupation of Okinawa since the last days of World War II was the most contentious and troublesome issue between the two governments, until it was resolved by the return of the island group to Japanese administration in 1972. No sooner had the Okinawa problem been amicably disposed of when a succession of trade disputes began to plague *Japan-U.S. relations. For more than two decades from the late 1960s to the early 1990s, as Japanese exports threatened one American industry after another and as the Japanese trade surplus and U.S. deficit increased, government and business leaders of the two nations repeatedly locked horns at negotiating tables. Japanese textiles, steel, color televisions, machine tools, automobiles, and semiconductors thus became subjects of a series of intense, and often acrimonious, negotiations, until both sides began to sound chauvinistic and even hostile. The tension further increased as Japanese direct foreign investment in the United States surged in the late 1980s in response both to the rise in the yen's value and in the prices of Japanese exports and to the protectionist movement in the United States. Half a century after Japan's surprise attack on Pearl Harbor, its relationship with the United States was once again increasingly strained and explosive.

The timing and manner of Japan's postwar "return" to individual Asian nations were dictated mainly by the history of Japan's colonial rule and wartime occupation and the imperatives of the Cold War. The intense anti-Japanese feeling among Korean leaders and people nurtured during the half-century of brutal Japanese rule, complicated by the division of the peninsula into a communist-ruled northern half and an anticommunist southern half and the 1950–1953 war between them, prevented normalization of Japan's relations with the Republic of Korea (South Korea) until 1965 and the Democratic People's Republic of Korea (North Korea) until an as-yet-unknown future date. The communist victory in the Chinese civil war and involvement of Chinese "volunteers" in the Korean War led Japan to sign a peace treaty with the Nationalist government on Taiwan in 1952 under intense U.S. pressure. The presence of that treaty and internal political instability in China, as well as the continuing Cold War, delayed normalization of Japan's relations with the People's Republic until 1972 and the formal conclusion of a peace treaty until 1978.

Postwar Japan reestablished political and economic relations with many Southeast Asian nations via reparations payments. In accordance with a provision of the 1951 Peace Treaty, Japan paid the bulk of these reparations, worth about US$1 billion altogether, in the form of technical services in the construction of power stations, roads, bridges, port facilities, irrigation systems, factories, and so on. This particular manner of its reentry into Southeast Asia helped Japan establish a predominant economic

position in the region in the next few decades. The recipients of Japan's postwar reparations rapidly shifted the main sources of their imports, foreign investments, and economic aid from their former colonial masters to Japan.

By the early 1990s, Japan had thus not only "returned" to Asia but had become the leading trading partner, investor, and aid giver for most nations of the region. Japan's economic relations with Australia, New Zealand, and other Pacific island nations also expanded rapidly in the 1970s and 1980s. It was as if, only a few decades after its defeat in World War II, Japan had successfully created by economic means the Greater East Asia Co-Prosperity Sphere that it had failed to create by military means during the war. Japan's expanding presence in the region, however, made nearly all of its neighbors concerned and nervous about its long-term political and strategic implications. Moreover, most nations in the region suffered from and complained about substantial and chronic trade deficits with Japan. Japan thus remained a discomforting, if not unwelcome, economic partner and an unacceptable political or military leader to most of its Asian and Pacific neighbors, as well as to most of those in other regions of the world.

(See also CONFUCIANISM; FINANCE, INTERNATIONAL; HIROHITO; MILITARISM; MODERNIZATION; PACIFIC REGION; PROTECTION; WAR CRIMES.)

Robert E. Ward, ed., *Political Development in Modern Japan* (Princeton, N.J., 1968). Bernard S. Silberman and H. D. Harootunian, eds., *Japan in Crisis: Essays on Taisho Democracy* (Princeton, N.J., 1974). Robert A. Scalapino, ed., *The Foreign Policy of Modern Japan* (Berkeley, Calif., 1977). Bradley M. Richardson and Scott C. Flanagan, *Politics in Japan* (Boston, 1984). Carol Gluck, *Japan's Modern Myths: Ideology in the Late Meiji Period* (Princeton, N.J., 1985). Akira Iriye, *The Origins of the Second World War in Asia and the Pacific* (London and New York, 1987). Peter Duus, ed., *Cambridge History of Japan*, vol. 6, *The Twentieth Century* (Cambridge, U.K., and New York, 1988). Takeshi Ishida and Ellis S. Krauss, eds., *Democracy in Japan* (Pittsburgh, Pa., 1989).

HARUHIRO FUKUI

JAPAN-U.S. RELATIONS. Relations between *Japan and the *United States have followed a regular fifty-year cycle alternating between cooperative and antagonistic phases. The first cooperative phase began in 1853, in the midst of Anglo-American competition for the China trade, when, with the four "Black Ships" of the U.S. Navy, President Millard Fillmore forced feudal Japan out of its 230-year self-imposed isolation. (The United States wanted Japan to provide coaling stations for American ships in the new age of steam-powered navigation. To this day, the Japanese use "Black Ships" as a metaphor for external pressures.) This first phase ended around 1905, when President Theodore Roosevelt mediated the peace treaty concluding the Russo-Japanese War, by which time the United States had become increasingly concerned about potential competition with

Japan for Pacific *hegemony. Already in 1903, President Roosevelt prophetically declared, "the United States will tolerate no other 'top dog' in the Pacific region. If Japan wants to be the top dog, she must be beaten."

After World War I, each nation became progressively more xenophobic. In 1924, the United States banned Japanese immigration, viewing Japan through the racist paradigm of the "Yellow Peril." Across the Pacific, militarist Japan adopted an equally racist paradigm of an "Anglo-Saxon–Jewish" conspiracy against Japan. In the late 1930s Japanese politics became totalitarian after a forty-five-year experiment with *constitutional monarchy. By 1940, alarmed by the aggressive behavior of the Axis powers in Europe, Africa, and Asia, the United States abandoned the *isolationism adopted after World War I, which led to a rupture in Japan-U.S. relations. Japan declared war on the United States on 7 December 1941. *World War II ended in Japan's defeat on 14 August 1945.

Under the relatively benign policies of the U.S. occupation, the second cooperative phase of Japan-U.S. relations began, a throwback to the late nineteenth century when Japan began to modernize. The United States helped Japan carry out long-overdue social, political, economic, and educational reform. The U.S. occupation also broke up the tight, hierarchical controls of family-owned industrial combines, *zaibatsu,* like Mitsui, Mitsubishi, and Sumitomo, over their member corporations. These moves paved the way for more dynamic, flexible groups of diverse firms that emerged after the mid-1950s. These newer corporate organizations and strategic alliances of managerially independent firms facilitated Japan's economic recovery in the 1950s and rapid economic growth in the 1960s. Strategic *alliances also fit better the borderless, high-tech-driven economies of the 1980s and beyond.

In the late-1940s, the *Cold War split the U.S.-led West from the Soviet-led East. Under the *Truman Doctrine, the United States helped revive Japan and the Federal Republic of Germany (West Germany) as new members of the Western bloc, a part of the American effort to contain the spread of *communism.

Although Japan regained political independence in 1951, the U.S.-Japan Mutual Security Treaty entrusted the United States with the responsibility for Japan's external security. Japan's preoccupation with economic interests at home and abroad fit well with the emerging "Pax Americana" of U.S. hegemony after World War II. In the late 1950s, the United States included Japan and West Germany in the economic order associated with Pax Americana. With freer access to the markets, raw materials, capital, and technology of the United States and other developed countries of the West, Japan performed its postwar economic miracle of the 1960s. However, Pax Americana has produced five fundamental changes in the world order, reducing Japan's dependence on the United States.

First, after the two oil crises in the 1970s, U.S. dollars glutted the world market and the dollar rate began sliding particularly against the deutsche mark and the Japanese yen. Since the mid-1980s, the United States has become increasingly dependent on Japan and West Germany to prop up the U.S. dollar. The *World Bank also became dependent on Japan's capital and technology to bail out internationally indebted countries in Latin America and Asia.

Second, by the 1980s, Pax Americana's *geopolitics had been replaced by a world of geoeconomics. Technological and economic strength mainly determines a nation's security, and, increasingly, economics drives politics. Military spending has become an economic and technological burden on the United States, while deterioration of public education and of social infrastructure like transportation have weakened its economic and national security. And in an era where technological innovations for civilian use often determines advancements in defense technology, the United States has become increasingly dependent on Japan even for defense-related technology. By the mid-1980s, the decline of the U.S. economy and technology vis-à-vis Japan triggered a more outward-looking foreign policy for the United States after a decade of self-doubt triggered by the *Vietnam War.

Third, from the mid-1970s to the 1980s, many U.S. manufacturing firms, seeking to reduce wages, moved their factories abroad. American management's disdain of workers and engineers accelerated the loss of various manufacturing skills and bases in the United States. The loss of higher-paying jobs in nondefense manufacturing industries gave rise to U.S. economic and technological *nationalism. As the United States mistakenly blamed Japan's alleged import restrictions for America's economic and social problems, Japan-U.S. relations became strained. Also, Japan was too slow in deregulating its economy and opening it to foreign business. Adding to that strain was the fact that with an anemic economy and reduced government revenues, the United States became dependent on foreign debt to finance its budget and trade deficits, while Japan emerged as its largest foreign creditor.

Fourth, the so-called Pacific Basin Club—Australia, New Zealand, China, Hong Kong, the Republic of Korea (South Korea), Taiwan, Japan, and the six nations of the *Association of Southeast Asian Nations (ASEAN)—began to trade and invest more and more among themselves rather than across the Pacific with the United States and Canada. By the end of the 1980s, Japan replaced the United States as the leading trade and investment partner of ,the other Pacific Basin nations. Japan's rise as the new economic and technological power reduced the political and economic hegemony of the United States in the Pacific. In 1941, Japan's GNP was about one-seventeenth that of the United States; as of 1991, the figure had risen to about sixty percent. With a growth rate in real GNP about double that of the United States, Japan stands to surpass the United States before the year 2010.

Fifth, by the early 1990s, the disintegration of the Soviet Union and the end of the Cold War reduced the Soviet threat in the Pacific. This challenged the basis of the U.S.-Japan Mutual Security Treaty that had made Japan a political and military ward of the United States for almost forty years.

As a consequence of these developments, "Contain Japan" thinking now seems to dominate the U.S. view of Japan. Fifty years after the end of World War II, Japan-U.S. relations once again have entered an antagonistic phase. In Japan, neonationalist sentiment has surfaced, encouraged by Japan's rising influence in the Pacific. This ideological turnabout is fueled by a generational change in Japanese society. Japanese who have no direct experience of the benign policies of the U.S. occupation are moving into leadership positions in business, government, and political circles. They were alarmed when Japan was caught unprepared for such sudden shifts in world politics as the end of the Cold War and the *Gulf War. They resented U.S. demands that Japan pay a share of war costs. Japan has started stonewalling America's requests to share the economic and military burdens of President *Bush's undefined, unexplained "new world order." In addition, the rise of neonationalist sentiment in the United States and Japan has further damaged bilateral relations and complicated international negotiations. For example, in December 1990, the United States openly blamed Japan for destroying the *General Agreement on Tariffs and Trade (GATT) by refusing to open its rice market to imports. What lies ahead for the Japan-U.S. bilateral relationship?

As Japanese influence in the Pacific expands, Japan will come to understand that its Asian neighbors' fears will be allayed by the U.S.-Japan Mutual Security Treaty that restrains Japan's political and military activities abroad. Japan needs the U.S. nuclear umbrella to prevent nuclear blackmail by the Democratic People's Republic of Korea (North Korea) and possibly China. The transformation of the U.S.-Japan Mutual Security Treaty from a Cold War tool to a political instrument in the Pacific Age will enhance U.S. influence in the Pacific.

Japan's economic and technological rise enabled it to sell more value-added goods and services to the United States. In the 1970s, the United States accounted for twenty to twenty-five percent of total Japanese exports; in the 1980s, the figure reached thirty-five percent. The rising value of the Japanese yen against the U.S. dollar spurred direct Japanese investment in the United States throughout the 1980s. By 1990, Japan's cumulative direct investment in the United States passed $110 billion. From electronics, automobiles, steel, and machine tools to telecommunications, U.S. nondefense manufacturing industries are being revitalized with massive infusions of Japanese capital, technology, and management know-how. As a result, Japan's renewed dependence on the U.S. market has also made it a political and economic hostage, which counteracts America's technological and economic dependence on Japan.

Without a global framework for multilateral trade, Japan will be isolated by emerging economic blocs like the *European Community and the emergent North American Free Trade Area. Japan will have to seek U.S. cooperation to create a new international treaty organization that oversees the freer international flow of technology, capital, and products. The "new world order" will likely include both Japan and Germany as permanent members of the Security Council of a reformed UN. With a mandate from the UN, Japan will find increased pressure to share the economic and military costs of this new world security and to assume a political role in world affairs commensurate with its growing economic power. Pressure will increase for greater cooperation and mutual understanding in Japan-U.S. relations, and the character of these bilateral relations will have enormous global repercussions.

(See also AMERICAN FOREIGN POLICY.)

David Halberstam, *The Reckoning* (New York, 1986). Robert B. Reich, *The Next American Frontier* (New York, 1986). Yoshi Tsurumi, "The U.S. Trade Deficit with Japan: Putting America's House in Order" *World Policy Journal* V, no. 2 (Spring 1987): 207–230. Yoshi Tsurumi, "U.S.-Japanese Relations: From Brinkmanship to Statesmanship" *World Policy Journal* VII, no. 1 (Winter 1989–1990): 1–33. Donald Calman, *The Origin and Nature of Japanese Imperialism* (New York, 1992).

YOSHI TSURUMI

JIHAD. Originally the doctrine of struggle against unbelievers for the expansion and protection of the Muslim community, jihad is closely linked with *hijra* or emigration from non-Muslim society. According to the doctrine, the sins of a person making jihad are remitted and death "on the path of God" is martyrdom which secures immediate entry to paradise. Scholars also have spoken of "the greater jihad" as the internal struggle against one's own sinful tendencies or as the personal struggle for the good against what is forbidden.

Jihad is a collective duty, but women, minors, and the sick are among categories legally excluded. It is also a personal duty, though not one of the five pillars of Islam. Shiʿi teach that jihad can only be under the leadership of the Imam, whereas Sunnis accept the proclamation of even an unjust ruler. Most believe jihad cannot be declared against fellow Muslims, though Ayatollah Ruhollah *Khomeini did so against the rulers of Iraq in the *Iran-Iraq War.

In the colonial period, wars against external forces were often regarded as jihad: for example, by the

Sanusi religious order who proclaimed it against the Italians in Libya in 1912, and by the Mahdi in the Sudan against the British and the Egyptians (1881–1885). More recently, guerrillas fighting the Russian occupation of Afghanistan in the 1980s saw themselves as mujahidin, as did certain groups opposed to the shah of Iran in the 1970s, and who later opposed the Ayatollah Khomeini.

Many authorities consider that if Muslims live in a society ruled by non-Muslims but are not under threat and can perform their ritual duties, then jihad is not obligatory. States are not constantly at war, and good relations and treaties with non-Muslim powers are permissible. This is most relevant in the modern period when many Muslims in Africa, Asia, and Europe live in nation-states that are neither under Muslims rulers nor, where the ruler is a Muslim, under the *shari'a.

Modern reformers, facing a world dominated by non-Muslim powers in which Muslims live with members of other communities in many distinct nation-states with their own secular interests, have emphasized the moral nature of jihad. They see military jihad only as defensive against oppression. Nationalist movements most often stressed the homeland rather than the Muslim community, even if they made *nationalism a quasi-sacred cause and used jihad rhetorically when they thought it opportune. Modernists such as President Bourguiba of Tunisia tried to appropriate the concept as meaning the struggle for national development.

Islamic radical movements scorn such interpretations and stress *Islam as an expansionist world order. Jihad is again a fundamental duty and active struggle for the global application of the shari'a. They also seek to "purify" Muslim societies of "corrupt" and "tyrannical" Muslim rulers, used by some in justification of the assassination of President *Sadat of Egypt in 1981.

The identification of sacred duty with violence or national wars is made in many political systems and states. Muslims *qua* Muslims are no more bellicose than followers of any creed, religious or otherwise. Jihad has been used in some Western writings to justify the view that all Muslims are aggressive fanatics, but this claim says more about Western views of others than about the behavior of Muslims, and is false.

(See also ARAB NATIONALISM; RELIGION AND POLITICS; SECULARIZATION.)

Rudolph Peters, *Islam and Colonialism: The Doctrine of Jihad in Modern History,* Mouton Religion and Society Series, no. 20 (The Hague, 1979).

MICHAEL GILSENAN

JOHN PAUL II. On 16 October 1978 the assembled crowd at St. Peter's Square heard the news: the newly elected Pope, after the brief reign of John Paul I, was from the East, a Polish man of 58 years, Karol Wojtyla, Archbishop of Cracow. This election marked, in many ways, a new stage in the history of Catholicism.

The new Bishop of Rome was born in Wadowice, near Cracow, on 8 May 1920, a little more than a year after the proclamation of Poland's independence. His mother died when he was 9 years of age, and he lost his elder brother four years later. He was raised by his father, a former soldier. A brilliant student, he passed his baccalaureate in 1938 and began his studies at the Jagiellonian University of Cracow. His taste for sports equaled his love for theater and poetry. The German invasion of September 1939 interrupted his university studies: the university was closed. The young Wojtyla enrolled as a student of the Polish language in a secret cell of the clandestine university and, in order to avoid deportation to a work camp in Germany, found employment as a worker, at first aboard a carrier, then at the Solvay factory of Borek Falecki. During those dark years, he continued to write poetry and participate, as actor and author, in the clandestine theater of Cracow. In the meantime, his father had died in 1940.

In 1942, he enrolled in the underground seminary of theology in Cracow. The end of the war allowed him to enter Jagiellonian University as a third-year student and to publish anonymously a book of poems, *Song of a Hidden God.* He was ordained a priest in 1946 and immediately began two years' study with the Dominicans at the Angelicum in Rome. There he discovered St. Thomas Aquinas and an interest in international affairs and left as Doctor of Philosophy with a thesis entitled "The Doctrine of the Faith of St. John of the Cross." He returned to the now-Soviet-ruled Poland in 1948, where he prepared a qualifying thesis, at the same time practicing his ministry in a parish in Cracow. He defended his doctorate entitled "The Possibilities of Founding Catholic Morality on the System of Max Scheler" in 1954, which opened the door to university teaching, and in 1956 he was assigned to the post of professor of moral theology at the University of Lublin. In 1958, when he was 38 years of age, he was named Coadjutor-Bishop of Cracow. On 20 December 1963, he was made Archbishop of Cracow by Paul VI, who elevated him to the rank of cardinal on 29 May 1967.

An untiring worker and enthusiastic athlete, he manifested a particularly lively pastoral interest in youths and intellectuals. His active participation in the *Vatican II Council and his care in promoting the application of aggiornamento (modernization) to the assembly of prelates in the Polish church marked his emergence as a senior cleric. If his pastoral style, as well as his ecclesiastical orientation, separated him from Cardinal Wysinski, nevertheless he firmly maintained his complete solidarity with the man who embodied the Polish resistance against the Communist regime and whose role in the practical and international scene largely eclipsed his own.

The entire personality and religious vision of Karol Wojtyla were formed by the dual experiences of the war and the Soviet annexation of Poland. His image of a culturally and religiously unified Europe capable of resisting the secular pressure of the states came to life in the idea that it was his role to restore moral authority and the symbolic power of the Church in a divided, chaotic world. This authority, with the support of his people, would be capable of ensuring the "Peace of God," as it had done during the most troubled periods of the Middle Ages. This conception of the Church's mission, which was specifically outlined in the encyclical *Slavorum Apostoli* of June 1985, was forged by constant reference to the Polish experience, in which the Church's resistance to the encroachment of the Communist government was progressively mixed with the nation's affirmation of its identity in the face of *totalitarianism. Strengthening the Messianic conscience of a Polish people who have been threatened for their entire history by the appetites of neighbors and who as a nation have been erased from the world map several times, the experience of religious resistance to the political totalization that was intended by the Communist regime found a symbolic end in the election of Karol Wojtyla to the papacy. On 17 October 1978, the Polish episcopate declared it a "reward" to "the entire body of Polish people" for their faith and religious fervor. The Pope himself, referring to the event (which was the first time a Slav had been elected Pope), spoke of it as a "sign."

An East European, intimate with the specificity of the Polish experience, a nation exemplary for its Catholicism, the new Pope was convinced that the Church had an irreplaceable mission to rid the world of its demons. John Paul II appeared difficult to classify into categories ordinarily used to differentiate the trends in the Catholic world. His traditionalism is expressed in his doctrinal, and above all in his moral, plans, where he affirms the classic teachings of the Church in matters of sexual and conjugal morals without the least concession to the evolution of the mores and desires of modern conscience. His continually repeated condemnations of divorce, abortion, and sexual relations outside marriage, and his firm opposition to recent progress in *in-vitro* fertilization and to the promotion of women in the Church contribute to the aggravation of conflicts within Catholicism. Otherwise, the reign of John Paul II is progressive. It has become noted for the exceptional commitment of the Roman pontiff to *human rights, for his affirmation without ambiguity of the "preferential option for the poor," and for his tireless appeals for universal access to education, health, a decent life, and the exercise of fundamental liberties, of which the first is religious freedom. This mission has taken John Paul II to all the continents; he has visited seventy-four countries, some several times, during the first ten years of his Papacy and covered some 600,000 kilometers.

This "contradiction," which confused the media, is only slowly becoming clarified. The liberties that the Pope defends under the double aegis of his spiritual authority and Polish origins are not the liberties inscribed in the Declaration of the Rights of Man and of the Citizen of 1789. The demand for *democracy, such as John Paul conceives it, is above all a call to the order inscribed by divine creation. This order is founded on the dignity of all individuals and their indivisible rights to affirm these human qualities in the context of society and local communities. This perfectly traditional position, rooted in the Catholic theology of natural right, resists any accommodation to modern positive theories of liberty and has much in common with contemporary conservative appeals. They join together in an effort to reduce the sprawling influence of the state on civil society and to limit its intervention into the lives of individuals and communities. This convergence can be observed in Western democracies where economic crisis, with its attendant inequalities, has sharpened the modern contradictions at the same time that the powerlessness of states to govern and control increasingly complex and interdependent economies becomes more apparent. This confluence between Catholic discourse on human rights and certain aspects of civil societies is even more pronounced in the non-Western world. There, the Church (often the sole organization that has succeeded in preserving its structures and contacts with the West during long periods of dictatorship) appears to be the only force able to offer a coherent language concerning liberation and the search for an autonomous path to political change and cultural affirmation. The Church under John Paul II plays this role in countries rendered politically and socially backward by years of corruption and despotism, such as the Philippines, Haiti, and the Republic of Korea (South Korea). It is in Eastern and Central Europe, however, that he has been most effective in championing an alternative to what he views as the false promise of modernism, with its mixture of atheism and totalitarianism.

Is it therefore unfair to conclude that John Paul II, ignoring late-twentieth-century skepticism, has simply updated the pre–Vatican II Catholic condemnation of the errors of the modern world. This would be a simplistic view of the matter, for John Paul II does not denounce the modern need for liberty. To the contrary, in line with Vatican II, he praises it. He even considers liberty one of the "positive temporal values" that mark the progress of humanity toward its perfection. What he underscores, however, is the powerlessness of the modern world to render concrete this hope for liberty—whether confronted by the totalitarian *modernity that triumphed for forty years in the East or by the materialistic modernity that has invaded, under the cover of liberalism, the West.

The first foreign leader invited to Czechoslovakia

by President Václav *Havel, John Paul II expressed in a particularly explicit manner his concern that the end of Communist totalitarianism might mean that all Europe might succumb to Western ways of thinking and living, under which liberty, according to him, has been degraded to "permissiveness." This radical rejection of modern *liberalism and individualism is at the heart of John Paul's plan of "new evangelization" that he has developed for Europe. It concerns nothing less than an effort to rediscover "the common Christian roots of Europe, roots which constitute a most firm foundation of which no attempt to reform the unity of the continent can be ignorant" (Slavorum Apostoli). The problem is to anticipate the political impact (not just the ethical-religious dimension) of the restructuring of Europe in a world where religion has become the private affair of individuals and no longer constitutes the primary organizing principle of social life. The rapidity of the changes that are affecting religious life in post-1989 Poland (the decline in religious practice and vocations, the rise of anti-clericalism, etc.) could well signify the limits of John Paul's vision.

(See also RELIGION AND POLITICS; ROMAN CATHOLIC CHURCH.)

Danièle Hervieu-Léger, "La Stratégie de Concentration Catholique" L'Année Sociologique (Paris, 1988): 212–231. Paul Valadier, L'Eglise en procès: Catholicism et société moderne (Paris, 1989). Brian Hehir, "Papal Foreign Policy" Foreign Policy 78 (Summer 1990): 26–48. Patrick Michel, "L'Eglise de Jean Paul II: Quel rôle sur la scène mondiale?" La Documentation Française 658 (June 1991).

DANIÈLE HERVIEU-LÉGER

JOHNSON, Lyndon Baines. Born on 27 August 1908 on a farm in the Texas Hill Country near the village of Stonewall, Lyndon Baines Johnson was the eldest of five children. His father, Sam Ealy Johnson, had served in the Texas legislature, and young Lyndon grew up in an atmosphere that emphasized politics and public affairs. Lyndon's mother, Rebekah Baines Johnson, encouraged her son's ambition and sense of striving. In 1913 the Johnsons moved to nearby Johnson City. Young Lyndon was educated in local schools in the area and graduated from high school in Johnson City in 1924.

During the next several years, Lyndon tried various jobs in California and Texas without success. In 1927 he entered Southwest Texas State Teachers College in San Marcos. A history and social science major, he was active in campus politics. He earned his elementary school teacher's certificate in 1928 and for one year was a principal and teacher at Cotulla in south Texas. His work with the destitute Hispanic students there had an important effect on his attitude toward poverty and the role of government.

Johnson received his B.S. degree in 1930. He had already taken part in several political campaigns. Late in 1931 he became the secretary to a member of Congress, Richard M. Kleberg of Texas. During the four years he held the position he gained valuable contacts in Washington. In 1934 he met and married Claudia Alta ("Lady Bird") Taylor, daughter of a prosperous planter and storeowner in Marshall, Texas. Two daughters were born to the Johnsons during the 1940s. Lady Bird Johnson proved to be an effective political partner. Her business acumen was an important element in the success of the radio and television stations that the Johnsons acquired in Austin during the 1940s and 1950s.

Johnson's first important political position was as director of the National Youth Administration (NYA) in Texas from 1935 to 1937. He established a system of roadside parks to put young Texans to work and quietly fostered the participation of *African Americans in some NYA programs. When the incumbent member for the Tenth Congressional District died in 1937, Johnson entered the race as a devoted supporter of Franklin D. *Roosevelt and the *New Deal. He spent eleven years in the House of Representatives and became intimately familiar with the legislative process. He was a follower of the programs and policies of Franklin D. Roosevelt and a close ally of Majority Leader (later Speaker) Sam Rayburn. He was the chair of the Democratic Congressional Campaign Committee in 1940 and helped the Democrats retain control of the House. In 1941 he ran for the Senate from Texas, but was narrowly defeated in a special election.

Upon the outbreak of World War II in December 1941, Johnson entered the Navy as a lieutenant commander. He saw combat during an inspection tour of the South Pacific in 1942. He left the Navy in response to President Roosevelt's directive that members of Congress should remain in Washington. Johnson made another race for the Senate in 1948 against the popular former governor, Coke Stevenson. Texas had lost its earlier affection for the New Deal and Johnson stressed his own *conservatism in the election. The runoff primary in August 1948 was very close. Amid charges of ballot box stuffing and other fraudulent practices, Johnson was declared the Democratic nominee only after extended legal battles. He easily defeated his Republican opponent in the general election.

Johnson was an effective senator who mastered the organization and rules of the upper house. His Democratic colleagues elected him majority whip within three years, and in 1953 he was chosen to be minority leader—the youngest such leader in the history of the Senate. Johnson won a second term in 1954. The Democrats regained control of Congress that same year, and in January 1955 he became the majority leader.

In his rush to power, Johnson had neglected his health. During the early summer of 1955, he had a severe heart attack. He returned to his duties in the Senate in late 1955. He pursued a strategy of bipartisan cooperation with the Republican administration of Dwight D. *Eisenhower. As majority leader

Johnson was instrumental in the passage of civil rights acts (the first in more than eighty years) in 1957 and 1960. He also played a large role in establishing the National Aeronautics and Space Administration (NASA).

Johnson wanted to be president throughout the 1950s. Power in the Senate did not mean that he could win delegate votes from the Democratic Party or surmount his party's reluctance to name a southerner as its national candidate. After his nomination campaign against John F. *Kennedy failed, Johnson agreed to become the vice-presidential candidate in 1960. Johnson campaigned hard across the South, and his ability to put Texas and other southern states in the Democratic column helped Kennedy gain a narrow victory.

The vice-presidential years from 1961 to 1963 were hard on Johnson. He carried out the assignments he received from Kennedy, including chairing the National Aeronautics and Space Council and the President's Committee on Equal Opportunity. Johnson resented the absence of any real power, and he was angered at the slights he received from the people around Kennedy.

Kennedy's *assassination in November 1963 brought Johnson to the *presidency in tragic circumstances. He conducted himself during the transition in a manner that reassured the nation and set his administration on a constructive course. The new president was particularly skilled with Congress, and he persuaded lawmakers to pass much of the stalled Kennedy legislative program. During the spring of 1964 Johnson set forth his domestic objectives, termed the *Great Society. He wanted to use the affirmative power of government to establish programs that would end poverty and racial discrimination. Congress readily approved his requests to increase foreign aid, reduce taxes, and pass conservation legislation.

The centerpiece of Johnson's achievements in this early phase of his presidency was the Civil Rights Act of 1964. The new law outlawed segregation in public accommodations and pursued fair employment practices. Johnson's administration was identified, more directly than that of any previous president, with the aspirations of African Americans. Another major domestic goal was the "war on poverty" that led to a food stamp system, a Job Corps for unemployed youth, and community action programs to deal with the local needs of poor Americans. The Office of Economic Opportunity directed these Great Society initiatives.

In foreign policy, Johnson inherited the commitment that Kennedy had made to the preservation of South Vietnam. He decided in late 1963 not to withdraw from Southeast Asia. During 1964 the Tonkin Gulf incident of August and the resulting Tonkin Gulf Resolution from Congress reflected popular support for Johnson's policy of cautious commitment to the future of *Vietnam. Johnson

used his moderation in foreign affairs to win an overwhelming electoral victory over his conservative Republican opponent, Senator Barry M. Goldwater of Arizona, in the 1964 presidential election.

With his popular mandate, Johnson pressed for the enactment of Great Society legislation during 1965–1966. Laws to deal with education, conservation, health care, immigration, and poverty poured out of Congress. The Voting Rights Act of 1965 safeguarded African-American voting rights and expanded black participation in southern politics. By the end of 1965, however, the momentum of the Great Society had slowed because of conservative opposition to the liberal programs and eroding public support for the *Vietnam War.

Johnson faced mounting foreign policy problems. A military intervention in the *Dominican Republic in 1965 produced congressional criticism. More important, escalation of the war in Vietnam during the summer through a bombing campaign and the full-scale combat role for U.S. troops led to popular protests in the United States. Antiwar demonstrators focused on Johnson and made it difficult for him to travel around the country. Social unrest at home compounded the president's difficulties. Riots with racial overtones began in 1965 and continued in major cities during the remainder of his presidency. The political skills that had taken Johnson to the White House proved of little help as his popularity declined.

The war in Vietnam seemed stalemated as 1967 ended. The Tet offensive in February 1968 was a defeat for North Vietnam militarily but a blow to Johnson's weakened standing at home. Faced with political challenges from Eugene McCarthy and Robert Kennedy in the Democratic Party, Johnson also worried about his own health if he ran again. On 31 March 1968, he announced that he was limiting the bombing of North Vietnam and was seeking negotiations. In a political surprise, he also announced that he would not be a candidate for reelection. Johnson left office on 20 January 1969 and died on 22 January 1973.

Unfriendly biographers have depicted Johnson as driven only by a lust for power. His personality could be abrasive and his methods were often crude. Nonetheless, Johnson was also a liberal nationalist who was impelled to improve the lives of Americans generally. Despite his foreign policy failure in Vietnam, Lyndon Johnson was one of the most important presidents of the period after World War II. His ambitious Great Society symbolized the expansive policies of U.S. *liberalism. The reaction to this program laid the basis for the conservative trend that followed him. The war in Vietnam called into question the ability of the *United States to exert its influence where it chose in the world. Johnson's broad concept of presidential power came under criticism because of the excesses of his White House years. Lyndon Johnson had tried to be a great president and achieved some impressive results. He also demonstrated the limits of the government and the presidency to produce social change and to pursue an activist foreign policy.

(See also AMERICAN FOREIGN POLICY; CIVIL RIGHTS MOVEMENT.)

Lyndon Baines Johnson, *The Vantage Point: Perspectives of the Presidency, 1963–1969* (New York, 1971). Vaughn Davis Bornet, *The Presidency of Lyndon B. Johnson* (Lawrence, Kans., 1983). Robert Dallek, *Lone Star Rising: Lyndon Johnson and His Times, 1908–1960* (New York, 1991).
LEWIS L. GOULD

JORDAN. The state of Jordan came into being after World War I, when Britain and France imposed their rule over lands of the defeated Ottoman Empire. In 1920, the British government took formal control of the territory as part of its Palestine Mandate. Soon afterwards, on 15 May 1923, the British accorded separate status to the territories east of the Jordan River, recognizing them as the Emirate of Transjordan and affirming Prince Abdullah, son of the Sherif Hussein of Mecca, as ruler.

Abdullah's family, the Hashemites, had sought to create a united Arab kingdom after the war, a project blocked by the British and French. Abdullah thus partly symbolized the movement for Arab unity and independence. Ironically, however, because of Transjordan's scant resources and small population, Abdullah remained heavily reliant on Britain for more than three decades. During that time, the British effectively controlled the country's army and finances, and British advisers virtually ran the government.

In 1946, Britain granted formal independence, the name of the country was changed to Jordan, and Abdullah took the title of king. In 1948, when *Israel was created, the Jordanian army joined in the ensuing *Arab-Israeli conflict, taking control of the Old City of Jerusalem and a substantial block of *Palestine to the west of the Jordan River—an area generally known as the West Bank.

Four hundred thousand Palestinian refugees entered Jordanian-controlled territory during the hostilities; afterwards, unable to return to their homes in the new Jewish state, they became long-term residents, the majority in squalid *refugee camps. When King Abdullah formally annexed the West Bank to his kingdom in 1950, he assumed rule over this explosive social and political situation.

Dependent on British and the West for financial and political support, Abdullah agreed to pursue a policy of nonbelligerency with Israel, the powerful new neighbor to the west, and sought to impose his authority over the Palestinians. This created many difficulties in an era of growing Arab and Palestinian nationalism and led to Abdullah's death in Jerusalem at the hands of a Palestinian assassin on 20 July 1951.

Abdullah's son Talal succeeded his father but reigned only briefly. His son Hussein then assumed the throne in 1953 at the age of 17. Hussein identified himself with *Arab nationalism, but he nonetheless maintained a close alliance with Britain and later the United States. Through the years, he survived radical nationalist opposition to his rule—an opposition that found one important base in the kingdom's Palestinian population and that drew support from various Arab regimes such as Egypt, Syria, and Iraq.

The early years of Hussein's rule were particularly stormy. In 1955, he bowed to popular pressure and refused to join the Baghdad Pact, a short-lived regional security group organized by Britain and the United States. Then, in 1956, parliamentary elections resulted in an outspokenly nationalist Parliament. Under pressure from the new government, the king dismissed General John Glubb, the British chief of staff of Jordan's army, and not long after annulled the British-Jordanian Treaty.

In spite of these early accommodations, Hussein eventually affirmed his rule and his alliance with the West, at the expense of political freedoms. In April 1957, Washington sent emergency economic and military assistance to Hussein and moved the Sixth Fleet to the eastern Mediterranean in response to an abortive military coup. Shortly thereafter, the king purged the government of nationalists and banned all political parties except the Muslim Brotherhood—a ban that was to remain in force for over thirty years. Freedom of expression was substantially curtailed at this time as well. In the West Bank, where many Palestinians questioned the *legitimacy of Jordanian rule, repression was particularly harsh.

The political balance in the kingdom shifted with the June War of 1967, when Israeli forces quickly defeated the royal army, capturing Jerusalem and the entire West Bank. More than 200,000 Palestinian refugees fled across the Jordan River during and immediately after the war. In dozens of camps, a Palestinian guerrilla movement took form, launching raids across the new border and touching off Israeli reprisals. When commandos of the *Palestine Liberation Organization (PLO) challenged the authority of the Jordanian government, the king cracked down with his army in September 1970.

Though Israel occupied the West Bank, the Jordanian government continued to exercise considerable authority in the territory, paying the salaries of teachers and civil servants and competing with the PLO and other political forces for legitimacy. But after the October War of 1973, the increasingly powerful PLO won the support of all other Arab states based on its claim to represent Palestinians. The emerging idea of an independent Palestinian state in the Israeli-occupied territories dealt another blow to King Hussein's claim to sovereignty over the Palestinians and their territory. The king responded by suspending Parliament in 1974; the body would remain suspended for the next ten years.

Jordan enjoyed an economic boom for over a decade after the 1973 war, thanks largely to soaring oil prices. Although the country was not an oil producer, it obtained large aid grants from oil-rich Gulf states, took in substantial remittances from Jordanians and Palestinians working in the Gulf oil economies, and profited from its role as a regional trade and financial center. When oil prices began to decline in the early 1980s, Jordan's economy found a new source of profits: its role as major transshipper for *Iraq during the *Iran-Iraq war. Prosperity muted political problems for a time. Thousands flooded into Amman from the countryside to participate in the boom, swelling the population of the capital to about 1.3 million—or nearly half the country's population—by 1985.

The Palestine question remained at the center of the kingdom's political agenda during the 1980s. Discussions between the king and the PLO led to temporary accords in 1985 for a Palestinian-Jordanian negotiating strategy and an eventual joint confederation, a formula responsive to pressures from the United States and Israel. This formula never won full support within the PLO, however, and in August of 1988, after the *intifadah in the Occupied Territories, the king publicly relinquished responsibility for the West Bank in favor of the PLO, losing much of his remaining leverage over the territories.

Meanwhile, tension at home was rising as the Jordanian economy faltered. The end of the Iran-Iraq War had removed the last big economic prop. A series of price increases on government-subsidized necessities in April 1989 set off antigovernment riots that swept the south, traditional bedrock of Hashemite rule. The king sought to rebuild his authority by offering a program of broad political liberalization—curbing the security forces, restoring Parliament, and calling parliamentary general elections for the first time in more than twenty years.

The elections, held in November 1989, resulted in a victory for the Muslim Brotherhood, which won a third of the eighty-seat Parliament. The king managed to integrate Islamic representatives into the government, however, without a major shift in the political system.

The *Gulf War of 1990–1991 revealed the kingdom's continued political and economic vulnerability. Throughout the crisis, King Hussein refused to join the anti-Iraq coalition, losing Jordan's large economic aid from the Gulf oil producers and the United States. The Jordanian economy was also swamped by 300,000 refugees—mostly Jordanians and Palestinians—who had fled or been deported from Kuwait and the Gulf states.

By 1992, much of the crucial aid flow had been restored (now from the Federal Republic of Germany and Japan), but the government of King Hussein continued to face serious problems. Most ominous was the possibility of continued conflict over the Palestine question, leading potentially to expulsion of more refugees from Israel or even another regional war.

Economic problems and Islamic fundamentalism also challenged the monarchy. Under these difficult circumstances, the king sought to build consensus around the throne by promising broader democratization. In June 1991 he rallied all political forces of the country behind a new "National Charter," proposing substantially enlarged *pluralism, including a legalized multiparty system and the repeal of martial law, which had been in effect since 1967. Whatever political arrangements emerge in coming years, the *monarchy will probably retain substantial power and authority, with firm backing from long-standing allies, Britain and the United States.

(See also BALFOUR DECLARATION; SYRIA; ZIONISM.)

P. J. Vatikiotis, *Politics and the Military in Jordan* (London, 1967). Naseer Aruri, *Jordan: A Study in Political Development* (The Hague, 1972). Peter Gubser, *Jordan: Crossroads of Middle Eastern Events* (London, 1983). Rodney Wilson, *Politics and the Economy in Jordan* (London, 1991).

LAMIS ANDONI

JUDICIAL REVIEW. The power of certain courts to invalidate laws or actions of governmental officials as unconstitutional is known as judicial review. In federal nation-states, such review applies both to state and national legislation. While a theory of judicial review was intimated in English law, most notably in Lord Chief Justice Edward Coke's decision in *Dr. Bonham's Case* (1610), judicial review of national legislation is usually traced to the *United States and especially to Chief Justice John Marshall's decision in *Marbury v. Madison* (1803). In denying Marbury's request for relief, Marshall ruled that the law under which Marbury appeared before the U.S. *Supreme Court violated the Constitution.

The U.S. Constitution of 1787 does not actually state the power of judicial review, but it has been accepted since 1803 and has been copied by many other nations, especially those liberated by the Allies and victims of the dictatorial excesses that led to World War II. Judicial review is consistent with the idea of a written *constitution, expressing the consent of the people, superior to ordinary acts of legislation, and unchangeable by ordinary legislative means. Accepting *parliamentary sovereignty and with no rigid constitution, Britain has no judicial review although a fair number of Britain's one-time colonies are among the approximately sixty-five nations that now do. Most such nations specifically state this power in their constitutions. In federal systems, where it is especially common, judicial review provides a peaceful means of resolving conflicts between the national government and the sovereign subunits. Judicial review also helps settle disputes among branches of the national government in systems employing *separation of powers.

The U.S. model of judicial review is "diffuse,"

enabling courts at all levels to exercise such review, albeit only in genuine "cases or controversies" where parties have established "standing." In such cases, trial court judgments may be reviewed by appellate tribunals, with the Supreme Court having final judgment. Countries with such systems—often with common-law backgrounds—include a number of Latin American nations as well as Greece, Australia, Canada, Japan, India, Pakistan, Burma, and most Scandinavian nations. Germany, France, Spain, Italy, and other countries—often with civil-law traditions—have a more "concentrated" mode of review that follows the Austrian example where a specific court or courts, sometimes separate from the regular judicial system, resolve constitutional questions. Some such nations have more relaxed requirements for standing than do American courts, even permitting advisory opinions. In the United States, the president appoints judges with the advice and consent of the Senate, and their service is contingent on good behavior. Nations where concentrated judicial review is exercised are more likely to vest appointments in the legislative branch and have fixed terms and/or mandatory retirement ages. Some nations, Portugal, Switzerland, and a number of Latin American countries, for example, have "mixed" systems blending elements of the concentrated and diffuse models.

Although positively linked to governmental stability and to free political systems with competitive political parties, judicial review may, as in the United States, pit the judgments of unelected magistrates serving for life against those of the people's representatives elected for fixed terms. U.S. courts, like others, have developed various maxims by which to defer or bypass controversial political issues, especially in the realm of foreign affairs where the need for quick action is often incompatible with judicial second-guessing and where constitutional limitations may be particularly difficult to define. U.S. courts also favor political and equal protection rights over others, modifying an earlier preference for property rights.

Even in countries like the United States where judicial review is firmly established, disputes arise as to how freely such review should be exercised. "Interpretivists" and advocates of judicial restraint believe courts should void only legislation which clearly violates the constitutional text. "Noninterpretivists" advocate judicial activism to remedy perceived injustices in society even where such rulings proceed from natural-law principles or the spirit and/or structure of the constitution rather than from a specific text. Judicial activists also downplay *stare decisis* (respect for precedent), preferring to remedy perceived judicial errors. In the United States, judicial decisions can be overturned only by the courts themselves or through the difficult constitutional amending process. In countries with such rigid constitutions, courts are sometimes urged to initiate changes, the line between alterations through amendment and changes through judicial interpretation often being a particularly fine one.

Allan R. Brewer-Carías, *Judicial Review in Comparative Law* (Cambridge, U.K., 1989).

JOHN R. VILE

JUNE WAR OF 1967. See ARAB-ISRAELI CONFLICT.

K

KAMPUCHEA. See Cambodia.

KAZAKHSTAN. See Commonwealth of Independent States.

KEMALISM. The name given to the *ideology that evolved during the 1920s and 1930s under the auspices of the Turkish national movement led by Kemal *Atatürk, the origins of Kemalism are to be found in the policies of the Young Turks who attempted to modernize and create a sovereign multinational empire. The Kemalists, freed of the imperial burden by the defeat of the Ottoman Empire, emphasized *nationalism. Influenced by the ideas of the French Revolution, they sought to create the "new Turk" (and the new *Turkey) to replace the "Ottoman." Because Turkish society lacked a developed, modern *class structure with a bourgeoisie and a working class, Kemalism adopted corporatist *populism, emphasizing the classless nature of Turkish society. Kemalism saw conflict only between the old, defeated ruling class and "the people" or "the nation," defined in terms similar to the French "nation" of 1789.

In the 1920s, Kemalism left the initiative for economic development to the private sector. But the failure of the wealthy classes to invest in economic *development, the onset of the world economic crisis in the West, which discredited *capitalism and *democracy, and the success of the Soviet and Italian experiments encouraged the Kemalists to use the state to engineer society. The full-blown ideology of Kemalism, in which the state and party became dominant in all spheres of life, was adopted by the ruling People's Republican Party (RPP) in 1931. The party defined the new Turkey as nationalist, republican, populist, secular, statist, and revolutionary. These "six arrows" became the guiding principles of the nation and were incorporated into the Constitution in 1937.

The ideological challenge of Italian *fascism forced the Kemalists to give a new twist to their ideology. Responding to Italian claims that their movement was fascist, Kemalists took the position of anticolonialists and argued that fascism was a variety of *imperialism. They claimed that Kemalism was an appropriate ideology for precapitalist societies struggling for their independence and striving for nationhood, whereas fascism was suitable only for semicapitalist societies in crisis. Here we find the first inklings of the "Third Worldism" which made Kemalism popular among *national liberation movements in Asia and Africa, a model for Reza Shah in contemporary Iran, and, later, *Nasser in Egypt.

At home Kemalism successfully mobilized Turkish society to promote socioeconomic development, although on a highly authoritarian basis. But its very success made it redundant after 1945. Its policies produced new classes which demanded the right to organize independently of the state and a bourgeoisie that insisted on a mixed economy. Once Kemalism gave way to multiparty politics in 1945, militant *secularism disappeared. Though all parties, especially the RPP, continued to profess their loyalty to Kemalism, it steadily dissolved as a coherent ideology and practice, although it became a useful weapon used by the establishment against ideological challenges from the left. The armed forces set themselves up as the guardians of Kemalism after the coup of 1960. But even they paid only lip service to its ideals. Since then, as *Nasserism and other similar radical nationalist ideologies have weakened, Kemalism as a coherent system has lost its capacity to inspire. But its emphasis on secularism, egalitarianism, and nationalism still defines goals which many Turks aspire to.

(Ali Kazancigil and Ergun Özbudun, eds., *Atatürk: Founder of a Modern State* (London, 1981). Jacob Landau, ed., *Atatürk and the Modernization of Turkey* (Boulder, Colo., 1984). Feroz Ahmad, *The Making of Modern Turkey* (London, 1992).

Feroz Ahmad

KENNAN, George. The epitome of the public figure, George Kennan's (b. 1904) contributions to both international relations and scholarship have had an effect on the world and how people think about it. His career has embraced four distinct fields: diplomacy, foreign policy-making, historical scholarship, and political criticism.

His diplomatic career began in 1926, a year after he graduated from Princeton University, with his appointment to the U.S. Foreign Service. He rose rapidly through the ranks and performed duties in key overseas posts, including Berlin, Moscow, Prague, and Vienna. Trained as one of a handful of

U.S. specialists on the *Soviet Union, Kennan was stationed in Moscow during much of the 1930s and between 1944 and 1946. His sure command of the Russian language and knowledge of the country's history, politics, and economy earned him the admiration of ambassadors under whom he worked in Moscow: William Bullitt (1933–1936), Joseph Davies (1936–1938), and W. Averell Harriman (1943–1946). While serving as the embassy's chargé d'affaires in 1946, Kennan composed the "Long Telegram," a seminal *Cold War document that helped alert President Harry S. *Truman's administration to ideological and security problems then posed by the Soviet Union. Kennan twice held ambassadorships: in 1952 to the Soviet Union, which ended unceremoniously when Joseph Stalin's government declared him persona non grata, and in 1961–1963 to Yugoslavia.

During the Cold War years 1946–1950, Kennan was a prominent policymaker in Washington. In this period he wrote the so-called "X Article," which appeared (July 1947) in the influential journal *Foreign Affairs*. In this article Kennan elaborated upon themes from the Long Telegram, and advocated measures to check and frustrate Soviet international ambitions: the *containment policy. The most controversial passage from the X Article, and the one whose meaning scholars have long disputed, was ambiguous even by Kennan's own later admission. He asserted: ". . . the Soviet pressure against the free institutions of the Western world is something that can be contained by the adroit and vigilant application of counter-force at a series of constantly shifting geographical and political points, corresponding to the shifts and maneuvers of Soviet policy."

However unclear the intentions of the X Article, government papers that he wrote at the time make plain that Kennan wanted containment to rely primarily on economic and political programs, and only secondarily on military strategies. The militarization of containment policy, exemplified by the founding of the *North Atlantic Treaty Organization and the acceleration of the nuclear arms race, seemed excessive and dangerous to him. As director of the State Department's Policy Planning Staff in 1947–1949, he was able to promote his preferred version of *American foreign policy through crucial work on the *Marshall Plan and attempts to rehabilitate postwar Japan. His dissatisfaction with the increasing military orientation of U.S. foreign policy under secretaries of state Dean *Acheson and John Foster Dulles helped lead to his resignation from the Foreign Service in 1953.

Kennan then joined the history faculty at the Institute for Advanced Study at Princeton and began a scholarly career that he interrupted only once—to represent the United States in Yugoslavia. Until his retirement in 1974 (and subsequent status as professor emeritus), Kennan wrote a number of important books analyzing such topics as early Soviet-U.S. relations, U.S. diplomacy, and the origins of World War I.

Kennan has not only distinguished himself as a man of belles lettres since the mid-1950s—twice he was awarded the Pulitzer Prize—but he has also won the attention of many statesmen and members of the politically literate public as a commentator on contemporary international affairs. His written statements, lectures, and expert testimony before congressional hearings have touched on a number of significant issues. These have included Soviet-U.S. disengagement from Europe, the folly of American involvement in Vietnam, the dangers of unbridled arms race, the need for accommodation with the Soviet Union, and the desirability of multilateral cooperation to solve global environmental problems.

Kennan has never developed a systematic political philosophy. But implicit in his pronouncements and recommendations over the course of more than six decades are a set of underlying assumptions that, taken together, constitute a theory of politics. This blends elements of realpolitik with ideas ultimately traceable to conservative thinker Edmund Burke and theologian Reinhold Niebuhr. At the core of Kennan's conception is a preoccupation with the continuity and intrinsic value of human civilizations and history. For him the United States must recognize that international problems are properly understood when viewed in historical context and that successful foreign policy requires taking the long view of both problems and solutions; to cultivate a world environment that will contain or prevent large-scale warfare, U.S. policymakers and citizens must also appreciate that their adversaries do not have a monopoly on evil but have a role to play within a vast scheme of history and ultimate purpose.

(See also DIPLOMACY; TRUMAN DOCTRINE.)

George Kennan, *Memoirs: 1925–1950* (Boston, 1967). George Kennan, *Memoirs: 1950–1963* (Boston, 1972). George Kennan, *Sketches From a Life* (New York, 1989).
DAVID MAYERS

KENNEDY, John Fitzgerald. The thirty-fifth president of the United States, John Fitzgerald Kennedy was born on 29 May 1917 in Brookline, Massachusetts. His father, Joseph Kennedy, was a hard-driving businessman who instilled in his sons a passion for power and achievement. Joseph Kennedy served President Franklin *Roosevelt in several capacities, most notably as ambassador to Britain in the years before World War II. John F. Kennedy fought in the Pacific in that war, and, shortly after his return to civilian life, won a seat in the House of Representatives in 1946. Elected senator from Massachusetts in 1952, Kennedy began to eye still-higher office. A successful run in the primaries brought him the Democratic Party presidential nomination in 1960. Defeating the Republican candidate, Vice President Richard *Nixon, Kennedy became the youngest person and the first Catholic ever to be elected to the *presidency.

Kennedy was determined to be an activist president. The centerpiece of his domestic policy was economic growth. Convinced that the American economy was lagging behind its potential, Kennedy proposed to stimulate the economy with taxation policies designed to foster greater investment by business and consumption by individuals. The resulting economic growth, he believed, would produce a shared abundance, ending conflicts between business and labor over the distribution of wealth. Kennedy's chief problem in economic policy was to persuade suspicious business elites that he genuinely wanted a partnership with them. Courting the business community throughout his presidency, he succeeded in inducing the investment to make the American economy grow faster. Higher rates of growth were, however, accompanied by an increase in economic inequality, since the prosperous were the biggest winners from Kennedy's policies.

During Kennedy's presidency, the *civil rights movement by black Americans gained increasing momentum. Kennedy was caught between the moral and political force of the civil rights movement and the congressional bastions of the white South in his own Democratic Party. Hoping to hold the support of both blacks and white southerners, Kennedy approached civil rights conflicts cautiously and sometimes reluctantly during his first two years in office. In 1963, however, civil rights demonstrations led by Dr. Martin Luther *King, Jr., in Birmingham, Alabama, created such a dramatic and explosive confrontation that Kennedy was compelled to take stronger action. Appearing on television, the president told the nation that equal treatment for black Americans was a moral issue. He also proposed major new civil rights legislation, which was passed by Congress after his death.

Although questions of economic growth and civil rights demanded Kennedy's attention, his paramount concern as president was foreign policy. Upon assuming the presidential office, Kennedy proclaimed that the *Cold War had entered a critical stage. "Each day," he said in his first State of the Union Address, "we draw nearer the hour of maximum danger. . . ." In Kennedy's grim analysis, a *United States that had drifted dangerously under the previous administration now faced a global offensive from an increasingly aggressive Soviet Union. Acting on the basis of this analysis, Kennedy urged upon Congress a massive buildup of U.S. military forces at all levels. Fortified by this buildup, he was prepared to take on what he believed was an intensified Communist threat, with a new zeal for American action that his admirers would applaud for its vigor and his critics would decry as reckless overreaching.

"The hour of maximum danger" was soon upon Kennedy. In the summer of 1961, the United States confronted the Soviet Union over the divided city of Berlin. Opposing Soviet Premier Nikita *Khrushchev's effort to break the long-standing impasse over Berlin on Soviet terms, Kennedy announced a new military buildup and employed martial rhetoric to summon U.S. citizens to a new test of their resolve. Although the confrontation ended inconclusively after the Communists constructed the Berlin Wall, it had awakened fears of war between the two *superpowers.

Those fears returned a year later, in much greater magnitude, in the *Cuban missile crisis. In October 1962, when the United States discovered that the Soviet Union had secretly deployed medium-range nuclear missiles on the island of Cuba, Kennedy and his advisers debated the proper U.S. response. Rejecting suggestions that the missiles might have been placed in Cuba to deter an invasion by the United States or to rectify an imbalance in strategic weaponry that left the Soviets far behind the United States, Kennedy interpreted the Soviet move as the supreme test of U.S. will. Demanding that the Soviets withdraw their missiles, Kennedy began a naval quarantine of Cuba and, through diplomatic channels, warned of further military action. The gravest nuclear crisis of the postwar era ended when Khrushchev acceded to Kennedy's demands and pulled out the missiles in exchange for a U.S. pledge not to invade Cuba. Seemingly sobered by this frightening confrontation, the United States and the Soviet Union negotiated a limited nuclear test ban treaty in 1963.

For Kennedy, the challenge of *communism had to be met in every corner of the globe. Part of Kennedy's strategy to deny the Third World to communism involved modernization efforts and attempts to secure friendly regimes, as exemplified by his Alliance for Progress in Latin America. The U.S. policy of providing financial assistance and promoting internal reforms and stronger police and military forces was intended to help *Third World nations through the turbulence that might foster the growth of insurgent movements. Where armed struggles by guerrilla forces threatened pro-U.S. regimes, the nation-building strategy relied on counterinsurgency warfare to suppress the guerrillas. Vietnam became the test case for the Kennedy administration's counterinsurgency approach. Although Kennedy was skeptical about the situation in Vietnam, he deepened American involvement there in an effort to prove that U.S. power could master any challenge.

Kennedy was assassinated in Dallas, Texas, on 22 November 1963. Popular during his presidency, he became a revered national hero after his tragic death. In retrospect, his brief administration was the apex of postwar U.S. globalism. Kennedy vigorously asserted the power and pride of a nation enthused by its preeminent role in the world. It would be left to his successors to confront the limits to U.S. power that Kennedy had not acknowledged.

(See also AMERICAN FOREIGN POLICY; ASSASSI-NATION; BAY OF PIGS INVASION; NUCLEAR WEAP-ONS; VIETNAM WAR.)

Herbert S. Parmet, *JFK: The Presidency of John F. Kennedy* (New York, 1983). Thomas G. Paterson, ed., *Kennedy's Quest for Victory: American Foreign Policy, 1961–1963* (New York, 1989).

BRUCE MIROFF

KENYA. The Republic of Kenya lies on the equator in East Africa astride the Rift Valley and flanking the Indian Ocean; its land area is 571,416 square kilometers (220,624 sq. mi.). Kenya has a current population of approximately 21.8 million with a 4.1 percent annual growth rate. Comprising this population are more than forty ethnic groups, the main ones being the Kikuyu, the Luhya, the Luo, the Kalenjini, and the Kamba. Accompanying the Africans are the numerically smaller Asian, European, and Arab populations.

The various African groups migrated into the area which would become known as Kenya long before the advent of colonialism. Groups such as the Maasai lived pastoral nomadic lives on the rangelands of Kenya while others such as the Kikuyu settled on the fertile cropland of the central forest regions and took up sedentary agriculture.

The area came under the suzerainty of the Imperial British East African Company in 1888 when the company received a royal charter to administer the territory. The British government took over formal administrative responsibilities of the East African Protectorate in June of 1895. The British colonial administration was noted for the building of a railroad between Mombasa and Lake Victoria and the subsequent leasing of vast amounts of land to white settlers: the belief being that only under settler control could the territory be developed economically. The leases dispossessed many Africans of their traditional land and provided the seeds for future social ferment.

The land loss hit the Kikuyu the hardest and in their desperation they sent a representative, Jomo Kenyatta, to London to lobby for their land. In this way the Kikuyu came into the forefront of the independence struggle. The land question was never resolved to the satisfaction of the Africans. Between 1952 and 1956, the Kikuyu led an ill-fated guerrilla war against the British—the Mau Mau rebellion. The African fighters were defeated militarily; however, the British decided to relinquish control of the colony.

Britain granted Kenya independence in December 1963 under the Majimbo constitution. This constitution formed a federal-type system to protect the smallest tribes: the effective power of the central government was reduced in favor of the regions. Jomo Kenyatta became the first prime minister of independent Kenya under the Kenya African National Union (KANU). As leader, he wanted to re-place the Majimbo constitution with one that put more power in the hands of the national government while also destroying the opposition party, the Kenya African Democratic Union (KADU).

Both of Kenyatta's goals were accomplished in 1964. KADU dissolved itself "in the interest of Kenya" and the leaders were absorbed into KANU. On 12 December of the same year, Kenya officially became a republic with Kenyatta as president, re-establishing the central administration of the colonial authorities and helping to strengthen a tempered Kikuyu dominance.

The one-party state was upset in May 1966 when the radicals in KANU left to form a new opposition party, the Kenyan People's Union (KPU). This state of affairs lasted only a very short time, however, and by 1968 state intervention in the political process marked the essential end to competitive politics. In October of 1969 KPU was declared illegal.

In general, under Kenyatta the day-to-day politics were dominated by factionalism which essentially amounted to Kikuyu versus non-Kikuyu, for tribal links were the basis for patronage and the Kikuyu dominated in economic terms. Kenyatta retained power until his death in 1978. He had always been able to remain above the dirty day-to-day politics and factionalism by his assumption of the role of Mzee—"the father of the nation"—and by the suppression of dissent.

Upon Kenyatta's death, the Vice President Daniel arap Moi peacefully and constitutionally succeeded into the presidential office. Moi strengthened his claim to office through subsequent elections. His tenure in office has been marked by the de facto one-party state becoming de jure in June 1982 when KANU was made the sole legal party and by increasing repression following the attempted coup by the Kenyan Air Force in 1982. By 1988, Moi amassed enough influence to push through other constitutional amendments. The secret ballot was abolished in primary elections, with voters required to line up in public behind pictures of candidates. In addition, the length of time a suspect could be held was increased from twenty-four hours to fourteen days, and the independence of the judiciary was undermined when the amendment separating the judiciary and executive branches was repealed.

The seeds of discontent which began with Moi's actions in the 1980s have erupted into a larger movement for *democracy in the early 1990s. Encouraged by changes across Eastern Europe, clergy, lawyers, students, and opposition politicians began to debate openly the merits of a multiparty system. Moi declared the debates unconstitutional and illegal and ordered any discussion to end. One cabinet minister even urged cutting off the fingers of those who raise two as a symbol for a two-party system. The influential *Nairobi Law Monthly,* one of the few voices of opposition, was banned and its editor jailed.

Protest has taken on a new form involving segments of the population previously not expressing public opposition to the Moi/KANU regime. As a result, Moi has become more antagonistic toward aid donors, particularly the United States and Norway, who have urged the government to improve *human rights conditions in the country. In November 1991, a consortium of donors assembled by the *World Bank in Paris finally decided to suspend aid to the Kenyan government for six months unless President Moi allowed multiparty elections. Three weeks later, President Moi legalized opposition politics in the country, opening the way for elections in 1992.

Since independence, the Kenyan economy has followed a path which is essentially a continuation and elaboration of policies established by the government during the closing days of colonial rule. The 1965 document "African Socialism and Its Application to Planning in Kenya" established the economic foundations—*capitalism, free enterprise, and controlled state participation in the economy.

Despite attempts to industrialize, the Kenyan economy is dominated by agricultural production and the sale of cash crops, coffee and tea being the most important, on the international market. Kenya sustains a flourishing tourist trade as well. There is a significant amount of manufacturing.

In East Africa, Kenya has pursued several cooperative economic ventures with other African countries. In June of 1967 Kenya, Uganda, and Tanzania signed the treaty for the East African Community (EAC) to provide closer integration in economic matters. However, Kenya was the main beneficiary of the intraregional trade because it was relatively more developed than the other partners, much in the same way South Africa dominates its neighbors. The EAC was finally disbanded in February 1977 because of growing conflict over unequal gains as well as political rift between the three heads of state: Kenyatta, Idi Amin, and Julius *Nyerere. Kenya joined another economic cooperation unit in 1978 when it, along with eleven other East and Southern African states, indicated the intent of establishing a Preferential Trade Area for Eastern and Southern Africa (PTA). Since that time, the PTA has grown to fourteen members.

Internationally, Kenya maintains a pro-Western foreign policy. Although it maintains ties to Britain, Kenya has developed closer ties with the United States. One of Kenya's main *security concerns has been in the security of its northeastern territory against Somali irredentism. Kenya has signed several agreements with Ethiopia, which has similar concerns, for cooperation in this matter. Kenya is a member of the UN and its specialized and related agencies while also belonging to the *Nonaligned Movement and the *Organization of African Unity.

(See also COLONIAL EMPIRES; DECOLONIZATION; GUERRILLA WARFARE; MAU MAU ANTICOLONIAL STRUGGLE; ONE-PARTY SYSTEM.)

Colin Leys, *Underdevelopment in Kenya: The Political Economy of Neocolonialism* (Berkeley, Calif., 1974). Gavin Kitching, *Class and Economic Change in Kenya: The Making of an African Petite Bourgeoisie, 1905–1970* (New Haven, Conn., 1980). Steven Langdon, *Multinational Corporations in the Political Economy of Kenya* (New York, 1981). Walter O. Oyugi et al., eds., *Democratic Theory and Practice in Africa* (Portsmouth, N.H., 1988).

FANTU CHERU

KEYNESIANISM. The term *Keynesianism* owes its origins to the thought of John Maynard Keynes (1883–1946), a prolific British economist whose most influential work was *The General Theory of Employment, Interest, and Money,* first published in 1936. Keynes's doctrine was at once a denunciation of the then-orthodox view that a modern economy, left to its own devices, would naturally tend to adjust to an operational level at "full employment," an analytic account of the way the economic system might instead be "stuck" at an underemployment equilibrium, and a prescription of the policy interventions needed to stimulate a depressed economy. The crucial argument of *The General Theory* rested on the claim that aggregate demand (primarily the sum of spending by the public on consumer goods, by producers on investment goods, and by governments) was the fundamental determinant of levels of national income and employment. In Keynes's view, aggregate demand during the years of the Great Depression was indeed deficient; hence, the remedy for the distresses of that time should be sought through measures to spur total spending. Monetary policy—directed toward reductions in interest rates to encourage investment spending—could play a role in this strategy, but its effectiveness was held to be limited. Far greater impact was expected from an activist fiscal policy in which governments would add to total demand by running deliberate deficits, particularly by adding to their outlays for public works. Keynes's analysis provided a theoretical rationale for the enlargement of government's role in the management of the economy—and it represented a clear and direct challenge to the long-standing view that the test of a government's "fiscal responsibility" was a balanced budget. Besides calling for a reorientation in conventional thinking about the scope and form of government intervention, *The General Theory* also called for a reorientation in formal economic theory. The subsequent development of "macroeconomics"—in which the aggregative behavior of such magnitudes as saving, investment, consumption, etc., are the focus of attention—is built on the foundations of Keynes's doctrine. Keynes was overly aggressive in his own claims for the "revolutionary" character of his findings. Others had arrived independently at similar conclusions, particularly with respect to the conduct of economic policy. Keynes succeeded, however, in introducing a novel technical vocabulary which captured the imagination of a budding generation of professional economists. Not only did this theoretical system seem to offer solutions to urgent practical problems presented by the Great Depression, it also provided a framework within which an intellectually exciting range of empirical investigations could proceed.

As originally constructed, the Keynesian "model" was intended to address the issue of persistent mass unemployment. Initially, however, its direct impact on the formulation of economic policy was slight. In *Britain, treasury officials were not notably sympathetic to Keynes's recommendations on remedies for unemployment. In the United States, his arguments had a mixed reception. President Franklin D. *Roosevelt did indeed reorient his administration's economic strategy in 1938 when he called for a deliberate program of deficit spending: although his administration had recorded deficits in each of its preceding years, the president had always insisted that balanced budgets remained his goal. This shift represented an intellectual conversion, but it is not clear that the analysis provided by *The General Theory* was decisive in bringing it about. The arguments which persuaded the president to rethink the role of an activist fiscal policy were packaged by aides who had already developed an analysis of changes in the "net contribution of government to spending" to account for the totally unanticipated downturn in the U.S. economy in 1937 (which occurred at a time when the economy was still well below its capacity). A number of the *New Deal economists were, however, delighted to invoke the authority of Keynes to reinforce positions they had reached on their own. Even so, by 1940—when "Keynesianism" had been well assimilated into official U.S. thinking—it still came through with an American accent. The central message, as read by Lauchlin Currie, the economic adviser to the president, was that aggregate demand management in the United States should focus on producing a "high consumption–low saving" economy. This could be accomplished through more aggressive programs of progressive taxation and transfer payments to those at the lower end of the income distribution. Thus, it was argued, the "social objectives of the New Deal" could be reconciled with "sound [i.e., Americanized "Keynesian"] economics." Deficit financing of public works—which had figured so prominently in Keynes's own policy prescriptions—was downplayed.

The "Keynesian" way of thinking came into its own in World War II. Shortly after the outbreak of hostilities, Keynes produced a pamphlet entitled *How to Pay for the War*. This was an application of the Keynesian apparatus of aggregative analysis to a problem quite different from the one it was originally designed to deal with. In wartime, the objective of demand management was to suppress private consumption and investment spending in the interests of releasing resources for military mobilization and to constrain upward pressures on prices. In both Britain and the United States, the tools provided by the Keynesian model proved to be invaluable in organizing the thinking of policymakers around the potential size of the "inflationary gap," with attention to measures necessary to contain it (i.e., some combination of increased taxes and borrowing from the public to drain off excessive purchasing power, direct controls over consumer prices, restrictions on access to materials normally used in private capital formation, etc.).

The "Keynesian" perspective further left its mark on planning for the postwar economic order. At the international level, the architecture of the Bretton Woods agreements—in which Keynes participated personally as a British delegate—owed much to his influence. The fruit of this work was the creation of two new institutions—the *International Monetary Fund (IMF) and the International Bank for Reconstruction and Development. Their purpose was to create a climate favorable to expansion of international trade and investment in which individual countries could also pursue "full employment" policies at home. The rigidities of the *gold standard—the rules of which implied that countries experiencing balance-of-payments difficulties should curtail domestic demand—were rejected. Instead, a debtor country could seek accommodation from the lending facilities of the IMF to cover its trade and payments deficits. In principle, the adjustments needed to correct its international accounts could be accomplished without resort to domestic deflation. This amounted to an extension of the Keynesian conception of aggregate demand management from the national to the international scene.

The Keynesian style of thinking also inspired the approach of a number of governments to the management of domestic economic affairs after World War II. Consensus was readily reached on one proposition: that a reversion to depression conditions was intolerable and unacceptable. Keynes's disciples were confident that his teachings could ensure a different—and much happier—result. This approach found its way into the blueprint for postwar Britain produced in the Beveridge Report *Full Employment in a Free Society* (published in 1944) and into the macroeconomic strategies pursued by the postwar Labour government. Keynesians in the United States were instrumental in promoting the Employment Act of 1946. Their original aspirations—contained in the initial versions of this bill—did not survive congressional scrutiny. They had hoped to enact legislation that would create a fiscal authority (staffed by economic experts of the "correct" persuasion) with discretionary powers to alter tax rates and government spending programs in light of the requirements of economic stabilization. This grand vision was frustrated: indeed there was a touch of naïveté in the expectation that elected officials would delegate the jurisdiction over spending and taxing to faceless "experts," however insistently the latter might assert their competence as "scientists." Even in watered-down form, the Employment Act was a victory of sorts. It put the U.S. government formally on record as responsible for maintaining "maximum levels of employment, income, and purchasing power." (The language of "full employment," however, had been struck.) In addition, it created a three-member Council of Economic Advisers within the Executive Office of the President. The council was charged only with the preparation of reports on the state of the economy and had no operational responsibilities. Nevertheless, it was expected that the "new economics" would henceforth have a hearing at the pinnacle of power.

In the 1950s, Keynesian doctrine was more widely dispersed. In Britain and the United States, it became the centerpiece of mainstream academic teaching. Not surprisingly, its absorption in countries cut off from Anglo-Saxon intellectual developments during the war—particularly Germany and Japan—came later and was never complete. The rallying cry of "full employment," however, was one that no government dependent on support from the electorate could afford to ignore. And whether it chose to endorse a Keynesian route toward that goal or not, the insistence of Keynesians that the goal was attainable meant that the message commanded attention. In many countries, Keynesianism—which, in its early iterations, had often been regarded as dangerously interventionist—came to be regarded as essentially conservative in the sense that its approach to aggregate demand management promised to stabilize a "mixed economy" and thus to undercut support for more radical structural changes in the economic system.

The 1960s in the United States witnessed a much-heralded "laboratory test" of applied Keynesianism in peacetime. The Kennedy administration's Council of Economic Advisers—composed of academic Keynesians and chaired by Walter Heller—successfully orchestrated a tax cut to attack unemployment and to raise the economic growth rate at a time when the federal budget was in deficit. The early results went according to expectation, and confidence in the ability of Keynesians to "fine-tune" the economy to a noninflationary full-employment track reached its all-time high.

Keynesianism fared less well in the 1970s, even though a conservative U.S. president—Richard M. *Nixon—proclaimed that "we are all Keynesians now." The stagflation of those years—in which unemployment coexisted with rising inflation rates—was a reality that could not readily be explained within the framework of the Keynesian model. Indeed, in the eyes of critics of Keynesianism, the very application of this doctrine was responsible for much of the discomfort in the world economy. According to such diagnoses, the "Keynesian era"—the end of which was now trumpeted—had led governments to lower their guard against inflation because of excessive concern for the evils of unemployment. In addition, the preoccupation of Keynesians with sufficient aggregate demand, it was alleged, had given too much emphasis to expanding consumption and too little to the encouragement of saving. The result was inadequate capital formation and declining productivity growth.

This disenchantment with Keynesianism provided a propitious environment within which alternative approaches to economic analysis and political management could flourish. The doctrine of *monetarism then took on fresh vitality with its claim that size of the money supply was the force driving the performance of the economy. Its advocates maintained that governments had been misled by the fiscal "fine tuners" and that a stable climate for noninflationary growth could be achieved only when central banks disciplined themselves to restrain expansion of the money supply to preannounced targets. Automaticity, not discretion, in policy-making should now be the order of the day. Few governments were immune from this shift in the tide—and certainly not those of Britain and the United States where the supremacy of Keynesianism had once seemed secure. Change also occurred in the conduct of international economic affairs: the fixed exchange rate feature of the Bretton Woods system was swept away in favor of a regime of floating rates in which the international value of national currencies would be determined by the allegedly impersonal forces of the marketplace.

Keynesianism as a political rallying point was dealt yet another blow by the electoral triumphs of Ronald *Reagan in the 1980s. In their rhetoric at least, the "supply-siders" of Reaganomics were determined to undo the "demand side" economics of Keynesianism.

Since the 1970s, Keynesianism may have lost much of its luster. But even its critics have paid it the ultimate tribute: they have defined their own positions in reaction to the doctrines associated with Keynesianism.

(See also BALANCE OF PAYMENTS; FINANCE, INTERNATIONAL; INTERNATIONAL POLITICAL ECONOMY; POLITICAL ECONOMY.)

Donald Winch, *Economics and Policy: A Historical Study* (London, 1969). John Maynard Keynes, *The Collected Writings of John Maynard Keynes*, 31 vols. (London, 1971–1989). David N. Worswick and James Trevithick, eds., *Keynes and the Modern World* (Cambridge, U.K., 1984). Peter A. Hall, ed., *The Political Power of Economic Ideas: Keynesianism across Nations* (Princeton, N.J., 1989). Mary O. Furner and Barry Supple, eds., *The State and Economic Knowledge: The American and British Experiences* (New York, 1990). Herbert Stein, *The Fiscal Revolution in America*, rev. ed. (Washington, D.C., 1990).

WILLIAM J. BARBER

KGB. The KGB (Komitet Gosudarstvennoi Bezopasnosti, or Committee of State Security) was established in March 1954 as the *Soviet Union's political police and intelligence apparatus. The KGB's origins date back to December 1917, when Vladimir *Lenin, leader of the new Soviet regime, created the first political police, called the Cheka, which had powers of summary justice and unleashed the "Red Terror" against Soviet opponents in 1918. After it was disbanded in the early 1920s, the Cheka was superseded by a succession of police organizations, all of which subjected Soviet citizens to extreme political repression under the ruthless dictatorship of Lenin's successor, Joseph *Stalin. Following Stalin's death and the creation of the KGB, the powers of the political police were curtailed, and it no longer employed violence on a wide scale. However, it still was used as an instrument of coercion to support a nondemocratic regime.

As a police organization the KGB was empowered by Soviet law to investigate certain state crimes, including treason, espionage, smuggling, organized crime, and certain forms of political dissent. In the past KGB investigators often circumvented Soviet laws of criminal procedure in dealing with political dissenters. Once Soviet President Mikhail *Gorbachev initiated his policy of *perestroika, however, the KGB's arbitrary powers were restricted, and it drastically curtailed political arrests.

The KGB, which was last headed by Chairman Vladimir Kriuchkov, combined the functions of counterintelligence and intelligence gathering in one body. Its First Chief Directorate was responsible for foreign operations, including espionage, while its Second Chief Directorate conducted political counterintelligence. Military counterintelligence was under the Third Chief Directorate. The KGB had three other numbered directorates: the Seventh, for surveillance and technical assistance; the Eighth, for communications interception; and the Ninth, for guarding high-level officials and government building. In addition the KGB had a Border Guards Directorate, which included some 250,000 troops for protecting Soviet borders, and a Directorate for the Protection of the Constitution, which focused on the growing problem of ethnic unrest and separatist movements. The KGB's overall manpower, according to Western estimates, was in the range of 700,000 full-time employees.

Although the KGB was a Soviet state committee, formally under government authority, the *Communist Party of the Soviet Union (CPSU) exercised de facto control over the KGB. As part of his program of perestroika, Gorbachev enhanced the powers of the government at the expense of the party, and CPSU control over the KGB was assumed by the USSR Supreme Soviet, headed by Gorbachev. The KGB then reported to the newly created Supreme Soviet Commission on Defense and Security, which consisted of elected delegates. However, this commission never took an active oversight role, and the main authority over the KGB rested with Gorbachev and his Presidential Council. Because of increasing political instability in the Soviet Union, Gorbachev and his colleagues continued to rely heavily on the KGB for support despite the overall trend toward a more open political system.

Following the attempted coup of August 1991 and the consequent break-up of the Soviet Union, the KGB was disbanded. Russian President Boris *Yeltsin established a new, reformed security and intelligence apparatus: the Russian Ministry of Security and a separate Foreign Intelligence Agency. Thanks to the Yeltsin government, these agencies have considerably less influence on the political process than had the KGB. But they could again become powerful if conservative forces were to defeat Yeltsin's reform program and attempt to reintroduce repressive measures. In the other former Soviet republics new security agencies have replaced the KGB and now serve the national interests of the new states rather than the interests of Moscow.

(See also CENTRAL INTELLIGENCE AGENCY.)

John Barron, *KGB Today: The Hidden Hand* (New York, 1983). Amy W. Knight, *The KGB: Police and Politics in the Soviet Union* (Boston, 1988).

AMY KNIGHT

KHOMEINI, Ruhollah. Ruhollah Musavi Khomeini (1902–1989), the most important leader of the *Iranian Revolution, was born in the small town of Khomein, located in central *Iran about 290 kilometers (180 miles) south of Tehran. Both his grandfather and father were Shi'i Islamic clergy. Because his father was killed while Khomeini was an infant, he was raised by an uncle, who provided him an early religious education. In 1918, Khomeini went to the nearby city of Arak to study in the seminary set up by the renowned theologian Ayatollah Abdol-Karim Haeri-Yazdi. In 1922, after Haeri-Yazdi had been invited to establish a major theological center in Qom, Khomeini moved there to continue advanced religious studies. After his mentor's death in 1936, Khomeini was recognized as one of Qom's religious scholars and taught in the prestigious Fayziyeh seminary.

Khomeini first acquired national prominence in 1944 with the publication of a book that attacked secular policies during the reign of Reza Shah (1926–1941). Although Khomeini raised the idea of an Islamic government in this early work, it would be another twenty-five years before his concept of rule by the clergy was fully developed. Two years after this book appeared, Khomeini became closely associated with Ayatollah Borujerdi, then regarded as the most distinguished cleric in the Shi'i world. Because Borujerdi opposed the clergy's participation in politics, Khomeini refrained from political activity, even during the turbulent National Front era (1949–1953), when some of his clerical colleagues were politically involved. Borujerdi's death in 1961, at a time when no single cleric was regarded as his equal, provided an opportunity for Khomeini to emerge as one of several contenders for Borujerdi's position as paramount Shi'i theologian while simultaneously obviating any need to show deference to the views of a senior religious figure.

Within two years, Khomeini had acquired a reputation as a senior cleric who was not afraid to criticize the government's domestic and foreign policies as contrary to Islamic principles. Khomeini's antigovernment sermons led to his arrest in June 1963, an incident that sparked several days of mass protests throughout the country which were forcibly suppressed with thousands of casualties. Khomeini refused to remain silent following his April 1964 release from prison, his opposition sermons focusing on legislation granting diplomatic immunity to U.S. military personnel in Iran. Khomeini's outspokenness led to his second arrest in November 1964, but this time the government sent him into exile to Turkey; a year later, Iraq permitted him to settle in the Shi'i pilgrimage and theological city of Najaf.

Khomeini and his supporters never forgot the violent events of 1963 and commemorated them annually, each year gaining more adherents to their cause, which by the early 1970s had become the overthrow of the shah's regime. During his thirteen-year stay in Najaf, Khomeini elaborated his theory of Islamic government. His original contribution to Shi'i political theory is *velayat-e faqih,* or rule by the clergy. Khomeini argued that the twelve saintly successors and descendants of the Prophet Muhammad transferred their political authority *(velayat)* to the Shi'i clergy, in particular to those trained in Islamic jurisprudence *(faqih)*. Monarchies and other forms of government that fail to defer to the clergy are illegitimate, and pious Muslims are obligated to overthrow them.

Khomeini's views on Islamic government gained broad appeal throughout the 1970s as the shah became more authoritarian and his foreign policies more aligned with those of the United States. Former students and political dissidents visited the increasingly revered ayatollah in exile and smuggled back into Iran cassettes of his sermons denouncing the shah's government. Khomeini acquired a charisma that derived from his reputation for honesty, moral rectitude, ascetic lifestyle, religious knowledge, and uncompromising opposition to the shah's dictatorship. The January 1978 forcible suppression of pro-Khomeini protests in Qom touched off a cycle of demonstrations that spread throughout the country and mobilized millions of people by the end of the year. The increasing momentum of the mass popular movement demoralized the security forces; the shah fled the country in January 1979, and his regime was soon toppled.

Following his own triumphal return to Iran in February 1979, Khomeini supervised the creation of an Islamic republic as the country's preeminent *faqih*. The success of the *revolution in Iran inspired

Islamic-based political opposition movements in other Middle Eastern countries and led to confrontation with the United States and the war with secular Iraq (1980–1988). Thus, during the last ten years of his life, Khomeini was as much preoccupied with foreign relations as he was with efforts to institutionalize clerical rule in Iran. His style of rule generally was to refrain from direct involvement in the day-to-day affairs of government, preferring to serve as arbiter of the differing political perspectives among the clergy.

(See also IRAN-IRAQ WAR; ISLAM; RELIGION AND POLITICS.)

Hamid Algar, ed. and trans., *Islam and Revolution: Writings and Declarations of Imam Khomeini* (Berkeley, Calif., 1981). Shaul Bakhash, *The Reign of the Ayatollahs: Iran and the Islamic Revolution* (New York, 1984).

ERIC HOOGLUND

KHRUSHCHEV, Nikita. Born into a peasant family in April 1894, Nikita Sergeevich Khrushchev would rise within the Soviet political system to become supreme leader from 1953 until his forced retirement in October 1964. With only a rudimentary education, Khrushchev brought opportunism, shrewdness, energy, commitment, and intelligence to his political career within the Communist Party.

During the years that Khrushchev was in power, the Soviet system changed from a Stalinist war economy and garrison state into a more relaxed regime in which the authorities no longer used mass terror to keep the population in line. Leadership politics evolved from terroristic despotism into a more orderly oligarchy. The losers in political conflict no longer lost their lives. The secret police was resubordinated to party control, and the pall of terror and fear that had hung over the population was lifted. Dogmatic restrictions on culture were relaxed to a degree, and Soviet society gained somewhat greater access to the outside world. Budgetary priorities were adjusted to permit greater attention to consumer goods and services, housing, and agriculture. Social security, wages, and pensions were improved, and the educational network was vastly expanded.

In its foreign relations, the Soviet Union developed the capability to deliver nuclear weapons at great distances and entered the space race with Sputnik and other earth-orbital devices. At the same time, *Soviet foreign policy broke out of its continental confines, seeking to curry influence, win friends, and prosecute the "anti-imperialist struggle" among newly decolonized or decolonizing territories throughout the world. In addition to these competitive tendencies, the Khrushchev era witnessed the development of a sustained effort by the Soviets to engage the United States in a bilateral association geared toward managing the nuclear relationship, harnessing the arms race, expanding East-West trade, preventing nuclear proliferation, ratifying the partition of Europe, and, more generally, inducing the United States to treat the Soviet Union as an equal in world affairs. The origins of *détente are to be found in the Khrushchev era.

Khrushchev made a substantial contribution to these redirections of Stalinist foreign and domestic policy. To be sure, moves away from the personal despotism, mass terror, consumer austerity, and war economy of the *Stalin era would likely have taken place in his absence, as would the development of an effort to manage the *superpower relationship. However, breaking through the obstacles to reform of the Stalinist system, and building coalitions on behalf of a change in assumptions about international politics, were no mean feats. They required the kind of energy, determination, and, most importantly, risk orientation that Khrushchev appears to have uniquely possessed among leading members of the post-Stalin leadership. Khrushchev's de-Stalinization campaign, including his anti-Stalin "secret speech" (1956), is the best example of boldness in the face of accumulating obstacles to change. Of course, boldness also drove him to initiate the *Cuban Missile Crisis as well, although in the service of goals with which most Westerners are less likely to identify.

Khrushchev faced basic dilemmas in trying to reform the Stalinist system. Convinced that an excess of bureaucratic centralism was stifling the public initiative required to revitalize both economy and society, Khrushchev pursued increasingly populist policies. This *populism threatened the privileges and power of the bureaucratic establishment, which used active and passive resistance to undermine his programs. In addition, however, many of Khrushchev's economic policies were ill conceived, based on a faith that popular initiative without market coordination could replace coordination through detailed directives from above. As his policies failed, Khrushchev sought to recoup by imposing organizational innovations and economic policies that made little administrative or economic sense. At the same time, he tried to reform the political order in order to purge the establishment and bring new generations into positions of authority. Before these innovations could purchase him a new base of support, Khrushchev was ousted by the elite representatives of the institutions threatened by his policies. By delegitimizing Stalinist methods of protecting his political power, Khrushchev himself had made possible the conspiracy that deposed him. And by relying more on the masses than on established institutions as his political base, he deprived himself of a power base within the establishment.

In foreign policy, Khrushchev promised both to compete with the "imperialists" and to collaborate with them, but from a position of strength. Only such a posture, he believed, would induce the United States, in particular, to treat the Soviet Union as an equal in world affairs. His goal was to create a collaborative relationship that he could then use to justify further development of the Soviet civilian and consumer economy. However, neither economically, nor militarily, nor in terms of international influence and alliance cohesion (as in the growing Sino-Soviet schism) was the Soviet Union anything approaching an equal of the United States. Hence, Khrushchev's competitive rhetoric and behavior tended to be interpreted in Washington as a sign of his determination to "bury" the West, while his collaborative initiatives were often misinterpreted or dismissed as disingenuous. The *Cuban Missile Crisis ultimately stunned both sides into a mutual search for accommodation. The resulting *détente of 1963–1964 was short-lived, however, owing to the combined impact of the assassination of John *Kennedy, the overthrow of Khrushchev, his replacement by leaders less inclined than he to be conciliatory, and Americanization of the war in Vietnam.

Khrushchev's major contributions to Soviet history lay in his willingness to take risks and seize the initiative on behalf of breaking out of the Stalinist mold in domestic and foreign policy. He succeeded in doing so. However, his vision of an alternative political, economic, and world order was never realized, in part because of his insufficient understanding of what needed to be done, in part because of the inherent immensity of the task. After twenty years of relative bureaucratic conservatism, Mikhail *Gorbachev again took up the challenge that Khrushchev had been willing to face. It is not coincidental that balanced and objective appraisals of Khrushchev's role in Soviet history began reappearing in Soviet publications even before the dissolution of the union.

(See also COMMUNIST PARTY OF THE SOVIET UNION; STALINISM.)

Roy A. Medvedev and Zhores A. Medvedev, *Khrushchev: The Years in Power* (New York, 1976). George Breslauer, *Khrushchev and Brezhnev as Leaders: Building Authority in Soviet Politics* (London and Boston, 1982).
GEORGE W. BRESLAUER

KING, Martin Luther, Jr. For many Americans, Martin Luther King, Jr., epitomizes the black freedom struggle in the United States during the 1950s and 1960s. Born in Atlanta, Georgia, on 15 January 1929, King was the second of three children of Martin Luther King, Sr., a prominent Baptist minister, and Alberta Williams King, a teacher in the city's Jim Crow (segregated black) schools. His early years were spent in the relative security of a middle-class family environment. Following his graduation in 1948 from Morehouse College in Atlanta, King abandoned a youthful notion of pursuing a career in medicine or law and, instead, enrolled at Crozer Theological Seminary in Chester, Pennsylvania. While at Crozer, he developed a fascination with the philosophy of Mohandas *Gandhi, who successfully employed passive resistance and civil disobedience (satyagraha) in his campaign to break the grip of British imperialism in India. King earned a bachelor of divinity degree in 1951. He continued his education at Boston University's Graduate School of Theology and received a Ph.D. in systemic theology in 1955. In Boston, he met Coretta Scott, whom he married in 1953. The union would produce four children.

In 1954, while completing his doctoral dissertation, King accepted a call to pastor the prestigious Dexter Avenue Baptist Church in Montgomery, Alabama. His return to the South placed him in the midst of a confluence of events that would push the young minister into the national spotlight. On 1 December 1955, Rosa Parks, a black seamstress, was arrested for refusing to relinquish her seat on a crowded city bus to a white man. This incident sparked a boycott of the city's bus lines by members of Montgomery's black community. Although initially reluctant to become directly involved in the proposed boycott, King eventually acceded to the request of his friend, the Reverend Ralph Abernathy, and Montgomery's most outspoken black activist, E. D. Nixon, that he assume the presidency of the Montgomery Improvement Association (MIA), an organization formed to sustain the protest. Under the auspices of the MIA, King directed a yearlong campaign which employed the strategy of nonviolent direct action to challenge the local bus segregation ordinance. The boycott ended in 1956 when the *Supreme Court upheld a federal appellate court order striking down bus segregation in Montgomery. As leader of the successful boycott, King found himself catapulted to national prominence. Capitalizing on the momentum generated by this victory, he organized the Southern Christian Leadership Conference (SCLC) in 1957. This organization, based in Atlanta, became the institutional center for King's civil rights activities for the next decade.

Although King neither directed nor participated in most of the nonviolent direct action protests of the early 1960s, his leadership at demonstrations in Alabama and Washington, D.C., focused national attention on the depth and persistence of racism in the South. In 1963, nonviolent efforts to eliminate segregation in Birmingham, Alabama, produced few immediate results, but the brutal assaults by local police on peaceful demonstrators under King's direction left searing images in the public mind. Responding to criticism from fellow clergy following his arrest in Birmingham, King penned "Letter from Birmingham Jail," in which he eloquently proclaimed the moral imperative of resisting unjust laws. In August of the same year, King participated in the historic March on Washington, organized to protest racial inequality in the United States and to promote federal civil rights legislation. Addressing the assembled throng from the steps of the Lincoln Memorial, King galvanized the audience with his "I

Have a Dream" speech, which evoked his vision of a future America freed from the psychic scars of racism. King's role in this mass demonstration probably assured both his selection as Time magazine's "Man of the Year" for 1963 and his receipt of the 1964 Nobel Peace Prize. Further, King's influence on the *Kennedy and (following Kennedy's *assassination) *Johnson administrations was instrumental in securing passage of the landmark Civil Rights Act of 1964. Turning his attention in 1965 to the political powerlessness of black southerners, King organized a march from Selma, Alabama, to the state capitol in Montgomery to demand the vote for disenfranchised black Alabamans. This event provided impetus for passage by Congress of the Voting Rights Act of 1965.

Despite his victories, King faced numerous challenges to his leadership. Many younger black activists complained that the strategy of nonviolent direct action had outlived its usefulness. They denounced King as too conservative and too willing to compromise with whites in positions of power. The new slogan of the day was "Black Power," a concept that King viewed as counterproductive to his dream of interracial harmony and peace. Others criticized him for ignoring the economic problems confronting millions of *African Americans, many of whom lived in desperate conditions in the major cities of the North and West. When he turned his attention to racial problems outside the South, as in Chicago in 1966, King often faced angry receptions by blacks and whites. Moreover, in 1967, King's public opposition to the United States' involvement in the *Vietnam War deprived him of further support from the Johnson administration. Finally, King endured unrelenting attempts to discredit his leadership by J. Edgar Hoover, director of the Federal Bureau of Investigation. Nevertheless, he forged ahead with a plan to conduct a "Poor People's March" to Washington for the purpose of emphasizing the economic plight of many blacks in the United States. In the spring of 1968, he traveled to Memphis, Tennessee, to lend his support to garbage collectors in that city who were striking for higher wages and improved working conditions. Here King was assassinated on 4 April, as he stood talking with friends on the balcony of a local motel.

In contrast to widespread attempts at apotheosis in the years immediately following his death, recent students of the *Civil Rights Movement have characterized Martin Luther King, Jr., as simply one among many men and women whose actions fueled the black protest movement. In fact, some scholars have argued persuasively that King's leadership was not essential to the success of the struggle for racial equality. King's legacy to the sociopolitical fabric of the United States, however, is substantial. According to historian August Meier, by emphasizing the power of redemptive love, King effectively played upon the guilt of many whites in the United States in order to increase their awareness of the needs and aspirations of the nation's African-American population. He forced the nation to respond to the existing contradiction between the ideal of the American dream and the reality of an obdurate system of caste that promoted racial inequality. He advanced the cause of freedom through his advocacy of nonviolent protest and his powerfully articulated vision of a color-blind nation. Martin Luther King, Jr., then, among the many leaders of the black freedom struggle, became for both blacks and whites in the United States a symbol of the concept of racial and social harmony.

(See also CIVIL DISOBEDIENCE; MALCOLM X; NONVIOLENT ACTION; RACE AND RACISM.)

August Meier, "On the Role of Martin Luther King" *New Politics* 4 (Winter 1965): 52–59. David Garrow, *Bearing the Cross: Martin Luther King, Jr., and the Southern Christian Leadership Conference* (New York, 1986). Clayborne Carson, "Martin Luther King, Jr.: Charismatic Leadership in a Mass Struggle" *Journal of American History* 74 (September 1987): 448–454.

JAMES M. SoRELLE

KIRGHIZSTAN. See COMMONWEALTH OF INDEPENDENT STATES.

KIRIBATI (GILBERTS). See PACIFIC ISLANDS.

KISSINGER, Henry. Few leaders have had as much influence on U.S. *foreign policy over as long a period of time as Henry Kissinger. Since the mid-1950s, Kissinger has helped shape the way people in the United States think about global politics through his eight books and innumerable articles, interviews, and public statements. He played a major role in American foreign policy by serving as adviser for national security affairs during President Richard *Nixon's first term (1969–1972), and as secretary of state in Nixon's aborted second term and the presidency of Gerald Ford (1973–1977).

Although Kissinger has achieved international recognition, many in the United States regard him ambivalently. They see his allusions to tragedy in history, his emphasis on power in international relations, and his esteem for leaders such as Prince Metternich of Austria, Otto von Bismarck of Germany, and Charles de *Gaulle of France as evidence of his European cast of mind.

Kissinger's achievements, including his 1973 Nobel Peace Prize, gain added significance when contrasted with the events of his early life. His birth in May 1923 to an Orthodox Jewish family in Fürth, Germany, coincided with the rise of Nazism in German politics. Many interpret his emphasis on order and limits as a reaction to the chaos of his youth. Kissinger's family fled Germany in 1938 for the United States.

Following his wartime service in the U.S. Army, Kissinger enrolled at Harvard University in 1947.

His undergraduate thesis, "The Meaning of History"—an idiosyncratic treatment of the philosophies of history of the English historian Arnold Toynbee, the German historian Oswald Spengler, and the German philosopher Immanuel Kant—provides a key to much of his later thinking. Kissinger completed his doctoral program in the Department of Government in 1954. He remained at Harvard, teaching and writing about international politics, for almost fifteen years.

Kissinger is linked with other realist scholars of international politics who achieved prominence in the United States after World War II, such as George *Kennan, Hans Morgenthau, and Reinhold Niebuhr. In contrast to the "legalistic-moralistic approach to international problems" (George Kennan, *American Diplomacy: 1900–1950,* Chicago, 1951), the realists regard conflict as inherent in the state system and emphasize the *balance of power as the primary means of maintaining order. Kissinger's doctoral dissertation concerning the Congress of Vienna, later published as *A World Restored: Metternich, Castlereagh and the Problems of Peace, 1812–1822* (Boston, 1957), presents a similar worldview. The balance of power and what Kissinger refers to as *legitimacy—i.e., acceptance of the existing order by the major powers—are its principal elements.

Throughout the 1950s and 1960s, Kissinger established his reputation as a scholar of international politics. His strength was his ability to synthesize political and military patterns of thought in novel forms. During this period, his affiliation with the Rockefeller Brothers Fund and the Council on Foreign Relations exposed him to the nation's business and government elites. His association with Governor Nelson Rockefeller of New York contributed to his own rise to power.

Kissinger's first book, *Nuclear Weapons and Foreign Policy,* New York, 1957), challenged the Eisenhower administration's reliance on massive nuclear retaliation to deter aggression. Kissinger believed this strategy left the United States paralyzed in the face of ambiguous challenges from Communist powers—no single one of which was worth an all-out war. In an eclectic work, *The Necessity for Choice* (New York, 1961), Kissinger continued to address U.S. defense policy, but he also dealt with the U.S. style in diplomatic negotiations, political evolution in the Soviet Union and the emerging nations, and the role of the intellectual in policy-making. The book provided a trenchant criticism of *American foreign policy. Kissinger's thinking on U.S.-European relations, including his description of the growing structural problems in the Atlantic Alliance, is presented in *The Troubled Partnership* (New York, 1965).

The Nixon-Kissinger years marked a period of fundamental transition in the U.S. role in world affairs. The Nixon administration's four "state of the world" messages (1970–1973), prepared under Kissinger's direction, defined this transition and provided a new conceptual basis for American foreign policy. Kissinger emphasized that the *Cold War era of rigid blocs had ended. An evolving balance among five major powers—China, Japan, the Soviet Union, the United States, and Western Europe—now dominated international life.

This perception of a new global order underlies Kissinger's actions as diplomat and policy architect as well as his portrayal of events in his memoirs *White House Years* (Boston, 1979) and *Years of Upheaval* (Boston, 1982). Kissinger's secret opening to China in July 1971 set the stage for more normal relations with Beijing and gave the United States added flexibility in a new triangular relationship with China and the Soviet Union. In place of the United States' economic and political dominance of Western Europe and Japan, Kissinger called for an era of partnership in which each would act more in its own interests. He supported relative strategic parity with the Soviet Union instead of military superiority.

Kissinger sought stability in political dealings with the Soviet Union. He was the major proponent of *détente—a policy that tried to transform U.S.-Soviet relations by emphasizing restraint and the negotiation of differences. The Strategic Arms Limitation Talks (SALT), in which Kissinger played an important role, were the centerpiece of détente.

Kissinger also helped define and implement the Nixon Doctrine—a doctrine that substituted for the postwar policy of *containment. No longer would the United States serve as the world's police force; rather, its allies and other regional powers would be encouraged to take responsibility for their own security. The Nixon Doctrine provided the basis for Kissinger's negotiation of the end of U.S. involvement in the *Vietnam War.

The 1960s and 1970s marked the passage of the United States from its post–World War II dominance of world affairs and the international economy to a more equal status with other countries. Kissinger's approach to global politics urged the nation to recognize the need for a transition between those two eras, as well as a sense of its own limits. This is his principal legacy as scholar, diplomat, and foreign policy strategist.

(See also DIPLOMACY; REALISM; STRATEGIC ARMS LIMITATION TREATIES.)

Stephen R. Graubard, *Kissinger: Portrait of a Mind* (New York, 1973). Peter Dickson, *Henry Kissinger and the Meaning of History* (Cambridge, 1978). Gregory D. Cleva, *Henry Kissinger and the American Approach to Foreign Policy* (Lewisburg, Pa., 1989).

GREGORY CLEVA

KOHL, Helmut. Helmut Kohl, chancellor of the Federal Republic of *Germany (FRG), was born in 1930 in Ludwigshafen in what is now the state of Rhineland-Palatinate. Kohl is considered the first "true" postwar chancellor, as he was only a teenager at the conclusion of *World War II in 1945. A career politician, Kohl was active in the Christlich Demokratische Union (CDU) in his home state, serving in many elected and appointed positions during the 1950s and 1960s for his moderately right-wing party. He was first elected to the position of minister-president of Rhineland-Palatinate in 1969 and served until 1976. In 1976 he was the chancellor candidate of the CDU and its sister party the Bavarian-based Christlich Soziale Union (CSU) against the center-left coalition of the left-wing Sozialdemokratische Partei Deutschlands (SPD) and the small, centrist Freie Demokratische Partei (FDP). Kohl lost that election to the Social Democrat Helmut Schmidt and did not stand as chancellor candidate at the next federal election in 1980, as former CSU leader Franz-Josef Strauss was the CDU-CSU choice. This election was also won by Schmidt and the SPD-FDP.

In October 1982 when the FDP decided to end its coalition with the SPD in favor of joining forces with the CDU-CSU, Kohl became chancellor by virtue of his leadership of the CDU. In order to ratify this change with the voters, Kohl's new coalition government called early elections in the winter of 1983, and the CDU-CSU-FDP achieved a strong majority position. Kohl was subsequently reelected in both 1987 and 1990 and thus became the second-longest-serving postwar chancellor, trailing only fellow Christian Democrat Konrad Adenauer, who was the chancellor from 1949 to 1963.

During his first term of office (1983–1987) Kohl's leadership was sometimes compared unfavorably to that of Margaret *Thatcher and Ronald *Reagan, who had also displaced center-left parties to win executive office. Moreover, the monolingual Kohl—unlike his predecessors Helmut Schmidt and Willy Brandt—seemed insufficiently cosmopolitan in the eyes of some critics. Eschewing sharp ideological rhetoric, however, Kohl relied on a pragmatic approach to leadership which drew on his long experience in party politics in the FRG. In fact, Kohl more closely resembled former U.S. President Gerald Ford, both in terms of long service to his party and the relative moderation of his policies. Unlike the effects of Reagan or Thatcher on politics in the United States or Britain, Kohl did not turn German politics sharply in a rightward direction during the 1980s.

During the first Kohl government there were no major changes in direction and few significant policy innovations. Some observers predicted that Kohl would either lose the 1987 election or face a challenge from within his own party grouping by having to face an opponent as chancellor candidate. However, Kohl's political skills within his party—he reportedly knows the name of every Christian Democratic mayor in the country—and institutional skills within his center-right coalition enabled him to both fend off internal opponents and to defeat the SPD and the other party of the German Left, the Greens, in the 1987 elections.

Kohl was helped in his reelection by the lack of effective opposition from the SPD and the Greens. He also benefited from his early embracing of European unity in the Single European Market which promised to increase economic and political unity by 1992. Acting more on pragmatic than ideological grounds, Kohl's endorsement of a more unified Europe helped solidify the FRG's position among its neighbors. This proved particularly important given the bitter memory of Germany's aggressive posture toward other European countries during World War I and World War II.

Despite the favorable short-term factor (the 1987 election) and the favorable long-term factor (1992 European unity), Kohl faced increasing criticism during the late 1980s. With its campaign against German-Polish borders as fixed in several post–World War II treaties—the Oder-Neisse line—a right-wing party, the Republikaner, won representation in several regional elections in the winter and spring of 1989. Kohl's apparent indecisiveness during this period only served to increase the challenge from both the Republikaner to the *Right and more moderate forces, whether inside and outside his coalition, to the center and *Left.

Kohl's extrication from these political troubles came with the surprising East German quest for freedom in the fall of 1989. Rather than playing on old ideological rhetoric from the *Cold War, Kohl and his center-right coalition embraced the rapid process of dissolution of the former *German Democratic Republic (GDR), as communist East Germany was called. Acting quickly and pragmatically, Kohl took his political opponents on both the left and right by surprise. By the spring of 1990, when events proceeded so rapidly in the GDR that demands for freedom were being surpassed by demands for unification of the two Germanies, Kohl quickly positioned himself as the "chancellor for Germany." He also instituted a currency reform which—against the wishes of Karl-Otto Pöhl, the leader of the Bundesbank (Federal Reserve Bank)—gave most favorable exchange rates to citizens of the former GDR.

Kohl's optimistic and enthusiastic endorsement of a unification process that promised to avoid hardship for former GDR residents resulted in electoral gains for the CDU-CSU-FDP coalition in regional voting in the former GDR prior to unification. It also carried over after formal German unification in October 1990 to electoral victories for his coalition in subsequent regional elections, as well as the Bundestag (parliamentary lower house) federal elections—the first all-German elections since 1933—in December 1990. Thus, in the space of a few short years, Kohl's image was transformed from that of an unexciting career politician to seemingly the most significant political figure in Germany since Konrad Adenauer and one of the most significant leaders in Europe.

By early 1991, however, the euphoria of unification had given way to the reality of the full dimensions and costs of German unification. In retrospect, many observers felt that Kohl had too cavalierly underestimated the material and social expenditure of such a huge undertaking. Having promised eastern Germans that their lives would be better, he was forced to concede that the process of transition would take several years of hardship. He also promised western German voters that no new taxes would be necessary to pay for the massive rebuilding costs, a promise he was also forced to rescind during the spring of 1991. In regional elections in early 1991, Kohl's Christian Democratic Party suffered sharp losses, the most surprising of which was the Social Democratic Party's victory in Kohl's home state of Rhineland-Palatinate for the first time in the post–World War II period. The losses of state elections by the CDU meant that the SPD opposition attained control of a majority of the sixteen state governments—which, under the German political system, gave the SPD control of the upper house of the German legislature, the Bundesrat. The upper house has considerable constitutional powers, as it must accede to all laws passed in the Bundestag; thus Kohl faced a less free political hand after losing control of the upper house.

Although his pragmatism proved effective for Germany and Europe in the short and medium term, it was unclear by the early 1990s whether Kohl had sufficient vision for the strategic tasks that a powerful and united Germany would face in an increasingly unified Europe. Despite these setbacks, however, Kohl still found himself in a relatively strong position in the early 1990s. He remained chancellor of the leading European country and did not face scheduled elections again until the fall of 1994.

(See also CHRISTIAN DEMOCRACY; GERMAN REUNIFICATION.)

Werner Haser, *Helmut Kohl: der deutsche Kanzler: Biographie* (Frankfurt, 1990). Gordon Smith, "The Resources of a German Chancellor" *West European Politics* 14, no. 2 (April 1991): 48–61.

CHRISTOPHER S. ALLEN

KOREA, DEMOCRATIC PEOPLE'S REPUBLIC OF. The Democratic People's Republic of Korea (DPRK), or North Korea, is a singular and puzzling nation that defies easy description. Because its leadership is secretive and unyielding to foreign attention, many basic facts about the country are unknown; thus pundits are able to project stereotypes onto it (a Stalinist attempt at creating "1984," a socialist basket case, a Confucian/Communist monarchy, etc.). In the night of ignorance, North Korea confirms all stereotypes.

Closer familiarity confounds simple expectations. Western travelers are ill prepared for the wide tree-lined boulevards of P'yŏngyang, a city of about 2 million in this country of 23 million people, with every street swept clean and traversed by determined, disciplined urban commuters. Visitors do not expect to find a population living in modern high rises, hustling out in the morning to a waiting subway or electric bus. Except for Singapore, P'yŏngyang is perhaps the most efficient, best-run city in Asia. If consumer goods are predictably slim, daily necessities seem ample.

North Korean villages are plain to the same degree that the capital is spectacular. Spartan but clean, with the agricultural work organized by socialist cooperatives, they recall the bucolic atmosphere of the Korean past so lacking in P'yŏngyang. On every square meter of land residents plant vegetables raised for home consumption or for sale on the small private market; electric wires run to all peasant homes, but TV aerials are much less visible than in the cities. Signs urge self-reliance ("regeneration through one's own efforts") on the locals, no doubt a reflection of state priorities which emphasize heavy industry, military preparedness, and the cities.

The DPRK was established on 9 September 1948. Emerging within the bowels of Soviet Red Army occupation, it thus took its administrative and industrial structure from Soviet models. Kim Il Sung and most of the top leadership, however, had been anti-Japanese guerrillas in northeast China in the 1930s; thus Soviet influence mingled with two others: the resistance to Japanese colonialism (slogans still exhort citizens to "live in the way of the anti-Japanese guerrillas") and that of Chinese communism. These two influences help explain DPRK domestic and foreign policy: the thought of *Mao Zedong competed with Soviet doctrines and gave the regime an internal "mass politics" emphasis, while externally the DPRK has based its strategy on close relations with and backing from China, while tilting toward Moscow from time to time for tactical reasons. With the demise of the Soviet Union in 1991, however, North Korea is more dependent on China than ever, and thus seeks to break its isolation vis-à-vis Japan and the United States.

Foreign influences, while significant, have been less important than the indigenous *political culture. The DPRK has been unique among socialist countries for its top-down leadership principle and its corporate organizational doctrine. This is a tightly held, total politics, with undoubted repressive capacity and many political victims—some reports suggest as many as 100,000 people may be held in prisons and reform-through-labor camps.

In city, town, and village there is Kim Il Sung: everywhere there is Kim Il Sung. Born on 15 April 1912 and now in power for almost five decades, no leader in the twentieth century has stamped a nation with his presence more than Kim. He is seen as the father of a family-nation, a body politic which returns fealty to him—a heritage from Korea's long history of Confucian statecraft. This is a kind of socialist *corporatism that appeals to a people with a strong extended family system, high consciousness of lineage, and deeply-inbred patriarchal moral codes. The 1972 DPRK constitution (the second since 1948) defines the family as the core unit of society. Marriages are still arranged, family themes are exalted in the arts, and the regime has never sought to break up the family unit. Accordingly, North Korea often impresses foreigners precisely in its cultural conservatism.

The ruling Korean Workers' Party (KWP) was designated a "mass party of a new type" at its inception in 1946. North Korea has always had the highest percentage of the population enrolled in the party of any *communist party state, fluctuating between twelve and fourteen percent. The Korean *revolution, far from polarizing the population exclusively into good and bad classes, pursued an inclusive, all-encompassing mass politics. The North Koreans have envisioned their society as a mass, the gathered-together "people," rather than a class-based and class-divided society.

Kim Il Sung's doctrine, known as *Juche,* is defined as self-reliance and independence in politics, economics, defense, and *ideology; it first emerged in 1955 as P'yŏngyang drew away from Moscow, and then appeared full-blown in the mid-1960s as Kim sought a stance independent of both Moscow and Beijing. On closer inspection, however, the term is opaque. The North Koreans say things like "everyone must have *Juche* firm in mind and spirit"; the closer one gets to its meaning, the more the meaning recedes. It might best be translated as "put Korean things first, always"; in this way it might best be seen as a type of *nationalism.

The North Koreans also adapted typical postcolonial *Third World policies to their indigenous political culture and to Soviet-style *socialism: an economic program of rapid industrialization through multiyear plans; *Lenin's notion of national liberation; *Stalin's autarky of socialism in one country. Autarky fit Korea's "Hermit Kingdom" past, and represented a kind of closure from the world economy after decades of opening under Japanese imperial auspices.

Familial succession to leadership, a long tradition among Korean kings, has now been institutionalized in the DPRK. In 1980 at the Sixth Congress of the KWP, Kim's son by his first marriage, Kim Jong Il, was publicly named to the Presidium of the Politburo, the Secretariat of the Central Committee, and the ruling Military Commission. In 1992 he took over supreme command of the armed forces. His rank was still second, however, behind his father and ahead of his father's old comrade-in-arms from the 1930s, O Chin-u. The ground was carefully laid for this succession from the 1960s onward: Kim Jong Il was immersed in party organizational work, and in a key campaign at the grass-roots level.

North Korea is the supreme example in the post-colonial developing world of conscious withdrawal from the capitalist world system—but withdrawal with development. Until recently its growth rates have generally been high, not just in industry, which might be expected given Japanese industrialization of northern Korea, but also in agriculture. Both Koreas now have an agrarian sector no larger than thirty percent of the population and twenty percent or less of GNP. According to a published Central Intelligence Agency report, North Korea's per capita GNP was the same as the Republic of Korea's (South Korea) in 1976. It probably kept pace up to 1983 in part because of South Korea's six percent loss of GNP in 1980. Its total production of electricity, coal, fertilizer, machine tools, and steel was comparable to or higher than South Korean totals in the early 1980s, despite its population being half that of the South. Since 1983 South Korea has forged ahead, however, as the North reaps diminished returns from an industrial system badly needing new infusions of technology.

Few countries have a more unfortunate geopolitical position than the DPRK, sharing a common border with China and Russia and with a still-tense confrontation with the United States and South Korea along the demilitarized zone. Defense expenditures account for thirteen to fifteen percent of the state budget officially, twenty to twenty-five percent according to U.S. figures.

In the early 1990s the DPRK has begun to open itself to the outside world. But there is nothing yet to suggest that the DPRK has departed from its long-standing policies of corporate politics and heavy-industry-first economics at home and self-reliance abroad.

(See also COMMAND ECONOMY; COMMUNIST PARTY STATES; CONFUCIANISM; KOREA, REPUBLIC OF; KOREAN WAR.)

Dae-Sook Suh, *Kim Il Sung: The North Korean Leader* (New York, 1988). Bruce Cumings, *The Two Koreas: On the Road to Reunification?* (New York, 1991). Chong-Sik Lee and Se-Hee Yoo, eds., *North Korea in Transition* (Berkeley, Calif., 1991).

BRUCE CUMINGS

KOREA, REPUBLIC OF. Occupying the southern half of a peninsula that juts from continental Asia toward Japan, the Republic of Korea (South Korea), despite its meager territory, is not a small country by other measures. The Republic of Korea has a population of 43 million, a GDP that equals Australia's, and a rate of economic growth almost un-

surpassed in the world; it is a developmental wunderkind of the late twentieth century. This achievement is all the more spectacular considering that the Republic of Korea was a global mendicant in the 1950s, an economic basket case sustained by the United States because of its strategic importance. The rapid pace of *development has contributed to political instability, however, and exacerbated Korea's tendency toward *authoritarianism. The Republic of Korea was in an authoritarian grip almost continuously from 1948 to 1988, when arbitrary rule gave way to parliamentary politics and limited *democracy.

The Korean propensity toward authoritarianism and state-centrism is often thought to have been overdetermined by its culture and history. In reality, the agrarian bureaucracy of the Yi dynasty (1392 to 1910), which preceded Korea's entry into the international system, was not strong; the state ostensibly dominated the society, but in fact landed aristocratic families could keep the state at bay and perpetuate local power for centuries. This pattern was broken when Japan colonized Korea in 1910, substituting a brutal and modern state for a decaying agrarian bureaucracy.

From 1910 to 1945, Japan created in Korea a web of centralized bureaucracies. the colonial government, in collaboration with semiofficial companies and conglomerates *(zaibatsu),* intervened systematically in the economy, creating markets, developing new industries, and suppressing dissent. The result of this colonial policy was a paradox: it spurred economic growth but immiserated the populace, increased agrarian output but also increased tenancy, and created a vibrant industrial structure that was an appendage of Japan's interests.

The political consequences of colonial rule were disastrous for Korea. When Japan surrendered to the Allied forces, a country that had been unified for thirteen centuries was divided at the thirty-eighth parallel, with the Soviet Union occupying the north (and then turning it over to Kim Il Sung) and the United States occupying the south until 1948, when the Republic of Korea was founded. This division was a calamity. It separated families, brought on the *Korean War (1950–1953), and produced a deadly politics that has stunted the free exchange of ideas in both the Democratic People's Republic (North Korea) and South Korea. The worst blight of the *Cold War has been heaped on the Koreans. But colonial rule also meant a new role for the central state, new sets of Korean political leaders, and a new breed of entrepreneurs *(chaebŏl),* and thus has deeply shaped the political and economic trajectory of postwar Korea.

The ravages of colonialism and war were devastating to the Republic of Korea, and the recovery, too, was slow, painful, and costly. In the 1950s, the United States poured close to $1 billion a year in military and economic aid into the Syngman Rhee regime (1948–1960) in order to sustain, in the end, a very modest growth. The generous aid was instead siphoned off to create a formidable state structure that included a very large bureaucracy and a dominating police and military. It also subsidized large industrialists, who in turn helped Rhee win elections. This coalition between bureaucracy, police, military, and *chaebŏl* would prove enduring in supporting successive authoritarian regimes.

The long-awaited economic spurt finally arrived in the mid-1960s, resulting from a fortuitous collocation of factors: a vigorous U.S. aid policy that liberalized the economic regime in Korea and emphasized exports, rapprochement with Japan as an additional source of aid, participation in and windfall gains from the *Vietnam War, and, finally, the emergence of a regime that was capable of harnessing these opportunities into an export push.

Park Chung Hee was a nationalist, anticommunist, and modernizer, and in the nearly two decades of his rule, from 1961 to 1979, the Republic of Korea was molded in his image: a vibrant, modern economy and a bulwark of anticommunism and the Cold War. This left little room for liberal democracy, and Park, after an experiment with limited parliamentary democracy in the 1960s, put an end to all such "inconveniences" in 1972. Through bureaucratic authoritarian measures known as the *Yushin*, he was made president for life, and the parliament became a rubber stamp; opposition parties were dissolved, their leaders sent either into exile or jail; dissenters, including students, intellectuals, and workers, were muzzled and terrorized; and the entire society was paramilitarized, equipped with one of the world's largest standing armies and a vast civilian reserve force. The tension created by the terror finally snapped in 1979, when, amid a growing economic crisis, workers, students, and common people poured into the streets of South Korea, and Park Chung Hee was assassinated by his own security police chief in what was probably a bungled coup attempt.

The exit of Park Chung Hee provided no relief for those who had hoped for democracy. In less than a month, a young officer named Chun Doo Hwan seized power within the military in a coup in which several high officers were killed. Chun had been a favorite of Park's, had commanded Korean troops in the Vietnam War, and was head of the powerful Army Security Command at the time of the assassination. In protest against the tightening grip of Chun, who now had himself made head of the Korean Central Intelligence Agency (KCIA), students and common people protested in ways unprecedented since 1960. This led to martial law, which then touched off province-wide rebellion in the southwest, centered in the provincial capital of Kwangju. Chun violently put down the rebellion and went on to become president of the republic, but he never transcended his role in the bloodletting in Kwangju. The Kwangju massacre remains a deep wound in the body politic.

In the first half of the 1980s, a new team of U.S.-educated economic managers proceeded to open up the economy, doing away with the *import-substitution policies of the 1970s, liberalizing imports, dismantling subsidies for exports and specific industries, privatizing banks, and developing an equity market. But the political system remained fundamentally authoritarian notwithstanding the emergence of new political elites and new political parties. In 1987 Chun sought to have the ruling party ratify Roh Tae Woo, his close friend, as his chosen successor, and this triggered massive urban demonstrations throughout Korea.

In late June 1987 big cities were paralyzed by demonstrators, newspapers were full of rumors of a military coup, and the world was riveted to television broadcasts showing chaos at the site of the 1988 Summer Olympics. Then Roh Tae Woo suddenly announced direct elections for the presidency and lifted previous restrictions on most political activities. He challenged the opposition, but it failed to seize the opportunity that had been so long in coming.

When the elections came in December 1987, Kim Dae Jung and the other major opposition figure, Kim Young Sam, were unable to agree on a single candidate to challenge the incumbents. They renamed their parties and ran separately, splitting the opposition vote (totaling fifty-three percent) and thus allowing Roh to stay in power with thirty-seven percent of the votes cast. They compounded the blunder in the 1988 assembly elections, splitting 101 seats between them while the ruling party got only eighty-six. The opposition parties in the Republic of Korea have not transcended their past as clientelist groupings around one strong leader.

In 1990 Kim Young Sam joined with the ruling group to form yet another new party, the Democratic Liberal Party, molded in the image of Japan's Liberal Democratic Party. The ruling groups thus hope to emulate the longevity and stability of Japan's one-party rule, but the likelihood of success was seriously called into question when the Democratic Liberal Party was denied a majority in the parliamentary elections of March 1992.

An important constraint on democratization in the 1990s remains the continuing power of the military, followed by the intelligence and national security bureaucracy. Despite the considerable improvement in civil liberties in the Republic of Korea, these authoritarian institutions continue to be used to suppress heterodox and dissenting views.

The real key to political stability, however, resides in the Republic of Korea's relations with the Democratic People's Republic. With the end of the Cold

War, there are perhaps reasons to hope for meaningful changes. The Republic of Korea is an important trade partner of both the Commonwealth of Independent States and China; and the Democratic People's Republic is expected to normalize relations with Japan. Prime ministerial talks between the two Koreas yielded major agreements in 1992, pledging both sides to nonaggression and wide-ranging exchanges. Real progress toward unification, however, will require full implementation of the accords.

(See also COLONIAL EMPIRES; DEMOCRATIC TRANSITIONS; FOREIGN AID; KOREA, DEMOCRATIC PEOPLE'S REPUBLIC OF; MILITARISM; NEWLY INDUSTRIALIZING ECONOMIES.)

Gregory Henderson, *Korea: The Politics of the Vortex* (Cambridge, Mass., 1967). Bruce Cumings,*The Two Koreas:* 2d. ed. (New York, 1991) Jung-en Woo, *Race to the Swift: State and Finance in Korean Industrialization* (New York, 1991).

MEREDITH WOO-CUMINGS

KOREAN WAR. The Korean War has gone through several reinterpretations since it was fought in the 1950s. For President Harry S. *Truman, Korea was a "police action" that began on 25 June 1950 when North Korean forces backed by the Soviet Union launched a full-scale, unprovoked invasion across the thirty-eighth parallel. The United States responded to this attack by invoking UN sanctions and leading some sixteen nations into battle. The war ended on 27 July 1953, when an armistice was signed at P'anmunjŏm, reestablishing the status quo ante.

By the 1960s Westerners had renamed the Korean conflict "the limited war," a conflict different from the world wars in being less than total and in being shaped by political decisions taken in Washington: mainly the controversy in which Truman sought to limit the conflict to the Korean peninsula while General Douglas MacArthur sought to extend the war to China. As a limited war, Korea was a success. But for MacArthur it was a failure, a stalemate yielding "a substitute for victory."

The *Vietnam War influenced another revision of meaning, as scholars in the 1970s increasingly came to see Korea as a civil war in which revolutionary *nationalism confronted a status-quo-oriented United States. Even the dates of the war were changed, its origins pushed back into Korea's colonial experience with Japan where the military leaderships of both the Democratic People's Republic of Korea (North Korea) and the Republic of Korea (South Korea) were formed. The northerners had been anti-Japanese guerrillas, while the high command of the South Korean forces had fought with Japan. New emphasis was also placed on political and guerrilla conflicts in 1945–1949 and small border wars in 1949–1950, with corresponding deemphasis on the "start" of the conventional fighting in June 1950; there was

likewise a spreading of responsibility for the origins of the war.

By the 1980s, however, Korea was "the forgotten war." Books and documentaries by that title proliferated, and the war entered an ambiguous realm: not *World War II, not quite Vietnam either, but something falling between the two, more a question mark than a known quantity. This was also a decade of new light on the war, however, as scholars exploited reams of declassified documents. Most now questioned the assumption that Joseph *Stalin launched the war for his own purposes, or in concert with Kim Il Sung; it is now thought that the conventional assault in June 1950 was Kim Il Sung's idea, with perhaps more Chinese than Soviet support. The direct U.S. role in suppressing left-wing politics in South Korea during its military occupation (1945–1950) was definitively proved. Captured documents showed that the origins of the North Korean regime were much more complex than had been thought, with significant indigenous and Chinese influence in addition to the Soviet role. Both Korean sides were implicated in the border fighting that ensued from May 1949 through early 1950.

New materials showed that the U.S. decision to march into North Korea was taken by Harry S. Truman, not Douglas MacArthur, under a frank "rollback" doctrine; Truman also thought long and hard about extending the war to China, and sacked MacArthur in April 1951 in part so that a reliable commander would be in place should that happen. The Truman administration also used atomic diplomacy to try to settle the war in 1951; heretofore this had been thought to be President Dwight *Eisenhower's strategy in 1953. New materials on the Chinese entry into the war in October 1950 show how difficult this decision was, with *Mao Zedong taking the lead; they also show a combined North Korean–Chinese strategy to lure UN forces deep into the interior of Korea after the famous amphibious landing at Inch'on in order to stretch supply lines and gain time for a dramatic reversal on the battlefield.

That reversal came as 1950 turned to 1951. Sino-Korean forces threw UN troops back well below the thirty-eighth parallel, capturing Seoul; General Matthew Ridgway organized a successful defense and then resumed the offensive, reestablishing a Korea divided roughly along that same line. The war could have ended here, but it continued through two years of difficult peace negotiations.

All these are Western views. For Koreans in North and South, the likelihood of war came with the division of the ancient integrity of the Korean nation through the unilateral action of the United States in mid-August 1945, to which Stalin later acquiesced. For the South it was a just war to recover "lost territories" in the North. For the North it was a just war "to resist American *imperialism and reunify the homeland." For Koreans and some 39,000 U.S.

soldiers stationed in Korea, the war continues today through a "cold peace" held only by the armistice, and with a "hot war" an ever-present possibility. More than a million soldiers still confront each other along the demilitarized zone.

Eventually the Korean War will be understood as one of the most destructive and one of the most important conflicts of the twentieth century. More than 4 million Koreans died, three-quarters of them civilians (Japan lost 2.3 million people in the Pacific War). The Korean conflict gave Japan's postwar recovery and industrialization a dynamic boost, which some have likened to "Japan's *Marshall Plan." China fought the United States to a stalemate and established itself as a major power. In the aftermath of war, two ideologically obverse Korean states competed toe-to-toe in economic development, and in the process both turned into modern industrial nations. Finally, it was this war and not World War II that established a far-flung American base structure abroad and a national security state at home, as defense spending nearly quadrupled in the first six months of the war. Four decades later, Koreans now seek reconciliation and eventual reunification of their torn nation, and Americans deal with a massive and expensive *military-industrial complex that has lost its raison d'être.

(See also AMERICAN FOREIGN POLICY; KOREA, DEMOCRATIC PEOPLE'S REPUBLIC OF; KOREA, REPUBLIC OF; UNITED NATIONS.)

Rosemary Foot, *The Wrong War: American Policy and the Dimensions of the Korean Conflict, 1950–1953* (Ithaca, N.Y., 1985). Keith D. McFarland, *The Korean War: An Annotated Bibliography* (New York, 1986). Bruce Cumings, *The Origins of the Korean War*, 2 vols. (Princeton, N.J., 1981 and 1990).

BRUCE CUMINGS

KU KLUX KLAN. From the post–Civil War Reconstruction era to the present, the Ku Klux Klan has been a loosely connected succession of racial terrorist societies in the United States. The first Klan was created in 1866. The name came from the Greek *kyklos,* meaning circle, to which was added the alliterative word "klan." In general terms, there have been five periods of Klan history: Reconstruction, the national Klan of the 1920s, the post–World War II rebirth, the late '70s revival, and the turn toward the Radical Right in the '80s and '90s, which Klansmen call "the Fifth Era." Variously the Klan has been a counterrevolutionary, a vigilante, and a resistance movement; a fraternal lodge; a money-maker for its leaders; a status society for Southern poor boy politics; and a hotbed of revolutionary violence. Unvaryingly, it has stood for white supremacy and has opposed other racial and ethnic minorities.

First organized as a social club, it soon became a means of controlling black people freed by the Civil War. Most active in the Southern Piedmont, where whites outnumbered blacks, the Klan and like organizations such as the Knights of the White Camellia spread across portions of the so-called "black belt" of the Deep South. Through intimidation and murder, the Klan sought to drive blacks out of politics, overturn the new Reconstruction state governments, control black labor, and restore black subordination. Members came from all levels of white male society, led by local elites. Its murders ran into many hundreds and the victims of its beatings and other intimidations numbered in the thousands. By the time the federal Enforcement and Ku Klux Klan Acts of 1870–1871, federal troops, and trials closed it down, the Klan had basically accomplished its goals.

D. W. Griffith's epic 1915 motion picture, *The Birth of a Nation,* based on Thomas Dixon's 1905 romanticized racist novel *The Clansman,* helped produce a revival. Organized in 1915 as a social lodge, after World War I the Klan spread rapidly as the defender of white Protestant small-town morality against social change, and became the great fraternal lodge of the 1920s. Anti-Catholicism and Prohibition were added to its white supremacist beliefs. Klan violence took place mainly in the South and Southwest, but the Klan drew support in many northern and western cities and helped elect more than twenty governors and senators, literally from Maine to California. Inept leadership, internal conflict and corruption, immorality and violence discredited the Klan which declined rapidly in the late 1920s. It hung on locally in the Southeast and died during World War II.

Revived after World War II, it has remained splintered into small competing units, hostile to organized labor, and unable to prevent desegregation in the South, despite church burnings, beatings, bombing, and murder. The 1964 disappearance of three civil rights workers in Philadelphia, Mississippi, and the 1965 murder of civil rights volunteer Viola Liuzzo led President Lyndon *Johnson to use the reluctant Federal Bureau of Investigation (FBI) against the Klan. The FBI undertook a secret illegal harassment program (COUNTERINTELPRO), federal juries sent Klansmen to jail under the Reconstruction era anti-Klan Acts and a new 1968 civil rights protection law (18 U.S.C. 245), and eventually state juries also began to convict.

At the end of the 1970s, there was a minor Klan revival as leaders competed for a blue-collar constituency that equated job uncertainty with affirmative action and government favoritism to *African Americans, but Klan membership remained below 10,000. Investigations and lawsuits by the nongovernmental Southern Poverty Law Center resulted in convictions of Klan members and heavy cash damage awards.

In the 1980s, while some Klans pushed recruitment of prison inmates and young street-violent skinheads, the former American Nazi and Klan leader

David Duke was elected to the Louisiana legislature on the issues of race and deep-seated populist resentment of government tax and welfare programs. (Duke subsequently failed in a gubernatorial bid in 1991, which he parlayed briefly into a campaign for the 1992 Republican nomination for the presidency.) Elsewhere, a portion of the Klan world became involved with the fiercely antisemitic Radical Right and its paramilitary militants and survivalists. The Klans had been historically revivalist, seeking to restore "lost" social and racial purity. The new revolutionary Radical Right of Christian Identity churches, Posse Comitatus, and The Order, sought to overthrow or secede from a "racially corrupt" America. Responding to growing racial harassment and violence, Congress, in 1990, passed a Hate Crime Statistics Act to keep track of bias-motivated crimes.

(See also Antisemitism; Civil Rights Movement; Race and Racism; Right.)

Allen Trelease, *White Terror: The Ku Klux Klan Conspiracy and Southern Reconstruction* (New York, 1971). David Chalmers, *Hooded Americanism: The History of the Ku Klux Klan,* 3d ed. (Durham, N.C., 1987). For current Klan information, consult Southern Poverty Law Center (Montgomery, Ala.), *Klanwatch;* Center for Democratic Renewal (Atlanta), *Monitor;* and the Anti-Defamation League of B'nai B'rith (New York).

David Chalmers

KURDISTAN. The name given to the homeland of the Kurds, a Muslim people numbering, in 1990, approximately 18 to 20 million, Kurdistan comprises most of eastern and southeastern Turkey, northern Iraq, parts of northwestern Iran, and a small slice of northeastern Syria. In all these states, Kurdistan has long been a peripheral and relatively underdeveloped area. Its most important natural resource is oil; the chief wells are near Kirkuk and Khaniqin, both in present-day Iraq and of essential importance for that country.

Most of Kurdistan is very mountainous; animal husbandry and small-scale agriculture are the major economic activities there, with smuggling as a third major source of income in the border zones. There are also a few large and fertile plains, such as those of Arbil in Iraq and Diyarbakir in Turkey, where large-scale capitalist agriculture is practiced. The mechanization of agriculture, starting in the 1950s, led to rapid *urbanization. The towns in and near Kurdistan, traditionally centers of crafts and trade, offer little industrial employment. Many migrants therefore moved on to cities or to areas of labor-intensive agriculture elsewhere in the same country or abroad.

There are no reliable counts of the Kurds (or other ethnic groups) in any of these countries, and only very rough estimates are possible. Turkey has the largest Kurdish population, between 8 and 11 million (out of a total population of 55 million). Then follow Iran, with 4 to 6 million Kurds (out of

around 50 million) and Iraq, where the Kurds, at 3.5 to 4 million, make up around a quarter of the population. Somewhat fewer than a million Kurds live in Syria (around ten percent of the population), while Kurdish enclaves in Caucasia number over a half million. Numerous Kurds, perhaps as many as thirty to forty percent, live outside Kurdistan proper now, as a result of deportations, labor migration, or flight.

The Kurdish ethnic identity is not based on unity of language or religion. The southern and northern Kurdish dialects (known as Sorani and Kurmanji, respectively) are not mutually understandable, while there are also several million speakers of more distantly related Zaza (in Turkey) and Gurani. These languages belong to the Iranian family and are therefore unrelated to Turkish or Arabic, although they contain numerous loanwords from them.

Most Kurds are Sunni Muslims, but a significant minority in Turkey belong to the heterodox Alevi sect, while smaller numbers adhere to other syncretistic sects. On the southern fringes of Kurdistan we finally find considerable numbers of Twelver Shi'a. In spite of this linguistic and religious diversity, there is a widespread awareness among all these groups of belonging to a larger common entity, and all have at times taken part in Kurdish nationalist rebellions. This is not to say that there has ever been a united Kurdish movement; division by personal, tribal, regional, and sectarian rivalries has been the rule rather than the exception. The geopolitical situation has moreover made the Kurds vulnerable to manipulation by outside powers. Iran and Syria have supported Kurdish parties active in Iraq and Turkey, while Iraq has supported the Iranian Kurdish parties.

Kurdish *nationalism first became a mass movement in Iraq. Qassem's left-wing military coup (1958) raised Kurdish expectations of more equal participation in the state: when these were frustrated, Kurdish leader Mulla Mustafa Barzani took to the mountains and started a guerrilla war. As this war dragged on, it politicized Kurdish society, inviting increasingly wider participation all over Iraqi Kurdistan. The *guerrilla warfare contributed to the fall of several governments and resulted in 1970 in a peace agreement promising autonomy as well as Kurdish participation in the central government. When the government failed to implement the agreement in full, fighting flared up again in 1974–1975, when the Kurds received considerable Iranian support (and secret U.S. aid). During the *Iran-Iraq War, 1980–1988, the Iraqi Kurds once again were supported by and cooperated with Iran, without any lasting gains and at great human cost. Iraq several times used chemical arms against Kurdish civilians as well as insurgents. More than half of Kurdish villages were razed to the ground, their inhabitants resettled in new towns and concentration camps or executed. As many as 100,000 may have been killed in what a UN report characterized as "genocide-type" operations. In fighting following the *Gulf War of 1991 between the U.S.-led coalition and Iraq, almost 2 million Kurds were displaced and unknown but large numbers killed.

The long struggle of Iraq's Kurds has also had its impact on the Kurds in the neighboring countries and strengthened their nationalism. In Iran there had been, in the aftermath of World War II, a short-lived independent Kurdish republic, centered around Mahabad. The central government, however, soon reasserted its authority and defeated the republic. Thereafter, the shah effectively suppressed all Kurdish political aspirations. In the year of the *Iranian Revolution (1978–1979), however, Kurdish nationalism proved capable of mobilizing large masses; the demand for some form of autonomy, put forward by Kurdish leaders, appeared to be almost universally endorsed. As the Shi'i character of the new regime became increasingly apparent, this demand only gained in strength. Government attempts to reimpose central authority led to protracted guerrilla warfare, the Kurdish fighters initially operating from bases in Iran, later from bases close to the Iraqi border.

In Turkey, where the very existence of the Kurds has long been denied, Kurdish demands were initially limited to recognition of the Kurdish language and culture and appeals for economic development of the Kurdish provinces. During the 1970s a new Kurdish awareness, first arising among the Kurds living in Turkey's large cities, spread over Kurdistan and developed into a rapidly radicalizing nationalism, including talk of independence. Kurdish parties and organizations, though illegal, brought entire districts more or less under their control. The Turkish military coup of 1980, followed by large-scale operations in the Kurdish provinces, cut short most of this Kurdish movement and ushered in a new period of forced assimilation. The military was challenged by the radical and extremely violent Workers Party of Kurdistan, which started a guerrilla war in 1984 and has since forced Turkish public opinion to admit, for the first time in history, that the country's Kurdish problem cannot be defined out of existence.

(See also Arab Nationalism; Ethnicity; International Migration; Kemalism; Nationalism.)

Chris Kutschera, *Le Mouvement National Kurde* (Paris, 1979). Martin van Bruinessen, *Agha, Shaikh and State: The Social and Political Structures of Kurdistan*, rev. ed. (London, 1992).

Martin van Bruinessen

KUWAIT. In the early 1700s Kuwait was founded by an alliance of tribes that migrated from central Arabia to the northern Gulf. One extended family, the Al-Sabah, soon captured a predominant position in local politics; by the end of the eighteenth century, senior Al-Sabah sheikhs regularly succeeded one another as leaders of the community. Each ruler's power nevertheless remained severely limited by the rich merchants who provided goods and revenues vital to the Kuwaiti economy. Influential merchant families punished overly capricious or exploitative rulers by emigrating to other Gulf ports. Furthermore, Kuwait's rulers faced challenges throughout the nineteenth century from Ottoman governors based in Basra who wished to annex the town, as well as from the Al-Sa'ud's attempts to extend its control along the Gulf littoral and British efforts to reorganize regional trade. In 1899, Sheikh Mubarak bin Sabah signed a treaty with the British Political Resident in the Gulf binding "himself, his heirs and successors not to cede, sell, lease, mortgage, or give for occupation or for any other purpose any portion of his territory to the Government or subjects of any other Power without the previous consent of His Majesty's Government."

British backing, along with the oil revenues that began flowing into the central treasury in the years after World War II, enabled the Al-Sabah to consolidate its hold over Kuwaiti politics at the expense of the merchant community. During the 1950s, Sheikh 'Abdullah bin Salim eased the commercial elite out of a variety of administrative and consultative posts in the government. In return, the Al-Sabah earmarked funds for improvements to the port, expanded the national health and education systems, and subsidized the purchase and development of unused land around Kuwait City by Kuwaiti citizens. Such programs created a wide range of mutual interests between the ruling family and the commercial elite, while dampening popular enthusiasm for *Arab nationalism.

With the end of the British protectorate in June 1961, the Kuwaiti regime promulgated a Constitution that provided for a fifty-member elected National Assembly and a council of ministers appointed by the ruler (emir), who was also empowered to select the prime minister, dismiss the Assembly, and rule by decree whenever it was out of session. Parliamentary politics during the 1960s largely pitted a bloc of liberal nationalist deputies critical of the regime's pro-Western foreign policy and restrictive labor regulations against bedouin allies of the ruling family and a smaller number of representatives of the country's Shi'i minority. Government attempts to encourage parliamentary agitation in support of the *nationalization of the Kuwait Oil Company set the stage for hotly contested elections in 1975, which resulted in victory for a number of vocal opponents of the regime's economic and social policies. When it became evident in the late summer of 1976 that the critics enjoyed widespread support among poorer citizens and the press, the emir dismissed the National Assembly and introduced a more stringent press law.

Kuwait's indigenous Shi'i community responded to the *Iranian Revolution of 1978–1979 by organizing a series of mass meetings and demonstrations.

The authorities countered by deporting a prominent Shi'i cleric with close ties to the Islamic Republic and expelling a large number of politically suspect expatriates. They then resurrected the National Assembly as a way of rallying support for the regime among Kuwaiti citizens. But the elections of February 1981 gave Sunni Islamists enough seats to dictate the agenda governing Assembly debates over the next four years, while Shi'i militants launched a wave of bombings and hijackings in an attempt to undermine the authority of the Al-Sabah. The ruling family turned to liberal nationalist and bedouin candidates as allies in the 1985 balloting, but the new Nasserist deputies soon joined forces with the Islamist opposition, and in July 1986 the cabinet asked the emir once again to dismiss the National Assembly on the grounds that its divisiveness threatened national security at a time when the *Iran-Iraq War was moving closer to the country's borders.

After the Assembly was dissolved, the ruling family and its rich merchant allies made greater use of the armed forces and security services to suppress the local Islamist movement. Shi'i military and police commanders were cashiered; Shi'i religious rituals and celebrations were increasingly circumscribed; surveillance was stepped up in Shi'i districts; and many longtime residents of the Kuwaiti Shi'a were deported to *Iran. These policies drove the regime into closer collaboration with *Iraq and the states of the Gulf Cooperation Council, and particularly enhanced ties between the Kuwaiti and Saudi security services. Militants loyal to the Islamic Republic responded by escalating their attacks against government offices and petroleum installations, at the same time that Iranian forces began targeting Kuwaiti oil tankers traversing the Gulf. The conjunction of these internal and external attacks caused government oil revenues to plummet, dramatically increasing the state's budget deficit. Consequently, the Kuwaiti leadership abandoned its traditional neutrality vis-à-vis the great powers and invited both the Soviet Union and the United States to escort its tankers past Iranian territory. This step aroused strong criticism in the local press, prompting the interior minister to announce in August 1987 that the government would refuse to grant bases to U.S. forces operating in the Gulf under any circumstances.

Throughout the winter and spring of 1990, prominent Kuwaitis called for the restoration of the National Assembly, petitioning the emir to abide by the terms of the 1962 Constitution and hold new elections. The ruler riposted by announcing the creation of a seventy-five-member National Council,

one-third of whom would be appointed and charged with amending the rules governing parliamentary action and debate. Leaders of the former National Assembly immediately rejected this proposal and pledged to boycott elections to the new body; seven notable pro-Parliament activists were arrested in early May. The elections held the following month evidenced neither the enthusiastic popular participation desired by the regime nor the general abstention urged by the opposition. Confronted with domestic unrest and falling world oil prices, the government stepped up petroleum production as a way of paying for its economic and social programs. This move provoked threats from Iraq, whose leadership blamed their own economic troubles on Kuwait's failure to abide by the oil production quotas mandated by the *Organization of Petroleum Exporting Countries (OPEC). When negotiations between Kuwaiti and Iraqi officials collapsed at the end of July, the Iraqi army overran Kuwait.

In the aftermath of the Iraqi invasion, the prime minister hinted on several occasions that an elected Assembly would be restored as soon as the Al-Sabah regained control of Kuwait. He told a group of Kuwaiti notables in mid-October that "the people of Kuwait can only be rewarded for their trust and loyalty by further trust," and that women, who were ineligible to vote in earlier elections, could expect to "play a greater role in liberated Kuwait." Reformers welcomed these remarks but expressed concern over intimations from other cabinet members that martial law would be imposed on the country during the initial period following an Iraqi withdrawal. When the Al-Sabah returned to Kuwait in March 1991, a state of emergency was indeed declared, and the cabinet appointed in mid-April included no critics of the government. Nevertheless, the ruler promised that new parliamentary elections would be held in October 1992, and the unexpected defeat of the regime's campaign to win control of the influential Chamber of Commerce and Industry in May 1992 highlighted the importance that pro-Parliament forces attached to their pledge.

(See also GULF STATES; GULF WAR; ISLAM; NASSERISM; SAUDI ARABIA.)

Jacqueline S. Ismael, *Kuwait: Social Change in Historical Perspective* (Syracuse, N.Y., 1982). Jill Crystal, *Oil and Politics in the Gulf: Rulers and Merchants in Kuwait and Qatar* (Cambridge, U.K., 1990).

FRED H. LAWSON

KYRGYZSTAN. See COMMONWEALTH OF INDEPENDENT STATES.

L

LABOR MOVEMENT. The term *labor movement* points in two directions. In its "union" sense it refers to efforts by wage workers in industrial societies to pursue collectively their interests at the workplace and in the labor market. Even when engaged in the most mundane of these concerns, however, unions have consistently run up against legal, ideological, and policy barriers which only self-conscious political organization, usually through labor-based parties, could confront. Labor movements, writ large, have thus acted in both market and political arenas. They have also traditionally constituted the major source of opposition to unrestrained free-market *capitalism.

The idea of individuals selling themselves on an open labor market at going market price is historically constructed, as are the legal prerogatives contained in notions of private property and contract, upon which this idea is premised. The rise and success of capitalism in Europe and elsewhere happened to workers with historical memories in which the effects of markets were limited by guilds, concepts like "just prices," and notions of communal solidarity. The marketization of human life and labor which the new order brought was thus hard to accept. It was quite natural, therefore, for early wage workers to organize themselves to resist the full effect of capitalist labor markets. It was quite as natural for capitalists, armed with self-justifying liberal economic theories, to try and prevent them doing so successfully.

From the beginning collective actions by workers, often involving strikes, challenged employers not only on essential issues of remuneration, working conditions (including the length of the working day), and control over the organization of work, but also on issues of de facto and legal recognition of workers' rights to organize into unions. These attempts to confront the effects of capitalism attracted the attention of rebellious intellectuals. A persistent pattern of alliance was thus established between workers, their unions, and such intellectuals, who often gave theoretical voice to working-class concerns. In the nineteenth century, when neither the permanence nor the basic structures of market-based capitalist societies were clear, this alliance produced a wide range of creative reflection about alternative, and more humane, ways of organizing society inspired by the writings of Robert Owen, Fourier, Blanqui, Bakunin, Lassalle, *Marx, Engels, and others. Various conceptualizations of *socialism, which would become the characteristic *ideology of the labor movement, came from this alliance.

The labor movements which emerged from the crucible of capitalist industrialization varied between and within countries. The pattern and rate of industrialization and the ways in which it mobilized labor were critical factors creating different mixes of different types of workers. The political settings in which industrialization occurred, particularly whether workers were granted the vote or not, were also very important. The outcomes, clear by the early twentieth century, were national labor movements with generally similar concerns, but with great differences about how to approach these concerns. Specific movements might be united or divided, more or less centralized, dominated by craft or industrial unions, be politically moderate or radical, or even apolitical in different ways—radical, anarchosyndicalist in some parts of Europe, or "Gompersist" in the United States.

The nationalist fervor of World War I dashed hopes that labor movements would become an international "resistance front" to capitalism. Labor's terrain was clearly national. Nonetheless the development of a vision of capitalist society as structured into classes in which the working *class was the central hope for progressive change was widespread, supported by libraries of intellectual argumentation. Moreover, most national labor movements, given *democracy and advancing industrialism, settled down to a quest for protecting workers in the market and humanizing capitalist societies through reformist political action, usually through social democratic parties.

In most cases, labor movements also elaborated a multidimensional program. There should be fully institutionalized collective bargaining in the labor market and trade union rights in the workplace. Politically capitalism should be democratized, often through public ownership of industry, increased state intervention and steering of the economy, plus the elaboration of a wide range of social policies to moderate harsh market outcomes. Most of these changes, which implied democratic political success by labor, were to be achieved by the resolute use of national states to regulate and supplement the market.

There were important exceptions to this. Certain labor movements, the U.S. case being the most prominent, eschewed explicit party strategies to achieve their goals. In addition, large parts of the revolutionary branch of the labor movement affiliated with the Communist Third International following the 1917 Russian Revolution. This step involved the subordination of national movements to an international strategy coordinated from, and very quickly by, Moscow. The Soviet Union's pursuit of brutal Stalinist economic *modernization and "socialism in one country" beginning in the later 1920s transformed Soviet unions themselves into instruments for supplying docile labor for purposes decided by the party and bureaucratic center (a model which was exported to Eastern and Central Europe after 1945). Communist labor movements elsewhere then found themselves obliged to devote most of their resources in very costly efforts to support Soviet international political purposes. The fundamental cleavages between Communists and Social Democrats internationally and within societies, particularly in Latin Europe, damaged labor movements almost everywhere.

The record of labor movement success in the interwar period was spotty. In a number of places, often following pitched battles—as in the Congress of Industrial Organizations campaign in the United States and the Popular Front in France—partial victories, particularly on the bargaining front, were achieved. But the devastating effects of the Great Depression of the 1930s in terms of unemployment and disrupted lives made labor action difficult. Moreover, the Social Democratic program, however reformist it had become, still struck fear into the hearts of the propertied and the conservative. Thus little was won in the political arena except in Scandinavia and, in very different ways, in *Roosevelt's *New Deal in the United States, where no Social Democratic Party existed. In societies where democracy itself had been but precariously established, antidemocratic opposition to labor gains, as in Weimar Germany, post-1918 Italy, and 1930s Spain, helped Nazism, Italian *Fascism, and other such illiberal movements to come to power, subsequently to destroy labor movement autonomy and abolish labor parties.

The three decades after World War II, in contrast, were the high point of the labor movement's history. The progress of "Fordist" mass-production industry was favorable for union organization and collective bargaining success—"webs of rules" were woven in the workplace which consecrated worker and union rights, particularly in the area of job security, and avenues of appeal. The immediate aftermath of the war also coincided with a simultaneous advance of political democracy and prolabor voting in a number of different societies. In the flurry of reformism which followed, the *welfare state was greatly extended and instruments for broad state intervention in the economy were elaborated.

In time it became clear that many labor movements had substantially and felicitously modified their programs in response to the Great Depression and wartime experiences. Labor thus embraced a vision of the "mixed economy" in which private corporations, themselves willing to accept labor presence at firm level, pursued profits in a context of greatly enhanced state economic steering of a Keynesian type targeted to moderate the business cycle and achieve stable growth and relatively full employment. The long postwar expansion transformed societies and individual lives, allowing the acquisition of a wide range of new consumer goods, extensive redistribution of profits into high wages and, through taxation, to social services like health care, pensions, and education. In many places Social Democratic ideas about economic management and trade union ideas about the contractual organization of workplace life became hegemonic, and where unions, Socialist parties, and capitalist firms were able to strike harmonious "neocorporatist" arrangements, like Sweden and Austria, great advances were possible. For the first time it seemed that the benefits of a capitalist market system could be obtained without paying the worst of its costs.

The contemporary period, beginning with the two oil shocks of the 1970s and the widespread turn of governments to *monetarism in the 1980s, has brought a swift end to these euphoric postwar decades. There has been a qualitative internationalization of economic development which has undercut the national premises of earlier approaches and transformed the entire planet into a single market for labor, products, and financial capital. In many places there has also been a decisive return to pre-Keynesian free market liberal and deregulatory economic ideologies according to which unions are sources of "rigidity" and state involvement in economies a major cause of inefficiency.

In this new context governments, even Social Democratic ones with ties to union movements, have had to abandon earlier *Keynesianism in favor of more restrictive economic management. Their highest policy priority has become a quest for international competitiveness for national firms. The pursuit of redistribution and relatively full employment have thus become secondary objectives. From the point of view of firms themselves the capacity to change technologies, the organization of production, and product offerings rapidly in response to accelerated market fluctuations has become paramount. Given these new priorities of "flexibilization" firms have moved to decentralize collective bargaining, to individualize its content, and, often, to avoid dealing with unions altogether. This has undercut earlier trade union strength in the workplace and made it vastly more difficult for unions to aggregate local concerns into a broader "labor movement" vision. Rising unemployment has also greatly weakened unions in both their market and political capacities.

These unfavorable policy and market movements have coincided with important sociological changes. The share of "classical" industrial workers in national work forces has declined in the face of the growing importance of new middle-strata administrative and "intellectual" workers, female labor-market participation, and *underclass labor-market sectors often occupied by deprived minorities. The place of labor in its traditional sense has thus been relativized. Simultaneously there has been a rise of new forms of political expression among salaried new middle strata and the intelligentsia, often of a new social movement type, which has further deprived the labor movement of allies, particularly among the intellectuals whose earlier help had been important.

After more than a century of complex growth and self-definition, not to speak of struggle, labor movements once again find themselves in a difficult new situation. The market capacities, mobilizational resources, and memberships of union movements have declined almost everywhere. Moreover, even where unions remain important social actors, nowhere do they retain the status which they had prior to the mid-1970s. Earlier they had been widely perceived as the very core of any progressive social and political project. Now, more often than not they are regarded as self-seeking *interest groups like any other. Social Democratic parties, where they themselves remain plausible political contenders, have attenuated their connections with unions and older labor movement outlooks to make new appeals to nonlabor constituents based on proclaimed new capacities as technocratic economic managers "with a human face." Ideas about class and class conflict have disappeared from political discourses everywhere. Moreover, much of the earlier policy repertory of trade unions and labor parties has been jettisoned. With the approach of the millennium there seems but slim hope that anything like the old labor movement can be reconstituted on new ground. Unless labor movements can miraculously find ways to forge the effective international labor market and political ties which so dramatically eluded their predecessors, "labor's century" appears to be over.

(See also AMERICAN FEDERATION OF LABOR AND CONGRESS OF INDUSTRIAL ORGANIZATIONS; CORPORATISM; FORDISM; NEW SOCIAL MOVEMENTS; POLITICAL ECONOMY; REFORM; STATE.)

Selig Perlman, *A Theory of the Labor Movement* (New York, 1928). Colin Crouch and Alessandro Pizzorno, eds., *The Resurgence of Class Conflict in Western Europe*, 2 vol. (London, 1978). David Brody, *Workers in Industrial America* (New York, 1980). Peter Lange, Maurizio Vannicelli, and George Ross, *Unions, Crisis and Change: French and Italian Unions in the Political Economy* (London, 1982). Richard Freeman and James Medoff, *What Do Unions Do?* (New York, 1984). Peter Gourevitch, Andrew Martin, and George Ross, *Unions and Crisis: Sweden, West Germany and the UK* (London, 1984). Gary Marks, *Unions in Politics* (Princeton, N.J., 1989). Frances Fox Piven, ed., *Labor Parties in Postindustrial Societies* (New York and Oxford, 1992).

GEORGE ROSS

LAND REFORM. The central idea of land reform—reflected in the rallying cry "land to the tiller"—is that the state will acquire agricultural land from landlords and plantation owners and transfer it to tenant farmers, agricultural laborers, and others who are landless. Land reform has been a highly important political and economic process during this century, with major land reforms carried out by at least twenty-five countries. Some of these reforms have followed communist *revolutions (as in the Soviet Union, the People's Republic of China, Cuba, and Vietnam); some have followed noncommunist revolutions (as in Mexico and Bolivia); and some have come in nonrevolutionary settings, such as the immediate postwar land reforms carried out with U.S. support by Japan, Taiwan, and the Republic of Korea (South Korea).

In the developing countries, land is still the principal source of livelihood, security, and status for a majority of the population, with six families out of ten engaged in agriculture. In a number of these countries, the issue of land ownership still looms large: over half a billion of the world's poorest and most powerless people still make their living from land they do not own. (A parallel problem arises in systems of mandatory *collectivization of farming under state control, although the largest such system, that of China, was decollectivized in the early 1980s.) The more classic problem of insecure tenants and ill-paid agricultural laborers is still found in a score of countries, including India, Pakistan, Bangladesh, the Philippines, Indonesia, most of Central America, Brazil, and South Africa.

Such landlessness underlies a number of persisting problems. Farmers with insecure tenure and poor remuneration lack incentive to make long-term improvements to the land. Because of their low productivity and lack of purchasing power, the village economy stagnates. Aggrieved, landless *peasants have, moreover, provided rank-and-file support for a series of bloody twentieth-century revolutions and continue to play a central role in ongoing civil conflicts in countries such as the Philippines and El Salvador.

Landlessness is also related to high birthrates, both for the landless and for the larger community influenced by their low productivity and poverty. Landless people face an insecure old age, for as their physical powers decline they are likely to be evicted from land they do not own. Many of their children die of hunger or disease, and female children have little prospect for schooling or jobs in the stagnant village economy. Where children are the only old-age security, these factors encourage bearing many children to ensure that some will survive to care for the parents. Finally, landlessness is implicated in both excessive urbanization and large-scale deforestation and erosion, as rootless and desperate people are increasingly forced into cities already bursting at the seams or onto steep forested hillsides and other marginal lands.

Successful land-reform programs can reverse these processes:

• They provide aggrieved peasants an alternative to revolutionary violence (and also can be acceptable to many landlords, if accompanied by reasonable compensation for their land). Simultaneously, they help lay the groundwork for evolutionary democratic change as peasants endowed with increased security, status, and power within the village participate with increasing effectiveness in the political life of their community and in voicing demands on the central government. ("Second-generation" reforms that decollectivize communist agricultures similarly help create grass-roots conditions more conducive to democratization.)

• They sharply increase agricultural productivity, as peasants assured of long-term rights to the land introduce irrigation and other capital improvements. Such prosperous small farmers become, in turn, the buyers of a wide range of locally produced goods and services (brick houses, clothes, radios, health care, and schooling), helping to create many new nonagricultural jobs. Indeed, ex-landlords can invest their compensation in the new enterprises.

• With increased prosperity and better nutrition, health care, and schooling, the stage is set for the "demographic transition": a steep decline in infant and child death rates is followed by an even larger decline in the number of births. Taiwan, a generation after land reform, has achieved the same low crude birthrate as the United States, and even lower infant mortality.

• Meanwhile, secure on their own land, families are far less likely to part for the city or push desperately onto marginal forestlands.

Yet the industrial democracies have supported *Third World land reforms only sporadically. The explanation, which is complex, includes a frequent focus on industrial development, competition for resources, and bureaucratic reluctance to tackle difficult or controversial problems.

(See also DEMOCRATIC TRANSITIONS; DEVELOPMENT AND UNDERDEVELOPMENT; ENVIRONMENTALISM; FOOD POLITICS; RURAL DEVELOPMENT; WOMEN AND DEVELOPMENT.)

Ronald J. Herring, *Land to the Tiller* (New Haven, Conn., 1983). Roy L. Prosterman and Jeffrey M. Riedinger, *Land Reform and Democratic Development* (Baltimore, 1987).

ROY L. PROSTERMAN

LAOS. The Lao People's Democratic Republic (LPDR) was proclaimed on 2 December 1975, thus putting an end to the 600-year-old *monarchy. This landlocked nation of 3.5 million people, sandwiched between China to the north, Burma and Thailand to the west, Cambodia to the south, and Vietnam to the east, was proclaimed a French protectorate in 1893. It regained its independence sixty years later, only to be torn by a drawn-out civil war pitting the Pathet Lao, a Marxist revolutionary movement, against the Royal Lao government. The victorious Pathet Lao established an orthodox Marxist-Leninist democratic centralist state directed by the Lao People's Revolutionary Party (LPRP). Up to an estimated ninety percent of the small educated middle class not undergoing political reeducation subsequently fled the country.

Under the terms of the Constitution promulgated in August 1991, political power remains the monopoly of the governing party. At the apex stands the Political Bureau, whose membership under Party Chairman Kaysone Phomvihane has remained remarkably stable and free of factions. It is elected by the Central Committee, which in turn is elected and answerable to the Party Congress. In reality, however, the Politburo is the seat of supreme power. Delegates to both the Party Congress and the Central Committee reflect regional and ethnic divisions within the country. The Fifth Party Congress in March 1991 abolished the party secretariat, leaving day-to-day party affairs in the hands of the chairman.

The 1991 Constitution considerably enhanced the powers of the state president, a position also held by Kaysone. It also enhanced the powers of the National Assembly, the supreme popularly-elected legislative body, which meets twice a year. The prime minister is appointed by the state president, but the government, which consists of some twenty ministries and state committees with ministry status, is answerable to the National Assembly. Considerable overlap has existed in Laos between the top echelons of the party and government, and this makes any clear definition of party-state relations an impossibility. Of the mass organizations that play a significant political role, the most important are the Lao Front for National Construction, the Federation of Lao Trade Unions, the Lao People's Revolutionary Youth, and the Union of Lao Women. Because Laos is still predominantly a Buddhist country, the Lao United Buddhists Association is also able to exert limited political influence.

The LPRP is described as "an avant-grade party of the worker and *peasant *class" rather than a party of the tiny Lao proletariat. The party is credited with having brought about a national democratic revolution in Laos. It claims to exercise a dictatorship on behalf of the proletariat and peasantry aimed at achieving the socialist transformation of Lao society. In fact, socialism, if it remains a goal at all, has been removed to the distant future. Politics in Laos presently depends more on family loyalties, region, and *ethnicity than on class or *ideology.

Historically the kingdom of Lan Xang (Laos) was divided from the early eighteenth century until the arrival of the French into three antagonistic principalities. This regionalism persists as an important political influence, which finds expression in a degree of political and economic decentralization unusual in a communist state. By official count there are sixty-eight "nationalities" divided into three broad groups—the politically and culturally dominant lowland Lao, numbering about fifty-five percent of the population; the mountain-dwelling hill tribes, who broadly supported the revolutionary movement (thirty-five percent); and the opium-growing Hmong (Meo), most of whom opposed it (ten percent). Whereas the political influence of the hill tribes is strong in the more mountainous provinces, they are underrepresented in the central government and upper echelons of the party.

Political change has occurred since 1975 through both internal and external pressures, including poor economic performance, the declining capacity of the socialist bloc to meet Lao requirements for aid and investment, and improved relations with Thailand. Low levels of anticommunist insurgency have posed no real threat to regime viability and have been easily contained by the Lao army.

Following Pathet Lao seizure of power the small industrial sector was nationalized, the market for goods and services closely regulated, and a program of agricultural collectivization initiated. Stiffening peasant opposition and plummeting production forced suspension of *collectivization in 1979 in anticipation of sweeping economic reforms. Five sectors of the economy were defined, including a capitalist component—tacit recognition that Laos could not hope to implement *socialism at its current low level of economic development. Further relaxation of orthodox socialist policies followed as the government launched the country's first five-year plan (in January 1981). Although plan targets remained unmet, economic performance did improve sufficiently for moderates within the LPRP to implement further reforms during the second five-year plan. As of 1988 Laos began actively soliciting foreign, particularly Thai, investment in timber, manufacturing, and tourism, while reprivatizing a number of nationalized enterprises.

The wartime dependence of the Pathet Lao on Vietnamese communist support continued after 1975 with the signing of a twenty-five-year Treaty of Friendship and Cooperation. With establishment of the People's Republic of Kampuchea (Cambodia) in 1979, Vietnam, Laos, and Cambodia formed a Vietnamese-dominated "solidarity bloc" in opposition to the *Association of Southeast Asian Nations (ASEAN). After 1986, relations remained close with Vietnam and the Soviet Union (which until 1991 provided most *foreign aid to the LPDR) even as relations with Thailand, China, and the United States improved. Thus, by the early 1990s, Laos had reverted to something approaching its traditional role in mainland Southeast Asia—an impoverished buffer state between Thailand and Vietnam concerned to obtain maximum levels of economic aid from any country willing to assist.

(See also BUDDHISM; COMMAND ECONOMY; COMMUNIST PARTY STATES; VIETNAM WAR.)

MacAlister Brown and Joseph J. Zasloff, *Apprentice Revolutionaries: The Communist Movement in Laos, 1930–1985* (Stanford, Calif., 1986). Martin Stuart-Fox, *Laos: Politics, Economics and Society* (London and Boulder, Colo., 1986).

MARTIN STUART-FOX

LATIN AMERICAN REGIONAL ORGANIZATIONS. There are two main types of Latin American regional organizations: groups aiming to promote economic integration and those purporting to coordinate Latin American responses to particular problems. Among the former, the most important organizations are the Latin American Free Trade Area (now evolved into the Latin American Integration Association, LAIA), the Andean Group, the Central American Common Market (CACM), the Caribbean Community (CARICOM), and most recently the Southern Cone Group (Mercosur). The latter include the Latin American Economic System (SELA) and the Group of Eight (G-8).

The regional integration groups originated in the 1960s, largely stimulated by the UN *Economic Commission for Latin America and the Caribbean, which saw regional or subregional integration as a way to resolve the problems of small markets. These organizations initially enjoyed some success in eliminating tariff barriers and increasing the volume of trade, but a number of problems worked against integration as envisioned in the various charters. Common difficulties stemmed from disparities in the nature of the different national economies. The benefits of increased trade and industrial growth were not shared equally by member states, and competing interests of the large, medium, and small economies inhibited mutually satisfactory equalization policies. The planned distribution of industrial production was particularly unsuccessful. Other problems occurred when products imported from other members were more expensive than, or inferior in quality to, similar products formerly imported from outside the region. In addition, national rivalries, long-standing boundary and territorial disputes, and changing governments with opposing political philosophies complicated cooperation.

Latin American economic integration is also marked by positive elements on which future developments may be based. A more cooperative intra–Latin American climate, and specific support for integration measures, has been created by the departure of military regimes and redemocratization in much of the region in the 1980s. The concept of economic integration was expanded to the entire continent in

June 1990, when President George *Bush proposed his Enterprise for the Americas Initiative, following the adoption of a U.S.-Canadian free trade area (FTA) and commencement of U.S.-Mexican FTA negotiations.

Although the second type of Latin American regional organizations—those designed to coordinate regional response—also began in the 1960s, they increased in importance during the last two decades. They have been largely based on the assumption that Latin American states will be more influential in the *international system if they adopt common positions and regional unity toward the rest of the world. Such efforts were seen as a parallel to economic integration; in the 1980s, they increasingly discussed prospects for some kind of political integration as well. The first transregional endeavor came in 1964 when most Latin American states joined the Special Latin American Coordinating Committee (CECLA). Although no formal agreement was signed or organizational apparatus created, CECLA periodically convened as a regional caucusing group before UN Conference on Trade and Development or other international meetings.

CECLA was superseded as the Latin American regional caucus by the Latin American Economic System (SELA), as part of the latter's broader agenda. In 1975, twenty-three states signed a charter establishing SELA, with a permanent secretariat located in Caracas; three new Caribbean states later joined. SELA's organizational structure is simple: a council of ministers meets at least once annually, with the power to appoint ad hoc action committees; and a permanent secretariat provides operational support and conducts staff studies. SELA has been active in a number of areas. It urges economic integration although it is not an integration scheme itself and does not propose to be one. It has put forward proposals to resolve the debt crisis, and it has done many studies on trade relations and capital flows between Latin America and the United States, Europe, and Japan.

Attempts to mediate the Central American conflicts led to a new and important multipurpose regional association that extended its agenda to include a number of seminal international issues. In December 1986, the foreign ministers of the eight countries involved in the Contadora and Support Group states met in Rio de Janeiro and adopted a declaration creating the Permanent Mechanism of Consultation and Political Coordination, known as the Rio Group or the Group of Eight (G-8). The declaration said that, based on their experience of joint action in the Contadora process, they had decided to strengthen and systematize their political coordination through regular consultation on topics of common interest. The declaration provided for regular meetings of foreign ministers. In addition, annual summit meetings of heads of state were begun in November 1987, and regular conferences of finance ministers were instituted in December 1988. In June 1988, representatives from SELA, the Inter-American Development Bank, the UN Economic Commission for Latin America and the Caribbean, and the Latin American Integration Association were invited to participate in the foreign ministers' meetings.

Central G-8 purposes have been made clear in the Rio declaration and the various meetings of ministers and presidents. They include efforts 1) to strengthen Latin American *democracy through sustained economic and social development and regional cooperation and integration; 2) to discuss all aspects of the Central American crisis and to reiterate support for the peace plan initiated by President Oscar *Arias of Costa Rica known as the Esquipulas agreements; 3) to prefer negotiated agreements with external creditors over a collective moratorium or "debtors' cartel" and to suggest specific measures; 4) to call attention to the problem of an unstable international financial system and the need to create a free and fair international trading system; 5) to work toward a Latin American common market, with full awareness of the limitations of existing integration schemes; 6) to cooperate for disarmament and scientific, technical, cultural, and educational interchange, and to deal jointly with problems of clandestine arms trade, *terrorism, *drug trafficking, and environmental degradation; and 7) to promote discussions with other nations and intergovernmental organizations in a climate of goodwill.

(See also DEMOCRATIC TRANSITIONS; ENVIRONMENTALISM; INTERNATIONAL DEBT.)

Altaf Gauhar, ed., *Regional Integration: The Latin American Experience* (Boulder, Colo., 1985). G. Pope Atkins, "Latin American Integration and Association," chap. 7 in *Latin America in the International Political System*, 2d ed. (Boulder, Colo., 1989). Instituto de Relaciones Europeo-Latinoamericanas/Institute for European-Latin American Relations (IRELA), "The Group of Eight: A New Regional Actor for Latin America?" Dossier No. 17 (Madrid, 1989).

G. POPE ATKINS

LATINOS. See HISPANIC AMERICANS.

LATVIA. See BALTIC REPUBLICS.

LAW OF THE SEA. The oceans have always had a dual character as medium of transportation and site of resources. The law of the sea is the set of treaty-based and customary rules that governments have established to regulate their own and their nationals' marine activities. This law reflects the balance of interests between maritime and coastal states, and between different groups of ocean users. Like other international *regimes, the regime for ocean use balances basic principles through an elaboration of rules defining the areas or interactions to which each applies.

Before 1900 the main exploitable ocean resource was fish, which were so abundant that they could be treated as a common pool freely exploitable by all. The main balance to be struck was thus between a general interest in open access and each coastal state's desire for *security against seaborne attack. The "traditional rules" developed among European states in the seventeenth through nineteenth centuries accomplished this by dividing the oceans into two zones. Coastal states were allowed full control, limited only by foreign ships' right of innocent passage, in the territorial sea—the waters and seabed within 3 nautical miles of shore. Beyond lay the high seas where ships of all countries had equal rights of free passage and fishing.

The oceans' resource aspect acquired equal prominence by the mid-twentieth century. Larger fishing fleets equipped with improved gear caused serious depletion of fish stocks in many areas. Invention of methods for extracting oil lying beneath the seabed created a new, and highly important, resource activity. Invention of new mining techniques led to expectations that the "manganese nodules" and metallic crusts of the deepest ocean floor would soon be exploited. By 1972, there was widespread awareness that both transportation and resource uses would have to be regulated to ensure protection of the marine environment. Thus the traditional concerns with security and open access were supplemented by concerns about resource management and environmental protection.

The abortive League of Nations conference in 1930, which allowed active participation by governments from all parts of the world, changed the terms of future discussion by reducing the major maritime powers' political advantage. At the same time, those directly engaged in ocean resource activities became powerful lobbies for extending national jurisdiction even in some traditionally maritime states. The owners of offshore platforms sought strong protection of property rights, and regarded national governments as the only entities capable of providing it. Their concerns were met by new doctrines establishing exclusive coastal state jurisdiction over resource activity on the continental shelf. These claims were first advanced by Venezuela and the Untied Kingdom in 1942, then by the United States in the Truman Proclamation of 1945. Other governments made similar claims so quickly that coastal state jurisdiction over the continental shelf had become part of customary *international law by the mid-1950s. Coastal fishers became concerned about foreign competitors, adding their voices to coastal state demands for greater national control. Yet efforts to assert such control provoked considerable controversy. In the late 1940s several Latin American governments claimed exclusive jurisdiction over all waters within 200 nautical miles of shore. These broad claims to "patrimonial" seas were rejected by the major maritime powers, which saw in them threats not only to traditional fishing rights but also to freedom of navigation and scientific research.

The First UN Conference on the Law of the Sea (1958) produced four multilateral conventions, but neither it nor the Second Conference (1960) resolved all disagreements about the extent of allowable coastal state jurisdiction. Three major areas of contention remained. The first was defining the breadth of the territorial sea. Most governments agreed that the widespread ownership of fast motor vessels necessitated having authority to enforce basic customs, fiscal, immigration, and sanitary rules as far as 12 nautical miles at sea. Yet there was no agreement on whether to keep the 3-mile limit and create a new contiguous zone for enforcing those regulations or to extend the territorial sea to 12 miles. The second concerned fisheries jurisdiction. Maritime states were willing to concede coastal jurisdiction within 12 nautical miles of shore, but would agree only to establishment of international management commissions involving both coastal and fishing states in areas further to sea. The third involved defining the seaward extent of the continental shelf. The result was an ambiguous provision that placed the limit at the 200-meter isobath or any greater depth at which commercial resource exploitation was possible.

Rapid improvements in ocean technology soon forced reconsideration of all these issues. By 1965 many observers feared that the exploitability criterion would be used to justify coastal state enclosure of the whole seabed. Improvements in trawlers and ocean-going processing ships allowed many countries, most notably Japan and the Soviet Union, to expand their fleets and increase their catches. The international fisheries commissions lacked the power to enforce effective limits on fishing. *Third World governments and coastal fishing communities in industrial states were both worried that continued open access would allow foreigners to take the lion's share of the resource. The push for broader coastal state control over resource activity raised fears in maritime and naval circles that navigation rights would also be curtailed.

Although a number of governments were reconsidering their positions in the mid-1960s, explicit discussion was precipitated by Malta in 1967. It proposed a new norm, neither national enclosure nor open access, establishing the deep seabed as "the common heritage of mankind" and creating an international agency to control mining activity there. This triggered negotiations culminating in a Third UN Conference on the Law of the Sea.

The Third UN Conference (1973–1982) produced the agreements at the base of current efforts to balance coastal and maritime state interests, and to simultaneously promote navigation, coastal state security, resource management, and environmental protection. Coastal and maritime interests in security and freedom of navigation were balanced in acceptance of a new 12-nautical-mile limit for the territorial sea, an additional 12 nautical miles of contiguous zone, a new regime of transit passage through straits that would otherwise be enclosed under the 12-mile rule, and special rules for waters lying between the islands of archipelagic states.

The new doctrines on resource management represented victories for a coalition of Third World governments seeking to limit the influence of the more advanced states and of coastal resource exploiters in industrial states. The new exclusive economic zone concept assured coastal state control over all resource activities, but not navigation, in waters within 200 nautical miles of shore. This places some ninety percent of current fishing under national control and triggered a major reallocation of catches in favor of local fishing fleets. Coastal state jurisdiction over the continental shelf was reaffirmed, and defined as extending at least 200 nautical miles or, where the geological continental margin is wider, up to 350 nautical miles from shore. Coastal states thus gained control over all likely hydrocarbon exploitation and some mining of metallic crusts.

The open access principle was retained for waters beyond 200 miles, but the new common heritage concept was applied to the ocean floor seaward of national zones. That area was to be held in common with a central agency, the International Seabed Authority (ISA), created to control resource activity. Third World governments hoped to gain the predominant say in management, a source of direct revenues for their development needs, and an international monopoly of deep seabed mining. Industrial states won concessions diluting Third World voting control and establishing a "parallel system" splitting exploitation rights between state-owned or private licensees and the ISA's own enterprise. Although much of the 1982 Convention enjoys universal acceptance, continued opposition to the deep seabed mining provisions by industrial states, particularly the United States, has delayed its entry into force. Efforts to strike additional compromises with the less adamant opponents and weaken the resolve of the most adamant continue.

Many of the rules expressed in the 1982 Convention are already being adopted. Formal acceptance of the 1982 Convention would facilitate this process by providing common legal formulations and common procedures for dispute settlement. Yet even with formal acceptance the 1982 Convention would be only one step in revising the law of the sea to meet contemporary needs. It is not exhaustive and many of its provisions are broad or ambiguous. Lacunae will need to be filled and more specific arrangements developed through additional negotiations or state practice.

(See also ENVIRONMENTALISM.)

D. P. O'Connell, *The International Law of the Sea*, 2 vols. (London, 1982–1983). Giulio Pontecorvo, ed., *The New Order of the Oceans: The Advent of a Managed Environment* (New York, 1986). Mark W. Zacher and James G. McConnell, "Down to the Sea with Stakes: The Evolving Law of the Sea and the Future of the Deep Seabed Regime" *Ocean Development and International Law* 21 (1990): 71–103.

M. J. PETERSON

LEAGUE OF NATIONS. The covenant of the League of Nations, the first permanent international organization charged with the task of preserving international *peace and *security, was drafted during the Paris Peace Conference in 1919, primarily under the influence of President Woodrow Wilson of the United States, Robert Cecil of Great Britain, and the French diplomat Léon Bourgeois. The core of the new covenant was Article 10, under which the members agreed to preserve each other's territorial integrity and political independence against external aggression. Articles 11 through 16 defined procedures for resolving international conflicts. All states were obligated to submit their conflicts to arbitration, judicial settlement, or to the League Council which could investigate, conciliate, and recommend terms of settlement. If the council unanimously recommended a course of action or terms of settlement, the parties could not subsequently use armed force. If there was no unanimity, then the parties could go to *war following a three-month cooling-off period. In the event that a state used armed force contrary to the procedures and prohibitions contained in the covenant, member states were obliged to employ economic *sanctions. The league could only recommend military sanctions.

The League of Nations comprised an assembly, to which all members belonged, and a council of permanent members (initially Britain, France, Italy, and Japan) and four (expanded to eleven by 1936) non-Great Powers elected for set terms by the assembly. The assembly in 1920 established the Permanent Court of International Justice, a legal body to which certain kinds of disputes could be referred for decision or advisory opinions.

The U.S. Senate did not approve the Treaty of Versailles, in which the covenant was embedded, so the United States remained outside the organization. Germany was admitted as a permanent member of the council in 1926, and the Soviet Union in 1934. In 1935, Japan and Germany withdrew from the organization. Throughout most of its history, the league contained no more than four of the seven Great Powers.

The League of Nations broke radically from eighteenth-century and nineteenth-century international practices. The idea of mutual guarantees and the statement (Article 11) that any use of armed force was a matter of concern to all members contravened the old principle of neutrality. The covenant also undermined the principle of a sovereign's right to employ force. War was not outlawed, but its legitimacy became highly circumscribed. Finally, the league inaugurated the idea of collective economic sanctions.

The league was unable to take effective measures against Japanese, Italian, German, and Soviet aggression between 1931 and 1939. It could deal with situations where the parties to a conflict generally wanted to avoid war, and where the obligations under Article 10 were taken seriously. The aggressive powers of the late 1930s had purposes that were fundamentally incompatible with the core ideas in the covenant.

Despite these shortcomings, the league's organs did consider sixty-six disputes and conflicts between 1920 and 1939. Twenty were referred to other agencies. Eleven cases involved conquest contrary to league principles and procedures. But in the remaining thirty-five cases (seventy-six percent), league procedures, recommendations, and decisions resulted in compromise outcomes. This level of achievement is substantially higher than the record of the UN since 1945. The organization employed plebiscites, mediation, conciliation, and fact-finding to fashion settlements in conflicts among its members. Economic sanctions collectively employed against Italy for its attack on Ethiopia in 1935–1936 were the first on behalf of the international community, and they almost worked.

The League of Nations also supervised the fast-growing network of private transactions between societies. It established or incorporated bureaus and committees dealing with disease, communications, traffic in arms, slavery, drugs, and conditions and protection of labor, women, and children. The specialized agencies collected statistics, disseminated information, sponsored conferences, and placed pressure on governments to observe international conventions or upgrade their domestic legislation on these issues. The league organized a mandates system, under which Imperial Germany's overseas colonies were administered by some of the *World War I victors. The mandatory powers were held responsible for promoting "the well-being and development" of the local populations. The league had a right to monitor the performance of this "trust." The covenant implied that the ultimate goal of the tutelary relationship was to educate the colonial peoples to political independence.

Governments and league officials debated during *World War II whether to reform the league or to launch a new international organization. The United States and the Soviet Union decided the debate in favor of creating a new *United Nations. Although some league committees continued to function dur-ing the war, in the security field the league ceased to operate in 1941. It was formally disbanded in April 1946.

(See also FORCE, USE OF; INTERNATIONAL LAW.)

Alfred Zimmern, *The League of Nations and the Rule of Law* (London, 1936). F. P. Walters, *History of the League of Nations,* 2 vols. (London, 1952).

KALEVI J. HOLSTI

LEBANON. During four centuries of Ottoman rule (1516–1918), the term *Lebanon* referred to a vaguely defined region centered on the Mount Lebanon range, near the eastern Mediterranean coast. The region's main inhabitants were Maronite Christians, as well as adherents of an offshoot of Islam known as Druze.

After World War I, France gained control of the area. In 1920, it created a state of Lebanon, with today's boundaries, by adding to Mount Lebanon various adjacent regions, inhabited mainly by Sunni and Shi'i Muslims and by various Christian groups, notably Greek Orthodox and Greek Catholics.

France ruled Lebanon through a system known as "confessionalism," which allocated seats in Parliament, cabinet offices, and civil service posts on the basis of religious affiliation. This colonial system gave preeminence to the Maronites, Lebanon's largest single religious community at that time, who had long-standing religious and economic ties to France. The system ensured that the country's various Christian communities (then a majority of the population) controlled the political system, disadvantaging the Muslims.

Lebanese increasingly opposed French rule and, overcoming their sectarian differences, fought together against the colonial power. In 1943, on the eve of independence, the leaders of the various communities negotiated an informal National Pact. It continued the confessional system and guaranteed a Christian majority in Parliament, even though Muslims accounted for a growing proportion of the population and were probably already in the majority.

In spite of the favored position of the Christians, and especially the Maronites, Muslim elites had a place in the new system too. The pact gave the presidency and the top army command to Maronites, but the prime minister was to be a Sunni, the chief of staff a Druze, and the Speaker of the Parliament a Shi'i. In the civil service and army commands, Christians were assured a majority, but Muslims had posts as well. Though Lebanon was independent, not merged with Syria as many Muslims preferred, the pact affirmed that Lebanon would orient itself toward the Arab world.

During the 1950s under conservative pro-Western governments, Lebanon became the commercial capital, banking center, and playground of the Arab world. However, the political system came under increasing strain, as the largely Christian elite amassed great wealth, while blocking basic social *reforms like public education, health care, and housing for the predominantly Muslim poor. Rich conservatives insisted on low taxes, ensuring a weak, underfunded central government. With few national institutions, many Lebanese identified more with their religious communities than with the nation as a whole.

In 1958, when President Camille Chamoun endorsed the *Eisenhower Doctrine, refused demands for reform, rigged parliamentary elections, and won an unconstitutional second term, the country exploded into civil war. *Nasser's Egypt supported left-wing and Arab nationalist rebels, while right-wing Maronite militias backed Chamoun. At Chamoun's request, U.S. military forces intervened. Eventually, the factions negotiated a settlement whereby General Fouad Chehab, the popular army chief who had stayed out of the fighting, assumed the presidency.

Chehab used his popular support and his control of the powerful security apparatus to promote social reform. He strengthened the educational system, built roads, and spurred economic development, giving priority to manufacturing over services. Most importantly, he tried to build a sense of Lebanese national identity that transcended sectarian loyalties. But neither Chehab nor his successor was able to break the power of the traditional sectarian politicians or significantly undermine the confessional system.

During the 1960s, the Lebanese economy boomed, especially financial services. By mid-decade, Lebanon had more bank deposits per capita than any country in the world. While bankers prospered, much of the countryside was transformed from small holdings into large commercial farms, driving thousands of peasants off the land and into the burgeoning slums of Beirut and other cities. A rising tide of protest against class disparities and inadequate social services strengthened left-wing forces, who demanded fundamental reform and called for a nonsectarian *democracy. Conservatives, especially the Maronite parties, rejected reform, and their militias prepared to fight against what they saw as foreign-inspired radical threats to the social order.

In 1970 the *Palestine Liberation Organization (PLO), driven out of Jordan, established its headquarters in Beirut and expanded its guerrilla bases in the south, near the Israeli border. The PLO found its main support among the 300,000 Palestinian refugees who lived without *citizenship rights in Lebanon, but it also enjoyed sympathy from many Lebanese who supported the Palestinian cause and saw it as a force for social change in Lebanon and the Arab world. Conservative Lebanese, however, viewed the autonomous armed Palestinian presence as an affront to Lebanon's sovereignty, a threat which exposed Lebanon to Israeli attack; they also perceived the PLO as a supporter of the Lebanese reformists.

In April 1975 tensions finally exploded into full-scale civil war between a largely Muslim and Druze coalition demanding reform and a predominantly Maronite alliance rejecting change and insisting that the Lebanese army clamp down on the Palestinians. As fighting intensified, the army broke up along sectarian lines, tax revenues dried up, and the Lebanese government nearly ceased to function. The PLO, which initially sought to avoid involvement, soon entered the civil war on the side of the reformist forces.

In the summer of 1976, Syrian military units, acting nominally as Arab League–sponsored peacekeepers, entered Lebanon in force. Seeking to prevent a victory of the reformist-PLO bloc, they threw their support initially to the Maronite militias. Later, consolidating their role as arbiter of the conflict, the Syrians shifted sides.

Syrian forces soon occupied more than half of Lebanese territory, gaining a growing leverage over the government and over most institutions of Lebanese society, including the economy and the press. Civil war continued, punctuated by innumerable truces and lulls. Religious-sectarian animosities increasingly displaced ideological quarrels as the driving force of the conflict. All sides perpetrated atrocities against noncombatants, including massacres, *torture, car bombs, and hostage taking. Gangs lacking any political program soon set up neighborhood protection rackets; meanwhile, foreign governments gave money, arms, and support to various Lebanese factions. By late 1976, the end of the first phase of the civil war, some 30,000 Lebanese and Palestinians had been killed, 60,000 wounded, and at least 300,000 displaced from their homes. Many neighborhoods, towns, villages, and refugee camps were badly damaged or destroyed.

The militias partitioned Lebanon into exclusive religious enclaves and took charge of local administration, collecting taxes, providing social services, and operating ports. For the first time, the country's impoverished Shiʿa built their own political and military force, demanding a political role commensurate with their new status as Lebanon's largest community. In the Syrian-controlled Beqaa Valley, farmers grew hashish and opium as staple export crops. Many Lebanese came to have an economic interest in the strife. All attempts to end the civil war failed.

From the earliest days of the fighting, *Israel had developed close ties with Maronite militias. In March 1978 Israeli forces invaded south Lebanon up to the Litani River; soon withdrawing, they left a Lebanese-manned "South Lebanon Army" under their control in a ten-mile-wide "security zone" adjacent to the border. In June 1982 Israel again invaded Lebanon. This time its forces, along with Maronite militias, besieged Beirut in an effort to annihilate PLO headquarters and destroy the powerful Palestinian combat units assembled to defend the city. After two months of intense Israeli bombardment and heavy civilian casualties, PLO leaders and fighters withdrew under a U.S.-brokered cease-fire.

With Israeli forces controlling much of the southern half of the country, a pro-Israel Lebanese government sought to reestablish central authority. U.S. land and naval forces lent their support to the postwar government and intervened directly in the continuing intercommunal fighting. The new government failed to gain control, however, and a violent Syrian-backed Lebanese resistance compelled the United States to withdraw its forces in 1983 and Israel to pull its troops back to the border zone in 1985. Intercommunal fighting continued fitfully, with occasional upsurges of intense violence. Syrian forces remained in control of large areas in the north and east, and Syria gained overwhelming influence over the political scene, including domination over the ineffective but still symbolically important central government.

Military stalemate, the collapse of Lebanon's economy, and growing war-weariness opened the way for the United States and Saudi Arabia to broker an agreement in October 1989, known as the Taif Accords. This agreement, reached by members of the Lebanese Parliament, amended the 1943 National Pact by giving Muslims equal parliamentary representation and by strengthening the powers of the prime minister. But otherwise the confessional system remained intact. With U.S. support, Syrian forces eventually crushed opposition to the accords and imposed a cease-fire among the combatants. A new pro-Syrian government began to disarm the militias and broaden its authority to include much of the country, though Israel continued to control the border region and launched military actions against the Lebanese resistance in the south.

Efforts to put Lebanon back together have made little headway. Sectarian identities and loyalties remain powerful, and the economy is a shambles. Despite growing public demands for action, the government of old-guard politicians and younger warlords seems paralyzed. Lebanon's prospects of overcoming the legacies of the civil war and achieving fully independent statehood remain in doubt.

(See also ARAB-ISRAELI CONFLICT; ARAB NATIONALISM; POLITICAL VIOLENCE.)

Walid Khalidi, *Conflict and Violence in Lebanon* (Cambridge, Mass., 1979). Jonathan C. Randal, *Going all the Way: Christian Warlords, Israeli Adventurers and the War in Lebanon* (New York, 1983). Helena Cobban, *The Making of Modern Lebanon* (London, 1985). Tabitha Petran, *The Struggle over Lebanon* (New York, 1987). Kamal Salibi, *A House of Many Mansions* (London, 1988).

JAMES A. PAUL

LEFT. As a political term, the *Left* derives from the practice of the French revolutionary parliament, where "radical" representatives sat to the left of the presiding officer's chair, while "conservatives" sat to the *right. Since the French Revolution the Left has been associated with demands for greater popular sovereignty and democratic control over political, social, and economic life. The Left has been identified with the belief that democratic movements are capable of transforming social institutions in a manner that improves the human condition. Conservatives, on the other hand, warn of the "perverse," unintended consequences of social change (or "social engineering") and praise the "prescriptive" wisdom of long-standing institutional and cultural practices.

In the nineteenth century the European Left consisted of an unstable coalition between an emergent working class and middle-class "radical" anticlerics who fought for universal suffrage and elimination of established state religions. Middle-class radicals largely rejected the demands of socialist parties for greater popular control over the capitalist economy. After World War II, the mainstream Right in industrial democracies accepted the Left's demand for universal political suffrage. But conservatives caution that *democracy should only extend to popular selection of competing elites whose rule is essential to any complex society.

The modern Right also contends that economic redistribution and state regulation promote inefficiency and a restriction of liberty. In contrast, the Left holds that the equal worth of liberty can only be guaranteed by universal, public provision of basic human needs such as education, health care, and child care. In addition, the Left believes that popular participation in workplace governance increases productivity, as does public expenditure on infrastructure, research and development, and job training. In sum, while the Right holds that equality and liberty inherently stand in tension, the Left believes that the two values are synergistic.

The Left has been severely divided over the requisite means to achieve the end of extending popular sovereignty to all social institutions. Since the *Russian Revolution, communists have argued that without the leadership of a revolutionary vanguard party the working class by itself would only demand incremental reforms of *capitalism. In addition, communists contended that only *nationalization of industry and a centrally planned economy could achieve rapid industrialization and economic efficiency. But in industrial democracies whose working class fought for universal suffrage and civil liberties, the majority of the Left has advocated parliamentary and gradualist strategies for democratization.

Western European social democratic, labor, and socialist parties were also divided over whether democratization was best achieved by humanizing capitalism or striving for *workers' control of production. After World War II most West European social democratic parties, as well as liberals in the United States, embraced a mixed capitalist, Keynesian *welfare state as the institutional means by which to achieve social justice. But in the 1960s the student

*New Left, as well as militant sectors of the trade unions, argued that only participatory democracy could alleviate workplace alienation. Many on the Left sought a "third way," a democratic *socialism which rejected both corporate dominance of the welfare state and the bureaucratic domination of the inefficient *command economies of Eastern Europe.

The Left's renewed interest in decentralized, democratized authority drew upon anarchist, syndicalist, and feminist traditions long ignored by most communists and social democrats. The economic stagnation and restructuring of the 1980s, however, both weakened the traditional trade union core of the Western Left and thwarted this search for a third way. As the crisis of a Keynesian welfare state identified with social democracy engendered a conservative upsurge in most Western polities, the Left found itself reduced to fighting defensive battles in support of the very welfare state reforms it had only recently hoped to move beyond.

This crisis of the welfare state, combined with the collapse of authoritarian *communism in Central and Eastern Europe and the failure of Soviet-style economies to achieve equitable and efficient development in the *Third World, has contributed to a (perhaps temporary) demoralization of the international Left. (Capitalist development in the Third World has also abjectly failed to serve popular needs, though the highly statist, "planned" capitalisms of East Asia are often, ironically, cited by the Right as examples of "free-market miracles.") Authoritarian communism's repression of independent life in civil society sensitized the Left to the central role in a free society of social movements independent of state and party control. In addition, most leftists now recognize that movements for emancipation often organize around nonclass identities such as *race and *gender. In light of the failures of command economies, most leftists now recognize that the market and regulated competition are useful mechanisms for coordinating the activities of decentralized, efficient firms. But the Left continues to advocate for worker participation in firm management, as well as for state regulation of economic activity through fiscal, monetary, and industrial policy. While such social and ideological transformations will influence the nature of a twenty-first century Left, its core values are likely to remain the democratization of political, economic, and cultural life.

(See also ANARCHISM; CONSERVATISM; FEMINISM; IDEOLOGY; KEYNESIANISM; LABOR MOVEMENT; LIBERALISM; NEW RIGHT; NEW SOCIAL MOVEMENTS; REVOLUTION.)

David Caute, *The Left in Europe Since 1789* (New York, 1966). Michael Harrington, *Socialism: Past and Future* (New York, 1989).

JOSEPH M. SCHWARTZ

LEGISLATURE. Although legislatures exist in virtually every nation, they vary greatly in their power and stability. The U.S. *Congress and the Brazilian Chamber of Deputies are both legislatures, but the former has played a central and enduring role in the U.S. policy-making process while the latter has had a variable, but at most marginal, impact on policy decisions made by others. But what defines both of these institutions and what separates them from those institutions that are not legislatures is a set of essentially democratic characteristics that govern their membership and operation.

Simply put, legislators are elected by a larger public to which they are formally responsible and in whose interests they are presumed to act. No special training or expertise is required for membership in the legislature, each member possesses equal voting power, and decisions are taken publicly and by majority vote. Thus, the legislature stands at the confluence between democratic theory and democratic practice; indeed, it is often regarded as the most visible indicator of a nation's commitment to democracy. It is no accident that the trend away from *authoritarianism and toward *democracy that went forward in Eastern and Central Europe, East Asia, and Latin America during the late 1980s involved in each nation a more prominent role for legislative institutions.

If these democratic characteristics unite legislatures, they are distinguished from each other, first, by the activities in which their members engage and, second, by their capacity to survive from year to year.

Although all legislatures are involved in making public policy, some legislatures play a more salient role than others. The U.S. Congress initiates and designs public policies affecting every economic, social, and international question on the nation's policy-making agenda. The Japanese Diet, in comparison, debates and occasionally modifies proposals the essentials of which have been decided by business, government, and party leaders. And, except for a brief period between *perestroika and the collapse of the Soviet Union, all the Supreme Soviet was able to do was to approve, with minimal discussion, a small number of decisions made by *elites outside the legislature.

Members of all legislatures act as representatives; they articulate the interests of constituents, political parties, and *interest groups, and they intercede with bureaucrats on behalf of those whom they represent. But in some legislatures this is virtually all that legislators do, and the effectiveness of such activities varies substantially across legislatures.

All legislatures, regardless of their policy-making capacities, affect a nation's political stability by providing representation for its significant political interests as well as a forum within which dissent can be heard and government policies explained and legitimized. But in some instances these activities are all that legislatures are expected to do, in others such activities are more latent and incidental to the performance of policy-making and representational activities, and in still others legislative activity seems to detract from rather than enhance stability.

Finally, some legislatures are more vulnerable than others to attacks on their existence and prerogatives. In the United States and Britain the policy-making role of the legislature had remained unaltered in its constitutional design and unthreatened for centuries, whereas in Argentina and Thailand military coups have produced frequent changes in the prominence, membership, and structure of the legislature.

(See also LEGITIMACY; POLITICAL PARTIES AND PARTY COMPETITION.)

Gerhard Loewenberg, Samuel C. Patterson, and Malcolm E. Jewell, eds., *Handbook of Legislative Research* (Cambridge, Mass., 1985).

MICHAEL L. MEZEY

LEGITIMACY. The concept of *legitimacy* refers to a political order's worthiness to be recognized. Because the reasons offered in support of an order can differ—the preservation of customary forms of social life, the continuity of a legally recognized dynasty, the maintenance of *peace and *security, the promotion of general welfare, etc.—one can also speak of different conceptions of legitimacy according to the kind of reason given. Even the general definition may be controversial, however, since it restricts the term to political orders and ties the concept to the idea of providing grounds (rather than simply equating legitimacy with the de facto acceptance of a political order by its citizens).

Legitimus, like the related *legalis*, derives from the Latin *lex* (law), and in its early usage in Roman jurisprudence no clear distinction is drawn between the legitimacy and legality of a regime: an *imperium legitimum* or *potestas legitimus* designated rule according to law in contrast to arbitrary rule or tyranny. Under the influence of Christian thought, in medieval jurisprudence the concept of legitimacy also remained closely tied to the ideas of natural law and a normatively ordered cosmos. With the rise of absolutism in the sixteenth century, the idea of a secular justification of political power spread rapidly (see Jean Bodin, *The Six Books of the Commonweal* [1576], Cambridge, Mass., 1962), and under the subsequent influence of social contract theory and Enlightenment thought the concept was gradually democratized and aligned with the idea of popular sovereignty: "Sovereignty resides with the people, the only legitimate source of power" (Simonde de Sismondi, *Observations générales sur le gouvernement actuel*, Paris, 1815). With the "legitimist" disputes between the ultramonarchists and constitutional monarchists (Charles de Talleyrand) over the restoration of the Bourbon dynasty in France, the concept finally entered into the mainstream of political discourse.

At the beginning of this century, Max *Weber's distinction between traditional, charismatic, and rational-legal forms of legitimate domination paved the way for a sociological conception of legitimacy (*Economy and Society*, Berkeley, Calif., 1978). His definition of legitimacy as "belief in the legality of enacted rules" contributed to the development of legal positivism and the decline of the classical connection between legitimacy and substantive values or worldviews. Weber's position has recently been advocated in an extreme form by the systems theorist Niklas Luhmann, whose defense gave rise to an influential debate in the 1970s with the critical theorist Jürgen Habermas.

If the concept of legitimacy is not severed from the need to provide reasons and narrowly reduced to the question of the *state's capacity to generate belief in its legitimacy, several distinct types of legitimation can still be identified. Substantive theories assume there is a normative natural order that provides a measure for the legitimacy of a political order. Only regimes whose policies conform to this "good old law" are worthy of recognition. The liberal-minimalist model, by contrast, rejects the idea that legitimacy must involve reference to substantive values in this manner. Legitimacy depends rather on the state's ability to maintain peace, under the rule of law, between individuals and groups who hold widely divergent and even conflicting conceptions about the ultimate value of life. This conception, which can be traced back at least to Benjamin Constant (1767–1830), construes legitimacy as a modus vivendi in which an expanded interpretation of religious toleration replaces the search for substantive moral truth. A third model, which may be called discursive or democratic-proceduralist, has its roots in Rousseau and Kant and has recently been defended by Habermas. Legitimacy is understood in terms of the counterfactual ideal ("regulative idea") of an agreement between free and equal citizens, and the task becomes that of designing political institutions to reflect that ideal while also leaving them open to future criticism in light of it. Although it does not presuppose the idea of a normative natural order, this model sees legitimacy as relying on more than a modus vivendi. Finally, it may be possible to identify a "postmodern" model in which the search for universal legitimating grounds is abandoned in favor of a return to narrative traditions. The idea is not to develop a global theory of legitimation but to practice more immanent and local forms of critique under the banner of plurality and innovation. Whether this approach, which can be found in the works of Jean-François Lyotard, Jacques Derrida, and Michel *Foucault, constitutes a distinct alternative remains to be seen. Much depends, of course, on the capacity of one or another of the alternatives to respond successfully to the dilemmas of legitimacy in an increasingly interdependent yet functionally differentiated and pluralistic world.

(See also CITIZENSHIP; POSTMODERNISM; SOVEREIGNTY.)

Jürgen Habermas, *Legitimation Crisis* (Boston, 1975). William Connolly, ed., *Legitimacy and the State* (New York, 1984). Athanasios Moulakis, ed., *Legitimacy/Légitimité* (New York, 1986).

KENNETH BAYNES

LENIN, Vladimir Ilich. The Russian thinker and political leader Vladimir Ilich Lenin articulated the primacy of political will in an age of total *war. Yet his political *ideology, *Leninism, promised an ultimate end to politics after a period of continuous warfare among *classes and nations. Heir to the ideas of many, including *Marx and *Clausewitz, Lenin saw politics as the continuation of war by other means. Politics, not economics, was the fundamental agent of historical change. But at the end of history lay true victory and peace, namely, the annihilation of all enemies and therefore of all politics. To build *socialism was to eliminate class struggle by eliminating all social classes but one, the proletariat.

Lenin's main political contribution was the theory of the omniscient vanguard party, made up not of workers, but of professional revolutionaries and intellectuals, the class from which he came and which he despised. Trained as a lawyer, Lenin denied the rule of law in favor of a higher apocalyptic historicism, dialectical materialism, an ideology of absolute truth understood correctly only by Lenin and his party.

Lenin adapted the economic theories of Marx and Engels to support the primacy of politics as a form of class war in which consciously organized individual wills could overcome the spontaneous forces of history. A continuous reviser of Marxist ideas to suit Russian political conditions, Lenin claimed an orthodoxy superior to his revisionist rivals, right and left. His Manichaean worldview divided friends and light from enemies and darkness. His metapolitics depended on the violent ultimate triumph of a single social class, the proletariat, over its historically doomed enemy, the bourgeoisie. In the end Lenin's own elusive personality dissolved into a militant political ideology.

"V. I. Lenin" was one of many revolutionary pseudonyms used by Vladimir Ilich Ulyanov to publish under the censorship conditions of Imperial Russia. Born 22 April 1870 (10 April, old style) in the Volga River town of Simbirsk, Lenin was the fourth of six children of a superintendent of schools and member of the hereditary nobility, Ilya Ulyanov. In 1887, Lenin's older brother, Aleksandr, was executed for his role in a plot to kill Tsar Aleksandr III.

After graduating from the law faculty of the University of Kazan in 1891, Lenin converted to *Marxism and engaged in the typical career of a professional revolutionary—arrest, prison, and political exile. He spent the years 1900–1917 in Munich, Paris, Geneva, Cracow, and Zurich as a radical journalist and leader of the Bolshevik faction of the Russian Social Democratic Workers' Party (RSDWP, founded 1898). In April 1917, after the collapse of the Imperial government during World War I, Lenin returned to Petrograd with hundreds of other political exiles transported by the German government to foment revolution. He masterminded the successful Bolshevik seizure of power in November 1917 and led the new Soviet government as chair of the Council of People's Commissars (Sovnarkom). After suffering a stroke in May 1922, Lenin died in Moscow on 21 January 1924. The father of the *Russian Revolution, and his wife, Nadezhda Krupskaya, left no children.

Lenin's political career began with the peasant-centered revolutionary conspiracy of Russian *populism in the 1880s and, after his brother's death, shifted from terrorism to Marxism. From Russian thinkers such as P. I. Pestel and P. N. Tkachev, Lenin inherited the Jacobin notion of a political seizure of power from above as the key to revolution. The scientistic, historicist, materialist, and economic ideas of Marx, combined with Russian populism, formed the basis of his emerging "Leninism" around 1900, expressed in the RSDWP journal *Iskra (The Spark),* of which Lenin was an editor.

As a Bolshevik after the RSDWP split of 1903, Lenin favored both legal participation in the Russian parliament (Duma) and illegal underground activity, mainly strikes and bank robberies. In 1907–1912, he nearly lost control of Bolshevism to rivals impressed with the concurrent rise of antiparliamentary syndicalism and trade unionism in Western Europe. In 1917, Lenin sharply opposed the liberal democratic provisional government and, with *Trotsky and others, called for a seizure of power in the name of the soviets, or workers' councils, as the prelude to world revolution and a classless society without state power. He then successfully defended Soviet rule during a bloody civil war (1918–1921) and created the organs of a new state.

Lenin's influence on domestic politics in the *Soviet Union derived from his political will, personal charisma, and ideology, not the offices he held. He founded both the *Communist Party of the Soviet Union (CPSU) and the Soviet Union, with its single-party political system and democratic centralist hierarchy of power. He originated the principles of antifactionalism, purge, and the banning of all opposition parties (after disbanding the freely elected constituent assembly in January 1918), on which *Stalin would later build his totalitarian police state. His voluminous writings became scripture defining the party line and the correct view of history. Lenin died, but Leninism survived, in his ideology and in the Red Square mausoleum, as a cult designed by rival Bolshevik "god builders" who viewed socialism as a surrogate religion for the masses.

Lenin's overall role in the political history of the Soviet Union was perhaps greater in death than in life. Leninist ideology defined the terms of political discourse and struggle for succession among Trotsky, *Bukharin, Zinoviev, and Stalin in the 1920s. Stalin, *Khrushchev, and Brezhnev all claimed Lenin's mantle. Leninism defined correct party policy against the ideological enemies of dogmatism, revisionism, and opportunism. It became the political language of the mass mobilization, industrialization, and militarization of Soviet society.

Beginning in the 1890s, Lenin in his writings revised Marxist theory to fit Russian conditions, borrowing ideas and using them as political weapons. In *The Development of Capitalism in Russia* (1899), he argued that industrialization made Russia ripe for proletarian revolution. In this, Lenin was more Marxist than Marx, who had observed the revolutionary potential of the Russian peasant commune in the 1870s. In *What Is to Be Done?* (1902), titled after the populist novel by his idol, N. G. Chernyshevsky, Lenin argued for the primacy of political organization and discipline over worker spontaneity and trade unionism. He expanded his authoritarian notion of democratic centralism in *One Step Forward, Two Steps Back* (1904) and defended absolute materialist truth against relativism and idealism in *Materialism and Empirio-Criticism* (1909). In *Imperialism* (1916), Lenin blamed finance capital for World War I and predicted inevitable international civil war.

During the summer of 1917, Lenin argued in *State and Revolution* for a necessary, but temporary, dictatorship of the proletariat, to be succeeded at some undefined future time by (in Engels's words) the "withering away of the state." Finally, in *Left-Wing Communism: A Childhood Disease* (1920), Lenin renewed his pre-1914 assault on European syndicalism for its direct action and worker spontaneity. Lenin's ideas were rarely original. They constituted a form of political warfare appropriate to the conditions of the day and were enormously influential both in the Soviet Union and abroad.

Lenin played a central role in the 1917 Revolution and the formation of the Soviet Union (1922). He turned the Bolsheviks from cooperation with, to hostility toward, the provisional government. His letters and articles prodded the Bolshevik central committee to seize power in November. He wrote the decrees on land reform and peace with the Central Powers that engineered short-term peasant support for an urban revolution and led to the Treaty of Brest-Litovsk (1918). He oversaw Soviet victory over the White Armies during the Russian Civil War and a "breathing-space" *New Economic Policy (1921–1928) that allowed limited capitalism to develop (whether this was a strategy or a tactic is still debated), and later served as an economic reform model for Khrushchev and *Gorbachev. Lenin's deathbed testament warned against the growth of excessive state and party bureaucracy and a centralization of political power which, in fact, simply extended his own ideas and which, because of illness, he was powerless to halt.

Lenin was also the most important figure in the Soviet experience of a violent attempt to achieve the transition from capitalism through socialism to communism. Both official Soviet historians and earlier Western critics saw Leninism as identical with Bolshevism and as the logical ancestor of Stalinism. More recently, Leninism has been recognized as distinct from both pre-1917 Bolshevism and post-1929 Stalinism. Yet Leninism has guided the politics and policies of many Soviet leaders. It provides a model for seizing and holding power in modernizing non-Western societies, even as it failed as a model in Western Europe after the two world wars. Only peasant societies of Eastern Europe and Asia adopted Leninism to suit their own revolutions in the wake of World War II. By 1990, however, Leninist centralism and single-party politics were in disarray in both the Soviet Union and Eastern Europe.

Lenin's significance outside the Soviet Union has generally followed success or failure by foreign communist parties in their own countries. Lenin was a well-known and thorny figure in international socialist politics under the Second International (1887–1914). His clarion call to turn World War I into a civil war became the basis of the Comintern, or Third International, founded in Moscow in 1919. The Comintern, through its links with communist parties in other countries, became a parallel arm of *Soviet foreign policy and its Council of Foreign Affairs. His writings, published in nearly every language, became international guidelines for world revolution. But Leninism remains only one variant of Marxism, whose appeal to intellectuals has generally been more analytical and critical than action-oriented. Lenin spawned no intellectual tradition in the manner of Marx or Freud, aside from a political ideological orthodoxy institutionalized in his own country.

Despite his cult status in the Soviet Union, especially in the 1920s and 1960s, Lenin ironically stands for the sacrifice of self to ideology. His revolution liberated individuals only for a one-man dictatorship that suppressed individual freedom in expectation of a future classless, stateless society. Revolution in the name of the people produced one-party rule in the name of a social class, the proletariat. The dream of international revolution gave way to the reality of Stalin's "socialism in one country," the Soviet Union. National liberation ultimately meant Soviet empire. Economic compromise led to a planned, command economy of state power, not consumer demand.

The genius of Lenin lay in his political ideology. He recognized that the most effective ideological myth of revolution is one that claims absolute, not relative, truth. But in the multipolar world of global interconnections and high technology, Leninism ultimately failed to provide either political liberation or the material benefits so often promised and postponed. His legacy, an ideological empire, has now been dismantled by his successors in his name.

(See also COMMUNIST PARTY STATES; RUSSIA.)

Rolf Theen, *Lenin: Genesis of a Revolutionary* (Princeton, N.J., 1973). Nina Tumarkin, *Lenin Lives! The Lenin Cult in Soviet Russia* (Cambridge, Mass., 1983). Robert C. Williams, *The Other Bolsheviks: Lenin and his Critics, 1901– 1914* (Bloomington, Ind., 1986). Philip Pomper, *Lenin, Trotsky, and Stalin: The Intelligentsia and Power* (New York, 1990).

ROBERT C. WILLIAMS

LENINISM. At its first major congress the Marxist movement that had begun to form in the Russian Empire during the last one or two decades of the nineteenth century split into two factions, Mensheviks and Bolsheviks, that came to disagree about revolutionary strategy, tactics, and organization. In the Bolshevik faction Vladimir *Lenin eventually emerged as the sole acknowledged leader, and after his death the legacy of ideas and practices that he left was given the name *Leninism*. This legacy is a unique blend of orthodox *Marxism, as accepted in Social Democratic parties around the turn of the century, with elements specific to Russian revolutionary populism. It is by no means unambiguous or internally consistent; but some general statements can nonetheless he made about it. Leninism offers prescriptions on two problems: first, how to bring about a proletarian *revolution in a country like Russia, and, second, how to govern the country once such a revolution has occurred.

Revolutionary Strategy. Like all Russian Marxists, Lenin took it for granted that a Russian revolution would have to come in two stages: the first, or bourgeois, revolution designed to replace the tsarist system with a bourgeois democratic one, and only the second revolution aiming to usher in a proletarian dictatorship leading to *socialism and *communism. For the initial revolution, he argued, the Marxist movement and the proletariat supposedly represented by it would need allies because the working class alone was too small. Lenin's program for the "democratic" revolution therefore sought to appeal to the peasantry and to Russia's national minorities.

Moreover, Leninism incorporates a thorough reexamination of the Marxist model of *capitalism. Instead of treating capitalism as the system prevailing in the most developed countries, Leninism sees it as a global system, called *imperialism; and in this global system all underdeveloped nations are regarded as potential allies in the revolutionary struggle, while the proletariat of the imperialist nations tends to be written off, superprofits having bribed it into acquiescence. At the same time, Leninism insists that in all political alliances the proletariat should play the leading role.

The Party. Leninism sharply distinguishes between two elements of the Marxist movement—the working class, which reacts against the exploitation of labor, and does so in uninformed, "spontaneous" fashion, and the small group of bourgeois intellectuals who join the movement because Marxist theory has made them "conscious." Both consciousness and spontaneity are essential driving forces of revolution. Spontaneity means that the exploited masses will be mobilized for revolutionary action, while consciousness is needed to guide this rebellion into political effectiveness. Leninism regards itself as the science of revolution making and therefore insists on the hegemony of consciousness over spontaneity: unguided revolutionary action will be futile and must be prevented because the working class by itself cannot be expected to understand its own interests.

Consciousness must be institutionalized in the party, which should function as the command center or general staff of the revolution. It should be a small organization recruiting only those who, armed with scientific knowledge (i.e., Marxist theory), will become professionals in revolution making. Like other organizations based on professional expertise, it should be organized according to principles of bureaucratic rationality, although Leninism stresses the importance of the authoritarian command structure and of strict discipline much more than the Weberian model does. Because the elitism of this arrangement runs counter to strong democratic traditions in the socialist movement, Leninism seeks to combine authoritarian and democratic principles in a form of party governance called democratic centralism. But in practice the centralist tendencies have always overwhelmed the democratic and participatory ones.

Nevertheless, yet this *elite party seeks to mobilize the masses. For this purpose it develops two means— organization and propaganda. To organize the masses it creates a vast network of auxiliary organizations modeled on those developed earlier by the German Social Democratic Party, and educational activity is divided into long-range indoctrination ("propaganda") and short-term arousal ("agitation"). According to Lenin, one of the most effective means of mobilizing the masses for revolutionary action is the heroic deed: once conditions have ripened for revolution, a small beginning anywhere will serve as the spark that will set off a general political conflagration. In 1917 he was confident that a communist revolution in Russia would serve as the beginning of an all-European proletarian revolution; and on the basis of this expectation he defended his party's seizure of power.

Tsarist rule had been overthrown in February/ March 1917. The left-of-center parties that tried to rule the country afterwards faced overwhelming problems that they were unwilling or unable to solve quickly. Impatient and angry, large masses of the poor supported the only party that promised quick and drastic solutions—the Bolsheviks; and thus by endorsing the utopian expectations and the bitter resentment of the Russian underclass, Lenin led his party to power.

The Soviet State. The Soviet state established in 1917 went through several distinct phases employing different policies and institutions. Yet certain principles remained more or less constant; they make up the Leninist pattern of government. Chief among them are the extension of democratic centralism over the entire system of government; the priority of economic growth; the cultural revolution; and the willingness to apply terror.

Leninist theory demands that the masses be drawn into participation in public life. For this purpose the Communist Party creates a vast network of mass organizations and associations. For the administration of the country, the relevant organization is the system of soviets (councils). At the same time, central control over this entire system is exercised by the Party, which regards itself as the repository of the genuine national interest and as the organization of the most enlightened citizens. The Party assures its control through a variety of methods, but ultimately through terror, i.e., through the threat of indiscriminate and unlimited violence against anyone suspected of dissenting from the Party's will. Readiness to apply terror is an acknowledged principle of Leninism.

The first priority of the Leninist state is the task of economic construction and reconstruction, for its ultimate goal, genuine communism, presupposes an affluent industrial society. One of the auxiliary tasks in this connection is a "cultural revolution," designed to transform a people steeped in traditional peasant culture and religion into literate, sophisticated city dwellers who know how to handle modern technology.

In its relations with the outside world, the Leninist state from its very beginning followed two mutually exclusive aims. One of them was the pursuit of the national interests of the Soviet state through fostering fruitful relations with governments of the capitalist countries. The other aim was to promote revolutions that would overthrow these capitalist governments. Pursuing both aims at one and the same time promoted chronic failure in both.

Stalinism. After Joseph *Stalin became the single most powerful leader of the Soviet Union and of international communism, his interpretation of Lenin's heritage became the orthodox version of Leninism. In this interpretation, Leninism demanded a commitment of the nation's total material and human resources to a crash program of industrialization, so that Leninism became entrepreneurship of a primitive but powerful sort. An essential element of this program was the imposition of a new serfdom on the peasantry by forcing them into collective farms. The control over the nation's organizational

and associational life was extended into all areas of human activity, including science, the arts, and entertainment. In every field of endeavor, orthodoxies were strictly enforced through censorship. Meanwhile the revolutionary terror endorsed by Lenin was institutionalized in the practice of prophylactic justice, through a system of police supervision and punishment designed to eliminate *potential* offenders and dissenters, including potential challengers high in the Party, the government, and other elites.

Leninism in its Stalinist version took pride in eliminating unemployment and in providing cheap housing, free medical care, free education, and similar social services. But it also rejected egalitarianism and endorsed a system of social stratification based on the value of a person's services to the state. It continued to declare the working class to be the leading class of Soviet society, but in reality allowed the workers to remain exploited by a managerial class.

By the mid-1930s, Stalin declared dogmatically that *socialism had been achieved, even though full communism was still in the very distant future. Thus his version of Leninism effectively eliminated the ideals and dreams in the name of which the revolution had been made—*Stalinism implied the withering away of utopia.

Alternatives to Stalinism. The Stalinist version of Leninism, which officially came to be called Marxism-Leninism, was challenged by many leaders within the Bolshevik movement. Nikolai *Bukharin, who was alert to the links between economic centralization and unchecked political power, advocated a policy of slower economic growth that would permit a gentler and more democratic political system. Aleksandr A. Bogdanov and others, criticizing the Party's exclusive attention to problems of economic growth and political control, suggested that it should also develop the cultural and spiritual aspects of the transition from capitalism to socialism. Leaders of the Workers' opposition interpreted Leninism in an anarcho-syndicalist spirit, demanding *workers' control of industry and grass-roots democracy through the unions and the soviets. Aleksandra M. Kollontai and other Bolshevik feminists sought to combine revolutionary Marxism with the demands for women's liberation, including liberation from conventional sexual morality.

Lev D. *Trotsky's ideas do not constitute an alternative to Stalinism. Instead, they were its precursors: Trotsky must be recognized as a major pioneer of Stalinism, although it probably required a Stalin to put his ideas into practice.

Leninism Worldwide. As long as the *Soviet Union was the only country governed by a Leninist party, its Stalinist dogma was acknowledged by all other communist parties as orthodox Leninism, although splinter parties analogous to the oppositions in the Soviet Union formed in many countries. When communist parties came to power in Eastern Europe in the wake of World War II, many of their leaders expected to apply Leninism in a more democratic and humane manner but were forced to adopt the strict Stalinist version. Nonetheless, reformers in the Eastern and Central European parties and also in the Soviet Union eventually repudiated Stalinism, appealing to neglected aspects of Lenin's heritage.

The Yugoslav party, excommunicated by Stalin, developed its own, Titoist version of reform Leninism. In China and Indochina, the revolutionary strategies of *Mao Zedong and *Ho Chi Minh led to a very different interpretation of Leninism, and so did the ideas and practices of Latin American communists. *Eurocommunism in Western Europe gave Leninism a rather social democratic interpretation, while in some African countries ruled by parties that called themselves Marxist-Leninist, Leninism meant little more than a commitment to revolutionary anticolonialism, economic planning, and government by a single party.

The collapse of communist regimes in Eastern and Central Europe as well as the dissolution of the Soviet Union have produced a crisis for Leninism, the outcome of which is uncertain. The people who ousted ruling communist parties from power have also removed statues and posters of the once-idolized Lenin, and some of them now repudiate every idea and every word once associated with him. In time, some parts of this heritage, especially his theory of imperialism, may, of course, come to be appreciated again.

(See also COMMUNIST PARTY STATES; PEASANTS.)

Herbert Marcuse, *Soviet Marxism: A Critical Analysis* (New York, 1958). Leonard B. Schapiro, *The Communist Party of the Soviet Union* (New York, 1960). Alfred G. Meyer, *Communism*, 4th ed. (New York, 1984). Alfred G. Meyer, *Leninism* (Boulder, Colo., and London, 1986).

ALFRED G. MEYER

LESOTHO. See BLS STATES.

LIBERALISM. A protean doctrine with views on matters as diverse as epistemology and *international relations, liberalism has been interpreted in different ways throughout history. We must begin by asking if there is a common core to liberalism that stands behind different facades. At a minimal definition we can say that liberalism considers individuals the seat of moral value and each individual as of equal worth. Hence, the individual should be free to choose his or her own ends in life. Liberalism may be morally neutral in regard to the ends people choose for themselves, but it is not morally neutral in its view that such individual choice is desirable and must be safeguarded from unwarranted interference from the *state. Liberalism is a view of the world, an *ideology, and to adopt it is to take a stand.

If we are to understand liberalism, we need to pay attention to its most determined critics. *Marxism sees liberalism as fatally flawed through association with *capitalism. Its central charge is that liberalism cannot fulfill its promise of every individual's freedom to pursue a life plan because it enshrines the rule of the propertied—something which, at least for orthodox Marxists, will lead both to class war and, after intensified trade competition among states, to world war.

Other critics charge that the liberal order is without moral substance, that it is soulless and mechanical. Stressing the significance of human sociability and the collectivities that constitute society, some say that "the individual" is a social construct, and that he/she depends upon and cannot survive without proper social mooring. By contrast, for instinctualist thinkers such as Nietzsche, liberalism is all-too-social; it is held to be a corrupt and timid set of moral constraints on real human desire and feeling. It is better to understand and confront the consequences of one's deep instinctual desires, according to this view, than to be chained by what is seen as a secularized theology. Although these two strands of criticism are very different, they have on occasion merged. Some of those who find liberalism soulless have been attracted to vitalist ideologies determined to place people firmly within a social context. Both sets of criticisms must be carefully evaluated.

This essay has three parts. It begins by distinguishing and examining the principal strands of thought within the liberal enterprise as a whole. The second part is concerned with the history of liberalism, considering both liberal institutions and liberal doctrine. The final part of the essay analyzes liberalism in postwar Europe—in both its geopolitical and domestic influences—and considers the stability of the advanced core of liberalism as well as the possibility of liberalization elsewhere.

The Philosophical Underpinnings. There have been two principal concerns within liberalism. One has centered on epistemology, reflecting the fact that liberalism has always had a particularly high regard for modern science. The second concern has been liberalism's relationship to capitalism. The stress on the human agent, as knowing subject or consumer, links these two categories—as do thinkers such as David Hume and Adam Smith, in whose work the theories of empiricism and capitalism are closely blended.

The key figures within the epistemological tradition are Hume and Kant, the latter moved to philosophize by his dissatisfaction with the former's conclusions. What is most striking about Hume's thought is its simplicity. Human beings can only build up a picture of the world, in his view, by means of their senses, for nothing exists except sensation. The trouble with this position is that it led Hume to something like despair: if we have only our senses, it is impossible to guarantee the reality of the external world, the regularity of nature, and even causation itself. While Kant did not try to disprove Hume, he did seek to remedy the situation. On the one hand, he sought to restore a sense of order by arguing that our minds could only approach reality by means of regular causal principles. On the other hand, however, he sought to guarantee the special status of humanity by arguing that reason is not simply, as Hume has it, "a slave to the passions."

These two views are important for liberalism insofar as Kantianism underwrites British empiricism in an absolutely necessary way. In its utilitarian guise, empiricism was open to the objection that the general happiness of a group of ten people might be increased if, say, the bodily parts of one healthy member were shared out to the other nine incapacitated members. This is in fact an academic objection: the British empiricists inhabited a society in which great respect was shown to individuals, and they did not themselves recommend such policies of dismemberment. Nonetheless, the Kantian position gives the firmest possible base for treating all human beings as ends rather than as means. Second, both views share the same enemies. Both mount attacks against superstition and authority, and individuals are left as masters of their fate.

If empiricism and Kantianism remain unsettling in the ways in which they diminish our certainty, the best-known defense of liberalism bravely seeks to make a virtue of necessity by praising doubt. As nobody can be completely sure of anything, John Stuart Mill argued, it is vital that every opinion have a hearing—albeit so that the best idea, in the light of current evidence, can win out. This striking view has implications for political life: if individuality of view is encouraged, a common culture of literacy and tolerance is crucial to sustain ordered debate. This opens the specter of relativism, of liberalism as but one option. That liberalism has to justify itself against its rivals tends to shift attention from pure doctrine to the efficacy of its social institutions in comparison to those of its rivals. With Adam Smith, liberalism turned to less lofty concerns.

A great novelty of Smith within the tradition of Western thought lies in his preference for wealth over virtue, that is, a society of abundance rather than a frugal one designed to encourage moral virtue. The basic justification was simple and democratic: the standard of life of normal people would be enhanced. But a more important issue was involved. The making of money, about which Smith had few illusions, had served historically in Europe as a counterbalance to the pursuit of *power, the former being a calm rather than a violent passion, and it remained the best guarantee of decent politics. Smith endorsed capitalism as a means to his ultimate value—control of arbitrary rule, a limit, as Montesquieu had it, to the fear which governments could impose on their citizens. Smith's highly sophisticated view is, of course, far removed for the naiveté of his neoclassical descendants, who turned the market from a means to an end in itself.

Nineteenth-century Manchester School thinking was equally naive about international relations. Politicians such as Cobden and Bright believed that *interdependence through the international division of labor would ensure *peace. Although there is probably something to this mechanism—the transmutation of the doctrine of free trade—the history of the twentieth century forces us to be aware that trade has not in itself been capable of controlling *militarism. But there is much more to be said for the supremely sophisticated liberal view of international relations expressed by Kant. While he too hoped that interdependence might help the cause of peace, his positive cause ultimately depended on liberal republican rule. As the people serve as cannon fodder for war, popular control is likely to limit aggression; still more importantly, a league between republican states may be able to prevent war between ideological partners. If the people have occasionally been militant and liberal states vicious in their wars against ideological rivals, we can see that there is something to Kant's view because of the brute fact that liberal states have not fought wars against each other.

The Rise and Fall of Liberalism. Intellectual doctrines are often codifications of social practices which may, in turn, then have an impact on social life. This principle most certainly applies to liberalism, and we need first to examine in turn the social bases that support liberalism before then turning to an analysis of its loss of hegemony in late-nineteenth-century Europe.

Comparative historians agree that the uniqueness of the West lies in the fact that power was held in many sets of hands. Where a Chinese empire had a settled status order (which distinctively sought to control the destabilizing forces of capitalism), Europe was much more varied. The Christian church provided a certain unity for Europe as a whole, and within that shell there was constant restlessness created by competition between states and in the market, and complicated interactions between political and economic forces. The character of the whole can be seen in the calling of parliaments—institutions unique to the West—in which nobles, church, and burghers (and peasants in the Swedish case) voted kings special funds, habitually for the conduct of war. The absence of a single center made experiments possible. One example was the autonomy allowed city-states in Flanders and in Northern Italy. It may be, as John Milton has argued, that the combination of Judaic law and the Greek emphasis on laws of nature favored the emergence of modern science; but the "materialist" fact of centers in which the burgher was king ensured a demand for technology, without which European intellectual and social progress would have been impossible.

If this social portfolio provided a baseline of *pluralism, a very long and varied set of events translated favorable circumstances into a liberal world. European pluralism prevented the triumph of any party in long wars of religion, and the crucial liberal doctrine of tolerance accordingly slowly struggled to the fore. The diversity of the system was such that restrictions imposed in one locale could not prevent advances elsewhere, and these later had, on pain of extinction, to be imitated by laggards. Particularly crucial in this respect was, as Barrington Moore has demonstrated, the slow conversion of the English aristocracy to commercial agriculture—a development which ruled out for Europe as a whole the creation of nonplural absolutist power systems. When England triumphed over France in the Napoleonic Wars, it seemed that liberalism would be triumphant.

But in the 1870s the English model—by that time insisting as much on free trade as on retrenchment and reform—came under widespread assault. Intellectually, counter-Enlightenment ideas accused liberalism either of providing insufficient support for the self or of standing in the way of true individuality, contradictory charges which, nevertheless, could blend into a single positive reenchanting ideology. The charges are not without foundation. But the critics of liberalism suffer from more serious problems. Intellectually, they create society as an abstraction hovering over the individual with potentially unconstrained powers. More importantly, the historical record has demonstrated that the worship of society in a form glorifying instinctualism—including the "will to power"—was most significantly effected at the Nuremberg rallies. It may be that individuality is not, as John Stuart Mill believed, easy. But to achieve individuality, through struggle and with some personal costs, seems far less expensive socially than any alternative available.

Did liberalism fall apart instead for institutional reasons? The key Marxist charge in this connection is that liberal society suffers from class conflict. It is indeed true that a revolutionary working class played a significant role in the *Russian Revolution of 1917, and the German workers had as their agent a political party with distinctive socialist goals. But what can now be seen clearly is that working-class militancy was by no means uniform within capitalist society: it was effectively absent in the United States, nearly absent in England, and strongly present only in the classical model in Germany, and, most militant of all, in tsarist Russia. Militancy resulted from autocratic and authoritarian old regimes seeking to exclude workers through antisocialist legislation of various sorts: where workers were free to organize under a liberal state, they naturally did not fight politically against the state which had given them *citizenship, but fought industrially, in the workplace, in order to achieve better pay and conditions from capitalists. Differently put, liberalism disperses

conflict throughout society, whereas the concentration of power tends to focus it. Insofar as some nation-states became politically unstable in the late nineteenth century, it was less because they were capitalist than because they were not yet liberal.

The same essential point applies to a second institutional failing held to follow from the relations of liberalism to capitalism, this time concerning liberalism or openness in international trade. It is indeed true that several states sought to protect their own producers from the world market at the end of the nineteenth century, and that this did lead to increased international trade rivalry. But such rivalry did not in itself lead to armed conflict. If we are to understand the origins of *World War I—as we must, because it (in combination with *World War II, which was occasioned by the social forces unleashed in World War I) created the world in which we now live—it is necessary to comprehend the nature of the German state, whose backing for Austria was the crucial determinant of war in 1914. What is crucial is that Wilhelmine Germany ended up with two policies: one directed worldwide, supported by intellectuals, the excluded middle class, some heavy industrialists, and Social Democrats, and another directed eastward, favored by the army and the traditional landed upper class. The presence of two policies meant that Germany alienated every major state, and thereby brought on itself a coalition that led to its greatest fear—that of having to fight on two fronts. How was such a blunder possible? The German state was a court: whoever had the ear of the kaiser was influential—the trouble was that the kaiser, without a Bismarck, listened to many and did not ensure that a single grand strategy was put into place. Again, it was the absence of liberalism—in the sense here of cabinet government and parliamentary control—rather than the presence of captalism which caused disaster.

Liberalism Triumphant? At the end of the twentieth century, some polemicists claim that liberalism is now triumphant. There is an uncomfortable amount of hubris involved in that claim. Liberalism spread in the heart of the advanced world less because of any inevitability than because the Anglo-Saxon power triumphed, none too easily, in two world wars. Equally, *decolonization, which has removed the illiberal character of European rule abroad, has not led, as hoped, to the spread of liberalism: the perceived need to centralize power to speed development has increased authoritarian and dictatorial rule. We need to make distinctions in order to establish the ways in which liberalism is more and less solidly in place at the end of the twentieth in comparison with the end of the nineteenth century.

The most famous argument asserting the primacy of liberalism was that made at the end of the 1950s proclaiming "an end to ideology." This assertion was both disingenuous and unhelpful in hiding the fact that liberalism is itself an ideology needing to be defended as such. However, there was then and is now much truth to the basic contention that the great ideologies of the twentieth century, from the fascist *Right to the Marxist *Left, have been massively discredited by historical events. The defense of the people against fear as well as the ability of liberal and capitalist societies to provide affluence for citizens in the prosperous core sustain liberalism's appeals. This is not to say that everyone accepts this state of affairs. Ideological hostility toward the soulless world of liberalism remains on the part of many intellectuals. More significantly, capitalism raises profound issues of *equality and inequality in global terms, even as the reach of liberalism beyond the wealthy core remains in doubt.

The core of liberal society has prospered to an extraordinary degree in the years since 1945. U.S. dominance of capitalist society as a whole led to the reconstruction of the Federal Republic of Germany and Japan, a very wide acceptance of a historic class compromise, and a promotion of multilateral free trade that was so successful as to finally create a genuinely international division of labor. In recent years, a certain diminution in U.S. economic hegemony has led to fears that trade rivalries between capitalist states may destabilize international relations. Although tensions certainly do exist—notably among Europe, Japan, and the United States—it would be a mistake to exaggerate them.

In domestic terms, since the late 1970s much debate has taken place as to whether the class compromise—an acceptance by conservatives of welfare, and an acceptance by socialists of the market—has come unstuck. More particularly, ideologists of the radical Right such as Hayek and Friedman have been proclaimed as the "true" liberals by politicians such as Ronald *Reagan and Margaret *Thatcher in an attempt to discredit social democracy. The claims of the radical Right are questionable, insofar as all states intervene in economic life, none "dismantle" the welfare state, and those which institutionalize state governance of the economy with the greatest sophistication (such as Japan and Germany) seem more competitive than the more laissez-faire Britain or the United States.

An important question of the age facing liberals concerns the fate of advanced but authoritarian regimes. Can regimes which industrialized by concentrating power, that is, that suffered "revolutions from above," make a successful transition to liberal democracy? In Eastern and Central Europe, there is no doubt but that the Soviet model has collapsed both because of external capitalist pressure and because of internal pressures exerted by ever more important educated labor. The states involved are faced with a double and simultaneous transition, to capitalism and to *democracy. This is an awesome task, and it is highly unlikely that all will make the transition successfully. Before the legislative elections of June 1992, one could hope for a Czechoslo-

vakia (with reliable memories of both democracy and industry), fear for a Poland (with memories of an alternate polity), and be scared by a Russia (never possessed of a civil society tradition and now bereft of basic peasant self-reliance). With Czechoslovakia apparently facing dissolution, the prospects for successful double transitions in postcommunist societies seem even bleaker. The fact that authoritarian capitalist regimes, in contrast, face a single transition to democracy gives them better prospects. But here, too, the result is likely to be variable. Latin American states have historically mobilized populations, and this can make the self-control required while decompressing an authoritarian regime difficult to achieve; faced additionally with debt, such states may continue to oscillate between demonstration and *military rule. The prospects in East Asia look correspondingly better, albeit they are better in Taiwan than in the Republic of Korea: the massive concentration of property in the latter undermines basic pluralist pressure.

The single most vital question facing liberals is, however, quite different. Societies such as Brazil and Argentina or Taiwan and the Republic of Korea deserve the appellation "*newly industrializing economies," that is, such countries are, with greater or lesser speed, becoming members of the advanced world. Many societies are not developing at present, and some look likely never to develop: they suffer from massive population increases, a lack of natural resources, corrupt bureaucracies, and, in striking instances, ecological catastrophe. That this is so, of course, offends the most utilitarian aspect of liberalism, that is, the desire to feed people; it rules out key questions of liberal political rule almost completely. A detailed examination of the world economy—in terms of resource, trade, and capital flows—decisively demonstrates that the advanced world does not depend upon most such states, and this explains why they are increasingly ignored. This cannot but worry liberals. If an oil-rich state such as Iraq can get its hand on advanced weapons technologies, it will not be long before even poorer regimes do the same. The misery of much of the world remains a threat as much as a disgrace to the liberal heartland; it is also a threat that must be confronted if liberalism is to survive.

(See also AUTHORITARIANISM; CONSERVATISM; DEMOCRATIC TRANSITIONS; DEVELOPMENT AND UNDERDEVELOPMENT; GEOPOLITICS; SOCIALISM AND SOCIAL DEMOCRACY.)

Barrington Moore, *Social Origins of Dictatorship and Democracy* (Boston, 1966). Robert Paul Wolff, *The Poverty of Liberalism* (Boston, 1968). Isaiah Berlin, *Four Essays on Liberty* (Oxford, 1969). Albert Hirschmann, *The Passions and the Interests: Political Arguments for Capitalism Before Its Triumph* (Princeton, N.J., 1977). Michael Howard, *War and the Liberal Conscience* (Oxford, 1978). Michael Sandel, *Liberalism and the Limits of Justice* (Cambridge, U.K., 1982). Michael Doyle, "Kant, Liberal Legacies, and Foreign Affairs" *Philosophy and Public Affairs* 12, nos. 3 and 4

(1983). Quentin Skinner, "The Idea of Negative Liberty: Philosophical and Historical Perspectives," in R. Rorty, J. B. Schneewood, and Q. Skinner, eds., *Philosophy in History: Essays on the Historiography of Philosophy* (Cambridge, U.K., 1984). John A. Hall, *Liberalism: Politics, Ideology and the Market* (Chapel Hill, N.C., 1988). Nancy Rosenblum, *Liberalism and the Moral Life* (Cambridge, Mass., 1989). José Merquior, *Liberalism: Old and New* (Boston, 1991).

JOHN A. HALL

LIBERATION THEOLOGY. A new current in Christian theology, mainly in Latin America, that first emerged in the 1960s, liberation theology argues that a central element in the message of the Bible is the special duty of the believing Christian to work for the liberation of the poor and oppressed in history. It also criticizes earlier theological writing and teaching as excessively abstract and too supportive of existing power structures.

The description of liberation theology given by the movement's founder, Gustavo Gutiérrez, as "critical reflection on Christian praxis in the light of the Word," contains three important elements in what is claimed to be a new way of doing theology— it is critical of the status quo, it is committed to action by and for the poor, and it is biblically based. In their original formulations, the writings of the liberation theologians emphasized the need for a new hermeneutic, developed out of the experience of the poor. They argued that the insights of social science should be used to identify the causes of oppression and the ways in which they can be removed. In keeping with the views of many Latin American social scientists of the time, the principal cause of Latin American poverty and oppression was seen to be "dependent *capitalism," and the remedy the socialization of the private ownership of the means of production. However, from the outset there was also a commitment to the promotion of "Christian base communities" among the poor in order to enable them to apply biblical insights to their situation of oppression. Liberation theology therefore is both a method of doing theology and an analysis of the social situation of the poor that combines elements of Marxist-influenced *socialism and of grass-roots *populism.

The emergence of liberation theology is rooted in the changes in worldwide Catholicism in the 1960s and the experience of Latin American Christians. The Second Vatican Council (1962–1965) brought the Latin American bishops to Rome for several months each year over a period of four years, and its effort to modernize the church culminated in the adoption of "The Pastoral Constitution on the Church in the Modern World" (*Gaudium et Spes*), which opened the church to other religions and points of view, including those of atheism and *Marxism. In Latin America the challenge of the *Cuban Revolution and the pressures for reform promoted by the Alliance for Progress created a ferment among intellectuals and students that led to an increasingly revolutionary outlook. When the former Catholic chaplain at the National University of Bogotá, Camilo Torres, joined a Marxist guerrilla movement in 1966 and was killed in a confrontation with the Colombian military, many Christians debated the morality of his commitment to *revolution. By 1968 when the Conferencia Episcopal Latinoamerican (CELAM) met at Medellín, Colombia, there was a significant group that considered the situation of the poor in Latin America to be an urgent concern for the church. In the Medellín documents, the bishops called on the church to give "effective preference to the poorest and most needy sectors" and described the situation in many parts of Latin America as one of "injustice that can be called institutionalized violence . . . violating fundamental rights," warning that "the temptation to violence is surfacing in Latin America."

Gustavo Gutiérrez, a Peruvian priest trained in Europe, was an advisor to the bishops and probably wrote the words quoted above. Armed with the legitimation derived from the bishops' statements, he argued that Latin America needed a social revolution and that violence might be required to liberate the poor. In *A Theology of Liberation*, the 1971 book that was the founding document of the movement, Guitérrez identified as the cause of Latin American underdevelopment the domination of the major capitalist countries, especially the United States. He argued that the class struggle was a central fact and neutrality impossible and called upon the church to recognize that loving one's enemies requires recognizing those enemies and the necessity of combatting them. The *class struggle was based on the "dichotomy of capital and labor and the exploitation of man by man" and the solution was social ownership of the means of production.

This revolution was not to be carried out by a Leninist revolutionary elite. Rather, the poor and the oppressed were to be agents of their own liberation through the grass-roots base communities that had already been organized in Brazil and endorsed by the Medellín meeting. Gutiérrez's writings thus combined both structuralist anticapitalism and populist communitarianism and linked both to biblical themes, especially the verse from Isaiah 61 quoted by Christ in Luke 4 when he says that he has come "to preach the good news to the poor (and) to liberate those who are oppressed."

The publication of the Gutiérrez book coincided with a heightening of revolutionary ferment in Latin America. In Chile, the election of Salvador *Allende, a Marxist socialist with the support of one and later two left Christian groups, seemed to typify the kind of cooperation between Marxists and Christians that liberation theology recommended. Other writers such as the Brazilian Hugo Assmann and the Argentinian José Miguez Bonino argued more strongly than Gutiérrez that socialist revolution was the only option for Christians, and the Christians for Socialism movement held a continent-wide meeting in Chile in April 1972. In *The Liberation of Theology*, Juan Luis Segundo of Uruguay endorsed the use of a "hermeneutics of suspicion" to unmask the ideological content of most theological writings.

The movement grew after the overthrow of elected governments in countries such as Chile and Uruguay in the mid-1970s, and it began to receive attention in Europe and the United States. An effort was made by more conservative church leaders to root out the liberation theologians from the CELAM bureaucracy and educational programs, but they demonstrated their influence at the next CELAM meeting in Puebla, Mexico, in 1979. Most of them were not invited to the conference, but operating from outside the meeting they prepared position papers that influenced the content of the Final Document of the Conference, which endorsed "the preferential option for the poor" and declared that "the Church has a duty to proclaim the liberation of millions of human beings among whom are many of the Church's own children." The document also attacked the "free market economy," which makes it possible for small groups, "often tied to foreign interests," to make large profits "while the vast majority of the people suffer."

Yet the bishops did not accept the liberationist position uncritically. Following statements made at the conference opening by *John Paul II, who had been made pope only three months before, the bishops warned of "the risk of ideologization run by theological reflection when it is based on a praxis that has recourse to Marxist analysis," and they denounced the "re-reading of the Gospel on the basis of a political option" involving "a strategic alliance between the Church and Marxism." The meeting also endorsed the Christian base communities but warned against "the theories of the People's Church, born of the people in opposition to the official or institutional church."

The warnings came none too soon, for five months later, on 19 July 1979, a popular uprising headed by the Frente Sandinista de Liberación Nacional (FSLN) ended the forty-year rule of the Somoza family in Nicaragua. In October 1979 a reformist coup in El Salvador overthrew the conservative military, initiating a period of revolutionary upheaval that plunged the country into civil war the following year.

In both countries liberation theology played a role. In Nicaragua it had inspired leading Catholic priests, intellectuals, and students to ally themselves with the *Sandinista movement, despite its known Marxist orientation, because they viewed the alliance as an exercise of the preferential option for the poor. Similarly in El Salvador, when the Frente Farabundo Martí de Liberación Nacional (FMLN) began *guerrilla warfare in 1980, leading Catholic intellectuals and the left wing of the Salvadoran Christian Democratic Party joined the Frente Democrático Revolucionario (FDR), which allied itself with the FMLN. In both countries, the base community movement had also taken on a clearly political character, and in Nicaragua the new Sandinista government supported the "church of the poor" that opposed Archbishop (later Cardinal) Miguel Obando y Bravo when he criticized the Sandinista government. It is possible to exaggerate the direct political influence of liberation theology in Latin America, but in small countries such as those in Central America, which are unstable and uncertain of their future, the conversion of a relatively small group of students, intellectuals, and labor and peasant leaders to the liberationist approach had a significant influence on their *political development. Fidel *Castro himself recognized this in a set of interviews he gave to a Brazilian liberation theologian in support of the establishment of long-term alliances between Marxists and progressive Christians.

In the 1980s the Vatican's Congregation for the Doctrine of the Faith, headed by Cardinal Josef Ratzinger, began to criticize liberation theology. The Brazilian Franciscan, Leonardo Boff, was summoned to Rome in 1984 to explain statements critical of the hierarchy in his book *Church, Charism and Power*, and despite widespread support in Brazil he was ordered to observe "penitential silence" for a year. In the same year the Vatican issued the first of two instructions on liberation theology, warning against the "risks of deviation damaging to the faith and Christian living . . . that are brought about by certain forms of liberation theology which use, in an insufficiently critical manner, concepts borrowed from various currents of Marxist thought," among them "a biblical hermeneutic marked by rationalism" and "a partisan conception of truth."

In 1986, a second Instruction on the subject took a more positive attitude toward aspects of liberationist thought, especially the base communities, "if they really live in unity with the universal church," and theological reflection based on experience, if it is done "in the light of the experience of the church itself." It also admitted that armed struggle might be legitimate "as a last resort to put an end to an obvious and prolonged tyranny" but warned that it could also be "a cause of new forms of slavery." Shortly after the second Instruction was issued, the pope wrote a letter to Brazilian bishops, many of whom had long been supporters of liberation theology, in which he described liberation theology as "not only timely but useful and necessary" provided that it is developed "in full fidelity to church doctrine, attentive to the preferential, but not excluding or exclusive, love for the poor."

The papal statement was a recognition that liberation theology had wide support in Latin America, and that, purged of its Marxist elements, it could be an important way to reach the poor and the oppressed. Leading liberation theologians such as

Gustavo Gutiérrez had already moved in their writings in a more spiritual and communitarian direction, abandoning the earlier calls for revolution. Leonardo Boff had accepted his (temporary) silencing, saying that "I would rather walk with the church than walk alone," and insisting on his orthodoxy on central doctrines such as the Eucharist, the Trinity, and devotion to the Virgin Mary.

In the 1980s elected civilian governments took office in nearly every Latin American country, following a decade of repression in which the hideous violations of *human rights under military regimes had given the Catholic *Left a new appreciation of the values of the "bourgeois" *democracy that they had earlier denounced. As the dreams of an alternative model of socialism perished in the upheavals of Eastern and *Central Europe and the electoral defeat of the Sandinistas, the liberation theologians, like much of the rest of the Latin American Left, gave renewed attention to the need for developing effective grass-roots organizations that could express the needs of the poor and oppressed through democratic institutions. The continuing influence of the movement was affirmed in Brazil in the late 1980s, when mayoral elections in several important cities saw victory go to products of the base community movement, and again in Haiti in 1990, with the landslide victory of Father Jean-Bertrand Aristide in the country's presidential election.

Why did liberation theology show so much more staying power than other comparable movements of the 1960s? One reason may be its proponents' insistence on remaining within the Catholic church (there are some Protestant liberation theologians such as José Miguez Bonino and Rubem Alves, but the overwhelming majority are Catholic), linking their political and economic radicalism with a continuing reliance on the Bible and traditional theological symbols and (reinterpreted) doctrines. Another reason may be that their core teaching, the special concern of Christianity with the poor and oppressed in opposition to the status quo, represented central—but often ignored—elements of the biblical message. Critics may attack the liberationists' flirtations with Marxism and their naïveté about the operation of national and international economics, but an approach that takes account of the radical implications of the Christian message and that is willing to learn, as liberation theology has done, from the experience of the poor and oppressed will have a continuing vitality and appeal.

(See also DEVELOPMENT AND UNDERDEVELOPMENT; RELIGION AND POLITICS; REVOLUTION; ROMAN CATHOLIC CHURCH; VATICAN II.)

Michael Novak, *Will It Liberate? Questions about Liberation Theology* (New York, 1986), Phillip Berryman, *Liberation Theology* (New York, 1987). Arthur F. McGovern, *Liberation Theology and its Critics: Toward an Assessment* (Maryknoll, N.Y., 1989). Paul E. Sigmund, *Liberation Theology at the Crossroads: Democracy or Revolution?* (New York, 1990).

PAUL E. SIGMUND

LIBERIA. By 1867, approximately 20,000 blacks from the United States had colonized this sub-Saharan country based on the American model. Since then Liberia, once a symbol of liberty for freed slaves, has gradually been transformed into one of the most underdeveloped nations in the *Third World. This phenomenon is largely attributed to the deterioration of a political economy structured on the institutionalization of privilege as determined by one's *ethnicity.

Participation in the early government and economic enterprises was confined to the American black elite. Economic activity was based in Monrovia, the capital, for fear that extension into the hinterland would threaten the hegemony of the Americo-Liberians. The signing of a loan agreement between the Firestone Corporation and the government of Liberia in 1927 marked the beginning of American financial supervision and resulted in an influx of investors scrambling for Liberia's cheap and abundant natural resources. By the turn of the century *multinational corporations (MNCs), which enjoyed minimal taxes and maximum repatriation, had practically depleted the major export earnings of iron ore, rubber, and cocoa. These companies whose investments totaled US$425 million as of 1980, began to seek buyers for their concerns and pulled out of the country, because of political instability and dwindling natural resources. The revenue generated from these MNCs had benefited only five to ten percent of Liberians. Increases in GNP were unaccompanied by infrastructural development.

The decline in Liberia's economic system is intertwined with the inconsistencies of its political system. The origins of the governing unit stem from the freed slaves who sought to realize their freedom by adopting and exaggerating Western values and even assumed the role of masters in their new country. A family dynasty evolved and dominated the political sphere well into the period of African *nationalism in the 1960s, when the contradictions of the Liberian elite were revealed. Historically, the Americo-Liberian government silenced the rumblings of discontent which the indigenous population expressed over resident taxes, increasing rice prices, erosion of local autonomy, and the failure to extend privileges. Fiscal mismanagement and nepotism during the administration of Tubman (1944–1971), followed by destabilization under Tolbert (1971–1980), led to *military rule. In spite of *human rights violations under the military regime of Samuel Doe (1980–1990), the United States extended over $50 million to sustain his ten-year tenure.

The displacement of familial rule and the organization of progressive Liberians led to the merging of the general population for a common purpose. That alliance was split through selective indigenous massacres by Doe, and later by rebel groups, so that each faction could gain a consensus of an identifiable stratum of the population. The civil war that ensued in 1990 has devastated the economy and destroyed the infrastructure. Over half of the 2.5 million Liberians have been killed or are displaced refugees in surrounding countries and abroad. A significant aspect of this war, moreover, is the involvement of the Economic Community of West African States (ECOWAS) and its newly created monitoring group, the Economic Community Monitoring Group (ECOMOG). What began as a peacekeeping force evolved into an offensive military intervention in their efforts to establish an interim government. The success of this strategy will have vast implications for the future of African politics.

(See also AFRICAN REGIONAL ORGANIZATIONS.)

Edward Lama Wonkeryor, *Liberia Military Dictatorship: A Fiasco Revolution* (Chicago, 1985).

IFE WILLIAMS-ANDOH

LIBERTARIANISM. Although sometimes used broadly to refer to a strong concern about liberty, irrespective of other political views, the term *libertarianism* is more narrowly applied (especially in the United States) to an intellectual-cum-political movement which revives and develops classical or European *liberalism. Libertarians espouse individualism and free markets. They emphasize the importance of "spontaneous" social order and share a moral repugnance to coercion and the predatory use of the *state. They typically favor a noninterventionist *foreign policy, not only because of their misgivings about foreign adventurism but also because of the link between *war, the growth of the state, and the loss of domestic freedoms. Some libertarians take their opposition to the state to the point of *anarchism.

Contemporary libertarianism, however, is complex. It might be understood as consisting of three loosely interrelated strands. First, there is the academic revival of classical liberalism after World War II. The work of Milton Friedman and Friedrich Hayek played a key role. Other important influences were James Buchanan and Gordon Tullock's *public choice critique of a "benevolent despot" model of government and their account of "rent seeking," as well as the work of many other market-oriented economists; Richard Posner and Henry Manne's work in "law and economics" and Richard Epstein's constitutional jurisprudence; Robert Nozick's *rights-based *Anarchy, State, and Utopia* and the contractarianism of Buchanan; and Thomas Szasz's powerful critique of the abuses of psychiatry.

Second, there is a strongly individualistic current in U.S. culture which has received reinforcement from a variety of intellectual sources. The typical

libertarian's views in the United States have a pedigree that runs variously through later Scholastic thought, the Levellers, John Locke, Thomas Paine, Thomas Jefferson, early French liberalism, Jacksonian social theory, the Manchester liberalism of Cobden and Bright, Herbert Spencer, and Benjamin Tucker. In the twentieth century, the most important sources are H. L. Mencken, Albert J. Nock, "Old Right" isolationism, Ludwig von Mises and "Austrian" free-market economics, and the novelist and philosopher Ayn Rand. An influential contemporary figure is the prolific Murray Rothbard.

Third, there is a more explicitly political libertarian movement. This draws upon a wide diversity of individualistic and nonstatist currents in U.S. life, from opposition to the *Vietnam War and the military draft, through tax resistance and the cause of "hard" money, to the often religiously inspired home schooling movement and those who wish to end the involvement of government in the control of "victimless crimes." A Libertarian Party candidate ran a distant third to the Republicans and the Democrats in the 1988 presidential election.

In the United States there is also an important network of libertarian policy or ideas-related organizations. Internationally, libertarianism has made its impact through the influence of academic work and through an international network of market-oriented public policy institutes. Ideas from such policy institutes—notably about *privatization—have been adopted by governments of a variety of complexions.

Politically, libertarianism is sometimes confused with modern, market-oriented *conservatism. There is a shared emphasis on the market and on the importance of voluntarism, and libertarians have provided an intelligentsia to which conservatives have had recourse, especially on economic issues. Outside the realm of economics, however, libertarians and conservatives have differed sharply regarding foreign policy and issues of individual liberty.

Norman P. Barry, *On Classical Liberalism and Libertarianism* (New York, 1987).

JEREMY SHEARMUR

LIBYA. A desert country in North Africa, Libya emerged as an independent state in 1951. The territory had been seized by Italy shortly before World War I and forged into a single colony during long military campaigns against local tribes between 1911 and 1927.

Over 100,000 Italians came to settle in Libya as part of a Fascist policy of "demographic colonization." The *Mussolini regime, which proudly spoke of Libya as Italy's *Quarta Sponda* or "Fourth Shore," spent 1.8 billion lira to build roads and other infrastructure to strengthen its hold on the colony.

When Allied forces defeated the Axis armies in North Africa in 1942, British and Free French forces occupied Libya and Italy's colonial control came to an end. Between 1942 and 1951, British military administrations controlled Tripolitania and Cyrenaica, while France controlled the Fezzan.

The new state, created as a monarchy at British insistence, was placed under the rule of the religious leader Idris al-Sanusi, a pro-British figure who had lived in exile in Egypt since 1923. At the time of independence, Libya was one of the world's poorest nations. Mostly desert, with only two percent of its territory arable, Libya's major exports were esparto grass and scrap iron from its World War II battlefields. The new state had to depend on foreign aid from Europe and the United States and to accept, in return, *foreign military bases on its soil and a foreign policy that espoused Western interests in the region.

Though Libya had a small population of just 1.1 million, it was not politically coherent or socially homogeneous. The urban mercantile classes of the two major cities—Tripoli and Benghazi—shared in the wider culture of Egypt and the Middle East, while the major tribes of Cyrenaica were still extremely narrow in their outlook: bound to the Sanusi religious order and the monarchy which was based on it.

Many Libyans were very poor and resented their government's subservience to the West. This bred political radicalism, especially among the youth who were increasingly influenced by the radical *Arab nationalism of neighboring Nasserist Egypt.

On 1 September 1969, a group of junior officers overthrew the monarchy; their leader was a young signals captain, Muammar *Qaddafi. The new Revolutionary Command Council was dominated by Qaddafi who, along with many of his comrades, came from the hitherto insignificant region of Sirtica. The new regime soon revealed the strong influence of *Nasserism.

For the next decade, the new political system was in constant evolution, as it changed from radical Arab nationalism tinged with *Islam to the idiosyncratic system of the *jamahiriyah* ("state of the masses"), as outlined in Qaddafi's political treatise, the *Green Book*. During the 1970s, the regime attempted to create a popular power base and to eradicate irredentist support for the previous system among rural populations and in Cyrenaica. In doing so, however, it also alienated large sections of Libyan society.

In 1969 and 1970, in the wake of two failed coup attempts and consequent trials, the royalists went into exile. In April 1973, the Libyan "cultural revolution," proclaimed at Zuwara, forced out the intellectuals and media personalities. In August 1975, a failed army coup led to arrests and executions of young officers who had originally been part of the regime's support base. In September 1976, business and commercial groups began to leave, as "popular sovereignty" and the *jamahiriyah* were proclaimed

to be the basis of Libya's Constitution and the economy was effectively nationalized. In 1977, the Islamic religious establishment and the Qaddafi regime disagreed violently over the role of Islam and in the *jamahiriyah*. By 1980, therefore, there was considerable opposition to the regime, both at home and abroad, as domestic political reform was pushed ahead.

The *jamahiri* system expresses the concept of "direct popular *democracy" and bans political parties as special interest groups that threaten the common purpose of the "people's authority"—Libyan society overall. All Libyans are members of one of the 2,150 Basic Popular Congresses (BPCs) through residential location or professional affiliation. The congresses discuss all local, regional, national, and international policy issues and mandate delegates to the General People's Congress (GPC), which is the equivalent of a parliament and usually meets twice a year, in March and September. The GPC elects the members of the General Popular Committee (cabinet) in which the members, the secretaries (ministers), have specific responsibilities for secretariats (ministries). Local administrative and executive responsibilities devolve into Local Popular Committees, appointed by the BPCs but linked to the appropriate secretariat, which carry out day-to-day administration.

The individual political commitment required by such a system—in which Qaddafi and his close associates have no formal role—was so great that it rapidly fell into decay. In 1978, therefore, the leader created the Revolutionary Committee movement, directly responsible to him and designed to galvanize and control the popular committee system and the armed forces. The Revolutionary Committees also became an instrument of repression and *terrorism when, after February 1980, they were instructed to "eliminate the stray dogs of the revolution," a policy which resulted in a diplomatic breach with Britain in May 1984. Its members were essentially young activists and regime supporters who now also occupy important formal governmental positions. Real power, however, resides in a third, informal level of national political structure, in which members of the tribes to which the leadership belongs—the Warfalla, the Maghara, and, particularly, the Qadadfa—occupy all crucial positions in the administration, economy, and security system.

This domestic radicalism was largely made possible by Libya's massive oil revenues, which reached US$22 billion by 1980, before declining steadily during the 1980s to around US$6 billion today. The revenues paid for development, consumer imports (Libya imports sixty-five percent of the food its 4-million-strong population consumes), arms (US$14 billion to the Soviet Union alone), and a radical foreign policy based on anti-imperialism and *populism, with support for national liberation movements in the Middle East and Africa, such as the *Palestine Liberation Organization, the Front de

Libération Nationale (FROLINAT) in Chad, or the Polisario Front in Western Sahara. Its apparent support for international terrorism and for Iran during the *Iran-Iraq War earned it Western hostility, exemplified by U.S. military attacks in August 1981 and March–April 1986, and isolation in the Middle East and Africa, particularly after defeat by Chad in a border war in March 1987.

Since 1987, Libya has attempted to recover from its diplomatic isolation. It joined the Maghreb Arab Union, alongside Tunisia, Algeria, Morocco, and Mauritania, in February 1989, and has dramatically improved relations with Egypt, Sudan, and Chad. Relations with European states, except Britain, also improved at the end of the 1980s, although the United States has maintained an economic blockade since 1986. Libya also cautiously supported the U.S.-led multinational coalition against Iraq in early 1991, despite considerable domestic opposition. However, U.S., British, and French claims of Libyan responsibility for terrorist attacks on aircraft (Flight PA 103 over the Scottish town of Lockerbie in December 1988 and a UTA DC-10 flight over Niger in September 1989) have ensured that international hostility to the Qaddafi regime endures, despite internal liberalization.

(See also IMPERIALISM; REVOLUTION.)

E. G. H. Joffe and K. S. McLachlan, eds., *Social and Economic Development in Libya* (Wisbech, U.K., 1981). John Wright, *Libya: A Modern History* (London, 1982). René Lemarchand, ed., *The Green and the Black: Qadafhi's Policies in Africa* (Bloomington, Ind., 1988).

GEORGE JOFFÉ

LIECHTENSTEIN. The Principality of Liechtenstein, between Austria and Switzerland, comprises 161 square kilometers (62 sq. mi.) and has a population of about 30,000, mostly Roman Catholic, who speak German in an Alemannic dialect. The economy has, within the last fifty years, changed from agrarian to highly industrialized and service-oriented.

The country was created in 1719 after a prince of Liechtenstein purchased and combined two earldoms, Vaduz and Schellenberg. Its sovereignty was recognized in 1806 as a member of the *Rheinbund* and of the German *Bund* a decade later. Close economic ties existed with Austria until 1919 and were then superseded by a customs union with *Switzerland. Although the Swiss monetary system and postal services are used, Liechtenstein has issued its own postage stamps since 1912. A member of the *International Court of Justice and the *Council of Europe, it has participated in the Helsinki *Conference on Security and Cooperation in Europe. In 1990, Liechtenstein became a member of the UN.

Liechtenstein is a *constitutional monarchy, with Prince Hans Adam II (b. 1945) succeeding his father Franz Josef II (1906–1989). The prince participates in the government and may veto laws passed by the *Landtag*, a parliament of twenty-five members elected by proportional representation. The differences between the two political parties of consequence, the Vaterländische Union and the Fortschrittliche Bürger Partei, are traditional and personality-centered rather than ideological. They have governed in coalition since 1938, with the majority party supplying the *Regierungschef*. Popular referenda are frequent, like the one in 1984 giving women voting rights (on the third attempt).

Walter Kranz, ed., *The Principality of Liechtenstein* (Schaan, Liechtenstein, 1969). Pierre Raton, *Liechtenstein: History and Institutions of the Principality* (Vaduz, Liechtenstein, 1969). Walter S. G. Kohn, *Governments of the German-speaking Countries* (Chicago, 1980).

WALTER S. G. KOHN

LITERACY. *Elites choose a language or languages for important functions, and then they decide how and where to promote literacy in the language just as they make other decisions for their societies and states. Their language policies change less frequently than their tax policies, for example, but both are subject to inputs of group interests and ideologies that change because of shifting social, economic, political, and religious forces from within and from without the society and state. No language policy can be separated from interests and ideologies.

The most important language choice is the officialization of one or more varieties of language, the designation of them as the means of communication with and among governmental institutions and the medium of instruction in state-supported schools. The second most important choice is who will receive institutional help in learning to read and write those languages. Self-instruction is possible, but most look to schools and organized programs for literacy. Elites in the private sector may promote other languages depending on world market forces and doctrines. Such complexity forces individuals to consider their own interests as they decide which languages to learn, if they have a choice.

Officialization is one important gateway to participation. Access to power, wealth, and prestige depends in part on one's ability to speak, read, and write the official tongue, but there other factors, too. High-ranking bureaucrats in Senegal use only French in their written communications. A letter in Wolof would go unanswered unless it were delivered by an emissary of a powerful marabout, or religious leader. If the marabout appeared suddenly in person because neither he nor his advisers could write a single word in any language, the bureaucrats would receive him courteously. His acolytes would not be accorded this reception even if they were literate in French.

Reading and writing the official language is important, but it is only one factor in participation. Put another way, illiteracy is not necessarily a barrier to power, wealth, and prestige. No one who believes in *democracy, human development, and *modernization will approve illiteracy, but it is necessary to moderate the deprecation of illiteracy and the claims made for literacy.

The strongest claims for the benefits of literacy come from scholars, politicians, and intellectuals, particularly those associated with UNESCO, who believe there is a "great divide" between the literate and the illiterate. By this dramatic metaphor they assert that literates have more fully developed intellectual skills: they are better able to analyze, to think abstractly, to plan logically, and to be politically free. Increased economic development or output is possible among literates, as is more equitable distribution. Such a view may serve to limit political *rights for illiterates and to promote a condescending missionary posture among literacy workers.

Countering the "great divide" idea, other scholars and intellectuals have insisted that literacy in and of itself is no guarantee of economic development; nor is there any proof of mental incapacity among illiterates. They have shown through historical example that literacy may be used to enforce conformity as well as to promote change. These scholars might, however, agree with the others that literacy is a human right that international and national institutions should promote when possible.

In fact, the UN and the *World Bank designated 1990 as International Literacy Year. UNESCO took the lead in providing advice and technical assistance to over 100 national committees and many more nongovernmental organizations set up to promote literacy. Beginning with its first literacy plan in 1947, UNESCO has played a key role in numerous efforts to promote reading and writing skills. Its goal now is to "eradicate" illiteracy by the end of the twentieth century—an enormous task given that there are an estimated 900 million illiterate adults, aged 15 and older, and 100 million children younger than 15 without access to schools. The highest rates are in South Asia (53.8%), sub-Saharan Africa (52.7%), and the Arab states (48.7%). Further, according to UNESCO, illiteracy in poor, rural areas exceeds that in urban areas, and women's rates are higher than men's.

Disappointing results of development programs and nation-building processes in these countries have affected the goals and definitions of literacy. Literacy defined as a technology involving the use of the written word is rejected by many. "Functional literacy," first used in 1956, related reading and writing to tasks important to the society; thus literacy depended on the ability to solve problems. Somewhat more than a decade later, "meaningful literacy" was linked with *development. The focus had shifted from the individual to the individual's contribution to the group.

More recent developments include Paulo Freire's concept of "political literacy" and "cultural literacy." According to this school of thought, true literacy comes only with consciousness of the shortcomings of one's society and political system. Increased literacy allegedly will empower citizens and will help free *Third World states from their economic and cultural dependence on industrialized states. Sponsored by the United Nations Development Program, UNESCO, the World Bank, and UNICEF, the March 1990 World Conference on Education for All affirmed the new claims for literacy and education.

These changing definitions and perceived tasks of literacy are a reflection of the shifting concerns and goals of different elites. A study of tax policy would yield similar results. Literacy is an important element in language policy, one of many efforts to shape states and societies according to values and ideals. It can serve the goals of conformity and redemption, socialist and capitalist development, and individual freedom and subordination. At their best such policies are a noble effort of humans to control their destinies.

(See also WOMEN AND DEVELOPMENT.)

Paulo Freire, *The Politics of Education: Culture, Power, and Liberation*, translated by Donald Macedo (South Hadley, Mass., 1985). Kenneth Levine, *The Social Context of Literacy* (London, 1986). Harvey J. Graff, *The Legacies of Literacy: Continuities and Contradictions in Western Culture and Society* (Bloomington, Ind., 1987). *Unesco: Worldwide Action in Education*, International Literacy Year (Paris, 1990). Brian Weinstein, ed., *Language Policy and Political Development* (Norwood, N.J., 1990).

BRIAN WEINSTEIN

LITHUANIA. See BALTIC REPUBLICS.

LOANS, FOREIGN. See INTERNATIONAL DEBT.

LOMÉ CONVENTION. Association between Africa and Europe became formalized in 1958, when France obtained the necessary agreement of its five European partners that its African colonies be granted preferential status under Part IV of the Treaty of Rome in terms of trade, aid, and investments. When the territories gained independence in 1960, it became necessary to renegotiate the association status between the six current member states of the European Economic Community (later the *European Community, or EC) and the eighteen (later nineteen) African Associated and Malagasy States (AAMS). While the first Yaoundé Convention (1964–69) reproduced the Part IV provisions with hardly any modifications, the second (1971–75) introduced minor innovations, still leaving the basic structure of the original agreement intact.

Britain's entry into the EC (January 1973) required that the original agreement, which involved only *Francophone African states, be extended to include its African, Caribbean, and Pacific (ACP) partners within the *Commonwealth. Following a year and a half of negotiations during which the ACP states demonstrated a remarkable degree of cohesion and bargaining skill, the first Lomé Convention was signed on 29 February 1975 between the nine (now twelve) EC member states and the forty-six (now sixty-nine) ACP states.

The Lomé Convention may be defined as a legally binding, contractual agreement of limited duration (initially five, now ten years) based on partnership, reciprocity, and equal benefits between the EC and the ACPs in the areas of trade, commodities, minerals, aid, and agricultural and industrial *development. The Lomé I Convention (1975–80) has since been renegotiated and renewed three times and was followed by the Lomé II (1980–85), Lomé III (1985–1990), and Lomé IV (1990–2000) conventions.

The institutional framework of ACP-EC cooperation includes the Council of Ministers, the Committee of Ambassadors, and the Joint Assembly. The Council of Ministers, whose decisions are binding, is the major decision-making organ of the Lomé Convention; it is composed of representatives of the EC Council of Ministers (plus one delegate of the EC Commission) and of representatives of the ACP governments, and meets annually. The Committee of Ambassadors, which monitors the implementation of the convention, is composed of representatives of each EC member state (plus a representative of the EC Commission) and of representatives of each ACP state; it meets twice a year. The Joint Assembly acts in a purely consultative capacity and is composed of members of the *European Parliament and ACP members of Parliament or other members of the legislature.

In the area of trade, the prevailing rule is that of free and nonreciprocal access to the EC market of almost all ACP export products, abolition of all quantitative restrictions, and gradual elimination of nontariff barriers (NTBs). Excluded from this rule are products subject to the EC's Common Agricultural Policy (such as beef, veal, and dairy products), as well as products falling under a special trade regime (such as bananas, sugar, rum, and textiles). Because of these restrictions and of the EC's restrictive definition of rules of origin, resort to safeguard clauses, and to a broad range of NTBs, ACP exports to the EC stagnated and even declined between 1975 and 1990. In the area of commodities, the system of stabilization of export earnings (STABEX) provides financial compensation to ACP countries in the event that fluctuations in the price or quantity of any of forty-nine stipulated products lead to sharply reduced export earnings. Since its creation, the STABEX system has been plagued by a number of problems and deficiencies: limited product coverage (restricted to unprocessed commodities); a complex and unfavorable method of calculation for transfer entitlement; extreme beneficiary country and product concentration; and insufficient financial allocation. The system approach has been extended into the area of minerals. Thus, the system of stabilization of mineral exports (SYSMIN) is designed to maintain the production capacity of the ACP countries' mining sectors at a viable level and operates when these countries experience a ten percent fall in production and/or export capacity as a result of exceptional events.

The main instrument of ACP-EC cooperation is the aid program subsumed under the label of "financial and technical cooperation." This program includes grants by the European Development Fund (EDF) and loans by the European Investment Bank (EIB) aimed at financing national and regional *development programs and projects in the areas of infrastructure, agriculture, industry, energy, and mining. Among the major problems of financial and technical cooperation are insufficient financial endowment (particularly with regard to the increased number of ACP states and rate of inflation), administrative and procedural problems, and a predominantly "colonial" sectoral distribution of aid (with eighty percent of total aid allocated to infrastructure and commodity production support).

Other areas of ACP-EC cooperation include the environment (including a convention banning the movement of hazardous and radioactive waste between the EC and the ACPs); agricultural cooperation, food security, and *rural development; development of fisheries; industrial development and cooperation (including facilitation of foreign private investment, information exchange, and industrial promotion through joint ventures); development of services (notably in the areas of tourism, transport, communications, and informatics); cultural and social cooperation; and regional cooperation.

Much in the spirit of the *New International Economic Order and of North-South cooperation, the Lomé Convention initially aimed at restructuring the traditional EC-ACP economic division of labor inherited from colonial times, whereby ACPs exported unprocessed commodities and raw materials to Europe in exchange for manufactured goods. Yet most analysts of Euro-African economic relations concur in their opinion that only incremental changes and marginal improvements on specific (formal or technical) aspects of the convention have been introduced over the years; and that the economic and political benefits derived by the ACPs from the arrangement are at best marginal and fall far short of the initial goals and expectations in terms of economic restructuring, transformation, and development. Given that the end of the *Cold War and the advent of the Single European Market in January 1993 are likely to translate into reduced levels of trade, aid, and investment from the EC to Africa, it is debatable whether the marginal economic benefits derived by the ACPs are sufficient to justify their maintaining a permanent and exclusive contractual arrangement with the EC beyond the year 2000.

(See also INTERNATIONAL POLITICAL ECONOMY; NORTH-SOUTH RELATIONS.)

John Ravenhill, *Collective Clientelism: The Lomé Conventions and North-South Relations* (New York, 1985). Alfred Tovias, *The European Communities' Single Market: The Challenge of 1992 for Sub-Saharan Africa*, World Bank Discussion Papers No. 100 (Washington, D.C., 1990). Michael Davenport, *Europe: 1992 and the Developing World* (London and Boulder, Colo., 1991).

GUY MARTIN

LUMUMBA, Patrice. Born in Katako-Kombe, *Zaire, on 2 July 1925, Patrice Lumumba was an autodidact. He began his career in the colonial postal service in 1954 before joining the Kinshasa-based BRACONGO brewery company as a sales manager. Meanwhile, he became a member of various native *elite circles and, later, cofounded and chaired the nationalist party Mouvement National Congolais (MNC). From then on he was a full-time politician, attending conferences such as the All African People's Conference in Accra, Ghana, in 1958, organizing political rallies, and participating as the MNC chief delegate to the Round-Table Conference on Zaire's Independence in Belgium.

After the MNC's victory in the national elections, Lumumba was invested prime minister and minister of defense of the coalition government to run the country at independence on 30 June 1960. Three months later, Lumumba faced the first constitutional crisis in a conflict opposing him to the head of state, Joseph Kasavubu, which prompted an attempt by Mobutu, then a colonel and the army's chief of staff, to neutralize both parties. Later, Mobutu ordered Lumumba's arrest, imprisonment, and transfer to the Katanga (now Shaba) province where he was summarily executed on 17 January 1961. He was 35.

Lumumba was a controversial person. While his friends admired him as a nationalist leader, his enemies simply considered him a communist, a demagogue, and a dangerous man. Lumumba's posthumous book *Congo, My Country*, however, portrays a gradually maturing politician whose ideas and experience changed as he faced new challenges and met new people.

Lumumba's closest friends and advisers divide his political life into three phases. During the first phase, Lumumba, like most *évolués*—the colonially created group of Zairian elite—believed in the "Belgian civilizing mission" in Zaire and wanted to achieve a constructive synthesis between Western and African values. The second phase began shortly before Zaire's independence. Disappointed by the Belgian reluctance to grant equal rights, Lumumba began to shift toward an increasingly nationalist position. He was then inspired by such radical African leaders as Kwame *Nkrumah of Ghana, Sékou Touré of Guinea, and Gamal Abdel *Nasser of Egypt. The last phase started at independence and ended with his assassination two hundred days later. During that time, Lumumba had become "a lonely man in power." Though democratically elected, he had to face numerous obstacles from internal rivals and major Western democracies. Among the latter were the Eisenhower administration in the United States and most European interests in Zaire.

It is hard to predict what Zaire would have been had Lumumba been able to consolidate his power. However, it is certain that his nationalist ideal, his struggle to keep his country unified, strong, and prosperous, his anticolonial and nonaligned stance, and his position in favor of a united Africa had a strong appeal throughout Africa and beyond. Lumumba's political philosophy still resonates in Zaire today.

(See also CONGO CRISIS; DECOLONIZATION; NATIONALISM.)

Patrice Lumumba, *Congo, My Country* (London, 1962). Thomas Kanza, *The Rise and Fall of Patrice Lumumba: Conflict in the Congo* (London, 1978).

MUSIFIKY MWANASALI

LUSOPHONE AFRICA. See ANGOLA; CAPE VERDE; GUINEA-BISSAU; MOZAMBIQUE; SÃO TOMÉ AND PRÍNCIPE.

LUXEMBOURG. The Grand Duchy of Luxembourg, which is a relatively recent entity (its title dates back to 1315, its current boundaries and independence to 1839, and the accession of the House of Nassau-Weilburg to 1890) has preserved from its more distant past a culture marked by its dual Romano-Germanic roots and by a strong attachment to Catholicism despite the upheaval caused by the Reformation. With 370,000 inhabitants, it is today the smallest member state of the *European Community (EC) and of the North Atlantic Treaty Organization (NATO).

History has not been kind to Luxembourg, whose existence has been called into question after each international crisis. This was particularly the case after the German occupation during World War I and the brutal Germanization at the hands of the Nazi regime between 1940 and 1944, when the Grand Duchess Charlotte and the government supported the Allies. After World War II, the Grand Duchy became an active participant in the process of forming economic and political union within Europe. As early as 1944, it joined with Belgium and the Netherlands to found an economic union (Benelux).

Modern metallurgy was the vector of the Industrial Revolution in Luxembourg. The iron and steel industry, initially dominated by family businesses, graduated to limited companies and then large industrial groups (Aciéries Réunies de Burbach, Eich et Dudelange [ARBED]). The iron and steel industry halted traditional emigration flows and then stimulated immigration, first of Italians and then of Portuguese. Consequently, the worldwide crisis in the steel sector in the 1970s hit the country extremely hard. All economic and social structures rested on this basic industry, and the very existence of the country was affected. A tripartite committee consisting of the ARBED management, the government, and the trade unions (the "Luxembourg model") coordinated orderly cutbacks, and modernization was achieved without recourse to dismissals of redundant employees.

The Luxembourg economy, which was the only one in the EC to survive the crisis without significant unemployment (it has never exceeded two percent) and with a relatively high per capita income, revolves around two other main sectors. Luxembourg is the headquarters for one of the major European telecommunications groups, the Compagnie Luxembourgeoise de Télédiffusion (CLT). It is also a leading financial market.

Luxembourg, which has a monetary union with Belgium (the Belgo-Luxembourg Economic Union), is a free exchange area for European currencies with no form of credit control. Although there is a great deal of concern about the effects of the forthcoming free movement of capital and tax harmonization within the EC, the Grand Duchy is counting on the country's calm labor situation and political stability to attract foreign investors.

Luxembourg is a *constitutional monarchy and a *parliamentary democracy. Universal suffrage for men and women was introduced in 1919. The political parties still bear the traces of the ideological struggles from which they emerged. Five parties are represented in Parliament. The Chrëstlech-Sozial Vollekspartei (CSV), the Letzeburger Sozialistesch Arbechterpartei (LSAP), and the liberals of the Demokratesch Partei (DP) are the traditional groups. They are joined by the Kommunistesch Partei vu Letzeburg (KPL)—which is a minority grouping rapidly dying out—and the ecologists Déi Greng Alternativ (GAP). The green movement, although divided and not so strong as in Germany, for example, reflects the concern of the general public about the French Cattenom nuclear power plant, built near the Luxembourg border.

Coalition governments are the rule. With two brief exceptions—in 1925 and in 1974–1979, when a liberal socialist government was led by Gaston Thorn—the CSV has led the government in coalition with either the LSAP or the DP. Since the 1984 elections, when Pierre Werner gave up his post of prime minister to Jacques Santer (his favored successor in the CSV), a Christian-Socialist coalition, which rewon public support in the 1989 elections, has formed the Luxembourg government.

Since the middle of the 1980s, the Luxembourg economy has been in excellent health, and even the steel industry has been profitable. On 19 June 1990, Luxembourg, Belgium, the Netherlands, France, and the Federal Republic of Germany signed the Schengen Convention, which is intended to abolish border controls for individuals between the five countries. But paradoxically, although the Grandy Duchy was one of the pioneers of European unification, the single market is a source of concern to Luxembourg because it threatens its status as a tax haven. In a more positive vein, however, the EC institutions, particularly the Court of Justice, add a further element to Luxembourg's character as a European melting pot. The Grand Duchy has, nevertheless, held on to its heritage and has built harmonious labor relations and a tradition of political consensus that it considers a model for its European neighbors.

Gilbert Trausch, *Le Luxembourg à l'époque contemporaine* (Luxembourg, 1981).

MATEO ALALUF

M

MACAO. Macao lies 50 kilometers (30 mi.) west of *Hong Kong, at the mouth of the Pearl River. Macao's harbor, unlike Hong Kong's, is very shallow; the lack of a good harbor was a key impediment to Macao's economic growth. The enclave was settled by the Portuguese in 1557 to provide a base for trade with *China. In 1951 it was declared an overseas province of Portugal.

In 1967 and again in 1974, the Portuguese tried to hand Macao back to China, but the offer was refused mainly out of fear of the repercussions in neighboring Hong Kong. Lisbon then redefined Macao as a Chinese territory under Portuguese administration.

The enclave has since come under heavy Chinese and local business influence, and the administration has become nothing more than a façade propped up by several hundred Portuguese officials. Essential welfare and educational facilities are primitive and inadequate. Corruption is rampant. The major economic activity is gambling.

In April 1987, the Chinese and Portuguese governments signed the Sino-Portuguese Joint Declaration on the Future of Macao, under which Macao would become a special administrative region of China in 1999. Although the accord contained guarantees of autonomy similar to that of the 1984 Sino-British agreement on Hong Kong, few find these guarantees believable.

In spite of past maladministration, the Portuguese government's handling of the future of Macao was praised by the international community, especially when measured against Britain's treatment of the people of Hong Kong. The 100,000 Macao people who are Portuguese citizens—one-quarter of the population—will continue to hold Portuguese nationality after 1999 and will retain the right to live in Portugal.

"Asia Yearbook," *Far Eastern Economic Review* (1991).
EMILY LAU

MACEDONIA. See YUGOSLAVIA.

MADAGASCAR. The Democratic Republic of Madagascar, located some 350 kilometers (220 mi.) east of Mozambique, is about the same geographic size as France and has a population of about 11 million. Despite a relatively diversified resource base in comparison with many African countries, Madagascar is still one of the world's poorest countries. Consumer welfare has been declining almost continuously since independence. Inflation, for example, has been high during the past decade as indicated by a doubling of the general price index during the 1980s. Conversely, food consumption per head has generally declined.

Madagascar became a French protectorate in 1890 and gained autonomy in the French Union in 1958. Madagascar made a peaceful transition to independence in 1960 under its first president, Philibert Tsiranana. By the early 1970s there was growing dissatisfaction with the conservative and somewhat authoritarian Tsiranana regime. After a series of strikes and riots in the capital, Antananarivo, Tsiranana turned over the government to the armed forces. By 1975 political unrest and a mutiny by the police in the capital, resulting principally from declining economic conditions, led to another change of government headed by Lieutenant Commander Didier Ratsiraka, who has retained power throughout the intervening period.

Following his major policy statement (the Charter of the Malagasy Socialist Revolution), Ratsiraka nationalized the banks, mines, oil refinery, and shipping company, and closed the U.S. satellite tracking station. He continued with a military-style government. The government has been organized around the head of state (the president), who is directly elected for a seven-year term. The Supreme Revolutionary Council is "the Guardian of the Malagasy Socialist Revolution," whose members are chosen by the president. The National People's Assembly is composed of members elected for five-year terms. The Military Development Committee oversees national security and economic development programs. Madagascar maintains an army of 20,000 personnel, a 500-person navy and air force, and military service of eighteen months is compulsory. Madagascar's local government is composed of six provinces and 110 prefectures.

Social and political unrest grew in the late 1970s, again due primarily to economic concerns, this time in the drought-stricken rural areas. Riots followed in 1981. The radical Ratsiraka regime began to eliminate organized dissent during this period. After the president announced his intent to run for a second term of office, Madagascar experienced increased social and economic unrest. Compliance with the strict terms of the *International Monetary Fund (IMF) caused higher prices in urban areas. After riots again broke out in the capital the government suppressed virtually all opposition. Food shortages again sparked riots in the rural areas, mostly in southern Madagascar in the late 1980s. In 1989 Ratsiraka was elected to a third term in a somewhat fair election, at least compared with the previous two. By 1990, and after considerable domestic and international pressures, Madagascar officially allowed other parties to contest elections and generally engage in political debate. Nevertheless, Madagascar's political stability remained precarious into the 1990s.

Madagascar's economic situation remains troubled. Madagascar ranks as one of the world's twelve poorest states. During the 1980s the GNP per capita declined by about 3.4 percent annually, with a current GNP per capita of perhaps US$200. During the same period, the population was increasing at about three percent. Madagascar's population has more than doubled since 1950, and by the year 2000 the population will reach an estimated 16 million. Probably half of the population is under 20 years old.

Almost three-fourths of the working population is engaged in agriculture, most at the subsistence level, although this percentage has declined slightly in recent years. Agriculture is the country's largest source of foreign exchange (as much as eighty percent of the total). It provides most of the population's food needs and also supplies much of the raw material for the manufacturing sector. Agriculture declined precipitously in the 1970s and 1980s due to inappropriate government agricultural policies, droughts, and four cyclones. Rice is the most important food crop; in fact, Madagascar has the highest per capita consumption of rice in the world. Production has fallen steadily behind consumption.

After three decades of state intervention and economic decline, Madagascar began to liberalize its economic policies in the mid-1980s. In 1986, it launched a new investment code which encouraged private foreign and domestic investment. The Malagasy franc has been devalued and the government has successfully negotiated agreements with its major official and private creditors at the London Club and the *Paris Club. The government also began to close state-run enterprises which were running at a loss.

Madagascar's *foreign policy has undergone significant changes of direction. Madagascar's initial foreign policy after independence was conservative, and it gave the West (particularly France) virtually uncritical support. It broke with France over only a few issues, such as maintaining diplomatic recognition of Taiwan even after France's acceptance of the People's Republic of China (PRC). After Tsiranana's regime ended in the early 1970s, the new government under Ratsiraka established diplomatic relations with the Soviet Union, PRC, and Arab nations and took on a radical stance regarding North-South and East-West issues. It withdrew from the Franc Zone in 1973. Ratsiraka's cornerstone policy was the "Indian Ocean Zone of Peace" initiative, supporting nonalignment and a demilitarization of the area. Madagascar moved closer to the Soviet Union, and generally supported the Eastern bloc in the UN and other international fora. Nevertheless, Madagascar did not grant naval rights to the Soviets at the major port of Diégo Suarez. Madagascar established close ties with the Democratic People's Republic of Korea (North Korea), and Ratsiraka even created a personal bodyguard composed mainly of Korean soldiers. Relations with the West in the early 1970s were cold, and Madagascar in fact broke relations with the United States over an alleged plot to overthrow the government. A new U.S. ambassador was not appointed until 1980.

Although it criticized the IMF, Madagascar negotiated standby agreements with the Fund in the early 1980s, with conditions requiring an opening up of the economy and a general move away from state intervention. Madagascar received economic support from multilateral institutions such as the *World Bank, and bilateral aid from some key Arab states (Libya and Algeria) and France. As an indication of how much Ratsiraka had moved from his previous radical position, the South African president made a visit to Madagascar in 1990 when the two countries concluded a commercial cooperation agreement.

Madagascar has accumulated sizable foreign debt, of which forty-two percent is owed to member countries of the *Organization for Economic Co-operation and Development, twenty percent to international organizations, and eleven percent to commercial banks. Madagascar's debt service ratio has worsened, from only four percent in 1978 to an estimated eighty-six percent by the early 1990s. Western nations are Madagascar's major trading partners. France alone accounted for thirty-three percent of Madagascar's exports and twenty-six percent of its imports in 1988.

(See also INDIAN OCEAN REGION; INTERNATIONAL DEBT.)

Nigel Heseltine, *Madagascar* (New York, 1971). Harold D. Nelson, *Area Handbook for the Malagasy Republic* (Washington, D.C., 1973). International Monetary Fund, *Madagascar—Recent Economic Developments* (Washington, D.C., 1984). Maureen Covell, *Madagascar: Politics, Economics and Society* (London, 1987).

DONALD L. SPARKS

MALAWI. A small landlocked country in southeast Africa, Malawi has a population of 8 million and a per capita income of US$160, making it one of the poorest countries in the world. Agriculture is the chief economy, accounting for ninety percent of export earnings. Its timely debt repayments and implementation of Western economic prescriptions enable Malawi to receive modest sums of foreign aid from Western governments and multilateral lending agencies.

An estimated thirty-five percent of the population observe African traditional beliefs, fifty percent are Christians, and fifteen percent Muslims. English is the official business language, while Chewa, one of about a dozen local languages, is the national language.

Britain declared the country a protectorate in 1891 under the name British Central Africa, but renamed it Nyasaland in 1907. In 1915 John Chilembwe, an American-educated reverend, fomented a rebellion in which three whites and forty blacks were killed. This marked the beginning of the nationalist struggle. In 1944 Africans formed the Nyasaland African Congress (NAC) to press for economic and social reforms, but not independence. That changed, however, when white settlers in Southern Rhodesia (now *Zimbabwe), Northern Rhodesia (*Zambia), and Nyasaland, with the endorsement of Britain, formed the Federation of Rhodesia and Nyasaland in 1953. The NAC quickly opposed it, fearing that the federation would further subjugate blacks under white rule, and seized the opportunity to demand secession and independence. Opposition increased when Hastings Kamuzu Banda, a physician and strong critic of the federation, arrived in the country in 1958, after forty years in the United States, Britain, and Ghana, to lead the struggle.

On 6 July 1964 the country became an independent state under the name Malawi, with Banda as prime minister. In 1966 Malawi became a republic under Banda's presidency. In 1971 Banda became president-for-life. Malawi is governed by a parliamentary system in which all candidates must be members of the single ruling Malawi Congress Party and must be approved by the president. Party policies are enforced mainly through the Young Pioneers and the Youth League, both paramilitary groups, and women's organizations.

Tension within the predominantly Chewa army, and between the army and the paramilitary groups, has been deftly defused by the president by playing the politics of tribalism, often targeting the well-educated northerners as the source of the nation's problems. The president denies the charges.

In 1964 a cabinet crisis over internal and external policies led the president to dismiss three ministers, and three others resigned in sympathy. In 1965 Henry Chipembere, former minister of education, led a coup attempt and subsequently escaped to the United States. In 1967 Yatuta Chisiza, former minister of home affairs, was killed while leading a guerrilla insurgency into the country. The three main

opposition groups in exile are: the Socialist League of Malawi (LESOMA), the Malawi Freedom Movement (MAFREMO), and the Congress for the Second Republic of Malawi. In June 1991 they became part of the United Front for Multiparty Democracy (UFMD), an umbrella organization formed in Lusaka, Zambia.

The military is composed of the army (7,000 members), marines (100), and air force (150). Military bases are in each of the nation's three regions.

In 1967 Malawi became the first African state to establish diplomatic relations with white-governed South Africa. Generally, the country keeps a low profile in international affairs and in international organizations of which it is a member, namely, the UN, the *Organization of African Unity, and the *Southern African Development Co-ordination Conference. However, because of gross human rights violations and the lack of a democratic government, Western donor countries cut off aid to Malawi in May 1992.

(See also SOUTHERN AFRICA.)

Robert I. Rotberg, *The Rise of Nationalism in Central Africa: The Making of Malawi and Zambia, 1873–1964* (Cambridge, Mass., 1965). Africa Watch Report, *Where Silence Rules: The Suppression of Dissent in Malawi* (New York, 1990).

WALUSAKO A. MWALILINO

MALAYSIA. Comprising Peninsular Malaysia, previously known as Malaya, which lies at the southeastern tip of the Asian continental landmass, and Sabah and Sarawak, which occupy the northwestern flank of the island of Borneo, to the east of Peninsular Malaysia, Malaysia has a population of about 18 million, of which about four-fifths is in Peninsular Malaysia. The indigenous Muslim-Malay community constitutes almost three-fifths of the population on the peninsula, with ethnic Chinese accounting for a third and ethnic Indians for a tenth. In Sabah and Sarawak, however, while the Chinese proportion is roughly the same, there are few Indians, and Muslim Malays are a minority. Instead, other non-Muslim indigenous minorities predominate.

The boundaries of the federation of Malaysia today have existed since 9 August 1965, when the island republic of Singapore seceded. The eleven states of the earlier Federation of Malaya gained independence from Britain on 31 August 1957. On 16 September 1963, Singapore and the Bornean states of Sabah (previously North Borneo) and Sarawak merged with Malaya to form Malaysia.

After centuries of Hindu-Malay rule, a Muslim maritime empire based in Malacca was established in the early fifteenth century. In 1511, Malacca was captured by the Portuguese before falling into Dutch hands in 1641. The British East India Company colonized Penang in 1786 and Singapore in 1819, and gained control of Malacca with the Napoleonic

Wars in Europe. The division of Southeast Asia into broad European spheres of influence dates back to the Anglo-Dutch Treaty of 1824 in which can be found the origins of contemporary divisions between Indonesia and the rest of "Malay" Southeast Asia.

Colonization of the peninsular hinterland, fueled initially by the British desire to control tin mining, began in 1874. Sarawak came under the control of the Brooke family while the North Borneo Chartered Company gained control of Sabah from the second half of the nineteenth century. The colonization process was completed by the outbreak of World War I.

Varied British administrative arrangements continued in Peninsular Malaysia until the Japanese invasion in late 1941. After the Japanese occupation, the British unsuccessfully tried to introduce a Malayan Union arrangement in 1946 after an initial period of British military administration. In 1948, the Federation of Malaya arrangement emerged instead and, in 1955, the first elections were held for a federal legislature in anticipation of independence in 1957.

Although Malaya, as the world's leading exporter of tin and rubber, had long been Britain's most lucrative colony, pressures from a communist-led insurgency, militant labor organizations, and other nationalist groups, in addition to the new postwar international situation, ensured independence from the British. Nonetheless, the relatively smooth transfer of power to the Malayan elite prepared the way for a heavy British imprint on postcolonial forms of government and political institutions.

Malaysia is a constitutional monarchy in which nine of thirteen states have hereditary rulers (sultans) dating back to the colonial era, often claiming legitimacy from the precolonial period. Since 1957, these rulers have taken turns serving as king, or *Yang Di Pertuan Agong*, for five-year terms. The remaining states have constitutional governors who are also appointed for renewable five-year terms.

At the federal level, there is a bicameral parliament comprising the *Dewan Rakyat* (Lower House) and the *Dewan Negara* (Senate). The *Dewan Rakyat* consists of elected members of parliament from constituencies greatly varying in size, both geographically and demographically, with the registered voting population in the largest constituencies more than ten times that in the smaller constituencies. Members of the Senate are nominated by the federal and state governments. The states have legislative assemblies, except for the Federal Territory of Kuala Lumpur, the national capital. Municipal elections, which were largely won by opposition parties, have been discontinued since the mid-1960s.

The executive is led by the prime minister, who invariably has also been president of the United Malays National Organisation (UMNO), which has dominated the National Front ruling coalition. Except for Sabah, Sarawak, and Penang, and, for a time, Kelantan (1959 to 1978) and Trengganu (briefly in the early 1960s), the state governments also have been led by state UMNO leaders appointed by the UMNO national president. Except for the Kelantan and Trengganu governments, which were once led by the Islamic Party (Parti Islam SeMalaysia, or PAS), all other state governments have belonged to the ruling coalition dominated by UMNO.

Public administration has been dominated by the civil service inherited from the colonial period, although there has been considerable Americanization since the mid-1960s. There are also professional services linked to many ministries and government departments as well as state civil services. Legally independent of the federal and state governments are various statutory bodies.

From independence and especially after the declaration of the New Economic Policy (NEP) in 1971, a number of government-financed enterprises—many of which were ostensibly committed to redistributive goals—were set up under the Companies Act. The second phase of British colonization in the late nineteenth century transformed Malaya into a major exporter of tin and then rubber. After independence, diversification was encouraged through *import-substitution industrialization and through other primary commodity exports such as palm oil, timber, petroleum, cocoa, and petroleum gas. Export-oriented industrialization became the priority from the late 1960s, except for a brief flirtation with heavy industrialization for the domestic market in the early 1980s.

Malaysia has enjoyed fairly rapid economic growth since independence, especially throughout much of the 1970s and late 1980s. However, the economic wealth of the country has been rather unevenly distributed along class, ethnic, and regional lines, which has led to dissatisfaction and ethnic and regional political mobilization, as well as to various policies ostensibly designed to ameliorate these inequalities. Post-election race riots in May 1969 opened the way to some political realignment and the introduction of the NEP, which aimed to create the socioeconomic conditions for national unity—defined primarily in terms of improved Malay/non-Malay relations—by reducing poverty and enhancing the economic position of Malays in order to reduce interethnic differences.

With the weakening of the communist-led insurgency in the mid-1950s and the repression of the parliamentary *Left in the mid-1960s, there has been virtually no opposition other than ethnic political mobilization. Despite significant poverty reduction and improvement of Malay economic status, the implementation of the NEP has exacerbated rather than reduced interethnic tensions. Uneven regional development has heightened regional resentment toward the federal government, especially in Sabah and Sarawak.

Meanwhile, rapid economic growth and capitalist

development have greatly increased the proportion of wage earners in the labor force, mainly at the expense of the self-employed peasantry. However, only a sixth of wage employees, mainly in the public sector, are unionized. Consequently, class-based and other social movements are rather weak, especially in the face of overriding ethnic divisions.

Both support for and opposition to the government have largely been channeled through ethnic mobilization. Since the 1970s, the opposition has centered around the ethnic Chinese–based Democratic Action Party (DAP) and the ethnic Malay–based Islamic Party (PAS), except for a brief period when the latter joined the ruling coalition in the mid-1970s.

However, division in UMNO since the mid-1980s and a court order in February 1988 declaring UMNO unlawful because of electoral irregularities resulted in the formation of a rival faction known as the Spirit of 46. The Spirit of 46 has, in turn, forged links with all existing opposition parties, resulting in the virtual emergence of a two-coalition situation. Hence, for the first time in postcolonial history, the opposition has a reasonable chance of posing a threat to the ruling coalition, which has governed without serious challenge at the federal level and in most states since independence. Ethnic and religious tensions, regional frustrations, and the new bipolar political situation will probably continue to animate Malaysian politics and culture for some time to come.

The Malay-dominated armed forces have not threatened political stability, and are unlikely to do so, at least as long as Malay political dominance continues. However, since the peace treaty with the communist-led insurgents in December 1989, the traditional concern of the army and the police with communist insurgency has undergone substantial reorientation.

U.S. influence has grown, especially since the mid-1960s. Malaysia supported important *Third World initiatives in the early and mid-1970s (e.g., Chinese entry into the UN, the call for a *New International Economic Order, and sanctions against the governments of Israel and South Africa). Malaysia also played a crucial role in the *Association of Southeast Asian Nations (ASEAN) declaration of Southeast Asia as a zone of peace, freedom, and neutrality (ZOPFAN).

Since the early 1980s, the government under Mahathir has favored Japan, particularly to support its industrialization efforts and to secure external financing. Since the late 1980s, there has been a strong interest in attaining a higher profile in international forums such as the UN, the *Commonwealth, the *Nonaligned Movement, the Muslim world, and ASEAN.

(See also ETHNICITY; ISLAM.)

Jomo K. S., *A Question of Class: Capital, the State and Uneven Development in Malaya* (Singapore, 1986). Gordon Means, *Malaysian Politics: The Second Generation* (Singapore, 1991).

JOMO KWAME SUNDARAM

MALCOLM X. More than a generation after his death, Malcolm X remains one of the most controversial black figures of the twentieth century. He was born in Omaha, Nebraska, on 19 May 1925, the seventh of eleven children. His father, Earl Little, was reportedly an enthusiastic supporter of Marcus Garvey's United Negro Improvement Association. Malcolm Little attended school in East Lansing, Michigan, but dropped out in the eighth grade when his family moved to Boston. Involvement in criminal activities in Roxbury and Harlem resulted in 1946 in a ten-year prison sentence for burglary and larceny. Prison was a transforming experience for Malcolm. While serving his sentence he was introduced by his younger brother Reginald to the Lost-Found Nation of Islam (known popularly as the Black Muslims) led by the Honorable Elijah Muhammad. Malcolm became a devout supporter of the Nation and changed his surname to X to symbolize his transformation into an "ex-smoker, ex-drinker, ex-Christian, ex-slave." In prison, he also embarked upon a process of self-education. Beginning by copying words out of a dictionary, he progressed to reading works on history, philosophy, and anthropology.

After being paroled in 1952, Malcolm became an eloquent member of the Nation of Islam, whose doctrines suggested that the white race was on the verge of being destroyed by God and that Elijah Muhammad would lead the black race to safety in a separate state. Malcolm founded mosques in Boston, Philadelphia, and Harlem and started the newspaper *Muhammad Speaks*. He was soon elevated to the position of national spokesman and awarded Mosque Number 7 in Harlem, the second most important mosque of the Nation of Islam. Courteous and soft-spoken in private, Malcolm proved to be a fiery and provocative public speaker. In spite (or perhaps because) of his message that all white people were "devils" and the satisfaction he took in stories of white suffering, many young whites as well as blacks responded sympathetically to his apocalyptic language, and he was frequently invited to speak before predominantly white audiences. Malcolm was extremely critical of black leaders. He denounced integration, the nonviolent philosophy of Martin Luther *King, Jr., and the more traditional *civil rights movement, which he characterized as a "mealy-mouth, wait-in, beg-in, plead-in kind of action." Instead, Malcolm defended the legitimacy of violent reaction by blacks against their common white oppressor and against racial injustice. Although in the last months of his life he made overtures of friendship to mainstream civil rights leaders, many continued until his death to be wary of him.

In 1963, a rupture developed between him and

Elijah Muhammad, allegedly because of Malcolm's remark that President John F. *Kennedy's *assassination in November of that year was a case of "chickens coming home to roost." Malcolm left the Nation of Islam in 1964 and founded his own organizations, the first of which was the Muslim Mosque, Inc. He made a pilgrimage to Mecca in 1964, followed by travels later that year to the *Middle East and Africa, where he was warmly received. As a result of his pilgrimage, he renounced his allegiance to the Nation of Islam and converted to orthodox *Islam. He adopted the Muslim name El-Hajj Malik El Shabazz and denounced Elijah Muhammad as a "racist" and "faker." In 1965, he founded the Organization of Afro-American Unity. Malcolm was assassinated while giving a speech at the Audubon Ballroom in Harlem on 21 February 1965. Three Black Muslims were convicted of his murder in March 1966. More than a decade later, one of them gave sworn testimony confirming that Malcolm had been assassinated by the Nation of Islam, although the Nation has continued to deny involvement in his death.

Malcolm's *Autobiography,* written with his co-operation by Alex Haley (author of *Roots*), appeared nine months after Malcolm's death. The book was instrumental in transforming Malcolm X in the public imagination from demagogue to the foremost spokesman of radical black nationalism, referred to generally as the "Black Power movement." The continuing controversy over and interest in Malcolm X reflects the complexity of the man himself: charismatic, restless, and articulate. Fascination with Malcolm X's life and thought continues, and by the early 1990s he had become an icon in American cultural life. A movie of his life was completed by the director Spike Lee in 1992.

(See also AFRICAN AMERICANS; NONVIOLENT ACTION; RACE AND RACISM.)

Alex Haley and Malcolm X, *The Autobiography of Malcolm X* (New York, 1973).

ROWENA OLEGARIO

MALDIVES. The Maldives has been a traditionally insular state in the Indian Ocean with a fragmented geography and an independent polity. In the 1970s, however, the Maldives dramatically increased its diplomatic contacts and active participation in international and regional forums. Such a significant expansion in Maldivian foreign relations underscores the imperatives of socioeconomic development and trade for a country that is among the least developed countries in the world. Additionally, it emphasizes the Maldives' need for establishing a politico-cultural identity as a modern, Islamic nation-state.

The Republic of Maldives has a population of approximately 214,000 and lies roughly 820 kilometers (512 mi.) southwest of India in a chain of 1,200 coral islands. Its geostrategic location in the *Indian Ocean region has given it the impetus to pursue a nonaligned policy and to support the declaration of the Indian Ocean as a zone of peace. As a member of the *South Asian Association for Regional Cooperation, the Maldives, under the guidance of President Maumoon Abdul Gayoom (reelected to a third term in 1988), has gained considerable political visibility and regional recognition.

Virtually independent throughout its history, the Maldives emerged as a sovereign nation in 1965, marking the end of its 1887 protectorate pact with the British. With the formation of the Second Republic in 1968, the sultanate, created with the conversion of the population to *Islam in 1153, was finally abolished. With this event, the Maldives entered its contemporary phase of national politics.

The present system of governance is highly centralized and has its roots in the oligarchic structure of the sultanate. For the most part, Maldivian politics is dominated by an elite drawn from a few influential families who frequently command considerable support among the population of the 200 inhabited islands.

The Gayoom administration follows the institutional framework outlined in the 1968 constitution, which calls for the functional separation of the executive, legislative, and judicial branches of government. The political infrastructure is a unique blend of traditional modes of governance and modern concepts of state, based primarily on Islamic principles. For instance, in the Maldivian criminal justice system, banishment, a customary form of punishment, continues to prevail along with imprisonment.

The president is the chief executive and, in the absence of political parties, is nominated by the members of the Citizens' Majlis—the unicameral legislature—and confirmed in a nationwide referendum. Forty-eight members serve five-year terms in the Majlis—two representatives from each of the nineteen administrative atolls, two from Malé (the capital), and eight appointed by the president. The cabinet ministers are presidential appointees, directly responsible to the president for the functioning of the ministries and departments under their control. Local atoll administrations have a hierarchical structure headed by the *atol veriya* (atoll chief), who is aided by the *khatib* (island headman) and the latter's deputy, the *kuda khatib.*

Socioeconomic inequities, an outcome of rapid development, and traditional rivalries have spawned pockets of political dissent against the present government. In response, President Gayoom has attempted to walk a political tightrope between factional groups, promoting a relatively consensual mode of governance that promises to be pivotal to the Maldives' democratic future.

Urmila Phadnis and Ela Dutt Luithui, *Maldives: Winds of Change in an Atoll State* (New Delhi, 1985).

SUDESHNA BAKSI-LAHIRI

MALI. The Republic of Mali (formerly French Sudan) is a Sahelian, land-locked former French colony in West Africa with a land area of approximately 1.24 million square kilometers (475,000 sq. mi.) and a population estimated at 8.2 million in 1990. During that year GDP stood at US$2.5 billion, while GNP per capita was $271. The capital city is Bamako (population 700,000), and *Islam is the dominant religion.

Mali gained independence from France on 20 June 1960 as the two-country Mali Federation (Senegal and Mali). The federation broke up on 20 August 1960, and on 22 September 1960 the dominant party, the Union Soudanaise–Rassemblement Démocratique Africain (US-RDA), led by Modibo Kéita, opted for *socialism. Kéita, as leader of the US-RDA and the country's first president, set about to nationalize the economy (through the development of state enterprises and the creation of a national currency, the Mali franc), to tighten the party's and administration's control over the polity and civil society, and to launch a nonaligned, Pan-African foreign policy with close ties to the Soviet Union and other Eastern-bloc countries, notably China and Cuba.

However, Mali was soon confronted with serious political, economic, and social difficulties, partly due to the West's latent hostility toward its ideological orientation and policies. The February 1967 monetary agreement with France brought Mali back into the Franc zone and signalled an economic rapprochement with France and the West. Capitalizing on deep-seated popular discontent owing to economic problems, political repression, and the excesses of the party's militia, a military *coup d'état toppled the Kéita regime on 19 November 1968. Fourteen junior army officers ruled through the Comité Militaire de Libération Nationale (CMLN), led by a young lieutenant, Moussa Traoré, who became the country's second head of state. The new military regime set out to further liberalize the economy and polity while basically maintaining the US-RDA's nonaligned foreign policy. From 19 November 1968 until 2 June 1974, the CMLN government ruled by decree. The constitutional referendum of June 1974 and the creation in March 1979 of a new party, the Union Démocratique du Peuple Malien (UDPM), contributed to the institutional legitimization of *military rule. The June 1979 legislative and presidential elections, followed by the dissolution of the CMLN, confirmed the UDPM's and Moussa Traoré's dominance of the Malian political system.

Opposition to the increasingly authoritarian, corrupt, and nepotic rule of the Traoré clan started to mount from various quarters, notably from disgruntled "Modibist" bureaucrats and from a fraction of the army (soldiers and mid-ranking officers) who felt excluded from Traoré's kleptocratic system. The growing and widespread political and social malaise finally culminated in an open and bloody confrontation between frustrated youths (mostly schoolchildren) and the army. Acting on behalf of the senior military officers, Lieutenant Colonel Amadou Toumani Touré intervened to stop the bloodshed (there were over 200 deaths), toppled the Traoré regime, and assumed power on 26 March 1991. Touré immediately set up a Conseil de Réconciliation Nationale (CNR), which appointed a broad-based Comité de Transition pour le Salut du Peuple (CTSP) as a government of transition from military-authoritarian to civilian-democratic rule. A National Conference (29 July–14 August 1991) which brought together forty-eight parties and some 700 associations adopted new political rules and institutions, notably a new electoral code, new party statutes, and a new Constitution. This popular and sovereign assembly also established the agenda and schedule for *democratic transition: constitutional referendum (12 January 1992); municipal elections (19 January); legislative elections (22 March and 5 April); and presidential elections (12 and 26 April). Of forty-eight political parties and movements initially registered, only four emerged from the electoral process: 1) the Alliance pour la Démocratie au Mali (ADEMA), led by Alpha Oumar Konaré; 2) the Comité National d'Initiative Démocratique (CNID), led by Mountaga Tall; 3) a rejuvenated US-RDA, split into two rival factions led by Tieoulé Konaté and Baba H. Haidara; and 4) the former UDPM with a new label.

On 26 April 1992, Alpha Oumar Konaré of the ADEMA won the presidential elections over challenger Tieoulé Konaté and eight other candidates. His five-year tenure, which begins in a context of chronic economic crisis, severe financial constraints, continuing social unrest, growing political conflict and factionalism, and uncertainty regarding the role of the army, promises to be a most difficult and challenging period.

(See also FRANCOPHONE AFRICA; SAHEL.)

Cheick Oumar Diarrah, *Le Mali de Modibo Kéita* (Paris, 1986). Joseph-Roger de Benoist, *Le Mali* (Paris, 1989). Pascal James Imperato, *Mali: A Search for Direction* (Boulder, Colo., 1989). Cheick Oumar Diarrah, *Mali: Bilan d'une Gestion Désastreuse* (Paris, 1990).

GUY MARTIN

MALTA. The Maltese archipelago is in the Mediterranean Sea between Sicily and the North African coast. Historically, Malta has played a significant part in international affairs because of its strategic importance, and its fine natural harbors have been beneficial to many nations.

In 1921 a constitution was granted that allowed for considerable self-government, but after political crises British crown colony rule was reestablished. In World War II Malta was awarded the George Cross for withstanding repeated enemy attacks.

After intense political debate, the island became

an independent state and a full member of the *Commonwealth in 1964. There is a sixty-five-member House of Representatives elected for a five-year term, with a president and prime minister as the chief officers of state. The longest-serving prime minister and most widely know Maltese political leader was Dom Mintoff, prime minister from 1955 to 1958 and from 1971 to 1984. Since independence a radical approach in general has been adopted with regard to political freedom, education, judicial reform, and nationalization. The Nationalist Party defeated the Labour Party in 1987, with the parties disagreeing on many issues, especially over the state appropriation of church property, as the country has one of the highest percentages of practicing Catholics in the world.

Today a nonaligned foreign policy is pursued, and a viable economy has been created based not on the islands' military value but on tourism, industry, and agriculture. Associate status within the European Community (EC) has been maintained since 1971, and in the interest of gaining full membership in the EC, trade liberalization and foreign investment are being actively encouraged.

B. W. Blouet, *The Story of Malta* (Valletta, 1981). John Richard Thackrah, *Malta* (Oxford, 1985).

JOHN RICHARD THACKRAH

MALVINAS/FALKLANDS WAR. The Malvinas/Falklands War (2 April–14 June 1982) was the world's first major naval missile conflict and presaged the emergence of the new post–Cold War era in pitting an emerging *Third World country against an established European power.

The dispute centered on issues common since World War II: a long-held claim of territorial rights by a developing country lodged against an ex-colonial power. The Argentine military junta—in an effort to distract its public from concern with the "dirty war," in which 15,000–30,000 Argentine civilians were killed or "disappeared," and from the economic failures of the military regime—made a nationalist appeal to recover the islands 300 miles off their coast. This territory had been lost to *Britain in the nineteenth century.

The British, led by Conservative Prime Minister Margaret *Thatcher, couched the dispute with *Argentina in terms of the right of self-determination on the part of the ethnically British Falkland Islanders. The British government, too, used the conflict as a unifying national issue in the midst of economic hardships resulting from conservative fiscal and economic policies.

*War erupted as the result of a series of miscalculations and the influence of the United States. Argentina claims that the United States intimated that it would not interfere with Argentine assertions of sovereignty over the islands. Subsequent U.S. assistance to Britain, in the form of *intelligence and material support, are viewed as a betrayal by

Argentines and other Latin Americans who expected, at best, a demonstration of hemispheric unity against a European interloper or, at worst, neutrality. The Argentines judge the U.S. role as critical, asserting that combat would not have broken out had Britain not had U.S. assurances. The *Organization of American States and Latin America in general supported Argentina, but U.S. influence thwarted any attempts at concrete action. The British expected assistance from the United States to liberate the oppressed Falklanders from a brutal military regime. The *European Community generally sided with Britain. France embargoed exports of arms to Argentina, which severely limited Argentine military capability.

The role of the UN was minimal. Negotiations over the status of the islands had been ongoing for decades; the failure to make progress in those negotiations is cited by Argentines as the motivation for military action.

The war progressed rapidly with continual British successes based upon their naval and ground force superiority, although the Argentine air forces inflicted heavy damage to British ships. Some five weeks of fighting in and around the islands resulted in the complete surrender and capture of all Argentine forces, which were then repatriated immediately through Uruguay. The British military commitment to the *security of the islands increased, presenting some problems for the British commitment to *North Atlantic Treaty Organization security forces, but those have been mitigated by the thaw in the *Cold War occurring in 1989–1990. The Argentine junta collapsed, leading to the longest continual civilian rule in Argentina since 1930, but the *sovereignty issue of the islands is still a sensitive one in Argentina. The end of hostilities was not recognized until the inauguration of President Carlos Saúl Menem in 1989.

(See also U.S.–LATIN AMERICAN RELATIONS.)

Rubén E. Moro, *The History of the South Atlantic Conflict: The War for the Malvinas* (New York, 1989).

BLAIR P. TURNER

MANDELA, Nelson. Born in Qunu, Transkei, on 18 July 1918, Nelson Rolihlahla Mandela was descended from the Thembu royal lineage. Suspended from Fort Hare University College in 1940 for leading a student strike, he traveled to Johannesburg, working initially as a compound policeman before beginning legal studies. Joining the *African National Congress (ANC) in 1942, Mandela helped to establish the Youth League, a group determined to recast the ANC's temperate philosophy in the mold of a militant, racially exclusive *nationalism. In 1949, the league persuaded the ANC to adopt its program of action. By 1951, however, Mandela's friendships with Indian activists and white Communists prompted him to revise his conviction that African nationalists should not cooperate across race lines. That year, Mandela helped plan a "defiance campaign" against "unjust laws." Appointed "volunteer-in-chief," Mandela was arrested on the first night of civil disobedience, 26 June 1952. Throughout the decade, as the ANC's deputy president, Mandela played a major role as an ANC strategist. In 1952 he founded an attorney's partnership with his comrade Oliver Tambo. He married twice, the second time in 1958 to Nomzamo Winifred Madikizda.

Following the 1960 *Sharpeville massacre, Mandela was detained five months and the ANC was outlawed. In 1961, elected secretary of a National Action Council, he led a nationwide general strike on 29–31 May and then disappeared from public view. In October, he helped form a sabotage organization, Umkhonto we Sizwe (Spear of the Nation). Mandela left *South Africa in January 1961 to tour the continent seeking financial support and military training facilities. He returned in July 1962 and was arrested on 5 August. While serving a prison term for incitement he was convicted again after the other Umkhonto leaders were captured in July 1963 at their headquarters in Rivonia, Johannesburg. Mandela received a life sentence on 11 June 1964. On 11 February 1990, he was unconditionally released to resume his post as deputy ANC president. Playing a commanding part in negotiations with the government, Mandela announced the suspension of the armed struggle in July 1990 and supervised the ANC's efforts to reconstruct itself as a mass organization inside South Africa. One year later he was elected president at the ANC's first national conference since 1959.

Nelson Mandela contributed significantly to the ANC's ideological formation and its internal restructuring during its development as a popular movement in the 1950s. He was a powerful proponent of the multiracial "Congress Alliance" and the architect of a highly localized neighborhood network, the ANC's cellular "M-Plan." Though influenced by *Marxism, he maintained an admiration for British *parliamentary democracy as well as supporting an ideal of a classless society modeled on precolonial institutions. Despite his advocacy of working class mobilization, Mandela fostered his social connections with the rural aristocracy, skillfully balancing different exhortations to the various constituencies within the ANC's popular following. After 1960, his personal courage and theatrical style were vital in retaining for the ANC the adherence of rank-and-file militants. He pioneered the ANC's transformation to a clandestine insurgent body and helped establish a tradition of moral restraint in its guerrilla tactics. His speech from the dock at the 1964 Rivonia trial enhanced a burgeoning international reputation as, in the words of the London *Times*, "a colossus of African nationalism." His political importance did not cease with his imprisonment. After the revival of mass opposition in 1976, Mandela became a symbolic figure of enormous weight, uniting the loyalties of several generations of black resistance behind the ANC. In consenting to his release in 1990, the South African government recognized his indispensability in legitimizing a negotiated transition to a reformed political order.

(See also APARTHEID; SOWETO REBELLION.)

Mary Benson, *Nelson Mandela* (Harmondsworth, U.K., 1986). Fatima Meer, *Higher than Hope: The Authorized Biography of Nelson Mandela* (New York, 1990).

TOM LODGE

MAO Zedong. By all reasonable standards of historical judgment, Mao Zedong must be counted among the half-dozen most important political actors in modern world history. Mao was the acknowledged leader of the greatest and most popular of modern revolutions. And almost unique among revolutionary leaders, he remained the dominant figure in the postrevolutionary regime for more than a quarter of a century, presiding over the beginnings of the modern industrial transformation of the world's most populous land. Certainly no one influenced more profoundly, for better or for worse, the lives of more people than did Mao Zedong by virtue of his person, his power, his policies, and his thought.

The son of a rich *peasant, Mao Zedong was born in the village of Shaoshan in Hunan province on 26 December 1893. During his early years, the old imperial Chinese order was rapidly disintegrating, radical reformist and revolutionary movements were rising, and newly introduced Western ideas and ideologies were undermining faith in traditional values and beliefs. Although the young Mao became well versed in classical Chinese texts and retained a strong attachment to certain aspects of tradition (especially historical novels and poetry), he soon became caught up in the radical political and iconoclastic intellectual currents that swept Chinese cities in the years preceding and following the Revolution of 1911 that overthrew the imperial system. As a student at the middle and normal schools in the provincial capital of Changsha during the years 1913–1918, Mao eagerly assimilated a broad range of Western ideas, briefly pursued a career as a teacher, and embarked upon his lifelong career as a political organizer, establishing the "New People's Study Society," one of the more important of the local groups that were to prove so politically and ideologically instrumental in the making of the radical May Fourth Movement of 1919. In Changsha, Mao became involved with *New Youth* magazine, that extraordinarily influential westernizing and iconoclastic journal of the new intelligentsia that molded the ideas of a whole generation of modern Chinese political and intellectual leaders. It was in *New Youth* that Mao's first published article appeared in 1917, "A Study of Physical Culture," which combined an ardent Chinese *nationalism with a no less ardent rejection of traditional Chinese culture—in this instance an attack on the Confucian separation between mental and manual labor. It was a uniquely modern Chinese combination of nationalism and cultural iconoclasm that very much reflected the radical spirit of the times and one that was to remain a prominent feature of the Maoist vision.

In late 1918, Mao Zedong left Changsha for Beijing. Beijing University had then become the center of radical Chinese intellectual and political life. Under the influence of radical intellectuals and their activist student followers, Mao became increasingly politicized. Even though he was unable to enroll as a regular student, he worked as an assistant librarian at the university and was first introduced to Marxist theory in the winter of 1918–19 as a member of a loosely organized Marxist study group. But Mao did not become an immediate convert to *Marxism. He later described his ideas at the time as a "curious mixture" of Western *liberalism, democratic reformism, and utopian *socialism or anarchism. It was only after his return to Changsha in the summer of 1919, under the influence of the increasingly radical and fiercely nationalistic currents then rising in *China, that Mao began to be attracted to the political message of the *Russian Revolution and its accompanying Leninist version of Marxism.

Yet Marxian influences are by no means apparent in Mao's prolific writings and frenetic political activities during the winter of 1919–20. Rather, what is most clearly evident is a powerful populist strain that celebrates the organic unity and inherent revolutionary potential of the Chinese people. Also celebrated, again in typically populist fashion, was a belief in the advantages of backwardness. Although the Chinese people had been oppressed and made impotent for "thousands of years," Mao wrote in his main treatise of the period entitled "The Great Union of the Popular Masses," this historic backwardness promised great political advantages for the future—for, as he confidently put it, "that which has accumulated for a long time will surely burst forth quickly." These populist-type beliefs were to remain enduring characteristics of the Maoist mentality, profoundly influencing Mao's reception and reinterpretation of Marxism.

Mao Zedong's actual conversion to Marxism, according to his own testimony, occurred only in the summer of 1920, following discussions with one of his political mentors in Shanghai. He then plunged into organizational activities, working to establish a labor union for miners in his native province of Hunan and organizing a small Communist group in Changsha, one of several such local groups in various parts of the country (and among Chinese students studying abroad) which coalesced into the *Chinese Communist Party. Mao was one of the thirteen delegates who attended the party's founding congress, secretly convened in Shanghai in July of 1921.

During the first, urban-based phase of the party's history (1921–1927), and especially during the period of the Soviet-fashioned Communist-Nationalist anti-warlord alliance (1924–1927), Mao's populist proclivities increasingly drew him from the cities to the countryside—and from the proletariat to the peasantry. Mao was not the only, nor the first, Chinese Communist to discover the revolutionary potentialities of the peasantry, but he did of course prove to be the most important. During the years 1925–1927, he devoted the greater portion of his prodigious energies to detailed investigations of rural socioeconomic conditions, to the organization of peasant associations, and (under Nationalist auspices) to the training of peasant organizational cadre. Mao's populist impulses found their fullest expression near the end of this period in his famous "Report on an Investigation of the Peasant Movement in Hunan," published early in 1927. Here, in what is perhaps the most pristine expression of what later came to be known as "Maoism," the young Mao celebrated the spontaneity of peasant revolt, an elemental force that he described as a tornado and a hurricane, one "so extraordinarily swift and violent that no power, however great, will be able to suppress it." Mao not only looked to the peasantry as the popular base of the *Chinese Revolution; he also attributed to peasants themselves all those elements of revolutionary creativity and standards of political judgment that orthodox Marxist-Leninists reserved for the Communist Party. For Mao, it was not the party that was to judge the revolutionary capacities of the peasantry, but rather peasants who were to judge the revolutionary sufficiency of the party. Throughout, the document emphasized, in most non-Leninist fashion, the creative revolutionary works that the peasants were accomplishing on their own and expressed hostility to all external organizational restraints.

The "Hunan Report," so heretical from an orthodox Marxist-Leninist point of view, no doubt would have earned Mao his expulsion from the Chinese Communist Party had it not been for the collapse of the Communist-Nationalist alliance just weeks after the publication of the document. It was in early April 1927 that Chiang Kai-shek turned his army to the task of destroying the Communists and their urban-based mass organizations. The relatively few Communists who survived the counterrevolutionary carnage were driven from the cities and sought refuge in the more remote areas of the countryside. The tie between the Communist Party and the urban working class was severed, and was to remain broken until 1949. The confinement of the *revolution to the rural areas was the essential condition that permitted Mao's political ascendancy in the Communist Party and the emergence of "Maoism" as the dominant Chinese version of Marxism.

The rise of Mao Zedong to party leadership in the mid-1930s was accomplished only after a long and bitter struggle against a Moscow-supported faction of Chinese Communists—and in direct defiance of *Stalin. During the entire Stalinist era of the world Communist movement, Mao was the only leader of a Communist party to achieve leadership without the blessings of the Soviet dictator. The Chinese party's de facto independence of Moscow sowed one of the seeds of the later Sino-Soviet dispute.

The Yanan era (1935–1945)—so called after the area in remote northwest China where the Communists established a base area to escape annihilation by Chiang Kai-shek's Nationalist forces—was the heroic and decisive phase in the history of the Chinese Communist revolution—and it was undoubtedly Mao's finest hour as a revolutionary leader and military strategist. Under Mao's leadership and through a combination of popular nationalist and social revolutionary programs, the Chinese Communists won enormous popular support, especially among the peasantry of north China, the essential basis for their eventual victory over the Nationalists. During the Yanan era the distinctive Chinese variant of Marxism-Leninism (canonized as "Mao Zedong Thought") crystallized as a formal body of doctrine. It was an ideology marked by powerful nationalist, populist, and voluntaristic impulses that greatly modified the inherited corpus of Marxist-Leninist theory. Indeed, "Maoism" implicitly defined itself, in large measure, by its *departures* from the main premises of Marxist theory. It was a doctrine that rejected the Marxist orthodoxy that capitalism is a necessary and progressive phase in historical development and thus the essential prerequisite for socialism. Accordingly, Maoism rejected the Marxist faith in the industrial proletariat as the necessary bearer of the new society, instead looking to the peasantry as the truly creative revolutionary *class in the modern world. Further, Maoism inverted the Marxist conception of the relationship between town and countryside in the making of modern history, rejecting the Marxist and Leninist assumption that the city is the source and site of sociohistorical progress. And reflecting the lack of any real Marxist faith in objective laws of historical development, Maoism placed a decisive emphasis on the role of human will and consciousness in molding social reality.

Such were some of the essential intellectual and ideological preconditions for the Maoist-led Chinese Revolution which took the historically unprecedented form of harnessing the revolutionary energies of the peasantry in the countryside to "surround and overwhelm" the conservative cities. That unique revolutionary process, with a now-semisacred Mao Zedong as its unquestioned leader, culminated in 1949 when the Red Army defeated the numerically superior armies of Chiang Kai-shek's Nationalists—and peasant soldiers victoriously marched into the cities to "liberate" an urban working class that had

been mostly politically passive since the defeats of 1927. On the basis of that victory, the People's Republic of China was formally established on 1 October 1949, unifying China after a century-long period of disintegration and humiliation. In 1949 Mao stood high atop the Gate of Heavenly Peace ("Tiananmen"), appearing as both national liberator and socialist prophet.

Mao Zedong dominated the history of the People's Republic for more than a quarter of a century, until his death in September of 1976, just as he had dominated the history of the rural-based revolution that had produced the new Communist state. Much of what is unique and distinctive about both the general pattern and the specific events of China's turbulent postrevolutionary history must be credited to—or blamed upon—the leadership of Mao Zedong. Rarely in world history has an entire historical era been so deeply stamped by the personality of a single individual.

In considering the thought and policies of Mao Zedong over "the Mao era" (1949–1976), one is struck by several enduring themes. First, it is a period animated by the notion of "permanent revolution." Although the Maoist theory of permanent (later "continuous") revolution was not explicitly set forth as part of "Mao Zedong Thought" until 1958, the essential components of the notion were present from the outset—an impatience with history that expressed itself in an ambivalent attitude toward the Marxist assumption that socialism presupposed *capitalism; a burning determination to pass through the Marxian-defined "stages" of history in the most rapid possible fashion; an ardent faith that people armed with the proper will and spirit can mold social reality in accordance with the dictates of their consciousness, regardless of the material circumstances in which they find themselves, and indeed a tendency to extol the advantages of backwardness as such for the advancement of socialism. The latter notion was to find its most extreme expression in Mao's celebration of the alleged Chinese virtues of being "poor and blank."

This utopian impulse to escape the burdens of history manifested itself in the brevity of the "bourgeois" or "New Democratic" phase of the history of the People's Republic, essentially terminated at the end of 1952 with the proclamation of the beginning of the period of "the transition to socialism." It further revealed itself in the 1955–1956 campaign to collectivize agriculture, accomplished in little more than a year. And it found its most fulsome expression in the disastrous Great Leap Forward campaign of 1958–1960, whose utopian *ideology envisioned a spiritually mobilized populace simultaneously bringing about the full-scale *modernization of China *and* its transition from socialism to *communism within a few short decades.

A populist modification of *Leninism is another strikingly pervasive feature of Mao Zedong's postrevolutionary theory and practice, one manifestation of which was a continuous tension between the person and persona of Mao, on the one hand, and the institution of the Chinese Communist Party on the other. The tension originated with the "Hunan Report" of 1927 when Mao drew a sharp dichotomy between the revolutionary spontaneity of the peasant masses and the conservative restraints that political parties (and intellectuals) attempted to impose upon them. A similar dichotomy reappears after 1949, with Mao presenting himself not simply as the chairman of the Communist Party but also as the embodiment of the popular will struggling against the conservatism of an increasingly bureaucraticized party apparatus. This tension between Mao the leader and the institution he led dramatically revealed itself in July 1955 when Mao personally overrode the collective decisions of the party leadership and appealed directly to "the people" in launching the accelerated campaign for agricultural collectivization. It is also apparent in the "Hundred Flowers" campaign of 1956–1957 when Mao encouraged nonparty intellectuals to criticize the Communist Party from without. And the tension culminated in the *Cultural Revolution which began (but did not end) with the extraordinary Maoist call for the masses to rebel against the authority of the party and its organizations.

Perhaps the most distinguishing feature of the postrevolutionary Mao Zedong was his historically unique (if ultimately unsuccessful) attempt to reconcile the means of modern economic development with the ends of socialism. Rejecting the inherited Stalinist orthodoxy that the combination of rapid industrialization with state ownership of the means of production would more or less automatically guarantee ever higher stages of socialism and eventually communism, Mao emphasized that the continuous socialist transformation of human beings and their social relations was essential if the process of modern economic development were to have a socialist outcome. This social radicalism was responsible, in part, for the adventures of the Great Leap and the Cultural Revolution—and Mao Zedong must bear the historical and moral responsibility for the enormous toll of death and suffering that resulted from these extraordinary events, however unintended those results may have been. But Maoist social radicalism also served to forestall the fully Stalinist institutionalization of the postrevolutionary order in China and perhaps served to keep alive, among some, the hope for the eventual realization of the ultimate socialist goals that the revolution promised. It certainly kept the postrevolutionary order in flux, providing Mao's successors with considerable flexibility for charting a new course of *development.

The conventional view of the Mao era is that Mao Zedong sacrificed modern economic development to "ideological purity" in a vain and costly quest for some sort of socialist utopia. Yet the actual historical record of the era suggests that Mao was more successful as an economic modernizer than as a builder of socialism. Over the Mao period (1949–1976), China was transformed from a primarily agrarian nation to a relatively industrialized one, the ratio of the value of industrial production to total production increasing from thirty to seventy-two percent. From 1952 (when industrial output was restored to its highest prewar levels) until the close of the Mao era, Chinese industry grew at an average annual rate of eleven percent, the most rapid pace of industrialization achieved by any major nation (developed or developing) during that time. Indeed, Maoist industrialization, however crude the process was in many respects, compares favorably with comparable decades in the industrialization of Germany, Japan, and the Soviet Union, hitherto generally regarded as the three most successful cases of modernization among major "latecomers" on the world industrial scene.

Rapid industrialization during the Mao period exacted enormous human and social costs, as had been the case with other late-industrializing countries, and most of the costs were borne by the peasantry. Agricultural production barely kept pace with population growth, and living standards in both town and countryside largely stagnated after 1957 as the state extracted most of the surplus product to finance the development of heavy industry. Yet although the blunders, deficiencies, inequalities, and imbalances that marked and marred the process were many and grave, future historians nevertheless will record the Mao era as the time when the basic foundations for China's modern industrialism were laid.

Far more questionable than Mao's status as a modernizer is his reputation as the creator of a socialist society. For what is most strikingly absent in both Maoist theory and practice is the elemental Marxist principle that socialism must be a system whereby the immediate producers themselves democratically control the products and conditions of their labor. In the Maoist system, by contrast, the control of labor and its fruits was left in the hands of an ever larger and more alien bureaucratic apparatus. Mao, to be sure, repeatedly conducted antibureaucratic campaigns, and there is no reason to doubt the genuineness of his antipathy to bureaucracy. But from those campaigns, he time and again failed to devise any viable means of popular democratic control over the powerful bureaucratic apparatus over which he uneasily presided. And if Mao broke, at least in some significant ways, with the Stalinist strategy of socioeconomic development, in the political realm the Maoist regime retained essentially Stalinist methods of bureaucratic rule and consistently suppressed all forms of intellectual and political dissent in Stalinist fashion. The Mao era was thus marked by a deep incongruity between its progressive socioeconomic accomplishments and its retrogressive political features, an incongruity that precluded any genuine socialist reorganization of Chinese society.

The Mao era in the history of the People's Republic was one of the most turbulent periods in modern world history, and it remains one of the most controversial. When the political passions engendered by the era have subsided, most future historians will likely evaluate Mao Zedong much in the fashion in which he is now ideologically portrayed by his successors in Beijing. First and foremost, Mao will be lauded as modern China's greatest nationalist, the leader of a revolution whose enduring achievement was to bring national unification and independence to the world's most populous land—after a century of repeated internal political failures and grave external impingements. Mao will also be seen as a great modernizer who, despite monumental postrevolutionary blunders, presided over the initial modern industrial transformation of one of the world's most economically backward lands, inaugurating a lengthy process destined eventually to make China a great world power. Ultimately, Mao Zedong's role as a pioneer of socialism will receive less attention and will appear far more problematic than his legacy as a nationalist modernizer.

(See also COLLECTIVIZATION; DENG XIAOPING; POPULISM; SINO-AMERICAN RELATIONS; SINO-SOVIET RELATIONS; STALINISM; ZHOU ENLAI.)

Benjamin I. Schwartz, *Chinese Communism and the Rise of Mao* (Cambridge, Mass., 1958). Mao Tse-Tung [Mao Zedong], *Selected Works of Mao Tse-Tung*, 4 vols. (Beijing, 1967–1977). Ross Terrill, *Mao: A Biography* (New York, 1980). Maurice Meisner, *Marxism, Maoism, and Utopianism: Eight Essays* (Madison, Wis., 1982). Stuart Schram, *The Thought of Mao Tse-Tung* (Cambridge, U.K., 1989).

MAURICE MEISNER

MAQUILADORAS. The Spanish term *maquila*—first used to designate the grain retained by *peasants as compensation for their work—has been extended to export-oriented factories operating in less developed countries as subsidiaries or subcontractors of transnational corporations. In the same way that tillers transform agricultural staples into milled grain, maquiladoras process raw materials and components into finished or semifinished goods that are then sold in world markets. In the late 1960s, the term applied to plants along *Mexico's northern border. At present, it is broadly used to name operations in all export-processing zones whether in Asia, Latin America, or the Caribbean.

Maquiladoras reflect the internationalization of the economy. Several political and economic factors led to their growth in border cities like Ciudad Juárez, Tijuana, and Matamoros. Unemployment and popular discontent in Mexico's northern border region followed the termination, in 1964, of the Bracero Program—a bilateral agreement that had allowed the entry of Mexican agricultural workers into the United States since 1942. By attracting foreign investment in the maquiladora sector, the Mexican government sought to create new jobs, neutralize political strife, and facilitate technological transfer.

At the same time, companies were exploring ways to reduce production costs by relocating manufacturing to less developed countries. Given its proximity to the United States, Mexico's northern border held a privileged geographical advantage. At the local level, Mexican entrepreneurs saw the benefits of mediating between a cumbersome Mexican bureaucracy and foreign firms. Maquiladoras were the result of these various converging interests.

Mexico's maquiladoras have been sustained by government stimuli that include customs-law changes authorizing the temporary entry of raw materials, machinery, and components. Foreign ownership restrictions of Mexican factories were waived. Other, less drastic, measures complemented the incentive package.

The expansion of the Mexican maquiladora program has been impressive. In 1968 there were fewer than 100 plants scattered along the U.S.–Mexican border; by 1991, there were more than 2,000 maquiladoras employing approximately 400,000 workers. Most assemble garment and electronics products, although the fastest-growing type of manufacturing in the 1980s was transport equipment. Mexico's maquiladora program is the world's largest export-oriented experiment of its kind and the fastest-growing sector of the Mexican economy. Since 1985, maquiladoras have surpassed tourism and trail only petroleum-related activities as a source of foreign exchange for the Mexican government. In the future, the growth and significance of the maquiladora sector will be influenced in important ways by the free trade area negotiations between Mexico and the United States.

The program has always had critics. Maquiladoras employ only ten percent of the Mexican labor force, and the majority of workers are women between 16 and 25 years of age, a particularly vulnerable segment of the labor force. Maquiladoras have been denounced as sweatshops that do not afford most workers seniority, safe working conditions, or adequate wages. Moreover, maquiladoras have not created significant linkages with domestic economies or fulfilled the hope of technological transfer. Finally, there are concerns about environmental pollution accentuated by types of production such as electronics. Despite these objections, maquiladoras are contemplated by governments in less developed countries as one of the few viable alternatives to create jobs and to integrate national economies into the world's system of production.

(See also MULTINATIONAL CORPORATIONS; U.S.–LATIN AMERICAN RELATIONS; WOMEN AND DEVELOPMENT.)

M. Patricia Fernández Kelly, *For We Are Sold, I and My People: Women and Industry in Mexico's Frontier* (Albany, N.Y., 1983). Leslie Sklair, *Assembling for Development: The Maquila Industry in Mexico and the United States* (Boston, 1989). Khosrow Fatemi, *The Maquiladora Industry: Economic Solution or Problem?* (New York, 1990).

M. PATRICIA FERNÁNDEZ KELLY

MARCOS, Ferdinand. Born on 11 September 1917 in Sarrat, Ilocos Norte, the *Philippines, Ferdinand E. Marcos rose to prominence to become the most controversial Philippine president in the country's history. The only president to win reelection, he extended his second four-year term by invoking the emergency provisions of the Philippine constitution and stayed another fourteen years in power. At the time of his fall in February 1986, he had ruled the country for half of its forty post-independence years. Five presidents shared the first half before him.

Accused of the 1935 murder of his father's political rival, Marcos became a celebrity for having undertaken his own defense, taking and passing the bar examinations during the trial, and winning his own acquittal in 1939. During World War II, he became a guerrilla fighter. His claim to be the most decorated Filipino soldier was based largely on undocumented wartime feats.

He began his meteoric rise to political power by winning the congressional seat in his home province; he would become senator, senate president, and, finally, Philippine president in 1965. In the meantime, in 1954, he had married a poor relation of the prominent Romualdez clan, the young and beautiful Imelda Romualdez.

Marcos was a consummate politician—bright, energetic, crafty, and ruthless. During his presidential campaign in 1965, for example, he commissioned Hartzell Spence to write his biography. *For Every Tear a Victory* (New York, 1964), focusing on the candidate's wartime feats and medals, was a brilliant political tool in a country much taken by heroes. Marcos later used this image to forge a partnership with the military in governing the Philippines under his authoritarian rule.

His twenty-year presidency saw the Philippines transformed from an "Asian showcase for democracy" with economic growth second only to Japan's in 1966 to a conjugal dictatorship of plunder and economic devastation. He built more infrastructure than all other Philippine presidents combined. He reoriented Philippine foreign policy by normalizing relations with socialist countries, improving relations with the United States, and strengthening links with Asian neighbors through membership in the *Association of Southeast Asian Nations.

During his second term in office he initially sought to shift to *parliamentary democracy through a new constitution, but this effort was aborted when he imposed martial law in September 1972. The martial law period saw the systematic destruction of democratic political institutions, the rise of the military,

plunder of the economy, the escalation of communist insurgency and Muslim separatism, and mounting poverty and violence.

His trusted associate, General Fabian C. Ver, chief of staff of the military, was suspected of leading the conspiracy to assassinate Marcos's principal political rival, former Senator Benigno ("Ninoy") Aquino, on 21 August 1983. The *assassination triggered massive protests against Marcos, culminating in his peaceful overthrow on 22–25 February 1986. He fled to Hawaii and remained in exile until his death on 28 September 1989.

His legacy of plunder and violence continued to haunt the country he claimed to have loved dearly. Imelda Marcos was remembered for excessive extravagance, ostentatious living, and indecent display of wealth. Their rule one day would be referred to as a "kleptocracy."

(See also AQUINO, CORAZON.)

Raymond T. Bonner, *Waltzing with a Dictator: The Marcoses and the Making of American Policy* (New York, 1987).

CAROLINA G. HERNANDEZ

MARIÁTEGUI, José Carlos. José Carlos Mariátegui was Latin America's most original and important socialist thinker. Although his work was centered on *Peru, it transcended the boundaries of that country and came to be studied throughout the continent. Indeed, the Argentine social critic José Aricó has called Mariátegui's magnum opus, *The Seven Interpretive Essays of Peruvian Reality*, the only significant theoretical work produced by Latin American *Marxism. In addition to journalism and theoretical essays, Mariátegui's activities included the organization of Peru's General Confederation of Workers and the Socialist Party.

Mariátegui was born into a humble family in Moquegua, Peru, on 14 June 1894. He had only a primary education and, at the age of 14, took his first job with a Lima newspaper. Moreover, he had continual health problems, owing to a childhood knee injury that led to several unsuccessful operations. Later an infection necessitated the amputation of his good leg. He died on 16 April 1930, at the age of 35.

In 1919, Mariátegui founded the journal *La Razón*, which was critical of the Peruvian government. When the journal was shut down, Mariátegui was sent abroad, ostensibly with a scholarship. In Europe, and particularly in Italy, he began his autodidactic education in Marxism through the Italian historicist perspective; at the same time, he acquired great familiarity with contemporary bourgeois culture. Having married a woman "and some ideas" (as he put it), he returned to Lima in 1923 and began his task of analyzing Peruvian society and building a *socialism that was "neither an imitation nor a copy." In this task, Mariátegui came into growing conflict with another young leftist leader, Víctor Raúl *Haya de la Torre.

His efforts resulted in the publication of *Amauta,* a vanguard theoretical journal on Peruvian issues; *Labor,* a workers' newspaper; and *The Seven Essays.* In terms of political practice, he founded the Socialist Party during the second half of 1928. For Mariátegui, use of the name *socialist* rather than *communist,* as well as the controversy his nonorthodox ideas would provoke at the conference of Latin American communist parties in Buenos Aires in 1929, were an expression of creative Marxism. The latter had to be based on concrete conditions within Peruvian society and as part of an effort oriented toward the consolidation of a vigorous workers' movement, the vanguard of the *revolution.

In his many works, Mariátegui emphasized that what characterized Peruvian society was its colonial heritage, racial heterogeneity, and incipient *capitalism. The racial heterogeneity of its predominant Indian population, far from being a disadvantage, provided two important political tools to transform Peruvian reality. First were the Indian communities which, according to Mariátegui, represented a concrete possibility for agrarian socialism in Peru. Second was the Andean tradition, which constituted an important component of Peruvian social consciousness and a mechanism for promoting the political mobilization of the popular classes. These ideas continue to have a following today, and several parties in Peru claim to be inheritors of Mariátegui's tradition.

Jesús Chavarría, *José Carlos Mariátegui and the Rise of Modern Peru, 1890–1930* (Albuquerque, N.Mex., 1979). José Aricó, *Mariátegui y los Origines del Marxismo Latinoamericano,* 2d ed. (Mexico City, 1980).
HERACLIO BONILLA

MARSHALL ISLANDS. See PACIFIC ISLANDS.

MARSHALL PLAN. Proclaimed in a speech by Secretary of State George Marshall at the Harvard University commencement on 5 June 1947, the Marshall Plan was the largest and most successful program of foreign assistance ever undertaken by the U.S. government. The harsh European winter of 1946–1947 brought home to Washington the failure of various interim aid programs to achieve sustained economic recovery. The British withdrawal from the eastern Mediterranean, which led to the *Truman Doctrine on 12 March 1947, also signaled the weakness of Western Europe. The failure of the United States at the Moscow Conference in late March and early April 1947 to reach agreement with the Soviet Union on such questions as German reparations encouraged U.S. leaders to search for a new policy. As Marshall put it, "The patient is sinking while the doctors deliberate."

Marshall's speech contained an offer of U.S. funding for a cooperative European recovery program.

The secretary of state set forth certain conditions, such as the need for a high degree of inter-European cooperation and the inclusion of Germany. Marshall even invited the Soviet Union to participate, arguing that "our policy is directed not against any country or doctrine but against hunger, poverty, desperation, and chaos." But he added that "its purpose should be the revival of a working economy in the world so as to permit the emergence of political and social conditions in which free institutions can exist."

British Foreign Secretary Ernest Bevin quickly seized upon Marshall's offer and called a conference in Paris for all the European countries to consider the proposal. The Soviet Union walked out of the meeting, refusing to accede to the American demand for disclosure of economic information and claiming that the terms of the plan were incompatible with the Soviet system of central *planning. The Soviets also took with them Poland and Czechoslovakia, and later in the year created their own trading organization, the *Council for Mutual Economic Assistance (COMECON), for Eastern Europe. The irony is that if the Soviet Union had chosen to participate, the chances of congressional acceptance of the plan would have decreased substantially.

The sixteen countries which remained at the Paris conference agreed to form the Committee on European Economic Cooperation (CEEC), to prepare a report on European economic capacities and requirements, and to devise a four-year program for economic recovery. At U.S. insistence, they included the Western zones of Germany, a critical step in the reintegration of the Federal Republic of Germany into the international community. The CEEC's program aimed to increase agricultural production to prewar levels and to push industrial production even higher. It also called for the elimination of the "dollar gap" through an increase in European exports, and for the creation of an organization to foster economic cooperation, what became the Organization for European Economic Cooperation (OEEC). The final goals of the CEEC were the creation of internal financial stability and a curb on inflation. Though the Europeans estimated their financial need at US$22 billion, this figure was later scaled back to US$17 billion.

The debate in Congress was a bitter one, with supporters such as the former isolationist Arthur Vandenberg pitted against an opposition led by Senator Robert Taft. To build support among the public, a group of influential private citizens organized the Committee for the Marshall Plan to Aid European Recovery. President *Truman worked to preserve bipartisanship by appointing Paul Hoffmann, a Republican businessman, to administer the program. Passage of the plan was further assisted by the Communist takeover of the Czechoslovakian government in February 1948. For many Americans the Marshall Plan became part of the *containment strategy against the Soviet Union. American leaders still envisioned containment as primarily a political and economic task; Congress prohibited the use of Marshall Plan assistance for military supplies.

The Economic Cooperation Administration (ECA), the organization which administered the Marshall Plan, did not "control" the Western European economies, though it did exert U.S. influence over the use of assistance. Aid most often took the form of food and raw materials, which the European governments would sell to their citizens. The money from these sales, called counterpart funds, remained in the local currency in a special account. These funds were then used for special projects or investments agreed on between the United States and the recipient country. Britain used the assistance to retire some of its debt, while France channeled funds into the Monnet Plan for the modernization of its infrastructure. The Germans eliminated production bottlenecks within their economy and supported the isolated city of Berlin.

Between 1948 and 1951, Congress authorized more than US$13 billion for the European Recovery Program. In its initial years of operation, Marshall Plan assistance amounted to approximately ten percent of the annual federal budget and between one and two percent of the national income. (In contrast, the United States devotes roughly 0.4 percent of its national income today to foreign aid.) After the outbreak of the *Korean War in June 1950, the United States reversed its earlier policy and encouraged the use of Marshall Plan assistance to provide for the rearmament of Western Europe within the North Atlantic Treaty Organization alliance. At the end of 1951 this change in emphasis became official as the ECA became the Mutual Security Administration.

Americans tended to overestimate the importance of their aid in the reconstruction of Western Europe, an overestimation which led them to call for Marshall Plans in other parts of the world, where conditions for success were much less favorable. The crucial argument for the role of the Marshall Plan assistance was less the sheer magnitude of aid than its key function in overcoming bottlenecks within the European economy and allowing rapid economic growth without imposing undue sacrifices on the Europeans. This made political stability under democratic institutions all the more probable. Western European production rose rapidly, and by 1950 production surpassed prewar levels by twenty-five percent. Inflation was largely brought under control, levels of employment increased, and the dollar gap decreased. European cooperation increased through such organizations as the European Payments Union and the European Coal and Steel Community. A final legacy of the plan was to further accentuate the division of Europe, breaking the traditional trading patterns between Eastern and Western Europe, and binding the Western European countries in closer political and economic relationships with the United States.

(See also COLD WAR; FOREIGN AID; ISOLATIONISM; MONNET, JEAN; WORLD WAR II.)

Alan Milward, *The Reconstruction of Western Europe* (Berkeley and Los Angeles, 1984). Michael J. Hogan, *The Marshall Plan: America, Britain, and the Reconstruction of Western Europe* (New York, 1987). Charles S. Maier and Günter Bischof, eds., *The Marshall Plan and Germany* (New York, 1991).

THOMAS ALAN SCHWARTZ

MARTÍ, José. To *Cuba and Spanish America, José Martí is considered to be the precursor of Cuba's political independence as well as the prophetic voice of the deep transformations that would occur in Cuba a century after his birth. Martí was born in Havana on 28 January 1853 into a humble Spanish family. He owed his humanist and patriotic tendencies to his mentor, Rafael María de Mendive. Imprisoned on 21 October 1869, Martí was deported to Spain on 15 January 1871, when a letter condemning those who defended the Spanish cause was discovered in his possession. In Spain, he studied law and philosophy. He also traveled in France, Mexico, and Guatemala. Upon his return to Cuba in 1878, he again pronounced himself against the colonial status of the island. Deported to Spain once again, he left shortly thereafter for New York, where he remained from 1881 to 1895.

In the United States, Martí's activities were fundamentally centered around journalism, disseminated throughout the continent, as well as the writing of poetry and a novel. At the same time, his long stay in the United States convinced him of the idiosyncrasy of "European America" and of the risks that it represented to Latin America. His knowledge and authority on the matter were increasingly geared toward promoting the definitive independence of Cuba, definitive not only vis-à-vis colonial Spain but also against neocolonial domination by the United States.

The product of his work in favor of the liberation of the island, *Bases del Partido Revolucionario Cubano*, was approved by the party on 5 January 1892. It declared that the party was founded to achieve "the complete independence of the island of Cuba" and "to encourage and assist with the independence of Puerto Rico." In addition, Martí contributed to the organization of the Cuban exiles and the creation of a military expeditionary force. At the end, he himself was involved in the military activities until his death in combat on 19 May 1895.

His premonitions about new threats menacing the American continent were expressed in the vibrant pages he wrote 10 January 1891, under the title *Nuestra América,* for the second Pan-American Congress, convened under U.S. initiative. In them, he prophetically cautioned about "the disdain of the formidable neighbor, which unknowingly is the major danger to our America."

Christopher Abel and Nissa Torrents, eds., *José Martí, Revolutionary Democrat* (Durham, N.C., 1986).

HERACLIO BONILLA

MARTIAL LAW. See MILITARY RULE.

MARX, Karl. Born in Trier, Germany, in 1818, Karl Marx saw his intended careers in university teaching and journalism frustrated by political suppression, and he moved to France and then Belgium. After the failure of the 1848 *revolutions (in which he took an active part), Marx settled in London in 1849. It was here that he produced his major works on political economy, including *Das Kapital.* He died in 1883.

Of all the nineteenth-century versions of socialism, it is Marx's that has proved intellectually the most influential and politically the most powerful. Drawing on the diverse traditions of German classical philosophy (G. W. F. Hegel), French utopian socialism, and Anglo-Scottish political economy (Adam Smith and David Ricardo), Marx's ideas centered around what he called his materialist conception of history. This allotted a central role throughout history to the development of the forces of production, which, together with their concomitant relations of production, formed a kind of economic base that determined the political and ideological superstructure of society. Whereas in the past the forces of production had been in the hands of successive minority classes, Marx believed that economic *development in his own time, and particularly deepening crises of *capitalism, meant the imminence of the conquest of the productive forces by the majority of society, who would be able to inaugurate a system of common ownership. Marx's theories are at their strongest in analytical/critical aspects, particularly in dealing with historical topics such as the transition from feudalism to capitalism or the role of the *state in contemporary capitalist society. In outlining a theory for future revolutions, however, Marx was less successful: he extrapolated too readily from contemporary trends, and his own theory precluded any detailed account of how, politically and economically, a future socialist society might be organized.

Marx's ideas were at first most influential among the German socialists, where they were assiduously propagated by his lifelong collaborator, Friedrich Engels, who survived him by thirteen years. But they came to world attention through the triumph of *Lenin and the Bolshevik Party in 1917—although it is worth remembering that two of the central tenets of *Leninism, the vanguard role of the party and the doctrine of *imperialism, are not to be found in Marx. With the emergence of *Stalinism, the ideas of Marx became transformed into an ossified and barren ideological system. In recent decades, the fuller publication of Marx's writings (and especially his earlier works) has revealed a more philosophical and humanist side to his theories. This aspect has been prominent in "Western" *Marxism, which has developed a thoroughgoing critique of capitalist society. In the *Third World Marx's ideas appear, usually modified by Lenin, as an ideology of *modernization calculated to appeal to elites. To date at least, attempts to put Marx's ideas into practice have not met with long-term success. To reverse one of his best-known aphorisms: he (and his followers) have been better at interpreting the world than at changing it.

(See also COMMUNISM.)

David McLellan, *Karl Marx: His Life and Thought* (New York, 1974). Saul Padover, *Karl Marx: An Intimate Biography* (New York, 1978).

DAVID MCLELLAN

MARXISM

In an era in which Marxism is now widely claimed to be discredited, it is useful to recall that a similar claim was made in 1882 by a French opponent of Marxism. In response, Friedrich Engels (1820–1895), the lifelong political companion of Karl *Marx (1818–1883), asserted: "so-called 'Marxism' in France is an altogether peculiar product, so much so that Marx said . . . what is certain is that for me, I am no Marxist." Marx meant, in other words, that he was clearly no adherent of what was then in France being called Marxism.

This essay argues that an examination of what Marx and Engels actually advocated and did reveals that most of what today is known as Marxism (or Marxism-Leninism) is such a "peculiar product" that, were they (and V. I. *Lenin [1870–1924]) alive, they would probably be leading the charge against it.

More than thinkers, they were, above all, people of action. It was through action as revolutionary democrats that Marx and Engels became Marxists or, as they preferred to be called, communists. While some debate their unanimity on "philosophical" issues, it is clear that in the sphere they took most seriously—politics—they spoke with a single voice.

From the first Marx and Engels differentiated themselves from the utopian socialists and their blueprints for the future by emphasizing that "communism is not a doctrine but a *movement;* it proceeds not from principles but from *facts* . . . insofar as it is a theory, [it] is the theoretical expression of the position of the proletariat in this struggle [between the proletariat and bourgeoisie] and the theoretical summation of the conditions for the liberation of the proletariat." The conflict between labor and capital is the specific form of the class struggle— "oppressor and oppressed—in constant opposition to one another"—in the era of *capitalism. Marxism, therefore, to the extent that it can be defined—in order to serve as the framework for this essay—is the discovery and application of the generalized lessons of the historical struggle between labor and capital in the interests of labor.

As communists, Marx and Engels sought immediately to win others to the lessons they had begun to draw about the *class struggle. This in turn led them to join the League of the Just in 1847—renamed, at the urgings of Marx and Engels, the Communist League. They were assigned to draw up a program that they would promote for their political current or, as they later called it, their "party," within the workers' movement, the *Manifesto of the Communist Party.* Written in 1848, it sought to persuade communists who had tended to function in a conspiratorial fashion to end their sectarian attitudes toward the working class and to see themselves as the most conscious layer of the proletariat. Its chief message was that labor's struggle against capital could only succeed if the proletariat conquered political power by overthrowing the bourgeoisie. In addition, it would only be on the basis of the working class in power that class exploitation would be eliminated.

The *Manifesto* was quickly put to the test of reality with the outbreak of *revolutions in France, Germany, Austria, Hungary, and Italy in 1848. These upheavals, in which Marx and Engels actively participated, especially in Germany, though unsuccessful from the viewpoint of the proletariat, became the basis for many of the lessons in political strategy they were to draw. Contrary to the forecasts of the *Manifesto,* however, socialist revolution, particularly in the case of Germany, was not on the immediate agenda at that time.

The 1848 revolutions also taught that the liberal bourgeoisie could no longer be counted on to lead its own bourgeois or liberal democratic revolutions. More fearful of its own small but growing proletariat than its traditional adversary, the feudal aristocracy, the liberal bourgeoisie was now an obstacle to the extension of democracy. If necessary it would look to a leader who appeared above the interplay of class forces—like Louis Bonaparte (also known as Napoleon III) (1808–1873) in France or Otto von Bismarck (1815–1898) in Germany—to protect its interests, even if this meant forfeiting its right to rule directly. Such a phenomenon, "bonapartism," was also characterized by a tendency for the *state to become increasingly autonomous, with the bureaucracy becoming the politically dominant force. Only when the bourgeoisie felt safe from the proletariat would it discard personalized leadership.

The 1848 experience also revealed to Marx that the proletariat had to be wary of reform-oriented socialists posing as friends of the working classes. The purpose of "social democracy," as Marx called this grouping in his most famous work about this

period, *The 18th Brumaire of Louis Bonaparte* (1852), was to blunt the class struggle, to convince workers that the interests of capital and labor could be reconciled. For Marx, "parliamentary cretinism"—the erroneous belief that workers' salvation was through parliamentary institutions—was the modus operandi of social democracy.

Marx and Engels concluded that the proletariat could avoid the trap of social democracy only by having its own party organized in the "most unanimous and independent fashion possible." In one of their most significant political statements, *Address of the Central Authority to the League, March 1850,* they outlined the strategy and tactics for a workers' party in order to ensure that a bourgeois revolution would become "permanent," i.e., move in the direction of a socialist revolution. Contrary to the oft-repeated claim that Marx and Engels ignored or deprecated the peasantry, both during and after 1848 they fought for an alliance of the proletariat with the peasantry in order for the proletariat to take power.

For Marx and Engels it was clear by 1852 that the revolutionary upsurge of 1848 had come to an end. The lessons of these events, along with the *Manifesto,* came to constitute the core ideas for what increasingly came to be known as the "Marx party." As the leaders of this small grouping, they saw that their primary task was to carry out the theoretical work to prepare workers for what would inevitably be another upsurge. Thus, a major accomplishment of these years was the publication in 1867 of the first volume of Marx's *Capital,* one of whose purposes was to provide workers with a "scientific" explanation of the capitalist system and why the interests of labor and capital are irreconcilable.

With the onset in 1863 of what Marx called "a new revolutionary era," the "Marx party" was able to throw itself once again into active political work. The following year working class leaders in London initiated the International Workingmen's Association (IWA), sometimes called the First International. Marx saw this as an opportunity for his "party" to win the proletariat over to communism. His activism at both the programmatic and organizational levels in the IWA was so extensive that Engels was later to comment that "to describe Marx's activity in the International is to write the history of the Association."

The IWA was the first international venue for workers to debate and reach programmatic conclusions about the class struggle. Marx and Engels waged a constant struggle within it to win adherents to their views. Their most important theme was that the proletariat had to conquer political power before it could liberate itself. Furthermore, proletarian internationalism was a necessary condition for success in the daily struggles of labor against capital.

Marx and Engels were vigilant against attempts by those with "parliamentary ambitions" who sought to take the IWA in a reformist (i.e., nonrevolutionary or social democratic) direction. To counter these forces they strove to transform it into a politically homogeneous body organized in a disciplined and centralized fashion. This resulted in one of the major fights inside the IWA, that between the Marxists and the anarchists led by Mikhail Bakunin (1814–1876). Marx believed the IWA should be an instrument for action—"the engine in our hands for the next revolution"—and not a "debating club." The success of their efforts can be seen from the fact that, of all the nineteenth-century European revolutionary currents, it was the "Marx party" that eventually emerged as the most influential. The IWA was decisive in this achievement.

The "next revolution" came in 1871 with the Paris Commune, the first working class seizure of political power. Following Prussia's defeat of Louis Bonaparte's armies (the Franco-Prussian War of 1870–1871), the masses of Paris established and proclaimed on 18 March a revolutionary government—the Commune—in opposition to what remained of the defeated regime. Although it lasted less than three months, the Commune's experience provided new and crucial lessons. Marx and Engels had accurately anticipated—on the basis of previous judgments—a revolutionary upsurge in France in the wake of the war.

Marx and Engels predicted that a revolutionary upsurge in France was not likely to succeed owing to the lack of capable leadership and an inadequate preparation of the working class. Thus, they counseled against such an uprising. Nevertheless, when the Commune began they became actively involved, through the IWA, in its defense before and after its defeat.

In spite of its defeat, the Commune's short existence confirmed the lessons of the 1848 revolutions—that in order to rule, the proletariat could not make use of the old state machinery associated with bourgeois rule. Rather, the Commune itself was "a harbinger of a new society," one in which a new and far more democratic form of government would emerge under proletarian rule. The Commune created a legislature, which was at the same time an executive body, with recallable deputies—to make them more accountable—who earned workers' pay. The Commune also taught that a working class revolution could only succeed if it took immediate measures to centralize authority and even to use force—including "terror"—to defend itself and subdue the defeated military, economic, and political powers who would invariably organize a counterrevolutionary force.

The defeat of the Commune and the resulting reactionary wave that swept over the continent convinced Marx and Engels that the revolutionary era that began in 1863 had come to an end. They concluded that the IWA was no longer useful and took steps to terminate it in 1874. A new organization, they believed, should not begin the way the IWA had, with a politically heterogeneous grouping. Engels predicted, rather, that "the next International—after Marx's writings have exerted their influence for some years—will be directly communist and will candidly proclaim our principles. . . ."

In the aftermath of the IWA the "Marx party" added to the previously drawn lessons. Anticipating, for example, by almost half a century the "iron law of oligarchy" of the German sociologist Robert Michels (1876–1936), Engels wrote to Marx in 1869 that "unfortunately it appears to be a law of the proletarian movement that everywhere a part of the workers' leaders necessarily become corrupted. . ." (Marx and Engels, *Collected Works*, vol. 43, Moscow, 1988, p. 336). Also, the tendency toward social democracy in the German party—already evident in 1894—was the "misfortune of all extreme parties when the time approaches for them to become 'possible'," i.e., to be the official party via the electoral road. Marx and Engels sought to counter these corrupting, oligarchic, and moderating trends by advising growing numbers of revolutionary leaders and their parties attracted to their perspective in such countries as Italy, the United States, and especially Russia on the strategy and tactics of revolution. Although there were no universal laws of the development of revolutionary movements (because each country had its own dynamic), the peaceful road to power was unlikely, except perhaps in England, Holland, and the United States, because the bourgeoisie would not permit such a course. Marx and Engels also advocated the worker-peasant alliance as crucial to a successful revolution and in 1894, eleven years after Marx's death, Engels wrote *The Peasant Question in France and Germany*, which provided their most detailed treatment of this topic.

Consistent with their critique of utopian socialism, Marx and Engels provided no blueprint for the socialist future. However, as part of their effort to exorcise reformist intrusions from the Marxist movement, in his *Critique of the Gotha Program* (1875) Marx identified some of the essential features of a socialist society. Only if the proletariat actually rules through *"the revolutionary dictatorship of the proletariat"*—as Marx and Engels occasionally referred to the form of working class power in the period of a revolutionary consolidation which contrasted to the prerevolutionary "dictatorship of the bourgeoisie"—can socialism be realized.

The defeat of the Paris Commune led Marx and Engels by the mid-1870s to expect that the next revolutionary upheaval would take place in Russia. They believed their ideas were more accepted and understood in that country than anywhere else. While the process of socialist revolution through the democratic revolution would begin in Russia, they also held that it could be consummated only by spreading westward to Germany. Clearly optimistic about prospects in Russia, Marx commented in 1881, two years before his death, "Nowhere my success is to me more delightful; it gives me the satisfaction that I damage a power, which besides England, is the true bulwark of the old society" (Saul Padover, ed., *The Letters of Karl Marx,* Englewood Cliffs, N. J., 1979, p. 402).

Marx and Engels's optimism about Russia challenges the standard charge that their perspective was meant to apply only to the advanced capitalist countries of Western Europe. Indeed, they did make clear in discussions about Russia in 1877 that their description of the rise of capitalism in Western Europe was not "an historico-philosophic theory of the general path of development prescribed by fate to all nations." At the same time, they felt theoretically and programmatically at home in analyzing an overwhelmingly peasant country like Russia. In his 1875 article "On Social Relations in Russia," Engels, with remarkable insight, argued that "Russia undoubtedly is on the eve of a revolution. . . . Here all the conditions of a revolution are combined, of a revolution which, started by the upper classes of the capital, perhaps even by the government itself, must be rapidly carried further, beyond the first constitutional phase, by the peasants. . . ." Although the preliminary steps were taken, with Engels's decisive assistance, to form in 1889 what eventually became the Socialist or Second International, Engels doubted the need for a new association in that period in the absence of a major political event. "Such events however are maturing in Russia where the vanguard of the revolution will engage in battle. This and its inevitable impact on Germany is what one must in our opinion wait for, and then will also come the time for a grand demonstration and the establishment of an *official,* formal International which however can no longer be a propaganda society but only a society for action" (Marx and Engels, *Selected Correspondence,* Moscow, 1975, p. 329). The next organized international "Marx party," in other words, would come into existence with the Russian Revolution.

Marxism after Marx and Engels. Engels's caution about forming a new International was ignored. Five years after his death, the Second International (SI) effectively came into being in 1900 with the establishment of a Secretariat. Although the vast majority of parties affiliated with it considered themselves to be Marxist, their self-appellation, owing largely to the post-Commune repression, was social democratic rather than communist. While Marx and Engels tolerated this usage, their earlier criticism of social democracy was still justified; the practice of most SI affiliates revealed that reform perspectives and, especially, reliance on parliamentary orientations had made greater inroads into their ranks than Engels could have imagined. As an organization the SI proved to be more of a debating club—with increasing distance between adopted policies and actions—than an activist association.

The wing of the SI that maintained the greatest fidelity to the ideas of Marx and Engels, particularly on the issue of proletarian internationalism, grouped around Rosa Luxemburg (1871–1919) of the German affiliate, the Sozialdemokratische Partei Deutschlands (SPD), and V. I. Lenin of the Russian Social Democratic Labor Party (RSDLP), although they too had their own differences on the question of national self-determination and the organization for a socialist revolution. For Lenin it was the colonial question that first revealed the differences within the SI. It was, in part, the failure of the sections from countries with colonial possessions to denounce unequivocally colonial rule that led him to charge that the SI "recognized only white-skinned peoples" (*Theses, Resolutions and Manifestos of the First Four Congresses of the Third International,* London, 1980, p. 124).

When the first revolutionary upsurge occurred in 1905 in the wake of Russia's defeat by Japan—the first revolution in Europe since the Paris Commune—during which soviets, councils of elected representatives, arose, Lenin saw parallels with the French uprising. Thus, for him, Russia's working class would be able to exercise rule in a governing alliance with the peasantry, by means of the soviets—"the democratic dictatorship of the proletariat and peasantry"—and carry out the fundamental tasks of the bourgeois revolution. Like Engels, Lenin saw the role of the peasants as decisive for the proletariat. Without them, especially in an underdeveloped and overwhelmingly peasant country like Russia, the proletariat could not hope to exercise political power.

Precisely because Lenin felt that the time for the proletariat had come—the position of the majority (Bolshevik) faction of the RSDLP—he followed Marx and Engels's advice that it was necessary that they be organized in the most independent and conscious way. This was the political basis, as he argued in his *What Is to Be Done?* (1902), for his call for a highly disciplined vanguard party in which decisions, having been agreed upon after debate, were to be carried out by every member—the principle of democratic centralism. A minority in the party, the Mensheviks, felt proletarian rule was not on the agenda and thus such organizational norms were unnecessary. These differences between the two factions eventually led to a split in the party. Outside the ranks of the Russian party, Luxemburg argued against such organizational norms on the ground, in part, that they were unnecessary because the masses would solve the leadership question in the course of their spontaneous uprisings. Leninist centralism, she also argued, would inevitably lead to the sectarian isolation of the party from the masses.

Another revolutionary upsurge began in February 1917, leading to the overthrow of the semifeudal tsarist government and the establishment of what Lenin termed "dual power"—power divided between the "democratic dictatorship of the proletariat and peasantry" through the soviets, which appeared once again, and the "dictatorship of the bourgeoisie" through the provisional government. As in 1905, Russia's defeat or near defeat in war, this time World War I (1914–1918), was the precipitating factor. Drawing on lessons from Marx and Engels, the SI anticipated such upheavals and adopted a resolution in 1912—the Basle Manifesto—instructing its affiliates to take advantage of the situation to lead socialist revolutions. Only the Russian, Serbian, and Hungarian sections actually sought to implement the decision. The others, and significantly the SPD in Germany, broke with Marxism and supported the war efforts of their respective governments. For Luxemburg, their violation of the basic norms of proletarian internationalism was the clearest evidence that the SI had become a "stinking corpse" of a once-Marxist organization.

Armed with essentially the same program they had derived from the 1905 experience and the lessons of Marx and Engels, the Bolsheviks successfully implemented the Basle Manifesto—the only SI affiliate to do so—leading in October 1917 to what would soon become a socialist revolution. At the heart of this overturn, and a major issue of disagreement between supporters and opponents of the revolution, was the substitution of the soviet for the liberal democratic form of government. With the Paris Commune as his model, Lenin had argued, on the eve of the October revolution in his most important political work, *State and Revolution* (1917), that only the soviet form ensured that workers and peasants—the majority—would actually exercise political power. Against its detractors Lenin also argued that the October revolution was not one imposed on the majority by a minority. As proof he pointed out that in the Bolshevik victory in the civil war (1918–1921) the peasants and workers voted with their feet on what form of rule they wanted. Also, the Bolsheviks understood that the October revolution did not usher in socialism but only the beginning of a prolonged transition whose ultimate success depended—just as Marx and Engels had assumed—on the revolution spreading to Germany and the other more industrialized centers of Europe.

In 1919, a new international, the Communist International, the organization whose formation Engels had predicted, came into being at the initiative of the Bolsheviks and in response to the revolution of 1918 in Germany. Calling itself "communist" in order clearly to indicate its aims, thus differentiating itself from the social democratic parties of the SI, Comintern (CI), as it became known, declared its fundamental pillar to be fighting to establish the dictatorship of the proletariat through the soviet form of power.

Coming in the wake of the victorious Russian Revolution as well as the failed socialist revolutions in Germany, Hungary, and Poland, this new Marxist association had a rich set of experiences from which it could draw lessons about the class struggle. It was in the first four congresses and other leadership meetings though 1923 that the most open and spirited discussions took place to arrive at programmatic conclusions. By the time of the Fourth Congress in 1922, the delegates of more than fifty countries participated in its deliberations, including those of twenty non-European nations.

Among the major programmatic stances of the CI was the defense of the Russian Revolution as the basis for its extension. A 1922 resolution on that revolution "reminds proletarians everywhere that the proletarian revolution can never triumph within the limits of a single country; it can triumph only internationally, by developing into a world revolution" (*Theses*, p. 428). The Russian Revolution revealed that no country was ordained to have to undergo capitalist development for some indefinite period before considering socialism. Also, the anticolonial and national liberation struggle was intertwined with the fight for socialism in the advanced capitalist countries.

Although the Russian Revolution was the basis for many lessons drawn by the CI, Lenin recognized that it was at best only a provisional model. He argued in *"Left-Wing" Communism—An Infantile Disorder* (1920) that while it was easier to begin the socialist revolution in Russia than in Europe, it would be far more difficult to complete it there than in the latter. In the same year, he wrote, "After the victory of the proletarian revolution in at least one of the advanced countries . . . Russia will soon after cease to be the model country" (Lenin, *Collected Works*, vol. 31, Moscow, 1965, pp. 21–22).

At the end of his last speech to a CI congress (1922), and about three months before he was totally incapacitated by a stroke, he criticized the previous congress for adopting organizational norms that, in his opinion, were "too Russian," reflecting too much the unique national experience. At the previous congress the year before, Lenin had disputed the claim of an Italian delegate that the October revolution was a model for revolutions by a minority. Perhaps it was he whom Lenin had in mind when almost prophetically he urged the delegates in 1922, foreign as well as Russian, to take the time to study the reality of the Russian revolution in order to understand what to emulate in it and avoid "hanging it in a corner like an icon and praying to it" (*Selected Works*, vol. 3, Moscow, 1977).

In the last months before his final stroke in 1923 Lenin waged an unsuccessful struggle against what was widely recognized as the increasing bureaucratization of the revolution. Rather than a socialist state, Lenin had in fact characterized the newly formed *Soviet Union as a "workers' state with bureaucratic distortions" (*Collected Works*, vol. 32, Moscow, 1965, p. 48). Lenin also sought to combat

"Great Russian chauvinism" vis-à-vis national minorities, which involved a failed attempt to have Joseph *Stalin (1879–1953) removed from his post of general secretary of the party. In his final months of political activity, Lenin offered the following reasons for the revolution's degeneration: ". . . firstly, because we are a backward country; secondly, because education in our country is at a low level; and thirdly, because we are getting no outside assistance. . . . Fourthly, our machinery of state is to blame" (*Collected Works*, vol. 33, Moscow, 1965, p. 428; the last reason referred to the absence of popular control over the bureaucracy). Once the revolution spread westward, these problems, he felt, would be overcome. In fact the revolution failed to extend itself after aborted attempts in Germany—three times between 1918 and 1923—Eastern Europe and China in 1927.

After Lenin's death in 1924, Stalin effectively used his post to block opposition to his growing power and that of the bureaucracy, and within five years he had silenced all internal opposition and substituted himself for the Bolshevik party which he eventually destroyed. In a claim that flew in the face of Marxist fundamentals, Stalin proclaimed in the 1936 constitution that "socialism" had been achieved in the Soviet Union. The most successful explanation within a Marxist framework of the degeneration of the Russian Revolution is that of one of its leaders, Lev *Trotsky (1879–1940). His "theory of *Stalinism," the most systematic treatment of which is in his 1936 book *The Revolution Betrayed*, has its roots in Marx and Engels's notion of bonapartism as well as in Lenin's explanation for the bureaucratization of the revolution. (He also employed the bonapartist concept to explain fascism.) Trotsky's thesis was that Stalinism constituted a counterrevolution in which the bureaucracy usurped political power that had momentarily been in the hands of the workers and peasants after October 1917. The toll of the civil war on the proletariat—which included the invasion of Russia by Western powers to overthrow the revolution—and the failure of the revolution to expand were the fundamental reasons for this overturn. The displacement of the dictatorship of the proletariat by the "dictatorship of the bureaucracy" meant that socialism could not be constructed in Russia.

Within the framework of this essay, the significance of Stalinism is that it ended Marxist continuity for the vast majority of would-be Marxists who emerged in its wake. Lenin's fear about the Russian Revolution becoming an icon was realized not only in the Soviet case but for Lenin himself and virtually the entire Marxist program. Stalin, whom Lenin had denounced and tried to have removed from his party post, became shortly afterwards the self-appointed guardian of "Leninism" and "orthodox Marxism-Leninism." Along the way, he either had killed or jailed virtually every other Bolshevik leader. Aside

from individuals such as the Italian revolutionary Antonio *Gramsci (1891–1937), no organized current of revolutionary activists—except for the relatively small number of supporters of Trotsky—could claim any longer an organic and programmatic link to the Bolshevik and, thus, to revolutionary Marxist tradition.

Just as the Bolshevik party was demolished by Stalin, the CI, certainly by the Sixth Congress in 1928, had ceased to be an arena for real discussion and debate for drawing programmatic conclusions about the class struggle—in other words, for practicing Marxism. By the Seventh Congress in 1935, it had become obvious that decisions on key issues had already been reached in Moscow prior to increasingly infrequent leadership meetings. Proletarian internationalism, once a hallmark of the Marxist movement, was replaced by the primacy of the needs of the bureaucracy in Moscow.

The Stalinization of the CI coincided with the greatest influx into its ranks of revolutionaries from the colonial and semicolonial world, for example, *Mao Zedong and *Ho Chi Minh. The prestige of the October revolution, the industrialization of an economically backward country, the victory over fascism in World War II, and the Red Army–made "revolutions" in Eastern and Central Europe after the war all made Stalinized Russia attractive to these new CI adherents. With state power in Moscow, the Stalinists were able to couple these appeals with material incentives to ensure fidelity from these disparate forces. Hence, it was through a Stalinized CI and its national sections—most of them having undergone purges in the late twenties or early thirties to ensure their loyalty to Moscow, as was, for example, the case in South Africa in 1931—that most new revolutionaries learned "Marxism." Many of these "lessons," in fact, such as the norm of a single-party state or the well-known "people's front" tactic, contradicted earlier CI policies.

Only with the victory of the *Cuban Revolution in 1959 did a new revolutionary tendency emerge that did not have roots in Stalinism. No one epitomized this break with Stalinism more than the Argentinian-born Cuban revolutionary Ernesto ("Che") *Guevara (1928–1967). What most distinguishes the Cubans as Marxists from almost everything done in the name of Marxism after the advent of Stalinism is their proletarian internationalism, i.e., their tendency to subordinate national interests to what they see as the international interests of workers and peasants, especially those in the *Third World. Yet the current "rectification" process under way on the island, which involves in part an effort to abandon models borrowed from Eastern Europe and the Soviet Union, indicates that the struggle between Marxism and Stalinism in the revolution is not a settled question.

The denouement of Stalinist communist parties in Eastern Europe and the Soviet Union is the most dramatic and profound manifestation of the disintegration which has been in process since the 1950s. While Marx and Engels certainly did not anticipate the existence of such regimes, their oft-stated position that socialism could only be built when political power rested in the hands of the proletariat was profoundly confirmed—admittedly in a negative way—by the Soviet and East European reality. The crisis of Stalinism undermines the popular belief—originating in the mid-1930s and once promoted by "intellectual Marxists" such as those of the Frankfurt School—that its totalitarian hegemony was impregnable. Trotsky's position that the Stalinist regime in the Soviet Union was an ephemeral phenomenon appears to have been more accurate.

The collapse of Stalinism and its icons is the necessary, if not sufficient, condition for working people of the former Soviet Union to return to political power; in Central and Eastern Europe it is the precondition for the people to take power for the first time. Such optimism is consistent with the unflinching faith that Marx and Engels had in the oppressed to liberate themselves through struggle. Marx and Engels expected that as long as capitalism, with all its contradictions, exists, there will be class struggle. They would not have been surprised at the resistance on the part of the working classes in the former Stalinist regimes to the attempts to reintroduce the capitalist mode of production. And as long as there is class struggle, there will be those who seek to explain and apply the lessons of that struggle in the interests of the oppressed. Whether they be called Marxists would probably matter little to Marx or Engels themselves.

(See also ANARCHISM; SOCIALIST INTERNATIONAL.)

Edward H. Carr, *The Bolshevik Revolution 1917–1923*, 3 vols. (London, 1966). Richard N. Hunt, *The Political Ideas of Marx and Engels*, 2 vols. (Pittsburgh, 1974, 1984). Stephen Cohen, "Bolshevism and Stalinism," in *Stalinism: Essays in Historical Interpretation*, edited by Robert C. Tucker (New York, 1977). Hal Draper, *Karl Marx's Theory of Revolution*, 3 vols. (New York, 1977, 1978, 1986). Farrell Dobbs, *Revolutionary Continuity*, 2 vols. (New York, 1980, 1983). Marcel Liebman, *Leninism under Lenin* (London, 1980). John Riddell, ed., *The Communist International in Lenin's Time*, 3 vols. (New York, 1984, 1986, 1987). Alan Gilbert, *Marx's Politics* (Boulder, Colo., 1989).

AUGUST H. NIMTZ, JR.

MASS MEDIA. See INFORMATION SOCIETY.

MAU MAU ANTICOLONIAL STRUGGLE. Soon after the end of World War II, there was a general nationalist upsurge in the British colonies in Africa. In *Kenya, the Kenya African Union (KAU), a nationalist political party, was formed in 1944; from 1947 it would be led by the legendary Jomo Kenyatta. The KAU demanded constitutional reforms to allow Africans to participate in the affairs of government so as to correct colonial injustices such as land deprivation. The white settler community, a strong political force in colonial Kenya, reacted negatively to the KAU's demands, arguing that Africans were not yet ready to understand the affairs of modern government, let alone take part in politics. In Central Province and the Rift Valley, the heartland of white settler agriculture where African peasants had been forcibly deprived of their land to facilitate white settlement, the KAU found its most ardent supporters among the Kikuyu squatters (tenants-at-will), landless *peasants and rural intelligentsia *(athomi)* such as school teachers, and demobilized soldiers who were regarded by the settlers as "hotheads." The KAU received support as well from the incipient trade union movements in Mombasa, Nairobi, Kisumu, and other urban areas.

But the KAU's politics of persuasion and discussion were soon viewed as too slow by the landless and the demobilized soldiers. The latter chafed at being treated unfairly by the colonial government—whereas white soldiers were given fertile land for farming on returning to Kenya, Africans were only given "a few shillings" and told "to start business," as one demobilized soldier put it. Only by force, concluded some radical Africans, would settlers and their government listen to African grievances, particularly with regard to land appropriations. An armed uprising of the masses against colonialism was advocated. It was led by the Kenya Land Freedom Army—an underground movement that precipitated what came to called "the Mau Mau." (The origins of the term *Mau Mau* are unknown, but historians concur that it was a derogatory expression coined by the white settlers themselves.)

On 7 October 1952, Chief Waruhiu, a Kikuyu chief known for his partisan views in defense of the colonial administration, was assassinated in Kiambu, a few miles outside Nairobi. This event finally united all shades of European opinion behind the settlers' demand for immediate and drastic action. On 20 October 1952, the governor signed a proclamation declaring a state of emergency in Kenya. The Mau Mau anticolonial struggle officially dates from this period.

Banning of the KAU followed; party leaders, arrested and tried on charges of having organized Mau Mau, ultimately would spend more than seven years in detention. In an accompanying military campaign, thousands of Africans lost their lives and the Kikuyu countryside was reorganized into village hamlets for purposes of control. By the end of 1953, Mau Mau was already militarily defeated. Nevertheless, the political, economic, and social conditions that led to its rise were as yet unsettled. The reforms carried out between 1953 and 1960 trace their origins to Mau Mau, and paved the way for independence in Kenya.

It may therefore be argued that Mau Mau had a significant, and perhaps decisive, impact on the struggle for independence in Kenya. It was encouraged by favorable changes in the international environment. Within Kenya, it forced intransigent settlers to concede to constitutional and peaceful reforms toward majority rule and finally independence.

(See also DECOLONIZATION; NATIONALISM.)

Jaramogi Oginga Odinga, *Not Yet Uhuru* (London, 1966). Carl Rosberg and John Nottingham, *The Myth of "Mau Mau": Nationalism in Kenya* (New York, 1966). Bildad Kagga, *Roots of Freedom, 1921–1963* (Nairobi, 1975).

PETER ANYANG'-NYONG'O

MAURITANIA. The Islamic Republic of Mauritania occupies a large area of the Sahara Desert and a portion of the Atlantic coast of West Africa. Because of its remoteness, Mauritania was one of the last places on the African continent to be effectively colonized. The French, who ruled the country from 1903 until independence in 1960, never really gained effective administrative control until the 1920s. Though still predominantly rural, the urban population has been growing rapidly, and over one-fifth of the total population now lives in Nouakchott, the capital city. At the beginning of the 1990s, the total population was about 2 million.

The Mauritanian economy is very narrowly based. During the 1960s, the "modern" economy was dominated by iron ore and, to a lesser extent, copper mining. These minerals were exploited by foreign-owned mining consortia. These mining activities did generate significant state revenue; however, they did little to diversify the economy. Offshore fisheries, some of the richest in the world, were exploited almost entirely by foreign fleets and contributed almost nothing to local development. The government made feeble efforts to establish industry during the 1960s and, especially, the 1970s, but these were poorly planned and unsuccessful. Agriculture was neglected throughout this period. Moreover, desertification (the result, according to some accounts, of ill-advised colonial policies) has gradually reduced arable land.

Economic conditions worsened significantly during the 1970s. First, a worldwide decline in the prices of Mauritania's mineral exports caused a substantial, and largely unexpected, drop in revenues. The accumulated foreign debt (now almost US$2 billion) became largely unpayable. Second, a drought devastated the countryside, destroying much of the cattle herd and the livelihood of a large segment of the population. Destitute herders converged on the already-crowded urban areas, generating extremely rapid urbanization. Third, Mauritania participated in a protracted war in the Western Sahara region during the years 1975–1978, which absorbed scarce economic resources.

All these problems exacerbated long-standing ethnic and regional tensions. Essentially, the country is divided between the northern Arabic-speaking peoples and several southern groups, mainly Wolofs and Peuls. The northerners account for about two-thirds of the population, and they have traditionally dominated national politics. With their political dominance, the northerners have attempted to Arabize the country and to promote Arabic, at the expense of French, in the educational system. The southerners, more oriented toward the French language, have long protested these efforts, leading to periodic riots and uprisings.

From the time of independence in 1960 until 1978, the country was ruled by Moktar Ould Daddah, under the official Parti du Peuple Mauritanien. During most of this period, the country functioned as a one-party state. The growing economic dislocations gradually discredited the Daddah regime, and it was overthrown in 1978. A succession of military councils have ruled since 1978. Recently, the military has introduced gradual democratization measures, with municipal elections held in 1986, followed by departmental and communal elections in 1988 and 1989. Multiparty national elections were held for the first time in January 1992.

With the assistance of the *International Monetary Fund, Mauritania has embarked on a substantial economic restructuring, which devalued the national currency, the ouguiya, and reduced restrictions on foreign investment. Agriculture, previously neglected, now receives augmented financial support, mostly through foreign aid. Substantial resources have also been invested in fisheries. In recent years, there has been modest economic recovery, with some GDP growth since the middle 1980s (although there is no information on the equity effects of this recovery).

(See also FRANCOPHONE AFRICA.)

M. Bennoune, "The Political Economy of Mauritania: Imperialism and Class Struggle" *Review of African Political Economy* 12 (1978): 31–52. David N. Gibbs, "The Politics of Economic Development: The Case of the Mauritanian Fishing Industry" *African Studies Review* 27, no. 4 (1984): 79–93.

DAVID N. GIBBS

MAURITIUS. See INDIAN OCEAN REGION.

MAY 1968. The term *May 1968* should be understood in two ways, literally and metaphorically. The "events of May," as the French called them, were first of all a cluster of large-scale social protests which shook the very foundations of French politics. At the same time, undoubtedly because of its amplitude, May 1968 became the symbolic nexus of an international contagion of student and new middle strata protests which marked the later 1960s and which in retrospect can be seen to have permanently changed the course of politics in most advanced industrial societies.

The "events of May" began early that month with a gigantic student protest against the regime of General Charles de *Gaulle. The roots of unrest lay in the *modernization over which de Gaulle's Fifth

Republic had presided and the difficulties which it had posed for French society and the French polity. Rapid economic growth, urbanization, consumerization, occupational and life-style changes came together with an unprecedented demographic boom to destabilize traditional French ways. Social discomfort in the earlier 1960s was contained by the charismatic Gaullist regime. Despite this, given its largely traditionalist social base and the benevolent *authoritarianism of its leader, the regime had limited capacities for understanding the new social concerns which modernization brought.

It was no surprise that the student and intellectual world provided the spark for explosion. Inept efforts to update the French educational system—expansion of university teaching without adequate budgets, poor and alienating facilities, and incompetent reflection about curricular organization and change—fed student and intellectual malaise. France's student milieus were traditionally prone to agitation and, moreover, had already been touched by the burgeoning international movement of protest against the *Vietnam War. The "events" themselves were provoked directly by a march, led by Daniel Cohn-Bendit ("Danny the Red"), from the Nanterre campus in suburban Paris to the Latin Quarter to protest against plans to bring student anti-Vietnam activists to trial.

After the marchers had held a rally in the Sorbonne courtyard, police moved in brutally for mass arrests. The interaction was prototypical. The authorities believed that a show of force would intimidate the student movement. Militant student leaders, acting in deliberately provocative ways, were quite as convinced that such repression, given the depth of student discontent, would provoke a mass movement. Barricades were thus repeatedly erected in the Latin Quarter. Pitched battles between excited students and ferocious-looking riot police occurred, replete with barrages of paving stones answered with tear gas. The student leaders proved the better strategists. In short order the totality of Paris's very large student population was mobilized while the movement spread through the provinces. An intense week of startling confrontation between government and students, broadcast live on French radio and television, polarized French adult society.

The ideological content of the student movement was an interesting combination of anarchistic "new culture" slogans—"bring imagination to power," for example—and the strident *Marxism and Third Worldism which led to the ritual singing of "l'Internationale" after big rallies. Indeed, the real objects of the student movement were difficult to discern. Some wanted to reform the educational system. Others wanted to strengthen opposition to the Gaullist regime. Still others, and probably the majority, thought that they were engaged in revolution. The social base of the movement was "new-middle-class youth" in profound intergenerational conflict on the cusp of France's modernization. Movement leadership, in contrast, was largely drawn from a preexisting universe of student leftist groups perpetually seeking out "masses" to direct.

On 11 May, after a week of student protest, French union leaderships called for a one-day strike of solidarity with the students in an effort to warn the Gaullist government away from its course of repression. This strike, meant to be brief, precipitated a decentralized brushfire among workers all over the country. Three days later France was completely shut down by a national strike movement which, at its peak, encompassed virtually the entire French working *class, perhaps the largest single strike in the history of modern societies. The workers sought redress for an entirely different set of grievances from the students', largely in the area of industrial relations (wages, employment security, union rights), to which the Gaullist regime and French employers had proved unwilling to respond over the years.

The contiguity of student and strike movements came very close to destabilizing France. When General de Gaulle, appreciated for a decade as a consummate political strategist, was unable to prevent the situation from deteriorating, French elites prepared for dramatic political changes. A solution was finally proposed by Prime Minister Georges Pompidou based on dividing students from workers by negotiating an end to the strike and then calling new legislative elections. After nearly a month of *Sturm und Drang*, the strike was finally settled. The student movement, which had itself degenerated toward utopian extremism, then began to wane as the impending elections led political elites back into tried-and-true campaign paths. In the heat of general social panic which May 1968 promoted, General de Gaulle's electoral coalition won a sweeping victory.

De Gaulle's career was nonetheless fatally compromised by May 1968. He ultimately resigned in April 1969. The course of French economic and social life was likewise profoundly changed by the "events." The strike settlement was costly, contributing to inflation and currency devaluations and ultimately to the economic difficulties which overtook France in the 1970s. The course of French social policy was changed after May in more generous and less authoritarian directions as well. Student leftists, convinced that *revolution was on the way, followed a course of exhausting agitation which wore them down by the early 1970s. Gathering its own strength in the aftermath of the "events," the French Left began to move decisively toward its 1980s successes, eventually providing a legitimate home for many of the May movement's more able leaders.

The symbolic role of May 1968 is quite as important. May in Paris was the most spectacular and eloquent moment of the broader parade of student upheaval of the 1960s. Because it had brought a major European society, if not to the verge of revolution, at least to an advanced stage of disorder, it was seen as a model for what student protest might achieve and a confirmation for the most committed student activists that they were a new vanguard of fundamental social change. At virtually the same moment the anti-Vietnam mobilization in the United States was reaching its peak—obliging President Lyndon *Johnson to renounce any attempt at reelection. With student activism paralyzing major campuses, rebellions against conscription and discipline in the armed services growing, and unprecedented violence marking public life, it looked as if American society were disintegrating. Likewise German students mobilized dramatically in the streets of Berlin and Frankfurt and the "*Prague Spring" pursued its tragic course in Czechoslovakia amid a tide of smaller movements almost everywhere in advanced societies. In the aftermath of the events in Paris, Italian students and workers initiated the long "Hot Autumn" which was to loom so large over Italian politics in the 1970s.

It would take some time for the deeper meaning of this international wave of protest, with the French May at its symbolic center, to become clear. In effect, the content of progressive politics in advanced societies was changing dramatically. Older, labor-centered political patterns would henceforth be challenged, and have to share their political space on the Left with the newer issues and ways of organizing characteristic of the educationally credentialed new middle strata, particularly those engaged in public-sector and "helping" professional occupational roles. A new feminism, "green" ecology movements, and other such mobilizations would come to share the Left political stage with and complicate the lives of social democratic and other older Left formations.

(See also GAULLISM; NEW LEFT; NEW SOCIAL MOVEMENTS; POSTMATERIALISM.)

Alain Touraine, *The May Movement: Revolt and Reform* (New York, 1971). George Ross, *Workers and Communists in France*, ch. 10 (Berkeley, Calif., 1982). Jacques Capdevielle and René Mouriaux, *Mai 68: L'entre-deux de la modernité* (Paris, 1988). David Hanley and Anne Kerr, eds., *May '68: Coming of Age* (London, 1989). Sidney Tarrow, *Democracy and Disorder: Protest and Politics in Italy, 1965–1975* (Oxford, 1989).

GEORGE ROSS

McCARTHYISM. The term *McCarthyism* was invented in late March 1950 by *Washington Post* cartoonist Herbert Block (Herblock). It referred to tactics employed by Republican Senator Joseph R. McCarthy of Wisconsin, who for some two months had been rocketing to international fame by charging that subversives in the federal government were influencing and setting national policy. The term rapidly became used to identify methods used by advocates of the Second Red Scare (1948–1957), who made reckless personal charges of Communist

and pro-Communist activities for the sake of political, psychological, and economic profit.

Postwar frustrations, especially associated with Soviet aggression in Western Europe, were largely responsible for the emergence of McCarthyism. Several politicians in the elections of 1946 learned that voters could be influenced by charges that their opponents were "soft" on the "Reds." But claims of Communists in high places began to appear in many areas of American life. In 1947, for example, the House Committee on Un-American Activities held widely publicized hearings on disloyalty in the film industry.

The 1948 presidential election saw the Democratic incumbent Harry S. *Truman record a stunning upset victory over the Republican Thomas Dewey. In the aftermath many Republicans became convinced that future victories could best be achieved by claiming that Democrats, especially liberals within the party, were aiding the Communist cause. Soon such events as the Judith Coplon case (in which a Department of Justice employee was arrested as a Soviet spy), the Communist takeover of China, the Soviet Union's unexpected development of the atomic bomb, and the sensational perjury conviction of the liberal Alger Hiss (which many interpreted as a vindication of charges that he had been a Red spy), persuaded many in the United States that something was definitely wrong in Washington.

Joe McCarthy entered the picture in February 1950, charging—without evidence—that there were 205 Communists in the State Department. The allegations grew more widespread, eventually resulting in the persecution and firing of people in all walks of life. The Second Red Scare, with the flamboyant, publicity-conscious McCarthy as its leader, was under way. Republicans eagerly—and successfully—employed McCarthyism in the elections of 1950 and 1952, culminating in the 1952 presidential race, won by Dwight *Eisenhower with the aid of McCarthy (a man he personally despised) and his supporters.

McCarthy quickly became a thorn in the side of the new administration by attacking Republicans, army leaders, and even the president himself. His shrill charges of subversive activity led to the televised Army-McCarthy hearings in 1954, in which McCarthy claimed unconvincingly that the military was riddled with Reds. In front of millions of viewers, McCarthy revealed himself to be an irresponsible bully. He was censured by the Senate later that year for offensive conduct toward colleagues.

Still, McCarthyism continued, in the nation's churches, libraries, schools, mass media, governmental bodies, and elsewhere. It began to fade in 1956, when Eisenhower easily won reelection, and it was buried the following year by the United States Supreme Court in several decisions including *Watkins v. United States* and *Jencks v. United States*.

The Second Red Scare directly affected only a

small minority of Americans, and few people, pollsters reported, considered the issue of major importance. Still, McCarthyism clearly had some negative impact on *American foreign policy, politics, the media, and intellectual freedom, and McCarthyism as a term denoting a politically motivated witchhunt to discredit ideological opponents has remained in the lexicon of U.S. politics.

(See also COLD WAR; COMMUNISM.)

Thomas C. Reeves, *The Life and Times of Joe McCarthy: A Biography* (New York, 1982). Thomas C. Reeves, ed., *McCarthyism*, 3d ed. (Malabar, Fla., 1989). Richard M. Fried, *Nightmare in Red: The McCarthy Era in Perspective* (New York, 1990).

THOMAS C. REEVES

MERCANTILISM. The early mercantilist writers of the sixteenth and seventeenth centuries never thought of themselves as such. The term' was largely unknown until, in the *The Wealth of Nations* (1776), Adam Smith criticized the mercantile system for its obsession with precious metals as the source of all wealth. His attack was largely confined to the commercial policies that flowed from this view, but later liberal economists have widened their understanding of mercantilism to include any government interference in the market of which they disapprove. In the nineteenth century, Friedrich List and the German historical school of political economists viewed mercantilism more favorably, arguing that active government management of the economy was an essential instrument of nation- and *state-building. Despite the intellectual dominance that liberal economics achieved during the twentieth century, most governments have continued to follow their advice.

The mercantile system was a product of the emergence of the early modern state with its centralized administration and standing army. Mercantilist policies varied from country to country, but their principal objectives were similar: to maximize the power of the sovereign and the well-being of his or her subjects. Under mercantilism power and wealth were synonyms not opposites.

These objectives were pursued within an intellectual climate which had two background features. The first was the belief that the state could only prosper by prevailing over its enemies: it had to be in a position to fight and win *wars. Since wars had to be paid for, governments needed a war chest, particularly as their tax base was narrow and financial credit in short supply. The second feature was the belief to which Adam Smith took such fierce objection, that wealth was fixed, residing in a finite stock of gold and silver. This zero-sum assumption meant that in any exchange, what one side gained, the other lost. It lay behind the export bounties and import prohibitions, the competition for bullion and colonies, and the mercantile wars of the early modern period. Indeed, mercantilism may be regarded as the economic dimension of the system of European power politics which developed after the signing of the Treaty of Westphalia in 1648.

The mercantilist worldview led to a preoccupation with *security and control in monetary and commercial relations between states. In monetary affairs a surplus was regarded as of paramount importance. Since wealth resided in money, a deficit meant impoverishment. A hoard of bullion was also necessary to fill the war chest, a consideration which weighed heavily on governments which often relied on mercenaries to fight their wars. The logical absurdity of all governments seeking a surplus at the same time was not perceived as a problem: within a zero-sum world, there had to be winners and losers. There was no difference, in principle, between the acquisition of territory through conquest and the acquisition of bullion as the result of an act of piracy on the high seas.

In commercial relations, the same "realist" logic applied. It led to protectionist attitudes toward foreign trade. Thus, for example, Johann Joachim Becher wrote: "It is always better to sell goods to others than to buy goods from others, for the former brings a certain advantage, and the latter inevitable damage." Hence, governments attempted to keep foreign goods out, a practice which was also good for local employment, and to subsidize the export of manufactures. Foreign trade was strictly controlled through the provision of royal charters, as a means of raising revenue. And since control was important, some mercantilist writers urged buying only from your own customers, i.e., bilateralism.

In his historical survey (*Mercantilism*, London, 1955) Eli Heckscher suggests that two events, the Boston Tea Party and the publication of *The Wealth of Nations*, doomed mercantilism as a social order. By the beginning of the nineteenth century it was no longer respectable to advocate practices in which there was no distinction between legitimate trade and plunder. Moreover, David Ricardo's *Theory of Comparative Advantage* undermined the conception of political economy as a zero-sum set of relations, while *imperialism and capitalist development led to the emergence of a global economy and an increasingly complex international division of labor. The liberal challenge to mercantilism, based on the advantages of relatively open foreign trade rather than economic *nationalism, was thus advanced on both practical and intellectual grounds. At first sight it was enormously successful. Yet, the fact that international society consisted of competitive sovereign states (not of individual profit maximizers) ensured the survival of many mercantilist policies. In the late twentieth century, these still provide the basis of national solutions (or attempted solutions) to the problems of *interdependence.

The ends of economic nationalism—the protection of the interests and welfare of the community—are not the same as those of mercantilism—the power and wealth of the sovereign state—but the means used to pursue these ends are often similar. In *The Closed Commercial State* (1800) Johann Fichte described in detail the principles on which a completely self-sufficient, autarkic national community should be based. These included the planning of production, investment, and employment and a total prohibition of foreign trade. Since states vary in their resource endowments, success required military expansion until the nation reached its "natural frontiers," at which point there would be no further need for either trade or war. Fichte's vision is the prototype of aggressive economic nationalism. Few governments have been tempted to follow his prescriptions, although his ideas probably influenced the economic policies of the Third Reich toward Eastern Europe during the 1930s. Between 1960 and 1980, many *Third World governments attempted to industrialize through *import-substitution policies. However, the postwar *international system offered few opportunities for territorial expansion, and none has pursued self-sufficiency with anything approaching the rigor envisaged by Fichte.

Throughout the twentieth century, a milder version of economic nationalism has established itself as the norm, even infiltrating the liberal international institutions (*International Monetary Fund, International Bank for Reconstruction and Development, and *General Agreement on Tariffs and Trade) which were established after World War II. This milder version, in which the right of governments to give preference to their own nationals is implicitly acknowledged, draws heavily on the legacy of mercantilism.

The early mercantilists had no conception of the business cycle. The final proof that the international division of labor could not safely be ignored came with the Great Depression of the 1930s: business failure and mass unemployment were transmitted from country to country in the manner of an epidemic. The cure which governments adopted was to fall back on a range of mercantilist measures for promoting exports and inhibiting imports, e.g., high tariffs, import quotas, export subsidies, currency manipulation.

After 1945 an attempt was made to insure against a repetition of these "beggar your neighbor" policies on the grounds that they had failed to bring about economic recovery and had contributed to the poisoning of political relations in Europe and the drift to war. Despite significant progress in trade liberalization under the General Agreement on Tariffs and Trade, it has not proved possible to abolish protectionism altogether. In the 1970s and 1980s there was a sharp increase in the use of export subsidies, voluntary export restraint, and organized marketing agreements, all neomercantilist measures. During the 1980s and early 1990s, many governments attempted to reduce their direct involvement in the market, but so long as their electoral fortunes depend largely upon the performance of the economy, it is doubtful whether democratic states can abandon mercantilist policies altogether.

(See also CAPITALISM; PROTECTION; REALISM.)

Friedrich List, *The National System of Political Economy* (New York, 1841, reprinted 1904). Jacob Viner, "Power versus Plenty as Objectives of Foreign Policy in the Seventeenth and Eighteenth Centuries" *World Politics* 1, no.1 (October 1948): 1–29. Eric Roll, *A History of Economic Thought* (London, 1961). David Baldwin, *Economic Statecraft* (Princeton, N.J., 1985). Robert Gilpin, *The Political Economy of International Relations* (Princeton, N.J., 1987). James Mayall, *Nationalism and International Society* (Cambridge, U.K., 1990).

JAMES MAYALL

MERCENARIES. Many of the new African states of the 1960s and 1970s were so weak that a few outsiders with modern weapons could hope to overthrow a government or tip the balance in a civil war. White mercenaries served as ground forces in Zaire, Nigeria, Sudan, and Angola, and as *coup d'état strike forces in Guinea, Equatorial Guinea, Benin, Togo, the Seychelles, and the Comoros, not always successfully.

Mercenaries appeared in *Zaire (the former Belgian Congo) in 1960. The officers and noncommissioned officers of the *gendarmerie* or army of secessionist Katanga were regular Belgian army personnel, but mercenaries were recruited in Belgium by the security police.

To avoid complete dependence upon Belgium, Katanga's leaders sought additional white mercenaries from Rhodesia, South Africa, and France. The English-speakers formed a separate unit under Colonel Mike Hoare of South Africa. Belgium prevented France's Colonel Roger Trinquier from entering Katanga to assume command of the *gendarmerie,* but most of the twenty officers he had recruited did serve there; one of them, Major Roger Faulques, led the fight against the UN. Other French recruits, including Bob Denard, joined the initial force. UN expulsion of most foreign "advisers" and military personnel eliminated most Belgian regular officers and left control of the *gendarmerie* to the mercenaries. When the UN ended the secession in 1963, Denard and former Belgian settler Jean Schramme led a hundred mercenaries and several thousand African *gendarmes* into Angola, where other "Katangans" later joined them.

In 1964, with supporters of Patrice *Lumumba controlling half the Congo, Tshombe returned from exile to head the central government. He summoned Schramme and 8,000 "Katangans" and gave Hoare the job of forming a white mercenary unit to be known as Five Commando. Congolese Army (ANC) units were "stiffened" by giving them a Belgian officer (regular or mercenary) as combat leader, but the all-white Five Commando was the spearhead of all attacks. A motorized column headed by Five Commando was nearing the Lumumbist capital of Kisangani when Belgian paratroops dropped from

U.S. planes to seize the city and rescue white hostages.

General Mobutu's coup of November 1965 was motivated in part by his desire to block President Kasavubu's effort to get rid of the white mercenaries before the Lumumbists were defeated. The mercenaries then played key roles in two efforts to restore Tshombe to power. In 1966, conspirators planned to call Hoare out of retirement as leader but the South African government showed no interest in supporting the conspiracy. The conspirators incited a revolt at Kisangani by ex-Katangans serving in the ANC, but Denard and Schramme helped to thwart the rising.

In 1967, French-speaking mercenaries led a revolt at Kisangani, following which a column led by Schramme left Kisangani and seized Bukavu. Colonel Monga, a Katangan accompanying Schramme, announced formation of a provisional government to replace Mobutu. The ANC (backed by the United States) blockaded Schramme and his men at Bukavu and forced them to retreat to Rwanda.

Mercenaries also served on both sides in the Nigeria-Biafra war. In 1967, the federal government hired South Africans, Britons, and Egyptians as pilots to attack Biafran targets. Mercenary contributions to the federal cause were minor except for their negative contribution of failing to close Biafra's Uli airstrip, thereby prolonging the war and keeping their paychecks coming.

*Biafra employed mercenaries (including Five Commando veteran Alistair Wicks) as pilots and as ground troops. At the end of 1967, Faulques brought in fifty-three mercenaries to fight on the ground for Biafra, but most left two months later, alleging that they had not received the modern arms stipulated in their contract. Sixteen other Frenchmen stayed in Biafra for one week in September 1968. Mercenaries and arms for Biafra apparently were arranged by Jacques Foccart, secretary-general for African affairs at the French presidency.

In 1975, Denard helped socialist Ali Soilih overthrow President Ahmed Abdallah of the Comoro Islands, just months after the archipelago gained its independence from France. Then he left the Comoros to engage in other escapades, including a bungled attempt to overthrow President Mathieu Kerekou of *Benin in 1977. In 1978, Denard invaded the islands with fifty white accomplices and reinstalled Abdallah (allegedly on behalf of Comoran business interests). When François Mitterrand vowed to rid the Comoros of the mercenaries in 1981, Denard apparently won South African support for the *Garde présidentielle* which he had formed to protect Abdallah. In 1989 South Africa and France agreed that Denard and his force should leave by the end of December. When Abdallah refused to renew the mercenaries' contract he was murdered by Denard's chief assistant. Following suspension of French and South African aid, local demonstrations, and a show

of French military force, Denard and his recruits flew to Johannesburg. Denard's activities, like Hoare's unsuccessful invasion of the Seychelles in 1981, seem to reflect South Africa's perceived security needs in the Indian Ocean.

Gerry S. Thomas's attempt to distinguish mercenaries from other operatives by three negative characteristics—including lack of support from their own government—is called into question by these cases, since South Africa, France, and Belgium all recruited and financed mercenaries, including their own citizens, for service in Africa. More basically, the mercenary era seems a by-product of the *Cold War.

(See also CONGO CRISIS; DECOLONIZATION; INDIAN OCEAN REGION; MILITARISM.)

Gerry S. Thomas, *Mercenary Troops in Modern Africa* (Boulder, Colo., 1984).

THOMAS TURNER

MEXICO. Throughout the post–World War II period, the Mexican political system has been characterized by a strong concentration of power. Decision making is dominated by a president, elected every six years, and his appointed elite within the bureaucracy. The electoral arena is controlled by an official party, the Partido Revolucionario Institucional (PRI), a vast and powerful patronage machine, and the corporatist apparatus of the state and party are used to co-opt and channel the activities of labor unions and other economic *interest groups. After the early 1970s, a degree of political liberalization began to expand the scope of public debate and to offer somewhat greater opportunity for opposition political parties. The most important of these was the Partido de Acción Nacional (PAN). Nevertheless, pluralist political institutions—the Congress, state and local government, the courts, and other formal institutions of the constitutional system—have continued to play an insignificant role.

In a continent characterized by frequent military coups and unstable civilian democracies, these arrangements have persisted for decades. Nevertheless, important social and political changes have created major pressures for both political *reform and economic adjustment. On the one hand, it has been increasingly difficult for the representative mechanisms of the dominant party to co-opt and manage the growing range of independent business and middle-class groups that seek participation in the political process. At the same time, the severe economic crisis beginning in the early 1980s has produced strong pressures for economic liberalization. These twin pressures, economic liberalization and democratic reform, constitute the challenges of the 1990s.

History. Although Mexico formally won its independence from Spain in 1821, it did not really emerge as a modern nation-state until the 1870s, when it became integrated into the world economy as an exporter of agricultural and mineral products.

The previous half century had been marked by civil war, economic turmoil, and foreign invasions in which, among other things, Mexico was forced to cede half of its original territory to the United States. As international trade opportunities expanded, however, President Porfirio Díaz (1876–1911) was able to consolidate an alliance among the local oligarchy, foreign capital, and the military; and for the first time since independence, the central government was able to establish a degree of control over population and territory. The economy grew during the Porfiriato, led by the continued expansion of commercial agriculture and mining. But these developments failed to provide political opportunities for the emerging middle class, and they were achieved at the expense of Indian and mestizo peasants. In 1911, an armed rebellion against Díaz, led initially by Díaz's opponents within the oligarchy and middle class, triggered a decade of civil war and the widespread political mobilization of the peasantry and small urban working class.

The contemporary Mexican political system emerged out of these struggles, from compromises and reforms among revolutionary generals and middle-class politicians who sought a formula for the political reconstruction of the state. The first decisive moment in this process came under the great populist reformer General Lázaro *Cárdenas, president of Mexico from 1934 to 1940. Cárdenas's administration left several major legacies for the Mexican system. First, a sweeping *land reform built a base of legitimacy for the system among the rural poor, while Cárdenas's bold expropriation of foreign-owned petroleum companies helped to rally nationalist sentiment. At same time, control over the popular base of the system was institutionalized through the organization of "corporatist" peasant and union organizations linked to the dominant revolutionary party. The contemporary framework of party organization in Mexico dates primarily from that period.

During the early 1940s Cárdenas's successors engaged in other steps fundamental to the consolidation of the contemporary Mexican system: reconciliation with the United States and the domestic business elite. A compensation agreement over the oil expropriations was the most important step in normalizing relations with the United States. With war breaking out in Europe, the Roosevelt administration had no wish to antagonize its neighbor and settled on terms comparatively favorable to Mexico. Rapprochement with business was based in part on *import-substitution policies which offered profitable subsidies to the private sector. More broadly, the dominant party and the official union organization served as important instruments of social control through which the regime could provide a safe climate for investment without overt and systematic repression of dissent.

The "golden age," at least in retrospect, was the so-called period of stabilizing development, which lasted from the mid-1950s until the late 1960s. Although the political elite was divided during this period into contending orthodox and populist factions, macroeconomic policymaking was controlled primarily by technocrats in the Bank of Mexico and Finance Ministry, who attached high priority to domestic price stability. Under their leadership, import-substituting strategies were combined with cautious fiscal and monetary policies, resulting in almost fifteen years of high growth, relatively low inflation, and rising real wages for segments of the population represented through the official union movement.

Social Change and Mounting Political Problems. Despite its successes, by the end of the 1960s the stabilizing development model was running up against serious limitations, and policy changes initiated during the presidency of Luis Echeverría (1970–1976) brought the period to a close. By that time, two important types of pressure had become sources of concern for much of the Mexican political elite.

First, there were broad social and demographic changes. During the 1950s and 1960s, Mexico had evolved into an urban, middle-class society, with groups seeking broader forms of representation and wider latitude for dissent and participation. At the same time, the corollary of the elite's accommodation with conservative business groups and the United States had been a deliberate scaling back of the revolutionary ideals that had provided the initial base of *legitimacy for the PRI. Governments during the early postwar era had become increasingly indifferent to growing income inequalities and to income lags among the system's traditional rural constituency.

These two issues were dramatized by the eruption of radical student protest in 1968, and the government's decision to order the massacre of hundreds of protesters in Tlatelolco Square in October of that year. For a wide segment of the political elite, these events provided shocking indications that the system had entered a "crisis of legitimacy" that demanded urgent new political responses. The approaches to these challenges under Echeverría and his successor, José López Portillo (1976–1982), were marked by important reforms and growing political conflicts, leading to the crisis and political changes of the 1980s.

Political liberalization and social reform were pushed by reformist and developmentalist factions of the elite critical of the policies pursued by the more orthodox technocrats. On the political front, their program included a partial relaxation of controls over the union movement, greater opportunities for opposition parties, and more freedom for debate in the press and the universities. Within the social sphere, Echeverría and López Portillo initiated agricultural reforms and development programs, expanded health and welfare expenditures, and increased public investment projects aimed at stimulating growth. By the end of the 1970s, these programs had done much to deradicalize and co-opt antisystem movements that had begun to emerge on the left.

At the same time, the reforms also carried a high economic and political cost. Although the business elite had profited substantially from lucrative subsidies and public contracts provided by the expanding public sector, it was deeply alienated by the *populism of the Echeverría government and was transformed during the 1970s into an increasingly independent and critical political force. Direct efforts to influence politics included the formation of new independent associations, financial backing for the opposition PAN, and the formation of privately backed media networks. The trump card, however, was the threat of capital flight to the United States, which provided business groups with a strong potential veto over policies that appeared to threaten their core interests.

Macroeconomic policy during the 1970s reflected these political contradictions. Business's veto power was wielded with greatest success against efforts to match expanding spending commitments with increased taxes. The result was growing fiscal and trade deficits, and increasing inflationary pressures, which eventually led to the debt crisis of August 1982.

Acute problems first emerged in the mid-1970s, when mounting trade deficits and capital flight forced the Echeverría administration into a stabilization program backed by the *International Monetary Fund (IMF). These pressures were temporarily relieved by the rapid expansion of petroleum exports from 1978 to 1981. Under López Portillo, the government again attempted to cope with social tensions through expansionist policies that were not sustainable over the long run—running up huge fiscal deficits, allowing the peso to become badly overvalued, and borrowing heavily in external commercial credit markets.

The bubble burst during 1982 after a series of external shocks forced Mexico into temporary default on its debt service. The turn to tight monetary policies in the United States dramatically raised interest payments on Mexico's external debt. Simultaneously, declining demand for petroleum reduced revenues. In effect, these developments combined to force the system into virtual bankruptcy, the rescheduling of external debt payments. and a very painful process of stabilization and adjustment. The next decade was the worst since the civil war, with growth rates near zero and real wages plunging over forty percent.

Economic and Political Adjustments under de la Madrid and Salinas. Major factional realignments within the Mexican elite shaped the response of the system to these problems, first during the presidency of Miguel de la Madrid (1982–1988) and then under his successor, Carlos Salinas. After the inauguration of de la Madrid, virtually all the old-guard developmentalists were pushed out of positions of power and replaced by a new generation of orthodox technocrats similar to those who had dominated the stabilizing development period. These new technocrats were by no means united around a detailed strategy of reform, and their response to the crisis was often characterized by internal debate and improvisation. They did, however, share broad ideological commitments to market-oriented economic adjustments, and over the course of the next decade this led to at least three profound changes in the Mexican political economy: an extensive program of macroeconomic stabilization and structural adjustment; the reconstruction of a close alliance between the state and business elites; and the normalization of relations with external creditors.

Stabilization and Adjustment. The extent of Mexico's orthodox stabilization and adjustment program was matched during the 1980s only by the *Pinochet regime in Chile. Stabilization efforts began in 1982 with a deep fiscal austerity program that was maintained, with some wavering in the mid-1980s, for the next ten years. When orthodox programs themselves failed to contain inflationary pressures, the government began to experiment with other measures as well. In 1988, a wage and price control program (the Economic Solidarity Pact or PSE) was negotiated with the private sector. Undertaken in conjunction with continuing fiscal austerity, it finally provided the basis for a durable stabilization of prices. When Salinas entered office at the end of the year, the groundwork had been laid for the resumption of growth during the 1990s.

Structural adjustment efforts began in the mid-1980s, in response to a new round of crisis associated with a drop in petroleum prices and conflicts with external creditors. In 1985, the government began a major trade opening, which was followed in 1988 by a further substantial reduction in tariffs. Salinas extended this trade liberalization program by seeking free trade agreements with the United States and Canada. By the early 1990s, he also sharply accelerated the pace of *privatization, with sales of the public telephone and airline companies and several of the large banks nationalized under López Portillo in 1982.

Rebuilding the Alliance with Business Elites. The legacy of state-business conflicts under Echeverría and López Portillo constituted a powerful impediment to rebuilding an alliance with the business elite; antagonisms had become especially sharp after the bank nationalization decision mentioned above. Gradually, however, these suspicions were allayed by the promarket polices consistently pursued after 1982, and by the realization among business elites that continuing conflict with the state could open the way to "dangerous" populist trends within the political system. The turning point came in December 1987 with the negotiation of the PSE. The pact did much more than simply stabilize prices; it also helped to contain the political problems associated with a dangerous period of transition from one president to another and to reaffirm the interests of the Mexican political elite and the business sector in the continuing stability of the political economy.

Rebuilding Ties to the External Sector and the Resumption of Growth. Normalization of relations with creditors faced a number of major obstacles that also persisted throughout most of the 1980s. These included the burdens of the debt service and adjustment itself, the unwillingness of commercial banks to resume voluntary lending, and serious conflicts with the U.S. government over Central American policy, drug trade, and immigration. Relations reached a crisis point during stalled efforts to renegotiate a new loan agreement with the IMF in 1985–1986, and the Mexican government began seriously to consider a unilateral suspension of debt service.

New approaches to these problems were launched principally in order to avert a confrontation that neither side wanted. The U.S. government, deeply concerned about the implications of turmoil in Mexico, began the move back from the brink by pressuring the IMF to respond with flexibility to Mexican demands. The conclusion of a new agreement in June 1986 opened the way to new commercial bank agreements, which brought US$4.5 billion in new money into Mexico during 1987. On the Mexican side, the government quietly backed away from its activist role in Central American diplomacy.

Changes of presidential administration in both the United States and Mexico during 1989 helped to consolidate this new, more cooperative course, and provided the spark for a new round of economic expansion in the early 1990s. The main elements were the conclusion of the "Brady Plan" negotiations in February 1990, which reduced Mexico's commercial bank debt by approximately thirty percent, and the mutual commitments to conclude a free trade treaty which opened important new opportunities for sales in the huge U.S. market. Building on the economic reforms already discussed, these developments led during the first half of the Salinas administration to an upsurge in economic optimism not seen since the debt crisis of 1982. While expectations were still subject to reversal, particularly in the event of the failure of the trade negotiations, finance capital and external direct investment began to flow back into the country and the economy appeared to be entering a new period of sustained expansion.

Political Prospects. By the early 1990s, Mexico was widely considered an economic success story—at least among government officials, bankers, and economists. There were much more serious questions, however, about Mexico's longer-term political future. Mexico's centralized state and party system had been crucial in permitting the de la Madrid

government to impose painful economic adjustment measures, control populist and union dissent, and transfer power to Carlos Salinas at the end of 1988. Yet it was increasingly clear that the dominant party and corporatist apparatus was itself becoming obsolete and unable to secure the cooperation of widening sectors of Mexican society. The 1988 election had produced an unprecedented protest vote in favor of the center-left movement headed by Cuauhtémoc Cárdenas, the son of Lázaro, and Salinas's victory was tainted with charges of fraud.

With the economic upturn of the early 1990s, Salinas's personal popularity surged markedly, and much of the controversy that surrounded the transfer of power to Carlos Salinas at the end of 1988 abated. At the same time, he took a number of important steps to relieve some of the political pressures on the system. Electoral laws were reformed to reduce opportunities for fraud, and after a series of street confrontations, the PAN was permitted to win two state governorships in the midterm election of 1992, an unprecedented event within the Mexican system. There have also been efforts to reform the dominant party itself. The most important step has been the creation of the Programa Nacional de Solidaridad (PRONASOL), a new mass organization charged with reallocating public resources toward locally directed health and education projects.

Nevertheless, as of the early 1990s, these changes had not fundamentally altered the basic hierarchies of elite power within the Mexican system, and the dilemmas of institutional reform remained. On the one hand, while the government groped toward accommodation with the PAN, it continued to harass and intimidate opponents on the left. Moreover, there were serious questions about whether the economic trajectory launched during the 1980s could be sustained within the framework of a more pluralistic political system.

On the other hand, the economic reforms themselves were likely to add to pressures already building for a political modernization of representative institutions. A reduction of the economic resources flowing through the public sector, for example, could be expected to reduce the scope of political patronage available to the traditional bosses that dominated the corporatist and party apparatus. Successful economic adjustments are also likely to increase middle-class and business pressure for a more open political system, while closer cultural and economic ties with the United States are certain to introduce important new political cleavages into the system.

(See also CORPORATISM; INTERNATIONAL DEBT; NATIONALIZATION; U.S.–LATIN AMERICAN RELATIONS.)

Roger Hansen, *The Politics of Mexican Development* (Baltimore, Md., 1971). Dale Story, *Industry, the State and Public Policy in Mexico* (Austin, Tex., 1986). Sylvia Maxfield and Ricardo Anzaldúa Montoya, eds., *Government and the Private Sector in Contemporary Mexico* (San Diego,

Calif., 1987). Stephen A. Quick, *Mexico's Economic Revolution: Implications for the United States*, Staff Study for Joint Economic Committee (Washington, D.C., 1988). Robert Kaufman, "Stabilization and Adjustment in Argentina, Brazil, and Mexico," in Joan M. Nelson, ed., *Economic Crisis and Policy Choice* (Princeton, N.J., 1990), pp. 63–113.

ROBERT KAUFMAN

MICRONESIA, FEDERATED STATES OF. See PACIFIC ISLANDS.

MIDDLE EAST. The region of the world which comprises Egypt, the Arabian Peninsula, and the states of the Fertile Crescent (Syria, Lebanon, Israel, Jordan, and Iraq) is known as the Middle East. It is also frequently said to include the Arab states of North Africa, as well as Turkey and Iran. In this larger sense, the region covers about ten percent of the earth's land surface and supports about five percent of the world population.

The name *Middle East* has a recent origin. For many centuries, European geographers used the term *Near East*. During World War II, the British designated their military headquarters in the region as the "Middle East Command." Thereafter, the term *Middle East* came into general usage, and today this Eurocentric term remains the name of choice for both scientific and popular discourse, not only in the West but also in the region itself.

The Middle East is not a concept rooted in physical geography. Natural boundaries do not mark it off unequivocally from other areas of habitation like Africa and Central Asia. Rather, the Middle East takes meaning from human history, geopolitics, culture, and *political economy. Though alternative regional conceptions exist for some of the same territories—among them the Arab world, the Islamic world, and the Mediterranean basin—the Middle East has proved in recent times to be the most useful and enduring analytical framework.

The Middle East enjoys great historical and cultural unity—even more so, perhaps, than Europe. Most of its lands were ruled for over four centuries by a single state—the Ottoman Empire—and in the eight previous centuries Arab-Islamic empires often held sway. As a result, the overwhelming majority of the population adhere to *Islam, and Arabic is spoken as the vernacular in most countries while it is honored as the language of religion in most of the remainder. Architecture, arts, and even cuisine have a marked similarity throughout the region.

A long history of competition and conflict with Europe defines the region. For over ten centuries, powerful Middle Eastern states clashed with European military forces and generally held the upper hand. As recently as 1683, an army from the Middle East nearly conquered Vienna. These conflicts, often considered in the West as a clash of Christianity with Islam, pitted neighboring civilizations and empires against one another and often had economic

roots. The long competition did much to form the states, institutions, and consciousness of the modern world.

In the past two centuries, and especially the past hundred years, the *balance of power shifted radically. European states came to dominate the Middle East economically and militarily and for a time ruled it directly through colonies and protectorates. Since World War II, the United States has supplanted Europe as the dominant power in the region. Though no colonies remain, the peoples of the region are inclined to resent their subordinate status and look back with wonder at an earlier age. In Europe and North America, on the other hand, the region is often portrayed as a dangerous, inhospitable place, marked by violence, corruption, fanaticism, and voluptuousness. Such ideas of history, of Self and of Other, are central to the notion of the Middle East.

Many relatively weak nation-states now divide the region. Created by European colonial powers, these states are often bitter rivals and their conflicts fuel regional instability—much as did the intense rivalries of European states. Two dozen border wars since 1945, including five conflicts between Arab states and Israel, have involved all but four of the region's twenty-two states, and most border claims remain unsettled. Under these circumstances, political movements seeking greater regional unity have achieved little progress, and neither Pan-Arabism nor Pan-Islamism have borne fruit. The *Arab League and the Islamic Conference Organization seek to establish closer ties between their member states, but they have gained little power. Efforts in recent years to promote regional ties through trade pacts have also been largely unsuccessful, and less than four percent of all Middle East trade is intraregional.

The Middle East is the world's most arid region, with desert covering more than half of its land surface. Heavy human use over a very long period and shifting climate have led to the steady spread of deserts and the destruction of human and animal habitats. Aridity has concentrated the rapidly growing population and created serious problems of agricultural development; the Middle East imports by far the highest proportion of food of any world region, and some large countries like Egypt and Iraq import between half and three-quarters of all their basic foodstuffs.

Since irrigated agriculture is in wide and growing use in the Middle East, competition for scarce ground and river water has created a number of sharp interstate conflicts. Turkey, Syria, and Iraq dispute the use of the waters of the Tigris and Euphrates river systems; Israel and its neighbors quarrel over underground aquifers and claims to the Jordan River system; while Egypt, Sudan, and Ethiopia differ over the Nile.

The geopolitical importance of the Middle East in today's world partly results from its location on the major trade routes between Europe and Asia. The

Suez Canal is the most important such corridor, linking the Mediterranean and the Red Sea and accounting for nearly eight percent of world trade. Other vital seaways include the Turkish Straits, the Strait of Hormuz at the mouth of the Persian Gulf, and the Bab al-Mandeb at the southern entrance to the Red Sea.

Even more important than transportation looms the role of the Middle East as an oil producer whose output fuels the industrial economies of Europe and Japan. Nine regional countries are major producers, and some, such as Saudi Arabia and Kuwait, have amassed great wealth through export earnings. The region now produces twenty-five to thirty percent of the world's oil and refines about five percent of the world's refined product. With a large proportion of the world's petroleum reserves—more than sixty percent by most estimates—the region will produce most of the world's oil in just a few decades. Oil production in the Middle East, far less costly than elsewhere in the world, has been enormously profitable. Military and economic control of the region is therefore considered a key to global power.

The heavy concentration of oil resources in the Middle East has sharpened international rivalry and wars in the past century and has led to political instability and conflict in the Middle East itself. Oil revenues, which have enriched the treasuries of unpopular regimes, are also believed to have strengthened the tendency toward authoritarian governments in a region where even partially democratic political systems are rare. Most regimes have spent heavily on military forces. The Middle East consequently imports more arms than any other region of the world and accounts for some twenty-five percent of world trade in major weapons.

Located on Europe's periphery, the Middle East will probably be drawn increasingly toward the *European Community and incorporated into the European trading network in the twenty-first century. Israel, Turkey, and the states of North Africa are furthest along this path. Expanded European direct investment is also likely in the near future. The influence of European culture and lifestyles can be expected to increase as well, especially as European television programming becomes more available across the region.

Will the Middle East become absorbed into Europe or will it move to affirm its own regional economy and culture? Regionwide Islamic movements have signaled a strong popular resistance to Europeanization. But whether the peoples and states of the Middle East will build common structures to affirm their mutual identity remains to be seen.

(See also ARAB-ISRAELI CONFLICT; ARAB NATIONALISM; COLONIAL EMPIRES; DECOLONIZATION; EISENHOWER DOCTRINE; FOOD POLITICS; ORGANIZATION OF PETROLEUM EXPORTING COUNTRIES; RELIGION AND POLITICS; SUEZ CRISIS.)

Charles Isawi, *An Economic History of the Middle East and North Africa* (New York, 1982). Alasdair Drysdale and Gerald Blake, *The Middle East and North Africa: A Political Geography* (New York, 1985). Gerald Blake, John Dewdney, and Jonathan Mitchell, *The Cambridge Atlas of the Middle East and North Africa* (Cambridge, U.K., 1987).

JAMES A. PAUL

MILITARISM. Although subject to a wide range of interpretation, militarism is usually defined as the excessive or illegitimate influence of military institutions, policies, and values on civil society. From the very beginning, the term has been used primarily in a pejorative sense—to paint as abnormal a nation or society in which the military leadership exercises inordinate control over national life—although some effort has been made in recent years to invest the concept with greater analytical precision. Even so, the term is generally reserved for regimes that engage in autocratic or atavistic displays of military power, as in the saturation of urban neighborhoods with armed guards (to deter unwanted political activity) or the ready use of *force to resolve international disputes.

The label of militarism was first used in the late nineteenth century in Europe to characterize the imperial pretensions of Emperor Napoléon III (ruler of France, 1852–1870) and the efforts of the Prussian Junkers to fashion a powerful, military-dominated German state. Similarly, in the interwar years, the term was commonly used to describe and deprecate the Fascist regimes in Italy, Germany, Spain, and Japan. More recently, in the postwar period, the term has been used by critics of governments of both East and West who have opposed the massive U.S. and Soviet investment in nuclear and non-nuclear forces.

In all of these cases, the term has been used to castigate what is seen as the encroachment of a nation's military sector onto the civilian sphere. The implication is that there is a natural boundary or divide between the legitimate functions of the military—that is, defense of the nation in times of *war and appropriate training in times of *peace—and all other human activities. When that boundary is crossed, when the military usurps any of the roles normally ascribed to civilian institutions, then a process or condition of militarism is said to exist.

This interpretation of militarism was given its fullest expression in the 1938 classic *A History of Militarism,* by the German-American historian Alfred Vagts. "Militarism," Vagts wrote, "has connoted a domination of the military over the civilian, an undue preponderance of military demands, and emphasis on military considerations, spirits, ideals, and scales of value, in the life of states."

A similar perspective was advanced in more recent years by Marek Thee of the International Peace Research Institute in Oslo. Militarism begins "with the abuse of the military of its legitimate function and its encroachment on political affairs," he wrote in 1980. As this process proceeds, "the military tends to usurp roles and prerogatives in society which go beyond democratic legitimacy, intervening in internal [affairs] and imposing its will in external affairs." Thee and his colleagues saw evidence of this process in the *Cold War behavior of the two *superpowers, entailing the creation of a vast *military-industrial complex devoted to the development and production of ever more sophisticated weapons, and a propensity for overt or covert intervention in regional *Third World conflicts.

This interpretation of militarism has also been extended to the analysis of military-dominated regimes in the Third World. For many observers, the tendency of Third World military elites to overthrow civilian governments and to exercise authoritarian control over civil institutions is a deplorable expression of classical militarism. "In the Third World particularly," Ruth Leger Sivard wrote in 1989, "the intrusion of military authority into the political arena has been a fast-growing exercise." In *World Military and Social Expenditures* (13th ed., Washington, D.C., 1989) she reported that sixty-four Third World countries (out of a total of 120) were ruled by "military-controlled governments," wherein senior military officers occupied key government positions and the *state *security forces possessed extrajudicial powers under martial law decree.

As manifested in the Third World, contemporary militarism tends to be closely associated with highly stratified societies that have been subjected to recurring internal struggles over the distribution of power, wealth, and status. In many of these countries, the military has used its power to protect the dominant group or class against demands from less privileged groups for a radical redistribution of national resources. Such crackdowns have often proved quite brutal, resulting in widespread civilian casualties and frequent roundups of political dissidents (who may then be subjected to torture, execution, or long-term detention).

Militarism, then, is generally seen as entailing an aberrant or atavistic use of military force. In contrast to this interpretation, a number of social scientists have recently attempted to develop an alternative understanding of militarism, one that views the expanded role of the military as a natural consequence of state formation in the modern world. As states evolve, they argue, there is a natural tendency of state authorities—whether military or civilian—to seek the concentration of political and economic power in the central government's hands, often by constructing civilian institutions on military models and/or by involving military elites in the management of state-run agencies and enterprises. Hence, in this analysis, there can be no clear-cut boundary between the military and civilian sectors of society, as each is routinely interpenetrated by the other.

Adherents to this perspective tend to prefer the term *militarization* to militarism, as the former bears less risk of inviting a normative impulse into the analysis of these phenomena. Whereas militarism has tended to be seen "as something exceptional, archaic, or even exogenous to modern society," John R. Gillis wrote in 1989, "militarization carries no such evolutionary presuppositions." Rather, militarization is a process that can be detected in all modern states, whether or not they exhibit the overt displays of military force associated with *Hitler's Third Reich and *Mussolini's Italy.

(See also FOREIGN MILITARY BASES; MILITARY RULE.)

Alfred Vagts, *A History of Militarism* (London, 1938; New York, 1959 and 1967). John J. Johnson, ed., *The Role of the Military in Underdeveloped Countries* (Princeton, N.J., 1962). Adam Yarmolinsky, *The Military Establishment: Its Impact on a Society* (New York, 1971). Asbjørn Eide and Marek Thee, eds., *Problems of Contemporary Militarism* (London, 1980). Nicole Ball, *Security and Economy in the Third World* (Princeton, N.J., 1988). John R. Gillis, ed., *The Militarization of the Western World* (New Brunswick, N.J., 1989).

MICHAEL T. KLARE

MILITARY-INDUSTRIAL COMPLEX. For nations in the industrial era, national defense has meant an industrialized defense and therefore a defense industry. In the United States, the defense industry includes corporations that produce for the civilian market as well as for the military one, but its core consists of firms whose primary customers are the military services. The defense industry needs the military services; it was brought into being by military contracts during World War II, and it has been sustained in the half-century since by military contracts. The military services, in turn, need the defense industry. The industrial firms put political pressure on Congress and the Executive to maintain defense spending and the budgets of the military services. This mutual, symbiotic relationship between military services and industrial corporations has given rise to the concept of the military-industrial complex (MIC). The phrase itself was first used by President Dwight *Eisenhower in January 1961 in his Farewell Address: "In the councils of government, we must guard against the acquisition of unwarranted influence, whether sought or unsought, by the military-industrial complex. The potential for the disastrous rise of misplaced power exists and will persist." Having commanded the allied armies in World War II and having institutionalized U.S. peacetime military spending during his presidency, Eisenhower was the highest-possible authority on the topic. His phrase described a reality that had only come into being during his own administration. The term has been used ever since because that reality has remained largely the same in the three decades since he spoke.

In the United States, the MIC is composed on the

military side by the services—the air force, navy, army, and marines. On the industry side it is composed principally of about two dozen corporations; the largest of these defense contractors are those engaged in the production of aircraft and missiles, which include McDonnell Douglas, Lockheed, Boeing, Grumman, and the three generals, General Dynamics, General Electric, and General Motors.

A crucial link in the MIC are the elected political officials, especially those who sit on the congressional committees dealing with the armed services and who vote the authorizations and appropriations for weapons systems. They benefit from having weapons contracts given to firms in their districts or states, and they both pressure and support the military in the awarding of these contracts. Some observers consider the congressional committees to be as important to the process as the military services and the defense corporations and speak of the three elements as an "iron triangle."

Critics of the MIC charge it with causing several distortions, or worse, in public policy: 1) higher defense budgets than have been reasonable or necessary, aggravating the *arms race with the Soviet Union from the late 1940s to the late 1980s; 2) within the general defense budget, procurement of destabilizing or inappropriate weapons systems (e.g., human-operated bombers and ballistic missiles, where cruise missiles could accomplish the same ends with less risk and less expense); 3) within a particular weapons system, inefficient production because of "waste, fraud, and abuse," resulting in fewer weapons at greater cost; 4) the weakening of the nondefense industrial base of the United States, making it less capable of competing in the world market for civilian consumer and capital goods, especially against those countries whose own defense industry is quite small (Japan and Germany).

The United States has the most well-known and well-examined MIC, but one can be found in other countries as well. It has been particularly important in the Soviet Union, France, and Britain. Some analysts think that the entire Soviet economy from Stalin to Brezhnev was a vast military-industrial complex. The Soviet military industry—the "metal-eaters" in *Khrushchev's words—was the only part of the Soviet economy that seemed to work, and it provided a model for the rest of the society. But over the long run, the expense of maintaining it (between fifteen and twenty percent of Soviet GNP) drove the Soviet Union into economic decline, political upheaval, the collapse of the *Warsaw Treaty Organization (Warsaw Pact), and eventually the dissolution of the Soviet Union itself. Although the United States, in contrast, spends only five percent of its GNP on defense, the Soviet Union provides a sobering warning about the possible long-term social costs of military spending.

France and Britain also have substantial defense industries. Their greatest impact on world politics probably comes from their dependence on large-scale exports to Third World countries. And since the 1980s, other countries, including China, Israel, and Brazil, have entered into the international arms trade with their own MICs.

Military needs helped foster industrial and technological innovation, including Eli Whitney's development in 1798 of the mass-production process for U.S. army muskets. For almost two centuries thereafter, military needs helped bring new industries into being (e.g., chemicals, aviation, computers, and semiconductors), and during the *Cold War military spending helped to stabilize the overall level of U.S. economic activity (in what has been called military *Keynesianism). Yet in the end military spending has diminished the capacity of the United States to compete in the world market with Japan and Germany, those very countries who were principal beneficiaries of U.S. military protection and therefore of U.S. military spending, and who thus had to undertake little military spending of their own. The two halves of the complex, the military and the industrial, have always been a dynamic and unstable equilibrium. In our own time, the real threat to a nation's industry may come not so much from another nation's military, but from its own.

(See also MILITARISM.)

Mary Kaldor, *The Baroque Arsenal* (New York, 1981). Thomas L. McNaugher, *New Weapons, Old Politics: America's Military Procurement Muddle* (Washington, D.C., 1989).

JAMES KURTH

MILITARY OCCUPATION. See FOREIGN MILITARY BASES.

MILITARY RULE. Armed forces have been influential actors in the countries of Asia, Africa, Latin America, and the *Middle East since World War II. Some *Third World countries under military rule are not "new." Ethiopia, Thailand, and Latin American countries were independent states long before 1945. Many countries in these areas hardly can be called "developing" ones either. In not a few, per capita income has stagnated or declined in recent decades. Thus we cannot take for granted that armed forces come to prominence in new states or in developing ones. Indeed, military forces have been significant actors in ancient Rome and in the empires that have grown up and disintegrated in Asia and the Middle East. What should interest us is how civil-military relations change over time within countries or differ from country to country at similar periods of history.

Armed forces have comparative advantages in moving people and material by virtue of their logistical abilities. They are usually, but not always, relatively well armed compared to other groups in society. This brings us to the distinction between the official and regular military forces of the state and bands of warring people, guerrillas, local police, and other organizations of force. These organizations may well compete with regular military forces; they may sometimes be heavily armed. Insurgents can become organized into regularized armed forces, as occurred during the Chinese and Vietnamese anticolonial and civil wars.

Also, the official armed forces may vary from huge armies with highly specialized service branches—India and China, for example, each have a million or more soldiers under arms—to the small, largely infantry units of some African countries. An armed force may expand very rapidly, as the Nigerian army did during the Nigerian Civil War when it grew from 10,000 to over 250,000 between 1968 and 1970.

It is striking, however, that in many non-Western states, both large and small, militaries play a powerful role in the politics of their countries. In the industrial countries of the West such as the United States and France, militaries are important interest groups, take significant shares of government budgets, and may have veto power over crucial public issues. In 1958–1960, in the aftermath of the *Algerian War of Independence, the French military posed a challenge to continued civilian rule. Military rule, however, in contrast to military influence, has been rare in the countries of Western and Eastern Europe since 1945.

Military rule may be defined by the fact that the head of state achieves a ruling position by virtue of a place in the military chain of command. True, junior officers may come to power. In Africa especially it has not been unknown for noncommissioned officers to seize power, as exemplified by Captain Marien Ngouabi's ascendancy in Congo-Brazzaville (1968), Sergeant Samuel Doe's *coup d'état in Liberia (1980), and Flight Lieutenant Jerry Rawlings's coup in Ghana (1979).

The military establishment itself may be highly fragmented, and an officer or noncommissioned officer may stage a coup as much against a segment of the army as against civilians. This pattern characterized Idi Amin's 1971 coup in Uganda and also occurred periodically in postwar Argentina. Moreover, it is a mistake to think that militaries rule without civilian allies. In fact, civilians often may try to provoke military takeovers in order to bolster their class or ethnic positions. The military coup of 1964 in Brazil is a case in point where business groups feared the growing *populism of civilian elites and growing working-class activism.

In the Middle East and in Africa, one ethnic group may act against others through military coups. Thus, for example, the prominence of Shiʿi officers has been striking in Syria under Hafiz Al-Assad since 1970. Coups and countercoups in Nigeria have had critical ethnic components.

To talk then of *the* military is something of a misnomer. Armed forces are split by service branch, ethnic group, rank, and often class background. It is a matter for empirical investigation as to how cohesive are military organizations. Similarly, it is a matter of empirical study to find out how professionalized are armed forces and whether or not they are distinctive corporate bodies marked off from civilians by education, training, and socialization processes. Militaries usually have specific codes, uniforms, and training, and their officers go to special academies. But whether this training and recruitment makes them cohesive and distinctive by attitude or policy preference as compared to civilians is an open question.

It is not always easy to decide whether a particular leader maintains power by virtue of place in the chain of command or the support of the armed forces. *Mao Zedong rose to power in China by forging the *Chinese Communist Party and leading a broad revolution, but during the *Cultural Revolution in the late 1960s and 1970s he came to rely on particular military units as well as components of the Communist Party and students. Both Gamal Abdel *Nasser and Anwar *Sadat tried to civilianize their leadership in Egypt in the 1960s and 1970s. Both were military figures, but they used civilian parties and interest groups to maintain their power and to give them freedom from their own militaries. Yet military support was critical to their continued rule.

The social science literature on coups and military rule has established few generalizations that we can put forward with great confidence with respect to why and when military coups take place or what are the consequences of military rule in terms of policy preferences and development outcomes. Coups have occurred in nations large and small, have been carried out by armies large and small. Clearly, however, it is difficult to stage a junior officer coup in a large army—Pakistan's, for example.

Within Asia, Africa, Latin America, and the Middle East, few countries have escaped at least some period of military rule. India has been one. But India does not have a relatively high per capita income even within developing countries. It has a tradition of British civilian supremacy—but so do many former British colonies. Nor has the Congress Party in India proved to be highly institutionalized and coherent over the last decade.

It is not true that militaries are more likely to be "modernizers" or more successful in bringing about economic development than are civilian counterparts. Indeed, both the case study literature on military rule and cross-national aggregate data work that has utilized statistics to test hypotheses show us that there is as much differentiation within the category of military rule as there is between military and civilian regimes. Personal leadership has been important to the evolution of specific patterns of military rule. As within civilian regimes, the class and ethnic composition of society has been a powerful factor within military rule.

If militaries have not been associated typically with higher growth rates or particular patterns of economic development, they frequently have tried to curtail *political participation by parties and interest groups only to find that they need allies in civilian society in order to extend their influence beyond the barracks or the statehouse. Sometimes these allies have been civilians with a bent for revolution, as in Ethiopia after 1975 or Peru during the early period of the Velasco-Alvarado regime (1968–1975). Often they have been elites with status quo tendencies, as in Brazil, Paraguay, or Pakistan.

Looking at *foreign policy outcomes, we do not find that military regimes align themselves in clearcut ways. The Argentine military came to grief after its failed invasion of the Malvinas/Falklands, as did the Greek colonels after their Cyprus fiasco. But military regimes have not proved to be more aggressive or nationalistic than civilian ones.

Idiosyncratic leaders such as Idi Amin in Uganda have destroyed their own militaries in order to stay in power. Others, such as General Evren in Turkey (1980–1983), have tried to guide their countries back to civilian rule.

One relatively understudied phenomenon is that of transitions from military rule. Chile, Argentina, Uruguay, and Brazil, among other Latin American countries, reverted to civilian rule in the late 1980s. A number of African countries have had oscillating periods of military and civilian rule, Ghana and Nigeria in particular. Where the armed forces have carried out bloody repression of civilians, as in Argentina and Chile, civilian rule is more difficult to achieve and to sustain, for the officers insist on protection against prosecution. Frequently, as in Brazil and Argentina, the armed forces have left civilians with large debt burdens and bloated state enterprises. The policies of expanding the state sector have not been unique to military regimes, but these regimes have been especially closed off from broad public scrutiny and accountability.

(See also DEMOCRATIC TRANSITIONS; DEVELOPMENT AND UNDERDEVELOPMENT; MILITARISM.)

Gavin Kennedy, *The Military in the Third World* (New York, 1974). Amos Perlmutter, *The Military and Politics in Modern Times* (New Haven, Conn., 1977). Henry Bienen, *Armies and Parties of Africa* (New York, 1978). Alain Rouquie, *The Military and the State in Latin America* (Berkeley, Calif., 1987).

HENRY S. BIENEN

MINORITIES. See RACE AND RACISM.

MITTERRAND, François. In 1964, six years after Charles de *Gaulle's return to power as leader of *France, an opposition politician wrote a fiery pamphlet, *Le Coup d'Etat permanent*, denouncing de Gaulle for overthrowing the Fourth Republic and creating a republic and powerful presidential office tailored to de Gaulle's own personality. Ironically, this same politician waged an unceasing and ultimately successful battle to replace de Gaulle as France's president. François Mitterrand finally was elected president in 1981 (after two unsuccessful presidential campaigns) and occupied the Elysée (the presidential palace) for well over the entire decade that followed, exceeding de Gaulle's record as the Fifth Republic president with the longest tenure in office. Indeed, Mitterrand is arguably second only to de Gaulle as the most powerful French politician of the twentieth century. Yet, in part because he has changed so often during his long political career, it is difficult to characterize the nature of his impact on France.

Mitterrand was born 26 October 1916 in the village of Jarnac, in Charente, a conservative and prosperous agricultural region in southwest France. The fifth of eight children in a quite affluent family whose wealth derived more from inherited land than from current income, Mitterrand's father was stationmaster in the nearby town of Angoulême. Although open-minded, Mitterrand's family was solidly anchored on the right of the political spectrum. For example, in 1936 his parents were squarely opposed to Léon Blum, France's first Socialist prime minister, whom Mitterrand later evoked as one of his great predecessors!

Mitterrand attended Catholic boarding school, where he was an above-average but not outstanding student. Like many talented middle-class provincial students, he pursued higher education in Paris, entering the School of Political Studies and the Paris Law School. His political convictions remained solidly anchored on the conservative side of the spectrum: he was a supporter and possibly a member of the Croix de Feu, one of the rightist paramilitary organizations that flourished in France in the 1930s.

During World War II, however, Mitterrand broke with conservative orthodoxy and embarked on the course that resulted in his becoming France's most influential Socialist politician. In 1938, he was drafted into the French army and, after war began, was wounded (and decorated). He was captured by the invading Nazi forces and, while in prison camp, was greatly influenced by the ideas and social commitment of fellow prisoners from the left secular *laïque* political tradition—the rival to the conservative Catholic milieu in which he was raised.

Mitterrand escaped from prison in 1941 and for two years led a double life: he was an administrator in the Commissariat of Prisoners in the puppet Vichy regime; at the same time, he forged identity papers for members of the Resistance. The Nazi invasion of unoccupied France in 1942 and the abolition of the Vichy regime put an end to this equivocal situation. Mitterrand participated full-time in the Resistance movement, displaying great courage and skill in helping to organize former prisoners of war for Resistance activity.

Mitterrand's first meeting with de Gaulle occurred at this time. Policy and personality differences separated the two men (Mitterrand resisted de Gaulle's attempt to establish his leadership over the entire Resistance movement), and a distance and rivalry developed that lasted until de Gaulle's death in 1970. After the Liberation of Paris in 1944, de Gaulle refused to offer the independent young Mitterrand a ministerial position in the newly created provisional government. Mitterrand soon broke openly with de Gaulle and briefly pursued a career as a journalist (he was a brilliant polemicist) and leader of France's largest organization of former war prisoners. He quickly returned to his real vocation, politics. In 1946, after one electoral defeat, he was elected to the National Assembly in the newly created Fourth Republic; he occupied elected office for most of the following half-century.

Mitterrand proved a brilliant tactician in the intricate parliamentary maneuvers of the Fourth Republic. Leader of a small centrist party whose support was often needed to form and sustain governments, he was handsomely rewarded. At the ripe age of 31, soon after his election to parliament, he was appointed to a junior cabinet post and began to figure among the handful of Fourth Republic politicians who appeared destined to become prime minister. Among his most important ministerial positions were overseas colonies, interior, and justice. His career was not without controversy: he was involved in several political scandals, although each time he managed to survive. In most respects, Mitterrand espoused the orthodox political beliefs of the time (for example, supporting the use of the French army to maintain control over France's empire in Africa and Asia). In sum, Mitterrand was among the inner circle of Fourth Republic politicians, but his reputation derived from a talent for political maneuver, not vision.

Mitterrand's political ambitions were abruptly checked when de Gaulle regained power in 1958, subverted the Fourth Republic, and created the constitutional framework of the Fifth Republic. Most Fourth Republic politicians reluctantly supported de Gaulle; Mitterrand was among the few who displayed total opposition, on the grounds that de Gaulle had violated constitutional procedures and republican traditions. In subsequent years, Mitterrand's opposition to the Gaullist governing coalition never wavered. As a result, his former image as a political operator was replaced by that of a principled leader. He now applied his formidable tactical skills to developing an effective opposition rather than rising within the ranks of the political establishment. Eventually, he succeeded in forging a major leftist opposition force that captured control of France's leading political institutions. He did so by rebuilding the divided Socialist Party—which he joined in 1971—and forming an alliance with the other major opposition on the *Left, the Communist Party. (In the process, he helped to subordinate the Communist Party.)

By 1980, after more than two decades in opposition and defeats in two presidential elections, Mitterrand began to appear as the perennial outsider. What reversed this situation was his tactical brilliance, the economic stagnation of the 1970s (for which the conservative governing coalition was blamed), and the political divisions and exhaustion of the incumbent forces. In 1981, Mitterrand's efforts were rewarded when he defeated President Valéry Giscard d'Estaing, who was running for reelection. Mitterrand swept in a strong Socialist majority on his coattails in parliamentary elections in 1981. After twenty-three years, the opposition gained control of the Fifth Republic, and Mitterrand and his associates enjoyed an extraordinary opportunity to reshape France.

Mitterrand's term as president, which rivals de Gaulle's in length and importance, can be divided into four phases. In his first two years in office, between 1981 and 1983, Mitterrand's Socialist government sponsored a whirlwind series of reforms, including decentralization of the state, liberalization of the judicial system, and restructuring industrial relations, the economy, and media. Mitterrand was the principal architect of the new course. Although not an original political thinker (his creative talents rather lay in the direction of literature and writing; he is author of numerous books of memoirs and essays), he firmly controlled the government and the Socialist parliamentary majority. The Socialist reforms helped to modernize antiquated, rigid bureaucracies, political institutions, and policies that the conservatives had put in place or accepted through decades of rule. In part, the reforms nudged France toward a more democratic society and economy. However, although audacious by French standards, the reforms were a pale version of those already implemented by Scandinavian and German Social Democratic governments.

The second phase began in 1983, when economic and political difficulties forced Mitterrand to moderate the earlier reformist course, and lasted until the conservative opposition won the 1986 parliamentary elections and gained control of the government. As a result of economic stagnation and the austerity measures adopted from 1983, Mitterrand's personal standing fell to record lows, and it appeared that he might even be forced from office before completing his seven-year term. However, in the third phase of his presidency, between 1986 and 1988 (when he was forced to share power with the conservative parliamentary majority—a situation referred to as *cohabitation*), he waged a remarkable comeback. Outmaneuvering his conservative opponents, he was triumphantly reelected president in 1988. From that point to the present—the fourth phase—he pursued a prudent and quite successful course, distinguished less for its reform impulse than for the economic growth and political stability occurring during these years. He capped this last phase of his presidency with an energetic attempt to secure French ratification of the Maastricht Treaty.

Mitterrand can be credited with three major accomplishments as president. First, he has demonstrated that the Left has the capacity to organize a responsible, capable government. In the process, he transformed the Socialist Party from a radical opposition movement to France's major governing force. Second, he has presided over the reduction of polarized political conflicts in France and assured political and institutional stability. Third, his leadership has enabled France to remain a major political and economic force within the world—ranking fourth or fifth by many measures. In particular, his vigorous efforts to strengthen European integration in the late 1980s and early 1990s have made him the most influential European political leader of the current period after German chancellor Helmut *Kohl.

(See also SOCIALISM AND SOCIAL DEMOCRACY.)

Catherine Nay, Le Noir et le Rouge, ou l'histoire d'une ambition (Paris, 1984). Philip G. Cerny and Martin A. Schain, eds., Socialism, the State and Public Policy in France (New York, 1985). George Ross, Stanley Hoffmann, and Sylvia Malzacher, eds., The Mitterrand Experiment (New York, 1987).

MARK KESSELMAN

MODERNITY

The word *modern* entered the center of West European intellectual debate in the seventeenth century (although it had been sporadically used as far back as the fifth century); ostensibly, it meant no more than "current" or "of recent origin." And yet the context of its appearance and fast-growing popularity suggest a deeper than merely technical meaning: the quality of "being of recent origin," being newly created, had suddenly become a matter of acute interest, apparently acquiring a thoroughly novel significance. That significance derived from changing values, which now, unlike in previous centuries, favored the new over the old, denied authority to the past, and approved of irreverence to tradition and readiness to innovate, to "go where no man dared to go before." From the moment of its triumphant entry into public discourse, the idea of the modern tended to recast the old as antiquated, obsolete, out of date, about to be (deservedly) sunk into oblivion and replaced.

The idea of the modern reappeared in the seventeenth century as a militant concept, as the focus of contention in the so-called "Quarrel of Ancients and Moderns" that lasted in France and England for almost a century. Arts and literature served as the initial battleground: after the spectacular achievements of scientists like Newton and Descartes, with

the Royal Society in England and more diffuse but no less influential *sociétés de pensée* in France valiantly promoting the unprecedented excellence of new science and philosophy, the question had to be asked sooner or later whether this upward movement was the lot of science alone or of all human endeavors—particularly of creations like painting and poetry. The Ancients (like Nicolas Boileau and Jean de La Fontaine in France, Sir William Temple and Jonathan Swift in Britain) defended the long-standing conviction that the peak of human achievement had been reached in Greek and Roman antiquity and that the inevitably inferior products of later generations could attempt no more than to struggle in vain to approximate its perfection. Earlier, such propositions were voiced routinely, seen as trivially true, and aroused no dissent. Now, however, inspired by the astonishing discoveries of the new science, opposing views began to spread and gain in popularity. The holders of the traditional views were redubbed Ancients—a concept, for the Moderns, tinged with contempt and derision. Charles Perrault and Bernard de Fontenelle were among the most pugnacious and vociferous advocates of the modern, daring attitude, which would draw its confidence from the belief that, as in science, so in all other fields of spiritual creation, the new may be better (truer, more useful, more right, more beautiful) than the old; that the potency of human reason and skill is unlimited; and that therefore human history has been and will forever remain a relentless march upward and forward.

The Quarrel was never conclusively resolved to everybody's satisfaction (a century later the Romantic movement resuscitated the ideas that the Moderns strove to put to rest once for all); it just fizzled out, as the philosophical edge of the issue was blunted by the rapid pace of practical cultural change. In retrospect, however, the Quarrel may be better appreciated as the condensed expression of a revolution taking place in the European mentality; of the new feeling of self-reliance and self-assurance, readiness to seek and try unorthodox solutions to any current trouble and worry, belief in the ascending tendency of human history and growing trust in the capacity of human reason. In the nineteenth century, the emergent mentality itself came to be described as modern, and the dominance of such mentality came to be seen as one of the crucial symptoms of the new age of modernity.

Modernity may be best described as the age marked by constant change—but an age aware of being so marked; an age that views its own legal forms, its material and spiritual creations, its knowledge and convictions as temporary, to be held "until further notice" and eventually disqualified and replaced by new and better ones. In other words, modernity is an era conscious of its historicity. Human institutions are viewed as self-created and amenable to improvement; they can be retained only if they justify themselves in the face of the stringent demands of reason—and if they fail the test, they are bound to be scrapped. The substitution of new designs for old will be a progressive move, a new step up the ascending line of human development.

Progress is, essentially, a human accomplishment. It consists in applying human reason (rationalizing) to the task of making the world better geared to serve human needs. Whatever is seen as a human need, as a condition of agreeable life, is accorded unqualified priority over all other considerations: the nonhuman part of the world (nature) is of itself meaningless, and any meaning it may be given can derive only from the human uses to which it is put. Designing an artificial, rational order of the human habitat is not an arbitrary choice; it is a necessity, an unavoidable human condition, for to be habitable the world must be made fit for the satisfaction of human needs through science-assisted technology. Science and its technological applications are therefore the principal sources and instruments of political, social, cultural, and moral progress. They are both the expression and the vehicle of human ascendancy over nature.

To modern Europe, conscious of its own historicity, styles of life and institutions that differed from those it currently approved were merely steps leading to its own, superior condition—survivals of its own past. Other cultures were seen as forms temporarily arrested in their development, and in this "frozen" state retarded. This belief gave modern Europe its characteristic self-confidence as a carrier of historical destiny, a collective missionary with the duty to spread the gospel of reason and to convert the rest of the world to its own faith and form of life. In case of resistance, the objects of prospective conversion could only be viewed as primitive, as victims of superstition and ignorance, whose authority (and particularly the ability to decide what was best for them) reason denied in advance. The modern period in European history (and the history of countries that underwent early the process of Europeanization) was therefore an age of proselytism, one marked by colonization of the non-European world and by repeated cultural crusades aimed at the regional, ethnic, or class-bound traditions within European societies themselves.

The modern *state was invested with functions never contemplated by premodern rulers. It had to impose a unified order on vast territories heretofore regulated by a variety of local traditions; by the same token, it had to make the creation and maintenance of social order a matter of deliberation, conscious design, monitoring, and daily management, rather than limit itself to the observance of traditional customs and privileges. (It had, one might say, to assume a gardener's, rather than a gamekeeper's, stance toward the society.) The new tasks involved standardization of law and legal institutions across the state; unification, and often direct administration, of the process of popular education; and securing the priority of unified legal discipline over all other, particularistic loyalties. It is for this reason that modern states engaged in the process of nation building, having assumed the form of nation-states rather than dynastic realms. They promoted national unity over ethnic differentiation, deployed *nationalism in the service of state authority, and adopted the promotion of national interests as the criterion and purpose of state policies. It is for the same reason that the modern state rejects and devalues traditional entitlements to rule (such as the longevity of rights) and charismatic rule (which is grounded on peculiar—and superior—personal qualities of a given ruler), demanding discipline to its own commands solely on formal, legal grounds: that is, referring to the fact that the commands have been issued by duly appointed incumbents of offices entitled to make rulings related to the given area.

By all historical standards, modernity (often referred to as "modern civilization," to locate it as a distinct type of social organization and culture among other civilizations, ancient, medieval, or contemporary) has been a remarkable success. It has come closer than any other known civilization to the status of genuine universality. It seems to be on the way to becoming the first global civilization in history. The states of the modern world may be politically and ideologically divided and even locked in mutual conflict, but they all agree on the superiority of the modern way of running human affairs and use modern methods and implements to assert themselves and pursue their ends. The modern form of life seems to have no serious competitors left among the forms it displaced; it has succeeded, moreover, in confronting its own difficulties and "developmental problems" in a way that strengthens the ascendancy of the worldview and pragmatic stance that are its own most characteristic traits. Thus modernity is usually described as the ultimate form of historical development. Inherently dynamic, modern civilization yet retains its own identity. It is capable of continuous creativity rather than, like other civilizations, ossifying and losing the capacity of creative adjustment to new challenges. With its arrival, the world has been split into a modern part and the rest, confronted with the challenge of *modernization.

Most theoretical models of modernity select inner dynamism and the capacity for change and self-improvement as the central characteristics and the ultimate sources of modernity's worldwide ascendancy and attractiveness. They also agree that to explain that dynamism is the most important task—and duty—of any theory of modernity. Beginning with the early nineteenth century, most analysts sought the secret of modern dynamism in the emancipation of human action from the shackles of custom, tradition, and communal obligations and in its subjection solely to the criteria of efficient task performance. In Karl *Marx's picturesque expression, "everything solid melts into air, everything sacred is profaned": once the authority of tradition has been sapped and denied, nothing can prevent human courage from setting ever more ambitious tasks and designing ever more effective ways of performing them. It is the match between means and ends that now decides which course of action is to be chosen. As the U.S. social theorist Talcott Parsons put it (elaborating on the ideas of the nineteenth-century German sociologist Ferdinand Tönnies), in modern times the traditional ways of assessing actors and their actions have been reversed. Action is now judged "out of context," independently of the socio-cultural setting in which it takes place and the social standing of its human objects—solely according to the universal rules of adequacy and efficiency. By contrast, actors are judged by their specific performances relevant to the task at hand, not by their general qualities. What truly counts is what is being done and how, not by whom and why. Selection of action is freed from all criteria—personal loyalties, political commitments, and moral norms, for example—that are irrelevant to the pursuit of the task at hand.

Division and separation are indeed constant themes in the theoretical discourse of modernity. The German sociologist Max *Weber proposed that the separation of business from household was the constitutive act of modern economy. Thanks to that separation, business decisions were emancipated from the pressure of moral obligations and personal commitments that guide family life. In still more general terms, the significance of separation was elaborated on by Immanuel Kant. In reference to his division between pure reason, practical reason, and judgment, many theorists of modernity (notably Jürgen Habermas in Germany and Ernest Gellner in Britain) consider the separation and mutual autonomy of the discourses of truth, moral norms, and aesthetic judgment (setting apart the spheres of science, ethics, and arts) as the most distinctive and decisive feature of modern mentality and practice. Beginning with Adam Smith, division of labor and splitting of complex functions into smaller and more manageable tasks has been seen as the most conspicuous factor of modern efficiency and productivity. Emile Durkheim, a French sociologist of the early 1900s, saw in the progressive, ever more minute division of labor the substance and the motive force of all aspects of historical development. The more complex is the division of labor, the simpler and more straightforward are separated functions; therefore they may be better mastered and more efficiently performed by specialists, who can now concentrate fully on effective means of "problem resolution." Expertise becomes a trademark of modern economy, science, art, and politics alike.

All fields of modern life, as Weber insisted, tend to become progressively rationalized. Action is rational (in the instrumental sense) insofar as it is oriented toward a clearly conceived and well-defined end, and thereafter based on the calculation of relative efficiency of alternative means to achieve it. Rational action is guided by motives and purposes, amenable in principle to conscious scrutiny and correction, and not determined by forces of which the actor is unaware or over which he or she has no control. Rational action splits the context of performance into ends and means and is guided solely by the effort to match the second against the first. Action is rational (again, in the instrumental sense) insofar as it consists in such decision-making and choice, even if a specific choice made by a given actor here and now is not the best conceivable or is even downright mistaken. Indeed, most choices stop short of the ideal. Means may be miscalculated because of inadequate or erroneous knowledge. Moreover, task-oriented activity is seldom free from interference by "impure" factors, irrational insofar as they are irrelevant to the task at hand—like the actor's uncontrolled habits and traditional loyalties, affections that get in the way, or commitment to values that interfere with the efficient performance of the given task. Rationality is therefore a tendency rather than the accomplished reality of modernity; a continuous, though by and large inconclusive, trend discernible in all fields of social life. For instance, according to Weber, the rule-governed, task-subordinated, impersonally acting organization, subjected to a meticulous division of functions, strict hierarchy of command, and scrupulous matching of personal skills of incumbents to the objective requirements of office, is the specifically modern, rational form of government.

The other side of rationalism is, of course, the taming or suppression of everything irrational—everything that interferes with the work of reason and detracts from the pragmatic effectivity of action. This irrational element in human behavior is called passion, which has been construed as the major obstacle on the road to the rule of reason. Modern civilization is prominent as much for its suppression of passions as for its promotion of the rationality of human conduct. More than in any other sphere, rational organization of society consists in controlling, defusing, incapacitating, or channeling away human instinctual drives and predispositions. A thorough analysis of this other, dramatic face of modernity is associated first and foremost with the work of Sigmund Freud. According to Freud, modern civilization substitutes the "reality principle" for the "pleasure principle"—the first being the necessary condition of peaceful, secure coexistence, the second being a natural predisposition of humans that clashes with the first. In practical terms, this substitution means constraint: pursuit of happiness is trimmed and limited by the consideration of what it is possible to achieve without paying costs too excessive to conceive of the effort as worthwhile.

Partial security is obtained in exchange for at least part of the individual's freedom. Adequately civilized behavior is marked by self-constraint; society, so to speak, "leaves a garrison in a conquered city" in the form of the socially trained individual conscience that prompts the individual to suppress such urges as may fall in conflict with the socially approved norms.

In his study of the modern condition—entitled *Civilization and Its Discontents*—Freud theorizes that modern civilization inevitably breeds discontent and resistance, and that its perpetuation thus involves an element of mental or physical coercion. The picture of modernity that emerges from Freud's analysis is far from peaceful and benign. The rule of reason has psychologically traumatic consequences. From the individual's point of view, it cannot be an unambiguous blessing, as it leaves quite a considerable part of human needs downgraded, unattended, or starved. This is why reason's rule is continuously resented and can never be complete; it will go on prompting rebellion against itself. Again and again, people pressed to abide by the cool and unemotional rules of calculation of costs and effects will rally instead to the defense of suppressed affections, natural urges, and the immediacy of human contact.

Another rendition of the inner contradiction and ambiguous impact of civilization (and modern civilization in particular) can be found in Friedrich Nietzsche's concept of a spontaneous and instinctual "Dionysian" rebellion as a constant, only barely tamed threat, ever again boosted by the "Apollonian" effort to construct a logical, rational, and harmonious world order. This theme, in its Freudian-Nietzschean rendition, is directly or implicitly present in virtually all of the numerous critiques of modernity as an ambitious, but in many respects abortive, project aimed at overall rationalization of social organization and individual human behavior. Two types of critique are particularly prominent. One (undertaken by the "mass politics" theoreticians inspired, in somewhat different ways, by the "elite" theory of Vilfredo Pareto, the concept of the "revolt of the masses" popularized by José Ortega y Gasset, and the "iron law of oligarchy" articulated by Robert Michels) points out that, contrary to rationalistic rhetoric, modern conditions promote a blatantly irrational, heavily aestheticized mass politics that hinders rather than promotes rational choice. Another (mainly associated with the Frankfurt School tradition of critical theory, established by the work of Theodor Adorno and Max Horkheimer, but going back for many of its ideas to the early twentieth-century German sociologist Georg Simmel) uncovers the irreparable conflict between the drive to rationalize supra-individual institutional structures and the promise to render individual decisions amenable to free rational choice.

All in all, resistance to rationalization has been as prominent a mark of modernity as has rationalization itself. The history of modernity is punctuated by criticisms of its excesses or even of the vanity or evil of its motives and historic ambitions. For every intellectual expression of enthusiasm for the breathtaking vistas opened by modern science, technological expertise, and political expediency, there has been a protest against the "drying up" of individuality and genuinely human affectivity. Against the modern promise of a human species empowered in its struggle to make the world more hospitable, critics have hastened to point out that even if the species as a whole gains in freedom, its individual members do not; they are denied true choice, having been "functionalized" and transformed into "cogs in the machine." Against the utility of reason-guided problem solving, the critics have defended the values of individuality, the indivisible whole, and the all-too-human right to be different, erratic, and altogether irrational. Beginning with the Romantic poetry of the early nineteenth century, through decadence, the militantly "modernistic" avant-garde of the early twentieth century, dadaism, surrealism, and up to present-day postmodern culture (which proclaims normlessness the only cultural norm and calls for resistance to all authority, declining even to supply a foundation for its own practice)—the modern rationalization drive has been accompanied by a stridently oppositional culture bent on the defense of individual freedom and emotional experience. Cultural rebellion against the reality of society, a virtually constant antagonism between social and political practices and advanced cultural creation, whether in philosophy, art, or literature, has been thus far a most astonishing—and apparently permanent—feature of modernity.

An explanation of this paradox is sought in the specifically modern structure of daily life and individual experience. The most salient attribute of the latter is its fragmentariness; cast into the densely packed urban environment and bound to spend most of his or her life among strangers, the individual finds its difficult, perhaps impossible, to integrate experience into a meaningful whole. Within the horizon drawn by individual experience, time seems to split into unconnected events and space into uprelated spots. If there is a bond of mutual dependence that unites them into a cohesive totality—such a link eludes the individual observer, facing but brief and spatially limited episodes of the drama. Modern experience, it was first pointed out by the French poet and critic Charles Baudelaire, is a sighting of a fleeting moment. To be in tune with modern experience, art ought to represent the world as fragmentary and transitory—as a collection of "fleeting moments."

As Georg Simmel indicated, the characteristic feature of modern experience is the lack of coordination and communication between civilization as total cultural product and the snippets of cultural achievement that individuals are capable of assimilating and using as the building material in constructing their own identities. The sum total of cultural products far exceeds individual absorptive capacity. This fact, on the one hand, frees cultural creation from its bonds with daily life and permits thereby an infinite specialization and infinite expansion within each specialized field (hence the logarithmic acceleration in the growth of science, technology, and the arts, which exacerbates still further the original conflict); on the other hand, however, it leaves to individuals the awesome task of patching together "meaningful lives" out of the subjectively meaningless splinters of other, unknown or invisible totalities. While performing this task, individuals must be able to compare the incomparable and combine elements that apparently do not belong together; for this they need a strategy that, so to speak, "imposes" comparability between wildly discrepant experiences, and thus allows them to make choices while neglecting the qualitative differences between the objects of choice. Hence the intellect (capacity for abstract, formal thinking) and money are simultaneously inevitably products and indispensable instruments of life under modern conditions. Both address themselves solely to the quantitative aspects of experienced phenomena, and downplay their qualitative characteristics.

These and related characteristics of human habitat have persisted throughout the modern era, constantly gathering force. They continue to mark present-day Western and Westernized societies and continue to spread into areas of the globe until recently seen as "traditional" or "premodern." Nonetheless, some observers suggest that modernity in its classic form has run its course and has been replaced, or is about to be replaced, by another sociocultural formation, which they call postmodernity. Descriptions of this allegedly new formation (meant to demonstrate its novelty and qualitative distinction from modernity) do not differ on the whole from the above description of the modern condition. There is, however, one significant difference on which the assertions about the "end of modernity" and the advent of postmodernity tend to found their credibility: if throughout the modern era the "messiness," ambivalence, spontaneity, and uncertainty inherent in social and individual life were seen as temporary irritants, to be eventually overcome by the rationalizing tendency, they are now seen as unavoidable and ineradicable—and not necessarily irritants. It now has been accepted that historical processes have no specific end or direction; that pluralism of values and forms of life is here to stay; and that the centers of political power, most notably state governments, have lost both the resources and the ambitions that characterize the "gardening stance." The all-inclusive designs of "rational society" and global social-engineering schemes and cultural crusades that backed them

seem to have fallen into disrepute and have been all but abandoned. The recent collapse of the communist command economies and all-regulating states has provided a most spectacular display of this tendency.

(See also POSTMODERNISM.)

Krishan Kumar, *Prophecy and Progress: The Sociology of Industrial and Post-Industrial Society* (Harmondsworth, U.K., 1978). Zygmunt Bauman, *Legislators and Interpreters: On Modernity, Postmodernity, and Intellectuals* (Cambridge, U.K., 1987). Jürgen Habermas, *The Philosophical Discourse of Modernity* (Cambridge, U.K., 1987). John F. Rundell, *Origins of Modernity: The Origins of Modern Social Theory from Kant to Hegel to Marx* (Cambridge, U.K., 1987). David Harvey, *The Condition of Postmodernity* (Oxford, 1989). Anthony Giddens, *Consequences of Modernity* (Cambridge, U.K., 1990). Agnes Heller, *Can Modernity Survive?* (Cambridge, U.K., 1990). Bryan S. Turner, ed., *Theories of Modernity and Postmodernity* (London, 1990).

ZYGMUNT BAUMAN

MODERNIZATION. The term *modernization* became prominent in the social sciences and in more general discourse in the years following World War II. Increasing attention was then being paid to the possibility that the so-called underdeveloped societies of the *Third World might attain levels of development—whether economic, social, or political—hitherto associated only with modern industrial societies. The studies of modernization that emerged in this period entailed a far-reaching shift in basic orientation compared with earlier, "classical" sociological approaches. Instead of stressing the specificity of European civilization and attempting to explain why *modernity developed only in the West, the postwar studies of modernization assumed that the development of modernity constituted the apogee of the evolutionary potential of humanity in general, the kernels of which are in principle to be found in most societies. These studies evaluated societies according to several indices of modernization and attempted to explain what societal factors facilitate or impede their development and the consequent emergence of a modern social order.

The most important types of such indices included sociodemographic, structural, cultural, and psychological characteristics. Among the major sociodemographic indices were *urbanization, industrialization, levels of *literacy and education, as well as openness to modern modes of communication. Structural characteristics were identified as a high degree of role specialization and differentiation; the availability of resources not committed to fixed ascriptive groups (such as kinship or territoriality); the predominance of achievement criteria rather than ascription in the allocation of the major social roles; and the development of and differentiation between large-scale, diverse, and functionally specific organizations on the one hand, and more informal interest-based groups on the other.

Culturally, the process of modernization was said

to involve a growing differentiation of the major arenas of cultural activity such as religion, philosophy, and education; the development of specialized intellectual and cultural roles; the spread of education and communications; and wider mass participation in the cultural arena. Finally, on the individual level, modernization was seen as giving rise to a new cultural-psychological outlook characterized by greater ego flexibility; the ability to adjust to wider societal horizons; a broadening of the spheres of interest; growing potential empathy toward other people and situations; and more emphasis on self-advancement and mobility.

In most of these studies modern and traditional societies were depicted as juxtaposed. Traditional societies were defined as basically restrictive and limited, whereas modern societies were seen as much more expansive and able to cope with a continually widening range of problems in their internal and external environments alike. Societies on the move from traditional to modern were designated as transitional.

Behind these theories there loomed a vision of the inevitability of progress toward modernity, toward the development of a universal modern civilization, and toward the convergence of industrial societies. Most of these theories implicitly took for granted that the Western European and U.S. experiences constituted the major paradigm of modern society and civilization. The institutional and ideological developments in the contemporary world, however, have not upheld this vision. The great institutional variability of different modern and modernizing societies—not only among the transitional but also among the more developed societies such as the United States, Western Europe, and Japan—became more and more apparent, giving rise by the late 1960s to new models of modernization.

Two major approaches to the problem may be identified. The first approach stressed the importance of the traditions of different societies for understanding the variability of modern or modernizing societies; this approach negated the dichotomy between modern and traditional societies and their dynamics. The second approach emphasized international factors, especially the global capitalist system, as the major explanatory variables in the process of modernization.

These approaches have certainly pointed to some important influences on the dynamics of modernization. They are not able, however, to explain all the patterns of change which have been taking place in different traditional and transitional societies in the contemporary world. These approaches have not faced squarely the problem of how different patterns of change arise in response to the sociodemographic, structural, and ideological aspects of modernization enumerated above. Accordingly, some of the assumptions of these approaches need reappraisal as did those of the initial model of modernization.

The starting point of such a reappraisal is the historical fact that modernization, or rather modernity in its basic institutional and cultural aspects, crystallized first in the West—in Europe and in the United States—from the sixteenth century on. This modernization then expanded by economic, military, political, and ideological means throughout the world and created a series of continually changing world systems. The original institutional formations and cultural contours of modernity as they developed in the West were closely related to the capitalist economy and civilization, which were characterized by the bureaucratization of different aspects of social life, a secular worldview, and the development of a distinctive cultural orientation toward modernity. This orientation emphasizes a scientific outlook (including the radical tendency to critique the world), individual autonomy and emancipation, an ideology of equality, and a conception of society as an object of active construction by conscious human action.

The construction of modern society gave rise in the West, especially in Europe, to nation-states and class societies, and to a strong emphasis on economic development. The expansion of modernity beyond Europe gave rise to the development of different types of modern societies and to a great variety of institutional constellations, as well as of cultural orientations toward modernity. This variety indicates the necessity to go beyond some of the assumptions of the initial studies of modernization, without however forgetting that such variety developed out of the interaction between the institutional forces and ideological premises of the first examples of modernity as developed in the West and the various societies on which they impinged.

The varieties of modernization suggest that different aspects of the process such as industrialization, urbanization, and political modernization are not necessarily interlinked. Furthermore, such variability can be seen not only, or even mainly, in different institutional patterns but in the combination of these with the different cultural contours of modernity. Such programs may entail different interpretations of many of the basic premises of modern civilization: the nature of equality; the extent of participation by wider social sectors in various aspects of public life; the relative importance of economic development in the panorama of human goals; the balance between productive and distributive economic priorities; the construction of new symbols and collective identities; and negative or positive attitudes toward modernity in general and to the West in particular.

These different orientations toward modernity were shaped by the continuous interaction between the "point of entry" of any society into the modern *international system and specific aspects of the society's traditional order, including the social, political, and economic formations already existing in these societies, the basic values of these civilizations, and the patterns of authority, hierarchy, and equality that prevailed in them. These varieties of modernization were the product of actions by elites and major counterelites, protest movements, and the overall historical experience of social change in these societies.

The multiplicity of types of modern societies does not negate the obvious fact that, in many central aspects of their institutional forms, such as occupational patterns and industrial structures, or in the organization of education and cities, very strong convergences are apparent in different modern societies. These convergences have indeed generated common problems. However, the means of coping with these problems differ greatly among nations, which again reflects how these different modern societies have been shaped by their specific institutional development and cultural contours and by their historical experiences.

(See also DEVELOPMENT AND UNDERDEVELOPMENT; POLITICAL CULTURE; POLITICAL DEVELOPMENT; SECULARIZATION; WEBER, MAX.)

S. N. Eisenstadt, *Modernization, Protest and Change* (Englewood Cliffs, N.J., 1966). S. N. Eisenstadt, *Tradition, Change and Modernity* (New York, 1973). A. Inkeles and D. H. Smith, *Becoming Modern: Individual Change in Six Developing Countries* (Cambridge, Mass., 1974).

S. N. EISENSTADT

MOLDOVA. See COMMONWEALTH OF INDEPENDENT STATES.

MONACO. Europe's second smallest country—the Vatican is the first—Monaco is a city-state covering 200 hectares (500 acres) between the mountains and the Mediterranean in the middle of the French Riviera. It has but 30,000 permanent residents, only a quarter actually citizens. Prince Rainier III, ruler for over four decades, is the most recent heir of the Grimaldi dynasty which has lasted for 700 years. The 1962 Constitution grants the prince a substantial amount of real power which he must share with a minister of state approved by the French government. There is an eighteen-member elected legislature *(Le Conseil National)*, plus a municipal government and judicial system. Monaco's self-government is constrained by its many treaty ties to surrounding France. It thus participates in a customs union with France—although it is not a member of the European Community—and France conducts Monaco's foreign relations, telecommunications, and postal services (an arrangement which has nonetheless allowed Monaco to do a brisk business selling postage stamps).

The principality's seaside location and temperate climate make it a mecca for chic tourism. Monaco's casinos are world-famous, but now account for only a relatively small part of its economic activities. The Société des Bains de Mer (SBM), controlled by Prince Rainier after a long takeover struggle with Aristotle Onassis in the 1960s, serves de facto as a Monegasque planning agency, using its substantial financial power to shape Monaco's economy. The keys to Monaco's great prosperity are its desirability as a market for very expensive second homes, its banking and financial services—themselves largely real-estate driven and drawn to the principality by tax breaks. Retailing to and feeding a wealthy clientele generate further income alongside a small component of light industry. Pursuing Monaco's comparative advantages, SBM has undertaken to expand land available for development by filling in areas in the harbor while guaranteeing the kind of public security which will attract well-off part-time residents. The formula has been remarkably successful.

Paul Marie de la Gorce, *Monaco* (Paris, 1963). Philippe Saint-Germain and François Rosset, *La Grande Dame de Monte Carlo* (Paris, 1981).

GEORGE ROSS

MONARCHY. The term *monarchy* refers to a form of government in which all aspects of a state, whether economic or political, are controlled by an individual with sovereign power, the individual's position being legitimized by the ideological assumptions of the social group from which the monarch is drawn. In its most common form these assumptions are that the office of monarch is hereditary within a particular family or kin group, In Europe, this has often been reduced to primogeniture—succession through the eldest child of the reigning monarch—although in medieval Germany, elective monarchy also existed. This appears to be a legacy from the earliest forms of the institution in Europe.

In fact, in the earliest forms of the institution, however, monarchs were often elected or were legitimized by their ability to seize power through main force. However, in these cases, the selection process was usually legitimized by the sacred quality associated with the role of monarch. Indeed, the monarch often became the guarantor for social survival and could be ritually sacrificed for that purpose. Alternatively, the monarch was seen as a divine reincarnation in earthly form, as was the case in prehistoric China, Persia, Mesopotamia, and Egypt. The European version of monarchy was derived from Greek and Roman archetypes, together with Germanic traditions of tribal kingship.

Even in Europe monarchy in the late medieval period tended to acquire a sacred character, with Christian doctrine being used to bolster the principle of "divine right" by which absolutist monarchical authority was given divine sanction. In the earlier medieval period, monarchy had been based on the principle of *primus inter pares* and, in northern Europe particularly, had been an extension of feudalism. This change in part arose from the decline of the authority of the Holy Roman Empire, which had contested rights to divine sanction for the temporal authority of the emperor with the papacy.

This sacred character still continued until modern times in the tradition of the "King's Evil" (scrofula), which the Stuart monarchs of Britain were supposed to be able to cure by touch.

Monarchy is to be distinguished from two other forms of monocracy; dictatorship and imperial rule. Dictatorship lacks the legitimizing principle inherent in monarchy and does not normally include a defined and accepted process of succession. Imperial rule implies the sovereign control of dispersed states and unrelated peoples, rather than the compact social order usually associated with monarchy. In this respect, monarchy represents a form of government between that of stateless societies, such as tribes, and that of the modern nation-state, in which governmental institutions derive their *legitimacy from sovereign power of the "nation" rather than from that of the individual ruler.

In the modern world, monarchy, at least in its absolutist form, has virtually disappeared, even though it transmuted in the eighteenth century, the "Age of the Enlightenment," into the concept of the "benevolent despot" in Prussia and Russia. It was effectively destroyed by the French Revolution in 1789. The first and second world wars removed its remnants, except for those few monarchies which had evolved toward *constitutional monarchy. The monarchies still found in the Muslim world are, in fact, theocratic institutions which, in theory, are elective and not absolutist in character.

Sigmund Freud, *Totem and Taboo* (London, 1950). *Encyclopaedia Britannica*, 15th ed., *Macropaedia*, s.vv. "Sacred Orders and Offices (Sacred Kingship)," "Monarchy," and "King."

GEORGE JOFFÉ

MONETARISM. The concept of *monetarism* was initially devised to describe a school of economic thought that emphasizes the impact of the money supply on the rate of inflation and economic output, and it is now widely used to describe the economic policies of governments that have been influenced by this school of thought.

The term *monetarism* was introduced in 1968 by the economist Karl Brunner to describe an approach to economics then being developed by economists in the United States, notably at the Federal Reserve Bank of St. Louis and the University of Chicago where Milton Friedman did much to popularize the doctrine. It built upon the quantity theory of money, initially used by the classical economists and formalized by Irving Fischer in 1926 to suggest that the price level varied directly with the amount of money in circulation, and it was subsequently extended by rational expectations theorists who argued that activist macroeconomic policy was likely to be ineffective because its impact would already be discounted by highly rational actors in the private economy.

From a political perspective, monetarism was most significant as a challenge to *Keynesianism, the doctrine that dominated economic policy-making in the capitalist world for thirty years after World War II. The two doctrines were based on quite different views of the economy. Whereas Keynesians saw the private economy as fundamentally unstable and in need of active macroeconomic management, monetarists regarded the private economy as inherently stable and government policy as likely to be destabilizing. Whereas Keynesians believed that an active fiscal policy could reduce the level of unemployment, monetarists argued that the "natural" rate of unemployment was fixed by structural imperfections in the labor market and relatively impervious to macroeconomic manipulation over the long run. While Keynesians argued that inflation was often generated by excess aggregate demand or wage militancy that might be addressed by an incomes policy (statutory or voluntary wage and price restraint), monetarists argued that the rate of inflation could be controlled best by the establishment of fixed targets for the rate of growth of the money supply.

Accordingly, monetarists tended to depreciate the effectiveness of fiscal policy, associated with changes in the budget balance, in favor of a focus on monetary policy. They opposed "discretionary" macroeconomic management in favor of a policy based on relatively fixed "rules." They preferred to use the rate of growth of the money supply, rather than the level of interest rates, as a monetary target. Where Keynesians emphasized government action to reduce unemployment, monetarists gave highest priority to reducing inflation. Although the views of individual monetarists varied on important points of detail, they tended to be ranged against Keynesians along these general lines, and their views were underpinned by a fundamentally different model of the economy that gave prominence to monetary variables.

In the political sphere, monetarism became an important doctrine during the 1970s largely as a consequence of two economic developments. First, rates of inflation began to rise more rapidly in the industrialized world from the end of the 1960s. Second, unemployment began to increase along with inflation during the 1970s. These developments called traditional Keynesian analyses into question. As political attention shifted to the problem of inflation, monetarist doctrines acquired more prominence because they were directly oriented to inflation, whereas Keynesian doctrines had initially been devised to explain unemployment. Moreover, Keynesian explanations for inflation turned heavily on the Phillips curve, which postulated an inverse correlation between the level of unemployment and the rate of inflation. That analysis seemed unpersuasive after 1974 when both variables began to rise simultaneously in many nations. As a result, initially contentious monetarist arguments about the importance of the rate of growth of the money supply and the limited effectiveness of fiscal policy were gradually incorporated into the analyses of mainstream economists during the 1970s and 1980s.

However, the political popularity of monetarist doctrine during the 1970s and 1980s was also a response to broader political developments. Many governments initially responded to rising rates of inflation with efforts to secure wage and price controls. These efforts drew politicians into protracted negotiations with trade unions and employers about complex distributional issues on which it was difficult to secure a consensus; and the compression of wage differentials that often accompanied income policies generated resentment among the work force. Such neocorporatist efforts strained the political authority of many governments, especially in nations such as Italy and Britain where it was difficult to mobilize consent among decentralized union movements. Thus, a monetarist approach that promised to reduce inflation without any need for an incomes policy began to seem increasingly attractive to many politicians and voters.

Monetarist doctrines also had a special appeal for conservative politicians because they provided a new rationale for policies that conservatives had long espoused, including reducing public spending and taxation, limiting state intervention and the power of trade unions in order to reinforce the role of market mechanisms in the allocation of resources, and renouncing the responsibility of governments for unemployment. Thus, monetarist arguments began to figure prominently in the market-oriented programs that conservative politicians promulgated during the 1970s and 1980s.

The impact of monetarist economics was greatest in Britain, where it was embraced by a small group of Conservative politicians led by Margaret *Thatcher, who became the leader of the party in 1975 and imposed many monetarist tenets on the government after she became prime minister in 1979. Largely as a result of her influence, monetarism is seen in Britain not just as an economic doctrine but also as a political doctrine closely associated with her efforts to give priority to reducing inflation rather than unemployment, to reduce the role of the state in the economy by privatizing many public enterprises, to limit the power of the trade unions in politics and the labor market, to reduce income taxes on higher incomes as well as public spending, and to make the control of the monetary aggregates the central target of macroeconomic policy. Paradoxically, the last of these efforts and the one most central to monetarist economic doctrine has been the least successful. By the end of the 1980s, the exchange rate and the level of interest rates had become more important targets of British policy, as the authorities found it exceedingly difficult to attain monetary targets.

Elsewhere in the world, monetarist doctrine has had the most influence on central banks and monetary authorities, who now tend to monitor and target the rate of growth of the money supply on the grounds that it feeds directly into the rate of inflation. Under its chair, Paul Volcker, the U.S. Federal Reserve Bank publicly embraced this approach in 1979. However, monetarist ideas have also contributed to a widespread view among economic policy-makers that the effectiveness of active fiscal policy against unemployment may be distinctly limited and that budget deficits should thus be avoided. Therefore, monetarism is closely associated with the collapse of the Keynesian consensus in the 1970s and the resurgence of conservative economics in the 1980s.

(See also CONSERVATISM; CORPORATISM; POLITICAL ECONOMY; TAXES AND TAXATION.)

Keith Cuthbertson, *Macroeconomic Policy: The New Cambridge, Keynesian and Monetarist Controversies* (London, 1979). John T. Woolley, *Monetary Politics: The Federal Reserve and the Politics of Monetary Policy* (Cambridge, U.K., 1984). Peter Riddell, *The Thatcher Government*, 2d ed. (London, 1985).

PETER A. HALL

MONGOLIA. The heartland of the empire of Genghis Khan (1162–1227) and his successors, Mongolia (the former Mongolian People's Republic) is a landlocked country of 1.5 million square kilometers (580,000 sq. mi.) and approximately 2.1 million people lying between Russia to the north and China to the south. The last of the Mongol khans was defeated by the Manchu leader Abahai, who was proclaimed khan of southern (Inner) Mongolia in 1636. The princes of northern (Outer) Mongolia submitted to the Chinese Manchu (Qing) dynasty in 1691. Following the republican revolution in China in 1911, the Manchu governor left Outer Mongolia, which declared its independence. The *Bogd Gegeen,* or spiritual leader of Mongolia's Lamaists, was proclaimed khan of Mongolia on 16 December, and the country's religious center, Urga, became the capital. Inner Mongolia remained part of China. The Chinese government refused to recognize Outer Mongolia's independence, and the Russo-Chinese declaration of 1913 spoke of Mongolian autonomy under Chinese suzerainty.

Two underground nationalist revolutionary groups formed in 1919 and joined forces in June 1920 as the Mongolian People's Party (MPP). The MPP sent delegates to Russia to seek the help of the Soviet leadership. Northern Mongolia was occupied by the Japanese-backed anti-Bolshevik "White" Russian forces in October 1920, and the MPP developed its political activities in the Siberian towns of Irkutsk and Kyakhta, where its first congress (March 1921) adopted an "anti-imperialist and antifeudalist" platform. Mongolian revolutionary troops crossed the border at Kyakhta on 18 March and with the help of the Soviet Red Army defeated the "Whites" and entered Urga on 6 July. A people's government under the limited monarchy of the *Bogd Gegeen* was proclaimed on 11 July, now celebrated as National Day.

After the death of the *Bogd Gegeen* in 1924, a national assembly, or People's Great Hural, was held to endorse a republican constitution. The Great Hural elected a standing legislature, called the Little Hural (abolished in 1950 but reestablished in 1990), which formed the government and its presidium. The third congress of the MPP in 1924 adopted *Lenin's formula for "bypassing capitalism" with Soviet help and proclaimed itself the ruling party, adopting the name Mongolian People's Revolutionary Party (MPRP). Urga was renamed Ulan Bator (Red Hero). The so-called "right" (petty-bourgeois nationalist) and "left" (communist extremist) deviations and the purging of leaders in the 1920s and 1930s left the country devastated by forced *collectivization of livestock herding and the ruthless destruction of Lamaism. Thousands of innocent people fell victim to the "personality cult" of the party leader, Horloogiyn Choybalsan (1895–1952).

Mongolia had entered a long period of political isolation, having treaty relations only with Soviet Russia and with Tannu-Tuva (part of Outer Mongolia until 1911 and absorbed into the USSR in 1944). When Japanese forces attacked Mongolia in 1939, Soviet troops forced them back. In World War II Mongolia aided the Soviet war effort with livestock, food, and clothing.

Following the *Yalta agreement of 1945 to preserve the status quo there, Mongolia voted 100 percent for independence in a plebiscite, which the Kuomintang government of China recognized. Mongolia joined the UN in 1961 and was recognized by Britain in 1963. By 1990 Mongolia had diplomatic relations with over 100 countries, including the United States.

On Choybalsan's death in 1952, Yumjaagiyn Tsedenbal became premier and then, in 1974, chairman of the Presidium of the People's Great Hural (head of state). Until his illness and removal from power in 1984, Tsedenbal had been concurrently MPRP general secretary for some forty years. Loyal to the Soviet leadership, Tsedenbal came to be depicted as a Brezhnev-like figure responsible for Mongolia's socioeconomic stagnation. Mongolia's traditional livestock economy had changed little, despite various attempts to alter the basis of ownership, but collectivization was completed in the 1950s. Grain-producing state farms enabled Mongolia to become self-sufficient in wheat in years not affected by soil erosion or inclement weather. Coal mining was developed for electric power generation, and the railway line across Mongolia linking Siberia and northern China was completed. The industrial complex built in Ulan Bator with Soviet aid in the 1930s to process animal products into food and clothing was expanded.

The pressures of the Sino-Soviet dispute and the Chinese *Cultural Revolution in the 1960s encour-

aged the Soviet leadership to invest more heavily in Mongolia's economy and defense. Mongolia joined the *Council for Mutual Economic Assistance (COMECON) in 1962. Many new industrial projects were started, including the building of several complete cities and mines. The number of Soviet technicians working in Mongolia grew rapidly. The Mongolian People's Army (MPA) was expanded and equipped with modern Soviet weapons. Soviet army and air force units were stationed in Mongolia. It was not until the restoration of Soviet and Mongolian relations with China at the end of the 1980s that the MPA was reduced in size and Soviet units began to leave.

As Soviet *perestroika and glasnost swept the communist world, Mongolia's leaders had to admit that industrialization had left the country bankrupt, with 9 billion rubles owed to the Soviet government and virtually no hard currency resources. Mongolia's economy was based on obsolete equipment and concepts and dependent on irregular Soviet supplies. It remained lacking in infrastructure, and its inadequacy threatened social disorder among a fast-growing and disillusioned population. Challenged by the vigorous development of alternative political movements, the MPRP was forced in 1990 to renew its own leadership, surrender its role as the ruling party, separate itself from purely government functions, and participate in the country's first-ever free elections. In the new People's Great Hural elected in July 1990, however, the MPRP received eighty-five percent (375) of the 430 seats with sixty-one percent of the ballot, while the Mongolian Democratic Party (MDP) received only four percent of the seats (16) with twenty-four percent of the ballot. The remaining seats went to the New Progress Party (NPP), the Social-Democratic Party (SDP), and independents. The first session of the People's Great Hural elected Punsalmaagiyn Ochirbat (MPRP) to the new post of president of Mongolia and reconstituted the State Little Hural (standing legislature) with proportional representation of political parties (MPRP, thirty-one members; MDP, thirteen; NPP, three; SDP, three). This second chamber then approved the appointment of Prime Minister Dashiyn Byambasuren and his cabinet.

MPRP Chairman Gomojavyn Ochirbat was replaced in February 1991 by Budragchaagiyn Dash-Yondon, who abandoned Marxism-Leninism as the party doctrine. By the end of 1991 the MPRP had split into several factions, the moderates founding the Party of Renewal. Meanwhile, Sanjaasurengiyn Dzorig, leader of the Democratic Union (parent organization of the MDP) left to establish the Mongolian Republican Party.

A new Mongolian Constitution, adopted by the People's Great Hural on 13 January for implementation from 12 February 1992, enshrined the Mongolian people's human rights, including ownership of land and other property, and declared that henceforth the Mongolian People's Republic would be known as Mongolia. Elections to a new single chamber seventy-six seat national assembly, the State Great Hural, were called for June 1992. The MPRP, which won seventy-one seats, formed a new government headed by Prime Minister Puntsagiyn Jasray.

(See also COMMUNIST PARTY STATES; SINO-SOVIET RELATIONS.)

Alan J. K. Sanders, *The People's Republic of Mongolia: A General Reference Guide* (Oxford, 1968). Alan J. K. Sanders, *Mongolia: Politics, Economics and Society* (London and Boulder, Colo., 1987).

ALAN J. K. SANDERS

MONNET, Jean. Born in Cognac, in the southwest of France, Jean Monnet (1888–1979) did not attend a university, instead entering the family cognac business at an early age. During World War I he persuaded the French government to organize a joint executive commission with Britain to coordinate nautical transportation of provisions and war materiel. Monnet served as deputy secretary-general of the *League of Nations between 1920 and 1923, and went on to pursue international business activities with large American firms.

During World War II Monnet presided over a French and British coordinating committee formed for the purpose of purchasing war materiel. He became a trusted adviser to President Franklin *Roosevelt in the launching of the program which would make the United States the "Arsenal of Democracy."

In 1945, Monnet was appointed head of the French Commissariat du Plan by General Charles de *Gaulle. He directed the establishment of the first French plan (for modernization and equipment). In 1950, he proposed to Robert Schuman, the French minister of foreign affairs, the basis for a new policy regarding the Federal Republic of Germany. The policy was founded on principles of equality of rights and European integration. It was adopted by the French government and made public on 9 May 1950 (the Monnet-Schuman Declaration). The policy was the foundation for the European Coal and Steel Community (ECSC) and the European Defense Community (EDC), presented by the French government in October 1950 for the purpose of placing the rearmament of Germany in a European context.

After the rejection of the EDC by the French National Assembly in August 1954, Monnet retired from public service, but he remained active, as a private citizen, in discussions and negotiations which led to the March 1957 conclusion of the *Rome Treaties (concerning the European Economic Community or Common Market and the European Atomic Energy Community or Euratom). In an "Action Committee for the United States of Europe" (October 1955), he brought together the leaders of the democratic parties and independent trade unions of the six member countries of the ECSC. Until 1973,

when Monnet withdrew from public life, the committee would defend the principles of European integration, would demand the expansion of the Communities to include Britain, and would support the work of European integration.

Drawing on his extensive network of personal relationships with leaders on both sides of the Atlantic, Monnet exerted an extraordinary influence during the decisive postwar years. In this he was aided by his capacity to imagine or identify new, clear, and attainable ideals, by the force of his belief in contacts at the highest level, and, finally, by his absolute lack of self-interest, as evident in his refusal of every office and public honor. The fixed principles of the Monnet-Schuman Declaration continue to guide the functioning and development of the *European Community: equality of the rights of all participants, transfer of powers to independent institutions, the establishment of a European judicial system, and democratic control by a parliamentary assembly.

(See also EUROPEAN COURT OF JUSTICE; EUROPEAN PARLIAMENT; PLANNING.)

Jean Monnet, *Memoirs* (New York, 1978). Douglas Brinkley and Clifford Hackett, eds., *Jean Monnet: The Path to European Unity* (New York, 1991).

EMILE NOËL

MONROE DOCTRINE. What came to be known as the Monroe Doctrine originated in President James Monroe's message to Congress on 2 December 1823. The enduring element of Monroe's statement was a warning to Europeans to keep "hands off" the Western Hemisphere and not to extend further their control in the Americas. The message articulated ideas already well established in U.S. foreign policy. The idea of geographic, political, economic, and social separation of the New World from the Old, with the Americas having distinct interests, dated from before U.S. independence; it complemented ingrained *isolationism. Monroe echoed these sentiments, in the specific context of perceived threats from Russia, France, and Spain, when he said that the political system of Europe was essentially different from that of America; and that the United States would consider any attempt by them to extend their system to any portions of the Western Hemisphere, or to control the newly independent Latin American countries, as dangerous to U.S. *peace and safety and "the manifestation of an unfriendly disposition towards the United States." Monroe assured Europe of U.S. reciprocity by promising that the United States would not interfere in its internal concerns. Unilateralism was indicated by the rejection of a prior British proposal for a joint declaration and by rebuffing subsequent Latin American suggestions for formal alliance against Europe.

Monroe's declaration was largely ignored as a policy guide during most of the nineteenth century, a period of U.S. military weakness and domestic preoccupations. A number of European military and other interventions and even colonizations in Latin America brought little response.

By the end of the nineteenth century, with the U.S. rise to great power status, the Monroe Doctrine had become the "cornerstone" of U.S. foreign policy. "Corollaries" appeared that further defined the doctrinal content. The broadest extension was the Roosevelt Corollary of 1904. President Theodore Roosevelt said that "chronic wrongdoing" or "impotence" in the Americas might force the United States, because of its adherence to the Monroe Doctrine, "to the exercise of an international police power." The United States invoked the Roosevelt Corollary for the next quarter-century in order to preempt European intervention and to justify U.S. *imperialism and coercive instruments. U.S. military intervention and occupation, formal protectorates, and increasing economic domination, all in the Circum-Caribbean, were inspired by geopolitical thinking regarding the Panama Canal. Latin Americans, even those not directly the targets of U.S. coercion, vigorously protested violations of their sovereignty and advocated nonintervention as an international legal principle.

The United States went through a series of steps that transformed the unilateral Monroe Doctrine into a multilateral inter-American policy of nonintervention and mutual *security. President Herbert Hoover's Under Secretary of State, J. Reuben Clark, wrote a memorandum in 1928 that was made public in 1930 dissociating the Roosevelt Corollary from the Monroe Doctrine. President Franklin D. *Roosevelt adhered to inter-American treaties in 1933 and 1936 that prohibited any intervention "directly or indirectly, and for whatever reason, in the internal or external affairs of the parties," a principle notably reaffirmed in the Charter of the *Organization of American States (1948) and the Inter-American Treaty of Reciprocal Assistance (*Rio Treaty, 1947).

During the *Cold War doubt was cast on the extent to which the United States truly considered the Monroe Doctrine to have been multilateralized and intervention made illegal. The Monroe Doctrine was referred to as the justification for the overthrow of the Guatemalan government (1954), the Bay of Pigs adventure (1961), and the Dominican Republic invasion (1965). In response to assertions by Soviet Premier Nikita *Khrushchev that the Monroe Doctrine was dead, the Department of State proclaimed that its principles were "as valid today as they were in 1823."

In the 1980s and 1990s, by contrast, the doctrine was rarely referred to regarding Central American conflict and was not used to justify the U.S. invasions of Grenada and Panama. The retirement of the Soviet Union from hemispheric affairs and its subsequent dissolution, plus the lack of other external threats, made the Monroe Doctrine irrelevant in the post–Cold War era.

(See also AMERICAN FOREIGN POLICY; GEOPOLITICS; INTERVENTION; U.S.–LATIN AMERICAN RELATIONS.)

Dexter Perkins, *The Monroe Doctrine, 1823–1826, 1826–1867,* and *1867–1907,* 3 vols. (Cambridge, Mass., 1927; Baltimore, 1933 and 1937). Dexter Perkins, *A History of the Monroe Doctrine* (Boston, 1963). Ernest R. May, *The Making of the Monroe Doctrine* (Cambridge, Mass., 1975).
                                                            G. POPE ATKINS

MOROCCO. Known in Arabic as *al-Maghrib,* Morocco is the most westerly Arab country. For many centuries, sultans ruled the land from the ancient capitals of Fez and Marrakesh. But in 1912, after nearly a hundred years of growing European pressure, Sultan Moulay Hafiz faced rebellion among his subjects with an empty treasury. French troops intervened, forcing him to turn over most of his territory to France, while Spanish forces took control of a zone along the northern coast.

Both powers installed protectorates, ruled nominally by the sultan but closely controlled by a European administration. Though rural Moroccans put up a fierce twenty-two-year resistance, nearly half a million Europeans eventually settled in Morocco, farming its best land and monopolizing its top posts.

The French protectorate installed a modern network of transportation and communication, light industries, and mechanized and irrigated farms. Casablanca, a small fishing village, became the country's largest city and its foremost port and financial center. From the new capital of Rabat, the French constructed a strong, highly centralized state which imposed domestic order and enforced a new legal system. Though the settlers lived well, most Moroccans faced harsh poverty and discrimination.

In the 1940s an anticolonial movement gathered strength, led by the Istiqlal Party under the leadership of Allal al-Fassi. Sultan Muhammad ben Youssef cautiously supported the movement and achieved great popularity among Moroccans as a result. By the mid-1950s, the French finally decided to withdraw, and Spain soon followed suit. The country attained a united independence in 1956 under the rule of the sultan.

Unlike most postcolonial states, Morocco's victorious independence movement did not assume power. The sultan, who crowned himself King Muhammad V in 1957, kept the upper hand, drawing on his personal prestige and the support he enjoyed from France and from conservative leaders in the Moroccan countryside. For a time it seemed that the Istiqlal might take power, but internal disputes soon weakened the party. A breakaway group formed the Union Nationale des Forces Populaires (UNFP) in 1959, and called for extensive *land reform and socialist initiatives to overcome poverty and bolster lagging economic *development.

Many of Morocco's urban poor and intellectuals, fierce opponents of the *monarchy and advocates of a united North Africa, rallied to the UNFP. The French, fighting a military campaign against independence in neighboring Algeria, provided aid and advisers which served to bolster the king's campaign against his radical nationalist opposition. In early 1960, only five months after the party was founded, police rounded up most UNFP leaders, citing evidence of a plot to kill Crown Prince Hassan. Many were tortured and eventually sentenced to prison, although little credible evidence was presented against them.

In February 1961, Muhammad V died and his son succeeded as Hassan II. Hassan pardoned the UNFP prisoners and eventually promulgated a constitution in December 1962. Local elections were followed by national parliamentary balloting the next year. The Constitution placed few restraints on the monarchy, however, and extensive official fraud marred the elections. The UNFP's electoral campaign had attracted more public support than the palace was willing to tolerate. In July, police arrested most UNFP leaders; confessions extracted under torture led to another dubious trial. Some, including leader Mehdi Ben Barka, fled into exile, and the party never fully recovered.

Morocco inherited many public enterprises from the colonial period, especially the large and profitable state phosphate-mining company. To these the government, in an effort to stimulate the economy, added fresh investments in chemicals, light industry, trade, and tourism. Though the regime was conservative and laissez-faire, it ironically built a heavily state-controlled economy. In the private sector, the king himself was the richest and largest investor, who built a portfolio of holdings throughout the economy.

Nearly half Morocco's population continued to face dire poverty; many lived in urban shantytowns; almost three-quarters were illiterate. A small middle class of professionals and civil servants lived modestly. By contrast, the king enjoyed fabulous luxury in ten palaces, while courtiers and ministers enriched themselves on bribes, payoffs, and other unchecked corruption.

With political parties weakened, spontaneous mass protests racked Morocco's cities. On 23 March 1965, when the government announced austerity measures, Casablanca exploded in riots, and Rabat and Fez soon followed. After several days, Interior Minister General Muhammad Oufkir crushed the uprisings with special security forces, leaving at least a thousand casualties. Soon the king dissolved Parliament and declared a state of emergency that continued for the next five years. In October, UNFP leader Ben Barka was kidnapped on the streets of Paris and never reappeared.

Five years from the armed forces. In July 1971, high army officers launched a nearly successful *coup on the king's birthday. Then, in August 1972, Moroc-

can air force jets tried unsuccessfully to shoot down the royal passenger plane. General Oufkir himself had been the leader of this second failed coup. The king sent many of the military rebels to the firing squad and jailed others in a notorious underground political prison.

Often described as a thousand-year-old institution, the Moroccan monarchy is best understood as a recent creation. Though the king is "Commander of the Faithful," and seems the incarnation of an oriental despot, he is French-educated and runs a strong, modern state with an efficient police apparatus. A staunch ally of the West in regional as well as international politics, the king has enjoyed the solid support of France and the United States. Both have given generous aid, as well as military and security assistance, and helped him defeat his domestic opponents.

In 1975, king and opposition found themselves curiously united. A desert colony to the south, ruled by Spain, had long been considered part of Morocco. As Spain's hold on this phosphate-rich territory weakened, the king led 350,000 Moroccans across the border in a "Green March" to claim the land. The following year, Spain signed over its colony.

Residents of annexed *Western Sahara formed a liberation movement called Polisario and with aid from Algeria began to fight Moroccan forces. Morocco eventually doubled the size of its army, devoting almost forty percent of its national budget to the widening conflict. When phosphate prices dropped in the late 1970s and European integration closed off key markets, growing war costs deepened the country's economic problems.

Real wages fell sharply in Morocco and a serious drought drove thousands off the land and into the cities. Meanwhile, the *International Monetary Fund pressed for austerity. When the government raised prices on necessities, trade unions called a general strike. On 20 June 1981, the poor of Casablanca rose in protest, setting fire to banks and nightclubs and taking control of the city; security forces struck back with armored cars and helicopters, restoring order after four days of fighting and many casualties. In January 1984, a second wave of riots swept the country, leading to another harsh counterattack, with hundreds of casualties and thousands of prisoners.

During the 1980s, as in other countries of the region, Islamic groups emerged as a major political force. Flourishing in urban slums and attracting a following in universities and even in the army, the Islamists called for a purified Islamic politics, and some played a leading role in the 1984 riots. After the riots, the king angrily accused Islamists of being pawns of foreign enemies and the police implacably hunted them down.

By the end of the 1980s, Morocco's population reached nearly 30 million, more than three times the number at independence. Casablanca, fed by rural migrants, became one of Africa's largest cities. Economic troubles, worsened by US$20 billion in foreign debts, plagued the country, even though wealthy patrons like Saudi Arabia and Kuwait offered extensive aid. Urgently seeking solutions, the government announced it would privatize more than 100 state enterprises and introduce new measures of austerity. In an effort to enhance his Islamic credentials, the king began building the world's largest and most lavish mosque on the shore of Casablanca.

The royal system continues to combine repression with nominally democratic institutions. Opposition newspapers criticize the government, *human rights committees function, elections allow a modicum of public discussion, and Parliament occasionally holds a serious debate. But the king rules, and individual Moroccans enjoy little ability to influence affairs of state.

(See also COLONIAL EMPIRES; DECOLONIZATION; ISLAM; POLITICAL VIOLENCE.)

John Waterbury, *The Commander of the Faithful* (New York, 1970). David Seddon, *Moroccan Peasants* (Folkestone, U.K. 1981). Tony Hodges, *Western Sahara: Roots of a Desert War* (Westport, Conn., 1983). I. William Zartman, *The Political Economy of Morocco* (New York, 1987). Gilles Perrault, *Notre Ami le Roi* (Paris, 1990).

JAMES A. PAUL

MOZAMBIQUE. A former Portuguese colony in southeast Africa, Mozambique gained political independence after more than ten years of a guerrilla war (25 September 1964–25 June 1975) that capped a long tradition of resistance to foreign rule. The war was led by the Mozambican Liberation Front (FRELIMO), under Eduardo Mondlane (1962–1969) and Samora Machel (1970–1986). Outside support for the war of liberation came from, among others, the African Liberation Committee of the Organization of African Unity; Tanzania (which shares a common border in the north); and the People's Republic of China, North Vietnam, the Soviet Union, and Eastern European countries. Many solidarity groups in the West (especially in the Scandinavian countries) also supported FRELIMO's efforts.

Started as a purely nationalist movement, FRELIMO transformed itself during the war by building alternative forms of economic, social, and political relations to those dominating the colonial society. This transformation would have been impossible without strong support from the poor peasantry in the northern provinces of Cabo Delgado and Nyassa. This support enabled FRELIMO to survive the assassination of its first leader, Eduardo Mondlane (in February 1969), and the Gordian Knot military offensive of 1970–1972. By April 1974, FRELIMO successes and growing popularity had generated discontent and demoralization among the young officers of the Portuguese colonial armies, and this led to an army coup in *Portugal. Negotiations led to

the Lusaka Agreement of 7 September 1974, which opened the way to political independence on 25 June 1975, headed by Prime Minister Joaquim Chissano. Taking the first major step toward a radical transformation of the colonial economy, FRELIMO nationalized land, education, and health care a month later.

At the Third Congress in February 1977, FRELIMO declared itself a Marxist-Leninist party and formally institutionalized a structure of government based on the Soviet model with executive and legislative powers concentrated in the central committee, the political bureau, and the presidency. Both bodies and the president are elected at the party congress which was to be held every five years. (In practice it has been every six years.)

Economically, socially, and politically, the government sought to pursue the transformations it had introduced in the "liberated zones" during its guerrilla war. The main objectives were to replace the colonial system based on the exploitation of cheap labor, racial discrimination, and undemocratic rule by a more democratic system in which wealth was more equitably distributed and access to health and education was considered a basic right and not a privilege of those who had the economic means.

Regionally, Mozambique committed itself to contributing to the end of the white minority regime in Southern Rhodesia. In 1976, following a vote at the UN, it imposed an embargo on goods to and from Rhodesia, and it supported Zimbabwean struggles for independence. Mozambique was never compensated for the economic and financial losses it suffered by closing Beira and Maputo harbors to Rhodesia.

Following Zimbabwe's independence, efforts toward regional cooperation for greater economic independence from the dominant economic power of South Africa led to the creation of the * Southern African Development Co-ordination Conference (SADCC). Mozambique worked to develop and coordinate the regional infrastructural transport network with particular emphasis on providing sea access to its landlocked neighbors: Zimbabwe, Zambia, Malawi, and Swaziland.

Mozambique's hopes of concentrating its resources on social and economic development were shattered with South Africa's decision to take over the white Rhodesian instrument of destabilization in Mozambique, the Mozambique National Resistance (RENAMO). Furthermore, the change of administration in the United States in 1980 signaled a move toward a more lenient attitude toward South Africa, as manifested by the "constructive engagement" policy of the Reagan administration.

In part as a result of poor economic performance (especially from 1981) and increased defense spending, the Fourth and Fifth congresses (1983 and 1989) witnessed a gradual retreat from the Eastern European model of social and economic transformation, as well as a process of decentralization of power. At the Fifth Congress, all references to *Marxism-*Leninism were dropped.

In January 1990, the draft of a radically rewritten constitution was formally presented for discussion by President Joaquim Chissano. Among some of the major new proposals were election of the president directly by the people (scheduled for 1991); president's term of office limited to three five-year terms; complete separation between the party and the government (i.e., no longer would the president of FRELIMO automatically be president of the country); freedom of association; independent trade unions; and abolition of the death penalty. The question of a multiparty system of government would be included in the discussions on the constitution as well. FRELIMO held an extraordinary Sixth Congress (12–20 August 1991) during which new statutes and programs were adopted, reflecting the drastic changes in the system of government and the demise of the one-party system. The new political bureau (now called the Political Commission) was selected by secret ballot. Taking advantage of the new Law on Political Parties (February 1991), the Partido Liberal e Democratico de Moçambique (PALMO) and the Movimento Nacional Moçambicano (MONAMO) registered in April and May 1991.

Genuine mistakes and inexperience notwithstanding, arguably the most important factor in the socioeconomic deterioration of Mozambique has been the relentless military attacks mounted and paid for by, first, the white Rhodesian regime (1969–1980) and, later (from 1980 through the early 1990s), the apartheid regime of South Africa. The human and economic costs of destabilization have been estimated at US$10 billion for the 1980–1990 period. Such estimates, however, do not provide an adequate means of measuring the long-term impact of RENAMO's strategy of destruction and terror, especially its psychic and psychological effect on the more than 250,000 children who are known to have been traumatized by the war. Moreover, persistent drought and famine have compounded these problems.

Despite the Nkomati Accord of 1984, and despite the new climate of *peace generated by the end of the *Cold War and the conversations between the *African National Congress (ANC) and the white South African government, all indications are that RENAMO continues to receive support from inside South Africa. Nevertheless, the Mozambican government continued to press for discussions toward a peaceful resolution of the war, and urged RENAMO leaders to join in the reconstruction of the country and participate in the ongoing discussions for a new constitution. It seems that persistence may have paid off finally, as, on 18 October 1991, both delegations met in Rome, Italy, and signed a peace protocol.

On the economic front, the leaders of the country are relying on the *International Monetary Fund and World Bank structural adjustment programs to rebuild the economy, while, on the social front, specialized UN agencies like UNICEF and numerous nongovernmental organizations (NGOs) from the West seek to give a "human face" to this adjustment process by providing or paying for some social services for the most vulnerable groups in Mozambican society. Since 1987, the government-sponsored National Executive Commission for the Emergency has responded to the urgent needs of the victims of war and famine and has coordinated investments in long-term projects.

(See also GUERRILLA WARFARE; NATIONAL LIBERATION MOVEMENTS; SOUTHERN AFRICA.)

Eduardo Mondlane, *The Struggle for Mozambique* (Harmondsworth, U.K., 1969; London, 1983). Joseph Hanlon, *Mozambique: The Revolution Under Fire* (London, 1984). Mamphela Ramphele and Francis Wilson, *Children on the Front Line: The Impact of Apartheid, Destabilization and Warfare on Children in Southern and South Africa,* A Report for Unicef, 3d ed. (New York, 1989). Alex Vines, *RENAMO: Terrorism in Mozambique* (Bloomington, Ind., 1991).

JACQUES DEPELCHIN

MULTINATIONAL CORPORATIONS. One definition of the multinational corporation (MNC) seems self-evident: a firm based in a single home country that invests in one or more other states (known as host countries). Even this simple definition, however, raises a central issue regarding the implications of foreign direct investment. Whose interests does the MNC represent: those of the home country, the host country, or the firm itself? This ambiguity has resulted in a debate over the appropriate labeling of the MNC. Is it in fact a *multinational* entity with stakes and interests in many different countries, or is it more accurately a *transnational* corporation that serves the interests of the home country with little regard for the host economies involved? Some argue that the real misnomer is the term *corporation,* which is in fact only one part of a larger entity more correctly called a multinational enterprise.

Although these may appear to be little more than semantic distinctions, they are indicative of a larger and more fractious debate over the broader political and economic impact of international investment. These issues have become even more complicated as the nature of production and international investment strategies have changed over time. Consequently, the MNC remains one of the most controversial actors in the *international political economy.

MNCs and the Changing Nature of Production. One of the earliest attempts to develop a theory of foreign direct investment was Raymond Vernon's product cycle model (*Sovereignty at Bay,* New York, 1971). Vernon argued that international investment was a stage in a cycle of production: new goods were first sold at home, but were exported abroad once domestic markets were saturated. These exports translated into foreign investment as international production became necessary to service overseas markets. Eventually, these foreign countries would begin to export the original product themselves. Vernon himself criticized this thesis later, arguing that as MNCs became more at ease with international production and market conditions in developed economies converged, domestic and foreign production would begin to occur simultaneously.

Differences between domestic and foreign manufacturing were further blurred by the changing organization of production within the firm. Frobel, Heinrichs, and Kreye (*The New International Division of Labour,* Cambridge, U.K., 1980) argued that as transportation and communications costs decreased, it became easier for the firm to divide up the production process and disperse it geographically. Firms could rationalize production by making certain technology-intensive components in the home country, shipping them abroad to be assembled in offshore operations in cheap labor countries, then reexporting them to other markets. Obviously, this marked a change in the role of the MNC's foreign subsidiaries. No longer were they intended merely to produce for the host country market; instead, they became an integrated part of the company's global production process.

With the introduction of robotics and the growing mechanization of production, the nature of production is again changing. In some sectors offshore assembly operations have become redundant as production becomes less labor intensive. In addition, labor in these "export processing zones" has in many cases reacted to harsh working conditions and low wages. As foreign labor unionizes and labor costs increase, there is an even greater incentive to repatriate assembly operations, to the detriment of this largely female work force.

Another important change in the nature of production is the actual investment strategies of MNCs. In the past, U.S. multinationals in particular tended to invest abroad in the form of wholly owned subsidiaries. Stephen Hymer argued that because a major motivation for foreign investment was the possession of a competitive advantage, the MNC did not want to risk losing this advantage or creating potential competitors by taking on joint venture partners or licensing the product to a local firm (*The International Operations of National Firms,* Cambridge, Mass., 1976). This trend is rapidly changing, as MNCs participate in joint ventures, research and development collaboration, and marketing and distribution agreements with other firms. Labeled strategic partnerships, these agreements are also a manifestation of the changing nature of production. In many industries, production has become so knowledge intensive and so competitive that it is impossible for a single firm to keep up with the product and process innovations taking place. As Japanese and European firms have grown to challenge U.S.

multinationals, this competition has intensified. Consequently, it is important that new products be commercialized and distributed worldwide immediately to cover costs and prevent competitors from usurping the firm's market share. Even the largest MNCs may need help in this regard. In some cases, companies that compete in one product area have banded together to jointly develop and distribute goods in another segment of the market.

MNCs and the National Interest. Critics in both home and host countries have argued that despite the MNC's huge profit-making capacity, international investment may not always be in a country's interest. Labor in the home country charges that international companies merely export jobs abroad, taking advantage of cheap labor in developing countries and leaving workers at home unemployed. They argue that this in turn reduces the bargaining power of trade unions at home and benefits countries that refuse their workers essential *human rights. Others argue that *security interests can be threatened by multinationals, particularly in the case of strategic partnerships. Many worry that MNCs collaborating with foreign firms may transfer strategic technology abroad—technology that has often been heavily subsidized by the state.

Others have made more structural arguments against foreign direct investment. On the basis of a historical comparison of Britain and the United States, Robert Gilpin (*U.S. Power and the Multinational Corporation,* New York, 1975) argued that massive outflows of foreign investment can lead to a neglect of productive capacities in the home economy. Rather than promoting qualitative improvements in productivity by ploughing profits into domestic operations, foreign investment allows MNCs to increase their profits *quantitatively* by setting up subsidiaries in new markets. The result is declining investment levels at home as well as stagnation and decreasing innovation and productivity.

Gilpin's argument may have applied in the case of Britain, but it appears less relevant to the United States today. Although U.S. economic superiority is being challenged by highly innovative foreign firms, it remains a relatively productive economy. An important consideration is that the United States is the world's largest host country as well as being the biggest foreign investor. The willingness of other companies to invest in the United States may counteract the tendency to stagnation evident in Britain. In any case, it indicates that unlike the British case, there are investment opportunities in the U.S. market.

Like Vernon, Gilpin argued that foreign investment ultimately disperses home country economic power because of the politics surrounding MNCs in the host country. Labeled the "obsolescing bargain," the argument is that when the MNC is considering an investment in a foreign market, it is in a powerful bargaining position. The host, usually a developing country, is anxious to attract new investment, and the MNC has the knowledge and resources it so desperately needs. Once the investment is sunk, however, bargaining power shifts to the host government. This is particularly true in raw materials industries, where large, up-front capital investments are necessary. As the technical knowledge of government officials grows over time owing to their interaction with the MNC, their need for foreign expertise decreases. In addition, since many of these investments provide the MNC with an enclave or mini-economy within the host market, their high profile and large profits create resentment among local citizenry. This in turn creates nationalist resentment that is often translated into political platforms. The result is a tendency for the original bargain to obsolesce, often leading to the *nationalization or expropriation of the MNC.

Critics have challenged this portrayal of foreign MNCs as the pawns of powerful host states. They argue that nationalizations were a phenomenon of the 1970s. In the 1990s, declining foreign investment levels to developing countries in particular have shifted bargaining power back to the MNCs and left host countries clamoring to offer incentives to potential investors. They also point out that this argument applies only to raw materials where large, relatively immobile investments are involved. In manufacturing, disgruntled firms can simply pick up and leave, taking their more sophisticated product and process innovations with them.

Despite the difficulty of regulating MNCs, many host countries have attempted to do so in order to address some of the disadvantages associated with foreign direct investment. For example, host countries complain that MNCs have an adverse effect on the national trade balance, because they tend to import components from other subsidiaries rather than sourcing locally. Similarly, parent companies at times will prevent their foreign subsidiaries from exporting if they are designed primarily to service foreign markets. Current account difficulties can also arise owing to the expatriation of profits and payments for services provided by the MNC. Because of this, many critics argue that foreign firms extract more from the host economy than they bring in. This trend is exacerbated by the tendency of MNCs to borrow locally in the host economy rather than bringing capital in from abroad. In broader economic terms, this local borrowing can crowd out domestic investors. These factors are of particular concern for developing countries anxious for foreign exchange.

Host countries also worry that MNCs may displace local producers who are unable to compete with large international firms. Thus it is not surprising that many efforts to regulate multinationals have come at the behest of domestic capital, and have led to an insistence in some states that MNCs take on local joint venture partners. A related point

is that because MNCs have concentrated their research and development in the home country in the past, the combined impact of large volumes of foreign investment and displaced local producers may lead to a decrease in the host economy's innovative capacity.

MNCs can also challenge the political sovereignty of the host country. For example, internal accounting procedures may allow the MNC to avoid paying higher taxes in the host country by transferring profits to other subsidiaries in lower tax havens. Political sovereignty is further threatened by the extraterritorial application of home country laws. The United States has infuriated Canada by periodically ordering Canadian subsidiaries of U.S. companies to avoid selling goods to U.S. "enemies" (such as Cuba and China) through its Trading with the Enemy Act.

Skeptics argue that efforts to regulate MNCs have met with little success, however, because of the high mobility of international firms. Although there is no clear correlation between investment flows and attempts to regulate MNCs, states with investment review policies worry that they may be deflecting investment elsewhere. Combined with an overall slowdown in world economic growth, these considerations prompted many states to dismantle their investment review programs in the 1980s. Frequently, they have been replaced by investment incentive packages including tax write-offs, subsidies, and real estate deals.

There is considerable evidence, however, that these incentive programs affect investment decisions only on the margins. Not only do they engage states in bidding wars against one another, surveys of MNCs indicate that in many cases the investment would have been made anyway. Changing international economic conditions and new investment strategies call for new approaches to regulating and attracting MNCs. Rather than considering investment policies in isolation, states must embed them in larger industrial strategies focusing on labor training, research and development policies, and sectoral targeting.

Obviously, the *interdependence between host countries, home countries, and firms that is created by the MNCs' global networks will continue to generate controversy in the future. While few countries are in a position to refuse international investment, they will continue to question the MNC's impact on the national interest.

(See also DEVELOPMENT AND UNDERDEVELOPMENT; NEW INTERNATIONAL ECONOMIC ORDER; NORTH-SOUTH RELATIONS; TAXES AND TAXATION; TECHNOLOGY TRANSFER.)

Stephen Guisinger, *Investment Incentives and Performance Requirements* (New York, 1985). Edward M. Graham and Paul R. Krugman, *Foreign Direct Investment in the United States* (Washington, D.C., 1989). Lynn Mytelka, ed., *Strategic Partnerships: States, Firms and International Compe-*

tition (London, 1991). Robert Reich, *The Work of Nations* (New York, 1991).

BARBARA JENKINS

MUNICH CONFERENCE. See WORLD WAR II.

MUSSOLINI, Benito. The founder and leader of Italian *fascism and the first successful European fascist dictator, Benito Mussolini served as prime minister of *Italy from 1922 to 1943. Mussolini (born in Predappio, 29 July 1883) was from the Romagna, a region known for its political radicalism. His father was an anticlerical, Socialist blacksmith, his mother a schoolteacher. Pugnacious, restless, and surly, the young Mussolini obtained a certificate as an elementary school teacher in 1902 and then spent nearly a decade as an itinerant teacher, journalist, and Socialist agitator in Switzerland, Austria, and Italy. In 1910 he began living with Rachele Guidi, whom he married in 1915; she bore him five children. The oldest daughter, Edda, eventually married Galeazzo Ciano, who became Mussolini's foreign minister in 1936.

The future Duce (Leader) of fascism and reviver of Italy's colonial ambitions began his political career as a revolutionary Socialist opposed to Italy's colonial war against Libya in 1911. His first major opportunity as a radical politician and journalist came in 1912 when he was appointed editor of the Partito Socialista Italiano newspaper *Avanti*. When World War I broke out, at first he advocated neutrality for Italy, then reversed himself and called for intervention on the Entente side. For this the party expelled him, and in November 1914 he launched his own newspaper, *Il Popolo d'Italia*, which later became the organ of the Fascist movement. He served briefly in the army until he was wounded in 1917.

On 23 March 1919, in Milan, Mussolini and a politically heterogenous collection of war veterans and radicals founded the revolutionary, nationalist Fasci di Combattimento ("Fighting Leagues"). In the 1919 national elections the Fascists did poorly. Mussolini capitalized on middle-class fears of a socialist revolution during the "Red Biennium" (1919–1920) and on the struggle of big landowners and industrialists in the Po Valley to beat back resurgent socialist labor organizations. This latter conflict spawned the notorious Blackshirt squads that carried on province-wide civil wars against socialists, communists, liberals, and Catholics. Mussolini's great triumph—a sign of his formidable political skills—came in October 1922. Backed by nothing more than his unruly, poorly armed Blackshirts, he threatened to "march on Rome." His bluff worked, and King Victor Emmanuel III invited Mussolini to form a coalition government (28 October 1922). Fascist violence, however, continued. Public outrage in 1924 over the murder of Socialist deputy Giacomo Matteotti by Blackshirt thugs nearly toppled the Fascist

government. Mussolini counterattacked and declared a dictatorship in January 1925.

Mussolini had no clearly defined program. In practice, he continued many projects and policies initiated by his Liberal predecessors. Despite the bombastic propaganda that accompanied them, his social programs of land reclamation, economic self-sufficiency, and population growth were largely failures. Among his most popular and enduring legacies were the 1929 Lateran Pacts with the Vatican.

Always the journalist, picturing the morning's headlines, Mussolini in the 1930s initiated an aggressive foreign policy. This included colonial expansion, with the conquest of Ethiopia (1935–1936) and the annexation of Albania (1939), and intervention on the Fascist side in the *Spanish Civil War (1936–1938). Mussolini's fatal mistake was to abandon Italy's traditional role as a balancing power between blocs and to commit himself to Nazi Germany by the Rome-Berlin Axis (1936) and the Pact of Steel (May 1939). In June 1940, with the fall of France, Mussolini, anticipating a short war, intervened on the side of his German ally in *World War II. A series of military defeats led to a no-confidence vote at a meeting of the Grand Council, the supreme Fascist decision-making body, on 25 July 1943. The following day Mussolini was deposed by the king and placed under arrest. He was rescued by the Germans, and in October 1943 was placed in charge of the puppet Italian Social Republic, headquartered at Salò on Lake Garda, until the German collapse in April 1945. Then, with his mistress, Claretta Petacci, the aging and beaten dictator attempted to flee into Switzerland. Italian partisans captured the couple, who were summarily executed on 28 April at Giulino di Mezzegra near Lake Como. The bodies were strung up by the heels and exposed to the public in Milan's Piazzale Loreto.

Within the Italian political tradition, Mussolini's regime was unprecedented for its violence, its repression of civil liberties, its aspirations to create a totalitarian state. Nevertheless, Mussolini's regime also recalled a long tradition of Machiavellian princes and petty tyrants, as well as the chain of powerful prime ministers, from Camillo Cavour and Francesco Crispi to Giovanni Giolitti, who ruled Liberal Italy.

Mussolini's regime has often been dismissed as a superficial one that left relatively few marks on Italian political life. Since the fall of fascism, Italy has unquestionably developed a strong democratic political system with a new constitution, a multiparty system, women's suffrage, and strong safeguards against political centralizaion. Nevertheless, aspects of Fascist legislation, including the Lateran Pacts, were incorporated wholesale into the Italian constitution of 1948. Traces of the corporativist (or corporatist) state are evident in the national structure of the Italian labor movement, in provisions regarding nationwide collective bargaining. Other influences include the persistence of state-owned and state-controlled public and semipublic enterprises like the Istituto per la Ricostruzione Industriale (IRI).

On the international level, until he fell under *Hitler's shadow in the late 1930s, Mussolini represented the prototype of the successful fascist dictator. The Duce was probably more typical of the classical fascism of the 1920s and 1930s than were Hitler and Nazism. In a world still reeling from the revolutionary effects of World War I, Mussolini appealed as a strong leader with an air of quasi-military efficiency about him, a man who could make the trains run on time even in a backward nation such as Italy. His slogans and programs appeared to offer a middle way between the extremes of communism and a discredited liberal capitalism. Aspects of the corporativist state were imitated in Spain and elsewhere. His theatrical oratorical style served as a model to aspiring politicians ranging from Argentina's Juan *Perón to Egypt's Anwar *Sadat.

(See also AUTHORITARIANISM; CORPORATISM; TOTALITARIANISM; VATICAN CITY STATE.)

Ivone Kirkpatrick, *Mussolini* (New York, 1964). Renzo De Felice, *Mussolini*, 7 vols. to date (Turin, 1965–). Denis Mack Smith, *Mussolini* (New York, 1982).

CLAUDIO G. SEGRÈ

MYANMAR. See BURMA.

N

NAMIBIA. One of the newest nations in the world, having achieved its independence on 21 March 1990, the southwest African territory of Namibia gained its independence following UN-supervised elections in November 1989 that ended a twenty-four-year war of liberation led by the South-West Africa People's Organization (SWAPO). Sam Nujoma, the leader of SWAPO, was inaugurated as the first president of Namibia.

The new government is a nonracial, unitary *democracy with a progressive bill of rights included in its constitution. Executive power is vested in a cabinet headed by a president who is head of state and commander in chief. The president is elected by direct universal suffrage to a five-year term. Legislative authority is possessed by a seventy-two-member National Assembly and a National Council consisting of two representatives from each region. An independent judiciary is headed by a Supreme Court. Women are accorded equal rights under the constitution, and capital punishment is prohibited. An ombudsman has power to investigate the government.

Germany took Namibia in 1883 following a series of treaties by F. A. E. Luderitz. Germany's control over "South-West Africa" (SWA) was recognized by other major powers at the Berlin Conference of 1884–1885. When German authorities met violent resistance from the Namibian people, Germany responded by pursuing a genocidal campaign against the Herero and the Nama. Between 1904 and 1906, the Herero were reduced from about 70,000 to 15,000. More than half of the 20,000 Nama also were eliminated.

With World War I, Britain ordered its South African dominion to seize SWA. In 1915 this mission was achieved. In 1919, upon the termination of the war, the League of Nations set up a mandate system allowing former German colonies to be administered by mandatory states. *South Africa was appointed the mandatory over SWA.

Following World War II, the UN assumed the responsibilities of the League, and a trusteeship system superseded the mandate system. South Africa was the only mandatory not to join the trusteeship system, arguing that the UN lacked the authority to supervise League mandates. South African proposals to annex SWA were rejected by the UN in 1946.

In 1966, the UN General Assembly voted to terminate South Africa's mandate for Namibia on the grounds of maladministration, and SWAPO (founded in 1957 as the Ovamboland People's Congress) began military actions against South African Defence Forces in Namibia.

In June 1971, the *International Court of Justice ruled that South Africa's continued occupation of Namibia was a violation of *international law. Members of the UN also were obligated to refrain from any acts supporting South Africa's administration in the territory.

In January 1988, the United States began negotiations with Angola and Cuba to implement a "linkage" policy that tied Namibian independence to the removal of Cuban troops from Angola. South Africa agreed in March 1988 to join these talks. In May 1988 South Africa suffered a major military defeat at Cuito Cuanavale, Angola, at the combined hands of Cuba, Angola, and SWAPO. South Africa agreed to a formal cease-fire on 8 August. On 22 December 1988 a formal treaty was signed by South Africa, Angola, and Cuba at UN headquarters providing for independence elections in Namibia and the evacuation of all Cuban troops from Angola by July 1991.

The UN Transitional Assistance Group (UNTAG) assumed a supervisory presence in Namibia on 1 April 1989, and began repatriating over 40,000 Namibian exiles. Independence elections were held from 6 to 11 November 1989. SWAPO won the election with fifty-eight percent of the vote. The Democratic Turnhalle Alliance (DTA) received twenty-seven percent, and eight other parties shared the remainder of the vote. Support for SWAPO was broad-based, but was especially solid in the northern war zones. The DTA had a strong showing among whites, Hereros, San, and other groups that had collaborated with South African authorities.

Namibia is an expansive country (824,292 sq. km.; 318,261 sq. mi.), about twice the size of California, but possessing a population of only about 1.4 million. Most of the infrastructure of the country is sandwiched between the Namib Desert along the Atlantic coast and the Kalahari Desert that straddles the Botswana border. Windhoek is the capital and largest city with a population of about 120,000. Walvis Bay, Namibia's principal port, possesses a population in excess of 20,000. The enclave of Walvis Bay (an area comprising 1,124 sq. km.; 434 sq. mi.) remains under the occupation of South Africa.

Namibia is a relatively prosperous country, possessing a per capita income of US$1,050. It is among the top twenty mining countries in the world; mining accounts for the largest part of the GDP and earns about seventy-five percent of total export revenue. The most important mines are the diamond concerns at Oranjemund controlled by De Beers, considered the richest gem diamond source in the world. The Rossing uranium mine, dominated by Britain's Rio Tinto-Zinc group, is one of the largest uranium mines in the world. The Tsumeb base metal mine, controlled by Gold Fields of South Africa, is Africa's largest producer of lead and zinc. Namibia also possesses a rich offshore fishing industry and a karakul fur industry. Under South African rule, about ninety percent of the goods purchased in Namibia were exported, whereas about eighty-five percent of the goods used in the territory were imported.

Although SWAPO has professed socialist goals, the new independent government has promised a mixed economy and has not nationalized mines or other major sectors of the economy. The new country is economically dependent on South Africa and is a member of the South African Customs Union. The South African rand is the official currency. Namibia has become the tenth member of the *Southern African Development Co-ordination Conference (SADCC), which fosters regional cooperation to offset dependency upon South Africa.

(See also ANGOLAN CONFLICT; SOUTHERN AFRICA.)

Andre Du Pisani, Namibia: The Politics of Continuity and Change (Johannesburg, 1985). Tore Linne Eriksen, The Political Economy of Namibia: An Annotated, Critical Bibliography (Oslo, 1989).

ALLAN D. COOPER

NASSER, Gamal Abdel. Born 15 January 1918 in the upper Egyptian village of Bani Murr, Gamal Abdel Nasser (Jamāl 'Abd al-Nāṣir) was educated mainly in Alexandria and Cairo. His father was a postal clerk. In November 1935, while a student at Cairo's al-Nahda School, known for its nationalist activism, Nasser was wounded by British soldiers during a demonstration demanding restoration of the constitution. He subsequently flirted with many political organizations and ideologies without committing himself fully to any of them, although he briefly joined the quasi-fascist Young *Egypt.

In March 1937, Nasser enrolled in the Military Academy, opened to middle-class boys as a result of the Anglo-Egyptian treaty of 1936. There, and at his first posting in upper Egypt, he made friends with 'Abd al-Hakim 'Amir, Zakariya Muhyi al-Din, and Anwar *Sadat—all future leaders of the Free Officers organization. Like many of Egypt's educated youths, these young officers had been radical-

ized by the failure of the leading nationalist party, the Wafd, to end the British military occupation of Egypt, and they were dismayed by Egypt's ineffective *parliamentary democracy and its weak response to Egypt's economic and political crisis. Nasser and the others were particularly offended when British tanks surrounded 'Abdin Palace on 4 February 1942 and forced King Faruq to install a Wafd government.

In 1943, Nasser became an instructor in the Military Academy, a post that enabled him to make contacts with future officers. Later, while commanding a battalion in the Arab-Israeli War of 1948–1949, his unit was encircled and besieged at Faluja. Like other nationalist officers serving on the same front, Nasser viewed this experience as a metaphor for Egypt's corrupt and inequitable internal regime, which he saw as the fundamental cause for the defeat. He was outraged by the lack of an adequate military plan, the political manipulation of the army by the palace, and reports that members of King Faruq's entourage had sold faulty weapons to the army.

Because the civilian nationalist opposition was too weak and disunited to take action, Nasser recruited discontented junior officers into the Free Officers organization—a disciplined and cohesive group that set as its goal the overthrow of the regime. The officers had only a vague program of national reform, influenced by the demands for social justice adopted by the post–World War II nationalist movement. On 23 July 1952 they executed a nearly bloodless coup and formed a Revolutionary Command Council (RCC) headed by General Muhammad Naguib. Three days later they deposed King Faruq.

On 9 September 1952 the RCC proclaimed a *land reform that limited agricultural holdings, regulated rents, and promised to distribute land to poor peasants. The economic goals of the land reform—stimulating industrial development and providing land for the landless—were incompletely realized; but it symbolized a break with the old regime and curtailed the power of its dominant class, the large cotton growers allied with the monarchy and the British. The RCC also raised the minimum wage, encouraged the formation of trade unions, and enhanced job security, though it also imposed corporatist control over the labor movement and prevented independent political action by workers. In 1953 the regime banned the old political parties and abolished the monarchy.

Though it dismantled parliamentary democracy and limited political expression, the military regime won genuine popular support. In 1954, Nasser consolidated his personal power by eliminating Naguib from the government. He then successfully concluded a treaty with Britain in October of the same year, securing the evacuation of British troops from the Suez Canal Zone by June 1956.

The popularity of the new regime was due in no

small measure to Nasser's political style and personal charisma. He spoke to the people in colloquial Egyptian rather than the standard Arabic that was imperfectly understood by the majority of Egyptians. A rhetorical master, he succeeded in making common people feel they had a stake in politics. His charisma and popularity extended beyond Egypt to the entire Arab world, where he became a symbol of independence and resistance to European colonialism and *imperialism.

Nasser assumed leadership of the pan-Arab national movement, and he also achieved international prominence as a pioneer in the *nonaligned movement of Asian and African states. His dramatic *nationalization of the Suez Canal on 23 July 1956, his support for Palestinian grievances against Israel, and his acquisition of arms from Czechoslovakia led to the *Suez Crisis. On 29 October 1956 Britain, France, and Israel attacked Egypt and sought to overthrow his regime. Despite Egypt's military defeat, the attackers were forced to withdraw and Nasser emerged a hero. The war prompted the regime to nationalize all enterprises owned by foreign nationals in Egypt, a precursor to more extensive nationalizations in 1961 and 1962, as well as other populist redistributive economic measures known as Arab socialism.

Nasser's rhetoric intensified as his pan-Arab commitments increased after 1956; yet he avoided military confrontations with Israel. In May 1967, Syrian criticism of his passive response to Israeli raids on Syria and Jordan convinced Nasser to mobilize his army and blockade the Straits of Tiran. In response, Israel launched a preemptive strike and devastatingly defeated Egypt, Syria, and Jordan. Nasser resigned in the face of the defeat, but millions of Egyptians came out into the streets and persuaded him to stay on.

Nasser died on 28 September 1970. At his death, Israel still occupied Egyptian territory captured in the June War of 1967, and a deepening crisis gripped the economy. Military and economic failure described the limits of Nasser's efforts to assert Egyptian independence and highlighted the undemocratic aspects of his regime, which had become increasingly repressive in the late 1960s. His successor, Anwar Sadat, abandoned many of his policies and established a close alliance with the United States.

(See also ARAB-ISRAELI CONFLICT; ARAB NATIONALISM; CORPORATISM; MILITARY RULE; NASSERISM.)

Jean Lacouture, *Nasser* (New York, 1973). P. J. Vatikiotis, *Nasser and His Generation* (London, 1978).

JOEL BEININ

NASSERISM. A radical nationalist political movement, Nasserism is associated with the regime of Egyptian President Gamal Abdel *Nasser (1952–1970). Nasserists saw their movement as an anti-imperialist challenge to continuing European political and economic influence in the *Middle East in the postcolonial era and to the interests of large landholders who were regarded as obstacles to industrial development because of their collaboration with European interests. At the same time Nasserism opposed Marxian conceptions of *class struggle and the revolutionary transformation of society. From the mid-1950s to 1967 Nasserism acquired a wide following in the Arab world as Nasser's personal charisma, militant *Arab nationalism, and skillful maneuvering between the two *Cold War great power blocs inspired enthusiastic popular support throughout the region. Nasserism has many similarities with Peronism in Latin America and with other varieties of radical, secular nationalism in the Middle East.

Nasserism was not a well-articulated philosophy developed before Nasser and the Free Officers seized power in the *coup d'état of 23 July 1952. Its two seminal texts—Nasser's *Philosophy of the Revolution* (1954) and the Egyptian National Charter (1962)—were composed after the actions they justify were substantially completed. The Free Officers had no previously existing social base of support outside the army; and despite the initial popularity of the new regime, it was undemocratic and did not tolerate collective action initiated by grass-roots activists. Its successive single parties—the Liberation Rally, the National Union, and the Arab Socialist Union—were bureaucratic, hierarchical organizations.

Nasserism gained great influence outside *Egypt because Nasser's anti-imperialist foreign policy established him as the dominant political figure in the Arab world. After signing a treaty in 1954 stipulating that the last British troops would leave Egypt by June 1956, thus ending an occupation begun in 1882, Nasser refused to join the anti-Soviet Baghdad Pact because it might have required Egypt to permit foreign troops on its soil once again. In April 1955 Nasser further angered the West by attending the Conference of Asian and African States in Bandung, Indonesia, where he emerged as a leading exponent of nonalignment and positive neutralism.

Because of Egypt's independent foreign policy orientation, the United States refused Nasser's requests to purchase arms. Egypt's ignominious defeat in the Arab-Israeli War of 1948–1949, its inability to thwart raids into its territory launched by Israel in reprisal for violations of its borders, and the regime's dependence on support of the army made military modernization an urgent matter. Hence, in September 1955 Egypt announced it would purchase weapons from Czechoslovakia. In retaliation, the United States and Britain withdrew their offers to assist in financing the construction of the Aswan High Dam—a critical economic development project. In response, on 23 July 1956, Nasser announced that Egypt would nationalize the Suez Canal and finance construction of the dam with the canal transit fees. An electrified Arab world rallied to Egypt's support.

*Nationalization of the Suez Canal and Egypt's support for the Algerian Front de Libération Nationale led Britain, France, and Israel to launch a joint attack against Egypt on 29 October 1956. The ensuing Suez-Sinai War ended in military defeat for Egypt, resulting in Israeli occupation of the Sinai Peninsula and the Gaza Strip. But Israel's withdrawal, under pressure from both the United States and the Soviet Union, gave a political victory to Nasser, who was hailed as the defiant hero of anti-*imperialism, anti-Zionism, and Arab nationalism.

Forces inspired by Nasser's actions were active in Syria, Lebanon, Jordan, Iraq, and the Arab Gulf states, although they were not politically or organizationally united. The election of a nationalist government in Jordan and the ouster of Glubb Pasha in 1956–1957, the unification of Egypt and Syria in the United Arab Republic (UAR) in 1958, the civil war in Lebanon in 1958, and the deposition of the Hashemite monarchy in Iraq in 1958 were all expressions of the radical nationalist upsurge in the Arab world that, inspired by Nasser's example, threatened pro-Western rulers and interests. However, despite the popularity of the slogan, Arab unity was not realized. Syria left the UAR following a military coup in 1961, motivated in part by opposition to the nationalization of banks and other large-scale enterprises that initiated the policies of Arab socialism.

The Baʿth Party, which also advocated Arab unity and socialism, saw itself as the natural organizational vehicle for Nasserism. But unity talks with Egypt held after the Baʿth came to power in Syria and Iraq in 1963 failed. Nasser refused to accept the ideological tutelage of the Baʿth; so despite the similarity between their views, the Baʿth and Nasser were rivals for the leadership of the radical pan-Arab movement of the 1960s.

The Movement of Arab Nationalists (MAN), a pan-Arab party founded by Palestinians after 1948 with branches in several Arab countries, looked to Nasser for leadership until the mid-1960s. The Palestinian MAN members eventually formed the Popular Front for the Liberation of Palestine and its splinter, the Democratic Front for the Liberation of Palestine—component organizations of the *Palestine Liberation Organization. The MAN branch in Aden became a key element in the National Liberation Front that expelled the British and established the People's Democratic Republic of South Yemen in 1967. Omani members launched a guerrilla war based in Dhofar province against the sultan of Oman that was crushed after the shah of Iran intervened in 1973.

Other political forces influenced by Nasser include: Kamal Junblat's Popular Socialist Party in Lebanon; the Murabitun, a Sunni militia active during the Lebanese civil war; and al-Ard, a movement of Palestinian Arab citizens of Israel in the late 1950s and early 1960s. When Muammar *Qaddafi executed his coup d'état ousting the king of Libya in 1969 he regarded Nasser as his model.

The demise of the UAR, the failure of the 1963 unity talks, Egypt's costly and indecisive intervention on the republican side in the Yemeni civil war (1962–1967), an economic crisis in Egypt beginning in 1965, and Israel's overwhelming victory in the June 1967 war diminished the mass appeal of Nasserism and other varieties of secular Arab nationalism. Many of Nasser's policies were reversed by his successor, Anwar *Sadat. His legacy in Egypt is claimed by small opposition groups—elements of the National Progressive Unionist Party and a Nasserist party.

(See also ARAB-ISRAELI CONFLICT; NONALIGNED MOVEMENT; PERÓN, JUAN DOMINGO; SUEZ CRISIS; ZIONISM.)

Malcolm Kerr, *The Arab Cold War: Gamal ʿAbd al-Nasir and his Rivals*, 3d ed. (London, 1971). Jean Lacouture, *Nasser* (New York, 1973).

JOEL BEININ

NATIONALISM

The history of the study of nationalism is closely intertwined with the history of its subject. When the forty-two founding members of the *League of Nations assembled in 1920, they inaugurated an era in which the nation became the only internationally legitimate *state form. The sudden appearance, out of the debris of the Habsburg, Hohenzollern, and Romanov empires, of many new nation-states in Central and Eastern Europe, all basing their sovereignties on ancient identities, immediately attracted the attention of comparative historians. It was the achievement of Carlton Hayes (New York, 1931) and Hans Kohn (New York, 1944) to show conclusively that, in spite of these claims to antiquity, nationalism was a late-eighteenth-century creation, and that exactly this *modernity was one reason for its recent spread to Asia and Africa. With different emphases, both argued that nationalism owed its origins to a *secularization of political thought generated by the Renaissance and the Enlightenment, to the egalitarian implications of *liberalism, and to the conceptions of republicanism and *citizenship popularized by the upheavals of the American and French revolutions.

After World War II the study of nationalism went into general eclipse. In Europe nationalism seemed profoundly discredited by its association with Nazism, *fascism, and *anti-Semitism. In Eastern Europe, most of the new states of 1920 had fallen under Moscow-controlled communist regimes at least formally committed to the concept of proletarian internationalism. In a battered Western Europe under U.S. domination, institutions were being initiated that would lead to a putatively supranational *European Community. Hence, although anticolonial nationalist movements were gaining ever-greater impetus in Asia and Africa, it was tempting to regard them as signs of these regions' backwardness, and to believe that nationalism was in the process of being historically superseded in civilized Europe.

In the 1970s, however, against most expectations, an explosion of new nationalisms broke out in Western Europe—above all Scottish and Welsh in Britain, Flemish in Belgium, Breton and Corsican in France, Basque and Catalan in Spain. In the late 1970s wars broke out between the communist regimes of China, Vietnam, and Cambodia. During the 1980s, revived nationalisms were breaking up Stalin's East European empire. At the start of the 1990s Yugoslavia had disintegrated, and the Union of Soviet Socialist Republics had divided into an uncertain Commonwealth of Independent States, as the heterogeneous populations once "united" by tsars and Bolsheviks moved rapidly toward separate independences. Still more puzzling was the fact that while the membership of the UN continued to rise—by 1991 it had four times the membership of the League of Nations of 1921—transnational corporations and electronic communications were creating a planetary economic system more intricately unified than ever before in history.

These extraordinary developments encouraged, in the 1980s, a scarcely less extraordinary proliferation of theoretically innovative and comparative studies of nationalism. Two basic assumptions held by the pioneers of the interwar years were, from differing perspectives, generally discarded. First was the idea that, at least in any simple way, nationalism represented a "stage" in some steady evolutionary march, as suggested by both liberal and Marxist theory. For violent Basque nationalism, arising in the most advanced industrial zone of Spain, appeared exactly contemporaneous with violent Tamil nationalism in agrarian northern Ceylon. Second was the conception that nationalism was primarily an *ideology— a political-philosophical creed analogous to liberalism or conservatism—a conception that had been nourished by the writings of nineteenth-century intellectuals and politicians such as Giuseppe Mazzini, Jules Michelet, Simón Bolívar, and Sun Yat-sen. By the 1980s, these texts had become period pieces of demonstrable intellectual shallowness.

The search for a more profound understanding of nationalism was guided by an awareness of its modernity and of its astonishingly rapid spread across the entire globe through dozens of different cultures, social orders, and political-economic systems. In this search two general tendencies have become plain, one emphasizing political and economic change, the other stressing transformations of technology and culture (or consciousness).

Miroslav Hroch's meticulous, cross-national analyses (Prague, 1968, Cambridge, 1985) of the rise and development of nationalism in Central and Eastern Europe pioneered the close sociological study of the different types of regional *elites, professional groups, and economic interests that took up nationalism and led nationalist movements in three distinct, successive stages: apolitical, romantic folklorizing, propagandizing of literate publics, and organizing of mass movements. Hroch's geographical frame and sociological perspective were subsequently widened by thinkers such as Tom Nairn (London, 1977), who tied the spread of nationalism directly to the "uneven *development" characteristic of the global onrush of industrial *capitalism. Just as weak and backward states attempted to protect themselves from external economic domination by erecting high tariffs around local industries, so groups whose interests and status were being undermined by powerful metropoles promoted nationalism among available masses in order to build political-cultural walls behind which they could defend and enhance their power. Nationalism's putative exclusivism, its emphasis on unique cultures, literatures, histories, and languages—and its absence of intellectual depth— made it an ideal instrument for building the vertical, cross-class alliances that such threatened elites most urgently required.

At the same time, other scholars began to explore the puzzling availability of mass publics for nationalist propagandizing. Why were so many very ordinary people willing to lay down their lives for nations of whom their grandparents had never heard? Generally speaking, provisional answers came from two directions. On the one hand, Ernest Gellner (Oxford, 1983), among others, explained this new availability in terms of the dislocations caused by modern industrial society, and by the development of new, highly centralized and standardized institutions of indoctrination, some of them agencies of the state, others of the mass market. Industrialism destroyed traditional, often face-to-face, rural communities and drove millions of people into wholly strange factories and urban slums. That same industrialism imposed an immense mechanical discipline—working hours, production rates, quality controls, transportation schedules, and so forth— unintelligible for all traditional cultures. Almost simultaneously came the modern state, with its program of standardized, hierarchical public education for everyone within its reach, and the mass market in communications (first books, then newspapers, radio, and television) which together appeared to make sense of modern life and to create the illusion of vast new "citizen" communities.

Gellner's somewhat functionalist approach to the appearance of nationalism did not directly explain either its emotional appeal or its attachment to a seemingly fabricated antiquity. Accordingly, other scholars, most notably Anthony Smith (especially New York, 1983, Oxford, 1986) and John Armstrong (Chapel Hill, N.C., 1982), turned to the religious, cultural, and political antecedents of nationalism—those earlier sentiments, memories, local attachments, and identities—which were, so to speak, the bricks out of which Nairn's protectionist walls were eventually to be constructed.

All these studies have their own important contributions to make to any considered understanding of what is certainly the single most powerful political force of modern times. The early work of Hayes and Kohn showed that the peculiarly limited, but conceptually egalitarian, notion of the nation could not come into existence without the intellectual overthrow of two long-standing, fundamental axioms about political life and human history. The first was that all societies were naturally ordered as hierarchies under sovereigns whose right to rule was divinely prescribed and sanctioned. The second was that human beings were, at bottom, members of vast religious collectivities, divinely directed and inspired, whose ultimate mission was to encompass the entire population of the planet. History began with the First Man, and would end with a Last Day. By the end of the eighteenth century divine monarchy was beginning a meteoric collapse, while the territorial stretch of the great world religions had stabilized, after centuries of conflict, into something close to their present limited extents. Meanwhile, divine, cosmological time was being rapidly undermined, initially in Europe, by the new sciences of geology and astronomy, and by capitalism's mass production of chronometers and clocks, as well as dated newspapers and magazines, inaugurating the mass acceptance of what the philosopher Walter Benjamin called "homogenous, empty time." Meanwhile, space was coming to be envisioned in a wholly new way, exemplified by the mass-produced Mercatorian map, which viewed the world, as it were from God's vantage point, as a flat plane whose most important markings, first longitude and latitude, then political boundaries, were impossible to see, on the ground, in everyday experience. To these deep changes, *liberalism and republicanism gave a political cast, invoking collectivities of bounded, mapped extent, and ruled by popular, no longer divine, consent.

Out of these changes emerged, between 1776 and 1830, the first substantial plurality of nation-states—not in Europe but in the Americas. The approaches of Hroch and Nairn suggest why nationalism was born first in the New World rather than the Old. Capitalism, chronometry, and shipbuilding technology had made possible, in the eighteenth century especially, the unprecedented transportation of millions of Europeans, fully aware of themselves as transoceanic migrants, to a huge, rich region thousands of miles away from Europe. Here were born Nairn's first "peripheries," Anglo-Saxon and Iberian creoles, who shared religion, language, customs, laws, and post-Renaissance worldviews with their respective metropoles, but who were devastatingly subordinated to them as mere "Americans" and "colonists." Here too were born, already in the seventeenth century, apolitical antiquarians who sought to connect Aztec Moctezuma with conquistador Cortés, Incan Atahualpa with the God-sent pirate Francisco Pizarro. After them came, as Hroch's model suggested, angry, elite political propagandists, whose life chances and worldviews were shaped by the contours of their peripheralization. Spanish or Anglo-Saxon they might in every way be, but they were barred from metropolitan careers, and confined within metropole-defined administrative units—the Thirteen Colonies, Brazil, Mexico, or Venezuela. Intensifying economic and political domination by the Bourbon monarchy in Spain and the Hanoverian in England drew creole planters, merchants, and professional elites into the propagandists' embrace. The North American slogan "no taxation without representation" expressed in exemplary fashion the emerging nationalist coalition. Soon after came social (and military) mobilizations made possible by the spread of the newspaper and other products of print capitalism, and by extraordinary political inventions such as José de San Martín's baptizing of Quechua-speaking Andeans as "Peruvians." By the 1820s, if not earlier, an international model of the nation-state was in place, which, over the next century and a half, spread, through print and school, all over the world.

Between roughly 1820 and 1920, the Old World became the next stage for nationalist movements. Initially, the French Revolution provided a powerful impetus in this direction, but first with Napoléon Bonaparte's assumption of an emperorship ruling most of continental Europe, and then the victory of the imperial Holy Alliance in 1815, monarchies remained the norm in Europe until the firm establishment of the Third Republic in France in 1871 in the wake of Louis Napoléon's crushing defeat by Bismarck's armies. Europe's monarchs, however, presided over realms which, built up over centuries by war and dynastic marriages, inevitably included communities speaking completely different languages and preserving widely divergent cultures and historical traditions. Close ties of royal kinship made it possible for Hohenzollerns to rule in Prussia and Romania, and Wittelsbachs in Bavaria and Greece; Queen Victoria was related to every significant royal house in Europe. Yet, at the same time, the long decline of Latin as the trans-European language of civilization had brought all monarchies to adopt one or other vernacular—English, Castilian, German—as a unifying language of administration and power.

Under these circumstances language came to serve in Europe, in the manner the Atlantic had earlier done for the Americas, as a profoundly peripheralizing force. Intensifying this force were three intertwined agencies of change. Industrialism's uneven spread produced historically unprecedented economic inequalities, huge population movements, as well as regional and cultural disparities, within each monarchical realm. The standardization, centralization, and proliferation of the state's activities brought traditionally quite isolated, self-contained communities into far closer, and often disagreeable, contact with one another. Along with military conscription, modern education had, as Gellner acutely argued, the most profound impact. For this state-sponsored education had an almost wholly novel character. It was fully standardized, it was minutely stratified, it used a single vernacular at its higher levels, and, in a way that classical education had scarcely been, it was functionally geared to the realm's economic and workforce needs. Increasingly, people were being differentially trained for jobs rather than educated to be civilized human beings.

Most significant of all, the rapid expansion of literacy and the development of mass newspaper readerships brought new, mediated, political communities into being; for while Sicilians and Venetians might not comprehend each other's speech, they had been made capable of simultaneously *reading* standardized, mass-produced printed Italian. These mediated, or imagined, communities were often very large, but they were necessarily limited to those capable of direct or indirect access to each printed language, and their stretch almost never coincided with the boundaries of Europe's dynastic realms. In this fashion, printed languages, tied as they were (actually or potentially) to occupationally orientated educational systems, and to the inmost mechanisms of industrial life, became available as strong "tariff walls" behind which emerging imagined communities could hunker down for protection and advancement. (Unsurprisingly, it was therefore always the privileged "metropolitans" who came last to nationalism—Germans in Austria-Hungary, English in the United Kingdom, Turks in the Ottoman Empire.) Thanks in part to the models provided by revolutionary France and the Americas, these communities envisioned themselves as popular, and usually republican, in opposition to dynasties which had no obvious nationality and whose *legitimacy was essentially based on preindustrial notions.

For the same kinds of structural reasons, nationalisms finally emerged in an Asia and an Africa subjected in the course of the nineteenth century to European *imperialism's military power, capitalist penetration, industrial civilization, and administrative and educational modernization. Just how important this conjuncture was can be seen from the history of the most ancient of Europe's Asian colonies. By the end of the sixteenth century Spaniards already controlled most of what is today the Philippines, but Philippine nationalism only appeared three centuries later. By the mid-seventeenth century the Dutch dominated the Indonesian archipelago, but Indonesian nationalism was born only at the start of the twentieth. Everywhere the historical timing of nationalism's birth was tightly synchronized with the appearance of vernacular newspapers, job-market education, industrial production and consumption, mass migration by railway, steamship,

and motor vehicle, and the spread of clock time and Mercator space.

Yet the Asian and African nationalist movements, developing after those in the Americas and Europe, and in various ways learning from them, had their own special characteristics. As in the New World, their early languages were those of the metropole, though these languages were secondary linguae francae rather than mother-tongues. In a manner similarly reminiscent of the Americas, the movements took the administrative units into which the caprices of rival imperialisms had bound them as the natural territorial stretch of the nation-states they were dreaming into existence—even where, as was usually the case, these territories bore no relationship to the domains of precolonial polities. But their attachments were no longer primarily secured by the bureaucratic and geographical limits set by the imperial center on the careers of their elites. For the age of mechanical reproduction brought the logoized map of the colony into classrooms, railway stations, magazines, and proliferating government offices. On the other hand, unlike the independence movements in the Americas, they were able to take advantage, early in the twentieth century, of all those organizational means for mass mobilization (centralized political parties, trade unions, peasant leagues, women's associations, etc.) which Europe had invented in the course of the nineteenth century. They benefited additionally from the fact even the metropoles were increasingly defining themselves in national terms, such that a League of Empires became unthinkable, and the House of Hanover belatedly nationalized itself as House of Windsor.

While the investigations led by Hayes, Kohn, Hroch, Nairn, and Gellner signally deepened and widened understandings of the historical sociology and *political economy of nationalism, they did not really explain the passions it aroused, the sacrifices it evoked, or the sense of antiquity which it so surprisingly conjured up. In this regard the studies of Anthony Smith, J. A. Armstrong, and an array of cultural historians and historically minded anthropologists made powerful contributions by investigating the antecedents of nationalism and the processes whereby "ethnicities" and what are now often called "identity politics" have emerged, especially in advanced industrial societies.

In its earliest manifestations in the Americas, nationalism had already shown a double face. The Declaration of Independence in 1776 made no mention of "America," Christopher Columbus, or the Pilgrim Fathers, and San Martín's Peruvianization of Incan peasants moved them into a limitless future rather than toward an immemorial past. But both invoked a kind of homeland or *patria* to which a loyalty was due on the basis of settled residence, landscape, and daily interaction: *nosotros americanos*, as Mexican patriots became accustomed to say. Contributing to this "identity" (which was both more and less than nationalism) was the proto-racist disdain of the metropoles, who often regarded the creoles as irremediably contaminated by their extra-European birth. If they did not conceal black or "Indian" ancestries, as surely many did, the very air of the American environment, its climate, flora and fauna were felt to produce a natural and fatal degeneration. Argentina, Venezuela, Peru—it made no difference: a creole was a creole, an identity rather than a nationality. In the course of the nineteenth century, as secularization, historicism, and print civilization grew steadily more powerful, these seeds developed intertangled vines.

It is likely that secularization played the most profound role, particularly in its unwitting encouragement of self-conscious, ideological racism. The conquistadors had justified their barbarous depredations by a Christianizing mission. Pious Jesuits devoting themselves to the spiritual care of African slaves could still view themselves as instruments of redemption. An idea that the ultimate core of each human being was a soul—God-given, genderless, classless, raceless, ageless—still prevailed. But as the soul gradually withered away, it was replaced by a variety of intramundane essences shaped above all by racism and sexism. It still made sense to fiercely Catholic, sixteenth-century Iberian rulers to convert (forcibly) their Jewish and Muslim subjects to Christianity. By the enlightened nineteenth century, however, true anti-Semitism had been born: a Jew was genetically a Jew, no matter what his or her beliefs, place of birth, gender, or political loyalty. Women were turned into "eternal woman," no longer eternal souls temporarily garbed in female flesh. From there it was but a step to the secular biologization of culture, traditions, language, and memory into excluded/exclusive "identities" for which nationalism's open-armed acceptance of "naturalization" was less and less possible.

Historicism, allied with print capitalism, made scarcely less important contributions. No better instance is afforded than the generous-minded, French-nationalist historian Jules Michelet (1798–1874), who was possibly the first major European intellectual to claim to speak on behalf of the dead precisely because they could not know what their lives really meant. In his conception, millions of "French" people (who did not know of themselves as such) had for hundreds of years labored (without understanding their mission), speaking languages which were often not French, to make possible the French Revolution and the liberation of the modern world. Confronted all over the France he knew with visible residues of ancient polities, religions, and languages, and, as a classically trained historian with access to documentary records stretching back 2,000 years, Michelet could only unify them, outside God's time, by an eternal France. Out of Michelet came the possibility of reading Peking Man as Chinese, the builders of Stonehenge as British, and the ancient Mayans as Mexicans. That this possibility soon became virtually a necessity was the result of three factors: 1) the physical presence in every zone of the world of multifarious relics of the past; 2) the immense, easily available documentation of a thousand pasts that print capitalism brought to the huge new reading publics; 3) a new inaccessibility to those pasts caused precisely by the revolutionary transformations engendered by industrialism, secularization, and nationalism itself. In the face of a suddenly remote prenationlist past, the nationalist was like the adult faced with his or her own baby photographs: the evidence seemed to imply an identity with someone unrecognizable and unremembered. Out of this forgetting/remembering came a historicized essentialism (as it were, an eternal Germanness or German "identity") first put in service to nationalism, but later fully available for the construction of "ethnicity" and "ethnic identity"—outside history. Hence, in due course, the Irish-American who lives in the United States, speaks no Gaelic, knows no Irish literature, wears no Irish clothes, and plays no Irish sports, but who, with an ethnicized Catholicism at his back, feels firmly Irish.

Contemporary anthropological studies show these processes at work today in even the most remote corners of the globe. The children of illiterate tribal parents (who lived by oral folk memory, practiced subsistence agriculture or nomadic hunting, and were connected by unmediated kinship networks) are sucked into schools, put into uniforms, sent into factories, haled into offices, and invited into cinemas. As Marx poignantly wrote: "All that is solid melts into air"—except that the parents may still be there, and the tribal group is inscribed ethnically in the national history textbooks.

Even *communism, which in its heroic early days believed that it was historically superseding nationalism—under the banner of proletarian internationalism—found that it was up against a force too deeply rooted in modern living to be overcome. *Lenin's Soviet Union did not regard itself a national polity, and for decades it commanded the loyalty of millions living beyond its borders. But after 1945 a plethora of new communist states came into existence, nationally defined, if under various degrees of Soviet influence. In 1978–1979 the communist states of China, Vietnam, and Cambodia went militarily at each other's throats. Today once-Communist Yugoslavia has disintegrated in bloody interethnic fighting, and the Soviet Union has ceased to exist. It seems unlikely that twenty years hence the territory now ruled by the Chinese Communist Party, heir of the Ch'ing emperors, will be united under a single *sovereignty.

It is possible, in fact, that the very way in which the early communist rulers attempted to solve "the national question" will prove to have exacerbated the contemporary crises. For they relied primarily on the secular power of communism's social doctrines and revolutionary global mission at the ideological level, and the organizational might of communist parties and their militaries and polices at the administrative-political level, while leaving, or even creating, imagined shells for latent "identity politics." Uzbekistan, Slovenia, Macedonia, and Azerbaidzhan, for example, remained formal units into which such states were territorially segmented, while their respective inhabitants were allowed no genuine political autonomy as such. A powerless Ukraine and an impotent Byelorussia even had token seats in the UN. At the same time, so-called nationalities (which one might read as "ethnic groups") were even, up to a point, encouraged to build museums, organize folk dance troupes, and publish traditional literatures, just so long as no political claims were made on such bases. But once the engine of the administered economy seized up, once trust in and fear of communist leaders declined, and confidence in the promised future decayed, the shells came quickly to be filled by frustrated nationalisms that were often warped by their forcibly ethnicized pasts. An "administrative Georgia," demarcated by Moscow and full of all kinds of peoples, including ethnicized Georgians, has become, almost in a flash, a territory from which all those unable to prove three generations of "biological" Georgian ancestors are being violently expelled. Georgians in this imagining are the polar opposite of San Martín's Peruvians.

Even in Western Europe comparable processes seem to be at work. Witness the nervousness arising from an impending integration which, because it threatens real sovereignties, has the potential to "ethnicize" what are now still nations. Even less than the Soviet Union does a European Community correspond to the deep-rooted imaginings of nationalism. From a Georgianized Germany and a Byelorussianized Britain little that is amiable can be expected. The irony of the present condition is that the world is today unified, at one level, by a capitalism more fluid and transnational than ever before, and that it is this unification that makes the republican sovereignty of the citizen nation so necessary.

(See also DECOLONIZATION; EQUALITY AND INEQUALITY; ETHNICITY; INTERNAL COLONIALISM; PERIPHERAL NATIONALISM; RACE AND RACISM; RELIGION AND POLITICS; UNITED NATIONS.)

Aira Kemilian, *Nationalism: Problems Concerning the Word, the Concept and Classification* (Jyvaskyla, 1964). Elie Kedourie, ed., *Nationalism in Asia and Africa* (New York, 1970). Hugh Seton-Watson, *Nations and States* (Boulder, Colo., 1977). John A. Armstrong. *Nations before Nationalism* (Chapel Hill, N.C., 1982). John Breuilly, *Nationalism and the State* (Manchester, U.K., 1982). Donald Horowitz, *Ethnic Groups in Conflict* (Berkeley, Calif., 1985). Partha Chatterjee, *Nationalist Thought and the Colonial World: A Derivative Discourse* (London, 1986). Ernest Gellner, *Nations and Nationalism* (Oxford, 1986). Anthony Smith, *The Ethnic Origins of Nations* (Oxford, 1986). Homi Bhabha, ed., *Nation and Narration* (London, 1990). Eric Hobsbawm, *Nations and Nationalism since 1788* (Cambridge, U.K., 1990).

BENEDICT R. O'GORMAN ANDERSON

NATIONALIZATION. Two distinct types of government policies may be referred to by the term *nationalization*. The first is public ownership: the state's possession and control of private property, particularly in key industries. The British Labour government asserted such control in the late 1940s and early 1950s when it nationalized the coal, gas, electricity, steel, and transport industries. French Socialists pursued similar policies in the early 1980s and offered a similar rationale: greater income equality, rationalized production, and greater state control over economic *planning. In Britain, many of the same industries were reprivatized in the 1980s, under Conservative Prime Minister Margaret *Thatcher. Thatcher not only stressed the costs and inefficiency of state control (also important issues to the French Socialists, who quickly abandoned their nationalization plans after an initial foray into banking and steel), but also her opposition in principle to such public ownership, even in cases of natural monopolies.

Nationalization can also refer more specifically to the seizure of *foreign* assets and their transfer to local ownership, usually to state firms. Such indigenization policies were pursued extensively in Latin America, Africa, and the Middle East in the 1960s and 1970s. They were focused largely in raw materials and extractive industries, in countries that were highly dependent on export earnings from those industries. The most vulnerable sectors, according to Raymond Vernon, where those that had already developed standardized products and processes, but where foreign investors had not yet adapted to their weaker bargaining position with host countries. The largest expropriations came in oil exporting countries, which replaced foreign oil companies with state-owned enterprises in production and refining. Foreign firms still had significant advantages in exploration, transport, and marketing and used them to maintain a major international role. Indeed, nationalized firms have continued to rely on them for final sales and sometimes for operations and management.

Nationalization is a sharply contested political process. At stake is control over the local economy and, more broadly, control over the direction of economic development and the role of foreign capital. It has been a focal point for economic controversy between rich and poor nations throughout the twentieth century. Foreign property was nationalized after political transformations in Mexico (1917), the Soviet Union (1917), Turkey (1923), Chile (1970), and Iran (1951, 1979), among others. These new governments had widely differing ideologies, but all stressed some form of economic *nationalism and all seized some foreign assets as part of their program. Capital-exporting states not only opposed the expropriations as such, they typically regarded them as part of a broader and more objectionable socialist movement. They responded with diplomatic protests and sometimes with economic *sanctions and force (both overt and covert). Multinational firms added their own important sanctions, especially in oligopolistic industries such as oil, where producers could isolate economic nationalists from world markets.

Compensation has often been a central issue in these disputes because investors are usually offered little or no payment. Host states generally claim their rights as sovereign powers to determine what payment, if any, is due to foreign investors. Multinational firms and their home states respond by citing traditional international legal standards, which require full and immediate compensation in hard currency. This controversy reached its apex in the 1970s, when many less developed states expropriated major foreign investments with little compensation. The same states, holding a majority in the UN General Assembly, passed a series of resolutions asserting their "National Sovereignty over Natural Resources."

By the late 1970s, the spread of these nationalizations had effectively changed their political meaning. Earlier, in postrevolutionary Mexico, in Atatürk's Turkey and Mossadegh's Iran, both the state and investors considered nationalization part of a wider attack on foreign capital and an assertion of socialized state control of the economy. In the 1970s, by contrast, nationalizations by member states of the *Organization of Petroleum Exporting Countries, such as those by Saudi Arabia and Venezuela, were understood by all participants as relatively narrow business disputes, fully consistent with foreign investment in other sectors.

The worst of these disputes have now subsided. One reason is that virtually all older foreign concessions in raw materials have been nationalized. Vulnerable firms, recognizing the changed environment, have abandoned their outmoded strategy of stiff political resistance, a strategy that relied on support from their home government and corporate allies. Instead, they have developed new, more flexible arrangements for working with state-owned firms, as well as a sharper concern for political risks. State-owned firms have also recognized the economic importance of sustaining these international commercial ties to ensure marketing and technological skills. Joint ventures, management contracts, and long-term trade partnerships have all proliferated, in part because they diminish the political risks of foreign investment. Moreover, new investments are typically concentrated in less vulnerable sectors, particularly manufacturing and service industries, which are difficult to operate effectively as nationalized industries. Major political goals of indigenization, such as local employment and export growth, are

now likely to be pursued through regulatory policies rather than by blunt threats of expropriation.

The long debt crisis in Latin America and Africa has also changed political attitudes toward foreign investment and lessened the threat of nationalization. In the 1970s, foreign capital was readily available as loans to larger economies among the less developed countries (LDCs). After 1982, when Mexico effectively declared itself insolvent, these voluntary financial flows stopped to nearly all LDC borrowers. Facing severe balance-of-payments pressures, major debtors such as Mexico slowly reversed their long-standing policies restricting foreign ownership and actively encouraged direct investments by multinational firms. The rhetoric of sovereign rights, public ownership, and indigenous control—so prominent in the 1960s and 1970s in mobilizing nationalist support for expropriations—was largely abandoned.

(See also DISINVESTMENT; FINANCE, INTERNATIONAL; FORCE, USE OF; INTERNATIONAL DEBT; MULTINATIONAL CORPORATIONS; PRIVATIZATION.)

Stephen J. Kobrin, "Expropriation as an Attempt to Control Foreign Firms in LDCs: Trends from 1960 to 1979" *International Studies Quarterly* 28 (September 1984): 329–348. Charles Lipson, *Standing Guard: Protecting Foreign Capital in the Nineteenth and Twentieth Centuries* (Berkeley, Calif., 1985).

CHARLES LIPSON

NATIONAL LIBERATION MOVEMENTS. Political organizations dedicated to the pursuit of political independence from foreign domination, economic independence, social revolution in an anticapitalist direction, and a cultural revolution to remove the influence of previously dominant external forces and to substitute an indigenous culture in their place are known as national liberation movements. The concept conflates *class struggle with national identity and self-determination by embracing the notion of "the oppressed nation" present in Leninist theory.

The principal targets of these movements have been the colonial powers. Yet as the process of *decolonization has approached completion, movements struggling to remove what they perceive to be exploitative and alien regimes within sovereign states (e.g., the Sendero Luminoso in Peru or the *African National Congress in South Africa) or to detach components of a sovereign state's territory (e.g., the Eritrean People's Liberation Front in Ethiopia) from control by the center have gained prominence.

The process of national liberation may be peaceful or violent, although self-styled liberation movements tend to adopt armed struggle and *guerrilla warfare as means of attaining their objectives. Generally these are only one part of a larger strategy for gaining power, involving the mobilization of social classes and groups previously outside national politics. This includes not only programs of political education but also the establishment of a broad array of socioeconomic and political organizations (trade unions, students' and women's organizations, and *peasant associations) tied to the liberation movement.

Although in theory such efforts expand considerably the social bases of politics, practice suggests that participation is limited in scope by the resistance of traditional populations to inclusion in politics. The substance of this participation is also limited by the hierarchical organization of liberation movements, the frequently personalistic nature of leadership, the claim of such movements to be the sole legitimate representatives of their peoples, and by their lack of tolerance toward alternative political organizations and programs. These characteristics leave little space for pluralism in the politics of opposition to colonial rule and—if these movements attain power—in the political activity of the states they rule. In this sense, despite their stated objectives, national liberation movements have tended to be vehicles for the replacement of external elites with internal ones who use their position in much the same way as their predecessors to appropriate resources from the people they rule.

The principal focus of liberation movements is the acquisition of state power. Yet because the enemy—*imperialism—is seen in critical respects to be an international phenomenon, these movements generally also conceive themselves to be participants in a universal struggle against political and economic oppression. As such, they have sought to develop international links among themselves and with states and groups who share their interest in weakening the hold of the West over the *Third World. Their struggles, consequently, frequently became entangled in the broader global competition between the United States and the Soviet Union and the blocs these powers represented. Struggles for national liberation became important vehicles for expansion of the Soviet role in the Third World. However, the deeply nationalistic inclinations of the leaderships of these movements and the frequent disparity between their concrete national and regional interests and the global agenda of the Soviet Union greatly constrained the Soviet capacity to build and sustain influence in this fashion. The recent deemphasis on global class struggle and universal bipolar competition in *Soviet foreign policy during the Gorbachev era, followed by the dissolution of the Soviet Union, weakened the link between struggles for national liberation and global politics.

(See also COLONIAL EMPIRES; LENINISM; NATIONALISM; REVOLUTION.)

S. NEIL MACFARLANE

NATIVE AMERICANS. When Europeans first settled in America north of the Rio Grande, the Native American (or American Indian) population, estimated at from 3 to 7 million persons, was divided into several hundred distinct, culturally diverse groups or "tribes." Indigenous political organization varied as well, from formalized hierarchical structures within clearly bounded groups to loose and informal associations of villages or bands.

For the most part, the European colonial powers recognized Indian groups as having *sovereignty over the lands they occupied. In subsequent years they and, later, the United States used a combination of diplomacy, purchase, guile, and warfare to force Indian nations to give up their lands. Beginning late in the eighteenth century, land dispossession usually was formalized in treaties signed between the United States and Indian nations. These treaties typically specified not only land cessions but tribal acceptance of increasing degrees of U.S. control over their external affairs and, eventually, their internal affairs as well.

Land dispossession was accompanied by a precipitous drop in aboriginal numbers owing to warfare, economic collapse, and, in particular, European-introduced diseases. By 1900, the indigenous population of what is now the lower forty-eight states had dropped below 300,000.

By then as well, most remaining Native Americans had been confined on reservations—lands typically unwanted by whites and reserved to the tribes by treaty, legislation, or executive agreement. A side effect of treaty making and the reservation system was the institutionalization of once relatively fluid Indian group boundaries, laying in place the political framework that has designated contemporary tribes as the primary political actors in Indian affairs.

Today these reservation lands, held in trust for tribes by the federal government, are all that remain of the original Native American land base. Indian numbers, on the other hand, have recovered dramatically. The 1990 U.S. census counted nearly 2 million Native Americans, widely distributed across the country.

At least some degree of Native American political power has been reestablished as well. In 1924, Congress affirmed that all Indians born within the territorial limits of the United States were citizens. While some jurisdictions opposed Indian voting well past mid-century, Indians' right to vote in federal, state, and other elections was largely secure by the 1950s. In 1934, responding to persistent reservation poverty and the communitarian and progressive ideals of some leading New Deal figures, Congress passed the Indian Reorganization Act (IRA). Among other things, this legislation gave formal recognition to tribal governments and encouraged their formation. While the powers of these governments were severely limited, by legitimizing them and opening the political arena to them, the IRA helped initiate a long process of Native American political resurgence.

In subsequent decades a wide assortment of Indian groups—not only tribes but pan-Indian organizations and single-issue constituencies—mobilized in pursuit of Native American political agendas, airing long-standing grievances over lands and *rights. One factor that significantly advanced this development was the gradual emergence of a politicized supratribal identity. Beginning in the 1940s, as growing numbers of Indians spent time in multitribal urban communities, reservation-based tribes came to recognize that their survival depended in part on cooperative effort. As a result, a generalized Indian identity increasingly appeared in Indian politics, representing a disposition to act not only on tribal but on supratribal terms, providing a basis for collective action on a larger scale.

At the same time, as Native Americans began to move into the mainstream of the larger society, migrating off the reservations to urban areas, and as that society made greater inroads on the reservations, new cleavages began to emerge within Indian communities. Following both cultural and class lines and overlaying aboriginal tribal differences, these cleavages complicated both tribal and supratribal politics. Nonetheless, Native Americans have managed to retain a substantial consensus over their broadest political goals, which emphasize a recurrent theme: the preservation of the politically sovereign, culturally distinct, land-based tribal communities that the original treaties guaranteed but that the United States repeatedly has tried to undermine. Much of the internal debate has had to do with the desired nature of those communities, the best ways to preserve them, and the distribution of economic and political benefits within them.

By the mid-1960s these various factors had come together in a diffuse but growing Native American political movement directed at the reassertion of Indian control over Indian communities and lives. As the claims of the disadvantaged penetrated the political arena in these years, Indian claims were heard as well, while Indian resources—including increased education, growing organizational networks, federal funds from the War on Poverty, and a willingness to engage in confrontational political action—gave those claims political teeth. Over the next decade and a half Native Americans seized the political initiative in Indian affairs, using litigation, protests, and assertions of tribal rights and powers to reverse the pattern of the previous two centuries.

Partly in response to this activism, in 1975 Congress passed the Indian Self-Determination and Education Assistance Act, which, along with other legislation and subsequent court decisions, placed enlarged power over their own affairs in the hands of Indian nations. Since 1980, consequently, much Native American political action reflects the efforts of newly empowered tribal governments to initiate their own programs of economic and social renewal and to solidify their political gains.

Despite these gains, American Indians continue to face widespread poverty, and remain subject to the will of Congress and the often-unpredictable decisions of the judicial branch. Indian nations today must struggle to protect their sovereign powers and their remaining lands. Many of the battles they face are over resources and entitlements. In an attempt to gain access to Indian-controlled resources such as water, fish, and minerals, non-Indian constituencies, particularly in the midwestern and western states, have organized to abrogate the *treaties that form the basis of Native American–U.S. relations, to undermine tribal sovereignty, and to force Indians to integrate as individuals into the economic and political mainstream. Many Indians have chosen, on their own, some degree of just such integration: today urban Indians significantly outnumber the reservation population. But even in the cities, most Native Americans remain fierce defenders of treaty rights, sovereignty, and the remaining land base.

Native Americans today occupy a unique political position in the United States, rooted in a treaty-based relationship that sets them apart from all other groups in American life. The preservation of that relationship and tribal sovereignty within it remains at the heart of Native American politics.

(See also ETHNICITY; NEW SOCIAL MOVEMENTS.)

Vine Deloria, Jr., and Clifford M. Lytle, *The Nations Within: The Past and Future of American Indian Sovereignty* (New York, 1984). Charles F. Wilkinson, *American Indians, Time, and the Law* (New Haven, Conn., 1987). Stephen Cornell, *The Return of the Native: American Indian Political Resurgence* (New York, 1988). Sharon O'Brien, *American Indian Tribal Governments* (Norman, Okla., 1989).
STEPHEN CORNELL

NATO. See NORTH ATLANTIC TREATY ORGANIZATION.

NAURU. See PACIFIC ISLANDS.

NAZISM. See FASCISM; HITLER, ADOLF.

NEHRU, Jawaharlal. One of modern *India's great political leaders, Jawaharlal Nehru (1889–1964) was prominent during India's nationalist movement against British *colonialism, and, although he differed from Mohandas *Gandhi on important political matters, he was Gandhi's designated political heir. Nehru was president of India's premier political organization, the Congress Party, several times and was actively involved in the negotiations over independence and the partition of India. He became the first prime minister of independent India in 1947 and remained in that office until his death in 1964.

Nehru was a political leader of international standing. His main achievement was to give the Congress, India's ruling party, a modernizing coherence that helped set India on a firm path of secular *democracy and self-sufficient economic *development. The three planks of his political outlook for

India were economic *planning, social *reform, and a nonaligned foreign policy.

Nehru was a self-proclaimed socialist. As an architect of Indian development, he steered India toward adopting a mixed economy with a large public sector and considerable state control of the private sector. Moreover, he favored heavy industry aimed at buttressing India's self-reliance. Although the economic impact of this strategy was mixed, there is no doubt that India during Nehru's reign achieved industrialization with considerable depth. He also attempted land redistribution with the hope of boosting India's agricultural production. Here his efforts met with little success. An overriding commitment to democracy meant a strong respect for fundamental *rights, including the right to private property, and this, in turn, often took precedence over such ambitious economic reforms as land redistribution.

Even though modern India was born amid religious strife, Nehru's strong commitment to a secular India helped India's minorities feel secure. In retrospect, it is clear that Nehru's success on this front, as on other fronts, was partial. Perhaps he assumed too readily that tolerance for minorities and social reform would result simply from the extension of the franchise. The result was that there remained an unbridgeable gap between his ideas and the religious and cultural aspirations of the groups in the society that he presided over, one that he could not quite overcome. Although Nehru's own example and charisma contributed to temporary political success, his death did not leave behind strong institutions to carry out his agenda.

In foreign policy, Nehru was a founder of the worldwide *Nonaligned Movement. He also laid down the basic tenets of Indian foreign policy that helped put India on the world map as a leading developing country. Nevertheless, in spite of considerable successes, he could not resolve India's border disputes with China and Pakistan. War with China in 1962 and the failure to find a lasting solution to the dispute with Pakistan over Kashmir are debits in Nehru's foreign policy record.

(See also MODERNIZATION; NATIONALISM; SOCIALISM AND SOCIAL DEMOCRACY.)

S. Gopal, *Jawaharlal Nehru: A Biography*, 3 vols. (London, 1975–1984). M. J. Akbar, *Nehru: The Making of India* (New York, 1985).

PRATAP MEHTA
ATUL KOHLI

NEPAL. Situated between China on the north and India on the south, Nepal is a landlocked country. Its topography is dominated by the Himalayas, except for a narrow area along its southern flank. Thus, geography has made Nepal dependent on India in economic, cultural, and various other ways.

Nepal's modern history has been shaped by geography, the colonial legacies of South Asia, and its own quest for national identity. Such a quest became intense following the conquest of Kathmandu valley by the Gorkhali king Prithvi Narayan Shah—generally considered to be the founder of modern Nepal—in 1768. Taking note of Nepal's difficult geopolitical location between China and India, Prithvi Narayan advised his successors not to get too close to either one in order to avoid domination. Internally his rule was inspired by a Hindu religious ethos and a brand of military chivalry that together would come to dominate the political culture of Nepal. A rigid caste hierarchy characterized the post-Shah political structure and social relations.

The Shah rule was supplanted by the Rana family oligarchy after Jang Bahadur usurped power in a violent coup in 1846. For 104 years, the Shah kings were relegated to the background and were treated as figureheads until they were restored by a successful anti-Rana movement launched jointly by the Nepali people, the king, and the government of India. Yet the restoration of monarchy in 1951 proved to be costly for Nepal's fledgling *democracy. The rise of monarchical absolutism, along with the declining influence of political parties, retarded the evolution of democracy. In December 1960, King Mahendra not only dismissed the elected government headed by the Nepali Congress but also ended multiparty democracy, which he denounced as divisive and antinational in character.

Masking personalized rule in the garb of a native political model, Mahendra banned the operation of parties. Despite extensive state-sponsored efforts to make the new system workable, it proved unable to attract widespread support for the regime. As a result, all major political groups remained an active source of opposition. The changing international environment of the late 1980s was crucial in promoting Nepal's democratic movement. The regime was isolated both internally and internationally, causing disquiet among the ruling circles. Eventually, King Birendra announced the end of the partyless system after the movement reached its climax on 8 April 1990.

One of the principal reasons for the survival of the partyless system for thirty years was the coercive state machinery and patronage distributed by the royal regime. The monarchy's commitment to establish a just society proved to be a sham. A two-percent average annual economic growth rate had been nullified by 2.6 percent population growth. The government's poor capacity to mobilize internal resources and growing dependence on *foreign aid (more than seventy percent of the national budget) increased the economic vulnerability of royal rule. The regime also could not get needed support from ethnic and regional groups because of their feelings of deprivation and the history of repression. Many of them felt that their cultural heritage and language were being discarded in a process of "Nepalization" that, according to these groups, promoted Gorkhali culture and language. Their grievances have become even more pronounced following the demise of the partyless system as freedoms granted to them have allowed them to articulate their demands.

The new government created by the mass movement inherited all the problems of the old regime. Its major task was to frame a democratic constitution for holding elections in March–April 1991. Political forces involved in the movement have yet to formulate their roles in the new system. The coalition of democratic and leftist forces is not likely to remain intact long after the announcement of elections. The coalition was running the government as of early 1991, but how they behave during and after the elections will have a great impact on the future of democracy in Nepal.

LOK RAJ BARAL

NETHERLANDS. A stable *democracy located in northwestern Europe, with 15 million people, the Netherlands is the most populous of the smaller democracies. Its location in the Rhine Delta makes the Netherlands highly dependent on trade with Germany and other members of the *European Community.

Although formally a *constitutional monarchy, the dominant traits are parliamentary government and a unitary system. Except for cabinet formations, the monarch's role is largely symbolic. Cabinets are responsible to a multiparty Parliament, and coalition government is the norm. The prime minister (minister president) leads but does not dominate the cabinet. Cabinet ministers are often experts in their own fields and enjoy considerable autonomy within their departments. Cities and provinces elect councils and assemblies, but mayors and provincial governors are appointed (in consultation with local leaders) by the Crown.

Elections must be held every four years. The Dutch system of *proportional representation effectively treats the entire country as a single national constituency; parties with as little as 1/150th of the national vote can secure a seat in Parliament. However, although as many as fourteen parties have been represented in the lower house (Second Chamber), the contemporary party system is dominated by four parties. Labor (PvdA), the Christian Democratic Appeal (CDA), and the Liberals (VVD) have roots in nineteenth-century class and religious divisions, while Democrats '66 (D'66) originated in protest against elite bargaining and cooperation. Heir to social-democratic traditions, the Labor Party favors a fairer distribution of wealth, knowledge, and power, but is torn between a defense of the public sector and acceptance of budgetary restraints. The Christian Democratic Appeal is a centrist force formed by the 1980 merger of the Catholic and two Protestant parties: the CDA and its predecessors have been consistently represented in the cabinet since 1918.

Except on moral issues, the Liberals are on the right, generally favoring more market and less state intervention. However, the party has eschewed extreme Thatcherite positions. Democrats '66 characterizes itself as a progressive force, favoring greater popular control (for example, direct election of mayors) and a pragmatic approach to politics. Once sharply defined by the articulation of Calvinist, Catholic, and Socialist "pillars" (cradle-to-grave networks of religious or ideologically based organizations), the class and religious base of party support is increasingly blurred. Although the Christian Democrats derive their core support from regular church attenders, the party casts its electoral appeal not in terms of religiosity but rather its ability to govern. The active cadres of the Labor Party and a portion of their electoral support come not from the working but from the middle classes. Liberals and Democrats '66 also draw support from the secular middle classes.

Proportional representation and persistent multipartyism have ensured that no single party has a majority. Cabinets usually include Christian Democrats (or their predecessors) and either Socialists or Liberals. Cabinets emerge from protracted negotiations that determine not only the composition but also the policies of the government. Forming a cabinet takes at least two to three months. Negotiations are overseen by the monarch, who may appoint one or more "informateurs" to seek out a basis for a majority government, but once established, cabinets frequently last a full four-year term. Parliamentary support is not automatic. Parliamentary parties are disciplined and cohesive but retain the freedom to criticize the government and demand changes in policy.

Cabinet and Parliament are at the apex of the policy process, but not the only actors involved in it. Governments draw on independent experts and try, not always successfully, to enlist the support of organized interests. Ministries often maintain formal and informal contacts with *interest groups, and the government meets semiannually with trade unions and employers' associations, organized in the bipartite Foundation of Labor. In addition, the cabinet is legally required to seek the advice of the Social and Economic Council (SER), made up of representatives of trade unions, employers' associations, and independent experts, on all matters of social and economic policy. However, SER recommendations are not binding and can be circumvented if the government chooses. Disagreements between social partners give the government considerable latitude to impose its own position.

In practice, the margins open to Dutch policymakers are not wide. Constraints come both from domestic interests, and from the international economy. Like many of its European counterparts, the Netherlands built up a complex array of social welfare programs intended to ensure minimum levels of subsistence. Sustaining these programs narrows the margins available for the introduction of new policies; cutting them risks the wrath of organized interests. Options are further narrowed by the position of the Netherlands in the international economy. Highly dependent on trade, the Netherlands is vulnerable not only to trends in the international economy, but in particular to the policies of its principal trading partner, the Federal Republic of Germany. The Netherlands Bank enjoys considerable autonomy from the government and aligns its monetary policies with those of the Deutsche Bundesbank. Dutch commitments to the integration of Europe further narrow policy options. Maintaining competitiveness and adjusting to international trends are central concerns.

The Netherlands has been classified as a *consociational democracy, a corporatist system, and more recently as a consensual democracy. None of these labels describes the contemporary Dutch system accurately. Characterization of the Netherlands as a consociational democracy, held together by the deliberate efforts of political *elites to reach compromises, stems from the segmentation of Dutch society into distinct pillars or subcultures and the apparent absence of cross-cutting ties among them. Consociational interpretations overstate both the severity of conflicts and the role which political elites may have played in ameliorating them and apply only to the Netherlands between 1918 and 1967. Since then, both the scope and impact of pillarization and the extent of elite accommodation have receded. Corporatist approaches emphasize regular consultations with trade unions and employers' associations but overstate the extent to which social partners determine policy. Trade unions and employers were intimately involved in shaping and administering the income policies central to the postwar industrialization of the Netherlands, but since the 1960s there has been little agreement on key issues. Governments have been more than willing to proceed with policies opposed by either employers (the mid-1970s) or, since then, the trade unions. Of the three labels, consensual democracy is the most appropriate, but only if we take this not to mean a system characterized by consensus but rather one in which consensus is sought but not always achieved.

(See also CHRISTIAN DEMOCRACY; CORPORATISM; SOCIALISM AND SOCIAL DEMOCRACY.)

Arend Lijphart, The Politics of Accommodation: Pluralism and Democracy in the Netherlands, 2d ed. (Berkeley; Calif., 1975). Hans Daalder and Galen A. Irwin, eds., Politics in the Netherlands: How Much Change? (London, 1989). Ken Gladdish, Governing From the Center: Politics and Policy-making in the Netherlands (DeKalb, Ill.,1991).
STEVEN B. WOLINETZ

NEUTRALITY. See FORCE, USE OF.

NEW DEAL. Franklin *Roosevelt promised "a new deal for the American people" in his speech accepting the 1932 Democratic nomination for president. The phrase survived as a name for his twelve-year presidency and, more specifically, for his administration's considerable domestic achievements. Eclectic, experimental, the New Deal defies easy classification. Many of its programs were stillborn; many others were failures. But some endured and made the New Deal the single most important episode in the shaping of the United States in the twentieth century.

The "First New Deal." The domestic policies of the Roosevelt presidency passed through three distinct phases. It took office at the lowest moment of the Great Depression and moved immediately to stabilize the economy. In its first year, the administration produced a major reform of the floundering U.S. banking system (which included federal insurance of bank deposits); a new federal agency to regulate the financial markets (the Securities and Exchange Commission); an ambitious experiment in flood control and regional planning (the Tennessee Valley Authority); and a federal program to protect farmers from fluctuating crop prices (the Agricultural Adjustment Administration). All these efforts survived, in one form or another, to become enduring parts of the federal government.

Other early New Deal efforts were less lasting. Federal relief agencies—all of them explicitly temporary—funneled assistance to the nation's estimated 15–25 million unemployed. More ambitious was the National Industrial Recovery Act (NIRA). It included a guarantee to workers of the right to bargain collectively through unions and a major new public works program. But its centerpiece was the National Recovery Administration (NRA), whose mission was to create a harmonious, vaguely corporatist economic order in which capital, labor, and government would cooperate to stabilize prices, wages, and production. By 1935, when the *Supreme Court invalidated the NRA, it was already a political and economic failure.

The "Second New Deal." By the spring of 1935, the New Deal faced new demands. The Depression continued. The trade union movement, invigorated by the collective bargaining provisions of the NIRA, pressed for new *reform legislation. Dissident politicians on the *Right and the *Left attacked the administration and, some believed, threatened Roosevelt's reelection. The administration responded with a new set of initiatives, frequently labeled the "Second New Deal."

Some of the most celebrated efforts of the Second New Deal were, like many of those in 1933, ultimately transitory: a major new work relief program, the Works Progress Administration; a highly publicized assault on utilities monopolies; a dramatic (if largely symbolic) effort to raise taxes on the wealthy. But the most enduring measures were the National Labor Relations Act (NLRA; better known as the Wagner Act) and the Social Security Act. The NLRA restored the collective bargaining protections that the now-invalidated NIRA had created in 1933, but added vital new enforcement mechanisms (most importantly the National Labor Relations Board) to ensure compliance by employers. Over the next several years, it contributed to successful unionization drives in the largest American industries. The Social Security Act established the framework of the modern U.S. *welfare state. It created two important social insurance programs: old age pensions and unemployment insurance, which offered potential support to most Americans. It also offered welfare benefits to more narrowly defined "categories" of people: the handicapped, the elderly poor, and dependent children. In doing so, it established a lasting and generally invidious distinction between federal "insurance" and "welfare" (public assistance) mechanisms.

The "Third New Deal." Roosevelt's landslide re-election in 1936 emboldened him to try to consolidate his own power within the federal government with a series of efforts some historians have labeled the "Third New Deal." But despite the apparent mandate, Roosevelt's second term was much less successful than his first. He proposed to reorganize the federal bureaucracy in ways that would enhance presidential power, but the plan floundered in the face of powerful opposition from congressional conservatives who charged him with wanting to create a "dictatorship." More important, the president tried to halt the succession of defeats his programs were suffering in the Supreme Court. He asked *Congress to allow him to appoint additional justices, and thus expand the Court's membership, to shift its ideological balance in his favor. The proposal ultimately failed in Congress. Before it did, however, two of the existing justices (almost surely in response to the "court-packing" threat) began voting to uphold New Deal measures, hence creating an effective liberal majority.

The most significant policy initiative of Roosevelt's second term was his response to the serious recession that began in the fall of 1937. The new crisis was at least partially a result of a premature effort in 1937 to balance the budget by reducing federal spending on relief. In the spring of 1938, the government announced a major new drive to investigate and police monopolies, which many liberals accused of having caused the recession. Of more lasting importance, it reversed its budget decisions of the previous year and launched a $5 billion spending program whose purpose was to stimulate economic activity by increasing mass purchasing power. Never before had the government made such explicit use of its fiscal powers to stabilize the business cycle. This approach to managing the economy would soon become known as *Keynesianism and would establish a lasting, if always controversial, place in public policy. Later that year, the administration won approval for the Fair Labor Standards

Act, which established a national minimum wage and set limits on hours of work. This was the last major domestic achievement of the New Deal. By early 1939, the government was beginning to turn its attention to the growing international crisis that would soon draw the United States into war and that would ultimately do what the New Deal itself was never able to accomplish: restore prosperity to the U.S. economy.

Legacies of the New Deal. The New Deal had a lasting impact on both government and politics. It contributed to the mobilization and organization of new economic groups—most notably farmers and industrial workers—who would henceforth play a major role in shaping public policy. The Roosevelt administration also established the outlines (and the limits) of the modern U.S. federal commitment to social provision. It expanded the regulatory functions of the state and, at the same time, ensured that capitalists would retain most of their traditional prerogatives. It produced a major *political realignment in party politics and a new Democratic coalition (often called the *New Deal coalition) large enough to dominate U.S. politics for nearly forty years. Not least, the Roosevelt administration also created a set of ideas, known as "New Deal *liberalism," that survived for more than a generation as the basis of reform experiments.

(See also CORPORATISM.)

Arthur M. Schlesinger, Jr., *The Age of Roosevelt*, 3 vols. (Boston, 1957–1960). William E. Leuchtenburg, *Franklin D. Roosevelt and the New Deal* (New York, 1963). Ellis Hawley, *The New Deal and the Problem of Monopoly* (Princeton, N.J., 1966). Anthony Badger, *The New Deal* (New York, 1988). Steve Fraser and Gary Gerstle, eds., *The Rise and Fall of the New Deal Order* (Princeton, N.J., 1988).

ALAN BRINKLEY

NEW DEAL COALITION. Combining Southern whites, Northern blacks, Catholics, Jews, wheat and dairy farmers from the Upper Midwest, and organized industrial workers into a national majority for the Democratic Party in the United States, the New Deal coalition was the closest approximation to a class-based social democratic party in U.S. political history. Yet the coalition's dependence on Southern support placed constraints on policy change.

The formation of the New Deal coalition began in 1924, when Midwestern farmers responded to agricultural depression by leaving the Republican Party to support the third-party presidential candidacy of Robert M. La Follette. The process of coalition formation continued through the election of 1936. Whether electoral change resulted from conversion (voters switching parties) or mobilization (new voters entering the electorate) remains controversial for the *New Deal no less than for other periods of partisan realignment.

The initial winning coalition of 1932, when voters punished the Republican incumbent, Herbert Hoover, for the Great Depression and elected the Democratic candidate, Franklin *Roosevelt, was less class-based than the coalition that reelected Roosevelt in 1936 and dominated American politics thereafter. New Deal policies altered Roosevelt's initial coalition and made it last. Unions of industrial workers, which grew under Section 7(a) of the National Industrial Recovery Act (1933) and its successor, the National Labor Relations Act of 1935 (the Wagner Act), provided votes, money, and organizational support for the Democrats. The Agricultural Adjustment Act of 1933 and later farm programs kept Southern farmers within the Democratic Party and added support from wheat and dairy farmers in the Upper Midwest.

Like the farm-labor alliance that began to govern Sweden in the 1930s, the New Deal coalition was held together by policies that combined high prices for farmers with high wages for industrial workers. However, New Deal policies were more conservative than those of the Swedish Social Democrats because the New Deal coalition depended on support from Southern Democrats, whose congressional representatives were closely tied to (or were themselves) large-scale planters.

Continuous Democratic control of the federal government ended with the election of a Republican *Congress in 1946, and Dwight *Eisenhower, a Republican, was elected president in 1952 and reelected in 1956. Yet the New Deal coalition was maintained during the 1950s: Democrats controlled Congress for most of the decade and a clear plurality of voters identified themselves as Democrats. The coalition began to dissolve after the Democrats sponsored the Civil Rights Act of 1964, the Voting Rights Act of 1965, and other civil rights legislation. White southerners, who had been solidly Democratic since the end of Reconstruction, defected to the Republican Party, which pursued a conscious "Southern strategy."

From 1932 to 1964, the Democrats won seven of nine presidential elections; from 1968 to 1988, the Republicans won five of six presidential elections. Under the New Deal coalition, Democrats had an electoral majority, but could not govern when Southern Democrats allied with Republicans to form a conservative coalition in Congress. The dissolution of the New Deal coalition made the Democrats a less contradictory minority party.

(See also POLITICAL REALIGNMENT.)

Kristi Andersen, *The Creation of a Democratic Majority, 1928–1936* (Chicago, 1979). James L. Sundquist, *Dynamics of the Party System*, rev. ed. (Washington, D.C., 1983).
KENNETH FINEGOLD

NEW ECONOMIC POLICY, U.S.S.R. Introduced in the *Soviet Union in the spring of 1921 as a response to the devastating consequences of civil war, the New Economic Policy (NEP) was not only successful in staving off the immediate *crisis but,

until it was eclipsed by the Stalinist onslaught against the peasantry in 1929, came to symbolize the entire strategic orientation of the Bolsheviks during the transition to socialism. The Bolshevik leaders saw NEP as a method for building socialism in a backward *peasant country. The backwardness of the peasantry consisted not only in its poverty and low level of productivity but also in its preference for small individual farms over large collective structures. NEP therefore implied toleration of market relations as the basic economic link *(smychka)* with the peasantry.

The Bolsheviks admitted that toleration of capitalist activity was in some sense a retreat, but they denied vehemently that they had lost interest in constructing socialism. A planned, nonmarket economy would be built gradually by raising the cultural level of the peasants and demonstrating the material advantages of socialism through organizations such as the cooperatives. NEP is sometimes called a mere "bivouac," with the implication that the Bolsheviks were just waiting to gather up enough strength to start a Stalin-type offensive against the peasantry. But there was a stark contrast between the pre-Stalinist consensus on the nature of the socialist offensive and the reality of *Stalin's forced collectivization, which meant the abandonment of NEP.

One reason for its failure was the unpopularity of much of the reality of NEP: the flashy lifestyles of the "NEP men" (the newly tolerated middlemen), the widespread crime and corruption, and the ever-present shadow of mass unemployment. Another reason was the difficulty in using market methods to mobilize resources for high-speed industrialization. In the late 1920s, problems in grain collection were interpreted by the Bolshevik leadership as sabotage by *kulaks* (rich peasants). This definition of the situation was incompatible with the gradualism and voluntarism of the NEP strategy. To this day, historians argue over whether the failure of NEP had deep structural roots or whether it could have been avoided by more rational decision making.

Far from being merely an emblem of a historical period, during the era of *perestroika NEP became a symbol of a possible strategy for socialists. Before perestroika, the official Soviet view was that NEP was a success story that could be recommended to anyone building socialism in a peasant country, whether in Eastern and *Central Europe or the *Third World. With the advent of perestroika and the rejection of the Stalinist heritage, NEP was seen as a genuine Bolshevik alternative to *Stalinism.

The attractiveness of NEP stems from its contrast with the civil war that preceded it and the Stalin era that followed it. The economic policies of the civil war—known after the fact as "war communism"—became the symbol of everything the reformers of perestroika did not like about original Bolshevism: the dogmatic rejection of the market, the bureaucratic over-centralization of the *command economy, hostility toward the peasants, and the class-war interpretation of social processes. An effort was made to show that *Lenin had rejected all of these in a series of articles written just before his debilitating stroke in 1923. These articles, known as Lenin's testament, came to be regarded almost as a charter for perestroika. In 1990, *Gorbachev called them "a revolution within the revolution, no less profound, perhaps, than the October [revolution of 1917]."

The NEP model was used to legitimize economic reform proposals in the early years of perestroika. But there were important limitations to NEP as a model for reform. The total contrast between NEP and war communism required more than a little historical myth making: war communism was not so bad nor was NEP so wonderful as the reformers claimed. Furthermore, the scope of perestroika soon went beyond the NEP model. NEP meant the toleration of the market on the road to socialism; if the reformers of perestroika were indeed on the same road, they were traveling in the opposite direction. Finally, in the political sphere, the 1920s saw not only one-party rule but a steady narrowing of pluralism and democracy within the party. By 1990, the reform process in the Soviet Union had clearly moved beyond the NEP model, and post-Soviet reforms have completely embraced the market system as a goal.

Edward Hallet Carr, *A History of Soviet Russia,* 4 vols. (London, 1950–1978). Stephen F. Cohen, *Bukharin and the Bolshevik Revolution* (New York, 1973).

LARS T. LIH

NEW INTERNATIONAL ECONOMIC ORDER. The success of the *Organization of Petroleum Exporting Countries (OPEC) in sharply raising oil prices in 1974 had profound effects on the rest of the *Third World. On the one hand, price increases of more than 500 percent in one year for a commodity without substitutes had devastating consequences for Third World importers. On the other hand, the Third World was also enormously pleased to see OPEC apparently turn the tables against the developed countries. A new era of "resource power" seemed to have opened and the Third World wanted to capitalize on it as quickly as possible, while the developed countries were in disarray, while fears of imminent resource shortages were widespread, and while their own needs for resource transfers were rapidly rising.

One result was a special session of the UN General Assembly in May 1974 to discuss resource problems. In the circumstances, there was obviously no time to develop new positions or policies on issues of concern to the developing countries. Instead, the developing countries simply grouped together in one package nearly all of the political and economic demands that they had been making over the previous decades. Not all of the demands were consistent, some were technically flawed, and the whole package was far from coherent. But questions of whether the demands were technically sound or politically feasible were overwhelmed by a shared sense of past and present grievances, by a new sense of power, and by the belief that the time had come for a radical restructuring of the old order. The demands, taken together, were described as the New International Economic Order (NIEO).

Most developed-country governments and most conservative neoclassical economists denounced the NIEO as "bad economics, worse politics." Some countries in the Western coalition (the Scandinavians and the Dutch) and some intellectuals and political figures on the left did support some or most of the NIEO demands, but usually on the presumption that acceptance of the NIEO necessarily implied acceptance by the developing countries of the need for parallel domestic changes. Conversely, in most of the Third World, there was so much hostility toward the international economic system and so strong a belief that domestic problems were a direct consequence of exploitative international economic relations that the case for the NIEO, whatever its imperfections, seemed unassailable. With pragmatists and conservative ideologues on one side and idealists and radical ideologues on the other side, the likelihood of agreement on the NIEO was never very high.

There were in the NIEO many controversial demands and statements. Nevertheless, conservative commentators who dismissed the NIEO as radical rhetoric or as a badly disguised political program to undermine the *liberalism of the Bretton Woods system were not entirely correct. The NIEO was not completely revolutionary; cooperation and *interdependence were emphasized as much as conflict and radical change; strong elements of continuity persisted in the analysis of many problems; and support for the NIEO varied greatly across countries, issues, and time. The latter point should not be surprising, given the diversity within the Third World and given the weakness of any coalition of the weak in trying to maintain a unified negotiating stance. In addition, the argument that the NIEO reflected an effort to seize political control of the international economic system so that global liberalism could be superseded by centralized control ignored the fact that many developing countries were doing very badly economically and desperately needed economic help as quickly as possible. In short, the ideological crusade (the "assault on global liberalism," in Stephen Krasner's interpretation) was never as profound, unrelenting, and sustained as critics would have it. Indeed, failed or failing economic performance has led many developing countries in the past decade to move, rapidly or hesitantly, toward the acceptance of some form of market economics.

The Third World felt that unity was its strongest

weapon. In this sense the NIEO could be conceived as an ideological bulwark of the quest for unity: it provided an interpretation of causality, a program of action, and a set of unifying themes. These were necessary on a psychological level because no program that focused solely on practical issues could have overcome conflicts of interest within the *Group of 77, the negotiating coalition of the Third World. This also explains why the leadership of the Third World continued to demand agreement on new principles as a necessary preface to detailed negotiations on specifics: any other strategy would have split the coalition. Moreover, if we conceive of the Third World as an international social movement that is both responding to change and seeking to implement changes favorable to its own interests, the NIEO might also be interpreted as a kind of guide through an uncertain and volatile international environment.

The proposals in the NIEO cannot be easily summarized. There are, however, at least two practical themes that cut across the diversity. The first is a consistent effort to seek protection for the Third World against adverse external trends, for which the Third World bears little responsibility but from which it usually suffers severely. Examples include sharp fluctuations in the demand for commodities, increases in inflationary trends, the rise of protectionism, and volatility in the international monetary system. The second theme is simply the desire to increase resource transfers to the Third World, both directly by increased *foreign aid and indirectly by using other proposals as a disguised form of resource transfer (for example, buffer stocks in commodities to raise prices as well as to stabilize them).

Almost none of the NIEO goals have been achieved, although some proposals are still being pursued. The mutual gains that might have been possible to achieve had both sides been willing to compromise were lost because of a combination of factors: the Third World focus on unity and negotiating principles before practicalities, as well as its overestimation of its "new" power; the developed world's ideological hostility and reluctance to risk change; and continued deterioration of the world economy. In short, the NIEO is a classic illustration of failed international reform.

(See also DEVELOPMENT AND UNDERDEVELOPMENT; INTERNATIONAL COOPERATION; INTERNATIONAL POLITICAL ECONOMY; NORTH-SOUTH RELATIONS; UNITED NATIONS CONFERENCE ON TRADE AND DEVELOPMENT.)

Robert L. Rothstein, "The North-South Dialogue: The Political Economy of Immobility" *Journal of International Affairs* 34, no. 1 (Spring/Summer 1980): 1–17. Stephen D. Krasner, *Structural Conflict—The Third World Against Global Liberalism* (Berkeley, Calif., 1985).

ROBERT L. ROTHSTEIN

NEW LEFT. The New Left in the United States was a movement of self-understood radicals, mostly students, in the 1960s. Larger and more diffuse than any distinct organizations, it aimed to galvanize a more general radical movement. Most of the central figures were in their twenties during that decade, and were born during or just before World War II; most of the rank and file were born after the war and were part of the so-called baby boom, which filled the expanding colleges and universities. Although the central figures began as student activists, the New Left grew into an intellectual tendency that included academics, principally in the social sciences and humanities; professionals (doctors, lawyers, social workers, etc.) who shared its concern for the rights of helpless and victimized people; and other radicals.

Two single-issue movements activated the New Left: 1) The *civil rights movement, beginning with the Montgomery bus boycott (1955–1956) and accelerating with student sit-ins and freedom rides (1960–1961), which stirred not only black students but white supporters in the North as well as the South; and 2) the movement against *nuclear weapons (1959–1963). Many of the original New Left activists were children of the Communist-dominated Old Left, and most of the others came from the homes of *New Deal liberals. Most shared the values of their parents but believed in direct action for change. They perceived the Old Left as having been fatally weakened both by *McCarthyism and Khrushchev's 1956 revelations about Stalin's crimes. They thought conventional *liberalism had been compromised by its commitment to the *Cold War. Many were stirred by the *Cuban Revolution (1958–1959) and by the cultural dissidence of the beat writers (principally Jack Kerouac and Allen Ginsberg).

Seeking intellectual coherence, student activists borrowed the term *New Left* from British intellectuals (including E. P. Thompson and Raymond Williams) who had left the Communist Party and helped form the Campaign for Nuclear Disarmament (1957). Unlike the Britons, most of the U.S. New Left were not Marxists. They disdained what the influential U.S. sociologist C. Wright Mills called "the labor metaphysic" and hoped to find other social constituencies with the social weight and commitment to transform society in an egalitarian and democratic direction. Hopeful about the prospects for radical politics under a liberal administration, they still, like the British, looked for a radical alternative to what they saw as staid or deadlocked party politics.

The foremost statement of New Left principles was the Port Huron Statement of Students for a Democratic Society (SDS), named after the town in Michigan that was the site of the group's first convention (1962). Most of the programs recommended by the Port Huron Statement and subsequent papers were staples of New Deal and social democratic traditions: the abolition of poverty, the elimination of racial segregation, the end of the Cold War, nuclear disarmament, the reform of universities in a democratic direction. But the main idea of the Port Huron Statement was "participatory democracy": direct participation in the decisions that affect people's lives. SDS insisted that anticommunism had been tainted by McCarthyism; they stood instead for anti-anticommunism.

From 1965 on, the main force that swelled the New Left was the *Vietnam War. Gathering strength, the New Left spun off a movement against the war, and in the popular mind became principally identified with that movement. SDS, which had nine chapters and some 600 members in 1963, grew to some 300 chapters and 100,000 members in 1969. National demonstrations against the war grew from 25,000 people (April 1965) to 500,000 (November 1969). As the war escalated, the New Left (or what increasingly called itself "the movement") became not only larger but more militant.

During this time, however, the core of New Left organizers came to regard themselves as more than a protest movement. They increasingly saw themselves as committed to a radical transformation with an antiauthoritarian spirit. Pragmatic, many were reluctant to call themselves "socialist" or "anarchist"; they borrowed elements from both traditions, as well as from liberalism. Toward that end, they experimented with community organizing among the poor; with projects in student-centered education; with attempts to radicalize factory workers. But their principal base was the university campuses. Best represented among elite universities in the early 1960s, their class base moved progressively downward by the early 1970s. By 1970, demonstrations against the draft, against military education, against corporate recruiters, against disciplinary rules, and in favor of ethnic studies departments took place on hundreds of campuses.

In the course of the decade, the New Left came to see itself as part of a worldwide movement of radical youth. New Left groups sprang up throughout Western Europe and Canada, usually also based on campuses, and militantly opposed to the Vietnam War—but only in the United States did the movement of ethnic minorities play such a large part in the the overall movement. In 1968, the New Left felt an affinity with Czechoslovakia's *Prague Spring, with the student revolutionaries of France and the Federal Republic of Germany, and with the radical students massacred by government troops in Mexico. By the end of the decade, however, its most intense identifications were with revolutionaries of the Third World, especially Vietnam.

By 1967, most of the New Left had moved (in the words of its own slogan) "from protest to resistance." Many, observing the massive disaffection of college-educated youth—as signaled in drug use, popular music, hippie clothing, long hair, and so forth—came to feel that a radical transformation of the society was necessary, although they had little

conception of a new order. By 1968, they saw institutions from university administrations to the Democratic Party as hopelessly oppressive.

In this setting, and in the context of an intensifying war, by 1969, a significant portion of the New Left considered itself revolutionary. As a growing number of students expressed opposition to the war, SDS was torn apart by a fight between two revolutionary factions, and disappeared.

In the early 1970s and continuing throughout the decade, New Left activists pursued radical politics by other means. Some moved into the left wing of the Democratic Party and were able to achieve local influence, though not national power or organization. Some tried to apply principles of radical democracy in their professional activities. Some transferred their passions into movements that extended some of the principles of the New Left—mainly the women's, gay, and environmental movements. Some, having "burned out," retired from public life and devoted themselves to private pursuits.

The New Left's impact is not simple. It helped end racial segregation and the Vietnam War, spawned important subsequent movements, contributed to antiauthoritarian tendencies throughout the society, left strong influences in the academy, and helped undermine the culture of the Cold War. But its excesses—along with the erosion of *liberalism—helped break apart the Democratic Party and to fuel the post-1960s *Right.

(See also LEFT; MAY 1968; NEW RIGHT; NEW SOCIAL MOVEMENTS; POLITICAL PARTICIPATION; SOCIALISM AND SOCIAL DEMOCRACY.)

Massimo Teodori, ed., *The New Left: A Documentary History* (Indianapolis, 1971). Kirkpatrick Sale, *SDS* (New York, 1973). Todd Gitlin, *The Sixties: Years of Hope, Days of Rage* (New York, 1987). James Miller, *"Democracy Is in the Streets": From Port Huron to the Siege of Chicago* (New York, 1987).

TODD GITLIN

NEWLY INDUSTRIALIZING ECONOMIES. The terms *newly industrializing economies* (NIEs) or *newly industrializing countries* (NICs) first appeared in the late 1970s to refer to a small group of developing countries that had been successful not only in industrializing rapidly but in expanding their exports of manufactured products. These countries fell into two groups. Several large countries in Latin America that had industrialized through high levels of tariff protection, particularly Mexico, Brazil, and Argentina, began at various points to promote exports of nontraditional products. The Latin American NICs did develop more diversified export structures that included labor-intensive light manufactures and even some intermediate and capital goods, but export-promotion policies were not always vigorously pursued and did not generate adequate foreign exchange to service rising external debt.

The term *NIEs* was often used to refer exclusively

to a second group of East Asian countries: the Republic of Korea (South Korea), Taiwan, Hong Kong, and Singapore. Korea and Taiwan industrialized in the 1950s through import-substitution, and Singapore and Hong Kong were initially commercial entrepôts. The transition to *export-led growth was somewhat different in the four cases, but there are important similarities in their growth paths. All initially exploited their comparative advantage in light, labor-intensive manufactures, gradually diversifying into technology-, skill-, and even capital-intensive goods. All depended heavily on the U.S. market and attempted to attract export-oriented foreign direct investment.

The emergence of the NIEs raised several important policy and political questions. The East Asian NIEs appeared to pursue a more market-oriented development strategy than other developing countries. Because of their rapid and relatively egalitarian growth they were held up by development economists and the international financial institutions as models of success. Yet there is substantial debate about how market-oriented the East Asian NIEs really are. Hong Kong never departed from a strong commitment to laissez-faire policies, but export-oriented industrialization in Korea and Taiwan involved a substantial degree of state intervention, such as continued protection and subsidies, as well as market-oriented reforms. Moreover, economic reform efforts in these countries were led by strong, authoritarian governments. These conditions cast some doubt on whether their experiences could be replicated elsewhere. Nonetheless, a "second tier" of countries attempted similar export-oriented growth strategies in the 1980s with some success. These countries included Thailand, Malaysia, and Turkey, and the NIE label was extended to them as well.

The second policy issue surrounding the emergence of the NIEs concerns trade. The rapid growth of manufactured exports from these countries, particularly the East Asian NIEs, created severe competitive pressures and contributed to adjustment problems in a range of mature industries in the advanced industrial states including textiles and apparel, footwear, and consumer electronics. As a result, the NIEs have been major targets of the so-called "new protectionism" in Europe and the United States: nontariff barriers designed to restrict trade with particular countries in particular products. In the 1980s, the larger NIEs also came under increasing pressures to liberalize their own markets and to "graduate" by giving up their developing-country status with reference to a number of preferences.

(See also DEVELOPMENT AND UNDERDEVELOPMENT; INTERNATIONAL POLITICAL ECONOMY; PACIFIC REGION; PROTECTION.)

Walter Galenson, ed., *Foreign Trade and Investment: Economic Development in the Newly Industrializing Asian Countries* (Madison, Wis., 1985). Stephan Haggard, *Path-ways from the Periphery: The Politics of Growth in the Newly Industrializing Countries* (Ithaca, N.Y., 1990).

STEPHAN HAGGARD

NEW RIGHT. The term *New Right* has gained usage since the mid-1970s in a number of advanced industrial democracies, especially the United States and Britain. In both these countries advocates of New Right arguments had been active since the early 1960s, but it was in the wake of the 1973–1974 economic crisis and the electoral success of Ronald *Reagan (1980) and Margaret *Thatcher (1979) that the term became commonplace.

Meaning. The term *New Right* refers to a range of conservative and liberal ideas including principally a commitment to individual freedom and the primacy of the free market in preference to *state policies. These fundamentals become the basis for policies such as privatizing the public sector, deregulation, reducing the *welfare state, monetarist macroeconomic measures, and, in some cases, a conservative moralism.

These principles give rise to two different approaches to politics. The first includes those who advocate traditional liberal values of personal freedom (defined negatively as protection from state intrusion), market processes, and minimal government. In this view, individuals are the most important units within society and their capacities must be maximized. Such liberal New Right theorists believe that political and economic freedoms are the most important values that can be realized in the polity and that they are best attained in that polity which confines itself to providing a legal framework and certain *public goods (infrastructure). The writings of F. A. Hayek, particularly *The Road to Serfdom* (London, 1944) and *The Constitution of Liberty* (London, 1960), and Milton Friedman's *Capitalism and Freedom* (Chicago, 1962) are influential statements of these principles.

The second New Right approach promotes the conservative values of inequality, social hierarchy, traditional moralism, and, in some cases, a strong state. Proponents of this position believe that many aspects of the welfare state have encouraged a breakdown of traditional values such as commitments to the family and religion, and undesirable social behavior such as bearing children outside of marriage. Exponents of these views include George Gilder in *Wealth and Poverty* (New York, 1981) and Roger Scruton in *The Meaning of Conservatism* (London, 1980).

Origins. The ideas of New Right theorists and activists are not especially new, enjoying a lineage with preindustrial conservative beliefs and nineteenth-century liberalism. However, such ideas were displaced from the political agenda of Western industrial democracies during the first three decades following World War II as social democrats captured the political initiative. Returning these ideas to the center of political debate became the self-proclaimed task of a number of interest groups and activists.

In Britain, the founding in 1957 of the Institute of Economic Affairs (IEA) was the key event. Through its publications (notably the Hobart and Occasional Papers series) and sponsorship of conferences this organization served as a conduit promoting the arguments of the *Right in economic and social policy. The IEA also introduced the basic tenets of *public choice theory to British policymakers and politicians, including the claim that bureaucracies are inefficient because bureaucrats are self-interested maximizers (William Niskanen, *Bureaucracy: Servant or Master?* London, 1973) and that politicians relying on Keynesian demand management have an inherent tendency to run budget deficits (James Buchanan et al., *The Economics of Politics,* London, 1978). The IEA was joined in the 1970s by the Adam Smith Institute and the Centre for Policy Studies. In the mid-1970s these groups won influential supporters within the Conservative Party and enjoyed direct access to policymakers after the 1979 electoral success of the Tories led by Margaret Thatcher.

In the United States, the *National Review,* founded in 1955 and edited by William F. Buckley, Jr., served as a key forum for the promulgation of conservative views opposed to the mainstream liberalism associated with the presidential administrations of the 1960s and 1970s. Opposition to the "liberal consensus"—the U.S. counterpart of the European social democratic consensus—was organized through the pages of Buckley's periodical, the editor's right-wing credentials having been established in *God and Man at Yale* (Chicago, 1955), an attack on collectivism and atheism (coincidentally the concerns of New Right liberals and conservatives respectively). Many of these ideas influenced the 1964 Republican presidential candidate Barry Goldwater, whose resounding defeat by President Lyndon Johnson seemed to augur poorly for the Right. But the success of Ronald Reagan in delivering a televised speech on Goldwater's behalf proved a glimpse of the future.

From the mid-1970s, the New Right in the United States enjoyed a revival parallel to that in Britain. Conservative intellectuals publishing in the *National Review* were joined by disillusioned radicals, notably Irving Kristol and Norman Podhoretz; self-proclaimed New Right conservative organizations including Howard Phillips's Conservative Caucus and Paul Weyrich's Committee for the Survival of a Free Congress and think tanks such as the Heritage Foundation proliferated and gained influence. In 1981 Richard Viguerie published *The New Right: We're Ready to Lead* (Falls Church, Va., 1981) and with his colleagues began to use direct-mail technology to raise funds and disseminate ideas. The religious Right, represented most vocally by Jerry Falwell's Moral Majority, was sympathetic with the aims of intellectual and populist conservatives. To-

gether these groups—intellectual conservatives, New Right and religious activists—provided an important part of the groundwork for Ronald Reagan's successful presidential candidacy in 1980.

Significance. New Right ideas have had considerable influence on public policy in Western democracies. Monetarist policy has been widely accepted as the key instrument for defeating inflation, although, as recent British trends illustrate, the policies implemented have varied in success. The policy of reducing the public sector through privatization and deregulation has become a general one. Many Western democracies have engaged in extensive privatization programs, and this strategy has extended to the new democracies of Eastern and Central Europe.

The New Right has had considerable significance in redefining the political agenda in Western democracies and in displacing social democracy. As a consequence the market has gained wide acceptance as an appropriate mechanism for resolving social and economic problems. The New Right has capitalized on a disillusionment with national economic planning and an acceptance of the important role of incentives in stimulating economic growth. Both the Labour Party in Britain and the Democrats in the United States have been placed on the defensive by the spread of these arguments and have been forced to revise their own programs. With the collapse of state *planning systems in Eastern and *Central Europe and the widespread adoption of privatization policy, New Right ideas have in important ways achieved dominance in the intellectual arguments informing public policy in Western democracies since the 1980s. This dominance is, of course, vulnerable to political change, and the growing problems of the new market-based economies in the postcommunist societies of Europe may raise important questions for the New Right.

(See also CONSERVATISM; LIBERALISM; MONETARISM; NEW LEFT; SOCIALISM AND SOCIAL DEMOCRACY.)

Kevin Phillips, *Post-Conservative America: People, Politics and Ideology in a Time of Crisis* (New York, 1982). Gillian Peele, *Revival and Reaction: The Right in Contemporary America* (Oxford, 1984). David G. Green, *The New Conservatism: The Counter Revolution in Political, Economic and Social Thought* (New York, 1987). Desmond S. King, *The New Right: Politics, Markets and Citizenship* (Chicago, 1987).

DESMOND KING

NEW SOCIAL MOVEMENTS. In the past decade most Western democracies have experienced a flowering of new groups concerned with *environmentalism, women's *rights, *peace, consumerism, and the other pressing issues of advanced industrial societies. These new social movements (NSMs) are now important and contentious actors in the political process of most advanced industrial societies, and similar political forces are growing in the emerging democracies of Eastern and *Central Europe and the Pacific Rim. The significance of these movements and their organizational representatives lies in translating the public's changing values and issue interests into a potential political force, challenging the influence of established *interest groups (such as unions and business associations), and channeling the energies of the movement into political action.

Although NSMs take on a wide variety of forms, they share a common political ideology that challenges the prevailing social goals and political style of Western industrial democracies. This alternative political ideology is especially strong among European movements, although the same themes appear in muted form among American groups. Environmentalists emphasize the theme of a sustainable society and economy as the underlying premise of environmental action; the women's movement stresses the dual goals of reshaping social norms about the role of women in society and equalizing life chances between men and women; the peace movement questions the basic premises of Western defense thinking by arguing that arms reductions hold the best potential for improving the security of nations. These distinct interests are bridged by a common political identity that emphasizes the quality of life for individual citizens, whether it is the quality of the natural environment, the protection of human rights, or peace in an insecure world. These groups also share certain libertarian themes: individuals must control society rather than the reverse, and personal fulfillment and self-expression should be maximized.

The structure and style of the political groups spawned by these social movements reflect their challenging ideology, and herein lies their larger significance for contemporary political systems. For example, the popular base of these groups differs from earlier progressive movements, such as the *labor movement or agrarian movement. The participants in NSMs are not drawn from the underprivileged of society, but from young, better-educated, middle-class citizens who share the postmaterial value orientations of NSMs. Participants are recruited into political activity by their own values and their ties to alternative political organizations, and there is a substantial overlap between the activists and supporters of the various movements. In terms of their numbers, by most accounts the number of citizens who belong to NSM organizations exceeds formal membership in the political parties for most Western democracies. While there is substantial public support for these same issues in Eastern and Central Europe and the developing nations in Asia, actual participation in these nations is much more limited.

One of the distinctive characteristics of NSMs is the wide variety of organizational forms they have spawned. Many movement organizations are large, complex bureaucracies, such as the Sierra Club or the National Organization for Women (NOW) in the United States; others are small elitist organizations or activist foundations, such as the Environmental Defense Fund. But the innovative aspect of these movements is the creation of new organizational structures that stress decentralization and participatory decision making and which sharply contrast to the oligarchic and bureaucratic tendencies displayed in most interest groups. This alternative organizational style is most visible among locally based citizen action groups or local branches of national organizations. The small size of these groups and their neighborhood locale make an extensive organizational structure unnecessary and undesirable. Similar organizational tendencies can be observed, however, even in larger NSMs. The women's movement in several European states is openly skeptical of an institutionalized women's lobby that might come to dominate the movement, and similar antiorganizational tendencies are apparent among peace groups and opponents of nuclear power. These movements are also distinguished by their development of multinational interest groups—such as Greenpeace, the World Wildlife Fund (WWF), or Friends of the Earth—that create an international basis for political action.

Another visible feature of NSMs is their expansion of the accepted methods of political action to include protests, spectacular actions, and other forms of unconventional activity. Because of their own values and status as challenging groups, NSMs place a greater reliance on unconventional political activities as a way to mobilize their potential supporters and exert public pressure on the political establishment: Environmental activists add dyes to industrial discharges to demonstrate the reach of pollution; peace groups assemble human chains connecting military installations; and women's groups organize large demonstrations on issues such as abortion rights. Early scholarship stressed only the unconventional nature of NSMs, but the practical demands of politics also involve these groups in established channels of interest group influence. But even as participants in the political process, NSM organizations advocate a change in the workings of the process. In Europe, the movement has criticized neocorporatist patterns of decision making and has pressed for expanding direct citizen input into policy making and policy administration. In the United States, these interests are pursued through a full range of political tactics, from demonstrations to litigation.

One clear example of the new political options created by NSMs has been the emergence of green political parties in recent years. Often established with formal assistance from NSM organizations, or at least informal support from the alternative social network comprising these movements, *green parties formed during the 1980s in most Western democracies. Green parties now hold seats in most Western European national parliaments as well as the parliament of the *European Community, and nascent green parties are forming in the emerging democracies of Eastern and Central Europe. These parties' alternative ideology, decentralized structure, and participatory style stand in sharp contrast to the established political parties in these same nations. Green parties try to epitomize the alternative values of the movement, and they differ so markedly from the established parties that they are sometimes described as the "anti-party parties."

The overall significance of NSMs is perhaps best illustrated by how political systems are responding to their challenges. Although these movements have not been successful in stimulating revolutionary change, they have produced broad-scale reforms in the policies of contemporary political systems. Nearly all democratic states now acknowledge the importance of the environmental issue, and most have responded with sincere efforts at policy reform. Global environmental problems—such as depletion of the ozone, disposal of toxic wastes, and acid rain—are creating a new international environmental awareness. Several forecasters expect the 1990s to be the environmental decade, foreseeing sweeping environmental reforms that will reach from issues faced by Western advanced industrial societies, to the severe environmental problems of Eastern Europe, to the loss of rain forests in less developed countries. Similarly, there have been far-reaching changes in the role of women in Western societies, and significant new legislation has been implemented to protect women's rights. Important and ongoing administrative reforms in Europe, Japan, and the United States are expanding the role of citizens within the political process. Thus, these movements have not created a new political order, but they have renewed the democratic process of advanced industrial societies.

(See also CORPORATISM; FEMINISM; GAY AND LESBIAN POLITICS; GENDER AND POLITICS; NEW LEFT; NUCLEAR FREEZE; PEACE MOVEMENT; POLITICAL PARTICIPATION; POLITICAL PARTIES AND PARTY COMPETITION; POSTMATERIALISM; REPRODUCTIVE POLITICS.)

Bert Klandermans et al., *From Structure to Action* (Greenwich, Conn., 1988). Herbert Kitschelt, *Logics of Party Formation* (Ithaca, N.Y., 1989). Bert Klandermans, *Organizing for Change* (Greenwich, Conn., 1989). Ferdinand Mueller-Rommel, ed., *New Politics in Western Europe* (Boulder, Colo., 1989). Russell Dalton and Manfred Kuechler, eds., *Challenging the Political Order* (New York and Cambridge, U.K., 1990).

RUSSELL J. DALTON

NEW ZEALAND. Situated in the South Pacific, midway between South America and Southeast Asia, part of the circum-Pacific volcanic "rim of fire," New Zealand is a former British settlement colony, now an independent state. The population of some 3.2 million people is predominantly of British extraction, although approximately thirteen percent is made up of indigenous Polynesians—the Maori.

Constitutionally, the British monarch—in her capacity as queen of New Zealand—is still head of state in New Zealand, although this is largely a formal position today, with the royal powers largely devolving upon the governor-general as the monarch's representative. As befits the country's evolution from colony through dominion status to independent state, since 1930 the governor-general has been appointed on the advice of New Zealand ministers, and since 1967 governors-general have all been New Zealand–born.

As the original inhabitants of the country, the Maori occupy a special position under the terms of the Treaty of Waitangi (1840), which formally ceded sovereignty to the British Crown. In return, the Crown (in the European version of the treaty) confirmed and guaranteed to the chiefs and tribes the full exclusive and undisturbed possession of their "Lands and Estates, Forests, Fisheries" so long as they wished to retain them, in addition to granting them "all the Rights and Privileges of British Subjects."

For much of New Zealand's history—and particularly following the Land Wars of the 1860s—the Treaty of Waitangi was largely ignored by successive New Zealand governments, but from the 1970s onward it has been central to attempts to forge a new and more equitable arrangement between *pakehas* (New Zealanders of European descent) and Maori.

Dating from 1854, the New Zealand Parliament enjoys a record of constitutional continuity second only to the U.S. Congress in the Pacific region. It is frequently cited as a prime example of the Westminster-type system. New Zealand has one of the world's strictest and most cohesive two-party systems, is highly centralized, has a parliament that has been unicameral since 1950, and is based on a simple majority electoral system with no formal constitution. A "Bill of Rights" was passed in 1990, but this is an ordinary statute rather than supreme law. This merely requires that the attorney general provide a certificate with the introduction of any measure that contravenes it.

Instead of the normal legal constitutional safeguards, heavy emphasis is placed on triennial general elections along with pragmatic devices and arrangements such as an ombudsman; an independent broadcasting authority; a race relations conciliator; the Waitangi Tribunal (set up in 1975 to consider claims made by the Maori people under the Treaty of Waitangi); an Official Information Act; and the courts. New Zealand follows the common law tradition of the United Kingdom with its own hierarchy of courts comprising district courts, high court, and court of appeal. In constitutional matters the courts are largely limited to the doctrine of *ultra vires*, judging whether a government agency has exceeded the powers granted to it under statute or regulation, although in recent times the courts have been given increasing responsibility for deciding a growing number of issues arising under the aegis of the Treaty of Waitangi.

The formal executive of the country is the Executive Council, made up of two or more cabinet ministers and normally presided over by the governor-general. The practical decision-taking center, however, is the cabinet, usually consisting of some twenty ministers of cabinet rank and supplemented by four to six noncabinet ministers. Emphasis is placed on both collective responsibility and collective decision-taking, and ministers often hold multiple portfolios.

In New Zealand, consideration of the executive cannot be divorced from the role of the parliamentary party caucuses, which represent an important part of the collective decision-making process. In the case of the Labour Party, the cabinet is elected by and from the parliamentary party caucus, and most important cabinet decisions are deemed to require caucus endorsement. The National Party, too, makes extensive, if less formal, use of its caucus. Both parties require their parliamentary leaders to be elected or reendorsed by caucus every three years.

A wide range of *interest groups represent capital, labor, environmental interests, peace groups, etc. Several of these groups have had close links with the Labour Party, and a number of trade unions are directly affiliated to it. On the other hand, third and minor parties have rarely flourished because of the nature of the electoral system. In 1984, for example, a newly founded third party won twelve percent of the total vote but no seats. By the mid-1980s constitutional reform had become an issue with a royal commission recommending a change to an electoral system similar to that of the Federal Republic of Germany that would combine *proportional representation and single member districts. After promising a referendum at the 1990 general election, Prime Minister David Lange subsequently declined to pursue the issue, but both parties later committed themselves to a referendum during the course of the 1990–93 term of parliament.

Socioeconomic and urban-rural differences are the predominant social cleavages. *Class is important but has always been a much less pronounced factor than in Britain, and, in common with many other countries, class-based voting has declined in the second half of the twentieth century. At the same time, considerations of *gender, and particularly of *race, have risen sharply. Religion has not played an important role in New Zealand politics.

Similarly, a shift has taken place in economic policies from those of a predominantly Keynesian complexion to a market-liberal stance with a heavy emphasis on user payment and the selling off of state enterprises. A rapidly developing free market with Australia, under the provisions of the Australia–New Zealand Closer Economic Relations Trade Agreement 1983 (CER), is projected to result in a single economic (but not political) entity.

New Zealand was unusual in building up what was a relatively affluent welfare state upon a predominantly agricultural base. There are limited natural resources (gold, coal, oil and natural gas). As a temperate agriculture producer, New Zealand was severely disadvantaged by Britain's accession to the *European Community (even despite useful transitional arrangements). Trade has been diversified extensively. In 1950, for example, sixty-six percent of New Zealand exports were sent to Britain. Britain now ranks fourth as an export market, following Australia, Japan, and the United States.

A small state with total armed forces of under 13,000, New Zealand was a loyal ally of both Britain and the United States until the prohibition of the visits of nuclear-armed and nuclear-powered ships led to the formal suspension of the *ANZUS alliance by the United States in 1986. New Zealand was a founding member of the UN in 1945, and has played an active role in peacekeeping from Korea to the Middle East as well as in the specialized agencies. Increasingly New Zealand has played an important role in environmental matters, ranging from protection of the ozone layer to the prohibition of whaling and drift-net fishing. The latter is a reflection in part of its growing involvement with the communities and interests of the smaller islands of the South Pacific.

(See also KEYNESIANISM; PACIFIC REGION.)

Geoffrey Palmer, *Unbridled Power*, 2d ed. (Auckland, 1987). *New Zealand Official Yearbook,* Department of Statistics (Auckland, 1990).

KEITH JACKSON

NICARAGUA. Strategically located astride the Mesoamerican isthmus, with waterways that facilitate transisthmian transit, Nicaragua has often held geopolitical significance greater than its size and population (around 4 million) would suggest. Since the nineteenth century the prospect of an interoceanic canal across Nicaragua has brought repeated external intervention in Nicaraguan affairs and has contributed to the turbulence of the nation's politics.

The emergence of a modern nation-state arguably continued into the last decade of the twentieth century as the *Nicaraguan Revolution (1979–1990) ended, although independence came in 1823. Despite periods of relative stability (1857–1893, 1936–1977), power conflicts between Liberal and Conservative elites were repeatedly violent from independence until the 1960s. Nicaraguans often experienced (sometimes themselves inviting) external intervention that intensified local conflict. Liberals invited U.S. filibusterer William Walker into a partisan squabble in 1856, and he then seized the entire country. The United States in 1911 installed a Conservative regime to protect the U.S. monopoly over the Panama Canal, then occupied Nicaragua (1912–1925) to contain Liberal rebellion. Liberal revolt again brought U.S. occupation (1927–1933); U.S.

Marines and the U.S.-trained Nicaraguan National Guard fought anti-imperialist guerrilla Augusto César Sandino.

National Guard commander Anastasio Somoza García seized power in 1936 and used the Guard, the Partido Liberal Nacionalista (PLN), and U.S. aid to rule Nicaragua until his assassination in 1956. Power passed to his sons Luis (1956–1967) and the more repressive Anastasio Somoza Debayle (1967–1979). The dictatorial dynasty promoted rapid economic *modernization characterized by *corruption, increased economic inequality, and deterioration of the PLN and Conservative parties. Spiraling repression eventually deepened opposition, spawned a revolutionary coalition headed by the Frente Sandinista de Liberación Nacional (FSLN), and caused widespread popular insurrection that toppled the regime in 1979.

The revolutionary government expanded the state, reorganized government, developed a new constitution (1987), and held democratic elections (1984, 1990). FSLN National Directorate member Daniel Ortega Saavedra, elected president in 1984, lost the 1990 election to the Unión Nacional Opositora (UNO—a twenty-party coalition) and transferred power to Violeta Barrios de Chamorro. Even in defeat, the FSLN retained widespread popular support and close ties to organized labor and the military.

Nicaragua's party system, political institutions, state structures, and political economy bear the imprint of its complex political history and revolutionary experiences. The Conservative and Liberal (later PLN) parties arose from regional/ideological conflicts before independence and became loose, nonideological, personalistic movements among the nation's agrarian bourgeoisie. Conservative dominance (1857–1893) was broken by rising middle-sector support for the Liberals. Conservative collaboration with U.S. occupation after 1912 and later with the Somozas further eroded and divided the party. The Somozas' PLN lost credibility, splintered, and eventually declined through its corruption. Liberal and Conservative splinter groups persisted throughout the revolution and several joined the victorious UNO coalition.

The FSLN, founded in 1961 by Marxist-Leninsts who had quit the Nicaraguan Partido Socialista (Communist Party), struggled as a tiny guerrilla movement until 1978, then emerged as the leader of the anti-Somoza coalition in the insurrection. Upon victory the FSLN marginalized its allies, took over the state, created a new party-based military, and dramatically broadened its popular base. Economic deterioration, the counterrevolutionary (*contra) war, and its abuses of power eroded FSLN support and brought electoral defeat in 1990. Other parties, most quite small, numbered over twenty by 1990; larger ones included the Partido Conservador, Partido Li-

beral Independiente, Partido Social Cristiano, and Partido Popular Social Cristiano.

Not only the party system but also the state institutions reflect Nicaragua's dramatic changes in power and regime type. The Somozas expanded the state but also captured and corrupted it. The Central Bank and the National Guard became the most modern and competent agencies because they helped the Somozas rule and enrich themselves and their allies. Revolutionary governmental reorganization further expanded the size and scope of the government in its management of the economy and provision of services. FSLN penetration of the bureaucracy replaced that of the PLN. The Central Bank remained strong while economic planning, presidential, and security ministries (interior, defense) grew rapidly. With special emergency powers and an FSLN majority during the 1980s, President Ortega overshadowed the unicameral National Assembly. However, during the UNO government after 1990 the Assembly gained new policy influence. The regular judiciary, largely corrupt under the Somozas, was politicized during the *revolution but sometimes acted with independence.

The National Guard, a combined police and military force with 14,000 troops at its peak, collapsed in 1979 and was replaced with the FSLN-dominated Ejército Popular Sandinista (EPS) and Policia Sandinista (PS). The EPS and PS were national institutions but also partisan—commanded by top Sandinistas, ideologically trained, and protective of the revolution. The EPS and PS received Soviet-bloc assistance and advice. The EPS and its conscripted militia grew to over 100,000 troops organized for counterinsurgency at the peak of the contra war but demobilized rapidly in 1990–1991 to some 25,000 troops. Violeta Chamorro's UNO government moved cautiously to reduce FSLN influence in the EPS and PS, retaining *Sandinista officers to avoid alienating either force. Loyalty of the EPS and PS to the post-Sandinista regime and the reduction of their partisanship appeared likely to remain major concerns for postrevolutionary governments.

A country burdened with enduring social cleavages, Nicaragua is divided between its fertile, volcanic Pacific littoral (approximately a third of the territory), with ninety percent of the population, and the wet Atlantic lowlands. The Pacific populace is fairly homogeneous ethnically and culturally (Spanish-speaking, Catholic, and mestizo) and dominates national life. The Atlantic zone's people, mostly Protestants, include English-speaking blacks and 100,000 indigenes. The Atlantic peoples generally resent politicoeconomic incursions from the Pacific. Such resentment fed the Miskitos' armed residence to the revolution in the 1980s and prompted a regional autonomy law enacted in the late 1980s. Nicaragua underwent a major surge of religious fervor (1970–1990s) that affected politics both among nominal Catholics (probably eighty-five percent) and Protestants—divided among many fast-spreading, largely evangelical denominations—and within the Catholic church, where an important minority, the "popular church," supported the Sandinista Revolution while the more conservative majority led by the hierarchy took an anti-Sandinista stand. Thus did social cleavages reinforce powerful political divisions that were fueled by economic forces and powerful international influences.

Nicaragua has historically exported coffee, cotton, and beef/hides; owners of the largeholds supplying most of these products constituted much of the political elite. The agro-export bourgeoisie diversified into manufacturing in the 1960s under the Central American Common Market (CACM). Political turmoil, deteriorating terms of trade, the CACM's collapse, capital flight, the contra war, the U.S. economic embargo, and revolutionary policy devastated the Nicaraguan economy in the 1980s. The contribution of agriculture and manufacturing fell, while much of the population turned to informal services. Divisions within the agro-export bourgeoisie and eroding popular living conditions helped motivate the revolution, but the Sandinistas themselves eventually lost power by alienating needed bourgeois allies, agrarian reform beneficiaries, and the huge new urban informal sector.

The U.S.-backed contra rebels fought the Sandinistas for several years but failed militarily. It was erosion of the FSLN's socioeconomic base that undermined the revolution in 1990. Subsequent stabilization of the polity is expected to require both a previously elusive consensus on political rules among Nicaragua's disparate elites and the tolerance of its masses. The severe 1973–1990s economic slide, dramatic declines in working-class and middle-class living standards, extraordinarily high inflation, and lack of capital all suggest that postrevolutionary economic recovery will be slow.

Throughout the twentieth century the United States has powerfully influenced Nicaragua, first with its occupations and then by supporting the Somozas. The Sandinista Revolution's Marxist leanings, sympathy for Salvadorean rebels, and friendliness toward the Soviet bloc brought U.S. hostility in the 1980s (contra war, economic and credit embargoes). Soviet/Cuban economic and military aid helped shore up the revolution, especially after the mid-1980s.

Nicaragua became a major focus of East-West and U.S.–Latin American tensions during the revolution. Although Nicaragua's neighbors expressed nervousness about the regime and at times cooperated with U.S. policy, Latin American powers generally opposed U.S. *intervention and sought to contain it through *diplomacy. Central American presidents negotiated a regional *peace process under which the contra war was ended and Nicaraguan domestic conflict reduced. The 1990 election—ob-

served by the UN, Organization of American States, and others at Nicaragua's behest—unexpectedly ended Sandinista rule and eased tensions among Nicaragua, its isthmian neighbors, and the United States.

(See also GUERRILLA WARFARE; LAND REFORM; LIBERATION THEOLOGY; REFORM; RELIGION AND POLITICS; U.S.–LATIN AMERICAN RELATIONS.)

Thomas W. Walker, *Nicaragua: Land of Sandino* (Boulder, Colo., 1981). John A. Booth, *The End and the Beginning: The Nicaraguan Revolution* (Boulder, Colo., 1985). Thomas W. Walker, ed., *Reagan Versus the Sandinistas: The Undeclared War* (Boulder, Colo., 1987).

JOHN A. BOOTH

NICARAGUAN REVOLUTION. On 19 July 1979, a coalition led by the Frente Sandinista de Liberación Nacional (FSLN) overthrew Anastasio Somoza Debayle and began an eleven-year revolution. The *revolution's *ideology and foreign alignments angered the Reagan and Bush administrations, which funded and guided *contra rebels in a militarily fruitless counterrevolutionary war against the *Sandinistas. The 1990 election ended both revolution and contra war when the FSLN relinquished power. The Sandinistas had greatly increased popular education and political mobilization and forged new political forces, but left the economy badly eroded. The revolution and contra *war increased inter-American tensions and inspired among Latin American nations a collective struggle to curtail U.S. intervention.

Opposition to the Somoza dynasty—Anastasio Somoza García (1936–1956), and his sons Luis (1956–1967) and Anastasio Somoza Debayle (1967–1979)—inspired the insurrection and revolution. Using the Partido Liberal Nacionalista and National Guard to rule, the Somozas aggressively promoted economic *development in *Nicaragua, forged shifting alliances (with conservatives, labor, and major capitalist sectors), and cultivated U.S. support. Growing corruption and repression in the 1970s, however, alienated most regime allies and spawned new opposition. Greatly expanded export agriculture and industrialization after 1950 benefited mainly the Somozas while increasing poverty and unemployment and eroding working-class and middle-class living standards; these trends were aggravated by Managua's 1972 earthquake and 1970s oil price rises. In the 1970s, the regime violently repressed labor, religious, and opposition party protests, leading its opponents to ally with the once-tiny FSLN, which, with broad popular support, militarily defeated the National Guard. *Human rights abuses led to the withdrawal of U.S. support in 1977 and to opposition to Somoza by other Latin American governments.

The Marxist-Leninist nine-member FSLN National Directorate directed revolutionary policy. A coalition junta ruled until the 1984 election, which installed President Daniel Ortega Saavedra (1985–90) and a National Assembly. A new constitution was adopted in 1987. Revolutionary policy sought to promote improved popular wages and human rights performance, agrarian reform, increased literacy, education, and popular health care, public ownership of almost half of the means of production (including the Somozas' vast holdings), foreign nonalignment, and solidarity with other Central American rebels. The FSLN drew support from among landless peasants, organized labor, high school and university students, the urban middle class including professionals and public employees, some sectors of the Catholic church, and several political parties.

The contra war led to heavy military mobilization for *counterinsurgency (with Soviet and Cuban support) that required an unpopular military draft. The war and a U.S. economic embargo badly undermined economic performance, public investment, and social programs, and brought increased political repression in the middle and late 1980s. Growing internal opposition by various political parties, families of draft-age youth, peasants, the private sector, and the Catholic hierarchy gradually undercut the FSLN's widespread support. The twenty-party Unión Nacional Opositora (UNO) coalition headed by Violeta Barrios de Chamorro defeated the FSLN in the February 1990 election. The FSLN survived electoral defeat as the strongest single party and kept great influence in organized labor and the armed forces, thus remaining a major force in postrevolutionary politics.

(See also GUERRILLA WARFARE; U.S.–LATIN AMERICAN RELATIONS.)

John A. Booth, *The End and the Beginning: The Nicaraguan Revolution* (Boulder, Colo., 1985). Donald C. Hodges, *Intellectual Foundations of the Nicaraguan Revolution* (Austin, Tex., 1986).

JOHN A. BOOTH

NIGER. With a population of more than 7 million and a land area of 1.27 million square kilometers (489,200 sq. mi.), Niger is the largest country in West Africa but one of the least densely populated. Poor resources, unstable and declining prices for exports, and severe periodic drought stand in the way of economic prosperity and provide the backdrop for developments in post-independence politics. Two-thirds of Niger consists of desert. Only three percent of the country is under cultivation, nearly all of it in the south. Since the 1970s, uranium has constituted the main source of foreign exchange. However, fluctuating prices have hampered government efforts to combat desertification, improve cereals storage and irrigated agriculture, restock herds, maintain public expenditures, pay civil servants, and repay debts.

The themes dominating domestic politics since independence include the monopoly of political power by a few individuals, corruption, a military reluctant to return to the barracks, ethnic tensions between the politically dominant Djerma and the numerically dominant Hausa, disaffection among the Tuareg, periodic but repressed student and worker opposition, and ambivalence over continuing French influence. However, *Islam, practiced by more than eighty-five percent of the population, is an important force in unifying Nigeriens. It sets the moral tone in public life and links the country, economically and politically, to powerful countries in the Islamic world.

Independence came in 1960 with the territorial head of the French-aligned Rassemblement Démocratique Africain, Hamani Diori, assuming the presidency. Assisted by a small council of ministers, Diori maintained tight control over a de facto one-party state until he was overthrown in a military coup in 1974. The coup occurred at the end of a severe drought that had begun in 1968 and had affected the entire Sahelian region. The loss of human life, livestock, pasture, and way of life, particularly among the Tuareg, was accompanied by charges (later proven true) that government officials hoarded food aid and sold it for profit.

The 1974 military takeover also coincided with the start-up of Niger's uranium export sector. The space created by the change of regime and improved economic conditions made possible a tentative political opening in the form of the 1978 appointment of a provisional parliament and constituent assembly, the release of several political detainees in 1980 and 1984, the gradual introduction of civilians into the cabinet, and the adoption by national plebiscite in 1987 of a national charter or provisional constitution for a second republic. Control of the ruling military committee, however, remained in the hands of a few individuals, and disaffection, including within its own ranks, was dealt with harshly. Unhappy with the government's response to the drought situation, a number of Tuareg dissidents accepted assistance from *Libya. The resulting tensions strained relations between the two countries and produced government reprisals against the Tuareg.

Political reform accelerated in the late 1980s and early 1990s, following a change at the top brought on by the sudden death of the leader of the 1974 coup. Nevertheless, old patterns of authoritarian and *elite rule persisted. Several categories of political prisoners were released, a general amnesty for exiles declared, and the hated political police dismantled. Political parties were unbanned in 1988, but the ruling military committee quickly established a single party that proclaimed its own compatibility with the "pluralistic expression of opinions and ideologies" within the country. The military committee was replaced by a twenty-two member civilian-dominated cabinet, but this new executive remained under the firm control of top military officers. In September 1989, Nigeriens approved a new constitution; in December of the same year the head of the former CMS was elected to a seven-year presidential term. Ninety-three deputies (including five women) were elected to a legislative assembly, ushering in Niger's second republic.

Formal liberalization was paralleled by increased informal dialogue and consultation with students, workers, and other sources of opposition. However, repression against Tuareg dissidents persisted (including military action, *torture, and deaths), and low uranium prices led to more forceful government intervention, with uranium and other workers suffering from reduced wages and employment, civil servants fearful of expenditure cuts, and students afraid of worsening living conditions on campus and bleak prospects for employment in the state sector. Many feel the political opening in Niger is still too narrow and leaves power concentrated in only a few hands.

(See also FRANCOPHONE AFRICA; SAHEL.)

BEVERLY GRIER

NIGERIA. With an estimated population of 105 million in 1990, Nigeria, which is on the west coast of Africa, is by far the most populous country in Africa. Approximately one of every four Africans is a Nigerian. It is a country of immense variety; its geographical zones range from tropical rain forest in the south to arid zones in the north, which is at the periphery of the Sahara. Over 250 languages are spoken by the numerous peoples and nationalities of which the largest are the Hausa in the north, the Yoruba in the west, and the Igbo in the east.

Nigeria's history as an independent nation-state began on 1 October 1960 when it gained political independence from Britain. It has been a rather eventful and troubled history of intense political competition, military coups, governmental instability, and a long, costly civil war. Nigeria has had eight governments, two civilian and six military, with an average tenure of only three years and nine months.

This history has to a considerable extent been shaped by its colonial legacy. The colonial state which Nigeria inherited at independence controlled the economy and was all-powerful; there was hardly an effective institutional check on its power. For the most part, the Nigerian political elite was divided along nationality lines, as was the political organization of Nigeria. The colonial policies of indirect rule and the tactics employed by the colonial government to weaken and split the nationalist movement had encouraged the regionalization of the political elite and the politicization of national and ethnic particularism. Thus the three political parties with which Nigeria came to independence were regional and nationality based: the Northern Peoples Congress (NPC) was the base of support of the Hausa in the north, the Action Group was based on the Yoruba in the west, and the National Council of Nigeria and the Cameroons (NCNC) based on the Igbo in the east. Once the political organizations

were instituted in this way, the dynamics of the struggle for power reproduced ethnic politics to the detriment of democratic political stability. Kinship and nationality groups are exclusive groups, and when politics is based on them, membership in political organizations is essentially exclusive, political differences become absolutized, and politics becomes a zero-sum game contested with passion.

It is not surprising that within two years of independence Nigeria was in deep political crisis. The immediate cause of the crisis was the controversy over the results of the national census of 1962. The results were keenly contested because of their potential effects on the balance of power between the major nationalities. Every attempt to reach a consensus failed. In 1963 another census was conducted with even more controversy. Amid the controversy, Nigeria went into a national election on 11 January 1965. The election ended in a constitutional crisis and extensive civil disorder, in the course of which the military took over power on 19 January 1966. Unfortunately, this only made matters worse because the coup makers, identified mainly as Igbo, were accused of killing mainly northern political leaders. A northern-led coup took place. In the wake of the coup Igbo resident in the north were attacked; many died, and the rest fled and decided to fight for secession. In July 1967 civil war broke out between *Biafra (the new name of the eastern region) and the federal government. The civil war raged until 13 January 1970. Military rule continued until 1979 when the second republic came into being after a fairly orderly military-supervised national election.

The constitution which was promulgated on 21 September 1978 tried to address the problem of political conflict and instability. It moved Nigeria from a parliamentary to a presidential system with considerable concentration of power on the presidency. The change in political system was designed to complement attempts already made to reduce the pressure on the center and to encourage pluralism by moving from three regions to a system of states. On 27 May 1967 Nigeria was divided into twelve states. The number of states was further increased to nineteen in April 1976. Changes in the constitutional framework improved the resiliency of the political system.

The problem of political stability in Nigeria seemed to worsen with the rising economic fortunes of Nigeria as a major producer of petroleum. Unfortunately the fragmentary political class failed to heed the lessons of the civil war and to capitalize on the opportunities of the oil boom. Rather its members competed even more recklessly for power, their appetites whetted by the large surplus from oil. The wealth was largely squandered as corruption rose to new heights in an orgy of conspicuous consumption. In 1973 at the peak of the oil boom Nigeria's imports increased sixfold from US$1.89 billion to $10.95 billion. Between 1975 and 1977 imports grew at the rate of sixty-five percent per annum while exports grew at seventeen percent; Nigeria moved rapidly from surplus to deficit and debt. By 1982, the deficit on current account was already $2.25 billion. By 1983 it had risen to the point where there were widespread shortages as Nigeria braced for a structural adjustment program. The civilian government was totally discredited and once again the military took over. In July 1992, Nigerians elected a new National Assembly, in which the Social Democratic Party (SDP) achieved majorities in both the Senate and House of Representatives, defeating the rival National Republican Convention (NRC). Nevertheless, with the powers of the National Assembly unclear, the military is expected to remain in power through 1992.

Nigeria has been under military rule for twenty of its thirty years of independence. The military has become one of Nigeria's problems rather than its solution as all the contradictions of Nigerian politics have penetrated and captured the military. It is now permeated by ethnic, religious, and regional conflicts and factionalization. The struggle for power has been transformed into a struggle for the capture of the military and, by extension, of state power. This has been manifest in a chain of coups and counter-coups. The Nigerian military is apparently no longer effective either as a military force or as a government, having been discredited as much as the civilian regimes.

On the surface, it appears that Nigeria's problem is governmental instability associated with ethnic parochialism. However, this is misleading. The governments in office have changed often, but the ruling class in power has not changed. The problem is that this class is not disciplined; it is factional and unable to instill a sense of national purpose. It is absorbed in the struggle for power and accumulation of wealth. It exploits regional and ethnic differences as a strategy of power to gain legitimacy, to reconnect itself with the masses and mask the class division of society.

It is not surprising that Nigeria has been unable to realize its potentialities as an African power despite its numerous natural resource endowments, considerable human capital, and large domestic market. It has been too unstable to play the important role that Africa and the world expect of the "giant of Africa."

In its region of immediate influence, West Africa, Nigeria's best achievement is that it has remained at peace with its neighbors and has not tried to use its power to dominate them. Nigeria along with *Togo spearheaded the formation of the Economic Community of West African States (ECOWAS) in 1975. It has put a lot of money into ECOWAS but little heart. Nigeria has violated the ECOWAS Protocols by expelling economic refugees from other West African countries in its own territory.

On the broader African field, Nigeria played a prominent role in the formation of the *Organization of African Unity (OAU) in 1963. It gave considerable financial support to the liberation movements in Angola, Mozambique, Zimbabwe, Namibia, and South Africa. But its support was restrained and ambiguous because of the conservative character of the Nigerian political class. Nigeria will not be able to play the important role expected of it until it makes significant progress toward resolving its considerable internal problems.

(See also AFRICAN REGIONAL ORGANIZATIONS; ETHNICITY; MILITARISM; MILITARY RULE.)

CLAUDE AKE

NINETEEN EIGHTY-NINE. As the year began in January 1989, the general consensus in the West was that *communism would maintain its hold over Eastern and *Central Europe and the Soviet Union well into the twenty-first century. Perhaps the most prominent proponent of this analysis was the former U.S. Ambassador to the United Nations Jeane Kirkpatrick, who advanced the thesis that communist societies were immune to change from within because of their rulers' success in atomizing citizens from one another. In the view of Kirkpatrick and her cothinkers, authoritarian societies such as *Pinochet's Chile could be transformed because they allowed room for action independent of the *state, but such autonomous activity was virtually impossible under totalitarian communism.

Yet by December 1989, Poland had held partially free elections in June in which the *Solidarity opposition won all but one of the contested seats; Hungary's communist leaders had conceded the right to completely free elections, which would take place in March of the following year; and the hard-line rulers of Czechoslovakia had resigned, with the Communist Party pledging to give up its monopoly on political power. The breathtaking changes of 1989 were symbolized by the fact that the Czech former dissident Václav *Havel, imprisoned for nine years under the old regime, became Czechoslovakia's new president.

Collapse was contagious: demonstrations in the German Democratic Republic (GDR, or East Germany), which had begun in the fall of 1989, grew larger and larger, while tens of thousands of East Germans poured out of the GDR, allowed in September by the still-communist Hungarian government to escape through their country. Budapest's willingness to grant passage to fleeing East Germans marked the end of the perverse solidarity of the East-bloc communist leaders, who had for decades helped keep their shared social system in place by forcing each other's citizens to return to their native countries if they were caught trying to leave. On 7 November, the infamous Berlin Wall separating East and West Germany fell, as GDR leaders tried desperately to conciliate their restive population with the concession of freedom to travel to the West. But to no avail—the days of communist leaders in East Germany were clearly numbered, though their final ouster did not take place until the following year. Finally, as 1989 drew to a close, Romania's Nicolae Ceauşescu, the most repressive of East European communist leaders, was overthrown in December.

In October 1989 Soviet foreign minister Eduard Shevardnadze had announced the Soviet Union's new policy of nonintervention in Eastern Europe, the so-called "Sinatra doctrine" (taken from the lyrics, "I did it my way," of a Frank Sinatra song). While at first it was unclear whether the Soviets meant what they said, it soon became apparent that they were serious, which effectively pulled the rug out from under the East German regime of Erich Honecker and Miloš Jakeš's Czechoslovak communist government.

The precise Soviet motives for adopting this new hands-off policy are still unknown. However, it is highly unlikely that Mikhail *Gorbachev and other leaders of the Soviet Union believed that they were setting in motion a process that would culminate in the collapse of communist leaderships throughout Eastern Europe, not only in the countries mentioned above, but within months in Albania and Bulgaria as well. It is even more unlikely that Soviet leaders deliberately set about to depose the Communist Party leadership of the Soviet Union itself.

Gorbachev's decision not to intervene in Eastern Europe was no doubt motivated by the hope that conservative, old-line leaderships would be replaced by communist reformers who could act flexibly enough to keep the system intact. Likewise, he probably hoped that within the Soviet Union a modernized and liberalized communist system could survive. Yet by August 1991, with the failure of the hard-line coup attempt in Moscow, the communist system was finished—at least in the countries of the old Soviet bloc—and the regimes of Cuba and China, while still in place two years later, seemed profoundly, possibly fatally, shaken by the events of 1989.

After the Euphoria. The collapse of communism in Central and Eastern Europe and the Soviet Union was greeted with euphoria by millions around the world. But by 1992, the elation had largely dissipated. The former Soviet Union was in chaos, and the new democracies of Eastern Europe were facing massive popular discontent. This discontent only sporadically manifested itself in the form of demonstrations or strikes; however, voter participation was often only fifty percent or less, and xenophobic and authoritarian appeals were finding increasing popular resonance. *Democracy was appearing more and more fragile throughout the former communist world.

The sources of discontent were both economic and political. People had hoped that the end of the old system would bring relief from the economic crisis of the communist system, which had been unable to deliver consumer goods at anything comparable to Western levels. Moreover, the vast majority of people had hoped not only for political liberties but also to be rid of the entrenched communist *elites. But the new postcommunist leaders adopted radical "free-market" programs, which meant "shock therapy" austerity measures for the bulk of the population in the old Soviet bloc. At the same time, the old communist privileged class, the so-called nomenklatura, often managed to retain its preogatives—either by holding on to its previous ministerial or management positions, or by manipulating the *privatization process so that they themselves became the new owners of property. This process was so typical that it became known widely as "spontaneous privatization" or "nomenklatura embourgeoisement."

For the most part, Western analysts believe that shock therapy is a necessary if painful requirement for destroying the old communist system, while Western-led international financial institutions such as the *International Monetary Fund (IMF) and the *World Bank have made the adoption of rapid privatization and radical austerity measures a precondition for Western aid, debt forgiveness, or debt rescheduling. This Western stance has reinforced the conviction of most of the first wave of postcommunist leaders of Central and Eastern Europe and the Soviet Union that state intervention in the economy is harmful, and that state ownership of enterprises is intrinsically inefficient.

Unfortunately, the social cost of the transformation process has been extremely high. In 1992 unemployment soared to thirteen percent in Poland and over thirty percent in the former East Germany; the threat of similar or even higher unemployment levels loomed over the whole region. Meanwhile, the cost of energy and consumer goods rapidly increased as postcommunist governments in Eastern Europe and the former Soviet Union freed prices, slashed subsidies, and held down wage levels. To make matters worse, domestic industry was severely weakened by the rush of Western imports that followed the abolition of import controls; meanwhile, in an effort to protect farmers and industries at home, Western governments maintained high levels of *protection against lower-priced goods from the East. The recessionary trends in the global economy of the early 1990s only served to exacerbate the predicament of countries emerging from communism.

Overt *nationalism has been on the rise throughout the region since the changes of 1989. In part this was inevitable, given the pent-up popular resentment against the artificial multinationalism of many of the communist states. Far from eradicating traditional national feelings, the domination by the "center" in countries like communist Yugoslavia or the former Soviet Union added new dimensions to old animosities. Moreover, the harsh economic and social conditions that followed the revolutions of 1989–90 intensified the inevitable conflicts.

The social frustrations that mounted in the aftermath of 1989 also encouraged a witch-hunting atmosphere toward any individuals suspected of responsibility for the oppression of the communist years. Economic and social insecurity fostered widespread popular resentment as people searched for scapegoats to explain their hardships. Moreover, many members of the old elite had been allowed to slip comfortably into positions of power and privilege under the new order. One reason the new leaders permitted this to happen was because they felt they needed the expertise of these old figures; another reason was that they desperately hoped to avoid risking the open social conflict that they feared would accompany a strong challenge to the prerogatives of the communist elite.

However, a high price had to be paid for routinely granting the old figures of power new positions of authority. *Human rights groups like the U.S.-based Helsinki Watch, which had played a critical role in monitoring human rights violations of communist regimes, expressed growing concern in the 1990s about such postcommunist practices as the uncritical use of old police files to determine if individuals in Central and Eastern Europe had been guilty of collaborating with the secret police, with no opportunity for accused individuals to challenge the contents or confront their accusers. Yet much of the population, exasperated by the growth of stark new inequalities and by the fact that communist bureaucrats were rising to the top regardless of their past roles, had little patience with civil libertarians who called for due process in deciding the culpability of former communists. As a consequence, there is a very real danger of a new *McCarthyism emerging out of this situation.

The Future of Postcommunist Societies. Democracy is fragile throughout Central and Eastern Europe and the former Soviet Union. In part this is because of the weakness of civic opposition movements in the communist years. Those who contended that communism was impervious to change from below because of its success in preventing the emergence of democratic movements overstated their case—witness the Hungarian Revolution of 1956, Czechoslovakia's 1968 *Prague Spring, the courageous Soviet dissidents, the Polish Solidarity movement of the 1980s, and the dramatic events of 1989.

Yet it was difficult to organize popular movements under communism, especially movements with any longevity and social depth. When the collapse of 1989 came, therefore, in most instances much of the population was newly involved in public life, with very little experience in democratic debate or participation. This legacy of the past contributed to the difficulty of building viable democratic institutions in Central and Eastern Europe and the former Soviet Union after the fall of communism.

The democratic initiatives that blossomed throughout the region in 1989–90 were an important, albeit frail, source of future civic vitality. If the West can be both generous and flexible toward Central and Eastern Europe and the former Soviet Union, if it can encourage an experimental and socially sensitive approach to building postcommunist society, it can help foster the economic conditions under which these tender initiatives can survive and flourish.

(See also COMMAND ECONOMY; COMMONWEALTH OF INDEPENDENT STATES; COMMUNIST PARTY STATES; DEMOCRATIC TRANSITIONS; PERESTROIKA; SOVIET DISSENT.)

Timothy Garton Ash, *The Uses of Adversity* (New York, 1989). Joanne Landy, "Politics and the Economy: What's to Come in the USSR?" *Social Policy* 22, no. 2 (Fall 1991): 17–31. Ivo Banac, *Eastern Europe in Revolution* (Ithaca, N.Y., 1992). John Feffer, *Shock Waves: Eastern Europe After the Revolutions* (Boston, 1992).

JOANNE LANDY

NIXON, Richard Milhous. The thirty-seventh president of the United States, Richard Milhous Nixon (b. 1913) remains the most durable yet polarizing American political figure of the second half of the twentieth century. He helped to launch the *Cold War that he also helped to end. He typified the McCarthy era that he also helped restrain. The man whose early career gave him the nickname "Tricky" eludes a final judgment.

Born of Ulster-Irish parents who had become Quakers, he grew up in Southern California, where his family had an adequate income, for which it nonetheless did conscious scrambling. In the town and at the college named after the Quaker poet John Greenleaf Whittier, Nixon was an industrious and successful student, debater, and amateur actor. He studied law at Duke University (1934–1937) on a scholarship; applied, unsuccessfully, for employment with the Federal Bureau of Investigation; and entered a law firm back in Whittier. In 1942, Nixon joined the war effort as a Washington bureaucrat (in the Office of Emergency Management). But after six months at this job he volunteered for the navy, which sent him to the South Pacific as a supply officer.

The year he was mustered out of the navy (1946), he ran the first of two vitriolic campaigns in California that established his reputation as a man always on the attack. In 1946, he defeated a popular incumbent, Jerry Voorhis, in a contest for the U.S. House of Representatives. The campaign was among the first to make an opponent's relation to communism the issue—Nixon alleged that Voorhis had ties with a Communist-influenced union (the CIO).

After an unchallenged reelection to his House seat in 1948, Nixon waged another ferocious campaign, this time against Helen Gahagan Douglas for the Senate, helping further to define Cold War electioneering (his campaign literature called Douglas a "pink lady," the name of a faddish cocktail). During his second term in the House, Nixon had been the most active member of the Committee on Un-American Activities in the investigation of Alger Hiss on a charge of espionage. Earlier in 1950, Hiss was convicted of perjury in his answers to that charge. This sent Nixon into the election year as the hero of anti-Communists; but he already was, and would forever be, a villain for those who believed that Hiss had been destroyed by the falsehoods of his accuser, Whittaker Chambers.

The year of the Hiss conviction and the Helen Douglas campaign was also the year when Senator Joseph McCarthy of Wisconsin began his melodramatic denunication of Communists in government. By 1952, Dwight *Eisenhower chose the young Senator Nixon as his running mate, hoping to bring Taft Republicans of the Right into alliance with the Eastern branch of the party led by Eisenhower's promoter, Thomas Dewey. Nixon was expected to address the concerns and control the excesses of the McCarthyites.

During the campaign, however, allegations about a "secret" Nixon campaign fund (an essentially innocent arrangement) made the Eisenhower team consider dropping him from the ticket. In a desperate bid to be retained, Nixon went on national television to make an emotional revelation of his financial status. The speech is called "the Checkers speech" after the dog he itemized among his belongings. The reaction to this speech forced Eisenhower reluctantly to embrace a man he still distrusted. In the self-abasements of the Checkers broadcast, Nixon revealed a knack for prevailing by being violated. As one of the world's aggrieved, he would know how to mobilize resentments.

As vice president, Nixon was more active than his predecessors in that office—discreetly so after Eisenhower's heart attack and later stroke. In his travels, Nixon was vilified by mobs in Latin America and by Nikita *Khrushchev in Moscow—to his political betterment at home. Nixon lost the presidency in 1960 by the closest margin in the history of presidential elections. Popular myth ascribes his loss to a poor showing in the first televised debate with his opponent, John F. *Kennedy. But Nixon blamed his loss on Eisenhower's unwillingness to manipulate the economy at election time—a mistake Nixon would not repeat in 1972.

Sent back to California by his defeat, Nixon ran a halfhearted and feckless race for governor, and gave a bitter "last press conference" after the loss that seemed to end his political career. His leaving California, his political base, to practice corporate law in New York seemed to confirm his demise. Yet, by an extraordinary political resurrection, Nixon forged a role for himself as party veteran, campaign adviser, and fund-raiser. He stayed loyal to the party during its disastrous defeat under Barry Goldwater in 1964, winning back conservatives who had grown cool to him during his service under Eisenhower (and who were looking with admiration to a new conservative star, Ronald *Reagan).

Nixon began his effort toward the 1968 Republican nomination as an apparent underdog to Michigan governor George Romney; but he defeated Romney, and fended off a last-minute bid by Reagan, to lead the Republican Party against an incumbent vice president (Hubert Humphrey) who was even more crippled by dependence on his own president, Lyndon *Johnson, than Nixon had been in 1960.

By choosing the aggressive Spiro T. Agnew as his running mate, Nixon kept many conservatives from drifting toward the third-party candidacy of Governor George Wallace of Alabama. Although Nixon beat Humphrey only by a plurality (43.4 percent to Humphrey's 42.7), the combined vote for Nixon-Agnew and for Wallace and his running mate, Air Force General Curtis LeMay, came to fifty-seven percent—a clear repudiation of the Johnson administration.

As president, Nixon was experimental in domestic affairs, although not insistent on the innovative programs he sponsored (e.g., the Family Assistance Plan). Yet Nixon's interest in domestic programs was dutiful. His enthusiasm and best skills were reserved for foreign policy. With great ingenuity he maneuvered toward goals he was not previously suspected of (or credited with) cherishing—normalized ties with the People's Republic of China, the easing of tensions (*détente) with the Soviet Union, and *arms control agreements (SALT I signed, SALT II negotiated). He used unorthodox methods in working for these accomplishments—secrecy, "back channel" communications outside customary diplomatic conduits, and the practical displacement of his secretary of state (William Rogers) by an all-purpose personal emissary (National Security Council aide Henry *Kissinger).

A right-wing revolt against these moves was contained by Nixon's prolongation of the *Vietnam War. Many conservatives, angered by the "sellout" of Taiwan and the limitation of nuclear weapons, were unwilling to desert a president while the Left was demonstrating against him in the streets. Nixon tried to turn the war over to South Vietnamese forces ("Vietnamization"), but had to support those forces' faltering efforts with ancillary technological interventions—the secret bombings of Cambodia (1969), followed by an open "incursion" into Cambodia (1970), ever-heavier bombing of North Vietnam's cities, followed by the mining of Haiphong's harbor (1972). Working for a peace "with honor" (i.e., without open abandonment of South Vietnamese allies), in 1969 Nixon rejected terms little worse (and far better enforceable) than he had to settle for in 1973—after 20,000 more American deaths and proportionally graver casualties to both sides in

Vietnam itself. When the South Vietnamese regime fell after U.S. withdrawal, Nixon blamed that on congressional unwillingness to resume the bombing and negotiating cycles.

The great domestic priority for Nixon was his own reelection. Determined not to repeat Eisenhower's mistake of facing an election with poor inflation and employment figures, he timed the 1971 imposition of wage and price controls (an abomination in the eyes of his early supporters) to bring about a spurt of renewal in 1972. He even wanted to replace Spiro Agnew on his 1972 election ticket with the wage and price manager, Secretary of the Treasury John Connally. Taking no chances on the election, Nixon arranged for the political surveillance and covert activities that led to a break-in at Democratic headquarters in the *Watergate Hotel and to the chain of revelations and attempted cover-ups that resulted in his resignation after a landslide reelection in 1972.

Although ready to abandon ideological consistency himself, Nixon managed to heat the ideological temperature around him in ways that will confuse all judgments made on him into the foreseeable future. Those who had admired him were dismayed at his reversals on subjects like China, détente, and arms control. These things were, in turn, his finest achievements in the eyes of his natural opponents who could not, despite these good works, forgive him his years of red-baiting, his conduct of the Vietnam War, and his attempts at the suppression of dissent. He survived by keeping all sides off balance—which makes it hard for a consensus to be reached among people so often inspired and disgusted by his acts (often in swift succession). Yet, just as Nixon worked at his own political resurrection after the electoral defeats of 1960 and 1962, he has spent his years since resigning office in a strenuous and partly successful attempt to rehabilitate his reputation. Denied control over his own presidential papers after his attempt to alter and suppress the record during the Watergate crisis, he nonetheless raised the money to build his own library in Yorba Linda, California, to whose opening Presidents Ford, Reagan, and Bush came in a kind of ritual of Republican reinstatement. Nixon will, no doubt, be respected but not liked, in death as in life; but always he will fascinate.

(See also MCCARTHYISM; POLITICAL BUSINESS CYCLE; PRESIDENCY, U.S.; STRATEGIC ARMS LIMITATION TREATIES.)

Richard Nixon, *Six Crises* (Garden City, N.Y., 1962). Garry Wills, *Nixon Agonistes* (Boston, 1970). Richard Nixon, *RN: The Memoirs of Richard Nixon* (New York, 1978). Stephen E. Ambrose, *Nixon, Volume I: The Education of a Politician* (New York, 1987). Stephen E. Ambrose, *Nixon, Volume II: The Triumph of a Politician, 1962–1972* (New York, 1989). Herbert S. Parmet, *Richard Nixon and His America* (Boston, 1990).

GARRY WILLS

NKRUMAH, Kwame. In the course of a career that spanned four decades and that saw him assuming variously the roles of intellectual, anticolonial fighter, pan-Africanist, nationalist, socialist, diplomat, and prime minister and president of *Ghana, Kwame Nkrumah distinguished himself as one of the greatest leaders of the twentieth century.

The humble circumstances of his birth in 1909 in a Ghanaian village contributed to his acute consciousness of, and lifelong struggle against, colonialism and exploitation. He was educated in Ghana and the United States. While in the United States, he became involved in the fight for *African Americans and in Marcus Garvey's movement; he helped Paul Robeson, W. E. B. *Du Bois, and the Council on African Affairs to promote African decolonization and self-determination as well.

Moving to London in 1945, he became co-organizer of the Pan-African Congress of 1945, from where he helped plan the subsequent anticolonial nationalist struggles in Africa and elsewhere. Later, in 1958, as the head of newly independent Ghana and torchbearer of African emancipation, he organized two historic conferences: the Conference of Independent African Nations and an All-African People's Conference. Ghana under Nkrumah became the training ground for anticolonial struggle and African unity in accordance with his belief in the "oneness of Africans" and the "total liberation of the continent."

Ghana owes much of its significance to the force of Nkrumah's personality and intellect. Forming the largest mass organization in Ghana's history, the Convention People's Party (CPP), in 1949, he led Ghana to independence in 1957, opposed by the middle-class professionals and intelligentsia who felt he had usurped their right to succeed the colonialists.

In the first few years of Nkrumah's rule, Ghana was relatively prosperous mainly thanks to its healthy export earnings and to Nkrumah's decision to invest in the social and economic infrastructure of the country—education, industrial projects, health clinics, factories, and housing. Nkrumah's preoccupation with the "political kingdom," however, came at the expense of a full-fledged socioeconomic revolution: before long, the realities of managing a neocolonial entity took hold. The CPP became a shell of itself; state institutions—among them the army, police, and civil service—retained their colonial character; more important, the economic structures in place before independence remained intact.

Steering Ghana in these times proved difficult. Nkrumah's political opponents became bolder and stronger, twice attempting his assassination. He, in turn, became more repressive—detaining without trial, and eventually creating a one-party state. The once-representative CPP became a vehicle for crude wealth accumulation and repression. It constructed a personality cult around "the redeemer" and "the leader who never dies." Coupled with the perils of dealing in an increasingly hostile external economic environment, an impasse was inevitable. Even though the armed forces, with external help, overthrew his regime in February 1966, Nkrumah continued to cast a long shadow over Ghanaian politics until his death in 1972.

One of Nkrumah's legacies is as a theoretician of the African *revolution. In ten books and numerous pamphlets, he laid out the historical, philosophical, theoretical, analytical, and prescriptive foundations of the struggle for liberation in Africa. He concretized the notion of the triple heritage of modern Africa: traditional, Islamic, and European.

Ultimately, his most enduring legacy for Africa's future will be his exemplary life of commitment and struggle. He was a patriot grappling with questions of emancipation, dependence, neocolonialism, and the creation of a genuine social revolution. His life is instructive in the seeming contradictions between his words and deeds, as an avowed anticolonialist yet managing a neocolonial economy, and for his ideological shifts dictated by specific historical circumstances. Throughout his life, however, Kwame Nkrumah remained the truest servant of genuine African unity.

(See also AFRICAN SOCIALISM; DECOLONIZATION; NATIONALISM; PAN-AFRICANISM.)

George Padmore, *Pan-Africanism or Communism?* (London, 1955). Basil Davidson, *Black Star: A View of the Life and Times of Kwame Nkrumah* (London, 1973). Erica Powell, *Private Secretary (Female)/Gold Coast* (New York, 1984).

AKWASI P. OSEI

NONALIGNED MOVEMENT. The Nonaligned Movement (NAM) is an international social movement of small and middle-sized states drawn mostly from former colonies in the developing world. In the post–World War II era, new states in Asia, Africa, the Caribbean, Latin America, and Europe found it difficult to preserve their political independence and choose their own path of economic and social development as the United States and the Soviet Union began to militarize the globe to further their *Cold War. Leaders of twenty-five states gathered in Belgrade in 1961 to discuss economic concerns and seek an end to East-West tensions and the nuclear arms race. They formed the NAM as an international coalition of states with members supporting certain fundamental principles of nonalignment.

Nonalignment is an integral part of the foreign policy of NAM members. It includes a commitment to peace and disarmament, especially an end to the Cold War and dangerous *superpower rivalries in the post–Cold War order; political independence, notably the right of self-determination of all colonial peoples; racial and economic equality, particularly

through a restructuring of the existing international economic and political orders; cultural equality, including an end to Western cultural imperialism and a reorganization of the world information and communications system that supports the current Western monopoly; and multilateral decision making on global matters through strong support for the UN system. The NAM's primary purpose is to change the existing global system, which nonaligned countries find unequal and exploitative of the "South" to the benefit of the "North." In its anticolonial and anti-imperialist orientation, it seeks to create a more just, equitable, and peaceful world order.

Over three decades, the NAM has grown to 102 members and developed a flexible organizational structure; it meets from time to time in different regional settings and at the UN. It is a new type of political formation—an international, state-centered, nonhierarchical, dynamic coalition of different political, economic, social, and religious systems. Leadership and meeting places are rotated and decisions are made by consensus. Along with ministerial meetings and special issue gatherings, there are summit meetings of heads of state at which major nonaligned policy statements are prepared for action within the UN system.

Each summit meeting has both responded to current international crises and addressed long-standing issues requiring change. For example, the 1961 Belgrade summit sought ways to prevent any potential nuclear holocaust that could result from heightened East-West tensions. Support for *decolonization and *national liberation movements were the focus of the second and third summits, in Cairo (1964) and Lusaka (1970). The 1973 Algiers summit, with its call for a *New International Economic Order, was a watershed—global economic disparities and underdevelopment, in the NAM analysis, were inextricably bound to the arms race.

The NAM became institutionalized as its membership grew extensively at the fifth, sixth, and seventh summits, in Colombo (1976), Havana (1979), and New Delhi (1983). During this period, its support for decolonization contributed to the emergence of many new African and Caribbean states choosing nonaligned status. This was also a period of destabilization of NAM. As the movement met more frequently to confront the economic pressures and regional conflicts throughout the *Third World, it had to contend with efforts by the West to thwart nonaligned activities through military *interventions and withdrawal of economic assistance.

At the eighth summit, in Harare (1986), the NAM called for the self-determination of *Southern Africa, especially the independence of *Namibia, the end of *apartheid, and the right of peoples in the region to choose a destiny outside of the East-West framework. At the ninth summit, in Belgrade (1989), nonaligned countries began to examine the global consequences of the dismantling of the Cold War system and the implications for regional conflicts.

Since its inception, the NAM has accomplished many of its objectives and continues to seek meaningful resolutions to international issues through the UN system. It contributed to the end of the Cold War through its continuous efforts to draw attention to the futility of the arms race and the relationship between disarmament and development. It initiated the UN Disarmament Conferences, supported the North-South dialogues, and devised action programs for a New International Economic Order. The NAM also pursued a UN settlement concerning the independence of Namibia, which has now been achieved. Similarly, the NAM has long sought a resolution to Middle East tensions that would include the recognition of the rights of the Palestinian people. Other activities have included such concerns as the return of cultural artifacts to their countries of origin, formation of a new international information order, support for the UN Decade for Women, protection of the global environment, and much more.

Facing the demise of the Cold War and the dissolution of the Soviet Union, the NAM will have to respond to a new world situation. First, the end of superpower rivalries calls for a reexamination of regional conflicts involving nonaligned countries and improves the prospect for each to be treated as a discrete problem. Second, military reductions resulting from the end of the Cold War will bring about fundamental economic changes. In particular, the North-South maldistribution of control of resources and pricing, as well as the production of goods and services, will require restructuring. Third, the NAM considers the destruction of the environment a global concern.

All these developments lead to a new theory of violence between states. Conflict resolution in the post-Soviet era shifts from an East-West to a North-South focus, where an unequal sharing of resources and power among states and regions persists. The NAM continues to approach global decision making through the UN and seeks a greater role for all small and middle-sized states in defining the world situation. Its principles and practices contribute to a new theory of *international relations.

(See also GROUP OF 77; INTERNATIONAL SYSTEMS.)

A. W. Singham and Shirley Hune, *Namibian Independence: A Global Responsibility* (Westport, Conn., 1985). A. W. Singham and Shirley Hune, *Non-alignment in an Age of Alignments* (London and Westport, Conn., 1986).

SHIRLEY HUNE
A. W. SINGHAM

NONPROLIFERATION, NUCLEAR. Since the 1940s, there has been concern that countries would acquire *nuclear weapons as soon as they were technologically capable of doing so. The first two decades of the nuclear age seemed to confirm this

fear. The United States, with assistance from foreign scientists, dropped atomic bombs on *Hiroshima and Nagasaki in August 1945; the Soviet Union in 1949 and Britain in 1952 successfully tested their own nuclear weapons. France became a nuclear power in 1960, and China followed suit four years later.

Yet, since India's self-proclaimed "peaceful nuclear explosion" in 1974, no non-nuclear weapons state (NNWS) has formally joined the "nuclear club" by testing a nuclear device. The major reason for this is the strength of the international nonproliferation *regime that has developed since the 1950s. This regime includes a number of legal arrangements between and among nuclear and non-nuclear weapons states. The 1968 Non-Proliferation Treaty (NPT) is widely viewed as the centerpiece of the regime. Under the NPT, which has over 140 members, NNWSs promise to refrain from acquiring nuclear arms in return for full access to nuclear technology for peaceful purposes and a reduction in the nuclear arsenals of the nuclear weapons states. The treaty thus attempts to codify the somewhat artificial distinction between peaceful and military uses of nuclear technology. In 1995, its members will determine whether the NPT should continue in force indefinitely or for a fixed time.

Other important pillars of the regime are atomic energy organizations and agreements that make it difficult for states to misappropriate nuclear technology: the Vienna-based International Atomic Energy Agency, which applies safeguard mechanisms to nuclear activities; the 1963 Partial Test Ban Treaty, which prohibits member states from testing nuclear devices in the atmosphere, in outer space, and underwater; the 1967 Treaty of Tlatelolco, which makes much of Latin America a nuclear-weapons-free zone; and the Nuclear Suppliers Group, a collection of fifteen countries that have agreed informally not to transfer particularly sensitive nuclear technology to NNWSs.

An additional element of the nonproliferation regime, the influence of which is less easy to assess, is world public opinion against nuclear weapons acquisition and use. Further, many countries have realized that a nuclear arsenal may be detrimental to their domestic policy objectives by requiring the diversion of scarce economic and scientific resources; *foreign policy objectives may be harmed as well by aggravating relations with neighbors, allies, and adversaries.

Not all countries have accepted the underlying premise of the nonproliferation regime, namely, that the spread of nuclear weapons would be destabilizing to regional and international *security. Rather, some countries regard these weapons as a prized scientific and engineering accomplishment, evidence of *modernity, a source of political influence, and the most potent symbol of military might. Israel, India, and Pakistan are strongly suspected of possessing nuclear arms. Iran, Iraq, and the Democratic People's Republic of Korea (North Korea) are thought to harbor nuclear aspirations. These countries have used nuclear technology allegedly acquired for peaceful purposes to improve their capability to build nuclear weapons. Their continuing, determined efforts to enhance their nuclear competence threaten the viability of the nonproliferation regime.

A new challenge to this regime is the expanded ease with which countries can obtain the technical knowledge and engineering skill to assemble nuclear weapons. Nuclear weapons acquisition has always been a function of both this technological expertise and political willpower. For the foreseeable future, then, political willpower will be the conclusive determinant for countries contemplating a nuclear weapons capability.

The tension between the constraints imposed by the nonproliferation regime and the nuclear ambitions of certain countries has produced three results. First, a few countries have found it more advantageous to acquire a "nuclear option" than to proceed further to testing and open deployment of a nuclear arsenal. Under this option, a country may surreptitiously develop the competence to construct nuclear weapons within months, weeks, or days, or even possess a clandestine nuclear arsenal. It has been thought that possession of a covert nuclear weapons capability will allow a country to receive the security benefits of a declared nuclear weapons capability without the attendant liabilities, such as provoking adversaries into acquiring a similar capability or impairing relations with key allies. In fact, however, because of the virtual impossibility of a country masking its nuclear intentions, these liabilities may outweigh the perceived benefits of the nuclear option.

Second, nonproliferation experts today have more sophisticated understanding of the spread of nuclear weapons than before. The path to nuclear weapons acquisition is now viewed as a series of discrete technological hurdles and political decisions, each of which must be addressed for a country to become a nuclear weapons state.

Finally, as countries have learned that nuclear weapons acquisition is much more problematic than originally anticipated, they have sought other, more easily obtainable lethal technologies, such as cruise and ballistic missiles and chemical and biological weapons. In the near term, threats to regional and international stability are more likely to come from the spread of these weapons than from the proliferation of nuclear weapons.

(See also ARMS CONTROL; STRATEGIC ARMS LIMITATION TREATIES.)

Mitchell Reiss, *Without the Bomb: The Politics of Nuclear Nonproliferation* (New York, 1988). Leonard S. Spector, *Nuclear Threshold: The Spread of Nuclear Weapons, 1991–92* (Boulder, Colo., 1991).

MITCHELL REISS

NONVIOLENT ACTION. A general technique of sociopolitical action applied by people and institutions through the use of symbolic protest, noncooperation, and nonviolent intervention, nonviolent action may also be called "nonviolent struggle" or "nonviolent sanctions." Since the 1986 struggle against the *Marcos dictatorship in the Philippines, this technique is frequently called "people power."

Role of Power. Nonviolent action is an application of a very simple truth: people do not always do what they are told to do, and sometimes they do that which has been forbidden. This technique is thus rooted more in human stubbornness than in a belief in turning the other cheek. When people refuse their cooperation, withhold their help, and persist in their disobedience and defiance, they are denying their opponents the basic human assistance and cooperation which any government or hierarchical system requires. If they do this collectively through their established independent social institutions or newly improvised groupings for a sufficient period of time, the power of that government or hierarchical system will weaken and potentially dissolve. The basic political principle underlying nonviolent action is that hierarchical systems and all governments, including dictatorships, are able to function only to the degree that they receive the submission and cooperation of the people and institutions within them—whether that assistance is freely given or induced by fear.

A Technique of Conflict. Nonviolent action is a way to conduct conflict. It is a response to the problem of how to act effectively in politics, especially how to wield *power. In this technique, however, people and institutions apply societal pressures other than physical violence. Nonviolent action may involve: 1) acts of omission—that is, people may refuse to perform acts which they usually perform, are expected by custom to perform, or are required by law to perform; 2) acts of commission—that is, people may perform acts which they do not usually perform, are not expected by custom to perform, or are forbidden to perform; or 3) a combination of acts of omission and commission.

Methods of Struggle. Three broad classes of methods are included in the technique. 1) Where the nonviolent group uses largely symbolic actions intended to help persuade the opponents or someone else, or to express the group's disapproval and dissent, the behavior may be called nonviolent protest and persuasion. Marches, parades, and vigils are among the methods of this class. 2) Where the nonviolent group acts largely by withdrawal or the withholding of assistance, submission, and cooperation, its behavior may be described as noncooperation. This class contains three subclasses: social noncooperation (such as social boycotts or ostracism), economic noncooperation (including many types of economic boycotts and labor strikes), and political noncooperation (among them noncooperation with government units, *civil disobedience, mutiny, and severance of diplomatic relations). 3) Where the nonviolent group acts largely by direct intervention its acts may be referred to as nonviolent intervention (disrupting usual routines psychologically, socially, economically, politically, or physically). The methods in this class include sit-ins, hunger strikes, nonviolent obstruction, nonviolent invasion, and parallel government. Some of the more visible manifestations of people power, such as blocking tanks, fall into this class.

Often in this technique people use their usual roles in the social system as means of direct resistance. This occurs, for example, when factory workers refuse to continue working because of a grievance, or when judges refuse to enforce the illegitimate orders of putschists. The impact of noncooperation will be influenced by the type or extent of the group's usual participation in the normal functioning of the system. The application of noncooperation by key groups and the use of multiple methods of nonviolent struggle have the potential to slow, halt, paralyze, or even disintegrate the institution or political system against which it is employed.

Such defiance will not be welcomed by the opponents, and they may apply extreme violent repression in attempts to force a resumption of passive submission and cooperation. That will not necessarily succeed, however. Nonviolent struggle has been demonstrated to be capable of operating successfully under such harsh repressive conditions.

Indeed, at times the use of extreme violence against disciplined nonviolent struggle may contribute to the success of the resisting population. Through a process of "political jujitsu" violent repression sometimes drives more people to join in the resistance, alienates some usual supporters of the opponents sufficiently that they too protest and resist, and causes third parties to oppose the opponent group and support the nonviolent struggle group.

Mechanisms of Change. The nonviolent technique has its own requirements for effectiveness. These include sound strategy, wisely chosen tactics and methods, persistent action despite repression, and nonviolent discipline. Physical violence, or the threat of it, is excluded in nonviolent action, for it disrupts the general dynamics of this type of conflict.

The technique possesses special mechanisms of change which must be implemented if a given struggle is to succeed. When successful, nonviolent action achieves results through one of four broad mechanisms of change or some combination of them. 1) In conversion, the opponents come around to a new point of view in which they positively accept the nonviolent actionists' aims. 2) In accommodation, the opponents choose to compromise and grant some of the resisters' objectives, adjusting to the new situation produced by the conflict but without changing their viewpoint. 3) Where nonviolent coercion operates, change is achieved against the oppo-

nents' will and without their agreement because they have lost control. Nevertheless, the opponents still retain their institutional positions and hold to their original opinions. However, the sources of their power have been so undercut by the nonviolent means that they no longer are able to deny the objectives of the nonviolent actionists. 4) Finally, in disintegration, the opponents' sources of power are so completely removed that the whole system or government simply falls apart. This occurred, for example, with the communist regimes in the German Democratic Republic (East Germany) and Czechoslovakia in 1989.

"War Without Violence." Nonviolent action is so different from milder peaceful responses to conflicts (such as conciliation, arbitration, and negotiation) that several writers have pointed to certain similarities of nonviolent action to military warfare. Nonviolent action is also a means of combat. It, too, involves the matching of forces and the waging of "battles," requires wise strategy and tactics, and demands of its "soldiers" courage, discipline, and sacrifice. The degree of bravery required, however, is no greater than that required by military means, and the casualty rates in nonviolent struggles repeatedly appear to be very much lower than those in comparable violent conflicts.

The Choice of Nonviolent Struggle. Nonviolent action has been overwhelmingly applied by groups that would have been willing to use violence in other circumstances. In most cases the choice to employ the nonviolent means has been made out of pragmatic considerations. These include assessments of the resisters' objectives and resources, the nature of the conflict, and the strengths and weaknesses of the opponents. Such action has seemed to be the obvious way to pursue certain objectives. In many cases nonviolent struggle has been consciously chosen because optional violent forms of action were seen in advance to be ineffective or unrealistic, or because violence had already been used and failed.

Nonviolent struggle has sometimes been practiced widely even when the rhetoric of resistance has been "armed struggle"—as was the case in South Africa in the 1970s and 1980s with the widespread use of school boycotts, rent strikes, and demonstrative funerals. A similar situation occurred in some European resistance movements during *World War II that used such forms as strikes, civil disobedience, and symbolic protests, although they supported the Allied military efforts.

Much more rarely, nonviolent means have been chosen over violence for religious or ethical reasons, or at times because of a mixture of normative and practical motives. In some cases, even when pragmatic political considerations were dominant in the choice of nonviolent struggle, the movement has taken on certain religious or ethical overtones. This was the case in the campaigns of the Indian National Congress for independence from Britain in the 1920s,

1930s, and 1940s. Those struggles, often under *Gandhi's leadership, and also the civil rights campaigns in the 1950s and 1960s in the Deep South of the United States, under the leadership of Martin Luther *King, Jr., and others, are very important, but they are not historically typical. In most cases, elements of religious or ethical nonviolence are much weaker or absent, and charismatic leaders are not present.

Scholarly Study and Preconceptions. Nonviolent action has in recent decades been subjected to the beginnings of research and analysis by social scientists. As a result, it is now clear that some common assumptions about this technique and various preconceptions about its requirements and limitations are not valid. As late as the 1960s, for example, it was sometimes assumed that nonviolent struggle in politics had been an innovation made by Gandhi. It is now clear, however, that nonviolent struggle has been widely practiced throughout history in all parts of the world.

The belief that nonviolent action usually requires much more time to produce success than does violence is not accurate. As with violence, the length of nonviolent struggles varies widely. In some cases, success has even come within days or weeks, as in the nonviolent revolutions against the military dictatorships of El Salvador and Guatemala in 1944 or in the noncooperation and defiance of the August 1991 coup in the Soviet Union.

Contrary to the view that nonviolent action can occur or succeed only under democracies, much nonviolent struggle has been practiced, sometimes successfully, against oppressive systems and extreme dictatorships. For example, nonviolent resistance was used with varying degrees of effectiveness during the Nazi occupations of Norway, Denmark, and the Netherlands. Nonviolent struggle even at times played a significant role in saving Jews from the *Holocaust, as in Berlin, Bulgaria, and Denmark. In communist-ruled Eastern European countries, nonviolent struggle was widely practiced, beginning in 1953 in East Germany, then in both Poland and Hungary in 1956. Czech and Slovak resistance to the 1968 Soviet-led invasion was a powerful case of improvised nonviolent struggle used for national defense which held off the Soviet objective of a hardline regime for eight months. The successful ten-year struggle of *Solidarity in Poland (1980–1990) exemplified the ability of people to carry on nonviolent resistance under the harsh conditions of martial law. In 1989–1990 nonviolent struggle contributed significantly to the collapse of communist rule throughout Eastern and *Central Europe.

Surprisingly, the preconception that this technique can operate only when both parties share common ethical norms, such as the Judeo-Christian heritage, still surfaces from time to time. Much contrary evidence exists, however. Nonviolent struggle has been widely practiced in diverse cultures of the world, including its use by Muslims, atheists, Hindus, Buddhists, Marxists, and people of other persuasions.

Scholarship on nonviolent struggle has also clearly separated the technique of nonviolent action from belief systems espousing ethical or religious "principled nonviolence" or "pacifism"—of which there are various types. Some groups of believers in "nonviolence" still view the nonviolent technique and moral or religious belief systems as necessarily closely tied. Some such believers even reject nonviolent action. Belief systems espousing ethical and religious nonviolence are clearly distinct phenomena from nonviolent action. Although nonviolent action is usually extraconstitutional (that is, it does not rely upon established institutional procedures of the state), it is possible to incorporate the technique into constitutional government at various points, and even to use it to defend an established government against attack.

Civilian-based Defense. Since 1964 serious explorations have been made into the potential of a refined, developed, and prepared use of the nonviolent technique for national defense, against both internal *coups d'état and foreign aggression. This policy is usually now called "civilian-based defense." It aims to block domestic usurpers or foreign aggressors from establishing illegitimate rule over the attacked society.

Opinions differ among policymakers and strategists of this policy as to its proper role in a country's defense preparations. Increasingly the disagreements are not about whether civilian-based resistance options have a role, but rather about what role that should be, and how large a role they are capable of playing. In 1986 the Swedish Parliament unanimously added such a "nonmilitary resistance" component to its overwhelmingly military "total defense" policy. Switzerland and Austria have similar components, officially at least. In 1991 the writings about civilian-based defense influenced the Lithuanian, Latvian, and Estonian defenses against attempted coups aimed to depose the independence-minded governments of those countries.

Civilian-based resistance components and full civilian-based defense policies are likely to receive increasing attention in the coming years. The development of these defense options could alter fundamentally certain aspects of *international relations and international *security.

Increased Knowledge and Practice. Knowledge about the nature, requirements, and strategic principles of the nonviolent technique is increasing and spreading at the same time that the practice and visibility of nonviolent action are expanding. During the twentieth century nonviolent struggle has grown, rising to unprecedented political significance throughout the world. This technique is now widely recognized as a potentially powerful alternative to violence for groups engaged in acute conflicts. Much more is yet to be learned about nonviolent struggle and its potential, but knowledge has already been expanded significantly. The development of research and policy studies on this technique itself marks a significant new stage in the historical development of the technique.

(See also CIVIL RIGHTS MOVEMENT; NINETEEN EIGHTY-NINE; PEACE; PEACE MOVEMENT; POLITICAL VIOLENCE; PRAGUE SPRING; REVOLUTION.)

Gene Sharp, *The Politics of Nonviolent Action* (Boston, 1973). Anders Boserup and Andrew Mack, *War Without Weapons: Non-Violence in National Defense* (New York, 1975). Joan V. Bondurant, *Conquest of Violence: The Gandhian Philosophy of Conflict*, rev. ed. (Princeton, N.J., 1988). Gene Sharp, *Civilian-Based Defense* (Princeton, N.J., 1990). Ronald McCarthy and Gene Sharp, eds., *Nonviolent Action: A Bibliography* (in press).

GENE SHARP

NORTH ATLANTIC TREATY ORGANIZATION. Founded in 1949, the North Atlantic Treaty Organization (NATO) has played a collective defense role for its member, allied states. The geographic scope of NATO was specified in Article 6 of the North Atlantic Treaty as including "the territory of any of the Parties in Europe or North America" as well as any "islands under the jurisdiction of any of the Parties in the North Atlantic area north of the Tropic of Cancer." In the event of attack upon any NATO member or "on the forces, vessels, or aircraft of any of the Parties" when operating in or over "the Mediterranean Sea" or elsewhere in "the North Atlantic area," *alliance members are committed under Article 5 of the same treaty to "assist the Party or Parties so attacked." More specifically, each member is pledged "individually, and in concert with the other Parties," to take "such action as it deems necessary" for restoring and maintaining "the security of the North Atlantic area." Such action may include "the use of armed force," although this is not a necessary response.

Beyond the collective-defense role of the NATO alliance, Article 2 identifies a much broader purpose. Alliance members are to pursue "further development of peaceful and friendly international relations by strengthening their free institutions, by bringing about a better understanding of the principles upon which these institutions are founded, and by promoting conditions of stability and well-being." Moreover, NATO countries "will seek to eliminate conflict in their economic policies and will encourage economic collaboration between any or all of them." From the start, NATO was understood to be more than just a military alliance.

NATO came into existence soon after the beginning of the *Cold War. Direct military response to Soviet closure of access routes to Berlin in the form of an airlift of supplies to the beleaguered city (1948–1949), *Marshall Plan aid to help rebuild the economies of Western European states (beginning in 1947), the *Truman Doctrine (announced on 12 March 1947) by which the United States pledged "to support free peoples who are resisting attempted subjugation by armed minorities, or by outside pressure," and formation of the *Council of Europe, the Western European Union (WEU), and NATO were among the Western responses to the changed international environment. NATO soon became an essential part of a new European security order that aimed to contain the Soviet Union and curb any expansionist tendencies it might have, to anchor in the West what would become the Federal Republic of Germany (FRG), and to assure an American commitment to the defense of Western Europe.

The charter members of NATO were the members of the WEU (Belgium, France, Luxembourg, the Netherlands, and the United Kingdom) plus Canada, Denmark, Iceland, Italy, Norway, Portugal, and the United States. Late accessions, bringing membership to its current sixteen, were Greece (1952), Turkey (1952), the FRG (1955), and Spain (1982).

In 1966, claiming independent control of its military forces as a national prerogative, France withdrew from the alliance's integrated military command structure; however, it retained its membership in NATO and remained a full participant in the North Atlantic Council. Military-to-military, bilateral coordination by France with other NATO members, including the United States, increased substantially during the 1980s with joint planning and exercises conducted outside of the NATO structure. France also continued to participate in the WEU (which had added the FRG and Italy as members in 1954), but the organization maintained a low profile until the 1980s when it came to be seen as a useful complement to NATO (or by some as a potential substitute for NATO). A new role for the WEU emerged in the early 1990s as it assumed the task of coordinating European participation with the United States and Canada outside of the NATO area. Out-of-area NATO commitments had long been controversial within the alliance; the WEU merely provided an alternative forum for managing this issue.

Another difficult issue for NATO has been persistent conflict between two alliance members, Greece and Turkey. Following the crisis over Cyprus in 1974, considerable progress was made under NATO auspices in managing, though not resolving, conflict between the two. Indeed, peaceful management of Greek-Turkish conflict is seen by some as a most important NATO success story.

Resource constraints and economic competition among the NATO allies in arms production and sales have produced tensions within the alliance. Feeling that it has borne a disproportionate share of NATO defense costs, the United States for many years repeatedly called for greater burden sharing—an irritant to European allies who argued that many of their contributions were overlooked in the U.S. calculus. Acquisition of weaponry for use by NATO allies has also been highly charged politically, given its implications for industrial competitiveness within the alliance. Joint production and licensing arrangements with offset payments are among the measures that have been adopted to manage this issue. Rationalization, standardization, and interoperability (RSI) also became goals for a more efficient allocation of resource by the NATO allies. As a practical matter, however, it has been extremely difficult to agree upon rationalization—a national division of labor among the allies—or standardization and interoperability of weapons, ammunition, and spare parts.

NATO's military strategy in the 1950s and 1960s was heavily reliant on the threat of massive nuclear retaliation as response to aggressions, conventional or nuclear, by the Soviet Union and its *Warsaw Treaty Organization (Warsaw Pact) allies. In 1967, NATO strategy shifted formally to flexible response, a posture that allowed for conventional *war–fighting options while still retaining a nuclear first-use option should that be deemed necessary. Forward defense—not trading space (particularly German territory) for time in any kind of planned, strategic retreat—was also an important element of the new NATO strategy. Both flexible response and forward defense were intended only as part of a *deterrence posture aimed at avoiding warfare altogether. In addition to deterrence and the purely military aspects of security, the 1967 Harmel Report recognized the continuing importance of diplomatic efforts to reduce tensions and create stable international relations conducive to maintaining *peace. As such, deterrence and *détente were seen as complementary approaches to security in the North Atlantic area.

The twin military-diplomatic track to security was also reflected in a 1979 decision to respond with a two-track approach to Soviet deployments of a new category of intermediate-range ballistic missiles. *Arms control negotiations were to be undertaken at the same time that NATO prepared to deploy its own ballistic and cruise missiles. Although NATO began missile deployments in 1983, the two-track approach did succeed in 1987 when the United States and the Soviet Union agreed to eliminate all intermediate-range ballistic missiles from their inventories. Throughout these negotiations the NATO allies consulted regularly as they have done in other arms control talks—strategic arms limitation talks (SALT) in the 1970s, strategic arms reduction talks (START) beginning in the 1980s, mutual and balanced force reductions (MBFR) conducted between 1973 and 1989, and conventional forces and confidence- and security-building measures in the 1980s and 1990s. The latter negotiations resulted in agreement on substantial reductions and ceilings with respect to conventional forces while providing for an extensive regime of notifications of exercises and troop movements and mutual inspections. Significantly, these negotiations were conducted under the auspices of the *Conference on Security and Cooperation in Europe (CSCE).

Reduction of the risk of war in Europe through arms control and confidence building has led to a major reassessment of NATO strategy and NATO's relation to other international organizations associated with European security. NATO's London Declaration (1990) made clear that changed circumstances had made reduced reliance on *nuclear weapons possible. Emphasis was also placed on the enduring political and economic aspects of collaboration among the NATO allies as elaborated in Article 2 of the North Atlantic Treaty, suggesting a reduced emphasis on the purely military aspects of the alliance. More recent developments include a major restructuring of military force commitments consistent with NATO's changed environment. A stronger "European pillar," an enhanced role for the WEU (particularly for commitments outside of the North Atlantic area), an enlarged security role for the CSCE, and the possibility of the *European Community's (EC) assuming a direct security function are alternatives under consideration as a new European security order is constructed. NATO will probably have a significant, albeit different, role in this new order.

(See also CONTAINMENT; GAULLE, CHARLES DE; SECURITY; STRATEGIC ARMS LIMITATION TREATIES.)

William T. R. Fox and Annette Fox, *Nato and the Range of American Choice* (New York and London, 1967). George Liska, *Nations in Alliance: The Limits of Interdependence* (Baltimore, 1968). Douglas J. Murray and Paul R. Viotti, eds., *The Defense Policies of Nations: A Comparative Study* (Baltimore, 1982, 1989). Catherine M. Kelleher and Gale A. Mattox, *Evolving European Defense Policies* (Lexington, Mass., 1987).

PAUL R. VIOTTI

NORTHERN IRELAND. A quasi-independent state within the United Kingdom, Northern Ireland's political *legitimacy has been contested by Irish nationalists since the 1920 partition of Ireland. Sectarianism and *nationalism have intersected throughout the modern history of this region, nourished by the coincidence between religious and political allegiances.

At the opening of the twentieth century, the northeast of Ireland was the major locale for internal opposition to constitutional efforts at home rule and to the nationalist republican movement. Although the execution of republican leaders after the failed Easter Rebellion of 1916 thrust much of Ireland into the nationalist camp, segments of the more industrialized sectors and especially Protestants in the northeast saw little economic advantage to independence and feared a loss of civil and religious liberties should the independence movement succeed. Partition under the 1920 Government of Ireland Act conceded the power of Unionist opposition to independence.

From 1920 to 1972, Stormont, the seat of local government, exercised relatively autonomous control over the internal affairs of the region. Westminster (the British parliament) retained control of fiscal and treaty powers. Throughout this period, Protestants—who constitute about two-thirds of the populace of Northern Ireland—dominated Stormont through the Unionist Party; Catholics, with about one-third of the populace, generally supported reintegration with the predominantly Catholic Republic of *Ireland through the Nationalist and Social Democratic Labor parties. The Irish Republican movement and its military arms (the regular and provisional IRA) have been almost entirely Catholic.

During the period of devolved rule, the leadership of the Unionist Party warded off internal conflicts among Protestants and effective opposition by nationalist Catholics. They adopted an electoral mechanism designed to reduce flexibility in voter choice (e.g., single-member constituencies, gerrymandered boundaries, and plurality rules); provided an official proportion of seats on the Unionist Council to delegates selected by the Protestant fraternal Orange Order; and, gave preferential treatment to Protestants in public housing, works, and employment. Unionists exercised control over regime opponents through repressive legislation such as an infamous Special Powers Act that permitted arrest and suspension of civil liberties to anyone suspected of nationalist activities, and through a three-tiered constabulary that virtually armed the entire Protestant male adult populace. In the face of such sectarian rule, the Nationalist Party frequently boycotted elections.

The political bases of this contested regime were eroded by developments in post–World War II *Britain, especially the growing *welfare state, the expansion of multinational *capitalism, and the declining power of Ulster's industry. In this context of Britain's more active role in Ulster's internal affairs, a civil rights movement developed in the mid-1960s. By means of sit-ins and marches, the civil rights movement, a coalition of Catholic professionals, university students, trade union activists, liberal Protestants, Labour members of Parliament, and supporters of the Irish Republican Army, directly challenged the system of political patronage and discrimination. But this movement was short-lived. Loyalist Protestant opposition to reform limited governmental concessions, and the subsequent interethnic conflict culminated in the dispatch of British troops throughout the province, ushered in the period popularly known as "the troubles," and ultimately the introduction, in 1972, of direct rule by Westminster. The protracted ethnic antagonisms and suspicions have been strengthened by British restrictions on civil liberties and *human rights. Hence, political and paramilitary opposition to power-sharing proposals have been strong among both loyalists and republicans.

The "troubles" have taken an enormous toll on the region. During the 1980s, staple industries declined significantly and average unemployment exceeded twenty percent. Industrial decline and unemployment were felt more sharply in continuing conflict and economic stagnation, as efforts at political reconciliation continued. In 1985, Westminster and Dublin signed an Anglo-Irish agreement which guaranteed that there would be no change in the status of Northern Ireland without the consent of the majority of the people in the region. Should such a majority clearly consent to the establishment of a United Ireland, both governments agreed to support such legislation in their parliaments. The accord also established an intergovernmental conference to regularly discuss political, security, and legal matters and to promote cross-border cooperation on security, economic, social, and cultural matters. Unionist opposition to this agreement surfaced quickly and has not declined considerably.

Interpretations of the conflicts and problems of governance of Northern Ireland constitute something of an academic cottage industry, frequently reflecting the political terrain. Some scholars, especially nationalists and neo-Marxists, view the conflict as resulting from processes of capitalism and *imperialism. They emphasize the historic consequence of the patterns of Protestant settler colonization and of uneven regional development of Ireland's economy under British rule. These patterns, it is argued, resulted in a more affluent and industrialized sector in the predominantly Protestant parts of the northeast and a rational shared interest between that sector and British Unionists. The Ulster and British elites collaborated in creating a material base for Protestant working-class loyalty to the Union. From this perspective, contemporary conflicts are engendered in part by the changing economic and political relations between Britain and Ireland. The economic need for better relations between these states necessitated some crown support for civil rights and nondiscrimination, undermined the hegemony of the Unionist Party, and set the stage for the last decades of volatile intergroup conflicts. For these scholars, the Unionist/Nationalist divide is an essential one—explained by the interplay of political and *class forces.

Other scholars, equally sensitive to the historical impact of the Union, emphasize the substantial cultural and institutional barriers between Catholics and Protestants. Although much research indicates that the two populations share common attitudes toward business, family, social class, and other dimensions of culture, there are important social processes that reinforce division. Educational and residential segregation, religious insulation, different leisure activities, and distinct voluntary associations all reinforce the sense of separate confessional identities and political values. Moreover, the privileged status of the *Roman Catholic church in the Republic of Ireland reinforces Protestant skepticism about the possibilities of a secular republic; and the continuing disadvantages of Catholics in the northern state and economy make consensus between these communities extraordinarily difficult. From this perspective, the essential divide is a communal/religious one rooted in the interplay of social and cultural forces. The richest analyses of Northern Ireland are located between these two perspectives, although few point to any immediate way to resolve the conflicts over regime legitimacy and to reform the state.

(See also ETHNICITY; INTERNAL COLONIALISM; RELIGION AND POLITICS.)

Katherine O'Sullivan See, *First World Nationalism: Class and Ethnic Politics in Northern Ireland and Quebec* (Chicago, 1986). Paul Teague, *Beyond the Rhetoric: Politics, the Economy and Social Policy in Northern Ireland* (London, 1987). Charles Townshend, ed., *Consensus on Ireland: Approaches and Recessions* (Oxford, 1988).

KATHERINE O'SULLIVAN SEE

NORTH KOREA. See KOREA, DEMOCRATIC PEOPLE'S REPUBLIC OF.

NORTH-SOUTH RELATIONS. Most analysts use the term *North-South relations* to refer to the multilateral aspect of relations between developed and developing countries, which have gone through major transformations over the last four decades. Initially, as the developing countries achieved independence and began to act as a group on international issues, there was great optimism about the future of the North-South relationship. The oil crisis and the economic turbulence of the 1970s and after marked a second and far more controversial stage of the relationship. Confrontation became the norm, implicit beliefs about a long-term harmony of interests between the two sides were challenged, and many analysts were pessimistic that a viable relationship could be established. A third stage of the relationship began to emerge during the 1980s as the oil crisis waned, the debt crisis gained in force, supporters of market approaches became dominant among developed (and some developing) countries, and political and economic problems—domestically and internationally—continued to grow. For many developing countries the 1970s and 1980s were lost decades for development and sharply increased resource transfers have become even more imperative. Whether the confrontational North-South relationship of the past can now be replaced by a more cooperative relationship is unclear, but there are only limited grounds for optimism. In any case, these three stages, while overlapping to some extent, have largely defined the nature of the North-South relationship, an evolutionary relationship that is in part autonomous and in part a reflection of wider trends and developments in *international systems.

Why was there so much optimism in the early stage of North-South relations? One reason was that in developed and developing countries political and intellectual elites tended to assume that economic development would be relatively easy, that political independence would ensure economic independence, and that relations between the two sides would be contentious in the short run but mutually beneficial in the long run. The developing countries would rapidly industrialize through import substitution and thus end dependence on raw materials exports whose terms of trade were declining. And what worked for the developed countries in the past would also work for the developing countries. For a while, until the oil crisis that began in 1973, the record of economic and political performance seemed to justify the optimism, although that record was greatly facilitated by extraordinarily high rates of growth in the world economy.

The second stage of North-South relations was dominated by the ascent of the *Organization of Petroleum Exporting Countries (OPEC), an unsettled world economy, and a major challenge by the *Third World—led by the *Group of 77, its negotiating entity in the UN system—to establish a *New International Economic Order (NIEO). OPEC's success in sharply raising oil prices energized the Third World, changing perceptions about relative power and the prospects for changing the international order. If other commodity producers could not emulate OPEC, because oil was indeed "different," it was at least hoped that the tacit threat of the oil weapon would induce the developed countries to make important concessions. But the OPEC "threat" was never implemented, largely because the main OPEC countries did not have much interest in undermining a system from which they were earning substantial benefits, and the developed countries could thus safely respond with a policy of delay and passive resistance. The developed countries also believed that the NIEO proposals were ideologically hostile to the liberal order they had created and in many cases economically unsound (even, in some instances, in terms of helping the Third World). Because the developing countries needed help quickly and because their effective power was largely limited to setting institutional agendas and passing resolutions—which could be ignored by the developed countries—the strategy of delay succeeded. But this meant that *both* sides lost an opportunity to negotiate useful changes.

The leadership of the Group of 77 clearly overestimated how much the configuration of power had changed in its favor and persisted in a strategy of confrontation, of demanding acceptance of new principles before discussing specific proposals, well past the point where confrontation had any chance of success. Still, because it was an article of faith in the Third World that unity was its only weapon (apart from the illusion that OPEC would sacrifice its own interests for the rest of the Third World), and because unity could be unraveled by compromises that did not promise benefits to all, the leadership was sharply constrained in its ability to alter negotiating strategies. Moreover, most of the Third World needed greatly increased international support not only to deal with the effects of rising import prices for oil, food, and manufactured goods, but also to deal with the growing domestic problems created by failures in political and economic development. This too made compromise difficult because only the presumed benefits of massive change seemed to promise enough additional resources to the Third World. Thus compromise was resisted and the Group of 77 continued to pursue a strategy that would have been appropriate only if underlying power relationships had in fact altered significantly and if in fact the postwar economic system was facing the "beginning of the end."

The second stage of North-South relations ended badly for the Third World. The arrival in power in several developed countries of conservative administrations that were even more hostile to the anti-market proposals in the NIEO, a continued decline in economic performance in most developing countries that undermined unity and forced an emphasis on immediate coping strategies, and the arrival of an era of interdependence that seemed only to promise increased dependence for developing countries marked the end of this difficult and confrontational period in North-South relations. If, however, we think of the South not merely as a coalition of the weak that won few benefits but also as an international social movement, responding to change and seeking to direct it in favorable ways, perhaps the balance sheet is not as bleak. The Third World did force consideration of its problems and perspectives, it did have some of its ideas and proposals incorporated into the mainstream discussion of the issues, and it did perhaps increase awareness of proper negotiating strategies and of both the limits and the possibilities of group bargaining. Debt, for example, began to be treated as a *development issue rather than a liquidity problem; the industrialized countries recognized the need for special programs to help the least developed countries; and issues such as trade, finance, and industrial development were linked in discussions, rather than treated as separate topics. But the South did not achieve the NIEO, which was largely a rhetorical goal.

The third stage of North-South relations has been and is dominated by a sense of crisis, even despair. The "descent" of OPEC, however transitory, the onset of the debt crisis, trade conflicts, the rise of protectionism, and instability in the world monetary system are among the factors that have contributed to the sense of crisis. Some parts of the Third World, especially in East and Southeast Asia, have done reasonably well over the past decade, but it is far from clear how they will cope with pressures for democratization or what effect democratization will have on trade and development strategies. Other parts of the Third World, especially in Africa but also elsewhere, have been barely able to cope, forced to cut imports, to impose austerity policies, and to become even more dependent on external resource transfers.

In the circumstances, common action by the Group of 77 in the multilateral arena has become even more problematic because splits within the coalition have become more salient, the ability to remain unified behind long-term restructuring goals has diminished, and the emphasis has turned to short-term coping strategies. The growing emphasis on market approaches, reflecting both pressures from the developed countries and the manifest failures of non-market approaches, has also undermined the ideological coherence of the NIEO policies. "Coalitions of sentiment," as in the past, are being replaced by shifting and perhaps unstable "coalitions of interests." Finally, the post-1989 transitions in Eastern and *Central Europe and the plight of Russia and the other members of the *Commonwealth of Independent States have raised fears that resources will be diverted and that attention will shift away from the Third World.

There are also other secular trends that are generating ominous forecasts about the prospects for much of the Third World. The most profound of these trends concerns escalating deterioration as a result of linked crises from population growth rates, declining agricultural productivity, water shortages, and environmental decay. In addition, the amount of raw materials in manufactured products has continued to decline, injuring prospects for the many raw materials exporters in the Third World. Even the highly successful newly industrializing countries (NICs), whose prosperity rested initially on exporting labor-intensive manufactured goods, may suffer as labor costs become an increasingly smaller component of the final cost of manufacturers. This trend will also make it even more difficult for other countries to emulate the success of the NICs.

As Third World states are increasingly differentiated by their ability to cope, as multiple pressures and rising demands compel an emphasis on nationalistic, short-run responses, and as the developed countries turn away from the Third World and offer primarily lectures about the market, will North-South disappear as a central axis of concern? A definitive answer is impossible because North-South is not autonomous and is dependent on developments in the world economy and on domestic performance. Much also depends on ideological interpretation as conservative realists, free market advocates, liberal reformers, and radical theorists all bring their own perspectives to past, present, and future. Given the complexity of the issues, the wide diversity within the Third World, and the absence of a general theory of North-South, the lack of consensus is not surprising.

North-South will surely continue to exist in a formal sense as multilateral negotiations continue and as the problems besetting the Third World require some degree of *international cooperation for resolution. But it is likely to be most salient only on issues where the Third World is genuinely united, issues such as institutional reform and increased resource transfers. The "grand strategy" of confrontation is unlikely to be revived as the world order is transformed by trends and developments that neither side foresaw or clearly comprehends. North-South's greatest weakness has been insufficient concern with domestic linkages, a point of importance because international policies create opportunities that can be grasped only by states pursuing appropriate domestic policies. Only if these linkages are understood will North-South become an arena for the pursuit of mutual benefits rather than one of confrontation or compensation for failed domestic policies.

(See also IMPORT-SUBSTITUTION INDUSTRIALIZATION; INTERNATIONAL DEBT; INTERNATIONAL POLITICAL ECONOMY; LOMÉ CONVENTION; NEWLY INDUSTRIALIZING ECONOMIES; NINETEEN EIGHTY-NINE.)

Robert L. Rothstein, *The Weak in the World of the Strong* (New York, 1977), Stephen D. Krasner, *Structural Conflict—The Third World Against Global Liberalism* (Berkeley, Calif., 1985). Robert L. Rothstein, "The Limits and Possibilities of Weak Theory: Interpreting North-South" *Journal of International Affairs* 44, no. 1 (Spring/Summer 1990): 159–181.

ROBERT L. ROTHSTEIN

NORTH YEMEN. See YEMEN.

NORWAY. A small West European state of about 4 million inhabitants, Norway is relatively homogeneous both in terms of ethnicity (except for a Lapp population of 40,000 in the north) and religion (eighty-eight percent of the population are members of the Lutheran state church). Norway has a very long coastline facing the North Atlantic. Its most sensitive border is with Russia in the far North, close to the Kola Peninsula, which contains the former Soviet Union's largest concentration of marine forces. In the *Cold War era, the northern part of the country was of crucial strategic importance as the northern flank of the NATO alliance, of which Norway has been a member since 1949.

A very poor and backward society in the early modern period, Norway has experienced considerable economic transformation since the mid-nineteenth century. Despite heavy dependence on the international economy, Norway avoided the pattern of underdevelopment often fostered by such dependence and became one of the world's richest countries per capita in the postwar period. Fish and timber were traditional export staples. Traditionally a seafaring nation, its merchant marine achieved success of international proportions. At the turn of the century, cheap energy could be generated by Norwegian waterfalls, and a sector of energy-intensive chemical industry (e.g., aluminum) became the new cornerstone of the economic structure. In the late 1960s, another energy-source—oil—was discovered on the continental shelf west of Norway.

An independent Norwegian state existed in medieval times, but from 1523 to 1814 Norway was a Danish colony. There was no indigenous aristocracy. In 1814 Norway was granted home rule in a union with *Sweden, an arrangement that lasted until 1905. The cabinet consisted exclusively of civil servants, supported by sections of the countryside, bureaucracy, and business interests. In the national assembly (Stortinget), the opposition consisted of rural groups—the 1814 constitution had enfranchised all farmers—with important support among the urban intelligentsia. These groups became the Conservative (Høyre) and Liberal (Venstre) parties, respectively. The Liberals led the struggle for parliamentary government (1884) and together with the Labor Party (Det Norske Arbeiderpartiet, founded in 1887) secured universal suffrage for men in 1898 and for women in 1913.

As industrialization spread in the early twentieth century, parties relating to special interests split from the Liberals: an Agrarian Party (Senterpartiet, 1920) and a Christian Party (Kristelig Folkeparti, 1933) supported by lay Protestant countercultures and those opposed to alcohol consumption. The bourgeoisie increasingly supported the Conservatives while the labor movement remained strong and unified. After some turbulence in the 1920s and the formation of a small Communist Party, Labor embarked on a reformist strategy. In 1961 an independent neutralist Socialist People's Party, or Sosialistisk Folkeparti (SF), broke away from Labor. Still, the basic structure of Norwegian postwar politics consists of a homogeneous social democratic Left facing a fragmented nonsocialist bloc. Labor was in power for nearly thirty years (1935–1965, except for united front governments during the German occupation of 1940–1945). Since then, collaborative governments of nonsocialist parties have alternated with Labor governments, but a social democratic approach, with economic *planning and an institutional *welfare state, has persisted.

Norway has a mixed economy, with little direct state ownership of industry. Until the 1980s, the financial system was thoroughly regulated, with state banks providing a large share of total credit. Many traits of the Norwegian social structure—no indigenous aristocracy, a historically weak bourgeoisie, strong state, united labor movement, small-scale owner-occupied farming—have bolstered equality as a basic norm. The social partners (workers, employers, farmers, and fishermen) have been organized in centralized bodies, and incomes policies have been consensual, although since the late 1970s separate confederations for academics and white-collar workers have challenged the traditional trade union confederation (Landsorganisasjonen).

Oil income relieved pressure on the economy in the difficult period since 1973. Unemployment was low until the late 1980s, and the welfare state enjoyed continuous support. The oil price slump in 1985, however, created severe adjustment problems. Politics has become more volatile in the last decades. In 1973, a right-wing populist tax-revolt party (the Fremskrittspartiet, or Progress Party) emerged. This, as well as a reorganized left-wing party, the Socialist Left Party, or Sosialistisk Venstreparti (SV), have gained support in the late 1980s, at the expense of Labor and the Conservatives. The Liberal Party, which had split over the issue of Norway's membership in the *European Community (EC) in 1972, lost its last seats in 1985. In 1972, a referendum decided that Norway would not be a full member of the EC. The anti-EC victory was taken as proof of the continued strength of grass-roots, counter-cultural movements in Norway. The EC question will reemerge as a crucial one in the 1990s.

(See also DENMARK; SCANDINAVIA; SOCIALISM AND SOCIAL DEMOCRACY.)

Stein Rokkan, "Norway: Numerical Democracy and Corporate Pluralism," in Robert Dahl, ed., *Political Oppositions in Western Democracies* (New Haven, Conn., 1966): 70–115. Fritz Hodne, *An Economic History of Norway, 1815–1970* (Trondheim, 1975). Jan Fagerberg, Ådne Cappelen, Lars Mjøset, Rune Skarstein, "The Decline of Social-Democratic State Capitalism in Norway" *New Left Review* 181 (May–June 1990): 60–94.

LARS MJØSET

NUCLEAR FREEZE. The nuclear freeze movement was spawned out of the antimilitarism and environmental efforts of the 1970s. It was formed in 1980 under the organizational leadership of the American Friends Service Committee, Fellowship of Reconciliation, and Clergy and Laity Concerned. These groups, along with local campaigns against *nuclear weapons research, production, and testing facilities, became the social base upon which the national movement was built. The movement reached its peak in 1982–1984 and faded from national visibility soon after the reelection of Ronald *Reagan to the White House in November 1984.

The policy proposal for a bilateral, mutual freeze on nuclear weapons and their delivery systems had been proposed by President Lyndon *Johnson's administration. Its reintroduction into popular discourse began in 1979 through the discussions and writings of Arthur Macy Cox, Randall Forsberg, and Richard Barnet.

The freeze movement's support rapidly expanded beyond the antinuclear and antimilitarist nucleus to include prominent citizens and professional and domestic policy organizations. By April 1982, U.S. citizens polled eighty-one percent in favor of the proposal. The freeze movement's rapid and expansive growth resulted in 11 million people voting in favor of it in fifty-three referenda (in nine states, plus the District of Columbia, and in a total of forty-three towns, cities, and counties) in the 1982 elections.

By September 1983, 156 national and international organizations had endorsed the freeze, including the U.S. Conference of Mayors, the Young Women's Christian Association, the American Nurses' Association, Friends of the Earth, the National Conference of Black Lawyers, and the American Association of University Women. Mainstream politicians also became visible advocates for the freeze despite a highly visible attack by President Ronald Reagan and others in the administration against the movement as "*KGB-inspired."

The freeze movement has had a permanent impact on public policy. The movement caused news coverage of *arms control and East-West issues to expand in breadth and depth. Foundation giving, academic programs, and government officials were influenced by the sophisticated self-styled citizen experts who organized in seventy-five percent of the congressional districts around the country.

The freeze movement left an infrastructure for the continued generation of domestic opinion on foreign and military policy matters. Professional organizations such as the Physicians for Social Responsibility, Lawyers' Alliance for Nuclear Arms Control, International Physicians for the Prevention of Nuclear War, and other professional organizations joined the established Catholic and mainline Protestant churches who made policy proclamations and made the freeze and nuclear war a priority for social action. Independent and unaffiliated groups of citizens at the local level were also established.

The freeze movement in the United States developed formal relationships with *peace movements throughout Western Europe and had some contact with independent movements emerging in Eastern and Central Europe and the Soviet Union. Regular meetings and coordination of events and strategy occured through the mechanism of the International Peace Coordination and Communications (IPCC) based in the Hague and staffed by the Interchurch Peace Council (IKV) in the Netherlands. The European Nuclear Disarmament (END) initiative, first articulated in "Protest and Survive," a statement by a group of British peace movement leaders led by historian E. P. Thompson, provided the intellectual and political framework within which a new European politics evolved. West European movements, working through a politics of "détente from below," engaged counterparts in Eastern and Central Europe. While the U.S. freeze movement stressed the dangers of nuclear war and technical issues of arms control, those in Europe stressed a vision for a new Europe beyond the military blocs. Domestic pressure within Europe caused heads of state in the *North Atlantic Treaty Organization to press President Reagan to alter war fighting rhetoric and began rattling the consensus around extended deterrence and for the deployment of the cruise and Pershing missiles.

The freeze movement altered public discourse and set in motion political changes beyond its intention. Confirmation of the emergence of a new framework for East-West relations and the delegitimization of nuclear deterrence came when Reagan addressed the nation in March 1983 and announced his plan for the Strategic Defense Initiative ("Star Wars"). Reagan condemned deterrence as immoral and committed himself to making nuclear weapons obsolete. His path was the technical fix of a military shield in space, but the political equivalent came two years later in Reykjavik, Iceland, when in October 1985 Reagan and Mikhail *Gorbachev agreed to the abolition of nuclear weapons. The staff and allies of the two leaders were unprepared for the declaration. However far off the implementation of the declaration as policy, the two leaders had ratified world opinion. Less than a decade later, the collapse of the Soviet Union and Russia's weakened situation in the post-Soviet era opened unexpected prospects for extensive reductions in nuclear arsenals.

(See also ARMS RACE; COLD WAR; INTEREST GROUPS; NEW SOCIAL MOVEMENTS.)

Pam Solo, *From Protest to Policy* (New York, 1988).
PAMELA A. SOLO

NUCLEAR WEAPONS. The first atomic weapons, including the two dropped on *Hiroshima and Nagasaki in 1945, derived their energy from fission, the splitting of atomic nuclei. Modern nuclear weapons, however, are based on fusion, the joining together of atomic nuclei at extremely high temperatures, the heat for which is created by an initial fission reaction. The subsequent chain reaction creates an enormous release of energy, causing massive destruction through the combined effects of heat, fire, shock, and wind. High levels of radiation are the by-product of the uranium and plutonium used in the fusion reaction.

The actual nuclear device, which can be the size of a small piece of luggage, is contained within a casing called a warhead. Strategic nuclear weapons are divided into four categories, according to the way in which the warhead is delivered to its target: intercontinental ballistic missiles (ICBMs), which carry the warhead into space and release it on a trajectory toward its target; submarine-launched ballistic missiles (SLBMs), which work in the same way, but are launched from submarines instead of land; bombers, which carry the warhead to its target; the cruise missiles, which reach their targets by air, flying a preprogrammed route close the ground. In principle, however, a nuclear device can reach its

target by virtually any means, including automobiles and even parcel post. Nuclear weapons have also been adapted to many other weapons systems, including artillery shells, land mines, short-range missiles, surface-to-air missiles, and depth charges.

Distribution. The vast majority of nuclear weapons are in the hands of the five nations known to possess them: the United States, Russia, China, France, and Britain (who, not coincidentally, are also the five permanent members of the UN Security Council). A portion of the formerly Soviet nuclear arsenal remained on Ukraine soil in the aftermath of the dissolution of the Soviet Union. In addition, several other nations are now assumed to possess nuclear weapons. India, which exploded a "peaceful nuclear device" in 1974, may have a small arsenal of nuclear weapons intended for Pakistan, which has vigorously pursued the development of its own nuclear weapons. In 1989, an Israeli technician confirmed that Israel has built as many as several hundred nuclear weapons as weapons of last resort in the ongoing *Middle East conflict. Other nations which are suspected to be developing nuclear weapons include Iraq and Libya. With the possible exception of Israel's, these arsenals are much outweighed by those of China, France, and Britain, each of which has many hundreds of weapons. Their arsenals, in turn, are dwarfed by those of the *superpowers, who maintain many thousands of weapons in their so-called "tactical" arsenals, while reserving many thousands more for their "strategic" arsenals.

In 1968, international negotiators concluded the Nuclear Non-Proliferation Treaty (NPT), intended to halt the spread of nuclear weapons to other countries and to create an international *regime for the development and oversight of peaceful nuclear technologies. By 1987, more than 100 nations had ratified the treaty or had agreed to abide by its safeguards. But that treaty has only a twenty-five-year life span. Any extension or renewal is not automatic, but must be renegotiated.

Deterrence between the Superpowers. The awesome destructive power of nuclear weapons has fundamentally transformed military strategy and the nature of *war in general. For the first time in the history of warfare, the destructiveness of the means of war far outweighs most ends for which a global nuclear war could be undertaken.

While the United States possessed an overwhelming nuclear superiority throughout the late 1940s and 1950s, by 1960 the Soviet Union had built a nuclear stockpile large enough to guarantee that any nuclear attack upon it could be met with a significant nuclear retaliation. In the years following, the Soviets added to their arsenal, reaching rough parity with the United States by the late 1960s. This novel balance gave rise to the theory of "mutual assured destruction" (MAD). The MAD theory holds that, if both nations have the ability to destroy each other's society, neither will use nuclear weapons for fear of bringing devastation upon itself. Under the conditions of MAD, the purpose of continuing to maintain nuclear weapons is to deter an attack by the other.

Policymakers, defense officials, and experts have long disagreed over what constitutes a credible threat to retaliate, and what level of destruction against the attacker must be "assured" in order for deterrence to be stable. At one extreme, some have argued that the guaranteed destruction of not more than a few major urban centers is a sufficient deterrent against attack. According to this view, a small number of nuclear weapons with a very high certainty of reaching their targets is all that is needed for *security. At the other extreme, some have asserted that a nation must be able to respond at a higher level of violence than its opponent, whatever its opponent's level is, for *deterrence to be guaranteed.

Deterrence, by its nature, is a highly symbolic process: it requires both parties to convince each other that they have the strength and the will to respond to threats against their vital interests. Deterrence has placed a high premium on demonstrations of resolve. During the *Cuban Missile Crisis of 1962, for example, both the United States and the Soviet Union felt that a symbolic defeat would undermine the credibility of their nuclear deterrent, to the detriment of their overall security and influence. During this crisis and others of the *Cold War, there were moments at which the commitment of national resolve was at least as important as the prima facie issues themselves.

One critique of MAD is its failure to provide a motive for retaliation: if a nation's society has been obliterated, what rational motive—other than sheer revenge—would prompt decisionmakers to launch the massive retaliation guaranteed by MAD? If a nation has ceased to exist, what national interest can it pursue by launching a retaliatory strike? Many have responded that even the slightest probability of retaliation is sufficient to deter attack—given the colossal stakes, any potential aggressor must fear that the victim will act out of revenge. But others have felt that decisionmakers need options other than massive retaliation after a nuclear attack. In order for deterrence to be convincing, they argue, a country which has been attacked must still be able to respond with selective, punitive retaliations. If the attacked country retains the ability to engage in cycles of increasing violence, an aggressor will not feel that it can gain a decisive advantage with a massive, sudden first strike. This argument became especially prominent in the United States in the late 1970s, and led to an emphasis on weapons and strategies for protracted nuclear warfare (often called "warfighting").

MAD had the effect of "wiring together" the security of the two superpowers, for they both relied upon the stability of deterrence to ensure their security. Thus, paradoxically, any attempt by one country to gain an absolute advantage might actually diminish its own overall security by undermining deterrence. The less stable the nuclear balance, the more precarious the situation was for both sides, even for the country favored by the imbalance.

The recognition of this interdependence led the United States and the Soviet Union to seek ways in which to ensure stability. Through *arms control, the superpowers sought to maintain an essential parity of nuclear forces and to limit the deployment of some especially destabilizing weapons systems (the Anti-Ballistic Missile Treaty, for example, limited national defenses against nuclear missiles). The two countries also negotiated an extensive array of "confidence and security-building measures" designed to facilitate communications in a crisis, prevent misunderstandings, and safeguard against accidental launches.

Utility of Nuclear Weapons. The enormous destructiveness of nuclear weapons, plus the absence of any kind of effective defense against them, gives them unique qualities. Three situations are worth distinguishing: wars between nations possessing them in quantity, wars between nations having only a few, and wars between a nation that has them and one that does not.

Consider the dramatic third possibility first. A nation possessing nuclear weapons in quantity that fights a war against one that does not possess them could, in principle, win that war absolutely and almost instantly, by using a portion of its nuclear arsenal.

Such a war has not been witnessed, however. In substantial measure it has not been because there also is a strong, worldwide "taboo" against any nuclear use. The Soviet Union did not use nuclear weapons in Afghanistan and the United States did not use them in Vietnam or Iraq. It is true that in the first two cases, an additional reason why the nuclear power eschewed their use was some fear of a reaction by the other superpower. But at least equally important was a fear of incurring universal ignominy by using weapons that are generally feared as hideous and hyperviolent, and that to many people even carry some air of the magical. The United States could not even consider the global consequences of using nuclear weapons against Iraq in the *Gulf War, even though the Soviets would have taken no immediate military action in response.

Any war between two nations that both possess nuclear weapons in quantity would carry consequences so colossal that anything like full-scale use would mean the annihilation of them both, and enormous damage to others as well. Between the United States and the Soviet Union such a war would have produced global environmental damage so profound that there is doubt whether humanity would have survived. Between heavily armed superpowers, however, the enormous inhibition of MAD came into play and, paradoxically, nuclear weapons had relatively little value. It is worth noting that in the future wars might become imaginable between other nations having substantial nuclear arsenals (China and India? Israel and Iraq? China and the independent Russian Republic?). Such twenty-first century possibilities have not yet been much considered.

The remaining case is war between nations that have only a few nuclear weapons. At present, many specialists would predict that this is the least unlikely case in the coming decades. (At the time of this writing, a nuclear war between India and Pakistan is seen by some as perhaps the most worrisome possibility.) One reason why this case seems the least unlikely is that the temptation may be great to strike against a weak enemy. If the other side has only a few weapons, and especially if those weapons are relatively vulnerable to attack, the desire may be great to remove a terrible danger by direct action.

Nuclear Weapons and the Cold War. Our chief experience, to date, of what nuclear weapons mean has been the East-West Cold War (roughly 1947–1989). Future generations may come to see that as a special case. For some fifteen years, one side in that Cold War was enormously superior to the other in nuclear capabilities, and through much of that time could have readily attacked and defeated the other, but forebore to do so primarily because of its own values. Subsequently, the other side also deployed nuclear weapons in quantity and made them relatively secure from attack. Thereby it created the situation of MAD, which, while uncomfortable, is one of the less dangerous nuclear configurations possible.

In the Cold War the United States explicitly extended its nuclear deterrent guarantee to Western Europe, via the *North Atlantic Treaty Organization (NATO), and the Soviet Union effectively extended its to Eastern Europe, via the *Warsaw Treaty Organization (Warsaw Pact). Western Europe also received significant protection by the development of first British and then French nuclear weapons. While it is impossible to be sure, many specialists believe that Cold War nuclear deterrence went a long way toward preventing the outbreak of World War III in Europe despite some intense East-West crises there. It has been otherwise rare for two great military alliances, in intense mutual competition, to avoid war. In this sense nuclear weapons surely promoted peace and stability during these decades. However, it can be argued that East and West, essentially stymied in Europe, turned to the *Third World to play out their competition and thereby caused, or at least enlarged, Third World conflicts beyond what they otherwise might have been. It also can be well argued that we are indebted to a substantial factor of good luck in having so far avoided an accidental (or "inadvertent") nuclear war, caused by computer malfunction or human error.

Nuclear Weapons in the Twenty-First Century. With the passing of the Cold War, humanity's experience of nuclear weapons and their meaning may turn to other regions. Some specialists fear that the twenty-first century may witness one or more Third World nuclear wars. Such wars would not only be locally devastating but also would cause worldwide ecological damage, perhaps severe damage.

In the coming decades, much may depend on whether the "taboo" against the actual use of nuclear weapons is strengthened or weakened. It could be stengthened by a renewed Nuclear Non-Proliferation Treaty and by further arms reductions by the existing nuclear powers. However, it could be gravely weakened if, after many decades of no actual use of nuclear weapons, they then are used, in the Third World or elsewhere. Especially it would be weakened if the first such fresh use was followed by a second, a third, and so forth. If the first aroused an intense worldwide revulsion, the world might thereafter move strongly toward nuclear disarmament and strict nonproliferation. But if the first was followed by a second nuclear use, and then by more, one of the grimmest of all possible futures might come into being—a world in which the use of nuclear weapons in warfare came to seem "normal."

(See also ARMS RACE; RULES OF WAR; STRATEGIC ARMS LIMITATION TREATIES.)

Donna Gregory, *The Nuclear Predicament: A Sourcebook* (New York, 1986). Herbert M. Levine and David Carlton, *The Nuclear Arms Debate* (New York, 1986). Richard Smoke, *National Security and the Nuclear Dilemma: An Introduction to the American Experience*, 2d ed. (New York, 1987). Philip Bobbitt, Lawrence Freedman, and Gregory F. Treverton, eds., *U.S. Nuclear Strategy: A Reader* (New York, 1989).

RICHARD SMOKE

NUREMBERG TRIALS. The Nazi and Japanese atrocities of *World War II were without precedent in modern times. After 1941, Allied leaders repeatedly warned the Axis powers that war criminals would be brought to trial. A UN War Crimes Commission was created in 1943, and the Soviets held sporadic *war crimes trials even while hostilities were going on. Naturally, however, the most highly placed individuals could not be apprehended and indicted prior to the unconditional surrender of Germany and Japan in 1945.

The principal trial of German war criminals following the war was held in Nuremberg, Germany, before an international military tribunal that had been established in the 1945 London Agreement for the Prosecution and Punishment of the Major War Criminals of the European Axis. The tribunal consisted of four judges and four alternates from the contracting states: the United States, the Soviet Union, Britain, and France.

Twenty-four defendants, headed by Hermann Göring, were indicted. Of these, one (Robert Ley) committed suicide before the trial commenced, and the proceedings against another (Gustav Krupp) were indefinitely suspended owing to his senile degeneration. One of the remaining twenty-two (Martin Bormann) was tried *in absentia*. The indictment also sought to declare as criminal seven groups and organizations.

The Nuremberg trial began in November 1945. After hundreds of sessions, in which many witnesses were heard and thousands of documents submitted, the tribunal delivered judgment on 30 September–1 October 1946. In all, nineteen defendants were convicted and three (Hans Fritzsche, Hjalmar Schacht, and Franz von Papen) acquitted. The sentences were death in twelve instances (Bormann *[in absentia]*, Hans Frank, Wilhelm Frick, Göring [who managed to commit suicide before execution], Alfred Jodl, Ernst Kaltenbrunner, Wilhelm Keitel, Alfred Rosenberg, Fritz Sauckel, Arthur Seyss-Inquart, Julius Streicher, and Joachim von Ribbentrop), life imprisonment in three (Walter Funk, Rudolf Hess, and Erich Raeder), and imprisonment for a fixed number of years in four (Karl Dönitz, Albert Speer, Konstantin von Neurath, and Baldur von Schirach). Of the seven groups, four (the SS, the SD, the Gestapo, and the Leadership Corps of the Nazi Party) were declared criminal organizations. The Soviet judge dissented from the acquittals of the three defendants and two of the three organizations, as well as from Rudolf Hess's life sentence.

Although proceedings against ordinary war criminals have many antecedents, the Nuremberg trial is the first to have been held before an international penal court. Moreover, the indictment (based on the charter of the tribunal, annexed to the London Agreement) went beyond traditional war crimes, and also encompassed crimes against peace and crimes against humanity. The international military tribunal pronounced the initiation of a war of aggression to be a crime under general *international law. The argument that this amounted to an *ex post facto* criminalization of the act was rejected by the tribunal.

It can scarcely be contested that the convictions of some of the accused at Nuremberg for crimes against *peace were innovative. However, the issue of the retroactive criminalization of aggressive wars at Nuremberg—hotly debated in the late 1940s—is no longer of great import. Undeniably, present-day international law endorses the position taken by the tribunal. Contemporary international law also validates the position taken by the tribunal in rejecting the defense of obedience to superior orders. By contrast, the concept of the criminal responsibility of organizations has gained much less support and remains doubtful.

The Nuremberg trial was conducted in a manifestly fair manner that impressed all impartial observers. The records of the proceedings, including the documentation of the Nazi atrocities, were published in a series of forty-two volumes. The irrefutable evidence of unprecedented horrors speaks for itself even after half a century.

(See also HOLOCAUST; WAR, RULES OF.)

Robert E. Conot, *Justice at Nuremberg* (New York, 1983).
YORAM DINSTEIN

NYERERE, Julius. Born in Butiama in the Lake Victoria region of Tanganyika in 1922 and maturing in the period of the Great Depression and World War II, Julius Kambarage Nyerere was educated in Catholic missionary schools and from 1943 to 1945 attended Makerere University in Kampala, Uganda. While he was a student at Makerere University Nyerere came into contact with the future nationalist leaders of Kenya and Uganda who articulated the opposition to colonialism. He was also exposed to Fabian socialism when he attended graduate school at the University of Edinburgh in Scotland in 1952.

The whole of the region of East Africa had seen a wave of general strikes, cash crop holdup, demonstrations, and uprisings, the most well known being the mass resistance of the Kenya Land and Freedom Army (sometimes called Mau Mau). In Tanganyika a small organization called the Tanganyika African Association (TAA) had agitated for self-rule since the 1920s. In 1953 Julius Nyerere, by then a secondary school teacher, was elected president of the TAA.

On 7 July 1954 the leading elements of the TAA along with the leaders of the trade union movement created a new political party called the Tanganyika African National Union (TANU). Nyerere was the first chairperson of TANU. Nyerere remained as leader of the party throughout its existence. In 1977 TANU was united with the party in Zanzibar, the Afro-Shirazi Party, to form the Chama Cha Mapinduzi (CCM). Nyerere was elected the chairperson of the party at its first congress in 1977 and was reelected at the two subsequent congresses in 1982 and 1987. He retired as leader in August 1990.

Tanganyika became independent on 9 December 1961, and Julius Nyerere was the first prime minister. After the Zanzibar revolution of January 1964 the two countries, Tanganyika and Zanzibar, joined together on 26 April 1964 to create the United Republic of *Tanzania. Julius Nyerere was the executive president of this Union.

The Arusha Declaration of 1967, which nationalized foreign property, was the basis for the promulgation of the ideas of Nyerere on a variant of socialism called *Ujamaa*. This concept of self-contained nucleated villages was also buttressed by a conception of "Education for Self-Reliance."

Nyerere was called *Mwalimu* ("teacher") both by the citizens of Tanzania and also by the leaders of the African liberation movements that had their base in Dar es Salaam, the capital of Tanzania. After 1975 Julius Nyerere became the chairperson of the leaders of the Frontline States—Angola, Botswana, Mozambique, Tanzania, Zambia, and Zimbabwe—who joined together in an anticolonial alliance. In 1978 Tanzania was attacked by Uganda and Nyerere took the decision that the Tanzanian army should not only repulse the Ugandan armed forces but also remove Idi Amin from future menacing of Tanzania.

Under the leadership of Julius Nyerere Tanzania was a stable one-party *democracy which held elections every five years. Nyerere decided not to campaign for the presidency in the 1985 elections, but he remained as the chairperson of the ruling party. He emerged as a leading critic of the *International Monetary Fund and called for a *New International Economic Order. At the 1986 meeting of the *Nonaligned Movement he was selected chairperson of the South-South Commission.

(See also AFRICAN SOCIALISM; DECOLONIZATION; MAU MAU ANTICOLONIAL STRUGGLE; ONE-PARTY SYSTEM; PAN-AFRICANISM.)

Cranford Pratt, *The Critical Phase in Tanzania, 1945–1968: Nyerere and the Emergence of a Socialist Strategy* (Cambridge, U.K., 1976).

HORACE CAMPBELL

O

OCCUPATION, MILITARY. See FOREIGN MILITARY BASES.

OCEANIA. See PACIFIC ISLANDS.

OCTOBER WAR OF 1973. See ARAB-ISRAELI CONFLICT.

OMAN. See GULF STATES.

ONE-PARTY SYSTEM. The term *one-party system* (sometimes referred to as *one-party state*) includes at its broadest two rather different types of regimes. In the Marxist-Leninist or "vanguard" party state, the party is distinguished by its restricted membership, highly structured internal organization, commitment to a Leninist *ideology, and direct supervision of the organs of state power. The second type of single-party state has a mass rather than elite membership and is generally rather weakly organized, with a variable level of ideological commitment, and exists alongside government organs rather than directly controlling them.

The origins of this type of one-party system lie in anticolonial nationalism and state consolidation in newly independent states, and classically it has arisen in Africa. In several cases, including Côte d'Ivoire, Guinea, Malawi, and Tanganyika (Tanzania), nationalism resulted in the formation of a single or overwhelmingly dominant movement, dedicated to the achievement of independence, that faced no appreciable internal opposition. At independence, a single party then monopolized political activity, regarding itself as the authentic expression of a new national identity. In other cases, such as Ghana, Kenya, Sierra Leone, or Zambia, two or more viable parties existed at independence, normally drawing their support from rival regional, ethnic, or factional groupings; a single party was deliberately created by the government in order to restrict opposition and to prevent the articulation of divisions that it regarded as dangerous to the stability of a new and often artificial state. This unity was sometimes achieved by the straightforward suppression of rival parties, but more often by inducing opposition leaders to join the governing party through the offer of ministerial portfolios.

These differences were reflected both in ideologies of one-party rule and in the ways in which such parties actually operated. All one-party systems shared an emphasis on the unity of the party, which in turn was taken to represent the unity of the nation, and on the dominant role of the party leader, who was rapidly elevated to the role of executive president; in some cases, as in Malawi, he became president for life. Party ideologies, such as "Nkrumaism" in Ghana or "humanism" in Zambia, reflected the personality of the leader; underlying them was a concept of democracy that owed much to Jean-Jacques Rousseau's ideal of the general will, articulated through a leader who took on many of the attributes of Rousseau's legislator. In the eyes of its most articulate defender, Julius *Nyerere of Tanzania, the one-party system was greatly superior to the divisive struggles of rival parties. He derisively compared a multiparty system to a sterile game of football, whereas the single party was likened to a "two-way all-weather road" through which popular wishes could be conveyed to the government, and government policies transmitted to the people. In other cases, such as Guinea and Mali, the insistence on unity and condemnation of enemies of party and nation at times approached paranoia.

In some cases, considerable efforts were made to achieve a measure of internal party democracy. In Tanzania, party elections were held in which two candidates, each carefully scrutinized and approved, competed for popular approval. In Kenya, where the party was the vehicle for a level of factional competition that would not have been tolerated in Tanzania, any number of candidates could stand for election to parliament. Sometimes, as with Kwame *Nkrumah's Convention People's Party (CPP) in Ghana, candidates were simply selected from the center and declared elected unopposed. Even where internal party competition was recognized, however, this was not allowed to challenge the position of the leader, and became instead a vehicle for factional conflict over patronage. The one-party system thus was ultimately irreconcilable with popular debate or choice over either national leadership or basic party policies.

The actual policies followed by one-party regimes have varied widely. Owing to the prominence of early leaders such as Nkrumah, Nyerere, and Sékou Touré in Guinea, they have often been associated with "populist socialist" development strategies, in which the state took over the reins of the economy and sought to use the government, aided by popular mobilization through the party, to promote rapid economic growth. In states such as Côte d'Ivoire, Kenya, and Malawi, however, one-party rule has accompanied explicitly capitalist development policies. The same was true of one of Africa's most distinctive single parties, the True Whig Party (TWP) of Liberia, which served as the vehicle for a capitalist oligarchy dominated by the immigrant Americo-Liberian segment of the population. The success of one-party systems has varied likewise. In some cases the party, atrophied by the absence of popular participation, decayed to a point at which it could readily be overthrown by a military coup. In Guinea, the one-party system lasted as long as its founder, Sékou Touré, and was overthrown immediately after his death. On the other hand, one-party regimes in Côte d'Ivoire, Kenya, Malawi, Tanzania, and Zambia have lasted for over a quarter of a century; the Liberian TWP, ousted in 1980, had by that time enjoyed more than a century of uninterrupted rule.

The one-party state remains an attractive option for regimes that wish to retain a measure (or at least an appearance) of party organization or popular participation yet are unprepared either to risk the dangers of multiparty competition or to commit themselves to the much more rigid framework of the Leninist party state. It thus can serve as a mechanism for the partial civilianization of military regimes, and can help a regime gain the support of elite groups in society. Only under conditions of exceptional national unity, however, such as those sometimes accompanying *decolonization, can the one-party system realize its stated goal of representing popular aspirations. The lack of accountability within such a system renders it inherently liable to corruption, and it may indeed prove most successful as a device for regulating the internal conflicts of an entrenched oligarchy. The creation of a genuinely participatory political structure must inevitably result in its demise.

(See also AUTHORITARIANISM; COMMUNIST PARTY STATES; LENINISM; MILITARY RULE.)

Immanuel Wallerstein, "The Decline of the Party in Single Party African States," in Joseph LaPalombara and Myron Weiner, eds., *Political Parties and Political Development* (Princeton, N.J., 1966). Aristide Zolberg, *Creating Political Order: The Party-States of West Africa* (Chicago, 1966).
                                          CHRISTOPHER CLAPHAM

OPEC. See ORGANIZATION OF PETROLEUM EXPORTING COUNTRIES.

ORGANIZATION FOR ECONOMIC CO-OPERATION AND DEVELOPMENT. The Organization for Economic Co-operation and Development (OECD) was founded in 1961 as successor to the Organization for European Economic Co-operation, the agency that had distributed *Marshall Plan funds in Western Europe. The organization now includes all major industrialized countries with market economies. The OECD is governed by a Council of Ambassadors; however, most of its work is carried out by a professional secretariat at its Paris headquarters or within committees and working groups that employ consultants throughout the industrialized world. Compared with international organizations such as the *European Community and the UN, the OECD has few ties to the public in member countries. The only nongovernmental organizations granted observer status are a Business and Industry Advisory Committee and a Trade Union Advisory Committee.

When the OECD began, it was envisioned in part as continuing the Marshall Plan, with developed market countries joining the United States as donors and with states in the developing world to be the recipients. This has remained one of the major tasks of the organization. Its Development Assistance Committee serves as a coordinating mechanism among donor countries. Within it, donors make pledges to each other about the levels of support they will provide to developing nations, and donors share information on their development activities. Building on this role, the OECD has become a caucusing group within UN agencies like the UN Conference on Trade and Development, where relations between more industrialized and less industrialized economies are discussed. In such forums OECD membership is often considered synonymous with "the North" facing the *Third World caucus, the *Group of 77, "the South."

The conflict between North and South over development assistance and the structure of the world economy brought about a major innovation within the OECD. In the 1973–1975 oil crisis the apparent influence of the *Organization of Petroleum Exporting Countries over the world price of oil led OECD members to create the International Energy Agency (IEA) to coordinate national stockpiles of oil and intervene in world markets when price increases threaten.

Third World critics point to the IEA and argue that the OECD has evolved away from the Marshall Plan precedent into an agency concerned only with the short-term self-interest of the wealthiest industrialized nations. It is certainly true that now most OECD activity, both of the secretariat and of various working groups, involves studying how economic cooperation among its members can be increased. The organization mainly studies individual OECD economies or sectors across all the industrialized market countries. The expertise of the OECD staff and the organization's role as one of a few that include all advanced capitalist states has given the OECD a role in preparing for the annual economic summits of the *Group of 7, an innovation in statecraft which also began after the first oil crisis.

(See also DEVELOPMENT AND UNDERDEVELOP-MENT; NORTH-SOUTH RELATIONS; UNITED NA-TIONS.)

Miriam Camps, *"First World" Relationships: The Role of the OECD* (New York, 1975).

CRAIG N. MURPHY

ORGANIZATION OF AFRICAN UNITY. The Organization of African Unity (OAU) was established in May 1963 amid much pomp and ceremony, at a time when the Pan-Africanist idea of continental unity was popular and during a period of momentous changes in international relations. The end of the European colonial era and the rise of the *Nonaligned Movement of *Third World countries occurred against a backdrop of a divided world of East-West rivalry for global control. Conceived as a harmonizing center of nations, the UN had instead become an ideological battleground between East and West with the emergence of blocs in which the Third World began to play a significant role.

Two basic points must be made regarding the UN and the OAU as *international organizations. First, the UN is a microcosm of the world's *state system, reflecting the interests of world governments. Governments, not people, are represented at the UN. The same is true of the OAU—it represents African governments, not peoples. Second, the modern African state system was shaped by colonial history: What became national boundaries were fixed by European rulers and crosscut ethnic lines in almost all cases.

At the second OAU summit in Cairo in 1964, African leaders accepted these boundaries over the objection of the Pan-Africanist minority voice led by Ghana's Kwame *Nkrumah. The latter advocated a "United States of Africa" that would transcend the colonial (and precolonial) legacy and transform the fragmented state system. Nkrumah contended that the postcolonial state system would be politically divisive and economically wasteful, a contention that proved to be prophetic. The tension between this Pan-Africanist idea and the fragmented state system is implicit in the compromise solution embedded in the OAU Charter, Article II of which advocates "the promotion of solidarity and cooperation" among African states as well as for the defense of their sovereignty and territorial integrity.

The OAU is clearly a creature of compromise which bridged the gap between a hitherto ideologically and geographically divided continent. This was no mean achievement. But, as a creature of compromise, the OAU tended to be all things to all governments, and its resolutions by and large have been ineffectual. Controversial issues have been continually postponed for fear of a split in the organization. The OAU thus has failed to exert moral authority to censure errant leaders or governments, even those engaged in grave violations of *human

rights, such as Idi Amin of Uganda, Mengistu of Ethiopia, and Siad Barre of Somalia.

On the credit side, the OAU can justly boast of some successful mediations of conflicts. The first such meditation concerned territorial dispute between Algeria and Morocco. It was followed by similar efforts in Congo (now Zaire) in the mid-1960s and in Nigeria in the late 1960s. In all cases the issues were clear-cut and the debates focused and coherent. The "OAU principles" of sovereignty and territorial integrity were applied with clarity and consistency.

Regarding Southern Africa and the *decolonization of the former Portuguese territories, the OAU's role was admirable as well. The establishment of the liberation committee, the channeling of financial, material, and military aid to the liberation fighters of those territories (the *African National Congress, the South-West Africa People's Organization, and the Zimbabwe African National Union—Patriotic Front), as well as the diplomatic campaigns conducted in support of their respective causes have been among the organization's best achievements.

The OAU fell far short of its stated objectives and periodic rhetorical commitments when it concerned the settlement of more complex interstate and intrastate conflicts. Its inability (or unwillingness) to mediate between Ethiopia and Somalia, or to confront the challenges posed by the developments in Eritrea and southern Sudan, are among its signal failures. On the other hand, it occasionally met challenges head-on, as it did, for example, in the Chad dispute by seating the Habré delegation to the exclusion of the Goukouni delegation in 1987. Again the divisive question of Western Sahara ended in the admission of the Sahrawi Arab Democratic Republic to OAU membership. That decision cost the OAU Morocco's membership, underscoring the risks which have caused the OAU to postpone the resolution of contentious issues for fear of a split.

The OAU's failure to apply a vigorous political will in search of lasting solutions to some of African's problems must be viewed in a larger historical perspective. To begin with, there is the fragmented postcolonial state system. Then there is the troubled economy, declining and distorted; there are political unrest, war, and famine, all of which have undermined Africa's confidence and dampened the earlier enthusiasm. In each state, perceived national or domestic needs have dictated harmful policy options including costly militarization. Such conditions do not foster bold moves in the settlement of disputes, but instead induce caution and inaction.

Nevertheless, some bold resolutions and plans of action have been adopted by the OAU. The Lagos plan of action of April 1980 is one such measure in the economic arena, together with the use of the UN *Economic Commission for Africa in working out alternative strategies for Africa's economic development. In the political sphere, the use of the Economic Community of West African States in the resolution of the Liberian conflict in 1991 was another example of how regional and subregional organizations might be used for economic and political objectives. In the realm of human rights, the OAU's adoption of the African Charter of Human and Peoples' Rights is another example of this promise and potential.

However, the gap between promise and performance is too wide for comfort. And in view of the prevailing international economic and legal order which does not favor developing nations, the Pan-Africanist aspiration of political unity, economic prosperity, and social progress remains a distant dream at best. In that context, it can be fairly said that the resolutions and plans of action will remain dead letters for the foreseeable future.

In sum, the OAU has played a useful role in Africa's liberation and in the settlement of some conflicts, but the failures far outweigh the successes. The OAU is a financially weak institution whose members cannot be compelled to pay their dues. There is no enforcement machinery to give its resolutions binding force and effect. And making dues payments compulsory and creating enforcement machineries have been entertained as alternatives, only to be abandoned because of the fear they might split the organization or drive member states out. This remains an unresolved dilemma.

Perhaps the current winds of democratic change will help foster a proper reappraisal and reorientation of policy and action to reflect the popular will. The central drama of Africa in the late twentieth and early twenty-first centuries will be seen in the response to this dilemma, and in this critical mission the OAU has a historic responsibility.

(See also AFRICAN REGIONAL ORGANIZATIONS; INTERNATIONAL SYSTEMS; PAN-AFRICANISM; UNITED NATIONS.)

Zdenek Cervenka, *The Unfinished Quest for Unity in Africa and the OAU* (New York, 1977). Yassin El-Ayouty and William Zertman, eds., *The OAU after Twenty Years* (New York, 1984).

BEREKET HABTE SELASSIE

ORGANIZATION OF AMERICAN STATES. The Organization of American States (OAS) is the preeminent institution in the Inter-American System of multilateral, multipurpose cooperation among the American states. The system, which traces its formal beginnings to 1889 through an uninterrupted ancestry of international conferences and organizational development, is today largely (but not exclusively) institutionalized in the OAS, the Inter-American Treaty of Reciprocal Assistance (*Rio Treaty), and the *Inter-American Development Bank. They are coordinated but have separate existences under their own conventions, as well as overlapping but distinct membership.

The charter of the OAS was agreed upon in 1948 to serve as the basic constitution for western hemispheric regional organization and to coordinate various organs and agencies. The OAS charter has been amended on two occasions, by a protocol approved in 1967 that entered into force in 1970, and another agreed to in 1985 that became operative in 1988.

In 1991 the OAS achieved universal regional membership of the thirty-five sovereign American states. Charter members in 1948 were the United States and the then-twenty Latin American states. Beginning in 1962, former British Caribbean dependencies gained independence and joined the OAS. Belize and Guyana, in accordance with original charter provisions, were not allowed to become members because of unsettled boundary disputes with member-states Guatemala and Venezuela, respectively; but the 1985 charter amendments dropped the membership-denial provision, and Belize and Guyana both joined in 1991. Suriname, a former colony of the Netherlands, adhered in 1975. Canada, invited since 1889 to join the Inter-American System, finally accepted membership in the OAS in 1990. Cuba technically remains a member; multilateral sanctions imposed in 1962, which remained in effect in 1992, denied "participation" to the *Castro government. The OAS has invited representatives from nonhemispheric states, the Holy See, and the UN to attend its meetings as permanent observers; as of 1991, eighteen entities had observer status.

The general purposes of the OAS have involved mutual security (coordinated with Rio Treaty procedures), economic cooperation and development (partly in concert with the Inter-American Development Bank), nonintervention and sovereign equality, peaceful settlement of disputes, and representative *democracy and *human rights. Various member states have assigned them different priorities and levels of commitment.

From the end of World War II to the mid-1960s, the United States primarily pursued mutual *security goals in the Cold War context and sought to convert the OAS into an "anti-Communist alliance." Latin Americans urged their own economic preoccupations, as well as the nonintervention principle as the institutional sine qua non. Interests temporarily converged under what came to be known as the Alliance for Progress when, from about 1959 to 1965, U.S. policies linked developmentalism to a definition of security that took into account economic and social progress. From the mid-1960s to 1979, the United States did not perceive serious security threats in Latin America and its interest in economic development declined; it did, however, address the issues of human rights. Latin Americans expressed dissatisfaction with U.S. regional dominance and insistence on an anti-Communist alliance, and resentments over U.S. trade and aid restrictions, intransigence in the Cuban issue, and violation of treaty-based pledges of nonintervention with unilateral coercive actions in Cuba, the Dominican Republic, and Chile.

The charter amendments of 1967 emphasized Latin American concerns by strengthening and broadening OAS economic and social functions; political and security purposes were relatively deemphasized as a consequence, although no treaty changes were made. Economic development activities were expanded, continuing into the 1980s, but the United States remained unwilling to commit significant resources to developmental programs. The most positive area of activity in the 1970s, continuing into the 1980s, was the reinforcement of human rights organization within the OAS. The American Convention on Human Rights, agreed to in 1969, finally went into effect in 1978 for the ratifying states; it expanded the authority of the Inter-American Commission on Human Rights and established the Inter-American Court of Human Rights.

During the decade after 1979 the importance of the OAS declined even further. The United States pursued its Central American policies with only peripheral reference to the OAS, and Latin Americans, in turn, went outside the system to make their most important multilateral peace proposals (the Contadora initiative and the peace plan, initiated by President Oscar Arias of Costa Rica, known as "Esquipulas II"). The United States invaded Grenada in October 1983, entirely ignoring the OAS charter. The OAS was only one of several forums, and not the most important, for dealing with the external debt crisis.

In the late 1980s, as inter-American cooperation progressed in the post–Cold War era, interest was revived in resuscitating the OAS. The principal effect of the 1985 amendments was to emphasize further Latin American economic concerns and to strengthen the policy role of the secretary general. Security issues involving threats from nonhemispheric entities were nonexistent, although a number of intraregional situations remained problematical. Pressing common problems, such as numerous economic questions, immigration and refugee policies, narcotics traffic, democracy and human rights, and environmental concerns, were increasingly prominent. The movement for an effective OAS was temporarily set back by the unilateral U.S. military intervention in Panama in 1989, but that event seemed to be transcended by an evolving consensus that hemispheric relations were best approached within established institutions designed to emphasize compatible interests and accommodate differences.

(See also INTERNATIONAL DEBT; LATIN AMERICAN REGIONAL ORGANIZATIONS; U.S.–LATIN AMERICAN RELATIONS.)

John D. Martz and Lars Schoultz, eds., *Latin America, the United States, and the Inter-American System* (Boulder, Colo., 1980). L. Ronald Scheman, *The Inter-American Di-*
lemma: The Search for Inter-American Cooperation at the Centennial of the Inter-American System (New York, 1988).
G. POPE ATKINS

ORGANIZATION OF PETROLEUM EXPORTING COUNTRIES. The Organization of Petroleum Exporting Countries (OPEC) was established in September 1960 by Venezuela, Saudi Arabia, Iran, Iraq, and Kuwait. Other countries which qualified for membership and joined later were Qatar (1961), Indonesia and Libya (1962), Abu Dhabi (1967, later transferred to the United Arab Emirates, 1974), Algeria (1969), Nigeria (1971), Ecuador (1973), and Gabon (1975).

The concept of an oil producers' organization began to take form at the first Arab Petroleum Congress in Cairo in 1959, and in the months following Pérez Alfonzo of Venezuela and Abdullah Tariki of Saudi Arabia worked toward its realization. Pérez Alfonzo's vision was for controlled use (conservation) of oil through a mechanism of production sharing (cartelization) by the main oil producers; in national terms this would simultaneously have upgraded the value of Venezuelan oil against the competition of lower-cost Middle East oil. Tariki was an Arab nationalist who saw an oil alliance with Pérez Alfonzo as a means to greater Arab strength and to the development of political change in Saudi Arabia. Their success in creating OPEC was due partly to the timing of Arab political developments in 1959–1960, and partly to an increasingly competitive oil market. The catalyst was the decision by the oil companies to reduce the posted price of Middle Eastern crude oils. This was precisely the trigger that Pérez Alfonzo was waiting for. Because of its direct effect on government revenues from oil, the price reduction was decisive in bringing Iran into the new organization.

For ten years OPEC achieved little in terms of its original underlying objectives, which were to improve its share of revenue from oil and ultimately to gain control over its natural resources. Production sharing, the vision of Pérez Alfonzo, was never acceptable to Iran nor, in spite of Tariki, to Saudi Arabia. Negotiations with the companies for improved terms were slow and only marginally effective.

During these first ten years, however, OPEC laid the groundwork for its later success; in the first place it gained experience on how to negotiate with the companies and how to present itself to a wider, often skeptical, audience; second, it obtained widespread practical, if never legal, acceptance of the principle that the law of changing circumstances applied to the concession contracts between oil-producing countries and the oil companies; and, third, in Resolution XV1.90 of June 1968, it agreed to a series of policy objectives for the organization.

OPEC's high noon was the period 1970–1973

when, from a position of market strength and political confidence, it negotiated with the oil companies new terms relating to revenue (split of profit and "rent") and to ownership ("participation"). Milestones were the Teheran and Tripoli agreements on price (1971) and the Riyadh agreement on participation (1972). The first phase of OPEC's activity ended in October 1973 when, in the euphoria of the Arab-Israeli war, OPEC doubled the oil price by its own decision, dismissing the oil companies from the negotiating table. This was quickly followed by a further doubling of price at a meeting in December in Teheran, taking advantage of the Arab oil embargo and production cutbacks that had also been imposed in October. It was followed with pressure for majority participation in the oil concessions, which the companies, even if they wished, were by now unable to resist. OPEC's original objective, to control its own oil resources, was thus achieved.

This success, however, had an important implication for OPEC; because it had in effect arrogated to itself the unilateral responsibility for oil price management, its relevance as an international organization was greatly enhanced—the more so, given that member countries of the *Organization for Economic Co-operation and Development (OECD) saw themselves challenged by a threat not only to their energy security but also to their *balance of payments and to the international monetary system. One result was the creation of the International Energy Agency within OECD.

Although OPEC had a high media profile, after 1973 it soon became apparent that its influence in international political terms was far less than it had at first seemed; nor did it in practice even have the ability to manage the oil market, although its members amassed vast revenues in the process.

In reality, the member countries of OPEC had no common objectives. Their different political attitudes, systems, and interests were such that even agreement on how to set or pursue an oil price objective was beyond their capability. In the context of international politics the objectives of, for instance, Iran, Saudi Arabia, Iraq, Algeria, and Venezuela were too much at variance to admit of any workable consensus. This was proved by the weakness of OPEC's summit declaration (Algiers, 1975), by the failure of the Conference on International Economic Cooperation (CIEC) or, as it was commonly known, the North/South Dialogue (1977), and by OPEC's inability to create a long-term strategy (1979). As for price management, in the years 1973–1979 the bitter arguments (often publicly expressed by Amuzegar of Iran and Yamani of Saudi Arabia) between the countries seeking higher prices and those preferring lower prices were only resolved by the unilateral use of its oil swing production capability by Saudi Arabia, with occasional additional support from Kuwait and Abu Dhabi. OPEC was frequently credited with the oil price increases

of 1973 and, after the *Iranian Revolution and the outbreak of the *Iran-Iraq War, with the increases of 1979–1980, when the price of oil again increased more than twofold, from US$12.50 to more than US$30 per barrel. In reality OPEC in both cases followed a market that was violently affected by external events; it then tried to use the new and higher price level created by those events as a base from which to operate irrespective of subsequent changes in market conditions. In the 1970s the result was to maintain nominal prices during a time of continuous high inflation (so that much of the initial increase was lost in real terms); in the 1980s the result was a price collapse as conservation policies and economic recession slashed OECD demand for oil. OPEC efforts to maintain prices in this period would have collapsed even more quickly if the production capacity of Iran and Iraq had not been drastically reduced by the effects of the war between them.

From 1982 OPEC efforts to maintain price levels by running itself as a cartel and setting production quotas for each member (thus meeting the original production-sharing objective of Pérez Alfonzo) failed. OPEC had no capacity to apply *sanctions against, or otherwise to police, members who broke the quota agreements they had undertaken. Moreover, the basic mistrust that existed between members (two of whom were by now at war with each other) and the diverse political and economic interests of member countries combined to erode OPEC's ability to set prices.

OPEC celebrated its thirtieth anniversary in 1990 with no consensus as to how to face the future. The international environment and the situations of individual members have so changed in the intervening years that to many OPEC seems outdated as an organization and ill prepared for the decades ahead. The capacity to expand oil production is now largely confined to the Gulf countries; the development of non-OPEC oil and alternatives to oil (gas, coal, nuclear power) have substantially weakened OPEC's market power; international alignments have altered the geopolitical importance of the Gulf; and the oil market is radically different as the influence of the major oil companies has been reduced and the commoditization of oil, based on spot, futures, options, and other financial derivatives, has developed. OPEC is likely to remain useful to the main oil producers as an umbrella organization, but, to the extent that oil producer decisions will be important, it will be the Gulf producers—and not OPEC—who will be playing the key role.

(See also ARAB-ISRAELI CONFLICT; ARAB NATIONALISM; FINANCE, INTERNATIONAL; INTERNATIONAL ORGANIZATIONS; INTERNATIONAL POLITICAL ECONOMY; NORTH-SOUTH RELATIONS.)

Fadhil J. al-Chalabi, *OPEC and the International Oil Industry: A Changing Structure* (Oxford, 1980). Ian Seymour, *OPEC: Instrument of Change* (London, 1980). Pierre Terzian, *OPEC: The Inside Story* (London, 1985). Mohammed E. Ahrari, *OPEC: The Failing Giant* (Lexington, Ky., 1986). Robert Mabro, ed., *OPEC and the World Market: The Genesis of the 1986 Price Crisis*, Oxford Institute for Energy Studies (Oxford, 1986). Ian Skeet, *OPEC: 25 Years of Prices and Politics* (Cambridge, U.K., 1988).

IAN SKEET

OSTPOLITIK. In its generic form, Ostpolitik comprised the Federal Republic of *Germany's (FRG) political relationships with its East European neighbors and the Soviet Union. Owing to the Federal Republic's location in the middle of the European continent and its hegemonic dominance over the area often referred to as *Mitteleuropa,* Germany's Ostpolitik assumed paramount importance for countries that remain beyond its immediate purview. For West Europeans and North Americans, too, Germany's Ostpolitik, though often welcomed, persistently caused some anxiety emanating from the fear and suspicion that Germany's (potentially excessive) rapprochement with the East would be forged at substantial cost to West European security. Developments such as Otto von Bismarck's finely honed balancing act between East and West *(Schaukelpolitik),* the conciliatory strategy vis-à-vis the Soviet Union via the Rapallo Treaty of 1922, and the Hitler-Stalin Pact of 1939 have given Ostpolitik a dubious reputation in certain Western quarters. It was precisely a consequence of this ambivalent legacy that the pejorative term "Genscherism" became commonplace in Western capitals during the late 1980s, denoting to its users yet another suspiciously cozy arrangement between an influential German politician (in this case the Federal Republic's foreign minister Hans-Dietrich Genscher) and the Soviet elite.

On a more positive note and more specifically, Ostpolitik stands for Willy Brandt's concrete measures to have the post-1945 European order fully accepted by the Germans and their neighbors, thereby making the Federal Republic one of the prime movers toward European reconciliation and global détente. Accompanied by a generally hostile attitude toward Eastern Europe and the Soviet Union among most West Germans, the 1950s and 1960s witnessed Konrad Adenauer's first initiative toward making Germany an integral member of the family of European nations by irretrievably anchoring the Federal Republic in Western Europe and the Atlantic Alliance. These measures comprised what subsequently came to be known as Westpolitik.

The second step in this conciliatory and integrative process—Ostpolitik—was taken by the Brandt-led Social-Liberal (Sozialdemokratische Partei Deutschlands–Freie Demokratische Partei) coalition in the early 1970s via extensive treaties between the Federal Republic and its Eastern and Central European neighbors, notably Poland, Czechoslovakia, the Soviet Union, and the *German Democratic Republic (GDR). Concretely, Brandt's Ostpolitik included specific moves in three distinct areas: (1) With regard to the Soviet Union, the Federal Republic pledged to increase its economic relations with that country and exchanged declarations of the nonuse of force. (2) With regard to Eastern European countries, the Federal Republic signed a similar agreement with Poland, which included German recognition of the Oder-Neisse line as Poland's permanent western border with Germany. Treaties with other East European countries, followed by international recognition of the GDR and the entry of both German states into the UN and other international bodies, completed the East European segment of Ostpolitik. (3) The most tangible and far-reaching aspects of Ostpolitik involved relations between the FRG and the GDR. A treaty between West Germany and East Germany established "special relations" between the "two states in Germany." Thus, for the first time, the FRG officially recognized the de facto existence of another German state. Above all, the treaty between the two German states called explicitly for an array of concrete measures to improve human relations between East and West Germans on a daily level. (4) Lastly, the so-called quadripartite agreement secured the status of West Berlin.

In short, Willy Brandt's Ostpolitik was nothing short of an unequivocal recognition of Germany's—indeed Europe's—postwar reality. As such, it represented a decisive, although long overdue, step in Germany's lengthy and arduous process of coming to terms with its National Socialist past. Only in this context do the bitter controversies surrounding Ostpolitik in the West German debate of the early 1970s make sense. Ostpolitik's ultimate triumph must be seen in the fact that through its normalization of East-West relations it contributed to an atmosphere of openness that ultimately destroyed the East's Stalinist dictatorships and thereby rendered Ostpolitik itself obsolete.

(See also GERMAN REUNIFICATION.)

William E. Griffith, *The Ostpolitik of the Federal Republic of Germany* (Cambridge, Mass., 1978). Helmut Kistler, *Die Ostpolitik der Bundesrepublik Deutschland 1966–1973* (Bonn, 1982). Peter Bender, *Neue Ostpolitik: Vom Mauerbau zum Moskauer Vertrag* (Munich, 1986). Wolfram F. Hanrieder, *Germany, America, Europe: Forty Years of German Foreign Policy* (New Haven, Conn., 1989).

ANDREI S. MARKOVITS

OUTER SPACE. See SPACE.

P

PACIFIC ISLANDS. Although the insular Pacific region (also referred to as Oceania) is not precisely defined, it is generally considered to comprise the three entities of Melanesia, Polynesia, and Micronesia (exclusive of Australia and New Zealand). The region consists of about 10,000 islands with a total land area of 982,555 square kilometers (379,365 sq. mi.) scattered across some 35 million square kilometers (13.5 million sq. mi.) of ocean. The population of the region is approximately 7.13 million (1990), about half of whom live in Papua New Guinea.

Thirty years ago all of the Pacific island nations were subject to some form of colonial administration: Indeed, the present political map of the Pacific islands is a product of the colonial divisions of the last century and early part of the present century. Today every country (except post-coup Fiji) operates on the basis of constitutional law and an independent judiciary. Elections are held on a regular basis and nearly everywhere (except Tonga and the French colonies) the head of government is chosen by the people.

The historical development of the region has been influenced by the cultural backgrounds of the Melanesian, Polynesian, and Micronesian peoples, and by the differing institutions brought about by the three major colonial traditions: British, U.S., and French.

The relatively large, mountainous islands of Melanesia in the western Pacific have considerable natural resources and potential for development. The much smaller islands of Polynesia to the east and Micronesia to the north (many of which are coral atolls) have fewer natural resources, compounded in many cases by problems of population pressure.

Pacific island communities are predominantly rural and communal societies in which relations with the extended family, the clan, and village are ubiquitous. Traditionally, Melanesians followed a consensus form of government; leaders would sit down to discuss issues until a compromise was achieved, which was then accepted universally. This grassroots democracy—known as the "Pacific way"—is still practiced, although centralized bureaucracies now exist in the capitals. The Polynesians and Micronesians have a tradition of powerful hereditary chiefs and kings; the king of Tonga is still the most powerful figure in his country.

Political stability characterized the early stages of the decolonization period, beginning with Western Samoa in 1962. In all but one case—Vanuatu (formerly New Hebrides)—the transition to independence was peaceful and smooth. In Vanuatu a serious problem arose in the final stage of decolonization in 1980 when minority dissent (led by external elements) sparked incidents of violence and an attempted secession by force on Santo and Tanna islands.

The 1980s witnessed uncharacteristic acts of violence and destabilization in the Pacific islands:

- The still-unsolved June 1985 assassination of Belau's first elected president, Haruo Remeliik, was followed three years later by the apparent suicide of Belau's second president, Lazarus Salii, in the wake of massive corruption charges.
- The July 1985 sabotage of the Greenpeace ship *Rainbow Warrior* by French *intelligence agents in New Zealand prevented the ship's attempt to protest ongoing French nuclear tests near Tahiti.
- The 1987 military coups in Fiji (the first in the region) deposed the democratically elected coalition government of Timoci Bavadra and installed an interim military-dominated regime amid continuing political instability.
- Violence recurred in New Caledonia in 1988, leading to the controversial French-created Matignon Accord, and the political assassination of indigenous Kanak independence leader Jean-Marie Tjibaou the following year highlighted the volatile situation there.
- Papua New Guinea has faced border incursions by Indonesian forces committed to suppressing an indigenous revolt in neighboring Irian Jaya, and a *secessionist movement exploded into violence in 1989 on the copper-rich island of Bougainville.

The Treaty of Rarotonga (also known as the South Pacific Nuclear Free Zone Treaty) was ratified in December 1986 by the Pacific nations and established the South Pacific (excluding Micronesia north of the equator) as a nuclear-free zone.

Following the UN's *Law of the Sea Treaty, the Pacific island nations in 1979 declared 200-mile exclusive economic zones (EEZs) around their archipelagoes in order to protect their valuable marine and mineral resources. These EEZs greatly enlarge the territorial size of these Pacific microstates and will become more important when the mining of strategic seabed minerals begins sometime in the twenty-first century.

The South Pacific Commission (based in New Caledonia), the region's first organization, was founded in 1947 by six metropolitan powers (Australia, France, the Netherlands, New Zealand, Britain, and the United States) to promote regional economic development (e.g., fisheries and agriculture) and social development in the Pacific island nations.

The South Pacific Forum, founded in 1971, grew out of dissatisfaction with the South Pacific Commission, which was perceived as being dominated by Britain and France. The forum currently comprises fifteen member nations and meets annually to discuss pressing issues in the region. In 1973 the forum created the South Pacific Bureau for Economic Cooperation (SPEC)—now called the Forum Secretariat and based in Suva, Fiji—which focuses on economic problems of the region. Since 1975 a Pacific-wide grass-roots organization—known as the Nuclear-Free and Independent Pacific (NFIP) movement and based in New Zealand—has worked toward the decolonization and demilitarization of the region.

The following section lists each Pacific island nation within its larger cultural grouping.

Melanesia. Fiji: independent republic (ind. 1970 from Britain); Irian Jaya: province of Indonesia (since 1962); New Caledonia: overseas territory of France (since 1853); Papua New Guinea: independent state (ind. 1975 from Britain); Solomon Islands: independent state (ind. 1978 from Britain); Vanuatu: independent republic (ind. 1980 from Britain and France).

Polynesia. American Samoa: unincorporated U.S. territory (since 1900); Cook Islands: self-governing in free association with New Zealand (since 1901); Easter Island: territory of Chile (since 1888); Eastern Polynesia (or French Polynesia; includes the Tuamotu, Society and Gambier islands): overseas territory of France (since 1842); Galápagos: province of Ecuador (since 1832); Niue: self-governing in free association with New Zealand (since 1900); Pitcairn Islands: dependency of Britain, administered by British High Commissioner in New Zealand (since 1838); Tokelau: dependency of New Zealand (since 1925); Tonga: independent monarchy (ind. 1970 from Britain); Tuvalu (formerly Ellice Islands): independent state (ind. 1978 from Britain); Wallis and Futuna: overseas territory of France (since 1887); Western Samoa: independent state (ind. 1962 from Britain).

Micronesia. Belau (formerly Palau): internally self-governing; last remaining territory under UN trusteeship (since 1947); Federated States of Micronesia (FSM, comprising Pohnpei, Kosrae, Yap and Chuuk): self-governing republic freely associated with U.S.

(since 1945); Guam: unincorporated U.S. territory (since 1898); Kiribati (formerly Gilberts, also includes Phoenix and Line islands): independent republic (ind. 1978 from Britain); Marshall Islands: self-governing republic freely associated with U.S. (since 1945); Nauru: independent republic (ind. 1968 from Britain); Northern Marianas: commonwealth with U.S. (since 1976).

David Stanley, *South Pacific Handbook,* 3d ed. (Chico, Calif., 1985). Luella S. Christopher, "Pacific Island Nations: Overview of Trends and Problems in the South and West Pacific," *Congressional Research Service Report* (Washington, D.C., 1990). Norman Douglas and Ngaire Douglas, eds., *Pacific Islands Yearbook,* 16th ed. (NSW, Australia, 1989). *Countries of the World and Their Leaders Yearbook,* vol. 1 (Detroit, 1990). *The European World Yearbook,* vol. 1 (London, 1990).

GLENN H. ALCALAY

PACIFIC REGION. Vigorous expansion in trade, investment, and other economic ties within the Pacific economy have been critically important to the region's extraordinary growth in the second half of the twentieth century.

East Asia's production, in the three decades after 1960, grew from less than one-quarter of North America's to rough equality with that of North America and about one-quarter of the world's. In this time, East Asia was a main source of dynamism in international and especially long-distance international trade. It became the most important source of world savings—larger than North America or Europe—and overwhelmingly the largest source of surplus savings for international investment.

In the period between 1965 and 1988, the share of the Pacific (here including East Asia, North America, and Australasia) in world trade grew from around thirty percent to forty percent. East Asian and Pacific countries transact sixty-six percent of their trade with each other. In 1965 intraregional trade was less than fifty percent of Pacific trade and more than half intraregional trade in the Pacific was with North America; by 1988, the largest proportion was among other East Asian and Western Pacific countries. The proportion of intraregional trade is now approaching seventy percent, matching that in Europe. The process of East Asian and Pacific economic integration is intensifying as Japanese corporations follow, in the 1980s and 1990s, the pattern of overseas expansion set by U.S. multinationals and private investors in the 1950s and 1960s.

The shift in the world's economic center of gravity toward East Asia and the Pacific brought with it huge changes in the international economic and geopolitical system, as well as in the analytic and ideological prisms through which people all over the world came to view reality. These developments were of particular importance in the conduct of international trade and economic *diplomacy. Asia-Pacific countries have not moved to form a European-style economic union or a discriminatory trading bloc. Such a development is viewed as inimical to the long-term interests of the region, which is critically reliant on rapid trade transformation and global market access. The political, economic, and cultural diversity in the region militates against such arrangements within the Pacific, except on a subregional basis as within North America, between Australia and New Zealand or among the *Association of Southeast Asian Nations (ASEAN) group of countries.

Compared with the elaborate mechanisms for consultation on economic policy matters that have evolved within Europe or that are incorporated in the *Organization for Economic Co-operation and Development (OECD), those in the Pacific are as yet quite rudimentary. Nonetheless, they have been built on common interest in economic cooperation and private efforts to encourage them and are uniquely suited to the problems of encouraging policy coordination among Asia-Pacific economies.

The process of establishing an infrastructure for closer economic cooperation was begun in September 1980, with what became the first Pacific Economic Cooperation Conference (PECC) in Canberra. PECC's forums and task forces, which deal with regional cooperation in trade, agriculture, fisheries, minerals and energy, and other issues, serve both policy and commercial strategic purposes. PECC has a tripartite structure, including government officials, industry representatives, and academic researchers. PECC has a small coordinating Secretariat in Singapore. Earlier regional forums had included a series of Pacific Trade and Development (PAFTAD) conferences, which had been bringing together economists since 1968, and the Pacific Basin Economic Council (PBEC), a regional business group founded in 1969. Both PAFTAD and PBEC are represented on the International Standing Committee of PECC.

At the end of the 1980s, Pacific economic cooperation activities underwent a significant change. In November 1989, a ministerial level meeting on Asia Pacific Economic Cooperation (APEC) was convened in Canberra. This was the most powerful and representative group of ministers responsible for foreign economic policy ever to assemble in Asia and the Pacific (from Japan, the Republic of Korea, the ASEAN countries, Canada, the United States, Australia, and New Zealand). The APEC ministerial group meets annually and, from November 1991, expanded to include participation from China, Chinese Taipei, and Hong Kong.

The emergence of stronger regional institutions is seen to be important in maintaining a liberal trading environment and promoting Pacific interests in the *General Agreement on Tariffs and Trade (GATT) trading system; in sustaining growth in East Asia; in constraining tensions between the United States and East Asia over trade and international payments; in managing the emergence of China, with its partially reformed economy, as a major Pacific partner; in advancing Pacific economic interests in global forums; and in providing coherence in the response of Asia-Pacific countries to changes in Eastern Europe and developments in the former Soviet Union.

(See also DEVELOPMENT AND UNDERDEVELOPMENT; GEOPOLITICS; MULTINATIONAL CORPORATIONS; NEWLY INDUSTRIALIZING ECONOMIES; PROTECTION.)

PETER D. DRYSDALE

PAKISTAN. In 1947, at the moment of the British withdrawal from South Asia, a movement orchestrated by the All-India Muslim League under Mohammad Ali Jinnah led to the emergence of Pakistan out of the predominantly Muslim northwestern and eastern extremities of the subcontinent. Although the nation was intended as a homeland for Muslims, less than three-quarters of the Muslims at the time of *India's partition became citizens of Pakistan. Since independence Pakistan has striven to reconcile its Islamic identity with the imperatives of a modern state structure. Despite a religious bond Pakistan's constituent units are characterized by linguistic, cultural, and economic disparities. Pakistan's socioeconomic heterogeneities and the ensuing political cleavages have forced the adoption of half a dozen constitutional frameworks—parliamentary and presidential—based on variations of *federalism. Yet the suspension of representative government for twenty-five years following independence fashioned a state structure more unitary than federal in form. Seven years before Pakistan's first military intervention in 1958, the military and the civil bureaucracy had registered their dominance within the state structure. The shift in the balance of power from elected to nonelected institutions has endured *military rule under General Ayub Khan (1958–1969) and General Yahya Khan (1969–1971), the "populist" era of Zulfiqar Ali Bhutto (1971–1977), the military and quasi-military *authoritarianism of General Zia-ul-Huq (1977–1988), and the return to *parliamentary democracy since 1988.

In the absence of well-organized political parties the clash between a centralized administrative structure and a regionally differentiated Pakistani society has strengthened provincial sentiments, confounding the task of forging an exclusively Islamic identity. The success of the Islamic Democratic Alliance (IDA) in the 1990 elections was hailed by some as an endorsement of the state-sponsored Islamization program initiated in the 1980s. Yet it is the long-standing structural imbalances within the state, polity, and economy, not the lack of a coherent religious ideology, which have been at the root of Pakistan's domestic instabilities.

The breakaway of *Bangladesh in 1971—the only successful secessionist movement in a newly independent state—was simply the most dramatic manifestation of the problems involved in basing national identity on religion alone. There have been continuing tensions in Pakistan's western provinces where the distribution of political power and economic resources favor the majority province of the Punjab, which also dominates the military and the civil bureaucracy. Of the minority provinces, the Northwest Frontier province has been relatively successful in staking a claim to state power and economic resources. The sense of alienation in Sind and Baluchistan, particularly among the linguistic minorities within them, has been sharpened by the prolonged suspension of representative government and selective political mobilization under direct or quasi-military rule.

Regional and international strategic requirements have exacerbated Pakistan's domestic dilemmas. Relations with India have been strained by memories of partition, two wars over Kashmir, and a third resulting in the dismemberment of Pakistan. Fears of India's hegemonic ambitions and disputes with *Afghanistan have seen the diversion of scarce financial resources into the defense effort and the ascendancy of a mainly Punjabi military establishment to the commanding heights of the state. By manipulating their connections with the centers of the international system in London and Washington, senior state officials during the *Cold War era sought to raise a viable shield of regional defense and to tip the domestic balance against elected institutions. Membership in the Southeast Asia Treaty Organization and the Baghdad Pact entitled Pakistan to U.S. military and economic aid. The full benefits of association with the United States eventually bore fruit once the Soviets invaded Afghanistan in December 1979. Washington set aside reservations about Pakistan's nuclear program and rewarded Zia-ul-Huq's military regime with billions of dollars of aid for supporting the Afghan resistance movement.

Western assistance in the 1980s spawned a parallel arms and drugs economy. The presence of 3 million Afghan *refugees and policies of political denial and differential economic patronage fueled social conflict, especially in Sind where unemployed youth armed with sophisticated weapons waged war against rival linguistic communities. The grafting of military officers into top positions within the state structure gave them privileged access to key sectors of the economy. Efforts to stretch the networks of political collaboration brought segments of the dominant socioeconomic strata—landlords and emergent commercial and industrial groups—within the state's orbit of patronage.

During the longest period of military rule in Pakistan's history the subservience of the political system to the nonelected institutions of the state became fully confirmed. Political parties were banned and support extended to local notables acceptable to the military-bureaucratic establishment. Massive infusions of funds swayed voting patterns; reliance on clan-based ties diluted party programs and the brazen use of state power ensured the success of favored candidates. In an overwhelmingly rural society where the winds of economic change were bringing about a gradual switch from agrarian to commercial relations of production, the monetization of politics, matched by concerns with local development issues, fostered the dependence of politicians on the state apparatus. Vast sums of money were distributed to assembly members elected on a nonparty basis in 1985, along with imprudent loans to the regime's supporters. This had grave implications for the fiscal health of the state. With debt reservicing charges outstripping revenue receipts and regional tensions foreclosing cuts in the defense budget, the state treasury was unable to redistribute resources more equitably between the center and the provinces or between the Punjab and the non-Punjabi provinces.

By the time of the 1988 party-based parliamentary elections Pakistan's economic woes were mirrored in the acute polarization of its political arenas. More than a decade of depoliticization and the IDA's access to state power and patronage restricted the success of Benazir Bhutto's Pakistan People's Party (PPP) in the general elections. Although the PPP, whose main power base was in Sind, managed to form a government at the center, stiff opposition from the IDA government in the Punjab greatly limited its room for political maneuver. Amid charges of corruption and mismanagement, embittered relations with the army high command, and administrative paralysis and deepening violence in Sind, Benazir Bhutto's government was dismissed in August 1990 by President Ghulam Ishaq Khan. Since the 1985 constitution aimed at perpetuating a quasi-military rule, the president had powers to override the prime minister. The installation of federal and provincial interim governments studded with IDA supporters once again proved the efficacy of access to state power and patronage in generating positive electoral results. With its 105 of 217 seats in the national assembly of 1990 and support from smaller parties, the IDA's landlord-dominated government, led by the Punjabi industrialist Mian Nawaz Sharif, could effectively check the forty-five PPP members. Whether the formation of the Sharif government accurately reflected a societal consensus on the political, economic, and ideological dilemmas facing Pakistan's 110 million people or merely represented the triumph of the military-bureaucratic state structure in imposing its imprimatur on the political process will continue to be debated.

(See also INTERNATIONAL DEBT; ISLAM; SOVIET-AFGHANISTAN WAR.)

Hasan-Askari Rizvi, *The Military and Politics in Pakistan: 1947–86*, 3d ed. (Lahore, 1986). Omar Noman, *The Political Economy of Pakistan: 1947–1985* (London, 1988).

Ayesha Jalal, *The State of Martial Rule: The Origins of Pakistan's Political Economy of Defence* (Cambridge, U.K., 1990).

AYESHA JALAL

PALESTINE. In the twentieth century, the region known as Palestine has been a field of intense conflict between peoples who have laid claim to it as their national home on grounds of long residence and historic and religious associations. Prior to the development of national states in the region after World War I, "Palestine" was not a separate political entity, but the name had long been in use. It was the name of a Roman province, and in the tenth century Arab geographers referred to "Filastin" (the Arabic name for Palestine) as one of the provinces of Syria. From the fifteenth century until World War I, Palestine formed part of the Ottoman Empire, and changing provincial boundaries blurred its separate status. However, for adherents of the three main monotheistic religions—*Islam, Judaism, and Christianity—"Palestine" remained the locus of holy sites of great significance: Jerusalem (al-Quds), Hebron (Khalil), Bethlehem, and Nazareth, to name only a few.

By the end of the Ottoman period (1914) the inhabitants of Palestine numbered approximately 650,000, the vast majority of whom were Arabs. Some ten percent of the Arabs were Christians and the rest Muslims; in addition there was a Jewish population of approximately 75,000. About three-quarters of the Arab population were settled cultivators. Only about five percent of the total population were nomadic pastoralists (bedouin).

The development of a separate and distinctive Palestinian identity was a consequence of two major historical developments which began in the late nineteenth century. The first was the growth of European economic, political, and military intervention in the *Middle East. This culminated after World War I in the division of the Middle East into spheres of control among the major European powers, primarily Britain and France, with Palestine falling under a League of Nations Mandate assigned to Britain. Arab nationalist and pan-Arabist movements had grown in response to Western intervention in the nineteenth century. With the drawing of new national boundaries under the post–World War I treaties, these *nationalisms took more specific forms.

A second cultural factor in the development of a separate Palestinian nationalism was the Zionist movement which sought to establish a "national home" for the Jews in Palestine under the aegis of British rule. Jewish settlement had begun during the late Ottoman period on a small scale, but the National Home policy agreed by the British administration explicitly facilitated immigration, settlement, and the acquisition of land in Palestine, and separate Zionist institutions. *Zionism aimed to create a Jewish homeland in Palestine, and therefore of its nature was unable to accommodate the demands and aspirations of the Arab population. The Jewish population grew, mainly through immigration, from eleven percent of the total in 1922 to thirty percent of the total population of 1,739,624 in 1944.

Prior to the period of British Mandate rule (1922–1948) Palestine's Arab inhabitants defined themselves mainly according to local, regional, and religious or family allegiances. While these continued to be important, the rise of *Arab nationalism had influenced some members of the Palestinian elite. However, it was the sense of threat generated by the new settler movement sponsored by the British that gradually created new consciousness of identity as Palestinians.

In the first years of the Mandate many looked to a union with Syria to bring about an end to the National Home project and British rule. As this hope faded, the Arab elites sought to change British policy through negotiation and appeals to Islamic solidarity in the Arab region to defend the holy places. By the 1930s the economic pressures created by Jewish settlement and land buying increasingly impinged on the lives of the majority of the Palestinian population. The nature of nationalist protest began to change as the strategies and self-interested infighting of the elites were challenged by new tendencies: among the intelligentsia by a more radical secular nationalism; and among the poor and dispossessed by a radical and redemptive Islam embodied in the movement of Shaikh al-Qassam, killed by the British in 1935. His attempted uprising and death were one of the triggers for the full-scale Palestinian uprising which took place from 1936 to 1939, against the Zionist movement and against British rule, crushed only by the use of massive force.

The 1940s found the popular Palestinian nationalist movement which had taken shape in the 1930s in ruins. The traditional leadership tried to reassert its position, but its status and effectiveness were diminished. In contrast, the Zionist movement, despite its own internal rifts, had consolidated its position over the decade since 1936. The Holocaust had united world Jewry behind Zionism and had created moral support in the West for a Jewish homeland. Greatly increased Jewish immigration to Palestine had also shifted the demographic balance of forces. The 1947 UN plan for the partition of Palestine into separate Jewish and Arab states was rejected by the Palestinians and the Arab world who refused to truncate Arab Palestine or to recognize a separate Jewish state. The ensuing impasse resulted in virtual civil war. The British prepared to pull out while the Zionists sought to gain control of as much territory as possible, including land beyond that assigned to them in the partition plan.

The war of 1948–1949 in which the forces of the

newly declared state of *Israel defeated Palestinian forces as well as armies sent from neighboring Arab states resulted in the obliteration of "Palestine" as a state. The state of Israel occupied a large part of the territory with the remainder held by *Jordan (the West Bank) and *Egypt (the Gaza Strip). Of the Palestinian Arab population, some 700,000, fleeing the fighting, had been barred from returning to their homes, or expelled beyond the boundaries of the new Jewish state by Israeli forces. Those who had fled were scattered in the West Bank, in the Gaza Strip, and in surrounding Arab countries, mainly Lebanon, Syria, and Jordan. Only a tiny percentage of the refugees were ever permitted to return to their homes inside Israel. In 1950, some 160,000 Palestinians remained under Israeli rule. During the June War of 1967, the map was again revised, with the Israeli occupation of all Jerusalem, the West Bank, the Gaza Strip, and the Golan Heights. Thus virtually the entire area of Palestine came under Israeli rule.

From 1949, Palestine became an idea, and Palestinian national identity took on a distinctive form, based on the loss of a homeland and the longing to return. The experience of dispossession, or of living under Israeli rule, has varied according to class, location, and circumstances. Divisions and resentments have developed over the years between social layers within the exiled community—in Jordan and Lebanon. The squalor of the refugee camps contrasted with the relative affluence, if not security, of middle-class urban dwellers. Differences arose between those who have established themselves in the Gulf or the United States and all others; and between those living under Israeli rule and those outside. Yet in times of crisis all are drawn together by the sense of identity through dispossession and by the insecurity of the stateless.

The *Palestine Liberation Organization (PLO) has embodied both this aspiration for return to Palestine and the sense of loss. Its appeal has been both to a secular nationalism—the right of the Palestinians to their own land and self-determination—and also at times to the idea of reclaiming Palestine's Islamic holy places, especially Jerusalem. The idea of the Palestinian "revolution" is a common reference point. Revolution here is a broad term connoting a redemptive nationalist struggle, not necessarily a class struggle. Islamic groups have placed much stronger emphasis on the liberation of the holy places, *jihad, and an Islamic Palestine. These groups have not, however, exercised a decisive influence on the direction of the movement.

The Israelis contributed to this sense of identity by their efforts to deny the Palestinians any cultural memory or political identity. For many years Israelis denied the very existence of "Palestinians" as a category distinct from "Arabs" and with a legitimate claim to identity and self-determination. This denial took the form of censorship, political repression,

and control over education. Palestinian citizens of Israel have lived the constant contradiction between the Israeli denial of their specific identity and history and its refusal to accord them equal treatment as citizens. The marginality, in the course of several generations, has reinforced rather than diminished a sense of Palestinian identity in the younger generation. In the occupied territories, attempts to repress political and cultural identity have similarly proved counterproductive. The *intifada, coming after twenty years of occupation, is clear evidence of the growth and consolidation, despite internal disputes, of national feeling in the territories.

The geographical definition of Palestine has been based on the boundaries under the British Mandate, but since the 1970s an increasing number of Palestinians have been willing to accept the idea of a Palestinian state "on a part of Palestine," thus allowing for the continued existence of an Israeli state. This position was embodied in the PLO's 1988 declaration of an independent state, followed by the explicit recognition of the Israeli state. This strategy, so far not accepted by the Israelis, envisages a Palestinian state based in the occupied West Bank and Gaza Strip.

However, several crucial questions remain. The first regards the status of Jerusalem, which contains sites holy to Islam, Judaism, and Christianity and is claimed by both Palestinians and Israelis. Second, the geographical discontinuity of such a Palestinian state would create strategic and economic problems. Third, after over twenty years of Israeli occupation, the economies of the territories have been made highly dependent on the Israeli economy. This dependence, whether on Israel or other neighboring states, would be difficult to break. Finally, there remains the question of what proportion of over 4 million Palestinians such a state could accommodate.

Palestinian nationalism has had a shifting relationship to Arab nationalism and pan-Arabism. Palestinians have invoked Arab nationalism and unity to help reclaim the territory of Palestine. However, in the last two decades Palestinians have expressed increasing bitterness that while the liberation of Palestine has served as a slogan to sustain pan-Arabism, the Arab states have provided only limited support to the Palestinian cause.

(See also ARAB-ISRAELI CONFLICT; RELIGION AND POLITICS; UNITED NATIONS.)

Gershon Shafir, *Land, Labor and the Origins of the Israeli-Palestinian Conflict* (Cambridge, U.K., 1969). Rosemary Sayigh, *Palestinians, from Peasants to Revolutionaries* (London, 1979). Edward Said, *The Question of Palestine* (London, 1980). Nels Johnson, *Islam and the Politics of Meaning in Palestinian Nationalism* (London, 1982).

SARAH GRAHAM-BROWN

PALESTINE LIBERATION ORGANIZATION. The Palestine Liberation Organization (PLO) was formed by the Arab summit conference in January 1964 in order to contain and channel renewed *nationalism among the Palestinians, displaced by *Israel's foundation in 1948. The 422-member *Palestine National Council (PNC), the PLO's policy-making parliament, first convened in Jerusalem in May 1964. The PNC elected a fifteen-member Executive Committee, which elected as chair the veteran diplomat Ahmad al-Shuqayri. The PNC endorsed a National Charter that sought to restore Palestine to Arab rule and formed the Palestine Liberation Army (PLA), whose units were attached to the armed forces of Egypt, Syria, and Jordan.

When Israel defeated those armies in June War of 1967, their leaders and the PLO officials were discredited. The lawyer Yahya Hammudah replaced Shuqayri as chair in December 1967. The Palestinian guerrilla movements, which had remained aloof from the PLO, swelled in size after they withstood Israel's attack on Karameh, Jordan, in March 1968. Yasir *Arafat, head of Fatah, the largest group, was elected chair at the fifth PNC (February 1969), at which more than half the members came from guerrilla forces. Fatah, formed in 1958, called for the establishment of a "democratic, non-sectarian Palestine state in which all groups will have equal rights and obligations irrespective of race, color and creed."

The PLO charter, amended at the fourth PNC (July 1968), reflected the guerrillas' emphasis on popularly-based armed struggle, rejected *Zionism and the partition of Palestine, termed Judaism "a religion . . . not an independent nationality" (Article 20), and called for "the total liberation of Palestine" (Article 21). The charter upheld Arab unity, but emphasized that just as the PLO would "not interfere in the internal affairs of any Arab state" (Article 27), it would also "reject all forms of intervention, trusteeship and subordination" (Article 28) by Arab governments. The charter could only be amended by a two-thirds vote of the total membership of the PNC, at a special session.

Arafat not only led Fatah but also, as PLO chair, commanded the PLA units. He formed the Palestinian Armed Struggle Command (PASC) in 1969 as a police force to maintain order in refugee camps in Jordan and Lebanon. By June 1970 the Unified Command of the guerrilla groups included Fatah, the largest group; the Popular Front for the Liberation of Palestine (PFLP), founded by Dr. George Habash in December 1967; the Popular Front-General Command (PF-GC), whose leader Ahmad Jabril broke away from PFLP in 1968; the Democratic Front for the Liberation of Palestine (DFLP), whose Jordanian head, Naif Hawatmeh, left the PFLP in February 1969; the Syrian-sponsored Saiqa, formed in 1968; and the Iraqi-sponsored Arab Liberation Front (ALF), formed in January 1969. The PLO provided an umbrella for the diverse groups, which often worked at cross-purposes. Fatah focused on freeing Palestine from Israeli rule and sought amicable relations with

Arab governments. In contrast, the PFLP and DFLP worked to overthrow conservative Arab regimes prior to liberating Palestine. Saiqa and the ALF were controlled by rival branches of the Ba'th Party, which emphasized Arab unity rather than Palestinian nationalism. They also differed on tactics: Fatah, Saiqa, and the DFLP denounced the PFLP and PF-GC for hijacking foreign airplanes in 1969–1970.

Disagreements with Arab host governments crystallized in mid-1970 when Egypt and Jordan accepted a U.S.-mediated cease-fire with Israel. In September 1970 Jordan's King Hussein used the occasion of the PFLP's landing hijacked planes on Jordanian soil to launch a military showdown with the PLO, accusing it of seeking to overthrow his government. All the guerrilla units were forced out of Jordan by late 1971. They regrouped in Lebanon, where the Cairo Agreement (November 1969) regulated their presence in the refugee camps and along the border with Israel.

The PLO established a complex institutional structure in Lebanon, which included hospitals and clinics run by the Palestine Red Crescent Society, handicrafts and light industries, and planning and research centers. Such affiliated organizations as the unions of workers, engineers, writers, journalists, teachers, students, and women ran activities throughout the *Middle East. The Palestine National Fund handled fund-raising and disbursement.

Palestinian despair in the early 1970s after the defeat in Jordan was signaled by desperate attacks by Black September commandos, including the assassination of Jordan's prime minister in Cairo in November 1971 and the kidnapping and murder of Israeli athletes at the Olympic Games in Munich in September 1972. Nonetheless, PLO leaders began to revise their political objectives. The eleventh PNC (January 1973) secretly resolved to form a Palestine National Front in the Israeli-occupied West Bank and Gaza Strip, which would work politically to end Israeli rule in those parts of Palestine. Following the October War (1973), the twelfth PNC (June–July 1974) advocated the establishment of an "independent combatant national authority . . . over every part of Palestinian territory that is liberated." (Even though the PNC rejected a permanent *peace with Israel, the PFLP viewed the resolution as tantamount to accepting Israel's existence and withdrew from the Executive Committee of the PLO, remaining only on the intermediate-level Central Council.)

The PLO's standing in the Arab world was consolidated in October 1974 when the Arab summit at Rabat affirmed "the right of the Palestinian people to establish an independent national authority under the command of the Palestine Liberation Organization, the sole legitimate representative of the Palestinian people, in any Palestinian territory that is liberated." The PLO's international role was enhanced in November 1974 when, following Arafat's address to the UN General Assembly, the PLO secured observer status at the UN. Furthermore, pro-PLO candidates swept the West Bank municipal council elections in 1976 and the thirteenth PNC (March 1977) stressed the Palestinians' "right to establish their independent national state on their own land." By then, Fatah had paramount influence within the PLO, since the PFLP had failed to mobilize other groups behind its Rejection Front and Saiqa had virtually collapsed in the wake of Syrian-supported attacks on Palestinians during the initial phase of the Lebanese civil war.

The PLO's strategic shift from the goal of reclaiming all Palestine to the goal of forming a state alongside Israel failed to have the intended diplomatic impact. It was sidetracked first by Egyptian President Anwar *Sadat's bilateral negotiations with Israel, which culminated in the March 1979 peace treaty, and then by the Israeli invasion of Lebanon in June 1982. The Egyptian-Israeli accord provided for a transitional period of self-rule on the West Bank and Gaza Strip that excluded the PLO and downplayed the prospects of Palestinian statehood. The Israeli invasion, designed to destroy the PLO's military and political infrastructure in Lebanon, was complemented by Israel's dismantling the municipalities on the West Bank and Gaza Strip. During the sixty-seven-day Israeli siege and aerial bombardment of Beirut, Arafat negotiated the withdrawal of Palestinian forces from the Lebanese capital. In August 1982, he moved the PLO headquarters to Tunis. Palestinians living in refugee camps near Beirut, no longer protected by PLO forces, suffered vengeful attacks by Israeli-protected Lebanese Forces the next month.

The PLO seemed severely weakened by the Israeli invasion, especially when several Fatah officers denounced Arafat in 1983, decrying the evacuation and calling for renewed combat with Israel. Syria hosted not only those dissidents but also the leaders of the PFLP, DFLP, and PF-GC. Nonetheless, Arafat reinvigorated his diplomatic efforts and formed a counterweight with his erstwhile antagonists Egypt and Jordan. The seventeenth PNC (November 1984), held in Amman, enabled Arafat to join King Hussein in February 1985 in calling for a confederation of Jordan and a Palestinian state on the West Bank and Gaza Strip. However, the PLO appeared to weaken and fragment further when Washington did not respond to the joint initiative, Israel bombed the PLO headquarters in Tunis in October 1985, dissident Palestinians launched terrorist attacks in late 1985, and King Hussein renounced the accord in February 1986. Despite these tensions, Arafat reconsolidated the movement at the eighteenth PNC (April 1987, Algiers). Despite Syrian opposition, the PFLP and DFLP resumed their seats on the Executive Committee, the Palestine Communist Party gained a seat for the first time, and only the numerically insignificant dissident Fatah and PF-GC remained outside the PLO's fold.

The PLO was thus well positioned to respond to the popular *intifada ("shaking off") that has swept the West Bank and Gaza Strip since December 1987. The Unified National Leadership of the Uprising contains the major groups within the PLO, and it helped propel the PLO to endorse the establishment of an independent Palestine state at the nineteenth PNC (November 1988, Algiers). That PNC endorsed, for the first time, both the UN General Assembly's partition plan of 1947 and UN Security Council *Resolution 242 of November 1967, and called for "security and peace for every state in the region." The next month Arafat explicitly recognized Israel's right to exist as a Jewish state and underlined the PNC's renunciation of *terrorism. The Central Council elected Arafat president of Palestine in April 1989.

The PLO has been transformed organizationally and politically since its formation in 1964. Originally the instrument of Arab governments and then the umbrella for guerrilla movements, the PLO is now a proto-state with ramified policy-making and bureaucratic structures. PLO aims, articulated by the authoritative PNC, have shifted from liberating all Palestine to establishing a state alongside Israel. The means for achieving that goal have altered from armed struggle to active *diplomacy. The PLO has maintained its autonomy in the face of efforts by Arab governments to co-opt and control it. The Israeli government has consistently refused to negotiate with the PLO and has branded it a terrorist organization, but virtually all other governments—including, from December 1988 to June 1990, the United States—have some diplomatic contact with the PLO and view it as the effective representative of the Palestinian people.

(See also ARAB-ISRAELI CONFLICT; GUERRILLA WARFARE; NATIONAL LIBERATION MOVEMENTS; REFUGEES.)

William Quandt, Fuad Jabber, and Ann Mosely Lesch, *The Politics of Palestinian Nationalism* (Berkeley, Calif., 1973). Bard O'Neill, *Armed Struggle in Palestine* (Boulder, Colo., 1978). Aryeh Yodfat, *PLO Strategy and Politics* (New York, 1981). Helena Cobban, *The Palestine Liberation Organization* (New York, 1984). Alain Gresh, *The PLO* (London, 1986). Rashid Khalidi, *Under Siege: PLO Decisionmaking during the 1982 War* (New York, 1986). Shaul Mishal, *The PLO under Arafat* (New Haven, Conn., 1986). Emile Sahliyeh, *The PLO after the Lebanon War* (Boulder, Colo., 1986).

ANN M. LESCH

PAN-AFRICANISM. The Pan-Africanist movement has been the principal agency for the self-definition of the African peoples in the twentieth century. This conception of self has been manifest both at the subjective level in the race consciousness of the African peoples in Africa and outside and at the objective level in the organizational forms which aspired to give expression to the ideas of African identity and African liberation. It is the organizational form which is more widely known, with six Pan-African Congresses and the *Organization of African Unity (OAU) representing formal unity. The Pan-African movement has gone through four main stages in this century.

Stage 1. Pan-Africanism and the quest for self-definition arose out of the concrete realities of the partition of Africa at the end of the nineteenth century and the rise of racism in the Americas. In this period the intellectuals were the main spokespersons for the ideas of African independence and racial dignity. At the level of organization this took the form of Pan-African Congresses which sought to bring together those with an agenda for the liberation of Africa from colonialism. There were five congresses between 1900 and 1945.

During this first period the major organization which combined both the subjective aspirations and the objective basis for Pan-African unity was the Universal Negro Improvement Association, whose president was Marcus Garvey. Garveyism took root in the United States where the ideas of African redemption provided a framework to combat the racism and lynching of the period after World War I. The UNIA has been the only Pan-African movement in this century to have more than 2 million members in Africa, the United States, the Caribbean, and South America.

The Italian invasion of Ethiopia in 1935 was another high point in the Pan-African movement. Before 1900 the movement called Ethiopianism could be seen as the precursor to Pan-Africanism; for Ethiopia, the oldest independent state in Africa, was a symbol for both spiritual and political independence. In this period the main thrust of Pan-Africanism came in the form of the writings by scholars of the ideas of Pan-Africanism and Negritude. W. E. B. *Du Bois, C. L. R. *James, George Padmore, Aimé Césaire, and Léopold Senghor were some of the noted writers. They brought to international attention the contribution of Africa to human transformation in the process of opposing colonialism. Others such as Cheik Anta Diop, Frantz *Fanon, and Walter Rodney were inspired by the earlier scholars and their writings deepened and broadened the understanding of Pan-Africanism.

Stage 2. This was the period of the anticolonial struggle, when the nationalist movement embraced the ideas of the intellectuals in developing concrete organizations for independence—the idea that the independence of one part of Africa would be meaningless until Africa was completely liberated. Kwame *Nkrumah had returned to Ghana and popularized these ideas in the struggle for Ghanaian independence. The first Pan-African meeting to be held on African soil was the All-African Peoples' Congress

held in Accra, Ghana, in 1958. It was here that the concept of the OAU gained force and where leaders such as Patrice *Lumumba became exposed to the potential international force of the Pan-African movement.

Stage 3. The OAU was formed in 1963 with its headquarters in Ethiopia. The OAU was committed to Pan-African liberation and supported the *decolonization process with military support for those fighting for liberation. However, as an organization of states this body was constrained by the principles of inherited colonial structures and boundaries which became the basis of the new states. A clause of noninterference in the internal affairs of states ensured that even with *human rights abuses in societies such as Uganda (under Amin), Zaire (under Mobutu), Nigeria (during the civil war and the expulsion of other Africans), Central African Republic (under Bokassa), and Equatorial Guinea, this body was silent.

A key tenet of Pan-Africanism was that Africans in one part of the world were responsible for the plight of other Africans. This tenet had developed in the solidarity of the slaves and made Pan-Africanism simultaneously a brand of *nationalism and internationalism. It was internationalism that was missing when the OAU was called upon to support the *civil rights movement in the United States and refused. This movement was another high point in the Pan-African movement in this century and spoke to the subjective and objective dimensions of Pan-Africanism. Spokepersons such as *Malcolm X linked the movement against racism in the United States to the liberation process in *Southern Africa.

In this period the principal spokespersons for the Pan-African movement were the cultural artists who through various media gave expression to the aspirations of Pan-African liberation. The Rastafari movement was an expression of Pan-Africanism at the grass-roots level and Bob Marley was one of the those who used music to carry the Pan-African and internationalist messages of emancipation. Eusi Kwayana, the Pan-African humanist from Guyana, was among a small group in North America and the Caribbean that planned the Sixth Pan-African Congress in Tanzania in 1974. However, contrary to the original intentions of the conference call, the actual meeting turned out to be a gathering of leaders of states—like a small-scale OAU. In the last phase of decolonization and with the narrow vision of the political leadership of the OAU there were appeals for a new conception of Pan-Africanism based on the cultural unity of Africa and leaving European models of development behind.

Stage 4. In the 1970s and 1980s, the promise and reality of African independence gave rise to a new conception of Pan-Africanism. While some organizations, such as the Pan-Africanist Congress of Azania, still held on to a conception of Pan-Africanism which derived from the anticolonial period, the movement had matured to a more internationalist phase. The quest for emancipation embraced those social groups most burdened by the economic retrogression of Africa while at the same time there was the search for new forms of interstate relations which broke the stranglehold of external powers over Africa. Small initiatives such as the *Southern African Development Co-ordination Conference (SADCC), the Preferential Trade Agreement (PTA), and the Economic Community of West African States (ECOWAS) reflected the search for economic independence. Most of these efforts were frustrated by the *destabilization of *apartheid. The concept of a larger economic unit in the region of Southern Africa after apartheid began to gain ground in the long search for economic independence. Thus was Pan-African liberation linked not only to a new form of economic organization but to a concept of Pan-African humanism to rise above the legacies of the Eurocentrism.

(See also AFRICAN REGIONAL ORGANIZATIONS; RACE AND RACISM.)

V. B. Thompson, *Africa and Unity* (London, 1969). Horace Campbell, *Pan-Africanism* (Toronto, 1975).

HORACE CAMPBELL

PANAMA. Geography is destiny on the isthmus between North and South America where the Pacific and Atlantic oceans are separated by a strip of land only fifty miles wide. Political developments since the Spanish Conquest have been marked by an ongoing struggle for access to and control over and the transit route—whether the gold, silver, and slave routes using mules or dugout canoes until 1739; the first transcontinental railroad, completed in 1855; the French canal effort of the 1880s; or the U.S.-built Panama Canal since 1903.

As a result, an urban commercial elite developed and predominated both in the economic and political realms, as opposed to a rural-based oligarchy as in most Latin American countries. *Alliances and conflicts with other groups, national or foreign, in this century have largely revolved around access to the Canal Zone, a process that intensified in the late 1980s, as the year 2000 approached, when full control of the canal and surrounding land reverts to Panama. The denouement was the invasion by the United States in December 1989 to replace a military government with statist and populist leanings by one that was friendly to the United States and favored a privatized and deregulated economy.

Much of Panama's economic activity traditionally centered on the transit zone—through servicing the civilian and military inhabitants of the Canal Zone and the highly-paid Panamanians employed there, in addition to providing some ancillary services to canal users—or on the banana export industry near the western frontier. During the 1970s the government promoted diversification of Panama's inter-national services, based on the establishment of an international banking center, taking advantage of the circulation of the U.S. dollar in Panama, and expansion of the Colón Free Zone, the world's largest free zone after Hong Kong. Along with other countries in Central America, Panama also became a *drug transshipment point, an activity that sporadically enjoyed official protection.

By 1988, Panama's 2.3 million inhabitants had a per capita income of over US$2,000, although they suffered one of the worst income distributions in Latin America. The expansion of the public sector through heavy borrowing in the 1970s helped contribute to eighty percent literacy rates and a decline in infant mortality to under thirty per thousand. Nearly half the population lives in the metropolitan area, in the Panama-Colón corridor.

Panama has a presidential form of government, under which elections for president and the Legislative Assembly are held formally every five years. Smooth transitions have been the exception, however, and since Panama's independence from Colombia in 1903, most presidents have been ousted before completing their term.

Political parties were banned for ten years following the October 1968 military coup against President Arnulfo Arias, Panama's most famous politician, who was first elected president in 1940 and reputedly won every election in which he ran through 1984. His espousal of support for the Axis powers during World War II ensured his swift removal from power, as the Panama Canal and the Canal Zone were vital elements in the war effort of the Allies.

General Omar Torrijos Herrera emerged as leader of the Revolutionary Process, as it was known, from 1969 until his death in an airplane crash in 1981. Under his leadership a new constitution was approved in 1972, providing for elections to a National Assembly of 505 representatives from municipal subdistricts and for a much-enhanced role for local councils. As a result, sectors that had been largely excluded from the political process—*peasants, Indians, women, and organized labor—were incorporated directly, albeit under the tutelage of the military. In this period Panama took on a regionally important role rallying support for modernization of its relations with the United States, as expressed in the *Panama Canal Treaty negotiations. Through the Contadora group, Panama continued to promote a Latin American stance toward regional problems of Central America in the 1980s.

Torrijos's chief of intelligence, Manuel Antonio Noriega, became commander in 1983 of the Defense Forces, taking a more direct role in state control, despite presidential elections held in 1984 and 1989. In 1984 the government candidate won by a suspiciously small margin, only to be ousted by Noriega a year later, and in 1989 the elections were annulled when it became obvious the opposition had a two-to-one victory.

Noriega's long association with branches of the U.S. federal government, the *Central Intelligence Agency since the mid-1960s and the Drug Enforcement Agency in the 1970s and 1980s, made him an unlikely figure to lead a genuine nationalist movement when relations with the United States deteriorated in mid-1987. His command of psychological operations gave him control with maximum use of fear and minimal violence. The U.S. invasion of Panama in December 1989 that ousted Noriega was welcomed locally, despite the more than 550 deaths and widespread destruction and looting that resulted.

The political forces in power in the post-invasion period had in common a favorable attitude toward U.S. policy, anticommunism, and dislike of the military. While some were interested in recovering access and privileges denied to them since 1968, commercial sectors that had benefited from the 1970s expansion of Panama's role as an international service entrepôt proposed dismantling all restrictions to free trade.

Organized labor, deliberately courted and favored by Torrijos in a labor code that guaranteed job stability and minimum wages, was weakened by the high unemployment rate resulting from *sanctions imposed by the United States in its efforts to remove Noriega. Public-sector employees were similarly demoralized by fiscal austerity and political manipulation. Other social forces and popular movements were co-opted or repressed during the period of military government, leading to their demobilization and fragmentation.

Threats to regime stability arose from a number of sources, including the large numbers of people dispossessed of jobs, income, and housing. Additionally doubts surrounded the nature of the Panama Public Forces—composed of members of the previous Defense Forces—and the legitimacy of the government, given its externally aided assumption of power.

(See also INTERVENTION; MILITARY RULE; U.S.–LATIN AMERICAN RELATIONS.)

Steve C. Ropp, *Panamanian Politics, From Guarded Nation to National Guard* (New York, 1982). George Priestley, *Military Government and Popular Participation in Panama: The Torrijos Regime, 1968–1975* (Boulder, Colo., 1986).
CHARLOTTE ELTON

PANAMA CANAL TREATY. The Panama Canal Treaties were signed by U.S. President Jimmy *Carter and *Panama's chief of government Omar Torrijos on 7 September 1977 at the Organization of American States. The main Panama Canal Treaty abrogated the 1903 Hay-Bunau-Varilla Treaty and mandated that the United States gradually turn over to Panama responsibility for the administration, operation, and defense of the canal until the year 2000—when Panama would have complete jurisdiction and operational authority over the canal. The Treaty on

the Permanent Neutrality of the Panama Canal granted to both the United States and Panama acting together or, if necessary, unilaterally, the right to defend the canal after the year 2000. The Neutrality Treaty was ratified by the U.S. Senate on 16 March 1978 and the Canal Treaty on 18 April, both by the same vote, 68–32.

Panama was a province of Colombia when the latter rejected a treaty with the United States to build a canal. The Panamanians, who frequently rebelled against Colombian rule, accurately judged that the United States would not come to Colombia's aid, as it had in the past, if the Panamanians rebelled. On 3 November 1903, Panama declared its independence. Within two weeks, the United States recognized Panama, and Secretary of State John Hay signed a treaty with Philippe Bunau-Varilla, an enterprising French citizen with interests in Panama. The treaty ceded "rights, power, and authority" to the United States to exercise jurisdiction as "if it were sovereign" over a zone ten miles wide—"in perpetuity"—and to construct, operate, and defend a canal.

Panamanians protested the treaty's provisions, but only after riots killed twenty-four people near the canal in 1964 did the United States begin to negotiate seriously the repeal of the 1903 treaty. Negotiations dragged on for thirteen years because U.S. presidents were aware of the political cost of "giving away" the canal. By 1977, the Panamanian "patience machine," in Torrijos's pungent phrase, "was running out of gas," and Carter judged that the greatest threat to the canal would occur if the United States did not negotiate new treaties. In addition, a number of Latin American presidents informed Carter that good relationships between the United States and their countries would depend on the United States negotiating new canal treaties.

Because polls showed that as many as eighty-seven percent of the U.S. public opposed a canal giveaway, Carter had to proceed carefully and only after developing a comprehensive strategy for helping senators to vote for the treaties. The ratification of the treaties (which required a two-thirds majority) by a single vote in the United States and a close vote in Panama indicates that there was a narrow band of common interest in both countries. Carter and Torrijos had worked skillfully and cooperatively to strengthen the forces that favored ratification.

(See also U.S.–LATIN AMERICAN RELATIONS.)

William J. Jordan, *Panama Odyssey* (Austin, 1984). George D. Moffett III, *The Limits of Victory: The Ratification of the Panama Canal Treaties* (Ithaca, N.Y., 1985).
ROBERT A. PASTOR

PAN-ARABISM. See ARAB NATIONALISM.

PAPAL STATES. See VATICAN CITY STATE.

PAPUA NEW GUINEA. See PACIFIC ISLANDS.

PARAGUAY. Lying between Brazil, Bolivia, and Argentina, Paraguay has developed socially and politically in a manner unlike that of the rest of Latin America. Lacking a coastline or a major natural resource, it was peripheral to Spanish colonization and never experienced an export boom in the nineteenth century. After independence (1811) Paraguay alternated between strong dictators and tumultuous civil wars. It entered decades of decline, and the population halved following a devastating war (1865–1870) with Argentina, Brazil, and Uruguay. From 1932 to 1935 it fought Bolivia, winning vast arid tracts known as the Chaco.

Today, only 2.5 percent of Paraguay's 4 million people are officially "Indian," the rest being of European and mestizo origin. But more Paraguayans speak the indigenous language, Guaraní, than speak Spanish. Most, however, speak both. There is a high *literacy rate—officially ninety-two percent—and a respectable life expectancy of 66.4 years. Only forty-one percent of Paraguayans live in urban areas and the country has few industries; per capita GDP was barely US$1,500 in 1988.

In this century, until 1954, Paraguay was famed for instability. Presidents lasted on average about a year, despite the well-established two-party system of Colorados and Liberals. After the Chaco War, the military became influential in politics, but attempts to create a military-backed corporatist system from 1940 to 1945 failed largely owing to opposition from party *elites.

In 1954, General Alfredo Stroessner seized power and forged an alliance between the armed forces and the Colorado Party, creating a one-party regime. A high degree of fusion between state, party, and military grew up that was typical of postrevolutionary political systems such as Mexico or Cuba. Stroessner purged the Colorado Party of rival factions, and the army of all Liberals. This "partyization" of the state and the armed forces made elections meaningless. Stroessner did not rule in a purely personalistic fashion; instead he built the army and party into powerful (if corrupt) institutions of domination.

Stroessner encouraged new medium-sized farms on virgin land in the east of the country and closely aligned Paraguay with Brazil, rather than Argentina as before. U.S. aid—both economic and military—was high in the 1950s and 1960s thanks to Stroessner's cooperative foreign policy. Hundreds of millions of dollars went to projects such as the vast Itaipú dam. From 1970 to 1981 Paraguay experienced ten percent growth per year. One consequence was that Paraguay's small middle class began to expand.

In the 1980s, Paraguay's boom ended. While the aging ruler was increasingly shaky, opposition grew and harsh repression was renewed. The ruling Colorado Party split as so-called "Traditionalists" battled "Militants," who insisted Stroessner be succeeded by his son. The latter used fraud and even violence to take over the apparatus of the Colorado Party. Their attempts to purge the Traditionalists eventually led to the February 1989 coup that brought General Andrés Rodríguez (a former close associate of Stroessner) to power.

Cleverly riding the wave of democratization in South America, Rodríguez called early elections and invited democratic dissidents to rejoin the Colorado Party. Mobilizing the vast patronage resources of the state, he was elected president in May 1989 by a massive margin; but it remained unclear how far the Stroessner system would be reformed.

(See also FOREIGN AID.)

Paul H. Lewis, *Paraguay under Stroessner* (Chapel Hill, N.C., 1980). Carlos A. Miranda, *The Stroessner Era* (Boulder, Colo., 1990).

CHARLES GUY GILLESPIE

PARASTATALS. Public enterprises formed in order to enhance the economic and social health of a nation, parastatals come into being through a variety of means and circumstances. A wealthy nation may transfer the ownership of its largest oil producers, utilities, and manufacturing concerns into public hands for ideological reasons, while a new, poorer nation is forced to take control of its vital interests soon after becoming independent.

In the latter case, the absence of an established entrepreneurial class to run parastatals or public enterprises (the terms are used interchangeably) necessitates government involvement. Parastatals have also been created out of privately owned enterprises in financial peril. To risk their complete failure could mean serious damage to the national economy; instead they are taken over by government. For example, the Philippine government nationalized major firms owned by former associates of Ferdinand *Marcos because they failed to repay government-guaranteed loans.

Ownership Typology and Revenue Sources. Public enterprises vary quite considerably in their rationale and function. They may differ in methods of incorporation, in their relationship to the central administrative structure, their source of capital funds, and the degree of management independence. Public enterprises, therefore, run the gamut between governmental departments and privately owned and controlled profit/nonprofit organizations. They are engaged in a whole spectrum of economic activities including agriculture, mining, construction, manufacturing, utilities, commerce, and financial and other services. In mixed economies, they compete with the domestic private producers for market share and may often be fully or partially exempt from tariffs for importing capital goods and raw materials.

Bearing in mind the variety of ideas and forms of state enterprises found in *Third World countries, a parastatal or public enterprise is an organization which:

- is owned by public authorities to the extent of fifty percent or more;
- is under the top managerial control of the owning public authorities, such as public control, including, *inter alia*, the right to appoint top management and to formulate critical policy decisions;
- is established for the achievement of a defined set of public purposes, which may be multidimensional in character;
- is engaged in activities of a business character;
- is consequently placed under a system of public accountability;
- involves the basic idea of investment and returns and services.

This delineation excludes non-profit-making public institutions which are purely concerned with providing social services such as fire departments, government relief organizations, public hospitals, regulatory bodies, and state organizations which have no economic or commercial functions but which, nonetheless, often are referred to as state enterprises.

Origin and Status. The origin of public enterprises in Third World nations can be traced, for the most part, to colonialism; many former European colonial nations utilized corporations as an arm of their government for seizing foreign territories (Fabrikant, 1976). Though they were privately owned, the British East India Company and the Hudson's Bay Company operated under charters granted to them by the British government and were used as an instrument of British colonial policy. During the colonial period, the colonial administration also participated in the distribution of goods through marketing boards. At the time of independence, for example, there were more public enterprises in India than there were in Britain.

As the colonial structures were being dismantled, existing infrastructures such as railways, postal and telegraph services, and a host of factories were inherited by the newly established governments. Assets abandoned by colonial powers were also transformed into the state enterprises of many developing countries. Furthermore, at independence, many former colonies adopted a policy which welcomed an uninhibited flow of foreign private capital into the Third World, mainly via multinationals. However, such development strategies were viewed by many *dependency theorists as inappropriate because they were creating dual economies, sluggish growth, and foreign dependency. Many developing countries, therefore, opted for a strategy of economic development based on state ownership and control of much of the industrial sector, which they hoped would bring about structural changes in their economies. Buying out of foreign and domestic assets was thus widely undertaken by most Third World nations as a matter of developmental strategy, and they were run by government.

Apart from ideological considerations, some developing countries took over companies that were incurring financial losses. While employment generation has rarely been the explicit objective for setting up state enterprises, though it might have been an implicitly expected result, governments may find it necessary to take over loss-making private companies to protect the employment of citizens working in those companies. Governments may also take over or establish business enterprises to provide goods and services deemed necessary for *development. However, by far the largest number of state enterprises in developing countries were established as a result of the government's development strategies.

Through monetary and fiscal policy and deficit financing, governments of industrialized countries can induce growth, increase employment, and affect interest rates and foreign exchange parity. They can also stimulate demand for their goods through *foreign aid to developing nations, and thus increase exports. Developing countries generally do not have such abilities, and if they wish to increase employment or induce growth, governments must engage in the production of goods and services via parastatals.

State ownership and control often involves projects with large capital outlays which may not be profitable. Such projects, therefore, may not appeal to the private investor. However, industries that provide vital products and services, including steel plants, fertilizer factories, and manufacturing plants, may have to be established by the government with no regard to their profitability. Such state enterprises are established with a conscious choice for security and self-reliance over profit, and the desire to control the major part of the national economy.

With goals as ambitious as these, there is a built-in tension between profitability and the social benefits parastatals contribute to the nation as a whole. When the public enterprises do not make a profit and require continued subsidies from the government to stay afloat, they become a target of criticism by those who question the validity of their social objectives.

In Britain during the 1960s, the Conservative Party was more receptive than the Labour Party to accepting higher levels of unemployment, withholding wage increases from government employees, freeing private initiative, modifying workers' protective practices to increase efficiency, and the restoration of laissez-faire principles. This philosophical tension between the two major political parties turned public enterprises into a political football used by one party against the other until many nationalized industries were privatized in the 1980s by the Conservative government of Prime Minister *Thatcher.

The tension between profitability and attaining national economic and social objectives became clearly visible in Chile. Salvador *Allende was elected president in 1970, leading the Popular Unity Coalition government. The government nationalized the copper industry and several other interests, resulting in a conservative backlash. The government lost access to credit in the international marketplace and soon became unstable. It is history how Allende's government fell under a military coup in 1973. The military government led by General *Pinochet moved quickly to privatize public enterprise in Chile. The literature is not clear on the outcome of *privatization policy in different countries. Yet, it can be fairly stated that governments that have privatized are not as overextended as those governments that have not privatized. Perhaps there is also less stress on the government's finance. Yet it is not apparent what the long-term impact of privatization on the government's budget is, nor what the ultimate political and social consequences may be.

The widespread privatization of parastatals in the industrial North in the 1980s has led to a privatization movement worldwide. The international banks (*International Monetary Fund and *World Bank) that have made loans to developing nations since World War II are now making evidence of privatization efforts a condition for aid. In struggling for an answer to the question "are parastatals a success" scholars can find as many examples of parastatals that make a financial and social contribution as those that have fallen short of their objectives.

A more comprehensive assessment of the situation must take into account the worldwide context in which parastatals have had to survive. Rising oil prices, serious recessions in the industrialized countries, and instability in the *Middle East have made development challenges more difficult.

An even bigger challenge is to create a public enterprise model that is managed autonomously and divorced from political squabbling and manipulation. Very often public enterprises are run by political appointees whose loyalties are politically constrained and decisions ideologically motivated. Hence, management decisions may not be consistent with the objectives of the enterprise. Furthermore, parastatals are often labor intensive and often are an integral component of the state budget instead of set up on their own terms and operated according to commercial principles.

Reform Measures. Several Third World governments have adopted reform measures designed to increase profitability and streamline management. Typical reform measures of parastatals include (Swanson and Wolde-Semait, 1989):

- Macroeconomic policy reforms that are designed to improve the competitive environment in which public and private enterprises coexist. Substantive reform strategies in this area focus on elimination of price control, protective trade policies, and state monopolies of the production and delivery of certain goods.
- Privatization, including contracting out, liquidation, sale of shares, and closing down of nonstrategic and nonviable public enterprises.
- Management reforms aimed at introducing management techniques such as standard accounting, procurement, and auditing procedures.
- Legal and institutional reforms aimed at strengthening the roles of management and governing boards of public enterprises.

It is too early to accurately assess the outcome of these reform measures. One thing that is apparent, however, is that many countries in the Third World have gone on a "privatization binge." In Africa alone, governments of many countries have sold their shares in public enterprises and many parastatals are up for sale. Government-owned hotels are signed off to management contracts. In short, the economic reforms undertaken in many Third World countries seem to have made the prospect for private investment more attractive and reasonably reduced the usual risks associated with investing in Third World countries. Yet, if privatization programs are to be carried through successfully, a number of conditions must be met. First, there must be a strong political commitment and support for privatization programs. Second, the privatization programs must be pragmatic and creative in approach, designed to exploit a country's specific opportunities for development. As Pfeffermann (1988) observed, parastatals cannot be arbitrarily privatized because the transaction costs associated with the privatization process can be even more burdensome than restructuring the enterprise to more efficient management practices.

The Debate Continues. In a recent study, Nayar (1991) compared the profitability and contribution to development of public and private aluminum and steel companies in India (for the period 1958–1988), and found that the private enterprise sector performed better. He also found that private firms were equally effective in backward-area development and meeting obligations to employees in terms of housing, benefits, and wages. In addition, he observed that the private sector's capacity utilization was superior to that of public enterprises. Nayar attributes the superior performance of private enterprises to property rights theory, which holds that the nature of ownership is the critical determinant of performance.

In contrast, Israel (1991), among others, favors state intervention in the marketplace but wants a more fluid relationship between state and private sector enterprises. He argues that government should be an effective enabler and negotiator, and put itself in a position to maximize public and private market potentials. He sees past government policy toward the private sector as inconsistent. It ignores the problem of small business while yielding to pressures from the larger ones. In the meantime, Israel observes that government policies of Third World countries have saddled public enterprises with an excessive number of often contradictory economic, political, and social objectives, making their effective management practically impossible.

The new role for the government that Israel advances, as negotiator and entrepreneur between the public and private sectors, seems to provide an optimal strategy for development that is rich with potential. In other words, the unnecessary dichotomization, and hence polarization, of public and private sector enterprises' activities in the Third World is not helpful to society. What may be helpful and productive, at this point in time, is an efficiency-oriented and less politicized public policy that will provide an interface and appropriate linkages between government enterprises and private businesses.

(See also COLONIAL EMPIRES; MULTINATIONAL CORPORATIONS; NATIONALIZATION; PROTECTION; THATCHERISM.)

R. Fabrikant, "Developing Country State Enterprises: Performance and Control" *Columbia Journal of Transactional Law* 15 (1976): 40–56. R. Millward, "The Comparative Performance of Public and Private Ownership," in Lord Hall of Ipsden, ed., *The Mixed Economy* (New York, 1982): 83–84. P. Dunleavy, "Explaining the Privatization Boom (in Britain): Public Choice versus Radical Approaches" *Public Administration* (Spring 1986): 13–34. B. Wilson, "The Public-Private Debate" *Africa Report* (July–August 1986): 93. Y. Aharoni, *The Evolution and Management of State Owned Enterprise* (Hagerstown, Md., 1987): 317–328. G. Pfeffermann, "Private Business in Developing Countries—Improved Prospects," Discussion Paper Number 1, International Finance Corporation (1988): 13–20. D. Axelrod, *A Budget Quartet, Critical Policy and Management Issues* (New York, 1989). D. Swanson and T. Wolde-Semait, "Africa's Public Enterprise Sector and Evidence of Reforms," World Bank Technical Paper Number 95 (1989): 23–25. W. T. Gormley, Jr., *Privatization and its Alternatives* (Madison, Wis., 1991). A. Israel, "The Changing Role of the State in Development" *Finance and Development* 28, no. 6 (June 1991): 41–43. B. R. Nayar, "Property Rights Theory and Government Efficiency: The Evidence from India's Public Sector" *Development Policy Review* 9, no. 2 (1991): 131–150.

BERHANU MENGISTU

PARIS CLUB. The Paris Club is not a club. It is a grouping of creditor governments which meets periodically to negotiate a rescheduling of debts owed them by individual debtor governments. These debts include export credits, concessional assistance, and military assistance. A debtor government will ask for a meeting of the Paris Club when it is unable to service fully its external public debt. A debtor is normally required by creditor governments to have negotiated a stabilization agreement with the *International Monetary Fund (IMF) before a Paris Club meeting takes place. Creditors are reluctant to agree to reschedule debts without some evidence that debtor governments are implementing economic reforms aimed at improving their future abilities to service their debts.

Paris Club meetings are normally chaired by an official of the French treasury, and staff work for those meetings is usually provided by the IMF. Debtor governments participating in Paris Club negotiations are almost wholly drawn from the developing world. Creditor governments participating in a Paris Club meeting typically include those of Western Europe, North America, and Japan. Participation by creditor governments varies according to which government's debt is being rescheduled. Creditor governments from the former socialist bloc in Eastern and *Central Europe have not participated in Paris Club reschedulings, but there is an expectation among Paris Club members that debts owed them will be subject to the same rescheduling arrangements negotiated for Western creditors. Private banks with credits outstanding to developing country governments do not participate in Paris Club negotiations. (They usually renegotiate their credits through the "London Club.") However, they are expected to provide debtors with terms comparable to those negotiated at the Paris Club.

The Paris Club first met in 1956 to reschedule the debt of Argentina. Until the end of the 1970s, it was involved primarily in rescheduling the debts of Latin American governments. By the late 1970s, African debtors began to seek Paris Club debt reschedulings in increasing numbers. Since that time, the largest number of debt reschedulings have been for African governments, some—like the government of Zaire—returning more than ten times to reschedule its public bilateral debts.

During the 1980s, the terms of Paris Club reschedulings for the poorest countries became progressively more favorable. The cancellation by many creditor governments of concessional credits reduced this element in reschedulings. An agreement at the economic summit in 1988 created a menu of alternative rescheduling terms for export credits, including concessional interest rates, repayment periods of up to twenty-five years, or a reduction in the value of the principal owed. Traditional terms had involved a consolidation of all the interest and principal owed in a new loan at market rates of interest, with three years grace and four years to repay the debt.

(See also DEVELOPMENT AND UNDERDEVELOPMENT; FINANCE, INTERNATIONAL; INTERNATIONAL DEBT; INTERNATIONAL POLITICAL ECONOMY.)

Alex Rieffel, *The Role of the Paris Club in Managing Debt Problems*, Essays in International Finance #161 (Princeton, N.J., 1985). Miles Kahler, ed., *The Politics of International Debt* (Ithaca, N.Y., 1986). Barry Eichengreen and Peter H. Lindert, eds., *The International Debt Crisis in Historical Perspective* (Cambridge, Mass., 1989).

CAROL LANCASTER

PARLIAMENTARY DEMOCRACY. Occasionally given a broad definition, parliamentary democracy connotes any form of representative *democracy, thus distinguishing it from forms of plebiscitary and direct democracies. In its narrower and more precise definition, it is a particular form of representative government: essentially, a democratic system in which government is drawn from and is regularly answerable to the elected national assembly. Commonly the executive is subject to dismissal on political grounds (as distinct from removal by impeachment) by that assembly. The concept itself has its origins in the nineteenth century, when the notion of democracy became allied with a parliamentary form of government.

The juxtaposition of the two words is significant. *Democracy* serves to distinguish the form of government from one-party and other states in which the national assembly—although it may formally constitute an elected parliament—is not elected on the basis of a free choice between candidates. *Parliamentary* distinguishes the form of government from that in which the executive is elected separately from the legislature (presidential government), a dichotomy well recognized by Bagehot. Some states, such as France, have a hybrid system, with an elected executive but with ministers drawn from, and dependent for support on, the national assembly.

Parliamentary democracy is a feature of West European states and, increasingly, of a number of post-Communist European states. It is also a feature of "old" *Commonwealth nations, notably Canada, Australia, India, and New Zealand. It is less prevalent in Africa, South America, the Middle East, and the Far East.

(See also PARLIAMENTARY SOVEREIGNTY.)

Walter Bagehot, *The English Constitution* (1867, reprinted London, 1963).

PHILIP NORTON

PARLIAMENTARY SOVEREIGNTY. With its origins in England, parliamentary sovereignty, in its English application, constitutes a judicially self-imposed doctrine under which the courts apply without challenge on grounds of being contrary to the provisions of the *constitution, all measures being passed by the Queen-in-Parliament. The doctrine was variously asserted by legal scholars before the late seventeenth century, but it was confirmed as a judicial rule by the Glorious Revolution of 1688. (Common lawyers allied themselves with Parliament in contending that the king must be subject to the law of Parliament, and that if the king must be so subject, then so too must be his subjects, including the courts.) The doctrine was given its most authoritative articulation in the nineteenth century by A. V. Dicey, Vinerian Professor of English Law at Oxford University. According to Dicey, the doctrine had three elements: 1) Parliament has the right to make or unmake any law whatever; 2) No person or body is recognized by the law of England as having a right to override or set aside the legislation of Parliament; and 3) The right or power of Parliament extends to every part of the Queen's dominions.

The definitions and scope of the doctrine have been variously challenged. To what extent can Parliament "unmake" acts conferring independence? Formally it could, and courts in Britain would apply such legislation, but in practice it would be unenforceable. The doctrine has limited use outside the United Kingdom, most *Commonwealth countries—often federal states—being subject to written constitutions and *judicial review.

(See also DEMOCRACY; FEDERALISM; PARLIAMENTARY DEMOCRACY.)

A. W. Bradley, "The Sovereignty of Parliament—in Perpetuity?" in Jeffrey Jowell and Dawn Oliver, eds., *The Changing Constitution* (Oxford, 1985), pp. 23–47. Philip Norton, "The Glorious Revolution of 1688 and 1689: Its Continuing Relevance" *Parliamentary Affairs* 42, no. 2 (April 1989): 135–147.

PHILIP NORTON

PATRIARCHY. Throughout its long history, the term *patriarchy* has denoted male authority in various contexts, notably religion, politics, and the family. In modern political thought in the West, the concept has lent itself to the debate about political *power and *legitimacy. For example, in *Patriarcha,* written in the seventeenth century by Sir Robert Filmer, paternal authority, monarchical privilege, and divine power were equated. Filmer was refuted by John Locke in his *Two Treatises of Government;* however, Locke's rejection of patriarchal domination in the public realm did not extend to the private realm of the family, a distinction that has been interpreted as an influential articulation of the emerging relationships between *capitalism, bourgeois male *citizenship, and the subjugation of women.

More recently, the sociologist Max *Weber used *patriarchy* to describe the form of social organization in which the father not only stood at the head of the kinship network but also controlled its economy. However, the most familiar and extensive usage of the term today emerges from *feminist theory in the West. Although earlier feminists, such as Virginia Woolf, had used the term, Kate Millett gave the concept its contemporary currency in her theoretical analysis of patriarchy, *Sexual Politics* (New York, 1970). Millett defined patriarchy as a gendered system of social control that pervaded all aspects of human existence, including politics, industry, the military, education, philosophy, art, literature, and civilization itself. This analysis enabled an expansion of traditional notions of politics to include the hitherto "private" spheres of love, sexuality, marriage, and children. The family was politicized as the foundation of patriarchal power. Millett argued that perceived differences between the sexes (women are passive and nurturing; men are active and ambitious) maintained the normative familial structure of a heterosexual male-headed household, in which the woman's primary tasks of childbearing and childrearing "naturally" constrained her free and equal participation in society. In the family, males and females were socialized into sex roles, thereby ensuring general complicity in inequality as well as the transmission of patriarchal ideology across generations. The longevity of this system of male dominance was aided by its methods of surveillance and rewards, which coerced or seduced women into accepting their secondary status. While Millett's theory acknowledged the violence of class and race, it insisted that patriarchy was more enduring, more comprehensive, more uniform, and therefore antecedent and more fundamental to understanding other forms of injustice.

The transhistorical universality of gender oppression suggested by this analysis has been problematic for feminist theory. Its assumption of similar structures of social domination in vastly different societies across millennia is undermined by the notion of a historically specific, context-bound, social construction of key concepts such as "power," "woman," "family," and "the state." Furthermore, women's experience of their sexual roles, social status, and economic options has varied widely depending on the material and ideological conditions of the time. Socialist feminists, among others, have called for a refinement of the concept of patriarchy to acknowledge the specific forms, characteristics, and boundaries within a mode of production. Consequently, the collaboration between sexual hierarchy and *class structure in the formation of patriarchy under capitalism has received extensive treatment, replacing an essentialist conception of patriarchy with a complex set of mutually constitutive, socially constructed relations of power. However, the notion of patriarchy remains limited as long as the complicated relationships between a plurality of human characteristics and social experiences such as gender, class, race and *ethnicity, nationality, and colonial experience, are muted in favor of one dominating concept, such as gender.

For women outside the intellectual mainstream from which these theoretical analyses of patriarchy have emerged, the struggle to translate conceptual understanding into political activism is particularly acute. Nonwhite and non-Western feminists are challenged by the many intersecting strands of oppression in their daily lives. On the one hand, these women are aware of the problematic gender relations within their communities. On the other hand, they feel compelled to unite with their menfolk against commonly experienced discrimination, such as racism, in the larger society. In addition, the global expansion of capitalism and Western neocolonialism has elicited nationalist or cultural nativist responses from the *Third World that, for the moment of resistance, suggest a solidarity between genders that transcends patriarchal relations. For example, the tendency of Western feminists to condemn out of hand certain unfamiliar practices, such as

arranged marriages and veiling, has prompted counterallegations of cultural insensitivity, arrogance, and racism from Third World women. To eliminate patriarchy, the feminist consensus calls for a redefinition of social practices, a transformation of assumptions about social reality, and an overturning of existing structures of domination.

(See also EQUALITY AND INEQUALITY; FEMINISM; GENDER AND POLITICS; RACE AND RACISM; WOMEN AND DEVELOPMENT.)

Zillah R. Eisenstein, ed., Capitalist Patriarchy and the Case for Socialist Feminism (New York, 1979). Heather Eisenstein, Contemporary Feminist Thought (London, 1984). Sonia Kruks, Rayna Rapp, and Marilyn B. Young, Promissory Notes: Women in the Transition to Socialism (New York, 1989). Kumkum Sangari and Sudesh Vaid, eds., Recasting Women: Essays in Colonial History (New Delhi, 1989). Chandra Talpade Mohanty, Ann Russo, and Lourdes Torres, eds., Third World Women and the Politics of Feminism (Bloomington, Ind., 1991).

ARATI RAO

PATRON-CLIENT POLITICS. The foundation of patron-client politics rests on an exchange between actors of unequal power and status: the more powerful, or patron, offers protection and access to scarce resources such as land or jobs to the client; the client in turn provides support and services such as labor or votes for the patron. Political structures based on such exchanges were first described by anthropologists studying Mediterranean societies, and persist in organizations such as the Mafia; but patron-client politics exists in a wide variety of systems, spread across the globe. The "*political machines" of American cities such as Chicago under Mayor Richard Daley provide an example, as do the party systems of many Third World states in which local political bosses such as landlords or traditional chiefs trade the votes of their subordinate peasantry for favors received from the central government. Patron-client relations readily infiltrate apparently bureaucratic organizations, such as the *Communist Party of the Soviet Union during the period it dominated Soviet society, in which powerful leaders sought to place their own personal supporters in key posts.

Despite variations in setting, patron-client systems are guided by a common logic. They arise in hierarchical societies, where individuals and groups compete at each level of the hierarchy, but where there is scope for collaboration between those at different levels. Marxists often criticize such collaboration for obscuring the "real" conflict between classes; but clientelism arises in situations where class politics is inappropriate, not because class differences and exploitation are absent (quite the contrary), but because they are so entrenched that it is rational to work within them. The link between patron and client is often expressed in terms of personal obligations (such as godparenthood) or communal solidarity: *ethnicity in its myriad forms provides a powerful vehicle for clientelism because it reinforces cross-class linkages as a basis for political action. Underlying it all, however, is an eminently rational struggle for control of political and economic resources that can also cut across ethnic barriers when the logic of competition requires. Patron-client links thus provide a flexible and effective tool, the persistence of which is not surprising. They extend into international relations, where the inequality of states, and their mutual need for protection and support, mirror the conditions in which they flourish in domestic politics. The patron state provides military protection or economic aid, in exchange for which the client state offers diplomatic support or economic opportunities. Such links, which readily involve personal relationships between national leaders, likewise cut across the unequal economic relations between industrial and underdeveloped states.

Clientelism nonetheless suffers crippling defects. It is inherently inefficient because it is geared to meeting particularistic rather than universal goals; jobs or development projects are allocated by patronage criteria rather than by qualification or need. It emphasizes distribution rather than production and is often parasitic on the productive economy. It erodes any appeal to common values while encouraging ethnic conflict and often leading to a pervasive cynicism. Such political stability as it provides depends more on buying the support of key groups than on establishing any basis for *legitimacy. Ultimately it must be seen as a barrier to *political development, even though its usefulness ensures that elements of clientelism persist even in the most sophisticated political systems.

(See also DEVELOPMENT AND UNDERDEVELOPMENT; MODERNIZATION; PEASANTS.)

S. N. Eisenstadt and Rene Lemarchand, eds., *Political Clientelism, Patronage and Development* (Beverly Hills and London, 1981).

CHRISTOPHER CLAPHAM

PEACE. The term *peace* can be interpreted narrowly as the absence of warfare, i.e., organized violence, between groups defined by country, nation (culture, *ethnicity), *race, *class, or *ideology. International or external peace is the absence of external wars: inter-country, inter-state, or international (in the sense of intercultural). Social or internal peace is the absence of internal wars: ethnic, racial, class, or ideological groups challenging the central government, or such groups challenging each other. As central governance came late in human history, so did *war among and against governments. Conclusion: many wars are avoidable, many types of peace are achievable.

This concept of peace is carried by the Latin *pax*, related to pact, as in *pacta sunt servanda*, "treaties must be observed." The implicit theory that peace is a contractual, conscious and mutually agreed upon relationship is the source of the Western *international law tradition.

Another Roman legacy is *si vis pacem, para bellum*, "if you want peace, prepare for war." This constitutes another strand in mainstream Western peace theory: peace through *deterrence of any potential aggressor, countering the aggressor with the deployment of military force. Mainstream occidental thought about peace has changed little during the past 2,000 years, apart from oriental elements during the Middle Ages.

Broader definitions of peace usually include the concept of *pax,* but extend it by asking, "What type of violence?," "Violence by whom?," and "Peace with whom?" The first question leads to a distinction between violence to the body and violence to the mind and spirit. An example of the latter in life under the threat of extermination in a war in which weapons of mass destruction are used (e.g., a nuclear war), extending the definition of peace to absence of war and the *threat* of war. The problem with offensive deterrence is that the same capability can be used to attack even if the motivation is defensive. Some argue that this is the best that can be hoped for.

The second question tries to identify the actor capable of inflicting damage and motivated to do so. Consider, however, the case when no such actor exists, yet harm is being done. Thus, 40,000 children die daily from avoidable causes such as malnutrition. To the extent that these deaths are not war-related, they occur under conditions of peace as narrowly conceived. Instead they can be attributed to structural violence, built into the structure within and between countries, and not necessarily intended by anybody. Twice as many children die annually from structural violence as there were people killed annually in the direct violence of World War II.

Structural violence differs from institutionalized direct violence that is perpetrated to vindicate honor or to revenge (vendetta), and from institutional violence linked to particular social institutions. Concretely, structural violence takes the form of economic exploitation and/or political repression in intra-country and inter-country class relations. In imperialist structures the two come together, with exploitation and repression so heavy that life expectancy in the periphery of the periphery countries is less than one-half of that at the top. Another form is violence to nature.

Structural violence may also be institutionalized, that is, deeply rooted and protected against reduction and elimination by countervailing social forces. The "military-bureaucratic-corporate-intelligentsia" complex, instrumental in modern warfare and in direct violence against any *revolution, violent or nonviolent, benefits from that protection.

Both direct and structural violence may be internalized, that is, cultural violence may be used to legitimate the exercise of violence, direct or structural, by one group against another. Examples include appeals to "chosen peoples" and "superior races." The notion of male gender superiority has been used to legitimate gender violence of both varieties—killing of unborn females, infanticide, circumcision, incest, family violence, rape, and widow-burning—in addition to exploitation and repression.

In comparison with the Roman *pax,* the Greek *eirene,* the Hebrew *shalom,* and the Arab *salām* seem to approach "peace with justice," including an absence of direct and structural violence. The question is which part has priority.

The third question—"peace with whom?"—is answered in new ways further east, by the Hindi *shanti* and *ahimsa,* also usually translated as "peace." *Shanti* means "inner peace," peace with oneself, with no part of body-mind-spirit doing violence to other parts. *Shanti* can be seen as complementing the occidental focus on "outer peace," and as a necessary condition for "outer peace."

Ahimsa means "no-harm," including to self (inner peace) and nature, bringing in the ecological dimension missing in the Occident (an exception being Saint Francis of Assisi). *Ahimsa* was the peace concept used by the leading peace practitioner of our times, M. K. *Gandhi, as the basis for nonviolent struggle, *satyagraha,* against such structural violence as racism, caste, and gender, industrialism and colonialism/imperialism, and as an alternative to communal, social, and international direct violence. Gandhi also tried to create an ecumenical peace culture, providing the most complete answer so far to the problem of achieving peace in a very broad sense by peaceful means. Aspects of his approach were taken up by the *civil rights movement in the United States (especially by Martin Luther *King, Jr.) and by the European dissident and peace movements in their struggle for a nonviolent end to the *Cold War in 1989.

Still further east the Chinese *ho p'ing/p'ing ho* and the Japanese *heiwa/wahei* point to inner, social, and international harmony; they complement the concepts of outer and inner peace, seeing harmony between the international, social, and personal spheres as a necessary condition for all of them to come true.

Coming full circle, we return to the narrow *pax,* well institutionalized and internalized in the Occident. Missing in that concept is attention to structural violence, inner peace, nonviolence, and harmony between the spheres of the human condition. But the concept of peace is open, like freedom and justice, with no culture having any monopoly on its definition. We have to draw on the human experience as a whole, not only on one gender, in one generation, in one corner of the world. All are aspects of a more universal concept of peace not yet defined.

(See also ETHNICITY; FORCE, USE OF; GENDER AND POLITICS; IMPERIALISM; INTERNATIONAL CO-OPERATION; PEACE MOVEMENT; POLITICAL VIOLENCE.)

A. C. Bouquet and K. S. Murty, *Studies in the Problems of Peace* (Bombay, 1960). Takeshi Ishida, "Beyond Traditional Concepts of Peace in Different Cultures" *Journal of Peace Research* 6, no. 2 (1969): 133–145. Johan Galtung, "Cultural Violence" *Journal of Peace Research* 27, no. 3 (1990): 291–305.

JOHAN GALTUNG

PEACE CORPS. The purpose of the U.S. Peace Corps, as stated in Executive Order 10924 signed by President John F. *Kennedy on 1 March 1961, was to "be responsible for the training and service abroad of men and women of the United States in new programs of assistance to nations and areas of the world." Such a charge placed the agency firmly within the established tradition of participatory development aid programs such as the British VSO (Volunteers in Service Overseas) and resurrected the model created by President William McKinley in 1901, when 1,000 volunteer teachers sailed to staff the newly created Department of Public Education in the Philippines. Its creation also realized earlier proposals of a similar nature proffered by Rep. Henry Reuss of Wisconsin under the Point Four Plan.

The distinctive ethos of the organization was evident from its earliest weeks, with emphasis laid on the volunteers' status as invited residents of their host nations, fully subject to local restraints of custom and law. This stress on becoming a part of each host society separated the Peace Corps personnel sharply from the majority of foreign assistance workers, with their expatriate communities and attitudes. Benefits for American culture were envisioned from the creation of a cadre of people possessing first-hand knowledge of world development problems and possibilities. They would serve to educate citizens back home about their countries of service and make the nation more aware of the experiences of other people and more flexible in adapting to rapidly shifting geopolitical realities.

The idea of the Peace Corps triggered diverse reactions. Domestic political opposition to the proposal ranged from a virtually unanimous resolution against it by the Daughters of the American Revolution to former President *Eisenhower's characterization of it as "a juvenile experiment" and a newspaper editorial in Rockford, Illinois, terming the agency "as silly a bit of political boondoggling as any American politician has ever devised." By contrast, the response of the international community was encouraging, if guarded. Given the fact that teams of Soviet technical advisers were already active in many *Third World nations, *Pravda*'s depiction of the Peace Corps as "a tool for spreading the notorious American way of life" was understandable.

Following his appointment as interim director in

1961, R. Sargent Shriver participated in congressional hearings on the viability of the Peace Corps as a continuing federal program and undertook a goodwill tour to prospective African and Asian host nations. With the exception of U Nu of Burma, most leaders visited expressed interest in the concept. Specific invitations for Peace Corps members were issued by presidents Kwame *Nkrumah of Ghana and Julius *Nyerere of Tanganyika (Tanzania), creating the now-traditional image of the Peace Corps volunteer living in a village setting among the people and speaking the local language.

Indeed, the unique nature of the terms of Peace Corps service gave all volunteers a dual political identity which made them potentially vulnerable to manipulation. Their rejection of privileged expatriate status, their willingness to immerse themselves in a new culture and its institutions and languages, and their open adoption of and often advocacy for their second homelands was completely in keeping with Kennedy's original vision. However, such behavior, atypical of U.S. government representatives abroad, also exposed them to charges of being agents provocateurs. Much of the initial questioning, skepticism, and outright hostility the early volunteers encountered stemmed from disbelief in the stated premises of the organization; no Americans would willingly contribute two years of their lives to help another nation unless as a cover for espionage. Such attitudes reflected the larger patterns of *Cold War thought and the role played by covert action. Although persistent intermittent rumors of Peace Corps links to the *Central Intelligence Agency have surfaced during the thirty years since its inception, no proof of this claim has ever been adduced. Lack of evidence did not change the view that the volunteers could be used in pursuing certain political agendas. Perhaps the best example of this was the total expulsion of Peace Corps workers from Bolivia in 1971 on charges of conducting sterilization and birth control programs and spreading drug addiction in the guise of health care assistance. Yet, paradoxically, this openness to challenge and question provided a heretofore absent channel for cross-cultural communication and a mechanism for questioning stereotypes on both sides. It was this quality that President George *Bush viewed as crucial in agreeing to send the Peace Corps to the restored democracies of Poland, Hungary, and Czechoslovakia in the early 1990s.

The legacy of Peace Corps service for the United States has been substantial, with alumni heading bodies such as Amnesty International and the Agency for International Development as well as contributing to virtually every field and profession in the United States. In what is perhaps the ultimate extension of the effect of returned volunteers on domestic life, a Peace Corps veteran of Ethiopia, Senator Paul Tsongas, declared his candidacy for the Democratic Party's presidential nomination in the 1992 election. The formation of the National Council of Returned Peace Corps Volunteers in 1986 is an indication that the agency's influence will continue to be felt on both the international scene and the field of American social change.

(See also AMERICAN FOREIGN POLICY.)

Robert B. Marks Ridinger, *The Peace Corps: An Annotated Bibliography* (Boston, 1989). Karen Schwarz, *What You Can Do for Your Country: An Oral History of the Peace Corps* (New York, 1991).

ROBERT B. MARKS RIDINGER

PEACE MOVEMENT. In the twentieth century the European continent has been the site of a repeated cycle of *arms races and *war scares. Each of these cycles has produced peace movements that seek a reduction of international tensions. The armament drives that preceded each of the two world wars produced vigorous movements particularly in the smaller European countries, where many hoped to avoid being drawn into big-power rivalries.

Peace movements between the wars were largely pacifist, seeking disarmament and an avoidance of international entanglements. The experience of World War II and the new realities created by the *Cold War and by nuclear *deterrence have made obsolete the idea of pacifist withdrawal from the international system. As a result, postwar peace movements have abandoned pacifism as a central aspect of their beliefs. But postwar peace movements have continued to flourish when international tensions have grown and when new types of armaments—especially *nuclear weapons—have been introduced.

Both of these conditions were met in the early 1980s. The immediate trigger for the peace movements that swept Europe at that time was the decision by the *North Atlantic Treaty Organization (NATO) in 1979 to deploy 572 Pershing II and cruise missiles in five NATO countries. This decision was made at a point when relations between the United States and the Soviet Union were as tense as they had been in twenty years. Twenty-eight percent of a sample of Europeans, and fifty percent of those who considered themselves members of the peace movement, went so far as to say that "we are heading directly toward world war" (*Eurobarometer 21: Political Cleavages in the European Community*, Brussels, April 1984). The peace movement that swept Western Europe as a result of these tensions was the largest political movement in Europe in this century. During the month of October 1983 alone, over 3 million people demonstrated in the cities of Western Europe against NATO's plans for new nuclear weapons.

Despite this great size, the protest tactics characteristic of political movements have been notoriously ineffective in altering public policies. One of the few concrete peace movement successes before World War II occurred in 1923 in the Netherlands, when a governmental plan to modernize the Dutch fleet led to a gathering in Amsterdam of a then unheard-of 80,000 demonstrators, followed by a petition campaign that gathered over one million signatures (twenty percent of the entire population) within a period of three weeks. Thanks to pressure from the opposition Social Democratic Workers Party, and from the socialist and Catholic wings of the trade union movement, the Dutch Parliament rejected the plan for a new naval fleet by a single vote.

The much larger peace movement of the early 1980s was not able to claim such success. Of the five countries that agreed in 1979 to accept the Pershing II and cruise missiles, all confirmed their commitment to deployment between 1983 and 1985 despite the massive demonstrations and petition campaigns during those years. It would be going too far to say that the peace movement had no policy impact. The Dutch government, for example, twice delayed its final decision on the new missiles, and the Belgians agreed to accept their forty-eight cruise missiles only in several stages. Yet the peace movement failed to attain its main objective, which was to prevent the nuclear modernization envisaged by NATO in 1979. Although cruise and Pershing II missiles were eventually removed from Europe under the provisions of the Intermediate-Range Nuclear Forces (INF) Treaty of 1988, peace movement pressure was only an indirect factor in obtaining the INF agreement.

The greater immediate impact of the peace movement was on domestic political alignments within the various West European countries. Social democratic parties in several countries were converted from support for the missile deployment to opposition. Because social democratic parties were not in power in the early 1980s, their opposition to the missiles proved fruitless. Yet the peace movement did manage to reawaken the more radical wing of the European social democratic parties as well as to revive the traditions of political activism in many churches and trade unions.

The greatest medium-term impact of the peace movement was to open a debate about nuclear weapons policy, which until then had been largely the province of a small group of experts, NATO officials, and top military and civilian leaders. The original plan to modernize NATO's intermediate-range nuclear forces in 1979 took shape in NATO's Nuclear Planning Committee and in a series of meetings of NATO foreign and defense ministers. When the British Parliament debated the INF plan in 1980, it was the first debate on nuclear weapons in fifteen years in the House of Commons. Across Europe, the subject of nuclear strategy went from being a technical issue to a political issue. Policies that had long been taken for granted were now being questioned, and alternatives were being proposed where it was once believed that none existed. The ability of the peace movements to demonstrate widespread public interest in the subject of nuclear weapons

gave parliaments an incentive to become more aggressive in demanding a role in *security policy.

The impact of this change in the political process on nuclear and security issues has become clear only in the 1990s, nearly a decade after the height of the peace movement mobilization. The democratization of the countries of Eastern and Central Europe and the dissolution of the *Warsaw Treaty Organization (Warsaw Pact) and of the Soviet Union have created an environment in which a fundamental rethinking of the ways and means of European security is needed. Two results of these changes are the absence of a threat from the East and much less U.S. involvement in European security. A Europe no longer divided between East and West is experiencing intensified, sometimes violent ethnic and nationalist conflict. It also faces new problems of defining the nature of potential threats to European security, and of developing international structures of alliance and cooperation that will respond to those threats.

The question of alternative means of guaranteeing security was addressed a decade ago only by those within peace movements and within such allied organizations as peace research institutes. It is remarkable today how much their ideas have now been brought into the mainstream of European debate. Collective security arrangements that bridge the entire European continent, defensive deterrence strategies, and the problems of converting military production into nonmilitary forms of productive capacity are all issues that ten years ago were discussed within the peace movement but dismissed by others as unrealistic. It is still far from certain what form post–Cold War security arrangements in Europe will take, but it is already clear that the ideas developed within peace movement circles will be important in structuring that debate.

(See also ARMS CONTROL; CONFERENCE ON SECURITY AND COOPERATION IN EUROPE; NEW SOCIAL MOVEMENTS; SOCIALISM AND SOCIAL DEMOCRACY.)

Diana Johnstone, *The Politics of Euromissiles* (London, 1984). Ulrike Wasmuht, *Friedensbewegungen der 80er Jahre* (Giessen, Germany, 1987). Thomas Rochon, *Mobilizing for Peace* (Princeton, N.J., 1988).

THOMAS R. ROCHON

PEASANTS. Often, peasants have been defined as low-status cultivators who are trapped in a double bind of material poverty and political marginality. Like other venerable definitions in the social sciences, this one has advantages and very real limitations. Its signal merit has been to focus our attention on the fact that peasants labor in a subsistence economy that is typically precarious and subject to predation by powerful *elites. As a result, peasants in otherwise diverse cultural and historical contexts share a common vulnerability to natural and human-made disaster that constrains peasant strategies in the direction of an emphasis on subsistence security and family survival. As many scholars have shown, the logic of peasant society cannot be easily translated into the more familiar categories of urban, industrial life.

However, the notion that the common predicaments of peasant societies imply a homogeneous peasant *class has become increasingly difficult to maintain in the face of a growing scholarly literature focused on the empirical dynamics of power and production in small-scale rural societies. Without always being explicit, scholarship suggests that the people we call peasants manifest extraordinary diversity and complexity in property rights, economic hierarchies, and relations to the forces and means of production. In this sense, peasants are quite unlike capitalists or proletarians, whose economic location and forms of stratification show much more commonality and coherence than the almost lush diversity of peasant societies. Indeed, as the otherwise quite distinctive work of political scientists like Samuel Popkin, James C. Scott, and Joel Migdal implies, class is much less significant as a basis for understanding peasant life than are convergent peasant political institutions and survival strategies rooted in the logic of subsistence cultivation. Seen from this perspective, peasants can no longer be understood as merely a subordinate class of backward marginals without history or politics. Instead, peasants have increasingly come to be understood as historical actors whose collective responses to nature and elite demands have significantly affected the transition to the modern world.

Political scientists have made a substantial contribution to the rediscovery of the peasant as ahistorical agent, and the remainder of this essay focuses on a synthetic overview of the empirical findings of their work. Those findings will be discussed under the three headings of localism, political invisibility, and the strategic flexibility of custom.

Localism refers to the universal tendency of peasants to define their primary collective interests and collective political action in terms of highly localized, small-scale territorial groups. Usually confined to a hamlet, village, or group of related villages, these microgroups are the most important organizations of peasant life, and the institutional arrangements they contain are central to rural politics, economic production and exchange, and ritual and religious practice. Similarly, when peasants engage in collective action, whether in moments of revolt or during more routine resistance, the goal of their project is usually the defense of the autonomy of local institutions against the claims of outside elites. Conversely, however, peasants rarely organize at national or even regional levels, and most large-scale peasant movements can be understood as temporary alliances of local communities that in the end will return to their component villages and localities. Even the spectacular events of the French, Russian, and Mexican *revolutions might best by interpreted as tremendous explosions of rural localism that drew their energy from an attempt by ordinary rural people to strengthen local cohesion and local control of subsistence resources. In this sense, the ubiquitous elite enemies of peasants, absentee landlords and tax collectors, are not so much class enemies as intrusive and unwanted outsiders who threaten the precarious equilibrium of local practices.

The intense localism of peasant life used to be understood as resulting from the blinding effects of false consciousness, unthinking traditionalism, and the general inability of peasant classes to act in a properly "class" (i.e., national, large-scale) fashion. However, much recent research indicates that this interpretation is unacceptable, for it denies the very real dependence of peasants on local institutions for whatever margin of wealth, status, and power they possess. Networks of neighbors and neighboring kin are the primary determinants of peasant well-being, and their help or hostility can mean the difference between disaster and comfortable survival. As a result, peasant localism is a "rational" adaptation strategy to a world in which large-scale, translocal institutions are either unavailable or unreliable as the basis for peasant welfare. This means that rural localism is unlikely to disappear until peasants are effectively integrated as citizens into national governments that are capable of underwriting rural welfare and that are responsive to popular demands. It can be argued that this process has thus far occurred only in the advanced industrial nations, and it is unlikely that even postrevolutionary regimes like that of the People's Republic of China have eliminated the salience and structural causes of peasant localism.

Although localism is the most important institutional characteristic of peasant societies, it is closely linked to what is best described as a politics of invisibility. Generations of field researchers have remarked on the reticence of peasants to speak openly and objectively about the ways in which they arrange their lives. This suspicion of outsiders is a rational response to a situation in which outsiders are typically trouble, especially when they make demands on scarce community resources. However, public reticence can also be seen as part of a broader strategy of disguising, or rendering invisible to outsiders, key dimensions of their lives. For example, it is often the case that the formal institutions of local government prescribed by central elites are less important to peasants than informal, customary means of decision making that are ignored or unknown by central bureaucrats. Similarly, peasants try to conceal the size of their harvests, the extent of their fields, and even the meaning of ritual events. All of this must be glossed as an attempt to create a barrier to the penetration of local institutions by potentially predatory elites. As James C. Scott argues, this sort of camouflage is vital if peasants are to retain a sufficient degree of local autonomy to meet the pressures of a subsistence-driven environment.

Moreover, by creating a network of institutions and resources that are invisible from the outside, peasants are able to construct a stable routine protected from the arbitrary interference of national states and their agents. Naturally, the extent of this invisibility varies across time and among societies, but the degree to which peasants actively conceal themselves is an important marker of the difference between peasant institutions and the visible politics of mass publics and *public opinion characteristic of industrial democracies.

The final important way in which peasant survival strategies intersect with peasant political institutions has to do with the subtle interplay between custom and peasant politics. It is a commonplace that peasants adhere tenaciously to customary norms governing everything from kinship and inheritance to work routines and community celebrations. To outsiders, the depth and persistence of such customs underscore peasant traditionalism and conservatism, particularly because rural customary codes change only slowly and incrementally in response to shifting constellations of opportunities and interests. Yet as political scientists have come increasingly to realize, peasant custom should not be seen solely as an index of conservatism or a brake on innovation. Instead rural custom must be understood as a strategic response to an unpredictable environment in which customary codes help to provide order and meaning in a disordered world. In addition, peasant custom is flexible in the sense that peasants are able and willing to renegotiate custom in reaction to changing incentives. For example, kinship practices that once favored partible inheritance may be collectively reformulated to favor primogeniture in response to shrinking land allotments and population growth. Once again, it is important to keep in mind that this strategic flexibility of custom is only possible because peasants are involved in local institutional networks that allow for collective deliberation and political redefinition of traditional norms and values. Custom is, in fact, one more resource that peasants have available in their enactment of strategies of subsistence and survival.

In sum, the study of peasant politics has become increasingly sophisticated. However, much work needs to be done, and future work may help us to arrive at a more complete analysis of the processes that dissolve peasant localism and that contribute to the development of genuinely integrated national societies. Only when that endpoint has been reached will we truly witness the vanishing of peasant society and the creation of a modern world on a global scale.

(See also GREEN REVOLUTION; LAND REFORM; PATRON-CLIENT POLITICS; RURAL DEVELOPMENT.)

Joel Migdal, *Peasants, Politics, and Revolution* (Princeton, N.J., 1975). James C. Scott, *The Moral Economy of the Peasant* (New Haven, Conn., 1976). Samuel Popkin, *The Rational Peasant: The Economy of Rural Society in Vietnam* (Berkeley, Calif., 1979). James C. Scott, *Weapons of the Weak: Everyday Forms of Peasant Resistance* (New Haven, Conn., 1985). Victor Magagna, *Communities of Green: Rural Rebellion in Comparative Perspective* (Ithaca, N.Y., 1991).

VICTOR V. MAGAGNA

PEOPLE'S REPUBLIC OF CHINA. See CHINA.

PERESTROIKA. According to authoritative Soviet sources, perestroika ("restructuring") may be defined as a "deep, revolutionary renewal of all aspects of the life of Soviet society, providing socialism with the most modern forms of organization, and disclosing to the fullest extent possible its merits in all respects: economic, sociopolitical and ideological" (*Kratkii politicheskii slovar'*, Moscow, 1989). Although the term was used by *Stalin and earlier Soviet leaders, it became most closely associated with the *reform program advanced by the *Gorbachev leadership in the *Soviet Union from 1985 to 1991.

At the outset of his administration Gorbachev's objectives were still fairly obscure, even at leading levels of the party. Gorbachev, unlike his main rivals for the leadership, had not addressed a party congress, and he had still (in March 1985) no published collection of writings to his name. He had made only a few visits abroad, to Canada in 1983 and to Britain in late 1984, on both occasions as the head of a delegation of Soviet parliamentarians. There were, however, several indications, in his biography and known policy positions, that his administration would be rather more than a continuation of those of his predecessors. Gorbachev was a relatively young leader (just 54 on his election, too young to have fought in the war or to have known the worst of *Stalinism); he was unusually well educated, with a law degree from Moscow University; and he was known to be open-minded, particularly by his university contemporaries.

There were also some clues in Gorbachev's speeches before his accession that his leadership would be an innovative one. The clearest indication of this was a lengthy speech to an *ideology conference in December 1984, not published in full at the time, in which the future general secretary made positive references to self-management and to social justice (in effect, an attack on the corruption of the later Brezhnev years) and called for the further development of socialist *democracy and glasnost ("openness") in the media and public life. There were further clues in Gorbachev's speech at the local elections in February 1985, made at a time when Konstantin Chernenko's illness was already well known. Gorbachev defined the Soviet system as a form of rule "of the workers for the workers," and called for the party "again and again to check its political course against the rich experience of the people." These and other speeches made it clear that a Gorbachev administration would continue the reforms of its predecessors but also place them within a broader framework of political and moral regeneration.

Of all the policies that were promoted by the new leadership after March 1985, glasnost was probably the most distinctive. Glasnost did not mean an unqualified freedom of the press or the right to information; nor was it original to Gorbachev. It did, however, reflect the new general secretary's belief that without a greater awareness of the real state of affairs and of the considerations that had led to particular decisions there would be no willingness on the part of the Soviet people to commit themselves to the program of perestroika. "The better people are informed," Gorbachev told the Central Committee meeting that elected him, "the more consciously they act, the more actively they support the party, its plans and programmatic objectives." This led to more open treatment of social problems such as drugs, prostitution, and crime; it also led to a more honest consideration of the Soviet past, including the repression of the 1930s and the corruption of the Brezhnev era.

The "democratization" of Soviet political life was a further part of perestroika. The political system established by the October revolution, Gorbachev told the Nineteenth Party Conference in 1988, had undergone "serious deformations," leading to the development of a "command-administrative system" that had become the main obstacle to perestroika. A limited experiment in electoral choice had taken place in June 1987; the Party Conference approved a more far-reaching "radical reform" of Soviet political life, and this led to a related series of constitutional changes in late 1988. These included an entirely new electoral law, on the basis of which the national elections in March 1989 were conducted on a largely competitive basis, and the establishment of a working parliament (the Supreme Soviet) elected by a larger and popularly elected assembly called the Congress of People's Deputies. Attempts were also made to democratize the operation of the Communist Party itself through competitive ballots for leading positions, greater information about all aspects of the party's activity, and (in the rules that were adopted at the Twenty-eighth Congress in 1990) greater respect for the rights of the minority.

Together with these changes, for Gorbachev, there had to be a "radical reform" of the Soviet economy. Levels of growth had been steadily declining since at least the 1950s, and by the late 1970s they had reached the lowest levels in Soviet peacetime history. Indeed, as Gorbachev pointed out in early 1988, if the sale of alcoholic drink and of Soviet oil on world markets were excluded, there had been no real growth in the Soviet economy for the previous fifteen years. Radical reform, as Gorbachev explained to the Party Congress in 1986 and to a Central Committee plenum the following year, involved a set of related measures. One of the most important was a greater degree of decentralization of economic management, leaving the state to set broad parameters but allowing factories and farms a much greater degree of operational autonomy. Retail and wholesale prices would gradually be reformed so as to eliminate indiscriminate subsidies, and enterprises that failed to pay their way might be liquidated. These objectives were gradually broadened to encompass a more far-reaching program of "destatification" and limited forms of private ownership as part of a transition to a "regulated market economy." Changes of this kind had led, at the close of the 1980s, to a more diverse but not necessarily a more dynamic and efficient economy. (In 1990, in fact, national income fell by four percent, the first such fall in Soviet postwar history.)

Despite a series of reforms of this kind, the nature and consequences of perestroika remained somewhat obscure. What, for a start, was its relationship to "socialism" and the longer-term objective of transition to a wholly communist society? *Khrushchev had promised that the Soviet Union would construct a society of such a kind by 1980 in the Party Program that was adopted under his guidance in 1961. His successors swiftly dropped that commitment and began to describe the Soviet Union, from the early 1970s, as a "developed socialist society," whose evolution into a fully communist one was a matter for an unspecified point in the fairly distant future. Brezhnev's successors in turn made clear that the Soviet Union was at the very beginning of the stage of developed socialism, and that its further evolution would require a "whole historical epoch." Gorbachev's original objective, as he explained it to the Central Committee that elected him, was the "acceleration of socioeconomic development and the perfection of all aspects of Soviet life." This soon developed into a larger view of a "new image" of socialism, one that (as Gorbachev explained to the Party Conference in 1988) would be free of the abuses of the Soviet past and open to the cultural achievements of other civilizations.

Gorbachev set out his thinking at greater length in an important article, "The Socialist Idea and Revolutionary Perestroika," which appeared in *Pravda* in November 1989. Drawing on a series of speeches over earlier weeks, the Soviet leader insisted there could be no detailed blueprint of the kind of society he and his colleagues wished to construct, nor would it come about quickly. Perestroika, rather, would be a "lengthy stage in the historical development of socialism," probably extending into the twenty-first century. It would, however, avoid both the "bureaucratic deformations" of the Soviet past and the gross inequalities of *capitalism. It would draw upon the experience of other countries, including social democratic parties in Western Europe. It would be a "genuinely democratic and self-governing social organism." And it would involve the greatest possible degree of cooperation between East and West to resolve their common problems, in line with the "new thinking" on international problems that had been a hallmark of his administration.

The Twenty-eighth Party Congress in July 1990 advanced these rather general guidelines with a "Programmatic Declaration," discussed in draft earlier in the year, which was intended to set out the party's intentions for the short and medium term. It indicated that the "essence of perestroika" was a transition from an "authoritarian, bureaucratic system to a society of humane, democratic socialism." However difficult, this was the "only way of securing a worthwhile life and realizing the [Soviet Union's] material and spiritual potential." A society of this kind would be one in which the "purpose of social development" was human development. There would be "diverse forms of property and management," and the sole source of political power would be the "sovereign will of the people." A society of this kind, finally, would "consistently work for peaceful and equal cooperation among nations."

Perestroika had consistently been clearer in its condemnation of the abuses of the past than in its specification of a Soviet future, and by the end of the Gorbachev era any such vision had a relatively limited appeal to a population whose actual experience was one of shortages, rising prices, and social inequalities. Indeed quite different interpretations could be offered of the whole project of perestroika. For an influential group of critics within the party, for instance, perestroika reflected the undue influence of a group of academic economists infected by "market euphoria." For critics of this kind, well represented in the Central Committee, collective forms of property were to remain dominant, glasnost was not to be exploited by "demagogues," and ordinary workers were to be protected from any move toward the market. For another group of critics, most of whom had left the party by 1990, and many of whom were to join with Boris *Yeltsin in leading post-Soviet *Russia, perestroika was much too limited in its objectives. Rather than "democratization," they wanted democracy; the party, they thought, should limit itself to a purely parliamentary function; and they insisted on the full "de-ideologization" of Soviet public life.

Perestroika could also be placed within the broader perspective of communist reform. It was, in this sense, one of a series of attempts that had been made to find a "middle way" between capitalism and the Stalinist form of socialism, one that respected individual rights but at the same time avoided the social inequalities that were associated with the market. There were many similarities, for instance, between Gorbachev's perestroika and the *Prague Spring of 1968, when reformers led by Alexander Dubček had sought to develop a "socialism with a human face." There were some similarities with developments in the Soviet Union itself in the 1920s, when a form of mixed economy had developed and a reasonably wide range of opinion had been reflected in the official media. By the early 1990s, however, no convincing "third way" had been found: the countries of Eastern and Central Europe had mostly opted for capitalism and liberal democracy, and at least one of those that remained under communist rule (China) had been compelled to preserve socialism by wholesale repression. By the early 1990s perestroika in its original form was widely agreed to have failed, and, with the collapse of the attempted coup in 1991, the removal of the Communist Party from its dominant position, and the demise of the Soviet Union, it became increasingly unlikely that any form of "humane, democratic socialism" would accommodate the future course of politics.

(See also COMMUNISM; COMMUNIST PARTY STATES; NEW ECONOMIC POLICY, U.S.S.R.; SOVIET–EAST EUROPEAN RELATIONS.)

Mikhail Gorbachev, *Perestroika* (New York and London, 1987). Richard Sakwa, *Gorbachev and His Reforms* (London, 1990). David Lane, *Soviet Society under Perestroika,* 2d ed. (Boston, 1991). Stephen White, *Gorbachev and After,* 2d ed. (Cambridge and New York 1991).

STEPHEN WHITE

PERIPHERAL NATIONALISM. The term *peripheral nationalism* refers to the manifestation of collective identity and/or mobilization on behalf of autonomist or separatist ends in culturally (especially linguistic or religious) distinctive territories that are subject to the rule of a central, culturally alien state apparatus. Whereas the bulk of scholarly attention has focused on peripheral nationalism in highly developed societies, such as Britain, Canada, Belgium, and Spain (Edward Tiryakian and Ronald Rogowski, *New Nationalisms of the Developed West,* Boston, 1985), the phenomenon is of central importance in societies at all levels of development.

Four different—though not mutually exclusive— theoretical approaches have been advanced to explain the timing and geographical distribution of peripheral nationalism. In chronological order of their development, these are a *diffusionist* theory, which holds that *nationalism ultimately withers in the face of the penetration of markets in peripheral regions; an *internal colonial* theory, which holds that it arises from a cultural division of labor that can be maintained in advanced capitalist social structures; a *competition* theory, which holds that it is most likely to develop when the cultural division of labor begins to break down; and a *rational choice* theory, which ascribes it to the nationalists' ability to secure private goods and thereby win adherents. Since systematic comparative data on peripheral nationalism are extremely difficult to obtain, no comprehensive tests of the four approaches exist. In *The Comparative Method: Moving beyond Qualitative and Quantitative Strategies* (Berkeley, Calif., 1987),

Charles C. Ragin presents a quantitative test of the first three theoretical perspectives; however, it indicates that the internal colonial and competition approaches are superior to the diffusion approach in thirteen Western European societies.

(See also INTERNAL COLONIALISM; SECESSIONIST MOVEMENTS.)

Karl W. Deutsch, *Nationalism and Social Communication* (Cambridge, Mass., 1966). Michael Hechter, *Internal Colonialism: The Celtic Fringe in British National Development, 1536–1966* (Berkeley, Calif., 1975). Susan Olzak and Joane Nagel, eds., *Competitive Ethnic Relations* (Orlando, Fla., 1986). Michael Hechter, "Nationalism as Group Solidarity" *Ethnic and Racial Studies* 10, no. 4 (1987): 415–426,

MICHAEL HECHTER

PERÓN, Juan Domingo. The most important and controversial political leader of twentieth-century *Argentina, Juan Domingo Perón sharply divided Argentines during and after his lifetime over the issues of distribution of income and political power. In historical retrospect, he may be seen as a leader who wanted to extend to the lower classes the standard of living and the political enfranchisement that Hipólito Yrigoyen and the Unión Cívica Radical had brought to the Argentine middle classes earlier in the century. One of the few South American leaders to be known throughout the world, Perón championed a "Third Force" in world politics and encouraged wider *political participation by Argentine women.

For the first five decades of his life, Perón showed little indication of his future accomplishments. Instead, he followed a rather typical military career. Born to a middle-class family in 1895, he graduated in 1913 from the Colegio Militar. After rising to the rank of lieutenant colonel, he studied mountain warfare techniques with the Italian Alpine troops in 1939 and 1940, having an opportunity personally to evaluate Italian, German, and Spanish *fascism while in Europe. In 1943, as a colonel, Perón worked with a group of officers to depose the incumbent government and share in collective power for two years. He headed the new Secretariat of Labor and Social Security, working to expand the size and influence of labor unions and to make their members loyal to him personally. Perón went on to become minister of war and vice president before other officers, sensing his expanding authority, deposed him in October 1945.

Perón's true assumption of power came on 17 October 1945 when a vast crowd of workers and other supporters assembled in the Plaza de Mayo in Buenos Aires, demanding his release from imprisonment on Martín García Island. Once released, Perón addressed the cheering crowd from the balcony of the Casa Rosada, where he would give a series of famous speeches in years to come.

In 1946, Perón was elected to the Argentine presidency in one of the freest elections in Argentine history; he was elected to a second term in 1951. A military coup in 1955 deposed him, sending him into exile first in Paraguay and ultimately in Madrid. For many years, historians and political leaders in Argentina tried to write Perón off as a has-been, but this ultimately proved impossible. In 1973, he returned triumphantly to Argentina and to the presidency after eighteen years in exile.

The basis for Perón's power was the Justicialista (Peronist) Party. Multiclass in nature, ranging over the ideological spectrum from far right to far left, it was an archetypal example of *populism. Peronism has been able to count consistently on support from ten percent of the upper classes and seventy percent of the lower classes. Perón built fierce and durable loyalty for the movement during his first presidency, during which he increased the proportion of national wealth going to the working class very substantially. By 1955, however, the real wages of many workers had fallen back to the levels of the 1940s, because economic growth was not strong enough to support the higher wage levels. More important than economic gains, members of the working class and trade unions had achieved a sense of political consciousness and economic entitlement that made them combative participants in Argentine politics for decades to come.

Juan Perón also had high ambitions in international politics. Quite accurately, he predicted that if the countries of Latin America did not join together, they would remain weak and put upon by more powerful nations. Often credited with originating the concept of the *Third World, Perón after 1945 dreamed of a coalition of states allied to neither the Soviet Union nor the United States. Argentine yearning for leadership of this movement appears in one of the most common Peronist slogans: *Ni yanqui, ni marxista—peronista* (Neither Yankee, nor Marxist—Peronist).

Much of Perón's popularity can be attributed to his fiery second wife, María Eva Duarte de *Perón ("Evita"). Evita campaigned for him in the 1946 election and later became the symbol of Peronism through her charismatic oratory and her advocacy of social welfare as president of the Fundación Eva Perón. Her death from cancer in 1952 was a major blow to Perón in political as well as personal terms. While in exile in Spain, he married María Estela Martínez ("Isabel"). When Perón returned to the presidency in 1973, she became his vice president and succeeded him after his death in office in 1974. Isabel, in turn, was overthrown by the military in 1976.

In perspective, the range of Perón's influence remains striking. Peronist President Carlos Menem reversed the traditional economic policies of Perón, working to privatize state enterprises and to encourage citizens' economic self-reliance rather than their dependency on the state, saying that Perón's policies were for the 1940s and 1950s but that another era had come to Argentina in the 1990s. Nevertheless, Menem carefully copies much of the personal lifestyle of General Perón, his mentor and role model. Even those who find Perón's policies dated and fallible continue to evoke his memory as a political symbol of the full enfranchisement of the working class.

Frederick C. Turner and José Enrique Miguens, eds., *Juan Perón and the Reshaping of Argentina* (Pittsburgh, 1983). Juan Domingo Perón, *Obras Completas,* Fermín Cháves, series ed. (Buenos Aires, in process).

FREDERICK C. TURNER

PERÓN, María Eva Duarte de. Better known as Evita, María Eva Duarte de Perón was the wife of Juan Domingo *Perón during his first term as president of *Argentina (1946–1952) and one of the most influential women in Latin American history. Born on 17 May 1919 in a hamlet of Buenos Aires province, she was the fifth illegitimate child of Juana Ibarguren and Juan Duarte. At 15, having completed her primary schooling, she left for Buenos Aires to pursue an acting career. She began playing silent parts on the stage, but by the early 1940s, Eva Duarte was a starlet who earned her living doing radio soap operas while waiting for her big role in a film. Her life began to change when she met Colonel Perón, head of the Labor Secretariat and soon-to-be minister of war as well as vice president. To the dismay of his fellow officers and Argentina's social and political elite, she openly became his mistress.

The transformation of the dark-haired actress into the fiery, blond, charismatic leader of the *descamisados* ("shirtless ones") was a slow process that began after the dramatic events of 17 October 1945, when thousands of workers gathered in Buenos Aires to demand the release of the imprisoned Perón. Contrary to the accepted belief, Evita neither helped to organize nor participated in the workers' demonstration—though she tried to obtain a writ of habeas corpus for Perón's release. Perón wrote her a loving letter from jail: he was concerned for her well-being and safety and promised to marry her. Indeed, on 21 October, in a quiet civil ceremony, Eva Duarte became the wife of Perón.

Shortly after the wedding, Perón began his campaign for the presidency. Though Evita could not vote because she was a woman, and as such was expected to remain in the background, she accompanied Perón in his tours of the provinces, took part in strategy meetings, stood by him waving to the enthusiastic crowds, and even addressed a women's rally in Buenos Aires.

Her interest in politics and her influence increased decisively after Perón took office in June 1946. She began to meet daily with workers' delegations, union leaders, and officials of the Secretariat of the Labor Confederation, thus continuing the work that Perón did as secretary of labor. She frequently addressed

Perón's supporters on his behalf and proved to be a rousing speaker. After a triumphant European tour which she undertook without Perón, she returned in time to urge the passage of a law granting women the vote.

Evita was never formally part of Perón's government, though she tried unsuccessfully to be the Peronist vice-presidential candidate in the 1951 elections. She was officially only Argentina's First Lady, but she was a one-woman propaganda ministry for Perón and his trusted liaison with labor. She was also president of the Eva Perón Foundation, a well-endowed social welfare organization. She used the foundation funds to build hospitals, schools, youth hostels, and low-income housing, and to buy thousands of goods that she distributed to the needy. In addition, she was president of the women's branch of the Peronist Party, which helped to reelect Perón in 1951 with an overwhelming female vote.

Evita's death from cancer on 26 July 1952 undermined the stability of Peronism. She was a crucial component of that political structure and irreplaceable—as Perón soon realized when his economic policies began to strain his relationship with the *descamisados*. On the other hand, her death transformed her into a powerful myth that became essential for the survival of Peronism after Perón's ouster in 1955 and, despite the repression of successive military dictatorships, its return to power in 1973 along with Perón's own reelection that same year.

Julie M. Taylor, *Eva Perón: The Myth of a Woman* (Chicago, 1979). Marysa Navarro, *Évita* (Buenos Aires, 1981).

MARYSA NAVARRO-ARANGUREN

PERSIAN GULF. See GULF STATES.

PERSIAN GULF WAR. See GULF WAR.

PERU. Politics in twentieth-century Peru have been shaped in many ways by events in the previous century: from reluctant independence in the 1820s and an overwhelming preponderance of military rulers to economic ruin imposed by loss to Chile in the War of the Pacific (1879–1883) and the subsequent expansion of British interests in Peru to pay off the war debt. A limited liberal *democracy finally became established between 1895 and 1919, to date Peru's most extended period of elected civilian rule. The major conflict from the 1930s through the 1960s was between the country's first mass-based political party, the Alianza Popular Revolucionaria Americana (APRA), and the army. APRA represented the middle class and newly organizing agricultural and industrial workers, while the military, at least until 1962, protected the interests of established elites.

From the 1880s into the 1960s, Peru's government was one of the smallest in Latin America, with an economy based on production and export of a number of primary products, including sugar, cotton, fish meal, copper, and other minerals. Economically, Peru was distinguished only by the diversity of its export products, by low inflation, and by modest but almost unbroken economic growth from the late 1940s until the mid-1970s.

A historic shift in Peruvian politics began with the military *coup d'état of 1968. Led by a reformist army and the commander in chief of the armed forces, General Juan Velasco Alvarado, the regime carried out substantial changes over twelve years in power in the name of national development for national security. Most notable were an agrarian reform benefiting over 375,000 farm families; the rapid expansion of unions along with legalization of the Marxist union confederation; and a threefold expansion in the size and scope of government.

The most significant political legacy of Peru's first long-term military government was the legitimization of the Marxist *Left as an actor. Economically, the regime's ambitious reforms far exceeded Peru's capacity and contributed directly to increased inflation, endemic debt crises starting in 1978, and stagnation or decline for most years after 1975. A consolidating coup led by General Francisco Morales Bermúdez in 1975 slowed the pace of reform and eventually committed an increasingly harassed military to the restoration of civilian rule.

Under the constitution of 1979, Peru returned to civilian rule the next year with the politically exhausted military's blessing. For the first time the country experienced universal suffrage—the vote was extended to illiterates, thereby enfranchising much of the Indian population (estimated at about thirty percent of Peru's 20 million people), and to those 18 and older. With successive presidential and congressional elections in 1985 and 1990, and local elections in 1983, 1986, and 1989, Peru experienced its most extended period of elected civilian rule since the early twentieth century. *Proportional representation ensured access to Congress and to municipalities of multiple parties and groupings, even though in 1980 and 1985 the parties of the presidential candidates won a majority in both houses and the first plurality in the next local elections following.

This meant that Fernando Belaúnde Terry (1980–1985), Acción Popular (AP), Alán García Pérez (1985–1990), and APRA were able to implement substantial portions of their legislative agendas. Alberto Fujimori (1990–) and his newly created Cambio 90 Party were not as fortunate, gaining less than a third of the congressional seats and being forced into a runoff election to win the presidency itself. Fujimori is the first president since 1963 who required coalition support in Congress for each component of his legislative agenda. Even so, he succeeded in getting much of his program implemented during his first twenty months in office. This included an economic shock program drastically reducing inflation and a major international reinsertion package to restore Peru's foreign credit standing.

However, frustrated by political machinations and corruption, Fujimori, a newcomer to politics, abruptly suspended the constitution, Congress, and the judiciary in a totally unexpected self-coup (autogolpe) on 5 April 1992. The armed forces continued to proclaim their support of the Fujimori government, but it would not be difficult to envision a shift back to *military rule should Peru continue to drift from crisis to crisis.

Among contemporary Latin American democracies, Peru has the most diverse array of parties. The Izquierda Unida (IU) coalition included six parties for most of the 1980s. While the fortunes of the Left ebbed and flowed—with a peak of twenty-nine percent of the vote in the 1978 Constituent Assembly—as late as 1989 IU appeared to have an excellent chance to win the 1990 national elections. A split between moderate and radical factions, however, led to the presentation of two candidates who captured only eleven percent of the presidential vote between them.

APRA, which straddled the center of the Peruvian political spectrum, gained thirty-seven of the Constituent Assembly seats before dividing after the death in 1979 of founder Víctor Raúl *Haya de la Torre and seeing their support fall significantly in the 1980 presidential election. Under the leadership of Haya's youthful protégé Alán García, APRA regained its dynamism and captured the presidency in 1985, with fifty-three percent of the vote and a majority in both houses. The dramatic failure of García's policies, however, meant that APRA was repudiated in the 1990 elections.

The Right coalition of Belaúnde's Acción Popular and Luis Bedoya Reyes's Partido Popular Cristiano (PPC) went from victor in 1980 to vanquished in 1985 to leading contender status again by 1989, with the entrance into politics of novelist Mario Vargas Llosa and his Movimiento Libertad. As the Frente Democrático (FREDEMO) with Vargas Llosa as its standard bearer, the *Right took more mayoralties in the November 1989 municipal elections than did any other party or coalition. Up until a month before the April 1990 presidential elections, Vargas Llosa and the Right appeared poised for victory.

Almost no one predicted the "Fujimori phenomenon." His candidacy grew from one percent support in a public opinion poll the first week of March to twenty-four percent in the first round of the presidential elections in April to fifty-seven percent in the June runoff against Vargas Llosa. Fujimori and his Cambio 90 Party, formed less than six months before the election, came to be seen as a popular alternative to the overconfident Right. Once in office, however, the new president surprised all by adopting much the same drastic economic measures proposed by his main opponent.

Fujimori justified this draconian approach because Peru's economic problems were so serious. Real incomes in 1990 were well below 1972 levels. Unemployment and underemployment reached almost seventy percent. Inflation totaled 7,650 percent in 1990; nominal prices were over 1,000 times higher than they had been in 1985. Net economic growth was negative in eleven of the fifteen years between 1976 and 1990. The foreign debt was over US$20 billion in 1990, with almost $6 billion in arrears.

Were it not for the large and dynamic "informal" sector (which is about forty percent of the urban population and accounts for a similar proportion of the goods and services generated in the country) and the "illegal" sector (Peru's Upper Huallaga Valley produces some sixty percent of the coca leaf used in the manufacture of cocaine, employs about 300,000 people, and generates over US$1 billion in foreign exchange, most of which makes its way to Lima), Peru would be economically prostrate. Through 1990 at least, the political manifestations of this new endemic economic crisis took shape primarily in the election of different parties rather than in more dramatic forms. Most of the population remained committed to democracy, according to opinion polls, despite continuing economic difficulties.

Even so, economic erosion played into the hands of Latin America's most radical guerrilla movement, Sendero Luminoso (SL). SL began in the 1960s as one more Marxist university group in the isolated and predominantly Indian department of Ayacucho. The military government's blundering with an agrarian reform imposed from the center in the 1970s contributed to increases in SL's local support. The movement began the armed struggle simultaneously with the return to democracy in Peru. During the 1980s political violence accounted for over 16,000 casualties and over $15 billion in damages to a $28 billion economy.

In spite of reverses and a patent lack of support among most of the populace owing to its uncompromising radical stance, SL continues to recruit among disaffected youth and to wreak havoc in diverse parts of the country. Beginning in 1990, SL shifted to a more urban strategy, particularly in the sprawling shantytowns of the capital city of Lima. SL's persistence in the use of violence and terrorism to advance its revolutionary cause even in an open civilian democratic system has lent a perverse legitimacy to other extremists.

The military has had both success and failure in its fight against the guerrillas, complicated in the Upper Huallaga Valley by the simultaneous waging, with U.S. assistance, of coca eradication and coca paste interdiction campaigns that drive many farmers into the hands of the guerrillas. Recently the military has also been affected by the economic crisis, which has substantially reduced funds for troops and officers in the field as well as for salaries. The broader problem is the long-standing one of overreliance on the central government in Lima for plans and resources, often inappropriate, inade-

quate, tardy, or nonexistent. This combines with urban-rural, worker-farmer, and white/mestizo-Indian cleavages to make a gulf between center and periphery that is very difficult to bridge. President Fujimori's April 1992 *autogolpe* was likely to contribute to Peru's problems rather than to solve them, even though constitutional rule was supposed to be restored within a year through an elected constituent assembly. It cut off political party ties between the Congress and local communities. It resulted in the suspension of about $700 million in economic assistance and the cancellation of the reinsertion package, dashing prospects for continued economic recovery. While it boosted Fujimori's public support in the short run, it reduced the legitimacy of central government by removing its democratic basis. All this played into SL's hands, as symbolized by July 1992 bombings that killed at least 25 and wounded over 300 in middle- and upper-class sections of Lima previously considered relatively safe.

In foreign policy, Peru has attempted with some success to forge an independent *Third World position over the past twenty years. It played major roles in the creation of the Andean Pact in 1969 with its precedent-setting posture on regulating foreign investment, profit remittances, and progressive reversion to domestic ownership. Peru led the effort among a number of Latin American countries to normalize relations with Cuba in the 1970s, hosted a meeting of the *Group of 77, nationalized a number of foreign companies, and played a significant role as moderator in the *Malvinas/Falklands War, the Contadora group, and the *Socialist International during the APRA government of 1985–1990. The forceful limited debt repayment plan of the García administration, intended to lead the way toward a more aggressive Latin American stance on their foreign debt burden, became an albatross around the country's neck as Peru fell further behind and found others unwilling to follow. Chastened by the failure of its aggressive Third World stance, Peru has become more willing to set a moderate course, hoping that a rise in international stature will ultimately benefit the country's now-perilous domestic situation.

(See also DEMOCRATIC TRANSITIONS; DRUGS; GUERRILLA WARFARE; LAND REFORM; MARXISM; U.S.–LATIN AMERICAN RELATIONS.)

Daniel M. Masterson, *Militarism and Politics in Latin America: Peru from Sánchez Cerro to Sendero Luminoso* (New York, 1991). David Scott Palmer, ed., *The Shining Path of Peru* (New York, 1992). James D. Rudolph, *Politics in Peru: The Evolution of a Crisis* (Stanford, Calif., 1992).

DAVID SCOTT PALMER

PHILIPPINES. The Philippines is an archipelago of 7,100 islands, islets, and atolls located southeast of the Asian mainland. It straddles the South China Sea and the Pacific Ocean and serves as a gateway to the international straits linking Northeast and

Southeast Asia to the Indian Ocean and the Middle East. Its strategic location has made it a prize asset in U.S. global strategy since the turn of the twentieth century. Covering nearly 300,000 square kilometers (115,300 sq. mi.), Philippine land territory sprawls over some 1.3 million square kilometers (500,000 sq. mi.) of oceanic waters and has a population of 60.5 million (1990). The islands are grouped into Luzon in the north, Visayas in the center, and Mindanao in the south. The country's premier city, Manila, which is located on Luzon Island, is its political, economic, and educational center.

The Filipinos are a blend of Malay, Chinese, Spanish, and American heritages, reflecting their long history of racial mixing through trade and colonialism. Spain created in the Philippines a centralized political structure bringing under the Spanish Crown independent Malay kingdoms and indigenous tribes already trading with Chinese merchants. Its defeat in the Spanish-American War (1896–1898) led to the imposition of rule by the United States after a bloody war (1898–1902) against the Filipinos, erstwhile U.S. allies, who fought fiercely but in vain to retain their independence.

These successive colonialisms produced the modern Filipino, mixed in race, primarily Roman Catholic in religion (eighty-five percent), conversant in English and in at least one of their eighty-eight distinct languages and dialects. Filipinos share the liberal democratic values of the West but remain burdened by socioeconomic structures shaped by colonialism which enable the rich minority to dominate the poor majority.

Social Bases of Politics. The social bases of politics were laid out during the country's colonial history when powerful local elites were co-opted by the Spaniards. In return, they were afforded the privilege and opportunity to amass land-based wealth. In some cases, their wealth came from marriage with rich but low-status Chinese merchants. They produced a class of leaders wielding both economic and political power who led the nineteenth-century reform movement seeking liberalization in the colony within the context of Spanish rule, who fought U.S. colonialism, rewon independence, and have ruled the country since then. The national hero, José Rizal, and the first Philippine president under U.S. rule, Manuel L. Quezon, as well as subsequent presidents, like Ferdinand E. *Marcos and Corazon ("Cory") C. *Aquino, were among their members.

The major ethnolinguistic groups that have shaped politics were the Tagalogs, Ilocanos, and Pampangans of Luzon, the Cebuanos of the Visayas, and the Muslim Maranaos and Tausugs of Mindanao. Close to the seat of power in Manila, Tagalogs have exerted the greatest political influence dating back to the nineteenth-century reformists and their revolutionary successors. They succeeded in making Tagalog the basis of a national language called "Pilipino" at a time when Cebuano-speakers constituted

the majority; by 1990 it was the language understood by most Filipinos.

Ethnolinguistic distinctions and consequent regionalism were reinforced by geographical fragmentation, posing physical difficulties for easy travel and communication. They contributed to a perception of a Manila-based, Tagalog-dominated "colonialism" by other groups. Nevertheless, ethnolinguistic rivalry has not erupted into large-scale violence except in two cases: Muslim separatism led by the Moro National Liberation Front in Mindanao, and the autonomy movement of ethnic communities in the Cordillera Mountains. Regional autonomy for these two groups is recognized in the 1987 Constitution.

Religion is not a central political issue, even in Muslim separatism whose real cause is socioeconomic-political domination of the Muslim minority by the Christian majority. Be that as it may, all Philippine presidents have been Catholics; some prominent leaders have been Protestants.

Philippine politics demands alliance making across the three island groups. Hence, presidential candidates from Luzon are careful to have vice-presidential teammates from either Visayas or Mindanao, and vice versa. Sometimes, marriages of politicians are contracted with this regional complementation in mind.

The politicization of the intelligentsia, farmers, and laborers since the 1930s led to the emergence of left-leaning organizations centering initially on the Soviet-oriented Philippine Communist Party and the *Hukbong Mapagpalaya Laban sa Hapon* (an anti-Japanese guerrilla group known as the Huks). An ideological split spawned the new pro-Chinese Communist Party of the Philippines and its armed wing, the New People's Army (CPP/NPA) in the late 1960s, which is still conducting an active insurgency against the government.

The Political System. *Authoritarianism and *democracy provide the experiential and ideological backdrop of the political system. Authoritarianism of traditional culture was reinforced by repressive colonial structures and processes including those under wartime Japanese rule. However, Philippine encounters with Western liberal ideas through the nineteenth-century reformists and its actual experience with U.S. democracy (1902–1942; 1946–1972) shaped Filipino political orientation. The experience of the fourteen years under Marcos made authoritarianism unpalatable to the majority. Hence, redemocratization under Cory Aquino followed the fall of Marcos in the "People Power Revolt" of 22–25 February 1986.

The 1987 Constitution restored a presidential-style republican government operating under separation of powers and checks and balances. The bicameral legislature consists of a twenty-four-member Senate elected nationwide and a 250-member House of Representatives largely elected through single-member constituencies. To secure the representation of minority groups, some seats are to be filled through a party-list system. Terms of office are six years for senators, three years for House members.

The president, who heads the executive branch, serves for a single six-year term. Executive powers are severely constrained, especially emergency powers including declaration of martial law, to prevent a repeat of authoritarian rule. Executive appointments require confirmation by the Commission on Appointments for heads of executive departments, ambassadors, and chiefs of mission, as well as military promotions from the rank of army colonel or navy captain and up.

Personality-oriented political parties have dominated Philippine politics. Until 1972 the Nacionalista (NP) and Liberal (LP) parties were the major organizations. Since then many new groups emerged such as Marcos's New Society Movement and the "pro-Cory" Philippine Democratic Coalition. A multiparty system is enshrined in the new Constitution. Apart from the left-oriented Alliance for New Politics, other parties and groups have very little ideological distinction among them.

The erosion of military professionalism during the Marcos era fractionalized and politicized the officers corps to the extent that military rebels became a major threat to political stability after 1986. Military factions loyal to Marcos staged six unsuccessful coups against the Aquino government between July 1986 and December 1989 and continue to threaten Philippine democracy. In May 1992 former defense secretary Fidel Ramos was elected president to succeed Corazon Aquino in a largely peaceful multiparty election.

Socioeconomic Policies. Both *import-substitution industrialization and *export-led growth have been tried as strategies for economic development. Neither seems to have worked as basic structural problems traceable to inequitable wealth distribution have not been addressed. Various agrarian reform programs from earlier presidents to Cory Aquino could not be implemented owing to landlord opposition in and out of Congress. An international debt burden of US$29 billion in 1990 tied up some forty percent of the national budget in debt service, diverting resources from development needs such as building job-creating enterprises for some 750,000 new entrants annually to the labor force.

Population, though growing relatively slowly at 2.3 percent annually during the 1980s, still increased by 12.4 million by 1990. The influential Catholic church remained opposed to a population program endorsing artificial birth control measures. A related problem is the incidence of poverty, which stood at 49.5 percent in 1989 (down from fifty-nine percent in 1983).

Internal Conflict. Social unrest since the conclusion of World War II has diverted national resources and energies from the task of nation building and economic development. The domination by the governing elite over the economy and the polity has prevented fundamental social restructuring, an essential component of moderating social conflict.

Consequently, the Philippines continued to be threatened by a communist insurgency, long after most of its Southeast Asian neighbors had neutralized this threat internally. Ethnic conflicts also remained unresolved because of earlier fear of exacerbating ethnic differences through decentralization and sharing of power, measures which could have allayed ethnic minorities' fear of Christian domination and assured their participation in forging a single nation out of the country's multiethnic society.

Foreign Policy and International Relations. Bilateral relations with the United States, which centered around the agreement which allowed American military bases in the Philippines, were transformed during 1991 by a series of events which culminated in the termination of those agreements. Oil imports and labor exports, the country's third-highest income producer, make relations with the Middle East crucial. A restructuring of relations with the United States in the aftermath of the scheduled closing of the military bases remains the major item on the foreign policy agenda in the 1990s, along with the maintenance of good relations with Japan and both China and Taiwan. The combination of international pressures and internal conflicts ensures that the challenge of building the Philippine nation is bound to continue into the 1990s.

(See also ASSOCIATION OF SOUTHEAST ASIAN NATIONS; COLONIAL EMPIRES; DEMOCRATIC TRANSITIONS; INTERNATIONAL DEBT; SOUTHEAST ASIA TREATY ORGANIZATION.)

Carl H. Lande, ed., *Rebuilding a Nation: Philippine Challenges and American Policy* (Washington, D.C., 1987). Daniel B. Schirmer and Stephen R. Shalom, eds., *The Philippines Reader: A History of Colonialism, Dictatorship and Resistance* (Boston, 1987). Stanley Karnow, *In Our Image: America's Empire in the Philippines* (New York, 1989).

CAROLINA G. HERNANDEZ

PINOCHET, Augusto. As the president who ended four decades of electoral *democracy and state expansion in *Chile, Augusto Pinochet Ugarte installed an unusually personalistic and durable authoritarian regime along with a market-driven economy. He saw his mission as ridding Chile of Marxist parties and excessive government intervention in the economy.

Pinochet was born in the port city of Valparaíso on 25 November 1915. He graduated from military school in 1939 and from the War Academy in 1952. In the latter institution, he subsequently taught geopolitics and military geography. He rose through the ranks until becoming commandeer-in-chief of the Army in 1973 during the climactic crises of the elected socialist government of Marxist Salvador *Allende Gossens. Pinochet led the junta that seized power on 11 September and thereafter ruled for seventeen years.

During his first three years in office, Pinochet alienated international opinion with massive *human rights violations. He shut down all democratic institutions. The security forces imprisoned, tortured, murdered, or exiled thousands of Chileans, especially members of leftist parties and labor unions.

Pinochet reversed not only Chile's democratic traditions but also its statist industrial and social welfare policies. He quickly returned to former owners their lands and factories expropriated under Allende. In 1975 he implemented a monetarist "shock treatment" to lower the triple-digit inflation unleashed by Allende. Advised by the technocratic "Chicago Boys" (so called because of their ties to the Economics Department at the University of Chicago), Pinochet then instituted Latin America's most drastic conversion to a neoliberal, free-market system. He moved decisively to liberalize trade, promote nontraditional exports, slash government spending, privatize public enterprises, reduce social services, and weaken labor unions. During 1976–1981, the results included high levels of growth, export diversification, stable prices and exchange rates, foreign indebtedness, *deindustrialization, regressive income concentration, and unemployment.

In the glow of his economic "miracle" in 1980, Pinochet institutionalized his rule through a controlled plebiscite to approve an authoritarian constitution. That charter kept him in the presidency until 1988, when another plebiscite would offer him the opportunity for eight more years in office. In 1981–1982, however, an international recession and debt crisis capsized the economy. By 1983, protests against the dictatorship by social organizations and the banned political parties convulsed the country.

Despite mounting domestic and foreign opposition, Pinochet revived the economy by 1985 and retained power. He barely survived an *assassination attempt by leftist guerrillas in 1986. Then in the 1988 plebiscite his candidacy was defeated by a coalition of seventeen centrist and leftist parties in favor of a full return to representative democracy. Those same parties, prevailing over candidates sympathetic to Pinochet in the subsequent presidential and congressional elections of 1989, took office in 1990.

Grudgingly but peacefully, Pinochet transferred the presidential sash to his opponents. He claimed that his mission to bring health to the polity and economy had been completed. At the same time, he remained commander of the Army. Most Chileans hailed the end of his harsh regime, but a minority continued to revere Pinochet as the strongman who had saved the country from Marxism and economic mismanagement.

(See also AUTHORITARIANISM; INTERNATIONAL DEBT; MILITARY RULE; MONETARISM.)

Genaro Arriagada, *Pinochet: The Politics of Power* (Boston, 1988).

PAUL W. DRAKE

PLANNING. Most human beings, whether individually or in association with others, prepare to affect the future. In other words, they plan. With the evolution of high-technology industrialism, competing planners have invented many separate planning methods, each with its own respected jargon, literature, interest groups, and high priests. Some make special efforts to coordinate the specialists and guide results. All are involved—despite frequent protestations to the contrary—in efforts to get, keep, and use some degree of *power or influence.

Much of the important planning in life has always taken place on a relatively small scale. Thus, parents may plan for the number and timing of children, students for learning certain subjects and preparing for future careers, and teachers for improving a curriculum or writing books. Managers of police departments, fire departments, and hospitals plan the deployment of their usually scarce resources. On a larger scale, governments plan to promote economic growth, to direct growth in particular sectors, and to cushion the effects of the business cycle. Government planning emerged in response to discontent with the effects of market competition in which governments only facilitated private transactions. During the twentieth century, planning has taken two distinct forms, central command and democratic planning.

Market Competition and Government. One of the great successes of industrial civilization has been the maturation of government-supported competitive markets. Over the centuries, small urban spaces for the display of goods by farmers and artisans have become part of national and transnational markets for the exchange of goods and services, including specialized facilities for labor, land, and finance. This maturation took place largely as the result of government policies in Western Europe and North America during the eighteenth and nineteenth centuries. On the one hand, as celebrated in the vast literature of laissez-faire, governments withdrew (often reluctantly) from various forms of state monopoly and control of private activities. On the other hand, as Karl Polanyi explains, governments took on the responsibility of "enormous increase in continuous, organized and controlled intervention" (*The Great Transformation*, New York, 1957). This has involved public action to protect private property, build police and military forces, create money and banking systems, regulate weights and measures, and maintain judicial machinery for enforcing contracts. Governments also enlarge opportunities for business investment by providing infrastructures of roads, water supply, public health and education, and by developing foreign policies that support business operations abroad.

With these supports, private companies can plan ahead for greater profits, market penetration, technological advance, and political influence. Vigorous efforts throughout an enterprise may be promoted through both fear of failure and the expectation of the greater rewards that can flow from success. This often leads to higher quality of output, an improved range of goods or services, and increased efficiency. Through mass production and reduced costs and profits per unit, companies may not only earn larger total profits but also facilitate long-term growth in the volume of goods and services available to a society. In seeking mainly his own gain, as Adam Smith observes with regard to an individual employing "his capital in support of domestic industry" (not industry as a whole), he may thus promote public interests that were "no part of his intention" (*The Wealth of Nations* [1776], New York, 1937, p. 423).

But as Robert Burns put it, "The best laid schemes o' mice an' men gang aft a-gley." Going astray may result from imperfect information, serious error, changing conditions, or being outsmarted by rivals. Successful planning may impose unforeseen damages upon employees, consumers, or the environment; these are rarely reflected in a firm's accounts. The healthy effects of market competition may be offset by mergers, cartels, or price leadership understandings, most of which are legitimated or tolerated by government. Such arrangements tend to concentrate economic and political power, keep or push selected prices up, or manufacture shortages by setting ceilings on production. In periods of seriously short supply, unregulated competition can lead to dangerous outbreaks of hoarding, speculation, profiteering, and political unrest.

In preindustrial or industrializing societies, competitive markets have enlarged the opportunities for businesspeople and landowners to live longer and accumulate more wealth. But aggregate growth of income and population has often been associated with an enormous growth in the number of poor people with few expectations of escaping absolute or relative deprivation. Low-paid jobs, joblessness, and massive underemployment provide too little of the purchasing power needed for profitable investment to meet domestic needs. The most disastrous by-products of competitive markets have been the sharp economic fluctuations of the "capitalist business cycle," and the political turbulence resulting therefrom, during problems which have been moderated but not eliminated by greater expansion of government intervention and coordination.

Central Command. One response to the ravages of competitive *capitalism was centralized government planning. During the period from Francis Bacon

to Saint-Simon (seventeenth to eighteenth centuries), the idea of unlimited progress through science-based central command became an article of faith among West European *elites. With rationality as their guide, redesigned governments would construct ideal societies. In this spirit, socialists promised that national control of economic affairs would end exploitation and promote economic justice. Poverty, colonialism, and *war would be replaced by prosperity, independence, and *peace. Revolutionary socialists argued that with the forceful expropriation of private property, the immense productive forces of technology, once freed from the fetters imposed by capitalism, would operate "in accordance with a common plan" (Karl Marx, *The Communist Manifesto*). Humankind could then gradually pass from scarcity to abundance, and the history of human freedom would begin. Evolutionary socialists disagreed. They campaigned instead for *welfare state reforms, which were slowly legitimated as an alternative to the specter (usually exaggerated) of violent *revolution. These reforms helped make market operations more productive, allowed increases in living standards, and, by alleviating poverty, joblessness, and urban decay, undermined support for revolutionary movements in developed societies.

In 1917, when the Bolsheviks seized power in Russia, they had no idea how to run an economy "in accordance with a common plan." At first, *Lenin thought that capitalism had reduced management to "the extraordinary simple operations—which any literate person can perform—of checking and recording, knowledge of the four rules of arithmetic, and issuing receipts" (*State and Revolution,* 1917). Later, he introduced "war *communism" modeled largely on German central planning during World War I. He then sponsored a state-led scientific management program avowedly based on U.S. corporate principles of promoting labor discipline and productivity. A dominant slogan was "American technique plus Soviet power." By the time that "American technique" was already oriented toward decentralization,*Stalin's Five-Year Plans were devised on the principle of running the economy like One Big Company—but with more concentration at the top than capitalist companies usually attempted. The Stalinists and their successors rivaled (some would say exceeded) anticommunist fascist regimes in concentrating political power, suppressing opposition, and building an empire. They counterbalanced the incompetence and corruption of their central bureaucracies with remarkably efficient mind control and public relations. They won international prestige for having abolished unemployment (allegedly), helping defeat the fascist Axis in World War II, supporting many anticolonial movements, and opposing *apartheid in South Africa. Although this was no part of their original intention, the Stalinists and their successors produced enough literate people, scientists, intellectuals, and artists to help dismantle the empire and fragment the system of central command.

Democratic Planning. In the West, the worldwide capitalist depression of 1929–1939 was so deep and long that it shook faith in laissez-faire *ideologies and led to greater expansion of government intervention and coordination. In 1939, as World War II began in Europe, many people saw that it was the war, far more than welfare-state planners, that would conquer the Great Depression. In the name of "winning the peace," postwar planning became a widespread activity. Books, conferences, "think tank" seminars, and government reports offered a plethora of ideas on both transitional reconversion and longer-term policies. Under the banner of planning for full employment, many governments accepted the responsibility of preventing another general mass depression. In the United States, a loose policy guidance system (abjuring the dangerous word *planning*) was set up under the Employment Act of 1946. In France, "indicative planners" brought business and labor leaders together to set national goals; these were then backed up by government credit policies. The Federal Republic of Germany, Japan, Switzerland, and Scandinavian countries went still further in getting business, banking, and labor elites together to promote overall growth and help tame "the business cycle."

Procedurally, democratic planners tend to follow John Dewey's earlier concept of "a continuously planning society" instead of one with fixed blueprints ("The Economic Basis of the New Society," *Intelligence in the Modern World,* New York, 1939). In diverse ways, they combine fiscal and monetary policy with government interventions on behalf of managed competition, a strategy advocated by Eugene V. Rostow for the United States (*Planning for Freedom,* New Haven, Conn., 1960). *Cold War military spending (the importance of which was exaggerated by radicals and denied by conservative economists) has also been a factor. Thus in countries of constitutional capitalism, downturns, now labeled "recessions," have been relatively short and mild. Mass depression has been confined to ethnic ghettoes and areas hit by plant closings, declining basic industries, or farm failures. In developing countries, the record is much more mixed. When national economic growth has occurred, it has often been accompanied by large-scale underemployment and inflation.

During the Cold War, the sustained tension between the United States and the Soviet Union seemed permanent. Thus, planning to "win the peace" rarely occurred. With the surprisingly sudden collapse of the Soviet empire in 1991, no government seemed prepared for either short-term conversion or longer-term growth. For the new regimes in former communist countries, the transition to welfare state capitalism has proved enormously difficult. *Priva-tization measures have placed former state properties under the control of former state oligarchs. Laissez-faire ideologies have diverted attention from the government activities and the intermediary organizations of civil society without which competitive markets cannot mature. Nowhere in the world docs central command wither away easily. In countries of high-technology capitalism, conversion of military industries to peacetime pursuits is particularly difficult under conditions of slow-growth stagnation or recession. In poor countries, development planners can no longer play one side of the Cold War against the other. Throughout the world, planners have begun to debate alternative approaches to a truly global *political economy.

The most intensive planning takes place at the higher levels of transnational corporations and such agencies as the *International Monetary Fund and *World Bank. The relevance of these efforts to the fulfillment of basic *rights and fundamental freedoms will long be a matter of debate. Truly democratic planning requires painful—although far from revolutionary—changes in the culture and power structure not only of government and political parties, but also of families, schools, workplaces, and organized religion. Major shifts would be essential within developing countries as well as in their relations with more industrialized societies. Yet any resulting release of intelligence and moral commitment would inevitably be resisted by the elites, technocrats, bureaucrats, and patriarchalists who regard democracy as too precious to be wasted on the many.

(See also COMMAND ECONOMY; INTERNATIONAL POLITICAL ECONOMY; REFORM; SOCIALISM AND SOCIAL DEMOCRACY.)

Mary Parker Follett, "Individualism in a Planned Society," *Dynamic Administration* (London, 1932). Donald N. Michael, *On Learning to Plan and Planning To Learn* (San Francisco, 1973). Otis Graham, Jr., *Toward a Planned Society* (New York, 1976). Charles E. Lindblom, *Politics and Markets* (New York, 1977). Bertram Gross and Kusum Singh, "Planning under Freedom," in Barry Checkoway, ed., *Strategic Perspectives in Planning Practice* (Lexington, Ky., 1986). Melville Branch, *Planning: Universal Process* (New York, 1990). United Nations Development Programme, *Human Development Report* (New York, 1990).

— BERTRAM GROSS

PLO. See PALESTINE LIBERATION ORGANIZATION.

PLURALISM. The term *pluralism* was created in legal studies and political science in the early twentieth century to designate theories that strongly emphasized the importance of human associations other than the *state. Previously, in its general though rarely employed usage in English, the word simply meant, as the *Oxford English Dictionary* defined it, "the character of being plural." It had been used more specifically in England since the fourteenth century to refer to the ecclesiastical practice according to which one person held more than one benefice at the same time; and especially after the work of the U.S. philosopher William James, it had also been applied to philosophical theories that recognized more than one ultimate principle, as in morals or ethics, for example. In the mid-twentieth century yet another meaning was attributed to the term by social scientists who employed it to refer to societies stratified along racial or ethnic lines.

In political science and law, however, pluralism came to be attached to theoretical and empirical work that stressed the role played in political life by associations, organizations, and groups that were relatively independent of the state and one another. Typically, pluralist work in this sense was both descriptive and prescriptive, empirical and normative. From a pluralist perspective, a diversity of autonomous associations is not only a fact (in democratic polities, at any rate) but also desirable. However, neither pluralist writers nor their critics have always sharply distinguished empirical from evaluative judgments: it is not always clear whether their statements about pluralism are meant to be purely descriptive and explanatory, or judgments about the desirability of the state of affairs described, or both.

Although efforts have been made to group different pluralist accounts into various categories, the variety of writings that might be called pluralist in orientation defies easy or simple classification. However, a historical perspective suggests three rough phases in the development of pluralism in legal and political thought, each of which can be better understood if it is seen in opposition to a contrary and more "monistic" point of view.

The first, to which the term *pluralism* was first explicitly attached, arose during the first two decades of the twentieth century in opposition to widely prevalent doctrines about the exclusive *sovereignty of the state. For convenience, this form can be called legal pluralism. Among its best known advocates were Léon Duguit, whose principal works appeared in France between 1911 and 1913, and Harold Laski in England, who shortly thereafter not only translated Duguit but also mounted his own attack on the idea of state sovereignty. Legal pluralists like Duguit and Laski insisted that the conception of the state as the single and wholly sovereign association was simply false as a matter of fact; moreover, no state that attempted to achieve absolute internal sovereignty would be morally justifiable.

In their attack on state sovereignty, legal pluralists echoed earlier views—Greek, Roman, and medieval—that had also emphasized the actual and proper existence of associations within a political society. By contrast, later conceptions of state sovereignty advanced by Jean Bodin (1530–1596), Thomas Hobbes (1588–1679), John Austin (1790–1859), and others stressed the overwhelming primacy of the state. Even the French Revolution, Duguit argued, had merely substituted the sovereignty of the

nation for that of the monarch, thereby creating a myth that thereafter gained hold widely throughout Europe. The myth, Duguit contended, implied not only an exact correspondence between state and nation but also the suppression in the national territory of all groups exercising independent control. Both implications, he pointed out, were denied by the facts of actual social and political life in many countries—not least in countries where decentralization or *federalism maintained vigor. Some legal pluralists, including Duguit, not only insisted on the rightful independence of associations other than the state but went even further, contending that the state was simply one association among many, neither more important nor necessarily more powerful (in all circumstances) than others.

In the 1920s, legal pluralism acquired a substantial body of intellectual supporters, including, in addition to Laski, A. D. Lindsay, Ernest Barker, J. N. Figgis, and G. D. H. Cole in Britain. During the next decade, however, interest in legal pluralism greatly declined, and thereafter it almost disappeared in Britain and the United States. Critics argued that the legal pluralists had overstated their case, misrepresenting the prevailing doctrines of sovereignty and exaggerating the relative strength and importance of associations in comparison with the state. Laski himself became a Marxist. The Great Depression of the 1930s and World War II lent greater credibility to the belief that strong central governments were necessary for general well-being, and even for the survival of democratic systems and national independence. However, the decisive blow to legal pluralism probably came from the rise of authoritarian and totalitarian ideas and systems in Italy, the Soviet Union, Germany, Italy, Austria, and Spain. For these systems demonstrated beyond much doubt that a highly centralized authoritarian state could virtually eradicate autonomous associations, and certainly could deny them a significant place in social, economic, and political life. Thus, while pluralism in associational life might be desirable, and a basic characteristic of liberal and constitutional political systems, the authoritarian systems demonstrated that it was definitely not an inherent feature of all modern political systems.

From the mid-1950s to the mid-1960s, pluralism reappeared in the view that a fundamental constituent of modern democratic orders is the existence of associations that are relatively independent of one another and of the state. This perspective (which we might call democratic pluralism) explicitly countered the older monistic argument, strongly endorsed by Jean-Jacques Rousseau in *The Social Contract* (1762), that associations were undesirable because they expressed interests narrower than the general good. Recent democratic pluralism had been foreshadowed by, among many others, Alexis de Tocqueville, who in his famous *Democracy in America* (1835–1842) implicitly rejected Rousseau in contending that a rich associational life was essential to *democracy.

With its federal system, *separation of powers, relatively decentralized political parties, and multiplicity of groups and associations, the United States furnished a setting that was unusually supportive of pluralist interpretations. In 1908 A. F. Bentley set out a theory of politics that focused on the primacy of small groups; in 1929 E. Pendleton Herring described the role of group interests in the U.S. Congress; the perspectives of Bentley and Herring on the importance of groups in U.S. political life were adopted and systematically developed and documented by David Truman in a highly influential work in 1951. The general thrust of these approaches was opposition to the common belief, espoused not only by Rousseau but many others, that for groups to advance their group interests was necessarily inimical to the public interest.

In the 1950s and 1960s, however, the monistic alternative to pluralism that democratic pluralists were more likely to contest was the view that a relatively unified ruling class or *elite dominated political decisions, even in ostensibly democratic systems. This monistic alternative was supported not only by writers who held that a ruling class was an inherent condition of social life and organization, like Vilfredo Pareto, Gaetano Mosca, and Robert Michels, but also by Marxists (and others) who contended that a ruling class was an inevitable consequence of capitalism. Democratic pluralists, in contrast, contended that while serious inequalities in political resources prevented full political equality among citizens, careful empirical study of local or national governments in democratic countries failed to show that political life was dominated by an identifiable ruling class. On the contrary, empirical work demonstrated that public policies and decisions were often significantly influenced by different groups with different and even conflicting interests and objectives. A multiplicity of relatively autonomous associations, democratic pluralists contended, was inevitable in a democratic system because of the rights and opportunities guaranteed in democratic systems, and the advantages such associations provided their adherents. What is more, like Tocqueville they argued that associations were a positive benefit to democracy: they served to educate citizens in political life, strengthened them in their relations with the state, helped to ensure that no single interest would regularly prevail on all important issues, and, by providing information, discussion, negotiation, and compromise, even helped to make public decisions more rational and more acceptable than they would otherwise be.

Antipluralist critics contended in turn that pluralist accounts neglected the defects of democratic pluralism in practice. Some critics insisted that pluralists described only the facade, behind which existed the reality of monistic rule by capitalists or business elites. Even if the ruling elite did not always control specific decisions, it indirectly maintained its domination by preventing matters adverse to its interests from being placed on the agenda of the official decision-makers. The elite, antipluralists argued, also manipulated *public opinion, creating a circularity in beliefs running from the elite to the public to elected officials.

While rejecting these claims, democratic pluralists agreed that social pluralism was not, by itself, a guarantee that democratic values were adequately achieved. Social pluralism, they said, was necessary to democracy; it was not sufficient. In some cases, associations might even tend to stabilize inequalities, deform civic consciousness by exaggerating group interests, distort the public agenda, and alienate some control over decisions from the general public to the groups themselves. Yet because social pluralism is necessary, inevitable, and desirable in a democratic order, associations cannot be destroyed without destroying democracy itself. As with individuals, so with associations: independence or autonomy, though necessary to a good life, also creates an opportunity for individuals to do harm. Like individuals, associations ought to possess some autonomy, and at the same time ways should be found to eliminate or reduce the harm they might cause. How best to achieve a desirable balance between autonomy and control is, then, a fundamental problem of pluralist democracy.

When democratic pluralists looked beyond the United States, they observed that no single solution to this problem had been adopted among democratic countries. Democratic countries vary greatly in their patterns of cleavages and the relative strength of associations in different spheres. Judged comparatively, the United States is a deviant case. Many factors, including the relative absence of class-based organizations, the weakness of trade unions, and the persistence of cross-cutting cleavages, make pluralism in the United States markedly different from that in many other countries. At the opposite extreme are countries where national bargaining between employers and unions that include most of the labor force leads to agreements supported by the government, and carried out by legislation if need be. This "corporatist" variant of democratic pluralism, so unlike the pluralist patterns in Britain and the United States, has existed not only in Sweden but in some form in the other Scandinavian countries, the Netherlands, the Federal Republic of Germany, and Austria as well. Thus because of historical and societal factors the shape of democratic pluralism comes in many varieties of which the United States provides only one, and probably a unique, example.

If pluralism is an inherent aspect of modern democracy, and at the same time the specific patterns of pluralism vary enormously among democratic countries, the critiques of democratic pluralists by antipluralists in the United States appear to have focused, more narrowly than they usually made clear, on the particular achievements and defects of democracy in the United States.

In the 1980s, the desirability of pluralism became a rallying cry for opponents of the theory and practice of authoritarian rule in *Communist Party states, particularly in Eastern and Central Europe and the Soviet Union. Like legal and democratic pluralists earlier, antiauthoritarian advocates of pluralism insisted on the need for independent associations in political, social, and economic life. Although they developed no single or systematic doctrine, in contesting the monopoly of power of the state and insisting on pluralism as a necessary ingredient of the democracy they aspired to, these antiauthoritarian pluralists could be understood as an amalgam of both legal and democratic pluralism.

Liberalization and democratization in these countries soon revealed the fundamental problem of democratic pluralism mentioned above. Through their newly formed associations many people gained a voice, an influence, and a degree of freedom in political life they had hitherto been denied; at the same time, the interests and goals advanced by some groups were seen by others as clearly harmful. Thus the introduction of pluralism inevitably brought with it the need to confront the inescapable dilemmas of pluralist democracy.

(See also AUTHORITARIANISM; CONSOCIATIONAL DEMOCRACY; CORPORATISM; EQUALITY AND INEQUALITY; INTEREST GROUPS; TOTALITARIANISM.)

Harold Laski, *Problems of Sovereignty* (New Haven, Conn., 1917). Léon Duguit, *Law in the Modern State* (New York, 1919). David B. Truman, *The Governmental Process* (New York, 1951). Robert A. Dahl, *Who Governs?* (New Haven, Conn., 1961). William E. Connolly, ed., *The Bias of Pluralism* (New York, 1971). Peter Hardi, "Why Do Communist Parties Advocate Pluralism?" *World Politics* 32 (July 1980): 531–552. Robert A. Dahl, *Dilemmas of Pluralist Democracy: Autonomy vs. Control* (New Haven, Conn., 1982).

ROBERT A. DAHL

POLAND. In 1918, as Poland emerged from World War I and over 120 years of foreign partition, its struggle for *democracy and independence was associated with and assisted by a relatively mature and stable left-center-right political spectrum. Seventy years later, as it once again seeks to rebuild independent nationhood, its fragmented political parties, argumentative *elites, and disenchanted populace point to a more burdensome political legacy inherited from forty-five years of *communism. Predispositions to *authoritarianism, *populism, and egalitarianism are just some of the ills predicted for Polish democracy. Clericalism vs. secularism and *nationalism vs. cosmopolitanism are likewise among the new dichotomies which make the elaboration of a left-right divide in Polish politics a precarious enterprise.

The present course of politics and the personal biographies of all political actors are rooted in a complicated past which includes the precommunist regime, forty years of involvement with the *Communist Party state, and the period of the 1980s marked by the *Solidarity social movement. The most recent period of "roundtable" transition and the attempted break with all previous legacies in favor of a "Polish" solution have introduced additional complications. These factors all intertwine in any analysis of *parliamentary democracy, presidential power, and the construction of a rule of law in Poland.

The unifying theme throughout the current period has been the transformation of Solidarity (Solidarność in Polish) from quintessential nationally-based social movement and vehicle for the emerging civil society, to parliamentary political party, to vestigial umbrella organization overseeing its own dissolution, and finally its return to its original function—one it had never really performed—as a trade union of fewer than 2 million members. Solidarity has been at once Poland's major political asset and in turn an obstacle to the creation of party politics. In particular, its passage from a force unifying society and confronting communism to one seeking to establish new forms of societal integration in a postcommunist order has proved difficult.

There can be little denying that Poland's variant of communism, apart from providing steady economic growth, new opportunities for upward social mobility, a large noncollectivized agricultural sector, and small-scale private economy, also ensured job security, subsidized health, housing, and food supply. It is not surprising, then, that during the recent years of uncertainty brought about by the economic "shock treatment" of the Balcerowicz Plan aimed at macroeconomic stabilization and restructuring, a third of the population should sigh for the comforts of Gomulka's, Gierek's, and even Jaruzelski's (mis)rule. The legacies of communist rule—international indebtedness of US$40 billion for a population of 37 million, rampant corruption, bureaucratization, and mismanagement, not to mention high mortality and morbidity rates linked to environmental poisoning and individual pathology such as alcoholism—all seem to be forgotten in the face of First World prices and Third World wages. More critically, the system of state redistribution bequeathed a set of reflexes and expectations whereby individual behavior was oriented to state paternalism rather than market opportunity. Passivity and the trained incapacity to take initiatives meant that the capitalist and democratic society would have no basis in any precommunist Polish tradition and would be further impeded by the negative inheritance of the single-party command economy.

Building on the first papal visit of *John Paul II to his Polish homeland a year earlier, the moral and then ideological rejection of communism found expression in the events of the summer of 1980 and the Solidarity movement. Ten million members demanded renewal, *reform, and recognition. An alternative organization led by a societally generated elite now confronted the communist party (Polish United Workers' Party, or PUWP). Autonomous association and self-government confronted the bureaucratic-centralist party state. Unable to find a formula for coexistence under the pre-Gorbachev international constraints, on 13 December 1981 the armed wing of the party fell back on the expedient of martial law, thereby demonstrating the irreformability of "real socialism."

During the 1980s the PUWP sought to don the mantle of reform and practice political co-optation and market reforms. Under the protection of Soviet *perestroika and in tandem with Hungarian reforms, the Jaruzelski regime went as far as it conceivably could without surrendering the fundamental tenets of socialized property and the leading role of the party. Repeated amnesties to leading figures of the Polish opposition, a referendum, consultation, and inclusionary tactics which almost permitted political *pluralism all failed, however, to confer the necessary legitimacy on a government facing growing indebtedness and international ostracism.

When the denouement to the social deadlock came, it did so with such rapidity that five years later the world is still unable to fully digest its significance. During the spring and summer of 1988, a series of Solidarity-led strikes culminated in an extraordinary gesture on the part of the Polish leadership, leading to the now-historic formula for what was to become the negotiated transfer of power, the April 1989 "roundtable" agreement. The relegalization of Solidarity, partially free elections for June 1989, and a commitment to far-reaching reforms in all spheres of life were agreed to by a party which must have believed that these gestures would earn it a measure of gratitude at the ballot box. On the contrary society spurned this offer of shared *legitimacy. The "Contract Parliament" which emerged, with its built-in sixty-five percent majority for the communists and their allies, became untenable, not least because Solidarity held ninety-nine percent of the seats in the freely elected Senate, or second chamber. The result was a Polish version of cohabitation between communist President Wojciech Jaruzelski, the soon-to-be redundant guarantor of Soviet interests, and Prime Minister Tadeusz Mazowiecki, the first noncommunist premier in the Soviet bloc.

Lech *Wałęsa, Solidarity's prime mover, was left on the margins of the democratic process, overseeing events from a distance at his union headquarters in Gdansk. These included tough anti-inflationary measures, supported by *International Monetary Fund (IMF) and *World Bank authority, which reduced inflation from nearly eighty percent per month in January 1990 to more manageable single figures in the second quarter. The concomitant drop in production and real living standards by twenty-five to thirty percent stretched the support for Solidarity past the breaking point.

By now all shades of political opinion were unanimous on the need for rapid *privatization, a massive legislative effort to end censorship and police power, and the institutionalization of the principles of civil, political, and social *rights. Nevertheless, the Citizens' Parliamentary Caucus, which brought together members of Parliament and senators elected from the Solidarity list in the June 1989 elections and had been first and foremost united in its opposition to "them," after September 1990 had to form a government which included some of "them," the excommunists. By November the caucus began to fracture internally with the exit of the *peasant lobby, and a conflict ensued between those who supported unity at any price as the only sure means of seeing through the reforms and those in favor of a looser federal structure. Within a year of its formation, the caucus contained at least eleven groupings, and by October 1990, with the announcement of presidenial elections with Wałęsa and the more reticent Mazowiecki as the chief candidates, the breakup of Solidarity as a political entity, assisted by vigorous election campaigning, was complete.

Wałęsa, who once again had engineered a major turn in the course of events, was elected president in December 1990, but not without a growing awareness of the instability of a revolution led by elites. These elites were now increasingly gathering around the Democratic Union of Mazowiecki, representing much of the old Solidarity intelligentsia, in favor of a nonconflictual transition to democracy without needless political and social casualties. On the other side, the original supporters of Wałęsa, the Center Alliance, were less prone to forgive and forget. "De-communization" was meant to cleanse both personnel and practices from Poland's institutions, regardless of the short-term effect this would have on institutional stability.

In all of this the *Roman Catholic church had become a major actor, whether willingly or not, on the political stage. Abortion law reform, religious education in schools, and the nature of church-state separation within the new constitution were no less divisive than the issue of past party membership. The unstable center-right coalition which emerged in January 1992 after two months of political haggling reflects this clash of ideological values rather than material interests, and there is concern that they may be more irreconcilable and therefore ultimately more destabilizing.

Clearly many other issues affecting Poland's long-suffering population were not addressed by these elites. A turnout of forty-three percent for the October 1991 general elections indicated that the 100 or so parties that had participated in the election were not connecting to key constituencies. Notably absent from the twenty-nine political parties that entered the new Parliament was a significant *Left or blue-collar representative. The discredited formerly communist Left, although it had made a better showing in all elections than had been anticipated, was not a viable partner in any coalition, whereas the post-Solidarity Left had failed dismally. Solidarity as a union had only a token presence in Parliament, the price of being associated, if only by name, with Poland's current predicament. The precariousness of the right-wing coalition is underlined almost every day. A major confrontation with the Wałęsa presidency is fought out in the language of attempted coups, corruption, charges, curious ministerial appointments, and a general souring of the whole political scene. Parliamentary stalemate holds up the key budget legislation and makes the likelihood of another general election grow ever greater. If this were to happen, then the extremes of the political spectrum would benefit at the expense of the overcrowded center.

In the meantime, the overarching imperative to support marketization, coupled with the incomplete rehabilitation of social democracy, have left the political balance badly skewed to the right, at least in rhetoric if not in principle. Whatever the long-term prospects for reconstructing a traditional Left-Right balance, in the short-term a neocorporatist solution based upon resurgent trade union power is more likely. A host of economic issues—union militancy, unemployment allied to privatization, cutbacks in budget-sector expenditure under the tutelage of the IMF and World Bank, the plight of pensioners—will be submerged in the need of a now-depoliticized Solidarity to fend off rival postcommunist unions and some radical competitors.

A neocorporatist solution would allow the interplay of politics to continue while Poland works to find its place on the European political map. It is bounded on one side by a united, increasingly powerful Germany, albeit within the *European Community, with which Poland has signed "good-neighbor" agreements and association agreements, respectively. On the other side is a nascent Ukraine, Belarus, and Lithuania with whom similar accords have been signed despite incipient tensions over national minorities. Although the departure of troops of what is now Russia has been slower than was hoped, trade and political relations between the countries of the former Soviet bloc have improved since the demise of the Soviet Union. But the specter of a powerful Germany to the west, regaining through economic means its hold over prewar territories (coupled with the presence in Parliament of a small but now more self-assured German minority), is one source of nervousness among Poles. To the east, meanwhile, lies the potential for border conflict with unstable but militarily powerful new nations. Thus it is difficult for Poles to see themselves as occupying a favorable position at the crossroads of the new Europe, far easier to imagine that they once again

will assume their traditional and peripheral role as buffer.

(See also CORPORATISM; DEMOCRATIC TRANSITIONS; GORBACHEV, MIKHAIL; INTERNATIONAL DEBT; NINETEEN EIGHTY-NINE; RELIGION AND POLITICS.)

GEORGE KOLANKIEWICZ

POLICY COORDINATION, ECONOMIC. Economic *interdependence among nations has grown dramatically in recent decades, as innovations in transportation and communication have lowered the transaction costs that bounded national markets, and as U.S. postwar dominance has given way to a world economy of several relatively equal major participants and a host of significant smaller ones. For governments, interdependence circumscribes the autonomy of domestic economic policy-making with new external constraints. Small, open economies typically adjust to these constraints, often developing distinctive patterns of policy-making. Similarly situated countries have occasionally coordinated their policies in order to combat the fragmentation of common interests that economic competition would otherwise induce: the *European Community and producer cartels in commodities, from oil to coffee, provide examples. Since the early 1970s, however, interest in economic policy coordination has focused on the major economies, especially those of the Federal Republic of Germany (FRG), Japan, and the United States (the Group of 3, or G3), as well those of the G3 nations together with Britain, Canada, France, and Italy (the *Group of 7, or G7), and the meaning of policy coordination has altered correspondingly. For the G3, the concern is with the possibility that their domestic policies will distort economic equilibria in other nations and in the world economy. (This is not to imply that coordination is motivated by altruism. If country A's domestic expansion stimulates inflation overseas, other countries can be expected to tighten their macroeconomic policy in response, thus weakening demand for A's exports: coordination can avoid such self-defeating cycles of retaliation.) In addition, coordination among the major economies is more complicated than other types of coordination: rather than implementing identical policies, contributors must actively orchestrate a set of complementary policy moves that balance national policy choices.

Calls for more economic cooperation have risen as the spillover effects of interdependence have multiplied, but successful joint policy actions have been few—the 1967 agreement to reduce interest rates, the 1978 bargain trading FRG and Japanese domestic stimulus for U.S. oil price deregulation, and the 1985 Plaza agreement on dollar depreciation, for instance. The failure of repeated attempts at coordination has stimulated a more careful look at the process of negotiating joint actions, and the different perspectives of economists and political scientists have produced cumulative insights but different recommendations about the promise of future initiatives.

Economic analyses pose the question of policy coordination by analogy with other collective action problems, treating countries as unitary actors with stable preferences, according to formal *game theory models. This perspective highlights two sorts of obstacles to coordination: enforcement and uncertainty. The enforcement problem occurs because, although a coordinated package would make each country better off than under a noncooperative *regime, a country could gain additional advantage if everyone else went along but it "cheated." This international version of the free rider problem has generated a great deal of theoretical interest, but in practice enforcement has seldom been a major stumbling block to economic policy coordination. Uncertainty, springing from disagreement among major econometric models of the world economy—even on such key issues as whether a monetary expansion overseas will stimulate or depress domestic trade and aggregate demand—poses a more severe problem. With no consensual model from which to predict outcomes, it is impossible for a country to know with certainty what policy moves it should ask of its trading partners or what concessions it should offer in return. In view of the weak informational base for international coordination (compared with that for setting domestic stabilization policy), economists have argued that international forums for sharing information and analysis will be less costly to arrange and often as beneficial as explicit attempts to coordinate policies. Where the need for coordination is especially strong, initiatives should focus on only one or two clear, simple indicators and countries' responsibilities to each other should be limited to avoiding interference rather than providing assistance.

Political scientists have been less concerned with theoretical formalization and more sensitive to the way institutions and contexts condition how negotiators view their countries' interests. Their more detailed empirical analyses of cases of policy coordination underline the importance of allowing for the interplay between domestic politics and international negotiations, and of evaluating international coordination against political as well as economic criteria. Although the "national interest" on any issue is always a concatenation of the preferences of parties, interest groups, bureaucratic agencies, and individual politicians, in many international negotiations a government's position follows directly from its established electoral coalition: here the unitary actor assumption clarifies theorizing at little empirical cost. Coordinating national economic policies, however, depends crucially on the malleability of domestic political coalitions. Concluding a bargain for joint action essentially requires that each negotiator voluntarily take other countries' interests into account in setting the home country's policy,

and this will be politically rational for an electorally accountable chief executive only if a domestic majority can be mobilized in favor of the policy the internationally coordinated bargain will require.

In short, the prospects for successfully coordinating national economic policies are greater if the governing coalition is not a stable, closed group but relatively open and flexible, and if the distribution of policy preferences in the country is not consensual but more evenly balanced and hence sensitive to shifts of position by a few pivotal interests. For instance, U.S. negotiators seeking to open Japanese markets might try to appeal to domestic consumer interests in Japan, and Japanese negotiators seeking U.S. efforts to right the trade balance might find allies among domestic U.S. interests who advocate reducing the federal deficit and raising the national savings rate. Economic policy coordination is, then, a distinctly political enterprise. At the international bargaining table, economic uncertainty requires negotiators to risk their own political capital on the trustworthiness of their opposite numbers; at the ratification stage, each chief executive is committed to mobilizing support for a policy course the nation would not have adopted solely out of short-run self-interest. The few successfully coordinated undertakings have relied on trust in the face of economic uncertainty and on political resourcefulness in building domestic support.

Although knowledge of the policy coordination process is in its infancy, considering its political aspect fosters two inferences about the most promising types of initiatives. First, forums for exchanging information, and even tentative attempts at coordination, should be encouraged, not so much because they promise economic gains as because they build familiarity and help develop reputations and trust. Second, because achieving domestic ratification may require side payments to a variety of interests, negotiation at the international table should not be narrowly defined in terms of macroeconomic policy trade-offs but should allow for the possibility for trades across multiple issue areas (as in the 1978 Bonn agreement).

Global interdependence in many realms challenges political elites to revise traditional conceptions of national *sovereignty. Both the cost of excessive self-interest and the potential benefits of coordination are unusually visible in the economic realm, and the emerging flexibility with which the major nations have recently sought common solutions in economic policy should provide useful lessons for arranging joint action on environmental problems and perhaps even *North-South issues.

(See also INTERNATIONAL POLITICAL ECONOMY; POLITICAL ECONOMY; PROTECTION.)

Martin Feldstein, *International Policy Coordination* (Chicago, 1988). Robert D. Putnam, "Diplomacy and Domestic Politics: The Logic of Two-level Games" *International Organization* 42 (Summer 1988): 427–460. Richard N. Cooper,

Barry Eichengreen, Gerald Holtham, Robert D. Putnam, and C. Randall Henning, *Can Nations Agree?* (Washington, D.C., 1989).

M. STEPHEN WEATHERFORD

POLITICAL ACTION COMMITTEES. A political arm organized by a corporation, labor union, trade association, professional, agrarian, ideological, or issue group to support candidates for elective office and, by inference, to defeat others is a political action committee (PAC). PACs raise funds for their activities by seeking voluntary contributions, which are pooled together into larger, more meaningful amounts and then contributed to favored candidates or political party committees. PACs are a uniquely U.S. phenomenon, although labor unions and business federations exist elsewhere.

The number of PACs climbed sharply after the 1974 amendments to the Federal Election Campaign Act imposed contribution limitations on congressional candidates. The act not only diminished the potential for big givers but also put emphasis on seeking out larger numbers of smaller contributors, a process effectively achieved through group efforts. Thus PACs are mediating structures legitimized by law. They act as an institutionalized outreach by providing a process to gather contributions systematically through groups of like-minded persons for whom issues are a cohering element in their political activity.

The growth of PACs has been helped along by the dramatic shift from neighborhood politics to nationalized socioeconomic and *interest group politics. Corporations and labor unions, for example, are socioeconomic units replacing geographic wards and precincts. The workplace and vocational specialty have come to attract the loyalty of politically active citizens, replacing loyalties once enjoyed by political parties. PACs are better able to adapt to these changes than are political parties because PACs can focus on single issues or give priority to emerging issues and still survive with limited but devoted constituents, whereas parties rely on broad-based consensus. The issue orientation of PACs leads a few to make independent expenditures, a form of parallel campaigning without the collaboration of the candidate favored.

As PACs have gained influence, they have become increasingly the object of criticism. Poll data indicate that a majority of U.S. citizens feel that too much money is spent on elections, and that those with money to spend have too much influence over government. Critics suggest that contributions give PACs undue influence over election results; that PACs favor incumbents and thereby decrease the competitiveness of election campaigns (74.2 percent of all PAC contributions in the 1987–1988 election cycle went to incumbents, and the percentage which incumbents received is even greater when PAC gifts to open seat candidates are subtracted from the total amount); that PAC sponsors enjoy extraordinary access to officeholders and exert decisive influence on legislative decisions, making it difficult for lawmakers to represent the interests of the public as a whole. Some critics further argue that PAC contributions are inherently corrupt, serving as legalized bribery of candidates for public offices. Such critics contend that election finance reform should move in the direction of restraining, not abolishing, PACs.

However, there is one common understanding among PAC supporters and detractors: that PAC growth has been substantial and that PACs will remain controversial as long as they continue to be a major supplier of campaign funds.

(See also CONGRESS, U.S.; ELECTIONS AND VOTING BEHAVIOR; POLITICAL PARTIES AND PARTY COMPETITION.)

HERBERT E. ALEXANDER

POLITICAL BUSINESS CYCLE. The term *political business cycle* refers to the efforts of politicians to manipulate the timing and outcome of phases in the business cycle. Because economic policymakers are held electorally accountable for economic performance, they have an incentive to shape short-run economic outcomes if they wish to remain in power. Theories of the business cycle call attention specifically to the *political* dimensions of economic policymaking, arguing directly against a purely technocratic image of the political process.

The earliest conception of how the cycle works was developed by the economist Michael Kalecki, who posited that capitalists believe that lasting periods of full employment are unsound because they strengthen the economic position of workers. Hence, they convince governments of the need for policies that increase unemployment when their economies approach full employment. Following Kalecki, more recent class-based models of the business cycle have been presented by Alexander Hicks, Douglas Hibbs, and others. Hibbs, for instance, contends that governments associated with parties of the *left tend to be more concerned with reducing unemployment than inflation, whereas center-right parties tend to prefer the opposite. The empirical results from tests of these *class/party-based models of the political business cycle have been mixed.

The dominant political business cycle model, initially put forward by William Nordhaus and Edward Tufte, does not focus on class conflict as the generator of the cycle but more simply on the desire of incumbent elected officials in democracies to be reelected. The government does this by taking advantage of lags between the implementation of macroeconomic policies and their effects on the economy. In the months preceding an election, governments can be expected to pursue expansionary policies that increase real disposable income and decrease unemployment. Voters, who are backward-looking in their electoral behavior, reward the incumbents. Because the inflationary consequences of such a policy show up only after the election, governments are then able to pursue policies that restrain economic activity. When inflation is brought under control, the government can then return to an expansionary policy in time for the next election.

Rigorous empirical tests have revealed scant empirical support for the existence of political business cycles. The notion that preelection upswings are the rule rather than the exception has been contradicted repeatedly. The model's assumption of an unsophisticated electorate and highly strategic politicians has been criticized as an oversimplified abstraction. The empirical evidence presented to support the models has been criticized as well. Initial research focused on outcomes (such as unemployment and growth rates), which governments influence only indirectly, ignoring shifts in the level of policy instruments (such as fiscal and monetary aggregates) that governments directly control. When variations in the latter have been examined, almost no support for the political business cycle has been found. There have been a variety of reformulations and refinements of the model, but these too have fared little better than the original Nordhaus-Tufte version.

Some have argued that the parsimony and abstractness of political business cycle models, upon which much of their appeal rests, may account for the disappointing empirical results. The models assume such a degree of knowledge about and control over policy instruments and outcomes as to enable policymakers to optimize their popular support. It is doubtful, however, that the state of economic knowledge and the political system's capacity are sufficient to produce precisely timed and carefully gauged outcomes. Such models also assume a narrow conception of economic policy, focusing exclusively on short-term macroeconomic policies while ignoring other kinds of policies (e.g., regulations, tax expenditures, subsidies) that affect economic performance. Similarly, the literature in this area oversimplifies the notion of political influences that are brought to bear on policy. It assumes that policy is driven by a simple, unalloyed compulsion on the part of policymakers to be reelected. The influence of a complex of other factors—policymakers' conceptions of what constitutes "good" economic policy, international actors, domestic organized interests, intramural competition among policymakers, and the structure of governmental institutions—are largely excluded from consideration.

(See also ELECTIONS AND VOTING BEHAVIOR; POLITICAL ECONOMY; RIGHT.)

M. Stephen Weatherford, "Political Business Cycles and the Process of Economic Policymaking" *American Politics Quarterly* 16 (January 1988): 99–136.

GARY MUCCIARONI

POLITICAL CULTURE. Involving both the ideals and the operating norms of a political system, po-

litical culture includes subjective attitudes and sentiments as well as objective symbols and creeds that together govern political behavior and give structure and order to the political process. Nations generally have both elite and mass political cultures, along with further subcultures that are rooted in regional, occupational, class, ethnic, and other differences.

Classical political theorists starting with Plato and Aristotle and continuing through Montesquieu, Rousseau, and Tocqueville all recognized the importance of custom, tradition, mores, and religious practices for explaining political differences. However, the formalizing of the concept of political culture had to await the convergence after World War II of three intellectual currents: advances in anthropology involving psychocultural theories; innovations in the technology of sample surveys, which made possible the quantification of attitudinal differences; and the emergence of area studies, which globalized the social sciences while preserving an appreciation of cultural differences. The adoption of the concept of culture, one of the most powerful in the social sciences, radically changed the study of political behavior. The political values of individuals and societies are no longer to be seen as mere random congeries of opinion but can be analyzed as having coherent patterns, based on psychologically identifiable human characteristics. Thus, political science is able to exploit important advances in psychology, anthropology, and sociology.

Political culture became an established concept in political science largely as the result of the impact of Gabriel A. Almond and Sidney Verba's classic study, *The Civic Culture* (Boston, 1963). Almond had earlier stimulated interest in the concept with his seminal article, "Comparative Political Systems" (*Journal of Politics* 18, no. 1 [August 1956]: 391–409), in which he observed that "every political system is embedded in a particular pattern of orientation to political action."

Political culture soon became a widely accepted concept, but there has been considerable variation in both method and focus in its study. The utilization of rigorous sample surveys was initiated by Almond and Verba (1963), repeated in their *The Civic Culture Revisited* (Boston, 1986) and carried on in many other important works since then. A second common approach has focused more on the socialization processes that are critical in both forming and transmitting political cultures. A third approach looks at historical traditions with special emphasis on continuities and changes during the modernization process. Finally, there are case studies that generally deal with significant theoretical or policy issues, such as the extent to which cultures can be changed by conscious policies or by the operations of specific institutions, such as the mass media.

Although there has been increasing appreciation of the merits of the different approaches and a noticeable retreat from the more extreme conceptual and methodological positions, there has been no decline in lively debates about the concept of political culture. Possibly the most fundamental of these debates has been over the issue of explaining political change in light of the presumed durability of cultures. In the late 1960s and early 1970s political culture was attacked as a conservative, if not reactionary, abomination. It was believed by some that *Mao Zedong, Fidel *Castro, and other revolutionary leaders had successfully changed the thinking of the masses in their respective countries, and therefore that the presumed constraints of culture represented merely the hegemonic domination of the feudal and bourgeois classes, which the arrival of the revolution would shatter. By the mid-1980s, however, it was apparent that communist claims about producing revolutionary "new human beings" was largely propagandistic pretention and that people in all the socialist countries have by and large continued to manifest their national cultures. Also, as the 1960s have receded into history, there is greater appreciation that the disorders of the 1960s in American life associated with the *Vietnam War and the *Civil Rights Movement represented not revolutionary changes in American political culture but the playing out of what Samuel Huntington has called the "disharmonies" inherent in the "American creed," which has always contained contradictions and dilemmas as a result of conflicting ideals (*American Politics: The Promise of Disharmony*, Cambridge, Mass., 1981).

The problem of change has also been raised from the opposite ideological perspective by rational choice theorists who insist that calculations of self-interest are generally stronger than cultural predispositions. Samuel Popkin ("Choosing Preferences by Constructing Institutions: A Culture Theory of Preference Formation" *American Political Science Review* 81, no. 1 [March 1987]: 3–21) and Robert Bates (*Rural Responses to Industrialization*, New Haven, Conn., 1976), for example, have shown that peasants in Third World countries will change their behavior in response to positive incentives. Aaron Wildavsky (*The Rational Peasant*, Berkeley, Calif., 1979) has argued, however, that the preferences on which decisions are based are the products of cultural learning, and hence the way people interpret their self-interest is rooted in culture.

Closely related to the rational choice argument is the challenge to political culture theory of those who stress the importance of structures in determining behavior. According to advocates of the "bring back the *state" school, attitudes and values are unimportant; it is the basic institutions of state and society that are decisive in shaping national development. Such institutions, including *class structures, are, in their view, the prime norms of history that shape cultures. It is not clear, however, that causation goes only in one direction. Perhaps a sounder view is that culture and structure are closely

interrelated, that each affects the other, and that it is impossible to decide which is more important.

By the late 1980s there was a significant revival of interest in political culture. The crisis of the communist states raised speculations not only about the reasons why national cultures were not homogenized under Marxist-Leninist rule, but also posed questions about the relative prospects for democratic development among the once-authoritarian systems.

The revival of interest in culture was also spurred by the conspicuously different patterns of development among Third World countries. The pronounced successes of the *newly industrializing economies with Confucian traditions as contrasted to the continuing stagnation of other less-developed countries has caused scholars to reexamine the relationship of culture to economic development. The remarkable economic successes of Japan also stimulated interest in the role of culture in the advanced industrial societies. Thus the study of *political economy which began with an emphasis on rationalistic policy analysis has increasingly returned to the type of culture and society issues first explored by Max *Weber, Emile Durkheim, and Talcott Parsons. Political culture has also come to play a larger role in the study of advanced industrial nations because, as Ronald Inglehart points out, when countries become more affluent, issues of cultural values tend to replace basic necessities as the focus of political life.

The 1990s will see sustained interest in the relevance of cultural factors because political agendas worldwide will be stressing *human rights, the rule of law, and "transitions to *democracy." In asking questions about the attitudes and values basic to democratic politics, contemporary political scientists will be returning to the central questions that Almond and Verba confronted in *The Civic Culture* at the beginning of systematic research into political culture.

(See also DEMOCRATIC TRANSITIONS; POLITICAL DEVELOPMENT; POSTMATERIALISM.)

Lucian W. Pye and Sidney Verba, eds., *Political Culture and Political Development* (Princeton, N.J., 1965). Sidney Verba, *Elites and the Idea of Equality* (Cambridge, Mass., 1988). Ronald Inglehart, *Changing Culture* (Princeton, N.J., 1989).

LUCIAN W. PYE

POLITICAL DEVELOPMENT. The study of stages of change in the structure of government is known as political *development. The basic notion is that human society and government become more complex over time, passing through successive stages. (For example, these stages might be called hunting and gathering, agrarian, and industrial—to give but one possible nomenclature.) Corresponding to changes in social or economic structure are changes in political organization. Although different theories of change may posit the importance of various factors in accounting for development, whatever the proposed sequence of stages and their underlying dynamic, the outcome of all the various conceptions of political development is that political organization varies in degrees of complexity and that the history of the species shows a tendency toward increased complexity.

A hypothetical sequence of stages may serve as an example of how this thinking works. At a first stage, a group coheres thanks to family bonds, religious consensus, and the leadership of an individual of outstanding capabilities. Nothing that resembles a government or *state exists as an institution apart from the group. Politics, or the social application of *power, is vested in the group or a specific individual. At a second stage, the diffused power of the group or of the single leader gives way to the rule of families or clans. A group of individuals now share in power, deciding among themselves how decisions are made and applied for the entire collectivity. At a still-later stage, family rule becomes more institutionalized in kingships with the help of bureaucracies—of which military, finance, courts, and religion are the most crucial. Here the ability to write is often seen as basic to a more advanced political form. Finally, in the current era, party systems appear, governmental functions proliferate, and the general population becomes politically more participatory.

What should be apparent from such an outline is that political development is related to stages of the increased complexity of the state, what is sometimes called the "institutionalization" of government. Different writers discuss the character of this complexity in their own ways, but what their definitions all have in common is the notion that the state becomes more varied in the functions it performs, more open to acquiring new roles in relation to society, and either more responsive to the variety of groups in society or more able to control their behavior directly. Corresponding to this increased complexity of functions, states acquire increased coherence. Institutions formed on the basis of regularized procedures tend to replace the dictates of personal preference or the interests of special groups, and the state as an entity acquires a formal role to such an extent that one can speak of the consolidation of the rule of law.

It must be understood that descriptions such as the foregoing are ideal types that correspond to historical reality only generally. No particular state ever corresponds perfectly to its ideal type, that is, to a schematic definition of its character of the kind provided here. Nevertheless, thinking of the state as evolving in its structure in correspondence with changes occurring in the economic and social dimensions of group life is the essence of conceptualizing the character of political development.

However necessary it may be to see the reality of political development, its actual definition is sometimes a contentious matter because of teleological meanings often ascribed to the term. When development is studied teleologically, the presumption is that there is an evolutionary design to the character of social change such that some forms of government proceed automatically and necessarily from others. Yet critics make three telling observations concerning any such supposition.

First, history shows that apparently more advanced stages of political development may suddenly be surpassed by seemingly more backward forms. For example, the more decentralized and feudal regimes of Britain and Japan proved better able to industrialize than the more centralized governments of France and China, yet the latter appear to have been more complex politically. Thus, as time passes, there may be "advantages to backwardness," such that an apparently more primitive form of political organization demonstrates a better ability to adapt to new historical conditions.

Second, the concept of political development may be ethnocentric when it imputes a linear form of development to history. For example, the suggestion by some writers that the future of agrarian societies today will be an imitation of the character already assumed by industrial, democratic Western countries and Japan is a problematic notion. The implicit assumption that somehow a more developed polity is also morally superior is especially debatable. The practice of slavery, for example, was a condition often imposed by more politically developed peoples on those less fortunate or powerful than themselves and may scarcely be thought to represent a morally superior form of behavior. In short, less developed states today are not inherently inferior morally to those more developed, and their future may be distinctively different from what the West has achieved.

Finally, while some states today may well be more developed than others, there is no final stage where development will stop. We need only think of the anarchy of international relations and the distance humans still have to go to achieve some modicum of institutionalized international government to see this point clearly. Those polities that congratulate themselves today on being "modern" or "developed" may appear primitive indeed to later observers. Is there a final point at which development will cease? There are those today who speak of liberal *democracy, for example, as if it will become the universal form of government after which nothing more advanced can be imagined. However, given the continuing anarchy in *international relations, it is hard to believe that the work of political development will not continue to confront us. Here the contemporary example of the integration of the *European Community (EC) serves as an inspiration to many of the way a collection of different peoples with a fratricidal past can evolve political institutions in common that may eventually result in their full integration. This case apart, the prospects for world government seem dim indeed.

Aside from these debates over the nature of political development, yet another reason the term presents difficulties is that no easy measurement is available to indicate how developed a polity is. By contrast, the concept of economic development is readily apparent: one may look either at the size of the GNP or the sectoral distribution of productivity and from these indices establish a relative ranking of a country's economic level. Yet given the considerations mentioned above, one must be cautious when asserting firm distinctions about relative levels of political development. Because the actual path of political development may vary so much from country to country, with a seemingly "advanced" country beginning to stagnate while a seemingly "backward" polity leaps forward, and because its features are less easily amenable to statistical measure, the level of development of the state is far less easy to ascertain than the level of economic development. Finally, although states at similar stages of development may in many ways resemble one another, there may be important differences among them as well, reflecting either their inherited political traditions or the expression of unique political forces that will give an individual stamp to the state in question. Which is more "developed" will then be an idle question.

Is development reversible? Of course it is; one need only think of the history of the Roman Empire. Nevertheless, the literature tends to deal with stages as if, once achieved, they represent gains in the character of the state such that disintegration to a lower form of political organization is unlikely although not impossible. For example, the consolidation of a stable form of modern government in France has been a lengthy process as various regimes have succeeded one another, with the threat of civil war often being raised. Students of political development therefore must be aware that the process may stagnate or reverse.

The question of why development occurs has stimulated a vast literature. Marxists see a dynamic to history in the forces of technology, leading societies to have higher and higher divisions of labor economically that call forth more advanced political structures. Other writers point to the forces of war or to the power of ideologies as giving birth to more complex forms of the state, which then in turn stimulate changes in the socioeconomic forces over which they rule. A blend of these various approaches is probably the most fruitful way to think about development, although on occasion one or another of the various theories may have superior insights into how economic, social, and political complexity increase and thus what we commonly refer to as development occurs.

The notion of political development is essential to the study of history. Yet both its causes and its very definition remain hobbled by serious debates that must be engaged, for the topic cannot be dismissed.

(See also MARXISM; MODERNIZATION; POLITICAL ECONOMY.)

Gerhard E. Lenski, *Power and Privilege: A Theory of Social Stratification* (New York, 1966). Leonard Binder et al., *Crises and Sequences in Political Development* (Princeton, N.J., 1971). Elman R. Service, *Origins of the State and Civilization: The Process of Cultural Evolution* (New York, 1975). Karl Marx and Friedrich Engels, *The Communist Manifesto* (Washington, D.C., 1982). Ikuo Kabashima and Lyn T. White III, eds., *Political Systems and Change* (Princeton, N.J., 1986). Myron Weiner and Samuel P. Huntington, eds., *Understanding Political Development* (Boston, 1987).

TONY SMITH

POLITICAL ECONOMY

The discipline termed *political economy* examines the relationship of individuals to society, the economy, and the *state. The concept emerged in the eighteenth century as an integrated field of theory challenging religious and corporatist modes of thought. It has subsequently fragmented into several strands of inquiry: the autonomous study of the economy based upon rational individualism, and the extension of this approach as a methodology for examining human behavior; the systemic study of the interaction of society and the economy; and debate over policy problems with an economic dimension. This essay examines the origins of the concept and its subsequent evolution.

Origins of the Concept—A Unified Theory. The doctrine of political economy emerged in the eighteenth century. It drew on the individualism of Hobbes and Locke, the pragmatism of Machiavelli, and the empiricism of Bacon. Its theorists desanctified social discourse. They removed the veil of religion, fought the invocation of God to explain events, and loosened the grip of tradition and precedent. They disliked any form of thinking which put social analysis beyond human reach. Governments, laws, procedures, associations were all to be thought of instrumentally, as devices formed by human beings to solve problems, as "efficient institutions." Political and social institutions are like machines: if they are broken, fix them. These standards of empiricism, pragmatism, and utility were in sharp contrast to the divine right of kings, the fighting words against which political economy railed.

Political economy stressed purposive action by goal-seeking individuals. Upon that conceptual foundation could be erected a substantial field of investigation and policy analysis. Adam Smith and David Ricardo used it to theorize about the market economy and to attack mercantilist policies. James Mill and Jeremy Bentham used it to integrate representative government with the calculus of utilitarianism, equating good policy with the aggregation of individual preferences—"the greatest good for the greatest number." Political economists wrote about everything: morals, prisons, freedom, wealth, art, goodness, virtue, constitutions, leadership, war, and peace. University chairs bore such labels as "Moral and Political Economy."

Evolution of the Concept: Fragmentation of Method. In contemporary usage, the concept of political economy has fragmented into discrete components so varied that users of the label do not necessarily communicate with or know anything about each other. We may identify two large limbs on the tree of political economy each stressing a different postulate of the founders: one branch focuses on the postulate of individual rationality, the other on the postulate of interconnectedness, or the interaction between economics and other forces.

The Postulate of Individual Rationality. For this line of inquiry, methodological individualism can be applied to any branch of human behavior (or nonhuman for that matter). Social analysis requires a secure "micro" foundation, and that can only be the individual. Scientific reasoning requires the assumption of a coherent goal (the maximization of welfare) and the capacity for ends-means calculations in pursuit of that goal. Preference functions are taken as given and human nature is held constant. What varies are incentives. The inducement for specific actions, or the sanctions against them, are shaped by incentives which derive from institutional arrangements. The variance of those arrangements explains the variability of human action.

These assumptions have led to various branches of work. *Contemporary neoclassical economics* has developed the largest, most extensive body of thought along these lines. At its most abstract, modern economics behaves like mathematics, drawing out the implications of a few key axioms as a deductive body of thought without any particular real-world reference. The ideas are tested solely by their internal logic, valued for beauty, elegance, coherence. In the more applied form, propositions about the economy are derived from theory and confronted with data from actual economies. The empirical debates have to do with such topics as *monetarism, *Keynesianism, inflation, market structure, rational expectations, and efficient institutions.

By and large, contemporary economics has been self-contained. It has not been interested in examining the influence upon economic behavior of variables which lie outside its logic: values, culture, history, politics, ideology. Prestige in research has gone to theory and to econometrics. Expertise specific to countries, historical periods, companies, and policy has had low prestige, as evidenced by the Nobel Prizes or appointments at leading universities.

While the economics profession has stayed within the boundaries of the substantive field of economics, economic reasoning itself, the presumption of methodological individualism, has been applied to many topics in other fields. *Social choice, *public choice, and *rational choice* are all labels used for these efforts. An important shift is made here. Economics assumes both "ends" rationality and "means" rationality; the end is wealth, the means is work to get wealth and keep it. The social choice approach assumes that there is a "rationale" behind action, that action is rational to the individual according to the goals, whatever these might be. By taking the origins of the goals and their rationality for granted, these theorists then explore the context of external incentives that induces the action in question. These concepts have been used to explore a broad range of action: In *Taking Chances* (Berkeley, Calif., 1975), Kristin Luker examines why teenagers fail to use contraception even when they know the consequences. Mancur Olson's *The Logic of Collective Action* (Cambridge, Mass., 1965) explores the obstacles to cooperative behavior which arise in the pursuit of public goods, when people are able to "free ride" by getting a benefit without exerting any effort to get it. In studying the organization of the modern firm, Oliver Williamson examines how "principals," those with power, delegate authority to their "agents" to attain desired goals; see his *Markets and Hierarchies* (New York, 1975) and *The Economic Institutions of Capitalism* (New York and London, 1985). Several social scientists interpret the structure of the federal bureaucracy in the United States as the solution by legislators of their own principal-agency problem, that of creating institutions which carry out the imperatives legislators face in getting reelected. Sam Popkin, in *The Rational Peasant* (Berkeley, Calif., 1979), and James Scott, in *The Moral Economy of the Peasant* (New Haven, Conn., 1976), explore the rationality and moral reasoning of peasants.

The Postulate of Interconnectedness, or the Interaction between Economics and Society. This approach rejects the autonomy and self-sufficiency of economics. The economy is seen as a societal output. Economic performance derives from political choices, social organization, culture, circumstances, history. The economy is constructed. That construction needs explanation.

Systems theorists such as Saint-Simon, Comte, Durkheim, and *Weber constructed integrated models of the way in which economy, politics, ideas, and society interact. In the middle of this century, Talcott Parsons, among other things a translator of Weber, influenced much social science with such a model. The Marxian tradition has gone in two rather contrasting directions. One branch stresses the primacy of economics, seeing all else as derivative, as epiphenomena, the superstructure upon an economic base; in so doing, these Marxists approach their ideological enemies, the neoclassicists. The other strand of *Marxism turns economic reductionism on its head, seeing as more interesting the notion of complete interconnectedness, that no element of culture or economy or social structure or institutions is ever independent of the other, that no social or individual action is "accidental"; culture shapes economics, and is also a way of reading about economics. Antonio *Gramsci is a notable contributor in this tradition, as are "critical theorists" such as Max Horkheimer and Theodor Adorno. Weber's *The Protestant Ethic and the Spirit of Capitalism* (London, 1989), seeing religion as shaping economics, is a classic non-Marxian statement of this genre.

Contemporary social science links positivist research techniques to these kinds of systemic questions in modern political economy. In *The Affluent Worker in the Class Structure* (London, 1969), John Goldthorpe and David Lockwood examine how prosperity affects the political behavior of the working class in capitalist society. In *The Second Industrial Divide* (New York, 1984), Charles Sabel and Michael Piore show the ways in which ethnicity, family, and religion facilitate a distinctive form of efficient capitalist economic organization, often known as the "Italian model." With his book *British Factory/Japanese Factory* (Berkeley, Calif., 1990), Ronald Dore brought the study of Japan into a broader framework of comparative capitalism. In *Dualism and Discontinuity* (Cambridge, U.K., 1980), Suzanne Berger explores the politics which favors small-scale enterprises in capitalist economies. As industrialization and the market have spread around the globe, leaving their Western roots, social science has found fabulous opportunities for exploring the interaction of markets, cultures, and institutions.

Policy Debates. These differing intellectual approaches to the relationship between politics and economics are reflected in policy debates. Three main arenas may be noted that involve all countries: a) the role of public policy in shaping market efficiency; b) the foreign economic policy each nation adopts to manage its relationship to the world economy; and c) the attainment of goals other than growth, such as equality, mobility, environment, and national strength.

The analytic separation of market and society entails a quarrel over the role of the state and public policy in producing growth and efficiency. The minimalist view sees least as best. The state need only be a "nightwatchman," keeping peace, preventing crime. By contrast, the "developmental state view" sees the market as requiring substantial provision of public goods, that is, items whose diffuse benefits fail to elicit enough private rewards to be provided by the market. These include education, research, public health, physical infrastructure, and uniform standards. Advocates of industrial policy argue that state policy can contribute to efficiency in the strategic promotion of selected industries. Theorists of regulation explore policies concerning market and firm structure to consider efficient institutions.

The policy disputes involve both highly advanced industrial economies and those at early stages of development. They arise from disagreement over the past, as well as the present. The minimalists claim that economic growth occurs when the prices are right, a condition best achieved with little state action, for which they offer British and U.S. growth as proof. State intervention leads to "rent-seeking," an extraction of wealth by officials who contribute nothing to efficiency, or to interest group distortion of policy, favoring inefficient sectors over potentially efficient ones (urban residents, for example, using political control to keep down food prices, thereby preventing farmers from earning income through exports).

The state activists dispute this interpretation of the U.S. and British past, noting state promotion of canal and railroad building and other infrastructure. Alexander Hamilton and Adam Smith are both cited as advocates of an active policy. And state activists point to Germany and Japan as examples of state-"involved" growth, a model now being taken up by the East Asian *newly industrializing economies (NIEs), particularly the Republic of Korea (South Korea), Taiwan, Hong Kong, and Singapore. The minimalists dispute this interpretation of those countries. Economists would see this as an argument over the volume and quality of public goods the state needs to supply; political scientists would see this as an argument over the political circumstances that produce growth-promoting policies, be they activist or minimalist; sociologists would see this as an argument about the determination of collective goals and social structures needed to sustain growth.

On the side of the minimalist state view lie a good portion of the economics profession and some economists located in places like the *World Bank and the *International Monetary Fund (IMF), who have urged extensive *privatization and expenditure cuts to developing countries. On the side of the developmental state view can be found many political scientists, sociologists, and some heterodox economists; two recent examples are Robert Wade, *Governing the Market* (Princeton, N.J., 1990), and Stephan Haggard, *Pathways from the Periphery* (Ithaca, N.Y., 1990).

Debates over the role of the state spill over into debates about managing a market economy. Modern economics seeks to provide the tools of management: money supply, fiscal policy, exchange rates. Modern economists divide over the application of these tools. Other social scientists treat these policies as dependent variables, whose determination requires political interpretation. Andrew Shonfield's *Modern Capitalism* (London, 1965) pioneered the comparative analysis of macroeconomic management. Other political economists have subsequently examined such topics as the influence of politics on the business cycle, the impact of international trade on domestic policies and politics, and the politics of state regulation of specific industries and companies. Particularly interesting are Peter Katzenstein's *Small*

States in World Markets (Ithaca, N.Y., 1985), Ronald Rogowski's *Commerce and Coalitions* (Princeton, N.J., 1989), and Peter A. Hall's *Governing the Economy* (New York, 1986).

Disputes within countries over state-society relations concerning the economy spill over into the international arena and into national policies toward the world economy. How should a nation relate to the international economy? The neoclassical argument champions the benefits of specialization, not only at home but abroad; the optimal policy for a country is to have open borders and free trade. This view has been challenged since the nineteenth century by conservative nationalists as well as political radicals. The nationalists sought self-sufficiency and political military strength. The radicals sought social transformation. Both doubted that these goals could be provided by free trade of a capitalist economy. In their view, the market would act to favor those already strong, the first industrializers. The market segments divide, and layer countries, as well as groups, into particular and by no means equal roles. The nineteenth-century version of these arguments bore the names of "national economics" (the conservatives) and "imperialism" (the radicals).

As the quarrels continued in the twentieth century, the arenas of debate shifted. The developing countries supported a set of arguments elaborated most systematically by Raúl *Prebisch of Argentina, working with the UN Economic Commission for Latin America, who argued that the unrestrained free market confines developing countries to an inferior role as suppliers of raw materials and markets for advanced industrial goods. Many countries around the world, both conservative and radical, sought to counter their position, which came to be characterized as *dependencia*, through active state policies, most easily described as *import-substitution industrialization (ISI); other elements often included *nationalization of railroads, public works, and natural resources.

A few countries, notably in East Asia, pursued export-oriented industrialization (ESI) strategies instead. State intervention was extensive, but oriented toward promoting industries that would export rather than toward replacing imports. ESI countries have grown faster than ISI, and in the 1980s many countries switched to that approach.

National strategy intersected with international policy and the national policy of other countries. In the 1950s, the United States and international agencies encouraged states to adopt import substitution. In the 1980s, these advisers switched positions to become champions of privatization, *deregulation, and economic liberalism both within their countries and in international institutions. They pressed governments in Latin America, particularly susceptible to international leverage because of substantial public debt, to undertake measures of fiscal reform and state-sector reduction. Thus the debates about international economic policy link back to the debates over national policies and the role of the state. Comparisons of the political economy of developing countries have broken down some of the intellectual barriers which isolated regions of the world into specialized subfields. See, for example, Robert Bates's *Markets and States in Tropical Africa* (Berkeley, Calif., 1981), particularly influential for his work on the subordination of agriculture in many developing countries.

These trends take place at a moment of growing stress in the international economic order. Policymakers after World War II sought to preclude a repetition of the instability of the interwar years. Their interpretation of the causes of that instability led to the formation of a stable monetary order through the IMF and a free trade system through the *General Agreement on Tariffs and Trade (GATT). Both were strongly championed by the United States, which at that time produced fifty percent of the world's gross product.

With the rivival of Europe and Japan, the end of empire, the spread of industrial capacity, the formation of the oil cartel, and other trends, the world has become economically multipolar. Theorists debate whether a multipolar world can be a stable free trade world. Does free trade require a hegemon to provide public goods? Can there be cooperation among egotists? The challenge to the trade regime has also changed. GATT has been moderately successful in lowering formal tariff barriers. Nontariff barriers, however, remain quite potent, and have if anything grown in importance as countries have learned instruments of policy regulation which escape the formal limits of GATT rules. Agricultural subsidies in the industrial countries of Europe, North America, and Japan produce immense surpluses. This greatly harms the developing countries, for whom food exports would be a major instrument for launching a successful export-oriented growth strategy, propounded, indeed, by the very countries urging privatization and market strategies. Regulation extends the debate over "improper" barriers to trade to include many aspects of society traditionally not on the international bargaining table. The United States and European countries accuse Japan of excluding products and investment through these instruments (leading to the "Structural Impediments Initiative"); Japan claims that the *keiretsu* and other forms of organization are simply efficient market instruments which are available to any country, and are therefore not valid elements of international regulation or dispute.

At this juncture, one can see the inescapable interconnection of elements of political economy. The debate over effective state policy blurs into arguments over foreign economic policy and the international economy, which in turn blur into arguments over the micro-organization of firms, which blur into arguments about culture and state policy, or back to the beginning of the chain.

A third category of policy disputes in political economy concerns the attainment of goals other than growth and efficiency. Arguments are made on behalf of equality of income, opportunity, and participation in public life; over notions of social justice, health, safety, housing, security, a good society, a protective "net" for each citizen; over the role of leisure, culture, and individual fulfillment; over gender, ethnicity, race, and other elements of social relationships; over environmental quality and preservation of resources; and finally, over values of national power, domination, attainment, glory, autonomy, and security. All of these goals have an economic component. At a minimum they involve resources and the allocation of resources. They involve the use of politics to interact with the economy in order to attain these goals.

The political economy tradition approaches these questions with a set of distinctive tools. It asks cost-benefit questions and considers incentives, markets, self-interest, institutions. It proposes solutions which take account of collective action problems, monitoring, "agency," delegation of authority. It examines values, culture, and community in the context of institutions and interests. It is willing to put a price on pollution, for example, or on a type of medical operation, or on disease prevention, and to ask, "How much is saving a life worth?"—an approach which often enrages analysts not trained in this tradition.

The Field Today. The fragmentation of political economy as an intellectual tradition interacts with disputes over policy. The "proper" definition of the economy mixes with issues over the "proper" goals of public policy. Some students of political economy are interested in economics but not politics; some are interested in politics and not economics; still others explore the elements of an interactive "system."

One may say that the pure economists—those who treat economics as purely autonomous either analytically or in policy reality—do not belong in the category of political economy, as there is no politics in their endeavor. Some who work on politics are not necessarily interested in economics, but rather in the rationality of economic reasoning about individuals. And those who integrate economics and politics may not agree on methods for doing so, nor on the policy consequences. All may claim, with some historical validity, the label "political economy." *Caveat lector.*

Only a very few contemporary authors succeed in reestablishing the historical linkage among morality, politics, economic reality, and economic reasoning with which political economy began more than two centuries ago. Jon Elster in *Ulysses and the Sirens*

(Cambridge, U.K., 1984), *The Cement of Society* (Cambridge, U.K., 1989), and *Solomonic Judgements* (Cambridge, U.K., 1989) pushes at the bounds of rationality by looking at a wide range of individual "moral" dilemmas. Amartya Sen in *The Political Economy of Hunger* (Oxford, 1990) and *Women, Technology, and Sexual Division* (New York, 1985) examines the moral and political economy of famines and the treatment of women in developing countries. Barrington Moore in *Social Origins of Dictatorship and Democracy* (Boston, 1966) and Perry Anderson in *Origins of the Absolutist State* (London, 1974) probe the interconnections among economic policy, institutions, and political development. Albert O. Hirschman, in addition to his pioneering contributions to the study of economic development in *The Strategy of Economic Development* (Boulder, Colo., 1988), proposed in *Exit, Voice, and Loyalty* (Cambridge, Mass., 1970) analytic tools for understanding the effects of how people express dissatisfaction. Hirschman has also become a historian of political economy through such work as *The Passions and the Interests* (Princeton, N.J., 1977), which examines changing attitudes toward the political consequences of market society. In the hands of theorists such as these, political economy evokes the power and forcefulness of its ancestors.

(See also CAPITALISM; CORPORATISM; DEVELOPMENT AND UNDERDEVELOPMENT; ECONOMIC COMMISSION FOR LATIN AMERICA AND THE CARIBBEAN; EXPORT-LED GROWTH; INTERNATIONAL DEBT; INTERNATIONAL POLITICAL ECONOMY; MERCANTILISM; PLANNING; PUBLIC GOOD; WOMEN AND DEVELOPMENT.)

PETER A. GOUREVITCH

POLITICAL MACHINE. The political machine has been an important form of grass-roots party organization in democratizing and industrializing countries. First appearing in the United States in the late nineteenth century in cities such as New York (Tammany Hall), machines in the twentieth century have spread to the cities and countryside of newly democratic *Third World nations. Today, however, local machines are in eclipse, overwhelmed by antiparty reform movements and by declining governmental resources.

Machines are *one-party systems in formally democratic states. They feature a political boss who employs a grass-roots party organization to dispense patronage jobs, social services, and other divisible benefits to voters. The clientele generally are poor immigrants. Nonideological in nature, machines serve as alternative distributional networks to the market, dispensing material benefits to the party's supporters.

In *comparative politics, the clientelist approach is the chief theory of machine dynamics. It suggests that machine politics flourishes in the democratic interstices separating traditional and modern society. First comes *democracy—participatory politics; later, urban/industrial development. Older patron-client ties linking landlord and peasant in predemocratic traditional society are replaced by newer party-sponsored patronage ties connecting political leaders and voters in urban/industrializing society. In this perspective, machine politics represents a transitional stage in democratic politics, destined to dissolve in the face of such modernizing forces as organized *interest groups, civil service reform, and the *welfare state.

Another theory—functionalism—addresses the machine's linkages to economy and society. It argues that machines both accelerated economic growth and promoted ethnic assimilation. In the early stages of economic development, urban bosses supposedly used corruption as a vital lubricant. Needing votes, city bosses had to rapidly mobilize immigrants from the countryside and overseas.

Recent research, however, has been critical of these two approaches. Regarding clientelism, studies of local machines in the United States and southern Italy have shown how these organizations have stayed in power by skillfully grafting themselves onto national economic development and welfare state programs. Far from weakening machines, reforms such as civil service have been cleverly circumvented.

Regarding functionalist theories, recent work has demonstrated the high economic cost of machine corruption. It also has shown that entrenched local party organizations were poor assimilation devices. Already having fashioned minimal winning voter coalitions, machines had little incentive to recruit and reward new voters. Instead, local bosses overrewarded their core ethnic constituencies. In the United States, the classic Irish-run big-city machines such as Tammany Hall naturalized Irish-Americans and placed them on the public payroll but did little to mobilize later-arriving Southern and Eastern European immigrants, blacks, and Hispanics.

Today machines are in decline. In the United States, reformers and minorities have toppled such once-vaunted big-city machines as those of New York, Chicago, Philadelphia, and Jersey City. The bosses of the aging Northern cities also were victims of growing fiscal crisis compounded by cutbacks in federal financial assistance. In less developed countries, local machines persist but have been likewise weakened by reform and ethnic and fiscal pressures.

(See also PATRON-CLIENT POLITICS; POLITICAL PARTICIPATION; PROGRESSIVE MOVEMENT, U.S.)

James C. Scott, "Corruption, Machine Politics, and Political Change" *American Political Science Review* 63, no. 4 (December 1969): 1142–1158. Judith Chubb, *Patronage, Power, and Poverty in Southern Italy* (Cambridge, 1982). Steven P. Erie, *Rainbow's End: Irish-Americans and the Dilemmas of Urban Machine Politics, 1840–1985* (Berkeley, Calif., 1988).

STEVEN P. ERIE

POLITICAL PARTICIPATION. The concept of *political participation* covers an extraordinary range of activity. Consider these images:

- *Tiananmen Square, Beijing, June 1989: tens of thousands of people, mostly young, peacefully but with intense commitment risk their lives to influence the leaders of the largest nation on earth to alter the rules of the political game;
- A committee of Sri Lankan rice farmers meet with irrigation officials to determine the timing of water release and review their respective responsibilities for supervising water use;
- A citizen of Kansas City argues with a policeman over a traffic ticket.

Despite their obvious contrasts, these scenarios share a core theme that constitutes a definition of political participation: action by private citizens seeking to influence governmental decisions. As the examples suggest, political participation can take the form of individual, small group, or mass action. It may be narrowly self-interested or breathtakingly self-sacrificing, sporadic or sustained, spontaneous or highly organized, cooperative or confrontational, legal or illegal, peaceful or violent. Participants may seek to influence policies or their implementation, to retain or change the decision makers, or (more rarely) to defend or alter the institutions and rules of the political game.

A great deal of political participation is rational problem-solving behavior. People vote, campaign, lobby, demonstrate, strike, or riot because they think that the government can solve some individual or group problems. Participation entails costs: at a minimum, participants spend time, money, and other resources; at a maximum, they may risk losing their jobs, their liberty, or even their lives. Who participates, through what modes, and for what goals therefore will reflect people's perceptions regarding:

- relevance: can the government help with the problem? (The answer is especially clear if the government is viewed as a major source of the problem, for example, by imposing burdensome regulations.)
- efficacy: are the authorities likely to respond positively?
- alternative means: given the specific problem and the expected government reactions, are the benefits of participation higher or its costs lower than available alternatives like aid from other sources, individual or group self-help, or waiting for others to take political initiative?

Mancur Olson (*The Logic of Collective Action*, Cambridge, Mass., 1965) argues that this last option, free-riding, is a formidable impediment to collective action of many types. Albert O. Hirschman (*Exit, Voice, and Loyalty*, Cambridge, Mass., 1970) adds "exit" as another alternative to "voice" or political action: the individual's best course may be to change occupation or neighborhood, or even to migrate abroad.

The rational self-interest perspective is powerful, but it deals inadequately with much political participation. "Other-regarding values" such as civic duty or group loyalties often affect voting levels. Protest ranging from antiwar or pro-ecology "green" demonstrations to popular uprisings against oppressive regimes are prompted less by calculated self-interest than by passionate commitment to values such as civil liberties, group self-determination, or long-run global welfare, and often also by rage against injustice and corruption.

Key issues regarding political participation are the determinants of varying levels and modes, the implications thereof for trends in participation, and the consequences for individuals, groups, and nations. The focus here is on fairly conventional participation in ordinary times, leaving discussion of mass movements and *revolution to other entries.

Determinants. Surveys in many countries demonstrate that better-educated and higher-status individuals are more likely to be politically active, especially for modes of participation that are more demanding and complex than voting. Virtually everywhere men tend to be more active than women, even after controlling for other factors such as education. People in middle age brackets are usually more active than youths or the elderly.

Organizational membership, identification with ethnic, regional, or religious groups in culturally diverse nations, and rural and small town residence all encourage participation, independent of (and often outweighing) the effects of individual traits. Strong identification with an organization or group may make political action seem more relevant or effective. Moreover, group loyalty (and fear of group disapproval of free-riding) heightens the incentive to participate. *Ethnicity has proved a particularly potent base for political participation in many ethnically diverse societies. *Religion is a powerful mobilizing force not only in the Middle East and Latin America but also elsewhere, as in Ireland, Poland, and Korea. *Class has proved less crucial in most of the world than many theorists expected.

Political traditions and institutions powerfully shape levels and modes of participation. Voting is an obvious example: between the extremes of compulsory voting and no elections are all shades of ease or difficulty in registering and voting. National or local laws and traditions may similarly facilitate or obstruct lobbying, contacting, and demonstrating, for all citizens or for particular groups.

Political circumstances swell or diminish participation. Closely contested elections or highly charged issues (for example, abortion in the United States) prompt previously passive citizens to vote, lobby, or demonstrate.

Trends. In the 1950s and 1960s, it was widely assumed that broadening political participation was an integral aspect of *modernization. Participation would increase naturally as education spread, communications improved, voluntary associations proliferated, and expanding government activity offered more benefits and imposed more regulation. As authoritarian governments took power in the late 1960s and 1970s in much of Africa, Asia, and Latin America, many political scientists discarded the earlier assumptions. But the unprecedented wave of popular pressure for more open political systems in the late 1980s suggests that the older analysis was not wrong, but partial: broad social trends, such as the spread of education and access to mass media, do strengthen the impetus for political participation in the long run. But elite goals and strategies usually powerfully constrain short-run options.

Moreover, patterns of participation change over time in particular countries, and some types of participation may decline. The secular fall in voting rates in the United States, for example, has been the focus of considerable concern. Since different modes of participation vary fairly independently, reduced voting need not imply reduced overall participation, but the trend nevertheless affects how the political system works.

Consequences. The turn or return to more open political systems in the early 1990s lends urgency to the question of consequences of broad-based or expanding participation. Classic liberal and conservative theories offer multiple—and conflicting—assumptions on the issue.

Liberal theory sees widespread participation as crucial to responsive and responsible government. Citizen involvement and a sense of shared responsibility in public choices will raise levels of information, moderate claims on government, and increase legitimacy and stability, it is argued. A stronger voice for ordinary people enhances equality. Opportunity to hear diverse views and gain fuller information on local conditions and popular priorities improves the design and efficiency of public programs. More stable and efficient government enhances economic growth.

Conservative critics have long challenged these assumptions, questioning the capacity of ordinary citizens to grasp the complexities of public affairs, to perceive their own long-term interests, and to compromise in the larger public interest. Indeed, they argue, widespread participation is likely to harden positions, escalate demands, intensify conflicts, and thereby threaten both stability and minorities' rights. Mass pressures may also result in paralysis or in conflicting and unsustainable policies.

Remarkably little research has seriously tested these competing visions. Much of the research on consequences, moreover, is weakened by using voting rates or indices of *democracy as proxies for the broader concept of participation. Efforts to link expanded participation rates to increased income equality across nations show little relationship. That outcome is not surprising, because relatively privileged groups, especially urban middle classes, are nearly always more active political participants than the very poor. Similarly, evidence on links between participation (or democratic forms of government) and rates of economic growth is inconclusive.

Assessing the effects of participation on stability poses special problems, because most measures of stability include indices of protest and *political violence, yet these are also modes of participation. Obviously not only the amount but also the modes and goals of participation bear on stability. In ethnically divided nations mass participation may well be disintegrative. But it is possible to structure political parties and other institutions to cut across cleavages and reduce their destabilizing effects. The impact of participation on legitimacy and stability also is strongly affected by popular expectations relative to governmental resources and capacity.

Participation is far too diverse a concept to permit easy generalizations. Some theorists have suggested the notion of an "optimum" level of participation that encourages governments to be responsive yet permits them to act consistently and decisively. But the idea of "optimum level" offers little practical guidance. As growing numbers of nations are affected by the global pressures for democratization so evident in the 1990s, each confronts complex interactions and some painful trade-offs between rapidly expanding participation, stable and effective government, economic revitalization, and equity. And all face formidable challenges to design institutions such as electoral laws or relations between legislature and executive that will channel participation constructively.

(See also CONSERVATISM; ELECTIONS AND VOTING BEHAVIOR; INTEREST GROUPS; LIBERALISM; NEW SOCIAL MOVEMENTS; PLURALISM; POLITICAL PARTIES AND PARTY COMPETITION; REPRODUCTIVE POLITICS.)

Samuel P. Huntington and Joan M. Nelson, *No Easy Choice: Political Participation in Developing Countries* (Cambridge, Mass., 1976). Sidney Verba, Norman Nie, and Jae-on Kim, *Participation and Political Equality: A Seven-Nation Comparison* (Cambridge, U.K., 1978). Jack Nagel, *Participation* Englewood Cliffs, N.J., 1987).

JOAN M. NELSON

POLITICAL PARTIES AND PARTY COMPETITION

Political parties play key roles in organizing the politics of the world, yet are rarely official government organizations. They take different forms under different kinds of regimes, and their degree of importance varies greatly, from nation to nation, from party to party, and from time to time. They may be of any size and any (or no) ideological persuasion. They may appeal only to the most narrow segment of the electorate, or assume the form of a "catchall party," which tries to do what its name implies. Parties' internal organization may be democratic or authoritarian. Because they are relational networks, composed of individuals who enter and leave more or less at will, their boundaries are constantly shifting. They use a wide range of campaigning techniques, with greater or lesser dependency on modern communications technology. They sometimes control the work of government, singly or in coalition with one another, and sometimes have no effective control even over their own elected representatives in legislative office. The general public may hold them in admiration or contempt, or an ambivalent blend of both. Existent parties grow stronger and weaker, sometimes disappear, and sometimes reappear in altered form, while new parties are constantly formed. Political parties' power and prestige may be in decline, yet the universal need for organizations capable of giving shape to popular elections and linking citizens to the work of their governments ensures they will continue to play an important role.

Political parties are political organizations that nominate candidates for public office under their own names. This definition separates parties from *interest groups; when a group runs a candidate for office under its own name, it becomes, at least temporarily, a political party, and when a political organization consistently fails to nominate candidates, it ceases to be a party. Aside from this fundamental and useful distinction, parties and groups often perform many of the same functions. In discussing the functions of political parties it is important to distinguish between the functions they perform for their own purposes, gaining power and making policy in accord with their programs, and those they perform within and for the polity, such as providing participatory, responsive, clientelistic, or directive linkage. With regard to the first, it is also important to remember that the motives of party activists vary, not only from party to party, but often within the same organization.

The Origins of Parties. The origins of particular parties can be traced, but the exact origins of the genus *party* are hopelessly lost in the history of factional strife. We know, however, that as power gradually concentrated in the evolving modern *state, groups (usually called "factions," sometimes "parties") formed around key leaders or families to struggle for its control. Such struggle commonly took place inside legislative bodies that were formed first to advise autocratic monarchs, then to share their power, and finally to replace them. The institutionalization of these groups did not begin until an expanding suffrage forced them to seek support outside the legislative arena, in order to win reelection to it. The external organizations thus created gradually assumed lives of their own, independent of the notables who had established them. At this point, which took place in most Western nations during the nineteenth century, the modern political party had been born.

Once those in power saw the need for parties to keep them in office, it followed naturally that those not in office began to see parties as a possible way to get there. Organization bred counterorganization, and by the end of the nineteenth century the mass membership party was born, a kind of party composed (at least at first) of outsiders rather than insiders, and depending less on the personal wealth and "natural aristocracy" of its leaders and more on the force of numbers, good organization, and an effective system for collecting dues.

New parties tend to form around the cleavages of the time. This was true in the earliest days of party politics, and remains true today, as new nations form, or new parties form in older polities. Those who have power and form parties to maintain it are different from those who lack power and form parties to acquire it. Although parties normally seek to differentiate themselves from each other in broadly philosophical terms, the principles each espouses are almost always consistent with the interests of the class, ethnic group, language group, and/or religious affiliation of those whose support they seek.

Some authors have suggested that early divisions fix a party's identity for decades to come, as it draws support from the same social groups, battles for the same principles, and maintains the same kind of internal organization (Lipset and Rokkan, 1967; Panebianco, 1988). But such stability has been less common in the larger catchall parties, such as the major British and U.S. parties, which constantly seek to redesign their coalitions to meet the shifting interests of potential majorities. Furthermore, as the rate of change has accelerated, the formerly stable parties of multiparty regimes have also often been forced to adjust or cede power to new organizations (Kay Lawson and Peter Merkl, *When Parties Fail: Emerging Alternative Organizations*, Princeton, N.J., 1988). The contemporary era—postmaterialist, post-industrialist, and globally interdependent—has clearly created new *class structures, eased old cleavages of language and *religion, drawn new racial lines, and confused formerly clear lines of philosophical difference (Russell J. Dalton, *Citizen Politics in Western Democracies*, New York, 1988). How rapidly and how well parties and their electorates are adapting to this change remains a subject of some dispute (Stefano Bartolini and Peter Mair, *Identity, Competition and Electoral Availability*, London, 1990).

A variable that no one disputes remains important in determining what kind of parties a nation will have—and how many of them there will be—is the electoral system. Where nations are divided for election purposes into single-member districts and all it takes to win is a plurality of the vote, there is a natural tendency for smaller parties to drop out and for a two or three party system to evolve. Where the districts are larger, multimember districts, with each party represented according to its strength (the system known as *proportional representation),

smaller parties are motivated to keep contesting, and a multiparty system is more likely (Duverger, 1959). Single member districts with runoff elections, as in France, fall in between: the supporters of the smaller parties can use the electoral process and the bargaining power of their votes on the second round to win important concessions, but the control of public office remains in the hands of the major parties. (Rein Taagepera and Matthew Shugart discuss electoral systems in *Seats and Votes*, New Haven, Conn., 1989.)

The Organization of Parties. Key questions regarding how parties are organized include how democratic the party is, what rewards it provides its most active members, how factional or cohesive it is, and where exactly it begins and ends (its *boundaries*).

Internal party democracy was the focus of Mosei Ostrogorski's *Democracy and the Organization of Political Parties* (New York, 1964; first English publication 1902) and Robert Michels's *Political Parties* (New York, 1959; first English publication 1915). Of the two, Michels has had the greater impact, proclaiming as he did the "Iron Law of Oligarchy" ("HE WHO SAYS ORGANIZATION SAYS OLIGARCHY"—the capital letters are his). Michels based his unhappy conclusion (he himself would have preferred to find internal party democracy possible) on the characteristics of organizations (which need speed and efficiency to be effective), members (who are lazy and hero-worshiping) and leaders (who become certain of their own indispensability).

The concept of oligarchy has been extended by contemporary analysts of parties. For example, Samuel Eldersveld (*Political Parties: A Behavioral Analysis*, New York, 1964) has argued that U.S. parties were characterized by *stratarchy*: layers of oligarchies consisting of the independent fiefdoms of machine politics loosely connected to equally elite-controlled state and national organizations. Although David Mayhew has demonstrated (in *Placing Parties in American Politics*, Princeton, N.J., 1986) that only thirteen states ever really had machines worthy of the name, his research suggests only the weakness, not the absence, of rules by the few in U.S. parties. Recent studies of parties in a wide range of nations confirm that oligarchic tendencies remain strong in parties throughout the world (Alan Ware, ed., *Political Parties: Electoral Change and Structural Response*, New York, 1987; Ronald Hrebenar, *The Japanese Party System*, Boulder, Colo., 1986; Hans Daalder, *Party Systems in Denmark, Austria, Switzerland, the Netherlands and Belgium*, New York, 1987).

Even if parties are almost always commanded by a few, the relationships party activists have with those few vary greatly, and depend on what rewards the party seeks for itself and for its followers. Programmatic parties focus on securing power in order to enact a set of policies and may offer their active members the chance to take part in formulating programs and choosing candidates, as well as working for electoral victory. Office-seeking parties are more pragmatic, seeking the rewards of power for their own sake and offering their activists a share of the patronage that will become available with success in exchange for the hard work and large donations required by modern campaigning. Not all activists demand either programmatic input or patronage payoff; some are content with the sense of belonging to a significant and comradely organization. Robert Salisbury characterized such followers as having *solidary* motives for activism, in contrast to those seeking the *material* rewards of patronage or the *purposive* rewards of program formulation (*Interest Group Politics in America,* New York, 1970).

Another key question regarding party organization is the extent, durability, and institutionalization of factions. As V. O. Key, Jr., demonstrated in his classic study *Southern Politics* (New York, 1949), the more secure a party's hold on power, the more likely it is to be riven by faction. The American South is no longer dominated by a single party, but the principle holds true in other nations: numerous studies of the ruling Liberal Democratic Party of Japan and Christian Democratic Party of Italy (most recently in T. J. Pempel, ed., *Uncommon Democracies,* Ithaca, N.Y., 1990) reveal these parties' strongly institutionalized factions contesting for control of an organization that itself seems invincible in the electoral arena. Parties that have not achieved hegemonic control but are serious contenders for power are also likely to reveal internal divisions, as different groups believe different tactics and promises will bring the party into office. The longevity of specific factions tends to be associated with the pragmatic versus ideological focus of the internal groups: factions in the pragmatic U.S. parties are likely to be transient and variable, whereas those in the more programmatic European Socialist parties will tend to be longer-lived and relatively fixed. (For an interesting example, see David Hanley's study of factions in the French Socialist Party, *Keeping Left?,* Manchester, 1986.) Parties whose prospects of achieving majority control are dim are more subject to schism and recombination with other parties than to permanent subdivision into factions.

The rise and fall and transformation of factions is related to another characteristic of the party as organization, its lack of fixed boundaries. Unlike most other organizations, parties can never quite say who or what they are. Frank Sorauf points out in *Party Politics in America* (Boston, 1984) that a party is always supplemented by "the party in the electorate" (nonactivist voting supporters) and "the party in government" (its elected representatives). Mildred Schwartz shows (in *The Party Network,* Madison, Wis., 1990) how shifting and indeterminate the nature of that supplement can be. Her research indicates that the ever-varying activities of members, elected representatives, interest group representatives, and major campaign donors make any party less a fixed entity than an ever-changing *network.* New parties (especially those being born in new or postrevolutionary polities) and dying parties (especially those struggling to survive in radically altered polities) appear particularly prone to indefinite perimeters. The totalitarian party, capable of controlling not only who enters and who leaves, but also of making membership essential for advancement in all domains, has often been able to establish a somewhat more stable identity, at least until the democratic revolt or coup d'état that succeeds in abolishing it altogether.

Parties at Work. The work of political parties in a democratic polity is twofold: they must place their representatives in government and they must try to run that government according to the plans they made before achieving office. To accomplish the first, they must win the loyalty of the voters either by serving as open participatory bodies or, more commonly, by proposing programs responsive to the perceived needs and wishes of those whose support they seek. To take control of the work of government, they must keep the loyalty of their own elected representatives, who must in turn succeed in prevailing over various other agents responsible for governing (particularly true in constitutionally divided governments or in *cabinet governments formed by political coalition).

Parties in authoritarian systems have a different double assignment: normally placed in office by a combination of military and demagogic power, they begin their real work only after carefully rigged elections have taken place. They are expected to keep their supporters in line (sometimes coercively, sometimes clientelistically, usually with a combination of stick and carrot) and to carry out the work of government as directed by other agents with greater power (the military, the demagogue and his personal entourage, sometimes a combination of both).

Parties in both kinds of states thus provide a form of linkage between citizen and state—participatory or responsive linkage in *democracies, directive or clientelistic linkage in more authoritarian systems— and parties in both kinds of political systems take part in the work of government, but never do it all (Lawson, 1980). Here we focus first on campaigns (in democracies), and then on how the work of parties in government varies according to kind of regime.

Parties in Campaigns. The modern political campaign has come full circle. The earliest campaigns were created by candidates, not parties; so are many of today's. The campaign function of parties began with an expanding suffrage; it may be ending with a shrinking globe. The characteristics of mass communications technology have not only made it easier to reach the electorate but have also placed greater emphasis on the personal characteristics of the candidates, a phenomenon which empowers candidates at the expense of their parties.

In the United States this has come to mean more reliance by candidates on their own organizations and less on the parties, whose labels are wrested from them via hard-fought primary battles, after which the winners conduct the general election contest, using but not relying exclusively on whatever aid the parties can provide. In Europe, where campaign costs are reduced by public funding, normally funneled through the parties, and by the provision of free media time, candidates are less likely to separate themselves so thoroughly from their parties: rather than replace them, strong candidates take them over (as Jacques Chirac took over the Union Pour la Défense de la République in France, renaming it the Rassemblement Pour la République, as Margaret *Thatcher took over the Conservative Party in Britain, and as Helmut *Kohl took over the Christian Democratic Union in the Federal Republic of Germany). In such cases, the party remains a powerful force, but one that tends to be at the beck and call of its currently most powerful candidate.

The tactics of modern campaigns, whether conducted by party or candidate or both, have changed dramatically, as Stephen Frantzich describes in *Political Parties in the Technological Age* (New York, 1989). The most important change is the tendency to rely more and more on the use of the mass media and direct mail, campaign methods that require the expertise of trained political consultants. It is no longer sufficient for experienced party leaders to pass on words of wisdom to their candidates. If parties wish to maintain a significant role in campaigns, they must attract positive free media attention for their candidates, and maximize positive voter response to paid advertising on the media (in nations where such advertising is allowed). They must develop computerized lists for every purpose, gather poll data, and target audiences for the receipt of appropriate messages by television, radio, telephone, or mail. They must train candidates (and their surrogates, such as family members or running mates) to perform well in all the new tasks of campaigning. And finally, if campaign costs are not limited by law and/or covered by public financing, they must raise the funds to pay for all these activities. This new style of campaigning appeared first in the United States, but parties throughout the modern world are rapidly being forced to face the same demands.

The change in the nature of modern campaigning has also affected the role of the party activist. Volunteers are now less necessary than before. In some nations, such as Japan, door-to-door campaigning is not allowed; in others, it is no longer considered cost effective. In most nations voter registration is performed by the government, not party volunteers.

Ballot counting is now likely to be as automated as the campaign itself, and those who might once have spent election night tallying the vote now wait at home to watch it on television. Parties are still active participants in campaigns, but that role is more specialized, and requires fewer people, with greater funding, than ever before.

Parties in Government. The role parties play in government varies from system to system. With some simplification, we may say that the key differences are whether the system is democratic or authoritarian; if democratic, whether the constitutional system is presidential or parliamentary; and if parliamentary, whether there are many parties or few and the relative strength of each.

Authoritarian systems are systems in which the general population takes little or no part in collective decision making. Decisions are made by a narrow *elite, and government becomes the tool for carrying out the will of that group. Where the elite has sought absolute (totalitarian) control over society, it has commonly used a single party to organize that control, placing itself in the top positions of both the party and the government. Subordinate but significant careers are made by joining the party, by becoming one of its candidates, and by carrying out the mandates of its leaders in the offices of government. In such systems, the role of the party man or woman in government has been largely indistinguishable from that of obedient bureaucrat.

Parties have played such roles in fascist and communist systems, but there are now no formally fascist systems and most formerly communist states have abandoned that philosophy of government. Remaining totalitarian systems, such as may be found in several Middle Eastern states, are more likely to rely on a combination of demagogic leadership backed up by military and religious personnel to maintain broad control over all aspects of the lives of their subjects. Such nations may use a single party to recruit and socialize civilian/secular servants to carry out some of the work of government, but the role of party *qua* party in totalitarian rule has been minimized. A notable exception is China, where party continues to play a powerful role along with other ruling forces in a state still committed to the direction of all aspects of its subjects' lives.

How totalitarian an authoritarian system seeks to be depends in large part on how large and how wealthy (or potentially wealthy) the polity is. Smaller and/or less developed states under elite rule are less likely to seek to guide every step in the lives of their subjects. In such states, military and paramilitary forces, sometimes backed by the Catholic church, maintain order, and appointed bureaucrats extort what taxes they can and provide what services they must to keep a largely indigent population under control. Parties are less significant in the governance of such states, long common in Latin America and now more typical in Africa. The power of African single parties at the time of independence, discussed by Gwendolyn Carter and her contributors in *African One-Party States* (Ithaca, N.Y., 1962), has been progressively bureaucratized and diminished. Now, once they have organized the show of support through managed elections, the parties' role in these states seldom extends beyond legislative rubber-stamping and the distribution of patronage.

Parties play a stronger role in government in the world's democracies, particularly those with a parliamentary system. A presidential system, in which the chief executive has powers independent of the legislature, poses difficult problems for parties seeking to govern. Directly elected presidents are former candidates who have succeeded in dominating their parties and winning election in the largest possible single-member district, the nation at large. Such an accomplishment is seldom conducive to humility, or to accepting the restraints of party discipline. Once in office, presidents commonly use the power of their mandates to reinterpret their parties' programs as they wish.

Legislators may nevertheless be able to bring presidential initiative into line with party promises, but that depends on what powers are reserved to them in the nation's *constitution as well as their strength in numbers. Furthermore, their willingness to *use* any power they may have to restrain a chief executive is likely to depend on the extent of party control over their chances for renomination to candidacy in winnable constituencies, and over campaign funding.

The democratic parliamentary system provides the best arena for political parties to carry out their programs, particularly those in which one party is able to win a majority of the seats in the lower house (Rose, 1980). In such a system "parliament is sovereign" and the majority party is the party that rules. Yet even then the party *qua* party may be hard-pressed to take a directing role in governmental affairs, and there is often a considerable gap between "visions and realities of party government" (the title of a volume of studies edited by Francis G. Castles and Rudolf Wildenmann, Berlin, 1986). The party ostensibly "in power" is limited by the tendency of that power to concentrate, first, in the hands of its own elected leadership, particularly the prime minister, and, second, in those of civil servants who know only too well how to circumvent the election-driven demands of probably transient politicians.

A party may temporarily wrest power back by changing its leadership, as the Conservatives did in Britain in 1990, but victory is likely to be short-lived if the new leader comes to feel sure of popular backing for the party's continued dominance: the Ironic Law of parliamentary party politics is that the greater the party's electoral success, the weaker it itself will be vis-à-vis its leadership.

Parliamentary elections do not always produce a majority for a single party, particularly if a system of proportional representation is used (see above). When coalition cabinets must be formed, small parties in the ideological center often exercise a disproportionate power over governmental affairs, a phenomenon well documented in Ian Budge and Hans Keman, *Parties and Democracy: Coalition Formation and Government Functioning in Twenty States* (Oxford, 1990), in Michael Laver and Norman Schofield, *Multiparty Government: The Politics of Coalition in Europe* (Oxford, 1990), and in Manfred J. Holler, ed., *The Logic of Multiparty Systems* (The Hague, 1987). Acceptable to those belonging to larger parties to the left and to the right, the *ministrable* leaders of such organizations sometimes find themselves occupying important cabinet positions so often that they develop an expertise and authority far beyond that warranted by popular support for their parties. Other unlooked-for effects are produced when a majority coalition must include—or negotiate the cooperation of—small extremist parties. Even when not invited into the cabinet, such parties may indirectly shape the course of policy.

Decline and Continuity. Originating in faction, thriving on contention, checked by constitutional and statutory law as well as by the strength of opposing forces, taken over by candidates contemptuous of their paltry offerings, and betrayed by the weakness and occasional corruption of their own leadership, parties have found it difficult not only to govern as they have promised, but to maintain a credible role of any kind in modern polities. *Public opinion polls show a greater disdain for parties and party politicians than ever before, while voters seem never to have been less willing to state a party affiliation or, having stated one, to vote consistently.

Nevertheless, the answer to whether or not parties are in decline is not a simple one. There is, for one thing, some evidence that the decline may have bottomed out, as rates of affiliation and evaluation scores tend to stabilize. More significantly, the parties themselves continue to function regardless of popular discontent with their performance. Old parties refuse to die, although names, tactics, and even ideologies may all be changed. Renascent subnationalism and increasing global interdependence serve not to stymie but rather to stimulate the creation of new parties, as new nations, or nations new to democracy, automatically channel their battles over policy, ideology, and the very shape of government into the parties they hasten to create, and transnational parties are formed to match the larger boundaries of supranationalism. Nothing seems to stop the parties; they endure and even prosper.

What accounts for the durability of the political party? Perhaps the same thing that accounts for its variability. If human beings are to live at all comfortably, some form of association to which all cede a share of their personal sovereignty is required. Yet the very institutionalization of government is a process that cuts it off from the common man and woman and makes of it something alien, threatening, distant, strange. Some way must be found to reach out to government, to keep it in touch with the rest of us, even, in democracies, to make it do our bidding. Some way must be found for those in government to reach out to us, to let us know what they have been doing and why, and to get from us expressions of support that permit them to count on our compliance. Parties are the organizations we have invented for those purposes. We disdain them and misuse them, we allow others to use them as instruments of corruption and tyranny, we try to ignore them, and we pretend their day is over. Yet nevertheless, again and again, we find we cannot do without them. If we did not have political parties, we would no doubt invent them tomorrow.

(See also AUTHORITARIANISM; CHRISTIAN DEMOCRACY; CITIZENSHIP; COMMUNIST PARTY STATES; ELECTIONS AND VOTING BEHAVIOR; INFORMATION SOCIETY; LEGISLATURE; ONE-PARTY SYSTEM; PARLIAMENTARY DEMOCRACY; PARLIAMENTARY SOVEREIGNTY; PATRON-CLIENT POLITICS; POLITICAL MACHINE; POLITICAL PARTICIPATION; POSTINDUSTRIAL SOCIETY; POSTMATERIALISM; SOCIALISM AND SOCIAL DEMOCRACY; TOTALITARIANISM.)

Maurice Duverger, *Political Parties* (New York, 1959). Seymour Lipset and Stein Rokkan, eds., *Party Systems and Voter Alignments* (New York, 1967). Giovanni Sartori, *Parties and Party Systems: A Framework for Analysis* (New York, 1976). Richard Rose, *Do Parties Make a Difference?* (Chatham, N.J., 1980). Kay Lawson, ed., *Political Parties and Linkage: A Comparative Perspective* (New Haven, Conn., 1980). Alan Ware, *Citizens, Parties and the State* (Princeton, N.J., 1987). Angelo Panebianco, *Political Parties: Organization and Power* (Cambridge, 1988). Vicky Randall, ed., *Political Parties in the Third World* (San Marcos, Calif., 1988).

KAY LAWSON

POLITICAL REALIGNMENT. Politics occurs, in most nations, within a context of long-standing institutions, processes, and patterns. Political realignments are cyclical, sharp, comprehensive, and durable shifts in these elements that alter the political situation in profound ways. In the United States and a number of other nations, they have been firmly rooted in popular voting behavior beginning with an intense reaction to some powerful, deeply felt, economic or social shock. Such shocks energize new issues, mobilize voters to come to the polls in greatly increased numbers, and cause some to change their previous political allegiances. That reaction usually occurs not in one election alone, but over several in succession.

For much of U.S. history, the major political parties have benefited from a remarkable partisan stability among voters—a rock-like support expressed at the polls in election after election and which allowed one of the parties to win most contests in an era and thus dominate government policy. These long periods of stability have been abruptly interrupted five times, beginning in *elections in 1800, 1828, 1854, 1894, and 1932. In each case, as old issues lost their force and new pressures emerged, a particular calamity—the depression after 1929, for example—unleashed forces strong enough to overturn and then realign the elements comprising the political world.

Realignments are followed by a new period of political stability. Before a realignment, the electorate behaved predictably. Once it ended, voters did so again, in their new configuration, with a new majority party controlling the government and enacting, in its turn, its policy agenda. Thus, in the United States, after 1932, the Democrats dominated the national government for a generation and enacted a range of unprecedented legislation. Similarly, in Britain, after the realigning election of 1945, the Labour Party, in a similar situation, successfully passed a new legislative program of its own design.

Realignments have thus clarified politics, marked precise dividing points between different eras, and supplied a critical dynamic for peaceful change within political systems. But in recent years, changes in the external environment of politics linked to broad economic and social transformations of society have led to increasingly volatile popular voting and no further realignments. Since the 1960s, election outcomes in the United States, Britain, and in much of Western Europe have reflected fluctuating short-term forces rather than stable, deeply imbedded, partisan loyalties. This voter dealignment from parties has significantly altered the rules of the game. Confusion and fragmentation reign as voters wander from candidate to candidate and from one party to the other in successive elections. In the United States, there have been few clear policy mandates. Government has been divided between Republicans and Democrats with neither able to control the policy arena in a sustained way. In Britain, the growth of nationalist parties in Wales and especially Scotland and the proliferation of center parties counterposed to both Labour and Conservative have vastly complicated politics and made electoral behavior less predictable. More generally in Western Europe, the development of *new social movements, the growth of xenophobic and neofascist parties, and the vitality of environmental issues and *green parties have vastly complicated elections and voting behavior.

This volatile voter pattern, and consequent decline in the realignment dynamic, has provoked questions as to whether these political systems any longer have the ability to relieve pressure on them and redirect government in a peaceful manner. Some are less bleak in their assessment, believing that many elements have realigned over the past generation in both the United States and Europe, albeit without the clarity of the consistent patterns in popular voting characteristic of the party-dominant eras of national politics.

(See also POLITICAL PARTIES AND PARTY COMPETITION.)

Walter Dean Burnham, *Critical Elections and the Mainsprings of American Politics* (New York, 1970). Bruce A. Campbell and Richard J. Trilling, eds., *Realignment in American Politics: Toward a Theory* (Austin, Tex., 1980).

JOEL H. SILBEY

POLITICAL VIOLENCE. Scholars have used the phrase *political violence* since the 1960s to refer to the use or threat of physical harm by groups involved in domestic political conflicts. Initially it was an inclusive term for all disruptive forms of internal opposition to governments, including political *terrorism and *assassinations, antigovernment riots and demonstrations, rebellions, and revolutionary warfare, also known as "civil violence." Later its usage expanded to include governments' acts of repression and violence against their own citizens, also known as "state violence."

Some peace researchers have criticized the narrow conception of political violence as physical injury, arguing that deprivation and social injustice also are forms of violence that they label "structural violence." Almost all conflict and peace researchers would agree that these three aspects of political violence are closely linked: structural violence is a major cause of civil violence, while state violence is both a common response to civil violence and a stimulus to intensified opposition.

Measures of various aspects of political violence have been used to compare civil conflict across regions and over time. Empirical distinctions are made among protest, rebellion, and state violence; and between the scope (extent of participation) and intensity (deadliness) of political violence. Data for the 1950–1980 period show that Western and *Third World democracies tend to have widespread protest but little rebellion or state violence and few conflict deaths. By contrast, the autocratic regimes of Africa, Asia, and the *Middle East tend to have high levels of state violence, rebellion, and many conflict deaths. Until recently the socialist states were largely successful in inhibiting both protest and rebellion. On the rare occasions when domestic resistance did occur it was suppressed with intense state violence, as happened in Hungary in 1956 and Beijing in 1989. After 1989 the patterns of political conflict and violence in Eastern Europe and the Soviet Union increasingly resembled those of the more turbulent Western democracies: protest became widespread and sometimes "revolutionary" in its objectives, but both dissidents and authorities were restrained in their use of violence.

The most deadly types of political violence are civil wars and government-sponsored campaigns of mass murder. About sixty sustained civil wars have been fought since 1945, resulting in more than 3 million battle-related casualties. There also have been more than forty episodes of genocide and politicide, for example in Tibet (1959), Equatorial Guinea (1969–1979), and Argentina (1976–1980), in which most victims have been unarmed civilian members of communal groups, classes, or political parties that were targeted for elimination by the state. At least 7 million and as many as 16 million people died in these campaigns of state-directed political violence, far more than were killed in all international wars fought since 1945.

Serious international repercussions often follow from political violence. More than half the world's 30 million *refugees in need of assistance in 1990 were fleeing from civil wars and politicides. Political violence also provokes military *intervention. From 1945 to 1988 the United States provided military support or combat units for governments or rebels in eighteen civil wars, the Soviet Union in fourteen. And in East Bengal (1971), Kampuchea (1977), and Uganda (1978) mass murder by repressive regimes triggered invasions by neighboring countries. Because of the potentially destabilizing effects of political violence, the major powers, regional organizations, and the UN have given increasing attention to mediation and peacekeeping in civil conflict situations.

(See also REVOLUTION.)

James B. Rule, *Theories of Civil Violence.* (Berkeley, Calif., 1988). Barbara Harff and Ted Robert Gurr, "Toward Empirical Theory of Genocides and Politicides: Identification and Measurement of Cases since 1945" *International Studies Quarterly* 32 (September 1988): 359–371.

TED ROBERT GURR

POPULATION POLICY. The practice of population policy seeks to influence the rate of growth, size, distribution, or composition of a human population or subpopulation within defined territorial boundaries. A population policy aims to act on one or more of the following major demographic variables: fertility, mortality, and migration. It potentially encompasses a broad range of measures affecting marriage and childbearing, levels of nutrition and health, rural and urban development, and internal or external migration. Actions of a government can be considered to be within the realm of population policy if policymakers consciously seek to serve demographic objectives, which themselves are generally linked with larger collective goals such as economic growth, social welfare, and environmental protection. This definition excludes policies that have unintended demographic consequences. Because health and migration traditionally have been accepted spheres of government involvement even without explicit demographic objectives, population policy as it has emerged in recent practice often refers to measures designed to influence birthrates and thereby the size and growth rate of a population.

As far back as Plato, the social implications of changes in population size and growth rates have captured the attention of intellectuals in both the Western and non-Western worlds. Much of the debate had revolved around the propositions advanced by Thomas Robert Malthus in *An Essay on the Principle of Population* (1798). Malthus contended that population growth inevitably outstrips the land and resources available to support additional people. Although Malthus himself did not advocate interventions other than individual "moral restraint," his intellectual descendants have used variations of his argument to justify policies to limit fertility. In a direct challenge to Malthus, Karl *Marx argued in *Das Kapital* (1883) that the emergence of a surplus labor force, and, hence, "overpopulation," was a consequence of the capitalist mode of production. According to Marx and most of his followers, overpopulation would be eliminated under socialism. Although other social thinkers, economists, and eugenicists prior to World War II expressed concern about population trends, the slow pace of population change and the relative infeasibility of policy interventions tended to keep it out of the forefront of public attention.

It was not until the 1940s, when death rates in developing countries were declining rapidly in response to improve nutrition and health conditions, that the idea of public policies to induce a corresponding decline in birthrates gained many adherents. In 1952, newly independent India was the first country to adopt a national population policy explicitly aimed at reducing fertility through the promotion of family planning and modern forms of contraception. Other Asian countries, such as Pakistan and the Republic of Korea (South Korea), were among the first to follow India's example in the 1960s in the belief that they could thereby improve their economic prospects. Since 1974, a number of African governments have adopted population policies, including Nigeria, Zimbabwe, and Niger. Latin American governments, with a few exceptions (e.g., Mexico in 1974), have been reluctant to articulate demographic objectives, although some, including Brazil, have supported provision of contraceptive services. As of 1989, governments from fifty-three countries, totaling sixty-three percent of the world's population, have reported to the UN that they have introduced policies to lower the rates of growth in their countries.

Explanations for the widespread adoption of population policies in recent decades include growing knowledge of population trends in all societies through periodic censuses and demographic analyses; the dominance of ideologies of state intervention in the economy and the institutionalization of development planning; improvements in contraceptive technologies, especially since the early 1960s; and, in most countries, the weakening influence of religious opposition to family planning. International coopera-

tion involving the UN system, development aid agencies, and private organizations has also played a critical role in assisting many developing countries to initiate population policies and programs. After 1965, the government of the United States became the leading supporter of this cooperation, a policy that has been modified since 1981 owing mainly to strong domestic opposition from anti-abortion groups.

National policies built around active promotion of family planning have been shown to have contributed significantly to fertility declines in a number of countries, including Mexico, Thailand, and Indonesia. Still other countries where a considerable financial investment has been made in population programs, such as Bangladesh, Kenya, and Egypt, have achieved minimal results on a national scale, although demonstration projects in certain areas have attained relatively high levels of contraceptive use. The country with the strongest fertility reduction policy is the People's Republic of China. Analysts agree that the policy explains much of the dramatic decline observed in birthrates in China since the early 1970s. In 1978, the government announced a "one-child policy," which has been at times rigorously enforced. In recent years, exceptions to the policy have been increasingly permitted, although accusations of *human rights violations continue.

In general, effectiveness in reducing fertility seems to have been associated with the commitment of political leaders to the policy, the stability and legitimacy of the government, the strength of the health care system, and the involvement of local community structures, as well as with more conventionally measured determinants of fertility such as levels of education and income, infant mortality, and the role and status of women.

Political mobilization in many developing countries, with greater participation of women and religious and ethnic groups, also affects the implementation of population policies. Population programs have often been impeded in countries where there is competition among tribal and ethnic groups such as Nigeria, Lebanon, and Sri Lanka. Changes of government, as in Iran (1979) and the Philippines (1986), have sometimes caused the rejection of previously adopted population policies. The defeat of Indian Prime Minister Indira *Gandhi in the 1977 elections, which observers believe was due in part to voters' reaction to compulsory sterilization policies, led to a substantial reorientation in the national family planning program. In China, continued political unrest may have a significant impact on the population policy and on fertility trends.

Policies to raise birthrates were adopted even before the end of World War II by some countries in Europe, including the Soviet Union, Germany under the Nazis, France, and Sweden. In Western Europe, family allowances and other benefits have been designed primarily as welfare measures, with pronatalist objectives ambiguous or absent, and with little long-term impact on fertility. In Eastern and Central Europe, in addition to positive incentives to raise fertility, some governments have restricted access to contraception and abortion. These measures were carried to their harshest extreme in Romania from the late 1960s until the government was overthrown in 1989. Political reforms in Eastern and Central Europe may be accompanied by an easing of pro-natalist policies although religious opposition and resource shortages are still likely to impede access to family planning services. Overall, twenty-one governments from both developed and developing countries, with four percent of the world's population, reported to the UN in 1989 that they have policies to raise growth rates. Another seventeen governments have policies under which they actively seek to maintain current rates.

On the international level, although governments have moved toward a weak consensus on the need for each country to adopt a policy it considers appropriate to its circumstances and on the right of individuals to have access to family planning services, agreement on population issues in the past was often hindered by East-West or North-South bloc politics. Even with the profound changes now under way in the international economic and political order, however, population policies are likely to remain relevant and no less a source of conflict.

(See also DEVELOPMENT AND UNDERDEVELOP-MENT; NORTH-SOUTH RELATIONS; REPRODUCTIVE POLITICS; WOMEN AND DEVELOPMENT.)

Gunnar Myrdal, *Asian Drama: An Inquiry into the Poverty of Nations,* 3 vols. (New York, 1968). John D. Montgomery, Harold D. Lasswell, and Joel S. Migdal, *Patterns of Policy: Comparative and Longitudinal Studies of Population Events* (New Brunswick, N.J., 1979). C. Alison McIntosh, *Population Policy in Western Europe* (New York, 1983).

BARBARA B. CRANE

POPULISM. Populist movements claim to represent the people as a whole: sometimes the entire nation, sometimes the majority of the people. Radical versions of populism that seek to represent and mobilize the poor or the underprivileged masses have therefore often begun as movements of protest and ended as parties. These have naturally been hostile to parties of the *Right, which are seen as defenders of the existing social order. Thus radical rural populists have often made common cause with organized Labor, seeing it as their counterpart in the cities.

Other populist movements, however, particularly agrarian-based ones, have mistrusted established parties of the *Left, viewing them as defenders of the entrenched sectional interests of organized urban workers only, i.e., as a relatively privileged "labor aristocracy." Hostile to the city in general, these movements celebrate farmer or *peasant values.

Yet other populist movements claim to represent a majority, hitherto deprived of any say in national politics, that is distributed across all social *class and other divisions. Finally, at its very loosest, the term has been applied to any political leader or movement able to mobilize support on a wide scale, for instance Margaret *Thatcher or Ronald *Reagan.

Historically, the term *populism* was used in the United States in the 1890s to describe the doctrines of the People's Party, the most powerful in a series of similar movements, such as the Grangers of the 1870s and 1880s, which sought to represent the interests of small farmers, especially in the West. Between 1860 and 1900, this sector nearly tripled in size. But their life chances were governed by the large institutions in the industrialized East who controlled the commodity markets and the prices that farmers had to pay for agricultural inputs: the banks that the farmers depended on for credit, the agencies that stored the grain, the grain exchanges that purchased it, and the railroads that transported it. The onset of the protracted depression of the last decades of the nineteenth century drove farmers into politics, since, to them, the two major established political parties, the Democrats and the Republicans, were simply corrupt agencies for putting the power of the state at the disposal of the dominant economic interest groups. In the 1892 presidential election, the People's Party polled a million votes. Four years later, in order to appeal to nonfarmers, the party platform was widened to include another populist theme that had been pioneered by movements like the Greenbackers—monetary reform. The addition of "free silver" to its program brought the People's Party candidate in the 1896 presidential election, William Jennings Bryan, to within a half a million votes of victory.

The second major movement to which the label *populist* has been applied was the *narodnichestvo,* or populism, of tsarist Russia, also in the late nineteenth century. This, however, was not a movement of the peasantry so much as a movement about the peasantry, primarily on the part of intellectuals fired with the idealistic belief that the authentic heart of Russian culture was the village, whose central institution was its ancient communitarian system of landholding. Though capitalist relations were beginning to penetrate the countryside, the *Narodniki* believed not only that this process could be halted but that a new social order based on the egalitarian principles embodied in the village community could be brought into being at the level of the state as a whole. The *ideology was thus anticapitalist, and therefore unacceptable to those who, like Stolypin, strove to bring into being a large new class of entrepreneurial peasants who would establish a solid basis for capitalism in the countryside. It was equally unacceptable to *Lenin, who considered that capitalism was already well established in the countryside. The proletarianization of ex-peasants would inevitably lead them to realize that their interests lay in an alliance with the urban workers. In 1874, large numbers of young *Narodnik* city intellectuals "went to the people," only to meet with incomprehension, mistrust, and even betrayal to the police. But in the years following World War I, the ideas of the *Narodniki* became a significant political force in several countries of Eastern Europe (Bulgaria, Poland, Romania): where the majority of the population were peasants, peasant parties came to power.

The dual hostility of populists to both capitalist "Big Business" and to "scientific" *socialism can be seen in two movements in adjoining provinces of Canada between the two world wars. Both were responses of farmers to the Depression of the 1930s, but the Cooperative Commonwealth Federation (CCF), which controlled the province of Saskatchewan until the post–World War II epoch, and Social Credit, in Alberta, were very different in orientation. The CCF brought not only grain-storage and agricultural supplies under provincial *parastatal agencies, but also organized insurance, transport, and much of general retail trade on a cooperative basis. Social Credit, by contrast, saw the solution to the province's problems in the monetary reform nostrums of Major Douglas. Again, whereas Getúlio *Vargas of Brazil developed themes borrowed from Italian fascist *corporatism into an ideology of national renewal, in Argentina the much more radical Peronist movement—which persists to the present day—based itself upon organizing the mass of the poor urban workers into powerful trade unions. The Peronist claim to represent the common people was expressed in Evita *Perón's idealization of the *descamisados*, the "shirtless ones."

By the 1960s, when nearly a score of new countries came into existence in black Africa, many observers saw resemblances between the ideologies of some of the new "single parties" and the classical nineteenth-century and earlier twentieth-century populisms on other continents. Like their predecessors, these parties claimed to embody an authentic Africanness, a cultural distinctiveness rooted in village culture that had only been interrupted during the colonial era. The towns implanted by the Europeans, the divisions between one African people and another fostered by colonialist policies of "divide and rule" through the emphasizing of tribal differences, and the Marxist conception of social class as the major component of social structure, were all denounced as Western distortions. Instead, the populist parties in power dedicated themselves to nation building. The new nation was to be founded on a modern restatement of a postulated traditional egalitarianism and solidarity of the village—*umoja* (unity) and *ujamaa* (literally, "family-ness"), for instance, in the rhetoric of East African ruling parties—though now at the level of the nation-state.

In the immediate euphoria of the post-independence period, these parties, which had led the independence struggle, commanded widespread popularity.

But as that power was used to eliminate opposition at all levels, and, in the case of Tanzania for instance, to enforce *collectivization of the villages overnight, popular support withered. Populist ideology had decreasing purchase on the minds of people who saw it simply as rhetoric disguising the reality of the monopolization of power—not so much economic power, as in the case of the classic European or American bourgeoisies or landowning classes, as that of a New Class which ruled because it controlled the political apparatus of the state, by making itself the only legal party.

Hence, the energies of those disillusioned with populism have more recently tended to be channeled into a more class-based radicalism or ethnic-based opposition. Yet the populist ideal of a society run in the interests of the common people by a party and government that will eliminate inequitable social divisions retains its appeal to a wide range of people, from idealistic socialists to authoritarian nationalists.

(See also AUTHORITARIANISM; ETHNICITY; ONE-PARTY SYSTEM; PERÓN, JUAN DOMINGO.)

Ghita Ionescu and Ernest Gellner, eds., *Populism: Its Meanings and National Characteristics* (London, 1969). Margaret Canovan, *Populism* (London, 1981).

PETER WORSLEY

PORTUGAL. Having emerged in the twelfth century, Portugal is among the oldest polities in Europe. The Atlantic archipelagos of the Azores and Madeira were colonized in the fifteenth century, a prelude to 500 years of multicontinental imperialism. Mainland and islands cover 92,082 square kilometers (approx. 35,550 sq. mi.), with a resident population in 1991 of 10,421,000.

LIberal constitutionalism was introduced in the 1820s and a centralized, French-style administrative system in the 1830s under the Braganza dynasty, which was overthrown on 5 October 1910. The First Republic suffered from political instability that encouraged military interventions, culminating in the movement of 28 May 1926, which inaugurated a military dictatorship. In 1932 the Catholic economics professor and Finance Minister António de Oliveira Salazar (1889–1970) was appointed prime minister, a position he held until incapacitated in 1968. In 1933 he introduced the "New State," an authoritarian corporative political system that had the support of Republican and Monarchist conservatives and Catholics offended by the anticlericalism of the preceding regime, which had separated church and state in 1911. Salazar kept Portugal neutral during World War II and seemingly liberalized his regime after 1945, but elections were rigged and his supporters filled the National Assembly.

Nationalist revolts broke out in the Overseas Provinces of *Angola, *Guinea, and *Mozambique in 1961–1964. The strain of these colonial struggles was the main preoccupation of Salazar's successor,

Marcello Caetano (1906–1980). He attempted political liberalization on the domestic front but opposition hardened and he was overthrown by the Movimento das Forças Armadas (MFA) on 25 April 1974.

This *coup ushered in seventeen months of semi-revolutionary turmoil. The first postcoup president, General António de Spínola, tried to reassert authority against the military and political *Left but resigned on 30 September 1974. Government was then dominated by the radical MFA, which engaged in rapid *decolonization. On 11 March 1975 a countercoup by Spínola failed and was followed by large-scale state confiscation of private banks and large companies as well as land occupations of large estates in the southern region.

After elections for a constituent assembly (25 April 1975) resulted in victory for the Partido Socialista (PS) of Mário Soares, the MFA split into revolutionary, pro-Communist and anti-Communist factions. The climax of this revolutionary process came on 25 November 1975 when an alleged revolutionary coup was foiled. The new constitutional regime formally began in July 1976. The Portuguese transition from dictatorship to *democracy was tortuous and sui generis, though contemporaneous with that in Greece and preceding that in Spain.

The constitution of 2 April 1976 instituted a democratic system in which the powers of the prime minister and single-chamber legislature (Assembly of the Republic), elected for a four-year term by citizens over 18 by *proportional representation, are balanced by those of the president, elected every five years by direct universal suffrage. General António Ramalho Eanes, operational commander of the antirevolutionary forces on 25 November 1975, was elected in 1976 and 1980. Soares was elected in 1986, the first civilian president for sixty years, and reelected in 1991.

The constitutional text of 1976, influenced by the MFA, committed Portugal to making the transition to *socialism and proclaimed the nationalizations and agrarian reform of 1975 irreversible. It also made the military the constitutional watchdog and allowed politico-administrative autonomy for the Azores and Madeira. The revision of 1982 ended the military's political role, replacing the Council of the Revolution by a civilian constitutional court. The second revision, in 1989, removed the commitments to socialism and the irreversibility of *nationalizations, thus sanctioning the reprivatization policies of Prime Minister Aníbal Cavaco Silva.

Since 1976, Portugal has enjoyed stability of regime but frequent changes of government (twelve in the first fifteen years of democracy). This instability resulted from constitutional bickering, rivalries between parties, and, until 1987, the reluctance of the electorate to give one party the majority.

The two strongest parties are the PS and the Partido Social Democrata (PSD). The PS, a democratic socialist party founded in 1973, largely the creation of Soares, was electoral leader until 1985. In opposition it recovered only some of its popularity. The PSD—founded in 1974, it was called the Popular Democratic Party until 1976—enrolled opponents and supporters of Caetano and is liberal-reformist in orientation. It governed alone under Cavaco Silva after 1985, obtaining 50.2 percent of the vote in 1987 and 50.6 percent in 1991.

Other parties include the Partido Comunista Português (PCP), founded in 1921, backbone of opposition to Salazar and traditionally strong among proletarians, but declining since 1979. Also in decline is the Centro Democrático Social (CDS), a conservative Christian Democrat party that was founded in 1974 and was the PSD's chief coalition partner from 1979 to 1983.

Unemployment was among the lowest in Western Europe in the 1970s and 1980s, but the rate of inflation was the highest. Portugal is dependent on imports for over four-fifths of its energy. An unfavorable trade balance is to an extent offset by tourism and money flowing back to Portugal from emigrants. Portugal's GNP was approximately US$69 billion and per capita GNP $6,610 in 1991.

Portugal, a founding member of the *European Free Trade Association in 1960, opted for a fully West European political future when, despite Communist opposition, it applied in 1977 to join the *European Community (EC), of which it became the eleventh member on 1 January 1986. Membership led to increased foreign investment, vastly stimulated trade with Spain (previously negligible), and secured significant development aid from the Community. A seven-year transition period was stipulated (ten years for agriculture). The Portuguese are divided in their opinions on European monetary and political union.

Portugal was a founding member of the *North Atlantic Treaty Organization in 1949 and is particularly valued therein for its possession of the Azores: the U.S. base at Lajes, on Terceira, provides a transatlantic staging post and center for maritime surveillance. The Portuguese armed forces, 217,000 strong in 1975 at the end of the colonial wars, numbered 62,000 in 1991 (mostly army).

The Portuguese remain proud of their imperial and cultural achievements and hope to be the EC's chief interlocutors with Lusophone Brazil as well as former African possessions. Portugal administers the territory of *Macao, which is to return to China on 20 December 1999, and is committed by its constitution to self-determination for East *Timor, its former colony, occupied by Indonesia in 1975.

(See also ANGOLAN CONFLICT; DEMOCRATIC TRANSITIONS.)

R. A. H. Robinson, *Contemporary Portugal: A History* (London, 1979). Walter C. Opello, Jr., *Portugal's Political Development: A Comparative Approach* (Boulder, Colo., 1985). Thomas C. Bruneau and Alex Macleod, *Politics in*

Contemporary Portugal: Parties and the Consolidation of Democracy (Boulder, Colo., 1986). Kenneth Maxwell, ed., *Portugal in the 1980s: Dilemmas of Democratic Consolidation* (Westport, Conn., 1986).

RICHARD A. H. ROBINSON

POSTINDUSTRIAL SOCIETY. Postindustrialism is an elusive notion. Formulated to explain fundamental discontinuities in social development and to delineate the principal characteristics and dynamics of a new type of society, it is resolutely oriented toward the future. Yet its very composition constitutes an admission that our knowledge of the institutions and processes ostensibly surpassed ("industrialism") remains far more complete than our understanding of the society replacing them ("post-"). In contrast with other macrosociological concepts that claim a systematic and unified apprehension of their object (industrial society, *capitalism), postindustrialism declares itself an inherently indeterminate notion poised between an obsolete past and a future still impervious to formal synthesis.

Concepts of postindustrialism attempting to assert a more rigorous scientific status have been rebuked by potent historical continuities. The idea of a "leisure society" in which the constraints of toil are transcended or an "*information society" in which the working class has dissolved is difficult to maintain given the effective expansion of average work time in many industrial societies and the perpetual absorption of new groups of workers into predominantly low-paying and insecure jobs within an integrated global economy. Continuing economic crisis, persistent unemployment, and widening divisions between rich and poor mock assertions about the incipient abolition of scarcity in a "posteconomic" society. An embryonic "postmaterialist" transformation in values has been countered, if not subverted, by a powerful global resurgence of belief in the virtues of classical market principles.

Daniel Bell's notion of postindustrialism, the most influential and most carefully circumscribed in its pretensions, is neither a theory nor a conceptual schema but merely a "speculative construct," a descriptive plotting of particular social tendencies to their logical limits. From this perspective, postindustrialism refers to the sociotechnical terrain, a limited focus excluding the political and cultural realms and not necessarily homologous with them. Within this sphere, postindustrialism is defined by a new "axial principle": if industrial society is propelled by material technique, postindustrialism is governed by the primacy of theoretical knowledge in both innovation and policy-making.

A new "intellectual technology" substituting rationality for trial-and-error judgment changes technical practice, occupational structure, and social organization. The centrality of theoretical knowledge is evident in science-based technological development (the shift from steel and autos to electronics), rationalized economic management (*planning,

modeling, forecasting), the diffusion of computer-based work, and the priority accorded research and development in social evolution. Postindustrial society witnesses a shift from the production of goods to the delivery of services: service employment may have been extensive previously (domestic service, distribution), but postindustrialism rests decisively on human and professional-technical services, particularly in health, education, research, and government. Management and labor are displaced by the preeminence accorded to professional, scientific, and technical strata, elites concerned primarily with the processing and exchange of information. If industrial society is defined by the quantity of goods produced, quality of life is the goal of postindustrial society.

This looser conception of postindustrialism resists premature theoretical closure and stimulates social investigation. But its virtues are dissipated by excessively speculative trend analysis based on artificially precise distinctions and unrestrained by substantive exploration of the connections among phenomena.

Although theoretical knowledge unquestionably has assumed a more important role, its social primacy is more problematic. Societies with the highest levels of expenditure on basic science (the United States, Britain) have registered low rates of economic growth while others (Japan) have attained industrial dominance while exhibiting comparative weakness in scientific research. Rather than issuing from a linear transfer of scientific knowledge, innovation tends to be incremental, derivative of "learning by doing," and dependent upon reciprocal information flows between all phases of production. The prior political determination of technological development or social structure remains opaque. Service employment growth in fact has been driven less by secular trends in income or consumption substituting services for manufacturing than by structural changes in industry fueling demand for intermediate services linked to goods production. Service employment, therefore, can expand without increasing consumption of services as a distinct category: indeed, even in the sphere of final consumption, demand for services (public transport) may be replaced by investment in goods (autos). The expansion of services reflects changes in occupational structure within all sectors of the economy as opposed to a shift in demand patterns between sectors. However, the increased service component of jobs does not necessarily entail a generalized application of sophisticated "information work": rapid rates of growth in scientific and technical occupations are offset by the greater quantitative weight of new, relatively routinized service jobs. The new power of the scientific intelligentsia has not demonstrably displaced existing political and economic elites.

In these and other respects, the putative distinctiveness of "postindustrial" trends appears illusory. The concept of postindustrialism serves a useful function in alerting us to incipient transformations worthy of more extensive analysis. Its vision of a science-based and technocentric future, however, ironically is undermined by its own speculative distance from the standards of scientific inquiry.

(See also DEINDUSTRIALIZATION; FORDISM; LABOR MOVEMENT; POSTMATERIALISM; TECHNOLOGY TRANSFER.)

Daniel Bell, *The Coming of Post-Industrial Society: A Venture in Social Forecasting* (New York, 1973). Jonathan Gershuny, *After Industrial Society?* (London, 1978). Krishan Kumar, *Prophecy and Progress: The Sociology of Industrial and Post-Industrial Society* (Harmondsworth, U.K., 1978). Fred Block, *Postindustrial Possibilities: A Critique of Economic Discourse* (Berkeley, Calif., 1990).

RICHARD GORDON

POSTMATERIALISM. Postmaterialist values give top priority to self-expression, belonging, and the nonmaterial quality of life—as opposed to materialist values, which give top priority to economic and physical security. Throughout industrial society, people's basic values and goals are gradually shifting from giving top priority to economic growth and consumption, to placing increasing emphasis on the quality of life. The incentives that once motivated the work force are becoming less effective than they were; the policies that once gave rise to broad political support no longer work as readily as they did; even the values that once shaped sexual behavior and child rearing are giving way to new norms. In large part, this reflects a process of intergenerational value change; it is invisible to the naked eye and tends to pass unnoticed unless it is measured by systematic, longitudinal survey research. But its impact is pervasive. It is changing social, political, and economic life. And because it is transforming entire life-styles, including consumer patterns, fertility rates, and the priority that people give to environmental protection, human activities have become a major factor influencing changes in the geophysical environment. It is also leading to less public support for *nationalism, less emphasis on military expenditures, and a declining willingness to fight for one's country. These changes are gradual, however, and subject to substantial short-term fluctuations.

Evidence of intergenerational value change began to be gathered on a cross-national basis in 1970 (Inglehart, 1971). It was hypothesized that, as a result of the rapid economic development and the expansion of the *welfare state following World War II, the formative experience of the younger birth cohorts differed from that of older cohorts in ways that were leading them to develop fundamentally different value priorities. Throughout most of history, the threat of severe economic deprivation or even starvation had been a crucial concern for most people. But the unprecedented degree of economic security experienced by the postwar generation in most industrial societies was leading to a gradual shift from "materialist" values (emphasiz-

ing economic and physical security above all) toward "postmaterialist" priorities (emphasizing self-expression and the quality of life).

In 1970, surveys were carried out in six West European nations to test this hypothesis. The results showed striking differences between the priorities of old and young. Among the oldest group (which had experienced the insecurity and devastation of World War I, the Great Depression, and World War II), those with materialist priorities outnumbered those with postmaterialist priorities by more than twelve to one; but, moving from the older to younger cohorts, the proportion of materialists shrank, and the proportion of postmaterialists rose. Among the youngest group—those born after World War II—there was a shift in the balance between value types, with postmaterialists becoming more numerous than materialists.

Cohort analysis of a twenty-year time series of surveys, in which exactly the same questions were administered to representative national samples, demonstrated that given birth cohorts did *not* become more materialist as they aged from 1970 to 1990—instead, most of these cohorts were actually a little *less* materialist at the end of this period than they had been at the start.

During the period from 1970 to 1990, the group that was aged 65+ became a group aged 85+, of whom very few survivors remained to be interviewed. They were replaced by younger individuals, who are much more postmaterialist than their elders. As a result, we would expect to find a net shift from materialist to postmaterialist values in the populations of these societies. Do we?

The answer is "yes." In each of the six societies first surveyed in 1970 (and also in the United States, which was first surveyed in 1972), a significant decline was found in the proportion of materialists, and an increase in the proportion of postmaterialists. The size of this shift varied from country to country, partly as a function of the economic and physical conditions that prevailed in the given country during this period, but all seven countries moved in the predicted direction. Similar results emerged from the much larger number of countries included in both the 1981 and the 1990 World Values surveys: in almost every case, there was evidence of an intergenerational shift from materialist toward postmaterialist priorities. This shift was taking place not only in Western countries but (very rapidly) in East Asia and (more slowly) in Eastern and Central Europe. It has not yet become an important factor in preindustrial societies but, theoretically, should become increasingly significant there too, as economic development takes place.

In industrialized societies, postmaterialist values are closely related to environmental attitudes and environmentalist behavior. For example, those with postmaterialist values are about twice as likely to express support for environmental protection as are materialists—and four or five times as likely to be active members of environmentalist groups, or to vote for *green parties, in countries where they exist. An intergenerational shift seems to be occurring toward giving higher priority to environmental protection (Inglehart, 1977).

Similarly, because the basic goals of postmaterialists differ from those that have long prevailed in their societies, they tend to support change-oriented parties—which are usually the parties of the *Left. But this fact does not guarantee the automatic success of the Left. On the contrary, the rise of postmaterialist issues such as abortion, *environmentalism, and gay and lesbian rights often tends to split existing Left parties, with the traditional working-class base sometimes being alienated by the stand advocated by growing postmaterialist elements.

Postmaterialist values turn out to be correlated with a surprisingly wide range of other values, relating to work, leisure, gender roles, and a variety of other social and political orientations. One example of the many dimensions that are correlated with materialist/postmaterialist values is sexual restrictiveness. In every one of the twenty-four countries surveyed in the 1981 World Values Survey, those with postmaterialist values were much less restrictive than those with materialist values. It may be that the two types of orientations go together because they reflect a common set of causes: the formative conditions that gave rise to postmaterialist values also give rise to an outlook which has less need for the security and predictability of absolute sexual rules (Inglehart, 1990). And the World Values Survey data suggest that sexual restrictiveness is not only correlated with the materialist/postmaterialist values dimension but is undergoing a similar process of intergenerational change, moving toward less restrictive orientations. Across those nations for which we have data, there is a clear and consistent tendency for the young and the postmaterialists to have less restrictive sexual norms than the old.

The rise of postmaterialism seems to be working to erode mass support for nationalism and patriotism. Publics have become accustomed to economic and physical security, and are less likely to feel threatened by neighboring peoples. But the decline of patriotism and nationalism goes beyond the postmaterialist syndrome, for it also reflects a historical change in Western publics' orientations toward *war—a change that seems linked with the experience of World War II, on one hand, and an awareness that modern technology would make a third world war vastly more destructive than even the cataclysm of 1939–1945. Finally, in Western Europe the emergence of *European Community institutions has contributed to making the perspective of the nation-state seem outmoded, giving rise to a faint but growing sense of European *citizenship.

(See also Gay and Lesbian Politics; Gender and Politics; New Left; New Social Movements; Peace Movement; Postindustrial Society; Postmodernism; Reproductive Politics.)

Ronald Inglehart, "The Silent Revolution in Europe: Intergenerational Change in Post-Industrial Societies" *American Political Science Review* 65, no. 4 (December 1971): 991–1017. Ronald Inglehart, *The Silent Revolution: Changing Values and Political Styles Among Western Publics* (Princeton, N.J., 1977). Ronald Inglehart, *Culture Shift in Advanced Industrial Society* (Princeton, N.J., 1990).

Ronald Inglehart

POSTMODERNISM. Postmodernism is a body of thought and sensibility that emerged in the late 1960s, and that appears alive and well at the start of the 1990s. Postmodernism has spread and thrived throughout Western Europe and the United States, especially in and around universities, among architects, artists, and performers, and in advertising and the mass media. The term *postmodern* has generated, and is still generating, an immense amount of discourse. It is often simply a vehicle for talking about "the spirit of the age," so that many people who doubt that it means anything besides chronology—say, work produced after 1965 or so—are still eager to come to symposia and conferences on it. The most original work done under a postmodern label has been in architecture, mainly in North America, and in social thought, mainly in France.

Postmodern architects and their publicists claim to have rediscovered the historic forms and styles—"the styles," in Le Corbusier's dismissive terminology—that the triumphs of Le Corbusier, Mies, and Gropius were supposed to have wiped out. But they are not just reactionary eclectics; they think they can twist and recombine architectural history in fresh and original ways that would have been unthinkable before modernism wiped the slate clean. Their sensitivity to the forms of the past enables them to design buildings and environments that are complex and ironic, contradictory and multivalent. Louis Kahn, Robert Venturi, Michael Graves, Aldo Rossi, Frank Gehry, Charles Moore, James Stirling, and Ricardo Bofill are among the stars of postmodern architecture, although all are not happy with the label.

Postmodern architecture presents various conceptual and human problems. Its way of blending past and present is in fact the central idea of modernism in literature and art: the principle of montage. This is not radical innovation, but what Harold Rosenberg called "the tradition of the new." Postmodern language explodes with images of radical breakthrough, subversion, and transgression and with claims to leave both Dada and revolutionary *Marxism far behind; but beneath the noise, one can hear a familiar refrain, a blatant, shameless self-promotion worthy of the great modernist hustlers Flaubert and Mark Twain. Philip Johnson put postmodernism over the top in the late 1970s and established it as *the* corporate idiom of the Reagan decade with his AT&T Building in New York. This skyscraper features an extravagant Chippendale top, an immense, dramatically lit stone arcade at the bottom (he said "Borromini," his critics said "Mussolini"), and fifty floors of lucrative real estate in between. Within a decade the giant AT&T was gone, and the building was reincarnated as the Sony Building, as solid an investment as ever. If this was postmodern irony, much of the public was ready for plain talk.

The most interesting postmodern social thought emanates from France, where it developed out of the Parisian uprising of 1968, the breakdown of that uprising, and the years of post-traumatic stress syndrome that French intellectuals went through. Among the most original postmodern thinkers have been Michel *Foucault, Jacques Lacan, Roland Barthes, Jean-François Lyotard, Jacques Derrida, Julia Kristeva, and Jean Baudrillard. These intellectuals had a distinctive aura in France: they were spectacular performers who could mesmerize large audiences with theatrical flair and they received an often frenzied public adulation. Many of their most ardent followers have been U.S. academics, who have arranged a constant round of transatlantic visits for them.

The intellectuals who began to identify themselves as postmodern in the early 1970s professed regrets for their radicalism in the 1960s, although they continued to define their work by the paradigms of resistance or revolution. The original sin of 1960s radicals, they said, was to have employed the wrong metaphysics—Derrida called it "the metaphysics of presence"—which posited the essential unity of human experience. This delusion was supposedly the source of the Western idea of *human rights. Postmodernists came to disparage the whole paradigm of human rights, because it discounted the differences between people, which they considered more important. The human differences most interesting to postmoderns so far have been sex/gender and race/ethnicity. They haven't shown much interest in class, national, or religious differences. They have been violently abusive toward Marxists who stress the importance of class-based differences.

Jean-François Lyotard is the paradigmatic postmodernist, the writer who has used the concept in the most ambitious and audacious ways. He says, "There is no longer a horizon of universalization, of general emancipation, before the eyes of postmodern man." The postmodern epoch is defined by "the failure of the universal" and "the disappearance of the idea of progress within rationality and freedom." To be in tune with the times (though he never explains just why we should be) is to be free from "grand narratives" (or "master narratives," "metanarratives"), from stories that supposedly give our individual or collective histories meaning beyond ourselves. We ought to give up the quest for transcendent meaning, and "just live," in a playful "eternal present." Lyotard (along with his whole generation in France) portrays Nietzsche as the prophet

and hero of this new morality. The other pillar of his postmodern edifice is Ludwig Wittgenstein. Lyotard offers a highly politicized version of the late Wittgenstein's "language games": language games are bound to be heterogenous and incommensurable with each other; truth and meaning can exist only in particular communities of belief and desire; no one can transcend the community into which he or she is born. Lyotard's signature is a radical skepticism, both about what people can know and about what they can do—"skepticism of metanarrative," he calls it—which passes abruptly into dogmatism and peremptory a priori decrees about what is and what is not possible. Some critics have argued that this leap from skepticism to dogmatism typifies postmodern thinking as a whole.

As French culture veered sharply to the right in the 1970s, postmodern attacks on Marxism gradually escalated into diatribes against the French Revolution and the Declaration of Rights. Before long, the Left Bank was saturated with tracts that showed how the mass murders perpetrated by Stalinism were actually simple corollaries of the Enlightenment. Parisian intellectuals who had finally learned (often at quite advanced ages) to see through Stalinism were carried along by a momentum that propelled them, in a remarkably short time, through *liberalism as well. By the time the revolution's bicentennial arrived, it was hard to find a French intellectual who would say a good word for it. French postmodernism today is marked by a ferocious contempt for the Enlightenment, for the revolution, for humanism, for the idea of human rights, for what sometimes seems to be the whole of modern life and thought. Its emotional violence, lack of intellectual balance, and learned ignorance of the traditions it condemns suggest echoes of the Action Française, or the pre-1933 German "politics of cultural despair." French postmoderns look longingly across the Rhine and celebrate Martin Heidegger as their intellectual hero, while German humanists like Habermas look nervously toward Paris and fear that once more the lights are going out all over Europe.

He need not worry. True, in denying human unity and human rights, postmodernism shows an affinity with the traditional post-1789 European Right (Burke, de Maistre, Müller, et al.). However, its activists come from the post-1960s Left, and their practical activity focuses almost wholly on causes and groups that today's Left has made its own: e.g., racial and sexual equality, local and global ecology, nuclear disarmament. Still, left-wing politics from the perspective of right-wing metaphysics is bound to generate trouble, though not exactly the kind of trouble Habermas fears. Postmoderns typically work in or for *new social movements: they fight oppression and injustice against women, homosexuals, people of color, et al. But if the ideas of justice, shared humanity, and human rights are groundless, why should anyone who isn't a member of these groups identify with them, accept their claims of victimization, or care about their fate?

Postmoderns have contributed brains and energy to feminist, gay, and ecological movements, and to the Greens. They have generally pushed their movements in the separatist and sectarian directions, away from broad civil rights coalitions and from human bonds that could transcend group boundaries. If there is coherent postmodern political vision, it is probably something like what U.S. political scientists call "interest group liberalism": an open, ever-growing aggregation of voluntary associations, some immensely powerful, others virtually powerless, none showing any concern for anyone beyond itself. French postmoderns present this view of the world as a spectacular discovery and as the key to freedom and happiness in the new pluralist, "polytheistic" world. Americans, who have lived in a political culture dominated by interest-group liberalism (at least since Tocqueville's time) and who are used to seeing vital public needs unrecognized and unfulfilled, should be forgiven if they cast a cold eye.

Both friends and enemies of postmodernism felt that it "fit" the sleazy glamour and flamboyant nihilism of the Thatcher-Reagan years. But there was one big thing that it did not fit: the struggle for human rights in Eastern Europe, and then in China, in 1989. When demonstrators in Prague went up against armed Soviet troops, bearing signs that said "Truth Will Prevail," when students in Beijing died with "We Shall Overcome" on their shirts, this wasn't in the postmodern repertory. It was too serious, too universal, too much of a "grand narrative": people weren't supposed to be doing this anymore! Postmodernism blanked out in 1989, in the face of one of the great political moments in history. On the other hand, their blankness positioned them perfectly for 1990: when revolutionary people and peoples fell apart into a hundred tribes and tribalisms, postmoderns could tell the world they'd told us so, that tribal identity and corporate privilege were all there was.

It would be foolish to predict postmodernism's fate in the twenty-first century. However, its ups and downs in 1989–1990 should make it clear that it is really less a theory than a mentality: arch sophistication, emotional flatness, weariness of life (even in the very young), certainty that everything that can happen has happened (hence the self is defined by being "post-"), talent for manipulating everything without meaning anything. In periods of political impasse and constriction, the postmodern mood appears to make sense of life. But it grows blind and dumb when men and women step into the foreground, grow innovative and resourceful in fighting for freedom, and actually create something new under the sun. When people manifest unexpected depths, postmodernism shows that deep down it's shallow.

(See also MAY 1968; MODERNITY; NINETEEN EIGHTY-NINE; POSTINDUSTRIAL SOCIETY; POSTMATERIALISM.)

Robert Venturi, *Complexity and Contradiction in Architecture* (New York, 1966). Michael Foucault, *Power/Knowledge: Selected Interviews and Other Writings, 1972–1977* (New York, 1980). Jean-François Lyotard, *The Post-Modern Condition: A Report on Knowledge,* translated by Geoff Bennington and Brian Massumi (Minneapolis, 1984). Jürgen Habermas, *The Philosophical Discourse of Modernity,* translated by Frederick Lawrence (Cambridge, Mass., 1987). Marshall Berman, "Why Modernism Still Matters" *Tikkun* 4, no. 1 (January–February 1989). Linda Nicholson, ed., *Feminism/Postmodernism* (New York, 1990). Fredric Jameson, *Postmodernism, or, the Cultural Logic of Late Capitalism* (Durham, N.C., 1991).

MARSHALL BERMAN

POTSDAM CONFERENCE. The last meeting of the *World War II Grand Alliance took place from 17 July to 2 August 1945 in Potsdam, near the destroyed German capital of Berlin. The future of Germany was the major issue facing the new president of the United States, Harry *Truman, Premier Joseph *Stalin of the Soviet Union, and Prime Minister Winston *Churchill of Britain. (After the election of 28 July, Labor Party leader Clement Attlee replaced Churchill.) The successful test of the first atomic bomb on 16 July also cast its shadow over future relations among the Big Three.

The key dispute at the conference concerned German reparations. The Soviet Union demanded significant reparations from Germany, both in industrial plant and from current production, on the scale of the US$20 billion figure established for discussion at Yalta. The Western powers favored reparations only through the dismantling and removal of industrial plant. The United States and Britain opposed reparations from current production, insisting that Germany must first become self-supporting from exports. The three countries reached a compromise that merely postponed the problem. Although Germany itself was to be treated as a single economic unit, each power was entitled to collect reparations from its respective zone. The Western zones were to provide the Soviets with one-quarter of all additional equipment not necessary for the peacetime functioning of the German economy. The zonal agreement on reparations was a first step leading to the division of Germany.

A related issue was the settlement of Germany's eastern frontier. Having already annexed a large section of eastern Poland, Stalin wanted the country to receive territorial compensation from Germany. He proposed a western border for Poland at the Oder and Neisse rivers. When asked about the millions of Germans in the territory, Stalin claimed that they had fled. Although the Western powers conceded the Oder-Neisse boundary as a "provisional solution" pending the final peace conference, the Soviets and the Poles made it permanent through the forcible expulsion of the German population.

Although word of the atomic bomb strengthened

Truman's confidence at Potsdam, there is little evidence that the weapon played any decisive role in conference diplomacy. Truman informed Stalin of the existence of the new weapon in only the vaguest terms, but the Soviet leader was already aware of it through his espionage network. Despite Truman's complaints, the Soviets did not change their policy in Eastern Europe. Truman was first and foremost determined to secure Soviet involvement in the war against Japan. For his part Stalin shared with Truman information about Japanese proposals for peace. Although the Big Three issued a general warning demanding that Japan surrender, there was no specific reference to the bomb. Less than two weeks after the conclusion of the conference, the United States used the atomic bomb against *Hiroshima and Nagasaki, the Soviets entered the war against Japan, and the Japanese surrendered.

(See also COLD WAR; NUCLEAR WEAPONS; YALTA CONFERENCE.)

Herbert Feis, *Between War and Peace: The Potsdam Conference* (Princeton, N.J., 1960). Martin J. Sherwin, *A World Destroyed: The Atomic Bomb and the Grand Alliance* (New York, 1975).

THOMAS ALAN SCHWARTZ

POUJADISM. A movement of artisans and shopkeepers (the Union de Défense des Commerçants et Artisans—UDCA), led by Pierre Poujade, Poujadism spread rapidly throughout *France after 1953. It emerged in the poorest, least urbanized areas of the country, among small shopkeepers who were being threatened by the expansion of larger commercial establishments and who were benefiting least from economic expansion in the country. (In 1953, four-fifths of small shopkeepers had a declared income that was lower than the working class average.)

The movement began as a tax protest as well as a revolt against existing trade associations dominated by larger enterprises, but the program of the UDCA was a broad attack against politicians, parliament, Jews (Pierre Mendès-France became prime minister in 1954), *modernization, collectivism, centralization, and, by implication, the Fourth Republic. By 1955, the UDCA had decided to go beyond protest and to present candidates in local and national elections as a political party (the Union et Fraternité Française—UFF). The party won 2.6 million votes (ten percent of those who voted) and fifty-three seats in the elections for the National Assembly in 1956. Within two years this "flash party" had both disintegrated as a parliamentary group and dissipated as an electoral force.

As an electoral phenomenon, Poujadism never revived after 1958. No party during the Fifth Republic (since 1958) has successfully mobilized voters by appealing to the interests of shopkeepers, although a movement of shopkeepers and artisans in the early 1970s did succeed in pressuring the government to pass legislation that delayed the spread of large supermarkets (at least in the short run).

Nevertheless, Poujadism has survived as a symbol and political concept long after Pierre Poujade and his organization have faded into history. Like "rank-and-file *fascism" in Germany and Austria and *populism in the United States, Poujadism defines the political mobilization of the self-employed lower middle class, caught between the organized working class, on one hand, and the *gros* (the dominant social elites), on the other. It also defines a coalition of voters from across the political spectrum, united more by protest and anger against change than by support for the specifics of the program elaborated by Poujade and his collaborators.

In the 1990s the Front National (usually considered to represent the extreme Right) has attracted an electorate that is sometimes referred to as Poujadist. Like Poujadism, it has drawn a popular following from many people who had previously voted for the Left and from voters whose attitudes toward key social issues (religion and birth control, for example) might be termed leftist. And as in the case of Poujadism, electoral support for the Front National rose rapidly (this time in the 1980s) and has been more unstable than support for more established parties. The comparison is only approximate, however. Voters for the Front National (about the same percentage of the electorate that voted for the UFF) are disproportionately from big cities, not small towns, and, in addition to shopkeepers and artisans, the party has attracted a disproportionately large number of factory and clerical workers. Moreover, these voters are not especially concerned with taxes or modernization of the economy. What concerns them and unites them most are two issues: fear of crime and fear of immigrants.

What links this party most with Poujadism is not the electoral coalition but its authoritarian, demagogic, and unstable leadership, in the person of Jean-Marie Le Pen. Like Poujade, Le Pen mobilizes his followers with violent verbal attacks on "the gang of four" (the leaders of the established parties) and immigrants, all of whom are "betraying" the real France. Like the Poujadist movement, the Front National can also be seen as a protest movement by vulnerable voters against a perceived danger ignored by established political leadership. What clearly differentiates the Front National from Poujadism, however, is that it has succeeded in sinking organizational roots, has begun to develop a stable electoral following, and has remained an electoral force in every election since 1984.

(See also AUTHORITARIANISM; INTERNATIONAL MIGRATION; NEW RIGHT; NEW SOCIAL MOVEMENTS; TAXES AND TAXATION.)

Stanley Hoffmann et al., *Le Mouvement poujade* (Paris, 1956). Pierre-André Taguieff, *Le National populisme* (Paris, 1989).

MARTIN A. SCHAIN

POVERTY. See DEVELOPMENT AND UNDERDEVEL-
OPMENT; EQUALITY AND INEQUALITY; FEMINIZA-
TION OF POVERTY.

POWER. In human behavior and society, and in the
social sciences, the concept of power is very widespread and diverse. It is usually defined as the ability
to get what is wanted, or to produce desired change.
This change may be in physical systems, as when
we dig a hole, drive a car, or make a pot. It may be
change in beliefs, knowledge, or know-how. It may
be change in laws or institutions, organizations,
boundaries, and so on. Power may be enhanced by
the means or instruments of power—tools, machines, weapons, communications, money or purchasing power, the ability to persuade, and so on.
The power to destroy and the power to create are
often allied in a single process. We destroy wheat to
make flour and destroy flour to make bread. Destructive power involves cost; constructive power,
benefit. Destructive power is usually justified on the
grounds that the benefits exceed the costs.

There are a great many varieties of power, each
of which has a dynamic of its own. There is no
standard terminology for classifying the varieties of
power. However, a number of authors apply three
major varieties: One is frequently called "force,"
which usually implies power over other people, as
when a crying child is lifted up and put in a crib, a
criminal is sent to prison or executed, or a city in
an enemy country is bombed. There is a distinction
here perhaps between force as restraint, as in the
case of the child, and force as victimization, out of
fear, hatred, or contempt for the victim. Force is
associated strongly with threat power, which consists of A saying to B, "You do something I want
or I'll do something you don't want." This is usually
associated with political structures such as governments. The dynamic that results from the threat can
be very complex and depends on the reaction of the
threatened and the counterreactions of the threatener. The threatened may submit, as when we pay our
income tax or, occasionally, obey a speed limit.

A second possibility is defiance on the part of the
threatened. This puts the system back in the hands
of the threatener as to whether to carry out the
threat. This is often expensive, and threats are frequently bluffs. A defied threat may collapse. If the
threat is carried out, the threatener also tends to be
injured.

A third possibility is flight on the part of the
threatened, for the power of a threatener always
declines as the distance from the threatener increases
because of some cost of transport. Decline in the
cost of transport of threats in the form of destructive
power, as we have seen dramatically in the twentieth
century, can profoundly affect the institutions that
rest on threat. Flight from threat probably counts
for a good deal of the expansion of the human race
around the globe.

A fourth possibility is counterthreat, when B says
to A, "If you do something nasty to me, I'll do
something nasty to you." This can lead into *arms
races and to mutual *deterrence. Mutual deterrence,
however, can only be stable in the short run. It must
have some positive probability of breaking down or
it will not deter. Living under mutual deterrence,
therefore, is rather like living in a floodplain with a
positive probability each year of a flood. There is
some evidence that prenuclear deterrence in the
modern world had a probability of breaking down
of about three to five percent per annum. The five
wars of the United States in the twentieth century
illustrate this principle rather well. A fifth response
to threat might be described as disarming behavior
on the part of the threatened: communications which
appeal to the potential community of the threatened
and the threatener. Even submission can be part of
this process, as when we pay our tax and vote out
a government that imposed it.

Surrounding the system of threat power, and sharing complex interactions with it, is a system of
economic power. This can perhaps best be defined
as that which the rich have more of than the poor.
The total of economic power in a society or in the
world is measured roughly by aggregates like the
gross national product or the gross world product.
This is a very imperfect measure, as it neglects
household production and includes the war industry,
which produces very little civilian benefit. The distribution of economic power among individuals,
groups, and nations is the result of a long historical
process that includes a certain amount of threat
power in terms of stealing other people's property,
but on the whole depends mainly on the differential
increases in productivity. Exploitation that rests on
the use of threat power only accounts for a small
proportion of the growth of riches of the rich, which
is mainly the result of a learning process such as
that which has enabled the rich countries to feed
themselves with a much smaller proportion of the
labor force than was required 200 years ago. There
is a good deal of evidence, at least from the middle
of the nineteenth century on, that the imperial powers in Europe sharply reduced their own internal
rate of economic development as a result of the
resources expended on empires and that nonimperial
countries like Denmark and Sweden got richer at a
much faster rate by devoting more of their resources
to the internal learning process.

The third form of power goes by many names. It
is the power of *legitimacy, loyalty, affection, community, identity, and so on. In the long run this
seems to be the dominant form of power, to which
perhaps can be given the name "integrative power."
Without widespread legitimacy, neither threat power
nor economic power can be very effective. In the
communist countries, the financial markets lost their
legitimacy for many decades but now seem to be
recovering it. Without legitimacy, these markets could

not function. Threat without legitimacy is also very ineffective. It is hard to get rich by mugging or by winning wars. Military defeat often leads to cultural and economic expansion, as in Paris after 1871, or in Christian Europe after the victory of the Turks in 1453. China seems always to have prospered after being conquered and to have had a remarkable capacity for turning its conquerors into Chinese. It is a very short-run view, therefore, that looks at threat and force as the ultimate form of power, although there are situations in which it is important, particularly when it is allied with integrative power, as in the case of the initial expansion of Islam.

From the middle of the nineteenth century on, we have seen a remarkable rise in the area of stable peace among independent nations, beginning perhaps with Scandinavia after the Danish defeat by the Germans in 1864. It spread to North America by the 1870s, to Japan, Australia, and the rest of Europe after World War II. This involves the abandonment of military threat as a means of changing frontiers and a reasonable restraint on the power to intervene in other people's affairs.

An interesting development of the twentieth century has been the rise of the power of organized nonviolence in achieving political change, most dramatically, of course, with *Gandhi in India, but also as we saw in Eastern Europe in 1989. This is a complex phenomenon, but it does appeal to the development of "positive-sum games," a dynamic in which both parties benefit. Economic power also rests very much on the principle that exchange is a positive-sum game, especially in competitive markets, although in monopolistic situations there may be recourse to threat and bargaining.

It is a curious irony that improvement in the means of destruction has often diminished the power of threat. It was the invention of the effective cannon that made the feudal castle and the city wall obsolete and created the nation-state, with its relatively widespread areas of internal peace. Similarly, the nuclear weapon and the long-range missile have probably done for the nation-state what gunpowder did for the feudal baron. Reliance on threat power may destroy it; the development of integrative power in the form of stable peace and a world community may save it. The more we appreciate the complexity of the concept of power, the better chance we have for survival.

(See also NINETEEN EIGHTY-NINE; NONVIOLENT ACTION.)

Dennis Wrong, *Power: Its Forms, Bases, and Uses* (New York, 1980). John Kenneth Galbraith, *The Anatomy of Power* (Boston, 1983). Kenneth E. Boulding, *Three Faces of Power* (Newbury Park, Calif., 1989).

KENNETH E. BOULDING

PRAGUE SPRING. Until *Gorbachev's *perestroika the Prague Spring was the most important Communist Party–led reform aimed at creating a democratic and pluralist socialism. The fact that this peaceful attempt at "within-system" reform came in *Czechoslovakia had much to do with the relatively deep roots of *socialism in that society, by comparison with the rest of Eastern and *Central Europe, as well as with the absence of strong anti-Soviet *nationalism.

The movement for radical change stemmed from a combination of economic and political factors. Economic performance began seriously to falter in the early 1960s when production actually declined. This fueled pressure for a decentralizing and marketizing economic reform that was introduced in 1967 as the New Economic System. As this fell short of what the economic reformers, led by Ota Šik, thought necessary, they lent their weight to the demands of the creative intelligentsia for political change, voiced at the writers' congress in June 1967. WIthin the Communist Party grievances focused on Antonín Novotný who was replaced in January 1968 as first secretary by Alexander Dubček.

A moderate Slovak party official, against whom nobody, notably Moscow, had any objections, Dubček found himself heading a motley coalition united only by opposition to Novotný and including conservatives such as Vasil Bilák as well as reformers like Josef Smrkovský. The reformers successfully encouraged what would now be called glasnost to magnify calls for the removal of conservatives from power, which hastened the replacement in March of Novotný as president (his state post) by Ludvík Svoboda. Taking advantage of the relaxation of censorship and police controls, intellectuals and students demanded more rapid and far-reaching democratization than the Dubček leadership, hampered by a largely conservative party central committee, anxious allies in Moscow, East Berlin, and Warsaw, and its own notions of acceptable reform, was able to provide. The party's action program, published in April, set out a somewhat more enlightened system of Communist Party rule. More radical political reform was outlined in theses prepared by a central committee team headed by Zdeněk Mlynář; these were to be submitted to the Fourteenth Party Congress, which was preempted by the Soviet invasion and held clandestinely in August. These proposals envisaged a staged transition to a more constitutional and pluralistic system in which a more democratic Communist Party might, within a decade, share power with interest organizations rather than compete on an equal basis with opposition parties.

Growing differences between the party leadership and radical, mainly non-Communist, groups centered on the distinction between the kind of gradual democratization allowing for oppositional activity the party advocated and the competitive democracy seen as vital by the radicals. Václav *Havel, for instance, called for the creation of a democratic party based on a national moral revival, something he helped bring about in 1989. In 1968 political activity was more fragmented, with the reinvigoration of the small non-Communist parties, the revival of the social democrats, and the establishment of quasi-political clubs, such as K231 (former political prisoners) and KAN (a non-party pressure group). Seeing the need by June for more forceful civic action, a group of intellectuals signed the 2,000 Words declaration, a clarion call to the grass roots to organize themselves, help oust the conservative officials still dominating party and government, and pressure the leadership for radical institutional change. The Dubček leadership found itself squeezed between the Scylla of public pressure for faster change and the Charybdis of domestic conservative resistance supplemented by warnings from East European and Soviet allies. Following a collective *Warsaw Treaty Organization (Warsaw Pact) ultimatum in June, the Czechoslovak party leaders, under pressure at meetings in Čierna nad Tisou (July) and Bratislava (August), made pledges to curtail democratization that they found difficult to fulfill. In retrospect some, like Mylnář, have argued that had tougher restraints been imposed, Soviet intervention might have been avoided.

The Soviet politburo, after much hesitation, decided that Dubček could not control the growing tide of radical reform, which was acquiring revolutionary proportions. Apart from their concerns about the Prague Spring setting up an alternative and attractive model of democratic and humane socialism, the Soviet leaders viewed with alarm the weakening of security links and military links. At a time when it was reversing reform at home, the Brezhnev leadership was averse to running even the slightest risk of Czechoslovak change spilling over into the western republics of the Soviet Union. While the 500,000 Warsaw Pact troops encountered no more than demonstrations, the invasion of 20 August 1968 failed to install a "workers' " government. The partial restoration of censorship did not extinguish reform: spurred by nationalist sentiment, workers started to give more active support to the "renewal" of political life, as the reforms were commonly termed. October saw the establishment of a federation of Czech and Slovak republics, a goal that had preoccupied Slovak attention in preceding months. As protest against the invasion, notably the self-immolation of Jan Palach, continued into 1969, Dubček was replaced in April as first secretary by Gustáv Husák, a Slovak politician with a moderately reformist reputation. Early hopes that he might emulate Hungary's János Kádár and renew change after restoring order went unfulfilled as the policy of "normalization" purged 500,000 Communists and ushered in two decades of moral and economic decay that bankrupted the chances of party-led reform. It was by human rights groups such as *Charter 77, which gave birth to Civic Forum, that society

was finally mobilized in November 1989 to carry through a peaceful *revolution that saw the Prague Spring as a proud symbol of free speech—Dubček became chair of the federal parliament—but an outdated political model. The most significant impact of 1968 was felt within the group of reform-minded members of the party establishment in the Soviet Union. It was from the Prague Spring that Gorbachev and his associates drew many of their ideas of democratization and from the invasion and its aftermath that they largely derived their determination not to use force in Eastern and Central Europe, a decision that made possible the *annus mirabilis* of 1989.

(See also COMMUNIST PARTY STATES; NINETEEN EIGHTY-NINE; SOVIET–EAST EUROPEAN RELATIONS.)

Galia Golan, *The Czechoslovak Reform Movement* (Cambridge, U.K., 1971). H. Gordon Skilling, *Czechoslovakia's Interrupted Revolution* (Princeton, N.J., 1976).

ALEX PRAVDA

PREBISCH, Raúl. Economist, policymaker, and diplomat, Raúl Prebisch (1901–1986) was among the most influential Latin Americans of the century. Prebisch had a major impact on Argentina, as the first director of the nation's central bank; on the region, as executive secretary of the UN Economic Commission for Latin America (ECLA; later the *Economic Commission for Latin America and the Caribbean, or ECLAC); on the *Third World as a whole, as the first director of the UN Conference on Trade and Development (UNCTAD); and globally, as a founder of development economics. In the postwar era, Prebisch's thesis on unequal exchange between "center" and "periphery"—his term for the industrial West and the primary-exporting Third World—has achieved wide recognition, if not universal acceptance, as the hallmark of the structuralist school of economics.

Born in Tucumán, Argentina, in 1901, Prebisch studied at the University of Buenos Aires. As a young economist, he gained favor with Argentina's political establishment, and led the country's new central bank from 1935 to 1943. The perceived inadequacy of neoclassical economics during the Great Depression of the 1930s led him to *Keynesianism, and then to his own center-periphery thesis on the world economy, developed between 1944 and 1949. Prebisch's instrument for elaborating, testing, and propagating his ideas was ECLA, which he directed from 1950 to 1962.

His first and most famous thesis appeared in *The Economic Development of Latin America and Its Principal Problems* (Spanish ed., 1949). Here he sought to explain the secular deterioration of the relative prices of primary goods in the world market. Prebisch argued that long-term productivity gains were greater and diffused more readily in industrial than in primary activities. If prices of industrial goods had fallen, Prebisch held, the effects of technical progress would have spread over the entire center-periphery system, and the terms of trade for agricultural and mineral goods would have improved. They did not do so, Prebisch asserted, because during the upswing of the business cycle, the center's working class absorbs real economic gains, but wage contracts make industrial prices "sticky" during the downswing. Because workers are poorly organized in the periphery (especially in agriculture), the periphery absorbs more of the system's income contraction during recession. (Although the terms-of-trade argument remains highly controversial today, econometric evidence of the last decade has tended to confirm secular deterioration.) Finally, Prebisch pointed to the center's monopolistic pricing of industrial goods as a cause of unequal exchange.

In the *Economic Survey of Latin America: 1949,* Prebisch further elaborated his thesis. An underlying cause of the deterioration in terms of trade was the creation of a surplus labor supply, as modern technique partially transformed the largely agricultural, precapitalist, and low-productivity sector of the periphery's economy. Such labor put downward pressure on wages and therefore on agricultural prices. For Prebisch, the very definition of "underdevelopment" was the heterogeneity of productivities.

Another reason for deterioration was that, with world income rising, the periphery demanded more industrial goods while the center wanted fewer primary goods as proportions of their total incomes. (H. W. Singer independently developed a similar thesis.) For Prebisch, a related problem was the periphery's high propensity to import, partly caused by income concentration, contributing to a perennial *balance-of-payments problem.

Thus Prebisch's analysis pointed to three negative features in the periphery's economy: structural unemployment, external disequilibrium, and deteriorating terms of trade—all of which a properly implemented policy of industrialization would help eliminate. Traditional export activities could be "taxed" for industrial development through state-directed exchange and commercial policies.

The *Economic Survey* was a point of departure for a "structuralist" school of development studies that would emphasize macroeconomics, the foreign exchange constraint, the role of the state, interdisciplinary approaches, and historical (transcyclical) changes. One such study was *Towards a Dynamic Development Policy for Latin America* (1963), in which Prebisch treated hitherto-subordinated social issues. He now called for reforms in agrarian structure and income distribution and pointed to structural problems whose recognition anticipated *dependency theory: First, income concentration in Latin America was accompanying industrialization; second, manufacturing was becoming more capital-intensive, owing to elite consumption patterns, and

consequently was absorbing less labor than anticipated.

Prebisch's work at ECLA ranged far beyond his theoretical contributions. He promoted Latin American economic integration and the creation of UNCTAD, of which he was appointed first director. During his years at UNCTAD (1964–1969), Prebisch traveled the globe, propagating his ideas on unequal exchange and seeking commodity price agreements between central and peripheral countries. Subsequently Prebisch returned to ECLA, where he remained an active theorist, policy advisor, and advocate for Third World interests until his death in 1986.

Prebisch's most important later book was *Peripheral Capitalism* (1981), which can be associated with the non-Marxist version of the "dependency" tradition. He now argued that the structural features of peripheral countries prevented the full development of capitalism owing to the large and growing share of income appropriated by the center-emulating privileged classes; unequal exchange with industrial countries; and "power relations" between center and periphery (and within the periphery).

(See also IMPORT-SUBSTITUTION INDUSTRIALIZATION; UNITED NATIONS CONFERENCE ON TRADE AND DEVELOPMENT.)

United Nations Economic Commission for Latin America, *The Economic Development of Latin America and Its Principal Problems* (Lake Success, N.Y., 1950). Raúl Prebisch, *Capitalismo periférico: Crisis y transformación* (Mexico City, 1981). Raúl Prebisch, "Five Stages in My Thinking on Development," in Gerald M. Meier and Dudley Seers, eds., *Pioneers in Development* (New York, 1984), 175–192.

JOSEPH L. LOVE

PRESIDENCY, U.S. Henry Jones Ford, in his classic 1898 work *The Rise and Growth of American Government,* quoted Alexander Hamilton's prediction to a friend that the time would "assuredly come when every vital question of the state will be merged in the question, 'Who shall be the next president?' " Ford cited this remark to support his argument that, in creating the presidency, the Constitutional Convention of 1787 had "revived the oldest political institution of the race, the elective kingship."

Although there is much truth in Ford's evaluation of the U.S. presidency, it also displays a certain measure of ambivalence on a fundamental issue. Is the presidency best understood as primarily a person ("Who shall be the next president?") or an office (an "elective kingship")?

Political scientists in the twentieth century have continued to grapple with Ford's conundrum but have not resolved it. The majority probably would agree that the best answer to the person-or-office question is both: person and office, president and presidency. The office has become important mostly because its constitutional design suited it well for national leadership in the changing circumstances of history. But because the U.S. Constitution invested so much responsibility in the person who is president, that person's background, personality, and leadership skills are also consequential.

Office. The Constitutional Convention created a government marked not by *separation of powers (the traditional formulation) but rather, in the political scientist Richard Neustadt's apt phrase, by "separated institutions sharing powers." Institutional separation meant, for example, that in stark contrast to political systems based on *parliamentary democracy, which draw their executive leadership from the legislature, the president was forbidden by Article I, Section 6, of the Constitution to appoint any sitting member of Congress to the cabinet or White House staff. These severely separated branches were, however, constitutionally enjoined to share in the exercise of virtually all the powers of the national government—the president is "Commander in Chief of the Army and Navy," but Congress has the power to "declare *war"; Congress is empowered to "make all laws," but the president may veto them, or more energetically, may propose "such Measures as he shall judge necessary and expedient"; the Senate may (or may choose not to) give "Advice and Consent" concerning presidential appointments to the executive branch and the judiciary; and so on.

Powers, of course, do not define power—over time the presidency has become increasingly powerful even though the formal powers of the office have remained the same. A second cluster of constitutional decisions, those concerning the number and selection of the executive, provides much of the explanation for the presidency's expanding influence. The framers of the Constitution, after much debate, created the presidency as a one-person, not a plural or committee-style, office and provided that the president would be elected by the entire nation, independent of Congress and the state governments. In doing so, they made the president the only national officer who can plausibly claim both a political mandate to speak for the people and their government and an institutional capacity to lead with what the Pennsylvania delegate James Wilson described as "energy, unity, and responsibility."

Lead, that is, when national leadership is sought, which, during the nineteenth century, it usually was not. Historically, it took a century and a quarter—from 1789 to 1913—for parchment to become practice, that is, for all of the constitutionally enumerated powers of the presidency to come to life. Treaty making and other matters of foreign affairs aside—who but the president could represent the *United States to other nations or lead it into war?—Congress seized the lion's share of the government's shared powers nearly from the beginning, dominating even the executive appointment process. When

it came to legislation, members of Congress treated with scorn most early presidential efforts to recommend or influence their consideration of bills and resolutions; nor, until Andrew Jackson in the 1830s, were presidents able to exercise the veto power without provoking a politically disabling storm of wrath on Capitol Hill.

Presidential disempowerment was, if long-lived, temporary, the logical consequence of the condition of weak national government that generally prevailed during the nineteenth century. The country, then a congeries of local economies and cultures, was not seeking what the presidential office was constitutionally designed to offer, namely, energetic leadership in behalf of national initiatives. But the conditions that sustained weak government began to change around the turn of the century. The broad extension of railroads and telegraph lines made all but inevitable the development of a national economy, and with this transformation came demands that the national government take measures variously to facilitate the spread and to tame the excesses of massive corporations. Early-twentieth-century presidents Theodore Roosevelt and Woodrow Wilson roused a popular mandate for the president to make full use of the office's constitutional powers to lead Congress and the executive branch. Franklin D. *Roosevelt, during the Great Depression of the 1930s, and more recent presidents such as Lyndon B. *Johnson and Ronald *Reagan also have played the role of chief legislator on a grand scale. The post–World War II rise of the United States to *superpower status in a then-bipolar, now-unipolar international system lifted the presidency to center stage not just in Washington but the world.

Person. Because the presidency is important, so is the person who is the president. What background characteristics do presidents typically acquire before taking office? What manners of personality? What skills of leadership?

As to background, presidents almost always have been drawn from the ranks of white, male, married Christians who already have held high governmental office. Women, African Americans, Jews, bachelors, even nationally prominent leaders from the realms of business, education, and elsewhere in the private sector have found it hard to rouse serious interest in their potential presidential candidacies. Recent historical trends indicate both an expansion (in social terms) and a contraction (in occupational terms) of the talent pool from which Americans choose their presidents. Until John F. *Kennedy's election in 1960, for example, Roman Catholics were effectively excluded from consideration; so, until Reagan was elected in 1980, were divorced men. *Public opinion surveys indicate a growing willingness among voters to select a black, female, or Jewish president. Yet the rosters of presidential candidates in recent elections have been composed almost entirely of sitting or former senators, governors, and vice presidents.

The personality, or psychological character, that a president brings to the White House is, considering the power of the office and the pressures that weigh upon its occupant, of obvious importance. Public interest in former Senator Gary Hart's sexual behavior, Senator Joseph Biden's plagiarism, Senator Robert Dole's temper, and the purported "wimpiness" of nominees George *Bush and Michael Dukakis in the 1988 presidential election illustrates the widespread concern about presidential character. So do the efforts of James David Barber and other political scientists to develop behavioral models that relate presidential personality to presidential performance. Regrettably, however, scholarly understanding of this matter has not kept pace with public concern. Personality theory is still too murky a field to explain, much less predict, presidential character.

The skills of leadership that a president requires may be more confidently described. In relations with the rest of the executive branch, the president is called upon to be a talented manager of authority, both of lieutenants on the White House staff (whose chronic sycophancy toward the president and hostility toward the president's critics perennially threaten to overwhelm the good effects of their loyalty, talent, and hard work) and of the massive departments and agencies of the bureaucracy, whose activities lie at the heart of the president's role as chief executive.

Presidential leadership of Congress requires different, more tactical political skills. Senators and representatives, no less than the president, are politically independent and self-interested. No one has described the challenge of leading them more precisely and pithily than Neustadt: to lead is to persuade, to persuade is to bargain, and to bargain is to convince individual members of Congress that their interests and the president's are (or can be made to be) the same.

Ultimately, a president's standing with Congress and the bureaucracy rests on the bedrock of public opinion, which makes the "presentation of self" (a phrase invented by the sociologist Erving Goffman) to the American people an important cluster of leadership skills. Presentation of self involves not just speechmaking, press conferences, and other forms of rhetoric, but dramaturgy as well. During Richard *Nixon's first term, for example, he reinforced a televised speech appealing for the support of the "silent majority" of blue-collar workers and their families by dramatically donning a hard hat before a cheering crowd (and a battery of observing cameras) at a New York construction site.

Perhaps a president's most important leadership skills involve a strategic sense of the historical possibilities of the time. These possibilities are defined both by objective conditions (such as the international situation, the budget, and the health of the economy) and by the public mood. Above all, the president must have a highly developed aptitude for what Woodrow Wilson called "interpretation"— that is, the ability to understand and articulate the varying, vaguely expressed desires of the American people for change or quiescence, material reward or moral challenge, isolation from or intervention in the problems of the world, and so on.

In the end, the background, personality, and leadership skills of the president are important because of the ways in which the Constitution and changing historical circumstances have made the presidency important. Person and office, although defined and often discussed separately, are in essence one.

(See also BUREAUCRATIC POLITICS; CARTER, JIMMY; CONGRESS, U.S.; CONSTITUTION; EISENHOWER, DWIGHT D.; INTERNATIONAL SYSTEMS; PSYCHOLOGY AND POLITICS; SUPREME COURT OF THE UNITED STATES; TRUMAN, HARRY S.)

Richard E. Neustadt, *Presidential Power* (New York, 1960). James David Barber, *The Presidential Character: Predicting Performance in the White House* (Englewood Cliffs, N.J., 1972). Erwin C. Hargrove and Michael Nelson, *Presidents, Politics, and Policy* (Baltimore and New York, 1984). Michael Nelson, ed., *The Presidency and the Political System* (Washington, D.C., 1984). Sidney M. Milkis and Michael Nelson, *The American Presidency: Origins and Development, 1776–1990* (Washington, D.C., 1990).

MICHAEL NELSON

PRISONERS' DILEMMA. See GAME THEORY; INTERDEPENDENCE.

PRIVATIZATION. The intersection of politics and privatization is volatile. When we analyze privatization in a global political perspective, we see that, far from being technical and narrow, it is political and broad. At its core "privatization" means shifting property and ownership rights from one party to another. It means taking property and power from civil servants and politicians and transferring it to local or foreign businessmen. Adam Smith, Karl *Marx, and many subsequent political theorists agree that property and the exercise of political power are intimately linked. The global process of privatization confirms this relationship. But if it is important for social scientists to understand privatization in the broad context of political economy, mastery of the the technical details of privatization is equally important. With both, one is properly prepared to account for and analyze its truly global incidence in the 1990s.

By privatization we mean a decrease in state ownership and/or state management and control of economic units. These two main aspects, ownership and control, often go together in privatization exercises, but not always. Government may choose to retain state ownership while contracting the management of the enterprise to a private company, as often happens with hotels. Alternatively, government may reduce its ownership and its management controls. Privatization typically means cutting back public corporations (also called public enterprises or *parastatals). Conversely, privatization encourages an increase in private ownership and control and a greater reliance on managers in private firms to make decisions about investment, production, distribution, and consumption. Although privatization has been used as an ideologically charged instrument by partisan political interests (as with Ronald *Reagan in the United States and Margaret *Thatcher in Britain), it is best understood, and most widely used, as an economic policy instrument like fiscal, monetary, or industrial policy. During the 1980s it lost much of its heavy ideological content as many governments, pressed by external debt problems, falling international markets, cutthroat competition, and domestic demands to improve public services, turned to privatization as one part of a national reform agenda. Some embraced privatization enthusiastically, others reluctantly, but by 1990 it was widely used in scores of countries.

Privatization can be understood in terms of its goals and its modalities. It has been used to increase economic efficiency and competitiveness; to reduce the burden of inefficient public enterprises; to restructure enterprises and the national economies; to attract foreign investment; and to satisfy the demands of multilateral lenders like the *World Bank or the *International Monetary Fund. Specific modalities used to implement privatization include the sale of state company shares through the stock market; private placements and competitive bidding for shares; sale of public enterprise assets; management contracts or leases; sale to employees or management; and outright liquidation. A government's choice of modality is shaped by the particular institutional, social, political, and economic conditions prevailing in the country, and by the goals the government wants to achieve. Furthermore, each modality tends to have particular strengths and weakness. For example, stock market sales of enterprise shares are relatively transparent, speedy, and can be used to encourage widespread share ownership. On the other hand, many less developed countries (LDCs) lack stock exchanges altogether. Furthermore, most exchanges have rules requiring companies quoted there to produce annual reports and to meet minimal performance standards that exclude the most inefficient and badly managed public enterprises. Competitive bidding and private sales are means of avoiding these problems. Being less transparent, however, they invite favoritism and abuse. They may also concentrate ownership in private hands in ways that undermine both efficiency and equity considerations. Rapid-fire private sales in Hungary in 1989 permitted well-placed public officials and Hungarian business elites to profit unfairly from privatization. Employee Stock Option Plans (ESOPs) are popular politically but often difficult to implement.

Privatization should be distinguished from other reforms that are similar or often used in conjunction with it. At the microeconomic level, public enterprise rehabilitation, restructuring, or commercialization are all policies that retain government ownership but seek to make public enterprises more efficient through improved management incentives, streamlined enterprise-government relations, and market-based pricing criteria. However, neither public ownership nor public management is reduced. At the macroeconomic level are policies that liberalize the strategic environment in which the privatized enterprises operate—general price deregulations, opening the economy to foreign competition, demonopolization, and so forth. These steps reduce barriers to entry and exit. Experience has shown that privatization works best when combined with these and other ways to free the market and promote competition. Without them, the process risks transforming public monopolies into private ones, with no increases in social welfare.

Privatization around the world occurs as a bumpy, protracted, and complicated process that is as politically sensitive as it is technically complicated. It is especially sensitive where the public-private division coincides with regional, ethnic, and religious cleavages. For example, northern Nigeria is populated by Muslim Hausa-Fulani who are relatively uninvolved in the modern market economy but relatively powerful in the civil service. Privatization is interpreted by some northerners as transferring power out of their region, tribe, and religious group. Privatization for the average Polish citizen may mean the sale of national assets to the nation's traditional antagonists, the Germans, or to politically connected party apparatchiks. Some multiethnic societies like Malaysia try to address this problem by specifying that, for example, the "target of ownership restructuring . . . is to have at least 30% Bumiputera (indigenous Malay) ownership, 40% other Malaysians, and 30% foreign interest by 1990" (Guy Pfeffermann, *Private Business in Developing Countries,* Washington, D.C., 1988).

Privatization can vary markedly in different regions of the world. In Africa, privatization, defined as actual public-to-private transfer of assets, has been slow and halting. It has been most seriously tried in West African countries like Nigeria and Côte d'Ivoire, which formally privatized about thirty enterprises each. In Asia, Singapore (thirteen privatizations, including public offering of shares of Singapore Airlines), Malaysia (eleven, including airline offerings) and Korea (eight, also including an airline) have been active. The Chilean government privatized many recently nationalized firms, and Brazil and Mexico moved slowly if steadily to privatize enterprises. In Europe, we saw early and consistent changes in Britain under Margaret Thatcher—British Aerospace (1981), Cable and Wireless (1982), British Oil (1982), British Telecom (1984), British Gas (1986), and Rolls-Royce (1987). Some subsequent flotations have been more difficult. France reduced state holdings in several sectors including industry (St. Gobain), oil (Elf Aquitaine) and banking (Banque Nationale de Paris, Paribas, Crédit Commercial de France).

It is generally agreed the gravest challenges ahead lie in Eastern and *Central Europe. Britain took a decade to reduce a state sector that accounted for only about 10 percent of its GNP; Poland, with around 8,700 state enterprises, and with no stock exchange or private banking system or other market infrastructures, hoped to achieve substantial reductions in far less time. Hungary, with a new privatization process launched in 1988, saw 1,600 new companies created out of existing state assets in 1988–1989. The Soviet Union began to permit "cooperatives" to compete with state enterprises, sometimes using "privatized" state assets. In Russia as in Poland, there remained profound political opposition to privatization, even as post-Soviet Russia embraced privatization and the market system in the *Yeltsin era.

Future attention should be directed toward assessments of the microeconomic and macroeconomic impacts of privatization programs in operation, as well as toward their impacts on social equity and political power. Privatization, like all controversial policies, requires strong leadership and consensus building if it is to be implemented and sustained. It remains an open question whether in Poland, Russia (and the other Soviet successor states), and China these necessary political components are in place. If privatization is shaped by the structure of politics, it also may in turn reshape the structure of politics and power. Privatization has everywhere meant new patterns of winners and losers. Where the potential losers (managers of public enterprises, civil servants, unions, and subsidized consumers) are powerful, they can substantially block it; where potential losers can be overridden or bought off, privatization has proceeded. The conventional wisdom, probably accurate, is that when used pragmatically privatization is one policy among several that can be used to promote economic reform, and as such is not an end in itself. The concomitant shifts in political and social power provide a rich laboratory for future social science research.

(See also THATCHERISM.)

ERNEST J. WILSON III

PROGRESSIVE MOVEMENT, U.S. Progressivism was a political movement that was not contained within any one party or organization. Its adherents were reformers who opposed the patronage-based *political machines that dominated many levels of government in the *United States. Progressives also shared a vision of a political community in which civically educated citizens were not divided by enduring *class, ethnic, or party conflicts, but by temporary, well-informed disagreements on public issues. Such a diffuse movement cannot be precisely dated, but progressivism had its greatest impact between the election of 1896 and U.S. entry into *World War I in 1917. Competing interpretations of the Progressive movement have portrayed it as a native-stock reaction to new immigrant groups, as a pro-capitalist alternative to agrarian populism and working-class socialism, as an ideology influenced by Protestant social activism, or as a manifestation of larger processes of *modernization and professionalization.

Progressivism moved from local to state to national government as individual leaders sought higher office. Support for Progressive candidates sometimes followed earlier class and ethnic divisions, and sometimes created new coalitions. Local Progressives were most successful when they could bring together machine opponents from different social classes and ethnic groups. A new conception of efficiency, which encompassed effective service provision as well as elimination of corruption, displaced the older reform ideal of "good government," which often meant government from which non-Anglo-Saxon or working-class politicians had been removed. Tom Johnson and Newton Baker (Cleveland), Hazen Pingree (Detroit), and Brand Whitlock (Toledo) were among the most enduring Progressive mayors. John Purroy Mitchel (New York) and George Alexander (Los Angeles) were more briefly successful.

At the state level, Progressives organized against what they believed were exploitative economic interests; opposition to the railroads was particularly important in the Midwest and West. Robert La Follette (Wisconsin) and Hiram Johnson (California) built farm-labor alliances to become governors of their states, and then U.S. senators. Charles Evans Hughes was elected governor of New York after leading an investigation into insurance company abuses.

Progressivism created chaos in national politics, but ultimately little was changed. In 1912, former President Theodore Roosevelt organized the Progressive Party after he lost the Republican nomination to incumbent William Howard Taft. The Republican split allowed Democrat Woodrow Wilson to win the election with a minority of the popular vote. Though Roosevelt's party claimed the label, all three candidates could be considered Progressives. In 1916, Roosevelt returned to the Republican Party, frustrating the hopes of the most radical Progressives for a new politics pitting a single Progressive Party against a single conservative party. Most Progressives followed Roosevelt and supported Charles Evans Hughes, the Republican nominee, but an estimated twenty percent, including leaders of the radical faction, supported Wilson as he won reelection. By 1920, the national Republican majority of 1896–1908 was restored. Progressivism had a more enduring impact on the House of Representatives: a 1910 revolt against Speaker Joseph G. Cannon by Republican Progressives produced decentralization as authority shifted from the Speaker of the House to committees.

World War I disrupted Progressive politics, exacerbating ethnic conflicts that Progressive coalitions had often cut across. Progressive coalitions in some cities and states survived the effects of war; in others, Progressive innovations were adopted by the party organizations they had displaced. In national politics, progressivism became more exclusively the movement of insurgent Republicans from the Midwest and West, who fought their party's dominant Eastern wing over the tariff and other issues. Robert La Follette, the leader of this faction, received seventeen percent of the popular vote as the Progressive Party candidate for president in 1924. Progressive ideas were among the many strains contributing to Franklin *Roosevelt's *New Deal, but there was no clear political continuity between the two eras of political change: most surviving Progressive leaders actually opposed Roosevelt's policies as excessively centralist.

Because Progressives disagreed over issues like business regulation, their legacy was less evident in new policies than in new ways of making and administering policies. The New York Bureau of Municipal Research provided a model for new semi-public institutions applying expertise to governmental problems. Progressives also enacted mechanisms to weaken party organizations: the direct primary (allowing voters to choose party candidates), the initiative (allowing voters to propose measures), the referendum (allowing voters to approve measures), and the recall (allowing voters to remove officials). Local antiparty measures included nonpartisan elections, at-large rather than ward-based (district) elections, and, especially in smaller cities, replacement of mayoral systems with government by commission or city manager.

Benjamin Park De Witt, *The Progressive Movement* (1915; Seattle, 1968). William S. Leary, Jr., and Arthur S. Link, *The Progressive Era and the Great War, 1896–1920* (Arlington Heights, Ill., 1978). John D. Buenker and Nicholas C. Burckel, *Progressive Reform* (Detroit, 1980).

KENNETH FINEGOLD

PROPAGANDA. See PSYCHOLOGY AND POLITICS.

PROPORTIONAL REPRESENTATION. Most common in continental Europe, proportional representation is a method of electing representatives in *parliamentary democracies. In the more commonly used list system, the intent is to provide for political parties the same ratio of seats in a parliamentary body that these parties received in an election. For example, if a political party received twenty percent of the vote in an election, under proportional representation this party would receive twenty percent of the seats in the legislative body. The much less widely used Hare system (named for the nineteenth-century British political reformer Thomas Hare) is a complicated mechanism wherein individual candidates can be ranked by the voters in an order of preference.

Proportional representation differs greatly from the nonproportional single-member-district, "first-past-the-post" electoral system used in Britain, the United States, and many other Commonwealth countries. Proportional representation's origins date from the late nineteenth and early twentieth centuries when the proliferation of political parties representing specific groups in continental European societies (nobility, peasants, industrialists, workers, religions) made the Anglo-American system impractical and unfair. For example, if several districts had individual candidates from five different parties and the leading party's candidate received twenty-five percent of the vote in each of them, under the Anglo-American "first-past-the-post" rule, that party would win one hundred percent of the seats with only twenty-five percent of the votes.

The Anglo-American preference for single-member-district, "first-past-the-post" electoral systems derives from the earlier introduction of *democracy, the greater role given to individual representation, and the smaller number of parties in those countries. In fact the relationship between the number of parties and the choice between proportional representation and the Anglo-American system is somewhat of a chicken-and-egg issue. With fewer parties, there is less likelihood of a perceived need for proportional representation. Yet an entrenched single-member-district, "first-past-the-post" system is biased in favor of only two parties and thus makes the effective formation of additional parties inherently more difficult.

Most countries using proportional representation today have the political parties provide a list of candidates so that voters may choose to give their vote to the party that most closely represents their ideological preference. In other words, the party as a collective entity is the primary vehicle for organizing political expression. This system encourages parties to place candidates whom they would most like to see elected near the top of the list, as the candidates are chosen for the legislature on the basis of the proportion of their party's votes that they receive. In multiparty systems, voters often have a wider range of political choices, which often correlates with higher voter participation than in Anglo-American systems. Some countries (Sweden and the Federal Republic of Germany [FRG]) provide a minimum threshold (four percent and five percent, respectively) to prevent the proliferation of a large number of tiny parties. Other countries (Italy and Israel) have minimal (one percent) thresholds, producing large numbers of political parties. There are also variations in how candidates are chosen. For example, the FRG uses a combination of single-member districts and proportional representation, but the allocation of seats in the Bundestag still depends on the proportion of the vote that the parties obtain in the votes by party list.

The primary criticisms of proportional representation by advocates of Anglo-American systems are that there is too great a proliferation of parties and that the formation of working majorities is made more difficult. As the above examples of the threshold provision suggest, however, problems associated with a large number of parties can be avoided by building safeguards into the system.

(See also ELECTIONS AND VOTING BEHAVIOR; POLITICAL PARTIES AND PARTY COMPETITION.)

Seymour Martin Lipset and Stein Rokkan, *Party Systems and Voter Alignments* (New York, 1967).

CHRISTOPHER S. ALLEN

PROSTITUTION. Financial or material compensation for sex may be differentiated as prostitution or may be integrated in relationships such as marriage or dating. A continuum of sexual-economic exchange between women and men is a culturally and historically persistent feature of social organization (Tabet, 1987). Almost exclusively men pay for sex (with money, goods, or other reimbursement) and largely women provide sex; male homosexuals and transvestites also provide sexual service in a minority of cases, but this does not change the gender pattern because, like women, they service men and their role is often feminine. Significantly, those who explicitly provide sex are defined by their activity as "prostitutes," a stigmatized and/or criminalized status, while those who buy sex are neither defined nor branded by engagement in the same activity. Although in principle some laws and attitudes do not privilege male prostitution customers above female prostitution workers, in practice men are rarely penalized or ostracized for buying sex whereas women service providers are labeled social outcasts and legal outlaws (see Frédérique Delacoste and Priscilla Anderson, eds., *Sex Work,* San Francisco, 1987, and Gail Pheterson, *The Whore Stigma,* The Hague, 1986).

The gender imbalance in prostitution has been explained within the general political economy of past and present societies wherein men as a social class are entitled to more money, material resources, sexual license, freedom of movement, and legal rights than are women and wherein women as a class are dependent upon male provisions and protections for survival. A conflicting explanatory paradigm dismisses such material considerations in favor of an essentialist claim that the sexes have inherently different natures which account for female sexual service to male sexual need. This latter position is criticized for ignoring evidence of the social construction of gender and for justifying the exploitation of women by men.

The relation between prostitute and customer is frequently mediated by a third party or establishment. Beginning with ancient societies, third parties have controlled the sexual-economic system for their own social or material benefit by recruiting women and by selling, transporting, or offering them as gifts to (other) men. For many centuries politicians, reformers, and religious and medical authorities have been debating whether the barter in women should be legitimized, prohibited, tolerated, regulated, or abolished. Within those debates the person of the prostitute serves as a symbol of social disorder, immorality, and disease.

Most contemporary societies combine inconsistent approaches to prostitution which both recognize the sex industry, often as a significant source of state revenue, and at the same time punish prostitutes for sexual transactions. In the United States, Canada, Thailand, Britain, France, and Queensland in Australia, laws technically prohibit facilitating or profiting from prostitution but not prostitution itself; in practice, it is prostitutes, more often than third party profiteers, who are pursued and punished under such laws for acts surrounding sex commerce such as renting a room or asking money for sex.

Some governments, such as those of the Federal Republic of Germany, Austria, Switzerland, and Ecuador, place the sex industry under police-controlled state regulations. Prostitution is then legal in certain places under specific conditions and illegal outside those guidelines. Medical authorities have historically advocated regulation in order to legitimize mandatory testing of prostitutes for venereal disease. Others, including some health scholars and activists, strongly oppose regulation; they claim that mandatory health surveillance detects rather than prevents disease, promotes an illusion of protection to customers demanding unsafe sex, and infringes on prostitute rights to medical privacy and choice. Historians have convincingly documented the failure of regulation as a public health measure; see especially Alain Corbin (*Misery and Prostitution in the 19th and 20th Century,* London, 1990), Mary Gibson (*Prostitution and the State in Italy, 1860–1915,* New Brunswick, N.J., 1986), and Judith Walkowitz (*Prostitution and Victorian Society,* Cambridge, U.K., 1980).

Despite certain regulations and prohibitions, some governments operate within a framework of toleration. In the Netherlands, for example, prostitution businesses are widely tolerated although they have been formally illegal for most of the twentieth century. Prostitutes are not persecuted, but they are also not given worker rights because prostitution is not recognized as legitimate employment. It should be noted that whether or not countries prohibit explicit sexual-economic exchanges, they nevertheless tolerate the sexual servicing of men by women within culturally prescribed codes.

Although prostitution is legislated predominantly on national levels, the realities of contemporary sexual economics are increasingly international in character. Since the 1970s there has been a dramatic and unprecedented augmentation of sex commerce between countries. A majority of prostitutes in many Western European cities are currently women from Asia, Africa, and Latin America. Millions of women migrate yearly especially from rural regions in developing countries to escape poverty and abuse. Criminal "trafficking" networks transport women and girls in great numbers from rural to urban areas and from *Third World to industrialized countries for purposes of prostitution (by deceit, by force, or by conscious individual or parental decision). A booming sex tourism provides entertainment to traveling and military men from industrialized countries, a meager income for millions of women, and significant revenue for developing countries. Given the poverty of women throughout the world, prostitution is often women's only work option. (See Thang-Dam Truong, 1990.)

International transactions have augmented not only profits and abuses of the sexual-economic system but also opportunities for self-organization among prostitutes. A political movement of prostitutes was begun in North America and Western Europe in the 1970s, notably by U.S. activist Margo St. James and Swiss activist Grisélidis Réal. By the mid-1980s, prostitutes' *rights advocates on all continents were protesting violence against women and coordinating their efforts in North and South America, Asia, and Africa. The international movement for prostitutes' rights is documented in *A Vindication of the Rights of Whores* (Gail Pheterson, ed., Seattle, 1989). In short, prostitute activists worldwide are claiming the right to the same social and political legitimacy as their customers and the right to decide for themselves how to survive and resist exploitation.

(See also GENDER AND POLITICS; WOMEN AND DEVELOPMENT.)

Paola Tabet, "Du Don au Tarif: Les Relations Sexuelles Impliquant une Compensation" *Les Temps Modernes* 490 (May 1987): 1–53. Gail Pheterson, "The Category 'Prostitute' in Scientific Inquiry" *Journal of Sex Research* 27, no. 3 (August 1990): 397–407. Thang-Dam Truong, *Sex, Money and Morality: The Political Economy of Prostitution and Tourism in South East Asia* (London, 1990).

GAIL PHETERSON

PROTECTION. Government policies that increase the price or decrease the availability of imported goods protect domestic producers. Although many policies can have protective effects, they are generally described as "protectionist" only when protection is intended or the protective effects are significant.

Economic theory prescribes the use of protective measures under some conditions. When a nation is relatively large and wealthy, it may exploit its market power by imposing import or export duties to shift the terms of trade in its favor. If workers are idle, then import restrictions can raise national in-

come, especially if foreign retaliation against exports is not prompt or severe. Strategic trade theory has identified circumstances where protection can be applied to imperfectly competitive industries with beneficial consequences not only for the industry but for the nation as a whole. Some economists have also suggested that protection serves the social value of stability and, in developed countries, raises the incomes of poorly paid workers. However, in the latter case, as well as most other cases where protection is a plausible policy, economists generally argue that intervention is either undesirable or else more efficiently accomplished through other means. For example, a direct wage subsidy for low-wage, import-competing industries would protect the welfare of their workers more efficiently than a tariff, and much more efficiently than quotas or so-called voluntary export restraints.

The actual imposition of protection can seldom be explained in terms of the implementation of these prescriptions. Protection is common in small countries that have negligible market power, and it is common in industries that do not fall within the scope of strategic trade theory. Although world tariff levels have declined substantially in the last twenty years, the least economically efficient forms of protection (quotas and voluntary export restraints) are an increasingly prevalent substitute.

While the economic efficiency of current protective practices is dubious, their political efficacy is not. One must therefore understand protection as a policy that is politically rational, i.e., it maximizes political support for the government in power. Economic conditions are important insofar as they affect the political demand and supply of protection. Models based on such an assumption need not assume that governments are attempting to maximize national income.

Most empirical work on the *political economy of trade policy deals with the inter-industry distribution of protection within a nation. A common approach is to explain variation in protection in terms of variation in political demand, and to argue that the characteristics which make industries strong and effective demanders are unevenly distributed. It is commonly hypothesized that declining import-competing industries which are moderately concentrated, labor-intensive, low-wage, and employ large numbers of workers are better able to achieve protection than industries which are not. Although there is a moderate degree of empirical support for such claims, other factors also have relatively strong effects: current protection is generally a function of previous protection, and it is also a function of reductions in protection offered by other countries in multilateral tariff negotiations.

How one analyzes the dynamics of protection depends on the time horizon one adopts. In the short run, economic resources cannot inexpensively redeploy to different activities. This implies that capital and labor within an industry are likely to take common positions on protective measures. (Labor's interest in protection becomes more producer-oriented as it acquires more bargaining strength and sector-specific skills. This, in addition to increasing exposure to the consequences of international wage disparities due to declines in transport costs and protection, may well account for the historic shift of labor movements in advanced capitalist states toward more protectionist positions.) In the short run the political effects of idle capacity caused by business cycle downturns can be pronounced, particularly in nations that are large and that have geographically concentrated industries. There is also some evidence that inflation reduces protectionist pressures. The business cycle is thus linked to a trade policy cycle so that recession engenders protection and prosperity leads to liberalization. Choices of monetary and fiscal policy therefore shape a government's trade policy choices.

Over a longer period, economic factors redeploy to new sectors, and neoclassical conceptions of factors become more realistic. The Stolper-Samuelson theorem (1941) argues that with two factors of production, the scarce factor in each nation will benefit from protection. If political dynamics followed these lines, commercial policy would invariably be an arena of antagonism between capital and labor: In capital-scarce economies, capital ought to favor protection, whereas under labor scarcity, the reverse should be true. The evidence suggests that capital-scarce nations are considerably more protectionist than nations in which capital is abundant, an asymmetry not easily accommodated within the confines of this theorem or its extensions to politics. (The relative ease of administering a bureaucracy that taxes external trade probably contributes to the heavy reliance on such taxes in poor countries, but this cannot account for their frequent resort to non-tariff barriers that let foreigners capture the rents.)

The extent to which a government can make credible commitments to maintain a policy can also affect the level of protection. When governments cannot change their policies, they have a strong motivation to take into account the distorting effects of factor reallocations induced by protection, but when they are relatively free to alter policies, this incentive is weaker. Thus, "committed" protection tends to be less than discretionary protection. Another way in which entry and exit dynamics affect policy-making is by shaping the nature and duration of protection. If "voluntary" export restraints are used when firms in countries not covered by the restraints face low barriers to entry, then protection will either become chronic and the agreements more and more encompassing and elaborate, or else protection will soon lapse. The outcome depends on the political strength of the domestic producers and the barriers to exit they face. If foreign producers not covered by a restraint agreement face substantial entry barriers, the analysis is similar, except that there is a larger "breathing space" for domestic producers to become more competitive.

Over the long run, factors accumulate within an economy at rates that are affected by national policies and by conditions in the world economy. For nations whose capital-labor ratios are close to the world ratio, differing growth rates of capital and labor imply the possibility that their relative scarcity and hence their trade policy preferences will reverse. Thus, political success can alter the economic conditions that created a winning coalition for a policy.

An entirely different approach to explaining changes in protection over an extended period has been developed by those who offer a *hegemony theory of protection. The gist of their argument is that open trade is a collective good, that the presence of one very large, dominant nation that benefits from openness will enhance prospects for an open global trading system, and that in its absence the prospects for openness are meager. (A variant of this argument is that when international trade is concentrated among a small set of trading nations, the trading system will be open.)

Hegemony theory is superficially attractive, but it possesses several weaknesses. Empirically, the relation between U.S. or U.K. supremacy and trading system openness is weak; in both cases, openness is not closely related to hegemony (or even concentration of capabilities in a small number of nations). The conceptual difficulties are also formidable. Market access is not a public good in two important senses. As the results of multilateral tariff bargaining make clear, nations reduce protection in such a way as to award relatively excludable benefits to those offering reciprocal cuts. In addition, the Soviet Union and other East bloc nations historically have been excluded from the *General Agreement on Tariffs and Trade (GATT) system—owing partly to the U.S. desire to do so. While this exclusion was obviously influenced by national security politics, it also had fewer negative economic consequences for the United States than for some of its allies and economic competitors in Western Europe.

Hegemony theorists have not yet offered a compelling reason why the hegemon should prefer an open trading system. If the hegemon were to forgo levying optimal tariffs in an attempt to get other nations to reduce their own, then other nations also must possess substantial market power, and it is not clear what distinguishes a hegemon from them except its somewhat larger size. On the other hand, if other nations do not possess market power, then their optimal tariff is zero, and they therefore cannot match reductions in the hegemon's optimal tariff with reductions in their own. The hegemonic state would then levy the optimal tariff, and other states would "grin and bear it." The simplest way to motivate the claim that hegemonic nations prefer open trade is to define such nations as capital exporters and then note that they must establish a trading system that permits borrowers to earn enough foreign exchange through exporting to be able to service their international debts.

Efforts to explain differences in the level of protection across nations have been quite limited. Aside from its relation to relative capital scarcity, protection is statistically associated with large land area, plentiful unskilled labor, a high ratio of government expenditures to national income, and low levels of per capita income. Such variables account statistically for about two-thirds of the cross-national variation in tariff rates, but only one-fourth to one-fifth the variation in the ratio of imports to GNP.

Other analysts explain cross-national differences in terms of different national institutions and ideologies. Work in this vein has been limited, and has primarily addressed U.S. commercial policy. These institutional and ideological explanations are often concerned with accounting for *lack* of change—in particular, the continued alleged adherence of the United States to a policy of openness. They suggest that government officials enjoy enough freedom from interest group, party, and public pressure to exercise discretion in their policy choices, but that these choices are also constrained by the institutional forms of national governments and international organizations and law, which change much more slowly than the short-run constellation of interests in civil society. These ideas are plausible, and there is some empirical support for the notion that politicians gratify their private preferences when making policy choices. However, the historical narratives favored by most exponents of this approach are better suited to illustrating the argument than to testing it. Such explanations must also confront the sources of changes in institutions and ideologies in order to explain policy shifts over the long run.

(See also INTERNATIONAL POLITICAL ECONOMY; MERCANTILISM.)

Arye L. Hillman, *The Political Economy of Protection* (New York, 1989). Stephen P. Magee, William A. Brock, and Leslie Young, *Black Hole Tariffs and Endogenous Policy Theory: Political Economy in General Equilibrium* (Cambridge, U.K., 1989). Robert E. Baldwin, ed., *Empirical Studies of Commercial Policy* (Chicago, 1991).

TIMOTHY J. McKEOWN

PSYCHOLOGY AND POLITICS. Because politics deals with relations among people, it is inevitably linked with psychology, which deals with human thinking and behavior. Political analysts throughout the ages and across civilizations have been interested in the reciprocal impact of personality characteristics and political environments. Although psychological insights have been applied to the study of numerous political phenomena for thousands of years, no overarching theories or coherent body of knowledge have emerged. Rather, diverse theories have been employed to explain why rulers and subjects think

and act as they do and how their thoughts and actions shape the course of politics.

In the pre-Christian era, for example, Confucius (551–479 B.C.E.) and Aristotle (384–322 B.C.E.) taught about the connection between psychology and politics. Aristotle's *Rhetoric* provides advice about motivating various publics to support political causes. To succeed, Aristotle said, politicians must know how to stir their audiences' emotions. Another early classic in the literature of political psychology is Niccolò Machiavelli's *Prince* (1513). Machiavelli believed that human nature is the one unchangeable element in politics. Rulers therefore must study it so that they can control political action by manipulating their subjects. *The Prince* is filled with practical advice about the art of political manipulation.

The Nature of Humans and Their Governments. Plans and proposals for the best ways to govern political entities hinge on perceptions about the psychological makeup of human beings. These perceptions have differed throughout the ages. They moved to the forefront of the political dialogue starting in the seventeenth century, when the question of citizen control of government agitated people in the Western world. Thomas Hobbes (1588–1679), a major contributor to the debate, saw human life as nasty, brutish, and short, in the absence of stern rulers. By contrast, later political philosophers like John Locke (1632–1704), the Baron de Montesquieu (1689–1755), and Jean-Jacques Rousseau (1712–1788) believed that ordinary citizens were capable of governing themselves and entitled to protection from the unbridled whims of fallible rulers. The nature of government therefore must be decided through negotiations between rulers and subjects and affirmed by contract. These later political philosophers laid the foundations for constitutional government in the Western world. It was based on the belief that the fallibility of all human beings, including rulers, required a system of checks and balances to forestall excesses and assure governance for the public good rather than private gain.

Karl *Marx (1818–1883) held a different view of human nature, believing that it conformed to the ideals prized by most societies. He ascribed the evils of human society to the patterns of human behavior fostered by capitalist economic systems based on private ownership of property. The overweening desire for domination of human and material resources could be eliminated through the abolition of property rights. Human nature would then emerge in all its glory. People would share resources equitably and would be harmonious and devoted to the collective good. Based on Marx's ideal vision of humanity, millions of people around the world embraced communist *ideology.

Not all visions of human nature were as optimistic as Marx's view. Eighteenth-century constitutional governments had been based on visions of people as mixtures of good and evil traits. In later years, psychologists like Sigmund Freud (1856–1939) pointed to irrational elements in human personality that required external control of human behavior. There was ample proof of irrational political behavior throughout human history, including genocide and war, directed against outgroups within nations or within the world community. Psychological explanations for such destructive behavior abounded. Freud believed that societal norms were required to control individual irrational drives. When these norms were internalized, they became the individual's superego or conscience. Civilizations and individuals advanced through a continuous process of interaction.

In the twentieth century, the study of the connection between psychology and politics became a scientific endeavor. Modern psychological theories and social science techniques became common for psychopolitical analysis, replacing mere assertions and speculations about the relation between human nature and politics. Using Freudian and neo-Freudian psychoanalytic concepts, the political psychologist Harold Lasswell wrote his pathbreaking book *Psychopathology and Politics* (Chicago, 1930). Lasswell contended that leaders rationalize their actions by claiming that they are performed in the public interest. In reality, the public behavior of political leaders is usually motivated by private concerns that they cannot admit to themselves or others. Political leadership, in Lasswell's view, is frequently coupled with psychological characteristics bordering on the pathological. To gather proof for his assertions, Lasswell examined psychiatric case studies of political activists.

The political consequences of the psychological make-up and motivations of major political leaders have been of particular interest to their subjects and to scholars. Psychobiographies based on Freudian and neo-Freudian notions have been written about leaders such as *Stalin, *Roosevelt, *Churchill, *Gandhi, *Mao Zedong, and *Hitler. In Hitler's case, for instance, biographers have tried to explain the psychological urges that made him willing to plunge the world into war to accomplish his political objectives. They have tried to fathom what made him capable of ordering the deliberate extermination of millions of human beings whom he deemed racially inferior and therefore worthless or dangerous. Even more puzzling, what allowed mild-mannered Harry *Truman, president of a society that prides itself on its high regard for human lives, to order that an atomic bomb be dropped on wartime enemies in full knowledge of the horrendous consequences for military and civilian targets alike?

Answers to such questions have been sought from psychoanalytic theories, from social learning theories, and from various behavioristic approaches to psychology. Are inborn traits or human drives the explanation, so that a leader is born with an au-

thoritarian personality or a compulsion for grandiose acts of violence? Or should one seek causes for the behavior of political leaders in societal influences that molded their personality, particularly during the formative years? Do circumstances create heroes and leaders as well as villains and mindless followers, or will these personality characteristics surface regardless of environmental contexts? Can political leaders mold the psyches of populations under their control to benefit the leaders' political purposes? What are the elements of charisma? These and many other questions about the psychological aspects of political leadership await definitive answers.

Political Socialization. Because political beliefs and perceptions are learned behaviors, political leaders everywhere are interested in political socialization. It entails the initial creation of basic political attitudes and the development of well-rounded shared *political cultures that generate allegiance and support for political entities. Depending on the prevailing political ideology, political socialization may strive to engender a high regard for *democracy or a high regard for authoritarian rule. Regardless of the ideological beliefs that are fostered, it is far easier to govern populations that willingly cooperate with the rules and regulations by which this governance takes place than to govern by force, contrary to the subjects' will.

Socialization efforts are based on psychoanalytic concepts and learning theories. They range from unwritten rules about the norms of political behavior that are passed to successive generations through parents and teachers, to formal prescription of the nature of civic education, to the elaborate indoctrination programs used in authoritarian societies throughout the life cycle. Because the reality of the world is filtered through human minds, political socialization guides the perceptions that are formed about this reality and the attitudes and opinions about these perceptions. Actions are then shaped by these attitudes and opinions. Besides conveying the political culture through the transmission of historical and ideological information, political socialization engages people's emotions through the use of stirring symbols, such as flags and patriotic music, and through public ceremonies.

Political socialization is usually designed to motivate people to engage in various types of political actions, such as voting in election campaigns, paying taxes, serving in the armed forces, or contributing to the society's economic development. In the international sphere, when political socialization fosters attitudes favoring international cooperation and peaceful conduct, it is more likely that international agreements can be reached and peace maintained. When attitudes are chauvinistic, or when other countries are routinely depicted as enemies, international conflict may ensue. This is especially true because mirror images are common. A nation that perceives its chief antagonist as a likely aggressor is apt to be perceived in exactly the same way by this antagonist.

Success of socialization efforts hinges on psychological predispositions of the socialized subjects as well as on the political environment in which socialization takes place. For example, when citizens lack achievement motivation, their societies are likely to lag in economic development (David McClelland, *The Achieving Society,* Princeton, N.J., 1961). Likewise, the fact that there are hierarchies of human needs that are satisfied sequentially explains a number of political behaviors that otherwise might seem irrational (Abraham Maslow, *Motivation and Personality,* New York, 1954). A major problem plaguing political socialization is the fact that misperceptions are common and are spread and perpetuated through socialization processes. Because major policies, including the decision to go to war, may hinge on these perceptions, the fear of misperception is great (e.g., Ralph White, *Nobody Wanted War,* Garden City, N.Y., 1970).

The fact that political socialization is largely a state function underlines that politics affects the individual as much as or more than the individual affects politics. It is therefore important to assess the impact that different political environments have on the political thinking and behavior of various publics. Comparative studies of the political attitudes and actions of people living under various types of regimes in different political cultures have disclosed marked variations in citizens' political attitudes and opinions (e.g., Junius Flagg Brown, *Psychology and the Social Order,* New York, 1936; Gabriel Almond and Norman Nie, *The Civic Culture,* Princeton, N.J., 1965). Citizens' attitudes and behaviors are also altered by major political upheavals such as wars, revolutions, and economic depressions. For example, the trauma of the worldwide economic depression of the 1930s left people everywhere fearful of losing their jobs and eager to support previously shunned social insurance policies.

The Context for Decision Making. Political leaders affect the fate of their nations and the world through the decisions they make. These decisions are shaped by the leaders' perceptions, attitudes, and opinions as well as the political context at the time of decision. Many psychological pressures arise during decision making, especially when it occurs under conditions of high tension and group pressure. The psychologist Irving Janis, for example, in *Victims of Groupthink* (Boston, 1972), described how U.S. policymakers bungled policies designed to overthrow Cuba's Communist government because group pressures supported flawed policy proposals. Understanding such psychologically debilitating pressures and developing remedial procedures can ease such problems.

Of course, leaders are not the only decision makers in politics. Individual citizens make voting decisions and decisions about supporting various policies and *interest groups. These decisions are important in all societies, but especially in democracies, because *public opinions and actions can be very influential in the political life of the nation. This is why leaders spend much time and effort to gauge the nature of these political perceptions and attitudes, to measure their prevalence, and to influence the psychological climate that provides the context for citizen decision making.

The Causes and Cures of Political Violence. *Political violence, such as civil war, revolution, terrorism, and international war, is a major political concern. These types of violence are widely condemned by many societies and glorified by others as the acme of patriotic fervor. Important psychological forces are involved in practicing political violence. For example, it is well established that people have fewer inhibitions about violent acts when they are acting as members of a crowd rather than acting alone. Mob psychology and crowd hysteria are common. It is also common for people who oppose committing acts of violence in their private behavior to willingly perform violent acts involving individual and mass destruction at the behest of their societies. Even organized religious bodies that fervently preach the sanctity of life to their constituents often pray for the success of their nation's military forces.

If it is true, as is often alleged, that political violence originates in the mind, then its eradication, if desired, may require the creation of more peace-inducing psychological environments. Political psychologists have devoted considerable thought and effort to this problem since the mid-1950s. Studies have focused on attitudes relevant to *international relations, including *nationalism, patriotism, images of other nations, public opinion, decision-making processes, and interactions during international conflicts. Psychologists have developed various models of international conflict, viewing it, for example, as a zero-sum aggressor-defender situation in which one party's gain is the other's loss. To frustrate the aggressor's plans, the defender must develop sufficient military capacity to intimidate and thereby deter the aggressor.

The political psychologist Charles Osgood discussed one possible approach to fostering peace based on a conflict-spiral model that postulates that tensions escalate in spiral fashion. In *An Alternative to War or Surrender* (Urbana, Ill., 1962), he suggested his "GRIT" plan, designed to lower tensions through "graduated reciprocation in tension-reduction." The process constitutes a positive-sum solution to international problems whereby all parties benefit. Other plans to forestall war, especially nuclear war, have tried to use psychological and social pressures to suppress jingoism (e.g., Edward

Tolman, *Drives toward War,* New York, 1942). Since 1957, *The Journal of Conflict Resolution* has featured studies that focus primarily on ways to forestall and resolve various types of conflicts. In 1983, the Center for Psychological Studies in the Nuclear Age was created in Cambridge, Massachusetts, to study the psychological dimensions of the global crisis created by the arms race and destruction of the environment. The center's conferences are designed to raise public consciousness about these dangers and promote efforts at resolving them.

(See also AUTHORITARIANISM; ELITES.)

J. David Singer, ed., *Human Behavior and International Politics* (Chicago, 1965). Joseph de Rivera, *The Psychological Dimension of Foreign Policy* (Columbus, Ohio, 1968). Alexander George, *Presidential Decision-Making in Foreign Policy* (Boulder, Colo., 1980). Robert Jervis, Richard Ned Lebow, and Janice Gross Stein, *Psychology and Deterrence* (Baltimore, 1985).

DORIS A. GRABER

PUBLIC ASSISTANCE. See WELFARE STATE.

PUBLIC CHOICE THEORY. According to the major text in the field, *public choice* "can be defined as the economic study of nonmarket decision-making, or simply the application of economics to political science" (Mueller, 1989). The subject, then, pertains to voters, politicians, bureaucrats, *interest groups, and the environment within which they interact to produce policy outcomes. That is the political science part; the economics part is a bit more difficult to specify. In brief, the economist's basic postulate is that the human actor is an egotistical, rational pursuer of utility or satisfaction. With this as the point of departure the public choice analyst proceeds to employ the rather formidable analytical tools of modern economics in search of truths about public or collective choice. Thus, the analyst might wish to explain voter choices; coalition formation; party electoral strategies; the choice of fiscal and monetary policies; seeking of market advantages by interest groups; the growth of government; budgetary behavior of bureaucrats; and so on.

Now a well-recognized cross-disciplinary field claiming two Nobel laureates (Kenneth J. Arrow and James M. Buchanan), the study is hardly more than forty years of age, having been created, independently, by Kenneth Arrow (1951) and Duncan Black (1948) in the late 1940s and early 1950s. Both economists were fascinated by the perplexities of elections and voting under simple majority rule. Arrow demonstrated through the use of symbolic logic that, under certain clearly specified conditions or norms, collective choices could not achieve outcomes consistent with the diverse preferences held by voters. The problem was not that a majority could not be formed, but that too many majorities would eventuate, each to negate the others; thus,

"cyclical majorities" resulted. This outcome, if true, was demoralizing to any committed democrat and believer in expanding government.

Countless commentators have since found or claimed to have discovered ways around Arrow's paradox, but the single best critique was actually written shortly before Arrow's monograph was published, namely the highly original work of Duncan Black. Black argued that groups using simple majority rule $[(N+1)/2]$ could achieve a stable equilibrium or outcome if the preferences of the voters were "single-peaked," i.e., if the rank-ordering of their preferences displayed a certain logic such as preferring more to less or less to more and not confusing the two by making one's second choice the very opposite of the first. Thus, a voter whose first choice is to have the largest budget possible but second choice is the smallest budget instead of the median budget is deemed inconsistent and has preferences that are not single-peaked. Black's early work produced an enduring result called the median voter theorem that says the median voter preference will, under certain oft-found conditions, win over other options, thus negating Arrow's paradox.

This proposition has important normative significance as well in that it can be shown that the result generates the most utility possible under the circumstances. In addition, Anthony Downs (1957) claimed that electoral competition among parties would also lead to policy positions closest to those preferred by median voters; thus, "Tweedledum and Tweedledee."

Although this branch of public choice has gone on to further explore the formal properties of elections and various constitutional rules, other less mathematical approaches have centered on other elements of politics including bureaucracy. James M. Buchanan has chosen to explore basic constitutional problems and "rent-seeking," i.e., the politically rational pursuit by interest groups of economic privileges. He has been particularly concerned with facilitating mutually beneficial exchanges among citizens and a more efficient fiscal constitution. His work has also emphasized the redistributional quest of the interests leading in the end to the growth of government and negative-sum games in which everyone becomes worse off. Much of his work as well as that of followers in the so-called Virginia School has produced a theory of governmental or political failure very much the logical opposite of the market failure school. Thus, Buchanan and colleagues have deromanticized politics and, indirectly, elevated appreciation for the market and other private institutions to new heights.

Although much of the substance of public choice can be stated in intricate mathematical terms, its basic findings are, like those of economics, simple. For example, democratic governments engage in a number of highly important monetary and fiscal activities that are inefficient and, often, inequitable. Among other things, 1)*political business cycles are produced in which inflationary policies are pursued during the months before elections while less inflationary or deflationary policies follow a successful campaign; 2) policies are enacted in which total costs exceed total benefits; 3) costs are usually diluted through time and over the general taxpaying population so they will be invisible politically, while benefits will be highly visible to those who enjoy them, i.e., shares will be substantial enough to be noticed and provided during the immediate period.

The political process that generates the above behavior differs dramatically from the market process, and therein resides the explanation of the various inefficiencies. Voters, politicians, and bureaucrats must all respond to peculiar and perverse political incentives and institutions, none of which facilitates optimal policies. Voters are constrained by having single votes that can only be cast at discontinuous elections while politicians must concern themselves with mobilizing majorities based on incompatible coalition interests. Bureaucrats must please legislatures rather than consumers in markets.

All the actors in politics maximize their own welfare but do so in different ways: thus, the politicians seek maximal votes while the voters attempt to obtain maximum flows of benefits paid by others, while the bureaucrats wish to ensure maximal flows of budget monies. But, whereas the market is able to integrate its diverse interests and make everyone better off, there is no efficient "hidden hand" in politics. In fact, politics might better be described as a veiled fist because politics is ultimately based on coercion if not by dictators, then by minorities or majorities consisting of temporary alliances among powerful interests. Such an image of politics is not reassuring, but it is the one set forth by public choice analysts (Mitchell and Simmons, 1992) during the past forty years and it is one that has gained increasing influence not only among academics but in politics itself.

(See also ELECTIONS AND VOTING BEHAVIOR; GAME THEORY; POLITICAL ECONOMY.)

Duncan Black, *The Theory of Committees and Elections* (Cambridge, U.K., 1948). Kenneth J. Arrow, *Social Choice and Individual Values* (New York, 1951). Anthony Downs, *An Economic Theory of Democracy* (New York, 1957). James M. Buchanan, *The Limits of Liberty* (Chicago, 1975). Dennis Mueller, *Public Choice II: A Revised Edition of Public Choice* (Cambridge, Mass., 1989). William C. Mitchell and Randy Simmons, *Markets, Politics, and Welfare* (New York, 1992).

WILLIAM C. MITCHELL

PUBLIC GOOD. A good characterized by two main properties, jointness of supply and nonexcludability, is a public good. If a good is characterized by jointness of supply, then the consumption of the good by one person does not affect the consumption of others in the group. If a good is characterized by nonexcludability, then it is impossible to prevent anyone in the group from consuming it. The classic example of a public good is a lighthouse: unlike a private good, the benefits of the lighthouse are joint and, once produced, are unsusceptible to exclusion.

The general idea of public goods and the problems which they pose for society have been present in political writings for several centuries. The contemporary interest in the concept originated in welfare economics in the work of Paul Samuelson ("The Pure Theory of Public Expenditure" *Review of Economics and Statistics* 36 [November 1954]: 387–389). Samuelson focused on how the properties of jointness and nonexcludability affected our ability to determine optimal levels of *consumption* of the good. For political analysis the problem of the *provision* of public goods was prominent in Mancur Olson's analysis of the logic of collective action (*The Logic of Collective Action,* Cambridge, Mass., 1965). These initial efforts to analyze the political and economic implications of public goods have led to extensive research on the subject.

To grasp the fundamental importance of the concept, one must relax the stringent criteria for what constitutes a public good. There are very few pure public goods, goods that are truly joint in supply and that are of a form which makes exclusion from consumption impossible. But a wide range of goods—known variously as "collective," "group," or "club" goods—have properties sufficiently similar to the pure case to create collective action problems. Examples in political analysis are numerous: international stability, national defense, tax revenues, environmental concerns, union activities, *interest groups, etc. For all of these goods the problem of nonexcludability is the key: the fact that members of a group cannot be excluded from enjoying the benefits of a good, either because exclusion is too costly or because it is technically infeasible, produces two fundamental problems. First, in the classic "free-rider" problem, if any member of the group pays the costs of producing the public good, then anyone else in the group can exploit the producer and consume the good for free. Second, the free availability of the good diminishes the incentive for any individual to contribute to its production, resulting in a collectively suboptimal provision of the good. Many of the strategic implications of these problems have been investigated through the use of *game theory. The basic conflict between individual and collective rationality characterized by the provision of public goods is analogous to the "Prisoners' Dilemma" problem: the choice of noncooperation dictated by individual self-interest leads to the production of a collective outcome which is suboptimal for all of the actors.

Much of the research has focused on the problem of suboptimal provision. Solutions can be divided into those which attempt to show that individual contribution is the rational self-interested action (such as Olson's by-product theory) and those which rely on external sanctions, typically by the state, to guarantee contribution.

(See also PUBLIC CHOICE THEORY.)

Duncan Snidal, "Public Goods, Property Rights and Political Organizations" *International Studies Quarterly* 23, no. 4 (December 1979): 532–566. Russell Hardin, *Collective Action* (Baltimore, 1982). Michael Taylor, *The Possibility of Cooperation* (New York, 1987).

JACK KNIGHT

PUBLIC INTEREST MOVEMENT. The history of the United States has been punctuated by periodic episodes of social protest, loosely organized and sometimes unruly citizen movements centered on political causes that have engaged deeply felt beliefs. Many of these movements—for example, the agrarian protest in the late nineteenth century or the *Civil Rights Movement of the 1950s and 1960s—involve self-interested demands by the dispossessed. Indeed, we often think of protest as the weapon of the weak, the only recourse available to those who command few of the conventional political resources. However, there is a long tradition of protest, usually rooted in the middle class, that is not narrowly self-interested, a tradition that encompasses, for example, historical movements on behalf of abolition, temperance, and progressivism, as well as more recent causes.

There is some controversy as to whether it is appropriate to label these public interest movements. One perspective holds that there is no such thing as the public interest apart from the sum of the private utilities of individuals. According to this view, citizen environmental activists who seek tougher regulations on toxic waste disposal are just as self-interested as the executives of a chemical manufacturing firm who seek to relax them. An alternative view, however, is that it is possible to distinguish political action that is narrowly self-interested from that which seeks a goal, the achievement of which would not benefit selectively either the members or the activists of a movement or organization. Ordinarily, such benefits are *public goods—peace, clean air, or good government—that are broadly available to all citizens. It is also possible to draw under this rubric activity undertaken on behalf of others—for example, the handicapped, children, or prisoners—seeking benefits that, while not generally available, would not selectively advantage those pursuing them. Public interest movements, although similar to other citizens' movements in their tactics, can be differentiated in terms of their objectives from other social movements—for example, the women's suffrage movement or the gay rights movement—that pursue goals that benefit selectively the adherents or leaders of the movement.

To make the distinction between self-interested and public-interested goals is not to claim that, in any particular political controversy, there is a single broadly available public interest at stake. On the contrary, in any given political conflict, there are usually competing generally available benefits at issue: environmental preservation versus economic growth; consumer product safety versus lower prices for consumer goods; the need for secrecy to protect national security versus the public's right to scrutinize what the government is doing. Individual citizens will differ in their taste for such competing public goods.

The 1960s ushered in a period of renewed mass action and protest movements of many kinds. Some of these movements—for example, the Civil Rights Movement and, later, the women's movement—involved the mobilization of citizens on their own behalf. Others involved pursuit of more broadly shared benefits. Although it would be difficult to document this assertion empirically, some have contended that social movement activity during the 1960s was more extensive than during earlier protest eras, the result of the convergence of the weakness of the political parties and the development of electronic technologies that facilitate both political mobilization and fund-raising. A number of the social movements of the 1960s and early 1970s—among them public interest movements seeking environmental and consumer protection—were successful in becoming institutionalized as organizations taking part in Washington pressure politics, thus contributing to the explosive growth of the organized interest community in Washington. These public interest movements left not only new organizations but also new policies in their wake. Although the links between citizen protest and policy innovation are always indirect at best, it is important to recognize the significance of the new policies—political reforms as well as consumer and environmental legislation—that emerged during these years.

The aftermath of this decade of social ferment and policy innovation was not so much an era of quiescence as a period in which the energy for citizen action emanated as much from the *Right as from the *Left. Public interest movements on behalf of public goods more congenial to conservatives—for example, lower taxes, economic development, economic freedom, and traditional morals—arose and flourished during the Reagan years and scored major policy successes.

Public interest movements, which have been so significant in U.S. politics, are characteristic of other contemporary democracies as well. Although present everywhere, there is diversity across democracies with respect to the specific issues they champion. Furthermore, there is a great deal of variation from country to country—even from movement to movement within a single country—in their success, in the degree to which they have desired and been able to penetrate mainstream politics, and in the strategies they have adopted for doing so. In some cases, such movements—for example, the environmentalist, antinuclear movement in Germany that became the basis for the Green Party—attempt to enter electoral politics on their own. In others, they find their concerns addressed by at least one of the established parties, thus obviating the need for a new party. In still others, they remain, by choice or necessity, outside the realm of electoral politics. Only in the United States, however, is a move into *interest group politics the ordinary route for a public interest movement that seeks to supplement mass action with more readily sustained forms of *political participation.

(See also ENVIRONMENTALISM; FEMINISM; GREEN PARTIES; NEW SOCIAL MOVEMENTS; POLITICAL PARTIES AND PARTY COMPETITION; POPULISM; PROGRESSIVE MOVEMENT, U.S.)

Andrew M. McFarland, *Public Interest Lobbies* (Washington, D.C., 1976). Jeffrey M. Berry, *Lobbying for the People* (Princeton, N.J., 1977). Kay Lehman Schlozman and John T. Tierney, *Organized Interests and American Democracy* (New York, 1986).

KAY LEHMAN SCHLOZMAN

PUBLIC OPINION. Students of politics agree that public opinion, broadly speaking, is an aggregate of individual opinions on issues of political relevance that can influence individual and group behavior and the actions of political leaders and governments. The term began to be used frequently in political discourse in the late eighteenth century, catalyzed by the French Revolution. Its earlier origins from ancient Greece and Rome are summarized, for example, by Wilhelm Bauer in his "Public Opinion" (in Edwin R. A. Seligman, ed., *Encyclopaedia of the Social Sciences,* vol. 12, New York, 1934).

There is less agreement about specific meanings of public opinion: that is, whether it refers to "mass public," "informed public," or to different "attentive" or "issue publics" in politics; to the opinions of *elites, organized groups, or other "opinion leaders" who ultimately influence widely held attitudes and beliefs; or to the "climate of opinion" that individuals perceive—correctly or incorrectly (the term *pluralistic ignorance* refers to the latter)—from the information that they get through interactions with others and directly or indirectly through the mass media and other sources. The last meaning, most notably, has been emphasized by Walter Lippmann (United States) and Elisabeth Noelle-Neumann (Germany), among others.

Notwithstanding this disagreement, public opinion as mass opinion has been considered an important and even "rational" force: political actors must respond to public opinion or confront it. This claim of rationality—in the face of charges that the mass public is ignorant and ideologically unsophisticated about politics—is based predominantly on empirical research in the United States, beginning with the research of Paul Lazardfeld and his associates at Columbia University and spurred on by voting studies at the University of Michigan and, especially, the writing of V. O. Key, Jr. The rational sources of opinion include: 1) the explicit pursuit of self-interest, which research has not found to be as predominant as economic theories about politics have expected; 2) the pursuit of more genuinely collective or national interests (e.g., the concern of individuals for the nation's economic and general well-being, not simply their own); 3) the influences of culture, core values, and identifiable ideological and symbolic concerns; 4) social characteristics and identification with social groups (i.e., race and ethnicity, economic status, gender, education, and so forth, which are directly related to political interests); 5) the influences of trusted opinion leaders, organizations, and institutions, ranging from national political elites and others whose opinions and interpretations may be conveyed through the mass media, to friends, peers, and family members from whom individuals take cues about political matters; and 6) events and changes in objective conditions themselves that may affect the public directly, independent of the interpretations offered by opinion leaders.

The conclusion that public opinion is rational in this sense, does not mean that the public is thought to be wise, because through processes of manipulation or deception (e.g., through propaganda, in the extreme case) the public may be misdirected from its true interests. In one sense this rationality offers support for greater *democracy, in which electoral accountability provides the incentive for government responsiveness; in another sense, the myth of rational public opinion may be exploited by governments and others in order to exert political control and remain in power. Regardless of whether public opinion influences government to do its bidding or whether the latter controls the former, public consensus or compliance is a necessary context for effective governance and policy making.

In such a context public opinion has visible influences. It provides *legitimacy or may serve as a legitimizing symbol. At times of elections in democracies, the influences on public opinion described above are reflected in electoral outcomes, and in this way public opinion provides a mechanism for change by replacing leaders who govern and by altering the bases of support for those who are elected. There is increasing evidence that public opinion not only constrains both domestic and foreign policy making from exceeding the bounds acceptable to the public but that on many salient issues public preferences can move governments in new directions, and that public opinion can also influence how government institutions formulate policies and adapt their own structures to take public opinion into account.

There have been many ways for government policymakers, political analysts, and academic researchers to learn about public opinion. These have included reliance on their own impressionistic observations; the use of elites, organized groups, or others as informants; reports in the mass media that are presumed to reflect or influence public opinion; and the documentary and other primary sources commonly used by social historians. By far the most important means for tracking and communicating public opinion, however, has been the scientific sample survey, which, thanks to George Gallup and others, first came into broad use in the United States in 1935 to study national opinion and has grown in significance ever since.

Two developments have suggested that public opinion polling is associated with the struggle for democratic political processes. First, since 1960, U.S. presidents in office have been as strongly concerned about public opinion as they had once been only during their electoral campaigns, which indicates their interest in responding to or trying to control public opinion. Second, the movement away from authoritarian government toward democratic processes around the world—from Latin America to Eastern and Central Europe, the Soviet Union, and parts of Asia—has been accompanied by public opinion polling. Survey researchers have emerged (or reemerged) in these countries. In some instances they have desired to help democracy along; in others, involving government-sponsored or controlled polling, they have hoped to confront democratic initiatives more effectively. As new and ostensibly free elections have occurred, political candidates worldwide have sought information from opinion polls, suggesting that concern for public opinion and use of survey research methods to track public opinion will increasingly accompany leaders into office, as has occurred in the United States and elsewhere.

Given these developments, there is currently more need than ever before for comparative analysis that examines public opinion and public opinion processes across nations. The number of mass opinion surveys conducted worldwide has reached record numbers, and partly in recognition of these developments and the desire to maintain the integrity of survey research, the World Association for Public Opinion Research, formed in 1947, began publishing in 1989 the *International Journal of Public Opinion Research*.

(See also ELECTIONS AND VOTING BEHAVIOR; IDEOLOGY; INFORMATION SOCIETY; POLITICAL PARTIES AND PARTY COMPETITION; PSYCHOLOGY AND POLITICS.)

W. Phillips Davison and Avery Leiserson, "Public Opinion," in David Sills, ed., *International Encyclopedia of the Social Sciences*, vol. 13 (New York, 1968). Donald R. Kinder and David O. Sears. "Public Opinion and Political Action," in Gardner Lindzey and Elliot Aronson, eds., *Handbook of Social Psychology*, 3d ed., vol. 2 (New York, 1985). Robert S. Erikson, Norman R. Luttbeg, and Kent L. Tedin, *American Public Opinion: Its Origins, Content, and Impact*, 3d ed. (New York, 1988). Samuel Long, ed., *Research in Micropolitics*, vol. 3, *Public Opinion* (Greenwich, Conn., 1990).

ROBERT Y. SHAPIRO

PUERTO RICO. In the twentieth century the story of Puerto Rico is of an ongoing effort to overcome almost 500 years of colonialism. Conquered in 1493 by Spain and acquired by the United States in 1898 during the Spanish-American War, this Caribbean island of 8,931 square kilometers (3,435 sq. mi.) has never been an independent state. Officially, Puerto Rico became a U.S. commonwealth in 1952, when the island was granted limited self-government. Earlier, the Foraker Act (1900) had provided for three branches of government, vested executive authority in a presidentially appointed government, and integrated Puerto Rico into the U.S. economy. The Jones Act (1917), perceived as a war measure to ensure loyalty, conferred U.S. *citizenship on island residents but denied them participation in national elections. Although the Puerto Rican Federal Relations Act (1950) authorized a locally drafted constitution, ultimate sovereignty over island affairs was retained by the U.S. Congress. Puerto Rico's lone representative to that body, a resident commissioner in the House, has a voice but no vote except in committees.

Puerto Rico has become a crossroads for some of the major ideologies of this century—*nationalism, *socialism, and *modernization—and for the principal Western cultural heritages—African, Hispanic, Antillean, and North American. Its 3.6 million Spanish-speaking inhabitants make it one of the most densely populated regions of the world.

Modernization and economic development, sometimes negatively perceived as Americanization, took off during the 1940s and 1950s led by Luis Muñoz Marín (1898–1980), the island's first elected governor. A charismatic populist leader, he blended nationalist, socialist, and modernization ideas into a new *populism centered around the Partido Popular Democrático (PPD). He temporarily rejected independentism and statehood, coopting these two movements into populist autonomism. Nationalist sentiment, variously expressed as independence, autonomy, and statehood, has been fueled by the still-unresolved colonial status. The island's economic dependency continues to overshadow U.S. efforts to portray it as a showcase of development.

Economic progress has been accompanied by wide income disparities and intractable social problems. The per capita income of $5,574 is among the highest in Latin America, but it is forty-seven percent below that of the lowest of the fifty states. In 1990 over sixty-two percent of the population had incomes below the federal poverty level. Socialist populism swelled the ranks of the autonomist PPD, making it the dominant party while increasing government size—twenty-three percent of the total workforce by 1988—and at the cost of encouraging outmigration. About 2.3 million Puerto Ricans live in the continental United States. The island's staggering federal dependency, $6.2 billion in 1988, or thirty-four percent of Puerto Rico's $18.4 billion GNP, rendered its economic model nonexportable. Its dynamic industrial economy is heavily dependent on exemptions from federal and local taxes. Over 625 U.S. corporations have received tax credits equaling $1.6 billion per year. With these incentives, industry surpassed agriculture and exports ($13.2 billion) exceeded imports ($11.8 billion) in fiscal year 1988. But unemployment recently has fluctuated between 23.5 percent and 15.9 percent. Besides poverty and unemployment, Puerto Rico faces a serious *AIDS epidemic, alcoholism, drug addiction with consequent crime, mental illness, and a host of other social problems, at rates among the highest in the nation.

Political inequality and lack of sovereignty have become both a national human rights and an international *decolonization issue in the 1990s. In 1972 the Decolonization Committee of the General Assembly of the United Nations recognized the inalienable right of Puerto Ricans to self-determination and independence. Although debate exists about whether the present commonwealth status qualifies as a decolonizing option, the United States has opposed subsequent efforts to discuss the Puerto Rican case at the General Assembly. In 1990, legislation was introduced unsuccessfully in the 101st Congress calling for a referendum on Puerto Rico's political status. The three options represented by the island's three principal political parties were defined as "enhanced" commonwealth status (the PPD position), statehood (the position of the Partido Nuevo Progresista [PNP]), and independence (the position of the Partido Independentista Puertorriqueño [PIP]). Although the respective voting strength in the 1988 elections was 48.6 percent to the PPD, 45.8 percent to the PNP, and 5.6 percent to the PIP, by 1990 public opinion polls showed 48 percent approval for statehood, a marked contrast to 12.9 percent approval in the 1952 elections, when 64.8 percent voted in favor of the commonwealth and nineteen percent voted for independence. Should a future referendum be held, this shift, if sustained in the 1992 elections, may signal an end to Puerto Rico's decolonization efforts in favor of statehood.

Henry Wells, *The Modernization of Puerto Rico: A Political Study of Changing Values and Institutions* (Cambridge, Mass., 1969). Arturo Morales Carrión, *Puerto Rico: A Political and Cultural History* (New York, 1983). Raymond Carr, *Puerto Rico: A Colonial Experiment* (New York, 1984). U.S. General Accounting Office, *Puerto Rico Information for Status Deliberations* (Washington, D.C., 1990).

LUIS G. RODRÍGUEZ

Q

QADDAFI, Muammar. Born in 1941 into a family of the Qadhafa tribe on the southern coastline of the Gulf of Sirte in *Libya, Muammar Qaddafi received a mosque-based early education in Misurata. Then, in the late 1950s, his family moved to Sabha, the main town of the Fezzan where Qaddafi attended secondary school. He soon became an active Arab nationalist, after contact with Ba'thist and Nasserist ideas, especially the radical nationalist propaganda of Radio Cairo.

At school, Qaddafi participated in a small group of politically active friends—a group which was eventually to form the nucleus of the Free Officers Movement. Finally, in October 1961, he was expelled from school by the authorities after organizing a demonstration against the monarchy.

Qaddafi and the majority of his circle then decided that the only way to pursue their political objectives was through the Libyan armed forces—the only institution in the country not dominated by traditional tribal influences and with a relatively modernist outlook. So in late 1961, Qaddafi became a student at the Benghazi Military Academy. Upon graduation in 1966, he joined the communications branch of the army—away from elite units such as the Cyrenaican Defense Force which were renowned for their firm support of the monarchy.

Qaddafi continued to develop the Free Officers Movement, despite senior commanders' occasional suspicion of his activities. Eventually he was sent to Britain for further training, but even at a distance, Qaddafi pursued his political work. His military career also prospered and he was promoted to the rank of captain. Finally on 1 September 1969, when King Idris was on holiday in Turkey, the Free Officers struck. Their *coup succeeded largely because the authorities did not realize how well-organized the military conspiracy had become. While the king took up a comfortable exile in Cairo, Qaddafi assumed the leadership of the new republican regime, becoming head of state in 1970.

Qaddafi came to power with an Arab nationalist perspective, tinged with the egalitarianism and puritanical morality of nomadic society. This political vision evolved throughout the 1970s and by the end of the decade his personal *ideology had been codified and published in a three-volume work, often known as the *Green Book*. This treatise described the "Third Universal Theory" which was to supersede capitalism and communism and which was based on the principle of "direct popular democracy." Qaddafi also considered the Third Universal Theory to be a prescription for political organization throughout the Third World. Although not explicitly Islamic, the underlying moral justification of the theory was drawn from Islamic thought.

The full rigors of the political system derived from the *Green Book* were put into operation by Qaddafi in Libya during the 1970s and 1980s. Political life in modern Libya is very much Qaddafi's personal creation.

The political radicalism of Libya under Qaddafi has made him personally a notorious figure, particularly in the West, although his antagonism to most established Middle Eastern governments has isolated him there as well. Qaddafi is the Middle Eastern politician most closely associated in the popular mind with international *terrorism, although up to 1986 Libya's terrorist links had been largely with extremist Palestinian organizations and, as a priority, directed against its own nationals in exile who were opposed to the Qaddafi regime. U.S. and British hostility toward the Libyan leader has been most marked since the mid-1980s, and since then he has often been inaccurately portrayed in the Western media as an irresponsible extremist and a threat to regional security and stability.

(See also ARAB NATIONALISM; ISLAM; NASSERISM.)

Frederick Muscat, *My President, My Son* (Valletta, Malta, 1974). J. Cooley, *Libyan Sandstorm* (London, 1984).
GEORGE JOFFÉ

QATAR. See GULF STATES.

QUEBEC. The 5.3 million French speakers of Quebec represent the overwhelming majority (eighty-two percent) of Quebec's population. At the same time, they constitute the only instance of a French-speaking majority within a Canadian province. The next-largest Francophone concentration, in the province of New Brunswick, numbers about 240,000 and constitutes less than one-third of the province's population. In all the other provinces, French speakers represent no more than four percent of the population—in most cases the percentage is far less.

This concentration of French speakers in Quebec has in recent decades provided the basis for a strong Québécois *nationalism which has spawned a movement for Quebec's political disengagement from the rest of *Canada. However, this Quebec-based nationalism is only the most recent variant of a longstanding nationalist sentiment among French speakers, born of a long history of cultural threat and economic inferiority.

The Francophone population of Quebec can be traced back to the colony of New France, founded in 1608. By the time the colony was conquered by the British, in 1759, its population had grown to 70,000. Although New France had such quasi-feudal institutions as a seigneurial system and entitlement of the Catholic church to collect tithes, the bulk of the population, concentrated in subsistence agriculture, displayed considerable independence from formal authority. And a certain number of residents amassed wealth on the basis of trade in furs with France (the precise significance of this element has been a long-standing issue of scholarly debate). Over time, the colonial residents developed a clear sense of identity, using the term *Canadiens* to distinguish themselves from not only the metropolitan French but the Indian and English-speaking populations of North America.

Initially, the British authorities planned to force the assimilation of the colony's French-speaking, Catholic population, following the directive of the Royal Proclamation. However, both practical and strategic concerns led them to abandon this plan. In 1774 the Quebec Act restored seigneurial rights, the tithe, and the Civil Code. In 1791, the Constitutional Act established a representative assembly, as the colony's growing English-speaking population had long demanded, but divided the colony into Lower Canada (the basis of present-day Quebec) and Upper Canada (the basis of present-day Ontario).

Within Lower Canada, French-speaking *Canadiens* composed the overwhelming majority of the population; they enjoyed a majority of seats within Lower Canada's assembly. Nonetheless, English speakers were predominant within two superior bodies, appointed by the colonial governor. As an emerging petite bourgeoisie of French-speaking lawyers, notaries, and doctors used the assembly to champion the interests of the largely agrarian *Canadiens,* the English-speaking colonial bourgeoisie, heavily involved in timber trade, land speculation, and banking, sought to use the upper bodies to promote canal construction and related projects. At the same time, English speakers regularly championed projects to force assimilation of the *Canadiens.* Out of this conflict there emerged a *Canadien* nationalist movement, *les Patriotes,* which led to an abortive rebellion against British rule in 1836–1837.

With the failure of the rebellions, leadership within French-Canadian society fell to the church and associated forces which articulated a conservative, apolitical version of French-Canadian nationalism, upholding Catholic spirituality and the preeminence of the church and extolling the rural life over commerce and industry.

After being merged into the United Canadas in 1840, Quebec and Ontario joined New Brunswick and Nova Scotia in 1867 to create a new confederation, the basis of present-day Canada. Despite the confederal referent, the Canadian system is in fact federal. Even this feature was largely the result of the insistence of French-Canadian delegates who feared that a unitary system would place distinctive French-Canadian institutions at the mercy of the overwhelming English-speaking majority. However, the designation of provincial jurisdictions was itself a reflection of the priorities of the conservative, clerical leadership which supported confederation. While provinces were granted jurisdiction over such matters as education, social welfare, and civil law (thus protecting traditional French-Canadian institutions), economic functions were firmly placed in federal hands. Defense of provincial autonomy became a constant of Quebec political life, faithfully intoned by all provincial governments. This Quebec autonomism was reinforced by the chronic underrepresentation of French speakers in federal institutions and the steady decline of the French-speaking communities in most other provinces (usually reinforced by repressive English-only laws).

With the turn of the century Quebec began the transition to an urban, industrial society. By the 1930s the bulk of French speakers were living in urban areas, many of them as members of an industrial working class. In the 1950s, there emerged a substantial new middle class of intellectuals, administrators, engineers, and other professionals. This class began to challenge clerical control of education and social services and to call for an end to the historical predominance of English speakers in both the ownership and management of the Quebec economy. These objectives necessarily entailed a more interventionist Quebec state.

During the 1950s the Union Nationale government of Maurice Duplessis largely resisted these demands. But with the 1960 election of Jean Lesage's Parti Libéral, the Quebec government was rapidly expanded, assuming direct control of education and social functions and creating a network of state enterprises. These initiatives were legitimized within a new variant of French-Canadian nationalism which defined the nation in terms of Quebec alone and called for the transformation of the provincial government into a national state.

This period of Liberal government (1960–1966), commonly known as the "Quiet Revolution," saw an escalation in tension between Quebec and the rest of Canada as Quebec neonationalists contended that the existing federal system could afford the Quebec government neither the powers nor the status which befit its new role as a national state.

Proposals proliferated for a new constitutional arrangement: special status for Quebec, the construction of the federal level along binational lines, Quebec sovereignty linked to a Canadian economic association, etc. Nonetheless, the federal government under the leadership of Pierre Elliott *Trudeau (1968–1979 and 1980–1984) roundly rejected any scheme which would recognize Quebec's specificity, instead championing the constitutional entrenchment of a variety of rights: political, legal, and linguistic. The protection of the French language minorities outside Quebec, through official bilingualism, was the centerpiece in the federal strategy for countering Quebec nationalism.

As the constitutional stalemate persisted, support steadily grew in Quebec for the Parti Québécois (PQ), founded in 1968 with René Lévesque as its leader. The PQ called for Quebec to assume political sovereignty, while remaining closely linked to the rest of Canada in an economic association. Upon its election to the Quebec government in 1976 the PQ undertook a series of social and political reforms and, in particular, reinforced through Bill 101 the law on French preeminence which had been put in place by the Liberal government of Robert Bourassa (1970–1976). But in a May 1980 referendum, the PQ government was unable to secure majority support for its proposal that it be given a mandate to negotiate sovereignty-association with the rest of Canada.

With the failure of the Quebec referendum, the federal government seized the occasion to pursue Pierre Trudeau's alternative vision of repatriating the Canadian Constitution and entrenched bill of rights. In the fall of 1981 the federal government succeeded in securing the approval of all provincial governments but Quebec to revision of the Constitution along these lines. Thus, the Constitution was revised without Quebec's formal approval. In the wake of this additional setback, Quebec nationalist forces appeared to have lost much of their drive. The Parti Québécois remained in power until 1985, but in the process was led to defer indefinitely its sovereignty objective.

With the return to power of the Bourassa Liberals in 1985 efforts were renewed to secure Quebec's formal adhesion to the Constitution. These efforts produced a new package of changes, commonly dubbed the Meech Lake Accord, which had the approval of all ten premiers and the Canadian prime minister. However, over the next three years, changes in provincial governments coupled with the rapid rise in English-Canadian opposition to the accord resulted in failure of two provincial legislatures to approve the accord within the three-year time limit.

This failure of the accord, coupled with the evident English-Canadian opposition to any recognition of Quebec's specificity, clearly has refueled the cause of Quebec sovereignty. Moreover, the continuing decline of the Francophone minorities outside Quebec has effectively undermined the federal government's efforts to counter Quebec nationalism through official bilingualism. Nonetheless, Quebec's accession to sovereignty is not a foregone conclusion.

(See also FEDERALISM; INTERNAL COLONIALISM; REFORM; RELIGION AND POLITICS.)

Denis Monière, *Ideologies in Quebec* (Toronto, 1981). Kenneth McRoberts, *Quebec: Social Change and Political Crisis*, 3d ed. (Toronto, 1988). Pierre Fournier, *A Meech Lake Post-mortem: Is Quebec Sovereignty Inevitable?* (Montreal, 1991). Philip Resnick, *Toward a Canada-Quebec Union* (Montreal, 1991).

KENNETH McROBERTS

R

RACE AND RACISM

The study of race and racism is a rapidly growing field in the social sciences. Over the past few decades there has been a flowering of studies of race and ethnic differences and their social meaning in various historical, social, political, and economic contexts. Theoretical and political debates have raged during this time, and have sometimes led to bitter conceptual and political arguments. At the same time the analysis of race and racism has become an established field of study in a number of social science disciplines, most notably in sociology, political science, economics, anthropology, cultural studies, and geography. The literature emanating from all these disciplines has multiplied over the years, particularly in the United States, Britain and other European societies, and South Africa.

There seem to be two major reasons for this growing interest in the study of race and racism. First, and most importantly, there has been an evident preoccupation with racial issues in a variety of societies, including the United States, South Africa, and a number of societies in Western Europe. Studies have shown that racial inequalities and injustices continue to be reproduced at a number of levels, ranging from the economic, social, and political to the cultural. Second, associated with this awareness of the persistence of racial inequalities there has been a realization that racism continues to be a vital, and some would say growing, force in contemporary societies.

Whatever the explanation for the recent flowering of interest in the study of race and racism, it is clear that current debates have led to the emergence of a variety of schools of thought. There is by no means agreement about the definition of the key concepts of race and racism, nor about their relevance for social analysis. Some scholars argue that the concept of race has no relevance for social analysis, while others have questioned whether racism exists as a unified category or is composed of a variety of political and social discourses and practices. Given these theoretical differences it is useful to explore diverse explanations of racial and ethnic phenomena in the contemporary political environment and their implications for sociopolitical change.

Theoretical and Conceptual Origins. The study of race as a field of social-scientific inquiry and research can be seen as originating in the work of a number of American social theorists, including most notably Robert E. Park, Charles S. Johnson, and E. Franklin Frazier. From a different perspective the work of black writers, most notably W. E. B. *Du Bois, helped to establish the centrality of race to the analysis of U.S. society. During the period from the 1920s to the 1950s the works of this group of writers helped to establish what came to be defined as the study of race relations, particularly through their studies of segregation, immigration, and race consciousness in the United States. During the interwar period the works of these authors helped to develop a body of sociological concepts which were later to be refined into a sociology of race relations.

Early sociological theorizing on race in the United States saw race as a relevant social category only to the extent to which cultural and social meanings were attached to the physical traits of a particular social group. This in turn helped to popularize notions about the origins of racial conflicts and prejudice which concentrated on situations of cultural contact. Emphasis in sociological studies of the race problem during these decades was on the origins of race prejudice, the interplay between prejudice and conflict, the impact of assimilation on the life of *African Americans, and the processes by which racial conflicts could be mediated or overcome.

These early studies of race did not actually talk about racism as such. This is a more recent concept and its usage was linked to the rise of Nazism in Germany. As the Nazis came to power and articulated and put into practice their ideas about racial superiority, the term *racism* came to be used to refer to ideas which defined some racial or ethnic groups as superior and others as inferior. This usage of the term was first suggested by Ruth Benedict in her book *Race and Racism* (London, 1942), which defined racism as "the dogma that one ethnic group is condemned by nature to congenital inferiority and another group is destined to congenital superiority." In this context racism was seen as referring to those sets of ideas that defined ethnic and racial groups on the basis of claims about biological nature and inherent superiority or ability.

In the post-1945 period a number of developments outside of the United States encouraged interest in the study of race and racism in other societies. An important development in this context was the emergence of migrant labor as an important social group in many West European societies. Migration from the ex-colonies and southern Europe led to the creation of racial and ethnic minorities in countries such as Britain, France, the Federal Republic of Germany (FRG), and the Netherlands. Another important development was the entrenchment of the *apartheid system in South Africa, a process which aroused the interest of both social scientists and political activists, particularly in relation to the role of the political and legal systems in enforcing racial segregation and the "separate development" of different racial groups.

In Britain and other European societies, the growth in the theorization of race and racism ran parallel to these developments. This work has provided a number of important and sophisticated analyses of the politics and *ideology of racism. There were two central concerns in these early European attempts to theorize racial and ethnic relations; first, the patterns of immigration and incorporation in the labor market of black and other ethnic communities; second, the role of colonial history in determining popular conceptions of color, race, and ethnicity in European societies. Most studies of this period concentrated on the interaction between minority and majority communities in employment, housing, and other social contexts.

Although many of these studies were influenced by the early American theories, they also included theoretical works of some significance. Michael Banton's book *Race Relations* (London, 1967) represents a good example of texts from this period. It looked at race relations from a global and historical perspective, concentrating particularly on situations of cultural contact, beliefs about the nature of race, and the social relations constructed on the basis of racial categories. By looking at the experience of changing patterns of interaction historically, Banton argued that six basic orders of race relations could be delineated: institutionalized contact, acculturation, domination, paternalism, integration, and pluralism.

Political Sociology of Racism. An important focus of research in recent years has been on the role of political institutions in shaping the position of racial minorities in particular societies. As William Julius Wilson has pointed out, political and legal frameworks are an important element in contemporary situations governed by racial domination and inequality. This is a theme which has been developed over the past three decades in the works of political sociologists who have looked at a variety of race relations situations, ranging from South Africa to Britain and the United States.

This concern with relations of *power and privi-lege has influenced the study of race and racism in a fundamental way. A clear example of this trend is John Rex's *Race Relations in Sociological Theory* (2d ed., London, 1983), which attempts to provide a broad theoretical framework for the study of race relations. According to Rex's analytic model, the definition of social relations between persons as race relations is encouraged by the existence of certain structural conditions: e.g., frontier situations of conflict over scarce resources, the existence of unfree, indentured, or slave labor, unusually harsh *class exploitation, strict legal intergroup distinctions and occupational segregation, differential access to power and prestige, cultural diversity and limited group interaction, and migrant labor as an underclass fulfilling stigmatized roles in a metropolitan setting. From this perspective the study of race relations is concerned with situations in which such structured conditions interact with actors' definitions in such a way as to produce a racially structured social reality.

Marxism, Racism, and Class Theory. The other main conceptual framework which has influenced the study of race and racism in recent years is *Marxism. Early Marxist work on racial and ethnic divisions concentrated particularly on race and class as modes of exploitation. Oliver Cox's *Caste, Class and Race* (New York, 1948) is an early example of this focus. Cox was primarily interested in the economic interests which produce racist exploitation and ideologies historically, and explained racial inequality as an outcome of the interest of the capitalist class in super-exploiting sections of the working class. Because he saw class divisions as the fundamental source of exploitation in society, the main thrust of his work was to conceptualize racial exploitation as a special form of class exploitation. This model was subsequently to exercise a deep influence on the work of Marxist writers on race in the United States and, to a more limited extent, in European and other societies.

The majority of recent Marxist studies, however, are critical both of the work of Cox and of classical Marxism. It has been pointed out, for example, that although the works of *Marx and Engels contain a number of scattered references to the pertinence of racial and ethnic relations in certain social formations (e.g., the reference to race as an economic factor in the slavery of the United States), they contain little historical or theoretical reflection on the role of such processes in the capitalist mode of production as a whole. Perhaps even more damaging, a number of critics have argued that several statements on race by Marx and Engels reveal traces of the dominant racial stereotypes of their time and an uncritical usage of common racist imagery. Additionally, a number of critics of Marxism have argued that the reliance by Marxists on the concept of class has precluded them from analyzing racial and ethnic phenomena in their own right, short of subsuming them under wider social relations or treating them as a kind of superstructural phenomenon.

Recent studies in the United States and Britain have focused more specifically on the role of the *state as a site for the reproduction of racially structured situations. Drawing partly on recent Marxist debates on the nature of the capitalist state, a number of studies have analyzed the interplay between politics and racism in specific historical settings. Studies of the role of state institutions in maintaining racialized structures in a number of societies, particularly the United States and South Africa, have highlighted the importance of the political context of racism. This has raised important questions and problems: What is the precise role of the state in the reproduction of racially structured social relations? How far can the state be transformed into an instrument of antiracist political actions? These and other questions are currently being explored and debated.

As mentioned earlier, the claim that racism is a source of division within the working class was central to the work of early Marxist writers such as Cox. This theme has once again become central to contemporary debates about racism and class formation. In their study of immigrant workers in the class structure of Western Europe, Stephen Castles and Godula Kosack (*Immigrant Workers and Class Structure in Western Europe,* London, 1973) deal with the way in which the state has intervened to create two distinct strata within the working class through the system of contract labor, which denies political rights to the essentially foreign lower stratum. This lower stratum is said to perform the function of a reserve army of labor.

In Britain, the work of Robert Miles represents the most fully developed Marxist analysis of racism as a social and historical phenomenon. His writings reflect a deep concern with overcoming the potentially divisive impact of racism on class organization and radical political action. His analysis was first articulated in *Racism and Migrant Labour* (London, 1982), which is perhaps the most sustained attempt to include the study of racism within the mainstream of Marxist social theory. His empirical research has focused specifically on the situation in Britain and in the rest of Western Europe, and has looked at the role of political, class, and ideological relationships in shaping our understandings of racial conflict and change in these societies.

A final aspect of recent debates about the pertinence of Marxism to the analysis of race and racism is the question of whether there is an intrinsic Eurocentric bias in the core of Marxist theory. This theme has been taken up in recent years by a number of critics of Marxism and by others who profess to be sympathetic to the Marxist tradition. Perhaps the most important statement of this position is Cedric Robinson's *Black Marxism* (London, 1983), which argues forcefully that Marxism is inextricably tied to Western European philosophical traditions which cannot easily incorporate the experience of racism and ethnic divisions. This and other studies seem certain to raise questions which will play a part in Marxist discussions for some time to come.

What seems clear is that Marxist discussion of race and racism is searching for a new agenda for the analysis of the dynamics of racial categorization, and there are some encouraging signs of development and renewal. Important contributions are being made to this debate from a number of countries, and these are helping to fashion new perspectives on the role of the state in maintaining racial domination. Good examples of such research are the numerous studies of the South African state and its part in institutionalizing the apartheid system since 1948. These studies have shown that the state and legal institutions played an integral role in the establishment and maintenance of apartheid. They have also suggested that the state must be included as a key actor in the study of racism in different national and political contexts.

Politics, Power, and Racism. Concern with the state and politics has been evident in studies of the United States and Europe as well. A key concern of a number of recent U.S. studies has been the interrelationship between relations of politics, power, and racism. As Michael Omi and Howard Winant argue, one of the most salient features of racial relations in contemporary societies is the role of political and legal relations in defining the existence of racial categories and defining the social meanings of notions such as racial inequality, racism, and *ethnicity.

This theme has been taken up in recent years in studies of the situation of black and other ethnic minorities in Europe. Such studies have looked particularly at the processes by which minority communities and migrant workers are often excluded from equal access to political institutions and are denied basic social and economic rights. It is interesting to note in this context that in countries such as the FRG and France a key point in recent political conflicts has been the question of whether migrant workers should be given greater political rights.

The position of black minorities in Britain represents something of a special case in this regard, and a key concern of a number of recent studies of the politics of race in Britain has been to develop a conception of racialization as a process which has specific effects on politics and ideology. Aspects of this process include the impact of racist ideologies and nationalist discourses, antiracist discourses, and the influence of black political action on political institutions and forms of political mobilization.

It is within this context that the concepts of racial categorization and racialization have been used to refer to what Robert Miles in *Racism* calls "those instances where social relations between people have been structured by the signification of human biological characteristics in such a way as to define and construct differentiated social collectivities." A number of writers have attempted to use these concepts to analyze the processes by which race has been socially and politically constructed in specific historical, political, and institutional contexts.

Good examples of such studies include attempts to critically analyze the role of race relations legislation, the emergence of black minority representation in political institutions, and the development of public policies dealing with specific aspects of racial inequality in areas such as employment and housing. The premise of such studies is that the processes by which race is given particular meanings are variable across and within national boundaries and are shaped by political, legal, and socioeconomic environments. Comparative studies of immigration policies in Europe have shown, for example, that the construction of legislation to control the arrival of specific groups of migrants was often the subject of intense political and ideological controversy.

Race, Culture, and Ethnicity. The changing form of racial ideologies in advanced industrial societies is perhaps best illustrated by the recent debates about the role of racial imagery and symbols in the mass media, literature, art, and other cultural forms. A growing body of work has been produced on the use of race as a symbol in various areas of cultural expression and experience. Reacting against what they see as the lack of an account of cultural forms of racial discourse, a number of writers have sought to develop a more rounded picture of contemporary racial imagery by looking at the role of literature, the popular media, and other cultural forms in representing changing images of race and ethnicity. As David Goldberg has pointed out (*Anatomy of Racism,* Minneapolis, 1990), "the presumption of a single monolithic racism is being displaced by a mapping of the multifarious historical formulations of *racisms.*"

This has led to growing interest in how racist ideologies developed and in the various forms such ideologies have taken at different stages of development. Although this issue had not received much scholarly attention in the past, the renewed interest in the analysis of culture and discourse has helped to overcome this neglect, and the historical, cultural, literary, and philosophical roots of ideologies of race are coming under scrutiny. Specifically, questions are being asked about the role that ideological relations can play in providing a basis for the articulation of racist discourses and practices.

The role of the press and other popular media in shaping social images about racial and ethnic minorities has been a particular focus. A number of detailed studies have examined how press coverage of racial questions can help to construct images of racial minorities as outsiders and as a threat to social cohesion (Teun van Dijk, *Racism and the Press,* London, 1991). One interesting illustration of this process was the furor over the response of Muslim communities to the publication of Salman Rushdie's *The Satanic Verses* (London, 1989). The attempt by some Muslim community leaders to use the affair as a means of political mobilization received extensive coverage in the media and led to a wide-ranging debate about the "future of race relations" in British society. Sections of the press used the events surrounding the Rushdie affair to question the possibility of a peaceful transition toward a multiracial society. Hostile media coverage of the events surrounding the political mobilizations around the Rushdie affair thus served to reinforce the view that minorities who do not share the dominant political values of British society pose a threat to social stability and cohesion. The affair also gave added impetus to debates about the multiple cultural and political identities that have been included in the broad categorization of "black and ethnic minority communities."

Another focus has been the role of race and ethnicity as symbols in a variety of cultural forms, including literature and the cinema. This had been a neglected area of research, but in recent years this has been remedied by the publication of a number of important studies of race, culture, and identity. Originating largely from the United States, such studies have looked at a number of areas, including literature, the cinema, and other popular cultural forms, such as television and radio, along with advertising. They have sought to show that within contemporary societies our understandings of race, and the articulation of racist ideologies, cannot be reduced to economic, political, or class relations. This line of argument is exemplified by Henry Louis Gates, Jr.'s *The Signifying Monkey* (New York, 1988), which attempts to outline a framework for the analysis of images of race within the context of literature in the United States.

Apart from studies of contemporary trends, there has also been a growing interest in historical research on the origins of ideas about race and in the dynamics of race, class, and *gender during the colonial period. This has been reflected in important and valuable accounts of the changing usage of racial symbols during the past few centuries and in accounts of the experiences of colonialism and their impact on our understandings of race and culture. The work of Gayatri Spivak (*In Other Worlds,* London, 1987) has helped to highlight, for example, the complex processes of racial and gender identification experienced by the colonized during the colonial and postcolonial periods. Other studies have sought to show that the oppressed themselves have produced their own discourses about race and identity in the context of their own experiences of domination and exclusion.

Conclusion. In the context of the current political environment it is likely that questions about racism will remain an important component of the political agenda in many societies. It is therefore important to analyze the changing discourses and practices about race in contemporary societies rather than assume that they can be subsumed under an ahistorical and unchanging category of racism. Developments in the United States, Europe, and South Africa point to the need to see racial ideologies as unstable and as liable to transformation and change. Indeed, in the contemporary European environment the transformations in Eastern and *Central Europe have introduced a new dimension to debates about race and ethnicity, and one which existing accounts of the Western European situation seem to be singularly incapable of dealing with.

The analytical models outlined above also point to the need to broaden existing research priorities to include a multidimensional view of racial discourses. Such a view will need to include perspectives about economic, social, political, cultural, and legal expressions of ideas about race and ethnicity. Indications are that recent theoretical contributions in this field have looked more seriously at the cultural dimension and have helped shed new light on contemporary racisms which have received little attention. But recent political trends worldwide point to the urgency for us to develop more adequate conceptualizations of the workings of racisms as sets of ideas and as practices if we are to be able to challenge and overcome them.

(See also CIVIL RIGHTS MOVEMENT; COLONIAL EMPIRES; DECOLONIZATION; EQUALITY AND INEQUALITY; IDEOLOGY; INTERNATIONAL MIGRATION; KING, MARTIN LUTHER, JR.; MALCOLM X.)

William Julius Wilson, *Power, Racism and Privilege* (New York, 1973). Henry Louis Gates, Jr., ed., *"Race," Writing and Difference* (Chicago, 1986). Michael Omi and Howard Winant, *Racial Formation in the United States* (New York, 1986). John Rex and David Mason, eds., *Theories of Race and Ethnic Relations* (Cambridge, U.K., 1986). Robert Miles, *Racism* (London, 1989).

JOHN SOLOMOS
LES BACK

REAGAN, Ronald Wilson. Fortieth president of the *United States, from 1981 to 1989, Ronald Reagan was born on 6 February 1911 in Tampico, Illinois, to Jack and Nelle Reagan. In 1920, the Reagans moved to Dixon, west of Chicago, and this remains, to Reagan, his hometown. Reagan's childhood centered on sports, especially football. Reagan attended Eureka College in Illinois from 1928 to 1932, where he played football and graduated with a degree in economics.

The future president initially pursued a show business career, and he landed his first job as a radio sports announcer in Des Moines, Iowa, in 1933. A 1937 screen test led him to Hollywood and a contract with Warner Brothers studios where Reagan began a thirty-year career in films and television. During his Hollywood years, Reagan married actress Jane Wyman, whom he later divorced, and in 1952 he married actress Nancy Davis.

The Hollywood years engendered Reagan's interest in politics. He was active in negotiations on behalf of the Screen Actors Guild and served six terms as its president. Reagan served in the Army Air Corps during World War II, achieving the rank of captain. After the war, Reagan began to speak against *communism in Hollywood, and he publicly renounced his lifelong affiliation with and support for the Democratic Party in 1952. As Reagan's film career waned, he moved to television, hosting "General Electric Theater," and making motivational and political speeches at GE plants throughout the country.

A 1964 speech on behalf of Republican presidential candidate Barry Goldwater brought Reagan national attention, and he was urged to run for public office. He did so successfully when, at the age of 55, he defeated incumbent Edmund G. ("Pat") Brown to become governor of California in 1967. Reagan's two terms as governor established a strategy later used as president: stark ideologically driven policy proposals that would be modified and compromised in order to gain passage. Hence, while governor the conservative Reagan signed legislation extending the availability of abortions and tightening the control of handguns. Reagan's staff operation was characterized by a decentralized and delegated management style; aides such as Edwin Meese and Michael Deaver played significant policy development and advising roles that would mirror later functions in the White House.

Reagan sought the presidency three times. In 1968 he made an aborted run that began and ended at the Republican National Convention in Miami. After completing his second term as California governor in 1975, Reagan mounted an unsuccessful challenge to President Gerald Ford for the 1976 Republican nomination. The 1980 presidential election saw Reagan gain the Republican nomination, defeating a field of challengers that included George *Bush (who had described Reagan's proposed supply-side economic plan as "voodoo economics"), but then chose Bush as his vice-presidential running mate.

Running against an incumbent President Jimmy *Carter, Reagan identified the economy, government growth, declining U.S. prestige abroad, and the increasing threat posed by the Soviet Union as the themes of his campaign. With Americans held hostage in Iran, high inflation, and a $60 billion budget deficit, Reagan won with fifty-one percent of the popular vote and 489 electoral college votes. Riding on Reagan's coattails was a new conservative majority in the Senate.

The first year of Reagan's presidency stands as his most significant domestically; his last years were most memorable with respect to *foreign policy.

Reagan survived an *assassination attempt in March 1981, and his vigorous and speedy recovery brought him goodwill from Congress and the nation. Although the president ran against Washington in his 1980 campaign, once ensconced in the White House, Reagan became the consummate insider, willing to strike deals, negotiate, and reward those in Congress voting for him. As a result, Reagan was able to gain passage from the Democratic House and Republican Senate of sweeping tax reductions that were designed to induce economic growth.

Reducing marginal tax rates to thirty-three percent (twenty-eight percent at the top of the income scale) and altering the corporate income scale from forty-six percent to thirty-four percent, the abatement of inflation, the reduction of unemployment, and tax simplification constitute significant changes. The nation's fortieth president presided over the longest peacetime economic expansion in history. Yet the Reagan tax cuts and defense spending transformed the United States into the world's biggest debtor. A conservative Republican president submitted a $1.15 trillion federal budget to Congress for fiscal year 1990.

The conservative social agenda Reagan pursued met with limited success. On *New Right issues such as abortion and school prayer, Congress refused to act and Reagan declined to push. With a Republican-controlled Senate, Reagan turned to using his power to appoint federal judges as a method by which some of his social agenda items could be achieved without the Congress. This was evident at all levels of the federal judiciary, including the four appointments Reagan made to the U.S. *Supreme Court. The president sought to appoint young conservatives who would follow traditions of judicial restraint and loyalty to Reagan's political and social agenda. The federal judicial appointments Reagan made, over sixty percent of all federal judges by the time of his 1989 departure, stand as a significant legacy.

In foreign affairs, the Intermediate Nuclear Forces (INF) treaty, the Moscow summit, and the Reagan-Gorbachev relationship placed Ronald Reagan in the role of "peacemaker"—a person who had once described his Soviet adversaries as an "evil empire." The Strategic Defense Initiative (SDI), or Star Wars, engendered great debate, and by 1988 over $12 billion had been committed to the SDI program. Reagan did not get all he wanted, but the program was on the table as a potential bargaining chip.

The Reagan doctrine of aiding anticommunist freedom fighters and replacing communist regimes with democratic ones found success and failure. Reagan's tough-line policy, which included selling Stinger missiles to the rebels, hastened the Soviet retreat from Afghanistan. The Reagan legacy in Central America is mixed, and the Iran-contra initiative should bring only an inheritance of chagrin. Reagan's fixation on the *contras as freedom fight-

ers left unresolved such issues as the serious international debt crisis.

U.S. military presence as a peacekeeping force in Lebanon and later in Grenada demonstrated Reagan's willingness to use the armed forces. His frustration with terrorist activities emanating from Libya and inability to rescue U.S. hostages being held in Lebanon culminated in an air raid over Libya in April 1986. The house of Libyan leader Muammar *Qaddafi was hit in the attack. Qaddafi has, since the attack, minimized further public criticism of the United States.

The first term defined Reagan's management and organizational style in the White House. As in California, Reagan chose to delegate much of his authority to aides and advisers, and predicated policy formulation and success on the appointment of like-minded, loyal followers. The extent of delegated authority elicited criticism as Reagan worked limited hours and vacationed frequently. Many charged that Reagan was inattentive to detail and delegated too much responsibility to his staff without the necessary oversight.

His use of staff stands out further in the manner in which Reagan became susceptible to the large and unaccountable institutionalized presidency. Several former staff assistants later drew devastating portraits of life inside the White House. Reagan's staff used the president's schedule to maximize policy agenda exposure, scripted the president's public appearances to minimize diversion from that agenda, and attempted to manipulate media coverage of the president. A widely agreed-upon Reagan legacy was his use of imagery, video, and in-house experts to maximize favorable exposure and minimize criticism. Hence, unscripted media events, such as news conferences, were infrequent. The Reagan style was one of detachment from White House staff operations, a disinclination to sustain the cerebral combat of press conferences, verbal gaffes, and inattentiveness to facts. The mangling of facts was often a cause of embarrassment: Reagan identified President Samuel Doe of Liberia as "Chairman Moe." He failed to recognize his secretary of housing and urban development, Samuel Pierce, and called him "Mayor."

Reagan won reelection in 1984 with a landslide victory over Democratic challenger Walter Mondale; he garnered 525 electoral votes, a record, and fifty-nine percent of the popular vote. On the heels of military success in Grenada, U.S. athletic triumphs at the Los Angeles Olympic Games, and economic recovery, Reagan proclaimed it was "morning again" in America.

Entering his second term, Reagan had yet to meet with a Soviet leader. As economic growth continued, Reagan turned his attention and priorities to foreign policy. The successful tax reforms of 1986 were the major domestic initiative attained during the second term. Reagan devoted most of his energy to forging a line of communication with new Soviet leader Mikhail *Gorbachev. The first of several summits between the two leaders occurred in November 1985 in Geneva. At that and subsequent meetings, Reagan and Gorbachev created a warm friendship. Gorbachev's open attempts to democratize Soviet society and create a free-market economy mandated military cuts; therefore, he and Reagan made substantial progress in arms reductions talks.

Indeed, *public opinion polls show that President Reagan received his strongest ratings in the area of reducing the chance of nuclear war with the Soviets. This stands in striking contrast to the greatest fear about Ronald Reagan in 1981: the likelihood of precipitating a nuclear confrontation with the Soviets. The images of Ronald Reagan and Mikhail Gorbachev strolling together through Red Square in May 1988 in the bliss of glasnost and *perestroika had a profound impact on the public.

Reagan retained high personal popularity in his second term, although the last two years were controversy-ridden. The 1986 midterm elections brought the Democratic Party back into control of the Senate. One result of that switch was the 1987 defeat of Reagan's Supreme Court justice nominee Robert H. Bork.

In late 1986, it was revealed that several members of Reagan's National Security Council staff had been engaged in illegal activities including selling arms to Iran and diverting the profits of those sales to the Nicaraguan contras who had been denied aid by Congress. The controversy resulted in a commission investigation, congressional testimony, and temporary damage to Reagan's popularity. Even as he left office, a majority of the public believed the full story on the Iran-contra affair had not been revealed.

During his final two years in office, Reagan found himself the target of criticism for his clean-desk management style and decentralized decision making. The last two years were devoted to stemming attempts to minimize or curtail Reagan's economic legacy and to the creation of a stronger one in foreign policy. By 1988, Reagan turned his attention to campaigning for his vice president, George Bush, and was able to hand the reins of power over to Bush in January 1989.

Reagan will be remembered for bringing a tide of *conservatism to U.S. politics. As a domestic president, Reagan changed the face of campaigning and governing with imagery, symbols, and video, emphasized personal warmth and charisma, and forged success in economic growth and tax cuts and tax reform. His legacy will be tempered by long-term budget deficits and national debt and the Iran-contra scandal. Many of the tenets of Reagan's 1980 campaign, including reducing the size and scope of government and balancing the federal budget, were not realized.

Reagan's relationship with Mikhail Gorbachev dominates his foreign policy legacy and seemed to usher in a new era of U.S.-Soviet relations. Reagan's success in other regions of the world, such as the Middle East and Latin America, was limited and not enduring. Reagan's promise to enhance U.S. power in the international arena was successful through the military buildup that occurred under his watch and his display of force in selected regional conflicts. The extraordinary allied military success in the *Gulf War of 1991 owes much to the massive Reagan military budgets of 1981–1989. When President Reagan left office in January 1989, sixty-eight percent of U.S. citizens approved of his overall job performance, seventy-one percent approved of his handling of foreign relations, and sixty-two percent gave approval to his handling of the economy.

(See also AMERICAN FOREIGN POLICY; COLD WAR; CONGRESS, U.S.; NICARAGUA; PRESIDENCY, U.S.; STRATEGIC ARMS LIMITATION TREATIES; TAXES AND TAXATION; THATCHERISM.)

Sidney Blumenthal and Thomas Byrne Edsall, eds., *The Reagan Legacy* (New York, 1988). Charles O. Jones, ed., *The Reagan Legacy: Promise and Performance* (Chatham, N.J., 1988). Larry Berman, ed., *Looking Back on the Reagan Presidency* (Baltimore, 1990).

LARRY BERMAN
SCOTT HILL

REALISM. Also known as Political Realism or Realpolitik, Realism remains one of the dominant schools of thought within the field of *international relations. With a long intellectual pedigree, dating at least from *Thucydides' (ca. 460–400 B.C.E.) history of *The Peloponnesian War* and the writings of Niccolò Machiavelli (1469–1527) and Thomas Hobbes (1588–1679), Realism is distinguished from contending approaches by three assumptions regarding the nature of international politics.

First, the *international system is anarchic and based on the principle of self-help. By *anarchy, Realists do not mean that international politics are chaotic. Indeed, some proponents argue that relations between nations do exhibit regularities and are even driven by widely accepted social norms. Rather, for Realists anarchy simply means that the international system lacks any political authority higher than the *state. Unlike domestic politics, where a hierarchical pattern of authority exists to enforce private agreements and public laws, sovereign states stand in relations of formal equality. As a result, states are ultimately dependent on their own resources to protect their interests, enforce agreements, and maintain order.

Second, states are the dominant actors in world politics. While both private actors, such as multinational corporations, and intergovernmental organizations, such as the UN, exist and influence international politics, Realists assume they are subordinate to states. Private entities and intergovernmental organizations act within the political arena, but they do so only with the consent of national political authorities.

Third, in Hans Morgenthau's classic statement (*Politics Among Nations: The Struggle for Power and Peace,* 5th ed., rev., New York, 1978, p. 5), "statesmen think and act in terms of interest defined as power," broadly conceived to include both material and psychological, military and economic capabilities. The "national interest," in this view, is to maximize *power. Because power exists only relationally, it follows that world politics is inherently conflictual; all countries cannot increase their power or satisfy their national interests simultaneously.

Kenneth Waltz (in *Theory of International Politics,* Reading, Mass., 1979, p. 118) has recently refined this third assumption, clarifying the ambiguity between power as a means and as an end. "At a minimum," he writes, states "seek their own preservation and, at a maximum, drive for universal domination." Only after survival is assured, he continues, can they afford to seek other goals; as a result, states act, first and foremost, to maximize *security.

Realism emerged in its modern form largely in reaction to *Idealism, a more normatively driven approach which held that countries were united in an underlying harmony of interest—a view shattered by the outbreak of World War II. Rather than study the world as it might be, Realists maintained that a science of international politics must study the world as it was—an insistence that resulted in the Realists' self-acclaimed appellation.

The generation of Realists writing immediately before and after World War II, now referred to as the classical Realists, shared an essentially pessimistic view of human nature. Reinhold Niebuhr (1892–1971), Nicholas Spykman (1893–1943), Hans Morgenthau (1904–1980), and others believed that the struggle for power was inherent in human nature. Viewing humankind as unchanging, these Realists held out little hope for any transformation of international politics. Rather, they focused on the principles of *diplomacy and mechanisms—such as the *balance of power, international morality and world *public opinion, and *international law—which regulated and restrained the inevitable clashes of interests between states.

Contemporary Realists, often called Neorealists or Structural Realists, have sought to inject greater theoretic rigor by defining concepts more clearly and deriving testable hypotheses. Neorealists have also focused on the international system, examining how different structures—defined in terms of ordering principles, the functional differentiation of the units, and distributions of capabilities—produce varying patterns of world politics which cannot be explained simply in terms of the interests and policies of individual countries. Most fundamentally, Neorealists derive the causes of international conflict not from innate human characteristics but from anarchy. Given the necessary reliance on self-help, a state must prepare to defend itself against potential threats from others. In so preparing, however, it (perhaps unwittingly) threatens others—thereby creating a vicious cycle of increasing threat and insecurity. Thus, even though all states may possess thoroughly pacific intentions, international competition and conflict may still arise.

In the approximately forty-five years since it emerged as a clearly defined school of thought, Realism has stimulated a diverse research program. In a recent review, John A. Vasquez (*The Power of Power Politics: A Critique,* New Brunswick, N.J., 1983) identifies five foci within Realism: the study of 1) *foreign policy, which has sought both to clarify the concepts of national interest and power in the context of past and present policy problems and develop models of national decision making; 2) systemic processes, especially those that regulate international conflict; 3) the causes of *war; 4) *deterrence and bargaining, with a particular emphasis on *nuclear weapons and strategy; and 5) supranationalism, including *international organizations and international regimes. Since the early 1970s, a Realist school of *international political economy has also emerged. Focusing on the interaction of power and wealth, this school has been particularly concerned with the relationship between *hegemony, or the presence of a single dominant state, and international economic openness and closure.

Critiques of Realism. No theoretical approach to international relations, especially one as central as Realism, is without its critics. Although by no means an exhaustive list, it is possible to identify five general criticisms.

First, the predictive power of Realism, and its status as a positive theory of international relations, rests on the objective determination of the national interest—whether it be defined in terms of power or security. Only if the national interest is clear and unambiguous can the theorist discern whether countries do, in fact, adopt appropriate policies. Yet, "the trouble . . . ," as Arnold Wolfers noted in "'National Security' as an Ambiguous Symbol" (*Political Science Quarterly* 67, no. 4 [December 1952], p. 484), "is that the term 'security' covers a range of goals so wide that highly divergent policies can be interpreted as policies of security." As a consequence, the predictive and, in turn, explanatory power of Realism is weakened.

Second, many Realists, and especially Neorealists who explicitly exclude domestic policies from their theories, have treated the state as a unitary actor. Critics have charged that even if this "billiard-ball" view was appropriate for describing international relations in an earlier era, it is of declining relevance today. With the growth of private cross-border communications and organizations, and with the rise of economic *interdependence, the "hard shell" of the state has crumbled. According to Robert Keohane and Joseph Nye in *Power and Interdependence:*

World Politics in Transition (2d ed., Boston, 1989), relations between some countries and in some issue areas are better characterized by "complex interdependence"—where multiple channels connect societies, no clear hierarchy exists between the "high" politics of military security and "low" politics of economic affairs, and military force is of less utility.

Third, Neorealists have recently been criticized for being "statists," that is, assuming that states are the primary actors in world politics without explaining why they emerged as the predominant form of political organization or considering how they might evolve in the future. Fourth, and closely related, Neorealists have been challenged for not developing a dynamic theory which can explain the evolution of the international system through time. Specifically, critics within the "agent-structure" debate have argued that Neorealism must incorporate how the actions of "agents," or decision makers operating within the constraints of the system, affect in turn the structure of the system. In "Reflections on *Theory of International Politics:* A Response to My Critics" (in Robert O. Keohane, ed., *Neorealism and Its Critics,* New York, 1986), Waltz recognizes both of these problems and accepts them as inevitable limitations of relevant, "problem-solving" theory.

Finally, Realism does not adequately ground the national pursuit of power or security, however defined, in the interests and incentives of individual foreign policy decision makers. Classical Realism was developed before many of the advances in modern political science, and Neorealism seeks to derive strictly systemic theories of international politics. From a public or rational choice perspective, which accepts the methodological individualism of neoclassical economics, there is no necessary reason why the interests of self-seeking politicians should coincide with the national interest. Given the difficulties of translating social preferences into public policy, a considerable gap will often exist between the interests of the people as a whole and actual policy. To the extent that such difficulties arise, the explanatory power of Realism is further weakened.

Despite these limitations, Realism remains a powerful, simple, and elegant theory of international politics. Rather than focusing on *ideology, national *regime types, stages of economic development, and other particularistic or time-bound factors, Realism builds its explanations on the most general and enduring features of international politics—the struggle for power and security by self-seeking states within an anarchic international system—and in doing so provides both a persuasive explanation for conflict within the international arena and a guide for managing such disputes.

Normative Critique. Realism is often criticized for being amoral, and perhaps even immoral, in its elevation of the national interest over other ethical principles. Realism, as defined above, is a positive theory of international politics, and as such is not motivated primarily by normative concerns. Yet, to the extent that Realists enter the policy arena, whether as direct participants or outside experts, this criticism is not entirely inappropriate.

Realists do consider standards of conduct at the international level to be different from those governing behavior within states. In an anarchic world, national leaders must, at times, adopt or countenance actions that would be legally or morally repugnant in relations among individuals. As the environment changes, Realists maintain, definitions of morality must change too. As George F. Kennan writes in "Morality and Foreign Affairs" (*Foreign Affairs* 64, no. 2 [Winter 1985–1986], p. 206), the "primary obligation [of a government] is to the *interests* of the national society it represents, not to the moral impulses that individual elements of that society may experience."

As always, Realists emphasize the importance of studying the world as it is rather than as we wish it to be. This commitment to "realism" carries over into the evaluation of policy. As Hans Morgenthau concludes in "Another 'Great Debate': The National Interest of the United States" (*American Political Science Review* 46, no. 4 [December 1952], p. 988), "The contest between utopianism and realism is not tantamount to a contest between principle and expediency, morality and immorality. . . . The contest is rather between one type of political morality and another type of political morality, one taking as its standard universal moral principles abstractly formulated, the other weighing these principles against the moral requirements of concrete political action, their relative merits to be decided by a prudent evaluation of the political consequences to which they are likely to lead."

Edward Hallett Carr, *The Twenty Years' Crisis, 1919–1939* (New York, 1939). Stephen D. Krasner, *Defending the National Interest: Raw Materials Investments and U.S. Foreign Policy* (Princeton, N.J., 1978). Robert Gilpin, *The Political Economy of International Relations* (Princeton, N.J., 1987). Alexander Wendt, "The Agent-Structure Problem in International Relations" *International Organization* 41, no. 3 (Summer 1987): 335–370.

DAVID A. LAKE

REBELLION. See POLITICAL VIOLENCE.

RECIPROCITY. In *international law the term *reciprocity* refers to the principle that the *rights claimed by one state accrue to other states; or more generally, that the rights of one party accrue to comparable entities. Reciprocity is implied by the concept of *sovereignty, as developed in the fifteenth and sixteenth centuries: legally independent states, claiming authority over their own territories and populations, could not deny similar rights to other states. Astute diplomats have for centuries conceded rights to other states when, through the principle of reciprocity, they could therefore obtain equivalent rights themselves, and have refrained from claiming rights when such claims would imply more valuable comparable claims by others. As secretary of state of the United States in the early 1790s, for example, Thomas Jefferson was careful to make such use of the principle of reciprocity in his negotiations with Britain and France.

Reciprocity also refers to situations of interaction resulting from the intersection of actor strategies. Specific reciprocity refers to balanced exchanges in which each party's actions are contingent on the other's, in such a way that benefits are exchanged for benefits, but are withheld in the absence of compensation. Diffuse reciprocity refers to the observance of norms prescribing that one contribute one's fair share, or behave well toward others, for the sake of obtaining benefits for a group of which one is a part, rather than for the sake of specific conditional rewards.

In bilateral situations involving a combination of mutual interest in cooperation and conflict of interest over the distribution of gains—specifically, in what is known in *game theory as Prisoners' Dilemma—strategies of specific reciprocity can promote cooperation. Such cooperation can be seen not only in experimental games but also on such issues as international trade and *arms control. Specific reciprocity is often an appropriate principle of behavior when norms of obligation are weak because it protects participants against severe exploitation.

However, even in bilateral situations, specific reciprocity can accentuate conflict. Even moderate levels of uncertainty and misleading information ("noise") can prevent reciprocal cooperation from emerging; and reciprocity can lead to "feuds" as well as to cooperation. In multilateral situations, reciprocity can cause further difficulties, because reciprocal agreements between two parties can affect the value of previous agreements, thus engendering demands for renegotiation of older bargains. For instance, the conditional most-favored-nation (MFN) clause in U.S. trade policy before 1923 exemplified specific reciprocity: a concession given to one trading partner was not offered to others automatically, but only for negotiated compensation. The clause was eventually abandoned largely because the resulting negotiations were tedious, mutually irritating, and often fruitless.

Specific reciprocity in contemporary international politics is also complicated by differences in internal regulations among countries. For instance, in the late 1980s some members of the *European Community demanded that in order for banks from nonmember countries to have access to the Single European Market, those countries must grant reciprocal access to European banks. But the United States does not have unitary arrangements for banking, which is regulated by the states. The United States could offer "national treatment," in which European banks suffer no more restrictions in Illi-

nois or California than New York banks do, but it could not offer specific reciprocity, providing that a New York subsidiary of a German bank could operate in Illinois or California. For its part, the European Community could not implement specific reciprocity by discriminating against U.S. subsidiaries in Germany without fragmenting the regulatory framework that it had been at pains to establish.

Specific reciprocity is not, therefore, a guarantee of cooperation. Diffuse reciprocity, in which members of a community follow accepted norms of behavior toward one another, requires much less negotiation. For example, unconditional MFN treatment provides that all benefits provided to one trade partner are immediately generalized, without compensation, to all other trade partners to which unconditional MFN applies (e.g., among members of the *General Agreement on Tariffs and Trade [GATT]).

However, governments following strategies of diffuse reciprocity may be exploited by partners that seek gains at their expense or by others attempting to benefit from general observance of norms without doing so themselves. Institutional arrangements such as GATT and the European Community incorporate elements of both specific and diffuse reciprocity in order to encourage mutually beneficial exchange while limiting opportunities for exploitation.

Reciprocity will remain a central principle of world politics as long as separate units engage in exchange in a nonhierarchical system. Under favorable conditions, either specific or diffuse reciprocity can promote cooperation, but under unfavorable conditions, conflict can result. The appropriateness of various strategies of reciprocity depends both on the configuration of actors' interests and on prevailing institutional arrangements.

(See also INTERNATIONAL COOPERATION; INTERNATIONAL POLITICAL ECONOMY; REGIME.)

Martin Wight, *Systems of States* (Leicester, 1977). Robert Axelrod, *The Evolution of Cooperation* (New York, 1984). Robert O. Keohane, "Reciprocity in International Relations" *International Organization* 40 (Winter 1986): 1–27. George W. Downs and David M. Rucke, *Tacit Bargaining, Arms Races, and Arms Control* (Ann Arbor, Mich., 1990).
ROBERT O. KEOHANE

REFORM. The goal, in some form, of countless political leaders and social movements throughout history, reform has also been a central focus of reflection for political theorists ranging from Machiavelli to Marxists of the twentieth century. Successful reforms may serve not only to reorient policy but also to change the balance of social power and the contours of political debate. Failed reforms not only ruin political careers but even, in extreme cases, set the stage for violent upheavals. It is thus important, as Machiavelli acknowledged centuries ago in *The Prince,* to understand the difficult and often dangerous process that ushers in a "new order of things."

The *Oxford English Dictionary* defines reform as "the amendment, or altering for the better, of some faulty state of things, especially of a corrupt or oppressive political institution or practice; the removal of some abuse or wrong." This definition is useful, but both its empirical and normative components are controversial. The normative issue concerns whether or not reform necessarily represents "altering for the better." In the eyes of many Marxists, for example, attempts at "reform" within the capitalist system have traditionally been viewed as futile or even counterproductive, given that they may well delay the coming of the socialist *revolution that is deemed the only genuine solution to the oppressive practices of the current system. Even within the Marxist camp, however, another strong current—the revisionists or social democrats—has argued that cumulative reforms might well be the most effective way of producing a humane socialist society.

The major empirical issue is how broad or dramatic the scope of "amendment" must be to qualify as reform. Where should one draw the line between incremental change and genuine reform? Many policymakers have been known to herald even modest changes (e.g., the restructuring of an agency) as reforms precisely because they believe attaching such a label may have symbolic value, enhancing the perceived importance of their actions. Arguably the term should be reserved for more substantial instances of policy change; classic examples would be the 1832 Reform Act that significantly expanded the suffrage in Britain or the administrative reforms resulting from the Progressive movement in the United States during the nineteenth century.

In recent years the term reform has also been used, as in the case of the Soviet Union under Mikhail *Gorbachev, to describe an even more ambitious project: a multifaceted campaign undertaken by the government to restructure key state institutions, revamp a host of public policies, shift the balance of social power, and ultimately even change fundamental social values. According to most dictionaries, a sweeping reform of this sort should more properly be termed a "reformation," but that label is seldom employed by contemporary political analysts, no doubt owing to its inevitable association with the religious Reformation of the sixteenth century. At the expense of analytical precision, such political reformation projects—whether or not they be deemed fully successful—are now frequently referred to as "revolutions" (e.g., see Peter Jenkins, *Mrs. Thatcher's Revolution*, London, 1987, and Martin Anderson, *Revolution: The Reagan Legacy*, Stanford, Calif., 1988). A less confusing term for such phenomena, and thus the one that will be used here, is simply "great reforms."

Unlike revolutions, great reforms traditionally have not been the focus of extensive comparative analyses. However, the profusion of dramatic reform experiments over the last decade—including *Deng Xiaoping's China, Gorbachev's Soviet Union, and Margaret *Thatcher's Britain, to mention only the most prominent—has recently inspired a number of social scientists to examine the origins, dynamics, and effects of great reforms in a comparative perspective. The following is but a brief summary of some of their central findings.

First, great reforms have tended to be launched in what can be broadly described as a context of crisis. Whether the crisis stems from external threats (as in Peter the Great's Russia), economic depression (as in Franklin D. *Roosevelt's United States), political malaise, or some combination of factors, it can serve to open a window of opportunity for reformers by making action seem urgent and thus increasing support for what would otherwise be seen as excessively bold or risky ventures. Important though the facilitating role of crises has been, two caveats should be noted here: not all nations in crisis experience great reform experiments, and not all major reforms are introduced in a burst during a crisis period (in twentieth-century Sweden, for example, it was primarily the extraordinary longevity of Social Democratic rule that allowed for the implementation of great reforms; see T. J. Pempel, *Uncommon Democracies*, Ithaca, N.Y., 1990).

Second, although some reform leaders may appear to be ideologues, they generally lack a coherent blueprint for social change and act in a rather pragmatic fashion. For example, Margaret Thatcher and Ronald *Reagan were reputed to be ideological in the extreme, but political prudence led them both to shy away from or limit cuts in popular social programs (the National Health Service in Britain, Social Security in the United States) that contradicted their conservative views. Thatcher became best known for her vast program of *privatization (selling state-owned industries to private shareholders), but it was barely mentioned in her 1979 manifesto and was developed gradually in an experimental manner. Deng's reforms have proceeded in a zigzag fashion, as innovations have often been curtailed to mollify opposition. Roosevelt was famous for his experimentation and improvisation during the *New Deal of the 1930s, and Gorbachev employed a similar style.

Third, reform governments generally find it extremely difficult to maintain the support of all elements of the coalition that backed them initially. Once vague promises of reform are transformed into concrete policy, and once laundry lists of programs are reduced to manageable or affordable priorities, many erstwhile supporters become disappointed or even actively opposed to the government. Thus the New Deal coalition began to collapse in 1937, Deng found himself faced with explosive demonstrations in 1989, Thatcher was rejected by her own Conservative Party in 1990, and Gorbachev was ultimately ousted by forces who had once applauded his programs of glasnost and *perestroika.

Fourth, the effects of great reform campaigns vary enormously and are hard to gauge while they are still in progress. The administrations of Lyndon *Johnson (1963–1969) and Reagan (1981–1989) in the United States enjoyed enormous success in their early years but then stalled so badly that many would question categorizing them as examples of great reform. The Socialist government of François *Mitterrand in France met with a similar fate from 1981 to 1986. More dramatically, Salvador *Allende's Unidad Popular government in Chile enjoyed a promising first year of reform in 1970, but by 1973 it had been ousted in a bloody coup that led to the reversal of its initiatives and the abolition of democracy. The governments of both Deng in China and Gorbachev in the Soviet Union experienced serious problems right after scholars were beginning to portray their reforms as irreversible, and it is still too early to assess their achievements accurately. The Thatcher government illustrated how tenuous the concept of "irreversible reform" really is by privatizing enterprises that had been nationalized forty years before and had seemed destined to stay in the public sector forever. As many scholars have noted, the most durable reforms are no doubt those instituted in such a manner as to create beneficiaries (e.g., strengthened trade unions or welfare recipients) willing and able to fight for their retention years after reforms are introduced.

(See also POLITICAL REALIGNMENT.)

Samuel Huntington, *Political Order in Changing Societies* (New Haven, Conn., 1968). Adam Przeworski, *Capitalism and Social Democracy* (Cambridge, U.K. 1985). Michael Oksenberg and Bruce Dickson, "The Origins, Processes and Outcomes of Great Political Reform," in Dankwart Rustow and Kenneth Erickson, eds., *Comparative Political Dynamics* (New York, 1991), pp. 235–261. John T. S. Keeler, ed., "The Politics of Reform in Comparative Perspective," *Comparative Political Studies* special issue (January 1993).

JOHN T. S. KEELER

REFUGEES. Since the beginning of human history, refugees have been both a cause and consequence of intercommunal conflict. Today there are an estimated 18 million refugees who have crossed an international frontier and even more internally displaced persons. The predicament of present-day refugees is reminiscent of the experiences of earlier forced migrants. For example, the flight of Huguenots from France after the revocation of the Edict of Nantes in 1685 involved religious persecution, pirate attacks on "boat people" at sea, emergency assistance, legal protection, integration problems, overseas resettlement, and repatriation.

The quest for communal homogeneity along religious, ethnic, and political lines with its attendant problems of minorities and statelessness, the persistent tendency toward the centralization of state power, and the assertion of hegemonic control of territory, resources, and populations by national groups or ruling elites remains today, as it has been for centuries, at the root of forcible expulsions. The refugee policies of receiving *states, meanwhile, have been and continue to be animated by a composite of domestic and foreign policy calculations: pressure from domestic compatriot constituencies, the labor requirements of industrialization, preservation of relations with allies, embarrassment of adversaries, and, to a certain extent, humanitarianism.

The current situation is problematic because of increased restrictionism toward foreigners generally since the declining demand for foreign labor resulting from the oil embargo of 1973–1974; great power intervention, either directly or through proxies, in Vietnam, Afghanistan, the Horn of Africa, Angola, and Central America; uneven economic development, dramatic changes in demography, and ecological decay in many regions; as well as the belated and still-embryonic development of international procedures and institutions for addressing the problems of refugees.

What is also novel in the current situation is that the world's poorest countries both produce and host each other's refugees. These governments are unable or unwilling to provide for the basic security or subsistence needs of their own populations, let alone those of refugees. Attention to the psychological and social trauma of forced migration is rare. In a world in which nation-states lay increasingly firm claim to sovereign territorial control, refugees often exist both at the geographic frontiers between states and at the conceptual margins of international politics and law; they are frequently at the mercy of the capricious benevolence of asylum states and vulnerable to the political calculations of regional and international powers.

Throughout the twentieth century, defining the term *refugee* has itself been a serious political and conceptual problem for states and *international organizations. Until the imposition of immigration controls by many European and North American states in the late nineteenth century, there was little reason to define clearly the term *refugee*, as refugees constituted an exception to the usual categories of legally sanctioned immigrants. Until then, open immigration, including that of refugees, was permitted and encouraged by most states. In contrast to the present, immigrants and refugees were not considered a problem. Instead, they were frequently considered crucial to economic growth and a valuable cultural and intellectual resource. Ironically, for persons on the brink of personal disaster, refugee status has always been a privileged position, for refugees alone of the world's destitute are considered an exceptional category of migrants eligible for various forms of assistance, including asylum or membership in the polity, otherwise reserved by receiving states for recognized immigrants, usually on the basis of kinship, professional skills, or capital investment.

As a concept of *international law, the term *refugee* has evolved considerably since its entry into international affairs after *World War I. The earliest international legal instruments concerning refugees date from the 1920s and assigned refugee status to specific national groups, for example to Russians fleeing the Bolshevik Revolution. Such national groups were viewed as lacking the protection of their country of origin and in need of international protection. The Evian Conference of 1938, which addressed the flight of Jews from National Socialist Germany, marked the first instance of international recognition of the refugee as victim of persecution.

The currently favored definition of *refugee* is to be found in the UN Convention Relating to the Status of Refugees, drafted in 1951 and now adopted by 106 states. The UN Convention defines refugees, in essence, as persons who are outside their homeland owing to a well-founded fear of persecution on the basis of race, religion, nationality, membership in a social group, or political opinion. Since 1951, several regional accords, notably the Organization of African Unity Refugee Convention of 1969, have defined refugees in broader terms to include persons fleeing external aggression, occupation, foreign domination, or events seriously disturbing public order. In recent years, many states, especially in Western Europe, have created new categories of protection, such as "Humanitarian Refugee Status," or "B Refugee Status," that seek to accommodate persons fleeing their homeland for compelling reasons other than individual persecution, though such status usually entitles its recipients to fewer opportunities for naturalization, family unification, employment, and social welfare benefits than is granted to those accorded full refugee status.

There exists increasingly broad recognition that a conception of refugee status linked to persecution arose as a consequence of the European war and *Cold War experiences and is poorly adapted to other regions and current circumstances. The common analytic assumption of all refugee definitions throughout the twentieth century has been that a normal bond of trust, loyalty, protection, and assistance constitutes the basic political link between the citizen and the state, the violation of which engenders refugees. Much of the current debate among states regarding refugee status, of which the regional conventions and alternatives to full status are symptomatic, questions whether persecution is the sole phenomenon by which the social contract can be severed or whether the absence of state protection can manifest itself in diverse ways, including the state's inability to provide public order or subsistence. It is widely agreed that even the UN's current persecution-based definition encompasses especially predatory, politically motivated economic policies, such as the denial on racial, religious, or political

grounds of any opportunity for employment, and that the rigid distinction between so-called political and economic refugees is politically motivated and on weak jurisprudential ground. The definition of refugee has been a fluid one for at least three generations, and there is little reason to think that the current definition, any more than its predecessors, will remain unaffected by changing political conditions.

Stemming both from humanitarian sentiments and from a perception that refugees adversely affect state interests, an international refugee "regime" has been developing throughout the twentieth century. Originally under the auspices of the *League of Nations and later under the UN, a series of international organizations have been established to address the refugee problem. These institutions, including the present-day office of the United Nations High Commissioner for Refugees (UNHCR), have pursued a strategy of attempting to depoliticize the refugee issue and to emphasize instead its moral and humanitarian dimensions. The alternative solutions to the refugee's predicament identified by UNHCR include asylum (either within the region of origin or overseas), permanent resettlement in a new society, or eventual voluntary repatriation to the country of origin.

As with so many international political issues, the politics of refugees was complicated by the Cold War. Owing primarily to conflicts between the Soviet Union and the Western powers over the repatriation versus Western resettlement of Russian, Ukrainian, and Baltic nationals, the Soviet Union declined to support the UNHCR, and control of the organization fell to the West by default, which in turn led to the politicization of the refugee issue by the West to its strategic and ideological advantage. The United States went still further by enacting legislation which, until 1980, identified refugees by definition as persons fleeing *communism.

In comparison with other transnational procedural and institutional arrangements for dealing with trade, monetary issues, security, communications, and transport, the international refugee regime remains primitive. Nation-states are especially reluctant to cooperate when the defining characteristic of their identity—community membership—is potentially at issue, as it always is when asylum and permanent resettlement are a possibility. Moreover, an influx of refugees frequently complicates domestic relations between various ethnic or national groups, requiring the diversion of resources away from national development; complicates class relations, especially with the indigenous poor; leads to hostile relations with the country of origin; and exacerbates regional tensions. For these reasons, states continue to approach the refugee issue with policies that are both ad hoc and unilateral, emphasizing traditional rights of *sovereignty, thereby perpetuating an environment poorly suited to the formation of a cooperative and sophisticated regime. This can be said generally of national approaches to *international migration, including labor migration, which raises the question of whether international economic integration, harmonization, and a "global economy" can be created when a core component of production, labor, is omitted from the overall economic regime. Calls for so-called "international burden sharing" are common, although rarely realized, largely because emphasis is usually placed upon humanitarian obligations—always a weak incentive for action—rather than upon either the political, economic, and cultural assets that refugees can provide, or, where indeed they are a liability, the foreign and domestic policy advantages to individual states of collective action.

(See also FOREIGN WORKERS; HUMAN RIGHTS; NATIONALISM; WORLD WAR II.)

Justine Wittenberger, comp., *A Basic Bibliography for Refugee Studies* (Oxford, 1989). Julian Davies, comp., *Displaced Peoples and Refugee Studies: A Resource Guide* (Oxford, 1990).

B. E. HARRELL-BOND
ANDREW SHACKNOVE

REGIME. In the second half of the twentieth century, the French word *régime*—referring to a set of rules recognized in *international law for the governance of a particular subject—was first anglicized by international lawyers, then adopted by social scientists studying international institutions. Regimes are sets of implicit or explicit principles, norms, rules, and decision-making procedures applicable to specific areas of international relations. Examples of international regimes include the international monetary arrangements established at the Bretton Woods Conference of 1944, regulations governing civil air transport and telecommunications, the rules and organizations established in the 1970s to monitor and control the proliferation of *nuclear weapons, and an emerging set of international environmental regulations. International regimes therefore operate in all major issue areas of world politics: *security, economic, environmental.

The concept of international regime helps observers to describe the rapid increase, since 1945, in the number of multilateral arrangements through which *states cooperate to regulate transborder activity. Most international regimes include at least one formal *international organization, with the tasks of providing particular services, monitoring members' compliance with rules, and serving as a forum for negotiations. Yet *international relations remains a "self-help" system, organized through interstate arrangements rather than hierarchically. International regimes are established by states to achieve state purposes, not to make them obsolete. The international organizations involved in regimes usually have quite restricted powers, and certainly do not act as miniature governments. When the rules of international regimes are enforced, they are enforced by states, not by international organizations themselves.

International regimes have problematic relationships to state power, and two questions are particularly debatable: 1) whether international regimes must rely on the support of a single dominant power; and 2) whether the rules of the regimes have significant effects apart from the influence exerted by their supporters.

International regimes thrived during the period after World War II, which was characterized both by increasing *interdependence and by the preponderance of the United States. It is therefore difficult to disentangle the relative contributions of interdependence and U.S. dominance to their success, and whether they can continue to flourish in a more multipolar world remains to be seen. Continued high levels of interdependence will provide incentives to cooperate, and cooperation in a complex, multipolar world will require regimes. On the other hand, economic and political competition among states in such a world is likely to limit the efficacy of international rules.

The rules of international regimes reflect not only the power of states but internationally accepted principles, such as that of *sovereignty. Furthermore, over time the relative power of actors may change, while rules remain relatively fixed. Thus the outcomes to be expected on the basis of power alone often differ from those observed within the framework of international regimes. To the extent that such differences persist, and states continue to comply with regime rules, international regimes matter. When their rules become too inconsistent with the distribution of state power, however, it is to be expected that the regimes will be bypassed, deprived of substantial funding, or otherwise rendered meaningless.

International regimes are created by states for their purposes, and they operate within limits set by states. Within these limits, however, they enable systematic cooperation to occur and affect the authority patterns and the distribution of benefits in world politics.

(See also HEGEMONY; INTERNATIONAL COOPERATION; INTERNATIONAL POLITICAL ECONOMY.)

Stephen D. Krasner, ed., *International Regimes* (Ithaca, N.Y., 1983). Robert O. Keohane, *After Hegemony: Cooperation and Discord in the World Political Economy* (Princeton, N.J., 1984).

ROBERT O. KEOHANE

RELIGION AND POLITICS

Religion relates to politics in a number of ways. First, it interacts in various ways with the nation-state, which is now the standard political arrangement throughout the global community. Second, many religions are powerful worldwide forces and thus affect international arrangements. Third, religious conflicts can intensify divisions within and between states. Fourth, religious values are often invoked to justify and legitimize political action and political arrangements, and this links in with ways in which it affects voting behavior and other manifestations of political behavior or political struggle. Fifth, religious institutions themselves play a role within nations. Sixth, the behavior of political leaders often owes something to their religious beliefs. All these points of course are often intertwined.

Whereas premodern arrangements varied widely between West and East and between North and South, the nation-state as understood today is roughly homogeneous, and by treating it in relation to religion we have a good way of surveying the global scene and preparing the path to longer historical analysis. In describing interactions I shall adhere to a rather traditional definition of religion, which emphasizes belief in the transcendent or supernatural, to distinguish religion from secular *ideologies such as *Marxism, though in fact such ideologies may function like religions.

The classical modern nation-state, as developed in nineteenth-century Eueope, was linguistically and culturally based. Regions such as Germany, Italy, Norway, and Poland acquired self-consciousness in part through the creation of modernized national languages and literatures. But religious affiliation could also stand as an additional marker of identity—for instance, Catholicism in Poland could help to define Polish identity, although this immediately created problems for minority groups. There could also be conflict between religion and *nationalism as with Italy, because Italian unification was bound to destroy the Papal States. Further, the ideology of much nineteenth-century nationalism was *liberalism, and the conservative traditionalism of the papacy resisted this. In Italy it was only after World War II, with the coming to power of the Christian Democrats (effectively a blend of Catholicism and liberal democratic ideology), that the Church was able or willing to play a fully effective role in Italian national politics.

In some cases the marker of national identity is itself religious or ideological. For instance, despite Protestant leadership in the nineteenth century, Ireland's nationalism has been defined through Catholicism, and in contemporary Northern Ireland the split occurs along religious lines between the two main ethnic groups. Even before the breaching of the Berlin Wall, the German Democratic Republic's raison d'être disappeared with the abandonment of Marxism-Leninism as its official ideology, given too that the masses were disillusioned with it.

Where religious divisions were significant, linguistic nationalism might serve to cement the nation, itself the focus of ultimate loyalty, as in nineteenth-century Germany. In the United States, things were different: Here was a nation defined through a constitution, where the separation of church and state came to be thoroughly realized despite the religiously homogeneous, primarily Protestant, character of its history up to the nineteenth century, when Catholic and Jewish migrants began to arrive in large numbers.

Japan, though mainly a Buddhist country, reshaped itself in a different key through the Meiji Constitution of 1889, which defined the national ethos as being summed up in *Shinto ritual (but freedom of religion was entrenched in the constitution, although it declared Shinto *not* to be a religion: the doctrinal dimension of Shinto, never strong, was eliminated, but nevertheless the myth of the imperial family and its divine descent was underlined). Shinto was seen as an integral part of the *kokutai,* or national essence.

The breakup of the Ottoman and Habsburg empires after World War I led to further national development, giving rise in Europe to a number of new linguistically shaped nations. The most significant long-term occurrence was the beginnings of the effective realization of a Jewish state. Although the Zionist movement was secular and socialist in ethos, the definition of Jewishness could not escape the religious question: Was it not because of the observance of Judaism that the Jews had come to be a separate people?

The position of minorities throughout the new, nationally oriented Europe was unhappy: and hypernationalism was a main factor in the growth of *antisemitism. Premodern religious epistemology also played its part: Lutheran and Catholic anti-Jewish thinking was predicated on the assumption that revelation was plain and so the Jews, in neglecting the Christian interpretation of the Old Testament, were willfully rejecting the truth.

The spread of colonialism contributed to the development of nationalist identity among subject peoples, taking various forms relative to religion. Pan-Arab nationalism tended toward secularism. In India a modernized Hindu ideology of tolerance of different religions as so many paths to the one truth provided the content of a new sense of India as a single, however diverse, people. After independence India's constitution was consciously pluralist, though in giving concessions to Muslims and other minorities it slowly began to provoke a backlash among Hindu nationalists. A large segment of India's Muslims, moreover, parted from the Republic of India, creating Pakistan. Like other predominantly Muslim countries it has experimented with a partial imposition of Islamic law (*shari'a) and consequently has caused some problems for minority groups. But religion was not strong enough to bind East and West Pakistan together: the Bengali-speaking eastern province became Bangladesh in 1971.

But when combined with nationalist sentiment, *Islam could be highly dynamic, most notably in the case of the Ayatollah *Khomeini's Islamic revolution in Iran in 1979. Although secular pan-Arabism has been a powerful force, attempts to unite countries on this basis have failed, whereas Islamic revival is a growing movement in various major Arab countries, from Algeria to Egypt. A soft ideology of religious unity has proved a major instrument in governing predominantly Islamic Indonesia, which because of its geographical and cultural configuration is prone to disunity.

Many formerly Buddhist countries have come under Marxist rule. Because Marxist ideology is aggressively antireligious, traditional religions have suffered greatly in these circumstances, and especially when, as in the case of Tibet, national consciousness is vitally religious as well as linguistico-cultural in nature. But in Vietnam, Laos, Cambodia, China, and the Democratic People's Republic of Korea (North Korea), traditional religious practice was mostly suppressed until the mid-1980s. On the other hand, a strong Sinhala Buddhist nationalism became evident not very long after the independence of Sri Lanka in 1948. In 1956 Solomon W. R. D. Bandaranaike campaigned under the slogan "Sinhala only." This linguistic enthusiasm overlay a concern to restore something like the glories of the medieval Buddhist state. It led to deteriorating relations with the Tamils, an uprising among young Sinhalese radicals (the People's Liberation Front) in 1971, and eventually civil war in 1985. Sinhalese Buddhist ideology did not have a suitable theory of the place of *Hinduism (practiced by Tamils) or other minority religions (Islam and Christianity) in a Buddhist Sri Lanka.

In sub-Saharan Africa the relations of religion to the nation are even more complex because of the ethnically irrational colonial boundaries. Because so many of the political elites were trained in mission schools, there is a presumption of Christianity as the ruling ethos; but in some areas the new states must try to balance Islamic, Christian, and indigenous African practices, as in Nigeria. An interesting evolution is that of South Africa. After the union in 1910 the humiliated Afrikaners systematically began to work for power, realized in 1948, and then for the imposition of *apartheid. They had constructed a language and literature (Afrikaans) and used the ethos of the Dutch Reformed church to underpin their conception of the political order.

Some of the effects of religion on nationalism can be seen operating in the successor states of the Soviet Union since 1989. Christianity helps to reinforce culture in the national struggles of Armenians and Georgians against contiguous Muslim groups. Revived Orthodoxy, after its taming during the high Marxist period, helps to intensify Russian identity, and so on.

In addition to the religious factor in the composition of national identities, there is the increasingly transnational character of major and minor religious traditions and ethnic groups. This often has great political significance, because diaspora migrants can use their economic and political influence abroad to help movements at home. For instance, in the 1980s, Sikhs in Britain, Canada, and the United States strongly supported the movement for an independent Sikh state (Khalistan) in the Punjab. Tamils abroad have taken part in the struggle for autonomy in Sri Lanka. Diaspora communities may be doubly effective: first, they are likely to be more prosperous than their coreligionists at home; and second, because their identity is ambiguous, they are likely to contain people more fanatically committed to tradition as a means of overcoming the ambiguity. This is one factor, for instance, in the migration of U.S. Jews to Israel, out of a hyperactive sense of renewed commitment to the faith, and this reinforces some of the groups, such as Gush Emunim, which combine nationalism and religious commitment.

In debating the concept of civil religion, Robert N. Bellah and others draw attention to the way in which the nation itself functions as a focus and vehicle of pieties that are analogous to those of traditional religion. Patriotism has the dimensions of religion: having a mythic or narrative dimension, an ethical, an experiential, a ritual, an organizational, and a material dimension. History as taught in high school textbooks sums up much of the myth of the nation and refers to its heroes and saints (successful generals, presidents, poets, artists, and so on). The national ethos is presented through civics and in the inculcation of the values of the good citizen (for example, willingness to fight, ability to raise a family, honesty). The experiential dimension is expressed through the feelings of glory and uplift found in the celebration of the nation. The ritual dimension is expressed through the flag, the national anthem, state ceremonies, television presentations on solemn occasions, tours of national monuments, etc. The organizational dimension is woven into the development of ritual (the military, the president, the schoolteacher, and others are significant members of the social pattern of the nation). The material dimension is found in the monuments, the land itself, the artwork and architecture of the nation, and military hardware. What is lacking in terms of the comparison is a highly developed doctrinal dimension, and this is why the nation-state, to justify the great sacrifices it demands of individuals (and we may note how the language of sacrifice pervades war memorials and political rhetoric), tends to fall back on the doctrines of religion or universal ideology (such as Marxism), and sometimes both. Consequently Britain could see itself in World War II as fighting for Christian and democratic values against paganism and *totalitarianism; the Soviet Union invoked its Marxist values, and in a more minor key the support of the Orthodox church.

The demand for religious or ideological justification for the nation-state arises simultaneously from the great sacrifices demanded and the weakness of mere nationalism as an ideology. But insofar as the doctrines designed to fill out the doctrinal dimension of nationalism tend to be universalistic, a contradiction can easily develop between them and patriotic values. Hence Margaret *Thatcher's anger at Saint Paul's for including the Lord's Prayer in Spanish in the memorial service after the *Malvinas/Falklands War. Hence too the struggles of a minority of Christians against the regime in Germany during World War II. Also, a ruling elite may try to impose an unpopular worldview at odds with the values of the majority of the population (e.g., in Poland up to 1989; in the Shah's Iran, with its ideology of *modernization and quasi-Fascist celebration of ancient glory; and in the blend of Calvinism and racism in the apartheid ideology of South Africa). But the most vital strain is represented by the essential contradictions between universal worldviews and the particularities of nationalism. So, for instance, the democratic worldview built into the U.S. Constitution and suffused palely with religious values comes into conflict with U.S. foreign policy in supporting authoritarian regimes such as that of Chile under *Pinochet and Iraq under Saddam *Hussein during the war in the 1980s against Iran, both out of fear of the supposed alternative. Jimmy *Carter tried to reconcile his own Christian and democratic values by beginning his presidency trying to align *foreign policy with the protection of *human rights. The takeover of universalistic values by nation-states helps to explain the paradox of nations' fighting each other under the flag of the same God (as with Germany and France in World War I). The Nazis overcame such contradiction by adopting a racially based ideology that undergirded a kind of nationalism writ large, and so could mobilize support among suitable ethnic groups beyond the German nation. But its intellectual power was weak, although partly compensated for by the Nazi mastery of ritual.

The universalism of religions often makes religious values a rallying point in the critique of regimes and in revolutionary movements. Thus Catholic *liberation theology has a revolutionary and reconstructive role in Latin America, modernized Shi'i Islam provided a platform for the *Iranian Revolution of 1979, and the Komeito has argued for the purification of Japanese politics. The prevalence of religious revitalization movements, ranging from the Islamic Brotherhood in Syria and Egypt to new independent churches in black Africa, and from the new Christian conservatism in the United States to the neo-Hindu nationalism of the Bharatiya Janata Party in India, is politically significant, and itself follows *secularization. Such movements are sometimes protests against religious changes consequent upon the adoption of liberal values (as in liberal Protestantism, post–Vatican II Catholicism, Islamic modernism, etc.); sometimes, as in the colonial world, revivalism represents a protest against the adventi-

tious Western trappings of modern methods; sometimes (as in India) it is also a backlash against a pluralism whereby minorities are seen as having privileges not accorded to the majority. Also, revival movements often aspire to reestablish religious or ethnic glory perceived to have existed in the past: in earlier Islamic civilization before the onset of the colonial period; in medieval Sri Lanka; in ancient India; and so on. This may sometimes cause tension between nationalism as more narrowly considered and a wider spiritual revival: this is most evident in relation to species of Arab nationalism (for example, Egyptian, Iraqi, and Algerian) and pan-Islamic values.

Traditional relationships between religion and the political order generally have not persisted into the contemporary era; some aspects of earlier arrangements, however, have survived, albeit in modernized form, as with the monarchy in England (where the queen is both constitutional monarch and head of the Church). In Thailand something akin to the old symbiosis between monarchy and Buddhist *sangha* (order) persists. Something of older arrangements was evident in the role of the emperor in prewar Japan. But by and large previous modes of conceiving the relation of political and religious power have disappeared. In different ways, political power used to be religiously sanctified, though in general religious institutions had some degree of independence. In Western Europe this independence was in part expressed through the papacy: by having a spiritual monarch the Catholic church protected its transnational status. But the feudal system also allowed for Church functionaries, for instance the abbots of powerful monarchies, to adopt something of a baronial role. The usual Buddhist schema involved a symbiosis between the *sangha* and the king. The latter was responsible for the economic well-being of the order and the purification of the system through the periodic purging of monks and nuns who did not live according to the rules. On the other hand, the *sangha* guaranteed the *legitimacy of the monarch. In modern times the disappearance of monarchs from many Buddhist countries means that the state functions to control the *sangha*, often ineptly because of the different basis of political power. The Buddhist system was adapted in Hindu contexts, where the king was seen as a divine being mediating between heaven and earth: his symbolic role was managed by brahmin priests, e.g., through coronation rituals. The deep entrenchment of sacred legal values interpreted by a priestly class placed some restraints on the monarchy's absolute authority. Sometimes the political and spiritual systems were fused, as in the traditional role of the Dalai Lama in Tibet. The Chinese emperor's role was for the most part conceived within the framework of Confucian values, which also served as an ideology for the unified imperial civil service. The Confucian examination system based on classical literary and sacred texts lasted over two millennia, until its abolition in 1905. Islamic monarchy was restricted by the necessity to adhere to sharī'a or law. In the Ottoman Empire a partially pluralist system was developed called *millet*, which gave Christian and Jewish leaders control over their own subcommunities, which could adhere to their separate systems of custom and law. By contrast, from the seventeenth century onward in Europe the usual political system was one of *cuius regio eius religio*—that is, every principality or state had its official religion to which citizens were expected to adhere, although they were not prevented from migrating to another state to practice their own religion. While fragments of such prior systems have carried over, even these have undergone profound modification. Established religion, associated with the monarchy, continues for instance in England, but effectively the country is pluralistic; the role of the Dalai Lama has been greatly spiritualized during his exile; the imperial functions of the Japanese emperor have been greatly diminished; the Indian maharajahs have in effect been privatized.

In modern times the influence of religious organizations on political life results in part from their weight within the interplay of institutional forces, from the ways religious values may influence voting, and from the motivations and policies of individuals among the political leadership. Instances of the first kind can be found in the effects of church lobbies on issues such as abortion and divorce in Ireland and the United States; the lobby in the United States on behalf of Israel; and revivalist Hindu pressures on the state in India. In relation to the second we may mention the historic nonconformist linkage with the emergence of the Labour Party in Britain, the tendency of pious Catholics in Italy to vote Christian Democrat, and Buddhist support for the Sri Lanka Freedom Party from 1956 onwards. Finally, among influential individuals whose politics were fired by religious belief we may include Mahatma *Gandhi in India; Martin Luther *King, Jr., in the U.S. *Civil Rights Movement; the Ayatollah Khomeini in the Iranian Revolution; Alcide De Gasperi in the restoration of Italian democracy after World War II; Solomon W. R. D. Bandaranaike, a convert to *Buddhism, in the revival of Sinhala Buddhist nationalism; Dag *Hammarskjöld, the mystic who was UN secretary-general; Desmond Tutu, archbishop of Cape Town, prominent in the anti-apartheid struggle; President Jimmy Carter; and Lech *Wałęsa. Also important, of course, is the impact of antireligious values, as seen in the lives of such as Kemal *Atatürk, *Mao Zedong, and Joseph *Stalin.

Modern communications elevate leading religious figures to global status and give them political influence in a wider context than would have been true even fifty years earlier: for instance, the extensive travels of Pope *John Paul II give him a political role beyond that implied by the leadership of the *Roman Catholic church; the same holds true for the Dalai Lama and Archbishop Tutu.

The globalization of institutions also affects traditional religions. The trend is toward the formation of spiritual blocs through such organizations as the World Council of Churches, the World Fellowship of Buddhists, and the Organization of the Islamic Conference. This accompanies a move toward a relative homogenization of faith and practice in the different religions. These moves enhance the power of traditions to influence events. Such power may reflect demographic developments: for instance, the shift of Christianity southward, with its relative decay in the North and increase in Africa and revival in Latin America, and the fact that the great majority of Muslims live in South and Southeast Asia (with Indonesia, Pakistan, Bangladesh, and India being by far the largest Muslim countries).

Until recently (the beginning of the 1980s) there was a tendency for political scientists to ignore or downplay the force of religion in politics. This was in part ideological—attributable to, for example, the influence of Marxian ideas—and in part due to a more general secular bias within the discipline as a whole. Conversely, scholars of religion tended out of a sense of idealism to neglect the political dimension of religions. Now we can perceive more realistically the range of patterns of interaction between the two critical aspects of human existence.

(See also CHRISTIAN DEMOCRACY; COLONIAL EMPIRES; CONFUCIANISM; JIHAD; VATICAN II; ZIONISM.)

Ernst Cassirer, *The Myth of the State* (London, 1946). Donald E. Smith, *Religion and Political Development* (Boston, 1970). Peter Merkl and Ninian Smart, eds., *Religion and Politics in the Contemporary World* (New York, 1983). James E. Wood, ed., *Religion and the State* (Waco, Tex., 1985). Richard T. Antoun and Mary Elaine Hegland, eds., *Religious Resurgence* (Syracuse, N.Y., 1987). Richard L. Rubenstein, ed., *Spirit Matters: The Worldwide Impact of Religion on Contemporary Politics* (New York, 1987). Ninian Smart, *Religion and the Western Mind* (Albany, N.Y., 1987). Gustavo Benavides and Martin W. Daly, eds., *Religion and Political Power* (Albany, N.Y., 1989).

NINIAN SMART

REPRODUCTIVE POLITICS. The domain of law, policy, public administration, and social action in modern societies in which groups and individuals contend over the means, and meanings, of controlling human fertility is known as reproductive politics. Because fertility intimately involves issues regarding gender division, the status of women, sexuality, health, population, and child welfare, reproductive politics necessarily encompasses all of these.

Although women have for centuries acted on the view that control over their bodies, fertility, and health ought to be in their hands, the formalization of this belief in the concept of "reproductive *rights" is a fairly recent development. The term first emerged in feminist struggles to defend access to safe, legal abortion and funding in North America and Europe during the 1970s. Organizations such as the Committee for Abortion Rights and Against Sterilization Abuse (CARASA), founded in New York City in 1977, and the Women's Global Network on Reproductive Rights (WGNRR), founded in Amsterdam in 1978, reflected the growing international concern with protecting women's control over reproduction from both pronatalist and antinatalist assaults. These avowedly feminist groups arose in response to three influences, also international: first, the emergence in the late 1960s of a broad-based women's rights movement, a major component of which focused on women's health; second, a growing opposition among women's and ethnic groups to the technological methods and population control objectives of medical and family planning interests; and finally, the increasing power, during the late 1970s and throughout the 1980s, of antiabortion, "profamily" groups associated with Catholic and fundamentalist Protestant clergy and allied with conservative politicians. In many countries with a strong Catholic church presence (the United States, Ireland, Brazil, Philippines, Chile, Peru, even Nigeria), these groups gained considerable momentum in this period.

Against both opponents of legal abortion and proponents of medically managed population control, feminist advocates of "reproductive rights" asserted "women's right to decide whether, when and how to have children—regardless of nationality, class, race, age, religion, disability, sexuality or marital status—in the social, economic and political conditions that make such decisions possible" (from WGNRR Statement of Purpose, 1989). They called for access to safe, effective contraception; safe, legal abortion services for all women, regardless of income; access to prenatal care and good-quality, comprehensive maternity and child health services for all women; an end to sterilization abuse and other coercive practices by health and family planning providers; and improved education for women of all ages about birth control, reproduction, sexuality, and medical risks. They affirmed women's right both to have and not to have children, and to live self-determined sexual lives, as basic *human rights.

By the time of the UN Decade of Women Conference in Nairobi in 1985, the promotion of reproductive rights as a fundamental basis for women's achievement of social and political equality had become a worldwide goal of women's rights activists. But the specific issues and strategies contained within this concept continue to stir debate among feminists, family planners, medical professionals, and demographers, as well as strong opposition from conservative religious and political groups. For the latter, the emphasis on women's reproductive freedom contravenes the interests of fetuses and children and the authority of husbands, fathers, and church

hierarchies. But even among different groups of feminists, the meanings of "reproductive rights" may differ depending on region, country, *class, race, *ethnicity, the particular balance of political forces in the society, and the extent to which those speaking or their communities must confront daily problems like *AIDS, drug addiction, and endemic poverty.

Two Different Approaches to Rights. We may approach the concept of "reproductive rights" from two different standpoints: that of formal human rights instruments and resolutions, or that of grassroots and international political struggles. These two standpoints are not mutually exclusive, but they do reflect different emphases. Since 1966, a series of UN-sponsored resolutions has endorsed the idea of "freedom of choice" in family planning as part of the framework of human rights universally recognized for all individuals. In 1968 the 157 participating governments at the UN International Conference on Human Rights in Tehran granted the "basic human right to determine freely and responsibly the number and spacing of their children" to "parents"; and in 1974 the World Population Plan of Action (Bucharest) applied it to "all couples and individuals." Subsequently, Article 16 of the UN Convention on the Elimination of All Forms of Discrimination Against Women (CEDAW) made not only rights over procreative decision making but also "access to the information, education and means to exercise these rights" a matter of "equality of men and women." (This information is summarized in The Human Right to Family Planning, published by the International Planned Parenthood Federation, London, 1989.)

These formal international expressions of procreative rights as human rights are a major advance over previous tendencies to restrict "rights" to more conventionally "civil" or "political" areas of human activity. Nonetheless, they have several serious limitations, reflecting the reality that international and national laws distill the lowest common denominator of (a) what those in power are willing to tolerate in the context of (b) the pressures exerted on them by organized political actors. First, human rights documents attempt to be "gender neutral" and to stress the "equality" of women and men in reproductive and procreative matters. But in doing so they ignore the *specificity* of women's reproductive situation; for it is still a fact that women, not men, get pregnant, and in most societies in the world women are still the ones mainly responsible for the care and rearing of children. Women have a much bigger stake in reproductive rights than men do and a much more direct and intimate concern with reproductive health.

Second, international resolutions from the 1960s to the present have remained silent regarding abortion, even though lack of access to legal, safe abortion is, according to the *World Health Organization, a major cause of maternal mortality and morbidity in the *Third World. At the World Population Conference in Mexico City in 1984, the U.S. government put forth its policy of denying foreign aid funds to any abortion-related services in recipient countries or to UN agencies involved in sponsoring such services. The impact of this "Mexico City policy" was evident when leaders of seventy of the world's countries met at the UN World Summit for Children in the fall of 1990 to call for, among other goals, a fifty-percent reduction in maternal mortality, yet declined once again to mention abortion.

Third, the major focus of most human rights instruments that deal with procreation and reproduction is on family planning in the narrow sense of "birth limitation." The broader issues of access to health care, economic resources, and social security, to say nothing of freedom from sexual abuse and discrimination, remain unaddressed, even though these conditions are directly tied to women's lack of reproductive self-determination. Even where international documents recognize the need for policies that guarantee "maternal and child health," the emphasis is overwhelmingly on "the child"; women and their health needs remain invisible.

Finally, recent history shows that there is often a large gap between formal resolutions or legislation guaranteeing women's "rights" (for example, the "constitutional right" to abortion declared by the U.S. Supreme Court in *Roe v. Wade [1973]; the Women's Health Charter [PAISM] passed by the Brazilian legislature in the mid-1980s but never funded; and CEDAW) and their practical implementation. This is particularly true for poor women and women of color in developed countries and most women in the Third World, for whom formal legal rights are all but useless in the absence of basic material resources.

In contrast to the formal human rights approach, women's grass-roots organizations, feminist advocates, and women's health activists around the world have worked to develop and implement a conception of reproductive rights whose starting point is the health, well-being, and empowerment of women. Their priority is to reduce women's morbidity and mortality related to reproduction and sex, as well as to maximize the conditions that make authentic choice—whether to have a child or not to have one—possible. As Sally Mugabe of Zimbabwe put it when addressing the UN Decade Conference in Nairobi, "Women must control their own fertility, which forms the basis for enjoying all other rights. First and foremost, our bodies belong to us."

The idea of "owning our bodies," or "bodily integrity," which provides the philosophical foundation of reproductive rights, is not merely a derivative of Western notions of private property. Rather, it reflects women's experience as childbearers and nurturers who must maintain control over the conditions of their reproductive activity in order to perform it well. It also resonates closely with religious and cosmological traditions that value women's bodies as the source of life and nourishment or that view the human body as an integral part of the self, not separate from (or below) the soul or spirit.

In addition, the idea that women have a "right to control over their bodies" is given unintentional reinforcement by medical practitioners, international family planning agencies, and government officials when they treat women's bodies as though they were incubators, pill receptacles, or polluters of the earth. Technological and managerial approaches to women's fertility by medical and family planning agents, whether in the service of policies to limit or policies to increase population, have provoked an awareness among women clients and patients about their need for reproductive autonomy. These two forces combined—traditional values celebrating women's bodies and nurturance, and responses to the insensitive, "assembly-line" treatment by family planners and clinic personnel—have made women throughout the world receptive to the ideas promoted in international feminist meetings and networks concerned with health and reproductive issues. In this way, the idea of reproductive rights—and of control over one's body as a fundamental right—has achieved a global resonance.

Putting Reproductive Rights and Health in an International Economic and Political Context. Since the UN Decade Conference in Nairobi, women's reproductive rights advocates have come a long distance toward developing a framework that puts women's needs, especially their health needs, at the center of international population and family planning discussions. They have broadened the meaning of "reproductive rights" to include a full range of health and social conditions; have united on the priority of ending maternal mortality and securing safe, legal abortion in all countries; and have challenged the persistent neo-Malthusian thinking that ties social development and a healthy environment to population targets (more or fewer births). But this progress confronts increasing barriers as the international political and economic context for recognizing reproductive rights *as rights* grows more and more precarious.

First, the continuing debt crisis (made worse by the *Gulf War of 1991) and calls by international lending organizations for "structural adjustments" will further shrink the proportion of public resources and basic services devoted to poor women and their children. This can only result in exacerbating the chain reaction of maternal and infant mortality, not only by deepening poverty and the lack of food and health care but by undermining the legitimacy of claims on the state. This deterioration of conditions is occurring not only in the Third World but in parts of Europe and the United States, where reports in mid-1990 indicated that over half the states had severely cut government nutritional allotments to poor women and their children.

Second, the hegemony of the market and market values throughout the world, since the demise of the socialist societies in Eastern and Central Europe, is likely to have a negative impact on reproductive rights and health in many countries. Despite the drawbacks of government bureaucracies as health care providers, women's experiences with private agencies that function according to the profit motive suggest that this model is far less reliable in meeting people's health needs, especially the needs of poor women. Where there is no system of public account-ability nor any commitment to criteria of social justice, reproductive health providers will become supermarkets for those who can pay.

Third, the resurgence of right-wing movements, racism, and ethnic hatred and violence in many countries is likely to influence population policies. Historically, such conditions have provoked the use of women's fertility as a weapon in the contest to "out-reproduce" a rival group and to cut off the reproduction of those considered "less fit." The result is often coercive policies promoting child-bearing among dominant groups and discouraging it among marginal or "outsider" groups. Evidence of such neo-Malthusian thinking began to resurface during the 1980s and early 1990s in the United States, India, China, Israel, South Africa, and else-where.

Fourth, continuing militarism, imperialist inter-vention, and war, despite the end of the Cold War, create devastating threats to women's reproductive health and well-being. Whether in the Philippines, El Salvador, Liberia, or the Middle East, military occupation or violence greatly increase the risk to women and children of abandonment, rape, sexual abuse, *prostitution, and other forms of sexual traf-ficking, unwanted pregnancy, and sexually trans-mitted disease. Meanwhile, the semblance of any public institutions to deal with these problems is torn apart.

Finally, the persistence of patriarchal culture in the family, religion, the medical profession, and the state reinforces social trends that undermine wom-en's reproductive health. These include the premium on producing sons; patrilineal marriage systems; resurgent fundamentalist tendencies in all major re-ligious groups, who work actively to condemn abor-tion and birth control; the increased medicalization of family planning and reproductive health care, with its focus on high-tech methods and on the "fetus as patient." Above all, women throughout the world continue to be stigmatized as "carriers"— of fetuses "at risk," environmental pollution, over-population, AIDS, and sexual taint.

Together, these conditions construct the larger context in which women's reproductive rights will continue to be difficult, if not impossible, to achieve. This means, first, that the analysis of reproductive

politics must take such structural constraints into full account; and second, that strategies to define and implement women's reproductive rights must aim toward a deeper level of social change than the language of "family planning" or even "reproduc-tive health" has yet envisioned.

(See also EQUALITY AND INEQUALITY; FEMINISM; GENDER AND POLITICS; INTERNATIONAL DEBT; NEW RIGHT; PATRIARCHY; POPULATION POLICY; RACE AND RACISM; RELIGION AND POLITICS; ROMAN CATHOLIC CHURCH; WOMEN AND DEVELOPMENT.)

Betsy Hartman, *Reproductive Rights and Wrongs: The Global Politics of Population Control and Contraceptive Choice* (New York, 1987). Carmen Barroso, "Maternal Mortality: A Political Question," in *Quando a Paciente e Mulher* (Brasilia, 1989). Marge Berer, Amparo Claro, and Ana Maria Portugal, eds., *Maternal Mortality and Morbid-ity: A Call to Women for Action* (Santiago, Chile, 1990). Rosalind P. Petchesky, *Abortion and Woman's Choice: The State, Sexuality and Reproductive Freedom*, 2d ed. (Boston, 1990). Ruth Dixon-Mueller, *Women's Rights and Popula-tion Policy: The Search for Common Ground* (Baltimore, 1991).

ROSALIND POLLACK PETCHESKY

RESOLUTION 242. UN Security Council Resolu-tion 242, passed in November 1967 in the wake of the Arab-Israeli War of June of that year, has be-come the internationally accepted basis for peace-making in the *Middle East. Drafted by Lord Caradon, the British ambassador to the UN, in consultation with the parties concerned, the resolu-tion was an attempt to bring Israeli demands for a final, formal *peace agreement together with those of Egypt, Syria, and Jordan for Israel's withdrawal from the territories—the Sinai Peninsula, Gaza Strip, Golan Heights, West Bank, and East Jerusalem— which it had occupied during the June war.

The resolution did this by a balanced emphasis on "the inadmissibility of the acquisition of territory by war and the need to work for a just and lasting peace." It therefore called for "withdrawal of Israel from territories occupied in the recent conflict," as well as for "termination of all claims or states of belligerency and respect for and acknowledgement of the sovereignty, territorial integrity and political independence of every state in the area and their right to live in peace." The resolution also called for "a just settlement of the refugee problem."

The resolution was accepted by Egypt, Jordan, and Israel from the outset, but was initially rejected by Syria. Only after the October War of 1973 did Syria accept the resolution, while all the Arab states (except Libya) accepted its principles at the Fez Arab summit conference in 1982. The most consistent rejection of Resolution 242 came from the *Palestine Liberation Organization (PLO), which from its in-ception in 1964 refused a peaceful settlement with Israel. After 1974, however, as the PLO moved toward the idea of a negotiated settlement with Israel, it increasingly based its objections to Resolution 242 on the fact that it dealt with the Palestinians as *refugees, rather than as a people with national rights. Finally, in 1988, the PLO formally accepted Resolution 242 as the basis for a Middle East settlement, thereby meeting one of the conditions posed by the United States for opening contacts with it.

In spite of apparently universal acceptance of Resolution 242 as a basis for an Arab-Israeli settlement, major problems remain. From 1977 until 1992, Israeli governments were dominated by the Likud bloc, which rejected the application of this resolution to the occupied West Bank, Gaza Strip, Arab East Jerusalem, or the Golan Heights. They claimed that its provisions regarding Israel's withdrawal were fulfilled with the 1982 withdrawal from Egypt's Sinai Peninsula. Over the years, moreover, a school of thought has grown increasingly influential in Israel and the United States, arguing that the principle of "land for peace" embodied in Resolution 242 is no longer relevant, and that the changes since June 1967 have become irreversible. This argument for the permanence of the status quo emerging from the 1967 war was undermined by the outbreak of the Palestinian *intifada in December 1987, which showed that the status quo in the occupied territories was untenable. If this is true, a negotiated resolution to the conflict is necessary, and when and if this occurs, it will most likely be on the basis of Security Council Resolution 242.

(See also ARAB-ISRAELI CONFLICT; PALESTINE; UNITED NATIONS.)

Arthur Lall, *The UN and the Middle East Crisis, 1967*, rev. ed. (New York, 1970). William B. Quandt, *Decade of Decisions: American Policy Toward the Arab-Israeli Conflict* (Berkeley, Calif., 1977).

RASHID I. KHALIDI

REVOLUTION

Since ancient times, governments have been changed by force. Plato and Aristotle commented on changes in the governments of Greek city-states from aristocracies and tyrannies to democracies (and back again) in the third through sixth centuries B.C.E. The Roman republic was founded in a revolution against Etruscan kings in the sixth century B.C.E. During the European Renaissance of the sixteenth century C.E., Italians introduced the word *revolutions* (in Italian, *revoluziones*) to describe the alternating victories of the popular and aristocratic factions who fought for control of Italian states, which sometimes became republics and sometimes duchies. And in the mid-seventeenth century, the philosopher Thomas Hobbes used the English word *revolution* to describe the circular transfer of power from England's King Charles I to the Puritan Parliament under Oliver Cromwell, and after Cromwell's death back to Charles's son, King Charles II. In all these cases, *revolution* meant a transfer of power and a recasting

of government, from one party and kind of government to another. But nothing in this change was necessarily permanent or progressive; power could be taken again by a group that was defeated. A *monarchy could be (and often was) restored.

This view of revolution as an alternation of governments was replaced in the eighteenth and nineteenth centuries by a new view of revolution, based on the Enlightenment faith in progress. In this new view, made popular in attempts to understand the French Revolution of 1789, writers argued that society was bound to progress toward more fair and productive forms of social organization, and that revolutions were necessary to destroy the institutions and individuals who maintained, and benefited from, an outmoded and unfair social order. Revolutions, therefore, were progressive and necessary. Instead of cyclical crises of governments, revolutions marked permanent, favorable transformations of entire societies.

This view of revolution was given an enormously influential presentation in 1848 by Karl *Marx and Frederick Engels in *The Communist Manifesto*. Marx and Engels argued that all of history showed a series of revolutions that were linked to economic progress. In each revolution, a backward and oppressive economic class which benefited from outmoded economic and political institutions was turned out by a new class whose power stemmed from more advanced forms of economic production. Revolutions, therefore, were as inevitable as the improvement of economic production. In this Marxist view, the French Revolution marked one revolutionary transition, in which more productive capitalist merchants and manufacturers overturned outmoded feudal landlords. A next step was bound to come, in which capitalists were themselves thrown out by workers. Free of the exploitation of capitalist masters, workers could then develop an unfettered system of production that would serve workers' needs better than any other system. The workers' revolution would thus usher in a lasting age of genuine utopia.

By the later nineteenth century (and through most of the twentieth century) the progressive utopian view of revolution, usually in its Marxist form, had become the dominant view of the meaning of *revolution*. People who described themselves as revolutionaries, as well as scholars who tried to understand revolutions, addressed themselves to the problem of the permanent transformation of entire societies. The notion of revolution as a simple crisis of government, leading to a not necessarily beneficial, and possibly reversible, change in leaders and institutions, was put aside.

However, actual historical experience has not always justified faith in the progressive utopian view. The American Revolution of 1776 began with a remarkable Declaration of Independence and led to a Constitution and *Bill of Rights that have inspired the struggle for freedom and citizenship for centuries. Yet while this freedom proved durable for many, African Americans and Native Americans long remained subject to slavery and conquest. The French Revolution of 1789 lost its way after Napoleon's defeats in 1812 and 1815, and France—from 1815 to 1848—was again ruled by kings (Louis XVIII, Charles X, Louis Philippe). The *Russian Revolution of 1917 and the *Chinese Revolution of 1949 promised both prosperity and freedom for millions of people, but in fact have led their populations down economic blind alleys, while suppressing political liberties.

By contrast, Prussia and England, which experienced not revolutions but major reform movements in 1806–1812 and 1828–1832, respectively, showed great progress in economic and political development. Both England and Prussia managed to extend citizenship, reduce the privileges of aristocrats, and reorganize their economies without revolutions.

Twentieth-century politics and scholarship has therefore remained divided. There is a vast body of believers in the "utopian view" of revolution—both revolutionaries and scholars alike—who consider revolutions to be the result of the collapse of outmoded *states and economies, and as necessary transitions for political and economic progress. There has also been a more modest body of skeptics and conservatives, who believe that revolutions are neither necessary nor progressive, but are costly, often tragic events, indicating only that a government has run into a crisis.

Much of twentieth-century politics reflects the efforts of believers in progressive revolution to transform their societies by carrying out revolutions. Such efforts resulted in major revolutions in Mexico (1910), Russia (1917), Turkey (1922), China (1949), Cuba (1959), Algeria (1962), Vietnam (1975), Iran (1979), and Nicaragua (1979), along with other revolutions and revolutionary movements in a host of African, Asian, and Middle Eastern societies. Yet these revolutions ran into fierce opposition from internal and international forces skeptical of any benefits, indeed fearful of great costs, of changes in the status quo. These revolutions also created opportunities for aggressive political factions and nations to struggle for control of populations and regions. Armed conflict, often on a massive scale, was the usual result. The history of revolution in the twentieth century is thus a history of widespread efforts at social transformation, accompanied by violent civil and international *wars.

A second, less deadly battlefront has arisen in the world of ideas. Scholars have sought to interpret the historical record of revolutions to determine whether they are indeed progressive and beneficial, marking permanent changes, or whether they are, as was long thought, merely cyclical crises of governments. As this century comes to a close, there are signs that the latter scholars, once overwhelmed by the progressive utopians, are winning their case.

Revolutions in the Twentieth Century. What is perhaps most striking about revolutions in this century is their sheer volume and variety. From the beginning to the end, in every area of the world, revolutions have shaped political life.

From 1900 through the 1920s, revolutions shook Mexico, Saudi Arabia, China, Turkey, Iran, and Russia. The Mexican Revolution led to a capitalist, populist, one-party state. Saudi Arabia's revolution was made by Islamic fundamentalists. In Turkey, Iran, and China, secular modernizers overthrew traditional monarchies and installed republican constitutions. In Russia, *Lenin's Communist Party created the world's first communist state. Clearly, from the beginning of the century, a wide range of revolutionary ideologies and outcomes is evident. This diversity would continue throughout the century.

Western Europe also felt the impact of revolution. The German revolution of 1918, following World War I, eliminated the reign of the kaiser and left in place a weak and divided government that paved the way for the rise of Nazism.

In the 1940s and 1950s, following World War II, communist revolutions in Eastern and Central Europe (secured by Soviet tanks) set the stage for the *Cold War, while the communist revolution in China (1949) transformed Asian politics. From 1945 through the 1960s, revolutions of national liberation and *modernization altered the maps of Africa, the Middle East, and Southeast Asia. Some of these revolutions were socialist, others capitalist; all were strongly nationalist. In the 1970s and 1980s revolutions overthrew semimodern personal dictatorships in Nicaragua, Iran, Portugal, and the Philippines. These revolutions ranged from socialist, to Islamic fundamentalist, to democratic-capitalist. Finally, the end of the 1980s were marked by revolutions against communist regimes in Eastern and Central Europe and the Soviet Union, whose outcomes are still unclear. Even experts on revolution are sometimes confused by the enormous range of forms and places in which revolutions have arisen.

Given this great variety, it is difficult to find simple, common factors that created this century of revolution. However, four major factors largely account for the rising revolutionary tide: 1) weak states; 2) conflicting *elites; 3) rapid population growth; and 4) erratic international intervention.

1. Weak States. Prior to the twentieth century, most large states were long-standing, well-financed, conservative organizations. They enjoyed a tradition of power, financial means appropriate to their goals, and stable relationships with supportive elites. However, in the twentieth century, international military and economic competition has greatly increased the pressures on states. The rate of economic growth in the leading countries in the twentieth century—three or four percent per year in the large advanced economies, and up to nine or ten percent per year in

rapidly developing states in Asia and Latin America—allowed successful states to leave states that grew more slowly trailing in the dust. Throughout this century, many states have therefore found themselves competing with more advanced economies—Russia competing with Germany, China with Japan, Iran and Afghanistan seeking to begin to catch up with Europe. As a result, leaders of traditional states undertook programs of rapid investment and restructuring, straining their finances to the utmost, alienating traditional elites, and becoming dependent on international borrowing. These conditions reduced the ability of states to maintain old loyalties, and to operate freely against internal and external opponents. Straining to overcome past disadvantages, these states struggled with their economies and lost political support.

In many other cases, twentieth-century states arose as recent creations or colonial impositions, with no long tradition or well-established supporters. Personalist dictators or unpopular colonial powers often found themselves isolated, opposed by entire populations, and with their armies becoming strained and unreliable.

Long-established, economically successful states do not have revolutions. Recently established or economically struggling states often do. In the twentieth century, both of the latter have become far more common.

2. Conflicting Elites. In every society certain individuals are more influential than others. They may have influence by occupying certain positions of leadership, or by expressing influential views through art, journalism, or speaking. Thus army officers, political leaders and high bureaucrats, cultural and religious leaders, labor and business leaders, and intellectuals form influential elites.

In stable states, elites compete for power but accept basic "rules of the game" for the distribution of power, wealth, and status. However, sometimes new factors emerge which upset those rules. The state may fall into the hands of one leader or one faction that seeks to exclude all others. Foreigners may displace domestic elites. Or rapid social mobility may undermine traditional pathways to office and wealth, creating challenges to established elites and opportunities for new ones. In any of these situations, elites may come into sharp conflict with each other or with the state. If the state is weak, a determined elite group, or coalition of groups, may seek to overthrow the state and change the "rules of the game"—that is, the basic political and economic institutions—in a direction they believe is better. Such elite leadership is always necessary for revolutions to become more than mere popular rebellions, which, as a rule, are readily suppressed.

The growth of international economic and military links in the twentieth century greatly increased the opportunities for elite conflicts. International investors, foreign aid donors, or military backers might support one person or faction in a country, excluding and alienating others. The growth of industrial and export enclaves gives new resources to business, labor, and trading elites, who might then challenge the prerogatives of landlords and rural elites. "Uneven" economic development, which favors one sector of the economy over others—industry over farming, urban over rural, factory over household manufacturing—can lead to violent elite conflicts if it makes no allowance for elites in the less favored sector to retain their positions of influence.

In sum, the explosion of international trade, investment, and foreign aid and military support in the twentieth century has greatly increased the potential for conflict among elites.

3. Rapid Population Growth. The twentieth century has seen exceptionally rapid population growth, particularly in the developing countries of the *Third World. A rapid fall in death rates, chiefly due to progress in vaccination and sanitation, combined with a continued high birth rate and large family size, has produced a rise in world population from 1.6 billion in 1900 to over 5 billion today.

Although population growth is usually cited for contributing to poverty and resource exhaustion, it has profound political effects as well. The growth of populations increases the difficulty of states in providing services to an expanding population, increases the competition among elite groups for positions of power and status, and undermines the position of workers and *peasants seeking jobs and adequate land. Population growth is also generally accompanied by shifts in the composition of the population: more people generally means more young people, and they are increasingly concentrated in cities. This increases the pool of people most likely to join revolts—single young people—and concentrates them where they can easily join to demonstrate or protest. Although population growth alone does not cause revolutions, population growth can intensify the pressures on weak states and conflicting elites, making it more likely that such states and elites will enter full-scale revolutionary struggles.

4. Erratic International Intervention. A stable international balance of power, with stable policies, as prevailed in Europe in the second half of the nineteenth century, can reduce the likelihood of revolutions. Governments know they can count on international support, and challengers know they cannot. But erratic international *intervention can lead to widespread revolutionary turmoil.

In the twentieth century, the erratic swings of the Cold War, and swings in U.S. policy between internationalism and isolationism, enhanced the instability of governments around the world. In the 1950s and 1960s, the Soviet Union, later aided by Cuban military support, sponsored revolutionary movements around the world, particularly in Asia and Africa. The United States resisted such movements steadfastly in the 1960s and early 1970s, less so in the late 1970s, but then actively—including support for counterrevolutionary movements in Central America and Africa—in the 1980s. The Soviet Union in the 1980s, in contrast, withdrew its support from many revolutionary movements and recently successful revolutionary states. As a result, the United States first supported, then declined to support, repressive governments in Nicaragua, Iran, and the Philippines. The Soviet Union first supported, then declined to support, revolutionary governments in Eastern Europe, Afghanistan, and Cuba. All these policy shifts contributed to revolutions, or are creating revolutionary situations, some of which may be exacerbated in the 1990s in the wake of the dissolution of the Soviet Union.

The four factors listed above—weak states, conflicting elites, rapid population growth, and erratic international intervention—have become widespread in this century. In many states, one or more of these conditions have arisen without leading to revolution. But where all four factors appear simultaneously in one society, revolution is the likely result. Such revolutionary conjunctures have become increasingly common over the course of this century, producing an extraordinary number of revolutions.

Interestingly, there is no one kind of *ideology behind this century's varied revolutions. Rather, when the four conditions noted above are all present, a revolutionary ideology emerges, combining elements of *nationalism and utopianism, plus whatever indigenous widespread beliefs can be used to oppose the ideology that supports the current regime. Thus, although there are some basic similarities among communist revolutions, or among Islamic revolutions, these are far from identical. Every revolution reflects its own custom-built revolutionary ideology.

The consequences of these revolutions for twentieth-century politics, especially since World War II, have been momentous. First, the communist revolutions in the Soviet Union and China led to a two-way, and sometimes three-way, competition for world influence between these states and the capitalist alliance of the United States and Europe. With world leaders often believing that revolutions could create a permanent move of countries into the "communist" camp, much of the world's international tensions and conflicts in the latter twentieth century revolved around whether various countries in Asia, Africa, and Latin America would "go communist." However, as the realization has grown that revolutions may in fact be only cyclical crises whose results may be altered with time, superpower concern over the form of other nations' governments has begun to diminish.

Second, the twentieth century saw so many states founded on the belief in revolutionary utopianism that an enormous amount of human and material energy was expended in trying to make revolutionary institutions "work." No doubt the greatest portion of human misery in this century came from World Wars I and II, which were rooted in traditional plans for territorial expansion by Germany in Europe and by Japan in Asia. But close behind in sheer volume of human misery caused were the attempts of revolutionary governments to remold human beings and societies—in spite of all evidence and human will to the contrary—to fit utopian ideals. In the Soviet Union, Eastern and Central Europe, China, various countries in Africa and Asia, and most recently in Cambodia, tens of millions of people were starved, imprisoned, or stripped of their livelihoods and dignity in failed efforts to create allegiance, efficiency, and harmony in revolutionary states.

Third, the large number of revolutions in the twentieth century has created regions of local instability and political competition in Africa, the Middle East, and South Asia, leading to continued international wars between regional rivals. In the Horn of Africa, on the Iran-Iraq border, in Afghanistan, and in Indochina, international conflicts involving revolutionary states and neighbors who either feared revolutionary expansion or sought to take advantage of revolutionary turmoil have led to decades of war, migration of *refugees, and hunger. Lack of governmental stability in these regions has made them continuous sources of international tension and military operations.

If revolutions are indeed passages on the path to progress, we should expect that the end of the twentieth century should show progressive results. Yet the historical record is dauntingly bleak. Those nations and regions most affected by revolutions—the Soviet Union, Eastern Europe, China, Cuba, Vietnam, Africa, the Middle East, Indochina—have shown remarkably little progress toward *democracy and economic prosperity, the twin goals of most revolutionary utopians. The nations and regions that have made greater progress in these respects—the Pacific Rim nations of Japan, the Republic of Korea, Taiwan, Singapore, and Hong Kong, and certain states in Latin America (Brazil, Chile, Venezuela, Mexico, Argentina)—have been relatively free of revolution, especially since World War II. This is not to say that revolutionary states have not made great progress in industrialization, literacy, and basic health care; only that their progress toward democracy and overall economic prosperity has been deeply disappointing to their leaders and their populations, and has generally lagged well behind comparable states which undertook less radical reforms. This outcome has led to a radical reevaluation of the causes and outcomes of revolution by scholars.

The Scholarly Analysis of Revolutions. In this century, scholarship on revolutions has itself turned in cycles. In the first half of the century, most scholars believed that revolutions were essentially state crises, and were skeptical as to whether they brought social progress—a view most elaborately presented in Crane Brinton's *Anatomy of Revolution* (1965), which described revolutions as being like a "fever." In the years from World War II to the late 1970s, however, scholars increasingly believed that revolutions were perhaps necessary to destroy traditional institutions and classes that impeded the development of modern social and economic organization. Communist revolutions were credited with promoting rapid industrialization in Russia and China, and it was hoped that in Cuba, and perhaps in Vietnam, Nicaragua, and Iran, revolutions would succeed in replacing repressive dictatorships by fairer, freer societies.

Yet the 1980s have been a decade of great disillusionment with revolutionary dreams. Cuba under Castro has become a showplace for economic crisis and a personalist, dominating state. Nicaragua and Iran have suffered from devastated economies and harsh repression. Given a chance, Nicaragua's population voted its revolutionary government out of power, a step also taken by the peoples of Eastern Europe and the Soviet Union. Indeed, the collapse of communist governments in Europe has shown that the Russian Revolution of 1917 did not mark a permanent transformation of Russian society, but rather was the breakdown of a particular state (Russia's traditional tsarist regime), which was followed by the overturning of the communist state itself several decades later.

As to the revolutions of 1989–1991 in Eastern and Central Europe and the Soviet Union, it would be equally unwise to assume that they mark a permanent transformation of their societies in a more progressive direction. The successors to the fallen communist regimes may well prove democrats, or they may found authoritarian states in a nationalist, populist vein. There is, in the early 1990s, strong evidence for possible movement in either direction.

If contemporary scholarship has become more skeptical of the utopian nature of revolutions, it has also become more certain of particular aspects of revolution. First, certain causal principles are widely recognized, largely as a result of the work of those scholars who have shown that several specific structural characteristics and processes make states vulnerable to crisis and revolution (Theda Skocpol, *States and Social Revolutions*, Cambridge, U.K., 1979, and Jack A. Goldstone, *Revolution and Rebellion in the Early Modern World*, Berkeley, Calif., 1991); these are the four elements mentioned above as becoming increasingly prevalent in this century. Only the industrial democracies of Europe and North America seem to have escaped these conditions. Weak states, conflicting elites, rapid population growth, and erratic international intervention are still frequently found in Asia, Africa, Latin America, Eastern Europe, and the former Soviet Republics; thus revolutions and revolutionary movements should continue to be common into the twenty-first century.

In addition, scholars have come to agree on certain outcomes of revolutions. First, revolutions lead to the strengthening of feelings of nationalism and self-assertion in new revolutionary states. Second, revolutions tend to increase the ability of states to mobilize people and demand sacrifices for military and economic efforts. Regrettably, this combination of assertive nationalism and mass mobilization increases the likelihood of wars, which are common by-products of revolution. This is why armed conflicts are likely to arise in the wake of the revolutions in the Soviet Union and Eastern Europe. Third, revolutions tend to lead to a concentration of power. This is the expected result when a new government faces the strains of war and mass mobilization. However, this tendency makes it difficult for revolutions to maintain democratic governments.

There is a nobility to the dream of revolution as a means to achieve utopia in a single stroke. Yet the twentieth century has been, as a century of widespread revolution, a harsh testing ground for that noble ideal. All too often, revolutions have revealed the decay and distress of one government only to erect, with great bloodshed and sacrifice, a state which made a mockery of utopian ideals. Indeed, with few exceptions the great anti-utopian, totalitarian police-states of the twentieth century have been not the work of small-minded dictators but the outcome of revolutions guided by progressive utopian visions.

In the twentieth century, revolutions have sometimes spread the ideals of democracy and justice but more often have spread the centralization of power, wars, and economic hardships. But as long as weak governments, divided elites, population increase, and international intervention continue, revolutions and their effects will continue to shape world politics.

(See also ALGERIAN WAR OF INDEPENDENCE; CLASS AND POLITICS; CUBAN REVOLUTION; GUERRILLA WARFARE; GUEVARA, ERNESTO; IRANIAN REVOLUTION; LENINISM; MAO ZEDONG; NATIONAL LIBERATION MOVEMENTS; NICARAGUAN REVOLUTION; POLITICAL VIOLENCE.)

Crane Brinton, *The Anatomy of Revolution*, rev. and exp. ed. (New York, 1965). Robert C. Tucker, *The Marxian Revolutionary Idea* (New York, 1969). John Dunn, *Modern Revolutions: An Introduction to the Analysis of a Political Phenomenon*, 2d ed. (Cambridge, Mass., 1989). Thomas Greene, *Comparative Revolutionary Movements*, 3d ed. (Englewood Cliffs, N.J., 1990). Barry M. Schutz and Robert O. Slater, *Revolution and Political Change in the Third World* (Boulder, Colo., 1990). James DeFronzo, *Revolutions and Revolutionary Movements* (Boulder, Colo., 1991). Jack A. Goldstone, Ted Robert Gurr, and Farrokh Moshiri, eds., *Revolutions of the Late Twentieth Century* (Boulder, Colo., 1991).

JACK A. GOLDSTONE

RIGHT. Generally used to characterize the conservative end of the political spectrum in modern polities, the Right as a concept may be defined in part by its opposition to its political counterpart, the *Left. Political parties, movements, and ideas sharing a commitment to the advancement of conservative economic, social, and political ideas may be referred to as being of the Right. Parties such as the British Conservatives, the U.S. Republicans, and many European Christian Democrats are seen as representing the arguments of the Right. These parties are to be distinguished from those of the extreme Right (such as the Front National in France) whose philosophies commit them to a level of radical change—often predicated on a social vision associated with racism and xenophobia—that in itself disqualifies them from consideration alongside more mainstream versions.

The Right is suspicious of the idea of progress and is generally committed to the status quo. Its preference for the existing order and resistance to substantial change can be traced to the work of the conservative thinker Edmund Burke, who, for example, rejected the principles of the French Revolution in 1789. Burke, strongly committed to personal liberty, believed that striving for liberty through revolutionary methods would inevitably fail and result in the undermining of the democratic institutions necessary for individual freedom.

Advocates of the Right reject rationalism and reason as a basis for political action, believing instead in tradition and custom as guides to behavior. Accordingly, institutional arrangements which have evolved gradually over the course of history are to be modified only with extreme prudence. Conservative principles of the Right also include the veneration of religion, loyalty, and a system of social hierarchy. In contrast to liberals and those on the Left, conservatives on the Right believe that the bases of political obligation lie in historical legitimacy and loyalty to the state and not in any sort of social contract.

Although some of its proponents look askance at changes associated with capitalist development, harking back to an era of clearly defined social and economic hierarchical allegiances, most modern advocates of the Right now accept the capitalist system. All members of the Right share a belief in the importance of private property (together with a legal system) as the foundation and enabling condition for political and economic liberty. They also share an antipathy to collectivist economic or political institutions, preferring those based in individualism.

As a political movement the Right has to some extent been eclipsed by the success of the *New Right, which has been due in part to the latter's greater attention to social issues concerning the family, for example, and women's abortion rights. In this sense, the Right has suffered a similar fate to that of the Left, as *new social movements have eroded the traditional bases of support. But democratic parties advancing arguments of the Right are still prominent electorally in Western democracies, and with the collapse of collectivist polities in East-

ern and Central Europe they have received a measure of vindication and have shown renewed vitality and purpose.

(See also CHRISTIAN DEMOCRACY; CONSERVATISM; LIBERALISM.)

Michael Oakeshott, *Rationalism in Politics* (London, 1962). Noel O'Sullivan, *Conservatism* (London, 1976).

DESMOND KING

RIGHTS. As a focus of moral, political, and legal theory, the concept of *rights* has assumed an ever-increasing importance in recent decades. This significance has generated debates of great sophistication about the nature and limits of rights, engaging the most impressive philosophic and theoretical energies of this period.

The idea of rights is closely associated with the existence of a claim, either to be protected in relation to activity, as in civil and political rights, or to be confirmed as entitled by law or morality to certain benefits, as in social rights. Rights can either be embodied in law or expressed aspirationally. The abortion debate illustrates contradictory conceptions of rights, focusing in one instance on the right to life of the fetus, and in the other on the right to choice of the mother. Government can resolve this debate legally, but the encounter of opposed moral conceptions is basically without any means of reconciliation, especially by advocates of unconditional positions. Those who conceive of such a controversy in less polar terms are often open to compromise as to the character of the right at stake.

The importance of rights reflects centuries of popular struggle against autocratic government and other modes of coercive authority, and yet the historic success of rights should not be confused with the rise of political *democracy. An emphasis on rights is also intended to guard minorities against the tyranny of the majority or to insulate individuals against societal and cultural practices based upon intolerance. The gradual acceptance of the Western liberal notion that only constitutional government is fully legitimate contributes to the wider conviction that the claims of the governed are worthy of consideration. The essence of this claiming process is the struggle to overcome avoidable human suffering in its many forms. Such an endeavor has resulted in societal demands for limits on the authority of the *state and other agencies of control (whether it be church or employer).

The rise of the idea of *citizenship has reinforced the notion that the individual has certain rights that should be upheld regardless of the source of encroachment. The U.S. *Civil Rights Movement of the 1960s illustrates this belief. This affirmative role of the state in protecting rights remains controversial in several respects. To begin with, it is less firmly established, especially in non-Western countries that reject strict separations of church and state and regard cultural and religious notions of ethical behavior as of greater relevance than "rights" derived from state action or by reference to international standards. Moreover, the role of the state as the custodian of human welfare is currently under attack by enthusiasts of market economics, who contend that there is a tension between efficiency in the allocation of resources and welfare rights.

The history of rights as a political language is properly associated with movements of resistance to royalism, culminating in the English, American, and French revolutions. In each instance, the idea of rights emerged as a principal means to mediate between the authority of the state and the autonomy of the people subject to governmental control. At stake from the nineteenth century onwards was the basic "right" of peoples to give their consent, whether by elections or otherwise. The notion of rights is linked to ideas of *legitimacy and *sovereignty within the frame of constitutional government. The depth of this linkage has been recognized through endorsing an inherent "right" of *revolution in response to tyrannical or oppressive rule. This understanding of a reciprocal relationship based on the duty to respect law and the authority of the state on the one side and the duty of government to act in accordance with principles of fairness and respect on the other gives rise to the concept of a social contract between government and governed. These ideas of contract—a historical fiction, as the bargain was never actually struck in real time, but only presumed—rest on an even deeper foundation in the Judeo-Christian tradition of a covenant between God and the Israelites acknowledging reciprocal duties.

The evolution of practices pertaining to rights exhibits the clear influence of political philosophy upon political behavior and institutions. John Locke's exposition of inalienable rights definitely influenced the founders of the American republic in the aftermath of the revolution against British colonial rule. Similarly, the writings of Voltaire, Rousseau, Diderot, and others were much in the minds of those who made the French Revolution, quite remarkably including those who constituted the mobs in Paris. The revolutionary spirit, carried to terroristic excess, was grounded on the need to establish a new governmental framework that would sweep away all at once the cruel and arbitrary excesses of the French monarchy, the Catholic church, and the inequities of feudal economic structures. This framework was anchored in the revolutionary espousal of "the rights of man" that took precedence over whatever stood in the way. In this regard, the eighteenth century ended with an acceptance of rights as the basis of constitutional limitation on the state.

The next phase of struggle centered on ways to impose limits on the market. The rise of labor and the challenge of *Marxism posed the issue in a variety of distinct settings. Marxist-Leninists avoided concern about rights by contending that justice and injustice were inevitable expressions of class rule,

and that seizure of power on behalf of the masses was the only relevant political goal—justice being impossible in a capitalist society, injustice being impossible in a classless society. The collapse of the Soviet Union has discredited such views almost everywhere and correspondingly reaffirmed the liberal emphasis on the need to avoid abuses of power, wherever situated, by the enumeration and implementation of rights.

The failure of Marxism-Leninism has also had some spillover effect on socialist values more generally and the notion of welfare rights in particular. The view is now prevalent in many societies that the market must be freed from undue constraints, which means "rolling back" some welfare rights. For example, Sweden, long a pioneer in according welfare to all of its people, seems in the 1990s to believe that its competitiveness in the world economy has been reduced by the conferral of excessive welfare rights.

In the period since World War II a new type of rights has achieved prominence, namely "*human rights." Starting in 1948 with the Universal Declaration of Human Rights, governments have come to affirm that all people are entitled to certain modes of protection as well as to provision of basic material needs. The impetus for human rights clearly reflected the ascendancy of an individual ethos associated with Western *liberalism, although international undertakings took some account of the more collectivist notions of *socialism as championed during the *Cold War period by the Soviet Union. The most comprehensive formulation of human rights is contained in two treaties that were opened for ratification in 1966—the International Covenant on Economic, Social and Cultural Rights and the International Covenant on Civil and Political Rights. Essentially, these documents set forth standards. There are no enforcement mechanisms, and many governments that adhered to such treaties did so despite their own gross violations. Others, including the United States, could never mobilize the political will to ratify such treaties, with opposition to adherence centering on supposed interferences of human rights with some understandings that a sovereign state should not be subject to external claims of authority. Despite these difficulties, the human rights movement has continued to gather momentum over the decades, finding expression in various treaties that, in elaborating more specialized rights, were in effect calling attention to categories of persons deemed especially vulnerable to abuse. An array of treaty instruments on such matters as racial discrimination, women, and children has resulted.

The effectiveness of human rights has surprised many observers. Governments were prepared to acknowledge that human rights generated *international law obligations, but many were not prepared to respect these rights in practice nor to negotiate arrangements that would impartially establish violations and provide for enforcement. Nevertheless, the existence of human rights embodied in international law standards came to matter in a variety of settings. For one thing, a vast network of transnational, nongovernmental organizations concerned with human rights emerged and used reliable information about gross violations to exert pressure on governments, many of which cared about their reputations. Further, *public opinion favored using economic leverage in relation to human rights, as has been the case with foreign economic assistance policy in the United States since the mid-1970s.

For another, broad currents of international politics coincided with the claims embodied in human rights standards. In the East-West setting, the *Helsinki Accords of 1975 were conceived at the time as important mainly because they officially recognized the post–World War II boundaries that existed in Europe. Provisions in the treaty relating to human rights accountability by countries in Europe were scornfully dismissed as exercises in Cold War propaganda. In operation, the annual inquiry into human rights failures in Eastern and Central Europe mandated by what came to be known as the Helsinki Process grew important both in strengthening the popular will of the people in these countries to resist and in undermining the belief of the leadership in their capacity to rule. These tendencies were strongly reinforced by the emergence of the *Gorbachev leadership in the Kremlin with its espousal of a commitment to human rights and democracy. In retrospect, the emancipation of Eastern and Central Europe and the Soviet Union reflects the relevance of human rights to political behavior.

The complexity of human rights as a topic of global scope is somewhat daunting. There is, to begin with, a variety of initiatives to carry human rights forward on a regional level, most notably in Europe, where an implementation structure enables individuals to mount certain claims against their own government. Further, there are many areas of protection in which existing standards remain insufficient or inappropriate, as in relation to the protection of indigenous peoples or with respect to gay and lesbian autonomy. Also, non-Western normative traditions are becoming more assertive, being both critical of claims of universality on behalf of human rights that hide alleged Western biases, and in some instances self-critical of cruelties embodied in hallowed cultural norms, as in the Hindu caste system or in Islamic views on corporal punishment or the status of women.

There is little doubt that the transnational ferment of recent years in relation to rights is likely to persist and influence the quality of political life. As we grow even more conscious of what it means to live in a global village, with cultures in constant contact through both modern communications and by way of intercultural migration, the pressure for tolerance and understanding will increase, and so will the appeals to rights in response to avoidable human suffering.

(See also CONSTITUTION; GAY AND LESBIAN POLITICS; LENINISM; REPRODUCTIVE POLITICS; ROE v. WADE; WELFARE STATE.)

Ronald Dworkin, *Taking Rights Seriously* (Cambridge, Mass., 1977). Joel Feinberg, *Rights, Justice, and the Bounds of Liberty* (Princeton, N.J., 1980). United Nations, Geneva Centre of Human Rights, *Human Rights: A Compilation of International Instruments* (New York, 1988).

RICHARD FALK

RIO TREATY. The Inter-American Treaty of Reciprocal Assistance, adopted in 1947 at a meeting in Rio de Janeiro, is known as the Rio Treaty. It is a mutual *security pact providing for the American states to respond to acts of aggression in the Western Hemisphere (given a precise geographic definition) with consultative procedures and, if agreed upon, certain types of assistance and *sanctions. The treaty placed on a permanent basis the prior temporary regional security arrangements adopted during World War II, with the scope of aggression broadened to include attack by other American states as well as non-American. Its procedures are closely coordinated with provisions in the charter of the *Organization of American States. The Rio Treaty began with twenty-one signatories, the United States and the then-twenty sovereign Latin American states. Cuba unilaterally abrogated the treaty in 1962, but Trinidad and Tobago later adhered, so that membership has remained at twenty-one states.

Except for one case, all treaty applications have entailed inter-American disputes; except for two, they have all involved the circum-Caribbean region. Eighteen situations were addressed between 1948 and 1979; sanctions were applied against the Dominican Republic in 1960 and Cuba in 1962 and 1964. The case of Panama versus the United States in 1964 over Canal Zone problems was the first involving a non–Latin American party. After 1979 security collaboration was minimal. Latin Americans were dissatisfied with what they viewed as U.S. domination of inter-American security processes. The Rio Treaty was not a significant factor in Central American conflict during the 1980s or involved at all in the settlement of the Beagle Channel dispute between Argentina and Chile (decided in 1984 with mediation by the Holy See). Treaty procedures were applied to armed conflict between Ecuador and Peru in 1981, and to the British-Argentine South Atlantic War (*Malvinas/Falklands War) in 1982, the only cases undertaken outside the Caribbean zone; the latter was the only one involving a non-American state. In the post–Cold War era, mutual security as defined in the Rio Treaty remained a low priority.

(See also U.S.–LATIN AMERICAN RELATIONS.)

General Secretariat of the Organization of American States, *Applications of the Inter-American Treaty of Reciprocal Assistance, 1948–1972*, 2 vols. (Washington, D.C., 1973).

G. Pope Atkins, "The Inter-American System," chap. 8 in *Latin America in the International Political System,* 2d ed. (Boulder, Colo., 1989).

G. POPE ATKINS

RIOT. See POLITICAL VIOLENCE.

ROE v. WADE. The U.S. *Supreme Court's 1973 decision, *Roe* v. *Wade,* is widely understood as granting women a constitutionally protected right to abortion. Although the decision was far more limited, it has served as the focal point for one of the most divisive social issues facing the United States in the last quarter-century.

Until the early nineteenth century, abortion was not a criminal act if it took place prior to "quickening." State legislatures began passing laws criminalizing abortion as a response to a conflicting series of interests, including efforts to professionalize and monopolize medical care by male doctors, and backlash against the assertion of women's rights by the nineteenth-century suffrage movement. Criminalization of abortion was not religiously based; the *Roman Catholic church did not declare abortion a mortal sin until 1869. Historically no concern for the fetus or its "*rights" was voiced until after contemporary efforts by women to secure the autonomous right to abortion.

By the turn of the century statutes criminalizing abortion existed in every state, and they remained unchallenged until the second wave of the women's movement in the 1960s. The early abortion movement insisted on abortion on demand, and worked to achieve this aim by providing referral services for then-illegal abortions, supporting development of technologies for self-abortion or menstrual extraction, and engaging in demonstrations and legislative lobbying.

Court-focused constitutional attacks on abortion laws came from a coalition of quite disparate elements. The women's movement was joined by the medical establishment, unhappy about legislative control over its practice, and population control groups like Planned Parenthood. In addition, conservatives who were alarmed by increases in out-of-wedlock births, particularly to women of color, considered abortion a necessary means to quell rising welfare rolls. After *Roe* was won, conservative members of the coalition, with liberal women's organizations and medical providers, controlled litigation and defined issues within a debate increasingly limited to legal rights discourse.

The Court's *Roe* decision rejected the fetus as a "rights-bearer," and instead called upon the "right of privacy" in the liberty clause of the Fourteenth Amendment to the U.S. Constitution to protect the choice to bear or beget free from unwarranted governmental interference. The Court identified two state interests—maternal health and protection of potential life—and developed a trimester framework which determined the time during pregnancy when those interests became sufficiently compelling to permit regulation, or even prohibition, of abortion.

For health, this was the end of the first trimester, after which regulations reasonably related to maternal health (frequently defined by reference to "standard medical practice") could be imposed to restrict abortions, despite burdens on choice. Preservation of potential human life became operative after the second trimester, understood as the time of fetal viability. During the last three months of pregnancy, the state was free to limit or prohibit abortion except where the pregnant woman's life or health was endangered.

In its medicalization of abortion, and identification of the medical profession as the locus for decision making, *Roe* gave very provisional and extremely limited support for women's reproductive rights. Even these limited rights, however, were characterized as extreme, and conservative and religious forces immediately mobilized to further limit *Roe* in the name of "unborn children." Although *Roe* did not originally animate the politics of abortion, it shifted the balance, forcing opponents to reassert their interest in increasingly and overtly political ways.

By exposing and, in a sense, facilitating women's claims to equality and control of their own sexuality, abortion became the perfect target for a diverse coalition of interest groups constituted as the "Right to Life." Their purpose was to restore the authority of the patriarchal family, reimpose substantial limitations on women's autonomy, and manipulate confusion over changing gender roles as part of a broader *New Right agenda.

One of the Right to Life coalition's most significant victories was the 1977 passage of the Hyde Amendment, a congressional funding restriction on Title XIX of the Social Security Act, which prohibited Medicaid funding for abortions for poor women. The Supreme Court upheld the Hyde Amendment and placed *Roe*'s limited right in stark relief—the woman's *choice* to have an abortion, not her actual access to abortion, which might be limited by its cost or availability. Over the next decade the Court approved additional limitations as the Reagan administration's abortion litmus test for judicial appointments moved the Court further right. By the spring of 1991, in *Rust* v. *Sullivan,* the Court upheld a federal law that prohibits employees of federally funded family planning clinics, including doctors, from providing any information about abortion to their patients.

In January 1992 a five-to-four Court decided *Planned Parenthood of Pennsylvania* v. *Casey,* the case in which the Reagan-Bush realignment of appointments was expected to result in an overruling of *Roe.* Instead, in a rare majority opinion authored by three Justices, the Court "preserved" the precedential effect of *Roe* in the name of institutional integrity while finally gutting the trimester framework and standard of review that was at the heart of *Roe*. The Court upheld a 24-hour waiting period, parental consent, and informed consent provisions that had previously been invalidated under *Roe*, striking down only a requirement that a woman seeking an abortion must notify her husband. Rather than requiring the state to show a "compelling interest" for its regulations, the majority shifted the burden to those challenging state regulation to show "undue burden" on the woman's choice. Justice Blackmun, the 83-year-old author of *Roe*, wrote that only one vote maintains even this limited protection of abortion rights, and predicted an increased politicization of future confirmation proceedings.

Although the availability of legal abortion for middle- and upper-class women was preserved, the decision made it constitutionally permissible to impose regulations that will make abortion virtually unavailable to many poor women, young women, and those living in rural and other areas distant from abortion providers. Neither legislative relief at the federal level nor state-by-state responses to *Planned Parenthood* can resolve the deeper problems of inequality and growing acceptance of restrictions on access to abortion.

Difficulties in abortion rights organizing in the United States follow in part from the unqualified support for *Roe* by many women, which implies acknowledgment of the legitimacy of legal restrictions on abortion. This approach fails to place abortion in the broader context of women's economic and sexual rights, which are powerfully limited by unwarranted pregnancy, and obscures the critical personal and sexual politics involved in reproductive rights. Even prochoice mainstream political discourse ignores the fact that abortion is a means, not the end, and obscures the argument of many feminists that reproductive freedom can be achieved only through a transformational politics which secures women's control over their bodies, within a changed social context in which the choice to bear children is not burdened by poverty, unemployment, and lack of housing or health and child care.

Critical understanding of this broader context was first raised by socialist feminists organizing against the Hyde Amendment. They made explicit connections, for example, between limitations on abortion and increasing sterilization abuse, particularly against poor women and women of color. By 1989 women of color had developed more powerful networks of resistance, including the National Black Women's Health Network, which made further linkages to the shamefully high rate of infant mortality in their communities, the need for universal health care, and other social provisions that would make real reproductive choice a reality. Finally, lesbian political activists stressed the importance of abortion as an element in the control of women's sexuality—and opposed restrictions as part of the "policing of gender."

These more far-reaching and liberatory claims for abortion rights are frequently obscured—and have never been judicially acknowledged—in the court-centered politics of abortion in the United States. Although Canada has also successfully employed a constitutional challenge to laws restricting abortion, and the Irish High Court has interpreted its absolute ban to provide a limited exception, recourse to judicial remedies is primarily a U.S. phenomenon. Its proven limitations may provide an important lesson for women engaged in the effort to secure reproductive rights elsewhere in the world.

(See also FEMINISM; GENDER AND POLITICS; PATRIARCHY; RELIGION AND POLITICS; REPRODUCTIVE POLITICS.)

Faye D. Ginsberg, *Contested Lives: The Abortion Debate in an American Community* (Berkeley, Calif., 1989). Marlene Gerber Fried, ed., *From Abortion to Reproductive Freedom: Transforming a Movement* (Boston, 1990). Rosalind P. Petchesky, *Abortion and Women's Choice: The State, Sexuality and Reproductive Freedom*, 2d ed. (Boston, 1990).

KRISTIN BOOTH GLEN

ROMAN CATHOLIC CHURCH. The Roman Catholic church has been an actor in world affairs for two millennia. The "Christian fact," a religious community which quickly assumed an institutional status, posed a double challenge to the Graeco-Roman world. First, the church's claim on the conscience of believers was a profound challenge to the classical world's conception of the power of the *state; now there was a new standard of behavior against which a state's prescriptions and prohibitions would be tested. Second, as a social institution the church quickly became a contending locus of *power in the Roman Empire.

The evolution of the relationship between spiritual and temporal power took several forms: the church and the Roman Empire, the church in the Republica Christiana of the High Middle Ages; the church and the Catholic and Protestant states of the post-Reformation period. The Treaty of Westphalia (1648), which ended the religious wars in Europe, also marked the emergence of the nation-state, the basic unit of world politics for the last three centuries. It is in the context of the "Westphalian system" that the issue of the Catholic church and international politics emerges in its modern form. The nation-state posed a theoretical and a practical challenge for Catholicism. On the one hand the claims of the sovereign state threatened fundamental Catholic teaching that bonds of human solidarity and responsibility to others exist in spite of state boundaries and these obligations must be honored in times of *war and *peace. In theory Catholic teaching on international affairs accorded the state real but relative moral value. The nation-state is recognized as a legitimate center of moral and political authority, but the activity of states is to be assessed in light of the moral order of *rights and duties. On the other hand, at the practical, diplomatic level, the church recognizes the role of nation-states and maintains formal diplomatic relations with over 100 states; this activity is directed by the Vatican's secretary of state, a cardinal who is the ranking official in the Roman Curia.

The modern diplomatic role of the Catholic church begins with Pius XII, elected to the papacy shortly before World War II began. A diplomat by temperament and training, he was deeply involved in the *diplomacy of the war and even more so in the postwar period, until his death in 1958. Using an extensive teaching ministry and a wide range of diplomatic contacts, Pius XII was particularly known for two aspects of his policy: an unyielding opposition to *Marxism and Soviet *communism, and an active role in the renewal of Christian Democratic parties in Western Europe. While these parties were lay organizations, the social teaching of Pius XII and the clear support of the Vatican for *Christian Democracy were essential contributions to the growth of the party in the Federal Republic of Germany (FRG), Italy, and the Low Countries.

The brief pontificate of John XXIII (1958–1963) produced profound changes in Catholic teaching and practice, the effects of which strongly influence the church today. From the perspective of international politics two dimensions of this papacy stand out: the inauguration of the "Vatican Ostpolitik" and the convocation of the Second Vatican Council (1962–1965).

The term *Ostpolitik* was never used by the Holy See, but it was appropriately applied by commentators to the change in policy of the Roman Catholic church toward the communist regimes of Eastern and *Central Europe (Hansjakob Stehle, *Eastern Politics of the Vatican, 1917–1979*, Athens, Ohio, 1981). Pius XII viewed these regimes as morally illegitimate and he followed a policy of refusing to deal with them diplomatically. By the early 1960s, it was judged by many in the church that the policy of isolating these governments also made it more difficult for the church to achieve key pastoral objectives. These included the appointment of trustworthy bishops, the increase in the number of seminarians allowed to prepare for the priesthood, and the establishment of religious education programs in parishes. John XXIII, relying upon the skillful diplomacy of Monsignor Agostino Casaroli (later cardinal-secretary of state), initiated a process of limited negotiations with states in Eastern Europe.

The policy was continued and expanded by Pope Paul VI (1963–1978) who had unsuccessfully advocated such negotiations in the 1950s. The purpose of engaging the communist regimes was to seek concrete practical steps which would improve the possibilities for Catholics to practice their faith. The diplomacy of both John XXIII and Paul VI not only changed the position of the church in dealing with communist governments, it also gave much greater weight in Vatican diplomacy to the countries of the *Third World.

The decisive contribution of John XXIII to the church, however, was his quite unexpected decision to convoke an ecumenical council. The council had a significant effect on Catholicism's relationship to the political order. Its two principal documents in this regard were the *Declaration on Religious Freedom* (*Dignitatis Humanae,* 1965) and *The Pastoral Constitution of the Church in the Modern World* (*Gaudium et Spes,* 1965). The influence of *Vatican II can be assessed in terms of its teaching, and in the way the teaching took shape in policies. The texts just named had the double effect of "depoliticizing" the church's role and "resocializing" its ministry. The document on religious freedom refashioned Catholic teaching on church-state relations. The basic principle of *Dignitatis Humanae* is that the church seeks one thing from the state, the freedom to fulfill its ministry. This position left behind the post-Reformation view that the state should acknowledge Catholicism as the religion of the state whenever possible. The concept of the Catholic state was designed to protect the status of the church in civil law, but it often had the consequence of tying the church to policies of states which were of dubious moral quality. *Dignitatis Humanae* "depoliticized" the church's role by distancing it from any specific government. The freedom the church gained from the policy of *Dignitatis Humanae* provided a more independent status from which to address the social issues within nations and among states.

The teaching of *Gaudium et Spes* "resocialized" the church's public ministry, providing new authority and impetus for Catholic social engagement from the parish to the papacy. The conciliar document provided the most expansive conception of the church's public role of any teaching document since the Reformation. Its decisive significance was not what it said about any specific social issue, but the way it defined the ministry of the church in the world. It tied the church's ministry to the defense of human dignity.

In the theology of Vatican II, the church's primary identity is as a religious community with a goal and purpose which are found beyond human history. But the church should pursue its religious ministry in history by contributing to four objectives: protecting human dignity, promoting *human rights, fostering the unity of the human family, and providing a sense of meaning to every area of human activity (*Gaudium et Spes,* #40–42). This conception of the church's role seeks a religiously based ministry which produces socially significant results.

The Second Vatican Council's impact can be found

in the deepening social engagement of the church at all levels of its life since 1965. This social involvement is evident in the "local church" in various parts of the world, and in the ministry of Pope *John Paul II (1978–).

Since Vatican II local churches in Latin America, Eastern Europe, and the United States have played significant social roles in quite different ways. The Latin American example is the best known and most analyzed. This region of the church, overwhelmingly Catholic and facing massive social and economic issues, was the first to undertake a systematic review of its life and ministry after Vatican II. The occasion was the Medellín Conference of Bishops in 1968; the results of the meeting set a direction for the church on human rights and social justice throughout Latin America, particularly in Brazil and Chile in the 1970s, and in Central America in the 1980s. The animating spirit for much of this activity was the Theology of Liberation, a method of understanding the church's role in society from the perspective of and with an "option" for the poor. The pervasive influence of the Theology of Liberation attracted the attention of the Holy See, which has supported some themes and criticized others.

Most of the church's confrontation in Latin America has been with governments of the right. Poland provides a counterexample from Eastern Europe. In the long postwar struggle with the communist regime, the Poles relied upon the institutional strength and pastoral support of the church. The crucial relationship of the Catholic church and *Solidarity in the 1980s (in which each played a distinct and different role) provided the internal leverage against the communist regime whose fate was sealed when Mikhail *Gorbachev refused to use Soviet troops to quell dissent.

In the quite different setting of the United States, where Catholics are about twenty-five percent of the population, Catholic bishops were highly visible actors in the policy debate of the 1980s on four questions: abortion, nuclear strategy, equity in the economy, and the U.S. role in Central America. The two pastoral letters on peace and the economy generated societal debate far beyond the confines of the church.

The engagement of the "local church" in social, political, and economic issues throughout the world is one of the most visible consequences of Vatican II. It should not be understood, however, as replacing the more traditional method through which Catholicism has addressed the international order, namely through the papacy. John Paul II has, in fact, become the most activist incumbent the papal office has known since the Middle Ages. John Paul has shaped a strategy of imposing tight internal discipline in the church, with a broad-ranging commitment to public issues of peace, human rights, and economic justice in the world. Continuing Vatican II, John Paul has stressed the need for the church to maintain its religious identity while simultaneously seeking to contribute to the solution of major social issues.

He has used three means to shape a very activist pontificate. First, he is committed to a ministry of the word, written and spoken. He has produced three explicitly "social encyclicals"—*Laborem Exercens* (1981), *Sollicitudo Rei Socialis* (1987), and *Centesimus Annus* (1991)—and scores of other statements and speeches on a remarkable range of social issues. Second, the pope has used over fifty trips to some of the most conflicted areas of the world to strengthen the church's social and pastoral ministry. One respected observer even credits the beginning of the collapse of *communism in Eastern Europe to the pope's first visit to Poland (Timothy Garton Ash, "Eastern Europe: The Year of Truth" *New York Review of Books*, Feb. 15, 1990).

Third, John Paul II has been willing to engage his office and the Holy See in direct diplomatic intervention under specified conditions. He approved the church's role in mediating the Beagle Channel dispute between Chile and Argentina. He personally intervened with George *Bush and Saddam *Hussein on the eve of the *Gulf War, arguing against the use of force, something he continued to do throughout the war. He attempted Vatican mediation in Lebanon and Yugoslavia without much success. Finally, he has an abiding commitment to the church's public role in the shaping of the European continent in the post–Cold War age. The combined influence of Vatican II and John Paul II has produced a church that understands its religious role as encompassing a broad and diversified public ministry in the world.

(See also LIBERATION THEOLOGY; RELIGION AND POLITICS; REPRODUCTIVE POLITICS; VATICAN CITY STATE.)

Ivan Vallier, "The Roman Catholic Church: A Transnational Actor," in Robert O. Keohane and Joseph S. Nye, Jr., eds., *Transnational Relations and World Politics* (Cambridge, Mass., 1973), pp. 129–152. Thomas M. Gannon, S.J., ed., *World Catholicism in Transition* (New York, 1988). J. Bryan Hehir, "Papal Foreign Policy" *Foreign Policy* 78 (Spring 1990): 26–48. Adrian Hastings, ed., *Modern Catholicism: Vatican II and After* (New York, 1991).

J. BRYAN HEHIR

ROMANIA. The first Romanian states emerged from independent shepherd communities in the Carpathian Mountains in the eleventh century, about eight centuries after the departure of the last Roman legions from the province of Dacia. Its people spoke a Latin language and were Orthodox Christians. In the thirteenth and fourteenth centuries, after the Mongol conquest and withdrawal, two principalities coalesced, Moldavia and Wallachia. North and west of the Carpathians, in Transylvania, Romanian speakers were ruled by the Hungarians as well as German merchant cities. Wallachia and Moldavia were indirectly ruled by the Ottoman Empire from the fifteenth to the nineteenth centuries, but by their own princes. Serfdom was the rule, but in a heavily pastoral economy serfs usually had only a light tribute to pay.

Russian military occupation between 1828 and 1834 created the first modern administration and opened up trade and cultural relations with Western Europe. This soon produced a nationalist movement, modeled on the French example, among educated noble youths. In Transylvania, ruled by the Hapsburgs since the late seventeenth century, Romanian nationalism also developed, but as a reaction against growing Hungarian, anti-Austrian *nationalism. Romanians were led at first by their Orthodox and Uniate (Eastern-rite Catholic) churches (whereas the Hungarian and German elements were mostly Catholic or Protestant). Nationalism led to the Union of Moldavia and Wallachia in 1859, and to the creation of an independent Romanian kingdom in 1878. The king and a parliament dominated by the landowning nobility shared power.

The growth of foreign trade turned the old nobility into grain-exporting landlords. Although serfdom was abolished in 1864, the lords kept the best lands, and in 1907 the peasants, transformed into sharecropping, overworked, resentful semiserfs, staged a massive but ultimately unsuccessful rebellion.

After *World War I the kingdom annexed Transylvania, Austrian Bukovina, and Russian Bessarabia. This brought large non-Romanian minorities into the country, particularly Hungarians who became about ten percent of the new Romania. There was a *land reform to head off peasant revolution, but this resulted in fragmented dwarf holdings and increasing poverty as industry failed to grow enough to absorb rural overpopulation. Economic and political problems mounted under Carol II's royal dictatorship. Aside from those brought on by the Great Depression of the 1930s, there was also the restiveness of the new class of university-trained intellectuals who resented the commercially and professionally successful minorities, especially the Jews (four percent of the population). The intelligentsia turned to a xenophobic, antisemitic fascist movement, the Iron Guard, which by the late 1930s had become the most dynamic political movement in the country.

During *World War II, led by a military dictatorship, Romania allied itself with *Hitler and invaded the Soviet Union. A victorious Soviet Army imposed a communist regime in 1945 even though the Communist Party was tiny. By 1948, the Communists were in full control.

From the late 1940s to the early 1960s, Romania was subservient to the Soviets and engaged in the usual Stalinist projects of massive industrialization and rural *collectivization. But then, pushed by nationalist Communists, Romania accelerated its industrialization, defying Soviet and other Eastern European wishes to have Romania specialize in light industry, agriculture, and mineral extraction. Romanian Stalinists led by Gheorghe Gheorghiu-Dej found the ultranationalism of the intellectuals, which had been dormant since 1944, useful to legitimize their rule.

This trend intensified under Romania's second Communist ruler, Nicolae Ceausescu, who took power in 1965. He made nationalism the central part of his program and opened trading relations with the West to free Romania of its dependence on the Soviet Union. But what was perceived in the West as liberalization was actually an effort to legitimize his regime so that he could extract more investment from his economy. Once in solid control in the early 1970s, Ceausescu retracted liberalizing measures and began to demand ever more sacrifices. By the early 1980s he had amassed a mountain of debts in his effort to purchase advanced technology, but his industry could not export enough to pay these back. Although this was a common enough problem in Eastern and Central Europe at the time, only Ceausescu took the draconian measure of forcing more food and fuel exports to pay back the debts while intensifying investment in huge and inefficient showcase industrial enterprises.

Because of the gradual disillusionment of the population and of the party in the late 1970s, as Ceausescu's schemes turned sour he undermined the party and replaced its leading members with his own family and cronies. By the early 1980s this had produced a grotesque cult of personality. He resurrected old mythologies about racial and national unity since the time of the Dacians (i.e., antedating the Roman Empire) and used the Hungarian minority as a scapegoat for Romania's ills. He and his wife Elena presented themselves as omniscient, benevolent demigods.

To boost population growth, Ceausescu prohibited birth control. As consumption fell to meet investment and export demands, there were food and fuel shortages along with increasing misery. The culmination was the initiation of a gigantic rebuilding project in Bucharest, the capital city, that displaced tens of thousands and threw them into suburban slums.

Neither *perestroika nor glasnost had any effect on Romania. The Ceausescu regime, already isolated from the Soviet bloc, refused to contemplate reform. In December of 1989, however, encouraged by the fall of *communism elsewhere in Eastern Europe and by assurances that the Soviets would not interfere, the Romanian people finally exploded in a brief, violent uprising. The army joined in, and the hated Nicolae and Elena Ceausescu were executed.

Unlike most other Eastern and Central European countries, Romania had no organized or active opposition with a program for change. Rather, former party administrators took power under the guise of being democrats. With inefficient industries, an increasingly restive, poor population, and no concrete plan of action, the new regime, headed by Ion Il-iescu, floundered. To keep order it turned to the army and the old secret police *(securitate),* the only cohesive forces in the country, and almost immediately began to exhibit authoritarian tendencies. Romania in the 1990s is facing a deteriorating economy, social discontent, extreme fragmentation, resentful nationalism, and ethnic tensions with the Hungarian and Gypsy minorities (there are almost no Jews or Germans left). At best, it will take years to recover from the damages inflicted under communism.

Many nationalist Romanians feel that their strategic position in the *Balkans will bring aid from the West. But the Eastern Balkans are no longer important to the world, and the fate of Romania's 23 million people is of little interest to either the troubled Russians or to the European Community, except that a Romanian majority in the former Soviet Moldavia wishing to rejoin Romania may become the source of a future border conflict. In 1992 there was serious ethnic violence between Slavs and Romanians in this former Soviet province, now the independent Republic of Moldova. As there are many Russians and Ukrainians in Moldova, Russia or Ukraine could become involved. Isolated and unstable, Romania in the twenty-first century is likely to repeat the sad political history of much of twentieth-century Latin America.

(See also AUTHORITARIANISM; COMMUNIST PARTY STATES; DEMOCRACY; ETHNICITY; FASCISM; NINETEEN EIGHTY-NINE; SOVIET–EAST EUROPEAN RELATIONS; STALINISM.)

Henry Roberts, *Rumania: The Political Problems of an Agrarian State* (New Haven, Conn., 1951). Kenneth Jowitt, *Revolutionary Breakthroughs and National Development* (Berkeley, Calif., 1971). Daniel Chirot, *Social Change in a Peripheral Society* (New York, 1976). Michael Shafir, *Romania: Politics, Economics and Society* (London, 1985).

DANIEL CHIROT

ROME, TREATY OF. The treaty that created the European Economic Community (EEC), the Treaty of Rome, remains the most historically significant instrument of regional integration. It was one of two treaties of Rome signed by Belgium, the Federal Republic of Germany, France, Italy, Luxembourg, and the Netherlands on 25 March 1957. The other created the European Atomic Energy Community (Euratom). Together with the 1951 Treaty of Paris, which created the European Coal and Steel Community (ECSC), these treaties form the basic constitutional documents of what is now the twelve-nation *European Community (Denmark, Ireland, Greece, Portugal, Spain, and the United Kingdom having subsequently acceded).

It is unusual for an international treaty to be compared to a constitutional document, but the treaties of Paris and Rome created central decision-making institutions (the European Commission, the Council of Ministers, and the *European Parliament) with the power to promulgate common legislation, plus a *European Court of Justice to rule on the interpretation of the community law that those institutions create. The court has insisted that community law must always override the national law of a member state wherever a conflict occurs, basing this view on the treaties. Thus the treaties limit the sovereignty of the member states, and in this they differ from conventional international treaties and more closely resemble constitutional documents.

Unlike more conventional constitutional documents, however, the treaties also contain commitments to specific policies. The most well-known provision of the EEC treaty is for the creation of a common market with no internal tariffs, with a common external tariff, and with internal free movement of labor, capital, goods, and services. There are also commitments, however, regarding the creation of a common agricultural policy and a common transport policy, and regarding the coordination of economic and social policy.

The treaties were a recognition of the interdependence of the economies of the participating states, but they also strengthened that interdependence. More significantly, perhaps, the EEC treaty was a response to the perception that a large, regional domestic market was necessary if the community states were to be able to compete economically with the United States. There was also an ambition among at least some of those involved with the drawing up of the treaty to move toward a politically united Europe. The framework of community law that the treaty created, as interpreted by the European Court of Justice, has assisted this development from economic to political unity.

One effect of the treaties was to create a new category of law: not domestic law, but, because it has direct applicability in member states, not international law either. Also, the demarcation of what were previously domestic policy areas as the subject of joint policy-making blurred the division between foreign and domestic policy for the member states. In creating the European Community, then, the treaties created a new type of international organization, one that remains the archetype for all efforts at regional integration and is a major new actor in international economic and political affairs.

Neill Nugent, *The Government and Politics of the European Community* (London, 1989).

STEPHEN GEORGE

ROOSEVELT, Franklin Delano. Thirty-second president of the *United States, Franklin Delano Roosevelt (1882–1945) is one of the most significant political figures of the twentieth century. He led the nation through the Great Depression of the 1930s, the most harrowing crisis in its history since the Civil War, and was the architect of the U.S. *welfare state and leader of the Allies in victory over *fascism in *World War II. His election to third and fourth terms as president was unprecedented (and now constitutionally prohibited), he was the first president to systematically utilize intellectuals in his administration (generically known as his "Brain Trust"), and he recast the electoral support for the Democratic Party through his *New Deal coalition. Yet during his lifetime FDR was a controversial figure in U.S. politics, beloved by many and referred to derisively by others as "that man in the White House." Today his personality and contributions are still contested by scholars.

Franklin Roosevelt was born in Hyde Park, New York, to a family of considerable inherited wealth. His parents, James and Sarah Delano Roosevelt, were descendants of Hudson Valley squires. Franklin was educated by private tutors, graduated from Groton School, and received a degree from Harvard University in 1904. A year later he married a distant cousin, Eleanor Roosevelt, who became the most politically prominent first lady in U.S. history and an important political figure on her own terms. A student with little intellectual commitment, Roosevelt entered Columbia Law School with the vague intention of becoming a corporate lawyer. Although he never graduated, he passed the New York bar examination in 1907. After a brief experience with a law firm, Roosevelt was elected to the New York State Senate in 1910 from a district that had not sent a Democrat to the state legislature since 1884. He received national attention by leading the opposition to the U.S. senatorial candidate supported by Tammany Hall, the Democratic Party machine in New York County, and for his sponsorship of labor and conservation legislation. President Woodrow Wilson selected him for the position of assistant secretary of the Navy in 1913, which he held until 1920 when he was nominated by the Democratic Party as its vice-presidential candidate.

In August 1921 Roosevelt was confronted with the most momentous event in his personal life: he was stricken by polio. FDR would never walk or stand again without crutches and braces. In political terms, however, his medical exile proved to be an advantage. Roosevelt's defense of the *League of Nations in the 1920 presidential campaign was now a political liability, and his low national profile left other Democrats to struggle in a period of Republican hegemony. Roosevelt nominated Al Smith for governor of New York in 1924 and for president in 1928 and gained attention for his rousing speeches in support of the "happy warrior of the political battlefield." Although Smith was defeated by Herbert Hoover, Roosevelt won the governorship of New York by the small margin of 25,564 votes. He proved to be an able administrator who responded quickly to problems created by the depression, which deepened dramatically during his second term. For

this precursor to the *New Deal Roosevelt recruited many figures who would later run bureaucracies in his presidential administrations, including Harry Hopkins, Adolf Berle, Jr., and Frances Perkins.

In 1932 the Democratic Party selected Franklin Roosevelt as its presidential nominee on the fourth ballot over his former mentor Al Smith. Roosevelt ran an aggressive campaign, promising to provide "a new deal for the American people" and calling for the formation of a "concert of interests" to fight the depression as Thomas Jefferson had done in 1800 to fight elite domination of the new federal government. While Hoover explained that the depression was an international phenomenon, Roosevelt insisted that the depression represented the failure of U.S. economic *elites. According to FDR, the president had presided over an era of profligate capitalism and people in the United States were being forced to bear the burden of this "obeisance to Mammon."

Elected by a landslide of 472 electoral votes to Hoover's 42, Roosevelt faced a demoralized nation with an economy on the verge of collapse when he took office in March 1933. In his inaugural address, the new president spoke of the "nameless, unreasonable, unjustified terror" that gripped the nation and assured the American people that "the only thing we have to fear is fear itself." Roosevelt spoke darkly of the possibility of employing dictatorial powers to meet this emergency that was as serious as invasion by a "foreign foe," and Congress delegated significant powers to the executive branch, especially in the first one hundred days of his presidency; but in the end the Roosevelt administration remained within the constitutional boundaries of the political system.

The depression proved to be a formidable challenge. Roosevelt employed a variety of measures, both cautious and bold in conception or implementation, to restore economic confidence and provide relief. Sometimes the president was pushed by Congress and by his own administrators to initiate programs, as in the case of labor and social security legislation. Frances Perkins, secretary of labor, contended that she had great difficulty in convincing the president to examine the ideological significance of unionization. Sometimes, however, the president would move in directions that surprised and angered his own advisors, such as his famous "left turn" in 1936 in which he attacked "economic royalists" who would "regiment people, their labor and their property." He contended that these same kind of elites had behaved similarly toward the populist President Andrew Jackson in the 1830s. As "it seemed sometimes that all were against him—all but the people of the United States," so too did he "welcome the hatred" of those who would "gang up against the people's liberties." It was from this democratic antielitism that FDR built ideological support for the welfare state. He once contended that the "spirit of the frontier husking bee is found today in carefully constructed statutes."

Roosevelt's power was seriously reduced after his landslide reelection over Alfred Landon, governor of Kansas and Republican Party candidate, by both congressional and public opposition to his "court packing" proposal in 1937 and his failure to "purge" conservative Democrats running in state primaries in 1938. In regard to the latter, Roosevelt abandoned his role of honest broker among party factions by campaigning for liberals in an attempt to reform the U.S. party system into clearly defined opposing ideologies. Although this reform effort did not succeed, to the considerable anger of both Republicans like Hoover and Democrats like Smith, Roosevelt did manage to redefine *liberalism as the belief that under modern conditions the national government can actively solve problems, notably in the realm of economic and social welfare policy.

The rise of fascism, however, provided the president with a new political arena as he began to focus on international issues. In the early 1930s Roosevelt's interests were almost entirely domestic ones, although he did promote the Good Neighbor policy for Latin America. He was an internationalist early in his career but did not actively oppose the Neutrality Act of 1935, which required an arms embargo when states of belligerency occurred, despite objections from his secretary of state, Cordell Hull. His Chautauqua address of 1936, in which he warned of pursuing "fool's gold" in seeking to trade with belligerents and described "men coughing out their gassed lungs," is one of the strongest antiwar speeches ever delivered by a U.S. president.

In October 1937, however, the president spoke of the "breakdown of all international law and order" and suggested the possibility that collective action might be necessary to "quarantine" aggressors. In his controversial decision to seek reelection to a third term, FDR warned that the world crisis involved an ethical choice of "moral decency versus the firing squad" and compared the crisis he faced to the one faced by Abraham Lincoln in 1860. He hired Robert Sherwood, the author of a Broadway play about Lincoln, as speech writer and encouraged the press to follow up his analogy that as Lincoln faced a nation half slave and half free, the president faced a world so divided. His Republican opponent Wendell Willkie rejected these comparisons to Lincoln and compared Roosevelt's ambitions to those of European dictators. Put on the defensive by Willkie's charge that his reelection would mean that the United States would be at *war in six months, Roosevelt pledged that "your boys are not going to be sent into any foreign wars."

After his reelection, however, in a series of measured steps the president prepared the people for war. Japanese forces bombed U.S. military installa-

tions at Pearl Harbor in December 1941. To defend nations fighting the Nazis in Europe, Roosevelt had extracted commitments from a reluctant Congress and an isolationist public in the six months before Pearl Harbor. He told the people in a fireside chat that the lend-lease arrangement with Britain was necessary to prevent its fall to the Nazis. FDR admitted that the United States risked war as it prepared to become the "arsenal for democracy." Roosevelt declared in 1941 that he was now "Dr. Win the War" instead of "Dr. New Deal," and that August, with British leader Winston *Churchill, he defined Allied war aims in the Atlantic Charter in terms roughly equivalent to his conception of freedom developed in the New Deal.

In his prosecution of the war, Roosevelt tended to follow the same honest-broker strategy that he had undertaken in his rebuilding of the Democratic Party. He extended lend-lease aid to the Soviet Union when it was invaded by Germany and added the Soviets to an Allied coalition with the British, gave assurances to the Soviets that the Allies would open a second front against Germany in 1942, and generally refused to deal with divisive questions during the war such as territorial disputes or questions of colonial independence. FDR envisioned a postwar world built on cooperation between the great powers. This would be the animating idea behind the creation of the UN.

During the war Roosevelt's opponents found it almost impossible to challenge his domination of the political agenda, despite some regrettable policies and dangerous threats. In 1942 by executive order he incarcerated U.S. citizens of Japanese descent and told Congress that should they fail to pass economic stabilization legislation he would act himself. Although reelected to a fourth term in 1944, Roosevelt was seriously ill, and he died on 12 April 1945, shortly after attending a meeting with Allied leaders at Yalta. Although there was initial congressional support for these accords, the almost immediate advent of the *Cold War led to a reevaluation of the utility and wisdom of FDR's policy of cooperation and compromise with the Soviet Union.

FDR's legacy is still a controversial one owing in part to the fact that the two major initiatives of his administrations, the welfare state and international intervention, remain contested policies in the United States. Moreover, Roosevelt's own personal capabilities continue to be scrutinized. Many scholars and even political allies, including in varying degrees Walter Lippmann, Rexford Tugwell, and Frances Perkins, insist that a careful examination of Franklin Roosevelt's policies suggests that his political *ideology never rose much beyond that of the "country squire" from Hyde Park with some progressive sensibilities. Roosevelt himself was generally reluctant to state his views in any systematic way, insisting as he did on one occasion that he was simply "a

Christian and a Democrat." Others, such as James MacGregor Burns, grant that he was a masterful politician with the characteristics of the lion and the fox that Machiavelli contended were the essential features of a leader, but maintain that he lacked any real political vision. There is certainly a sense that even in the context of political compromise there was an especially ad hoc and gimcrack quality to many New Deal programs. Still others, including Arthur Schlesinger, Jr., contend that his pragmatism itself constituted a democratic theory and that he had built a "middle way" of governance between fascism and communism. Whatever assessment is offered of Roosevelt's leadership, he clearly was a superb reader of U.S. *political culture who managed to apply all the great symbols in the American experience (both of past presidents like Jefferson, Jackson, and Lincoln and of dearly held values such as social justice and fairness) to the art of political crisis management.

(See also CONGRESS, U.S.; ISOLATIONISM; PRESIDENCY, U.S.; UNITED NATIONS; YALTA CONFERENCE.)

James MacGregor Burns, *Roosevelt: The Lion and the Fox* (New York, 1956). Rexford G. Tugwell, *The Democratic Roosevelt* (Baltimore, 1957). Philip Abbott, *The Exemplary Presidency: Franklin D. Roosevelt and the American Political Tradition* (Amherst, Mass., 1990). Frank Freidel, *Franklin D. Roosevelt: A Rendezvous with Destiny* (Boston, 1990).
PHILIP ABBOTT

RULES OF WAR. See WAR, RULES OF.

RURAL DEVELOPMENT. The term *rural development* implies a process of increasing productivity and improving standards of living in rural areas. It is a term used most frequently with reference to developing countries. In most such countries, rural areas exhibit not only very low levels of productivity but also persistent evidence of dire poverty. In the decades after World War II, many governments introduced public policies to relieve constraints on agricultural growth and to improve conditions of life in rural areas. Nongovernmental organizations (NGOs) also experimented with a variety of means to stimulate more dynamic and equitable rural economies. Despite such interventions, rural underdevelopment proved difficult to overcome whether in socialist or capitalist economies of the *Third World. Among ongoing problems were urban bias in national *development strategies, increasing population pressure on land and water resources, growing incidence of landlessness and underemployment, and low investment in human resource development.

Rural areas in developing countries were strongly affected by the impact of colonial economic exploitation. Before World War II, rural areas were often characterized by an emphasis on commercial production for export, great inequalities in the distribution of productive assets, and large portions of the population producing only for subsistence. Colonial governments, through marketing boards and taxes, captured significant benefits from export trade. Colonial economies, however, were strongly conditioned to monocrop production and were buffeted by strong boom and bust cycles. In most countries, lack of infrastructure, low life expectancy, and high rates of infant mortality, ill health, malnutrition, and illiteracy also combined to discourage rural economic growth.

After independence, many governments and development specialists anticipated that the *modernization of rural areas would follow from urban and industrial growth in the process of economic development. Modernization was expected to draw excess labor out of the agricultural sector and increase demand for food and industrial inputs that would then be reflected in greater agricultural production and potential for rural growth. The modernization of the rural sector would thus be a consequence of the normal process of industrial development, much as it had been in the United States and other industrializing countries a century earlier. Many governments in the 1940s, 1950s, and 1960s sought to stimulate rural transformation through policies to encourage technological innovation in agriculture, particularly in areas of high productive potential. This emphasis was spurred in both capitalist and socialist economies through investment in physical infrastructure and efforts to encourage the adoption of new seed varieties and more extensive use of chemical fertilizers and irrigation, basic components of the *green revolution.

By the 1960s, critics of the urban and industrial bias of this "trickle-down" model were pointing to evidence that only a small sector of the rural population was benefiting from government-assisted efforts to increase productivity through agricultural research, extension, credit, and infrastructure. Moreover, they pointed to increasing evidence that urban and industrial development was not absorbing excess rural labor. Concern over the apparent failure of modernization to stimulate a process of rural development, along with increased sensitivity to the potential for rural political protest, led to new emphases in government policies and the efforts of NGOs. In many countries, the problems of peasant producers and rural communities were given more focused attention. During the late 1950s and 1960s, even while governments continued to invest in ongoing agricultural modernization efforts, they also introduced community development and agrarian reform programs to encourage greater equity and more dynamic rural growth.

Such efforts sought to unleash the productive potential of rural villages and communities through identification of felt needs, local organization, and self-help efforts, in the expectation that such activities would overcome the fatalism, powerlessness, and traditionalism thought to characterize the lives of the rural poor. A critical component of this approach was the village-level worker, who was to be a catalyst in unlocking local potential for development.

At the same time, several strands in development thinking encouraged a redistributive approach to stimulate agricultural productivity and rural development, especially in Latin America and parts of Asia. Among many development specialists, inequity in the distribution of productive assets was increasingly viewed as the cause of the failure of technological modernization to reach poor rural villages. The rapidly growing economies of Taiwan and Japan supported the argument that greater equity in land distribution was needed before the productive potential of rural areas could be unleashed. A radical critique of modernization policies emphasized the feudal and semifeudal relations of production that encouraged landlords to eschew productivity in favor of security, status, and power and that forced *peasants into exploitative relationships, stifling their initiative. More conservative supporters of redistributive policies anticipated increased rural political stability if peasants were to become small market-oriented producers. In a number of countries, agrarian reform legislation was passed and agrarian reform institutes established to address difficult issues of land tenure, to redistribute land, and to build infrastructure for agrarian reform beneficiaries.

In most countries, however, agrarian reform affected only a small portion of the rural population. In practice, governments proved unwilling or unable to expropriate large landholdings, many of which had modernized and were providing an important source of foreign exchange to the country. The capacity of both traditional and more capitalist landowners to resist the redistributive efforts of even committed governments was considerable. In addition to the political constraints of a redistributive path toward rural development, the difficulties of financing and administering access to green revolution technology, extension, and markets were among factors that helped dampen optimism about the potential of agrarian reform to respond effectively to rural underdevelopment. Agrarian reforms that emerged from revolutionary upheavals also faced severe organizational, administrative, and financial constraints that limited their economic and political success. Theoretical arguments for the importance of agrarian reform remained generally intact, while practical experience increased awareness of its political, administrative, and financial demands. Increasingly, government-sponsored agrarian reform initiatives were targeted only for areas where rural unrest or insurgency threatened.

The early 1970s brought new efforts to address persistent evidence of rural underdevelopment. Keynoted by *World Bank President Robert McNamara in a 1973 speech in Nairobi, "the poorest forty percent," most of whom lived in rural areas, took on new importance. Significant shortfalls in food grain production and high international commodity prices in the early 1970s focused attention on a "world food crisis" and increased interest in the provision of national food security. The decade demonstrated greater concern for peasants and villagers and new regard for their contributions to agricultural production, particularly of basic food grains. There was much increased attention to the role of women in the rural development process as well as new emphasis on the importance of nutrition, health, and education to improved standards of living. Basic human needs and integrated rural development approaches sought to counterbalance the inequities and inefficiencies introduced by ongoing modernization efforts. The *basic needs approach indicated the importance of social development in the countryside if rural poverty were to be addressed, and governments sought to generate programs, often funded by international loans, to deliver increased education, health, and sanitation services to rural dwellers. Integrated rural development programs focused on the provision of social, productive, and infrastructural services in packages designed to be appropriate to the diverse needs and conditions of specific rural regions. This approach, which at times acknowledged the need for land redistribution, placed greater emphasis on the potential for technological innovation to increase peasant productive potential even on very small holdings.

Basic needs and integrated rural development approaches were widely adopted in developing countries in the 1970s, often bringing new vigor to ministries of planning, agriculture, public works, and social services as well as to diverse agencies for research, extension, credit, and marketing. Heavy foreign borrowing often accompanied these efforts, encouraged by the programmatic concerns of many international agencies and the wide availability of easy credit during the decade. Disillusion with these new approaches to rural underdevelopment began to emerge within a few years of their adoption, however. Governments experienced great difficulty in meeting the heavy demands they made on administrative capacities for coordination and timely delivery of effective services. Moreover, evidence accumulated of the frequent appropriation of program and project benefits by better-off sectors of the rural population, leaving the poorest untouched or relatively worse off. In the wake of an international debt crisis in 1982, many governments retreated rapidly from rural investment commitments under the dual impact of foreign exchange shortages and the need to impose strict austerity on public sector budgets.

Rural development initiatives in the 1980s were dominated by concerns about the macroeconomic contest of agricultural sector development and the impact of prices on incentives for production. Prior initiatives, particularly those at the sectoral level such as modernization and integrated rural development, were heavily criticized for having been pursued in macroeconomic contexts that were highly unfavorable to agriculture in general and for having introduced a variety of unsustainable subsidies that distorted national economic interactions. Throughout the decade, the potential for rural development was associated with efforts to alter rural-urban terms of trade and to introduce competitive market prices for agricultural inputs (particularly fertilizer and credit) and outputs. Considerable efforts were undertaken, often as the result of conditions set by international financial institutions, to weaken or dismantle agricultural marketing boards and to remove subsidies that had been introduced in the 1960s or 1970s to stimulate technological innovation and greater productivity. In Africa, where communal landholding systems were increasingly imperiled by poverty and population pressures, new emphasis was placed on tenure reforms thought to be essential to the stimulation of dynamic smallholder production.

Just as the rural development initiatives of the 1970s were criticized for being less concerned with price incentives and macroeconomic terms of trade than they should have been, so the emphasis on macroeconomic and pricing policies of the 1980s engendered criticism for their failure to encourage investment in social and physical infrastructure, research and extension, and poverty alleviation. Increasing concerns were voiced about natural resource degradation caused by inappropriate government policies and the interrelated impact of poverty and population pressure. Similarly, greater attention was focused on the problem of rural employment. The 1990s witnessed a renewal of concern about persistent poverty, natural resource degradation, research and extension, and employment as factors that needed to be addressed if rural development were to occur.

Four or more decades of efforts to address problems of rural areas were characterized by changing analyses of the constraints on rural economic development. These were reflected in altered approaches to stimulating productivity and raising standards of living by governments and NGOs. In most cases, rural inhabitants were not the principal initiators of these interventions. International agencies and ministries of planning or finance often took the lead in defining the problems and designing the solutions. To the extent that rural interests were represented in national policy making, they were often those of larger, commercially oriented farmers and of village elites who continued to benefit from unequal resource distribution and preferential access to public goods and services. With sporadic exceptions, the majority of most rural populations continued to be not only poor but also powerless in national politics. Rural development continued to be an elusive goal in many countries, the achievement of which implied

changes in international economic exchanges, domestic political relationships, macroeconomic and agricultural sector policies, and access to productive and social assets among the rural poor.

(See also COLLECTIVIZATION; FOOD POLITICS; LAND REFORM; WOMEN AND DEVELOPMENT.)

Robert Bates, *Markets and States in Tropical Africa* (Berkeley, Calif., 1981). Carl Eicher and John Staatz, eds., *Agricultural Development in the Third World* (Baltimore, 1984). Merilee S. Grindle, *State and Countryside: Development Policy and Agrarian Politics in Latin America* (Baltimore, 1986). Jean Dreze and Amartya Sen, *Hunger and Public Action* (Oxford, 1990).

MERILEE S. GRINDLE

RUSSIA. In December 1991 the Russian Federation (or Russia) declared the *Soviet Union dissolved and claimed the status of sole legal successor. For the first time since 1922 an independent Russian state came into being. Over the previous two years, Russian society had changed at an extraordinary pace. Glasnost transformed Russia from a tightly controlled dictatorship into a writhing civil society. Competitive elections to the republic's Parliament in February 1990 brought the first noncommunist government in seventy-three years to power. The successful efforts of that government to assert its sovereignty vis-à-vis the Communist-dominated center eventually led to the attempted *coup d'état of August 1991 and, in the wake of the coup's failure, to the collapse of the Soviet Union and the banning of the Communist Party.

Yet, in spite of the dizzying speed of change, the extent to which the new Russia marks a distinct break from the old remains unclear. *Public opinion polls show a surprisingly high level of acceptance of democratic values for a society that has never before experienced political democracy. But Russians still display a relatively low level of tolerance for political *pluralism. Voter turnout in the February 1990 elections for the 1,068 seats of the Russian Congress of People's Deputies was relatively high (seventy-seven percent). Candidates backed by Democratic Russia, a liberal electoral coalition, won approximately a third of the seats and were able to control the body by forming an alliance with reform-minded Communists. Support for Democratic Russia was strongest in urban areas and among the younger generation. In May 1990, the Parliament selected a 152-member Supreme Soviet to act as a permanently operating legislature, with Boris *Yeltsin as its chair. A year later the Russian state was transformed into a presidential system of government, and in June 1991 Yeltsin ran in a contested election against five other candidates for president, winning fifty-seven percent of the vote. But by then electoral participation had dropped to seventy percent, and extremist right-wing candidate Vladimir Zhirinovsky, who advocated his personal dictatorship and the use of force to hold the Soviet Union together, won almost eight percent of the vote.

Many of the institutions characteristic of functioning democracies remain weak in postcommunist Russia. The Parliament is split into thirteen fractions of roughly equal size, making legislative coordination difficult. Yeltsin was granted temporary emergency powers (subject to legislative override) in November 1991. At that time he abolished the Council of Ministers and replaced it with a smaller State Council, consisting of his most important advisers and ministers. Yeltsin dispatched presidential envoys throughout the country in an effort to root out local resistance to his reforms. But these acts remained controversial, leading to accusations of excessive concentration of power in the executive branch.

Russia suffers as well from an excess of weak political parties. With the revision of Article 6 of the Soviet Constitution in March 1990 to allow multiparty activity, hundreds of new political parties formed. Among the larger parties to emerge were the People's Party of Free Russia, the Democratic Party of Russia, the Social Democratic Party, the Republican Party, and the Russian Christian-Democratic Movement. But in general Russian parties were poorly represented in legislative institutions, have small memberships, and have been plagued by innumerable splits. Umbrella coalitions like Democratic Russia or the Movement for Democratic Reforms have been unstable. The phenomenon of Russian *populism—i.e., direct ties between politicians and citizens unmediated by political organization—has weakened parties. Indeed, many of Russia's prominent politicians remain unaffiliated with any political party. Surveys indicate that sixty to seventy percent of the population support no political party, and only two to four percent identify strongly with one. This may change as future rounds of elections are held. Conservatives are as divided as liberals; since the permanent banning of the Communist Party in November 1991, dozens of small neocommunist parties have emerged to claim the role of successor, none establishing itself as a legitimate heir.

The Russian economy is in a state of collapse. Yet it is only beginning to experience the enormous stresses and strains that accompany the transition to a market economy. Since October 1991, the Yeltsin government has pursued radical policies aimed at rapid marketization and *privatization of the economy. The freeing of prices in January 1992 led to immediate consumer price increases of 300 to 350 percent, pushing 90 percent of the population below the poverty level. Most economists expect that marketization and privatization, if they proceed apace, will leave approximately 8 million unemployed (10 percent of the work force) by the end of 1992. In addition, the Russian government is saddled with an enormous budget deficit and has pledged to pay the lion's share of the former Soviet Union's US$100 billion in outstanding foreign debt. Economic collapse and price liberalization have been accompanied by outbreaks of strikes, although tripartite negotiations among representatives of labor, business, and government have sought to contain labor unrest.

The territorial integrity of the Russian republic has been subject to question since the collapse of the Soviet Union, as representatives of some minorities sought independent statehood. Of Russia's 147 million people, eighty-one percent are ethnic Russians. The remainder consist largely of thirty-six groups with populations of 100,000 or more. The largest of these, the 5.5 million Volga Tatars, voted in a vaguely worded referendum in March 1992 to recognize Tatarstan as a "sovereign state" and "a subject of international law." The authoritarian government of the 900,000-strong Chechen minority, headed by former air force general Dzhakhar Dudaev, declared its independence from Russia in fall 1991, although the Russian Federation refuses to recognize Dudaev's authority. In March 1992 eighteen minority republics signed a federal treaty with Russia, with only Tatarstan and Chechnia refusing to participate.

The fate of the 26 million Russians living beyond Russia's borders in the former republics of the Soviet Union has attracted the attention of Russian politicians across the political spectrum. Some, such as Vice-President Aleksandr Rutskoi, have provocatively called for remaking Russia's borders in line with patterns of Russian settlement. The Russian Parliament formally requested that Crimea, ceded to Ukraine in 1954 in spite of its majority Russian population, be returned to Russia. This dispute threatens to bring an end to the *Commonwealth of Independent States, founded by Russia, Ukraine, and Belarus in December 1991. Restrictive *citizenship legislation in some former republics could cause a massive in-migration of displaced Russians, significantly altering the political alchemy of Russia and providing strength to extremist nationalist movements.

There is considerable consternation as well surrounding the role of the former Soviet military in Russian politics. The post-Soviet era has confronted the predominantly Russian officer corps with a stark reduction in power, status, income, and living conditions, as well as with rival claims to its control by post-Soviet governments. This has led to dissatisfaction among officers with the Yeltsin government and speculation about a possible military coup.

In short, Russia has entered upon a most unpredictable stage in its democratization process. Some observers speak of "Weimar Russia," foreseeing collapse into dictatorship in the face of insurmountable problems. Others argue that liberal values and orientations have sunk deep roots into Russian society and that a return to the authoritarian ways of the past is not possible. The last decade of the twentieth century will undoubtedly provide the answer as to which of these points of view is correct.

(See also GORBACHEV, MIKHAIL; NATIONALISM; PERESTROIKA.)

Azade-Ayse Rorlich, *The Volga Tatars* (Stanford, Calif., 1986). Hedrick Smith, *The New Russians* (New York, 1990). Boris Yeltsin, *Against the Grain* (New York, 1990). Jeffrey W. Hahn, "Continuity and Change in Russian Political Culture" *British Journal of Political Science* 21, part 4 (October 1991): 393–421. Robert T. Huber and Donald R. Kelley, eds., *Perestroika-Era Politics* (Armonk, N.Y., 1991).

MARK R. BEISSINGER

RUSSIAN REVOLUTION. The *revolution that took place in Russia in 1917 was actually a series of overlapping revolutions occurring in rapid succession, each transforming those that preceded it. First, early in 1917, the Liberal or Political Revolution of the middle classes and part of the intelligentsia attempted to create a constitutional order. A provisional government, self-selected by leading members of the old tsarist parliament, the Duma, attempted to govern the country and guide the revolution along a moderate track while keeping Russia in the *war against Germany. Social polarization and growing discontent with the war and the policies of the provisional government led to an increase of support among workers and soldiers for the radical wing of Social Democracy, the Bolshevik party, led by Vladimir *Lenin. The Workers' Revolution of October 1917 led to the establishment of Soviet power and a government under Lenin. Among its first acts, the new government encouraged the growing peasant movement to seize the lands and eliminate the economic and social power of the old aristocracy. The Peasant Revolution of 1918 culminated in massive land seizures, the expropriation of the nobility, and the leveling of landholding. Finally, the multiple revolts of the non-Russian peoples of the empire—the Revolutions of the Nationalities—left the Bolsheviks isolated in central Russia and led to the separation of these peoples from Russia and the establishment of nation-states.

The revolutions of 1917 changed the face of both Russia and the world. Not only was the three-hundred-year-old autocratic state apparatus, along with its army and bureaucracy, destroyed in the Liberal or Political Revolution of February 1917, but after a long civil war the old dominant classes (*tsentsovoe obshchestvo*), the nobility and the propertied middle classes, were eliminated in a radical social revolution. Legal private capitalism was replaced briefly by state capitalism (1917–1918) and then by a system of nationalized economy later called "War Communism" (1918–1921). Within the new Soviet republic ordinary people, particularly workers, were brought into government, the army, and the state apparatus, and they eventually became part of a new ruling class of bureaucrats and party officials. Out of the chaos of the first revolutionary year the Bolsheviks succeeded in creating a new and authoritarian state, which they considered to be "the

dictatorship of the proletariat," and which overwhelmed the radical democracy that had begun to flourish in 1917.

The origins of the revolution lay in deep structural tensions in the tsarist political and social order. The autocratic system resisted articulation of the interests of social groups in the making of state policy, and by the early twentieth century large numbers of liberal and radical intellectuals, workers, and townspeople desired political reform (or revolution) to create a more representative and responsive polity. At the same time a significant part of the landed nobility, the social class on which the tsar depended most immediately for support and high state personnel, became increasingly resistant to political reform, changes in the patterns of landholding, or ideas of constitutionalism.

Peasant dissatisfaction with their small plots exploded in the revolution of 1905–1907, and workers, living under a harsh regime of all-powerful bosses and no legal expression for their grievances, responded to the radical messages of socialist revolutionaries. By the eve of World War I society was polarizing. At one extreme were the tsar and his few supporters; at the other, much of society ready for radical change. But at the same time the top and bottom of society were also pulling apart, with the most radical workers alienated from both liberal and moderate socialist politicians. Internationally, tsarist Russia was engaged in a desperate competition with the economic and military power of Imperial Germany, and in the bloody test of strength from 1914 to 1918 Russia's technological and productive backwardness proved inadequate to stand up to its enemies. The war was the final blow to the fragile structure of the empire, which was unable to carry on the war and supply its cities with fuel and food.

The events of the February Days, well-described in the memoir-histories of Nikolai Sukhanov and Lev *Trotsky, began when illegal meetings of women workers were held in several textile mills in the Vyborg district of Petrograd (St. Petersburg). The women decided to go on strike and marched to other factories shouting "bread." By noon twenty-one factories and 50,000 workers had joined the strike. Bread shortages inflamed those in breadlines, and they joined the strikers. By the second day, 24 February (March 9 new style), 200,000 workers—half the industrial workers of Petrograd—were on strike. Cossacks refused to shoot the workers. In the Duma the liberals now called for a government responsible to the Duma. Some workers, more radical than their socialist, even Bolshevik, leaders, called for an armed insurrection, but the Russian Bureau of the Bolsheviks opposed that demand. Soon the workers' rebellion was joined by the soldiers' mutiny, and tsarist power collapsed in a few days.

Liberals in the Duma were fearful of the spontaneous rebelliousness of the masses (*stikhiia*). Pavel Milyukov, leader of the liberal Constitutional Democratic Party (Kadets, Partiia Narodnoi Svobody) later admitted: "We did not want this revolution. . . . And we had desperately struggled so that this would not happen." They formed their own government, while the workers created a Soviet ("Council") of Workers' Deputies (Soviet Rabochykh Deputatov). Instead of a single center of power in Russia, the February Days ended with two rival centers—one holding formal power and representing the middle and upper classes, as well as liberal public opinion; the other holding real, physical power, commanding the soldiers and workers. The polarization of prewar tsarist society was reproduced in the new political institutions of "dual power" (*dvoevlastie*).

The first clash between the two powers occurred in April over disagreements about the continuation of the war. The provisional government wanted to carry war to a victorious end and acquire the imperial fruits of war (e.g., control over the Bosporus and the Dardanelles) promised by the Allies to the tsar. But the Soviet demanded a "democratic peace" with no annexations or indemnities. When demonstrators surged into the streets to protest Foreign Minister Milyukov's note on war aims, the government fell. A coalition government was formed with a number of Soviet representatives from moderate socialist parties. The Bolsheviks remained outside the government and championed the notion of Soviet power, a government made up only of representatives of the lower classes.

Through May and June workers became more discontented with rising prices and falling real wages. The initial cooperation of the factory owners dissipated, and workers blamed the owners for their worsening situation. Soldiers were tired of the war and turned against the government when it attempted to launch an offensive in the late spring. In early July radical workers and soldiers attempted a coup in Petrograd, but the Soviet, led by the Mensheviks and Socialist Revolutionaries, managed to put it down. Bolsheviks were arrested, and Lenin went into hiding. But this short-lived decline in Bolshevik support ended with the attempt by General Lavr Kornilov to seize power and reestablish discipline in the army. By early September Bolsheviks held majorities in both the Moscow and Petrograd Soviets, and Lenin urged his followers to seize power. On 25 October 1917 (7 November new style), the Bolsheviks overthrew the provisional government, now led by Aleksandr Kerensky, and proclaimed a Soviet government.

The Russian Revolution has been the classic example for Marxists of a successful workers' revolution. Indeed, the February Revolution particularly was carried out by a largely spontaneous workers' movement, aided at key moments by the soldiers of the Petrograd garrison. The October Revolution was much more a planned, military operation, initiated by the Bolshevik leadership, but it was widely supported in Petrograd by workers and soldiers and did not fit the image of an unpopular, conspiratorial coup d'état of an earlier historiography. The broad alliance of social forces—workers, soldiers, some local middle-class elements in the towns, and a part of the peasantry—that had come together to support Soviet power in the fall of 1917 soon disintegrated as Russia withdrew from the war, soldiers left for home, and industrial erosion took its toll on an already-weakened working class. For many analysts, especially those who were more sympathetic to the aspirations of the Bolsheviks, the subsequent drift from a more democratic form of Soviet rule to the one-party dictatorship of 1918 and the Civil War years was rooted in the traumatic circumstances of international isolation, the loss of a broad social base for Bolshevism, and the collapse of the old economy. For others, particularly Western liberal and conservative writers, dictatorship was inherent in the Leninist theory of party organization, the vanguardism of the cadre party, and Bolshevik suspicion of Western parliamentary forms.

Unlike later twentieth-century revolutions—in China, Vietnam, Cuba, and elsewhere in the Third World—Russia's revolutions were primarily urban. The success of the Bolsheviks required, in their own understanding, the mobilization of the peasantry, which would make restoration of monarchical and aristocratic power impossible, and an international revolution to help backward Russia grow into socialism. Lenin repeatedly insisted that revolution either in the West or in the colonial world, along with an alliance between workers and peasants, was the sine qua non for the survival of Soviet power. When those revolutions failed to materialize, the party fell back on those elements that supported it most completely and curtailed the range of free expression and political action. Key to their survival after 1917 was the organization of a militant party and effective army that could wage war against socialism's enemies.

For Third World Marxists the Bolsheviks were not only the founders of the "first socialist state" and the "party of a new type," but model revolutionaries committed to the anti-imperialist struggles of the colonial peoples. The legacy of Bolshevism went beyond the development of the powerful revolutionary weapon of the Leninist party. It included, most importantly, a view of history that saw socialism of the Soviet type, complete with party dictatorship and a nationalized economy, as a higher stage of development beyond capitalism, the market, and a democratic, representative political order of the Western type. That legacy of the Russian Revolution and Civil War would first be radically revised by the heirs of the Bolsheviks themselves in the late 1980s and only later by their descendants in other postrevolutionary societies.

(See also Chinese Revolution; Communist Party States; Leninism; Marxism; Soviet Union.)

William G. Rosenberg, *Liberals in the Russian Revolution: The Constitutional Democratic Party, 1917–1921* (Princeton, N.J., 1974). Alexander Rabinowitch, *The Bolsheviks Come to Power: The Revolution of 1917 in Petrograd* (New York, 1976). Allan K. Wildman, *The End of the Russian Imperial Army*, 2 vols. (Princeton, N.J., 1980, 1987). Ronald Suny and Arthur Adams, eds., *The Russian Revolution and Bolshevik Victory: Visions and Revisions* (Lexington, Mass., 1990).

RONALD GRIGOR SUNY

RWANDA. A small country in the highland lake region of east-central Africa, Rwanda has a history of state organization that long predates the period of European colonial rule. In precolonial Rwanda the *mwami* (king) ruled through a dense hierarchy of officials; pervasive patron-client relations provided the essential mechanisms of control over land, cattle, and people. The kingdom's three major ethnic groups—Hutu (about eighty-four percent of current population), Tutsi (fourteen percent), and Twa (less than one percent)—were distinguished by status and wealth but shared a common language and many other cultural features.

The monarchy was retained during colonial rule, under Germany before World War I, and thereafter under Belgium as a League of Nations mandate and UN Trust Territory. Belgian policies expanded the power and prerogatives of chiefs, while imposing taxes, labor exactions, and obligatory cultivation which fell heavily on Hutu. While not all Tutsi were rich and powerful, virtually all those who became rich or powerful during the colonial period were Tutsi.

Resentment over these *class and ethnic inequalities fueled popular protests during the 1950s. In the revolution of 1959–1961, rural Hutu repudiated the authority of Tutsi chiefs, and the Belgian administration shifted its support to the majority Hutu. Both Hutu and Tutsi died in the violence; many more Tutsi fled to Uganda, Tanzania, Burundi, and Zaire. Local elections in 1960 gave an overwhelming victory to Hutu parties; in 1961 a referendum abolished the monarchy and Hutu candidates won a large majority in the new National Assembly.

On 1 July 1962, Belgium ceded power to a Hutu-dominated republic headed by President Grégoire Kayibanda. Although revered among Hutu for his role in the revolution and his dedication to the interests of the rural masses, Kayibanda is faulted by his critics for having introduced single-party rule, for concentrating power in the hands of individuals from his home region (central Rwanda), and for failing to dampen ethnic conflicts. Regional and ethnic tensions erupted into violence in 1972–1973, precipitated in part by the massacre of many thousands of Hutu in Burundi under a Tutsi-dominated government. In a *coup d'état on 5 July 1973, Major General Juvénal Habyarimana, a Hutu from the north, overthrew Kayibanda's government.

Rwanda faces severe structural constraints. Population density is among the highest in Africa, with nearly 7 million people in a country of only some 26,000 square kilometers (10,000 sq. mi.), where more than ninety percent of the population depends on agriculture for their livelihood. The Second Republic tried to address these realities by improving the transport network, promoting extensive reforestation, expanding export crop production (coffee and tea), establishing small-scale manufacturing, and energetically soliciting foreign aid. Habyarimana's government also reorganized primary school education, encouraged the construction of rural health clinics, and promoted the proliferation of local associations working for *development.

Many of these programs benefited rural dwellers, and Rwanda achieved an enviable record of providing price incentives to rural producers and improving rural infrastructure. But toward the end of the 1980s, a series of crises dramatized contradictions in Rwanda's development efforts. Precipitous decline in the world price of coffee undermined government revenues and wreaked havoc with the local economy. Famine caused several hundred deaths. Revelations in the press exposed corruption and land accumulation by government officials, drawing attention to favored treatment in employment and foreign scholarships for northerners. Initially the government responded by arresting journalists, but in July 1990 Habyarimana launched a process of political renewal designed to lead toward multiparty elections.

In October 1990, the Rwandan army turned back an invasion of several thousand well-armed Rwandan exiles from Uganda; but guerrilla attacks continued throughout 1991 and early 1992; these were seen by many as a tool of monarchist (Tutsi) exiles. The aftermath of the invasion both accelerated and complicated the process of political liberalization. Massive mobilization for military service, tight security throughout the country, and the polarization of ethnic relations seemed hardly conducive to open debate and fair multiparty elections. Opposition critics claimed that Habyarimana proposed only superficial changes, while manipulating the reform process to insure the survival of incumbents. Meanwhile, a structural adjustment program including a sharp currency devaluation in November 1990, caused hunger and deprivation among both rural and urban poor.

By mid-1992 the position of Habyarimana and his single ruling party, the Mouvement National Rwandais pour le Développement (MNRD), was severely weakened. Parades in support of the opposition parties, workers' strikes, the inability of the government to end the war, and revelations of official complicity in massacres of Tutsi in Bugesera region (eastern Rwanda) and elsewhere had undermined MNRD claims to legitimacy. Under strong pressure from Western donor countries, in April 1992 Habyarimana agreed to a transition government with representatives of three major opposition parties as well as the MNRD. The new prime minister, Dismas Nsengiyaremye of the Mouvement Démocratique Rwandais, promised to negotiate with the guerrilla movement (the Rwandese Patriotic Front) for an end to the war and to lead the country to democratic elections in 1993. Meanwhile, his transition government struggled to control intense regional animosities between northerners and southerners, unrest in the army at the prospect of demobilization should the war end, and terrorist violence (bombs, land mines, and assaults on prominent persons) apparently perpetrated by MNRD supporters.

Whatever the outcome of this political liberalization process, the government of the early 1990s will face daunting challenges: how to achieve democracy and improved governance in conditions where there is too little land for too many people, where inequality is growing rapidly, and where external economic and political environments can so sharply intensify internal difficulties.

(See also ETHNICITY; FRANCOPHONE AFRICA.)

René Lemarchand, *Rwanda and Burundi* (London, 1970). Donat Murego, *La Révolution Rwandaise, 1959–1962* (Louvain, 1975). Ian Linden and Jane Linden, *Church and Revolution in Rwanda* (New York, 1977). Jean-Paul Harroy, *Rwanda: de la féodalité à la démocratie* (Brussels, 1984). Filip Reyntjens, *Pouvoir et droit au Rwanda* (Tervuren, Belgium, 1985). Catharine Newbury, *The Cohesion of Oppression: Clientship and Ethnicity in Rwanda, 1860–1960* (New York, 1988). Fernand Bézy, *Rwanda, Bilan socio-économique d'un régime (1962–1989)* (Louvain, 1990).

CATHARINE NEWBURY

S

SADAT, Anwar. Born to a modest peasant family, Anwar Sadat (1918–1981) rose through the army to play a prominent part in Egyptian political life, first as a key figure in the anti-British military conspiracies of the 1940s and later as an influential government official in the 1950s and 1960s. However, Sadat did not reveal his potential for political leadership until his imposing predecessor, Gamal Abdel *Nasser, passed from the scene on 28 September 1970 and Sadat assumed the presidency in a smooth constitutional transfer of power.

Sadat soon made his own distinctive bid for leadership, breaking with Abdel Nasser's radical nationalist policies. Only six months after assuming power, he imprisoned many of his opponents on the Left, claiming that they had been plotting against him. He soon released from *Egypt's jails thousands of Islamic fundamentalists, using them as a counter to the remaining power of the Nasserist Left.

Sadat then launched an economic and political liberalization called the *infitah or "Open Door"— a policy that tried to tie Egypt's economy to the West and to give the regime a democratic face. Realizing that a full accommodation with the West remained blocked by the state of *war with Israel, Sadat expelled Egypt's Soviet advisers in 1972. Then, in October 1973, he launched a war against Israel in order to prepare the way for a peaceful settlement. Egypt's initial battlefield successes gave Sadat the prestige of "victory" in the war and enabled him to make a dramatic bid for *peace with Israel, including a personal trip to Jerusalem in November 1977. Though excoriated by many in the Arab world, Sadat continued to seek peace with Israel, eventually signing the Camp David Accords and sharing the 1978 Nobel Peace Prize with Israeli Prime Minister Menachem Begin. Continued negotiations led to a formal peace treaty in March 1979.

Many Egyptians, especially the upper classes, welcomed Sadat's economic liberalization, his relaxation of Nasserist *authoritarianism, and his achievement of peace with Israel. However, by the late 1970s limited democratization proved no substitute for real economic progress and domestic discontent mounted. When the government cut back state subsidies in 1977, riots swept several Egyptian cities, reflecting popular anger at the new rich and their foreign-influenced lifestyle, while so many Egyptians had barely enough to eat. Such policies drew critical attention to Sadat's own family: his brother had made millions on shady business deals and his wife Jihan often hosted lavish international social events.

Sadat's peace agreement with Israel had increasingly become a liability. His critics accused him of betraying the Palestinians and of gaining little substance in return. Throughout the Arab world he was an outcast. Abroad, his prestige as a Nobel laureate obscured these difficulties. The illusion was shattered on 6 October 1981 when members of an Islamic fundamentalist cell in the army assassinated the president while he was reviewing a military parade. Sadat's supporters in the West, expecting the kind of outpouring of grief that met Abdel Nasser's death, found instead that Cairo was unmoved.

Husni Mubarak, Sadat's successor, has adhered to the main lines of his predecessor's policies. The historic peace with Israel and ties to the West have held. Yet Sadat's achievements will remain problematic until a broader *Middle East peace has been achieved and Egypt's economy and political life fulfill the initial promises of Sadat's liberal reforms.

(See also ARAB-ISRAELI CONFLICT; ARAB NATIONALISM; ASSASSINATION; ISLAM; NASSERISM; NATIONALISM; REFORM.)

John Waterbury, *The Egypt of Nasser and Sadat: The Political Economy of Two Regimes* (Princeton, N.J., 1983). Raymond William Baker, *Sadat and After: Struggles for Egypt's Political Soul* (Cambridge, Mass., 1990).

RAYMOND WILLIAM BAKER

SAHEL. Arabic for "border" or "edge," the Sahel refers to West African countries located at the edge of the Sahara desert. Characterized by little or no rainfall, the Sahel includes *Burkina Faso, *Cape Verde, *Chad, The *Gambia, *Guinea-Bissau, *Mali, *Mauritania, *Niger, and *Senegal. To varying degrees, the Sahelian countries grapple with ethnic, regional, caste, and *class conflicts that colonial powers exacerbated by drawing boundaries that divided coherent ethnic groups. These conflicts are mostly nonviolent. Virulent conflicts, however, have occurred in Chad and Mauritania. In the former, racial, religious, and regional conflict has erupted in periodic civil war; in the latter, slavery continues though officially outlawed in 1979. In the Sahel, religious traditions are strong and divided among animism, Christianity, and Islam. Islam, a major religious force, accounts for over eighty percent of the population of Mauritania, The Gambia, Senegal, Mali, and Niger. Despite its potentially unifying force, in Mauritania, Islam has neither prevented the periodic outbreak of violence between blacks and "whites" (Arabs) nor, in 1989, the expulsion of 110,000 Senegalese and black Mauritanians.

Before colonialism, political organization throughout the Sahel was based on small clans, kingdoms, and, in a few cases, empires. The modern nation-state system began essentially at the moment of independence with the creation of democratic political systems that quickly deteriorated, for the most part, into authoritarian or mildly authoritarian, one-party regimes. The exception is The Gambia, which has maintained a multiparty system; however, due to the resources of the ruling elites and the ineffectual nature of the opposition, President Jawara has held on to power. Throughout the region, executive power is strong, and the Western notion of legislative and judicial checks and balances is virtually nonexistent, with the exceptions of Senegal, Burkina Faso, and The Gambia. In Mauritania, Islamic law (*sharī‘a) is in place. Throughout the Sahel, interest group politics representing workers, students, women, intellectuals, the landed elite, and traditional, religious, and ethnic groups exist, but the governments work to eliminate, co-opt, or weaken them.

In recent years major dissatisfaction with one-party governance, government corruption, and bureaucratic inefficiency has made government co-optation of civic groups more difficult. Instead, rejuvenated civic associations have employed strikes, demonstrations, and other methods to signal their lack of support for the ruling regimes. The demand for democratic *pluralism has touched all Sahelian states. Beginning the democratic trend, in 1981, Senegal legalized multiparty *democracy. The most significant development took place in Cape Verde when, in 1991, in the first elections held in the country since independence, the opposition group, the Movement for Democracy, democratically removed the government. Two major developments of 1991 included replacing the military-ruled government of Mali by a civilian-military government and weakening the power of the president of Niger through persistent public protests. Mali and Mauritania held multiparty elections in 1992; Niger scheduled multiparty elections for November 1992. Elsewhere, Chad, Burkina Faso, and Guinea-Bissau have accommodated demands for democracy by legalizing opposition parties, guaranteeing trade union and press freedoms, and by promising to implement multiparty democracy. The ultimate question is whether democracy will prevail under economic crisis.

The economics of the Sahel are heavily dependent upon cash crops, protein products, and minerals. Since independence, governmental development strategies privileged the industrial and services sectors in urban areas over the agriculture sector and the rural areas, even though seventy-five percent of the population resides in the rural areas. Urban food prices were kept deliberately low and party patronage swelled the state bureaucracies and *parastatals. Compounded by declining terms of trade for agricultural exports and rising import costs, these policies have spelled economic disaster. To counter the severe economic crisis facing the countries, the governments have implemented *International Monetary Fund– and *World Bank–sponsored structural adjustment reforms. Nevertheless, despite several years of these reforms, economic recovery has failed to materialize.

Efforts to overcome these economic and political difficulties have included unification and regional integration schemes such as the Senegambia Confederation (1982–1989) and Guinea-Bissau and Cape Verde's unification plan (1975–1980). Political integration schemes have not fared well in the Sahel.

A critical challenge for the Sahelian governments is the deteriorating natural environment. In 1973, to make the region less vulnerable to drought, the governments formed an international organization, the Permanent Inter-State Committee on Drought Control in the Sahel (CILSS). CILSS works closely with the Club du Sahel, an organization that brings together the donor community and the Sahel governments to identify solutions to environmental problems and to mobilize funding to implement development projects. The creation of CILSS has allowed the region to reduce significantly its heavy dependence on bilateral aid from the French. More than ever dependent upon international development aid, the Sahel receives monies from a diversity of bilateral and multilateral sources. Since CILSS's formation official development assistance to the Sahel went from US$756 million in 1974 to almost US$2 billion in 1985. Today the Sahel, in commitments, receives more aid per capita than any other region of the world. Despite this surge in official development assistance and private sector aid, the Sahel remains marginalized from the world economy. Present scenarios for the Sahel's future remain bleak.

(See also AFRICAN REGIONAL ORGANIZATIONS; ETHNICITY; FRANCOPHONE AFRICA; LOMÉ CONVENTION.)

Carolyn M. Somerville, *Drought and Aid in the Sahel: A Decade of Development Cooperation* (Boulder, Colo., and London, 1986). Organization for Economic Co-operation and Development, *The Sahel Facing the Future* (Paris, 1988).

CAROLYN M. SOMERVILLE

SAINT KITTS AND NEVIS. See ENGLISH-SPEAKING CARIBBEAN.

SAINT LUCIA. See ENGLISH-SPEAKING CARIBBEAN.

SAINT VINCENT AND THE GRENADINES. See
English-Speaking Caribbean.

SALT. See Strategic Arms Limitation Treaties.

SAMOA. See Pacific Islands.

SANCTIONS. In their dealings with one another,
*states often use sanctions to pursue various *for-
eign policy goals. Economic sanctions are defined as
interruptions in, or threats to interrupt, "customary" economic relations between countries in order
to bring about a change in the policies of the target
country. Sanctions can take the form of denial of
imports (trade boycotts) or of exports (embargoes).
Restrictions on financial interactions, such as denial
of economic or military assistance or limitations on
access to financial assets held overseas, are another
common form of sanctions. Sanctions can be applied
unilaterally (by just one state) or on a multilateral
basis. Multilateral sanctions may or may not involve
management by *international organizations. Sanctions are actions taken by governments and directed
against other states. Thus, the appropriate unit of
analysis in understanding the role of economic sanctions is the state. However, entities both above and
below the level of the state, such as *multinational
corporations or international organizations, influence the effectiveness and scope of sanctions.

The use of sanctions has deep historical roots.
*Thucydides, in his history of the Peloponnesian
War, describes a trade boycott imposed by Athens
against Megara, an ally of Sparta, in 432 B.C.E.
During the Napoleonic Wars, France organized much
of continental Europe to limit sales of grain to
Britain. In the twentieth century, the use of economic
sanctions has escalated in frequency. The *League
of Nations imposed a boycott and a limited embargo
against Italy for its invasion of Ethiopia in 1935.
Since World War II, the UN has organized sanctions
against a number of countries, most notably Rhodesia and South Africa to protest their apartheid
policies. However, the United States has utilized
economic sanctions more frequently than any other
state or group of states in the postwar era.

The primary debate about economic sanctions
centers on their effectiveness. Can sanctions actually
bring about desired changes in target countries' policies? If so, is their impact on the target worth the
cost of sanctions to the state responsible for imposing them (the "sender")? Studies of individual cases
of sanctions have typically come to the conclusion
that these measures do not have the desired impact
on the target country. For example, League of Nations sanctions did not force Italy to pull out of
Ethiopia, and a U.S. grain embargo against the
Soviet Union in 1980 did not induce that country
to end its occupations of Afghanistan. Given this
evidence about effects on target countries, the utility
of sanctions deserves further attention.

Opponents of the use of sanctions argue that the
sender incurs higher costs than the target, making
sanctions counterproductive. However, others argue
that the relevant comparison is not between the costs
of sanctions to different countries, but between the
costs and benefits of sanctions and the costs and
benefits of alternative policy tools. States pursue a
wide range of foreign policy goals, and sanctions
are properly seen as one tool in the kit of statecraft.
Thus, governments do not simply ask whether they
should impose sanctions in response to objectionable
policies, but ask whether sanctions are the best
possible response to certain situations. Other potential responses range from diplomatic protests to
covert or military intervention. Diplomatic measures, although less costly than sanctions, send a
weaker signal of commitment to the target and thus
are less effective in bringing about policy change.
Military measures, although perhaps more likely to
succeed in transforming the target's policies, are far
more costly and risky than sanctions. Thus, states
frequently find that, despite the costs involved and
the relatively low probability of success, sanctions
are an appropriate means of carrying out their foreign policies. In difficult foreign policy decisions,
economic sanctions may be the least unattractive
response in an array of unattractive policy options.

Recent studies have called into question earlier
assumptions about the failure of sanctions to have
an impact on target policies. In one study of 103
cases of twentieth-century sanctions, Gary Hufbauer
and Jeffrey Schott (*Economic Sanctions Reconsidered,* Washington, D.C., 1985) find that approximately one-third of the time, sanctions led to at least
a minor change in the target's policies. The probability of success decreases as the goals of the sender
become more ambitious. For example, sanctions
rarely lead to major reversals in military policies or
to a change of government in the target. However,
they can be effective if goals are more modest, such
as protesting the expropriation of property or violations of agreements on the use of nuclear fuels.
This study also refutes the claim that sanctions are
an expensive tool of statecraft. Because sanctions
frequently take the form of reducing foreign assistance or short-term interruptions in trade, their costs
to the sender are often minimal. In the case of
financial sanctions, these actions may even result in
a net economic benefit for the sender. Thus, recent
analyses put sanctions into a more positive light
than did earlier studies.

When sanctions fail, it is usually because the target
has found alternative markets or suppliers to offset
the sender's actions. For this reason, governments
prefer multilateral to unilateral decisions to use
sanctions. Along with actions directed against the
target, cases of economic sanctions usually include
strenuous efforts to gain the cooperation of other
states. For example, when the United States imposed
a grain embargo against the Soviet Union in 1980,

it attempted to organize cooperation from other grain exporters, including Canada, the European Community, Australia, and Argentina. If these states would not actively participate in the embargo, Washington desired at a minimum commitments to avoid increasing grain exports to offset the U.S. embargo. While some states initially cooperated, Argentina took advantage of the situation to increase profitable exports to the Soviets, leading to the unraveling of the entire sanctions effort. This example illustrates the absolute necessity of *international cooperation if sanctions are to be effective, making sanctions a matter of multilateral as much as bilateral diplomacy.

(See also DIPLOMACY; FOREIGN AID; UNITED NATIONS.)

Margaret P. Doxey, *Economic Sanctions and International Enforcement*, 2d ed. (New York, 1980). David A. Baldwin, *Economic Statecraft* (Princeton, N.J., 1985).

LISA L. MARTIN

SANDINISTA FRONT. Founded in 1961, the Frente Sandinista de Liberación Nacional (FSLN) came to power in July 1979 at the head of a broadly supported insurrection that toppled Nicaraguan dictator Anastasio Somoza. The FSLN's early leaders were young Marxists disenchanted with the cautious tactics of Nicaragua's stodgy, Moscow-line Partido Socialista Nicaragüense and inspired by the *Cuban Revolution. Pragmatic revolutionaries, they accepted revolutionary Christians into their ranks and sought out upper-class political allies. Nationalists, they named their party after Augusto Sandino, who led a peasant-guerrilla army against U.S. Marines (1927–1933).

The Sandinista leadership conceived of the *revolution as a two-stage process, designed around the needs of a politically backward, ecnomically dependent society. The popular democratic stage would emphasize national liberation, economic development within a mixed economy, social *reform, and mass mobilization. The first stage was to lay the basis for the socialist stage, about which there was little consensus. A strong vanguard party was required to keep this gradualist program on track.

Always more unified politically than ideologically, the Sandinistas built a formidable Leninist organization—selective, disciplined, and hierarchical. Power was centralized in the nine-member National Directorate (DN), formed in March 1979. DN members, including President Daniel Ortega, held the key positions in the revolutionary government, army, and security forces. Other party leaders, down to the local level, were appointed from above. In the mid-1980s, many of the party's roughly 30,000 militants were government officials, army officers, or leaders of the Sandinista mass organizations, to which hundreds of thousands of Nicaraguans belonged.

In the early 1980s, heavy investment in social programs helped the Sandinistas consolidate their mass following, even as their government lost the support of business and church leaders who had backed the insurrection. Recognizing the FSLN's popularity and organizational strength, the Right boycotted national elections in 1984, undercutting the legitimacy of the anticipated Sandinista victory. But the FSLN's popular support was already eroding as as result of economic troubles and the multiple strains of the U.S.-sponsored contra war. In the countryside, the collective emphasis of early Sandinista agrarian policies alienated *peasants, thousands of whom joined the contra army.

In the late 1980s, the Sandinistas leaned toward market-oriented economics and peasant-oriented rural policies. But the economy grew worse and the war persisted, while the Sandinistas' Soviet-bloc backers went into abrupt decline. The FSLN was defeated in the 1990 elections by a U.S.-supported conservative coalition, but remained a formidable political force, retaining over forty percent of the seats in the legislature, the only organized popular base, and control of the army.

In the wake of an unexpected defeat, the FSLN began a period of critical self-examination, admitting that it had been internally undemocratic and sometimes abusive in its exercise of power. In open elections for all posts below the DN, the majority of party leaders were replaced. A new, more democratic party constitution was adopted by the First Party Congress in July 1991. The document described the FSLN as a vanguard party—revolutionary, democratic, anti-imperialist, and committed to *socialism.

(See also NICARAGUA; NICARAGUAN REVOLUTION.)

Dennis Gilbert, *Sandinistas: The Party and the Revolution* (New York, 1989).

DENNIS GILBERT

SAN MARINO. An independent microstate with a territory of only 60.5 square kilometers (approx. 23 sq. mi.) and a population of 23,000, San Marino lies entirely within *Italy. Tradition has it that the state was founded on its mountainous site in the third century by Christians fleeing from persecution under Diocletian. Its constitution as an independent commune dates from the ninth century. San Marino aided the nineteenth-century campaign for Italian unification, and the victorious Italian nationalists rewarded the republic by affirming its independence. Relations between San Marino and Italy have been maintained by a series of treaties of friendship and cooperation beginning in 1862.

The economy of the republic is based on tourism, although governments since World War II have tried to diversify by attracting light industry. San Marino shares a customs union with Italy and is thus, effectively, part of the *European Community's economic area. In 1988 the republic solidified its identity with Europe's Western-oriented market economies by joining the *Council of Europe.

Nevertheless, the republic's greatest distinction may be that it is was the first of the Western nations to elect Communist-led governments. San Marino's political parties reflect those of Italy. However, unlike in Italy, a Communist-Socialist coalition government ruled from 1945 until 1957. Then for the next twenty years San Marino followed the Italian pattern of domination by the Christian Democrats. From 1978 to 1986 there was another round of Communist-led coalition governments of the Left. In 1986 Communists and Christian Democrats agreed to form a government based on the idea of a "*historic compromise" between the Right and Left, which had animated political debate in Italy for a generation but had never become a reality there.

J. Theodore Bent, *A Freak of Freedom: The Republic of San Marino* (London, 1979).

CRAIG N. MURPHY

SÃO TOMÉ AND PRÍNCIPE. Located in the Gulf of Guinea off the coast of West Africa, the islands of São Tomé and Príncipe achieved political independence from Portugal in 1975 under the leadership of the Movimento de Libertação de São Tomé e Príncipe (MLSTP). Following constitutional reform which abolished the post-independence single-party state, 1991 elections gave the Partido da Convergência Democrática–Grupo de Reflexão (PCD-GR), founded by MLSTP dissidents, a solid parliamentary majority, with veteran politician Miguel Trovoada ousting Manuel Pinto da Costa as president. The MLSTP redefined itself as the Movimento de Libertação de São Tomé e Príncipe–Partido Social Democrático, or MLSTP-PSD; other legal parties included the Coligão Democrática de Oposição, or Codo, originally a coalition of Lisbon-based opposition grouplets, and the Frente Democrata Cristã (FDC), headed by a businessman with ties to South Africa.

The islands were not populated prior to the 1470s when Portuguese settlers began importing slaves from the mainland, transforming São Tomé into the world's largest sugar producer in the 1600s. Today's population of 120,000, who speak a Portuguese creole and consider themselves Catholic, fall into two broad categories. There are the *forros,* descendants of slaves freed in the nineteenth century, who have survived as small farmers, artisans, and civil servants; from this group come the national leadership. There are also the descendants of plantation workers brought as contract laborers from Angola, Mozambique, and Cape Verde, known as *tongas,* some of whom have begun to farm for themselves. A small fishing community of *Angolares* is said to be descended from shipwrecked Angolan slaves.

Cocoa estates covering ninety percent of the land have provided eighty to ninety percent of export earnings since the early 1900s when São Tomé produced one-sixth of the world's crop under conditions similar to those of capitalist slavery. Following independence, production fell due to the flight of European planters, tumbling international prices, and difficulty in contracting cocoa workers. On the plantations, housing and social services steadily declined during the 1980s; and 1990 wages were actually lower than those during the colonial era. The islands are highly dependent on food imports; in 1990, the UN found that ninety percent of the islands' children were suffering from nutritional diseases.

In the mid-1980s, the government began licensing previously nationalized plantations to European capital. Outright sale of the estates to foreigners met with domestic resistance, as did European plans for tourist enterprises, opposed by a local environmentalist group concerned with preservation of the rain forest. Full privatization was intended as a measure to cope with external debt, estimated at three times GNP in 1991.

Closer ties with Gabon, Portugal, and South Africa have supplanted post-independence relations with the governments of the former Soviet bloc. Angola supplies the islands with fuel at concessionary prices. São Tomé is an active member of the Lusophone community as well as the Economic Community of Central African States (ECOCAS).

Tony Hodges and Malyn Newitt, *São Tomé and Príncipe, from Plantation Colony to Microstate* (Boulder, Colo., and London, 1988).

LAURA BIGMAN

SAUDI ARABIA. The Kingdom of Saudi Arabia is the third state formed by the Saʿud family. The first—born in the mid-eighteenth century—expanded to include most of the Arabian peninsula and even some parts of modern Iraq and Jordan. It was defeated and eradicated by an Egyptian expedition in 1818. A second state reappeared a few decades later, when a Saudi prince succeeded in reestablishing his family rule, but this second endeavor disappeared in 1881 after a civil war among Saudi princes triggered Ottoman and British intervention.

The present Saudi state dates from 1902, when Prince ʿAbd al-ʿAziz ibn ʿAbd al-Rahman (Abdelaziz) and a few dozen men captured Riyadh from another tribal chief. Abdelaziz then spent twenty-five years conquering the Saudi domain, occupying and annexing the various provinces—Najd, Hassa, Asir, and finally the Hijaz with its pilgrimage city of Mecca. These provinces were officially united and proclaimed as the Kingdom of Saudi Arabia on 21 September 1932. Abdelaziz signed his first oil concession agreement the following year.

This new state had been welded together by a powerful form of Islamic fundamentalism, called Wahhabism, which called for a return to the letter of the Quran. This simple, literal interpretation of

Islam was attractive to the Bedouins as well as the settled populations in the oases, and they had flocked to the banner of Abdelaziz and his holy war, sweeping him to one victory after another. These fearless troops wanted to continue their conquest beyond the borders of the present country, but the British warned Abdelaziz that he could go no further. He finally turned on his own followers and defeated them in a bloody desert battle in 1929.

Today, Saudi Arabia remains a kingdom with a monarch as its active chief of state. Abdelaziz ruled for fifty-one years after his capture of Riyadh. At his death in 1953 he was succeeded by his eldest living son, Sa'ud, who was replaced by his brother Faisal in 1964. Since then, two of Faisal's brothers have reigned: Khalid and the present ruler, Fahd. It is an unusual—and an extremely flexible—system of succession.

The Saudi *monarchy is not "constitutional," since the Saudis have refused to grant the country a written constitution. The king's authority is not unlimited, however. Major decisions have to be taken with the assent of leading members of the royal family, who hold major positions in the cabinet (defense minister, interior minister, etc.) and are governors of various provinces. Some decisions are arrived at only after a long process of consensus-building within the royal family.

The royal regime has totally banned political parties, professional associations, and trade unions. Several times, the king has promised to appoint a consultative body with a substantive mandate, but he has never implemented his promise. From time to time, though, opposition has surfaced. The regime has periodically quelled discontent within the royal family itself (including an attempt in 1962 by a group of "Free Princes" to establish a *constitutional monarchy). It has also clamped down on dissent by workers (notably in the Eastern Province oil fields in 1955) and in the armed forces (during the Yemen war, and later in 1969). In the wake of the *Gulf War discontent surfaced again and led the monarch to promise a limited form of consultation in the future.

This large country, covering more than 2 million square kilometers (775,000 sq. mi.), has a very small native-born population, usually estimated at 6–8 million (there has never been a published census). To staff its burgeoning oil-based economy, the kingdom has recruited a large number of *foreign workers, mostly from the Middle East and South Asia. Nearly all of the country's wage labor is done by these foreigners, whose lives are tightly controlled. The government has not hesitated to deport them en masse during strikes and international disputes, and it has refused to grant naturalized *citizenship, even to those "foreign" families who have lived many decades in the country. During the Gulf War of 1991, a million Yemeni workers were deported

because of policy differences between the Yemeni and Saudi governments. By contrast, generous subsidies and modest work responsibilities ensure a comfortable life for all Saudi nationals.

Ever since the first oil began to flow in 1938, Saudi Arabia has been a state built on oil revenues. In the first decade, its oil production and revenues were relatively modest, but geologists then already knew that under the Saudi sands lay the world's largest petroleum deposits. When rising Saudi production met soaring prices in the period after 1974, revenues increased astronomically.

The enormous income to the kingdom each year from its oil sales has been used for many purposes. Some has supported the fabulous lifestyle of the royal family, some has enriched Saudi nationals and funded the Saudi welfare state, some has been spent on elaborate military weapons and on foreign aid, some has built luxurious new airports, cities, and universities, some has been used to create new industries and economic infrastructure, and some has been invested abroad—largely in the United States and Britain. These uses have all set off social changes in the kingdom which have undermined its traditional society and given rise to pressures for more change.

Every year, Saudi Arabia gives away several billions of dollars in grants, loans, and other kinds of foreign aid, mainly to Islamic recipients. It supports not only governments in Muslim countries but also Islamic political groups, Muslim minority movements in countries such as the Philippines, and Muslim international organizations such as the Islamic Conference. The Saudi government also spends large amounts of money to make the Haj (pilgrimage to Mecca) a successful event each year. All these efforts seek to promote the Saudi government's own particular version of *Islam, a version that many Muslims disagree with. When Iranians demonstrated in Mecca against the House of Sa'ud in 1987, Saudi security forces opened fire, killing 400 and wounding many more.

Saudi Arabia has coordinated its foreign aid programs with the United States and has funded political movements that the U.S. government could not afford to support or preferred to keep at arm's length. During the 1980s, the Saudis supported the Mujahidin guerrillas in Afghanistan, the RENAMO guerrillas in Mozambique, and the contra guerrillas in Nicaragua. Over the years, the Saudis have consistently used their wealth to defend the status quo and to defeat revolutionary movements.

In 1981, Saudi Arabia became the de facto leader of the Gulf Cooperation Council (GCC), a group of six Gulf oil monarchies. The GCC sought to build a military system for mutual defense. Despite very high spending for sophisticated arms imported from the West, the GCC remained militarily weak. The group supported Iraq during the Iran-Iraq War, because Iran was then the most destabilizing actor in Gulf policies. But the GCC was unable to defend Kuwait against the Iraqi invasion of 2 August 1990.

That crisis made it clear that Saudi Arabia could not defend itself without the support of the United States. In fact, the United States has been the patron of the Saudi state since the 1940s, when U.S. wartime aid helped keep the royal family's budget in balance. The House of Sa'ud, suspicious of the British, helped U.S. oil companies obtain and keep a monopoly of the kingdom's oil production—a source of very large profits and great geostrategic leverage for the United States ever since.

To protect the Saudi state (and monarchy), the United States has consistently provided military and security assistance. During the 1980s, the United States built a network of major military bases in the kingdom designed to accommodate foreign forces in a *crisis, and it organized a powerful U.S.-based Gulf intervention force which was actively deployed in 1990–1991.

Today, Saudi Arabia accounts for as much as twenty-five percent of the world's proven oil reserves. Though its current production is far less than its potential, the country plays a key role in the oil market, especially within the *Organization of Petroleum Exporting Countries (OPEC). During the Arab-Israeli War of 1973, King Faisal employed the "oil weapon," refusing for a short time to export oil to countries supporting Israel. Since then, Saudi Arabia has shown great moderation and has been reluctant to use such a boycott again. As the world comes to rely more heavily on Gulf oil in the 1990s, Saudi Arabia will have an even more critical role to play in regulating the oil market and influencing prices.

The Saudi monarchy today faces an uncertain future. Its viability will depend on how it can adjust to new circumstances and how the royal family responds to calls for participation from the expanding middle class. It will also depend on how successfully the Sa'uds maneuver in a turbulent regional environment, amid violent conflicts and radical ideologies. U.S. political and military support, more visible than ever after the Gulf War, may eventually prove a serious political liability. But for the time being, the United States is the greatest prop for the Saudi throne.

(See also FOREIGN MILITARY BASES.)

Tim Niblock, ed., *State, Society and Economy in Saudi Arabia* (London, 1982). Anthony H. Cordesman, *Western Strategic Interests in Saudi Arabia* (London, 1987).

GHASSAN SALAME

SCANDINAVIA. The five Nordic countries of *Denmark, *Finland, *Iceland, *Norway, and *Sweden together constitute Scandinavia. The Nordic-Teutonic people inhabited the Nordic areas from ancient times, sharing a single language. The Viking age (800–1000 C.E.) was marked by a number of connected petty kingdoms, and during this period Iceland, the Faroe Islands, and Greenland were settled. Another group, distinct both ethnically and linguistically, settled the Finnish area (100 C.E.); later, Swedes settled there as well. In 1389, the Swedish-Finnish area fell under the rule of the queen of Denmark. This arrangement, called the Kalmar Union, broke up in 1523 and was followed by numerous Nordic wars. The two main adversaries—Denmark and Norway opposing Sweden and Finland—sided with different great powers during the Napoleonic Wars (1807–1814). In the postwar settlement, Denmark lost Norway to Sweden, which had lost Finland to Russia in 1809. Full independence was attained by Norway in 1905, Finland in 1917, and Iceland in 1918. The Faroe Islands and Greenland were granted home rule by Denmark in 1947 and 1979 respectively.

Language is a unifying factor, as Danish, Norwegian, and Swedish are mutually intelligible languages. Finland has been integrated into the Nordic world in the twentieth century, despite the language barrier. (Swedish is still an important second language there.) Religion is also a source of commonality: Christianity was adopted during the Viking age, and Lutheran Protestantism replaced Catholicism around 1530. There is also a common legal tradition: medieval Scandinavian law was a separate branch of Germanic law. *Things* (meetings of all freemen) established laws, which were recorded from the eleventh to the thirteenth centuries, then supplemented and codified in the early modern period.

Modern Nordic development has been characterized by a peaceful transition to liberal democracy. The aristocracy was too weak to block the consolidation of peasant property rights in the preindustrial period. An independent peasantry on small family farms formed autonomous farmers' parties. The industrial working class, with some rural support, formed social democratic parties. Their achievement was universal franchise and parliamentary democracy. In the 1930s labor movements won the support of the poorest farmers. The Nordic party systems all display a nonsocialist side, split between agrarian, liberal, conservative, and Christian populist parties. The Left is more homogenous, dominated by social democratic parties with close connections to centralized trade union organizations. The Finnish case varies from the Scandinavian model in important ways. First, it experienced a bloody civil war in 1917–1918. In addition, its Left was split equally along communist and social democratic lines, and the trade union movement was splintered as well. Recent developments, however, bring it closer to the general Nordic pattern. Iceland's Left is also divided.

Nordic cooperation in the modern age began during the mid-nineteenth century. A monetary union existed between Denmark, Norway, and Sweden from 1873 to 1914. During *World War I, bilateral trade between the three countries expanded significantly. But Finnish preoccupation with the Soviet Union, its eastern neighbor, ties to German industry in the case of Sweden, and a Norwegian orientation toward its western trade partner, Britain, blocked further integration. In the interwar period, much collaboration took place within the *League of Nations. With the threat from Nazi Germany in the late 1930s, a Nordic defense union was discussed, but *World War II precluded its realization. In 1948 the idea was resurrected. The Danish, Norwegian, and Icelandic governments, however, wanted support from Western great powers and opted for North Atlantic Treaty Organization (NATO) membership instead. Sweden maintained neutrality. Finland concluded a Treaty of Friendship, Cooperation, and Mutual Assistance according to which it was to be defended by the Soviet Union if invaded by foreign troops.

Nordic collaboration has also been complicated by the effects of unequal economic development. Negotiations toward a Nordic common market began in 1948, but the process of European integration delayed the proposal until May 1959, and at that juncture the *European Free Trade Association (EFTA) was seen as a more interesting alternative. Extensive Nordic economic cooperation developed within EFTA. A more ambitious plan, Nordek, was launched in the late 1960s, inspired by the increase of intra-Nordic trade during that decade, but suddenly new prospects for extension of the *European Community (EC) emerged. Finland backed out, owing to its links to the Soviet Union. Sweden believed EC membership to be incompatible with neutrality. Norway decided to withdraw its membership application following a referendum in 1972. Only Denmark joined the EC in 1972. Finland, Iceland, Norway, and Sweden later concluded trade treaties with the EC.

In 1991, the Nordic countries became more closely linked to the single market of the European Community through the European Economic Area agreement between the EC and EFTA. But Sweden and Finland have already submitted applications for full EC membership, arguing that the disappearance of the *Cold War made it less urgent to guard neutrality. In Iceland and Norway, the question of whether to join the EC will be the most important political topic of the early 1990s.

Nordic collaboration may, however, point to some achievements. The Nordic Council, a yearly gathering of delegations of legislators and government ministers, was founded in 1952. (Later, a separate council of ministers was set up.) Subcommittees meet more often. Finland joined in 1955. The Nordic Council is an advisory body, not mandated to deal with foreign policy, although there is some coordination of policies in the UN, in the *Council of Europe, and regarding *North-South relations. The Nordic Council adopted the Nordic Convention on Cooperation (the Helsinki convention) in 1962 (extended in 1970), an international treaty that codified the results and aims of Nordic cooperation. A cultural agreement (1971), a transportation treaty (1972), and the Environmental Protection Convention (1974) were subsequently added. The Nordic Investment Bank (1975), a network of electrical power lines linking all Nordic countries except Iceland, and the Nordic Industrial Fund (1973) are features of Nordic collaboration as well.

Cooperation on laws implies negotiation of uniform solutions, while the member countries independently formulate actual law. Since the mid-1950s there has been a common labor market (Iceland excluded) for all unlicensed occupations and some licensed ones. The Nordic countries all established welfare states in the postwar era. Basic social security is provided independently of labor market participation, but supplementary pensions are indexed to wages. Health and educational services are provided for all at low cost. In the case of inter-Nordic migration, pensions and social insurance are transferred. There are uniform laws regarding citizenship: a resident becomes a citizen after seven years in another Nordic country, and can run for municipal offices after only three years.

(See also SOCIALISM AND SOCIAL DEMOCRACY.)

Erik Allardt et al., eds., *Nordic Democracy* (Copenhagen, 1981). Franz Wendt, *Cooperation in the Nordic Countries—Achievements and Obstacles* (Stockholm, 1981).

LARS MJØSET

SECESSIONIST MOVEMENTS. Secession entails the breaking of connections between an administrative unit and the *state to which it is joined. Frequently ethnically inspired, the seceding entity rejects measures of reform within the state as insufficient for its purposes (the internalist solution) and chooses instead to struggle for political independence, control of vital resources, and sovereign statehood (the externalist solution). Secession, therefore, represents a radical effort on the part of societal interests to achieve self-determination, transforming the political structure of the existing state relationship in the process. Not surprisingly, the uncompromising and far-reaching nature of secessionist demands brings on a sharp response from state authorities determined to maintain the state's territorial integrity against all challengers. Because the demands and counterdemands of secessionist and state elites are presented in nonnegotiable terms, they often prove difficult to mediate. In many instances, therefore, the consequence is intense and intractable conflict.

Secessionist movements tend to reflect both the desire for an aligning of a nation and a fully autonomous state and the will to resist what are perceived as illegitimate rules on the part of the existing state of which they are a part. Despite the enormous resources potentially at the disposal of ruling authorities, secessionist movements have been skillful in using a variety of means to mobilize their constituents to oppose extensions of state power to their region: nonpayment of taxes, unwillingness to enlist for military service, boycotts, work stoppages, emigration, sabotage, and armed violence. Ungovernability (that is, the breakdown of reciprocities and political exchanges between state and societal elites) is frequently viewed by secessionist leaders as a precondition for radical change. Whereas the Lithuanian Parliament in 1990 proclaimed independence and authorized its leaders to open negotiations with the *Soviet Union regarding future relations, achieving full political autonomy in 1991, other secessionist movements in *Kurdistan, Kashmir, and the southern Sudan in the 1960s and 1970s, heavily outnumbered by government troops and lacking equipment and comparable logistical support, have resorted to *guerrilla warfare tactics to achieve independence, with less success to date. In some of the most dramatic conflicts of our times, ethnoregional fears of central government domination have led to battles between standing armies, resulting in the crushing of the opposition in *Biafra, heavy fighting in Croatia and Bosnia-Herzegovina, and victory by secessionist forces in *Bangladesh. The emergence of a sovereign state of Bangladesh has been something of a secessionist exception in postcolonial times. In Eritrea, the protracted Eritrean People's Liberation Front struggle to regain self-determination also resulted in a successful outcome in May 1991; at a national conference of representative Ethiopians in July, an agreement was reached in principle to hold a UN-supervised referendum in two years to determine the issue of Eritrea's full sovereignty. Nevertheless, despite the evident fragility of many states in postcolonial years, they still have had sufficient military, political, and economic resources at their disposal—including international recognition—to ward off effective counterclaims by internal challengers.

In the postcolonial era, then, the international state system has proved decisive in preserving the state against counterstate challengers. This is not to imply that the international community has remained neutral in such conflicts. Although the tendency of most governments is to refuse to extend recognition to secessionist regimes, in some cases (Biafra) recognition by a limited number of important countries in the region has assured a wider audience for the airing of counterelite grievances. In addition, external aid to secessionist movements (Belgian support for Katanga; Ethiopian and Israeli aid to the southern Sudan in the 1960s and 1970s) has served to prolong encounters. More significantly, the UN, determined to bring an end to the fighting in Croatia and Bosnia-Herzegovina, put pressure on authorities in Belgrade by placing sanctions on trade and by authorizing the use of force to protect shipments of humanitarian aid; in the

case of Bangladesh, moreover, the role of a supportive Indian army was critical in thwarting efforts by the Pakistani army to regain control over this noncontiguous region.

However, if the forces of local *nationalism have generally lacked the capacity to wrest independence from a reluctant political center, there are signs that such movements may fare better in the future. The disastrous economic performance of many Third World countries, the weakening of their institutions and infrastructures, and the growing indications of fatigue on the part of the Western donor community in the post–Cold War period all point to the prospect of a new fluidity in interstate relations. Nationalist aspirations in Eastern Europe and the formerly Soviet republics have precipitated the break-up of a superpower, the collapse of *Yugoslavia into civil war, and the dissolution of the Czechoslovak union. The force of nationalism appears to be broadening in scope at the very point in history when the state as currently manifested seems unable to meet the minimal expectations of the public in many lands. Paradoxically, then, global communications and economics may bring about a weakening of state sovereignty as traditionally understood, opening up new opportunities for state formation in the period ahead.

(See also ERITREAN WAR OF INDEPENDENCE; ETHNICITY; NATIONAL LIBERATION MOVEMENTS; PERIPHERAL NATIONALISM.)

Donald Rothchild and Victor A. Olorunsola, eds., *State Versus Ethnic Claims: African Policy Dilemmas* (Boulder, Colo., 1983). Donald L. Horowitz, *Ethnic Groups in Conflict* (Berkeley, Calif., 1985).

DONALD ROTHCHILD

SECULARIZATION. The origin of the term *secularization* goes back to the Middle Ages. First used to indicate the process of alienation of Church property to the state, it soon came to be applied to the loss of temporal power by the Church. Later its meaning was extended to include the process by which priests abandoned or were forced to leave their clerical role and become laymen. Overall, then, secularization involves a transition from the religious to the nonreligious—to the secular—world.

In order for such a transition to take place, it must be possible to differentiate clearly between the two spheres, to distinguish the lay and civilian from the religious and sacred. Consequently, and inevitably, secularization implies increasing reliance on worldly criteria in the process of decision making, the jettisoning of religiously based or inspired doctrines, the rationalization of attitudes and behaviors, and the Weberian imperative to apply rationality to the goals selected and to the means utilized. Accordingly, rulers will no longer follow religious doctrines but will structure their decisions according to secular criteria. Then, in its social and political behavior, the population at large will no longer feel bound to the teachings of the Church and dependent on its representatives and their religious principles. Finally, all *ideologies, and not just religious doctrines and beliefs, will be abandoned and replaced by secular, rational behavior. Because some political ideologies have a quasi-religious character, de-ideologization may therefore come to coincide with the process of secularization.

Taken for granted and considered irresistible and irreversible, the process of secularization has encountered serious obstacles. Religious principles and criteria continue to play a significant role in the life of many individuals who generally abide by them in their social and political behavior. They can still serve as justifying principles of more than passing significance. Political ideologies may have crumbled away, but they are not necessarily replaced by rational criteria and rational processes of decision making. More important, powerful religious beliefs are still used to shape and justify the behavior of rulers both domestically and on the international scene.

Twentieth-century fundamentalism has acted as a drag on secularizing tendencies. Fundamentalist thought aims directly at the reconstruction of temporal power for religious organizations and their leaders. It denies the separation of the religious sphere from all other spheres and especially from the political, social, and cultural domains. Indeed, fundamentalism affirms the supremacy of the religious sphere over all others and the supremacy of its interpreters over all other sociopolitical actors. It claims that religious criteria must be not only the dominant criteria but the exclusive arbiter of behavior. Thus all major principles of thought and behavior must be sought, and can be found, in the books of the prophets. Any action whatsoever should be inspired by those principles and evaluated according to those criteria. Muslim fundamentalism worldwide and, to a lesser degree, Jewish and Christian fundamentalism are contemporary phenomena that underscore the fact that secularization has not been completed. The proliferation of religious sects all over the world testifies to the resurgence of fundamentalism and throws doubt on the prospect that complete secularization will ever be accomplished. Encircled and endangered minorities may always resort to some immutable, fundamental principles to take hope, to strengthen their faith, to survive in a hostile world, and to justify death for a holy cause.

The fundamental contradictions of Western rationalism and the corresponding process of secularization are exposed by current challenges. The continued significance of fundamentalism calls into question a conventional modernist view of history as continuous progress, with secularization an important constituent process. A different conception of history seems to be in order, one that makes room for the reversal of processes, the resurgence of ideas, and the basic spiritual needs of individuals. A more subtle understanding is required of different principles and criteria for different realms of individual life, thinking, and activities. An awareness is developing that religious criteria are not the only, nor even the dominant, criteria to be used. At the same time, secular, rational criteria are not the only criteria people will apply in their behavior. Secularization, although a powerful and still-unfolding process, is not all-encompassing.

(See also MODERNITY; MODERNIZATION; RELIGION AND POLITICS; WEBER, MAX.)

Harvey Cox, *The Secular City: Secularization and Urbanization in Theological Perspective* (New York, 1966). Wolfgang Schluchter, *The Rise of Western Rationalism. Max Weber's Developmental History* (Berkeley, Calif., 1981).

GIANFRANCO PASQUINO

SECURITY. Although a concept that is crucial to an understanding of international politics, as is the case with most fundamental concepts, *security* is ambiguous and elastic in its meaning. In the most fundamental sense, to be secure is to feel free from threats, anxiety, or danger. Security is therefore a state of mind in which an individual, whether the highest political leader of the land or the average citizen, feels safe from harm by others. Used in this way, a *state (or its leaders and citizens) believes itself secure when it fears that nothing adverse can be done to it by other states or by other foreign nonstate actors. To define security in this fashion is to see that it is a subjective state of mind, not an objective condition of being. It describes how people feel, not whether they are justified in feeling the way they do. In this sense security depends on the perceptions people have of their position in their environment, not on an objective view of that environment.

This subjectivity explains why security can encompass so many things: what makes one individual feel secure may not be sufficient to make another feel so. Individuals differ in their tolerance for uncertainty, their ability to live with anxiety, and their capacity to cope with pressure. One person's security can well be another's insecurity.

Furthermore, although individuals differ in what makes them feel secure or insecure, most experience neither perfect security nor absolute insecurity. Rather, the subjective sense of security or insecurity varies along a continuum. Security, therefore, is not a matter of either/or—either one has it or one does not; rather, it is a matter of degree, of feeling more or less secure, more or less insecure. What is true of individuals is true of states. States are not perfectly secure or completely insecure, but rather experience either condition in degrees. For both individuals and states, then, security is a condition that comes in shades of gray, not hues of black and white.

The concern that states have for their security stems from the nature of the international political environment in which states exist. International politics is characterized by the absence of an effective government above states that has the authority and the power to make laws, to enforce them, and to resolve disputes among states. International politics is anarchic because there is no world government. In such an anarchic realm, states must be concerned first and foremost with their security—the extent to which they feel unthreatened by the actions of others. With no government to look to for protection, they must rely on their own efforts. A concern for survival thus breeds a preoccupation with security.

At the minimum, the ability to enjoy a reasonable degree of security requires that a state be certain either that it can dissuade other states from attacking it or that it can successfully defend itself if attacked. A concern for security immediately gives rise to a focus on the military power the state has relative to that of others. In a condition of *anarchy, therefore, the pursuit of security requires that states be watchful about both the balance of military *power that obtains among them and the intentions of other states.

The concern for relative power is best illustrated by what is probably the oldest, and many say still the best, book on international politics—*Thucydides' The Peloponnesian Wars. Thucydides saw the root cause of the Peloponnesian Wars to be the growing power of Athens relative to that of Sparta and to the danger which that growing imbalance posed to the security of Sparta. If Sparta allowed Athenian power to grow too great, Sparta would be at risk because Athens could have attacked and defeated her. Even if not attacked by Athens, its growing power, if left unchecked, could intimidate Sparta because Athens could threaten to attack and destroy Sparta whenever Athens chose. If the imbalance of power grew too great, Athens could have easily defeated Sparta and could simply threaten to do so in order to bend Sparta to its will. What was thus at stake for Sparta, if Athenian power grew too great, was not simply safety from military attack but also the protection of Sparta's moral values, its way of life, and the material prosperity of its citizens. In this sense, Sparta's security was not an end in itself; rather, what was at stake were all the things that being physically secure from attack enables a state to enjoy.

The case of Athens and Sparta demonstrates that a concern for security must ultimately focus on the potential physical danger to a state that is posed by imbalances in military power. But the case also shows why a concern for security cannot be restricted simply to military power. A state fashions the military power it deploys from many elements: the economic wealth of a nation, the quality of its political leadership, the cohesiveness of the polity, the motivation of the citizenry, the nature of its military leadership, its access to food and raw materials, and so on. It was the growth in Athenian wealth and financial and naval power, together with the democratic nature of Athens, that enabled Athens to deploy an ever-more-threatening military force. Athens was a more dynamic society than Sparta, and that was reflected in the growth of its overall power. At the end of the day, security demands military power sufficient to dissuade or defeat an attack; but so many nonmilitary elements are required to generate effective military power that a concern for security can never be restricted solely to the final military end product.

Taken together, these two factors—the nonmilitary elements required to fashion an effective military instrument and the subjective nature of security—demonstrate why security has been such an ambiguous and elastic term. Not only is there a large degree of variability in what makes individuals and states feel secure; there are also many elements required to fashion an effective military instrument. Both factors explain why states historically have never restricted their security purview simply to their armies. In the name of security, great empires have been founded and relentlessly expanded, hegemonic wars have been waged, economic self-sufficiency has been sought after, crushing armaments races have been entered into, innumerable interventions into the affairs of other states have been undertaken, alliances have been formed and broken, and great religious and ideological crusades have been launched.

For example, in the nineteenth century, Britain developed a huge empire in northeast Africa in order to protect its sea route to India that ran through Egypt via the Suez Canal, all in the name of protecting the security of the British Isles and its overseas empire. In the twentieth century, Japan annexed Korea, conquered Manchuria, waged war against China, conquered Southeast Asia and the Dutch East Indies, all in the name of creating an autarkic "Greater East Asia Co-Prosperity Sphere" that would make her secure against external threats. In the post–World War II era, the Soviet Union conquered and ruled for forty-five years Eastern and Central Europe in the name of security against another attack from the West; and the United States waged two land wars in Asia—in Korea and Vietnam—in the name of security for itself and its allies against Communism. Finally, the United States and the Soviet Union developed nuclear arsenals of tens of thousands of warheads each, all in the name of making each secure against nuclear attack by the other. In the grand sweep of history, almost the entire range of state behavior has been, in one way or another, justified in the name of security.

In the contemporary world, security has come to include two additional elements. The first involves protection of the environment from irreversible degradation by combating, among other things, acid rain, desertification, forest destruction, ozone pollution, and global warming. In a world in which environmental degradation crosses national borders with abandon, environmental security has impelled states to find cooperative rather than competitive solutions. The second element has to do with the revival of the UN and the brighter prospects for collective security. The end of the *Cold War has brought an end to the paralysis of the UN and has cleared the way for the institution to develop beyond its traditional peacekeeping role to a war-deterring one. Rather than simply sending troops and inserting them between two warring parties that have agreed to cease fighting (its peacekeeping role), many hope the UN can now create a standing military force to threaten, and punish if necessary, potential aggressors in order to stop aggression in the first place (its war-deterring or aggression-punishing role). If its collective security role worked well, its peacekeeping role would diminish dramatically.

Viewed in analytical and historical perspective, security is an all-encompassing concept. It is inevitable that it be so both because of its subjective nature and the varied elements that make it up.

(See also ALLIANCE; BALANCE OF POWER; DETERRENCE; ENVIRONMENTALISM; FORCE, USE OF; INTERNATIONAL RELATIONS; UNITED NATIONS.)

Arnold Wolfers, *Discord and Collaboration* (Baltimore, Md., 1962). Robert Jervis, *Perception and Misperception in International Politics* (Princeton, N.J., 1976). Robert Gilpin, *War and Change in World Politics* (Cambridge, U.K., 1981). Barry Buzan, *People, States and Fear* (Chapel Hill, N.C., 1983).

ROBERT J. ART

SECURITY DILEMMA. The term *security dilemma* appears to have been coined by John Herz ("Idealist Internationalism and the Security Dilemma" *World Politics* 2 [January 1950]: 157–180). He referred to the condition in a "self-help" anarchic society (one without government or superordinate authority) in which groups or individuals, striving to attain *security from attack, "are driven to acquire more and more power to escape the impact of the power of others." Insecurity among the others increases, and this motivates stepped-up preparations: the "vicious circle of security and power accumulation is on." *International relations is in most respects an anarchic society, and the security dilemma is often credited as the source of *arms races and the escalation of diplomatic crises into *war, even though neither of the adversary states may have aggressive intentions toward the other.

The security dilemma operates only under particular conditions of international relations. It stems primarily from leaders' perceptions of the military circumstances, specifically whether the offense has substantial advantages over the defense and whether defensive capabilities can be distinguished from offensive ones. Geographically, mountains and bodies of water (e.g., the situations of Switzerland and Britain) facilitate defense and ease the security dilemma; plains (e.g., the western region of the former Soviet Union) exacerbate it. Technologically, strong land fortifications ease the security dilemma, and highly accurate but vulnerable *nuclear weapons exacerbate it.

In 1914 most military and civilian commanders thought that the extant technology favored an offense which could mobilize and move rapidly; these expectations contributed to rapid competitive mobilizations and war even among those who in principle preferred peace. Offensive and defensive strategies thus could not easily be distinguished. Ironically, the course of the war soon showed that perceptions of the strategic circumstances were erroneous, and that trench warfare favored the defense. Perceptions of the adversary's hostile intent and of changing strategic circumstances can also aggravate the security dilemma. German leaders in 1914 perceived a certain "window of opportunity" before expansion of the French army and modernization of the Russian army were consolidated, after which their own security dilemma would be aggravated.

Neither threats nor concessions are likely to ease a security dilemma. Threats will enhance the adversary's sense of insecurity; concessions will probably enhance one's own. Changes of strategic postures and weapons procurement in favor of the defense can help, as can better means to monitor the adversary's intentions and capabilities—if the adversary likewise has largely defensive aims. *Arms control agreements that provide for the destruction of vulnerable "first-strike" weapons, the provision of demilitarized buffer zones, and inspection procedures are helpful. The dissolution of the Soviet Union and the *Warsaw Treaty Organization have considerably eased the security dilemma in Europe. So too have arms control and *disarmament agreements to reduce offensive forces, and agreements for prior notification of maneuvers and exchange of information in crisis.

(See also ANARCHY.)

Robert Jervis, "Cooperation under the Security Dilemma" *World Politics* 30 (July 1978): 167–212.

BRUCE RUSSETT

SELF-DETERMINATION. From its first formulation in the second half of the eighteenth century until today, the principle of the self-determination of peoples has had several meanings. It has been variously understood as a criterion to use in the event of territorial changes of sovereign *states (interested populations should through plebiscites have the right to choose which state to belong to); a democratic principle legitimating the governments of modern states (the people should have the opportunity to choose their own rulers); an anticolonialist principle (peoples subject to colonial rule should have the right to secure independence or at any rate to choose their international status freely); a principle of freedom for ethnic or religious groups constituting minorities in sovereign states (these groups have the right to create an independent state or to join groups existing in another state); and a prohibition against the occupation or invasion of the territory of other states.

The French Revolution proclaimed the principle of self-determination, both as a ban on territorial annexations or changes without regard for the wishes of the populations concerned as well as a criterion for the democratic legitimation of governments. It was also the French Revolution that trod the principle underfoot. In 1917 the principle was proclaimed anew, by two opposed figures: Woodrow Wilson and *Lenin. The former conceived of it primarily as a criterion for the breakup of those empires defeated at the end of the *World War I (the Austro-Hungarian, German, and Ottoman empires); Lenin conceived of it essentially as an anticolonialist and anti-imperialist postulate.

Until World War II, the self-determination of peoples remained a political principle that some believed should inspire the action of governments. In 1945, at the insistence of the Soviet Union, the principle was for the first time given legal status in the UN Charter, as one of the organization's guidelines for action. Because of Western resistance, the anticolonialist connotation advocated by the Soviets was diluted, and the principle was adopted in its minimal sense of "self-government." Subsequently, various international documents (among them the UN General Assembly resolution on the independence of colonial peoples [1960]; two UN covenants on *human rights [1966]; the UN General Assembly Declaration on Friendly Relations among States, [1970]; and the Final Act of the *Conference for Security and Cooperation in Europe [1975]) have gradually transformed self-determination into a general legal principle of the international community.

Of the possible meanings of this political principle, which have been accepted in *international law? Above all the anticolonialist one; indeed, it was from this angle that the principle proved most effective and incisive after 1950. Self-determination was also consecrated legally as a principle rendering illegitimate occupations or invasions of foreign territories (and imposing, in the event of territorial changes freely agreed by sovereign states, the consultation of the populations concerned). The presence in the international community of so many despotic states has, however, prevented full acceptance of the principle as a criterion for the democratic legitimation of governments. Trends are slowly emerging that might lead to such acceptance, particularly the steadily increasing spread of norms and institutions relating to human rights. On the other hand, there are few prospects for the legal acceptance of the principle as implying a right of independence for ethnic groups or religious minorities: the multiethnic composition of many states, or the presence in them of large minorities, have induced the international community to exclude the right of secession, that is, to deny groups and minorities any right whatever to independence.

Apart from legal affirmations by international bodies, the principle of self-determination frequently remains unapplied, whether for geopolitical reasons bound up with the attitude of one or more Great Powers (for instance, the problem of the Palestinian people) or because of intrinsic difficulties in resolving the contradictory claims of states (the cases of, for instance, Eritrea, the *Malvinas/Falklands, or Gibraltar). For these cases as well, international law—even if it is unable to dictate, still less to impose, an appropriate solution—at least suggests the method to pursue: political negotiation toward a peaceful solution based on the wishes and desires of the populations involved.

(See also DECOLONIZATION; ERITREAN WAR OF INDEPENDENCE; IMPERIALISM; LEGITIMACY; RIGHTS; SECESSIONIST MOVEMENTS; UNITED NATIONS.)

A. Rigo Sureda, The Evolution of the Right of Self-determination: A Study of the U.N. Practice (Leyden, 1973). Y. Alexander and R. A. Friedlander, eds., Self-determination: National, Regional and Global Dimensions (Boulder, Colo., 1980). S. K. N. Blay, "Self-determination Versus Territorial Integrity in Decolonization" NYU Journal of International Law and Politics 18 (1986): 441–472. Nathaniel Berman, "Sovereignty in Abeyance: Self-Determination and International Law" Wisconsin International Law Journal 7 (1988): 51–105. Hurst Hannum, Autonomy, Sovereignty and Self-Determination (Philadelphia, 1990).

ANTONIO CASSESE

SELF-MANAGEMENT. See INDUSTRIAL DEMOCRACY; WORKERS' CONTROL.

SENEGAL. Small in size (approximately 197,000 sq. km.; 76,000 sq. mi.) as well as in population (7 million people), Senegal is a peasant-dominated society overwhelmed by problems of poverty and illiteracy. It is notable for having been able to maintain a multiparty system—a rarity in Africa until recently.

Senegal borders on both the Sahara desert and the Atlantic Ocean. Because of the early advent of Islam, most Senegalese are Muslims (eighty-three percent), and Muslim religious leaders, called Marabouts, play an important role in the political process. Although the Marabouts do not make policy, and attempts to build an Islamic party have failed in Senegal, the support of the Marabouts is essential to the stability and even the viability of any government.

Senegal also has had long and continuous contact with Europe by way of the Atlantic, particularly since the country was a French colony from 1850 to 1960. As early as 1879, the residents of the major cities along the coast were granted French *citizenship and were allowed to elect their own mayors and municipal councils and a representative to the Chamber of Deputies in Paris. After World War II, voting privileges and rights of free association were extended throughout the country. Through this process, the Senegalese acquired the habit of political debate and the skills of political mobilization, organization, and management.

Civic understanding of modern politics and the existence of a turbulent intellectual and commercial bourgeoisie explain why the Senegalese avoided the *authoritarianism that appeared elsewhere in Africa. After a brief period of de facto one-party rule following independence, Senegal's domestic political history has been pluralistic: four parties between 1974 and 1981, and since 1981, seventeen political parties competing at the local, regional, and national levels. The system cuts across ethnic and religious lines and offers choices across the ideological spectrum. Moreover, the electoral system of proportional representation encourages the representation of diverse interests.

The government is headed by a president who is elected every five years. The president selects the members of the cabinet, who are responsible to him rather than to the national assembly. The Senegalese assembly is unicameral and is elected at the same time as the president. The judicial system, which is separate from the legislative and executive branches, is headed by a supreme court that judges the constitutionality of laws.

The recent history of the country indicates that these achievements are not enough and that sustained economic progress is critical to containing growing frustrations. When Abdou Diouf came to power in 1981 following the voluntary resignation of President Léopold Sédar Senghor, he inherited an economy in a state of chaos. A series of severe droughts, declining prices of the nation's major exports—peanuts and phosphates—poor management of an oversized public sector, a rise in oil prices, and a steady population increase all served to lower the annual income of the average Senegalese. The decline of the rural economy fueled a rural exodus, swelling the slums of Dakar, the capital, and exacerbating existing problems.

Diouf has responded to these critical problems by attempting to rewrite the social contract between the government and the population in effect since independence. With the help of the *International Monetary Fund and the *World Bank, he launched an economic recovery program designed to reduce quite radically the role of the government in the allocation of resources. This has meant a substantial reduction of the bureaucracy, a gradual erosion of subsidies on foodstuffs, and an increased role for the private sector.

Economic housecleaning has not been painless, especially in urban areas. Furthermore, national income has been inadequate to repay the country's burdensome debts. Servicing of the debt has absorbed about one-fifth of total exports the last several years. In addition, the gap between the government, composed mostly of technocrats, and the rest of the population has increased, severing the link that had been maintained in the past by the populist regional leaders who had held positions in both government and party.

The erosion of domestic support for the government, however, has had little effect on the prestige of Senegal abroad and its influence in international organizations and meetings. This influence remains because Senegal is unusual—a multiparty democracy in Africa—and is a voice of moderation in such bodies as the *Organization of African Unity and the UN.

(See also FRANCOPHONE AFRICA; PLURALISM; SAHEL.)

Donal Cruise O'Brien, *Saints and Politicians: Essays on the Organizations of a Senegalese Peasant Society* (London, 1975). Rita Cruise O'Brien, ed., *The Political Economy of Underdevelopment: Dependence in Senegal* (London, 1979). Sheldon Geller, *Senegal: An African Nation between Islam and the West* (Boulder, Colo., 1982). Mark Gersovitz and John Waterbury, eds., *The Political Economy of Risk and Choice in Senegal* (London, 1982). Robert Fatton, *The Making of a Liberal Democracy: Senegal's Passive Revolution 1975–1985* (Boulder, Colo., 1987).

SAMBA KA

SEPARATION OF POWERS. Seeds of the separation of powers principle can be found in ancient Greek and Roman notions of the mixed regime, which provided for representation of the dominant social orders in distinct branches of government that could check and balance one another with the end of securing internal harmony through compromise. The writings and developments most relevant to the modern doctrine, however, arise from the struggles in England during the seventeenth century between the Parliament and monarchy. Of particular importance is John Locke's *Second Treatise* (1690) wherein the ordering principle of mixed government is replaced by a differentiation between legislative and executive functions or powers. Locke's connection of functions with separate departments of government constitutes an indispensable theoretical step in the development of the modern version of the separation of powers.

Baron de Montesquieu, who built upon Locke's writings and the English experience, set forth in some detail the requirements and purposes of the separation of powers. His principal work, *The Spirit of the Laws* (1748), had a profound impact on American political thinking during the founding era, particularly those portions which linked the separation of powers to liberty and the rule of law. In *The Federalist,* James Madison acknowledges the role of the "celebrated Montesquieu" in propagating "this invaluable precept in the science of politics," and he skillfully uses certain of Montesquieu's teachings in defending and explaining the constitutional provisions for the separation of powers.

The almost-universal acceptance of the separation of powers doctrine by Americans during the founding period arose from the belief, advanced by Montesquieu, that the combination of any two of three powers—legislative, executive, or judicial—in the same hands would constitute tyranny. In this context, tyranny assumes the attributes of slavery; any such concentration was viewed as rendering the people subject to the arbitrary and capricious will of their rulers, a condition manifestly contrary to the rule of law. Moreover, because the meaning and execution of the laws might vary according to the caprice of the rulers, so that the citizens could never be certain of the limits of permissible conduct, any concentration of functions was seen as a mortal threat to liberty (i.e., the right of the individual to do that which is not forbidden by the law).

Although many *constitutions embody some features of the separation of powers doctrine, the U.S. Constitution is universally regarded as embodying its principles in their purest form. The provision for three separate branches, each entrusted with primary responsibility for one of the three functions of government (legislative, executive, and judicial), the prohibitions against overlap of personnel among the departments, and—in its original form—the specification of different modes of selection for the members of each branch are among the more salient of these principles. The founders can even be credited with an original contribution to the doctrine, the complete separation of the judiciary from the executive department and its establishment as a coordinate branch of government.

The U.S. experience points to problems of implementing a system of divided powers, a critical one being how to prevent one branch from completely dominating another. The answer provided by the framers was a limited blending of powers, commonly associated with the principle of "checks and balances," that would provide each branch the power to resist or repel the unconstitutional intrusions of another (e.g., judicial tenure during good behavior, the qualified presidential veto of legislation).

(See also CONGRESS, U.S.; PRESIDENCY, U.S.; SUPREME COURT OF THE UNITED STATES; UNITED STATES.)

William B. Gwyn, *The Meaning of Separation of Powers* (New Orleans, 1965). M. J. C. Vile, *Constitutionalism and the Separation of Powers* (Oxford, 1967).

GEORGE W. CAREY

SERBIA. See YUGOSLAVIA.

SEYCHELLES. See INDIAN OCEAN REGION.

SHABA WARS. In March 1977 and May 1978 an opposition group to the government of President Mobutu invaded *Zaire's Shaba province (formerly Katanga), located in the the southeastern part of the country. Rich in mineral resources, Shaba produces about six percent of the world's copper and fifty percent of its cobalt supply, in addition to manganese, tin, zinc, uranium, and other mineral products. Minerals constitute seventy percent of Zaire's export reve-

nues. The 1977 invasion (Shaba I) was repelled by a joint military effort by Zairian and Moroccan forces after eighty days. The 1978 invasion (Shaba II), the more devastating of the two, was ended by a joint military intervention by French and Belgian paratroopers. In both wars the United States provided logistical support for the joint operations.

The invading group, the Front pour la Libération Nationale du Congo (FLNC), was made up of former members of the Katangan gendarmerie that served as the formal army of secessionist Katanga from 1960 to 1963 under the leadership of Moïse Tshombe. After serving Katanga up to the end of the secession in 1963, the gendarmes were incorporated into the national army and the Katanga provincial police by Tshombe, who had become prime minister in 1964. Tshombe's subsequent removal from power, the army's takeover in 1965, and the massive repression against the former gendarmes forced the latter to flee to Angola. They formed the core of the FLNC and were later joined by youths from Katanga and other neighboring provinces. There is evidence that the FLNC received military training and equipment from the Angolan government and, probably, from Angola-based Cuban forces.

Shaba I and Shaba II resurrected the buried demons of the Katanga secession of 1960. The ethnic and regional composition of the FLNC lent credence to the view that the group sought to control Shaba province and to secede from the rest of Zaire. There is no evidence to support this view. The FLNC's own declarations and actions, the presence of people from regions other than Shaba in its fighting units, the Zairian government's reluctance to unequivocally accuse the FLNC of secessionist designs, and, most important, the FLNC's contacts with other Zairian opposition groups all attest to the erroneous character of the secessionist thesis. Like other opposition groups, the FLNC sought to effect change in Zaire as a whole outside the constitutional and institutional limits of the state.

Indeed, in the authoritarian context of Mobutu's regime, any opposition could be voiced only outside the established institutions in the form of open *political violence. The FLNC was part of such opposition. The socioeconomic policies favoring political coalitions that buttressed the Mobutu regime had deeply impoverished the masses by diverting crucial resources from them and by destroying and preventing the erection of social and economic infrastructures. This pattern of the pauperization of the masses explained their easy collusion with the FLNC's invading forces. The FLNC-led Shaba I and Shaba II offered avenues for the masses seeking change in an authoritarian state.

With respect to world politics, the Shaba wars shed light on the relationship between the world powers, the Zairian state, and the latter's chances for change. France, Belgium, the United States, Morocco, and other "moderate" African countries were the more visible actors on the Western side, joined by China. Although the Western powers displayed conflictual national and superpower interests in Zaire, they sought to preserve them as a bloc, united by the specter of the Soviet-Cuban "communist threat." The joint French-Belgian-American military intervention in the Shaba wars bore testimony to such an attempt. Given that the protection of Western interests was predicated on the support of the Mobutu regime that had made Shaba I and Shaba II unavoidable, real changes in Zaire after the Shaba wars were almost impossible. This situation explains why attempts at changes, even those proposed by the West, did not work.

(See also AUTHORITARIANISM; CONGO CRISIS; SECESSIONIST MOVEMENTS.)

Jean-Claude Willame, "La Seconde Guerre du Shaba" Enquêtes et Documents d'Histoire Africaine (Louvain, 1978). Jean-Claude Willame, "Contribution à l'Étude des Mouvements d'Opposition au Zaïre: le F.L.N.C." Cahiers du CEDAF 6 (1980). Crawford Young and Thomas Turner, The Rise and Decline of the Zairian State (Madison, Wis., 1985).

S. N. SANGMPAM

SHARĪ'A. The generic term for Islamic law, sharī'a is to be distinguished from *fiqh*, jurisprudence, and from *qānūn*, which refers to law as statute and as legal rules in actual operation in the contemporary *Middle East. Strictly speaking, the sharī'a derives from two written sources: the Quran, the Book revealed to the Prophet Muhammad in the sixth century C.E., and the *sunna*, which is the compilation of the words and deeds of the Prophet. In actual fact, the sharī'a was formed in later centuries through arduous and systematic scholarship, developed by jurists of competing schools. Although formally based on the Quran and the *sunna*, the sharī'a generated a logic of its own as jurists had to articulate a system with internal coherence, responsive to social interests, needs, and customs.

As late as the 1970s, scholars of the contemporary sharī'a described it as being an ever more restricted domain of the law, confined essentially to matrimonial and inheritance jurisprudence. But with the advent of the Islamic revolution in Iran in 1979, traditional Islamic jurists (known as the *Āyāt Allāhs*) took over the Iranian state and sought to establish the rule of Islamic law in all walks of life. At the same time, the leaders of neighboring Pakistan tried to introduce strict sharī'a rules, while political *Islam all over the Muslim world called for the comprehensive and strict implementation of Islamic law.

In this context, the sharī'a became significant on two levels. First, because of a tradition which was rich with more than ten centuries of sophisticated writings, the sharī'a came to be associated politically with the quintessence of Islam, and the projected Islamic state was defined as a state ruled by the sharī'a. The sharī'a therefore served as the rallying point of Islamic forces across the Muslim world,

even in the more conservative states like Saudi Arabia and Jordan.

Second, although the content of this Islamization was vague, significant efforts were exerted to expand the application of the sharī'a from the restricted areas of family law to wider legal subjects. Chief among these were constitutional and economic law. In the first case, the Iranian constitution became the model for governmental institutions. In economic law, the two most urgent areas for the adaptation of the sharī'a were the regulation of the production and distribution of goods in the light of a reconstruction of legal precedents, and the conception and establishment of an Islamic banking system in which interest would be banned. Various efforts in these fields have met with only mixed results, but the sway of the sharī'a has nonetheless been significantly extended.

(See also RELIGION AND POLITICS.)

Noel Coulson, A History of Islamic Law (Edinburgh, 1964). Joseph Schacht, Introduction to Islamic Law (Oxford, 1964). Norman Anderson, Law Reform in the Muslim World (London, 1976). Chibli Mallat, ed., Islamic Law and Finance (London, 1988). Chibli Mallat and Jane Connors, eds., Islamic Family Law (London 1990). Chibli Mallat, The Renaissance of Islamic Law (Cambridge, U.K., in press).

CHIBLI MALLAT

SHARPEVILLE MASSACRE. On Monday, 21 March 1960, in Sharpeville, Vereeniging, thirty South African policemen fired into a crowd of 5,000, killing sixty-nine and wounding 186. The crowd had been summoned by the Pan-Africanist Congress (PAC), an assertive rival to the *African National Congress (ANC), formed in 1959 from Congress dissidents who contended the ANC was deradicalized by cooperation with Communists, white democrats, and Indian Gandhists. The PAC proposed an offensive against the pass laws, urging its supporters to surrender themselves without passes outside police stations. Believing that rhetorical emphasis on race pride was by itself sufficient to evoke a large following, the PAC undertook little systematic preparation. Its branches were concentrated around the steelmaking center of Vereeniging and in the African communities of Cape Town. In Sharpeville, high rents, unemployment among school dropouts, and authoritarian administration generated angry discontent, particularly among young people. The ANC was weak in Sharpeville and PAC activists constructed a strong network. In Cape Town, the PAC constituted its base among squatters and migrant laborers, the principal targets of fiercely applied influx control intended to reduce to a minimum the African presence in the western Cape.

After the massacre, a volatile mood prevailed. Responding to a strike call by the ANC, on 28 March teenagers invaded the streets of Soweto, burning public buildings, stoning commuters, and destroying the public radio system. The most drama occurred in Cape Town, where the PAC succeeded in mounting a "stay-at-home" from 21 March and headed a series of demonstrations climaxing on 30 March in a procession of 30,000 people. The demonstrators marched from the African townships to the city center, intent on assembling outside Parliament. Police authorities persuaded the young Pan-Africanist Philip Kgosana to divert the marchers toward police headquarters; subsequently promised an interview with the minister of justice, Kgosana led his supporters home. Later Kgosana was arrested and soldiers and police occupied the townships. By the date of the PAC and ANC's prohibition, 8 April, the "Sharpeville crisis" was over.

For many, these events confirmed the vulnerability of minority rule. On 25 March, the government temporarily suspended the pass laws. A cabinet minister was moved to announce that "the old book of South African history was closed." In eighteen months there was a net capital outflow of 248 million rands (£124 million), and exchange reserves were halved. On 1 April, the UN Security Council passed its first condemnation of *South Africa. As Nelson *Mandela observed, the suppression of African political organizations convinced their leaders that "it would be unrealistic . . . to continue preaching peace and nonviolence." During the crisis the Congresses dispatched representatives abroad and the first efforts to build exile movements began.

White South Africa's crisis was more apparent than real. Active support for the Congresses was socially and geographically uneven and their organizations too weak to survive underground for long. ANC and PAC insurgencies failed to ignite popular rebellions. State violence inspired fear, not defiance. In the 1960s, the police gained intimidating legal and institutional powers, the military budget expanded tenfold, and an armaments industry was established to counter the 1963 UN arms embargo. The resettlement of 3.5 million people under influx control and the demolition of the trade unions contributed to industrial and political stability, attracting massive foreign investment after 1963. Through the decade GNP growth averaged 5.9 percent, much of the increase accumulating around advanced manufacturing.

The Sharpeville massacre heralded South Africa's international isolation, it prompted a major reorientation in African politics, and it opened an era of profound social change accompanied by the consolidation of the modern *apartheid state.

(See also RACE AND RACISM; SOWETO REBELLION.)

Tom Lodge, "The Sharpeville Crisis," in Tom Lodge, ed., *Black Politics in South Africa Since 1945* (London, 1983), pp. 201–230. Philip Kgosana, *Lest We Forget: An Autobiography* (Johannesburg, 1988).

TOM LODGE

SHINTO. Japan's oldest indigenous *religion, centering on the worship of deities called *kami*, Shinto

was the sacral basis of ancient Japanese society. It interacted for centuries with the immigrant cult of *Buddhism but successfully retained its identity until they were separated by law at the Meiji Restoration (1868) when purist State Shinto *ideology was enforced to unify the nation. State Shinto was formally abolished in 1946 during the Allied occupation of *Japan as part of constitutional separation of state and religion.

Controversy still surrounds the status of the emperor and the Yasukuni shrine for the war dead. The ruling Liberal Democratic Party has tried five times to have this Shinto shrine nationalized in blatant violation of the Constitution. Various Buddhist, Christian, and some Shinto groups oppose what is conceived as a move to revive State Shinto.

Further controversy ensued over the funeral of Emperor *Hirohito in 1989 and the accession rites of Emperor Akihito in 1990. The government divided the ceremonies into the secular state portion and the private Shinto rituals of the imperial household but followed the prewar Ordinance of Ceremonies. Widespread criticism resulted.

The crucial issue is whether Shinto should be classified as a religion. The prewar nationalist argument that it was a folkway that could be mandatory for citizens without violating their freedom of religion has been revived to justify nationalizing certain shrines. Serious repercussions could follow such a program of state support including a shift in political orientation. The outcome is uncertain and is complicated by the active lobbying of associations of war-bereaved, right-wing groups, and revisionists within the Ministry of Education.

Helen Hardacre, *State and Shinto: 1868–1989* (Princeton, N.J., 1989).

STUART D. B. PICKEN

SIERRA LEONE. Contemporary Sierra Leone is a product of its history as a haven from conflicts elsewhere in Africa and from slavery in the Americas; the legacy of colonialism; the economic imperatives of a mining and agricultural economy; and politics since independence in 1961. Competitive party politics reached its zenith with the victory of the opposition All People's Congress (APC) over the ruling Sierra Leone People's Party (SLPP) in 1967. A new democratic Constitution was approved in a referendum in August 1991.

The modern nation-state builds on the highly centralized and personalized executive presidency established under Siaka Stevens, who headed the government from 1967 to 1985 (except for a brief military interregnum in 1967–1968). By 1973 political activity was heavily influenced by violence and intimidation, and economic success was increasingly tied to patronage. Constitutional changes in 1978 made the APC the only legal party. Stevens brought political stability and managed to balance regional, ethnic, and elite demands. The cost was growing inequality with a disproportionately heavy burden falling on the rural population and urban poor.

Peaceful succession occurred in 1985 with Stevens's choice (and the only candidate), army commander General Joseph Momoh, elected president. From 1985, the state became increasingly democratic in the context of a one-party parliamentary system in which there were competitive elections for members of Parliament. The 1991 Constitution legalized multiparty competition, paved the way for new elections, and enhanced civil and *human rights.

On 29 April 1992, President Momoh was overthrown in a *coup d'état. Captain V. E. Strasser became chairman of the National Provisional Ruling Council (NPRC), promising to end the war caused by the invasion of Charles Taylor's forces (and their allies) from Liberia, root out corruption, and rebuild the economy. The military forces (estimated at 4,000) are dominated by the army. Their support, and continued unity, are essential to stability.

About seventy percent of the 4.2 million people of this West African nation are primarily involved in agriculture, producing about one-third of the GDP. Mining contributes approximately seventy-five percent of the exports and fifteen percent of GDP. Economic difficulties, apparent in the mid-1970s, became acute by 1980. Total public debt increased tenfold by 1987 to more than half of GNP. Budget deficits grew with expenditures exceeding revenue by as much as 100 percent in the mid-1980s. Shortfalls have been met by deficit financing and increases in the money supply. Inflation averaged fifty percent a year during the 1980s with a decline in the real GDP. Economic problems have been exacerbated by a sharp decrease in diamond production, dramatic growth of the parallel market, and stagnation of the agriculture sector compounded by state policies that have discouraged agricultural production.

Despite its early lead in education, including Fourah Bay College (1827), literacy is now only fifteen percent and the once-outstanding educational system is in danger of collapse. Sierra Leone has not been a major actor in the international arena beyond the region. Its external links have been strongest with Europe and the United States.

Among the most vocal critics of government policies are professionals, students, and the press. Increasingly frequent shortages of rice and other essentials have led to demonstrations and violence. Ethnicity became an important factor in politics in the mid-1960s under Prime Minister Albert Margai, who favored southerners, and has remained an issue as the economy declined and northern ethnic groups were seen to dominate at the expense of southerners. Similar tensions developed between northerners. Ethnic tensions have been exacerbated under the NPRC, which is perceived as dominated by southerners and creoles at the expense of northerners. Religion has not been a source of conflict.

Until the dismal performance of the economy is reversed, there is a risk of continued political instability. Given the traditions of mass participation, the push for democracy in the 1990s grew out of the desire of citizens to have a choice between political parties. Multiparty elections for Parliament were expected in 1992, but campaigning has been suspended following the coup.

John R. Cartwright, *Politics in Sierra Leone: 1947–67* (Toronto, 1970). Fred M. Hayward and Jimmy Kandeh, "Perspectives on Twenty-five Years of Elections in Sierra Leone," in Fred M. Hayward, ed., *Elections in Independent Africa* (Boulder, Colo., 1987), pp. 25–59. Fred M. Hayward, "Sierra Leone: State Consolidation, Fragmentation and Decay," in Donal Cruise O'Brien, John Dunn, and Richard Rathbone, eds., *Contemporary West African States* (Cambridge, U.K., 1989), pp. 165–180.

Fred M. Hayward

SINGAPORE. A dominant-party state ruled by the People's Action Party (PAP) since the island achieved internal self-government in 1959, Singapore was part of Malaysia between 1963 and 1965 and became an independent country on 9 August 1965. Lee Kuan Yew served as prime minister from 1959 to 1990. He retains a cabinet post as second-generation PAP leaders take power.

Singapore is a republic with a unicameral parliament. A ceremonial head of state, the president, is chosen by Parliament for a four-year term. Beginning in 1993, the president will be popularly elected and will have veto power over the budget and public appointments. Parliament has 81 elected seats and voting is compulsory. The PAP won 77 of 81 seats and 61.0 percent of the popular vote in the August 1991 elections. Between 1968 and 1981 the PAP held all parliamentary seats.

Final political authority resides with the elected prime minister and his cabinet. Up to three oppositional candidates can be invited to become nonconstituent members of Parliament (MPs) if fewer than three opposition candidates are elected. A 1990 law provides for up to six nominated MPs, and the single-member constituency format was modified shortly before the 1988 elections. There are now fifteen Group Representation Constituencies (GRCs), each with four MPs, and twenty-one single-member districts.

Judicial authority rests with the High Court, the Court of Appeal, the Court of Criminal Appeal, and twenty-three subordinate courts. Judges are appointed by the president. Jury trial was abolished in 1970. Persons suspected of endangering security of the country can be detained without trial under the Internal Security Act (ISA) for renewable two-year terms. ISA detentions are few, but they cause considerable negative foreign publicity when they occur.

Singapore's meritocratic society has a highly trained, efficient, and well-paid civil service. The integrity of the civil service and politicians is ensured by the Corrupt Practices Investigation Bureau.

Singapore's racial breakdown is: Chinese, 77.7 percent; Malay, 14.1 percent; Indian, 7.1 percent; other, 1.1 percent. Some eighty-six percent of Singaporeans live in government-built multiracial housing estates. Electoral districts in which Malay and Indian communities are concentrated have disappeared.

Singapore is a city-state of 2.7 million persons (1989) on a diamond-shaped island of 619 square kilometers (239 sq. mi.). By the year 2000 land reclamation will expand the land area by three percent. Per capita income is over US$14,000. Singaporeans' average life expectancy surpasses 71 years, about the same as that of Austria or Scotland. Family planning has been too successful, and the population has not been replacing itself since 1975. It now depends on 150,000 foreign workers to meet its labor needs.

Since the early 1960s, Singapore has followed unswerving commitment to *export-led growth. The first economic objectives after independence were to create political stability, attract investor confidence, and recruit *multinational corporations (MNCs). In 1960, nearly ninety percent of the manufacturing output was for domestic consumption, whereas today two-thirds of the output is exported.

The Second Industrial Revolution (SIR) was introduced in 1979. The National Wages Council increased employee compensation fourteen percent for three years. SIR was intended to encourage plant upgrading and automation and relocation of labor-intensive industries.

The government has subsequently pushed programs to make Singapore more attractive for MNC investment, particularly in terms of regional headquarters and as a servicing center. During the 1980s over half the workers in manufacturing were employed in foreign-owned firms, and more than eighty percent of direct exports came from these firms. Today, seventy percent of the GDP comes from the service sector, with just over twenty-eight percent from the manufacturing sector.

Political stability and orderly political transition are the foundation of Singapore's political continuity and change. Lee Kuan Yew and the PAP government have basically succeeded in meeting Singaporeans' material needs. In 1991, official foreign reserves were US$34 billion, and throughout the 1980s real GDP increased at 6.6 percent annually. Singapore remains heavily dependent on external economic forces to maintain its prosperity and growth. Stability and prosperity are the first task of the second-generation leaders.

Singapore's military strategy is geared toward deterrence. Defense spending is 5.5 percent of GDP. The 55,000-member Singapore Armed Forces (SAF) is a highly mobile, technologically sophisticated force with the most capable air force in the *Association of Southeast Asian Nations (ASEAN). Mandatory two-year military service beginning at age 18 or official exemption is required for employment. The SAF is externally oriented, and has a minimal internal security role.

The pillars of Singapore's foreign policy include trade with any state for mutual benefit, close cooperation with fellow ASEAN neighbors, and a non-aligned foreign policy. Singapore was a founding member of ASEAN in 1967. It has offered expanded facilities to the U.S. military, while emphasizing that expanded facilities were not a substitute for the Philippine bases. The foreign minister has applauded the stabilizing impact of the United States in Asia during the past two decades and urges a continued U.S. presence.

(See also CONFUCIANISM; NEWLY INDUSTRIALIZING ECONOMIES.)

Thomas J. Bellows, *The People's Action Party of Singapore: Emergence of a Dominant Party System* (New Haven, Conn., 1970). R. S. Milne and Diane K. Mauzy, *Singapore: The Legacy of Lee Kuan Yew* (Boulder, Colo., 1990).

THOMAS J. BELLOWS

SINO-AMERICAN RELATIONS. The relationship between the United States and *China became a significant factor in world politics only during World War II. Over the past half-century, the ebb and flow of Sino-American conflict and cooperation has had a major impact on the Asian regional balance of power, and on the global strategic balance as well. In recent years, questions of international trade, *arms control, *human rights, *population policy, global ecology, and natural resources have appeared on the agenda of Sino-American relations, largely supplanting the security issues of the early postwar decades.

Underlying the growing importance of Sino-American relations was America's postwar rise to global superpower status and the establishment in 1949 of the People's Republic of China (PRC), a revolutionary communist government that succeeded in unifying the country, mobilizing its people, and expanding China's international role. During the *Cold War decades of the 1950s and 1960s, the United States and China, lacking formal diplomatic relations, viewed each other as mortal security threats as well as irreconcilable ideological enemies. The status of the Republic of China on *Taiwan, a territory that the PRC claimed as its province and that the United States protected as an anticommunist bastion under Chinese Nationalist rule, became and remains to this day a point of contention.

In the 1970s Sino-American hostility dissipated owing to the emergence of a shared concern about what the United States and China both viewed as a greater threat emanating from the Soviet Union. After the establishment of diplomatic relations between Washington and Beijing in 1979, a rapid expansion of political, economic, cultural, and other relations took place. For a few years, a Sino-American strategic alignment began to take shape, but by the mid-1980s, as Washington and Beijing separately patched up their relations with Moscow, the Sino-American marriage of convenience eroded. A burgeoning economic relationship in which China saw the United States as a major contributor to Chinese modernization seemed for a while to provide a new basis for stable long-term relations. By the beginning of the 1990s, however, the future of Sino-American relations was clouded by American revulsion at the bloody *Tiananmen Square incident of June 1989 and the Chinese leadership's perception of the United States as a source of cultural contamination and threat to Communist Party authority.

From the onset of the Cold War, U.S. policymakers and analysts tended to view Sino-American relations in the context of a tripartite relationship involving China, the Soviet Union, and the United States that by the 1970s came to be known as the strategic triangle. In February 1950, the PRC and the Soviet Union signed a thirty-year Treaty of Friendship and Alliance. Washington assumed incorrectly that Moscow lay behind China's decision to intervene in the *Korean War (1950–1953), which marked the first time that American and Chinese troops had ever met in battle. Nevertheless, pursuing a long-term strategy of splitting the Sino-Soviet alliance, Washington was gratified by the bitter Sino-Soviet conflict that erupted in the early 1960s.

Yet while improving relations with the Soviet Union, the United States passed up opportunities to ameliorate relations with China and supported Chinese Nationalist attempts to destabilize the Chinese Communist regime. U.S. domestic political opinion in the 1950s and 1960s viewed China as an aggressive, expansionist power that had to be kept out of the UN and contained through a system of military alliances. Since the early 1950s, when Republicans blamed President Harry *Truman and the Democrats for the "loss of China," U.S. policy toward China had been a partisan political issue; to advocate better relations with the PRC was presumed to entail insupportable political costs. In the PRC a parallel consensus condemned the United States as the chieftain of world imperialism and the implacable enemy of the *Chinese Revolution. In the Taiwan Straits crises of 1954 and 1958, the United States and the PRC came to the brink of war over Chinese attempts to reclaim several offshore islands that the Chinese Nationalists controlled.

The Soviet Union's rise to global power status in the early 1970s and its attainment of rough strategic nuclear parity with the United States impelled Washington and Beijing to reassess their heretofore hostile relations. President Richard M. *Nixon's dramatic journey to China in February 1972 and his meetings with Chairman *Mao Zedong and Premier *Zhou Enlai laid the groundwork for a new Sino-American relationship. Fear of Soviet expansionism overcame

the continuing political and ideological differences between the United States and the PRC. Formal Sino-American diplomatic relations were established in 1979 under the guidance of China's paramount leader *Deng Xiaoping and U.S. President Jimmy *Carter. Sino-American strategic cooperation included U.S. arms transfers to the PRC as part of an effort to contain the perceived Soviet threat. For its part, Moscow viewed the new U.S.-China relationship as a threat to its own *security and interests.

In 1978 Mao's successors initiated an era of rapid reform in domestic and foreign policy, and China was opened to foreign investment, trade, tourism, and Western culture. While several billions of dollars of U.S. investments flowed into China and Sino-American trade greatly expanded, tens of thousands of Chinese students went to study in the United States. In urban China, a materialist, proto-consumer society displayed a tremendous interest in American popular culture. American democratic values began to permeate the intellectual elite, particularly students and younger intellectuals who lost their faith in *Marxism-*Leninism and viewed China's socialist system as an obstacle to development and democracy.

These developments alarmed old-guard Chinese Communist leaders who, fearful of losing power, periodically warned of the dangers of cultural subversion emanating from the West, particularly the United States. They repeatedly denounced U.S. efforts to influence Chinese public policy choices on such issues as internal governance, population, nationality affairs (*Tibet), and human rights. The bloody suppression of China's student-led democracy movement in June 1989 plunged U.S.-China relations into crisis. At the same time, dramatic improvements in U.S.-Soviet relations appeared to eliminate the need for Sino-American cooperation in the security realm. As international economic issues, particularly America's declining position in the world economy vis-à-vis its major trading partners (e.g., Japan, the *European Community), increasingly occupied the attention of the United States, the salience of U.S.-China relations decreased, at least in the short term.

By this time, however, the PRC had become a major actor in both the global and regional political arenas, and China's policies on a wide range of matters such as regional conflicts, arms control, the environment, and food and population issues could not be ignored. The network of societal linkages between the United States and China established during the 1980s seemed certain to survive the chill in official relations. The increasing integration of China into the world economy and the continuing attraction that younger Chinese felt toward Western culture and values suggested that U.S.-China relations would continue to flourish at many levels even in the face of Chinese Communist doubts and constraints. The collapse of communist regimes in Eastern Europe and the Soviet Union put Chinese Communist leaders on guard and widened the gap between the communist regime and Chinese society. How this political impasse is eventually resolved is certain to affect both the scope and intensity of Sino-American interactions in the coming years.

(See also AMERICAN FOREIGN POLICY; CONTAINMENT; SINO-SOVIET RELATIONS; SOVIET FOREIGN POLICY.)

Warren I. Cohen, *America's Response to China*, 3d ed. (New York, 1989). Gordon H. Chang, *Friends and Enemies: The United States, China, and the Soviet Union, 1948–1972* (Stanford, Calif., 1990).

STEVEN I. LEVINE

SINO-SOVIET RELATIONS. It is no exaggeration to say that Sino-Russian relations is the second most important bilateral international relationship after that between Russia and the United States. *China and Russia are two nuclear-armed neighbors with a long history of animosity interspersed with periods of cooperation. Their dealings with one another, only complicated by the coming of *communism to the *Soviet Union and then to China, took yet another turn in the early 1990s with the rollback of communism in and the death of the Soviet Union. Thus, with communist structures still in place in China, an additional element was introduced into a relationship that was already an unstable mixture of competition and coexistence.

The Soviet Union was geographically the largest state in Asia (as is its successor, Russia), largely the result of the expansion of the Russian Empire in the past four centuries. For much of that time, China, the traditionally dominant power in Asia, fought Russia for control of Central Asia, Mongolia, and Manchuria. But as the Chinese Empire collapsed, especially in the century before 1949, various powers, including Russia and Japan, maneuvered for influence. During the 1930s and early 1940s China sought Russian support when Japan was perceived as the main enemy. Following the defeat of Japan in 1945, the communist forces in China under the leadership of *Mao Zedong came to power in 1949, albeit without much assistance from their comrades in Moscow.

Although the Soviet Union was unable to offer lavish assistance, if only because it too was recovering from the devastation of World War II, China and the Soviet Union did grow closer in common cause against the capitalist states of East Asia and their supporters across the Pacific in the United States. China fought alongside the communist Democratic People's Republic of Korea (North Korea), with Soviet arms, in the *Korean War of 1950–1953. By the mid-1950s China was experimenting with the "Soviet model," whereby Soviet-style central *planning and *modernization was adopted in all walks of Chinese life. The model soon proved unsuitable to the conditions of poor, *peasant China,

and experiments with such radical strategies as the Great Leap Forward of the late 1950s led to Soviet suspicions that China was seeking its own revolutionary path. Indeed, Soviet suspicions about Chinese intentions were deepened by various disputes in foreign policy. China wanted to take a more forceful stand against Western states and the Soviet Union increasingly became convinced that there would have to be *détente with the West in order to avoid the risks of nuclear war.

By the late 1950s the skilled reader of Russian and Chinese tea leaves knew that the two communist giants were falling out, and in 1963 the dispute went public over the Soviet signature on the Partial Nuclear Test Ban Treaty with the United States and Britain. In the ensuing years China and the Soviet Union expended scarce resources on building up military forces along the frontier, and as China descended into the radical depths of the *Cultural Revolution in the second part of the 1960s, the Soviet Union feared that China was becoming a dangerous neighbor. In 1969 China provoked a major series of military clashes along the frontier and the Soviet Union responded with devastating conventional forces and threats to destroy China's fledgling nuclear capability.

In the wake of this Asian version of the Cuban Missile Crisis, the United States finally recognized that the Sino-Soviet split was such a serious problem for the Soviet Union that it might even provide possibilities for American gain. As China and the United States improved relations in the 1970s, the Soviet Union spent heavily to fortify its military position in East Asia. As Western nations, and most notably Japan, improved relations with China, the Soviet Union tried to bolster its position by improving relations with Vietnam, whose own relations with China were deteriorating.

But as China found itself locked in extreme anti-Soviet positions, for example in supporting anti-Soviet forces in Africa and even Chile, Beijing began to reassess its options. The death of Mao Zedong and the coming to power of a more pragmatic regime under *Deng Xiaoping in the late 1970s laid the groundwork for a more pragmatic foreign policy. China slowly reassessed its anti-Soviet attitude and by 1982 announced a more independent position between the two superpowers. As China focused on the needs of modernization at home, it sought to reduce tension with the Soviet Union and make more friends around the world.

Although Chinese domestic politics were a crucial motivation for the reform of Sino-Soviet relations, it was the coming to power of reformers in the Soviet Union that made real détente possible. Yury Andropov in 1983, and especially Mikhail *Gorbachev in 1985, placed a priority on improving relations with China. Gradually, trade increased, cross-border contacts multiplied, troops were withdrawn from the frontier, and high-level delegations were exchanged. China had become the Soviet Union's second-largest trade partner in the Pacific, and some 30,000 Chinese were staffing farms and factories in the Soviet Far East. In May 1989, Mikhail Gorbachev arrived in Beijing to mark the normalization of Sino-Soviet relations and the restoration of party-to-party ties.

Yet this was to be the briefest of honeymoons, for 1989 was the year of the brutal crushing of reforms in China in June and the collapse of communism in Eastern and Central Europe. As the Soviet Union de-communized in subsequent months and China reinforced Communist Party rule, the two countries drifted further apart. To be sure, the state-to-state level of relations remained basically stable, although trade was not increasing at the expected rate and there were continuing problems in reaching arms control accords. But both sides recognized that even if they no longer had a shared ideology, there were sound reasons for them to get along.

This new definition of détente—competition and coexistence—had a beneficial impact on East Asia and even farther afield. Both states sought improved relations with the Republic of Korea (South Korea) and refused to give North Korea room to play off one patron against the other. China and the Soviet Union encouraged their respective friends in Indochina to come to the negotiating table. Both the Soviet Union and China were also increasingly interested in participating in the economic prosperity of the Pacific and therefore helped create a more peaceful international environment. Both countries also joined with the West in agreeing to tough UN Security Council action against Iraq in the crisis leading to the *Gulf War in 1991.

Yet reasons remain for continuing competition in the Sino-Russian relationship. The demise of communism in the Soviet Union was a threat to the ruling regime in China. Moreover, as the Soviet Union collapsed, China saw both opportunities and dangers, especially from restive Muslims in Central Asia. In East Asia, as Russian power wanes, China continues to spend more on its armed forces and seems likely to be involved in regional conflict, especially in Southeast Asia. In such times of major shifts in the global *balance of power, the future of the Sino-Russian relationship is both more important and more uncertain than ever.

(See also CHINESE REVOLUTION; NINETEEN EIGHTY-NINE; SINO-AMERICAN RELATIONS; SOVIET FOREIGN POLICY.)

Gilbert Rozman, *A Mirror for Socialism* (Princeton, N.J., 1985). Gerald Segal, *Sino-Soviet Relations After Mao* (London, 1985). Thomas Hart, *Sino-Soviet Relations* (London, 1987). Gilbert Rozman, *The Chinese Debate About Soviet Socialism* (Princeton, N.J., 1987).

GERALD SEGAL

SLOVENIA. See YUGOSLAVIA.

SOCIAL INSURANCE. See WELFARE STATE.

SOCIALISM AND SOCIAL DEMOCRACY

Socialists of all stripes criticize *capitalism—a combination of private ownership of productive resources with their decentralized allocation by markets—claiming that this system cannot simultaneously achieve rationality in allocating scarce resources to alternative uses and justice in distributing material welfare. Yet the specific diagnoses and the proposed remedies have been sufficiently distinct to have generated at least three alternative socialist projects: communitarian, Marxist, and social democratic. Communitarian socialism emerged in the 1830s and withered as a serious alternative when socialist *ideology became fused with Marxist theory and the working-class movement around 1890. The Second International split in the aftermath of World War I over the issue of *democracy, but Marxist socialism continued uncontested in the economic realm until the middle 1930s, when the Swedish Social Democrats first formulated their strategy. Between World War II and 1989, command socialism and social democracy offered alternative and highly antagonistic projects. With the fall of command socialism in Central and Eastern Europe, the demise of the social democratic model in Scandinavia, and the dissolution of the Soviet Union, socialists can only ask, "What is left?"

Since this question organizes my essay, the approach I adopt is not historical. Indeed, to set the framework of analysis, I begin in the first section by recouching socialist critiques of capitalism in a deliberately anachronistic language of contemporary economic theory. In the second section I briefly review the blueprints, and the weaknesses, of command socialism, social democracy, and market socialism. The concluding part gropes for an answer.

Socialist Critiques of Capitalism. Let me first restate the fundamental views of *Marx and Engels and their followers concerning capitalism. The main conclusion of their analysis, which became the guiding theory of the Second International (1889–1914), was that capitalism was at the same time irrational and unjust. It was irrational because it necessarily inhibited the development of productive resources and regularly caused a waste of already-produced assets. And it was unjust because it distributed material welfare as a function of initial wealth rather than contributions or needs.

Viewed in retrospect, socialist critiques of capitalism frequently appear quaint, often incoherent, and at times bizarre. They bear the imprint of the nineteenth century: the very notion that any decentralized social system can function in an orderly way still baffles the imagination of many socialist critics of capitalism. And they are frightfully ignorant: they dispose of arguments for capitalism with a wave of a hand. Yet paradoxically, as all variants of the really-existing socialisms have plunged into disrepute, some central arguments for the irrationality of capitalism are regaining their theoretical force.

To formulate socialist critiques in a modern way, we need to reconstruct the capitalist blueprint. The model is simple: individuals know that they need, they have endowments, they exchange and engage in production whenever they want. Moreover, in equilibrium all markets clear. Hence, the prices at which individuals exchange reflect their preferences and relative scarcities; these prices inform individuals about all the opportunities they forsake. As a result, resources are allocated in such a way that all gains from trade are exhausted, no one can be better off without someone else being worse off, and the resulting distribution of welfare would not be altered under a unanimity rule.

Reasonable socialist critiques of this model all converge on the assertion that capitalism generates "waste." Yet they evoke several alternative reasons: 1) the "anarchy" of capitalist production, 2) the "contradiction" between individual and collective rationality, and 3) the "contradiction" between forces of production and relations of production. Moreover, the waste involved in each of these explanations is different: anarchy causes waste of existing endowments and even of commodities already produced, while the waste caused by the two remaining contradictions is of opportunities. My view is that the first of these criticisms is valid but we do not know whether it is remediable under any economic system, that the second critique fails to draw some important distinctions and is misdirected once these are made, and that the third one is valid and fundamental.

The anarchy critique concerns 1) the efficiency of the competitive equilibrium and 2) the feasibility of costless adjustment to a state where the expectations under which individual agents make their decisions are simultaneously fulfilled. Both are complicated issues.

First, in the light of recent developments of neoclassical theory, markets cannot be expected to generate efficient allocation of resources. Even under perfect competition, labor and capital are underutilized and final goods markets do not clear in equilibrium because employers, lenders, and consumers must pay rents to assure that, respectively, employees, borrowers, and sellers will deliver goods and services of contracted quality. Capitalism is thus inefficient even in a competitive equilibrium.

Second, even if the competitive equilibrium were efficient, as the capitalist blueprint maintained, a costless adjustment to this equilibrium may be unfeasible either because decentralized economies are never in equilibrium or because the adjustment is gradual. Marx himself seems to have wobbled about the first point, and he firmly adhered to the second. On the first point, he asserted that capitalist markets

do sometimes clear but only by accident. And he developed an elaborate theory of crises of overproduction and underconsumption that became the mainstay of the economic theory of his followers. In these crises, capital and labor lie idle and the final goods markets do not clear. The waste is of the already-available factors of production and commodities.

Hence, the anarchy critique seems vindicated by recent developments of economic theory. Yet whether this critique establishes the irrationality of capitalism depends on whether the anarchy characteristic of the capitalist markets can be remedied by some alternative economic organization. And since I doubt it can be, I do not see this critique as crucial.

The claim that under capitalism individually rational actions lead to collective suboptimality confuses two situations, and is false about the first one and misdirected concerning the second. Marx thought that competition forces individual firms to invest in such a way that the general rate of profit falls. This particular argument has been shown to be false. In general, if consumption is rival and if there are no externalities, no increasing returns to scale, and no myopia, then there is no conflict between individual and collective rationality. Only if any of these assumptions are violated does individual rationality diverge from the collective one.

In real economies, these assumptions are violated: about this much no one disagrees. But all this implies is that any reasonable blueprint of capitalism must have some ways of coping with situations under which individual and social rates of return diverge— and all such blueprints do treat this situation. One way is to introduce corrective fiscal intervention, another is to reassign property rights. Hence, even under capitalism, markets may do only what they do well, and the state may have to step in where markets fail. This observation gives comfort to many socialists who gleefully observe that capitalism cannot exist without state intervention. But in fact it dulls the critique: capitalism is not any less, or more, capable than socialism of handling all the situations in which social rates of return diverge from private ones.

Having cleared the underbrush, we arrived at the claim that capitalism leads to a systematic underutilization of the productive potential. My version of this argument asserts that capitalism is irrational because it cannot access some technically feasible distributions of welfare even if these are normatively and politically desirable. We may have technological and organizational means to feed everyone on earth, we may want to feed everyone, and yet we may be still unable to do it under capitalism. Here is the argument.

Imagine an economy in which there are two agents, capitalists and workers. If the output does not depend on rates of return to the endowments controlled by these agents, then under a given state of technology all distributions of welfare that sum up to this level of output are accessible. But under capitalism output does depend on the rates of return to endowments. If capitalists receive the entire return from capital and workers the entire return from labor, then resources will be efficiently allocated and the distribution of income will reflect marginal productivity of the two factors. But if either capitalists or workers receive less than the entire return, that is, if the distribution of income diverges from the competitive market, they will withdraw capital or labor and resources will be underutilized.

Under capitalism, endowments—capital and labor power—are privately owned, and the agents who decide whether and how to utilize them are self-interested. Private property implies that owners have the right to withdraw their endowments from productive uses if they do not expect to receive an adequate rate of return. Hence, when the final distribution of welfare diverges from the allocation that would be generated by competitive markets, resources will be underutilized, and capitalism will lead to an inefficient, that is, collectively irrational allocation.

Suppose that, instead of wasting already-produced food, we distributed it to the poor. Then the price of food would fall, farmers would be getting a lower rate of return, and they would produce less. Moreover, some people who produce food for themselves would find it more profitable to do something else and get free food. Or suppose that we paid farmers to produce, supported farm prices out of taxes, and distributed food to the poor. Then the rate of return would fall throughout the economy, and the output of other commodities would decline. In fact, we do some of both, out of compassion or other motivations. But under capitalism we do it at the cost of reducing output below its potential level.

Hence, capitalism is irrational in the sense that under this system we cannot use the full productive potential without rewarding those who control the productive endowments. Technically feasible distributions of welfare are inaccessible under the capitalist system. If a society decides that the allocation of resources or the distribution of income should obey criteria other than maximization of profit, resources will be underutilized or underdeveloped.

"Command" Socialism. According to Marx, Engels, and their followers within the Second International, the irrationality and injustice of capitalism are intrinsic to the combination of private ownership and market allocation. Capitalism cannot be reformed. In turn, these deleterious effects of capitalism, as well as many others, ranging from war through prejudice to prostitution, would be automatically eliminated by abolishing private property. Hence, when *Marxism, socialism, and the *labor movement became briefly fused in Europe between 1891 and 1914, the economic program of socialist parties consisted of one demand: to nationalize the means of production, so that all resources at society's disposal could be rationally administered to satisfy human needs.

At the same time, it is important to remember that until 1919 Marxists did not develop any blueprints for implementing this system. Only in the aftermath of World War I, as the triumph of the *Russian Revolution and the massive insurgency of workers in several European countries confronted the socialist movement with the real possibility of realizing its ideas, did several detailed proposals for administering socialist economies develop.

The central claim of the "command" model was that the dynamic potential could be fully developed only if resources were centrally allocated to satisfy human needs. This model was based on several explicit assumptions: as co-owners of the means of production, "socialist men" would truthfully reveal their needs and their productive potential and would exert effort independently of reward while planners would behave as perfect agents of the society, simply solving problems of optimal allocation.

To analyze what went wrong, we must first restate the socialist blueprint. Households have needs. Firms have the capacity to produce objects that satisfy needs. The planner learns about the needs of households and the production capacities of firms and calculates how to allocate resources among firms and how to distribute the output among households in order to satisfy needs to the extent possible given the resources. The result is rational administration of things to satisfy needs.

The critiques of this model of socialism fall into three categories: 1) Even if the planner had truthful information, the sheer complexity of the problem would make it impossible to handle. 2) If individuals are self-interested, without a market mechanism the planner cannot learn about the true needs of households and the true capacities of firms. 3) There are no incentives and no monitoring mechanisms that would force the planner to promote general welfare.

Even if the planner's problem can be resolved in principle, the task facing planners is enormous. Soviet economists envisaged a few years ago that under the reformed price system, between 1,500 and 2,000 prices of basic products would be fixed by Gosplan (the State Planning Commission), another 20,000 to 30,000 prices would be administered by specialized agencies, and the remaining prices would be determined by contracts between suppliers and users. It is difficult to imagine how so many prices could be "gotten right," even with the use of computers.

Even if the planner is able to solve the calculation problem, the case for the feasibility of socialism hinges on the assumption that once economic agents—households, firms, and planners—become coproprietors of productive wealth, they act spontaneously in ways that support collective welfare. Specifically, households truthfully reveal to the planner their needs and firms their productive capacities, while planners act as perfect agents of the public.

None of these assumptions has worked under really-existing socialism. This may not be a decisive argument, for it is easy to claim that the nondemocratic nature of economic decision making in the socialist countries subverted the very notion of social ownership. But it is obvious that this notion ignores "free rider" problems (i.e., individuals trying to avoid paying their share of the cost of providing public goods).

If individuals continue to be self-interested even when they co-own the productive wealth, households overreport their needs. True, the planner need not rely on revealed preferences to decide what to produce and how to distribute. In a poor country, the urgency of some needs is apparent to any observer. The planner can rely on some theory of needs to decide that minimal calorie consumption should be assured to everyone first, followed by shelter, medical attention, education, etc. This was the original intuition behind physical *planning. These methods will not work, however, once needs become more differentiated. And if the planner relies on revealed preferences, households have an incentive to misrepresent their needs.

Likewise, firms have powerful incentives to hide some of their productive capacities, and individuals may shirk in production. At least thus far, arguments for the feasibility of socialism must rest on the assumption that socialization of the means of production causes individuals to adopt socialist preferences, and this assumption is unrealistic. Since collective ownership does create free rider problems, the hope that it would alter preferences is tenuous. Hence, command socialism is unfeasible.

When planners are misinformed and self-interested and the immediate producers shirk, the output may be inferior to capitalism at any distribution of welfare. Under socialism, we may be unable to feed everyone because we cannot produce enough.

Social Democracy. The fundamental premise of social democracy is that *nationalization of the means of production is not necessary to overcome either the irrationality or the injustice of capitalism. Governments that want to eradicate poverty while minimizing losses of efficiency are not helpless in capitalist economies. They can counteract economic fluctuations, they can steer investment, they can facilitate labor mobility, and they can deliver welfare services and maintain incomes. The degree of irrationality of capitalism is not given: governments elected with a mandate to assure the material security of all citizens do have instruments with which to pursue their mission. They can implement "functional socialism," even if ownership of productive resources remains private.

Since this understanding emerged only gradually, as a reflection on successful practice rather than implementation of prior blueprints, it may be useful to trace its origins. Ever since the 1890s, socialists had thought their irreversible electoral progress would culminate one day in a parliamentary majority that would allow them to take office and legislate their societies into socialism. They were completely unprepared for what ensued. In several countries, parties bearing social democratic, labor, or socialist labels were invited to form governments by default, without winning the majority that would have been necessary to pursue the program of nationalization, because the bourgeois parties were too divided to maintain their traditional coalitions. Indeed, the first elected socialist government in the world was formed by the Swedish Social Democrats in 1920 just as they suffered their first-ever electoral reversal.

Once in office, socialists found themselves in the embarrassing situation of not being able to pursue the only program they had—nationalization—and not having any other program that would distinguish them from their bourgeois opponents. They could and did pursue ad hoc measures designed to improve conditions for their electoral continuency: the development of public housing; the institution of unemployment relief; and the introduction of minimum wages, income and inheritance taxes, and old-age pensions. But such measures did not differ from the tradition of conservative reforms associated with Bismarck, Disraeli, or Giolitti. Socialists behaved like all other parties: with some distributional bias toward their own constituency but full of respect for the golden principles of the balanced budget, deflation, the *gold standard, etc. They formed commissions to study the feasibility of nationalization and stopped there.

By the 1930s, the problem was that resources lay fallow: engines stood idle while people were out of work. At no time was the irrationality of capitalism more blatant. As families starved, food—already-produced food—was destroyed. Coffee was burned, pigs were buried, machines rusted. And according to the economic orthodoxy of the time, this state of affairs was simply natural; the only recourse was to cut the costs of production, which meant wages. Some relief measures to assist the unemployed were obviously urgent, but such measures were not considered advisable from the economic point of view. In Britain, the Labour government actually proposed to reduce unemployment compensation: this was the condition for being bailed out by the thirties' version of the *International Monetary Fund (IMF), where the "M" stood for the Morgan Bank. But in Sweden the Social Democratic Party, having won the elections of 1932, broke the shell of orthodox monetary policy. As unemployment climbed sharply with the onset of the Great Depression, the party stumbled upon an idea that was truly new: instead of assisting the unemployed, the Swedish Social Democrats employed them.

As this new policy appeared to have generated a spectacular success, it became theoretized. Socialist parties had acquired a reason to be in office under capitalism. There was something to be done: the economy was not moving according to natural laws, the economic crises could be attenuated, the waste of resources and the material deprivation could be alleviated if the government pursued anticyclical policies. Full employment became a realistic goal that could be pursued at all times. Moreover, since the economy would be stimulated by distributing incomes to people who consume most of it, the distributional bias of the Left found a rationalization in a technical economic theory.

It was Keynes who could reconcile private ownership of the means of production with democratic management of the economy. Whether or not the Swedish Social Democrats were following Keynes's recipes when they launched their policies, this has become the credo of social democracy. The practical question that social democrats have tried to solve ever since is how simultaneously to regulate investment and income. An appropriate government policy, combining a particular tax system with a social policy, would generate a level of welfare equal to the one attainable had workers jointly owned the capital stock.

The closest this general posture came to an explicit blueprint was the so-called Rehn-Meidner Plan, which was developed in Sweden between 1951 and 1958. In this model, the unions were to keep their private wages at the competitive level, given by the increase of productivity and the rate of inflation in export-receiving countries, and to reduce wage differentials, in part to put pressure on less efficient firms. In turn, the role of the government was to maintain full employment, devalue the currency whenever wage drift pushed wages above the competitive level, facilitate labor mobility by an active labor market policy, and supply social services on a universalistic basis. The tax system, which combined a high rate of taxation on consumption and selective incentives for investment, was the main policy instrument.

There is no question that this model has been successful in practice. Statistical analyses of developed capitalist countries show repeatedly that lower income inequality, more extensive welfare services, a more favorable trade-off between employment and inflation, a more favorable trade-off between wages and investment, and a more favorable trade-off between growth and social policies are to be found in those countries that combine strong unions with social democratic control over the government. To put it simply, the only countries in the world where almost no one is poor after taxes and transfers are the countries that have pursued social democratic policies.

Yet there are several indications that the social democratic model is no longer viable. At the institutional level, it is apparent that the two cornerstones of the social democratic strategy—centralized bargaining and continued tenure in office of social democratic parties—have crumbled. Formal centralized bargaining disintegrated in Sweden and is maintained only by the insistence of governments in Norway, while electoral support for social democratic parties declined drastically, forcing them out of office. At the economic level, it is apparent that the performance of the social democratic countries deteriorated in relative terms during the 1980s.

While it is not easy to separate cause and effect, several deficiencies endogenous to the social democratic model are cited to explain this demise: 1) A high degree of regulation and discretionary interventions by governments distorted the price system and weakened incentives to save and to work. In particular, governments tended to maintain full employment by unproductive employment in the public sector. 2) Universalistic welfare programs led to excess of demand over supply and thus to the rationing of access by administrative rules. 3) High marginal tax rates led to capital flight. 4) Wage drift, which was unresponsive to economic conditions, undermined the centralized bargains.

Exogenous factors may also elucidate the demise of social democracy: 1) The changing composition of class structure, especially the numerical decline of manual labor, undermined both the traditional electoral base of socialist parties and their ability to recruit voters among other sectors of society. 2) Increasing international competition undermined the initial rationale for centralized bargaining and forced governments to align their tax policy with those of competitors.

Yet, while explanations of the collapse abound, thus far the retreat from traditional social democratic policies has been limited. It is most visible in the abandonment of the full employment policy, the adoption of the "flat" tax model, and in fiscal and monetary policy. Thus far at least, it has not extended to welfare or labor market policy.

Market Socialism. The combination of full employment, a reasonable level of investment, and material security is possible only when encompassing centralized unions cooperate with socialist governments that enjoy long tenure in office. When these political conditions are absent, the efforts of particular groups of workers to raise wages result in unemployment and inequality, while governments have no incentives to assure material security for everyone.

The case for "market socialism"—a system in which workers own their firms but resources are allocated by markets—is a political, not an economic one. That is, we still do not know if 1) forms of property have consequences for firm performance and 2) the observed distribution of forms of property, in particular the paucity of employee-owned cooperatives, is due to their performance. In spite of the popularity of the idea of market socialism, we still do not have a theory of the firm that would justify this preference.

Therefore, the putative advantages of market socialism rest on distributional considerations, which have in the past provided and in many countries continue to furnish an important impulse toward socialism of some sort. One way to see the distributional cost of capitalism to wage earners, suggested long ago by Paul Samuelson, is to look at the proportion of net income consumed by owners of capital. The net output in any capitalist economy can be partitioned into consumption of wage earners, investment, and consumption of capitalists. The last part is forever lost to wage earners; it is the cost they pay for the private ownership of productive wealth. This cost varies enormously among capitalist countries. In 1985, for every dollar of value added in manufacturing, the consumption of capitalists ranged from about ten cents in Austria and Norway to well under forty cents in Britain and the United States to about sixty cents in Brazil and seventy cents in Argentina. Hence, in purely distributional terms, Austrian and Norwegian wage earners have little to gain from nationalization or socialization. Since nationalization has some inevitable costs, they are best off relying on their market power and electoral influence. British and U.S. workers have more to gain by squeezing profits or owning productive wealth directly: they end up striking more. In turn, the distributional effect of nationalization in Argentina and Brazil would be enormous. If income differentials between the top and the bottom quintile would be limited at the factor of five in socialist Brazil, the income of the poorest twenty percent would increase tenfold. Hence, in Argentina and Brazil nationalization is attractive to wage earners for purely distributional reasons.

Yet the paradox is that those working-class movements that may have the political muscle to bring about some form of socialism by legislation have no incentives to do so, while those movements that have much to gain by transferring productive wealth into the public realm have no power to do it. Hence socialism as the program of public ownership of productive wealth is the political project only of those movements that cannot bring it about.

In the end, market socialism does appear attractive on distributional grounds. Even if we cannot exactly anticipate its effects on employment, investment, and labor productivity, a combination of cooperatives with markets would be superior to capitalism in equalizing income distribution. If we think of market socialism as a system in which there is a labor-cum-capital market, that is, if being a shareholder in a co-op constitutes simultaneously a right and the obligation to work in it and these rights-obligations can be traded, then in equilibrium the rate of return to total endowments will be uniform throughout the economy. The distribution of income associated with this equilibrium will be more egalitarian than under capitalism since employees receive the entire net income of the firm.

However, the claim that market socialism would be a system of *industrial democracy, in the sense that the process of production would be democratic, seems unfounded. If worker-owned firms compete and if one way of organizing production maximizes profits, then they will be forced to choose this organization. In turn, if more than one organization of production maximizes profits, then capitalists would be indifferent between them, and if workers prefer one, capitalists would adopt it. Hence, workers' co-ops would have nothing to change.

Moreover, since under market socialism the utilization of resources would depend on rates of return, this system would suffer from the social inaccessibility of technically feasible allocations of welfare, the same irrationality that characterizes capitalism. Hence, market socialism would be still at odds with democracy. The principle that everyone has equal economic rights is not sufficient for democracy either in production or in the economy as a whole.

What Is Left? The capitalist economy, in which owners of wealth and of the capacity to work make decentralized decisions about allocation of their endowments, regularly generates a number of effects that are experienced as profound deprivations by large segments of society. The combination of market with private ownership limits the collective sovereignty, does not assure the material security of anyone who does not own wealth, and generates drastic inequalities, including the inequality of opportunity. This has been the traditional socialist critique of capitalism. The perennial question of various strands of socialism has been what, if anything, can be done about it. And, as this review shows, none of the answers survived intact the test of time.

What is then left? By posing the question in this manner, I want to inquire whether any socialist ideals continue to 1) conform to the traditional normative commitments of socialism, 2) remain economically feasible, and 3) appeal to movements or parties that would be capable of realizing them.

Imposing these three constraints on the potential answers evokes a sense of a paradox. If a Martian were asked to pick the most efficient and humane economic systems on earth, it would certainly not choose the countries with unfettered markets. The United States is a stagnant economy in which real wages have been constant for more than a decade and the real income of the bottom forty percent of the population has declined. It is an inhumane society in which 11.5 percent of the population, some 32 million people, including twenty percent of all children, live in absolute poverty. It is a political system with the lowest voting rates among democracies and the highest per capita prison population in the world. Yet the message about the virtues of market economy it emanates finds receptive echoes all around the world. This is even more perplexing when we observe that the worldwide turn toward a reliance on markets and away from state intervention during the 1980s has been accompanied by an equally widespread economic stagnation and increasing inequalities among and within nations.

Moreover, faith in the virtues of unfettered markets is being increasingly undermined by recent developments in the very neoclassical economic theory that used to provide theoretical foundations for the belief that markets allocate resources efficiently. As long as belief in the efficiency of market allocation was sustainable, justifications of socialism were limited either to those cases where the private and the social rates of return diverged or to claims that market allocation, while efficient, leads to other normative undesirable outcomes. Today, the observation that a complete set of markets is unfeasible and information is inevitably imperfect places political institutions at the very core of any debate about economic systems. Yet again, despite these theoretical developments, market ideology is enjoying today an unprecedented and almost uncontested hegemony.

Given the current flux of economic theory and the puzzling divergence between economic realities and economic ideologies, this is not the moment to speculate about the future of socialism. Critiques of an exclusive reliance on markets cannot be used as a vindication of the traditional socialist models analyzed above. With all their faults, markets are the only mechanism we know today for eliciting private information and for providing private incentives. Command socialism is dead. Moreover, while social democracy was an unquestionable historical success, the conditions that made it feasible have been undermined by its own dynamic or by changes in the world economy. Hence, no return to the models of the past is feasible. Let me thus limit this conclusion to normative considerations that render continuing relevance to socialism.

The fundamental motivation of socialism is the ideal of collective sovereignty. People, that is, individuals acting on the bases of their current preferences, are collectively sovereign if the alternatives open to them as a collectivity are constrained only by conditions independent of their collective capacities and by individual rights. Specifically, people are sovereign only if there exist some procedures through which they can alter the existing institutions, including the state and property, and they can allocate available resources to all feasible uses.

But why juxtapose individuals and society: is not the choice by the "society" the same as the choice by the competing individuals? The warrant for claiming that capitalism is irrational stems from the fact that individuals are simultaneously market agents and citizens. The allocation of resources they prefer as citizens does not in general coincide with that at which they arrive via the market. Capitalism is a system in which scarce resources are owned privately. Yet under capitalism property is institution-

ally distinct from authority. As a result, there are two mechanisms by which resources can be allocated to uses and distributed among households: the market and the *state. The market is a mechanism in which individuals cast votes for allocations with the resources they own, and these resources are always distributed unequally; the state is a system which allocates resources it does not own, and where the rights to decide are distributed differently from market. Hence the two mechanisms lead to the same outcome only by a fluke.

Democracy in the political realm exacerbates this divergence by equalizing the right to influence the allocation of resources. Indeed, distributions of consumption used by the market and those collectively preferred by citizens must differ since democracy offers those who are poor, oppressed, or otherwise miserable as a consequence of the initial distribution of endowments an opportunity to find redress via the state.

Hence, if "the people" are sovereign, they may prefer an allocation and distribution of resources that differs from the market outcome. It is this preference that cannot be reached when endowments are allocated in a decentralized way. Even when individuals express as citizens their collective preference for a particular allocation and when all the material conditions are present to implement this preference, the democratically chosen allocation is unreachable under capitalism. Society, by which I always mean all individuals through a democratic process, can decide collectively that needs different from those maximized by the market should be the goal of development. It is this insistence that the allocation of resources and the distribution of incomes should fall under collective control that renders continuing relevance to socialism.

Nonetheless, the notion of "the" socialism, socialism as the end of history, is untenable. The democratic process in which all individuals are equally empowered in the collective decision making is necessarily open-ended, and its verdicts are continually reversible. It cannot be based on any assumptions about human nature, and it cannot be expected to lead to predetermined outcomes. The outcome of political conflicts—and conflict is what all politics is about—may be to direct societal resources to maximize free time, maximize employment, seek beauty, or maximize consumption. Moreover, continuing disagreements about the manners in which any of these goals can be implemented, including the organization of states and markets, are inevitable and desirable.

Given that we live in an age of doubt not only about decentralized but also collective mechanisms of decision making, neither the design of markets nor of democratic institutions is obvious. Yet at the level of practical politics, this quest for collective sovereignty has two immediate consequences, both concerning the status of citizenship. One is the traditional emphasis on equality of access to the democratic process, access that entails real empowerment of individuals to participate in public affairs in an enlightened manner. This is both a call for political institutions that open a space for deliberation and for educational institutions that do not limit the knowledge of pubic affairs to those who enjoy a privileged position in the economic structure. The second is the insistence that full membership in a political community entails social *citizenship: security and opportunity for all. These two practical principles continue to distinguish socialism.

(See also COMMAND ECONOMY; COMMUNIST PARTY STATES; EQUALITY AND INEQUALITY; KEYNESIANISM; NINETEEN EIGHTY-NINE; TAXES AND TAXATION; WELFARE STATE.)

Karl Marx, *Capital,* 3 vols. (New York, 1967). Maurice Dobb, *Welfare Economics and the Economics of Socialism* (Cambridge, U.K., 1969). G. A. Cohen, *Karl Marx's Theory of History: A Defense* (Princeton, N.J., 1978). Alec Nove, *The Economics of Feasible Socialism* (London, 1983). Michael Burawoy, *The Politics of Production: Factory Regimes under Capitalism and Socialism* (London, 1985). Adam Przeworski, *Capitalism and Social Democracy* (Cambridge, U.K., 1985). Brian Barry, *Democracy, Power and Justice: Essays in Political Theory* (Oxford, 1989). Jon Elster and Karl Ove Moene, eds., *Alternatives to Capitalism* (Cambridge, U.K., 1989). Pranab Bardhan and John Roemer, *Market Socialism: A Case for Rejuvenation,* East-South System Transformations Working Paper #9 (Chicago, 1991). Peter Murell, "Can Neoclassical Economics Underpin the Reform of Centrally Planned Economies?" *Journal of Economic Perspectives* 5 (1991): 59–76.

ADAM PRZEWORSKI

SOCIALIST INTERNATIONAL. Today's Socialist International (SI) was founded in Frankfurt in 1951. Headquartered in London, its members include socialist and social democratic parties from over sixty countries, as well as a number of "fraternal" and "associated" organizations such as the International Union of Socialist Youth and the Jewish Labor Bund. While never explicitly stated, the SI perceives itself as continuing the ideological legacy and historical mission of the famous Second International of the pre–World War I era (1889–1914) and its interwar incarnation known as the Labor and Socialist International (1923–1940).

From its founding congress, the SI has consistently defined its role as helping the global struggle for a third way between the political *totalitarianism of *communism on the one hand and the economic inequities and social injustices of *capitalism on the other. Anti-Leninist in its views, the SI has considered socialism and *democracy perfectly compatible, and indeed has always supposed that neither could be achieved without the other. The SI's positions vis-à-vis communism and communist parties remained among the most controversial within its ranks until the late 1980s.

The SI's anti-Leninist *Marxism and staunch anticapitalism bore the unmistakable imprint of social democracy in the Federal Republic of Germany (FRG) and its leader, Kurt Schumacher. Very much the dynamo of the founding congress, the West German social democrats have remained far and away the most critical actors within the organization. The dominance of the West German, Austrian, and Swedish parties in the SI and in the larger world of social democratic politics was consolidated in the 1970s by the ascendance of the FRG's Willy Brandt to the organization's presidency in 1976 and the unchallenged power exerted by the triumvirate of Brandt, Austria's Bruno Kreisky, and Sweden's Olof Palme. In terms of financial commitments as well as political influence these three parties leave the Italian, British, Norwegian, Dutch, and French comrades far behind.

Under Willy Brandt's leadership, the SI made special efforts to shed its Eurocentric activities and address global problems more actively. Thus, the SI has been in the forefront of restructuring *North-South relations in favor of the poor countries of the Southern Hemisphere. Being particularly keen to assist *Third World movements with socialist *and* democratic aims and methods, the SI provided important diplomatic assistance on behalf of such movements, especially in Central America and South Africa.

Global *peace and *disarmament were also central topics of SI involvement during the Brandt incumbency. Indeed, they assumed such paramount importance for the SI's German-dominated leadership that the organization barely supported *Solidarity in Poland and other logical SI allies in Eastern and Central Europe, lest such support appear as a *Cold War–style challenge to the Soviet Union. This "appeasement" toward Soviet domination of Eastern Europe was sharply challenged by the Mediterranean members of the SI, most notably the French. This marked a total role reversal on the issue of socialists' relations with communism, for it was the French members of the SI who favored close collaboration with the Portuguese communists during the mid-1970s when the Germans were vehemently opposed.

Although wielding absolutely no power, the SI has undoubtedly established itself as a major voice in today's international arena. Its opinions matter; its pronouncements have the weight of moral suasion. Lastly, its success can also be measured comparatively, in that it is the only party international that enjoys worldwide attention. Most certainly this cannot be said of the Christian democratic/conservative, liberal, or communist internationals that exist in nearly total obscurity.

(See also CHRISTIAN DEMOCRACY; LENINISM; SOCIALISM AND SOCIAL DEMOCRACY.)

Karl-Ludwig Günsche and Klaus Lantermann, *Kleine Geschichte der Sozialistischen Internationale* (Bonn, 1977). Rolf Steininger, *Deutschland und die Internationale nach dem Zweiten Weltkrieg* (Bonn, 1979). Wolfgang Höpker,

Sozialistische Internationale: Aufschluß über eine unbekannte Größe (Zurich, 1982). Hugues Portelli, ed., *L'Internationale Socialiste* (Paris, 1983).

ANDREI S. MARKOVITS

SOCIAL MARKET ECONOMY. The social market economy (*soziale Marktwirtschaft* in German) is the term used to describe the set of economic policies in the post–World War II Federal Republic of *Germany (FRG). It drew its intellectual origins from the Economics Department of the University of Freiburg during the 1920s and 1930s as well as from Christian social and economic teachings characteristic of the European Catholic church. The most well-known Freiburg School theorists and practitioners of the social market economy were Wilhelm Röpke, Walter Eucken, Egon Tuchtfeldt, Ludwig Erhard, and Alfred Müller-Armack. The social market economy is often considered the linchpin in the rapid economic growth of the FRG during the 1950s and early 1960s, the period also known as the *Wirtschaftswunder* (Economic Miracle). These social market principles have also continued to shape German economic policy during the 1970s, 1980s, and 1990s.

The social market economy is sometimes referred to as simply a combination of free market economy with a considerable layer of social benefits. In reality, this set of economic policies is more complex; just situating it on a continuum between laissez-faire and state-centered policies does not do justice to the concept. In fact, its authors wanted a set of economic policies that sidestepped the shortcomings of Nazism, communism, laissez-faire, and the post–World War II set of Keynesian policies. Specifically, the primary principle behind the social market economy is one of a market system, but one in which the market is organized by a comprehensive framework that defines the boundaries of competition. Moreover, these framing policies produce a stable set of market policies that are implemented by coordination among public and private sector actors and improve—not impede—economic competitiveness. The social market economy does not lie "halfway between state and market," but represents a qualitatively different approach.

The "social" component of the social market economy also differs from those of other countries. Although the FRG has always been generous with benefits, they serve more than just distributive income transfer purposes. For example, two of the most important provisions, government savings subsidies to individuals and a comprehensive vocational education system, have direct and positive benefits for the competitiveness of the German economy.

The best way to convey the vision of the social market economy may be through the words of one of its founders, Wilhelm Röpke:

[Our program] consists of measures and institutions which impart to competition the framework, rules, and machinery of impartial supervision which a competitive system needs

as much as any game or match if it is not to degenerate into a vulgar brawl. A genuine, equitable, and smoothly functioning competitive system can not in fact survive without a judicious moral and legal framework and without regular supervision of the conditions under which competition can take place pursuant to real efficiency principles. This presupposes mature economic discernment on the part of all responsible bodies and individuals and a strong impartial state. ("The Guiding Principles of the Liberal Programme," in Horst Friedrich Wünche, ed., *Standard Texts on the Social Market Economy*, p. 188.)

(See also KEYNESIANISM; POLITICAL ECONOMY; WELFARE STATE.)

Horst Friedrich Wünche, ed., *Standard Texts on the Social Market Economy* (Stuttgart and New York, 1982).

CHRISTOPHER S. ALLEN

SOCIAL MOBILITY. Societies in the modern world are divided into social classes that rank people according to the *power, privileges, and prestige that they have. Whereas the number and kinds of social classes in a society change little over time, the membership in those social classes does change. Social mobility is the movement of some people from one social *class to another. Mobility can be upward or downward along society's rank ordering. Some socially mobile people move up from underprivileged classes to privileged ones; others move down from more to less privileged classes. People whose social class position remains the same over time are immobile.

The rates of upward and downward mobility reflect both opportunity and inequality in society. Opportunity fosters mobility by creating more professional and managerial positions that can be filled by upward mobility. *Equality fosters mobility by allowing the higher and lower classes to compete equally for whatever positions opportunity has created. Societies with few opportunities and much inequality have low rates of both upward and downward mobility. The privileged and the poor are locked into their social class positions throughout their lives, and children grow up to inherit the privilege or poverty of their parents.

Many Americans think of the United States as a country with more opportunity and equality than others have. Since the 1950s researchers have sought to test that perception by comparing mobility rates in the United States with mobility rates in other industrial societies. Early comparisons by researchers such as Seymour Martin Lipset and Reinhard Bendix found no evidence of "American exceptionalism." Later comparisons, based on data from the 1970s, also found few differences between the United States and other industrial societies.

Although the question of cross-national differences has been leading to consensus, other work has shown that mobility patterns in the United States have changed substantially. Opportunity and equality increased rapidly between 1962 and 1973. Since the stagflation of 1975–1982, however, opportunity has ceased to be a major source of upward mobility. Equality has continued to contribute to mobility throughout that period, however. One important measure of inequality—the strength of the statistical association between a person's social class while growing up and his or her social class as an adult—decreased fifty percent between 1962 and 1985. This is a dramatic and unprecedented change over roughly twenty years. Shrinking inequality (growing equality) in the United States reflects the expansion of higher education between 1955 and 1975. The future of mobility in the United States is uncertain because some measures of participation in higher education among poor and working-class youths show that conditions worsened between 1975 and 1990.

*African Americans had a very distinctive pattern of blocked social mobility up until 1962. African-American families that succeeded in accumulating some advantages during one generation could not pass them on to succeeding generations the way white families could. This pattern exacerbated the effects of discrimination and poverty. Since the mid-1960s, mobility patterns among African-American families have become more like those of white families, increasing the social distance between the African-American middle class and *underclass and at the same time reducing the social distance between African-American and white middle classes.

*Gender is not a major factor in social mobility. Despite vast (but shrinking) differences between men's and women's labor force participation and their representation in many occupations, the social distance between two women of one social class and another is the same as the social distance between two men of those same classes.

Public policy is rarely focused on enhancing social mobility directly. Some policies advance opportunity; others foster equality. Indirectly they create mobility. Case studies of public policy in Sweden and Hungary show two dramatically different approaches to opportunity and equality that have affected mobility. In Sweden, social democratic programs to promote equality have been largely successful. They have resulted in a lower association between social class background and adult social class in Sweden than anywhere else that has been studied closely. In Hungary, a politically motivated policy of advancing the children of the working class (favored by the Communist leadership) dramatically reduced the association between class background and adult social class between 1956 and 1973. The U.S. case shows the consequences of far more diffuse state-level policies. Despite a near-absence of federal policies designed to promote social mobility, support for public higher education in most large states contributed to the fifty percent reduction in inequality of mobility chances between 1962 and 1985.

Robert Erikson and John H. Goldthorpe, "Commonality and Variation in Social Mobility in Industrial Nations" (Parts I and II) *European Sociological Review* 3 (1987): 54–77, 145–66. Michael Hout, "Expanding Universalism, Less Structural Mobility: The American Occupational Structure in the 1980s" *American Journal of Sociology* 93 (1988): 1358–1400.

MICHAEL HOUT

SOCIAL MOVEMENTS. See CIVIL RIGHTS MOVEMENT; LABOR MOVEMENT; NEW SOCIAL MOVEMENTS.

SOCIAL POLICY; SOCIAL SECURITY; SOCIAL WELFARE. See WELFARE STATE.

SOLIDARITY. With its coordination of a mass workers' movement in *Poland against a putative workers' state and its crucial role in facilitating the collapse of communist systems in Eastern Europe, Solidarity is rightly regarded as one of the most important and innovative social movements of the twentieth century. It began as a trade union movement in August 1980, when Polish workers (particularly in large industries like shipbuilding and steel) staged massive strikes protesting price increases and demanding the right to form trade unions independent of state and Communist Party control. When general strikes in Gdańsk and Szczecin threatened to engulf the entire country, the government, already weakened by a severe economic crisis, capitulated and signed the Gdańsk Accord on 31 August, legalizing independent union activity. On 17 September, activists nationwide voted to create the "independent self-governing trade union 'Solidarity,' " led by Lech *Wałęsa of Gdańsk.

Solidarity survived as a legal trade union and social movement until December 1981, when state authorities declared martial law and outlawed Solidarity. Nevertheless the organization retained a powerful hold on the popular imagination, and, in 1989, as the government faced new economic difficulties and new social protests, the authorities negotiated a power-sharing deal with the former union leaders. Elections intended to sanction the deal, however, showed so little support for the Communist Party that Solidarity representatives themselves formed a government in September 1989, a development that helped trigger the collapse of *Communist Party states throughout Eastern and *Central Europe over the next few months.

Solidarity has been interpreted variously as a militant trade union, a *new social movement, a democratic political opposition, and a Catholic fundamentalist movement for national revival—and in some sense it was all of these things, for so many people with so many different views joined Solidarity. "State vs. society" is how both Solidarity *and* the government spoke of the conflict in 1980–1981, and although such language is a sociologist's nightmare, it revealed the unusual set of social cleavages produced by communist government. By nationalizing all industry and controlling social life, the ruling party made employees out of virtually the entire population. And nearly 10 million of these employees joined the union, including skilled workers, manual laborers, teachers, doctors, lawyers, engineers, even storekeepers. Whereas in market societies citizens can strive to improve their own conditions at the expense of others (as in the capital-labor relationship), in communist society all claims are directed only against the state. And so these disparate social groups all entered Solidarity, which promised to vigorously defend their interests before a common employer.

But while workers dominated the union numerically, they did not always do so politically. For insofar as Poland was also a political monopoly, all political oppositions entered Solidarity too, as the only legal institution, besides the Catholic church, with a right to present an alternative vision of a just social order. The interconnectedness of politics and economics in communist society thus had two important consequences: it made Solidarity much larger than it would have been in a market society (indeed, in the new conditions of the early 1990s, Solidarity had about one-fourth the members of 1981); and it made it impossible for Solidarity to be a trade union alone, for when the employer is the state, every economic strike is necessarily a political strike as well.

In its first months, Solidarity *tried* to be a simple trade union, seeking basic gains for its members, such as wage increases and reduced working time, and leaving "politics" to the state. Yet it quickly became clear that Solidarity's very existence threw the entire system into crisis. A planned economy cannot function when an independent union asserts workers' interests irrespective of plan provisions, and a single-party government cannot effectively govern when the majority of citizens speak freely and publicly against it. Solidarity therefore had no choice but to become a political opposition movement. Although many tendencies competed for influence, the dominant line at the national level was a rather moderate one. At the same time that it supported a fully democratic system, the national leadership did not fail to recognize geopolitical realities (possible Soviet intervention). Thus it proposed only a neocorporatist power-sharing arrangement whereby Solidarity would uphold the party's right to hold state power in return for governmental guarantees of Solidarity's right to determine key areas of social policy.

Solidarity also exhibited a profound moral dimension, which played itself out in two different ways. For some, particularly radical intellectuals, Solidarity was above all a new social movement whose primary aim was neither to defend workers' interests nor to win state power, but to build a vibrant civil society with an active citizenry and a flourishing public sphere. The early days of Solidarity most closely approximated this vision, as embodied in the union's original password, *podmiotowość,* meaning *citizenship, autonomy, self-determination, and dignity, all rolled into one.

For others, however, Solidarity's moral mission meant making Poland a true Catholic country. This nationalist-fundamentalist tendency became increasingly strong, particularly in poorer industrial areas, in the second half of 1981, when political and economic reform appeared stalled. Scorning "compromises with Communists" and "phony geopolitical constraints," this tendency in Solidarity, harking back to the prewar era, demanded free elections to oust the Communists and favored a clericalization of public life.

The government imposed martial law in December 1981 ("to protect the country from anarchy"), and Solidarity was driven underground. But with political stalemate continuing to paralyze the country, the party declared a general amnesty in 1986 and cautiously renewed ties with Solidarity. The party now favored market reform but lacked the *legitimacy needed to implement it. Solidarity, meanwhile, now also favored the introduction of radical market reform, and it alone did have legitimacy. The basis of the neocorporatist deal began to reappear. After a series of wildcat strikes in 1988 threatened to overtake both the government *and* Solidarity, the two sides convened roundtable talks in early 1989 and struck the deal that led to parliamentary elections, a Solidarity government, and proof to other Eastern Europeans that the Soviets would no longer intervene to keep Communist parties in power.

In the end, Solidarity led a *sui generis* *revolution: nonviolent, evolutionary, but leading to a radical change in government and economic policy. Although "*socialism" was rejected in favor of "*capitalism," many collectivist values persisted, as can be seen in Solidarity's desires that capitalism be beneficial to all and that the state still intervene to make life better. Solidarity therefore leaves a very rich and diverse legacy, having proved that state socialism could be radically transformed without violent revolution.

Its role for the future is very uncertain. By 1990 the political groups that emerged from Solidarity ceased being directly associated with the union, particularly after Lech Wałęsa was elected president in December. Solidarity became a trade union again, albeit one that claims to support both radical market reform and the defense of workers' interests. No other workers' organization has managed to do this, particularly during austere economic times such as lie ahead for Poland, and thus it is likely that Solidarity will continue to fragment in the years ahead.

(See also CORPORATISM; NINETEEN EIGHTY-NINE; ONE-PARTY SYSTEM; RELIGION AND POLITICS; ROMAN CATHOLIC CHURCH.)

Timothy Garton Ash, *The Polish Revolution* (New York, 1983). Abraham Brumberg, ed., *Poland: Genesis of a Revolution* (New York, 1983). David Ost, *Solidarity and the Politics of Anti-Politics* (Philadelphia, 1990). Lawrence Goodwyn, *Breaking the Barrier: The Rise of Solidarność in Poland* (New York, 1991). Michael D. Kennedy, *Professionals, Power and Solidarity in Poland* (Cambridge, U.K., 1991).

DAVID OST

SOLOMON ISLANDS. See PACIFIC ISLANDS.

SOLZHENITSYN, Aleksandr. Born in Kislovodsk in the southern Caucasus region of Russia on 11 December 1918, Aleksandr Solzhenitsyn was educated in mathematics and literature, and during his years in college he also became a Marxist and joined the Communist Party. After the German invasion in 1941, Solzhenitsyn entered the Red Army, where he became a battery commander and a captain in the artillery. But he was arrested near the end of the war and charged with "anti-Soviet agitation and propaganda" and "the founding of a hostile organization." The principal evidence against him was a series of letters he had written from the front in which he alluded critically to *Stalin and proposed establishing a political party to oppose the Communists. He received an eight-year term in the Soviet gulag—an experience that inspired all his subsequent creative work.

After Stalin's death in 1952, Solzhenitsyn was soon released and permitted to live in Ryazan, where he taught physics in a high school and devoted himself to writing. His first published work, *One Day in the Life of Ivan Denisovich*, landed like a bombshell in Soviet society. Nikita *Khrushchev read the novella and gave his personal approval for it to appear in November 1962. The story captured the world's attention, as did Solzhenitsyn's subsequent novels, most notably *Cancer Ward* and *The First Circle*, which, like *Ivan Denisovich,* are autobiographical treatments of his years as a prisoner under Stalin.

In the 1960s, Solzhenitsyn was closely identified with exposing the full truth of Stalin's extensive labor camp system and with attempts to challenge the Kremlin's harsh censorship of literature. As a result of this defiance, Solzhenitsyn was expelled from the Union of Soviet Writers in 1969. A year later, he was awarded the Nobel Prize for literature.

By that time, a small but vigorous *human rights movement was emerging inside the Soviet Union. One of its leading figures was the physicist Andrei Sakharov, with whom Solzhenitsyn was often linked in the eyes of the West. But in 1973 Solzhenitsyn published "Letter to the Soviet Leaders." This long essay, together with subsequent public statements, made clear that Solzhenitsyn, unlike Sakharov and many other dissidents, had no use for *parliamentary democracy or political parties. Solzhenitsyn's ideas resembled the views of the nineteenth-century

Russian Slavophiles, who opposed serfdom and other such harsh dimensions of tsarist autocracy but also mistrusted Western forms of government.

In February 1974, Aleksandr Solzhenitsyn was arrested and charged with treason for his book *The Gulag Archipelago,* a mammoth account of Stalin's labor camp system. He was immediately expelled from the Soviet Union and deprived of his *citizenship. With his family, Solzhenitsyn soon moved from Europe to Vermont, where he has lived a secluded existence, concentrating on a cycle of novels about *World War I and the Bolshevik revolution.

Under Mikhail *Gorbachev, all of Solzhenitsyn's works were published in the Soviet Union and his citizenship was restored. His unique status in Soviet society was confirmed on 18 September 1990, when two Soviet newspapers, with a combined circulation of more than 22 million readers, published his long essay *Rebuilding Russia: Toward Some Formulations* (New York, 1991). With characteristic eloquence and anger, Solzhenitsyn denounced the Soviet regime for bringing catastrophe onto the country. And he repeated his mistrust of a Western parliamentary system. He then urged the breakup of the Soviet Union—the secession of eleven of fifteen republics. Solzhenitsyn contended that a new, more vigorous Russian state, made up of the Ukraine, White Russia, Russia proper, and the northern portion of Kazakhstan—which is heavily populated by people of Russian origin and where Solzhenitsyn himself spent three years in exile—could then emerge.

Solzhenitsyn's ideas were debated in the Soviet media for several weeks. Although Mikhail Gorbachev publicly acknowledged Solzhenitsyn "to be a great man," he concluded that Solzhenitsyn was "immersed in the past." During the Gorbachev era, Solzhenitsyn accepted the end of the Soviet Union's imperial claims. Even before the dissolution of the Soviet Union, however, he considered his country to be more Russia than the Soviet Union, and believed it had little to gain from contact with the West.

(See also SOVIET DISSENT.)

Michael Scammell, *Solzhenitsyn* (New York, 1984).

JOSHUA RUBENSTEIN

SOMALIA. Situated at the extreme corner of northeastern Africa, contemporary Somalia is a direct product of European colonialism during the second half of the nineteenth century. Prior to this, and over many centuries, the highly homogeneous pastoral Somalis had roamed, with their livestock, the breadth of the *Horn of Africa. This autonomy was undermined with the inception of British rule over northern Somalia (as the Somaliland Protectorate) in 1886 and Italian claims over southern Somalia in 1905. The French established their own colony (French Somaliland) in 1888; Ethiopia was ceded the Ogaden in 1897; and, later, the Northern Frontier District became part of colonial Kenya.

This trauma of partition ignited Somali indignation. However, before a common counterattack could be marshaled, Somalis of the region, notwithstanding their one language, one religion (*Islam), and one ethnic base, had to overcome two factors: the disparate nature of a pastoral way of life and the absence of any measure of collective consciousness.

A source of inspiration for the Somali response to colonialism was sought primarily in Islam and secondarily in the extension of kinship to include all Somalis—a form of protonationalism. Basing his cause on the concept of *jihad (disciplined and millenarian struggle against "infidels"), a fiery and poetically gifted Sayyid Muhammad Abdille Hassan led twenty years of fierce resistance to colonial rule, particularly by the British and Ethhiopians. In the end, however, his forces were defeated.

With the conclusion of World War II, a new spirit of Somali nationalism came to the force. The vectors for this revival were anticolonial organizations such as the Somali Youth League (SYL) and the Somali National League (SNL), established in 1945 and 1947 respectively. The collaborative agitation of these two organizations and other smaller ones culminated in independence for British Somaliland on 26 June 1960. Five days later, on 1 July, British Somaliland joined southern Somalia to become the new nation of the Somali Republic. In one of the first acts of union, representatives of the two regions elected Aden Abdille Osman, a key figure in Italian Somaliland politics, as the new president.

The Somali Republic began its new political life as a multiparty parliamentary state. Abdulrashid Ali Sharmarke, a leading member of the SYL, was sworn in as the first prime minister. But this initiation of democratic institutions was soon undercut by the weight of a weak civil society, tension between northerners and southerners over the new dispensation, a border war with Ethiopia in 1964, and the overall frailty of the Somali economy. This created a situation among political elites where high premiums were put on securing a strategic position in the postcolonial state.

In the general elections of 1964, eighteen parties took part, with the SYL emerging as the majority party. Sharmarke was replaced as prime minister by A. H. Hussein. The Hussein government lasted until 1967, when President Osman lost his bid for reelection to Sharmarke. Somalia descended deeper into corruption and bickering among its state elite, resulting in more than 65 parties competing for 122 seats in the 1969 parliamentary elections. This process came to a halt on 15 October 1969 with the assassination of Sharmarke. Six days later, the armed forces stepped in, bringing to a close Somalia's experience with electoral, multiparty politics.

The new military government, named the Supreme Revolutionary Council (SRC), dismissed the Parliament, banned political parties, canceled the 1960 constitution, and promised, among other things, a rejuvenation of democracy in the near future. Chaired by the senior member of the military, Major General Siyad Barre, the SRC renamed the country the Somali Democratic Republic, with socialism as its official ideology. Despite some notable accomplishments (e.g., the development of an official orthography for the Somali language), after six years of unilateral rule the SRC came under pressure from its main patron, the Soviet Union, to enlarge its political base. In July 1976, the Somali Revolutionary Socialist Party was proclaimed with Barre as secretary general. Whatever the form of government, however, Somalia faced increasing economic pressures.

The most fundamental and immediate element of Somali material life is the harshness of its ecological base. The climate is arid to semiarid, with annual precipitation of less than 430 millimeters (17 in.) a year and less than thirteen percent of the land (about 8 million hectares, or about 19.75 million acres) suitable for agriculture and farming. This Sahelian environment is deteriorating fast, with severe droughts expected about every eight years.

Somalia's economy is a hybrid. Much like the postcolonial state itself, this is a consequence of a continuing clash between an ancient and indigenous kin-based production and trade system and the commodity-ordered world economy. Pastoralism is consistent with reciprocal social systems in which production, despite its austere nature, is essentially organized for collective consumption. The commodity-ordered economy is driven by a very different logic of exchange and private control and use of resources. The articulation of these two systems has created an asymmetric relationship in which the indigenous economy has underwritten the modern sector, including the state, and continues to do so. About sixty percent of Somalia's population earn their living by raising livestock, which in turn contributes over eighty percent of the country's exports. The agricultural sector, the second largest, suffers from neglect. Of the available productive land, less than ten percent is under cultivation, and most of this is being appropriated by the ruling elite and foreign concerns. Development expenditures for the rural economy have not surpassed twenty percent of total government allocations, whereas security and general administration costs usually claim well over seventy percent. Funds for loans and credit have overwhelmingly gone to a small cluster of traders who dominate the export/import market.

In short, a worsening ecological foundation, inadequate investment in productive sectors, a rising birthrate, unwise and bloated state expenditures, an inauspicious international order, and a rising debt burden have created harrowing circumstances for most Somalis. Average living standards continue to decline while Somalia's dependency has deepened to the extent that virtually all development funds and nearly half of the government's annual budget come from external donors. All of these limiting conditions are exacerbated by two other factors with long-term consequences: war with Ethiopia and the conditions for more loans set by the *International Monetary Fund (IMF). The war, which took place in 1977–1978, cost thousands of lives, left behind many displaced people, and skewed the political economy toward militarism. The direct hostilities between the two states have subsided since the signing of a nonaggression treaty in 1988. One outcome of the war was the change in patrons from the Soviet Union to the United States. IMF interventions started in the early 1980s. These liberalizing and reform policies have generated some growth (particularly in agriculture) but have also induced inflation (over 300 percent), the decay or disappearance of social services, growing unemployment, and immiseration.

The most critical issue in contemporary Somali political economy is the intensifying combat over the state. A new threshold of confrontation was reached in the summer of 1988, when insurgents of the Somali National Movement (SNM) attacked Hargeysa, the regional capital of the north, and other settlements. More than 30,000 people are reported to have died and nearly 400,000 civilians sought refuge across the border in Ethiopia. These clashes soon spread to southern Somalia. By January 1991, Mogadishu exploded. After fierce fighting for three weeks, Siyad Barre and his regime collapsed. SNM forces moved into northern Somalia, forming an independent state. In the south, internecine wars competed with the replacement of Barre as the most critical issue.

The Somali conflict is essentially a contest among Somali *elites over the most coveted of all national institutions, the state. However, this intraclass struggle is interlaced with clannish loyalties. Such a complication renders the construction of a national front elusive. Somalia approaches the end of the twentieth century with very few friends, while it descends deeper into fragmentation, general pauperism, and mutual predacity.

I. M. Lewis, *A Pastoral Democracy: A Study of Pastoralism and Politics Among the Northern Somali of the Horn* (Oxford, 1961). Saadia Touval, *Somali Nationalism: International Politics and the Drive for Unity in the Horn of Africa* (Cambridge, 1963). Said S. Samatar, *Oral Poetry and Somali Nationalism: The Case of Sayyid Mohamed Abdille Hassan* (Cambridge, 1982). A. I. Samatar, *Socialist Somalia: Rhetoric and Reality* (London, 1988). Abdi I. Samatar, *The State and Rural Transformation in Northern Somalia, 1884–1986* (Madison, Wis., 1989).

AHMED I. SAMATAR

SOUTH AFRICA. Since white settlers came to South Africa in 1652, and especially following the constitution of the Union of South Africa in 1910 as a white dominion in the British Empire, the maintenance of whites as a dominant estate exploiting black labor has been the first priority of what is called South Africa's Native Policy. There are other aims as well, such as mediation and adjustment of the differences between English and Afrikaners, be-

tween white workers and their employers, and between mining and farming interests, but these contradictions are pursued in the context of the major goal, which is "making South Africa a white man's country."

The population of South Africa is made up of 28 million Africans, 5.4 million whites (2.9 million Afrikaners, 2.5 million English and other whites), 3.2 million colored, and 1 million Asian Indians. The official languages are English and Afrikaans; Zulu, Xhosa, north and south se-Sotho, and se-Tswana are spoken widely by Africans. Christianity is the dominant religion, with Hinduism, Islam, Judaism, and traditional African practices also observed.

The spirit out of which the Native Policy was born is inherent in the nature of settler colonization and the priorities of South Africa's capitalist development. A succession of laws was instrumental to the formation of a white minority regime and the systematic exclusion and exploitation of blacks. The Mines and Works Act of 1911 excluded blacks from all skilled jobs in the mining industry. The 1913 Land Act imposed territorial segregation in a way that eliminated African farmers as competitors with white farmers while at the same time it increased landlessness among African *peasants and thus increased the supply of labor to the mines and white farms. Under the terms of the act, eighty-seven percent of South Africa was declared a "white area" and the remaining thirteen percent African. The Native Affairs Act of 1920 set up segregation in local government for "natives" and, by creating the Native Affairs Commission, emphasized the fact that Africans were a "separate community." The Native Urban Areas Act of 1923 established the principle of residential segregation in cities and towns. The Native Taxation and Development Act of 1927 instituted a "segregation in revenues"; the Immorality Act of 1926 "imposed criminal sanctions against what G. Heaton Nichols called 'the unwritten law of vital segregation' "; the Native Administration Act of 1927 "ensured segregation in the administration of the law"; and, finally, the 1936 Representation of Natives Act and the Native Land Act removed African voters from the common roll in the Cape and, as an alternative, gave seven white representatives in the House of Assembly the power to vote on measures affecting Africans only. These measures, according the the Native Affairs Commission, supplemented by the amendment to the Urban Areas Act, "completed the legislative plan." These laws constitute the essence of the policy of segregation rooted in the fact of conquest.

In 1948 the National Party, led by Dr. D. F. Malan, a minister in the Dutch Reformed Church, won the election in a campaign that not only introduced *apartheid as a new slogan but emphasized the danger that postwar *decolonization represented to the white minority. For the first time since union,

Afrikaners had an exclusive hold on the South African state. In the next forty years South Africa experienced a major counterrevolution, as state power was increasingly turned against any opposition to white domination. In the process, every legal norm was trampled underfoot as the regime assumed extraordinary powers to enforce its will. It summoned anticommunist hysteria in reversing, by legislation and penal sanctions, those processes of an industrializing society that put black and white in a position of social equality.

In 1960, following the *Sharpeville Massacre, the *African National Congress, formed in 1912 to unify African people who were not represented in the newly created union, and the Pan Africanist Congress (PAC) were banned. The apartheid laws covered every aspect of social life and closed every loophole that could be used as "a thin edge of the wedge" to undermine white minority rule. A long series of laws defined apartheid, including the Prohibition of Mixed Marriages Act (1949), forbidding marriage between "a European and a non-European," and the Immorality Act of 1950 (amended in 1957), which criminalized sexual relations or any "immoral or indecent act" between black and white persons. Faced with international abhorrence of apartheid, the regime abolished the two acts in June 1985 and thus could claim that apartheid was "dead." The Population Registration Act of 1950 froze South African "racial" divisions by establishing three classifications: white, colored, and native. The act set forth who belonged to which "race" and the community was set as arbitrator; that is, if the community accepted a person as "white," the person was to be categorized as "white."

In 1950 the Suppression of Communism Act became law. The definition of communism was so broad as to make criminal any challenge to white supremacy. The Group Areas Act of 1950 imposed residential segregation in cities and affected mostly coloreds and Indians. Thus, the National regime eliminated all vestiges of black franchise and self-determination. To crown their victory, in 1961 the Republic of South Africa Act established South Africa as a republic outside the *Commonwealth. By 1970 apartheid had codified racism into an elaborate and rigid infrastructure which seemed all but impregnable.

In 1969 the premier role of the National Party was challenged by the appearance on the political scene of a new party, the reconstituted (Herstige) National Party led by Dr. Albert Hertzog, son of General Hertzog, who controlled several well-endowed funds entrusted to him in the 1930s for the furtherance of the Afrikaner cause. In 1983, the Conservative Party led by Dr. Treurnicht, who defected with seventeen other National MPs, joined in opposing the National Party. These are extremist parties which viewed Prime Minister Vorster, who succeeded Dr. Verwoerd after the latter had been assassinated as a "liberal" who was leading Afrikanerdom down the river.

The crisis of Afrikanerdom was accelerated in 1970–1980 by the collapse of Portuguese colonization in Mozambique and *Angola in 1975, the creation of an independent *Zimbabwe in 1980, the escalating conflict in *Namibia (which became independent in March 1990), the *Soweto uprising of 1976, and the escalating struggle waged by Umkhonto Wesizwe (the armed wing of the ANC), mass resistance organized by the United Democratic Front, and working-class resistance that began in Durban in 1972–1973, continuing to the formation of the Congress of South African Trade Unions. Added to this was growing international isolation and pressure to change. In the late 1970s the regime appointed a series of commissions (Schlebush, Riekert, Wiehahn) whose conclusions paved the way for the abortive reform strategy of the early 1980s.

The *reform strategy included several developments. The Presidential Council gave dictatorial powers to the executive presidency in case of a stalemate. Preferential treatment in jobs was also granted to Africans in urban areas and in the Bantu homelands where Africans were expected to have *citizenship. It was to oppose the attempt to divorce coloreds and Indians from Africans that the United Democratic Front was formed. The popular revolt that swept the country from 1984 to 1986 marked a watershed in the long history of African resistance. The state of emergency imposed in 1985 and suspended in June 1990, except in Natal, failed to suppress the uprising.

The cumulative effect of the popular masses, combined with external pressures (for instance, the defeat of South Africa's expeditionary forces in Angola, and the imposition of *sanctions by the *European Community and the U.S. *Congress) convinced sections of the National Party that it was time to negotiate. Despite Pretoria's attempt to play down the impact of sanctions, the effects of sanctions and divestment are being felt. The South African economy is suffering from a rapidly shrinking trade surplus. The value of the rand declined by more than two-thirds between 1985 and 1990, consumers suffer from higher interest rates, and defense expenditures are increasing. All this combines to reveal the fragility of the economy.

The Conservative Party, which broke away from the National Party in 1982 over Botha's plan to create a tricameral power-sharing plan with coloreds and Indians, has grown in strength, and in the whites-only election of 1987 it polled over thirty percent, while the "left-wing" Democratic Party, led by Wynand Malan, another National Party MP, won twenty-two percent. The Conservative Party relies for its support on blue-collar working people, farmers, the lower echelons of the civil service, the police and the army. Many downwardly mobile Afrikaners who find themselves squeezed by inflation and black competition have abandoned the National Party, which in 1948 could claim to be the standard-bearer of all Afrikaners. This means that the National Party no longer represents the Afrikaner bloc. In this respect, it resembles the United Party, which, when the coalition it formed with middle-class English voters could no longer hold, lost power to the National Party in 1948.

The release of Walter Sisulu and his compatriots in September 1989 and de Klerk's announcement, on 1 February 1990, of the release of Nelson *Mandela on 11 February 1990, along with the lifting of the thirty-year ban on the ANC and other organizations, opened the way for three days of talks in May 1990 and enhanced the prospect for fundamental political change. The talks reflected how the white minority regime had come to the realization that the ANC could not be wished away. At the start of the 1990s, South Africa was witnessing the rise of an armed right-wing movement—the Afrikaner Resistance Movement, which wears swastika-like symbols—on the white side, and, on the African side, the upsurge of the Mass Democratic Movement organizing strikes and protest marches. Amid much-heralded efforts for a negotiated transition to majority rule, processes of political polarization proceed unabated.

(See also DISINVESTMENT; RACE AND RACISM; SOUTHERN AFRICA.)

Brian Bunting, *The Rise of the South African Reich* (London, 1969). H. J. Simons and R. Simons, *Race and Class in South Africa, 1850–1950* (London, 1969). John W. Cell, *The Highest Stage of White Supremacy: The Origins of Segregation in South Africa and the American South* (New York, 1982). T. R. H. Davenport, *South Africa: A Modern History,* 3d ed. (Cambridge, U.K., 1987). Bernard Magubane, *The Political Economy of Race and Class in South Africa,* 2d ed. (New York, 1990).

BERNARD MAGUBANE

SOUTH ASIAN ASSOCIATION FOR REGIONAL COOPERATION.
The South Asian Association for Regional Cooperation (SAARC) was instituted in December 1985 primarily as a vehicle for evolving a viable economic order in the region. Recognizing the necessity of delinking South Asia's political conflict from the process of economic cooperation, its seven member states—Bangladesh, Bhutan, India, Maldives, Nepal, Pakistan, and Sri Lanka—adopted the principle of unanimity in selecting multilateral questions for debate. Nevertheless, the course of socioeconomic progress in the region has remained hostage to South Asia's turbulent political history and prevalent interstate tensions that are frequently fueled by traditional hostilities.

The association's inception is, in itself, unique given the extreme volatility of the South Asian geopolitical environment. India's bilateral disputes with Pakistan, Sri Lanka, Bangladesh, and Nepal, coupled with its formidable size, population, industrial output, technological capability, and overall power potential, have created an atmosphere of suspicion and distrust regarding its regional role. Such negative strategic perceptions are compounded by South Asia's cultural, ideological, and ethnic heterogeneity. However, despite its vulnerability to regional politics, the association has inadvertently provided an informal, but crucial service: a forum for mitigating the very conflicts that threaten to disrupt its functioning.

Progress toward realistic socioeconomic goals via the SAARC process has been limited despite frequent consultative committee meetings. It may be too early, however, to evaluate the success of SAARC in promoting regional economic prosperity. Nevertheless, it is clear that the future of SAARC will be bleak if the member states do not transcend their political differences in the interest of forging the promised new regional economic alliance.

Rasul B. Rais, "Politics of Regional Cooperation in South Asia" *Journal of South Asian and Middle Eastern Studies* 11, no. 3 (Spring 1989): 57–72.

SUDESHNA BAKSI-LAHIRI

SOUTHEAST ASIA TREATY ORGANIZATION.
The French defeat and withdrawal from Indochina in 1954, following in the wake of the 1949 communist victory in China, led to greater U.S. involvement in the security affairs of Southeast Asia. One result of this was the South-East Asia Collective Defense Treaty, signed in Manila, the Philippines, on 8 September 1954, by Australia, France, New Zealand, Pakistan, the Philippines, Thailand, Britain, and the United States. This treaty served as the basis for the Southeast Asia Treaty Organization (SEATO). Headquartered in Bangkok, Thailand, SEATO was designed to be one of a series of military treaties initiated by U.S. Secretary of State John Foster Dulles to contain communist expansion. The main geographic focus was Vietnam, Cambodia, and Laos, which, although not signatories, were included under a separate protocol. A separate U.S. understanding limited the treaty to communist aggression, excluding many of the other conflicts relevant to the member states.

SEATO served as an umbrella for, but not as an active participant in, the U.S. involvement in the Vietnam War up to 1973. This was due in part to disagreements among the Western members concerning the conduct of the war, but also to the treaty's focus on conventional forms of military threat. SEATO only slowly developed an explicit focus on counterinsurgency techniques, which were applied largely in Thailand and the Philippines. A program of economic assistance to its members was the major significance of SEATO, but its effect on the military *containment of communism can only be judged a failure. Following the U.S. withdrawal from Vietnam in 1973, the economic programs were no longer sufficient to sustain SEATO, and the organization was formally disbanded in June 1977.

Leszek Buszynski, *SEATO: The Failure of an Alliance Strategy* (Singapore, 1983).

DONALD K. CRONE

SOUTHERN AFRICA. A region in Africa which includes the nations of *Angola, Botswana, Lesotho, *Malawi, *Mozambique, *Namibia, *South Africa, Swaziland. *Zambia, and *Zimbabwe, Southern Africa is bordered on the west by the south Atlantic Ocean and east by the Indian Ocean. It includes a territory of 5.8 million square kilometers (2.25 million sq. mi.), or about two-thirds the size of the United States. The population of the region is about 102 million. The ethnic background of the people of Southern Africa is predominantly Bantu. Other groups include whites (Dutch, British, German, Portuguese, Greek, Italian origin), mixed race (Coloureds), Asians (predominantly from India), and Khoisan (or, in colonial usage, Bushmen). The predominant religious affiliations are Christianity (50 percent), traditional African religions (46.5 percent), Hinduism (0.5 percent), and Islam (3 percent).

The region is an important contributor to the world economy. Regional economic growth in 1988 (4.5 percent) exceeded population growth (3.3 percent) for the first time in fifteen years. Among the exports from the region are asbestos, beef, chromium, coffee, cobalt, copper, cotton, coal, corn, crude petroleum, diamonds, fertilizers, fish, gold, hides, iron ore, karakul pelts, livestock, manganese, nickel, platinum, sugar, tea, tobacco, vanadium, and uranium. When taken separately, South Africa dominates the economic picture. It has the strongest and most diversified economy in all of Africa.

The ten countries of the region form a variety of political and economic patterns. The political and economic status of the region has been largely dominated by South Africa and the legacy of colonial domination by white settler regimes in Angola, Mozambique, Zimbabwe, and Namibia. While independence from British colonialism in Botswana, Lesotho, Malawi, Swaziland, and Zambia came by the mid-1960s, other countries in the region fought difficult and protracted struggles for national liberation. The former Portuguese colonies of Mozambique and Angola won their independence in the mid-1970s. Zimbabwe and Namibia fought against the entrenched settler colonial regimes, gaining their independence in 1980 and 1990, respectively. The Frontline States of Angola, Botswana, Mozambique, *Tanzania, Zambia, and Zimbabwe banded together as a political force of support against the forces of colonial domination and as a forum for debate and negotiation.

The *national liberation movements in Mozambique, Angola, Zimbabwe, Namibia, and South Africa gained inspiration from Marxism-Leninism and other socialist ideologies. Many of the new nations have attempted to use the socialist framework as a model for political and economic development during the postcolonial period. The regimes were faced with the challenge of economic *development, providing for the social welfare of the majority population that had been neglected during the colonial period, and weathering efforts at *destabilization by South Africa. It has been difficult for the new nations to initiate new political and economic patterns and therefore socialist development models have not been successful.

In South Africa, political strife has been a continuing feature of the political scene. *Reforms to the system of racial separation (*apartheid) characterized the 1980s and the early 1990s. The release in 1990 of political prisoners such as Nelson *Mandela and thousands of others, the unbanning of African political organizations such as the *African National Congress (ANC) and Pan Africanist Congress (PAC), and the repeal of some apartheid laws bolstered the hopes of the international community that change to the system of racial segregation, repression, and white hegemony in South Africa was imminent.

The peoples of Southern Africa have been united in the common goal of fighting apartheid and the remnants of colonialism in the region. However, as the nations emerge from systems of colonial domination, cleavages based on ethnic background and ideological differences concerning strategies for development have emerged.

There have been challenges to the regimes in Angola, Mozambique, Zambia, and Zimbabwe concerning the concept of *democracy and the one-party state. These challenges have been based on dissatisfaction with the lack of diversity in the political elites. Much of the leadership of the countries of Southern Africa are veterans of the difficult wars of national liberation. Hence, they see themselves as the protectors of those newly won freedoms. The extent that these regimes can open and allow political opposition will determine their viability in the future.

The South African policy of destabilization of the regimes of the independent countries of the region has created a situation of turbulence spawning organizations that have had an adverse effect on stability of the region. Mozambique, Zimbabwe, Angola, Botswana, Lesotho, and Swaziland have all been subject to destabilizing efforts by the South African regime. Organizations such as RENAMO (Mozambique Resistance Movement), UNITA (Angola) and armed bandit groups in Zimbabwe have wreaked havoc in the countries that they have operated in with military support from South Africa. South Africa in the mid-1980s intruded militarily into the territorial space of surrounding independent countries in "hot pursuit" of forces they claimed were threatening its existence.

In the 1990s, the reforms inside South Africa have created a shift of emphasis from destabilizing its neighbors. As South Africa looks inward, the years of war and strife are having considerable effect on the political arenas in the countries of the region. Armed groups that were responsible for destruction and havoc are organizing themselves into political parties that will vie for political power. Challenges to the regimes of Southern Africa will come from those groups that have been South African–inspired, from ethnic divisions and competition, and from groups who challenge the regimes on ideological grounds. To the extent that the regimes are able to provide for the material needs of their populations, the challenges will remain insignificant.

The fate of the region in both economic and political terms holds immense global significance. Several factors account for the significance of the region in the international sphere: the large population, political dynamics, strategic location, and the vast storehouse of important minerals and resources. The countries of Southern Africa have been affected by such factors as the legacy of a long colonial history, economic dependency on South Africa, continued war and strife into the 1990s, and periodic drought. These factors have affected adversely the region's ability to maintain institutions and infrastructure for sustained economic and political development.

As white minority rule is phased out in the region, the peoples of Southern Africa will increasingly turn their attention to the challenges of development in an interdependent world political economy, and their success will say a great deal about the contemporary world order.

(See also BLS STATES; DECOLONIZATION; LENINISM; MARXISM; SOCIALISM AND SOCIAL DEMOCRACY; SOUTHERN AFRICAN DEVELOPMENT CO-ORDINATION CONFERENCE.)

Basil Davidson, *The People's Cause: A History of Guerillas in Africa* (Essex, 1981). Malyn Newitt, *Portugal in Africa: The Last Hundred Years* (Essex, 1981). Ann Seidman, *The Roots of Crisis in Southern Africa* (Trenton, N.J., 1985). Phyllis Johnson and David Martin, *Destructive Engagement: Southern Africa at War* (Harare, 1986). Moeletsi Mbeki, *Profile of Political Conflicts in Southern Africa* (Harare, 1987). Ibrahim Msabaha and T. Shaw, eds., *Confrontation and Liberation in Southern Africa* (Boulder, Colo., 1987). Nzongola-Ntalaja, *Revolution and Counter-Revolution in Africa* (London, 1987). Kevin Shillington, *History of Southern Africa* (London, 1987). John Saul, *Socialist Ideology and the Struggle for Southern Africa* (Trenton, N.J., 1990).

DEBORAH A. SANDERS

SOUTHERN AFRICAN DEVELOPMENT CO-ORDINATION CONFERENCE.

In April 1980, nine independent nations in Southern Africa (Angola, Botswana, Lesotho, Malawi, Mozambique, Swaziland, Tanzania, Zambia, and Zimbabwe) established the Southern African Development Co-ordination Conference (SADCC) with the major objective of decreasing regional economic dependence on South Africa. Other objectives included the reduction of economic dependence in general, the forging of links to create a genuine and equitable

regional integration, the mobilization of resources to promote the implementation of national, interstate, and regional policies, and concerted action to secure international cooperation within the framework of the strategy outline for economic liberation. On independence in 1990, Namibia became the tenth member of the organization.

The strategy adopted by SADCC, the Lusaka Program of Action, involves regional cooperation, designed to enhance the economies of member states through the *development of the major regional sectors: transport and communications; food, agriculture, and natural resources; industry and trade; energy; human resources; mining; and tourism.

With the exception of Botswana and Namibia, the SADCC countries are also members of the Preferential Trade Area for East and Southern Africa (PTA). The major objective of the PTA is to integrate the economies of the subregion. It is argued by both SADCC and non-SADCC officials that there is duplication in the goals and objectives of SADCC and the PTA, especially in the area of intraregional trade.

SADCC has served as a unifying force in the region against apartheid South Africa. Its greatest impact, however, has been political, largely owing to South Africa's policy of regional *destabilization. At the international level, the organization is recognized as an important conduit for regional development and therefore receives most of its economic support from the United States and Western Europe.

Although meetings among various SADCC officials take place throughout the year, the two most important meetings are the annual consultative conference and the annual summit. At the former, SADCC's international cooperating partners meet with SADCC officials to discuss financial pledges to the organization. During the latter, SADCC officials, including the heads of state and government, meet to review the progress from the previous year and make future plans.

The major weakness of the SADCC Program of Action is that while the member states attempted to decrease their economic dependence on South Africa, they became more dependent on the Western industrialized nations. In addition, as a result of South Africa's regional destabilization of major sectors, including transportation, energy, and agriculture, the SADCC member states were hampered in their efforts to circumvent the apartheid regime. For example, the destabilization of the regional transportation network forced SADCC members to continue to use the South African transport system.

This increased *dependency on South Africa, coupled with increased dependency on the West, has meant that no significant progress has been made toward economic structural transformation in the region. There have been gains despite South Africa's regional destabilization, however, especially in the area of transport and communications.

It appears that as long as *apartheid in South

Africa exists, SADCC will not make significant progress toward meeting its objectives. The greatest potential for the organization rests with postapartheid *Southern Africa.

Joseph Hanlon, *SADCC in the 1990s: Development on the Frontline* (London, 1989). Margaret D. Lee, *SADCC: The Political Economy of Development in Southern Africa* (Nashville, 1989).

MARGARET C. LEE

SOUTH KOREA. See KOREA, REPUBLIC OF.

SOUTH PACIFIC. See PACIFIC ISLANDS.

SOUTH-SOUTH COOPERATION. The aim of South-South cooperation is to strengthen economic ties among the developing countries of Africa, Asia, and Latin America by such mechanisms as regional economic integration, mutual trade preferences, *development assistance, direct investment, technical cooperation, and collective bargaining in international economic negotiations. The intention is to reinforce and expand the mutual benefits that can be derived from growing collective self-reliance among the developing and underdeveloped economies of the *Third World. The quest for cooperation has been propelled by the slow overall expansion in South-North trade, growing Northern resistance to Third World industrial and agricultural imports, the creation of trading blocs in Europe and North America which portends new obstacles to Third World exports, and the ineffective North-South dialogue regarding the establishment of a more equitable global economic order. South-South cooperation is seen as a way to stimulate economic growth in Third World countries, while reducing dependency on Northern markets and investment capital and placing Third World countries in a position to take greater control of their economic fortunes.

Despite the difficulties of transforming aspirations into tangible accomplishments, South-South cooperation is a growing reality. Notable achievements have been realized regarding economic integration, joint research and development, the transfer of appropriate technology, food security, agricultural development, transport and communications, transfers of development aid from the capital-surplus Gulf states to debt-burden economies of Africa, and the development of joint negotiating positions. Commitments to South-South cooperation have been reiterated in the current period of rapid international political and economic transformations. Notwithstanding the growth of economic relations among Third World states, however, South-South cooperation has yet to have a marked impact on the overall character of the international economic order. The South remains overwhelmingly dependent on the North for export markets, manufactured goods, commercial and concessionary finance, and access to technology. Moreover, commitment to South-South cooperation must contend with increasing economic differentiation among Third World states, the seemingly intractable Third World debt problem, often intense regional political conflicts and rivalries, and new efforts by competing industrial Northern economies, seeking to position themselves for the twenty-first century, to more fully integrate regions of the developing world into their economic spheres.

The origins of South-South cooperation lie in the coming together of the newly independent African and Asian countries and the developing countries of Latin America in the 1950s and early 1960s to argue for basic reforms in the organization of world trade and finance and to fashion a political stance independent of the *Cold War polarization. Notable among the early regional and interregional conferences that laid the intellectual and political foundations for South-South cooperation were the Afro-Asian Conference, held in Bandung in 1955, the First Summit of Non-Aligned Countries, in Belgrade in 1961, and the Conference on Problems of Developing Countries, in Cairo in 1962. New international institutions emerged. For example, between 1955 and 1964 the *Nonaligned Movement, the *Organization of Petroleum Exporting Countries, the *Group of 77, and the *United Nations Conference on Trade and Development were established as organs for defining and promoting Third World political cooperation and economic development needs and strategies.

The landmark Declaration and Programme of Action on the Establishment of a *New International Economic Order adopted at the UN Sixth Special Session in 1974 provided the impetus for strengthened commitment to South-South cooperation as an integral part of the effort to fundamentally restructure global economic relations. Among the subsequent declarations regarding the importance and substance of South-South cooperation were the Arusha Programme for Collective Self-Reliance and Framework for Negotiations, 1979, the Caracas Programme of Action on Economic Cooperation among Developing Countries, 1981, and the 1988 Mexico City agreement on a Global System of Trade Preferences among Third World countries. These and similar declarations and concrete agreements have sought to strengthen South-South cooperation in the areas of finance, the transfer of technology, preferential trade, food and agriculture production and research, energy, raw materials, and industrialization.

Inspired by the successful examples of the *European Community and the *European Free Trade Association, economic integration among groups of neighboring Third World states is the most prominent feature of South-South cooperation. Subregional and regional free trade and preferential trade associations, common markets, and lake and river basin development arrangements are proliferating. The future promises deepening Third World economic integration. For example, at the 1991 summit of the *Organization of African Unity (OAU) African leaders signed a treaty committing the continent to the establishment of the African Economic Community (AEC), to be achieved in stages over the next three decades. Among current Third World economic integration associations are the Economic Community of West African States (ECOWAS), the *Southern African Development Co-ordination Conference (SADCC), the Preferential Trade Area for Eastern and Southern African States (PTA), the Maghreb Union, the *Association of Southeast Asian Nations (ASEAN), the *South Asian Association for Regional Cooperation (SAARC), the Gulf Cooperation Council (GCC), the Latin American Integration Association (LAIA), and the Caribbean Community (CARICOM).

It deserves reiterating that regardless of the clear and widespread commitment among Third World countries to integrate their economies and to pursue other aspects of South-South cooperation, major obstacles have to be confronted. Increasing economic differentiation within the Third World is making questionable some of the central assumptions underlying South-South cooperation. It is becoming clear, for example, that the trade of the more industrialized Third World countries (the Republic of Korea, Singapore, Brazil) with the majority of primarily agricultural and mineral-extracting developing economies is often as unequal as the North-South trade it is replacing. The heyday of South-South commitment may also have passed. There appears to be a resigned but growing sentiment among many Southern states that in the current era of global economic and political realignments, increasing protectionist pressures, and European and North American economic integration, continued *dependency on the North is to be preferred to the danger of becoming totally marginalized in the evolving world economic and political order.

(See also AFRICAN REGIONAL ORGANIZATIONS; INTERNATIONAL DEBT; LATIN AMERICAN REGIONAL ORGANIZATIONS; NORTH-SOUTH RELATIONS; PROTECTION; TECHNOLOGY TRANSFER.)

Beverly May Carl, *Economic Integration among Developing Nations* (New York, 1986). Jerker Carlsson and Timothy M. Shaw, eds., *Newly Industrializing Countries and the Political Economy of South-South Relations* (New York, 1988).

HASHIM T. GIBRILL

SOUTH YEMEN. See YEMEN.

SOVEREIGNTY. A concept central to modern political thought, sovereignty's importance is bound up with specifying the essential character of the territorial *state. Sovereignty, a complex and somewhat contested conception, combines a description of attributes with various emotive concerns for or against limitations on the internal and external dis-

cretion of the state. According to most influential lines of interpretation, sovereign states remain the primary political actors in international society, although in a condition of relative decline as compared to international institutions, transnational corporate and financial actors, and transnational citizens' associations. To varying extents, these nonstate actors are controlled by sovereign states, and cannot be properly regarded as completely independent actors. For instance, only sovereign states are eligible to become full members of the UN and most other important international organizations.

In origins and evolution, sovereignty is definitely a Western concept, and was not shared by other regions until this century. (Certain non-Western parallels do exist, however.) In contemporary discussion, the concept of sovereignty is accepted as an indispensable term in both academic and diplomatic discussions of political life throughout the world. Its importance is confirmed in Marxist, realist, and liberal political discourse, but the range of usage varies widely, reflecting differences in *ideology and political priorities.

The very centrality of sovereignty ensures its contested character. In each setting, meanings are attributed to sovereignty that accord with the interpreter's project. There is little neutral ground when it comes to sovereignty.

It is possible, of course, to throw one's weight behind a particular definition or to obscure the difficulty of providing a definition that is at once clear and authoritative. Surely, some definitions are more influential than others, and to some extent, there exists a mainstream tradition with a distinguished roster of adherents. This lineage can be traced to the classical works of Machiavelli, Bodin, Hobbes, Locke, Rousseau, and Bentham, and was carried forward by such thinkers as Max *Weber, Hans Morgenthau, Bertrand de Jouvenal, F. H. Hinsley, and Hedley Bull. Despite this corpus of distinguished scholarship, sovereignty has a history of conceptual migration. Early usage, perhaps most prominently in Jean Bodin's great work, *Six Books of a Commonwealth* (1576), was almost exclusively devoted to state/society relations, the internal dimensions of sovereignty. The doctrine of sovereignty provided a way of locating the center of authority in relation to domestic conflict, and, in the end, was a means to uphold the claims of the state as against rival feudal and ecclesiastical claimants. The state became "sovereign" because it generally succeeded in upholding this final power of decision, or as later put so influentially by Weber, because the state enjoyed a monopoly over the legitimate use of *force. Sovereignty in early modern Europe was a secularizing terminology that reflected the decline of universalist religious authority and actively encouraged belief in the territorial supremacy of the state.

Hobbes extended these aspects of sovereignty in *Leviathan* (1651), interpreting sovereignty as a status, conferring upon the state an absolute prerogative to impose its will via law on civil society, an authority derived from a hypothetical social contract that overcame the ravages of life in a state of nature. The people in any society were, in effect, protected by the sovereign against their own aggressive natures, but in exchange relinquished much of their freedom to obtain the order and serenity of a well-administered civil society.

This Hobbesian view of sovereignty was challenged by John Locke, among others. Locke feared much of what Hobbes favored. If human nature was as flawed as Hobbes believed, then it would be a disastrous error to concentrate authority in the state, or in any single place. Locke, although more positive about human nature, was concerned with establishing a government as clear about the limits of its authority as about its extent. It is from Locke, and Montesquieu as well, that we owe ideas about the *separation of the powers of government, notions of checks and balances, and, most of all, the idea that citizens enjoy certain inalienable *rights which, if not upheld, lead finally to a right of *revolution that inheres in the citizenry. For Locke the locus of sovereignty was suspended somewhere between the state and society, a constitutionalist nexus that has become associated with the inner nature of legitimate government at the level of the sovereign state. So conceived, sovereignty is compatible with citizen rights and the accountability of government and officialdom, including the head of state.

Indeed, some formulations of sovereignty, tracing their lineage to Rousseau, especially those imbued with democratic ideology, go much further. They locate sovereignty in civil society or in the people, giving rise to the terminology of popular sovereignty and an associated enthusiasm for the will of "the people." This line of thinking underlay the radicalism of the French Revolution. At least rhetorically, Abraham Lincoln endorsed such a view of sovereignty when he spoke of government "of the people, by the people, for the people."

Whether or not the state is sovereign, or how to construe sovereignty in relation to civil society, is no longer an important focus of debate except when it comes to *foreign policy. Domestic controversy about governance has shifted its ground: the key concerns now revolve around the way the state is constituted, especially relations between the center and other administrative units, and the modes by which governing authority is constrained and held to account. In this regard, the idea of sovereignty as such has been generally displaced in political discourse by an emphasis on rights and duties, by arguments about the nature of *democracy, and by discussions of how to maintain political and economic independence in relation to outside forces. One partial exception to this generalization has to do with state building in the non-Western world as a preoccupation in the immediate postcolonial period. Especially in Africa and the Middle East, the idea of making the state truly "sovereign" and upholding "sovereign rights" retains relevance as a central project of both governmental and oppositional forces.

Sovereignty as a basic idea and ideal in *international relations persists. Implicit in discussions since Machiavelli and Hobbes is the conviction that the state is the ultimate arbiter of its own fate in relation to the outside world. The clash of sovereign wills in international life gives rise to ceaseless conflict, as scarcity in relation to relative power and prestige, as well as with respect to resources and markets, leads to fierce competition among states, giving international relations its zero-sum history and reputation, and accounting for the prominence of *war.

Because there is no state beyond the state—no superstate—there is no human agency capable of establishing a shared morality or an effective legal order. Each state is "sovereign" in international society, a law unto itself. By and large, such formulations of sovereignty in international relations have been associated with realist thinking, which tends to regard law, morality, and conscience as irrelevant, or of marginal relevance, to the external conduct of states.

Despite the continuing prevalence of *realism as the approach of choice among diplomats and academic specialists, conceptual and policy tensions exist, and are mounting. For several centuries the states system has needed to endow agreements among its sovereign members with reliability. Sovereignty, if carried too far as a guide to behavior, undermined the reliability of mutually beneficial interaction among distinct states, whether the subject matter was diplomacy, tourism, or commerce. *International law arose to regulate such relations among states, and has expanded steadily over time in response to the growing complexity of international life. But an effective international law is not easily reconcilable with conceptions of sovereignty that underlie realist thought about international relations. Realist thinking erodes the authority of treaties as binding obligations of states and casts doubt upon the rules protecting foreign diplomats and citizens.

The recent emphasis on the international protection of *human rights is a particular challenge to sovereignty, implying that a state is not territorially supreme even with respect to the manner in which a government treats persons resident within its boundaries. Such challenges to the conventional understanding of sovereignty arise from both normative and functional pressures. The experience of Nazi persecution of the Jews and the disclosures about the *Holocaust after World War II generated a political consensus that the internal relations of state and society were no longer a matter exclusively within domestic jurisdiction, but had become a subject of legitimate international concern under certain specified conditions of abuse. This consensus has been reinforced by the rise of influential grass-roots and transnational nongovernmental organizations dedicated to the promotion and protection of human rights.

On a functional level, interdependence and globalization have made it impractical to view the world as consisting of territorial units each exerting supreme authority within its borders, but not elsewhere. Technological capacity gives many states the possibility of operating beyond boundaries, including *space. Ocean activity has long been a feature of international relations. Protecting the global commons against environmental decay is widely acknowledged as taking precedence over a purely territorial conception of authority, as is the complementary need to protect the health and well-being of territorial communities against damage from extraterritorial toxic releases.

A second type of conceptual tension is also of recent origin. Sovereignty and sovereign rights are emphasized as a means to protect the weak against the strong, yet the notion of sovereignty as placing the actor beyond accountability has been relied upon by the strong to impose their will on the weak. The UN Charter illustrates the tension in theory and practice. In Article 2(1) the principle of "sovereign equality" is endorsed, and Article 2(7) affirms that even the UN is bound to respect the "domestic jurisdiction" of states; thus territorial supremacy is privileged over the enforcement of international obligations. Yet the charter, especially as combined with UN practice, undertakes to save succeeding generations from the scourge of war, to promote human rights, and to uphold the principle of *self-determination.

Recent trends in international relations are contradictory and confusing. All states, including the most powerful, give lip service to ideas of sovereign equality, nonintervention, and respect for international law. Yet the experience of international relations includes the theme of the strong exerting their will upon the weak, of repeated interventions, aggressive wars, and of indirect penetration of sovereign territory by way of capital, *diplomacy, propaganda, and culture. Even if a few states can still defend their territory against an invading army, not even the most powerful can protect its people and cities against a devastating surprise attack by guided missiles, and none can control the flow of images and ideas that shape human tastes and values. The globalized "presence" of Madonna, McDonald's, and Mickey Mouse make a mockery of sovereignty as exclusive territorial control. A few governments do their best to insulate their populations from such influences, but their efforts are growing less effective and run counter to democratizing demands that are growing more difficult to resist.

There have been many attempts in the history of political and legal thought to reconcile these conceptual and operational tensions between sovereignty as an idea and law as a source of constraint on the behavior of governments. Even Bodin, the seminal modern theorist of sovereignty, conditioned his theory of sovereignty on an acceptance of the embedded applicability of natural law to the affairs of state. Jurists and others have written about notions of "auto-limitation" as inherent in sovereignty, or that sovereign authority can be flexibly redirected to satisfy state interests. Yet in the end such attempts at reconciliation seem more ingenious than convincing. Doubt persists, and properly. The fundamental claim of sovereignty is its emphasis on unrestricted governmental authority within territorial boundaries. If such authority exists, then wider obligations of the state are problematic. If such authority is denied, then sovereignty itself seems abridged or qualified. Indeed, if the state no longer is entitled to exercise such authority or fails to do so in practice, then it becomes misleading to retain sovereignty as a descriptive term.

Undoubtedly, sovereignty will continue to be used in the public discourse of international relations for the foreseeable future. It provides diplomats with a hallowed concept by which to carry on political debate, and it represents in a variety of situations the ongoing struggles of a given people for self-determination and independence. Nevertheless, its continued use in academic work seems more questionable, except possibly in the setting of describing "contending notions of sovereignty." Interdependence and the interpenetration of domestic and international politics, the mobility and globalization of capital and information, and the rising influence of transnational social movements and organizations are among the factors that make it anachronistic to analyze politics as if territorial supremacy continued to be a generalized condition or a useful fiction. In particular, sovereignty, with its stress on the inside/outside distinction as between domestic and international society, seems more misleading than illuminating under current conditions. If the role of political ideas in academic pursuits is to clarify tendencies and patterns, then the viability of sovereignty as concept and project seems increasingly dubious. When the polemical function of a concept outweighs its empirical referent, it may be time to consider scuttling the concept itself, or at least severely circumscribing its use.

(See also ENVIRONMENTALISM; INFORMATION SOCIETY; INTERNATIONAL SYSTEMS; INTERVENTION; LEGITIMACY; NATIONALISM; TREATY; UNITED NATIONS.)

Harold J. Laski, *Studies in the Problem of Sovereignty* (New Haven, Conn., 1917). Bertrand de Jouvenal, *Sovereignty: An Inquiry into the Political Good* (Chicago, 1957). Hedley Bull, *The Anarchical Society: A Study of Order in World Politics* (New York, 1977). Hans Morgenthau, *Politics Among Nations: The Struggle for Power and Peace*, 6th ed., edited and revised by Kenneth W. Thompson (New York, 1985). F. H. Hinsley, *Sovereignty*, 2d ed. (Cambridge,

U.K., 1986). David Held, *Political Theory and the Modern State* (Stanford, Calif., 1989).

RICHARD FALK

SOVIET-AFGHANISTAN WAR. The invasion of *Afghanistan on 27 December 1979 marked the first use of the Soviet Red Army outside the territory of the *Warsaw Treaty Organization (Warsaw Pact countries). For nine years, the *Soviet Union deployed an army of 120,000 men to battle the Afghan resistance, bringing death to more than a million Afghans and forcing more than a third of the population to seek refuge in Iran and Pakistan. Yet it failed to subdue the Afghan people; on 14 April 1988 in Geneva, the Soviet Union agreed to withdraw its troops from Afghanistan. The withdrawal was completed on 15 February 1989, presaging the end of Soviet *hegemony in Eastern Europe. An assessment of Soviet reasons for invading Afghanistan will have to await the release of documents from the period, but the impact of the invasion on international and regional relations is clear. Sports were the first casualty of the invasion, as many countries boycotted the 1980 Moscow Olympics. A more enduring loss was the shattering of the carefully nurtured image of the Soviet Union as the ally of the *Third World in general and the *nonaligned countries in particular. Year after year, the UN General Assembly became the arena where an ever-larger number of countries voted for the withdrawal of foreign forces from Afghanistan.

The invasion also deepened the already-existing rift between the Soviet Union and China and paved the way for further rapprochement between China and the United States. Soviet-American relations were severely strained. Allowing the SALT II treaty, which had been signed but not yet ratified, to go into abeyance, President Jimmy *Carter also imposed an embargo on the grain trade with the Soviet Union. President Ronald *Reagan, while lifting the embargo, embarked on an ambitious plan of military buildup and increased U.S. support for forces engaged in regional conflicts against *communism and the Soviet Union.

To help the Afghan resistance combat the Soviet army of occupation, the Reagan administration reassessed its priorities in Southwest Asia. The United States had lost its privileged position in Iran following the Islamic revolution of January 1979. Therefore, it turned to Pakistan, treating it as "frontline state" against Soviet expansionism. General Zia of Pakistan, who had seized power in a military coup in 1977, was shored up with substantial economic and military assistance. His country's role in sustaining the Afghan resistance was deemed vital, and the Reagan administration hardly protested Pakistani efforts to pursue the development of *nuclear weapons or the emergence of Pakistan as a major center for drug trafficking. Displeased with the U.S. posture in support of Pakistan, India drew closer to the Soviet Union and refrained from condemning the invasion of nonaligned Afghanistan.

Pakistan retained control of the resistance even when financial support from the United States and Saudi Arabia reached massive levels. The increase in aid had come in response to the successes scored in the field by the resistance, particularly after the United States supplied it with Stinger ground-to-air missiles in the summer of 1986. To preempt the Afghan resistance from consolidating control over certain provinces, becoming a state within a state, the Pakistani regime relied on its intelligence agencies to divide and rule. The strategy, however, backfired. When the Soviets withdrew their troops in 1989, the resistance was unable to offer a unified leadership that could form a credible government. Contrary to U.S. and Pakistani expectations, the Soviet-backed regime in Kabul has been able to maintain a precarious existence by presenting itself as a nationalist force opposing Pakistani designs on Afghanistan.

The emergence of Mikhail *Gorbachev as leader of the Soviet Union in March 1985 and the willingness of the Soviet leadership to end the *Cold War were crucial to the disengagement of the Red Army from Afghanistan. But the UN played a critical role in diplomatic negotiations, initiated in August 1981 and culminating, after twelve rounds, in the Geneva agreement of April 1988. This agreement, however, did not bring an end to the war in Afghanistan, as the Soviet and U.S. governments were left free to supply their Afghan clients with arms and weapons. Today, Soviet troops are out of Afghanistan, the Soviet empire in Eastern and Central Europe has been dismantled, and the Soviet Union itself has collapsed. But Afghans are still dying. The UN secretary-general has spoken of an international consensus for finding a political solution to the conflict in Afghanistan. Whether this consensus can bring peace to Afghanistan and prosperity to its people remains to be seen.

(See also SINO-SOVIET RELATIONS; SOVIET FOREIGN POLICY; STRATEGIC ARMS LIMITATION TREATIES.)

Henry Bradsher, *Afghanistan and the Soviet Union* (Durham, N.C., 1983). Olivier Roy, *Islam and Resistance in Afghanistan* (New York, 1986).

ASHRAF GHANI

SOVIET DISSENT. For nearly two decades, beginning in the mid-1960s, Soviet *human rights activists demanded a dialogue with their own government over the country's growing social, economic, and political problems. Dissent involved a broad range of nonconformist opinion. Nationalists in several republics pressed Soviet officials for cultural autonomy for their peoples. Religious activists wanted freedom to practice their faiths. Many Jews petitioned for the right to emigrate. Human rights activists in Moscow and Leningrad defended all these movements as well as insisting that the regime obey its own laws, relax censorship, end the abuse of psychiatry for political purposes, and dismantle its harsh labor camps for political prisoners. The Kremlin responded with arrests, harassment, and, in many cases, forcible banishment from the *Soviet Union.

In the mid-1970s, two leading dissident figures, Andrei Sakharov and Aleksandr *Solzhenitsyn, carried out a momentous debate over the future of the Soviet Union. Sakharov advocated the need for law, greater contact with the West, and the development of a *parliamentary democracy. Solzhenitsyn rejected this idea, preferring to see Russia ignore Western models of pluralism and what he considered to be messy parliamentary arrangements. The regime, at least officially, paid no attention to this debate.

The death of Anatoly Marchenko on 8 December 1986 marked the end of this era. After a prolonged hunger strike and inadequate medical care, Marchenko, one of the most well-known human rights activists of the Brezhnev period, died in Chistopol Prison, bringing to a close his fourth term of confinement.

Marchenko's death provoked widespread international alarm. Mikhail *Gorbachev by that time had been in power for almost two years. But he was still burdened with the legacy of harsh repression he had inherited from his predecessors. Gorbachev turned the tragedy to his advantage. Within ten days, he called Andrei Sakharov in Gorky, where he was forcibly confined, and invited him to return to Moscow a free man.

In one dramatic gesture, Gorbachev broke with the policies of the Brezhnev era and unleashed a new program of glasnost. Sakharov's release was the first of many hundreds. In February 1987, the regime announced its readiness to release all prisoners of conscience. At the same time, glasnost permitted the official Soviet press to explore historical subjects and contemporary social and political issues and to publish long-banned works of Russian and Western literature. Books that once circulated by clandestine means could now be published in mass circulation journals. The official press became a genuine mirror of Soviet society as newspapers and television began to report on hitherto forbidden topics such as pollution, prostitution, crime, and homelessness.

Gorbachev's *reforms allowed many former prisoners and activists to move from positions of dissent to what might be called the "loyal opposition." Andrei Sakharov, of course, was elected to the Congress of People's Deputies where, until his death in December 1989, he defended the same democratic principles that guided his years as a leading figure among the Moscow dissidents. When the Estonian nationalist Mart Niklus was released from a labor camp in 1987, his train was greeted by a crowd of thousands of people, who carried him—he was still wearing his prison uniform—from the train station

to his home in Tartu. Niklus soon became a prominent voice in the Estonian struggle for independence, and was able to do so openly, with the determined support of his people.

Other former dissidents were elected to republican legislatures. Sergei Kovalyov, who had earlier served a twelve-year term for "anti-Soviet agitation and propaganda," sat in the legislature of the Russian republic, while Genrikh Altunyan, a veteran human rights campaigner from Kharkov, represented constituents in the Ukrainian legislature. And Vyacheslav Chornovil, a long-term prisoner and Ukrainian nationalist, was elected chairman of the regional council in Lvov in the Western Ukraine; Chornovil led a group of decidedly anti-Communist officials.

The life of Larisa Bogoraz exemplifies the changes that took place in Soviet society. The widow of Anatoly Marchenko, Bogoraz began her career as a dissident when her first husband, Yuli Daniel, was brought to trial in February 1966 for publishing his short stories in the West. It was this trial that originally provoked the cycle of arrest and protest that led to the human rights movement. Larisa Bogoraz herself was arrested in Red Square in August 1968 for demonstrating against the Warsaw Pact invasion of Czechoslovakia and sentenced to four years of internal exile. For years afterward, her telephone service was disrupted and she could not receive mail from abroad. By 1989, her life turned upside down. She was permitted to travel to Europe and the United States. Today, she participates in a new organization, Memorial, which has millions of adherents and advocates proper documentation of the *Stalin period and a suitable monument to Stalin's victims. And when Czech president Václav *Havel visited Moscow in March 1990, he made a point of visiting Larisa Bogoraz and expressing the gratitude of the Czech people for her courageous act of witness in August 1968. A year later, in August 1991, she was invited to Prague along with other veterans of the 1968 demonstration, where she was honored by an enormous crowd in the capital's central square.

Not all former dissidents, however, assumed roles in the official opposition during the Gorbachev era. Members of the Moscow Bureau of Information Exchange maintained a large collection of unofficial documents, helping scholars and journalists cover issues that the official press, even in its expanded and candid metamorphosis, had yet to explore. Other activists, like Aleksandr Podrabinek, produced unofficial journals. Podrabinek's weekly and daily *Express Chronicle* circulated information on labor camps and details of ethnic strife, for example, that the official press still could not bring itself to publish— only after glasnost Podrabinek, among many others, operated openly, with correspondents throughout the country and direct access to Western supporters.

Gorbachev affirmed his determination to turn the Soviet Union into a country of laws, to dismantle the power of the Communist Party, and even to remake the economy through a program of market incentives. He helped dig the country out from under *Stalinism before being pushed aside himself. The dissidents, by their example of nonviolent, principled resistance to tyranny, helped to inspire Gorbachev's "revolution from above," as they helped inspire resistance to the ill-fated coup of August 1991. Many continue to press for democratic reform.

(See also PERESTROIKA.)

Joshua Rubenstein, *Soviet Dissidents, Their Struggle for Human Rights* (Boston, 1985). Ludmilla Alexeyeva, *Soviet Dissent, Contemporary Movements for National, Religious, and Human Rights*, trans. John Glad and Carol Pearce (Middletown, Conn., 1987).

JOSHUA RUBENSTEIN

SOVIET–EAST EUROPEAN RELATIONS. The Soviet Union's designs on Eastern Europe were clearly stated as early as 1944. At the 1945 *Yalta Conference *Churchill and *Roosevelt reluctantly accepted the Soviet demand that Eastern Europe become a Soviet "sphere of influence." As it turned out, this term denoted unlimited control by the Soviet Union over the nations of Eastern Europe. The peoples of Eastern Europe showed no enthusiasm for the imposition of Soviet-type communism. Several nations of the region shared long-standing anti-Russian and anti-Soviet sentiments (East Germans, Hungarians, Poles, and Romanians); others (Bulgarians, Czechs, and Slovaks) more sympathetic toward the Russians were soon to learn the grim realities of Moscow's domination.

The Soviet army liberated much of the region from German occupation and proceeded to extend Soviet control. In this undertaking Moscow was assisted by several actors: first, by the Soviet army occupying several states in the region and providing tacit support to Soviet activities; second, by East European communists who spent years in the Soviet Union working for various communist organizations; third, by the thousands of Soviet "advisers"—along with Soviet *intelligence operatives and diplomatic personnel—installed in virtually all areas of political, economic, and social affairs. In addition, the states of Eastern Europe and the Soviet Union made long-term bilateral "friendship and cooperation" treaties with each other. In 1949 the *Council for Mutual Economic Assistance (COMECON), an organization that choked Eastern Europe's traditional trade relations with the West, was founded as a response to Western Europe's Common Market and to coordinate trade within the Soviet bloc.

By the time of *Stalin's death (1953) the countries of Eastern Europe were completely "Sovietized." Most significant aspects of Soviet-style *totalitarianism were ruthlessly implemented in the region, although the extent and intensity of political repression and economic transformation showed impor-

tant variations. In foreign affairs, too, the nations of the region were obliged to obey Moscow's dictates. The first major schism occurred in the late 1940s between Yugoslavia and the Soviet Union. The Yugoslav leaders strongly protested Moscow's unabashed meddling in their country's domestic affairs, and the escalating tension culminated in an open break between Belgrade and Moscow. The friction between Yugoslavia and the Soviet bloc was significantly reduced only after a new Soviet leader, Nikita *Khrushchev, succeeded Stalin.

Particularly in the latter part of Khrushchev's tenure (1953–1964), uniformity in the domestic political and economic affairs of Soviet-bloc countries was deemphasized; unity on major points of foreign policy and ideology was stressed instead. In May 1955, the *Warsaw Treaty Organization (WTO) was established with Albania, Bulgaria, Czechoslovakia, the German Democratic Republic (GDR), Hungary, Poland, Romania, and the Soviet Union as its members. Throughout its existence the WTO remained a thoroughly Soviet-controlled institution. The 1969 reorganization of the institutional structure of the WTO did little to change Moscow's preponderance in the organization.

After Stalin's demise a number of anticommunist and anti-Soviet revolts took place in Eastern Europe. Moscow reinforced its control of the region by quelling several uprisings with military force. The Soviet Union's direct involvement was necessitated by the fact that native armed forces could not be trusted to turn their weapons against their fellow citizens. In June 1953 workers in the GDR rioted in hundreds of cities only to be suppressed by Soviet tanks. In the summer of 1956 a political crisis erupted in Poland that was resolved domestically. In the fall, the Hungarian Revolution developed into the greatest challenge yet to Soviet-type communism in the bloc. The widespread popular revolt was crushed by the Soviet army but not without heavy casualties suffered by both sides.

The decade following the uprisings of 1956 was perhaps the most tranquil in postwar Soviet–East European relations. Soviet foreign policy objectives were assisted by the states in its sphere of influence in several ways, including vocal support for Moscow in international organizations (primarily the UN) and in the international communist movement as well as the dispatching of economic and military aid to Soviet client-states in the *Third World. By the end of the Khrushchev era, however, the Soviet Union had to deal with another malcontent within the bloc: Romania. Bucharest—rejecting Soviet interference in Romania's internal affairs—became and remained a reluctant participant in the bloc's international organizations (e.g., COMECON, WTO) and succeeded in distancing its foreign policy to a certain degree from that of Moscow, thereby earning the reputation of a maverick in the West.

Under the leadership of Leonid I. Brezhnev (1964–

1982) Moscow had to deal with further disturbances in the bloc. The *Prague Spring (1968), Czechoslovakia's attempt to establish "socialism with a human face," endangered the political monopoly of the local communists and therefore occasioned armed interference. Aside from the Soviet Union, its WTO allies (minus Romania and Albania, the latter unilaterally withdrawing from the WTO in protest after the invasion) also participated in the August 1968 invasion, albeit with token forces. The Brezhnev Doctrine—Moscow's declaration of limited sovereignty of East European states—was issued quickly after the invasion.

Although on the surface Soviet–East European relations appeared to be unclouded during Brezhnev's leadership, several events showed that the bloc was far from united. Disagreements between Moscow and at least some of its allies emerged regarding the Sino-Soviet crisis in 1969, the Soviet invasion of Afghanistan in 1979, and during the Polish crisis of 1980–1981, to mention only a few instances. In the latter, Soviet intervention was avoided only because of the Warsaw communist leadership's willingness and ability to contain the crisis in preference to facing Soviet weapons. In the 1970s, the reluctance of some WTO states—primarily Hungary, Poland, and Romania—to increase their defense outlays according to Soviet desiderata in the face of their deteriorating economic situation became another bone of contention. In addition, COMECON proved unable to perform as a mutually advantageous regional economic organization.

Few changes occurred in Soviet–East European relations during the short tenures of Yury Andropov (1982–1984) and Konstantin Chernenko (1984–1985). Under Mikhail *Gorbachev's leadership (1985–1991) Soviet–East European relations were gradually and radically transformed. Initially (1985–1986), it appeared that Gorbachev wanted to "reestablish order" within the bloc, calling for enhanced cooperation within COMECON and increased defense expenditures from Eastern Europe. Moscow warned its allies—particularly Hungary and to a lesser extent Poland—about the political and economic "dangers" of too friendly relations with the West. Beginning in 1986, however, the Soviet Union, facing enormous political and economic problems of its own, became more sympathetic to manifestations of limited independence, particularly in the economic sphere. In fact, Gorbachev emerged as a reformer who supported domestic political liberalization in Eastern Europe. Although Soviet leaders continued to stress the importance of intra-bloc political, economic, and military cooperation, their own problems received priority in their policies and shifted their attention away from the affairs of the region.

During the 1989 revolutions in Eastern Europe Moscow played the role of an interested but not terribly concerned spectator. In the new international political situation evolving in the late 1980s and the early 1990s the Soviet Union relinquished its dominant role over Eastern Europe. In 1989 Gorbachev denounced the Brezhnev Doctrine and declared that East European nations were free to pursue their own political agendas. Moscow agreed to German reunification and to the withdrawal of its troops from the eastern part of Germany by 1994. In 1990 Moscow began the pullout of its armed forces from Czechoslovakia and Hungary, a process that was completed in 1991. Also in 1991 COMECON was disbanded, as was the WTO, and ultimately, the Soviet Union itself disintegrated. Political democratization in the former Soviet Union and the clear rejection of socialism by the peoples of Eastern Europe resulted in the drastic diminution of Russian influence in the region.

(See also NINETEEN EIGHTY-NINE; PERESTROIKA; SOVIET FOREIGN POLICY.)

Christopher D. Jones, *Soviet Influence in Eastern Europe: Political Autonomy and the Warsaw Pact* (New York, 1981). Sarah Meiklejohn Terry, ed., *Soviet Policy in Eastern Europe* (New Haven, Conn., 1984). Karen Dawisha, *Eastern Europe, Gorbachev and Reform* (Cambridge, U.K., 1988). J. F. Brown, *Eastern Europe and Communist Rule* (Durham, N.C., 1988). Zbigniew Brzezinski, *The Grand Failure: The Birth and Death of Communism in the Twentieth Century* (New York, 1989). William E. Griffith, ed., *Central and Eastern Europe: The Opening Curtain?* (Boulder, Colo., 1989). Charles Gati, *The Bloc That Failed: Soviet–East European Relations in Transition* (Bloomington, Ind., 1990).

ZOLTAN D. BARANY

SOVIET FOREIGN POLICY. Two events in *Russia (and until 1991, the *Soviet Union) played a crucial role in shaping world politics in the twentieth century: the October Revolution in 1917 and the selection of Mikhail *Gorbachev as general secretary of the *Communist Party of the Soviet Union (CPSU) in February 1985. The October Revolution brought the Bolshevik Party to power (renamed the Communist Party of the Soviet Union in 1952) and set in train events that resulted, after *World War II, in the division of Europe and much of the rest of the world into two hostile blocs confronting one another in a *Cold War. On Gorbachev's accession to the leadership, he initiated domestic and *foreign policy reforms that led to the dismantling of that division and the disintegration of the Soviet Union. A brief examination of East-West relations before 1985 will highlight how dramatically world politics have been transformed since then.

Sources of East-West Conflict. Nonsocialist governments have always suspected that subversion and aggression, directed at fomenting and exporting revolution, were the real goals of Soviet foreign policy. Many analysts believed that Soviet foreign policy was motivated by *ideology. But even those who thought that it was based upon national interest distrusted the Soviet government, maintaining that traditional power-political interests made Soviet foreign policy expansionist.

The Bolsheviks were no less distrustful of nonsocialist governments. Foreign intervention in the civil war in 1918 and enforced diplomatic isolation in its aftermath appeared to confirm their prediction that capitalist states would attempt to destroy socialism. Thus long before World War II suspicion and apprehension had become entrenched in the perceptions of both East and West. Although Britain, the United States, and the Soviet Union were allies after 1941 (when Germany attacked the Soviet Union and the United States joined the war), cracks began to appear in their alliance even before the war had ended. Joseph *Stalin, mindful of how easily the western part of the country had been occupied during both world wars, was determined to create a politically reliable defense glacis in Eastern Europe. The Allies, committed to the establishment of democracy in the liberated countries, perceived Soviet actions as aggressive and feared that Stalin's ambitions would extend to Western Europe.

The term *Cold War* usually refers to the intense enmity short of "hot" war that characterized relations between the Soviet Union and its erstwhile allies from the end of World War II until the 1960s (there was a temporary lessening of hostility when Nikita *Khrushchev modified Soviet policy after Stalin's death in 1953). The Cold War divided Europe into two highly armed, antagonistic blocs, each containing a portion of a divided Germany. The *North Atlantic Treaty Organization (NATO), formed in 1949, ensured U.S. participation in the defense of Western Europe. When the Federal Republic of Germany (West Germany) joined NATO in 1955, Soviet leaders feared German remilitarization. The *Warsaw Treaty Organization (Warsaw Pact) was established, consolidating Soviet military control over Eastern and Central Europe. The Soviet bloc was far from monolithic, however. Yugoslavia had been expelled in 1948; the Sino-Soviet dispute became public in 1963 and briefly turned into a military conflict at the end of the 1960s. Albania left the bloc at the same time. Soviet troops crushed an uprising in Hungary in 1956, and Warsaw Pact troops suppressed an attempt to create "socialism with a human face" in Czechoslovakia in 1968. Soviet intolerance of East European diversity became known as the Brezhnev Doctrine.

Breaking the U.S. atomic monopoly had been an urgent goal of Soviet policy after World War II. Soon the arms race turned the United States and the Soviet Union into nuclear *superpowers. The *Third World became at best an arena for competition between them, and at worst the locus of proxy wars (for example, in Korea and Vietnam) between East and West. The bipolar *balance of power and the confrontational atmosphere of the Cold War meant that all *international relations were perceived as a function of East-West hostility.

Détente. At the beginning of the 1970s the international climate became more relaxed as the Cold War was replaced by *détente, a short period of East-West cooperation. Having achieved approximate military parity at the end of the 1960s, the superpowers began to negotiate *arms control (the first Strategic Arms Limitation Treaty was signed in 1972; a second was signed in 1979 but never ratified). The Final Act of the *Conference on Security and Cooperation in Europe (CSCE) in 1975 seemed to imply general acceptance of the division of Europe and to promise further improvements in East-West relations.

Almost immediately, however, détente began to decline. Some analysts blamed Soviet defense and foreign policy, arguing that under cover of détente the Soviet Union had adopted an aggressive policy in the Third World and built up its military forces in Europe. Others explained the military buildup as a response to NATO's strategy of flexible response and believed that Soviet intervention in the Third World was intended to aid friendly socialist-orientated regimes threatened by armed insurgencies. Soviet leaders attributed the problem to U.S. policy, in particular the linking of better political and commercial relations to demands for human rights concessions in the Soviet bloc. Relations became increasingly tense, although both sides avoided the crises that had characterized the Cold War.

Domestic Reform and Foreign Policy. The domestic reform program initiated in the Soviet Union in 1985 was directed at halting the progressive economic decline that had begun to affect living standards and to threaten Soviet superpower status. The new leaders diagnosed that the socialist economies had reached the limits of extensive development. They prescribed a switch to intensive development that required capital investment to modernize industry and agriculture. There were obvious foreign policy implications.

First, defense consumed a large proportion of the Soviet budget. Reducing defense spending could provide capital for modernization. But military expenditure could only be cut if better relations were established with the Soviet Union's traditional enemies. Second, sophisticated technology for modernization would have to be imported. But there was an embargo on exporting to communist countries goods that could be used for military purposes, and Gorbachev and his colleagues knew from experience that it operated more strictly in times of international tension. An improvement in East-West relations might make it easier to import the necessary technology. Third, the reform program envisaged an increase in foreign trade and the attraction of foreign investment and know-how. Better East-West relations would facilitate these plans. Finally, better terms of trade with East European and Third World allies would provide capital for domestic investment. The link, therefore, between domestic economic reform and foreign policy change was very direct.

Domestic needs were the primary but not the only reason for altering Soviet foreign policy. When the Soviet Union invaded Afghanistan in 1979 East-West relations deteriorated badly. But the invasion also had other negative consequences. The Chinese government made withdrawal from Afghanistan, together with the reduction of Soviet troops on the Sino-Soviet border and the withdrawal of Vietnam from Cambodia, a precondition for improving *Sino-Soviet relations. Moreover, previously friendly Third World governments objected to the invasion. The costs to important foreign policy goals might have been worthwhile if the initial aim—ending the Afghan civil war and stabilizing the pro-Soviet government—had been achieved. In fact, however, Soviet intervention intensified the civil war.

The Afghan government was not the only Soviet client that appeared unable to survive without military support. Socialist-orientated governments in Ethiopia and Angola required military aid and the intervention of Cuban troops to deal with rebel forces, and insurgencies threatened the governments of Mozambique and Nicaragua. Moreover, the economic predicament of many Third World clients was desperate and the Soviet Union could not afford the amount of aid they required. Nor could the countries of Eastern Europe, since their economies had begun to display the same symptoms of stagnation that afflicted the Soviet economy.

Furthermore, Soviet military *security seemed less assured in 1985 than it had been a decade before. After new multi-warhead, mobile SS-20 missiles were deployed by the Soviet Union, Western leaders had begun to station intermediate-range Cruise and Pershing-2 missiles in Europe in 1983. The Soviet military perceived them as a serious threat to security. When their objections were ignored, Soviet negotiators terminated the current nuclear and conventional arms control talks. President Ronald *Reagan's commitment to developing a Strategic Defense Initiative was perceived as a further threat to Soviet security. In short, Soviet foreign policy had reached an impasse by the time Gorbachev took over the leadership.

Foreign Policy Principles of Perestroika. *Perestroika affected East-West relations as well as relations within the Soviet bloc and policy towards the Third World. It was some time, however, before the new policies produced tangible results. But there was an immediate change in the style of Soviet foreign policy, brought about in part by the appointment of new personnel. The replacement of Andrei Gromyko, foreign minister since 1957, by Eduard Shevardnadze was accompanied by many new appointments at lower levels of the Ministry of Foreign Affairs and the Central Committee departments responsible for foreign policy.

The message that the new officials conveyed to domestic and foreign publics contributed to the changed style. Called the "New Political Thinking," it purported to represent the essential foreign policy principles of perestroika. Among its novel elements was the recognition, first, that to be effective, security must be mutual and international, and second, that the *security dilemma makes it impossible to achieve security by military means. Soviet policymakers advocated mutual political efforts and progressive arms reductions to levels of "reasonable sufficiency" for defense to enhance international security.

A second important principle concerned conflict: to avert the danger of escalation to superpower nuclear confrontation, political settlements, underwritten, if necessary, by the superpowers, should be sought for regional conflicts. Third World conflicts that had previously been supported because they were "national liberation struggles" were now called regional conflicts. Furthermore, Soviet policymakers began for the first time to accept that incompatible national interests could cause conflict between socialist states and to insist that the principles of noninterference in domestic affairs and respect for sovereignty should prevail in intersocialist relations.

A third aspect of the New Political Thinking related to Third World underdevelopment. Previous claims that socialist orientation offered a speedy and painless path to economic development were dismissed. Third World poverty, Soviet officials now maintained, was a global problem, requiring interdependent solutions. The concept of interdependence was central to the New Political Thinking. Used to define the nature of security and problems of pollution, resource depletion, and ecology, it also referred to the relationship between the economies of socialist and capitalist states. In effect it implied the replacement of a view of a conflict-ridden world sharply divided into two social and economic systems with a vision of a unified, cooperative international system.

New Policies. At first the New Political Thinking was regarded by many as empty rhetoric or dangerous propaganda. Within five years, however, world politics had changed dramatically: U.S.-Soviet détente had revived, Germany was reunited, the Soviet bloc had dissolved, the Third World was no longer an arena of competition, and the Sino-Soviet dispute had ended. But at the same time there was a precipitous decline of Soviet power as the domestic reforms caused economic chaos instead of efficiency, and as glasnost, or openness, revealed how empty previous claims of progress had been.

In East-West relations negotiations and summitry replaced confrontation and hostile rhetoric. By 1991 seven Soviet-American summits had taken place, interspersed by frequent meetings at foreign minister and lower levels and intensive negotiations about arms control. The most concrete results of better U.S.-Soviet relations were the Intermediate-range

Nuclear Forces (INF) Treaty (December 1987), which abolished Soviet SS-20s and U.S. Cruise and Pershing-2 missiles deployed in Europe, and the agreement to reduce strategic nuclear arms (START) by thirty-five percent on the Soviet side and twenty-five percent on the U.S. side. The negotiation of START proved very complex, in part because of the difficulty of verifying reductions in mobile missiles. Gorbachev did not, however, succeed in obtaining substantial U.S. financial assistance for his reform. But continuing Soviet-American discussions of a range of issues culminated at the end of 1990 in unprecedented cooperation within the UN Security Council, where in the past the two superpowers had habitually vetoed one another's resolutions, first to impose economic sanctions, and then to approve the use of force, in response to Iraq's invasion of Kuwait.

The Soviet leadership looked to Western Europe for trade, investments, technological imports, and new security arrangements. Gorbachev radically improved bilateral relations with individual European countries. In December 1988 he announced a unilateral cut in the Soviet armed forces of 500,000 soldiers and significant reductions in conventional weapons, particularly those that could be used for surprise attack. Shortly afterwards multilateral Warsaw Pact–NATO conventional arms negotiations began. The Conventional Forces in Europe treaty was signed at a CSCE meeting in Paris in November 1990. In the final analysis, however, European investment in the Soviet Union and financial assistance were lower than the Soviet government had hoped.

Toward the end of the Soviet era, foreign policy in the Third World concentrated on disengagement. However, applying the new theory about regional conflict proved rather difficult. When Soviet troops finally left Afghanistan in February 1989 the conflict was far from resolved. In the case of Angola, the withdrawal of Cuban troops did not end the civil war. But the determination to reduce Soviet military commitments to the Third World even if this led to the collapse of friendly regimes was clear. Financial aid also was drastically cut and Third World clients (with the exception of the Democratic People's Republic of Korea [North Korea], Vietnam, and Cuba) introduced economic and political reforms. At the same time the Soviet Union sought economically beneficial relations in the Third World by establishing diplomatic and commercial relations with richer capitalist states, for example, the Republic of Korea (South Korea) and Saudi Arabia.

The new Soviet policy (and subsequent Russian extensions of this approach) caused considerable consternation in parts of the Third World. Radical movements and governments could no longer take Soviet military aid for granted. More generally the opportunity was lost to play the two sides in the Cold War off against one another to obtain better terms of aid and trade.

Relations with China improved steadily when Gorbachev began to fulfill the conditions for normalization. Trade increased, border negotiations resumed, and in May 1989 Gorbachev visited China for the first Sino-Soviet summit in thirty years. But his visit was overshadowed by the *Tiananmen Square massacre and the subsequent reversal of political reform in China.

Of all the changes in Soviet foreign policy none was more portentous than the repudiation of the Brezhnev Doctrine. Until 1989 it seemed that Soviet observance of the principles of noninterference and respect for sovereignty would work in favor of the more conservative socialist governments of Eastern Europe. East European leaders were advised to introduce domestic reforms, but the Soviet government displayed no intention of imposing them. It seemed that those leaders who disapproved of perestroika could safely ignore it. However, they could not ignore the demands of their own people because they could no longer rely on Soviet forces to repress them. When popular protests began in Eastern Europe in 1989, the Soviet government tacitly withdrew its support from the governments that refused to reform, and they were overthrown. When socialism itself was rejected without Soviet opposition the effects of perestroika on Eastern and Central Europe became irreversible.

The Berlin Wall, symbol of the division of Europe and of the Cold War, was pulled down and in 1990 the Soviet Union reluctantly agreed to the reunification of Germany. At the beginning of 1991 the institutions of the Soviet bloc crumbled: the *Council for Mutual Economic Assistance dissolved in January and the Warsaw Pact ceased to be a military organization in February. By then, however, the Soviet bloc had ceased to exist.

Prospects. The cruel irony of perestroika was that economic reform, democratization, and glasnost produced economic disintegration, violent ethnic hostility, and demands for secession. Domestic instability reduced Gorbachev's popularity and credibility at home and abroad. Foreign policy changes, on the other hand, particularly the loss of Eastern Europe and arms control concessions, were welcomed abroad, but they undermined Gorbachev's domestic authority. As a result, the influence of the conservative opposition to reform increased and a protracted power struggle took place which culminated in an abortive coup d'état in August 1991. When the complicity of high officials of the CPSU in the failed coup became apparent, the power of the CPSU was destroyed and, with it, strong central government. In the aftermath of the coup the disintegration of the Soviet Union gathered pace. In December 1991 Gorbachev resigned, and the Soviet Union was dissolved. The eleven republics that had not entirely seceded signed a treaty forming the *Commonwealth of Independent States. However, there remained a strong possibility that the commonwealth would dissolve into separate states.

Since the former Soviet Union remains a nuclear power, what is the danger that Russia (or other successor states) might revert to the previous aims and methods of Soviet foreign policy? A number of factors make this unlikely. First, even if perestroika turns out to be reversible, many of the transformations that followed elsewhere (for example in Eastern and Central Europe) are not. Second, even if changes of leader or policy occur, getting the domestic situation under control will be the main preoccupation for some time to come. Third, with the exception of the nuclear dimension, all aspects of Soviet power have been diminished. A central government would be unable to expand its power beyond its borders for the foreseeable future. Nor would it have a credible ideology to export. And if there are fifteen separate governments, they will have to concentrate on their relationships with one another. As for the vast arsenal of nuclear weapons, using or threatening to use them could neither restore the status quo ante nor achieve any conceivable foreign or domestic policy aim.

(See also AMERICAN FOREIGN POLICY; GERMAN REUNIFICATION; INTERNATIONAL SYSTEMS; NINETEEN EIGHTY-NINE; RUSSIAN REVOLUTION; SOVIET-AFGHANISTAN WAR; SOVIET–EAST EUROPEAN RELATIONS; STRATEGIC ARMS LIMITATION TREATIES.)

Roy F. Laird and Erik P. Hoffmann, eds., *Soviet Foreign Policy in a Changing World* (New York, 1986). Margot Light, *The Soviet Theory of International Relations* (Brighton, 1988). Joseph L. Nogee and Robert H. Donaldson, *Soviet Foreign Policy since World War II*, 3d ed. (Oxford, 1988). Rajan Menon and Daniel Nelson, *Limits to Soviet Power* (Lexington, Mass., 1989). Michael McGwire, *Perestroika and Soviet National Security* (Washington, D.C., 1991).

MARGOT LIGHT

SOVIET REPUBLICS. See COMMONWEALTH OF INDEPENDENT STATES.

SOVIET UNION. From the end of World War II until the late 1980s, the Soviet Union was regarded, alongside the United States, as a *superpower, competing for influence by projecting a distinctive political system based on and justified by the *ideology of *Marxism-*Leninism (*communism), introduced into the Russian Empire by the Bolshevik-led "Great October Socialist Revolution" of 1917. From the mid-1980s, the system experienced induced change, in a process of *modernization that has parallels and echoes in Russian history. Under the dynamic leadership of Mikhail *Gorbachev, the country underwent a renewed search for identity, provoking contradictions and conflicts that at times bordered on chaos and anarchy. The search for new political and economic institutions and practices led at the end of 1991 to the collapse and dissolution of the Soviet system and its replacement by a series of new entities, including the *Commonwealth of Independent States, that attempted to continue some of the coordinating functions of the former union.

In its seven-decade existence, the Soviet Union possessed what appeared to be a new and distinctive type of political system, dedicated to the creation of a classless and stateless society. While the whole enterprise was justified in the terminology of Marxist theory, the principal feature was the elimination of spontaneity, accomplished in practice by the frequent use of forced methods. As such, it was copied and imposed in various parts of the world, including some very remote from *Russia. "Soviet communism" thus served as a model for emulation, which gave the land of its birth a powerful leading role in the world in the twentieth century.

There were two principal influences on the formation and functioning of the Soviet political system, now seen as a phase of Russian history: first, the inheritance of the Russian Empire, with its enormous landmass—some 22.4 million square kilometers (8.65 million sq. mi.), or one-sixth of the earth's land surface, and the problems and opportunities it presented; its large and growing population—reaching 290 million during 1990; its multiplicity of national and ethnic groups, with their varieties of tradition, language, and culture; and its peculiar historical experiences, including the failure to absorb the invigorating experiences of the Renaissance and the Reformation that prompted the values and concepts that inform modern Europe; second, the ideology of revolutionary communism, which created a powerful tradition in its own right. These two forces sometimes reinforced each other, sometimes were in tension.

Within each main tendency there were further strands. The Russian heritage was ambiguous about the nation's place in the world, and specifically its relationship with Europe (or more broadly the West). The Marxist-Leninist tradition embraced both humanistic, liberating goals and cruel methods, including some unique to Russia's experience. These ambiguities and tensions emerged in the political struggle over the heritage of *Lenin and *Stalin, whose influence in the first two decades of Soviet power shaped the system and reshaped the society using novel forms of rule backed by the ancient one of cruel repression. In few modern societies had the burden of history so dominated current politics.

Origins of the System. The Soviet system appeared for several decades to represent a new type of polity. It has been identified as a form of *totalitarianism, along with (notably) the Nazism of *Hitler's Germany, but other terms have focused on particular features, such as ideology or the *one-party system, characterizing it as an ideocracy or partocracy; more recent comparisons with other communist-ruled countries have identified a distinct political system typical of the "Second World." The system was established in the late 1920s and the 1930s by Joseph Stalin (1879–1953) on the basis of a legacy of ideology, political precepts, and practices bequeathed by Vladimir Lenin (1870–1924).

Its most obvious characteristic, almost from the beginning, was the Communist Party's political monopoly. The Constituent Assembly, convened in January 1918 to devise a new constitution, was broken up on Lenin's orders, and all other parties were subsequently prohibited. From March 1921, when the Bolsheviks' tenth congress banned organized factions within the party, that principle together with "democratic centralism" (the idea that discussion of a topic should cease once a decision has been taken and that orders from the center are binding) led to the establishment of an orthodox interpretation of the ideology. Marxism-Leninism was susceptible of only one "scientific" (and therefore "correct") interpretation—that presented by the wielder of supreme political power. This authoritative figure then used the prerogative of ideological innovation to brand political opponents as "un-Marxist" or "enemies of the people" and remove them from office.

From the mid-1960s, that tradition was used to stifle dissenting opinion by condemning as dissidents those who thought differently. Only from the mid-1980s, under Mikhail Gorbachev, did a fresh approach permit the discussion of alternative perspectives and the creation of fresh channels of political expression.

The Goal of "Communism." The ideology not only justified the revolution and the system to which it gave birth: it also posited certain goals. Given Russia's undeveloped condition, economic modernization was stressed under the phrase "building a communist society." Following Stalin's policy of "*socialism in one country," the Soviet Union set about industrializing the economy, partly to defend "socialism" but also because "communism" envisaged an industrial society. In 1931, Stalin warned that the country was 50 or 100 years behind the advanced countries: the lag must be overcome in ten years or the Soviet Union would be crushed. The principal purpose of the political system therefore became economic growth, with particular emphasis on heavy industry. Successive leaders sustained this. In the early 1960s, Nikita *Khrushchev (1894–1971) boasted that the country had embarked on the rapid building of communism: within two decades the United States would be overtaken on many economic indicators. Such promises were quickly abandoned by his successors, Leonid Brezhnev and Aleksei Kosygin, as attempted economic reforms failed and stagnation set in. Under Gorbachev, from 1985, the aim of "acceleration of social and economic development" was replaced by that of placing the economy on a market footing—an extremely controversial goal, given the values of Marxism-Leninism, which depended on the questionable existence of an appropriate pool of managerial skills and entrepreneurial values in society and on the

willingness of the bureaucracy to surrender its commanding position. The attainment of "communism," meanwhile, was postponed indefinitely, its definition less certain than at any time before.

Political Structures. In pursuit of this goal, political institutions were established in which control was the principal characteristic. The precise balance of power and influence varied, although the fundamental principles of rule remained constant. Under Stalin, the leader, surrounded by a cult, was dominant; the Communist Party that he led was used to discipline key sectors of society and to move reliable supporters into managerial and administrative positions through a system known as *nomenklatura;* the country was governed through the powerful ministerial empires, coordinated by Gosplan (the State Planning Committee); the representative institutions—Soviets of Workers' Deputies—were essentially decorative and ceremonial; other institutions, including the Komsomol (Young Communist League) and the trade unions, functioned as "transmission belts" for the center's policies; and the repressive agencies, notoriously the "secret" or political police, were virtually a law unto themselves. For many, this system has retained its authenticity as "socialism," referred to in the 1970s as "developed," "mature," or "real" socialism.

Under Stalin's successors, the party moved to the center of the political stage, its numbers expanded rapidly, and it came to embrace the best educated and trained. By the mid-1980s, this institution had some 19 million members, of whom 31.8 percent possessed higher education and a mere 45.0 percent were workers. As its own propaganda boasted, the working *class party had become the party of the whole people. A major political force, a significant employer, owner of substantial property including a dozen or more publishing houses, a large bureaucracy, and an institution from which millions of members and their families acquired a certain social status: such was the *Communist Party of the Soviet Union (CPSU) in the 1980s. Its monopoly was enshrined in Article 6 of the 1977 Constitution, which declared it to be "the leading and guiding force of Soviet society and the nucleus of its political system, of all state institutions and public organizations." It was described as a coordinator, a catalyst, a vanguard, but whatever the metaphor, the significance remained: the CPSU was a monopolistic ruling party and dominated the Soviet state, which converted party policy into law and then implemented the law under close party supervision, with party members placed in all sensitive positions throughout society. Such was the CPSU's "leading and guiding" role.

That constellation of institutional forces ensured discipline and directed the nation's efforts along channels deemed appropriate for economic development. The industrial sector was almost entirely state-owned and hence politically controlled; agriculture was controlled by the forced creation of collective and state farms. The *planning process established politically motivated production goals, which were made law and implemented under extreme pressure from the control agencies. This pressure included purges, show trials, and the labor camps that Aleksandr *Solzhenitsyn evocatively characterized as the Gulag Archipelago.

Politics consisted essentially in *mobilization:* an attempt to change behavior patterns in compressed time as society underwent a massive transformation. Before Stalin's imposition of "socialism in one country," the Soviet Union had a rural, agrarian, *peasant-dominated social and economic structure, its people characterized by a premodern lifestyle, poverty, cultural inertia, and lack of formal schooling and of participatory political experience, mitigated by strong cultural traditions and a native wiliness; within a generation it acquired an urban, industrial, and educated population, bullied into shape but galvanized to withstand the Nazi onslaught in World War II.

The positive attainments of the Stalin era laid the groundwork for a much more complex, educated, and sophisticated society that, by the 1980s at the latest, made demands on the political system beyond its capacity. The methods used, however, had an impact on the system's ability to modify its responses to societal developments and on the capacity of the society to sustain reform. That legacy, defined as genuine "socialism" and embracing both an institutional configuration and a set of attitudes and values (a particular *political culture), served to inhibit the whole country. Attempts to break out repeatedly proved inordinately difficult.

The Culture of Soviet Politics. For Lenin politics was about victory and defeat, in the final analysis about *kto kogo?* (Who whom?—who shall defeat whom?); compromise with the "class enemy" (political opponents) could be at most a tactic. Stalin applied this principle severely, arguing that the "class struggle" would intensify as "communism" approached, and the "class enemy" would have to be identified and rooted our mercilessly. He promoted administrators whose lack of sentimentality matched their sycophancy and devotion to the very simply understood cause: these set the ethos of the system, making up rules as they went along, petty dictators in their territory, but subject to the whims of their own superiors. Their object was to achieve fulfillment of central directives using whatever means necessary and to report successes to the center.

The population's political role was to turn out regularly and cast ballot papers into voting urns in favor of the party-selected candidates, including loyal and exceptionally diligent workers for whom this was a reward. The mass media were strictly censored. Contacts with the outside world were heavily restricted. Autonomous associations were replaced by regime-sponsored, party-led "public organizations" whose essential purpose was to control the expression of opinion. The secret police penetrated

all groups, apart from a number of "islands of separateness" (Carl J. Friedrich and Zbigniew K. Brzezinski, *Totalitarian Dictatorship and Autocracy,* 2d ed., New York, 1965), such as the family and the churches—and even these were far from sacrosanct. Public opinion was irrelevant; political debate took place behind closed doors; representative institutions simply could not function. In consequence, the population failed to acquire political experience for use when reform-minded leaders attempted to induce fundamental political change. Yet many came to regard the traditional ethos as quite authentic for a "socialist" system: this too caused political controversy in modern times.

Stalinism and Modern Soviet Politics. Many of the values, practices, and customs of the system came under sustained attack by freethinking intellectuals and by establishment figures in the Academy of Sciences and universities from the mid-1960s, most tellingly on the grounds that they now hampered further economic, scientific, and political advance (see, notably, Andrei Sakharov, *Progress, Coexistence and Intellectual Freedom,* London, 1968). The dogmatic application of the ideology; democratic centralism used to control the lower administration; the ban on factions in the Communist Party (when no alternative channels for political expression existed); the practice of party-controlled appointment to positions of responsibility and authority through *nomenklatura;* the censorship of all printed materials and the restrictions on imported publications: all these were seen as unnecessary obstacles in modern Soviet society. Nevertheless, so strong was the traditional hostility to spontaneity in favor of planning, organization, and discipline that it took a further generation before new leaders were prepared to act.

Meanwhile, many administrators, party members, and conceivably ordinary citizens retained allegiance to the ideals symbolized by these practices and principles. The critique of certain aspects of *capitalism remained powerful in a society with strong collectivist traditions. Moreover, the policies of the past had worked: the society *had been* transformed in a generation; countless millions *had* benefited from the new opportunities for education and for geographic and social mobility; the nation's health and welfare *had* improved within living memory. Politically it may not have mattered that such opportunities have accompanied modernization in other societies. Some drew the lesson that, if organized and told what to do, the Soviet people could move mountains—literally, if necessary. What was required, therefore, was a return to discipline.

Another interpretation acknowledged past attainments and even might have justified some of the harshness in terms of "backwardness" and absence of the appropriate culture. However, the society, and the problems and tasks facing it, were quite different from what had existed sixty years ago.

Rapid modernization was replaced by the task of managing a complex society. The demands on the resources of government and society were far greater than ever, and standard Western theory about interests and their articulation in the political process had been commonplace in Soviet literature well before Brezhnev became the first Soviet leader to use such language in the late 1970s.

Furthermore, new possibilities for participatory politics were presented by rising education standards and acquired experience. By 1989 some 20.2 million Soviet citizens had higher education; a further 35 million had special secondary education. In the three decades since Stalin's death, increased contacts with foreign countries—government-to-government and similar official contacts and cultural exchanges that brought Soviet citizens to the West in small but steadily expanding numbers—had ended the isolation and with it the profound ignorance of the outside world. As living standards rose, the invention of the transistor radio, television, and other communications technology opened the airwaves to Western information sources, including the highly influential broadcasts of Voice of America, the British Broadcasting Corporation, and Radio Liberty. Private channels, notably émigrés in the United States, Israel, and Western Europe, further educated Soviet citizens about their own condition compared with other nations and affirmed other effective ways of organizing society. Finally, by the mid-1980s the bulk of the population (all under the age of 45) had lived their adulthood in a society that, despite its limitations on freedom, was far less brutally repressive than that of their parents. Unlike the Brezhnev generation, they were no longer prepared to look back complacently at glorious past victories: in comparison with their contemporaries elsewhere, living standards were slipping, and they wanted to catch up.

When Gorbachev, through glasnost, allowed such concerns to be voiced, the Soviet people demonstrated their capacity to use political means to press their case, and they responded to offers of a more participatory *democracy. In December 1988 new representative institutions intended to perform a genuine political role, and accompanying electoral reform, gave opportunities to express dissatisfaction with the Communist Party's stewardship over seven decades.

The results were clear: in many cases, including some at the very top, party and state officials were voted out of office, even when running unopposed. In republican elections in 1990, nationalist movements, generally dedicated to withdrawal from the Soviet Union, won resounding victories, particularly in Lithuania ("Sajudis") and Georgia, but also in Estonia, Moldavia, and parts of the Ukraine; democrats also won control of soviets (councils) in key areas, including Leningrad and Moscow. Such councils, acting with the authority of a popular mandate,

set about redefining not only their policies but their relationship with the political center, leading to constitutional crises. The lessons were obvious: despite the lack of experience of competitive elections, and despite attempts by the apparatus to control the nomination procedures, the voters were able to use the electoral mechanism to express their political will. Moreover, the broad-ranging attempts over several generations to imbue citizens with the ideology-derived values of community, "proletarian internationalism," support for the Communist Party, and so forth, had manifestly failed.

Under glasnost the mass media had undermined the credibility of the party and state *apparatchiki* by exposing incompetence, privileges, and corruption; and old aspirations to self-determination, particularly among certain nationalities, resurfaced as hostility to the center's mismanagement led to demands for separation. This was exacerbated by the central authorities' blunders in heavy-handed repression of various nationalist demonstrations from late 1986 onwards. The program of rolling reforms led to fundamental questions about the nature of the system, its governability, and its integrity: its very survival was thrown in doubt. By the end of 1991 the Soviet Union as a world power disintegrated under internal political and economic pressures.

The Crisis of Perestroika. On attaining office as general secretary of the CPSU Central Committee in March 1985, Mikhail Gorbachev inherited a society suffering from the general complacency of the late Brezhnev era, whose fundamental weaknesses were partly masked by the formidable projection of military power. According to careful Western estimates, in 1983 the country had over 5 million troops in the regular armed forces, plus border guards and special troops of the interior ministry deployed in an army of some 1.8 million (including 1.4 million conscripts), an air force of 365,000, air defense forces numbering half a million, 325,000 in the strategic rocket forces, a naval air force of 60,000, aviation armies numbering 100,000, over half a million strategic rocket reserves, 14,500 marines, and a civil defense force of 150,000. They were equipped with massive firepower and delivery systems, including well over 1,000 intercontinental ballistic missiles capable of launching the 5,500 nuclear warheads; almost 1,000 ship-launched missiles, supplied with nearly 3,000 warheads; and powerful new intermediate-range missiles. The naval forces were deployed far from Soviet shores in the Indian, Pacific, and Atlantic oceans and Mediterranean Sea, with nuclear-powered submarines frequently cruising close to the North American and West European coasts. Some half a million troops were stationed in the *Warsaw Treaty Organization allies in Eastern and Central Europe; 100,000 troops had been engaged in combat duty in Afghanistan since 1979; a further 75,000 were stationed in Mongolia; and small numbers of military advisers were in various countries of Southeast Asia, Africa, and the Middle East. Such capacity had caused constant concern to the Soviet Union's ideological opponents, with whom relations had deteriorated sharply following the military intervention in Afghanistan in December 1979 (estimates from the annual volume *The Military Balance, 1983–84*, London, 1983).

However, Soviet leaders after Brezhnev's death in 1982 knew that this military might was supported by an ailing economy and a population whose level of satisfaction, although never tested in an election, could not be assumed to be high. Falling life expectancy and rising infant mortality (reversing trends typical of developing countries, including the Soviet Union) indicated major failures in policy or its application, as did the growing environmental degradation: atmospheric pollution in the industrial cities and soil erosion and salination resulting from excessive irrigation in large areas of Central Asia and the south. Moreover, as the Western world forged ahead with the capital-intensive modernization of its industrial economy using the microchip and computers, the Soviet Union fell behind its technically innovative rivals in the sophistication and efficiency of industrial production and the wealth of its citizens. A political system that had prided itself on using planning to match society's needs and capabilities could not manage resources as efficiently as its ideological opponents: in short, a principal claim for world attention collapsed. Without significant reforms, the country faced an extended period of "muddling down" (Seweryn Bailer, *Stalin's Successors: Leadership, Stability, and Change in the Soviet Union*, Cambridge, U.K., 1980, p. 305.)

Gorbachev's original goal of "acceleration" of social and economic development was swiftly replaced by *perestroika (restructuring). It was progressively extended in scope to embrace economic reform and, from January 1987, "democratization" of the political system.

The Meaning of Reforms. On one level the reforms were a rational response to the social, economic, and international developments of previous decades. The planning and command system's inability to cope with the demands of a consumer-oriented economy required new energy and enterprise in economic management, involving foreign companies to bring capital and technical and managerial expertise. That, in turn, necessitated a fresh approach to information control in a world increasingly dependent on instantaneous global communication. The expansion of the range of information and the opportunities for expression also reflected the society's own growing sophistication. Contested elections, a highly important symbol of political development, also had practical consequences for the articulation and incorporation of interests in policy-making. The establishment of new representative bodies—the 2,250-member Congress of People's Deputies and the quasi-parliamentary USSR

Supreme Soviet of 542 almost full-time deputies—to replace the previous rubber stamp was also vital for the effective incorporation of interests in policy-making and particularly for winning public confidence. Without institutions in which the representatives could perform a genuine political role, contested elections would have amounted to a very hollow gesture. Finally, and equally significant, the creation of a state governed by law—a socialist *Rechtsstaat*—was also vital if the electorate's alienation were to be overcome and if the new representative bodies were to perform their designated roles.

These measures reflected the needs of a demanding society and the prescriptions of the ideology, which attacked (among other things) the state's bureaucratic nature: the transfer of authority to elected bodies aimed to bring the bureaucracy under control. It also risked loss of power by the Communist Party, which was not the principal goal. As a policy of radical reform, perestroika was intended to secure the party's ruling position by winning confidence rather than by imposing authoritarian rule.

However, the bureaucrats—the *apparatchiki,* or people of the apparatus, appointed through *nomenklatura* and, in the eyes of many, forming the ruling class—resisted attempts to remove their privileges and the power that accompanied control over economic management. Glasnost therefore served a further purpose: under the searchlight of publicity, the privileged lifestyles and the often criminal activity of the entrenched bureaucracy became unsustainable. The political aim was to win popular support through a vigorous attack on privilege; the political risk was that it might severely erode residual support for the party responsible for appointing these bureaucrats and for ignoring, if not encouraging, their corruption and complacency. At worst, support for the system might be completely undermined.

The reforms were also intended, however, simply to consolidate Gorbachev's position, first by appealing for popular support by offering greater freedom of expression, opportunities for participation, and economic benefits. Power consolidation also entailed circumventing the bureaucracy by creating new law-making bodies that possessed authority derived from popular elections. Third, consolidation entailed the creation of a powerful presidency, with substantial authority to make nominations to important state positions. By the end of 1990, the president of the Soviet Union had concentrated enormous power, including the power to govern by decree in economic affairs and to declare direct presidential rule. Meanwhile, at the Communist Party's Twenty-eighth Congress, in July 1990, leading figures failed to secure membership of the Central Committee, and the Politburo—formerly the country's policy-making body—was revamped, expanded, and rendered incapable of performing its traditional role. With neither the party nor the highest state bodies effectively able to limit the president–general secretary, the fate of democracy relied heavily on the incumbent's sense of restraint. The potential for exploitation of the office by an authoritarian leader caused great concern to liberals and democrats—and to the outside world. In response to this and other trends, the political struggle acquired a further dimension in an attempt to circumscribe the powers of the central government, of which the president was head. The early 1990s witnessed attempts from below, taking advantage of the opportunities offered in the "revolution from above," to assert popular authority against the center.

Sources of Political Conflict. In the climate of open discussion generated by glasnost, various forms of dissatisfaction were expressed that acquired unprecedented political salience following the revitalization of the electoral system and the representative institutions, the abolition of the Communists' political monopoly in March 1990, and the creation of a spectrum of new parties and political movements. Public dissatisfaction with dismal economic performance was compounded by the reemergence of various national grievances; there was an ideological clash between traditionalists wishing to retain much of the experience of "building socialism," and democrats, who wished to introduce essentially Western standards of political behavior; and finally, certain long-term consequences of Russian imperial expansion were being played out.

A key feature of Soviet society as the heir of the Russian Empire was its exceptionally complex ethnic mix. Over 100 nationalities were recognized, ranging in size from the Russians (at 145.2 million, some 50.8 percent of the population), Ukrainians (44.2 million, 15.5 percent), and Belorussians (10 million, 3.5 percent), through 16.7 million Uzbeks, 4 million Georgians, 3 million Lithuanians, and 6.9 million Tatars, to 263,000 Uigurs, 15,000 Chukchi, and about 900 Orochi (1989 census figures). They varied in their levels of cultural, linguistic, economic, and political development and were beset with rivalries and animosities, in some cases based on religion or language. Some groups shared ethnic affinities with nations outside the Soviet Union, or indeed were part of external nations; in other cases, notably the Baltic peoples, a compact nation was incorporated into the Soviet Union after a period of independent statehood. Elsewhere, boundary adjustments by the early Soviet regime had created enclaves in which national minorities, separated from their compatriots, were surrounded by traditional rivals (for example, the Christian Armenians in Nagorno-Karabakh, surrounded by the Muslims of Azerbaijan.)

Some nationalities were identified during World War II as hostile and deported to Central Asia and elsewhere—the Volga German community, the Crimean Tatars, and the Meskhetians of Georgia are three prominent examples. More generally, however, ideology and other considerations prompted a policy of playing down ethnic identity and treating the whole Soviet Union as an economic unit with freely encouraged interregional migration. Frequently Russians and Ukrainians moved into non-Slavic areas as teachers, managers, administrators, and government and party officials, the latter often appointed through *nomenklatura* to positions over the indigenous population. In development areas such as the new industrial cities in the east or the virgin lands of Kazakhstan, worker recruitment created multiple diasporas, and the ability of ethnic populations to retain their own identity was frustrated. Finally, even those ethnic groups that possessed their own "statehood" in the form of union republics, autonomous republics, or national areas were never granted the rights that a genuinely federal state would confer. The Soviet Union functioned as a unitary state; there was some devolution in certain policy areas such as cultural affairs, education, and family law, but usually Soviet standards were imposed regardless of local traditions and popular wishes.

Glasnost allowed the expression of antagonisms long suppressed—and indeed repressed—as the central authorities attempted to demonstrate that the "Soviet people" constituted "a fraternal family of nations." Hostility to Soviet or Russian rule in some areas was compounded by hostility to local cultural dominance in others, while elsewhere nations organized in movements that enjoyed spectacular electoral success. Led by the *Baltic states of Lithuania, Estonia, and Latvia, many regions declared their "sovereignty" in a development that by late 1990 challenged the center's authority and called into question the Soviet Union's integrity. As economic reform failed, new political forces from below sought to gain control over republics, cities, or districts in response to the wishes of the increasingly diverse electorates. A mighty political struggle—a struggle for power in the most basic sense—thus developed that is likely to take some time to resolve, even following the collapse of Soviet power.

The third element in the struggle reflected a resurgence of arguments concerning the appropriate road for Soviet development, overlaid with Marxist-Leninist rhetoric. At its starkest, the question was: what should Russia—or the Soviet Union—learn from the West? what are the lessons of the West's experience? For some, the best hope lay in bringing the country into the mainstream of Western civilization. That would have entailed accepting modern techniques of economic management and ownership, along with democratic and libertarian political values and procedures, to release the energies of individuals. For others, however, the country had a distinct destiny, to be realized by creating a new society along different lines from the West, building on Russia's collectivist traditions and distinctive qualities: individualism is alien to Russian thinking, will not work, and is positively harmful to the greater needs of society. In this struggle it was difficult to identify a middle way.

Recent Soviet political life thus reflected old and new tensions and old tensions in new guises. As they played themselves out the effects on the system proved devastating. Authoritarian regimes can effectively direct a nation's energies into certain prestige projects, such as industrialization and militarization. But in a society with the level of education, the range of skills and talents, the experience, and the aspirations of the former Soviet population, effective channels for involvement are required if performance is to match potential. Ultimately the Soviet Union's communist system proved unable to restructure itself, and by the summer of 1991 its communist *elite had been so weakened and undermined by the effects of its own reforms that it could not sustain a crude attempt to restore "normality" through a coup. The Communist Party was disinherited and later banned, the system began to disintegrate with the secession of the three Baltic republics, and before the end of the year the Soviet system had been dissolved and replaced by the Commonwealth of Independent States.

While the communist structures and symbols have been eliminated, and public opinion was glad to have the whole experiment abandoned as a colossal failure, the legacy of Soviet rule is complex and in a number of ways uncertain. On the plane of theory, the failed experience of communist rule in Russia does not necessarily demonstrate the falsity of the Marxian analysis: what it certainly does demonstrate, however, is the failure of particular methods of attaining the vision of a communist society. More practically, the Soviet experience, presented as "real socialism," may have destroyed any confidence in collective ideals in that society and internationally.

However, the legacy is ambiguous in its effects on the post-Soviet societies that are proceeding to rebuild their systems according to different principles. The Communist Party exists no more, but given the scale of its dominance in politics, the economy, and society, its influence may still be felt for some time to come in the norms, values, and attitudes embraced by the political culture. A number of pertinent questions arise in this context. For example, are former communists—who are still likely to form an active segment of society—capable of accepting the restraints and conventions of a democratic process? How will other parties relate to former communists? Will former communists in the state service accept the ethic of a neutral administration? How will the population react to future unemployment, price rises, and the withdrawal of welfare benefits they have taken for granted? What are the prospects for a smooth transition to a stable, democratic political process in such circumstances? Following the breakup of the union into independent states (based on the borders of the former Soviet republics), it is not certain that the territory and its peoples can be effectively governed without, perhaps, special provision for national minorities, embracing a range of forms to accommodate different traditions and cultural distinctions. Indeed, there are strong grounds for apprehension as new states are born at war with each other and newly independent nations explore facets of their identity—religion and language, for example—that had been largely suppressed under communist rule.

Over the medium term, the painful and exhilarating experiences of the twentieth century may perhaps be seen as a time of formation. The period of Soviet rule created the economic and social basis for modernity, gave citizens new skills and values that could not be contained within the structures that gave them birth, and made possible a new variety of politics.

(See also AUTHORITARIANISM; COMMUNIST PARTY STATES; ETHNICITY; RUSSIAN REVOLUTION; SOVIET DISSENT; STALINISM.)

Stephen F. Cohen, *Rethinking the Soviet Experience* (Oxford and New York, 1985). Moshe Lewin, *The Gorbachev Phenomenon* (Berkeley, Calif., 1988). Ronald J. Hill, *The Soviet Union: Politics, Economics and Society*, 2d ed. (London and New York, 1989). Geoffrey Hosking, *The Awakening of the Soviet Union* (London and Cambridge, Mass., 1990). Stephen White, *Gorbachev and After* (Cambridge, U.K., 1991). Stephen White, Alex Pravda, and Zvi Gitelman, eds., *Developments in Soviet and Post-Soviet Politics* (London and Durham, N.C., 1992).

RONALD J. HILL

SOWETO REBELLION. One of the satellite cities of Johannesburg, *South Africa, where cheap African labor was segregated and transported daily for this vast industrial area, Soweto (South West Town) was carved out of the forced removals and Bantustan policy of *apartheid. Soweto grew to be a major area for urban Africans, and the rebellions against the dehumanization of Africans has been continuous there since the massive student rebellion in 1976.

On 16 June 1976 students of the Orlando High School took to the streets to demonstrate against the enforced use of Afrikaans as the medium of instruction in the inferior school system. The educational system reproduced the alienation and deformities of the system of Bantu education under apartheid, and the march was part of a new period of mass opposition to the absence of basic social and human rights.

The students, who had organized the march without the support of established liberation movements, were met with violence. As a peaceful demonstration ended in brutal police violence, images were beamed across the world by television so that the Soweto rebellion became known internationally. The revolt spread rapidly across the country beyond Soweto as students across the country demonstrated against the system. Police violence was buttressed by military intervention, and by the end of the year over 284 persons had been killed and over 2,000 wounded.

In an effort to combat the police raids and shootings the students broadened their base of support to involve working people. Major strikes involving hundreds of thousands of workers created a new phase in the politics of the self-organization of the people. The weapon of the community strike, called "stayaway from work," was developed in this period. The worker-student alliance which was forged became the base for the numerous organizations which developed into the Mass Democratic Movement in the period 1976–1990.

At the outset, Black Consciousness was the principal inspiration for the demonstration. The Black Consciousness Movement (BCM) for a short period spoke in the language of race consciousness, but the demands of the working people for decent housing, better conditions and safety at work, a living wage, and the right to form trade unions soon superseded the ideas of racial identity. The leaders of the BCM faced constant persecution, and hundreds died at the hands of the police. One of the more well known cases was that of Steve Biko, who died in police custody under questionable circumstances.

In aftermath of the Soweto rebellion those youth who were in the forefront of the uprisings matured as leaders in numerous organizations committed to fighting against apartheid. They formed trade unions, cultural groups, community organizations, sports clubs, youth groups, and educational groups, engaging the state to the point where the mass democratic alliance made South Africa ungovernable and apartheid unworkable.

Soweto was the venue of one of the longest rent strikes in the period of the militant uprisings. In the period after the unbanning of the liberation movements Soweto was the home of Nelson *Mandela. In 1990 the town of Soweto and the city of Johannesburg became one municipality.

(See also AFRICAN NATIONAL CONGRESS; POLITICAL VIOLENCE; RACE AND RACISM; SHARPEVILLE MASSACRE.)

Archie Mafeje, "Soweto and its Aftermath" *Review of African Political Economy* (1978). Baruch Hirson, *Year of Fire, Year of Ash: The Soweto Revolt* (London, 1979).

HORACE CAMPBELL

SPACE. Since the Soviet Union launched the first artificial Earth-orbiting satellite on 4 October 1957, nine additional countries (the United States, France, Australia, China, Japan, the United Kingdom, India, Israel, and Iraq) and the European Space Agency have launched at least one satellite. Twelve humans have walked on the surface of the moon, several people have stayed in space for a year at a time, automated spacecraft have landed on Venus and Mars, and close-up images of five of the remaining six planets and of Halley's comet have been obtained. Earth observation satellites have obtained

data essential for national *security purposes as well as for environmental management, resource location, and weather forecasting. Communications via satellite have become both a multibillion-dollar business and a vital link between military forces and their command structures.

Five international treaties have come into force to provide a framework for the conduct of activities in space; the most fundamental and influential of these is the Outer Space Treaty of 1967, which set forth the basic principles that outer space was the province of all mankind, that the moon and other celestial bodies were not subject to claims of national sovereignty, and that weapons of mass destruction should not be stationed in space. A number of international and regional organizations have been formed to operate space systems, particularly communication satellites. The global International Telecommunications Satellite Consortium (INTELSAT) had 119 members at the end of 1990.

Underpinning the extension of humanity's sphere of activities to outer space (a sphere without clear legal definition) have been a variety of motivations. The particular mix of factors leading a nation to be active in space has varied across countries and over time, but the political-military foundations of space policy have been paramount throughout.

The United States and the Soviet Union have carried out comprehensive civilian and national security space programs and are the only two countries to have developed the capability of launching humans into space. Both have orbited not only their own citizens but individuals from several other countries. The budgets for the U.S. and Soviet space programs from 1960 to 1990 were of roughly the same size, and an order of magnitude or more greater than the space spending of Europe, Japan, or China, the next tier of spacefaring countries. All three of these have identified autonomy as a longrange space goal, i.e., the ability to carry out any space activity they choose, including putting humans into space, using means under their own control. Whether any or all make the commitment of human and financial resources to achieve such autonomous capability early in the twenty-first century remains to be seen. Until they do, they will remain secondlevel space powers except in those cases where they target their investments into particular areas of specialization. Even in the United States and Russia (as successor to the Soviet program), questions are increasingly raised about the benefits of continuing to support across-the-board space programs at a high budget level.

Neither the Soviet Union nor the United States deployed complete weapons systems in space, although there is no treaty between them preventing such an action. However, space systems have become an essential part of planning for and fighting a modern *war, because they are used for early warning of attack, target identification and location, damage assessment, strategic and tactical communications, position location, and weather forecasting. Space systems are also used for optical and electronic *intelligence. Given the high military value of space systems, it is perhaps surprising that the United States and the Soviet Union (with minor exceptions) denied themselves the ability to destroy or disable the space systems of an opponent in event of warfare.

Other countries use, or plan to use, space for military purposes. For example, Britain has launched military communication satellites and China and France use observation satellites for national security objectives. The very possession of a launch vehicle capable of putting a sizable payload into orbit is an indication of the capability to launch a warhead (nuclear or non-nuclear) over significant distances in time of war.

Observation satellites also play a critical role in verifying arms control agreements; the 1972 Strategic Arms Limitation Treaty forebade the signatories from interfering with "national technical means," i.e., photointelligence satellites used to verify compliance. There have been frequent proposals for a regional or international satellite agency to monitor military activities around the world and to add confidence to various *arms control agreements.

Scientists around the world have taken advantage of the opportunity to put their instruments into space; space science has become a major arena for international technical cooperation. Objects of scientific investigation include the universe beyond the Earth's solar system, the origins, evolution, and current condition of the moon, other planets, comets, asteroids, the physical character of space itself, and the Earth's surface and atmosphere. Some suggest that a comprehensive scientific study of the Earth from space can provide the information and insights required for understanding and effective management of global environmental changes.

Certainly the single most significant space achievement to date was Project Apollo, carried out by the United States between 1961 and 1972. President John F. Kennedy, in response to Soviet successes in launching the first satellite and the first human, in May 1961 set a manned lunar landing as a high-priority U.S. goal. The Soviet Union also attempted a lunar landing program in the 1960s, but several failures convinced it to withdraw from the moon race. Having won that race, the United States launched six more lunar landing missions, five successfully, but then chose not to continue human exploration beyond Earth orbit. Both the United States and the Soviet Union in the 1970s and 1980s confined their crewed space flights to the immediate vicinity of humanity's home planet. The experience to date of putting humans into space has not provided convincing evidence of tangible benefits from human involvement. The United States, in particular, has carried out an expensive national security space

research and utilization program with minimal presence of humans in space.

There is no doubt that the utilization of space for various Earth-bound purposes—communication of voice, video, and data for a variety of purposes, Earth observation, and potentially new applications such as space manufacturing, navigation services, generating electrical power from solar energy, among others—will continue. Various entrepreneurs and larger firms continue to attempt to develop profit-making enterprises based on launching payloads into orbit and using them for established and new applications. The very high costs of both access to space and space operations mean that space utilization must produce high benefits or unique advantages leading to economic return. Only if access and operating costs are lowered dramatically are activities in space likely to become economically much more significant. Military utilization of space will continue, and could expand, as the focus shifts from bipolar to multipolar conflict.

The political competition that fueled humanity's first steps on another celestial body has largely dissipated, and three decades of experience with human operations in Earth orbit have demonstrated few advantages beyond the symbolic and motivational of putting people into space, particularly given the high additional costs of life support for human crews. Yet the idea of human travel to other planets and of eventual establishment of permanent outposts on the moon, Mars, and perhaps beyond remains potent. Whether space activities to date are the precursor to humanity becoming a multiplanet species in the twenty-first century remains to be determined.

(See also STRATEGIC ARMS LIMITATION TREATIES.)

Walter J. McDougall, . . . the Heavens and the Earth: A Political History of the Space Age (New York, 1985). Radford Byerly, ed., Space Policy Reconsidered (Boulder, Colo., 1988). John Noble Wilford, Mars Beckons (New York, 1990).

JOHN M. LOGSDON

SPAIN. The current political regime of Spain (population 39 million) is a consolidated *democracy. The relative stability of the constitutional monarchy established in the aftermath of nearly four decades of right-wing authoritarian rule under Francisco *Franco (who died in November 1975) stands in contrast with the preceding century of Spanish history, in which several cleavages (involving conflict between anticlericals and those who defended the traditionally privileged position of the Catholic church, between regional nationalists and defenders of a centralized state, between *Left and *Right, and, in industrial areas of the north and northeast and in latifundist agricultural regions of the south, between classes) contributed to the instability and breakdown of semidemocratic and democratic regimes, the most recent culminating in the outbreak of civil war in 1936.

The origins of several of these cleavages can be seen in the emergence of the Spanish state itself. Certainly, the multilingual, multicultural, and, depending upon one's perspective, multinational aspects of Spanish society can be traced back to the *Reconquista*—the expulsion of Islamic Moors from the Iberian Peninsula—a process that lasted over 700 years. Even though by 1492 a large and internationally powerful Spanish state could be said to have come into existence, the heterogeneity of Spain's population and the absence of a single political culture meant that nation building would be difficult, protracted, and only partly successful. Since the *Reconquista* had been undertaken by peoples with different languages and cultures, one product of this state-building process was considerable linguistic pluralism. In Galicia (in the northwest corner of the country), the language spoken by over eighty percent of the population is a dialect of Portuguese. The languages spoken by between seventy and eighty percent of the populations of the east-coast regions of Valencia and Cataluña, respectively, as well as the languages of the Balearic Islands (Mallorca, Menorca, and Ibiza), were medieval derivatives from the language spoken in the French region of Languedoc. And the Basque language (spoken by about one-quarter of the population of Euskadi, near the Bay of Biscay) is not even an Indo-European language. While virtually all of the population of present-day Spain speak Castilian Spanish, defense of regional languages and cultures has been manifested in micronationalist movements that are today institutionalized as Basque and Catalán nationalist parties, as well as much smaller regionalist parties in Galicia and Valencia.

The political impact of this linguistic and cultural pluralism has been magnified by differing preferences concerning the proper structure of the state—a legacy of the earlier decentralized structure of the Spanish state. Basques and Cataláns, in particular, have consistently preferred considerable regional autonomy (and about one-quarter of Basques favor outright independence) from the traditionally centralized Spanish state. Indeed, five civil wars over this basic institutional issue have been fought between the Castilian center and the peripheral regions of the north and northeast over the past three centuries (1640, 1700–1715, 1833–1841, 1873–1876, and 1936–1939). The Spanish nationalist Francisco Franco, who emerged victorious from the civil war of the 1930s, presided over a rigidly centralized, authoritarian state and crudely attempted to suppress regional languages and cultures. One of the key issues addressed during the transition to a new democratic regime involved redressing the grievances of these regional minorities. The result was establishment of an unevenly decentralized structure of government called the *estado de las autonomías*

(the state of the autonomies), within which the various autonomous communities formed regional governments and legislative bodies. Created through a protracted series of bilateral negotiations between representatives of the Spanish state and each individual region, this gave differing levels of autonomy to different regions. While administratively awkward and conducive to annual disputes between regions and central government over such matters as the distribution of budgetary resources, it satisfied the demands of all micronationalist parties and movements except some Basques. In Euskadi, some Basque nationalists continue to favor secession from Spain, merger with three neighboring French departments, and formation of an independent nation-state. These aspirations have fed a terrorist campaign by the clandestine ETA (Euskadi ta Askatasuna—Basque Homeland and Liberty) which, by the end of 1990, had claimed the lives of over 700 persons.

This unresolved conflict notwithstanding, the Spanish transition to democracy must be regarded as enormously successful. Unfolding largely through negotiations among representatives of the key parties (in contrast with the mass-mobilization and revolutionary tumult of the transition in neighboring *Portugal), a constitutional order was established under which traditionally divisive issues such as monarchy versus republic and church-state relations were satisfactorily resolved. All significant nationwide political parties, ranging from Communists and their allies within the coalition Izquierda Unida to the Partido Popular (formerly Alianza Popular, founded by conservatives and former supporters of the Franco regime), have consistently behaved as responsible democratic parties. Only the anti-system stance maintained by the small revolutionary Basque nationalist party, Herri Batasuna, and the semiloyal stance initially adopted by the two more centrist Basque nationalist parties, Partido Nacionalista Vasco and Eusko Alkartasuna, represent departures from this overall pattern of firm support for the new regime and its institutions.

Success in this *democratic transition can largely be attributed to the responsible, stabilizing leadership of Spain's political elites, in particular: the first post-Franco democratic prime minister, Adolfo Suárez, a product of the Franquist National Movement, but who, along with King Juan Carlos, engineered the dismantling of the old regime; the Communist leader Santiago Carrillo, who led his party from clandestine opposition to Eurocommunist moderation; Manuel Fraga, a prominent former Franquist minister who led his party, Alianza Popular, and the overwhelming majority of former supporters of the Franco regime to fully support the new regime; and Felipe *González, leader of the Partido Socialista Obrero Español (PSOE), who transformed that party into one of the most centrist social democratic parties in Europe.

The first democratic governments (1977–1982) in this parliamentary system were formed by the center-right Union of the Democratic Center. Following the breakup of that party, the center-left PSOE came to power under the leadership of Felipe González. Given an electoral law that somewhat magnifies parliamentary representation of the largest party, single-party governments were formed uniformly from 1977 onward, even though no party has received a majority of popular votes cast in any parliamentary election. The dynamics of partisan competition in Spain are characterized by moderation and centripetal drives toward the center of the political spectrum; they stand in sharp contrast with the rancorous, polarized interparty conflicts of the ill-fated Second Republic (1931–1936).

Democratic stability has been facilitated by profound processes of change that have moderated important cleavages and transformed Spain into a fundamentally modern European society. The rapid economic development that began in the early 1960s led to substantial urbanization and restructuring of the labor force. In 1930, half of the labor force was employed in agriculture, and fifty-seven percent of all Spaniards lived in towns or villages with fewer than 10,000 inhabitants. By 1989, only 12.6 percent of workers were active in the agricultural sector (with forty-eight percent in the service sector), and only one-quarter of the Spanish population lived in towns of 10,000 inhabitants or less (with forty-two percent living in cities with over 100,000 residents). Economic development also raised the living standards of most Spaniards to typically West European levels. Although unemployment increased to extremely high levels in the early 1980s (resulting, in part, from Socialist-government neoliberal economic and industrial policies, designed to streamline the economy in preparation for entry into the *European Community), the existence of social welfare programs and the increasing participation of females in the labor force (amounting to over one-third of the economically active population by 1989) softened the social and political impact of these policies over the short term, while the return of rapid rates of economic growth in the late 1980s further ameliorated social and economic conditions.

Reduced *class polarization has been accompanied by a decrease in the divisive potential of conflict over the proper role of the Church in Spanish society and politics. The conscious choice by the Church hierarchy and by party leaders in the mid and late 1970s to avoid linking religion with partisan politics helped to avoid a repetition of the divisive conflicts of the past (and also to differentiate the postauthoritarian experience of Spain from those of Italy and Germany, where large Christian Democratic parties were established). The divisive potential of religious-related conflicts has also been substantially reduced by a profound process of *secularization: between 1965 and 1983 the number of Spaniards describing

themselves in public opinion polls as "practicing Catholics" or "very good Catholics" declined from nearly eighty percent to thirty-one percent, and between 1976 and 1983 those describing themselves as "nonpracticing," "indifferent," or "atheist" increased from seventeen percent to forty-five percent of those polled.

In addition to these social-structural, economic, and political changes, Spain has undergone a substantial shift in foreign policy. Traditionally seeing itself as a bridge to both Latin America and the Arab world, Spain shifted decisively toward European integration in the 1980s. Previously nonaligned, Spain joined the North Atlantic Treaty Organization (NATO) in 1981. Although this decision by the Union of the Democratic Center government of Leopoldo Calvo Sotelo was initially controversial and provoked a partisan battle with the Socialist and Communist parties, the succeeding PSOE government of Felipe González changed its attitude toward the alliance, and, by successfully supporting a positive vote in a 1986 referendum on continued membership in NATO, laid this issue to rest. In that same year, Spain formally entered the European Community, quickly adopting a pro-integrationist stance.

(See also AUTHORITARIANISM; EUROCOMMUNISM; ROMAN CATHOLIC CHURCH; SPANISH CIVIL WAR.)

Richard Gunther, Goldie Shabad, and Giacomo Sani, *Spain After Franco: The Making of a Competitive Party System* (Berkeley, Calif., 1986). Stanley G. Payne, ed., *The Politics of Democratic Spain* (Chicago, 1986). Stanley G. Payne, *The Franco Regime, 1936–1975* (Madison, Wis., 1987).

RICHARD GUNTHER

SPANISH CIVIL WAR. On 17 July 1936, Spanish armed forces in Morocco rose up against the legitimate government of the republic, accusing it of promoting both the "disintegration of the fatherland" and the cause of Bolshevik revolution. The uprising, proving to be only partially successful, ushered in a three-year civil war. Forces loyal to the republic, supported by working-class militias, retained control over the republic's key industrial zones of Madrid, Catalonia, Levante, and the Basque Provinces; nationalist rebels, meanwhile, consolidated their position in the agricultural, food-producing areas of the peninsula, causing chronic food shortages throughout the war in republican *Spain.

The working-class revolution that the rebel generals warned against was in fact unleashed by their own rebellion. As a result of what can be termed a spontaneous *revolution, improvised worker committees and militias surged throughout much of the republican territory, assuming the administrative functions of the government and the military role of the army that had just been dissolved by the republican government. In the social and economic sphere, hundreds of farms and factories were collectivized. The European left-wing romantics who came to

Spain to fight for the "last great cause" believed they were witnessing the rise of a new working-class civilization.

The vital dilemma of republican Spain was this: was it possible to win the war through this spontaneous revolutionary momentum, or was it imperative to create a centralized military machine as demanded by the communists? The latter believed that the social revolution should be postponed until after the military victory. The communist thesis predominated because the Soviet Union was the main supplier of arms to the republic and the Partido Comunista de España exercised sole control over these weapons. Also, their defense of private property and of a "bourgeois" order as the best way to win the war turned the communists into a barrier against social revolution and, consequently, into the champions of the middle classes. The need to create a central government and an efficient army became the principal issue in the struggle for political power in republican Spain. In the fall of 1936, the anarchosyndicalist Confederación Nacional del Trabajo joined Francisco Largo Caballero's government, but in May 1937 the coalition was dissolved owing to the communist attempt to break up the militias and curb the social revolution. Largo Caballero's affinity with the revolutionary unions and his opposition to the communist strategy of gaining full control over republican Spain in the service of the Soviet Union's foreign policy led to his downfall.

The new government, headed by the socialist Juan Negrín, was a coalition between communists and socialists bent on destroying the power of the unions. Negrín followed the communist logic: the militias were inefficient; a disciplined army was necessary to win the war, or at least to resist until a change in international conditions would motivate France and Britain to assist the republic. Only the Soviet Union could guarantee the resources needed to implement this strategy.

Indalecio Prieto, the defeatist defense minister of the republic, maintained that "the side that has the healthier rear guard will win the war. Ours is festering in plain sight." Political unity and the morale of society in nationalist Spain were of course vital for victory. In the end, however, the winning side was the one that had the better-trained and better-supplied army, under the undisputed leadership of a prestigious general.

The core of the nationalist army were the elite African units that, led by Francisco *Franco, crossed the Strait of Gibraltar during the first critical days of the war. A disciplined recruiting and training system enlarged the nationalist army, turning it into a war machine superior to that of the republicans. When in 1937 Franco merged the Falange (the Spanish fascist party) with other right-wing political forces, thus creating a unified movement under his leadership, nationalist Spain was definitely consolidated.

Even though the origins of the Spanish Civil War were strictly internal, its development clearly depended on the attitudes of the major foreign powers. France and Britain followed a nonintervention policy more as a way to prevent a large-scale European war than as a mechanism to save the Spanish republic. On the other hand, Germany and Italy did not hesitate to break the nonintervention agreements; *Hitler and *Mussolini supplied considerable military help to Franco. In exchange for economic concessions, the Germans sent the Condor Legion, a force of one hundred combat aircraft, to Spain. Mussolini was more generous than his German colleague and sent sizable infantry forces, tanks, and artillery.

Aid by the Soviet Union to the Spanish republic was more a foreign policy instrument aimed at restoring a European system of collective *security against Germany than an effort to uphold the cause of democracy or social revolution in Spain. Also, the Communist International recruited and organized the International Brigades. The Brigades mobilized an army of antifascist workers, progressive authors, communist activists, and middle-class intellectuals; the war in Spain gave them a cause. Many came with the hope of turning Spain into the graveyard of European *fascism.

The Spanish Civil War had a significant effect on the Western conscience; its impact on the intellectuals was considerable. Very few of them, like T. S. Eliot, refused to take sides. A small minority of conservative and Catholic intellectuals defended "Franco's Crusade." The majority supported the republic as the cause of freedom and democracy. The war in the trenches was indeed accompanied by a war of pens.

The International Brigades played a decisive role in the defense of Madrid in November 1936, and also in two later campaigns (Jarama in February 1937 and Guadalajara in March of the same year) initiated by the nationalists with the objective of isolating Madrid from the rest of the republican territory. Franco's failure to bring the war to a quick end by a sweeping assault on the capital forced him to shift his efforts to the north. In the fall of 1937, the Basque Provinces succumbed to the nationalists in a campaign that had its most tragic moment in the bombardment of Guernica by the German air force. The republic attempted its own offensives in Brunete, Aragón, and Teruel but was always unable to exploit its initial gains. Franco, on the other hand, knew how to turn his counteroffensive in Teruel (early in 1938) into the beginning of his thrust toward the eastern coast and Valencia with the purpose of splitting republican Spain. In an effort to save Valencia, the republic launched its last great offensive of the war when its forces crossed the Ebro River on 24 July 1938. But as in earlier cases, the republican army failed to take advantage of the initial success of its offensive.

The last phase of the war took place in Catalonia.

Weary and worn, the republican army was unable to withstand the nationalist offensive that would end with the taking of Barcelona on 25 January 1939. The military options left to the republic were practically nil, and as a result the insistence by Negrín and his communist allies on continuing the war effort was futile. On 7 March 1939, as a prelude to its surrender, Madrid witnessed a new, yet brief, civil war between those advocating an agreement with Franco in order to end the war and communists who wanted to continue the struggle. On 28 March, the nationalist army entered the capital. The civil war between the two Spains, in which hundreds of thousands of Spaniards lost their lives, ended with Madrid's surrender.

Stanley Payne, *The Spanish Revolution* (London, 1970). Gabriel Jackson, *The Spanish Republic and the Civil War* (Princeton, N.J., 1972). Jesús Salas Larrazábal, *Intervención extranjera en la guerra de España* (Madrid, 1974). Raymond Carr, *The Spanish Tragedy: The Civil War in Perspective* (London, 1977).

SHLOMO BEN-AMI

SRI LANKA. The island-nation of Sri Lanka, with a population of around 17 million, lies 46 kilometers (29 mi.) off the southeastern coast of India. The British unified the island in 1815 and governed it as the colony of Ceylon until independence in 1948. The country's name was changed to Sri Lanka in 1972.

The parliamentary system, which had been in place since independence, was replaced in 1978, when a new constitution put power in the hands of an executive president in addition to the Parliament. The executive president is elected directly by universal adult suffrage, and the Parliament is chosen by a system of proportional representation. In the 1980s violence and intimidation increasingly affected election campaigns, but the actual vote counts are generally thought to be accurate. The judiciary has some independence, but in the 1970s and 1980s it became increasingly susceptible to political pressures. The state has been highly centralized, with all power resting in the capital city, Colombo, but a constitutional amendment passed in 1987 gives significant political powers to provincial councils. The extent to which this devolution of power will take place remains uncertain.

All governments since independence have been led by one of the two main political parties, the United National Party (UNP) or the Sri Lanka Freedom Party (SLFP). Policy differences between the two major parties have often been minimal, but the UNP has generally followed a more pro-Western and pro-business line than the SLFP. At each of the six elections held between 1956 and 1977 the incumbent government was defeated, but since 1977 the UNP has solidified its hold on political power. UNP governments since 1977 have reversed the earlier policy of tight state regulation of the economy and pursued a program of economic liberalization, which has been supported generously by the international aid community. Exports have been diversified away from the traditional crops of tea, rubber, and coconuts; the massive Mahaweli irrigation project has gone ahead at a great pace; and the nation is now self-sufficient in rice when the weather is favorable. On the other hand, welfare programs have been cut back, and the very poor have experienced a decline in their standard of living. The nation is also saddled with a large foreign debt.

Ethnic divisions have played an important role in politics since independence, but began to threaten the integrity of the polity only after 1972, when the first republican constitution entrenched the position of the Sinhalese majority and took little account of minority interests, especially those of the Sri Lanka Tamils. In the 1970s a small number of Sri Lanka Tamils launched violent attacks against representatives of the state, and civil war broke out after anti-Tamil riots in the majority-Sinhalese areas in 1983. Sri Lanka Tamil groups claimed a Tamil homeland (Eelam) in the northeast, and most of the fighting has been confined to this area. The separatists received some support from India, but in 1987 the Sri Lankan and Indian governments concluded an agreement to end the violence. Under this pact the government made concessions to some Tamil demands, including the devolution of power to the provinces. An Indian peacekeeping force was stationed in the northeast, but the most powerful Sri Lanka Tamil group, the Liberation Tigers of Tamil Eelam (LTTE), believed that the agreement did not go far enough. Fighting soon broke out between the LTTE and the Indians and continued on and off until the Indian withdrawal in March 1990. After a brief period of peace, the war between the government and the LTTE then resumed.

In addition to the Sri Lanka Tamils, there are two other Tamil-speaking ethnic minorities, the Indian Tamils (descendants of immigrants who came to work on the plantations during the British period) and the Moors (Muslims). The Indian Tamils have generally managed to stay out of the current ethnic violence, but the Moors have been drawn in because they contest the LTTE's claim to represent all Tamil-speaking groups.

In addition to ethnic cleavages, there are class and generational tensions. The LTTE wages its campaign not only against Sinhalese dominance but against other Sri Lanka Tamil political groups, including those dominated by the English-speaking elite. Moreover, beginning in 1987 a Sinhalese group, the Janatha Vimukthi Peramuna (JVP), waged a violent campaign against the government. The JVP resented the Indian presence on the island and believed that the peace agreement went too far in meeting Tamil demands. It received support from young Sinhalese in rural and semiurban areas who felt excluded from the political process. The security forces succeeded in killing most JVP leaders in late 1989, and the threat to the government receded. However, the social and economic forces that bred support for the JVP remain, and further challenges to the state from Sinhalese acting outside the democratic system are likely, in part because the government's struggle with the LTTE and JVP has led to massive human rights violations and undermined confidence in Sri Lankan democracy.

(See also ETHNICITY; INTERNATIONAL DEBT; SOUTH ASIAN ASSOCIATION FOR REGIONAL COOPERATION.)

K. M. de Silva, *Managing Ethnic Tensions in Multi-Ethnic Societies: Sri Lanka 1880–1985* (Lanham, Md., 1986). Stanley J. Tambiah, *Sri Lanka: Ethnic Fratricide and the Dismantling of Democracy* (Chicago, 1986).

JOHN D. ROGERS

STALIN, Joseph. General Secretary of the *Communist Party of the Soviet Union from 1922 to 1953 and effective dictator of the country from 1929 to 1953, Joseph Stalin was born Iosif Vissarionovich Dzhugashvili on 9 December 1879 (21 December, Western style) to a working-class family in the town of Gori in the Republic of Georgia. Stalin was abused as a child, and at the Orthodox seminary where he was sent to study he was considered willful and rebellious. Expelled from the seminary at the age of 19, he joined the nascent Social-Democratic Workers' Party and became a professional revolutionary, following the radical, Bolshevik wing led by V. I. *Lenin after the split of 1903. His conspiratorial activity in Transcaucasia (including the organization of bank robberies to finance the party) brought him to Lenin's personal attention, and in 1912 he was coopted to be a member of the Central Committee of the Bolshevik Party and an editor of the party newspaper *Pravda*.

Arrested in 1913, Stalin was released from detention in Siberia after the fall of Tsar Nicholas II in February (March, Western style) 1917, and resumed his place in the Bolshevik leadership. Following the Bolshevik seizure of power in October (November) 1917 he was made Commissar of Nationalities in the new Soviet government. During the Civil War of 1918–1920 he served as political commissar with the southern army and as Commissar of the Workers' and Peasants' Inspection. He was chosen a member of the Politburo of the Communist Party when it was set up in 1919.

In 1922, at Lenin's suggestion, Stalin was elevated to the new post of general secretary of the party. In his "Testament" of January 1923 Lenin judged Stalin "too rude," but failed to secure his removal.

In the period 1923–1927 Stalin collaborated with the cautious faction of Communists led by Nikolai *Bukharin who favored continuation of the semicapitalist *New Economic Policy (NEP, 1921–1928), to fight Lev *Trotsky and the "Left Opposition," who urged a more proworker line. Meanwhile he built a personal power base in the professional bureaucracy or "apparatus" of the party. After expelling the Left Opposition from the party in 1927, he ousted Bukharin and the "Right Opposition" from the leadership and launched the radical programs that linked his name with the basic principles of the Soviet system for the next half century.

The "Stalin Revolution," ostensibly furthering the revolutionary program of 1917, included forcible *collectivization of the peasants, with arrest or deportation to Siberia of the "kulaks" (allegedly rich peasants) who resisted; rapid expansion of heavy industry under the central direction of the Five-Year Plans, together with *nationalization of residual small-scale private enterprises; a vast increase in the labor camp system; and the imposition of political controls and propagandistic standards in all areas of cultural and intellectual life. Challenged within the Communist Party leadership over the economic privation and famine (claiming millions of lives) that his policies had brought on, Stalin used the assassination of his heir apparent Sergei Kirov in December 1934 (perhaps arranged by Stalin himself) as the excuse to launch the Great Purge of 1936–1938. This included the "Moscow Trials" that condemned his rivals of the 1920s, and the secret execution or imprisonment of one to two million members of the Soviet bureaucracy, intelligentsia, and military leadership.

In 1928 Stalin revived the revolutionary confrontation with the capitalist world that had prevailed from 1917 to 1921 but had abated in the 1920s. In the mid-1930s, responding to the rise of the Nazis in Germany and the militarists in Japan, he sought alliances with the Western democracies in the name of "collective security" and ordered foreign Communist parties to support democratic governments through the "Popular Front." Then, to buy time, he concluded the German-Soviet Nonaggression Pact of August 1939 that set the stage for *World War II. In 1939–1940, under cover of the pact, Stalin advanced Soviet borders at the expense of Poland, Finland, and Romania, and annexed the Baltic Republics of Lithuania, Latvia, and Estonia. At the same time, he tried to placate Adolf *Hitler and refused to heed intelligence warnings of German plans to attack.

Soviet forces were taken by surprise and suffered crushing initial defeats when Germany invaded in June 1941. Stalin at first panicked, but then assumed direct personal control over military operations and over relations with his new allies, Britain and the United States. At war's end the Red Army had pushed all the way back to Berlin, occupying the entire band of East-Central and Southeastern European countries that had collaborated with the Nazis or had been occupied by them. Despite his promise at the *Yalta Conference of January–February 1945 to respect democratic principles in this region, Stalin proceeded to install the local Communists in power, thereby helping to bring on the

*Cold War between the *Soviet Union and the Western powers.

Stalin took the victory of 1945 as vindication of his *command economy, and intensified his dictatorial control instead of relaxing as most of his subjects had hoped. He continued mass arrests and occasional purges, directed particularly against national minorities, foreign influences, and Jewish cultural figures, and continuing to the eve of his death with the announced "doctors' plot" of mostly Jewish physicians charged with planning the medical murder of the Communist leadership. Further purges were cut short by Stalin's death of a stroke on 5 March 1953.

Stalin was survived by a son, Vasili, an air force officer who later died of alcoholism, and a daughter, Svetlana Allilueva, who defected and now lives in England. These were children of his second marriage, to Nadezhda Allilueva, who died in 1932, reportedly by suicide brought on by her husband's cruel behavior and the horrors of the collectivization drive. An older son, Yakov, was the child of Stalin's first marriage to Ekaterina Svanidze, who died in 1907; Yakov died in German captivity during World War II after Stalin refused a prisoner exchange for him. A rumored third marriage to the sister of his long-time lieutenant Lazar Kaganovich has never been authenticated.

Stalin's place in history has been subject to widely differing interpretations, though all accounts agree on his extraordinary personal impact on the development of the Soviet Union and its relations with the outside world. The official Communist line while Stalin was still living was that he continued the proletarian revolution begun by Lenin, led the Soviet Union to the victorious building of *socialism, crushed the "enemies of the people" who allegedly fought this ideal, and inspired every area of Soviet life and thought with his genius. This view was totally repudiated, in part by Nikita *Khrushchev in his de-Stalinization campaign of 1956–1961 emphasizing the terror of the purges, and more systematically by Mikhail *Gorbachev and his supporters from 1985 through 1991, rejecting *Stalinism as a "command-administrative system" that only created "barracks socialism."

Western, non-Communist, evaluations of Stalin have divided particularly over the question whether he merely implemented the tyranny inherent in the Bolsheviks' violent seizure of power and the one-party Communist dictatorship (the more conservative view), or whether he fundamentally betrayed the Communist revolution by creating a bureaucratic dictatorship over the workers (the view of the non-Communist Left, notably of Trotskyists). Both these schools of thought equate Stalin with the totalitarian system of rule, although after Stalin's death Western revisionist scholars rejected the "totalitarian model" as allegedly sustaining the Cold War mentality of international confrontation.

A more historically grounded approach puts Stalin in the context of revolutionary events in Russia. Thus he drew on the psychology and philosophy of the revolution's early years of fanatical utopianism under Lenin, but applied them at a time when the genuine revolutionary spirit was ebbing, in order to fashion the system of despotic personal rule and the centralized, bureaucratic control of economic and social life with which his name is permanently associated. In this view, Stalin built on Lenin's heritage in some respects and contradicted it in others, as he worked out the Russian version of the postrevolutionary dictatorship that synthesizes the worst of the revolution and the old regime and combines revolutionary rhetoric with old nationalist ambitions. The totalitarian model serves to describe regimes of this sort that arise in the wake of revolution but ultimately succumb to military defeat or (in the Soviet case) to internal stagnation, generational change, and a revival of reformist hopes.

By most accounts, Stalin was a person of extraordinary evil. George F. *Kennan has called him "a man of incredible criminality . . . , a criminality effectively without limits" (*Russia and the West under Lenin and Stalin,* Boston, 1960), and the Soviet historian Viktor Danilov has called him "even worse than Hitler." Not a charismatic leader in public, Stalin was adept at the behind-the-scenes politics of intrigue and divide-and-conquer. He harbored implacable vindictiveness toward anyone who had disagreed with him or outshone him, save Lenin (and there are theories, unsubstantiated, that he was somehow responsible for Lenin's death in 1924). Foreign leaders and diplomats who dealt with Stalin credited him with much personal charm as well as shrewdness, though he enjoyed humiliating his own loyal entourage. In retrospect his paranoid tendencies are clear, though this is an occupational disease of dictators. Khrushchev, in his "secret speech" to the Twentieth Party Congress in February 1956, attributed Stalin's purges to "his capricious and despotic character," but many Marxists, including the Italian Communist leader Palmiro Togliatti, questioned how the Soviet political system could permit such individual tyranny, and this reasoning led the Gorbachevian reformers to repudiate Stalin's system altogether.

Stalin's attitude toward the *ideology of *Marxism-*Leninism is still not widely understood. Most authorities assume either a doctrinaire belief that goaded him on, or a totally cynical, propagandistic manipulation of doctrine. More likely he combined an intense need for legitimation and personal acclaim with the ability to adopt any policy he chose, to label it correct Marxism-Leninism, and to destroy anyone who called this reasoning into question. He always cloaked his actions in Marxist-Leninist garb while reserving to himself the exclusive authority to interpret what Marxism-Leninism meant. Instead of deciding his policy choices on the basis of ideology,

Stalin tailored the meaning of ideology to suit his policy choices, while the party's monopoly of public discourse made it seem to friend and foe alike that the ideology was being followed undeviatingly.

The most striking episode of such transformation of policy under cover of ideological continuity was Stalin's systematic shift to traditionalist norms in social and cultural policy in the mid-1930s. This took place after he had accomplished his "revolution from above" and consolidated his postrevolutionary dictatorship, and embodied the synthesis of traditional policy norms with revolutionary language and institutions that is characteristic of this phase of the revolutionary process. In economic life, Stalin rejected equalitarianism as "leveling" and endorsed the hierarchy of salaries and authority, though he claimed to have achieved the classless society of socialism. He returned to traditional, disciplinarian education and to conservative family norms (divorce made difficult, abortion illegal, "heroine mothers" rewarded). He repudiated literary and artistic experimentation as "bourgeois formalism" and endorsed the style of "socialist realism," i.e., conventional form and propagandistic content. Identifying himself with the Great Russian majority of the Soviet population, Stalin called for the nationalistic rewriting of history and rehabilitated such figures as Ivan the Terrible (1533–1584) and Peter the Great (1689–1725), on whom he modeled himself. Finally, he abandoned the Marxian doctrine of the "withering away of the state," and quashed serious Marxist social analysis. He shared the Marxist antireligious attitude and persecuted all religions in the 1930s, but in 1943 he granted a measure of toleration to the Russian Orthodox Church in order to use it for patriotic support. In sum, Stalin went beyond the consolidating function of the postrevolutionary dictatorship, to effectuate a social and mental counterrevolution, the functional equivalent of an imperial restoration.

Stalin had earlier toned down the Communist doctrine of world proletarian revolution, beginning with his theory of "socialism in one country" (1924). Nevertheless, he pressed successfully for more discipline and Soviet control among the parties of the Communist International, which he used as agents of influence (and recruitment of spies) in the service of *Soviet foreign policy. He did not attempt to promote Communist revolutions until after World War II, and then only as a means of consolidating Soviet influence over the nations of East-Central Europe. The artificial revolutions in Poland, Czechoslovakia, Hungary, Romania, and Bulgaria (and the establishment of the separate Communist regime of the German Democratic Republic in the Soviet occupation zone of East Germany) all incorporated Stalin's system of totalitarian dictatorship and planned economy, as well as subservience to Soviet foreign policy and Russian cultural hegemony. Local Communists as well as non-Communists who resisted this fate were purged, with the exception of *Tito's Yugoslavia, where the Communists had come to power independently through guerrilla warfare; in 1948 Stalin expelled Yugoslavia from the Communist Information Bureau (Cominform) that linked the new Communist governments, but he failed to overthrow Tito.

Stalin's model of government and economy was copied in China, the Democratic People's Republic of Korea (North Korea), North Vietnam, and Cuba. The term *neo-Stalinism* is generally applied to the antireform government of Leonid Brezhnev that followed the overthrow of Khrushchev in 1964, and to the other Communist governments that followed the lead of the Brezhnev regime. They did not revive the worst of Stalin's terror, and softened his conservatism in cultural and labor policy.

(See also COMMUNIST PARTY STATES; RUSSIAN REVOLUTION; TOTALITARIANISM.)

Isaac Deutscher, *Stalin: A Political Biography* (New York and London, 1949). Robert C. Tucker, *Stalin as Revolutionary, 1879–1929,* and *Stalin in Power* (New York, 1973 and 1990). Roy A. Medvedev, *Let History Judge: The Origins and Consequences of Stalinism* (rev. ed., New York, 1989). Robert V. Daniels, ed., *The Stalin Revolution: Foundations of the Totalitarian Era* (3d ed., Lexington, Mass., 1990). Dmitri Volkogonov, *Stalin: Triumph and Tragedy* (New York, 1991).

ROBERT V. DANIELS

STALINISM. Joseph *Stalin had become undisputed leader of the *Soviet Union by 1929 and remained so until his death in 1953. Stalinism is the name given to the system that developed during those tumultuous years and to the attitudes that sustained and defended it. The salient features of Stalinism vary according to the point of view of the observer. The major themes of Stalinism's own self-presentation were:

1. Unity. The Bolsheviks were obsessed with unity, and they had good reason to be: only their own unity and the disunity of their many powerful opponents gave them hope for survival. Stalin emerged victorious from the leadership competition after *Lenin's death not only because of "machine politics" but because the party felt that would guarantee this unity at whatever cost.

2. Vigilance. The will to unity had an exclusive and punitive side that expressed itself as "vigilance" in unmasking "enemies of the people." This outlook was apparent already in the revolution of 1917, when accusations of sabotage were a vital aspect of popular militancy and class hatred.

3. "There are no fortresses Bolsheviks cannot storm." This slogan typified the sense of urgency of the early 1930s, when Stalin made clear that he would go to any lengths to build up the country's strength in the shortest period of time. The ensuing violent attempts at social engineering engendered mass confusion that brought the country to the brink of ruin.

4. Construction of Socialism. Out of the chaos of breakneck industrialization and forced *collectivization arose a system of highly centralized control that reduced market forces to a minimum. In 1936, Stalin announced that the country had achieved *socialism, the first milestone on the road to full communism. During the *perestroika period, the system built up in the 1930s was labeled the administrative-command system, amid passionate debates about whether the country had ever really achieved genuine socialism.

5. Patriotism. Stalin increasingly stressed "the moral and political unity of the Soviet people" and the importance of the Russian national tradition. This feature became even more prominent during the war against *Hitler. Patriotism was part of a larger dimension of Stalinism to which Nicholas Timasheff gave the name "the great retreat"—the progressive abandonment of revolutionary values in favor of traditional values such as *nationalism, family, and hierarchy.

Besides these features, outside observers tended to stress the following:

1. Gulag Prison-Camp System. "Gulag"—an acronym for *Glavnoe Upravlenie Ispravitel'no-Trudovykh Lagerei* ("Main Administration of Corrective Labor Camps")—is a term made world-famous by the writings of Aleksandr *Solzhenitsyn. During the Stalin years, millions of people from all levels of Soviet society were arrested on false charges and subjected to treatment that reached extremes of inhumanity.

2. Cult of the Leader. The term *cult of personality* was used in the Soviet Union after Stalin's death as a euphemism for various sins of the Stalinist period, from the replacement of collective leadership by one-man rule to the many "violations of socialist legality." But what struck foreign observers was the quasi-religious cult of Stalin, which reached dizzying heights in the postwar period.

3. Cultural Repression. The Stalinist authorities maintained strict control over intellectual life of all kinds; two episodes in particular symbolize Stalinism's aggressive intellectual provincialism. One was the career of Trofim Lysenko, the charlatan who managed to convince the leadership that rejection of Mendelian genetics would lead to miraculous spurts of agricultural productivity. The other episode was Andrei Zhdanov's denunciation of two of the greatest writers of the time, Mikhail Zoshchenko and Anna Akhmatova.

4. One crucial aspect of Stalinism is almost forgotten: the "grand alliance." During *World War II, the Western democracies willingly accepted Stalin as an ally. The viciousness of the war on the eastern front was incomparably greater than the war in the west: Western Europe and the United States survived with their material and moral values more or less intact partly because the Soviet Union took the brunt of the casualties and devastation. In a 1943 cover story on Stalin and the Soviet Union, the editors of *Life* wrote: "It is safe to say that no nation in history has ever done so much so fast. If the Soviet leaders tell us that the control of information was necessary to get this job done, we can afford to take their word for it for the time being." But a convenient historical amnesia has removed from popular consciousness the fact that the Western powers were once Stalin's grateful allies.

Stalinism covered a period of intense change, during which the Soviet Union went from defeated pariah state to world *superpower. Many of the foregoing features of Stalinism are more appropriate to some periods than others. This point can be illustrated by two novels that have done more than any amount of scholarly analysis to fix the Western image of Stalinism. Arthur Koestler's *Darkness at Noon* was an attempt to solve the mystery of why former party leaders confessed to imaginary crimes during the show trials of the late 1930s. George Orwell's *1984* was inspired by postwar Soviet society, with its mind-numbing barrage of xenophobic and mendacious propaganda combined with the gray poverty of a country devastated by the war.

After the war, the Stalinist system was exported more or less intact to the communist countries of Europe and Asia. *Mao Zedong's radical policies in China were sometimes seen as an alternative to Stalinism. The implied contrast, however, was to postwar Soviet society, which seemed bogged down in terminal stodginess; observers forgot about the Soviet Union's own "great leap forward" of the 1930s.

The process of de-Stalinization in the Soviet Union started immediately upon Stalin's death, beginning with the release of political prisoners and with denunciations of other flagrant crimes of the Stalin period. During the *Khrushchev years the scope of the critique steadily widened, until it threatened to subvert some of the fundamental features of the Soviet system. Under Brezhnev, this process of critical rethinking was silenced. (To call the result "neo-Stalinism" is misleading; Lysenko, for example, was discredited only after Khrushchev was replaced by Brezhnev.) Under *Gorbachev, the critique was renewed and widened to include the entire system of centralized command *planning. This was as far as de-Stalinization could go, however—the positive program it implied had always been "Back to Lenin!" De-Stalinization has been transcended to the extent that Leninist values themselves were ultimately rejected by Soviet society.

A phenomenon as complex and dramatic as Stalinism has naturally given rise to many interpretive debates. One debate arises out of the question: "When did Stalinism become inevitable?" Some have argued that something like Stalinism is inherent in any real-world attempt to apply the teachings of *Marx. Much discussion has also centered on whether any valid alternatives to Stalinism existed within *Leninism. Two of Stalin's defeated opponents— Lev Trotsky and Nikolai *Bukharin—have become symbols of this possibility. The main themes of the Trotsky alternative were internal democratization for the working class leading to overthrow of the repressive bureaucracy, combined with world revolution leading to a benign international environment. Bukharin stressed the gradual and voluntary socialist transformation of agriculture. The difficulty is to account for the failure of these leaders without subverting their status as genuine historical alternatives.

The most serious attempt to place Stalinism in a larger comparative framework has been the concept of *totalitarianism. This concept grew out of two basic perceptions: first, that there was an essential similarity between Nazism and Stalinism, and, second, that these systems differed vastly from ordinary authoritarian dictatorships. The unprecedented monopolization of all social activity by the central leadership meant the elimination of independent alternatives in every area from politics to literature. In each sphere the leadership not only silenced opposition but demanded enthusiastic and sincere acceptance.

Opponents of the totalitarianism concept argue that it encourages a view of Soviet society as merely the passive victim of the party elite. They also point to the great convenience of the term for *Cold War propaganda battles. Supporters argue that the term brings out essential features of the system and note that critics so far have not proposed any valid alternatives. The debate over the term itself has obscured the necessity of preserving what is valuable and rejecting what is inadequate in the writings of earlier scholars who used the concept.

Another debate has been over the role played by Stalin himself. Some students of Stalinism argue that Stalin was personally responsible for many key features of the system. Others feel that the influence of the top political leadership has been vastly overestimated and that social history holds the key to real understanding. This debate has been quite productive in terms of the historical research it has generated, but no theoretical framework has yet been devised that incorporates the valid insights of both sides.

The collapse of communism in Eastern Europe and the Soviet Union conclusively demonstrates that Stalinism was a historical dead end, and our heightened awareness of this may lead us to underestimate the seriousness of the dilemmas that gave rise to it. Any full account of Stalinism would have to give due weight not only to Bolshevik policies but also to the heritage of the Russian past, the utopian dreams of Marxist socialism, the murderous international pressures of the twentieth century, and the contradictions of forced-pace economic and cultural *modernization.

(See also COMMAND ECONOMY; COMMUNIST PARTY STATES; MARXISM; RUSSIAN REVOLUTION; SOCIALISM AND SOCIAL DEMOCRACY; SOVIET FOREIGN POLICY.)

Leon Trotsky, The Revolution Betrayed: What Is the Soviet Union and Where Is It Going? (1937; rep. New York, 1972). Nicholas S. Timasheff, The Great Retreat: The Growth and Decline of Communism in Russia (New York, 1946). Merle Fainsod, Smolensk Under Soviet Rule (Cambridge, Mass., 1958). Aleksandr Solzhenitsyn, The Gulag Archipelago: An Experiment in Literary Investigation, 3 vols. (New York, 1973–1978). Roy A. Medvedev, Let History Judge: The Origins and Consequences of Stalinism, revised and expanded edition (New York, 1989).

LARS T. LIH

STATE

There is a great deal of agreement among social scientists about how the state should be defined. A composite definition would include three elements. First, a state is a set of institutions which possess the means of violence and coercion. The state staffs such institutions with its own personnel; the continuity of such personnel over time distinguishes the state from the more transient government or administration as used in the context of U.S. politics. Second, these institutions in principle control a geographically bounded territory, usually referred to as a society. Crucially, the state looks inward to its own society and outward to larger societies in which it must make its way; its behavior in one area often can only be explained by its activities in the other. Third, the state monopolizes rule-making within its territory. This tends toward the creation of a common political culture shared by all citizens. Differently put, the historical record witnesses an increasing merging of nation and state. Sometimes national sentiment is created by the state, but sometimes the national principle can call into existence new states.

It must be stressed that statehood is often an aspiration rather than an actual achievement. On the one hand, most historic states have had great difficulty in controlling their civil societies, and in particular in establishing their own monopoly of the means of violence. On the other hand, the *security of the state is compromised to an extent by broader forces which it cannot control. One such force— ably theorized recently by writers such as Raymond Aron, Kenneth Waltz, and Robert Gilpin—is that of the system of states, present for a thousand years in European history and now characteristic of what is genuinely a world polity. A second force, *capitalism, clearly has laws of motion all its own. Much interesting and important work is now being done in modern social science on the interrelations of capital and state, both domestically and internationally. If we are to understand the behavior of states, however, as much attention must be paid to a third variable, that of political regime, which has complex relations both to capital and to the state system.

Contesting the State. The nature of the state has been the subject of intellectual and political debate, especially in the twentieth century. The most obvious opposing views are those of Anglo-Saxon *liberalism, *Marxism, and a looser school best dubbed Germanic *realism.

While there are many versions of liberalism, most are suspicious of the activities of the state. All that is virtuous is seen as residing in society; state forces are seen as obstacles ideally to be avoided. The most active role for the state envisaged by some liberals is that of a night watchman, protecting a framework within which market forces can then operate according to their own logic. This is the philosophy of laissez-faire; its explanations are society-based rather than state-centered because no independent reality is accorded to the polity. More sophisticated liberals emphasize the need for restrictions on state intrusion into society, but are much more aware of the visceral qualities of political *power. They seek to protect the individual against fear and arbitrariness—a position which means that the market, when it is accepted at all, is endorsed more for its capacity to create *pluralism and wealth than as something to be affirmed in and of itself. A similar distinction between naïveté and sophistication can be seen at work in liberal attitudes to *geopolitics. The laissez-faire "Manchester School" insisted that *peace would be assured by the growing interdependence of the world economy; trade rather than territorial conquest was held to be the route to progress and prosperity. Less naive liberals, following the lead of Immanuel Kant, have suggested that the era of peace will depend not just on trade but on other states recognizing the principles of *nationalism and of *democracy.

Quite clearly, Marxism displays characteristics of the naiver versions of liberalism. This can be seen most generally in the fact that Marxism offers society-based accounts of politics, and more particularly in its doctrines of eventual universal peace and of the "withering away of the state." The originality of Marxism lies in its belief that society is structured by the presence of social classes whose characters depend upon the particular mode of production in which they are embedded. This stress on *class society means that Marxist hopes for both peace and the end of the state are on a different time scale than those of the naiver sort of liberal: these dreams cannot be realized until property relations are abandoned. The transition to *socialism will be difficult, Marxists maintain, precisely because the modern state looks after the interests of capitalists: domestically state power is used to break working class bids for power while internationally the fact that different states seek markets for their national capitalists leads to *war.

A third perspective, Germanic realism, sees the state as an actor in its own right, able to represent the general interest in an "asocial" world of state competition. Externally, the state is seen as the guarantor of survival. Social thought in general was massively influenced by the long peace between 1815 and 1914 in which the brute social transformation of industrialization seemed all-important. But Germans achieved statehood in part because of war, and hence in the work of thinkers such as Max *Weber and Otto Hintze the impact of geopolitical transformation upon social life acquired particular prominence.

Since the 1970s, renewed interest in the state has been at the forefront of the social sciences. The exact reasons why this should be so are complex, although they certainly include modern Marxists' attempt to move beyond the instrumentalism generally characteristic of *Marx's own theory to understandings, most of which proved to be unsatisfactory, of "the relatively autonomous powers" of the state. Whatever the intellectual history of the matter, there is no doubt about the outcome: the state is back.

Recent Theoretical Developments. Contemporary political analysis concerning the state will be better understood by first considering some pertinent empirical material. First, it is now generally recognized that the history of economic *development beloved by both Marxists and liberals was rudely interrupted by geopolitical conflict between 1914 and 1945, and that this period profoundly changed social life. The different organization of social class in the German Democratic Republic and Federal Republic of Germany (East and West Germany) for a full half century, to cite but a single example, was the result of geopolitical settlement rather than of any logic of class formation itself. Similarly, *revolutions tend to occur in regimes which have been debilitated by excessive participation or actual defeat in war. State breakdowns give revolutionary *elites their chance.

Second, social scientists increasingly realize that the form of social movements often results from the characteristics of the state with which they interact. Working classes tend to be militant when a state excludes them from participation in civil society, i.e., workers take on the state when they are prevented from organizing industrially and confronting their immediate capitalist opponents. Thus a liberal state with full *citizenship sees no working-class revolutionary movement, whereas authoritarian and autocratic regimes see the emergence of Marxist-inspired workers: this principle helps explain the difference in working class behavior in the United States and Tsarist Russia at the end of the nineteenth century. The same principle—that political exclusion breeds militancy—helps explain the incidence of revolution within the *Third World since 1945. Central American societies share a mode of production, but only a few witness revolutions. The possibility of participation in a Costa Rica diffuses social conflict;

its absence in Nicaragua under Somoza led to the creation of a revolutionary elite with popular support.

Contemporary analysts of the state also point to two dimensions of state power. Traditional theory concerned itself with the extent of the state's arbitrary powers, that is, the polar opposition between despotic and constitutional regimes. However, studies of agrarian states show that claims to universal power were more pretension than reality because the state had relatively few servants to penetrate and organize social life. Hence, a second dimension of state power, infrastructural power, concerns actual state capacities. Differently put, states are not free-floating. State strength is often the result of a state's ability to cooperate with groupings in civil society, and such cooperation is often ensured by some limitation on a state's despotic powers. Thus in the eighteenth century, the absolutist French state may have been autonomous in the sense of being "free from" parliamentary constraint, but it was nonetheless weaker—as the test of warfare showed—than its constitutional rival, Britain. In Britain, agreement between the upper classes and state actors allowed for higher levels of taxation and greater general efficiency, so the British state was "free to" do much more. This paradox applies equally well to the modern world: the war mobilization of Britain in *World War II exceeded that of Germany, and recent scholars of the Japanese state have stressed that its great strength results from a "politics of reciprocal consent."

Modern social science is at its best when tracing the ways in which state power influences and is influenced by other sources of social power. An appreciation of the state complements previous understandings of socioeconomic forces, but it need not improperly seek to establish a monolithic state-centric view. We can appreciate some of the advances that have been made by scholars by turning first to historical and then to contemporary realities.

Origins of the State. Two processes have been responsible for the rise of states. Irrigation agriculture is the first. Whereas pastoralists or slash-and-burn agriculturalists can literally run away from an incipient state, the fixed investments of irrigation systems necessitate stability and thereby allow taxation, the lifeblood of the state. Second, the first states were based on temples, and recent scholarship has suggested that service of a demanding god may account for acceptance of the state.

Pristine state formation took place on only a few occasions, typically in geographically diverse places. But even early state power was so great that secondary state formation became an evolutionary necessity. Societies which did not have the protection of a state fell before those so endowed. Once the state was invented, it could not be forgotten.

As important a breakthrough in social evolution

as the emergence of pristine states was the rise to world *hegemony of northwestern Europe, due to a dynamic broadly capitalist in spirit. Why this should have happened has long haunted social scientists, not least because much of the European pattern came to dominate the world. Recent research has made it possible for us to understand the role of the state and of the state system in the initial emergence of capitalism.

The European continent saw the emergence of states whose structures were conducive to the emergence of capitalism. Limits to arbitrariness meant that the state could not finally control capitalist actors, and the greater state revenue that resulted from cooperation with upper classes working through parliaments allowed for the provision of regularized justice and, in time, a revenue base.

This European development is largely explicable as the result of forces external to any single state. European states were long-lasting, and in consequence engaged in endless competition with each other. The pressure of interstate rivalry led to an increase in bureaucracy (the central development of the modern state), and in time to the creation of genuine nation-states. Under these circumstances, it was in the interest of rulers to limit predatory behavior toward capitalists whose flight would only result in an increase in the tax revenue of geopolitical rivals.

European development was exceptional in that it allowed for the emergence of capitalism and of a pluralistic society at one and the same time. This, of course, involved a long process, with extensive citizenship *rights only coming in the nineteenth and twentieth centuries. To mention this fact is to point to a darker side to the picture. The development of the modern state did not always encourage the growth of political rights. Imperial Germany sought to develop its economy and to keep its old regime in power; the people were to be integrated essentially through social rather than political citizenship, given that the state could not be controlled by parliamentary means. *Authoritarianism in tandem with a mobilized populace proved a dangerous brew. So too was the presence in multiethnic states such as Austro-Hungary of those who, convinced they could not advance through access to the imperial state, chose to play the national card so as to form their own. All in all, the dynamic which had proved so beneficial to the rise of Europe proved disastrous in 1914.

*World War I opened an era of geopolitical conflict, during the course of which it was by no means always apparent that this liberal legacy would survive. But in World War II force of arms destroyed *fascism, although it vastly enhanced—at least for nearly half a century—state socialism as well.

Liberal and Authoritarian States in the Modern World. The core of capitalist society was extended and consolidated in the settlement occasioned by the end of World War II. Japan and West Germany had liberalism imposed upon them, and they have thereafter preferred to advance via trade rather than conquest. More generally, the postwar world has seen the removal, in part at the behest of the United States, of extreme *Left and extreme *Right within the nations at the heart of capitalist society: liberalism seems triumphant. Does this mean that this core now operates on Anglo-Saxon principles—such that a concern with the state is losing much relevance? That question has gained in salience over time, for both intellectual and institutional reasons. Intellectually, a radical Right has sought to undo those elements of statist organization that had been retained, largely in Europe, against American wishes. Institutionally, the creation of a genuine international division of labor in combination with recent freeing of financial markets from governmental regulation has suggested to many that capitalism, rather than states, now runs the world.

However, the ability of a national society to succeed within capitalism depends upon its state's ability to coordinate both workers and capitalists and to provide the necessary infrastructure such that citizens have the capacity to respond flexibly to international economic change. The practices of states in this regard are quite varied. Late industrial society does seem to benefit from high standards of education at every societal level, and increasing attention to this point is being given by economic leaders. Involvement of workers can be guaranteed in different ways, by the microcorporatism of German and Japanese firms or the macrocorporatism familiar from the Swedish model. States do not have a good record of managing firms themselves, not least because nationalized industries become powerful actors that are often able to prevent flexible responses. There is, however, every reason to believe that states can help business in myriad ways, for example by providing information about international market conditions, as is done particularly skillfully in Japan and the Republic of Korea (South Korea).

Thus, despite changes in the organization of capitalism, the evidence overwhelmingly goes against the assertion that states do not matter. They do, and any loss of their salience in certain areas of policy has been compensated for by their increased intervention in others. Competitive advantage is still created by nations. Organization internally and nationally enables a modern citizenry to swim in the larger sea of capitalist society; differently put, organization is needed internally because the principles of Adam Smith work externally. Anglo-Saxon countries, most notably Britain and the United States, which seek to marketize the insides of their society look, on current evidence, doomed to continuing economic decline.

Meanwhile, the overwhelming reality for most states in the world remains that of underdevelopment. The attempt to modernize quickly has placed

liberalism at a discount. Both state socialist regimes and authoritarian regimes inside capitalism have sought to achieve development by means of centralizing power. The fate of such nations in contemporary circumstances is one of the questions of the age.

The most striking fact about state-planned industrialization is that it proves to be ineffective, even counterproductive, once the earliest stages of economic growth have been achieved. This is the fundamental fact behind attempts to liberalize authoritarian regimes. Such liberalization attempts are driven by pressures from above and from below, the exact mix between the two varying according to national circumstance: rulers wish to gain *legitimacy (and modern weaponry) through economic growth while newly educated middle-class elements, functionally ever more important in late industrial society, consistently join reformist parties. It is becoming possible to distinguish between different types of liberalization. The fact that a double transition to democracy and to capitalism has to be made in postcommunist societies makes for very profound difficulties, with the distinct possibility that popular pressure might make it impossible for state leaders to implement necessary economic reforms. In this world, however, chances of success are highly variable. If biology is not, *pace* Freud, destiny, history often is: on this basis, Czechoslovakia (democratic and industrial in the interwar years) might be expected to fare better than Romania and Poland, but for the ethnic-nationalist tensions spurring dissolution of the union.

In contrast, the transition from authoritarian regimes within capitalist society is, in principle, easier. But here too variable outcomes, again often dictated by historical legacies, can be expected. An East Asian state such as South Korea has benefited from fundamental *land reform pushed through at the time of the *Korean War, a tradition of literacy and of a state, created by Imperial Japan, concerned with infrastructural affairs; furthermore, as the result of its geopolitical vulnerability it has gained a good deal—from loans to trading privileges—from the United States. Whereas one can hope for successful liberalization there, great fears attend the "openings" in countries such as Brazil and Argentina. Racked by debt, possessed of ruling classes with reference points abroad (to which they often export capital), and bereft of a state tradition concerned with infrastructural services, it seems possible that the oscillation between democracy and *military rule will continue, at least in the near future.

In fact, the majority of states within the less developed world do not look as if they are liberalizing at all. India is exceptional in retaining democracy in such circumstances. More typical are state apparatuses which are overly developed, that is, possessed of sophisticated weapons used internally against their own people—or, as in Africa, against ethnic elements other than those comprising the ruling elite.

System of States and the Question of Hegemony. The theorists of the interstate system have in recent years added a striking coda to traditional theory. Once capitalist society becomes industrial, a leading state is needed to provide key services for capitalism as a whole—particularly a common currency and an insistence on free trade. Both Britain and the United States are held to have provided such services; the fact of disputed hegemony after 1870 is held to be the underlying reason for international trade rivalry and full-scale geopolitical conflict thereafter.

This theory is not much of a guide to history: Britain had an economic lead but always faced genuine geopolitical rivals, but German expansionism is best explained in terms different from those suggested by the theory. The United States, on the other hand, was a genuine hegemon in 1945 in terms of both economic and military might; and it makes sense to see the theory in question, dubbed "hegemonic stability theory," as the *ideology of the postwar U.S. state elite.

U.S. hegemony has been exercised in two ways. In the period whose end was symbolized by the dollar "going off gold" in 1971, U.S. hegemony was benign. The *interdependence of the world economy increased both because the United States insisted on free trade and because it provided the defense for all of capitalist society. But the glories of this period—at least for the core of capitalist society—have been replaced by much more predatory behavior on the part of the United States. The leading state has refused to balance its budget, and in the last decade has absorbed most of the world's excess capital—something that bodes ill for both developing and liberalizing countries. Equally importantly, the United States has exported the inflation it created by refusing to finance the *Vietnam War by taxation. All this has created great resentment among the allies of the United States.

At present, however, it does not seem that resentment will lead to a new age of geopolitical confrontation. *Nuclear weapons make recourse to war less rational for state actors, while trading is, as attested by Mikhail *Gorbachev, Boris *Yeltsin, and their colleagues in the Soviet Union and its successor states, quite widely recognized as the best avenue to success. Furthermore, given the widespread realization that economic growth depends upon participating in an ever-larger and ever-faster international market, withdrawal from that market via protectionism (and, in consequence, trade wars) is relatively unlikely. In short, the world *political economy looks set to "muddle through."

The optimism of these last remarks amounts to saying that we can hope that there will be no World War III. But this optimism must be tempered. If major war is less likely, regional wars of ferocious intensity look ever more likely, particularly after the *Gulf War of 1991. Large parts of the Third World possess formidable armed forces, and some will possess nuclear weapons soon; and many such countries have not benefited from economic growth. This is a dangerous mix. It suggests that war will continue to affect the historical record.

Future of the State. A current claim in scientific and political discourse is that the state is likely to lose its importance in the future. Two forces seem to have occasioned this speculation. On the one hand, the state seems to be losing its powers, in a process of "hollowing out" due to the greater globalization of various international forces. The interdependence of the world economy, and in particular the growing share of world production taken by transnational corporations, is seen as withering the state's economic functions. In political terms, moreover, the emergence of supranational authorities, from the *International Monetary Fund and the *General Agreement on Tariffs and Trade (GATT) through, ever more dramatically, the *European Community, is seen as curtailing the state's authority in significant ways. To this we can add, as noted, the fact that the advanced nations have lost some of their geopolitical autonomy because of the nature of nuclear weapons.

There is some truth to these assertions, but they need to be qualified. Full-scale state sovereignty was never available in the European dynamic which was thereafter largely extended to the rest of the world: states always had to contend with the forces of capitalism and of interstate rivalry. The principal thrust of this essay is that the state has in myriad ways not lost its salience. Third World countries most certainly are states, and if their power is often greater in despotic than in infrastructural terms, it certainly shows no sign of diminishing. Equally, success within capitalist society seems to depend on national organization by the state. It may be that states, whether liberal or postcommunist, are now less attracted to actual central *planning of industries; but a loss of state direction in that quarter is often more than made up for by an increasing emphasis on state provision of other services, from education to seed money for infant industries. Finally, capitalist society is not, so to speak, pure: its institutions are not genuinely supranational since they were created and are still controlled by the United States. Most important of all, the behavior of the United States—still half preferring to change the rules of the *international system which it dominates rather than to adopt a genuine trading strategy of its own—remains that of a great state. The world may be more complex than before, but we cannot understand it without an appreciation of the workings of the state.

(See also BUREAUCRATIC POLITICS; CORPORATISM; DEMOCRATIC TRANSITIONS; INTERNATIONAL

DEBT; INTERNATIONAL POLITICAL ECONOMY; MODERNIZATION; MULTINATIONAL CORPORATIONS; PLURALISM; PROTECTION; REFORM; TAXES AND TAXATION.)

Kenneth Waltz, *Man, the State and War* (New York, 1959). Charles Tilly, ed., *The Formation of National States in Western Europe* (Princeton, N.J., 1975). Gianfranco Poggi, *The Development of the Modern State* (London, 1978). Theda Skocpol, *States and Social Revolutions* (Cambridge, U.K., 1979). Mancur Olson, *The Rise and Decline of Nations* (New Haven, Conn., 1982). Peter Katzenstein, *Small States in World Markets* (Ithaca, N.Y., 1985). Michael Mann, *States, War and Capitalism* (Oxford, 1988). John A. Hall and G. John Ikenberry, *The State* (Milton Keynes, U.K., 1989).

JOHN A. HALL

STRATEGIC ARMS LIMITATION TREATIES. Even before the explosion of the first nuclear device in 1945, scientists and policymakers sought ways to control the development and deployment of *nuclear weapons. Through the 1950s, the *United States and the *Soviet Union explored a variety of proposals for nuclear *disarmament and the control of fissionable materials required for the production of nuclear weapons. While these efforts had gained some momentum by 1957, the then-rapid pace of technological change, plus the substantial overall superiority of the United States, foreclosed grounds for agreement.

Negotiations in the early and mid-1960s were directed toward a number of issues which, while significant, did not directly address the U.S.-Soviet arms buildup: the Limited Test Ban Treaty (1963), which prohibited atmospheric nuclear detonations; two treaties prohibiting the placement of nuclear weapons in outer *space and on the ocean floor; and the Nuclear Non-Proliferation Treaty (1968), an attempt to create an international *regime to prevent the spread of nuclear weapons to other nations.

In 1967, President Lyndon *Johnson and Premier Alexei Kosygin held a summit in Glassboro, New Jersey, which laid the foundation for the Strategic Arms Limitation Talks (SALT). The strategic talks, which were delayed until 1969 as a result of the Soviet invasion of Czechoslovakia in 1968, continued almost without interruption throughout the 1970s and 1980s, and gave birth to several major *arms control treaties.

By 1972, U.S. and Soviet negotiators had concluded the first major treaty of the SALT process: the Antiballistic Missile (ABM) Treaty, which sharply restricted national defenses against nuclear missiles. The ABM Treaty stemmed from a recognition by both superpowers that attempts to build defenses against nuclear missiles could greatly intensify the *arms race. By the late 1960s, the Soviet Union had obtained a rough parity of strategic nuclear forces with the United States. The resulting nuclear balance guaranteed that the United States and the Soviet Union were in a state of "mutual assured destruction" (MAD), in which either country's society could be destroyed and still possess sufficient nuclear forces to retaliate. Deterrence under these conditions would be maintained by the certainty that an attack by one side would be met with a massive counterattack by the other. The rudimentary defensive systems that both the United States and the Soviet Union were constructing in the late 1960s threatened to undermine this deterrence with the prospect of a country possessing the ability to attack without fear of retaliation. The *superpowers were concerned that a new cycle of offensive and defensive buildups would begin, in which both nations would seek to build enough missiles to overwhelm the other's defenses, while fortifying their own.

The ABM Treaty not only prevented this dangerous new cycle in the arms race but, just as importantly, recognized that both nations had a common interest in preserving the stability of the nuclear balance. Coming at a time of nuclear parity between the United States and the Soviet Union, the treaty was an affirmation of the paradoxical security of MAD.

The first set of SALT talks also produced an interim agreement on limiting strategic nuclear missiles, which then served as the basis for the SALT II negotiations (1973–1979). The purpose of SALT II was to negotiate limits on the numbers and types of offensive strategic forces. The negotiations, among the most complicated ever undertaken, were plagued throughout by numerous technical and political obstacles. Disparities in the composition, technology, and strategy of each nation's nuclear forces prevented ready comparisons and trade-offs. New technologies such as the cruise missile and the multiple-warhead missile outpaced the negotiations and created tremendous challenges for verification. In the United States in the 1970s, a political tide was turning against the entire SALT process, while the gradual demise of *détente cast a shadow over the future of U.S.-Soviet relations in general.

By 1979, negotiators had reached agreement on a complicated set of ceilings and subceilings on the deployment of strategic nuclear forces, limiting each side to an aggregate of 2,250 launch vehicles (missiles and bombers). The limits imposed by the SALT II Treaty, however, were barely distinguishable from existing and planned deployments by both nations, prompting critics to charge that the agreement had failed to place any significant brake on the arms race (and, indeed, had the effect of sanctioning the existing nuclear stockpiles). The agreement's emphasis on numerical ceilings, furthermore, did not take into account the increasingly qualitative nature of developments in the arms race. For instance, targeting accuracy and mobility had become important factors in the strategic equation, as significant as the raw numbers of nuclear weapons possessed by each nation.

Despite these shortcomings, the SALT II Treaty represented an important step in laying the framework for discussing more significant reductions in strategic nuclear weapons. Although the treaty was never ratified by the U.S. Senate, the two countries adhered to its terms until President Ronald *Reagan breached the treaty's ceiling on cruise missile bombers in the mid-1980s.

Strategic arms control was mostly dormant in the early 1980s, the victim of the Soviet invasion of Afghanistan in 1979 and the conservative shift in U.S. politics beginning with the election of Ronald *Reagan in 1980. Negotiations made little progress until 1985. Then serious bargaining got under way in the Strategic Arms Reductions Talks (START), which had begun fruitlessly several years earlier. Their name reflected a new goal of reducing, rather than merely limiting, existing strategic arms. Mikhail *Gorbachev, the new leader in Moscow, was more determined than his predecessors to achieve nuclear reductions, and he also succeeded in establishing a personal and political rapport with President Ronald Reagan. Even so the issues were intricate, and negotiations continued for years in what were formally renamed the Nuclear and Space Talks.

The START negotiations, as they were still generally called, continued under the *Bush administration. Finally the remaining issues were settled, and the agreement was signed in July 1991 during a visit by President George Bush to Moscow. The START agreement reduces each side's strategic nuclear delivery vehicles by about forty percent, and each side's nuclear warheads by about thirty percent. Although thousands of nuclear weapons will be eliminated, the thousands remaining are still ample to destroy the United States and the former Soviet Union many times over.

The aborted coup in Moscow in August 1991, the dramatic decline in the authority of the central Soviet government, and the dissolution of the Soviet Union thereafter threw into question whether any further strategic arms limitation treaties would follow, with any Soviet-successor governments. But these events also opened the door to further reductions. To avoid the highly time-consuming process of negotiating treaties, President Bush announced within weeks major American nuclear reductions, beyond those required by START, to be carried out unilaterally. He invited similar action by the Soviet government, which President Gorbachev announced within days.

The decades of strategic arms control during the *Cold War produced a mixed record. The ABM Treaty was outstandingly successful in contributing to the stability of the nuclear balance. By essentially prohibiting any effective defense, it forestalled what could easily have become an intense race between offensive and defensive forces on both sides. But efforts to constrain, still less reduce, offensive forces proved far more difficult. The SALT I and II Treaties

essentially ratified offensive force levels then existing. Only START was able to reduce them, and START could be signed only when the Cold War was already over.

Coit D. Blacker and Gloria Duffy, eds., *International Arms Control* (Stanford, Calif., 1984). Arms Control Association, *Arms Control and National Security: An Introduction* (Washington, D.C., 1989).

RICHARD SMOKE

STRATEGY. The term *strategy* refers to the means that policymakers choose to attain desired ends. Strategy is, in effect, a course of action, a plan for achieving specified goals. Although the term can be used to describe a plan for applying means to attain ends in any realm of political life, it is most frequently used in military affairs, a usage that became common during the eighteenth century.

When used in the realm of warfare, strategy refers to the art of using force to bring about desired outcomes on the battlefield. It refers to the broad questions of how, when, and where to bring *force to bear against an adversary. While the goal of a given strategy may be the destruction of the enemy's war-making potential, countries that engage in *war often pursue objectives that fall far short of destroying the enemy's military capability. The goal of a successful military strategy is to attain, in the most efficient and least costly fashion, a country's military objectives, whatever those objectives may consist of.

There are three broad types of military strategy. Offensive strategies involve taking the battle to the adversary, often to the end of destroying the enemy's fighting capability or compelling the enemy to retreat or surrender. Defensive strategies involve blocking the adversary's attack and denying the enemy its objectives. Deterrent strategies attempt to raise the cost to the adversary of continuing the battle, seeking to convince the enemy to abandon its aggressive intentions. Whereas offensive and defensive strategies focus on wearing down the enemy's military capability, deterrent strategies focus on wearing down the enemy's will. In any given campaign, military commanders may well use a mix of these strategies to attain their objectives most effectively.

Military planners formulate strategy at differing levels of generality. The term *grand strategy* refers to overarching plans that seek to balance a country's resources with its global military commitments. Formulating grand strategy involves determining the set of military objectives that devolve from a country's national interests and the threats that exist to those interests, identifying geographic and functional missions, and allocating available military resources to those missions.

During the nineteenth century, for example, British grand strategy involved maintaining a *balance of power on the European continent largely through shifting its political alignments with other European countries, while relying on the unrivaled Royal Navy to protect imperial lines of communication. During the *Cold War, U.S. grand strategy was based on the notion of *containment: preventing the Soviet Union from gaining control over the main industrial centers of Eurasia while restricting the spread of Soviet influence in the *Third World.

Grand strategy is distinct from theater strategy, which refers to planning for military operations in a specific geographic area. Theater strategy specifies how many and what types of forces are needed in a given region and how those forces would be used in battle. For example, the infamous Schlieffen plan— the strategy used by Germany at the outset of *World War I—called for German forces to hold defensive positions on the eastern front against Russia while mounting a decisive attack against France on the western front. During the Cold War, the *North Atlantic Treaty Organization's strategy for defending Western Europe against a Soviet attack called for forward defense with conventional weapons in Germany and escalation to the use of *nuclear weapons should conventional forces fail to halt the Soviet advance.

Strategy is distinct from tactics, which focus more narrowly on the actual placement and movement of troops on the battlefield. Whereas strategy seeks to identify how best to attain military objectives through the course of a campaign, tactical considerations focus on day-to-day prosecution of the battle: how to take advantage of the terrain, whether to attempt to penetrate the enemy's defensive line or to attack from the flanks, whether to retreat when under fire or to hold one's position, etc.

Military planners and scholars of military affairs have long searched for fundamental rules to govern the formulation of strategy. Inquiry has focused on a broad range of questions, including the following: What level of numerical superiority is necessary to ensure military victory? Is it preferable to be on the offensive, or does the defender enjoy tactical advantages that offset the attacker's ability to choose the time and place of battle? How important is the element of surprise?

Although some generalizations about strategy have emerged from inquiry into these questions, understanding the nature of warfare remains an intractable problem. The obstacles to a better understanding of war and a more scientific approach to formulating strategy stem in part from the unique nature of each battle. The quality and morale of opposing forces, the terrain, the climate, the technological sophistication of weaponry—these factors vary widely from case to case. Furthermore, the "fog of war"—the confusion and uncertainty that often pervade the battlefield—makes it very difficult, if not impossible, to transform the art of strategy into a science.

The term *strategic weapons* is commonly used to refer to intercontinental missiles armed with nuclear warheads. *Strategic studies* refers to scholarly inquiry into military affairs, broadly defined. In the context of *game theory, an analytic technique used to model bargaining between parties, strategy refers to the pattern of play that a given side pursues in order to attain its preferred outcome. If following a "tit-for-tat" strategy, for example, a player simply responds in kind to its opponent's move in each round of play.

(See also ALLIANCE; CLAUSEWITZ, CARL VON; DETERRENCE; FOREIGN POLICY.)

Edward Mead Earle et al., eds., *Makers of Modern Strategy* (Princeton, N.J., 1971).

CHARLES KUPCHAN

SUDAN. The rising tide of *nationalism in the 1940s reflected in the Graduates' Congress—a liberation movement led by Ismail el-Azhri—forced Anglo-Egyptian rulers to accommodate greater participation by Sudanese in government institutions such as the Advisory Council and the Legislative Assembly. Among the Sudanese members of these bodies were the founders of the new political parties: the Nationalist United Party (NUP), associated with Ali el-Marghani, leader of Khatmiya, a religious sect; and the Umma Party under the patronage of Abdel-Rahman el-Mahdi, the son of Mahdi, leader of another religious sect that ruled Sudan from 1881 to 1898. A larger measure of self-government was accorded in 1953 when Sudan's first Parliament was opened with Premier el-Azhri heading an NUP government.

Full independence of what is physically the largest country in Africa—2.5 million square kilometers, or 967,500 square miles—was achieved on 1 January 1956, when el-Azhri and the NUP rejected union with Egypt. Political rivalry led to uncertainty and speculation over the composition of a coalition government. That led, in turn, to neglect of administration and the southern problem, which had originated in 1930 when the south was isolated culturally and linguistically from the north.

Amid political uncertainty, General Ibrahim Abboud led a military *coup d'état on 17 November 1958. A state of emergency was declared, political parties were dissolved, and the press was controlled. Unlike the military regime in neighboring Egypt, Abboud's regime was too conservative to introduce radical changes that might have won it popular support. The regime remained unstable as many coups were unsuccessfully attempted, and the southern conflict deepened as a federation for the south proved to be illusory. The Anya Nya, southern guerrilla groups, resisted the regime, attacking military targets following the closing of two schools in the south. The continued civil war led to the October Revolution of 1964 when a Khartoum University student meeting held on 21 October to discuss the civil war was interrupted by gunfire, killing one student. Public demonstrations and a general strike forced the junta to surrender power. However, the protection of the coup leaders from any public accountability for their period in office encouraged future army interventions, trapping Sudan in a cycle of ineffective civilian and military regimes.

A broad civilian transitional government headed by a neutral premier, Siralkhatim el-Khalifa, was formed. Divisions among political parties and revolutionary leaders were exacerbated by north-south tensions, resulting in inactive government. The 1965 elections brought to power a coalition of Umma, the NUP, and the Southern Front—a political party founded in 1962 by southern politicians—under Umma premier Mohamed Ahmed Mahjoub. A year later the Umma Party split and a new coalition was created under Sadiq el-Mahdi. However, the 1968 elections returned the former coalition. The continuance of unstable coalition building resulted in five governments between 1965 and 1969, and reflected the deep historic rivalries between the two sects. The instability led to neglect in designing policies for ending the civil war and for developing a new constitution.

Because of this breakdown, the military coup of 25 May 1969, led by Colonel Ja'afar Nimeiri, was not entirely unexpected. Once again, political parties were dissolved. However, lacking a mass political organization and for reasons of ideological sympathy, Nimeiri aligned himself with the Communists. Their influence on policy was obvious. More arms and advisers from the Soviet Union and Eastern Europe arrived following the *nationalization of foreign and domestic private enterprises. Nevertheless, tensions between the Communists and Nimeiri's Revolutionary Command Council (RCC) arose in 1971 when two Communist members of the RCC, Hashim el-Atta and Babikir el-Nour, were ejected. El-Atta retaliated by leading a military coup on 19 July 1971. The coup, which was seen by the two sects as a complete Communist takeover, failed after three days, and the coup leaders were executed. Nimeiri's problems were not solved by the elimination of the Communists, however, for the unstable army faced a continuing war against the Anya Nya. Lacking allies, the Nimeiri regime was left with no other option than to end the civil war. Western support was rendered to consolidate Nimeiri following his break with the Communists and the Soviet Union. The Addis Ababa Agreement of 1972 ended the civil war by granting the south a unique status within Sudan.

Nevertheless, opposition increased and the regime remained unstable, surviving four subsequent overthrow attempts. Negotiations toward national reconciliation were entered into with the opposition in exile but these proved unsuccessful. Given the refusal to cooperate of the leaders of the two sects, Hassan el-Turabi, Muslim Brothers leader, seized the opportunity and built the National Islamic Front (NIF) under the patronage of Nimeiri's regime. Ideologically, the regime was transformed when *shari'a (Islamic law) was decreed in September 1983. The predominantly non-Muslim south witnessed a wave of mutinies, led by former army colonel John Garang, leader of what became the Sudan People's Liberation Army (SPLA). Supported by Ethiopia, Libya, Israel, and even Cuba, Garang's attacks forced the abandonment of work on oil fields in the south.

Nimeiri was seen as a reliable U.S. ally, providing a valuable counterweight to the threat posed by Ethiopia and Libya to U.S. interests in the Red Sea and the *Horn of Africa. Consequently, during the period 1980–1985 only Egypt among African nations received more U.S. economic and military aid than did Sudan. Nevertheless, economic conditions deteriorated and Western aid came with its conditions: liberalization of prices, trade, and other economic policies that took little consideration of the structure of the economy. Social unrest developed as the economic crisis deepened, with stagnant national income, double-digit inflation, and foreign debt amounting to US$8 billion.

Nimeiri's downfall after a popular uprising in April 1985, the return of liberal *democracy, and the continuing war in the south closely resembled events surrounding the overthrow of Abboud. But unlike the complete withdrawal of the army in 1964, a transitional military government headed by General Siwar el-Dhahab, one of Nimeiri's officers, provided a relatively smooth transition by holding elections in 1986. However, the government was, like the first transitional one, largely inactive, with no plans to reform the economy or to address the southern conflict. It was compelled to transfer power to civilians.

The unstable Umma-NUP coalition was threatened in the 1986 elections when the NIF won fifty-one seats as compared with the NUP's sixty-three and Umma's 100. Consequently, many successive coalitions (including the May 1988 coalition in which the NIF was included) swiftly collapsed. The problem of maintaining a government at all became the central issue, whereas urgent issues—the economy and the south—appeared largely beyond the capacity of the government. Premier Sadiq el-Mahdi's negotiations with Garang in 1987 and NUP-SPLA meetings in 1988 failed to end the civil war, which continued to drain the budget by US$1 million per day. Economic conditions continued to deteriorate as inflation and shortages worsened. Foreign debt accumulated to US$10 billion. A once-prosperous state that rejected a major U.S. aid package in 1956 is now an increasingly dependent recipient of aid. Again, the military coup of 30 June 1989 led by Brigadier Omer Hassan el-Bashir was regarded by many people as inevitable. By 1992 the el-Bashir junta was still running the country, but under the influence of the NIF.

(See also ETHNICITY; INTERNATIONAL DEBT; MILITARY RULE; SECESSIONIST MOVEMENTS.)

Mohamed Omer Beshir, *The Southern Sudan: Background to Conflict* (London, 1968). Tim Niblock, *Class and Power in Sudan: The Dynamics of Sudanese Politics, 1898–1985* (London, 1987). Peter Woodward, *Sudan, 1898–1989: The Unstable State* (Boulder, Colo., 1990). Fareed Mohamed Ahmed Hassan, *Impact of Structural Adjustment Program on the Sudanese Economy* (Khartoum, 1991).

FAREED MOHAMED AHMED HASSAN

SUEZ CRISIS. The Suez crisis of 1956 began with President Gamal Abdel *Nasser's speech of 26 July 1956 announcing the *nationalization of the Suez Canal. This itself was a response to the U.S. decision, supported by the British, to withdraw the offer of financial assistance for *Egypt's proposed Aswan High Dam. Nationalization was bitterly resented by the British and French governments, which saw it as an act of self-aggrandizement on President Nasser's part and a threat to their vital interests. Both prepared their forces to invade Egypt while going through the motions of trying to negotiate the international management of the canal.

The crisis culminated in the coordinated military attack by Britain, France, and Israel beginning on 29 October 1956. British and French forces occupied Port Said but were forced to withdraw under intense U.S. economic pressure. A UN Emergency Force was hastily established to replace the invading armies. The canal was then cleared of the obstacles sunk by the Egyptians and reopened to traffic in April 1957. Meanwhile, Israel was forced to withdraw its forces from the Sinai Peninsula in March 1957, also under U.S. pressure.

The response of Sir Anthony Eden's British government to the crisis was dictated by its determination to use force to overthrow Nasser. But it was also anxious to do this in a way which would neither offend the United States nor the many Britons who were bitterly opposed to an attack on Egypt. Eden's mismanagement of the crisis led to his resignation as prime minister in January 1957 and his replacement by Harold Macmillan. Both Macmillan and President Dwight *Eisenhower were quick to restore the Anglo-American partnership. The Conservative Party under Macmillan then went on to win the general election of 1959 in which the Suez issue played little role. For Macmillan and his colleagues the main lessons of the crisis concerned the extent of British dependence on the United States and the lack of support from major *Commonwealth countries like India. Many were now persuaded that Britain's future lay not with its Empire but Europe.

Unlike the British, French public opinion was almost unanimous in its belief that force should be used against Egypt, which was widely seen as the main supporter of the Algerian rebellion begun in 1955. However, the government of Guy Mollet realized that it had to act in concert with the British, and it was for this reason that, in October 1956, it suggested the idea of cooperation with Israel, to which it was already supplying arms. Many in France,

including senior officers, were unhappy at being forced to stop military action before it had either secured the whole of the canal or led to the overthrow of Nasser. In this way, failure at Suez was one of the major factors exacerbating the political divisions which encouraged the collapse of the Fourth Republic in 1958, the return of President Charles de *Gaulle, and the decision to grant Algeria its independence. A second result was the belief that it was unwise to allow France to remain dependent on Britain and the United States, something which did much to stimulate the development of France's independent deterrent (the *force de frappe*) and its entry into the European Economic Community as a founding member in 1957.

U.S. policy toward the Suez crisis was guided by President Eisenhower's desire to secure a peaceful settlement without alienating his British and French allies. Once the invasion had begun, Eisenhower's aim was the immediate withdrawal of the Anglo-French force under UN auspices, followed by the reconstruction of the Western alliance. To this end, during a major run on the British pound, he held up U.S. financial assistance until military evacuation was complete. He was similarly adamant about Israeli withdrawal. Soviet and Arab reaction to the crisis then persuaded him that swift action was necessary to prevent the communists and their allies from filling the vacuum left by the retreating British and French. The result was the so-called *Eisenhower Doctrine, which stated that the United States was willing to use armed force in the Middle East in the event of communist aggression. As a result, Washington lost much of the credit that it had obtained in the Arab world for its strong stand against the invasion.

The one Great Power which was not directly involved with the crisis was the Soviet Union. This was partly because it was engaged in putting down the revolt that had broken out in Hungary just before the invasion, partly because the Soviets could derive great benefit from the affair by simply identifying themselves with a Third World country subject to imperialist aggression. Moscow's only major political intervention was on 5 November 1956 when it proposed joint action with the United States against Britain and France, accompanied by an unspecified military threat if a cease-fire was not immediately accepted. The Soviet Union was also quick to provide economic and military aid to Egypt, followed by an offer to finance Egypt's new development program and then, in October 1958, to assist in the funding and the construction of the Aswan Dam. In this way the Soviets were able to use the crisis to establish themselves as a major rival to the United States in the region and the primary source of assistance to important Middle Eastern states like Egypt, Syria, and Iraq.

In the Middle East itself, the person who benefited most from the crisis was President Nasser. Not only had he kept the canal in Egyptian hands but he also became the focus for widespread Arab support. His immediate response was to try to increase inter-Arab cooperation as well as to extend his influence into countries like Jordan, Saudi Arabia, and Iraq, which he identified as allies of the West. But the most immediate result was his acceptance of Syrian requests for political union, which culminated in the creation of the United Arab Republic (UAR) in February 1958. On the domestic front, the nationalization of British, French, and Jewish property which accompanied the invasion provided the spur to a large extension of state enterprise and, ultimately, to the move to a centrally planned economy in 1961.

Israel also derived benefit from the crisis. It obtained the right of free passage through the Gulf of Aqaba, denied by Egypt since 1948, and so commercial access to the countries of Africa and Asia. There was also a considerable decline in the number of armed incursions from the Gaza Strip and elsewhere until the mid-1960s. More problematic was the partial security guarantee which the Israeli government obtained from the United States at the time of its military withdrawal from the Sinai Peninsula. This was not honored during the Arab-Israeli crisis which preceded the June War of 1967.

As far as the *Middle East was concerned, the Suez crisis of 1956 accelerated the decline of British and French influence and paved the way for the Soviet and U.S. domination which lasted until the decline of the Soviet position in the early 1970s. It provided an important but temporary victory for President Nasser and his type of secular *Arab nationalism and transformed the dispute between Israelis and Palestinians into one between Israel and the surrounding Arab states.

(See also ALGERIAN WAR OF INDEPENDENCE; ARAB-ISRAELI CONFLICT; NASSERISM.)

Donald Neff, *Warriors at Suez: Eisenhower Takes America into the Middle East* (New York, 1981). Mohamed H. Heikal, *Cutting the Lion's Tale: Suez Through Egyptian Eyes* (London, 1986). Wm. Roger Louis and Roger Owen, eds., *Suez 1956: The Crisis and its Consequences* (Oxford, 1989). Keith Kyle, *The Suez Crisis: Thirty Years After* (London, 1991). Ilan Troen and Moshe Shemesh, eds., *The Suez-Sinai Crisis: Retrospective and Reappraisal* (London, 1990).

ROGER OWEN

SUPERPOWER. During the post–*World War II era, the United States and the Soviet Union have been called superpowers because of their predominant military power. The term became widely used after the publication of William Fox's *The Super-Powers* (New York, 1944). Superpowers are distinguished from traditional great powers because of the absolute and relative size of their military predominance. In absolute terms, both the United States and the Soviet Union developed nuclear arsenals capable of massive destruction. In relative terms, U.S. and Soviet military might far surpassed that of other powers. This relative predominance led to the emergence of a bipolar international structure after 1945. Competition between these two poles produced the *Cold War and led to the formation of the *North Atlantic Treaty Organization and the *Warsaw Treaty Organization—military alliances that effectively divided Europe into two opposing blocs.

While the military arsenals of the United States and Russia (after the dissolution of the Soviet Union) still qualify them as superpowers, a combination of factors—principally Russian reliance on Western economic assistance—radically undermine Russian global influence. The gradual proliferation of military capability to other countries and the *arms control initiatives associated with the waning of the Cold War have moved the *international system toward a more multipolar structure. Furthermore, the end of hostile East-West relations serves to decrease the importance of military capability and increase the importance of economic capability as determinants of international influence. In this respect, the waning of the Cold War enhances the influence of economic powers such as the Federal Republic of Germany and Japan.

(See also DÉTENTE; NUCLEAR WEAPONS.)

Anton Deporte, *Europe Between the Superpowers: The Enduring Balance* (New Haven, Conn., 1979).

CHARLES KUPCHAN

SUPREME COURT OF THE UNITED STATES. The U.S. *Constitution of 1787 sketched a bare outline of the federal judicial power. Article III established only one federal court—the Supreme Court—leaving *Congress, in the Judiciary Act of 1789, to create the lower federal courts, to fix the number of justices on the high court, and to set its appellate jurisdiction. The Constitution provided that the president would appoint the justices with the advice and consent of the Senate, leaving their specific qualifications (should they be lawyers? should they have previous judicial experience? should they be native-born citizens?) undefined. This open-ended process invited the president to consider political and not just professional legal qualifications. The delegates to the Philadelphia convention also clothed the justices with substantial independence by granting them tenure during good behavior and providing for their removal from office only after impeachment by the House of Representatives and conviction by the Senate.

In response to complaints by states' rights advocates that the proposed Constitution granted too much autonomy to the Court, Alexander Hamilton formulated his classic nationalist defense of judicial independence. Hamilton proclaimed in *Federalist 78* (1787) that "the judiciary . . . will always be the least dangerous to the political rights of the Constitution" (Clinton Rossiter, ed., *The Federalist Papers*,

p. 465). Because the Court commanded only the authority of its legal judgment instead of the power of the purse and the sword, the justices would be able to consult "nothing . . . but the Constitution and its laws" (p. 471). Accordingly, he asserted that an independent federal judiciary, generally, and the Supreme Court, specifically, offered the best protection for the *rights of citizens under the new Constitution. Hamilton's arguments remain compelling, even though today the justices exercise far greater influence over political issues than Hamilton anticipated.

The growth of the Supreme Court's power is attributable at least as much to the exigencies of U.S. *political culture as to any effort on the part of the justices to broaden their authority. As Alexis de Tocqueville observed in the 1830s, law in the United States is an extension of political discourse, so much so that "scarcely any political question arises in the United States that is not resolved, sooner or later, into a judicial question" (*Democracy in America*, vol. 1, ed. Phillips Bradley [1945], p. 290). The justices, however, have also played a decisive role in expanding their influence over public affairs, often doing so by disavowing that they either wanted or should have such influence. For example, in addressing a directive from Congress to seat federal judges as pension claims commissioners, Chief Justice John Jay stated in *Hayburn's Case* (1793) that Congress could only assign judges to judicial and not administrative duties. In the same year, Jay refused President George Washington's request for an advisory interpretation of the 1778 Franco-American treaty. By limiting the Court to actual rather than hypothetical disputes, the justices sought to assure themselves that when they spoke they did so in ways that would have direct rather than imagined consequences.

Chief Justice John Marshall (1803–1835) built upon this early foundation by establishing the authority of the Court to interpret conclusively the meaning of the Constitution. He did so by establishing the institution of *judicial review, doing so for federal legislation in *Marbury* v. *Madison* (1803), in which the Court declared a portion of the Judiciary Act of 1789 unconstitutional, and for state legislation in such cases as *McCulloch* v. *Maryland* (1819), which voided a Maryland law imposing a tax on the Second Bank of the United States. The cost of this heightened judicial authority over constitutional interpretation was inevitably the judiciary's greater involvement in the political system.

Throughout the remainder of the nineteenth century, Marshall's successors expanded the scope of judicial review and the prestige of the Court at the same time that they refused to adjudicate so-called political questions. In *Luther* v. *Borden* (1849), Chief Justice Roger B. Taney held that the question of which of two competing governments in Rhode Island was legitimate was entirely "political in na-

ture." Therefore, Taney concluded, the political branches of the federal government, not the courts, could best determine whether Rhode Island or any other state had met the mandate of the Guarantee Clause of Article IV that each state have a republican form of government. The judiciary, Taney observed, had no role to play; its business was legal, not political.

As in the nineteenth century, the Court also deferred in the twentieth century to the legislative and executive branches in matters involving war and foreign affairs. In *Korematsu* v. *United States* (1944), for example, the justices invoked national security to approve the relocation of Japanese-American citizens based solely on their ancestry. The Court's actions echoed decisions during World War I that affirmed the power of the national government to proscribe political dissent to a degree unthinkable in peacetime (e.g., *Schenck* v. *United States* [1918]). In a dispute arising out of President Jimmy Carter's termination of a treaty with Taiwan, the justices in *Goldwater* v. *Carter* (1979) refused to determine whether Congress's approval of the termination was required by the Constitution. The Court did reluctantly enter the foreign policy arena in *Dames & Moore* v. *Regan* (1981), upholding an executive order, issued after Iran's release of American hostages, that effectively prevented the petitioner's recovery of assets from the government of Iran. Stressing the narrowness of its decision, the Court precluded further action on the case as precedent.

The justices themselves have recognized that regulating the standards granting litigants access to the Court can influence its power. The Court has found a textual limit to its power of review in the "cases and controversies" clause of Article III. Accordingly, suits must be justiciable before the Court will decide them, and the party bringing the suit must have standing to do so. The Court will not accept friendly or collusive controversies, moot causes, and disputes lacking in ripeness. For instance, in *Muskrat* v. *United States* (1912), the justices dismissed a suit paid for by the defendant, the U.S. government, because the action was a friendly controversy meant to gain an advisory opinion on the constitutionality of federal legislation. Similarly, a cause was found moot in *Atherton Mills* v. *Johnson* (1922) where the plaintiff, who initiated the suit to challenge the regulation of minor laborers, was no longer governed by the law's age limits when the case came before the Court. The action in *United Public Works* v. *Mitchell* (1947) was also beyond the Court's "judgment" because the law banning political campaigning by federal employees was challenged by plaintiffs who had not been charged with violating the statute in question. According to Justice Robert H. Jackson, a "hypothetical threat" to the plaintiffs' constitutional rights was insufficient to confer jurisdiction, and the suit was dismissed because it had not "ripened" into an actual contest.

Despite these examples, the justices have often honored the concept of judicial restraint more in word than deed. In *Dred Scott* v. *Sandford* (1857), for example, Chief Justice Taney attempted to settle the highly explosive political issue of slavery in the territories by declaring that persons of African descent were not citizens of the United States and that they had no rights that white men were bound to respect. Taney's position stirred outrage among free-state Republicans on the eve of the Civil War. In *Pollock* v. *Farmers Loan and Trust Company* (1895), a bare majority of the Court declared the federal income tax unconstitutional, a position that was not reversed until the passage of the Sixteenth Amendment in 1913.

The Court, moreover, is hardly a self-regulating institution; instead, its agenda is shaped by the character of the litigation that comes before it, which is in turn the product of shifting social demands. Until 1937, for example, the justices invoked the doctrines of liberty to contract and substantive due process of law to limit government intervention in the economy. The Great Depression shattered the myth of laissez-faire constitutionalism and free-market economics that supported these doctrines, but even so the Court refused to extend constitutional support to Franklin D. *Roosevelt's innovative *New Deal economic programs. Initially, the justices struck down several pieces of Roosevelt's legislative program. Eventually, however, they reversed field, deciding in *West Coast Hotel* v. *Parrish* (1937) and *Jones & Laughlin Steel Corporation* v. *National Labor Relations Board* (1937) that state legislatures and Congress had broad power over the economy. Having changed course, however, the Court did not go out of business; instead, civil-liberties and civil-rights activists, represented by the American Civil Liberties Union and the National Association for the Advancement of Colored People, demanded an increased portion of the Court's time.

Under the leadership of Chief Justice Earl Warren (1953–1969), for example, the Court became a judicial engine of social reform. Beginning with *Brown* v. *Board of Education* (1954), the justices made a permanent imprint on race relations in the United States by ordering an end to separate-but-equal public schools. Opponents of the Court retaliated by claiming that Warren and his colleagues were unelected, and therefore unaccountable, judges who sought to substitute their personal preferences for that of legislative majorities.

The dramatic expansion of judicial "judgment" for the sake of racial equality was followed by the Court's equally bold venture into the once-taboo field of "political questions." In the interest of electoral fairness, the Court in *Baker* v. *Carr* (1962) refashioned the political questions doctrine to permit judicial review of state apportionment plans. The Warren Court also departed from the historic practice of permitting the president and Congress to operate according to their own rules. In *Powell* v. *McCormack* (1969), the justices responded to an attempt, under House of Representative rules, to exclude a duly elected member, Adam Clayton Powell, from sitting in the House. The Court held that, regardless of the House's internal procedures, the Constitution gave Congress only the power to remove a member, not the power to exclude.

The modern Court has also become more directly engaged in policy making by exercising greater selectivity than in the past over the cases that it hears while simultaneously easing some of the traditional barriers to access. Through the course of the twentieth century Congress has substantially broadened the Court's certiorari jurisdiction, enabling the justices to select those cases that they deem most important. While the traditional barriers of justiciability such as ripeness and mootness remain in force, the justices in certain areas have narrowed them somewhat. For example, the ripeness doctrine of *Mitchell* was modified in *Steffel* v. *Thompson* (1974) where a policeman's threat to arrest the plaintiff for distributing antiwar literature sufficed to confer standing to challenge the relevant statute. Similarly, in the landmark abortion case of *Roe* v. *Wade* (1973), a majority of the justices concluded that the mootness doctrine did not apply, even though the petitioner had already terminated her pregnancy by the time the Court accepted the case.

By design and circumstance, the seemingly apolitical Supreme Court has emerged over the past two centuries as more than a court but less than a full-blown political institution. Hamilton believed that certain constraints on the Court would permit the justices to transcend politics and devote themselves exclusively to guarding the Constitution. For Hamilton, the Court's independence from direct political accountability guaranteed both its limited power and its subordination to the legislative and executive branches. Yet as Tocqueville observed, the tendency of U.S. politics to elevate crucial issues to the plain of constitutional struggle has necessarily made the Court more politically aggressive and more constitutionally innovative than Hamilton anticipated. To remain the supreme arbiter of the Constitution, the Court, paradoxically, has had to be of the world of politics without being in that world. One measure of the Court's historic success is how well it has cultivated its institutional strength by fulfilling this difficult task.

(See also CIVIL RIGHTS MOVEMENT; PRESIDENCY, U.S.; UNITED STATES.)

Robert G. McCloskey, *The American Supreme Court* (Chicago, 1960). Alexander Bickel, *The Least Dangerous Branch: The Supreme Court at the Bar of Politics* (Indianapolis, 1962). Kermit L. Hall, *The Supreme Court and Judicial Review in American History, 1789–1981* (Washington, D. C., 1985). William M. Wiecek, *Liberty Under Law: The Supreme Court in American Life* (Baltimore, Md., 1988). Alfred H. Kelly, Winfred A. Harbison, and Herman Belz,

The American Constitution: Its Origins and Development, 7th ed. (New York, 1991).

KERMIT L. HALL
MITCHELL S. RITCHIE

H. E. Chin and H. Buddingh'. *Surinam: Politics, Economics and Society* (London, 1987).

EDWARD M. DEW

SURINAME. Once a member, together with the Netherlands Antilles, of the Tripartite Kingdom of the Netherlands, Suriname achieved its independence on 25 November 1975. For five years this small country on the north coast of South America—its population is approximately 400,000—was governed as a parliamentary republic by a largely black ("Creole") government counterposed by a largely East Indian ("Hindustani") opposition. The existence of a number of other fairly sizable ethnic groups (Indonesians, Bush Negroes, Amerindians, Chinese, Syrians, and Dutch) meant that neither of the two largest groups could control the government without a multiethnic alliance of some kind. Nevertheless, the Creole-Hindustani rivalry paralyzed the system and precipitated a military coup on 25 February 1980.

Seven governments in as many years followed, as the military leader, Desi Bouterse, shuffled civilians in and out of office. Enthusiasm at the possibility of transcending ethnic politics turned to dismay as misgovernment, corruption, and human rights violations followed. A guerrilla war of Bush Negroes (descendants of escaped slaves) broke out in the summer of 1986. This, together with financial pressure from the *Netherlands and student and other demonstrations in the capital, Paramaribo, led Bouterse to restore democracy in 1987. A constitution was approved on 30 September, and elections followed on 25 November with a coalition of the Creole, Hindustani, and Indonesian parties driving the promilitary party from power.

This new government, headed by President Ramsewak Shankar and Vice President Henck Aaron, is a cross between French and German models. Both the president and vice president are selected by and accountable to the fifty-one-member National Assembly. The vice president serves as head of the cabinet and directs the government. Yet the president's powers to force legislative reconsideration and to take other initiatives make him more than a ceremonial figure. Even more powerful, it seems, is Desi Bouterse, who remains the military's commander in chief. In the years since democracy's restoration, Bouterse has blocked all initiatives to end the guerrilla war and has placed a cloud of suspicion over the country for alleged use of airstrips in the interior for the transshipment of drugs to Europe and the United States.

On 24 December 1990, the Shankar-Aaron government was overthrown by the military. New elections were held in May 1991. The same multiethnic coalition emerged victorious. Heading the new government are Ronald Venetiaan (president) and Jules Adjodhia (vice president).

(See also GUERRILLA WARFARE.)

SWAZILAND. See BLS STATES.

SWEDEN. A small, affluent nation located in *Scandinavia in northern Europe, Sweden is commonly considered the archetype of the modern *welfare state. Its 8.3 million inhabitants enjoy one of the highest per capita incomes in the world. The Swedish economy is highly dependent on the export of manufactured goods, and its manufacturing sector is dominated by a small number of large, private firms. Alongside these capitalist features, Sweden has the highest rate of taxation of any country in the *Organization for Economic Co-operation and Development (OECD). In 1990 government expenditures equaled sixty percent of GDP (down from sixty-seven percent in 1982). The public provision of welfare encompasses a wide range of services as well as cash benefits, and public employment accounted for twenty-eight percent of total employment (working hours) in 1988. Centralized, economy-wide wage bargaining constitutes another distinctive feature of the "mixed economy" that Sweden developed in the postwar era.

The size of the welfare state and the centralization of wage bargaining are related, as both effect and cause, to the strength of the Swedish labor movement. With unions organizing more than eighty-five percent of all wage earners, Sweden stands out as the most thoroughly unionized country in Europe. Closely tied to the powerful confederation of blue-collar unions (*Landsorganisationen,* or LO), the Social Democratic Party has dominated Swedish politics since the 1930s. From 1932 to 1976, Sweden had but three prime ministers (Per Albin Hansson, Tage Erlander, and Olof Palme), all Social Democrats. Following a brief stint in opposition (1976–1982), the Social Democrats scored three successive election victories in the 1980s. Their economic policy successes unraveled in 1989–1991, however. With the Social Democrats polling only 37.6 percent of the popular vote, their worst election score since 1928, the election of 1991 ushered in the formation of a non-Socialist, four-party coalition government headed by the Conservative leader, Carl Bildt. In the aftermath of this historic election, the future contours of Swedish politics are uncertain.

The Social Bases of Politics. By comparative standards, Sweden industrialized late and rapidly. The industrial revolution did not begin in earnest until the 1890s, and thirty-five percent of the economically active population were engaged in agriculture as late as 1930. Feudalism was much weaker in Sweden than on the European continent, and the class of small farmers that emerged through the enclosure movement of the nineteenth century inherited a political tradition of peasant independence vis-à-vis the nobility. This tradition provided the basis for a reformist coalition of workers and farmers in the twentieth century: in the 1930s, and again in the 1950s, the Social Democrats governed in coalition with the Farmers' Party.

As foreign demand for Swedish raw materials (iron and timber) drove the industrialization process in its initial phase, the distinctive working-class culture of scattered mill towns shaped the outlook of the early labor movement. The experience of the struggle for democracy also contributed to the formation of a labor movement characterized by a mixture of political pragmatism and class solidarity.

The period from the 1930s to the mid-1970s witnessed a dramatic *urbanization process, promoted by Social Democratic governments. Today, roughly twenty-five percent of the population lives in three major conurbations (Stockholm, Göteborg, and Malmö). Following the general pattern of advanced capitalist countries, the growth of blue-collar and industrial employment slowed down as white-collar and service employment began to expand in the postwar period. Blue-collar employees constituted fifty-three percent and white-collar employees twenty-six percent of the electorate in 1956. By 1988, the former figure had fallen to forty-one percent and the latter figure had risen to forty-seven percent. By the late 1980s, the rate of unionization among white-collar employees had nearly caught up with that of blue-collar employees, but white-collar unions have their own separate confederal organizations (the Central Organization of Salaried Employees, or TCO, and the Central Organization of Professional Associations, or SACO), and postwar changes in the structure of employment have contributed to growing tensions between LO and the Social Democratic Party. To maintain their electoral position, the Social Democrats have had to mobilize increased support among white-collar voters.

Political Institutions. Sweden became a hereditary monarchy and a national state with a unitary structure in the sixteenth century. Ever since, the central government has enjoyed complete lawmaking authority. While there exists a long tradition of municipal self-government within the framework of national legislation, regional authorities have always played a minor role in the Swedish system of government. At the central level, the most distinctive feature of the Swedish state is the fact that ministries are small and have very few administrative responsibilities. The task of implementing government policy rests with state agencies (*ämbetsverk*) run by civil servants, and the ability of elected politicians to influence their activities is strictly limited. The autonomy and professionalism of the civil service constitutes an important feature of the consensual cast of Swedish politics.

Adopted in 1809, Sweden's first constitution checked the exercise of royal authority by affirming civic rights of citizenship. Originally an assembly of estates, the *Riksdag* became a bicameral parliament in 1866, but the principle of parliamentary government did not become institutionalized until 1917. The latter reform was closely linked to extension of suffrage, which occurred in two steps: male suffrage in 1907–1909, and universal suffrage in 1919–1921. The electoral reform of 1907–1909 introduced *proportional representation.

The constitution of 1809 survived the introduction of *parliamentary democracy. In 1974, the *Riksdag* finally adopted a new constitution, which formally reduced the role of the monarch to that of a figurehead. As part of the rewriting of the constitution, a unicameral Parliament was introduced in 1970. Since 1976 Parliament has comprised 349 seats, all of which are contested every three years. To be represented in Parliament, a party must gain four percent of the national vote or twelve percent of the vote in any one of twenty-eight electoral districts.

From 1921 to 1988, there were five parliamentary parties in Sweden. These five parties are commonly conceived as forming two separate blocs: on the one hand, the "socialist bloc" of the Social Democrats and the Communists (known since the 1960s as the Left Party); and, on the other hand, the "bourgeois bloc" of the Agrarians (known since 1957 as the Center Party), the Liberals, and the Conservatives (known since 1969 as the Moderate Unity Party). The two blocs have always been deeply divided among themselves, however, and compromises across the socialist-bourgeois divide have been common. Although the Social Democrats have dominated Swedish politics since the 1930s, they have held a parliamentary majority of their own on only two occasions (1940–1944 and 1968–1970).

Having entered Parliament in 1988, the Environment Party again fell below the four-percent threshold in 1991, but two other parties entered Parliament in 1991. The Christian Democrats increased their share of the vote from 2.9 percent to 7.1 percent, and the New Democrats, commonly characterized as a right-wing populist party, came out of nowhere to capture 6.7 percent of the vote. The rise of these parties introduces new divisions within the bourgeois bloc, and renders parliamentary politics even more unpredictable.

The proliferation of parties since 1988 reflects voter disaffection with the established parties. While voter turnout declined, the number of voters who switched their party preference from one election to another increased in the 1980s. Both trends appear to have continued through the 1991 election. (In 1988, the turnout was eighty-six percent, and switch voters accounted for twenty percent of votes cast). Several concomitant developments account for the destabilization of the party system: 1) the growing salience of new postmaterialist issues, such as the environment; 2) the growth of tax resentment, especially among bourgeois voters; and 3) growing tensions between the Social Democratic government and the LO unions over economic policy.

The Political Economy of Class Compromise. The welfare state constructed by the Swedish Social Democrats during their forty-four-year tenure in government (1932–1976) is first and foremost distinguished by universalism, i.e., the welfare state provides benefits and services as a matter of citizen rights and caters to the needs of the middle class and skilled workers as well as more disadvantaged strata. This would seem to account for the broad political consensus behind welfare-state expansion in the postwar era and for the resilience of this consensus in the face of the worldwide economic crisis of the 1970s. The bourgeois coalition governments of 1976–1982 kept the lid on unemployment (which peaked at 3.5 percent in 1982) and essentially continued the expansion of the welfare state. The upshot of this policy orientation was a huge government deficit (thirteen percent of GDP in 1982).

When the Social Democrats returned to power in 1982, they opted to boost private profits through a sixteen percent currency devaluation (on top of a ten percent devaluation in 1981) and public expenditure cuts that did not entail encroachments on basic welfare entitlements. Rapid private-sector growth yielded surpluses in the *balance of payments and the government budget by 1987–1988. However, full employment and high corporate profits gave rise to inflationary wage pressures and to growing tensions between the unions and the government. Increasingly, the bourgeois parties, and many economists, have come to argue that unemployment must be allowed to rise in order to keep wages in check. Although the Social Democrats reject this argument, they have failed to articulate a coherent alternative strategy for continued growth.

Invented in the 1950s, the "Swedish model" of wage bargaining pivoted on peak-level negotiations between LO and the Employers' Confederation (SAF). LO agreed to exercise wage restraint in return for employer acceptance of its solidaristic wage policy (raising relative wages for its lowest-paid members). In the course of the 1980s, the government became increasingly involved in wage bargaining. At the same time, private employers sought, with some success, to decentralize wage bargaining. These developments can partly be explained in terms of the growing importance of white-collar unions and public-sector wage bargaining. The number of actors involved in wage bargaining has rendered the voluntary exercise of wage restraint more difficult. The decentralization of wage bargaining can also be seen as part of employer efforts to develop more flexible forms of industrial organization and to reward their employees for productivity and quality improvements.

More broadly conceived, the "Swedish model" involved a national bargain between labor and business, premised on the ability of the national government to regulate the Swedish economy. The parameters for the politics of class compromise have changed as the Swedish economy has become increasingly integrated into a European-wide economy and large Swedish firms have become multinational in their operations. In relation to domestic industrial employment, employment abroad by Swedish manufacturing businesses increased from twelve percent in 1960 to twenty-six percent in 1973 and thirty-seven percent in 1987.

Sweden in the International Order. Since 1815, Sweden has consistently avoided military conflict with other states. Whereas neutrality was primarily a matter of convenience for the Conservative governments of the nineteenth century, the Social Democrats and Liberals argued for neutrality on principled grounds. A broad foreign policy consensus, based on a combination of pragmatic and principled considerations, emerged as part of the democratic breakthrough at the end of World War I. Because of its neutrality, Sweden became a member of the *European Free Trade Association (EFTA) rather than the European Economic Community (later the *European Community, or EC) in the late 1950s. Nonetheless, its trade with EC member states continued to increase; by 1985, half of Swedish exports were sold within the EC.

The single market program adopted by the EC in the mid-1980s, and the subsequent collapse of the erstwhile Eastern bloc, led Sweden to reevaluate its relationship to the EC. In the summer of 1991, the government formally applied for EC membership. At the same time that the formation of a single market has rendered EC membership more attractive from an economic point of view, the new political situation has rendered membership more compatible with neutrality policy.

The implications of joining the EC are uncertain. Arguably, the government's ability to pursue its own macroeconomic policy priorities has already been decisively constrained by economic interdependence. There is no obvious reason why EC membership would require Sweden to lower its standards on environmental protection or the rights of workers, women, and immigrants. The crucial question is perhaps whether EC membership will force Sweden to align its rate of taxation more closely to that of the large EC states, as this would require massive cuts in public expenditure. The issue of tax harmonization within the EC remains unsettled. As Sweden moves toward the EC, it naturally comes to partake of the uncertainties surrounding the 1992 project.

(See also LABOR MOVEMENT; POSTMATERIALISM; SOCIALISM AND SOCIAL DEMOCRACY; TAXES AND TAXATION.)

Gøsta Esping-Andersen, *Politics Against Markets: The Social Democratic Road to Power* (Princeton, N.J., 1985). Hugh Heclo and Hendrik Madsen, *Policy and Politics in Sweden: Principled Pragmatism* (Philadelphia, 1987). Jonas

Pontusson, *The Limits of Social Democracy: Investment Politics in Sweden* (Ithaca, N.Y., 1992).

JONAS PONTUSSON

SWITZERLAND. Landlocked Switzerland, in the Alpine region of Western Europe, has an area of 41,273 square kilometers (15,940 sq. mi.) and a population of between 6 and 7 million. Most of the inhabitants speak a German dialect, but French and Italian are also recognized as official languages, and Romansh, spoken by a tiny minority, is a fourth national tongue. The population is about evenly divided between Protestants and Roman Catholics, a division that caused a number of bloody conflicts until the middle of the nineteenth century.

The origin of Switzerland can be traced to 1291, when three small forest communities, Uri, Schwyz, and Unterwalden, concluded a defensive alliance in order to preserve their local independence and individual customs. Five more cantons joined them during the following century, and an additional five by 1513. The Peace of Westphalia of 1648 officially recognized Swiss independence from the Holy Roman Empire and acknowledged frontiers that have not changed much since that time. The Napoleonic period led to some border rearrangements and brought the number of Swiss cantons to twenty-two, of which three, at various times, split into half-cantons. In 1979 the largely French-speaking Catholic part of the old canton of Bern (mainly German-speaking and Protestant) broke away, forming a separate twenty-third canton, Jura.

Early in their history the Swiss were frequently involved in wars. Following some victories, such as Morgarten in 1315 against Austria, they seemed likely to play a major military role in European affairs, but after decisive defeats two hundred years later, the concept of Swiss nonintervention and neutrality prevailed, even though Swiss mercenaries continued to participate in many foreign battles. Aided by a terrain that is largely mountainous and a highly trained army in which nearly all able-bodied males serve most of their adult lives, neutrality has become a major pillar of Swiss *foreign policy. Switzerland joined the League of Nations, whose headquarters were in Geneva, but regards membership in the UN as incompatible with its neutrality. However, it has joined various UN agencies, is part of the *European Free Trade Association (EFTA) and the *Council of Europe, and has participated in the *Conference on Security and Co-operation in Europe. Joining a lengthening queue, in May 1992 the government announced its intention to apply for membership in the *European Community. Important international organizations are still based on Swiss soil, and various international conferences, including summit meetings, are held there from time to time.

All the cantons originally had their own ways of governing and strongly desired to retain their tra-

ditions. As the alliance gradually grew into a federation, the many cantonal and communal differences led to frequent disputes and armed conflicts. The constitution of 1848 eventually provided a viable modern government. It was revised in 1874 and is still, with amendments, the blueprint of the present-day Swiss political structure. It emphasizes democracy, decentralization, and the sovereignty of individual cantons, which give much autonomy to individual communities. All powers not specifically granted to the federal authorities in the federal constitution are reserved to the cantons. These include schools, police, and affairs of church. The people also have a direct say in the running of their political affairs, and in some areas there still exist town meetings with legislative powers, as in Appenzell Inner-Rhodes where, in April 1990, local suffrage for women was overwhelmingly defeated by a show of (male) hands. Local, cantonal, and federal questions are frequently determined by referendum, as were such national issues as joining the UN (rejected in 1985), joining the *International Monetary Fund and the *World Bank (approved in 1992), limiting the number of foreign workers (rejected in 1988), and allowing women to vote in federal elections (rejected in 1959 but approved in 1971).

Emphasizing the concept of *federalism and following the example of the United States, the Swiss national parliament, the *Bundesversammlung*, is bicameral. In the 200-seat *Nationalrat* every canton and half-canton is represented according to its population, with each guaranteed at least one member. Elections are held every four years under a rather complicated list system on the principle of *proportional representation. In the forty-six-member *Ständerat* every canton has two seats and every half-canton one. Methods of election and length of term are left to the discretion of each canton. Both chambers usually meet four times a year for about three to four weeks; their members are part-time legislators and receive merely a per diem compensation for their services.

The executive branch, the *Bundesrat*, or federal council, is chosen by the *Bundesversammlung* for a four-year period. Each of the seven councillors is responsible for one of these departments: finance and customs; foreign affairs (called the political department); interior; justice and police; military; public economy; and transportation and energy. Incumbents are usually automatically reelected as often as they wish, and there is no way for them to be voted out of office during their term, although some have resigned under pressure. The president of Switzerland is named by the *Bundesversammlung* from among the councillors on an annual rotating basis and holds this office in addition to any other portfolio. He may not be immediately reelected. No canton may have more than one member on the executive, and there are various additional rules to ensure that some of the larger cantons are always represented and that the non-German-speaking cantons are not neglected.

Lists of candidates for parliamentary elections are developed in each canton by the individual parties. Although as many as fifteen or twenty different lists may be presented at any given election, most of them have no chance of success. However, communists have in the past acquired a few seats, as have right-wingers who cashed in on such emotional issues as the alleged overabundance of *foreign workers. In recent years the Greens have also managed to enter the legislature. But the overwhelming majority of the *Bundesversammlung* is usually made up of a combination of members of the Freisinnig-Demokratische Partei, the Christlichdemokratische Volkspartei, the Sozialdemokratische Partei, and the somewhat smaller Schweizerische Volkspartei. Since 1959, the *Bundesrat* has been composed of representatives of these four parties in what amounts to a permanent coalition, thus assuring a high degree of stability.

George Arthur Codding, Jr., *The Federal Government of Switzerland* (Boston, 1961). Christopher Hughes, *Switzerland* (New York, 1975). Walter S. G. Kohn, *Governments and Politics of the German-speaking Countries* (Chicago, 1980). James Murray Luck, *A History of Switzerland* (Palo Alto, Calif., 1985).

WALTER S. G. KOHN

SYRIA. Syria has a geopolitical importance out of all proportion to its relatively small population, area, resource base, and economic wealth because of its formidable military power, assertive foreign policy, and location at the heart of the *Middle East, bordering Israel, Lebanon, Turkey, Iraq, and Jordan. As a result, it plays a central role in most of the Middle East's key disputes and has been one of Israel's foremost adversaries.

Syria has one of the world's richest and longest recorded histories, but the modern state was created only in 1920, when the Western powers carved it out of the Ottoman Empire, and it remained under French colonial rule until independence in 1946. The state originated through no felt need among those who lived in it, and its arbitrary boundaries bore no relationship to underlying cultural patterns or historical relationships within the region. From its inception, Syria lacked legitimacy among its inhabitants, who aspired to be part of a larger pan-Arab state. Between 1958 and 1961, Syria erased itself from the map altogether, merging with *Egypt to form the United Arab Republic. Although pan-Arabism still plays an important role as a legitimating ideology for Syrian regimes, it has lost some of its power, and a coherent Syrian state, with a powerful political center and distinctive identity, has gradually emerged.

The nominally pan-Arab, socialist Ba'th (Resurrection) Party has ruled Syria without interruption since 1963, although a *coup d'état in 1966 brought a leftist faction led by Salah Jadid to power and another one in 1970, led by Hafiz al-Asad, resulted in a swing back to the center. This continuity, which contrasts sharply with the chronic instability between the late 1940s and early 1960s, has come at a high cost to civil liberties. The Ba'thist regime is, at root, an authoritarian military dictatorship in which President Asad stands supreme and in which members of the minority 'Alawi sect dominate key positions within the elite. The president, after a pro forma nomination by Parliament, is popularly elected to a seven-year term (Asad received more than ninety-nine percent of all votes in the 1991 election). In theory the Ba'th shares power with six kindred small parties in the National Progressive Front (NPF), but the non-Ba'thist parties are clearly subordinate members: they lack autonomy, genuine constituencies, and the right to recruit followers in the armed forces and the universities, which are exclusively reserved for the Ba'th. Beneath the presidency, the main formal political institutions are government cabinets, within which all key cabinet portfolios are awarded to Ba'this, and the People's Assembly, which is elected by popular vote every five years. Despite their high visibility, neither commands much actual power. As a sop to those demanding a more open political system, the number of seats in the People's Assembly was increased in the May 1990 elections to allow greater representation of "independents." Roughly half of the 250 seats were reserved for workers and peasants. The NPF won two-thirds of all seats and independents the rest, but the elections were neither free nor open: the Ba'th controls who gets on the ballot and, through its control of the media, who gets heard.

The Ba'th has approximately 600,000–700,000 members and a formal presence in virtually every village, as well as in all large institutions, workplaces, and organizations. The party is organized hierarchically: the Regional Command is the top authority as well as the center of power within Syria. Despite its ubiquity, the Ba'th Party shows evidence of enervation and decay. Discipline has declined as the party has attracted careerists and fallen victim to the corruption that infests all of public life in Syria.

Real power in Syria rests with the armed forces and internal security and intelligence agencies, which are largely commanded by officers from the 'Alawi sect. Most of the Ba'this who seized power in 1963 were officers from villages and small provincial towns, and many came from the peripheral 'Alawi and Druze communities. They replaced a traditional elite composed mainly of Damascus- and Aleppo-based large landowners and merchants, most of whom were from the majority Sunni community. Initially the putschists were inspired by class differences, not sectarian ones. However, since 1963 the regime's greatest vulnerability has been the perception that it is essentially an 'Alawi one, although Sunnis are represented within the regime at all levels. In this heterogeneous country, in which Sunni Muslims account for seventy percent of the population of 13 million (1991) and Arabs for eighty-five percent, sectarian and ethnic differences remain the source of some of the sharpest political cleavages.

After seizing power, the Ba'th, in accordance with its socialist ideology, implemented land reform and nationalized all major industrial, commercial, and financial institutions. The regime also embarked on an ambitious program of industrialization and infrastructural development, which transformed and integrated Syria's economy. The Ba'th's social development policies were equally far-reaching: an enormous expansion of education and health care opened up new opportunities and improved living conditions for many Syrians, especially in the countryside. In the 1970s, Asad liberalized the economy, which grew rapidly because of an influx of petrodollars and *foreign aid. When these sources of revenue declined in the late 1970s, growth dropped sharply. In addition, rampant corruption, a bloated bureaucracy, an inefficient public sector, foreign exchange shortages, and a military machine that regularly consumed over half of the ordinary budget combined to produce severe economic problems, which the growth of oil exports in the late 1980s ameliorated only slightly. Despite the collapse of socialism in the Eastern bloc and growing demands for economic liberalization, the regime has shown little interest in structural economic reform, maintaining that Syria already has an active private sector alongside the mixed and public ones.

Periodically, the regime has faced open opposition, particularly by the Muslim Brotherhood. Shortly after Syria's intervention in Lebanon in 1976, a wave of bombings and assassinations rattled the regime, whose harsh response fueled even more discontent. In 1980, the army was called into Aleppo and other leading cities to quash strikes and demonstrations that threatened to blossom into an insurrection. Two years later the regime virtually destroyed the city of Hama and killed as many as 20,000 people while suppressing a Muslim fundamentalist uprising. Since then, the opposition has been in disarray and the regime has felt more secure, but *human rights violations continue on a large scale. Prospects for political liberalization are bleak because the regime fears it would be repudiated in genuinely free elections.

Under Asad, Syria has emerged as a major power in the Middle East. Syria's foreign policy has largely evolved in the context of its sense of territorial impairment, its self-conception as the birthplace of *Arab nationalism, and its conflict with Israel, with which it has fought wars in 1967, 1973, and 1982. Pan-Arabism and anti-Zionism have traditionally been the twin guiding principles of its policies in the region, as well as the justification for most of its actions. One of the overriding goals of the Asad regime's foreign policy has been to regain the Golan Heights, which Israel occupied in 1967, and restore Palestinian rights. Despite Syria's rhetoric about Arab unity, its relations with other Arab countries have been stormy. Its alliance with Egypt in the 1973 war quickly collapsed after Egypt pursued a separate peace agreement with Israel. Relations were not restored until 1989. At least since the mid-1970s, Syria has been a bitter enemy of Iraq, where a rival wing of the Ba'th Party holds power. Syria's support for Iran in its war with Iraq between 1980 and 1988 was denounced throughout the Arab world, and its deployment of forces in Saudi Arabia following the Iraqi invasion of Kuwait in 1990 was also controversial within the region. From the mid-1970s, Syria tried unsuccessfully to bring Lebanon, Jordan, and the Palestinians into its orbit to increase its leverage. The limits of its power were clearest in Lebanon, where Syria intervened militarily in 1976 to bring an end to civil war: it has been bogged down ever since, unable to impose its will but unwilling to withdraw.

Syria's close relations with the Soviet Union were based on its need for military and diplomatic support in its conflict with Israel. Asad exploited *Cold War tensions to his advantage and used Soviet backing to build Syria into the powerful state that it is. The relationship between the two countries changed profoundly after Mikhail *Gorbachev came to power. The Soviet Union indicated that it would not support the Asad regime's quest for military parity with Israel, undermining its central strategic doctrine. By the close of the 1980s, Syria's doubts about the reliability of the Soviet Union as an ally and recognition that only the United States could persuade Israel to withdraw from the Golan Heights prompted it to seek better relations with the United States, a pattern that intensified during the *Gulf War and continued in the postwar discussions about the Middle East.

(See also ARAB-ISRAELI CONFLICT; DECOLONIZATION; IRAN-IRAQ WAR; MILITARY RULE; SOVIET FOREIGN POLICY; ZIONISM.)

Tabitha Petran, Syria (London, 1972). Nikolaos van Dam, The Struggle for Power in Syria (London, 1981). John Devlin, Syria (Boulder, Colo., 1983). Moshe Ma'oz, Asad: The Sphinx of Damascus (New York, 1988). Patrick Seale, Asad: The Struggle for the Middle East (Berkeley, Calif., 1988). Raymond A. Hinnebusch, Authoritarian Power and State Formation in Ba'thist Syria (Boulder, Colo., 1990).

ALASDAIR DRYSDALE

T

TAIWAN. Comprising one major and several smaller islands (36,000 sq. km. or 14,000 sq. mi., about the size of the Netherlands; 1991 population 20 million), Taiwan is located 160 kilometers (100 mi.) east of the Chinese mainland. Both the Communist Chinese government based in Beijing and the Nationalist Chinese government based in Taipei, Taiwan, claim it is only a province of *China, not an independent country.

China's Qing dynasty ceded Taiwan to Japan after losing the Sino-Japanese War in 1895. At the end of World War II, it was retroceded to the Republic of China (ROC) government under the Kuomintang (KMT; Nationalist Party) under Generalissimo Chiang Kai-shek.

Driven off the mainland by the Communists, in 1949 the KMT "temporarily" moved its capital to Taipei. It brought along its governmental institutions: the five *yuan* (legislative; executive, i.e., cabinet, under the premier; control; judicial; and examination); the national assembly (which elects the president and vice president and amends the constitution); and the army. It suspended the 1946 constitution and ruled by martial law. It decreed that no elections for national bodies could be held prior to the government's return to the mainland. It held local elections from 1950, but forbade citizens to organize new political parties.

The corruption of the first post-retrocession governor sparked the February 28 incident in 1947, a popular uprising that was ruthlessly suppressed, creating a deep division between the "Taiwanese" (those Chinese whose ancestors had come to the island prior to the Japanese occupation) and the "mainlanders," the 1.5–2 million Chinese who came after 1949. The latter virtually monopolized power in the party, state, and army, and the state became the major actor in the modern sector of the economy.

A peaceful three-stage *land reform (1949–1953) compensated landlords with shares of stock in government enterprises and rice and sweet potato bonds, selling their surplus land to tenants on easy terms. The government assisted farmers with credit, technology, and marketing while compelling them to trade rice for state-produced chemical fertilizer. A few landlords used their enterprise shares to become wealthy industrialists.

The United States had abandoned the KMT as it lost the civil war, but revived military and civilian support after the outbreak of the *Korean War in June 1950. Through its U.S.-assisted planning agencies and its ownership of the banking system and upstream enterprises, the state played a multifaceted role in Taiwan's economy. In the 1950s, it followed an import substitution policy, focusing on textiles and food processing. The United States compelled the regime to dismantle some protectionist policies such as high tariffs, multiple exchange rates, and disincentives to export and to shift to an export-oriented strategy around 1960.

In the 1960s, the government devised incentives to encourage foreign investment, including the export processing zone at Kaohsiung. This was a port with factories where imported parts were to be assembled for export. Jobs in these labor-intensive industries attracted thousands of young women from farms. American and then Japanese multinationals, particularly in consumer electronics, flocked to the island. The government assisted local businesses in establishing supply and subcontracting relations with foreign capital. Other local manufacturers produced to foreign buyers' specifications for export. Taiwan's economy took off, growing at an average annual rate of 10.8 percent from 1963 to 1972.

The 1973 oil shock hit the imported energy–dependent island hard. To maintain growth, the government supported major infrastructural projects including transportation, energy, and heavy industry. After the second oil shock hit in 1980, state planners began efforts to integrate the economy vertically and to shift into knowledge-intensive industries such as computers. The government built a science-based industrial park in Hsinchu to attract local and foreign capital. By the late 1970s, Taiwan was widely regarded as a *newly industrializing economy (NIE). In 1991 Taiwan inaugurated a US$303 billion Six-Year Development Plan to modernize infrastructure and improve the environment and social life.

Taiwan's social structure underwent a fundamental transformation as the population shifted from agriculture to industry and services, moved from rural areas to the cities, attained a literacy rate above ninety percent, enjoyed nine years of free compulsory education, lived longer, and achieved a 1991 per capita income of US$8,800 while maintaining remarkable income equality.

However, political change did not keep pace, although in 1969 the government permitted supplementary elections to the legislative *yuan* and national assembly while letting those elected on the mainland in 1947 retain their seats. In the 1970s, the ROC's international fortunes dived as it lost its seat in the UN to the People's Republic of China, most nations shifted their diplomatic relations to Beijing (neither government permits dual recognition), and Richard *Nixon went to the mainland.

Throughout the 1970s and 1980s, an anti-KMT political movement took shape, coordinating election campaigns, demanding reforms, and trying to establish a new party. Violent demonstrations in 1977 and 1979 were the first such outbursts since 1947.

Chiang Kai-shek died in 1975, and his son, Chiang Ching-kuo, took power over the party and state. Originally a hard-liner, he ironically oversaw the regime's transition from hard to soft *authoritarianism. He promoted younger and more professional cadres, including many Taiwanese. He selected an American-trained Taiwanese agricultural economist, Lee Teng-hui, as his vice president in 1984, and Lee succeeded him on his death in January 1988. Chiang did not crack down when oppositionists established a new party, the Democratic Progressive Party (DPP), in 1986. He promoted the passage of a new law on social organizations. He lifted martial law in July 1987, which opened the floodgates of unprecedented social movements of all kinds. In November 1987, Chiang permitted visits to the mainland, and millions of people went to see relatives and check on trade and investment opportunities. In December 1989, the now-legal DPP made significant inroads in Taiwan's first multiparty elections for the legislative *yuan*, county magistrates, and provincial assembly. Many candidates openly called for Taiwan's independence, an act officially considered sedition. All members of the National Assembly, legislative *yuan*, and control *yuan* elected on the mainland were compelled to retire at the end of 1991. KMT candidates received seventy-one percent of the popular vote for the new, smaller National Assembly in December 1991. New legislative and control *yuan* elections are scheduled for 1992 and 1993 respectively.

(See also CHINESE REVOLUTION; CONFUCIANISM; SINO-AMERICAN RELATIONS.)

Thomas B. Gold, *State and Society in the Taiwan Miracle* (Armonk, N.Y., 1986). Hung-mao Tien, *The Great Transition: Political and Social Change in the Republic of China* (Stanford, Calif., 1989).

THOMAS B. GOLD

TAJIKISTAN. See COMMONWEALTH OF INDEPENDENT STATES.

TANZANIA. Led by a philosopher-president who translated Shakespeare into Swahili and walked the countryside to mobilize *peasant support, contemporary Tanzanians have experienced both remarkable improvements in their quality of life and recurring economic reverses. A stepchild of the colonial era, Tanganyika was colonized by Germany and then ruled by Britain as a League of Nations Mandate and subsequently a UN Trusteeship Territory. Independent on 9 December 1961, Tanganyika united with Zanzibar in 1964 to create the modern United Republic of Tanzania.

Tanganyika's integration into the European sphere of influence was uneven: while new crop and market opportunities permitted some regions to flourish, others became labor reservoirs with disintegrating local institutions and a shredded social fabric. At independence, Tanganyika had little developed infrastructure, even less industry, and few educated citizens.

European rule ended far less violently than it had begun. Negotiators, not guerrillas, assumed power. Still dependent on external advice and personnel, the new leadership quickly recognized the fragility of both government and party, the Tanganyika African National Union (TANU). Prime minister scarcely a month, Julius *Nyerere resigned in January 1962 to address divisions within the country, reinvigorate the party, and elaborate a *development *ideology. Victorious in the election held under a new republican constitution later that year, Nyerere became Tanzania's first president.

Optimistic projections and *World Bank advice spawned a liberal development strategy: relatively open economy, emphasis on export production, successful farmers, pilot projects, an increasing but still limited state role, and maintenance of friendly relations with the major powers. Events soon deflated the optimism. Popular opposition to Britain's transfer of authority to a minority Arab government in Zanzibar in December 1963 provided fertile ground for a brief but bloody coup on the islands. Shortly thereafter an army mutiny on the mainland led a vulnerable government to summon foreign troops. Before the gunsmoke had fully cleared, Nyerere and the new Zanzibar leader, Abeid Karume, negotiated the union of the two states.

Sharply declining world prices for sisal exports delayed or aborted several projects. Diplomatic ruptures with Britain and the Federal Republic of Germany and conflict with the United States reduced external support and encouraged expanded relationships with socialist Europe and China. University students' dramatic 1966 protest against conscription into the National Service led Nyerere to reduce both his own and other leaders' salaries, expel the students involved, and rethink the role and organization of education.

Social services expanded rapidly. Although one of the world's poorest countries, Tanzania achieved nearly universal primary education and provided clean water to more of its citizens than most other African countries. Infant and maternal mortality declined, life expectancy increased, and adult illiteracy was largely eliminated.

Yet, the liberal development strategy had failed. The 1967 Arusha Declaration and related papers analyzed the failure, identifying the major problem as external dependence. Self reliance and *ujamaa*—Tanzanian *socialism loosely based on historical patterns of mutual support—became the guiding principles for a radical development strategy. The open economy was increasingly closed: new policies included *nationalizations, import restrictions, foreign exchange controls, and constraints on foreign investment. Other measures severely restricted individual accumulation and consumption, gave preferential treatment to cooperatives and socialist villages, assigned priority to basic industries, and accelerated indigenization. *Foreign policy became more sharply critical of international *capitalism and more Africa-oriented.

Party supremacy was institutionalized. The 1965 Interim Constitution introduced an innovative pattern of single-party competitive elections, seeking to reconcile control and participation. In government and party elections held regularly since independence, voters choose among competing candidates and vote for or against the party's presidential nominee. While support for Nyerere was always very high, its regional and national variation did register discontent. Though formally superior in the parallel party and government institutions, in practice the party ruled but did not govern. Potential alternative power bases—unions, women, youth—were incorporated into the party and, like the reorganized and politicized military, guaranteed representation in the party National Executive Committee. In 1977 TANU merged with its Zanzibar counterpart, the Afro-Shirazi Party, becoming the Chama cha Mapinduzi (CCM), or Revolutionary Party.

With no dominant regional/ethnic group and an official language, Swahili, that is also national, Tanzania's heterogeneous population has only infrequently experienced conflicts organized around racial, religious, and ethnic identities. A major source of continuity and *legitimacy, Tanzanian elections facilitated the presidential transition in 1985 from Nyerere to Ali Hassan Mwinyi, a Zanzibari whose broad support reflected the national integrative ethos.

Reorganization of local government also reflected the tension between control and participation. The 1972 decentralization relocated central officials to regional capitals and strengthened regional government but at the same time eliminated elected district and urban councils. Earlier regarded as the appropriate model for introducing rural socialism, cooperatives were eliminated in 1976. Dismantling locally responsive institutions was expected to improve efficiency and coordination. In practice, it achieved

neither. In the severe economic crises of the early 1980s, both elected local government and cooperatives were reconstituted.

Drought and sharply increased oil prices in the mid-1970s jarred the radical development strategy. A further increase in oil prices, drought, the collapse of East African economic cooperation, and war compounded the economic problems at the end of the decade. Starved of foreign exchange, industries operated below capacity. Depressed commodity prices and efforts to protect urban consumers stimulated extralegal trade. Successive emergency economic recovery plans in the early 1980s neither brought rapid improvements nor satisfied the policy reform demands (including devaluation, decontrol, and *privatization) of the *International Monetary Fund and external development assistance agencies. Nyerere's retirement from government in 1985 facilitated renewed external support. By the end of the decade, inflation had slowed and the growth in production resumed. But the gap between the most and least affluent, progressively reduced over a quarter century, began to expand, and social services were increasingly jeopardized.

Tanzania's internationalist leadership attempted to preserve the East African cooperation developed under British rule and simultaneously to reduce Kenya's regional advantage. Nyerere's commitment to self-determination and democracy was reflected in Tanzania's recognition of Biafra during the Nigerian Civil War and opposition to Idi Amin Dada's dictatorial rule in Uganda. When Ugandan troops invaded northwestern Tanzania in 1978, Nyerere unsuccessfully sought *Organization of African Unity (OAU) support. Ostensibly no match for the relatively well supplied invaders, Tanzanian soldiers traversed the country from their distant bases, largely on foot. Quickly expelling the Ugandans, they drove the retreating army across Uganda, exiled Amin, and remained in Uganda until mid-1981 to support the transition to civilian rule.

Since independence Tanzania has provided significant support to African nationalist and liberation movements, both independently and through regional and continental organizations, including the OAU's Liberation Committee. Staunchly opposed to minority rule in South Africa, Tanzania undertook major investments—an oil pipeline, a railway, and improved roads—to reduce landlocked Zambia's dependence on the Southern African infrastructure. It also provided settlements and training, communication, and education facilities to Mozambique's nationalist movement and other Southern African liberation groups.

Frustrated by the halting pace of economic growth and encouraged by the dramatic transitions in Eastern and Central Europe and the Soviet Union in the late 1980s, Tanzanians in the 1990s began to consider reforming their single-party system. A national commission considered instituting multiparty competition, critical newspapers expanded their circulation, and the national leadership sought to broaden its political base. Still, Nyerere's challenge remained appropriate: "We must run while others walk."

(See also AFRICAN SOCIALISM; ONE-PARTY SYSTEM.)

Julius K. Nyerere, *Freedom and Socialism/Uhuru na Ujamaa* (Dar es Salaam, 1968). Haroub Othman, ed., *The State in Tanzania* (Dar es Salaam, 1980). Joel Samoff, "Single-Party Competitive Elections in Tanzania," in Fred Hayward, ed., *Elections in Independent Africa* (Boulder, Colo., 1987), 149–186. Rodger Yeager, *Tanzania: An African Experiment*, 2d ed. (Boulder, Colo., 1989).

JOEL SAMOFF

TARIFF. See PROTECTION; TAXES AND TAXATION.

TAXES AND TAXATION. It is impossible to overestimate the importance of taxation. Indeed, without taxation there can be no government. But whom governments tax, what kinds of taxes they levy, and how much they take in taxes are some of the most difficult issues faced by governments anywhere. They are also issues that are settled quite differently in different polities. Even at the most basic measure of difference (total tax revenue as a percent of GDP) the variance is enormous: in 1990, in the most heavily taxed nation (Sweden) the tax level reached fifty-four percent of GDP, whereas in the least heavily taxed nation (Uganda) the government took less than 2.6 percent of GDP in taxes.

Taxation in the Developing World. Generally, the poorer the nation, the smaller its tax base, and, consequently, the less revenue the government will have at its disposal. The average tax burden across all nations was approximately thirty percent of GNP in 1986, with industrial countries collecting an average of thirty-eight percent of GNP and developing countries collecting an average of twenty percent of GNP. In the poorest nations nearly two-thirds of the population live at or near the subsistence level; taxing the poor heavily could drive them to starvation. In very poor nations, moreover, the economy is largely based on subsistence agriculture, and thus in those nations income taxes (the most popular form of taxation among governments elsewhere) comprise only approximately ten percent of all tax revenue, or two percent of GDP.

The highly unequal distribution of income in most developing nations does not necessarily imply that these governments will tax the wealthy (or the small middle classes) heavily. Even in developing countries whose tax codes do include steeply progressive wealth or income taxes, actual collection is often extremely difficult. Tax administration in poor countries tends to be weakly administered and inefficient. Taxing authorities, moreover, are often corrupt.

Governments in the less developed world are thus left with fewer choices about whom to tax and how

much to tax than are governments in more prosperous countries. Countries in which multinational corporations are a substantial presence tend to generate a large share of state revenues through corporate income or profits taxes. These taxes are easier to collect than income taxes and (sometimes) easier to levy. Countries that have large extractive industries (especially oil) tend to rely the most heavily on corporate profits taxes. These taxes contribute an average of 16.5 percent of total revenue (3.5 percent of GNP) in the developing world, as compared to 7.8 percent of revenue (2.8 percent of GNP) in the rich countries. In twelve poor countries corporate income taxes make up over one-quarter of all revenues, and in six they make up over half.

But for most developing countries the largest sources of revenue are taxes on goods and services (such as tobacco taxes or petroleum taxes) and taxes on foreign trade. On average, these taxes respectively contribute twenty-five percent to thirty-five percent of total tax revenues in developing countries. Import taxes are by far the most important single source of revenue, accounting for nearly twenty-five percent of all revenues. The poorer the country, the more likely it is to rely heavily on import taxes as a major source of revenue because these taxes are relatively easy to collect and quite simply monitored.

Taxation in Industrial Democracies. Although governments in advanced democracies have substantially larger economies from which to draw taxes, it does not follow that raising tax revenues is necessarily easy. Democratization generates greater demands for public spending, but it also gives citizens who oppose taxes more power to resist tax increases. Most citizens want more public spending and tax cuts at the same time. This fundamental dilemma has shaped the development of all modern tax systems.

One hundred years ago all governments collected the vast bulk of their revenue from property taxes, import/export taxes, and special levies (on, for example, salt, tea, tobacco, men's hair powder, number of windows or number of female servants per residence). These taxes, however, are very visible and thus difficult politically to increase or even maintain; they are very inefficient and thus expensive to administer; finally, because they focus on particular groups of items and activities, they raise comparatively little revenue. Advanced countries have therefore come to rely on the four "modern" taxes: personal income tax, corporate profits taxes, value added taxes (VAT), and social insurance contributions. These taxes are preferred because they are very broad based (i.e., virtually everyone pays them and they generate a great deal of revenue even with relatively low rates) and because revenues from them increase "automatically" with inflation and economic growth. Progressive income taxes are the most heavily utilized taxes—accounting for thirty-two percent of revenue yield—in part because of "bracket creep" (i.e., as their incomes increase taxpayers move into higher tax brackets and therefore pay a larger share of their income in taxes). The "automatic growth" of these taxes has allowed democratic governments to increase government revenues a great deal over the past hundred years even while citizens have consistently clamored for tax reductions. In 1990 these four taxes contributed an average of eighty percent (and often more than ninety percent) of total government revenues in the advanced countries.

Although all advanced countries tend to rely broadly on the same types of taxes, there is huge variation in both the structure of these taxes and the degree to which they are used. The United States, for example, relies mostly on progressive income taxes and social security taxes and has no national VAT. The absence of a national consumption tax helps explain why it is the lowest-taxed of countries belonging to the *Organization for Economic Co-operation and Development (OECD). Several other countries collect comparatively little in progressive income taxes and instead rely quite heavily on social security taxes or a national VAT or both.

It was once widely assumed that taxation would be a major instrument of income and wealth redistribution in the democratic world. It is reasonable, therefore, to expect countries that have been dominated by *Left governments to rely heavily on progressive taxes and those dominated by the *Right to have regressive tax structures. Closer examination does not bear out these expectations. There appears to be no correlation between the degree to which a country relies on progressive taxes to finance its *welfare state and the actual progressiveness of that welfare state. Indeed, the countries that have gone the furthest toward income and wealth redistribution do not have particularly progressive tax systems. The most advanced welfare states have instead chosen to increase consumption and social security taxes substantially and then spend this money in progressive ways.

World Tax Reform. The globalization of the world economy is affecting the tax policy choices of developing and developed societies alike. As capital has become more mobile virtually every country has responded by cutting income and corporate tax rates. In 1986 the United States, for example, reduced its top personal income tax rate to thirty-three percent (as recently as 1980 it had been seventy percent). Almost all other countries have followed suit. In Sweden, the Social Democratic finance minister announced recently that "progressive taxes no longer work." The government then passed a tax reform that cut its top income tax rate from eighty percent to fifty percent and replaced these revenues by increases in consumption taxes. As states continue to compete for investment by lowering taxes and tax

rates, it seems inevitable that they will have less revenue to continue financing their welfare states at current levels.

(See also POLITICAL ECONOMY.)

Richard Musgrave and Peggy Musgrave, *Public Finance in Theory and Practice*, 3d ed. (New York, 1980). David Newbery and Nicholas Stern, eds., *The Theory of Taxation for Developing Countries*, World Bank Research Publication (New York, 1987). Joseph Pechman, *World Tax Reform: A Progress Report* (Washington, D.C., 1988).

SVEN STEINMO

TECHNOLOGY TRANSFER. In the twentieth century technology has entered the foreground of history—not so much (as theorists have pointed out) because human beings are subordinated to technology as because technology tends to reconfigure human reality. Of course, technology is able to confer benefits only to the extent that a society has access to it. Yet technology is not simply a piece of hardware or software to be transported from one place to another, from one society to another. Technology is tied to particular traditions of technical behavior and reflects social, cultural, and even political and economic arrangements.

Transferring a particular machine or even the knowledge to use it comes much more quickly and easily than does applying that technical activity so as to make it useful in a particular setting. New technology can open doors—but the choice of whether to enter remains. To accept or reject a technology, and the implications of accepting or rejecting it, still depend very much on the condition of the society in question. History is replete with examples of societies that accepted or rejected technologies. Typically, the choice is based not on technical but on social, political, and economic considerations. Society determines the uses of technology, just as society determines the transfer and adoption of technology derived from an alien terrain.

Despite the global civilization of technology, people continue to live in largely distinct societies. The impact of technology and the capacity to adapt it to local needs are not predetermined. For a less-developed country, the promise of technology represents an enormous opportunity to catch up, to improve the quality of its citizens' lives in the space of a generation or two. Imported technology also entails huge risks, however. Once transferred, technology can quickly become dangerous to the country that is unable to control and manage it. It can be destructive of the natural environment, for example, or may even undermine the most deeply held values of the society.

Pertinent statistics are compiled and analyzed by the *Organization for Economic Co-operation and Development (OECD) and its largely industrialized member countries, and by the UN Educational, Scientific and Cultural Organization (UNESCO). Although such statistics are never fully up-to-date, they indicate the magnitude of the imbalance between the major industrial countries and the rest of the world. The seven major OECD countries (the United States, Japan, Germany, France, the United Kingdom, Canada, and Italy) account for ninety-one percent of total OECD research and development (R&D). OECD countries in turn constitute about eighty-five percent of global R&D. Of the world scientific and engineering community, moreover, the United States accounts for forty-three percent, the *European Community for twenty-eight percent, and Japan for twenty percent. Equally illuminating data record the scientific and technical expertise available per million population in various societies. In the mid-1980s developed countries as a group numbered 70,000 researchers per million population, compared to only 8,000 per million in the less-developed countries as a group. Europe as a whole had 48,000 per million population, compared to Africa's 3,000 per million. Such huge disparities speak volumes regarding relative capacity to do research and to make national policy.

Patent data also shed light on the extent to which countries produce and disseminate technology. The largest disseminators of technology abroad are the United States, Germany, France, the United Kingdom, and Japan. Although governments still financed forty percent of R&D (albeit much of it military) during the 1980s, there has been a noticeable swing from the public to the private sector. In the commercial sector technology is transferred in essentially three ways: through the export of goods that incorporate technology; through direct investments by corporate subsidiaries; and by the sale of disembodied technology in the form of licenses and know-how, much of it lodged in patents. Increasingly in North-South conflicts, industrial states wanting to protect knowledge acquired through R&D are pitted against less-developed states desiring free, or at least freer, trade of knowledge. Even among OECD members, less-developed states like Turkey, Yugoslavia and its successor states, Portugal, Greece, and Spain largely depend on the import of foreign technology. Outside OECD membership, dependence on technology generated by a half-dozen states is overwhelming.

Global policy issues include the one-way flow of R&D from a few states to the rest of the world, the cost of transfer to those states least able to pay for it, and the relative capacity of less-developed states to select, manage, and control technologies and their societal impacts. A clear case can be made that each state must develop at least enough R&D capacity to select wisely from the international marketplace of technology, that only in this way will transfers take place that are appropriate for a given context. To narrow the gap in the next century between the "have" and the "have-not" states of the world requires access to knowledge at an affordable cost.

Each state will also have to develop the national capacity to select and manage imported technology. The economic and environmental qualities of life among the developed and the less-developed societies of the world are connected by the umbilical cord of technology transfer.

(See also DEVELOPMENT AND UNDERDEVELOPMENT; ENVIRONMENTALISM; NORTH-SOUTH RELATIONS.)

Volker Rittberger, ed., *Science and Technology in a Changing International Order* (Boulder, Colo., 1982). Organization for Economic Co-operation and Development, *R&D Production and Diffusion of Technology*, Science and Technology Indicators Report No. 3 (Paris, 1989).

ISEBILL V. GRUHN

TERRORISM. The concept of *terrorism* has been a category of political discourse since the late eighteenth century. Its central meaning is the use of terror for the furthering of political ends, and it was originally used to denote the use of terror by the French revolutionary government against its opponents. This is also the sense in which it was used, and on occasion justified, by the Bolsheviks after 1917. This usage of the term, to cover terror by governments, has now become less common, though by no means irrelevant, and in most contemporary usage the term covers acts of terror by those opposed to governments. The range of activities which the term covers has been wide, but four main forms of action tend to be included: *assassination, bombings, seizures of individuals as hostages, and, more recently, the hijacking of planes. In the 1970s the term *international terrorism* began to be used to cover acts of violence committed by political groups outside the country in which they were primarily active. The other term that emerged at the same time, *state terrorism*, referred to encouragement, or alleged encouragement, by *states of such acts of violence.

Taking terrorism in its second, anti-state, sense, there can be said to be three main phases of its history. There is first a prehistory of terrorism, in the sense of acts which would today be called terrorist. The main form this took were acts of assassination for political and politico-religious ends: the tyrannicides of Greece and Rome, the Zealots of Palestine, the Hashashin of medieval Islam. It is significant that many of these cases were often regarded as morally legitimate. The second phase of terrorism was the use of violence by political groups in the nineteenth century, especially by anarchists and some nationalists. The assassinations of Tsar Alexander II in 1881 and of Archduke Franz Ferdinand in 1914 were perhaps the most famous cases, but there was widespread endorsement of bombing by anarchists in Europe and the United States, as "propaganda of the deed," and a number of nationalist groups, notably the Irish and the Armenians, practiced assassination, bombing, and various forms of violent seizure and destruction of property.

A third and more complex phase of terrorism dates from the end of World War II. In a range of nationalist conflicts in the *Third World—Israel, Kenya, Cyprus, South Yemen, Algeria—officials and citizens of the colonial state were attacked as part of what in the end were successful campaigns for national independence. In other cases nationalist movements that did not succeed also used it—for example, in Palestine, the Basque region of Spain, and South Molucca. At the same time, political groups seeking various forms of revolutionary political and social change within their own countries also resorted to acts of terror: this was widespread with the urban guerrillas of Latin America—in Argentina, Brazil, Uruguay—and on a more spasmodic basis in some of the developed democracies—the Red Army Faction in the Federal Republic of Germany, the Red Brigades in Italy, the Weathermen in the United States. Most of these revolutionary groups claimed affiliation with the political *Left: but in the 1970s and 1980s there were also major campaigns of terror by right-wing groups, notably in France and Italy.

Terrorism in this specific sense generated widespread concern in the societies affected, and, as a result of the spread of so-called international terrorism, in the world as a whole. The publicity given to certain dramatic events, such as hijackings, and the administrative and financial costs of searching and monitoring international travel from the late 1960s onward underlined this. During the late 1970s the U.S. Congress and government made concern with terrorism a major part of its *foreign policy and compiled a list of those countries that were deemed to be supporting it. Special units were set up to cover antiterrorism, that is, measures to prevent terrorist acts, and counterterrorism, that is, measures to respond to, and where deemed appropriate retaliate against, terrorism.

Distinct as these phenomena appeared to be, there were, however, a number of ways in which the public and international concern of the 1970s and 1980s obscured the issues involved. First, the scale of the phenomenon was distorted by the focus on international terrorism. Acts of this kind certainly occurred and were likely to continue. But the numbers of people affected were small—most plane hijackings ended without bloodshed. The far more important and costly phenomenon was not international terrorism but terrorism within communal situations, largely in Third World countries. This involved situations where people of different ethnic or religious character, who had often lived side by side for centuries, came to be locked in situations of violence and retribution, often involving massacres, mass kidnappings, forcible displacements, and so forth. Cases of this were in the conflicts between Christian and Muslim in Lebanon, between Tamil

and Sinhalese in Sri Lanka, between Hindu and Sikh in Punjab. Despite its Third World focus, however, there were a number of cases in Europe as well—in Cyprus, Northern Ireland, and, with the breakdown of Communist authority during the late 1980s, in the Soviet Union and Eastern Europe as well. The most pervasive and, in the long term, dangerous aspect of terrorism was this spread of communal terrorism as a product of social and economic tensions in ethnically mixed societies.

A second area of confusion concerned what were and were not acts of terrorism. Here those who opposed states and were victims of state violence were quick to revive the original, 1790s definition of the term and to argue that most of the acts of terror for political ends committed in the contemporary world were carried out by states: the victims of Nazism and *Stalinism, and of many repressive regimes in the post-1945 period, were testimony enough of that. Those who analyzed forms of oppression and coercion outside the framework of state power also argued that terror played a part in establishing and maintaining these forms of domination: the use, actual and threatened, of violence by men against women was an evident case.

There was also considerable room for debate on the way in which the term *terrorist* was used to define, as distinct from merely qualify, specific political groups. Many of those involved in nationalist campaigns questioned the use of the term *terrorist* to disqualify not just specific acts but the overall *legitimacy and goals of their movements. Some revolutionary groups in developed countries appeared to have no other strategy than that of planting bombs and killing individuals, but this was not the case in the nationalist contexts where the goal, national independence, was distinct from the tactics used, of which terror was one but by no means the only one. That the Zionists, Algerians, and Palestinians used, among other tactics, terror as an instrument in independence struggles did not necessarily mean that their broader goals were illegitimate.

Two further issues raised in discussions of terrorism were those of cause and efficacy. The search for a cause of terrorism ranged from social and economic conditions to theories based on psychology, "the terrorist personality," and religion. Given the variety of forms taken by terrorist phenomena and the diversity of conditions in which it originated, this was a fruitless exercise. The one characteristic common to terrorist acts against states was a belief, usually mistaken, that individual acts of violence could in some way accelerate change and achieve goals that other, more conventional forms of political action could not. The association with individual religions, most recently Islam, does not survive historical comparison. Assessments of the efficacy of terrorism have tended to show that, beyond publicity, it usually achieved very little, unless the goals were very specific—the release of particular prisoners, the appropriation of some money. Indeed the main result of terroristic acts was not to inflect governments in the direction the terrorists wanted but rather to harden them in the opposite direction—as Russia after 1881 and Argentina after 1975, to name but two cases, demonstrated.

(See also ANARCHY; DECOLONIZATION; INTERNATIONAL LAW; NATIONAL LIBERATION MOVEMENTS; POLITICAL VIOLENCE; REVOLUTION; RIGHT.)

Walter Laqueur and Yonah Alexander, *The Terrorism Reader: A Historical Anthology* (New York, 1987). Richard Rubenstein, *Alchemists of Revolution: Terrorism in the Modern World* (London and New York, 1987). Walter Laqueur, *Terrorism,* 2d ed. (New York and London, 1988).

FRED HALLIDAY

THAILAND. Located in mainland Southeast Asia, Thailand is bordered by Burma on the west and north, by Laos and Cambodia on the east, and by Malaysia on the south. Its northern borders are only 160 kilometers (100 mi.) from China, while Vietnam is less than 160 kilometers to the east. About the size of Texas and with a population approaching 60 million, Thailand can be divided into four geographic regions: the central plain with its rich alluvial soil and relatively high standard of living; the northeast where poverty and arid conditions prevail; the north with its mountains and varied ethnic hill groups; and the southern peninsula, characterized by a Malay-speaking minority.

Thailand's capital city, Bangkok, with a population of 8 million, is located in the central plain near the Gulf of Siam. Bangkok, dominating every aspect of Thai society, is the kingdom's unchallenged center of political, economic, cultural, educational, and social activity.

Although seventy percent of the Thai people are in the agricultural sphere of the economy, the number in rice farming is decreasing as Thai farmers have diversified into crops such as vegetables, fruits, maize, tapioca, coffee, flowers, sugar, rubber, and livestock. As *modernization has arrived, Thai farmers have become more sophisticated economic actors, moving from subsistence to surplus agriculture. Although farming areas have not developed economically as rapidly as urban areas in the past twenty years, the standard of living in the countryside has improved. Manufacturing now is responsible for a larger share of the GDP than is agriculture. The average yearly per capita income in Thailand is US$1,600.

For most Thais, the family is the most important unit of identity, although the movement toward a more urban population has undermined the traditional closeness of extended families. Rural Thais also identify with their village, a community of about one to three hundred households, characterized by an agricultural economy, a Buddhist temple, and patron-client bonds that act as the integrative web of society.

The key element in the structure of Thai society is that of superior-subordinate relationships. These relationships are reciprocal and personal with the superior (patron) having power over the subordinate (client). Patron-client bonds stem from personal relationships such as kinship groupings, official ties within the bureaucracy, school ties, or common village origins, and are based largely on personal loyalty.

The superior is expected to be compassionate and kind and to manifest these qualities by protecting, aiding, complimenting, and giving generously to those whose status is inferior. In return, the subordinate, or client, is expected to act deferentially and to cause his patron the least amount of trouble.

At every level, from the village to the central government in Bangkok, patron-client groups perform the functions of disseminating information, allocating resources, and organizing people. These groupings form a link in a network of personal relations that extends throughout Thai society and that traditionally has formed the heart of Thai politics. Although both personalism and patron-client relationships remain important, in the past several decades, Thai politics has evolved in the direction of decreased personalism and more formalized participation in the political structures.

Since 1932, when a group of civilians and military officers overthrew the absolute monarchy, the Thai military has played the dominant role in Thai politics. Of the forty-six cabinets during the period 1932 to 1990, twenty-three were classified as military governments, eight as military-dominated, and fifteen as civilian. Civilian governments, which were the most unstable, were often replaced by military regimes following army *coups d'état. Because communist insurgency has ended and because there is no viable external threat to Thai *security, the major rationale for military intervention into governmental affairs has been undermined. Nevertheless, the February 1991 coup is an example of continuing military dominance.

For most of the contemporary era, Thailand has been a bureaucratic polity with the military holding the key positions. Although the highest-level leaders may change, often by extraconstitutional means such as military coups, the sustained role of the bureaucracy has assured a high degree of policy continuity. The formerly exclusive role of the bureaucracy has been widened in recent years by the new role of technocrats who are highly trained and educated officials concerned more about the public good than the traditional values of hierarchy, patronage, and security. Moreover, institutions such as Parliament, political parties, and interest groups are playing a more effective role in determining public policy.

The Parliament is no longer just a rubber stamp of the prime minister. In the present semidemocracy the appointed higher chamber, the Senate, is still dominated by the military. However, the members of the lower chamber, the Assembly, are chosen in free elections featuring multiple candidates representing many political parties. The organizational apparatus for the major parties has strengthened in the last two decades compared to the past when political parties centered around individual personalities. In the last several elections, parties have been fewer in number, more coherent in structure, and better able to represent citizens' demands. Chatichai Choonhavan, leader of the conservative Chat Thai Party, became prime minister when his party won the largest plurality of votes in the 1988 election. Following the overthrow of Chatichai's administration in 1991, the military appointed Anand Panyarachun as prime minister. In May 1992 the Thai citizenry demonstrated against the military leaders, forcing them to retreat and to accept the return of civilian rule.

Theoretically above politics, the Thai monarch is the national symbol, the supreme patron who reigns over all, and the leader of the Buddhist religion. The prestige and veneration of the monarchy have grown since the 1950 coronation of King Phumiphol Adunyadej, who recently became the kingdom's longest-reigning monarch. In the 1980s, the king became more involved in Thai politics. His strong stance against coups d'état, for example, has helped to stabilize politics in Thailand.

Traditionally, the Chinese-Thai minority (about ten percent of the population) has dominated the Thai economy while the Thai majority has prevailed in politics. However, a fundamental change has occurred in Thai politics with the Chinese-Thai becoming more involved. The new Parliament includes an unprecedented number of Chinese-Thai business executives.

Since the 1960s, Thailand has sustained a seven percent growth rate, a rate equaled by few other developing nations. More remarkably, the kingdom's economic growth in the late 1980s was ten percent, the highest of any country. Coincident with these high growth rates was the increase in the export sector, which in the late 1980s grew about twenty-four percent each year. Foreign investment has grown at a similarly rapid rate, with Japan, Taiwan, the United States, Hong Kong, and the Republic of Korea the leading investors.

The factors responsible for the kingdom's economic successes include a commitment to free-market, export-driven policies, carried out by highly trained, and generally conservative, technocrats. These new officials are not as steeped in personalistic, clientelist politics as their predecessors. The vital involvement of Thailand's Chinese minority and the fact that Thai politics has adhered to a consistent set of economic policies also help explain the vibrancy of the economy.

The greatest obstacles to continued economic growth are the poor state of infrastructural facilities and the depletion of natural resources, especially forests. Thai universities graduate only a third of the students needed in engineering and related "hard" sciences and technology. One further difficulty stems, ironically, from the nation's economic success. Foreign investment and trade have made the Thai economy vulnerable to the vagaries of the world economy. Thus far, imports and exports are sufficiently diversified to assure that a downturn in one sector will not cripple the overall economy.

Thailand has evolved into a semidemocracy with new institutions available for more effective political participation. There is open participation, a free press, and free elections. Nevertheless, Thai society is still dominated by a small proportion of the society that controls the military, economic, and political spheres. The prospects for continued *parliamentary democracy depend on the capacity of the government to meet the needs of the people, to continue the high level of economic development, to restrain the military, and to provide for a smooth monarchical succession. Prospects are also contingent on the ability of the state to strengthen institutions such as the Parliament and political parties and to decrease the role of patronage and *corruption.

Thailand is fundamentally different from just a decade ago, when the military-dominated bureaucracy controlled society. As democratization and economic *development have emerged, Thai society has evolved into a more independent, confident, stable, and vibrant nation. Except during periods of military control, Thais do not feel oppressed by their government leaders. Thailand's continuing capacity to cope with changing demands and to assert its own destiny remains intact.

(See also ASSOCIATION OF SOUTHEAST ASIAN NATIONS; BUDDHISM; DEMOCRATIC TRANSITIONS; MILITARY RULE; PATRON-CLIENT POLITICS; SOUTHEAST ASIA TREATY ORGANIZATION.)

Clark D. Neher, ed., *Modern Thai Politics* (Rochester, Vt., 1981). John L. S. Girling, *Thailand: Society and Politics* (Ithaca, N.Y., 1981). David Morell and Chai-Anan Samudavanija, *Political Conflict in Thailand: Reform, Reaction, Revolution* (Weston, Mass., 1981). Clark D. Neher and Wiwat Mungkandi, eds., *Thailand-U.S. Relations in the New International Era*, Institute of East Asian Studies Research Papers (Berkeley, Calif., 1990).

CLARK D. NEHER

THATCHER, Margaret. The first woman prime minister in a major West European state, Margaret Thatcher is remarkable also for being the first British prime minister to win three successive general elections since Lord Liverpool in the early nineteenth century, as well as for being the longest continuously serving prime minister in twentieth-century *Britain, holding the post from May 1979 to November 1990. She has lent her name to an "ism"—*Thatcherism. This refers both to her political style—which is abrasive and direct—and her policies—tax cutting and encouraging the free market. In Britain she has also made a mark for her proclaimed break with the postwar consensus policies which she thought had produced the relative economic decline of the country.

She was born in 1925, the daughter of a shop-keeper in Grantham. She read chemistry at Oxford and later qualified as a barrister, specializing in taxation. She entered Parliament for Finchley, North London, in 1959, a seat which she held until her retirement from the House of Commons in 1992. It is interesting that she chose such male-dominated careers; at the time the Conservatives had only a handful of women members of Parliament (MPs). The Conservative Party was also dominated in these years by people from upper-class backgrounds. In this company Margaret Thatcher, although she married a well-off divorcé, Denis Thatcher, was something of an upstart. Even in 1990 she could still speak dismissively of "toffs" in the party. She also publicly referred to middle-class "guilt," which she thought held back earlier Conservative governments from taking necessary but unpopular actions to combat inflation, social indiscipline, and abuses of trade union power. She dismissed these as "wet" Conservatives.

In the new Conservative administration of 1970 Thatcher was appointed secretary of state for education, the only female member of the cabinet. In that post she gained extra resources for her department and oversaw an expansion of the service. But she was never close to the prime minister, Edward Heath, or closely involved in major decisions. The Heath government was controversial for its adoption in 1972 of a statutory prices and incomes policy to combat inflation—in spite of an election pledge not to do so. When the Conservatives lost two general elections in 1974 Heath's position as leader came under pressure. Thatcher was the only heavy-weight figure to challenge him in a leadership election in February 1975. It was a shock when she defeated him and went on to win the leadership on a second ballot among Conservative MPs. As leader of the opposition she increasingly espoused free market economic policies, in contrast to those both of the previous Conservative government and the then Labour government.

As prime minister in 1979 she broke new ground in economic policy. Income tax cuts, tough monetary targets, a reduced growth of planned public spending, and the abandonment of Keynesian fine tuning signaled a new approach. These policies were maintained despite a subsequent sharp rise in unemployment and fall in production. Measures to privatize publicly owned undertakings and weaken trade unions were also introduced. Yet soaring inflation and sharply rising unemployment made the government and the prime minister deeply unpopular. The reputation of both was helped by the recapture in June 1982 of the Malvinas/Falkland Islands from Argentina and the recovery of the economy. In the June 1983 general election, Thatcher gained a landslide election victory.

In the new Parliament the government continued with the *reforms of trade unions, *privatization, and tax cuts. Industrial action by trade unions was defeated, notably a yearlong strike by miners. Inflation and unemployment turned down, thus preparing the ground for another handsome election victory in 1987.

In foreign affairs Margaret Thatcher was so assertive of British interests that she was sometimes dismissed as a "little Englander." In contrast to Edward Heath she was more of an Atlanticist than a European. Her relations with most *European Community (EC) leaders were marred by acrimonious disputes over Britain's budgetary contribution and her resistance to measures to speed integration. The special relationship with the United States was largely a function of her close rapport with President Ronald *Reagan. In 1986 she courted unpopularity by allowing U.S. planes to take off from Britain to mount bombing raids in Libya.

She reduced the size and challenged the culture of the civil service and sharply reduced the role of local government, but she did little else to reform political institutions. Opinion surveys showed that she was not a much-liked figure but was much respected as a strong, decisive leader. As party leader she reasserted a long-dormant neoliberal strand in the Conservative Party and stood for a unique blend of liberal economics—a greater role for markets, income tax cuts, and less government intervention in the economy—and *authoritarianism—regarding law and order and freedom of information.

As a peacetime prime minister she was distinctive. The most dominant personal premierships in this century were the wartime tenures of Lloyd George and Winston *Churchill. As party leader and prime minister, Thatcher was more of a mobilizer than a conciliator, determined to take radical measures to turn the country around. For a Conservative she was oddly impatient with the state of things. She was so closely involved in pushing so many radical policies on privatization, income tax cuts, education reforms, industrial relations changes, local government finance, and resistance to British membership in the EC Exchange Rate Mechanism that it can be argued she made a difference to policy outcomes.

Thatcher appointed her supporters to key economic posts and intervened energetically in the work of departments. In this she was helped by a strengthened policy unit and above all by her own stamina, inquisitiveness, and self-confidence in the correctness of her opinions on so many issues. What she achieved at the center of British government she did largely by herself rather than through institutions. Remarkably, in a political system with a collective executive (the cabinet) she was less an advocate for the team than a figure apart, forcefully presenting her own views.

There was some irony in that her cabinets contained few true Thatcherites. Some of her close allies, notably Nigel Lawson, chancellor of the exchequer, Norman Tebbit, party chair, and Nicholas Ridley, secretary of state for trade and industry, all left in stormy circumstances. In November 1990 Sir Geoffrey Howe suddenly resigned. Sir Geoffrey was the only other member, apart from Margaret Thatcher herself, to have survived from the first government in 1979. In his resignation speech he condemned Thatcher's leadership style and forcefully repudiated her approach to Britain's relationship with the EC. The speech was seen as a challenge to Thatcher's leadership, a challenge that was accepted by her old foe Michael Heseltine. Although she won the first ballot for the party leadership her majority was not sufficient to avoid the need for a second ballot. Concerned cabinet colleagues warned that she would lose the leadership and appealed to her to stand down. This she did, and in the ensuing leadership ballot John Major was elected party leader and became prime minister.

Two questions remain for historians. First, why has the Conservative Party achieved such dominance throughout the 1980s and the first years of the 1990s? In part it was a consequence of the first-past-the-post electoral system which translated a forty-two percent share of the popular vote into some sixty percent of the seats in the House of Commons in 1983 and 1987. In part it was also due to the decline of the Labour Party and the trade unions, and in part to the division of the non-Conservative vote between the Alliance and Labour parties. Second, if Thatcher undoubtedly helped to dismantle so many of the institutions and policies of the postwar consensus, how successful was she in laying the outlines of a new settlement? Although the Labour Party has moved to accept many Thatcherite policies and Major continues many aspects of her policy agenda, the extent to which Thatcher left an enduring political legacy is not yet clear.

(See also CONSERVATISM; LIBERALISM; MALVINAS/ FALKLANDS WAR; MONETARISM; NEW RIGHT; TAXES AND TAXATION.)

Anthony King, "Margaret Thatcher: The Style of a Prime Minister," in *The British Prime Minister,* 2d ed., Anthony King, ed. (London, 1985). Dennis Kavanagh, *Thatcherism and British Politics* (Oxford, 1989). Hugo Young, *One of Us* (London, 1989). Dennis Kavanagh, "Making Sense of Thatcherism," in *Politics and Personalities,* Dennis Kavanagh, ed. (London, 1990).

DENNIS KAVANAGH

THATCHERISM. The political phenomenon known as *Thatcherism* flourished in *Britain from the mid-1970s to the early 1990s. It can be viewed both as a dominant current in British politics and as a term introduced to interpret diverse contemporary British trends. It has also had some influence internationally—both as a real political force and as an ideological exemplar. The term *Thatcherism* was coined after the surprise victory of Margaret *Thatcher in the Conservative Party leadership ballot in October 1975. First used by leftist critics, it soon became part of everyday discourse across the political spectrum. Initially the term served to characterize Thatcher's distinctive style of campaigning and political leadership of right-wing "authoritarian populism" and her programmatic commitment to a "free economy and strong state." After her translation from opposition leader to prime minister in 1979, it acquired other, often contested, meanings. These include a) Margaret Thatcher's personal qualities and values; b) a particular style of prime ministerial and party leadership; c) a distinctive set of neoliberal policies; and d) the changing economic and political strategic line pursued by Thatcher and her close advisers during the Thatcher premiership. Some commentators question whether the term has any analytic value and others deny that there is much distinctive about Thatcher governments.

Margaret Thatcher became prime minister when her party defeated the outgoing Labour government in the June 1979 election. Her own administration soon adopted a monetarist economic program based mainly on securing tight control over the money supply, public spending cuts, attacking trade union privileges, and trusting in the regenerative powers of market forces. Monetary targeting had mixed success and the overall impact of Thatcher's policies was likewise mixed—they produced a severe recession, mounting unemployment, and growing unpopularity. Yet her government still managed to consolidate its power during 1982. The British defeat of Argentinian forces in the *Malvinas/Falklands War helped by making Thatcher unassailable within her cabinet and party. Possibly more important were a covert relaxation of monetary policy, an electioneering boom, and a suicidally split opposition. Together these factors secured another general election victory in 1983, which encouraged the Conservatives to embark on a more radical economic program. *Privatization in various guises was intensified, further steps were taken to shackle organized labor economically and politically, six Labour-controlled metropolitan councils were abolished, and the government triumphed in a grueling yearlong miners' strike. They gradually evolved a novel economic and political strategy to rescue Britain from a decline they attributed to a Keynesian commitment to full employment and a social democratic commitment to the *welfare state. Under Thatcher the Conservatives pursued an economic strategy based on supply-side flexibility and a political strategy based on popular capitalism. Yet many Conservatives regarded these as years of drift and, from October 1986, Thatcher committed them to a more radical, neoliberal project aimed at restructuring the whole society. A year after a third decisive general election victory in 1987, Nigel Lawson introduced a radical tax-cutting budget that was extraordinarily favorable to the rich.

This seems to have been the high point of Thatcherism. Thereafter economic trends moved against the government: inflationary pressures fueled by an escalating money supply (which were partly masked by rising imports and were made palatable by rising asset prices) were expressed in continued growth in the trade deficit, rising interest rates, resurgent wage demands, and then falling house prices. Political matters also turned sour. A shocking defeat in the 1989 elections for the *European Parliament and Lawson's resignation as chancellor were followed by growing discontent with the handling of such diverse issues as National Health Service reform, road and rail transport, and privatization of water and electricity. The final straw was the massively unpopular and clearly Thatcher-inspired "poll tax" introduced to replace the local property tax. Thus 1989–1990 proved to be the beginning of the end for Thatcherism. It became increasingly defensive, faced growing disenchantment, and feared the resurgence in Labour fortunes. November 1990 saw Thatcher's resignation as party leader and prime minister and her replacement by John Major after a bruising leadership battle.

The social basis of Thatcherism changed over time. Support initially stemmed from Thatcher's ability to give expression to hitherto unvoiced petit bourgeois discontent with the postwar settlement as well as more general disillusion with the Labour government, the unions, and visible economic decline. More generally, from Thatcher's first days in opposition almost to her final days in Downing Street, most of the press provided massive support for Thatcherism. Once in office, the Conservatives used government resources to consolidate this support—notably among skilled manual workers in the private sector and among the small business and self-employed sectors. Key elements here were: the discounted selling of publicly owned housing, tax cuts, ending restrictions on private-sector collective bargaining, and petty gains from privatization issues. Support was particularly strong in the prosperous south of England rather than in Scotland, Wales, and the declining north. Between elections working class support was volatile, however, and support from the professional middle class declined steadily—especially in the public sector. Although the appeal of Thatcherism was often explained at first in terms of its successful hegemonization of political discourse, there is scant evidence that the Thatcher governments shifted public opinion in a Thatcherite direction. Moreover, as signs of economic crisis multiplied and the full horror of the poll tax emerged, instrumentally motivated support began to crumble across the board. Thatcherism had

been damaged by a fatal contradiction in its strategy: the political pursuit of popular capitalism when high interest rates were its main macroeconomic instrument.

Thatcherism's overall impact is hard to assess because key evidence is still lacking or disputed. But some effects are undeniable: the massive program of privatization extending beyond disposal of state-owned enterprises to include the contracting out of public services, introducing market proxies into the state sector, and higher charges; the diversion of resources from public investment into private consumption; a redistribution of the incidence of taxation from direct to indirect and of its burden from rich to poor; the abolition of exchange controls and financial deregulation; major changes in trade union legislation; the abolition of metropolitan councils and the severe weakening of local government; and so on. There is mounting evidence that the Thatcher regime failed to preside over an improvement in the long-run international viability of the British economy at full employment levels of demand despite its tenth-anniversary celebrations of an economic miracle. This can be attributed in large measure to continuing and massive neoliberal neglect of the economic and social infrastructure. But Thatcherism did force the Labour Party to launch its own socialist perestroika and move toward a left-conservative program.

Part of Thatcherism's ultimate economic and political difficulties can be attributed to Thatcher's Atlanticist political instincts and distrust of Europe. At a time when Britain's trading future lay with Europe, Thatcher clung obstinately to the special relationship with the United States and opposed any significant progress toward European unification—economic as well as political. This alarmed and disillusioned the British establishment as well as her erstwhile U.S. allies. Her isolation increased as events in Eastern Europe and the *European Community reinforced German and French influence. Thatcherism presided over the ever-greater integration of Britain into the world economy, but many of its policies seemed to push Britain further down the global economic hierarchy into a low-wage, low-investment, low-productivity economy with at best a protected and thriving international business and financial services sector.

(See also CONSERVATISM; KEYNESIANISM; MONETARISM; NEW RIGHT.)

BOB JESSOP

THIRD WORLD. In the late twentieth century, the concept *Third World* refers to a dynamic and multifaceted phenomenon. The revolutions of 1989, the disintegration of socialist regimes, the end of the *Cold War, and the globalization process all have profound implications for the group of countries said to constitute the Third World. To assess the contemporary significance of this concept for *international relations, the place to begin is with its origin and alternative definitions.

Coined by French authors, the term contains an allusion to the Third Estate of prerevolutionary France—that is, to social groups other than the most privileged groups of the day, the clergy and the nobility (the First and Second Estates, respectively). Analogously, then, *Third World* refers to the marginalized strata of the international system.

Another interpretation equates the Third World with poverty in general. For the *World Bank, the Third World comprises low-income countries. These may be subdivided according to GNP per person. But this definition is replete with empirical contradictions. Some Middle Eastern countries have a higher average per capita income than does the United States, and there is a greater incidence of poverty in some U.S. inner cities than in many parts of the Third World. Furthermore, emphasis on statistical indicators such as per capita income often deflects attention from qualitative social conditions. From a slightly different perspective, the term *Third World* means oppressed nations, suggesting the existence of states that are exploited and of others that are exploiters.

In common usage, the Third World comprises all countries not included in the First World and the Second World. The Western capitalist countries plus Japan, Australia, and New Zealand, and often Israel and South Africa as well, are widely regarded as constituting the First World. The Second World—a construction of the Cold War era—consisted of the socialist countries of Eastern and Central Europe, what was called the Soviet bloc. The Third World encompasses the nations of Africa, Asia, and Latin America, most of them former colonies which to varying degrees could be characterized as underdeveloped.

The ambiguities associated with the term *Third World* are manifold. One complication is the role of oppressed peoples outside the three continents. Are African Americans part of the Third World? Native Americans? Australian aborigines? In addition, ethnocentrism may be detected in assigning first place to the countries that rank ahead of the others according to an economic and technological yardstick. The Third World would be first if the criteria were the chronology of the human species (which begins with Africa) or total population.

Yet another snag is the disagreement over whether China belongs to the Third World. The Chinese position is that the United States and the Soviet Union make up the First World, the other developed countries form the Second World, and, with the exception of Japan, the whole of Africa, Asia, and Latin America constitute the Third World. Although China has proclaimed itself to be part of the Third World, Beijing's view of the matter has been treated with skepticism at meetings of the *nonaligned nations. Although China may not qualify as a super-power, a country with one billion people, bountiful natural resources, and nuclear hardware is, by any standard, a great power.

Ambiguities aside, some observers reject the term *Third World* altogether. An influential commission headed by Willy Brandt, former chancellor of the Federal Republic of Germany, preferred a dichotomy, as indicated by the title of its report: *North-South: A Program for Survival* (Cambridge, Mass., 1980). This distinction is between two hemispheres, a more economically advanced "north" and a less developed "south." However, there are well-to-do nations *south* of the equator (Australia, New Zealand, and, more problematically, South Africa) as well as several poor countries in the "north": India, with fifteen percent of the world's population, the rest of South Asia, most of Southeast Asia, the Caribbean, Central America, and the northern region of South America. Another viewpoint is that the world should be analyzed in more unitary terms. World systems theorists such as Immanuel Wallerstein reason that there is a single world economy and that it is capitalist. The analysis that follows from this presupposition identifies three tiers of the world economy: core, periphery, and semiperiphery. The danger, however, in employing such broad strokes lies in omitting the fine detail, which is precisely what in substance must be discerned.

Clearly, the division of the world into zones is a reality. But the components are changing. Most important is the disintegration of the Second ("socialist") World. Moreover, the global political economy is increasingly differentiated, with important distinctions between the first generation of countries to have penetrated Japanese and Western markets (the "Four Dragons"—Taiwan, the Republic of Korea [South Korea], Singapore, and Hong Kong), possible competition from a second generation of *newly industrializing economies, and, on the other end of the spectrum, sub-Saharan Africa, which is the most marginalized area in the mosaic of globalization.

In sum, the Third World is a geographical and political category referring broadly to the three continents of Asia, Africa, and Latin America, not a precise analytical concept. The main drawbacks to Third Worldist thinking are sentimentality, the tendency to romanticize struggles waged by "the wretched of the earth," and the impression that only the advanced countries are the oppressors without due emphasis on locally dominant forces and transnational coalitions. Despite its pitfalls, the term *Third World* is a convenient shorthand to depict the group of countries struggling to escape from underdevelopment. As a metaphor, it describes the disadvantaged position of peoples, most of whom are of color and live in poverty in postcolonial societies, within the ambit of a rapidly changing global political economy.

(See also DEVELOPMENT AND UNDERDEVELOP-

MENT; INTERNATIONAL SYSTEMS; MODERNIZATION; NINETEEN EIGHTY-NINE; NORTH-SOUTH RELATIONS; RURAL DEVELOPMENT; WOMEN AND DEVELOPMENT.)

Allen H. Merriam, "Semantic Implications of the Term 'Third World' " *International Studies Notes* 6, no. 3 (Fall 1979): 12–15. James H. Mittelman, *Out from Underdevelopment: Prospects for the Third World* (London and New York, 1988).

JAMES H. MITTELMAN

THUCYDIDES. Considered the greatest of the classical Greek historians because of his authorship of an unfinished, untitled history of the Peloponnesian War, Thucydides evidently was trained in the dialectical modes of argument of the Sophists and influenced by the diagnostic practice of early Greek medicine. Sensitive to many themes in the Greek culture of his time, he wrote his book to be, in the rendering of his first English-language translator, Thomas Hobbes, "an everlasting possession."

His immortality as a historian derives from an exemplary commitment to descriptive accuracy, analytical depth in probing the conditions and possibilities of the human condition, and the dramatic power of his account. The book can be read as a tragic account of the rise and fall of imperial Athens, as a painfully accurate account of the dismemberment of the unifying alliances and the civilized standards of conduct of the Greek city-states in general and Athens in particular, and as a scientific history of the Peloponnesian war (431–404 B.C.E.) between Athens and Sparta, each supported by a changing coalition of allies, colonies, and even former enemies.

Ironically, his failings as a general facilitated his detailed investigation of the actions and rationales of both sides during the *war. The son of Olorus, Thucydides was an Athenian who had Thracian roots, including an interest in gold mines there. From textual evidence, Thucydides is estimated to have been born around 460 B.C.E. Having been elected one of Athens's ten *strategoi* in 424 with responsibility for the Thracian region, Thucydides unfortunately lost the important city of Amphipolis that winter to the Spartan general Brasidas's surprising winter campaign and his effective anti-imperialist appeals. Returning to Athens, Thucydides was tried and convicted for his loss, and exiled from Athens. He appears to have returned some twenty years later, at the end of the war, and to have died shortly thereafter.

Thucydides shares with Sun Tzu and Kautilya the role of cofounders of a global discipline of international politics. In each case these writers emphasized the "realistic" importance of power politics, within a theoretical and cultural framework that acknowledged as well the importance of cultural ideals such as justice, moderation, and appropriateness. Modern Western writers have identified him with the Realist tradition of international theorizing and prudent diplomacy, citing Machiavelli, Hobbes, *Clausewitz, and Morgenthau as important successors. Except for revolutionary, anti-imperialist, or communitarian regimes, this school of international political practice has had tremendous influence—if not always great public acclaim—among the leading statesmen and stateswomen of the modern era. As Hobbes tried to justify his absolutist antidemocratic politics with references to the horrible civil strife in Corcyra, so Thucydides' insights and interpretive visions have been fitted with Neorealist, Marxist, communitarian, and even postmodernist perspectives.

(See also BALANCE OF POWER; INTERNATIONAL RELATIONS; POSTMODERNISM; REALISM.)

Donald Kagan, *The Outbreak of the Peloponnesian War* (Ithaca, N.Y., 1969). Donald Kagan, *The Archidamian War* (Ithaca, N.Y., 1974). Donald Kagan, *The Peace of Nicias and the Sicilian Expedition* (Ithaca, N.Y., 1981). W. Robert Connor, *Thucydides* (Princeton, N.J., 1984). Donald Kagan, *The Fall of the Athenian Empire* (Ithaca, N.Y., 1987).

HAYWARD R. ALKER, JR.

TIANANMEN SQUARE. The spontaneous demonstrations that filled Tiananmen Square, the symbolic capital of China's communist *revolution, in the spring of 1989 were unprecedented in the history of the People's Republic of *China. They revealed a high level of disillusionment with the reform program initiated in the late 1970s and exposed deep divisions within *Chinese Communist Party leadership about future development.

The specific cause of the demonstrations was the death of the reforming ex–General Secretary Hu Yaobang. But frustrations among key sectors of the urban population meant that the student actions quickly found widespread support. The stop-and-go urban economic reform program launched in late 1984 failed to turn around the urban economy and was extremely destabilizing. The industrial working class saw its privileged position coming under threat from market-based reforms; intellectuals and students were frustrated by insufficient political reform; and all were affected by inflation.

The students were the social group that first took to the streets and remained the driving force. They were alienated from the mainstream of the party-dominated society and were not concerned so directly with the financial and social problems that beset the rest of Beijing's urban population.

On 26 April, the Beijing Students Autonomous Federation was formally founded, the first such organization in the history of the People's Republic. This represented a fundamental challenge to traditional party dominance of social organizations, a challenge that was increased by the founding of the Beijing Workers Autonomous Federation in mid-May.

The stress on combating official corruption gave

the movement the feel of a moral crusade, and this was important for creating broader public support. This moral image was heightened by the launching of the hunger strike on 13 May. However, the original leaders found it increasingly difficult to coordinate actions. The fragmented organizational structure made decision making cumbersome and hampered the students' capacity to act flexibly and decisively.

The party's reaction was no more coherent. The movement exposed deep divisions within the party about the reform program. The resultant inner-party struggle between conservative leaders and reformers gathered around General Secretary Zhao Ziyang had to be resolved before the students could be dealt with. Zhao was marginalized and martial law was invoked on 20 May. The conservative group saw the establishment of autonomous organizations as a fundamental challenge to party rule and were unwilling to accept any political agenda that was not set by the party itself. This refusal to recognize the organizations shut out the possibility for genuine dialogue, making conflict inevitable. The decision to call in the army to crush the demonstrations on 4 June highlighted how out of touch the conservative leaders were with the process of change that the economic reforms had unleashed. Estimates of the number killed in the crackdown range from a few hundred to over 1,000.

Tiananmen Square has become an important symbol for all involved. Conservatives see it as a test that the party has passed with flying colors. From their perspective, a counterrevolutionary uprising was crushed and the party's commitment to socialism was reconfirmed. Their opponents see the demonstrations as signifying a key break with the past and an important step on China's road away from a party-dominated political agenda. At the same time, Tiananmen Square stands in vivid contrast to the events of 1989 in Eastern and *Central Europe and is a source of considerable criticism of China abroad. Any future leadership will have to deal with these different interpretations and foreign policy repercussions.

(See also DENG XIAOPING; NINETEEN EIGHTY-NINE; SINO-AMERICAN RELATIONS.)

Tony Saich, ed., *The Chinese People's Movement: Perspectives on Spring 1989* (Armonk, N.Y., 1990). Suzanne Ogden, Kathleen Hartford, Lawrence R. Sullivan, and David Zweig, eds., *China's Search for Democracy: The Student and Mass Movement of 1989* (Armonk, N.Y., 1991).

TONY SAICH

TIBET. From rival tribes, the Tibetans were united in the sixth century; they were led by strong tribal leaders until the thirteenth century, when Mongol khans created a theocracy under their Buddhist spiritual advisors. These Dalai Lamas held absolute power, although at times Tibet was ruled by monk regents or by agents *(amban)* sent by the Chinese

government. From 1913 to 1950 Tibet was de facto independent. In 1950 Tibet was incorporated into the People's Republic of *China (PRC), and since 1 September 1965 has been known as the Tibet Autonomous Region (TAR).

The Chinese constitution stipulates that in areas where ethnic minorities make up a majority of the population, local governments will be run by the ethnic minorities and have relatively broad powers in comparison with similar regions where the majority Han Chinese predominate. The TAR represents about one-third of the total area of ethnic Tibetan inhabitation and corresponds to the area of political control maintained by the Dalai Lamas. Outside of the TAR, where about half the Tibetans live (the Chinese government counts 3 million Tibetans; the Dalai Lama counts 6 million), there are twelve autonomous prefectures and counties with a Tibetan majority in the provinces of Gansu, Qinghai, Sichuan, and Yunnan.

From 1950 until an abortive revolt in 1959, the fourteenth, and current, Dalai Lama continued ruling in conjunction with Chinese officials. After the revolt, the Dalai Lama and approximately 50,000–60,000 Tibetans fled into exile in India and the surrounding region. An ad hoc government replaced the Dalai Lama until the establishment of the TAR in 1965.

The TAR government, always led by a Tibetan, is in charge of enforcing laws, making local policies, administering local finance and economic development, and has responsibility in the areas of, for example, education, tourism, and public health. August 1979 saw the establishment of a Tibet Regional People's Congress, also led by Tibetans, with similar parliamentary groups at the county and municipal levels. There is a local court system and police force. All major decisions must be approved by the authorities in Beijing.

Real power lies in the hands of the local *Chinese Communist Party (CCP) organization, which has never had a Tibetan leader. There are CCP branches at every level of government. In addition, Chinese military forces have considerable sway in the region owing to Tibet's strategic position, a plateau averaging 4,880 meters (16,000 feet) above sea level looking down onto the frontier with India (with whom China fought a brief war in 1962). There are also border police units and a sizable local militia. Because of recent disturbances, the central government has introduced armed police forces as well. All military units are ultimately controlled by the authorities in Beijing.

Tibet is riven by religious and ethnic animosity. Chinese policies of the 1960s attempted to destroy religion and imposed arbitrary rules on the Tibetans. The Dalai Lama was portrayed as a traitor in exile. Tibetans are devout Buddhists who universally look upon the Dalai Lama as their spiritual leader, and Chinese policies have found few followers while creating deep divisions between the two peoples. A recent influx of Chinese into the TAR has exacerbated the cleavages as the immigrants have received privileges beyond those available to the Tibetans.

These divisions are further aggravated by an effective worldwide campaign conducted by the Dalai Lama in India and his supporters in the West to achieve Tibetan independence. China believes Tibet was never independent, and the issue is historically murky. Initially aided by the Central Intelligence Agency, the Tibetan exile movement has gained a momentum of its own, and in 1990 the Dalai Lama won the Nobel Peace Prize. The exile community has been able to operate clandestinely inside Tibet as well. In 1987 violence erupted in Tibet, resulting in many Tibetan casualties and the declaration of martial law in the capital, Lhasa, in 1989, only to be lifted more than a year later.

Tibet was a feudal state until 1959 and desperately poor. Beginning in 1951 the Chinese built roads, hospitals, schools, factories, tourist facilities, airports, and the like. However, these additions for the most part have had little effect on the local Tibetan population, and it appears that the Chinese have benefited more than the Tibetans. Tibet remains a poor, traditional, agricultural economy with little prospect for growth without a railway, which to date has remained a technological impossibility over the permafrost and 4,900-meter (16,000-foot) mountain passes.

In recent years the Dalai Lama and the Chinese government have held informal talks on various levels to negotiate the cleric's return to Tibet in order to ease ethnic strains. Many Tibetan exiles oppose the Dalai Lama's return until Tibet has achieved independence. The Dalai Lama believes that under certain conditions he can return and work with the Chinese government as he did in the 1950s and serve as a force for political stability and economic development.

Currently the hostility that Tibetans feel toward the Chinese is palpable, and this tension makes any prospect of economic and political progress unlikely. Chinese officials have admitted that political autonomy has been a sham yet do little to change the situation. Military force is still deemed the best way to maintain order and stability.

(See also BUDDHISM; ETHNICITY.)

A. Tom Grunfeld, *The Making of Modern Tibet* (London and New York, 1987). Melvyn C. Goldstein, *A History of Modern Tibet, 1913–1951: The Demise of the Lamaist State* (Berkeley, Calif., 1989).

A. TOM GRUNFELD

TIMOR. An island in the Indonesian archipelago, Timor is inhabited by people of mixed Austronesian-Melanesian ancestry. European involvement dates from the sixteenth century, and diplomatic negotiations between 1839 and 1914 partitioned the island into West (Dutch) Timor and East (Portuguese) Ti-

mor, including the enclave of Ocussi Ambeno on the northwest coast. After Japanese occupation during World War II, West Timor became part of independent *Indonesia, with the east remaining a Portuguese overseas territory. After the 1974 armed forces coup in Portugal, the options for East Timor of independence, continued association with Portugal, and integration with Indonesia or *Australia were explored with increasing acrimony among the small mestizo elite. This culminated in a brief civil war in August 1975 in which the left-wing pro-independence Frente Revolucionária do Timor Leste Independente (Fretilin) defeated the conservative associationist forces. Fearing Fretilin's left-wing connections, Indonesia used volunteers to invade the territory in September. Fretilin declared an independent Democratic Republic of East Timor on 28 November, but was forced from the capital, Dili, after an Indonesian airborne attack in December 1975. The UN General Assembly called on Indonesia to withdraw and the Security Council condemned the invasion, but many observers believe that the invasion initially had the tacit approval of the United States and Australia. Indonesia formally annexed the territory on 15 July 1976 as its twenty-seventh province under a governor appointed by Jakarta. *Guerrilla warfare under a succession of Fretilin leaders continued in the mountains. The disruption of agriculture by the war and the resettlement of villagers by Indonesian authorities as a *counterinsurgency measure led to famine in which perhaps 100,000 people (of an original population of 650,000) died. Indonesian rule is now firmly established and Indonesia has ignored further General Assembly resolutions calling for self-determination in the region.

Jill Joliffe, *East Timor: Nationalism and Colonialism* (St. Lucia, Australia, 1978).

ROBERT CRIBB

TITO. Josip Broz, known as Tito (1892–1980), was president of *Yugoslavia (1953–1980), general secretary (later president) of the Communist Party (League of Communists) of Yugoslavia (1939–1980), and marshal of Yugoslavia. He was born in the village of Kumrovec, northwest of Zagreb, Croatia, to a peasant family. Having completed his apprenticeship as a locksmith, he worked in Zagreb, where he joined the Social Democratic Party of Croatia-Slavonia in 1910, and later in Austria and Germany. During World War I he served as a sergeant in the Austro-Hungarian army on Serbian and Russian fronts. Wounded and captured by the Russians in 1915, he was a prisoner of war until 1917, when he joined the Red Guard unit in Omsk, Siberia. He returned to the newly founded Yugoslavia in 1920 as a convinced communist. Having joined the Communist Party of Yugoslavia (KPJ), he worked as a trade union organizer and in 1928, as a result of his work against party factions, became the political secretary of the Zagreb party organization.

After the assassination of Stjepan Radić, the leader of the Croatian national movement, in 1928, Tito stirred up demonstrations against the Belgrade government. In line with the growing Communist militancy of the time, he apparently planned terrorist actions (bombs were discovered in his apartment). His defiant defense at the trial increased his standing in the KPJ. After serving a prison term, he was released in 1934 and was co-opted into the KPJ's exiled Politburo in December 1934, when he assumed the pseudonym Tito. After 1937, when *Stalin decimated the exiled leadership of the KPJ, Tito increasingly emerged as the Comintern's choice for general secretary. His appointment was formalized in 1939 and received internal confirmation at the Fifth Land Conference of the KPJ, held in Zagreb, in October 1940. Tito was already noted as a leftist who put little stock in Popular Front arrangements with non-Communists. Moreover, he was a strong federalist, seeing the solution of the nationality question in Yugoslavia in a Soviet-style federation. This led him to ignore Soviet pleas for cooperation with anti-Communist and Great Serbian Chetniks during the war and prompted him to emphasize the revolutionary seizure of power. This was contrary to Soviet policy of wartime alliance with the Western Allies and their local adherents.

In line with his insurrectionary strategy, Tito organized the Yugoslav Partisan army during the Axis occupation and dismemberment of Yugoslavia. This guerrilla force was not meant to be auxiliary to the Allied military effort, but to conduct offensive operations of its own. Concurrent with the strengthening of Partisan operations, Tito also fostered the growth of Communist-dominated administrations on the local level and in the future federal republics. As a result of his military successes and the expansion of the territory held by the Partisans, the Western Allies recognized Tito in 1943 as the leader of Yugoslav resistance, obliging the exiled government of King Peter II to come to terms with him. With the entrance of Soviet army and Partisan detachments into Serbia in October 1944, Tito established his headquarters in Belgrade and proceeded to mount mop-up operations against the remnants of German and collaborationist unites. Communist power was established throughout Yugoslavia by May 1945, usually with a level of ruthlessness that was unique in Eastern Europe. In essence, unlike the countries of Eastern Europe which were occupied by the Soviet Army, Yugoslavia underwent a domestic revolution that established a regional and very militant Communist center.

After fully consolidating his power by purging non-Communists from the provisional government (in which he served as premier), holding bogus elections on the status of the monarchy, and proclaiming the federal people's republic (all in summer and fall of 1945), Tito proceeded to tighten Communist control through trials of ecclesiastic dignitaries, oppositional notables, and even dissident Communists. In the immediate postwar period, under Tito's leadership, Yugoslavia became the most communized country of Eastern Europe. In the early years of the *Cold War Tito's militancy in the *Balkans (Albania, Greece) irritated the Soviet leadership, which was afraid that Tito might provoke a premature war with the West. Tito's independent views and base ultimately provoked the Soviet leadership to plot his overthrow. This failed, but in June 1948, after the promulgation of the Cominform resolution, Yugoslavia was expelled from the Communist family and briefly floundered in total isolation, exposed to internal challenges by pro-Soviet Communists.

After 1949, Western countries came to the aid of Tito, having determined that his "national communism" was a toxin that ought to be encouraged within the increasingly monolithic Soviet camp. For his part, Tito moderated his policies and by 1950 started introducing workers' councils into enterprises. These were meant to be the institutional basis for a return to authentic Marxist "self-management" by the producers in all areas of decision making. In fact, this was a pragmatic attempt to find an ideological alternative to Soviet *socialism without embracing Western *pluralism and a market economy. Though he was himself least of all an ideologist, Tito occupied this diminishing middle ground between the Soviets and the West. Self-management, nonalignment in foreign policy, and self-reliance in defense policy were the three pillars of his system. From 1962 he increasingly favored Yugoslavia's decentralization, the high point of this effort being the semiconfederalist constitution of 1974, which was, however, predicated on the lasting rule of the Communist Party.

Having reconciled himself with the Soviet leadership in 1955, Tito continued to clash with Moscow, notably after the Hungarian uprising in 1956 and the invasion of Czechoslovakia in 1968. His relations with the West, notably with the United States, were on the whole good, with occasional cooling, as in the early 1960s. Most of his energies in foreign policy were devoted to the Third World countries, whereby he became an acknowledged leader of the nonaligned. Tito's last years were a period of deepening malaise, noted for growing conflicts between the constituent nationalities, and recourse to repression. His style of charismatic personal dictatorship was increasingly anachronistic and his ideological solutions an obstacle to needed reform.

(See also COMMUNISM; COMMUNIST PARTY STATES; INDUSTRIAL DEMOCRACY; NONALIGNED MOVEMENT; SOVIET–EAST EUROPEAN RELATIONS; WORKERS' CONTROL.)

Phyllis Auty, *Tito: A Biography* (New York, 1970). Duncan Wilson, *Tito's Yugoslavia* (Cambridge, U.K., 1979).

IVO BANAC

TOGO. A small West African state (55,995 sq. km.; 21,620 sq. mi.) located between Ghana and Benin, Togo stretches inland 320 miles from a thirty-two-mile coastline along which its capital, Lomé, is located. Discovered by Europeans in 1471, Togo's port of Aného played an important role in the slave trade. Contested by several European powers, Germany established a protectorate in 1884 and laid much of the country's infrastructure, including railroads. In 1914 Togo fell to Anglo-French forces in the first Allied victory of World War I. Divided into two League of Nations mandates (later UN trusteeships), British Togoland opted in a 1956 plebiscite (with dissent, intermittently irredentist, among the Ewe) to merge with Ghana. French Togoland became independent on 27 April 1960 under Sylvanus Olympio, leader of the more developed southern populations.

The country's roughly three million people comprise some thirty ethnic groups. The largest are the upwardly mobile, originally animist (now heavily Christianized) Ewe, Ouatchi, and Mina in the south, who live in decentralized village groups that were developed, proselytized, and favored by Germans and French alike; and the northern (some Muslim) Kabre, Kotokoli, and Moba, amongst whom several small precolonial chiefdoms emerged, and who were neglected socially and economically until 1967.

In 1963, Olympio, who had erected a harsh single-party system and espoused fiscal orthodoxy, rejected demands by northern troops just demobilized from France's colonial armies for integration into the new Togolese army. Olympio was murdered in an armed confrontation and power passed to a northern party (under Nicholas Grunitzky) that accepted the insurgents' demands. (The army in due course tripled in size.) Grunitzky, however, was incapable of either consolidating his rule or legitimizing himself among coastal groups; in 1967 Captain Gnassingbe Eyadema, the Kabre assassin of Olympio, seized power and set up an initially benign and development-oriented administration.

Until 1965, Togo had the lowest economic growth rate of all twelve former French African colonies, exporting primarily cocoa and coffee. Eyadema's reign coincided with the initiation of phosphate exports, of which Togo is today the world's fifth-largest producer. Swollen state revenues (especially after nationalization of the industry) alleviated Togo's fiscal problems, consolidated Eyadema's rule, and permitted sustained development of the north without neglect of the south. However, patronage (used as a societal glue) led to massive *corruption; state enterprises turned chronic deficits owing to inefficiency and embezzlement; and efforts to project an image of Eyadema's popularity gave birth to a personality cult. As commodity prices fell in the 1980s, revenues contracted, the debt-servicing burden (second-highest in Africa) brought the economy

under intense pressure, and conspiracies arose, including some involving Olympio's sons.

Throughout his lengthy rule Eyadema maintained a numeric equality in the north-south ethnic balance in his cabinet. In 1969, for the first time, a national political party was introduced. A partly rigged referendum in 1972 formally "civilianized" and legitimated Eyadema's presidency. And in 1979, a plebiscite gave the country a new constitution and a sixty-seven-seat (single-party) national assembly. Eyadema himself was reelected in 1986, allegedly winning approval by margins approaching 100 percent. (Surprisingly, free local elections took place the next year.) Despite Eyadema's relatively benign rule, his northern and military origins continue to be rejected in the south (although many cooperated out of self-interest), intermittent conspiracies were detected, and the (mostly Kabre) armed forces remained the true prop of the regime.

The end of the *Cold War in 1989 saw pressures for the redemocratization of Africa that did not bypass Togo. Initial demands for the end of military rule and multiparty elections were met with brutal repression that in turn triggered riots and demonstrations in the coastal cities. Finally in July 1991 a National Conference was convened that promptly declared its sovereignty and set up an interim dual executive with most powers passing to a prime minister, and Eyadema retained as head of state. The (mostly northern) army was displeased with the eclipse of their leader and northern hegemony, a fact which was reflected by a number of attempted power-grabs on behalf of Eyadema, who, however, supported the interim constitutional array of power. Free multiparty elections, and the presumed final eclipse of Eyadema, are anticipated in 1992–1993.

(See also FRANCOPHONE AFRICA; MILITARY RULE.)

Robert Cornevin, *Histoire du Togo* (Paris, 1959). Samuel Decalo, *Historical Dictionary of Togo*, 2d ed. (Metuchen, N.J., 1987). Samuel Decalo, *Coups and Army Rule in Africa: Motivations and Constraints* (New Haven, Conn., 1990).

SAMUEL DECALO

TONGA. See PACIFIC ISLANDS.

TORTURE. From the Latin *torquere* (to twist), torture is best defined as a deliberate, sanctioned procedure by which official authority inflicts pain. According to *Amnesty International's 1989 report, torture was practiced by ninety-three countries to obtain information, provoke confessions, induce detainees to implicate third parties, and, above all, to humiliate and destroy the victim's personhood.

Although torture occurred in the Ottoman Empire and Imperial Japan, its institutionalization is especially European: it flourished in the Greek city-republics, the Roman Empire, and the Renaissance. Under Greek civil procedure in the fifth and fourth centuries B.C.E., free citizens were not tortured, but a coerced kind of evidence was extracted by force from noncitizens—slaves and foreigners—if they had been accused of a crime. The first major Western legal provisions for torture appeared during the Roman Empire: Title 48 of the *Digest* and Title 9 of the *Code*. With these came a vastly expanded definition of treason that included injuring or diminishing the majesty of the emperor *(crimen laesae maiestatis)* and granted the imperial order extraordinary legal powers when the imperial safety was (or was imagined to be) in danger. As a result, disgraced free citizens, originally protected from torture, were increasingly vulnerable to interrogation and punishment, as Edward Peters *(Torture,* New York, 1985) describes.

Torture declined in Europe between the ninth and twelfth centuries, only to become an integral part of criminal procedures of the Latin church and of most European states between 1250 and 1800, with confession elevated to "the queen of proofs" and crimes of heresy aligned with crimes of treason. During this period torture became an integral part of criminal jurisprudence in much of Europe.

In 1754, all torture was abolished in Prussia, with Saxony, Denmark, and Poland following suit. On the heels of the 1789 French Declaration of the Rights of Man (forbidding torture "forever") and the U.S. Bill of Rights (forbidding "cruel and unusual punishment"), the practice disappeared as a legally authorized procedure in the nineteenth century. John Langbein *(Torture and the Law of Proof,* Chicago, 1977) argues that this attitudinal shift was due to the rise of prisons and workhouses, which offered alternatives to death as a punishment for serious crimes and thus diminished the need for full proof—the underpinning of torture.

Torture was revived in World War I, when state secrets became more closely guarded by state security police, such as the Deuxième Bureau in France and Scotland Yard in Britain, and by military intelligence, which became increasingly unanswerable to civilian jurisprudence. The fear of conspiracy engendered paranoia toward the enemy; accused spies and prisoners of war were tortured for information in the recesses of a new labyrinth of prisons. Secret political police used torture on suspected enemies of the state, party, and people in Mussolini's Italy after 1929, in the Stalinist Soviet Union of the 1930s, and in Nazi Germany, where torture was practiced on communists and socialists, religious and cultural prisoners, and above all on Jews, and was transformed into a medical specialty (Robert Jay Lifton, *The Nazi Doctors,* New York, 1986) and a routine part of extrajudicial procedure. During World War II, the practice of torture spread among the Allied and Axis armed forces in Europe and Asia, although the Germans and Japanese used it more often, not only because their ideologies justified it more easily

but also because they had initially conquered more foreign territory and had to contend with strong movements of resistance. Some of the most terrifying incidents of torture were perpetrated against the French Resistance in German-occupied France, and were carried out under the direction of Klaus Barbie, the "Butcher of Lyon" (who would help train Bolivian security forces in the 1950s and 1960s).

After World War II, the international community hoped to abolish torture. In 1948, the UN adopted the Universal Declaration of Human Rights, with Article 5 stating, "No one shall be subjected to torture or to cruel, inhuman, or degrading treatment or punishment." The 1949 Geneva Convention forbids combatants, prisoners, or civilians to be tortured; Article 3 of the 1950 European Convention on Human Rights prohibits torture and inhuman, degrading punishment.

Nonetheless, European forces fighting national resistance and liberation movements in Africa and Asia increasingly practiced torture. Refinements in the technology and psychology of torture occurred in French Indochina and Algeria, where in the 1950s the French army and police modernized the science of torment, particularly the use of electricity on and in the body. In South Africa (where torture was used routinely by the Dutch on blacks and whites in the 1600s but abolished with the British conquest in 1795), emergency powers and security legislation enacted to mask the routine torture of black political detainees by the police have led to the destruction of the rule of law, as Anthony Mathews *(Freedom, State Security and the Rule of Law,* Cape Town, 1986) documents. In Latin America (where the Spanish Crown instituted the Inquisition in 1571), torture was part of legal proceedings until independence in the 1810s and 1820s. Its reinstitution occurred in the 1960s beginning with the military coup in Brazil in 1964. Torture became a routine part of state policy in Argentina between 1976 and 1983.

The United States became interested in torture as a result of an increased interest in national security doctrine and counterinsurgency. The U.S. Agency for International Development and the Office of Public Safety became the cover under which the *Central Intelligence Agency (CIA) developed experts in torture in the 1960s and 1970s. At the Latin American Defense College, School of the Americas, International Police Academy, and U.S. Border Patrol Academy, courses in interrogation, anatomy, and basic electricity were offered. Jaime Wright et al. *(Nunca Mais,* New York, 1986) describe incidents of U.S. advisors and U.S.-trained Latin American officers using prisoners as guinea pigs in torture classes in Brazil. In the 1980s, U.S. military and CIA officials paid Salvadoran army death squads to torture and kill citizens they identified as politically dangerous. Moreover, U.S. arms firms and the U.S. government, among other countries such as Britain, are deeply involved in the sale or transfer of torture equipment.

Similar to the expansive justifications for torture, ranging from *crimen laesae maiestatis* in the Roman Empire to heresy and treason by the Vatican and most European states between 1250 and 1800, today the doctrine of national security views all dissent as subversive and terrorist and focuses on the danger of the enemy within. Therefore, despite efforts by Amnesty International, the UN, and other international bodies to eliminate the practice, torture has not died out. It is clear that, far from being the eccentric practice of deranged and psychotic military commanders or governments, torture remains routine in many states. Medieval and early modern torture was applied by the judiciary and restricted in its application, purpose, and technology. Today, unfortunately, it has become an official procedure of the state, unrestricted in application, purpose, or technology.

(See also HUMAN RIGHTS; INTERNATIONAL LAW; WAR CRIMES.)

Michel Foucault, *Discipline and Punish* (New York, 1979). Ximena Bunster, "Surviving Beyond Fear: Women and Torture in Latin America," in June Nash and Helen Safa, eds., *Sex and Class in Latin America* (South Hadley, Mass., 1985), 297–325. Nigel Rodney, *Treatment of Prisoners and International Law* (New York, 1990).

JENNIFER SCHIRMER

TOTALITARIANISM. The term *totalitarianism* might best be defined as participatory despotism, i.e., a tyranny exercised in the name and with the active participation (voluntary or coerced) of the entire citizenry. The term, which originated as a boastful self-description of fascist regimes after World War I, has since then been used primarily to characterize fascist and communist systems in order to bring out their similarities as well as their distinctiveness from other forms of *authoritarianism. Because it is evaluative as well as descriptive, the term has lent itself readily for use in political polemics.

Participatory despotism develops in reaction to perceived inequities or widespread discontent that make broad segments of the population ready for drastic action, revolutionary violence, and assertive leadership. The founders of totalitarian regimes may promise to change the world according to some utopian ideal, to prevent change, or to restore an idealized past. Some scholars have identified personality traits that predispose individuals to totalitarian politics, such as conformism, proneness to use violence, ego weakness, self-righteousness, dogmatism, and the tendency to find scapegoats for all social ills.

The standard theoretical model of totalitarianism includes rule by a single party that claims to speak for the entire nation and tolerates no rival parties. The single party rules absolutely and often arbitrarily, although its instruments of government include a system of laws and judicial institutions as well as a government apparatus run according to bureaucratic rules. At the peak of the power pyramid there is a leader whose judgments are declared to be infallible and whose word is law.

The single party not only determines the structure, personnel, and policies of the government but also governs the entire associational life of society, making all organizations and institutions, down to sports clubs and stamp collectors' organizations, auxiliaries of the party and obedient to its guidelines. The administrative apparatus required for this universal coordination takes the form of a huge, top-heavy, poorly coordinated bureaucracy. The entire nation turns into one vast command structure in which every citizen is a functioning member and promotion to any position of authority requires party approval.

The party or its leader are declared to be the sources of truth, and no rival interpretation of reality or goals is tolerated. All forms of expression are controlled for content and form. By using the prescribed language, therefore, all citizens confirm party dogma, both in daily discourse and in frequent public ceremonies. Totalitarian regimes use pageantry to mobilize shows of mass support and enthusiasm. Politics here turns into mass participation theater and political events turn into photo opportunities.

Language control works because it is backed up by terror. Totalitarian regimes govern with the help of both laws and lawlessness. The secret police function as the extralegal enforcers. Their function is to survey public opinion, detect the earliest manifestations of dissent, and serve "prophylactic" justice by detaining and punishing anyone who might some day commit acts of disloyalty. The entire system is designed to instill fear and universal suspicion in all citizens.

The *ideologies of totalitarian systems typically include theories of human nature, history, and politics, a definition of the society that is to be created and the new noble human being that is to be reared, and an identification of the enemies allegedly standing in the way of these goals. Preaching and teaching these ideologies is designed to legitimize the regime. Citizens are exhorted to be patriotic and obedient, disciplined and hard-working, and ready for heroic self-sacrifice. Totalitarian ideologies emphasize citizens' duties toward the state, not rights against it.

Another source of *legitimacy is performance. Successes in war, foreign policy, economic growth, science, and athletic competitions are often cited as evidence of legitimacy. Totalitarian regimes also reward their citizens. For those whose services they value the most, there is a promotion ladder; and at various times there may be a great deal of room near the top of the pyramid of authority, status, and affluence, so that there may be periods of rapid upward social mobility. For all citizens, totalitarian regimes typically provide certain basic goods or protections that constitute a floor underneath the living standards. Consumerism, careerism, and welfare state policies thus are important legitimation devices.

In communist systems virtually the entire economy is administered by the state. While in fascist systems the economy largely remains in private or corporate hands, it is nonetheless subject to many regulations and restrictions. Emphasis on industrial growth, large defense budgets, and a striving for autarky are typical policies of totalitarian systems. Excessive regulation often leads to the development of a "second economy," i.e., of illegality and *corruption.

Because only organizations and associations sponsored or controlled by the single party are permitted to exist, the conclusion might be drawn that totalitarianism implies the withering away of politics. Indeed, compulsory voting without choice and other forms of coerced participation cannot be considered political acts, and opposition parties cannot form. Nonetheless there are decision-making processes that involve disagreements over alternative interpretations of reality and alternative courses of action. Factions or clientelistic groups within the party may fight each other over such issues; and as in every complex bureaucracy there is *bureaucratic politics. Underneath the show of unanimity, solidarity, and control, much conflict reigns in totalitarian systems.

It used to be assumed that totalitarian systems are constructed and controlled so tightly that they can be removed only from the outside by war. Defeat in war, indeed, was needed to destroy the Nazi regime in Germany, and defeat in war emboldened the king of Italy to oust the fascist dictator *Mussolini. But in communist countries totalitarian governments have reformed themselves and ultimately been removed by combinations of events that included elite conflict and genuine reform movements within the ruling parties, organized protest by various civic organizations that formed despite the ban against them, as well as mass rebellion.

Once a nation has rid itself of a totalitarian regime, the obstacles against creating a participatory system that is constitutional and liberal may be overwhelming if a democratic culture has been destroyed or was absent to begin with. Moreover, the removal of totalitarian rule is likely to promote the eruption of hitherto-suppressed ethnic, national, and class antagonisms.

Like other models of political systems, totalitarianism is an abstraction to which no actual state fully conforms. Many despotic regimes of our century display some traits of the model: Latin American death squad regimes, one-party regimes rising in former colonies, and personal tyrannies by rapacious dictators promoting their self-enrichment. Totalitarianism thus is less unique than many scholars suggest. Nor is it an explicitly modern phenomenon. The Puritan dictatorship in Massachusetts, Calvin's rule in Geneva, and the all-pervasive terror of the Holy Inquisition under Charles V or in thirteenth-century France are obvious examples; numerous others could be adduced. Within liberal-constitutional systems, moreover, there are islands of totalitarianism, namely those institutions that Erving Goffman calls "total" (such as prisons, mental health facilities, and some units of the armed forces), as well as highly coercive families, clans, or mafias.

Totalitarianism may not be a thing of the past. No less a hero of democratic politics than Václav *Havel has warned repeatedly that totalitarianism may be the wave of the future, especially in the Western world. He has cited the technological imperative, bureaucratization, the ungovernability of modern societies, techniques of manipulation and persuasion, consumerism, and conformism as possible seeds of totalitarianism. The decline of the superpowers and the lowering of living standards in societies that have for generations nurtured ever-rising expectations might also produce a fascist backlash of major proportions.

(See also COMMUNIST PARTY STATES; FASCISM; ONE-PARTY SYSTEM; PSYCHOLOGY AND POLITICS.)

Hannah Arendt, *The Origins of Totalitarianism* (New York, 1951). Czesław Miłosz, *The Captive Mind* (New York, 1953). Carl Joachim Friedrich and Zbigniew K. Brzezinski, *Totalitarian Dictatorship and Autocracy* (Cambridge, Mass., 1956).

ALFRED G. MEYER

TRADE. See GENERAL AGREEMENT ON TARIFFS AND TRADE.

TRANSNATIONAL CORPORATIONS. See MULTINATIONAL CORPORATIONS.

TRANSNATIONAL RELATIONS. See INTERNATIONAL SYSTEMS.

TREATY. A formal written agreement between *states or intergovernmental organizations that creates legal rights and duties for the contracting parties is known as a treaty. The wide variety of names for treaties, such as convention, covenant, charter, and accord, is unimportant; what matters is that the agreement is considered by the parties to be legally binding. To be cited before a UN organ, a treaty must be registered with the UN, whose treaty series now lists over 30,000 entries.

The other major source of *international law is customary law, which, although unwritten, is accepted as binding by all states. However, treaties are listed first in Article 38 of the Statute of the *International Court of Justice, which sets out the sources of law that the court will apply.

Treaties ending wars, promising friendship, and making territorial and other dispositions have been known since antiquity. In the modern world they are indispensable for the orderly conduct of *international relations in economic and social spheres as well as in areas of high politics. Treaties can be bilateral or multilateral and deal with single or multiple issues. They can also establish organizations such as the UN or the *European Community. In addition to defining relationships between parties in specific terms and providing a basis for claims of nonperformance and possibly sanctions, treaties may have a "legislative" function, establishing normative *regimes for the benefit of the world community. The UN Charter has a "law-making" character: it sets out principles of state conduct and, in particular, proscribes the use of *force except in self-defense against armed attack.

Principles governing treaty law were well understood in international customary law and reflected in state practice. Of particular importance are the rules that treaty obligations must be fulfilled *(pacta sunt servanda)*, that third parties may not be bound without their consent, and that treaties must be interpreted in the light of the intentions of the parties. These principles are now codified in the Vienna Convention on the Law of Treaties (1969), in force since 1980 for those who have ratified it and accepted as generally declaratory of international customary law by those who have not. The Convention also establishes that coercion during negotiation invalidates a treaty and—more controversially—that it may be rendered inoperative by a fundamental change of circumstances.

The trend since 1945 has been to codify customary law, which has entailed revision as well as restatement. Besides the law of treaties, conventions were drawn up on diplomatic immunity and the *law of the sea. And to meet ethical concerns and technological imperatives, entirely new codes have been developed on *human rights, air and outer space, and the environment. The UN sponsors this ongoing process, which found favor with its *Third World majority of members, who felt they had "inherited" an inequitable system of "Western" international law. Consensus on new universal law is hard to achieve, however, and codification is not problem-free. Ambitious rules of humanitarian law that set standards of conduct for states within their own borders may not be implemented by governments and are generally unenforceable, while the failure of major powers to ratify multilateral treaties makes the status of new rules uncertain. This has been the fate of the comprehensive 1982 Law of the Sea Treaty, rejected by the United States and other Western powers.

Ian Sinclair, *The Vienna Convention on the Law of Treaties,* 2d ed. (London, 1984).

MARGARET P. DOXEY

TREATY OF ROME. See ROME, TREATY OF.

TREATY OF VERSAILLES. See WORLD WAR I.

TRIBALISM. The use of the concept of *tribalism* would seem to imply acceptance of a term which requires scientific reevaluation. To avoid any possible misunderstanding, it is extremely important to draw a distinction between tribalism as a concept and as a putative social phenomenon. Some controversy centers on the latter, depending on the ideological and professional background of the onlooker. For historical reasons, Westerners generally take for granted the existence of "tribalism" in Africa. In contrast, African intellectuals generally believe that this usage reflects the usual European or colonially derived stereotypes about Africa. This represents both an ideological and an espistemological disjuncture between the two points of view. It is therefore not without significance that since the 1970s African social scientists have dispensed with the concept of tribalism and have displayed great hostility to its continued use by Westerners. This is partly a subjective reaction against the Eurocentric ideological supposition that, sociologically speaking, everything African is tribal. It is also a result of an increasing awareness of the complexity and range of social formations in both precolonial and postcolonial Africa. The incongruity between this and anthropological tribal stereotypes has become a source of exasperation among African intellectuals.

Yet there are historical predispositions which account for the reflexes of apparent African detractors as well as for the demand by African intellectuals for the decolonization of African history and social science. Therefore, we do well by starting from the beginning, because all social thought is befogged by prevailing historical circumstances.

Historical Origins of the Concept of the Tribe. The tribe as a concept dates back to Greek and Roman antiquity, ending in Europe with what Karl *Marx referred to as "Germanic tribes." According to this classical view, tribes were supposed to represent a particular stage of human development characterized by the existence of self-contained, autonomous groups based on kinship or principles of consanguinity and practicing subsistence economy.

Although this concept is questionable even for ancient societies in that "self-contained" societies are an historical rarity, it is most important to grasp that according to classical notions tribes were a particular stage of political and economic organization wherein there was neither subjugation to an external authority nor reliance on external exchange. However, there was recognition of internal authorities such as chiefs and elders.

This is what European evolutionists brought with them to Africa. Their intellectual predispositions were confirmed by the reports of the early European explorers. Images of African rulers, adorned with all sorts of symbols of rank, holding court with tribal elders, with plumed warriors, prancing about in their fur anklets as symbols of power, came to typify social organization in the "Dark Continent." Colonial anthropologists succeeded in bestowing respectability upon this stereotype. In *African Political*

Systems (Evans-Pritchard and Fortes, eds., 1947), an otherwise sympathetic, albeit paternalistic collection of essays, a wide range of African political formations is reduced to one denominator. But inconsistencies in terminology betray an awareness among the authors of certain differences. For instance, the presiding "tribal" authorities are variously referred to as "king," "paramount chief," and "chief," and the units they govern as "kingdom" and "chiefdom," respectively. What is not questioned, despite the implicit awareness of differences in scale and quality, is the basic assumption that they all represent tribal formations.

This is what African intellectuals and politicians have come to object to not only as a distortion of African history but also as an expression of European arrogance, if not racism. In doing so, some have gone so far as to deny the existence at all in Africa of things called tribes. Subjective responses aside, it would be premature to reject all existing concepts without first testing them rigorously. A careful analysis of African social formations would indicate that tribal formations *did* exist in Africa but that they were not characteristic of *all* regions of the continent. For instance, the kingdoms of West Africa, riverine Sudan, Ethiopia, the interlacustrine region of East Africa, and the Congo Basin had long passed the tribal stage. Far from being self-contained, their economies were mercantile or predatory. Likewise, far from being based on kinship, their polities were distinguished by well-established formal bureaucracies which depended on revenues and exploitation of servile or slave labor.

In other parts of Africa such as East, Central and Southern Africa, with a few exceptions here and there, it can be said that tribal formations in the classical sense were the norm. But once again, all this refers only to different types of centralized political formations. Yet there existed noncentralized social formations as well, ranging from the hunters and food gatherers of Southern Africa and the Congo forest to the "Nilotic" herders of East Africa and southern Sudan. It was in recognition of the latter that David Tait and John Middleton edited the volume *Tribes Without Rulers* in 1953. The title of the book itself is a contradiction in terms because the concept of tribe refers to a particular level of political centralization, as we have seen. Under the impact of colonial ideology the most the anthropologists were able to do was to distinguish between different types of "tribes" in Africa. Indeed, it could be surmised that the obsession with tribalism in Africa among Westerners derives from the colonial ideological fixation with tribes in Africa.

Tribalism: A Basic Misconception. If the application of the concept of tribe in Africa had been flawed from the beginning, then the concept of tribalism could not but perpetuate the original fallacies. Second, having emerged, the concept is incapable of distinguishing between nationalities, regionalism, *ethnicity, and *class conflicts, especially in the urban or modern context. If we proceed from the assumption that colonial impositions undermined tribal organization in Africa by incorporating all and sundry into a broader political entity, the colonial state, then "tribalism" cannot be interpreted as a harking back to a nonexistent past. Its reference point must be something post-tribal and postcolonial. This means that it has nothing to do with tribes but rather with modern African political and economic exigencies, whose drama is largely played out in the urban areas.

This interpretation would favor the concept of ethnicity at the expense of tribalism. The former, unlike the latter, has no organic connotations but rather diffuse cultural and linguistic connotations which are subject to more than one form of expression. Unlike intertribal relations, ethnic representations are not total. They are partial, intermittent, and nontranscendental, i.e., they are subject to class manipulation, they are evoked opportunistically, and are not aimed at overthrowing the whole system. They are a conscious maneuvering for relative advantage within the established order. If they become transcendent, as has happened in some African countries, then we must think of the problem of nationalities within given African states, the best example of which so far is Ethiopia. There might be other, less clear-cut cases such as Nigeria during the Biafran War, Uganda during the Buganda rebellion, or Chad in its period of civil war. But these would seem to be still within the realm of ethnic conflict and a by-product of the concept of a unitary nation-state which Africans inherited from the Europeans.

It may be concluded that the concept of tribalism is erroneous in its general foundations and consequently obscures a number of issues in Africa which could be understood otherwise. The concept militates against cross-cultural comparisons regarding certain social phenomena which obtained in but are not peculiar to Africa, e.g., ethnic and class conflicts or manipulation of these in the interests of certain identifiable strata within African society at large. The persistence of ethnic identities is almost universal, as current history shows in both Western and Eastern Europe, the New World in general, and, of course, most of sub-Saharan Africa.

Therefore, the problem is not to decry a spurious category called "tribalism" but to confront the problem of *cultural pluralism* within modern nation-states which, deriving from the European historical antecedent, are supposed to be unitary. What is called "tribalism" in Africa is often an attempt by disadvantaged sociocultural groups to gain more social space within the given political and economic setup. In the circumstances democratic *pluralism is at issue rather than a dictatorial insistence on misconceived unitarism. Ethnolinguistic groups have existed throughout history but have not forestalled the emergence of different cross-cultural political and social formations over the last two thousand years. Why should they be a problem in the modern era which is supposed to be more enlightened, more rational, and certainly more affluent than previous ages? Africa is part of the modern world, even if not by its own choice. It has to be treated as such, irrespective of any colonial prejudices or Western ideological or racist suppositions. "Tribalism" is one of those, and should be dispensed with in scientific discourse regarding Africa so as to facilitate cross-cultural comparisons or the development of more universalistic concepts for dealing with contradictions among the different peoples of the world.

(See also COLONIAL EMPIRES; RACE AND RACISM; SECESSIONIST MOVEMENTS.)

N. Paden, ed., *Values, Identities and National Integration: Empirical Research in Africa* (Evanston, Ill., 1980). C. Coquery-Vidrovitch, "A Propos des Racines Historiques du Pouvoir: Chefferie et Tribalisme" *Pouvoir* 25 (1983): 51–56. C. Young, "Ethnicity and the Colonial and Post-colonial State in Africa," in P. Brass, ed., *Ethnic Groups and the State* (London, 1985), 57–93. A. D. Smith, *Ethnic Origin of Nations* (Oxford, 1986).

A. B. M. MAFEJE

TRILATERAL COMMISSION. Formed in 1972–1973 by U.S. banker David Rockefeller and a group of establishment figures, the Trilateral Commission (TC) is the most important "private" international relations council (IRC). Major predecessors include the (Anglo-Saxon) Round Tables of the interwar years and the secret Bilderberg meetings, originating in 1954 (mainly Euro-American). The TC is unique in including in its membership of 350 (originally 180) the Japanese as equals with Americans, Canadians, and *European Community nationals. Recruited from top elite positions, members are politicians (mainly liberal and conservative); big business and bank moguls; a few trade unionists; and media, civic, and intellectual leaders. It is organized by a steering committee, with three regional chairs and secretariats.

The TC gained notoriety when U.S. President Jimmy *Carter was elected in 1976 and TC members filled virtually all senior positions in his administration. Carter acknowledged that the TC provided his "foreign policy education," with National Security Adviser Zbigniew Brzezinski (ex-TC director) his personal tutor. TC members have filled key positions in other member countries. Measured simply in terms of members in office in the United States, the TC lost influence during the first *Reagan administration (although Vice President George *Bush and Secretary of Defense Caspar Weinberger were former TC members), regaining it in Reagan's second and in the Bush administration.

Nevertheless, the TC's influence has been mainly indirect—especially on the climate of opinion in economic policy. This is because its membership reflects a dynamic set of "transnational" economic and political forces that are becoming more powerful in the domestic politics of the Trilateral countries. TC interests are committed to stronger collective management of global problems ("the management of *interdependence"), to sustaining political preconditions for maximum international mobility of goods, services, capital and knowledge, and to promoting global economic welfare according to liberal economic principles.

Forces associated with the TC are often challenged domestically by socialist, nationalist, and statist forces. For example, mercantilist forces seeking *protection from international economic competition, often in alliance with elements in the state and security complex, seek to reassert control over strategic industries and national economic welfare. Elements in the developing world oppose the prerogatives of the ruling classes of the wealthiest countries of the world: the TC is a "rich man's club" (nearly all members are men).

What is the lasting significance of the TC and other IRCs? They are not only elite networks of interest and identity but also debating chambers for questions of world order that reflect and reinforce the interface between "public" and "private" power and influence at the domestic and international levels. Thus TC agendas anticipate and in some ways parallel those of the *Group of 7 (G7) summits (meetings of the leaders of the seven richest nations), which were conceived in task force reports to the TC in 1973–1974. TC networks are bound up with the internationalization of the state system, the development of a global civil society, and the rise of a more integrated global political economy.

(See also HEGEMONY; INTERNATIONAL POLITICAL ECONOMY; INTERNATIONAL SYSTEMS; MERCANTILISM.)

Stephen Gill, *American Hegemony and the Trilateral Commission* (Cambridge, U.K., 1990).

STEPHEN GILL

TRINIDAD AND TOBAGO. The Republic of Trinidad and Tobago comprises two main islands, located off the coast of Venezuela. It is the second-largest of the *English-speaking Caribbean states with a population of 1.2 million. The two main racial groups are Africans and East Indians. Trinidad was a Spanish colony from 1498 until the British captured the island in 1797. Tobago was disputed by the Dutch, French, and English until it was ceded to Britain in 1814. The two islands were administratively joined in 1888; British Crown Colony government lasted until independence in 1962.

Until self-government was granted in 1956, Trinidad and Tobago's politics was characterized by personalism. In that year, the first mass party—the People's National Movement (PNM)—was formed by Dr. Eric Williams. The PNM remained in power until 1986, when charges of *corruption and mismanagement and general discontent fed by a declining economy led to its defeat at the polls. A new party, the National Alliance for Reconstruction (NAR), a merger of various opposition groups, was swept into power on a platform of economic and social *reform.

Trinidad and Tobago's economy is heavily dependent on oil. It is among the wealthiest of the English-speaking Caribbean countries, with a per capita GNP over US$3,500. During the oil boom of the 1970s, Trinidad and Tobago disbursed more than US$250 million to its Caribbean neighbors in loans and technical assistance. Despite problems in the 1980s, the country remains one of the most industrialized of the Caribbean area. After years of economic nationalism, it is now encouraging foreign investment, privatizing state enterprises, and actively promoting exports.

Trinidad and Tobago plays a particularly important role in the region. Social ties and geographical proximity have engendered a close relationship with the eastern Caribbean islands, and its relatively advanced economy has made the country into the major market for Caribbean Community (Caricom) products. Traditionally noninterventionist and nonaligned in its foreign policy, Trinidad and Tobago has recently adopted a more active regional and international posture.

Selwyn Ryan, ed., *Trinidad and Tobago: The Independence Experience, 1962–1987* (St. Augustine, Trinidad, 1988).
JACQUELINE ANNE BRAVEBOY-WAGNER

TROTSKY, Lev. Born Lev Davidovich Bronstein, Lev Trotsky (1879–1940) was a man of numerous talents: a theorist of revolutionary *Marxism, a gifted historian, a cultural and literary critic, and a spellbinding orator. Critical of centralized party organization, he did not join the Bolsheviks until 1917. In that year he was elected president of the Petrograd Soviet and coordinated the Bolshevik seizure of power. During the civil war he organized and commanded the Red Army. After the death of V. I. *Lenin in 1924, he led the party's left opposition in the struggle against Stalinist reaction. Deported from the *Soviet Union in 1929, Trotsky escaped Joseph *Stalin's purge trials of the 1930s. In 1940 he was assassinated in Mexico by an agent of Stalin's secret police.

Trotsky interpreted the *Russian Revolution from an internationalist perspective. In 1906 his theory of "permanent revolution" analyzed Russian history as a contradiction between backwardness and modernity (Leon Trotsky, *Permanent Revolution* and *Results and Prospects,* London, 1962). The Russian capitalist class was weak relative to the level of economic development, for the tsarist state depended on imported capital. At the same time, the workers were stronger than their numbers suggested, being concentrated in large factories that facilitated political strikes. Trotsky concluded that the workers must overthrow the autocracy and make the *revolution permanent in two respects: the workers'

government would pass immediately from political to socialist reforms; and, by repudiating foreign debts, it would also precipitate a revolutionary crisis in Europe.

Trotsky expected the revolution to create a socialist "United States of Europe" and a planned international division of labor. When the European revolution failed to come to Soviet Russia's assistance, he turned to centralized *planning and military discipline in the factories to sustain socialist prospects within the "capitalist encirclement." Authoritarian "War Communism" provoked widespread opposition both to Trotsky and to the Soviet government, leading to the *New Economic Policy (NEP) in the spring of 1921. Trotsky accepted the return to market relations but also believed state industry must be supported by planning. His political opponents argued that further attempts at planning would disrupt the market and prevent agricultural recovery.

By the mid-1920s, N. I. *Bukharin led the right wing of the *Communist Party of the Soviet Union in arguing that agriculture must have priority over industry and generate voluntary savings for new investments. Trotsky replied that continued agricultural growth depended on material incentives and manufactured consumer goods. He believed a solution to the "goods famine" lay in Soviet Russia's reintegration into the world economy: like its tsarist predecessor, the Soviet economy remained dependent on foreign investments and imports of machinery and goods. By planning relations with the capitalist countries, Trotsky hoped Soviet Russia might forestall a crisis of the NEP and orient industrialization strategy on expanding foreign trade (Richard B. Day, *Leon Trotsky and the Politics of Economic Isolation,* Cambridge, U.K., 1973). With accelerated economic growth, he believed the working class would reconstitute itself as a political force capable of resisting Stalinist bureaucracy.

The struggle between the left and right wings of the party exhausted the two antagonists to the benefit of the Stalinist "center." Bukharin claimed that "permanent revolution" denied Soviet Russia's capacity for independence; Trotsky discredited Bukharin as an exponent of capitalist agriculture and an enemy of socialist industry. Stalin defeated them both by sweeping aside the real issue—how to utilize market relations to reconcile industry with agriculture. Appropriating Bukharin's slogan of "socialism in one country" and Trotsky's emphasis on industry, Stalin minimized the need for consumer goods and decided that heavy industry must receive priority as the guarantee of economic self-sufficiency. For material incentives Stalin substituted forced labor; for voluntary savings he substituted the fiscal apparatus of forced collectivization.

Trotsky thought the Stalinist system was inherently unstable: it was a contradictory combination of nominally socialist property with primitive productive forces. The resulting bureaucratic regime could lead either to capitalist restoration or to a new political revolution. Looking ahead, Trotsky anticipated in the 1930s many themes of Mikhail *Gorbachev's *perestroika half a century later. Observing that arbitrary plans necessarily reproduced a black market, he became one of the first Marxists to contemplate market *socialism. He believed that effective planning must incorporate both a market and political democracy. To determine plan priorities required independent trade unions, flexible prices, and multiparty politics. Condemning the revolution's degeneration, Trotsky hoped it would yet redeem its socialist promise. In 1940, as in 1906, he linked the ultimate fate of the Russian Revolution with the world economy and the international struggle for socialism.

(See also LENINISM; STALINISM.)

Isaac Deutscher, *The Prophet Armed* (New York, 1965). Isaac Deutscher, *The Prophet Unarmed* (New York, 1965). Isaac Deutscher, *The Prophet Outcast* (New York, 1965).
                                                                                            RICHARD B. DAY

TRUDEAU, Pierre. Born in Montreal on 18 October 1919, Pierre Elliott Trudeau was prime minister of *Canada from 1968 until 1979, when the Liberal Party which he led was defeated, and from 1980 until 1984, when he retired from office. His tenure was longer than any, save those of prime ministers Sir John A. MacDonald and Mackenzie King. Like them, he profoundly shaped the direction of Canadian politics.

Raised and educated in *Quebec, Trudeau was part of the important postwar generation of progressives drawn from the trade union movement, intellectual circles, and left Catholicism that determined to turn traditional elites out of power and create a modern Quebec. He played a central intellectual role in the 1950s as one of the founders of *Cité Libre,* a reliable source of critical commentary on Quebec society, and as the editor of a politically influential book about the landmark strike at Asbestos in 1949. Nevertheless, in his writings on democratic theory and Quebec society Trudeau exhibited a deep fear of all *nationalisms and a mistrust of his compatriots' commitment to what he considered fundamental democratic values. Therefore, when the nationalist movement emerged with force in the new Quebec of the mid-1960s, Trudeau—with Gérard Pelletier, a journalist, and Jean Marchand, a unionist (a group termed the Three Wise Men)—moved into politics at the national level in order to present an alternative to that movement.

Combining his stance on nationalism with a profound commitment to a liberal society, Trudeau set out to translate his vision into legislative and constitutional reality. As minister of justice and then prime minister he engineered a liberalization of the criminal code (1969), which legalized abortion and contraception, decriminalized homosexual acts be-

tween consenting adults, and relaxed the grounds for divorce. Even more important, the Official Languages Act (1969) announced the federal government's commitment to bilingualism throughout the country. Finally, the 1982 Constitution Act entrenched not only language rights but also a Charter of Rights and Freedoms in fundamental law. Having worked to defeat the 1980 referendum on sovereignty-association for Quebec in the name of "renewed *federalism" and having pushed through constitutional reform, Trudeau retired to private law practice in Montreal in 1984.

Trudeau's policies were never uncontested, of course. Significant opposition existed among provincial politicians in Quebec, who found him too federalist and individualist, and among popular opinion in the western provinces, which tagged him too pro-French. Regional tensions, especially, increased mightily throughout his years in office.

In the realm of economic policy Trudeau demonstrated little consistency. He objected to economic programs developed for nationalist reasons (to reduce the influence of the United States in Canada), but his governments also sometimes tried to develop more active industrial strategy and policy for trade diversification. Such half-measures had little success, however, and he left office in 1984 after pressure from the United States, most of the provincial governments, much of *public opinion, and a major recession forced the dramatic repudiation of a series of interventionary economic programs. The government led by his successor, John Turner, presided over the first stages of the move to a Free Trade Agreement with the United States in the context of neoliberal economic thinking.

By the 1980s Pierre Trudeau had become the longest-serving leader in the West and, as such, tried to encourage a better *North-South dialogue and an easing of East-West tensions. After leaving office he undertook a personal peace initiative to countries in both the Eastern and Western blocs, arguing for reduction of nuclear weapons and an end to the *Cold War. He was awarded the Albert Einstein Peace Prize for these efforts.

(See also U.S.-CANADA FREE TRADE AGREEMENT.)

Pierre Elliott Trudeau, *Federalism and the French-Canadians* (Toronto, 1968). Pierre Elliott Trudeau, ed., *The Asbestos Strike* (Toronto, 1974).
                                                                                            JANE JENSON

TRUMAN, Harry S. The thirty-third president of the *United States, Harry S. Truman has become a national hero. Although he might not agree with the present estimate, he clearly rejected the very different evaluation that reigned during his *presidency.

Truman, like some of his predecessors, rose to high office from humble circumstances. Descended from English and southern stock, he spent his early years at the intersection of the South, the Middle West, and the Far West—in Lamar, Missouri, his birthplace on 8 May 1884, and in Grandview and Independence, Missouri. The first child of John and Martha Truman, Harry attended the Independence public schools. Unable to afford college, he worked for several years in Kansas City and then farmed from 1906 to 1917 on the Grandview place established by his maternal grandfather, Solomon Young. Service at the front in France in 1918 affected his outlook on himself and the world and was followed by an unsuccessful business venture in downtown Kansas City.

Before the business episode, Harry had married Bess Wallace in 1919 and settled into his mother-in-law's house in Independence, and in 1924, Bess gave birth to the couple's only child, Margaret. By then he had embarked upon his political career. Raised a Southern Democrat, he had joined Kansas City's Pendergast organization before the war, and with the backing of the *political machine he was elected to the county court (an administrative agency) in 1922, defeated in 1924, and elected presiding judge in 1926. Serving two four-year terms as Jackson County's top administrator, he distinguished himself as a road builder.

Still backed by the Pendergast machine, Truman moved up to the U.S. Senate in 1935. There he supported *Roosevelt's *New Deal and promoted regulation of the transportation system. Coming close to defeat in 1940 following the collapse of the organization, he gained fame in his second term as chair of a *World War II Special Committee to Investigate the National Defense Program, and his new prestige and his ability to get along with a wide range of Democrats, along with the hostility of some leaders and factions to Vice President Henry A. Wallace, led to Truman's selection for the vice presidency in 1944.

With Roosevelt's death on 12 April 1945, Truman ascended to the presidency. As president, he saw himself basically as decision-maker-in-chief, the person to whom his aides brought major matters for final resolution. Although capable of vacillation, he functioned in ways that pleased many of his subordinates, especially two of his secretaries of state, George C. Marshall and Dean *Acheson.

International relations dominated Truman's presidency. World War II still raged when he became president, and the major decisions about defeating Germany and establishing the UN had already been made, but he carried those tasks to completion and then made a major decision of his own concerning Japan: he decided that atomic bombs should be used to end the Pacific War (and also to influence the Soviet Union, now behaving in troubling ways in Eastern Europe).

The *Cold War soon commanded Truman's attention, and he was ultimately responsible for the decisions on U.S. contributions to it. Those decisions included the dismissal of Henry Wallace as secretary of commerce in 1946, aid to Greece and Turkey,

and the promise of similar assistance to other countries faced with similar pressures (the so-called *Truman Doctrine). The decisions of 1947–1948 to help economically depressed Western Europe (the *Marshall Plan) and to airlift supplies to blockaded Berlin also came to his desk, and he played a similar role in recognizing the new state of Israel in 1948 and in restraining U.S. participation in the Chinese Civil War.

By 1949, the United States was enjoying more success in Western Europe than in China, and in the next four years, with Truman functioning as decision maker, Washington enlarged and militarized its policy of *containment. In this process, Truman approved of U.S. membership in the *North Atlantic Treaty Organization and authorized the development of a hydrogen bomb. For a time, he withheld endorsement of a plan for a vast expansion of U.S. military spending (NSC 68) but then gave the go-ahead for U.S. military intervention in the war in Korea, which began in 1950. He now endorsed a military buildup and decided, in 1951, that U.S. troops should be dispatched to Europe to strengthen a developing NATO force. He gave his stamp of approval to U.S. financial assistance to France in its battle against revolution in Indochina as well as to a U.S. alliance with Japan. And he made the decisions against General Douglas MacArthur, refusing MacArthur's proposed widening of the *Korean War and removing him from command.

Although significant chiefly in international affairs, Truman's presidency also affected domestic developments. His economic decisions helped the nation avoid a postwar depression. A series of decisions to establish a Civil Rights Committee, begin Justice Department cooperation with the National Association for the Advancement of Colored People, deliver a special presidential message on civil rights, and issue two executive orders on the treatment of minorities in the civil service and the military assisted black Americans in their escalating efforts to change race relations in the United States. Although *Congress did not pass civil rights legislation, the *Supreme Court handed down decisions that favored black claims, and the military and civilian bureaucracies altered their racial practices. Congress accepted only a few items on Truman's reform agenda, labeled the Fair Deal, but his efforts prepared the way for legislative victories in the 1960s.

Truman also played roles of some importance in the Red Scare. He fanned the flames with his loyalty program, established in 1947, his Justice Department's prosecution of communist leaders in the United States, and his rhetorical attacks upon both Republicans and Henry Wallace in the 1948 election. And when the scare reached new heights in his last years in office, he tried to contain it by vetoing legislative manifestations of it and criticizing Senator Joseph R. McCarthy, the most prominent proponent of the charge that communists inside the United States seriously threatened the nation.

Proud to be president and regarding presidential leadership as essential, Truman had an impact on his office. He enlarged and strengthened it, increasing the number of presidential advisers, employing the veto power more often than all but two other presidents, sending troops to Korea and to Europe on his own authority, and putting down MacArthur's challenge to the presidency.

Yet Truman was not popular. He did enjoy an unexpected victory in the presidential election of 1948, but even then he obtained less than fifty percent of the popular vote. By late 1951, only twenty-three percent of the people approved of his performance as president, and the next year he failed to maintain Democratic control of the national government. When he left office, only thirty-one percent of the people approved of his handling of the job.

In the eyes of many in the United States, Truman seemed too small, but, as his farewell address in January 1953 suggests, he regarded himself as unusually successful. Emphasizing his decisions in foreign affairs, he proposed that he had prevented a repetition of the mistakes made from 1919 to 1941 that he held responsible for World War II. Henry Wallace had portrayed him as a major contributor to the coming of the Cold War; revisionist historians later repeated the charge, and they were right. But Truman regarded the Cold War as the best of the available alternatives. The leading competitor was World War III, and a combination of Wallace-like weakness and MacArthur-like rashness, rather than the decisions he made, would, he maintained, have produced that war.

Truman did not live long enough to see himself become a national hero. Returning to Independence in 1953, he was an active ex-president for a decade until his health, which, except for stress, had been robust, began to decline. He died in a Kansas City hospital on 26 December 1972, and his rise to hero's rank began soon thereafter.

(See also AFRICAN AMERICANS; AMERICAN FOREIGN POLICY; HIROSHIMA; McCARTHYISM; UNITED NATIONS.)

Richard S. Kirkendall, ed., *The Truman Period as a Research Field* (Columbia, Mo., 1967, 1974). Richard S. Kirkendall, ed., *The Harry S. Truman Encyclopedia* (Boston, 1989). Michael J. Lacey, ed., *The Truman Presidency* (Cambridge, U.K., 1989).

RICHARD S. KIRKENDALL

TRUMAN DOCTRINE. The Truman Doctrine, as set forth by President Harry S. *Truman in 1947, committed the U.S. government to a global policy aimed at stopping the spread of *communism. The seeds of the doctrine were planted on 21 February 1947, when Britain informed U.S. officials that it no longer could aid conservative forces in Greece who were fighting the National Liberation Front (which contained Communist leaders), nor Turkey, which the Soviets were pressuring for treaty concessions.

Realizing that the British Empire was collapsing, Truman and Under Secretary of State Dean *Acheson (who wrote the doctrine message) also realized the president himself had been weakened by economic problems and a Republican landslide victory in the 1946 congressional elections. They further believed that communist political victories could occur in war-devastated Western Europe unless vast U.S. aid was quickly extended. Truman therefore decided to ask Congress for $400 million for Greece and Turkey, but also to frame an open-ended policy that stressed how communism had to be stopped globally by "the free peoples of the world." The Republicans, pledged to cut taxes and expenditures, would then have to choose publicly whether to appropriate large amounts in Congress to fight communism wherever Truman saw the threat existing.

Internal opposition appeared. Secretary of State George Marshall and his top advisers on Soviet affairs criticized the strong anticommunist rhetoric and also noted that Yugoslav Communists, not Soviet, supplied the Greek Front. Truman overruled Marshall. Acheson convinced congressional leaders privately by arguing that if communists won in Greece they would extend their power throughout the Middle East and Europe. Acheson thus anticipated the later *domino theory. Congressional critics who feared that a new global commitment could lead to huge expenditures, if not war, and to a vast expansion of presidential powers, were a small minority.

Truman announced his doctrine before a congressional joint session on 12 March 1947. Congress accepted his argument by appropriating the $400 million and did so again in 1948 when it passed the $12 billion *Marshall Plan to rebuild Western Europe. Greece finally quieted in 1949 only when the Yugoslavs, for internal reasons, quit aiding the Front; nevertheless, the doctrine was seen as triumphant in its first test. Later presidents tried to revive it to conjure up domestic support for their beleaguered policies. Lyndon *Johnson, 1964 to 1967, in *Vietnam; Jimmy *Carter, 1980, in the Persian Gulf; and Ronald *Reagan, 1983, in Central America were among those presidents. Truman had used a regional crisis to increase presidential power, create a powerful anticommunist consensus in U.S. politics, and make global commitments that transformed *American foreign policy.

(See also CONTAINMENT.)

Lawrence C. Wittner, *American Intervention in Greece 1943–1949* (New York, 1982).

WALTER LaFEBER

TUNISIA. A small North African nation, Tunisia borders strategic narrows between the western and eastern Mediterranean. The capital city of Tunis, occupying the site of ancient Carthage, has had a long history as a major trading port.

Beginning in 1574, the Ottoman Empire controlled the area, and its military governor, known as the bey, eventually became a hereditary ruler. In 1881, as Ottoman power waned and European colonialism expanded, France invaded and imposed a protectorate. The French established internationally recognized boundaries and created a modern state. Though the bey continued to rule, France exercised real power through a parallel administration. After World War II, an anticolonial movement known as the Neo-Destour (New Constitution) gathered force. Led by lawyer Habib Bourguiba and supported by a growing trade union movement, it effectively mobilized the population behind the cause of independence.

France finally withdrew in 1956, leaving Tunisia under the rule of the bey, who appointed Neo-Destour members to his cabinet and named Bourguiba as first prime minister. Bourguiba and his colleagues did not want to share power, however. They soon deposed the bey and proclaimed a republic. Their new constitution created a presidency endowed with very strong powers, while a new legislature was little more than a rubber stamp. The leaders affirmed a virtual monopoly of power for their Neo-Destour Party, the Parti Libéral Constitutionnel. Backed by the powerful Union Général des Travailleurs Tunisiens (UGTT), they barred other parties from elections and claimed to represent the unity of the new nation.

Bourguiba, who was very influenced by French ideas, became known for his modernizing *reforms—some of the most far-reaching in any Arab or Islamic country. He nationalized religious landholdings, dismantled religious schools and courts, and sought to abolish the Islamic fast of Ramadan. He also improved the status of women with legal and social reforms, including a campaign to end the practice of veiling.

Tunisia, unlike its neighbors Libya and Algeria, possessed no oil fields. With Western aid, the Bourguiba regime developed the country's large phosphate deposits, and it promoted tourism and light industry. But agriculture lagged. Irregular rainfall and subsistence landholdings held back agricultural development plans, and crops failed to feed a growing population. Tunisia had one great economic advantage over most other *Third World countries: it had a very small army and so was not burdened with high military costs; a very high proportion of state revenues could therefore be spent on social services, including education. For at least twenty-five years after independence, military influence in politics remained slight.

During the first years after independence, as French settlers and French capital pulled out of the country, the economy foundered, creating demands for more state intervention. In 1963 the ruling party changed its name to the Parti Socialiste Destourien (PSD), and the regime undertook many economic reforms, bringing more than half the economy under state control by the end of the decade. The most ambitious reform program, led by former labor chief Ahmad Ben Salah, sought to bring all private farms into state-sponsored agricultural cooperatives. In 1970, amid fierce criticism from the farmers, the president changed his mind, abruptly dismissing Ben Salah and jailing him for treason. A new government team dismantled many of the reforms and returned the cooperative land to private ownership.

The socialist turn in politics further concentrated power in the hands of the state and of its top leadership, opening the way for new abuses. Many politicians, along with their families and friends, became wealthy through patronage and corruption. Bourguiba—increasingly powerful, isolated, and intolerant of criticism—banned all opposition political activities in 1973; though his health was failing (he had suffered a stroke in 1967), he refused to prepare the way for a successor.

The turn away from socialism did not lead to democratization. In 1973, when unions went on strike to protest falling real wages, the government outlawed strikes and imposed fines and prison sentences on strikers. The president (often referred to in the press as the "Great Combatant") purged the ranks of the party and had himself elected "president for life" in 1974. Four years later, when the UGTT called a general strike to protest government repression, Bourguiba ordered out the army; military and security forces savagely attacked the strikers, killing dozens and arresting hundreds more, including UGTT chief Habib Achour and all major leaders of the union.

The Tunisian economy grew rapidly in the 1970s. Oil was discovered in sufficient quantity to meet domestic needs and begin exports, producing nearly half of all export earnings by the end of the decade. Tunisia also attracted investments from European *multinational corporations. But continuing agricultural problems led to heavy migration from the countryside; for the first time, urban dwellers comprised more than half of the total population. In spite of new jobs, many created by the burgeoning tourist industry, urban unemployment remained high and thousands of workers emigrated to Europe in search of work.

In international relations, Tunisia continued its close relations with the West. It also assumed a more prominent role in the Arab world during the 1980s as Tunis became headquarters of the *Arab League from 1979 to 1991 and headquarters of the *Palestine Liberation Organization in 1982. In 1988, Tunisia joined in forming a regional trade and development body, the Union du Maghreb Arabe (UMA). If effective, the union could give wider markets to Tunisian enterprises, now constrained in an economy of only about 8 million people (1990).

In 1981, the government experimented with limited democratization, allowing a few officially sanctioned parties to run for office for the first time since independence. But social peace proved elusive. Sagging foreign investments, a slump in oil prices, and onerous foreign debts dragged down the economy. Unemployment reached very high levels. Finally, the *International Monetary Fund (IMF) imposed austerity measures, forcing the government to raise the price of bread and semolina in late 1983. Protest riots broke out almost immediately in villages and towns in the south, then swept into the major cities. The government restored order only after massive intervention by the army. Though the protests were largely spontaneous, the Mouvement de la Tendance Islamique (MTI) came to the fore as the greatest challenge to the regime.

The shaken regime blamed the riots on foreign plotters and accused the MTI of being a puppet of Iran; it disbanded the UGTT, closed down critical newspapers, and jailed many thousands of dissidents, especially Islamists. General Zin al-Abidin Ben 'Ali, minister of the interior and former director of military security, organized the crackdown. A major trial of Islamist leaders, some of whom received the death sentence, threatened to ignite further protests. The ailing Bourguiba insisted he would "eradicate the fundamentalist poison."

In October of 1987, the president named Ben 'Ali as prime minister. Just one month later, the premier deposed the 85-year-old Bourguiba in a bloodless *coup; by claiming the president was no longer physically or mentally competent to rule, Ben 'Ali became the constitutional successor. Though Bourguiba departed, the Bourguibist political system remained largely intact. One difference stood out: Ben 'Ali brought many army and security officers into top political positions, including General Habib 'Amar, commander of the National Guard, who was named minister of the interior.

Ben 'Ali promised reforms and set in motion a modest liberalization, declaring a general amnesty for political prisoners and inviting political exiles home. He pushed through constitutional reforms limiting the presidency to two terms, with no candidate allowed over age 70. He pardoned Sheikh Rashid al-Ghannushi, the imprisoned MTI leader, and began talks to placate the Islamists. As a gesture to the religious forces, the new government started to build mosques, broadcast the call to prayer over state radio, and refounded the old Islamic university. Ben 'Ali also undertook a new round of *privatization of state-controlled enterprises; he eliminated price controls and devalued the currency, in line with demands of the IMF and other international creditors.

Though single-party states were unraveling elsewhere, the Tunisian Destour proved remarkably durable. In 1989 elections, Ben 'Ali ran unopposed for the presidency while Destourian candidates won all seats in the Parliament. But the MTI and its successor party al-Nahda were banned from the political contest, and Islamist leaders soon again faced jail

and exile. Liberalization gave way to increasing repression as even the long-established human rights league dissolved under government pressure. Political Islam continued to challenge the regime, while economic difficulties aggravated social discontent.

(See also COLONIAL EMPIRES; DECOLONIZATION; ISLAM; MODERNIZATION; ONE-PARTY SYSTEM.)

Harold D. Nelson, *Tunisia: A Country Study* (Washington, D.C., 1979). Lisa Anderson, *The State and Social Transformation in Tunisia and Libya* (Princeton, N.J., 1987).
MONCEF M. KHADDAR
JAMES A. PAUL

TURKEY. One of the successor states that emerged from the ruins of the Ottoman Empire after World War I, the new state of Turkey was created after a protracted nationalist struggle (1919–1922) against an invading Greek army supported by the Western powers, as well as a civil war that pitted the nationalists against the forces of the Sultan. Turkey is strategically located at the crossroads between Europe and Asia. Its control over the vital straits which join the Black Sea to the Aegean and the Mediterranean give the country a permanent and vital strategic significance. Its population (estimated at around 55 million in 1990) and size (780,575 sq. km.; 301,380 sq. mi.) make Turkey one of the largest powers in the region.

After the Treaty of Lausanne (July 1923) had confirmed their victory, Turkish nationalists began to resolve the question of the new regime. In the struggle that followed, the radicals, led by Kemal *Atatürk, defeated the conservatives and established a republic on 29 October 1923. The Republican People's Party (RPP), founded by Atatürk and his followers in 1923, became the major instrument in the battle against conservatism. The 1924 Constitution vested virtually all power in a unicameral legislature; owing to an indirect system of elections, this body was dominated by the country's *elites. The Assembly never passed laws (regarding, for example, *land reform) which might have changed the social structure. But it gave its backing to major institutional changes. In 1924 it abolished the caliphate, setting off a program of secular *reforms which made Turkey the first Muslim country to disestablish *Islam.

By their secularizing reforms in the twenties the Kemalists sought to create a rational society associated with Western capitalism. When private business interests failed to take the initiative, the Kemalists decided that the state would carry out reform from the top. This was especially true after the world economic crisis of 1930 when—under the new ideology of *Kemalism—the state began to intervene actively in the economy in order to create an industrial infrastructure.

The policy of statism continued until the end of World War II, when a powerful group of merchants, industrialists, and intellectuals emerged from within the RPP to challenge the hegemony of the single-party state. President Ismet Inönü and most of the Turkish elite agreed that the time had arrived for competitive multiparty politics. In 1946 the dissidents formed the Democrat Party, which went on to defeat the ruling RPP in the general election of 1950.

The Democrats ruled from 1950 to 1960. Instead of democratizing the system, however, they continued to use institutions inherited from the single-party period. However, aided by the Korean War–era boom, they transformed the economy, opening it to private enterprise. *Marshall Plan funds financed highway construction and provided tractors, undermining traditional agriculture and setting off a major migration of peasants to the towns and cities. Commerce also flourished as goods were imported at very favorable rates of exchange, allowing merchants to make fortunes and accumulate capital for investment.

These policies touched off inflation that especially harmed salaried civil servants and soldiers; they lost ground not only financially but also in terms of status. The young officers became dissatisfied with the performance of their politicians. Ultimately, however, it was the Democrats' impatience with the opposition and their repressive and autocratic policies that led to military intervention on 27 May 1960.

The soldiers had intervened in order to break the deadlock between the parties, but their allies in the universities persuaded them to oversee the restructuring of the entire political system. Before elections were held in October 1961, Turkey had a new, liberal Constitution which guaranteed virtually all civil rights, an election law which permitted direct elections and *proportional representation (thereby breaking the grip of the old elites), and a political parties law which allowed the founding of a socialist party. Under these conditions the country began an ideological debate beyond the narrow confines of Kemalism. In 1961, trade unionists formed the Workers' Party of Turkey (WPT) and within two years the Assembly passed laws which gave unions the right to engage in collective bargaining and to strike.

The junta had shut down the Democrat Party and arrested and tried its leaders, three of whom were executed for violating the Constitution. Neo-Democrat parties, the most important of which was the Justice Party (JP), emerged to take its place. The 1960s began with coalition governments, but the JP, under Süleyman Demirel's leadership, won the elections of 1965 and 1967, and Turkey was back to a two-party system.

Perhaps the most important political development of this period was the integration of the armed forces into the political system as the guardian of the status quo. The armed forces set up a mutual fund which soon became a huge business-industrial conglomer-ate, the officer corps got new privileges, and a new military intelligence network came into being—all of which made a coup from below virtually impossible. Any future military intervention would be to defend stability, not to promote change.

Under the watchful eye of the newly created State Planning Organization, the economy averaged a growth rate of almost seven percent between 1963 and 1973. Turkey began to industrialize, which had important political and social repercussions. On the one hand, it led to the rise of a militant working class, represented by the WPT, and a radical union movement known by the acronym DISK. On the other hand, small businesses and industries went bankrupt as a few large holding companies established their sway over the economy. As a result, the Right was fragmented; groups broke away from JP to form parties to represent their own narrow interests. The late 1960s witnessed the rise of several small parties including the neofascist Nationalist Action Party (NAP) and the Islamist National Order Party, later renamed the National Salvation Party (NSP). The center-right JP government was trapped between the criticism of an increasingly anti-U.S. Left (after the *Cyprus crisis of 1964) and a Right which demanded *protection for small enterprise. The ensuing political instability—marked by strikes, the massive workers' demonstration of 15–16 June 1970, and acts of urban *terrorism by the student Left—led to another military intervention on 12 March 1971.

Turkey lived under martial law until the elections of October 1973. During that period, the generals attempted to restore political stability by ruthlessly crushing the Left and bolstering the Center-Right with constitutional amendments. The Workers' Party was shut down; its supporters coalesced around the RPP, now social democratic and led by the charismatic Bülent Ecevit. In the elections of 1973, the RPP emerged as the strongest party but with insufficient seats to form a government on its own. It therefore formed a coalition with the Islamist NSP.

Intervention in Cyprus (July 1974) enhanced Ecevit's popularity, and he calculated that he would win a large majority in an early election. He resigned, but found that the opposition would not permit early polling. His coalition was replaced by a coalition of the Right in which the neofascists were partners. As the two major parties could never win sufficient seats to form governments on their own, they were forced to depend on the small parties of the Right. Chronic political and economic instability throughout the 1970s, including increasing terrorism, prepared the way for a third military intervention on 12 September 1980.

The 1970s also witnessed the triumph of social democracy, which established itself in the cities and among the unions. The Right came to see this as the main threat to the established order. The generals who seized power in 1980 decided to restructure the politics, economy, and society of Turkey so as to put an end to any such threat in the future. They abolished the 1961 Constitution and replaced it by a quasi-presidential charter which eliminated virtually all previous rights guarantees. All parties were dissolved and ex-politicians disqualified from politics for from five to ten years. The universities lost their autonomy and professional associations were not permitted to engage in political activity—the medical association could not even lobby against the death penalty. The general's aim was to depoliticize the entire society by restricting politics to a tiny minority. Meanwhile, supported by the *International Monetary Fund and the *World Bank, Deputy Prime Minister Turgut Özal was charged with managing the economy. He implemented a free-market policy designed to bring down inflation by curbing demand at home and encouraging exports.

When political activity was partially restored in 1983, the generals found that depoliticization had not worked. Their party failed to win a managed election in November. The voters elected Özal's Motherland Party because it promised the swiftest return to *democracy. That trend continued throughout the 1980s, but the Constitution and new laws prevented a more rapid transition to democratic politics. By 1989 the Social Democratic Populist Party (SHP, formerly the RPP) had again become the first party in the country, although not in the Assembly. Meanwhile, Özal saw that his party was likely to lose the next general election. He therefore had himself elected president, but this only increased political disaffection in the country. When an early general election was held in October 1991, Demirel's True Path Party won the most votes but did not win enough seats to rule on its own. Demirel formed a coalition government with SHP, now the third party, and the Motherland Party, led by Mesut Yilmaz, went into opposition. Turkey had not yet found political stability, but it had learned at great cost that military regimes could not provide it.

(See also DEMOCRATIC TRANSITIONS; MILITARY RULE; ONE-PARTY SYSTEM; SECULARIZATION.)

Kemal Karpat, *Turkey's Politics: Transition to a Multi-Party System* (Princeton, N.J., 1959). Niyazi Berkes, *The Development of Secularism in Turkey* (Montreal, 1964). Bernard Lewis, *The Emergence of Modern Turkey,* 2d ed. (Oxford, 1968). Feroz Ahmad, *The Turkish Experiment in Democracy, 1950–1975* (London, 1977). I. C. Schick and E. A. Tonak, eds., *Turkey in Transition* (New York, 1987). Feroz Ahmad, *The Making of Modern Turkey* (London, 1992).

FEROZ AHMAD

TURKMENISTAN. See COMMONWEALTH OF INDEPENDENT STATES.

TUVALU (ELLICE ISLANDS). See PACIFIC ISLANDS.

U

UGANDA. The configuration of historical forces that have molded Ugandan politics may be attributed to the geography of the country and to governmental policies pursued since the turn of the twentieth century. These have given Uganda its particular brand of politics, which in turn have been shaped by the pattern of uneven socioeconomic development across the country; the manipulation of ethnic consciousness; religious loyalties and ideologies; and reliance on the military as the mainstay of power. The course of political events in Uganda has borne a direct relationship to the existence or absence of a viable national *ideology or ethos and the degree of internal *legitimacy of the authorities. Yet although socioeconomic conditions have in large measure influenced the patterns of politics in the country, their tempo has been affected by the factor of leadership or personality, and this in turn has been conditioned by the international climate.

The nation-state of Uganda came into existence as a result of territorial surgery performed by European colonial powers in Eastern and Central Africa during the heyday of the new European *imperialism between 1890 and 1914. The delimitation of Ugandan territory by European colonial powers brought together an African population composed of about fifteen different ethnic groups with various socioeconomic and political characteristics. These ethnic groups can be categorized into four main language clusters: Bantu, Nilo-Sudanic, Lwo, and Atesot. In Uganda's contemporary history, both ethnic and linguistic factors have played a significant role in politics.

The relevance of *ethnicity and language to Ugandan politics is derived from economic and political policies pursued by successive administrations in the country since the beginning of the twentieth century. Although during the period of its rule over Uganda the British government was committed to developing the country as a single political unit, in practice its economic and political policies fostered uneven *development between regions, leading to structural imbalances which have exercised an enduring impact on Ugandan politics. In addition, the sociopolitical policy of ethnic compartmentalization pursued in the colonial period, combined with economic policies, militated against territory-wide social cohesion. Thus, to this day, different social groups do not

perceive that they have common national interests, and political mobilization has therefore tended to be along ethnic and regional lines.

Preferential treatment of Buganda and Busoga by the British colonial administration allowed for the first formal political organizations on the national scene to emerge in that region of the country. After World War II Africans began political agitation, first to demand their rights in the political process and then to challenge the pyramidal racial power structure in the country, creating a stir for a quasi-national approach to politics. In Buganda, the Bataka Party was formed in 1946 and the Uganda African Farmers' Union was inaugurated the following year; for the remainder of the 1940s these two organizations became the organs through which the African population articulated its grievances. After an insurrection by Africans in 1949, the British colonial government granted Africans in Buganda the right to elect their representatives to the Colonial National Legislative Council, on which hitherto only Europeans and Asians had sat. The action proved to be a watershed in Ugandan history and heralded populist politics against the colonial authorities in Buganda; in the decade of the 1950s, it spread to other parts of the country.

Postwar politics in Buganda—and later the rest of Uganda—grew out of an increasing awareness of the principles and practices of *democracy and African consciousness of *race and *class. The first mass political party, the Uganda National Congress (UNC), was founded in March 1952 during the liberal era of Governor Cohen and was a lineal descendant of the Bataka Party and the Uganda African Farmers Union. Although the UNC was initially a Buganda-based political party, its leadership identified itself with the broad aspirations of Africans across the country and it made concerted efforts to draw in representatives from the various parts of Uganda. As it expanded, its leadership became dominated by Protestants. This caused apprehension among Roman Catholics, and in 1956 they recast nationwide the Democratic Party (DP), which had been launched in Buganda in 1954 by Catholic Action to represent their interests. The formation of the DP to represent the interests of Roman Catholics reawakened the religious dimension in Uganda politics. The binding force of Catholicism was to enable the DP to win followers throughout the country.

Although the UNC was arguably the most broad-based nationalist party in the country, it was, after the formation of the DP, torn by internal division and personal bickering; this introduced the element of personality in Uganda politics. As a result of the internal disharmony within the UNC, a number of splinter parties emerged, one of which was the Uganda Peoples Union (UPU). In March 1960, the UPU and A. Milton Obote's faction of the UNC amalgamated to form the Uganda Peoples Congress (UPC), which adopted a Pan-Africanist posture at the same time that it exhibited antipathy toward Buganda; in fact two groups were bound together by common fear of domination of the rest of the country in Buganda in a postcolonial Uganda. The emergence of the UPC as an expression of anti-Kiganda nationalism has since then colored the perception of the UPC in Buganda and has injected the theme of center versus periphery into Ugandan politics, which has endured to the present time.

In October 1958, the first general elections on the basis of qualified franchise were held to elect African representatives to the Legislative Council. However, in the event, only eighteen constituencies in Uganda participated; the Buganda Lukiiko (traditional parliament), fearing the erosion of its privileged status and committed to Kiganda nationalism, together with the districts of Ankole and Bugisu, dissociated themselves from the elections. This gesture demonstrated the lack of national consciousness while it highlighted ethnic and regional awareness, which has continued to plague Ugandan politics; it also reflected social disequilibrium in the country.

The lack of a perceived common national interest again surfaced in March 1961 when a second general election, conducted by the British colonial authorities on common rolls and with a broadened qualified franchise based on income, was held. Although the general elections brought a substantial majority of elected African representatives to the Legislative Council, and although throughout Uganda about eighty percent of the electorate in seventy-six rural and urban constituencies exercised their right of franchise, only three percent turned out in Buganda to vote in the twenty-one rural constituencies there. The results of the election, favoring the Democratic Party (DP) over the UPC by forty-three seats to thirty-five, pointed to the emergence of an ideological alliance in the country along ethnoregional and religious lines. After the win by the DP, the Colonial government asked the leader of the DP, Benedicto Kiwanuka, to form an administration and become the first African chief minister in the Legislative Council during the transitional period of self-government, while the leader of the UPC, A. Milton Obote, was recognized as leader of the opposition. The results also demonstrated that there were now only two dominant political parties in the country,

and in the future they would be the locus of Ugandan politics. But because only a minuscule proportion of the population in Buganda participated in the elections, there was the distinct possibility that the Buganda Lukiiko could constitute a third force in Ugandan politics. That possibility became a reality when late in 1961 a political party representing the interests of the Buganda Lukiiko and opposed to the Catholic-based DP, the Kabaka Yekka (KY—"the King Alone"), was formed for the principal purpose of allying itself with the non-Kiganda but predominantly Protestant party, the UPC.

The dominance of the two political parties—DP and UPC—was underlined the following year when in April 1962 another general election was held to presage the granting of juridical independence to Uganda. In this election, the UPC gained 52.4 percent of the total poll, while the DP won 45.5 percent; this gave the UPC forty-three seats and the DP twenty-four, in a parliamentary National Assembly of ninety-one seats. The remaining twenty-four seats were claimed, in accordance with a provision in the constitution, by the Buganda Lukiiko for its political party, the KY, which then entered into an alliance with the UPC. Thus when Britain granted political independence to Uganda on 9 October 1962, it was the UPC-KY alliance which formed the first postcolonial government of the country. By the terms of the UPC-KY coalition, the leader of the UPC, Obote, became prime minister and thus executive head of state, but his position was offset by the appointment of the *kabaka* as president—the titular head of state. The UPC and the KY were ill-matched partners, since on virtually every policy issue the two parties were opposed; but they were held together by their common resentment of the Catholic-dominated DP. The UPC-KY alliance poignantly demonstrated how religion can be manipulated to shift the balance of power in Ugandan politics.

But precisely because the UPC-KY alliance was constructed less around any positive aims than on mere resentment of the DP as a Catholic-inspired party, it was bound to prove both deceptive and futile. Within a year of the formation of the coalition, strains in the UPC-KY relationship quickly developed when the UPC began to establish political branches in Buganda. A year later, in 1964, the "unholy" alliance broke down irretrievably when the UPC, in accordance with a constitutional provision, resolved to settle a territorial issue—that of the "lost counties of Bunyoro"—while the *kabaka* attempted to secure Buganda's retention of two of the countries at issue by settling Buganda's ex-servicemen there. The termination of the UPC-KY alliance after 1964 led to a bloody military confrontation between the *kabaka*'s forces and those of Obote in 1966 and the resultant demise of the Kiganda monarchy.

The end of the UPC-KY tactical political alliance both betrayed the inadequacy of religion as a cohesive factor in Ugandan politics and brought into greater prominence the divisions between center and periphery in the country. Equally significant, the absence of UPC strongholds in Buganda, where Kampala, the seat of government, is situated, compelled it to rely on the military as a mainstay of power. The use of the military by Obote to settle political differences between the UPC and the KY emboldened the army to intervene directly in politics. This was, among other things, a precondition of the *coup d'état of 25 January 1971, led by General Idi Amin Dada. And since then, the equation of power has rested on the determination of the military, which in July 1985 overthrew the second government of the UPC, and was in turn ousted on 25 January 1986 by another military organization, the National Resistance Army (NRA), led by Yoweri Kaguta Museveni.

The usurpation of power by Yoweri Museveni's NRA has ushered in a new era of *militarism in Ugandan politics. At the same time, President Museveni has shown himself to be a man of political cunning, shrewdness, and clear military ability. Significantly, although in 1986 Museveni won the contest for power with the military junta of Tito Okello Lutwa, he still has neither won peace nor created the climate for political *pluralism in the country.

Although any leader must be held responsible both for his or her government's policies and for their impact, many of the actions of Ugandan leaders and politicians have been molded by the historical circumstances of the country. In brief, Ugandan history has been largely characterized by uneven socioeconomic development in different areas of the country, competition and conflicts along ethnic and regional lines, loyalties and divisions derived from religion, and political reliance on the military. In all likelihood this situation will continue.

(See also COLONIAL EMPIRES; MILITARY RULE; PAN-AFRICANISM.)

Kenneth Ingham, *The Making of Modern Uganda* (London, 1958). F. B. Wellbourn, *Religion and Politics in Uganda* (Nairobi, 1965). G. S. K. Ibingira, *The Forging of an African Nation: The Political and Constitutional Evolution of Uganda from Colonial Rule to Independence, 1894–1962* (New York, 1973). Nelson Kasfir, *The Shrinking Political Arena: Participation and Ethnicity in African Politics, with a Case Study of Uganda* (London, 1976). Mahmood Mamdani, *Politics and Class Formation in Uganda* (New York, 1976). Samwiri Karugire, *A Political History of Uganda* (Nairobi, 1980). T. V. Sathyamurthy, *The Political Development of Uganda, 1900–1986* (London, 1986). Amii Omara-Otunnu, *Politics and the Military in Uganda, 1895–1985* (London, 1987). K. Rupesinghe, *Conflict Resolution in Uganda* (Oslo, 1989).

AMII OMARA-OTUNNU

UKRAINE. See COMMONWEALTH OF INDEPENDENT STATES.

UNDERCLASS. The term *underclass* has been used to refer to the persistently poor, whose economic resources and behavioral patterns differentiate them from their fellow citizens. Although the term has primarily been used in the United States to refer to the poor in black and Hispanic urban ghettos, it has also been applied in European nations, where economic restructuring and immigration combined to produce concentrations of poverty during the 1980s.

The Swedish social scientist Gunnar Myrdal first drew attention to the term in 1962, when he warned that economic progress threatened to leave behind a sector of the population who were either unemployed or unemployable. Such people, he feared, would become increasingly marginal to the mainstream of modern society. By the late 1970s, high rates of unemployment, teen pregnancy, and increases in urban crime helped to popularize arguments about the emergence of an underclass within U.S. ghettos. The violence that accompanied the spread of drugs in the 1980s gave further credence to the notion of an American underclass.

The popular use of the term *underclass* sparked efforts to define this group more precisely. Most definitions identify four characteristics of underclass neighborhoods: high rates of school dropouts, female-headed households, welfare dependency, and irregular attachment to the labor market. Depending on how these indicators are defined, estimates of the size of the underclass in the United States have varied widely.

There is also little agreement about the causes of the existence of an underclass in the United States. Debate has centered around two contending explanations. The first argues that cultural and behavioral factors account for the existence of the underclass. In this view, the deviant behavior of the poor—including an unwillingness to work, stay in school, and postpone childbearing until marriage—creates an underclass. The second explanation highlights the role of social and economic structural forces in creating an underclass. The most prominent exponent of this perspective, William Julius Wilson, has argued that the shift from a manufacturing to a service-based economy created severe economic dislocations in the 1970s that disproportionately affected poor and minority urban communities. Combined with the gains of the *Civil Rights Movement, which allowed middle-class *African Americans to move out of inner-city ghettos, these economic forces stripped minority inner-city areas of the resources needed to sustain communities.

Despite disagreement about the causes of the existence of the underclass, the term has most often been used in public debate to signal behavioral, not economic, factors. This development has led some analysts to abandon the term altogether.

During the 1980s, rising poverty and concentrations of ethnic minorities in European cities raised concern about the growth of an underclass in some European nations. Arguments have been made most strongly in Britain, where economic decline and sharp cuts in social programs have created a new group of very poor citizens. In other nations, concentrations of poor ethnic minorities have been compared to the U.S. underclass. However, the distinctive history of race and the comparatively small *welfare state in the United States suggests that the sharp social isolation and persistent poverty characteristic of the U.S. underclass is less likely to develop in European nations.

(See also INTERNATIONAL MIGRATION.)

Christopher Jencks and Paul E. Peterson, eds., *The Urban Underclass* (Washington, D.C., 1991).

MARGARET WEIR

UNDERDEVELOPMENT. See DEVELOPMENT AND UNDERDEVELOPMENT.

UNION OF SOVIET SOCIALIST REPUBLICS. See SOVIET UNION.

UNIONS, LABOR. See LABOR MOVEMENT.

UNITED ARAB EMIRATES. See GULF STATES.

UNITED KINGDOM. See BRITAIN.

UNITED NATIONS. The United Nations (UN), born on 24 October 1945, has been the most important *international organization of the period since *World War II, and the center of a wide-ranging network of international bodies. The UN emerged from the anti-Axis coalition of World War II. On 1 January 1942 in the Washington Declaration twenty-six Allied countries, which came to be called the "United Nations," had pledged to employ their full resources against Germany, Italy, and Japan. Thus World War II not only showed the need for an effective international organization to replace the unsuccessful *League of Nations (1919–1946) but also highlighted the possibilities of *international cooperation as a basis for resisting threats to the *peace. In its early years, the new body was often known as the United Nations Organization (UNO), in order to distinguish it from the wartime alliance out of which it had grown.

Charter and Structure. The formal basis for the UN's activities was, and remains, the UN Charter. The product of careful consideration and intensive diplomacy on the part of the leading Allied powers in World War II (especially the United States, the United Kingdom, and the Soviet Union), the charter was finally adopted by the representatives of fifty states meeting at San Francisco on 26 June 1945, formally entering into force on 24 October of the same year. The charter reflected the view that an *international system, if it is to be stable, has to take account of the demands not just of international *security narrowly conceived but also of justice and *human rights. The 111 articles of the UN Charter established not only the purposes and principles of the organization but also its structures, tasks, finances, and procedures. Membership was confined to states (as distinct from nongovernmental or international entities). Thus, although the charter begins with the ringing words "We the peoples of the United Nations," the UN has always had the character of being an association of governments of sovereign states. In accord with article 7 of the charter, there are six "principal organs" of the UN: the General Assembly, the Security Council, the Economic and Social Council, the Trusteeship Council, the *International Court of Justice, and the Secretariat.

The General Assembly, established under chapter IV of the charter, is the plenary body, controlling much of the UN's work. Meeting in regular session for the last quarter of every year, it approves the budget, adopts priorities, calls international conferences, oversees the work of numerous subsidiary bodies, and adopts resolutions on a wide range of issues.

The Security Council, established under chapter V of the charter, has "primary responsibility for the maintenance of international peace and security." It was originally specified as having eleven members: the "big five" permanent members (China, France, the United Kingdom, the United States, and the Soviet Union) plus six others to be elected for two-year terms by the General Assembly. In 1965, following the growth in UN membership, the council was enlarged to fifteen members, ten of whom are elected, its decisions requiring an affirmative vote of nine members. Each of the "big five" has a power of veto. It meets frequently throughout the year, and is empowered to take decisions binding on all UN members. Under the charter's crucial chapter VII (articles 39–51) it has extensive powers to take "action with respect to threats to the peace, breaches of the peace, and acts of aggression."

The Economic and Social Council (ECOSOC), established under chapter X of the charter, supervises the work of numerous commissions, committees, and expert bodies in the economic and social fields, including the Commission on Human Rights, and seeks to coordinate the activities of UN specialized agencies in these areas. Originally consisting of eighteen members elected for three-year terms by the General Assembly, it was progressively enlarged, in 1965 and 1973, to its present size of fifty-four.

The Trusteeship Council, set up under chapter XIII of the charter, superintended the transition to self-government of trust territories. Because most cases of *decolonization did not involve trust territories, the UN was involved, if at all, through different bodies, such as the Special Committee on Decolonization, set up by the General Assembly in 1961.

The International Court of Justice (ICJ) in The Hague was constituted by the Statute of the ICJ, adopted at San Francisco on 26 June 1945 at the same time as the UN Charter. All UN member states are also parties to the statute. The ICJ, recognized by chapter XIV of the charter as "the principal judicial organ of the United Nations," actually came into existence in 1946, as successor to the Permanent Court of International Justice (1922–1946). It consists of fifteen judges, elected by the General Assembly and the Security Council for nine-year terms. It considers cases brought to it by states, and it also gives advisory opinions on legal questions put to it by the UN General Assembly, the Security Council, and other UN bodies. By the end of 1991 it had dealt with fifty-three contentious cases between states, and also delivered twenty-one advisory opinions.

The Secretariat, established by chapter XV of the charter, was intended to consist of "international officials responsible only to the Organization." It has grown to comprise some 16,000 people at UN headquarters in New York and at other offices, the largest of which is Geneva. It is headed by the secretary-general. The holders of this post have been Trygve Lie (Norway, 1946–1953), Dag Hammarskjöld (Sweden, 1953–1961), U Thant (Burma, 1961–1971), Kurt Waldheim (Austria, 1972–1981), Javier Pérez de Cuéllar (Peru, 1982–1991), and Boutros Boutros-Ghali (Egypt, 1992–).

The "UN system" comprises not only the six principal organs of the UN outlined above but also the numerous subsidiary bodies and specialized agencies that operate under the UN's auspices. There are sixteen specialized agencies, each with its own constitution, membership, and budget. Apart from the main financial agencies (the *International Monetary Fund [IMF] and the *World Bank), the "big four" are the *International Labor Organization (ILO) in Geneva, the Food and Agriculture Organization (FAO) in Rome, the UN Educational, Scientific and Cultural Organization (UNESCO) in Paris, and the *World Health Organization (WHO) in Geneva. Many other intergovernmental organizations, including the International Atomic Energy Agency (IAEA) and the *General Agreement on Tariffs and Trade (GATT), are closely associated with the UN.

The number of member states of the UN, fifty-one at the beginning, increased dramatically in its first four decades, mainly owing to the ending of European empires. By March 1992 membership was 175. No member state has ever been expelled from the UN; nor has any left, although in 1965–1966 Indonesia temporarily withdrew, and from 1949 to 1971 China was represented only by the Nationalist government in Taiwan.

Role and Influence. The actual role and influence of the UN have differed significantly from what was foreseen in 1945. In particular, peacekeeping and observer forces, not mentioned in the charter, have been an important aspect of UN action in numerous conflicts and crises; various issues not addressed in the charter, such as environmental management,

have become more central to the work of the organization; and the secretary-general's functions have grown, especially the use of the position's "good offices" to mediate between members.

For much of the UN's first forty-five years of existence, East-West hostility prevented the Security Council from taking action on certain major issues: by the end of 1989, the Soviet Union had vetoed 114 resolutions, the United States 67, the United Kingdom 30, France 18, and China 3. The majority (103) of the Soviet vetoes were in the years to 1965; all the U.S. vetoes occurred after that, reflecting a growing U.S. perception of the organization as being dominated by hostile groupings of *Third World and communist states.

In 1950 the UN did support decisive action, over Korea. At that time the Soviet Union had unwisely absented itself from the Security Council (in protest against China's being represented by the Nationalist delegate), so it could not use the veto. On 25 June 1950, the Security Council condemned the armed attack by the Democratic People's Republic of Korea (North Korea) on the Republic of Korea (South Korea). Two days later, Security Council Resolution (SC Res.) 83 recommended that UN members "furnish such assistance to the Republic of Korea as may be necessary to repel the armed attack." Then on 7 July 1950 SC Res. 84 approved a unified command in Korea under the United States, authorizing it to use the UN flag. When the Soviet Union resumed its place in the Security Council, the Western powers secured the passage of the "Uniting for Peace" resolution through the General Assembly, which enabled the General Assembly to act in cases where the Security Council was hamstrung by the veto.

The "Uniting for Peace" procedure was used again in 1956—against two of its original sponsors, Britain and France, after they had vetoed any Security Council action over their attack on Egypt. The General Assembly called for an immediate cease-fire and the withdrawal of forces from the Suez Canal. Britain, followed by France, acquiesced, partly owing to U.S. pressure. Another General Assembly resolution at that time called for a withdrawal of Soviet forces from Hungary: this was ignored.

The Middle East crisis of 1956 gave rise to a major innovation in UN practice: peacekeeping, or the use of multinational forces under UN command to help control and resolve conflict between hostile states or between hostile communities within a state. Since 1948 there had been a small UN Truce Supervision Organization (UNTSO) in the Middle East. This was complemented in November 1956 by the dispatch of a UN Emergency Force (UNEF-I) to the Suez Canal area, Sinai, and Gaza, by agreement with the Egyptian government. Some 6,000 soldiers drawn from many countries helped keep a precarious peace between Israel and Egypt: their withdrawal at Egypt's request in 1967 was part of the process that led to the outbreak of the June 1967 war.

In the decades after 1956, many other peacekeeping forces were created under UN auspices—all in the postcolonial world, where political systems and borders often lacked legitimacy. They were deployed in Lebanon, West Irian, Yemen, Cyprus, Sinai, and the Golan Heights. The largest and most controversial was the UN operation in the Congo, which in 1960–1964 sought to support the central authorities in the newly independent Congo (now Zaire) against secessionist and other threats.

One method of pressure provided for in the UN Charter (article 41) is mandatory economic *sanctions, but these have been used only rarely. From 1966 onward the Security Council applied them, with very limited effect, against Rhodesia in response to its unilateral declaration of independence: however, the eventual settlement leading to the creation of Zimbabwe in 1980 owed little to UN pressure and less to UN mediation. In November 1977 an arms embargo was imposed on South Africa. In August 1990 sanctions were imposed on Iraq following its invasion of Kuwait.

In the many conflicts and crises of the post-1945 era the UN's record has been mixed. In some, especially those involving Security Council members on both sides, the UN could achieve little. This was true of the wars in Vietnam between 1946 and 1975, of the 1979 Sino-Vietnamese war, and of the long armed confrontation in Europe between the *North Atlantic Treaty Organization and the *Warsaw Treaty Organization (Warsaw Pact) states. On the other hand, in many cases the UN did enunciate important principles, as for example in SC Res. 242 of 22 November 1967, on the Arab-Israel problem; and SC Res. 502 of 3 April 1982, on the Argentine invasion of the *Malvinas/Falkland Islands. Through mediation and good offices the UN contributed to the 1988 cease-fire ending the *Iran-Iraq war, to the 1989 Soviet withdrawal from Afghanistan, and to securing Namibia's independence from South Africa in 1990.

With the changes in the Soviet Union in the late 1980s, the collapse of communist rule in central and eastern Europe in 1989, and the ending of the Cold War, new possibilities of cooperation within a UN framework began to emerge. The UN was put to a severe test by Iraq's invasion of Kuwait on 2 August 1990. The Security Council condemned this strongly the same day, and in an unprecedented series of resolutions imposed on Iraq extensive economic sanctions. On 29 November 1990 SC Res. 678 authorized the use of "all necessary means" if Iraq did not quit Kuwait by 15 January 1990. In subsequent military action in January–February 1991 a large coalition of countries led by the United States forced Iraq to withdraw from Kuwait. The Security Council then imposed tough peace terms on Iraq, including measures of nuclear and chemical disarmament. The implementation of these terms, requiring detailed verification on a long-term basis, posed many problems. The whole episode was exceptional in many ways, especially because it originated in an unusually blatant act of aggression. Yet it reinforced hopes, and also fears, that the UN might become much more active and interventionist in the post–Cold War era. The subsequent UN action in offering temporary protection to Kurds in northern Iraq, and then in 1992 in sending UN peacekeeping forces to Cambodia and Yugoslavia to bring largely internal wars to an end, reinforced the idea that the UN was now playing a more significant, intrusive, and also risky role.

Apart from action in particular crises, the UN—through General Assembly resolutions, conferences, specialized agencies, and subsidiary bodies—has been involved in a wide range of other activities. It has assisted the development of various international agreements on human rights, and established monitoring machinery; it has played a key part in the development of *international law and legal institutions; it has become increasingly associated with the causes of *arms control and *disarmament, and has been instrumental in securing and reviewing the operation of some multilateral agreements in this field, including the 1968 Treaty on the Non-Proliferation of Nuclear Weapons; and it has provided an important venue for discussion of trade, aid, economic development, and the environment.

The UN has been criticized from several different directions. In its early years it was seen by the Soviet Union as an instrument of Western hegemony. Later, the General Assembly, often dismissed as a talking shop, came to be viewed in the United States as hostile and as promoting rather than resolving conflict on certain issues. The relentless growth of UN bureaucracy led to strong attacks on waste and inefficiency. As a protest against particular activities and practices, both the Soviet Union and the United States have at times been among the many states withholding assessed contributions to the UN budget.

Despite its weaknesses and perennial financial crises, the UN has become the first genuinely global international organization, bringing almost all sovereign states together under one set of principles—those of the UN Charter. States find membership of the UN and its many associated bodies indispensable and value the functional cooperation it facilitates. It is probably wrong to see the UN as a nascent world government, but it remains central to the survival and advancement of the idea that states exist as part of a universal international society.

(See also ARAB-ISRAELI CONFLICT; CONGO CRISIS; ECONOMIC AND SOCIAL COMMISSION FOR ASIA AND THE PACIFIC; ECONOMIC COMMISSION FOR AFRICA; ECONOMIC COMMISSION FOR LATIN AMERICA AND THE CARIBBEAN; FORCE, USE OF; GULF WAR; KOREAN WAR; RESOLUTION 242;

SOVIET-AFGHANISTAN WAR; SUEZ CRISIS; UNITED NATIONS CONFERENCE ON TRADE AND DEVELOPMENT.)

United Nations, *Yearbook of the United Nations* (New York, annually). Inis Claude, *Swords into Ploughshares: The Problems and Progress of International Organization*, 4th ed. (New York, 1971). Thomas M. Franck, *Nation Against Nation: What Happened to the UN Dream and What the US Can Do About It* (New York, 1985). Adam Roberts and Benedict Kingsbury, eds., *United Nations, Divided World: The UN's Roles in International Relations* (Oxford, 1988). Paul Taylor and A. J. R. Groom, eds., *International Institutions at Work* (London, 1988).

ADAM ROBERTS

UNITED NATIONS CONFERENCE ON TRADE AND DEVELOPMENT. In 1964 the United Nations Conference on Trade and Development (UNCTAD) was established by the General Assembly as one of its permanent organs. The developing countries at the time were not entirely happy either with certain developments in the world economy or with the norms, principles, and practices of postwar economic institutions (the *International Monetary Fund, the *World Bank, and the *General Agreement on Tariffs and Trade), often referred to as the Bretton Woods system. They felt, in particular, that the latter institutions reflected essentially Western, liberal perspectives that were not wholly appropriate for developing countries and that the international economy itself was biased against their interests and needs. There was thus strong support among intellectual and political leaders of developing countries for the creation of an international economic institution that would articulate and promote their views and facilitate and accelerate their economic *development. Despite opposition from Western nations, which disagreed with the need to create a new institution and with the ideas being propounded, the *Third World prevailed and UNCTAD became the institutional embodiment of a specific Third World perspective on international economic relations. UNCTAD was established as an organ of the UN General Assembly rather than as a specialized agency, largely to ensure that it would receive adequate budgetary support.

Raúl *Prebisch, the Argentine economist who subsequently became the first secretary-general of UNCTAD, developed or popularized many of the ideas that lay behind UNCTAD's creation. In brief, Prebisch argued that Third World raw material exports were facing a continuing decline in their terms of trade, that the Third World had to adopt a strategy of *import-substitution industrialization in order to develop, and that relations between the developed "center" and the developing "periphery" were inherently exploitative. These ideas were sharply challenged by many economists but, to practitioners and intellectuals in the Third World, they seemed intuitively correct. In any case, Prebisch's ideas, which were also the basis of *dependency theory in

many of its variations, were transformed into UNCTAD's leitmotifs: suspicions about the fairness of the Bretton Woods system, pessimism about the prospects for raw materials exports and thus an emphasis on the need to stabilize and raise prices by interventions in the markets, demand for preferential access to Western markets for Third World manufactures, and free or freer access to Western technology. These ideas were of course anathema to conservative developed-country governments strongly committed to the market—as long as they benefited from open markets—and guaranteed that UNCTAD would become an institution of confrontation, the developed countries' least favorable multilateral setting.

UNCTAD, by international standards, is not a very large organization in terms of either budget or staff (less than 400 professionals). It is, however, one of the most universal organizations as it has almost 170 member states—more than the UN itself. The conference usually meets every four years to set policy guidelines and to attempt to resolve major disputes on the issues. Between conferences, the Trade and Development Board is largely responsible for providing direction and guidance. The Board, which usually meets annually, also operates through standing committees that correspond to divisions within the staff bureaucracy: committees dealing with manufactures, commodities, transfer of technology, development finance, economic and technical cooperation among developing countries, and the like. The committees provide direction to the staff and also review reports and papers prepared by the staff, but what the committees request is also heavily influenced by what the staff itself wants to do. Informal channels of communication between the staff and representatives of key Third World governments are thus powerful and pervasive.

Measured against the desire of the developing countries to restructure the international economic order, UNCTAD has not been a success. It did succeed in its early years in gaining support for the General System of Preferences, but the benefits were relatively limited and largely concentrated in a small group of newly industrializing countries. Indeed, many economists have argued that the emphasis on a combination of preferential access to Western markets and relatively closed Third World markets was itself mistaken, as it hindered or delayed efforts to make the manufactured exports of the developing countries internationally competitive. On other issues, such as commodities, transfer of technology, and shipping, UNCTAD did some useful work in its early years, largely in forming a common Third World position, but achieved limited practical results.

UNCTAD's influence surged in the 1970s as it became the major institutional setting for the Third World's effort to establish the *New International Economic Order. With the *Organization of Petroleum Exporting Countries seemingly dominant and perhaps willing to use some of its power to achieve gains for other developing countries, and with the developed countries in disarray, the odds on a successful challenge to the existing order by a coalition of weak countries seemed to be as short as they were likely to get. Thus the *Group of 77 in UNCTAD demanded major changes in a number of key areas, especially commodities and the transfer of technology. The developed countries successfully resisted or diluted these demands, partly from ideology, partly from conflicts of interest, and partly because of technical weaknesses in some of the demands.

UNCTAD's role diminished in the 1980s and after. UNCTAD's interventionist principles were increasingly out of fashion among conservative Western countries, new problems in debt and the trading regime were dealt with largely by the old Bretton Woods institutions, and sharply declining economic performance in much of the Third World tended to deflect attention from multilateral to bilateral or regional relations. UNCTAD still performs some useful functions as the "voice" of the Third World, as a source of some useful research, and as a provider of technical assistance for the least developed countries and for cooperation among developing countries. If UNCTAD were to change its principles and become less confrontational, it would probably seem redundant; if it were to continue to demand radical changes without success, it would become irrelevant. Without stronger Third World leadership, more genuine Third World unity, and a more stable international economic order, UNCTAD is most likely to remain a minor player in the North-South arena.

(See also INTERNATIONAL DEBT; INTERNATIONAL POLITICAL ECONOMY; NEWLY INDUSTRIALIZING ECONOMIES; NORTH-SOUTH RELATIONS; TECHNOLOGY TRANSFER; UNITED NATIONS.)

Branislav Gosovic, *UNCTAD: Conflict and Compromise* (Leiden, 1972). Robert L. Rothstein, *Global Bargaining: UNCTAD and the Quest for a New International Economic Order* (Princeton, N.J., 1979).

ROBERT L. ROTHSTEIN

UNITED STATES. From their early history, the United States and its politics have been described, in the words of Alexis de Tocqueville, as "exceptional," qualitatively different from other nations. The distinction still holds. The American polity is the only one dominated by two loosely structured coalition parties, weaker as national organizations than those elsewhere. It is the only democratic system without an electorally viable socialist, social democratic, or labor party. The correlation between social *class (high to low, middle-class and working-class) and party voting present in all electoral democracies is weaker than in other industrial nations. The United States is the oldest continuing *democ-

racy (the Democratic Party has existed longer than any party in the world), and the most populist, in that over 500,000 offices are filled in elections. Nevertheless a smaller percentage of the eligible electorate vote than in other democracies, roughly fifty percent in presidential *elections, thirty-five percent in non-presidential-year congressional contests, and even less in many local ones. The American polity is also differentiated from others in having state-conducted primary elections, in which voters who select to register in a political party choose nominees for the general elections.

Institutional Principles of American Government. The American *Constitution, the oldest in the world, established a divided form of government, the *presidency and two houses of *Congress, which differs from those of Europe and the *Commonwealth and reflects a deliberate decision by the country's founders to create a weak and internally conflicted political system. The leaders of the Revolution, with their opposition to a powerful monarchical regime, strongly distrusted the state. The first constitution, the Articles of Confederation, provided for a Congress to pass laws, but *not* for an executive.

The second and continuing one, which went into effect in 1789, divided the government into many units, each selected differently for varying periods of office. The president was to be elected every four years by an electoral college, basically local *elites. Senators, two from each state, were to be chosen by the state legislators for six-year terms, with one-third of the seats open every two years, and the popularly elected House of Representatives was to be filled every two years, with the number from each state roughly proportionate to its share of the national population. The president may veto legislation passed by Congress, but the veto can be overridden by two-thirds of each house. Changes to the Constitution require a two-thirds vote in both houses of Congress and ratification by three-quarters of the states. The Constitution provides for *Supreme Court justices who are appointed by the president for life, but their nomination, like those of other federal justices, cabinet members, and high ranking officeholders, must be ratified by the Senate. The terms of office are still the same today, but the system of selecting the electoral college has been changed so that the contest for president is practically by popular vote, as is the election of senators.

Almost all other democratic nations, those in Latin America apart, have a much more unified government, with a prime minister and cabinet who must have the support of the majority of the elected members of parliament. Given that the executive must be backed by the parliamentarians who place it in office, prime ministers are much more powerful, particularly in the domestic field, than presidents.

The American system laid down in the late eighteenth century is basically intact. As noted, it has been amended to provide for direct popular election of senators, but each state still has two, regardless of differences in population size. The procedures for nominating presidential and other candidates have also become more populist. Potential nominees must run in party primaries (elections among registered party members) held some time before the general election. These first emerged in some western states around the turn of the century. They became prevalent for almost all posts after *World War II. Nominees were previously chosen by party conventions, often controlled by "machines" or cabals of professional politicians. These developments were paralleled by the emergence in state and local governments of initiatives and referenda, which require the electorate's direct involvement in the passage of legislation and state constitutional amendments. These *reforms reflect a commitment to *populism, to the belief that the public, rather than professional politicians, should control as much of the policy-formation processes as possible.

Political Structure and Political Culture. Comparing causes and consequences of the divided authority presidential system with that of the more common parliamentary unified government points up the way in which values and institutions interact to produce distinct *political cultures. The American system has intensified the commitment to individualism and concern for the protection of *rights through legal action. The *Bill of Rights, unique until recently, is designed to protect the citizenry against governmental abuse of *power. It has engendered an emphasis on personal rights and thus fosters litigiousness. As a result, Americans have a greater propensity than other peoples to go to court not only against government but against each other. The emphasis on constitutionally protected rights has led to a steady enlargement of basic freedoms in the areas of speech, assembly, and private behavior and to a variety of legal defense organizations to sustain such efforts, the most prominent of which has been the American Civil Liberties Union. The rights of blacks and other minorities, of women, even of animals and plants, have grown extensively since World War II through legal action as well as mass protest. American litigiousness may be seen in the greater frequency of appeals against convictions, as well as more malpractice, environmental, and occupational safety suits than occur elsewhere. The country has more lawyers per capita than other nations.

The disdain for authority, for conforming to the rules laid down by the state, has been related by some to other unique American traits, such as the highest crime rate, as well as the lowest level of voting participation, in the developed world. Basically the American tradition does not encourage obedience to the state and the law. This point may be illustrated by reference to efforts by the U.S. and Canadian governments to change the systems of measurements and weights, that is, to "go metric" and drop the ancient and less logical system of miles and inches, pounds and ounces. Two decades ago, each country told its citizens that in ten years only metric measurements would be used, although both systems could be used until a given date. The Canadians, whose Tory-monarchical history and structures have made for much greater respect for and reliance on the state and who have lower per capita crime, deviance, and litigiousness rates than Americans, deferred to the decision of their leaders and now follow the metric system. Americans largely ignored the new policy, and the government abandoned the effort to change. Distances still refer to yards or miles, weights are in pounds and ounces, and temperature readings are in Fahrenheit.

The cross-national variation in voting rates may be explained in part by the different reactions of Americans and Canadians to fulfilling the obligations or duties of good *citizenship. Many voters everywhere take the time to cast a ballot for the same reason they obey a sign not to walk on the grass, wait at a red light even if no car is approaching, or do not break the law in other ways when there is little or no chance that they will be caught in a violation. Many potential voters, knowing that they will rarely, if ever, determine the outcome of an election, recognize that to devote time to cast a ballot is not rational behavior. Voting is simply encouraged as an expression of good citizenship. Americans, being less conformist, less law-abiding, than Canadians or Europeans, may be expected to vote less.

The greater emphasis on populism also appears to contribute to low turnout. In the United States, unlike Canada or other parliamentary countries, voters are asked to cast a ballot for many offices and referenda. In most states they are called on to vote twice every year in primary and general elections, sometimes more frequently if local and state balloting occurs at different times. In almost every other country, national elections are held only every four or five years. At these and in municipal or provincial elections, the ballot contains candidates for only one office, member of parliament, or legislator.

Conformism and populism do not exhaust the factors related to low voter turnout in America. Although Americans express greater interest in politics than those polled in other democracies, it is more difficult to vote in the United States than in Canada or Europe. Americans must register to vote some time before the election, a requirement which does not exist in other countries. Adult citizens elsewhere are usually placed on a voting roll. But, although the requirement to register reduces turnout, it is not the predominant cause of low voter turnout. Some midwestern states, like North Dakota and Minnesota, have practically eliminated voter registration and, while the proportion voting there is higher than in other states, it is still lower than in most of Europe and Canada.

Religion and American Political Culture. Individualism and resistance to authority in America are also fostered by the predominant religious institutions, the Protestant sects. The United States is the *only* country in Christendom the majority of whose inhabitants adhere to *sects,* voluntary, non-state-related institutions, mainly Methodist and Baptist, but also hundreds of others. The sects are predominantly congregational; each local unit adheres voluntarily to its national denomination, which has little or no control over it. Youths are asked to make a denominational choice on reaching the age of decision, i.e., they are not members automatically by family affiliation. Ministers do not have power over their parishioners. Elsewhere *churches,* Anglican, Catholic, Lutheran and Orthodox, dominate. They are hierarchical in structure, and membership is a birthright; parishioners are expected to follow the lead of their priests and bishops. Outside of the United States, churches have been state supported; their clergy are paid by the state, their hierarchy is formally appointed or confirmed by the government, and their schools are subsidized by taxes.

The United States was the first country in which religious groups became voluntary associations. American ministers and laity recognized that they had to foster voluntary commitments both to maintain support for the church and to foster community needs. Tocqueville concluded that voluntarism is a large part of the answer to the greater popular strength of organized *religion, a phenomenon still documented by cross-national opinion polls, indicating Americans are the most God-believing, churchgoing, and fundamentalist people in the West.

These emphases in American Protestant sectarianism have both reinforced and been strengthened by social and political individualism. The sectarian is expected to follow a moral code, as determined by his or her own sense of rectitude, through a personal relationship to God, one not mediated by bishops or dictated by the state. The sectarians in Britain, who are in a minority, have been known as "dissenters" and "nonconformists," dissenting from, rather than conforming to, the doctrines of the Church of England, the established state religion.

The strength of sectarian values and their implications for the political process may be seen in reactions to the supreme test of citizenship and adherence to the national will, *war. State churches have not only legitimated government (e.g., the divine right of kings), they have invariably approved of the wars their nations have engaged in, calling on the populace to serve and obey. And the citizens have done so. Americans, however, have been different. In every war in which the United States has participated, with the exception of World War II, when the country was attacked by Japan, there has been a major antiwar movement. During the war of 1812, the New England states threatened to secede because of their opposition to the conflict. Thou-

sands of American soldiers, including some West Point graduates, deserted during the Mexican War and joined the opposing army because they believed the Mexicans were right and the United States wrong. In the Civil War, both sides witnessed major opposition to their causes from behind the lines. There were hundreds of thousands of conscientious objectors and a large vote for antiwar Socialist Party candidates during *World War I. Polls revealed massive opposition to the *Korean War. The strength of the antiwar protest movement to the *Vietnam War, which helped to end it, is well known. In his comparative historical study of opposition to American wars, Sol Tax reported that, as of 1968, the anti–Vietnam War movement only stood *fourth* on the list of significance of such efforts.

Many of the antiwar movements have had direct links to Protestant sectarianism. Conscientious objection to military service has its roots there, and the phenomenon has been much more prevalent in America than elsewhere. Still it may be recognized that a great deal of antiwar activity in the United States does not have direct Protestant sectarian origin. Jews, Catholics, and secularists, particularly political leftists, have played major, sometimes predominant, roles in such movements. But it may be argued that sectarianism has affected non-Protestants who, like foreign immigrants, have been socialized and assimilated to the prevalent ethos. Studies of American Catholicism by foreign Catholic scholars have noted the extent to which their American coreligionists, including church functionaries, have taken over the cultural patterns and individualist moralistic emphases of Protestant sectarianism. A French Dominican, R. L. Bruckberger, observes that to European Catholics, American Catholics resemble Baptists and Methodists more than they do their Continental coreligionists. Similar points have been made about Jews. American socialists during World War I and *New Left antiwar activists in the Vietnam War followed scenarios laid down by Protestant sectarians.

Protestant-inspired moralism has affected not only opposition to wars. It has determined the American style in foreign relations generally, including the ways the country goes to war. Patriotism, including support for wars, is as moralistic as resistance to participation. To endorse a war, Americans must see a conflict as on God's side against Satan, for morality against evil. When Ronald *Reagan defined the struggle against *communism as an effort to destroy the "evil empire," he was as American as apple pie. The United States only goes to war against evil empires, not, in its self-perception, to defend material interests. And in such conflicts, no compromise is possible. Hence it demands "unconditional surrender" from the enemy, not negotiated *peace. When it cannot destroy the satanic opponent, it tries to refuse to do business with it. Thus the United States did not recognize the Soviet Union for a decade and a half after its creation. It refused to recognize the communist People's Republic of China for over two decades. It still does not deal with *Castro's Cuba or with Vietnam.

The passion of American opposition to *communism, prior to *Gorbachev's reforms, was interpreted by some as reflecting the fact the country is capitalist and conservative. But equally capitalist and conservative nations and leaders like *Churchill in Britain, de *Gaulle in France, and *Franco in Spain had little difficulty in coming to terms with, and trading with, communist states that the United States would not recognize. Francisco Franco, rightwing dictator, who won a bloody struggle identified by him as against atheistic communism, recognized Castro shortly after he took power in Cuba. As church, rather than sectarian, Christians, Churchill, de Gaulle, and Franco believed human beings and institutions are inherently corrupt, are never perfect. Countries with such views go to war to protect state interests, not to create the good society or eliminate evil.

The Two-Party System. The political institutions and basic values of the United States account for another aspect of American exceptionalism mentioned earlier: its two-party system, the absence of effective and electorally viable third parties. As various political scientists, notably E. E. Schattschneider, have emphasized, the American presidential system seriously discourages more than two parties. Given that only one party and person can win the presidency, voters recognize that realistically they must choose between the two strongest candidates running for office. Support for weaker third or fourth nominees or parties is a wasted choice. Hence voters who are not enthusiastic about the two major candidates still wind up supporting one of them as "the lesser evil." It is much easier for minor or new parties to gain votes in parliamentary systems, where voters elect individual members in constituencies. They do not take part in national or statewide elections for the head of government, as in the United States. The former permit smaller parties to concentrate their energies in districts in which they can win. The latter requires significant national support to be visible.

The pressure to back a potential winner produced the two-party coalitional system. Highly diverse groups have come together under the rubric of the Democratic and Republican parties. For historical reasons related to issues around the Civil War, the white South, which sought to hold down blacks, was Democratic until the post–World War II era. Blacks supported the Republicans, the party which ended slavery, until the Great Depression of the 1930s. Economic conditions led them to shift to the Democrats, who furthered state economic assistance to the poor, particularly the unemployed and sharecropping farmers. The Democrats historically have been the party of the "have-nots," which included those of recent immigrant background, Catholics, Jews, as well as organized labor. The Republicans, and before them the Whig and Federalist parties, have been the party of the "haves," the economically privileged, and those of higher-status, white Anglo-Saxon Protestant, background. Yet, prior to the Great Depression, the Republican Party included near-socialist agrarian radicals in the Midwest as well as most impoverished blacks.

What makes such heterogenous coalition parties possible has been the absence of party discipline, of the obligation of candidates and officials to follow a party line and support party leaders. This diversity is facilitated by the *separation of powers, the fact that unlike a prime minister, who must resign from office and usually call a new election if he or she loses a vote in parliament, a president stays in office no matter how many proposals are defeated in Congress. Parliamentary parties, like the British or Canadian Conservatives or the Scandinavian Social Democrats, must maintain discipline if the system is to work. Members of parliaments are expected, almost required, to vote with their party. They may have to vote for policies favored by their party leaders even when these are very unpopular in the districts they represent. An American congressperson, however, is only concerned with winning the district.

The American separation of powers allows and encourages members of Congress to vote with their constituents against their president or dominant party view. Allen Gotlieb, Canadian ambassador to the United States during the 1980s, has noted that American legislators, including congressional leaders, will vote against and help to kill bills to carry out major international agreements in response to pressure from small groups of local constituents, such as those in the scallop fishing industry or logging concerns. As former House Speaker Thomas P. (Tip) O'Neill once put it, in Congress "all politics is local."

The inability of party organizations to nominate and control legislators running and elected under their label has increased greatly since liberal reforms designed to weaken party "machines" took effect. The unanticipated results, however, were to increase the number and strengthen the influence of lobbyists and to make elected officials much more dependent on financial contributions produced by *interest groups, as the costs of campaigning have mounted in the television age.

Presidents normally have a great deal of difficulty with Congress, even when their party controls a majority of both houses, as Franklin *Roosevelt did after he won reelection by a landslide in 1936. In recent years the American electorate has divided control of the government between the two parties; the Republicans win the presidency, the Democrats dominate Congress. By so doing the voters seemingly reinforce the Founders' desire to have the different branches of government check and balance each other. Under such conditions, the presidency is a much weaker office than the prime ministership whose party has a parliamentary majority. An American president controls *foreign policy and can order troops overseas, but cannot get drafted budgets or much proposed legislation passed by Congress.

The heterogeneity of the major American parties has been enhanced by a primary system that allows representatives of antagonistic factions within the respective parties to run against each other in partywide elections. Thus in 1972, George Wallace, the former right-wing segregationist governor of Alabama, contested the Democratic Party presidential primaries. His successful rival in that year was George McGovern, a leftist populist, who was subsequently defeated by Richard *Nixon in the general election. Nixon had secured the Republican nomination by defeating a liberal, Governor Nelson Rockefeller. Jesse Jackson, a militant black and leftist on economic issues, ran in the Democratic presidential primaries in 1984 and 1988, as did a number of moderate and liberal whites. George *Bush, running as a moderate Republican, lost to Ronald Reagan, perceived as a right-winger, in the primaries in 1980.

During periods of national crisis, left-wing near-socialist groups won control of major party nominations on state levels. Thus the Non-Partisan League formed by socialists captured the Republican Party primaries and then elected state officials and senators in North Dakota from 1916 until World War II. A similar group took control of Oklahoma, running in the Democratic primary, in the early twenties. During the Great Depression of the 1930s, organized factions in which socialists or communists played a major role controlled the Democratic Party in California, Oregon, and Washington. While overt factions have not contested primaries since World War II, candidates representing different orientations continue to compete. During the eighties and nineties, self-defined conservative caucuses and organizations have operated within the Republican Party inside and outside of Congress. The moderate and more liberal Republicans are less well organized, but they exist. Among Democrats, the moderate and more conservative forces are organized in the Democratic Leadership Council. The more numerous liberals among party activists are divided among the Americans for Democratic Action, the Coalition for Democratic Values, and Jesse Jackson's Rainbow Coalition. Interests and ideological groups function in both parties, e.g., civil rights supporters, feminists, farm blocs, labor unions, environmentalists (greens), pro- and anti-choice advocates, etc.

Why No Socialism in America? Political structures explain the absence of significant third or minor parties in America, but they do not account for the absence of social democratic and leftist class-conscious groups as political forces. A number of factors have been suggested by students of the sub-

ject, such as the strength of the classically liberal (anti-state) tradition in America and a more egalitarian social class structure, i.e., one based in status rather than economic or power terms, than exists elsewhere.

The most general approach, associated with English author and Fabian H. G. Wells and the American political scientist Louis Hartz, emphasizes the extent to which the distrust of a strong state that was the core of the revolutionary ideology continues to influence the way Americans look at politics. *Socialism, which assumes the need for a powerful state-controlled economy, is antithetical to this outlook. The radicalism which stems from the Jeffersonian view that the less government the better is close to *anarchism. Therefore, it should not be surprising that the major American *labor movement, the American Federation of Labor (AFL), was syndicalist and anti-statist rather than socialist, favoring independent workers' action. Its founding president, Samuel Gompers, who held the office for four decades, described himself as a near anarchist. The most important American radical labor movement, the Industrial Workers of the World (IWW), was anarcho-syndicalist.

Conversely, the monarchical tradition in Europe and Canada fostered Tory statism. Tory *conservatism meant belief in the *monarchy, the alliance between church and state, *mercantilism, i.e., state intervention in the economy, and noblesse oblige. The emergence of the *welfare state in Europe is associated with two conservative figures, Disraeli in Britain and Bismarck in Germany. Classical liberalism, anti-statism, laissez-faire, which has dominated American political thinking, has been a minority movement in Europe. The socialist emphasis on using the state for economic and social reforms was legitimated there by statist conservatism. Americans today are less supportive of welfare state policies than the citizens of any other nation, and, not surprisingly, their government provides less.

The failure of socialist parties and the weakness of economic class as a base for partisan cleavage have also been linked to the special character of the American status system. Unlike most European countries, with a feudal aristocratic tradition of hierarchy, where deference has been given and expected, American society, as Tocqueville noted in the nineteenth century, has been more egalitarian in terms of respect. He emphasized that *equality in America also means meritocracy, a stress on equality of opportunity among individuals regardless of social origins. The United States, of course, has always been highly inegalitarian in economic and power terms, but much less so in status, social ranking, terms. In contrast to Japanese and most European languages, there are no words which must be used in America to reflect the relative status of the speakers. Lower-strata Europeans did not have to be propagandized or educated to think politically in class terms, they were socialized by their postfeudal, more status-conscious societies to react that way. In the United States the value-generating and value-sustaining institutions have negated class consciousness among whites. As political scientist Walter Dean Burnham sums up the political consequences: "No feudalism, no socialism."

While class-based movements have been weak in the United States, and the correlation between class position and party voting has been lower than in almost all other industrialized societies, the salient social bases of partisan cleavage in America, as elsewhere, have been stratification variables. As noted, the Democrats for much of their history have drawn disproportionate support from the have-not strata in occupational, ethnic, and religious terms. The Republicans represented the more socioeconomically dominant elements. However, these linkages were rarely presented in class terms until the Great Depression, when Franklin Roosevelt and the *New Deal wing of the Democratic Party appealed openly to the labor unions, the workers, the poor, the unemployed, and the less affluent rural population against the rich and economically powerful.

The association between class and party was greatly strengthened in that era. The labor organizations strongly backed the Democrats, and trade unions flourished with the help of the Roosevelt administration. Those business elements, a minority, which had previously been Democratic because of ethnic, religious, or sectional economic ties, shifted to the Republicans. The New Deal introduced, in historian Richard Hofstadter's words, "a social democratic tinge" into American politics. America now had its own welfare state, though one which never reached the proportions in other industrialized polities during this century.

Werner Sombart noted almost a century ago in his *Why No Socialism in the United States?* that the country's greater wealth undermines the socialist appeal and reduces the emphasis on class. This continued to be the case during the prolonged prosperity after World War II. America became even more affluent. It is still the richest industrialized nation in terms of per capita income, close to $20,000 per year. Although a significant population, disproportionately black and Hispanic, lives in poverty, consumption goods are more evenly spread among the remainder, particularly the white population, than is true elsewhere. The postwar increase in wealth, which continued through the 1960s, negated the stress on class divisions brought about by the Great Depression. Trade-union membership declined steadily from thirty-five percent of the employed labor force in 1955 to sixteen percent in 1991, one of the lowest such proportions in any industrialized economy. Republicans, the party identified with anti-statist laissez-faire ideologies, were able to win the presidency in five of the six presidential elections between 1968 and 1992.

Political Parties and Divided Government. During this period, the Democrats, as noted, have captured at least one, usually both, of the houses of Congress. It is puzzling why a majority of the American electorate selects different parties for the presidency and Congress. Part of the answer seems to be that presidential contests involve issues of national style and morality: patriotism, defense, crime, family. Alternatively, congressional campaigns focus more on interests: tax policy, entitlements and welfare provisions, health and education. But this is inference, not knowledge.

There is now renewed distrust of government and approval in principle of divided government by a solid majority of those polled. When survey researchers inquire whether it is better to have the presidency and both houses of Congress in the hands of one party or divided, sixty to seventy percent of the respondents reply "different parties."

This does not mean that many voters consciously opt for a president of one party and a congressperson of the other in order to check them. Rather, as in the constituency by-elections and provincial elections held elsewhere, those who vote for the governing party nationally frequently choose the opposition in special or local elections, which cannot remove the government from power. These lesser contests are used to express discontent with some policies of those who control the national administration, even though voters do not wish to remove their leaders. In the United States, the electorate behaves similarly. In off-year contests (those in which a president is not elected), the president's party almost invariably loses congressional seats. The nonpresidential party also wins by-elections and in recent presidential election years has gotten many more votes for its congressional than presidential candidates. In Canada, the party which wins federal office tends to lose in provincial contests, held soon after the national elections. Divided government, federal and provincial, does not weaken the power of the national administration in parliamentary systems such as Canada, the Federal Republic of Germany, or Spain. But in America, it produces a divided and sometimes ineffectual federal government, because Congress shares governing power with the president.

The Third Century of American Politics. As the United States moves into its third century under the same Constitution, it seemingly has the same divided form of government and, compared with the Euro-Canadian polities, value emphases. It is still classically liberal (libertarian), distrustful of government, and populist. The electorate still has more power to choose its leaders than in other democracies, which depend on unified governments to fulfill economic and welfare functions and which have fewer offices and policies directly open to electoral choice.

Yet America has obviously changed greatly since 1789. From a nation of thirteen states and 4 million people hugging the Atlantic seaboard, it has grown to a continent-spanning federation of fifty states and 250 million people. Close to 30 million live in California, a state nonexistent in 1789. It began as an overwhelmingly agrarian society with more than ninety percent of its work force on the land, many as impoverished subsistence farmers. As it approaches the twenty-first century, only two percent are farmers; the great majority live in sprawling metropolitan regions. From an underdeveloped rural economy which relied heavily on Britain for its manufactured goods, it became in the latter decades of the nineteenth century the most prosperous industrial power on earth. In real consumer income terms it still holds this position, although the emergence of other industrial countries and the reexpansion of Europe have reduced its proportion of the world's production from two-fifths immediately after World War II to a quarter. The character of its labor force has changed, first with the decline of agriculture and the expansion of industry, and more recently with the falloff in unskilled manual jobs and growth of high-tech and scientific activities accompanied by an increase in white-collar and service jobs and in positions requiring college education.

On the international scene, the United States moved from being a small, militarily weak country far from the major power centers and proud of its isolation to the strongest nation on earth, the focus of military and economic alliances and agreements. Domestically, the Civil War resolved the issue of states' rights versus federal power and resulted in a shift from the original loosely integrated federation to a highly centralized one. During and after the Great Depression and World War II, the country became an increasingly nationalized polity with funds and power concentrated in the center. Under Ronald Reagan, the Republicans tried to reverse the trend, but succeeded only in stopping its growth. The country's military and international responsibilities remain a major factor in maintaining the enhanced role of the national government.

Although the American government, as noted, remains the least involved in welfare activities and government ownership and influence on the economy of any developed country, it has moved greatly since the 1930s in the direction of providing assistance to the less privileged through programs like Social Security, unemployment insurance, bank deposit insurance, medical aid, aid to single mothers, and college student loans. The federal and state governments are deeply involved in legislation to protect the environment, provide occupational safety, and remove economic discrimination against blacks, ethnic minorities, women, and older people.

Despite these developments, which make governing the United States infinitely more complex than in the late eighteenth and nineteenth centuries, the *form* of government has not changed. The presidency remains a much weaker office than the prime ministry and cabinet in the rest of the democratic world. Congress is much more powerful than any parliament, but, as planned by the Founders, it is a divided body. The Supreme Court, with its powers to negate legislation as unconstitutional and to limit laws, regulations, and administrative decrees with reference to the Bill of Rights and other portions of the Constitution, is the most powerful court in the world. It can and does legislate major public matters such as the suffrage, racial and gender equality, abortion, and the death penalty. And the constitutional and individualistic elements in American culture which foster litigiousness contribute to further inhibition of the powers of government.

The question is increasingly raised by political observers whether these constraints on the government will permit the United States to deal with the problems posed by a global economy; challenges from Japan and the newly industrialized countries of East Asia, European unification, disruption of communist strength east of the Elbe, and the attempted industrialization of the impoverished nations of South Asia and Africa. To these may be added the domestic difficulties involved in handling the urban-based problems of housing, pollution, transportation, education, and minorities and immigrant placement. But it is not clear that a more united parliamentary system would work better under conditions of geographic and cultural heterogeneity. Canada, which has a parliamentary system and a Tory emphasis on government responsibility for welfare, also has severe governance problems. Its provinces are demanding and obtaining much more power than American states and, as noted, their electorates in recent decades have almost invariably chosen governments that are in opposition to the party in federal control.

The United States is a difficult place to govern. It is divided along sectional, economic, ethnic, racial, and religious lines. Mass immigration, close to 10 million in the 1980s, continues. Racial polarization has not eased. The country's international responsibilities have not declined. Yet its people continue to exhibit more distrust of centralized government than do any other, and, as noted, prefer divided and conflicted government. Viewed cross-nationally, Americans are the most Whiggish, most classically liberal population among the democratic nations. They continue to stand with Thomas Jefferson in believing the less government the better. It is not surprising, therefore, that the country retains the internally divisive system established in the late eighteenth century.

(See also AFRICAN AMERICANS; ALLIANCE; AMERICAN FEDERATION OF LABOR AND CONGRESS OF INDUSTRIAL ORGANIZATIONS; AMERICAN FOREIGN POLICY; CARTER, JIMMY; CIVIL RIGHTS MOVEMENT; EISENHOWER, DWIGHT D.; ETHNICITY; FEDERALISM; GREAT SOCIETY; HISPANIC AMERICANS; INTERNATIONAL MIGRATION; JOHNSON, LYNDON BAINES; KENNEDY, JOHN FITZGERALD; LIBERALISM;

NATIVE AMERICANS; NEW DEAL COALITION; PAR-
LIAMENTARY DEMOCRACY; POLITICAL MACHINE;
POLITICAL PARTIES AND PARTY COMPETITION; TRU-
MAN, HARRY S.)

E. E. Schattschneider, *Party Government* (New York, 1942).
Seymour Martin Lipset, *The First New Nation* (New York,
1963, 1979). Sol Tax, "War and the Draft," in Martin
Fried, Marvin Harris, and Robert Murphy, eds., *War* (Gar-
den City, N.Y., 1968). Raymond Wolfinger, *Who Votes?*
(New Haven, Conn., 1980). Samuel Huntington, *American
Politics* (Cambridge, Mass., 1981). Nelson Polsby, *Conse-
quences of Party Reform* (New York, 1983). Byron Shafer,
*Quiet Revolution: The Struggle for the Democratic Party
and the Shaping of Post-Reform Politics* (New York, 1983).
James Q. Wilson, *Bureaucracy* (New York, 1989). Seymour
Martin Lipset, *Continental Divide: The Values and Insti-
tutions of the United States and Canada* (New York, 1990.
                                    SEYMOUR MARTIN LIPSET

URBANIZATION. The development of modern societies is inextricably linked to the process of urbanization throughout the world. Any understanding of
the politics of the world must therefore take stock
of this agglomerative process insofar as it has shaped
the cultures, economies, and social institutions of all
societies.

As a process, urbanization commenced with the
Neolithic revolution in food production, some ten
thousand years ago or so. The mastery over food
production freed a number of persons from direct
subsistence activities and created a basis for a more
complex division of labor, the concentration of population in one place, and the emergence of new
forms of social inequality. As the stock of human
knowledge increased through inventions and cultural diffusion, more sophisticated tools were not
only used to harness the forces of nature but were
also transformed into the means of generating surplus by conquest and plundering, enslavement and
levying tribute. In this manner, the city-states of
classical antiquity came to develop and prosper, first
in the area that is roughly coterminous with the
contemporary *Middle East, and then the rest of
the world.

The ancient city-states and feudal societies which
followed them were incapable of maintaining the
continuity in socioeconomic development, despite
their impressive cultural accomplishments. This was
due to a number of reasons, including their low level
of technological development, territorial rivalries and
conflicts, and the extreme methods of exploitation
and political control. The development of *capitalism in Europe ushered in a new era in human history. The initial phase of *mercantilism facilitated
capital accumulation through trade, imperialist conquests, forced labor, and plundering. This phase
soon gave way to the era of competitive capitalism
in the nineteenth century, in which industrial cities
flourished as centers of capitalist production.

The laissez-faire philosophy of competitive capitalism translated into untold misery for the laboring
classes in industrial cities. Low wages, unemployment, poverty, homelessness, and crime became part
of the urban landscape. This situation was compounded by the limited scope of government intervention. It was in this context that workers, progressive and left intellectuals, and women coalesced
into social movements that began to agitate for
social justice. Fearful of this ground swell of opposition, the ruling classes and their political surrogates
were forced to grant concessions, which eventually
became institutionalized as *welfare state measures.

In all the imperialist countries, such as Britain,
Germany, France, and the United States, part of the
resources that have been used to finance domestic
development and welfare measures have been extracted from *Third World countries through the
agency of colonial and neocolonial relations. These
relations have been articulated spatially by a specific
geography of *dependency. The resulting hierarchical spatial structure has extended downwards, from
the national metropolis as a center of capital accumulation, technological diffusion, conspicuous consumption, and political power to the smaller regional urban centers, whose functions are to mediate
the flow of goods and services, labor, and political
influence between the national metropolis and the
rural hinterland. In turn, the national metropolis has
served as an "urban mechanism" for transferring
surplus to the imperialist countries.

In the major as well as the regional urban centers
of the Third World countries, the economic and
social structural distortions are borne out by the
extreme disparities in wealth, between the "haves"
and the "have-nots." This in turn has prompted the
development of the so-called "informal sector," which
complements the formal one by lowering the costs
of reproduction of the urban labor force through
the provision of low-cost goods and services. Given
the high rate of Third World urbanization, the informal sector also absorbs a large number of in-
migrants as low-wage workers and petty commodity
producers. This sector therefore serves to mitigate
the conditions of inequality and poverty and thus
engenders some semblance of political stability.
However, the chronic explosive political and economic *crises precipitated by extreme inequalities
have necessitated the installation of very repressive
regimes in a number of Third World countries.

Following a long period of post–World War II
prosperity, the economies of the advanced capitalist
countries have been caught in a structural crisis that
has prompted regressive methods of urban restructuring. While capitalist economic integration tends
to transmit throughout the system any shocks occasioned by periodic crises, it is the local areas that
bear the brunt of adverse consequences. In the more
centralized state systems such as Britain and France,
social groups adversely affected by urban restructuring have greater political leverage in influencing
national policies that can mitigate local conditions.
In highly decentralized and fragmented political sys-

tems such as that of the United States, local areas are left largely to their own resources. As a result, cities are locked in a feverish competition to attract private development using subsidy inducements that they can ill afford, given their shrinking revenue bases. Often these subsidies are financed with resources that have been withdrawn from social programs. This not only creates groups that are outside the labor market, thanks to, among other things, *deindustrialization, but groups that have fallen through the "safety net" of social insurance and welfare programs, notably the urban poor.

While there is little information available on the urbanization experiences of the socialist countries, the vista created by *Gorbachev's glasnost revealed within the urban microcosm a number of problems that are at the heart of the politics of consumption and the quality of life in these societies. In the competition between the two world systems of *socialism and capitalism, a long-term strategy of socialist industrialization emphasized the development of heavy industry and the expansion of productive capacity. This strategy took place in the context of the *Cold War abroad and bureaucratic distortions of economic and political processes at home. The cumulative impact of these developments is evident today in the form of chronic shortages of consumer goods, problems of housing, deterioration of the urban infrastructure, and pollution. Factories were built indiscriminately in residential areas, without much concern over such externalities as pollution. Today, urban populations are reaping the bitter fruits of this shortsightedness as health problems begin to mount.

In their own version of restructuring, the socialist countries have instituted measures aimed at revitalizing their economies and societies by promoting political and economic competition. Among some of the measures that will have far-reaching political consequences is the shift from an administered to a market price system. Muscovites are experiencing the effects of these measures in the form of radical shortages in food products and consumption goods. If the process of restructuring continues along these lines, new forms of inequality will appear that will raise fundamental issues regarding the character of these societies, as market pressures collide with receding socialist traditions.

Urbanization is an integral part of the process of socioeconomic development, one that has shaped the cultures and institutions of all societies, both historical as well as contemporary. Urban problems furnish insights into the connection between national and international politics, on the one hand, and the spatial articulation of economic, political, and ideological relations, on the other.

(See also DEVELOPMENT AND UNDERDEVELOPMENT; EQUALITY AND INEQUALITY; MODERNIZATION.)

Lewis Mumford, *The City in History* (New York, 1961). David Harvey, *Social Justice and the City* (Baltimore, 1973). Peter Michael Smith and Joe R. Feagin, eds., *The Capitalist City: Global Restructuring and Community Politics* (Oxford and Cambridge, Mass., 1987). United Nations Department of International Economic and Social Affairs, *Prospects of World Urbanization* (New York, 1989).

RONALD S. EDARI

URUGUAY. Formerly a province of Argentina, Uruguay won independence in 1828 following British intervention to create a buffer state with Brazil. Occupying 176,215 square kilometers (68,035 sq. mi.), Uruguay is dominated by the capital and port city of Montevideo, where half the people live. Ninety percent of the country is fertile prairie, and beef, hides, and wool constitute the country's traditional exports. Since ranching requires little labor, Uruguay is highly urbanized and has no peasantry. It was long Latin America's most stable *democracy, with a large middle class and the most egalitarian income distribution. Per capita GDP was almost US$3,000 in 1988, literacy ninety-six percent, life expectancy 70.3 years.

From 1836 Uruguay was rent by civil wars that pitted the more cosmopolitan and centralist Colorados against the more rural and clerical Blancos (officially known as the National Party). This struggle gave rise to the oldest two-party system in Latin America, which prospered in this century on the basis of clientelism and government patronage. In 1971, Uruguay's disparate left-wing parties united to form a viable third option, the Broad Front.

After 1865, continued Blanco uprisings alternated with dictatorship by Colorado *caudillos* (military strong men). A parliamentary tradition gained strength, however, and the Blancos' final defeat in 1903–1904 completed the process of state formation. Uruguay's greatest president, the radical Colorado José Batlle y Ordóñez (1903–1907 and 1911–1915), preceded to pacify the country and pass early welfare reforms. Batlle also nationalized many public services and campaigned for the introduction of a collegial executive along Swiss lines. Electoral registration was liberalized in 1910, and universal male suffrage with secret ballot fully achieved in 1916.

From 1918 to 1933 the directly elected nine-member National Council of Administration shared executive power with the president, taking responsibility for domestic affairs. The opposition (in practice the Blancos) was guaranteed one-third of its councillors. After the 1933 civilian coup, Uruguay returned to a unipersonal presidency until 1951. Then, for a period of fifteen years, a nine-member National Council of Government with a rotating presidency constituted the sole executive. In 1967 a single presidency was again restored by referendum, and the powers of the National Assembly curtailed.

In addition to its exotic constitutional experiments, Uruguay developed a unique electoral system early in this century: "double simultaneous vote." By a complex arrangement, both traditional parties run competing candidates for the presidency, each of which is supported by an array of rival lists of candidates for Senate and House of Deputies. The party with the most overall votes wins the presidency, and the candidate with the most votes from that party is elected. This is sometimes likened to holding a primary at the same time as the general election, but voters face an uncertain choice, not knowing which candidate may pull ahead in the party they choose to support. Blancos and Colorados typically run a spectrum of candidates with differing ideologies to maximize their total vote.

In the 1940s the Batllistas pursued renewed welfare reforms and encouraged industrialization by means of high tariffs, but declining exports of beef and wool in the 1950s created a severe recession. In 1958 the more conservative wing of the Blancos (known as Herreristas) won control of the National Council of Government. They attempted a conservative economic stabilization plan backed by the *International Monetary Fund that favored export ranchers; it proved unpalatable to the voters.

In 1966 the Colorados won the election and the presidency was restored. General Oscar Gestido was inaugurated in 1967, only to die the same year. He was succeeded by Vice President Jorge Pacheco, who turned out to be a tough and at times authoritarian leader. Economic decline in the 1960s produced mounting inflation and labor militancy, and the government responded with repression from 1968. Youth rebellion and international trends combined to create growth among Uruguay's left-wing parties and the emergence of an urban guerrilla movement, the Tupamaros.

Uruguay's military had long been subordinate to civilians, but their use by Pacheco to break strikes in the late 1960s began to politicize them. With U.S. training, in 1971 they were put in charge of the fight against the guerrillas, who were defeated the following year. Yet many young colonels and generals were dissatisfied with the politicians' handling of the country's growing social and economic crisis and felt they could do better. Following a rebellion in February 1973 they became the country's effective rulers; in June they closed the National Assembly.

Military rule in Uruguay lasted until 1985, during which time the level of repression was extremely high and the number of political prisoners among the highest in the world per capita. Conservative but heterodox economic policies of wage compression and export promotion were pursued. Under the *Carter administration (1977–1980), traditionally good relations with the United States deteriorated, and the United States suspended military and economic aid in protest at *human rights violations. In 1980 the military lost their own plebiscite called to introduce a tough new authoritarian constitution. The next year they announced the Blancos and Colorados would be legalized, although they tried to legally "ban" most former leaders from returning to politics.

Changing strategy in 1984, the generals legalized most left parties in order to split the opposition vote between the Broad Front and the Blancos. Having imprisoned their archenemy, Blanco leader Wilson Ferreira, they concluded the so-called Naval Club Pact with the Colorados and the Left. In the November elections the Colorados won a plurality, and moderate Julio María Sanguinetti was inaugurated in March 1985—the first elected president since 1972. His administration granted an immediate political amnesty and, with the support of most Blancos, passed a Law of Limitations (1986) ending all legal proceedings against the military for past human rights violations. This was upheld by referendum in April 1989.

The major parties are all multiclass, the Blancos being strong in the interior, the Colorados among women and pensioners, the *Left among organized labor and intellectuals. In 1989 the Blancos again won the presidency, but the Broad Front took control of the powerful city government of Montevideo despite having lost its center-left wing, which formed an alliance known as "New Space." An uneasy period known as "cohabitation" and renewed labor unrest ensued that threatened to slow progress toward democratic consolidation.

(See also DEMOCRATIC TRANSITIONS; MILITARY RULE; U.S.–LATIN AMERICAN RELATIONS.)

Charles Gillespie, "Political Parties and Redemocratization" (Ph.D. diss., Yale University, 1987). Martin Weinstein, *Uruguay: Democracy at the Crossroads* (Boulder, Colo., 1988).

CHARLES GUY GILLESPIE

U.S.-AFRICA RELATIONS.

The independence of African countries from European colonialism and their attempt to establish stable political regimes and developing economies provided the major post–World War II context for their international relations. The vast continent of Africa, a geopolitically important landmass connected to Europe and the Middle East, contains a critical supply of the raw materials needed for military and industrial purposes. As such, it remains strategically important, but because the European countries were often preoccupied with their own reconstruction, the *United States assumed an important role in Africa in pursuit of its own interests as well as those collectively of the postcolonial West.

The objectives pursued by the United States involved the preservation of its access to strategic resources and geographical position. For example, U.S. policy was designed to maintain friendly relations with North African states in order to have access to military facilities that would buttress the southern flank of its NATO commitments in the Mediterranean. This position would also provide stability for American allies in the Middle East and security for oil exports from certain Arab countries. Thus, when the United States was expelled from Libya after its revolution in 1969, U.S. policy for a considerable period was directed toward securing military base rights in Somalia, Kenya, and the Indian Ocean, and toward containing Libyan military pressure on states in the region.

Likewise, the basis for American involvement in the *Congo crisis of 1960–1964 was its dependence on the Congo for critical strategic minerals such as cobalt and uranium, utilized in its growing nuclear weapons program. The legacy of early U.S. relations with the Congo (now Zaire) initiated a long period of U.S. support for the regime of President Mobutu Sese Seko (formerly General Joseph-Désiré Mobutu), who reciprocated by helping to facilitate U.S. interests in *Southern Africa.

Equally important, American relations in West Africa have been anchored by Nigeria, the most populous African nation and the second-leading exporter of oil to the United States in the early 1970s. Nigeria has influenced the politics of West Africa and other parts of the continent, for example, by providing economic assistance to Angola and being an aggressive foe of South African *apartheid, actions that occasionally conflicted with British and *American foreign policy, especially during Richard *Nixon's administration. Nigerian relations with the United States only began to improve through the diplomacy of President Jimmy *Carter, and have more recently been complemented by Nigeria's adoption of a federal, multiparty, bicameral governmental structure similar to the American model.

U.S. policy has focused on Southern Africa mainly because of its desire to protect American business investments, to maintain access to a superior supply of strategic minerals (especially diamonds, manganese, chromium, and platinum-group metals), and to protect oil routes around the Cape of Good Hope and along the eastern and western shores of the region. Thus, the foreign policy of the United States has been designed to manage the emergence of independent states in this region in a way that would not threaten its own basic interests. U.S. *diplomacy shaped the preliminary issues in negotiations leading to the independence of Zimbabwe from the British in 1980 and, more recently, in multiparty negotiations to implement UN Resolution 435 establishing the independence of Namibia from South Africa in 1989–1990.

The difficult cases have been those of Angola and South Africa. Because of its use of Cuban troops in a continuing civil war with the National Union for the Total Independence of Angola (UNITA), the South African–sponsored guerrillas, and in response to military incursions by South Africa itself, the government of Angola has yet to receive diplomatic recognition by the United States. The American policy suggests that a strongly held anticommunist ideology remains a central aspect of American foreign policy.

The factors cited above were significant in the historically good relations between the United States and South Africa, and laid the groundwork for the modern high point of "constructive engagement" in Ronald Reagan's administration. These interests, however, which led to closer relations with South Africa, have been interpreted by the American public as supporting apartheid. Thus, the worldwide movement in opposition to apartheid that emerged within South Africa found considerable support in the United States, and the result was the passage of the Anti-Apartheid Act of 1986.

The "national interest" that shapes foreign policy is often governed by such factors at the intensity of public opinion, the influence of decision-making institutions, or a combination of these elements. Since racial and ethnic mobilization has traditionally been an important aspect of American *public opinion, it is significant to note that in the United States there are 30 million citizens of African descent. *African Americans have maintained an active interest in Africa since the nineteenth century, and these concerns have evolved naturally to include an interest in national policy toward African countries. Consequently, the African-American community has provided leadership in the civil mobilizations that have changed public opinion and influenced foreign policy on such issues as the allocation of substantial resources for drought relief in the *Sahel in the early 1970s; repeal in 1977 of the Byrd Amendment allowing the United States to trade with the Rhodesian regime of Ian Smith in contravention of UN *sanctions; the increase in economic assistance for Southern African regional development in 1987; and the passage of the Anti-Apartheid Act of 1986. However, only recently, with the spread of black elected and appointed officials, have African Americans had some measure of institutional influence on American foreign policy.

The salutary changes in American foreign policy toward Africa in the future will undoubtedly be affected by a lessening of hostilities between the United States and Russia (as successor to the Soviet Union), until recently a critical factor in American foreign policy decision making. In addition, recent regional settlements could facilitate a normalization of relations in the region, ensuring U.S. access to strategic resources and geographical position. Conceivably, then, U.S. interests in the arena could shift from the containment of political conflict to maintaining a more wholesome environment within which African states and the United States might achieve common foreign policy goals.

(See also ANGOLAN CONFLICT.)

Vernon McKay, *Africa in World Politics* (New York, 1963).
Frederick S. Arkhurst, ed., *U.S. Policy Toward Africa* (New

York, 1975). Gerald J. Bender, James S. Coleman, and Richard L. Sklar, eds., *African Crisis Areas and U.S. Foreign Policy* (Berkeley, Calif., 1985).

RONALD WALTERS

U.S.-CANADA FREE TRADE AGREEMENT. The U.S.-Canada Free Trade Agreement (FTA), which came into force in January 1989, will establish a bilateral free trade area between the signatory countries. The agreement will progressively reduce trade restrictions such as tariffs, nontariff barriers (NTBs), and institutional policies that hinder free flows of trade and investment. The FTA was negotiated pursuant to a provision in the *General Agreement on Tariffs and Trade (GATT) that allows GATT signatories to establish free trade associations while at the same time maintaining their GATT obligations. In some areas, such as tariffs, the FTA has simply reduced restrictions a bit further than GATT has already achieved. In other areas, such as services or investment, the FTA has broken new ground compared with other international trade agreements.

Free trade is not without precedent in Canada-U.S. relations. The earliest agreement was the Reciprocity Treaty of 1854, initiated by *Canada when it began to lose preferential trading relations with Britain. Trade flourished under the Reciprocity Treaty, but in 1866 the *United States abrogated the agreement in the aftermath of the Civil War. Although attempts were made over the years to negotiate a new free trade agreement, until recently a mixture of protectionism and economic *nationalism on the Canadian side militated against the reestablishment of such close trade links with the United States. In the 1980s, however, the Canadian business community became significantly less protectionist, while at the same time a Canadian royal commission recommended in favor of free trade with the United States. The Conservative government of Prime Minister Brian Mulroney took the opportunity to negotiate free trade and successfully defended the agreement in the bitterly contested 1988 election.

The FTA required important concessions from both countries. On investment, the United States sought free investment as a corollary to free trade, and the Canadian government eventually accepted more liberal rules on foreign acquisitions and an obligation to treat new U.S. investors on the same basis as Canadian investors. On dispute settlement, Canada sought strong judicial procedures to lessen the impact of U.S. retaliation against alleged unfair trade actions by Canada. The U.S. government resisted any abridgment of its right to take unilateral action against Canadian unfair trade practices such as government subsidies or sales at less than full market value (i.e., dumping). The final agreement established the right of individuals in one nation to participate in judicial reviews of actions against unfair trade taken by the other nation. This is a small but important reduction of unilateral policy making and is a step toward a more rules-based international trade regime.

Proponents of the FTA in Canada argued that the economic effects of the agreement would advantage the nation, while opponents objected to the reduction of the government's capacity to intervene in the economy. In the United States, the agreement was supported because it maintained momentum toward trade liberalization, although critics contended that it would weaken commitment to the multilateral GATT system. In both Canada and the United States, the FTA was a manifestation of the philosophy of the 1980s of reducing government regulation over the economy.

(See also PROTECTION.)

Marc Gold and David Leyton-Brown, *Trade-offs on Free Trade: The Canada-U.S. Free Trade Agreement* (Toronto, 1988). Gilbert R. Winham, *Trading with Canada: The Canada-U.S. Free Trade Agreement* (New York, 1988). Peter Morici, ed., *Making Free Trade Work: The Canada-U.S. Agreement* (New York, 1990).

GILBERT R. WINHAM

U.S. FOREIGN POLICY. See AMERICAN FOREIGN POLICY.

U.S.–LATIN AMERICAN RELATIONS. The history of U.S.–Latin American relations generally confirms *Thucydides' observation that large countries will do what they will and small countries will accept what they must, and so the analysis of inter-American relations must begin with the identification of U.S. interests in the region. These interests were first identified early in the nineteenth century, when England threatened to seize Spanish Florida and use it as a base to attack the *United States. As an act of national defense, in 1811 Congress responded by adopting the No-Transfer Resolution, the first substantial statement of U.S. policy toward Latin America. What began as an effort to keep the British out of Florida soon expanded when, in the early 1820s, the Holy Alliance authorized France to assist Spain in recovering her American colonies. This led to the *Monroe Doctrine, the cognitive bedrock of U.S. policy toward Latin America. Since that time the fundamental interest of the United States in its relations with Latin America has been to exclude extrahemispheric rivals from the region. Within this geopolitical paradigm of strategic denial, other interests—many motivated by the drive for economic advantage—have been subordinate but often complementary.

Because strategic denial has directed the attention of U.S. officials to the analysis of the intentions and behavior of extrahemispheric rivals, Washington's policy toward Latin America has rarely focused upon Latin Americans per se, but upon what extrahemispheric rivals might do in Latin America that would affect the *security of the United States. This view made good sense early in the nineteenth century, when Latin America was not much more than a large hunk of territory: sparsely populated by a few million humans divided into several mutually incomprehensible castes, the notoriously unstable nations of the region lacked all but the most rudimentary forms of political organization.

Over the years since the early nineteenth century, however, Latin American states have slowly emerged as independent actors on the world stage. The principal U.S. response has been to create an inter-American system to enlist the support of Latin Americans in preserving the paradigm of strategic denial. Although the initial steps were taken in the final quarter of the nineteenth century, the experience of *World War II was especially important in convincing U.S. policy makers of the need for the cooperation of Latin Americans to exclude extra-hemispheric rivals. It led to the first formal U.S. peacetime mutual security alliance, the 1947 Inter-American Treaty of Reciprocal Assistance, which firmly attached Latin America to the U.S. pole. In return for their nominal allegiance, Latin Americans extracted from the United States 1) a formal pledge of nonintervention, and 2) consent to the creation of institutions to regulate the inter-American system. Foremost among these institutions was the *Organization of American States (OAS), created in 1948 by the Act of Bogotá to replace the amorphous Pan American Union.

Although the United States has continued to intervene regularly in Latin America, and although the OAS and its ancillary organizations are weak, the result of these two concessions has been to strengthen Latin Americans when conflicts arise with the United States. They have redefined how members *should* act, and made deviations from expected behavior increasingly costly. One cost has been to galvanize Latin American resistance to deviations in U.S. policy, as the Contadora and Esquipulas peace processes suggest.

Formed at a summit meeting held on the Panamanian island of Contadora in early 1983, the Contadora Group (Colombia, Mexico, Panama, and Venezuela) pointedly excluded the United States; indeed, many of the twenty-one Contadora principles ran directly counter to U.S. policy in Central America. Although Contadora was designed in large measure to structure the process of diplomatic bargaining between the U.S. and *Sandinista Nicaragua, it had the effect of restricting Washington's freedom of maneuver in Central America. Similarly, the "Procedure for the Establishment of a Firm and Lasting Peace in Central America" (known as the Esquipulas II accords after the Guatemalan town where the five Central American chiefs of state met in mid-1987 to plan a process of political reconciliation) also pointedly excluded the United States and restricted Washington's freedom by designating, *inter alia*, a date after which it became illegal for any

state to assist insurgent movements such as the Nicaraguan *contras.

Latin America's growing autonomy can also be seen in the content of the post–Cold War inter-American policy agenda, which consists of issues such as *drug trafficking, *international debt, illegal migration, *democratic transitions, *human rights, poverty, economic *development, and trade. Given the continuing revolutions in communications and transportation, the 450 million people in the region will be in ever-more-intimate contact with U.S. citizens. Latin America is no longer an inert piece of territory.

In addition to emerging Latin American autonomy, a second structural change has also been occurring: a long-term process of democratization in U.S. public policy making. The rapidity of change since World War II has been especially striking. It was not easy to identify this process during the 1940s and 1950s, however, and it was only in the 1960s that sufficient space existed in public opinion for disaffected citizens to criticize Washington's tendency to interpret instability in the *Third World as an example of communist adventurism. Opposition to the *Vietnam War became the principal manifestation of this disaffection, but the erosion of support for *containment was also evident elsewhere.

The partisan debate that reached a fever pitch in the 1980s over the content of U.S. policy toward Central America was part of this process of democratization. It was produced by the slow incorporation of new groups of U.S. citizens into the policy-making process. Only a few decades ago, a small handful of officials in Washington were the only relevant participants. Today, even a minor policy issue is likely to involve a bewildering array of official participants, and major policy issues involve the public at all levels of government.

Because there are more participants, there is more diversity of opinion. This diversity may not seem immediately evident, for the policy-relevant ideological spectrum remains fairly narrow in Washington. But when *foreign policy goes beyond those issues that are amenable to a quick fix, as it did in Central America in the 1980s, then the diversity becomes increasingly obvious. The longer time frame permits the mobilization of the liberal foreign policy community—the citizens who emerged in the 1960s to anchor the left end of the U.S. political spectrum, creating institutions (like *Amnesty International, Americas Watch, the Washington Office on Latin America, and dozens of church groups) to structure their dissent. These liberals invariably lose simple up-or-down votes on issues like the 1989 invasion of Panama. When given sufficient time, however, they now have the power to stymie virtually any major foreign policy initiative to which they are strongly opposed.

Quite apart from the growing autonomy of Latin America and the democratization of the U.S. policy-making process, changes in *international relations also challenge the utility of strategic denial. One of these is the nature of warfare, whose history can be written as a continuous adjustment between technological change, on the one hand, and the significance of geographic proximity, on the other. Our most distant ancestors needed to be within an arm's distance of an adversary in order to inflict physical damage, but soon wooden clubs permitted rivals to strike one another from a slight distance. Not long thereafter the availability of rocks led to the discovery that one could launch a weapon rather than swing it, and with that the die was cast: all military history since then is little more than a discussion of the changing tactics and strategies surrounding the introduction of ever-more-sophisticated projectiles.

One consequence of the increased sophistication of offensive weapons has been the increased sophistication of defensive strategies. In the 1820s, the United States was vulnerable to attack from Latin America, and at this historical moment strategic denial earned its status as a paradigm by providing policy makers with a framework to address a problem they considered acute. Over two centuries, however, the changing nature of warfare has slowly but inexorably rendered less compelling the significance of geographic proximity and, hence, the rationale behind strategic denial.

A second change in international relations lies in the shifting standards of "success" in international relations. For most of human history, the tribe or nation that could bring the largest amount of physical power to bear on a battlefield could carry the day. For nearly half a century after the end of World War II, the Soviet Union and the United States were content to define "success" in terms of this strategy, with the focus upon the use of limited force to subdue a militarily primitive Third World nation allied with a rival *superpower. In the United States during the 1980s, this strategy was called the Reagan Doctrine.

Meanwhile, other important nations decided to define success differently. Instead of investing in physical power, these nations placed their resources in civilian research and development, education, health care, and other programs to improve the productivity and the quality of life of their citizens. The results of this redefinition are evident: the United States retains the largest arsenal on earth, but its citizens no longer even pretend to have the best medical care, the highest education levels, or the longest life expectancy. By committing its resources to the outmoded global version of strategic denial—containment—the United States has slowly dropped down the list of developed countries.

In sum, several changes in the structure of inter-American relations have combined to render strategic denial an anachronistic paradigm for U.S. policy toward Latin America at the end of the twentieth century. The 1990s is therefore a transitional decade, as officials in Washington develop a new paradigm to orient U.S.–Latin American relations in the twenty-first century.

A realist would argue that the only appropriate framework would be one that focuses upon protecting contemporary U.S. interests as they are affected by Latin Americans. That would imply the development of a policy toward Latin America similar to that which guides U.S. relations with the industrialized countries of Europe—a policy of patient *diplomacy based upon mutual respect but frequently conflicting interests.

Standing squarely in the way of the development of such a policy is an important residual aspect of strategic denial, however: a denigration of Latin Americans. For nearly two centuries, U.S. policy makers had to get Latin Americans out of the way so that they could focus upon the designs of extra-hemispheric rivals. This was accomplished by conceiving of Latin Americans as inferior human beings with inferior social systems: economies that are always in disarray, politics that are always chaotic, and a general level of culture that has been in decline since pre-Columbian times. At its intellectual core, the traditional paradigm of strategic denial rests upon this premise of cultural inferiority: because Latin Americans are disorganized and degenerate, they cannot defend themselves from outside attack or subversion; they need the help of the United States.

Although the *Cold War is over, this cultural prejudice remains as a daunting obstacle to the replacement of strategic denial with a framework similar to the realist paradigm that governs U.S. policy toward Europe. While the structural changes described above cannot be ignored, they will be filtered by a cultural prejudice that strongly influences the style and methods used by the United States to protect its interests in Latin America. Just as President George *Bush's characterization of Nicaraguan President Daniel Ortega as "an unwelcome dog at a garden party" indicates how close U.S. cultural prejudices lie to the surface, so the U.S. invasion of Panama in 1989 indicates how difficult it will be to change established patterns of behavior.

(See also AMERICAN FOREIGN POLICY; BAY OF PIGS INVASION; CUBAN MISSILE CRISIS; INTERVENTION; LATIN AMERICAN REGIONAL ORGANIZATIONS; REALISM.)

Samuel Flagg Bemis, *The Latin-American Policy of the United States: An Historical Interpretation* (New York, 1943). James W. Gantenbein, ed., *The Evolution of Our Latin-American Policy: A Documentary Record* (New York, 1950). G. Pope Atkins, *Latin America in the International Political System*, 2d ed. (Boulder, Colo., 1989).

LARS SCHOULTZ

UZBEKISTAN. See COMMONWEALTH OF INDEPENDENT STATES.

V

VANUATU. See PACIFIC ISLANDS.

VARGAS, Getúlio. *Brazil's foremost political leader in this century, Getúlio Vargas governed for over two decades and left a strong legacy. He wrought basic changes in Brazil's politics, economy, and society, while his own style of leadership evolved from traditional to populist.

Born in 1883 in Rio Grande do Sul, Vargas was raised in a prominent family. Disillusioned as an army cadet, he enrolled in law school. Upon graduation in 1907, he was appointed district attorney in Porto Alegre by party chiefs, and soon he won election to the state legislature.

Vargas took his first federal post in 1923, when he entered Congress, and a year later he was named chief of the state delegation because of his loyalty and skills of conciliation. After several years in national politics, Vargas was chosen to be governor of Rio Grande do Sul in 1928. His administration was remarkable for its bipartisan character and experiments with economic *planning.

In 1930 Vargas decided to run for president on a ticket supported by Rio Grande and Minas Gerais. When their candidate lost to the government candidate, younger politicians in the two states mounted an armed revolt. A reluctant revolutionist, Vargas nonetheless assumed leadership of the successful revolt and was sworn in as provisional president in November 1930.

During his first administration (1930–1937) Vargas was severely challenged by the depression, praetorian forces, a civil war in São Paulo, and former allies in Rio Grande. He remained in power by forming a new national alliance based on the army, loyal governors, and labor. During most of his first term, Vargas attempted to rule democratically, holding elections in 1933 and 1934, promulgating a liberal constitution in 1934, and working with Congress. Still, *democracy appeared chaotic in the mid-1930s and Vargas conspired to increase his own powers.

After convincing the army high command that he needed greater authority to preserve the nation, Vargas executed a coup in November 1937. He disbanded Congress, deposed a few state governors, and gave the country a new regime, named the Estado Novo after Salazar's in Portugal. He burned state flags to symbolize federal dominance and promulgated a *constitution pieced together from fascist models. In fact, Vargas did not use the Constitution but governed autocratically. His lawyers reworked labor legislation into a code, and social security expanded to cover most urban workers. Big business received favored treatment, as the government sought to spur the economy by all possible means. These measures alienated liberals but won Vargas the support of industrialists and workers alike.

After the outbreak of World War II, Vargas initially flirted with the Axis but eventually entered the war on the side of the Allies in 1942 and sent an army division to Italy in 1944. His aim was to reap economic benefits for Brazil in terms of trade, foreign investment, and lend-lease assistance. Meanwhile, politicians at home criticized the dictatorship and called for elections. Vargas agreed in early 1945 and soon founded two parties. But before the campaign could get under way, the army high command deposed Vargas and held elections without him.

From his self-imposed exile at the family ranch, Vargas easily won election to the Senate. He soon tired of defending his administration in a hostile Congress, however, and decided to run for president. After an arduous campaign—the first modern one in Brazil's history—Vargas won a landslide victory, largely on his reputation as "father of the poor" and defender of Brazil's patrimony. When inaugurated in 1951, Vargas pledged his administration to an ambitious program of economic growth and independence from foreign capital. He stressed government planning, higher income for labor, and ownership of basic industries. He created Petrobras, a government petroleum monopoly, and several development agencies. Vargas soon ran into balance-of-payments problems, however, and found himself stymied by political opponents. The country had grown too complex for his traditional administrative style. Threatened with a military coup in August 1954, he committed suicide rather than suffer another disgrace. The working and lower middle classes believed him a martyr and revered his memory.

The Vargas era brought major changes to the country. Brazil industrialized rapidly with official encouragement, a stance called "developmental nationalism." The work force moved to cities and became unionized. São Paulo, Rio, and Belo Horizonte formed an urban-industrial heartland. Governmental authority centralized in Rio, and the army gained a monopoly on the use of violence. Women and 18-year-olds gained the vote in 1932, and by the 1950s mass electoral politics had replaced the previous limited democracy. Although national parties mediated elections and managed congressional alliances, presidential elections became contests between populists—charismatic leaders pledged to help the masses and reform society. Vargas initiated most of these changes, and as late as the 1980s younger politicians still invoked his name. Vargas's long career embodies Brazil's transition from a backward, rural society to a modern industrial one.

(See also POPULISM.)

John W. F. Dulles, *Vargas of Brazil: A Political Biography* (Austin, Tex., 1967). Paulo Brandi, *Vargas: da vida para a história* (Rio de Janeiro, 1983).

MICHAEL L. CONNIFF

VATICAN CITY STATE. The *Roman Catholic church is a peculiar type of society in that its international juridical standing rests on its spiritual sovereignty. There are three distinct yet interdependent realities: the Vatican City State, the Holy See, and the Universal Church.

Until 1870, the temporal domain of the Church included the Papal States, which ceased to exist from 1870 to 1929. The Lateran Treaty, signed between *Italy and the Holy See on 11 February 1929, created the Vatican City and "recognizes the sovereignty of the Holy See" (Art. 2) over this atypical state. The function of this quasi-symbolic, tiny temporal sovereignty is to ensure that the Catholic church has the minimum autonomy necessary in order to freely exercise its spiritual mission. To this end, the Italian government "guarantees" its territorial integrity. As such, the Vatican City State is a member of nine intergovernmental organizations and of many nongovernmental organizations. Nevertheless, this minuscule state is only a recent development in the history of the papacy: it is not because he is the representative of a state of forty-four hectares (109 acres) that the Sovereign Pontiff is welcomed abroad and maintains diplomatic relations, but rather because he is at the head of the Holy See, which owes its sovereignty in the international order to its spiritual mission. This state is not a nation, for one does not belong to it by *jus sanguinis* or *jus soli,* but by *jus officii.* The Holy See enjoys a status *sui generis* in *international law.

According to Canon 361 of the new Code of Canon Law promulgated in 1983 by *John Paul II, the Holy See designates "not only the Roman Pontiff, but also . . . the office of the Secretary of State . . . and the other institutions of the Roman Curia." These are the official organs of the Vatican City State.

Following changes instituted in 1988, the office of the Secretary of State, which is directed by a cardinal chosen at the Pope's discretion, was divided into two sections. The first, called the Section of General Affairs, is responsible for relations with international organizations as well as with the personnel of the pontifical administration. The other section is in charge of "relations with states," thus replacing the Council for Public Affairs of the Church. Today 117 states have diplomatic representatives assigned to the Holy See: the U.S. representative is among the most recent arrivals, having been named by the Reagan administration.

Since 1929, numerous conventions attached to the Lateran Treaty have been signed. In addition, Article 7 of the Constitution of 27 December 1947 of the Italian Republic recognizes the validity of the accords agreed to by the Kingdom of Italy. Over the years, this agreement has passed from the status of a treaty giving the Vatican "guarantees" that could always be taken back by the Italian state to a bilateral accord regulated by international law.

More recently, a revision of the Lateran Accords was drafted and was signed on 18 February 1984. This agreement abrogates the first article of the treaty, which made Catholicism "the only religion of the [Italian] state." This formulation is in accord with what one finds in the accords passed during the same period with Spain, Colombia, and Ecuador. The Catholic religion asks to be recognized as a social reality of the highest importance not only because of the weight of history but also owing to its current vitality. Nevertheless, it no longer seeks to be treated as a monopolistic religion; henceforth, in a pluralist society the Catholic religion acknowledges respect on a juridical level for those who profess another religion or who manifest different ideological convictions.

(See also RELIGION AND POLITICS; SECULARIZATION.)

Higinus Cardinale, *The Holy See and the International Order* (Gerrards Cross, U.K., 1976). Pierre Blet, *Histoire de la Représentation Diplomatique du Saint-Siège, des origines à l'aube du XIXe siècle,* Collectanea Archivi Vaticani 9 (Città del Vaticano, 1982). Roland Minnerath, *L'Eglise et les Etats concordataires (1846–1981). La souveraineté spirituelle* (Paris, 1983).

HENRI MADELIN

VATICAN II. When on 25 January 1959 Pope John XXIII announced plans for a convocation of the ecumenical council, cardinals in attendance listened in stupefied silence. After the proclamation at the Vatican I council nearly a century earlier concerning the infallibility of the pope, the era of councils had seemed to be at an end.

On 11 October 1962 the Second Vatican Council was opened at Saint Peter's in Rome; its four annual sessions would bring together, by December 1965, over 2,000 "conciliar fathers" with voting rights as well as observers and lay experts. Vatican II was an extraordinary process of self-reflection for the church and proof of the cultural diversity of a Catholicism in which the Western churches had become the minority. Delegations prepared 70 books and 2,100 printed pages of documents to submit for the approval of the council. The votes that took place revealed a profound separation between the majority of 1,800 to 1,900 voters who wished to rethink the church's role in the modern world and a minority of 300 priests (at the most) who relentlessly opposed any reformation of the institution. This fundamental conflict concerning fidelity to tradition continues to divide the church nearly thirty years after Vatican II.

Conforming to the position sketched by John XXIII and assumed by his successor, Paul VI, the majority gave the council a resolutely pastoral and ecumenical (rather than doctrinal) style. The entire work of the council centered on the fundamental question "What is the church?" This question brought to the fore two distinctions between central theological traditions. The first and oldest, following the Pauline tradition, presents a mystical conception of the church as a spiritual community. The second, which became dominant in the thirteenth century during the papal struggle to contain the expansion of royal powers, was solidified during the French Revolution into a radically antimodern vision of the institution as a hierarchical society with a calling to exercise its authority directly over all of society. The dogmatic constitution *Lumen Gentium* attempted to transcend this contradiction by developing a vision of the church as the "people of God," in whom the fullness of God's gifts are realized. The council introduced this theological definition of the church nourished by a return to biblical and patristic tradition. In this way, it sought to reorient the functioning of the Roman church and its balance with the modern world.

Among the positions espoused at Vatican II, three deserve particular attention. First, the ecumenical council placed new emphasis on the communal characteristics of the church. It justified in particular the rehabilitation of the role of the laity and stressed the priestly qualities of all baptized Catholics. It also renewed the concept of collegiality, in particular the communion of bishops, to be used to encourage unity among culturally diverse churches.

Second, Vatican II renewed the conception of the church's mission to induce a positive and optimistic view of the world as it moves toward human fulfillment. The pastoral document *Gaudium et Spes* develops forcefully the idea of the "solidarity of the church" across the entire human family.

The third and certainly most original position affirmed by Vatican II was the limitless right of each person to behave according to the dictates of personal conscience, the source of innate knowledge of the good and true. The *Declaration of Religious Liberty* thus inaugurated a new rapport between Catholicism and other religions, Christian and non-

Christian, and atheism. This concept remains at the center of the most serious conflict within the Roman church. The doctrinal change opened a troubled period for the church, one stemming not only from the sometimes clumsy rapidity with which certain reforms were instituted (for example of liturgical matters) or from resistance from institutional structures and those with traditional outlooks, but most significantly from the new ambiguity that marks the relationship between the church and the contemporary world.

In Vatican II the church abandoned its radical condemnation of the world that was born of the Reformation and the Enlightenment and opened itself to the "signs of the times," opposing those who, like Monsignor Lefèbvre, challenge each instance of the church's recognition of positive values in the modern world. Nevertheless, the church did not entirely accept the modern conception of individual autonomy and institutional democracy. Rather, it affirmed in the last instance an account of individual freedom and liberation that comes from God alone. The sensitivity of *John Paul II, an Eastern European pope, to the failure of a *modernity allied to atheism and *totalitarianism leads him to stress this crucial dimension of the modern world. In this sense, his defense of *human rights is certainly bolstered by the ecclesiastical experience of Vatican II, in which he played an active role.

(See also RELIGION AND POLITICS; ROMAN CATHOLIC CHURCH.)

Gustave Martelet, *Les Idées Maîtresses de Vatican II* (Paris, 1985). Peter Hebblethwaite, *Jean XXIII, le Pape du Concile* (Paris, 1988). Joseph Thomas, *Le Concile Vatican II* (Paris, 1989).

DANIÈLE HERVIEU-LÉGER

VENEZUELA. During the nineteenth century, Venezuela was a poor and politically undeveloped state. A series of regionally based strongmen, or *caudillos,* backed by private armies, controlled the central government in Caracas, but never without sporadic challenges from other *caudillos.* Most of the population lived in poverty, ignorance, and fear, although a small elite class amassed some wealth from import businesses or the export of coffee, cocoa, or hides, and negotiated an uneasy coexistence with each government.

Fundamental transformations of Venezuelan politics and economy began during the dictatorship of Juan Vicente Gómez (1908–1935), who finally defeated all other *caudillos* and created an effective national military force. Oil production also began during his rule and expanded so rapidly that Venezuela became the world's largest oil exporter and second-largest producer by 1928. The resulting inflow of wealth strengthened state capacities but also contributed to the growth of a small middle class that began to demand greater participation in politics. These demands were met with brutal repression until the relatively liberal dictatorship of General Medina Angarita (1941–1945), who permitted the rapid organization of mass political parties, trade unions, and peasant leagues. The largest of the new parties, Acción Democrática (AD), joined with junior military officers to overthrow Medina and oversee the country's first popular elections. This democratic regime failed, however, because the Catholic church and conservative interests felt threatened by the anticlerical policies, social *reforms, and electoral dominance of the AD government, and encouraged the military to overthrow it in 1948.

As a result, Venezuela experienced ten more years of dictatorship, this time under Marcos Pérez Jiménez. This government coincided initially with continued oil-fueled economic expansion, which accelerated industrialization, urban migration, and infrastructure development. But when the economy slumped and the dictator was discredited by charges of corruption and electoral fraud in 1957, he was replaced by a military-civilian junta, which inaugurated the current democratic regime.

Since 1958, all Venezuelan presidents have been chosen in fair, direct elections with universal adult suffrage. The first government of this democratic regime faced frequent coup attempts but survived them all. The regime was also threatened by an armed insurgency movement beginning in 1961, but the guerrillas were mostly defeated by 1965 and returned to electoral politics in 1967. *Democracy was fully consolidated by 1969, when the ruling Acción Democrática party recognized its electoral defeat and handed over the presidency to Rafael Caldera of the Partido Social Cristiano (COPEI). These two parties alternated in the presidency for the next three terms.

The success of the transition to democracy owes much to the leadership of Rómulo Betancourt and Rafael Caldera, the founders of AD and COPEI, respectively. In order to prevent a repeat of the polarization that doomed democracy during the 1945–1948 period, the two leaders persuaded their parties to support the Pact of Punto Fijo, which calmed partisan rivalries, removed contentious issues from the political agenda, produced broad support for a common program of reforms, and committed the first presidential candidates to a national unity coalition regardless of the election results.

The stability of Venezuelan democracy also owes much to the nature of the two main parties. While the Social Democratic AD and Christian Democratic COPEI nominally reflect the cleavage between a hegemonic reformist, anticlerical government and its conservative opposition, both parties have since moved towards the center and are now best described as overlapping center-left and center-right parties. There is greater ideological distance between these two parties and the smaller parties, particularly the Movimiento al Socialismo (MAS), a pluralistic splinter from the Communist Party. However, as

AD and COPEI have shared around eighty percent of the legislative vote and ninety percent of the presidential vote since 1973, the cleavage between them is the dominant one. These two parties are also remarkably similar in the support they draw from all regions, classes, ages, and occupational groups. Their ideological proximity has helped preserve the spirit of interparty consultation and consensus established in the Pact of Punto Fijo.

AD and COPEI have also been aggressive in enforcing party discipline in Congress and in controlling other organizations for partisan purposes. Almost all leaders of trade unions, student governments, professional associations, and most other organizations are nominated and elected by party slates and tend to defer to their national party leaders' directives when asked. At first only the church, the military, and business associations escaped party penetration, but in recent years neighborhood associations, environmental groups, and *human rights lobbies have attempted to establish their independence. Thorough party penetration helped party leaders achieve their aim of moderating conflict in the interests of stability, but it also bred frustration with the nation's stifled organizational life. Despite reforms instituting direct elections for governors and mayors in 1989, frustration continued and, coupled with bitterness toward corrupt government officials during an extended economic decline, led to widespread rioting in 1989 and an unsuccessful coup attempt in February 1992.

Although Venezuela's socioeconomic inequalities are still pronounced, its per capita GDP has been by far the highest in Latin America for several decades thanks to the oil industry, which provides ninety percent of its export earnings and fifty to seventy-five percent of its central government revenues. *Nationalization of the oil industry in 1976 did not change this basic fact. The public sector grew quite large during the years of high oil prices (1974–1976, 1979–1981) in order to create jobs for party supporters, subsidize producers and consumers, expand social benefits, and finance ambitious industrialization and infrastructure projects, but without taking adequate precautions to prevent indebtedness or wrenching adjustment during years of falling oil prices (1977–1978, 1981–1987). Venezuela has remained at peace with its neighbors, although it has lingering border disputes with Guyana and Colombia and there is considerable resentment of the many illegal Colombian and West Indian immigrants. It has become an influential leader in Central America and the Caribbean Basin by placing investments there, offering mediation, granting economic assistance, subsidizing oil shipments, and providing air links to remote islands. Relations with the United States have been friendly, as the United States views Venezuela as the model of a democratic, reformist alternative to Cuba.

(See also DEMOCRATIC TRANSITIONS; ORGANI-

ZATION OF PETROLEUM EXPORTING COUNTRIES; U.S.–LATIN AMERICAN RELATIONS.)

David Eugene Blank, *Venezuela: Politics in a Petroleum Republic* (New York, 1984). John D. Martz and David J. Myers, eds., *Venezuela: The Democratic Experience,* 2d ed. (New York, 1986).

MICHAEL COPPEDGE

VERSAILLES, TREATY OF. See WORLD WAR I.

VIETNAM. The Socialist Republic of Vietnam (SRV), with a population estimated to number over 66 million in 1991, is the world's twelfth most populous state. The SRV was formed following military reunification in April 1975 and national elections held in July 1976, which formally united north and south.

Vietnam is situated on the rugged eastern part of the Indochinese peninsula. Laos and Cambodia lie to the west, China to the north. Vietnam's population is concentrated in two rice-growing areas, the Red River delta in the north and the Mekong River delta in the south. These are joined by the Annamese Cordillera range, which has been likened to a bamboo carrying pole from which the two rice baskets—the river deltas—are suspended.

Vietnam is an agrarian society with over three-quarters of the population living in rural areas and engaged in agricultural pursuits. An estimated eighty-five percent of the total population are ethnic Vietnamese. Vietnam's minority population consists of Chinese, Khmers, and a variety of highland ethnic groups. The Vietnamese people adhere to a syncretic religious tradition which is a mixture of Mahayana *Buddhism, Taoism, and *Confucianism. There is a substantial Catholic minority and a small Islamic community. Most of the highlanders are animists. Vietnam has also developed its own unique religious traditions, that of Hoa Hao and Cao Dai, which are strong in the Mekong delta and the area northwest of Saigon.

The emergence of a communist regime in Vietnam has been the end product of a prolonged process of socioeconomic transformation and *modernization precipitated by the corrosive impact of French colonialism on traditional Vietnamese society. In 1930 *Ho Chi Minh founded the Vietnam Communist Party (VCP), a modern political organization dedicated to revolutionary ends. In August 1945 Ho seized power and proclaimed the formation of the Democratic Republic of Vietnam (DRV). France opposed this move and a bitter eight-year war ensued.

In 1954, Vietnam was partitioned and the VCP took charge in the north. The VCP quickly established a "people's democracy." This was a mono-organizational state in which the party penetrated and controlled all organizations including the bureaucracy and the military. Society at large was grouped into mass organizations (for *peasants,

workers, women, and youth) and special interest groups (for artists, journalists, intellectuals, and various religions) which formed the constituent parts of the Vietnam Fatherland Front, an umbrella organization controlled by the VCP.

After assuming state power, the VCP moved to organize production along lines laid out by earlier *Communist Party states. In 1954–1955 Vietnam conducted a Chinese-style *land reform program which went badly off course. In addition to many innocent victims whose land was confiscated, an estimated 15,000 persons were executed. In 1956–1957, the regime admitted its mistakes, dismissed the officials concerned, and launched a "rectification of errors" campaign. The VCP then resumed its advance toward Marxism-Leninism. In the 1960s, peasant farmers were organized into agricultural production cooperatives in which the major means of production were collectivized. At the same time all heavy and light industry was nationalized and placed under central state control. Handicraft production was likewise organized collectively. The constitutional structure of the DRV initially drew its authority from the 1945 independence constitution. This was replaced by a more orthodox socialist state constitution in 1960. This document enshrined the leading role of the party and Marxist-Leninist *ideology. It also established a state structure which copied from Chinese and Soviet constitutional practice. The highest legislative body, the National Assembly, was in fact a rubber stamp controlled and directed by the VCP. All facets of the economy were placed under rigid central control under a State Planning Commission.

In the mid- to late 1950s North Vietnam became the beneficiary of large-scale Chinese and Soviet aid. Priority was now placed on developing an industrial base, and this emphasis was reflected in the First Three-Year Plan (1958–1960) and the First Five-Year Plan (1961–1965). In September 1960, the VCP's Third National Congress decided to step up support for the Communist-led "war of national liberation" in the south. This led eventually to retaliation by the United States, and much of North Vietnam's industry and infrastructure was destroyed in air attacks during 1965–1968.

After the end of the *Vietnam War in 1975, Vietnam's Communist leaders moved quickly to integrate the south into existing northern political structures. The 1960 DRV constitution served as the legal basis for rule until replaced by a new document in 1980. Former members of the Republic of Vietnam and its armed forces were placed in reeducation camps. Southern industry was nationalized and efforts were made to collectivize southern agriculture. In 1976, the VCP adopted Vietnam's Second Five-Year Plan, which once again gave priority to industrialization. The plan was later criticized by party reformers for reflecting a "hasty Great Leap Forward mentality." The south has never been fully incorporated into the SRV economically, and the north-south divide remains an important factor in contemporary Vietnamese politics.

Vietnam's endeavor to build *socialism in the post–Vietnam War years was short-lived. Relations with neighboring Cambodia and its ally, China, deteriorated to the point of open war. Natural disasters in 1977 and 1978, coupled with gross economic mismanagement, produced an economic crisis of mammoth proportions. Large numbers of ethnic Chinese and southern Vietnamese began to flee the country by boat or by land into southern China.

In late 1978 Vietnam invaded and occupied Cambodia. In early 1979 China retaliated by attacking and laying waste Vietnam's northern frontier region. Vietnam was also subject to an aid and trade embargo by neighboring states. This was supported by Western countries formerly sympathetic to Vietnam. As a result, Vietnam became totally dependent on the Soviet Union and Eastern Europe.

Just prior to its invasion of Cambodia, Vietnam and the Soviet Union signed a twenty-five-year Treaty of Friendship and Cooperation. In the aftermath of China's attack on Vietnam, the Soviet Union greatly increased its military aid to Vietnam. In short order, the regular Vietnamese army grew in size to the fifth largest in the world, numbering over 1.2 million. Vietnam's air and naval forces were also modernized at this time. However, the military remained primarily an infantry force ill suited for conventional offensive operations. The air force was best suited for a defensive role, while the navy never developed a blue water capacity.

The combined effects of the Third Indochina War, coupled with distortions in the Vietnamese economy caused by dependence on Soviet subsidies and misguided economic priorities, further deepened Vietnam's socioeconomic crisis. This provoked cries for *reform from within the party itself as early as August–September 1979. In the early 1980s some members of the VCP pushed for a reform package based on market mechanisms and price incentives. These efforts faced stiff opposition from party conservatives, and it was only in 1986, at the VCP's Sixth National Congress, that Vietnam formally endorsed "renovation" as national policy. Vietnam's shift to the reformist path followed similar developments in the Soviet Union and was encouraged and reinforced by *Gorbachev's policies.

Vietnam's efforts to reform the economy have resulted in restructuring of the central planning apparatus, greater decentralization, and increased emphasis on the market mechanism and individual initiative. Efforts to attract foreign investment and aid have met with limited success for two main reasons. First, despite Vietnam's withdrawal of its regular military forces from Cambodia in September 1989, it is still subject to an aid embargo. The restoration of *foreign aid, as indeed normal relations, is contingent upon a comprehensive political settlement of the Cambodian conflict. Second, economic assistance to Vietnam has fallen drastically as the former Soviet Union itself faces mounting economic problems. Vietnam has been forced to demobilize nearly half of its standing army and to conduct trade with Moscow in hard currency at world market prices.

Following the dramatic upheavals in Eastern and Central Europe in 1989, Vietnam has taken steps to clamp down on dissent from within. Party leaders have declared their opposition to *pluralism and multiparty *democracy. While there is evidence that the VCP is facing a crisis of *legitimacy, there is little evidence of the emergence of a movement of sufficient scope and popularity to bring about a change in regime. The prime advocates for political change are members of the party itself, and they have been either imprisoned or expelled. The average Vietnamese, it would appear, is more concerned with the economic well-being of the family group and in this respect is increasingly emboldened to act without reference to party direction in economic matters.

Vietnam once prided itself as being Southeast Asia's first outpost of socialism and proclaimed that relations with the Soviet Union were a cornerstone of its *foreign policy. Vietnam signed treaties of friendship and cooperation with neighboring Laos and Cambodia and proclaimed these "special relations" as a "law of development." These claims ran directly counter to China's self-perceived interests and role in the region and lie at the heart of Sino-Vietnamese differences. The crumbling of the Soviet cornerstone has meant that Vietnam can no longer rely on the former Soviet Union to counterbalance Chinese pressures. In order to avoid becoming an isolated outpost of socialism in Southeast Asia, Vietnam's leaders have set for themselves the task of developing a more omnidirectional foreign policy for the 1990s, one which would see the normalization of relations with all important external actors—especially China, Japan, and the United States.

(See also COMMAND ECONOMY; COMMUNISM; DECOLONIZATION; LENINISM; MARXISM; NATIONAL LIBERATION MOVEMENTS; REVOLUTION; SOVIET FOREIGN POLICY.)

Melanie Beresford, *Vietnam: Politics, Economics and Society* (London, 1988). David G. Marr and Christine P. White, eds., *Postwar Vietnam: Dilemmas in Socialist Development*, Cornell University Southeast Asia Program (Ithaca, N.Y., 1988). Carlyle A. Thayer, *War by Other Means: National Liberation and Revolution in Viet-Nam* (Boston, 1989).

CARLYLE A. THAYER

VIETNAM WAR. Fashioned from stark slabs of black granite, the Vietnam Veterans Memorial in Washington, D.C., perfectly represents America's collective memory of its longest *war and first defeat. The memorial, like the memory, is both somber and ambiguous.

On the polished face of the memorial appear the names of some 58,000 U.S. military personnel who died in Indochina. This was the greatest cost of the war to the *United States. There were others as well: the bitterness of over 3 million *Vietnam veterans who returned to more scorn than gratitude from their fellow citizens; the inflation that followed years of deficit financing to help cover more than $150 billion in war expenses; bruising divisions within American society about responsibility for the nation's defeat and the devastation of the peoples and lands of Indochina; and a public cynicism about government, reinforced by the *Watergate scandal, that was to mark U.S. politics for many years.

American involvement in the conflicts of Indochina was driven by a doctrinal commitment to the *containment of *communism. The goal was absolute, but it was pursued through incremental, compromise measures. From Harry *Truman to Richard *Nixon, no president could find a formula for victory at a cost in lives and resources he thought the public would endure or U.S. interests would justify. Yet throughout the war, even after it became broadly unpopular, *public opinion always opposed withdrawal if it would lead to defeat. Thus, from 1950 until 1975, as the military and political tide ran first against the French and then against a series of non-Communist governments in Vietnam, Cambodia, and Laos, American actions were sufficient only to postpone defeat.

American ambivalence about the French colonial war in Vietnam turned to active support after the triumph of communism in China in 1949. As Washington intervened in Korea in June 1950, President Truman ordered the first significant military aid to the French forces in Indochina. By 1954, the United States was covering some eighty percent of their costs.

As the French neared defeat at Dien Bien Phu in April 1954, French and American military leaders recommended a massive U.S. air strike to relieve the besieged garrison. After consulting with congressional leaders, President Dwight D. *Eisenhower refused unless Paris accelerated the independence of its Indochinese colonies and the British agreed to join in the operation. Neither condition was fulfilled.

While acquiescing in the French defeat and agreeing not to disturb the Geneva Accords (July 1954) that divided Vietnam pending elections two years later, the Eisenhower administration soon moved to buttress the anti-Communist government of Ngo Dinh Diem in the south. It formed the *Southeast Asia Treaty Organization (SEATO); sent American military advisers and massive quantities of military and economic aid to the Republic of Vietnam (South Vietnam); and backed Diem's stand against holding the scheduled 1956 elections.

Like his predecessor, President John F. *Kennedy avoided sending U.S. combat troops to Vietnam. But the unpopular Diem government faltered in its war against a burgeoning insurgency and Washington greatly increased its assistance and the number of American military advisers. As U.S. advisers began to accompany government battalions into combat and took casualties, Vietnam emerged as a public issue in the United States.

By the late summer of 1963, the strategic hamlets program (modeled on a successful British *counterinsurgency program in Malaya) was failing, military operations were mixed in their results, and Diem was under increasing pressure from Buddhist groups. Kennedy encouraged a *coup d'état by South Vietnamese military leaders. Diem was assassinated during the coup (1 November 1963). His removal produced an extended period of political instability in Saigon, lasting until the presidency of Nguyen Van Thieu (1967–1975).

President Lyndon B. *Johnson cautiously increased the number of U.S. advisers in 1964 and, in August, responded to an attack by North Vietnamese patrol boats on an American destroyer in the Tonkin Gulf with the first U.S. bombing raid against the Democratic Republic of Vietnam (North Vietnam). (The raid followed claims of a second PT boat attack that were never substantiated.) Johnson used the incident to gain from *Congress a nearly unanimous resolution authorizing him "to take all necessary measures" to defend U.S. forces and prevent further aggression in the region.

After his landslide reelection in 1964, Johnson moved more vigorously to head off a developing military defeat of Saigon's forces by the National Liberation Front, which was receiving increasing assistance from the North Vietnamese. In December, American bombing of infiltration routes in Laos (Operation Barrel Roll) was initiated. In February 1965, Johnson ordered a bombing campaign against North Vietnam (Rolling Thunder). This campaign was escalated incrementally over the coming years, in an effort to break Hanoi's will as well as to interdict the flow of supplies and soldiers to the south. The bases for U.S. airplanes were vulnerable to attack, and Johnson soon ordered two marine battalions to guard duty. By late spring 1965, Saigon's forces in central Vietnam were near collapse. Washington sent more American troops and by summer they were in combat.

During 1966 and 1967, American forces were gradually increased to some 500,000, matched by increasing numbers of North Vietnamese forces infiltrating the south. Each, with its southern allies, waged a brutal main force war of attrition designed more to inflict casualties than to gain and hold territory. Meanwhile, a *guerrilla war in the villages was opposed by a massive, American-supported pacification program that relied on local militia and economic aid efforts. As a result of both wars, well over one million Vietnamese were forced to leave their ancestral homes for the crowded, economically pressed cities. Throughout this period, both Hanoi and Washington proclaimed their willingness to negotiate an end to the conflict, but each insisted on its own terms.

As casualties mounted, U.S. public opinion began to turn against the war. On 31 January 1968 (the Vietnamese lunar New Year, called Tet), the National Liberation Front and the North Vietnamese army launched attacks throughout the south, including a dramatic assault on the American embassy in Saigon. While the offensive fell short militarily, it shocked an American public already skeptical of Johnson's claims of progress. Attacked by the *Left for intervention and by the *Right for a failure to prevail, in late March Johnson announced that he would not seek reelection. He ordered new efforts at a negotiated solution and put a cap on the U.S. force level at under 550,000.

Promising to end the war on honorable terms, Richard Nixon won the *presidency of a nation bitterly divided over the war. For the next four years, Nixon pursued a complex strategy. To convince the American public that the end was in sight, he pursued a policy of "Vietnamization" that attempted to strengthen Saigon's military forces while gradually withdrawing American troops.

To convince Hanoi to settle the war on acceptable terms, he ordered a series of military measures: increased bombing in Vietnam; the secret bombing of North Vietnamese sanctuaries in Cambodia; the April 1970 invasion of Cambodia by American and South Vietnamese troops to disrupt these sanctuaries (leading to widespread antiwar demonstrations in the United States and the fatal shooting of four student protesters at Kent State University); a disastrous invasion of Laos (to interdict North Vietnamese supply routes) in early 1971 by South Vietnamese troops; and heavy bombing as well as the mining of Hanoi's harbor, Haiphong, after a new North Vietnamese offensive in April 1972. And to help achieve a settlement, Nixon sought the assistance of Moscow and Beijing, Hanoi's patrons.

The key to ending the war were secret talks in Paris with North Vietnamese representatives. In the summer of 1969 Nixon's national security adviser, Henry *Kissinger, threatened them with punishing, new American military measures if there were no diplomatic breakthrough by 1 November. It did not move Hanoi and Washington failed to follow through on its threat. But the talks continued intermittently for the next three years, producing a compromise agreement between the two exhausted sides in October 1972. Hanoi abandoned its insistence that President Thieu be removed from power and agreed to return U.S. prisoners of war. Washington dropped its long-standing insistence that Hanoi withdraw its forces from South Vietnam when American troops left.

President Thieu balked at these terms. But after Nixon's reelection in November, a renewed bombing attack on North Vietnam in late December, and

a new aid package for the South Vietnamese, the American president insisted that Thieu acquiesce in a renegotiated settlement on essentially the same terms. An ill-defined cease-fire was declared in January 1973 and the remaining American forces were withdrawn.

Both the cease-fire and talks among the Vietnamese on the political future of South Vietnam collapsed, however. In early 1975, hindered by its own poor morale and dwindling American aid, the South Vietnamese army crumbled in the face of a new North Vietnamese offensive. On 30 April 1975, Saigon fell to the Communist forces. The remaining Americans fled before them, without having arranged for the escape of most of the hundreds of thousands of South Vietnamese who had worked with them. Soon thereafter, Phnom Penh, the capital of Cambodia, was taken by the genocidal Khmer Rouge.

For a few years after the war, "Let Us Forget" better described the collective attitude of Americans than "Lest We Forget." But by the 1980s, a series of films and television programs addressed the Vietnam experience. Some found only horror in the war; others found glory in the actions of American soldiers.

Similarly, during the war and after, analysts and political leaders found very different explanations and lessons in the experience. Some found an explanation in their view of a United States bound by its drive for economic advantage in the *Third World and the power of a *military-industrial complex in Washington. Others believed there had been a simple failure of will by American presidents.

Supporters of the presidents who had engaged America in the conflict argued that the war came through an inadvertent stumbling into the Vietnam quagmire. The bureaucracy either misled its leaders or failed to warn them. But critics of this view pointed to the information available within the government, from the start, about the difficulties of engagement.

Supporters of Congress blamed an "imperial presidency" for the disaster. But critics of Congress, arguing that it must share in the blame, pointed to the passage of the Tonkin Gulf Resolution and the failure of Congress to use the power of the purse to influence presidents' behavior.

The two most influential lessons of the war helped shape the general policies of the first two postwar presidencies. For President Jimmy *Carter and many of his advisers, Vietnam was primarily a conceptual error, the result of a rigid American commitment to the containment of communism everywhere, without due regard to local realities and specific U.S. interests. Vietnam tragically illustrated the limits of American power in a changing world. To President Ronald *Reagan and many of his advisers, the United States had been right to intervene in Vietnam. The failure was not conceptual but political: a liberal press and Congress had helped create a national loss of will that made the pursuit of victory impossible. The limits to American power were primarily self-imposed.

A crucial difference between them was thus the question of whether the war was winnable. Many conservatives, pointing to the incremental nature of U.S. military involvement, Johnson's limits on the bombing campaign, and the failure of Congress to allow generous quantities of aid to the anti-Communist governments in Vietnam and Cambodia in the months before their defeats, argued that the war could and should have been won. Liberal analysts pointed to Pentagon studies showing the limited effects of the bombing on a society with few industrial targets; to the ability of the North Vietnamese to match every American troop increase; to the dependency of the South Vietnamese government on American aid, demonstrating its lack of popular support in a war that would be decided as much by political as by military strength; and to the evident determination of Hanoi and the National Liberation Front to prevail and reunite their nation on their terms. For much of the public, the lesson was simple but ambiguous: "Win quickly or stay out," with some emphasizing the former and some the latter.

After UN forces had routed the Iraqi army in Kuwait in early 1991, President George *Bush im-mediately proclaimed that the specter of Vietnam had been buried forever in the desert sands of the Arabian Peninsula. To some, however, his impassioned reference to an earlier war showed how strongly it still weighed. Like the memorial on the mall in Washington, D.C., Vietnam continued to occupy a haunting place in the American memory.

(See also AMERICAN FOREIGN POLICY; BUREAU-CRATIC POLITICS; COLONIAL EMPIRES; DECOLONI-ZATION; GULF WAR; KOREAN WAR; NATIONAL LIB-ERATION MOVEMENTS; NEW LEFT.)

The Pentagon Papers (New York, 1971). Leslie H. Gelb with Richard K. Betts, *The Irony of Vietnam: The System Worked* (Washington, D.C., 1979). George C. Herring, *America's Longest War: The United States and Vietnam, 1950–1975* (New York, 1979). Stanley Karnow, *Vietnam: A History* (New York, 1983).

ANTHONY LAKE

VIOLENCE, POLITICAL. See ASSASSINATION; PO-LITICAL VIOLENCE; TERRORISM; TORTURE.

VOLUNTARY EXPORT RESTRAINT. See PRO-TECTION.

VOTING BEHAVIOR. See ELECTIONS AND VOTING BEHAVIOR.

W

WAŁĘSA, Lech. Born 29 September 1943 in the village of Popowo near Lipno in northwest *Poland, Lech Wałęsa will forever be associated with the Gdansk shipyard. For many he is still the charismatic tribune of the people who on 14 August 1980 jumped over the gates of that shipyard in which he had worked as an electrician since 1967 to set in motion a series of events that culminated in the dismantling of the Berlin Wall and the collapse of the Soviet empire. In the process his creation, *Solidarity (Solidarność), has become on the one hand a tangle of bickering parties unable to form a workable government and on the other a trade union with no clear idea of how it is to cope with the poverty, unemployment, and social dislocation caused by the policies its own governments have initiated during recent decades.

The recognition Wałęsa has gained has always been greater abroad than at home. A Nobel Peace Prize, an impressive address to both houses of the U.S. Congress, and in 1992 a successful visit to a reunited Germany are just some of the signs of respect he evokes from the international community. They are difficult to square with the criticism he constantly faces from domestic politicians and pundits, particularly since his election as president in December 1990. The same homespun philosophies, the common touch, the political instincts and straightforward manner that so impressed outsiders are seen as *populism, anti-intellectualism, and latent *authoritarianism by his detractors.

Married and the father of eight children, Wałęsa is by all accounts a lonely man, isolated from both the cutthroat political world of Warsaw and his roots in the shipyard. That he has retained such a high profile and considerable influence on the political stage is due as much to the disintegration and paralysis of the latter as to his successful transition from trade union leader to the "highest representative of the Polish State in internal and international relations and head of the armed forces." In particular, he is seen, unfairly according to some, as responsible for much of the political malaise that characterizes the "coalition carousel" of Poland's elite politics. From the time of his acrimonious break with Tadeusz Mazowiecki, propelled by Wałęsa in 1989 into the position of the Soviet bloc's first noncommunist prime minister, to his purposeful fracture of Solidarity into competing parties (in the interests of *democracy, as he saw it), to the bitter presidential election campaign in which he ironically profited from the emergence of the populist émigré Tyminski, receiving many votes that otherwise might not have been his, Wałęsa is seen as inexorably rising to power. This he is accused of doing at the expense of the economic and political cohesiveness of a country leading the way in the difficult transition out of *communism.

As a typical charismatic leader, Wałęsa has little time for procedures, statutes, or the complexities of the democratic process. His critics would quickly point to statements containing colorful metaphors such as the need for a president "with an axe." They would portray him as someone who spoke without thinking, who was unable to grasp difficult issues, and who was unpredictable and irresponsible. However, the record must speak for itself, and much of the rhetoric associated with his language of determined action, acceleration, and the like has remained just that. Undoubtedly Wałęsa was better equipped to be a precipitator of the collapse of communism than he was to be an astute politician overseeing the birth pangs of a new democracy. In particular, Wałęsa is a party to the struggle between those who wish Poland to become a full-fledged *parliamentary democracy and those who argue for the need for a strong executive, preferably rooted in a presidential system, as being the only guarantor of a successful transition to the market. That he sees such a system being built around him is demonstrated by the characteristic quote, "To attempt to propose today what the future office of the president should be is like choosing a hat and adjusting the size of the head to fit the hat."

The most popular historical analogy leveled at Wałęsa is the interwar president and dictator Josef Pilsudski, who took power in conditions very similar to those current in Poland. A political impasse, economic crisis, corruption, and scandals, as well as military discontent at civilian interference, all appear to set the scene for a reenactment of the coup of May 1926. However, this is to diminish the democratic sensibilities of a man who after 12 December 1981 spent nearly a year in internment and who for the following seven years fought a tactically sophisticated struggle, with no small cost to his health, against the post–martial law regime of General Wojciech Jaruzelski, which culminated in the "roundtable" agreement of 4 April 1989 and the subsequent emergence of the Solidarity-led government.

His closest opposition colleagues are now his political opponents, his working-class power base is increasingly disaffected, and the support of the church is now not as unambiguously decisive as it was. But these same politicians ultimately look to him to resolve their differences, his societal standing as judged by opinion polls has held firm, and *International Monetary Fund (IMF) and *World Bank confidence would be appreciably lower than it already is if he were to leave the scene.

GEORGE KOLANKIEWICZ

WAR

Aptly and very broadly defined by Malinowski (1968, p. 28), war in general is an "armed contest between two independent political units, by means of organized military force, in the pursuit of a tribal or national policy." The more restricted definition used here is Levy's (1983, p. 51) conception of international war as "a substantial armed conflict between the organized military forces of independent political units." International war excludes domestic conflict regardless of magnitude because populations of two or more nations are not prominently involved. Thus, the American Civil War (1861–1865) and the *Russian Revolution (1917–1921), despite enormous casualties, are considered domestic conflicts and not wars. War so defined also excludes guerrilla activities (e.g., the *Cuban Revolution, 1958); terrorist campaigns (e.g., the conflict in Northern Ireland, 1969–); crises resulting in border incursions (e.g., the Sino-Soviet conflict, 1959 and 1969); limited punitive strikes (e.g., Israeli border incursions against Palestinian forces, 1967–); or protracted rivalries that do not escalate to direct military confrontations (e.g., the *Cold War between the United States and the Soviet Union, 1946–1989). By contrast, *peace is the lack of militarized contest among nations. Nations are at peace when no contests arise, when disputes are resolved by accommodation, or, frequently, when one side yields to the demands of another without resort to force.

The systematic study of war has developed because key concepts have been defined and data collected. Despite shortcomings, data on attributes of war and their corollaries have allowed scholars to test existing propositions about war and to replicate results. Thus, for the first time since antiquity, when Kautilya and *Thucydides attempted to provide systematic explanations of war, contending propositions are undergoing empirical scrutiny.

War defies easy categorization. It is symmetric when one side uses force and the opponent fights back, asymmetric when one side intervenes and the opponent offers limited resistance. Symmetric wars need not be severe or protracted (e.g., the *Malvinas/Falklands War, 1982), but can directly escalate to a total, severe conflict among regional powers (e.g., the *Iran-Iraq War, 1980–1988). Asymmetric wars generally are more limited and less severe (e.g., the U.S. war in Panama, 1989) because of the disparity of capabilities among the contenders. Yet symmetry and asymmetry are not reliable guides for predicting the eventual escalation, diffusion, or severity of a conflict. When alliances are present, asymmetric wars can through diffusion become symmetric and severe (e.g., the Iraqi intervention in Kuwait in 1990 escalated to symmetric war against the U.S.-led alliance, 1990–1991). Indeed, global wars, which are multilateral contests that involve major powers on both sides, have devastating effects on world resources and populations, and threaten the very foundations of the international order, can be sparked by symmetric (e.g., *World War I, 1914–1918) or asymmetric (e.g., German intervention in Poland, 1939, leading to *World War II, 1939–1945) conflicts.

Much of the existing systematic study of war has concentrated on global war. Despite the fact that only three such wars—the Napoleonic Wars, World War I, and World War II—have been waged in the last two centuries, and only a handful have been fought in recorded history, particular attention has been paid to these conflicts because they are the most destructive of economic infrastructure, leave lasting scars in the population profile of the international community, and mark the beginning of major transformations in the *international system. Moreover, since 1945 the *deterrence of global nuclear war has dominated writing in the field.

One long-standing explanation of global war comes from the realist tradition in world politics. Realists propose that the distribution of power among nations is directly related to the likelihood of global war. *Balance of power, as the term implies, contends that an equal distribution of power leads to peace and an imbalance brings about the necessary conditions for war. This thesis is based on the assumption that under *anarchy, distributions other than a balance of power will, as Kenneth Waltz (1959, p. 232) argues, lead to war "because there is nothing to prevent them." In an anarchic international order, all nations wish to increase their relative power. The chief way in which this can be accomplished is by imposing one's preferences on weaker opponents. Hence, war is expected when one side or *alliance gains a power advantage over another. Alliances function to preserve parity among contending coalitions and provide weaker nations with sanctuary. Under conditions of equal power a major nation and its coalition cannot attack other major powers and their allies because the costs of war are prohibitive. Following the dictum of *Clausewitz that "war is the continuation of politics by other means," balance of power concedes that asymmetric conflict of limited severity cannot be prevented. Such conflicts produce minor adjustments among contending coalitions (e.g., the Soviet intervention in Hungary, 1956, and the U.S. intervention in Panama, 1989) but do not disturb the international order. Balance of power, however, contends that equality among contending coalitions prevents global war, ensures stability in the international order, and avoids the dismemberment of key members of contending coalitions.

In the nuclear era, balance of power has evolved into "mutual assured destruction," a "balance of terror" that ensures peace not because nations are satisfied with the status quo—none is in an anarchic world—but because the costs of nuclear war are prohibitive and indeed unthinkable. Deterrence retains the general structure of balance of power, picturing the international order as an anarchic, intrinsically competitive system in which nations seek to maximize *security by acquiring more power but are restrained from expansion because opponents are equally strong. The reason for stability in our time is simply that the costs of war are too high; in a perverse sense, the obsolescence of major war is due to the effectiveness of the means of mass destruction. A logical but controversial implication of the balance of terror is that nuclear proliferation will enhance the chances for peace. Indeed, as more members of the international community acquire a veto power over their opponents, the chances of war, particularly a total or global war, diminish because the absolute gains from a challenge pale in comparison with the potential destruction associated with a nuclear exchange.

Despite its wide acceptance and influence, empirical tests of balance of power theory have produced mostly negative or contradictory results. Formal reviews of the internal logic of balance of power strongly suggest that although peace is possible under power equality, very stringent conditions that do not prevail in world politics (e.g., leaders unwilling to take risks, complete information about the ultimate outcome of a war, or commitment to the international status quo) must be met to ensure stability. In the nuclear era, fortunately, there are no viable tests of the balance of terror, but the lack of congruence between the predictions of balance of power theory and international reality is at best disturbing.

A search is under way for alternatives within the framework of national competition over power. The current debate is vibrant but not new. Following World War I, Woodrow Wilson argued that power *hegemony rather than equality preserved peace in world politics. Frustrated with the dire consequences of anarchic competition among unconstrained nations, Wilson proposed the creation of a *League of Nations to ensure the absence of global war. The new legal structure would institu-tionalize a collective security alliance binding the major powers to jointly punish, with overwhelming force, departures from established conventions by all "aggressors." Wilson, incorrectly branded as an idealist, proposed institutionalization of a power hierarchy in world politics that would force nations to play by new rules or suffer punishment. Once national self-determination established the legitimate distribution of contested territories, Wilson proposed to use overwhelming force against any violator of existing agreements. In his view, preponderance of power could ensure peace where balance had failed. Asymmetric wars most likely would occur more frequently under collective security, but these were necessary to prevent the outbreak of much more dangerous global wars. Even though vestiges of collective security remain and are used to justify asymmetric interventions (e.g., the *Korean War, 1950–1952, and *Gulf War, 1990–1991), collective security has not been applied or tested in confrontations among major powers. (The League of Nations died for lack of membership of major powers, and the UN Security Council has been a largely ineffective instrument of collective action because all major powers can veto decisions to resist aggression.) In practice, collective security today relies on agreement among major powers to restrict their own behavior, a far cry from Wilson's conception of hegemonic preponderance that imposed established rules when aggression was detected.

A different challenge to the conception of balance of power comes from theories of power parity. Power transition, and more recently hegemonic theory, describe the international system in sharply different terms from balance of power and directly challenge the implication that equality leads to peace. Power transition, proposed by A. F. K. Organski (1958) and extended with some modifications by Robert Gilpin (1981), contends that the international order is not anarchic but hierarchical. Nations accept their position in the international hierarchy and recognize influence based on differences in the distribution of power. At the top of the hierarchy is the dominant hegemonic power that for most of its tenure is the most powerful actor in the international order. Below the hegemon are the other major powers, with potential to overtake the dominant country. Below them are the medium and small nations that cannot challenge for control of the global order. Most of the major and lesser powers support the status quo established by the hegemon. For this reason, alliances are stable and reliable instruments that cannot be easily altered. Yet one (or more) among the major powers, dissatisfied with the existing regime, can become the challenger and attempt to alter the status quo. Conditions for global war emerge when the challenger reaches parity with the hegemon and seeks to use its newly acquired power to establish a new place for itself in the international order. Power transition contends that balance of power sets the necessary conditions for global war, while gross inequality assures peace or, in the worst case, an asymmetric, limited war.

Empirical evaluations have tended to substantiate theories of power transition and hegemony. In the last two centuries, global wars occurred only when a contender achieved parity with the dominant power. Although there is disagreement about the need for a transition or a speedy overtaking to trigger war, recent work consistently associates parity of power among major nations with global wars and with serious, symmetric confrontations involving major powers (Houweling and Siccama, 1988; Kim and Morrow, 1990). Moreover, formal extensions of the internal logic of power parity are now able to explain why power parity provides only the necessary but not sufficient conditions for war (Bueno de Mesquita and Lalman, 1992). Under equality, empirical results show that war occurs only in half of the known parity periods, and peace is maintained in the remaining half. Formal work shows that when leaders are willing to take risks under parity, war should follow, but when they are risk-averse peace should be maintained (Kugler and Zagare, 1987). Complete information detracts from war under parity, but uncertainty can enhance either war or peace. Finally, commitment to the international status quo increases stability, but rejection diminishes the prospects for peace (Kugler and Zagare, 1987; Bueno de Mesquita and Lalman, 1992). War and peace seem to be tenuously in balance when parity is achieved, and national *elites play a critical role in determining war or peace.

An important but untested implication of power transition or hegemony is that with nuclear parity even the "balance of terror" becomes tenuous. This perspective is borne out by the historical record in the nuclear era. Nuclear war did not occur during the so-called period of massive retaliation (approximately 1949–1970), when the United States had a preponderance of *nuclear weapons, precisely because preponderance ensures that no global wars will occur. Extensions of power transition suggest that this stability may have been shattered after the necessary conditions for a global nuclear war were met in the late 1970s, when the Soviet Union achieved rough nuclear parity with the United States. Under these circumstances peace is not ensured by the costs of nuclear weapons or improvements in technology but rather is in the hands of elites of nuclear nations who must choose to avoid risk, minimize uncertainty, and—perhaps most important, as the *Gorbachev era suggests—maintain the status quo. However, if this logic is correct, then as nuclear proliferation proceeds, the danger of nuclear confrontation should rise because more nations will achieve parity at a global or regional level.

A final systemic reaction to the empirical challenges to balance of power comes from a long-term perspective on the phenomenon of war. The notion of a war cycle is firmly embedded in traditional work on war. Arnold Toynbee (1954) proposed a simple cycle in which a generation had to pass after a major war before national leaders could once more convince their citizens to join in another act of supreme carnage. A leading exponent of long cycle theory is Nikolai Kondratieff, a Russian economist, who proposed that wars are the result of long global economic cycles. He conceived of nations as passengers on a wave of global economic success and failure, driven to severe conflicts by forces beyond their control. George Modelski (1987) revived and restructured the long cycle theory, suggesting connections between economic and military cycles. Tests by Joshua Goldstein (1985), Modelski (1987), and William R. Thompson (1988) show that the empirical record thus far is mixed.

Challenges to well-entrenched balance of power explanations of war have led many to explore the role that national elites have in the initiation of war. Systemic theories can at best provide necessary but not sufficient conditions for war: individuals make the final decision to wage or avoid war. The search for understanding of such decisions has not been widespread. Some, like Graham Allison (1971) and Bruce Russett (1988), approach the decision to go to war from a domestic perspective and explore the process leaders follow to initiate war; others, such as Robert Jervis (1976), contend that the calculations leading to war reflect many misperceptions by decision makers that affect relative power calculations. Others follow Irving Janis (1972), who argued that the decision to wage—and more important, to escalate—a war is determined by "groupthink" that enshrines early, distorted positions perpetuating the waging of war long after such conflict is justified by impartial evaluations of reality. Still others adopt the decision making perspective, pioneered by John Steinbrunner (1974), which holds that decisions to join and escalate wars follow a cybernetic process confounded by prior expectations and motivated by a learning process based on prior experience. Convincing case studies suggest that these approaches hold promise, but little systematic work has been done in the area, and attempts at the explicit modeling of interesting alternatives using artificial intelligence are only beginning.

The exception is the rational decision making perspective. This approach, which has roots in microeconomic theory, has generated much formal work and has received extensive empirical testing. This relatively new and very dynamic literature suggests that if one assumes that national elites attempt to maximize net gains, war is a rational act used to resolve disputes where compromise is the inferior outcome. Substantial success is attributed to the expected utility that assumes independent decisions by each actor, but emerging solutions using *game theory that allow for interaction among the participants suggest the possibility of a general theory of war that can extend to all conflict. Unlike the models in the realist tradition, decision making approaches promise that decision making models can ultimately provide a general theory of conflict initiation, escalation, and management. Empirical results seem to support this contention. These new formal and empirical strides augur well for the future understanding of conflict. However, a major limitation in all decision making approaches is the shortened angle of vision and the detail required for effective evaluations. Few systematic data sets meet the requirements of the theories, and thus there is much debate about the validity of the reported findings.

Another approach to the understanding of war follows the seminal work of Richardson (*Arms and Insecurity,* 1960) and explores the relation between arms races and war. Nations threatened with conflict are expected to overreact to the arms expenditure of an opponent, generating an *arms race. Unless such a race is arrested through negotiations, the gap between the two contenders widens, prompting the weaker side to initiate conflict out of fear that the armament gap will become too large to overcome. Evaluations by Huntington (1958), Richardson (*Statistics of Deadly Quarrels,* 1960), and more recently by Wallace (1979) supported the connection between arms races and war. However, extensive empirical tests of this classic proposition suggest that arms expenditures are driven largely by domestic and not external factors. More important, most of the recent evidence indicates that wars are not directly associated with the presence or absence of arms races. This classic model has also received much formal scrutiny. Scholars have shown that minor changes in parameters lead to quite different outcomes than those expected by Richardson. Indeed, the distinction between an externally-driven arms race and an internally-driven arms buildup is very difficult to draw. However, because the arms race model justifies the need for *arms control and has important implications for nuclear *disarmament, much research continues in this area in the hope of discovering more complex relations that would once more justify the original connection between arms races and war, and arms control and peace.

Beyond theorizing on the causes of war, much has been learned about the characteristics and effects of war. Ongoing work now allows us to distinguish patterns of war diffusion that characterize international conflicts. Extensive explorations of the consequences of war show that, paradoxically, nations defeated in war, like the proverbial Phoenix, rise again; they erase dramatic but short-term losses in their industrial and demographic resources in two decades, and they do so whether victors impose reparations on the vanquished or whether they provide aid for their recovery. Moaz and Abdolali (1989) show that democracies do not fight democracies, but are no less prone than others to engage in conflict with nondemocratic members of the international order. This work is receiving scrutiny, with mixed results. Rummel (1963) demonstrates a relationship between domestic instability and international war, suggesting that elites may choose to solve domestic dissension by exporting violence and consolidating power. This plausible hypothesis, again, has received mixed empirical support but has generated intense interest regarding the connection between domestic and international conflict (James, 1987). Finally, the literature on just war that can be traced to Saint Augustine and Saint Thomas Aquinas continues to grow, and has acquired additional urgency because of the development of nuclear weapons.

What can be said from this short exploration of the vast literature on war? The paradigm used to explore war is still directly related to the work of Thucydides, but increasingly theory and evidence are moving the field further and further from broad generalizations. Empirical work has developed comprehensive, systematic, and generally accepted data banks for the study of war. The result is that many long-held beliefs about war have been discredited while very few propositions have emerged unscathed. As we move into the future, new data sets driven by theoretical demands will become increasingly available. Improvements in theorizing driven by the interaction between empirical reality, formal deduction, and inductive insights will vastly expand our knowledge of war. This generation, however, can take credit for being the first to face the scientific challenge of exploring propositions produced by generations of students of war and peace.

(See also FORCE, USE OF; REALISM; WAR, RULES OF.)

Pitirim A. Sorokin, *Social and Cultural Dynamics,* vol. 3, *Fluctuations of Social Relationships, War and Revolution* (New York, 1937). Arnold J. Toynbee, *A Study of History* (London, 1954). Samuel P. Huntington, "Arms Races: Prerequisites and Results" *Public Policy* 18, no. 1 (Spring 1958): 41–86. A. F. K. Organski, *World Politics* (New York, 1958). Kenneth N. Waltz, *Man, the State and War* (New York, 1959). L. F. Richardson, *Arms and Insecurity* (Pittsburgh, 1960). L. F. Richardson, *Statistics of Deadly Quarrels* (Pittsburgh, 1960). Inis Claude, *Power and International Relations* (New York, 1962). Rudolph Rummel, "Dimensions of Conflict Within and Between States" *General Systems* 8, no. 1 (Spring 1963): 1–50. Bronislaw Malinowski, "An Anthropological Analysis of War," in Leon Bramson and George Goethals, eds., *War* (New York, 1968), pp. 245–268. Graham Allison, *The Essence of Decision* (Boston, 1971). Irving Janis, *Victims of Groupthink* (Boston, 1972). John Steinbrunner, *The Cybernetic Theory of Decision* (Princeton, N.J., 1974). Robert Jervis, *Perception and Misperception in International Politics* (Princeton, N.J., 1976). M. D. Wallace, "Arms Races and Escalation: Some New Evidence," in J. David Singer, ed., *Explaining War* (Beverly Hills, Calif., 1979), pp. 240–252. A. F. K. Organski and Jacek Kugler, *The War Ledger* (Chicago, 1980). Robert Gilpin, *War and Change in International Politics* (New York, 1981). Jack Levy, *War in the Great Power System, 1495–1975* (Lexington, Ky., 1983). Joshua Goldstein, "Kondratieff Waves as War Cycles" *International Studies Quarterly* 29, no. 2 (December 1985): 411–444. Patrick

James, "Externalization of Conflict: Testing a Crisis-Based Model" *Canadian Journal of Political Science* 20, no. 3 (September 1987): 573–598. Jacek Kugler and Frank Zagare, *Exploring the Stability of Deterrence* (Boulder, Colo., 1987). George Modelski, *Long Cycles in World Politics* (Seattle, 1987). Hank Houweling and Jan Siccama, "Power Transition as a Cause of War" *Journal of Conflict Resolution* 32, no. 1 (March 1988): 87–102. Bruce Russet, *Controlling the Sword: The Democratic Governance of National Security* (Cambridge, Mass., 1988). William Thompson, *On Global War: Historical-Structural Approaches to World Politics* (Columbia, S.C., 1988). Zeev Moaz and Nasrin Abdolali, "Regime Types and International Conflict" *Journal of Conflict Resolution* 33, no. 1 (March 1989): 3–36. John Mueller, *Retreat from Doomsday* (New York, 1989). Woosang Kim and James D. Morrow, "When Do Power Transitions Lead to War?" paper presented at the annual meeting of the Midwest Political Science Association, Chicago, April 5–7, 1990. J. David Singer and Paul Diehl, eds., *Measuring the Correlates of War* (Ann Arbor, Mich., 1990). Bruce Bueno de Mesquita and David Lalman, *War and Reason* (New Haven, Conn., 1992).

JACEK KUGLER

WAR, RULES OF. The rules of warfare are established by *international law with a view to regulating the conduct of belligerents in the course of international armed conflicts. These rules (known in the aggregate as *jus in bello*) must be distinguished from the law governing the commencement of hostilities *(jus ad bellum)*. Comtemporary international law prohibits the use of *force in *international relations. Nevertheless, once *war breaks out (in violation of the *jus ad bellum*), the same rules of warfare *(jus in bello)* apply to all belligerents. There must be no discrimination in the implementation of the rules of warfare between the armed forces or the civilians of the aggressor state(s) and those of the victim(s) of aggression. Aggressor(s) and victim(s) alike are equally bound by the obligations ensuing from the rules of warfare and equally entitled to benefit from the corresponding rights.

The rules of warfare are premised on the dual notion that the adverse effects of war should be alleviated as much as possible (given military necessities), and that the freedom of the parties to resort to methods and means of warfare is not unlimited. Some rules—e.g., the protection of heralds arranging truce—have their roots in ancient practice. Most, however, are a product of modern humanitarian concepts: they were devised in the last two centuries and have no antecedents in the past.

Certain rules of warfare have evolved as customary law and remain uncodified, but much of the law is currently incorporated in numerous international conventions, preeminently the two sets of the Hague Conventions, dating from 1907, and the Geneva Conventions, concluded in 1949. The latter, four in number and supplemented by a partly controversial Additional Protocol of 1977, are usually referred to as the Red Cross Conventions and labeled as "international humanitarian law." In reality, there is

scarcely any justification for a substantive differentiation between the law of Geneva and the law of The Hague. The two sets of conventions are complementary, and many important provisions are actually interchangeable. All rules of warfare reflect a balance between humanitarian considerations, on the one hand, and the requirements of military necessity, on the other.

The rules of warfare draw a fundamental distinction between combatants and civilians. Civilians enjoy a qualified protection against dangers arising from military operations. Although they face the perils of warfare in many unavoidable ways (for instance, when they work in a munitions factory, which, as explained below, is a legitimate target for strategic bombing), they must not be the object of either a deliberate or even an indiscriminate attack. Special and detailed protection is offered to civilians living in territories occupied by the enemy in the course of the war.

Combatants, provided that they comply with the rules of warfare and satisfy prerequisite conditions, are entitled to the status of prisoners of war. This status is of paramount significance when combatants fall into the enemy's hands, either by choice (laying down their arms) or by force of circumstances (being wounded, sick, or shipwrecked). Prisoners of war are guaranteed their lives, health, and dignity, although they lose their liberty. During captivity, the detaining power must treat them humanely pursuant to numerous directives spelled out in the Third Geneva Convention of 1949. As a rule, prisoners of war are to be released and repatriated only after the cessation of active hostilities.

A number of weapons have been been expressly forbidden for any use in warfare on the grounds that they are deemed to be excessively injurious to the immediate victims or have potentially harmful effects for others. There are various conventions prohibiting chemical, biological, and bacteriological weapons; poisons; weapons modifying or causing damage to the environment; specified types of floating mines in maritime warfare; "dumdum" (i.e., expanding) bullets; explosive or inflammable projectiles under a prescribed weight (except in air warfare); and weapons causing injury by fragments not detectable by X rays. The employment of several other weapons (primarily land mines, booby traps, and incendiary weapons) is also restricted where civilians are concerned.

Recourse to some weapons is controversial. This is particularly true of nuclear devices. The rationale for proscribing them is obvious: they are not only excessively injurious to the immediate victims but have long-standing harmful effects to others as well. However, as yet, there is no comprehensive interdiction of *nuclear weapons that is legally binding. A series of conventions in force, wherein nuclear weapons are excluded from use in specific areas (for instance, Latin America), can be construed as implying that otherwise the employment of such weapons is permissible.

There are multiple rules concerning lawful and unlawful methods of warfare. Belligerents are allowed to resort to espionage, although, if caught in the act, the spy will not be accorded prisoner-of-war status. Siege on land, maritime blockade, and the seizure of contraband at sea are permissible. Conversely, the use of privateers at sea has been abolished. There are also injunctions against forms of deception considered perfidious (chiefly, feigning an intent to surrender; feigning noncombatant status; improper use of enemy or neutral uniforms; and abuse of emblems like the Red Cross). But there is no sweeping ban of deception in warfare. For example, there is no impediment to ambushes, camouflage, or false codes (other than distress signals). Occasionally, there are striking dissimilarities between the rules governing land and maritime warfare. Thus, whereas it is legitimate to fly a false (enemy or neutral) flag at any time prior to opening fire at sea, the equivalent tactics on land would be regarded as perfidious.

The general protection accorded to civilians has engendered a distinction between military targets (which can be attacked at discretion) and civilian objects (which are exempt from attack). This is a crucial issue in the context of strategic bombing. It is generally agreed that military targets encompass not merely military forces and installations (including depots, vehicles, aircraft, and warships) but also factories engaged in the manufacture of military supplies or central lines of communication. The presence of civilians does not shield industrial plants, airports, harbors, railroad stations, or major highways. Moreover, if a number of military objectives that are not clearly separated and distinct are located in a city or any other site inhabited by civilians, they can be looked upon as a single "target area" for the purpose of bombing. This is the juridical underpinning of the saturation bombings of the Ruhr basin in Germany during *World War II. By contrast, air raids purely designed to terrorize the civilian population or break its morale are manifestly illicit. Hence the enduring controversy relating to the legality of the overall strategic bombing policy carried out by the Allies in the course of War World II. The only possible justification was that of reprisals in response to previous violations of the law by the Axis air forces.

At all events, the following objects must not be attacked, as long as they are not used by the enemy for military purposes: hospitals, medical installations, ambulances, hospital ships, and medical aircraft; places of religious worship; cultural property, such as museums and historical monuments; undefended places (although it is debatable whether this term has much meaning in the context of strategic

bombing); unarmed merchant ships not traveling in an escorted convoy (but exemption from attack does not preclude the seizure of enemy merchant ships and cargoes as prize); crops and drinking water indispensable to the survival of the civilian population; dams, nuclear electrical generating stations, and other installations containing dangerous forces; and civil defense organizations. It is also forbidden to harm the wounded and sick; medical or religious personnel; envoys bearing flags of truce; and, of late, even journalists. Pillage and the wanton destruction of enemy private property are prohibited.

In the nature of things, the evolution of the rules of warfare cannot always keep pace with technological advances in weapon systems. Unless a new convention is concluded to cope with state-of-the-art devices, they are subject to the application of traditional legal concepts (although these may be perceived by some as outdated). Interestingly enough, even when new conventions emerge—e.g., the instruments adopted in the 1930s to deal with submarine warfare—they often leave the classical legal standards essentially intact.

After every major war, all preexisting rules of warfare must be reassessed in the light of the actual practice of states. For example, the use of "exclusion zones" in maritime warfare in the 1980s, both in the *Malvinas/Falklands War and in the *Iran-Iraq War, has left several open questions. It is not always easy to determine whether persistent breaches of the rules of warfare reflect the emergence of new legal norms or should be stigmatized as violations of international law (and, in grave cases, *war crimes).

(See also GENOCIDE; NUREMBERG TRIALS.)

D. Bindschedler-Robert et al., "The Regulation of Armed Conflicts," in M. Cherif Bassiouni and Ved P. Nanda, eds., *International Criminal Law*, vol. 1 (Springfield, Ill., 1973), pp. 293–452. Richard B. Baxter, "The Duties of Combatants and the Conduct of Hostilities (Law of the Hague)," in *International Dimensions of Humanitarian Law* (Dordrecht, 1988), pp. 93–133.

YORAM DINSTEIN

WAR CRIMES. Grave offenses against the laws of warfare entailing criminal responsibility of individuals are known as war crimes. It is frequently asserted that every single violation of the laws of warfare amounts automatically to a war crime, but in actuality individual criminal responsibility is more restricted in scope. A war crime is typically committed by members of armed forces, but it can also be perpetrated by civilians.

There is no comprehensive and binding definition of the term *war crimes*. The basic, albeit incomplete, definition appears in Article 6 of the 1945 Charter of the International Military Tribunal (annexed to the London Agreement for the Prosecution and Punishment of the Major War Criminals of the European Axis), which also sets forth two independent categories of "crimes against peace" and "crimes against humanity." Under this provision, war crimes include—but are not limited to—"murder, ill-treatment or deportation to slave labour or for any other purpose of civilian population of or in occupied territory, murder or ill-treatment of prisoners of war or persons on the seas, killing of hostages, plunder of public or private property, wanton destruction of cities, towns or villages, or devastation not justified by military necessity."

The International Military Tribunal at Nuremberg emphasized that other acts not mentioned in Article 6—such as the employment of poisoned weapons or the improper use of flags of truce—have historically been treated as war crimes. In fact, a number of war criminals tried after *World War II were convicted of offenses not covered by the London charter (e.g., breach of surrender terms).

The four Geneva Conventions of 1949 for the Protection of War Victims (Articles 50/51/130/147) list "grave breaches" involving specified acts committed against persons or property protected in each convention, chiefly, the wounded and sick, prisoners of *war, and civilians. Other grave breaches are enumerated in Article 85 of the 1977 Protocol Additional to the Geneva Conventions Relating to the Protection of Victims of International Armed Conflicts (Protocol I). Paragraph 5 of the latter clause proclaims that grave breaches of both the conventions and the protocol "shall be regarded as war crimes."

War crimes are punishable severely: in extreme cases the penalty can be death. However, verdict and sentence must be pronounced after a fair trial by a duly formed judicial tribunal. The performance of the International Military Tribunals at Nuremberg and Tokyo demonstrates the feasibility of the creation of international courts for the trial of war criminals. These tribunals operated on an ad hoc basis, however, and as yet no permanent international penal court has been established. In the absence of an international tribunal, the trial of war criminals must take place before national courts.

When states suppress war crimes committed by members of their own armed forces, trials are generally conducted pursuant to the pertinent domestic military law. But should other states wish to institute penal proceedings, they can only do so by virtue of *international law. Under customary international law, war crimes are subject to universal jurisdiction so that all states are entitled to bring offenders to trial.

Since the *Nuremberg Trials, it has been acknowledged that war criminals cannot relieve themselves of criminal responsibility by citing official position or superior orders. Even obedience to explicit national legislation provides no protection against international law. Additionally, war crimes are not subject to the application of ordinary rules of statutes of limitations. Hence, there is no time limit on prosecutions, which can commence after many decades.

War crimes trials date back at least to the fifteenth century, but the issue of war crimes came to the fore mainly as a result of the countless Nazi and Japanese atrocities perpetrated in the course of World War II. Apart from the two major trials conducted by the international military tribunals, thousands of lesser war criminals were prosecuted before national courts in more than a dozen countries.

Notwithstanding the overall success of the post–World War II trials, none of the multiple regional armed conflicts following it has spawned prosecutions of war criminals. Threats of indictments have been made on several occasions but have not been carried out. There are various reasons for the prevailing reluctance to proceed with war crimes trials subsequent to regional wars. But the key element is the lack of trust that national courts, although vested with jurisdiction, would be morally capable of administering justice to former enemy personnel. Only the establishment of an impartial international tribunal for the prosecution of war crimes can overcome mutual suspicions in this sphere.

(See also GENOCIDE; WAR, RULES OF.)

Jordan J. Paust and Albert P. Blaustein, "War Crimes Jurisdiction and Due Process: The Bangladesh Experience" *Vanderbilt Journal of Transnational Law* 11, no. 1 (Winter 1978): 1–38. Yoram Dinstein, "The Distinction between Unlawful Combatants and War Criminals," in Yoram Dinstein, ed., *International Law at a Time of Perplexity* (Dordrecht, 1989), pp. 103–116.

YORAM DINSTEIN

WAR ON POVERTY. See GREAT SOCIETY.

WAR POWERS RESOLUTION. The War Powers Resolution was enacted over President Richard *Nixon's veto in November 1973. As a joint resolution, the measure has the force and effect of law. It was the product of an increasing congressional sentiment, spurred largely by *Watergate and the *Vietnam War, that the executive branch had come too frequently to disregard legislative prerogatives in general and the congressional war power in particular. Final enactment came after the Senate's adoption of the National Commitments Resolution in 1969 and the passage of differing versions of war powers legislation (left unreconciled) during intervening years. At the time of its enactment the resolution was seen by many as a significant reclamation of the congressional war power.

The law contains six major provisions. First, it sets forth *Congress's opinion of the breadth of the president's power to use armed force without prior congressional approval. This, it provides, may be done in the event of a national emergency created by an attack on the United States, its territories or possessions, or its armed forces. The provision is nonbinding (unlike a similar, obligatory provision in the Senate version of the resolution that was dropped by the conference committee). Second, the resolution requires that the president consult with Congress before the U.S. armed forces are "introduced into hostilities or into situations where imminent involvement in hostilities is clearly indicated by the circumstances." Third, it requires that in such circumstances the president transmit a written report to Congress within forty-eight hours. Fourth, the resolution requires the president to withdraw the armed forces from hostilities within sixty days after a report is transmitted or required to be transmitted (ninety days in the event of unavoidable military necessity incidental to the withdrawal), subject to three exceptions: a declaration of *war, specific statutory authorization, or statutory extension of the time period. Fifth, the resolution requires the president to withdraw the armed forces from hostilities when Congress so directs through the adoption of a concurrent resolution (which is not presented to the president for his signature or veto). Finally, the resolution precludes any inference of authority to introduce the armed forces into hostilities from any treaty or statute not containing specific authorization.

Presidents generally have complied with the reporting requirement of the War Powers Resolution. Consultation, however, has been more uneven, and President Ronald *Reagan arguably declined to comply with the sixty-day time period during the 1988 escort operation to protect Kuwaiti shipping in the Persian Gulf. The courts have dismissed as political questions this and other legal challenges regarding alleged presidential violation of the reporting requirements. A 1983 *Supreme Court case casts serious doubt on the validity of the concurrent resolution withdrawal provision of the resolution. For all practical purposes, the resolution has thus proved judicially unenforceable.

Politically, the resolution has not worked as many had expected, in part because key provisions are vague. The term *hostilities*, for example, is undefined, leaving room for good faith disagreement over whether or when hostilities have occurred. Also, presidents have transmitted reports under other provisions of the resolution, creating doubt whether the sixty-day time period was triggered. A number of remedial amendments have been proposed, but none has been adopted.

(See also PRESIDENCY, U.S.; SEPARATION OF POWERS.)

Michael J. Glennon, *Constitutional Diplomacy* (Princeton, N.J., 1990).

MICHAEL J. GLENNON

WARSAW TREATY ORGANIZATION. The Warsaw Treaty Organization (WTO), also often referred to as the Warsaw Pact, was created pursuant to a treaty signed on 14 May 1955 by the Soviet Union, Albania, Bulgaria, Hungary, the German Democratic Republic (GDR), Poland, Romania, and Czechoslovakia. The treaty followed by only nine days the accession of the Federal Republic of Germany (FRG) to the *North Atlantic Treaty Organization (NATO). The treaty established an organization comprising a joint command of the armed forces of the member states and a political consultative committee; other military and political bodies were added later. While nominally all members were equal, the Soviet Union held a dominant and controlling position in the WTO until the end of 1989.

The WTO was originally established for a period of twenty years, to be automatically extended for ten years for all members who did not denounce its continuance. Albania ceased to participate in the WTO in 1961 and withdrew in 1968. In April 1985 the WTO was extended again for twenty plus ten years by all the other members. However, as a consequence of the revolutionary transformation of its members, the GDR withdrew on the eve of its own absorption into the FRG in August 1990, the military organizational elements of the alliance were abolished as of 31 March 1991, and on 1 July 1991 the WTO was dissolved by consensus of its members.

The WTO was designed both to be a political counter to NATO and to justify continuing Soviet military presence on the territory of various WTO members. The WTO coordinated the armed forces of its members (Romania only nominally after 1963), and joint military exercises were held from 1961 through 1989.

In 1956, Soviet military intervention prevented Hungary from leaving the WTO. In 1968, military forces of the Soviet Union and several other members, although not the WTO itself, intervened in Czechoslovakia to ensure communist orthodoxy, implementing what in the West came to be called the "Brezhnev Doctrine" (after Soviet leader Leonid Brezhnev).

With a new leadership in the Soviet Union under Mikhail *Gorbachev willing to permit freedom of choice to the nations of Eastern and *Central Europe, both the internal political systems of the member states and their external relations changed suddenly and drastically beginning in November 1989. For a time, with Soviet *hegemony ended and Soviet forces beginning their withdrawal, several of its members saw an interim role for a "new" WTO based on equality to serve their interests pending creation of pan-European *security arrangements. The Soviet Union encouraged such a transformation of the WTO from a military-political alliance under its control to a political consultative one. This prospect, however, proved ephemeral. The speed of *German reunification and the initiation of steps to establish a new European security order in 1990, coupled with the burdens of the pact's past role as an instrument of Soviet domination, doomed the WTO to a demise by 1991.

The WTO reflected the changing relationship of the Communist-ruled states of Eastern Europe with the Soviet Union in its origins, throughout its existence, and in its dissolution. The WTO was born of the *Cold War and died with it.

(See also CONFERENCE ON SECURITY AND COOPERATION IN EUROPE; NINETEEN EIGHTY-NINE; SOVIET–EAST EUROPEAN RELATIONS; SOVIET FOREIGN POLICY.)

Robin Alison Remington, *The Warsaw Pact: Case Studies in Communist Conflict Resolution* (Cambridge, Mass., 1971). David Holloway and Jane M. O. Sharp, eds., *The Warsaw Pact: Alliance in Transition?* (Ithaca, N.Y., 1984). General of the Army P. G. Lushev, ed., *Varshavskii dogovor: istoriia i sovremennost'* [The Warsaw Treaty: History and the Present Day] (Moscow, 1990).

RAYMOND L. GARTHOFF

WATERGATE. The most serious political scandal in modern U.S. history has come to be known as Watergate. In June 1972, burglars hired by the Committee to Re-elect the President to engage in political espionage were arrested at Democratic National Committee headquarters, located in the Watergate Hotel in Washington, D.C. The ensuing judicial proceedings, congressional investigations, and press coverage culminated in the resignation of President Richard M. *Nixon on 9 August 1974. Nixon had been forced to surrender tape recordings of conversations that he had had with several of his top aides, which revealed that he had conspired with them to obstruct justice by attempting to thwart the investigation of the burglary. The pardoning of Nixon by his successor, Gerald R. Ford, precluded criminal proceedings against him. Over thirty Nixon administration officials, campaign staff, and contributors, however, were indicted, convicted, and served jail sentences for their roles in the scandal.

Watergate encompassed wrongdoing on a wide scale, including the misuse of campaign donations and the unlawful and unethical use of the Federal Bureau of Investigation, the Internal Revenue Service, and the *Central Intelligence Agency by Nixon and his aides against their political "enemies." From 1969 to 1971 the Nixon administration authorized, without court approval, the wiretapping of government officials and journalists to uncover the sources of leaked news about the bombing of Cambodia and other "national security" matters. The "Huston plan," approved by Nixon in 1971, contemplated burglaries and the opening of mail to detect security leaks. Also in 1971, Nixon created the Special Investigations Unit (the "plumbers") to carry out such operations as breaking into the office of Daniel Ellsberg's psychiatrist. Ellsberg had given copies of the secret "Pentagon papers," documenting U.S. involvement in Indochina, to newspapers. Nixon's objective was to find derogatory information about Ellsberg before Ellsberg's espionage trial.

Scholars continue to debate the significance and long-term consequences of Watergate for the functioning of the U.S. political system. Most view it less as an aberrant event attributable to the character flaws of Nixon and his associates than as symptomatic of more deeply rooted problems of U.S. political development. One prominent view is that Watergate was the culmination of a decades-long trend toward an "imperial *presidency." With the growth of the federal government's domestic and international responsibilities, increased power, discretion, and prestige was (misguidedly) lodged in the presidency. This occurred through presidential initiative and *Congress's delegation of its powers or abdication of its responsibilities. The results included a greatly enlarged White House staff; an increase in secrecy, deception, and evasion of congressional controls in the conduct of military and covert operations abroad; the use of executive agencies to monitor and discourage political opponents and interfere in the electoral process; and the impoundment of funds appropriated by Congress. In short, along with the *Vietnam War, Watergate signaled for many the extent to which growing presidential power had endangered civil liberties and the constitutional balance between legislative and executive authority.

Watergate affected U.S. politics in a variety of ways. First, along with the war in Vietnam, it gave fresh impetus to the public's growing mistrust of government. Although the decline in trust began before Watergate and Vietnam, the largest single increase in mistrust occurred between 1972 and 1974, the period in which Watergate was a salient event. Second, Watergate, again like Vietnam, changed the relationship between the mass media and government, particularly the executive branch. The post-Watergate period has seen the demise of "objective journalism" as a professional standard, and in its place the rise of a more interpretive, skeptical, and aggressive style of reporting. For many journalists, Watergate signaled the need for a more adversarial relationship toward those in power; it also showed that such a relationship could reap professional rewards.

Third, Watergate led to changes in the internal workings of Congress. Coming on the heels of Nixon's resignation, the 1974 elections resulted in significant Democratic gains in Congress. The "Watergate babies" brought to Washington that year spearheaded a variety of reforms intended to decentralize authority by decreasing the power, in particular, of committee chairs chosen by seniority. The young cohort pushed Congress further in the direction of a legislature dominated by more individualistic, activist, issue-oriented, national politicians.

Finally, and perhaps most importantly, Watergate spurred Congress to reassert its authority vis-à-vis the president. Congress legislated a host of reforms intended to prevent a repeat of the criminal and unethical activities undertaken during the Nixon years, and to redress the perceived erosion of congressional powers that many believed had helped give rise to the aggrandizement of presidential power. Congress passed campaign finance reforms in 1974 that set a limit on how much a person or a person's family could spend on his or her candidacy, set a limit of $1,000 on the amount individuals could contribute to a candidate in any given election, outlawed cash contributions in excess of $100, and prohibited foreign contributions. All but the first provision have been upheld by the *Supreme Court. To put an end to usurpations of presidential power in foreign affairs, Congress passed the *War Powers Resolution in 1973. Its intent was to guarantee that the president could not commit troops without consulting Congress, and that if such a commitment extended beyond sixty days, Congress would be required to give its explicit approval. In domestic policy, Congress passed the Budget and Impoundment Control Act of 1974. The purposes of this legislation were to bring appropriations decisions closer to revenue decisions by centralizing the budgetary process in Congress, to give Congress the expertise (through the creation of budget committees and the Congressional Budget Office) that would allow it to operate independently of the president and his Office of Management and Budget.

The optimistic view of Watergate is that it represents a blessing in disguise. It ought to deter future presidents from breaking the law, and arrests the compulsion toward enlarging the powers and prestige of the presidency at the expense of the other branches. The ways in which the scandal was uncovered and resolved serve as a vindication of the U.S. system of institutional checks and balances and of such principles as "no one is above the law." A more pessimistic view is that, while future presidents may be deterred from acting criminally and unethically (or at least take greater care not to get caught), the presidency remains a problematic institution. Watergate did nothing to change the plebiscitary nature of the presidency, in which the public's unrealistic expectations (fueled in part by presidents themselves) create tremendous pressures on presidents to deliver. Yet presidents' capacity to control events is limited, despite the considerable, disproportionate resources and power at their disposal. As expectations inevitably outstrip their capacity, they will continue to disappoint themselves and the public, and be tempted to abuse their powers.

(See also SEPARATION OF POWERS; UNITED STATES.)

Carl Bernstein and Bob Woodward, *All the President's Men* (New York, 1974). Richard Ben-Veniste, *Stonewall: The Real Story of the Watergate Prosecution* (New York, 1977).
GARY MUCCIARONI

WEBER, Max. Although Max Weber (1864–1920) is regarded as one of the founders of twentieth-century sociology, Weber's university appointments were all in political economy (at Freiburg in 1894, Heidelberg in 1896, and Munich in 1919), and it was the mutual interaction between economic systems and law, culture, and politics that formed the subject of his major academic studies. His works stood out for their methodological sophistication, breadth of historical scholarship, and increasingly abstract conceptualization, culminating in his enormous theoretical compendium *Economy and Society* (1921). Although his reputation in his own time owed something to his controversial interventions in the political issues of Wilhelmine Germany, Weber came to articulate an ideal of value-free social science that has been highly influential on subsequent scholarship.

Weber's importance for political science and political sociology lies in his early recognition of key developments emerging in the social structure and politics of capitalist societies at the beginning of the twentieth century, and in the theoretical categories he provided for their analysis. In the field of social stratification, his threefold distinction between "class, status, and party" has provided a powerful instrument for analyzing the complexities of social structure. Weber himself used it to explain the position of an emergent middle *class of white-collar, technical, and administrative personnel between capital and labor, whose share of the economic product depended on skill and educational status rather than on the ownership of property or the power of collective organization. In opposition to Marxists, he contended that the terms of systematic class conflict in mature *capitalism could be set and regulated at the political level, and therefore was dependent for its containment on the character of the political system. At the same time he acknowledged the importance of status groups, especially those of *ethnicity and nation, in providing a basis of political allegiance and mobilization cutting across class lines.

Weber's most notable contribution, however, lay in identifying the importance of bureaucracy to modern politics. His definition of bureaucracy, not as a type of political *system,* but as a continuous, professionalized, and rule-governed form of administration, showed it to be increasingly prevalent—thanks to its being uniquely equipped to handle increasingly various and complex organizational tasks—in all spheres of modern life. On the basis of this analysis he demonstrated that the socialist ideal of a society without domination was utopian, and predicted that the replacement of the capitalist entrepreneur by the state administrator would create a monolithic power structure as oppressive as that of ancient Egypt and as economically stagnant as that of late imperial Rome. In Weber's view, the key concern about bureaucracy was not that it be replaced but that it be checked, on the one hand, within a framework of mutually limiting power structures and, on the other, by ensuring that bureaucratic organizations were themselves subordinate to the control of individual leaders selected on the basis of nonbureaucratic principles and acting under such principles.

Weber's theoretical analysis of the dangers as well as the indispensability of bureaucracy was put to practical effect in his criticisms of the Wilhelmine constitution during World War I. He was one of the most outspoken advocates of democratization, in the interests of coherent military policy and decisive national leadership alike. After the war this critique was developed into a theory of democratic politics as "competitive leadership democracy." Weber was among the first to recognize that the advent of universal suffrage had undermined the independence of the individual member of parliament in favor of the party machine, and had ensured the subordination of both to the party leader capable of winning a mass following in the struggle of an electoral campaign. In arguing that the chief function of parliaments lay in ensuring the public scrutiny of government and in providing a training ground for political leadership, he anticipated the relative decline that would take place in their importance during the course of the twentieth century.

Weber can best be characterized as a political liberal whose achievement was to provide a reformulation of *liberalism in sociological terms that were appropriate to a new age of capitalist combines, bureaucratic organization, mass politics, and working-class advance. Although he deplored the demise of the era of classical individualism, his perspective was forward- rather than backward-looking, and it was to the individual leader at the head of organizations that Weber turned to embody the creativity and dynamism that were always associated in his mind with the individual rather than the collectivity. This opposition provides the most convincing rationale for his famous antithesis between bureaucracy and charisma.

(See also BUREAUCRATIC POLITICS; MARXISM; MODERNITY.)

Max Weber, *Economy and Society,* ed. Guenther Roth and Claus Wittich (New York, 1968). Wolfgang Mommsen, *The Age of Bureaucracy* (Oxford, 1974). David Beetham, *Max Weber and the Theory of Modern Politics,* 2d ed. (Cambridge, U.K., 1985). Wolfgang Mommsen, *Max Weber and German Politics, 1890–1920* (Chicago, 1985).

DAVID BEETHAM

WELFARE STATE

In the past one hundred years welfare states have emerged both in Western Europe and in North America as only the most recent stage in the long-term process of *state formation in the West. Although widely different in their legal character, ideological legitimation, institutional structure, level and scopes of benefits, and overall share in the national income, all contemporary welfare states display significant similarities in their development and functioning.

In Western capitalist *democracies, national, collective, and compulsory arrangements have emerged in order to cope with the adversities and deficiencies that affect individual citizens in industrial society. Social security constitutes the hard core of the welfare state—a system of insurance under the direct or indirect control of the national government, intended to cover the risks to wage earners and their dependents of income loss when it is impossible for them to work because of disease, disability, lack of employment opportunity, old age, or death. Levies and benefits are job-related, and accordingly the system rests on the assumption that the vast majority of the healthy, adult, male population is regularly employed from adolescence to old age. Dependents are assumed to share in the wages and, if necessary, in the benefits paid to breadwinners or their survivors.

Social security represents a functional equivalent of the providential aspects of private saving. Payroll taxes are deducted from wages and serve to finance the benefits to those who cannot work: a compulsory accumulation of transfer capital. The obligation is imposed especially on wage earners. The self-employed are usually left out of social security, and salaries are often exempt from levies beyond a certain limit. As a result, social security taxes tend to be fiscally regressive, increasing income inequality, while benefits may have a progressive effect. The most important redistributive result, however, is an overall income transfer from the young to the old.

Modern welfare states complement their social security systems with some form of social assistance (or "welfare" in the strict sense as it used in the United States). These benefits are financed from general tax funds and reserved for those who are in no position to claim social security benefits on the basis of their past working career. The main beneficiaries are single parents and aged persons (both groups largely women) and those who have been disabled before reaching working age.

In many countries family allowances are paid, increasing with the number of children, so as to correct a wage system based on individual achievement to ensure that the needs of wage earners' dependents are met. Finally, a variegated array of "human" or "welfare services" provides manifold forms of assistance, such as social work, community work, legal counseling, psychotherapy, rehabilitation, and so on.

Closely connected to the web of welfare state benefits and services are the sectors of health care and education. In most countries wage earners are insured for the costs of medical treatment, hospitalization, and medication, with varying degrees of legal compulsion and of government intervention in the delivery of care. Only in the United States has insurance against medical expense remained mostly private, although the government fully funds Medicare (1956) for the elderly and Medicaid (1965) for welfare clients; also there is no national insurance scheme for income loss resulting from disease, although such plans function at the state level in New York and California, among others. In Britain, at the other extreme, all medical personnel and facilities were brought under direct government control through the National Health Service (1946).

Elementary education is compulsory up to early adolescence in all welfare states, and everywhere it is closely regulated and in large part subsidized by government. The development of basic skills and vocational training in principle enables all adult citizens to earn a living, reducing dependence on welfare provisions to specific conditions of hardship.

Many welfare states have carried out, at the national or the municipal level, large public housing programs aimed at providing adequate workers' dwellings at low rents. In the periphery of the welfare state, a multitude of government-initiated benefits, subsidies, and prevention, training, or treatment schemes provide for specific needs of separate population categories.

There is no single common denominator to define the area of the welfare state. Even within one country, a panoply of legal, ideological, and institutional characteristics intermingle to produce a conglomerate of arrangements. Private associations, church agencies, and governmental services compete and collaborate at every level, constituting a transitional zone between the private and the public realm: this coalescence is itself typical of modern welfare states.

The complexity and variety of contemporary welfare arrangements present social scientists with a challenge to establish some order and seek a systematic theoretical approach. Welfare state institutions may be analyzed from the perspective of the functions they perform. As philanthropic aid and insurance benefits were increasingly tied to a past of regular employment, they tended to reinforce the pressure on able workers to accept steady wage labor. As a consequence, social policy has been instrumental in "transforming non-wage-workers into wage-workers" (Claus Offe, *Contradictions of the Welfare State,* London, 1984) and thus has contributed to a process of "active proletarianization" by compelling already-dispossessed workers to sell their labor for a wage. Unemployment benefits and social assistance served the function of "regulating the poor" by maintaining a reserve labor force during slack periods and forcing it into employment as demand for labor picked up again (Frances Fox Piven and Richard A. Cloward, *Regulating the Poor: The Functions of Public Welfare,* London, 1972).

If these views stress the functions of the welfare state in creating and maintaining the supply of wage labor, other approaches accentuate the contribution of welfare state institutions to the maintenance of public order and the formation of modern citizens

by simultaneously eradicating extreme poverty and the rebellious nonconformism of the "dangerous classes." Madhouses, workhouses, and jails all served to "punish and discipline" (Michel Foucault, *Discipline and Punish: The Birth of the Prison,* London, 1977); schoolteachers, visitors to the poor, housing supervisors, and social workers became the infantry in the campaign for "social control" (Stanley Cohen and Andrew T. Scull, eds., *Social Control and the State,* Oxford, 1983) or even a veritable "family police" (Jacques Donzelot, *The Policing of the Families,* New York, 1979).

Not only regular employment but also decent conduct; abstinence from promiscuous sex, gaudy pleasures, alcohol, and illicit drugs; and parental discipline and children's school attendance became conditions for entitlement to welfare benefits. It was expected that workers who contributed to national insurance throughout their working lives and came to rely on its benefits in times of need would strengthen their initially tenuous bonds to the national state—a foremost consideration in Bismarck's Germany and a function served most explicitly by the veterans' schemes developed in the United States after the Civil War (Theda Skocpol and John Ikenberry, "The Political Formation of the American Welfare State in Historical and Comparative Perspective" *Comparative Social Research* 6 [1983]: 87–148) and in France after World War I.

The manifold institutions of the emerging welfare state did indeed serve these functions more or less effectively, and from the early nineteenth century on large employers or concerned members of the urban middle class had in fact been motivated in growing numbers by such considerations. Moreover, overcrowding, filth, and epidemics in the sprawling inner cities strongly heightened their concern with urban industrial poverty. The twofold objectives of labor supply and public order and the corresponding motivations among the entrepreneurial and urban *elites are necessary elements in the explanation of the emergence of welfare states, but by themselves they are not sufficient. Even when major social actors agreed on the objectives to be realized and on the means to bring them about, they were still divided by conflicts about the distribution of burdens and still had to overcome the paralyzing dilemmas of collective action that, time and again, have stood in the way of concerted action on the part of established elites.

In some important respects, the history of the welfare state is a continuation of the development of care for the poor in medieval and early modern Europe. During the Middle Ages, in periods of weak local and regional government and in the absence of effective central authority, the vagrant poor presented a major threat to the security of landholding *peasants. They could easily destroy harvests, set fire to barns, or cast equally terrifying magic spells (a power attributed especially to elderly women who were helpless in all other respects). Those poor who could walk, and thus roam about from one village to another, could also fight and work, which made them both fearsome and potentially useful. The vagrant poor therefore represented both a threat and an opportunity to the established ranks of society. But the established villagers could not on their own ward off the danger or exploit the potential of the poor in their midst. Generous peasants might find their farms overcrowded by beggars, whereas more miserly neighbors would profit from the relative quiet and safety thus brought about at no cost to themselves.

Under these conditions, itinerant or village priests operated as charitable entrepreneurs: by exhorting the villagers to charity and threatening ostracism and damnation, they succeeded in increasing the peasants' confidence that their neighbors would be equally generous. Ritualized and ostentatious giving provided a setting for mutual control of charitable effort. The mutual suspicion that peers might abstain from charitable effort was initially overcome by manipulating these reciprocal expectations, and once collective action got underway, it was gradually superseded by mutual confidence and the informal sanctions that operate within an emerging collectivity.

In this sense, the virtue of charity rests on expectations of the virtuousness of others. A more or less precarious charitable equilibrium might thus come into existence, provided no major external disturbances, such as harvest failure, plague, invasion, or war, interfered to undo it again. Village charity accordingly came about as the result of a process in which collective action produced both a collectivity, the parish community, and a collective good, pacification of the poor in the parish area.

In this perspective, the dilemmas of collective action belong to a phase of transition: the actors concerned are interdependent and already aware of their interdependence, but there is as yet no agency for effective coordination of their efforts. The collectivizing process may be set in motion through manipulation of expectations, by illusory expectations, or through outside intervention, and once it is underway, collective action may bring about a collectivity that can more effectively coordinate the members' efforts at creating collective goods.

A next round of the collectivizing process with respect to the care of the poor occurred at a higher level of integration in early modern Europe, when towns found themselves confronted with bands of vagrant beggars roaming the countryside and threatening their supplies. Again, municipalities hesitated to provide food and shelter lest they be overrun by the needy, and every town hoped it could profit from the efforts of its neighbors. The town walls served as much to keep out the poor, who plundered the harvests, as to defend against enemy armies. This time the dilemmas of collective action were overcome by an illusion: the workhouse, which was expected to take in the sturdy (that is, the able and dangerous) poor and make them work for their own keep without cost to the town. Although these high hopes soon proved illusory and the workhouses ended up operating at a loss, rarely succeeding in keeping the worst offenders behind their walls, the expectations prompted many municipalities in the sixteenth and seventeenth centuries to found workhouses. As workhouses spread, especially in the large cities, they absorbed a considerable number of vagrants. Although still relatively weak, central governments could persuade local authorities to continue operating their workhouses by judiciously distributing grants (e.g., the seventeenth century French *don royal*). Central governments also intervened by establishing general rules for the allocation of the poor (to their locality of birth or of residence) and, by enforcing these rules, increased the confidence of local authorities that neighboring towns would accept their shares of the burden, thus encouraging them to do likewise (e.g., the Elizabethan poor laws in England, 1601). As the central government intervened, local authorities competed in demanding its support, in the process both intensifying central intervention and promoting the expansion of the central state apparatus. By the end of the eighteenth century, European national states were deeply, albeit indirectly, involved in the care of the poor, which continued to be implemented by local authorities.

The spread of popular education in the nineteenth century represented another major advance in central state intervention in the lives of the poor and laboring classes. At its core, the elementary curriculum consists of a code for national communication, permitting any two strangers in the realm to effectively manage their encounter. A major impetus for the development of mass elementary education came from the conflict between, on the one hand, metropolitan elites, oriented toward the national state and the national market, who sought direct access to potential consumers, workers, taxpayers, recruits, and voters in the country at large, and, on the other hand, elites with a regional base who attempted to maintain their monopolistic mediation functions for their local clientele. Bureaucratic innovations such as the inspectorate, teacher certification, school subsidies, and enforcement of attendance constituted so many ramifications of the administrative apparatus into the remotest parts of the territory and into aspects of life hitherto considered outside the pale of public life. Mass education did increase the mental aptitudes and the social opportunities of the poor, but it also helped to form a state apparatus that would be equal to the intricacies of managing millions of people in contemporary social welfare systems. The experience of mass mobilization and large-scale warfare also prepared the bureaucracy for subsequent massive social interventions.

Throughout the nineteenth century the position of industrial workers was considered an anomaly, a transitory phenomenon. The established citizenry reasoned that if only laborers would learn to save, they would be able to provide against adversity and perhaps even establish themselves as independent entrepreneurs. Moral improvement and a "civilizing campaign" would teach them foresight and self-discipline. Within the radical wing of the workers' movement, on the other hand, the situation of the proletariat was equally regarded as transient—soon to be superseded by a socialist or syndicalist order in which either the state or workers' councils would run the factories and distribute the proceeds among those who had worked for them.

Only when industrial wage employment came to be considered a permanent and pervasive phenomenon of modern society did the notion of some kind of collective insurance against income loss take hold definitively. During the second half of the nineteenth century, workers' mutual funds spread rapidly, a transitory phenomenon between small, voluntary, private saving (albeit in groups and under mutual pressure) and large-scale, compulsory, collective provision. But mutual funds tended to exclude the neediest and to suffer from an accumulation of risks owing to their homogeneous membership, which was exposed to the same epidemics, laid off en masse, and reached pensionable age in the same period.

As industrialization proceeded and wage workers increased in number, attempts at solving the "social question" became the subject of intense contestation at every turn. First, there was the matter of distribution of the financial burdens that any kind of workers' insurance would entail. Second, the small bourgeoisie resisted all inroads by big business, big government, and big unions, and certainly the compulsory accumulation of transfer capital in lieu of private savings (Henri Hatzfeld, *Du Paupérisme à la Sécurité Sociale; Essai sur les Origines de la Sécurité Sociale en France, 1850–1940*, Paris, 1971). And, finally, the workers' movement was deeply divided on the issue of social insurance and government intervention—the American Federation of Labor (AFL) and the European radical socialist unions vehemently opposed the idea, whereas other unions supported it on condition that the state or the employers pay the costs.

Any lasting and adequate solution would have to match the scale of the problem: it would have to redistribute income from younger generations of workers to the retired, encompass an entire industrial sector so as not to unduly favor competitors, and maintain solvency into the distant future. Unions adamantly resisted company insurance because it tied the workers to the firm and might become insolvent with the company's demise. Management equally vehemently opposed union insurance as it would strengthen the union's grip on the workers and allow it to have a say in shop floor discipline. Both workers and employers wanted the other side to pay for the scheme. If the scheme was to be redistributive, older workers might find it even harder to get a job, for it was feared that they would soon qualify for retirement benefits from the common fund.

Employers faced the familiar dilemma of collective action: a cooperative course would weaken their position vis-à-vis their competitors, whereas an uncooperative stance would leave the overall situation at least as bad as before. External compulsion might solve the dilemma for them by forcing each and everyone to collaborate and by relieving fears that, by staying out of the insurance plan, some would improve their competitive position at others' expense.

Under these conditions an activist reformist regime might initiate legislation for social insurance, seeking the support of either progressive large entrepreneurs or moderate unions, or both. Bismarck did the former in Germany in the early 1880s, Lloyd George the latter shortly before World War I in Britain, and Franklin Delano *Roosevelt followed the third course in the early 1930s in the United States (Wolfgang J. Mommsen and W. Mock, eds., *The Emergence of the Welfare State in Britain and Germany, 1850–1950,* London, 1981; Maurice Bruce, *The Coming of the Welfare State,* London, 1961, 1968 [on the United Kingdom]; Martha Derthick, *Policymaking for Social Security,* Washington D.C., 1979 [on the United States]; Margaret Weir, Shola Orloff, and Theda Skocpol, eds., *The Politics of Social Policy in the United States,* Princeton, N.J., 1988).

The aftermath of World War II saw an extension and intensification of social security schemes throughout Western Europe, inspired by the Beveridge plan in Britain and similar schemes promising soldiers and workers a better future after the war. The appeal of the victorious Soviet Union and of communist parties throughout Europe helped to persuade centrist and conservative parties in the West that the time had come for adequate workers' insurance, if only to erase the memories of the misery that the Great Depression had caused for millions of unemployed workers, radicalized by their experience.

As a result of mobilization for total warfare, the state apparatus had increased enormously in capacity. During wartime large unions and big business had learned to cooperate with government, and afterwards this "wartime triangle" remained in place. After 1945, democratic society everywhere seemed to imply a welfare state.

In the early 1950s, once the devastations of war had been repaired, economic growth was used to finance expansion of welfare provisions. A second period of rapid growth occurred in the late 1960s and early 1970s. Throughout the postwar period "welfare state politics could lie in repose while the engine of economic growth did its work" (Hugh Heclo, "Toward a New Welfare State?" in Peter Flora and Arnold J. Heidenheimer, eds., *The Development of Welfare States in Europe and America,* New Brunswick, N.J., and London, 1981, pp. 383–406). The clientele of welfare provisions expanded accordingly. Even voters who opposed in principle public spending and high taxation tended to oppose much more strenuously cuts in benefits that profited them personally than they supported retrenchments in general and in the abstract. In this manner, strongly motivated minorities combined to defend their interests succesfully every time they were threatened by a necessarily less determined and cohesive opposition.

The second consequence of this expansion was the emergence of a stratum of professional experts and administrators who depended on collective arrangements for employment and advancement. These "new middle classes" constituted a formidable array of interest groups promoting the expansion of welfare arrangements.

A third consequence was a broad transformation of mentality among citizens of contemporary welfare states: 1) An increase in valuation of what experts and the welfare state have to offer—health, knowledge, and protection from income loss. People increasingly defined events in their daily lives in terms of the basic concepts of the professions that they expected to provide these values: a process of "proto-professionalization." 2) Increasing orientation toward the future, by deferring immediate gratification through greater self-constraint or through the acceptance of compulsion, for example, in schooling and social insurance. 3) Increasing awareness of the generalization of interdependency in modern society, a transition from a perception of events mainly in terms of religion or morality to a consciousness of the "lengthening chains of dependency"—an awareness of the ways in which the adversities and deficiencies that afflict one group affect others indirectly.

In this transition from charitable feeling to social consciousness, a sense of responsibility for the plight of others is combined with the conviction that it is not the duty of the individual to ameliorate the condition of the stranger in need. The state has become the abstract, universal, and anonymous caretaker of all members of society. Yet this "social consciousness" is not at all gratuitous. It implies silent consent to a considerable tax burden and to a significant redistribution of income between generations, between sexes, and between the active and nonactive populations. In short, social consciousness relates to charity as transfer capital to alms and as industrial production to craftsmanship.

By the mid-1970s, the powerful forces for expansion of the welfare state were checked—mainly by the budgetary deficits they helped to cause. In the following years left-wing governments such as that of François *Mitterrand in France found themselves incapable of continuing expansionist policies. Meanwhile, rightist regimes, such as Margaret *Thatcher's in Britain and Ronald *Reagan's in the United States, mostly failed in cutting back health, education, or social security expenditures. In multiparty systems, coalition politics even reinforced spending patterns: where bourgeois and social democratic parties alternated in government, as in the Netherlands, Scandinavia, and Italy, social expenditure nevertheless continued to increase (Harold L. Wilensky, "Leftism, Catholicism, and Democratic Corporatism: The Role of Parties in Recent Welfare State Development," in Flora and Heidenheimer, eds., *op. cit.,* pp. 345–382). After a period of exponential expansion from the mid-1940s to the mid-1970s, the welfare state has not broken down, but its growth has been slowed or halted.

The main problem in the further development of welfare arrangements is the gradual erosion of the dominant pattern of a full-time, lifelong working career. Persistent unemployment, the feminization of the work force, and part-time or casual work combine to undo the close relation between past earnings and subsequent entitlements that was at the core of the social security system. Increasingly elaborate regulations tend either to provoke evasion or to prompt inspection, thus undermining both civil confidence and civil liberties. Universal schemes, modeled after national pension plans, that require no means test and cannot easily be defrauded, such as the minimum income or negative income tax, appear to be promising but costly new avenues.

State-controlled arrangements for social security and health care exist in many developing countries as well. But these schemes tend to be restricted to those in regular wage employment, especially the military, the civil service, professionals, and workers in indispensable industries, such as mines or railroads. Domestic workers, the self-employed, and agricultural workers are generally excluded from membership. As a consequence, the overall redistributive effect is regressive—contributions and services are paid in large part by the general taxpayer or the consumer, and benefits accrue to a small, highly-paid, urban minority (Stewart MacPherson and James Midgley, *Comparative Social Policy and the Third World,* New York, 1987).

The Western welfare state stands at the end of a collectivizing process that in the course of many centuries has expanded in scale from the rural village to entire nations. But the process has not gone beyond that level, and the arrangements remain national in scope. Transnational social policy measures, implying an enforced accumulation of transfer capital and its redistribution from rich to poor nations, so far remain utopian.

(See also CITIZENSHIP; FEMINIZATION OF POV-

ERTY; GREAT SOCIETY; LABOR MOVEMENT; POLIT-
ICAL ECONOMY; SOCIALISM AND SOCIAL DEMOC-
RACY; TAXES AND TAXATION.)

Richard M. Titmuss, *Essays on "The Welfare State"* (London, 1958). Harold L. Wilensky and Charles N. Lebaux, *Industrial Society and Social Welfare* (New York, 1958). T. H. Marshall, *Social Policy in the Twentieth Century* (London, 1965). Catharina Lis and Hugo Soly, *Poverty and Capitalism in Pre-industrial Europe* (Brighton, U.K., 1979). Michael B. Katz, *In the Shadow of the Poorhouse; A Social History of Welfare in America* (New York, 1986). Peter Flora, ed., *Growth to Limits: The Western European Welfare States Since World War II*, 5 vols. (Berlin and New York, 1987). Abram de Swaan, *In Care of the State; Health Care, Education and Welfare in Europe and the USA in the Modern Era* (New York and Cambridge, 1988). Gøsta Esping-Anderson, *The Three Worlds of Welfare Capitalism* (Cambridge, U.K. 1990).

ABRAM DE SWAAN

WESTERN SAHARA. A territory claimed by *Morocco, Western Sahara is a former Spanish colony (1884–1976) located in northwest Africa. The territory is about 260,000 square kilometers (100,000 sq. mi.). In 1974, there were reportedly about 74,000 Sahrawis, the native Arabo-Berber-speaking people; owing to the nomadic character of the Sahrawis and the growth of the population since then, the actual figure today may reach more than 250,000. Although Western Sahara is one of the most inhospitable places in the world because of the scorching temperatures, this desert land contains considerable mineral deposits, mainly phosphates (reserves are estimated at 1.7 billion tons), and enjoys extremely rich fishing waters on the Atlantic coast.

Although the UN has called, since 1966, for the holding of a referendum on *self-determination for the Sahrawi people, Spain ceded her former colony to Morocco and *Mauritania in November 1975 before officially withdrawing from the territory in April 1976. The Frente Popular para la Liberación de Saguia el-Hamra y Rio de Oro (POLISARIO), the Sahrawi liberation movement, formed in May 1973 to liberate the land, immediately proclaimed the creation of a new state, the Sahrawi Arab Democratic Republic (SADR). The SADR became a member of the *Organization of African Unity (OAU) in 1984 and was recognized by seventy-six countries as of 1991. The territory, however, was occupied by Moroccan and, until 1979, Mauritanian troops. Morocco has since maintained and strengthened its military and administrative occupation, and controls about two-thirds of the land (including the Mauritanian sector, which it annexed following Mauritania's withdrawal).

Even though the *International Court of Justice stated in its 1975 report that Morocco, despite the ties of allegiance Sahrawi tribes had with Moroccan sultans in the past, had no rights of sovereignty over the territory, Moroccans continue to claim that Western Sahara is part of the Kingdom of Morocco.

The latter has strengthened its hold over the territory by positioning several thousand troops inside electronically protected earthen walls. Settlements of Moroccans have also been encouraged by the government in spite of the disputed status of the territory and the illegal character of its occupation. Morocco's occupation of Western Sahara led to tension with *Algeria, which has sheltered thousands of Sahrawi refugees in the Tindouf area and has provided military, diplomatic, and logistical support to POLISARIO and to the government-in-exile of the SADR.

In May 1988, Morocco and Algeria reestablished diplomatic relations, which Morocco had broken off in 1976. In August 1988, Morocco and POLISARIO accepted the UN secretary-general's peace plan which included the holding of a referendum on self-determination. Hopes for a peaceful resolution grew following the meeting between Morocco's King Hassan and POLISARIO leaders in January 1989. However, Morocco refuses to continue the direct dialogue despite calls put forth by the UN and the OAU. The United States, which has traditionally supported Morocco through substantial military and economic aid, has also encouraged a negotiated settlement. But, whereas the U.S. Congress has been more forceful in its demand for a resolution of the conflict, the Bush administration, despite its support for UN resolutions on Western Sahara, has been reluctant to put similar pressure on Morocco as it did on Iraq during its occupation of Kuwait because of Morocco's participation in the U.S.-led coalition during the *Gulf War.

In 1991, the situation remained stalemated. Morocco refused to withdraw its military and administrative forces, a decision which prevented the referendum from being held without constraints. Thanks to Morocco's improved relationship with Algeria and to the creation in 1989 of the Arab Maghreb Union (Algeria, Morocco, Tunisia, Mauritania, and Libya), in which the SADR is unrepresented, King Hassan felt less pressured to hold a fair referendum whose outcome may be favorable to the Sahrawi people. More seriously, in August and September 1991, Morocco forced the displacement and killed hundreds of Sahrawis through air raids only a few days before the cease-fire and also reneged on the conditions of the peace plan by insisting on adding several thousand individuals to the list of voters initially agreed upon. Furthermore, although the king agreed to the holding of a referendum in January or February 1992, Moroccan authorities created many hurdles for UN officials in charge of organizing the referendum. As a result, the date of the referendum has been postponed indefinitely. The question of Western Sahara is the UN's last decolonization issue, but its final resolution remains uncertain. Unless international pressure is applied effectively (similar to the *European Parliament's position), it is very unlikely that Morocco will relinquish its hold over Western Sahara or will even take the risk of allowing a fair referendum to be held.

(See also MILITARY RULE.)

John Damis, *Conflict in Northwest Africa* (Stanford, Calif., 1983). Yahia Zoubir and Daniel Volman, eds., *The International Dimensions of the Western Sahara Conflict* (Westport, Conn., 1992).

YAHIA H. ZOUBIR

WESTERN SAMOA. See PACIFIC ISLANDS.

WEST GERMANY. See GERMANY, FEDERAL REPUBLIC OF.

WOMEN AND DEVELOPMENT. The linking of the subjects of "women" and "development" was one of the outcomes of the UN Decade for Women (1975–1986). The Decade, with its themes of *equality (women's rights), *development (alleviation of poverty), and *peace (elimination of all forms of violence), must be seen within the framework of the concern of the international community with the issue of development in the years following World War II. The assumption underlying the launching of the first Development Decade (1960–1970) was that the process of capital accumulation and ensuing increases in the GNP would lead to the alleviation of poverty and to sustained economic growth. However, the failure of the benefits of economic growth to "trickle down" to the poor led to calls for a "new development approach," one that would focus on people, and to the "discovery" of women's role in development.

The recognition that women, as a specific social group, required special attention was supported by the seminal work of the Swedish economist Ester Boserup's *Women's Role in Economic Development* (New York, 1970), which drew attention to the importance of women's work in agriculture in many *Third World countries and to the "invisibility" of much of this work to economic planners and policymakers. Women's "invisibility" in the processes of production led to their marginalization, and to the notion that they were "outside" of development. Strategies for the "integration of women in development as beneficiaries and contributors" became the major theme for the Decade for Women, and an element in the overall strategies for the achievement of development goals in the Second Development Decade (1970–1980). The designation of 1975 as International Women's Year and the subsequent launching of a Decade for Women provided the framework for a variety of policies, programs, and projects aimed at the "integration of women in development" (WID for short), and the term entered the vocabulary of the discourse on development.

Over the past twenty years a number of different approaches to "increasing the participation of women in development" have been identified—from the "welfare" approach of the 1950s to 1970s, through the "equity" approach (the original WID approach, linked to the goal of equality) and the "anti-poverty" approach (linked to the goal of development). Currently, "efficiency" and "empowerment" have become the most commonly used concepts.

In the literature it is also possible to identify three approaches—Women in Development (WID), Women and Development (WAD), and Gender and Development (GAD). Although they are not mutually exclusive they represent slight but significant differences in approach: WID focuses on women's programs, WAD attempts to explore the relationship between these programs and development programs, while GAD considers the link between women and development issues in the context of the relationships between men and women embedded in the social relations of *gender. The increasing replacement of the word *women* by *gender* is a cause of concern among some feminists not only because of the fear that women will again become "invisible" but also because they see in this approach the tendency to obscure women's subordination as an issue. The use of gender as a feminist tool has, however, prevented this.

Another approach worth noting is that of "mainstreaming." Since 1985, despite the ending of the UN Decade for Women and the reduced resources available for women's development programs and projects, WID programs have continued, and indeed, gained new momentum with the thrust toward mainstreaming of women's projects by the United Nations Fund for Women (UNIFEM). Mainstreaming is a strategy for linking women's projects into the processes of development planning and delivery systems so that women gain access to development resources. The chief analytical tool for achieving this has been gender analysis, an analytical framework for identifying the differences in the (gender) roles of women and men, and elucidating the complexity of women's multiple roles and the implications of this for development planning.

The insights, knowledge, and analyses generated by the research and action stimulated by the Decade for Women have led to major challenges to the traditional discourse on development itself, and increasingly to the call for a new paradigm based on the reality and perspectives of women. At the cutting edge of this debate is the emerging network of Third World feminists—women involved in research and analysis, policy-making and action—promoting Development Alternatives with Women for a New Era (DAWN).

In a sense it was the achievement of many of the short-term goals of the Decade that revealed their limitation: for despite the changing of laws, the establishment of policies and programs, special mechanisms, and projects for ensuring the increased participation of women in development, the situation of women deteriorated, in the North as well as in the countries of the economic South, as the Decade progressed.

It is now increasingly recognized that the ideas and concepts guiding the policies and programs for the Decade emerged within a system that did not question the existing development model and which failed to recognize the interrelation between the cultural, social, and political factors which place women in positions of subordination and perpetuate this situation. The major assumptions of this model have been called into question: first, the "trickle-down" theory itself; second, that women were "outside" this model and that "integration into the mainstream" would improve their situation; third, that if women's contribution to development could be made visible to policymakers and planners they would be ensured access to benefits and resources; and fourth, that governments would introduce policies and programs which could enhance the role and status of women.

The research and analyses carried out throughout the Decade showed that industrialization and *modernization often had an adverse effect on women's lives, jeopardizing traditional *rights and livelihoods, "domesticating" them, limiting their role and status yet giving them additional burdens as modernization and commercialization replaced family-support systems and the mutual exchange of goods and services.

Feminist scholarship also exposed the existence of gender-based hierarchies, even at the level of the poorest household, determining women's access to critical resources and services. Moreover, it was recognized that far from being outside development, the exploitation of women's time, labor, and sexuality was central to the process of capital accumulation, and that women had in fact incurred a disproportionate cost of the evolution of the world capitalist system. Their marginalization, feminists argued, was not necessarily the product of ill-conceived development planning but a logical consequence of an economic system based on the exploitation of the most vulnerable by the most powerful.

Third, people began to acknowledge that development was not a purely technical issue but one that was deeply political and ideological. Political and ideological considerations were even more significant in issues concerning women and gender roles, rendering rational argument at times impossible and research findings irrelevant. Finally, the global economic crisis of the 1980s and the policies of structural adjustment adopted by most Third World countries to deal with the debt crisis exposed the apparent inability of governments locked into this global system to protect their countries from the devastating effects of the policies.

In fact, these policies emphasize the reallocation of government expenditures away from social services (so-called nonproductive sectors) to the "pro-ductive" sectors, and the privatization of these services, which tends to shift responsibility to "households" (i.e., women) and nongovernmental organizations. These patterns demonstrate, as nothing else has done, the gender and class biases inherent in a model that is focused on economic growth, and that ignores the social, cultural, and political factors that shape the lives of people. Indeed, cuts in social services jeopardize women in three ways: first, by reducing employment, because it is women who predominate in the social sector; second, by reducing their access to services that are essential if they are to manage their dual roles in production and reproduction; and third, by increasing the demand on their time, as they are expected to fill the gaps created by the cuts.

Similarly, on the production side of the equation, the export-oriented production models focus in many instances on the creation of export-processing zones dependent on large supplies of a cheap and compliant female labor force. The emphasis on export-oriented agriculture, meanwhile, jeopardized the production of food, the chief area of women's involvement in the field of agriculture.

But the negative impact of these policies on women also served to highlight how policies that hurt women spill over to the whole society. The centrality of women's role in reproduction, and the link between reproduction (all those tasks essential to the maintenance and sustenance of people who are also the labor force) and production, mean that policies which fundamentally harm women undermine the economy and society in far-reaching ways. Failure to take account of gender roles can therefore lead to faulty analysis and to ill-conceived policies.

All of this has led to a crisis in development itself, and to an increasing call for "development alternatives" that focus on the experience of women. One such alternative is the "empowerment" approach, a feminist approach based on a definition of *feminism as a consciousness of all the sources of women's oppression and a commitment to challenge and change the situation. The empowerment approach would build women's capacity to control resources by focusing on ensuring that they have the self-confidence and skills to access resources, and the analytical tools to understand the linkages between their situation and the larger structures—economic, social, cultural, and political—that so perversely affect their lives. It asserts that only a strong women's movement with the (feminist) consciousness and commitment to change can promote the achievement of a more equitable and humane world. In fact, from a narrow concern for "women's" issues, an increasing number of women see feminism as a "transformational politics" with the capacity to transform all oppressive structures.

For networks like DAWN, issues of *race/ethnicity, class, and *imperialism/neocolonialism must all be addressed along with gender, if women are to make their full contribution to the process of change. The network has shown the systemic linkages between debt, growing impoverishment, food insecurity and nonavailability, environmental degradation, growing demographic pressure, and *militarism. As Gita Sen and Caren Grown point out (*Development, Crises and Alternative Visions: Third World Women's Perspectives,* New York, 1987), "even as resources to strengthen women's economic opportunities are shrinking, women have begun to mobilize themselves, both individually and collectively, in creative ways. It is only by reinforcing and building upon their efforts in such vital sectors as food production, commerce, and trade that the needed long-term transformation to more self-reliant national development strategies can be achieved." They argue that development models which seek to place people at the center must therefore pay special attention to women and to the factors that constrain their participation in development, not only on grounds of equity (the goal of equality) and expediency (the goal of development), but because women's perspectives, strengths, and visions are essential if the planet is to survive (the goal of peace).

Thus, in the past two decades the linking of issues of development with that of women not only has led to a better understanding of women's contribution to development but has offered clues to the paths that need to be taken if the goals of a more holistic, participatory, and sustainable model of development are to be achieved: the shift from a focus on "integrating" women into an existing (and fundamentally inequitable) economic order to "empowering" women to change that order both summarizes the evolution and underlines the significance of the movement stimulated by the UN Decade for Women.

(See also FEMINIST THEORY; INTERNATIONAL DEBT; PATRIARCHY; REPRODUCTIVE POLITICS.)

Catherine Overholt, Mary B. Anderson, Kathleen Cloud, and James E. Austin, *Gender Roles in Development Projects* (West Hertford, U.K., 1984). Gita Sen and Caren Grown, *Development, Crises and Alternative Visions: Third World Women's Perspectives* (New York, 1987). Rita S. Gallin, Marilyn Aronoff, and Anne Ferguson, eds., *The Women and International Development Annual,* vol. 1 (Boulder, Colo., 1989). Ann Leonard, ed., *Seeds: Supporting Women's Work in the Third World* (New York, 1989). Caroline Moser, "Gender Planning in the Third World: Meeting Practical and Strategic Gender Needs" *World Development* 17, no. 11 (November 1989): 1799–1825.

PEGGY ANTROBUS

WORKERS' CONTROL. As David Montgomery has most cogently argued in *Workers' Control in America* (New York, 1979), workers' control over production has manifested itself from the beginnings of industrial capitalism in the chronic battles and everyday struggles of workers to control their own pace and style of work, to determine their own work group relations, and to resist the imposed routines of the clock and disciplines of the boss. In the nineteenth and early twentieth centuries, actual conflicts over control, as well as oppositional organizations and ideologies, such as anarcho-syndicalism, were most often rooted in craft cultures of skilled male workers. While challenging capitalist control, craft vision and practices were often quite traditional and exclusivist vis-à-vis less skilled and women workers.

With the political crises of World War I, however, as well as its acceleration of mass production and scientific management techniques threatening to further erode craft autonomy and shop floor discretion, skilled workers led mass movements for workers' control that included the less skilled more fully in a democratic challenge to capitalist authority in the workplace, and often in the political sphere as well. In Britain, the shop stewards movement was inspired by revolutionary syndicalism, as well as the guild *socialism of G. D. H. Cole, and helped articulate a vision of socialism based on democratic workers' control of industry, in contrast to statist control emerging in the Soviet Union. In Italy, Antonio *Gramsci and other Marxists around the journal *L'Ordine Nuovo* helped radicalize the unions' internal commissions and develop a movement for revolutionary workers' control through factory committees. Much like the Dutch council communist thinker Anton Pannekoek, Gramsci argued that the unions' function of bargaining for better conditions for the sale of labor power under capitalism prevented them from effectively representing workers' interest in democratic control of production and the abolition of labor as a commodity. In this view, unions invariably enforce bureaucratic discipline among workers, and only independent factory committees can lead the struggle to democratize the workplace.

In Germany and Russia, mass movements for workers' control in the factories and mines developed in the course of political revolutions at the end of the war, and these were often supported by workers' councils and soviets that took over local political power. The Bolsheviks' theoretical and practical ambivalence to workers' control was profound, however, as I have argued in *Workers' Control and Socialist Democracy: The Soviet Experience* (London, 1982), and along with the conditions generated by years of a devastating war followed by civil war (1918–1921), this ambivalence doomed workers' control in the new regime.

But as much as the early Soviet experience continues to define for many either the myth of democratic possibilities of revolutionary workers' control or the lessons of political betrayal, it is the experiences in other major European countries that defined limits relevant for the rest of the century. Even under the tremendous strains of war-induced political crises and rapid organizational growth, unions proved resilient and often able to accommodate modified demands for workers' control, and autonomist factory council movements proved incapable of generating effective leadership and organization to preempt or displace them. Neither the craft ideal nor resistance to Taylorism could be realistically sustained (contra Michael Piore and Charles Sabel, *The Second Industrial Divide,* New York, 1984), and industrial unionism was able to provide forms of representation and material benefits that enhanced the rights and conditions of the less skilled while compensating the more skilled. In cases such as Germany, the state was able to institutionalize works councils (1920) with modest powers and thus helped to undercut more radical demands for workers' control. In the post–World War II period, patterns of institutionalization through unions and the state became even more pronounced and were repeated even in some less developed societies. Challenges to these patterns emerged once again during militant shop floor struggles in the late 1960s and early 1970s, and the heritage of Gramsci, Cole, and others of the earlier period was revived and widely debated. Although these shop floor protests had an important impact on union organization, the revolutionary ideologies and vocabularies of workers' control were yet again displaced, this time by a much richer array of managerial, union, and state initiatives around worker participation and *industrial democracy. And more than in previous periods, these initiatives have aimed to reorganize the work process itself, utilizing the capacities of new information technologies to do so.

(See also ANARCHISM; INFORMATION SOCIETY; LABOR MOVEMENT.)

Carmen Sirianni, "Workers' Control in Europe: A Comparative Sociological Analysis," in James Cronin and Carmen Sirianni, eds., *Work, Community and Power* (Philadelphia, 1984), pp. 254–310.

CARMEN SIRIANNI

WORLD BANK. The World Bank, an enduring legacy of the postwar global economic order, is the foremost international *development institution. As the largest single source of lending for development, it is a principal intermediary between the advanced industrial countries and the less-developed countries. As the center of development orthodoxy, it is the primary actor in the propagation and dissemination of ideas about development. The financial and intellectual resources at its command, coupled with a steady growth of its roles in coping with economic adversity, have given it an increasingly influential and intrusive position in shaping policy choices of many countries. Its greatest impact in the *international political economy is one of system maintenance: it is a strategic mechanism for keeping developing countries engaged in the existing structures of world investment finance, technology, production, and exchange.

Formally the International Bank for Reconstruction and Development (IBRD), the World Bank was a product of the Bretton Woods conference of 1944. However, since the dominant concern of the architects of Bretton Woods was the postwar global monetary regime and the role of the *International Monetary Fund (IMF) in that regime, the bank was a sideshow in the epic negotiations at that conference. While the IMF was the object of many compromises between the United States and its European allies, the bank was in almost every respect an exclusively American creation, an institution that reflected the triumph of U.S. preferences and embodied a U.S. vision of world order. Practically the entire spadework for the organization had already been done by the U.S. Treasury Department. Given the fundamental asymmetry in which they found themselves in relation to the United States, other countries could only bargain for greater benefits and fewer burdens. Ultimately, it was the United States that determined the range of issues that would be subject to bargaining. On such issues as the lending capacity and the governing structure of the bank, the only relevant debate was that within the United States.

U.S. hegemony in the organization was consummated in the selection of its headquarters. John Maynard Keynes, Britain's senior foreign economic policy statesman, initially insisted that both the bank and the IMF be located outside the United States. Encountering U.S. opposition, he fought to have them located in New York City in the hope that they could be kept at a safe distance from "the politics of Congress and the nationalistic whispering galleries of the Embassies and Legations of Washington" (Roy F. Harrod, *The Life of John Maynard Keynes,* New York, 1951). The outcome was a foregone conclusion. The headquarters of the bank to this day is only two blocks from the White House, a location that not only ensures that few aspects of its operations escape political scrutiny but also one that gives the United States an inestimable degree of influence over the agency.

The paramount conception held by the creators of the World Bank was that of an organization that would perform compensatory and catalytic functions. The bank was designed to reduce the element of risk in foreign lending at a time when international capital markets were still reeling from the disastrous experiences of the interwar decades. Its own financing activities were expected to establish an international standard for sound loans and to improve the quality of information about international investment opportunities.

Although the developing countries succeeded in securing at Bretton Woods the injunction that development would command an equal priority as reconstruction, the primary mission initially assigned to the bank was to rebuild the economies of Europe ravaged by the war. When the bank began to shift its focus to the developing countries, it adopted an extremely cautious stance on who could be considered a creditworthy borrower and on what might qualify as a sound loan. In effect, its preoccupation with securing the confidence of investors dictated adherence to conservative conventions of banking on its part and an insistence on exacting standards of economic rectitude on the part of its clients.

Organizational Structure and Decision Making. From the very start, the sources of financing of the IBRD have confronted it with an exceptional amalgam of constraints and opportunities which, in turn, have intimately affected many aspects of its operations. The IBRD's equity consists of capital subscriptions from its shareholders—the member countries, currently 155 in number, who literally own the bank. However, the most important source of the IBRD's loanable funds comes from the sale of securities to private investors and central banks. It is the largest nonsovereign borrower in the international capital markets. Its modalities of financing give the IBRD a substantial degree of operational latitude and administrative discretion. At the same time they make the bank, perhaps more than any other * international organization, dependent on its standing in the financial markets. It is the judgment of bondholders, as much as the predilections of its leaders or the bidding of the United States, that defines the outer limits of what is permissible.

IBRD loans are concentrated on higher-income developing countries, borrowers commonly regarded as more creditworthy. Two organizational affiliates have been established to circumvent some of the limitations inherent in IBRD lending: the International Development Association (IDA) and the International Finance Corporation (IFC). The IDA was set up in 1960 in response to pressures from developing countries for a soft-loan agency under the control of the UN. It provides credits with maturities of up to forty years with 10-year grace periods and no interest (but a service charge of less than one percent). This concessional assistance is directed toward the poorest countries, most of which cannot attract commercial financing. What sets the IDA apart institutionally from the IBRD is its financial structure: aside from transfers from the IBRD (about US$100 million annually in recent years), the IDA derives its lending resources through periodic donations from wealthy countries.

The IFC, founded in 1956, is dedicated to the spread of private enterprise across the world and assists developing countries in attracting venture capital, both foreign and domestic, for that purpose. Like the IBRD, the IFC raises most of its resources through the capital markets. However, unlike the bank, the IFC makes not only loans but also equity investments. While its financial contributions have been modest relative to the bank's—in its thirty-five years of operation, the IFC has provided less than US$10 billion in financing—its larger impact is cat-

alytic. The IFC uses its own funds to mobilize project financing from other investors and lenders through syndications, underwritings, and cofinancing.

The concern with private capital led to the formation in 1988 of yet a third affiliate of the IBRD (and a fourth component of what is often designated as "the World Bank Group"), the Multilateral Investment Guarantee Agency (MIGA). The MIGA's mandate is to stimulate the flow of foreign direct investment to developing countries by providing guarantees against political risk such as armed conflict and civil unrest, * nationalization and expropriation, restrictions on currency transfer, and breaches of contract by host governments.

Formally, all powers of the World Bank are vested in a board of governors, consisting of one governor from each member country. As that body meets only once a year, most of its authority is delegated to a twenty-two member board of executive directors who meet in permanent session at the headquarters of the bank in Washington, D.C. The stratification of power among states in the bank is readily apparent in the composition of the executive board. While the five largest shareholders appoint their own directors, in effect occupying permanent seats on the board, the other members combine into more or less compatible caucuses to produce enough voting power to elect the remaining seventeen directors.

As in the IMF, voting is weighted: the voting strength of each member of the IBRD, as well as in its affiliates, is closely related to financial contributions. The United States, which initially commanded a plurality of thirty-five percent, has seen its voting power in the IBRD shrink by more than one-half. However, the dominant coalition of advanced industrial countries remains intact. In the IBRD, both the shares and the votes of the Big Five—the United States, Japan, Germany, France, and the United Kingdom—are more than forty percent. For the countries of the North as a whole, the proportion exceeds sixty percent.

The United States, moreover, continues to enjoy the preponderant influence among national actors in determining what issues do and do not dominate the organization's agenda. Although the United States has not always prevailed in preventing the bank from denying loans to individual countries (e.g., numerous countries singled as human rights violators in the 1970s) or for particular projects (e.g., agricultural projects considered to pose a threat of injury to U.S. producers in the 1980s), no programmatic initiatives are undertaken by the bank in violation of the preferences of the United States, nor are any likely to be pursued in the absence of the support of the United States. Because the United States does not face hegemonic contenders who espouse fundamental alternatives to the bank, the United States does not confront serious challenges to the traditional prerogatives it has enjoyed in the

Table 1. The World Bank's Largest Borrowers: Cumulative Lending through 30 June 1990
(Amounts in US$billions)

IBRD Loans[a]		IDA Credits[b]		Total IBRD/IDA Financing[c]	
1. India	$18.32	1. India	$16.96	1. India	$35.27
2. Brazil	17.98	2. Bangladesh	5.25	2. Brazil	17.98
3. Mexico	17.36	3. China	3.93	3. Mexico	17.36
4. Indonesia	14.83	4. Pakistan	3.24	4. Indonesia	15.76
5. Turkey	10.16	5. Tanzania	1.77	5. Turkey	10.34
6. South Korea	7.15	6. Ghana	1.45	6. Pakistan	7.41
7. Philippines	6.75	7. Kenya	1.40	7. South Korea	7.26
8. Colombia	6.53	8. Sudan	1.34	8. Philippines	6.87
9. Yugoslavia	5.81	9. Sri Lanka	1.32	9. Colombia	6.55
10. Nigeria	5.59	10. Ethiopia	1.26	10. Nigeria	5.85
11. China	5.28	11. Uganda	1.09	11. Yugoslavia	5.81
12. Morocco	5.18	12. Zaire	1.06	12. Morocco	5.23
13. Argentina	5.12	13. Nepal	1.06	13. Argentina	5.12
14. Thailand	4.19	14. Madagascar	1.00	14. Thailand	4.31
15. Pakistan	4.18	15. Egypt	0.98	15. Egypt	4.10

[a] IBRD lending began in 1947. Loans by the end of FY1990 totaled $186.66 billion. [b] IDA lending began in 1961. Cumulative credits made by the end of FY1990 amounted to $58.22 billion. [c] Details may not add to totals because of rounding. Compiled from data in World Bank, *Annual Report, 1990*.

organization, although such challenges could be forthcoming, especially from the European Community and Japan. It is still taken for granted that the president of the World Bank will be a U.S. national designated by the White House, even though they have seldom turned out to be subservient instruments of the U.S. government. During its first five decades the bank has had eight presidents: Eugene Meyer (1946–1947), John J. McCloy (1947–1949), Eugene R. Black (1949–1962), George D. Woods (1963–1968), Robert S. McNamara (1968–1981), A. W. Clausen (1981–1986), Barber Conable (1986–1991), and Lewis T. Preston (1991–).

Despite, and in part because of, the preeminence of the North in the World Bank, much of what the organization does is not the product of demands dictated by any single state or of bargains struck by a like-minded coalition of states. The distribution of voting rights sparks intermittent altercations among shareholders, but those votes are seldom exercised. Typically, decisions by the executive board have been consensual. Only rarely is there opposition to a lending proposal presented by the president to the board; even rarer is a proposal that is turned down by the directors.

The ascendancy of the "management," as the secretariat of the organization is called, was established in the early years after Eugene Meyer, the first president, resigned in a showdown with the executive directors over the issue of who would run the bank. The operational decisions that determine the day-to-day activities of the bank have since remained in the hands of the management, led by its president, whose resources today include a staff of more than 3,000 development professionals. The economic and technical expertise of this staff helps to ensure considerable administrative autonomy, as does the complex repertory of decision rules the organization has crafted over the years to govern its most tangible product, development projects.

Development Strategies: From Trickle-Down to the Magic of the Market. World Bank lending for development has gone through three major phases. While there are important continuities, each phase has been marked by different sets of policy goals and policy tools. Each phase has also reflected a different body of ideas about the role of the state and the market in development.

In the early years of development financing (1950–1965), the bank concentrated on "hard-hat," large-scale, and capital-intensive projects in economic infrastructure—power plants, highways, railways, ports, dams, and telecommunications facilities. The bulk of its loans were spent on the foreign exchange costs of such projects, whose financial and economic benefits could be measured with relative certainty. The bank became a steadfast champion of the view that investment in "physical overhead" sectors was the prerequisite for successful development. The proper role of the state in development it regarded as compensatory: to provide the institutional framework that would allow private enterprise, domestic and foreign, to function effectively. In addition, the bank pressed developing countries at every turn to rely on market incentives and market constraints. The emphasis on laissez-faire notwithstanding, the bank's activities from the very outset had a barely veiled Keynesian thrust. Its lending underwrote a more activist role for the state in developing economies. As early as the 1950s, the bank even gave its blessing to development * planning, maintaining that a visible hand was needed to guide investment decisions in order to ensure a sounder allocation of resources.

A major shift in its development strategy came in the 1970s under the leadership of Robert Mc-Namara, when the agency formally espoused a new hierarchy of objectives centering on the reduction of poverty and inequality. The new objectives, which found expression in such doctrines as "redistribution with growth" and "basic human needs," reflected misgivings both in and out of the bank about the consequences of the growth models it had peddled in earlier years. In particular, there was a widely shared conviction that trickle-down approaches of the past had worsened the syndrome of immiseration, marginalization, and inequality in many parts of the * Third World. McNamara personally took up the cause of alleviating the plight of the "bottom forty percent"—the 1 billion people thought to be living in conditions of absolute poverty.

The bank embarked on massive lending for * rural development, a sector that at one point became the largest in IBRD and IDA allocations, displacing even transportation. The bank also launched projects in other areas that previously had been neglected, especially population planning, health, nutrition, water, sanitation, small-scale enterprises, and sites and services for squatters in urban slums. The so-called "new-style" rural and urban projects were explicitly aimed at benefiting masses of the rural and urban poor. Yet, despite the rhetoric, the bank never benefits the truly poor of the world. The intended and actual beneficiaries of its poverty-oriented projects seldom reach below an upper crust of the poor, who, in contrast to the rural landless and the urban unemployed, were thought to be in a better position to pay back their loans. The new-style projects were still oriented toward increasing production. Hence, the original purposes of bank financing were not recast. Rather, new objectives and new components were tagged onto the old. Moreover, these projects, despite their novelty and complexity, were not subjected to a different set of evaluative criteria. Instead, the bank applied its traditional panoply of criteria for project evaluation. The thrust of the new-style projects remained reformist through and through. In the final analysis, therefore, the newly found concern about poverty did not amount to a wholesale departure for the bank, although it was instrumental in overturning many of the conventional assumptions once held by the bank about the process of development. It also put the bank at the forefront of global efforts to combat poverty in developing countries. The McNamara years are remembered as the golden era of this phase of the organization's history.

In the third phase, ushered in by the 1980s, the programmatic innovations of the 1970s were de-moted in favor of a yet more ambitious undertaking: rescuing developing countries from economic perversity. The World Bank began to gear its lending to a broad array of policy reforms that fall under the rubric of "structural adjustment." These reforms have included exposing protected economies to international competition and steering them toward outward-oriented policies; reducing distortionary government interventions in virtually all areas of economic activity; privatizing state-owned enterprises and, short of that, curbing their hold on the state budget and their access to domestic credit; and creating a decent "enabling environment" through a system of legal and regulatory institutions to facilitate economic activity. In pursuit of this agenda, the bank crafted a new lending vehicle, structural adjustment loans. In return for such balance-of-payments support, the bank wrested a commitment to a sweeping program of reform, with conditions that went greatly beyond the stipulations typically associated with project financing. Later in the decade, the bank deployed another instrument of policy-based lending, "sector adjustment loans." As they concentrate on policy and institutional reforms in a particular sector—such as finance, trade, agriculture, or energy—these loans are somewhat narrower in scope than structural adjustment loans, but they share many of the same objectives. By the end of the decade, adjustment lending surpassed twenty-five percent of the organization's lending commitments.

A complex array of factors pushed the World Bank to recast its strategy in the 1980s. The ascendance of neoclassical orthodoxy in the bank, as in the IMF, in many respects echoed the stances of its dominant shareholders, who have constantly pressured the two institutions to extend the scope and level of conditionality. The venture into balance of payments financing was also designed to compensate for the ponderous rhythms of the project cycle and to speed up the flow of resources to distressed borrowers. Institutional concerns over avoiding a lapse into irrelevance became particularly acute with the intensification of the economic travails of the 1980s, particularly as commercial creditors retreated from Third World lending in the wake of the debt crisis. There also were widespread admissions that projects once hailed as the cutting edge of development were less-than-adequate means for inducing policy reforms and that they might prove less than consequential in an overall framework of ruinous economic policies. Yet another contributor to the shift in strategy was the questioning within the bank regarding the open-ended support the organization gave to solidifying the role of the state in developing economies in the 1960s and 1970s, especially after it shed its inhibitions about lending to state-owned enterprises. Finally, while many disputes remained about such matters as the sequencing and pacing of reforms, the appropriate roles of the state and the market, and ways of mitigating political and social costs, a remarkable (albeit less than universal) consensus emerged on the central tenets of reformist packages. Few policy makers would challenge the need to adhere to monetary and fiscal prudence, to move away from inward-looking paths of development, to place a greater reliance on market forces, or to allow more leeway for the private sector.

Policy-based lending gave the World Bank a seat at the highest echelons of economic decision-making in developing countries. Henceforth, it would no longer consort merely with agricultural ministers and planning deputies; it became an interlocutor to finance ministers and central bankers as well. This higher profile inevitably embroiled the bank in some of the same political controversies that had plagued the IMF all along. These controversies intensified when the bank tightened and expanded conditionality to include not only economic but political liberalization (under the guise of such sobriquets as "governance").

Adjustment lending also increasingly pitted the bank against the IMF as the division of labor charted for the two agencies at Bretton Woods began to erode. Traditionally, the two agencies had complementary functions and close relations. Membership in the IMF has always been a prerequisite for membership in the World Bank. The notion that the IMF would assume responsibility for short-term reforms of a macroeconomic nature while the bank would occupy itself with long-term reforms of a microeconomic nature might have been credible at one time; it all but ceased to be so when the IMF began to pay more attention to "supply side" factors (e.g., enhancement of productive capacities in specific sectors and more efficient use of public revenues) that traditionally were the preserve of the bank, while the bank infused into its lending programs a host of macroeconomic concerns hitherto confined largely to the "wish lists" contained in its country economic reports and otherwise commonly regarded as falling within the competence of the IMF. As they were drawn into greater collaboration with one another, the bank and the IMF found themselves at odds over such policies as the amount of exchange rate devaluation and the size of public investment programs to be negotiated with borrowing countries. Partially, the conflicts are expressions of turf wars, including the jockeying for leadership in the lingering debt crisis, but they also suggest more fundamental differences in objectives and orientations between the two agencies.

Despite the narrowing of alternatives available to its economically troubled borrowing members and the greater leverage it has acquired over them as a consequence, the World Bank has not been particularly successful in achieving the objectives it has sought in adjustment lending. Its own evaluations provide only modest and highly qualified support to the notion that the average growth record of countries receiving adjustment loans is superior to that in countries that do not. These evaluations suggest improvements in external accounts, thanks to increased exports, although less than originally expected. On the other hand, the impact on indicators of living standards such as health, nutrition, and education has been at best negligible. Investment, which showed a marked decline, was one of the casualties of adjustment programs. These mediocre results are not a product of a general failure to adhere to the conditionality of adjustment loans; on the contrary; studies suggest that there has been substantial and increasing rates of compliance by borrowers (World Bank, *Adjustment Lending: An Evaluation of Ten Years of Experience,* Washington, D.C., 1988, and *Report on Adjustment Lending, II,* Washington, D.C., 1990).

Retrospect and Prospect. An analogy often used by World Bank staffers to describe their own organization is that of a supertanker that needs several nautical miles before it is able to modify its course. The tanker analogy seems apt when one considers the bank's response to the issue of the environment. As early as the mid-1970s, some bank officials acknowledged that they could no longer treat ecological destruction as just another inevitable but necessary externality. In subsequent years, others expressed the need to address ecological concerns explicitly in project design. Yet until the late 1980s these sentiments had only an episodic impact on project choice. What triggered internal policy reforms—including the establishment of a full-scale environment department, the creation of subunits within each of the regional offices (which are the mainstay of lending operations), and the adoption of a comprehensive environmental assessment directive—was external pressure from a coalition of environmental groups acting in concert with congressional critics of the bank who publicized the damage to the Brazilian Amazon and other environmental disasters caused by projects financed the bank (Bruce Rich, "The Emperor's New Clothes: The World Bank and Environmental Reforms" *World Policy Journal* 7, no. 2 [Spring 1990], pp. 305–329).

Such a pattern of behavior is hardly unique to the World Bank. Some of its responses are defensive and predictable reactions to the operational constraints it faces. The hesitation about undertaking a more assertive position in the debt crisis sprang in part from fears of jeopardizing its preferred creditor status and its standing in the capital markets. Yet, other responses by the bank involve creative and surprising adaptations to shifting opportunities. Ironically, the bank is not only becoming greener in its thinking and behavior but is also becoming the key player in the financing of environmental protection in developing countries.

Over the long run, the agency has been quite adept at recasting its policies in order to expand its domain. Indeed, it is probably one of the few multilateral organizations in the field of development whose authority has grown consistently. As its fiftieth anniversary approached, it faced more claimants and more demands than ever before. It proclaimed anew its commitment to poverty reduction in the Third World as its primary mission. Yet even as it reaffirmed the centrality of that task, it was faced with a new one: shepherding economic liberalization in the former republics of the Soviet Union who rushed to join the organization.

In the final analysis, the record of the World Bank has been profoundly contradictory. As the debt crisis suggests, the bank has been hostage to an economic environment over which it has little control. While the majority of its Third World members remained mired in the throes of the crisis, its flow of resources to them first shrank and then turned negative. Among the most severely distressed borrowers, in many years the World Bank, like the IMF, took out more through repayments than it put in through new loans. These negative transfers eroded the "money-moving" function that the bank regarded as integral to its identity and posed nothing less than a crisis of relevance for the institution. In many respects, development has proved to be a receding target. In the 1970s the bank failed in its attempt to create multisectorial and multicomponent projects that would combine the objectives of increasing productivity, reducing poverty, and enhancing equity. In the 1980s it had little more success in the daunting task of devising adjustment programs that would be economically, socially, politically, and administratively sustainable. And all along it managed to draw the fire of critics on both the Left and the Right: from the Left, "the bank thwarts socialist alternatives"; from the Right, "it bankrolls them."

For the foreseeable future, however, the World Bank will remain a linchpin of international collaboration in the area of development. It remains the leading channel of multilateral assistance for development. Among international organizations, it remains a principal protagonist in the process of economic reform in developing countries. And it remains the leading voice in the debate about development, its pronouncements, though seldom commonly heeded, always commanding attention throughout the developing world.

(See also BASIC NEEDS; ENVIRONMENTALISM; EQUALITY AND INEQUALITY; FINANCE, INTERNATIONAL; FOOD POLITICS; INTERNATIONAL DEBT; KEYNESIANISM; MODERNIZATION; NORTH-SOUTH RELATIONS; POPULATION POLICY.)

Edward S. Mason and Robert E. Asher, *The World Bank Since Bretton Woods* (Washington, D.C., 1973). Cheryl Payer, *The World Bank: A Critical Analysis* (New York, 1982). Judith Tendler, *Rural Projects Through Urban Eyes*, World Bank Staff Working Paper No. 532 (1982). Robert L. Ayres, *Banking on the Poor: The World Bank and World Poverty* (Cambridge, Mass., 1983). Richard E. Feinberg et al., *Between Two Worlds: The World Bank's Next Decade* (Washington, D.C., 1986). Paul Mosley, Jane Harrigan,

and John Toye, *Aid and Power: The World Bank and Policy-Based Lending*, vols. 1 and 2 (New York, 1991).

DON BABAI

WORLD COURT. See INTERNATIONAL COURT OF JUSTICE.

WORLD HEALTH ORGANIZATION. The World Health Organization (WHO) came into existence in 1948, taking over the functions of the Office International d'Hygiène Publique (established 1907) and the Health Organization of the League of Nations (established 1919). WHO's aim is the attainment by all peoples of the highest possible level of health, to be achieved through technical collaboration with its members in the areas of disease eradication, nutrition, environmental hygiene, and health service administration. To this end, WHO maintains epidemiological and statistical services, promotes scientific cooperation, proposes international conventions, conducts research, and develops international standards for food, biological, and pharmaceutical products. A publications program ensures the wide dissemination of statistical data and policy recommendations. Membership in the organization, which is open to all, has grown from the original sixty-one signatories to the Constitution in 1948 to 166 members in 1991.

Like other specialized agencies of the UN, WHO raises its budget from annual assessments of members. The projected 1992–1993 budget is US$764 million, but income from other sources such as the trust funds for *AIDS, tropical disease research, and onchocerciasis (river blindness) control more than doubles that sum, bringing the 1992–1993 total to US$1.69 billion.

WHO consists of three constituent bodies: the large, comprehensive World Health Assembly, which meets annually to decide policy and approve the program and budget; the smaller, representative Executive Board, which meets semiannually to prepare the assembly's agenda; and the Secretariat, which is the staff. Unlike other UN specialized agencies, WHO is a decentralized organization. It maintains headquarters in Geneva, Switzerland, but vital work of the organization is performed in six regional offices, which formulate regional policies and monitor regional activities—in Brazzaville, for the African region; in Washington, D.C., for the Americas; in Alexandria, Egypt, for the Eastern Mediterranean region; in Copenhagen, for Europe; in New Delhi, for Southeast Asia; and in Manila, for the Western Pacific region.

In the mid-1970s, under the leadership of Halfdan Mahler, a social democrat from Denmark, WHO stepped into the political limelight espousing the cause of the world's sick and poor. It successfully eradicated smallpox, the first disease ever to be eliminated through human effort. It gave *Third World nations useful instruments enabling them to negotiate with multinational corporations and, for those with the political will to do so, a handle on planning their services. It challenged the infant formula industry, for example, by producing a code that restricts sales practices in the Third World, and it took on the pharmaceutical industry by publishing a list of 200 essential drugs to substitute for the average 3,500 to 5,000 marketed to underdeveloped countries.

In 1978, the organization issued a challenge: "Health for All by the Year 2000." To reach this goal, WHO proposed a primary health care service model—a package of preventive and curative services to be delivered by auxiliary personnel. This strategy seemed revolutionary coming from an organization that, until 1975, subscribed to the medical doctrine that the proper response to human health needs in developing countries was the transfer of Western biomedical technology. Primary health care thus represented progress over most of WHO's previous programs, which relied on the delivery of curative services by physicians and nurses in urban hospitals. But the strategy failed to address the real health problems of the Third World poor and led only to the "medicalization" of underdevelopment. By the end of the 1980s, it was abandoned in favor of a multiplicity of microprojects run by nongovernmental organizations, which donors control more easily than direct aid to allegedly corrupt governments.

At the beginning of the 1990s in Latin America and Africa, tens of thousands of lives were claimed in outbreaks of cholera—the disease that instigated European cooperation in international public health in the nineteenth century. The current epidemic, which has killed the poorest of the poor living without the most elementary services in polluted, overcrowded shantytowns, underscores WHO's failure to alleviate the root causes of ill health. Basic concerns with the provision of latrines, safe water supplies, and adequate nutrition have yielded to preoccupation with AIDS, the new, communicable autoimmune disease syndrome that is potentially much deadlier than cholera.

Under Hiroshi Nakajima of Japan, the present director-general who assumed the post in July 1988, the organization appears to be shifting its viewpoiint. Though it worked closely with the UN Children's Fund (UNICEF) on the development of the primary health care strategy in 1978, WHO was not associaated with that agency's efforts a decade later to redress the decline in maternal and child health that followed in the wake of structural adjustment programs promoted by the *World Bank and the *International Monetary Fund.

Like other specialized agencies and the UN itself, WHO tends to mirror and transmit through its programs the balance of world power and the dominance of North over South. Smallpox eradication was carried out at the request of the United States,

which largely funded and staffed the program; not all Third World countries felt it was their highest priority or that it would improve overall health as measured by death rates, which failed to decline. Similarly, the Global Programme on AIDS corresponds to U.S. interests. The United States accounts for half of the world's cases of AIDS, and the U.S. government promotes research on heterosexual transmission of human immunodeficiency virus (HIV) rather than on care of people with AIDS under conditions of poor and scarce health resources; it also cooperates in vaccine trials with Third World governments that lack the health infrastructure needed to vaccinate their populations against HIV. WHO respected the UN Security Council embargo on Iraq during the 1991 *Gulf War and played no role in the provision of essential medical supplies or care to the civilian population, which it left to nongovernmental organizations, led by the International League of Red Cross and Red Crescent Societies.

If this trend continues, it seems unlikely that WHO will make a lasting change in the social inequalities between North and South, including inequalities in health care and chances of survival.

(See also DEVELOPMENT AND UNDERDEVELOPMENT; NORTH-SOUTH RELATIONS; UNITED NATIONS.)

Meredeth Turshen and Annie Thébaud, "International Medical Aid" *Monthly Review* (December 1981): 39–50. Meredeth Turshen and Annie Thébaud-Mony, "Combattre le SIDA au nom de la 'civilisation'?" *Le Monde Diplomatique* (April 1991): 24. World Health Organization, *The Work of WHO, 1990–1991: Biennial Report of the Director-General* (Geneva, 1991).

MEREDETH TURSHEN

WORLD SYSTEM. See INTERNATIONAL SYSTEMS.

WORLD WAR I. The fateful march toward the beginning of World War I started on 28 June 1914 in Sarajevo, Bosnia, with the assassination of Archduke Franz Ferdinand, heir to the throne of Austria-Hungary, and his wife. This terrorist act, planned in Belgrade with the knowledge of some Serbian officials, convinced Habsburg decision makers in Vienna that only a military defeat of the Serbs would curb South Slav appeals threatening the multinational state. Determined to take action, the Habsburg leadership in early July quickly gained German assurances of military support in case of a major *war. Berlin hoped this act of loyalty to its longtime ally (since 1879) would deter Russian intervention. The Austrian ultimatum, delivered on 23 July 1914 in Belgrade, was deliberately framed to be rejected. On 25 July Austria-Hungary broke diplomatic relations with Serbia; three days later Vienna declared war. The Habsburgs believed they had launched the Third Balkan War.

Russia's actions, meanwhile, were guaranteeing the war would not be localized. From the start Saint

Petersburg resolved to protect its Serbian client and its own *Balkan amibitions. Russia's assertiveness during the July crisis—not surprisingly—collided with Vienna's desire for revenge and the German commitment to support its ally. On 30 July Russia ordered general mobilization, the first Great Power to do so. This decision sparked German countermeasures. The step also thwarted Britain's belated efforts for mediation. Berlin then ordered mobilization and shortly thereafter began its offensive against France. Germany's deliberate violation of Belgian neutrality convinced the British cabinet to support France against Germany. By 5 August 1914 World War I had begun, even though the major fighting was still days away.

Europe's system of *alliances (the Triple Alliance of Germany, Austria-Hungary, and Italy) and ententes (the Triple Entente of Russia, France, and Britain) had managed for a decade to avoid a direct confrontation involving all of the partners. Now after two years of constant Balkan tension, the Sarajevo murders brought all but Italy into a continental war. Rampant *militarism, press agitation, fanatical *nationalism, untested military and naval forces, and boredom combined to end a century of European stability and *peace.

The shooting had scarcely begun when the war became a genuine world war. On 23 August Japan declared war on Germany, fulfilling its alliance commitment to Britain and seizing some German holdings in the Far East. Before long, a tortuous campaign began among German and Birtish colonial troops in Africa. Closer to Europe, the Ottoman government first proclaimed its neutrality in August, then in October joined the Central Powers (Germany and Austria-Hungary).

The Search for Allies. Both sides now started a desperate search for additional allies. The most fateful interventions would be those of Italy and the United States. From August 1914 to May 1915 Rome negotiated with both sides over possible entry. Italy's goal was unambiguous: it wanted Habsburg lands in which Italians lived transferred to Italy. To offset the claim of Italian irredentism Vienna and Berlin had little to offer but Habsburg territory. Yet Vienna's offers were never enough. Finally, on 23 May 1915, Italy entered the war against its former allies. Ultimately the Italian dead would outnumber the Italians living in the areas transferred after the war. Bulgaria and Romania remained aloof from the initial fighting. Each was courted assiduously. Eventually, in late 1915 Bulgaria entered the war to defend itself against an Anglo-French-Greek effort in Macedonia. Then in the summer of 1916 Bucharest joined the Triple Entente, only to find itself quickly routed by Austro-German forces. Neither intervention altered the course of the war.

U.S. intervention in April 1917 would be far more important. Through the war's first three years, Washington opted for neutrality while profiting handsomely from the sale of war goods to the Triple Entente powers. But in early 1915 Berlin's decisions about submarine warfare threatened to entangle the United States. The sinking of the *Lusitania* in May 1915 with the loss of 128 American lives jeopardized German-American relations, though subsequent German pledges eased the tension. Then in January 1917 Berlin resumed unrestricted submarine attacks. The Germans also launched a maladroit effort to entice Mexico into the war, exposed by the Zimmermann telegraph affair. President Woodrow Wilson believed he had no option but war. On 6 April 1917 Congress declared war on the Central Powers. The European *international system found itself fundamentally changed; henceforth, U.S. participation (or failure to do so) would be decisive. By November 1918 and the armistice, the American presence had become paramount in every phase of war and peace.

The Fighting, 1914–1917. As the diplomats added coalition partners, the military and naval leadership fought stubbornly and wastefully on land and sea. The German offensive in the west stalled in September 1914 at the Battle of the Marne. Within weeks trenches extended from Switzerland to the North Sea and cut off a substantial part of northern France and virtually all of Belgium. Horrendous efforts failed to break through the defensive positions in late 1914, then again in 1915. Each attack was seen as bringing a victory; none did. Then in 1916 came two costly efforts: Verdun and the Somme. The German high command resolved to take Verdun; the Anglo-French forces wanted to crash beyond the Somme River. Neither attack succeeded save in death and destruction; 2 million men on both sides were casualties in the Verdun-Somme battles. By late 1916 the fighting on the western front had altered almost nothing militarily, while prompting increasing domestic morale problems.

The war at sea was unspectacular. Allied blockade policies isolated Germany. Sporadic naval clashes in the North Sea brought no advantage. The admirals kept hoping for a major clash of capital ships instead of submarine warfare. But the long-awaited showdown of dreadnoughts in the Battle of Jutland on 31 May–1 June 1916 was inconclusive. Confusion, miscalculation, and hesitation produced a draw. Britain's naval blockade continued, while the Germans edged closer to an all-out submarine policy.

On the eastern front and in the Balkans the war was more dramatic. In 1914 Vienna had quickly lost territory to the Russians, only to regain some of it by 1915 with German assistance. Germany's great victory over the Russians at Tannenberg in September 1914 stemmed the Slavic tide. The Serbs retreated in 1914, then advanced, and then finally in mid-1915 were decisively routed. Bulgaria and Romania fought, lost, fought again, and the fighting along the Macedonian front altered little.

The most spectacular peripheral campaign, in failure and imagination, came with the British effort to open a second front against the Ottoman Empire in early 1915. Seizure of the Straits at Constantinople might, it was hoped, offset the stalemate in the west. From the start the Gallipoli campaign saw British and British imperial troops suffer from indecisive leadership and confusion of execution. Eventually in 1916 London abandoned the effort, just as the battles of Verdun and the Somme began.

As the stalemate in the west continued, new weapons systems emerged. None succeeded in bringing a decisive advantage. Heavy artillery pounded the trenches; airplanes fought and delivered some bombs; poison gas was tried with terrible physical and psychological damage; the truck became the tank. Still the trenches proved supreme. In the west in 1917 the armies remained deadlocked, the British and French awaiting the American troops. The Germans focused their attention eastward where events in Russia steadily dissolved the tsarist government. Everywhere discontent, malaise, and domestic hardship were commonplace. The war now consumed everything it touched.

War Aims, 1914–1917. From August 1914 to the spring of 1917 policymakers in each capital struggled to define their minimum war aims. As the casualties mounted, so also did the war aims. This vicious interaction meant that only total victory could make the increasingly fearful human cost worthwhile. In September 1914 Germany's expected victory led to schemes—east and west—that ensured Germanic hegemony on the Continent. Nor would those aims be entirely abandoned even late in 1918 with the German collapse. For France survival came first, then the expulsion of German troops from France and the return of Alsace-Lorraine, lost in 1871 to Berlin. For London, German colonies, a new *balance of power on the Continent, and protection from Russia emerged as goals. Vienna's perspective veered erratically from banishment of the Serbian menace in 1914 to mere survival by 1917–1918.

In 1914 Russia's aims had also been expansive: Constantinople, a Balkan sphere of influence, and predominance in eastern Europe. The war's continuing reverses eventually put the tsar's government on the defensive. In March 1917 the cumulative effect of court intrigue, the presence of the strange mystic Rasputin, food shortages, and mounting domestic discontent finally erupted. Within days the Romanov dynasty was gone. Ill-advised Allied and Russian attempts to prolong Russia's war effort merely condemned the country to mounting chaos. Guided by *Lenin's organizing genius and utter lack of scruples, the Bolsheviks in November 1917 seized control of the remaining organs of Russian authority. The Treaty of Brest-Litovsk on 3 March 1918 took Russia from the world war into the travail of civil war. The treaty extended German (and Austrian) power in the east almost beyond their earlier ambitions; the Ukraine, Russian Poland, the Baltic states, and Finland moved into the German orbit. Equally important, Russia had been ousted from the balance of power, at least for the moment.

In the Balkans French, British, and Greek forces continued to occupy German and Habsburg divisions. In the sands of Arabia, British efforts to dismantle Ottoman power began to succeed. On the Italian front Italians and Austrians continued to slaughter each other, with more Habsburg gains than losses but no decisive defeat of the former Italian ally.

On the western front, in early 1918, the German military, now thoroughly in command of the German government, opted for a final offensive to crush Anglo-French forces before America's full potential would be felt. The new German effort started on 21 March 1918; it nearly succeeded, only to falter once more at the Marne. Thereafter the military tide turned quickly. The arrival of U.S. forces made the difference. By September German forces were retreating. Later that month the German military asked the civilians to negotiate a respite. The German diplomats tried, only to be outmaneuvered by Woodrow Wilson who insisted on an armistice and a new German government. With their armies retreating and the populace near open rebellion, Berlin and Vienna concluded an armistice on 11 November 1918. The Habsburg and Hohenzollern dynasties abdicated, following the Romanovs. Six months later, on 28 June 1919, a civilian German government guided by a socialist president, Friedrich Ebert, not the kaiser or his generals, signed the Treaty of Versailles. Five years after the first two deaths on the streets of Sarajevo, at least 13 million had fallen in the Great War—and possibly there were that many unknown deaths as well. The old order in Europe was forever destroyed.

Peace Treaties and the War's Consequences. The treaties of Paris ending the war ratified the collapse of the Habsburg monarchy, while spelling out the details of Germany's defeat. The latter were more important. Germany's military and naval power was drastically curtailed; Allied soldiers could occupy the left bank of the Rhine for up to fifteen years; Alsace and Lorraine were returned to France; German colonies were divided among the victors; East Prussia was separated from Germany proper by the new Poland. The German government was obliged, moreover, to pay reparations for the physical and human suffering of the war, reparations that soon became a major political and economic stumbling block to Europe's recovery and stability. Further intensifying German resentment, Article 231 of the Treaty of Versailles assigned "war guilt" to Berlin and its allies for causing the war. That historical judgment, juxtaposed with the German military's allegations that the civilians and not they had lost the war, would frame the German agenda for the 1920s.

The war also destroyed the prevailing pattern of European *diplomacy. The monarchical governments of eastern Europe disappeared, as did the Ottoman regime. Successor governments displayed few of the aristocratic traits of the old regimes. Of these the new Soviet Union was the most radical. Elsewhere in eastern and central Europe small democratic states emerged, their nationalist ambitions amply fulfilled: Poland, Czechoslovakia, Yugoslavia. The residual survivors—Austria, Hungary, Romania, Bulgaria—were also more democratic and nationalistic. Yet in none of the governments, as the interwar years revealed, were democratic roots strong. Instead authoritarian regimes would soon come to power in most.

Germany, though defeated, remained basically intact as a country. France recovered its lost provinces but was stunted for a generation by wartime population losses. Britain obtained German colonies and full command of the European seas. Yet London also faced staggering debt problems. The Italians had fought on the winning side but felt and behaved like losers. The most significant alteration came, of course, from the effect of the American presence: in the fighting, in the peacemaking, and in its future relationship to Europe, whether intimate or not. Washington had become the supreme power.

The war effort also prompted calls for the creation of a *League of Nations, a formalized collective *security system to preserve the victory against Germany and to address the evils of the old diplomacy. The balance of power would be enshrined in a new, open diplomatic system in which the great powers would seek to protect the weaker. This new structural approach dramatically affirmed the new volatility of international politics without, however, changing much actual state behavior.

If the League appeared to alter the practice of diplomacy, the economic transformation wrought by the war did so in fact. The United States had replaced Europe's traditional economic dominance. War debts, reparations issues, social and human costs, and a dispirited work force were outcomes that made every European government, victor or defeated, dependent on the United States. New York replaced London as the center of the world economy. Henceforth, the House of Morgan and the U.S. Treasury were key players—whether openly or in secret—in the new international system.

Even in the imperial arena things had changed. To be sure, the Anglo-French victors kept and expanded their colonial holdings at German and Ottoman expense. But Wilson's talk of self-determination and the creation of the mandate system for colonial administration put finite limits on imperial holdings. The troops furnished by Britain's colonial governments, moreover, ensured the end of the empire and the creation of the *Commonwealth. In East Asia, meanwhile, the Japanese, with their new colonial possessions, were awakened to impe-

rial ambitions. From that development much mischief would come.

If nationalism had been a principal cause of the war, the four-year struggle had merely intensified its importance and worsened its debilitating effects. The collapse of the multinational Habsburg monarchy foreshadowed intensive national rivalries in eastern Europe. What had previously been contained under one sovereign monarch now existed in many. And the sheer bellicosity of the peace meant that German, French, and British nationalism was also strengthened, while that of the Italians became easily susceptible to Benito *Mussolini's bombast. While Lenin talked of the supranational idea, *communism appeared to many a more dangerous form of Russian nationalism and far more threatening to the economic order.

On the domestic side, the war's impact was as significant as on the international, perhaps more so. Death removed a generation of actual and potential leaders. State power grew at an extraordinary rate; the centralization of economic life continued. The character of the work forced changed, with more women present and with more demands for shared power. Socialism and unions were more appealing in an era of malaise, whether in the victor or the defeated states. *Democracy had won, but democratic values had received scant encouragement. Political stability was not only more difficult to achieve, it was far more difficult to maintain. The European governments of the 1920s were like revolving doors, forever changing and with little sense of persistent direction.

Perhaps most importantly, World War I and the peace treaties transformed the agenda of international politics. For Germany the abrogation of the Treaty of Versailles now became its abiding passion; for France and the new governments in the east, the containment of Germany became their principal agenda. Britain sought to preserve its empire while slipping back into its pre-1904 balance of power stance vis-à-vis the Continent. The United States, now the effective arbiter, reverted to political but not economic isolation; this contradictory stance left a dangerous vacuum which *Hitler would carefully exploit. Everywhere the fear of Bolshevism and the Soviet Union acted as a backdrop against which diplomacy was conducted. The League of Nations represented a new approach to international politics. But with Germany, the Soviet Union, and the United States outside the League, at least initially, collective security remained bilateral and intermittent. World War I had merely set the stage for *World War II.

(See also COLONIAL EMPIRES.)

Luigi Albertini, *The Origins of the War of 1914,* translated and edited by Isabella Massey, 3 vols. (London, 1952–1957). Marc Ferro, *The Great War, 1914–1918* (London, 1973). Fritz Fischer, *War of Illusions: German Policies from 1911 to 1914,* translated by Marian Jackson (New York, 1975). James Joll, *The Origins of the First World War*

(London, 1984). David Stevenson, *The First World War and International Politics* (Oxford, 1988). Samuel R. Williamson, Jr., *Austria-Hungary and the Origins of the First World War* (London and New York, 1991).

SAMUEL R. WILLIAMSON, JR.

WORLD WAR II. The term *World War II* is conventionally applied to the series of overlapping military and political conflicts which began on 1 September 1939, when the armies of Nazi Germany invaded Poland, and ended on 2 September 1945, when representatives of Germany's main ally, Japan, signed an instrument of surrender. During this six-year period fighting took place on six continents and on every ocean, and 40–50 million people, most of them civilians, lost their lives. World War II was not *an* event. It was, more accurately, a nexus, a giant knot in which the strands of several preexisting conflicts and crises became entangled. Though each of these conflicts and crises had a history of its own before 1939 and many continued their course after 1945, the process of entanglement and disentanglement was a transformative one. In international politics and in the domestic politics of most of the participating *states, the *war was a moment of transition, in which existing relationships were reshaped and existing trends accelerated or reversed.

The "Last European War." Although the case has been made against the Eurocentrism of dating a world war by Germany's aggressions in Europe rather than by Japan's prior aggressions in Manchuria (1931) and China (1937), most historians still treat Germany's attack on Poland and the British and French governments' formal declarations of war on Germany as the starting point of the conflict. In those terms, it began as an exclusively European war. The analogy with the events of 1914–1918, implicit in the very term *World War II,* is misleading, because the second war was far more global than the first, but it does convey at least a partial truth: the issues at stake in the original crisis of September 1939 were recognizably akin to those at stake in *World War I. In the most immediate sense, war came as a result of the German regime's drive to create a territorial empire in continental Europe and the Western powers' refusal to allow the *balance of power to be altered in that way.

In a broader perspective, however, *Hitler's actions and British and French reactions must be seen within the context of a fundamental *destabilization of the European system of interstate relations which occurred in the late nineteenth–early twentieth century and created the conditions for both world wars. The sources of this destabilization were, among others, the decay of long-established multinational empires in Central and Eastern Europe, the rise of a unified German state, and the wide dissemination of nationalist, imperialist, and social-Darwinist *ideologies. Historians have debated long and hard as to whether the settlement that followed World War I could ever have succeeded in remedying this

destabilization, but the undeniable fact is that it did not succeed, and in 1933 a man who was committed to overturning the settlement came to the head of the German state.

However one explains Adolf Hitler's foreign policy—and it has been variously interpreted as the systematic application of an ideological blueprint, the ad hoc improvisations of a skilled opportunist, or the inexorable working out of the regime's own inner logic—the objective consequences of the policy were clear. By absorbing Austria and Czechoslovakia (1938–1939) and by invading and occupying Poland (September 1939), Denmark and Norway (April 1940), and the Netherlands, Belgium, and France (May–June 1940), while signing a non-aggression pact with the Soviet Union (August 1939) and keeping the United States out of the war, Hitler accomplished much of what the German imperial government had sought but had never been able to achieve in the first war.

Operation Barbarossa and the Holocaust. At what point this traditional European conflict was transformed into something quite different is open to interpretation. Some would argue that the nature of Hitler's regime and ideology made it different from the start. Others would point to Hitler's decision to postpone invasion of the British Isles and transfer resources for an invasion of the Soviet Union (Operation Barbarossa) as a turning point. Certainly the launching of Operation Barbarossa in June 1941 dramatically expanded the scale of the conflict. It also introduced into it a more pronounced ideological and racialist dimension: the aim of the invasion was not just to expand German territory but to clear so-called inferior races from this territory and destroy the Bolshevik regime, which Hitler had long identified with Jewry. That said, Operation Barbarossa could also be fitted within the framework of traditional geopolitical and strategic calculations. On the one hand, Hitler was fulfilling a long-standing aspiration of German *nationalism (which he himself had expressed in his autobiography *Mein Kampf*) by extending the German empire into the open spaces of the Ukraine, White Russia, and the *Baltic republics; on the other hand, he was taking a strategic gamble to knock the Soviet Union out of the war before the United States was drawn in on Britain's side.

It is much more difficult to fit within any traditional framework the decision that accompanied Barbarossa to proceed with a more systematic persecution of European Jews. Historians of the *Holocaust have not reached a total consensus as to when and how the Nazis' "final solution of the Jewish problem" was agreed upon, but most would accept that during the second half of 1941, with the blocking of further Jewish emigration from German-controlled Europe and with the drawing up of plans for death camps, the Nazi leadership moved decisively toward the actual elimination of all Jews. The creation of the German territorial empire had created the conditions for a quite distinct war within a war—which the historian Lucy Dawidowicz has aptly termed "the war agains the Jews." This genocidal campaign, unprecedented in the totality of its objectives and the methodical bureaucracy of its procedures, was inexplicable in purely military terms and, indeed, toward the end of the war diverted scarce resources away from the campaign against the Red Army.

Pearl Harbor, the Asian Crisis, and Global War. In its initial stages Operation Barbarossa was a stunning success in rational-military as well as irrational-genocidal terms. However, by November 1941, the German advance had slowed and on 5 December it came to a halt on the outskirts of Moscow. Two days later, Japan launched a surprise attack on the U.S. Pacific Fleet at Pearl Harbor, and within a few days the United States found itself at war not only with Japan but also, as a result of Hitler's precipitate declaration of war, with Germany. By the end of 1941 the metamorphosis of European war into global war was complete.

Even though the European crisis had certainly influenced events in Asia and the Pacific, this new strand in the conflict had distinct origins of its own. The underlying conjuncture had emerged in the late nineteenth century: a huge but vulnerable Chinese empire being challenged by an emerging Japan, while other powers (European colonial powers, Russia, and the United States) attempted both to exploit Chinese weakness and forestall Japanese expansionism. After World War I, the region's stability had been restored with mechanisms comparable to those employed in Europe, i.e., multilateral, international agreements that were intended to provide for peaceful and gradual change within the framework of the status quo. But, as in Europe, this status quo proved unacceptable to a significant segment of the elite and the general public within the leading revisionist state, in this case Japan. From 1931 onwards Japan attempted to establish a territorial and economic empire at the expense of China. This expansionism increasingly alienated Japan from the Western powers and from the Soviet Union and encouraged the Japanese to cooperate with the anti–status quo powers in Europe.

By September 1939, with Japan's two-year war in China continuing and its international isolation deepening, some form of further conflict in the region was highly likely, irrespective of events in Europe. However, there was nothing predetermined about the form that war would take in December 1941. Japan's civilian and military leadership was torn between a northern strategy, which gave priority to conflict with the Soviet Union, and a southern strategy, which favored expansion into European colonial territories, especially resource-rich ones like the Dutch East Indies and British Malaya. It was only in July 1941, when Japanese troops entered the southern half of French Indochina and the United States responded by organizing a Western embargo on trade with Japan, that the configuration of the future conflict became apparent. The Japanese military and civilian leadership saw two alternatives: they could either submit to economic pressure, withdraw from China, and give up their vision of a Greater East Asia Co-Prosperity Sphere; or they could follow Berlin's promptings and prepare for war against the United States and Britain. By early September 1941 they had opted definitively for the latter course.

In December 1941, then, the two sides in the global war were fixed, and, in the opinion of most historians and many contemporaries, so was the outcome. The superiority in human and material resources enjoyed by the anti-Axis alliance of the United States, the Soviet Union, and the British Commonwealth and Empire was simply too great for the Axis powers to win the war. On the other hand, both the Germans and the Japanese (who within months of Pearl Harbor had taken control of Malaya and Singapore, the Dutch East Indies, the Philippines, and Burma) were well entrenched in their positions. To dislodge them, even with all the advantages that the anti-Axis alliance had at their disposal, was bound to take a considerable time, especially once the Allies had committed themselves to accepting nothing short of unconditional surrender. That created the conditions for long and bloody campaigns over the next three and a half years—in Russia, North Africa, Italy and the Balkans, France and Poland, the Pacific islands and the Philippines, Burma and China.

Domestic Conflict: Resistance and Collaboration. The protracted nature of the struggle to defeat the German and Japanese empires had implications beyond the international and military realms. While societies under Axis occupation were essentially spectators to the global conflict, individuals within these societies were engaged in their own struggles. Their war took place not on conventional battlefields but in the political and paramilitary skirmishing that pitted occupying authorities and those who collaborated with them against those who, in one form or another, resisted.

It appears that the majority of collaborators were motivated by impulses other than slavish admiration for the invaders or their ideology. In Europe they were often products of home-grown authoritarian traditions, with personal and political agendas that carried over from the prewar period. In Asia, the strongest common denominator among those who welcomed and tried to work with the Japanese was anti-Western nationalism. Resisters, who were generally motivated in the first instance by opposition to occupation and united in their efforts to sabotage it, nonetheless came to the struggle with agendas and motives that similarly predated the war. In both theaters resistance was often politicized by splits between communists and noncommunists or by attempts to develop reformist or revolutionary ideologies for the postwar future. In Asia, even more than in Europe, resistance entailed not just opposition to the current occupation, but rejection of the prewar status quo. These triangular conflicts, involving occupiers, collaborators, and resisters, would obviously not have occurred without the larger war between the Axis and the anti-Axis powers. But the forms that such conflicts took primarily reflected local conditions, and their reverberations lasted long after the foreign occupations had come to an end. In this sense, these domestic conflicts must be recognized as distinct from the international conflict that spawned them.

Impact of the War. States fight wars in order to resolve what they perceive as problems. From the perspective of the victors in World War II, this conflict solved the basic problem of the 1930s. By 1945 German and Japanese power had been utterly destroyed and the threat that these two nations posed to the international order eliminated for the foreseeable future. In virtually every other respect, however, the war seemed as much a starting point as an end point. It transformed military and political realities, but resolved remarkably little. Perhaps the two most graphic symbols of this in 1945 were the mushroom clouds hanging over *Hiroshima and Nagasaki and the political clouds hanging over Poland, for whose independence, ironically, the West had gone to war in 1939.

The transitional character of the war was nowhere more apparent than at the level of the *international system. In three respects, World War II hastened a transition which had been under way for many decades. First, it facilitated the accumulation of political, economic, and military might in what became known as *superpower states. There was nothing unexpected about the fact that this occurred where it did: the emergence of American and Russian superpowers had been predicted on numerous occasions over the course of the preceding century. But the war's global scale and protracted denouement after 1941 forced the pace of change by placing a premium on those nations (first and foremost, the United States) with the industrial, military, and demographic resources to fight such a war successfully. By the end of 1943, for example, the United States was producing almost as many arms as all the other belligerents combined and was the only power in the world capable of waging conventional war in both Europe and Asia while simultaneously investing heavily in the development of an atomic bomb.

The second element in the transition was a further decline in the status of the old system's dominant powers (something which had been going on well before 1939 but had been partially masked by the self-imposed isolation of the United States and the Soviet Union). The remarkable triumphs of the Axis in 1939–1942 had the unanticipated consequence of hastening the eclipse of all "middle" powers— not just Germany, Italy, and Japan, which were subsequently crushed under the weight of the opposing coalition, and not just France and the other states humiliated by the Axis in the early stages of the war, but even Britain. For the British, victory came at the cost of colossal economic dislocation and sacrifice, not to mention the political cost involved in surrendering remnants of global leadership to stronger allies and making concessions to colonial populations. Like their former foes, Britain and France were left with no alternative but to integrate themselves into a new system structured around the superpower rivalry—the same system into which the formerly independent powers of Central and Eastern Europe were integrated more forcefully.

Third, the war accelerated the emergence of newly independent states, especially in Asia and Africa, where the collapse of the European *colonial empires entered a critical stage. The easy successes that Japan and Germany achieved in 1939–1942 burst the bubble of European prestige outside Europe. In Asia, Japanese occupation encouraged the development of nationalist and regional consciousness and gave firsthand experience in self-rule. The economic disruptions that the war produced not only weakened the strategic capacities of the European states, but in many regions (particularly in Africa) fostered rapid economic development, which had significant political and social ramifications after the war. And, of course, the change in the global balance of power elevated two states which, from their different ideological perspectives, were both fundamentally opposed to colonialism.

In most of these respects, the transforming effect of World War II is more obvious in retrospect than it was at the time. The inevitability of Europe's decline or of *decolonization was far from universally recognized in 1945. Furthermore, it could legitimately be argued that the postwar system owed at least as much to the events of the immediate postwar era as to the events of 1939–1945. The problem of German power, for example, was not so much solved by 1945 as transcended after 1945, with the emergence of a greater and more threatening "problem," that of superpower rivalry. One might make a similar argument about the long *peace that the new international system produced among developed nations (though not between developed and less developed countries) aftrer 1945. The superpower confrontation and the unprecedented destructive power of *nuclear weapons were probably more significant deterrents to renewed conflict than the memories of World War II, however painful they might be.

Whereas the war's impact on the international system was more profound than at first recognized, its imapct on state behavior has been less profound than people in 1945 might have expected (or hoped). The war prompted a renewed internationalism in many quarters, but the *international organizations that were created at the end of the war (above all the UN, founded at San Francisco in June 1945) did not fulfill these high hopes, essentially because states refused to surrender their *sovereignty to such organizations. Similarly disappointed were the hopes of those who assumed that the development of an atomic bomb, which had so revolutionized the character of warfare, would also revolutionize diplomatic realities, for example by forcing an end to the anarchic relationship between sovereign states. In fact, the actual changes proved much more modest: states possessing the bomb have tended to manage their relations with one another in a more cautious and prudential manner, but the primacy of the state has not been fundamentally altered by nuclear weapons.

The impact of the war on the domestic politics of the various states involved is the largest and most difficult question of all. The war inevitably reshaped political agendas, altered political preferences, and changed the balance of political forces. The extent of its influence and the degree to which it reinforced or reversed prewar trends are issues that historians have to assess country by country and study by study. What one can say is that in every society that experienced the war firsthand it left an enduring mark on the collective memory. In some countries, like Britain and the Soviet Union, the collective memory could be a socially cohesive one. In others, particularly those which experienced the schisms of resistance and collaboration, the memory was often bitter and divisive.

(See also CHURCHILL, WINSTON; FORCE, USE OF; GENOCIDE; HIROHITO; MILITARISM; MUSSOLINI, BENITO; NUREMBERG TRIALS; ROOSEVELT, FRANKLIN DELANO; STALIN, JOSEPH; UNITED NATIONS; WAR CRIMES.)

Gordon Wright, *The Ordeal of Total War, 1939–1945* (New York, 1968). Christopher Thorne, *The Issue of War: States, Societies, and the Far Eastern Conflict of 1941–1945* (New York, 1985). Akira Iriye, *The Origins of the Second World War in Asia and the Pacific* (London, 1987). John Keegan, *The Second World War* (New York, 1989). R. A. C. Parker, *Struggle for Survival: The History of the Second World War* (Oxford, 1990).

ANDREW SHENNAN

Y

YALTA CONFERENCE. The Black Sea resort of Yalta was the setting for the last summit conference of the original "Big Three" alliance leaders during *World War II. Winston *Churchill, Franklin *Roosevelt, and Joseph *Stalin met from 4 February to 11 February 1945 to resolve their differences over the shape of the postwar order. Soon after the conference ended, Yalta became a controversial symbol in international politics and in the domestic politics of the United States.

Battlefield conditions influenced the relative strength of the participants. The Red Army occupied much of Eastern Europe and Poland; the Americans and British had not yet crossed the Rhine. To minimize U.S. casualties in attacking Japan, the U.S. military—not knowing that the still-untested atomic bomb would make unnecessary an invasion of Japan—wanted Soviet help in dislodging the large Japanese armies in Manchuria, northern China, and Korea. Fearing that allied discord might encourage isolationism, Roosevelt placed great emphasis on good relations with Stalin, preferring to leave critical issues unsettled rather than invite public disunity. He appreciated Soviet concessions on the United Nations: Stalin agreed that permanent members of the Security Council could not block the consideration of issues although they could veto UN actions. The Soviets also received additional seats in the General Assembly for their Ukraine and Belorussian Republics.

Summit participants postponed major decisions about the future of Germany. They decided to award a zone of occupation to France, and agreed that the Soviet Union was entitled to half of all reparations, with US$20 billion as a "basis for discussion." The future of Poland received the most attention. Churchill protested Soviet repression in Poland and insisted that Stalin allow noncommunist Poles to participate in the government. Roosevelt, referring to his millions of Polish-American constituents, also urged Stalin to make some gesture, though he was unwilling to press the issue. Stalin vigorously defended Soviet policy in Poland, making reference to the Soviet Union's *security and the Western powers' dominance in Italy. His only concession was to agree to include an unspecified number of other "democratic leaders from Poland itself and from Poles abroad" in the procommunist Lublin government. Along with the "Declaration of Liberated Europe," which "guaranteed" democratic governments and free elections in Eastern Europe, these concessions brought about little change in Soviet policy, because there was no attempt to define the particular procedures or principles underlying these concepts.

The Far Eastern agreements were equally controversial. The United States obtained Stalin's commitment to enter the war two or three months after Germany's surrender. In return the Soviets received the southern half of Sakhalin, which Japan had taken from imperial Russia in 1905, and the Kuril Islands, which had never been Russian possessions. In return for a vague commitment to negotiate with the Nationalist Chinese government, the Soviets also received leaseholds on Port Arthur and Dairen, control of the main Manchurian railways, and recognition of a Soviet-controlled regime in Outer Mongolia.

Despite the hopes raised by Yalta, disillusionment developed rapidly when it became clear that the Soviet Union would impose communist rule over Eastern Europe. After the Communist victory in China, Senator Joseph McCarthy charged that Roosevelt's concessions at Yalta betrayed the Nationalists. French President Charles de *Gaulle later claimed Yalta was proof of American designs to divide and weaken Europe. Only with the *Gorbachev revolution in *Soviet foreign policy did Yalta gain the chance to retreat into history.

(See also AMERICAN FOREIGN POLICY; COLD WAR; MCCARTHYISM; POTSDAM CONFERENCE.)

Athan Theoharis, *The Yalta Myths: An Issue in U.S. Politics, 1945–1955* (Columbia, Mo., 1970). Robert Dallek, *Franklin D. Roosevelt and American Foreign Policy, 1932–1945* (New York, 1979). Russell D. Buhite, *Decisions at Yalta: An Appraisal of Summit Diplomacy* (Wilmington, Del., 1986).

THOMAS ALAN SCHWARTZ

YELTSIN, Boris. In 1991, Boris Yeltsin became the first elected national leader in Russian history; shortly thereafter he became a driving force behind the final dissolution of the *Soviet Union. In the light of this achievement, Mikhail *Gorbachev's *perestroika seems no more than the prelude to the real historical turning point of 1991.

Yeltsin was born in 1931 in the Urals region of *Russia. After an apolitical childhood and youth, he joined the Communist Party in 1961 as a necessary step in a career as industrial manager. He soon became involved in full-time party work and in 1976 became a provincial party secretary in the important industrial region of Sverdlovsk (now Ekaterinburg). Yeltsin was an early beneficiary of Gorbachev's *reform program: he was promoted in 1985 to the position of party chief of Moscow and was also made a candidate member of the ruling Politburo that same year.

The drama of Boris Yeltsin began in the fall of 1987, when he tended his resignation from the Politburo because of his unhappiness with the slow pace of perestroika. His resignation was a clear violation of the rules of the Soviet political game: no previous Soviet politician had openly resigned on a matter of principle. Yeltsin's 1987 resignation was a leap into the unknown that in some ways was more heroic than his dramatic defiance of the attempted *coup in August 1991.

Yeltsin was promptly subjected to an old-style ritual denunciation. Gorbachev offered him a government post but warned him that he would not be allowed back into politics. At the same time, Gorbachev was busy creating a situation in which he could no longer unilaterally determine who was or was not allowed to play a leadership role. In 1989, Yeltsin ran for a seat in the newly created national legislature. Despite, or rather because of, the opposition of the party apparatus, Yeltsin won in an overwhelming landslide. In 1990 Yeltsin was elected to the Russian Parliament; in 1991, he won a solid majority in a direct election for the presidency of the Russian Republic. The newfound power of electoral legitimacy (along with the party's renunciation of its monopoly status) allowed Yeltsin to become the first prominent political leader to leave the Communist Party (June 1990).

In 1990 the rivalry between Gorbachev and Yeltsin took a new turn as each became identified with a different approach to the problem of reconstituting the multinational Soviet state on a more secure basis. Gorbachev was committed to a vertical, or topdown, approach that would preserve the old center while allowing greater autonomy to the republics. From his base as president of the Russian Republic, Yeltsin started to implement a horizontal approach that aimed at building a new center by means of agreements with his counterparts in other republics. This approach became known as "the union of presidents against the president of the Union [Gorbachev]." At the end of 1991, Yeltsin's approach triumphed with the declaration of a new *Commonwealth of Independent States, the dissolution of the old center, and Gorbachev's resignation.

Yeltsin's political style—his ability to take personal responsibility, his gamble on electoral legitimacy, and his horizontal approach to reconstitu-tion—is more significant than the content of his programs. A few underlying themes can be discerned in his political outlook. One might be called antimonopolism: Yeltsin blames the failures of the old system on the ideological monopoly of the party and the economic monopoly of the centralized planning system. Another continuing theme is a contempt for Gorbachev's "half-measures"; for Yeltsin, perestroika was no more than the last phase of the era of stagnation. He has also expressed a deep anger at the old system for pushing Russia off the path of advancing Western civilization.

Up to January 1992, Yeltsin owed his popularity to his role as leader of the opposition to the Communist Party and the old center. He is now in a position of power and responsibility that will magnify the defects of his leadership style: a delight in brusque improvisation, a Reaganesque inattention to detail and inability to discipline his administration, and a tendency to indulge in "populist" grandstanding. Yeltsin now faces the problems that Gorbachev was unable to solve. He needs to preserve his democratic legitimacy while implementing unpopular reform measures; he must respond to the passions of ethnic self-assertion while avoiding both repression and anarchy. Relations among independent states will prove more difficult than a "union of presidents" against an unpopular central government. Whatever the future may bring, it is already apparent that Yeltsin's courage and political imagination have transformed Russian politics.

(See also COMMUNIST PARTY OF THE SOVIET UNION.)

Boris Yeltsin, *Against the Grain* (New York, 1990). John Morrison, *Boris Yeltsin: From Bolshevik to Democrat* (New York, 1991).

LARS T. LIH

YEMEN. The Republic of Yemen was created in May 1990 as a result of the merger of two previously separate entities, the Yemen Arab Republic, or North Yemen, and the People's Democratic Republic of Yemen, or South Yemen. This union, achieved peacefully by agreement between the governments, brought together two rather disparate states, whose over 11 million inhabitants represented more than half the total population of the Arabian Peninsula.

The North. The mountains of Yemen have been the site of settled agricultural civilizations for thousands of years and of a succession of states claiming control of much of southern Arabia. Occupied by the Turks in 1870, who defined the area of the modern state, North Yemen emerged as a separate independent entity when the Turks withdrew in 1918. Society was divided between the tribal forces in the north of the country, loyal to the Zeidi branch of Shi'i Islam, and the Shafei population in the central and southern regions, loyal to a branch of Sunni Islam. Up to 1962 power lay in the hands of the Zeidis, whose leaders, the Hamid al-Din Imams, insulated North Yemen from the outside world and maintained an autocratic grip on the country.

In 1962 the Imamate was replaced by the Yemen Arab Republic in a nationalist coup, but resistance from the tribes, aided by Saudi Arabia and Britain, led to a civil war. Egyptian forces fought, until 1967, on the side of the republic. In 1970 a compromise peace was reached, but there was intermittent resistance from left-wing guerrillas until 1982 and from tribes opposed to the growing strength of central government. In 1978 power was assumed by Ali Abdullah Salih, a Zeidi artillery officer, who proceeded to strengthen the power of the army and the state. Although elections for a General People's Congress were allowed, parties were banned and power rested with the armed forces. In addition to left-wing and tribal resistance, there was also from the early 1980s onward widespread Islamist opposition.

In 1988 the population stood at 8.5 million. The Yemeni economy relied heavily on external funding, in particular from the remittances of hundreds of thousands of workers in the oil-producing states and from foreign aid. There has been some industrial and agricultural development, and in 1984 oil was discovered in commercial quantities by the Hunt Corporation. Estimated per capita income in 1988 was US$640.

After the end of the civil war in 1970, Yemen pursued a neutral policy in regional and international affairs. It cultivated relations with Saudi Arabia, on whom it was economically dependent and with whom there was a disputed frontier, but remained on good terms with Arab radicals. It continued to receive arms from the Soviet Union but gradually improved relations with the United States.

The South. The state of South Yemen was created as a result of the occupation by Britain of the port of Aden in 1839 and subsequently of the adjacent hinterland. Until the 1950s British attention focused almost entirely on Aden, for strategic reasons, but an attempt was then made to weld the various political entities encompassed by British rule into a Federation of South Arabia. This was finally achieved in 1962 but came under increasing pressure from radical nationalists, aided by the newly created republic in North Yemen and by Egypt. When Britain withdrew in November 1967 power was assumed by the National Liberation Front, who created a radical, *one-party state.

The National Front proceeded over the ensuing two decades to try, with Soviet support and guidance, to apply socialist transformation to South Yemen. In 1970 the country was renamed the People's Democratic Republic of Yemen (PDRY). The Front itself was gradually changed to become in 1978 the Yemeni Socialist Party and the economy was subjected to centralized *planning. Education, culture, and the press were brought under state control. Reforms were introduced to spread health and education services and to improve the position of women. Islam was given a "progressive" and "anti-imperialist" interpretation. This process was, however, fraught with problems: South Yemen had a very meager economic base, and the leadership was repeatedly rent by factional differences. In the most serious of these, in January 1986, several thousand officials and party members lost their lives after two weeks of fighting.

The economy of South Yemen was precarious, with the port of Aden having lost its previous prosperity and only one percent of the land area cultivable. In 1988 the population stood at 2.4 million and per capita income at US$430. Domestic productions included fish and cotton, but the state relied on workers' remittances and foreign aid to a considerable degree. However, after 1988, oil in commercial quantities was discovered.

In foreign policy, the PDRY built close relations with the Soviet Union and relied on the Soviet block for much military and economic support. Aden was in the first post-independence period committed to support for radical forces in the Arabian Peninsula, including left-wing guerrillas in Oman and in North Yemen. Relations with the West were poor and those with Washington were broken in 1969, only to be restored in 1990. In the late 1970s and 1980s, however, Aden gradually improved its relations with the West and with the rest of the Arab world.

Yemeni Unity. Both Yemeni leaderships had remained committed to union of the two Yemeni states: despite their fighting wars in 1972 and again in 1979, the two Yemens pursued this policy and in May 1990 agreed on full union of the two states, into a new Republic of Yemen, to be achieved after a thirty-month transition period. For the North this represented an opportunity, now that it had oil reserves, to enhance its power, while for the Southern leadership it was a means to offset growing economic problems and the collapse of the Soviet bloc. Development of the country was, however, soon disrupted by the impact on Yemen of the Iraqi occupation of Kuwait, in August 1990, and the *Gulf War that followed: Yemen inclined toward Iraq and, as a result, many Yemenis in Saudi Arabia were expelled and all aid from oil producers was cut. The consequences of this crisis, within the new republic and in relations with other states, were to last for some time.

(See also GUERRILLA WARFARE.)

Robert Burrowes, *The Yemen Arab Republic: The Politics of Development, 1962–1986* (Boulder, Colo., 1987). Gregory Gause III, *Saudi-Yemeni Relations: Domestic Structures and Foreign Influence* (New York and Oxford, 1990). Fred Halliday, *Revolution and Foreign Policy: The Case of South Yemen, 1967–1987* (Cambridge and New York, 1990). Manfred Werner, *The Yemen Arab Republic: Development and Change in an Ancient Land* (Boulder, Colo., 1991).

FRED HALLIDAY

YUGOSLAVIA. Established in 1918 as the national home for all the South Slavs except Bulgarians,

Yugoslavia represented the union of the previously independent kingdoms of Serbia and Montenegro and most of the South Slavic lands of Austria-Hungary (Slovenian Carniola, with portions of Styria and Carinthia; Croatia-Slavonia, Dalmatia, and Bosnia and Herzegovina; and portions of the former counties of Baranja, Bačka, and the Banat, collectively known as the Vojvodina). After *World War II, state territory expanded to include Istria, Rijeka, Zadar, and the Adriatic islands that Italy had earlier received in three unequal agreements with Yugoslavia (1920–1925).

The population in 1921 was 12,017,323, of which Serbs (including Montenegrins) constituted 38.8 percent, Croats 23.8 percent, Slovenes 8.5 percent, Bosnian Muslims 6.1 percent, Macedonians, 4.9 percent, Germans 4.3 percent, Hungarians 3.9 percent, and Albanians 3.7 percent. By 1981 the population had risen to 22,427,585, but the proportions of constituent nationalities (with exceptions) remained similar: Serbs 36.3 percent (Montenegrins, counted separately, 2.6 percent), Croats 19.8 percent, Slovenes 7.8 percent, Bosnian Muslims 8.9 percent, Macedonians 6.0 percent, Hungarians 1.9 percent, and Albanians 7.7 percent, Germans having been expelled as a group after the war.

The principal religious communities in 1921 were Eastern Orthodox (Serbs, Montenegrins, Macedonians, Vlachs) 46.6 percent; Roman and Greek Catholics (Croats, Slovenes, Germans, Hungarians) 41.2 percent; Sunni Muslims (Bosnian Muslims, Albanians, Turks) 11.1 percent; Protestants (Hungarians, Germans, Slovaks) 1.8 percent; and Jews 0.5 percent. The religious affiliation of the population became much more difficult to gauge under the postwar Communist regime. The country was unevenly developed, the industrial base before the war being largely in the northwest (Slovenia, northern Croatia), but with significant potential in grain production (northern Croatia, Vojvodina), mining (Bosnia, Serbia), and maritime transportation (southern Croatia).

Internal divisions of the Yugoslav state would have been difficult to overcome under the best of circumstances. Matters were complicated by a permanent clash of national ideologies that governed the aspirations and behavior of the principal national groups. For the Serbs, notably the governing Radical Party of Nikola Pašić, Yugoslavia was not a new state but the final product of Serbia's wars (1912–1918) for the unification of all Serbs within a single state. It was therefore only natural that Serbia's state institutions (monarchy, army, administrative apparatus) should be extended to the "newly liberated territories" of former Austria-Hungary, enabling Serbia to dominate in the political affairs of the Yugoslav state just as it did in military affairs; moreover, this new state should be administered from a single center, without recourse to any federal arrangements. *Federalism would be permitted only

after a redrawing of internal frontiers, meaning that the Serbs would then incorporate, by a combination of demographic and historical arguments, practically all areas of Yugoslavia, with the exception of Slovenia and northwestern Croatia, within their federal unit. This was clearly not to the advantage of Croats and the unrecognized Slavic groups that the Serbs treated as assimilable (Bosnian Muslims, Macedonians, Montenegrins). The Serbian view was reinforced by the Yugoslavist unitarists, who viewed centralism as an instrument that could aid the construction of an integral Yugoslav supranation. Jointly, Serbian centralists and Yugoslavist unitarists prevailed, and brought about the centralistic Vidovdan Constitution of 1921, which was passed by a bare majority over the boycott and opposition of most Croat, Slovene, and left-wing parties.

As the most important non-Serb group with a history of limited statehood within the Habsburg Monarchy, the Croats became the leaders in the struggle against the Serbian state project. Unlike the Serbs, who were divided among several major parties, the Croats were led by the agrarian-based Croat Peasant Party (HSS) during the interwar period. The party boycotted the Constituent Assembly and opposed the installation of Serbia's Karadjordjević dynasty for the whole country, opting rather for a loose confederal arrangement in which all the historical units (Serbia, Croatia, Slovenia, Bosnia and Herzegovina, Montenegro, Macedonia, Vojvodina) would be self-governed. The party was repressed and outlawed, but in 1925 the Pašić government exacted the recognition of the dynasty and the Constitution from imprisoned Radić, leading to the HSS's accession to the cabinet under a semblance of power holding. The arrangement did not last long. By 1927, no outstanding issues having been solved, Radić withdrew from the cabinet and pursued a new oppositional course, this time in alliance with the Serbs of Croatia. After his assassination in 1928 by a Radical deputy on the floor of the Parliament, the Vidovdan system seemed on the verge of collapse. In response, on 6 January 1929, King Alexander suspended the Constitution, the Parliament, and political parties and proclaimed his personal rule.

King Alexander's dictatorship, vestiges of which remained even after the king's assassination by Croat and Macedonian nationalists in 1934, was predicated on the ideology of Yugoslavist unitarism but effectively favored Serbian predominance. The rough handling of the opposition accomplished little. Since the successive quasi-dictatorial governments of prime ministers Bogoljub Jevtić and Milan Stojadinović (1934–1939) failed to reach an agreement with the Croats and other disaffected nationalities, Regent Paul increasingly took personal charge of the negotiations. These were all the more pressing owing to the rise of German and Italian influence in Central and southeastern Europe. In August 1939 Prince Paul accepted the agreement (Sporazum) between his prime minister Dragiša Cvetković and Vladko Maček, Radić's successor at the helm of the HSS. The agreement created an autonomous Croatian banate (a military district under the jurisdiction of a ban, or governor) whose territory encompassed most of Croatia-Slavonia, Dalmatia, and portions of Bosnia and Herzegovina. Maček became vice-president in the Cvetković cabinet and the HSS took over the regional and local administration in the banate. The agreement was opposed by various nationalist currents among the Serbs and Croats, the former having targeted the regency of Prince Paul as a culprit in the arrangement. After the Cvetković-Maček government acceded to the Axis in March 1941, the government was overthrown in a military putsch, the regency dissolved, and King Peter II proclaimed of legal age. In response, the Axis countries invaded Yugoslavia in April 1941, quickly overwhelmed its defenses, obliged the government and the king to flee abroad, and proceeded to dismember the country.

The Axis partners and their satellites (Germany, Italy, Hungary, and Bulgaria) either partitioned the territory of Yugoslavia among themselves or established their special occupation zones (Serbia, Banat, Montenegro). The unannexed portions of Croatia (with Bosnia and Herzegovina) formally became a new Axis ally—the Independent State of Croatia. This was, in fact, an Italo-German condominium, garrisoned by Germany and Italy, and ruled through the Ustašas (Insurgents), a miniscule Croat Fascist organization, which excelled in anti-Serb violence. (On the whole, Yugoslavia lost 1,014,000 people in the course of the war, or 5.9 percent of its population, not all because of internecine violence. The Serbs lost 487,000, or 6.9 percent; Croats 207,000, or 5.4 percent; Bosnian Muslims 86,000, or 6.8 percent; and Jews 60,000, or 77.9 percent, of their conationals.) For their part, the predominantly Serb guerrillas, or Chetniks, were themselves increasingly collaborating with the occupiers and, though ostensibly the army of the London-based Yugoslav government-in-exile, pursued a program of anti-Croat and anti-Muslim violence. Hence the inability of the London Yugoslavs to project a broader-based Yugoslav—rather than Serb—image, and the unwillingness of the non-Serbs to acknowledge this government as their own. The principal beneficiary of these troubles was the Communist Party of Yugoslavia (KPJ) under the leadership of Josip Broz (*Tito). The party's strengths were united and militant leadership; appeal to the disaffected peasantry, youth, and women; and, most importantly, a vision of an egalitarian future based on the equitable solution of the nationality question.

The Communists stressed the equality and individuality of the South Slavic nations (instead of nondescript nationalities or ethnicities) in the opposition to Serbian supremacy and Yugoslavist unitarism, thereby overthrowing the two pillars of the

interwar order. They proposed to build a Soviet-style federal state based on the minor modifications of historical borders. As their military successes increased and their political authority received Allied support, they extended their power at the expense of the exiled king, whose support was significant only in Serbia. After the conquest of Serbia by the Soviet army and Yugoslav Communists in October 1944, Tito encountered no significant obstacles on the road to power. The new constitution of 1945 dethroned the king and established a federal *Communist Party state. Though the Communists initially allowed for little self-rule, the existence of the six republics (Serbia, Croatia, Slovenia, Macedonia, Montenegro, and Bosnia and Herzegovina) and two additional autonomous provinces within Serbia (Vojvodina and Kosovo) created the framework for the affirmation of genuine statehood after the passing of administrative centralism. Still, strong central controls could not be removed at once. After the Soviet leadership expelled Yugoslavia from the Cominform (1948), thereby punishing Tito for an independent and excessively revolutionary policy while simultaneously initiating the wave of thoroughgoing Sovietization of Eastern Europe, Yugoslav Communists responded with innovative ideological measures, such as the introduction of workers' councils and self-management in the enterprises, which were predicated on a modicum of decentralization. In addition, after *Stalin's death, Yugoslavia restored some of its systemic ties with the Soviet bloc while simultaneously pursuing a nonaligned *foreign policy, which brought it into growing interaction with the *Third World countries.

In 1962, when the dispute between the reformers (Edvard Kardelj) and dogmatists (Aleksandar Ranković) threatened the unity of the Yugoslav Communist leadership, Tito sided with the reformers and thereby initiated a new wave of decentralization. In 1966 he toppled Ranković, the leading Serbian Communist and centralist, and permitted the transfer of significant powers to the republics and autonomous provinces. Despite reversals in this policy (the purge of the Croat nationalist Communists in 1971), Tito institutionalized his decentralization course in the Constitution of 1974, which raised Vojvodina and Kosovo to the level of virtual republics while simultaneously introducing a system of absolute parity and proportionality in the relations among the republics and in their participation in the federal organs. The Constitution had two major structural weaknesses: 1) it was predicated on the permanent rule and unity of the Communist Party, and 2) it could be changed only by absolute consensus.

Tito's perpetuum mobile kept rotating during the stagnant 1970s. After Tito's death in 1980, Serbian Communists started a campaign against Tito's Constitution. They found their pretext in Kosovo, where they exaggerated the supposed "counterrevolutionary activities" of the province's Albanian majority in order to abolish the autonomous status of Kosovo. Slobodan Milošević, leader of the Serbian Communist Party since 1987, put together a coalition of Serbian forces, representing the Orthodox church, intelligentsia, and apparatus of the party state, with the aim of hammering through the constitutional changes. With pressure and mass mobilization he succeeded in changing the leaderships of Kosovo, Vojvodina, and Montenegro. With four votes in Yugoslavia's federal presidency in his pocket, and with the Yugoslav People's Army (JNA) on his side, he was able to neutralize the influence of the four remaining republics—Slovenia, Croatia, Bosnia and Herzegovina, and Macedonia.

The Communists of these four republics repeatedly demonstrated their weakness in failing to resist Milošević's demolition of the Yugoslav federal system. As a result of their timidity, as well as communism's collapse throughout Eastern Europe in 1989–1990, the federal Communist Party split in January 1990. Successor parties failed to retain power in Slovenia and Croatia (March–April 1990) as well as in Bosnia and Herzegovina and Macedonia (November–December 1990). In Serbia and Montenegro, however, renationalized Communists won elections (December 1990). The new leaders, notably Franjo Tudjman of Croatia, then tried to negotiate a confederal arrangement for Yugoslavia. Milošević rejected these proposals on the grounds that the *sovereignty of the republics as confederal or independent states was possible only if their borders were changed to accommodate the Serb minorities that were unwilling to live outside a unitary Yugoslav or Serbian state. In order to underscore this point, Milošević stirred up Serb insurgency in Croatia, whose government played into his hands by failing to find common ground with its Serb minority (531,502, or 11.6 percent, of Croatia's population in 1981). Although the Serbs constituted a greater presence in neighboring Bosnia and Herzegovina (1,320,644 Serbs represented 32 percent of the republic's population in 1981), where they participated in the coalition government, here as in Croatia the Serb minorities were increasingly armed by the JNA.

In the spring of 1991, after negotiations between the presidents of the six republics collapsed, Serbia initiated a constitutional crisis by refusing to seat the Croat representative as chair of the federal presidency. Slovenia had already held a plebiscite on independence in December 1990, and Croatia followed suit in May 1991. In both cases overwhelming majorities opted for separation from Yugoslavia. With all the federal agencies paralyzed, Croatia and Slovenia proclaimed their independence in June 1991. The JNA staged a limited assault on Slovenia and was repulsed. In September 1991 it initiated a full-scale war against Croatia. By this time the JNA was deserted by non-Serb officers and was being supplied more and more by Serb irregulars. The growing disarray of the JNA accounts for the savagery of its assault throughout the inner rim of Croatia (Vukovar, Karlovac, Zadar, and Dubrovnik) as this predominantly Serb force carved out a third of Croatia's territory, causing vast destruction, loss of life, and emigration.

The war in Croatia prompted growing international mediation. Unprepared for a local crisis of this magnitude, practically all international agencies and individual governments failed to restrain the conflict. A UN mission, headed by former U.S. Secretary of State Cyrus Vance, won an agreement on the establishment of United Nations Protected Areas in the predominantly or significantly Serb-inhabited areas of Croatia, but its larger success is in doubt. The recognition of Slovenia, Croatia, and Bosnia and Herzegovina, initially by the *European Community countries and then by the United States and most major powers (January–April 1992), did not prevent a Serbian assault on Bosnia and Herzegovina (beginning in April–May 1992) with consequences even graver than those during the war in Croatia. With the recognition of Macedonia virtually assured, the Milošević government in Belgrade initiated the constitution of a rump Yugoslav state consisting of Serbia and Montenegro. The fragmentation of former Yugoslavia will certainly continue as the successor states and their neighbors position themselves for the lasting post-Yugoslav order that is bound to emerge.

(See also INDUSTRIAL DEMOCRACY; NATIONALISM; NINETEEN EIGHTY-NINE; NONALIGNED MOVEMENT; WORKERS' CONTROL.)

Stevan K. Pavlowitch, Yugoslavia (New York, 1971). Jozo Tomasevich, War and Revolution in Yugoslavia: The Chetniks (Stanford, Calif., 1975). Dennison Rusinow, The Yugoslav Experiment, 1948–1974 (Berkeley, Calif., 1977). Ivo Banac, The National Question in Yugoslavia: Origins, History, Politics (Ithaca, N.Y., 1984). Ivo Banac, With Stalin against Tito: Cominformist Splits in Yugoslav Communism (Ithaca, N.Y., 1988). Christopher Cviic, Remaking the Balkans (New York, 1991). Sabrina Ramet, Nationalism and Federalism in Yugoslavia (Bloomington, Ind., 1992).

IVO BANAC

Z

ZAIRE. With a territory of 2,345,406 square kilometers (905,562 sq. mi.), Zaire is the third-largest country on the African continent. Zaire's strategic location in the middle of Africa and its fabulous natural endowment of minerals and other resources unfortunately ensured that it would serve as a theater for the playing out of first colonial, and then *superpower, ambitions on the continent. This historical legacy not only undermined the possibility of independence and *development in the immediate postcolonial period but continues to impede *democracy and economic progress in the post–Cold War era.

First Republic and "Congo Crisis" (1960–1965). Faced with the worldwide phenomenon of anticolonialist struggles following World War II, the more enlightened colonial circles in Belgium recognized the inevitability of independence for their colony, the Belgian Congo; however, they supported a plan calling for a thirty-year *decolonization process. But the surge of African *nationalism after 1956; the rapid political development of the peasantry, the workers, and the elite *évolués* of Congolese society; and finally, the anticolonial riots in Léopoldville (Kinshasa) on 4 January 1959 convinced the Belgian authorities to accept the militant demand for "immediate" independence, and on 30 June 1960 King Baudouin proclaimed the independence of the new state, the Democratic Republic of the Congo. The Mouvement National Congolais (MNC) and its coalition of radical nationalist parties had captured the majority of seats in the lower house of Parliament, and the MNC's leader, Patrice *Lumumba, became the country's first and only democratically elected prime minister, with Joseph Kasavubu the first president.

This victory of a militantly nationalist leader with a strong national constituency was viewed as a major impediment to the Belgian neocolonialist strategy, particularly by its proponents in the business community, who hoped to preserve intact their economic dominion over the country's resources. Within a month after formal independence, Prime Minister Lumumba was faced with both a mutiny by the army and a *secessionist movement in Katanga (Shaba) Province led by Moïse Tshombe, both revolts instigated and bankrolled by Belgian mining interests. Belgium soon deployed its own troops to the Congo on the pretext of protecting European lives and property.

In the hopes of obtaining the evacuation of Belgian troops and white *mercenaries, and thus ending the Katanga secession, Lumumba appealed to the UN Security Council to send a UN force to the Congo. However, the UN general secretary, Dag *Hammarskjöld, interpreted the UN mandate in accordance with the United States' *Cold War imperative of preventing Soviet expansion in the *Third World. Citing the provisions of the UN Charter forbidding involvement in "internal conflicts," UN officials emphasized the troops' law-and-order functions, and placed greater value on the restoration of the economic and social infrastructure of the country than on confrontations with Katanga leader Tshombe and the Belgians. When Lumumba then requested and received aid from the Soviet Union in August, his removal from power under U.S. and Western pressure and his eventual assassination on 17 January 1961 by his Congolese rivals, with help and encouragement from the *Central Intelligence Agency (CIA), were all but insured.

No sooner had the external patrons resolved the crisis of decolonization than the client state itself was plunged into a new and more severe crisis. The Western-backed government of Prime Minister Cyrille Adoula was faced with widespread popular resistance against the state because of its failure to satisfy the deepest aspirations of ordinary people for more freedom and a better standard of living. The resistance began to manifest itself in January 1964 as popular insurrections for a "second independence" led by Pierre Mulele and other radical nationalists. The rebels were eventually defeated in 1965 by Prime Minister Tshombe's Katanga gendarmes, reinforced by white mercenary troops, Belgian advisers, and U.S. logistical support. The U.S.-Belgian military intervention of 24 November 1964 at Stanleyville (Kisangani) had already broken the back of the insurrection. Parliamentary elections held in 1965 failed to produce a resolution of the political crisis or a clear mandate for Kasavubu's newly designated prime minister, Evariste Kimba. In the context of this political impasse, and with the Western powers newly alarmed by Kasavubu's overtures to African nationalists in the *Organization for African Unity (OAU), General Joseph Mobutu, the army chief, carried out a *coup d'état on 24 November 1965, with the support of the CIA.

Second Republic, or the Mobutu Era (1965–1990). The Mobutu regime began as a military dictatorship with the entire army high command making up the junta. But it soon acquired all the characteristics of personal rule as found elsewhere in Africa: a one-party dictatorship under the authoritarian control of a single individual. Mobutu's power was so absolute that he could do anything his heart desired. He gave the country a new currency and a new name—both are now called "Zaire"—in 1967 and 1971, respectively; he seized expatriate-owned small and medium enterprises and distributed them to members of the Zairean *elite in 1973; and he encouraged the latter to plunder the public treasury and state enterprises, which made them into the most voracious "kleptocracy" on the African continent. An accomplished Machiavellian, he used his ill-gotten wealth and his powers of patronage to outfox potential opponents and to keep wavering officials in line. At the same time, he did not hesitate to use *force when it could best serve his purposes. And he did so with such ferocity and regularity that in addition to corruption, gross violation of *human rights is one of the defining characteristics of the Mobutu regime. Space does not allow to detail here his shameful record of *assassinations, extrajudicial executions, massacres of unarmed civilians, *torture, arbitrary arrests, banishments to remote penal colonies, and other acts of brutality.

Mobutu kept himself in power by eliminating all opposition to his rule through the ruthless repression of dissent by the security police and the armed forces. But no regime, however brutal and repressive it might be, can retain power exclusively through the use of force. As a neopatrimonial ruler with delusions of grandeur, Mobutu had an insatiable desire to be surrounded by as many admiring retainers as he could manage to appoint to ministerial and other top positions in an ever-expanding state sector. He relied for the most part on younger and better-educated individuals with no political base, people who had earned university degrees after independence. His quest for absolute power required the destruction of the political strength of the preindependence nationalist leadership. After the coup, he won support among university graduates and students with a pledge to supplant the "corrupt and incompetent" politicians with technocrats. At the same time, older politicians did not altogether disappear from the political scene. They were kept quiet with appointments to the boards of directors of various *parastatals and thus were provided with the means of pursuing lucrative business careers through the privileges and contacts resulting from these positions and from membership in various party-state organs like Parliament and the Central Committee.

Through frequent cabinet reshufflings and constant change of high-ranking officials, Mobutu gave as many people as possible the chance to enrich themselves, thereby developing a stake in the survival of the regime. A corrupt and degenerate ruling group, Mobutu's "kleptocracy" has blocked economic growth and development by depriving the state of those essential means and resources required for satisfying the *basic needs of the population. By privatizing the state itself, they succeeded not only in abolishing the distinctions between state and personal property but also in destroying the country's economic infrastructure and social fabric. Zaire today is a country in ruins, after a quarter-century of the Mobutu dictatorship.

Political Changes since 1990. The collapse of the East-West paradigm of geopolitical relations removed the realpolitik reason for international toleration of the corruption and human rights abuses of the Mobutu regime, and opened a space for Mobutu's foreign critics and internal opponents to be heard. A crucial shift in the U.S. Congress away from support for his regime in 1988 and 1989, and the victories of the democracy movement in Eastern Europe (in particular, the fall from power and execution of Mobutu's close ally, Nicolae Ceausescu), were probably factors in Mobutu's decision to institute a process of "national consultation" in January 1990 as an attempt to co-opt the growing popularity of the internal democratic opposition. This consultation process elicited over 6,000 memoranda (including a stern letter from Zaire's Episcopal Conference), almost all of them devastatingly critical of the regime. Prodded by this response and by pressure from his Western allies, Mobutu announced limited political reforms on 24 April 1990, including the end of one-party rule.

This moderate liberalization touched off a wave of political activities, including party-building, mass demonstrations, and strikes, which in turn provoked both political retrenchment by the regime and renewed repression of the democratic opposition. The most egregious example of such repression was the 11–12 May 1990 massacre of unarmed students at the University of Lubumbashi by commandos of Mobutu's own Division Spéciale Présidentielle (DSP), an incident that provoked worldwide condemnation of his regime.

Given the vastness of the country and the decay of the transportation and communications systems, effective political organizing by parties without access to the state treasury was confined to the capital city of Kinshasa and a few major regional urban centers. In this context, party organizing remained precarious, and the best gauge of support for a party was the number of people it managed to attract to its rallies and demonstrations. By this criterion, the most viable and independent opposition parties were the Union pour la Démocratie et le Progrès Social (UDPS) and the Parti Lumumbiste Unifié (PALU).

The UDPS had its origins in a 1980 rebellion by

thirteen members of Parliament, including Etienne Tshisekedi wa Mulumba, who wrote a fifty-two-page letter to Mobutu demanding political reforms. The "Group of 13" were immediately and brutally repressed. But in spite of repeated jailings and the defection of some of its original members, the group persisted in its opposition to the regime, defying Mobutu's laws against opposition parties by creating the UDPS in 1982. Thus, the UDPS could claim a long history of resistence prior to Mobutu's April 1990 legalization of political parties and has become associated in people's minds with the democracy movement in Zaire.

Under the leadership of Thérèse Pakasa, known affectionately as the "Iron Lady" of Zaire because of her militancy, PALU also demonstrated, on a smaller scale, its ability to mobilize masses of people for political action. Founded in 1964 by Antoine Gizenga, who served in the first postindependence government as Lumumba's deputy prime minister, PALU has its antecedents in the progressive wing of the Parti Socialiste Africain (PSA), which included Gizenga and Pierre Mulele.

In a move to strengthen the unity of the opposition in the face of Mobutu's attempts at manipulation, the major opposition parties formed a united front in July 1991, called the Union Sacrée. Under the leadership of the UDPS and Joseph Ileo's Parti Démocrate Social Chrétien (PDSC), the Union Sacrée's fundamental demand was for the convening of a Sovereign National Conference that would be representative of all sectors of Zairean society, and whose decisions would have executive force. The tasks of the Sovereign National Conference, following the example set in 1990 in Benin, would be to form a transitional government capable of elaborating such new institutions as are necessary to lead the country to multiparty elections and democracy. Recognizing in the Sovereign National Conference not only a threat to his continued hold on power but also the potential for *déballage,* or an extended inquisition on the abuses of his regime (and possible calls for retribution), Mobutu employed every means at his disposal to first delay and then disrupt the conference. In February 1992 government troops killed at least thirty-two people during a peaceful demonstration for the resumption of the national conference, which had been summarily adjourned by Mobutu the previous month. This massacre provoked international pressure on Mobutu to allow the conference to resume its work in April 1992. However, the continued political support Mobutu received from the *Bush administration and the *Mitterrand regime in France produced a political stalemate in Zaire that resulted in worsening the deplorable state of Zaire's economy, causing the population to sink further into misery in a country that has the potential to be the most prosperous in Africa.

For all practical purposes, the Mobutu era ended in 1990, although the wily dictator was still hanging on to the helm of his sinking ship of state two years later. By 1992 the regime had been reduced to its bare essentials as a band of bloodthirsty thieves who survive by looting and thuggery. Mobutu, the band's chief, was reluctant to set foot in the capital city, preferring instead to live on the presidential yacht anchored upstream on the Congo River, some 55 kilometers from Kinshasa. His was a government that could no longer govern, for lack of *legitimacy at home and of support abroad, and an administration that could no longer administer, given its lack of funds and the frequent strikes of its discontented employees. There was no better measure of both Mobutu's diminishing authority and his cynical penchant for political manipulation than the fact that he had five different prime ministers in 1991. His staying power was a function of the effectiveness of his praetorian guard, the DSP, in protecting him from an angry population, on the one hand, and of the weakness of the democratic opposition, on the other. Given current trends in Africa and around the world, there is a brighter future for the forces of change and democracy than for relics of *authoritarianism like Mobutu.

(See also CONGO CRISIS; FRANCOPHONE AFRICA; UNITED NATIONS.)

Jonathan Kwitny, *Endless Enemies* (Chicago, 1984). Crawford Young and Thomas Turner, *The Rise and Decline of the Zairian State* (Madison, Wis., 1985). Georges Nzongola-Ntalaja, *The Crisis in Zaire: Myths and Realities* (Trenton, N.J., 1986). Georges Nzongola-Ntalaja, *Revolution and Counter-Revolution in Africa* (London, 1987).

GEORGES NZONGOLA-NTALAJA
DEBORAH A. GREEN

ZAMBIA. Located in the center of the African continent, landlocked Zambia is best known for its copper mines, its vast dry plateau, and the dramatic Victoria Falls. Four cultural/linguistic groups have dominated its history: the Bemba, the Tonga, the Ngoni, and the Lozi. In 1898, the British South Africa Company annexed the territory, which became known as Northern Rhodesia. After some initial skirmishes, the company managed to entrench its rule, often through the authority of amenable local rulers. Company officials concentrated on collecting taxes, which drove adult males into migrant labor, and established Northern Rhodesia as a labor pool for its more affluent southern neighbors. On taking over in 1924, the colonial office initiated few changes; however, the territory's fortunes improved when its copper ores became commercially exploitable. By the mid-1930s, Northern Rhodesia was one of the world's leading copper producers. A dual economy developed, characterized by rural decline and increasing dependence on urban wage labor.

African nationalist activities initially relied on the leadership and support of African workers (particularly the mine workers) as well as the emerging urban middle class. However, trade union and nationalist goals clashed in the late 1950s, and trade unionists for the most part withdrew from the nationalist leadership. The educated African elite came to dominate both the United National Independence Party (UNIP) and the older but less popular African National Congress (ANC) of Zambia—not to be confused with the * African National Congress of South Africa.

In 1964 Northern Rhodesia, now Zambia, became a republic within the * Commonwealth. Kenneth Kaunda, the head of the UNIP, became the head of state as well as the chief executive. The UNIP dominated parliament, holding sixty-five of seventy-five seats, and ANC members rarely criticized the government. However, competition over political power exacerbated political divisions, opposition parties flourished, and political conflicts were fomented by economic difficulties.

Historically Zambia's economic ties had been with the south, and Kaunda's decision to cut those ties in an effort to help end white rule in * Southern Africa had serious economic repercussions. Between 1963 and 1968, high copper prices enabled the government to pursue this policy at little cost to its citizens. However, the subsequent slump in copper prices, combined with widespread economic mismanagement, reduced the new nation's capacity to deliver promised improvements. Political discontent increased as the economy weakened.

In an effort to contain these problems, the government nationalized the copper mines in 1969 and began to move against political opposition. It introduced the ideology of "Humanism," which emphasized national unity and commitment to the national good. Blaming Zambia's problems on political patronage and factionalism, especially by the opposition parties, in 1972 Kaunda and the cabinet set up a constitutional committee to establish a one-party state. The Second Republic was inaugurated the next year, with Kaunda as president. Henceforth, elections were to be contested within the UNIP. The populace accepted the change without comment, but participation in elections dropped precipitously. This apathy may have been due partly to the absence of rival parties, but it may also have reflected widespread discontent with UNIP rule. This discontent was particularly noticeable in the Copperbelt.

Since the mid-1970s, declining commodity prices, especially for copper, declining agricultural production, and blatant mismanagement have combined to bring about an economic crisis that the country has not been able to overcome. Despite regular infusions of financial assistance from the * International Monetary Fund (IMF) and adoption of IMF structural adjustment policies, the economy has continued to falter. Education, health, and welfare for the citizenry have declined precipitously. A number of attempted coups have occurred, primarily supported by members of the business community, the army,

and the trade unions. No coup has yet succeeded, but discontent continues to grow, increasingly centered around demands for a multiparty democracy and an end to the * one-party system.

Although Kaunda remained in control until 1991, the forces against him grew in strength. Intellectuals, businesspersons, students, trade unionists (particularly the still-powerful and articulate mine workers' union), and some dissident members of the armed forces become increasingly disillusioned with Kaunda's rule. The mass of the people lost faith in the UNIP government as well. This discontent led to the formation of the Movement for Multiparty Democracy (MMD) and to pressure for elections. In October 1991, UNIP was decisively defeated, the Second Republic ended, and a new government led by Frederick Chiluba of the MMD was installed.

(See also COLONIAL EMPIRES; DESTABILIZATION; NATIONALISM; SOUTHERN AFRICAN DEVELOPMENT CO-ORDINATION CONFERENCE.)

Andrew Roberts, *A History of Zambia* (London, 1976). Douglas G. Anglin and Timothy M. Shaw, *Zambia's Foreign Policy: Studies in Diplomacy and Dependence* (Boulder, Colo., 1979). Cherry Gertzel, Carolyn Baylies, and Morris Szeftel, *The Dynamics of the One-Party State in Zambia* (Manchester, U.K., 1984).

JANE L. PARPART

ZHOU Enlai. A veteran Chinese communist leader, Zhou Enlai (1898–1976) was premier and the foremost diplomat of the People's Republic of *China (PRC). Zhou Enlai was born into a family of local gentry in Zhejiang province. After his father's death, Zhou was sent to live first with his grandfather in northern Jiangsu and later with his father's elder brother in Shenyang. He attended Nankai Middle School in Tianjin in 1913 and went to Japan as an extramural student in 1917.

In the wake of the May 4th Movement of 1919, which had strong anti-Japanese overtones, Zhou returned to China and enrolled at Tianjin University, where he was a leader of students' anti-Japanese demonstrations. Later that year, he joined the Group for the Study of Marxist Theory under the guidance of some of China's leading intellectuals, many of whom became early leaders of the *Chinese Communist Party (CCP). His involvement in an anti-Japanese demonstration led to his arrest and six months' imprisonment.

After his release from jail, he left for France as a worker-student. There he founded the Chinese Communist Youth League with other Chinese student leaders. In 1924, he returned to China and was appointed director of the Political Department of the Whampoa Military Academy, then headed by Chiang Kai-shek. After the anti-warlord united front between the Nationalists and the CCP collapsed and Chiang launched a purge of the communists in the spring of 1927, Zhou went to Nanchang to lead the

Nanchang Uprising of 1 August 1927, a date that would become the anniversary of the founding of the People's Liberation Army (PLA). The same year, he was elected a member of the CCP Political Bureau, and in 1931 he joined other communists in the Jiangxi Soviet Area. At an enlarged meeting of the Political Bureau held in January 1935, in the midst of the epic Long March during which communist forces were pursued by those of Nationalists, Zhou yielded to *Mao Zedong chairmanship of the CCP Central Military Committee. Zhou subsequently became Mao's faithful subordinate and staunch backer. During the Xian incident in 1936 in which Chiang Kai-shek was kidnapped by a warlord who hoped to force Chiang to fight Japan rather than the Communists, Zhou was instrumental in Chiang's release; he then negotiated with Chiang to establish a new anti-Japanese alliance between the CCP and the Nationalists. During the next ten years he played a major role in dealing with the Nationalists and in mobilizing support for the communist cause.

After the founding of the PRC in 1949, Zhou served as premier of the new government, a position he kept until his death in 1976. He was also minister of foreign affairs until 1958 and a major architect of the PRC's foreign policy. He visited numerous countries and represented the PRC in many important international conferences. Richard Nixon, Henry Kissinger, and many other world leaders were impressed by Zhou's diplomatic skills. He also played a major role in China's opening to the United States and Japan in 1972.

Zhou was a master in the art of political survival and had the superb political acumen to vote with the winning side. Unlike other Chinese communist leaders, such as Liu Shaoqi and Lin Biao, who were disgraced during the *Cultural Revolution, Zhou weathered political storms through his intelligence and resourcefulness, combined with his Machiavellian talent for compromise and keen political instinct for knowing when to yield and when to stand firm. At once a Maoist and a pragmatist, Zhou assisted Mao in every political campaign but also tried to curb the excesses of Maoist leadership. Toward the end of his life, Zhou strived to restore political stability in China and launched a program for China's modernization. He died of cancer in January 1976 in Beijing. Unlike Mao, Zhou remains quite popular among the Chinese people.

(See also CHINESE REVOLUTION; SINO-AMERICAN RELATIONS.)

Dick Wilson, *Zhou Enlai: A Biography* (New York, 1984).
PARRIS H. CHANG

ZIMBABWE. Since it gained its independence in 1980, Zimbabwe has become one of the most important nations in *Southern Africa. The nation is situated in south central Africa between the Lim-

popo and Zambezi rivers and bordered by Zambia to the north and northwest, by *South Africa to the south, by Mozambique to the east, and by Botswana to the southwest. Zimbabwe has a population of 10.3 million. The ethnic distribution is Shona (71 percent), Ndebele (16 percent), others (12 percent), and whites (1 percent). The principal religions are Christianity combined with traditional beliefs (51 percent), Christianity (24 percent), traditional beliefs (24 percent), and Islam (1 percent).

Zimbabwe has a diversified economy relying on its chief exports of minerals and agricultural goods. The main exports are tobacco, gold, iron products, sugar, and nickel. The country is landlocked and depends heavily on South Africa and neighboring Mozambique for transport routes to ship its goods to the international market. The government has increasingly advocated greater emphasis on public sector involvement in the economy.

Zimbabwe was colonized by the British South Africa Company under Cecil Rhodes in the 1890s. The territory became part of the Federation of Rhodesia and Nyasaland in 1953. When the federation broke up in 1963 with the independence of Malawi and Zambia, the white minority of Rhodesia unilaterally declared independence from Britain. This move effectively prevented the institution of majority African rule in Rhodesia. The Rhodesian government instituted *apartheid-like policies and maintained racial discrimination in all sectors of life. In response, African liberation movements developed to protest the intransigence of the Rhodesian regime and resorted to *guerrilla warfare when all other tactics failed to produce any change. The combined forces of two main groups, the Zimbabwe African National Union (ZANU) and the Zimbabwe African Peoples Union (ZAPU), brought about a negotiated settlement and an end to the war in 1979.

Zimbabwe became independent on 18 April 1980 under the Lancaster House Constitution, the negotiated agreement between Britain, the African liberation movements, and the Rhodesian regime. Elections were held resulting in an overwhelming victory for ZANU. The Constitution provided for a Westminster-style government with a bicameral Parliament, a president who serves as the figurehead leader of the executive, a prime minister who has the responsibility of administering government, a forty-member Senate and a 120-member House of Assembly.

Key provisions in the Lancaster House Constitution ensured the whites of government support. The "willing buyer–willing seller" clause guaranteed that no lands would be confiscated by the state for at least the first ten years after independence. The state would have to pay current market rate for the land, making nationalization impractical and expropriation of the land unconstitutional. The clause that allowed for "reserved seats" for whites in Parliament ensured for the first seven years of independence that the white minority would be overrepresented in the legislative body. These aspects of the Constitution have expired and one person—one vote is now a feature of the Zimbabwe Constitution.

The ZANU Party remains in power as a result of elections held in 1985 and 1990. The government instituted two major constitutional changes in 1987. An executive presidency was instituted and racial representation in Parliament was abolished. The president has an unlimited term of office. These constitutional changes led to the consolidation of power by the ZANU Party and a call by the party for the implementation of a *one-party system.

The relationship between party and government is important in the Zimbabwean political structure. The party is defined as the body that establishes the general direction of government and has major influence in government. Key government leaders are also key party leaders, and the line between party and government is not always clear.

The Unity Accord signed in March 1986 between ZANU and ZAPU signaled movement toward a merger of the two major parties and the achievement of the goal of a one-party state. However, dissatisfaction among intellectuals, students, workers, and the peasantry with the concept of a one-party state and revelations of widespread corruption in 1988 presented serious challenges to the ZANU government.

The failure of government since independence to provide the social, economic, and political changes that were expected to result from an African-dominated government has fostered considerable opposition. Government has made progress in providing social services such as primary health care and universal education. However, other programs such as resettlement of the multitudes who were displaced during the war and land redistribution to the Africans who were dispossessed during the colonial period has not occurred.

Rising costs for basic goods and widespread corruption have led to serious protest in which groupings have reemerged along ethnic lines. The extent to which the current regime handles the questions of leadership, democracy, and economic development will determine its strength or weakness in the future.

Zimbabwe's *political economy has been dominated by economic dependency on South Africa and the South African policy of *destabilization, which refers to concerted efforts by the South African government to subvert *development efforts in neighboring countries that were outspoken critics of apartheid policies. The dependency of Zimbabwe on South African transport routes, the continuing war in Mozambique that affects Zimbabwe's transport routes to the east, and the dominance of the South African economy have presented serious challenges to the development of Zimbabwe.

As a method to lessen *dependency on South Africa, the *Southern African Development Coordination Conference (SADCC) was established in 1980. Its purpose is to promote economic cooperation among the independent Southern African states by coordinating development plans and reducing economic dependence upon the Republic of South Africa. The governments of the region have banded together to support continentally and internationally the call for an end to apartheid and reforms to bring about one person—one vote in South Africa.

Zimbabwe's future development is tied to the events taking place in South Africa. A lessening of hostilities in the region has resulted from internal reforms inside South Africa. However, Zimbabwe's landlocked situation will make it dependent upon cultivating good relations with its neighbors. The commitment of troops to Mozambique to aid in the defense of the Beira Corridor and to assist the Mozambique government against dissident forces is motivated by Zimbabwe's need for a stable transport outlet to the sea. A lessened dependency on South Africa by ensuring a more stable situation in Mozambique is desirable for Zimbabwe. However, the size, diversity, and strength of the South African economy make it a force that Zimbabwe will have to deal with at present and into the post-apartheid era.

Zimbabwe is a major actor in the regional and international order. It has taken stands that have been outspoken against South Africa and for *human rights at the United Nations that have criticized some of the most powerful nations of the world. It has been a constant voice against racism and colonialism. As colonial domination fades from the African scene, Zimbabwe will increasingly turn its attention to issues concerning the economic and *political development of its people.

(See also COLONIAL EMPIRES; DECOLONIZATION.)

David Martin and Phyllis Johnson, *The Struggle for Zimbabwe* (Harare, 1981). Michael Schatzberg, ed., *The Political Economy of Zimbabwe* (Westport, Conn., 1984). Carol Thompson, *Challenge to Imperialism: The Frontline States in the Liberation of Zimbabwe* (Boulder, Colo., 1985). Ibbo Mendaza, ed., *Zimbabwe: The Political Economy of Transition, 1980–1986* (1986).

DEBORAH A. SANDERS

ZIONISM. Although premodern Judaism idealized the "Land of Israel" and Jewish messianism promised restoration of the ancient homeland, over the centuries the trickle of Jews who actually immigrated to *Palestine had no notion of a state-building project. Modern Jewish *nationalism, in the form of Zionism (from the Hebrew *Tziyon*, a synonym for Jerusalem), emerged only in the last third of the nineteenth century, mainly among the Jewish masses of eastern Europe, for whom it was one of several responses to socioeconomic crisis and virulent *antisemitism (manifested in officially sponsored pogroms in tsarist Russia in 1871 and 1881), which together blocked most avenues of individual or collective integration or advancement. In this period millions of Jews sought to escape their plight by emigrating not to Palestine but to western Europe and the Americas, and above all to the United States. While most of those who did not emigrate westward clung to traditional ways, sought assimilation, or turned to socialism, which promised the eradication of antisemitism, the example of other European peoples' turn toward nationalism and a midcentury Hebrew-language cultural revival paved the way for the emergence of a small "Love of Zion" movement, promoting emigration to Palestine and Jewish national-cultural revival there. This first wave of Jewish immigration to Palestine, from 1881 to 1903, led to the establishment of a number of Jewish agricultural settlements in Palestine, which survived thanks largely to the financial support of western European Jewish philanthropists.

As an organized and explicitly political nationalist movement, however, Zionism emerged only after 1896, when Theodor Herzl (1860–1904), a Viennese journalist, published his influential pamphlet *The Jewish State* and a year later convened the first Zionist Congress at Basel, Switzerland. The antisemitism which the Dreyfus affair brought to the surface even in "enlightened" France had convinced Herzl, an assimilated Jew from an affluent family, that the only solution to the "Jewish problem" was emigration to some territory in which the Jews could establish their own sovereign state. Herzl transformed a diffuse proto-Zionism into a modern international mass political movement, the Zionist Organization (ZO), whose main focus during his lifetime was to secure from the Ottoman Empire, which then ruled Palestine, or from one or more of the European powers, a "charter" granting the Jews the right to settle in and develop Palestine. Over time the ZO developed a comprehensive network of institutions, including elected decision-making bodies, a financial apparatus, and an agency to acquire land in Palestine for Jewish settlement (the Jewish National Fund).

The main premises on which Zionism as an *ideology rests include the definition of all Jews everywhere as constituting a single nation; the inevitability of antisemitism wherever Jews and non-Jews live together, and its ineradicability by means of education or social change; the irredeemable abnormality of Jewish life in "exile," a result of Jewish rootlessness and powerlessness; and the necessity of achieving the territorial concentration of all or most of the world's Jews in Palestine, where Jewish national rebirth and *sovereignty are to be realized.

Zionism was influenced by, and has many similarities with, other contemporary European nationalisms. However, because Jews did not constitute a compact majority in any specific territory in Europe wherein they could seek sovereignty, Zionism could be realized only through large-scale Jewish immigration to, and settlement in, an extra-European territory, an undertaking which the contemporaneous "new *imperialism" made both conceivable and feasible. Zionism was thus not simply a national but also a colonial-settler project, and its attitude toward Palestine's substantial indigenous Arab population, on the verge of its own national "awakening," was profoundly influenced by contemporary European colonial discourse. The famous early Zionist slogan, "A land without a people for a people without a land," reflected a conception of Palestine as empty, because not inhabited or developed by Europeans. Later, when the existence of Palestine's Arab population and its opposition to the Zionist project became unmistakably obvious, most Zionists denied the authenticity of Palestinian *Arab nationalism while asserting a superior Jewish claim to Palestine based on historical precedence, divine promise, urgent need, and/or invested labor.

Zionism has never been a monolithic movement: from its very inception it has comprised distinct and often conflicting tendencies. Herzl's "political" Zionism and its successor, the bourgeois and secular "General Zionist" tendency, were challenged by "labor Zionism" (or "socialist Zionism"), which stressed not big-power diplomacy but immigration and settlement work leading to the creation in Palestine of a social-democratic Jewish society; among this tendency's outstanding figures was David *Ben-Gurion (1886–1973). Though most orthodox rabbis initially denounced Zionism as false messianism and state-worshiping idolatry, a religious Zionist movement also emerged, in uneasy partnership with the ZO's secular majority. In the 1920s a right wing emerged within the Zionist movement, led by Vladimir Jabotinsky (1880–1940). Jabotinsky's "Revisionist" Zionism rejected the gradualism of the ZO's leadership, its reluctance in certain periods to explicitly demand a sovereign Jewish state, and its talk of compromise with the Palestinian Arabs. Initially influenced by contemporary European *fascism, the Revisionists demanded the immediate establishment, by force if necessary, of a sovereign Jewish state in all of Palestine and Transjordan.

The General Zionists played the leading role in the ZO from its inception into the early 1930s, when labor Zionism emerged as the strongest tendency. For the following four decades, with the General and religious Zionist parties as junior partners, labor Zionism dominated the ZO, the yishuv (the Jewish community in Palestine), and later *Israel. The labor-Zionist movement played a crucial role in laying the economic, social, cultural, and political foundations of the future State of Israel, implementing a strategy that was shaped by conditions on the ground in Palestine itself and that stressed immigration and settlement work, the gradual development of a self-sufficient yishuv, rhetorical moderation toward the Palestinians without substantive concessions, and the importance of international support.

By the 1970s, however, political, social, and cultural developments within Israel (including the 1967 conquest and occupation of the West Bank and Gaza, and the Right's ability to capitalize electorally on the resentment felt by many Jews originally from Arab countries about discrimination at the hands of the labor-Zionist establishment) converged to undermine labor Zionism's dominance, and in 1977 Jabotinsky's disciple Menachem Begin (1913–1992) formed Israel's first government not dominated by labor Zionists. For the next fifteen years the direction and tone of Israeli politics were set largely by the Zionist Right.

Given Ottoman, and later Palestinian and other Arab, opposition to the Zionist goal of creating a Jewish state, the Zionist movement required a powerful European patron to provide protection and support. Only in November 1917, when Britain issued the *Balfour Declaration, did such a patron finally come forward. British support for and protection of the Zionist project lasted until 1939, when British efforts to conciliate the Arabs led to a breakdown in the alliance. By that time, however, the yishuv was, in demographic, economic, political, and military terms, almost strong enough to stand on its own, thanks in part to increased Jewish immigration during the 1930s stimulated by the spread of European antisemitism (particularly the Nazi assumption of power in Germany) and channeled to Palestine when the Western democracies shut their doors.

By 1942 the Zionist movement was openly proclaiming that its goal was a Jewish state in all of Palestine, but it was only after World War II that an all-out political, diplomatic, and military campaign was launched to achieve statehood, in uniquely favorable circumstances: shocked by the Nazi extermination of some six million European Jews, the world community was sympathetic as never before to Zionism as a response to antisemitism; for reasons of their own, both the United States and the Soviet Union endorsed Jewish statehood; the UN, to which Britain referred the Palestine problem in February 1947, still had few Third World members who might have been more receptive to the Arab case; Jewish communities worldwide (in which Zionism now won widespread support) were effectively mobilized; and within the yishuv itself the groundwork for statehood had been laid. In November 1947 the UN General Assembly voted to recommend the partition of Palestine into independent Arab and Jewish states, touching off intercommunal warfare. In May 1948 the State of Israel was proclaimed, and when the ensuing Arab-Israeli War of 1948–49 came to an end the following year, the new Jewish state was in control of seventy-seven percent of Palestine.

Although after 1948 some Israeli leaders (including Ben-Gurion) argued that there was no further need for a Zionist movement, the World Zionist Organization (as it is now officially called) has continued to function, promoting and raising money for Jewish immigration to Israel, carrying on Jewish educational and cultural work in the Diaspora, and lobbying on behalf of Israel. Within Israel various attitudes toward Zionism coexist, ranging from a strong commitment to the continuation of Israel's task of "ingathering the exiles" to indifference among many younger Israelis, in whose slang the word *Zionism* is a synonym for bombast. Nonetheless, Israel remains in theory and practice a Zionist state, in that it officially defines itself not as a state of its citizens, Jews and Arabs, but as the state of all Jews everywhere, who under Israeli law have the automatic right to immigrate to Israel, acquire citizenship, and enjoy privileges denied to Israel's non-Jewish citizens. This self-definition and the practices which flow from it, along with Israeli military rule over Palestinians in the West Bank and Gaza, were cited as justification for the controversial 1975 UN General Assembly resolution classifying Zionism as a form of racism (repealed in 1991).

Although since 1948, and especially since 1967, identification with Israel has come to be the main content of secular Jewish identity for many Jews in the Western democracies, and especially the United States, which has the world's largest Jewish community, that identification is unencumbered by any personal sense of obligation to move to Israel. In fact, very few Jews from these countries have chosen to live in Israel; for most, Zionism continued to be, as the old joke goes, a matter of "an American Jew donating money to a French Jew to fund a Russian Jew's immigration to Israel." Indeed, generally speaking, large numbers of Jews have gone to Palestine (and later to Israel) only when confronted with inequality of rights and opportunities, discrimination, or persecution in their own countries, and only when other options have been closed; even Soviet Jews emigrating in the 1970s and 1990s, if given a choice, usually evinced a preference for the United States or other Western countries. Before 1948 the Jewish communities in the Arab countries had been largely ignored by, and were generally unreceptive to, Zionism, a thoroughly European Jewish movement in leadership, orientation, and ethos; their massive immigration to Israel between 1948 and the early 1960s was the result not of Zionist conviction but of the Palestine conflict, which made their situation in their countries of origin untenable.

In one obvious sense, Zionism can be judged a tremendous success: the utopian dream of a Viennese journalist was realized some five decades later in the creation of a new nation-state which has repeatedly demonstrated its durability. Some qualification of that judgment may be in order, however. Although Zionism promised to establish a safe haven for Jews, its failure, despite repeated military triumphs, to induce the Palestinians to abandon their own drive for statehood, or to compel most Arab states to accept Israel's terms for peace, has meant that the yishuv, and then Israel, have always been embattled. Ironically, of all the world's Jewish communities, it is today in Israel that Jews face the gravest threat of physical annihilation. The apparently ineradicable persistence of the Palestinians also suggests that, even if Israel's present military superiority endures, the Zionist achievement after 1948 of a Jewish majority in Palestine is impermanent: barring mass expulsions, Arabs will once again be a majority in Palestine within a few decades, while the Palestinian minority within Israel's 1967 borders grows increasingly unwilling to accept the burdens of second-class citizenship imposed by the state's Zionist self-definition.

Nor have other goals of Zionism as originally envisioned—Jewish independence, unity, territorial concentration, and cultural revival—been fully realized. In conflict with much of the population over which it rules and most of the region in which it is situated, Israel's strength, if not its very survival, depends in large measure on the military, economic, and political support of a distant superpower, the United States. However, the end of the *Cold War and post–Gulf War realignments in the *Middle East may put that close relationship into question by depriving Israel of its former role as a key U.S. ally against Soviet-backed regimes and radical-

nationalist forces in the region. Israeli Jewish society is divided by deep and often bitter conflicts along ethnic, class, ideological, and religious/secular lines, conflicts that subside only when a grave external threat is perceived. Only a minority of the world's Jews live in Israel, though the new wave of Soviet (and post-Soviet) Jewish immigration that began in 1989 is likely to increase that proportion and will certainly have important (if unpredictable) effects on Israel's political, social, and cultural complexion. Israel-Diaspora relations are often troubled, and despite the danger of assimilation, many observers believe that the Diaspora fosters greater cultural vitality than Israel, where clericalist and chauvinist forces exert a growing influence. As a result, despite having overcome enormous obstacles and successfully created a strong state that enjoys widespread loyalty among Jews, the long-term prospects of the Zionist project remain uncertain.

(See also ARAB-ISRAELI CONFLICT; COLONIAL EMPIRES; GULF WAR; HOLOCAUST; INTERNATIONAL MIGRATION; UNITED NATIONS.)

Arthur Hertzberg, ed., *The Zionist Idea* (New York, 1959). David Vital, *The Origins of Zionism* (Oxford, 1975). David Vital, *Zionism: the Formative Years* (Oxford, 1982). David Vital, *Zionism: the Crucial Phase* (Oxford, 1987). Gershon Shafir, *Land, Labor and the Origins of the Israeli-Palestinian Conflict, 1882–1914* (Cambridge, U.K., 1989).

ZACHARY LOCKMAN

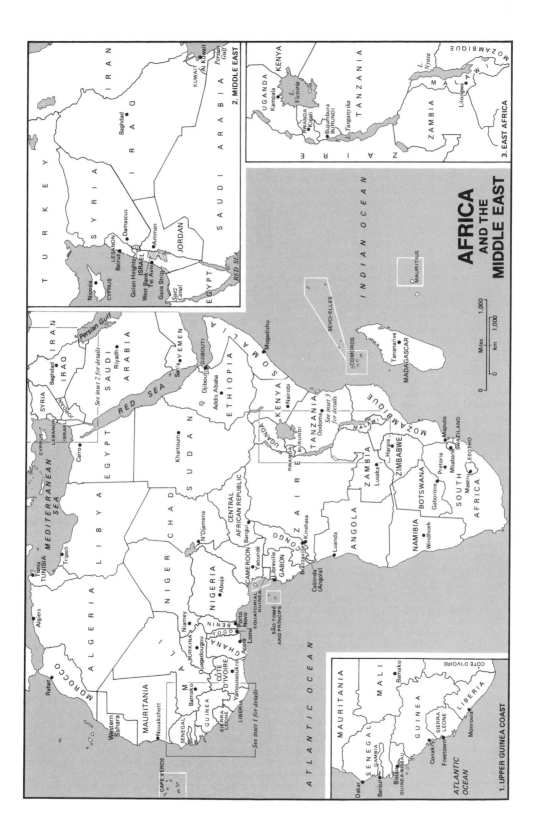

AFRICA
AND THE
MIDDLE EAST

2. MIDDLE EAST

IRAN
KUWAIT
Al Kuwait
Persian Gulf
IRAQ
Baghdad
SAUDI ARABIA
TURKEY
SYRIA
Damascus
LEBANON
Beirut
Golan Heights
West Bank
Tel Aviv
ISRAEL
Gaza Strip
JORDAN
Amman
Nicosia
CYPRUS
EGYPT
Suez Canal
RED SEA

3. EAST AFRICA

MOZAMBIQUE
KENYA
UGANDA
Kampala
L. Victoria
RWANDA
Kigali
BURUNDI
Bujumbura
L. Tanganyika
TANZANIA
ZAMBIA
MALAWI
L. Nyasa
Lilongwe
Z A I R E

INDIAN OCEAN
SEYCH-ELLES
COMOROS
MAURITIUS
Miles
1,000
km
1,000
0

IRAN
Persian Gulf
IRAQ
Baghdad
SYRIA
JORDAN
LEBANON
ISRAEL
CYPRUS
Cairo
EGYPT
MEDITERRANEAN SEA
TUNISIA
Tunis
Tripoli
LIBYA
ALGERIA
Algiers
MOROCCO
Rabat
Western Sahara
MAURITANIA
Nouakchott
SENEGAL
Dakar
See inset 1 for details
MALI
Bamako
NIGER
Niamey
BURKINA
Ouagadougou
CÔTE D'IVOIRE
Yamoussoukro
GUINEA
SIERRA LEONE
LIBERIA
GHANA
Accra
TOGO
BENIN
Lomé
Porto Novo
NIGERIA
Abuja
CHAD
N'Djamena
CAMEROON
Yaoundé
EQUATORIAL GUINEA
SÃO TOMÉ AND PRÍNCIPE
GABON
Libreville
CONGO
Brazzaville
Kinshasa
Cabinda (Angola)
ZAIRE
CENTRAL AFRICAN REPUBLIC
Bangui
SUDAN
Khartoum
RED SEA
SAUDI ARABIA
Riyadh
YEMEN
Sana
DJIBOUTI
Djibouti
ETHIOPIA
Addis Ababa
SOMALIA
Mogadishu
UGANDA
RWANDA
BURUNDI
KENYA
Nairobi
TANZANIA
Dodoma
See inset 3 for details
MALAWI
ZAMBIA
Lusaka
ANGOLA
Luanda
ZIMBABWE
Harare
MOZAMBIQUE
Maputo
BOTSWANA
Gaborone
NAMIBIA
Windhoek
SOUTH AFRICA
Pretoria
Mbabane
SWAZILAND
Maseru
LESOTHO
SEYCHELLES
COMOROS
Tananarive
MADAGASCAR
MAURITIUS

ATLANTIC OCEAN
CAPE VERDE
See inset 1 for details

1. UPPER GUINEA COAST

MAURITANIA
SENEGAL
Dakar
GAMBIA
Banjul
GUINEA-BISSAU
Bissau
GUINEA
Conakry
SIERRA LEONE
Freetown
LIBERIA
Monrovia
MALI
Bamako
CÔTE D'IVOIRE
ATLANTIC OCEAN

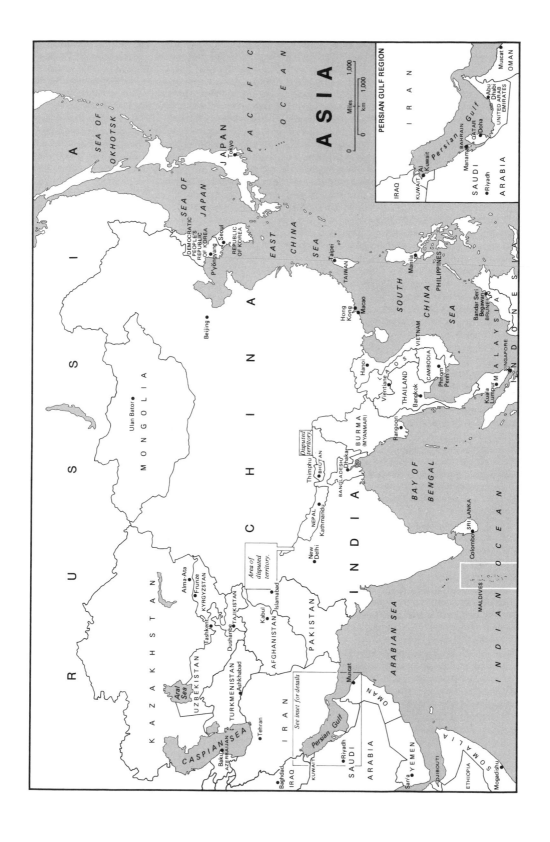

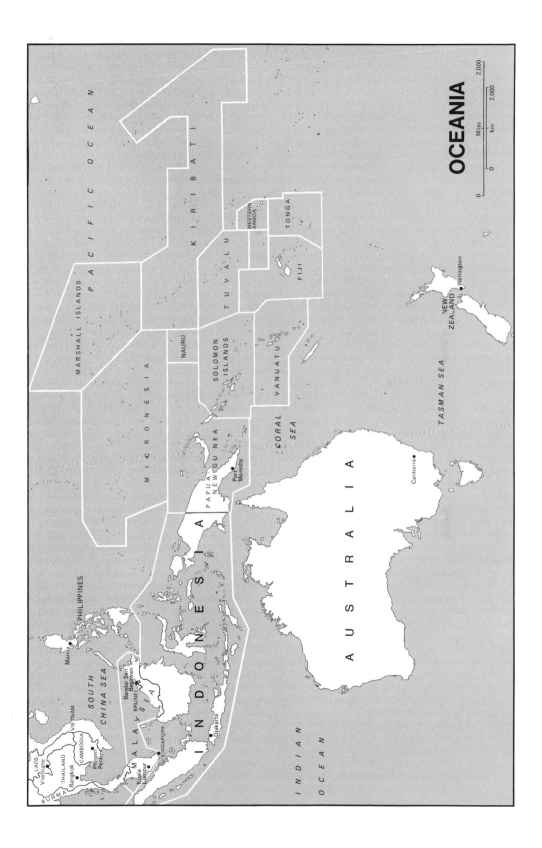

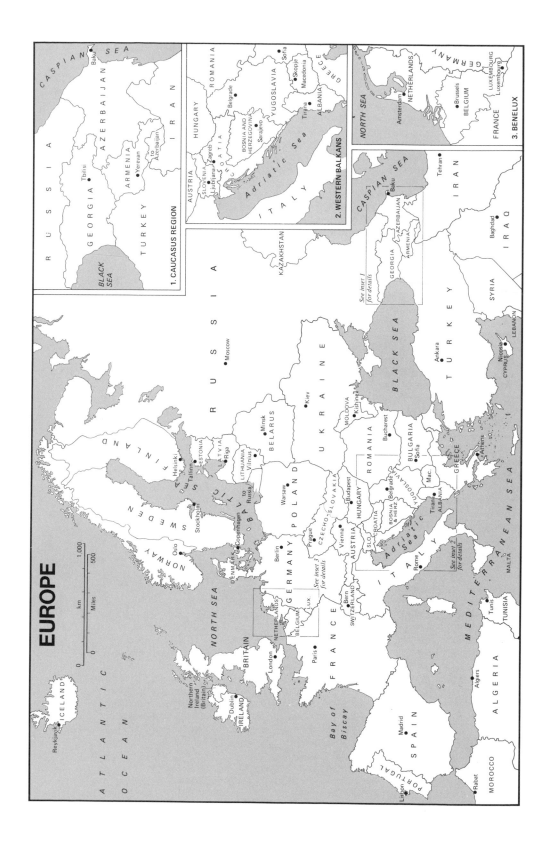

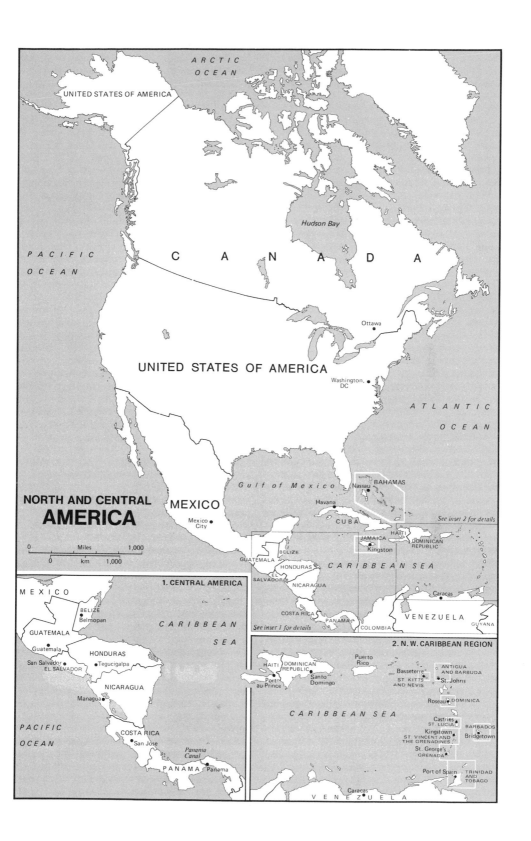

ARCTIC OCEAN

UNITED STATES OF AMERICA

CANADA

Hudson Bay

PACIFIC OCEAN

Ottawa

UNITED STATES OF AMERICA

Washington, DC

ATLANTIC OCEAN

Gulf of Mexico

BAHAMAS
Nassau

MEXICO

Havana

CUBA

See inset 2 for details

NORTH AND CENTRAL
AMERICA

Mexico City

JAMAICA
Kingston

HAITI

DOMINICAN REPUBLIC

0   Miles   1,000

0   km   1,000

GUATEMALA

BELIZE

HONDURAS

EL SALVADOR

NICARAGUA

CARIBBEAN SEA

Caracas

COSTA RICA

PANAMA

VENEZUELA

GUYANA

See inset 1 for details

COLOMBIA

1. CENTRAL AMERICA

MEXICO

BELIZE
Belmopan

CARIBBEAN SEA

GUATEMALA

Guatemala

HONDURAS

San Salvador
EL SALVADOR

Tegucigalpa

NICARAGUA

Managua

PACIFIC OCEAN

COSTA RICA

San Jose

Panama Canal

PANAMA Panama

2. N. W. CARIBBEAN REGION

HAITI

DOMINICAN REPUBLIC

Port-au-Prince

Santo Domingo

Puerto Rico

Basseterre
ST. KITTS AND NEVIS

ANTIGUA AND BARBUDA
St. Johns

Roseau DOMINICA

CARIBBEAN SEA

Castries
ST. LUCIA

BARBADOS
Bridgetown

Kingstown
ST. VINCENT AND THE GRENADINES

St. George's
GRENADA

Port of Spain

TRINIDAD AND TOBAGO

Caracas

VENEZUELA

CARIBBEAN SEA

ST. LUCIA

ST. VINCENT AND
THE GRENADINES

BARBADOS

GRENADA

ATLANTIC

OCEAN

Port
of Spain

Panama

Caracas

TRINIDAD
AND TOBAGO

PANAMA

V E N E Z U E L A

Georgetown

Paramaribo

G U Y A N A

Santa Fe
de Bogotá

French
Guiana

SURINAME

C O L O M B I A

Quito

ECUADOR

B   R   A   Z   I   L

P

E

R

U

Lima

La Paz

Brasília

B O L I V I A

PACIFIC

OCEAN

C

H

I

L

E

PARAGUAY

Asunción

A

R

G

E

N

T

I

N

A

URUGUAY

Santiago

Buenos Aires

Montevideo

SOUTH AMERICA

0   Miles   1,000

0   km   1,000

INDEX